# Handbook
# of Mental Health
# and Aging

*Associate Editors*

William Bondareff

Irene Mortenson Burnside

Louis Lowy

K. Warner Schaie

Alexander Simon

and

Judy L. Aklonis, Project Coordinator

# Handbook
## of Mental Health
## and Aging

JAMES E. BIRREN and R. BRUCE SLOANE

*Co-Editors*

Prentice-Hall, Inc. Englewood Cliffs, N.J. 07632

*Library of Congress Cataloging in Publication Data*

MAIN ENTRY UNDER TITLE·

HANDBOOK OF MENTAL HEALTH AND AGING.

Bibliography: p.
Includes indexes.
1. Geriatric psychiatry. 2. Aged—Mental health.
3. Aged—Psychology. !. Birren, James E.
II. Sloane, Robert Bruce. [DNLM: 1. Aging
2. Mental disorders—In old age. WT150 H2355]
RC451.4.A5H38 618.9'76'89 79-23648
ISBN 0-13-380261-2

# Handbook of Mental Health and Aging
Co-Editors
JAMES E. BIRREN AND R. BRUCE SLOANE

© 1980 by Prentice-Hall, Inc., Englewood Cliffs, N.J. 07632

Printed in the United States of America
10 9 8 7 6 5 4 3 2 1

Editorial/production supervision by JOYCE TURNER
Interior design by TOM PENDLETON
Cover design by A GOOD THING, INC.
Manufacturing buyer: HARRY P. BAISLEY

Prentice-Hall International, Inc., *London*
Prentice-Hall of Australia Pty. Limited, *Sydney*
Prentice-Hall of Canada, Ltd., *Toronto*
Prentice-Hall of India Private Limited, *New Delhi*
Prentice-Hall of Japan, Inc., *Tokyo*
Prentice-Hall of Southeast Asia Pte. Ltd., *Singapore*
Whitehall Books Limited, *Wellington, New Zealand*

# Contents

# V

# Pathology:

# Diagnosis and Assessment

# Foreword

## BRINGING KNOWLEDGE TO BEAR
## ON THE MENTAL DYSFUNCTIONS ASSOCIATED WITH AGING

A national health problem which is most severe in terms of its prevalence and cost is a group of mental disorders and dysfunctions which are associated with aging. Either because somatic mechanisms are more robust or, being simpler and easier to comprehend, are more readily preserved or restored as the result of progress in medical science, a substantial segment of the population can now look forward to a longer life, but one which may unfortunately be hampered by mental disability. This is a prospect that is both troubling to the individual and costly to society. Since mental handicap makes an individual increasingly dependent on the help and care of others, the cost of these services and perquisites to other members of the family and to the whole of society as well,

represents a burden which has been estimated at 36.78 billions of dollars per year in the United States. More important, perhaps, is a cost that cannot be measured or tabulated: the loss of human potential and of the affected person's capacity for adaptation and ability to contribute to human welfare.

A valuable characteristic of human societies is that their evolution is based more on cultural than on genetic transmission. The wisdom of experience can benefit not only the individual, which it does in all species which have well-developed memory systems, but also the group as a whole, to which experience can be communicated. In *Homo sapiens* particularly, language permits the transmission of individual experience to younger and future generations, so that adaptive progress can be accelerated by several magnitudes over the rate that would be possible through genetic mutation and natural selection. It may be more than a co-incidence that such cultures as the Chinese or the Jewish, which have for several thousand years respected and honored their older members, have also been characterized by sustained high levels of intellectual achievement.

For society to benefit, however, from the experience and wisdom of its elder members, optimal integrity and functioning of the biological, psychological, and social processes that determine mental function are required. Where these become severely disturbed and mental function is in serious disarray, there is a loss in the potential contribution.

Our ability to ameliorate this situation will depend upon more effective utilization of the knowledge we now have and also upon an augmented research effort to acquire the knowledge we will need in order to understand, to treat, and, best of all, to prevent the mental handicaps which too often accompany the aging process.

This *Handbook of Mental Health and Aging* is what a handbook should be—a comprehensive compilation of the state of our knowledge about the many facets of a problem, each written by a particularly qualified author. Its scope is multidisciplinary, as the study of mental health and illness must be. Its Co-Editors, a psychologist and a neuropsychiatrist, exemplify the interface and the continuous interaction between mind and brain.

James Birren was one of the expert and motivated scientists who joined me in the organization of the Intramural Program of the National Institutes of Mental Health and Neurological Disorders in Bethesda, Maryland more than twenty-five years ago. That program was organized around the fundamental biological, psychological, and sociological disciplines in order to maximize the opportunity for creative research by individual scientists, but there was every opportunity and encouragement to form collaborative, multidisciplinary efforts in addressing important clinical problems. The first of these efforts was organized by Birren, who drew together a unique consortium representing psychology, psychiatry, statistics, biology, and sociology; this group collaborated for more than a decade of research on the psychobiological aspects of aging. In addition to their individual publications

in the field, they produced a landmark compilation of their collaborative research in the volume *Human Aging. A Biological and Behavioral Study*, edited by James E. Birren, Robert N. Butler, Samuel W. Greenhouse, Louis Sokoloff, and Marian R. Yarrow, published as Public Health Service Publication No. 986, Government Printing Office, Washington, 1963.

Bruce Sloane, who began his career in internal medicine and neurology, has long been concerned with investigations of the interface of higher cortical function. In 1978–79 he was Visiting Professor at the Universities of London and Cambridge in England, supported by the Foundations' Fund for Research in Psychiatry. There he focused on geriatric and psychogeriatric research and clinical programs, with particular emphasis on dementia, and he has now initiated a study of Alzheimer's disease. Currently, he is spearheading curricular changes to incorporate knowledge of, and care of, aging processes into medical education, as well as facilitating the University of Southern California Medical School's participation with the Inter-University Group for Geriatrics and Gerontology, which is involved with medical education and health services for the aged.

The present volume, coming nearly twenty years after *Human Aging*, no longer confines itself to the work of a single group but reaches to the large body of knowledge that has accumulated in the entire field. It will make that knowledge available to those in the various professions concerned with health care and with the resolution of the medical, psychological, and social problems of the aged. It will also serve the important purpose of indicating the even larger areas of our ignorance. Each chapter tacitly or explicitly points out the limitations of our present knowledge. There is much that we need to know in the adjacent fields if we are to treat and serve the aging population more effectively. There is also much more that we need to learn in the wide-ranging areas of fundamental science from which will eventually come, as it has come repeatedly in other areas, a more complete understanding of the origins of health problems and how they may appropriately be prevented.

Seymour S. Kety
Harvard University

# Preface

The purpose of organizing this *Handbook of Mental Health and Aging* is to provide an important and growing, but still relatively unorganized, area of scientific and professional activity with an authoritative reference work. Since the research on mental health and aging has developed in many separate, even scattered, fields, the task of collecting information has been enormous. An attempt has been made to secure the assistance of a wide spectrum of specialists in preparing reviews of the relevant scientific and professional literature. The result is a book intended for use by professionals, researchers, graduate students, and others who have need for a definitive reference source for the literature of a complex emerging field.

There is little doubt that the ever-increasing numbers of older adults in developed countries will prompt more research and teaching in areas related to mental health and aging, as well as more organized services for the older adult. In addition, rising personal standards on the part of a better educated older population, as well as family concerns for its older members, will increase the numbers of older adults who will seek the services of mental health professionals. Such services should be based upon recent research findings as well as upon values which will encourage efforts to raise the standard of living and to develop individual potentials, regardless of age.

A basic question about the course of human life deals with how behavior is organized and how it changes with the conditions of adult life in its many facets. In order to judge and treat deviation from the norms of biological and psychological processes, we must have a firm grasp of "normal" ontogeny; and at this point our knowledge about development in adult life is still far from complete. This field will prosper to the extent that it can keep in touch with the explosive developments in the neurosciences and with discoveries in the behavioral and social sciences.

In return, it seems highly likely that research and service related to mental health and aging will provide the sciences and professions with insights that will strengthen our understanding of the essential processes of human existence. Until now, the field of mental health and aging has been small in comparison to what was viewed as mainstream scientific and professional activity. This seems destined to change. In the process, once-useful metaphors about the human organism and about the organization of behavior will have to be replaced with more definitive models that will reflect new discoveries in many different areas.

It is hoped that the publication of this *handbook* will encourage teaching, research, and services related to the mental health of aging people. The future well-being of entire societies, and of millions of individuals, was among our concerns as this book was planned. It is probable that many philosophical issues, even beyond those of which the authors and editors were fully aware, are latent in the following chapters. One way of increasing our sensitivity to issues in this field is to juxtapose differing information and points of view. As editors we considered several areas of scientific inquiry—biological, behavioral, and social—as being relevant to our subject. In addition, we saw many professions as having relevant information and skills: psychiatry, neurology, social work, nursing, psychology, and pharmacology, among others. We believe that this breadth reflects a healthy eclectic approach that keeps the field alert to advances and promotes an intellectual climate that will lead to progress in many areas, from the laboratory to the bedside, from society to individuals.

The Editorial Committee for this volume was William Bondareff, Irene Mortenson Burnside, Louis Lowy, K. Warner Schaie, and Alexander Simon, together with the two Co-Editors. Judy Aklonis served as Project Coordinator, and her efforts made the project "go." The Editorial Committee selected the areas of subject matter to be included and chose the authors. In some instances there were several potential choices of talented persons to prepare the same chapter. In other areas there were voids, both of information and of colleagues to call upon. For some topics the literature was so large that the authors had to be selective, so that

reference lists could not be exhaustive. On still other subjects data are sparse and conceptualization was, and is, necessary as a prelude to organized inquiry. As a whole, this field is not well-articulated; but that is the continuing and exciting task that faces us.

In part, the organization of this volume reflects the fields in which active research interests have already developed; but it also reflects opinion about new areas in which work should be encouraged. In addition to being broadly multiprofessional and multidisciplinary in character, we felt that the *Handbook* should support the linkage of the sciences and professions in such a way as to encourage the flow of information between fields and to increase the probability of its being used for human betterment. The planning and production of this volume were carried out with the hope that it would provide both a basis and a stimulus for new directions and developments in research and in service, leading to the increased well-being of millions of mature and older adults.

The support of the National Institute of Mental Health for the preparation of this manuscript (Contract No. 278-76-0056 [SM]) is gratefully acknowledged. We believe that this support reflects real foresight and that it will result in accelerated developments that will be widely beneficial.

The assistance of several individuals should be acknowledged here. Phoebe Liebig made the path smooth at many turning points in the planning and execution of the project. *Handbook* staff members included Janet Merritt (Project Assistant); Kathy Richkind (Copy Editor); Mary Lou Bianco and Louise Boer (Bibliographic Assistance); and Anita Woods (Acting Project Assistant). In addition, we are most grateful to the colleagues who, in addition to our Editorial Board, served as outside reviewers: Edward Beck, Caleb E. Finch, William Grings, David Krantz, Ivan Mensch, Edward Mongan, Pauline Ragan, Barbara Silverstone, George Simpson, Gordon Streib, Frances Wilkie, and Steve Zarit. We appreciate the assistance and cooperation of the many persons who contributed to the successful completion of this project.

James E. Birren
R. Bruce Sloane
University of Southern California

# Contributors

**Raymond D. Adams,** M.D., D.Sc. (Chapter 7) is Bullard Professor Neuropathology, emeritus, Harvard Medical School. He has published over 225 articles, chapters, and ten books. Recent publications include "Principles of Neurology"; "The Pathological Reactions of the Skeletal Muscle Fiber" (with K.E. Astrom) in *Handbook of Clinical Neurology* (in press); and "Cerebrovascular Diseases" in *Harrison's Principles of Internal Medicine.* Dr. Adams is a Fellow of American College of Physicians; American Academy of Arts and Sciences; Royal Society of Medicine, Sweden; and Royal Society of Medicine, England.

**Janet Kaplan Belsky,** Ph.D. (Chapter 23), is an Assistant Professor of Psychology at Lehman College, City University of New York, Bronx, New York. She received a U. S. Public Health Service Traineeship for graduate study from 1969 to 1973. Dr. Belsky's special areas of interest are psychotherapy and life-span development.

**Vern L. Bengtson,** Ph.D. (Chapter 17) is currently Visiting Professor at the Sociological Institute, University of Stockholm, Stockholm, Sweden; and Professor of Sociology, University of Southern California, Los Angeles, California. His publications include *The Social Psychology of Aging,* and *Youth, Generations and Social Change,* as well as over 40 articles in professional journals. Dr. Bengtson has conducted research on the social psychology of aging; family relations across the lifespan; the sociology of social change; and methodology of social-psychological research.

**Klaus Bergmann,** M.D., Ch.B., D.P.M. (Chapter 2) is a Consultant Psychiatrist at the Bethlem Royal Hospital and the Maudsley Hospital, and a Recognized Clinical Teacher at the University of London, London, England. In addition to numerous articles, Dr. Bergmann has published a chapter, "Neurosis and Personality Disorders in

Old Age," in *Studies in Geriatric Psychiatry*, edited by Isaacs and Post; and a book: *The Aged, Their Care and Understanding*. Dr. Bergmann's main concentration in research and teaching is the psychiatry of old age.

**James E. Birren,** Ph.D. (Chapters 1, 14) is Executive Director of the Andrus Gerontology Center, and Dean, Davis School of Gerontology, University of Southern California, Los Angeles, California. He has published over 150 papers, book chapters, and books, among which are: *Handbook of the Psychology of Aging* (with K. W. Schaie); *The Psychology of Aging;* and "Health Behavior, and Aging" (with V. J. Renner) in *Proceedings,* Institut de la Vie, Paris (in press). Among the honors he has received are the Distinguished Scientific Contribution Award, American Psychological Association, 1968; the Gerontological Society Award for Meritorious Research, 1966; and the CIBA Foundation Award for Research on Problems of Aging, 1956. His primary research and teaching interests include: psychophysiology of aging; speed of behavior and aging; psychology of aging; and the psychology of adult development.

**William Bondareff,** M.D., Ph.D. (Chapter 4) is currently Professor of Anatomy at the Northwestern University Medical School, Chicago, Illinois. His numerous publications, concerned with the neurobiology of aging and neurocytology, have appeared in a variety of scientific journals. In 1965–1970 Dr. Bondareff received the NIH Career Development Award; and in 1967–1968 he received a Fulbright Award as a Visiting Scientist at the Institute of Neurobiology, Goteborg, Sweden.

**Irene Mortenson Burnside,** R.N., M.S. (Chapter 30) is currently a Research Associate in the Gerontological Nurse Specialist Program, San Jose State University, San Jose, California. In addition to numerous chapters in books and journal articles, she has edited three books— *Psychosocial Nursing Care of the Aged, Nursing and the Aged,* and *Working With the Elderly: Group Process and Techniques*—and has co-edited a fourth, *Psychosocial Caring Throughout the Life Span*. The honors she has received include the Meritorious Service Award, American Association of Homes for the Aging (1976), and the Lulu Hassenplug Award, California Nurses' Association (1979). Irene Burnside's interests in aging include psychosocial care of the elderly, short term education, and group work with the elderly.

**Gene D. Cohen,** M.D. (Chapter 41) is Chief of the Center for Studies of the Mental Health of the Aging at the National Institute of Mental Health. He is author of a number of publications and papers in the fields of Psychiatry and Aging, and is on the Editorial Board of "The Gerontologist." Dr. Cohen is a member of the Committee on Aging of the Group for the Advancement of Psy-

chiatry, and Vice-Chairman of the Council on Aging of the American Psychiatric Association. His main area of research is in clinical work with older people.

**Alex Comfort,** M.B., B.Ch. (Chapter 36) is a Fellow at the Institute for Higher Studies at Santa Barbara, California, and a Consultant in geriatric psychiatry at the Brentwood Veterans Administration Hospital, Los Angeles, California. His many publications cover a wide range of topics, from human sexuality to gerontology; and his primary research interests include gerontology, geriatric medicine, and human biology.

**Nan Corby,** Ph.D. (Chapter 37) is Research Assistant Professor, Leonard Davis School of Gerontology, and Academic Coordinator for Geriatric Medical Education, School of Medicine & Andrus Gerontology Center, University of Southern California, Los Angeles, California. Her publications include chapters on the unmarried aged and assertiveness training with the elderly. She has received an NIMH training grant for doctoral studies and the National Research Service Award for postdoctoral research in sex and aging. Dr. Corby's research, teaching, and consulting areas range from sex and aging to memory training, assertiveness training, clinical geropsychology, stress management, and long-term care.

**John M. Davis,** M.D. (Chapter 31) is Director of Research, Illinois State Psychiatric Institute, Professor of Psychiatry, University of Chicago, Chicago, Illinois. In addition to over 600 scientific papers, Dr. Davis has published several books, among which are, *Diagnosis and Drug Treatment of Psychiatric Disorders* (with D.F. Klein); *Practical Clinical Psychopharmacology* (with W.S. Appleton); and *Drug Treatment of Psychiatric Disorders*. A member of numerous editorial boards for professional journals, he has received the Taylor Manor Hospital Award, the Keese Prize, and has been a consultant to the President's Commission on Mental Health, the FDA, the AMA, and the National Commission on Marijuana and Drug Abuse. He has a strong clinical interest in better treatment for seriously disturbed mental patients; his major research interests are in psychiatric treatment, both using drugs effectively, understanding side effects, and avoiding misuse of drugs.

**David A. Drachman,** M. D. (Chapter 21) is Professor and Chairman, Department of Neurology, University of Massachusetts Medical Center, Worcester, Massachusetts. His publications focus particularly on the neurobiology of memory and dizziness. Among his papers are "The Central Cholinergic System and Memory" in *Psychopharmacology: A Generation of Progress* and "Dizziness and Disorders of Equilibrium" in *Cecil: Textbook of Medicine* (in press). Dr. Drachman does research on the neurology of aging; disorders of memory; dizziness and human spatial orientation; and computer diagnosis in neurologic disease.

**Maurice W. Dysken,** M.D. (Chapter 31) is a Research Associate at the Illinois State Psychiatric Institute, and a Research Associate (Assistant Professor of Psychiatry) at the University of Chicago, Chicago, Illinois. He has written numerous articles and chapters in journals and books, among which are, "Beta-adrenergic Receptor Function in Affective Illness" (with others) in *American Journal of Psychiatry;* "Clinical Usefulness of Sodium Amobarbital Interviewing" (with others) in *Archives of General Psychiatry;* and "Serial Postdexamethasone Cortisol Levels During ECT: A Case Study" (with others) in *American Journal of Psychiatry.* Dr. Dysken's major research interests are in the field of the psychopharmacology of antipsychotic drugs.

**Arthur V. Everitt,** Ph.D. (Chapter 5) is Associate Professor of Physiology, University of Sydney, New South Wales, Australia. He is the author or co-author of 51 research papers and 35 reviews and chapters in books, and he is the co-editor of the book *Hypothalamus, Pituitary and Aging.* Dr. Everitt is a Fellow of the Gerontological Society (Biological Sciences). His primary area of research is the role of hormones and nutrition in aging phenomena in the rat; and his major teaching field is endocrinology.

**Marjorie Fiske** (Chapter 15) directs the research and Doctoral program in Human Development and Aging at the University of California, San Francisco. She is special adviser of a book series and serves as consultant and Advisory Board member of several educational organizations. Among Professor Fiske's publications are, *Aging and Mental Disorder in San Francisco: A Social Psychiatric Study* (with others); *Four Stages of Life: A Comparative Study of Women and Men Facing Transitions* (with others); and *Middle Age: The Prime of Life?* She has received the Robert W. Kleemeier Award for Outstanding and Meritorious Contribution to Research in Aging. Her major theoretical and research interests are in stress and adaptation across the adult life course, and psychosocial change in relation to societal changes.

**H. Harris Funkenstein,** M.D. (Chapter 31), an Associate in Medicine (Neurology) and Chief, Cortical Function Laboratory, Peter Bent Brigham Hospital; Assistant Professor of Neurology, Harvard Medical School; Assistant Neurologist and Director, Learning Disabilities Clinic, Children's Hospital Medical Center; and Consultant in Neurology, Massachusetts Mental Health Center, Boston, Massachusetts. Dr. Funkenstein received a Rhodes Scholarship in 1961. His major research and teaching interests are in neuropsychology, especially acquired language disorders and attentional disorders; and neurology of behavior.

**Charles M. Gaitz,** M.D. (Chapter 40) is the Head of Patient Care Division and the Department of Applied Research, Texas Research Institute of Mental Sciences; and Clinical Professor of Psychiatry, Baylor College of Medicine, Houston, Texas. He has over 64 publications to his credit and is Past President of the Gerontological Society. He was a participant in the 1971 White House Conference on Aging, and Chairman of the Committee on Aging of the Group for the Advancement of Psychiatry. Dr. Gaitz is Director of the TRIMS training program in Geriatric Psychiatry and Psychology. His major areas of research are in the relationship of leisure and mental health; and clinical evaluation of drugs.

**K. Gunnar Götestam,** M.D., Ph.D. (Chapter 32) is Professor of Psychiatry, University of Trondheim, Institute of Psychiatry, Ostmarka Hospital, Trondheim, Norway. He has authored over 100 articles in professional journals and, in addition, has written, *Reinforcing Properties and Abuse Potential of Amphetamine Analogues; Drug Dependence and Behaviour Therapy; Aldrandets psyhiska sjukdomar* (Psychiatric Disturbances in the Elderly, in Swedish and in Norwegian). Dr. Götestam is a Member of the Royal Norwegians Society of Sciences and Letters. His major areas of research and teaching are in human drug addiction; evaluation of psychotherapy; environmental planning for the institutionalized elderly; biological psychiatry; alcohol and drug abuse; and clinical psychology.

**Barry J. Gurland,** M.D. (Chapter 28) is Director of the Columbia University Center for Geriatrics and Gerontology of the Faculty of Medicine, and Associate Professor of Clinical Psychiatry, Columbia University, New York; and Principal Investigator of the United States-United Kingdom Cross-National Project. He has published numerous scientific papers on psychiatric diagnosis and in the field of geriatrics. Dr. Gurland has served on several scientific and policy-making national committees on aging, and is a member of the Royal College of Physicians and the Royal College of Psychiatrists.

**David Gutmann,** Ph.D. (Chapter 18) is Chief, Division of Psychology; and Director, Older Adult Program, Northwestern University Medical School, Department of Psychiatry and Behavioral Sciences, Chicago, Illinois. Among his many publications are "Developmental Issues in the Masculine Mid-life Crisis" in the *Journal of Geriatric Psychiatry;* and "The Cross-Cultural Perspective: Notes Towards a Comparative Psychology of Aging" in *Handbook of the Psychology of Aging.* Dr. Gutmann is a Fellow, Society of the Sigma Xi, and a recipient of Career Development Award, Level II, NIMH, 1964-1974. His major areas of research and teaching are in the comparative (cross-cultural), developmental, and clinical psychology of middle and later life.

**Beni Habot,** M.D. (Chapter 29) is Head of the Geriatrics and Chronic Diseases Division of the Health Ministry of Israel, and Chief of Geriatrics and Geriatric Rehabilitation of the "ASSAF-HAROFEH" Hospital associated with Tel-Aviv University. His publications include "Cardiovascular Complications in Matched Pairs of Low and Normal Renin Hypertensive Patients" in *Israel Journal of Medical Sciences* (with others) and "Separating Cardiac from Pulmonary Dyspnea" (with V. Portnoi) in *Journal of the American Medical Association.* Dr. Habot was chosen as Chaim Sheba Prize Physical of the Year on 1975 (Israel). His primary research interests include the medico-psycho-socio-economic needs of the elderly in Israel; the etiology of nonarteriosclerotic dementia; and geriatric medicine.

**Margaret E. Hartford,** Ph.D. (Chapter 33) is Professor of Gerontology and Social Work, Leonard Davis School of Gerontology, Andrus Center; and the School of Social Work, University of Southern California, Los Angeles, California. Among her publications are, *Groups in Social Work; Social Processes in the Community or the Group* (with G. Coyle); "Changing Approaches to Social Work with Older Adults" (with others) in *Changing Roles in Social Work Practice.* Dr. Hartford has received the Dart Award for Innovative Teaching from the University of Southern California, and her main interests in research and teaching are in the use of education by gerontology practitioners; self-assessment in later years; and working with groups of elderly in the institutions and the community.

**Robert Hicks,** M.D. (Chapter 31) is Clinical Psychopharmacologist and Director of Research, Section on Geriatric Psychiatry, University of Texas Medical School at Houston. He wrote this chapter while Research Associate (Assistant Professor) at the Illinois State Psychiatric Institute and University of Chicago School of Medicine. He is also editor of the "Clinical Psychiatric Case Conferences" in the *Journal of Clinical Psychiatry.* In the last year he has written 13 articles or chapters on geriatric psychopharmacology and is working on a book on the subject.

**Chen Ya Huang,** M. Med. (Chapter 5) is a Consultant Neurologist at the Department of Neurology, Lidcombe Hospital, Lidcombe, New South Wales, Australia. His publications include: "Spinal Cord Tumors in the Elderly" in the *Australia and New Zealand Journal of Medicine;* "The Sympathetic Nervous System in Diabetic Neuropathy—A Clinical and Pathological Study" in *Brain;* and "The Confused Geriatric Patient" in *Proceedings of the Australian Association of Gerontology.* In 1979 Dr.

Huang received the M.B.E. (Member of the Order of the British Empire) from the Australian government. Geriatric neurology is his primary research focus.

**Lissy F. Jarvik,** M.D., Ph.D. (Chapter 6) is a professor in the Department of Psychiatry and Biobehavioral Sciences at the University of California, Los Angeles, and is Chief of the Psychogenetic Laboratory at the Brentwood Veterans Administration Medical Center. She is the author of many articles and has edited *Aging into the 21st Century* and co-edited *Psychiatric Symptoms and Cognitive Loss in the Elderly* and *Intellectual Functioning in Adults.* Dr. Jarvik is one of two appointed representatives of the American Gerontological Society to the International Association of Gerontology for 1978–1981 and a member of the Council on Aging of the American Psychiatric Association, 1979–1982. Her major areas of research are in the psychobiology and psychopathology of aging, with particular concern in genetics, psychopharmacology, cognitive and affective functioning in old age.

**Stanislav V. Kasl,** Ph.D. (Chapter 20) is Professor of Epidemiology, Yale University School of Medicine, New Haven, Connecticut. His many publications cover topics including: the effects of the work environment on mental and physical health; psychosocial factors associated with rheumatoid arthritis; effects of plant closing, job loss, and retirement; and the health effects of residential environments. Dr. Kasl has been a member of the Epidemiologic Studies Review Committee, NIMH, and the Epidemiology and Disease Control Study Section, NIH. Presently, his research interests are focused on "stress and disease," including the health and mental health effects of job loss, residential relocation, imprisonment, illness and death of a spouse, and mental health effects of residental environments.

**David W. K. Kay,** F.R.C.P., F.R.C. Psych. (Chapter 2) is a Professor of Psychiatry at the University of Tasmania in Australia. He has published papers on the mental disorders of old age, anorexia nervosa, the classification and treatment of affective disorders, and on the familial aspects of schizophrenia. Dr. Kay was awarded a Leverhulme Research Fellowship to study the genetics of psychoses. His major interests are in teaching and in epidemiological research.

**Frances S. Kobata** (Chapter 19) is Program Manager, Community Programs Division, Andrus Gerontology Center, University of Southern California, Los Angeles, California. Among her publications are, "The Influence of Culture: The Asian Experience" in *Aging Parents;* and "The Role of the Church as a National Support System" in *Retirement: Concepts and Realities.* Her major interests in research and teaching are in technical assistance and consultation with community organizations, and aging network in Program Planning/Development and Administration.

**M. Powell Lawton,** Ph.D. (Chapter 23) is the Director of Behavioral Research at the Philadelphia Geriatric Center, Philadelphia, Pennsylvania. In addition to many other publications, he is the author of *Planning and Managing Housing for the Elderly,* and *Environment and Aging.* Dr. Lawton is Past President of Division 20 of the American Psychological Association and Past Chair of the Behavioral and Social Sciences Section of the Gerontological Society. He has also received the Kesten Award from the Andrus Gerontology Center, University of Southern California (1978). The environmental psychology of later life, clinical geropsychology, and the assessment of wellbeing comprise Dr. Lawton's primary research interests.

**Leslie S. Libow,** M.D. (Chapter 29) is Medical Director, Jewish Institute for Geriatric Care at Long Island Jewish-Hillside Medical Center, Long Island, New York, and Professor of Medicine, School of Medicine, State University of New York at Stony Brook, New York. His publications include over 30 papers, and he is presently preparing a book on geriatric medicine. Dr. Libow is a Fellow of the American College of Physicians, and a Consultant to the Director of the National Institute on Aging. His primary research interest is geriatric medicine.

**Shirley A. Lockery,** M.S.W., M.P.A. (Chapter 19) is currently the recipient of a Council of Social Work Education Fellowship as a doctoral student in Social Work at the University of Southern California. From 1974 to 1978 she was on the faculty of the Center on Aging, School of Social Work at San Diego State University, and she coordinated three National Institutes on Minority Aging and was Associate and Assistant Editor of the Institute Proceedings. Her main area of research interest is minority aging and social welfare policy.

**Louis Lowy,** Ph.D. (Chapter 34) is Professor of Social Work and Associate Dean, School of Social Work, and member in the Department of Sociology, Boston University, Boston, Massachusetts. His numerous publications include seven books, among which are: *The Challenge and Promise of the Later Years: Social Work with the Aging* and *The Function of Social Work in a Changing Society.* Among the honors he has received are the distinguished Award for Outstanding Contribution in Social Work Education, National Association of Social Welfare (Massachusetts Chapter) and Boston University's Metcalf Award for Teaching-Scholar Excellence. Dr. Lowy's main research interests are in attitudes towards aging, delivery of service to the elderly, career choices, and curriculum design and development in general, and gerontology in particular.

**Steven S. Matsuyama,** Ph.D. (Chapter 6) is Research Geneticist, Brentwood Veterans Administration Medical Center, Los Angeles, California; and Assistant Research Geneticist, Department of Psychiatry and Biobehavioral Sciences, UCLA, Los Angeles, California. Among his publications are, "Chromosomes in Old Age: A Six-Year Longitudinal Study," (with others) in *Human-genetik;* "Immunoglobulin Levels and Intellectual Functioning in the Aged" (with others) in *Experimental Aging Research;* and "Hypodiploidy and Serum Immunoglobulin Concentrations in the Elderly" (with others) in *Mechanisms of Aging and Development.* His major areas of research are in chromosome changes with age in lymphocyte and glial cell cultures; the relationship between immunoglobulin levels and cognitive performance in the elderly; and effects of psychoactive agents on human chromosomes.

**Henry J. Michalewski,** Ph.D. (Chapter 8) is a Research Associate in Developmental Psychology at the Andrus Gerontology Center, University of Southern California, Los Angeles, California. His primary research interests include psychophysiology, brain (EEG) and behavior correlates of aging, and evoked potentials and aging.

**Edgar Miller,** Ph.D. (Chapter 22) is a Consultant Clinical Psychologist at Addenbrooke's Hospital, Cambridge, England. In addition to numerous papers and chapters dealing with dementia and other aspects of neuropsychology, Dr. Miller has written three books: *Clinical Neuropsychology; Clinical Aspects of Dementia* (with J. Pearce); and *Abnormal Aging.* He is primarily interested in clinical practice and in research in neuropsychology, especially into the behavioral aspects of dementia and the rehabilitation of patients with severe head injuries.

**Vincent Mor,** Ph.D. (Chapter 35) is Senior Research Scientist at Brookdale Institute for Gerontology and Adult Human Development in Jerusalem, Israel; and Senior Research Associate in the Department of Social Gerontological Research, Hebrew Rehabilitation Center for Aged, Boston, Massachusetts. He has co-authored a number of monographs and articles including *Transportation for the Institutionalized; A Recreational Therapeutic Need* (with I. Ginsberg); *Clinical Assessment of Interviewable Rhode Island State Mental Health Clients* (with others); and *The Impact of a Friendly Visitor Surveillance Program on Discharged Rehabilitation Patients* (with others). Dr. Mor's primary research and teaching interests are in the areas of the impact of social and rehabilitation programs on the lives of recipients; the development and psychometric testing of research instrumentation used for classifying clients with histories of psychiatric impairment; and alcoholism and long-term care.

**Sharon Y. Moriwaki,** Ph.D. (Chapter 19) is Assistant Director of the Hawaii Gerontology Center, Honolulu,

Hawaii. She has published over 15 papers, chapters, or monographs, such as "Ethnicity and Aging" in *Nursing and the Aged;* "The World of the Elderly Asian American" (with R.A. Kalish) in *Journal of Social Issues;* "Self-disclosure and Psychological Well-being in Old Age" in *Journal of Health and Social Behavior;* and "Self-destructive Crises in the Older Person" (with N. L. Faberow) in *Gerontologist.* Dr. Moriwaki received the National Institute of Child Health and Human Development Fellowship (1967—1971) and a Biomedical Sciences Support Grant, National Institutes of Health (1970—1971). Her research and teaching are focused on aging, mental health, ethnicity and aging, and services for, and service delivery to, Pacific Asian elderly.

**James A. Peterson,** Ph.D. (Chapter 38) is Director of the Emeriti Center, and Director of the Journey's End Foundation, University of Southern California, Los Angeles, California. His publications include a number of books, among which are: *An Introduction to Gerontology;* (with A. Schwartz) *Widows and Widowhood;* (with Michael Briley) *Love in the Later Years;* (with Barbara Payne) and *Marriage and Family Counseling: Perspective and Prospect.* Dr. Peterson was President of the American Association of Marriage Counselors; and his areas of primary research interest include housing for the elderly, the family, and the style of life of retired professors.

**Felix Post,** M.D., F.R.C.P., F.R.C. Psych. (Chapter 25) is Emeritus Physician, The Bethlem Royal Hospital and the Maudsley Hospital, London. He has published numerous papers and monographs, dealing primarily with the psychiatry of late life. Dr. Post was Secretary of the Geriatric Section of the World Psychiatric Association, and Chairman of the Section for the Psychiatry of Old Age of the Royal College of Psychiatrists. His teaching and research interests are centered on general psychiatry, with special interest in the problems of late life.

**Pauline K. Ragan,** Ph.D. (Chapter 16) is the Laboratory Chief for Social Organization and Behavior, Andrus Gerontology Center; and Research Associate Professor, Leonard Davis School of Gerontology, University of Southern California, Los Angeles, California. Her main areas of teaching and research interest are sociology of aging, work and retirement, law and aging, and research methodology.

**Richard W. Redick,** Ph.D. (Chapter 3) currently doing private consultation work. From 1969 to 1977 he was Assistant Chief of the Survey and Reports Branch, Division of Biometry and Epidemiology, National Institute of Mental Health, and he served as Acting Chief from 1977 to 1978. Dr. Redick has authored or co-authored over 50 publications; among them are: "Epidemiology of Mental Illness and Utilization of Psychiatric Facilities Among Older Persons" in *Mental Illness in Later Life;* "Patterns of Use of Psychiatric Facilities by the Aged" in *Psychology of Adult Development and Aging;* "A Quarter Century of Psychiatric Care, 1950–1974" in *Hospital and Community Psychiatry;* and a series of government publications dealing with utilization of psychiatric facilities and mental health resources. Dr. Redicks' major research and consulting interests are in needs assessment for mental health services; demographic aspects of the aged; mental health needs of children, adolescents, and the aged; and urban ecology.

**V. Jayne Renner,** Ph.D. (Chapters 1, 14) is a Postdoctoral Fellow in the Department of Pharmacology, School of Medicine, University of Southern California, Los Angeles, California. Her publications include "Developments in Research on the Biological and Behavioral Aspects of Aging and Their Implications" (with J. E. Birren) in *Care of the Elderly;* "Research on the Psychology of Aging: Principles and Experimentation" (with J. E. Birren) in *Handbook of the Psychology of Aging;* and "Objectives and New Directions in the Study of Stress, Disease and Aging" (in press). Dr. Renner's research is focused on the biochemistry and psychology of stress.

**Sarah Rosenfield,** Ph.D. (Chapter 20) is a postdoctoral fellow in epidemiology at Yale University, New Haven, Connecticut. Her major research areas include social psychiatry, sex roles, and social psychology.

**Ronald E. Saul,** M.D. (Chapter 8) is Director of the NeuroBehavior Unit and Chief of the EEG Laboratory, Rancho Los Amigos Hospital, Downey, California; and Associate Professor of Clinical Neurology, University of Southern California, Los Angeles, California. His publications include: "Evoked Potential Correlates of Information Processing in Commissurotomy Patients" in *Cerebral Localization;* "CNS Arousal Level in MBD Children" in *Psychopharmacology of Childhood;* and "Age Differences in Cortical Evoked Potentials" in Senile Dementia: *A Biomedical Approach.* Dr. Saul was an Examiner for the American Board of Neurology and Psychiatry in 1974 and 1978. His primary research interests include aphasia and related higher function disorders, and electroencephalographic and behavioral studies.

**K. Warner Schaie,** Ph.D. (Chapter 12) is Professor of Psychology and Director, Gerontology Research Institute, Ethel Percy Andrus Gerontology Center, University of Southern California, Los Angeles, California. In addition to over one hundred chapters and articles in professional books and journals, Dr. Schaie has published five books, among which are: *Theories and Methods of Research on Aging; Life-span Developmental Psychology* (with P. B. Baltes); and *Handbook of the Psychology of Aging* (with J. E. Birren). He is past President of the Division of Adult Development and Aging, American Psychological Association; past Chair, Developmental Behavioral Sciences Study Section, Division of Research Grants, NIH. Dr. Schaie's primary research interests are in cognitive development across the adult lifespan; methodological issues in developmental psychology; and psychological test construction.

**A. E. David Schonfield** (Chapter 10) is Professor of Psychology at the University of Calgary, Calgary, Alberta, Canada. He has over 70 publications, among which are: "Memory Changes with Age" in *Nature;* "Mental Health and the Elderly" in *Mental Health in Alberta;* "Age Limitation of Perceptual Span" in *Nature;* and "Retirement and the Commitment to Activity—Motivation" in *Functional Disorders of Memory.* Dr. Schonfield's honors include the Province of Alberta Achievement Award and the Queen's Jubilee Medal (Canada); and he is First Vice President of the Canadian Association on Gerontology. His main areas of research and teaching interests are in age differences in learning and remembering, industrial retraining, and values.

**Sylvia Sherwood,** Ph.D. (Chapter 35) is Director of Social Gerontological Research, Hebrew Rehabilitation Center for the Aged, Boston, Massachusetts; and Clinical Professor of Community Health Research at the Brown University Program in Medicine. She has authored or co-authored several chapters and monographs, among which are, "Sociological Aspects of Learning and Memory" in *Experimental Studies in Adult Learning and Memory;* "A Multivariate Non-Randomized Matching Technique for Studying the Impact of Social Interventions" (with others) in *Handbook of Evaluation Research;* and "Institutions for Adults" in *Encyclopedia of Social Work.* Dr. Sherwood is Associate Editor of *Aging and Human Development,* and was a co-editor of *Research Planning and Action for the Elderly.* The major focus of her research is on the impact of alternatives of long-term care on the quality of life of different types of elderly populations.

**Alexander Simon,** M.D. (Chapter 27) is Professor of Psychiatry emeritus at the School of Medicine, University of California, San Francisco, California. His many publications cover a wide range of areas, from the comparative roles of physical health and social, economic, and psychological factors in the development of emotional and mental disturbances in the elderly, to the care and treatment of the aged mentally ill. Dr. Simon was the Director of The Langley Porter Neuropsychiatric Institute from 1956 to 1974; a delegate to the White House Conferences on Aging in 1961 and 1971; received the Royer Award for outstanding contributions in the field of psychiatry (San Francisco, 1968); and was President of the Western Gerontological Society (1968–1969). His research is centered on geriatric psychiatry and mental

illness in the aged, especially diagnosis, assessment, treatment, and care-giving services to the aged.

**R. Bruce Sloane,** M.D. (Chapter 24) is Professor and Chairman of the Department of Psychiatry and the Behavioral Sciences, University of Southern California School of Medicine, Los Angeles, California. He has published numerous articles and four books on outcome of treatment, especially psychotherapy and correlations of physiological, biochemical, and psychological parameters with behavior; and psychiatric problems of the aged. He has been a Fulbright Travelling Fellow, and a Nuffield Visiting Scientist to the Medical Research Council of Great Britain. He received a Foundations' Fund for Research in Psychiatry Senior Fellowship and was a Visiting Professor at the Universities of London and Cambridge in England in 1978/79. There he studied geriatric and psychogeriatric research and clinical programs, with particular emphasis on dementia. He is presently Chairman of the American Psychiatric Association Council of Aging's Task Force on Fellowships and Career Development in Geriatric Psychiatry.

**Robert. L. Solnick,** Ph.D. (Chapter 37) is presently a clinical psychologist with the La Paz Psychological Group in Mission Viejo, California. His publications include *Sexuality and Aging,* which he edited. Dr. Solnick's main areas of teaching and research interests are with the changing male sexual responsiveness with age, and human sexuality and sexual dysfunction with an emphasis on age factors.

**Asser Stenback,** M.D. (Chapter 26) is Professor of Psychiatry (retired) at the University of Helsinki, Finland. Since 1979 he has been a member of the Parliament in Finland. He served as President of the Finnish Psychiatric Association from 1958 to 1965, and was President of the Scandinavian Psychiatric Committee from 1965 to 1969. Since 1966 he has been a member of the Section of Geriatric Psychiatry of the World Psychiatric Association. Dr. Stenback's main areas of research interests are psychosomatics, depression, and aging,

**Carl A. Taube,** (Chapter 3) is Deputy Director, Division of Biometry and Epidemiology, National Institute of Mental Health. His publications include numerous reports issued by the Department of Health, Education, and Welfare, as well as book chapters and articles in professional journals. Studies of the mental health delivery system are his primary research interests.

**Hans Thomae,** Ph.D. (Chapter 13) is Professor of Psychology at the University of Bonn, Bonn, Federal Republic of Germany. Among his more than 150 publications are: *Patterns of Aging. Findings from the Bonn Longitudinal Study on Aging; Psychologie in der modernen*

*Gesellschaft; Konflikt, Entscheidung, Verantwortung;* and *Das Individuum and seine Welt. Eine Personlichkeitstheorie.* Dr. Thomae served as Scientific Director of the Bonn Longitudinal Study on Aging (1964–1977), and his research is centered on personality and motivation.

**Larry W. Thompson,** Ph.D. (Chapter 8) is Professor of Psychology, Department of Psychology, and Director of the Adult Counseling Center, Andrus Gerontology Center, University of Southern California, Los Angeles, California. His primary research interests are the psychosocial treatment of depression in the elderly and the EEG correlates of aging.

**Judith Treas,** Ph.D. (Chapter 17) is Assistant Professor of Sociology at the University of Southern California, Los Angeles, California. Her publications include "Family Support Systems for the Aged: Some Social and Demographic Considerations" in *The Gerontologist;* "The Occupational and Marital Mobility of Women" (with A. Tyree) in *American Sociological Review;* and "Socialist Organization and Economic Development in China: Latent Consequences for the Aged" in *The Gerontologist.* She is Book Review Editor of *Sociology and Social Research* and since 1978 has been a member of the Editorial Board of *The Gerontologist.* Dr. Treas's primary research interests include sociology of aging, population, family, and statistics.

**Roy V. Varner,** M.D. (Chapter 40) is Chief, Geriatric Services, Texas Research Institute of Mental Sciences, Texas Medical Center, Houston, Texas. Among his publications are, "The Training of Psychogeriatricians" (with A. Verwoerdt) in *Perspectives in the Psychiatry of Old Age;* "Clinical Assessment, Expectations, and Total Management of Organic Brain Syndromes in the Elderly" in *Southern Medicine;* "Pharmacotherapy of Age-Associated Brain Syndromes" (with C.M. Gaitz) in *Interdisciplinary Topics in Gerontology.* Dr. Varner is Clinical Assistant Professor of Psychiatry, University of Texas Medical School at Houston and is on the Psychiatric Consulting Staff of St. Anthony Center, Houston. His major area of research is in geriatric psychopharmacology.

**Jeffrey B. Wales,** Ph.D. (Chapter 16) is Director of Research and Evaluation for the Palliative Treatment Program at the Veteran's Administration's Wadsworth Medical Center in Los Angeles, California. His publications include: "Ethical and Legal Issues of Preretirement Counselling" in *Policy Issues in Aging, Work and Retirement;* "Recent Legislative Trends Toward Protection of Human Subjects: Implications for Gerontologists" (with D.L. Treybig) in *The Gerontologist;* and "Sexuality in Middle and Old Age: A Critical Review of the Literature" in *Case Western Reserve Journal of Sociology.* Dr. Wales received a Traineeship in Gerontology from the National

Institute of Aging (1972–1976). His major research interests are in the long term care of the aged, in health care services evaluation, and in the sociology of age.

**A. T. Welford,** Sc.D. (Chapter 9) is a Fellow of the Academy of Social Sciences in Australia, the British and Australian Psychological Societies, the Ergonomics Society of Australia and New Zealand, and the Gerontological Society. He is also an Honorary Member and Founder Member of the Ergonomics Society and was the first editor of its journal, *Ergonomics.* Dr. Welford's publications include *Ergonomics of Automation; Fundamentals of Skill; Christianity: a Psychologist's Translation;* and *Skilled Performance: Perceptual and Motor Skills.* Among the awards he has received are the Kenneth Craik Award for Physiological Psychology, the Vernon Prize for Applied Psychology, and he was Williams Lecturer to the Royal College of Physicians of London. From 1968 until his retirement in 1979, he was Professor of Psychology at the University of Adelaide.

**William M. Whelihan,** Ph.D. (Chapter 23) is Chief Clinical Research Psychologist at the Philadelphia Geriatric Center, Philadelphia, Pennsylvania. His recent publications include: "Levodopa and Psychometric Test Performance in Parkinsonism—Five Years Later" (with M. Riklan and T. Cullinan) in *Neurology;* "Psychological Assessment in Geriatric Settings" in *Proceedings of the Annual Meeting of the National Association of Jewish Homes for the Aged;* and "Geriatric Psychotherapy: A New Frontier" (with J. K. Belsky) *Perspectives on Aging.* Neuropsychology, life-span developmental psychology, and clinical geropsychology are Dr. Whelihan's major research interests.

**Blossom T. Wigdor,** Ph.D. (Chapter 11) is Director of the Programme in Gerontology and Associate Professor of Psychology, University of Toronto, Toronto, Ontario, Canada. Among her publications are *Recent Advances in Behaviour Change* and *Canadian Gerontological Collection I. Selected Papers, 1977.* Dr. Wigdor was appointed for two terms to the Science Council of Canada (beginning in 1973). Among her research interests are: intellectual, cognitive, and memory changes with age; and investigation of the relationship between behavior (especially coping styles) and health.

**Robert Allen Wiswell,** Ph.D. (Chapter 39) is an Assistant Professor of Physical Education and a Research Associate, Andrus Gerontology Center, University of Southern California, Los Angeles, California. He has published in the areas of aging and physical performance, exercise in preventive medicine, and cardiopulmonary physiology. His teaching interests include developmental physiology and aging; physiology, nutrition, and aging; respiratory physiology; and research design and statistics.

# Handbook
# of Mental Health
# and Aging

# I
# Background

# 1

# Concepts and Issues
# of Mental Health
# and Aging

*James E. Birren & V. Jayne Renner*

Despite the fact that our knowledge about the biological, psychological, and social processes associated with growing old has greatly increased, particularly in the last twenty years, and despite the surge of publications in the field, our understanding of the mental health problems of aging remains diffuse, particulate, and uncoordinated. Thus, the purpose of this chapter is to present the issues and concepts which are central to the topic of mental health and aging.

This chapter will first trace some of the historical origins and developing conceptual bases of mental health and aging. Since the aged in contemporary, technologically developed societies are often thought to be particularly alienated and normless, a section of our discussion is devoted to these topics. Morale of the aged is next discussed in terms of socialization and life styles. A perspec-

tive is then presented on maturity and integration of life experiences. Finally, implications are drawn for the training of mental health professionals.

The emergence of the field of mental health and aging has been slow. Until now the field has not been well charted, but increased activity at all levels can be expected, in research, theory, training, and in the demand for and provision of professional services to the middle-aged and older adult. If the increasing number (in the millions) of older adults does not in itself lead to increased mental health services, then at least the growing advocacy by retired and older adults will result in them being given a greater share of professional attention. The facts from epidemiological surveys will be discussed later.

Mankind seemingly has always looked forward to having labor lightened and years added in which to look back upon life, to interpret and integrate experiences, and to do this with peace of mind. Now with our physical labor indeed made lighter by machines and with our lives extended, more thought needs to be given to making old age the best gift of life, a significant vein of thought to which the field of mental health should contribute. The survival of a large number of persons to old age is a contribution of twentieth century technological society.

A long life offers the proving ground for the significance of events, decisions, and activities. The lives of people range from the most abject to ones which show such exemplary qualities that they become models for the aspirations of others and set higher expectations for the quality of all lives. The subject matter of mental health and aging embraces both the highs and lows of human existence. It encompasses full health or crippling and terminal disease; vivacity and buoyance of mood or depression; inviting conviviality or loneliness and alienation. Large numbers of older persons do go over the hurdles of life and through the separating sieves of experience in such ways as to experience the later years of life as a satisfying present with an anticipated tomorrow.

As has been the case with society as a whole, there has been a "youth centered" quality to the mental health movement, with major concepts arising for the most part from close study of the neonate and his subsequent career through the school years to late adolescence. To overcome this chronological handicap the "culture" of mental health research must become more cumulative so that data are conserved and passed on to other investigators. A task of the new generation of investigators is to remain sensitive to long-term effects, particularly to sleeper effects wherein some feature regarded as positive for early development may turn out to have deleterious effects later in life. These matters are not trivial either practically or scientifically, but they are very difficult to examine due to the fact that the span of years over which to judge or measure the consequences of events is so great.

There has not been much activity on the part of universities, medical schools, professional and scientific organizations and other responsible groups that enables one to write a complimentary picture of the past. Our educational institutions are extensions of the values of society, and if old age is repressed or denied in society we should perhaps not be surprised that our teaching institutions and research laboratories have not given the subject a high priority. With the maturing of America it may

be hoped that our institutions will come to embrace what is now a long second half of life. In so doing, there may be a renaissance of views about the nature of the human life cycle.

## CONCEPTS OF AGING

The concepts of *aging* and of *mental health* belong to a group of broad and significant concepts with which modern man is concerned. Although the concept of aging is partly a product of recent scientific advances, it also incorporates ideas about old age from antiquity. Aging refers to processes of change in organisms which occur after maturity, whereas old age refers to the last phase of life about which mankind has thought for centuries.

The definition of aging favored by the authors is:

> Aging refers to the regular changes that occur in mature genetically representative organisms living under representative environmental conditions as they advance in chronological age (Birren and Renner, 1977, p. 4).

This definition allows for expansion of function with age as well as decrement. More narrow biological definitions characteristically focus on limitation of function. Examples of such definitions are: "Senescence is a change in the behaviour of the organism with age, which leads to a decreased power of survival and adjustment" (Comfort, 1956, p. 190), and "aging is the deterioration of a mature organism resulting from time-dependent, essentially irreversible changes intrinsic to all members of a species, such that with the passage of time, they become increasingly unable to cope with the stresses of the environment, thereby increasing the probability of death" (Handler, 1960, p. 200).

Not all aspects of the human organism are necessarily in close synchrony in the processes of aging. While an individual may be declining physically in the later years, he may show an expansion in the psychological domain. Therefore, in describing an individual it may be useful to distinguish three ages: *biological age*, referring to life expectancy; *psychological age*, referring to the adaptive behavioral capacities of the individual; and *social age*, referring to the social roles of an individual with regard to the expectations of his group and society for someone of his age (Birren and Renner, 1977, p. 5). Clearly these "ages of mankind" interact and the processes must to some extent be interdependent but, within limits, one may be old in body and young in spirit. Such interactions as well as the relative autonomy of functions form an important part of the subject matter of mental health and aging.

## HISTORICAL BACKGROUND OF CONCEPTS OF AGING

Thoughts about aging become closely linked with thoughts about immortality. Evidence for this is found in Gruman's (1966) review of the history of ideas about longevity and ways of extending the life span prior to 1800. Age, death, and immortality have been linked in legends and myths throughout history. For Gruman, "at the very dawn of history, man is seen struggling with the problem of death. Two basic attitudes come to the fore—rebellion or submission . . ." (1966, p. 11). One of the earliest pieces of literature, the epic of Gilgamesh, appears to go back to around 3000 B.C. In this Babylonian poem, the hero becomes obsessed with the thought of immortal life and finding the secret to its possession.

Legends about death and immortality are still active today in our cultural heritage and they influence the related topic of growing older. It is remarkable that the legends of *healing waters* or *curing fountains* have been found in the literatures of many people and still seem alive in the appeal of water spas today. There is also the "antediluvian" theme that people lived longer in the past and perhaps lost the secret when they fell from grace. Another theme suggests that there are people living in remote parts of the world who are very long-lived. The elements of such myths live on and are found in contemporary thought about aging.

Gruman (1966) wisely divides his history of ideas about the length of life at the year 1800. It is in the 1800s when modern experimental science begins to make older ideas testable, that a systematic sorting out of myth and fact about aging could begin. Early thought emphasized the replacement of lost characteristics. Thus, if an old animal became cold in the process of dying, one might rejuvenate it by introducing heat.

In the last century one of the pioneers of objective thought about aging was Quetelet, who published his book *Man and the Development of his Faculties* (*Sur l'homme et le développement de ses facultés*) in 1835. This book had a major impact on thinking and put the life span of man in a natural science context. It is not until the twentieth century that one finds systematic development of research and theory about aging, although there is still perhaps

no other contemporary field of inquiry where subjectivity is so dominant.

The publication of Cowdry's *Problems of Ageng* (1939) ushered in the modern period of thought about aging. The volume was a multiscientific and multiprofessional view of the processes of aging covering a wide range of topics, from plants, through insects and vertebrates, to the aging of mankind in society. The book reflected an interdisciplinary approach, which came shortly thereafter, to characterize the mental health movement (United States Public Health Service, 1943). The history of modern psychological concepts of aging was reviewed by Birren in 1961. Many of these ideas from history form the substrate of much of our thinking about aging and mental health.

## CONCEPTS OF MENTAL HEALTH

### ORIGIN OF CONCEPTS OF MENTAL HEALTH

In America, since the late 1940s when the National Institute of Mental Health was founded, the term *mental health* became commonplace, both in professional literature and in daily speech. The earlier term used to refer to the same general subject was *mental hygiene*. The term mental health is much broader than mental hygiene and presumably not only embraces the absence of mental illness, difficulties, and frustrations, but also reflects the ability or capacity of an individual to deal with the issues of life in an effective, if not pleasurable or satisfying, manner.

There have been relatively few students of human development who viewed the life span. Most of our concepts of the mental health of the elderly are rooted in common sense and have found expression in the intuitions and wisdom that come from the cumulated experiences of an observant person, e.g., an old farmer or a country doctor. As a consequence, present concepts of life span mental health are more often bound to metaphor than to data. As the field of mental health proceeds toward increasing sophistication it will become more data-oriented, but *en route* society need not throw away its cultural intelligence about what is good for people and what makes for the good life throughout the life span. Since older adults are more likely than young persons to have physical illness, the interweaving of physical and mental problems is a greater conceptual, as well as a practical, problem in the later years.

There are roughly four components in our concept of mental health:

1. presence or absence of mental disease,
2. presence or absence of deficits or limitations in behavior,
3. the satisfaction or contentment that is derived from one's life as it is lived or has been lived,
4. some approximation to an ideal person.

Measuring up to a personal and to a cultural yardstick also enters into consideration. Judgments cannot be made about mental health without taking into account the cultural background and current environment of the individual.

*Cultural Relativism.* Early discussions of mental health gave rise to the concept of cultural relativism, the idea that cultures differ in the approved manner of expressing aggression and in their use of the symbols for acceptance and reverence. For example, differences in culture make it particularly difficult for older immigrants who leave their country of origin and spend their later adult years in a foreign country. The extent to which the later years have been ignored is shown by a book on the problems of relativism and culture in mental disease which does not even mention older adults as an issue in cultural relativism (Soddy, 1961).

Different cultures place different stresses on the individual in kind, quantity, and quality. The content of the symbol system in different cultures varies, something immigrants must learn to keep in mind as they grow old in foreign countries. The range of tolerated expression and the kind and degree of repression also varies, as does the cultural tolerance and acceptance of deviation from norms. The problems of cultural differences are especially important in a country like America where immigrants, as they grow old, may have few ties with reference groups either here or in their countries of origin. Ethnic identity thus seems to present special problems for older adults in a pluralistic society.

## COMPONENTS AND CRITERIA OF MENTAL HEALTH

Problems arise when we consider "normality" as the single criterion of mental health, since what is regarded as acceptable or unacceptably deviant behavior changes with time. Using a yardstick of normality encompasses four different things.

1. It is a statistical concept expressing the mean or central tendency of a group.

2. It is an imagined or believed frequency of the statistical type which amounts to social value opinions.
3. It is the functioning morality, ethical standards and social customs governing group life, or the ideas of conforming behavior; that is, that behavior which is acceptable to society.
4. It is biologically typical of the species or within typical physiological limits with respect to age.

Thus, if we use normality in any definition of mental health, there is the problem of choosing which of these criteria we will use. Those people who present behavior patterns which deviate from those which are common in a society often seek or are sent for therapy; homosexuality is a case in point.

Good adjustment as a criterion of mental health presents difficulties by also requiring that the situational context of the individual be taken into account. In western society, *happiness* is often thought of as an aspect of mental health, as though one could not be judged to be mentally healthy if one were not happy. There are difficulties when defining mental health in terms of a state of well-being, such as happiness, contentment, efficiency, satisfaction or sense of achievement. Such states are difficult to assess and they fluctuate according to the situation. They even fluctuate according to age (Campbell, 1976). This is not to deny that happiness and related moods may not be necessary and desirable consequences of good mental health, but so also may be pain, sadness, and unhappiness, and the ability to deal with such states. Williams (1972) makes the following relevant comments:

> There is a danger in confusing the mental disorders with suffering and mental health with happiness. A person who is clinically depressed is unhappy and suffers. But one can be unhappy and suffer without being clinically depressed, and, indeed, without any impairment in the capacity to act within the confines of one's natural abilities (p. 4).

Loss of parents, spouse, and friends from death become unavoidable as we grow old; the pain of bereavement is a natural emotion. Such suffering may or may not result in clinical depression. The question with respect to mental health then becomes, how does a mentally healthy person, without becoming clinically depressed, cope with bereavement?

There appears to be an implicit hierarchy of components, none of which alone provides the necessary and sufficient condition for good mental health; one seems to move from somatic factors, through levels of emotions and cognition, and ultimately to some philosophical or spiritual level.

While we have begun operationalizing our concepts of mental health in mature and older adults, measurement is difficult, as the chapters of this book illustrate, and agreement on the components is far from established. For example, adaptability or flexibility appears to be a reasonable component of good mental health, but under what circumstances is adaptation to be exercised? Complying with brainwashing as a captured prisoner, avoiding death and coping with religious persecution by feigning conversion, joining or not joining communal religious groups, or committing acts of violence against non-involved people on the basis of a political rationalization are matters of adaptation, but they may carry negative implications.

## CONCEPTS AND CRITERIA OF POSITIVE MENTAL HEALTH

Jahoda (1958) has been widely quoted for her attempts to identify the positive features of mental health. Her six criteria of positive mental health were:

1. positive self-attitudes,
2. growth and self-actualization,
3. integration of the personality,
4. autonomy,
5. reality perception, and
6. environmental mastery.

In the pursuit of the signs of positive mental health, Jahoda suggested the following principles:

1. The idea of any single criterion of mental health should be abandoned. Good mental health cannot be confined to a single concept and a single item of behavior.
2. The terms we use to define mental health may seem to be abstract, but they should be reduced to definite operational procedures and there is a need to have scales and measures for each criterion.
3. Each of the criteria should be thought of as a continuum or as continua since there are unhealthy trends for otherwise healthy persons.
4. These criteria of mental health should operate at any point in time to define the state of the individual, or they can be thought of as indicative of trends in the individual toward health or disease. Implicit in the criteria is the concept of gradients of mental health.
5. The criteria are regarded as relatively enduring attributes of the person. They are not merely functions of a particular situation in which the individual may find himself.

6. The criteria are set up as the optimum of mental health. They are not to be regarded as absolute and the minimum standard for any individual to achieve has yet to be determined and may change with age.

Each individual has limits and no one reaches the ideal in all the criteria. However, the assumption is made that most people can approach the optima. Below a yet-to-be-determined minima, most, if not all, people will have some mental illness.

Because of difficulties experienced in measuring the prevalence of mental ill health in the United States, a symposium was organized by the National Center for Health Statistics in 1966 (Sells, 1968). A wide range of scholars were represented in the symposium, from such fields as psychiatry, psychology, sociology, biometry and epidemiology. The conclusion to the symposium is pertinent to the present volume: "Our conclusion rejects preemption of the field by any one discipline and views the definition of mental health in a broader reference . . . The range of human effectiveness defines the content of mental health in our contemporary dynamic society and the perspective in which it is most appropriately measured" (Sells, 1968, p. 267). Although attention was given to issues which concerned the mental health of children, no parallel consideration was given to the concerns of adult mental health in the second half of life. While much of what was presented in the symposium about the concepts of mental health, mental illness, and about the relationships of mental health and illness, has relevance to older adults, the lack of attention to the issues of aging is to be regretted. The conceptual dichotomies which were discussed—health and illness, competence and incompetence, and intrapsychic and interpersonal processes—seem, in the minds of the present authors, to have rather different implications for older adults in which there can be many coexisting features.

Lurking behind these concepts of mental health is the implicit idea of maximizing the potentials of the individual in relation to abilities, resources, and the demands of the group with regard to social customs and conforming behavior if not ethical standards. One of the heritages from the study of children is the tendency to regard adults as passing through stages. The idea of stages in development is attractive and draws its plausibility from the clearly physical transitions that an organism undergoes in maturation, e.g., puberty. Successful biological, social, and psychological transitions presumably equip the individual to move forward into the next stage. This approach to individual development suggests a trajectory which involves continuous personal growth and self-actualization. By this process the individual becomes increasingly more self-determined and autonomous. Moving forward implies that the individual has a sense of identity and an acceptance of self so that the ambiguities of the future can be negotiated with a sense of security and optimism.

The competent older adult was described by Goldfarb (1974, p. 823) as follows:

> The well–adjusted aged appear to have carried into late life the capacity to gain gratifications, to relieve their tensions—both the biologically determined and those acquired through enculturation and life experience—so as to maintain their self-esteem, self-confidence, purposivity, and a satisfying sense of personal identity and social role despite losses that may occur with aging. This differs from the maladjusted who, either because of earlier influences upon their personality development or differences in life experience at whatever age, do not have the resources to deal constructively and efficiently with life problems.

Erikson (1959) has described the middle and later years of life in terms of stages which have definite goals. The goal of middle age is to develop generativity or expand productively and creatively, and to identify with a goal of making contributions to the future. In the last stage of life, the goal according to Erikson is to resolve the problem of attaining ego integrity; that is, if the individual cannot accept his life as it has been lived as being appropriate, worthwhile, and meaningful, the result will be despair, depression, bitterness, and fear.The delineation of stages of adult life and the characterization of their origin in biological, psychological, and social processes has not been researched seriously or with credibility, since the approach largely borrows from studies of development in children and varies with the theorist.

Negotiating the expected and unexpected issues of life implies some notion of competence. White (1959) introduced the concept of competence in which the effective adjustment of the individual requires some ability to manipulate, control, and interact with one's environment and interpersonal relationships. Symonds (1949) used the term ego development or effective intelligence which closely parallels White's idea of competence. For Symonds a mentally healthy person has learned to apply his intelligence to problems of living and to deal efficiently with issues of work, deriving at the same time feelings of life satisfaction. It is apparent in all of these concepts that the individual is viewed as an organism adapting to changing in-

ternal needs and a changing environment. The term developmental tasks is commonly used to refer to the characteristic demands which his environment makes on a developing child. This term is equally appropriate to apply to the middle-aged and older adult; however, the nature of the major tasks differ with age. For example, one of the important developmental tasks of the later years is to integrate one's life experiences (Birren,1964; Birren and Renner, in press; Bühler and Massarik, 1968; Butler, 1963; Erikson, 1959; Hall, 1922; Jung, 1962). To regard mental health in the later years as being only a projection of the issues of youth misses the point that aging is a moving toward something, not just a moving away from the period of youth.

Adapting to developmental tasks requires that there be an active dialogue going on within the individual involving the various parts of the self, including an awareness of the needs of the body. Such a dialogue within the self might have been called by Riegel a dialectic exchange. For Riegel, the pattern of dialectical reasoning was the highest stage of cognitive development (1973). The concept has some appeal in the present discussion of mental health since dialectical reasoning involves a process of change where one reasons between the opposing positions and demands of interacting forces.

It is too early to say whether the concept of dialectical reasoning will prove to be a useful bridge between areas of research on mental health, cognition, ego development, and personality structure and needs. One would presume that individuals who use a form of dialectical reasoning about the self will have better mental health than those who, in the sense of Riegel (1973), use more primitive forms of reasoning for decision making. The dialectical reasoning of the older person must involve levels other than the one used to deal with information. The decision to move one's place of residence is not only a rational decision to maximize certain physical and social exchanges, but since a long-term residence has considerable emotional and symbolic value it also represents a decision of affect. What is rationally desirable on the surface may in fact be undesirable if the emotional attachments of the older individual are considered.

*Opportunities for Positive Mental Health.* One of the newer criteria used to judge mental health in the later years is the measure of the extent to which an individual takes advantage of environmental opportunities. It is an often overlooked fact that the later years of life offer the individual new opportunities for satisfaction and fulfillment. For example, since older adults have fewer obligations to other persons they are in a position to relate to people in terms of choice rather than the more demanding obligatory relationships that follow from the roles of active middle years. Also, for the older adult there is more opportunity to act with impunity in the sense that one does not have to maintain a social facade or front as is often required during the competitive work years. The older adult may also try new things, since his social risks may now be smaller. Old age may bring the opportunity to be more self-directed, since older adults can have the opportunity to select interactions with friends and relatives for their own sake, and to engage in new activities because of their direct or intrinsic properties, rather than for some competitive or indirect gain. Admittedly, not every older person is surrounded by such opportunities, but for some this can be a period of relative decompression from obligatory behaviors and roles. The negative images of old age suggest restricted opportunities, life is over, or that the individual has "had it," and contrast with the view of later life as an opportunity for new experiences.

Unfortunately, many individuals cannot take advantage of the opportunities of the later years to engage in activities for their own sake, and to achieve a greater degree of personal integration and self-realization. There are those with developmental arrests in which their goals, motivations, and emotional responses are oriented to an earlier period of life. They may be unduly fixated upon a competitive work model and may be unaware that they are not using their economic returns for any particular personal advantage. An important element of mental health in later life is having the flexibility to take advantage of opportunities for new learning in the major areas of skills, emotions, and interpersonal relationships.

*Internal–External View of Mental Health.* Another dimension in the complex equation of mental health in the later years is that of the internal and external costs of the pattern of behavior. If, for example, there has been a wide separation between the ideal to which the individual has aspired and his concept of his actual self, the individual will often be in a tense and unstable position. Thus the degree of internal stress that the individual lives with is an aspect of mental health, as is the degree of morale or life satisfaction. For the individual who is relatively unaware and unskilled in the management of his own anger and anxiety, the cost may be social isolation from other persons. Or, as the longitudinal study of Wigdor and Morris (1977) suggests, the cost to depressed persons may

be a high incidence of somatic disease. A paradox exists, however, for unlike the depressives, paranoid individuals were found to have relatively greater freedom from somatic disease (Wigdor and Morris, 1977). Paranoid individuals remain highly isolated from neighbors and relatives since they are fairly difficult people to deal with socially in view of their constant projection of anger. They may present late-life problems to themselves other than those involving their somatic health (Post, 1966).

Thus, an aspect of mental health of the older person relates to his effectiveness in interpersonal relationships. Some older adults remain attractive to both their peers and to younger adults. They are sought after because they may raise the self-esteem of other persons who are in their company. They instill a feeling of hope and cheerfulness. Some older adults achieve this partly by being good raconteurs, telling stories in such a way as to reach the life themes of individuals of different ages and life circumstances. The interpersonal relationships of aged persons involve questions about the implicit costs and benefits to others who are involved with them. That is, it is a question of the extent to which other persons experience high emotional stress, high cognitive load and/or a blocking of their own goal-seeking while in the company of the older adult.

## THE NEED FOR A BALANCED PROFESSIONAL PERSPECTIVE

The professional's picture of the mental health problems of later life and the self-perceptions of the average older person are contrasted by Cohen in Chapter 41 of this volume. He points out some important facts, e.g., that mental illness is more prevalent in the elderly than in the young; that serious mental illness such as the psychoses are more than twice as common in persons over 75 than in individuals 20 to 35; that suicide occurs more frequently among the elderly than in the younger age groups; and that senile dementia is coming to be the fourth leading cause of death. The essential point is that a distortion of perspective occurs if older persons themselves are defined as the problem.

The dramatic growth of the older population in America has been met by a lack of social systems for taking care of, or preventing the dependency of, selected older persons. This contrasts with the health care system in Great Britain, where only 4.5 percent of those over 65 are in hospitals compared with 7 percent in the United States (Exton-Smith and Evans, 1977). British physicians and nurses make home visits. This suggests that in the United States a reduction in the need for costly hospital care would result if there were more provisions for home care. Apparently in America we have professional orientations which over-define the sick role and the requirements for hospitalization. In assessing the constellation of psychological and social problems of older persons, the individual is too often defined as being "sick" and then cared for in an expensive health care institution. We especially tend to over-use the most expensive system, which is the hospital complex. Since care facilities for mental illnesses are few relative to services for physical problems, such as arthritis, cardiac and stroke disorders, the individual with mental health problems often will be seen in the context of a somatic health problem.

An important point to keep in focus is that, while there will be increasing numbers of older persons who will require attention for physical and mental problems, there will be even larger numbers of competent older persons who will be able not only to help themselves but to help other persons as well. For example, volunteer work and peer counseling of the elderly by the competent retired is an intriguing prospect (Alpaugh and Haney, 1978). Our concepts of mental health must be able to embrace concern for the dependent elderly as well as for the capabilities and potentials of an increasingly competent portion of the older population.

In Western society we should not lose track of the fact that there are older persons who understand their own needs and their own insecurities. They know how to secure information and utilize knowledge in such a way that decisions are made that optimize their life circumstances as well as those of others. However, there are also the dependent elderly who need professional mental health care. To distinguish between the competent and the needy and to optimize the psychological health of both groups cannot be accomplished through naive idealism but demands better knowledge and informed services than we have available at the present time.

For the frail elderly a period of dependency may arise after a life-time of autonomy, and this may be a very difficult position for them. Not only may they have difficulty in accepting their limitations, but their families may also find it difficult to deal with the dependency of a person who has always been a provider and a dominant force in the family. Thus, there may be a secondary loss of competence in such a dependent elderly person, due to loss of pride, dignity, and even identity. The point is that some individuals move into a period of dependency in the older years for which they are ill-prepared by virtue of their personalities and earlier roles in families and communities.

These are some of the problems which have to be understood in greater detail if the mental health professions are to help older adults and progress is to be made on the broader issues of mental health, aging, and society.

*Mental Health in Relation to Mental Illness.* One of the reasons for dependency of older persons is the development of chronic brain syndromes. Chronic organic brain syndromes occur in a large number of older adults. Whether such individuals are cared for in their homes or in institutions depends upon their pre-morbid personalities as well as on the nature of their current social supports and living arrangements, since the occurrence of late-life organic brain deterioration can be superimposed upon a pre-existing mental illness (functional or organic) and/or physical disabilities (Isaacs and Post, 1978).

Since senile dementia may occur in a previously well-adapted and competent person, the discordancy between the pre-morbid social and personality characteristics of the individual and those associated with the disease state require considerable readjustment in family members and friends. Given the fact that most chronically disabled persons receive care from family and friends, it is important that supporting persons understand the course of illness in organic brain syndromes so that they might have a more realistic and, therefore, a more helpful grasp of the needs of the ill individual.

Depression in the older person may mimic organic brain syndrome, and the term *pseudo dementia* has been applied to those persons whose behavior associated with depression resembles that of chronic organic brain syndrome. There may be a co-existing condition of chronic organic brain syndrome and a previous history of depression, which may also co-exist with somatic illness, e.g., cardiovascular disease. Such factors and the individual's life-long personality may relate directly to the ease with which humane treatment of his condition is forthcoming from those in the immediate environment or institution. Aggressive paranoid reactions on the part of an older adult may make the individual less acceptable to the family and community. The result would be a tendency to move such a person into an institution more readily than would occur if the same conditions involved a passive and perhaps mildly depressed person.

A point in summary should be made here: a variety of factors within and outside the individual contrive to exacerbate or minimize the conse-

quences of physical or mental illness in the later years. Some individuals are simply more trouble to themselvs and to others despite greater potential resources and less organic disability. It is logical to think of maximizing the mental health of an older person who may have organic brain change. It is perhaps not even unrealistic to undertake individual therapy in individuals with senile dementia, since one can maximize or minimize the quality of life at any point from birth to death. Grotjahn (1940) undertook psychotherapy with a deteriorating older man. Therapeutic excursions may indeed lead to principles by which we can maximize the well-being of such persons by psychological and social supports, so that their participation in life can be maximized while minimizing the excessive cost of dependency on other persons, by reducing such side effects as anger and guilt.

Staff members of institutions that care for the aged may tend to minimize their estimates of elderly patients' capacities for being mentally, physically, and socially active. In so doing, they reduce for themselves the responsibility for providing opportunities for older adults to exercise their capabilities, however limited. Dismissing old patients as incapable and dying, is a self-protecting attitude of staff members which reduces their professional obligations.

An elderly person's nearness to death may suggest to institutions, staff members, and family members that they pull back their investment in the declining person. The task of dying can occur in the context of severe physical disability and senile dementia, or it can occur in an alert, lucid individual. The death of the individual may evoke anxiety in young staff members and relatives who may project their perceptions onto the dying individual to avoid confronting their own concepts of mortality. While death may seem to be biologically appropriate in a declining individual and may appear as a reasonable outcome of severe and pressing life problems, there are better and poorer ways to die and to participate in the final days of another person. Perhaps when we have resolved some of the uncertainties about our own mortality and about our concept of our own death, we can be more helpful to others.

*The Environmental Context—The Family.* Mental health, as is true for genetic characteristics, is displayed in an environment. Often a species of animal may be exposed to an environment which has different conditions than that under which genetic selection originally operated. In the same sense, older adults may find themselves in a different environment than that in which they grew up and

were socialized. It seems worthwhile, therefore, to use an expression such as the "mental health context of the older individual" to refer to the living circumstances of an older adult. This "context" can be more or less supportive of good mental health.

It is within the mental health context that the individual faces the developmental tasks of the later years, such as the deaths of close relatives and friends, economic retrenchment, changes in physical health, and change in place or residence. When these events are viewed from the perspective of theories of stress, they become the stressors which require the individual to react in some manner. The individual may react using coping strategies from earlier life but, at the same time, the current context of the individual will influence the interpretation of the events, the types of actions taken, the emotional response and, accordingly, the physiological and social consequences. The job, the family, the neighborhood, and other social roles and institutions have an effect on the individual which must all be considered along with his personality predispositions.

Perhaps the most important of the context influences is the family. One stereotype about older persons is that they are often isolated from their families, yet a substantial amount of social research reveals that older persons have frequent contact with their children (Shanas, 1961, 1967, 1979). Most older persons live near one or more of their adult children. In our society there is actually a considerable amount of intergenerational flow of assistance to family members, e.g., money, advice, services, visitation, and participation in holidays and ceremonial occasions (Sussman and Burchinal, 1962). The basis of such exchanges and intergenerational family bonds may rest solely on obligation or they may rest on choice and/or sentiment. In the exchange between the generations the character of the exchange or "balance of trade" between generations and individuals may shift when the aged person becomes extremely disabled or taxing to the family for emotional reasons.

Blau (1973) suggests that as adult children move into their own responsibilities, their continuing relationships with aged parents may lead to a conflict in priorities with the result that the affectional involvement of the child with the parent declines, but a sense of familial obligation remains. The question may be asked whether the parental generation is more important to adult children or adult children to the parents. Parents rate the significance of their relationships with their children higher than the children rate their relationships with their parents (Johnson and Bursk, 1977).

A study by Weishaus (1978) examined the

determinants of the affective relationships of middle-aged women with their aging mothers. Weishaus alludes to the onset of filial crises when daughters move into middle age and mothers move toward requiring more care with fewer rewards for their daughters. Little evidence was found in the longitudinal study of Weishaus of the direct influence of the early childhood years upon the later years of the mother–daughter relationship. The research also revealed that memories from childhood about the mother–daughter relationship may undergo a transformation in which the memories of the earlier years are modified to fit current perceptions of the relationship. In this way altered childhood memories provide a rationalization for the present affective relationship and the individual's role in it. In the study of Weishaus it appears that the daughter's relationship with her mother is one heavily influenced by issues of responsibility and dependency, whereas mothers are more emotionally involved with daughters. The father–son, mother–son, father–daughter relationships over the life span still remain to be studied. There is no reason to believe that they will be less dynamic in nature than the mother–daughter relationship, but the directions and the content of the changes are important to know.

Past views of the family have concentrated on the psychodynamic aspects of relationships. With regard to older members there is not only a psychodynamic aspect of family relationships to be considered, but also the structural nature of the family and the interaction patterns between family members. Herr and Weakland (1979), for instance, are concerned with the fact that attention to the "problems" of the older individual, rather than to the social system of the family, may limit attempts to improve the mental health of the aging individual as well as the mental health of younger persons in the family. They maintain that the nature of the communication and interactions between the family members powerfully affect the behavior of every individual involved, as well as their thinking, feelings, and actions. Family relations also have the characteristics of habits which "develop, more or less rapidly, and then persist not because any particular behavior is fixed or inherent in itself, but largely because of reciprocal reinforcements" (Herr and Weakland, 1979, p. 51).

This leads to a concern with circular interactions or circular causation, which is important in the family because of its long-standing and ubiquitous relationships. Herr and Weakland believe that the resolution of "problems" of older family members requires either a change in behavior or a change in the participants' evaluations of their behavior. The primary task of the family counselor is thus either to help people to change their behavior or to change their interpretations of their behavior. A notion of family therapy begins with the idea that a problem is a problematic interaction among the members of the family. Alternatively, one can begin from the point of view taken by Guttmann (1978) that older persons have decisions to make and that the problem may be in how they go about making decisions.

Often family members select a scapegoat who is cast in the role of causing all the trouble. Thus, an unhappily married middle-aged couple can avoid the problems of their own relationship by blaming the family's problem on an adolescent child or on an aged parent. In this context, long-standing styles of interaction and alliances may be formed in which a father and son might align against the mother, or a mother and daughter might align against a son or the father.

According to the review of literature by Herr and Weakland (1979), Miller and Harris (1967) regard the family as moving toward homeostasis. That is, the family adopts strategies and interactions which are designed to maintain the status quo of the family. Thus a subsequent improvement in the behavior of a deviant adolescent or in the physical health of an older person may result in deterioration in the behavior or health of other family members. While the traditions of dynamic psychology have given us a great deal of insight into the homeostatic mechanisms within the psychodynamics of the individual, one must place such mechanisms within the context of a family which also has a system homeostasis and long-standing habits of interaction. One aspect of family interactions is their influence on decision making in which family members may become excessively cautious and refuse to entertain risks. Botwinick (1977) and Arenberg and Robertson-Tchabo (1977) have viewed older persons as generally cautious in their approach to decision making in the later years. However, an important study by Guttmann (1977) indicates that people over the age of 60 do make decisions about important aspects of their lives. Apparently, most older people have sufficient internal and external resources at their disposal to manage such decisions. However, as implied earlier, because of some inordinate investment in an aspect of life that is changing, such as work, and the character of the social support and information system available, an individual may develop a crisis after retirement. Such crises, however, are in the zone in which some form of transient intervention is likely to have high success, since these individuals may always have been coping with the demands of life with a reasonable degree of success.

Guttmann (1977) reviewed the literature on decision making and pointed out that theories of decision making assume "that individuals will make choices in such a way that the maximum value or utility or the minimum of disutility related to various levels of objective or subjective probability will follow from the chosen alternative" (Guttmann, 1977, p. 50). A point to be made about the decision making of older adults is that the utility of a decision may be viewed very differently by different family members. An older person might regard the utility of a decision as that which will increase the probabilities of interactions with children, whereas the adult children might regard the utility of a decision as that which maximizes the independence of the older adult.

Some evidence indicates that older people require more information than do young adults before making a decision and are more concerned with being correct. This can be related to a general disposition on the part of the older adult to be cautious, although there is a wide range of individual differences in cautiousness among old persons. Aged persons as well as young adults should be provided with maximum information about situations requiring decisions. Such a provision would encourage an approach to problem solving that is both rational and possible, is relatively free from habitual homeostatic adjustments in the family to maintain power and face, and is free from blocking and resistance. Guttmann (1977) lists nine stages in the decision-making process. The description of these steps in rational decision making is perhaps different from a list of steps in the emotional components of decision making, since the affective components of decison making appear to follow a different course with time. Adjustments to grief after the death of a close person is an example. The decision to move one's place of residence following the death of a spouse is a complex decision involving rational as well as irrational components. Apart from the grief associated with death, a long-term place of residence has considerable emotional symbolic value. For this reason, participation of the older person at levels other than rational decision making is necessary, since what may, on the surface, seem to be the most rational decision, may, in fact, be the least desirable if the emotional attachments of the older individual are considered.

*Intrapsychic and Intrapersonal Aspects.* The evidence from a considerable amount of research suggests that there are a variety of pathways to life satisfaction in the later years (Bühler, 1961; Neugarten et al., 1964; Reichard, Livson, and Peterson, 1962). Apparently there is no direct relation between intrapsychic patterns, psychopathology, and competence in interpersonal relationships (Neugarten et al., 1964). Individuals may be judged to be very effective and sought after in interpersonal relationships, but study of their intrapsychic states may reveal considerable psychopathology and tension plus a disproportional effort at striving to be socially attractive and sought after by others. While their striving to be universally liked or loved may yield some returns, the individual may not accept the external evidence and may remain essentially driven in his quest.

Paradoxical relationships from earlier life (such as the fear of incompetence on the part of the highly-driven, competent individual; high self-doubting in the successfully competitive person; or fear of being dependent on the part of those with high autonomy needs) are not necessarily relieved by aging. One may not go directly from intrapsychic assessments of the individual, in terms of abilities and personality traits, to the prediction of their likely effectiveness in interpersonal relationships or their probable satisfaction with life.

Fozard and Thomas (1975, p. 160) suggest that the interdependence between a person and his particular environment tends to increase with age. If with age there is stability in personality traits and an increased interaction between the individual and his environment, predictions about the well-being of the individual are better based upon the particular environmental interactions than on a consideration of the psychological make-up of the individual.

A thoroughgoing environmental view of older persons would perhaps view their behaviors as almost totally determined by the environment. A behavioristic view of aging would, therefore, concentrate on the particular reinforcement systems of the environment (Skinner, 1971). The problem with highly environmentalist or behaviorist views of aging is that they neglect the internal changes of the organism to which the individual also is reacting. Changes in predisposition to mood states may be expected if there are alterations in brain chemistry, e.g., levels of monoamines and peptide hormones. The individual is not only reacting to external events but also to internal events, and this results in shifts in the intensity of needs, e.g., achievement, sexual behavior, and physical activity. In addition to a supportive environment, the concept of mental health appears to embrace the notion of a self-aware person who is trying to maximize his existence in terms of pleasures, rewards, avoidance of pain and discomfort and, for the most part, to increase his probability of survival. The individual, while being heavily determined by biological and social forces, is nevertheless viewed as having a significant degree of control over his actions and the choices he makes. He is viewed as trying to maximize the outcomes of interactions between many simultaneous factors.

If this concept is valid it should be expected that there will be interactions between mental health, mental illness, and the environment in the later years. For example, an individual may suffer progressive organic brain deterioration and yet, within the limits of decreasing self-awareness and ability, be able to maximize the effectiveness of his behavior. One area of concern is the cost of the ill individual's demands on other persons. Presumably the more mentally healthy individual, with a late-life organic mental illness, will maintain the emotional, social, and physical demands on the environment at a more tolerable level than would be the case of the less mentally healthy individual.

It does not seem possible to remain content with a simple theoretical orientation about the mental health of later life; what seems to be called for is an interactionist point of view. The interactionist point of view recognizes as important not only characteristics of the environment and the biological status of the individual, but also what the individual believes and thinks about himself and the environment. Thus, small elements of the environment can be disproportionately important to an older person. The associations which an object has for a person—a book, a vase, or an old photograph connected with one's family or origins, for example—can be very important, and the loss or damage of such an object can have a large impact on an older person. Such objects may serve as symbols of permanence.

Distance from the familiar and permanent can be a significant issue for some older persons. The extent of separation from objects, institutions, and other persons has often been mentioned in relation to older persons. The question arises as to whether the increasing distance between society and the individual can lead to alienation and anomie. It is this area of conceptual development and research to which we now turn.

## ALIENATION AND ANOMIE IN RELATION TO MENTAL HEALTH AND LATER LIFE

INTRODUCTION

The concepts of alienation and anomie have for a long time occupied central roles in the study of human relations and social science. Indeed, Kahler (1957) went so far as to state that "The history of man could very well be written as a history of the alienation of man" (p. 43). The validity of this statement could be challenged, but in view of the all-pervading theme of alienation and anomie in the literature and in everyday thought, it seems imperative to include such a discussion in this *Handbook.* We not only have to determine the meaning of these concepts, but in particular we need to know to what extent they are applicable to the aged and to mental health. In addition it is necessary to distinguish between the social-structural and the social-psychological dimensions of the alienation anomie themes. The social-structural view looks upon the conditions of society or part of society. In contrast, psychological approaches look at these conditions as a state of the mind. Thus, alienation or anomie may be regarded as characteristic of social conditions or alternatively as psychological states. Such a distinction between societal conditions and psychological states cannot be stressed too often, for much of the apparent confusion in the alienation/anomie literature is due to lack of differentiation between the two.

Hegel usually is regarded as the father of the modern use of the term *alienation*, whereas Durkheim was the first writer to use the term *anomie*. It should be emphasized from the start that these terms refer to different although related phenomena, which will become apparent as this discussion continues. A review of the literature has led the present authors to the following definitions of alienation and anomie:

*Alienation* implies detachment, the avoidance or prevention of emotional identification, objectification of things and others related to self, and estrangement from the self involving separation from one's "true" self and transformation into a "thing." These meanings apply whether one is referring to social-structural conditions or a psychological state, although it is important to distinguish the two orientations.

*Anomie* implies normlessness, loss of social values, a loss of norms or absence of regulative forces by which society (the social-structural view) or the individual (psychological view) makes decisions or evaluations. Again, there is a need to distinguish from what perspective one is applying the term.

In order to reduce the ambiguity associated with the term alienation, Keniston (1965) suggested that four questions should be asked when we apply the term. The first question considers the issue of what a person is alienated from. "Alienation always has an object or a focus" (p. 453). If an older person is described as alienated, does this mean that he is alienated, for example, from the political structure, the economy, family, a former religious life, or an ideal concept of himself? It is necessary to specify the object from which the individual is estranged, whether it be an external condition, another person or group, or himself.

Second, it is necessary to specify "what alienation consists of" (Keniston, 1965, p. 453). The concept implies that something of value, such as some former esteemed relationship, has been lost. One needs to specify if some other relationship or bond making has replaced the one that has been lost, or whether a detachment occurs so that a lapsed, empty condition results. There are cases where alienation involves an absence of a valued positive relationship and which is characterized by detachment and lack of emotional identification. However, there are also cases where a substitute relationship or activity takes the place of the old relationship. Such a substitution may have positive or negative consequences for the individual. An example of a negative consequence would be where a person replaces a lost relationship by resorting to alcoholism or drug addiction. Disruption of relationships is frequent for the aged since, in particular, the probability of losing one's spouse through death increases with age. Is the widower or widow necessarily alienated? To answer such a question one needs to know how the person adapted to bereavement and whether some other positive relationship was able to fill the void.

The third question to be asked about alienation is in what way the alienation is manifested or expressed. Keniston (1965, p. 454) classifies alienation according to whether the mode is "alloplastic" (involving a person endeavoring to alter his society or the world) or "autoplastic" (which involves a "self-transformation").

An alloplastic expression of alienation implies that the individual has rejected the norms of his society. Manifestation of this mode of alienation could be said to have existed among those older adults who fought to abolish the retirement age of 65 when the norms of society dictated that the appropriate role of people at this age was to cease their career activities. Whether or not this struggle for the abolition of the traditional retirement age constitutes good or bad mental health obviously depends on the reader's value system. This brings up an important issue with respect to alienation, for to be alienated has been typically viewed as being undesirable. It is quite possible that some form of alienated behavior, when the circumstances seem to warrant it, may have positive value, such as resistance against a government which violates human rights.

An autoplastic expression of alienation also implies a rejection of values, but in this case the rejection is expressed within the individual himself. Typically it describes some form of self-estrangement which involves a retreat into mental illness. This has a parallel with the Middle English use of the term alienation, meaning a form of mental disorder (Schacht, 1971).

Finally, Keniston (1965, p. 454) claims that we should describe the agent or the source of the alienation. It is necessary to know what aspect of society is involved in the rejection process, and whether the alienation is "imposed" by the external agent or consciously or unconsciously decided upon as a course of action by the individual himself. As a survey of the literature will show, many writers on alienation, particularly Marx (1962) and Fromm (1955), believe that the individual usually is unaware of his alienated condition. Many elderly are estranged from the political government due to limited access to public officials which means that from a social-structural point of view, alienation exists. However, if such older people are unaware of estrangement or are content despite their lack of involvement and identification, the term alienation is not applicable from a psychological point of view.

Thus, Keniston (1965) advises that in using or applying the term alienation, four specific parameters should be considered, namely those of "focus," "replacement," "mode," and "agent." In describing the use of the term alienation by other scholars the present authors will utilize these specifications as part of their evaluation of each writer's contribution toward an understanding of this complex syndrome. A selection of the alienation and anomie literature will be presented in order to illustrate the meaning and applicability of these concepts.

*Sociological Concepts of Alienation.* For Hegel, the focus of his first form of alienation (termed alienation 1 by Schacht, 1971) was the "social substance," the cultural, political, and social institutions and mores of which man is a part. Replacement took the form of a self-identification whereby the individual perceived himself as separate from the "social substance" and as a result became estranged from what Hegel saw as man's essential nature. The form or mode of the manifestation might have been either alloplastic or autoplastic, but it resulted in a discordant relationship between the individual and society. The person no longer conceived of his identity in terms of the roles he had to function in or the group with whom he lived, but rather, limited his identity to his own self-determined characteristics. The agent or source of such an alienation was the individual himself. The alienation was self-imposed although the individual may not necessarily have been aware of it (Schacht, 1971).

There is a very strong parallel between Hegel's view of alienation 1 and the disengagement theory of Cumming and Henry (1961) which proposes that as an individual becomes older, his involvement with others in his society decreases and he becomes increasingly preoccupied with himself.

For Hegel, this kind of self-determination and preoccupation with one's self would amount to what he meant by alienation 1, for man in so separating himself from social institutions becomes estranged from his essential nature. Such estrangement involves a loss of the universality which is required by man's essential nature, and involves a balance or harmonization between man as an independent person and the more abstract "social substance." Hegel viewed the ideal development of man as involving his ability to sufficiently balance individuality and universality, acknowledging his own existence and yet able to participate in the political, cultural, and social community without becoming dependent on other persons (Schacht, 1971). In other words, for man to be able to fully realize his essential nature, he must be aware of himself as a discrete entity but at the same time be able to identify with the broader aspects of humanity.

Marx was also concerned with the problem of alienation, which dominated most of his writings, but he examined alienation as a social phenomenon rather than as a philosophical issue concerned with the essence of man (Bottomore and Rubel, 1964). This does not mean that Marx was not concerned with man's essential nature; he was, but he approached it in terms of life activities in which labor and production as means of self-fulfillment and self-realization were given the greatest emphasis (Schacht, 1971).

Marx was particularly concerned with the alienation of the "working" man and he focused on the means of production, the product, and economic decisions. Alienation was manifested by a form of separation or surrender. As explained by Schacht (1971, pp. 91–92), "The separation to which the term 'alienation' refers is related in some way to a certain surrender: namely, the surrender of one's control over one's product and labor."

Interrelated with this separation from labor, Marx saw the consequences of man's becoming separated from his society, his neighbors or fellow workers, and eventually himself, which become yet other foci of alienation. With reference to this self-estrangement, if man has become separated from the source through which he finds self-fulfillment, such self-realization fails to materialize and man is thus alienated from his essential nature (which is to realize this self-fulfillment).

Alienation, as conceived by Marx, is imposed on the individual by an external social force. The agent responsible for such separation is the capitalistic state, as ruled by property owners and entrepreneurs; for the most part the proletariat are unaware of their alienated state (Bottomore and Rubel, 1964; Marx, 1962).

Once man has become separated from labor, society, and his essential nature, Marx asserts there is no substitute or alternative social bonding. Such an alienated man becomes reduced to the abstract in his work. His labor and the labor product become objectified, thereby becoming autonomous or independent of him, and eventually opposing him as a hostile obstacle (Bottomore and Rubel, 1964).

Thus, Marx essentially viewed man as living in a world in which his work, other people, and even himself have become objects. Extending such a premise further, objectified man becomes a commodity for whom the state would have no use if he no longer performed to produce the required product. Although Marx did not discuss the aging worker, the implications of his social theory for the elderly living in such a society are devastating. Remarkably, as this chapter will later discuss, the majority of older people have survived psychologically without manifesting apparent signs of self-estrangement or objectification. However, as Marx points out, most people are unaware of their alienated state, so that the alienation he sees is strictly a social-structural phenomenon. If people become aware of, and troubled by, feelings of self-estrangement and valuelessness (features which would make the alienation a psychological state) some manifestations of mental illness are likely outcomes.

Rarely considered a writer about alienation, Georg Simmel (1950) was, however, one of the first philosophers to evaluate the effect of mass culture or the metropolis on the human psyche. He took his perspective from the social-structural viewpoint. In particular he examined the effect industrial societies had on cultural values (Josephson and Josephson, 1962). The urban culture is a money-based economy which imposes an essentially impersonal character on the metropolis. Although Simmel does not specifically use the term alienation, it is implied in the way he describes the effect the metropolis has on people who live in it.

The focus of alienation for him is the metropolis and, in particular, the money economy which reduces the individual and his life to an "exchange value. . . man is reckoned with like a number, like an element which is in itself indifferent" (Simmel, 1950, p. 411). Evaluations and judgments are made according to objective measures which characterize an individual's working relationships and other social interactions. "Money . . . becomes the common denominator of all values" (Simmel, 1950, p. 414). The source or agent of alienation is thus an external one, of which the individual may or may not be aware. It is the character of metropolitan life—with its demarcations, differentiations, and divisions of labor—which dominates mass urban existence and which in turn is responsible for man's becoming alienated from others, himself, and his inner spirit.

Alienation is expressed in the way in which man adapts to this impersonal situation. He responds with intellectualization rather than emotionality, and by adopting attitudes of indifference and impersonality. The amount of "nervous stimulation" that the metropolitan man has to cope with would be threatening and destructive to him unless he were able to rigorously discriminate among the stimuli with which he is confronted. So man learns to govern his life through his head or intellectual powers, rather than through his heart or emotions. This results in a high degree of impersonality and indifference which Simmel describes as the "blasé" attitude that characterizes metropolitan man. Discrimination among stimuli in this way becomes blunted so that the things that are experienced are perceived as essentially "insubstantial."

The old, close, intimate relationships with others which characterize a rural existence are not replaced. Instead, in order that the individual may survive, a devaluation of the objective world often occurs which inevitably injects feelings of worthlessness into the individuals themselves. The negative attitudes which tend to characterize an individual's relationships with others, Simmel (1950) designates as "reserve." This not only involves indifference but may extend to feelings of aversion and antipathy or overt antagonism toward others if social contacts become too intimate. Each individual becomes highly individualistic, and his withdrawal means that close interpersonal relationships are rare. Consequently, there is a decay of spiritualism and idealism so that, although man achieves an individual independence, he becomes devoid of personal and emotional life which, in Simmel's terminology, involves an estrangement of man from his essential spirit.

These themes pervade other modern writings. Whyte (1956) depicted the organization man who became overwhelmed in the bureaucratic machinery of large corporate organizations. Mills (1953, 1962) concluded that the mass of the population who were not part of the power elite had few opportunities for meaningful activities, having been manipulated by the mass media to such an extent that they became powerless to influence effectively either institutions or events. In addition metropolitan people, because of the work ethic in our society, typically attempt to manipulate others, "to make an instrument" of them; which in time results in the individual's making "an instrument of himself," and finally self-estrangement results (Mills, 1953, p. 188).

In a more popular vein, Slater (1976) claimed that technological advance, the pursuit of individualism, the increased mobility of metropolitan people, and other characteristics of urban, bureaucratic life have eroded close, intimate relationships so that man loses a sense of himself, a sense of what his meaningful worth is in this world. One of the replacement mechanisms to compensate for this inability to create a meaningful place for himself is the individual's obsession with large, powerful others. "Americans love bigness, mostly because they feel so small. They feel small because they're unconnected, without a place" (Slater, 1976, p. 11).

Weber (1968) also perceived that the focus of alienation was derived from several different aspects of cultural and social life. Alienation, withdrawal, or estrangement could occur in a diverse arena of institutions, organizations, and interpersonal relationships. Within such an arena there is the possibility for freedom and creative, responsible enterprise. On the other hand, the constrictive forces, which occur as these institutions and social organizations become rationalized into legitimate authority, also may cause its participants to lose contact with the roots of their former social creativity. For Weber, the particular focus of such alienation is the bureaucratic organizations which evolve as a functional, rational outgrowth in the process of translating authority into a legitimate form and as a means of reducing economic and social differences.

The agent or source of alienation is the growth of legal, rational organizations which replace the more traditional or charismatic forms of authority. Old, more intimate relationships are replaced by a number of legally sanctioned patterns of roles, positions, and statuses which, as the bureaucracy grows, are subject to complex patterns of authorities which become further and further removed from the individual. Resentment, tension, and particularly, feelings of powerlessness, are the inevitable manifestations of this. It should be emphasized that Weber was discussing the social-structural events that caused the alienation of which many people were aware.

The present authors note that feelings of degradation also are likely to be manifested as the individual becomes subjected to increasing distances between himself and the sources of authority. The bureaucratization complex in our medical system is one example of the operative processes inducing alienation, in this instance in a patient. The aged, who are more frequently recipients of such bureaucratic treatment, from not one but multiple governmental agencies, and whose needs are dependent on these sources, are very susceptible to this alienating process.

Fromm extended the use of the term alienation, to make it a ubiquitous concept, although the focus of his attention was the individual who became estranged from his work, his products, other people, his life, and himself. The breadth of Fromm's use of the concept can be seen in his book *Escape from Freedom* (1941). He thought that man, despite his seeming increased mastery over nature, had become estranged from the world which he built, since he was in reality no longer the master of this world, but rather its servant. Fromm was particularly addressing himself to man in a capitalistic society in which man had become the instrument of the products he himself produced. As a result, man suffered from feelings of isolation, powerlessness, and insignificance. These qualities extended to his interpersonal relationships which "assumed a spirit of manipulation and instrumentality" (p. 118). Indifference is yet another manifestation of such alienation: relationships between people "assume the character of relations between things" (p. 119). Even more devastating for Fromm was that the alienation finally came to apply to man's own self: "man does not only sell commodities, he sells himself and feels himself to be a commodity" (p. 119). Although a man derives value from what he produces or from the services he provides, this value is lost once the commodity is no longer required.

This thesis then becomes extended in *The Sane Society* (Fromm, 1955). In particular, the emphasis is on self-estrangement where man is "out of touch with himself " and with others (p. 111). The theme is repeated that man is no longer the active master of his own world or his own fate. The working population and the management class are both subject to this alienation, the former being manipulated by the owner, the latter as an instrument of the product he "appears" to own. Impersonality characterizes human relationships, the growth of bureaucratization further reduces people into things. Man as compensation becomes obsessed with his role as a consumer, acquiring more and more material things. This attachment to possessions is likely to be abandoned if something newer appears. Interpersonal relationships become degraded into a state of two machines using each other, and eventually man loses the sense of his self and his identity beyond that of the roles he has to play. It is the discovery of "nothingness" in oneself—if these roles should disappear and one's usefulness is no longer required—that is likely to

result in mental illness. From this aspect, an older person, who has retired from work and who no longer has family responsibilities, is more likely to be vulnerable.

The foregoing discussion on alienation can be regarded as a sample of the major classical exponents of the themes of alienation from a social-structural point of view. There are other theories of alienation, which, together with the ones already described, have been extensively reviewed in recent literature (Geyer and Schweitzer, 1976; Israel, 1971; Johnson, 1973; Schacht, 1971). Alienation from a psychological viewpoint has rarely, in the authors' opinion, been discussed in a form which is completely distinct from the social-structural context.

*Psychological Concepts of Alienation.* Etzioni (1968), for example, attempted to bridge the two approaches. For him alienation is derived from the social structure but expressed in personal feelings. The focus of the alienation is the outside world which is unresponsive to the person interacting with it. This then becomes expressed in feelings of resentment, disaffection, and a subjection to objective conditions which render a person powerless to either understand or control. The alloplastic expression, seen in the active-alienated person, is an attempt to change the conditions. In contrast, the autoplastic mode, seen in the passive-alienated person, is one of being non-committal and of giving in to societal forces. Moreover, mental illnesses are most likely to occur in societal conditions which appear, to the individual concerned, to be unresponsive to his personal needs, leading him to be uncertain about his own identity and his social status. American society would appear to make the elderly vulnerable to such a fate, since in so many ways our public institutions remain unresponsive to an older person's needs (a societal condition described by Etzioni as one of "inauthenticity").

Nisbet (1970) described alienation as a form of behavior. In particular, it was behavior which was characterized by a "lack of commitment to norms and roles" and which was expressed by a "withdrawal of energy from social ends and purposes" (Nisbet, 1970, p. 264). The alienated individual is one who feels powerless, meaningless, and estranged in one or several aspects of life, such as the political, economic, and technological world or, at a more domestic level, in the neighborhood, school, and family.

Rotter (1966) linked the term alienation to the concept of powerlessness, a term earlier introduced by Seeman (1959) as one of the variables associated with this syndrome. Such feelings were likely to occur when the individual was dependent for reinforcement of behavior on outside forces around him, which Rotter (1966) designated as "external control." This contrasted with those who were able to regulate their behaviors according to internalized or inner forces, a reinforcement pattern which Rotter termed "internal control." In reference to this, Niederehe (1977) found that there was an interaction of stressful events with locus of control in depressions among older people. Those individuals with a strong internal locus of control tended to show less depression than those whose reinforcement was external and dependent on the vicissitudes of life.

Both these approaches to alienation approximate the concept of anomie, which signifies that there is an absence of regulative norms either within society or within the individual.

*Sociological Concepts of Anomie.* The introduction of the term anomie is usually attributed to Durkheim, who applied the term to a state of society rather than to a psychological state (Durkheim, 1951). Anomie is a state of normlessness or a lack of regulative forces within society which could affect the decision making and behavior of its members. It should be stressed that this condition of normlessness is not a property of the individuals themselves, but rather it is derived from the social or cultural structure.

In order for man to function constructively and meaningfully society needs to act as the collective regulator or conscience, or else man can become subject to a state of purposeless and meaningless. Expectations under these circumstances have no boundaries. With the absence of rules or constraints, man tends to strive toward indefinite goals, being unable to recognize his legitimate needs or determine the direction in which his efforts should be invested. Disillusionment often is the inevitable consequence, for man "cannot in the end escape the futility of an endless pursuit" (Durkheim, 1951, p. 256). When societal conditions are characterized by these conditions of anomie, the suicide rate tends to become high, a phenomenon Durkheim (1951) carefully analyzed for a number of countries.

The interpretation of Durkheim's concepts has been elaborated upon by several writers including the sociologist Parsons (1949) who concluded that man's appetites had to be controlled by disciplinary forces imposed by society rather than by the individual. In the absence of these regulative or normative rules and codes an individual finds himself in a state of "personal disequilibrium, which results in various forms of personal breakdown" (Parsons, 1949, p. 336). Suicide is an extreme example of what man might do if he finds

himself in the disorganized state of anomie, where the norms that control his behavior have broken down.

Merton (1968) is regarded as another major contributor to the concept of anomie. Again he stressed the social-structural elements of the anomie situation, distinguishing it from a psychological concept which implied a mental set. Two aspects of the structure of society are involved. One of these is the cultural fabric which is defined as that "organized set of normative values governing behavior which is common to members of a designated society or group" (Merton, 1968, p. 216). The other element involves the social structure, "an organized set of social relationships." Anomie occurs when there is "a breakdown in the cultural structure, occurring particularly when there is an acute disjunction between the cultural norms and goals and the socially structured capacities of members of the group to act in accord with them" (Merton, 1968, p. 218).

This failure in integration or the occurrence of this dissociation between the cultural and social structure, particularly between culturally derived values and the availability of appropriate social outlets, leads to a breakdown of norms or anomie. In particular, anomie applies when the aspirations of man, which are derived from cultural sources, are dissociated from realistic opportunities. In other words, a state of incongruity between a person's aims and socially institutionalized opportunities to achieve these aims can lead to aberrant behavior or personal disorganization. One such response that an individual might make in such a situation is to retreat. Merton (1968) cites a study done by Blau (1956) in which retreatism was found to be one type of response found among older individuals who had lost some form of social status, either through retirement or by becoming widowed. Such people became nostalgic for the past and apathetic about the present. Finding themselves isolated from a former major role, retreatists would withdraw from further social interaction.

Unfortunately, social organizations have a tendency to engage in labeling procedures for the aged, which can result in several negative consequences. If these interact with certain negative social events, such as loss of roles, absence of reference groups or lack of appropriate normative information, social conditions which amount to anomie, the elderly individual may internalize feelings of incompetence. The incompetence which is experienced may embrace his participation in social roles, his abilities to cope or adapt to environmental demands, and his felt capacities to influence, control, or master his environment (Kuypers and Bengtson, 1973). Social withdrawal may be a response pattern, and such a reaction has a high correlation with mental illness among the old (Lowenthal, 1964; Lowenthal, Berkman and Associates, 1967).

These fates, however, are not inevitable consequences of old age, and some investigators have found that age norms are operable over a wide range of behaviors which many older people have accepted (Neugarten, Moore, and Lowe, 1965). When the older individual perceives that his role, status, and behavior are appropriate and when the event he has to cope with is anticipated, the impact is less traumatic (Neugarten, 1969, 1970). In this sense, Neugarten argues, for instance, that death of a spouse will have less disruptive consequences on an older person's life, since at this age such an event is a more expected one than it is for the young adult. For some older adults, however, as we have already seen, changes in social relationships, roles, and status are associated with anomie conditions.

*Psychological Concepts of Anomie.* The psychological state of anomie, like alienation, has received less attention than the social structural aspects. Merton (1968), for instance, was aware that the psychological concept of anomie had a definite reference point corresponding to feelings of purposelessness, anxiety, tension or isolation, but he felt that this approach could not substitute for the sociological conceptual analysis of which the psychological state was a counterpart.

Riesman (1950) applied the term anomie to a form of behavior which was "maladjusted" in the sense of individuals being unable to conform to the normative values of the society in which they live. Such maladjustment obviously may not be negative in some cultures. In contrast, Nisbet (1970) defined anomie as behavior which arises when a person perceives that there is a "conflict" of social and cultural norms. The behavior is dependent on the social conditions but anomie, in these terms, is described as the response. Such a response consists of tension and "conflict-ridden behavior" (p. 275). It occurs because two or more obligations or goals arise that are "irreconcilable *within the framework of response of the individual concerned*" (Nisbet, 1970, p. 274).

McClosky and Schaar (1965) attempted to define anomie beyond mere behavior, isolating it as a psychological state which intervenes between the social conditions and the behavioral consequences. Furthermore, these investigations isolated psychological dimensions of the state of anomie which they found to be correlated with, but distinct from, the social conditions associated with it. Among these cognitive and personality factors which were associated with this "state of normlessness" were bewilderment, anxiety, lack of confidence, defensiveness, hostility, inflexibility and decreased cognitive capacity. Reduced or impaired interaction with others and consequent mental distress resulted.

## AN INTEGRATION OF THE SOCIOLOGICAL AND PSYCHOLOGICAL CONCEPTS OF ALIENATION AND ANOMIE

There have been few attempts to coordinate theoretically both the social and psychological approaches of alienation or anomie. However, one major contributor to this attempt at integration in the area of alienation has been Seeman (1959, 1976) who has approached the topic from a social-psychological point of view. He does this by describing various components of the alienation syndrome.

Powerlessness involves having limited feelings of mastery over social or life events. Meaninglessness is defined as feeling that there is little comprehensibility to events or relationships. Normlessness is conceived of as "commitment" to achieving one's goals in a "socially unapproved" manner. Cultural estrangement, called value isolation in Seeman's 1959 description, implies that the individual rejects the values that are held by his society or he rejects "group standards." Self-estrangement occurs when the individual pursues activities that are not "intrinsically rewarding." Social isolation implies that there is "an exclusion or rejection" of the individual from his society or group (Seeman, 1976, p. 268).

A large number of empirical studies have been done with reference to these parameters. Most of these, as reviewed by Seeman (1976), are concerned with young adults. Few such studies have concerned themselves with the aged, except with reference to social isolation. It is erroneous, however, to believe that all the aged are socially isolated. Indeed, Townsend (1962) points out that we should distinguish between objective isolation and a more subjective condition of loneliness in old age. Isolation implies that the individual has few social interactions either with his family or the community. However, such circumstances do not necessarily imply loneliness, which indicates that there are unwanted feelings of being alone or not having companionship.

Martin, Bengtson, and Acock (1974) took the social-psychological parameters of powerlessness, meaninglessness, normlessness, social isolation, and self-estrangement and investigated these in three different age generations within the social context of politics, the economy, education, religion, and the family. The most alienated group was the young adults. The least alienated group was the middle-aged. Thus, the relationship between alienation and age is curvilinear; the young who have not yet reached their socialized goals feel more alienated than the aged, who have realized some of their aspirations but have had to retire from many of their former roles. Although the aged had the highest scores on powerlessness and meaninglessness, they had low alienation scores on social isolation and self-estrangement. Indeed, their scores on these modes of alienation were lower than those attained by the middle-aged group.

Although the study by Martin *et al.* (1974) is significant in that the aged were less alienated than might have been predicted from the theories described in this chapter, it must be remembered that this represents only one sample of 182 males of whom 90 percent of the older group were then currently married. More investigations of this nature are required to determine the extent of alienation and anomie among the elderly. Indeed as the next section shows, some writers believe that people are poorly socialized into old age, a situation which would leave them normless and alienated.

It is possible that, among the aged who are estranged from different social sectors in the political, economic, and domestic spheres, the degree of alienation experienced is the result of spiraling, negative, social circumstances. The most likely individuals to be so affected are the elderly with low socioeconomic status. Low income, poor education, poor health, and social isolation would then interact not only to constitute social circumstances of alienation and anomie but also to produce their psychological-state counterparts.

Against such a premise we have to balance the evidence that, although there is a high suicide rate among the aged population as a whole, it is highest among males over 65, with high socioeconomic status. Alienation and particularly the social and psychological states of anomie are possibly most acute in those aged persons who have had the highest degree of investment in the norms and values of their society.

## SOCIALIZATION, MORALE, AND LIFE STYLES

### SOCIALIZATION

Sociologists interested in mental health and behavior in relation to age tend to trace the issues back to the social structure of the society in which the older persons live. That is, analysis is made in terms of assigned age statuses, age roles, norms of behavior with age, and the rights and rewards of having lived a long time and having occupied a particular position in society. The thesis that individuals in American society are not effectively socialized to old age has been developed by Rosow (1974). If one agrees with Rosow that the processes of socialization into old age are weak then one expects greater alienation with age, since the aged are faced with lack of role clarity by moving into what has been described as the roleless role, that of being old.

Rosow develops the idea that changes of status during the course of life are marked by recognized transitions such as starting school, leaving school, marrying, and changing jobs. Such changes in status are accompanied by changes in roles, relationships and, indeed, one's sense of identity. Rosow emphasizes that the norms in old age are weak and that the normative vacuum results from the fact that there is a weak process of socialization into old age in our society. However, there appear to be many forces which socialize the individual into the position of being old: family; church; work (employer, union professional group); the communication media, including television, movies, books, newspapers and magazines; fraternal groups, neighbors and others. An individual clearly does not cease to be free of all of these socializing influences when he arrives at the age of 65. In fact, by then older individuals have incorporated a great deal of influence and values that lie behind their decisions and behaviors. From the evidence it appears that the interpersonal network of many individuals continues to exist into later life.

Rosow's thesis should be examined in the light of what has been shown by the Harris poll (Harris and Associates, 1975) and the Guttmann survey (Guttmann, 1977). These studies did not find a grossly disproportionate number of older persons being lonely or otherwise regarding themselves as being distant from other persons in society. While alienation increases somewhat with age, the majority of older persons do not appear to be alienated. It seems likely that there is implicit socialization into old age going on in society through frequent discussions with neighbors, family, and friends.

However, Bengtson believes that, generally, there is a normlessness of old age in which " . . . there are fewer and fewer clear-cut obligations of appropriate behavior as one passes into the socially defined stage of old age" (Bengtson, 1973, p. 25). Rosow also feels that the lack of norms places the aged in a disadvantaged position, since individuals are not provided a set of expectations that structure activities and roles. As a result there is little motivation to become old and no basis for judging the success or failure in being an older person. A contrasting view holds that normlessness of old age may be an advantage in that older persons are freer to manipulate behavior and opportunities to better advantage since fewer persons are looking over their shoulders as compared for example with adolescent high school students.

Growing old and alienation may be greater problems for immigrants and minorities since America has a heterogeneous culture. Many older individuals are first-generation or second-generation Americans whose ties with a subgroup remain intact. Younger members of these ethnic and cultural groups are moving more toward participation in the social roles of society at large. Thus, to grow old as a Mexican-American, or an Italian-American, or a Polish-American, may be a more tenuous process than would have been growing old in the country of origin where there are more commonly shared values.

The study by Martin *et al.* (1974) showed that alienation is relatively high in adolescence when individuals are not yet into the dominant social roles of society and again in old age when, presumably, individuals are coming out of the dominant roles. The fact that the surveys by the National Council on Aging and Guttmann showed that older people maintain a rather high level of morale indicates that most persons make the transitions from the dominant roles of middle age to old age, and into the normless or roleless state of old age with poise and feeling of control. In this process, however, some individuals must experience a high level of anomie. Certainly the increase in suicide in old age would suggest that the transition is a difficult one for many older persons; again, not for most old persons, but for some (see Stenbach, Chapter 26 in this volume).

## Morale

Professionals are not immune to stereotypes and, in fact, they may be more prone to stereotypes about the aged than are members of the general public. One reason for this is that physicians mostly see sick old people, social workers see indigent old people, clergy see spiritually concerned older people, and lawyers see older people with legal problems. Other professionals also have biased contacts with selected members of the older population leading to a negative stereotype in which older people are viewed as sick, poor, lonely, and confused, among other negative features.

Since professional persons rarely have contact with well-adapting older people they tend not to be aware of the largest proportion of the older population which is doing quite well in managing their lives in relation to their resources and needs. Two facts are simultaneously true: that dependency rises with age, particularly in those over 85, and, at the same time, that the average person in the upper age range is not excessively dependent and does not have poor morale.

A substantial survey on age and the quality of life was undertaken by the American Institutes of Research (Flanagan, 1978). Nationally representative cohorts of one thousand 30-year-olds, one thousand 50-year-olds, and one thousand 70-year-olds were interviewed about the quality of their lives. There were only slight differences between the 50-year-old and 70-year-old groups with regard to the overall quality of their lives. About 85 percent indicated that the quality of their lives was good or better, that is, "good, very good, or excellent." An analysis was made of the overall judgments of the quality of life in relation to individual reports of how well needs and wants were being met in 15 different areas of life. A factor analysis yielded three relevant factors. The first factor included material comforts, work, and health and would appear to be identified as external or relatively impersonal or pragmatic contributions to the quality of life. The second factor included close friends and socializing, and appears to involve intimacy. The third factor included learning and creative expression, and the opportunity to use one's cognitive capacities.

Self-perceptions of well-being by persons over 65, as well as perceptions by the general public about persons over 65, were examined in a national survey conducted by Harris and Associates for the National Council on Aging in 1974 (Harris and Associates, 1975). There were 4,254 persons involved in household interviews and the sample was regarded as a representative cross-section of the American public over the age of 18.

Only about one half of the respondents indicated that the 60s and 70s were the least desirable ages or time of life. Those who did consider the older years to be the worst years had many reasons. The most commonly cited by the general public were: *bad health* 22 percent, *financial problems* 10 percent, *can't get work* 9 percent, and *loneliness* 6 percent. Over 27 different items were indicated, but the range from 22 percent for the maximum number of responses concerning *bad health* down to the minimum percentages of responses concerning *being in old age homes* (1 percent) indicates that there is not too much consistency in what are viewed as the worst things about being over the age of 65.

When asked which of the problems were *serious ones,* persons over 65 indicated that the fear of crime was the most serious problem (23 percent). Other major problems included poor health (21 percent), not having enough money (15 percent), loneliness (12 percent), and not enough medical care (10 percent). Items which might relate specifically to mental health included: *not enough things to do to keep busy* (6 percent), *not enough friends* (5 percent), *not feeling needed* (7 percent), and, of course, *fear of crime* (23 percent).

Two reversals of image between the general public and people over 65 were revealed in one item. Persons between 18 and 64 believed that most people over 65 are very warm and friendly; those over 65 were less favorable. The majority of those over 65 regarded themselves as being very good in getting things done (55 percent), while only 35 percent of the general public had this view. While the differences are not startling, it seems to be a safe generalization that the general public's view of the efficiency and competence of older persons is somewhat more negative than the view held by persons over 65 about themselves. This is perhaps reassuring in the sense that it suggests that older persons are more self-confident than the general public image of older persons assumes. Perhaps even more optimistic is the fact that about 32 percent of persons over 65 indicated that life now is better than expected, whereas only 11 percent found life worse than expected. Thus, there were three times as many people of 65 and over who found that life is better than expected than those who found life worse than expected. Individuals over 65 have a reasonably positive concept about themselves, although there was a clear tendency for persons in the lower income levels to be less positive in their self-regarding attitudes.

More than half of the older people were still planning for their future and 56 percent of those over 65 believed that they were just as happy as when they were younger. Three out of four persons over 65 believed that life was still as interesting as it had ever been. A total of 72 percent believed that "things I do are as interesting to me as they ever were" and a total of 57 percent "expect some interesting and pleasant things to happen to me in the future" (Harris and Associates, 1975, p. 154). Also, there was a belief that a trend exists toward improvement in the quality of life in the later years, with persons over 65 being better off than they were 10 to 20 years earlier.

On the negative side, 23 percent of persons over 65 agreed with the statement, "this is the dreariest time of my life." Before concluding, however, that this is of overwhelming importance, this statement should be compared with the sample of persons under 65, of whom 13 percent said, "this is the dreariest time of my life." While there is a large and important segment of the older population who finds life dreary, it is a gross error to identify the majority of persons over 65 as having such a bleak outlook. The general picture of morale and contentment among older persons is that most of them are deriving considerable satisfaction from their present lives and are looking forward to the future.

One implication of the survey is that adults before retirement tend to have a stereotyped view of the years after 65 which would not lead them to look forward enthusiastically to the later years. Yet, there is no reason why young adults could not have a positive image of old age in which the years after 65 could be looked upon as years for rest, relaxation, reflection, and personal choice. This has a bearing upon mental health in the middle years during which many persons may consciously avoid the thought of growing old or may experience feelings of fear of being old.

A concluding observation of the survey is worth quoting for its perspective. "Not only do four in five older people look back on their past with satisfaction, three in four feel that their present is as interesting as it ever was, and over half are making plans for their future. Granted, life could be happier for 45 percent of older people, but an even higher 49 percent of those under 65 feel the same" (Harris and Associates, 1975, p. 155).

A view often held about the aged is that they are lonely. The proportion of persons under 65 in the Harris survey who said they had no close person to talk to was 5 percent; those over 65 had a comparable proportion of 8 percent. While the difference between the two age groups may be important, it is not dramatic. If the question whether they would like to have someone to talk to, is asked, 41 percent of the 18–64 group said they would, whereas only 28 percent of those over 65 said they would.

There may be a condensation effect on morale in which some older adults accumulate multiple problems, each of which may have a low positive correlation with age but which, by their interaction, produce a selected group of highly dependent persons. The interaction between poor health, low income, poor housing and social isolation results in a pattern of low morale (Kutner, Fanshel, Togo, and Langner, 1956). Any one factor taken alone does not lead to gross dissatisfaction with life. Thus, health problems in the high-income, highly educated population do not lead to low morale as they do in the low-income, low-educated population. For the appearance of dependency to occur, there is likely to be a precipitating crisis in which the older person becomes incapacitated by an overload of interacting issues. One element in the constellation of factors is, of course, the pre-crisis or premorbid personality of the individual, as well as the kinds of decisions the individual has made in meeting perceived needs.

A major study was conducted by Guttmann (1977) on the decision making of adults over 60 and the degree of satisfaction they derived from their decisions. The independent variables of the study were: 1) subjective needs, 2) knowledge of resources, 3) ability to make decisions, 4) living arrangements and 5) age. The dependent variables were satisfaction or dissatisfaction with the decisions made and the nature of the actual decisions made.

The Guttmann study consisted of 447 interviews with persons over the age of 60 who were ambulatory and living in the community. Their average age was 71.9 years. Respondents were asked about important decisions made in the year prior to the first interview. Important decisions made by the groups were: 1) in relation to work, 6.9 percent; 2) housing and living arrangements, 8.9 percent; and 3) matters of health and illness, 4.5 percent. The self-perceptions of the health of this sample was such that 54.2 percent said their health was good, 29.5 percent said their health was average and 16.3 percent said their health was poor. The subjects interviewed were reinterviewed six months later as a follow-up. It is of interest that, over the six-month interval, 85 of the subjects said their health had improved and 60 said it had deteriorated; 265 indicated that their health remained the same.

More relevant to considerations of mental health are the findings that 60 percent of the subjects regarded their relationships with their family as *very* satisfactory and 27.3 percent regarded these relationships as satisfactory. Only 2.9 percent reported either partly unsatisfactory or unsatisfactory relationships between their families and themselves. During the period of the study, 77 subjects reported that their family relationships were improving, 73 reported such relationships were deteriorating, and 351 reported that they had remained the same.

The degree of local interpersonal involvement is revealed by the fact that two-thirds of the subjects visited or talked with neighbors five time or more in a month and only 11 percent said they never visited or talked to their neighbors. More than 40 percent of the respondents talked on the telephone or in person with relatives or friends

more than once a day. Only 4.4. percent reported that they did not have relatives or friends to talk with during the day.

Guttmann and his associates (1977) put their findings on loneliness in the context of other surveys. In their sample, loneliness was perceived to be felt sometimes by 18.5 percent and 11.2 percent stated that they felt lonely "very often," whereas 70 percent "almost never" felt lonely. Previous studies reviewed by Guttmann reported the percentage of individuals in different metropolitan areas who experienced loneliness often, e.g., 4 percent in Denmark and 7 percent in England. Loneliness experienced "sometimes" by subjects was reported by 13 percent in Denmark, 21 percent in England and 21 percent in the United States.

The attribution of a high level of loneliness to the older population is, therefore, not valid, a fact commented upon in the previous discussion of the Harris poll results. The availability of someone with whom to talk over intimate matters also was not a problem for the majority of the Guttmann sample, that is, only 6.1 percent said they had no one to confide in or to trust.

In answer to a question about satisfaction with their present life circumstances, 89.9 percent of the respondents said that they were satisfied and 12 percent reported that they were dissatisfied with their current situations. In answer to the related question, "would you consider this time of your life as your best time, worst time or no better or worse than usual?" 23.7 percent of the respondents said "best time," 55.9 percent said "no better or worse than usual," and 15.4 percent said this is "the worst time" of their lives (5.1 percent did not respond to the question). In a comparison of the life satisfaction responses between the initial and followup interviews, 22 subjects reported being more satisfied by the time of the second interview and 21 reported that they were more dissatisfied.

Those persons who took action on their own behalf differed from nonaction-takers in a number of characteristics. Those taking action were more likely to be living with their spouses or with their friends while the nonaction-taking persons were more likely to be living with their children or other relatives. Also, action-takers were healthier and economically better off than the nonaction persons. In this study, a positive relationship was found between decision satisfaction, family relations, and life satisfaction.

Findings indicate that most individuals are able to adjust to changes in role and expectations with age and to accommodate comfortably to the interactions between their needs and the opportunities of their environment. Indeed, for many older persons growing older is accompanied by an increasing sense of personal mastery and social recognition from family and other reference groups. While for some older persons increasing competence may be experienced, there is a cycle of decreasing competence for others in dealing with the environment.

Bengtson (1973) describes the positive cycle of events leading to increasing competence in older persons: 1) reducing susceptibility and increasing self-confidence; 2) reducing dependence and increasing self-reliance; 3) self-labeling as able; 4) building up and maintaining coping skills; and 5) internalizing the self as being an effective agent. There are three inputs to this cycle, from Bengtson's point of view: 1) liberation from the functionist ethic together with an evolution of alternative evaluations; 2) improved maintenance conditions such as housing, health, nutrition and transportation; and 3) encouragement of an internal locus of control and building adaptive problem-solving abilities. It is these characteristics which typify the sample investigated by Guttmann (1977).

While an optimistic point of view about the mental health of the older population in general is justified, there is every reason to be deeply concerned about the large numbers of older persons who are living lives in distress, for there are relatively more of them than in younger groups. Our professional service providers have not been trained to deal with these issues, nor are our institutions well geared to providing easy access to professional services for the older adult, since they have been primarily oriented toward the needs of children and young adults.

## LIFE STYLES IN THE LATER YEARS

The earlier quoted study of Kutner et al. (1956) indicated that morale and life satisfaction were highest for the more highly educated, higher income and higher role-participating individuals. This seems paradoxical when one considers the fact that, in relation to their social class, doctors are more prone to drug addictions and psychiatrists more prone to suicide. Perhaps some professional individuals are so highly specialized that secondary weaknesses appear in their personal systems. In such specialized individuals there may be a vulnerability in which an ego-threatening disruption may occur if their central role cannot be continued. All things being equal, however, the educated person living in an involved style of life is exposed to a full stream of information. Being embedded in a rich and varied stream of information, the individual is presented with useful information, op-

tions, and opportunities to maximize decisions. A question can be raised about how much of the variance in mental health is explained by the stream of information in which individuals are embedded and how much is explained by the personality predispositions of the individuals.

The research of Williams and Wirths (1955) describes six life styles in a sample of 168 individuals. They divided the sample into the following categories: a) world of work, 15 percent; b) familism, 33 percent; c) living alone, 13 percent; d) couplehood, 20 percent; e) easing through life with little involvement, 7 percent; f) living fully, 13 percent. In relating these styles of living to a global measure of successful aging they found that there were successful and unsuccessful individuals in each of the categories though the styles of "familism" and "living fully" showed a higher proportion of individuals with successful aging. Apparently each style of living has its own strengths as well as its own vulnerabilities. This is not unlike the study of personality and retirement of Reichard et al. (1962) which showed that individuals with different types of personality may derive life satisfaction in retirement. Perhaps life styles as well as personalities might be viewed in terms of the particular vulnerabilities and strengths they bring.

Another aspect of mental health which should be emphasized is the cost of the life style and personality of the individual to himself and to others, that is, the consequences for other persons who are dependent on the older adult as well as individuals on whom the older adult is dependent. The group of older persons described by Reichard et al. (1962) as self-haters, for example, are constantly blaming themselves for their limitations; they are a depressed group. Interpersonal involvement of the self-haters with others clearly results in a high drain on other people. Similarly, involvement with angry persons, those who are constantly projecting their lack of successes on others, would be taxing. All things being equal, the self-haters and the angry ones take more from other persons in an interpersonal exchange than, for example, do integrated persons or passive-dependent persons.

It is a truism, but perhaps useful to point out that individuals who have multiple affective attachments would probably do better in dealing with the losses of the later years than would those who have single affective investments. Similarly, those who have more social roles and a broader stream of information will be in a more advantageous position with regard to decision making than would those who are involved in a circumscribed life. The life styles of individuals, their personalities, the information streams in which they live and their abilities all constitute variables in the matrix which determines their competence in meeting the transitions of age.

To summarize the foregoing points with regard to the vulnerabilities of old age, it would seem that the most vulnerable older person is one who has a limited affective investment, lives in a narrow information stream, functions in highly specialized social roles, and has very high personal expectations in relation to his self-concept.

## A PERSPECTIVE ON MATURITY AND INTEGRATION OF LIFE EXPERIENCES

### MATURITY AND MENTAL HEALTH

One senses with age a growth of "maturity" with the appearance of greater mastery of self and the environment. Over a lifetime of experience many individuals have the opportunity to integrate their experiences in such a way as to modify the various components of their self-evaluation which results in lower tension. Specifically, experience over a lifetime may modify the ideal to which the individual aspires, and self-appraisal may change. Thus, in the mature person in the later years, the ideal self and the actual self may more closely approximate each other than they did earlier, e.g., in adolescence. Similarly, the individual's concept of what his public image is may become more realistic. The social image, therefore, may also be more congruent with the ideal self and the actual self. In this perspective a greater congruence or diminished distance between these different concepts of the self would result in greater internal stability in the self-structure. In this view of "normal development over the adult years" there would be less cause for the high defensiveness of young adults and adolescents and the related rapid changes in mood. The basic proposition is that there is, for the normally developing older adult, a more stable self-structure than existed in early life.

We may infer from the studies described, that the perceived quality of life will vary with environmental opportunities for intimacy with other persons, with opportunities for learning and creative expression, and with opportunities for material comforts and freedom from health disabilities. However, the role of the individual in creating and utilizing opportunities for meeting needs and wants is also a most relevant issue. While environmental opportunity is an independent variable, in mental health it does not act alone. The adaptive style and capacity of the individual to create and

utilize opportunity is an important contributor to well-being and the outcome of events over the life span. Vaillant (1977) has put the point well in his statement, "If you have not the strength to accept the terms life offers you, you must, in self-defense force your own terms upon it. If either you or your environment is distorted too much in the process, your effort at adaptation may be labeled mental illness" (p. 13). Vaillant finds that some strategies are more effective than others in bringing about a workable adaptation to the circumstances of life. Perhaps one should also consider the cost-effectiveness of different adaptive strategies which in ego terminology are called defense mechanisms.

Vaillant studied the lives of 95 men who were followed for twenty-five years from the time they were undergraduates in college. A total of 30 men showing the best outcomes in terms of social adjustment to life were compared with 30 men who had the worst outcomes. The worst outcomes were found to be related to a greater use of what Vaillant regarded as immature ego defenses. He believed that "defenses that channel rather than block inner life and affect—namely suppression, anticipation, altruism and displacement—were more common among the best outcomes. Defenses that removed, denied, or dammed inner life—reaction formation, dissociation, and the immature defense mechanisms—were far more common among poor outcomes" (Vaillant, 1977, p. 276). Of interest is the fact that with age fewer immature, and more mature, defenses were used by the men providing evidence of adult development in which the ego becomes less likely to function in an infantile manner.

There is a tendency to identify ego defenses with personality and not to ascribe any cognitive components to individuals' adaptive styles. Yet it is difficult to think of the processes of maturation in older adults without attention to the roles of learning and the extinction of less adaptive mechanisms. Highly creative adolescents appear to show an interaction between their cognitive style and personality (Welsh, 1977). It seems likely that individuals who can focus in a convergent way on problems that need to be solved and control their mental processes en route to solution will be adaptive. On the other hand, individuals who can shift from a convergent and controlled mode to a divergent and spontaneous mode when situations require novel and original behavior, may be most generally competent in adapting. Singlemindedness may work but the capacity to shift situationally may provide optimum mental health outcomes. Heath (1977) preferred to use the term *competence* rather than either mental health or self-actualization in describing the processes of optimum maturation in order to avoid confusion of issues but also to be able to draw into consideration cognitive skills, self-concept, values, and interpersonal relationships. Good mental health or competence would seem to be related to the capacity to recognize when what one is doing is not yielding optimum results and it therefore seems appropriate to add cognition, along with the affective elements of personality and reaction patterns, to that complex blend of variables we call mental health.

It is customary to regard self-acceptance and a positive self-concept as important in successful aging. It is difficult to know, however, whether to characterize positive self-regarding attitudes as a cause of, or as a result of, good mental health. Generally speaking, older persons with high self-regarding attitudes presumably will adapt better to changes of later life than individuals who are self-depreciating. One of the tasks of growing old is adaptation to change in self and others, and adaptation to environmental demands, so that there will be congruence between such demands and competence. The basic hypothesis being suggested is that the *ideal self*, the *actual self* and the *social image* of the self are more congruent in the later years for the successfully adapting persons. Such congruence could be expressed in many ways: reduction in motivational conflict, greater ability to regulate one's own life and increased flexibility in dealing with change and unexpected demands. By comparison, adolescents are often in a relatively unstable internal state because of high goals, ideals and achievements yet out of reach; adolescents often have low opinions of themselves with regard to actual circumstances. Furthermore, many adolescents interpret the feedback from other persons ambiguously, alternately regarding themselves as attractive or unattractive. Thus, an adolescent may oscillate rapidly between mood states because of instability and high tension within himself resulting from the large differences between the alternative views of the self. If the hypothesis is correct, a successfully aging person should show less oscillation in mood states as the congruency and stability of the different self-images increase.

Presumably, the processes of socialization and experience over a lifetime bring the individual to later life so that the ideal self has been adapted to correspond to the realities of life rather than to early life fantasies or abstractions. With age and with good mental health it is proposed that one's view of the actual self improves, since one becomes a master of more social roles. All things being equal, the middle-aged individual feels a greater sense of mastery and competence than does the late adolescent (Birren, 1967). Healthy older adults also learn to manage their interpersonal relationships in such a way as not only to convey their attitudes to others but also to seek realistic feedback from others. Maturity would seem to bring with it competence in managing interpersonal relationships so as to be mutually satisfying.

Writing one's autobiography and sharing it with others may be a facilitating process by which greater development of maturity and integration of the self is reached for older adults. Not only studies of autobiographies but other research, such as that undertaken at the University of Bonn (Thomae, 1976), is needed to uncover more facts about the processes through which the successfully adapting aged maximize the potentials of their lives. The "elite aged" appear to have some inner structure that enables them to be strong yet flexible, feeling yet controlled, living in the present yet planning for tomorrow, and less needing to justify their past views and behavior—a condition which brings them into the present with pride and strength. More research needs to be done to contrast the intrapsychic structure of the incompetent aged and of well-adapting older persons. Such information has its place along with the studies of the environment and the physiological status of the individual. The present perspective is comprehensive and one which an investigator may find excessively demanding, but it is the kind of understanding that is required about mental health in the later years if we are going to maximize the potentials of older adults for constructive decision making on their own behalf while minimizing limiting coping patterns. Also to be pursued are the issues of the types of interventions that are most likely to be successful in providing assistance to older persons at a time when they may be facing emotional and cognitive overload, e.g., following bereavement, illness, loss of finances or required change in living arrangements. Inappropriate intervention may lead an older person to become excessively dependent and limited while considerable personal potentials for a potentially productive life lie fallow.

An obvious point may be made about the adaptations of older persons; it has to do with the attractiveness of their behavior. A smiling, cheerful, enthusiastic older person leads others to interact or serve them cheerfully. In exchange for the physical, economic and personal services older persons may receive, they may in turn give their adult children a feeling of security and hope which can be an important part of the "balance of trade" between the generations. Persons reacting depressively to loss, or individuals who are narcissistically self-involved, are not likely to show the kind of interactive behavior which would induce other persons to seek to spend time with them.

The personal adjustments in the later years, as at any time of life, are attempts to maximize a complex life equation with many simultaneous variables. Into the set of simultaneous life equations are not only to be entered the stressors of daily life but also the individual's grasp of his own personality, temperament, abilities, skills, and the goals and values of a lifetime. In this vein, to judge an individual as aging successfully or as showing good mental health in the later years, one must have a grasp of the individual's goals in order to sense what it is he is trying to maximize internally and in relation to the environment. A low adjustment or productivity may, in fact, be a high level maximization of potentials if one understands the individual's origins and available resources. Earlier the individual was described as being immersed in a stream of information that may vary in quality and quantity. It is perhaps not surprising that individuals from middle or high socioeconomic status derive relatively better morale from life in the later years in the sense that it is difficult for them to avoid competent advice and alternative opportunities.

The older adult, on average, is less economically and socially powerful. Older adults do, however, retain many options in control over their own lives and it is from this that they should derive increasing satisfaction rather than from being controlling over the lives of others. How to bring the experience of the older adult to bear upon the lives of younger persons without seeming to preach or depreciate, how to bring up the relevant past in such a way that it is not a simple clinging to old rewards but an attempt to enrich the balance of trade between the generations, should be one of the cultivated arts of growing old with grace and wisdom. It is clearly suggested in the work of Thomae and his colleagues (1976) that many older adults negotiate these changes in status with age and derive satisfaction and plan new activities. Clearly a wise, attractive, and forward-looking older person will be sought after by others even though he may have reduced social power in a primary economic sense. Indeed Williams and Wirths (1965) believe that the later years of life can be a time for securing new kinds and levels of returns as well as new social goals.

INTEGRATION OF LIFE EXPERIENCES

A number of writers have suggested that the later years are appropriately concerned with integrating one's past experiences. In 1922 the developmental psychologist G. S. Hall, who had previously studied adolescence, examined the issues of late life. On the point of integration he said,

> Perhaps the chief suggestion is that every intelligent man, as he reaches the age of senescence, should thus pass his life in review and try to draw his lesson, not only for his own greater mental poise and unity, but for the benefit of his immediate descendents, for whom such a record must be invaluable. Thus the writing of an autobiography will sometimes become a fifth hygienic prescription for a well-rounded out old age (Hall, 1922, p. 117).

Bühler (1968) suggested that adding up one's life was a normal goal of the older adult. For her, fulfillment of one's life was a process of integration. Butler (1963) gave emphasis to the tendency of older adults to review their lives and he noted the additional point that proximity to death was the motivating force behind such life review. Birren (1964) commented also on the fact that reconciling one's life apparently becomes an increasing concern of the older adult. Jung (1962) spoke about the shift from the middle-aged man to the older man as evolving from one of outer-direction and striving for achievement to more serious attention to the inner life. For Jung, the later years are not a simple addition to youth, but have their own purpose and significance.

The foregoing implies that some older individuals have managed to extract wisdom from life, which includes mastery of self and situations that have resulted in emotional and cognitive overload. A wise person can be viewed as having a balanced investment in self as well as in others, and as having moved from concerns with things to ideas and from actions to meanings. Experience, reflectiveness, and emotional balance are characteristics which come to mind in association with an image of a wise old person.

A balance between active striving and reflection should exist throughout life, but a *shift* in this balance may occur over the life span. An acceptance of one's life as one *has lived* it, rather than as one *is living* it, involves a major shift in orientation. For such a task to be accomplished there first has to be a recognition that an evaluation of the events of life, the solving of one's unsolved conflicts, and integrating them into a meaningful context, is a necessary part of good mental health in old age. Birren and Renner (in press) suggested an expansion of earlier proposals, namely those of life review (Butler, 1963) and also reconciliation (Birren, 1964). To these Birren and Renner added the principles of: (a) relevance to a set of values, (b) reverence (or feeling of self-esteem and self-worth) for a set of ideals and for one's own life, and (c) a release in the sense that the active mind can rest, since the reconciliation of the content of one's life with one's ideals is stress-reducing. The five R's of *review, reconciliation, relevance, reverence* and *release* are especially pertinent to the aged. If cultivated, they may help to avoid or reduce the feelings of alienation or anomie, despair, regret, and perhaps fear of death.

The present authors suggest that to be mentally healthy a person of any age needs the ability *to respond to other individuals, to love, to be loved, and to cope with others in give-and-take relationships.* He should be able to retain intimate relationships, make new friendships, refrain from being destructive in relationships, and have satisfactory social groups. There are times when an individual should break a relationship, if it is becoming destructive. The management of separation from others when necessary without excessive distress is also a component of good mental health; coping with bereavement by older individuals is a good example. In addition, an individual of any age should have the essential quality of being able to cope with loneliness, aggression, and frustration without being overwhelmed. Such concepts may seem idealistic goals but they are not trivial, for unless we incorporate them into a philosophy not only for ourselves, but for those who have seen 65 years or more, is *real* progress in mental health possible?

## IMPLICATIONS FOR EDUCATION AND TRAINING

A major problem has been that our knowledge of the mental health problems and the frequency of psychiatric disturbances in the elderly has a weak information base. Epidemiologists such as Redick, Kramer, and Taube (1973) and Kramer (1976) point out that we still have few operational guidelines to use to estimate the exact number and types of patients, the kinds of dependency and disability in the population, and the types of manpower required, as well as how many or in what types of facilities or various community situations these services might be best delivered. Kramer, in discussing the present lack of services, emphasized the point that, if reliable estimates of manpower are going to be made and if existing manpower is going to be used most effectively, "then it is essential that a high priority be given to the design and implementation of the research that will yield the required facts" (1976, p. 198).

In 1967, Lowenthal, Berkman and associates reported that three million elderly people, i.e., 30 percent of the aged population, suffered from moderate to severe psychiatric problems; 10 percent of these were said to require hospitalization.

If we take only the minimum figure of 10 percent of the population 65 years of age and over, who may require the services of mental health professionals, then the number of people requiring attention and the number of staff required become quite alarming. Kramer (1975a, 1976) estimated that, at this level of need, there were 2,217,000 older adults requiring psychiatric services during 1975. In 1980 those in need would total 2,405,300 and in 1985 (when the population over 65 is projected to be 26,659,000) those requiring mental health services would number 2,665,900 if we maintain an estimated 10 percent level of need. Kramer goes on to state that, if we work on the assumption that a psychiatrist works 1500 hours per year (involving 50 weeks of the year and an average of 30 hours per week), the number of psychiatrists required, based on the above estimates of need, to provide six hours per patient per year, ranges from 8,860 in 1975 to 9,621 in 1980 and 10,664 in 1985. The increase of 1,804 in the number of psychiatrists between 1975 and 1985 is due to the 20 percent increase expected in the number of persons in this age group.

The number of psychiatrists estimated to provide these 6 hours of services per year per needing aged person in 1975, i.e., 8,860, was about 32 percent of the approximately 25,000 psychiatrists available. If we think beyond a meagre 10 percent minimum need to provide intensive care it is obvious that we will just not have enough psychiatrists. For instance, if we use a 20 percent demand level and calculate that 12 hours per patient per year are needed, then the required number of psychiatrists for the older population in 1975 was 35,400 and in 1985 would be 42,656. An even bleaker picture is painted when we realize that geriatric psychiatry in the US is still so embryonic that Butler (1975) estimated that there were fewer than 20 psychiatrists in the entire country who could be regarded as expert in the field. But there are many other mental health professionals who serve the aged, such as psychiatric nurses, social workers and clinical psychologists. The same shortages of trained personnel face these fields as well.

Kramer (1975a, 1976) estimated that the same number of psychologists as psychiatrists would be needed for this age group, yet Storandt (1975) estimated, after making a survey of clinical psychology programs associated with aging, that there were only 100 individuals who by virtue of their graduate training could be regarded as having some appropriate qualifications for work with the aged.

What, then, has our society typically done with its population over 65 who have psychiatric problems since there are so few trained professionals? Birren and Renner (1979) reviewed the historical trends in this area and pointed out that early management of elderly people who presented problems involved custodial care on "poor" farms. This era was succeeded by a heavy dependence on state mental hospitals. Kolb (1956), in analyzing admission rates to these hospitals, found that there appeared to be an excessive admission rate in those over 65 years of age. For first admissions per 100,000 persons the rate increased from 166.6 in 1936 to 214.5 in 1951. This involved an increase of 95.3 percent during this period, since the actual increase in population for this age group was only 57.5 percent. Clearly, mental hospitalization was being over-done and most likely many of the elderly were being admitted to these institutions for a variety of social reasons. Many people became concerned that the state mental hospitals were becoming inadequate homes for the aged.

The reaction to this trend could be seen between 1955 and 1972 when the rate of first admissions to mental hospitals for those over 65 dropped dramatically to the 1936 figure of 166.4 per 100,000 population (Kramer, 1975b).

During this time, outpatient psychiatric services, community health centers and similar facilities were growing rapidly. Yet, in 1969, only 2.6 percent of those admitted to day care services in community health centers were 65 years and over. In community health centers, with their range of inpatient and outpatient facilities, only 4 percent of total admissions were in this age group (Kramer, Taube, and Redick, 1973). In 1971 the number of elderly being seen in outpatient clinics was only 2.4 per 100,000 (National Institute of Mental Health, Mental Health Statistics, 1974) while, for the general population, there had been an increase in the use of these services from 241 to 620 per 100,000 population between 1963 to 1971, an increase of 157 percent.

Certainly the number of the aged in the general population was increasing; indeed it increased by 36 percent between 1955 and 1968. Trends indicate that mental health problems among the older population are not diminishing (Kramer *et al.*, 1973; Kramer and Redick, 1975; U.S. Department of Health, Education and Welfare, 1971). This is dramatically illustrated by figures given for completed suicides. In 1970, 23,480 persons (16,639 men and 6,851 women) committed suicide in the United States and, of these, 7,399 (4,171 men and 3,226 women) or 31.5 percent were 65 years of age or more (Pfeiffer, 1977). Thus the question can reasonably be asked where the elderly were and are receiving help? *A complete answer would undoubtedly give a picture of the inadequate state of mental health services for the aged at the present time.* The major locus of care of the elderly now is in nursing homes and related care facilities where medical and psychiatric services are limited. As Birren and Renner (1979) comment:

> The pendulum has thus swung again from mental hospitals back to a 'poor farm' concept, where although many of these facilities are much more sophisticated and better organized than their earlier counterparts, the principle remains that admission to these nursing homes is likely being abused and the type of care available is restricted to that of a custodial nature.

An Anglo-American conference on the care of the elderly was held in 1976 (Exton-Smith and Evans, 1977). From the evidence it is apparent that it is difficult and artificial to consider mental health problems of the aged apart from those of internal medicine and welfare, and a broader conceptual approach is required. Renner and Birren (1976) and Birren and Renner (1979) suggest that part of any therapeutic program for the elderly must not only embrace the adequate leadership and training of professionals, but also a sound theoretical and empirical framework from which therapeutic applications can be made. Whatever his age, a man should feel he has worth and dignity. By neglecting mental health services for the older adult we are robbing him of that human right.

# REFERENCES

ALPAUGH, P., AND HANEY, M. 1978. *Counseling the Older Adult: A Training Manual for Paraprofessionals and Beginning Counselors.* Los Angeles: Andrus Gerontology Center, University of Southern California Press.

ARENBERG, D., AND ROBERTSON-TCHABO, E. A. 1977. Learning and aging. *In,* J. E. Birren and K. W. Schaie (eds.), *Handbook of the Psychology of Aging,* pp. 421–449. New York: Van Nostrand Reinhold.

BENGTSON, V. L. 1973. *The Social Psychology of Aging.* New York: Bobbs-Merrill.

BIRREN, J. E. 1961. A brief history of the psychology of aging. *Gerontologist, 1*, 69–77, 127–134.

BIRREN, J. E. 1964. *The Psychology of Aging.* Englewood Cliffs, N.J.: Prentice-Hall.

BIRREN, J. E. 1967. Age and decision strategies. *In*, A.T. Welford and J. E. Birren (eds.), *Decision Making and Age*, pp. 23–36. New York: S. Karger.

BIRREN, J. E., AND RENNER, V. J. 1977. Research on the psychology of aging: Principles and experimentation. *In*, J. E. Birren and K. W. Schaie (eds.), *Handbook of Aging and the Individual*, pp. 3–38. New York: Van Nostrand Reinhold.

BIRREN, J. E., AND RENNER, V. J. 1979. *A Brief History of Mental Health and Aging.* Washington, D.C.: National Institute of Mental Health. In press.

BIRREN, J. E. AND RENNER, V. J. A biobehavioral approach to theories of aging. Paper presented at Symposium No. 5, Society, Stress and Disease, 1976. Stockholm. In press.

BLAU, Z. S. 1956. Old Age: A study of change in status. Unpublished doctoral dissertation, Columbia University. As cited by Merton, R. K, 1968, *Social Theory and Social Structure*, pp. 242–243. New York: The Free Press.

BLAU, Z. S. 1973. *Old Age in a Changing Society.* New York: New Viewpoints.

BOTTOMORE, T. B., AND RUBEL, M. 1964. *Karl Marx. Selected Writings in Sociology and Social Philosophy.* New York: McGraw-Hill.

BOTWINICK, J. 1977. Intellectual abilities. *In*, J. E. Birren and K. W. Schaie (eds.), *Handbook of the Psychology of Aging*, pp. 580–605. New York: Van Nostrand Reinhold.

BÜHLER, C. 1961. Meaningful living in the mature years. *In*, R. W. Kleemeier (ed.), *Aging and Leisure*, pp. 345–387. New York: Oxford University Press.

BÜHLER, C. 1968. Fulfillment and failure of life. *In*, C. Bühler and F. Massarik (eds.), *The Course of Human Life*, pp. 400–403. New York: Springer.

BÜHLER, C., AND MASSARIK, F. (eds.), 1968. *The Course of Human Life.* New York: Springer.

BUTLER, R. N. 1963. The Life review: An interpretation of reminiscence in the aged. *Psychiatry, 26*, 65–76.

BUTLER, R. N. 1975. *Why Survive? Being Old in America.* New York: Harper & Row.

CAMPBELL, A. 1976. Subjective measures of well-being. *American Psychologist, 31*, 117–124.

COMFORT, A. 1956. *The Biology of Senescence.* London: Routledge and Kegan Paul.

COWDRY, E. V. (ed.), 1939. *Problems of Ageing.* Baltimore: Williams & Wilkins.

CUMMING, E., AND HENRY, W. E. 1961. *Growing Old. The Process of Disengagement.* New York: Basic Books.

DURKHEIM, E. 1951. *Suicide: A Study in Sociology.* Translated by J. A. Spaulding and G. Simpson. New York: The Free Press.

ERIKSON, E. H. 1959. *Identity and the Life Cycle. Psychological Issues*, Monograph I. New York: International Universities Press.

ETZIONI, A. 1968. Basic human needs, alienation and inauthenticity. *American Sociological Review, 33*, 870–885.

EXTON-SMITH, A. N., AND EVANS, J. G. (eds.). 1977. *Care of the Elderly: Meeting the Challenge of Dependency.* London: Academic Press.

FLANAGAN, J. C. 1978. A research approach to improving our quality of life. *American Psychologist, 33, 138–147.*

FOZARD, J. L., AND THOMAS, J. C. 1975. Psychology of Aging: Basic Findings and Their Psychiatric Applications. *In*, J. G. Howells (ed.), *Modern Perspectives in the Psychiatry of Old Age*, pp. 107–169. New York: Brunner-Mazel.

FROMM, E. 1941. *Escape From Freedom.* New York: Rinehart.

FROMM, E. 1955. *The Sane Society.* Greenwich, Conn.: Fawcett.

GEYER, R. F., AND SCHWEITZER, D. R. (eds.), 1976. *Theories of Alienation.* Leiden: Martinus Nijhoff, Social Sciences Division.

GOLDFARB, A. V. 1974. Minor maladjustments in the aged. *In*, S. Arieti and E. B. Brody (eds.), *American Handbook of Psychiatry, 3*, pp. 820–860. New York: Basic Books.

GROTJAHN, M. 1940. Psychoanalytic investigation of a 71-year-old man with senile dementia. *Psychoanalytic Quarterly, 9*, 80–97.

GRUMAN, G. J. 1966. *A History of Ideas About the Prolongation of Life: The Evolution of Prolongevity Hypothesis to 1800.* Philadelphia: American Philosophical Society.

GUTTMANN, D. (ed.), 1977. *The Impact of Needs, Knowledge, Ability and Living Arrangements on Decision Making of the Elderly.* Washington, D.C.: National Catholic School of Social Service, Catholic University of America.

HALL, G. S. 1922. *Senescence.* New York: Appleton-Century Crofts.

HANDLER, P. 1960. *Radiation and aging. In*, N. W. Shock (ed.), *Aging*, pp. 199–223. Washington, D.C.: American Association for the Advancement of Science.

HARRIS, L., AND ASSOCIATES. 1975. *The Myth and Reality of Aging in America.* Washington, D.C.: The National Council on Aging.

HEATH, D. H. 1977. *Maturity and Competence.* New York: Gardner Press.

HERR, J. J., AND WEAKLAND, J. H. 1979. *Counseling Elders and Their Families.* New York: Springer.

ISAACS, A. D. AND POST, F. (eds.), 1978. *Studies in Geriatric Psychiatry.* New York: John Wiley.

ISRAEL, J. 1971. *Alienation: From Marx to Modern Sociology.* Boston: Allyn and Bacon.

JAHODA, M. 1958. *Current Concepts of Positive Mental Health.* New York: Basic Books.

JOHNSON, E. S., AND BURSK, B. J. 1977. Relationships between the elderly and their adult children. *Gerontologist, 17,* 90–96.

JOHNSON, F. (ed), 1973. *Alienation. Concept, Term and Meanings.* New York and London: Seminar Press.

JOSEPHSON, E., AND JOSEPHSON, M. (eds.), 1962. *Man Alone: Alienation in Modern Society.* New York: Dell.

JUNG, C. G. 1962. *Modern Man in Search of a Soul.* Translated by W. S. Dell and C. F. Baynes. London: Routledge and Kegan Paul.

KAHLER, E. 1957. *The Tower and the Abyss.* New York: Braziller.

KENISTON, K. 1965. *The Uncommitted Alienated Youth in American Society.* New York: Harcourt, Brace and World, Inc.

KOLB, L. 1956. The mental hospitalization of the aged: Is it being overdone? *American Journal of Psychiatry, 112,* 627–635.

KRAMER, M. 1975a. Psychiatric services and the changing institutional scene. Paper presented at the President's Biomedical Research Panel, November 25. Unpublished manuscript.

KRAMER, M. 1975b. Historical tables on changes in patterns of use of psychiatric facilities, 1946–1972–1973. Bethesda, Md.: Biometry Branch, National Institute of Mental Health (mimeograph).

KRAMER, M. 1976. Issues in the development of statistical and epidemeological data for mental health services research. *Psychological Medicine, 6,* 185–215.

KRAMER, M., AND REDICK, R. W. 1975. Epidemeological indices in the middle years. Unpublished manuscript.

KRAMER, M., TAUBE, C. A., AND REDICK, R. W. 1973. Patterns of use of psychiatric facilities by the aged: Past, present, and future. *In,* C. Eisdorfer and M. P. Lawton (eds.), *The Psychology of Adult Development and Aging,* pp. 428–528. Washington, D.C.: American Psychological Association.

KUTNER, B. S., FANSHEL, F., TOGO, A. M., AND LANGNER, T. S. 1956. *Five Hundred Over Sixty.* New York: Russell Sage.

KUYPERS, J. A., AND BENGTSON, V. L. 1973. Social breakdown and competence. *Human Development, 16,* 181–201.

LOWENTHAL, M. F. 1964. Social isolation and mental illness in old age. *American Sociological Review, 29,* 54–70.

LOWENTHAL, M. F., BERKMAN, P. L., AND ASSOCIATES. 1967. *Aging and Mental Disorder in San Francisco: A Social Psychiatric Study.* San Francisco: Josey-Bass.

MARTIN, W. C., BENGTSON, V. L., AND ACOCK, A. C. 1974. Alienation and age: A context-specific approach. *Social Forces, 53,* 266–274.

MARX, K. 1962. Alienated labor. *In.* E. Josephson and M. Josephson (eds.), *Man Alone: Alienation in Modern Society,* pp. 93–105. New York: Dell.

MCCLOSKY, H., AND SCHAAR, J. H., 1965. Psychological dimensions of anomy. *American Sociological Review, 30,* 14–40.

MERTON, R. K. 1968. *Social Theory and Social Structure.* New York: The Free Press.

MILLS, C. W. 1953. *White Collar.* New York: Oxford University Press.

MILLS, C. W. 1962. The mass society. *In,* E. Josephson and M. Josephson (eds.), *Man Alone,* pp. 201–227. New York, Dell.

NATIONAL INSTITUTE OF MENTAL HEALTH, MENTAL HEALTH STATISTICS. 1974. *Outpatient Psychiatric Services 1971–1972.* D.H.E.W. Publication No. (A.D.M.) 69–74. Washington, D.C.: Government Printing Office.

NEUGARTEN, B. L. 1969. Continuities and discontinuities of psychological issues into adult life. *Human Development, 12,* 121–130.

NEUGARTEN, B. L. 1970. Dynamics of transition of middle age to old age: Adaptation and the life cycle. *Geriatric Psychiatry, 4,* 71–87.

NEUGARTEN, B. L., BERKOWITZ, H., CROTTY, W. J., GRUEN, W., GUTMANN, D. L., LUBIN, M. I., MILLER, R., PECK, F., ROSEN, J. L., SHUKIN, A., TOBIN, S. S., AND FALK, M. (eds.), 1964. *Personality in Middle and Late Life.* New York: Atherton Press.

NEUGARTEN, B. L., MOORE, J. W., AND LOWE, J. C. 1965. Age norms, age constraints, and adult socialization. *American Journal of Sociology, 70,* 710–717.

NIEDEREHE, G., 1977. Interaction of stressful events with locus of control in depressions of later life. Paper presented at the 30th Annual Scientific Meeting of the Gerontological Society, San Francisco, California, November 20.

NISBET, R. A. 1970. *The Social Bond. An Introduction to the Study of Society.* New York: Knopf.

PARSONS, T. 1949. *The Structure of Social Action.* New York: The Free Press.

PFEIFFER, E. 1977. Psychopathology and social pathology. *In,* J. E. Birren and K. W. Schaie (eds.), *Handbook of the Psychology of Aging,* pp. 650–671, New York: Van Nostrand Reinhold.

POST, F. 1966. *Persistent Persecutory States of the Elderly.* New York: Pergamon Press.

QUETELET, A. 1835. *Sur l'homme et le développement de ses facultés.* Paris: Bachelier.

REDICK, R. W., KRAMER, M., AND TAUBE, C. A. 1973. Epidemeology of mental illness and utilization of psychiatric facilities among older persons. *In,* E. W. Busse and E. Pfeiffer (eds.), *Mental Illness In Later Life.* pp. 194–231. New York: American Psychiatric Association.

REICHARD, S., LIVSON. F., AND PETERSON, P. G. 1962. *Aging and Personality: A Study of 87 Older Men.* New York: John Wiley.

RENNER, V. J., AND BIRREN, J. E. 1976. The concepts and criteria of mental health and their application to aging. Paper presented at the Western Psychological Association, Los Angeles, April.

RIEGEL, K. F. 1973. Dialectical operations: The final period of cognitive development. *Human Development, 16,* 346–370.

RIESMAN, D. 1950. *The Lonely Crowd.* New Haven: Yale University Press.

ROSOW, I. 1974. *Socialization to Old Age.* Berkeley, Ca.: University of California Press.

ROTTER, J. B. 1966. Generalized expectancies for internal versus external control of reinforcement. *Psychological Monographs, 80,* 1–28.

SCHACHT, R. 1971. *Alienation.* New York: Doubleday.

SEEMAN, M. 1959. On the meaning of alienation. *American Sociological Review, 24,* 783–791.

SEEMAN, M. 1976. Empirical alienation studies. An overview. *In,* R. F. Geyer and D. R. Schweitzer (eds.), *Theories of Alienation,* pp. 265–305. Leiden: Martinus Nijhoff, Social Services Division.

SELLS, S. B. (ed.) 1968. *The Definition and Measurement of Mental Health.* Washington, D.C.: U.S., D.H.E.W., National Center for Health Statistics.

SHANAS, E. 1961. *Family Relationships of Older People.* New York: Health Information Foundation.

SHANAS, E. 1967. Family help patterns and social class in three countries. *Journal of Marriage and Family, 29,* 257–266.

SHANAS, E. 1979. Social myth as hypothesis: The case of the family relations of old people. *Gerontologist. 19,* 3–9.

SIMMEL, G. 1950. The metropolis and mental life. *In,* K. H. Wolff (ed.), *The Sociology of Georg Simmel,* pp. 409–424. Glencoe, Ill.: The Free Press.

SKINNER, B. F. 1971. *Beyond Freedom and Dignity.* New York: Knopf.

SLATER, P. 1976. *The Pursuit of Loneliness: American Culture at the Breaking Point.* Boston: Beacon Press.

SODDY, K. (ed.). 1961. *Identity, Mental Health and Value Systems.* London: Tavistock Publications.

STORANDT, M. 1975. Graduate education in gerontological psychology. Paper presented at the American Psychological Association, Washington, D.C.

SUSSMAN, M. B., AND BURCHINAL, L. 1962. Kin family network: Unheralded structure in current conceptualizations of family functioning. *Marriage and Family Living, 24,* 231–240.

SYMONDS, P. M. 1949. *Dynamic Psychology,* New York: Appleton-Century-Crofts.

THOMAE, H. (ed.). 1976. *Patterns of Aging. Vol. 3. Contributions to Human Development.* Basel, Switzerland: S. Karger.

TOWNSEND, P. 1962. Isolation, loneliness and the hold on life. *In,* E. Josephson and M. Josephson (eds.), *Man Alone: Alienation in Modern Society,* pp. 326–329. New York: Dell.

U.S. DEPARTMENT OF HEALTH, EDUCATION AND WELFARE, 1971. *Physical and Mental Health.* Report of the 1971 White House Conference on Aging. Washington, D.C.: Government Printing Office.

U.S. PUBLIC HEALTH SERVICE. 1943. *Mental Health in Later Maturity.* Washington, D.C.: Government Printing Office. Suppl. 168, U.S. Public Health Service Reports.

VAILLANT, G. E. 1977. *Adaptation to Life.* Boston: Little Brown.

WEBER, M. 1968. *On Charisma and Institution Building, Selected Papers.* Edited and with an Introduction by S. N. Eisenstadt. Chicago: The University of Chicago Press.

WEISHAUS, S. 1978. *Determinants of affect of middle-aged women towards their aging mothers.* Unpublished Doctoral dissertation, Department of Sociology, University of Southern California.

WELSH, G. S. 1977. Personality correlates of intelligence and creativity in gifted adolescents. *In,* J. C. Stanley, W. C. George, and C. H. Solano (eds.), *The Gifted and the Creative: A Fifty-year Perspective.* Baltimore: The Johns Hopkins University Press, pp. 197–221.

WHITE, R. W. 1959. Motivation reconsidered. *Psychological Review, 66,* 297–331.

WHYTE, H. W., Jr. 1956. *The Organization Man.* New York: Simon & Schuster.

WIGDOR, B. T., AND MORRIS, G. 1977. A comparison of twenty-year medical histories of individuals with depressive and paranoid states: A preliminary note. *Journal of Gerontology, 32,* 160–163.

WILLIAMS, R. H. 1972. *Perspectives in the Field of Mental Health.* Rockville, Md.: National Institute of Mental Health.

WILLIAMS, R. H., AND WIRTHS, C. C. 1965. *Lives Through the Years.* New York: Atherton Press.

# 2

# Epidemiology
# of Mental Disorders
# Among the Aged in the
# Community

*David W. K. Kay & Klaus Bergmann*

Epidemiology may be defined as the study of the distribution of morbidity in time and place, and of the factors which influence this distribution. Morbidity may be studied from hospital statistics or case registers, in general practice, or by carrying out field surveys. The field survey is the method used for detecting unreported illness in the community, and its aim is to assess, more or less intensively, the health of every person, either directly or indirectly. Field studies among the aged constitute the main topic of this chapter. The majority of them have been carried out in the aging populations of northern Europe and Japan.

The results of field surveys are expressed as rates of incidence and prevalence of a disorder within a defined population, or in the case of general practice studies as consultation rates. The *incidence (or inception)* rate refers to the number of persons falling ill within a specified time either with

first-ever illnesses or with new episodes, while the *prevalence rate* refers to the existing number of cases who are ill at any given time (point prevalence) or during a given period (period prevalence) irrespective of time of onset. The number of ill persons forms the numerator, the number at risk the denominator, and the ratio is expressed as a percentage, or as a rate per 1,000 or other convenient unit. When the frequency of an illness changes rapidly with age, it is essential to calculate the rates for each age group separately (age-specific rates).

Another index is the *morbid risk* or *disease expectancy*. This is the chance a person has of falling ill with a given disorder during his lifetime or up to a specified age. Of these indices, incidence and expectancy are the more biologically fundamental since they measure the actual rate of occurrence of a disorder and how it changes at different periods of life or varies in time and place, while prev-

34

alence is a function of incidence and *duration* of illness and is mainly of utilitarian interest. One survey suffices to estimate the prevalence of a disorder but to estimate its incidence it is necessary to survey a population on two separate occasions to determine the number of cases identified on the second survey who were not identified as ill on the first survey. Retrospective accounts of morbidity must be regarded as unreliable, particularly as the onset of many psychiatric disorders is difficult to date precisely. Expectancy may be estimated by the birth cohort method (see below) or from the cumulative incidence rates in consecutive age groups. Because of the difficulties comparatively few studies of incidence and expectancy of psychiatric disorders have been attempted.

## AIMS AND LIMITATIONS OF EPIDEMIOLOGICAL STUDIES

In general the aims of epidemiological studies of mental disorders may be utilitarian, clinical or scientific (Cooper and Shepherd, 1973). Surveys of the aged have had one or more of the following aims:

1. At a utilitarian level to assist in the *planning and evaluation of services*. This is specially important for brain damaged persons, who have special needs (Kay, Bergmann, Foster, McKechnie, and Roth, 1970), and for whom existing services may be inadequate (Foster, Kay, and Bergmann, 1976).
2. To examine the *social characteristics* of representative groups of mentally ill persons, exemplified by studies of marital status (Bellin and Hardt, 1958; Nielsen, 1962), social class (Kay, Beamish, and Roth, 1964b), and the environment (Gruenberg, 1961).
3. To identify disorders in the *early stage of development*, with a view to making predictions, and eventually to prevention and treatment (Kay, Bergmann, Foster, and Garside, 1966).
4. To examine the *age distribution* of the onset of disorders to identify those that are related to aging and those that are not (Hagnell, 1970b).
5. To investigate the *genetics* of senile and arteriosclerotic psychoses (Åkesson, 1969) and of senile dementia (Larsson, Sjögren, and Jacobson, 1963).
6. To permit better estimates of *disease expectancy* of the common disorders (T. Helgason, 1973; Larsson *et al.*, 1963).
7. Finally, to be able to make valid comparisons of the characteristics of well and ill persons with given disorders, and of communities with high or low rates of incidence or prevalence, both nationally and cross-nationally, and over periods of time.

Although a certain amount of information has accumulated about the prevalence of chronic brain syndrome which has drawn attention to the needs of the extramural aged and their families, most of the aims just listed have remained largely unfulfilled. Before considering the reasons for this and the special problems facing field investigators, two general limitations of the epidemiological method may be mentioned. The first lies in the impossibility of drawing conclusions about cause and effect from correlational data alone, an example of this being the association between social isolation and mental disorder. Secondly, the multiplicity of factors involved in the etiology of psychiatric disorders makes it difficult to isolate one from another. For instance, the proneness of the aged to depression may be due to factors that are not themselves intrinsic to aging but often accompany it in modern societies.

## EPIDEMIOLOGICAL METHODS

### DEFINING THE POPULATION AT RISK

The first step in carrying out an epidemiological study at any level is to define the denominator or population at risk, to which the number of ill persons are to be put into relation. There are two main methods.

In the *birth cohort or longitudinal method* all the persons born in a defined region over a certain period constitute the denominator. The whole cohort is traced till death or until it reaches a specified age, and the past and present psychiatric morbidity of all the members ascertained, so far as this is possible. Theoretically, this is the ideal method for determining the incidence and expectancy of disorders, but it is impossible to carry out except in geographically isolated communities, such as Iceland (T. Helgason, 1973), where there is continuity of records and little movement of the population. The *limited period longitudinal survey* is more practicable and has been used in Iceland (L. Helgason, 1977), Sweden (Åkesson, 1969; Hagnell, 1966) and England (Bergmann, Kay, Foster, McKechnie, and Roth, 1971).

In the *census method* a defined population is studied on a certain date or over a short period, such as six months or one year, to determine the numbers and proportions of ill and well people in the community. This is the most widely used method, but requires accurate information about the size and demographic characteristics of the population to be surveyed, and, if a sample is to be studied, the securing of an unbiased sample.

In some countries there may be difficulties in ascertaining who the aged members are. The method used will depend on what sources of information are locally available, for example, parish registers, electoral rolls, general practitioners' lists, social security files, or a combination of these methods (Gilmore and Caird, 1972). It may however be necessary to carry out household surveys to locate old people before the morbidity study can begin.

## DETERMINING THE NUMERATOR

*Psychiatric Case Registers.* In hospital statistics inpatients constitute the numerator for calculating rates. The limitations of this procedure have often been pointed out (Lemkau, 1955; Terris, 1965). To make up for some of the selective biases of hospital figures special *Psychiatric Case Registers* were set up. Their aims and characteristics have been described by Wing, Wing, Hailey, Bahn, Smith, and Baldwin (1967). These registers record contacts not only with inpatient facilities but with a wide variety of psychiatric services, such as day and outpatient clinics and in some areas social agencies and private psychiatrists. However, they do not usually incorporate data from general hospitals, nursing homes or residential homes even though many mentally ill old persons are known to reside in these places.

*General Practice Studies.* General practice studies fall between the studies based on psychiatric referrals and field surveys. General practitioners in both the US and UK see many more people with psychological problems than they ever refer to psychiatrists (Mazer, 1976; Shepherd, Cooper, Brown, and Kalton, 1966; Watts, Cawte, and Kuenssberg, 1964). However, field surveys have shown that there remains a large amount of illness among the aged including some severe illness, that even in countries where no charge is made for consultation, is unknown to general practitioners (Parsons, 1965; Williamson, Stokoe, Gray, Fisher, Smith, McGhee, and Stephenson, 1964). General practitioners' patients evidently do not constitute a random sample of ill persons.

*Field Surveys.* Unlike studies based on contact with existing agencies, field surveys have to generate their own data. The methodological problems include the scope and intensity of the case finding process, the techniques to be used in contacting and interviewing respondents, and the criteria chosen for the actual identification of "a case"

WHOLE POPULATION SURVEYS. In the earlier studies, summarized by Lin (1953), whole populations of defined regions were surveyed. This was done by a two or multistage process of screening, followed by closer examination of suspected cases. The aged were included only as a part of the population, and there was an interest in whether psychiatric disorder in general, or a particular type of disorder, increased or decreased with age (Lemkau, Tietz and Cooper, 1942; Pasamanick, Roberts, Lemkau and Krueger, 1957). Probably only the more severe cases were identified. In fact the prevalence rates for senile and arteriosclerotic psychoses were about 10 times lower that those found later when attention was focussed on cognitive functioning rather than gross behavioral disturbances. The rates for neuroses were also very low. The survey by Åkesson (1969) was also of this kind but was restricted to the aged population, and explicit criteria of severity were used.

In the Syracuse survey (New York State Department of Mental Hygiene, 1961), which was also restricted to the aged, each person was interviewed by trained lay interviewers, and the protocols were interpreted later by clinicians for evidence of severe mental disorder. Diagnoses were not made, however. In the Stirling County study (Leighton, Harding, Macklin, MacMillan, and Leighton (1963), the method was similar but all age groups were surveyed. Samsø, the Danish island, constitutes a case register and special project area in which the psychiatric morbidity of the whole population has been studied over a number of years but particular attention has been paid to the aged (Nielsen, 1962, 1976).

PSYCHIATRIC INTERVIEW METHOD. In this method there is no screening stage and the psychiatric state of every member of the population or of the sample is personally assessed by a psychiatrist or by the general practitioner (Bentsen, 1970; Bremer, 1951; Primrose, 1962). When all age groups are included rates of illness at different ages can be compared in the knowledge that the same methods of assessment have been used. The Lundby study is unique, in that a survey of the 2,550 inhabitants of a Swedish town was repeated after a 10 year interval (Essen-Möller, 1956; Hagnell, 1966) and the rate of incidence of disorders could be estimated. Although the neuroses and milder deviations of personality were the authors' main interest the incidence of psychotic disorders in the aged was noted to be very high (Hagnell, 1970a).

Other surveys in which this method was used were concerned solely with the aged. For instance, Bollerup (1975) was concerned with the "hidden morbidity" of the aged, that is with the amount of unknown and untreated illness in the community, and with the proportions of psychotic and demented persons who were living outside institutions. Kay, Beamish, and Roth (1964a) were interested in this question, and also in the detection of illness in its early stages. Bergmann (1970, 1971) made a special study of the neuroses of old age. Williamson *et al.* (1964) surveyed the patients attached to some general practices to discover how much mental disorder was unknown to the general practitioners. Parsons (1965) wished to establish the prevalence of serious psychiatric illness in the elderly living at home for service purposes, and did not examine hospitalized patients. Jensen (1963) was interested in the psychiatric problems of residents in homes for the aged but also conducted an enquiry about all aged persons living in the parish. Although the personal interview method appears to be the ideal method for surveys among the aged, the size of the samples has usually been small and the yield of cases correspondingly few. The method might be combined with a screening procedure to enable more ill persons to be studied.

*Questionnaire Methods.* A different approach to the assessment of psychiatric morbidity in the general population is the use of questionnaires. These are designed to detect the presence of symptoms, not to generate diagnoses. The questionnaire may consist of a check list of symptoms administered by lay interviewers (Comstock and Helsing, 1976; Gaitz and Scott, 1972; Hare and Shaw, 1965; Schwab, Holzer, and Warheit, 1973) or they may be self-rating scales such as the self-rating Depression Scale (Zung, 1965) or the General Health Questionnaire (Goldberg, 1972), both of which have been used with the elderly (Finlay-Jones and Burvill, 1977; Zung, 1967). Important limitations of self-rating scales are that they cannot be used to identify psychotic or demented persons and further, that it may be difficult to separate psychological symptoms from those with a physical basis.

## SPECIAL PROBLEMS OF FIELD SURVEYS

PROBLEMS OF CASE IDENTIFICATION

*The Reliability of Psychiatric Diagnosis and the Development of Standard Interviewing Techniques.* Whether some method of screening is used or not, the problem of who is to be categorized as ill and counted as a "case" remains crucially important in epidemiological studies. In the past, becoming a patient of a psychiatrist was the usual case-finding method, and the psychiatrist's evaluation was the ultimate criterion of diagnosis. When case finding moved into the community it was assumed that the making of a diagnosis would adequately identify cases. However, questions soon arose concerning both the reliability of psychiatric diagnosis and the categorizing of cases.

Until recently, no systematic studies of the reliability of psychiatric diagnosis in the aged appear to have been made. The reliability of the diagnoses in the studies reported later in this chapter is unknown. Gunner-Svensson and Jensen (1976), after reviewing nine investigations into the prevalence of mental disorder in the aged, concluded that the results were difficult to compare and stressed the need for more standardized methods of investigation and diagnosis in the future.

As part of the US/UK Diagnostic Project, Copeland, Kelleher, Duckworth, and Smith (1976) administered the Geriatric Mental Status (GMS) interview to hospitalized patients and were able to show that good agreement between raters could be achieved when the diagnoses were grouped into six main categories. These were: schizophrenia and paranoid states; affective disorders; neuroses and personality disorders; alcoholism and addiction; organic brain syndromes; and other diagnoses. There is little doubt that the use of modern interviewing techniques of known reliability will be obligatory in the future. Preliminary studies have already shown that they can be used effectively in community surveys (Gurland, Copeland, Sharpe, Kelleher, Kuriansky, and Simon, 1977-78; Wing, Mann, Leff, and Nixon, 1978).

*The Concept of a "Case" and the Objectives of the Study.* The making of a reliable diagnosis does not automatically identify a "case" in field surveys, because other criteria may be required. For example, social criteria are often regarded as specially relevant in the disorders of the aged. As Lin (1953) remarked on his Taiwan study, the identification of a case as one of senile psychosis may depend on the threshold of tolerance of the family and the community towards deviant behavior in the aged. However, whether social criteria are relevant to case identification or not should depend upon the purposes for which the study is being carried out.

An alternative to employing social criteria for case definition in field surveys is to count only those cases in which the intensity of symptoms reaches a certain level. For example, the intensity may have to be at least as great as the minimal intensity found in actual patients (Ingham and Miller, 1976; Wing, 1976; Wing *et al.*, 1978). Similarly, in studies using questionnaires, potential cases may be identified by using a cut-off point which has been shown to misclassify the smallest number of patients and normals (Goldberg, 1972). In the case of brain syndromes this is what many authors have done, at least implicitly. In other studies, however, different criteria have been employed. Åkesson (1969) required the presence of constant disorientation in time and place, and in the Syracuse study the cases had to be certifiable according to the state laws. Some authors have created a category of "mild dementia" applicable mainly to nonhospitalized persons.

These considerations suggest that psychiatric syndromes, in the absence of any pathological lesion, may have no universal meaning except in terms of operational criteria and the specific objectives of the investigation.

### INTERVIEWING PROBLEMS

If the old persons are to be interviewed at home, the manner in which they are approached and the interview carried out is important because too many refused or uncompleted interviews make it difficult to draw conclusions about the population as a whole, fruitless or unproductive calls are wasteful, and the accuracy of the information obtained and the reliability of the clinical assessment depend on using a suitable method. Methods of sampling older persons and differences between respondents and nonrespondents were described by Milne, Maule, and Williamson (1971) and some interesting comments on the human element in survey research among the aged were made by Dean, Teresi, and Wilder (1977-78).

Four decisions have to be made. How is contact to be made? Who is to carry out the interviews? What form should the interview take? And fourth, should any rewards or inducements be offered?

Contact may be established either by a letter seeking an appointment or by making an unannounced call. If the former method is used, the letter may be unanswered or misunderstood, or a relative's and not the old person's decision may be the one to be communicated. This is most likely to happen when the respondent is very old, physically ill, blind, illiterate, or suffers from a brain syndrome. According to Dean et al. (1977-78), it may take 10 hours of work to obtain an appointment for one interview. There is some anecdotal evidence (Parsons, 1965) that introductory letters cause more anxiety and a higher refusal rate than unheralded visits. Moreover, personal contact, even when brief, still permits some observations to be made. The choice may depend on the importance attached to seeing a random sample, at the expense of some incomplete interviews.

If no appointment is to be made, many calls will be fruitless and there may be failure to establish contact in up to 10 percent of the sample, as occurred in the Syracuse survey. However, respondents with whom interviews fail are probably not a homogeneous group. Some of them will not be at home because they are vigorous and active, while others are protected by relatives because they are very old and enfeebled. The presence of others in a household in which the old person has an inferior status may reduce the chances of a successful interview (New York State Department of Mental Hygiene, 1961).

When contact is made, it is essential to allay the old person's anxiety. A common fear is that the caller has come about the pension, tax, rent, or the collection of debts. The idea of a formal interview is forbidding to many old people and, instead, the aim should be to have a relaxed dialogue. The purpose of the visit should be explained in general, rather than specific, terms. The pros and cons of offering inducements or services are discussed by Dean et al. (1977-78) who conclude that an eclectic approach is best.

The next question is whether to use lay or professional interviewers. If the size of the sample to be interviewed is large, considerations of cost and time may settle the question in favor of lay interviewers. In the Syracuse survey the lay interviewers were specially trained for the task, but their protocols were interpreted by clinicians, a procedure the validity of which may be questioned (Dohrenwend, Egri, and Mendelsohn, 1971). Finally, the age and sex of the interviewer may be relevant but no actual information seems to be available on this point.

Interviews in private homes take place under widely differing conditions, and the technique must be adaptable and acceptable to people of varying background, education, and physical and mental health. Many aged persons are easily fatigued, and some are offended by questions which seem tactless or intrusive. The semistructured type of interview requires all the relevant areas to be covered, but allows the interviewer to take them in any order and to phrase them in words which seem to be most appropriate on each occasion (Copeland, Kelleher, Kellett, Gourlay, Gurland, Fleiss, and Sharpe, 1976). The items themselves are best committed to memory and the protocol completed after the interview. In our experience people who refused usually claimed they did so on grounds of "principle". However, the refusal rate is affected by the amount of effort and time which the respondent is asked to give. It rises, for instance, when psychological tests (Kuriansky, Gurland, and Cowan, 1976) or physical examination (Williamson et al., 1964) are included.

The interview should be conducted with the old person alone, without interference from relatives, but when memory is impaired or there are signs of neglect, independent information from another person may be essential in reaching a firm diagnosis.

## THE PREVALENCE AND INCIDENCE OF MENTAL DISORDERS IN THE COMMUNITY AGED

### CASE REGISTERS

The *one-day prevalence rates* for all kinds of mental disorder in the aged which have been reported from the case registers in Aberdeen, Baltimore and Camberwell (Wing et al., 1967) are about 10 times lower than the rates found in field surveys, where they are of the order of 15–20 percent (Bollerup, 1975; Essen-Möller, 1956; Kay et al., 1964a). In all three registers the rates rose steadily and reached a peak in the oldest age group, suggesting that there is an accumulation of cases throughout life.

*Incidence rates* show a different pattern. The one-year rates of new episodes of contact with registers for all diagnoses are lowest after the age of 65 in two of the three registers, varying from 5 to 9 per 1,000. The rates from Aberdeen show a second peak above the age of 60 in both sexes, and the rates reported from the Samsø special project (Nielsen, 1976) are very similar to those in Aberdeen (Wing et al., 1967). In the Lundby survey (Hagnell, 1970b) the incidence rates at most ages are somewhat higher than the rates found in Samsø in females though not in males. The most striking feature of this survey, however, is the very large increase in new episodes of illness occurring after the age of 70, diagnosed mostly as psychotic, and untreated by psychiatrists. This points to a serious gap in the registration of brain syndromes in the aged.

Incidence rates for different diagnoses by age are available from four case registers (Figure 2–1). These rates are not strictly comparable with each other, but show some common patterns, and also some differences. In Aarhus (Juel-Nielsen, Bille, Flygenring, and Helgason, 1961) the rates are for a new episode during one year; in Camberwell, UK (Wing, Hailey, Barnsby, and Fryers, 1972) they are for a first episode during the 5-year existence of the register; in Salford, UK (Adelstein, Downham, Stein, and Susser, 1968) they refer to first-ever referrals to a psychiatric agency; and in Iceland (L. Helgason, 1977) they are for first-ever psychiatric consultations. The Aarhus figures given

for neuroses refer to depressive neuroses and psychogenic psychoses; in the other registers neuroses refer to all forms of neurosis. The data on treated illness obtained from registers may be compared with the results of field surveys to provide estimates of the extent of unreported illness in the community.

### GENERAL PRACTICE STUDIES

General practice studies are of most interest for the information they give about minor psychiatric morbidity. They have shown that, unlike referrals to psychiatrists, general practice consultations for neuroses remain at a high level throughout life (Figure 2–2) in the UK (Kessel and Shepherd, 1962) and in Norway (Bentsen, 1970), as did consultations for all kinds of psychiatric disorder in the US (Mazer, 1976). Watts (1966) found that depression was common among his elderly patients and that, in males, the highest rate of episodes was in the decade 65 to 75 years.

### FIELD SURVEYS

Most authors of epidemiological surveys have paid special attention to separating organic brain syndromes from functional psychoses but have also identified cases of neuroses and personality disorder, and less often alcoholism. In this chapter the mental disorders of the aged will be considered under the following six headings:

1. Acute organic brain syndrome (ICD code 293).
2. Chronic organic brain syndrome (ICD codes 290, 294).
3. Schizophrenia and paranoid psychoses (ICD codes 295, 297).
4. Affective psychoses (ICD codes 296, 298.0).
5. Neuroses and personality disorders (ICD codes 300, 301).
6. Alcoholism (ICD code 303).

Unresolved problems in psychiatric classification exist which cannot be altogether avoided by broad groupings. The most serious of these concerns the distinction between the affective psychoses (ICD 296) and the depressive neuroses (ICD 300.4). A complication is the presence in Scandinavian nomenclature of the group of psychogenic psychoses which is intermediate between the psychoses and neuroses. However, psychogenic psychoses comprise only a small proportion of disorders in old age.

*Acute Organic Brain Syndrome.* About 15 percent of old persons admitted to geriatric or acute general medical wards show signs of acute brain syndrome at some stage (Bergmann and Eastham, 1974;

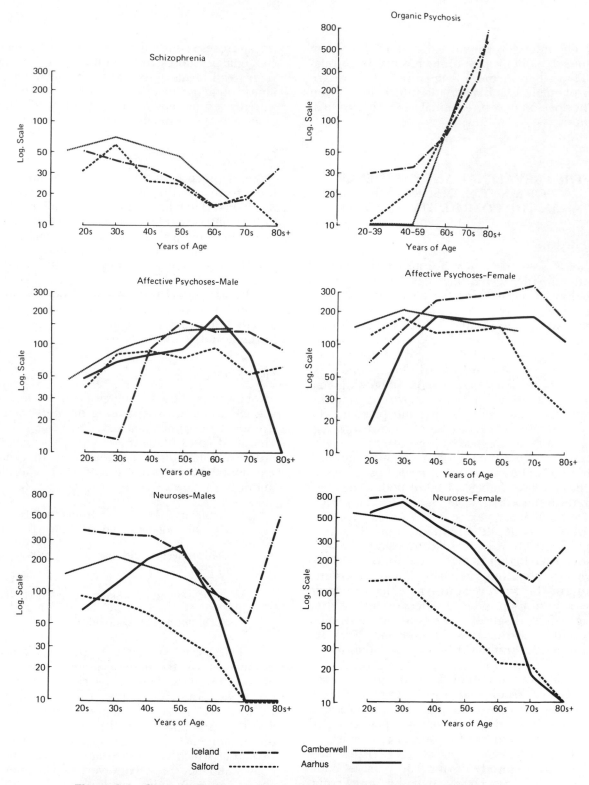

**Figure 2-1** One-year incidence rates for various disorders in four case register areas: Aarhus (Juel-Nielsen *et al.,* 1961), Camberwell (Wing *et al.,* 1972), Iceland (L. Helgason, 1977), and Salford (Adelstein *et al.,* 1968). The points for the Camberwell study have been calculated by the authors from the graphs published by Wing *et al.* (1972), and for the other studies, from the figures provided by the authors.

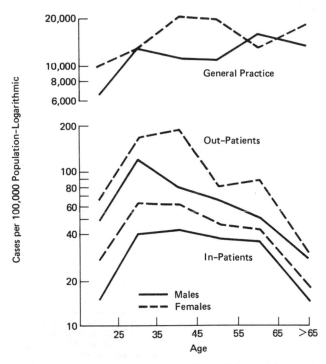

**Figure 2–2** Age prevalence of neurosis studied during one year. From Kessell and Shepherd (1962). The authors wish to acknowledge permission from Professors W. Kessell and M. Shepherd and the Editor of the British Journal of Psychiatry.

Hodkinson, 1973), but the incidence in the general population has not been studied, no doubt because of difficulties in operational definition, the short duration of episodes, and the close association with physical illness and mortality. Also, a code for acute brain syndrome (293) only appeared in the last edition of the International Classification of Diseases (WHO, 1977). Clinical experience, however, shows that the incidence of symptoms due to acute brain syndrome sharply increases at ages over 60 years, often on the basis of a chronic brain syndrome (Simon and Cahan, 1963).

*Chronic Organic Brain Syndrome.* The chronic brain syndrome is the disorder causing most concern in the aging populations of Europe and North America. The aims of field surveys have been to delineate the size of the problem, to locate the cases and to provide a rationale for planning. They also provide the unusual opportunity to study or treat the disorder in the early stages, and to obtain normative data on the cognitive functioning of random samples of the aged (Savage, Britton, Bolton, and Hall, 1973).

The chronic brain syndrome may be subdivided according to the severity of the dementia,

the presumed pathological condition present, or whether the place of residence is institutional or noninstitutional.

PREVALENCE OF DEMENTIA BY SEVERITY. Table 2–1 summarizes the results of a number of recent studies of prevalence in most of which all of those at risk were personally interviewed and including studies in which severity was not stated. Studies in which fewer than 200 aged persons were interviewed are excluded. The authors used different numbers of grades of severity and defined them in different ways, but a combination of the severe and moderate categories (figures in brackets) probably gives roughly comparable results across some of the studies at least. This category comprises persons who are unable to care for themselves and are therefore potential hospital cases (Akhtar, Broe, Crombie, McLean, Andrews, and Caird, 1972; Kay *et al.*, 1964; Nielsen, 1962; Parsons, 1965). The rate is generally between 5 and 8 percent. In the Syracuse study the rate was 6.2 percent, but the criterion was "certifiability" (New York State Department of Mental Hygiene, 1961), and some of the cases may have been suffering from functional psychoses and not brain syndromes (Gruenberg, 1961). When severe dementia is defined as "total disorientation" or "needing almost constant care" the prevalence rates are 1–2 percent (Åkesson, 1969; Bollerup, 1975; Jensen, 1963) which is fairly close to the rates for ages 60 or over reported in the earlier studies from the US (Lemkau *et al.*, 1942), Germany (Brugger, 1931), Taiwan (Lin, 1953) and Tokyo (Tsugawa, 1942).

Table 2–2 shows the prevalence of moderate or severe forms of chronic brain syndrome by age and Table 2–3 by sex. The overall rates for the sexes are very similar though there may be an earlier onset in males. In both sexes there is a progressive rise in rates with age. After the age of 80 the combined rate approaches 20 percent.

Most authors report a category of "mild dementia" which with one exception affects from 6 to 22 percent of the aged persons interviewed. Table 2–2(b) shows the prevalence of mild dementia by age in the three surveys in which this was reported. There is a marked difference between the rates found in Scandinavia and in Japan: in fact the concepts seem to have been different.

There is no code for mild dementia in the ICD (WHO, 1977) and at the present time it must be regarded as an experimental concept rather than a definite syndrome. Further study of the clinical picture and followup are needed to determine the status of this condition. Information on outcome is so far very limited, but Nielsen, Homma,

**Table 2–1** Prevalence Rates (Per Cent) of Dementia According to Severity

| AUTHOR | COUNTRY | AGE | N | SEVERE | MODERATE* | MILD | REMARKS |
|---|---|---|---|---|---|---|---|
| Lin (1953), | Taiwan | 60+ | 1,096 | – | – | (0.5) | – | Enquiry + interviews |
| Essen-Möller (1956), | Sweden | 60+ | 443 | 5.0 | – | (5.0) | 10.8 | Severe: impaired comprehension of speech; disorientation. Mild: impaired memory |
| Nielsen (1962), | Denmark | 65+ | 978 | 3.1 | 2.9 | (6.0) | 15.4 | Severe: inability to care for self. Moderate: cerebrovascular disease with mental symptoms. Mild: decline in performance, fluctuating level. 6-month prevalence rates |
| New York State Dept. Mental Hygiene (1961) | United States | 65+ | 1,805 | – | – | (6.8) | – | Degree: Potentially "certifiable." Includes functional psychoses. |
| Primrose (1962), | Scotland | 65+ | 222 | – | – | (4.5) | – | International Classification of Diseases, 1955 (WHO, 1957) |
| Jensen (1963), | Denmark | 65+ | 546 | 1.1 | 7.1 | (8.2) | – | Severe: total disorientation. (Nonhospitalized) |
| Leighton et al. (1963), | Canada | 60+ | 270 | – | – | (5.9) | – | Degree not specified. Lay interviewers |
| Kay et al. (1964a), | England | 65+ | 297 | 5.6 | – | (5.6) | 5.7 | Severe: disorganization of personality and failure in activities of daily living. Mild: deterioration in faculties greater than would be expected from age |
| Williamson et al. (1964) | Scotland | 65+ | 200 | 1.5 | 6.5 | (8.0) | 15.5 | Grades of severity not defined |
| Parsons (1965), | England | 65+ | 228 | 4.4 | 9.6 | (14.0) | 21.9 | Severe: self care impossible. Moderate: definitely forgetful. Mild: slightly impaired memory. PALT administered. (Nonhospitalized) |
| Balier et al. (1968), | France | 65+ | 985 | – | – | (3.8) | – | Interview method (Nonhospitalized) |
| Åkesson (1969), | Sweden | 70+ | 1,869 | 2.1 | – | (–) | – | Constant disorientation for time and place |
| Kaneko (1969), | Japan | 65+ | 531 | 0.6 | 6.6 | (7.2) | 52.7 | Severe: severely impaired memory, information and orientation, some habit deterioration. Moderate: intellect and recent memory impaired, partial disorientation. Mild: slight or doubtful dementia without obvious clinical symptoms |
| Helgason, T. (1973), | Iceland | 74–76 | 2,642 | 5.0 | – | (5.0) | 6.9 | Grades of severity not defined |
| Gilmore (1974), | Scotland | 65+ | 300 | 0.6 | 13.0 | (13.6) | – | Based on scores on a Memory and Information Test. (Nonhospitalized) Moderate includes mild cases |
| Bollerup (1975), | Sweden | All 70 | 626 | 1.6 | 3.4 | (5.0) | – | Severe: needing almost constant care |
| Bentsen (1970), | Denmark | 60+ | 798 | – | – | (6.3) | – | 4-year period prevalence study in general practice |

*Figures in brackets are the sums of severe and moderate categories, or the rates when no grade of severity is given by the author.

and Björn-Henriksen (1977a) followed 151 aged persons with mild dementia previously studied (Nielsen, 1962) for 15 years and found that, in each age group over 70, their duration of life was significantly shorter than that of persons without any mental disorder, but longer than in persons with severe dementia. Bergmann et al. (1971) made a similar observation but noted that only six of their 20 cases with mild or questionable dementia had developed definite dementia after an average pe-

**Table 2–2** Prevalence (Percent) of Organic Brain Syndromes by Age Groups

*(a) Moderate or severe dementia*

| STUDY | 65–69 | 70–74 | 75–79 | 80–84 | 85(+) | ALL AGES |
|---|---|---|---|---|---|---|
| Kaneko, 1975[a] N=531 | 1.9 | 2.7 | 11.3 | 9.9 | 33.3 | 7.1 |
| Nielsen, 1962 N=978 | 2.1 | 4.0 | 7.8 | 12.6 | 21.4 | 5.9 |
| Syracuse Study, 1961[b] N=1805 | 3.7 | 5.4 | 9.3 | 8.8 | 23.7 | 6.8 |
| Kay et al., 1970[a] N=758 | 2.4 | 2.9 | 5.6 | 22.0 | | 6.2 |
| Essen-Möller, 1956[c] N=443 | 0.9 | 5.1 | | 21.8 | | 5.0 |

*(b) "Mild dementia"*

| | | | | | | |
|---|---|---|---|---|---|---|
| Kaneko, 1975[a] | 44.3 | 62.6 | 55.7 | 48.7 | 52.7 | |
| Nielsen, 1962 | 4.2 | 12.1 | 23.8 | 37.1 | 15.4 | |
| Essen-Möller, 1956[c] | 3.5 | 16.6 | | 25.5 | 10.8 | |

[a]Persons living at home only

[b]Includes some functional psychoses

[c]Age groups 60–69, 70–79, 80+

riod of three years. It is probable that persons thought to manifest mild dementia are a heterogeneous group.

PREVALENCE OF DEMENTIA ACCORDING TO PATHOLOGY. The validity of subdividing chronic brain syndrome into senile and arteriosclerotic forms has long been questioned. However, it appears from recent neuropathological (Roth, 1971; Terry and Wisniewski, 1977; Tomlinson, Blessed, and Roth, 1970) and clinical studies that vascular or multi-infarct dementia and dementia associated with Alzheimer's neuronal degeneration are separate conditions, and that it is important to distinguish between them.

The distribution of cases diagnosed as senile or arteriosclerotic dementia by age and sex as reported in four studies is shown in Table 2–4. All the authors refer to the criteria proposed by Roth (1955).[1] The following generalizations seem possible. (1)Before the age of 75, arteriosclerotic dementia is more common than senile dementia in males, and both types of dementia are rare in females. (2)After the age of 75, senile dementia is as frequent as or more common than arteriosclerotic dementia in both sexes, except in Japan where the latter diagnosis is still considerably more common in females. (3)Senile dementia is a disease occurring mainly in the over 75 age group, while arteriosclerotic dementia also mainly affects this age group in females, but occurs earlier in males.

PLACE OF RESIDENCE OF PERSONS WITH CHRONIC BRAIN SYNDROME. It is of interest to see where the persons with chronic brain syndrome were residing. Of 751 persons in the five surveys in which this question was examined (Bollerup, 1975; Jensen, 1963; Kay et al., 1964a; New York State Department of Mental Hygiene, 1961; Nielsen, 1962)

**Table 2–3** Prevalence (percent) of Organic Brain Syndromes by Sex

| | Pooled Data[a] | | | | |
|---|---|---|---|---|---|
| | MALES N = 1008 | | FEMALES 1259 | | BOTH SEXES 2267 |
| AGE | % | S.E.[b] of % | % | S.E.[b] of % | % |
| 65- | 3.9 ± 0.97 | | 0.5 ± 0.35* | | 2.1 |
| 70- | 4.1 ± 1.21 | | 2.7 ± 0.85 | | 3.3 |
| 75- | 8.0 ± 1.99 | | 7.9 ± 1.67 | | 8.0 |
| 80- | 13.2 ± 2.64 | | 20.9 ± 2.68* | | 17.7 |
| All Ages | 6.2 ± 0.76 | | 6.3 ± 0.68 | | 6.3 |

[a]From Nielsen (1962), Kay et al. (1970), Kaneko (1969).

[b]S.E. = standard error.

*Difference between males and females is statistically significant (p < .01).

[1]Arteriosclerotic dementia is "associated with focal signs and symptoms indicative of cerebrovascular disease, or a remittent or markedly fluctuating course at some stage of the dementing process . . . combined with any one of the following features: emotional incontinence, the preservation of insight, or epileptiform seizures." Senile dementia is defined as "a condition with a history of gradual and continually progressive failure in the common activities of everyday life and a clinical picture dominated by failure of memory and intellect and disorganization of personality" when these are not attributable to specific causes.

**Table 2–4**  Distribution of Senile and Arteriosclerotic Dementia by Age and Sex (Number and Percent)

| Age group | Country | MALES | | | FEMALES | | | BOTH SEXES | | |
|---|---|---|---|---|---|---|---|---|---|---|
| | | Arterio-sclerotic dementia | Senile dementia | Total N(%) | Arterio-sclerotic dementia | Senile dementia | Total N(%) | Arterio-sclerotic dementia | Senile dementia | Total N(%) |
| 65–74 | Japan[a] | 5 | 1 | | 1 | 0 | | 6 | 1 | |
| | Denmark[b] | 12 | 1 | | 2 | 3 | | 14 | .4 | |
| | England[c] | 4 | 1 | | 1 | 3 | | 5 | 4 | |
| | Sweden[d] | 1 | 0 | | 2 | 2 | | 3 | 2 | |
| | **Total** | 22(24%) | 3(3%) | 25(27%) | 6(5%) | 8(7%) | 14(11%) | 28(13%) | 11(5%) | 39(18%) |
| 75 and over | Japan | 5 | 4 | | 16 | 6 | | 21 | 10 | |
| | Denmark | 4 | 13 | | 10 | 13 | | 14 | 26 | |
| | England | 6 | 4 | | 4 | 16 | | 10 | 20 | |
| | Sweden | 12 | 18 | | 16 | 27 | | 28 | 45 | |
| | **Total** | 27(30%) | 39(43%) | 66(73%) | 46(38%) | 62(51%) | 108(89%) | 73(34%) | 101(47%) | 174(82%) |
| All ages | | 49(54%) | 42(46%) | 91(100%) | 52(43%) | 70(58%) | 122(100%) | 101(47%) | 112(53%) | 213(100%) |

[a]Kaneko (1975). Criteria not stated.

[b]Nielsen (1962). Senile dementia includes some cases of arteriosclerotic dementia "in a late undifferentiated phase." Arteriosclerotic dementia = "cerebrovascular disease with mental symptoms."

[c]Kay et al., (1964a), Roth's (1965) criteria. Åkesson (1969) Roth's criteria, but with "constant temporal and spatial disorientation."

only 148 or 25 percent were living in institutions while 75 percent were living at home (Table 2–5).

STUDIES OF INCIDENCE OF CHRONIC BRAIN SYNDROME. Information about the incidence of chronic brain syndrome is scanty but several approaches have been made (Table 2–6). It may be seen that there is good agreement between the three case registers, and between them and the field survey carried out by Åkesson (1969). The average annual incidence ranged from 0.2 to 0.4 percent after the age of 60 and from 0.7 to 1.4 percent after 80. In the field surveys by Bergmann et al. (1971) and by Hagnell (1970a), in which all the individuals at risk were personally interviewed, the rate was several

times higher. Hagnell's figures, however include all kinds of psychosis, and some of Bergmann's subjects were suspected of being demented at the first interview and perhaps should be excluded. The revised estimate would be 1.1 percent per annum after the age of 65.

Estimates of disease expectancy over a lifetime, based on referred or hospitalized cases, have been made by Larsson et al. (1963) for senile dementia, and for senile and arteriosclerotic psychoses combined by L. Helgason (1977). The risks are in the range 1.3–2.1 percent, and they may be compared with the risk found by T. Helgason (1973) in his birth cohort study in which the primary sources of information were the general prac-

**Table 2–5**  Percentages of People with Psychoses of Old Age Living at Home and in Institutions.

| | NIELSEN[a] (1962) | | NEW YORK STATE DEPART OF MENTAL HYGIENE (1961)[b] | | KAY ET AL.[c] (1964a) | | BOLLERUP[d] (1975) | | JENSEN[e] (1963) | |
|---|---|---|---|---|---|---|---|---|---|---|
| | N | % | N | % | N | % | N | % | N | % |
| Hospitals Welfare Homes | 24 | 41.4 | 41 | 33.3 | 68 | 13.5 | 4 | 20.0 | 11 | 24.4 |
| At home | 34 | 58.6 | 82 | 66.7 | 437 | 86.5 | 16 | 80.0 | 34 | 75.6 |
| Total No. ill | 58 | 100% | 123 | 100% | 505 | 100% | 20 | 100% | 45 | 100% |
| Total Sample size | 978 | | 1805 | | 297[c] | | 626 | | 546 | |

[a]Includes severe dementia, and cerebrovascular disease with mental symptoms.

[b]"Certifiable" or certified cases. General hospitals not included in survey.

[c]Random sample of 297 out of population of 9,031 were interviewed at home; another 208 were located in institutions. No. ill at home is an estimated number.

[d]Senile and arteriosclerotic dementia, all aged 70.

[e]Severe and mild. Hospitals were not included.

**Table 2–6**  Estimated Annual Incidence Per 1,000 of Chronic Brain Syndrome

| AUTHOR, AND COUNTRY | PERIOD OF STUDY | N & SEX | AVERAGE ANNUAL INCIDENCE PER 1,000 | | | ALL AGES OVER 60 | REMARKS |
|---|---|---|---|---|---|---|---|
| | | | 60–69 | 70–79 | 80+ | | |
| L. Helgason (1977), *Iceland* | 2 years | 22,206 M | 0.8 | 2.6 | 9.4 | 2.3 | Case register study. First-ever consultations for senile or arteriosclerotic psychoses. |
| | | 25,130 F | 0.7 | 2.8 | 8.3 | 2.5 | |
| Adelstein et al. (1968), *Salford, UK* | 5 years | 9,228 M | 1.1 | 2.4 | 6.9 | 1.9 | Case register study. First referrals with senile and organic disorders. |
| | | 15,581 F | 0.8 | 2.8 | 6.7 | 2.1 | |
| Wing et al. (1972) *Camberwell, UK* | 5 years | 6,860 M | – | – | – | 1.5 | Case register study. First contacts with the register for dementia. |
| | | 13,000 F | – | – | – | 3.0 | |
| Åkesson (1969), *Sweden* | 3 years | 2,071 M | 0.3 | 4.8 | 8.6 | 2.6 | Census and enquiry method with followup. Senile and arteriosclerotic psychoses with constant disorientation. |
| | | 2,127 F | 1.2 | 3.6 | 13.7 | 3.5 | |
| Bergmann et al. (1971), *Newcastle, UK* | 2½–4 years Av. 3 years | 760 | – | – | – | 15.0 | Random sample personally interviewed and followed up. Dementia from any cause. |
| Hagnell (1970a), *Sweden* | 10 years | 455 | 8.4 | 21.5 | 34.0 | 15.6 | Personal interviews with whole population. Incidence of new cases of "senile psychoses" during 10-year period. Rates given are uncorrected for deaths. |

titioners. This was about five times higher, and the discrepancy suggests that only some 10 to 25 percent of cases of chronic brain syndrome in Iceland are ever actually referred to a psychiatrist.

*Schizophrenia and Paranoid Psychoses.* The prevalence of schizophrenia and related psychoses will depend on whether only hospitalized patients are counted or whether "inactive" cases living in the community are included. The number of former patients living outside hospitals is substantially greater than in the past. However, various authors (Bentsen, 1970; Bollerup, 1975; Bremer, 1951; Essen-Möller, 1956; Nielsen, 1962; Primrose, 1962; Strömgren, 1938) have found age specific prevalence rates of active cases in the region of 3–5 per 1,000 population at risk, which agrees well with the rates reported in psychiatric case registers and suggests that most of the cases are known to psychiatric agencies. Variation in prevalence after the age of 60 or 65 probably depend on the alternative types of care provided in different regions. Table 2–7 shows prevalence rates for the functional psychoses combined (i.e. schizophrenic plus affective psychoses).

Studies of incidence are of interest because of the widely held view that the period of risk for schizophrenia ceases at about the age of 45. However, case register data (Adelstein *et al.*, 1968) show that new referrals still occur after the age of 70. In Iceland, L. Helgason (1977) found that 15 percent of the risk in males and 37 percent of the risk in females remained to be passed after the age of 50. The incidence and prevalence of paranoid psychoses of late onset are probably underestimated

because they are often diagnosed as organic brain syndromes (Gurland, Fleiss, Goldberg, Sharpe, Copeland, Kelleher, and Kellett, 1976).

*Affective Psychoses*  As in the case of schizophrenic psychoses, field surveys have been on too small a scale to be informative about the relatively rare affective states diagnosable as psychotic. Most of the active cases are probably known to psychiatric agencies. However, this may not be true after 60 when the incidence of reported cases falls off both in case registers (Figure 2–1) and in first admissions to mental hospitals (Kay, 1976). In the Salford register, after the age of 70, the rate declined less in males than in females, and there seemed to be a reversal of the sex incidence (Adelstein *et al.*, 1968). This was not found in the Aarhus register, however (Juel-Nielsen *et al.*, 1961). In Iceland, the lifetime expectancy for affective psychosis is nearly three times higher for females than for males, and the incidence continues to be higher in females after the age of 60 (L. Helgason, 1977). A differential use of psychiatric facilities was suggested. The incidence of affective psychosis at advanced ages is worth further study.

The question is complicated by the unresolved problems of psychiatric classification whereby depressive neuroses may be included either with affective disorders (i.e. affective psychoses + depressive neuroses) or with neuroses. It appears from the data, however, that the clinical form of treated depression changes with age. Relatively more older persons are under treatment for depressive psychoses and fewer for reactive depressions and depressive neuroses. However, as ap-

**Table 2–7** Prevalence Rates (Percent) for Neuroses + Personality Disorders, Functional Psychoses and Chronic Alcoholism

| AUTHOR | N | AGE | NEUROSES AND PERSONALITY DISORDERS | FUNCTIONAL PSYCHOSES[a] | CHRONIC ALCOHOLISM | REMARKS |
|---|---|---|---|---|---|---|
| Essen-Möller (1956) | 443 | 60+ | 12.0 | 1.4 | M 16.1 (60–69) M 3.9 (70+) | Interview with psychiatrist |
| Kay et al.[b] (1964a) | 505 | ;65+ | 12.5 | 2.4 | – | Interview with psychiatrist |
| Williamson et al.[c] (1964) | 240 | 65+ | 16.5 | 12.0 | – | Interview with psychiatrist |
| Bollerup (1975) | 626 | All 70 | 7.4 | 1.4 | M 1.3, F 0.6 | Interview with psychiatrist |
| Parsons (1965) | 220 | 65+ | 4.8 | 2.6 | – | Interview with psychiatrist |
| Hagnell & Turving (1972) | 443 | 60–69 70+ | – | – | M 16.2 M 6.0 | Interview with psychiatrist |
| Nielsen (1962) | 978 | 65+ | 6.8 | 3.7 | M 1.0, F 0.5 | Case register and some interviews |
| Helgason, T. (1973) | 2,642 | 74–76 | 9.9 | 3.7 | – | Birth cohort. Records, including those of general practitioners and some interviews |
| Leighton et al. (1963) | 270 | 60+ | 27.0 | 1.5 | M 8.0, F 0 | Lay interviews and interpretation by clinicians |
| Bentsen (1970) | 500 | 60+ | 23.2 | 1.2 | M 2.9, F 0 | 4-year period prevalence survey in general practice |
| Bailey et al. (1965) | | 65–74 75+ | – | – | M + F 2.2 M + F 1.2 | Household survey in U.S.A. |

[a]Schizophrenia, paranoid psychoses, affective psychoses.

[b]N is an estimated number.

[c]Functional psychoses included unspecified depressive states.

pears from the next section, field surveys indicate that depressive neuroses are quite common in the elderly.

*Neuroses and Personality Disorders.* These conditions are numerically important in psychiatry and though usually regarded as minor, they may be associated with much unhappiness, social disturbance, suicidal behavior or drug or alcohol abuse. The age for their appearance was believed to be early adult life (Shepherd and Gruenberg, 1957). Statistics from hospitals and case registers showed a decline in the incidence of neuroses with age (Figure 2–1), and elderly persons were known to make little use of outpatient facilities where neurotic illness might be found (Kramer, 1969). There was also evidence that neuroses ameliorated with age (Ciompi, 1969). Despite the evidence from general practice, neuroses and personality disorders in the elderly tended to be regarded as of little importance.

PREVALENCE OF NEUROSES IN FIELD SURVEYS OF THE AGED. When old persons are personally interviewed and psychiatric symptoms elicited, neurotic disorders are generally reported to be present in 4 to 9 percent, with a marked preponderance in

females. If personality disorders are added, the overall rate for minor, functional psychiatric morbidity may be as high as 7 to 12 percent, though in the survey by Leighton *et al.* (1963) the rate was about twice as high, presumably due to the use of different criteria. These rates are similar to those found over the age of 60 in general practice studies (Bentsen, 1970; Kessel and Shepherd, 1962).

Direct comparisons across age groups can be made in the Stirling County study (Leighton *et al.*, 1963), the general practitioner studies (Bremer, 1951; Primrose, 1962), and the psychiatrists' survey of the town of Lundby, Sweden (Essen-Möller, 1956; Hagnell, 1966) in which all age groups were studied by the same methods. Although the results of these four surveys cannot be compared with each other, individually they each show that neuroses and related disorders continue to be found at the same or only slightly lower rates after the age of 60 years than before that age. The frequency of personality disorders also hardly alters with age (Essen-Möller, 1956).

INCIDENCE. For observations on the incidence of neuroses we are almost entirely indebted to Hagnell (1966, 1970b). Hagnell showed that the average annual incidence both of neurotic episodes in general and of first-ever episodes after the age of 60 was about one-half to one-third of the peak incidences in both sexes. Hagnell (1970b) also found that neurotic episodes occurring after the age of 70 usually lasted longer than episodes occurring earlier.

One of the difficulties in assessing Hagnell's findings concerns the reliability of recollections of neurotic episodes and their dates of onset and termination over a 10-year period. There are no other sets of data with which Hagnell's can directly be compared. Bergmann (1971) found that rather over one-half the neuroses in his aged sample had probably begun after the age of 60 but he did not try to estimate their rate of occurrence. However, T. Helgason (1973), in his birth cohort study, succeeded in tracing the members of his cohort from the age of 60-62 years for a further 14 years, and found a crude average annual incidence of new neurotic illness during this period of 2.7 per 1,000. This is about half that found by Hagnell (1966) after the age of 60. Hagnell (1970b) himself concluded after considering various other possibilities that the cause of the lower rate of incidence of neurosis with increasing age might actually be an improvement in mental health and adaptation.

DEPRESSIVE NEUROSES AS THE NEUROSES OF OLD AGE. In England and Wales first admission rates for both depressive neuroses and unspecified depressions increase with age relative to other forms of neurosis (Kay, 1976). In the field survey carried out by Bergmann (1971) depressive neuroses were found to replace anxiety neuroses as the commonest form of neurosis beginning in old age. Four percent of males and 11 percent of females manifested a depressive neurosis beginning after 60 and rated as of at least moderate severity. A prevalence study on the island of Samsø (Sørensen and Stromgren, 1961) showed that 1.5 percent of males and 4.8 percent of females over the age of 60 years were being treated for depression on the census day, the difference between the sexes being due to depressive neuroses. In the Stirling County study depressive neurotic symptom patterns were found in 9 percent of both males and females over the age of 60 (Leighton *et al.*, 1963). This was a period prevalence study lasting five years, in which past as well as present symptoms were enquired into, but Essen-Möller and Hagnell (1961) concluded from their Lundby study that recollection was not a reliable basis for making estimates of the expectancy of depressive illness. From the incidence rates in successive age

groups, these authors estimated the lifetime expectancy of developing a depression diagnosable as such by a psychiatrist as 18 percent for females and 8 percent for males.

QUESTIONNAIRE STUDIES OF DEPRESSIVE SYMPTOMS IN THE AGED. Field surveys tend to support the general practice finding that neuroses continue to be found in old age, and show that they have a measurable incidence. Questionnaire studies have shed some light of their own on this question. These studies will not be reviewed individually here; they are summarized in Table 2–8. One of the most striking features in several of these studies is that the highest depressive responses were obtained from the oldest and youngest age groups. However, the responses of the aged are not consistently unfavorable. Most intriguing, perhaps, are the studies by Comstock and Helsing (1976), Finlay-Jones and Burvill (1977), and Warheit, Holzer, and Schwab (1973), in which the oldest persons either scored more favorably that the younger respondents, or they did so after other variables such as income, socioeconomic status, and sex were held constant. It is possible that the association of age with indices of depression in some of the studies may be a consequence of the social changes that accompany aging rather than due to the aging process itself. Comstock and Helsing (1976) even suggested that age alone may reduce the tendency to feel depressed!

*Alcoholism.* Most of our scanty knowledge of the epidemiology of alcoholism comes from the Scandinavian countries (Bentsen, 1970; Bollerup, 1975; Nielsen, 1962) and from the US study by Bailey, Haberman, and Alksne (1965). These surveys mostly show (Table 2–7) that 1–3 percent of males aged 60 or over are suffering from chronic alcoholism. The two Lundby surveys (Essen-Möller, 1956; Hagnell and Turving, 1972) show a much higher prevalence; in fact the peak rate of 16 percent in males was in the decade 60–69 but it fell abruptly after the age of 70. The cause of this is unknown. Less than one quarter of the cases were known to the official agency.

## CHARACTERISTICS OF THE MENTALLY DISORDERED AGED IN THE COMMUNITY

One of the major aims of epidemiology is to give an account of the characteristics which distinguish the mentally ill persons in a population. Field surveys have added little to what was already known

**Table 2–8** Studies in Which Questionnaires Have Been Used to Detect Psychiatric Symptoms Across Age Groups

| AUTHOR (YEAR) | PLACE | TOTAL | INSTRUMENT | RESULTS |
|---|---|---|---|---|
| Hare & Shaw (1965) | Croydon, U.K. | 2,000 | Symptom Questionnaire | Over-64 group gave highest number of depressive symptom responses. |
| Zung (1967) | U.S.A. | 1,468 | 20 item self-rating depression scale (SDS) | Over-64 group scored higher than middle-aged and similar to under-20 age group. |
| Berkman (1971) | California, U.S.A. | 6,928 | 8-item Index of Psychological Well-Being. | Over-64 group and youngest groups worse than middleaged |
| Benfari, et al. (1972) | New York City, U.S.A. | 1,531 | Self-reporting Q of 53 neurotic symptoms, and Factor Analysis | Over-60 group had low score on 'self-esteem factor' but 'topically-oriented depression' and 'anxiety depression' decreased with age. |
| Gaitz & Scott (1972) | Houston, U.S.A. | 1,441 | (1) 22-item Langer screening scale (2) Affect Balance scale (3) Self-appraisal | No significant overall increase of symptoms with age but increase in 'depression' factor with age. Middle-aged groups intermediate between extremes. |
| Scott & Gaitz (1975) | Houston, U.S.A. | 1,441 | " | Despite reporting lower health ratings, aged gave higher ratings of self-satisfaction than younger age groups. |
| Warheit et al. (1973) | S.E. Co., U.S.A. | 1,642 | Depression Q of 18 items given by trained raters | Age was related to the score before but not after SES and sex were partialled out. |
| Schwab et al. (1973) | S.E. Co., U.S.A. | 1,642 | " | Over-60 group and young group report symptoms of depression more than middle-aged group. |
| Finlay-Jones & Burvill (1976) | Perth, Australia | 2,324 | G.H.Q. (Goldberg, 1972). Response rate 66% | 60–69 group scored *lower* than younger age groups for minor psychiatric morbidity. |
| Comstock & Helsing (1976) | Kansas, U.S.A. | 3,845 | 20-item symptom Q. Nonmedical interviewers | Over-64 group score *lower* than younger age groups after correction for other variables (e.g. income). |

about the functional psychoses but have contributed to our understanding of organic syndromes and of neuroses in the elderly.

## ORGANIC BRAIN SYNDROMES

The sexes appear to be about equally at risk for senile dementia (Larsson *et al.*, 1963) but brain syndromes from other causes such as chronic alcoholism and neurosyphilis are more common in males. Cerebrovascular disease, as such, seems to be equally distributed but may have an earlier onset and a more disturbing effect on mental function and behavior in males than females (Hagnell, 1970a). The importance of physical disease, both intra- and extracerebral, in aged persons with acute and chronic brain syndrome was shown in the Newcastle (Kay *et al.*, 1964b) and San Francisco (Lowenthal, Berkman *et al.*, 1967) surveys. In the Syracuse survey (New York State Department of Mental Hygiene, 1961) the association between physical illness and mental disorder was specially close in males. Mortality is high in chronic brain syndrome even in unselected samples (T. Helgason, 1973; Nielsen *et al.*, 1977a).

The associations found between brain syndromes and social factors are difficult to interpret. In Syracuse, there was a correlation between high rates of first admission to mental hospitals for se-

nile and arteriosclerotic psychoses and areas of the city with high concentrations of multifamily dwellings, and with high percentages of people living alone (Gruenberg, 1954). However, rates of certifiable mental disorder in the community could not be definitely related to these areas, although they were related to the socioeconomic ratings of the homes in which the residents lived. Fisch, Goldfarb, Shehinian, and Turner (1968) found that old persons with brain syndrome who remained in the community tended to be strongly independent individuals who rejected care-giving agencies.

In Newcastle, no relationship could be found between social class or electoral tract and rates of organic mental disorder, while a number of social variables such as poverty, poor home amenities, and unemployment that were related to mental illness, appeared to be more its consequences than its cause, or were probably associated with the advanced age of many of the cases. Social isolation might have indirectly aggravated the illness in some solitary females by permitting self-neglect to go unchecked.

Many of the studies showing that the rates of mental illness among the married are lower than those among the single or widowed, refer to hospital figures and not to community surveys. Bellin and Hardt (1958) studied the relationship between marital status and mental disorder in the noninstitutionalized aged population in Syracuse. They showed that while rates of mental disorder, mostly organic psychoses, were significantly higher among the widowed than the married, this was no longer so after age, physical health, and socioeconomic status were held constant. By taking account of these factors, it was possible to identify subgroups of married or widowed with relatively high or low rates of mental disorder. The number of risk factors present correlated highly with the rate of mental disorder.

As regards ethnic or cultural differences the Taiwan surveys (Lin, 1953; Lin, Rin, Yeh, Hsu, and Chu, 1969) have produced consistently low rates for senile and arteriosclerotic psychoses, and a cross-national study using comparable methods of ascertainment would be of interest. In Japan the overall rates for these conditions are very similar to those found in the western world but there appears to be a relatively higher rate of arteriosclerotic dementia (Kaneko, 1969).

## CHARACTERISTICS OF AGED PERSONS WITH NEUROSES

Females predominate as they do at all ages, but the characteristics of elderly male and female neurotics appear to differ (Bergmann, 1970, 1971). In males, physical illness is often present, particularly when the neurotic symptoms are of recent onset, and mortality is increased (Kay and Bergmann, 1966). In females, personality factors seem to be more important.

Neurotic symptoms were also found to be related to a reduction in social contacts and to feelings of loneliness, self-pity, and dissatisfaction with life. In some persons complaining of loneliness, however, no actual reduction in social contacts had occurred. The relationship between loneliness, social isolation, and mental disorder was complex (Kay et al., 1964b). Lowenthal (1968) found no evidence that extreme lifelong isolation was associated with psychiatric illness, though lifelong marginal social adjustment possibly was. There appears to be a personality factor which in earlier life makes it difficult to form close relationships and later results in unwanted isolation. This may however be more felt than real, since loneliness is a state of mind and is not synonymous with actual isolation. Feeling lonely may, indeed, be regarded as a symptom of neurosis.

When an old person becomes isolated for the first time late in life, it is more likely to be a consequence than a cause of mental illness. Physical disability may, however, be a cause of the isolation of the aged. When combined with physical illness and bereavement, isolation may increase the risk of suicide during an episode of depression (Barraclough, 1971).

Bergmann (1971) found that persons with neuroses beginning late in life tend to be of anxious and hysterical, or rigid and insecure personality, and that this might be connected with the marital disharmony, late marriage, or failure to have married that were also characteristic of them. Vispo (1962) also showed that adjustment in old age depended on the previous personality. In a psychometric study of a subsample of the same population, Nunn, Bergmann, Britton, Foster, Hall, and Kay (1974) found that the persons independently diagnosed by the psychiatric interviewers as suffering from neurosis tended to obtain low intelligence test scores, as measured by the Wechsler Adult Intelligence Scale. They suggested that persons with low educational or intellectual resources might have special difficulty in adjusting to the changes that accompany aging. Somewhat surprisingly, however, no evidence that bereavement was an important cause of depressive neuroses was forthcoming from the Newcastle surveys (Garside, Kay, and Roth, 1965). Heyman and Gianturco (1973) in a longitudinal study of aging volunteers carried out in the US also concluded that the aged, by and large, adapt to the loss of a spouse without psychiatric morbidity. Nevertheless, during the first year of widowhood there is a high incidence of psychological and physical symptoms (Clayton, 1974), an increase in inception rates to psychiatric services (Stein and Susser, 1969), and higher risk of suicide in elderly males (MacMahon and Pugh, 1965), all of which suggests that the period is one of increased vulnerability.

## SPECIAL DIAGNOSTIC PROBLEMS IN THE COGNITIVE ASSESSMENT OF ELDERLY PEOPLE AT HOME

Field surveys covering the aged are usually undertaken with the identification of cases with dementia as one of the major aims, and the diagnostic problems met with deserve some attention. This account is based mainly on experience gained during surveys in Newcastle upon Tyne, in which one of the chief aims was to detect organic brain syndromes in its early stages. The samples studied were followed for a number of years, which resulted in several of the original diagnoses being revised. The conditions discussed below were some of the causes of diagnostic uncertainty.

### Subnormal or Borderline Intelligence

The presence of a number of aged people of subnormal or borderline intelligence living in the community may pose diagnostic difficulties in field surveys. If the old person is living in conditions of personal neglect and domestic squalor (perhaps for physical or social reasons), the presence of a brain syndrome may seem to be confirmed.

In the Newcastle survey a subsample was tested on the WAIS by psychologists (Savage *et al.*, 1973), and it was possible to examine the relationships between the diagnosis of chronic brain syndrome, WAIS scores, and socioeconomic status based on occupational history. The conclusion was reached that the diagnosis of dementia depended basically on evidence that cognitive ability had deteriorated, not on actual level of performance. The occupational history was very important, but without an informant, reliance might have to be placed on the demonstration of an impairment in memory and orientation greater than would be expected in an aged person of borderline intelligence. For this purpose, a simple test of memory and orientation may be helpful but there is still a need to develop more discriminating tests of cognitive function to separate the aged dull and subnormal from those who are suffering from dementia.

### Acute Brain Syndromes

The number of cases met with during an investigation restricted to one day (as in a point-prevalence study) is likely to be small, because episodes of disturbed behavior resulting from clouding of consciousness are generally short in duration, ending in either death or recovery. However, the diagnosis may be in doubt when a reliable history cannot be obtained, specially when the acute syndrome is superimposed on a preexisting chronic brain syndrome.

### Functional Psychoses and Neuroses

Self-neglect in the absence of primary cognitive deterioration may result from extreme suspiciousness and self-isolation. In severely depressed old persons, the presence of dementia may apparently be confirmed by the history of social withdrawal and loss of interest. Complaints of memory difficulty or poor concentration may be regarded as confirming the diagnosis, whereas when not corroborated by objective testing memory complaints are usually part of a depressive syndrome rather than symptoms of dementia (Gurland *et al.*, 1976). This shows the importance of testing cognitive functions objectively when diagnosing dementia in the elderly.

### Physical Disabilities and Sensory Defects

Physical illnesses and disabilities may restrict the old person's mobility to an extent which makes it uncertain what tasks he would be able to carry out if he were physically capable. Defects of sensory deficits also have to be taken into account, since presumably they make correct orientation more difficult, impair registration of current events, and hinder communication. Severe sensory deficits may make it impossible to administer standardized psychological tests such as the WAIS, and physical disabilities such as severe tremor, arthritic deformities, or hemiplegia may leave the interpretation of performance tests open to doubt. However, no systematic study of the effect of physical or sensory defects on the cognitive functioning of aged persons seems to have been made.

### Normal Aging

Finally, chronic brain syndrome has to be distinguished from the mental changes accompanying normal aging. In the aged person some difficulty of recall and slowing of thinking may be expected, but impaired registration of ongoing events or disorientation for season or for year imply the presence of more than normal aging. Acute brain syndrome, however, must be excluded.

## THE USE OF STANDARD PROCEDURES IN COMMUNITY SURVEYS

The problems of diagnosis and case definition in community surveys and the urgent need for comparability of data have made it necessary to develop standard procedures for assessment and diagnosis.

### Psychological Tests of Brain Damage

Several psychological tests have been used to separate brain damaged from normal or functionally ill persons in field surveys among the aged.

The Paired Associate Learning Test (PALT), which is a measure of verbal learning ability (Inglis, 1959), was used by Parsons (1965) in Swansea and by Savage *et al.* (1973) in Newcastle-upon-Tyne in their studies of representative samples of old people living at home. However, Savage *et al.* (1973) found the Modified Word Learning Test (MWLT) (Walton and Black, 1957) to be more acceptable as a measure of verbal learning ability and superior as an aid to diagnosing generalized brain damage than the PALT.

The use of the PALT and other standardized psychological tests (WAIS vocabulary, digit copying, Bender-Gestalt) in community studies of psychiatric morbidity in the elderly was evaluated by Kuriansky *et al.* (1976). These authors also described some of the difficulties which may hinder the administration of psychological tests to old people in domestic surroundings, or produce false organic-type responses. Since the simple clinical measure of disorientation seemed to distinguish between diagnostic groups as satisfactorily as the more complicated psychological test battery, their conclusion that the latter is not the instrument of first choice in community studies seems justified.

STANDARD PSYCHIATRIC PROCEDURES

One of the earliest procedures proposed for the evaluation of mentally ill geriatric patients was the test battery of Goldfarb (1964). This included a psychiatric examination using a symptom checklist, a *Mental Status Questionnaire* (MSQ) focussing on recent memory and orientation, the face-hand test (Kahn, Goldfarb, Pollack, and Peck, 1960), and scales of physical functional status, psychomotor performance, and physical independence. The battery was developed for use with institutionalized patients.

*The Geriatric Mental Status.* (GMS) (Copeland, Kelleher, Kellett, Gourlay, Gurland, Fleiss, and Sharpe 1976) is a development of the Present State Examination (PSE) (Wing, Cooper, and Sartorius, 1974) and the Mental Status Schedule (MSS) (Spitzer, Fleiss, Burdock, and Hardesty, 1964) for use with the aged; it incorporates some of Goldfarb's (1964) tests. The GMS has already been used in field surveys among the aged (Gurland, Copeland, Sharpe, Kelleher, Kuriansky, and Simon 1977–78). The Comprehensive Assessment and Referral Evaluation (CARE) is a new assessment technique which includes the GMS and covers the psychiatric, medical, nutritional, economic, and social problems of the older person (Gurland, Kuriansky, Sharpe, Simon, Stiller, and Birkett, 1977–78).

*The Psychogeriatric Assessment Schedule.* (Bergmann, Gaber, and Foster, 1975) was designed as a screening instrument to identify elderly persons with organic or functional psychiatric symptoms. The principles governing its development were that it should be applicable to elderly persons living at home, should not require any special psychiatric training in its use, and should be acceptable to a wide range of older people from the fittest and most active to the severely disabled.

Four major areas of enquiry are employed: (1) social competence and self-care; (2) assessment of impaired communication and contact, and deficits in memory and orientation; (3) an enquiry into attitudes and self-regard; and (4) an enquiry into the presence of functional symptoms. Subjects who show a high level of social competence and self-care and also positive attitudes are not subjected to the more detailed psychiatric inquiries. Preliminary study shows that cut-off points derived from discriminant function analysis permitted 96 percent of organics, 75 percent of functionals and 80 percent of normals to be correctly placed.

## SUMMARY AND CONCLUSIONS

The early efforts of the 1950s and 1960s succeeded in drawing attention to the high prevalence of psychiatric morbidity among the aged in the community and to the large amount that was unreported. The available methods of case finding and diagnosis were, however, not reliable enough to make comparative studies possible, or to arrive at conclusions concerning etiology. There was difficulty in separating causes and effects of illness. Incidence proved particularly difficult to study.

The most consistent finding to emerge so far concerns the prevalence of chronic brain syndrome in persons aged 65 or over. Of these 1–2 percent are severely and 3–4 percent moderately impaired, the proportions increasing with age. The majority are at any one time living at home rather than in institutions, and being cared for by relatives or neighbors. With a few exceptions (Kay, Roth, and Hall, 1966; Nielsen, 1965; Nielsen *et al.*, 1977b), surveys do not appear to have had much effect on the organization of geriatric services locally or nationally.

The great majority of cases are diagnosed as suffering from senile or arteriosclerotic dementia, but there is need for further study of the distribution of these conditions by age and sex, and for confirmation of the diagnosis by neuropathological studies and followup. Chronic brain syndrome has to be distinguished from acute brain syndrome, functional psychoses, the effect of sensory and physical impairments, mental subnormality, and normal aging.

Little has been achieved as regards the early diagnosis of chronic brain syndrome, and "mild dementia" remains an enigmatic category needing further investigation and clearer definition. Normative data on the cognitive performance of representative groups of aged persons (Savage *et al.*, 1973) may lead to improved prediction of incipient brain syndrome, and give a better opportunity of early treatment.

Intensive field surveys have been carried out on too small a scale to add much to our knowledge of the functional psychoses, and, in particular, the incidence of affective disorders with increasing age needs further investigation.

One of the most consistent and important findings that has come from community surveys is the very large number of old persons with neuroses, especially depressive neuroses. Most of them are not receiving any formal psychiatric treatment, and their potential response to treatment is not known. This gap in our understanding of these conditions would be worth trying to remedy in future studies.

The causes of the neuroses of the aged have not been adequately studied but acute and chronic physical illness, adverse social conditions, isolation, and widowhood, personality difficulties, problems in family relationships and previous psychiatric illness appear to be important. Local registers of the aged would serve as a basis for surveys and for prospective studies of high-risk groups.

In future the objectives of each survey will need to be clearly formulated. Different case-finding methods will be required for different purposes. Broadly, three types of survey may be envisaged: (1) Local surveys undertaken to identify mentally ill persons, particularly those with brain syndromes, who are in need of geriatric services, and to evaluate the existing services. Such surveys would be oriented towards intervention. (2) Research into the incidence of the different mental disorders in different age/sex groups using case-finding methods of known reliability and validity, with the aim of studying etiology. Techniques appropriate for the detection of each of the three main groups of symptoms (neurotic, psychotic and organic) will have to be included. (3) The third type of survey would be concerned primarily with the clinical and psychological manifestation of age-related changes in the brain, with the aim of studying the biological processes involved in aging and death.

# REFERENCES

ADELSTEIN, A. M., DOWNHAM, D. Y., STEIN, Z. AND SUSSER, M. W. 1968. The epidemiology of mental illness in an English City. *Social Psychiatry, 3,* 47–59.

ÅKESSON, H. O. 1969. A population study of senile and arteriosclerotic psychoses. *Human Heredity, 19,* 546–566.

AKHTAR, A. J., BROE, G. A., CROMBIE, A., McLEAN, W. M. R., ANDREWS, G. R., AND CAIRD, F. I. 1972. Disability and dependence in the elderly at home. *Age and Ageing, 2,* 102–111.

BAILEY, M. B., HABERMAN, P. W., AND ALKSNE, H. 1965. The epidemiology of alcoholism in an urban residential area. *Quarterly Journal of Studies of Alcoholism, 26,* 19–49.

BALIER, C., BOURGERON, J. P., BOURGERON, G., AND PERRY, M. 1968. Enquête sur les besoins médicaux et sociaux des personnes agées du XIIIe arrondissement de Paris. *Bulletin de l' I.N.S.E.R.M., 23.* 439–510.

BARRACLOUGH, B. M. 1971. Suicide in the Elderly, *In,* D. W. K. Kay and A. Walk (eds.), *Recent Developments in Psychogeriatrics,* pp. 87–99. Ashford: Headley Bros.

BELLIN, S. S., AND HARDT, R. 1958. Marital status and mental disorders among the aged. *American Sociological Review, 23,* 155–162.

BENFARI, R. C., BEISER, M., LEIGHTON, A. H., AND MERTENS, C. 1972. Some dimensions of psychoneurotic behaviour in an urban sample. *Journal of Nervous and Mental Disease, 155,* 77–90.

BENGTSEN, B. G. 1970. *Illness and General Practice.* Oslo, Norway: Universitetsforlaget.

BERGMANN, K., 1970. Sex differences in neurotic reactions of the aged. *Journal of Biosocial Science,* Suppl. No. 2, 137–145.

BERGMANN, K. 1971. The neuroses of old age. *In,* D. W. K. Kay and A. Walk (eds.), *Recent Developments in Psychogeriatrics,* pp. 39–50. Ashford: Headley Bros.

BERGMANN, K., AND EASTHAM, E. J. 1974. Psychogeriatric ascertainment and assessment for treatment in an acute medical ward setting. *Age and Ageing, 3,* 174–178.

BERGMANN, K., GABER, L. B., AND FOSTER, E. M. 1975. The development of an instrument for early ascertainment of psychiatric disorder in elderly community residents: A pilot study. *In,* R. Degwitz, H. Radebold and P. W. Schulte (eds.), *Freiburg Gerontopsychiatrie, 4* Janssen Symposien, pp. 84–119.

BERGMANN, K., KAY, D. W. K., FOSTER, E. M., McKECHNIE, A. A., AND ROTH, M. 1971. A follow-up study of randomly selected community residents to assess the effects of chronic brain syndrome and cerebrovascular disease. *Psychiatry* Part II: Excerpta Medica International Congress Series No. 274. Amsterdam: Excerpta Medica.

BERKMAN, P. L. 1971. Measurement of mental health in a general population sample. *American Journal of Epidemiology, 94,* 105–111.

BOLLERUP, T. R., 1975. Prevalence of mental illness among 70-year-olds domiciled in nine Copenhagen suburbs. *Acta Psychiat. Scand., 51,* 327–339.

BREMER, J., 1951. A social psychiatric investigation of a small community in northern Norway. *Acta Psychiat. Scand.,* Suppl. 62.

BRUGGER, C. 1931. Versuch einer Geisteskrankenzahlung in Thüringen. *Zeitschrift fur Neurologie und Psychiatrie, 133,* 352–390.

CIOMPI, L. 1969. Follow-up studies on the evolution of former neurotic and depressive states in old age. Clinical and psychodynamic aspects. *Journal of Geriatric Psychiatry, 3,* 99–106.

CLAYTON, P. J. 1974. Mortality and morbidity in the first year of widowhood. *Archives of General Psychiatry, 14,* 151–157.

COMSTOCK, G. W., AND HELSING, K. J. 1976. Symptoms of depression in two communities. *Psychological Medicine, 6,* 551–563.

COOPER, B., AND SHEPHERD, M. 1973. Epidemiology and abnormal psychology. *In,* H. J. Eysenck (ed.), *Handbook of Abnormal Psychology,* 2nd. ed., pp. 34–66. London: Pitman.

COPELAND, J., KELLEHER, M., DUCKWORTH, G., AND SMITH, A. 1976. Reliability of psychiatric assessment in older patients. *International Journal of Aging and Human Development, 7,* 313–322.

COPELAND, J. R. M., KELLEHER, M. J., KELLETT, J. M., GOURLAY, A. J., GURLAND, B. J., FLEISS, J. L. AND SHARPE, L. 1976. A semi-structured clinical interview for the assessment of diagnosis and mental state in the elderly: the Geriatric Mental State Schedule. I. Development and reliability. *Psychological Medicine, 6,* 439–449.

DEAN, L. L., TERESI, J. A., AND WILDER, D. W. 1977–78. The human element in survey research. *International Journal of Aging and Human Development, 8,* 83–92.

DOHRENWEND, B. P., EGRI, G., AND MENDELSOHN, F. S. 1971. Psychiatric disorder in general population: a study of the problem of clinical judgment. *American Journal of Psychiatry, 127,* 1304–1312.

ESSEN-MÖLLER, E., 1956. Individual traits and morbidity in a Swedish rural population. *Acta Psychiat. Scand.,* Suppl. 100.

ESSEN-MÖLLER, E., AND HAGNELL, O. 1961. The frequency and risk of depression within a rural population

group in Scandinavia. *Acta Psychiat. Scand.,* Suppl. 162, 28–32.

FINLAY-JONES, R. A., AND BURVILL, P. W., 1977. The prevalence of minor psychiatric morbidity in the community. *Psychological Medicine, 7,* 425–489.

FISCH, M., GOLDFARB, A. I., SHAHINIAN, S. P., AND TURNER, H. 1968. Chronic brain syndrome in the community aged. *Archives of General Psychiatry 18.* 739–745.

FOSTER, E. M., KAY, D. W. K., AND BERGMANN, K., 1976. The characteristics of old people receiving and needing domiciliary services: the relevance of psychiatric diagnosis. *Age and Ageing, 5,* 245–255.

GAITZ, C., AND SCOTT, J. 1972. Age and the measurement of mental health. *Journal of Health and Social Behaviour, 13,* 55–67.

GARSIDE. R. F., KAY. D. W. K., AND ROTH, M. 1965. Old age mental disorders in Newcastle-upon-Tyne. Part III. A factorial study of medical, psychiatric and social characteristics. *British Journal of Psychiatry, 111,* 939–946.

GILMORE. A. J. J., AND CAIRD, F. I. 1972. Locating the elderly at home. *Age and Ageing, 1,* 30–32.

GOLDBERG, D. P. 1972. *The Detection of Psychiatric Illness by Questionnaire.* Institute of Psychiatry, Maudsley Monographs No. 21. London: Oxford University Press.

GOLDFARB, A. I., 1964. The evaluation of geriatric patients following treatment. *In.* P. H. Hoch and J. Zubin (eds.), *Evaluation of Psychiatric Treatment,* pp. 291–308. New York: Grune and Stratton.

GRUENBERG, E. M. 1954. Community conditions and psychoses of the elderly. *American Journal of Psychiatry, 110,* 888–896.

GRUENBERG, E. M. 1961. A mental health survey of older persons. *In,* P. H. Hoch and J. Zubin (eds.), *Comparative Epidemiology of the Mental Disorders,* pp. 13–23. New York: Grune and Stratton.

GUNNER-SVENSSON, F., AND JENSEN, K. 1976. Frequency of mental disorders in old age. *Acta Psychiat. Scand. 53,* 283–297.

GURLAND, B., COPELAND, J., SHARPE, L., KELLEHER, M., KURIANSKY, J., AND SIMON, R. 1977–78. Assessment of the older person in the community. *International Journal of Aging and Human Development, 8,* 1–8.

GURLAND, B. J., FLEISS, J. L., GOLDBERG, K., SHARPE, L., COPELAND, J. R. M., KELLEHER, M. J., AND KELLETT, J. M. 1976. A semi-structured clinical interview for the assessment of diagnosis and mental state in the elderly: the Geriatric Mental State Schedule. II. A factor analysis. *Psychological Medicine, 6,* 451–459.

GURLAND, B., KURIANSKY, J., SHARPE, L., SIMON, R., STILLER, P., AND BIRKETT, P. 1977–78. The comprehensive assessment and referral evaluation (CARE)—rationale, development and reliability. *International Journal of Aging and Human Development, 8*(1), 9–42.

HAGNELL, O. 1966. *A Prospective Study of the Incidence of Mental Disorder.* Lund: Scandinavian Universities Books, Norstedts New York: Humanities Press.

HAGNELL, O. 1970a. Disease expectancy and incidence of mental illness among the aged. *Acta Psychiat. Scand.* Suppl. 219, 83–89.

HAGNELL, O. 1970b. The incidence and duration of episodes of mental illness in a general population. *In,* E. H. Hare and J. K. Wing (eds.), *Proceedings of the Aberdeen Symposium on Psychiatric Epidemiology,* pp. 213–224. London: Oxford University Press.

HAGNELL, O., AND TURVING, K. 1972. Prevalence and nature of alcoholism in a total population. *Social Psychiatry, 7,* 190–201.

HARE, E. H., AND SHAW, G. K. 1965. *Mental Health in a New Housing Estate.* New York: Oxford University Press.

HELGASON, T. 1973. Epidemiology of mental disorder in Iceland, a geriatric follow-up (preliminary report). *Excerpta Medica International Congress Series No. 274,* 350–357. Amsterdam: Excerpta Medica.

HELGASON, L. 1977. Psychiatric services and mental illness in Iceland. *Acta Psychiat. Scand.* Suppl. 268.

HEYMAN, D. K., AND GIANTURCO, D. T. 1973. Long term adaptation by the elderly to bereavement. *Journal of Gerontology, 28,* 356–362.

HODKINSON, H. M. 1973. Mental impairment in the elderly. *Journal of the Royal College of Physicians of London, 7,* 305–317.

INGHAM, J. G., AND MILLER, P. MC. C. 1976. The concept of prevalence applied to psychiatric disorders and symptoms. *Psychological Medicine, 6,* 217–225.

INGLIS, J. 1959. A paired associate learning test for use with elderly psychiatric patients. *Journal of Mental Science, 105,* 440–443.

JENSEN, K. 1963. Psychiatric problems in four Danish old age homes. *Acta Psychiat. Scand.,* Suppl. 169, 411–419.

JUEL-NIELSEN, N., BILLIE, M., FLYGENRING, J., AND HELGASON, T. 1961. Frequency of depressive states within geographically delineated population groups. 3. Incidence (the Aarhus County investigation). *Acta Psychiat. Scand.* Suppl. 162, *37,* 69–80.

KAHN, R. L., GOLDFARB, A. I., POLLACK, M., AND PECK, A. 1960, Brief objective measures for the determination of mental status in the aged. *American Journal of Psychiatry, 117,* 326–328.

KANEKO, Z., 1969. Epidemiological studies on mental disorders of the aged in Japan. *In, Proceedings of 8th International Congress of Gerontology, 1,* Abstracts of Symposia and Lectures, pp. 284–287. Washington D.C.: International Association of Gerontology.

KANEKO, Z. 1975. Care in Japan. *In,* J. G. Howells (ed.),

*Modern Perspectives in the Psychiatry of Old Age,* pp. 519–530. New York: Brunner/Mazel.

KAY, D. W. K., 1976. The depressions and neuroses of late life. *In,* K. Granville-Grossman, (ed.), *Recent Advances in Clinical Psychiatry,* pp. 52–80. New York: Churchill Livingtone.

KAY, D. W. K., BEAMISH, P., AND ROTH, M. 1964a. Old age mental disorders in Newcastle-upon-Tyne, I. A study of prevalence. *British Journal of Psychiatry, 110,* 146–158.

KAY, D. W. K., BEAMISH, P., AND ROTH, M. 1964b. Old age mental disorders in Newcastle-upon-Tyne, II. A study of possible social and medical causes. *British Journal of Psychiatry, 110,* 668–682.

KAY, D. W. K., AND BERGMANN, K. 1966. Physical disability and mental health in old age. *Journal of Psychosomatic Research, 10,* 3–12.

KAY, D. W. K., BERGMANN, K. FOSTER, E., AND GARSIDE, R. F. 1966. A four-year follow-up of a random sample of old people originally seen in their own homes. A physical, social and psychiatric enquiry. *Proceedings of the 4th World Congress of Psychiatry,* pp. 1668–1670. Excerpta Medica International Congress Series No. 150. Amsterdam: Excerpta Medica.

KAY, D. W. K., BERGMANN, K., FOSTER, E. M. MCKECHNIE, A. H., AND ROTH, M. 1970. Mental illness and hospital usage in the elderly: a random sample followed up. *Comprehensive Psychiatry, 11,* 26–35.

KAY, D. W. K., ROTH, M., AND HALL, R. P. 1966. Special problems of the aged and the organization of hospital services. *British Medical Journal, 2,* 967–972.

KESSEL, N., AND SHEPHERD, M. 1962. Neurosis in hospital and general practice. *Journal of Mental Science, 108,* 159–166.

KRAMER, M. 1969. *Applications of Mental Health Statistics.* Geneva: World Health Organization.

KURIANSKY, J., GURLAND, B., AND COWAN, D. 1976. The usefulness of a psychological test battery. *International Journal of Aging and Human Development, 7,* 331–342.

LARSSON, T., SJÖGREN, T., AND JACOBSON, G. 1963. Senile dementia. *Acta Psychiat. Scand.* Suppl. 167.

LEIGHTON, D. C., HARDING, J. S., MACKLIN, D. B., MACMILLAN, A. M. AND LEIGHTON, A. H. 1963. *The Character of Danger: Psychiatric Symptoms in Selected Communities.* New York: Basic Books.

LEMKAU, P. V. 1955. The epidemiological study of mental illnesses and mental health. *American Journal of Psychiatry, 111,* 801–809.

LEMKAU, P. M., TIETZE, C., AND COOPER, M. 1942. Mental hygiene problems in an urban district. *Mental Hygiene, 26,* 100–119.

LIN, T. 1953. A study of the incidence of mental disorder in Chinese and other cultures. *Psychiatry, 16,* 313–336.

LIN, T., RIN, H., YEH, E.-K., HSU, C.-C., AND CHU, H. M.

1969. Mental disorders in Taiwan fifteen years later. *In,* W. Caudill and T. Lin (eds.), *Mental Health Research in Asia and the Pacific,* pp. 66–91. Honolulu: East-West Center Press.

LOWENTHAL, M. F. 1968. Social isolation and mental illness in old age. *In,* B. Neugarten, (ed.), *Middle Age and Aging.* Chicago: University of Chicago Press.

LOWENTHAL, M. F., BERKMAN, P., AND ASSOCIATES. 1967. *Aging and Mental Disorders in San Francisco.* San Francisco: Jossey-Bass, Inc.

MACMAHON, B., AND PUGH, T. F. 1965. Suicide in the widowed. *American Journal of Epidemiology, 8,* 23–31.

MAZER, M. 1976. *People and Predicaments.* Cambridge, Mass.: Harvard University Press.

MILNE, J. S., MAULE, M. M., AND WILLIAMSON, J. 1971. Method of sampling in a study of older people with a comparison of respondents and non-respondents. *British Journal of Preventive and Social Medicine, 25,* 37–41.

NEW YORK STATE DEPARTMENT OF MENTAL HYGIENE. 1961. *A Mental Health Survey of Older People.* Utica, New York: State Hospitals Press.

NIELSEN, J. 1962. Geronto-psychiatric period-prevalence investigation in a geographically delimited population. *Acta Psychiat. Scand., 38,* 307–330.

NIELSEN, J. 1965. Geronto-psychiatric treatment in a rural community. *Geront. Clin., 7,* 148–170.

NIELSEN, J. 1976. The Samsø project from 1957 to 1974. *Acta Psychiat. Scand., 54,* 198–222.

NIELSEN, J., HOMMA, A., AND BJØRN-HENRIKSEN, T. 1977a. Follow-up 15 years after a geronto-psychiatric prevalence study. *Journal of Gerontology, 32,* 554–561.

NIELSEN, J., HOMMA, A., AND BJØRN-HENRIKSEN, T. 1977b. Follow-up 15 years after a geronto-psychiatric prevalence study in Samsø. I. Geriatric service by the general practitioners, and local hospital, and the community psychiatric clinic. *Comprehensive Psychiatry, 18,* 533–544.

NUNN, C., BERGMANN, K., BRITTON, P. G., FOSTER, E. M. HALL, E. H., AND KAY, D. W. K. 1974. Intelligence and neurosis in old age. *British Journal of Psychiatry, 124,* 446–452.

PARSONS, P. L. 1965. Mental health of Swansea's old folk. *British Journal of Preventive and Social Medicine, 19,* 43–47.

PASAMANICK, B., ROBERTS, D. W., LEMKAU, P. M., AND KRUEGER, D. 1957. A survey of mental disease in an urban population. I. Prevalence by age, sex and severity of impairment. *American Journal of Public Health, 47,* 923–929.

PRIMROSE, E. J. R. 1962. *Psychological Illness: A Community Study.* Springfield, Ill.: Charles C Thomas.

ROTH, M. 1955. The natural history of mental disorders in old age. *Journal of Mental Science, 102,* 281–301.

ROTH, M. 1971. Classification and aetiology in mental disorders of old age: some recent developments. *In* D. W. K. Kay and A. Walk (eds.), *Recent Developments in Psychogeriatrics,* pp. 87–89. Ashford: Headley Bros.

SAVAGE, R. D., BRITTON, P. G., BOLTON, N., AND HALL, E. H. 1973. *Intellectual Functioning in the Aged.* London: Methuen.

SCHWAB, J. J., HOLZER, C. E., AND WARHEIT, G. J. 1973. Depressive symptomatology and age. *Psychosomatics, 14,* 135–141.

SCOTT, J., AND GAITZ, C. 1975. Ethnic and age differences in mental health measurements. *Diseases of the Nervous System, 36*(7), 389–393.

SHEPHERD, M., COOPER, B., BROWN, A. C., AND KALTON, G. W. 1966. *Psychiatric Illness in General Practice.* London: Oxford University Press.

SHEPHERD, M. AND GRUENBERG, E. M., 1957. The age for neuroses. *Milbank Mem. Quart. 35,* 258–265.

SIMON, A., AND CAHAN, R. B. 1963. The Acute Brain Syndrome in geriatric patients. *In,* W. M. Mendel and L. J. Epstein (eds.), *Acute Psychotic Reaction.* Psychiatric Research Reports of the American Psychiatric Association, No. 16, pp. 8–21, Washington, D.C.: American Psychiatric Association.

SØRENSEN, A., AND STRÖMGREN, E. 1961. Frequency of depressive states within geographically delineated population groups. 2. Prevalence (the Samsø investigation). *Acta Psychiat. Scand.,* Suppl. 162, pp. 62–68.

SPITZER, R. L., FLEISS, J. F., BURDOCK, E. I., AND HARDESTY, A. 1964. The Mental Status Schedule; rationale, reliability and validity. *Comprehensive Psychiatry, 5,* 384–395.

STEIN, Z., AND SUSSER, M. 1969. Widowhood and mental illness. *British Journal of Preventive and Social Medicine, 23,* 106–110.

STRÖMGREN, E. 1938. Beitrage zur psychiatrischen erblehre. *Acta Psychiat. Scand.,* Suppl. 19.

TERRIS, M. 1965. Use of hospital admission in epidemiological studies of mental disease. *Archives of General Psychiatry, 12,* 420–426.

TERRY, R. D., AND WISNIEWSKI, H. M. 1977. Structural aspects of aging and the brain. *In,* C. Eisdorfer and R. O. Friedel (eds.), *Cognitive and Emotional Disturbance in the Elderly,* pp. 3–9. Chicago: Year Book Medical Publishers Inc.

TOMLINSON, B., BLESSED, G., AND ROTH, M. 1970. Observations on the brains of demented old people. *Journal of Neurological Sciences, 11,* 205.

TSUGAWA, T. 1942. Über die psychiatrische Zensusuntersuchung in einen Stadtbezirk von Tokyo. *Psychiat. und Neurol. Jap., 46,* 204–218.

VISPO, R. H. 1962. Premorbid personality in the functional psychoses of the senium. A comparison of ex-patients with healthy controls. *Journal of Mental Science, 108,* 790–800.

WALTON, D., AND BLACK, D. A. 1957. The validity of psychological tests of brain damage. *British Journal of Psychology, 30,* 270–279.

WARHEIT, G. J. HOLZER, C. E., AND SCHWAB, J. J. 1973. A community study. An analysis of social class and racial differences in depressive symptomatology. *Journal of Health and Social Behaviour, 14,* 9–15.

WATTS, C. A. H. 1966. *Depressive Disorders in the Community.* Bristol: John Wright & Sons.

WATTS, C. A. H., CAWTE, E. C., AND KUENSSBERG, E. W. 1964. Survey of mental illness in general practice. *British Medical Journal, 2,* 1351–1359.

WHO (WORLD HEALTH ORGANIZATION. 1957. *International Classification of Diseases 1955.* Geneva: World Health Organization.

WHO (WORLD HEALTH ORGANIZATION). 1977. *International Classification of Diseases 1975 Revision.* Geneva: World Health Organization.

WILLIAMSON, J., STOKOE, I. H., GRAY, S., FISHER, M., SMITH, A., McGHEE, A., AND STEPHENSON, E. 1964. Old people at home: their unreported needs. *Lancet, 1,* 1117–1120.

WING, J. K. 1976. Preliminary communication. A technique for studying psychiatric morbidity in in-patient and out-patient series and in general hospital samples. *Psychological Medicine, 6,* 665–671.

WING, J. K., COOPER, J. E., AND SARTORIUS, N. 1974. *The Measurement and Classification of Psychiatric Symptoms.* London: Cambridge University Press.

WING, J. K., HAILEY, A., BRANSBY, E. R., AND FRYERS, T. 1972. The statistical context: comparisons with national and local statistics. *In,* J. K. Wing and A. M. Hailey (eds.), *Evaluating a Community Psychiatric Service. The Camberwell Register 1964–1971,* pp. 77–99. New York: Published for the Nuffield Provincial Trust by the Oxford University Press.

WING, J. K., MANN, S. A., LEFF, J. P., AND NIXON, J. M. 1978. The concept of a 'case' in psychiatric population studies. *Psychological Medicine, 8,* 203–217.

WING, L., WING, J. K., HAILEY, A., BAHN, A. K., SMITH, H. E., AND BALDWIN, J. A., 1967. The use of psychiatric services in three urban areas: an international case register study. *Social Psychiatry, 2,* 158–167.

ZUNG, W. W. K. 1965. A self-rating depression scale. *Archives of General Psychiatry, 12,* 63–70.

ZUNG, W. W. K. 1967. Depression in the normal aged. *Psychosomatics, 8,* 287–292.

# 3

# Demography
# and Mental Health Care
# of the Aged

*Richard W. Redick & Carl A. Taube*

Presented in this chapter is an examination of trends and patterns of change in selected demographic/socioeconomic characteristics of the aged (65 and older) population; a discussion of trends in and current patterns of use of various types of psychiatric services by the aged; some prediction of future use of and need for mental health services by this population group; and some consideration of what implications the demographic/socioeconomic changes in the aged population and their patterns of utilization of psychiatric services may have relative to the future mental health care of the elderly.

## DEMOGRAPHIC/SOCIOECONOMIC CHARACTERISTICS

Today, approximately 22.5 million Americans or a little over ten percent of the population are 65 years of age or older. This represents a 2.5 million increase over the number of elderly enumerated in the 1970 US census. Some of this growth can be attributed to the fact, as stated in a recent edition of *Health USA*,[1] that:

> ... Americans are living longer today than ever before in history. Mortality rates among the elderly have been declining during the past several years. Even without further reductions in mortality, persons currently reaching their 65th birthday will, on the average, live 16 more years.

Current projections of the US population, prepared by the US Bureau of the Census, show the population 65 and over increasing to over 27

[1] U.S. Department of Health, Education, and Welfare. *Health, United States, 1976-1977*. DHEW Publication No. (HRA) 77-1232. U.S. Government Printing Office, Washington, D.C. p. 3.

million by 1985 and to almost 32 million by the year 2000 (Appendix Table 1 at the end of this chapter), resulting in higher rates of increase in this segment of the population than that noted for other broad age groups, namely, the under 18 and 18–64 year age groups. Also, to be noted is that rates of increase over the time intervals 1975–1985 and 1985–2000 for the older segments of the 65 and over age group, that is 75–84 and 85 and over, are greater than that for the 65–74 year age group (Figure 3–1 and Appendix Table 1), such that the proportion of persons aged 65–74 is expected to get smaller while that for persons 75 and over is expected to become larger.

The ratio of males to females is quite low in the elderly population because death rates at every age are higher for males. Currently among persons 65 and over there are 69 males per 100 females

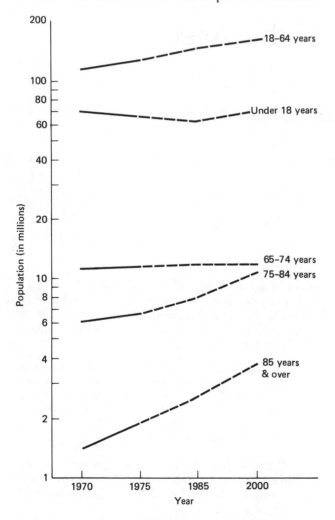

**Figure 3–1**  Number of population by broad age groups, United States, 1970, 1975 and Projections to 1985 and 2000. Source: See Appendix Table 1.

(Table 3–1). The ratio is higher for the 65–74 age groups, being 77, and drops to 62 in the 75–84 age group, and to only 48 for the age group 85 and over. Ratios of males to females in all of the age groupings 65 and over are lower today than in 1970.

All regions[2] of the United States experienced increases in population 65 and over between 1970 and 1975 with regions of the south (Region IV), southwest (Region VI) and the far west (Regions IX and X) experiencing the most significant percentage increases over this time interval (Table 3–2). Increases in the elderly population were also noted in every state except Pennsylvania between 1970 and 1975, with Florida and Arizona, as might be expected, having the largest percentage increases.

A racial-breakdown of the 65 and over age group shows that races other than white constituted only about 9 percent of this age group in both 1970 and 1975, (Table 3–3). This proportion was somewhat smaller than the percentage that all other races of all ages were of the total population at both time periods (approximately 12–13 percent). A more detailed age breakdown of the elderly whites and all other races show relatively little differences between the two race groups in 1975, with whites having just a slightly higher percentage in the age groups 75 and over.

Marital statuses of women 65 years and over in the 5 year period 1971–1976 showed proportionately little change with slightly over one-third being married and over half being widowed at both time periods (Table 3–4). For males, the shift toward higher percentage of marrieds was more in evidence, 72 percent in 1971 as compared to 77 percent in 1976, accompanied by some decline in widowed and single. Whereas widowhood was the more predominant marital status for elderly females, especially in the 75 and over age group where 70 percent were in this category, married was the predominant status for elderly males, with, for example, 70 percent of the 75 and over age group in this category.

The living arrangements of males and females 65 and over are reflective to some extent of the marital status patterns just noted. In 1976 about four-fifths of males 65 and over were heads of families and for almost all of these a wife was present. Among females only 36 percent were living in families as wife of the head of the family, with another 13 percent classified as "living with

[2] Regional breakdowns are those used by the U.S. Department of Health, Education, and Welfare which consists of 10 regions. States comprising each region are shown in footnote a of table 2.

**Table 3–1**  Ratio of males per 100 females, population 65 years and over, by race, United States, 1970 and 1975.

| | MALES PER 100 FEMALES | | | | | |
| | Total | | White | | All other races | |
| Age | 1970 | 1975 | 1970 | 1975 | 1970 | 1975 |
|---|---|---|---|---|---|---|
| 65 years & over | 72.1 | 69.3 | 71.5 | 68.7 | 79.2 | 76.1 |
| 65–74 | 77.7 | 76.8 | 77.3 | 76.4 | 82.0 | 80.4 |
| 75–84 | 66.2 | 61.5 | 65.5 | 60.6 | 75.8 | 72.1 |
| Total-85 + | 53.2 | 48.5 | 52.1 | 47.4 | 66.7 | 59.1 |

*Source:* U.S. Bureau of the Census, Current Population Reports, Series P-25, No. 614, tables 2 and 14.

other relatives." Only 5 percent of males were classified as "other relative" (Table 3–5). Considerably higher proportions of elderly females than males were seen to be living alone. Thirty-six percent of women 65–74 and 48 percent of those 75 or older were living alone in 1976 compared to 13 percent of males 65–74 and 20 percent of men 75 and over. Although the proportionate distributions of males and females by type of living arrangement have not changed to any large extent between 1971 and 1976, there is some evidence that the proportion of elderly maintaining their own household (i.e., heads of households, wife of head, primary individuals) has increased somewhat over this 5 year period and the proportion classified as "living with

other relatives" (i.e., residing in families of which they are neither head nor wife of head) has decreased.

This evidence of some increase in numbers of elderly maintaining their own household with less dependence on "other relatives" must be looked at relative to the financial status of the elderly. In 1976, males 65 and over had a median income of $4,961 which was about one-half that of males of all ages ($8,853). For females 65 and over, the median income in 1976 was only $2,642, approximately half that of males in this age group (Figure 3–2 and Appendix Table 2). For many of the elderly living alone or with nonrelatives, the financial situation appears to be particularly acute.

**Table 3–2**  Number, percent distribution and percent change in number of population 65 years and over by HEW Region[a], United States, 1970 and 1975.

| HEW REGION[a] | NUMBER (in thousands) | | PERCENT DISTRIBUTION | | PERCENT CHANGE IN NUMBER |
| | 1970 | 1975 | 1970 | 1975 | 1970–1975 |
|---|---|---|---|---|---|
| US Total | 20,082 | 22,287 | 100.0% | 100.0% | 11.0% |
| Region I | 1,264 | 1,370 | 6.3 | 6.1 | 8.4 |
| Region II | 2,645 | 2,797 | 13.2 | 12.6 | 5.7 |
| Region III | 2,347 | 2,363 | 11.7 | 10.6 | 0.7 |
| Region IV | 3,215 | 3,938 | 16.0 | 17.7 | 22.5 |
| Region V | 4,201 | 4,517 | 20.9 | 20.2 | 7.5 |
| Region VI | 1,899 | 2,199 | 9.5 | 9.9 | 15.8 |
| Region VII | 1,355 | 1,444 | 6.7 | 6.5 | 6.6 |
| Region VIII | 508 | 567 | 2.5 | 2.5 | 11.6 |
| Region IX | 2,028 | 2,380 | 10.1 | 10.7 | 17.4 |
| Region X | 620 | 712 | 3.1 | 3.2 | 14.8 |

[a]Region I   Conn., Maine, Mass, N.H., R.I., VT.
 Region II   N.J., N.Y.
 Region III   Del., D.C., Md., Pa., Va., W.Va.
 Region IV   Ala., Fla., Ga., Ky., Miss., N.C., S.C., Tenn.
 Region V   Ill., Ind., Mich., Minn., Ohio, Wis.
 Region VI   Ark., La., N.M., Okla., Tex.
 Region VII   Iowa, Kan., Mo., Neb.
 Region VIII   Colo., Mont., N.D., S.D., Utah, Wyo.
 Region IX   Ariz., Cal., Hawaii, Nev.
 Region X   Alaska, Ida., Ore., Wash.

*Source:* U.S. Bureau of the Census, *Current Population Reports,* Series P-25, No. 619, table 1 and 3. (Note: Data for individual states were combined into above regional figures).

**Table 3–3** Number and percent distribution of population 65 years and over by race, United States, 1970 and 1975.

| AGE | TOTAL 1970 | TOTAL 1975 | WHITE 1970 | WHITE 1975 | ALL OTHER RACES 1970 | ALL OTHER RACES 1975 |
|---|---|---|---|---|---|---|
| | *Number (in thousands)* | | | | | |
| 65 & over | 19,971 | 22,401 | 18,272 | 20,383 | 1,701 | 2,020 |
| 65–74 | 12,442 | 13,874 | 11,299 | 12,566 | 1,143 | 1,308 |
| 75–84 | 6,121 | 6,649 | 5,680 | 6,114 | 443 | 537 |
| 85+ | 1,408 | 1,878 | 1,293 | 1,703 | 115 | 175 |
| | *Percent distribution* | | | | | |
| 65 & over | 100.0% | 100.0% | 100.0% | 100.0% | 100.0% | 100.0% |
| 65–74 | 62.3 | 61.9 | 61.8 | 61.6 | 67.2 | 64.7 |
| 75–84 | 30.6 | 29.7 | 31.1 | 30.0 | 26.0 | 26.6 |
| Total 85+ | 7.1 | 8.4 | 7.1 | 8.4 | 6.8 | 8.7 |

*Source:* U.S. Bureau of the Census, *Current Population Reports,* Series P-25, No. 614, tables 2 and 14.

As seen in Table 3–6, over one-fourth of the males and almost one-third of the females living alone were below the poverty level. Two-fifths of both males and females 65 and over living with non-relatives were seen to be below the poverty level.

## PATTERNS OF UTILIZATION OF MENTAL HEALTH SERVICES

Currently, it is estimated that at any one point in time approximately 10 percent of the total US population may have a mental disorder (point preva-lence), and that over a one year period of time as much as 15 percent of the population may have a mental problem in need of treatment services (period prevalence).[3] Up to the present time, there have been no studies or surveys which could be used as a reliable and valid basis for estimating the prevalence of mental disorders among the population 65 years of age and over. If the above cited period prevalence rate of 15 percent, estimated for

[3] Regier, Darrel A., Goldberg, Irving D., Taube, Carl A. "The DeFacto U.S. Mental Health Services System." *Archives of General Psychiatry,* Vol. 35, June 1978, pp. 685-693.

**Table 3–4** Percent distribution of population 65 years and over by marital status and sex, United States, 1971 and 1976.

| MARITAL STATUS & SEX | TOTAL 65 & OVER 1971 | TOTAL 65 & OVER 1976 | 65–74 1971 | 65–74 1976 | 75 & OVER 1971 | 75 & OVER 1976 |
|---|---|---|---|---|---|---|
| Total–both sexes | 100.0% | 100.0% | 100.0% | 100.0% | 100.0% | 100.0% |
| Single | 7.2 | 5.3 | 7.8 | 5.2 | 6.4 | 5.6 |
| Married | 50.8 | 53.9 | 59.5 | 62.2 | 36.8 | 39.2 |
| Widowed | 38.5 | 36.7 | 28.5 | 27.7 | 54.2 | 52.4 |
| Divorced/ separated | 3.5 | 4.1 | 4.2 | 4.9 | 2.6 | 2.8 |
| Total–males | 100.0% | 100.0% | 100.0% | 100.0% | 100.0% | 100.0% |
| Single | 7.1 | 4.4 | 7.7 | 4.2 | 6.2 | 4.9 |
| Married | 71.8 | 77.4 | 77.6 | 82.2 | 61.4 | 67.8 |
| Widowed | 17.1 | 13.8 | 10.0 | 8.9 | 29.5 | 23.5 |
| Divorced/ separated | 4.0 | 4.4 | 4.7 | 4.7 | 2.9 | 3.7 |
| Total–females | 100.0% | 100.0% | 100.0% | 100.0% | 100.0% | 100.0% |
| Single | 7.3 | 5.9 | 7.8 | 5.9 | 6.5 | 6.0 |
| Married | 35.3 | 37.3 | 45.4 | 47.0 | 20.9 | 22.1 |
| Widowed | 54.2 | 52.8 | 43.0 | 42.0 | 70.3 | 69.7 |
| Divorced/ separated | 3.2 | 4.0 | 3.8 | 5.1 | 2.3 | 2.2 |

*Sources:* 1971–U.S. Bureau of the Census, *Current Population Reports,* Series P-20, No. 225, table 1. 1976–U.S. Bureau of the Census, *Current Population Reports,* Series P-20, No. 306, table 1.

**Table 3–5** Percent distribution of population 65 years and over by a household status by sex, United States, 1971 and 1976.

| HOUSEHOLD STATUS BY SEX | TOTAL 65 & OVER 1971 | 1976 | 65–74 1971 | 1976 | 75 & OVER 1971 | 1976 |
|---|---|---|---|---|---|---|
| Total–Males | 100.0% | 100.0% | 100.0% | 100.0% | 100.0% | 100.0% |
| Head of household | 90.6 | 94.5 | 92.7 | 96.8 | 86.8 | 90.1 |
|   Head of family | 75.4 | 78.9 | 80.1 | 83.5 | 66.8 | 69.6 |
|   Primary individual | 15.3 | 15.7 | 12.7 | 13.3 | 20.1 | 20.5 |
|     Living alone | 14.5 | 14.9 | 12.0 | 12.6 | 19.0 | 19.7 |
|     Living with non-relatives | 0.8 | 0.7 | 0.7 | 0.7 | 1.0 | 0.8 |
| Not head of household | 9.4 | 5.5 | 7.3 | 3.2 | 13.2 | 9.9 |
|   In family (other relative) | 7.3 | 4.6 | 5.3 | 2.5 | 11.2 | 8.8 |
|   Secondary individual* | 2.0 | 0.9 | 2.0 | 0.8 | 2.0 | 1.1 |
| | | | | | | |
| Total–Females | 100.0% | 100.0% | 100.0% | 100.0% | 100.0% | 100.0% |
| Head of household | 47.1 | 50.0 | 42.5 | 45.1 | 54.2 | 57.7 |
|   Head of family | 9.1 | 8.8 | 7.9 | 8.7 | 11.0 | 8.9 |
|   Primary individual | 37.9 | 41.2 | 34.5 | 36.4 | 43.2 | 48.8 |
|     Living alone | 36.5 | 40.3 | 33.3 | 35.6 | 41.4 | 47.7 |
|     Living with non-relatives | 1.5 | 0.9 | 1.2 | 0.8 | 1.8 | 1.1 |
| Not head of household | 52.9 | 50.0 | 57.5 | 54.9 | 45.8 | 42.3 |
|   In family | 51.2 | 49.1 | 55.7 | 54.1 | 44.2 | 41.1 |
|   Wife of head | 35.5 | 36.1 | 44.9 | 45.9 | 21.1 | 20.6 |
|   Other relative | 15.8 | 13.0 | 10.9 | 8.2 | 23.2 | 20.5 |
|   Secondary individual* | 1.7 | 0.9 | 1.8 | 0.8 | 1.6 | 1.2 |

*Excludes inmates of institutions

*Sources:* 1971–U.S. Bureau of the Census, *Current Population Reports*, Series P-20, No. 225, table 6. 1976–U.S. Bureau of the Census, *Current Population Reports*, Series P-20, No. 306, table 6.

the total population, is applied to the 65 and over population as a minimum estimate of prevalence for this age group, then approximately 3.4 million of the elderly population would currently be estimated to have a mental disorder requiring some form of mental health care in a one year period. However, in all likelihood the prevalence of mental disorder among this age group is considerably higher.

When one examines data on utilization by the elderly of the major group of psychiatric care services in the US (including inpatient services of state and county mental hospitals and of private psychiatric hospitals, general hospital psychiatric inpatient units, community mental health centers, and outpatient psychiatric services),[4] it becomes evident that only a relatively small percentage of the aged population estimated to be in need of mental health care are using these services. In 1975, of the 3.4 million admissions of all ages to this group of psychiatric services, approximately 162,000 or only 5 percent of these admissions were 65 years or older (Appendix Table 3). If it were possible to provide an unduplicated count of admissions, the number of persons represented by these admissions would be fewer than the 162,000 count. Despite the small proportion of elderly

admissions to psychiatric services in 1975, there has been an increase in both number and rate of admissions 65 and over during the period 1971–1975, with the number of admissions experiencing a 40 percent increase from 116,000 to 162,000, and the admission rate increasing 27 percent from 568 to 721 per 100,000 population during the interval (Appendix Table 3). However, as seen in Figure 3–3, these increases were seen not to be uniform across all types of services. For state and county mental hospital inpatient services the number and rate of admissions 65 years and older declined substantially between 1971 and 1975, and for general hospital psychiatric inpatient units the changes were relatively small. For the other types of psychiatric services, namely, private psychiatric hospital inpatient services, community mental health centers and outpatient psychiatric services, the number and rates of admission for the 65 and over age group experienced increases. These were of particularly substantial magnitude for the latter two types of services. However, in none of these types of services did the percentage of elderly admissions exceed 10–12 percent of all admissions to these services at either time period, with the percentages being smallest for community mental health centers and outpatient psychiatric services (4–5 percent).

Accompanying the substantial decrease in admissions 65 years and over to state and county mental hospital inpatient services noted above,

[4] Excluded are admissions to psychiatric services of the Veterans Administration and persons seen by office-based private practice psychiatrists for which data are not available.

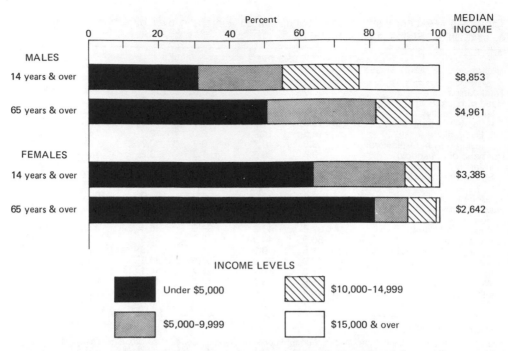

**Figure 3-2** Percent distribution of income recipients 14 years of age and over, and 65 years and over; by income level by age, United States, 1975.
Source: See Appendix Table 2.

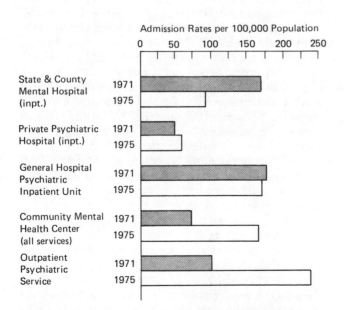

**Figure 3–3** Admission rates per 100,000 population for admissions 65 years and over to selected mental health services, United States, 1971 and 1975. Source: See Appendix Table 3 for data sources and for footnotes concerning these data.

there has been an equally substantial decline in the number and rate of elderly resident patients in these hospitals. In 1975 there were about 54,000 resident patients 65 and over compared to 140,000 ten years earlier (1965) and 88,000 in 1971. Corresponding resident patient rates per 100,000 population for these same years were 773 in 1965, 431 in 1971 and 242 in 1975.[5] There is some evidence to indicate that nursing homes may be becoming more and more an alternate locus of care for the chronic mentally ill elderly. Over the period 1969-1973, Table 3–7 shows that a decline of 38 percent occurred in the number of residents 65 years and over in the so-called long-term care psychiatric hospitals (state and county, private and Veterans Administration), whereas residents 65 and over with chronic conditions of mental disorder in nursing homes more than doubled according to surveys of these homes conducted by the National Center for Health Statistics (NCHS) at both time periods. Furthermore, the 1973-74 NCHS nursing home survey showed that living arrangements prior to admission for 53,000 of the 963,000 nursing home

[5] Milazzo-Sayre, Laura. "Changes in the Age, Sex, and Diagnostic Composition of the Resident Population of State and County Mental Hospitals, United States 1965-1975." *Statistical Note 146*. National Institute of Mental Health, March 1978. DHEW Publication No. (ADM) 78-158.

**Table 3–6** Percent distribution of population 65 years and over of all income levels and below the poverty level, and percent that those below poverty level are of all income levels, by family status by sex, United States, 1975.

| FAMILY STATUS | PERCENT DISTRIBUTION ALL INCOME LEVELS | PERCENT DISTRIBUTION BELOW POVERTY LEVEL | NUMBER BELOW POVERTY LEVEL AS % OF ALL INCOME LEVELS |
|---|---|---|---|
| Total–Males | 100.0% | 100.0% | 11.4 |
| Head of family | 79.0 | 57.7 | 8.3 |
| Other family member | 4.5 | 1.9 | 4.8 |
| Living alone | 14.9 | 34.8 | 26.5 |
| Living with non-relatives | 1.6 | 5.6 | 39.0 |
| In household | 1.5 | 5.1 | 39.1 |
| In group quarters | 0.1 | 0.4 | 33.3 |
| Total–Females | 100.0% | 100.0% | 18.1 |
| Head of family | 8.8 | 6.2 | 12.7 |
| Wife of family head | 36.1 | 16.3 | 8.2 |
| Other family member | 12.9 | 3.0 | 4.1 |
| Living alone | 40.3 | 70.4 | 31.6 |
| Living with non-relatives | 1.9 | 4.1 | 40.1 |
| In household | 1.6 | 3.3 | 35.9 |
| In group quarters | 0.2 | 0.9 | 69.0 |

*Source:* U.S. Bureau of the Census, *Current Population Reports,* Series P-60, No. 106, table 15.

**Table 3–7** Number of resident patients 65 years of age and over in psychiatric hospitals by type of hospital, and number of residents 65 years and over with chronic condition of mental disorder[a] in nursing homes; United States, 1969 and 1973.

| TYPE OF FACILITY | 1969 | 1973 | PERCENT CHANGE 1969–1973 |
|---|---|---|---|
| State and county mental hospitals | 111,420[d] | 70,615[f] | −36.6 |
| Private mental hospitals | 2,460[d] | 1,534[f] | −37.6 |
| VA hospitals[b] | 9,675[d] | 5,819[f] | −39.9 |
| Nursing homes[c] | 96,415[e] | 193,900[g] | 101.0 |

[a]Includes mental illness (psychiatric or emotional problems) and mental retardation but excludes senility.

[b]Includes VA neuropsychiatric hospitals and general hospital impatient psychiatric services.

[c]Data on residents with chronic condition of mental disorder used rather than data on residents with primary diagnosis of mental disorder at last examination, since latter data were not available by age in 1969.

[d]Source: Selected publications of Division of Biometry and Epidemiology, National Institute of Mental Health

[e]*Source:* National Center for Health Statistics. "Chronic Conditions and Impairments of Nursing Home Residents: United States—1969." DHEW Publication No. (HRA) 74-1707. Washington, D.C.: U.S. Government Printing Office.

[f]*Source:* Unpublished data, Division of Biometry and Epidemiology, NIMH.

[g]*Source:* National Center for Health Statistics, *Profile of Chronic Illness in Nursing Homes, United States: National Nursing Home Survey August 1973-April 1974.* Vital and Health Statistics-Series 13, No. 19, DHEW Publication No. (PHS) 78-1780.

residents 65 and over (6 percent) had been a mental hospital or other long-term specialty hospital.[6]

The foregoing discussion gives some indication of a shift in the locus of care of the aged mentally ill from the state and county mental hospitals, which at an earlier time had been the primary locus of care, to community-based settings such as community mental health centers, outpatient psychiatric services and nursing homes and homes for the aged. Despite these shifts, the data indicate that only a very small percentage of the estimated number of elderly with mental disorders in the population are receiving mental health care in psychiatric inpatient or outpatient services or in nursing homes. Moreover, little national data exist in order to be able to ascertain to what extent this population group may be receiving help for their mental and emotional problems in such settings as halfway houses or other community based group residences, private psychiatrist offices, and in nonpsychiatric medical care settings. For example, data from the 1975 National Ambulatory Medical Care Survey (NAMCS) conducted by the National Center for Health Statistics indicates that of the 93 million visits made to office-based physicians by persons 65 years and older, only 2.3 million or 2.5 percent were for mental disorder. The number of

[6] National Center for Health Statistics. *Characteristics, Social Contacts, and Activities of Nursing Home Residents, United States: 1973-74 National Nursing Home Survey.* Vital and Health Statistics-Series 13, No. 27, DHEW Publication No. (HRA) 77-1778.

persons represented by these visits, however, is not reported.[7]

Along with an examination of the patterns of utilization of the different types of psychiatric services by the aged mentally ill and trends in these patterns of utilization, this chapter will also examine which segments of the elderly population are utilizing which types of psychiatric services.

Among patients of all ages as well as those 65 and over admitted to the various types of psychiatric services in 1975, as shown in Table 3–8, it is seen that in all but state and county mental hospitals, female admissions outnumber male admissions. With respect to the aged admissions the greatest difference is seen to occur in outpatient psychiatric services where there are only 28 males for every 100 female admissions 65 and older. In contrast, for state and county mental hospitals, there are 156 male admissions 65 and over for every 100 female admissions in this age group.

A racial breakdown of admissions 65 years and older to the various types of mental health services show that admission rates to state and county mental hospital inpatient services, community mental health centers and outpatient psychiatric services are higher for all other races than for whites, in some cases being double or more (Figure 3–4). For private mental hospital inpatient services and general hospital psychiatric inpatient units, the reverse is noted with white rates being considerably higher than those for all other races. These patterns of differentials in rates among the two race groups are seen to hold for both male and female admissions (see Appendix Table 4).

When the admissions 65 and older are broken down into two age subgroups, namely, 65-74 and 75 years and older, it is seen for each of the types of mental health services shown in Table 3–9 that admission rates per 100,000 population generally tend to be higher for the younger than the older age group. Two exceptions are noted to this pattern, one among male admissions to general hospital psychiatric inpatient units where the rate for the 75 and over age group is slightly higher, and the other among female admissions to outpatient psychiatric services where 75 and over admission rate is substantially higher than that for the 65-74 age group.

A number of differences are noted in the diagnostic composition of persons 65 and over admitted to the various types of psychiatric services which reported these data in 1975. One of the most

[7] National Center for Health Statistics. *Office Visits by Persons Aged 65 and Over: National Ambulatory Medical Care Survey, United States, 1975.* Advance Data, No. 22, March 1978.

**Table 3–8**  Number of male admissions per 100 female admissions for all ages and age group 65 and over to selected mental health services, United States, 1975.

| TYPE OF SERVICE | TOTAL ALL AGES | 65 YEARS & OLDER |
|---|---|---|
| | Sex ratio | |
| State & county mental hospital (inpatient) | 183 | 156 |
| Private psychiatric hospital (inpatient) | 75 | 56 |
| General hospital psychiatric inpatient unit[a] | 70 | 58 |
| Community mental health center (all services)[b] | 92 | 76 |
| Outpatient psychiatric services[c] | 82 | 28 |

*Source:* Unpublished data, Division of Biometry and Epidemiology, National Institute of Mental Health.

[a]Data shown are for discharges. Discharges approximate number of admissions due to short lengths of stay in these units. VA general hospital psychiatric units are excluded.
[b]Includes inpatient, outpatient and partial care services.
[c]Includes freestanding outpatient clinics and outpatient services affiliated with other types of psychiatric facilities. Excludes VA outpatient services, CMHC outpatient services and private mental health practitioners.

notable differences is the large proportion of admissions to state and county mental hospitals diagnosed with organic brain syndromes—these are predominantly chronic brain syndromes associated with cerebral arteriosclerosis and senile brain disease. Almost one-half of state and county mental

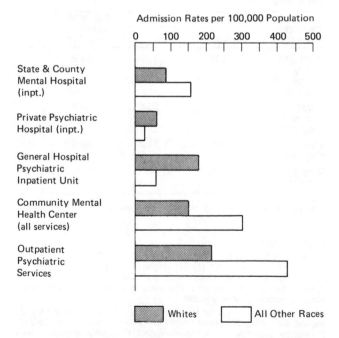

**Figure 3–4**  Admission rates per 100,000 population for admissions 65 years and over to selected mental health services by race, United States, 1975. Source: See Appendix Table 4 for data sources and for footnotes concerning these data.

**Table 3–9** Number of admissions 65–74 years and 75 years and older and admission rates per 100,000 population to selected mental health services by sex, United States, 1975.

| TYPE OF SERVICE | MALES | | FEMALES | |
| --- | --- | --- | --- | --- |
| | 65–74 YEARS | 75 & OVER | 65–74 YEARS | 75 & OVER |
| *Number* | | | | |
| State & county mental hospital (inpatient) | 10,173 | 2,340 | 5,679 | 2,367 |
| Private psychiatric hospital (inpatient) | 3,191 | 1,423 | 5,596 | 2,707 |
| General hospital psychiatric inpatient unit[a] | 9,044 | 4,900 | 15,415 | 8,781 |
| Outpatient psychiatric services[b] | 8,142 | 3,587 | 22,721 | 18,637 |
| *Rate per 100,000 population[c]* | | | | |
| State & county mental hospital (inpatient) | 168.8 | 74.4 | 72.4 | 44.0 |
| Private psychiatric hospital (inpatient) | 52.9 | 45.2 | 71.3 | 50.3 |
| General hospital psychiatric inpatient unit[a] | 150.1 | 155.8 | 196.4 | 163.2 |
| Outpatient psychiatric services[b] | 135.1 | 114.1 | 289.6 | 346.3 |

*Source:* Unpublished data, Division of Biometry and Epidemiology, National Institute of Mental Health.

[a]See footnote a, table 8.

[b]See footnote c, table 8.

[c]Base population used to compute rate was U.S. civilian population as of July 1, 1975.

hospital admissions were diagnosed in this category compared to only 25-28 percent of the admissions to the other types of psychiatric services shown in Table 3–10. Also to be noted is that anywhere from 40-50 percent of the aged admissions to these other types of services were diagnosed with depressive disorders, whereas only 18 percent of state and county mental hospital admissions of 65 and over had this diagnosis. Alcohol disorders were proportionately more predominant among elderly admissions to state and county mental hospitals than to the other services, while outpatient psychiatric services had a larger proportion of elderly admis-sions diagnosed with transient situational disturbances compared to the other types of services.

Admission rates by marital status for the elderly to three of the four types of psychiatric services shown in Table 3–11, namely inpatient services of state and county mental hospitals and of private psychiatric hospitals, and outpatient psychiatric services, were highest for the separated/divorced category followed by those for the never married. For general hospital psychiatric inpatient units the pattern was reversed but with little differential seen between the rates for these two marital status groups. In all four types of services widowed el-

**Table 3–10** Percent distribution of admissions 65 years of age and older to selected mental health services by primary diagnosis, United States, 1975.

| PRIMARY DIAGNOSIS | STATE & COUNTY MENTAL HOSPITAL (INPT.) | PRIVATE PSYCHIATRIC HOSPITAL (INPT.) | GENERAL HOSPITAL PSYCHIATRIC INPATIENT UNIT[a] | OUTPATIENT PSYCHIATRIC SERVICES[b] |
| --- | --- | --- | --- | --- |
| All mental disorders—number | 20,559 | 12,917 | 38,140 | 53,087 |
| All mental disorders—percent | 100.0% | 100.0% | 100.0% | 100.0% |
| Alcohol disorders | 16.2 | 7.5 | 6.0 | c |
| Organic brain syndromes (excl. alcohol & drug) | 47.1 | 25.1 | 28.9 | 23.8 |
| Depressive disorders | 18.3 | 51.1 | 46.1 | 38.4 |
| Schizophrenia | 10.1 | 4.6 | 3.3 | 6.2 |
| Psychoneuroses | c | 2.7 | 5.1 | c |
| Transient situational disorders | c | 1.8 | c | 11.4 |
| All other | 6.5 | 7.2 | 8.8 | 16.3 |

*Source:* Unpublished data, Division of Biometry and Epidemiology, National Institute of Mental Health.

[a]See footnote a, table 8.

[b]See footnote c, table 8.

[c]Based on 5 or fewer sample cases, data does not meet standards of reliability.

**Table 3–11** Percent distribution of admissions 65 years and older and admission rates per 100,000 population to selected mental health services by marital status, United States, 1975.

| MARITAL STATUS | STATE & COUNTY MENTAL HOSPITAL (INPT.) | PRIVATE PSYCHIATRIC HOSPITAL (INPT.) | GENERAL HOSPITAL PSYCHIATRIC INPATIENT UNIT[a] | OUTPATIENT PSYCHIATRIC SERVICES[b] |
|---|---|---|---|---|
| Total number of admissions | 20,559 | 12,917 | 38,140 | 53,087 |
| | *Admission rate per 100,000 population* | | | |
| Total | 97.3 | 61.1 | 180.5 | 251.3 |
| Married | 65.2 | 46.2 | 152.7 | 137.9 |
| Never Married | 249.4 | 92.5 | 239.1 | 507.3 |
| Widowed | 89.1 | 72.8 | 209.0 | 340.4 |
| Separated/divorced | 439.4 | 134.7 | 227.4 | 684.2 |
| | *Percent distribution by marital status* | | | |
| Total | 100.0% | 100.0% | 100.0% | 100.0% |
| Married | 36.5 | 41.3 | 46.2 | 30.0 |
| Never married | 13.6 | 8.0 | 7.0 | 10.7 |
| Widowed | 33.4 | 43.5 | 42.2 | 49.4 |
| Separated/divorced | 16.5 | 7.2 | 4.6 | 9.9 |

*Source:* Unpublished data. Division of Biometry and Epidemiology, National Institute of Mental Health.
[a]See footnote a, table 8.
[b]See footnote c, table 8.

derly ranked third in terms of magnitude of admission rates. Although the widowed and married elderly had the lowest admission rates, they constituted anywhere from 70 to 90 percent of the admissions to each of the types of services with approximately equal proportions of admissions in both marital status groups, the exception was in outpatient psychiatric services where the percentage of widowed was considerably higher (49 percent) than that for married (30 percent). Also to be noted is that state and county mental hospital inpatient services have a substantially higher percentage of separated/divorced admissions 65 and over than do the other types of psychiatric services (Table 3–11).

Data on length of stay of elderly patients admitted to the inpatient services of state and county and private mental hospitals and followed up three months after admission, and of elderly patients discharged from general hospital psychiatric inpatient units show that those receiving services in state and county mental hospitals had by far the longer stay. For this latter group the median length of stay was 53 days which was about double the length of stay (26 days) for admission of all ages to state and county mental hospitals (Figure 3–5). In contrast, the length of stay of the elderly in private mental hospitals was similar to that for all admissions to these hospitals, i.e., 21 days, while for general hospital psychiatric inpatient units the length of stay for discharges 65 and over was 18

days compared to 12 days for all discharges. To further contrast these differentials, it is seen from Appendix Table 5, that at the end of three months (43-84 day interval) only 58 percent of the elderly admissions to state and county mental hospitals had been discharged compared to 94 percent for pri-

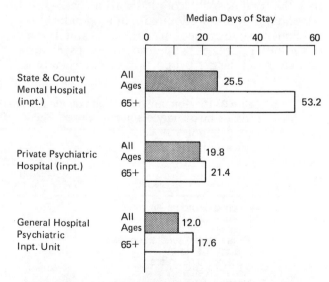

**Figure 3–5** Median days of stay of discharges from state and county mental hospital and private psychiatric hospital inpatient services and from general hospital psychiatric inpatient units, all ages and age group 65 years and older, United States, 1975. Source: See Appendix Table 5 for data sources and for footnotes concerning these data.

vate mental hospitals. For general hospital psychiatric inpatient units, 78 percent of the discharges 65 years and over had been released one month after admission.

Of the elderly discharged from these three types of inpatient services, the type of referral made on discharge showed some variations. Almost two-fifths of the males discharged from state and county mental hospital inpatient services received no referral compared to only one-fifth of the elderly males discharged from each of the other two types of inpatient services-private mental hospital and general hospital psychiatric inpatient unit (Table 3–12). In comparison, only a small proportion of female discharges had no referral, 6 percent for state and county mental hospitals and 14 percent each for private mental hospitals and general hospitals. Of discharges with referral from state and county mental hospitals, the highest proportion, two-fifths for both males and females, were to an outpatient psychiatric service; whereas, for discharges of both sexes from private mental hospitals and general hospitals the highest percentages were referred to a private psychiatrist. It is of interest to note that there was little variation in the percentage of discharges, whether male or female, from each of the three types of inpatient services that were referred to nursing homes, in each case the proportion was at or near one-fifth. Moreover, in every case, nursing homes ranked as the second most frequent place of referral.

## ASSESSMENT OF FUTURE NEEDS FOR, AND EXTENT OF USE OF, MENTAL HEALTH SERVICES BY THE AGED

The preceding discussion has provided some background data on demographic/socioeconomic trends with respect to the population 65 years and older, as well as on trends in patterns of use of various types of psychiatric facilities and of nursing homes by the aged, and on patterns of use during 1975 of a universe of mental health services including state and county mental hospital and private psychiatric hospital inpatient services, general hospital psychiatric inpatient services, community mental health centers, and outpatient psychiatric services.

With respect to demographic/socioeconomic trends and the current pattern of utilization of mental health services, there are several indicators which have implications relative to the future needs of mental health services for this age group. First of all, the elderly population has been increasing and is expected to continue to grow in the

future, with most of the increase occurring in the older segment (75 years and over) of this age group which is at greater risk of needing care. This growth in the population 65 and older, to date, has been more predominant in the female segment, as evidenced by the decline in the ratio of males to females between 1970 and 1975. Continuance of this pattern into the future has implications for needs for mental health services, since elderly females tend to use these services to a much greater degree than elderly males, particularly the more community-based type of services such as general hospitals and outpatient psychiatric services.

Of particular concern to the development of mental health services for the aged is the sizeable number of elderly in the population who either have had no marital ties or whose marital ties have been broken through divorce, separation or death of spouse, and who either live alone, or with non-relatives, or as "other relative of head" (excluding wives and children of head) in a family. Widowhood and living alone are particularly predominant among aged females. Further, it has been seen that anywhere from one-fourth to one-third of the elderly living alone are classified as being below the poverty level. These are all subgroups of the elderly population that must be considered to be at high risk of developing mental health problems and of needing mental health services, as evidenced, in part, by the higher rates of admission to psychiatric services, noted in the foregoing Table 3–11, for divorced/separated, never married and widowed compared to the married elderly. Although there was relatively little change in the proportions of elderly in these high risk marital status and living arrangement groupings between 1971 and 1976, there is little reason to believe the proportions would decrease in the future. In fact, with the projected larger increases in the population 75 years and older, it is more than likely these "risk" groups, particularly the widowed and those living alone, will increase.

Geographically, the continued growth of elderly population in the regions of the south, southwest and far west will require those areas to be particularly perceptive of the mental health needs of this population and to plan for the necessary mental health care services to meet such needs.

Lengths of stay of elderly in inpatient psychiatric services have been shown to be of relatively short duration now. Assuming the majority of elderly coming under care in these settings will need further follow-up care on release, as evidenced by the high proportions of discharges with referrals shown in Table 3–12, it seems incumbent that services need to be made available for such care

**Table 3–12** Percent distribution of patients 65 years and older discharged from selected types of psychiatric impatient units, by type of referral and by sex, United States, 1975.

| TYPE OF REFERRAL | STATE & COUNTY MENTAL HOSPITAL INPATIENT SERVICES | | PRIVATE PSYCHIATRIC HOSPITAL INPATIENT SERVICES | | GENERAL HOSPITAL PSYCHIATRIC INPATIENT UNIT | |
|---|---|---|---|---|---|---|
| | MALE | FEMALE | MALE | FEMALE | MALE | FEMALE |
| Total discharges—number | 7,705 | 3,915 | 4,400 | 7,550 | 13,944 | 24,196 |
| Total discharges | 100.0% | 100.0% | 100.0% | 100.0% | 100.0% | 100.0% |
| Discharged without referral | 39.8 | 5.7 | 18.8 | 13.6 | 21.1 | 13.5 |
| Discharged with referral to:[a] | 60.2[a] | 94.3[a] | 81.2[a] | 86.4[a] | 78.9[a] | 86.5[a] |
| Psychiatric inpatient facility | 1.0 | 6.9 | 3.5 | 2.9 | 5.9 | 4.1 |
| Nursing home | 20.3 | 20.4 | 18.1 | 16.6 | 17.6 | 21.9 |
| Other inpatient care | 4.2 | 7.6 | 9.2 | 6.9 | 9.1 | 2.2 |
| Outpatient psychiatric service | 39.3 | 41.8 | 11.2 | 11.9 | 13.0 | 10.3 |
| Private psychiatrist | 0.3 | 6.9 | 35.4 | 45.0 | 28.7 | 50.2 |
| Other physician | 7.7 | 10.1 | 14.6 | 13.2 | 8.2 | 9.0 |
| Other referral | 2.3 | 2.6 | 4.6 | 1.1 | 4.3 | 2.2 |

*Source:* Unpublished data, Division of Biometry and Epidemiology, National Institute of Mental Health.

[a]Subparts will not add to this total since a discharge may have had more than one type of referral.

whether it be in a nursing home, or extended care facility, or in some type of ambulatory care setting. Unfortunately the data on referral of elderly patients cannot be supplemented with any national surveys or studies which follow this group of patients discharged from inpatient psychiatric services into the community to ascertain what happens to them subsequent to their release, that is, whether recommended referrals are followed through, whether other types of further care or services are sought, what type of care or services are received, and how effective is that care or service. Some states and/or localities within states have after-care programs for those elderly needing further mental health related services, and studies or reports relative to the strengths and weaknesses and/or the success or failure of some of these programs do exist. In the absence of any national surveys encompassing all of these programs, it would be encouraged that a summary review of these studies and reports be undertaken, in order to provide leads as to which types of programs seem to be the most promising to meet the future mental health needs of the elderly.

The trend data on utilization of mental health services, presented earlier in the chapter, give further indication that the role of mental hospitals and psychiatric units of general hospitals for the care of the aged mentally ill is decreasing while that of nursing homes, community mental health centers and outpatient psychiatric services is on the increase. However, in the case of the latter two types of services, although the number of elderly being served has increased substantially, their percentage of the total caseload of these services has not changed appreciably over time and remains small, at 4–5 percent. Unless a strong impetus is given to the development and expansion of programs for the aged within these services, as for example, recent Congressional legislation mandating community mental health centers to provide special services to the elderly, they may continue to furnish care to only a relatively small proportion of this age group.

It is almost impossible to predict with any degree of accuracy the numbers and types of mental health facilities that will be required by the aged in the 1980s and beyond. This is because future trends will depend not only on the expected increases in the size of the aged population and their actual needs but also on a series of political, administrative, and clinical decisions that will determine: how many facilities of various types will be available; how their construction and staffing will be financed; how much manpower will be trained to staff these facilities; who will be admitted to what services; and how persons using these services will pay for them. These factors can be further influenced by: what effect various programs instituted by state and/or local agencies (both governmental and nongovernmental) to modify patterns of use of mental hospitals by the aged will have on the mental hospital *per se* and on other facilities and services; whether the trends in patterns of use of mental health facilities which were set in motion by the community mental health centers, and Medicare and Medicaid legislation will continue into the future; what effect legislation that may be enacted to establish a national health insurance plan and to provide more effective delivery of health services will have on the delivery of mental health services and the use of psychiatric facilities; what breakthroughs, if any, are likely in etiologic research that may reduce incidence of mental disorders of the aged, and, in therapeutic research, that may lead to more effective treatment of these disorders; and what effect current styles of life, economic conditions, problems resulting from social and political unrest will have on the physical, mental, and social well-being of persons who will enter the ranks of the aged, as well as on the aged who are growing older.

## APPENDIX TABLES

**APPENDIX TABLE 1**   Number, percent distribution and percent change in number of population by broad age groups, United States 1970, 1975, and projections to 1985 and 2000.

| AGE | Number (in thousands) | | | | Percent distribution | | | | Percent change | | |
|---|---|---|---|---|---|---|---|---|---|---|---|
| | 1970 | 1975 | 1985 | 2000 | 1970 | 1975 | 1985 | 2000 | 1970-1975 | 1975-1985 | 1985-2000 |
| All ages | 203,235 | 213,137 | 232,880 | 260,378 | 100.0% | 100.0% | 100.0% | 100.0% | 4.9 | 9.3 | 11.8 |
| Under 18 | 69,689 | 66,294 | 62,293 | 68,977 | 34.3 | 31.1 | 26.7 | 26.5 | -4.9 | -6.0 | 10.7 |
| 18–64 | 113,574 | 124,444 | 143,283 | 159,579 | 55.9 | 58.4 | 61.6 | 61.3 | 9.6 | 15.1 | 11.4 |
| 65 & over | 19,972 | 22,400 | 27,305 | 31,822 | 9.8 | 10.5 | 11.7 | 12.2 | 12.2 | 21.9 | 16.5 |
| 65–74 | 12,443 | 13,874 | 16,545 | 17,436 | 6.1 | 6.5 | 7.1 | 6.7 | 11.5 | 19.3 | 5.4 |
| 75–84 | 6,122 | 6,650 | 8,172 | 10,630 | 3.0 | 3.1 | 3.5 | 4.1 | 8.6 | 22.9 | 30.1 |
| 85+ | 1,408 | 1,877 | 2,588 | 3,756 | 0.7 | 0.9 | 1.1 | 1.4 | 33.3 | 37.9 | 45.1 |

*Sources:* 1970 and 1975—U.S. bureau of the Census, *Current Population Reports,* Series P–25, No. 614, tables 2 and 4, 1985 and 2000—U.S. Bureau of the Census, *Current Population Reports,* Series P–25, No. 704, table 8.

**APPENDIX TABLE 2**   Percent distribution of income recipients 14 years old and over and age group 65 years and over by income level by sex, United States 1975.

| INCOME LEVEL | MALES | | FEMALES | |
|---|---|---|---|---|
| | 14 YEARS & OVER | 65 YEARS & OVER | 14 YEARS & OVER | 65 YEARS & OVER |
| Total income recipients | 100.0% | 100.0% | 100.0% | 100.0% |
| $1–1,499 (or less) | 10.1 | 3.2 | 24.6 | 18.2 |
| $1,500–2,999 | 8.9 | 19.5 | 20.7 | 39.6 |
| $3,000–4,999 | 11.3 | 27.8 | 18.8 | 23.2 |
| $5,000–6,999 | 10.4 | 17.4 | 13.2 | 8.8 |
| $7,000–9,999 | 14.6 | 13.8 | 12.5 | 5.6 |
| $10,000–14,999 | 21.8 | 10.4 | 7.8 | 3.1 |
| $15,000 & Over | 22.9 | 7.9 | 2.4 | 1.5 |
| Median income | $8,853 | $4,961 | $3,385 | $2,642 |

*Source:* U.S. Bureau of the Census, *Current Population Reports,* Series P.60, No.105, table 46.

**APPENDIX TABLE 3** Number of admissions, admission rates per 100,000 population and percent change in number and rates to selected mental health services[d] by broad age groups (under 65 and 65 and over), U.S. 1971 and 1975.

| TYPE OF SERVICE AND AGE OF ADMISSIONS | NUMBER OF ADMISSIONS 1971[a] | 1975[b] | PERCENT CHANGE 1971–1975 | ADMISSION RATE PER 100,000 POPULATION 1971[a] | 1975[b] | PERCENT CHANGE 1971–1975 |
|---|---|---|---|---|---|---|
| All services-all ages[d] | 2,407,487 | 3,355,708 | 39.4 | 1,178.6 | 1,587.0 | 34.6 |
| Under 65 | 2,291,119 | 3,194,098 | 39.4 | 1,246.7 | 1,689.6 | 35.5 |
| 65 & over | 116,368 | 161,610 | 38.9 | 568.0 | 721.4 | 27.0 |
| State & Co. ment. hosps. (inpt)-all ages | 407,640 | 385,237 | −5.5 | 199.6 | 182.2 | −8.7 |
| Under 65 | 372,996 | 364,678 | −2.2 | 203.0 | 192.9 | −5.0 |
| 65 & over | 34,644 | 20,559 | −40.6 | 169.1 | 91.8 | −45.7 |
| Private psych. hosps. (inpt)-all ages | 87,000 | 129,832 | 49.2 | 42.6 | 61.4 | 44.1 |
| Under 65 | 77,038 | 116,915 | 51.8 | 41.9 | 61.8 | 47.5 |
| 65 & over | 9,962 | 12.917 | 29.7 | 48.6 | 57.7 | 18.7 |
| General hospital psychiatric inpatient units-all ages[c] | 519,926 | 515,537 | −0.8 | 254.5 | 243.8 | −4.2 |
| Under 65 | 483,787 | 477,397 | −1.3 | 263.3 | 252.5 | −4.1 |
| 65 & over | 36,139 | 38,140 | 5.5 | 176.4 | 170.3 | −3.4 |
| CMHCs (all services)-all ages | 411,548 | 919,037 | 123.3 | 201.5 | 434.6 | 115.7 |
| Under 65 | 396,613 | 882,130 | 122.4 | 215.8 | 466.6 | 116.2 |
| 65 & over | 14,935 | 36,907 | 147.1 | 72.9 | 164.8 | 126.1 |
| Outpatient psychiatric services-all ages[e] | 981,373 | 1,406,065 | 43.3 | 480.5 | 665.0 | 38.4 |
| Under 65 | 960,685 | 1,352,978 | 40.8 | 522.8 | 715.7 | 36.9 |
| 65 & over | 20,688 | 53,087 | 156.6 | 101.0 | 237.0 | 134.6 |

[a]Source: National Institute of Mental Health. *Utilization of Mental Health Facilities 1971* in Mental Health Statistics, Series B, No. 5 (DHEW Publication No. NIH-74-657) 1973.

[b]Source: Unpublished data, Division of Biometry and Epidemiology, NIMH.

[c]Data shown are for discharges. Discharges approximate the number of admissions due to short lengths of stay in these hospitals.

[d]Includes inpatient services of State and county mental hospitals and of private psychiatric hospitals, general hospital psychiatric inpatient units, all services of community mental health centers, and outpatient psychiatric services. Excluded are VA services and those of residential treatment centers for emotionally disturbed children.

[e]Affiliated and freestanding.

**APPENDIX TABLE 4** Number of admissions 65 years and older and admission rates per 100,000 population to selected mental health services by sex and race, United States, 1975

| TYPE OF SERVICE | TOTAL WHITE | ALL OTHER RACES | MALES WHITE | ALL OTHER RACES | FEMALES WHITE | ALL OTHER RACES |
|---|---|---|---|---|---|---|
| | | | Number | | | |
| State & county mental hospital (inpatient) | 17,383 | 3,176 | 10,861 | 1,652 | 6,522 | 1,524 |
| Private mental hospital (inpatient) | 12,357 | 560 | 4,349 | 265 | 8,008 | 295 |
| General hospital psychiatric inpatient unit[a] | 36,959 | 1,181 | 13,281 | 663 | 23,678 | 518[d] |
| Community mental health center (all services)[b] | 30,757 | 6,150 | 13,204 | 2,677 | 17,553 | 3,473 |
| Outpatient psychiatric services[c] | 44,411 | 8,676 | 10,719 | 1,010[d] | 33,692 | 7,666 |
| | | | Rate per 100,000 population | | | |
| State & county mental hospital (inpatient) | 85.3 | 157.3 | 130.9 | 189.2 | 54.0 | 133.0 |
| Private mental hospital (inpatient) | 60.6 | 27.7 | 52.4 | 30.4 | 66.3 | 25.7 |
| General hospital psychiatric inpatient unit[a] | 181.3 | 58.5 | 160.0 | 75.9 | 196.0 | 45.2[d] |
| Community mental health center (all services)[b] | 150.9 | 304.6 | 159.1 | 306.6 | 145.3 | 303.1 |
| Outpatient psychiatric services[c] | 217.9 | 429.7 | 129.2 | 115.7[d] | 278.9 | 668.9 |

Source: Unpublished data. Division of Biometry and Epidemiology, National Institute of Mental Health.

[a]See footnote a, text table 8.

[b]See footnote b, text table 8.

[c]See footnote c, text table 8.

[d]Based on 5 or fewer sample cases—figure shown does not meet standards of reliability.

**APPENDIX TABLE 5** Percent distribution of admissions discharged (excluding deaths) within selected time intervals after day of admission from state and county mental hospital and private psychiatric hospital inpatient services[a] and of discharges from general hospital psychiatric inpatient units, all ages and age group 65 years and older by length of stay, United States, 1975

| LENGTH OF STAY | STATE & COUNTY MENTAL HOSPITAL INPATIENT SERVICES[a] | | PRIVATE MENTAL HOSPITAL INPATIENT SERVICES[a] | | GENERAL HOSPITAL PSYCHIATRIC INPATIENT UNITS[b] | |
|---|---|---|---|---|---|---|
| | ALL AGES | 65 & OVER | ALL AGES | 65 & OVER | ALL AGES | 65 & OVER |
| Total number discharged | 381,589 | 19,197 | 129,536 | 12,712 | 515,537 | 38,140 |
| *Percent distribution* | | | | | | |
| 7 days or less | 23.5 | 15.0 | 23.2 | 15.5 | 34.4 | 19.1 |
| 8–14 days | 15.0 | 6.8 | 17.3 | 19.2 | 23.4 | 23.0 |
| 15–28 days | 14.7 | 15.3 | 25.3 | 31.1 | 25.7 | 35.6 |
| 29–42 days | 10.6 | 10.3 | 13.7 | 15.7 | 16.5 | 22.3 |
| 43–84 days | 15.1 | 10.2 | 13.0 | 12.5 | | |
| 85 or more days | 21.1 | 42.4 | 7.5 | 6.0 | | |
| *Cumulative percent distribution* | | | | | | |
| 7 days or less | 23.5 | 15.0 | 23.2 | 15.5 | 34.4 | 19.1 |
| 8–14 days | 38.5 | 21.8 | 40.5 | 34.7 | 57.8 | 42.1 |
| 15–28 days | 53.2 | 37.1 | 65.8 | 65.8 | 83.5 | 77.7 |
| 29–42 days | 63.8 | 47.4 | 79.5 | 81.5 | 100.0% | 100.0% |
| 43–84 days | 78.9 | 57.6 | 92.5 | 94.0 | | |
| 85 or more days | 100.0% | 100.0% | 100.0% | 100.0% | | |
| Median days of stay | 25.5 | 53.2 | 19.8 | 21.4 | 12.0 | 17.6 |

*Source:* Unpublished data, Division of Biometry and Epidemiology, National Institute of Mental Health.

[a]Based on 1975 sample survey of admissions to these services in which a 3 month follow-up of these admissions was made.

# II
# Neurosciences

# 4

# Neurobiology
# of
# Aging

*William Bondareff*

## INTRODUCTION

Attempts to identify changes in the brain which underlie behavioral differences between adult and senescent animals often begin with the assumption that the number of functional units, i.e., nerve cells, decreases as animals grow older. In a recent study, for example, in which computerized tomography was used to outline cerebrospinal fluid ventricles in living subjects, it was found that the ventricular volume increases with age (Barron, Jacobs, and Kinkel, 1976). The significance of this observation to behavioral changes in the aged depends upon the assumption that an increase in ventricular volume necessarily foretells a compression of the soft adjacent brain tissue and that a thinning of the cerebral cortical mantle is readily demonstrated in the tomograms. Yet, in this instance, the loss of nerve cells which cortical thinning implies

is probably epiphenomenal and has little to do with aging. Rather, it is more likely to be secondary to vascular or other pathology which unbalances the normal ratio between production and absorption of cerebrospinal fluid or interferes with its normal flow. In either case, by affecting the neuronal microenvironment and neuron-neuron interrelationships, behavior can be affected long before the advent of cortical thinning.

A loss of nerve cells may be due to an age-related change in some gross anatomical structure of the brain. It may also be due to some ill-defined insidious process, perhaps one that is secondary to a change in the vascularization of the brain that results in a slow but progressive decline in neuronal numbers with aging. Such changes imply: that with increasing age there will be increasing brain damage; that the brain damage, due to loss of nerve cells, will be irreversible; and that the effect of such nerve cell loss will depend upon the number of nerve cells lost and the region of the brain from which the loss occurs.

In this chapter I shall review the changes that have been ascribed to aging in the brain in which neuronal loss is a direct consequence. I shall then describe other neuronal changes with age which, although progressive, are not destined to result in neuronal loss, but which lead to functional impairment which may be modifiable or reversible throughout life.

Whereas studies of the aging brain may be extraordinarily difficult, studies of the aged brain are relatively simple and there are many which compare the gross anatomy, microscopic anatomy, cytology and chemistry of the brains of adult and senescent animals. They are, however, often difficult to interpret because potentially contributing factors are seldom known. These include nutritional factors at the time of death and during development, cardiovascular status, respiratory function, the possible presence of neoplasms, and the use and possible effects of alcohol and drugs, especially during the later years of life. As these factors are too often not considered in human studies it is often impossible to know with any degree of certainty whether a given observation is age-related or more directly the consequence of disease or environment. In animal studies similar problems arise and pose similar, although more controllable problems of interpretation. A compilation of selected reports which may truly reflect age-related differences in the brains of young and old animals, including man, is presented in tabular form (see Table 4–1 at the end of the chapter), in which differences are presented qualitatively, as being either increased or decreased in senescent, as compared to non-senescent, animals.

A decrease in brain weight, size and volume seems to be typical of many senescent animals, with the possible exception of certain rodents (Bondareff, 1959). It is known that brain weight increases steadily during the adult life of the rat and there is some indication that it might continue to increase throughout senescence. But in most animals there appears to be a real decrease in brain mass, which in man is probably associated, at least in part, with atrophic changes that are readily apparent at autopsy. It is not surprising, then, that a decrease in neuronal numbers has long been considered a characteristic of the senescent brain. Although this was once assumed to be a characteristic, *sine qua non,* of aging and thought to involve the brain globally, more recent studies suggest that it may, in reality, be a highly selective process.

# AGE-RELATED CHANGES IN NEURONAL STRUCTURE

## LOSS OF NEURONS

Neuronal loss in senescence was described at the turn of the century by Hodge (1894) who found the number of cerebellar Purkinje cells to be decreased in an aged man. Purkinje cells are large nerve cells distributed in a one-cell thick layer in the cerebellar cortex. They are readily visualized and the age-related loss of Purkinje cells has been confirmed several times, most recently by Corsellis (1976) and by Hall, Miller, and Corsellis, (1975). Purkinje cells, which were counted in a large number of human brains with an automatic cell counting apparatus, were found to be significantly decreased in number after the sixtieth year. In the cerebral cortex, which structurally is more complex than the cerebellar cortex, a loss of neurons in old animals (including man) is less reliably demonstrated (Brody, 1955, 1973; Brizzee, 1975; Tomlinson and Henderson, 1976). But few would doubt that such a loss does indeed occur. This loss does not involve the entire cortex. It is selective, although the degree of selectivity is not known because only very small areas of the cerebral cortex have been studied and because structural complexity makes the results of automatic counting methods difficult to interpret.

In the cerebral cortex of aged humans neuronal numbers appear reduced in the external and internal granular layers of the superior temporal and superior frontal gyri (Brody, 1955, 1973), although this finding cannot be considered conclusive (Cragg, 1975). Neuronal populations in other brain areas appear to be more stable. In the brain stem, in which it is sometimes possible to define the boundaries of specific nuclei and sample an entire neuronal population, no age-related decrease in neuronal numbers was found in the facial nucleus (Van Buskirk, 1945), the ventral cochlear nucleus (Konigsmark and Murphy, 1970, 1972), or the trochlear, abducens and inferior olivary nuclei (Brody, 1973; Monagle and Brody, 1974; Narayanakurup and Brody, 1977). The locus coeruleus, a pontine nucleus from which the major norepinephrine-containing axons terminating in the cerebral cortex originate, may be exceptional in showing cell loss (Brody, 1976). An age-related loss of locus coeruleus neurons has been reported but the limits of this nucleus are not so readily defined in the human brain and these data are therefore questionable.

Neuronal loss is not found in the senescent

rat dentate gyrus which, in routine electron micrographs, is difficult to differentiate from that of the young adult (Bondareff and Geinisman, 1976; Geinisman and Bondareff, 1976; Geinisman, Bondareff, and Dodge, 1978a). In random sections of the dentate gyrus of the senescent rat there is no noticeable involvement of blood vessels, no intimal thickening of arteries such as found in the brains of elderly humans (Klassen, Sung, and Stadlan, 1968). Granulovacuolar degeneration, neurofibrillary degeneration, neuritic plaque formation, and deposition of amyloid, which some believe to be characteristic of the senescent human brain, are not apparent in the dentate gyrus of 25-month old rats, nor is there apparent gliosis and dendritic atrophy as are commonly found in senescent brains (Geinisman, Bondareff, and Dodge, 1978a; 1978b).

The Fischer-344 male rat, which is bred and maintained by the Charles River Breeding Laboratories (Wilmington, Massachusetts) under contract with the National Institute on Aging, may provide a particularly suitable animal model for studies of aging of the brain. The natural history and pathology of aging in this animal have, to some extent, been characterized (Coleman, Barthold, Osbaldiston, Foster, and Jonas, 1977). Until 20 months of age, the mortality rate is negligible, but afterwards it increases sharply and rapidly. The 50 percent mean survival age is 29 months and maximal survival appears to be about 35 months. Although the incidence of nephropathy and testicular interstitial tumors is high in Fischer-344 rats more than 20 months of age, the incidence of pathological changes in the nervous system generally is rare, the most common being the formation of nonstaining vacuoles within neurons or within neuropil of the brain stem and cerebellum (Coleman et al., 1977). The senescent animal appears generally healthy and essentially free of overt neuropathology, yet there are significant changes with age and these can be found by morphometry.

## LOSS OF SYNAPSES

Of particular interest is a loss of synapses, which was unexpected in the dentate gyrus because an electron microscope study of synapses in the human cerebral cortex (Cragg, 1975) had failed to uncover any change in synaptic numbers. However, in a study of synaptic populations in the middle third of the molecular layer in the rostral portion of the dentate gyrus, an age-related change was found (Bondareff and Geinisman, 1976). There was a 27 percent decrease in the number of synapses per unit of neuropil square area in se-

nescent rats as compared with young adults. There were no age-related changes in synaptic size, tissue volume or number of post-synaptic granule cells which could have accounted for this loss (Geinisman and Bondareff, 1976). An almost identical loss of axodendritic synapses was found in the supragranular layer, which represents a population of synapses different from those found in the middle third of the molecular layer (Geinisman, Bondareff, and Dodge, 1977). This age-related change in neuronal connectivity in a region of the hippocampal formation which many believe to make an important contribution to cognitive function in man and to spatial orientation in the rat (Olton, Walker, and Gage, 1978) might have a considerable behavioral effect, even though the number of neurons does not change with age.

In addition to the dentate gyrus of the hippocampal formation, in the rat a loss of synapses has been demonstrated in the arcuate nucleus of the hypothalamus (Arai and Matsumoto, 1978) and the nuclei cuneatus and gracilus of the medulla oblongata (Fujisawa and Shiraki, 1978). A loss of synapses has also been found in the visual area of the cerebral cortex (Feldman, 1976) and in the cerebellar cortex of the Fischer-344 rat (Glick and Bondareff, 1979). Feldman (1976) compared numbers of synapses involving dendritic spines and shafts of pyramidal cells in layers I and IV of the visual cortex in 3- and 36-month old rats. Axospinous synapses appeared to be preferentially lost in layer IV in the senescent group; synapses involving shafts and spines were reduced about equally in layer I. In the cerebellar cortex of 25-month rats a 33 percent decrement in total synaptic numbers was found to represent a loss only of axospinous synapses involving dendritic spines of Purkinje cells (Glick and Bondareff, 1979). In the senescent Fischer-344 rat, then, a loss of synapses has been demonstrated in three brain regions of two different embryonic derivations: telecephalon (cerebral cortex and hippocampus) and metencephalon (cerebellum). It is not known how many different afferent systems of neurons lose their synaptic terminals in senescence and, although synaptic loss may be widely spread, the highly selective loss of axo-spinous synapses in the cerebral and cerebellar cortices suggests the impairment of selective populations of presynaptic neurons. In the cerebellum, it appears that granule cells, the axons of which form the majority of synaptic contacts with dendritic spines of Purkinje cells (Palay and Chan-Palay, 1974), may be affected preferentially by aging. Although this selectivity also suggests the impairment of specific populations of postsynaptic neurons, in the case of Purkinje cells which decline in number in the aged human cerebellum (Dayan, 1971; Hall *et al.*, 1975; Corsellis, 1976), this would not explain loss of synapses in the rat dentate gyrus.

Neuronal mechanisms underlying the loss of synapses in senescent animals have received little attention. Our studies of the process have focused upon structural changes occurring in the dentate gyrus of the Fischer-344 rat in which we have demonstrated significant decrements in the numbers of synapses per unit of tissue square area in both the middle third and the supragranular portions of the molecular layer in 25-month old animals. It is apparent that three different populations of presynaptic neurons are involved in this loss of synapses, since synapses in the middle third of the molecular layer are formed by entorhinal afferents and those in the supragranular portion are formed by commissural, associational and probably septal afferents (Raisman, 1966; Mosko, Lynch, and Cotman, 1973). It is also apparent that the loss of synapses in the dentate gyrus is not secondary to a loss of neurons or their complement of postsynaptic dendritic shafts or spines. Were it otherwise, a decrease in the number of granule cells in the dentate gyri of senescent rats would be anticipated. But no significant difference was found when the numbers of granule cells were counted in three-and 25-month old rats (Geinisman and Bondareff, 1976).

In addition, it appears unlikely that the loss of synapses depends upon an antecedent loss of dendritic shafts and/or spines by a constant population of postsynaptic neurons. Although the numbers of dendritic branches and spines have been shown to be diminished in senescence, it is unlikely that the loss of synapses is associated solely with the loss of dendrites. This is indicated by the fact that synaptic loss in the dentate gyrus is not only significant when expressed in terms of tissue square area, but is equally significant when expressed in terms of unit length of dendrites. When all axo-dendritic synapses involving dendritic spines within 1.5 μm of longitudinally sectioned segments of dendrites were counted along 10 μm long segments of dendrites, the number of synapses per unit length was found to be significantly lower in 25-month old rats than in three-month old rats (Geinisman, Bondareff, and Dodge, 1977). This means that the loss of synapses in the senescent brain cannot depend exclusively upon the prior loss of dendrites. If it did, the number of synapses would disappear as the amount of dendritic surface disappeared and the number of synapses per unit length of dendrite would not change. We have found that it decreases significantly (Geinisman, Bondareff, and Dodge, 1977).

## ATROPHY OF DENDRITES

Other changes in neuronal connectivity in senescence indicated by changes in postsynaptic elements have been found in other parts of the brain and in other animals. Scheibel, Lindsay, Tomiyasu, and Scheibel (1975, 1976) examined the dendritic trees of neurons in Golgi preparations and found, in the superior frontal and superior temporal gyri, the hippocampus and the entorhinal cortex of aged human brains, that certain pyramidal neurons underwent a deterioration of dendrites. In particular, there was a disruption of horizontal dendrites from the basilar portions of the neuron. If these horizontally distributed dendrites are, as has been suggested, involved with modulating aspects of cortical physiology, their disruption during aging might have a disrupting effect on many aspects of behavior. The Scheibels and their associates found, similarly, that pyramidal cells of the aged human hippocampal formation lose dendritic spines and that their horizontal dendrites undergo a progressive degeneration which first involves horizontally distributed dendrites.

A whittling away of the dendritic tree of neurons appears to be a fairly generalized characteristic of aging. It is characteristic of the aged human brain (Scheibel *et al.*, 1975) and the aged rodent brain. In the latter it is unlikely to be secondary to some age-related encephalopathy such as that which is often associated with dementia in man. In rodents it may also be somewhat subtle, appearing as a decreased density of dendrites in the auditory cortex (Feldman and Dowd, 1975). Both indicate a loss of neuronal connectivity and, in all probability, both are related to synaptic loss. Loss of synapses has been shown to be coincident to the loss of dendritic spines in the rodent visual cortex (Feldman, 1976) and a loss of dendritic surface area and volume has been found coincident with the loss of axo-dendritic synapses in the rodent dentate gyrus (Geinisman *et al.*, 1978a).

The number and the shape of dendritic spines have been shown to be unusual in the cerebral cortical neurons of children with certain types of mental retardation (Marin-Padilla, 1972, 1974; Purpura, 1974) and the degree of spine abnormality appears to vary, in part, with age (Purpura, 1974). It is probable, although it has not been shown in humans, that the number of dendritic spines is not static in normal individuals at any age.

It changes during development and it has been suggested that density of dendritic spines is reflective of normal functional capacity (Purpura, 1974). Accordingly, in the rat cerebral cortex, both the branching of higher order dendrites (Holloway, 1966) and the number of dendritic spines (Globus, Rosenzweig, Bennett, and Diamond, 1973) are increased by exposure to a hyperstimulatory "enriched environment." Any change in the number of dendritic spines, each of which is the postsynaptic component of a synapse, must equate with a change in the number of synapses. Indeed, it is well-established that the integrity of postsynaptic structures, in particular dendritic spines, depends upon an intact presynaptic innervation and functional coupling of pre- and postsynaptic elements at synapses. The number and distribution of dendritic spines is not however, totally dependent upon an intact afferent connection, since it has been shown that deafferentation of cerebellar Purkinje cells at an early stage of development does not totally prevent the appearance of dendritic spines later in development. This indicates that, to some extent at least, the capacity to form dendritic spines is inherent in the postsynaptic neuron.

Loss of a dendritic spine means loss of a point of interneuronal contact (i.e., a synapse) and, although the interrelationships of presynaptic elements, postsynaptic elements and synaptic clefts are not well known, it can be anticipated that synaptic numbers, too, are not static. In the cat visual cortex, the number of synapses has been shown to increase rapidly and regularly in the postnatal period from day 8-37 and then to decline in adulthood (Cragg, 1975). Synapses, whether or not they involve dendritic spines, may also be constantly remodeled during adult life (Sotelo and Palay, 1971) and the change in number and distribution of synapses in adulthood may be irregular and reflective of changing functional capacity. It should be noted that in the dentate gyrus of the senescent Fischer-344 rat the actual process of degeneration has never been observed; neither degeneration of the synaptic cleft nor of the axonal or dendritic terminals which encompass the cleft. Neither has there been any report of ongoing formation of synapses. It is, therefore, not known whether the age-related loss in neuronal connectivity is primarily a loss of pre- or postsynaptic elements; however, whether primary or secondary, there can be little doubt that there is an atrophy of both dendritic spines and shafts with age. The disintegration of neuronal dendrites in senescence has been shown in experimental animals (Feldman, 1976; Hinds and McNelly, 1977; Vaughan, 1977) and in man

(Scheibel et al., 1975, 1976). Its cause, time course and the cellular events by means of which it is accomplished, however, are not known. In the dentate gyrus of the Fischer-344 rat, the loss of dendrites in the supragranular layer has been carefully analyzed (Geinisman, Bondareff, and Dodge, 1977). Not only is there a decrease in the number of dendritic profiles in electron micrographs but there is a significant decrease in both the volume fraction and the surface area of dendrites in senescent animals. This decrease, which is not associated with an age-related change in the dimension of the molecular layer, appears to reflect an absolute loss of dendritic substance.

The mechanism of this dendritic loss is not known (Bondareff, 1978). It has been speculated that dendritic atrophy begins in the most distal tips of dendritic trees and gradually works its way back toward the neuron cell body (Vaughan, 1977), but there is little evidence for this. Yet, dendritic atrophy in the higher order dendritic branches (Feldman, 1976; Geinisman, Bondareff, and Dodge, 1978a; Vaughan, 1977) and in man appears to involve horizontally distributed basal dendrites preferentially (Scheibel et al., 1975). Because of the latter it has been speculated that dendritic atrophy may result from the accumulation of neurofibrils in nerve cell bodies that in effect "strangle" basal dendrites (Scheibel et al., 1975). Although it has been claimed that an alteration of neurofibrils (i.e., neurofibrillary change) is characteristic of neuronal aging (see Bondareff, 1959), the occurrence of twisted tubules, neurofibrillary tangles and senile plaques such as are found characteristically in Alzheimer's disease (see Terry and Wisniewski, 1972) are probably not so much reflective of aging as they are of a deteriorative encephalopathy (Birren, 1972). Neurofibrillary materials do not accumulate in the neurons of the Fischer-344 rat, although dendrites are lost.

## AGE-RELATED CHANGES
## IN THE METABOLIC FUNCTIONS
## OF NERVE CELLS

Temporal relationships between the loss of dendrites and the loss of synapses in the senescent dentate gyrus have not been revealed but there is good reason to believe that the age-related loss of synapses represents a process of partial deafferentation—a loss of axonal terminals by presynaptic neurons, which are unable to maintain the integrity of synapses in senescence (Bondareff, 1979). In the dentate gyrus it appears to be related to a diminution in axonal transport of glycoproteins destined for axonal terminals (Geinisman, Bondareff, and Telser, 1977). This was shown by labeling the medial septal nucleus of young adult and senescent Fischer-344 rats with $^3$[H]-fucose and comparing the times of arrival of $^3$[H]-fucose-labeled glycoproteins in the hippocampus as a function of age. Although the rates of $^3$[H]-fucose incorporated into glycoproteins in the septum were the same in young adult and senescent rats, the arrival times differed significantly, reflecting a reduction in amount and/or in the rate of axonal transport of glycoproteins via the septo-hippocampal pathway of the senescent rat. The amount of labeled glycoproteins transported to the dentate gyrus in a 30-minute period was decreased by 53 percent in senescent rats and the rate of axonal transport, estimated to be about 288 mm/day in young adults and 221 mm/day in senescent rats, was decreased by about 25 percent. These findings are coincident with the loss of synapses in the dentate gyri of senescent Fischer-344 rats. It is not known why axoplasmic transport of glycoprotein declines in the septo-hippocampal pathway but there is no reason to believe that any one system of presynaptic neurons is uniquely involved. Although the ubiquity of synaptic loss is not known, certainly synapses other than those in the dentate gyrus are lost with age.

## The Mechanism of Intraneuronal Transport

Glycoproteins and certain other proteins have been shown to be synthesized in the cell bodies of neurons. Their synthesis and subsequent packaging for transport through axons have been shown to involve intracytoplasmic organelles such as the Golgi complex. They are transported to cellular sites, both proximal and distal to the cell body, where they are utilized in the renewal of plasma membranes, presynaptic membranes and intracellular membranes such as those of presynaptic vesicles. The intraneuronal transport of fucose-labeled glycoproteins through axons of the septo-hippocampal pathway at rates of 221-228 mm/day represents rapid axoplasmic transport by a mechanism that requires enzymatic utilization of energy. The mechanism is not known. It may involve the subplasmalemmal cytoplasm, axonal plasma membranes or the smooth endoplasmic reticulum (Droz, Rambourg, and Koenig, 1975). However, it is more generally believed to depend upon intact microfilaments to which the transported material is bound and intact microtubules along which the

neurofilaments are moved by a sliding filament mechanism similar to that which characterizes the contraction of muscle (Ochs, 1972). A decrease in the axoplasmic transport of glycoproteins in the senescent brain suggests that something happens which interferes with the normal interaction between microtubules and microfilaments.

Neurofibrillary degeneration of certain neurons has long been recognized as characteristic of senile dementia (Terry and Wisniewski, 1972; Wisniewski and Terry, 1976). It is commonly found in neurons of older persons which are examined at autopsy and in some series it occurs with astonishing frequency. In a series of Japanese autopsied more than 70 years old at the time of death, Matsuyama, et al., (cited by Terry and Wisniewski, 1972), found neurofibrillary degeneration in 99 percent. The tangles of so-called neurofibrils which are readily impregnated with silver salts and visualized with the light microscope are thought by some to be neither microtubules nor microfilaments but a group of twisted filaments with their own unique ultrastructural characteristics. Chemically, they appear to be closely related to the microfilaments of normal neurons but their relationship to the microfilaments and microtubules of normal neurons is not known (Iqbal, Grundke-Iqbal, Wisniewski, Korthals, and Terry, 1976). In some neurons, especially certain pyramidal cells of the human cerebral cortex, structurally altered neurofibrils appear to accumulate, first in neuronal cell bodies at the base of dendritic shafts (Scheibel, Lindsay, Tomiyasu, and Scheibel, 1975). Because the clogging of these basilar dendrites appears to precede atrophy, it is thought that intracellular blockage by clumps of neurofibrillary tangles might interfere with normal intracellular transport mechanisms and lead progressively to the atrophy of dendritic processes and eventually to the death and loss of neurons.

Actually it is not known how these tangles form. Whether they in some way develop from normal neurofilaments or represent a unique species of filament is not known. Similar tangles of neurofibrils are found in diseases with other causes and the relationship between tangles found in human senile dementia (Tomlinson and Henderson, 1976) to neurofibrillary tangles found in certain viral diseases or toxic encephalopathies, such as the neurofibrillary degeneration associated with aluminum toxicity (Crapper, 1976), are not well understood (for review see Wells, 1978). Although some would argue to the contrary, the relationship between normal aging and the neurofibrillary degeneration found commonly in the brains of old humans examined after death from a wide variety of causes which are rarely even defined is at best tenuous.

Neurofibrillary degeneration is not found in neurons of the rat. There is no reason to suggest that neurotubules change with age, and the life history of neuronal microfilaments, which are a heterogeneous group of filaments not well defined in neurons, is not known. There is little, then, that substantiates the supposition that age-related changes in neuronal microtubules or microfilaments are related causally to the decrease in axoplasmic transport in senescence. But axoplasmic transport is an active process that depends upon oxidative metabolism. It is soon arrested by agents which induce anoxia, block oxidative phosphorylation or the citric acid cycle, or compromise the accessability of ATP. It is reasonable, then, to seek other indications of neuronal pathology which might interfere with the metabolism of neurons in senescence.

## ORGANELLES OF PROTEIN METABOLISM

Lipofuscin pigment accumulates in certain neurons and neuroglial cells as a function of age (Bondareff, 1959). It appears to result from the fusion of a primary lysosome, a membrane-bound cytoplasmic body which contains a number of acid hydrolysases, with an autophagosome, another membrane-bound cytoplasmic body into which various cytoplasmic components have been sequestered (Sekhon and Maxwell, 1974). With time and incomplete degradation of the contents of this liposomal complex, a residual body results. It is not known whether lipofuscin pigment is beneficial or detrimental to the neurons in which it accumulates, although it has traditionally been thought of as a slowly accumulating resultant of "wear and tear" with which neurons become progressively stuffed. It is usually considered to be an indigestable material which, as it accumulates, eventually causes a slowing down of metabolic processes and results eventually in neuronal death. However, in the human brain at least, one of the heaviest accumulations of lipofuscin pigment occurs in the inferior olivary nucleus which appears to function normally and from which no neurons are lost in senescence (Brody, 1973).

*Accumulation of Lipofuscin Pigment.* Lipofuscin is a peculiar substance, the formation and composition of which are still not understood. It is claimed by some to have highly selective properties by means of which it can be differentiated from other intracellular pigments (Siakotos and Koppang, 1973). But the differentiation is, in actuality, difficult to

make. Lipofuscin belongs to a family of intracytoplasmic, pigmented substances (lipochromes) which are autofluorescent (Siakotos and Koppang, 1973; Strehler, 1964). Their fluorescence properties are similar; they contain acid phosphatase and a variety of proteases, glycosidases, lipases and other enzymes which are typically found in lysosomes but which differ in different types of cells and in different conditions. Whereas the significance of these differences in specific intracytoplasmic lipochrome pigments is unknown, it is significant that all appear to be lysosomal derivatives. They appear to arise in some way from the fusion of primary lysosomes, which contain the various enzymes, with autophagosomes and/or lipid droplets. These primary lysosomes, containing acid hyrolases and oxidases, are transformed through intermediary stages which may involve other cytoplasmic bodies associated with phagocytic or autophagocytic activity, into residual bodies (Sekhon and Maxwell, 1974).

The ultrastructure of the resulting lipofuscin granule is distinctive. It is characterized by three components: one dense, one vacuolar and one which appears to be a lipid droplet. It suggests that at some time during the formation of lipofuscin, incorporation of a lipid body occurs. In some way, which is not understood, the formation of the residual lipofuscin body is related to the amount of cytoplasmic lipofuscin, the lipid and protein components of which are not subject to digestion by lysosomal enzymes (Barden, 1970). Next, with the effective removal or inactivation of other enzymes, potentially cytotoxic substances can accumulate in the cytoplasm; we see, for example, the accumulation of peroxides associated with the loss of peroxidase activity. Although it has not been shown that lipofuscin is detrimental to neurons, the intracellular accumulation of ceroid (another lipochrome pigment) does appear to be associated with neuronal disease. In addition, it has been shown that Vitamin E, an autoxidant, decreases the amount of lipochrome pigment in WI-38 cells *in vitro* and increases survival times (Packer and Smith, 1974), presumably by increasing the amount of peroxidase activity.

*The Golgi Complex.* The accumulation of lipofuscin pigment in all probability heralds a change in the availability or activity of lysosomal enzymes, but it is far from clear what this change might be. It may or may not be associated with age-related changes in other organelles, for example, the Golgi complex or the rough endoplasmic reticulum. The Golgi complex, which consists of stacks of agranular cisternae and a variety of closely associated vesicles, tends to be as well-developed in neurons as in secretory cells. It has a convex, forming or entry face which is continuous with the rough endoplasmic reticulum through a variety of vesicles. It has a concave, mature or exit face which is continuous with saccules of the smooth endoplasmic reticulum, called GERL (Golgi-endoplasmic reticulum-lysosomes). These GERL saccules contain acid phosphatase and appear to be involved in the formation of lysosomes and the packaging of secretory materials into granules (Novikoff, Novikoff, Quintana, and Hauw, 1976). Their function and that of the rough endoplasmic reticulum of nerve cells is concerned with synthesis of complex carbohydrate-containing proteins as well as the production of lysosomes. Acid hydrolases are found in the cisternae of the Golgi complex and GERL from which they are transferred to lysosomes and eventually are incorporated into lipofuscin pigment. Glycoproteins and glycosaminoglycans also are found in Golgi complex cisternae in which it appears they are assembled following their synthesis in the rough endoplasmic reticulum. These macromolecules, about which more will be said later, contribute to the composition of plasma membranes and perhaps also to the extraneuronal microenvironment.

Fucose is incorporated into newly synthesized glycoprotein, which is either packaged for secretion or transported intracellularly to plasma membranes in nerve cells in a manner presumed to be similar to that described in other types of cells. It is believed that synthesis of these glycoproteins destined for incorporation into neuron plasma membrane begins on ribosomes associated with the lamellae of the rough endoplasmic reticulum. Core sugars appear to be added within the cisternae of the rough endoplasmic reticulum and terminal residues of sugars such as fucose are added to the molecule in the Golgi complex (Jamieson and Palade, 1977; Leblond and Bennett, 1977). In nerve cells some of these newly synthesized glycoproteins are transported actively through the cytoplasm of axons and dendrites to sites on plasma membranes (including sites on pre- and postsynaptic membranes) where they are incorporated.

The Golgi complex, is, therefore, very much involved in neuronal metabolism, especially those aspects of it which appear to be altered during aging. Yet there is little evidence to link changes in the Golgi complex with aging, although such a link has long been suspected. Certain lamellae of the Golgi complex are readily impregnated by osmium tetroxide and it is well known that eventually deposits of reduced osmium can be built up so as to make the Golgi complex, or Golgi apparatus as it is more traditionally known, visualizable with the light microscope. It appears as a coarse reticulum with a perinuclear distribution in certain nerve cells. It has been observed by several investigators that the Golgi apparatus, visualized with the light microscope in sections of osmium impregnated tissue, fragments in the brains of senescent animals (see Bondareff, 1959).

*The Rough Endoplasmic Reticulum.* The role of the Golgi complex in neuronal metabolism, although obviously important, is not so well understood as that of the rough endoplasmic reticulum. In neurons, the granular or rough endoplasmic reticulum consists of stacks of cisternae, the membranes of which are covered with ribosomes. These stacks, between which are free ribosomes, are interconnected and closely ordered to form discrete bodies—Nissl bodies—which are visible with the light microscope. Most of a neuron's RNA is localized in its Nissl bodies which, because of this, have an affinity for certain aniline dyes such as thianin or gallacyanin. Nissl bodies, because they are stained with these dyes, constitute a chromidial substance in the neuronal cytoplasm.

A decline in neuronal metabolism would be suggested by a decrease in stainable Nissl substance (chromatolysis) in neurons in senescence, and such a decrease has been reported. A microspectrophotometric study of human brains obtained at autopsy showed an inverse relationship between lipofuscin pigment and Nissl substance in neurons of the inferior olivary nucleus and anterior horns. Lipofuscin increased progressively in neurons from individuals from the first through the ninth decades while cytoplasmic RNA progressively decreased (Mann and Yates, 1974a). After age 80 the loss of RNA became disproportionately greater and neurons appeared overtly chromatolytic, suggesting that the accumulation of lipofuscin, at least after a certain point, is deleterious to neuronal well-being. Chromatolysis related to age, however, is not always found and for a variety of technical reasons its significance, especially in human brains, is questionable. Although conclusive analysis of this question awaits a carefully controlled microspectrophotometric study of a reliable animal model, current evidence favors the conclusion that the content of cytoplasmic RNA decreases and protein metabolism fails in nerve cells of senescent animals.

Hydén (1967) has published intriguing data on age-related changes in neuronal RNA content. By means of microdissection, Hydén isolated neurons from the ventral horns of the spinal cord of human traffic accident victims and found the RNA content of these cells to fall after age 60. With similar methods, RNA has also been measured in pyramidal cells of rats isolated from the CA3 zone of the hippocampus (Ringborg, 1966). In pooled specimens of 5–10 neurons each, total RNA was determined microspectrophotometrically. A significant decrement in the rate of RNA synthesis in hippocampal neurons of senescent rats comparable to that found in ventral horn neurons of elderly men was found. This age-related decline in the rate of RNA synthesis suggests that there may be fewer ribosomes available for protein synthesis in neurons of old animals. The age-related decline in neuronal protein synthesis indicated by these studies of specific isolated neurons is difficult to interpret and must be considered with considerable caution. It is supported, on the one hand, by a methodologically different study of Purkinje cells and anterior horn cells *in situ* in which less ($^3$H) cytidine was incorporated by neurons of 20-month old animals than by 1.5-month old animals (Wulff, Quastler, Sherman, and Samis, 1965). On the other hand, no age-related difference was found in the rates of protein turnover by spinal motor neurons isolated from young adult and senescent rats (Jakoubek, Gutmann, Fischer, and Babicky, 1968).

It is impossible to summarize adequately these data derived from studies of neurons under widely varying conditions. Unfortunately, the complexity of the central nervous system encourages the use of model systems which may be difficult to compare. The use of neurons isolated by free-hand dissection permits study of a single, specific type of neuron under uniform laboratory conditions but necessitates the use of neurons variously damaged during the isolation procedure. Especially since the nature of this damage may be unknown, it is not possible to compare such a neuron with one isolated by some other method or one studied *in situ* under conditions which may not be controllable. Methods which are essentially morphological are difficult to compare with those that are essentially biochemical and it is often difficult to attempt to compare putative age changes in a rat or mouse brain with those found in man. Although they may not be convincing in themselves, taken collectively experimental animal studies and observational data from studies of man suggest rather strongly that neuronal metabolism in general (Ferendelli, Sedgwick and Suntzeff, 1971; Patel, 1977) and protein metabolism in particular fail in the senescent nervous system. If neuronal protein metabolism deteriorates in senescence, it is reasonable to anticipate deterioration of various enzyme systems and a few examples of this have been found. One of the more interesting concerns synthesis and storage of certain neurotransmitter substances.

## THE PRODUCTION OF NEUROTRANSMITTERS.

The amount of gamma aminobutyric acid (GABA), a putative neurotransmitter substance with inhibitory properties, was found to be greater in whole brain fractions of senescent rodents than in those of young adults (Davis and Himwich, 1975). Acetylcholine esterase activity, an important determiner of acetylcholine levels, was less in whole brains and cerebral cortical fractions of senescent, as compared with young adult, rodents (Frolkis, Bezrukov, Duplenko, Shchegoleva, Shevtchuk, and Verkhratsky, 1973; Hollander and Barrows, 1968; Samorajski, Rolsten, and Ordy, 1971). Amounts of catecholamine and indoleamine appear also to be decreased and amounts of norepinephrine, dopamine and serotonin are decreased in the brains of senescent mice (Finch, 1973; Samorajski, Rolsten, and Ordy, 1971). A decrease in striatal dopamine appears to be associated with the signs and symptoms of Parkinson's disease which are alleviated by replacement therapy with L-dopa.

Not only are the amounts of brain catecholamines reduced in senescence, but it has been shown that the uptake of dopamine, which is energy dependent, is also reduced in the senescent brain. (Jonec and Finch, 1975). The reduction in dopamine uptake by a synaptosome fraction of mouse striatum and hypothalamus, but not in the uptake of serotonin or norepinephrine, appears to represent a highly selective, age-related change in neuronal metabolic activity, which may be associated with a loss of dopaminergic neurons and/or synapses (Jonec and Finch, 1975). Such age-related changes in dopamine uptake and in the turnover of hypothalamic norepinephrine and striatal dopamine (Finch, 1973) signals a functionally significant decline in monoamine synthesis, which has been demonstrated in the brain stem, hypothalamus and straitum of senescent rats (Ponzio, Brunello, and Algeri, 1978). It is, therefore, of some interest that the accumulation of DOPA following electroconvulsive shock is reduced in the brains of senescent, as compared with young, and adult rats, suggesting a decline in the functional capacity of dopaminergic neurons in the senescent brain (McNamara, Miller, Benignus, and Davis, 1977).

Other indications of neuronal activity declining with age might reasonably be anticipated, but have proved difficult to demonstrate. Especially difficult to demonstrate have been indications of depressed synaptic activity, which are predictable in senescence because synthetic machinery in neuronal perikarya, upon which synaptic activity depends, fails in the senescent brain. Age-related changes in synaptic activity have long been suspected (Wayner and Emmers, 1958). They were believed to contribute to the decreased reaction times regarded as functional hallmarks of the aging organism. Such changes, although they are suspected and were predicted by Birren and Wall (1956), who studied conduction velocity changes in sciatic nerves of senescent rats, have never been actually documented, mainly because it has proved technically difficult to design experiments by means of which such changes might be reliably demonstrated.

An interesting model system, by means of which it may be possible to compare directly synaptic activity in young and senescent neurons was recently introduced (Landfield and Lynch, 1977; Landfield, McGaugh, and Lynch, 1978). It makes use of slices of rat hippocampus maintained in a controlled artificial medium, in which microelectrodes were positioned under direct visual control in specifically identified neurons and interneuronal pathways. By monitoring potentials evoked in CA1 pyramidal neurons by the repetitive stimulation of Schaffer collaterals, post-tetanic responses were compared in young and senescent (24-27-month old) Fischer-344 rats. Potentiation of these post-tetanic responses, indicating an increase in synaptic response after the termination of a repetitive stimulus, was found in slices from both young and old animals, but a significantly smaller frequency potentiation was recorded from the latter. This suggests that synapses in the aged animals may be unable to respond to repetitive stimulation and, because frequency potentiation decreased only at the end of a train of stimuli, not at the beginning, this decreased potentiation appears to represent a depression of synaptic activity. Depressed synaptic activity almost certainly results from a decrease in the availability of effective neuro-transmitter molecules at postsynaptic receptor sites.

The nature of depressed synaptic activity in senescence, although not known, undoubtedly represents a failure of neuronal metabolism. This might be expressed as an insufficiency in the neuro-transmitter substance within presynaptic vesicles or as an unavailability of neurotransmitter to recharge presynaptic vesicles once they had been emptied in response to an appropriate stimulus. It might also find expression in a deficiency of membrane proteins resulting in a qualitative or quantitative fault in presynaptic membranes or in the membranes of presynaptic vesicles.

## GLYCOPROTEIN SYNTHESIS AND PLASMA MEMBRANES

Either a failure in synthesis, which might be secondary to the lack of some essential substrate or precursor, or a failure to transport synthesized materials to intracellular sites of utilization might result in there being insufficient neurotransmitter in axon terminals to support normal synaptic activity. A deficiency in the protein component of membranes involved in transmitter release might, of course, have similar consequences, and changes in the composition of cytoplasmic organelles and in the efficiency of axoplasmic transport, on which transmitter release depends, have been described. Nothing is known of how synaptic vesicles might be changed in senescence. Similarly, there has been no demonstration of an age-related change in synaptic membranes. But age changes in the constituent glycoproteins of perikaryal plasma membranes have been demonstrated and prompt the speculation that comparable changes may extend to specialized plasma membranes, such as pre- and postsynaptic membranes.

Although pre- and postsynaptic membranes are of particular interest, they are not easily examined *in vivo* and a suitable *in vitro* model has yet to be developed. Tissue culture systems, which have been particularly useful in many experimental studies, are not well suited to studies of aging because the neuron is no longer in its normal microenvironment and the meaning of age becomes hypothetical. Isolation of whole neurons or parts of neurons containing synaptic membranes (synaptosomes) representing inhomogeneous neuronal populations of unknown origin, requires that isolated membranes or cells be exposed to a variety of nonphysiological forces and fluids for extended periods of time. Isolation of neurons by free-hand dissection tears neuronal processes but does allow a reasonably intact neuronal perikaryon to be isolated. Although neurons isolated by free-hand dissection are not ideally suited for studies of plasma membrane constituents in neurons of senescent animals they do provide a useful model system by means of which selected properties of neurons from young and old animals can be compared under controlled conditions. Neurons of the lateral vestibular nucleus can be quickly collected and isolated in incubation media under direct microscopic visualization. They appear to have intact plasma membranes (Bondareff and Hydén, 1969) and are capable of carrying on normal neuronal function *in vitro* including maintenance of a membrane potential and growth of new neuronal processes (see Bondareff and Hydén, 1969). They provide a specific, fully defined, homogeneous population of neurons which have aged *in vivo* prior to their isolation.

Perikaryal plasma membranes of such isolated neurons can be compared with the help of fluorescamine-labeled Conconavalin A (Bennett and Bondareff, 1977). This plant lectin binds to specific carbohydrate moities of glycoproteins and under appropriate conditions can induce clustering of carbohydrate-containing receptor sites, reflecting their mobility in plasma membranes. Lateral vestibular nucleus neurons, which are unusually large and therefore ideally suited to isolation by free-hand dissection, were isolated from three and 24-month old Fischer-344 rats and incubated in Conconavalin A labeled with fluorescamine. These neurons fluoresced with an intensity which varied with their age. They were scanned with a microdensitometer and a relative measure of neuron-associated fluorescence was obtained. The pattern of Conconavalin A binding and the intensity of fluorescence associated with neuronal plasma membranes indicated that neurons from young adult animals were about a third as fluorescent as were those from senescent animals. Furthermore, while the fluorescent material was evenly distributed over the surface of the majority of neurons isolated from young adult animals, it was bound in patches or in one discrete region of the neuronal surface (a cap) by neurons from senescent animals.

Incubation with a-methyl-D-glucoside prior to incubation in Conconavalin A prevented the appearance of fluorescence, thereby demonstrating that it was dependent upon the presence in the plasma membrane of specific glycosides. These glycosides are glycoprotein constituents, and an age-related difference in fluorescence intensity due to the reaction with Conconavalin A indicated that senescent rat neurons have more glycoprotein-containing receptor sites available in their plasma membranes for Conconavalin A binding than do young adult rat neurons. Incubation of neurons in trypsin or neuraminidase prior to incubation in Conconavalin A resulted in a very significant increase in the intensity of fluorescence of neurons from young adult animals but had no noticeable effect on fluorescence of neurons from senescent animals. This suggests that although Conconavalin A binding sites may be present in the plasma membranes of young adult rats they are masked or altered and not available for binding.

The presence of caps and the patchy distribution of fluorescent material in the plasma membranes of neurons isolated from senescent animals makes it reasonable to predict a greater mobility of receptor sites than that characteristic of young adults. This prediction follows from the fluid mosaic model of plasma membrane structure propounded by Singer and Nicholson (1972) which suggests that mobility of receptor sites and membrane fluidity may be directly dependent upon structural differences in plasma membrane glycoproteins. Treatment of isolated neurons with trypsin or neuraminidase results in a relatively greater change in the binding pattern of Conconavalin A receptors in young adult than in senescent neurons and suggests that binding sites on glycoproteins on the surface of young adult neurons may be masked by sialic acid or by glycoprotein interactions (cf. Nicholson, 1974). This may result from qualitative or quantitative differences in the distribution or characteristics of plasma membrane—associated microfilaments. By virtue of their capacity to deform plasma membranes, a change in neuronal microfilaments (or in microtubules) could alter the configuration of membrane-associated glycoproteins. It seems, however, more likely to result from a decrease in the amount of sialic acid—containing glycoproteins due to a synthetic decline in the senescent brain or to a failure in the transport of glycoproteins from sites of synthesis to sites of utilization in plasma membranes of senescent neurons.

Although there are no other reports of a change in the neuronal plasma membrane receptor sites in senescence, an increase in insulin-binding sites in the plasma membranes of "senescent" human fibroblasts *in vitro* has been reported (Rosenbloom, Goldstein, and Yip, 1976). Cellular mechanisms underlying this are no more understood than those underlying the altered binding of Conconavalin A to "senescent" rat neurons. Both phenomena undoubtedly reflect changes, not yet recognized, in cellular metabolism and there is ample evidence that the metabolism of neurons (at least some neurons) fails in senescence. (Lassen, Feinberg, and Lane, 1960; Meier-Ruge, Reichlmeier, and Iwangoff, 1976). Changes in organelles that support protein synthesis and changes in axonal transport of glycoproteins are well documented, but whether such changes are primary or secondary is moot and the events which lead to them in senescence are virtually unknown. A failure in neuronal metabolism may, of course, result from an intrinsic change in the genome, as has been hypothesized from various theoretical considerations.

It has been thought, for example, that chromosomes might become inactivated due to the accumulation of somatic mutations during a lifetime (Szilard, 1959); and that errors in translation might result in enzyme mutations (Orgel, 1963). In either case, a spontaneous change in the genome could decrease neuronal adaptability and lead to neuronal malfunction and perhaps neuronal death. There is, at present, little evidence of an intrinsic change in the genome in the senescent neuron. There is more evidence that metabolic failure might result from changes in the vascular or extracellular compartments that are extrinsic to the neuron.

## EXTRACELLULAR DETERMINANTS OF NEURONAL AGING

The relationship of vascular change to aging is difficult to assess (Thompson, 1976), although changes in small vessels in the cerebral cortex (Fang, 1976) and in regional blood flow (reviewed by Thompson, 1976) have been described in the aged human brain. In rodents, alterations of the cerebral vasculature are typically not found in senescence and a recent study of $^{14}$[C]-sucrose permeability indicates that the blood-brain barrier of 28-month old Fischer-344 rats is intact (Rapoport, Ohno, and Pettigrew, 1978). Contrarily, the relationship of change in the extracellular space to aging is more readily accessed, at least in rodents.

### THE BRAIN EXTRACELLULAR SPACE

The extracellular space of the brain, however, is a poorly defined tissue compartment. It is certainly extrinsic to the neuron anatomically but, because some of its contents may be of neuronal origin, the question of whether an age-related change in the extracellular space is properly an extrinsic change or an intrinsic one reflective of some change in the genome of neurons (or neuroglia) is unanswerable. In the brain the extracellular space constitutes a part of the neuronal microenvironment. It is bounded by the externalmost part of the plasma membranes of nerve cells and neuroglia which border upon it and, therefore, it contains plasma membrane-associated carbohydrates in addition to a variety of unidentified extracellular substances. In electron micrographs of brain prepared by conventional methods of chemical fixation, it appears as a gap about 15-20 nm wide. It is apparent, al-

though the relationships are unclear, that the blood and the cerebro-spinal fluid must contribute to the composition of the extracellular space and so to the neuronal microenvironment.

The biology of the extracellular space of brain is poorly understood. Much of what is known about it in the mammalian brain indicates that it is comparable to the extracellular compartment of other organs, and comprises about 20-30 percent of the volume of the brain in adults (Van Harreveld, 1966). It contains an ill-defined extracellular substance, believed to be a non-lipid, anionic material, which can be preserved and demonstrated by means of certain histochemical reactions. These reactions rely upon the selective distribution of dense metallic compounds within the extracellular space, including phosphotungstic acid, silver methenamine, saccharated iron oxide and ruthenium red (for review see Bondareff, 1976a). There are compelling reasons to believe that these metallic compounds react with glycoproteins and glycosaminoglycans, both of which have been isolated from brain (Brunngraber, Brown, and Aro, 1975; Margolis, 1967; Margolis and Margolis, 1970). Both have also been associated with synapses and nerve ending fractions.

Little is known of the histophysiological contribution of these complex macromolecules to the neuronal environment, but proteoglycans isolated from the cerebral cortices of Fischer-344 rats appear to contain keratan sulfate, the concentration of which varies during life (Vitello, Breen, Weinstein, Sittig, and Blacik, 1978). It was found to triple from one to three months, after which it decreased progressively to 25 months of age. Because charge density and water binding capacity appear to vary with sulfation (Bettelheim and Plessy, 1975), it can be anticipated that a decrease in the keratan sulfate concentration of brain proteoglycans will be accompanied by a significant change in the composition and functional capabilities of the extracellular spaces in the senescent brain, assuming, of course, that these sulfated proteoglycans and the polyanions visualized by electron microscopy are one and the same.

The relative volume of the brain extracellular space has been shown to decrease to about half the young adult level in the senescent rat brain (Bondareff and Narotzky, 1972). Coincidentally, there is a significant decrease in the depth of penetration of ruthenium red from the free ventricular surface into the substance of the dentate gyrus of the Fischer-344 rat (Bondareff and Lin-Liu, 1977). Because the depth of penetration of the highly charged ruthenium red molecule appears to depend upon the binding of charged macromolecules with the extracellular spaces, this change in depth of penetration indicates a change in the charge density of intercellular polyanions in the senescent brain. The nature of this change is not known. It might result from a change in the composition of brain proteoglycans, as suggested by changing concentrations of brain keratan sulfate; a net increase in polyanion concentration; or a change in the conformation of intercellular polyanions. Whatever the cause, a relative increase in the charge density of polyanions within extracellular space is likely to affect the passage of ions and charged metabolites through them. Although no such change has been directly demonstrated in the senescent brain, it has been shown that exogenous catecholamines injected directly into brain tissue spread about half the distance through senescent brain as they do through young adult brain (Bondareff, Narotzky, and Routtenberg, 1971).

The data discussed in this review prompt the speculation that nerve cells are affected at some time in later life by regional changes in their extracellular environment. As a consequence of these changes they become less able to maintain a variety of functions which normally support neuronal activities in younger animals. If sustained, these might lead to structural changes such as decrements in the numbers of dendritic processes and synapses. Because the number of dendritic spines (and presumably the number of synapses also) is known not to be static but to increase or decrease as the environment is "enriched or deprived" (Diamond, 1978; Globus et al., 1973) these changes in the senescent brain are likely to be reversible, at least initially, before an irreversible loss of neurons occurs.

Although the temporal sequence of these changes has not been elucidated, age-related changes in the dimensions and distributions of neuronal processes and their terminals appear to be compensated for by a redistribution of structural elements (Bondareff, 1979). An analysis of this process in the dentate gyrus of three- and 25-month old Fischer-344 rats indicates no change in the overall dimensions of the molecular layer but a decrease in the volume of the dendritic compartment from 41 to 36 percent (Geinisman, Bondareff, and Dodge, 1978b). This atrophy of neuronal processes is accompanied by an hypertrophy of astrocytes (Geinisman, Bondareff, and Dodge, 1978b) which does not involve any increase in the number of astrocyte cell bodies but an increase in the number and/or the dimensions of astrocytic processes. The result is an increase in the relative volume occupied by astrocytic processes, about 45 percent, which compensates for the volume lost by dendritic atrophy. Whether this astrocytic hypertrophy is compensatory for an actual loss of neuronal substance in senescence (comparable, perhaps, to the formation of a glial scar) in response to a brain-tissue-destroying lesion or whether it is compensatory to functional changes resulting from a decrement in the total mass of functional neuronal units is not known.

A decrease in the relative volume of the extracellular compartment in the senescent brain has been demonstrated electron microscopically, by morphometric analysis of brain tissue preserved by freeze-substitution (Bondareff and Narotzky, 1972). By similar means it has also been possible to document changes in relative volume of the extracellular space during maturation and as a consequence of experimental manipulation. A decrease in the volume of the extracellular space in the senescent brain, like the accumulation of lipofuscin pigment, appears to be a reliable herald of senescence. Considering that the extracellular space appears to be the site of important metabolic transactions involving ions and small metabolites, a contracted extracellular space is likely to have significant functional consequences. Unfortunately, its submicroscopic dimensions and the fact that it is thoroughly comingled with cellular processes of similar dimensions have, thus far, made a direct analysis of extracellular space functions impossible.

Extracellular space appears to accommodate diffusion of: (1) neurotransmitters from axon terminals where they are released to synaptic receptor sites with which they interact; (2) products secreted from axonal and dendritic terminals which appear to modulate neuronal activity; (3) potassium ions which are released from active neurons and taken up by neuroglial cells with the result that membrane potentials of both cell types are affected; and (4) nutritive products from capillaries to neurons and waste products from neurons to cerebral spinal fluid. The diminished spread of exogenous catechalamines found when norepinephrine or dopamine are injected intracerebrally into senescent rats (Bondareff, Narotzky, and Routtenberg, 1971) justifies the speculation that a decrease in brain extracellular space in senescence would effectively block transport of metabolites to and from neurons. It can be anticipated that such a block would compromise neuronal (and neuroglial) metabolism leading, through a cascading sequence of neuronal pathology, to the loss of synapses, dendrites and even nerve cells that is found characteristically in the senescent brain (cf., Bondareff, 1976b).

## AGE-RELATED CHANGES IN NEUROGLIA

Actually, the effect of aging on the neuroglia and the role of the neuroglia in the aging process are difficult to define because the role of the neuroglia in normal neural function is so poorly understood. Yet the neuroglia, which are even more numerous than neurons, are important contributors to the constancy of the neuronal microenvironment and they are altered in the senescent brain. In most attempts to estimate numbers of neuroglia in senescence, an increase has been found in various regions of the brain in man, monkey and rodents (Blinkov and Glazer, 1968; Brizzee, 1975; Sturrock, 1977), although a decrease was found in the anterior commissure of mouse (Sturrock, 1976). More specifically, an increase in the number of microglia was found in the cerebral cortex of the senescent rat (Vaughan and Peters, 1974) and in the indusium griseum of the senescent mouse (Sturrock, 1977). Because microglia are, in large part, phagocytes of extracerebral origin which invade central nervous tissue from its vasculature in response to infectious or degenerative processes, an increase in the number of microglia suggests a response to the neuronal, dendritic or synaptic degeneration which presumably has preceded the loss of these elements in the senescent brain.

Comparable changes in the number of oligodendrocytes have not been found and there is some question as to whether the number of astrocytes changes with age. They apparently do not in the rat cerebral cortex (Vaughan and Peters, 1974) and they may (Landfield, Rose, Sandles, Wohlstadter, and Lynch, 1977) or may not (Geinisman, Bondareff, and Dodge, 1978a) be increased in the rat hippocampus. Although there may be no actual increase in the number of astrocytes in the rat hippocampus in senescence there does appear to be a significant hypertrophy of astrocytes in the dentate gyrus of the senescent Fischer-344 rat (Bondareff, in press; Geinisman, Bondareff, and Dodge, 1978a). This is of particular interest because, in senescent animals, both the total volume fraction and the total surface area of astroglial processes increase in the supragranular zone coincidently with the loss of synapses and dendritic processes. This increase in the astroglial compartment is not associated with an increase in the volume of individual astroglial processes; it represents, therefore, not only a relative increase in the total astroglial compartment but one due specifically to the proliferation of astrocytic processes.

There is no explanation for this increase in the astrocytic compartment. Astrocytic processes in the dentate gyri of senescent rats are morphologically indistinguishable from those of younger animals. There are no apparent changes in the amounts of glycogen or microfibrils and there is, therefore, little reason to equate the astrocytic hypertrophy of senescence to the reactive hypertrophy of astrocytes in "scars" formed in response to the injury and death of normal brain tissue.

An increase in the volume of the astrocytic compartment may be a response to age-related changes in the neuronal microenvironment and reflect the role that astrocytes presumably play in maintaining its constancy. This includes preventing ions and neurotransmitters from accumulating in the extracellular space, which appears to be affected by astrocytes (Grossman and Seregin, 1977; Martinez-Hernandez, Bell, and Norenberg, 1977). Because the accumulation of $K^+$ and neurotransmitter substances released by discharging neurons are capable of depolarizing neurons, an expansion of the astroglial compartment in the senescent brain could affect neuronal firing patterns, which do appear to change in the dentate gyrus of senescent rats (Landfield and Lynch, 1977; Landfield, McGaugh, and Lynch, 1978). Astroglial hypertrophy in the senescent brain is a reality. It probably is a compensatory response to something more meaningful than a change in space-occupying structure and as such may relate to some poorly understood, suspected aspect of astroglial function, such as the maintenance of a homeostatic neuronal microenvironment. But it is not known whether maintenance of microenvironmental constancy requires uptake from the extracellular space into astrocytic cytoplasm of neuroactive ions and molecules such as $K^+$, $Na^+$, GABA, catecholamine and acetylcholine.

## NEUROBIOLOGICAL PROCESS OF AGING: AN HYPOTHESIS

Results of some of the more reliable published studies of the brains of aged and aging animals have been summarized. Most of the data considered, especially those which concern the aging (as opposed to the aged) brain, are derived from studies of experimental animals because man often grows old gracefully and, although functional deficits do occur in the aged, they usually are not so disruptive as to cause sudden death. As biopsy and suitable necropsy specimens of brain from senescent humans are not readily available, the relationship of pathology, especially neuronal pathology, to functional decline in the aged has been inadequately studied and poorly understood in man. It is, to some extent, clear that cerebrovascular disease and neuronal pathology such as the occurrence of neurofibrillary tangles, senile plaques and neuronal loss may be correlated with the appearance of a clinically apparent organic brain syndrome characterized by dementia in persons over 65 years (reviewed by Wells, 1978). It is less clear how such pathology relates to so-called involutional brain syndromes characterized by depression or paranoia, the neurobiological bases of which are not understood. Still less understood are neurobiological substrata of behavioral changes in the aged, some of which involve abnormalities of perception (for example, pain, touch and the modalities of vision, audition, olfaction and taste).

Studies of the brain in aged and aging animals suggest that aging is associated with a number of changes in the structure and composition of brain, which do not correlate well with behavioral symptomatology. It can only be assumed that such changes may correlate with minimal behavioral deficits such as demonstrated by Gold and McGaugh (1975) in retention performance tested by a one-trial passive avoidance task. No attempt was made to correlate this deficit in retention performance, which suggests an age-related decline in the learning/memory capacity of senescent Fischer-344 rats, with biochemical or morphological changes in the brain. It is, however, reasonable to assume that changes in the structure and chemical composition of the brain may underlie such behavioral deficits in experimental animals and comparably subtle behavioral changes that characterize the later years of man. Such age-related changes, which appear to result in a partial deafferentation of selected populations of neurons in senescent animals, appear similar to changes produced by deafferentation secondary to other natural events and by experimental manipulations. They appear similar to changes brought about by intellectual impoverishment of the environment. Because partial recovery from experimentally produced deafferentation has been described (Globus, 1975), and the reversibility of changes wrought by environmental impoverishment has been noted (Diamond,

1978), age-related changes can be expected to be similarly reversible.

Age-related changes in neural structure and chemical composition are not well-known, especially as regards their temporal interrelationships, and it may be premature to propose a course of events by which extracellular and cellular events can lead to morphological changes in neurons and result in alterations in neuronal connectivity in senescent animals. Yet it is tempting to propose sequential, age-related interactions between extracellular and intracellular phenomena (Bondareff, 1976b). These interactions appear to depend upon changes in the extracellular space, which may be secondary to as yet undefined alterations in cerebral vasculature or to changes programmed in cells that affect the composition of the extracellular space. These extracellular events presumably have a deleterious effect on neuronal metabolism and set in motion a cascading series of cellular events which eventually present as changes in neuronal structure and function. Such changes may compromise the ability of certain neurons to sustain the intracellular transport of materials, such as glycoproteins which are required to maintain the integrity of neuronal plasma membranes. Deteriorating axoplasmic transport of glycoproteins, by disrupting plasma membranes in general and pre- and postsynaptic membranes in particular, may result in the partial deafferentation of certain neurons in senescence.

Although the time course of changes in neuronal structure is but sketchily known during the period of adulthood, these changes appear eventually to result in the loss of synapses in senescence. This loss of synapses may, at first, be reversible because neurons remain capable of considerable plasticity and functional adaptation throughout adult life (Watson, 1976), and it has been suggested that synapses may be continually formed and reformed during adult life (Sotelo and Palay, 1971). At some age, not yet accurately determined, but in the Fischer-344 rat presumed to be in the vicinity of the 24th month, the capacity to replace and/or redistribute synapses appears to be lost. Neuronal inter-connections become permanently disrupted and functions which depend upon specific interconnections between neurons become altered. Consequent upon these structural changes in neurons there appears to be a compensatory redistribution of tissue elements in affected regions of the brain. When these compensatory mechanisms fail, neurons may die. Synaptic interactions will then become permanently lost and senility will ensue.

**Table 4–1** AGE-RELATED CHANGES IN THE MAMMALIAN CENTRAL NERVOUS SYSTEM: A SELECTED BIBLIOGRAPHY IN TABULAR FORM.

| I. GROSS ANATOMY | ANIMAL | STRUCTURE | AGE RANGE FROM | AGE RANGE TO | CHANGE | REFERENCE |
|---|---|---|---|---|---|---|
| A. *Brain Weight* | rhesus | whole brain | 3–4 yr | 15–16 yr | increase | Davis and Himwich, 1975 |
| | mouse | | 1 yr | 2 yr | | |
| | hamster | | 6 mo | 2 yr | | |
| | rat | | 1 yr | 2 yr | no change | Horrocks, Sun, and D'Amato, 1975 |
| | mouse | whole brain | 3 mo | 26 mo | decrease | Ordy and Schjeide, 1973 |
| | rhesus | whole brain | 12 yr | 24 yr | decrease | Burge (quoted by Himwich and Himwich, 1959) |
| | | | 21–30 yr | 81–90 yr | decrease | Appel and Appel, 1942 |
| | man | whole brain | 30–34 yr | 85–96 yr | | Blinkov and Glazer, 1968 |
| | | | 12–19 yr | 90 yr | | Arendt, 1972 (also see Peress, Kane, and Aronson, 1973 |
| | | | 18–20 mo | 60–70 yr | decrease | |
| | | | 70–80 yr | 70–80 yr | | |
| B. *Dimensions* | man | cerebellum | 20–30 yr | 80–90 yr | decrease | Blinkov and Glazer, 1968 |
| | | cerebrum | | | | |
| | | cerebral cortex | | | | |
| | | hippocampus | | | | |
| | | diencephalon | | | | |
| | rat | | 26 d | 650 d | decrease | Diamond et al., 1975 |
| length and width | man | pons | 21–30 yr | 60–90 yr | no change | Blinkov and Glazer, 1968 |
| height | man | cerebellum | 21–30 yr | 60–100 yr | decrease | |
| C. *Volume* | man | brain | 20–29 yr | 80–89 yr | | Boning (quoted by Brizzee, 1975) |
| | | vent. cochlear nucl. | 50 yr | 90 yr | decrease | Konigsmark and Murphy, 1972 |
| | man | dentate nucl. | 24 yr | 99 yr | | Blinkov and Glazer, 1968 |
| D. *Ventricles* volume | man | lateral ventricles | 20–29.9 yr | 80–89.9 yr | increase | Blinkov and Glazer, 1968 |
| area | | | 9 mo | 90 yr | | Barron et al., 1976 |
| dimensions | | | adult | senium | | Heinrich (quoted by Arendt, 1972) |
| E. *Gyri (width)* | man | brain | adult | > 75 yr | increase | Brizzee, 1975 |
| F. *Arteries* thickness of intima | man | brain | 1 yr | 90 yr | increase | Klassen et al., 1968 |
| G. *Enzymes, activity* acetylcholine esterase | rat[12] | forebrain, cerebral cortex | 3 mo | 24 mo | decrease | Hollander and Barrows, 1968 |
| | rat | whole brain | 8–10 mo | 26–28 mo | decrease | Frolkis et al., 1973 |
| | mouse[10] | whole brain | 3 mo | 28 mo | decrease | Samorajski, Rolsten and Ordy, 1971 |
| H. *Monoamines* norepinephrine | | striatum (synaptosoma) | | | decrease | |
| dopamine | mouse[13] | hypothalamus, striatum | 8–10 mo | 28–30 mo | decrease | Jonec and Finch, 1975 |
| uptake of | | striatum (synaptosoma) | | | | |

| | Species | Region | Age (young) | Age (old) | Change | Reference |
|---|---|---|---|---|---|---|
| tyrosine, serotonin | mouse[10] | hypothalamus, striatum (synaptosoma) | 3 mo | 28 mo | no change | Samorajski et al., 1971 |
| norepinephrine | mouse[13] | whole brain | 12 mo | 28 mo | decrease | Finch, 1973 |
| serotonin | | | | | | |
| norepinephrine turnover | mouse[13] | hypothalamus | 12 mo | 28 mo | decrease | Finch, 1973 |
| dopamine, amount | | | | | | |
| dopamine turnover | | | | | | |
| **II. HISTOLOGY AND CYTOLOGY** | | | | | | |
| A. Neuron, numbers of | mouse[2] | whole brain | 8 mo | 29 mo | decrease | Johnson and Erner, 1972 |
| | mouse[3] | whole brain | 4 wk | 158 wk | no change | Franks, Wilson, and Whelan, 1974 |
| | rat | dentate gyrus, granule cells | 3 mo | 25 mo | no change | Bondareff and Geinisman, 1976 |
| | | cerebellum[14,15] | 3 mo | 36 mo | decrease | Geinisman and Bondareff, 1976 |
| | | cerebral cortex | 3.6 mo | 21.6 mo | no change | Morsett, Braakman, and James, 1972; Diamond, Johnson and Ingham, 1977 |
| | rhesus | cerebral cortex | 4–6 yr | 18–20 yr | decrease | Brizzee, 1975 |
| | | cerebral cortex: superior frontal gyrus, superior temporal gyrus | 41 yr | 87 yr | decrease | Brody, 1955, 1973 |
| | man | cerebral cortex | 15–54 yr | 65–89 yr | no change | Cragg, 1975 |
| | | cerebellum[14] | 60 yr | 100 yr | decrease | Hall et al., 1975 |
| | | inf. olivary nucl. | Birth | 89 yr | no change | Monagle and Brody, 1974 |
| | | locus ceruleus | Birth | 86 yr | decrease | Brody, 1973 |
| | | facial nucleus | Birth | 75 yr | no change | Van Buskirk, 1945 |
| | | vent. cochlear nucl. | 0.3 yr | 90 yr | no change | Konigsmark and Murphy, 1970 |
| | | trochlear, abducens nuclei | Birth | 89 yr | no change | Brody, 1973 |
| B. Neuroglia, numbers of | rat[4] | cerebral cortex, microglia | 3 mo | 29.5 mo | increase | Vaughan and Peters, 1974 |
| | mouse | indusium griseum, micro- and astroglia | 5 mo | 18 mo | increase | Sturrock, 1977 |
| | mouse | ant. commissure, oligodendroglia | 5 mo | 18 mo | decrease | Sturrock, 1976 |
| | man | cerebral cortex | 25 yr | 72 yr | increase | Blinkov and Glazer, 1968 |
| volume fraction | rat[15] | brain stem nuclei | 26–27 yr | 61–82 yr | increase | Geinisman et al. 1978b |
| | rat[17] | dentate gyrus | 3 mo | 25 mo | | Fujisawa and Shiraki, 1978 |
| | | gracile and cuneate nucl. | 3 mo | 26.8 mo | | |
| C. Synapses, numbers of | rat[5] | dentate gyrus | 25 mo | 25 mo | decrease | Bondareff and Geinisman, 1976 |
| | | cerebellar cortex | 25 mo | 25 mo | | Glick and Bondareff, 1979 |
| | rat | cerebral cortex | 3 mo | 36 mo | decrease | Feldman, 1976 |
| | | gracile, cuneate nucl. | | 26.8 mo | | Fujisawa and Shiraki, 1978 |
| | man | cerebral cortex | 15–54 yr | 65–89 yr | no change | Cragg, 1975 |

**Table 4–1** (cont.)

| II. HISTOLOGY AND CYTOLOGY | ANIMAL | STRUCTURE | AGE RANGE FROM | AGE RANGE TO | CHANGE | REFERENCE |
|---|---|---|---|---|---|---|
| D. Lipofuscin, amounts of | rat[6] | spinal ganglion anterior horn | 3 mo | 24 mo | increase | Bondareff, 1959 |
| | mouse[7] | inferior olive | 6 mo | 21 mo | increase | Sekhon and Maxwell, 1974 |
| | man | inferior olive | 11 d | 91 yr | increase | Mann and Yates, 1974 l |
| | man | cerebral cortex, cerebellum, brain stem | 3 mo | 70 yr | increase | Brody, 1973 |
| | rhesus | | 1 yr | > 20 yr | increase | Brizzee et al., 1974 |
| | guinea pig | brain stem, cerebral cortex, cerebellum hypothalamus | 4 yr | 6yr | increase | Nandy and Bourne, 1966 |
| E. Melanin, amount | man | substantia nigra | birth | 60 yr | increase | Mann and Yates, 1974b |
| F. Cytoplasmic basophilia | rabbit | brain stem, cerebellum | 9 mo | 42 mo | decrease | Cammermeyer, 1963 |
| (relative amount of cytoplasmic RNA estimated in sections) | dog | autonomic ganglia cerebellum | 0 / 9 wk | 18 yr / > 50 yr | decrease / decrease | Sulkin and Kuntz, 1952 / Andrew, 1938 |
| | man | inferior olive | 11d | 91 yr | decrease | Mann and Yates, 1974,a,b |
| | rat[8] | spinal ganglion | 3 mo | 24 mo | no change | Bondareff, 1957, 1959 |
| | mouse[9] | anterior horn | 6 wk | 21 mo | decrease | Sekhon and Maxwell, 1974 |
| G. Neurofilaments, numbers of | mouse[10] | pyramidal tract axons (medulla) | 8 mo | 26 mo | increase | Samorajski et al., 1971 |
| H. Microtubules, numbers of | " | " | " | " | " | " |
| I. Neurofibrillary tangles and senile plaques, numbers of | man | cerebral cortex | 70–80 yr | 90–100 yr | increase | Matsuyama et al., 1966 (see discussion in Terry and Wiesniewski, 1972) |
| J. Plasma membrane, availability of Conconavalin receptors | rat[5] | lat. vestibular nucl. neurons | 3 mo | 25 mo | decrease | Bennett and Bondareff, 1977 |
| K. Dendrites no. spines diameter | rat[5] | cerebral cortex[16] | 2 mo | 29.5 mo | decrease | Feldman and Dowd, 1975 |
| no./cluster volume fraction surface area | rat[5] | dentate gyrus | 3 mo | 25 mo | decrease | Geinisman et al., 1978a |
| no. shafts integrity | man | cerebral cortex[16] | 58 yr | 96 yr | decrease | Scheibel et al., 1975 |
| L. Axons number of axons | rat[11] | sciatic nerve | 50–250 d | > 650 d | no change | Birren and Wall, 1956 |
| myelin thickness | mouse | pyramidal tract (medulla) | 3 mo | 26 mo | increase | Samorajski et al., 1971 |

| | Species | Region | Age | Age | Change | Reference |
|---|---|---|---|---|---|---|
| M. *Golgi complex, fragmentation* | mouse | cerebellum[14] | 160–324 d | 698–733 d | increase | Andrew, 1939 |
| | rabbit | spinal ganglion | birth | 4 yr | increase | Sosa and deZorrilla, 1966 |
| | dog | autonomic ganglia | 0 | 18 yr | increase | Sulkin and Kuntz, 1952 |
| N. *Nucleus,* inclusions Feulgen + chromatin | chinchilla | cerebellum (glia) | 8½ mo | 145½ mo | increase | Cammermeyer, 1963 |
| | rabbit | brain stem, cerebellum | 9 mo | 42 mo | decrease | |
| numbers | mouse[3] | whole brain | 4 wk | 158 wk | no change | Franks et al., 1974 |
| O. *Extracellular space* volume | rat[4] | cerebral cortex | 3 mo | 24 mo | decrease | Bondareff and Narotzky, 1972 |
| charge density | rat[5] | dentate gyrus | 3 mo | 25 mo | increase | Bondareff and Lin-Liu, 1977 |
| III. BIOCHEMISTRY | | | | | | |
| A. *Protein* protein nitrogen | man | whole brain | 16–20 yr | 81–90 yr | decrease | Burger, 1957 (quoted by Davis and Himwich, 1975) |
| ³H-cytidine incorporation | mouse[3] | anterior horn neuron (cervical) Purkinje cell Spinal ganglion neuron | 68 d | 610 d | decrease | Wulff et al., 1965 |
| protein, half life | rat[12] | whole brain | 12 mo | 24 mo | decrease | Menzies and Gold, 1972 |
| | rat[12] | anterior horn cell (L₄–S₁) | 6 wk | 24–27 mo | decrease | Jakoubek et al., 1968 |
| ³⁵S-methionine incorporation | man | whole brain | 31–40 yr | 71–80 yr | decrease | Burger, 1957 (quoted by Davis and Himwich, 1975) |
| | hamster | | 1 yr | 2 yr | decrease | Himwich, 1973 |
| total protein | mouse[3] | | 4 wk | 158 wk | no change | Franks, Wilson, and Whelan, 1974 |
| S-100 protein | mouse[13] | cerebellum cerebral cortex hippocampus, hippocampus, hypothalamus, striatum | 6 mo | 30 mo | increase | Cicero, Ferrendelli, Suntzeff, and Moore, 1972 |
| 14-3-2 protein | | | | | no change | |
| B. *Water, o/o* | guinea pig | whole brain | 1 yr | 6 yr | increase | Himwich, 1973 |
| | mouse | | 1 yr | 2 yr | decrease | |
| | hamster | | 1 yr | 2 yr | decrease | |
| | rabbit | | 1 yr | 8 yr | decrease | Burger, 1957 (quoted by Davis and Himwich, 1975) |
| | man | | 31–40 yr | 81–90 yr | increase | |
| C. *Lipids* cholesterol & phospholipid | mouse[10] | whole brain, myelin | 3 mo | 26 mo | increase | Sun and Samorajski, 1972 |
| fatty acids, total | man | whole brain | 33 yr | 98 yr | decrease | Yamamoto and Rouser, 1973 |
| | man | whole brain | 21–30 yr | 85–90 yr | decrease | Burger, 1957 (quoted by Davis and Himwich, 1973) |
| phosphatidyl ethanolamine (half life) | mouse[13] | whole brain mitochondria | 2.5 mo | 25 mo | increase | Huemer, 1971 |
| cholesterol, cerebrosides, prosphplipids | man | whole brain | 20 yr | 100 yr | decrease | Horrocks, Sun and D'Amato, 1975 |

# Table 4-1  (cont.)

| BIOCHEMISTRY | ANIMAL | STRUCTURE | AGE RANGE FROM | AGE RANGE TO | CHANGE | REFERENCE |
|---|---|---|---|---|---|---|
| III. |  |  |  |  |  |  |
| D. *DNA, amounts of* | rhesus | cerebral cortex (parietal, temporal) cerebellum) | 3–4 yr | 15–16 yr | decrease | Himwich, 1973 |
|  | mouse | whole brain | 4 wks | 158 wk | no change | Franks *et al.*, 1974 |
| E. *RNA, amounts of* | rat | hippocampus; CA$_3$ neurons | 6–8 wk | 36–38 mo | decrease | Ringborg, 1966 |
|  | man | anterior horn cells | 40 yr | > 60 yr | decrease | Hydén, 1967 |
|  | rhesus | cerebral cortex, cerebellum, medulla, hippocampus, hypothalamus | 3–4 yr | 15–16 yr | decrease | Himwich, 1973 |
| F. Amino Acids, amounts of glutamic acid | rat mouse hamster rabbit | whole brain | 1 yr | 2 yr 7 yr 2 yr | decrease increase increase | Himwich, 1973 |
| GABA | rat mouse hamster | whole brain | 1 yr | 2 yr | no change no change | Davis and Himwich, 1975 |
| glycine, alanine, serine | rat | whole brain | 1 yr | 2 yr |  |  |
| G. *Enzymes, activity* glutamic acid decarboxylase | rat | cerebellum, brainstem | 2 mo | 26 mo | increase | Epstein and Barrows, 1969 |
| tyrosine hydroxylase | rat | caudate nucleus | 2 mo | 29 mo | decrease | McGeer *et al.*, 1971 |
| monoamine oxidase | man | hindbrain | 45 yr | 65 yr | increase | Robinson *et al.*, 1971 |
| hydroxy-O-methyl transferase, monoamine oxidase, histamine-N-methyl transferase | man | pineal | 50–55 yr | 55–70 yr | no change | Wurtman *et al.*, 1964 |
| tyrosine hydroxylase | man | putamen | 20 yr | 80 yr | decrease | McGeer and McGeer, 1975 |

[1] Long-Evans  
[2] Swiss albino  
[3] C57BL  
[4] Sprague-Dawley  
[5] Fischer-344  
[6] Sprague-Dawley  
[7] Wobbler  
[8] Sprague-Dawley  
[9] Wobbler  
[10] C578L/10  
[11] Norwegian  
[12] Wistar  
[13] C57B1/6J  
[14] Purkinje cell  
[15] Granule cell  
[16] Pyramidal Cell  
[17] Wistar-Imamichi  
Restricted Diet

164

# REFERENCES

ANDREW, W. 1938. The Purkinje cell in man from birth to senility. *Zeit. f. Zellforsch., 28,* 294–304.

ANDREW, W. 1939. The Golgi apparatus in the nerve cells of the mouse from youth to senility. *Am. J. Anat., 64,* 351–375.

APPEL, F. W., AND APPEL E. M. 1942. Intracranial variation in the weight of the human brain. *Human Biol., 14,* 48–68.

ARAI, Y., AND MATSUMOTO, A. 1978. Synapse formation of the hypothalamic arcuate nucleus during aging process and its synaptic plasticity to estrogen. *Int'l. Cong. of Gerontol., XI, Abstract BM–30.*

ARENDT, A. 1972. Altern des "Zentral nerven Systems." *In: Handbuch der Allgemeinen Pathologie V 1/4.* Springer-Verlag, Berlin, 490–542.

BARDEN, H. 1970. Relationship of Golgi thiamine pyrophosphatase and lysosomal acid phosphatase to neuromelanin and lipofuscin in cerebral neurons of the aging rhesus monkey. *J. Neuropath., 29,* 225–240.

BARRON, S. A., JACOBS, L., AND KINKEL, W. R. 1976. Changes in size of normal lateral ventricles during aging determined by computerized tomography. *Neurol. 26,* 1011–1013.

BENNETT, G., LEBLOND, C. P., AND HADDAD, A. 1974. Migration of glycoprotein from the Golgi apparatus to the surface of various cell types as shown by radioautography after labeled fucose injection into rats. *J. Cell Biol., 60,* 258–284.

BENNETT, K. D., AND BONDAREFF, W. 1977. Age-related differences in binding of Conconavalin A to plasma membranes of isolated neurons. *Am. J. Anat., 150,* 175–184.

BETTLEHEIM, F. A., AND PLESSY, B. 1975. The hydration of proteoglycans of bovine cornea. *Biochem. Biophys. Acta., 381,* 203–214.

BIRREN, J. E. 1972. Toward an interdisciplinary approach. *In,* C. M. Gaitz (ed.), *Aging and the Brain,* pp. 221–224. New York: Plenum.

BIRREN, J. E., AND WALL, P. D. 1956. Age changes in conduction velocity, refractory period, number of fibers, connective tissue space and blood vessels in sciatic nerve of rats. *J. Comp. Neurol., 104,* 1–16.

BLINKOV, S. M., AND GLAZER, I. I. 1968. *The Human Brain in Figures and Tables.* New York: Plenum.

BONDAREFF, W. 1957. Genesis of intracellular pigment in the spinal ganglia of senile rats. An electron microscope study. *J. Gerontol., 12,* 364–369.

BONDAREFF, W. 1959. Morphology of the aging nervous system. *In,* J. E. Birren (ed.), *Handbook of Aging and the Individual,* pp. 187–215. Chicago: University of Chicago Press.

BONDAREFF, W. 1976a. Extracellular space in the aging cerebrum. *In,* R. D. Terry and S. Gershon (eds.), *Neurobiology of Aging,* pp. 167–175. New York: Raven Press.

BONDAREFF, W. 1976b. The neural basis of aging. *In,* J. E. Birren and K. W. Schaie (eds.), *Handbook of the Psychology of Aging,* pp. 157–176. New York: Van Nostrand Reinhold.

BONDAREFF, W. 1979. Synaptic atrophy in the senescent hippocampus. *Mech. Age. Develop., 9,* 163–171.

BONDAREFF, W., AND GEINISMAN, Y. 1976. Loss of synapses in the dentate gyrus of the senescent rat. *Am. J. Anat., 145,* 129–136.

BONDAREFF, W., AND HYDÉN, H. 1969. Submicroscopic structure of single neurons isolated from rabbit lateral vestibular nucleus. *J. Ultrastruct. Res., 26,* 399–411.

BONDAREFF, W., AND LIN-LIU, S. 1977. Age-related change in the neuronal microenvironment: Penetration of ruthenium red into extracellular space of brain in young adult and senescent rats. *Am. J. Anat., 148,* 57–64.

BONDAREFF, W., NAROTZKY, R., AND ROUTTENBERG, A. 1971. Intrastriatal spread of catecholamines in senescent rats. *J. Gerontol., 26,* 163–167.

BRIZZEE, K. R. 1975. Gross morphometric analyses and quantitative histology of the aging brain. *In,* R. D. Terry and S. Gershon (eds.), *Neurobiology of Aging,* pp. 401–424. New York: Plenum.

BRIZZEE, K. R., ORDY, J. M., AND KAACK, B. 1974. Early appearance and regional differences in intraneuronal and extraneuronal lipofuscin accomulation with age in the brain of a nonhuman primate (Macaca mulatta). *J. Gerontol, 29,* 366–381.

BRODY, H. 1955. Organization of the cerebral cortex. III. A study of aging in the human cerebral cortex. *J. Comp. Neurol., 102,* 511–556.

BRODY, H. 1973. Aging of the vertebrate brain. *In,* M. Rockstein (ed.), *Development and Aging in the Nervous System,* pp. 121–134. New York: Academic Press.

BRODY, H. 1976. An examination of cerebral cortex and brainstem aging. *In,* R. D. Terry and S. Gershon (eds.), *Neurobiology of Aging,* pp. 177–182. New York: Raven Press.

BRUNNGRABER, E. G., BROWN, B. D., AND ARO, A. 1975. Distribution and age-dependent concentration in brain tissue of glycoproteins containing N-acetylgalactosamine. *Neurobiol., 5,* 339–346.

CICERO, T. J., FERRENDELLI, J. A., SUNTZEFF, V., AND MOORE, B. W. 1972. Regional changes in CNS levels of the S–100 and 14–3–2 proteins during development and aging of the mouse. *J. Neurochem., 19,* 2119–2125.

COLEMAN, G. L., BARTHOLD, J. W., OSBALDISTON, G. W.,

FOSTER, S. J., AND JONAS, A. M. 1977. Pathological changes during aging in barrier-reared Fischer-344 male rats. *J. Gerontol., 32,* 258–278.

CORSELLIS, J. A. N. 1976. Some observations of the Purkinje cell population and on brain volume in human aging. *In,* R. D. Terry and S. Gershon (eds.), *Neurobiology of Aging,* pp. 205–210. New York: Raven Press.

CRAGG, B. G. 1975a. The density of synapses and neurons in normal, mentally defective and aging human brains. *Brain, 98,* 81–90.

CRAPPER, D. R. 1976. Functional consequences of neurofibrillary degeneration. *In,* R. D. Terry and S. Gershon (eds.), *Neurobiology of Aging,* pp. 405–432. New York: Raven Press.

CREPEL, F., MARIANI, J., AND N. DELHAYE-BOUCHARD. 1976. Evidence for a multiple innervation of Purkinje cells by climbing fibers in the immature rat cerebellum. *J. Neurobiol. 7,* 567–578.

DAVIS J. M., AND HIMWICH, W. A. 1975. Neurochemistry of the developing and aging mammalian brain. *In,* J. M. Ordy and K. R. Brizzee (eds.), *Neurobiology of Aging,* pp. 329–358. New York: Plenum.

DAYAN, A. D. 1971. Comparative neuropathology of aging. Studies on the brains of 47 species of vertebrates. *Brain, 94,* 31–42.

DIAMOND, M. C. 1978. The aging brain: Some enlightening and optimistic results. *Am. Sci, 66,* 66–71.

DIAMOND, M. C., JOHNSON, R. E., AND INGHAM, C. A. 1975. Morphological changes in the young, adult and aging rat cerebral cortex, hippocampus, and diencephalon. *Behav. Biol., 14,* 163–174.

DROZ, B., RAMBOURG, A., AND KOENIG, H. L. 1975. The smooth endoplasmic reticulum: Structure and role in the renewal of axonal membrane and synaptic vesicles by fast axonal transport. *Brain Res., 93,* 1–13.

ELLIS, R. S. 1920. Norms for some structural changes in the human cerebellum from birth to old age. *J. Comp. Neurol., 32,* 1–34.

EPSTEIN, M. H., AND BARROWS, C. H., JR. 1969. The effects of age on the activity of glutamic acid decarboxylase in various regions of the brains of rats. *J. Gerontol., 24,* 136–139.

FANG, H. C. H. 1976. Observations on aging characteristics of cerebral blood vessels, macroscopic and microscopic features. *In,* R. D. Terry and S. Gershon (eds.), *Neurobiology of Aging,* pp. 155–166. New York: Raven Press.

FELDMAN, M. L. 1976. Aging changes in the morphology of cortical dendrites. *In,* R. D. Terry and S. Gershon (eds.), *Neurobiology of Aging,* pp. 211–227. New York: Raven Press.

FELDMAN, M. L., AND DOWD, C. 1975. Loss of dendritic spines in aging cerebral cortex. *Anat. Embryol., 148,* 279–301.

FERENDELLI, J. A., SEDGWICK, W. G., AND SUNTZELLF, U. 1971. Regional energy metabolism and lipofuscin accumulation in mouse brain during aging. *J. Neuropath. Exptl. Neurol., 30,* 638–649.

FINCH, C. 1973. Catecholamine metabolism in the brains of ageing male mice. *Brain Res., 52,* 261–276.

FRANKS, L. M., WILSON, P. D., AND WHELAN, R. D. 1974. The effects of age on total DNA and cell number in the mouse brain. *Gerontol., 20,* 21–26.

FROLKIS, V. V., BEZRUKOV, V. V., DUPLENKO, Y. K., SHCHEGOLEVA, I. V., SHEVTCHUK, V. G., AND VERKHRATSKY, N. S. 1973. Acetylcholine metabolism and cholinergic regulation of functions in aging. *Gerontol., 19,* 45–57.

FUJISAWA, K., AND SHIRAKI, H. 1978. Study of axonal dystrophy. I. Pathway of the neuropil of the gracile and cuneate nuclei in aging and old rats: A stereological study. *Neuropath. Appl. Neurobiol., 4,* 1–20.

GEINISMAN, Y., AND BONDAREFF, W. 1976. Decrease in the number of synapses in the senescent brain: A quantitative electron microscopic analysis of the dentate gyrus molecular layer in the rat. *Mech. Age. Devel., 5,* 11–23.

GEINISMAN, Y., BONDAREFF, W., AND DODGE, J. T. 1977. Partial deafferentiation of neurons in the dentate gyrus of the senescent rat. *Brain Res., 134,* 541–545.

GEINISMAN, Y., BONDAREFF, W., AND DODGE, J. T. 1978a. Hypertrophy of astroglial processes in the dentate gyrus of the senescent rat. *Am. J. Anat. 153,* 537–544.

GEINISMAN, Y., BONDAREFF, W., AND DODGE, J. T. 1978b. Dendritic atrophy in the dentate gyrus of the senescent rat. *Am. J. Anat., 152,* 321–330.

GEINISMAN, Y., BONDAREFF, W., AND TELSER, A. 1977. Transport of ($^3$H) fucose labeled glycoproteins in the septo-hippocampal pathway of young adult and senescent rats. *Brain Res., 125,* 182–186.

GLICK, R., AND BONDAREFF, W. 1979. Loss of synapses in the cerebellar cortex of the senescent rat. *J. Gerontol.*

GLOBUS, A. 1975. Brain morphology as a function of presynaptic morphology and activity. *In,* H. Riesen (ed.), *The Developmental Neuropsychology of Sensory Deprivation,* pp. 9–91. New York: Academic Press.

GLOBUS, A., ROSENZWEIG, M. R., BENNETT, E. L., AND DIAMOND, M. C. 1973. Effects of differential experience on dendritic spine counts in rat cerebral cortex. *J. Comp. Physiol. Psych., 82,* 175–181.

GOLD, P. E., AND MCGAUGH, J. L. 1975. Changes in learning and memory during aging. *In,* J. M. Ordy and K. R. Brizzee (eds.), *Neurobiology of Aging,* pp. 145–158. New York: Plenum.

GROSSMAN R. G., AND SEREGIN, A. 1977. Glial-neural interaction demonstrated by the injection of Na$^+$ and

Li⁺ into cortical glia. *Sci., 195,* 196–198.

HALL, T. C., MILLER, A. K. H., AND CORSELLIS, J. A. N. 1975. Variations in the human Purkinje cell population according to age and sex. *Neuropath. and Applied Neurol., 1,* 267–292.

HIMWICH, W. A. 1978. Neurochemical patterns in the developing and aging brain. *In,* M. Rockstein (ed.), *Development and Aging in the Nervous System,* pp. 151–170. New York: Academic Press.

HIMWICH, H. E., AND HIMWICH, W. A. 1959. Neurochemistry of aging. *In,* J. E. Birren (ed.), *Handbook of Aging and the Individual,* pp. 187–215. Chicago: University of Chicago Press.

HINDS, J. W., AND MCNELLY, N. A. 1977. Aging of the rat olfactory bulb: Growth and atrophy of constituent layers and changes in size and number of mitral cells. *J. Comp. Neurol., 171,* 345–367.

HOLLANDER, J., AND BARROWS, C. H., JR. 1968. Enzymatic studies in senescent rodent brains. *J. Gerontol., 23,* 174–179.

HOLLOWAY, R. L., JR. 1966. Dendritic branching: Some preliminary results of training and complexity in cat visual cortex. *Brain Res., 2,* 393–396.

HORROCKS, L. A., SUN, G.Y., AND D'AMATO, R. A. 1975. Changes in brain lipids during aging. *In,* J. M. Ordy and K. R. Brizzee (eds.), *Neurobiology of Aging,* pp. 329–358. New York: Plenum.

HYDÉN, H. 1967. Dynamic aspects on the neuron-glia relationships—a study with micro-chemical methods. *In,* H. Hydén (ed.), *The Neuron,* pp. 179–220. Amsterdam: Elsevier.

IQBAL, K., GRUNDKE-IQBAL, I., WISNIEWSKI, H. M., KORTHALS, J. K., AND TERRY, R. D. 1976. Chemistry of neurofibrous proteins in aging. *In,* R. D. Terry and S. Gershon (eds.), *Neurobiology of Aging,* pp. 351–360. New York: Raven Press.

JAKOUBEK, B., GUTMANN, E., FISCHER, J., AND BABICKY, A. 1968. Rate of protein renewal in spinal motorneurons of adolescent and old rats. *J. Neurochem., 15,* 633–641.

JAMIESON, J. D., AND PALADE, G. E. 1977. Production of secretory proteins in animal cells. *In,* B. R. Brinkley and K. R. Porter (eds.), *Int'l. Cell Biology, 1976–1977,* pp. 308–317. New York: Rockefeller University Press.

JOHNSON, H. A., AND ERNER, S. 1972. Neuron survival in the aging mouse. *Exptl. Gerontol., 7,* 111–117.

JONEC, V., AND FINCH, C. E. 1975. Aging and dopamine uptake by subcellular fractions of the C57 B1/6J male mouse brain. *Brain Res., 91,* 197–215.

KLASSEN, A. C., SUNG, J. H., AND STADLAN, E. 1968. Histological changes in cerebral arteries with increasing age. *J. Neuropath., 27,* 607–624.

KONIGSMARK, B. W., AND MURPHY, E. A. 1970. Neuronal populations in the human brain. *Nature, 228,* 1335–1336.

KONIGSMARK, B. W., AND MURPHY, E. A. 1972. Volume of the ventral cochlear nucleus in man: Its relationship to neuronal population and age. *J. Neuropathol. Exptl. Neurol., 31,* 304–316.

LANDFIELD, P. W., AND LYNCH, G. 1977. Impaired monosynaptic potentiation in *in vitro* hippocampal slices from aged, memory-deficient rats. *J. Gerontol., 32,* 523-533.

LANDFIELD, P. W., MCGAUGH, J. L., AND LYNCH, G. 1978. Impaired synaptic potentiation processes in the hippocampus of aged, memory-deficient rats. *Brain Res., 150,* 85–101.

LANDFIELD, P. W., ROSE, G., SANDLES, L., WOHLSTADTER, T. C., AND LYNCH, G. 1977. Patterns of astroglial hypertrophy and neuronal degeneration in the hippocampus of aged, memory-deficient rats. *J. Gerontol., 32,* 3–12.

LASSEN, N. A., FEINBERG, I., AND LANE, M. H. 1960. Bilateral studies of cerebral oxygen uptake in young and aged normal subjects and in patients with organic dementia. *J. Clin. Invest., 39,* 491–500.

LEBLOND, C. P., AND BENNETT, G. 1977. Role of the Golgi complex in terminal glycoslation. *In,* B. R. Brinkley and F. R. Porter (eds.), *Int'l. Cell Biology, 1976–1977,* pp. 326–336. New York: Rockefeller University Press.

LEVAY, S. 1971. On the neurons and synapses of the lateral geniculate nucleus of the monkey, and the effects of eye enucleation. *Z. Zellforsch., 113,* 396–419.

MANN, D. M. A., AND YATES, P. O. 1974a. Lipoprotein pigments—their relationship to aging in the human nervous system. I. The lipofuscin content of nerve cells. *Brain, 97,* 481–488.

MANN, D. M. A., AND YATES, P. O. 1974b. Lipoprotein pigments—their relationship to aging in the human nervous system. II. The melanin content of pigmented nerve cells. *Brain, 97,* 489–498.

MARGOLIS, R. U. 1967. Acid mucopolysaccharides and proteins of bovine whole brain, white matter and myelin. *Biochem. Biophys. Acta., 141,* 91–102.

MARGOLIS, R. K., AND MARGOLIS, R. U. 1970. Sulfated glycopeptides from rat brain glycoprotein. *Biochem., 9,* 4389–4396.

MARIN-PADILLA, M. 1972. Structural abnormalities of the cerebral cortex in human chromosomal aberrations. A Golgi study. *Brain Res., 44,* 625–629.

MARIN-PADILLA, M. 1974. Structural organization of the cerebral cortex (motor area) in human chromosomal aberrations. A Golgi study. I. D₁ (13–15) Trisomy, Patau Syndrome. *Brain Res., 66,* 375–392.

MARTINEZ-HERNANDEZ, A., BELL, K. P., AND NORENBERG, M. D. 1977. Glutamine synthetase: Glial localization in brain. *Sci., 195,* 1356–1358.

MEIER-RUGE, W., REICHLMEIER, K., AND IWANGOFF, P. 1976.

Enzymatic and enzyme histochemical changes of the aging brain and consequences for experimental pharmacology on aging. *In*, R. D. Terry and S. Gershon (eds.), *Neurobiology of Aging*, pp. 379–387. New York: Raven Press.

McGeer, E. G., and McGeer, P. L. 1975. Age changes in the human for some enzymes associated with metabolism of catecholamines, GABA and acetylcholine. *In*, J. M. Ordee and K. R. Brizzee (eds.), *Neurobiology of Aging*, pp. 287–306. New York: Plenum Press.

McGeer, E. G., Fibiger, H. C., McGeer, P. L., and Wickson, W. 1971. Aging and brain enzymes. *Expt. Gerontol.*, *6*, 391–396.

McNamara, M. C., Miller, A. T., Jr., Benignus, V. A., and Davis, J. A. 1977. Age-related changes in the effect of electroconvulsive shock (ECS) on the *in vivo* hydroxylation of tyrosine and tryptophan in rat brain. *Brain Res.*, *131*, 313–320.

Menzies, R. A. and Gold, P. H. 1972. The apparent turnover of mitochondria, ribosomes and sRNA in young adult and aged rats. *J. Neurochem.*, *19*, 1671–1683.

Monagle, R. D., and Brody, H. 1974. The effects of age upon the main nucleus of the inferior olive in the human. *J. Comp. Neurol.*, *155*, 61–66.

Morsett, A. F. W., Braakman, D. J., and James, J. 1972. Feulgen-DNA and fast-green histone estimations in individual cell nuclei of the cerebellum of young and old rats. *Acta histochem.*, *43*, 281–286.

Mosko, S., Lynch, G., and Cotman, C. W. 1973. The distribution of septal projections to the hippocampus of the rat. *J. Comp. Neurol.*, *152*, 163–174.

Nandy, K. and Bourne, G. H. 1966. Effect of centrophenoxine on the lipofuscin pigments in the neurons of senile guinea-pigs. *Nature*, *210*, 313–314.

Narayanakurup, V., and Brody, H. 1977. A study of aging in the human abducens nucleus. *J. Comp. Neurol.*, *173*, 433–438.

Nicholson, G. L. 1974. The interactions of lectins with animal cell surfaces. *In*, G. H. Bourne and J. F. Daniell (eds.), *Int'l. Rev. of Cytology*, Vol. 39, pp. 89–190. New York: Academic Press.

Novikoff, P. M., Novikoff, A. B., Quintana, N., and Hauw, J. J. 1976. Golgi apparatus, gerl, and lysosomes of neurons in rat dorsal root ganglia, studied by thick section and thin section cytochemistry. *J. Cell Biol.*, *50*, 859–885.

Ochs, S. 1972. Fast transport of materials in mammalian nerve fibers. *Sci.*, *176*, 252–260.

Olton, D. S., Walker, J. A., and Gage, F. H. 1978. Hippocampal connections and spatial discrimination. *Brain Res.*, *139*, 295–308.

Ordy, J. M., and Schjeide, O. A. 1973. Univariate and multivariate models for evaluating long-term changes in neurobiological development, maturity and aging. *Prog. in Brain Res.*, *40*, 25–52.

Orgel, L. E. 1963. The maintenance of accuracy of protein synthesis and its relevance to aging. *Proc. Natl. Acad. Sci. (U.S.A.)*, *49*, 517–521.

Packer, L., and Smith, J. R. 1974. Extension of the life span of cultured normal human diploid cells by vitamin E. *Proc. Natl. Acad. Sci. (U.S.A.)*, *71*, 4763–4767.

Palay, S. L., and Chan-Palay, V. 1974. *Cerebellar Cortex, Cytology and Organization*. New York: Springer-Verlag.

Patel, M. S. 1977. Age-dependent changes in the oxidative metabolism in rat brain. *J. Gerontol.*, *32*, 643–646.

Peress, N. S., Kane, W. C., and Aronson, S. M. 1973. Central nervous system findings in a tenth decade autopsy population. *Prog. in Brain Res.*, *40*, 473–484.

Ponzio, F., Brunello, N., and Algeri, S. 1978. Catecholamine synthesis in the brain of ageing rat. *J. Neurochem.*, *30*, 1617–1620.

Purpura, D. P. 1974. Dendritic spine "dysgenesis" and mental retardation. *Sci.*, *186*, 1126–1128.

Raisman, G. 1966. The connections of the septum. *Brain*, *89*, 317–348.

Rapoport, S. I., Kikuo, O., and Pettigrew, K. D. 1978. *Blood-brain barrier in aged rats*. Society for Neuroscience Abstract.

Ringborg, U. 1966. Composition and content of RNA in neurons of rat hippocampus at different ages. *Brain Res.*, *2*, 296–298.

Robinson, A. J., Nies, A., Davis, J. N., Bunney, W. E., Davis, J. M., Colburn, R. W., Bourne, H. R., Shaw, D. M., and Coppern, A. J., 1972. Aging, monoamines, and monoamine oxidase levels. *Lancet*, *1*, 290–291.

Robinson, D. S., Davis, J. M., Nies, A., Ravaris, C. L., and Sylwester, D. 1971. Relation of sex and aging to monoamine oxidase activity of human brain, plasma, and platelets. *Arch. Gen. Psych.*, *24*, 536–539.

Rosenbloom, A. L., Goldstein, S., and Yip, C. C. 1976. Insulin binding to cultured human fibroblasts increases with normal and precocious aging. *Sci.*, *193*, 412–414.

Samorajski, T., Rolsten, C., and Ordy, J. M. 1971. Changes in behavior, brain, and neuroendocrine chemistry with age and stress in C57B1/10 male mice. *J. Gerontol.*, *26*, 168–175.

Scheibel, M. E., Lindsay, R. D., Tomiyasu, U., and Scheibel, A. B. 1975. Progressive dendritic changes in aging human cortex. *Exp. Neurol.*, *47*, 392–403.

Scheibel, M. E., Lindsay, R. D., Tomiyasu, U., and Scheibel, A. B. 1976. Progressive dendritic changes in the aging human limbic system. *Exp. Neurol., 53,* 420–430.

SEKHON, S. S., AND MAXWELL, D. S. 1974. Ultrastructural changes in neurons of the spinal anterior horn of aging mice with particular reference to the accumulation of lipofuscin pigment. *J. Neurocytol., 3,* 59–72.

SIAKOTOS, A. N., AND KOPPANG, N. 1973. Procedures for the isolation of lipo-pigments from brain, heart and liver, and their properties: A review. *Mech. Age. Devel., 2,* 177–200.

SINGER, S. J., AND NICHOLSON, G. L. 1972. The fluid mosaic model of the structure of cell membranes. *Sci., 175,* 720–731.

SOSA, J. M. AND DE ZORRILLA, N. B. 1966. Morphological variations of the Golgi apparatus in spinal ganglion nerve cells related to aging. *Acta. Anat., 64.* 475–497.

SOTELO, C., AND PALAY, S. L. 1976. Altered axons and axon terminals in the lateral vestibular nucleus of the rat: Possible example of axonal remodeling. *Lab. Invest., 25,* 653–671.

STREHLER, B. L. 1964. On the histochemistry and ultrastructure of age pigment. *In,* B. L. Strehler (ed.), *Advances in Gerontol. Res., 1,* pp. 343–384. New York: Academic Press.

STURROCK, R. R. 1976. Changes in neuroglia and myelination in the white matter of aging mice. *J. Gerontol., 31,* 513–522.

STURROCK, R. R. 1977. Quantitative and morphological changes in neurons and neuroglia in the indusium griseum of aging mice. *J. Gerontol., 32,* 647–658.

SULKIN, N. M., AND KUNTZ, A. 1952. Histochemical alterations in autonomic ganglion cells. *J. Gerontol., 7,* 533–543.

SUN, G., AND SAMORAJSKI, T. 1972. Age changes in the lipid composition of whole brain homogenates and isolated myelin fractions of mouse brain. *J. Gerontol., 27,* 10–17.

SZILARD, L. 1959. On the nature of the aging process. *Proc. Natl. Acad. Sci. (U.S.A.), 45,* 647–658.

TERRY, R. D., AND WISNIEWSKI, H. M. 1972. Ultrastructure of senile dementia and of some experimental analogs. *In,* C. M. Gaitz (ed.), *Aging and the Brain,* pp. 89–116. New York: Plenum.

THOMPSON, L. W. 1976. Cerebral blood flow, EEG, and behavior in aging. *In,* R. D. Terry and S. Gershon (eds.), *Neurobiology of Aging,* pp. 103–120. New York: Raven Press.

TOMLINSON, B. E., AND HENDERSON, G. 1976. Some quantitative cerebral findings in normal and demented old people. *In.* R. D. Terry and S. Gershon (eds.), *Neurobiology of Aging,* pp. 183–204. New York: Raven Press.

VAN BUSKIRK, C. 1945. The seventh nerve complex. *J. Comp. Neurol., 182,* 303–334.

VAN HARREVELD, A. 1966. *Brain Tissue Electrolytes.* Washington, D.C.: Butterworth.

VAUGHAN, D. W. 1977. Age-related deterioration of pyramidal cell basal dendrites in the rat auditory cortex. *J. Comp. Neurol., 171,* 501–516.

VAUGHAN, D. W., AND PETERS, A. 1974. Neuroglial cells in the cerebral cortex of rats from young adulthood to old age: An electron microscope study. *J. Neurocytol., 3,* 405–429.

VITELLO, L., BREEN, M., WEINSTEIN, H. G., SITTIG, R. A., AND BLACIK, L. J. 1978. Keratan sulfate-like glycosaminoglycan in the cerebral cortex of the brain and its variation with age. *Biochim. Biophys. Acta, 539,* 305–314.

WATSON, W. E. 1976. *Cell Biology of Brain.* London: Chapman and Hall.

WAYNER, M. J., AND EMMERS, R. 1958. Spinal synaptic delay in young and aged rats. *Am. J. Physiol., 194,* 403–405.

WELLS, C. E. 1978. Chronic brain disease: An overview. *Am. J. Psych., 135,* 1–12.

WISNIEWSKI, H. M., AND TERRY, R. D. 1976. Neuropathology of the aging brain. *In,* R. D. Terry and S. Gershon (eds.), *Neurobiology of Aging.,* pp. 265–280. New York: Raven Press.

WULFF, V. J., QUASTLER, H., SHERMAN, F. G., AND SAMIS, H. V. 1965. The effect of specific activity of $H^3$-cytidine on its incorporation into tissues of young and old mice. *J. Gerontol., 20,* 34–40.

WURTMAN, R. J., AXELROD, J., AND BARCHAS, J. D. 1964. Age and enzyme activity in the human pineal. *J. Clin. Endocrinol., 24,* 299–301.

YAMAMOTO, A., AND ROUSER, G. 1973. Free fatty acids of normal human whole brain at different ages. *J. Gerontol., 28,* 140–142.

# 5

# The Hypothalamus, Neuroendocrine, and Autonomic Nervous Systems in Aging

*Arthur V. Everitt & C. Y. Huang*

Until recently most aging research has been concerned with studying age differences in peripheral organs such as blood vessels, heart, or gonads. Now researchers are turning their attention to aging changes in the brain (Nandy and Sherwin, 1977; Ordy and Brizzee, 1975; Terry and Gershon, 1976) and the hypothalamic-pituitary complex (Everitt and Burgess, 1976). There are two reasons for this change of direction: to find the physical basis of mental disorders in the aged and to search for the postulated central regulators of aging, the so-called aging centers, clocks, or pacemakers.

## ORGANIZATION OF THE HYPOTHALAMUS, NEUROENDOCRINE, AND AUTONOMIC NERVOUS SYSTEMS

The hypothalamus, neuroendocrine, and autonomic nervous systems control the vegetative or involuntary functions necessary for living, and in so doing play an important role in meeting the challenges of an ever-changing environment.

### THE LIMBIC SYSTEM AND THE HYPOTHALAMUS

The limbic system is composed of areas 9, 10, 11, and 12 of the frontal cortex, septal nuclei, the cingulate gyrus, hippocampus, temporal lobe, amygdala, hypothalamus, the reticular formation of the brain stem, and their interconnecting pathways (Figure 5–1).

External stimuli arriving through the peripheral nervous system are received by the reticular formation. If the stimuli threaten the individual's survival or well-being, the reticular system alerts the higher brain centers. The reticular formation thus helps to focus on emotional and general responses to the environment in a selective manner.

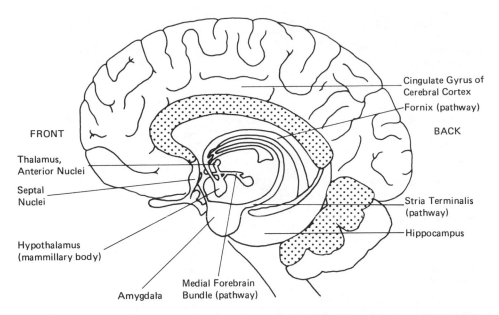

**Figure 5–1** The limbic system shown in gray. (Modified from Morgan, C. T., and King, R. A. 1975. *Introduction to Psychology.* 5th Edition. New York: McGraw-Hill Book Company. Used with permission of McGraw-Hill Book Company.)

When the information reaches the hypothalamus, endocrine activity and autonomic nervous system activity are altered to change the internal environment in response to the external stimulus. For example, digestion may be slowed down, the heart rate and blood flow increased, and epinephrine output elevated in response to a threatening stimulus. The hypothalamus affects a variety of vegetative functions (Figure 5–2). The cortical structures of the limbic system are responsible for organizing the emotional response more efficiently, and, depending on the past experiences, for determining the emotional and intellectual response most appropriate to the particular situation.

Bilateral lesions of the temporal lobe including the amygdala, uncus, and hippocampus will lead to a lack of emotional response; the subject displays no anger or fear and becomes hypersexual and docile. Stimulation of the amygdala and many parts of the hypothalamus causes aggressive behavior and heightened sympathetic activity in animals. Similar results are seen with lesions of the septal area. In man hypothalamic stimulation causes anxiety and autonomic excitation. However, stimulation of the human amygdaloid does not consistently cause aggressive behavior. Both amygdalotomy and hypothalamotomy have been reported to have a calming effect on patients with aggressive behavior (review, Goldstein, 1974).

The highest control of behavior and emotion rest in the prefrontal and frontal association areas of the limbic system. Destruction of these areas leads to changes in intelligence and personality. Prefrontal lobectomy causes the person to be less creative, less anxious, and more passive.

## The Neuroendocrine System

The neuroendocrine system is broadly defined as those structures of the brain that are implicated in the regulation of endocrine function (Siegel and Eisenman, 1972). The most important structures influencing endocrine function are found in the limbic system. According to the neurovascular hypothesis (Harris, 1955), neurohormones synthesized in the hypothalamus are liberated from nerve endings in the median eminence, enter the hypophyseal portal vessels, and then pass directly into the anterior pituitary where they regulate its secretions. (Figure 5–3).

The hypothalamic areas which influence adenohypophyseal functions are collectively termed the hypophysiotropic area. Special neurons in this area synthesize and secrete peptides called the hypothalamic releasing and release inhibitory factors (or hormones) that control the secretion of adenohypophyseal hormones. For each pituitary hormone there is a corresponding hypothalamic re-

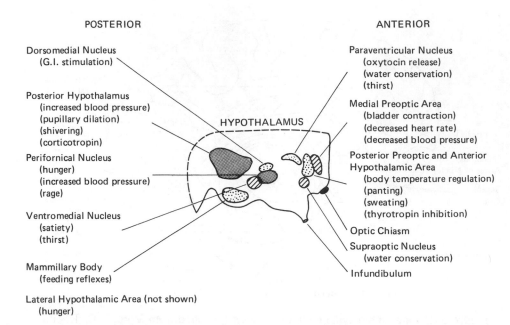

POSTERIOR

Dorsomedial Nucleus
(G.I. stimulation)

Posterior Hypothalamus
(increased blood pressure)
(pupillary dilation)
(shivering)
(corticotropin)

Perifornical Nucleus
(hunger)
(increased blood pressure)
(rage)

Ventromedial Nucleus
(satiety)
(thirst)

Mammillary Body
(feeding reflexes)

Lateral Hypothalamic Area (not shown)
(hunger)

ANTERIOR

Paraventricular Nucleus
(oxytocin release)
(water conservation)
(thirst)

Medial Preoptic Area
(bladder contraction)
(decreased heart rate)
(decreased blood pressure)

Posterior Preoptic and Anterior
Hypothalamic Area
(body temperature regulation)
(panting)
(sweating)
(thyrotropin inhibition)

Optic Chiasm

Supraoptic Nucleus
(water conservation)

Infundibulum

HYPOTHALAMUS

**Figure 5–2**  The autonomic control centers of the hypothalamus. (From Guyton, Arthur C., *Textbook of Medical Physiology,* 5th ed., © 1976 by the W. B. Saunders Co., Phila, Penna.)

leasing hormone or liberin, e.g., thyrotropin releasing hormone or thyroliberin which causes release of thyrotropin or the thyroid stimulating hormone. In addition, in the case of growth hormone and prolactin, there are hypothalamic release inhibitory hormones, viz., growth hormone inhibitory hormone (or somatostatin) and prolactin inhibitory factor.

The secretion of hypothalamic releasing and release inhibiting hormones appears to be controlled by neurotransmitters, but the mechanisms involved are complex (Brownstein, 1977; Frohman and Stachura, 1975). For example, pharmacologic studies indicate that basal adrenocorticotropic hormone (ACTH) secretion is maintained by cholinergic, noradrenergic, dopaminergic, and serotonergic influences, while ACTH stress responses appear to be determined by cholinergic and catecholaminergic mechanisms (Ordy and Kaack, 1976).

By controlling the release of pituitary tropic hormones, the hypothalamus determines the level of function of the thyroid, adrenal cortex, ovary, and testis. By the mediation of hormones, the hypothalamus thus exerts a major influence on many metabolic and morphological activities of the body, including the processes of growth, development, reproduction, and, presumably, aging.

## THE AUTONOMIC NERVOUS SYSTEM

The autonomic nervous system is responsible for control of body temperature, pupillary reaction, gastro-intestinal motility and secretions, and respiratory and cardiovascular functions. It is mobilized not only by an immediate physical change which requires a fight-or-flight response, but also by the everyday experiences which evoke anger, fear, anxiety, or pleasure. The integration of the autonomic nervous system into behavior is achieved by fiber tract connections between the hypothalamus, limbic system, and brainstem centers, to the frontal lobe and sensorimotor areas. Thus, stimulation of the cerebral cortex in the sensorimotor, supplementary motor, or secondary sensory regions can lead to alteration of autonomic functions (Penfield and Jasper, 1954). The limbic system, which has intricate connections between the cingulate gyrus, hippocampus, amygdala, anterior thalamic nucleus, hypothalamus, and parts of the basal ganglia, forms the center of integration for emotional expression and reaction, all of which have autonomic components. The integrated messages from the hypothalamic center are then sent down to the individual nuclei in the midbrain, pons, and medulla, which are responsible for the separate functions of respiration, pupil dilatation

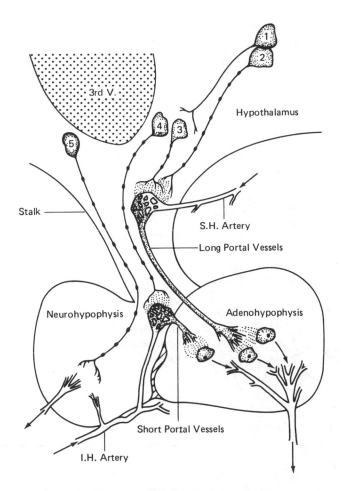

**Figure 5–3** The neural control of the pituitary gland. Neurons 2, 3 and 4 secrete peptides called releasing hormones (e.g. thyrotropin releasing hormone) which are conveyed by the portal blood vessels to the adenohypophysis where they stimulate the release of specific pituitary hormones (e.g. thyrotropin). Neuron 1 secretes monoamines (dopamine, norepinephrine or serotonin) which regulate peptidergic neurons. Neuron 5 secretes peptide hormones (vasopressin and oxytocin) in the neurohypophysis, without the mediation of portal vessels (From Gay, V. L. The hypothalamus: physiology and clinical use of releasing factors. *Fertil Steril 23;* 50, 1972. Reproduced with the permission of the publisher, *The American Fertility Society.*)

or constriction, vomiting, and vasomotor control.

Some of the efferent controls exit through the ventral spinal root to form the preganglionic autonomic fibers (Figure 5–4). The fibers of the sympathetic system enter the paravertebral sympathetic ganglionic chain which is continuous in the cervical, thoracic, lumbar, and sacral segments. The postganglionic fibers exiting from these ganglions are reponsible for vasoconstriction, the stim-

ulation of adrenal medullary secretion, cardiac acceleration, sweating, pilo-erection, and dilatation of pupils. The peripheral ganglia of the parasympathetic system are situated near their target organs and the postganglionic fibers are responsible for constriction of pupils, secretion from lacrimal and salivary glands, cardiac slowing, gastrointestinal peristalsis and secretion, bladder contraction, and erection of the penis and clitoris.

## AGING AND ITS MEASUREMENT

Most definitions of aging include two components: *physiological aging,* the decline in functional capacity after maturity, and *pathological aging,* the rising incidence of disease which increases the probability of death. However, some workers are prepared to accept aging as "any time-dependent change which occurs after maturity . . . and which is distinct from daily, seasonal and other biological rhythms" (Rockstein, Chesky, and Sussman, 1977).

Aging reveals itself as a deterioration in physical appearance such as hair graying and skin wrinkling. There is also a progressive functional decline with age in the cardiovascular, respiratory, digestive, renal, skeleto-muscular, nervous, immunological, endocrine, and reproductive systems (Everitt, 1976c; Finch and Hayflick, 1977; Goldman and Rockstein, 1975). Behavioral age decrements are observed in sensory processes, learning, intelligence, memory, motivation, and psychomotor skills (Birren and Schaie, 1977; Botwinick, 1975). These age changes are accompanied by a large increase in the incidence of disease, including mental illness, and a steep rise in mortality especially from cardiovascular and/or renal disease and neoplasms (Kohn, 1963).

In order to assess the physiologic or biologic age of the individual, a number of test batteries have been proposed (Comfort, 1969; Furukawa, Inoue, Kajiya, Inada, Takasugi, Fukui, Takeda, and Abe, 1975; Hollingsworth, Hashizume, and Jablon, 1965; Webster and Logie, 1974). Measurements used include tests of visual acuity, hearing loss, reaction time, vibratory sense, skin elasticity, hair graying, muscular strength, systolic blood pressure, and serum cholesterol. Using batteries of these tests it has been possible to compare the rates of aging in human populations living in different environments (Watthana-Kasetr and Spiers, 1973). However these tests of biological age have been criticized on the grounds that indices are selected solely on the basis of high correlation with chronological age, and do not predict age at death or years until death (Brown and Fobes, 1976).

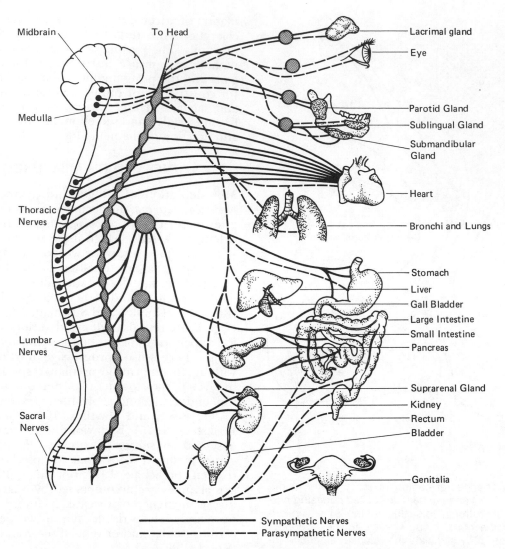

Midbrain

To Head

Lacrimal gland

Eye

Medulla

Parotid Gland

Sublingual Gland

Submandibular Gland

Heart

Thoracic Nerves

Bronchi and Lungs

Stomach

Liver

Gall Bladder

Large Intestine

Small Intestine

Pancreas

Lumbar Nerves

Suprarenal Gland

Kidney

Rectum

Bladder

Sacral Nerves

Genitalia

———— Sympathetic Nerves
— — — — Parasympathetic Nerves

**Figure 5–4**  From *Psychology: A Concise Introduction to the Fundamentals of Behavior,* by C. W. Telford and J. M Sawrey. Copyright © 1968 by Wadsworth Publishing Company, Inc. Reprinted by permission of the publisher, Brooks/Cole Publishing Company, Monterey, California.

## THE HYPOTHALAMUS AND AGING

Since the hypothalamus plays a commanding role in the regulation of most essential involuntary functions, age changes in this organ may have far-reaching effects on peripheral aging. At the present time there is a paucity of data on aging phenomena in the hypothalamus, despite the tremendous growth of neuroendocrinology during the last 25 years.

### MORPHOLOGIC CHANGES

There is little or no evidence for neuron loss with age in the hypothalamus of human subjects (Butt-

lar-Brentano, 1954) although this phenomenon occurs in the cerebral cortex, cerebellum, and thalamus (Brizzee, 1975; Brody, 1976). However, studies of the supraoptic and paraventricular nuclei in aging man indicate a marked enlargement of neurons to 8–10 times the size in young subjects, and the appearance of multinucleated cells with hyperchromasia in some nuclei (Buttlar-Brentano, 1954). Similar changes have been observed by Blumenthal (1976), who believes that they reflect *in vivo* aging changes, although he could not exclude the possibility of postmortem artifacts. Blumenthal suggests that these changes may be due to age changes in the negative feedback of hormones or other blood constitutents which act on the hypothalamus.

In human material there is no evidence for the age-related accumulation of lipofuscin pigment in the hypothalamus (Azcoga, 1965; Buttlar-Brentano, 1954), although this pigment accumulates in the hypothalamus of the guinea pig (Spoerri and Glees, 1975).

In the old rat there is a decrease with age in the nuclear volume of hypothalamic neurons in both sexes (Frolkis, 1976; Lin, Peng, Peng, and Tsen, 1976) and an accumulation of neurosecretory material in the supraoptic and paraventricular nuclei (Frolkis, Bezrukov, Duplenko, and Genis, 1972). These changes are interpreted by Frolkis (1976) as a reduction in neurosecretory activity in the hypothalamus of the aging rat. It must be emphasized that most morphologic studies are based on qualitative descriptions and are subject to artifacts in processing which lead to inconclusive findings (Ordy and Kaack, 1976).

*Metabolism.* Oxygen consumption of the rat hypothalamus decreases progressively throughout life (Peng, Peng, and Chen, 1977). The decreased oxygen consumption in old age appears to be a primary age change in the brain since this decrease is not affected by either hypophysectomy or castration (Peng *et al.*, 1977). Significant age differences in the metabolism of neurotransmitters in the hypothalamus have been recorded (Finch, 1973a; Simpkins, Müller, Huang, and Meites, 1977).

*Neurotransmitters.* All hypothalamic functions, including the secretion of the releasing factors for pituitary hormones, are dependent on neurotransmitters. Finch (1976) has proposed that age-related changes in catecholamine transmitters may trigger a cascade of aging changes.

Human data are presently limited to the finding of age differences in the enzymes associated with neurotransmitters. Significant decrements with age are found in enzymes associated with the metabolism of catecholamines, gamma-aminobutyric acid (GABA) and acetylcholine (McGeer and McGeer, 1975). Catecholamine systems, particularly dopaminergic ones, are highly vulnerable to age change (Finch, 1976; McGeer and McGeer, 1975).

The norepinephrine content of the hypothalamus declines significantly with age in the rhesus monkey (Ordy, 1975) and the male rat (Figure 5–5) (Miller, Shaar, and Riegle, 1976; Simpkins *et al.*, 1977). In the C57BL/6J male mouse, Finch (1973a) found no change with age in norepineph-

rine content of the hypothalamus, but the turnover was reduced 50 percent. Significant age-related declines are reported in the hypothalamic content of dopamine in the male rat (Miller *et al.*, 1976; Simpkins *et al.*, 1977), and of serotonin in the rhesus monkey (Ordy, 1975). There is evidence for depressed catecholamine and enhanced serotonin metabolism in aging male rats (Simpkins *et al.*, 1977).

*Hypophysiotropic Hormones.* The neurotransmitters appear to control the production of the hypophysiotropic or releasing hormones by the hypothalamus. Only a few studies have been made of age changes in these hormones. In the rat hypothalamus, there are significant reductions in the content of growth hormone (GH) releasing factor (Pecile, Mueller, Falconi, and Martini, 1965), luteinizing hormone (LH) releasing factor (Clemens and Meites, 1971; Riegle, Meites, Miller, and Wood, 1977) and prolactin inhibiting factor (Riegle *et al.*, 1977) and increases in follicle stimulating hormone (FSH) releasing factor (Clemens and Meites, 1971). The human LH releasing hormone is increased in the plasma of post-menopausal women (Seyler and Reichlin, 1973).

*Response to Stimuli.* The hypothalamus receives nervous inputs from both the periphery and higher centers, as well as chemical inputs of metabolites (e.g. glucose) and hormones (e.g. cortisol and estradiol). The hypothalamic response to

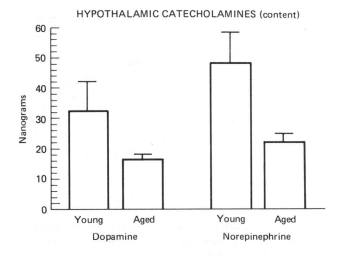

**Figure 5–5**  The age-related decline in the hypothalamic content of dopamine and norepinephrine (ng ± S.E.M. per hypothalamus) between ages 4 months and 24–26 months in male rats. From A. E. Miller, C. J. Shaar, and G. D. Riegle, *Exp. Aging Res.*, Vol. 2 (5), 1976, p. 478.

many stimuli is reduced in old age. However the studies of Frolkis and his coworkers (1972, 1976) on aging rabbits emphasize the lack of uniformity of age changes in the sensitivity of different areas of the hypothalamus to electric stimulation and to the direct effects of epinephrine, norepinephrine, and acetylcholine. Each area of the hypothalamus apparently has its own characteristic aging pattern.

The data of Dilman (1971, 1976) on human subjects suggest that the hypothalamus becomes less sensitive to glucose and glucocorticoids with increasing age. Corresponding studies in rats show that the hypothalamic pituitary responsiveness to glucocorticoid and gonadal steroid negative feedback is reduced in old age (Riegle, 1973; Shaar, Euker, Riegle, and Meites, 1975). In the rat there is also reduced hypothalamic-pituitary responsiveness to L-dopa treatment (Watkins, McKay, Meites, and Riegle, 1975). The reduced responsiveness of the hypothalamus to hormones may be due to a loss of hormone receptors. The uptake of tritiated estradiol by the hypothalamus is significantly less in old female rats (Peng and Peng, 1973). However the binding of corticosterone in the cytosol of the hypothalamus is not affected by age (Nelson, Holinka, Latham, Allen, and Finch, 1976).

Osmoreceptor response to fluid deprivation in elderly patients is reported to be subnormal (Mukherjee, Coni, and Davison, 1973). Similarly in old rats there is an impaired response to water deprivation as shown by a diminished secretion of antidiuretic hormone (Turkington and Everitt, 1976).

*Role of the Hypothalamus in Aging.* Only in the area of the hypothalamic control of endocrine function is it possible to relate age differences in the hypothalamus to the deterioration of peripheral functions with age. This will be discussed in the next section on neuroendocrine changes. Relatively little is known about age changes in other hypothalamic functions. This is especially unfortunate in the case of the control of food intake and body temperature, which are major determinants of the rate of aging.

No significant age changes in the mechanisms that control food intake in the rat have been revealed by studies of response to starvation, to changes in caloric value of food, or to ambient temperature (Jacubczak, 1976). However, in older animals the palatability of food is found to influence their response and this may lead to over- or under-eating (Jacubczak, 1976; Nisbett, Braver, Jusela, and Kezur, 1975). Aging is associated with less effective satiety mechanisms leading to obesity and finickiness (Kennedy, 1950). This suggests some failure of the behavioral and physiological mechanisms that control energy balance (Le Magnen, Devos, Guadilliere, Louis-Sylvestre, and Tallon, 1973; Mayer and Thomas, 1967). It has been suggested by Rothchild (1967) that the "syndrome of old age" is due to decreased activity of the ventromedial nucleus. It is well known that destruction of the ventromedial nucleus in rats increases food intake, leading to obesity, an early onset of renal disease, and a shortening of life (Kennedy, 1957). Obesity in man is associated with various chronic diseases in middle and old age (Mann, 1974; Stunkard, 1976).

Thermoregulatory behavior is a life-protecting mechanism which is largely intact in old age. However some impairment is seen in old rats and mice, and in elderly people (Finch, Foster, and Mirsky, 1969). Old rats immersed in iced water for 3 minutes take longer times to restore body temperature to normal than do young ones (Segall and Timiras, 1975). About 10 percent of elderly people living at home in the English winter of 1972 were found to have deep body temperatures below 35.5°C (Fox, Woodward, Exton-Smith, Green, Donnison, and Wicks, 1973). Although such people are at risk of developing hypothermia, it is also possible that the drop in body temperature would slow their rate of aging. Animal studies show that the rate of aging decreases as body temperature falls (Liu and Walford, 1972). Serotonin appears to be an important neurotransmitter in thermoregulation (Myers and Yaksh, 1972) and is normally derived from the metabolism of dietary tryptophan. Rats kept on a tryptophan deficient diet were found to grow at a slower rate and to show less evidence of aging in the thermoregulatory process (Segall and Timiras, 1975). Since there are many loci involved in temperature regulation, tryptophan deficiency need not necessarily be acting on the hypothalamic thermoregulatory center.

## NEUROENDOCRINE SYSTEM AND AGING

The brain and the endocrine system are the two major interrelated control systems which enable the individual to adapt to changing environmental conditions. These two systems, working together as the neuroendocrine system, control the level of function in almost all tissues of the body, not only acutely but also over long periods of time. Because of their far-reaching effects on body function, these two systems are ideally placed to exert a regulatory action on the many processes of aging. Furthermore any impairment of nervous or endocrine function in old age would have widespread consequences throughout the entire body.

## NEURAL AGING

The role of the neuroendocrine system in neural aging is largely unknown, although the actions of hormones on the development of the central nervous system are well documented (Balász, 1976; Dörner, 1976; Grave, 1977). During the latter part of the central nervous system (CNS) development, growth hormone, androgens, thyroxine, glucocorticoids, estrogens, and catecholamines exert specific metabolic effects (Schjeide, 1975). In the rat, steroid hormones bind to receptors in the brain, whose numbers increase during early postnatal development, plateau in adulthood, and finally decline in old age (Kanungo, Patnaik, and Koul, 1975; Roth, 1974; Roth, 1976). Corticosterone receptor studies in the old mouse brain show that high affinity binding capacity decreases in the hippocampus, whereas it increases in the hypothalamus (Finch, 1975). The affinity of receptors for triiodothyronine in the cerebral hemispheres is also reported to increase with age (Timiras and Bignami, 1976). Reductions in the number and/or affinity of brain hormone receptors suggest that age-related neural decrements may occur without evidence of neuron loss or brain disease. An increase in receptor binding suggests some compensatory phenomenon (Finch, 1975). It would be of great interest to study the long-term effects of ovariectomy, hypophysectomy, and food restriction on these age changes in steroid receptor binding in the brain. For example, hemiovariectomy accelerates ovarian aging in a number of mammals, but whether this is due to an action of estrogen in the hypothalamic control of ovarian aging (estrogen receptors studies would help here) or to another mechanism remains to be determined.

The discovery that peptide hormones affect learning processes (deWied, 1977a) and have other behavioral effects (Kastin, Plotnikoff, Schally, and Sandman, 1976; deWied, 1977b) again raises the question of possible hormonal control over CNS development and aging. There is growing evidence for neuroendocrine abnormalities in major mental illnesses (Sachar, 1975a; Sachar, 1975b; Sachar, 1976).

The role of nervous factors in neural aging has received little attention. In the case of neural diseases associated with aging, such as Parkinson's disease and Huntington's chorea, defects develop in the neurons of the cerebral cortex as well as in the hypothalamus and brain stem. The dopamine content of dopaminergic neurons of the substantia nigra are decreased in Parkinson's disease and in aging rats (Schjeide, 1975). Age-related changes in the monoaminergic neurons of the CNS are associated with age changes in sex drive, sleep, thermoregulation, and pituitary gonadotropin secretion (Finch, 1973b; Finch, 1976).

## ENDOCRINE AGING

As discussed earlier it appears that age-related decrements in a number of endocrine functions either have their origin in or are greatly modified by age changes in the hypothalamus (Aschheim, 1976; Dilman, 1976; Finch, 1976; Riegle, Meites, and Miller, 1977). In other words, age changes in the hypothalamic hypophysiotropic area may lead to secondary age changes in the endocrine system.

*Anterior Pituitary.* There is relatively little effect of age on the weight of the pituitary in the human adult (Bakke, Lawrence, Knudtson, Roy, and Needman, 1964; Calloway, Foley, and Lagerbloom, 1965), although the earlier studies of Rasmussen (1938) indicated a decrease in males after age 35.

Microscopically there is decreased vascularity accompanied by increased amounts of connective tissue (Shanklin, 1953). The gonadotropin cells become vacuolated in post-menopausal women (Sevringhaus, 1944).

Only recently has it become possible with radioimmunoassay techniques to measure the circulating level of pituitary hormones with sufficient accuracy to detect age changes. Apart from the increase with age in gonadotropic hormones (follicle stimulating hormone [FSH] and luteinizing hormone [LH]), there appears to be no major age change in the basal plasma levels. The use of provocative and inhibitory tests of pituitary function provides no evidence of major age-related defects in the feedback or neural control of pituitary hormone secretion except for the gonadotropins.

Prolactin cells do not regress in old age (Kovacs, Ryan, Horvath, Penz, and Ezrin, 1977) and normal serum prolactin levels are found in elderly subjects (Yamaji, Shimamoto, Ishibashi, Kosaka, and Orimo, 1976). However, reduced prolactin levels have been reported in post-menopausal women (Vekemans and Robyn, 1975).

## GROWTH HORMONE (GH) AGE CHANGES

Basal plasma growth hormone levels show little or no change with age (Blichert-Toft, 1975), although, GH production rates per 24 hours in elderly subjects are reduced significantly (Table 5–

1) due to the diminished secretion of GH during sleep (Carlson, Gillin, Gordon, and Snyder, 1972; Finkelstein, Roffwarg, Boyar, Kream, and Hellman, 1972). On the other hand, the GH secretory response to insulin hypoglycemia (Kalk, Vinik, Pimstone, and Jackson, 1973) and arginine infusion (Dudl, Ensinck, Palmer, and Williams, 1973) appears to be intact in elderly subjects. One interpretation of these findings is that the hypoglycemia- and arginine-mediated GH release CNS pathways are intact while the sleep pathway is defective in old age.

*Role of Growth Hormone in Aging.* It was earlier postulated that aging is a consequence of growth cessation (Lansing, 1948; Kohn, 1965). Since GH is strongly anabolic, its declining secretion during sleep in old age could account for some of the catabolic changes so characteristic of old age. In elderly subjects human GH has anabolic effects but there is some loss of responsiveness (Root and Oski, 1969). However, in old rats, long-term GH therapy which increased body weight failed to prevent the terminal age changes and did not increase survival (Everitt, 1959). Indeed, oversecretion of GH in acromegaly is associated with reduced life expectancy and increased mortality from cardiovascular, cerebrovascular, and respiratory disease (Wright, Hill, Lowy, and Fraser, 1970) as well as with diabetes mellitus (Lawrence, Tobias, Linfoot, Barn, Lyman, Chong, Manougian, and Wei, 1970). Thus GH therapy does not appear to be the answer to the problem of catabolic breakdown in old age.

Depression in postmenopausal women is clearly associated with a reduction in the GH response to insulin hypoglycemia (Gruen, Sachar, Altman, and Sassin, 1975). Since the GH response to hypoglycemia appears to be catecholaminergically mediated, this observation is consistent with the hypothesis of a functional depletion of hypothalamic catecholamines in depressive illness (Sachar, 1975b).

## AGING IN THE HYPOTHALAMIC-PITUITARY-THYROID AXIS

Many functions of the thyroid decline with age, but, according to Gregerman and Bierman (1974), "the thyroid of even very elderly persons appears to function adequately and maintain its reserve capacity." Histologically the thyroid shows signs of diminished function, such as atrophy of follicles, decreased mitotic activity, and fibrosis (Andrew, 1971; Charipper, Pearlstein, and Bourne, 1961). There is a diminished uptake of radioactive iodine by the thyroid in old age (Oddie, Myhill, Pirnique, and Fisher, 1968). Estimates of thyroxine secretion rate from the turnover of radioactive thyroxine in the circulation show a 50 percent decrement between ages 20 and 80 (Gregerman, Gaffney, Shock, and Crowder, 1962). The reduced turnover of thyroxine was attributed to the decreased mass of metabolically active tissue in old age. Despite the diminished secretion, the blood level of total thyroid hormone remains unchanged with increasing age (Gaffney, Gregerman, and Shock, 1962). However, the level of triiodothyronine (the more potent form of thyroid hormone occurring in much lower concentration) shows a significant decrease with age (Figure 5–6) (Rubenstein, Butler, and Werner, 1973; Snyder and Utiger, 1972). Triiodothyronine ($T_3$), which is formed mainly from thyroxine ($T_4$), appears to be the physiologically active hormone.

The fall in $T_3$ must reduce the feedback con-

**Table 5–1** The Secretion of Growth Hormone in Young and Older Adults During a 24-Hour Period.

| Group | Age (years) | Sex | Secretory Episodes Awake | Secretory Episodes Asleep | Secretion Rate (µg/day) |
|-------|-------------|-----|--------------------------|---------------------------|--------------------------|
| Young | 23 | F | 189 | 73, 344 | 606 |
|       | 24 | M | 0 | 328 | 328 |
|       | 24 | M | 79, 114 | 398 | 491 |
|       | 28 | F | 65, 76 | 74 | 215 |
|       | 33 | F | 76, 41, 238, 111 | 190, 113 | 769 |
| Older | 47 | F | 0 | 0 | 0 |
|       | 51 | F | 0 | 0 | 0 |
|       | 51 | F | 109, 146, 81, 54, 115 | 0 | 505 |
|       | 62 | M | 0 | 57 | 57 |
|       | 62 | M | 0 | 0 | 0 |

From Finkelstein, J. W., *et al.*, 1972. Age-related change in the twenty-four hour spontaneous secretion of growth hormone. *J. Clin. Endocrinol.*, 35(5), pp. 665–670.

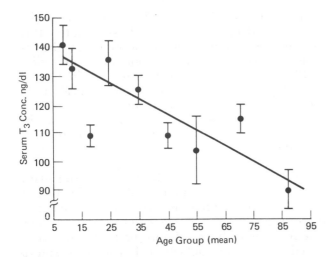

**Figure 5–6**   The age-related decline in serum triiodothyronine in human subjects. (From Rubenstein H. A., Butler V. P. Jr., and Werner S. C., 1973. Progressive decrease in serum triiodothyronine concentrations with human aging: radioimmunoassay following extraction of serum. *J. Clin. Endocrinol., 37,* 247–253.)

trol on the hypothalamus and hypophysis (Blichert-Toft, Hummer, and Dige-Petersen, 1975). This should lead to a compensatory increase in TSH secretion. However, studies on TSH changes with age have yielded conflicting results. Investigations on 170 healthy subjects aged 18–94 years showed no significant age change in the fasting morning level of serum TSH (Blichert-Toft *et al.,* 1975). There is some evidence that the pituitary gland may be less responsive to the hypothalamic thyrotropin releasing hormone (TRH) in old age. A relatively large dose (400 µg) of TRH produces a smaller rise in plasma TSH in elderly subjects than in young (Sakoda, Fukuda, Mori, Tateiwa, Kusaka, and Baba, 1975; Snyder and Utiger, 1972), but with smaller doses there is no age difference (Blichert-Toft *et al.,* 1975; Sakoda *et al.,* 1975).

Thus in old age there is a decrement in thyroid function which appears to be a consequence of multiple age changes, occurring not only in the thyroid but in the peripheral tissues and probably also in the hypothalamus and the pituitary.

THYROID HORMONE AND AGING. Old age has many features in common with hypothyroidism, such as low metabolic rate, cold intolerance, dry skin, diminished motor activity, sparseness of hair, atherosclerosis, and hypercholesterolemia (Korenchevsky, 1961; Zellmann, 1968). Consequently it was earlier postulated that a deficiency of thyroid

hormone contributes to aging phenomena (Lorand, 1904; Lorand, 1921). Certainly the thyroid gland secretes less thyroxine in old age, but whether this affects aging phenomena is unsettled. In the case of patients with myxedema (adult hypothyroidism), the aging-like changes are largely reversible by treatment with thyroid hormone, even in long-standing cases (Boyd, 1958). Nevertheless if we accept that aging changes are irreversible (Strehler, 1959), then these aging-like changes of myxedema are not true aging changes. Interest in the hypothyroidism hypothesis has been rekindled as a result of the observation that a pituitary factor decreases the response of peripheral tissues to thyroid hormone with increasing age (Denckla, 1973).

Patients with Graves' disease (hyperthyroidism) are reported to develop premature senescence by age 40 (Curshmann, 1929). Such observations are in accord with animal data relating hyperthyroidism to increased aging of collagen and kidney (Everitt, 1976d; Giles and Everitt, 1967), and to shortened life duration (Robertson, 1928). This is consistent with the observation in animal studies that high metabolic rates are associated with shortened life span (review Everitt, 1976d). High food intakes accompanying high metabolic rates are also associated with a short life. Since thyrotropin releasing hormone injected into the third ventricle of the rat can inhibit feeding behaviour (Vijayan and McCann, 1977), this hypothalamic hormone may play an important role in regulating aging phenomena.

Thyroid hormone has important behavioral effects. The thyroid gland is necessary for the normal development of the central nervous system (Grave, 1977) and thyroid dysfunction is associated with behavioral changes (Prange, 1974). A lack of thyroid hormone in childhood results in mental deficiency, which can be corrected by early treatment by thyroxine. In the adult, hypothyroidism leads to depression and mild cognitive deficits (Whybrow, Prange, and Treadway, 1969) similar to those seen in old age. The syndrome of "myxedema madness" occurs more frequently in the elderly (Pitts and Guze, 1961; Rullo and Allan, 1958). There is an increased susceptibility to psychosis in these patients who may have a combination of psychotic depression, dementia, irritability, and paranoia. Since thyroid hormones act synergistically with catecholamines the behavioral changes associated with aging and thyroid function may be due to changes in brain catecholamines (Eisdorfer and Raskind, 1975).

In conclusion, the role of thyroid hormones in aging in not clear since increased aging has been reported in both hypo- and hyper-thyroid states.

## AGING IN THE HYPOTHALAMIC-PITUITARY-ADRENOCORTICAL AXIS

In order to survive in an ever-changing environment it is essential to have a normally functioning hypothalamic-pituitary-adrenocortical axis. Although age-related decrements are detectable at different points in this axis, the healthy subject is still able to withstand moderate stress in old age.

Basal plasma glucocorticoid levels show no significant change with age between maturity and old age (Grad, Kral, Payne, and Berensen, 1967; Jensen and Blichert-Toft, 1971). In addition, the nyctohemeral variation (high values in the morning and low in the evening) is seen in most elderly subjects (Grad, Rosenberg, Liberman, Trachtenberg, and Kral, 1971). Estimation of cortisol secretion rates per day from the excretion of specific cortisol metabolites reveals a 25 percent reduction between maturity and old age (Figure 5-7), (Romanoff, Morris, Welch, Rodriguez, and Pincus, 1961). Cortisol removal from circulating blood is much slower in old age (Samuels, 1956; West, Brown, Simons, Carter, Kumagai, and Englert, 1961), so a lower cortisol secretion rate can maintain a normal plasma cortisol level in aged subjects.

Mineralocorticoid secretion also decreases with age. Plasma aldosterone and renin activity levels are significantly reduced in healthy normotensive subjects above age 60, compared with young adults (Noth, Lassman, Tan, Fernandez-Cruz, and Mulrow, 1977).

The responsiveness of the adrenal cortex to ACTH stimulation does not appear to change with age in man (Blichert-Toft, Blichert-Toft, and Jensen, 1970; Romanoff, Baxter, Thomas, and Ferrechio, 1969; Solomon and Shock, 1950). However, when allowance is made for the decreased disposal rate of cortisol in the elderly, an equal plasma cortisol response to ACTH stimulation in young and aged subjects implies that the old adrenal cortex secretes less cortisol (West *et al.,* 1961).

Plasma ACTH levels are difficult to measure. In the largest series so far studied (25 young and 28 elderly subjects aged 70–94), Blichert-Toft (1975) could find no significant difference in morning ACTH levels between youth and old age. Provocative tests with arginine and metyrapone also failed to reveal any age differences. Major surgery also produced a normal ACTH response and showed that the hypothalamic-pituitary-adrenocortical secretory mechanism was not affected by age (Blichert-Toft and Hummer, 1976).

Animal studies indicate a decreased sensitivity of the hypothalamic-pituitary ACTH control mechanism to the feedback of adrenocortical steroids in old age (Riegle, 1976; Riegle and Hess, 1972). The data of Dilman (1976) suggest that this may also be true in man. He showed that the inhibitory effect of dexamethasone on the excretion of 17-hydroxysteroids declines with age in man.

Hypothalamic-pituitary-adrenocortical function in man, although undergoing some age-related changes, shows no evidence of exhaustion in healthy old age, even under conditions of prolonged stress.

*Adrenal Cortex and Aging.* The adrenal cortex plays a major role in the adaptation of the individual to his environment. There is no doubt that the adaptive capacity declines with age (Timiras, 1972), but whether this is due to diminished adrenocortical function or to age deficits in hormone receptors in target organs or to age changes in other systems is not known. Adrenocortical steroids increase the life span of hypophysectomized rats (Everitt, 1976b) short-lived mice (Bellamy, 1968), and human dip-

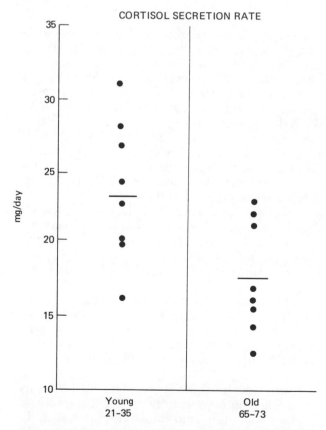

**Figure 5–7**  The age-related decline in cortisol secretion rates per day in human subjects (Drawn from the data of Romanoff, Morris, Welch, Rodriguez, and Pincus, 1961). *J. Clin. Endocrinol., 21,* pp. 1416, 1417.

loid W1-38 cells in tissue culture (Cristofalo, 1975).

When young animals are chronically exposed to stress, they develop behavioral, physiological, biochemical, and morphological changes similar to age-related changes in older animals (Birren and Kay, 1958; Paré, 1965; Wexler, 1976). According to the stress theory of aging (Selye and Prioreschi, 1960), old age is the result of the cumulative effects of stresses and strains that the organism is subjected to throughout life. There is considerable evidence to show that the life style and hence the amount of stress to which an individual is exposed influences his susceptibility to certain diseases. The compulsive, striving and deadline-conscious individual with the so-called type A personality has a much higher incidence of hypertension and coronary heart disease than the more passive individual (Abrahams, 1976; Friedman and Rosenman, 1974; Russek and Russek, 1977).

The hypothalamic-pituitary-adrenal axis has been extensively studied in relation to affective disorder (Ettigi and Brown, 1977). Patients suffering from depressive illness have a hypersecretion of cortisol, which is not simply a response to stress (Sachar, Hellman, Roffwarg, Halpern, Fukishima, and Gallagher, 1973). The hypersecretion of cortisol is not suppressed by dexamethasone, suggesting a continuing increased ACTH secretion in these subjects (Carroll, 1976). The abnormal lack of suppression in the depressed state returns to normal with clinical improvement.

## AGING IN THE HYPOTHALAMIC-PITUITARY-OVARIAN AXIS

With increasing age there is a progressive decline in all aspects of sexual behavior and reproduction. With the approach of the menopause estrogen levels become very low and this inevitably leads to loss of libido, sexual behavior, fertility, and reproduction.

In the ovary at birth there are one million oocytes, but only 400 of these will mature into ova and be ovulated, the remainder producing follicles which become atretic. Even by age 40, the number of follicles is low (Block, 1952) and at this time anovulatory cycles appear and reproductive performance declines (Francis, 1970). As a consequence of the reduced secretion of ovarian hormones, there is general involution of the female reproductive system soon after the menopause.

Associated with the loss of follicles is the decline in the secretion of estrogens and progesterone in women approaching menopause (Adamopoulos, Loraine, and Dove, 1971). Estradiol blood levels decline by over 90 percent (Figure 5-8), (Korenman, Perrin, and McCallum, 1969; Long-

cope, 1971). The main source of estrogens in circulating blood of postmenopausal women is from the conversion of plasma androstenedione to estrone, since no estrogen is secreted by the ovary (Grodin, Siiteri, and MacDonald, 1973).

The serum levels of both pituitary FSH and LH are elevated in postmenopausal women (Coble, Kohler, Cargille, and Ross, 1969; Kohler, Ross, and Odell, 1968; Wise, Gross, and Schalch, 1973). The production rate for FSH rises 15-fold (Coble et al., 1969) and for LH 5-fold (Kohler et al., 1968). The levels of both FSH and LH decline significantly 20 years after the menopause (Chakravarti, Collins, Forecast, Newton, Oram, and Studd, 1976).

High levels of pituitary gonadotropins suggest that the primary aging change is in the ovary, since there is a failure of the ovary to increase estrogen secretion in response to these high gonadotropin levels. Furthermore, high plasma titers of hypothalamic gonadotropin releasing hormone are found in postmenopausal women (Seyler and Reichlin, 1973). It has been suggested that the hypothalamic receptors for estrogen feedback lose their sensitivity with age, and that this leads to a compensatory increase in gonadotropin releasing hormone and pituitary gonadotropin secretion (Dilman, 1971; Dilman, 1976; Van Look, Lothian, Hunter, Michie, and Baird, 1977). A comparison

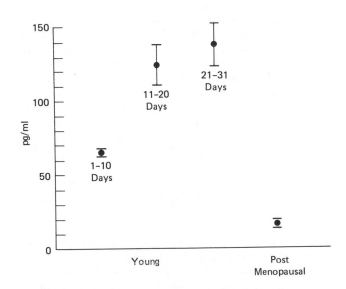

**Figure 5–8** Plasma estradiol levels in young women during 1–10, 11–20 and 21–31 days of the menstrual cycle and in postmenopausal women (Drawn from the data of Korenman, Perrin, and McCallum, 1969). *J. Clin. Endocrinol., 29,* p. 881.

has been made of the acute response of LH and FSH in four pre- and three postmenopausal women induced by infusing varying doses of 17β-estradiol (Tsai and Yen, 1971). The response was slightly greater in younger women. It is apparent that the hypothalamic receptors in older women are still responsive. Elevation of plasma FSH (with or without a rise in LH) in perimenopausal women may result from a decreased ovarian secretion of FSH release inhibiting substance (Sherman and Korenman, 1975).

On present evidence it appears that the reproductive decline in the human female is due to primary aging of the ovary. However in the rat there is now good evidence to show that the primary aging change occurs in the hypothalamus (Aschheim, 1976; Clemens and Bennett, 1977).

*Effects of Reproductive Aging in the Female.* The relationship between the cessation of reproductive function at the menopause and the subsequent aging of the entire organism has attracted considerable attention. Menopause refers to the cessation of menstrual cycles, which occurs at a mean age of 50 years in women in highly industrialized Western countries (Burch and Gunz, 1967; Jaszmann, 1973; Jaszmann, 1976). Climacteric or "the change of life" refers to the psychologic and physiologic changes in the body which can be traced to the cessation of ovarian function (Sharman, 1962) between ages of 45 to 55.

The female secondary sex organs (uterus, vagina, fallopian tubes) shrink and their epithelial linings atrophy in postmenopausal women (Timiras and Meisami, 1972). There is also thinning of pubic and axillary hair and loss of subcutaneous fat. The breasts become flaccid, the alveoli disappear, the ducts diminish in size, and the nipples become smaller and less erectile (Paschkis, Rakoff, Cantarow, and Rupp, 1967). Many of these postmenopausal changes can be reversed by sex hormone therapy (Masters, 1957), but eventually the organs become less responsive.

Symptoms experienced by many women during the climacteric are often called the menopausal syndrome (Jaszmann, 1976; Neugarten and Kraine, 1967; Paschkis *et al.*, 1967; Vara, 1970). The changes consist principally of genital atrophy and vasomotor instability due to estrogen lack (Ross and Vandewiele, 1974). The association of psychologic disturbances specifically with the menopause is controversial (Brown and Brown, 1976). In the premenopausal and menopausal phase (age 40 to 50 years) Vara lists the common symptoms as hot flashes, sweats, palpitation, nervousness, insomnia, frigidity, depression, fatigue, and weight increase. The nature of the menopausal syndrome varies from woman to woman. In one study it was reported that 15 percent of women experienced no symptoms at all, 10 percent felt incapacitated, 62 percent experienced "hot flashes", 45 percent headaches, and 30 percent nervous instability (Paschkis *et al.*, 1967). Estrogen replacement therapy is remarkably effective in abolishing autonomic vascular reactions such as hot flashes, sweating, and dizziness. Several studies indicate that only the symptoms of vasomotor instability are correlated with the menopause and estrogen lack (Thompson, Hart, and Durno, 1973; Utian, 1972).

The behavioral effects of estrogen are discussed by Eisdorfer and Raskind (1975). Estrogen therapy is believed by experienced clinicians to promote a "sense of well being" in older women (Eisdorfer and Raskind, 1975). This impression is supported by data on premenopausal women (Glick, 1967; Hamburg, Moos, and Yalon, 1968). On the other hand there have been several reports of depression associated with the use of oral contraceptives (Kane, Daly, Ewing, and Keeler, 1967; Lewis and Hoghughi, 1969), although these reports have not been confirmed by others (Goldzieher, Moses, Averkin, Scheel, and Taber, 1971; Weissman and Slaby, 1973).

The behavioral effects of sexual inadequacy in the elderly have been described by Weg (1975). The need for intimacy and love does not cease with the menopause, but continues on into later years especially as friends and relatives move away or die (Lowenthal and Berkman, 1967; May, 1969). About 60 percent of marital partners aged 60 to 74 and about 30 percent older than 75 years remain sexually active (Weg, 1975). Cessation of sexual activity is most often due to decline of physical health of one or both of the partners (Weg, 1975). The loss of sexual activity is not due to a lack of estrogen. However as a result of vaginal involution due to estrogen deprivation, the act of coitus may prove unsatisfying and even painful to some postmenopausal women (Weg, 1975). Although sexual arousability does not decline with advancing age (Kinsey, Pomeroy, Martin, and Gebhard, 1953), the intensity of the physiologic response to effective stimulation decreases in all four phases of the cycle (Masters and Johnson, 1970).

In conclusion, estrogen lack is the only known instance of marked hormone deficiency in old age. Estrogen replacement therapy will certainly reverse age changes in the genital organs and is clearly indicated for the emotionally distressing vasomotor instability during the climacteric. However, in long term estrogen therapy the risks of malignancy and cardiovascular disease must be kept in mind (Dewhurst, 1976; Greenblatt and Stoddard, 1978; Rust, Langley, Hill, and Lamb, 1977; Shoemaker, Forney, and MacDonald, 1977).

## AGING IN THE HYPOTHALAMIC-PITUITARY-TESTICULAR AXIS

Reproductive function in the male gradually declines with age (Baker, Burger, de Kretser, Hudson, O'Connor, Wang, Mirovics, Court, Dunlop, and Rennie, 1976; Stearns, MacDonnell, Kaufman, Padua, Lucman, Winter, and Faiman, 1974; Vermeulen, 1976). There is no dramatic failure in middle age as in the female.

Age-related changes in sexual behavior and reproductive function are more readily demonstrable in men than in women. There is a progressive decline in sexual activity with age such that at 80 years approximately 75 percent of men are impotent (Kinsey, Pomeroy, and Martin, 1948). Frequency of intercourse, speed of erection, intensity and force of erection, and frequency and intensity of orgasm all decline with age in men (Ordy and Kaack, 1976). Decreases in the volume and viscosity of seminal fluid and reduction in the force of ejaculation are also reported (Weg, 1975). These changes apparently result from the involution of the seminal vesicles and prostate in late middle age (Steward and Brandes, 1961), due to the declining secretion of testosterone. Spermatogenesis may be normal even in extreme old age, but generalized hypospermatogenesis is common (Baker, Burger, deKretser, and Hudson, 1977).

Plasma testosterone levels decline progressively from age 50 (Figure 5–9), (Baker *et al.* 1976; Vermeulen, 1976; Vermeulen, Rubens, and Verdonck, 1972). Free testosterone declines rapidly after age 20 (Baker *et al.*, 1976). Low levels of the active hormone dihydrotestosterone are found in old age (Giusti, Gonnelli, Borrelli, Fiorelli, Forti, Pazzagli, and Serio, 1975). There is an increase with age in the binding capacity of testosterone binding protein in plasma (Vermeulen *et al.*, 1972) and this may account for the age-related decrease in free testosterone.

Increases occur in serum FSH (Figure 5-10) and LH in aging men (Baker *et al.*, 1976; Vermeulen, 1976), but these are not as marked as in postmenopausal women. Although the pituitary secretes increased quantities of FSH and LH in aging men, its response to the hypothalamic gonadotropin releasing hormones is actually diminished (Haug, Aakvaag, Sand, and Torjesen, 1974; Snyder, Reitano, and Utiger, 1975).

On present evidence the association of low testosterone production with high FSH and LH

levels indicates that the age-related reproductive decline in men is due to primary aging of the testis (Baker, Burger, deKretser, and Hudson, 1977), and not to age changes in the hypothalamus or pituitary.

*Effects of Reproductive Aging in the Male.* Early workers believed that aging phenomena were due to declining testicular function. Some of the sensational rejuvenative experiments of that era were injections of testicular extracts (Brown-Séquard, 1889), ligation of the vas deferens (Steinach, 1920) and transplantation of monkey testes (Voronoff, 1926). There is no doubt that there is a decrease with age in testosterone secretion which contributes to the decline in sexual activity.

A male climacteric in which there is a sudden loss of sex function has been reported (Werner, 1939) but this affects only a small number of men, usually in their sixties. In these cases hypofunction of the testis is associated with a loss of potency and

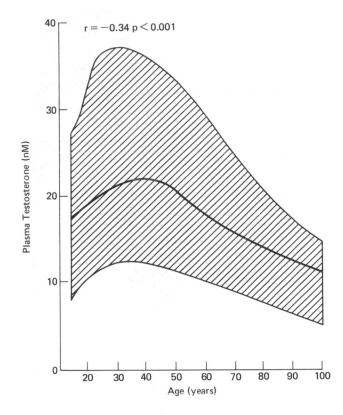

**Figure 5–9** Plasma testosterone levels in human subjects at different ages (From Baker, H.W.G., Burger, H.G., de Kretser, D.M., and Hudson, B. 1977. Endocrinology of aging: pituitary-testicular axis. *In,* V.H.T. James (ed.), *Endocrinology,* Vol.2, pp. 479–483. Amsterdam-Oxford: Excerpta Medica.)

libido, hot flashes, tachycardia, chills and sudden perspiration, and emotional instability.

Eunuchs and castrated men are said to age prematurely and frequently resemble senile women in appearance (Timiras and Meisami, 1972). The skin becomes yellowish and wrinkled; the shoulders narrow and the pelvis widens; movement is sluggish and there is a general lack of vigor. These changes are generally ascribed to androgen deficiency. However, it cannot be asserted that androgen depletion is the cause of aging processes generally. Certainly a lack of testosterone in old age leads to atrophy of accessory sex glands.

Although many studies emphasize the role of psychological factors in the loss of sexual vigor, other studies suggest that the decline in plasma testosterone levels with age may also contribute. It has been reported that young or middle-aged subjects suffering from psychogenic or constitutional impotence have reduced testosterone levels (Cooper,

Ismail, and Smith, 1970). It has been suggested that testosterone production may be related to sexual activity. In two sexually abstinent normal men the resumption of coitus produced marked increases in the basal testosterone level (Ismail and Harkness, 1967). Thus lower testosterone levels in the elderly may be a function of decreased sexual activity, which in turn may be dependent on various social and psychological factors (Pfeiffer and Davis, 1972). However, the relationship between circulating testosterone levels and sexual activity has been questioned (Monti, Brown, and Corriveau, 1977).

Impotence in the diabetic has been correlated with degeneration of autonomic innervation (Faerman, Glocer, Fox, Jadzinsky, and Rapaport, 1974). This relationship has not been studied in the healthy aging male and therefore the autonomic contribution to impotence is unknown.

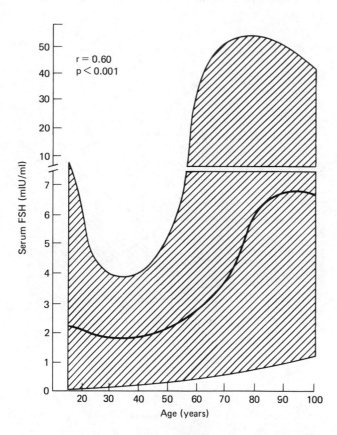

**Figure 5–10**  Serum follicle stimulating hormone (FSH) levels in human subjects at different ages (From Baker, H.W.G., Burger, H.G., de Kretser, D.M., and Hudson, B. 1977. Endocrinology of aging: pituitary-testicular axis. *In*, V.H.T. James (ed.), *Endocrinology*, Vol.2, pp. 479–483. Amsterdam-Oxford: Excepta Medica.)

## THE AUTONOMIC NERVOUS SYSTEM AND AGING

### ANATOMICAL AGE CHANGES

Very few studies have been made regarding anatomical changes in the autonomic nervous system. No significant change was found in the unmyelinated nerve fiber population of the vagus nerve with age (Sharma and Thomas, 1973) or in the myelinated fiber population of the greater splanchnic nerve, which is formed by the preganglionic sympathetic fiber of the thoracic segment (Huang and Walsh, 1974). However, Appenzeller and Ogin (1973) found reduction in internodal lengths in myelinated fibers of the human paravertebral sympathetic chain, and interpreted this as Wallerian degeneration and segmental demyelination occurring with increasing frequency with old age. Nevertheless it would appear that there are at least no marked degenerative changes in the preganglionic parasympathetic and sympathetic trunks with normal aging. However, there is evidence of a progressive decrease in the intermediolateral column neuron count with age (Low and Dyck, 1978).

Despite the fact that maximal degenerative changes are seen in the limbic areas in Alzheimer's disease (Brun and Gustafson, 1976), no studies on autonomic function have been noted in dementia.

*Role of the Autonomic Nervous System in Aging.* The significance of the autonomic nervous system in aging has not been studied systematically or adequately. Our knowledge of the contribution of autonomic failure to normal aging is, therefore, undecided and speculative. Part of the problem is due to the methodological difficulties of studying autonomic functions. Most of the studies depend on indirect rather than direct measurement of autonomic activity. Direct measurement of autonomic neuronal activity has not as yet reached the reliability or accuracy of electrical studies of the peripheral nervous system. Many of our concepts rest on extrapolations from indirect evidence and are subject to errors.

*Bladder Function.* Whether autonomic nervous system failure contributes to deterioration in bladder function with age is unknown. Uninhibited neurogenic bladder is common in elderly people (Brocklehurst and Dillane, 1966). Since incontinence in the elderly is a major social and medical problem, it obviously requires more study.

*Thermoregulation.* Thermoregulation depends on the integrity of skin receptors which inform the brain of temperature changes, the autonomic system which then takes corrective vasoconstriction or vasodilatation, and the somatic motor responses of shivering. Normal aging may lead to impaired shivering, with an unimpaired central temperature response to cold. However, some old patients do develop poor thermoregulatory responses and are at risk from accidental hypothermia (Horvath, Radcliffe, Hutt, and Spurr, 1958).

*Behavior.* Whether changes in the autonomic nervous system contribute to behavioral changes with age is similarly unknown. Immuno-sympathectomy causes rats and mice to be somewhat less reactive to threatened aversive stimuli, but somewhat overreactive to other stimuli which may not be aversive. General activity in the cage and open field did not appear to be altered, nor was social behavior altered. Learning ability did not seem impaired (Wenzel, 1972). In man, autonomic conditioning of galvanic skin response was substantially less for the old than for the young. In contrast the EEG was more responsive. However, the age changes in the skin may interfere with the response noted. Magnitude of the heart rate deceleration prior to a stimulus and the acceleration subsequent to the response is also less.

*Blood Pressure.* Pathological changes in the autonomic nervous system giving rise to orthostatic hypotension certainly occurs mainly with aging.

The role of the autonomic nervous system in the genesis of essential hypertension still remains an unresolved problem. In spontaneously hyper-tensive rats, the level of activity of splanchnic nerves is elevated above that of normotensive rats (Okamato, Nosaka, and Yamori, 1967). However, no difference was recorded in the lumbar nerves, which may perhaps more accurately reflect the discharges to blood vessels (Lais, Bhatnager, and Brody, 1975), nor in the peripheral nerves of hypertensive subjects (Wallin, Delius, and Hagbarth, 1973). On the other hand, central catecholamine neurons are altered in the spontaneously hypertensive rats, even before the onset of hypertension, suggesting that the autonomic nervous system may be implicated in the onset of the hypertension (Sarvedra, Grobecker, and Axelrod, 1977). Further aspects of the problem are reviewed by Brody and Zimmerman (1976) and reported in the Second Pan American Symposium on Hypertension (deQuattro, Barbour, Campese, Finck, Miano, and Esler, 1977; Frohlich, 1977; Weinshilboum, 1977). Blood pressure does not necessarily rise with age, but in normal subjects arterial baroreceptor sensitivity progressively decreases with increasing age (Gribbin, Pickering, Sleight, and Peto, 1971).

## NEURAL AND ENDOCRINE THEORIES OF AGING

The brain and endocrines, as the major interrelated control systems in the body, must exert a significant influence on the course of aging. Primary age changes in the brain and the neuroendocrine system would be expected to produce widespread secondary age changes. Further, the brain and the neuroendocrine system play a unique role in mediating the effects of the environment on the body. Biological theories of aging have emphasized genetic or environmental factors as single causes of aging. They have proposed that aging may result from changes in genes, somatic mutations, crosslinking of proteins and nucleic acids, formation of free radicals, loss of cells, connective tissue changes, rate of metabolism, stress, nutrition, and exercise (Rockstein, 1974). The neural and endocrine theories however, emphasize the control aspect of aging. They propose that aging is controlled by aging centers or pacemakers, or that aging is due to the breakdown of control by these centers, or that hormones and neurotransmitters have aging effects.

### THE AGING CLOCK HYPOTHESIS

It has been proposed that the aging program is precisely timed by means of an "aging clock" (Figure 5-11) which is probably located in the hypothalamus (Everitt, 1973; Everitt, 1976a; Hasan, Glees, and El-Ghazzawi, 1974; Samorajski, 1977). With this hypothesis development and aging consist of an orderly sequence of changes which appear to be programmed from the time of fertilization when the genetic code is laid down. The precise timing of events in the life program may be controlled by separate clocks for each body function. A gonadotropin aging clock governing the secretion of the gonadotropin releasing hormone may control the secretion of pituitary gonadotropins which, by stimulation of the ovary, lead in turn to the onset of puberty, successive menstrual cycles, and finally to exhaustion of the ovary at the menopause. Such a clock would probably have only a modulating influence on intrinsic aging in the ovary, since hypophysectomy (which abolishes gonadotropin production) retards but does not prevent oocyte loss from the ovary of the mouse (Jones and Krohn, 1961). Denckla (1975) has proposed that the lifespan is regulated by a biological clock which acts on the endocrine glands to produce failure of the immune and circulatory systems. Aging clocks or pacemakers have been postulated to exist in the pineal (Quay, 1972) and in the thymus (Burnet, 1974). The location of pacemakers of aging has been discussed by Finch (1973b). Intrinsic pacemakers may reside in every cell, as in the case

of fibroblast cells from human lung which in culture have a span of 40 generations (Hayflick, 1970). The mitochondrion is the likely site of an intrinsic clock (Harman, 1972). An example of an extrinsic pacemaker is the loss of ovarian hormones at the menopause, producing involution of the reproductive tract.

### THE HYPOTHALAMIC DISREGULATION HYPOTHESIS

Any breakdown or impairment of the endocrine or neural control mechanisms in the hypothalamus, whether it be due to neuron loss, to reduced sensitivity of receptors to feedback, or to neurotransmitter deficiencies, must have widespread effects on body function (Figure 5-12). There are thirty trillion cells in the human whose functions are coordinated principally by the actions of the vegetative part of the brain, including the hypothalamus (Still, 1969). In his cybernetic theory of aging, Still emphasizes message transmission failure. He postulates that the decreased redundancy of nerve cells, coupled with decreasing nerve conductive velocities, leads to differing times of message arrival at the control centers and subsequent loss of coordination. Shock (1974) suggests that in the whole animal aging is probably a reflection of the breakdown of control mechanisms.

Frolkis (1976) produces evidence showing that the pattern of hypothalamic aging varies with the region under study. He believes that the lack of uniformity in hypothalamic aging causes unequal changes in regulatory processes that deter-

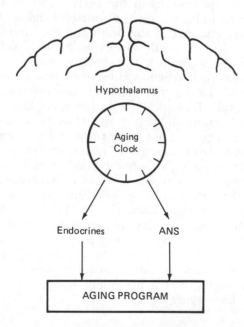

**Figure 5–11**   The aging clock hypothesis. It is proposed that the aging program from conception until death is timed by an "aging clock," probably located in the hypothalamus with aging processes driven by nervous and endocrine impulses having their origin in the hypothalamus.

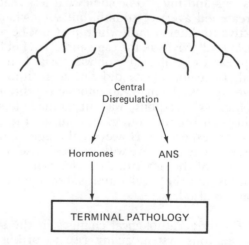

**Figure 5–12**   The central disregulation hypothesis. It is proposed that terminal aging and pathological processes are due to the breakdown of central endocrine and neural control mechanisms.

mine the pattern of aging and age-related pathology (Frolkis *et al.*, 1972).

## THE HYPOTHALAMIC ELEVATION HYPOTHESIS

Dilman (1971) suggests that the age-related loss of sensitivity of the hypothalamus to the negative feedback of hormones is the key process in aging. According to his view, gradual elevation of the hypothalamic threshold to feedback suppression leads to oversecretion of hormones which accelerate aging phenomena. Compared with young controls, blood hormone levels are increased for gonadotropins in postmenopausal women (Coble *et al.*, 1969), for cortisol after surgery in elderly patients (Blichert-Toft, 1975) and for growth hormone after glucose loading in middle-aged patients (Dilman, 1976). These differences may be due only partly to hypothalamic changes. For example, the high gonadotropin levels in postmenopausal women are largely due to the sharply reduced secretion of ovarian hormones. Although Dilman's work is open to criticism because of the use of data from hospital patients rather than from healthy subjects, it has the support of animal data. In the rat, an age-related elevation of the hypothalamic threshold to negative feedback has been demonstrated for corticosteroids (Riegle, 1973) and gonadal steroids (Shaar, *et al.*, 1975).

Recently Dilman observed a lowering of the threshold of sensitivity of the hypothalamic-pituitary complex to $T_3$ and $T_4$ suppression during the course of development and aging. This has led Dilman to modify his concepts, which are explained in a new monograph, *The Law of Homeostatic Deviation and Diseases of Aging.**

## NEUROENDOCRINE DEFICIENCY HYPOTHESES

A defect developing at any stage in the neuroendocrine pathway would be expected to produce aging-like changes. There are several hypotheses implicating changes in neurotransmitters or a lack of pituitary or thyroid hormones in aging (Figure 5-13).

## THE NEUROTRANSMITTER HYPOTHESIS

It is proposed that changes in the synaptic level of neurotransmitters may be implicated in aging phenomena (Samorajski, 1977). There appears to be general acceptance in the concept of dysfunction

*Manuscript in preparation. PSG Publishing Company, Littleton, Mass.

in the biogenic amines concerned in neurotransmission as a basis of affective disorder (Ettigi and Brown, 1977; Schildkraut, 1970). For example, depression is associated with a deficiency of catecholamines (Schildkraut, 1965). This hypothesis can be logically extended to include aging phenomena. It has been suggested that age-related changes in the metabolism of catecholamine neurotransmitters in certain regions of the brain which lead to deficiencies of catecholamines could trigger a cascade of secondary aging changes (Finch, 1976; Finch, 1977; Simpkins *et al.*, 1977). Hindbrain norepinephrine content decreases with age in man (Robinson, 1975) and deficiencies of dopamine

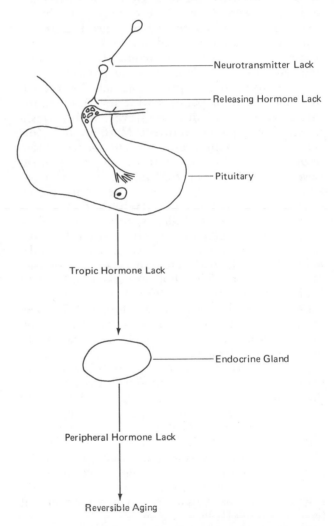

**Figure 5–13** The neuroendocrine deficiency hypotheses. Deficiencies of a vital component at any stage in the neuroendocrine pathway, be it neurotransmitter, hypothalamic releasing hormone, pituitary tropic hormone, or peripheral hormone, can lead to aging changes which may be reversed with appropriate replacement therapy.

occur in the basal ganglia in Parkinson's disease, a major age-related disease in man (Bernheimer, Birkmayer, Hornykiewicz, Jellinger, and Seitelberger, 1973). Age-related decreases in the norepinephrine content of the hypothalamus occur in male rats (Miller *et al.,* 1976) and in the rhesus monkey (Ordy, 1975). The secretion of the releasing factors for pituitary hormones is dependent on neurotransmitters in the hypothalamus. Therefore age-related decrements in hypothalamic catecholamines or other neurotransmitters could account for many of the age-related changes in pituitary and peripheral endocrine functions. For example, ovarian cycles in many old rats can be reinitiated by the administration of L-DOPA, epinephrine, and iproniazid (Quadri, Kledzik, and Meites, 1973; Huang and Meites, 1975). Since L-DOPA is converted to dopamine and norepinephrine in the brain, these drugs may overcome the age-related deficiency of catecholamines in the hypothalamus.

Neurotransmitter precursors have been tested in elderly human patients with severe dementia due to Alzheimer's disease (Meyer, Welch, Deshmukh, Perez, Jacob, Haufrect, Mathew, and Morrell, 1977). Data implicating the cholinergic system in aging have also appeared. Choline acetyltransferase is selectively depleted in Alzheimer's disease, and muscarinic binding sites in the frontal cortex decrease with advancing age (White, Hiley, Goodhart, Carrasco, Keet, Williams, and Bowen, 1977). One possible explanation for this is that there is a selective loss of cholinergic neurons with Alzheimer's disease, with retention of normal density of receptor sites. The cholinergic system has also been found to have a specific role in memory and cognitive function in man (Drachman, 1977). Deterioration in the cholinergic system with aging may therefore account for the prevalence of memory defects in the aged.

The feeding of tryptophan deficient diets to young rats reduced serotonin levels in all areas of the brain (Segall, Ooka, Rose, and Timiras, 1978) and delayed the maturation of the neuroendocrine axis. Pituitary function was arrested and thyroid activity depressed (Ooka, Segall, and Timiras, 1978). Since this treatment also delayed both the age of tumor onset and the age of cessation of reproductive function (Segall and Timiras, 1976), it was hypothesized that thyroid deficiency might have life-long effects on aging.

## The Hypopituitary Hypothesis

This hypothesis states that aging phenomena are due to a lack of pituitary hormones. Senile changes are found to occur prematurely in a number of patients whose pituitary has been destroyed by disease (Herman, 1976; Pribram, 1927; Simmonds, 1914). Similar changes were reported in hypophysectomized rats (Smith, 1930). Thus severe hypofunction of the pituitary produces involutional changes similar to those of senescence. Many of these changes in reproductive organs, muscles, and metabolic processes can be reversed by appropriate hormone replacement therapy (Taylor, 1956). Since these "senile" changes are reversible, they cannot be regarded as true aging changes if we are to accept progressiveness as a criterion of aging. (Strehler, 1959).

## Hypothyroid Hypothesis

Lorand (1904) proposed that many of the features of aging are due to hypothyroidism. The signs of hair graying, skin dryness, decreased motor activity due to impaired muscle strength, decreased resistance to cold, and low basal metabolic rate are seen in young patients with hypothyroidism. Thyroid replacement therapy can reverse these signs of aging in young patients, but is not effective in the elderly unless there is thyroid deficiency (Boyd, 1958). Interest in the hypothyroid hypothesis has been reawakened by the work of Denckla (1973, 1976). On the basis of rat studies, Denckla postulates that after maturity the pituitary secretes a factor which progressively blocks the effects of thyroid hormones on peripheral tissue. Thus a state of hypothyroidism may develop in the older organism due to the secretion of a pituitary factor. Alternatively these age changes could be due to a loss of tissue receptors to thyroid hormone.

## Neuroendocrine Overstimulation Hypotheses

Several hypotheses implicate hormones and stress in aging phenomena (Figure 5-14). Excessive hormone levels are associated with increasing aging.

## The Pituitary Hypothesis

According to this hypothesis, pituitary hormones accelerate aging processes and lead to an early onset of age-related pathology. The strongest evidence supporting this hypothesis is the observation that hypophysectomy in the rat retards aging phenomena (Table 5-2) in tail tendon collagen, kidney, aorta, skeletal muscle, bone, and ovary (Everitt, 1976b; Everitt, 1978). The retarded aging is presumably due to the withdrawal of pituitary hormones that stimulate these processes. Almost all of the anterior pituitary hormones and their target gland hormones (thyroxine, cortisol, estrogen, testosterone) have been shown to have aging effects in one or other organ (Everitt, 1973). Consequently, situations which chronically increase the secretion of pituitary hormones (e.g. stress, low temperature, pregnancy) accelerate aging phenomena (Everitt, 1973).

### THE STRESS THEORY

According to this theory, exposure to stressful stimuli accelerates the process of aging (Selye and Prioreschi, 1960; Selye and Tuchweber, 1976). Selye postulates that individuals are born with a fixed quantity of adaptive energy, which is progressively consumed with each exposure to stress. In other words, most stresses cause some permanent damage to the organism and accumulation of these small residual injuries is responsible for aging.

This theory is not supported by the work of Curtis and Gebhard (1958) in which doses of tetanus toxoid or tetanus toxin given every 14 days throughout life did not significantly shorten the life of mice. Furthermore, in another mouse study, repeated stresses actually extended the life duration significantly (Ordy, Samorajski, Zeman, and Curtis, 1967).In other studies, the physiologic aging of collagen fibers in rat tail tendon was increased by exposure of animals to various stresses (Arvay, 1976; Paré, 1965). In addition, there is a growing body of clinical, epidemiologic and experimental data showing that repeated exposure to stresses over lengthy periods produces serious damage, particularly to the cardiovascular system but also to the digestive, immune, nervous, and skeletal-muscle systems (Dodge and Martin, 1970; Friedman and Rosenman, 1974; Gunderson and Rahe, 1974; McQuade and Aikman, 1976; Selye and Tuchweber, 1976; Tanner, 1976).

### THE CATECHOLAMINE STRESS HYPOTHESIS

Carruthers (1969) postulated that high levels of catecholamines are maintained through the stresses of modern living and, in conjunction with other factors, are capable of producing atheroma. Emotions such as anxiety and aggression are contributing factors. It was found that individuals with a psychiatric disorder had a significant excess of coronary heart disease over those without a psychiatric disorder (Eastwood and Trevelyan, 1971).

### CONCLUSION

There are many hypotheses about the central control of aging processes. These hypotheses are not mutually exclusive, but probably all contribute to our overall picture of the neuroendocrine regulation of aging. Aging phenomena are clearly under primary genetic control, which may act by mediation of one or more aging clocks or centers in the brain. Deficiencies of a vital component at any stage in the neuroendocrine pathway, be it neurotransmitter, hypothalamic releasing hormone, pituitary tropic hormone, or target gland hormone, can lead to "aging" changes which may be reversed with the appropriate replacement ther-

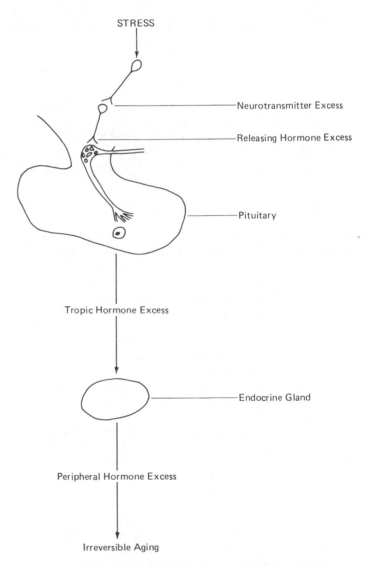

**Figure 5–14** The neuroendocrine overstimulation hypotheses. It is proposed that excessive stimulation of organs, by hormones and neurotransmitters, due to stress or to life events such as pregnancy or diseases like diabetes, produces permanent tissue damage which resembles aging phenomena.

**Table 5-2** A Comparison of Aging Parameters in Control Wistar Male Rats and in Rats Hypophysectomized at Age 2 Months.

| Parameter | Controls aged | | | Hypophysectomized aged 28–35 mo. |
|---|---|---|---|---|
| | 2 mo. | 10 mo. | 28–32 mo. | |
| Number of rats | 10 | 10 | 10 | 12 |
| Collagen fiber breaking time (minutes ± S.E.M.) | 4 ±0.3 | 46 ±1 | 523 ±24 | 132 ±12 |
| Protein excretion (mg/day ± S.E.M.) | 1.3 ±0.2 | 20 ± 3 | 163 ± 25 | 35 ± 7 |
| Abdominal aorta thickness (mm ± S.E.M.) | 0.18 ±0.013 | 0.225 ±0.009 | 0.28 ±0.016 | 0.18 ±0.007 |
| Hind leg paralysis % incidence | 0 | 0 | 70 | 0 |

apy. Long-term excessive production of hormones due to life events such as pregnancy, or diseases such as diabetes, or chronic environmental stress, can accelerate the aging process.

## STRESS AND AGING

Any harmful environmental factor which acutely threatens the individual produces changes in brain catecholamines (Usdin, Kvetnansky, and Kopin, 1976), causes a prompt rise in the secretion of pituitary ACTH and adrenocortical hormones, stimulates the sympathetic nervous system, and markedly increases the epinephrine and norepinephrine secretion by the adrenal medulla. The nervous and hormonal response produces an immediate increase in heart rate, blood pressure, and blood glucose. The circulation delivers glucose and oxygen to the muscles and brain, and mobilizes energy for meeting the threat, whether it be a mugger attacking an elderly man, a bill which a young married woman has just received and cannot pay, sitting for a difficult examination, the death of a near relative, a painful illness or an attack of influenza. For many people there may be only one stressful episode per week, but for others with more aggressive personalities their whole life is a continual battle against a multitude of stresses. Some people adapt well to chronic stress and are not greatly affected by it. Others, however, may be hard-driving, competitive types who are prime candidates for coronary heart disease, hypertension, duodenal ulcers, asthma, emphysema, arthritis, ulcerative colitis, migraine, diabetes mellitus, or involvement in traffic accidents (Matthews, Glass, Rosenman,

and Bortner, 1977; McQuade and Aikman, 1976). It is not known if these signs of breakdown are also indications of accelerated aging. A number of animal studies show that chronic exposure to stress leads to the premature development of age-related changes (Paré 1965; Selye and Tuchweber, 1976). However, under certain conditions, stress may be beneficial and has been found to prolong life in a life-long stress study on the mouse (Ordy *et al.*, 1967).

### AGE AND ADAPTATION TO STRESS

With increasing age there is a decreased ability to adapt to environmental change, leading ultimately to the development of mental and physical illness and increasing the mortality rate.

A young subject exposed to a cold environment (5°C-15°C) for 45 to 120 minutes increases his heat production by shivering and so maintains his body temperature, whereas an elderly subject does not shiver so much and in consequence his rectal temperature falls 0.5°C or more (Krag and Kountz, 1950). The elderly subject is also less able to adapt to high temperatures. It is well known that mortality rates in institutions for the aged increase during periods of prolonged high temperatures (Friedfield, 1949; Schuman, Anderson, and Oliver, 1964) and also on cold winter days (MacPherson, Ofner, and Welch, 1967).

Recovery after exposure to stress is much slower in the elderly than in the young. For example, after physical exercise old men require a longer time for the heart rate to return to normal than do young subjects (Norris and Shock, 1960). Similarly the return of the blood sugar level to normal after oral glucose loading is slower in elderly men (Streeton, Gerstein, Marmor, and Doisy, 1965).

Old people respond to psychological stress with higher rates of suicide and mental illness than do younger age groups. The poorer adjustment to the stresses of retirement, widowhood, and other losses in the elderly may be because grief is more personal and is not shared with others as it was in earlier life (Rosow, 1973). In other words loneliness can kill and hence companionship is a preventive medicine (Lynch, 1977).

*Internal Stresses.* Not all stresses have their origin in the external environment. The best known of the internal stresses are the diseases. Almost any disease, whether it be a coronary occlusion, cancer, pneumonia, or a mental illness such as schizophrenia, produces a stress response with increased sympathetic activity and hypersecretion of ACTH, adrenocortical steroids, epinephrine, and norepinephrine (Selye and Tuchweber, 1976). The body has to adjust to the abnormal situation and in so doing pays the price of increased aging, according to the stress theory of aging (Selye and Prioreschi, 1960)There are however, no direct data to show that disease accelerates the aging process. In the case of the aging brain, cerebrovascular disease would be expected to exert a deleterious effect on aging by interfering with normal circulation to the brain (O'Brien, 1977).

Pregnancy and aging are examples of internal stresses which are not diseases. In pregnancy, hyperadrenocorticism and other hormonal excesses can lead to the degenerative and metabolic changes typically seen in diabetes mellitus (Baird, 1969) and cardiovascular disease (Wexler, 1976). At the psychologic level, the increasing awareness of growing old and the eventual approach of death are examples of internal stresses to which the individual must adapt.

*Scaling of Life Events.* By means of life event questionnaires (Holmes and Rahe, 1967; Horowitz, 1977), it may be possible to quantitate the exposure and adjustment to the stresses of life events (Grant, Gerst, and Yager, 1976).

## MODULATION OF THE AGING PROGRAM BY ENVIRONMENTAL FACTORS

### THE AGING PROGRAM

It is generally agreed that aging is an intrinsic process which is genetically determined. The orderly sequence of changes during the life span appears to be programmed from the time of conception when the genetic code of the individual is laid down. Some of the more important events in the aging program starting from conception are embryonic development, birth, growth, puberty, maturity, physiological and behavioral decline, menopause, immunological decline, old age pathology, terminal disease, and finally death.

It has been proposed that an aging program which is so precisely timed is controlled by an aging "clock" or "center". The hypothalamus is the most likely site of a clock which controls the whole course of aging from conception to death (Everitt, 1973). Presently it is only possible to speculate about the existence of clocks or pacemakers of aging. There may be a single clock or a whole multitude of clocks, each controlling one aspect of aging such as body temperature, metabolism, feeding behavior, secretion of hormones, arterial blood pressure, cardiac function, etc. The program of aging may be driven or accelerated by a hormone in certain cases. For example the gonadotropin releasing hormone produced by the hypothalamus could determine the rate of development and aging of the ovary by controlling pituitary gonadotropin secretion and thence ovarian function. Hypophysectomy, which removes the supply of gonadotropin, slows aging of the ovary in the mouse (Jones and Krohn, 1961). Similarly catecholamines or other neurotransmitters could drive or accelerate aging processes in organs principally under neural control, such as the heart.

An alternative concept is that aging phenomena are determined by primary age changes in the hypothalamus, such as elevation of the threshold to feedback inhibition (Dilman, 1971) or changes in the metabolism of catecholamines (Finch, 1973b). Intrinsic age changes in the hypothalamus would set the aging program in motion. It has been postulated that the terminal age changes are caused by the breakdown of central homeostatic control mechanisms due to heterogeneous age changes in the hypothalamus (Frolkis *et al.*, 1972). The rate at which programmed age changes develop appears to be modulated by environmental conditions, both external and internal.

*External Environmental Factors.* The external environment varies enormously and the capacity of the organism to adapt to environmental change is dependent on the proper functioning of the nervous and neuroendocrine systems. Adaptation is mediated by the brain and nervous system through reflexes, conditioning, and learning, and by hormones secreted by the endocrine system, which maintains homeostasis principally by metabolic mechanisms. The hypothalamus and the pituitary probably play an important role in mediating the effects of extrinsic factors on programmed aging. The biochemical mechanisms have been investigated mainly in stress experiments on animals.

Hormones such as epinephrine and cortisol, which prolong life in a hostile environment, probably exact a price in the form of accelerated aging and early onset of pathological lesions (Selye and Tuchweber, 1976). In young animals, hormones secreted during exposure to stress (ACTH, corticosteroids, growth hormone, and catecholamines) produce pathologic lesions similar to those seen in old age.

Exposure of the rat to low temperature for long periods leads to an early onset of the diseases of old age and shortens life (Johnson, Kintner, and Kibler, 1963). In order to survive at low temperatures, the rat has to increase its heat production by raising its secretion of thyroxine (Johnson, Kibler, and Silsby, 1964) and other hormones such as catecholamines and adrenocortical steroids. Once again the price of adaptation is an early onset of pathology.

In human populations physical and social factors in the environment, particularly the life style, determine the pattern of physical and mental disease. A rural subsistence community in Papua, New Guinea, has a heavy burden of infectious disease but is relatively free of the cardiovascular diseases and psychiatric illnesses occurring in an urbanized community in Australia (Sinnett and Whyte, 1978).

*Internal Environmental Factors.* The microenvironment of the cell is normally maintained within narrow limits for pH and certain ions which are essential for physiological and biochemical processes. There are, however, quite large fluctuations in the internal environment with regard to blood hormonal levels. These levels vary according to requirements throughout the day (cortisol, ACTH), throughout the menstrual cycle (estradiol, progesterone, gonadotropins), during pregnancy (hormones of the ovary, pituitary, thyroid, adrenal cortex, placenta), during stress (cortisol, ACTH, growth hormone, epinephrine), and throughout the life cycle (sex hormones, gonadotropins, growth hormone). Similar large fluctuations occur in the local concentrations of neurotransmitters in muscles and glands during nervous stimulation. If aging processes are influenced by environmental factors, then hormonal and neurochemical stimulants probably play a significant role. Hormones have been shown to modify aging phenomena in a number of organs (Everitt, 1973).

When an organ ages, the body adapts to the declining function. For example, aging of the ovary reduces its secretion of estradiol. This leads to a compensatory rise in the secretion of pituitary gonadotropins in an effort to stimulate the aging ovary. Adaptation to aging in a non-endocrine organ such as the heart, would be only partly mediated by the neuroendocrine system. Hypertrophy of the heart and the kidney, which occurs in the majority of old rats in response to declining function of those organs, does not occur if the animals are hypophysectomized early in life. This suggests that the pituitary plays a role in the adaptation process (Everitt, 1976b).

Pregnancy places large demands on the mother, leading to increased secretion of many hormones and major physiological adjustments in metabolism and in cardiovascular and respiratory functions. There is evidence that pregnancy increases the incidence of age-related cardiovascular pathology and diabetes mellitus (Wexler, 1976).

The onset of age-related pathology such as diabetes also requires major adjustments in function. Many of the diseases of old age appear prematurely in the diabetic (Shagan, 1976). Diabetics experience an earlier onset of peripheral arterial disease, arteriosclerotic heart disease, stroke, senile cataract, osteoporosis, osteoarthritis, and loss of vibratory sensation. The vascular diseases may develop early due to a connective tissue defect. Tendon collagen from three juvenile diabetics was found to be 50 years older than normal on the basis of enzyme digestibility studies (Hamlin, Kohn, and Luschin, 1975). Although patients with diabetes experience the diseases of aging prematurely and exhibit accelerated collagen aging, they do not show early aging of all organs and tissues.

Undoubtedly any disease process acts as a stress. This stimulates the hypothalamus and pituitary, leading to increased secretion of adrenocortical hormones and catecholamines, which then accelerate the rate of programmed aging in the target organs for these hormones. These concepts are presented diagrammatically in Figure 5-15.

*Higher Brain Centers.* In man the higher centers play an important role in rendering the environment less hostile (Everitt, 1975). Man is able to shield himself from many external environmental factors (stress, temperature extremes, malnutrition, infectious diseases) which accelerate aging or shorten his life. Man uses his higher brain centers in medical research to find ways of identifying and treating the diseases which impair his health and shorten his life. Research on aging will inevitably

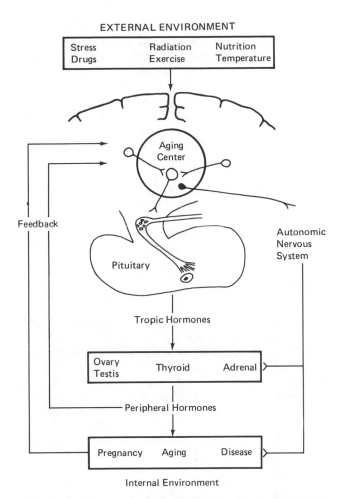

EXTERNAL ENVIRONMENT

| Stress | Radiation | Nutrition |
| Drugs | Exercise | Temperature |

Aging Center

Feedback

Pituitary

Autonomic Nervous System

Tropic Hormones

| Ovary Testis | Thyroid | Adrenal |

Peripheral Hormones

| Pregnancy | Aging | Disease |

Internal Environment

**Figure 5–15** Environmental modulation of the aging program. It is proposed that environmental factors, both external (stress, drugs, radiation, exercise, nutrition, and temperature) and internal (pregnancy, aging, and disease) modify the rate of aging set by the genes. These factors are believed to act on an "aging center" probably located in the hypothalamus, which modulates the rate of aging by the neuroendocrine and autonomic nervous systems.

improve the mental and physical health of elderly people and significantly extend their life.

## CONCLUSIONS

Adaptation to environmental challenges is achieved by the coordinated activity of the nervous system through reflexes, conditioning, and learning, and of the neuroendocrine system, through homeostatic regulation of metabolism. As the link between the brain and the neuroendocrine system the hypothalamus occupies a key position in the regula-

tion of vegetative functions. Consequently this organ has been proposed as the most likely site for a center to regulate aging processes throughout the body. Breakdown of central homeostatic regulation in old age may account for terminal aging phenomena. However, much work remains to be done to evaluate this hypothesis.

Considerable advances have been made in understanding the effects of age on the secretion of hormones. With increasing age there is a decline in the daily secretion rates of pituitary growth hormone, thyroxine, cortisol, testosterone, and estradiol, along with a compensatory rise in pituitary gonadotropin secretion. Presently available evidence indicates that these changes are due to primary aging of the ovary and testis, reduced tissue requirement for cortisol and thyroxine, and the loss of sleep-induced growth hormone secretion in old age.

Stress plays a significant role in aging. There is a growing body of evidence showing that high levels of catecholamines from sympathetic overstimulation, and corticosteroids from the hyperactive adrenal cortex have damaging effects on the cardiovascular, digestive, immune, and nervous systems. Whenever the individual has to adapt to a hostile environment, the very hormones which facilitate survival produce an early onset of the breakdown phenomena that are loosely associated with aging.

Information regarding the contribution of autonomic nervous system malfunction or degeneration to aging, or to mental health, is relatively scant. Much more will have to be learned with the aid of direct neurophysiological or anatomical studies of this system.

## REFERENCES

ABRAHAMS, J. P. 1976. Psychological correlates of cardiovascular disease. *In*, M. F. Elias, B. E. Eleftheriou, and P. K. Elias (eds.), *Special Review of Experimental Aging Research*, pp. 330–350. Bar Harbor, Maine: EAR, Inc.

ADAMOPOULOS, D. A., LORAINE, J. A., AND DOVE, G. A. 1971. Endocrinological studies in women approaching the menopause. *J. Obstet. Gynaecol. Brit. Comm., 78*, 62–79.

ANDREW, W. 1971. *The Anatomy of Aging in Man and Animals.* New York: Grune & Stratton.

APPENZELLER, O., AND OGIN, G. 1973. Myelinated fibres in the human paravertebral sympathetic chain: Quantitative studies on white rami communicantes. *J. Neurol. Neurosurg. Psychiat., 36*, 777–785.

ARVAY, A. 1976. Reproduction and aging. *In,* A. V. Everitt and J. A. Burgess (eds.), *Hypothalamus, Pituitary and Aging,* pp. 362–375. Springfield, Ill.: Charles C Thomas.

ASCHHEIM, P. 1976. Aging in the hypothalamic-hypophyseal ovarian axis in the rat. *In,* A. V. Everitt and J. A. Burgess (eds.), *Hypothalamus, Pituitary and Aging,* pp. 376–418. Springfield, Ill.: Charles C Thomas.

AZCOAGA, J. E. 1965. *Arch. de Histologia Normal y Pathologia* 9: 40–48. Cited by Brizzee, K. R., Klara, P., and Johnson, J. E. 1975.

BAIRD, J. D. 1969. Some aspects of carbohydrate metabolism in pregnancy with special reference to the energy metabolism and hormonal status of the infant of the diabetic woman and the diabetogenic effect of pregnancy. *J. Endocrinol., 44,* 139–172.

BAKKE, J. L., LAWRENCE, N., KNUDTSON, K. P., ROY, S., AND NEEDMAN, G. H. 1964. A correlative study of the content of thyroid stimulating hormone (TSH) and cell morphology of the human adenohypophysis. *Am. J. Clin. Pathol., 41,* 576–588.

BAKER, H. W. G., BURGER, H. G., de KRETSER, D. M., AND HUDSON, B. 1977. Endocrinology of aging: pituitary-testicular axis. *In,* V. H. T. James (ed.), *Endocrinology,* Vol. 2, pp. 479–483. Amsterdam-Oxford: Excerpta Medica.

BAKER, H. W. G., BURGER, H. G., de KRETSER, D. M., HUDSON, B., O'CONNOR, S., WANG, C., MIROVICS, A., COURT, J., DUNLOP, M., AND RENNIE, G. C. 1976. Changes in the pituitary testicular system with age. *Clin. Endocrinol., 5,* 349–372.

BALÁZS, R. 1976. Hormones and brain development. *Progress Brain Res., 45,* 139–159.

BELLAMY, D. 1968. Long-term action of prednisolone phosphate on a strain of short-lived mice. *Exp. Geront., 3,* 327–333.

BERNHEIMER, H., BIRKMAYER, W., HORNYKIEWICZ, O., JELLINGER, K., AND SEITELBERGER, F. 1973. Brain dopamine and the syndromes of Parkinson and Huntingdon. Clinical, morphological and neurochemical correlations. *J. Neurol. Sci., 20,* 415–455.

BIRREN, J. E., AND KAY, H. 1958. Swimming speed of the albino rat. I. Age and sex differences. *J. Geront., 13,* 374–377.

BIRREN, J. E. AND SCHAIE, K. W. 1977. *Handbook of the Psychology of Aging.* New York: Van Nostrand Reinhold.

BLICHERT-TOFT, M. 1975. Secretion of corticotrophin and somatotrophin by the senescent adenohypophysis in man. *Acta Endocrinol., 78,* Suppl. 195, 15–154.

BLICHERT-TOFT, M., BLICHERT-TOFT, B., AND JENSEN, H. K. 1970. Pituitary-adrenocortical stimulation in the aged as reflected in levels of plasma cortisol and compounds. *Acta Chir. Scand., 136,* 665–670.

BLICHERT-TOFT, M., AND HUMMER, L. 1976. Immunoreactive corticotrophin reserve in old age in man during and after surgical stress. *J. Geront., 31,* 539–545.

BLICHERT-TOFT, M., HUMMER, L., AND DIGE-PETERSEN, H. 1975. Human serum thyrotrophin level and response to thyrotrophin-releasing hormone in the aged. *Gerontol. Clin., 17,* 191–203.

BLOCK, E. 1952. Quantitative morphological investigations of the follicular system in women. *Acta Anat., 14,* 108–123.

BLUMENTHAL, H. T. 1976. Immunological aspects of the aging brain. *In,* R. D. Terry and S. Gershon (eds.), *Aging,* Vol. 3, *Neurobiology of Aging,* pp. 313–334. New York: Raven Press.

BOTWINICK, J. 1975. Behavioral processes. *In,* S. Gershon and A. Raskin (eds.), *Aging,* Vol. 2, pp. 1–18. New York: Raven Press.

BOYD, W. 1958. *Pathology for the Physician.* Philadelphia: Lea and Febiger.

BRIZZEE, K. R. 1975. Gross morphometric analyses and quantitative histology of the aging brain. *In,* J. M. Ordy and K. R. Brizzee (eds.), *Neurobiology of Aging,* pp. 401–423. New York/London: Plenum.

BROCKLEHURST, J. C., AND DILLANE, J. B. 1966. Studies of the female bladder in old age. III. Micturating cystograms in incontinent women. *Geront. Clin., 9,* 47–58.

BRODY, H. 1976. An examination of cerebral cortex and brainstem aging. *In,* R. D. Terry and S. Gershon (eds.), *Aging,* Vol. 3, *Neurobiology of Aging,* pp. 177–181. New York: Raven Press.

BRODY, M. J., AND ZIMMERMAN, B. G. 1976. Peripheral circulation in arterial hypertension. *Progr. Cardiovasc. Diseases, 18,* 323–340.

BROWN, J. R. W. C., AND BROWN, M. E. C. 1976. Psychiatric disorders associated with the menopause. *In,* R. J. Beard (ed.), *The Menopause,* pp. 57–79. St. Leonard's House, Lancaster, England: MTP Press.

BROWN, K. S., AND FORBES, W. F. 1976. Concerning the estimation of biological age. *Gerontology, 22,* 428–437.

BROWN-SÉQUARD, C. E. 1889. Des effects produits chez l'homme par des injections sous-cutanées d'un liquide retiré des testicules frais de cobayes et de chiens. *Compt. Rend. Soc. Biol., 41,* 415–422.

BROWNSTEIN, M. 1977. Neurotransmitters and hypothalamic hormones in the central nervous sytem. *Federation Proc., 36,* 1960–1963.

BRUN, A., AND GUSTAFSON, L. 1976. Distribution of cerebral degeneration in Alzheimer's disease. A clinico-pathological study. *Arch. Psychiat. Nervekr., 233* 15–33.

BURCH, P. R., AND GUNZ, F. W. 1967. The distribution of menopausal age in New Zealand; an exploratory study. *N.Z. Med. J., 66,* 6–10.

BURNET, F. M. 1974. *The Biology of Ageing.* Auckland: Auckland University Press Oxford University Press.

BUTTLAR-BRENTANO, K. 1954. Zur Lebengeschichte des Nuclear basilis, tubermammalaris, supraopticus und paraventriculus unter normalen und pathogenen Bedingungen. *J. Hirnforsch., 1,* 337–419.

CALLOWAY, N. O., FOLEY, C. F., AND LAGERBLOOM, P. 1965. Uncertainties in geriatric data. II. Organ size. *J. Am. Geriat. Soc., 13,* 20–28.

CARLSON, H. E., GILLIN, J. C., GORDON, P., AND SNYDER, F. 1972. Absence of sleep-related growth hormone peaks in aged normal subjects and in acromegaly. *J. Clin. Endocrinol., 34,* 1102–1105.

CARROLL, B. J. 1976. Psychoendocrine relationship in affective disorders. *In,* O. W. Hill (ed.), *Modern Trends in Psychosomatic Medicine,* Vol. 3, pp. 121–153. Boston: Butterworths. Cited by Ettigi and Brown, 1977.

CARRUTHERS, M. E. 1969. Aggression and atheroma. *Lancet, 2,* 1170–1171.

CHAKRAVARTI, S., COLLINS, W. P., FORECAST, J. D., NEWTON, J. R., ORAM, D. H. AND STUDD, J. W. W. 1976. Hormonal profiles after the menopause. *Brit. Med. J., 2,* 784–786.

CHARIPPER, H. A., PEARLSTEIN, A., AND BOURNE, G. H. 1961. Ageing changes in the thyroid and pituitary glands. *In,* G. H. Bourne (ed.), *Structural Aspects of Ageing,* pp. 265–276. London: Pitman Medical Publications.

CLEMENS, J. A., AND BENNETT, D. R. 1977. Do aging changes in the preoptic area contribute to loss of cyclic endocrine function? *J. Geront., 32,* 19–24.

CLEMENS, J. A., AND MEITES, J. 1971. Neuroendocrine status of old constant estrous rats. *Neuroendocrinology. 7,* 249–256.

COBLE, Y.D., JR., KOHLER, P. O., CARGILLE, C. M., AND ROSS, G. T. 1969. Production rates and metabolic clearance rates of human follicle-stimulating hormone in premenopausal and postmenopausal women. *J. Clin. Invest. 48,* 359–363.

COMFORT, A. 1969. Test battery to measure ageing rate in man. *Lancet, 2,* 1411–1415.

COOPER, A. J., ISMAIL, A.A., SMITH, C. G., *et al.,* 1970. Androgen function in "psychogenic" and "constitutional" types of impotence. *Brit. Med. J., 3,* 17–20.

CRISTOFALO, V. J. 1975. Hydrocortisone as a modulator of cell division and population life span. *In,* V. J. Cristofalo, J. Roberts, and R. C. Adelman, (eds.), *Explorations in Aging,* pp. 57–79. New York/London: Plenum.

CURSHMANN, H. 1929. *Endocrine disorders.* London: Oxford University Press. Cited by Korenchevsky (1961).

CURTIS, H. J., AND GEBHARD, K. L. 1958. *In, Proceedings* on the 2nd UN International Conference of Peaceful Uses of Atomic Energy, Vol. 22. *Biological Effects of Radiation,* pp. 53–57. New York: United Nations. Cited by Shock (1974).

DENCKLA, W. D. 1973. A pituitary factor inhibiting the effects of the thyroid: its possible role in aging. *In,* C. Eisdorfer and W. E. Fann (eds.), *Psychopharmacology and Aging,* pp. 77–80. New York: Plenum.

DENCKLA, W. D. 1975. A time to die. *Life Sciences, 16,* 31–44.

DENCKLA, W. D. 1976. Pituitary-thyroid axis and aging. *In,* A. V. Everitt and J. A. Burgess (eds.), *Hypothalamus, Pituitary and Aging,* pp. 703–705. Springfield, Ill.: Charles C Thomas.

de QUATTRO, V., BARBOUR, B. H., CAMPESE, V., FINCK, E. J., MIANO, L., AND ESLER, M. 1977. Sympathetic nerve hyperactivity in high-renin hypertension. *Mayo Clin. Proc., 52,* 369–373.

de WIED, D. 1977a. ACTH effects on learning processes. *In,* V. H. T. James (ed.), *Endocrinology,* Vol. 1, pp. 51–56. Amsterdam-Oxford: Excerpta Medica.

de WIED, D. 1977b. Pituitary adrenal systems hormones and behaviour. *Acta Endocrinol., 85,* Suppl. 214, 9–18.

DEWHURST, C. J. 1976. The effects of estrogen replacement therapy on the risk of cancer during the post-menopausal years. *In,* S. Campbell (ed.), *The Management of the Menopause and Post-Menopausal Years.* pp. 339–344. St. Leonards House, Lancaster, England: MTP Press.

DILMAN, V. M. 1971. Age-associated elevation of hypothalamic threshold to feedback control, and its role in development, ageing and disease. *Lancet, 1,* 1211–1219.

DILMAN, V. M. 1976. The hypothalamic control of aging and age-associated pathology. The elevation mechanism of aging. *In,* A. V. Everitt and J. A. Burgess (eds.), *Hypothalamus, Pituitary and Aging,* pp. 634–667. Springfield, Ill.: Charles C Thomas.

DODGE, D. L., AND MARTIN, W. T. 1970. *Social Stress and Chronic Illness.* Notre Dame, Ind.: University of Notre Dame Press.

DÖRNER, G. 1976. *Hormones and Brain Differentiation.* Amsterdam: Elsevier-North Holland.

DRACHMAN, D. A. 1977. Memory and cognitive function in man. Does the cholinergic system have a specific function? *Neurology, 27,* 783–790.

DUDL, R. J., AND ENSINCK, J. W. 1977. Insulin and glucagon relationships during aging in man. *Metabolism, 26,* 33–41.

DUDL, R. J., ENSINCK, J. W., PALMER, H. E., AND WILLIAMS, R. H. 1973. Effect of age on growth hormone secretion in man. *J. Clin. Endocrinol., 37,* 11–16.

EASTWOOD, M. R., AND TREVELYAN, H. 1971. Stress and

coronary heart disease. *J. Psychosom. Res. 15,* 289–292.

EISDORFER, C., AND RASKIND, M. 1975. Aging, hormones and human behavior. *In,* B. E. Eleftheriou and R. L. Sprott (eds.), *Hormonal Correlates of Behavior,* Vol. 1, pp. 369–393. New York/London: Plenum.

ETTIGI, P. G., AND BROWN, G. M. 1977. Psychoneuroendocrinology of affective disorder: An overview. *Am. J. Psychiatry, 134,* 493–501.

EVERITT, A. V. 1959. The effect of pituitary growth hormone on the aging male rat. *J. Geront., 14,* 415–424.

EVERITT, A. V. 1973. The hypothalamic-pituitary control of aging and age-related pathology. *Exp. Geront. 8,* 265–277.

EVERITT, A. V. 1975. The role of the brain in ageing and longevity. *Proc. Australian Assoc. Geront. 2,* 137–139.

EVERITT, A. V. 1976a. Conclusion: Aging and its hypothalamic-pituitary control. *In,* A. V. Everitt and J. A. Burgess (eds.), *Hypothalamus, Pituitary and Aging,* pp. 676–701, Springfield, Ill.: Charles C Thomas.

EVERITT, A. V. 1976b. Hypophysectomy and aging in the rat. *In,* A. V. Everitt and J. A. Burgess (eds.), *Hypothalamus, Pituitary and Aging,* pp. 68–85. Springfield, Ill.: Charles C Thomas.

EVERITT, A. V. 1976c. The nature and measurement of aging. *In,* A. V. Everitt and J. A. Burgess (eds.), *Hypothalamus, Pituitary and Aging,* pp. 5–42. Springfield, Ill.: Charles C Thomas.

EVERITT, A. V. 1976d. The thyroid gland, metabolic rate and aging. *In,* A. V. Everitt and J. A. Burgess (eds.), *Hypothalamus, Pituitary and Aging,* pp. 511–528. Springfield, Ill.: Charles C Thomas.

EVERITT, A. V. 1979. Pituitary function and aging. *In, Aging, A Challenge to Science and Science Policy.* Paris: Institut de la Vie, in press.

EVERITT, A. V., AND BURGESS, J. A. 1976. *Hypothalamus, Pituitary and Aging.* Springfield, Ill.: Charles C Thomas.

FAERMAN, I., GLOCER, L., FOX, D., JADZINSKY, M. N., AND RAPAPORT, M. 1974. Impotence and diabetes. Histological studies of the autonomic nervous fibers of the corpora cavernosa in impotent diabetic males. *Diabetes, 23,* 971–976.

FINCH, C. E. 1973a. Catecholamine metabolism in the brains of ageing male mice. *Brain Res., 52,* 261–276.

FINCH, C. E. 1973b. Monoamine metabolism in the aging male mouse. *In,* M. Rockstein and M. L. Sussman (eds.), *Development and Aging in the Nervous System,* pp. 199–213. New York: Academic Press.

FINCH, C. E. 1975. Aging and the regulation of hormones. A view in October 1974. *In,* R. C. Adelman, J. Roberts, and V. J. Cristofalo (eds.), *Explorations in Aging,* pp. 229–238. New York/London: Plenum.

FINCH, C. E. 1976. The regulation of physiological changes during mammalian aging. *Q. Review Biology, 51,* 49–83.

FINCH, C. E. 1977. Neuroendocrine and autonomic aspects of aging. *In,* C. E. Finch and L. Hayflick (eds.), *Handbook of the Biology of Aging,* pp. 262–280. New York: Van Nostrand Reinhold.

FINCH, C. E., FOSTER, J. R., AND MIRSKY, A. E. 1969. Aging and regulation of cell activities during exposure to cold. *J. Gen. Physiol., 54,* 690–712.

FINCH, C. E., AND HAYFLICK, L. 1977. *Handbook of the Biology of Aging.* New York: Van Nostrand Reinhold.

FINKELSTEIN, J. W., ROFFWARG, H. P., BOYAR, R. M., KREAM, J., AND HILLMAN, L. 1972. Age-related change in the twenty-four hour spontaneous secretion of growth hormone. *J. Clin. Endocrinol., 35,* 665–670.

FOX, R. H., WOODWARD, P. M., EXTON-SMITH, A. N., GREEN, M. F., DONNISON, D. V., AND WICKS, M. H. 1973. Body temperatures in the elderly; a national study of physiological, social and environmental conditions. *Brit. Med. J. 1,* 200–206.

FRANCIS, W. J. A. 1970. Reproduction at menarche and menopause in women. *J. Reprod. Fertility, Suppl. 12,* 89–98.

FRIEDFIELD, L. 1949. Heat reaction states in the aged. *Geriatrics, 4,* 211–216.

FRIEDMAN, M., AND ROSENMAN, R. H. 1974. *Type A Behavior and Your Heart.* New York: Knopf.

FROHLICH, E. D. 1977. The adrenergic nervous system and hypertension. State of the art. *Mayo Clin. Proc., 52,* 361–368.

FROHMAN, L. A., AND STACHURA, M. E. 1975. Neuropharmacologic control of neuroendocrine function in man. *Metabolism, 24,* 211–234.

FROLKIS, V. V. 1976. The hypothalamic mechanisms of aging. *In,* A. V. Everitt and J. A. Burgess (eds.), *Hypothalamus, Pituitary and Aging,* pp. 614–633. Springfield, Ill.: Charles C Thomas.

FROLKIS, V. V., BEZRUKOV, V. V., DUPLENKO, Y. K., AND GENIS, E. D. 1972. The hypothalamus in aging. *Exp. Geront., 7,* 169–184.

FURUKAWA, T., INOUE, M., KAJIYA, F., INADA, H., TAKASUGI, S., FUKUI, S., TAKEDA, H., AND ABE, H. 1975. Assessment of biological age by multiple regression analysis. *J. Geront., 30,* 422–434.

GAFFNEY, G. W., GREGERMAN, R. I., AND SHOCK, N. W. 1962. Relationship of age to the thyroidal accumulation, renal excretion and distribution of radioiodide in euthyroid man. *J. Clin. Endocrinol., 22,* 784–794.

GAY, V. L. 1972. The hypothalamus: physiology and clinical use of releasing factors. *Fertility Sterility, 23,* 50–63.

GILES, J. S., AND EVERITT, A. V. 1967. The role of thyroid and food intake in the ageing of collagen fibres. I. In the young rat. *Gerontologia 13,* 65–69.

GIUSTI, G., GONNELLI, P., BORRELLI, D., FIORELLI, G., FORTI, G., PAZZAGLI, M., AND SERIO, M. 1975. Age-related secretion of androstenedione, testosterone and dihydrotestosterone by the human testis. *Exp. Geront., 10,* 241–245.

GLICK, I. D. 1967. Mood and behavioral changes associated with the use of oral contraceptive agents. *Psychopharmacologia, 10,* 363–374.

GOLDMAN, R., AND ROCKSTEIN M. 1975. *The Physiology and Pathology of Human Aging.* New York: Academic Press.

GOLDSTEIN, M. 1974. Brain research and violent behaviour. *Arch. Neurology, 30,* 1–35.

GOLDZIEHER, J. W., MOSES, L. E., AVERKIN, E., SCHEEL, C., AND TABER, B. Z. 1971. Nervousness and depression attributed to oral contraceptives: a double-blind, placebo-controlled study. *Am. J. Obstet. Gynecol., 111,* 1013–1020.

GRAD, B., KRAL, A., PAYNE, R. C., AND BERENSEN, J. 1967. Plasma and urinary corticoids in young and old persons. *J. Geront., 22,* 66–71.

GRAD, B., ROSENBERG, G. M., LIBERMAN, H., TRACHTENBERG, J., AND KRAL, V. A. 1971. Diurnal variation of the serum cortisol level of geriatric subjects. *J. Geront., 26,* 351–357.

GRANT, I., GERST, M., AND YAGER, J. 1976. Scaling of life events by psychiatric patients and normals. *J. Psychosom. Res., 20,* 141–149.

GRAVE, G. D. 1977. *Thyroid Hormones and Brain Development.* New York: Raven Press.

GREENBLATT, R. B., AND STODDARD, L. D. 1978. The estrogen-cancer controversy. *J. Am. Geriat. Soc., 26,* 1–8.

GREGERMAN, R. I., AND BIERMAN, E. L. 1974. Aging and hormones. *In,* R. H. Williams (ed.), *Textbook of Endocrinology,* 5th ed., pp. 1059–1070. Philadelphia: Saunders.

GREGERMAN, R. I., GAFFNEY, G. W., SHOCK, N. W., AND CROWDER, S. E. 1962. Thyroxine turnover in euthyroid man with special reference to changes with age. *J. Clin. Invest., 41,* 2065–2074.

GRIBBIN, B., PICKERING, T. G., SLEIGHT, P., AND PETO, R. 1971. Effect of age and high blood pressure on baroflex sensitivity in man. *Circulation Res., 29,* 424–431.

GRODIN, J. M., SIITERI, P. K., AND MACDONALD, P. C. 1973. Source of estrogen production in postmenopausal women. *J. Clin. Endocrinol., 36,* 207–214.

GRUEN, P. H., SACHAR, E. J., ALTMAN, N., AND SASSIN, J. 1975. Growth hormone response to hypoglycemia in post-menopausal depressed women. *Arch. Gen. Psychiatry, 32,* 31–33.

GUNDERSON, E. K., AND RAHE, R. H. 1974. *Life Stress and Illness.* Springfield, Ill.: Charles C Thomas.

GUYTON, A. C. 1976. *Textbook of Medical Physiology.* 5th edition. Philadelphia: Saunders.

HAMBURG, D. A., MOOS, R. H., AND YALOM, I. D. 1968. Studies of distress in the menstrual cycle and postpartum period. *In,* R. P. Michael (ed.), *Endocrinology and Human Behavior,* pp. 42–63. London: Oxford University Press.

HAMLIN, C. R., KOHN, R. R., AND LUSCHIN, J. H. 1975. Apparent accelerated aging of human collagen in diabetes mellitus. *Diabetes, 24,* 902–904.

HARRIS, G. W. 1955. *Neural Control of the Pituitary Gland.* London: Edward Arnold.

HARMAN, D. 1972. The biologic clock: The mitochondria? *J. Am. Geriat. Soc., 20,* 145–147.

HASAN, M., GLEES, P., AND EL-GHAZZAWI, E., 1974. Age-associated changes in the hypothalamus of the guinea pig: effect of dimethylaminoethyl p-chlorophenoxyacetate on electron microscopy and histochemical study. *Exp. Geront., 9,* 153–159.

HAUG, E., AAKVAAG, A., SAND, T., AND TORJESEN, P. A. 1974. The gonadotrophin release to synthetic gonadotrophin-releasing hormone in males in relation to age, dose, and basal serum levels of testosterone, oestradiol–17β and gonadotrophins. *Acta Endocrinol., 77,* 625–635.

HAYFLICK, L. 1970. Aging under glass. *Exp. Geront., 5,* 291–303.

HERMAN, E. 1976. Senile hypophyseal syndromes. *In,* A. V. Everitt and J. A. Burgess (eds.), *Hypothalamus, Pituitary and Aging,* pp. 157–170. Springfield, Ill.: Charles C Thomas.

HOLLINGSWORTH, J. W., HASHIZUME, A., AND JABLON, S. 1965. Correlations between tests of aging in Hiroshima subjects—an attempt to define "physiologic" age. *Yale J. Biol. Med., 38,* 11–26.

HOLMES, T. H., AND RAHE, R. H. 1967. The social readjustment rating scale. *J. Psychosom. Res., 11,* 213–218.

HOROWITZ, M. 1977. Life event questionnaires for measuring presumptive stresses. *Psychosomat. Med., 39,* 413–431.

HORVATH, S. M., RADCLIFFE, C. E., HUTT, B. K., AND SPURR, G. B. 1958. Metabolic response of old people to a cold environment. *J. Appl. Physiol., 8,* 145–148.

HUANG, C. Y., AND WALSH, J. C. 1974. Pathologic changes in the greater splanchnic nerve of subjects with diabetic peripheral neuropathy. *Proc. Australian Assoc. Neurologists,* 13–18.

HUANG, H. H., AND MEITES, J. 1975. Reproductive capacity of aging female rats. *Neuroendocrinology, 17,* 289–295.

ISMAIL, A. A., AND HARKNESS, R. A. 1967. Urinary testosterone excretion in man in normal and pathological conditions. *Acta Endocrinol., 56,* 469–480.

JACUBCZAK, L. F. 1976. Behavioral aspects of nutrition and longevity in animals. *In,* M. Rockstein and M. L. Sussman (eds.), *Nutrition, Longevity, and Aging,* pp. 103–122. New York: Academic Press.

JASZMANN, L. 1973. Epidemiology of climacteric and post-climacteric complaints. *In*, P. A. van Keep and C. Lauritzen (eds.), *Ageing and Estrogens. Front. Hormone Res. 2*, pp. 22–34. Basel: Karger.

JASZMANN, L. J. B. 1976. Epidemiology of the climacteric syndrome. *In*, S. Campbell (ed.), *The Management of the Menopause & Post-Menopausal Years*, pp. 11–24. St. Leonards House, Lancaster, England: MTP.

JENSEN, H. K., AND BLICHERT-TOFT, M. 1971. Serum corticotrophin, plasma cortisol and urinary excretion of 17–ketogenic steroids in the elderly (age group 66–94 years). *Acta Endocrinol., 66*, 25–34.

JOHNSON, H. D., KIBLER, H. H., AND SILSBY, H. 1964. The influence of ambient temperature of 9°C and 28°C on thyroid function of rats during growth and aging. *Gerontologia, 9*, 18–27.

JOHNSON, H. D., KINTNER, L. D., AND KIBLER, H. H. 1963. Effects of 48°F (8.9°C) and 83°F (28.4°C) on longevity and pathology of male rats. *J. Geront., 18*, 29–36.

JONES, E. C., AND KROHN, P. L. 1961. The effect of hypophysectomy on age changes in the ovaries of mice. *J. Endocrinol., 21*, 497–509.

KALK, W. J., VINIK, A. I., PIMSTONE, B. L., AND JACKSON, W. P. U. 1973. Growth hormone response to insulin hypoglycemia in the elderly. *J. Geront., 28*, 431–433.

KANE, F., DALY, R., EWING, J., AND KEELER, M. A. 1967. Mood and behavioural changes with progestational agents. *Brit. J. Psychiat., 113*, 265–268.

KANUNGO, M. S., PATNAIK, S. K., AND KOUL, O. 1975. Decrease in 17β–oestradiol receptor in brain of ageing rats. *Nature, 253*, 366–367.

KASTIN, A. J., PLOTNIKOFF, N. P., SCHALLY, A. V., AND SANDMAN, C. A. 1976. Endocrine and CNS effects of hypothalamic peptides and MSH. *In*, S. Ehrenpreis and I. J. Kopin (eds.), *Reviews of Neuroscience*, Vol. 2, pp. 111–139. New York: Raven Press.

KENNEDY, G. 1950. The hypothalamic control of food intake in rats. *Proc. Roy. Soc. London, 137B*, 535–549.

KENNEDY, G. C. 1957. Effects of old age and overnutrition on the kidney. *Br. Med. Bull., 13*, 67–70.

KINSEY, A. C., POMEROY, W. B., AND MARTIN, C. E. 1948. *Sexual Behavior in the Human Male*. Philadelphia: Saunders.

KINSEY, A. C., POMEROY, W. B., MARTIN, C. I., AND GEBHARD, P. H. 1953. *Sexual Behavior in the Human Female*. Philadelphia: Saunders.

KOHLER, P. O., ROSS, G. T., AND ODELL, W. D. 1968. Metabolic clearance and production rates of human luteinizing hormone in pre- and postmenopausal women. *J. Clin. Invest., 47*, 38–47.

KOHN, R. R. 1963. Human aging and disease. *J. Chronic Diseases, 16*, 5–21.

KOHN, R. R. 1965. Aging as a consequence of growth

cessation. *In*, M. Locke (ed.), *Reproduction: Molecular, Subcellular and Cellular*, pp. 291–324. New York: Academic Press.

KORENCHEVSKY, V. 1961. *Physiological and Pathological Ageing*. Basel/New York: Karger.

KORENMAN, S. G., PERRIN, L. E., AND McCALLUM, T. P. 1969. A radio-ligand binding assay for estradiol measurement in human plasma. *J. Clin. Endocrinol., 29*, 879–883.

KOVACS, K., RYAN, N., HORVATH, E., PENZ, G., AND EZRIN, C. 1977. Prolactin cells of the human pituitary gland in old age. *J. Geront., 32*, 534–540.

KRAG, C. L., AND KOUNTZ, W. B. 1950. Stability of body function in the aged. I. Effect of exposure of the body to cold. *J. Geront., 5*, 227–235.

LAIS, L. T., BHATNAGER, R. K., AND BRODY, M. J. 1975. Role of the sympathetic nervous system in development and maintenance of spontaneous hypertension. *In*, S. Julius and M. D. Esler (eds.), *The Nervous System in Arterial Hypertension*, pp. 76–95. Springfield, Ill.: Charles C Thomas.

LANSING, A. I. 1948. Evidence for aging as a consequence of growth cessation. *Proc. Nat. Acad. Sci., 34*, 304–310.

LAWRENCE, J. H., TOBIAS, C. A., LINFOOT, J. A., BARN, J. L., LYMAN, J. T., CHONG, C. Y., MANOUGIAN, E., AND WEI, W. C. 1970. Successful treatment of acromegaly: metabolic and clinical studies in 145 patients. *J. Clin. Endocrinol., 31*, 180–198.

LE MAGNEN, J., DEVOS, M., GUADILLIERE, J., LOUIS-SYLVESTRE, J., AND TALLON, S. 1973. Role of a lipostatic mechanism in regulation by feeding of energy balance in rats. *J. Comp. Physiol. Psychol., 84*, 1–23.

LEWIS, A., AND HOGHUGHI, M. 1969. An evaluation of depression as a side effect of oral contraceptives. *Brit. J. Psychiatr. 115*, 697–701.

LIN, K. H., PENG, Y. M., PENG, M. T., AND TSENG, T. M. 1976. Changes in the nuclear volume of rat hypothalamic neurons in old age. *Neuroendocrinology, 21*, 247–254.

LIU, R. K., AND WALFORD, R. L. 1972. The effect of lowered body temperature on lifespan and immune and non-immune processes. *Gerontologia, 18*, 363–388.

LONGCOPE, C. 1971. Metabolic clearance and production rates of estrogens in postmenopausal women. *Am. J. Obstet. Gynecol., 111*, 778–781.

LORAND, M. A. 1904. Quelques considérations sur les causes de la sénilité. *C. R. Soc. Biol., 57*, 500–502.

LORAND, A. 1921. *Old Age Deferred*, 5th ed. Philadelphia: Davis.

LOW, P. A., AND DYCK, P. J. 1978. Effect of age and disease on the splanchnic outflow in man. *Neurology, 28*, 391.

LOWENTHAL, M., AND BERKMAN, P. L. 1967. *Aging and*

*Mental Disorder in San Francisco.* San Francisco: Jossey-Bass. Cited by Weg 1975.

LYNCH, J. L. 1977. *The Broken Heart: The Medical Consequences of Loneliness.* New York: Basic Books.

MACPHERSON, R. K., OFNER, F., AND WELCH, J. A. 1967. Effect of prevailing air temperature on mortality. *Brit. J. Prevent. Social Med., 21,* 17–21.

MANN, G. V. 1974. The influence of obesity on health. *New Engl. J. Med., 291,* 178–185, 226–232 (2 parts).

MASTERS, W. H. 1957. Sex steroid influence on the aging process. *Am. J. Obstet. Gynecol., 74,* 733–742.

MASTERS, W. H., AND JOHNSON, V. 1970. *Human Sexual Response.* Boston: Little, Brown.

MATTHEWS, K. A., GLASS, D. C., ROSENMAN, R. H., AND BORTNER, R. W. 1977. Competitive drive, pattern A, and coronary heart disease; a further analysis of some data from the Western Collaborative Group Study. *J. Chronic Diseases, 30,* 489–498.

MAY, R. 1969. *Love and Will.* New York: Norton. Cited by Weg, 1975.

MAYER, J., AND THOMAS, D. W. 1967. Regulation of food intake and obesity. *Science, 156,* 328–337.

MCGEER, E. G., AND MCGEER, P. L. 1975. Age changes in the human for some enzymes associated with metabolism of catecholamines, GABA and acetylcholine. *In,* J. M. Ordy and K. E. Brizzee (eds.), *Neurobiology of Aging,* pp. 287–305. New York: Plenum.

MCQUADE, W., AND AIKMAN, A. 1976. *Stress. How to Stop Your Mind Killing Your Body.* London: Hutchinson.

MEYER, J. S., WELCH, K. M. A., DESHMUKH, V. D., PEREZ, F. I., JACOB, R. H., HAUFRECT, D. B., MATHEW, N. T., AND MORRELL, R. M. 1977. Neurotransmitter precursor amino acids in the treatment of multi-dementia and Alzheimer's disease. *J. Am. Geriat. Soc., 25,* 289–298.

MILLER, A. E., SHAAR, C. J., AND RIEGLE, G. D. 1976. Aging effects on hypothalamic dopamine and norepinephrine content in the male rat. *Exp. Aging Res., 2,* 475–480.

MONTI, P. M., BROWN, W. A., AND CORRIVEAU, D. P. 1977. Testosterone and components of aggressive and sexual behavior in man. *Am. J. Psychiatry, 134,* 692–694.

MORGAN, C. T., AND KING, R. A. 1975. *Introduction to Psychology.* 5th Edition. New York: McGraw-Hill.

MUKHERJEE, A. P., CONI, N. K., AND DAVISON, W. 1973. Osmoreceptor function among the elderly. *Gerontol. Clin., 15,* 227–233.

MYERS, R. D., AND YAKSH, T. L. 1972. The role of hypothalamic monoamines in hibernation and hypothermia. *In,* F. E. South, J. P. Hannon, J. R. Willis, E. T. Pengelley, and N. R. Alpert (eds.), *Hibernation and Hypothermia, Perspectives and Challenges,* pp. 551–575. New York: American Elsevier.

NANDY, K., AND SHERWIN, I. (eds.), 1977. *The Aging Brain and Senile Dementia.* New York: Plenum.

NELSON, J. F., HOLINKA, C. F., LATHAM, K. R., ALLEN, J. K., AND FINCH, C. E. 1976. Corticosterone binding in cytosols from brain regions of mature and senescent C57BL/6J male mice. *Brain Res., 115,* 345–351.

NEUGARTEN, B. L., AND KRAINE, R. J. 1967. Menopausal symptoms in women of various ages. *In,* L. Gitman (ed.), *Endocrines and Aging,* pp. 218–230. Springfield, Ill.: Charles C Thomas.

NISBETT, R. E., BRAVER, A., JUSELA, G., AND KEZUR, D. 1975. Age and sex differences in behaviors mediated by the ventromedial hypothalamus. *J. Comp. Physiol. Psychol., 88,* 735–746.

NORRIS, A. H., AND SHOCK, N. W. 1960. Exercise in the adult years—with special reference to the advanced years. *In,* W. R. Johnson (ed.), *Science and Medicine of Exercise and Sports,* pp. 466–490. New York: Harper.

NOTH, R. H., LASSMAN, N., TAN, S. Y., FERNANDEZ-CRUZ, A., AND MULROW, P. J. 1977. Age and the renin-aldosterone system. *Arch. Int. Med., 137,* 1414–1417.

O'BRIEN, M. D. 1977. Vascular disease and dementia in the elderly. *In,* W. L. Smith, and M. Kinsbourne (eds.), *Aging and Dementia,* pp. 57–76. Jamaica, New York: Spectrum.

ODDIE, T. H., MYHILL, J., PIRNIQUE, F. G., AND FISHER, D. A. 1968. Effect of age and sex on the radioiodine uptake in euthyroid subjects. *J. Clin. Endocrinol., 28,* 776–782.

OOKA, H., SEGALL, P. E., AND TIMIRAS, P. S. 1978. Neural and endocrine development after chronic tryptophan deficiency in rats: II. Pituitary-thyroid axis. *Mech. Age. Dev., 7,* 19–24.

OKAMATO, K., NOSAKA, S., AND YAMORI, Y. 1967. Participation of neural factors in the pathogenesis of hypertension in the spontaneously hypertensive rat. *Jap. Heart J. 8,* 168–180.

ORDY, J. M. 1975. Neurobiology and aging in nonhuman primates. *In,* J. M. Ordy and K. E. Brizzee (eds.), *Neurobiology of Aging,* pp. 575–597. New York/London: Plenum.

ORDY, J. M. AND BRIZZEE, K. R. 1975. *Neurobiology of Aging.* New York/London: Plenum.

ORDY, J. M., AND KAACK, B. 1976. Psychoneuroendocrinology and aging in man. *In,* M. F. Elias, B. E. Eleftheriou, and P. K. Elias (eds.), *Special Review of Experimental Aging Research,* pp. 255–299. Bar Harbor: EAR, Inc.

ORDY, J. M., SAMORAJSKI, T., ZEMAN, W., AND CURTIS, H. J. 1967. Interaction effects of environmental stress and deuteron irradiation of the brain on mortality and longevity of C57BL/10 mice. *Proc. Soc. Biol. Med. 126,* 184–190.

PARÉ, W. P. 1965. The effect of chronic environmental stress on premature aging in the rat. *J. Geront., 20,* 78–84.

PASCHKIS, K. E., RAKOFF, A. E., CANTAROW, A., AND RUPP, J. J. 1967. *Clinical Endocrinology,* 3rd edition. New York: Harper & Row.

PECILE, A., MÜLLER, E., FALCONI, G., AND MARTINI, L. 1965. Growth hormone releasing activity of hypothalamic extracts at different ages. *Endocrinology, 77,* 241–246.

PENFIELD, W. G., AND JASPER, H. H. 1954. *Epilepsy of the Human Brain.* Boston: Little, Brown.

PENG, M. T., PENG, Y. I., AND CHEN, F. N. 1977. Age-dependent changes in the oxygen consumption of the cerebral cortex, hypothalamus hippocampus and amygdaloid in rats. *J. Geront., 32,* 517–522.

PENG, M. T., AND PENG, Y. M. 1973. Changes in the uptake of tritiated estradiol in the hypothalamus and adenohypophysis of old female rats. *Fertility Sterility, 24,* 534–539.

PFEIFFER, E., AND DAVIS, G. C. 1972. Determinants of sexual behavior in middle and old age. *J. Am. Geriat. Soc., 20,* 151–158.

PITTS, F. N., AND GUZE, S. B. 1961. Psychiatric disorders and myxedema. *Am. J. Psychiat., 118,* 142–147.

PRANGE, A. J. JR. 1974. *The Thyroid Axis, Drugs and Behavior.* New York: Raven Press.

PRIBRAM, B. O. 1927. Zur Frage des Alterns. Destruktiv Hypophyseo-thyreoditis. Pathologisches Altern und pathologischer Schlaf. *Virchows Arch. Path. Anat., 264,* 498–521.

QUADRI, S. K., KLEDZIK, G. S., AND MEITES, J. 1973. Reinitiation of estrous cycles in old constant-estrous rats by central-acting drugs. *Neuroendocrinology, 11,* 248–255.

QUAY, W. B. 1972. Pineal homeostatic regulation of shifts in the circadian activity rhythm during maturation and aging. *Trans. N.Y. Acad. Sci., 34,* 239–254.

RASMUSSEN, A. T. 1938. The proportions of the various subdivisions of the normal human hypophysis cerebri. *Res. Publ. Assoc. Nerv. Ment. Dis., 17,* 118–150.

RIEGLE, G. D. 1973. Chronic stress effects on adrenocortical responsiveness in young and aged rats. *Neuroendocrinology, 11,* 1–10.

RIEGLE, G. 1976. Aging and adrenocortical function. *In,* A. V. Everitt and J. A. Burgess (eds.), *Hypothalamus, Pituitary and Aging,* pp. 547–552. Springfield, Ill.: Charles C Thomas.

RIEGLE, G. D., AND HESS, G. D. 1972. Chronic and acute dexamethasone suppression of stress activation of the adrenal cortex in young and aged rats. *Neuroendocrinology, 9,* 175–187.

RIEGLE, G. D., MEITES J., MILLER, A. E., AND WOOD, S. M. 1977. Effect of aging on hypothalamic LH-releasing and prolactin inhibiting activities and pituitary responsiveness to LHRH in the male laboratory rat. *J. Geront., 32,* 13–18.

ROBERTSON, T. B. 1928. The influence of thyroid alone and of thyroid administered together with nucleic acids upon the growth and longevity of the white mouse. *Aust. J. Exp. Biol. Med., 5,* 69–88.

ROBINSON, D. S. 1975. Changes in monoamine oxidase and monoamines with human development and aging. *Federation Proc., 34,* 103–107.

ROCKSTEIN, M. 1974. *Theoretical Aspects of Aging.* New York: Academic Press.

ROCKSTEIN, M., CHESKY, J. A., AND SUSSMAN, M. L. 1977. Comparative biology and evolution of aging. *In,* C. E. Finch and L. Hayflick (eds.), *Handbook of the Biology of Aging,* pp. 3–34. New York: Van Nostrand Reinhold.

ROMANOFF, L. P., BAXTER, M. N., THOMAS, A. W., AND FERRECHIO, G. B. 1969. Effect of ACTH on the metabolism of pregnenolone 7$\alpha^3$H and cortisol -4-$^{14}$C in young and elderly men. *J. Clin. Endocrinol., 29,* 819–830.

ROMANOFF, L. P., MORRIS, C. W., WELCH, P., RODRIGUEZ, R. M., AND PINCUS, G., 1961. The metabolism of cortisol-4-$^{14}$C in young and elderly men. *J. Clin. Endocrinol., 21,* 1413–1425.

ROOT, A. W., AND OSKI, F. A. 1969. Effects of human growth hormone in elderly males. *J. Geront., 24,* 97–104.

ROSOW, I. 1973. The social context of the aging self. *Gerontologist, 13,* No. 1, 82–87.

ROSS, G. T., AND VANDEWIELE, R. L. 1974. The ovaries. *In,* R. H. Williams (ed.), *Textbook of Endrocrinology,* pp. 368–422. Philadelphia: Saunders.

ROTH, G. S. 1974. Age-related changes in specific glucocorticoid binding by steroid responsive tissues of rats. *Endocrinology, 94,* 82–90.

ROTH, G. S. 1976. Reduced glucocorticoid binding site concentration in cortical neuronal perikarya from senescent rats. *Brain Res., 107,* 345–354.

ROTHCHILD, I. 1967. The neurologic basis for the anovulation of the luteal phase, lactation and pregnancy. *In,* G. E. Lamming and E. C. Amoroso (eds.), *Reproduction in the Female Mammal,* pp. 30–54. London: Butterworth.

RUBENSTEIN, H. A., BUTLER, V. P. JR., AND WERNER, S. C. 1973. Progressive decrease in serum triiodothyronine concentrations with human aging: radioimmunoassay following extraction of serum. *J. Clin. Endocrinol., 37,* 247–253.

RULLO, F. R., AND ALLAN, R. N. 1958. Psychosis resulting from myxedema. *J. Am. Med. Assoc., 168,* 890–891.

RUSSEK, H. I., AND RUSSEK, L. G. 1977. Behavior patterns and emotional stress in the etiology of coronary heart disease: sociological and occupational aspects. *In,* D. Wheatley (ed.), *Stress and the Heart,* pp. 15–32. New York: Raven Press.

RUST, J. E., LANGLEY, I. I., HILL, E. C., AND LAMB, E. J. 1977. Panel discussion. Estrogens: Do the risks outweigh the benefits? *Am. J. Obst. Gynecol., 128,* 431–439.

SACHAR, E. J. 1975a. Evidence for neuroendocrine abnormalities in the major mental illnesses. *Res. Publ. Assoc. Nerv. Ment. Dis., 54,* 347–358.

SACHAR, E. J. 1975b. Neuroendocrine abnormalities in depressive illness. *In,* E. J. Sachar (ed.), *Topics in Psychoendocrinology,* pp. 135–156. New York: Grune & Stratton.

SACHAR, E. J. 1976. *Hormones, Behavior, and Psychopathology.* New York: Raven Press.

SACHAR, E. J., HELLMAN, L., ROFFWARG, H. P., HALPERN, F. S., FUKUSHIMA, D. K., AND GALLAGHER, T. F. 1973. Disrupted 24-hour patterns of cortisol secretion in psychotic depression. *Arch. Gen. Psychiatry, 28,* 19–24.

SAKODA, M., FUKUDA, T., MORI, H., TATEIWA, M., KUSAKA, T., AND BABA, S. 1975. The pituitary reserve of thyrotropin secretion in aged subjects. *Kobe J. Med. Sci., 21,* 61–67.

SAMORAJSKI, T. 1977. Central neurotransmitter substances and aging: a review. *J. Am. Geriat. Soc., 25,* 337–348.

SAMUELS, L. T. 1956. Effects of aging on steroid metabolism. *In,* E. T. Engle and G. Pincus (eds.), *Hormones and the Aging Process.* pp. 21–38. New York: Academic Press.

SARVEDRA, J. M., GROBECKER, H., AND AXELROD, J. 1977. Biochemical and morphologic study of catecholamine metabolism in spontaneously hypertensive rats. *Mayo Clin. Proc., 52,* 391–394.

SCHILDKRAUT, J. J. 1965. The catecholamine hypothesis of affective disorders: a review of supporting evidence. *Am. J. Psychiatry, 122,* 509–522.

SCHILDKRAUT, J. J. 1970. *Neuropsychopharmacology and the Affective Disorders.* Boston: Little, Brown.

SCHJEIDE, O. J. 1975. Relation of development and aging; pre- and postnatal differentiation of the brain as related to aging. *In,* J. M. Ordy and K. R. Brizzee (eds.), *Neurobiology of Aging,* pp. 37–83. New York/London: Plenum.

SCHUMAN, S. H., ANDERSON, C. P., AND OLIVER, J. T. 1964. Epidemiology of successive heat waves in Michigan in 1962 and 1963. *J. Am. Med. Assoc., 189,* 733–738.

SEGALL, P. E., OOKA, H., ROSE, K., AND TIMIRAS, P. S. 1978. Neural and endocrine development after chronic tryptophan deficiency in rats: 1. Brain monoamine and pituitary responses. *Mech. Age. Dev., 7,* 1–17.

SEGALL, P. E., AND TIMIRAS, P. S. 1975. Age-related changes in thermoregulatory capacity of tryptophan-deficient rats. *Fed. Proc., 34,* 83–85.

SEGALL, P. E., AND TIMIRAS, P. S. 1976. Patho-physiologic findings after chronic tryptophan deficiency in

rats: a model for delayed growth and aging. *Mech. Age. Dev., 5,* 109–124.

SELYE, H., AND PRIORESCHI, P. 1960. Stress theory of aging. *In,* N. W. Shock (ed.), *Aging. Some Social and Biological Aspects,* pp. 261–272. Washington, D.C.: American Association for the Advancement of Science.

SELYE, H., AND TUCHWEBER, B. 1976. Stress in relation to aging and disease. *In,* A. V. Everitt and J. A. Burgess (eds.), *Hypothalamus, Pituitary and Aging,* pp. 553–569. Springfield, Ill.: Charles C Thomas.

SEVRINGHAUS, A. E. 1944. Cytology of the anterior pituitary of the postmenopausal woman. *J. Clin. Endocrinol., 4,* 583–588.

SEYLER, L. E. JR., AND REICHLIN, S. 1973. Luteinizing hormone-releasing factor (LRF) in plasma of postmenopausal women. *J. Clin. Endocrinol., 37,* 197–203.

SHAAR, C. J., EUKER, J. S., RIEGLE, G. D., AND MEITES, J. 1975. Effects of castration and gonadal steroids on serum LH and prolactin in old and young rats. *J. Endocrinol., 66,* 45–51.

SHAGAN, B. P. 1976. Is diabetes a model for aging? *Med. Clin. N. Am., 60,* 1209–1211.

SHANKLIN, W. M. 1953. Age changes in the histology of the human pituitary. *Acta Anat.* (Basel), *19,* 290–304.

SHARMA, A. V., AND THOMAS, P. K. 1973. Quantitative studies on age changes in unmyelinated nerve fibres in the vagus nerve in men. *In,* K. Kunze and J. F. Desmedt (eds.), *Studies in Neuromuscular Diseases, Proc. Int. Symp. Giessen,* pp. 211–219. Basel: Karger.

SHARMAN, A. 1962. The menopause. *In,* S. Zuckerman (ed.), *The Ovary,* Vol. 1, pp. 539–551. New York: Academic Press.

SHERMAN, B. M., AND KORENMAN, S. G. 1975. Hormonal characteristics of the human menstrual cycle throughout reproductive life. *J. Clin. Invest., 55,* 699–706.

SHOEMAKER, E. S., FORNEY, J. F., AND MACDONALD, P. C. 1977. Estrogen treatment of postmenopausal women. Benefits and risks. *J. Am. Med. Assoc., 238,* 1524–1530.

SHOCK, N. W. 1974. Physiological theories of aging. *In,* M. Rockstein, M. L. Sussman, and J. Chesky (eds.), *Theoretical Aspects of Aging,* pp. 119–136. New York: Academic Press.

SIEGEL, G. J., AND EISENMAN, J. S. 1972. Hypothalamic-pituitary regulation. *In,* R. W. Albers, G. J. Siegel, R. Katzman, and B. W. Agranoff (eds.), *Basic Neurochemistry,* pp. 341–364. Boston: Little, Brown.

SIMMONDS, M. 1914. Ueber Hypophysisschwund mit tödlichen Ausgang. *Deutsche Med. Wochenschrift, 11,* 322–323.

SIMPKINS, J. W., MUELLER, G. P., HUANG, H. H., AND

MEITES, J. 1977. Evidence for depressed catecholamine and enhanced serotonin metabolism in aging male rats—possible relation to gonadotropin. *Endocrinology, 100,* 1672–1678.

SINNETT, P., AND WHYTE, M. 1978. Life style, health and disease: A comparison between Papua New Guinea and Australia. *Med. J. Australia, 1,* 1–5.

SMITH, P. E. 1930. Hypophysectomy and replacement therapy in the rat. *Am. J. Anat., 45,* 205–273.

SNYDER, P. J., REITANO, J. F., AND UTIGER, R. D. 1975. Serum LH and FSH response to synthetic gonadotropin-releasing hormone in normal men. *J. Clin. Endocrinol., 41,* 938–945.

SNYDER, P. J., AND UTIGER, R. D. 1972. Response to thyrotropin releasing hormone (TRH) in normal man. *J. Clin. Endocrinol., 34,* 380–385.

SOLOMON, D. H., AND SHOCK, N. W. 1950. Studies of adrenal cortical and anterior pituitary function in elderly men. *J. Geront., 5,* 302–313.

SPOERRI, P. E., AND GLEES, P. 1975. The mode of lipofuscin removal from hypothalamic neurons. *Exp. Geront., 10,* 225–228.

STEARNS, E. L., MACDONNELL, J. A., KAUFMAN, B. J., PADUA, R., LUCMAN, T. S., WINTER, J. S. D., AND FAIMAN, C. 1974. Declining testicular function with age. Hormonal and clinical correlates. *Am. J. Med., 57,* 761–766.

STEINACH, E. 1920. *Die Verjungung durch experimentelle Neubelebung der alternden Puberstätsdrüsen.* Berlin: Springer.

STEWARD, V. W., AND BRANDES, D. 1961. The accessory male sex glands and their changes with age. *In,* G. H. Bourne (ed.), *Structural Aspects of Ageing,* pp. 399–414. New York: Hafner.

STILL, J. W. 1969. The cybernetic theory of aging. *J. Am. Geriat. Soc., 17,* 625–637.

STREETON, D. H. P., GERSTEIN, M. M., MARMOR, B. M., AND DOISY, R. J. 1965. Reduced glucose tolerance in elderly human subjects. *Diabetes, 14,* 579–583.

STREHLER, B. L. 1959. Origin and comparison of the effects of time and high energy radiations on living organisms. *Q. Rev. Biol., 34,* 117–142.

STUNKARD, A. J. 1976. Nutrition, aging and obesity. *In,* M. Rockstein and M. L. Sussman (eds.), *Nutrition, Longevity and Aging,* pp. 253–284. New York: Academic Press.

TANNER, O. 1976. *Stress.* New York: Time-Life Books Inc.

TAYLOR, S. G. 1956. Endocrine therapy in the aged patient. *Med. Clin. N. Am., 43,* 135–144.

TELFORD, C. W., AND SAWREY, J. M. 1968. *Psychology. A Concise Introduction to the Fundamentals of Behavior.* Belmont, California: Brooks/Cole.

TERRY, R. D., AND GERSHON, S. 1976. *Neurobiology of Aging, Aging,* Vol. 3. New York: Raven Press.

THOMPSON, B., HART, S. A., AND DURNO, D. 1973. Meno-pausal age and symptomatology in a general practice. *J. Biosoc. Sci., 5,* 71–82.

TIMIRAS, P. S. 1972. *Developmental Physiology and Aging.* New York: Macmillan.

TIMIRAS, P. S., AND BIGNAMI, A. 1976. *In,* M. F. Elias, B. E. Eleftheriou, and P. K. Elias (eds.), *Special Review of Experimental Aging Research,* pp. 351–378. Bar Harbor: EAR, Inc.

TIMIRAS, P. S., AND MEISAMI, E. 1972. Changes in gonadal function. *In,* P. S. Timiras (ed.), *Developmental Physiology and Aging.* pp. 527–541. New York: Macmillan.

TSAI, C. C., AND YEN, S. S. C. 1971. Acute effects of intravenous infusions of 17β-estradiol on gonadotropin release in pre- and post-menopausal women. *J. Clin. Endocrinol., 32,* 766–771.

TURKINGTON, M., AND EVERITT, A. V. 1976. The neurohypophysis and aging with special reference to the antidiuretic hormone. *In,* A. V. Everitt and J. A. Burgess (eds.), *Hypothalamus, Pituitary and Aging,* pp. 123–136. Springfield, Ill.: Charles C Thomas.

USDIN, E., KVETNANSKY, R., AND KOPIN, I. J. 1976. *Catecholamines and Stress.* Oxford: Pergamon Press.

UTIAN, W. H. 1972. The true clinical features of postmenopause and oophorectomy, and their response to oestrogen therapy. *S. Afr. Med. J., 46,* 732.

VAN LOOK, P. F. A., LOTHIAN, H., HUNTER, W. H., MICHIE, E. A., AND BAIRD, D. T. 1977. Hypothalamic-pituitary-ovarian function in perimenopausal women. *Clin. Endocr., 7,* 13–31.

VARA, P. 1970. The climacterium from the gynecologist's point of view. *Acta Obstet. Gynecol. Scand., 49,* Suppl. 1, 43–55.

VEKEMANS, M. AND ROBYN, C. 1975. Influence of age on serum prolactin levels in women and men. *Brit. Med. J., 2,* 738–739.

VERMEULEN, A. 1976. Leydig-cell function in old age. *In,* A. V. Everitt and J. A. Burgess (eds.), *Hypothalamus, Pituitary and Aging,* pp. 458–463. Springfield, Ill.: Charles C Thomas.

VERMEULEN, A., RUBENS, R., AND VERDONCK, L. 1972. Testosterone secretion and metabolism in male senescence. *J. Clin. Endocrinol., 34,* 730–735.

VIJAYAN, E. AND McCANN, S. M. 1977. Suppression of feeding and drinking activity in rats following intraventricular injection of thyrotropin releasing hormone (TRH). *Endocrinology, 100,* 1727–1730.

VORONOFF, S. 1926. *Study of Aging and Rejuvenation by Grafting.* Paris: Doin.

WALLING, B. G., DELIUS, W., AND HAGBARTH, K. E. 1973. Sympathetic activity in peripheral nerves of normo- and hypertensive subjects. *Clin. Sci. Mol. Med., 45,* Suppl. 127S.

WATKINS, B. E., McKAY, D. W., MEITES, J., AND RIEGLE, G. D. 1975. L-dopa effects on serum LH and prolactin in old and young female rats. *Neuroendocrinology, 19,* 331–338.

WATTHANA-KASETR, S. AND SPIERS, P. S. 1973. Geographic mortality rates and rates of aging—a possible relationship? *J. Geront., 28,* 374–379.

WEBSTER, I. W., AND LOGIE, A. R. 1974. An assessment of aging based on screening data. *J. Am. Geriat. Soc., 22,* 360–364.

WEG, R. B. 1975. Sexual inadequacy in the elderly. *In,* R. Goldman and M. Rockstein (eds.), *The Physiology and Pathology of Human Aging,* pp. 203–227. New York: Academic Press.

WEINSHILBOUM, R. M. 1977. Serum dopamine-β-hydroxylase activity and blood pressure. *Mayo Clin. Proc., 52,* 374–378.

WEISSMAN, M. M., AND SLABY, A. E. 1973. Oral contraceptives and psychiatric disturbance: Evidence from research. *Brit. J. Psychiat., 123,* 513–518.

WENZEL, B. M. 1972. Immunosympathectomy and behavior. *In,* G. Steiner and E. Schönbaum (eds.), *Immunosympathectomy,* pp. 199–219. Amsterdam: Elsevier.

WERNER, A. A. 1939. The male climacteric. *J. Am. Med. Assoc., 112,* 1441–1443.

WEST, C. D., BROWN, H., SIMONS, E. L., CARTER, D. B., KUMAGAI, L. I., AND ENGLERT, E. JR. 1961. Adren-ocortical function and cortisol metabolism in old age. *J. Clin. Endocrinol., 21,* 1197–1207.

WEXLER, B. C. 1976. Comparative aspects of hyperadrenocorticism and aging. *In,* A. V. Everitt and J. A. Burgess (eds.), *Hypothalamus, Pituitary and Aging,* pp. 333–361. Springfield, Ill.: Charles C. Thomas.

WHITE, P., HILEY, C. R., GOODHART, M. J., CARRASCO, L. H., KEET, J. P., WILLIAMS, I. E. I., AND BOWEN, D. M. 1977. Neocortical cholinergic neurons in elderly people. *Lancet, 1,* 668–671.

WHYBROW, P. C., PRANGE, A. J., AND TREADWAY, C. R. 1969. Mental changes accompanying thyroid gland dysfunction. *Arch. Gen. Psychiat., 20,* 48–63.

WISE, A. J., GROSS, M. A., AND SCHALCH, D. S. 1973. Quantitative relationships of the pituitary gonadal axis in postmenopausal women. *J. Lab. Clin. Med., 81,* 28–36.

WRIGHT, A. D., HILL, D. M., LOWY, C., AND FRASER, T. R. 1970. Mortality in acromegaly. *Quart. J. Med., 39,* 1–16.

YAMAJI, T., SHIMAMOTO, K., ISHIBASHI, M., KOSAKA, K., AND ORIMO, H. 1976. Effect of age and sex on circulating and pituitary prolactin in humans. *Acta Endocrinol., 83,* 711–719.

ZELLMANN, H. E. 1968. Unusual aspects of myxedema. *Geriatrics, 23* (II), 140–148.

# 6

# Genetics
# and Mental Functioning
# in Senescence

*Steven S. Matsuyama & Lissy F. Jarvik*

## INTRODUCTION

As discussed in the preceding chapters, aging may be viewed as a time-dependent process whereby the body gradually loses the ability to cope successfully with environmental stress and to maintain homeostasis. Since both the ability to cope and its loss vary from individual to individual, the involvement of genetic factors is likely.

In this chapter, evidence for the role of genetic factors will be discussed in both normal and pathological mental functioning with advancing age. Basic genetic principles as well as the methods of investigating them will be presented. In addition, the available genetic studies on pathological conditions specific to the last period of life will be reviewed as will data on genetic influences upon the preservation of intellectual functioning during old age.

## BASIC PRINCIPLES AND METHODOLOGY

### HEREDITARY TRANSMISSION

Genetics is the science concerned with the understanding of the transmission of biological characteristics from parent to offspring. The primary observation that led to the study of heredity was that "like begets like". However, to develop a knowledge of heredity there must be variability, and the first step in the analysis of inheritance is the identification of clear and definite differences between individuals of the same species.

### MENDELIAN GENETICS

Gregor Mendel's work with garden peas forms the basis for modern genetics. The results of carefully

134

planned and controlled experiments were published in 1865 but went unnoticed and neglected until 1900 when rediscovered independently by DeVries in Holland, von Tschermak in Austria, and Correns in Germany. This rediscovery some 35 years later marks the beginning of genetics. Mendel chose plants with definite and differing characteristics that were constant and readily identified. Through controlled matings and complete records of the different types of progeny obtained, Mendel was the first to approach the problem quantitatively. His success was due to looking at each character separately. Thus, Mendel's laws are statistical laws based on proportions of different types of offspring resulting from various matings. As a result of his experiments, Mendel postulated that the hereditary characteristics (e.g., tall or short pea plants) were determined by unit characters and that these occur in pairs which separate from each other on germ cell formation. Only one member of the pair is transmitted by a gamete and a new combination, or pair, is restored on fertilization, as stated in Mendel's first law or the Law of Segregation.

Mendel further proposed in his second law, or the Law of Independent Assortment, that in the case of two or more pairs of unit characters, members of a given pair segregate independently of each other. Both of these laws, though based on results obtained in peas, are equally applicable to other organisms, including humans.

Another concept to emerge from Mendel's work is that of dominance. Thus, in a mating of tall and short plants, the resulting hybrid plants were all tall, tall being dominant and short recessive.

While Mendel's laws provide a description of what happens as a result of various matings, they do not provide information on how it happens, hardly surprising at a time when chromosomes were not known to exist. Indeed, the word "chromosome" was not coined until 1888 (Waldeyer, 1888) and the role of chromosomes as carriers of hereditary information was not recognized for several years after that. Then, it was proposed independently by Sutton (1903) and Boveri (1904) and has become known as the Sutton-Boveri hypothesis.

## CYTOGENETICS

The rediscovery of Mendel's work together with the discoveries in cytology led to the composite science of cytogenetics, the study of chromosomes in relation to inheritance. The study of human chromosomes began in 1956 when Tjio and Levan, utilizing modern cell culture techniques, correctly defined the chromosome number in man as 46 (the diploid complement), consisting of 22 pairs of autosomes and two sex chromosomes. Abnormal chromosome numbers involving either autosomes or sex chromosomes do occur (e.g., Down's syndrome is caused by an extra G-group chromosome) and have been implicated in or associated with oncology. Chromosome changes have also been related to advancing age, the percentage of aneuploid cells (cells with more or less than the normal 46 chromosomes) increasing with increasing chronological age (as discussed later in this chapter).

The importance of specific chromosomes could not be addressed until recently when techniques became available to distinguish between morphologically similar chromosomes (banding techniques). These techniques produce distinct staining differences which serve to distinguish each and every homologous pair of chromosomes. Moreover, they allow for the detection of structural changes in chromosomes which produce abnormal banding patterns. However, these methods can detect only gross changes and no insight is provided at the level of the gene where single base pair changes (point mutations) occur.

## MOLECULAR GENETICS

Although the chromosomal basis of heredity had been firmly established, the chemical identity of the genetic material was as yet unresolved. As a result of a number of ingenious experiments carried out in independent laboratories (Avery, MacLeod, and McCarty, 1944; Griffith, 1928; Hershey and Chase, 1952), deoxyribonucleic acid (DNA) was identified as the genetic material of man and most other organisms (with rare exceptions, e.g., RNA viruses). DNA is a polymer of nucleotide monomers, each nucleotide consisting of one pentose sugar of deoxyribose, one phosphate group, and one organic base, either a purine (adenine or guanine), or a pyrimidine (cytosine or thymine). However, the structure of DNA was not known. Based on X-ray diffraction findings and the chemical findings of equimolar concentrations of adenine and thymine as well as guanine and cytosine, a double helical model for DNA containing two strands of polynucleotides running parallel to each other but in opposite directions was proposed by Watson and Crick in 1953. The backbone of each strand was said to be the sugar phosphate chain with the organic bases lying perpendicular to the chain and projecting into the center. With bases aligned such that adenine was always hydrogen bonded to thymine and guanine to cytosine, the structure would readily satisfy one of the primary functions of a gene, the ability to exactly duplicate itself. The Watson and Crick model for DNA proposes that replication occurs by complementary base pairing. As the double helix unwinds, each chain acts as a template for the formation of a new double helix identical to the original. This semi-conservative replication scheme for DNA was confirmed in an elegant experiment carried out by Meselson and Stahl (1958) utilizing the heavy isotope of nitrogen ($N^{15}$).

The second essential requirement of DNA (as the genetic material) is that it serve as a source of genetic information for the development and functioning of the organism. The information encoded in DNA by the sequence of bases (unique for each gene) is expressed in the synthesis of proteins either enzymatic, structural or regulatory. DNA, which does not serve directly in protein synthesis, acts as a template for messenger RNA (ribonucleic acid) synthesis. This process is called transcription. RNA is similar in composition to DNA with the exception that the pentose sugar is ribose instead of deoxyribose and uracil is substituted for thymine as one of the pyrimidine bases. Messenger RNA is then translated into polypeptide chains which are involved in cellular activity (e.g., enzymatic catalysis of biochemical reactions).

The individuality of the different types of cells is determined by the types of protein the cell synthesizes. All cells within the organism are endowed with identical genomes yet do not produce the same set of proteins because of differences in gene expression. A significant contribution toward elucidating the molecular mechanisms controlling gene expression was made by Jacob and Monod (1961), who (as a result of experiments with the lactose systems in the bacterium *E coli*) proposed a model for the regulation of gene activity by means of "regulator" genes which could initiate or repress polypeptide chain synthesis. A more extensive model for gene regulation in higher cells was proposed by Britten and Davidson (1969). Both models are restricted to gene regulation at the level of transcription from DNA to RNA. Gene regulation may play a major role in aging based on the evidence for genetic factors in life span determination. Other aspects of the molecular genetics of aging (e.g., mutation theory) have recently been reviewed (Sinex, 1977).

Our concept of the genetic organization in higher organisms is currently undergoing a revolution. The stability of the genetic structure is now being contradicted by evidence showing that genetic elements are transposable, i.e., capable of moving from one site to another on the same chromosome, or from one chromosome to another chromosome. When inserted into another site, these transposed elements are capable of controlling the expression of the adjoining genes. Further, the concept of "one-gene one polypeptide chain" is being replaced by that of a long transcriptional unit containing alternating regions of nonexpressed (or silent) and expressed DNA from which the silent DNA regions have been excised in the final mature messengers. The terms intron for silent DNA and exon for the expressed DNA have been proposed by Gilbert (1978). Thus, the molecular picture of the gene is a mosaic of exon sequences in an intronic matrix and it is these sequences which may play a key role in evolution and differentiation, and as an extension, in the biology of aging.

## POPULATION GENETICS

*Demographic Approach.* One approach to understanding longevity is demography. This type of study utilizes actuarial and census methods to obtain a limited amount of information on a large number of individuals and is especially useful for detecting associations on the basis of enumerative procedures such as age, sibship size, birth order, vital statistics and differential mortality rates. These data are then subjected to analysis of variance and correlational statistical methods. Population surveys have provided information on the association of certain blood groups and histocompatibility antigens with disease, as well as on sex differences in longevity.

The reason for the sex difference in life span is as yet unknown although it has been hypothesized that females live longer because they have a more sheltered life protected from the stresses of competitive civilization. To test this hypothesis, Madigan and Vance (1957) studied 9,813 brothers and 32,041 sisters in American Catholic teaching orders who led relatively sheltered lives and faced equally negligible occupational hazards. Yet, they found a sex difference in life expectancy which was approximately the same as that for the general population. Further data may be forthcoming from the natural experiment presently being carried out in society with more and more women exposed to the stresses of competitive civilization. Meanwhile, it would appear that explanations for the differential life span must be sought elsewhere.

One such explanation may come from the different chromosome constitution of males and females; females having two X chromosomes while males have only a single X chromosome and in addition, a Y chromosome. While women have two X chromosomes, only one is required postembryonically, the other being inactivated. Nonetheless, taking the organism as a whole, X-linked deleterious recessive genes on one X chromosome in women are neutralized by the normal genes on the second X chromosome. Thus, in sex-linked conditions such as hemophilia, generally only the male manifests the abnormal condition (except in those rare situations where both chromosomes carry the same gene). Another possible mechanism may operate via hormonal differences directly related to the difference in sex chromosome constitution (e.g., estrogens protecting against atherosclerosis).

Demographic studies, however, are neither economical nor fruitful when it comes to genetic problems presenting difficulties in diagnosis or ascertainment and do not elucidate underlying genetic mechanisms. However, they may serve to identify potentially vulnerable individuals for more intensive study.

*Pedigree Approach.* The study of individual family histories is one of the oldest methods of genetic investigation in humans. Whereas demographic studies rely on large numbers of individuals for whom a limited amount of data is obtained, pedigree studies rely on a small number of intensively investigated individuals by means of individual family histories and construction of genealogies. The basis of these investigations is the assumption that in a genetically determined disorder there should be a correlation between the condition under investigation and the degree of genetic relatedness. First-degree relatives (parents, siblings, and children) share, on the average, 50 percent of the genetic material with the index case while second-degree relatives (grandparents, aunts, uncles, nieces, and nephews) share, on the average, 25 percent of their genetic material. Emphasis is usually on the parents and siblings. By combining a number of family investigations, morbidity risks can be computed for different groups of relatives. If affected individuals are easily recognizable, that is, if all affected individuals manifest the illness (complete penetrance) and if every affected person exhibits the same range of characteristic symptomatology (constant expressivity), the construction of individual pedigrees may provide presumptive information on the mode of inheritance, especially in cases of single gene defect.

The limitations of the pedigree method are dictated by small family sizes, the difficulties in gathering accurate information, and the biases of selection, i.e., a tendency to report only those pedigrees characterized by a high familial incidence of the disorder. Thus, in an autosomal dominant trait (such as Huntington disease) transmission is from parent to child, on the average 50 percent of the children being affected, regardless of their sex. In a sex-linked recessive disorder (such as Duchenne muscular dystrophy), only males are affected, while the females, who are carriers, transmit the trait to half their sons and the carrier status to half their daughters.

However, as pointed out by Cohen (1964), combining several genealogies ignores the influence of social factors and differential mortality among different socioeconomic strata and, therefore, is not well suited to the investigation of hereditary factors in longevity. Nonetheless, the first hypothesis concerning the inheritance of longevity was proposed on the basis of family histories. Bell (1918) studied the relationship of offspring to parental longevity among some 4,000 descendants of William Hyde. He found that when both parents died prior to the age of 60 years, the average lifespan of the descendants was nearly 20 years shorter than that for the individuals whose parents had both died at an age greater than 80 years. Pearl (1931) introduced the concept of "total index of ancestral longevity" (TIAL) as an indicator of the genetic contribution to increased life span and this TIAL was used by Pearl and Pearl (1934) to describe a longevous family where a centenarian index case had six direct ancestors who also reached an average age near 100 years.

*Twin and Twin-Family Studies.* The twin study method as a genetic research tool was introduced by Galton in 1876 and relies on the natural occurrence of two genetically different types of twins, monozygotic (one-egg or identical) and dizygotic (two-egg or fraternal). Monozygotic twins are genetically identical, while dizygotic twins are no more alike than ordinary siblings. Since monozygotic twins are of the same sex while dizygotic twins may be of the same or opposite sex, comparisons are often restricted to monozygotic and same-sexed dizygotic twins.

The concept behind the twin study method is that if hereditary factors play a role in the etiology of a well defined trait or disorder, monozygotic twins will have a much greater similarity (higher concordance) than dizygotic twins. If only one member of a given twin pair develops or expresses the characteristic under study, the twin pair is termed discordant. Since it is assumed that monozygotic twins have the same genotype in a similar environment while dizygotic twins represent somewhat different genotypes (on the average sharing 50 percent of the genes) in a similar environment, comparison of monozygotic twins allows assessment of environmental effects on identical genotypes while dizygotic twins reflect interaction of genotype and environment. If genetic factors are of minor importance, similar concordance rates are expected for the two types of twin pairs. Significantly higher concordance rates in monozygotic compared to dizygotic pairs indicate the existence and strength of hereditary components but provide no information with regard to the genes involved, their action, or their mode of transmission. Since monozygotic twins can be dissimilar (discordant), environmental factors clearly are also important. Moreover, concordance rates are useful primarily in studying traits or disorders appearing as all-or-none phenomena and not in examining continuously graded variables such as height, intelligence, or longevity.

Objections to the twin study method are numerous and some of them are overcome by investigating monozygotic twins separated at birth; unfortunately, only a very small number of such pairs are available and even they shared similar prenatal environments (e.g., maternal health and exposure to infection). Another version of the twin study method is the co-twin control method which entails the observation of a group of monozygotic twins when the twin partners are exposed to different experimental conditions (Gesell and Thompson, 1941).

An extension of the twin study method, overcoming other limitations of the original method, is the twin-family method which increases the number of genotypes available for comparison. In this method, a random sample of monozygotic and dizygotic twin pairs as well as their sibs, half-sibs, step-sibs and parents are studied. The main advantage is the effectiveness of this method as a sampling technique; the main disadvantage is the difficulty in filling all the cells. The twin-family method has been used in the evaluation of genetic factors in longevity. In the New York State Psychiatric Institute Study of Aging Twins started in 1946 by Kallmann and Sander (1948, 1949) and continued to the present time by one of the authors (Jarvik, Falek, Kallmann, and Lorge, 1960; Jarvik, Yen, Fu, and Matsuyama, 1976), data were collected on 2,356 senescent twin index cases as well as their relatives and revealed significantly greater mean intrapair differences in life span for same-sex dizygotic twin pairs than for monozygotic twin

pairs. Females outlived males regardless of zygosity (Jarvik *et al.*, 1960).

## GENETIC FACTORS IN GERIATRIC MENTAL DISORDERS

The methods of genetic investigation described above have been utilized not only in the evaluation of genetic factors in longevity but also in the study of diseases commonly afflicting the elderly. In such geriatric studies difficulties are encountered in assessing the role of hereditary factors since subjects are often intellectually impaired and make poor historians; relatives who could have served as key informants have died or are not readily accessible, or relatives may not have lived long enough to reach the risk period for the development of geriatric disorders.

### PRESENILE DEMENTIAS

*Huntington Disease.* Huntington disease is included in this section because of its importance in the differential diagnosis of presenile dementias and the fact that detrimental treatment may be instituted if the disease goes unrecognized. First described by Huntington in 1872 as a hereditary chorea, early clinical symptoms include a change in personality with a variety of nonspecific cognitive, affective, behavioral, or psychotic symptoms, followed by the appearance of involuntary movements which usually but not always progress to choreic movements, and eventually profound dementia (Whittier, 1963). The mean duration of life after onset of symptoms is approximately 16 years (Reed and Chandler, 1958).

Overall prevalence rates range from 4 to 7 per 100,000 population (Myrianthopoulos, 1966). Onset is insidious although the age is highly variable, ranging from 5 to 70 years with the greatest risk period between 35 and 40 years (Myrianthopoulos, 1966). Further, because of the variability of symptomatic expression, it is difficult to make an accurate diagnosis. Huntington disease may mimic other psychiatric illnesses such as schizophrenia (Van Putten and Menkes, 1973) or in the elderly, may be regarded as a dementia associated with aging (Heathfield and MacKenzie, 1971). This disease must also be differentiated from neurologic disorders with hyperkinetic symptoms. It is essential that an accurate diagnosis be established for a number of reasons, including the institution of appropriate therapy should the disease be other than Huntington disease or, in the case of a positive diagnosis, for purposes of genetic counseling of younger relatives who may wish to alter their child-bearing plans (cf. Jarvik, 1976). In the latter case, early detection of carriers (i.e., those with the gene for Huntington disease but who have not passed through the risk period) has been attempted (e.g., Falek and Glanville, 1962; Klawans, Paulson, Ringel, and Barbeau, 1972) but so far sucesses have not been reported.

The principal neuropathological feature is neuronal fallout, particularly in the striatum and cerebral cortex although cell loss is also seen in other regions of the brain. In areas of neuronal loss, there is extensive astrocytic gliosis.

Huntington disease is unique among the dementias, showing a clear genetic pattern of simple Mendelian autosomal dominant inheritance so that, on the average, half the offspring of those afflicted with this disease are similarly affected.

Despite the clear genetic picture presented by Huntington disease, little is known of its etiology and pathogenesis. At the present time, biochemical, cell culture, and immunological studies are at the forefront of research investigations. Enna, Bird, Bennett, Bylund, Yamamura, Iversen, and Snyder (1976) have reported changes in neurotransmitter receptors in the brains from patients with Huntington disease. Two laboratories have independently reported that cell cultures from patients with Huntington disease grew to a statistically significantly higher maximal density than matched control cultures (Barkley, Hardiwidjaja, and Menkes, 1977a; Goetz, Roberts, and Comings, 1975). According to recent immunologic studies utilizing the production of migration inhibition factor as a correlate of cellular immune response, lymphocytes from patients with Huntington disease but not from normal donors respond to brain antigens from affected patients. Further, lymphocytes from patients with Huntington disease respond only rarely to brain antigens from control brains, leading to the postulate of the existence of a late-appearing gene product consisting of a partial multiple sclerosis viral genome which is activated in middle life (Barkley, Hardiwidjaja, and Menkes, 1977b). The specificity of the consequent immune response suggests that Huntington disease is not an autoimmune disease (Barkley, Hardiwidjaja, Menkes, Ellison, and Myers, 1977). Other areas of research investigations have been reviewed by Heathfield (1973).

*Creutzfeldt-Jakob Disease.* This disorder was first reported by Creutzfeldt (1920) with a more detailed description provided a year later by Jakob (1921).

It is a rare, rapidly progressive neurological disease which occurs throughout the world, affects both sexes equally, and shows a highly variable age at onset. In a review of the world literature, May (1968) found cases as young as 21 years and as old as 79 years. Clinical symptoms too are variable and Slater and Roth (1969) have discussed two different types of Creutzfeldt-Jakob disease, one being characterized by a rapidly developing dementia with death ensuing within 3–6 months, and the second typically showing a longer course terminated by death within one to two years. At initial presentation there may be fatigue, dizziness, apathy, irritability or confusion, memory impairment, and speech disturbances. Dementia is accompanied by the development of a variety of neurological disturbances including cerebellar ataxia, myoclonus, seizures, pyramidal and extrapyramidal signs. With respect to gross changes in the brain, Malamud (1972) states that they "are relatively inconspicuous, although in some instances there may be severe localized atrophy."

Most cases occur sporadically with about 10 percent showing a familial pattern (Traub, Gajdusek, and Gibbs, 1977). Published pedigrees (Bonduelle, Escourolle, Bouygues, Lormeau, Ribadeau-Dumas, and Merland, 1971; Ferber, Weisenfeld, Roos, Bobowick, Gibbs, and Gajdusek, 1974; Gajdusek, 1977; May, Itabashi, and DeJong, 1968; Rosenthal, Keesey, Crandall, and Brown, 1976) extending over several generations are consistent with an autosomal dominant mode of inheritance. Thus, genetic predisposition appears to play a role in the etiology of Creutzfeldt-Jakob disease.

Recently Creutzfeldt-Jakob disease has been the subject of special interest because of its transmissibility to other animals (Gibbs, Gajdusek, Asher, Alpers, Beck, Daniel, and Matthews, 1968). In the first experiment, brain tissue from a patient with Creutzfeldt-Jakob disease was intracerebrally innoculated into a chimpanzee who, 13 months later, developed the characteristic spongiform encephalopathy (Gibbs *et al.*, 1968). Following this initial successful transmission, Creutzfeld-Jakob disease has been regularly transmitted to chimpanzees as well as to other animals, including New and Old World Monkeys, domestic cats and guinea pigs. This line of research indicates that Creutzfeldt-Jakob disease may be transmitted by a slow virus (Gajdusek, 1977).

However, the mode of transmission is unknown although the eating of hog and sheep brains and raw shellfish have been suggested as possibilities. Recently there has been concern among medical and laboratory personnel inspired by the reported accidental transmission via a corneal transplant in one case (Duffy, Wolf, Collins, DeVoe, Steeten, and Cowen, 1974) and neurosurgically implanted electrodes in two cases (Bernoulli, Siegfried, Baumgartner, Regli, Rabinowicz, Gajdusek, and Gibbs, 1977). There is also a suspicion of transmission to a neurosurgeon from one of his patients (Gajdusek, Gibbs, Earle, Dammin, Schoene, and Tyler, 1974). There is increased anxiety also, because of the unconventional nature of this virus—resistant to boiling, UV irradiation, formaldehyde, proteases, nucleases, etc. (Gajdusek, 1977). Indeed, the infective agent has been shown to survive for many months in formalin fixed tissue.

To summarize, evidence suggests that a significant portion of Creutzfeldt-Jakob disease may be related to a slow virus, transmissible to other animals, but the mode of transmission remains unknown. Traub *et al.*, (1977) have suggested that familial cases may be due to a slow virus infection superimposed on a preexisting genetically determined dysfunction which allows for invasion and/or activation of the agent. In familial Creutzfeldt-Jakob disease, the agent might be incorporated in the genome of the family members and transmitted in this manner until activated.

*Pick Disease.* Pick disease, first described as a form of senile dementia (Pick, 1892), is a rare disorder; Sjögren, Sjögren, and Lindgren (1952) estimated the morbidity risk in Sweden at a fraction of a tenth of a percent. Early symptoms are lack of energy and blunting of emotion with insidious onset of memory loss, impaired judgment, and confusion. Affected individuals show a progressive decline with development of a severe dementia and eventual death. The clinical symptoms are similar to those of another presenile dementia, Alzheimer disease, and the differential diagnosis is difficult, many researchers believing that the differentiation can be made only on postmortem examination. In Pick disease there is localized cerebral atrophy involving the frontal and temporal lobes with neuronal loss, gliosis and the distinctive Pick cell. In contrast to Alzheimer disease, however, senile plaques, neurofibrillary tangles and granulovacuolar degeneration are lacking.

An extensive pedigree study with longitudinal followup demonstrated direct parent to child transmission (regardless of sex) for five generations, approximately half of the offspring at risk becoming afflicted (Schenk, 1959). An autosomal dominant mode of inheritance has, therefore, been suggested. There appears to be genetic heteroge-

neity, however, since symptomatology varies between families, but is similar within families. And Sjögren *et al.* (1952), in a systematic investigation of patients with presenile dementia in Sweden, identified 44 patients with Pick disease (18 histopathologically confirmed). An increased morbidity risk for presenile dementia was found among their parents (19 percent) and siblings (6.8 percent). They concluded that a dominant major gene with modifiers was the most likely mode of inheritance.

*Alzheimer Disease.* Alzheimer disease, manifested between the ages of 45 and 64 years, is a dementia of insidious onset with a progressively deteriorating course. Early clinical symptoms include loss of memory, in particular for recent events, and inefficiency in social or occupational functioning. Later on, judgment and abstract thinking become impaired and there may be changes in personality. The progressive deterioration continues until the individual is reduced to a vegetative state and lifespan is generally reduced to only a few years following onset of symptoms. Pathologically, Alzheimer disease is characterized by diffuse cerebral atrophy, senile plaques, neurofibrillary tangles and granulovacuolar degeneration (Brun and Gustafson, 1976; Corsellis, 1976, Malamud, 1972; Terry and Wisniewski, 1972).

Genetic factors in the etiology of Alzheimer disease have emerged from a number of pedigree studies, summarized by Feldman, Chandler, Levy, and Glaser (1963). However, as mentioned earlier, caution is indicated in relying on pedigree information as the sole basis of evaluating genetic influence since pedigrees usually come to attention because they contain a strikingly high accumulation of affected individuals.

The first systematic study of Alzheimer disease, taking advantage of detailed hospital records maintained in Sweden, as well as files at two university pathology departments, was carried out by Sjögren *et al.* (1952) who collected a series of 36 index cases with Alzheimer disease, 18 of them with histopathologically verified diagnoses. Genealogical data were then collected from parish records and personal visits made to the families of the index cases and to secondary cases. In addition, all individuals suspected of having a mental disorder were psychiatrically evaluated or hospital records were reviewed for those who had died prior to the investigation. From these data, morbidity risks for Alzheimer disease were calculated at 10 percent for parents and 3.8 percent for siblings. The general population rate in Sweden being 0.1 percent, first-degree relatives exhibited a 38–100 fold increase in risk. On the basis of their data, the authors suggested a polygenic mode of inheritance.

Constantinides, Garrone, and deAjuriaguerra (1962) reviewed family history data derived from hospital records of individuals with Alzheimer disease admitted to the Bel Air Clinic in Geneva, Switzerland, between 1901 and 1958 and arrived at a 3.3 percent risk for siblings and 1.4 percent for parents. Their data appeared most compatible with an autosomal dominant mode of inheritance with reduced penetrance. While the risk for siblings was similar in both the Swiss and Swedish studies, the risk for parents was much lower in the former, possibly due, at least in part, to the fact that Constantinides and associates relied on hospital records while Sjögren and colleagues carried out personal psychiatric interviews.

Recently, Heston (1976) and Heston and Mastri (1977) reported on a family study of 30 well-documented index cases with Alzheimer disease. This sample was collected from a consecutive series of autopsies in the Minnesota State Psychiatric facilities between 1952 and 1971 and confirmed by a complete review of hospital records. Relatives of the index cases were then contacted, at least one member of each family was interviewed, and a medical history was compiled. Recurrence risks were found much higher than those previously reported (23 percent for parents and 10 percent for siblings), possibly because Heston and Mastri regard Alzheimer disease and senile dementia of the Alzheimer type as a single entity (the only difference being the age at onset) and, therefore, included both when calculating their risk figures. Heston and Mastri (1977), for the first time, reported a marked increase in the frequency of Down syndrome and myeloproliferative disease among the families of Alzheimer patients. Aside from this association, it had been known that patients with Down syndrome, if they survive, develop dementia at relatively early ages (i.e. in their 30s and 40s) with characteristic Alzheimer type brain changes (Jervis, 1970; Olsen and Shaw, 1969) and also have an increased risk of leukemia (Ager, Schuman, Wallace, Rosenfeld, and Gullen, 1965). On the basis of these associations, Heston and Mastri (1977) hypothesized a defect in the spatial organization of microtubules as a common pathological mechanism. Their data were compatible with both an autosomal dominant (low penetrance) and a polygenic model.

There is, then, evidence for a significant genetic component in the etiology of Alzheimer disease and Heston and Mastri have provided the first hypothesis concerning a mechanism. The mode of transmission may vary between families, both autosomal dominant with reduced penetrance and polygenic models having been proposed. Genetic markers which could help to identify persons at increased risk have not as yet been detected. The attempt to do so by analyzing blood groups, dermatoglyphics and chromosomes (Feldman et al., 1963) was unsuccessful. A promising lead is the report by Op den Velde and Stam (1973) that the gene frequency of haptoglobin 1 (Hp1) is significantly increased in Alzheimer disease compared to normal age-matched controls (0.70 vs. 0.35). Further work in this area may be anticipated.

## SENILE DEMENTIAS

*Senile Dementia, Alzheimer Type.* As mentioned earlier, senile dementia of the Alzheimer type is pathologically indistinguishable from the presenile Alzheimer disease. Clinically, onset is usually after age 70.

At the present time, general opinion favors the view that Alzheimer disease and senile dementia, Alzheimer type, are a single entity differing only in age at onset. Nonetheless, it is our opinion that the question has not been unequivocally resolved. Further, nearly all genetic investigations have distinguished between the two and for this reason Alzheimer disease and senile dementia, Alzheimer type, are treated separately. Clinically, onset is usually after age 70, with a uniformly progressive unremitting deterioration of mental functioning accompanied by personality changes. Early clinical symptoms include memory impairment, particularly recent memory, inefficiency in activities of daily life, and purposeless hyperactivity accompanied by perplexity and agitation; later there is disorientation for time, place, and person. Neither the etiology nor the precipitating factors are known and no specific treatment is presently available.

There is a fairly large literature with regard to its pathology. Among the most prominent distinguishing features are senile plaques, neurofibrillary tangles, and granulovacuolar degeneration (Ball, 1976; Ball and Lo, 1977; Malamud, 1972; Terry and Wisniewski, 1972). Although both senile plaques and neurofibrillary tangles are present in increasing number with increasing age (Matsuyama, Namiki, and Watanabe, 1965), their concentrations are significantly higher in demented than in nondemented patients (Blessed, Tomlinson, and Roth, 1968; Dayan, 1970a, b; Morimatsu, Hirai, Muramatsu, and Yoshikawa, 1975). Neuronal loss, particularly in the cortex and hippocampus, is thought to occur (Brody, 1973), and Ball (1977) has reported a diminished density of pyramidal neurons in the posterior region of the hippocampus in the brains of dementia patients as compared to those of normals. Other preliminary findings using computer counts of cortical cells did not show greater cell loss in senile persons than in the normal aged (Tomlinson and Henderson, 1976).

Evidence for genetic factors in the etiology of senile dementia come from family studies and twin studies. Family studies date back over 50 years when Meggendorfer (1925) studied the families of 60 histopathologically verified cases of senile dementia and among 16 families found 19 secondary cases of senile dementia. In one case there was direct inheritance through three generations and in another four cases through two generations. At about the same time Weinberger's (1926) investigation yielded 12 secondary cases among the families of 51 probands without increased morbidity for psychoses other than senile dementia. Cresseri (1948) who reported six instances of direct transmission of senile dementia, did not find an increase in the frequency of other psychoses either.

Constantinides *et al.* (1962) also reported an increased familial risk for senile dementia. Despite the small sample sizes in these early studies, they do give evidence of a familial incidence of senile dementia and that the hereditary factors are specific and do not come to expression in some individuals as senile dementia and in others as schizophrenia or other psychoses.

In the monumental study of senile dementia by Larsson, Sjögren, and Jacobson (1963), 15 years of records from two large mental hospitals in Stockholm were screened for patients diagnosed as senile dementia. These case records were carefully analyzed and only those meeting Roth's (1955) diagnostic criteria were included in the study. In this way 377 index cases were identified with 3,426 relatives; 2,675 of them were field investigated and led to the identification of 55 additional cases of senile dementia. The cases identified among the relatives did not deviate from the index cases with regard to onset, symptoms, or course of the disease. The morbidity risk for senile dementia among first degree relatives was assessed at 4.3 times that in the general population. By contrast, there was no increase in the frequencies of other mental disorders. Not a single case of the presenile Alzheimer or Pick diseases was said to have been discovered among the relatives, suggesting to the authors that presenile Alzheimer disease and senile dementia of the Alzheimer type were separate entities. Actually, based on general population figures, one would not expect to find any in a sample of so small

a size, and other studies did report both Alzheimer disease and senile dementia of the Alzheimer type within the same family. No evidence for sex linkage was found and sociomedical factors did not appear to influence the morbidity risk for senile dementia in this or any other study so far.

In another study an entire population in a well-defined area of islands off the coast of Sweden was studied in an attempt to identify every case of severe dementia (Akesson, 1969). Although the prevalence rates were lower than any previously reported, there was a markedly elevated risk for parents and siblings. In this study of 47 patients with the diagnosis of senile psychosis, nearly 20 percent of siblings 60 years of age or older (23 out of 125) also suffered from senile psychosis, the frequency increasing by age. The rate for those siblings 60–70 years was 7.1 percent and rose to 30.8 percent for those over 80 years of age. Fifteen percent of the 80 parents who survived past 60 years of age were also affected, and again, there was an age related increase in frequency (60–70 years, 5.6 percent; 70–80 years, 8.7 percent; and over 80 years, 23.1 percent).

In addition to the above family studies, there is one twin study in the literature (Kallmann, 1953). In that study concordance rates were 8 percent for dizygotic twins and 42.8 percent for monozygotic twins, with frequencies of 6.5 percent for siblings and 3 percent for parents.

Taken together, the family and twin studies provide strong evidence that genetic factors play a role in the etiology of senile dementia although the mode of inheritance is not yet known. However, investigators have speculated on possible modes of transmission. Larsson *et al.* (1963), while admitting that their data were not sufficient for the selection of any one mode over any other, favored an autosomal dominant over a recessive mode while Kallmann suggested a multifactorial etiology.

Additional evidence for genetic determinants in senile dementia stems from chromosomal findings. Women with senile dementia but *not* with cerebrovascular (multi-infarct) dementia, showed a significant increase in chromosome loss when compared to normal women of comparable age (Jarvik, Altshuler, Kato, and Blumner, 1971; Nielsen, 1970). These findings have not been duplicated for men, but the data base for men is small. The importance of chromosomal abnormalities has received further support from Heston's (1976) report of an increased frequency of Down syndrome and hematologic malignancy in the families of patients with Alzheimer disease including senile dementia. Other evidence is provided by the work of Op den Velde and Stam (1973) concerning haptoglobin (Hp) distribution. An increased Hp 1 gene frequency was found among patients with senile dementia (0.49 vs. 0.35 in controls). So far no linkage between the haptoglobin locus and the gene for Alzheimer disease or senile dementia has been proposed.

Exogenous influences in senile dementia have been proposed by Albert (1968) who suggested that what is inherited is a "special cerebral sensitivity." Such special sensitivity may involve immunologic factors, the latter having been suggested by a number of different observations, including the following:

Yugoslavian investigators (Janković, Jakulić, and Horvat, 1977), utilizing the delayed skin hypersensitivity reaction to human brain protein, found a higher proportion of positive responders (69 percent) among their patients with cerebral atrophy, than among schizophrenics (35 percent) or controls (2.5 percent). Autoimmune reactions have been suggested as having a role in the neuronal degeneration observed with advancing age. Nandy and colleagues (cf. review by Nandy, 1977), have identified brain-reactive antibodies in the gamma globulin fraction of serum from old but not young mice. These brain-reactive antibodies increase progressively with age, and were found to react equally with neurons from young and old mice. However, when sera from young mice were tested, no immune reaction developed. The report by Ingram, Phegan, and Blumenthal (1974) of an age-associated increase in a neuron binding gamma globulin fraction in human serum suggests that a similar brain-reactive antibody exists in aged humans. Nandy has extended his immunologic studies to humans and recently (1978) reported that preliminary data show an increase with age in brain-reactive antibodies in elderly controls and, further, that the levels in persons with Alzheimer disease (presenile) and senile dementia of the Alzheimer type exceeded those in control subjects of similar ages.

Immune changes are also consistent with the postulated involvement of an infectious agent in the etiology of senile dementia. There is the previously mentioned report of an increased frequency of Down syndrome and myeloproliferative disorders among the relatives of Alzheimer patients (Heston, 1976; Heston and Mastri, 1977) and viral agents have been implicated in both Down syndrome and leukemia. And there is tentative evidence pointing to a viral etiology for Alzheimer disease in the recent report (DeBoni and Crapper, 1978) that cultured neurons from fetal human cerebral cortex, exposed to an extract of Alzheimer brain, developed the paired helical filaments char-

acteristic of neurofibrillary tangles. Caution is indicated in interpreting these results, not only in terms of reproducibility, but also because brains damaged by some other underlying pathology may be attacked by a transmissible viral agent not directly involved in the pathogenesis of the final disorder. The findings pointing to an intimate involvement of the immune systems, must be regarded as tentative rather than definitive but represent leads worthy of further pursuit in our search for etiologic factors in senile dementia.

The major difficulty in genetic research on senile dementia is that of diagnostic accuracy. Multiple syndromes present as senile dementia (Bergmann, 1975) suggesting genetic heterogeneity. There is also the major question of the genetic relatedness of Alzheimer disease (presenile) and senile dementia. Larsson et al. (1963) consider them to be separate entities while Constantinides' group (Constantinides, 1968; Constantinides, Garrone, Tissot, and de Ajuriaguerra, 1965; Constantinides, Tissot, Richard, and de Ajuriaguerra, 1972) as well as Heston and Mastri (1977) believe them to be the same disease.

*Multi-Infarct Dementia.* Multi-infarct dementia is dementia secondary to cerebral arteriosclerosis. Previously, this dementia has been referred to as cerebrovascular disease, arteriosclerotic organic brain syndrome, and arteriosclerotic psychosis. Characteristic features include focal neurological signs, patchy deterioration, and a stepwise decline in intellectual function. Diagnosis is difficult since both multi-infarct dementia and senile dementia of the Alzheimer type are known to coexist (e.g., Morimatsu et al., 1975). Thus, clinically the diagnosis is usually restricted to those individuals in whom a clear-cut succession of strokes has destroyed a sufficient amount of brain tissue to cause dementia. Onset may be sudden, in association with stroke, and generally is said to be more rapid than that of senile dementia of the Alzheimer type. It is currently thought that the dementia is not the result of atheromatous changes within the cerebral vessels but that multiple infarcts (many of them small) produce the dementia by a reduction in cerebral blood flow and brain oxygen utilization (Hachinski, Lassen, and Marshall, 1974). Neuropathological studies carried out by Corsellis (1962; 1975) revealed severe cerebrovascular change in both large and small vessels, particularly in the middle cerebral artery and its branches.

A sex difference has been reported for multi-infarct dementia, the disorder being more common in men than in women. In a study of an elderly population in Newcastle-upon-Tyne, Kay,

Beamish, and Roth (1964) reported prevalence rates for arteriosclerotic organic brain syndrome of 8.7 percent for men and 1.0 percent for women. Nielsen (1962) studied a well-defined Danish elderly group and found lower prevalence rates of cerebrovascular dementia (3.2 percent for men and 2.5 percent for women) but still a sex difference. Constantinides *et al.* (1962), by contrast, did not find a sex difference in their family investigation of 423 patients with the diagnosis of cerebral arteriosclerosis which yielded morbidity risks of 7.3 percent for siblings and 3.9 percent for parents. They felt their data were consistent with an autosomal dominant mode of inheritance with reduced penetrance. Further, among the patients' relatives, the morbidity risk for senile dementia of the Alzheimer type was lower than expected.

Åkesson's (1969) study too provided data supporting the role of genetic factors in arteriosclerotic psychosis. Among the families of patients with this diagnosis, he calculated a morbidity risk of 5.6 percent for siblings 60 years of age or older and 9.6 percent for parents who lived to be 60 years of age or over compared to the population incidence figure of 0.52 percent.

Despite the evidence for hereditary factors in multi-infarct dementia, it must be borne in mind that the dementia is secondary to vascular disease and that the latter is believed to be related to environmental factors, as well as other conditions with genetic components, e.g., hyperlipidemia (Motulsky, 1976) and hypertension (Page, 1976). It may be difficult, therefore, to separate out the genetic factor(s) specific to multi-infarct dementia.

## GENETIC FACTORS AND MENTAL FUNCTIONING IN NORMAL AGING

A decline in intellectual performance is frequently found with advancing age. While the associations between hereditary determinants and survival have been extensively explored, there are but limited data on the association between genetic factors and mental functioning. The extent of the genetic contribution to the decline or preservation of intellectual performance was studied by Kallmann and his colleagues as part of the New York State Psychiatric Institute Study of Aging Twins, a longitudinal twin study carried out to assess hereditary influences on aging and longevity (Kallmann and Sander, 1948, 1949). In this long-term investigation, 1,603 twin "index cases" 60 years of age and over were initially selected and a subset of 134 intact pairs were used for psychological assessments. These subjects have been followed for approximately 30 years with ex-

aminations on repeated occasions (cf. review Bank and Jarvik, 1978). The initial psychometric test scores demonstrated that the mean intrapair differences in test scores were smaller for monozygotic twins than for dizygotic twins (Feingold, 1950; Jarvik, Blum, and Varma, 1972; Kallmann and Sander, 1949). For the sexes separately, this difference was significant for women, but for men, although there was a similar trend, the difference did not reach statistical significance, possibly because changes in the intellectual abilities studied may occur earlier in men than in women. Upon analyses of results obtained in later testing, the differences were no longer statistically significant (Falek, Kallmann, Lorge, and Jarvik, 1960; Jarvik, Kallman, Falek, and Klaber, 1957), perhaps due to the smaller sample sizes and increasing homogeneity of the dizygotic twin group.

Longevity and psychological test scores were also found to be positively correlated suggesting a possible relationship between genetic factors in survival and intellectual performance (Jarvik, Kallman, and Falek, 1962; Jarvik *et al.*, 1972). A common underlying biological mechanism responsible for these interrelated associations might be chromosomal. It is now well established that the proportion of hypodiploid cells (cells with 45 or fewer chromosomes instead of the normal 46) increases with advancing age (cf. review by Galloway and Buckton, 1978; Jarvik *et al.*, 1976), particularly in women, where older women have a significantly higher frequency of hypodiploidy than younger women with greater loss of C-group chromosomes (which include the X chromosome) than expected by chance. For men, most investigations failed to detect an increase in hypodiploidy, but nonetheless there is general agreement of increased loss of G-group chromosomes (which include the Y chromosome) with age. These cross-sectional findings have recently been confirmed in the only longitudinal study on aged subjects, a six-year followup of aged twins (Jarvik *et al.*, 1976).

Chromosome loss has been reported to correlate significantly with mental functioning, specifically with loss of certain cognitive functions, such as memory (Bettner, Jarvik, and Blum, 1971; Jarvik and Kato, 1969). Further, chromosome loss has been associated with senile dementia (Jarvik *et al.*, 1971; Nielsen, 1970). Again the above associations have been found only in women and not in men. It is established that women live longer than men and the possibility exists that the mental impairment associated with chromosome loss in women is an undesirable accompaniment of a successful mechanism for survival through the loss of an X chromosome.

Recent evidence suggests that the relationship between chromosome loss and intellectual impairment may be mediated through the immune system. The possible role of immunologic factors mediating age- and pathology-related changes in cognition is only just beginning to be explored. First reported by Roseman and Buckley (1975) was an inverse relationship between serum immunoglobulin (Ig) concentrations and certain measures of intelligence. Subsequently, Cohen, Matsuyama, and Jarvik (1976) reported a direct relationship between serum Ig levels and vocabulary score in aging twins. Similarly, a positive association between Ig levels and cognitive performance in nursing home residents as well as community elderly was reported by Eisdorfer and colleagues (Cohen and Eisdorfer, 1977; Eisdorfer, Cohen, and Buckley, in press), who suggest that a curvilinear function may best describe the relation between immune response and cognition. There is also the relationship between chromosome changes and levels of serum immunoglobulins recently observed in a small pilot study of aging twins (Matsuyama, Cohen, and Jarvik, 1978).

To summarize, genetic factors are implicated in the preservation of mental functioning into old age. Intellectual performance and survival are positively correlated and a common underlying mechanism may be through chromosome changes. Finally, there is the interrelationship between chromosome changes, serum immunoglobulin levels, and cognitive performance. While many of these reports are preliminary, they do represent new leads which deserve further attention.

# REFERENCES

AGER, E. A., SCHUMAN, L. M., WALLACE, H. M., ROSENFELD, A. B., AND GULLEN, W. H. 1965. An epidemiological study of childhood leukemia. *J. Chronic Diseases, 18,* 113–132.

ÅKESSON, H. O. 1969. A population study of senile and arteriosclerotic psychoses. *Human Hered., 19,* 546–566.

ALBERT, E. 1968. Discussion contribution to "epidemiology and genetics of senile dementia." *In,* C. Müller and L. Ciompi (eds.), *Senile Dementia,* pp. 65–68. Bern, Switzerland: Hans Huber.

AVERY, D. T., MACLEOD, C. M., AND MCCARTY, M. 1944. Studies on the chemical nature of the substance inducing transformation of pneumococcal types. Induction of transformation by a deoxyribonucleic acid fraction isolated from pneumococcus type III. *J. Exp. Med., 79,* 137–158.

BALL, M. J. 1976. Neurofibrillary tangles and the pathogenesis of dementia-quantative study. *Neuro. Appl. Neurobiol, 2,* 395–410.

BALL, M. J. 1977. Neuronal loss, neurofibrillary tangles and granulovacuolar degeneration in the hippocampus with ageing and dementia. *Acta Neuropathol.* (Berl.), *17,* 111–118.

BALL, M. J., AND LO, P. 1977. Granulovacuolar degeneration in the ageing brain and dementia. *J. Neuropathol. and Exp. Neurol., 36,* 474–487.

BANK, L., AND JARVIK, L. F. 1978. A longitudinal study of aging twins. *In,* E. L. Schneider (ed.), *The Genetics of Aging,* pp. 303–330. New York: Plenum.

BARKLEY, D. S., HARDIWIDJAJA, S., AND MENKES, J. H. 1977a. Abnormalities in growth of skin fibroblasts of patients with Huntington's Disease. *Annals of Neurol., 1,* 426–430.

BARKLEY, D. S., HARDIWIDJAJA, S., AND MENKES, J. H. 1977b. Huntington's Disease: delayed hypersensitivity *in vitro* to human central nervous system antigens. *Science, 195,* 314–316.

BARKLEY, D. S., HARDIWIDJAJA, S., MENKES, J. H., ELLISON, G. W., AND MYERS, L. W. 1977. Cellular immune responses in Huntington's Disease (HD). *Cellular Immunol., 32,* 385–390.

BELL, A. G. 1918. The duration of life and conditions associated with longevity: a study of the Hyde genealogy. Washington, DC: Genealogical Record Office.

BERGMANN, K. 1975. The epidemiology of senile dementia. *Br. J. Psychiat., 9,* 100–109.

BERNOULLI, C., SIEGFRIED, J., BAUMGARTNER, G., REGLI, F., RABINOWICZ, T., GAJDUSEK, D. C., AND GIBBS, C. J. 1977. Danger of accidental person-to-person transmission of Creutzfeldt-Jakob disease by surgery. *Lancet, i,* 478–479.

BETTNER, L. G., JARVIK, L. F., AND BLUM, J. E. 1971. Stroop color-word test, non-psychotic organic brain syndrome, and chromosome loss in aged twins. *J. Gerontol., 26,* 458–469.

BLESSED, G., TOMLINSON, B. E., AND ROTH, M. 1968. The association between quantative measures of dementia and of senile change in the cerebral grey matter of elderly subjects. *Br. J. Psychiat., 114,* 797–811.

BONDUELLE, M., ESCOUROLLE, R., BOUYGUES, P., LORMEAU, G., RIBADEAU-DUMAS, J. L., AND MERLAND, J. J. 1971. Maladie de Creutzfeldt-Jakob familiale, observation anatomoclinique. *Revue Neurol., 125,* 197–209.

BOVERI, T. 1904. *Ergebnisse über die Konstitution der chromatischen Substanz des Zellkerns.* Jena: G. Fischer.

BRITTEN, R. J., AND DAVIDSON, E. H. 1969. Gene regulation for higher cells: a theory. *Science, 165,* 349–357.

BRODY, H. 1973. Aging of the vertebrate brain. *In,* M.

Rockstein, (ed.) *Development and Aging in the Nervous System,* pp. 121–133. New York: Academic Press.

BRUN, A., AND GUSTAFSON, L. 1976. Distribution of cerebral degeneration in Alzheimer's Disease. A clinico-pathological study. *Archiv fur Psychiatrie und Nurven Krankheiten, 223,* 15–33.

COHEN, B. H. 1964. Family patterns of mortality and life span. *Quart. Rev. Biol., 39,* 130.

COHEN, D., AND EISDORFER, C. 1977. Behavioral-immunologic relationships in older men and women. *Exp. Ag. Res., 3,* 225–229.

COHEN, D., MATSUYAMA, S. S., AND JARVIK, L. F. 1976. Immunoglobulin levels and intellectual functioning in the aged. *Exp. Ag. Res., 2,* 345–348.

CONSTANTINIDES, J. 1968. The familial incidence of degenerative cerebral lesions, histologic substrate of senile dementia. *In,* C. Müller and L. Ciompi (eds.), *Senile Dementia,* pp. 62–64. Bern, Switzerland: Hans Huber.

CONSTANTINIDES, J., GARRONE, G., AND DE AJURIAGUERRA J. 1962. L'hérédité des démences de l'age avancé. *Encéphale, 51,* 301–344.

CONSTANTINIDES, J. GARRONE, G., TISSOT, R., AND DE AJURIAGUERRA, J. 1965. L'encidence familiale des altérations neurofibrillaires corticales d'Alzheimer. *Psychiat. et Neurol.* (Basel), *150,* 235–247.

CONSTANTINIDES, J., TISSOT, R., RICHARD, S., AND DE AJURIAGUERRA, J. 1972. Le role de l'heredité dans le developpment de la démence présenile d'Alzheimer et la démence sénile Alzheimeirsée (a propos de 9 observations familiales). *In,* C. Perez de Francisco (ed.), *Dimensiones de la Psiquiatria Contemporanea,* pp. 328–339. Mexico: Editorial Fournier.

CORSELLIS, J. A. N. 1962. *Mental illness and the ageing brain: The distribution of pathological change in a mental hospital population.* Maaudsley Monographs, No. 9. London: Oxford University Press.

CORSELLIS, J. A. N. 1975. The pathology of dementia. *Br. J. Psychiat.,* Special Publication No. 9, 110–118.

CORSELLIS, J. A. N. 1976. Ageing and the Dementias. *In,* W. Blackwood and J. A. N. Corsellis (eds.), *Greenfield's Neuropathology,* pp. 796–848. London: Edward Arnold.

CRESSERI, A. 1948. L'Ereditarietà della Demenza Senile. *Boll. Soc. ital. Biol. sper., 24,* 200–201.

CREUTZFELDT, H. G. 1920. Ueber eine eigenantige herdförmige Erkrankung des Zentralnerrensystems. *Ztschr. Neurol. Psychiat., 56,* 1.

DAYAN, A. D. 1970a. Quantitative histological studies on the aged human brain. I. Senile plaques and neurofibrillary tangles in "normal" patients. *Acta Neuropathol., 16,* 85.

DAYAN, A. D. 1970b. Quantitative histological studies on the aged human brain. II. Senile plaques and neurofibrillary tangles in senile dementia. *Acta Neuropathol., 16,* 95.

DE BONI, U., AND CRAPPER, D. R. 1978. Paired helical filaments of the Alzheimer type in cultured neurones. *Nature, 271,* 566–568.

DUFFY, P., WOLF, J., COLLINS, G., DE VOE, A. G., STEETEN, B., AND COWEN, D. 1974. Possible person-to-person transmission of Creutzfeldt-Jakob disease. *New Engl. J. Med., 290,* 692–693.

EISDORFER, C., COHEN, D., AND BUCKLEY, C. E. Behavioral-serum immunoglobulin relationship in the cognitively impaired elderly. Workshop Conference on Senile Dementia. Alzheimer's Disease, and Related Disorders. In press.

ENNA, S. J., BIRD, E. D., BENNETT, J. P., BYLUND, D. B., YAMAMURA, H. I., IVERSEN, L. L., AND SNYDER, S. H. 1976. Huntington's Chorea. Changes in neurotransmitter receptors in the brain. *New Engl. J. Med., 294,* 1305–1309.

FALEK, A, AND GLANVILLE, E. V. 1962. Investigation of genetic carriers. *In,* F. J. KALLMANN (ed.), *Genetics in Psychiatry,* p. 136. New York: Grune & Stratton.

FALEK, A., KALLMANN, F. J., LORGE, I., AND JARVIK, L. F. 1960. Longevity and intellectual variation in a senescent twin population. *J. Gerontol., 15,* 305–309.

FEINGOLD, L. 1950. A psychometric study of senescent twins. Unpublished doctoral dissertation, Columbia University.

FELDMAN, R. G., CHANDLER, K. A., LEVY, L., AND GLASER, G. H. 1963. Familial Alzheimer's disease. *Neurology, 13,* 811–824.

FERBER, R. A., WEISENFELD, S. L., ROOS, R. P., BOBOWICK, A. R., GIBBS, C. J., AND GAJDUSEK, D. C. 1974. Familial Creutzfeldt-Jakob disease: transmission of the familial disease to primates. *In,* A. Subriana, J. M. Espadaler, and E. H. Burrows (eds.), *Proceedings of the 10th International Congress of Neurology, Barcelona,* pp. 358–380. Amsterdam: Excerpta Medica International Congress Series.

GAJDUSEK, D. C. 1977. Unconventional viruses and the origin and disappearance of Kuru. *Science, 197,* 943–960.

GAJDUSEK, D. C., GIBBS, C. J., EARLE, K., DAMMIN, C. J., SCHOENE, W., AND TYLER, H. R. 1974. Transmission of subacute spongiform encephalopathy to the chimpanzee and squirrel monkey from a patient with papulosis maligan of Kohlmeier Degos. *In,* A. Subriana, J. M. Espadaler, and E. H. Burrows (eds.), *Proceedings of the 10th International Congress of Neurology, Barcelona,* pp. 390–392. Amsterdam: Excerpta Medica International Congress Series.

GALLOWAY, S. M., AND BUCKTON, K. E. 1978. Aneuploidy and aging: chromosome studies on a random sample of the population using G-banding. *Cytogenet. Cell Genet., 20,* 78–95.

GALTON, F. 1876. The history of twins, as a criterion of the relative powers of nature and nurture. *J.R. Anthropol. Inst. Gr. Br. Irel., 6,* 391–406.

GESELL, A., AND THOMPSON, H. 1941. *Twins T and C from infancy to adolescence: a biogenetic study of individual differences by the method of co-twin control.* Princetown, Mass.: The Journal Press.

GIBBS, C. J., GAJDUSEK, D. C., ASHER, D. M., ALPERS, M. P., BECK, E., DANIEL, P. M., AND MATTHEWS, W. B. 1968. Creutzfeldt-Jakob disease (spongiform encephalopathy) transmission to the chimpanzee. *Science, 161,* 388–389.

GILBERT, W. 1978. News and Views—Why genes in pieces? *Nature, 271,* 501.

GOETZ, I., ROBERTS, E., AND COMINGS, D. E. 1975. Fibroblasts in Huntington's Disease. *New Engl. J. Med., 293,* 1225–1227.

GRIFFITH, F. 1928. The significance of pneumococcal types. *J. Hygiene, 27,* 113–159.

HACHINSKI, V. C., LASSEN, N. A., AND MARSHALL, J. 1974. Multiple infarct dementia. A cause of mental deterioration in the elderly. *Lancet, ii,* 207–210.

HEATHFIELD, K. W. G. 1973. Huntington's chorea: a centenary review. *Postgrad. Med. J., 49,* 32–45.

HEATHFIELD, K. W. G., AND MacKENZIE, I. C. K. 1971. Huntington's chorea in Bedfordshire, England. *Guy's Hosp., London, Reports, 120,* 295–309.

HERSHEY, A. D., AND CHASE, M. 1952. Independent functions of viral protein and nucleic acid in growth of bacteriophage. *J. Gen. Physiol., 36,* 39–56.

HESTON, L. L. 1976. Alzheimer's disease, trisomy 21, and myeloproliferative disorders: associations suggesting a genetic diathesis. *Science, 196,* 322–323.

HESTON, L. L., AND MASTRI, A. R. 1977. The genetics of Alzheimer's disease: associations with hematologic malignancy and Down's syndrome. *Arch. Gen. Psychiat., 34,* 976–981.

INGRAM, C. R., PHEGAN, K. J., AND BLUMENTHAL, H. T. 1974. Significance of an aging-linked neuron binding gamma-globulin fraction of human sera. *J. Gerontol., 29,* 20–27.

JACOB, F., AND MONOD, J. 1961. Genetic regulatory mechanisms in the synthesis of proteins. *J. Molecular Biol., 3,* 318–356.

JAKOB, A. 1921. Über eigenartige Erkrankungen des Zentralnervensystems mit bemerkenswertem anatomischen Befunde. *Ztschr. Neurol. Psychiat. 64,* 147.

JANKOVIĆ, B. D., JAKULIĆ, S., AND HORVAT, J. 1977. Cerebral atrophy: an immunological disorder. *Lancet, ii,* 219–220.

JARVIK, L. F. 1976. Genetic modes of transmission relevant to psychopathology. *In,* L. F. Jarvik and M. A. Sperber (eds.), *Psychiatry and Genetics,* pp. 3–40. New York: Basic Books.

JARVIK, L. F. AND KATO, T. 1969. Chromosomes and mental changes in octogenarians. *Br. J. Psychiat., 115,* 1193–1194.

JARVIK, L. F., BLUM, J. E., AND VARMA, A. O. 1972. Genetic components and intellectual functioning during senescence: A 20-year study of aging twins. *Behav. Genet., 2,* 159–171.

JARVIK, L. F., KALLMANN, F. J., AND FALEK, A. 1962a. Intellectual changes in aged twins. *J. Gerontol., 17,* 289–294.

JARVIK, L. F., ALTSHULER, K. Z., KATO, T., AND BLUMNER, B. 1971. Organic brain syndrome and chromosome loss in aged twins. *Diseases of the Nerv. System, 32,* 159–170.

JARVIK, L. F., FALEK, A., KALLMANN, F. J., AND LORGE, I. 1960. Survival trends in a senescent twin population. *Am. J. Hum. Genet., 12,* 170–179.

JARVIK, L. F., KALLMANN, F. J., FALEK, A., AND KLABER, M. M. 1957. Changing intellectual functions in senescent twins. *Acta Genet. et Statist. Med., 7,* 421–430.

JARVIK, L. F., YEN, F. S., FU, T. K., AND MATSUYAMA, S. S. 1976. Chromosomes in old age: a six year longitudinal study. *Human Genetics, 33,* 17–22.

JERVIS, G. A. 1970. Premature senility in Down's syndrome. *Annals New York Academy of Sciences, 171,* 559–561.

KALLMANN, F. J. 1953. *Heredity in Health and Mental Disorder.* New York: Norton.

KALLMANN, F. J., AND SANDER, G. 1948. Twin studies on aging and longevity. *J. Heredity, 39,* 349–357.

KALLMANN, F. J., AND SANDER, G. 1949. Twin studies on senescence. *Am. J. Psychiat., 106,* 29–36.

KAY, D. W. K., BEAMISH, P., AND ROTH, M. 1964. Old age mental disorders in Newcastle upon Tyne, part I: a study of prevalence. *Br. J. Psychiat., 110,* 146–158.

KLAWANS, H. L., PAULSON, G. W., RINGEL, S. P., AND BARBEAU, A. 1972. Use of L-dopa in the detection of presymptomatic Huntington's chorea. *New Engl. J. Med., 286,* 1332–1334.

LARSSON, T., SJÖGREN, T., AND JACOBSON, G. 1963. Senile dementia: a clinical sociomedical and genetic study. *Acta Psychiat. Scand. (suppl. 1967), 39,* 1–259.

MADIGAN, F. C., AND VANCE, R. B. 1957. Differential sex mortality: a research design. *Social Forces, 35,* 193–199.

MALAMUD, N. 1972. Neuropathology of organic brain syndrome. *In,* C. M. Gaitz (ed.), *Aging and the Brain,* pp. 63–88. New York: Plenum.

MATSUYAMA, S. S., COHEN, D., AND JARVIK, L. F. 1978. Hypodiploidy and serum immunoglobulin concentrations in the elderly. *Mechanisms of Ageing and Development, 8,* 407–412.

MATSUYAMA, H., NAMIKI, H., AND WATANABE, I. 1965. Senile changes in the brain in the Japanese. Incidence of Alzheimer's neurofibrillary change and senile plaques. *In,* F. Luthy and A. Bischoff (eds.), *Proc. 5th International Congress of Neuropathology,* pp. 979–980. *Excerpta Medica,* Series No. 100.

MAY, W. W. 1968. Creutzfeldt-Jakob disease: I. Survey

of the literature and clinical diagnosis. *Acta Neurol. Scand., 44,* 1–32.

MAY, W. W., ITABASHI, H. H., AND DE JONG, R. N. 1968. Creutzfeldt-Jakob disease: II. Clinical pathologic and genetic study of a family. *Arch. Neurol., 19,* 137–149.

MEGGENDORFER, F. 1925. Über familiengeschichtliche Untersuchungen bei arterioskerotischer und seniler Demenz. *Zbl. ges. Neurol. Psychiat., 40,* 359.

MENDEL, G. 1866. Versuche über Pflanzen Hybriden. *Reprinted in,* J. A. Peters (ed.), *Classic Papers in Genetics,* 1959, pp. 1–20. Englewood Cliffs, N.J.: Prentice-Hall.

MESELSON, M., AND STAHL, F. W. 1958. The replication of DNA in *Escherichia coli. Proc. Nat. Acad. Sci., 44,* 671–682.

MORIMATSU, M., HIRAI, S., MURAMATSU, A., AND YOSHIKAWA, M. 1975. Senile degenerative brain lesion and dementia. *J. Am. Geriat. Soc., 23,* 390–406.

MOTULSKY, A. G. 1976. Current concepts in genetics: the genetic hyperlipidemias. *New Engl. J. Med., 294,* 823–827.

MYRIANTHOPOULOS, N. C. 1966. Huntington's chorea: review article. *J. Med. Genet. 3,* 298–314.

NANDY, K. 1977. Immune reactions in aging brain and senile dementia. *In.,* K. Nandy and I. Sherwin (eds.), *The Aging Brain and Senile Dementia,* pp. 181–196. New York: Plenum.

NANDY, K. 1978. Neuroanatomical changes in the aging brain. Presented at South Central RMEC symposium entitled "Biomedical Aspects of Senile Dementia and Related Disorders." St. Louis, Missouri.

NIELSEN, J. 1962. Geronto-psychiatric period -prevalence investigation in a geographically delineated population. *Acta Psychiat. Scand., 38,* 307–330.

NIELSEN, J. 1970. Chromosomes in senile, presenile, and arteriosclerotic dementia. *J. Gerontol., 25,* 312–315.

OLSEN, M. I. AND SHAW, C. M. 1969. Presenile dementia and Alzheimer's disease in mongolism. *Brain, 92,* 147–156.

OP DEN VELDE, W. AND STAM, F. C. 1973. Haptoglobin types in Alzheimer's disease and senile dementia. *Br. J. Psychiat., 122,* 331–336.

PAGE, L. B. 1976. Epidemiologic evidence on the etiology of human hypertension and its possible prevention. *American Heart Journal, 91,* 527–534.

PEARL, R. 1931. Studies on human longevity IV. The inheritance of longevity. *Human Biol., 3,* 245–269.

PEARL, R., AND PEARL, R. D. 1934. *The ancestry of the longlived.* Baltimore: John Hopkins Press.

PICK, A. 1892. Uber die Beziehungen der senilen Hirnatrophic zur Aphasic. *Prog. Med. Wochschr., 17,* 165.

REED, T. E., AND CHANDLER, J. H. 1958. Huntington's chorea in Michigan: demography and genetics. *Am. J. Hum. Genet., 10,* 201–225.

ROSEMAN, J. M. AND BUCKLEY, C. E. 1975. Inverse relationship between serum IgG concentrations and measures of intelligence in elderly persons. *Nature, 254,* 55–56.

ROSENTHAL, N. P., KEESEY, J., CRANDALL, B., AND BROWN, W. J. 1976. Familial neurological disease associated with spongiform encephalopathy. *Arch. Neurol., 33,* 252–259.

ROTH, M. 1955. The natural history of mental disorders in old age. *J. Ment. Sci., 101,* 281–301.

SCHENK, V. W. D. 1959. Reexamination of a family with Pick's disease. *Annals of Human Genetics, 23,* 325–333.

SINEX, F. M. 1977. The molecular genetics of aging. *In,* C. E. Finch and L. Hayflick (eds.), *Handbook of The Biology of Aging,* pp. 37–58. New York: Van Nostrand Reinhold.

SJÖGREN, T., SJÖGREN, H., AND LINDGREN, A. G. H. 1952. Morbus Alzheimer and Morbus Pick. *Acta Psychiat. et Neurol. Scand.* (suppl.), *82,* 1–152.

SLATER, E., AND ROTH, M. 1969. *Clinical Psychiatry,* 3rd edition. Baltimore: Williams & Wilkins.

SUTTON, W. S. 1903. The chromosomes in heredity. *Biol. Bull., 4,* 213–251.

TERRY, R. D. AND WISNIEWSKI, H. M. 1972. Ultrastructure of senile dementia and of experimental analogs. *In.,* C. M. Gaitz (ed.), *Aging and the Brain,* pp. 89–116. New York: Plenum.

TJIO, J. H. AND LEVAN, A. 1956. The chromosome number of man. *Hereditas, 42,* 1–6.

TOMLINSON, B. E., AND HENDERSON, G. 1976. Some quantitative cerebral findings in normal and demented old people. *In,* R. D. Terry and S. Gershon (eds.), *Aging, Vol. 3: Neurobiol. of Aging.* New York: Raven, pp. 183–204.

TRAUB, R., GAJDUSEK, D. C., AND GIBBS, C. J. 1977. Transmissible virus dementia: The relation of transmissible spongiform encephalopathy to Creutzfelt-Jakob disease. *In,* W. L. Smith and M. Kinsbourne (eds.), *Aging and Dementia,* pp. 91–172. Jamaica, N.Y.: Spectrum.

VAN PUTTEN, T., AND MENKES, J. H. 1973. Huntington's disease masquerading as chronic schizophrenia. *Diseases of the Nervous System, 34,* 54–56.

WALDEYER, W. 1888. Ueber Karyokinese und ihre Beziehungen zu den Befruchtungvorgangen. *Arch. Mikr. Anat., 32,* 1.

WATSON, J. D., AND CRICK, F. C. 1953. Molecular structure of nucleic acids. A structure for deoxyribose nucleic acids. *Nature, 171,* 737–738.

WEINBERGER, H. L. 1926. Über die hereditaren Beziehungen der senilen Demenz. *A. ges. Neurol. Psychiat., 106,* 666–701.

WHITTIER, J. E. 1963. Research on Huntington's chorea: problems of privilege and confidentiality. *J. of Foren. Sci., 8,* 568–575.

# 7

# The Morphological Aspects
# of Aging
# in the Human
# Nervous System

*Raymond D. Adams*

In the interests of clarity and precision in the following pages the term "aging" will refer to changes occurring after the peak of activity of the human organism and particularly after the end of its reproductive period. Aging is assumed to be synonymous with natural decline in the functional efficiency of the organism, and our present knowledge of the morphological bases of this decline will be reviewed in the following pages.

The term "degenerative" is often thought to be equivalent to aging but it is much too general. There are, for example, degenerative changes that occur during embryogenesis wherein certain excesses of cells are eliminated as the brain and spinal cord are molded into the mature organ.

Aging affects all parts of the body and, in view of the interdependency of organs, there is a certain artificiality in discussing the changes in the nervous system in isolation. Aging in the pituitary and endocrine glands, the liver, heart, and lungs are all capable of altering the function and structure of the brain.

Of course there are many diseases that become more frequent with the passing of years and in this sense bear a relationship to age. The most important of these are neoplasia and the cerebrovascular and degenerative diseases. They, too, are an aspect of aging and of the increasing mortality in late life. But since they are to be understood mainly in terms of special causes and mechanisms, there is no advantage to considering them as part of the aging process.

Emphasis in this chapter will focus largely on the fate of nerve cells, not just the nerve cell bodies (perikarya) but their dendrites, axons, myelin sheaths, and synaptic surfaces. The reason for this orientation is that the neurons, the most uniquely "postmitotic" cells in the human body, are present in full number at birth and they must last the lifetime of the individual. If destroyed during aging or by disease, the loss is permanent for there appears to be no possibility of regeneration and replacement.

There are some who would question whether aging of the nervous system should be considered only in terms of neurons. Are not the blood vessels and supporting tissues and organs known to play a most important role in maintaining the homeostasis of neurons? With this point of view the author agrees and feels compelled, therefore, to review changes in these latter structures as well.

A preliminary word of caution—many of the statements that follow must be regarded as tentative. Certain of the cellular changes presently declared to be aging effects may in another decade or two be traced to some recondite disease process.

## MACROSCOPIC CHANGES IN THE BRAIN ASSOCIATED WITH AGING

Probably the most indubitable fact about the aging brain is that it appears to have lost weight and to have become smaller with advancing years. This is true of man as well as of several mammalian and submammalian forms. As a reflection of this atrophy, the surface of the brain is separated from the skull by a wider space and the ventricles of the brain are enlarged. Reports of atrophy by various pathologists have differed rather widely, which is not surprising in view of the fact that the cerebral tissue may swell in the last hours of life because of heart and respiratory failure and other agonal causes of hypoxia. Hence, postmortem measurements are variable and not altogether valid. It is pointless to burden the reader with the innumerable references on this subject. Valuable source materials are to be found in the publications of Braunmühl (1957) and Blinkov and Glezer (1968). But taking the accumulated data on brain weight as a whole, a rough rule of thumb may be derived—a 5 percent loss by the age of 70, 10 percent by age 80, and 20 percent by age 90 (Arendt, 1972; Ordy and Brizee, 1975). These figures, unfortunately, are obtained from series of brains of elderly individuals whose mental status at the time of death was not known. The series of cases studied by Tomlinson, Blessed, and Roth (1968) were the only ones known to be competent mentally at the time of death and they showed a lesser degree of atrophy.

The cerebellum, which is an easily measured part of the brain, also loses weight with age in parallel to the cerebrum, the proportion of part to whole remaining more or less the same in each decade of life. The same general pattern of volumetric decline occurs in the pituitary gland and the adrenals.

Another gross parameter of brain atrophy with age is a volumetric decrease (Böning, 1925; Himwich, 1959). The normal adult male brain is observed to diminish from a volume of 1,329$cc$ to 1,100$cc$ from the age of 20 to 80 years and the extracerebral space to increase correspondingly from 100$cc$ to 200$cc$. Widening and deepening of sulci and narrowing of gyri and enlargement of the ventricles are other marks of this volumetric change. Last and Tomsett (1953) showed this increasing ventricular size by making casts of the ventricular system and measuring their volume. The study of Baron, Jacobs, and Kinkle, using computerized axial tomography, also shows a steady but slow increase in ventricular size from the tenth to the seventieth year and then a very rapid increase from the seventieth to the ninetieth year. These data were obtained from planimetric measurements of the lateral ventricles. Unfortunately, no information concerning the neuropsychiatric function of the older patients is given.

The progressive weight loss with age is known to be accompanied by changes in the chemical composition of the cerebral tissue, a topic reviewed by Brante (1949) and Himwich and Himwich (1959). There is an enormous literature on this subject. Suffice it to point out that the water content of the brain increases as lipids fall, the latter mostly in relation to myelin. Ribonucleic acid is reduced, as is potassium (K), reflecting loss of intracellular substance, and the content of iron (Fe) and calcium (Ca) increases.

In a similar time frame, cerebral blood flow decreases 20 percent by the age of 80+ years according to Kety (1956); presumably blood flow accommodates to the number of functioning neural elements.

Brain atrophy, when viewed in its microscopic dimensions, is attributable to neuronal loss and replacement by fibrous astrocytes. There is more or less general agreement among morphologists on this point even though the many attempts to count neurons at different age periods have yielded results that are somewhat conflicting. This is not surprising when one considers the difficulties in applying a purely quantitative methodology to structures such as the poorly demarcated areas of the cerebral cortex, which indeed have no finite boundaries. In point of fact, there is no complete consensus even on the number of neurons in the human cerebral cortex (figures range from 2.6 × 10$^9$ to 16.5 × 10$^9$). And, even in the most circumscribed cytoarchitectonic region such as motor area 4, the number cannot be ascertained because the boundaries are difficult to affix. The morphologist must therefore be content to count the number of neurons in representative parts of an indeterminate total. The method usually has been to calculate the number of neurons in .01cm³ of cortical tissue, but this has an obvious inherent error if the cell loss has led to shrinkage and a secondary approximation of cells. The available data are reviewed by Brizee (1973) and need not be reproduced here. He estimates, from a collation of the findings of several investigators, a reduction in the cerebral cortical neurons of about 20 percent from early to late adult life with a corresponding increase in glial density. Arendt (1972) records similar changes in the aged guinea pig, rat, dog, cat, and horse. Numeration of Purkinje and granule cells of cerebellum, neurons of basal ganglia and thalamus and of particular nuclei of brainstem, of dorsal-root ganglion and anterior horn cells of spinal cord, all reveal some degree of depletion with age. Burns (1958) deduced from studies such as these that the average adult loses 100,000 neurons per day. These data gain credibility by the fact that the reduction in neuronal number parallels loss in brain volume and weight. However, this conclusion has not passed uncontested. In a detailed analysis of the neurons in the ventral cochlear nucleus, Konigsmark and Murphy (1970) found no evidence of a loss of neurons with age and questioned whether there is any proof that loss of brain weight in general is due to depletion of neurons. Hanley (1974), who has reviewed this subject, decided that a nerve cell degeneration is not a universal phenomenon (i.e., occurring in all nuclear structures), but he allows the possibility that certain systems of neurons might be more vulnerable to age effects than others, a conclusion reached earlier by Brody (1955).

In an attempt to overcome some of the inconsistencies of numeration methods that depend on the human eye, other parameters of neuronal populations have been sought. The DNA and RNA per unit of nervous tissue has been measured and found to be reduced, but this method does not separate glial from neuronal elements. "Automated cell counting" (i.e., by machine) has been attempted to give more accurate quantitation, but here the results have not proved to be accurate because of the difficulty in separating small neurons from glial cells. The use of butyryl cholinesterase as a marker of glial cells has been used in an attempt to overcome this error, but again with limited success.

Of course, reliance on nerve cell bodies (peri-karyon), disregarding axons and myelin sheaths, gives only one parameter of brain atrophy. The nerve cell body, even if lost, would account for only a fraction of the volumetric change. Here another theoretical problem arises if one concentrates on numbers of myelin sheaths and axis cylinders, for it is known that each of these structures has its own susceptibilities to all manner of pathological states. It is possible that they or the dendritic processes of neurons might be destroyed by aging or disease while the "soma" of the nerve cell escapes.

With all these reservations in mind, as a working premise the author suggests, nonetheless, that brain atrophy and nerve cell loss be accepted as valid findings related at least in part to age. Further, it is probable that not all systems of neurons suffer the same degree of numerical attrition. Certain functionally related systems of neurons are probably affected more than others. One must agree with Brizee (1973) that there is still need for rigorous quantitation of different systems of nerve cells (i.e., a kind of differential analysis, in aging brains free of disease).

## ALTERATIONS OF NEURONS THAT COULD LEAD TO NEURONAL DEGENERATIONS IN THE AGING BRAIN

It is logical next, to inquire into the nature of the cytologic changes that could result in neuronal death. Histologists have grappled with this problem for nearly a century and the final answer still cannot be given. The following histopathological changes have been observed with increasing frequency in the later period of life and are thought by various pathologists to be related in some manner to the aging process(es):

1. Changes in organelles in neurons;
2. Accumulation of lipofuscin or lipochrome in nerve and glial cells;
3. Neurofibrillary changes of Alzheimer;
4. Granulo-vacuolar changes;
5. Pick, Hirano, and other bodies;
6. Senile plaques;
7. Congophilic angiopathy and amyloid bodies (Corpora amylacea);
8. Capillary fibrosis.

### CHANGES IN ORGANELLES IN NEURONS

Concerning progressive cellular changes, leading authorities are more or less agreed that neurons undergo visible age-linked changes. The size of many of the neurons diminishes. The blocks of cytoplasmic chromatin (Nissl bodies) become depleted and more variable in size and shape. The nuclei diminish in size and are more irregular in outline and the nuclear chromatin becomes more dispersed. And, as in the cells of many other organs there is a steady accumulation of lipofuscin within the cytoplasm.

Under the electron microscope it is seen that the chromidial substance (rough endoplasmic reticulum) and minute granules (ribosomes) in the cytoplasm of aged neurons have become more sparse. This corresponds to the reduced basophilia observed by light microscopy. There appears to be a rough parallel between the loss of Nissl substance and the accumulation of lipofuscin. Further, the nuclear membrane is invaginated (indicative of shrinkage). The Golgi apparatus of nerve cells becomes loosened and fragmented. Mitochondria are often swollen and have a degenerated appearance. In some of the latter, cristae disappear and central deposits of opaque material are seen. Metallic elements in the form of large or small particles accumulate in the cytoplasm of ancient neurons. Copper and iron are two of the elements that are identifiable in the lysosomes of nerve cells. Also, iron appears in astrocytes. Melanin granules are also reduced in the pigmented nerve cells of the brainstem (particularly the locus coeruleus and substantia nigra), and remnants (melanosomes) are seen free in the tissue or in microgliacytes, serving as markers of neuronal degeneration. Iron and calcium increase in the walls of small vessels in the lenticular nuclei and cerebellum. Feulgen-stainable proteinaceous material increases in the nuclei of aging nerve cells.

The synaptic and dendritic surfaces of neurons in the aging brain have been examined by Scheibel and Scheibel (1975), who describe the following sequence of alterations. In the third layer of the prefrontal and superior temporal cortex, the profile of the aging neurons and proximal dendrites is found to be "swollen and lumpy." There is a progressive loss of horizontally oriented dendritic systems (especially the basal dendrites); the apical shafts of dendrites are degenerated.

Axons become thinner and have a higher content of neurofibrils and neurotubules. Myelin sheaths are said to thicken as axons diminish in size. Spheroids are visible in axons in the neuropil of the brain. They are particularly prominent in the nuclei of Goll and Burdach. Axo-somatic and axo-dendritic synapses are reduced in number, and the number of spines on the dendrites diminishes. As astrocytes increase in number, their glial fibrils increase in stainability. Oligodendroglial satellites around nerve cells are said to be more evident—a finding we cannot confirm. The cellular components of capillary walls become fluorescent and in some places bundles of filaments course over the surface of such vessels. The size of the extracellular space is reduced.

A number of synthetic enzymes decline in parallel with these age changes in neurons. Those that facilitate the formation of catecholamines, such as tyrosine hydroxylase, glutamic acid dehydroxylase choline, acetyltransferase, and dopa decarboxylase, are reduced and noradrenaline diminishes. Others such as monoamine oxidase are said to increase with age. It has been shown that their rate of turnover is reduced and also that the lipid content of the aging brain diminishes.

## LIPOCHROME (LIPOFUSCIN) ACCUMULATION

For nearly a century, neuropathologists have observed the increased deposition of a fatty pigment in the cytoplasm of aging nerve cells. This material takes the form of fine granules that collect in the cytoplasm of neurons as well as of astrocytes, in the former between nucleus and apical dendrite. It stains variably but usually brownish (hence the term "fuscin" or "lipofuscin") with the common aniline dyes used in microscopic preparations; it is acid-fast, PAS-positive, and exhibits autofluorescence. Histochemical studies reveal protein, carbohydrate, and lipid moieties. For a time these granules were confused with ceroid, another fatty complex that forms in cells in certain diseases, but more recent chemical analyses have shown them to be different. Such age-linked pigments occur in the cells of all organs and are referred to by pathologists as "wear and tear" pigment.

More detailed biochemical studies trace the lipofuscin granules to primary lysosomes—special cytoplasmic particles that contain a wide variety of acid hydrolases (cf. reviews by Adams, 1965, and Pearse, 1972). The steps by which lysosomal enzymes and degeneration products are sequestered in autophagic vacuoles and deposited as residual bodies have been outlined by a number of workers. Currently, one of the widely entertained theories is that, during aging, free chemical radicles, and/or peroxides appear in the cell and damage subcellular enzymes, membranes, and nucleic acids. The latter ultimately become auto-oxidized, cross-linked, and formed into tertiary lysosomes or lipopigment granules. The cause of the failure to remove these peroxides during cellular metabolism is postulated to be a deficiency of peroxidase, catalase and glutathione peroxidase, enzymes that are shown to become depleted with age.

There is still a dispute as to the significance of lipopigment formation, whether it reflects a gradual impairment of essential biosynthetic processes in neurons or is a compensatory and potentially beneficial mechanism whereby toxic levels of cations and other elements are inactivated and extruded from the cell. The author favors the former interpretation since, in the pigment-laden areas, as was stated above, there is a decrease in RNA and ribonuclease (Hydén and Lindstrom, 1950; Morel and Wildi, 1952a).

As to the neuroanatomical localization of the first and most prominent intracellular accumulations of lipofuscin, Vogt and Vogt (1946) stated that each nuclear aggregate of cells has its own characteristic time course. Actually lipofuscin has been seen at birth and it is fairly obvious in the inferior olivary nerve cells by the sixth to the tenth year. Wahren (1957) finds lipofuscin formation to be prominent in the nucleus tuberolateralis of the hypothalamus as early as the fifth and sixth decades and in the pallidum by the seventh to eighth.

Brody (1960) observed an increasing proportion of cortical neurons to contain pigment with increasing age. The highest percentage was in the precentral gyrus. In contrast the Purkinje cells and some of the smaller nerve cells in brainstem nuclei show little if any tendency to lipochrome deposit at any age.

## NEUROFIBRILLARY TANGLES

These structures, named after Alzheimer (1907a) who first described them in a case of senile dementia, consist of skeins and whorls of intracytoplasmic microtubules. These microtubules proliferate and form compact parallel bundles that displace the neuronal nucleus as they fill out the cytoplasmic envelope. In the initial phase a thick band is seen to course from the apical dendrite to axon hillock alongside the nucleus; other bands are added. The tangles in the cerebral cortex tend to be elongate or triangular; those of the hippocampus more in the shape of a torch; and those in the subcortical nuclei, globose. The affected part of the cell lacks chromidial substance, and in the aniline stains (Nissl, H and E) only an altered refractility reveals its presence. The neurofibrillary tangles are brilliantly demonstrated by silver stains.

According to the electron microscopic studies of Terry and Wiesnewski (1970 and 1972), the constituent microtubules are abnormal in size as well as in number. Along their length there are regular constrictions suggesting a rotation every 80 mm. Another feature is their birefringence in polarized light.

It is believed that the fibrillary tangles reflect an abnormality of protein metabolism, but this is speculative. Eventually their elaboration leads to neuronal death, and the wicker-basket-like skeins may persist like a skeleton for a time after the rest of the cell has disappeared.

In the opinion of Alzheimer (1907b), this neurofibrillar change involves neurofibrils already present in the neuron. Bielschowsky (1932) disagreed because the abnormal argentophilic strands and particles seem to have little relationship to normal neurofibrils. Divry (1927) raised a further objection in that the argyrophilic material has staining reactions like those of amyloid. The latter substance was, in his view, deposited first on the surface of the cell and later on the neurofibrillary tangles themselves. It was this assumed congophilia of the substance that linked it in his mind to the senile plaque (as will be discussed below), and suggested a common origin of the two abnormalities. However, electron microscopy, while confirming the existence of amyloid in the senile plaque, does not do so for the neurofibrillary tangles.

The most frequent sites of the neurofibrillary change are the hippocampus, the temporal and the frontal lobe cortices, but in certain diseases it is seen in the mesencephalon, rostral rhombencephalon, and rarely the cerebellum, basal ganglia, and spinal cord. When present in the cerebral cortex there are usually senile plaques and granulovacuolar changes in the pyramidal cells of the hippocampus. Strangely, neurofibrillary tangles are not seen in sensory neurons of the dorsal-root ganglia, spinal cord, and brainstem.

## GRANULOVACUOLAR DEGENERATION

First described by Simchowicz (1910) in the cytoplasm of the hippocampal pyramidal neurons in senile brains, this alteration consists of the formation of dense basophilic granules 0.5–1.5µ in diameter, surrounded by vacuoles. The granules are not seen in Nissl stain but are readily visualized in H and E, Lendrum's phloxine-tartrazine, and in silver stains. They are PAS negative. As they increase in number, the Nissl substance is displaced and the cell outline becomes more irregular. Under the electron microscope these vacuoles are seen to be surrounded by a membrane, and the body in the center of the vacuole to consist of electron-dense granular material. The granulovacuolar bodies may be numerous in the cytoplasm of the neuron or there may be only one or two. They are more frequent in cases showing senile plaques and fibrillary changes. Indeed, they may be seen in neurons showing neurofibrillary tangles, which led Morel and Wildi (1952b) to believe that they are an early stage of neurofibrillary degeneration. However, the latter occurs all through the cortex and other parts of the brain and the granulovacuolar change is more or less restricted to the hippocampal pyramidal neurons which, as Corsellis (1976) points out, would disprove this relationship. Although a prominent feature of Alzheimer's disease and senile dementia, they are also observed in normal aging brains. Tomlinson and Kitchener (1972) rarely saw them in patients less than 60 years of age but they were present in 75 percent of cases age 80 or older.

Although increasing with age more or less in parallel with neuronal loss, there is no proof that granulovacuolar change is a stage of neuronal degeneration.

## PICK BODIES AND HIRANO BODIES

Inflated neurons with homogeneous cytoplasm are shown to contain dense argyrophilic bodies (Pick bodies) in Pick's disease and, rarely, in the normal aged brain. In such neurons, neurofibrillae and Nissl bodies appear to have virtually disappeared. Under the electron microscope Schochets, Lampert, and Earle (1968) noted in swollen cells with and without Pick bodies a loose aggregate of neurofilaments and neurotubules and the endoplasmic reticulum was vesiculated. The change is considered nonspecific. Spatz (1972) suggested that it is a reaction to distal axonal degeneration, a view accepted by Wisniewski and Terry (1971). However, one may question the authenticity of this interpretation since alterations of this type do not occur in Betz cells whose axons have been destroyed by capsular lesions. Such neuronal alterations are to be found in the cerebral cortex, basal ganglia, and midbrain.

The Hirano bodies, first observed by Hirano, Demlitzer, Kurland, and Zummena (1968) in the Guam Parkinson dementia disease, are also most often observed in the hippocampus. They consist of eosinophilic, nonargyrophilic, paracystalline, laminated structures which, by electron microscopy, are shown to consist of alternating sheets and rows of fibrils. Although localized mainly in the perikaryon, a few can sometimes be seen in the axon. Hirano and others have found them in amyotrophic lateral sclerosis, Alzheimer's disease, Pick's disease, and in the normal aging brain. Although they resemble the sheets of microfilaments in the Alzheimer fibrils, they are distinguished by their lack of argyrophilia, of birefringence, and of congophilia. Where numerous, there is usually a loss of some of the neurons, but it cannot be said that these intracellular changes are responsible for neuronal death.

## SENILE PLAQUES

These amorphous structures, first identified by Blocq and Marinesco (1892), are also thought by many to reflect neuronal degeneration. They are known to occur in small numbers in most old brains of man and some animals. Most of them are localized to the cerebral cortex (including the marginal layer) but a few may be seen in the amygdaloid nuclei, corpus striatum, thalamus, brainstem, and cerebellar cortex. Several types have been described. The most frequent and common type consists of a central homogenous core surrounded by an irregular cleared halo outside of which is a ring of fibrillar material. There may be a few microgliacytes in them and fibrous astrocytes may surround them. Others consist of round patches of granular or filamentous debris and some appear only as rounded homogeneous spheres that displace nerve fibers to one side. In size they vary from 5 to 100 μ, are nearly always spherical but with rather irregular outlines. Wisniewski and Terry (1972) postulate a developmental relationship between the types. In the first stage in development of the so-called primitive plaque, there is a central deposit of amorphous debris surrounded by a few glial cells. As it evolves, the plaque acquires the appearance of the more classic form, in which a more or less spherical central deposit of amorphous granular-fibrillary material is surrounded by particles, with a peripheral microglial reaction. The central, dense, argyrophilic central core contains at this stage a deposit of amyloid. The fibrillar material around the plaque still exists and is believed to be remnants, as in the beginning, of degenerated neuronal processes. The final or end stage, called the "burned-out" plaque, is composed mainly of amyloid with a few microgliacytes and astrocytes, but no dystrophic neurites are left.

The origin of the senile plaque has been a subject of controversy. One view is that the plaque begins as one or several degenerated neurons, or a disintegration of the peripheral processes of a group of neurons. A condensation (syneresis) of the ground matrix of the neuropil is another hypothetic explanation; and still another postulation is that congophilic deposits in capillary walls extend perivascularly into the tissue and form a nidus for plaques. Redlich (1898) and Alzheimer (1902) traced them to changes in glial reticulum, and Soniat (1941) and Liss (1960) believed them to start from an aggregate of neurofibrils from degenerating neurons. Divry (1927) was the first to identify amyloid in the center of the plaque and he postulated that it was deposited on condensed areas of ground substance in the neuropil. The attraction of microgliacytes and activation of astrocytes, according to his view, were secondary.

Senile plaques are seen most often in the temporal, frontal, and occipital cortex and the hippocampus; they are most numerous in patients dying with senile dementia. They increase in frequency with age and but few individuals over 90 years fail to have at least a few of them. In general they correlate with neurofibrillary neuronal changes and granulo-vacuolar degeneration.

## AMYLOID DEPOSITS AND CORPORA AMYLACEA

As was remarked above, amyloid is found in the center of many senile plaques and accounts for the congophilic property of their centers. And in some cases, as first pointed out by Scholz (1938), there is amyloid in the walls of small vessels in older individuals, a condition that he termed "drusige Entartung." This type of CNS amyloid has no relationship to that which occurs in the well-known primary systemic or secondary amyloidosis or in the pseudoamyloid masses that may form at the sites of gamma radiation.

In the typical congophilic angiopathy, a term given by Pentelakis (1954) which seems apt, the first deposit is in the basement membrane and perithelium and spreads to involve the whole of the vessel wall. It imparts a homogeneous or hyaline appearance, and the material stains pink in H and E and Nissl preparations. The vessels in the cerebrum are most disposed to this deposit, but those in the meninges may be affected and occasionally those of pancreas and heart as well. Although thought by Scholz (1938) to be related to senile plaques, others such as Krucke (1950) believe this association to be rare.

The amyloid in senile plaques has been studied under the electron microscope by Terry (1964), Kidd (1963), and others, all of whom find it to be composed of fibrils 300 to 100,000 Å in length and 70 to 100 Å in width to which is attached a second plasma component.

*Amyloid bodies* (corpora amylacea) are entirely unrelated spherical structures 10–75 μ in diameter, with a slightly denser core. They appear in increasing number with age in the brain and spinal cord,

being most numerous beneath pia and the ependyma.

Recent electron microscopic studies by Ramsey (1965) traces them to intracytoplasmic bodies in the processes of fibrous astrocytes. A glycogen-like substance with bound phosphate and sulfate radicals accounts for their staining reactions according to Strain and Roukema (1973). They have no particular association with the amyloid of senile plaques or congophilic vessel changes.

## OTHER ALTERATIONS OF VESSELS

Of course atherosclerosis, lipohyaline change, and hypertensive arteriolosclerosis increase with age and produce a variety of focal ischemic and hemorrhagic lesions. But they are conceded to have a recognizable pathogenesis unrelated to aging per se.

It was pointed out above that there are also age changes in capillaries and arterioles. The basement membrane thickens, the outer media is infiltrated, and the adventitial cells (pericytes) react. Small amounts of amyloid are not infrequently deposited in these parts of the vessel or impregnate all coats of the vessel in old age. Here the amyloid is deposited in "brush-like and stellate patches" in the adventitia or perivascular space of cortical and meningeal arterioles. Morel and Wildi (1952b) found such changes most frequently in the cerebral cortical area 17 and they termed the condition "dyshoric angiopathy." Such deposits have also been reported in the choroid plexuses, infundibulum, and in the vessels of the area postrema, subpial zones in pons, medulla, and spinal cord. In the latter sites they appear as nodular patches extending along fiber tracts and into the molecular area of cortices, where they are surrounded by rows of microgliacytes and astrocytes. When extending perivascularly the amyloid rarely will form the center of a senile plaque. However, we agree with Krucke (1950) that in the usual form of pure congophilic angiopathy no senile plaques or Alzheimer fibrillary changes are to be observed.

Gellerstedt (1933) called attention to an increasing number of perivascular fibroblasts and reticulum fibers with age, but most neuropathologists have not found this change to be consistent. Other vessel changes are age-linked, however. There are duplications and thickenings of the internal elastic lamina, increased fibrous tissue, and the deposit of hyaline-like, basophilic globules along small vessels in the basal ganglia and central parts of the cerebellum. These latter formations contain calcium (calc) and iron (hence called "ferrocalc") as well as other metallic ions. Extreme degrees of it may be visible in x-rays of the skull, and only then are there slight parenchymal changes and gliosis. Similar deposits have been observed in several other mammalian forms.

## THE SIGNIFICANCE OF CYTOLOGIC AND VASCULAR CHANGES WITH REFERENCE TO NEURONAL LOSS AND BRAIN ATROPHY

The aforementioned changes are all observed with increasing frequency in the brains of older humans and in some animals. The author has not described them in great detail for the reason that there are numerous authoritative articles devoted to each of them, which are cited in the bibliography. Of more general interest are such matters as the significance of these changes and their relation to the neuronal degeneration of aging, and whether or not there is evidence that they alter neuronal function.

Of all the changes, certainly lipofuscin deposits have been the most completely studied. For a time, after ceroid was identified, lipofuscin and ceroid were confused and it was common practice to discuss both in connection with degenerative diseases (e.g., the Jansky-Bielschowsky late infantile lipidosis and the Batten-Spielmeyer juvenile lipidosis). Reference has already been made to the origin of the lipofuscin from lysosomes and the suggestion (not universally accepted) that it represents a degradative change (resulting in a kind of neuronal slag) that impairs function and ends eventually in cell death. The older neuropathologic literature contains innumerable references to "lipoid degeneration" and contrasts it to simple neuronal atrophy. The evidence that this lipochrome formation results in the destruction of neurons is scanty. Certainly one may observe gradual nerve cell loss without lipofuscin deposit and also extreme degrees of lipofuscinosis with little loss of neurons. Hence, the correlation is inexact. Moreover, there is no real indication at present that the function of neurons which have accumulated lipofuscin is in any way altered. These remain key problems yet to be solved.

The significance of the Alzheimer neurofibrillary change as an age-linked change has been brought into question by a number of recent discoveries. It is noted to be a frequent finding in the neurons of the substantia nigra in encephalitis lethargica (von Economo's disease) presumably caused by a slow virus, and it is extremely prominent in the neurons of the upper brainstem in supranuclear ophthalmoplegia described by Steel, Richardson, and Olszewski (1964). Aluminum salts induce a proliferation of microtubules and the formation of neurofibrillary tangles in animals, and colchicine also stimulates their formation. Such data suggest that this change, originally thought to be unique in Alzheimer's disease and senile dementia, hence a degenerative age effect, may have multiple causes. Again there are no data concerning the effect of such microtubular alterations on neuronal function. Presumably neurofibrillary changes lead to neuronal degeneration in Alzheimer's disease, but there is no evidence that the more general neuronal losses throughout the nervous system begin this way.

The granulovacuolar change, which is more or less restricted to the pyramidal cells of the hippocampus, is poorly understood, as are also cytoplasmic formations (Pick bodies, Hirano bodies, Lewy bodies) that are thought to characterize a number of neurological diseases. Again their relation to the more common widespread and age-linked neuronal losses are to be doubted.

The meaning of amyloid is also obscure. It certainly has nothing to do with the hereditary and immunologic diseases that cause deposits in viscera, muscle, and so on. The origin of the senile plaque with which it is obviously associated appears not to begin with amyloid deposit but rather with the degeneration in small foci of the distal processes of neurites. How and why they attract the amyloid is unknown.

The hyaline-calcium-iron conglutinations along capillary walls in certain parts of the brain are known to be increased in certain diseases such as hypoparathyroidism, Fahr's disease, and Hallevorden-Spatz disease, which brings into question their specificity or age-linkage. This change and the perithelial fibrosis have never been incriminated in neuronal loss even though the idea that subtle changes in capillary perfusion might have a deleterious effect on the brain parenchymal is plausible. And, even if such changes are to be demonstrated, an equally acceptable theory would be that they are secondary to neuronal loss.

We can state, at the time this chapter is being written, that all the nerve cell changes described above occur in increasing degree with age but each one appears under other conditions so that there is a theoretical possibility of pathogenic mechanisms other than age being operative in its production. Further, neurofibrillary neuronal changes and senile plaques develop in increasing number in advancing years in individuals who are relatively well preserved with respect to mental function. One of the most carefully studied series is that of

Tomlinson, Blessed, and Roth (1968) who compared a group of 28 brains from individuals who were mentally competent with 50 from another group who were demented (1970). Their aging control group ranged from 56–92 years. They observed only quantitative differences between the two groups but the degree of change was far more advanced in the demented group. Thus, in over 70 percent of the demented patients the pathologic changes were more severe than in any one of the control cases. Dayan (1970) made similar observations. He noted that a few senile plaques were found in 40 percent of the controls whereas all of the demented cases exhibited large numbers of them. Neurofibrillary changes and granulovacuolar changes were apportioned in the same way between control and demented groups.

From these and other studies it would appear that if an individual lives long enough (90 years), the possibility of there being some degree of senile plaque formation, neurofibrillary and granulovacuolar changes approaches 100 percent. These then must be accepted as the histologic markers that correlate most perfectly with senility but not with senescence. They stand apart from other types of neuronal degeneration. The conditions under which these same tissue alterations may develop early in life, even in childhood and adolescence, and be associated with profound dementia and death within a few years are presently unknown. Special forms have been observed in the punch-drunk pugilist (Brandenberg and Hallervorden, 1954), and in midadult life in the individual suffering from Down's syndrome (Jervis, 1948).

## PATHOLOGIC CHANGES IN THE SENILE BRAIN AND THEIR RELATION TO DEMENTIA

Age and dementia go together. This idea is as old as the hills and is familiar to laity and medical scientists alike. But the morphological basis of this late-life decline in mental function has been elusive. For a long time two groups of changes in the brain—arteriosclerosis and brain degeneration and atrophy—have been associated with dementia.

Since arteriosclerosis is known to become increasingly prominent in middle and late adult life, it seemed reasonable to assume that if it had led to multiple small and large infarcts this could adequately explain a loss of mental function. And, since infarcts are often found in "quiet areas" of the brain, the dementia might not be accompanied by strokes. These observations and interpretations are incontrovertible and the literature is full of remarkable cases where one or a few strokes had resulted in profound mental changes. For example, occlusion of the inferior temporal branches of both posterior cerebral arteries with infarction of the hippocampal-parahippocampal regions has caused a severe Korsakoff amnestic defect, as in the well-studied case by Victor, Angevine, Mancall, and Fisher (1961). Border-zone infarcts in the parieto-occipital regions have been observed to give rise to severe agnosic and apraxic defects. Occlusion of frontal branches of one or both anterior cerebral arteries has produced striking frontal lobe defects.

But in these and other cases the clinical syndromes have differed in that there was not a general disintegration of all intellectual functions but a disproportionately severe impairment of one or other mental functions such as memory, speech, reading, visual perception, and praxis. Moreover, rather than a gradual and progressive decline in mental function, in nearly all instances, an apoplectic or strokelike onset of at least part of the syndrome had occurred. Rothchild (1942) and Marchand (1949) came to the conclusion that it was the involvement of small vessels causing minute, silent lesions in the lenticular nuclei and thalamus that causes more serious effects on mental function than does occlusion of larger ones. No doubt they were referring more to the lacunar state in hypertensive-atherosclerotic and diabetic patients, often with pseudobulbar symptomatology. Interestingly, Tomlinson, Blessed, and Roth (1970) could not confirm a greater involvement of small vessels in their cases of arteriosclerotic dementia; and Corsellis (1976) states that he was unable to corroborate the pathogenesis put forward by Fisher (1951) that stenosis of neck vessels could cause dementia by gradually reducing the blood supply to the brain.

Unfortunately, many of the reports of arteriosclerotic dementia are so inadequate from the standpoint of detailed clincial analysis and anatomic study that generalizations are impossible. One cannot really ascertain from the reports the status of cerebral function just prior to death or what neuronal systems were found to be destroyed at the time of the postmortem examination. What is much needed are single well-studied cases. These are of greater value than a series of poorly studied cases.

As a working clinical principle, we have taught our resident staff that any individual who shows a gradual decline in all measurable intellectual functions (verbal, memory, calculation, visual and auditory perception, and in problem solving), in short, in intelligence, will almost invariably be found to have a degenerative disease of the brain.

The relation of cerebral atrophy to dementia has been difficult to determine, again because of the inadequacy of the clinicopathological studies. There have been a number of studies comparing the brain of cases of Alzheimer's disease and senile dementia to the aging brain of mentally normal individuals. One of the most frequently quoted studies is that of Gellerstedt (1933) who described the brains of a series of old individuals whose minds were allegedly normal. However, the clinical examinations were carried out months or years before death and one did not know their mental status shortly before they died. In the aforementioned series of Tomlinson *et al.* (1968), this source of error was recognized and, indeed, this was the motivation for the study of a series of cases whose level of mental competence was being assessed at regular intervals, and also within a few months of demise. In those who were living an independent existence and fully able to cope with their environment up to the time of death, they found atrophy to be minimal in the males and almost nonexistent in females. A considerable number had a few senile plaques, and neurons showing neurofibrillary changes and granulovacuolar degeneration; but, when present, they were always slight in degree in contrast to the series with dementia. Hence one must conclude that if dementia has become evident in the older person, either vascular lesions or plaque-fibrillary abnormality or both are usually present and severe.

There are, however, other dementing degenerative diseases of obscure etiology in which brain atrophy is not accompanied by senile plaques and Alzheimer neurofibrillary changes. Presumably the neuronal degeneration and gliosis have some other cause. In some of these the disease is surely a variant of Huntington's chorea, i.e., a dementia without chorea. Creutzfeld-Jakob disease is another example, now believed to be due to a slow virus. In others dementia has been combined with Parkinson's syndrome and in some instances with amyotrophic lateral sclerosis where there are lesions in the cerebral cortex, substantia nigra, and anterior horn cells of nonspecific type. Widespread cortical neuron degeneration and gliosis without senile plaques and fibrillary neuronal changes have been reported in the rapidly advancing dementia and psychosis of Kraepelin's disease (cf., summary by Corsellis, 1976). But in all these and other ill-defined degenerations of late life, it would be incorrect to conclude they are due to the aging process per se.

## EXPERIMENTAL APPROACHES TO THE MORPHOLOGIC ASPECTS OF AGING

The processes leading to the degeneration of neurons appear to be basic and need to be the focus of future research. They are manifestly operative at all ages from the embryonal period to old age and are more prominent in the first than latter half of life. And although they may represent different processes at these two extremes of life, their pathogenesis may differ, a point that must be proven by further study. Since the neuronal degeneration occurs in both the developing and aging animal, the entire sequence can be studied under the controlled conditions of the laboratory.

There is also unequivocal evidence that many of the subtle neuronal alterations associated with aging can be found in the macaque and other primate and mammalian forms. This is true of lipofuscin deposit, senile plaque formation, and many alterations of chromidial substance, mitochondria, axo-dendritic and axo-somatic synapses, axons, myelin, and nuclei. Of these, only the neurofibrillary change has not been seen as a naturally occurring phenomenon in the animal. But, as was remarked above, comparable changes have been induced in the experimental animal by the administration of aluminum hydroxide and colchicine. Hence, the study of this change under experimental conditions becomes possible.

## CONCLUSIONS

The sum and substance of what has been stated is that despite a prodigious amount of work that has been done on the aging brain, there are remarkably few solid conclusions that can be drawn. The author believes the assembled facts justify acceptance of certain ideas—that there is a definite atrophy and functional weakening with age of many systems of neurons at all levels of the nervous system, from peripheral to central and from spinal to brainstem and cerebral. These are more or less universal and the deficits are gradual all through adult years and increase in late life. Their functional and anatomical quantitation in individuals free of disease still requires much study and documentation. It seems likely that the time sequences and safety factors in different systems of neurons vary.

Some of the most carefully studied neuronal alterations unquestionably increase with age. However, proof is lacking that such changes as lipofuscin deposit, neurofibrillary proliferation and condensation, granulovacuolation, intracellular bodies, and plaque formation are related to the neuronal losses in various systems of nerve cells. Nevertheless certain combinations such as the Alzheimer fibrillary changes and argyrophilic plaques, when widespread and severe, may result in failure of cerebral associative functions. Here a series of changes normally common to advanced age obviously assumes the form of a pathological syndrome indicative of a disease of multiple etiologies. The same may be said of Pick's lobar sclerosis, progressive supranuclear palsy and the Guam Parkinson-dementia complex. Whether these latter diseases which tend to have their onset in late middle-adult life and the senium involve a predisposing age factor is not known.

A fundamental pathologic principle must not be forgotten in these and other cerebral conditions—that disease states are delineated not merely by a single histologic feature but by a combination of changes of particular topography and temporal course, and often by the presence of other denominative factors, such as a virus or genetic background. Finally, in some instances the final pathologic picture is a combination of age changes and totally unrelated disease(s).

# REFERENCES

ADAMS, C. W. M. (ed.), 1965. *Neurochemistry.* London: Elsevier.

ALZHEIMER, A. 1902. Du Seelenstörungen auf arterioskerotisher Grundlage. *Allg. Ztschr. Psychiat., 59,* 693.

ALZHEIMER, A. 1907a. Ueber eine Eigenartige Erkrankung der Hirnrinde. *Cbl. Nervenheilk. Psychiat., 18,* 177–179.

ALZHEIMER, A. 1907b. Ueber eine Eigenartige Erkrankung der Hirnrinde. *Allg. Ztschr. Psychiat., 64,* 146.

ARENDT, A. 1972. Altem des Zenhalnervensystems. *In,* H. Gottfried (ed.), *Handbuch de Allgemeiner Pathologie,* pp. 49–542. New York: Springer.

BARON, S. A., JACOBS, L., AND KINKLE, W. R. 1976. Changes in size of normal lateral ventricles during aging determined by computerized tomography. *Neurol., 26,* 1011–1013.

BIELSCHOWSKY, M. 1932. Histopathology of nerve cells. *In,* Penfield, W. (ed.), *Cytology & Cellular Pathology of the Nervous System,* pp. 145–188. New York: Paul B. Hoeber.

BLINKOV, S. M., AND GLEZER, I. 1968. *The Human Brain in Figures and Tables.* New York: Plenum.

BLOCQ, P., AND MARINESCO, G. 1892. Sur les lésions et la pathologie de l'épilepsie dite essentiale. *Semin Med.*

*Paris, 12,* 443–446.

BÖNING, H. 1925. Zur Kenntnis des Spielraums zwischen Gehirn und Schädel. *Ztschr. Neurol. Psychiat. (Berl.), 94,* 72–84.

BRANDENBERG, W., AND HALLERVORDEN, J. 1954. Dementia pubilistica mit anatomischen Befund, *Virchow Archiv. für Pathol., Anat., und Physiol. und für Klinische Medizin, 325,* 680–709.

BRANTE, G. 1949. Studies of lipids in the nervous system with special reference to quantitative determination and topical distribution. *Acta Physiol. Scand. (Suppl.), 18*(63), 1–189.

BRAUNMÜHL, A. VON. 1957. Alerserkrankungen des Zentralnervensystem. *Archiv. für Psychiat. Nervendrank, 191,* 419–449.

BRIZEE, K. R. 1973. Neurobiological aspects of maturation and aging. *In,* D. H. Ford (ed.), *Progress in Brain Res., Vol. 40,* pp. 73–92. Amsterdam: Elsevier.

BRODY, H. 1955. Organization of the cerebral cortex: III. A study of aging in the human cerebral cortex. *J. Compar. Neurol., 101,* 511–556.

BRODY, H. 1960. The deposition of aging pigment in the human cerebral cortex. *J. Gerontol. 15,* 258–261.

BURNS, R. D. (ed.), 1958. *The Mammalian Cerebral Cortex.* London: Edward Arnold.

CORSELLIS, J. A. N. 1976. Aging and dementia. *In,* W. Blackwood (ed.), *Greenfield's Neuropathology,* pp. 796–849. London: Edward Arnold.

DAYAN, A. D. 1970. Quantitative histological studies of the aging brain. *Acta Neuropath., 16,* 85.

DIVRY, P. 1927. Etudes histochimiques des plaques séniles. *J. Belg. Neurol. Psychiat., 27,* 643–657.

FISHER, C. M. 1951. Senile dementia: A new explanation of its causation. *Canad. Med. Assoc. J., 65,* 1–7.

GELLERSTEDT, N. 1933. *Zur Kenntnis der Hirnveranderungen bei der Normalen Altersinvolution.* Uppsala: Almquist & Wiksells Boktryckeri A–B.

HANLEY, T. 1974. Neuronal fall-out in the aging brain: A critical review of the quantitative data. *Age & Ageing, 3,* 133–151.

HIMWICH, H. E. 1959. Biochemistry of the nervous system in relation to the process of aging. *In,* J. E. Birren, H. A. Innus, and W. F. Windle (eds.), *The Process of Aging in the Nervous System,* pp. 101–126. Springfield, Ill.: Charles C Thomas.

HIMWICH, W. A., AND HIMWICH, H. E. 1959. Neurochemistry of aging. *In,* J. E. Birren (ed.), *Handbook of Aging and the Individual,* pp. 187–197. Chicago: University Chicago Press.

HIRANO, A., DEMLITZER, H. M., KURLAND, L. T., AND ZUMMENA, H. M. 1968. The fine structure of some intraganglionic alterations. *J. Neuropath. Exp. Neurol., 27,* 167–181.

HYDÉN, H., AND LINDSTROM, B. 1950. (See Discussion-Faraday Soc. 9, 436–440, 1950.

JERVIS, G. A. 1948. Early senile dementia in mongoloid idiocy. *Amer. J. Psychiat.*, *105*, 102–106.

KETY, S. S. 1956. Human cerebral blood flow on oxygen consumption in relation to aging. *Res. Publ. Assoc. Nerv. Ment. Disease, 35*, 31–41.

KIDD, M. 1963. Paired helical filaments in electron microscopy of Alzheimer's disease. *Nature, 197*, 192.

KONIGSMARK, B. W., AND MURPHY, E. A. 1970. Neuronal populations in the human brain. *Nature, 228*, 1335–1336.

KRUCKE, W. 1950. Das Zentralnervensystem bei generalisierter Paramyloidose. *Arch. Psychiat. Nerven., 185*, 1662–1666.

LAST, R. J., AND TOMSETT, D. H. 1953. Casts of cerebral ventricles. *Brit. J. Surg., 40*, 425–445.

LISS, L. 1960. Senile brain changes. Histopathology of ganglion cells. *J. Neuropath. Exp. Neurol., 19*, 599–571.

MARCHAND, L. 1949. L'artériosclérose cérébrale: les aspects mentaux. *Annales Medico-psychologiques, 107*(1), 433–438.

MOREL, F., AND WILDI, E. 1952a. Clinique pathologie générale et cellulaire des alterations séniles et préséniles du cerveau. *In, Proc. First Internat'l. Neurol. Cong. Neuropathol.*, (Rome) *2*, 227–247.

MOREL, F., AND WILDI, E. 1952b. General and cellular pathochemistry of senile and presenile alterations of the brain. *In, Proc. First Internat'l. Neurol. Cong. Neuropathol. 2*, 347–374.

ORDY, J. M., AND BRIZEE, K. R. 1975. *Neurobiology of Aging.* New York: Plenum.

PEARSE, A. G. E. (ed.), 1972. *Histochemistry: Theoretical and Applied*, 3rd Edition, Vol. 2. London: Churchill Livingstone.

PENTELAKIS, S. 1954. Un type particulier d'angiopathie sénile du système nerveux: l'angiopathie congophile. *Monatsch. Psychiat. Neurol., 128*, 219–256.

RAMSEY, H. J. 1965. Ultrastructure of corpora amylacea. *J. Neuropath. Exp. Neurol., 24*, 25–39.

REDLICH, E. 1898. Ueber miliäre Sklerose der Hirnrinde bei seniler. *Atrophie Jahrbücher für Psychologie und Neurologie, 17*, 208–216.

ROTH, M., TOMLINSON, B. E., AND BLESSED, G. 1966. Correlation between score for dementia and counts of senile plaques in the gray matter of elderly subjects. *Nature* (London), *209*, 106.

ROTHCHILD, D. 1942. Neuropathological changes in arteriosclerotic psychoses and their psychiatric significance. *Arch. Neurol. Psychiat., 48*, 417–436.

SCHEIBEL, M. E., AND SCHEIBEL, A. B. 1975. Morphological and neurochemical aspects of the aging nervous system. *In*, H. Brody, D. Harma, J. M. Ordy (eds.), *Structural Changes in the Aging Brain*, Vol I., pp. 11–37. New York: Raven Press.

SCHOCHETS, S., LAMPERT, P. W., AND EARLE, K. M. 1968. Neuronal changes induced by intrathecal vincristine sulphate. *J. Neuropath. Exp. Neurol., 27*, 645–658.

SCHOLZ W. 1938. Studien zur Pathologie der Hirngefässe II. *Zeitschr. Gesampte Neurol. Psychiat., 162*, 694–715.

SIMCHOWICZ, T. 1910. Histologische Studien uber die Senildemenz Nissl-Alzheimer. *Arbeiten, 3*, 268.

SONIAT, T. L. L. 1941. Histogenesis of senile plaques. *Arch. Neurol. Psychiat., 46*, 101–144.

SPATZ, H. 1972. La maladie de Pick: les atrophies systématisées progressives et la sénéscence prématurée localisée. *Proc. First Internat'l Neurol. Cong. Neuropathol.*, 375–406.

STRAIN, F. C., AND ROUKEMA P. A. 1973. Histochemical and biochemical aspects of corpora amylacea. *Acta Neuropath.* (Berl.), *25*, 95–102.

STEELE, J. C., RICHARDSON, J. C., AND OLSZEWSKI, J. 1964. Progressive supranuclear palsy. *Arch. Neurol., 10*, 333–359.

TERRY, R. D. 1964. The fine structure of neurofibrillary tangles in Alzheimer's disease. *J. Neuro. Path. Exp. Neurol. 22*, 629–642.

TERRY, R. D., AND WISNIEWSKI, H. M. 1970. The ultrastructure of the neurofibrillary tangle and the senile plaque. *In*, G. E. W. Wolstenholme and M. O. O'Connor (eds.), *Alzheimer's Disease and Related Conditions*, pp. 145–165. London: J. A. Churchill.

TERRY, R. D., AND WISNIEWSKI, H. M. 1972. Ultrastructure of senile dementia and of experimental analogues of aging and the brain. *In*, C. M. Gaitz (ed.), *Advances in Biology*, Vol 3, pp. 89–116. New York: Plenum.

TOMLINSON, B. E., BLESSED, G., AND ROTH, M. 1968. Observations in the brains of nondemented old people. *J. Neurol. Sci., 7*, 331–356.

TOMLINSON, B. E., BLESSED, G., AND ROTH, M. 1970. Observations in the brains of demented old people. *J. Neurol. Sci., 11*, 205–242.

TOMLINSON, B. E., AND KITCHENER, D. 1972. Granulovacuolar degeneration of hippocampal pyramidal cells. *J. Path., 106*, 165–185.

VICTOR, M., ANGEVINE, J. B., MANCALL, E. L., AND FISHER, C. M. 1961. Memory loss with lesions of hippocampal formation. *Arch. Neurol., 5*, 244–263.

VOGT, C., AND VOGT, O. 1946. Aging of nerve cells. *Nature* (London), *158*, 304.

WAHREN, W. 1957. Neurohistologischer Beitrag zu Fragen des Alterus. *Z. Alterusforsch., 16*, 343–357.

WISNIEWSKI, H. M., AND TERRY, R. D. 1971. *Advances in Behavioral Biology*, Vol. 3. New York: Plenum.

WISNIEWSKI, H. M., AND TERRY, R. D. 1972. Re-examination of the pathogenesis of the senile plaque. *In*, H. M. Zimmerman (ed.), *Progress in Neuropathology*, Vol. 2, pp. 44–56. New York: Grune & Stratton.

# III

# Behavioral Sciences

# 8

# Use of the EEG and Evoked Potentials in the Investigation of Age-Related Clinical Disorders

*Henry J. Michalewski, Larry W. Thompson, Ronald E. Saul*

Anyone embarking upon the electrophysiological examination of brain and behavior relationships will encounter a rich variety of investigative efforts. Our focus here is upon the electrical activity that can be recorded from the scalp and the information that can be derived from such recordings. Aside from the many methodological and technical problems associated with collecting these scalp signals in normal subject populations, a tremendous challenge exists for the application of these techniques to patient groups and in clinical situations. Although the use of more advanced computer techniques offers promise in the refinement of assessment or diagnostic tools for the physician or clinician, direct application of this technology is only starting.

The topics emphasized in the following pages include the relation of health and age-related dis-

orders to the ongoing electroencephalogram, the clinical electroencephalogram, and, particularly, to event-related or evoked potentials. It is not possible in a single chapter to discuss all topics as completely as one might find desirable for complete understanding, but it is hoped that the information presented here will encourage further interest and work in this important area of endeavor.

The electrical potentials which are recorded from the scalp of the normal resting adult include most commonly the alpha rhythm (8–13 cycles per second), prominent over occipital and parietal regions, theta waves (4–7 cps), delta waves (approximately .5–3.5 cps) and beta waves (13 cps and above). Mean ranges for the alpha rhythm in the young adult are 10.2 cps to 10.5 cps (Lindsley, 1938), whereas individuals over 60 years of age demonstrate a decline in the alpha frequency to approximately 9.0 cps to 9.7 cps (Obrist and Busse, 1965). Besides the predominant rhythmical activity of the ongoing electroencephalogram, other features of interest include amplitude differences, synchronous and asynchronous discharges, hemispheric asymmetries, slow wave complexes, phase shifts, intermittent periods of electrical silence, and D.C. or very slow wave electrical activity. The origins of these potentials near the scalp are attributed to graded dendritic responses sensitive to a range of input intensities. The periodic rhythmic activity of the scalp represents the summated synaptic potentials generated within the cerebral cortex; this scalp activity, in turn, is influenced and is modulated by activity in thalamic and brainstem centers (Andersen and Andersson, 1974; Schlag, 1974). A detailed analysis of the sources of the scalp EEG is beyond the scope of the present chapter; however, a comprehensive treatment on the origins of the EEG is given by Creutzfeldt and Houchin (1974).

The generators of the electroencephalogram are particularly sensitive to psychoactive and pharmacological agents that alter electrical patterns in prescribed ways (Fink, 1968, 1974; Itil, 1974). Several very excellent texts exist, which the reader should consult for information regarding recording methods and procedures, and examples of clinical EEGs (see, for example, Cooper, Osselton, and Shaw, 1969; Gibbs and Gibbs, 1950; Hill and Parr, 1950; Kiloh, McComas, and Osselton, 1972; Kooi, 1971).

Alpha wave slowing is a consistent feature observed in the EEG records of the elderly (Obrist, 1976), a change which occurs quite gradually over the life span (Friedlander, 1958). Slightly lower mean alpha frequencies are observed in older males than in age-matched females (Mundy-Castle, 1962). The reasons for alpha slowing with increased age are not yet exactly determined, but vascular disorders (Obrist, 1963, 1964) may be implicated.

Focal abnormalities over the temporal, and especially left anterior temporal areas (3–5 cps), are a frequent observation in the electroencephalograms of older individuals (Busse, Barnes, Silverman, Shy, Thaler, and Frost, 1954; Harvald, 1958). The cause of this temporal slowing is most likely attributed to impaired cerebral circulation and does not appear to have been associated with any specific intellectual disturbances (Busse and Obrist, 1963). Indeed, in general, for healthy older individuals there is little relation between measures of intellectual functioning and the EEG (Busse, Barnes, Friedman, and Kelty, 1956). Irregularities

in the EEG are detected more readily at the extremes of the life span, that is, under 15 years and over 55 years of age, than for early and mid-adult ranges (Greenblatt, 1944). Severely demented patients often display bursts of EEG activity different in either frequency or amplitude from the dominant EEG rhythm (Frey and Sjogren, 1959).

Other features in the EEG of the elderly include increases in frontal bicentral fast activity and in some instances, increases in diffuse slow activity. Diffuse slowing is most closely associated with intellectual deterioration and can be viewed as more pathological than normal. There is a relative absence of beta activity in senile patients with intellectual deterioration, which suggests that the presence of beta activity in the EEG of an older person may be regarded as a favorable sign.

## EEG CHANGES OBSERVED IN SELECTED CEREBRAL DISORDERS ASSOCIATED WITH AGING

In evaluating the elderly for central nervous system disorders, the EEG remains as an important noninvasive diagnostic procedure. This is particularly true for the assessment of progressive disease processes occurring over time. Although the recent development of the computerized axial tomogram (CAT) is now considered the definitive test for demonstrating structural alterations in the brain tissue, this advance has not made electroencephalographic techniques obsolete. The dynamic sensitivity of the EEG to brain function, especially in the absence of gross pathology, makes EEG testing a most valuable diagnostic tool in evaluating patients with confusion, dementia, or depression (Andriola, 1978; Wilson, Musella, and Short, 1977).

Wilson has suggested four ways in which the EEG may be useful in patient evaluation (Wilson *et al.*, 1977):

(1). The EEG may help to define a disorder as either organic or functional. However, a normal EEG does not automatically indicate normal brain function, and conversely, the EEG may be normal in dementing disorders especially when the dementia is mild and in the early stages of onset. An abnormal EEG, on the other hand, is a strong indicator of organic impairment and suggests the need for additional examinations to identify the specific disease responsible for the clinical picture.

(2). In the organic patient, the EEG can provide evidence for focal or diffuse pathological processes. The need, as well as the choice of additional diagnostic procedures, frequently depends upon whether a focal or diffuse lesion is suspected.

(3). The EEG repeated on two or more occasions assists the physician in determining the temporal characteristics of the disease process whether progressive, stable, or resolving.

(4). And on occasion, a characterisic wave pattern will strongly suggest a particular diagnosis, for example, the periodic sharp wave complexes in Jakob-Creutzfeldt's disease and the distinctive triphasic waves in metabolic encephalopathy.

There are diagnostic limitations. A recognized EEG abnormality does not necessarily imply a relationship to observed clinical dysfunction. The disturbances in brain function producing the EEG abnormalities may occur for more than one disease process, and the EEG patterns, although useful in assessing localization and extent of the functional disorder, cannot be expected to predict the exact nature of the underlying pathology. Harner (1975) has emphasized the value of the EEG as an early screening procedure in the work-up for dementias, for there are occasions when it is sometimes possible to detect electroencephalographic abnormalities early in the course of dementing-type illnesses which are potentially reversible and treatable.

## EEG in Diffuse Encephalopathies and the Dementias

Gloor, Kalabay, and Giard (1968) have described the electroencephalogram in diffuse encephalopathies with respect to the EEG correlates of gray and white matter lesions. In disorders involving the cerebral white matter, irregular widespread theta-delta slowing is the characteristic abnormality; epileptiform discharges are uncommon. In contrast, the encephalopathies with predominately cortical gray matter involvement often have epileptiform abnormalities (sharp waves, spikes, or spike wave discharges) in the EEG. Bisynchronous slow waves and spike-and-slow wave patterns are frequently observed if gray matter involvement is diffuse with pathology at both the cortical and subcortical levels.

The waking EEG of demented patients shows no specific pattern and may vary from normal to diffusely slow activity with or without focal discharges. The evolution of the pathologic process responsible for the mental impairment, rather than the degree either of the brain damage or of the dementia, determines the degree of abnormality. The slight EEG changes observed in dementias of prolonged and slow evolution are hardly distinguishable from the physiological changes associated with aging. Normal EEGs may at times be observed in severe dementias from chronic brain disease or injury. The EEG in this instance may represent a secondary normalization parallel to the anatomical or physiological stabilization of the initial lesions. On the other hand, in progressive dementias or those due to acute, subacute, or repetitive brain lesions, the awake EEG shows diffuse abnormalities that parallel in intensity both the degree of brain damage and mental deterioration (McAdam and Robinson, 1956; Weiner and Schuster, 1956). As described earlier, focal slowing in the anterior temporal region, usually on the left, is quite consistent with normal intellectual functioning in elderly individuals. If the slowing, however, involves adjacent areas such as the frontal, the midtemporal, or the posterior temporal region, or is associated with a diffuse disturbance, an organic mental syndrome is the more likely diagnosis. In one study, 79 percent of the patients with diffuse slow activity had an organic brain syndrome, whereas 80 percent of those with normal EEG had a functional disorder (Obrist and Henry, 1958). The most prominent changes in the EEG observed in senile dementia (most likely Alzheimer's disease occurring in elderly individuals) as outlined by Markand (1977) include: (1) a slowing of the alpha rhythm to below 8 Hz; (2) the occurrence of low amplitude diffuse theta and delta slow waves; (3) a decrease or absence of low amplitude beta activity; and, (4) frontal rhythmic delta activity, usually bilateral and intermittent.

Epileptiform discharges are rare in senile dementia. Muller and Kral (1967) found that in senile dementia the normal fast EEG background activity, often rather sharp in appearance, becomes intermingled with diffuse slow waves and is gradually replaced by slow activity and sharp slow wave complexes in serial recordings. Severely demented patients, with autopsy evidence of senile or presenile dementia, displayed symmetrical episodic slow wave discharges that were maximal in the posterior head regions. These waves often had an initial sharp component that resulted in a triphasic appearance, not unlike the triphasic discharges associated with metabolic encephalopathy. The triphasic wave forms occurred at a fairly regular rhythm with a repetition rate ranging between 0.5–1.0 cps. Some of the severely demented patients also showed a prominent evoked response consisting of a sharp or triphasic wave-form with slow photic stimulation. The triphasic waves also occurred with arteriosclerotic dementia; the prognosis for these patients was poor. Wilson, however, was unable to confirm these observations (Wilson et al., 1977). Almost all patients with triphasic waves in his laboratory had a metabolic encephalopathy, most likely the result of liver failure. An example of the triphasic patterns due to liver involvement is shown in Figure 8–1. An investigation by Muller (1978) reviewed cases with triphasic waves. Confirmed autopsy results were available for only two cases. In the majority of the cases, the abundance of the triphasic waves varied with the intensity of a systemic disorder; however, triphasic waves were also observed in uncomplicated senile-Alzheimer's disease.

The central EEG feature of senile-Alzheimer's disease is progressive diffuse slowing followed by disorganization. A posterior 7 to 8 Hz alpha rhythm is generally considered slow; however, slowing from 11 or 12 Hz to the 8 or 9 Hz range may represent a significant deterioration of the EEG, which only serial EEG studies would detect. Harner (1975), in his review of 661 EEGs recorded on patients 60 years of age or older, observed that patients with increasingly serious neurological symptoms had a progressively increasing incidence of EEG abnormalities. EEG abnormalities, for instance, were found in only 17 percent of patients with nonspecific minimal complaints; however, abnormal EEGs were found in 75 percent of patients with dementia of varied etiology. As expected, abnormal EEGs were almost always associated with seizures, confusion, stroke, and coma. Overall, diffuse slowing is the most characteristic EEG finding in elderly patients with dementia, its severity being well correlated with the degree of functional loss. With the possible exception of the triphasic waves described earlier, the presence of EEG rhythms other than diffuse slowing suggest a nondegenerative etiology.

### ALZHEIMER-TYPE OR PICK-TYPE DEMENTIAS

Electroencephalographic abnormalities in presenile dementia of the Alzheimer-type or Pick-type are similar to those observed in senile dementia, but more severe. Several generalized EEG changes have been described for these conditions (Letemendia and Pampiglione, 1958; Liddell, 1958). The alpha rhythm is slowed or absent in association with diffuse low-to-medium amplitude irregular theta activity which dominates the background. Irregular random diffuse delta waves may occur or there may be high amplitude generalized runs of semi-rhythmic delta waves most prominently seen in the frontal-temporal regions. As in senile dementia, spontaneous or barbiturate-induced fast activity is reduced or absent in the frontal-central regions. The slow activity displays a minimal response to external stimuli, and sleep activity is disorganized in the advanced cases. Records from a demented elderly individual with monomorphic frontal delta patterns are shown in Figure 8-2.

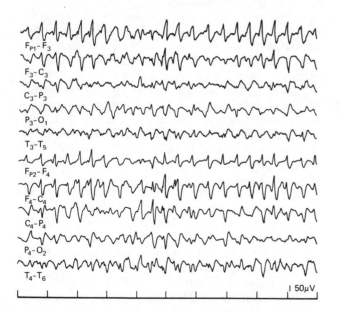

**Figure 8–1**   An example of the characteristic triphasic sharp wave patterns resulting from a liver disorder recorded from a male patient 50 years of age. (T. C. = 0.16 sec; time segments = 1 sec; negative is up).

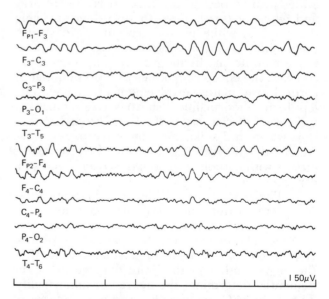

**Figure 8–2**   EEG tracing demonstrating monomorphic frontal delta activity (2–3 Hz) in a 79-year-old female diagnosed with dementia. (T. C. = 0.16 sec; time segments = 1 sec; negative is up).

The EEG does not reliably differentiate between Alzheimer's disease and Pick's disease. There are, however, differences in the severity of the EEG abnormalities between the two disease states. The EEG is almost always abnormal even in the early stages of Alzheimer's disease. The EEG may be abnormal in the early stages of Pick's disease, but if so it is usually less severe. These observations were reported in a study of 61 cases of presenile dementia with cerebral biopsy information by Gordon and Sim (1967). The normal or mild EEG findings in Pick's disease may reflect the localization of the disease process to the frontal and temporal regions in contrast to the involvement of the parietal and occipital regions in Alzheimer's disease. A normal EEG in the face of well-established presenile dementia, therefore, favors the diagnosis of Pick's disease (Markand, 1977). The relationship between the degree of dementia, the duration of illness, and the severity of the EEG changes is negligible.

A paper by Johannesson and his colleagues reported on the EEG and regional cerebral blood flow in neuropathological autopsy data in 17 patients with presenile dementia (Johannesson, Brun, Gustafson, and Ingvar, 1977). Separation of the cases into Alzheimer's or Pick's disease was based on the severity and regional distribution of the neuronal degeneration as seen on microscopic section. There was slow progression of the EEG abnormalities in the Alzheimer's cases, whereas the Pick's patients had normal EEGs even when the signs of dementia were marked and late in the course of the disease process. There was a tendency for measures of regional cerebral blood flow to correlate positively in precentral regions with the degree of EEG abnormality but negatively in postcentral areas. In addition, a number of patients showed bifrontal delta bursts that were related to degenerative changes in the brainstem. A reduction of cerebral blood flow in the temporal parietal areas is associated with memory deficits, speech, and perceptual disturbances (Gustafson, Risberg, Hagberg, Hougaard, Nilssen, and Ingvar. 1972). 1972).

The relationship between EEG abnormalities and regional pathology, for which a sufficiently large and representative sample of psychiatric elderly patients was included, is supported in the few studies relating autopsy findings and EEG disturbances (Leroy, Brion, and Soubrier, 1966). The presence of alpha activity was related to the anatomical intactness of subcortical gray nuclei rather than the anatomical integrity of the cortex, but a study of the correlation between diffuse EEG abnormalities and cerebral atrophy in senile dementia was essentially negative (Stefoski, Bergen, Fox, Morrell, Huckman, and Ramsey, 1976). The EEG, at least for the population investigated, was not a reliable aid for the detection of cerebral atrophy. Muller (1978) in a study of 100 autopsy reports and EEGs obtained during the last 12 months of the patients' lives reported significant correlations between the degree of diffuse EEG slowing and pathological findings indicative of senile and Alzheimer's disease. These findings, however, were considered tentative because of certain methodological limitations and the fact that a number of variables, namely the presence of severe physical illness and drug effects, may have influenced the EEG. Nevertheless, it was of interest that patients with confirmed Alzheimer's disease (intense plaque and tangle formation) showed abnormal tracings, while the EEG was normal in some patients with nonspecific atrophy. Deisenhammer and Jellinger (1974) previously reported a significant correlation between slowing of the alpha rhythm and the number of senile plaques in dementia. Studies of sleep patterns in the presenile and senile dementias are sparse. Feinberg (1976, 1978) has reported positive correlations between various stages of sleep and measures of cognitive functioning.

## CEREBROVASCULAR DISORDERS

The EEG abnormalities associated with generalized cerebral arteriosclerosis (multi-infarct dementia) can be remarkably similar to those described for senile dementia (van der Drift and Kok, 1972). The most common features include: (1) slowing of the resting waking alpha rhythm; (2) runs of bilateral anterior delta waves in drowsiness; (3) frequent and abrupt changes in the level of awareness; and (4) minor, sharp and slow activity in the anterior and midtemporal region. These latter patterns, generally inconspicuous, consist of brief trains of 3 to 8 Hz waves of medium voltage mixed with moderate sharp waves, nearly always lateralized, but at times shifting from side to side with a left emphasis. They are seen in the waking state and in very light drowsiness. These temporal abnormalities may well reflect ischemia of the hippocampus, which derives its blood supply from the basilar vertebral posterior circulatory system. Memory deficits are often associated. Drachman and Hughes (1971) compared EEG results and psychological test scores of normal aged subjects ($n = 15$, 51–69 years) and of patients with circumscribed bilateral hippocampal lesions ($n = 5$, 18–44 years). Aged subjects and patients were contrasted to a control group of normal young subjects ($n = 20$, 18–44 years). Psychological tests included the WAIS, Wechsler Memory Scale, extended auditory digit span, and visual paired-light span. In contrast to the patients with temporal lesions, the EEG and cognitive findings in the normal aged reflected a more diffuse degenerative process rather than hippocampal pathology. Hippocampal patients performed poorly on tests requiring memory storage but were approximately equal to the aged normal group in cognitive nonmemory tests.

Although many reports have concluded that the differentiation of multi-infarct dementia from senile dementia was difficult, if not impossible, electroencephalographically, Muller (1978) has provided guidelines consistent with the findings in his autopsy series. Sclerosis of cerebral arteries was found in all cases with lateralized episodic slow waves. In contrast, occipital alpha was often well preserved; in fact, those with background slowing showed additional pathological evidence for senile brain disease. Intermittent lateralized slow waves or slow waves alternating between the hemispheres most likely reflected intermittent vascular insufficiency. Symmetrical slow waves, particularly if sinusoidal or triphasic, were usually not caused by vascular disease but by systemic disease and the presence (or absence) of advanced senile brain disease. Thromboembolic lesions often produced abnormalities that were asymmetrical and persistent. Whether or not EEG abnormalities resulted was a function of the size of the lesion, proximity to the cortex, and acuteness. Small chronic subcortical lesions, for example the lacunes associated with hypertensive vascular disease, may have no effect at all on the EEG.

Chatrian, Shaw, and Leffman (1964) have described an EEG abnormality, termed periodic lateralized epileptiform discharges (or PLEDs), which has been associated with vascular disease in a large percentage of cases. These periodic discharge patterns were related to altered states of consciousness, psychosis, and confusion-disorientation. Additionally, these discharges were often associated with focal epileptic seizures and a grave prognosis. Autopsy studies revealed diffuse lesions with a cortical predilection, predominately parietal-temporal-occipital. It is now recognized that these lesions reflect acute or subacute vascular insufficiency in the border zone region between the territories of the large cerebral arteries. This occurs almost exclusively in elderly arteriosclerotic patients with long-standing chronic circulatory insufficiency. With chronic border zone insufficiency, the EEG findings are less dramatic; focal intermixed slow and sharp activity appears diffusely over the involved hemisphere, but always

predominating at the parietal-temporal-occipital junction. An example of the characteristic discharges associated with PLEDSs is illustrated in Figure 8-3. Patients may exhibit a variety of memory, perceptual-motor, or speech disorders, symptoms of which in the aggregate closely resemble a global dementia. The periodic EEG pattern described in association with chronic circulatory failure may also reflect an anoxic encephalopathy following an acute cardiac or respiratory arrest.

## JAKOB-CREUTZFELDT'S DISEASE AND HUNTINGTON'S CHOREA

If the periodic discharges consist of bilateral bursts of spikes and slow wave activity at regular intervals in a patient over 40 years of age with progressive dementia, the most likely diagnosis is Jakob-Creutzfeldt's disease. These highly characteristic patterns are found at a moderately advanced stage of the disease. Initially a nonspecific progressive slowing is observed, followed after a number of months by the suppression of background rhythms and evolution of the characteristic periodic sharp wave complexes (Burger, Rowan, and Goldensohn, 1972; Lee and Blair, 1973). Myoclonic jerks and changes in level of consciousness are present in advanced stages of this disorder.

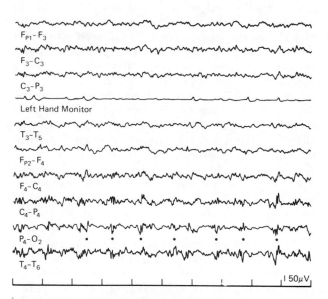

**Figure 8–3**   Acute ischemia of the parietal-occipital vascular boundary zone producing electrographically periodic epileptiform discharges (PLEDS) in a 68-year-old male patient. Prominent periodic discharges are indicated by dots in the illustration. (T. C. = 0.16 sec; time segments = 1 sec; negative is up).

The characteristic EEG pattern in Huntington's chorea consists of an absence of rhythmic activity in association with low voltage random intermittent slow activity in the theta and delta range. There is minimal or no change with hyperventilation, a finding noted in other hereditary degenerative disorders. Altered sleep patterns of low voltage with few sigma rhythms (or sleep spindles between 12 and 14 cps) and a poor response to sound stimuli are also noted. In an EEG-neuropathological study, Scott, Heathfield, Toone, and Margerison (1972) described a positive correlation between a low voltage EEG and generalized cortical atrophy.

In summary, gross EEG abnormalities are usually not observed at the onset of presenile dementia (Alzheimer's disease), Huntington's chorea, or senile dementia. There might be a slight slowing of alpha frequency or a slight excess of delta activity (Harner, 1975). In the course of one or more years, diffuse progressive slowing and loss of fast activity occur; clinical symptoms lag behind until the late stages of the disorder when paroxysmal or triphasic activity can be recorded. The value of the EEG in patients with dementia depends, therefore, on the stage of symptom development. In the early stages, a normal EEG provides good evidence against an infectious, metabolic, toxic, or focal disorder. The presence of diffuse slowing in the later stages helps to differentiate between organic causes of dementia and psychotic disorders of functional origin. As mentioned, focal weakness, language disturbance, or seizures may occur in the course of a degenerative disorder, with associated focal slow waves or irritative activity (sharp waves, spikes) in the EEG. Diagnosis may be difficult in such cases, as focal features can occur in as many as 10 percent of patients with degenerative disorders. This, however, should not delay the search for a focal and treatable lesion.

Although the incidence of EEG abnormality in the early stages of intellectual impairment due to degenerative disorders is low, the reversible and treatable secondary metabolic and related encephalopathies are usually associated with mild to more severe degrees of slowing. The EEG slowing usually antedates the onset of mental symptoms and correlates well with the degree of mental impairment. Hypothyroidism, hypoxia, hypoglycemia, hepatic or renal disease, collagen vascular disease, pernicious anemia, uremia, pulmonary insufficiency, trauma, increased intracranial pressure, low pressure hydrocephalus, CNS infections, and post-seizure states may all produce diffuse slow activity in the elderly.

## DRUG EFFECTS AND HYDROCEPHALUS

Muller (1978) has emphasized the lability of the geropsychiatric EEG and its sensitivity to many influences, which indicates a decreasing efficiency of homeostatic mechanisms. This would suggest that drugs or ingestion of other substances affecting metabolism may have a more pronounced effect on the EEG. Phenothiazines, anticonvulsants such as phenytoin and carbamazepine, may produce slowing of the waking background rhythms. This is part dose-related, the slowing more evident with increasing toxicity (Andriola, 1978). Ingestion of barbiturates, alcohol, and related drugs will produce a predominately low or moderate voltage fast EEG often associated with confusion and unresponsiveness. Tricyclic antidepressants (such as imipramine, amitriptyline), phenothiazines, and lithium may also increase epileptiform activity; however, the increase is usually minimal and clinically insignificant. Other drugs, such as L-dopa and amantadine, and occasionally the antidepressants, may make a slow EEG appear more normal. Such frequency shifts may also result from functional psychiatric disorders, for example, during a change from a depressed to a manic phase or vice versa (Muller, 1978).

Much attention has recently been focused on the syndrome known as "normal pressure hydrocephalus," a potentially treatable dementing disorder. Brown and Goldensohn (1973) reported the EEG findings in eleven cases which met strict criteria for diagnosis. Six patients had normal records; of the patients, however, five had EEG abnormalities ranging from focal delta to diffuse theta and delta activity that were considered nonspecific.

## FOCAL LESIONS

The clinical EEG can be a useful screening procedure for the detection of localized brain lesions, in particular for those that grow sufficiently large to produce symptoms of dementia. Rapidly growing primary brain tumors and metastatic lesions are most easily detected (Harner, 1975). The scalp EEG electrodes generally reflect cortical activity over the hemisphere convexity. Lesions involving the deep and basal portions of the brain may remain undetected until they become large enough to produce increased intracranial pressure as well as dementia and (or) obtundation. Precise EEG localization of the focal lesion, therefore, is usually correct by hemisphere, but weak in regard to extent and exact lobar placement (Andriola, 1978).

The diagnosis of a subdural hematoma, frequently occurring with only minor or no head trauma, is especially difficult in the elderly. Unilateral or bilateral slow activity is generally present; however, the depression of the rhythmic fast and medium frequency activity gives the best clue as to diagnosis and localization. Slowing and decreased voltage are also observed over areas of unilateral brain infarction associated with thrombo-embolic arterial disease. These abnormalities improve over a period of several months in contrast to the persistent and increased focal slowing observed in the EEG of a patient with a mass or space-taking lesion (tumor, hematoma, or abscess).

Transient ischemic attacks are not usually associated with EEG abnormalities; slow activity in the occipital and posterior temporal areas supplied by the posterior cerebral artery may suggest vertebrobasilar vascular disease. Bilateral diffuse slowing or minimal or no change in the scalp EEG has also been reported in this condition.

Seizure activity may be the major or first manifestation of a space-taking lesion, or less frequently, cerebral vascular disease. The EEG may assist in the localization of epileptiform activity and associated abnormalities. These discharges (sharp waves and spikes) may occur in the absence of clinical seizures. The interictal EEG also may be normal in the presence of clinical seizures. An EEG recorded during the transition from waking to drowsiness to light sleep often enhances visualization of epileptiform activity. A well-defined sharp wave or spike focus suggests the presence of clinical epilepsy, especially when localization is frontal-temporal, or basal, when they arise from a large area, are of high voltage, and have short spikes and a polyphasic configuration. They must be differentiated from the isolated monophasic sharp waves seen so commonly in the midtemporal regions of the normal aged. Likewise, random focal low to moderate voltage slow discharges in the temporal region, especially on the left, may be difficult to assess with respect to their clinical significance when clinical symptoms suggest a focal brain lesion. In contrast to the fleeting, intermittent temporal slow and sharp wave activity associated with normal aging, intrinsic brain lesions generally produce a suppression or alteration of cortical background rhythms as well as lateralized or localized slow activity.

As with diffuse brain disorders, the EEG remains a useful screening procedure for the detection of focal lesions, prompting the clinician to order further neurodiagnostic evaluation, for example, a CAT scan for precise anatomical localization.

## RESPONSIVENESS OF THE ELECTROENCEPHALOGRAM

On occasion the resting EEG does not disclose potential irregularities or abnormalities unless stressed. Techniques commonly used by electroencephalographers to alter resting records include hyperventilation, photic stimulation, acoustic stimulation, sleep, and drug administration (Wells, 1963). Liberson (1944) introduced the technique of delivering sensory stimulation to the resting EEG in order that changes in the ongoing EEG may become visible, a technique that led to the concept of functional electroencephalography.

### ALPHA BLOCKING

Alpha blocking is a reaction observable in the EEG in which the rhythmic frequency pattern of alpha activity is desynchronized and reduced as the result of the presentation of pulsed trains of photic stimulation. The alpha blocking response is thought of as a sign of cortical arousal probably dependent upon the brainstem reticular activating system (Lindsley, 1956; Lindsley, Schreiner, Knowles, and Magoun, 1950; Moruzzi and Magoun, 1949). The diminished ability of the nervous system to react to photic stimulation, or demonstrate an alpha blocking response, may indicate age-related changes in the brain. Obrist (1965) presented evidence that habituation to repetitive flashes was significantly reduced for older individuals, indicating less cortical reactivity in terms of alpha blocking, than for younger individuals. Using alpha blocking measures, Liberson (1944) observed more alpha attenuation in patients with functional psychosis (depression, anxiety) than schizophrenic patients or patients with arteriosclerosis.

When elderly subjects are divided according to learning ability, for instance, poor learners versus good learners, overall differences in alpha activity are not observed; however, good learners tend to have more beta activity during conditions of eyes open and photic stimulation than poor learners (Thompson and Wilson, 1966). The manner in which EEG activation patterns might relate to measures of reaction time and mental set (or expectancy) was tested by Thompson and Botwinick (1968) in a group of elderly persons and compared with a group of young adults. Electroencephalographic recordings were collected simultaneously during experimental sessions of fixed and variable foreperiod reaction intervals. In both age groups, the greatest change in the EEG (desynchronization, EEG amplitude change) occurred during the 0.5-second preparatory duration of the fixed series of reaction time trials (foreperiods tested ranged from 0.5 sec to 15 seconds). For the irregular presentation mode, however, elderly subjects displayed the maximum EEG alteration with the shortest preparatory interval, whereas for younger subjects the minimum EEG change occurred at this interval. Reaction times for older subjects were significantly slower than for younger subjects, but preparatory duration did not produce a differential effect between the two groups. These results suggest, to the extent that desynchronization can be considered as a nervous system sign of arousal, that activation patterns based upon preparatory set were differentiated by age factors.

Auditory stimulation can also produce alpha blockage provided that the auditory presentation is conditionally paired with a bright flash of light. In order to determine the anatomical structures that might be responsible for this blockade phenomenon, Wells (1962) investigated conditioned blockade in neurologically normal subjects and in patients with various disease entities (e.g., cerebral vascular disease, seizure disorders, intracranial neoplasms). The conditioning was induced by presentation of a tone followed one second later by a long bright flash. Conditioning was scored as a reduction in the alpha rhythm after tone presentation but before the occurrence of the flash from EEG tracings. Results for 50 presentations of the tone-flash pair was 10.2 blockades for normals but only 6.1 blockades for the patient group. Patients with brainstem lesions and hemispheric disorders produced fewer conditioned alpha blocks than the normal group. An analysis of single flash responses showed more attenuating effects in normal controls than in the patient group. Responses to 100 flash presentations demonstrated greater habituation effects (that is, diminished alpha blocking responses) in patient groups than in the normals. In another study of tone-flash pairings, patients with varying degrees of organic damage exhibited fewer suppressed alpha responses than controls. When blocks of paired presentations were compared, brain damaged individuals showed less capacity for alpha blockade than normal individuals (Wells and Wolff, 1960).

Some evidence suggests that schizophrenic patients show a lack of alpha responsiveness similar to that found for patients with organic brain damage (Blum, 1957). No relationship has been observed between background EEG activity and estimated strength of the contingent or alpha blockage response. Yet high alpha frequency is positively related to strength of the blockage response, while a negative relation exists between the quantity of alpha and responsiveness in tone-flash pairings (Visser, 1961).

## TIMING MECHANISMS AND THE EEG

Surwillo (1963a, 1963b) hypothesized that the ongoing cyclic fluctuations of the EEG represented a basic timing or clock mechanism of the central nervous system. The EEG cycle was thought of as a fundamental unit of time by which events were programmed by the nervous system. Reaction times, for instance, were a function of the time or number of cycles needed to execute a particular response. Surwillo found a highly positive correlation between reaction time and the average period (frequency = 1/period) of the EEG for subjects between the ages of 29 and 99 years. Variability of reaction times was also related to differences in brain wave period. More complicated behavioral situations demonstrated that longer decision times were indeed correlated with slower brain wave activity and, conversely, that shorter decision times were associated with faster brain wave patterns (Surwillo, 1964a). The experimental manipulation of an individual's brain rhythm to speed of response was also shown by Surwillo (1964b).

## EVOKED POTENTIALS

Research during the past decade has suggested that the evoked potential (EP) may be helpful in the assessment of central nervous system disorders. A review by Starr (1978) has emphasized the use of EP technology in the determination of various sensory and neurological disorders, including hearing and visual disturbances, multiple sclerosis, and more recently, the evaluation of possible brainstem lesions. Evoked potentials have also been used in other clinical investigations, including the study of vascular disease (Crighel and Sterman-Marinchescu, 1971; Noel and Desmedt, 1975; Tsumoto, Hirose, Nonaka, and Takahashi, 1973), Jakob Creutzfeldt's disease (Lee and Blair, 1973) and age-related dementias (Schenkenberg, Dustman, and Beck, 1972; Straumanis, Shagass, and Schwartz, 1965; Visser, Stam, Van Tilburg, Op Den Velde, Blom, and DeRijke, 1976), to mention a few. While in some instances EPs have proven to be more effective than the ongoing EEG in assessing CNS disorders (Miyoshi, Luders, Kato, and Kuroiwa, 1971; Oosterhuis, Ponsen, Jonkman, and Magnus, 1969), the many ambiguities in the literature indicate a need for continued clinical research to clarify the importance of technical and methodological differences among studies. Greater attention to age as a variable may be helpful in reconciling conflicting findings.

Before discussing the interrelationship of EP measures with age and behavioral disorders, it might be helpful to elaborate briefly on the technical aspects of this methodology. Evoked potentials are small amplitude changes superimposed on EEG scalp potentials that occur as a result of some sensory stimulus or other related event. These responses can vary in amplitude from less than 1 μ V to approximately 25 or 30 μ V depending on the stimulus parameters and experimental paradigm being used. Since the background EEG is usually of higher amplitude, it is difficult to discern responses to single stimuli in the EEG tracing and virtually impossible to make any reliable measurements of these potentials. Traditionally, a process of signal averaging has been used to identify stable evoked responses that have identifiable characteristics. Essentially, this involves sampling short segments of EEG that are time-locked around a stimulus presentation, and then summing across these segments for repeated stimulus presentations. This procedure is based on the principle that the minute changes in potential synchronized to the stimulus sum additively with successive presentations or trials, whereas background activity, lacking such synchronization, will fluctuate in a random fashion and thus be canceled out in the summing process. An example of this process is illustrated in Figure 8-4. Separate trials to individual brief tones recorded from the vertex ($C_z$) are overlaid along with the derived averaged potential. While some features of the EP are visible in single trials, these are influenced by background activity and do not reflect a stable response pattern.

Scalp recordings gathered in response to brief stimulus presentations result in a characteristic wave form, as the one illustrated, made up of several components or waves consisting of both positive and negative deflections. A brief tone burst, for example, can produce a brain response that may persist for 250 to 300 msec, or longer. These are variously referred to as EPs, evoked responses, averaged evoked responses, event-related potentials, and so on. Measures derived from EPs may include the latency of various prominent components from stimulus onset as well as amplitude measures, either peak-to-peak or relative to an averaged prestimulation baseline period. An accurate procedure for calculating amplitudes involves averaging a calibration pulse of some known voltage (e.g., -10μV), along with the evoked response. The difference between the peak of the calibration

pulse and baseline period before stimulation yields a scaling factor that can be used to determine component amplitudes of the evoked response.

Components of the evoked response waveform are thought to reflect input from sensory receptors and the electrical activity of higher cortical centers. Each sensory modality elicits characteristic wave forms specific of that modality. Much attention has been devoted to the careful examination of brain responses to simple flashes (Cigánek, 1975), auditory stimulation (Storm van Leeuween, 1975), and somatosensory stimulation (Halliday, 1975). Evoked response components are sometimes separated into primary and secondary components based on latency or time from stimulus onset. Primary components occur shortly after onset up to approximately 50 msec, whereas secondary components range between 50 and 100 msec. Researchers have hypothesized that different neural structures are involved in the division of the components. Primary components are thought to involve thalamocortical pathways to primary sensory areas of the cortex while secondary components are polysensory in character resulting from extralemniscal pathways and nonspecific tha-

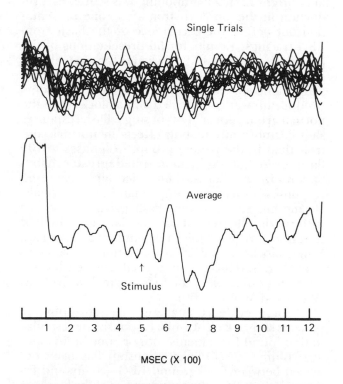

**Figure 8–4** Responses to simple brief tones are collected and averaged from a vertex ($C_z$) recording site referenced to the right earlobe. A–25μV calibration signal is shown at the beginning of the record.

lamic nuclei. Considerable controversy exists over the exact sources of the secondary or late responses and Beck (1975) has discussed evidence weighing different experimental positions. An excellent discussion of EPs and their neurophysiological and neuroanatomical correlates is given by Goff, Allison, and Vaughan (1978). Some difficulty has also arisen over the nomenclature of the various wave forms and components that may be encountered in EP research. In the auditory evoked potential, for instance, fifteen components can be identified from scalp averages (Picton, Hillyard, Krausz, and Galambos, 1974). Components that were once thought of as early are now classified as middle (up to 50 msec) since the discovery of brainstem potentials (1 to approximately 10 msec). Because the latencies of the various components can extend over a range of 500 msec and sometimes more, some confusion might occur. Such a vast literature has evolved concerning scalp-related potentials that the reader is advised to consult many of the excellent publications available for specific methodological details, analysis and treatment of results, and the many investigations collecting various EP measures (e.g., Callaway, 1975; Donchin and Lindsley, 1969; Perry and Childers, 1969; Regan, 1972; Shagass, 1972; Thompson and Patterson, 1973–1974).

A prominent theme throughout this literature emphasizes the importance of both stimulus and cognitive factors in influencing evoked response measures. Representative studies illustrating this are presented here to provide a framework for the consideration of clinical and aging research to be presented later. Two other types of EP, the contingent negative variation and the brainstem evoked response, are discussed separately.

## ATTENTIONAL FACTORS AFFECTING EPs

A striking feature of evoked responses to simple flashes, brief auditory clicks, or shock stimuli is the sensitivity these responses display to factors of attention (Garcia-Austt, Bogacz, and Vanzulli, 1964; Picton and Hillyard, 1974; Satterfield, 1965). Larger responses, particularly in the later components, are generally evoked to attended stimuli while unattended stimuli, or stimuli inducing distraction, decrease the amplitude of the response. A vigilance experiment described by Spong, Haider, and Lindsley (1965) illustrates one type of task controlling short-term attention. In their paradigm, recordings of visual and auditory evoked responses were collected from occipital and temporal regions, respectively. The experimental conditions consisted of (1) attending to a brightness change or an in-

tensity change, (2) a key-pressing task in which either flashes or clicks were attended, and (3) a counting task, attending either flashes or clicks and pressing a key after 50 stimulus presentations. The stimuli consisted of simple flashes and clicks alternately presented. For the brightness change (or an intensity change) and key-pressing situations, visual responses over the occipital area were larger for flashes than for clicks. When the subjects attended to clicks, however, they displayed larger auditory responses in the temporal area than when attending flashes. For the counting task no similar changes in the evoked responses were observed, and it was suggested that counting itself may be distracting and alter the attentive state of the subject. The findings demonstrated that even simple perceptual discriminations between sense modalities, demanding some degree of focused attention, easily alter the amplitude of the evoked response wave form.

Sutton, Tueting, and Zubin (1967) reported on the significance of a large positive wave in the evoked response which appeared dependent upon the information content delivered by simple stimuli. This large positive deflection occurred approximately 300 msec after the stimulus was presented and was related to the resolution of some uncertainty. If the subject was required to make a response to a stimulus which resolved some uncertainty, this late component or $P_{300}$ wave, was generally of larger amplitude than when the response did not resolve any uncertainty, as for example, when the subject had prior knowledge of the forthcoming stimulus.

In a typical vigilance task subjects probably attend equally to all the stimuli that are presented. Evoked responses may not always register changes in subject attention under these circumstances. However, Ritter and Vaughan (1969) found that small stimulus changes randomly embedded in a series of repetitive stimuli consistently elicited a prominent late positive component ($P_{300}$) in the averaged response. The appearance of the $P_{300}$ wave was considered the result of attentional shifts or orienting responses. In their report Ritter and Vaughan used both visual and auditory stimulation. For the visual condition, flashes were repetitively presented every three seconds; interspersed among the regular flashes a slightly dimmer signal flash was randomly presented. The subject's task was to monitor the flashes and press a switch whenever the dimmer signal flash was detected. For the auditory condition, brief tones were delivered at a fixed or standard level of intensity; embedded in the series of regular tones a signal tone of lower intensity was presented. Again the subject's task was to monitor the tones and press a switch whenever a signal tone was detected. Averaged scalp responses showed that vertex ($C_z$) and occipital sites exhibited a late positive component to the detected signals, whereas nonsignals did not have this deflection. If the discrimination between signals and nonsignals was made difficult, a late positive component was identified for both types of stimuli. Making the discrimination easy resulted in late components for both signal and standard stimuli in the early trials only to diminish with additional trial presentations. These results were interpreted as demonstrating the role of central processing mechanisms in assessing the cognitive significance of the stimuli.

Visual evoked responses are determined not only by receptor stimulation and attentional processes, but also by the perceptual context of the stimulus. Evoked responses are different for a blank field versus a field containing a geometric shape, as well as for dissimilar figures of equal area; geometrical figures of identical construction but unequal areas, however, produce visual responses that are very similar to each other ( John, Herrington, and Sutton, 1967). Visual evoked responses are also sensitive to parameters of stimulation including site of retinal stimulation (Eason, Groves, White, and Oden, 1967; Eason and White, 1967), intensity and wavelength (Eason, Oden, and White, 1967), and target structure and binocular interactions (Lehmann and Fender, 1967). The tachistoscopic presentation of more complicated stimulus patterns, for example a checkerboard pattern, produces visual evoked responses that are sensitive to movement, visual field stimulated, image sharpness, and the size and number of checkerboard elements (White, 1974). Extensive consideration of the methodology of patterned visual stimulation, especially with regard to application and clinical evaluation of the visual system, is presented in a text by Desmedt (1977) and a review by Sokol (1976).

Luders (1970) investigated somatosensory evoked potentials with subjects between the ages of 19 and 69 years. Response amplitudes described a V-shaped function with age. Generally smaller potentials were recorded for the 30-45 year age group than for either earlier or later age levels. An earlier study by Shagass and Schwartz (1965) reported similar findings. Liberson (1966) collected averaged cortical potentials in patients who suffered thrombosis of the left middle cerebral artery. In these patients right hemiplegia was also accompanied by aphasia. The results of somatic responses to median nerve stimulation were related in degree to speech impairment. Patients with only

slight verbal impairment displayed diminished responses over the ipsilateral hemisphere whether stimulated from the left or right sides. For a patient with severe aphasia, right median stimulation showed that essentially no response was recorded from either hemisphere, whereas left median stimulation showed little or no ipsilateral response while a contralateral wave was evident.

Visser *et al.* (1976) investigated visual evoked responses in groups of senile and presenile (Alzheimer-type) dementia patients. The patients tested ranged between 52 and 88 years of age. The common clinical symptoms of the patients included disorientation, various memory disturbances, intellectual deterioration, and language impairments. Scalp electrical potentials were collected from left and right parietal-occipital derivations and left and right occipital sites referred to an average reference. Stimulation consisted of brief flashes delivered at irregular intervals with eyes closed. Generally six waves in the averaged response were identified. Latency and amplitude measures were computed from the different peaks. Compared to normal controls, the evoked response results indicated that senile and presenile patients had longer latencies for all peaks except for an early wave around 70 msec. Amplitude measures revealed some increases in the later peaks.

## AGE-RELATED DIFFERENCES IN EVOKED POTENTIALS

While comparatively few studies have investigated EPs during the late adult range, there is clear evidence of reliable differences with age. These have been discussed in detail in earlier reviews (Klorman, Thompson, and Ellingson, 1978; Marsh and Thompson, 1977). In summarizing this literature, it is useful to distinguish between experimental paradigms in which individuals are responding to stimulation in a passive manner and those in which individuals are actively attending to information conveyed by stimulus presentation.

In passive situations where exogenous factors provide a major influence on EP wave forms, the most distinguishing differences related to aging are found with visual stimulation (Beck, Dustman, and Schenkenberg, 1975; Schenkenberg, 1970). Amplitudes of early components (<100 msec) have been observed to increase slightly over the middle and late adult years (Dustman and Beck, 1969; Straumanis *et al.*, 1965), while later components show substantial decreases in amplitude (Schenkenberg, 1970). Latencies of various components, particularly those after 70 msec poststimulus are significantly longer during the late adult age range

(Celesia and Daly, 1977; Schenkenberg, 1970; Straumanis *et al.*, 1965). The pattern for amplitude and latency differences to auditory stimuli is less clear, but there is reliable evidence of increased latencies in the later components ($P_2$, $N_2$, and $P_3$), of older individuals (Brent, Smith, Michalewski, and Thompson, 1976; Goodin, Squires, Henderson, and Starr, 1978; Smith, Tom, Brent, and Ohta, 1976). With regard to somatosensory EPs, there appear to be systematic declines in amplitude of later components across the middle and late adult age ranges (Luders, 1970; Schenkenberg, 1970); latency measures of later components also increase with age (Luders, 1970; Shagass and Schwartz, 1965; Schenkenberg, 1970).

The pattern of age differences is somewhat different when individuals are required to process the stimuli being presented. This is particularly apparent in the later components as reflected in the representative studies discussed below.

The paradigm used by Ritter, Vaughan, and Costa (1968) has been particularly useful in studying the effects of age on those components that are heavily influenced by cognitive processes. Brent *et al.* (1976) studied 10 old (X̄ age = 71 years), and 10 young (X̄ age = 21 years) healthy community volunteers using a modification of this design. Fifteen blocks of 30 pure tones (900 Hz) per block were presented to each subject. Ten percent of the tones in each block were higher in frequency (3300 Hz), and these were randomly presented between the 3rd and 27th tone. A rest break was introduced between each block. The nature of this design permitted an evaluation of habituation in the EP across 30 tone presentations and also provided for the analysis of the EP to the presentation of a rare or novel stimulus. The tones were presented under two conditions. In the nonattend condition, subjects read excerpts from *Newsweek*; in the attend condition they counted the number of common tones in each block.

Figure 8-5 shows the age differences associated with stimulus change during the attend condition. Amplitudes and latencies of 6 major components of the EP are depicted for the tones occurring immediately before rare tones (N-1), rare tones (N), and tones immediately following the rare ones (N + 1). It is clear that $N_2$ and $P_3$ are more prominent and that age differences in amplitude are enhanced when the rare tone is presented ($p < 0.05$ and 0.001, respectively). During the frequent tones there were no significant age differences for amplitudes of the later components ($N_2$, $P_3$), but the latencies for $N_2$ and $P_3$ were significantly longer for the older volunteers ($p < 0.01$ for both).

It is noteworthy that while $N_1$ and $P_2$ were unaffected by the presentation of rare tones (see Figure 8-6), both became significantly smaller in amplitude across each block of 30 tones. This habituation effect in these two components was more pronounced in the young than in the older group ($p < 0.05$ for both components.)

Goodin *et al.* (1978) have completed a similar study in which they extended the age range through adolescence and childhood. They also presented more tone trials, but did not separate them into discrete blocks. There was little evidence

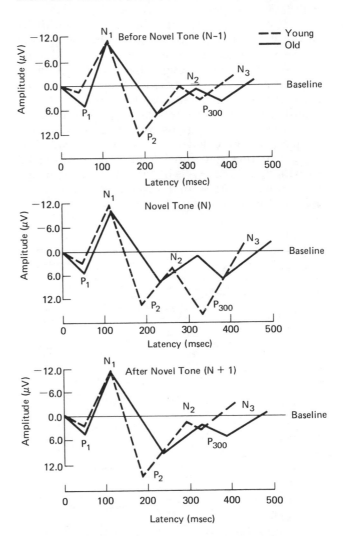

**Figure 8–5**  The effects of stimulus change on the auditory evoked potential in young and old community volunteers. Mean amplitudes and latencies for each EP component are illustrated for before Novel (N–1) trials, Novel (N) trials, and after Novel (N + 1) trials. Significant effects were observed for $N_2$ and $P_{300}$ components when the rare tone was presented. Thompson, L. W., Michalewski, H. J., and Saul, R. E. 1978, p. 143.

of the later components ($N_2$ and $P_3$) in the EPs of frequent tones, but these were quite prominent for rare tones during the attend condition. Latencies of these components showed significant linear trends across the adult age range ($p < 0.001$ for both). Age differences in $N_2 - P_3$ amplitude were also apparent, but these were not as marked ($p < 0.05$). The authors emphasize the systematic trend of the age differences in latency, suggesting that whatever is responsible for the change may be a long-term gradual process. They also emphasize the importance of obtaining age normative data for clinical purposes.

Both of these studies illustrate the sensitivity of the $P_3$ component to the informational content of the stimulus. Sutton, Braren, Zubin, and John (1965) developed a design that enabled them to study this component specifically by manipulating the certainty of a stimulus event. This was used by Smith *et al.* (1976) to evaluate age differences in $P_3$. Briefly paired signals were presented to the subjects, interspersed by a variable interval. The nature of the first signal (e.g., 1, 2, or 3 clicks) provided varying levels of information regarding the nature of the second signal (e.g., high or low tone). The subject's task was to predict the nature

of the second signal after being exposed to the first.

Seven old ($\bar{X}$ age = 68.5 years) and 7 young ($\bar{X}$ age = 23.4 years) community volunteers were presented 50 pairs of signals with 3 levels of certainty regarding the nature of the second signal. There were no significant age differences in the amplitudes of the later components, and changes as a function of certainty were comparable for both age groups. Latencies for $P_2$ and $P_3$ were significantly longer for the old than for the young ($P < 0.01$ for both).

Although age differences in amplitudes were apparent for the habituation study, they were minimized in the certainty paradigm. Marsh and Thompson (1977) have reported that age differences in both amplitude and latency measures were decreased in more complex auditory discrimination tasks. While more work is needed to clarify the nature of the interaction between age and type of cognitive processing, the available data indicate that age differences can vary as a function of processing demands. This limits the generality of findings in investigations of EP correlates of age and calls for specific attention to the kind of task being employed, particularly when studying age-related clinical disorders. Precise control of cognitive processing is not always possible when working with patients, because of differences in their ability to participate in experimentation.

## EVOKED POTENTIAL CORRELATES OF CLINICAL DISORDERS IN THE ELDERLY

In a comprehensive analysis of EP technology and its use in psychiatry, Shagass (1972) has stated that the two most important subject variables in EP research are age and sex. Goodin *et al.* (1978) have also reminded us that the majority of neurological patients are well beyond the young adult age, and therefore age differences in the EP must be considered in interpreting data obtained from clinical groups. Surprisingly, only a handful of studies has dealt with this issue in the EP literature. Some perceptive researchers do attempt to account for age by making clinical and control groups comparable on this variable (cf. Shagass, 1972, for a review of these studies). Yet, even in many instances where the age range of the subjects would make it seem feasible, there have been minimal attempts to evaluate age by clinical condition interactions.

One of the earliest studies to evaluate an age-related clinical condition using the EP focused on the diagnostic category of chronic brain syndrome presumed due to arteriosclerosis (Straumanis *et al.*, 1965). Twenty patients with this di-

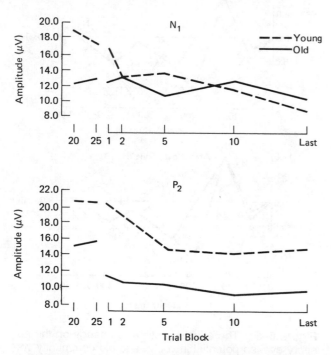

**Figure 8–6**   The mean amplitudes of components $N_1$ and $P_2$ represented across trial blocks for both young and old community subjects. Habituation effects were more pronounced in the younger than in the older subjects. Thompson, L. W., Michalewski, H. J., and Saul, R. E. 1978, p. 146.

agnosis were compared with 18 healthy old (X age = 71.8 years) and 18 healthy young ($\bar{\text{X}}$ age = 24.1 years) controls. Visual evoked responses were obtained from parietal-occipital electrodes in the midsaggital plane.

A comparison of patients and age-matched controls revealed that patients had a significantly higher amplitude in a component at 40 msec; amplitudes for other peaks were not significantly different. Latencies were significantly longer for the patient groups in all peaks after 100 msec. There was also significantly less rhythmic after-activity in the patient group than in the older group. A comparison of the old and young control groups revealed that the old subjects had larger amplitudes for the early components than the young, but that the latencies of peaks before 120 msec were slightly shorter for the young than for the old. No comparisons were reported for components later than 180 msec.

It appears that the major differences between old and young individuals occurred before 100 msec, whereas the primary differences between older patients and age-matched controls occurred in components after 100 msec. Straumanis *et al.* (1965) feel that these early events in the evoked potential are connected with transmission of information while the later events are implicated in processing and storing of information in the brain. Significant changes in the later components of the patient groups are consistent with the increased impairment in cognitive processes and clouded sensorium observed in these individuals.

Tsumoto *et al.* (1973) reported upon somatosensory responses in patients with unilateral lesions at or above the level of the thalamus. Electrical stimulation was delivered randomly either to the left or right median nerves at the wrist. Either 50 or 100 responses were collected with a sweep time of 250 msec. The patient responses were in general markedly different compared to a group of normal controls. In patients with sensory loss in all modalities, stimulation to the affected or damaged side resulted in early and later components that were greatly diminished in amplitude; however, stimulation of the nonaffected or intact side showed responses that were normal over both hemispheres. Combined cases of complete sensory loss and hemiparesis showed no visible response from the damaged side but normal bilateral responses from the nonaffected side. This close correspondence between sensory loss and somatosensory response was also demonstrated earlier by Williamson, Goff, and Allison (1970). Lee and Blair (1973) recorded serial EEGs from three patients with Jakob Creutzfeldt's disease. The patients eventually became severely demented. In one patient, evoked responses to somatosensory stimulation and auditory stimulation were of low amplitude even with high levels of stimulus intensity. Visual evoked responses collected over a six month period paralleled the progression of the disease state. Initially, abnormally large visual responses were recorded which gradually diminished over time. Later stages showed increasing latencies and changes in the evoked response wave form.

Visual evoked potentials have also been recorded in patients with presenile or senile dementia of the Alzheimer type (Visser *et al.*, 1976). Nineteen patients ($\bar{\text{X}}$ age = 71.2 years) were compared with a young control group comprised of subjects between 19 and 25 years of age. Recordings were obtained from bilateral placements at the standard occipital recording sites ($0_1$ and $0_2$) referred to a common averaged potential reference. No significant differences were observed for a positive peak occurring at approximately 60–70 msec. Latencies of all components measured following this were significantly longer in the patient group. Two components had significantly larger amplitudes in the patient group than in the control group; a positive peak with a latency of 112 and 155 msec for the control and patient groups, respectively, and a negative peak with a latency of 256 and 346 msec, respectively. No age-matched controls were used in this study, but the authors felt that the group differences observed were consistent with findings in other types of dementia (e.g., Jakob Creutzfeldt) and were not due to age alone.

Schenkenberg *et al.* (1972) have evaluated EPs in geriatric patients hospitalized in a long-term nursing care facility. Three patient groups with a clear diagnosis of arteriosclerosis, chronic brain syndrome (senile dementia), and alcoholism were presented with visual (10 μsec flash), auditory (0.25 msec click), and somatosensory (0.25 msec electric pulse to right index finger) stimuli. Age-matched controls were also run.

Visual EPs recorded from the occipital region showed generally lower amplitudes for the patient groups with a near absence of a positive-negative-positive going complex at about 100–150 msec. In visual EPs recorded from a left central lead, amplitudes of early components were lower in the arteriosclerotic group and higher in the dementia group. Latencies were longer in both leads for all three patient groups. The auditory EP showed higher amplitudes for early components in the dementia group, but not in the arteriosclerotic and alcoholic groups. In the somatosensory mode, the usual components could not be identified in the arteriosclerotic and alcoholic groups, but appeared to be near normal level in the dementia group. Thus, the results suggested that differential patterns could be identified in the three patient groups if intermodality comparisons were made.

For the most part, the above studies focused on differences in the early, stimulus-related components of the EP. Squires (1978) has emphasized that the later components, which are related to cognitive processes, might be particularly useful in the assessment of dementia in the elderly. Using the paradigm of his co-workers (Goodin *et al.,* 1978), Squires compared senile dementia patients with age-matched patients who did not have dementia and with healthy controls. Both amplitude and latency of $P_3$ were determined from vertex recordings referred to linked mastoids.

The results show significantly longer latencies for $P_3$ in the dementia group when compared with the nondementia group. The magnitude of the difference was illustrated by the fact that an arbitrary cutoff point of 2 standard deviations from the mean of the normal control group provided for near complete separation of the two groups. Several of the nondementia patients had neurological disease (e.g., multiple sclerosis), but, with one exception, their latencies were within the normal range. This suggests that impaired cognitive processes may be a primary behavioral correlate of very long latencies for $P_3$.

Several patients of the nondementia group were diagnosed as depressed, and the latencies for these individuals were all well within two standard deviations of the mean for the appropriate age-matched controls. These observations should encourage continued exploration of the reliability and validity of this paradigm for the assessment of dementia. Older patients frequently complain of memory loss and decreased intellectual abilities, and it is often difficult to determine whether these complaints are due to psychological factors such as anxiety or depression or to organic problems. Similarly, since some decline in certain specific cognitive abilities is anticipated with age, the question is often asked whether the change in a given patient is consistent for his/her age. Unfortunately, it is not always possible to resolve these questions with behavioral assessment. Elderly individuals are inclined to become at least mildly distressed when confronted with evidence of cognitive slippages, and the resulting psychological distress may aggravate the impairment. This can lead to increased awareness of cognitive problems which in turn precipitates increased distress, and so on. In such instances it is often difficult to determine the contribution of psychological versus organic factors using traditional assessment devices. However, if the findings reported here are supported in more extensive studies, then $P_3$ latency may serve as an objective assessment device, unhampered by psychological reactions.

## CONTINGENT NEGATIVE VARIATION

Another scalp potential that is readily recorded from the scalp is the contingent negative variation, or CNV, first reported by Walter and his colleagues in 1964 (Walter, Cooper, Aldridge, McCallum, and Winter). This very slow potential is recorded using amplifiers which are D.C. (direct current) coupled or have very long time constants (5 to 12 seconds). The CNV potential is usually elicited in a warned foreperiod reaction time situation where there is a brief signal ($S_1$), such as a tone, followed 1 or 2 seconds later by repetitive flashes ($S_2$) to which the subject must usually respond. The CNV builds up in the interval between $S_1$ and $S_2$ and is returned to pretrial resting levels by the response to $S_2$, commonly a simple button press. Although the CNV may attain -10 to -20 microvolt levels in the raw EEG tracing (and up to -50$\mu$V in some instances), CNV potentials are normally computer averaged for 8 to 16 trials (or presentations of the $S_1$–$S_2$ sequence) in order to lessen the fluctuations of background activity superimposed on the development of the slowly building wave.

The distribution of the CNV is normally symmetrical between the hemispheres with maximum amplitudes recorded at frontal and central placements. Walter (1968) suggested that massive depolarization of the apical dendrites in the frontal cortex was most likely involved in generation of the CNV. The slow wave develops shortly after $S_1$ (approximately 0.5 seconds) and can be sustained for prolonged intervals lasting several seconds (Walter, 1967). The expectancy created in the individual by the $S_1$–$S_2$ situation appears more critical in generating the CNV than any particular stimulus parameters, sense modality, or specific $S_1$–$S_2$ time interval. Shape of the CNV may be distinguished for different individuals determined by the rising portion of the CNV potential following the $S_1$ signal. Tecce (1972) called a rapid rise in the negative wave a Type A CNV, and contrasted this form of buildup with a slow or ramp-like development of the CNV called a Type B CNV. There is also some evidence suggesting that frontal CNVs are different from either vertex ($C_z$) or parietal CNVs in both amplitude and wave form (Weinberg and Papakostopoulos, 1975). More complicated CNV paradigms involving different processing strategies may also affect the normal anterior to posterior gradients of the CNV (Jarvilehto and Fruhstorfer, 1970; Poon, Thompson, Williams, and Marsh, 1974). Larger amplitude CNVs are generally related to faster reaction times to $S_2$ stimuli (Gaillard and Naatanen, 1973; Loveless, 1973; McAdam, Knott, and Rebert, 1969; Waszak and Obrist, 1969).

Investigations by Loveless and Sanford (1975) and Weerts and Lang (1973) have suggested that the normal CNV is a composite wave made up of an initial orienting complex at $S_1$ and a readiness or motor-related potential prior to the occurrence of $S_2$. At longer CNV intervals, four seconds or more, components of an orienting response and readiness potential are sufficiently separated to become apparent (Rohrbaugh, Syndulko, and Lindsley, 1976).

In most situations CNVs recorded from young adults and older individuals are quite comparable with respect to both measures of amplitude and wave form (Thompson and Nowlin, 1973). The CNV potentials for an older individual are shown in Figure 8–7 from EEG raw tracings. Loveless and Sanford (1974) analyzed the effects of interval durations (0.5 seconds to 15 seconds) on the CNVs of young and old subjects. For longer intervals, there was a marked difference in the shape of the CNV between the two age groups. Younger subjects showed an anticipatory response during long $S_1$–$S_2$ intervals which was indicated by an increasing shift of negativity near $S_2$. Older subjects, however,

did not show this increase near $S_2$, but displayed an even level of shifting throughout the CNV interval. Other evidence suggests that with longer CNV intervals well-defined negative shifts prior to $S_2$ can indeed be recorded in the elderly (Schaie and Syndulko, 1977). For simple $S_1$–$S_2$ task situations, older individuals demonstrate an inverse relationship between reaction time and CNV magnitude similar to younger subjects; in more demanding situations, however, this relationship breaks down for the older subjects (Bowman, Thompson, Michalewski, and Smith, 1978).

Only limited attention has been given to the CNV in clinical situations and its usefulness and application are still being weighed (Weinberg, 1975). Psychiatrically hospitalized patients are distinguishable not only in terms of the CNV (morphology and amplitude), but also by a sustained or prolonged negativity after the $S_2$ signal (Timsit-Berthier, Delaunoy, Koninckx, and Rousseau, 1973; Timsit-Berthier, Koninckx, Dargent, Fontaine, and Dongier, 1970).

The value of using the CNV technique in the evaluation of brain-damaged individuals appears favorable, although, this judgment is based on a limited number of reports. McCallum and Cummins (1973) studied the effects of an assortment of brain lesions on the development of the CNV. The patients tested included those with documented lesions (tumors, head injuries), localized lesions (cerebrovascular involvement), and patients with diffuse lesions extending over areas of one or both cerebral hemispheres (hydrocephalus, Parkinson's disease). The records of brain-damaged patients were compared to the records of normal subjects and psychiatric patients without damage. Findings indicated marked asymmetries in the CNV associated with brain-injured areas. The CNVs were reduced or suppressed over lesion sites. Diffuse cerebral impairment resulted in a general reduction of the CNV over the entire scalp. For those patients in which it was possible to compare recordings prior to and after surgery, CNV wave forms were observed to increase in amplitude and symmetry with the process of patient recovery.

## AUDITORY BRAINSTEM EVOKED POTENTIALS

An area of research that is gaining widespread attention and interest involves the recording of very early evoked potentials which are related to the initial stages of auditory processing, the auditory brainstem or auditory far-field potentials. The source of this interest is derived from the work of Jewett and his colleagues (Jewett, 1970; Jewett, Romano, and Williston, 1970; Jewett and Williston,

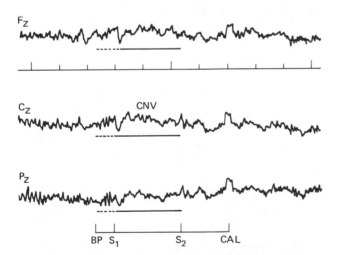

**Figure 8–7**  Single trial raw EEG tracing of the CNV in a healthy woman 82 years of age. The brief $S_1$ warning tone was followed by an $S_2$ signal tone. For this particular situation, a button press (BP) by the subject also initiated the $S_1$–$S_2$ sequence. Electrodes were referenced to linked mastoids. (T. C. = 12 sec; time segments = 1 sec; cal = –25 µV; negative is up).

1971) and the investigations of Sohmer and Fein-messer (1967). These very early brain responses are now known to reflect neural generators along successive stages beginning at the auditory nerve and proceeding through the brainstem. The practical clinical use of these potentials lies in the fact that each of the components of the brainstem wave form has been related to structures within the brainstem, and to the fact that these brainstem potentials are sensitive to intensity and frequency functions. It is important to realize that the total period analyzed in recording brainstem potentials seldom exceeds 10 or 12 msec, making the time perspective quite different from the recording of other scalp evoked potentials. Also, since the amplitudes of these potentials are in the submicrovolt or nanovolt range, some special care and recording techniques are needed in order to gather these potentials in a reliable manner.

Before considering some of the findings in recent brainstem research, it might be instructive to examine some wave forms and discuss some of the methods used in eliciting these far-field potentials. First, the distinction between far-field and near-field potentials should be mentioned. Jewett and Williston (1971) operationally defined far-field potentials and near-field potentials on the basis that far-field responses were not sensitive to small changes in electrode placement (that is, within a few cm) because of the supposed distances of the neural generators involved (i.e., the brainstem), whereas near-field responses, the generators of which may be closer to the surface of the scalp, can differ greatly in wave form and polarity with electrode placement. A representative brainstem wave form from our laboratory is illustrated in Figure 8–8 for a young female subject with normal hearing. Since the brainstem signal-to-noise ratio is poor, it is necessary to collect a large number of responses, typically 1024 to 2048 trials or more, depending upon the purpose of the experimentation. Brief auditory clicks produce the best brainstem responses, although tone pips and tone bursts can also elicit forms of the brainstem response. Because only a brief period of electrical activity of the brain is collected, fast presentation rates are possible and the collection of a relatively large number of trials does not become troublesome.

Frequently, the wave forms reported in the brainstem literature are not generally true averages but represent the successive summation of each of the individual trials. A useful feature to incorporate into the brainstem recording system is the capability of artifact rejection. Generally, this technique involves determination as to what constitutes an acceptable range for the EEG during a resting state; once a level is decided upon, the computer automatically rejects electrical activity exceeding the specified ranges or levels during stimulation sequences. Although not a completely satisfactory method, artifacts due to subject movements or muscle activity are not summed into the final average. Artifacts falling within the adjusted levels, of course, are not excluded from summation.

Jewett and Williston (1971) labeled the successive components of the brainstem wave form with roman numerals I–VII. Their original work used 2048 binaural click stimuli delivered at levels of 60 to 70 dB (SL) and summed from a vertex (C$_z$) site by an analog capacitor averager. Based on their original work, faster click rates (5/sec or more) tended to obscure the early components (I–IV) while slower rates (2.0–2.5/sec) produced more distinct wave forms. The fact that these small potentials were not artifact introduced by the electronics of the recording situation was demonstrated in control runs with both ear canals plugged. With the canals blocked, summed responses indicated no visible brainstem response.

The supposed origin for each of the brainstem components is as follows:

(I) acoustic nerve
(II) cochlear nuclei
(III) the superior olivary complex
(IV) lateral lemniscus
(V) inferior colliculus
(VI) possibly medial geniculate
(VII) possibly auditory radiations traversing the thalamus to the temporal cortex.

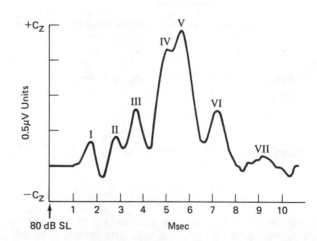

**Figure 8–8**  Sample brainstem evoked potential in a 27-year-old female with normal hearing. Brainstem components are labeled with Roman numerals. Binaural auditory clicks were presented at 80 dB (SL) at a rate of 15 clicks per second for 1024 presentations.

The small amplitude of the early peaks of the brainstem wave form are sometimes difficult to identify. Replications of the experimental conditions can at times help (e.g., Rowe, 1978) but extend recording sessions considerably. A method that we are presently developing involves preserving successive blocks of trials during data acquisition. The summed responses to blocks of 128 trails are stored in computer memory until a total of 1024 sweeps are collected. The ordered succession of block sums is then displayed and plotted. Stacked plotting automatically results from the summed responses and is easily implemented on a computer or averager. Figure 8–9 illustrates the process and the resulting plot. It should be noted that clear responses are evident with as few as 128 trials with higher levels of stimulus intensity.

*Stimulus Factors Affecting Brainstem Components.* Jewett and Williston (1971) inferred that the source of Wave I was most likely the eighth nerve. Thornton (1975a) gathered simultaneous recordings from each mastoid to monaural click stimuli and demonstrated that, as might be expected of far-field generators, contralateral records of brainstem activity lacked the first early wave, whereas ipsilateral records clearly exhibited the early, or presumed eighth nerve activity. There is a progressive increase in the latency of all brainstem components with decreased levels of intensity; at low levels,

however, Wave V is the most consistently observed brainstem component which can be detected near threshold (Starr, 1977). Pratt and Sohmer (1976) examined the effects of click rate (5, 10, 20, 40, and 80 clicks per second) and intensity (from 0 to 70 dB HL) on brainstem responses. Of the five early potentials considered, increased rates of presentation decreased the amplitude of the earliest wave; also, the increased rates did not appreciably affect the latency of this early component, whereas the latencies of later waves in the response were increased with higher rates. Over the range of intensities tested, the maximal latency shift in components of the brainstem response was about 2 msec.

Don, Allen, and Starr (1977) used relatively low click levels to investigate the shift effects due to presentation rate and stimulus intensity on the largest of the brainstem potentials, Wave V. Six adults were tested monaurally with rates that included 10, 30, 50, and 100/sec in combination with intensities of 30, 40, 50, and 60 dB above sensation level. Summed responses to 2048 clicks indicated a decrease in the latency of the Wave V component from stimulus onset with increased click intensity. For the sensation levels used, each 10 dB increment resulted in an approximately 0.4 msec decrease in the latency of Wave V. At faster click rates, and independently of intensity levels, the latency of Wave V was observed to increase. This prolongation of Wave V latency with faster rates of presentation suggested to the investigators that this effect may result from incomplete recovery of the neural structures involved or to an alteration in the synchronization pattern of these structures. The intensity shift is easily visualized from our records and is illustrated in Figure 8–10 for intensities of 60, 70, and 80 dB (SL) for a normal hearing subject.

The possible clinical use of the shift effect for Wave V at faster rates of presentation was studied by Fujikawa and Weber (1977). The subject groups tested included infants (7–8 weeks), young normals (18–24 years), and geriatric adults (69–81 years). Infant and older groups were selected for this study on the basis that each might serve as a representative model of altered or differing brainstem activity when compared to normals. The effects of high click presentation rates were used in order to evaluate each of the separate groups based on the latency of Wave V. The stimulus rates used were 13/sec, 33/sec, 50/sec, and 67/sec. For each of the click rates, intensity was set at 50dB above a normal young group threshhold. Responses to 1024 clicks composed each of the brainstem wave forms. Using 13/sec as a reference rate, difference scores were

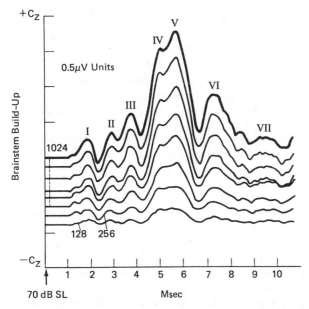

**Figure 8–9**  Build-up of the brainstem potential over successive blocks of 128 trials. Binaural click stimulation was presented at 70 dB (SL) at a rate of 15 clicks per second.

calculated for each of the faster rates and the reference. Results indicated that only the 67/sec rate differentiated both infant and geriatric groups from the young normals. However, in the infant group longer shifts occurred only at the 67/sec rate, whereas greater shifts occurred at all presentation rates for the older group.

Rowe (1978) investigated possible age differences in brainstem potentials in young (X̄ age = 25.1 years) and older subjects (X̄ age = 61.7 years). Click stimuli presented at 60 dB SL were delivered monaurally at rates of 10/sec and 30/sec. The EEG was recorded from a vertex-mastoid configuration. A major portion of the results were analyzed in terms of interpeak conduction times for selected components and combinations of components of the brainstem response. In general, interpeak latencies were not affected by changes in stimulus presentation rate. The major age effects observed by Rowe between the two age groups did, however, show that Wave I–III times increased with stimulus rate and increased age. Wave III–V times were not affected by either rate changes or age factors. Because absolute measures of brainstem amplitudes are highly variable between individual subjects, peak-to-peak measures of brainstem components are favored and lessen the effects of slower waves which may be superimposed on the brainstem responses (Thornton, 1975b).

The scalp distribution of the early auditory responses was investigated by Martin and Moore (1977) with five normal hearing subjects. Potentials to binaurally delivered clicks were collected from 13 sites based on the 10–20 placement system. The chin was used as the reference location. Clicks were presented at a rate of 9.2/sec and at a level of 70 dB (SL). Waveforms were composed of 2048 click presentations. Along the midline ($F_z$, $C_z$, and $P_z$), five or six components (I–VI) were readily identified from the recordings collected. Wave I started approximately 1.4 msec after click arrival. The second (II) and third (III) waves peaked at 2.5 msec and 3.6 msec, respectively. Wave IV, which was sometimes difficult to detect or frequently absent, appeared as a slight inflection on the larger Wave V component. The combined latency of the IV–V complex was approximately 5.5. msec. Wave VI was more apparent at lateral sites ($F_4$, $C_4$, $P_3$, and $T_4$) than at midline locations, yet earlier waves (I, II, and III) were sometimes obscured and of lower amplitude at these same lateral placements. Although the amplitude of each of the components varied, no significant differences were found among the different electrode sites. Similarly, latencies were generally not different among the electrode sites used.

A difficulty associated with using click stimuli exclusively is that much of the energy of the stimuli is concentrated at the high end (2 KHz–4 KHz) of the frequency spectrum. This limits the use of brainstem testing in audiometric applications, especially if high frequency hearing losses are present with normal low frequency thresholds. These considerations led Brama and Sohmer (1977) to use filtered clicks (250, 500, and 1000 Hz) in order to elicit low frequency responses and examine brainstem responses. Normally hearing individuals displayed the shortest latencies with the unfiltered clicks. A patient with a high frequency hearing loss exhibited brainstem responses to filtered clicks and not to the unfiltered high frequency clicks. Brainstem potentials were detected with filtered clicks at levels around 35 dB (HL) whereas responses to 1 KHz filtered and unfiltered clicks registered at approximately 10 dB (HL). Brama and Sohmer hypothesized that the longer latencies found with the filtered clicks were likely caused by the traveling wave delay induced by stimulating the low frequency region of the cochlea. Low frequency tone pips produce brainstem responses similar to high frequency tone pips except that low frequency pip responses do not yield as clear a wave form as high frequency pips (Jewett and Williston, 1971).

An intriguing feature of brainstem potentials which has not received a great deal of attention is

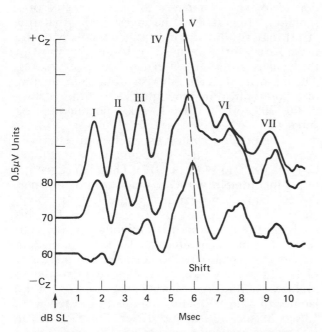

**Figure 8–10**   Brainstem potential shift (dotted line) of Wave V with intensity. Binaural click stimulation presented at 10 clicks per second; each wave form represents the summation of 1024 click presentations.

the amplitude relation between the stimulation of one or both ears. In an investigation of summation effects and brainstem potentials, Blegvad (1975) tested 14 normally hearing individuals with both monaural and binaural stimulation at intensities ranging from 10 dB (SL) to 90 dB (SL). Peak-to-peak measurements of various brainstem components showed consistently larger amplitudes with binaural click stimulation as opposed to monaural stimulation. Binaural responses at 50 dB (SL) approximated monaural stimulation at 90 dB (SL).

Patients with conductive hearing losses display essentially normal brainstem response patterns but with components delayed (Galambos and Hecox, 1977). Patients with sensorineural losses, for example Ménière's disease, demonstrate Wave V latency functions closely approximating their perceptual responses, especially when auditory recruitment is present (Galambos and Hecox, 1977). Action potentials recorded from the promontory of the middle ear of presbyacusic patients are prolonged compared to normal subjects (Bergholtz, Hooper, and Mehta, 1977).

*Clinical Findings.* Essentially normal brainstem responses can be recorded from patients in coma (due to drug overdose, metabolic disorders, or traumatic incidents), whereas brainstem tumors (e.g., glioma, acoustic neuroma) and demyelinating diseases produce highly abnormal brainstem potentials depending upon the structures involved (Starr and Achor, 1975). For example, an illustrative case was described by Starr and Achor in which the presumptive diagnosis was brainstem glioma. Brainstem recordings failed to disclose any waves after Component III. Postmortem examination revealed damaged regions in the midbrain and portions of the pons with the VIIIth nerves and cochlear nuclei left intact. Since absolute measures of amplitude are difficult to compare between subjects, a more clinically relevant measure used by Starr (1977) has been the IV–V/I ratio. Normal ratios are greater than 1.0 from levels of threshold to 75 dB SL.

A positive relation between brainstem responses and patients with neurological lesions of the brainstem has been established. Starr and Hamilton (1976) examined in detail the brainstem responses of a series of patients for which autopsy information was available. The appearance of the brainstem wave form depends upon the orderly succession of nervous information through the brainstem. The appearance of Wave II and III rests on the integrity of the cochlear nucleus and superior olives, respectively, while Waves IV to VII depend on the healthy condition of midbrain struc-

tures. Given that a normal sequence for Waves I to V can be recorded, no discrete lesion sites corresponding to Waves VI and VII have yet been reported.

A case of "locked-in" syndrome in which an occulsion near the basilar artery resulted in complete paralysis showed normal brainstem Waves I, II, and III, but with delayed and reduced amplitudes for Wave IV and V (Gilroy, Lynn, Ristow, and Pellerin, 1977). The slowed speed and reduced size of Wave V implicated the pons which was confirmed by arteriographic findings of infarction of the ventral pons. Similar positive findings in patients with suspected central pontine myelinolysis were described by Stockard, Rossiter, Wiederholt, and Kobayashi (1976). Increased latencies (that is, I–V difference latencies) corresponded to the presumed involvement of the pons. Repeated brainstem recordings demonstrated a reduction in the latencies to more normal values paralleling therapeutic treatments.

Binaural or monaural presentation modes have little effect on measures of latency in normally hearing individuals (Starr and Achor, 1975). Interaural measurements of Wave V differences in normal listeners to monaural click stimulation have ranged between 0 and 0.2 msec, suggesting that the latencies are distributed bilaterally; in cases of acoustic tumor, interaural latencies are observed to increase and are related to the size of the abnormal tissue (Selters and Brackmann, 1977). Selters and Brackmann also noted that larger tumors may act to compress the brainstem and cause delays and alterations in the Wave V complex. Daly, Roeser, Aung, and Daly (1977) discussed the possibility that tumor size (as for example in acoustic neuroma) and amount of displacement could be estimated using brainstem recording techniques.

One of the few studies examining early (0–8 msec), middle (8–50 msec), and long latency (50 msec and above) components to auditory stimulation both in normal controls and multiple sclerosis patients was reported by Robinson and Rudge (1977a). Although patients with multiple sclerosis seldom have hearing complications, a process of demyelination within the brainstem which may affect fiber tracts including auditory pathways, may also alter the transmission of brainstem potentials. Control subjects ranged from 20 to 56 years of age. The prolonged latencies of Wave V in MS patients were quite noticeable, whereas amplitude measures were of lesser value. Middle responses (8–50 msec) indicated some latency differences between controls and patients were significant but not for measures of amplitude. Late responses (50 msec and above) did not differentiate, by either latency or amplitude measures, controls from patient groups. Interestingly, an alteration in one of the early components of the brainstem response did not automatically affect middle components of the auditory response. Very evident changes in the brainstem responses of pathologic ears are recorded from patients with diagnosed cerebello-pontine angle tumors (Terkildsen, Huis in't Veld, and Osterhammel, 1977; Rosenhamer, 1977). The sensitivity of the brainstem response in detecting abnormalities can be enhanced by the presentation of closely paired click stimuli such that two sets of responses are recorded (Robinson and Rudge, 1977b). Multiple sclerosis patients in whom single click responses produce almost normal brainstem responses were found to have aberrant brainstem responses when paired clicks were presented. Brainstem responses to successive bursts of four clicks show adaptation of early components by the third or fourth click (Thornton and Coleman, 1975).

*Developmental Aspects of Brainstem Potentials.* The use of brainstem potentials in assessing hearing functions in high-risk newborn infants was investigated by Schulman-Galambos and Galambos (1975). Premature infants ranging from 34 weeks gestational age through term exhibited longer Wave V latencies (approximately 0.4 msec) with 10 dB decrements in stimulus levels from 60 dB SPL. At a given stimulus level, however, this Wave V latency decreased systematically with increased age, presumably reflecting maturational changes in the periphery. The latency of Wave V for infants appears to stabilize at 12 to 18 months of age to adult ranges; infant latencies for Wave V vary inversely with intensity in a manner comparable to adult recordings (Hecox and Galambos, 1974). Brainstem responses have also been successfully recorded from infants and children who have been classified as difficult-to-test subjects (Mokotoff, Schulman-Galambos, and Galambos, 1977). Early maturational changes in the brainstem response have been extensively investigated by Salamy and McKean (1976). In their work, Waves I and V were present for the ages tested (newborns to adulthood). Waves I and II were apparent in the records of six-week-olds while the first three waves (I, II, and III) were easily distinguished by three months of age. The pattern in the third month closely resembled the adult brainstem wave form. Further differences in the wave form were minimal from six months to one year of age. Although continuous stimulation sequences do not appear to show habituation effects, lower rates of stimulus presentation (e.g., 5 clicks per second) do improve infant brainstem wave forms (Salamy, McKean, and Buda, 1975). Leiberman, Sohmer, and Szabo (1973) recorded brainstem potentials in infants and were usually able to identify five components with the first wave appearing at approximately 1.8 msec and the fifth at 8 msec, respectively. Overall, the amplitudes for the infants ranged between .1 $\mu$V and .2 $\mu$V which are reduced compared to more mature subjects. Neuronal recovery functions are apparently present at birth as measured by high rates of presentation (Salamy, McKean, Pettett, and Mendelson, 1978).

## OVERVIEW

The literature indicates that the clinical EEG has become a useful tool in the assessment and management of age-related disorders. While it typically does not provide specific information regarding the nature of cerebral lesions and their precise locations, it frequently is helpful in making inferences regarding the integrity of the central nervous system. This can assist the clinician in determining the potential contribution of psychological versus organic factors in the presenting complaint. In view of the increased incidence of neurological disorders in the elderly, as well as increased psychological distress due to situational factors, the need to make this distinction often arises.

The sensitivity of the EEG in its present stage of development is such that it seldom results in false positive errors, but frequently shows a false negative picture. Thus, while evidence of organic pathology in the EEG may quickly lead to a diagnosis, absence of pathology in the EEG must be viewed with caution. Activation techniques have improved the sensitivity of the EEG to detect some disorders (e.g., epilepsies), and continued exploration in this direction may improve the usefulness of this tool in working with the elderly. Simple procedures, such as alpha blocking to visual stimulation, have shown promise and deserve further attention.

Evoked potentials have also been found useful in detecting some neurological problems, and the few studies focusing on age-related disorders suggest that various types of evoked response techniques when combined with the EEG may enhance the sensitivity of electrophysiological measures in the assessment process. The limited results have been sufficiently encouraging to argue strongly for support of continued research in this area.

The limited data available emphasize that a priority in future clinical research should be the development of normative data for various cohorts across the adult age range. Research paradigms need to be expanded, and where possible should follow along the lines of basic research designs that elicit strong EP-behavior relationships. Squires' (1978) use of the Ritter *et al.* (1968) paradigm is a good illustration of how basic research designs can be helpful in the clinical setting. More patient groups need to be studied and the number of patients within groups increased. This effort can be greatly facilitated if standard procedures and paradigms are adapted across laboratories. Of particular importance is the need to attend carefully to the criterion information used in establishing various groups. For the most part, behavioral variables are implicated in establishing criteria for classification. The reliability of behavioral assessment procedures frequently are suspect and deserve continued critical scrutiny. Exploration of the topographic distribution of EPs and their interrelationship should also be encouraged. The potential value of complex analysis of multi-site recordings has been suggested in earlier research (Gerson, John, Bartlett, and Koenig, 1976). An approach suggested by John (1977) utilizes a collection of EEG measures and a variety of psychometric profiles which are together or separately submitted to multivariate-type factor analysis and/or cluster-type analysis. Since no single evaluation of EEG frequency or EP measure may yield a diagnostically meaningful statement, the technique employed by John extracts the significant features of a number of variables to define or characterize a diagnostic entity. Although still in its beginnings, the technique may differentiate heterogenous populations with behavioral and perceptual problems and may delineate important areas of research for further consideration.

Only the surface has been touched in determining the usefulness of this technology. Evoked potential components are extremely sensitive to biological, psychological, and stimulus manipulations, and therefore the burden of sorting out the complex interactions of these measures is immense and time consuming. By the same token, this same sensitivity may well be a strength in clinical work, as we learn more about the various mechanisms which influence these scalp potentials.

# REFERENCES

ANDERSEN, P., AND ANDERSSON, S. A. 1974. Thalamic origin of cortical rhythmic activity. *In,* A. Remond, Editor-in-Chief, *The Handbook of Electroencephalography and Clinical Neurophysiology.* O. Creutzfeldt (ed.), *The Neuronal Generation of the EEG, Part C.,* pp. 90–118. Amsterdam: Elsevier.

ANDRIOLA, M. A. 1978. Role of the EEG in evaluating central nervous system function. *Geriatrics, 33,* 55–65.

BECK, E. C. 1975. Electrophysiology and behavior. *In,* M. R. Rosenzweig and L. W. Porter (eds.), *Annual Review of Psychology, Vol. 26,* pp. 233–262. Palo Alto: Annual Reviews.

BECK, E. C., DUSTMAN, R. E., AND SCHENKENBERG, T. 1975. Life span changes in the electrical activity of the human brain as reflected in the cerebral evoked response. *In,* J. M. Ordy and K. R. Brizzee (eds.), *Neurobiology of Aging,* pp. 175–192. New York : Plenum.

BERGHOLTZ, L. M., HOOPER, R. E., AND MEHTA, D. C. 1977. Electrocochleographic response patterns in a group of patients mainly with presbyacusis. *Scandinavian Audiology, 6,* 3–11.

BLEGVAD, B. 1975. Binaural summation of surface-recorded electrococheleographic responses. *Scandinavian Audiology, 4,* 233–238.

BLUM, R. H. 1957. Alpha-rhythm responsiveness in normal, schizophrenic, and brain damaged persons, *Science, 126,* 749–750.

BOWMAN, T. E., THOMPSON, L. W., MICHALEWSKI, H. J., AND SMITH, D. B. D. 1978. Age-related changes in ANS and CNS responses as a function of task difficulty. *Psychophysiology, 15,* 270. (Abstract)

BRAMA, I., AND SOHMER, H. 1977. Auditory nerve and brain stem responses to sound stimulus at various frequencies. *Audiology, 16,* 402–408.

BRENT, G. A., SMITH, D. B., MICHALEWSKI, H. J., AND THOMPSON. L. W. 1976. Differences in the evoked potential in young and old subjects during habituation and dishabituation procedures. *Psychophysilogy, 14,* 96–97. (Abstract)

BROWN, D. G., AND GOLDENSOHN, E. S. 1973. The electroencephalogram in normal pressure hydrocephalus. *Archives of Neurology, 29,* 70–71.

BURGER, L. J., ROWAN, A. J., AND GOLDENSOHN, E. S. 1972. Creutzfeldt-Jakob disease. An electroencephalographic study. *Archives of Neurology, 26,* 428–433.

BUSSE, E. W., BARNES, R. H., FRIEDMAN, E. L., AND KELTY, E. J. 1956. Psychological functioning of aged individuals with normal and abnormal electroencephalograms. *Journal of Nervous and Mental Diseases, 124,* 135–141.

BUSSE, E. W., BARNES, R. H., SILVERMAN, A. J., SHY, G. M., THALER, M., AND FROST, L. L. 1954. Studies of the aging process: Factors that influence the psyche of elderly persons. *American Journal of Psychiatry, 110,* 897–903.

BUSSE, E. W., AND OBRIST, W. D. 1963. Significance of focal electroencephalographic changes in the elderly. *Postgraduate Medicine, 34,* 179–182.

CALLAWAY, E. 1975. *Brain Electrical Potentials and Individual Psychological Differences.* New York: Grune & Stratton.

CELESIA, G. G., AND DALY, R. F. 1977. Effects of aging on visual evoked responses. *Archives of Neurology, 34,* 403–407.

CHATRIAN, G. E., SHAW, C. M., AND LEFFMAN, H. 1964. The significance of periodic lateralized epileptiform discharges in EEG: An electrographic, clinical and pathological study. *Electroencephalography and Clinical Neurophysiology, 17,* 177–193.

CIGÁNEK, L. 1975. Visual evoked responses. *In,* A. Remond, Editor-in-Chief, *The Handbook of Electroencephalography and Clinical Neurophysiology,* P. Buser (ed.), *Electrical Reactions of the Brain and Complementary Methods of Evaluation,* pp. 33–59. Amsterdam: Elsevier.

COOPER, R., OSSELTON, J. W., AND SHAW, J. C. 1969. *EEG Technology.* London: Butterworths.

CREUTZFELDT, O., AND HOUCHIN, J. 1974. Neuronal basis of EEG-waves. *In,* A. Remond, Editor-in-Chief, *The Handbook of Electroencephalography and Clinical Neurophysiology.* O. Creutzfeldt (ed.), *The Neuronal Generation of the EEG, Part C,* pp. 5–55. Amsterdam: Elsevier.

CRIGHEL, E., AND STERMAN-MARINCHESCU, C. 1971. Flash-evoked responses in acute cerebro-vascular diseases. The correlation with the clinical electroencephalographic course. *Revue Roumanine de Neurologie, 8,* 275–284.

DALY, D. M., ROESER, R. J., AUNG, M. H., AND DALY, D. D. 1977. Early evoked potentials in patients with acoustic neuroma. *Electroencephalography and Clinical Neurophysiology, 43,* 151–159.

DEISENHAMMER, E., AND JELLINGER, K. 1974. EEG in senile dementia. *Electroencephalography and Clinical Neurophysiology, 36,* 91. (Abstract)

DESMEDT, J. E. 1977. *Visual Evoked Potentials: New Developments.* London: Oxford.

DON, M., ALLEN, A. R., AND STARR, A. 1977. Effect of click rate on the latency of auditory brain stem responses in humans. *Annals of Otology, Rhinology, and Laryngology, 86,* 186–195.

DONCHIN, E., AND LINDSLEY, D. B. 1969. *Average Evoked Potentials: Methods, Results, and Evaluations.* Washington, D. C.: U. S. Government Printing Office.

DRACHMAN, D. A., AND HUGHES, J. P. 1971. Memory and the hippocampal complexes, III. Aging and temporal EEG abnormalities. *Neurology,* (Minneapolis), *21,* 1–14.

DUSTMAN, R. E., AND BECK, E. C. 1969. The effects of maturation and aging on the wave form of visually evoked potentials. *Electroencephalography and Clinical Neurophysiology, 26,* 2–11.

EASON, R. G., GROVES, P., WHITE, C. T. AND ODEN, D. 1967.

Evoked cortical potentials: Relation to visual field and handedness. *Science, 156,* 1643–1646.

EASON, R. G., ODEN, D., AND WHITE, C. T. 1967. Visually evoked potentials and reaction time in relation to site of stimulation. *Electroencephalography and Clinical Neurophysiology, 22,* 313–324.

EASON, R. G., AND WHITE, C. T. 1967. Averaged occipital responses to stimulation in the nasal and temporal halves of the retina. *Psychonomic Science, 7,* 309–310.

FEINBERG, I. 1976. Functional implications of changes in sleep physiology with age. *In,* R. D. Terry and S. Gershon (eds.), *Neurobiology of Aging,* pp. 23–41. New York: Raven Press.

FEINBERG, I. 1978. Sleep patterns in dementia: Evidence, issues and strategies. *In,* K. Nandy (ed.), *Senile Dementia: A Biomedical Approach,* pp. 155–167. New York and Amsterdam: Elsevier.

FINK, M. 1968. EEG classification of psychoactive compounds in man: Review and theory of behavioral associations. *In,* D. H. Efron (ed.), *Psychopharmacology: A Review of Progress 1957–1967,* pp. 497–507. United States Public Health Service Publication No. 1836.

FINK, M. 1974. EEG profiles and probability measures of psychoactive drugs. *In,* T. M. Itil (ed.), *Psychotopic Drugs and the Human EEG,* pp. 76–98. Basel, Switzerland: S. Karger.

FREY, T. S., AND SJOGREN, H. 1959. The electroencephalogram in elderly persons suffering from neuropsychiatric disorders. *Acta Psychologica et Neurologica* (Scandinavia), *34,* 438–450.

FRIEDLANDER, W. J. 1958. Electroencephalographic alpha rate in adults as a function of age. *Geriatrics, 13,* 29–31.

FUJIKAWA, S. M., AND WEBER, B. A. 1977. Effects of increased stimulus rate on brainstem electric response (BER) audiometry as a function of age. *Journal of the American Audiology Society, 3,* 147–150.

GAILLARD, A. W., AND NAATANEN, R. 1973. Slow potential changes and choice reaction time as a function of interstimulus interval. *Acta Psychologica, 37,* 173–186.

GALAMBOS, R., AND HECOX, K. 1977. Clinical applications of the brain stem auditory evoked potentials. *Auditory Evoked Potentials in Man. Psychopharmacology Correlates of EPs. In,* J. E. Desmedt (ed.), *Progress in Clinical Neurophysiology,* pp. 1–19. Basel, Switzerland: S. Karger.

GARCIA-AUSTT, E., BOGACZ, J., AND VANZULLI, A. 1964. Effects of attention and inattention upon visual evoked response. *Electroencephalography and Clinical Neurophysiology, 17,* 136–143.

GERSON, I. M., JOHN, E. R., BARTLETT, F., AND KOENIG, V. 1976. Average evoked response (AER) in the electroencephalographic diagnosis of the normally aging brain: A practical application. *Clinical Electroencephalography, 7,* 77–91.

GIBBS, F. A., AND GIBBS, E. L. 1950. *Atlas of Electroencephalography.* Reading, Mass: Addison-Wesley.

GILROY, J., LYNN, G. E., RISTOW, G. E., AND PELLERIN, R. J. 1977. Auditory evoked brain stem potentials in a case of "Locked-in" syndrome. *Archives of Neurology, 34,* 492–495.

GLOOR, P., KALABAY, O., AND GIARD, N. 1968. The electroencephalogram in diffuse encephalopathies: Electroencephalographic correlates of gray and white matter lesions. *Brain, 91,* 779–802.

GOFF, W. R., ALLISON, T., AND VAUGHAN, H. G. 1978. The functional neuroanatomy of event related potentials. *In,* E. Callaway, P. Tueting, and S. H. Koslow (eds.), *Event-Related Brain Potentials in Man,* pp. 1–91. New York: Academic Press.

GOODIN, D. S., SQUIRES, K. C., HENDERSON, B. H., AND STARR, A. 1978. Age-related variations in evoked potentials to auditory stimuli in normal human subjects. *Electroencephalography and Clinical Neurophysiology, 44,* 447–458.

GORDON, E. B., AND SIM, M. 1967. The EEG in presenile dementia. *Journal of Neurology, Neurosurgery, and Psychiatry, 30,* 285–291.

GREENBLATT, M. 1944. Age and electroencephalographic abnormality in neuropsychiatric patients. *American Journal of Psychiatry, 101,* 82–90.

GUSTAFSON, L., RISBERG, J., HAGBERG, B., HOUGAARD, K., NILSSEN, L., AND INGVAR, D. H. 1972. Cerebral blood flow, EEG, and psychometric variables related to clinical findings in presenile dementia. *Acta Neurologica Scandinavica* (Supplementum), *51,* 439–440.

HALLIDAY, A. M. 1975. Somatosensory evoked responses. *In,* A. Remond, Editor-in-Chief, *The Handbook of Electroencephalography and Clinical Neurophysiology,* P. Buser (ed)., *Electrical Reactions of the Brain and Complementary Methods of Evaluation,* pp. 60–67. Amsterdam: Elsevier.

HARNER, R. N. 1975. EEG evaluation of the patient with dementia. *In,* D. F. Benson and D. Blumer (eds.), *Psychiatric Aspects of Neurologic Disease,* pp. 63–82. New York: Grune & Stratton.

HARVALD, B. 1958. EEG in old age. *Acta Psychologica et Neurologica* (Scandinavia), *33,* 193–196.

HECOX, K., AND GALAMBOS, R. 1974. Brain stem auditory evoked responses in human infants and adults. *Archives of Otolaryngology, 99,* 30–33.

HILL, D., AND PARR, G. 1950. *Electroencephalography.* London: MacDonald.

ITIL, M. 1974. Quantitative pharmaco-electroencephalography. Use of computerized cerebral potentials in psychotropic drug research. *In,* T. M. Itil (ed.), *Psychotropic Drugs and the Human EEG,* pp. 43–75. Basel, Switzerland: S. Karger.

JARVILEHTO, T., AND FRUHSTORFER, H. 1970. Differentiation between slow cortical potentials associated with motor and mental acts in man. *Experimental Brain Research, 11,* 309–317.

JEWETT, D. L. 1970. Volume conducted potentials in response to auditory stimuli as detected by averaging in the cat. *Electroencephalography and Clinical Neurophysiology, 28,* 609–618.

JEWETT, D. L., ROMANO, M. N., AND WILLISTON, J. S. 1970. Human auditory evoked potentials: Possible brainstem components detected on the scalp. *Science, 167,* 1517–1518.

JEWETT, D. L., AND WILLISTON, J. S. 1971. Auditory evoked far-fields averaged from the scalp of humans. *Brain, 94,* 681–696.

JOHANNESSON, G., BRUN, A., GUSTAFSON, I., AND INGVAR, D. H. 1977. EEG in presenile dementia related to cerebral blood flow and autopsy findings. *Acta Neurologica Scandinavica, 56,* 89–103.

JOHN, E. R. 1977. *Neurometrics: Clinical Applications of Quantitative Electroencephalography, Vol. 2.* New York: John Wiley.

JOHN, E. R., HERRINGTON, R. N., AND SUTTON, S. 1967. Effects of visual form on the evoked response. *Science, 155,* 1439–1442.

KILOH, L. G., McCOMAS, A. J., AND OSSELTON, J. W. 1972. *Clinical-Electroencephalography.* New York: Appleton-Century-Crofts.

KLORMAN, R., THOMPSON, L. W., AND ELLINGSON, R. J. 1978. Event-related brain potentials across the life span. *In,* E. Callaway, P. Tueting, and S. H. Koslow (eds.), *Event-Related Brain Potentials,* pp. 511–570. New York: Academic Press.

KOOI, K. A. 1971. *Fundamentals of Electroencephalography.* New York: Harper & Row.

LEE, R. G., AND BLAIR, R. D. G. 1973. Evolution of EEG and visual evoked response changes in Jakob-Creutzfeldt disease. *Electroencephalography and Clinical Neurophysiology, 35,* 133–142.

LEHMANN, D., AND FENDER, D. H. 1967. Monocularly evoked electroencephalogram potentials: Influence of target structure presented to the other eye. *Nature, 215,* 204–205.

LEIBERMAN, A., SOHMER, H., AND SZABO, G. 1973. Cochlear audiometry (electrocochleography) during the neonatal period. *Developmental Medicine and Child Neurology, 15,* 8–13.

LEROY, C., BRION, S., AND SOUBRIER, J. P. 1966. Corrélation anatomoélectrique dans les démences séniles entre le rythme alpha et les lésions anatomiques. *Rivista di Neurologia, 36,* 191–193.

LETEMENDIA, F., AND PAMPIGLIONE, G. 1958. Clinical and electroencephalographic observations in Alzheimer's disease. *Journal of Neurology, Neurosurgery, and Psychiatry, 21,* 167–172.

LIBERSON, W. T. 1944. Functional electroencephalography in mental disorders. *Diseases of the Nervous System, 5*, 357–364.

LIBERSON, W. T. 1966. Study of evoked potentials in aphasics. *American Journal of Physical Medicine, 45*, 135–142.

LIDDELL, D. W. 1958. Investigations of EEG findings in presenile dementia. *Journal of Neurology, Neurosurgery, and Psychiatry, 21*, 173–176.

LINDSLEY, D. B. 1938. Electrical potentials of the brain in children and adults. *Journal of General Psychology, 19*, 285–306.

LINDSLEY, D. B. 1956. Physiological psychology. *Annual Review of Psychology, 7*, 323–348.

LINDSLEY, D. B., SCHREINER, L. H., KNOWLES, W. B., AND MAGOUN, H. W. 1950. Behavioral and EEG changes following chronic brain stem lesions in the cat. *Electroencephalography and Clinical Neurophysiology, 2*, 483–498.

LOVELESS, N. E. 1973. The contingent negative variation related to preparatory set in a reaction time situation with variable foreperiod. *Electroencephalography and Clinical Neurophysiology, 35*, 369–374.

LOVELESS, N. E., AND SANFORD, A. J. 1974. Effects of age on the contingent negative variation and preparatory set in a reaction-time task. *Journal of Gerontology, 29*, 52–63.

LOVELESS, N. E., AND SANFORD, A. J. 1975. Slow potential correlates of preparatory set. *Biological Psychology, 2*, 217–226.

LUDERS, H. 1970. The effects of aging on the wave form of the somatosensory cortical evoked potential. *Electroencephalography and Clinical Neurophysiology, 29*, 450–460.

MARKAND, O. N. June, 1977. EEG in degenerative CNS diseases. Course syllabus of the American EEG Society "Perspectives in Clinical EEG," Miami, Florida.

MARSH, G. R., AND THOMPSON, L. W. 1977. Psychophysiology of aging. *In*, J. E. Birren and K. W. Schaie (eds.), *Handbook of the Psychology of Aging*, pp. 219–248. New York: Van Nostrand Reinhold.

MARTIN, M. E., AND MOORE, E. J. 1977. Scalp distribution of early (0 to 10 msec) auditory evoked responses. *Archives of Otolaryngology, 103*, 326–328.

MCADAM, D. W., KNOTT, J. R., AND REBERT, C. S. 1969. Cortical slow potential changes in man related to interstimulus interval and to pre-trial prediction of interstimulus interval. *Psychophysiology, 5*, 349–358.

MCADAM, W., AND ROBINSON, R. A. 1956. Senile intellectual deterioration and the electroencephalogram: A quantitative correlation. *Journal of Mental Science, 102*, 819–825.

MCCALLUM, W. C., AND CUMMINS, B. 1973. The effects of brain lesions on the contingent negative variation in neurosurgical patients. *Electroencephalography*

*and Clinical Neurophysiology, 35*, 449–456.

MIYOSHI, S., LUDERS, H., KATO, M., AND KUROIWA, Y. 1971. The somatosensory evoked potential in patients with cerebrovascular diseases. *Folia Psychiatica et Neurologica Japonica, 25*, 9–25.

MOKOTOFF, B., SCHULMAN-GALAMBOS, C., AND GALAMBOS, R. 1977. Brain stem auditory evoked responses in children. *Archives of Otolaryngology, 103*, 38–43.

MORUZZI, G., AND MAGOUN, H. W. 1949. Brain stem reticular formation and activation of the EEG. *Electroencephalography and Clinical Neurophysiology, 1*, 455–473.

MULLER, H. F. 1978. Senile dementia and related disorders. *In*, K. Nandy (ed.), *Senile Dementia: A Biomedical Approach*, pp. 237–250. New York and Amsterdam: Elsevier.

MULLER, H. F., AND KRAL, V. A. 1967. The electroencephalogram in advanced senile dementia. *Journal of the American Geriatric Society, 15*, 415–426.

MUNDY-CASTLE, A. C. 1962. Central excitability in the aged. *In*, H. T. Blumenthal (ed.), *Medical and Clinical Aspects of Aging*, pp. 575–595. New York: Columbia University Press.

NOEL, P., AND DESMEDT, J. E. 1975. Somatosensory cerebral evoked potentials after vascular lesions of the brain-stem and diencephalon. *Brain, 98*, 113–128.

OBRIST, W. D. 1963. The electroencephalogram of healthy aged males. *In*, J. E. Birren, R. N. Butler, S. W. Greenhouse, L. Sokoloff, and M. R. Yarrow (eds.), *Human Aging I: A Biological and Behavioral Study* (USPHS Pub. No. 986), 79–93. Washington, D.C.: U. S. Government Printing Office.

OBRIST, W. D. 1964. Cerebral ischemia and the senescent electroencephalogram. *In*, E. Simonson and T. H. McGavack (eds.), *Cerebral Ischemia*, pp. 71–98. Springfield, Ill.: Charles C Thomas.

OBRIST, W. D. 1965. Electroencephalographic approach to age changes in response to speed. *In*, A. T. Welford and J. E. Birren (eds.), *Behavior, Aging and the Nervous System*, pp. 259–271. Springfield, Ill.: Charles C Thomas.

OBRIST, W. D. 1976. Problems of aging. *In*, A. Remond, Editor-in-Chief, *The Handbook of Electroencephalography and Clinical Neurophysiology*, G. E. Chatrian and G. C. Lairy (eds.), *The EEG of the Waking Adult*, pp. 275–292. Amsterdam: Elsevier.

OBRIST, W. D., AND BUSSE, E. W. 1965. The electroencephalogram in old age. *In*, W. P. Wilson (ed.), *Application of Electroencephalography in Psychiatry*, pp. 185–205. Durham, N. C.: Duke University Press.

OBRIST, W., AND HENRY, C. 1958. Electroencephalographic analysis of aged psychiatric patients. *Electroencephalography and Clinical Neurophysiology, 10*, 621–632.

OOSTERHUIS, H. J. G. H., PONSEN, L., JONKMAN, E. G., AND

MAGNUS, O. 1969. The average visual response in patients with cerebrovascular disease. *Electroencephalography and Neurophysiology, 27*, 23–34.

PERRY, N. W., AND CHILDERS, D. G. 1969. *The Human Visual Evoked Response.* Springfield, Ill.: Charles C. Thomas.

PICTON, T. V., AND HILLYARD, S. A. 1974. Human auditory evoked potentials. II: Effects of attention. *Electroencephalography and Clinical Neurophysiology, 36*, 191–199.

PICTON, T. W., HILLYARD, S. A., KRAUSZ, H. I., AND GALAMBOS, R. 1974. Human auditory evoked potentials. I: Evaluation of components. *Electroencephalography and Clinical Neurophysiology, 36*, 179–190.

POON, L. W., THOMPSON, L. W., WILLIAMS, R. B., AND MARSH, G. R. 1974. Changes of anterio-posterior distribution of CNV and late positive component as a function of information processing demands. *Psychophysiology, 11*, 660–673.

PRATT, H., AND SOHMER, H. 1976. Intensity and rate functions of cochlear and brainstem evoked responses to click stimuli in man. *Archives of Otology, Rhinology, Laryngology, 212*, 85–92.

REGAN, D. 1972. *Evoked Potentials in Psychology, Physiology and Clinical Medicine.* New York: John Wiley.

RITTER, W., VAUGHAN, H. G., JR., AND COSTA, L. D. 1968. Orienting and habituation to auditory stimuli: A study of short term changes in average evoked responses. *Electroencephalography and Clinical Neurophysiology, 25*, 550–556.

RITTER, W., AND VAUGHAN, H. G. 1969. Averaged evoked responses in vigilance and discrimination: A reassessment. *Science, 164*, 326–328.

ROBINSON, K., AND RUDGE, P. 1977a. Abnormalities of the auditory evoked potentials in patients with multiple sclerosis. *Brain, 100*, 19–40.

ROBINSON, K., AND RUDGE, P. 1977b. The early components of the auditory evoked potential in multiple sclerosis. *Auditory Evoked Potentials in Man. Psychopharmacology of EPs. In,* J. E. Desmedt (ed.), *Progress in Clinical Neurophysiology,* pp. 58–67. Basel, Switzerland: S. Karger.

ROHRBAUGH, J. W., SYNDULKO, K., AND LINDSLEY, D. B. 1976. Brain wave components of the contingent negative variation in humans. *Science, 191*, 1055–1057.

ROSENHAMER, H. J. 1977. Observations of electric brainstem responses in retrocochlear hearing loss. *Scandinavian Audiology, 6*, 179–196.

ROWE, M. J. 1978. Normal variability of the brain stem auditory evoked response in young and old adult subjects. *Electroencephalography and Clinical Neurophysiology, 44*, 459–470.

SALAMY, A., AND MCKEAN, C. M. 1976. Postnatal development of human brainstem potentials during the first year of life. *Electroencephalography and Clinical Neurophysiology, 40*, 418–426.

SALAMY, A., MCKEAN, C. M., AND BUDA, F. B. 1975. Maturational changes in auditory transmission as reflected in human brain stem potentials. *Brain Research, 96*, 361–366.

SALAMY, A., MCKEAN, C. M., PETTETT, G., AND MENDELSON, T. 1978. Auditory brainstem recovery processes from birth to adulthood. *Psychophysiology, 15*, 214–220.

SATTERFIELD, J. H. 1965. Evoked response enhancement and attention in man: A study of responses to auditory and shock stimuli. *Electroencephalography and Clinical Neurophysiology, 19*, 470–475.

SCHAIE, J. P., AND SYNDULKO, K. 1977. CNV component and cardiac correlates of time estimation and reaction time performance in the elderly. *Psychophysiology, 14*, 92. (Abstract)

SCHENKENBERG, T. 1970. Visual, auditory and somatosensory evoked responses of normal subjects from childhood to senescence. Unpublished doctoral dissertation, University of Utah, 1970.

SCHENKENBERG, T., DUSTMAN, R. E., AND BECK, E. C. 1972. Cortical evoked responses of hospitalized geriatrics in three diagnostic categories. *Proceedings of the 80th Annual Meeting of the American Psychological Association, 671–672.*

SCHLAG, J. 1974. Reticular influences on thalamo-cortical activity. *In,* A. Remond, Editor-in-Chief, *The Handbook of Electroencephalography and Neurophysiology,* O. Creutzfeldt (ed.), *The Neuronal Generation of the EEG, Part C.* pp. 119–134. Amsterdam: Elsevier.

SCHULMAN-GALAMBOS, C., AND GALAMBOS, R. 1975. Brain stem auditory-evoked responses in premature infants. *Journal of Speech and Hearing Research, 18*, 456–465.

SCOTT, D. F., HEATHFIELD, K. W. G., TOONE, B., AND MARGERISON, J. H. 1972. The EEG in Huntington's Chorea: A clinical and neuropathological study. *Journal of Neurology, Neurosurgery, and Psychiatry, 35*, 97–102.

SELTERS, W. A., AND BRACKMANN, D. E. 1977. Acoustic tumor detection with brain stem electric response audiometry. *Archives of Otolaryngology, 103*, 181–187.

SHAGASS, C. 1972. *Evoked Brain Potentials in Psychiatry.* New York: Plenum.

SHAGASS, C., AND SCHWARTZ, M. 1965. Age, personality, and somotosensory cerebral evoked responses. *Science, 148*, 1359–1361.

SMITH, D. B. D., TOM, C. E., BRENT, G. A., AND OHTA, R. J. 1976. Attention, evoked potentials, and aging. Paper presented at the meeting of the Western Psychological Association, Los Angeles.

SOHMER, H., AND FEINMESSER, M. 1967. Cochlear action potentials recorded from the external ear in man. *Annals of Otology, Rhinology, and Laryngology, 76*, 427–435.

SOKOL, S. 1976. Visually evoked potentials: Theory, techniques, and clinical applications. *Survey of Ophthalmology, 21,* 18–44.

SPONG, P., HAIDER, M., AND LINDSLEY, D. B. 1965. Selective attentiveness and cortical evoked responses to visual and auditory stimuli. *Science, 148,* 395–397.

SQUIRES, K. C. 1978. Auditory evoked potentials in development, aging and dementia. A paper presented at the 58th Annual Meeting of the Western Psychological Association, April 19–22, San Francisco, California.

STARR, A. 1976. Auditory brain stem responses in brain death. *Brain, 99,* 543–554.

STARR, A. 1977. Clinical relevance of brain stem auditory evoked potentials in brain stem disorders in man. *Auditory Evoked Potentials in Man. Psychopharmacology Correlates of EPs. In,* J. E. Desmedt (ed.), *Progress in Clinical Neurophysiology,* pp. 45–57. Basel, Switzerland: S. Karger.

STARR, A. 1978. Sensory evoked potentials in clinical disorders of the nervous system. *Annual Review of Neurosciences, 1,* 103–127.

STARR, A., AND ACHOR, J. 1975. Auditory brain stem responses in neurological disease. *Archives of Neurology, 32,* 761–768.

STARR, A., AND HAMILTON, A. E. 1976. Correlation between confirmed sites of neurological lesions and abnormalities of far-field auditory brainstem responses. *Electroencephalography and Clinical Neurophysiology, 41,* 595–608.

STEFOSKI, D., BERGEN, D., FOX, J., MORRELL, F., HUCKMAN, M., AND RAMSEY, R. 1976. Correlation between diffuse EEG abnormalities and cerebral atrophy in senile dementia. *Journal of Neurology, Neurosurgery, and Psychiatry, 39,* 751–755.

STOCKARD, J. J., ROSSITER, V. S., WIEDERHOLT, W. C., AND KOBAYASHI, R. M. 1976. Brain stem auditory-evoked response in suspected central pontine myelinolysis. *Archives of Neurology, 33,* 726–728.

STORM VAN LEEUWEN, W. 1975. Auditory evoked potentials. *In,* A. Remond, Editor-in-Chief, *The Handbook of Electroencephalography and Clinical Neurophysiology,* P. Buser (ed.), *Electrical Reactions of the Brain and Complementary Methods of Evaluation,* pp. 71–85. Amsterdam: Elsevier.

STRAUMANIS, J. J., SHAGASS, C., AND SCHWARTZ, M. 1965. Visually evoked cerebral response changes associated with chronic brain syndromes and aging. *Journal of Gerontology, 20,* 498–506.

SURWILLO, W. W. 1963a. The relation of simple response time to brain wave frequency and the effects of age. *Electroencephalography and Clinical Neurophysiology, 15,* 105–114.

SURWILLO, W. W. 1963b. The relation of response-time variability to age and the influence of brain wave

frequency. *Electroencephalography and Clinical Neurophysiology, 15,* 1029–1032.

SURWILLO, W. W. 1964a. The relation of decision time to brain wave frequency and to age. *Electroencephalography and Clinical Neurophysiology, 16,* 510–514.

SURWILLO, W. W. 1964b. Some observations of the relation of response speed to photic stimulation under conditions of EEG synchronization. *Electroencephalography and Clinical Neurophysiology, 17,* 194–198.

SUTTON, S., BRAREN, M., ZUBIN, J., AND JOHN, E. R. 1965. Evoked potential correlates of stimulus uncertainty. *Science, 150,* 1187–1188.

SUTTON, S., TUETING, P., AND ZUBIN, J. 1967. Information delivery and the sensory evoked potential. *Science, 155,* 1436–1439.

TECCE, J. J. 1972. Contingent negative variation (CNV) and psychological processes in man. *Psychological Bulletin, 77,* 73–108.

TERKILDSEN, K., HUIS IN'T VELD, F., AND OSTERHAMMEL, P. 1977. Auditory brain stem responses in the diagnosis of cerebellopontine angle tumors. *Scandinavian Audiology, 6,* 43–47.

THOMPSON, L. W., AND BOTWINICK, J. 1968. Age differences in the relationship between EEG arousal and reaction time. *The Journal of Psychology, 68,* 167–172.

THOMPSON, L. W., MICHALEWSKI, H. J., AND SAUL, R. E. 1978. Age differences in cortical evoked potentials: A comparison of normal older adults and individuals with CNS disorders. *In,* K. Nandy (ed.), *Senile Dementia: A Biomedical Approach,* pp. 139–153. New York: Elsevier/North-Holland Biomedical Press.

THOMPSON, L. W., AND NOWLIN, J. B. 1973. Relation of increased attention to central and autonomic nervous system states. *In,* L. F. Jarvik, C. Eisdorfer, and J. E. Blum (eds.), *Intellectual Functioning in Adults,* pp. 107–123. New York: Springer.

THOMPSON, L. W., AND WILSON, S. 1966. Electrocortical reactivity and learning in the elderly. *Journal of Gerontology, 21,* 45–51.

THOMPSON, R. F., AND PATTERSON, M. M. 1973–1974. *Bioelectric Recording Techniques,* Vol. 1, Parts A, B, and C. New York: Academic Press.

THORNTON, A. R. D. 1975a. Bilaterally recorded early acoustic responses. *Scandinavian Audiology, 4,* 173–181.

THORNTON, A. R. D. 1975b. The measurement of surface-recorded electrocochleographic responses. *Scandinavian Audiology, 4,* 51–58.

THORNTON, A. R. D., AND COLEMAN, M. J. 1975. The adaptation of cochlear and brainstem auditory evoked potentials in humans. *Electroencephalography and*

*Clinical Neurophysiology, 39,* 399–406.

TIMSIT-BERTHIER, M., DELAUNOY, J., KONINCKX, N., AND ROUSSEAU, J. C. 1973. Slow potential changes in psychiatry. I. Contingent negative variation. *Electroencephalography and Clinical Neurophysiology, 35,* 355–361.

TIMSIT-BERTHIER, M., KONINCKX, N., DARGENT, J., FONTAINE, O., AND DONGIER, M. 1970. Variations contingentes négatives en psychiatrie. *Electroencephalography and Clinical Neurophysiology, 28,* 41–47.

TSUMOTO, T., HIROSE, N., NONAKA, S., AND TAKAHASHI, M. 1973. Cerebrovascular disease: Changes in somatosensory evoked potentials associated with unilateral lesions. *Electroencephalography and Clinical Neurophysiology, 35,* 463–473.

VAN DER DRIFT, J. H. A., AND KOK, N. K. D. 1972. The EEG in cerebro-vascular disorders in relation to pathology. *In,* A. Remond, Editor-in-Chief, *The Handbook of Electroencephalography and Clinical Neurophysiology,* J. H. A. van der Drift (ed.), *Cardiac and Vascular Diseases,* Part A, pp. 12–64. Amsterdam: Elsevier.

VISSER, S. L. 1961. Correlations between the contingent alpha blocking, EEG characteristics and clinical diagnosis. *Electroencephalography and Clinical Neurophysiology 13,* 438–446.

VISSER, S. L., STAM, F. C., VAN TILBURG, W., OP DEN VELDE, W., BLOM, J. L., AND DERIJKE, W. 1976. Visual evoked response in senile and presenile dementia. *Electroencephalography and Clinical Neurophysiology, 40,* 385–392.

WALTER, W. G. 1967. Slow potential changes in the human brain associated with expectancy, decision, and intention. *In,* W. Cobb and C. Morocutti (eds.), *The Evoked Potentials,* pp. 123–130. Amsterdam: Elsevier.

WALTER, W. G. 1968. The contingent negative variation: An electro-cortical sign of sensori-motor reflex association in man. *In,* E. A. Asratyan (ed.), *Progress in Brain Research, Vol. 22, Brain Reflexes,* pp. 364–377. Amsterdam: Elsevier.

WALTER, W. G., COOPER, R., ALDRIDGE, V. J., MCCALLUM, W. C., AND WINTER, A. L. 1964. Contingent nega-

tive variation: An electric sign of sensorimotor association and expectancy in the human brain. *Nature, 203,* 380–384.

WASZAK, M., AND OBRIST, W. D. 1969. Relation of slow potential changes to response speed and motivation in man. *Electroencephalography and Clinical Neurophysiology, 27,* 113–120.

WEERTS, T. C., AND LANG, P. J. 1973. The effects of eye fixation and stimulus and response locations on the contingent negative variation. *Biological Psychology, 1,* 1–19.

WEINBERG, H. 1975. The contingent negative variation: Its clinical past and future. *American Journal of EEG Technology, 15,* 51–67.

WEINBERG, H., AND PAPAKOSTOPOULOS, D. 1975. The frontal CNV: Its dissimilarity to CNVs recorded from other sites. *Electroencephalography and Clinical Neurophysiology, 39,* 21–28.

WEINER, H., AND SCHUSTER, D. B. 1956. The electroencephalogram in dementia—some preliminary observations and correlations. *Electroencephalography and Clinical Neurophysiology, 8,* 479–488.

WELLS, C. E. 1962. Response of alpha waves to light in neurologic disease. *Archives of Neurology, 6,* 478–491.

WELLS, C. E. 1963. Alpha responsiveness to light in man. *In,* G. H. Glaser (ed.), *EEG and Behavior,* pp. 27–59. New York: Basic Books.

WELLS, C. E., AND WOLFF, H. G. 1960. Formation of temporary cerebral connections in normal and brain-damaged subjects. *Neurology, 10,* 335–340.

WHITE, C. T. 1974. The visual evoked response and patterned stimuli. *In,* G. Newton and A. H. Riesen (eds.), *Advances in Psychobiology, Vol. 2,* pp. 267–295. New York: John Wiley.

WILLIAMSON, P. D., GOFF, W. R., AND ALLISON, T. 1970. Somato-sensory evoked responses in patients with unilateral cerebral lesions. *Electroencephalography and Clinical Neurophysiology, 28,* 566–575.

WILSON, W. P., MUSELLA, L., AND SHORT, M. J. 1977. The electroencephalogram in dementia. *In,* C. E. Wells (ed.), *Dementia,* 2nd edition, pp. 205–221. Philadelphia: F. A. Davis.

# 9

# Sensory, Perceptual, and Motor Processes in Older Adults

*A. T. Welford*

At first sight, the psychiatric significance of sensory and motor changes with age may appear questionable. Yet anyone who has studied middle-aged and older people closely and sympathetically will know that comparatively small changes of these kinds can often have quite disproportionate effects. Thus, many people resent the need to use spectacles or a hearing aid in later middle age, and their resentment can color their attitudes to a wide range of activities. Difficulty in comprehending what is said seems often to encourage paranoid tendencies. Fear of falling when walking over rough ground, or lack of confidence in being able to make the rapid observations and decisions required for driving on busy roads can lead to severely restricted life-styles, which may in turn cause inertia and lack of interest. Failing ability to meet the demands of one's job may be present not only as physical symptoms of stress, but as irritability both at work and at home. Anyone who is concerned with the psychiatric care of middle-aged or old people, or responsible for maintaining their morale, can therefore benefit from at least an outline knowledge of the sensory and motor changes that are normal in the course of the adult years, and of how to foster those changes which are beneficial and mitigate those which are not. This chapter aims to sketch such an outline. For those who may wish to pursue the topics dealt with in more detail, it provides an introduction to the fuller treatments contained in such sources as the relevant chapters of the *Handbook of the Psychology of Aging* edited by Birren and Schaie (1977).

Sensory-motor performance is characterized by a chain of processes involving the conversion of incoming physical stimuli into nerve impulses by the sense organs, the central perceptual analysis and integration of sensory data, the further integration of these data with material from memory which gives them meaning, the use of the information thus gained for the choice of response, and the execution of phased and coordinated actions by various effector organs. These processes will be considered in three main groups: first, those concerned with the acquisition of information—processes of sensation and perception; second, processes involved in the use of this information as a guide to, and basis for, action; and third, certain processes which exert regulatory functions upon both the other groups.

Probably the best recognized of all age changes are those in visual and auditory performance which are appreciable in the thirties and progress into old age. They appear to result in part from anatomical and physiological changes in the sense organs, and partly from changes in central perceptual processes. The two interact to a considerable extent but will, for convenience, be dealt with separately.

## SENSORY FUNCTIONS

### VISION

Visual acuity declines substantially with age, especially in conditions of poor lighting or low contrast between details and their background that cause difficulty with fine visual tasks (e.g., Fortuin, 1963, Weston, 1949). The decline can be mitigated, although not entirely eliminated, by increased intensity of lighting. Both static acuity in terms of the finest resolution and dynamic acuity in terms of least perceptible movement, are affected (Hills, 1975; Hills and Burg, 1977). At the same time, tolerance of glare diminishes, making night driving unpleasant for older people, and dark adaptation is slower so that old people take longer to recover vision when going from a well-lighted room to semidarkness (e.g., McFarland, Domey, Warren, and Ward, 1960). Also, the area of the effective visual field diminishes in the sense that the size or intensity of stimuli presented in the peripheral parts of the field need to be increased if they are to be seen, and events occurring away from the center of the visual field may fail to be observed.

These trends are largely due to changes in the eye which reduce the quality or intensity of light reaching the retina. Thus, reduction of pupil size and absorption of light in the eye media mean that older people are effectively operating under poorer lighting conditions than are younger. Opacities in the lens which scatter light and thus reduce contrasts at the retina increase with age, producing the blinding effects of glare, and the lens itself becomes more rigid and less capable of adjustment to bring objects at different distances into focus. This last difficulty can be reduced by wearing spectacles: those over 40 commonly require spectacles, or if they already wear them, different lenses for close work. Any one power of spectacle lens, however, will bring only a limited range of distances into focus, so that middle-aged and old people can often be seen moving an object nearer or further away in order to bring it to the optimum distance for viewing. Where this cannot be done, they are likely to operate with poorer focus than younger people. If bifocal or trifocal spectacles are used, an additional problem arises because, at the junction of the lenses, a small band of visual field is missing and objects falling within it may not be seen. Also, the lenses for close work magnify and make objects in the lower part of the field appear larger and therefore nearer, causing difficulty when negotiating stairs. The former problem can be eliminated by using lenses of continuously increasing power from top to bottom. They will not overcome the second problem although the fact that they make the visual field continuous may reduce it, especially if the field is well structured.

In extreme old age these changes are often supplemented by degenerative changes in the retina. These changes cause much more severe difficulties in seeing, and aids such as large-print books and magnifiers are needed.

### HEARING

Various changes in the ear, such as thickening of the eardrum, stiffening of the ossicles, and degeneration in the structures of the inner ear, produce impairments of hearing which include loss of sensitivity, poorer pitch discrimination especially above about 1000 cycles per second, tinnitus or "singing in the ears," and "recruitment." This last denotes a condition in which the range of intensities between sounds heard as soft and loud is shortened, so that while low-intensity sounds appear quieter to an older person than to a younger, high-intensity sounds appear just as loud.

Some but not all of these changes can be compensated by wearing hearing aids, especially if two aids are balanced to correct for each ear separately. If they are not balanced, or if only one aid is used, the subtle differences of phase and intensity at the two ears, which enable the locations of different sound sources to be identified, are lost. It is largely on the basis of location that we are able to attend to one conversation and ignore others at a party, or attend to significant sounds and ignore those which make up the background noises of daily life. If, therefore, the ability to discriminate location is lost, both wanted and unwanted sounds seem to combine together in a great confusion. The effect is described by many who wear a hearing aid when they complain that "all it does is to bring in noise."

Other attempts to compensate for loss of hearing in middle and old age, such as placing a hand to the ear or turning towards a speaker so that hearing can be supplemented by lipreading, seem often, at least in the early stages, to be largely unconscious. They are probably of greater importance than is commonly recognized.

### OTHER SENSES

Evidence regarding age changes in other senses is much less than for vision and hearing, but indications are that similar declines of sensitivity occur. In the case of taste and smell, the changes are of little practical importance —some gourmet enjoyment may be blunted and some danger may arise from failure to smell toxic gases, but there may be advantages in not noticing some unpleasant smells as intensely as when young. Changes of tactile sensitivity are again of little significance, and an increased tolerance of pain found in older people could be regarded as an advantage (Schludermann and Zubek, 1962). Loss of kinesthetic sensitivity can be important when actions must be carried out without the aid of vision, and is perhaps part of the reason for the minor clumsiness often shown by older people when carrying out rapid actions. It may also contribute to loss of precision of body image in old people, although it is difficult to be sure how far this is due to kinesthetic loss and how far to a central failure to coordinate data from different parts of the body.

## RANDOM ACTIVITY IN THE CENTRAL NERVOUS SYSTEM

Sensory changes are to be understood not only in terms of anatomical deterioration of the sense organs but also, and in many ways more importantly, as due to signals in the form of nerve impulses resulting from incoming stimuli having to be discriminated from spontaneous background neural activity in the sense organs, afferent pathways, and brain. The level of this neural activity—"neural noise" as it is termed—is assumed to vary randomly from moment to moment so that, over a period of time, the momentary levels constitute an approximately normal distribution as shown in Figure 9–1. Signals are thought of as adding a constant to the noise and so shifting the whole distribution to a greater level of neural activity. The subject is conceived as setting a "criterion level" or "cutoff point" and as treating any level of activity which falls above this as "signal," and any level of activity below it as "noise alone." As a result, weak signals may be ignored while occasionally an unusually high momentary level of noise may be mistaken for a signal (for reviews see Green and Swets, 1966; McNicol, 1972; and, more briefly, Welford, 1968, 1976a).

Discriminability thus depends on the ratio of signal to noise, and is therefore reduced if either the strength of the signal is lowered or the level of noise is increased. The signal-to-noise ratio for the case shown in Figure 9–1 can be expressed as:

$$d' = \frac{\text{Strength of signal}}{\substack{\text{level of noise in terms of the standard} \\ \text{deviation of the noise distribution}}} \quad (1)$$

The criterion is measured in terms of $\beta$ where

$$\beta = \frac{\substack{\text{height of the ordinate of the} \\ \text{"signal + noise" distribution}}}{\substack{\text{height of the ordinate of the} \\ \text{"noise alone" distribution}}} \quad (2)$$

both measured at the criterion point, so that $\beta$ is greater than one if the criterion is high and a fraction of one if it is low. The calculation of $d'$ and $\beta$ in these ways requires a testing procedure in which, on a series of occasions, subjects are pre-

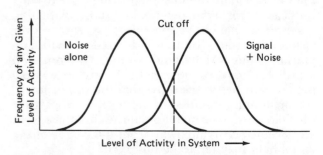

**Figure 9–1** Spontaneous neural activity ("noise alone") and increase in neural activity when a signal is added ("signal + noise"). Activity above the cutoff point is treated as a meaningful signal, and activity below the cutoff point is interpreted as noise.

sented with a signal or with no signal and so have the opportunity of making two types of error: failing to recognize that a signal has occurred, and regarding a signal as having occurred when it has not. A high criterion—high value of β—will result in a large number of errors of the first type but relatively few of the second, while the reverse will be true of a low criterion. The overall number of errors of both types will diminish as the signal-to-noise ratio increases.

The factors already surveyed clearly tend to reduce signal strength as age advances. There is also evidence that neural noise tends to increase (Gregory, 1974; Wenger, 1977). For example, Vickers, Nettelbeck, and Willson (1972) argued that when a pair of lines is shown, neural noise has the effect of making their momentary central effects variable, so that if the two lines are only slightly different in length, the central effect of the shorter may sometimes exceed that of the longer and lead to an error being made. They calculated from data obtained by Botwinick, Brinley, and Robbin (1958a) that when pairs of lines were shown briefly—for 0.15 second—the standard deviation of the variation due to noise averaged about 0.14° of visual angle for a group of subjects aged 18–35 and about 0.21° for a group aged 65–79. Subjects can, however, compensate for poor signal-to-noise ratio by accumulating data over a longer period, thus building up the signal and averaging out some of the noise. This they appear to do if the opportunity is present: when the lines were exposed for 2 seconds—that is, until in almost all cases subjects had responded—both age groups, but especially the older, took longer to respond but did so more accurately. Vickers *et al.* (1972) calculated that, as a result of taking more time, the average standard deviation of the variation due to noise was reduced in both groups to about 0.10°.

Similar relations between signal-to-noise ratio and age have been found for hearing (Gregory 1974; Rees and Botwinick, 1971), and the signal-to-noise ratio for pain has been found to be lower in older women (Clark and Mehl, 1971). Doubtless these relations could be found in many discrimination tasks if the appropriate methods of measurement were used. This, however, has seldom been done so far, and doubts therefore exist about the meaning of many commonly assumed falls of sensory performance with age. Are they due to a true fall of discriminability—that is of d'—or to the adoption of higher criteria—that is a rise of β? From what little is known so far, it appears that both occur, but which is the more substantial effect is often open to question. The answer is important

because, while there is usually little that can be done about a fall of d', which represents a lowering of capacity, criteria can be influenced by incentives and training (Craik, 1969). Failure to distinguish between true discriminability and criterion level is also a criticism of most standard clinical tests of vision and audition. These tests have the further shortcoming that they take no account of the time taken to make judgments. There is, in fact, a need for thorough overhaul of clinical tests of sensory functions, not only to clarify age changes but to give precision to diagnostic indications in general.

Any increase of neural noise with age implies that the performances of older and younger people cannot be fully equated. However, two observations suggest ways in which its effects could be to some extent prevented or mitigated. First, Nettelbeck (1972) showed that noise levels increased under the stress produced in subjects by giving them electric shocks at random intervals. Second, Wenger, (1977) found noise levels in his subjects aged 40–60 higher than in either younger or older groups, and suggested that this was because the 40–60 group was under chronic stress—they were drawn from administrative office staffs, and many complained of being greatly overworked and appeared tense. His older subjects, however, came from an old people's home where life was more peaceful. It seems reasonable to suppose that, just as Nettelbeck found noise to be increased over a short period by acute stress, so its level can be raised over longer periods by chronic stress. Such stress is a likely result of incipient failures of capacity with age if the individual tries to compensate for them by increased effort (Richardson, 1953). If so, there seems to be scope for minimizing neural noise by careful attention to conditions of work and of living generally so as to reduce stress, and by adjustment of aims and ambitions to take account of changes in capacity with age. Treatment of stress symptoms by means of tranquilizers is unlikely to help because these seem to reduce signal levels as well as noise, leaving the signal-to-noise ratio either unchanged or actually impaired (see Welford, 1978).

## PERCEPTUAL FACTORS

The concepts of signal-to-noise ratio and criterion levels for decision form a convenient framework within which to consider some more complex aspects of perception in relation to age. The great majority of research in this area has been in vision and hearing, and treatment will be confined to these.

## ALTERNATION IN AMBIGUOUS FIGURES

Vickers (1972) suggested that the rate of alternation between the two views of ambiguous figures such as that of Figure 9–2 depends upon random variation from moment to moment—that is, noise—in the central effects in favor of one or the other view. The viewer is assumed to accumulate evidence until a criterion level for one view is reached, whereupon that view is perceived and the process of accumulation starts again, resulting in either a continuation of the same view or a change to the other, whichever criterion is reached first. Either a fall of signal-to-noise ratio or a rise of criterion would lead to the accumulation taking longer time and account for the slower alternations shown by older observers. Heath and Orbach (1963) noted that the rate of reversals of the Necker cube in subjects aged 65–90 was comparable with that of patients having frontal lobe damage.

An auditory analogy to reversible figures shows fewer alternations among older subjects. The evidence for this comes from Warren (1961), who studied differences between groups aged 18–25 and 62–86 using a technique in which a word or short phrase is repeated over and over again

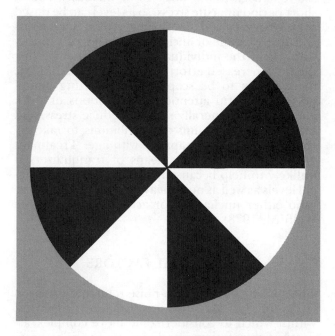

**Figure 9–2**  Example of reversible figure used by Vickers (1972). Subjects see either a white cross on a black disc or a black cross on a white disc.

for 3 minutes. During this period the word or phrase, *as heard,* undergoes a number of changes, for instance the word *"trice"* was heard not only accurately but sometimes as "tries," "price," "twice," "triced," "ter-ice," "try," "Christ," "right," "cry," or "tripe." Changes occurred suddenly during the course of listening, and were very much fewer among the older subjects, who tended most of the time to hear the word correctly. Warren (1968) suggested that the phenomenon is not analogous to visual reversal because the changes are more varied. It seems fair to argue, however, that while ambiguous visual figures have been constructed so as to be seen in only two or three ways, associations and similarities between words are such that any one word could, if its trace were disturbed by neural noise, be mistaken for several others. Whatever the cause, Warren's result provides an example of older people being at an *advantage* compared with younger.

## MASKING EFFECTS

If a visual pattern is exposed briefly and then, after a short interval, another visual stimulus is given, perception of the first pattern may be impaired or prevented: the second stimulus has "masked" the first. Presumably it takes time for the data from the initial pattern to build up to a critical level at which they trigger a judgment and so become immune to interference by further stimulation (see Welford, 1968, chapter 4). In the absence of a masking stimulus, data from the initial pattern can continue to be accumulated from some kind of iconic image for up to at least 0.5 second or so after the initial exposure has ceased, and it has been suggested that the time over which this can occur lengthens with age (see Fozard, Wolf, Bell, McFarland, and Podolsky, 1977). Both Kline and Szafran (1975) and Walsh (1976) obtained results which indicated that, in order to see the pattern initially presented, subjects in their sixties required either a longer exposure or a longer interval before the masking stimulus than did those in their twenties. The increased interval over which masking occurred in older subjects can be taken to imply that a longer time is needed for sensory and perceptual data to build up to criterion levels at which judgments are made.

## IRRELEVANT MATERIAL

Rabbitt (1965), using a task in which cards had to be sorted into piles according to letters printed on them, found that adding irrelevant letters to the cards produced greater slowing of performance in subjects aged 65–74 than in those aged 17–24. Irrelevant material appears to reduce effective signal strength (Welford, 1977c). A similar explanation can perhaps be given for the results of studies which have shown older people to be less able than younger to detect figures embedded in larger designs (e.g., Crook, Alexander, Anderson, Coules, Hanson, and Jeffries, 1958; Cohen and Axelrod, 1962). Inability to abstract a part from an integrated whole pattern is also a reasonable explanation of the tendency for the Müller-Lyer illusion shown in Figure 9–3A to increase with age (see Fozard *et al.* 1977).

Difficulty for older people caused by irrelevant material implies a need for careful design of displays to provide only essential information without extra confusing detail or "clutter." The need is emphasized by the finding of Murrell and Tucker (1960) that older engineering workers had greater difficulty than younger when interpreting involved working drawings. Other examples likely to repay care in design are symbols on industrial and domestic machines, road signs (see Figure 9–4), notices, and the layout of accommodation.

**Figure 9–4** To park or not to park? That is a question older people may find difficult to answer in this case.

## Degraded Signals

Reduced signal strength can also account for the finding that perception of degraded signals is more difficult for older people than for younger. For example, Verville and Cameron (1946) found that subjects aged 35–56 were slower than those aged 16–23 at identifying incomplete pictures of the type shown in Figure 9–5. They seemed to have difficulty in integrating the separate parts into a

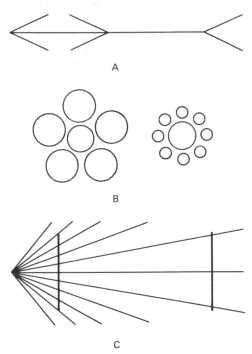

**Figure 9–3** (A) Muller-Lyer illusion (B) Titchener Circles illusion (C) Ponzo illusion. A and B are from S. Wapner, H. Werner, and P. E. Comalli, *Journal of Gerontology,* 1960, *15,* 413. Reproduced with the permission of the publisher. C is from H. W. Leibowitz and J. M. Judisch, *American Journal of Psychology,* 1967, *80,* 106. Reproduced with the permission of the University of Illinois Press.

**Figure 9–5** Example of incomplete figure. (From E. Verville and N. Cameron, "Age and sex differences in the perception of incomplete pictures by adults." *Journal of Genetic Psychology,* 1946, *68,* 151.)

whole. It is tempting to link this finding with the fact that, although susceptibility to the Müller-Lyer illusion of Figure 9–3A rises with age, it has been found to fall with age for the Titchener Circles illusion of Figure 9–3B: in the latter case the older subjects' perception of the center circle was less influenced by the other circles that were not attached to it. It is reasonable to suppose that difficulty of integration would also show when perceiving an object too large to be observed as a whole in a single glance, or a scene larger than the field of view at any one moment. The occasions on which this would occur would become more frequent if any impairment of movement or stiffness of the neck slowed the succession of glances required, or if, as already noted, retinal changes restricted the effective visual field, making more separate glances necessary.

Analogous age changes have been found in the hearing of complex sounds such as words and sentences which, although they bear some relation to pure tone thresholds, are not fully accounted for by them (Bergman, 1971; Corso, 1977; Farrimond, 1961). Thus, while there is little decline in the ability to hear sentences under good listening conditions between the twenties and the seventies, there is appreciable decline at later ages. Declines are much more severe and begin earlier—they are appreciable in the thirties and substantial by the fifties or sixties—under unfavorable conditions which impair or degrade the signals, such as when there is a long reverberation time, or speech is interrupted 8 times per second, or when words are overlapped, or when the normal presentation rate of 140 words per minute is raised to 350. Such findings imply that learning difficulties for older people could often be minimized if careful attention were given to securing good listening conditions and improving acoustic properties of buildings. Clearly, there is scope for care in speed of presentation when speaking to older people.

CONTEXTUAL FRAMEWORKS

Normally objects are not perceived alone but in a context or perceptual framework of other objects. In the case of vision this contains gradients of illumination, color, and spatial perspective. It is in this way that perceptual constancies operate and three-dimensional perception occurs (see Welford, 1976a, chapter 3). Since these frameworks are built up over a time which far exceeds any particular glance and commonly amounts to at least several seconds, it is understandable that little change with age has been found in perceptual constancy or three-dimensional perception, and no consistent

age changes have been found in the extent of the Ponzo illusion of Figure 9–3C. However, one might expect some decline with age in the ability to integrate the data from changing binocular disparities, as the eyes fixate first one object then another within distances of a few meters. Declines in the accuracy of depth perception over distances of about 1 meter have indeed been found after the age of about 40 (see Fozard *et al.*, 1977). Such declines are especially likely to affect performance in situations where changes of distance have to be judged rapidly, as during the visual guiding of hand movements, and may well contribute to the minor clumsiness and accidents due to misjudging distances, that seem to increase with age.

In the case of hearing, analogous contextual effects can be seen in the greater ease of comprehension when verbal statements continue a line of previous discussion or thought than when they mark a new departure. Older people often tend to request repetition of what has been said, especially if there has been a sudden change in the topic of conversation. To some extent this is understandable in terms of hearing deficit requiring the accumulation of data until an adequate criterion for response has been attained. However, in everyday life, it often seems as if the first time a remark is made, its effect is not to convey a meaning but merely to alert and orient the older listener to the speaker, and that once full attention has been secured, the message is heard well (R. M. Belbin, personal communication). If so, there is room for the development of special techniques for talking to the aged: when a conversation is to be started, the first remark should be a purely alerting one such as "I say!" or "Listen to this!" and any change of topic should be prefaced by a remark such as "Changing the subject" or "On quite a different point." Many who deal with old people constantly, adopt these techniques unconsciously, but awareness of the need for them could substantially improve communication with the elderly by others with whom they have to deal in normal everyday life.

## INTEGRATION OF PERCEPTUAL DATA WITH MEMORY

The factors in perception outlined so far have been concerned with the automatic functioning of the visual and auditory mechanisms, both peripheral and central, in which maturation and use may play some part but specific memories do not. Consideration must now be given to the role of memory in perception. For visual perception, the basic fact is that older subjects require longer exposures to achieve accurate identification of material presented (e.g., Wallace, 1956). The fundamental cause is supposed to be that older people often have difficulty in searching through their memory "store" to find a match for any incoming data. However, recent indications suggest that this is not so (Welford, 1979). Rather, the difficulty is due to the signal-to-noise ratio of the memory traces being lower in older people, either because the traces themselves are weaker, or because of a general increase of neural noise in the brain. In some cases, such as that mentioned by Verville and Cameron (1946), the difficulty is at least partly due also to deficient signals. In others, such as that reported by Wallace (1956), the range of possible identifications is confounded with the complexity of the pattern of the material to be identified. Generally, performance in identification changes less with age under good viewing conditions of lighting and contrast than under poor ones. All these cases are understandable in the sense that a clear and unambiguous signal is likely to be matched accurately with the appropriate memory trace, even if the trace itself is relatively weak, whereas a weaker signal will be likely to be inaccurately matched unless the traces themselves are strong and well differentiated from each other.

Similar principles can be assumed to apply to hearing. If so, hearing loss for meaningful material cannot be considered in terms of either peripheral or central factors alone: both are important.

A further indication of difficulty for older people is that an identification made of one object may be applied to others presented subsequently. Both Verville and Cameron, and Wallace found that older subjects who identified one picture correctly as, say, an animal tended to identify the next also as an animal and, if told this was wrong, to try further animals before changing to other categories of object. Comparable results have been obtained with series of pictures in which one object is gradually transformed into another (Korchin and Basowitz, 1956): older subjects attain the new identification later in the series than do younger. The age difference tends to be less when the second object is in the same general category as the first—for example when a jug becomes a teapot—than when the categories are different—for example mouse and car (Kirby, Nettelbeck, and Goodenough, 1978; O'Doherty, 1958). It is reasonable to suppose that when a particular trace has been activated by the identification of the first object, other closely related traces will be partially activated and thus be more readily available than those of less closely related objects. The partially activated traces would be those more likely to trigger identifications under conditions such as those of old age, when memory traces are weak or poorly differentiated. Similar considerations can be applied to the finding that older subjects perform less well than young on the Stroop test, in which words denoting colors are printed in different colors—for example, the word *green* may be printed in blue ink—and the subject has to say the color of the ink rather than read the word (see Fozard *et al.*, 1977).

At the same time it must be emphasized that, whatever difficulties older people may have in identifying objects quickly, no identification is possible unless material is available in memory with which a match can be made. Memory depends upon experience, and in this respect older people are at an essential advantage. The increasing experience that comes with age not only adds to the stock of traces available, but seems also to arrange them in broader groupings, perspectives, or frames of reference, so that events and objects can be seen in a wider and more coherent context than they would be otherwise. The process has been vividly described for high-level executives by Birren (1969). The broader integration may not always occur, but it obviously cannot do so without the material that experience provides.

The approach that has been outlined is obviously consistent with the fact that older people find it easier to identify familiar rather than unfamiliar objects and sounds: presumably the pattern of traces is more readily available when it has been kept strong by continual use. The approach also implies some means of making identification easier for old people—for example, by ensuring standardization and continuity with past conventions of signs, symbols, and other ways of conveying information. It also implies a need for explicitness, in order to avoid the kind of confusion shown by the elderly lady who, when confronted by two doors, one marked "G" and the other "L," chose "G" on the assumption that the letters meant "Girls" and "Lads."

Identification usually implies the integration of present data with material stored in relatively long-term memory. Of equal or greater importance from the psychological point of view, especially for hearing, is the integration of present data with material brought from the immediate past by ephemeral, running short-term memory. It is on this kind of integration that orientation in both space and time depend. These result from the short-period storage of vast amounts of data in plastic, developing schemata; it is the breakdown of these schemata that appears to underlie most of the confusion and disorientation seen in senility.

Under stable conditions of living, some compensation for loss of short-term retention can be made by using frames of reference built up in the course of long experience and carried in long-term memory. The loss of these frames of reference can severely aggravate tendencies to disorientation among old people when they move from familiar surroundings to new ones, as when they go from the home they have occupied for many years to an institution or when, as happens often in new countries such as Australia, aged parents migrate from continental Europe to live near their children in a country where the language is strange to them. In the former case, difficulty may perhaps be reduced by straightforward design which would enable newcomers to understand the layout of the institutional accommodation with as little problem as possible. In either case, difficulty is likely to be substantial unless the move is made before the ability to build up new frames of reference has been seriously impaired.

## INDIRECT EFFECTS OF SENSORY AND PERCEPTUAL CHANGE: THE EXAMPLE OF DEAFNESS

It was stated at the beginning of this chapter that changes of capacity with age may have not only obvious direct results on performance, but also results which are seemingly remote but understandable in the sense that the changes occur within a complex interacting system. These effects are well illustrated by way of example, in the results of hearing losses.

Severe deafness which is congenital or occurs early in childhood leads to a serious inability to use words for communication or to read fluently. Partial deafness beginning in middle or old age when these skills have been thoroughly acquired is obviously less disabling, but can nevertheless have widespread and serious results. At least six effects appear to be significant:

1. Scores for a number of the subtests of the Wechsler Adult Intelligence Scale, especially but not only those relying on words, have been found to be correlated with hearing losses in such a way as to suggest that some of the lowering of scores with age are the result of impaired hearing rather than age as such (Granick, Kleban, and Weiss, 1976).

2. Distress can result from the recognition that one's powers are failing, especially if work and life generally have previously depended heavily on verbal communication, or other activities such as music in which sound is essential. Attempts to deny the failure are prob-

ably the reason why many people in middle and old age who could benefit from using hearing aids refuse to do so.

3. The lack of music and everyday sounds means that many sources of variety, interest, and pleasure are either lacking or muted.

4. Experiments in which subjects have been kept for periods of hours or days with a minimum of sensory or perceptual stimulation have produced acute emotional distress and hallucinations (for a review see Zubek, 1964). While the deprivations of deafness are obviously less severe, they could be expected to lead either to a sagging of arousal, and thus to a dull inertia, or alternatively, in an attempt to compensate for this, to efforts aimed at securing stimulation of any kind available. Such efforts seem often to result in aggressiveness.

5. It has already been emphasized that what is perceived depends not only on data coming in through the senses, but also upon interpretation in terms of past experience. This not only provides factual knowledge, but also affects interests, attitudes, hopes, and fears. Any reduction in the strength of incoming sensory data tends to allow these interpretative tendencies to operate unchecked, so that biases due to interests, personality characteristics, and other such factors tend to have freer play than they would otherwise in the perception of events. It seems likely that this is why some deaf people show paranoid tendencies—suspicious traits in their personalities lead them to believe that the people around them, whom they can see but can not hear, are denigrating or plotting against them.

6. Probably the most serious effect of deafness is its impairment of social communication, leading to isolation. It is seemingly for this reason that deafness is often regarded as more distressing than blindness. The task of communicating with a deaf or partially deaf person is more laborious than with one having normal hearing. In consequence, it is undertaken less willingly and readily, so that deaf people tend to become lonely and neglected by others. If communication has to be maintained, failures to hear clearly, which lead either to misinterpretation of what is said or to requests for repetition, are annoying to both speaker and listener and can lead to hostility. If these consequences are to be avoided, obligations lie upon both parties: upon the deaf to use whatever aids are available, either electronic hearing aids or techniques such as lipreading, and upon the public at large to recognize that clear speaking is not an affectation but a social duty.

## FACTORS INVOLVED IN THE TAKING OF ACTION

Processes of perception trigger further central processes concerned with the choice of action, or rather of patterns of action, and these in turn give rise to phased and coordinated activity by groups of muscles. Peripheral and central factors can thus again be distinguished and will be dealt with in turn. Before doing so, however, one suggestion frequently made must be countered. Actions typically become slower during the adult years, and it often used to be argued that this was due to older people being less motivated than younger—less willing to exert themselves to the full. Changes of motivation may indeed occur with age, as the balances between demands of life and capacities to meet them change (Welford, 1976b), but age trends found in laboratory studies that have specifically examined the effects of motivation cannot be accounted for in this way. For example, studies of reaction time by Botwinick, Brinley, and Robbin (1958b) and by Weiss (1965), in which electric shocks were given following slow reactions, found that subjects reacted faster than when no shocks were given, but that there was little difference with age in the extent to which this occurred.

## PERIPHERAL MOTOR FACTORS

Brief tests of muscular strength have shown that the force that can be exerted by several muscle groups is maximal in the twenties and thereafter declines slowly so that by the sixties it has fallen by between 15 and 35 percent (see Welford, 1977a). A similar decline has been shown for longer maintained grip by the hand (Burke, Tuttle, Thompson, Janney, and Weber, 1953). Such falls of strength can be attributed to loss of muscle units, changes in the metabolism of those that remain, and higher thresholds for neural energization of muscles (Frolkis, Martynenko, and Zamostyan, 1976; Gutmann and Hanzlikova, 1976).

Amounts of heavy muscular work achieved over a period of time also fall with age owing to declines in various phases of metabolism within the muscles, respiratory, and circulatory systems, which reduce oxygen supply to the muscles. Astrand (1960) provides a nomogram for predicting work capacity from pulse rates and oxygen uptake, which takes account of sex and age. Physiological measures may not, however, provide a full picture of age changes: subjective assessments of exertion for any given exercise-induced heart rate have been found to increase with age, slightly between groups aged 30 and 45, and more substantially between these and groups aged 60 (Arstila, Antila, Wendelin, Vuori, and Välkimäki, 1977).

Maximum strength and capacity for continued exertion may well be important factors limiting energetic pursuits and work involving heavy muscular effort by older people. This is likely to be true even though the average workload is less than maximum: workload inevitably fluctuates from moment to moment and hour to hour, and the limitations will apply to the peaks rather than to the average. It is generally assumed as a rule of thumb that a muscular workload of about 50 percent of maximum is supportable over long periods (Åstrand, 1960). For lighter work and most everyday activities, maximum capacity for muscular effort is likely to be of little importance until well into old age. In line with this, Birren and Spieth (1962) found little relationship between speed of performance and either blood pressure or pulse rate, either before or after exercise.

Various other effector limitations, for example, stiffness of joints leading to difficulty of action, or reduced mobility of the neck resulting in the need to turn the whole body to see sideways, doubtless affect some performances, although the extent to which they do so has not, so far as the author is aware, been studied. There are also factors which enter into gait and posture which show well-known changes with age. Insofar as these changes result from arthritic conditions which cause pain during movement, they are likely to set up a vicious circle: because of the pain involved, activity is avoided; this leads to wastage of muscles, which in turn imposes extra stress on joints, leading to increased pain. On the other hand, Scheibel and Scheibel (1979) have suggested that some apparent stiffness of muscles is due to the loss of certain giant cortical Betz cells which become active just before the onset of voluntary action and inhibit tonic postural muscular activity which might be antagonistic to the action. If this inhibition does not occur, the muscles involved in the voluntary action may be working against those involved in maintaining posture. If so, action is slowed, and relatively weak postural muscles opposed to strong voluntary ones may be strained.

Any stiffness of joints or opposition between muscles will reduce the mechanical efficiency of action. This is especially so when the loading imposed by the task is low, since the internal resistances to movement will form a larger proportion of the total loading than when the loading from the task is high. It is consistent with the age trends noted in the previous paragraph that Åstrand (1960) found a fall of mechanical efficiency with age in a group ranging from age 20 to 68, especially at relatively low levels of loading. One might, therefore, expect that although older people may not be limited by such factors to any great extent in normal everyday performance, they might show a greater tendency to fatigue for any given effective physical achievement.

## CENTRAL FACTORS IN THE CHOICE AND CONTROL OF ACTION

Until the 1940s, it was commonly assumed that changes in sense organs, muscles, joints, heart, and lungs, together with changes in the demands of living, could account, either directly or indirectly, for virtually all normal changes of performance with age, and that mental powers remained virtually unchanged throughout normal adult life. The importance of central factors first became clear when detailed studies were made of sensory-motor performance in relation to age. These and subsequent studies have been surveyed by the present author (Welford, 1977a). Let us take as an example a serial reaction task the results of which are shown in Figure 9–6. Subjects had to move a lever as fast as possible from a central position (A) to a choice-point (B) and then to one of two end positions (C1 and C2) according to which of two signal lights had been illuminated. As soon as the end point had been reached, the light went out and the

lever had to be returned to A as fast as possible. On reaching A another signal light appeared and the cycle began again. The task continued until 64 responses had been made (Singleton, 1955). The signal lights were clear enough not to have caused any sensory limitation. If there had been serious motor limitation among older subjects, it should have shown in the times spent moving between the various points A, B, and C1 or C2. These times rose very little with age, however, compared with the times spent stationary at A, B, C1, and C2. In other words, the main slowing with age was not in the execution of movements, but in the central processes involved in deciding what movements to make. An industrial parallel to Singleton's results was obtained by Murrell and Forsaith (1960), who made detailed time studies of industrial work and found that slowing with age lay not so much in the speed at which actual movements were executed as in the times required to plan and decide actions to be taken.

In line with these results are those for three types of movement: first, simple unaimed movements which show substantial slowing from the twenties onwards (Pierson and Montoye, 1958); second, repetitive movements of tapping between two targets which show little change with age (Morikiyo and Nishioka, 1966; Welford, Norris, and Shock, 1969); and third, more elaborate movements as when writing digits or letters or tracing over a complex pattern, which again become substantially slower with age (Birren and Botwinick, 1951a; Brown, 1958). Percentage changes found between the twenties and sixties have been about 90 for the first, 8–16 for the second and 60–120 for the third. In the first case the limitations are muscular. In the third, speed of performance is largely determined by decisions about what movements to make at each point in the pattern. In the second case, neither of these limitations applies since the movements, being aimed at targets, are made relatively slowly and are well within muscular limitations, while their repetitive pattern means that little decision is required about each movement individually.

Similar principles apply to reaction times. When a prepared response can be given on the appearance of a predetermined signal, little decision is required, and there is usually little rise of reaction time, at least until the seventies (see Welford, 1977a). When, however, a choice is required between two or more responses to different signals, and it is uncertain which signal will appear, the amount of decision involved, and the increase of reaction time with age, are greater. Reaction time commonly rises approximately linearly with the

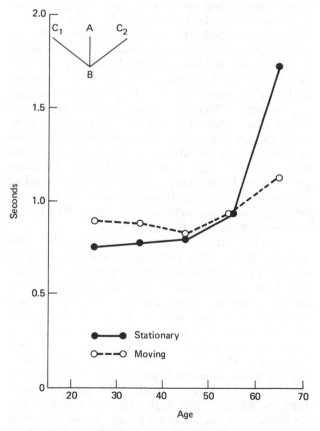

**Figure 9–6**  Results of a serial reaction task by Singleton (1955), showing that movement times rise less than decision times with age. The pattern of movement that was required is indicated by the diagram in the top left corner.

logarithm of the number of choices. The exact relationship has been a matter of controversy but recent indications are that it is well expressed by the equation

$$\text{Reaction time} = K \log \left( n \, \frac{C}{E} + 1 \right) \qquad (3)$$

where $K$ is a measure of the rate at which reaction time increases with degree of choice, $n$ is the number of (equiprobable) signals and their corresponding responses, $C$ is the criterion for responding—high when the subject is cautious, lower when he is wi ling to risk errors—and $E$ denotes the signal strength (Smith, 1977). The signal strength $E$ is assumed to accumulate with time until the level $C$ is reached and a response is triggered. $E$ and $C$ are conceived in terms of signal-to-noise ratio and the formulation is thus linked to the type of approach considered in relation to sensory functions. Age changes in different studies have taken the form of a rise attributable to either $C/E$, $K$, or both. Rises of $C/E$ cause an approximately equal rise of time for all degrees of choice and probably mean that the older subjects are accumulating more data before making a decision. If so, the results are in line with those discussed by Vickers *et al.* (1972) and suggest that, if they can, older subjects compensate for low signal-to-noise ratio by taking more time.

## Causes of Slowing with Age

The concept of signal-to-noise ratio appears to be fundamental to several types of cause which have been suggested for the slowing with age of reaction times and of decisional processes generally.

*Cardiac disabilities.* These might impair cerebral circulation and thus signal-to-noise ratio. They are associated with slowing of several types of performance, both motor and intellectual, and the likelihood of these impairments increases with age (Welford, 1977a). Szafran (1966), using a choice-reaction task, found that among subjects in good health the change with age was of a kind wholly attributable to a rise of $C/E$, but that among subjects showing cardiac deficiency after exercise, there was also a rise of $K$ with age. Similarly Abrahams and Birren (1973) found slowing of the types attributable to increases of both $K$ and $C/E$ among subjects judged to be predisposed to coronary heart disease by Friedman's Standard Situation Interview. The rise of $K$ in these cases is difficult to understand, but implies that older people with coronary deficiencies, have relatively greater difficulty with high degrees of choice than do those in good health.

*Lack of Physical Fitness.* This might be expected to impair signal-to-noise ratio, and thus tend to lengthen reaction time. It has been suggested that some of the slowing with age is due to older people tending to be less fit. Results are conflicting: Spirduso (see Stelmach and Diewert, 1977) found differences of reaction time associated with amount of exercise normally taken to be greater among older adults than among young, but Botwinick and Storandt (1974) found the reverse. In neither case could differences of exercise account for the whole age effect.

*Brain Deficiency.* This might be expected to lower signal-to-noise ratio. Hicks and Birren (1970) have surveyed relationships between age changes in psychomotor performance and the symptoms of various kinds of brain deficiency, and several authors have studied relationships between changes of EEG and of reaction time with age. Surwillo (1961, 1963, 1964) has shown a close correlation between reaction time, both simple and choice, and the frequency of the alpha rhythm, and has argued that the slowing of this can account for the lengthening of reaction time with age.

*Impaired Ability to Prepare Reactions, Hold States of Readiness or Formulate Expectations.* These could be indirect results of a lowered signal-to-noise ratio. What appears to be an example is the finding that when the interval is relatively short between a warning and a signal to respond, or between one signal and the next in a series, lengthening of reaction time tends to be greater among older subjects. For example, in a two-choice task using light signals and key-pressing responses, the slowing with age between subjects in their late teens or twenties and their grandparents aged 67–87 was found to average 24 percent when each signal followed 2 seconds after the completion of the previous response, but 36 percent when it followed immediately (Welford, 1977b). It has also been shown that when subjects have to guess which will be the next signal in a choice-reaction task, the older tend to guess less accurately (Sanford and Maule, 1973), and that the slowing of heart rate while waiting for a signal, commonly taken as an indicator of preparation, is less among older subjects than among younger, implying that older subjects do not prepare as *intensively* as do the young (Morris and Thompson, 1969). In line with this view, Loveless and Sanford (1974) found that older subjects failed to show an anticipatory electrocortical potential between a warning and a signal to respond. Also, Rabbitt (1964) found that a warning which conveyed information, such as that one of four out of a possible eight responses would be called for, shortened reaction times for younger but not older subjects.

*Noise Produced as an Aftereffect of the Decision-Making Process.* This is a plausible interpretation of the slowing of reaction time among older subjects when the interval between signals is very short. This aftereffect may increase with age, continué for a brief period, and act as noise, blurring any decision process which follows shortly after (Welford, 1965b). Such aftereffects could be expected to impair performance less when the following response is the same as the one just made: they should rather facilitate it since the processes for initiation of the response would already be operating to some extent. If this is the correct explanation of the disproportionate rise of reaction time with age in continuous tasks mentioned in the last paragraph, responses which are repeated should be relatively faster than others among older subjects in these tasks. However, scrutiny of the results revealed no such tendency. Instead, repeated responses tended to become progressively slower than others with age.

*The Greater Tendency of the Elderly to Monitor Their Responses.* This is a more likely reason for the slower performance of older people in continuous tasks. It has been found that while such monitoring is in progress, immediate attention cannot be given to new signals (see Welford, 1968). The tendency has frequently been noted for older people to monitor their performances in the sense of looking at what they are doing (e.g., Szafran, 1958). This is often done voluntarily, although it may become automatic as a result of habit. In the experiment discussed in the last two paragraphs (Welford, 1977b), the monitoring appeared to be an *involuntary* result of the older subjects being slower than the younger at perceiving new signals: feedback from the response seems to compete with new signals for attention and the first to arrive tends to secure attention to the exclusion of the other. Any slowing of older people's perception of new signals, even by a few milliseconds could, therefore, render attention more likely to be captured by feedback from a previous response and thus delay decision about the response to an ensuing signal. Greater tendencies of older people to monitor movements to the exclusion of immediate attention to new signals have also been observed by Rabbitt and Rogers (1965) and by Rabbitt and Birren (1967).

## SOME IMPLICATIONS OF SLOWING WITH AGE

Findings regarding age changes in speed of performance have widespread implications. For instance, they imply that work which older people are likely to find difficult will be that which calls for rapid decision and control of action rather than sheer muscular strength. Especially difficult are likely to be jobs where the worker has to keep pace with a conveyor line or other machinery which makes it necessary to decide upon and carry out an action within rigid time limits. This is not only because the average time required will rise with age so that an older worker has less margin to spare, but also because increased variability will mean an increasing proportion of occasions when the action required will take longer than the time available. Studies of industrial operatives have shown this to be so. Relatively few men or women over the age of 50 are found on work which is rigidly paced or which has to be carried out under severe pressure for speed or with a high piece-rate system of payment (Belbin, 1953; Heron and Cunningham, 1962; Welford, 1958, 1966). Many more older people are found on jobs which can be done at a pace they determine for themselves. Surprisingly, older people do a great deal of relatively heavy muscular work with evident success. It is true that people tend to move away in the late forties and fifties from the most strenuous jobs such as tunneling and working as colliers in coal mines (Powell, 1973), but they have been found in relatively large numbers on a wide range of jobs involving moderate physical effort (Barkin, 1933), and in some cases have seemed to prefer these when given a choice (Belbin, 1955). The reason appears to be that, except on the most strenuous jobs, speed is a greater limitation than muscular effort for older people.

Similar indications of the decline of speed of decision with age come from studies of industrial accidents. Whitfield (1954), in a study of coal miners, found that those aged 42–66 who sustained accidents were superior to their more fortunate contemporaries with respect to visual and auditory acuity, but were inferior in a task involving the rapid control of light hand movements. The opposite correlations were found, however, for miners aged 20–27. King (1955), in a study of accidents among agricultural workers, found that all the types of accidents which increased significantly in frequency with age—falls, being hit by moving objects, and so on—could be explained by slowness in getting out of the way of hazards, or in recovering lost balance. It should be noted in passing that slowness in taking the actions required to recover balance is a possibility that needs to be considered in all falls by older people. In line with the industrial accident findings is the trend of road accidents and offenses. Accidents typically sustained by older drivers seem to be due to slowness and tendency to confusion (McFarland, Tune, and Welford, 1964). Offenses characteristic of older drivers can be construed as due to slowness in reacting to rapidly changing situations (Johinke, 1977; Road Traffic Board of South Australia, 1972).

RELATIONSHIPS BETWEEN SIGNALS
AND RESPONSES

Performance at all ages becomes slower and often also less accurate when complex intermediate steps are required in order to relate signals to their corresponding responses, and the effects are disproportionately greater among older people. Certain factors such as ability to conceptualize relationships and to manipulate data in the abstract, which exert relatively little limitation in the twenties, appear to have much greater effects in later middle and old age. The types of intermediate step required can be divided into two broad classes: *spatial transpositions* and *symbolic translations* or recodings.

Spatial transpositions are required when the spatial layout of a display or set of signal sources is different from that of the corresponding responses as, for instance, when movements have to be made in relation to objects seen in a mirror, or when a signal on the left has to be responded to by pressing a key on the right and vice versa. In one such case, the increase of reaction time from the straightforward or so-called "compatible" arrangement to the reversed was 53 percent for a group aged 17–26 but 79 percent for the same subjects' grandparents aged 67–86 (Welford, 1977b). In an experiment where straightforward and reversed relationships were compared under two-, four-, and eight-choice conditions, the slope $K$ of Equation 3 rose by 74 percent in a group aged 20–28 years and by 82 percent in a group aged 48–62 years (Griew, 1964). The effect is illustrated in everyday life by the finding that, as one grows older, it becomes more difficult when traveling south to read a map without turning it upside down!

Symbolic translations typically involve making manual responses in relation to signals which are in the form of digits, letters, or other symbols. They are in many ways akin to the translations involved in digit-symbol and other substitution tasks. The magnitude of the effects is well illustrated in a choice-reaction task by Birren, Riegel, and Morrison (1962). Subjects were confronted by a row of ten signal lights, under each of which was a button. When the response required was to press the button immediately under the light that was on, subjects aged 60–80 took about 27 percent longer than those aged 18–33. When, however, the lights and buttons were numbered in different random orders so that subjects had to find the button that bore the same number as the light that was on—a button *not* immediately under the light—the older subjects took 51 percent longer than the younger.

Increases when the two types of "incompatibility" are combined can be dramatic. For example, in a twelve-choice reaction task of relating lights to response buttons by Kay (1954, 1955; see also Welford, 1958, 1977a), the increase of reaction time between groups aged 25–34 and 65–72 for a fully compatible arrangement was 13 percent. When the lights were placed three feet away across the table, necessitating a spatial transposition between lights and buttons, the increase of reaction time was 25 percent, and with a symbolic translation—relating light to key by number–it rose to 56 percent. When both the transposition and the translation were combined, the rise was no less than 299 percent.

Why incompatibility has these effects is not clear, and the question is an intriguing one for the psychology of sensory-motor performance in general. What is clear, however, is that the effects of incompatibility emphasize the need for straightforwardness in the design of articles to be used by older people. For instance, other things being equal, direct manual operations using hand tools are likely to be easier for older people than operations using complex machine tools. With machine tools, control panels of industrial plants, vehicles, and household articles such as radio and television sets, it is important that meters, dials, and other indicators should be placed in positions in which they are directly and obviously related to any controls that need to be used in conjunction with them. In view of Kay's results, it seems to be specially important to examine tasks to see whether two or more difficulties are stacked one on another: if so, removal of one could dramatically ease the task for older people.

COMPENSATORY FACTORS

Two factors tend to offset age changes in sensory-motor performance when conditions permit: balance between speed and accuracy, and practice and familiarity.

*Balance Between Speed and Accuracy.* With relatively simple tasks there is usually a compensatory relationship between speed, accuracy, and age such that older people tend to be slower but more accurate—presumably caution and extra time taken more than offset any tendency to error that would result from a lower signal-to-noise ratio. For example, in the spatially transposed condition of Kay's task mentioned in the previous section, the older groups made 43 percent *less* errors than the younger. Such compensation can, however, take place only within limits. For instance, it seems to fail as incompatibility rises: in the condition requiring a symbolic recoding, the older group made 129 percent *more* errors than the younger, and in the combined condition 458 percent more!

These results suggest, however, that within limits older people engaged in work or other activities they can do at their own pace may be slower than younger people but will tend to waste less time making errors and may, indeed, on balance be *more* efficient and effective—for instance, in cases where a single error can spoil a product which has taken a long time to make or can cause danger. The trouble is that older people may carry the shift too far and become unnecessarily meticulous. However, as was noted in the case of visual discrimination, excessive caution may be eliminated by suitable training.

*Practice and Familiarity.* Laboratory experiments have shown that both absolute and relative differences between the performances of older and younger adults tend to be greater initially than they are after some practice. Indeed, LaRivière and Simonson (1965), who studied speed of writing by men in several occupations, found no slowing from the forties to the fifties or again to the sixties among those engaged in clerical duties, although they found progressive slowing amounting to about 21 percent between the forties and sixties among those whose work did not lay so much stress upon writing. However, cross-sectional comparisons such as theirs between occupations are hazardous because, as Belbin (1953) showed, people tend to move from jobs which become unsuitable for them as they grow older: the older clerks may therefore have been a selected group. A further indication that decline with age tends to be less for familiar than for unfamiliar tasks is provided by Hellon, Lind, and Weiner (1956), who compared groups of mine rescue workers exercising by stepping on and off a stool under hot and humid conditions. They found that, compared to a younger group, those aged 39–45 were later in starting to sweat and had faster pulse rates and slightly higher body temperatures, and that these effects took longer

to die away during a subsequent period of rest. However, when the same men undertook a simulated mine rescue under the same hot and humid conditions, endurance did not differ with age (Lind, Hellon, Weiner, and Jones, 1955). The greater experience of the older men appeared to enable them to adopt more efficient methods of working in the familiar task.

It seems clear that many skills, especially motor skills, acquired when young can be maintained into later years far more readily than they can be acquired at that date. Also, older people have been shown to display various subtle patterns of performance which are indicative of skill which comes with long experience. For instance, Griew and Tucker (1958) found that the skill resulting from experience seemed to enable older machine-tool operators to use their machines more efficiently. Again King (1955) found that, of the agricultural accidents he studied, those which declined with age were of types associated with lack of experience and skill. Much the same can be said of the types of road accidents and traffic offenses that decline with age.

Facts such as these have led some to suppose that all declines of performance in middle and old age are due to older people being "out of training" for the tasks concerned. Certainly some industrial training procedures have shown themselves capable of bringing the performances of middle-aged people close to those of young adults (Belbin, 1965, 1969; Belbin and Downs, 1966; Chown, Belbin, and Downs, 1967). However, the fundamental nature of age changes in the brain and other bodily mechanisms, the fact that age changes occur in the performance of relatively simple tasks and cannot be eliminated by incentives, and the fact that practice curves suggest that asymptotic levels would still differ with age, all make it unreasonable to assume that lack of recent exercise of skills can account for the trends of performance seen during the adult years.

Nevertheless, the effects of familiarity and practice do indicate that older people have much to gain from careful standardization in the equipment they use, so that, for example, they do not have to learn a new layout or mode of operation of controls when they buy a new car, cooking stove, radio, or television set. Any change from what is familiar is liable to cause errors. These may not matter when operating a radio or television set, but can obviously be serious with a car. Even if the use of new equipment has been mastered sufficiently for performance to be error-free in normal circumstances, errors may still occur and cause accidents in emergencies or under conditions of stress.

STIMULATION, ACTIVITY, STRESS,
AND AROUSAL.

Sensory stimulation, besides signaling specific messages to particular parts of the brain, also activates the reticular formation in the brain stem, which in turn sends a stream of diffuse impulses to the cortex. These have an arousing effect, rendering the cortex more sensitive and responsive than it would otherwise be. Similar effects seem to result from activities within the brain involved in making decisions, and from the recognition of any situation implying danger or otherwise causing stress.

As arousal level rises, performance improves up to a point, but thereafter it deteriorates again. There is thus an optimum level below which the subject tends to be inert and above which he tends to be overactive. Level of arousal is commonly assessed by various indices of autonomic nervous system activity such as heart rate, sinus arrhythmia, pupil dilation, free fatty-acid level in plasma, skin resistance, and galvanic skin response. Attempts have also been made to link arousal with various EEG indices, although interpretations have been questioned (see Marsh and Thompson, 1977).

Relationships between arousal, signal, noise, and criterion levels can be broadly represented as in Figure 9–7 (Welford, 1973). Increased arousal is likely to raise the level of the signal and the standard deviation of the noise roughly in proportion. The signal-to-noise ratio will be little if at all altered unless levels of arousal become so high that a substantial number of cells in the cortex, instead of being merely rendered more sensitive and responsive, begin to fire. If this happens, noise might increase more than signal, and lead to a fall of signal-to-noise ratio. Short of this extreme, if the criterion point remains constant as shown in Figure 9–7, increasing arousal will raise the proportions both of correct responses and of false ones and lead to a lowering of β in the Equation (2). Lowering of arousal level will have the opposite effect, reducing the proportion of both correct and false responses and raising β. Other things being equal, the reduction of sensory stimulation in middle and old age could be expected to result in somewhat lower levels of arousal, and it is perhaps consistent with this that older subjects have been found to show less EEG reactivity to stimulation.

High values of β which have been found among older subjects are consistent with the view that their arousal levels are relatively low. Also consistent with this is the finding by Surwillo and Quilter (1964) that subjects aged 60–82 showed greater decline of performance in a "vigilance" task than did those aged 22–59. So-called vigilance tasks in-

volve watching for faint and infrequent signals in monotonous conditions. It has been found with subjects of all ages that the number of signals observed declines rapidly during a watch of half an hour or so, and that the decline is accompanied by a rise of β and various autonomic indications of lowered arousal (for a review see Davies and Tune, 1970). Surwillo (1966) showed that declines of vigilance between groups aged 22–45 and 69–85 were associated with changes of autonomic activity indicating lowered arousal. It is true that Griew and Davies (1962) and Davies and Griew (1963), using a different type of task, failed to find an age difference in vigilance, but their older subjects—aged 41–66—were considerably younger than those studied by Surwillo. Other studies of autonomic changes which support the view that arousal levels are lower among older people have been surveyed by Marsh and Thompson (1977). Taking the results together, it seems fair to suggest that any lowering of arousal with age does not become substantial until after the age of about 60–70. If arousal does fall, it is worth bearing in mind that a powerful method of overcoming low arousal in vigilance tasks has been found in the provision of "knowledge of results" of performance (see Davies and Tune, 1970), and that a possible cause of low-

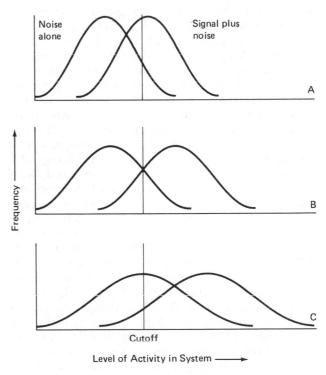

**Figure 9–7**  Distributions similar to those of Figure 1 for three levels of arousal: A low, B optimal, C high.

ered arousal among old people, especially those living in institutions, is that they do not see enough result for any effort they make.

On the other hand Eisdorfer (1968) and his colleagues (for references see Elias and Elias, 1977; Marsh and Thompson, 1977) studying performance during serial learning and in a vigilance task somewhat similar to that of Davies and Griew, found, in their older subjects, poorer performance together with higher free fatty acid levels which were slower to fall after the task had been completed. These results suggested that their older subjects were *more* aroused than their younger and that their performance was impaired by *over*-arousal. Impairment of performance under conditions that can be presumed to cause very high levels of arousal has been demonstrated experimentally, and is well recognized in cases of extreme fear or anger, in many cases of anxiety and schizophrenia, and in many depressive states where an outward inertia masks an underlying tension.

Further suggestions that older people, even if not overaroused, are not underaroused comes from the observed failure of their performance to improve following the administration of stimulant drugs (Eisdorfer, Conner, and Wilkie, 1968; Kleemeier, Rich, and Justiss, 1956). Similar suggestions are contained in the finding by Heron and Chown (1967) of a tendency towards unsociability with age in a personality test measuring a trait similar to introversion which, as will be noted shortly, is associated with relatively high arousal levels.

In seeking to resolve the conflict of evidence regarding older people, it must be borne in mind that arousal is not a single state with a unitary cause producing only one result, but is many faceted (Lacey, 1967). Again a distinction needs to be drawn between arousability in the sense of tendency for arousal to rise under stimulating or stressful conditions, and chronic arousal level. High degrees of arousability have been coupled with Eysenck's personality dimension of Neuroticism and high scores on the Taylor Manifest Anxiety Scale, while high chronic arousal levels have been associated with Eysenck's dimension of Introversion (see Eysenck, 1970; Welford 1965a, 1973, 1976a). Optimum arousal levels are lower for difficult than for easy tasks, and the various indices of arousal do not always agree. Further, the effects may be anomalous in the sense that a subject's reaction to situations in which arousal is higher or lower than optimum may be an effort, either conscious or unconscious, to bring it to optimum. Thus an introvert's seeking for solitude and quiet can be interpreted as an attempt to avoid overarousal re-sulting from social stimulation, while an extrovert's liking for loud sounds, bright colors, and social situations can be construed as an attempt to raise an arousal level that would otherwise be too low. Again, loss of sleep, which tends to lower arousal level, may inspire efforts to combat its effects and thus produce indices of autonomic activity associated with high arousal levels (Wilkinson, 1965).

These many variables make it understandable that changes of arousal with age vary in different studies. Not only might they differ with the type of task used and the conditions under which it was done, but it is likely that changes would differ according to the population from which subjects were drawn. For example, as Wenger's (1977) results mentioned previously suggest, middle-aged men at the peak of their careers who begin to notice age changes that could affect their working capacity, are likely to feel themselves to be under some chronic stress and thus to be more chronically aroused than those who have retired or are inmates of an institution for the aged. For the present, therefore, it seems appropriate not to assume that either under- or overarousal is necessarily associated with age. This is not to say that arousal should be neglected: the characteristic errors in performance, of omission in states of underarousal and commission in states of overarousal, mean that arousability and chronic arousal level are potentially important predictors of certain types of accident, and of the types of work and environment suitable for particular people (McEwen, 1973). The need is to examine carefully the individuals concerned. Failure to do so could have serious effects if those with a tendency to chronic overarousal or high arousability were given stimulating treatments or placed in a nosiy, lively environment, or if those chronically underaroused were placed in unstimulating conditions or sedated.

## THE SYSTEM AS A WHOLE

The various sensory, central, and motor mechanisms whose operation has been surveyed here work not in isolation but as a complex interacting system. In consequence, some events such as falls or accidents have many different possible contributing causes, including visual and kinesthetic sensory deficit, muscular weakness, and slowness of perception and decision making to recover balance. At the same time, the age changes in any one mechanism may have widespread indirect as well as more obvious direct effects. It has, for instance, already been noted that loss of auditory sensitivity may not only make hearing difficult, but may affect social interaction and lead to lowered levels of arousal and lack of motivation. Further indications of the interaction of different elements in the system come from studies which have shown correlations between the changes with age in different types of performance (for a brief review, see Welford, 1977a). Of these correlations some, such as that between auditory reaction time and depression (Botwinick and Thompson, 1967), collapse when age is held constant, implying that they are due to independent factors both of which change with age. Other correlations remain stable as age increases, implying that both the variables are affected by some common factor which changes with age. Other correlations again, such as that between writing speed and rate of addition (Birren and Botwinick, 1951b), increase with age, implying that some limiting factor which affects both tasks is of trivial importance when young but becomes more serious as age advances. For example, neural noise in the brain which, in young persons, would have minor effects compared with differences in the efficiency of particular sensory and central mechanisms, might increasingly come to have a blanket effect upon them all as age advanced.

More important for everyday living and from the psychiatrist's point of view are the means adopted for relating age changes of capacity to the demands of life. The environment makes demands upon the individual which are met with more or less success by use of the capacities he possesses. In order to relate demands to capacities, he develops a range of techniques and methods of coping or, as they have come to be termed, "strategies." These strategies are to some extent flexible, so that a fall in one capacity can often be compensated by a change in the method or manner of performing a task. If so, a substantial change in a particular capacity may have little effect on overall achievement. At the same time, performance employing any particular strategy is usually limited by one capacity while others involved are not used to their full extent. A relatively small change in the one limiting capacity may, therefore, cause either a substantial change of overall achievement or, alternatively, a radical change of method.

Strategies differ in range and time scale. Some are concerned with limited, detailed performance, others with broader aspects of living, and it is these latter that are of special importance and interest from a psychiatric standpoint, particularly strategies for coping when one or more capacities begin to fail. It seems fair to suggest that four broad strategies of this type are possible.

## INCREASED EFFICIENCY

A realistic reaction to an incipient fall of capacity is to ensure that all detailed strategies of performance are as efficient as possible so as to maximize the demands that can be met by the capacity still available. One adjustment for this purpose would be to optimize the relationship between speed and accuracy. Another is to develop routines that enable larger sequences of action to be carried out as unified wholes in which each item flows from the last with a minimum of fresh decision. One can also adjust by ordering sequences so as to cut out unnecessary actions, and by pacing oneself so as to avoid hurry and unnecessary expenditure of physical effort. These efficiencies come as the result of experience and can be regarded as ways in which experience compensates for age changes of capacity. This type of broad strategy is obviously important and valuable. It can, however, be effective only within limits, and has the danger that reliance on routines can reduce the flexibility needed if methods have to be changed because circumstances have altered.

## INCREASED EFFORT

Workers on conveyor lines and other jobs where speed is stressed, have been observed to cut down idle time and generally to make increasing efforts as they reach the late forties (Belbin, 1953; Richardson, 1953). The tendency is probably a more widespread reaction to changes in middle age than is commonly recognized, and often leads to increasingly desperate efforts to "keep young." The danger of such a strategy is that, if carried to excess, it leads to stress and anxiety syndromes, overarousal, increased neural noise, errors, and ill-considered actions, all of which are likely to reduce efficiency and thus exacerbate the effects of the very deficiencies it is attempting to overcome. Increased effort can be a sound strategy for short periods over special issues or during emergencies, but appears to be dangerous if wide-ranging or chronic.

## RECRUITMENT OF THE AID OF OTHERS

This is a reasonable strategy for short periods in case of emergency and, perhaps, in moderation for longer periods when the individual can call upon the paid services of others, for instance by going out to occasional meals to ease the burden of housekeeping or by moving into an old people's home when running one's own home is no longer possible without undue effort. Its danger is that, having once accepted the services of others, the recipient will become dependent. Especially when services are demanded from relatives or neighbors, dependency can lead to serious impairment of social relations: donors of services become increasingly unwilling to do what is demanded and as a result, in accordance with well-recognized principles of motivation, the demands become more insistent. Eventually the donor develops hostility and tries to minimize contact with the recipient who, as a result, becomes lonely (Welford, 1976b).

MODIFICATION OF AIM

This strategy essentially involves the phasing out of pursuits for which capacities are no longer adequate, in favor of interests and activities suited to those that remain. An obvious example is that most older people cease to play vigorous games or to go dancing, in favor of watching sport and engaging in less energetic forms of social intercourse. The danger in this course of action is of going too far and narrowing interests and activities to such an extent that life lacks the variety needed to ensure adequate arousal and motivation (Welford, 1976b). Maintenance of not only breadth but also quality of interest appears to be important: for instance, failure to preserve interest in, and concern for, other people can lead to isolation, loneliness, and, again in consequence, to lack of stimulation, arousal, and motivation.

It is perhaps not the business of a chapter concerned with sensory and motor performance to advise on life-styles, but it seems fair to add, having come thus far, that obviously no strategy is foolproof and none can fully restore certain powers of youth. Probably the optimum broad strategy is a mixture of all four: attempts to secure efficiency coupled with a selective modification of aim, concentrating on those aims which are in line with capacities that have changed relatively little with age in the individual concerned and which exploit the fruits of experience; a willingness to make extra efforts on occasion; and readiness to accept gratefully the help of others at times, without succumbing to the pleasures of feeling oneself to be in command of slaves. It is impossible to lay down any universal, precise prescription; individuals differ in the rates at which their various sensory, central, and motor mechanisms age, so that a person who is old in one respect may still be young in others—no unitary index of aging has any valid or useful meaning. All that can be urged is that each individual needs to be studied in detail in order to decide upon the mixture of strategies that will for him or her be optimum.

# REFERENCES

ABRAHAMS, J. P., AND BIRREN, J. E. 1973. Reaction time as a function of age and behavioral predisposition to coronary heart disease. *J. Gerontol., 28,* 471–478.

ARSTILA, M., ANTILA, K., WENDELIN, H., VUORI, I., AND VÄLIMÄKI, I. 1977. The effect of age and sex on the perception of exertion during an exercise test with a linear increase in heart rate. *In,* G. Borg (ed.), *Physical Work and Effort,* pp. 217–221. Oxford: Pergamon Press.

ÅSTRAND, I. 1960. Aerobic work capacity in men and women with special reference to age. *Acta Physiol. Scand., 49,* Supp. 169.

BARKIN, S. 1933. *The Older Worker in Industry.* New York Legislative State Document No. 60. Albany: Lyon.

BELBIN, R. M. 1953. Difficulties of older people in industry. *Occupational Psychol., 27,* 177–190.

BELBIN, R. M. 1955. Older people and heavy work. *Brit. J. Industr. Med., 12,* 309–319.

BELBIN, R. M. 1965. *Training Methods for Older Workers.* Paris: O.E.C.D.

BELBIN, R. M. 1969. *The Discovery Method: An International Experiment in Retraining.* Paris: O.E.C.D.

BELBIN, E., AND DOWNS, S. 1966. Teaching paired associates: the problem of age. *Occupational Psychol., 40,* 67–74.

BERGMAN, M. 1971. Hearing and aging. *Audiology, 10,* 164–171.

BIRREN, J. E. 1969. Age and decision strategies. *In,* A. T. Welford and J. E. Birren (eds.), *Decision Making and Age,* pp. 23–36. Basel: Karger.

BIRREN, J. E., AND BOTWINICK, J. 1951a. The relation of writing speed to age and to the senile psychoses. *J. Consult. Psychol., 15,* 243–249.

BIRREN, J. E., AND BOTWINICK, J. 1951b. Rate of addition as a function of difficulty and age. *Psychometrika, 16,* 219–232.

BIRREN, J. E., RIEGEL, K. F., AND MORRISON, D. F. 1962. Age differences in response speed as a function of controlled variations of stimulus conditions: Evidence of a general speed factor. *Gerontologia, 6,* 1–18.

BIRREN, J. E., AND SCHAIE, K. W. (Eds.) 1977. *Handbook of the Psychology of Aging.* New York: Van Nostrand Reinhold.

BIRREN, J. E., AND SPIETH, W. 1962. Age, response speed, and cardiovascular functions. *J. Gerontol., 17,* 390–391.

BOTWINICK, J., BRINLEY, J. F., AND ROBBIN, J. S. 1958a.

The interaction effects of perceptual difficulty and stimulus exposure time on age differences in speed and accuracy of response. *Gerontologia, 2,* 1–10.

BOTWINICK, J., BRINLEY, J. F., AND ROBBIN, J. S. 1958b. The effect of motivation by electrical shocks on reaction-time in relation to age. *Amer. J. Psychol., 71,* 408–411.

BOTWINICK, J., AND STORANDT, M. 1974. Cardiovascular status, depressive affect, and other factors in reaction time. *J. Gerontol., 29,* 543–548.

BOTWINICK, J., AND THOMPSON, L. W. 1967. Depressive affect, speed of response, and age. *J. Consult. Psychol., 31,* 106.

BROWN, R. A. 1958. See Welford, A. T. 1958, pp. 70–74.

BURKE, W. E., TUTTLE, W. W., THOMPSON, C. W., JANNEY, C. D., AND WEBER, R. J. 1953. The relation of grip strength and grip strength endurance to age. *J. Appl. Physiol., 5,* 628–630.

CHOWN, S., BELBIN, E., AND DOWNS, S. 1967. Programmed instruction as a method of teaching paired associates to older learners. *J. Gerontol., 22,* 212–219.

CLARK, W. C., AND MEHL, L. 1971. Thermal pain: a sensory decision theory analysis of the effect of age and sex on d', various response criteria, and 50% pain threshold. *J. Abnorm. Psychol., 78,* 202–212.

COHEN, L. D., AND AXELROD, S. 1962. Performance of young and elderly persons on embedded-figure tasks in two sensory modalities. *In,* C. Tibbitts and W. Donahue (eds.), *Social and Psychological Aspects of Aging,* pp. 740–750. New York: Columbia University Press.

CORSO, J. F. 1977. Auditory perception and communication. *In,* J. E. Birren and K. W. Schaie (eds.), *Handbook of the Psychology of Aging,* pp. 535–553. New York: Van Nostrand Reinhold.

CRAIK, F. I. M. 1969. Applications of signal detection theory to studies of ageing. *In,* A. T. Welford and J. E. Birren (eds.), *Decision Making and Age,* pp. 147–157. Basel: Karger.

CROOK, M. N., ALEXANDER, E. A., ANDERSON, E. M. S., COULES, J., HANSON, J. A., AND JEFFRIES, N. T. 1958. Age and form perception. U.S. Air Force School of Aviation Medicine Report No. 57–124.

DAVIES, D. R., AND GRIEW, S. 1963. A further note on the effect of aging on auditory vigilance performance: the effect of low signal frequency. *J. Gerontol., 18,* 370–371.

DAVIES, D. R., AND TUNE, G. S. 1970. *Human Vigilance Performance.* London: Staples Press.

EISDORFER, C. 1968. Arousal and performance: Experiments in verbal learning and a tentative theory. *In,* G. A. Talland (ed.), *Human Aging and Behavior,* pp. 189–216. New York: Academic Press.

EISDORFER, C., CONNER, J. F., AND WILKIE, F. L. 1968. The effect of magnesium pemoline on cognition and behavior. *J. Gerontol., 23,* 283–288.

ELIAS, M. F., AND ELIAS, P. K. 1977. Motivation and activity. *In,* J. E. Birren and K. W. Schaie (eds.), *Handbook of the Psychology of Aging,* pp. 357–383. New York: Van Nostrand Reinhold.

EYSENCK, H. J. 1970. *The Biological Basis of Personality.* Springfield, Ill.: Charles C Thomas.

FARRIMOND, T. 1961. Prediction of speech hearing loss for older industrial workers. *Gerontologia, 5,* 65–87.

FORTUIN, G. J. 1963. Age and lighting needs. *Ergonomics, 6,* 239–245.

FOZARD, J. L., WOLF, E., BELL, B., MCFARLAND, R. A., AND PODOLSKY, S. 1977. Visual perception and communication. *In,* J. E. Birren and K. W. Schaie (eds.), *Handbook of the Psychology of Aging,* pp. 497–534. New York: Van Nostrand Reinhold.

FROLKIS, V. V., MARTYNENKO, O. A., AND ZAMOSTYAN, V. P. 1976. Aging of the neuromuscular apparatus. *Gerontology, 22,* 244–279.

GRANICK, S., KLEBAN, M. H., AND WEISS, A. D. 1976. Relationships between hearing loss and cognition in normally hearing aged persons. *J. Gerontol., 31,* 434–440.

GREEN, D. M. AND SWETS, J. A. 1966. *Signal Detection Theory and Psychophysics.* New York: John Wiley.

GREGORY, R. L. 1974. *Concepts and Mechanisms of Perception.* New York: Charles Scribner's Sons.

GRIEW, S. 1964. Age, information transmission and the positional relationship between signals and responses in the performance of a choice task. *Ergonomics, 7,* 267–277.

GRIEW, S., AND DAVIES, D. R. 1962. The effect of aging on auditory vigilance performance. *J. Gerontol., 17,* 88–90.

GRIEW, S., AND TUCKER, W. A. 1958. The identification of job activities associated with age differences in the engineering industry. *J. Appl. Psychol., 42,* 278–282.

GUTMANN, E., AND HANZLIKOVA, V. 1976. Fast and slow motor units in ageing. *Gerontology, 22,* 280–300.

HEATH, H. A., AND ORBACH, J. 1963. Reversibility of the Necker cube: IV responses of elderly people. *Percep. Mot. Skills, 17,* 625–626.

HELLON, R. F., LIND, A. R., AND WEINER, J. S. 1956. The physiological reactions of men of two age groups to a hot environment. *J. Physiol., 133,* 118–131.

HERON, A., AND CHOWN, S. 1967. *Age and Function.* London: Churchill.

HERON, A., AND CUNNINGHAM, C. M. 1962. The experience of younger and older men in a works reorganisation. *Occupational Psychol., 36,* 10–14.

HICKS, L. H., AND BIRREN, J. E. 1970. Aging, brain damage, and psychomotor slowing. *Psychol. Bull., 74,* 377–396.

HILLS, B. L. 1975. Some studies of movement perception, age and accidents. Crowthorne, Berkshire: Transport and Road Research Laboratory. Report No. 137UC.

HILLS, B. L., AND BURG, A. 1977. A reanalysis of California driver vision data: general findings. Crowthorne, Berkshire: Transport and Road Research Laboratory. Report No. 768.

JOHINKE, A. K. 1977. An age analysis of traffic accidents and offences. Proceedings of the 13th Annual Conference of the Australian Association of Gerontology, Adelaide 1977, p. 31 (abstract)

KAY, H. 1954. The effects of position in a display upon problem solving. *Quart. J. Exp. Psychol., 6,* 155–169.

KAY, H. 1955. Some experiments on adult learning. *In, Old Age in the Modern World,* pp. 259–267. Report 3rd. Cong. Internat. Assn. Gerontol., London, 1954. Edinburgh: Livingstone.

KING, H. F. 1955. An age-analysis of some agricultural accidents. *Occupational Psychol., 29,* 245–253.

KIRBY, N. H., NETTELBECK, T., AND GOODENOUGH, S. 1978. Cognitive rigidity in the aged and the mentally retarded. *Int. J. Aging and Hum. Devel., 9,* 263–272.

KLEEMEIER, R. W., RICH, T. A., AND JUSTISS, W. A. 1956. The effects of alpha-(2-piperidyl) benzhydrol hydrochloride (Meratran) on psychomotor performance in a group of aged males. *J. Gerontol., 11,* 165–170.

KLINE, D. W., AND SZAFRAN, J. 1975. Age differences in backward monoptic visual noise masking. *J. Gerontol., 30,* 307–311.

KORCHIN, S. J., AND BASOWITZ, H. 1956. The judgment of ambiguous stimuli as an index of cognitive functioning in aging. *J. Personal., 25,* 81–95.

LACEY, J. I. 1967. Psychophysiological approaches to the evaluation of psychotherapeutic process and outcome. *In, E. A. Rubenstein and M. B. Parloff (eds.), Research in Psychotherapy,* pp. 160–208. Washington, D. C.: American Psychological Assoc.

LARIVIÈRE, J. E., AND SIMONSON, E. 1965. The effect of age and occupation on speed of writing. *J. Gerontol., 20,* 415–416.

LEIBOWITZ, H. W., AND JUDISCH, J. M. 1967. The relation between age and the magnitude of the Ponzo illusion. *Amer. J. Psychol., 80,* 105–109.

LIND, A. R., HELLON, R. F., WEINER, J. S., AND JONES, R. M. 1955. Tolerance of men to work in hot, saturated environments with reference to mines rescue operations. *Brit. J. Industr. Med., 12,* 296–303.

LOVELESS, N. E., AND SANFORD, A. J. 1974. Effects of age on the contingent negative variation and preparatory set in a reaction-time task. *J. Gerontol., 29,* 52–63.

McEWEN, J. C. 1973. Working conditions with different types of disability. *Ergonomics, 16,* 669–677.

McFARLAND, R. A., DOMEY, R. G., WARREN, A. B., AND WARD, D. C. 1960. Dark adaptation as a function of age: I. A statistical analysis. *J. Gerontol., 15,* 149–154.

McFARLAND, R. A., TUNE, G. S., AND WELFORD, A. T. 1964. On the driving of automobiles by older people. *J. Gerontol., 19,* 190–197.

McNICOL, D. 1972. *A Primer of Signal Detection Theory.* London: George Allen & Unwin.

MARSH, G. R., AND THOMPSON, L. W. 1977. Psychophysiology of aging. *In, J. E. Birren and K. W. Schaie (eds.), Handbook of the Psychology of Aging,* pp. 219–248. New York: Van Nostrand Reinhold.

MORIKIYO, Y., AND NISHIOKA, A. 1966. An analysis of the control mechanism on simple movement of hand (2). *J. Sci. Lab., 42,* 238–243.

MORRIS, J. D., AND THOMPSON, L. W. 1969. Heart rate changes in a reaction time experiment with young and aged subjects. *J. Gerontol., 24,* 269–275.

MURRELL, K. F. H., AND FORSAITH, B. 1960. Age and the timing of movement. *Occupational Psychol., 34,* 275–279.

MURRELL, K. F. H., AND TUCKER, W. A. 1960. A pilot job-study of age-related causes of difficulty in light engineering. *Ergonomics, 3,* 74–79.

NETTELBECK, T. 1972. The effects of shock-induced anxiety on noise in the visual system. *Perception, 1,* 297–304.

O'DOHERTY, B. 1958. See Welford, A. T. 1958, pp. 182–183.

PIERSON, W. R., AND MONTOYE, H. J. 1958. Movement time, reaction time, and age. *J. Gerontol., 13,* 418–421.

POWELL, M. 1973. Age and occupational change among coal-miners. *Occupational Psychol., 47,* 37–49.

RABBITT, P. M. A. 1964. Set and age in a choice-response task. *J. Gerontol., 19,* 301–306.

RABBITT, P. M. A. 1965. An age-decrement in the ability to ignore irrelevant information. *J. Gerontol., 20,* 233–238.

RABBITT, P., AND BIRREN, J. E. 1967. Age and responses to sequences of repetitive and interruptive signals. *J. Gerontol., 22,* 143–150.

RABBITT, P. M. A., AND ROGERS, M. 1965. Age and choice between responses in a self-paced repetitive task. *Ergonomics, 8,* 435–444.

REES, J. N., AND BOTWINICK, J. 1971. Detection and decision factors in auditory behavior of the elderly. *J. Gerontol., 26,* 133–136.

RICHARDSON, I. M. 1953. Age and work: A study of 489 men in heavy industry. *Brit. J. Industr. Med., 10,* 269–284.

ROAD TRAFFIC BOARD OF SOUTH AUSTRALIA. 1972. The Points Demerit Scheme as an Indication of Declining Skill with Age. Adelaide, South Australia: The Road Traffic Board.

SANFORD, A. J., AND MAULE, A. J. 1973. The concept of general experience: Age and strategies in guessing future events. *J. Gerontol., 28,* 81–88.

SCHEIBEL, A. B., AND SCHEIBEL, M. 1979. Structural alteration in the aging brain. *In, Ageing: A Challenge* to Science and Social Policy. Oxford University Press (forthcoming).

SCHLUDERMANN, E., AND ZUBEK, J. P. 1962. Effect of age on pain sensitivity. *Percep. Mot. Skills, 14,* 295–301.

SINGLETON, W. T. 1955. Age and performance timing on simple skills. *In, Old Age in the Modern World,* pp. 221–231. Report 3rd Cong. Internat. Assn. Gerontol., London, 1954. Edinburgh: Livingstone.

SMITH, G. A. 1977. Studies in compatibility and a new model of choice reaction time. *In,* S. Dornic (ed.), *Attention and Performance VI,* pp. 27–48. Hillsdale, N. J.: Erlbaum.

STELMACH, G. E., AND DIEWERT, G. L. 1977. Aging, information processing and fitness. *In,* G. Borg (ed.), *Physical Work and Effort,* pp. 115–136. Oxford: Pergamon Press.

SURWILLO, W. W. 1961. Frequency of the 'Alpha' rhythm, reaction time and age. *Nature, 191,* 823–824.

SURWILLO, W. W. 1963. The relation of simple response time to brain-wave frequency and the effects of age. *EEG Clin. Neurophysiol., 15,* 105–114.

SURWILLO, W. W. 1964. The relation of decision time to brain wave frequency and to age. *EEG Clin. Neurophysiol., 16,* 510–514.

SURWILLO, W. W. 1966. The relation of autonomic activity to age differences in vigilance. *J. Gerontol., 21,* 257–260.

SURWILLO, W. W., AND QUILTER, R. E. 1964. Vigilance, age, and response-time. *Amer. J. Psychol., 77* 614–620.

SZAFRAN, J. 1958. See Welford, A. T. 1958, pp. 186–189.

SZAFRAN, J. 1966. Age, cardiac output and choice reaction time. *Nature, 209,* 836.

VERVILLE, E., AND CAMERON, N. 1946. Age and sex differences in the perception of incomplete pictures by adults. *J. Genet. Psychol., 68,* 149–157.

VICKERS, D. 1972. A cyclic decision model of perceptual alternation. *Perception, 1,* 31–48.

VICKERS, D., NETTELBECK, T., AND WILLSON, R. J. 1972. Perceptual indices of performance: the measurement of "inspection time" and "noise" in the visual system. *Perception, 1,* 263–295.

WALLACE, J. G. 1956. Some studies of perception in relation to age. *Brit. J. Psychol., 47,* 283–297.

WALSH, D. A. 1976. Age differences in central perceptual processing: A dichoptic backward masking investigation. *J. Gerontol., 31,* 178–185.

WAPNER, S., WERNER, H., AND COMALLI, P. E. 1960. Perception of part-whole relationships in middle and old age. *J. Gerontol., 15,* 412–416.

WARREN, R. M. 1961. Illusory changes in repeated words: Differences between young adults and the aged. *Amer. J. Psychol., 74,* 506–516.

WARREN, R. M. 1968. Verbal transformation effect and auditory perceptual mechanisms. *Psychol. Bull., 70,* 261–270.

WEISS, A. D. 1965. The locus of reaction time change with set, motivation, and age. *J. Gerontol., 20,* 60–64.

WELFORD, A. T. 1958. *Ageing and Human Skill.* Oxford Univ. Press for the Nuffield Foundation. (Reprinted 1973 by Greenwood Press: Westport, Conn.).

WELFORD, A. T. 1965a. Stress and achievement. *Austral. J. Psychol., 17,* 1–11.

WELFORD, A. T. 1965b. Performance, biological mechanisms and age: A theoretical sketch. *In,* A. T. Welford and J. E. Birren (eds.), *Behavior, Aging and the Nervous System,* pp. 3–20. Springfield, Ill.: Charles C Thomas.

WELFORD, A. T. 1966. Industrial work suitable for older people: Some British studies. *Gerontologist, 6,* 4–9.

WELFORD, A. T. 1968. *Fundamentals of Skill.* London: Methuen.

WELFORD, A. T. 1973. Stress and performance. *Ergonomics, 16,* 567–580.

WELFORD, A. T. 1976a. *Skilled Performance: Perceptual and Motor Skills.* Glenview, Ill.: Scott Foresman.

WELFORD, A. T. 1976b. Motivation, capacity, learning and age. *Int. J. Aging Hum. Dev., 7,* 189–199.

WELFORD, A. T. 1977a. Motor Performance. *In,* J. E. Birren and K. W. Schaie (eds.), *Handbook of the Psychology of Aging.* pp. 450–496. New York: Van Nostrand Reinhold.

WELFORD, A. T. 1977b. Serial reaction times, continuity of task, single-channel effects and age. *In,* S. Dornic (ed.), *Attention and Performance* VI, pp. 79–97. Hillsdale, N. J.: Erlbaum.

WELFORD, A. T. 1978. Mental work load as a function of demand, capacity, strategy and skill. *Ergonomics, 21,* 151–167.

WELFORD, A. T. 1979. Perception, memory and motor performance in relation to age. *In,* Ageing: A Challenge to Science and Social Policy. Oxford University Press (to be published).

WELFORD, A. T., NORRIS, A. H., AND SHOCK, N. W. 1969. Speed and accuracy of movement and their changes with age. *Acta Psychol., 30,* 3–15.

WENGER, L. E. 1977. Estimation of "Inspection Time" and "Noise" in the visual system and age. Proceedings of the 13th Annual Conference of the Australian Association of Gerontology.

WESTON, H. C. 1949. On age and illumination in relation to visual performance. *Trans. Illum. Eng. Soc., 14,* 281–297.

WHITFIELD, J. W. 1954. Individual differences in accident susceptibility among coal miners. *Brit. J. Industr. Med., 11,* 126–139.

WILKINSON, R. T. 1965. Sleep deprivation. *In,* O. G. Edholm and A. L. Bacharach (eds.), *The Physiology of Human Survival,* pp. 399–430. London: Academic Press.

ZUBEK, J. P. 1964. Effects of prolonged sensory and perceptual deprivation. *Brit. Med. Bull., 20*(1), 38–42.

# 10

# Learning, Memory,
# and
# Aging*

*A. E. David Schonfield*

A reasonably good case could be made for subsuming almost all aspects of mental health under the general rubric of learning and remembering. If learning is defined as a change of behavior resulting from experience, and remembering is defined as long-term effects of such learning, both appropriate and inappropriate conduct are encompassed. The term behavior, nowadays, covers a wider variety of activities than in the heyday of behaviorism and is understood to include private psychological processes underlying overt behavior. Thus, alterations in attitudes, strategies for problem solving, associative mediators for

*The help of Dr. M. J. Stones in preparing the chapter is gratefully acknowledged.

The author is indebted to his University for the award of a Killam Resident Fellowship while writing this chapter.

memory retrieval, and modes of adjustment can be considered as exemplars of learning. Even the emphasis on experience as a necessary qualification for entitlement to the label of learning does not permit clear-cut demarcation lines between learned and nonlearned activities. A change in behavior due to the aging of the nervous system, for example, will usually be codetermined and interact with previous experience. Nevertheless, proclivities for colonial raids on the part of a gerontology-remembering-learning empire have to be curtailed because of the limited areas where the appropriate flag has been raised or planted. Comparatively few relevant experiments have been performed, and only tenuous generalizations about age changes can be derived from most of those studies. The very nature of the typical controlled, reductionist, in-and-out laboratory investigations makes it somewhat hazardous to extrapolate findings to the compound, complex, changing, and diversified variables influencing mental health.

Theoretical approaches of the experimentalist should not be disparaged on the grounds that applications in the mental health field tend to be farfetched. The primary aim of theorists or modelers is not an immediate translation of findings to everyday life situations. Their objective is rather to pinpoint the loci of age differences through analysis of component processes in learning and remembering. Such analyses, as well as the types of studies undertaken, are greatly influenced by prevailing contemporary idiosyncrasies in the progenitor discipline of experimental psychology (Arenberg and Robertson-Tchabo, 1977; Craik, 1977). Whether or not findings can properly be transferred to applied situations will depend on the degree of similarity between laboratory and the extralaboratory conditions. This similarity dimension is itself a matter of judgment and may be age-related, since a newly introduced or excluded feature could affect one age group but not another. Honing laboratory procedures to obtain consistent or reliable results might perforce exclude almost every normally occurring event in the "real world." This reservation has been at the forefront of discussions about the ecological validity of psychological experiments (Neisser, 1976). On the other hand, ideal theoretical formulations have widespread applications, and it is indeed sometimes true to say that there is nothing so practical as a theory.

A blinkered theorist with circumscribed aims often sacrifices possible valuable practical implications of findings. This frequently occurs in one of the most fruitful approaches to gerontological theory when variables are manipulated within an experiment. If age differences are substantial in one condition but disappear, or are greatly reduced, in another condition, the investigation is deemed successful. If, however, the manipulations result in equivalent age effects for all conditions, the outcome is uninformative for theoretical purposes. From an applied standpoint, however, modifications of procedure that produce improvement in the performance of older age groups are always of importance. Whether or not such improvement is greater at one age than at another may be inconsequential, since any suggested method for reducing learning or remembering difficulties of the aged could be of help to a practitioner. The following hypothetical results serve as an example. Assume that, on the average, a younger group required fifty trials and an older group seventy trials

to master a task without rest intervals, but with spaced learning, the young needed only twenty trials, and the aged forty trials. Analysis of variance, the most popular of prevalent statistics, would show no significant age-by-treatment interaction. Indeed, even a reduction to thirty trials for the aged group in spaced learning would probably not produce a statistically significant interaction, given the large standard deviation typically found among older groups. The constant age difference over conditions implies failure in the search for the locus of loss. Not only does the theorist lose interest, but the study may remain unpublished because a null hypothesis has not been disproven. And yet, the hypothetical finding should be of help to older people having to learn a task similar to that used in the experiment, and perhaps also in the case of dissimilar tasks. People trying to learn might give up before reaching the seventieth massed trial, but not before the fortieth spaced trial. The difference between success and failure in learning could have all sorts of implications for mental health, although it has no import for theory.

Whenever an interaction between age and condition is uncovered, support is provided for the rather obvious proposition that age differences are not necessarily consistent across tasks. Some learning and remembering tasks show deficits from the age of thirty, others show little if any loss, even in the sixties. There is no reason to assume that any specific example of learning—be it one that shows an age loss or not—should be evoked as the quintessential representative of all learning. Nevertheless, many authorities seem to succumb to the naming fallacy and generalize the results from one learning situation to every other. Controversies about one or many, and if many, how many categories of learning there are, have appeared intermittently in the general psychological literature, as shown by titles of papers and chapters such as: "There Is More Than One Kind of Learning" (Tolman, 1949), "The Representativeness of Rote Verbal Learning" (Underwood, 1964), and "Varieties of Learning" (Gagné, 1965). The temptation to universalize experimental findings is probably particularly strong when translating experimental results to applied areas. It would be wrong, however, to go to the other extreme and conclude that every learning situation is uniquely different from all others. The basic assumption of gerontological investigations is that general principles can be formulated about some variables which increase or decrease age differences.

There have been at least five recent surveys of the literature on age differences in learning and remembering (Arenberg, 1973; Arenberg and Robertson-Tchabo, 1977; Craik, 1977; Kausler, 1970; Schonfield and Stones, 1979), all from a pronounced theoretical perspective. One conspicuous gap in the surveys is any mention of classical conditioning, and that paradigm of learning, therefore, deserves consideration in this chapter. The output of new empirical findings does not justify updating those résumés, and the only excuse for replowing the same fields is an attempt to harvest a slightly different crop. The present venture is primarily designed to bring the crop to market, to suggest how results can be translated into everyday concerns. A set of precise maxims with reasonably wide applications would be the most valuable contribution, but, unfortunately, the choice is often between being vague or wrong. The bases of any proposed maxims have to be expounded, so that their limitations are recognized. Tentative rules should have as their aim the reduction of learning or remembering difficulties for older people. The emphasis must, therefore, include both the areas where there is presumptive evidence for special difficulties and where age differences seem to be negligible. A realization of special difficulties can, of course, create the danger of self-fulfilling prophecy, thereby accentuating problems. However, that particular hazard seems much less than the frustrations caused by unexplained failures. A realization that some learning situations often become disproportionately hard with increasing age may allow instructors to minimize difficulties by altering formats and, certainly, should alert both learner and instructor to the need for patience. Knowing that certain kinds of remembering deficiencies are common in older people, and that these do not presage mental illness, can have incalculable effects on mental health. On the other hand, those procedures which show no learning and memory age losses offer special opportunities for older people to demonstrate their abilities to themselves and to others.

Of fundamental importance to the practitioner is the age at which changes are likely to occur. Unfortunately, most experiments include only two age groups—usually a young group in their early twenties and an elderly group of over sixty-five. Results from the studies are summarized as, "with age, such and such occurs," whereas, in fact, the outcome only provides information about differences between the old and young. Nothing is known about the forty intervening adult years. Do the middle aged resemble the young group or the elderly group? It is certainly improper to assume that there is, on average, an equal decline in each decade between the twenties and seventies. All of the purported decline may normally occur in one or two decades, with a plateau, or even improvement, during the remaining periods. If the term aging rather than the aged is to be taken seriously as the subject matter of gerontology, much more needs to be known about stability and change in learning and remembering during the middle adult years.

One of the most intractable problems concerning learning, memory, and mental health in the later years is the question of differentiating normal aging from pathological symptoms. Organic brain syndromes, which include senile dementia and cerebral arteriosclerosis, are manifested by impairment of orientation, memory, and "all intellectual functions such as . . . knowledge, learning, etc." (American Psychiatric Association, 1968). Because mild impairments and more severe temporary impairments in these processes are also shown in normal aged persons, there is a clear involvement of the cognitive specialist. The reverse side of the coin is that learning difficulties shown in pathological states and perhaps in normal aging, may be expected to reduce the likelihood of successful psychotherapy, since all such therapies are themselves forms of learning. Some observations about the relevant studies on both differential diagnosis and therapeutic intervention will, therefore, be included in this chapter.

## CLASSICAL CONDITIONING

Classical conditioning, because of its tie-in with the autonomic nervous system, and, therefore, with emotional learning (Mowrer, 1960) bears a special relationship to mental health. Evidence that successful instrumental conditioning of human autonomic reactions (Katkin, 1971) may also be possible, with or without mediating conscious cognitive processes, does not alter the preeminence of classical conditioning. Stimulus substitution in eliciting a response is the most primitive form of learning, and that, too, makes putative age effects worthy of consideration. The popularity of classical conditioning as an area of study in the general field of human learning has waned in the last decade, and gerontological investigations have mirrored this loss of esteem. Whereas in the first Handbook (Birren, 1959) classical conditioning experiments received detailed coverage, in the second Handbook (Birren and Schaie, 1977) they do not even rate an index entry. Perhaps the diminution of interest is also due to a decision that the paradigm is not quite so simple as it seems, and, of necessity, introduces age-associated confounding variables.

The most difficult issue is a possible change with age in the strength and frequency of unconditioned responses during repeated presentations of the unconditioned stimulus. If such reactions are weaker and/or not as prevalent among elderly people, the conditioned stimulus has less opportunity for hooking on to responses. The consistent evidence for reduced levels of acquisition could not, therefore, be interpreted as demonstrating that older organisms tend to be less competent hookers, but rather that the latch is deficient. There is considerable evidence to support such a position. Kimble and Pennypacker (1963) reported that the amplitude of the blinking unconditioned response decreased much more in their elderly group than in their young group during the course of an experiment. That study also showed a significant correlation between the magnitude of the unconditioned response and the frequency of conditioned responses. Shmavonian, Miller, and Cohen (1968, 1970) emphasize the weakness in older groups of both conditioned and unconditioned responses on a variety of autonomic measures. Indeed, the whole question of poorer classical conditioning seems to have been sidetracked into a controversy about whether older humans are underaroused or overaroused compared to younger age groups (Marsh and Thompson, 1977). Both habituation to unconditioned responses and poorer conditioning are said to support the underarousal position.

Other features of the classical conditioning procedures may also contribute to age effects. The strength of the unconditioned stimulus should influence the likelihood, as well as the amplitude, of an unconditioned response, and the influence may not be consistent over age groups. In one study, the level of administered shock was the highest that individual members of each age group could tolerate (Shmavonian, Yarmat, and Cohen, 1965), while in another experiment, the level was the lowest amount necessary to produce a galvanic skin response (Caird, 1966). Age differences in conditioning might be affected not only by the strength of the unconditioned stimulus, but also by that of the conditioned stimulus, as suggested in the results of Solyom and Barik (1965). Another conditioned stimulus problem arises in the elaborate Kimble and Pennypacker (1963) arrangements. In order to reduce voluntary responses and conscious intervention, participants were led to believe that the study was on reaction time. Subjects were in-

structed to press a left-hand key when a light appeared on the left, and the right-hand key for a light on the right. Either light acted as the conditioned stimulus, and was followed by a puff of air as the unconditioned stimulus. The presence of alternative conditioned stimuli, rather than one, might well reduce the rate of acquisition for the elderly more than for the young. The interval between onset of conditioned and unconditioned responses, as well as the time within this period for a response to be labeled as conditioned, might also influence apparent age differences. Kimble and Pennypacker (1963) required that a blink occur between 300 and 500 milliseconds following the conditioned stimulus for the response to be reckoned as conditioned. At the other extreme in the Shmavonian experiments (Shmavonian et al. 1968, 1970), the conditioned stimulus began ten seconds before the shock was administered. In the former case, the interval may have been too short for the elderly, and in the latter case the delay may have been too long. Canestrari and Eberly (1964) attacked the problem of optimum interval between conditioned and unconditioned stimuli in a study confined to elderly veterans. No differences were found for intervals ranging from .3 seconds to 1 second in finger withdrawal when a buzzer acted as conditioned stimulus and a shock as unconditioned stimulus. However, the results of this experiment are difficult to interpret because few participants showed any evidence of conditioning. The published report is so sketchy that the outcome may have been due to some veterans thinking that they were not supposed to withdraw their hands, but to tolerate the shock. Lastly, the question of number of acquisition trials should not be completely ignored, since these have varied from fifteen (Botwinick and Kornetsky, 1960) to eighty (Braun and Geiselhart, 1959). Braun and Geiselhart specifically mention that two of their thirteen elderly subjects started responding after forty trials. In the Kimble and Pennypacker (1963) study, it seems that the young subjects had reached their asymptote after about fifty trials, whereas the elderly group were still increasing their average frequency of conditioned responses at the end of the sixty-fifth trial. Notwithstanding the foregoing inventory of reservations about individual classical conditioning experiments, it is still possible and proper to draw some tentative generalizations.

When all has been said and done, the covey of classical conditioning experiments is surprisingly consistent in showing very much poorer acquisition among elderly groups than young groups. The very fact of variations in procedures, measures, and responses can be viewed as supporting the notion that a real age-linked phenomenon has been uncovered. When very different samples of the universe of possible methodologies all show the same age difference, the conclusion that most of the elderly cannot readily be classically conditioned is strengthened. It is important to emphasize, however, that the elderly subjects in all the relevant experiments have been over sixty years old, with only an occasional underaged participant in the late fifties. The mean ages of the groups have often been in the seventies. It is also important to note that the spread of acquisition scores tends to be large in these elderly groups. Some individuals show little evidence of any conditioning, while a few may acquire the response to the new stimulus almost as readily as younger people.

The evidence for age effects in extinction is much more equivocal. This is, of course, mainly because it is pointless to compare extinction rates for an elderly group who have not acquired a response with rates of a young group who have. When Botwinick and Kornetsky (1960) equated old and young subjects for initial conditioning of a galvanic skin response, no difference was found in the number of extinction trials required to reach a criterion of response absence to four out of five conditioned stimuli. On the other hand, Canestrari and Eberly (1964) reported that a few of their elderly group failed to extinguish or extinguished only after many trials. The number of trials required for habituation to the to-be-conditioned stimulus before the experiments proper begin is also reported in a number of papers, and that, too, is a measure of extinction. These almost invariably show quicker habituation among the elderly than among the young, with Solyom and Barik (1965) providing an exception for a galvanic skin response to a faint tone. In this kind of adaptation, there seem to be especially large individual differences. Perhaps the best evidence for the variability among the aged comes from Botwinick and Kornetsky (1960), who give a mean of 11.9 but a median of 8.0 trials for extinction by their elderly group of a galvanic skin response to sound. Clearly, the mean in that study was raised by a handful of elderly subjects who responded like the young. These indications for average faster habituation by the elderly are, however, once again confounded by the probability of initial weaker responses.

The most striking feature of the classical conditioning literature is the absence of studies comparing middle-aged groups to either the young or to the elderly. Certainly, there are no grounds for assuming that the potential for conditioning in the middle years is midway between the young and the aged. It seems much more probable that changes in conditioning do not usually occur until the late sixties. Using a group approaching middle age, Gendreau and Suboski (1971) report no statistically significant difference between prisoners with mean ages of 21.2 and 36.8 (range 30–55), although the absolute number of conditioned responses was fewer in the higher age group. In any case, that experiment examined differential conditioning to reinforced and nonreinforced stimuli as well as the effect of inhibitory, facilitatory, and neutral instructions, which would make it difficult to draw any conclusions about straightforward conditioning. Because the alteration in conditionability is postponed until late in life, it seems probable that changes in the central nervous system are implicated. Evidence showing that the incidence of conditioning is even less among patients suffering from senile dementia and cerebral arteriosclerosis (Solyom and Barik, 1965) supports this position. An environmental or experiential explanation for the reduction of conditionability in old age was proposed by Braun and Geiselhart (1959), who suggested "that in the course of many years of living the eyelid response, as well as probably other responses have been adapted out and thus less susceptible to subsequent conditioning" (p. 388). However, it seems unlikely that such an adapting process would require some seventy years to become manifest. Until some experiments show that the prevalence of conditioning is reduced during middle age, the adaptation hypothesis should be rejected.

Implications of reduced conditionability in the elderly must be matters of conjecture until studies are performed on the correlates of this change. It might be anticipated that elderly people who do not condition readily—and that seems to include the majority of those over sixty-five—are less generally aroused and less prone to extreme emotional reactions. They should not demonstrate intense happiness or unhappiness. When happiness or unhappiness is experienced, environmental associations that might resuscitate the emotions in the future are less likely to be established automatically. Most important of all, because it contradicts the accepted wisdom, reliance on thinking and understanding might increase in old age. Notwithstanding deficits in these cognitive processes compared to earlier years, understanding may be as fundamental as emotional support for coping with new situations. Confirmation of this view can be claimed from rather disparate aging studies. The enforced relocation mortality effect seems greatly reduced when the people concerned are given adequate preparation and explanations

(Lawton, 1977). On a completely different experimental plane, it has been found that absence of meaningfulness, as in the case of learning nonsense syllables or equations, accentuates age losses (Botwinick, 1973). It is easy to assume that understanding and comprehension matter less in old age because they take longer. The exact opposite is likely to be true.

## CONSUMERS OF INFORMATION AND THE SCHEMA EXCHANGE

On most days of our lives, each individual operates in physical and social environments which are not very different from environments encountered on previous occasions. However, one or other feature of our surroundings is likely to change day by day—a light bulb might have burned out, a friend may behave in an uncharacteristic way, a new boss may have been appointed, and the news read in the newspaper is, at least by definition, new. Noticing alterations in the environment, or, for that matter, noticing stability, requires that appropriate records of the past be retrieved from a personal warehouse of knowledge for comparison purposes. These memories of the past provide a guide for the present—what to expect, as well as what to do— just as the newly registered information may provide a guide for the future. Processing new information involves exchanges with the memory store, so that confirmation of the expected is recorded and suitable corrections are registered when the unexpected occurs.

Paradoxically, when the unexpected does happen, reliance on memory is especially striking. A search for other relevant information is made in the memory store, which might explain the unexpected. When a light is not illuminated after the switch is turned on, minimal memory search leads to the conclusion or hypothesis that the bulb is burned out. This in turn determines the action needed to solve the problem—change the bulb! Sometimes that action can be accomplished readily, sometimes not. A person may not have a bulb, or the money to buy one, or even if she has one, she may be too frail to mount a ladder and unscrew the burned bulb. In unfamiliar surroundings, when visiting a different country or moving to a nursing home, where almost everything seems strange, it becomes even more satisfying when parallels are recognized with previously stored knowledge.

It is useful to distinguish between the memory of an isolated happening, such as a light failure, and the memory of general rules, such as switches turn on lights. Elsewhere (Schonfield and Stones, 1979) these have been labeled as episodic memory and generic memory, respectively. The term episodic follows Tulving's usage (Tulving, 1972), but his opposing category of semantic memory seems too confined, since it only deals with rules regarding the use of language. Semantic memory can be taken as a major subclass of generic memories, overlearned generalizations which have no special reference to temporally dated events. Generic memories themselves are formed from repeated series of episodic memories, and each episodic memory is a potential generic memory—hot stoves burn, thunder follows lightning, shop B comes after shop A, red lights mean stop. An episodic memory trace established as a result of a person's temporally and spatially defined experience will have reciprocal links with any number of generic memories. As time passes since an event occurred, its episodic trace probably becomes more difficult to access in a memory search and is also more susceptible to disintegration unless it has special emotional significance. The search route to an episodic trace will often commence with its linked generic memories. This is probably what Bartlett (1932) implied in his proposal that schemata provide the basis for reconstructing specific memories. If a specific trace is not contacted, the schema is embellished through imaginative processes which eventuate in a sensible pseudomemory. But even if the trace is accessed, the trace itself may be incomplete and schematized, rather than a representation of the whole truth about the original event.

Generic memories of concepts and the environment are invaluable in coping with relatively stable physical surroundings, and their importance probably increases with age. They allow reliable predictions to be made in our ongoing activities, and, therefore, also permit prior preparation of appropriate responses. Dealing with the environment was considered by Woodworth as the "all pervasive primary motivation of behavior" (Woodworth, 1958, p. 125), and Bartlett (1932) emphasizes the same point in his discussion of effort after meaning.

The desire or need to understand and to predict applies, of course, not only to stable physical environments, but also to more mutable, less consistent, social environments. Self-understanding, too, with its prodigious emotional significance, requires fixed anchor points for organizing incoming information. It is, therefore, appropriate to postulate the presence of generic memories concerned with social environments and the internal psychological environment, although these must be more malleable than other generic memories. The generic memory of an environmental map showing that shop B follows shop A, for instance, has to be altered when shop A burns down; but once the correction is made, the new generic memory mirrors the changed physical environment. The behavior of individual human beings is more variable and less readily identifiable than physical environments. The same person sometimes changes from being unselfish to selfish and reverts to unselfishness according to mood and circumstances. Other changes in human beings, especially age changes, occur gradually without any sudden alerting of attention that the relevant generic memory requires correction. These special problems do not detract from the usefulness of separating episodic from generic memories in psychosocial spheres. The postulated psychosocial generic memories resemble the personal constructs espoused by Kelly (1955), the self-schemata discussed by Markus (1977), and the conceptual prototypes of personality traits examined by Cantor and Mischel (1977).

Experiments on age differences in learning have concentrated on the establishment of episodic memories, and those studies provide the basis of most of the relevant formulations in this chapter. Closely linked with them are the reports of industrial gerontologists on longer training sessions in the acquisition of perceptual-motor skills by middle-aged workers. The meager knowledge available about controlled changes in social and self-related generic memories is derived, in the main, from accounts of therapeutic intervention among elderly groups in residential settings. These groups seem to suffer, because they consume insufficient information, and their existing schema become undernourished.

## PHASES OF LEARNING PROCESSES

A learning situation can be conceptually divided into phases, and the gerontological investigator can then examine the extent of age differences or age changes at each phase. Following this, attempts may be made to manipulate variables which could increase or decrease age effects at any of the phases. In the previous section, it was made clear that incoming information coalesces with existing knowledge, and, more specifically, with the generic memories which an individual brings into the learning situation. A pre-acquisition phase of learning, therefore, deserves consideration. What happens during the acquisition process itself is the next phase, and the final one occurs following acquisition. The latter post-acquisition phase necessarily involves consideration of possible influences on age changes in remembering and forgetting. The acquisition phase—beginning just before the initial intake of information and ending with storage in long-term memory—has been divided into micro-stages (Craik, 1977; Welford, 1977), and most recent studies have been concerned with analyzing variables which interact with age during those stages.

Middle-aged and older people usually complain of problems at the post-acquisition phase; they report that they forget more frequently than when they were younger. Psychologists, however, are inclined to attribute any apparent memory loss to a deficiency in acquisition. The literature suggests a strong disposition among many psychologists to deny age-associated deterioration of remembering following learning. Certainly, if a younger group is known to have acquired more information or stronger habits than an older group in an experiment, the fact that the young also perform better on a so-called test of memory merely demonstrates superiority at the acquisition phase and not the post-acquisition phase. In order to implicate memory, presumptive evidence for age equivalent acquisition must first be adduced. Nevertheless, one form of the reasoning for poorer acquisition, rather than poorer remembering, with increasing age can become circular. This argument, rarely made explicitly, runs as follows. The amount remembered is one of the many possible measures of acquisition strength. Therefore, data showing that older people remember less well ipso facto demonstrates poorer acquisition. The opposing proposition of acquisition depending on remembering seems more tenable. Why do older people have greater difficulty during the acquisition phase? Because their susceptibility to forgetting operates at that time as well as during the post-acquisition phase. These convoluted polemics lead to the conclusion that the division of a learning episode into phases does not necessarily parallel the underlying psychological processes. Both remembering and registration occur during the acquisition phase, while the post-acquisition phase is affected not only by the ability to remember, but also by the strength of original learning.

The applied gerontological implications of the foregoing discussion happily converge on the same major point. Whether age-associated problems arise in the pre-acquisition, acquisition, and post-acquisition phases or just during one of those, the aim should be stronger habit formation, overlearning, and improved procedures at the time of registering information. There are no exceptions to the general rule for all organisms of all ages that better learning produces better remembering. The acquisition phase is fundamental, even though the major difficulty may stem from some other phase. Be it a question of retraining middle-aged workers, of university courses for senior citizens, of a physiotherapist teaching an elderly woman to walk after breaking a hip, or of moving from one's own home to a nursing home, a feeling of competence or incompetence is awakened during the attempt to learn. Paramount aspects of mental health are affected when an individual reaches the conclusion on the one hand that disabilities can be mastered through learning or on the other hand that it is hopeless to attempt to learn.

## ACQUISITION PHASE

### MOTIVES, EMOTIONS, AND ANXIETY

Whenever older age groups show a decrement in learning or remembering compared to the young, it is possible, in principle, to explain the difference in terms of reduced motives. Motivation should be thought of as an intervening variable, and in this context implies that a less motivated person performs fewer of the various psychological processes which enhance learning. These would include attending, reviewing, analyzing material, and planning for retrieval. There is a danger in any discussion of motives to succumb to the temptation of treating the strength of the motive as if it were a relatively permanent individual attribute, rather like height. Clearly, the strength of the motive to learn will vary with the task, and may even change during a single learning session. Feelings of success, attitudes of an instructor, and the presence or absence of knowledge of results have effects on the motive to master new material or to acquire new skills. Thus, the average strength of motives might be stronger or weaker among an older group compared to the young at the outset of a training session, with a reversal later on.

Anyone who has carried out experiments with older volunteers or participated in industrial training programs can bear witness that the urge to succeed is often very strong. Welford described the typical situation many years ago:

> After being tested, older subjects almost always ask how they have done and demand to know how their results compare with the average or with those of younger subjects or of any friends known to have been tested previously. ... This strong interest in the relationship of one's performance

with that of others is seldom shown by subjects in their twenties, although one may suspect it is sometimes present but unexpressed. Visible relief and pleasure are frequently shown by older subjects upon being told they have "done well." Yet even when told this many criticize their performances. ... Frequently, their actual performances in no way merit this self-criticism. ... It has certainly been my experience that although many older subjects are unwilling to be tested, once they consent they approach their task with every intention of putting forth their best efforts and are fully as well motivated as those younger (Welford, 1958, p. 49).

That description certainly does not suggest low motivation, although attitudes might well be rather different when participants in an experiment are obtained from a captive population, such as a veterans' hospital. For middle-aged and older people who want to learn, instead of a difficulty caused by low motivation, there might be a problem of overzealousness.

The experimental approach would appear ideally suited to circumstances where two opposing hypotheses—undermotivation versus overmotivation—are propounded. And, indeed, a number of relevant experiments have been performed, usually in the framework of underarousal versus overarousal, to which we referred on page 217. The evidence from the classical conditioning studies strongly supports the underarousal position. However, a conclusion that age is associated with underarousal for classical conditioning is not at odds with the suggestion of overarousal for intentional learning. It is also worth reemphasizing that overarousal on entering a learning situation may switch to underarousal—"couldn't care less"—as learning progresses, or at least when learning does not progress. Degree of arousal or motivation is likely to interact with other situational variables.

Direct evidence on the question of arousal or anxiety during learning is provided in an oft-quoted experiment performed by Eisdorfer (1968). He measured autonomic nervous system arousal by collecting samples of free fatty acid in the plasma component of blood. Younger (mean age 38.1; range 20–48) and older (mean age 71.4) male patients were given fifteen learning and test trials for free recall of eight common words. Only total error scores were reported, and these averaged 44.3 for the "young" and 70.1 for the "old." Other data, using the same task, suggest that even after fifteen trials the old were managing only four out of eight correct responses, whereas at least some of the younger group were making no errors.

Plasma-free fatty acid levels were taken nine times: half an hour, quarter of an hour, and immediately before learning; after the fifth, tenth, and fifteenth learning trial; and every fifteen minutes during the hour succeeding learning. The results of these measures are shown in Figure 10–1. It is obvious that the level of free fatty acid was higher in the older than the younger group at all points of the study. Nevertheless, the rise at the commencement of learning is greater for the younger than for the older group, which contraindicates increased anxiety about the learning as such among the old. Eisdorfer himself, as well as other commentators, have given great prominence to the continued rise in free fatty acid levels during and after learning among the aged group, as opposed to the stability and drop among the younger group. A possible alternative interpretation might be that this difference is not so much due to dissimilar effects of learning, but to dissimilar *success* in learning. Other learning curves presented by Eisdorfer suggest that after five trials (45 point on the graph), the older group was only managing to produce two out of eight correct responses. The continued increase of autonomic nervous system arousal could, therefore, be attributed to the increased frustration. Even after learning had ceased, many members of the older group might be expected to feel angry with themselves about their poor performance. Imagine looking at eight words appearing one at a time in a memory drum and not managing to anticipate more than half of them after fifteen trails! On the other hand, at least some of the younger group would feel all the satisfaction of a job well done, with a resultant reduction of autonomic nervous system arousal.

The suggestion derived from the Eisdorfer experiment, that his younger group became comparatively more aroused than the aged when learning started, cannot be generalized to those who are usually considered young. The typical group described as young is generally made up of adults in their early twenties, whereas Eisdorfer's "young" have a mean age approaching forty. In an industrial or university setting, most of them would be conspicuous because of their age and would be regarded as older students. Many of them might be expected to feel uncomfortable in a strange learning situation, and to anticipate their own poorer performance, compared to when they were really young. It is quite possible, and indeed probable, that the big difference in anxiety during a learning situation is between people in their twenties and forties, rather than between people of forty and seventy.

In another important experiment, Eisdorfer, Nowlin, and Wilkie (1970) examined the effect on learning of chemical modification of autonomic nervous system activity. Propranolol, a drug which blocks autonomic receptor sites in peripheral end organs, was administered to one group of subjects before learning commenced, while the control group was injected with a placebo. Both groups consisted of male volunteers over sixty years of age. Free fatty acid blood sampling times replicated (almost) exactly the design of the study described above during the serial learning of the same words. The results showed much higher free fatty acid levels with placebo treatment than in the propranolol group. The average number of errors over fifteen trials was also statistically significantly greater in the placebo group—about 71 against 54. Although the difference is slight, averaging about one error per trial, definite support is provided for the hypothesis that poorer learning in older men is associated with heightened autonomic arousal and that some improvement can be obtained by blocking autonomic nervous system activity.

A few experimenters have tried to manipulate motives, tension, or attitudes within a learning situation and then assessed the effects on learning for various age groups. Ross (1968), for example, gave what she called neutral, supportive, or chal-

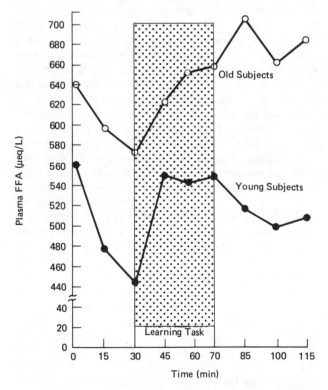

**Figure 10–1** Plasma-free fatty acid levels before, during, and after learning. See text for explanation. Reproduced with permission from Eisdorfer (1968, p. 203) and Academic Press.

lenging instructions to different groups of young (age range 18–26) and old (age range 65–75) non-institutionalized males. Each subgroup learned ten easy and ten difficult paired associates with identical stimulus terms to a criterion of two perfect scores within thirty trials, order of difficulty between difficult and easy associates being counterbalanced. Relearning was required after an interval of half an hour. The aged needed more trials to learn and to relearn than the young, with every type of instruction and both kinds of material. A statistically significant effect of instructions was confined to the initial learning of the old group with the difficult associates, the neutral, supportive, and challenging groups requiring 16.40, 13.20, and 22 trials respectively, before reaching criterion. Although the results for difficult associates were affected in accordance with the hypothesis, the labeling of the different instructions may be somewhat misleading. The supportive instructions de-emphasized learning aspects and asked for the help of the subject in a study concerned with the characteristics of words. Compared to the neutral instruction group, participants were placed in a supporting position vis à vis the experimenter, rather than the experimenter being supportive of the subject. The ultimate effect seems to have been to reduce worry about the learning situation, but it should be noted that the overlap of scores with the neutral group was rather large. The challenging instructions were as follows: "The ability to learn this material is a good test of your intelligence, not of what you know, but of how well you can learn *new* things. It's to your advantage, then, to do your best to show how capable you are, how bright you are in relation to people of your own age. Listen carefully and do your best, for your score will be compared with those of other subjects" (Ross, 1968, p. 263). The impact of these types of remarks on active members of clubs, who had volunteered their time—presumably to help the great science of gerontology—is a moot point. Some males might feel challenged, others might have a more negative reaction to a young lady who talked in this fashion. Nevertheless, the study shows conclusively that the aged are extremely sensitive when faced with a difficult task, and that the attitudes shown by the person in charge affects their learning accomplishments. It is still possible, however, that even the young might have exhibited volatile motives had they required twenty-five minutes, rather than ten minutes, to learn a few paired associates.

Using a slightly different approach, Lair and Moon (1972) compared middle aged (age range 33–51) and elderly (age range 55–76) on the re-

peated performance of the same timed coding test. Following every fifth trial, some members of each age group were told that they had done well and much better than most men of their age, while others were told that they had done poorly and worse than most men of their age. A control group who were told nothing was also included. There was no statistically significant effect of treatment in either age group, probably because of large standard deviations. Mean scores for both the middle-aged and elderly suggest detrimental effects of censure, but no beneficial effects of praise compared to the controls.

A study by Bellucci and Hoyer (1975) in the instrumental conditioning-Skinner-behavioral modification tradition is also pertinent. They manipulated noncontingent positive feedback which, in simple English, means that some of the participants in the experiment were told that they were doing better than people of their age, whether they were, in fact, performing well or abominably. Others were faced by a silent experimenter throughout the course of six trials on a cancellation task, six trials on a copying task, and six trials on a coding task. An additional variable included in the experiment was that half of the groups without feedback on the first two tasks were given feedback on the third task, and, vice versa, half of the groups with feedback on the first tasks were given no feedback on the third task. Participants in the experiment were undergraduate females from an introductory psychology class and an old (age range 60–74) college-educated female sample. Not surprisingly, both young and old feedback groups obtained higher scores than their respective nonfeedback groups on all tasks, and there was no age interaction. The authors interpret their findings as demonstrating the value of feedback, but it seems at least as likely that the cause of the treatment difference was due to the "blank wall" portrayed by the experimenter. Constantly reiterating to an intelligent subject after each trial that she was doing better than her peers—"what a good girl you are"—seems more condescending than rewarding or reinforcing. On the other hand, when an experimenter refrains from any sign of approval and minimizes social interaction, it might be interpreted as punishment rather than a neutral absence of praise.

This view of the situation receives some confirmation from a highly original aspect of the Bellucci and Hoyer experiment. Following each trial, subjects were asked to take between 0 and 25 S&H green stamps, the number taken to reflect self-assessment of performance on the basis of: 0–4 stamps, poor: 5–9 stamps, weak: 10–14 stamps, fair; 15–19 stamps, good: 20–25 stamps, excellent. Both young and old took more stamps when praised than when there was no feedback. Following praise, young and old demanded almost exactly the same number of stamps, but after consistent disregard by the experimenter, far fewer stamps were taken by the aged than by the young. Further, the effect of the switch from feedback on the first two tasks to praise on the last task and vice versa seemed age-related. The results are shown in Table 10–1. After being consistently patted on the back, witholding of praise seems to become almost rewarding for the old group. On the other hand, after being more or less ignored on the twelve trials of two tasks, the signs of recognition affected the old, but not the young. Whatever interpretation is placed on the study, it is clear that equivalent objective treatment can affect young and old very differently.

Detrimental effects of anxiety and the introduction of methods to counteract tension have been given major emphasis by Belbin (1965, 1969) and Belbin and Belbin (1972) in their discussions of industrial retraining of adults. On the basis of a wealth of experience and empirical studies, those authors make numerous suggestions, ranging from how to advertise so that the middle aged are not frightened of applying for posts to the improved design of equipment in order to reduce backache. R. M. Belbin calls his technique "The Discovery Method," which, as its name implies, requires that the learner be active and find out for himself/herself, with minimal intervention by the trainer. Belbin has incorporated into his system many processes which have been shown to reduce the problems of older workers. He, thus, rightly assumes that difficulties, especially at the outset of learning, intensify the individual's already existing concern about his/her own capabilities. Although the Belbins' work has been mainly in the field of acquiring perceptual motor skills among healthy middle-aged workers, their general approach is appropriate for practitioners in other settings with responsibilities for the frail elderly. Continued self-belief on the part of the learner in his or her own ability to master the task is a primary aim, and that demands real patience—not the pretense of patience—by all

those involved in learning situations. Building on a learner's assets, and, therefore, tailor-made programs, are two of the implications of the need to maintain confidence. It is not necessarily the elderly learner who demonstrates rigidity, but the young professional who is unable to change techniques in order to suit different people and situations.

Evidence obtained from experienced observers, as well as from some of the controlled studies, make it unnecessary to question the basic proposition that middle-aged and elderly people often have exaggerated beliefs about their own inadequacies. The resulting tension in a strange learning situation is almost certainly greater than among young adults, and the motive to learn is more easily squelched. Any procedures which increase the anxiety should obviously be avoided, whether or not the resulting intervention would also benefit younger groups. An appropriate motto for someone who wishes to help older people to learn and to minimize their anxiety is: "Nothing succeeds like success." The following sections provide some hints on how to enhance the prospects of success, thereby creating a sense of achievement and avoiding feelings of failure among older learners.

TIME AND PACING

Assessment of learning ability always involves a time element and, insofar as such ability declines with age, the implication is that older people are slower at acquiring information or skills. Many learning studies have, in fact, shown that the time taken to reach a specified level of performance and/or the number of errors made in a set time do increase with age. Confirmation of this finding is a pointless exercise, so that relevant experiments have usually been devoted to the discovery of stages in the acquisition process which are disproportionately slow or fast among different age groups, as well as uncovering variables which differentially influence speed of learning.

Pacing refers to the period allowed for completing a task or components of a task, and one of the better-documented gerontological generalizations is that fast, externally controlled paced situ-

**Table 10-1**  Mean Number of Stamps Taken on Third Task

| Treatment on previous task → | PRAISE | | NO PRAISE | |
| Treatment on third task → | Praise | No Praise | Praise | No Praise |
|---|---|---|---|---|
| Young | 23.02 | 21.58 | 18.77 | 18.37 |
| Old | 22.79 | 23.48 | 13.75 | 6.73 |

Adapted with permission from Bellucci and Hoyer (1975).

ations tend to cause special problems as people grow older. Belbin (cited in Welford, 1958) seems to have been the first to remark on this age-associated variable, but his observations mainly concerned the performance of acquired skills in an industrial setting, rather than the acquisition of new skills. Belbin reported that the proportion of males and females on time-stressed jobs showed a decrease in the 30–40 age range, with a precipitous drop thereafter. Most of the subsequent research shifted away from perceptual-motor tasks and concentrated on the learning of paired associates or serial lists. Considerable effort and ingenious methodology have gone into teasing out the locus of the pacing difficulty in verbal learning, its causes and effects. A major issue has been whether the enemy is the speed of presenting the material to be learned or the demand for quick responses (Botwinick, 1973). The quest for evidence to allow a firm conclusion on this point has been complicated by the fact that members of younger age groups are also handicapped by very fast pacing. There is by now little doubt that extra time for responding is usually especially advantageous to older groups. Slowing of presentation speed, however, is considered by most authorities to be equally beneficial for all ages, although careful examination of the evidence (Hulicka and Wheeler, 1976; Monge and Hultsch, 1971) suggests a verdict of not proven. In any case, such finer points are of little consequence from the applied point of view, and those who are involved in helping middle-aged and elderly people to learn should avoid time pressure, whether this would or would not assist other groups in a parallel fashion.

Unfortunately, a more-haste-less-speed guideline cannot be prescribed as an absolute rule to cover all learning situations. Completely independent self-pacing does not seem the ideal strategy for the not-so-young, since there comes a point where some members of older generations are slower than is warranted by their own level of potential efficiency (Botwinick, Brinley, and Robbin, 1958). Increasing age tends to be associated with increasing caution, and this may reach the stage of overcaution. One way of displaying such caution during learning is by withholding responses, in preference to chancing a possibly wrong answer—errors of omission rather than errors of commission (Canestrari, 1963; Leech and Witte, 1971). Extra time for an overt reaction, or even for covert rehearsal, becomes uneconomic unless responses increase. A tutor has to urge some students to risk errors and not to aspire to too high a level of confidence before venturing a response. The stage when a teacher needs to exert pressure on individual learners and to set time limits is a matter of judgment based on experience. Certainly, the outcome of verbal experiments tied to the rather primitive apparatus of memory drums does not provide much assistance. A memory drum, and its sibling, the projector, usually have a fixed common time allotted for the display of each item of learning material and a fixed response time. The consequence of this is unnecessary lengthening of the period allowed for reviewing already acquired items and, possibly, too brief a period for the difficult items. Kay (1966) reports an attempt to overcome this particular problem through an on-line computerized learning programme. Be that as it may, it has to be accepted that each learning situation for each individual differs somewhat from every other learning situation. The ideal universal solution would combine pacing with a tutorial nudge where appropriate. A human facilitator of learning has to be more than a technician, and to accept the professional duty of discretionary intervention (Belbin and Belbin, 1972).

Links and interactions with other hypothesized aging deficiencies form the bases for explaining the pacing difficulty. Thus, retrieval problems (see p. 229) would justify the need for extra time, and the anxiety (see above) is probably accentuated under time pressure. Eisdorfer (1968), for example, provides convincing evidence that a fast pace results in overarousal and thereby reduces optimal learning efficiency in older people. The involvement of both cognitive and noncognitive processes can be assumed, and it seems reasonable to conclude that the two interact. When very difficult material or skills are to be acquired and this is combined with time pressure, the elderly will usually be at their worst.

It is valuable to emphasize that pacing difficulties occur from about the age of 40 (Monge and Hultsch, 1971) and that the problem of speed stress is not confined to formal learning situations (Welford, 1977). Anyone conversing with an elderly person should attempt to create an unhurried atmosphere, and that advice applies especially to professional consultations. Finally, those who denigrate cross-sectional studies, whether out of wishful thinking or for metaphysical reasons, will wish to examine the longitudinal study reported by Arenberg and Robertson-Tchabo (1977) which has confirmed that pacing is not a unigenerational phenomenon.

TRANSLATION AND TRANSFER

In everyday life and in laboratory experiments, environmental cues determine not only when to act, but also how to act. Different cues have to be translated into different actions. When the relationship between a signal and its response is "natural," or in accord with previous experience, this is referred to as compatible. For example, pushing a lever on the right-hand side when the signal is on the right and vice versa for the left are highly compatible relationships. The label incompatible would be assigned if a signal on the right required a response on the left and a signal on the left required a response on the right. A simple and direct relationship between signals and actions is, of course, easier for people of all ages, but incompatibility causes disproportionate difficulty in older age groups (see, for example, Simon, 1967). Almost the same point is made in Thorndike *et al.* (1928) generalization that susceptibility to negative transfer increases with age. Customary ways of responding to a stimulus or display become more difficult to suppress when a new response has to be mastered. The incremental obtrusion of negative transfer applies to verbal learning as well as to perceptual motor skills. Typically, the aged are more encumbered than the young while replacing learned responses by different responses in a paired associated task. An important practical implication is to avoid repetition of errors, since habitual mistakes are more difficult to surmount in the not-so-young.

The concept of translation covers any transformation from one language to another, and we also talk of translating thoughts or words into actions. That, too, involves different languages—a conversion from the semantic modality to the kinesthetic modality. The disparity between these languages is best appreciated by attempting the reverse translation, i.e., describing in words the movements produced in exercising a well-versed skill. It is easy to state the outcome of the movements in the external world, but not so easy to state sequential positioning of limbs, body, fingers, and the distances/directions moved. During the initial stages of acquiring a perceptual-motor skill, the meaning of a display will usually be translated into words subvocally, and this will be followed by an implicit verbal command on the actions to be taken. With increasing proficiency, these verbal mediators drop out. We cease saying to ourselves when driving that this particular road sign means slow down, and that therefore the pedal on the left has to be depressed. The foregoing description applies to people of all ages, but there seems to be a special problem as people grow older in coping with new tasks which require translation processes. Welford (1977) provides an extensive discussion of many investigations, suggesting that even relatively simple spatial and symbolic translations can cause difficulties among members of older groups. And it appears that the greater the number of discrete translation operations, the greater the difficulty.

Belbin's (1969) discovery method of training older workers in industry, with its minimal reliance on verbal instruction, attempts to avoid some of the translation pitfalls. Emphasis on performance from the outset allows the establishment of direct links between specific aspects of the display and the appropriate responses at the genesis of skill acquisition. This will make it easier to relinquish verbal mediators as proficiency increases. Physiotherapists, occupational therapists, and other rehabilitation specialists, who are also involved in training, have to face the extra complications of translation processes when dealing with middle-aged and, especially, elderly patients. Verbal instructions cannot be avoided, and even demonstrations by a therapist will often be translated into words and from words into actions. Employing a mirror as an aid adds an extra incompatible relationship to translation, and should, therefore, be used warily. What at least can be attempted is to subdivide complicated tasks, so that a patient can master a component of the skill to be learned through his/her own kinesthetic sensations, thereby increasing the chances of feeling successful before advancing to the next component.

## ATTENTION AND THE IRRELEVANT

Two opposing tendencies related to attention seem to become more prevalent in old age. The first is a longer time lag and increased difficulty in switching concentration from one aspect of a situation to other aspects (Schonfield, Trueman, and Klein, 1972). Second, the elderly are reported to be easily distracted by irrelevant details (Rabbitt, 1965), but that entails a relatively fast switch in concentration. Elsewhere (Schonfield, 1975) it has been suggested that the contradiction can be synthesized, or perhaps merely concealed, by a more general principle. This states that stronger associations in a hierarchy, including a strong temporary association at the focus of attention, tend to become disproportionately powerful, as age increases. The statement tries to deal with the two-way traffic from the external world and from memory into the central processing junction. It is being suggested that the relative strength of items in a stored hierarchy changes with age in that the strong become comparatively stronger. Morever, an item can receive disproportionate strengthening by remaining at the center of attention.

The principle is probably overambitious in attempting to integrate many disparate findings.

Two of its implications in the present context are that irrelevancies are not equal in their potential for invading consciousness, and that it is more difficult for the elderly to "surrender" whatever is at the focus of attention. The probability of intrusions into consciousness of either external stimuli or stored memories is in part a function of frequency of prior experience with the percept or idea, but is also dependent on psychophysical properties of an external stimulus, such as its intensity and whether it is moving or not. By including interfering ideas, in addition to interfering stimuli, the principle can cover the proverbial tendency of some older people to give all the unnecessary details when recounting or re-recounting an experience or story. The hypothesized increment in strength of the content of attention ties in with Botwinick's (1973) stimulus persistence theory and earlier proposals concerning perseveration (Schonfield, 1975).

One significant conclusion from the foregoing discussion is that the intrusion of irrelevant material into ongoing cognitive processes is doubly harmful to the aged. Not only does the irrelevant occupy the central mechanism at the expense of the relevant, but the lengthened aftermath—stimulus trace persistence—increases the difficulty of switching to, and reinstatement of, the relevant. Distractions during learning are clearly to be avoided. Unfortunately, important communications to the elderly, even instructions prepared by investigators experienced in the field of learning, often transgress the law of avoiding the inconsequential. It is useful to bear in mind that because of the communicator's own age, there may be a tendency to dot every "i" and cross every "t." It would, however, be wrong to go to the other extreme and treat every communication as if it were important. The elderly, just like people of any age group, enjoy normal social intercourse, where discussions of the trivial are not out of place, and nothing is really irrelevant.

The age-associated difficulty of switching attention is found in every task which demands coping with two or more relevant features at the same time or in swift succession. Multiplicity may occur at input or output and also with respect to mental operations. Any translation process (see previous section) would be considered a mental operation, and this partly explains why special problems arise for the elderly when consecutive translations are required while learning a skill. However, the number of separate translations and mental operations depends not only on the nature of the task, but also on the proficiency and past experience of the performer. As was stated earlier, verbal mediators

tend to become excised when a perceptual-motor skill is mastered, and direct hookups between stimuli and responses have been strengthened. But, insofar as the middle aged and elderly are less competent hookers (p. 217), translation processes will continue longer than for the young. The aged may, thus, labor under an extra handicap during learning—the added mental operations which cause them especial difficulty persist over a lengthy period.

The absence versus presence of additional mental operations clarifies part of the differential age effects on learning a skill and performing a learned skill. There is slowing in later years while carrying out the skill learned in earlier years, but in general one can say that skills neither die nor fade away. So long as an elderly person can continue to use direct linking between display and response, the special age impediment of the intervening translation process is avoided. Although little hard evidence on the point is available, direct links developed in overlearned skills seem to be maintained forever. A major contribution for improved mental health among the elderly would come from increasing the opportunities available for the performance of well-established skills.

## LEARNING LOADS AND PART LEARNING

Increasing the number of units that have to be learned, other things being equal, reduces the learning level achieved for individual units. Although that generalization requires some qualifying clauses, including a submemory span restriction, it represents a fairly accurate summary of many experimental and everyday observations. The effect in verbal learning of additional loads under limited time conditions is to reduce the frequency of rehearsing, and perhaps also the depth of processing individual items (Craik and Lockhart, 1972). Partly because of this, but almost certainly due in addition to increased encroachments from extra learning material, proportionately fewer individual items are retained. It is important to emphasize that immediately following presentation of an item, recall is usually possible, so that some forgetting occurs while other items receive attention. This shows that the acquisition phase is not confined to acquisition (p. 220), but includes a post- and pre-acquisition stage for particular units. The very same item can have already been learned and forgotten, therefore deserving the label of postacquisition, but because the item will be relearned on later trials, a preacquisition label is also appropriate.

The crux of the matter is that forgetting takes place during learning. And since the number of trials required to learn equivalent amounts of material usually increases with age, it can be concluded that forgetting also increases. No investigation seems to have been reported which compares different age groups on trials to reach criterion with varying numbers of items in a paired-associate or serial-learning paradigm. However, an unsystematic survey of relevant studies suggests that the aged require disproportionately more trials, and, therefore, forget more, as the amount of material to be mastered increases.

Rather surprisingly, dividing an exercise into sections, as one obvious way of easing learning loads for aging individuals, has rarely been studied. A part learning approach was used by Kay (1951) on a task requiring the discovery of appropriate buttons for extinguishing ten different lights, but the problem-solving emphasis of that investigation differentiates it from typical learning assignments. Downs (1965) reported that her younger post office trainees (mean age 27), but not the older trainees (mean age 43), benefited from a progressive part method compared to whole learning. That finding contraindicates aging advantages through segmentation, and may be the reason why this avenue of research has not been pursued. However, the methods Downs employed do not justify widespread generalization. She allowed participants twelve minutes to learn the counties where twenty villages were situated. In her progressive part condition, the trainees were told to decide for themselves when they had mastered one part and were ready to go on to the next. The age-associated predilection for certainty may well have resulted in older trainees' overlearning earlier parts of the task and never reaching the later parts. The progressive part group also seemed to have been required to take cards out of boxes, and this extra manipulation compared to the condition of whole learning, might have reduced overall acquisition time and proved detrimental to the older trainees. All in all, therefore, the Downs' results cannot be considered as conclusive.

A more promising picture of the value derived from progressive part learning is obtained in Smith's (1974) study of the acquisition of twelve paired associates to a criterion of one perfect test trial. In the various progressive part conditions, a few paired associates were learned until the responses were mastered, followed by acquisition of the next few paired associates, then the two parts were combined until they were mastered, and so on with each part. Presentation rates were always of 3-second duration. Young (age range 20–30) and middle-aged (age range 45–55) women were assigned to one of four conditions: "12"—the usual

whole learning where each pair was studied and tested on every trial, and three part conditions— "4–4–4," "3–3–3–3," and "4–3–3–2," the digits signifying how many paired associates were presented in each successive part. Mean study times taken to reach criterion, but not including the unpaced testing times, are presented in Table 10–2. The figures speak for themselves. Clearly, the "4–3–3–2" condition is a much more economic form of acquisition than whole learning for both age groups. Although the reduction in acquisition time was slightly greater for the older than the young group, interactions between age and conditions did not approach significance. Nevertheless, from a practical, as opposed to a theoretical, perspective, the outcome of the study strongly suggests that a progressive part method is likely to reduce the burden of learning new material at least as much for the older population as for the young.

**Table 10-2**  Mean Study Times, by Age Group, for Progressive Part and Whole Learning (in seconds)

| | LEARNING CONDITION | | | |
|---|---|---|---|---|
| Age Group | 4–3–3–2 | 3–3–3–3 | 4–4–4 | 12 |
| 20–30 | 104 | 121 | 229 | 248 |
| 45–55 | 164 | 207 | 316 | 328 |

Adapted with permission from Smith (1974).

## POST-ACQUISITION AND PRE-ACQUISITION PHASES

Why do organisms forget? Do remembering mechanisms work less efficiently as human beings grow older? The first question can probably be considered as the central theme in the history of experimental psychology, and, as in all scientific endeavor, the quest for causes of memory loss becomes a search for variables influencing such losses. The second question—a central concern of gerontological psychology—is factual, and it ought to be simple to decide whether older people remember less well than the young. Yet, as was mentioned earlier (p. 220), the experts do not agree. Protagonists of the equal-forgetting-with-age position take the view that the mechanisms involved in acquisition, including remembering during acquisition, are deficient as people grow older, but on this point the opposition also agrees. Protagonists of the more-forgetting-with-age position would usually take the view that whatever causes forgetting becomes more influential as people grow older. Theoretical formulations concerning the determinants of forgetting seem unanimous in rejecting the idea that time of itself can have an effect. One is, therefore, left with the idea that some kind of encroachment must occur, either from material processed following acquisition or from learned material already present in the memory store—retroactive encroachments or proactive encroachments. Time, as such, may, however, interact with encroachments, so that a longer period since acquisition could increase the effects of previously stored traces.

The dispute between more forgetting and equal forgetting with age is confined to what is termed secondary memory, since the evidence seems irrefutable that there is no deterioration in primary memory or memory span until late in life, and even then the loss is negligible (Craik, 1977). Scanning the memory span does become slower with age (Anders, Fozard, and Lillyquist, 1972; Eriksen, Hamlin, and Daye, 1973) and that may have implications for transferring material to secondary memory, as well as for subsequent retrieval. The absence of age impairment in digit memory span even extends to the ability to suppress irrelevant material (Chatfield, 1977).

Explanations of forgetting are usually derived from classical interference theory, with its more recent exegeses (Postman and Underwood, 1973). (Because the term "interference" has been usurped by the theory, it is advantageous to use a vague and neutral expression, such as "encroachment," when the discussion is not within that specific theoretical framework.) The major postulate of interference theory implies that learning two different responses consecutively to each of a number of different stimuli, as in the AB–AC paradigm, constitutes one of the most forgetful learning situations, due to the presence of response competition. It has, therefore, been argued that if indeed more forgetting is associated with increased age, susceptibility to interference in the AB–AC paradigm should also increase with age. There have been very few tests of this hypothesis with respect to retroactive interference, and even fewer for proactive interference. The relevant studies, according to Schonfield and Stones (1979), do not demonstrate greater memory loss in older than younger subjects, compared to their respective controls. A more important point is that the older controls almost invariably do show a greater memory loss than young controls and thereby seem to contravene the canons of interference theory. Schonfield and Stones also conclude that even without a prior or succeeding *laboratory* learning assignment, the evidence strongly suggests that within about one half an hour of acquistion, increasing age is associated with increased forgetting. Craik

(1977) had earlier decided that older subjects were no more vulnerable to interference than the young, but that they might suffer from a cue overload which hindered retrieval (Schonfield and Robertson, 1966). A neutral spectator would probably say that the beginning of the end of the factual arguments is in sight, but that the end of the beginning of the theoretical disputes has not been reached.

From a practical perspective as it applies to middle-aged and older learners, it is best to assume that encroachments from stored information and later learning are likely to reduce recall. Whether the susceptibility to forgetting or interference is less or equal among younger people does not affect ways to enhance retention. It is obvious that two similar assignments should not be undertaken in close sequence. Mastering, and if possible overlearning, of one task should precede attempting the other. Methods of helping the learning process, such as semantic cues (Smith, 1977) and mnemonic aids (Robertson-Tchabo, Hausman, and Arenberg, 1976), will also assist recall following acquisition when memory may be weakened. Most important of all, the idea that some forgetting both during and following learning is to be expected, but that temporary failures can be overcome, provide the foundation for a healthy mental attitude towards acquiring new knowledge and skills.

## DIFFERENTIAL DIAGNOSIS

### METHODOLOGICAL ISSUES

Classification of illnesses based on symptoms promotes effective communication among practitioners and has as its constant objective the provision of beneficial treatment regimes through the understanding of underlying disease entities. Medical diagnosis thus assumes that independent disease entities exist and that they are distinguishable by differences in symptomatology. These assumptions have been questioned in the case of psychiatric illness (Costello, 1970; Goldenberg, 1977), mainly because of the empirical evidence demonstrating interpsychiatrist disagreement in assigning diagnostic labels (Kellett, Copeland, and Kelleher, 1975; Ley, 1970). Across national frontiers, the divergence between diagnostic practices may be especially pronounced, as has been shown, for example, by the tendency of British geriatricians to assign elderly patients to an organic psychosis category less readily than their American counterparts (Kramer, 1969). One important factor causing the discrepancies is the inadequacy of classification systems, and, in particular, the difficulty of separating primary (first order) from non-primary symptoms. Deficiencies in learning or remembering are the symptoms of concern in this chapter. Such deficiencies constitute part of the syndrome of many emotional disturbances and, as has been discussed in the earlier sections, also accompany normal aging processes.

Two overlapping assignments have, therefore, been accepted by specialists in the area. There has been an attempt to devise tests which reliably differentiate normal from pathological aging and which can also distinguish among diagnostic groupings. This leads to, or is derived from, the second task of explaining, understanding, and pinpointing the loci of deficiencies in specified pathological states. Any experimental procedure which separates normal from pathological aged groups can, in principle, be transformed into a psychometric test for differential diagnosis. However, the literature is replete with criticism of instruments developed by overoptimistic designers (Erickson and Scott, 1977), while the clinician recycles and re-psychles the instruments, faute de mieux. Part of the difficulty seems to be that there is usually only one way of being wrong on any one test, and pathology of every kind may reduce an overall score. Thus, a reasonably valid test designed for differentiating normal aged from chronic brain syndrome patients may not adequately separate the latter from elderly depressives. And a test suitable for labeling middle-aged Korsakov patients does not perform the same trick for the elderly Korsakov. An article by Saccuzzo (1977), enumerating parallels between cognitive deficits found among younger schizophrenics and normal aged populations, nicely illustrates the problem. Attempting to refine an instrument by standardizing different cutoff points for different psychiatric illnesses will usually only be possible with very lengthy tests. Unfortunately, a test of learning or memory requiring multitudinous repetitions of the same material can rouse antagonism and may defeat its own purpose, however high the initial validation index may be.

Imperfect reliability of diagnoses greatly complicates the problem of creating adequate psychometric tests. Cross-cultural differences in diagnostic practices compound problems of generalizing findings obtained from a single culture. In standardizing new tests, medical diagnoses are normally used as validation criteria, but any departure from perfect reliability inevitably causes misclassification across groups. There is not even uniformity among psychologists about the choice of the medical label for validating tests serving identical functions. Sometimes a test of memory has a criterion group of patients described as organic; sometimes only those with diffuse, but not focal, brain damage are included; sometimes it is patients with the amnesia syndrome, and sometimes patients with memory disorder. Employing objective tests to define organic involvement can cause even more confusion, as demonstrated by a report (Hilbert, Niederehe and Kahn, 1976) that out of eleven patients assessed as having "altered brain function," only one patient was so rated on both the two instruments in use. The proportion excluded from a sample, because of being judged as untestable, also varies greatly and can reach over fifty percent (Klonoff and Kennedy, 1966). To some extent, difficulties may be overcome through confining criterion groups to extreme and unmistakable cases. This manipulation aids in the delineation of drastic impairments, but tends to exaggerate the extent of population differences among diagnostic categories and between the "normal" aged and psychopathological groups. The resulting inflated validities frustrate clinical practitioners and lead to Williams' (1970) assertion that psychometric tests are of little help in the differential diagnosis of geriatric patients, except in the most clearcut cases.

## WECHSLER MEMORY SCALE

This battery of seven subtests (Wechsler, 1945), each tapping various cognitive functions which could be loosely categorized as memory-related, is described by Erickson and Scott (1977) as having a virtual monopoly in an important area of clinical assessment. Included in the tests are: questions demanding remote memories likely to be reviewed in everyday life, such as "Who is the present President of the United States?" "the previous President?" and "the name of the town where the test takes place?"; digit span; immediate memory of paragraphs ("logical memory") and visually presented figures; and three presentations, each followed by a recall trial, of ten paired associates, half of which are rather easy. Wechsler's manual gives age score corrections, with an upper limit of sixty-five, although no one in the standardization sample was, in fact, above fifty years old.

Norms for older samples—community living, institutionalized, or both—are provided by Klonoff and Kennedy (1965, 1966), Hulicka (1966), and Cauthen (1977), all adding useful information, but the later investigators omitting reference to, and apparently not knowing of, the earlier papers. Klonoff and Kennedy, with samples over eighty years of age, show lower scores for hospitalized patients than for parallel groups living in the community. The suggested deteriorating outcome of institutionalization is confirmed in a longitudinal study of patients over sixty by Howard (1966). He found a greater reduction in scores for nonorganic patients than for those diagnosed as organic after fifteen years in hospital, although no account was given of probable differences in mortality rates. Hulicka (1966) reported correlations of about .70 between Wechsler Memory scores and vocabulary for the aged decades above sixty. These were much higher than the intertest correlations and raises the perennial problem (Erickson and Scott, 1977; Eysenck and Halstead, 1945) of whether memory test batteries measure anything other than intelligence. Hulicka found that memory for paragraphs, memory for figures and paired associate learning were the subtests most sensitive to age changes. She also reported slightly higher correlations between these three tests and an independent measure of acquisition (paired pictures of people and names) than between the tests and the retention scores on the paired associates. Hulicka, in keeping with her general view that it is learning and not memory deficits that plague the aged (see p. 220), considers that the Wechsler Memory Scale measures acquisition rather than retention. She emphasized the need for a test of retention following acquisition to various criteria. Cauthen (1977) gives norms at three I.Q. levels in each of the memory subtests for people in their sixties, seventies, and eighties. He required the participants in his study to recall the two paragraphs (of the logical memory subtest) one hour after initial presentation and found both age and intelligence to be negatively correlated with delayed recall, when initial levels of acquisition were ignored. The norms provided by Klonoff and Kennedy (1965), Hulicka (1966) and Cauthen (1977) agree fairly well with each other.

The Memory Scale was intended by Wechsler (1945) to serve as an instrument for detecting memory deficits in case of organic impairment. A review of the relevant studies led Erickson and Scott (1977) to conclude that the scale "appears to offer little by way of helpful or unique information with organic patients" (p. 1133). Nevertheless, there is some evidence suggesting that the logical (paragraphs) memory, visual reproduction and paired associate learning subtests tap a factor which differentiates severely demented patients from others (Kear-Colwell, 1973). These subtests, it should be noted, are the same as those which Hulicka (1966) has fingered as sensitive to age differences. Earlier versions of such tests had been included in Babcock's (1930) battery and Gilbert

(1935) had already shown pronounced age differences on them. Later versions of clinical tests of immediate memory for designs (Graham and Kendall, 1960; Benton and Spreen, 1964) have not always proven themselves as valuable diagnostic instruments for elderly populations (Erickson and Scott, 1977; Newcombe and Steinberg, 1964), while memory for short narrative texts has produced ambivalent results (Newcombe and Steinberg, 1964; Shapiro, Post, Lofving, and Inglis, 1956). The acquisition of associates (see Inglis, below) has had a more successful history.

## LEARNING THE MEANING OF UNKNOWN WORDS

When comparisons are made between the learning ability of individuals or groups, it is important to try to ensure that there are no inherent aspects of the material itself, that are likely to make the task more difficult for one group or individual than for another. Ebbinghaus' invention of nonsense syllables is the most famous attempt to cope with this problem. Shapiro and Nelson (1955) offered an ingenious approach to the issue of equating difficulty on the vocabulary test. The New Word Learning and Retention Test used the meaning of the first five consecutive words previously failed on the Terman and Merrill Vocabulary as the material to be acquired and to be recalled twenty-four hours later. Definitions were repeated by the examiner with slight changes of wording until the respondent could give the correct meanings on three consecutive trials without help. Learning the meaning of a few words just beyond one's own vocabulary level will probably seem a reasonable task to most people, especially as the material is unlikely to be completely strange, and, therefore, motivation should be quite high. Shapiro and Nelson reported that the retention part of the test successfully differentiated among most psychiatric categories and between those and normals in the age range between twenty and fifty. However, as so often happens, the New Word Learning Test was found wanting in later studies (Shapiro et al., 1956).

The Shapiro and Nelson approach begat new diagnostic instruments, which have retained some, but not all, of its advantages. Walton and Black's (1959) Modified Word Learning Test uses the meaning of the ten consecutive failed words on the Terman and Merrill Vocabulary for material to be learned, with six out of ten correct responses in one trial as the criterion for success. Less than six correct definitions on one trial requires additional learning and test trials for all ten words, up to a limit of ten trials. A six-out-of-ten approach is also employed in the Synonyms Learning Test (Kendrick, Parboosingh, and Post, 1965), which offers yet another variation on the theme. Here it is one specific synonym from each of ten failed words on the Mill Hill Vocabulary, which is repeated in up to thirty learning trials, with six successes in one trial as the learning criterion. As opposed to other word-learning tests, the exact specification of a correct response on the Synonyms Test makes it similar to rote learning of paired associates and raises theoretical issues concerning retrieval (Schonfield and Stones, 1979). Scores on both the Modified Word and Synonym Learning Tests have usually been successful in identifying elderly patients with brain damage (see reviews by Erickson and Scott, 1977; and Savage, Britton, Bolton, and Hall, 1973), although there are problems with elderly depressives, especially those with low verbal intelligence. Newcombe and Steinberg (1964) found no significant differences between organic and functional disease groups on the Walton and Black test, which they considered as too tiring and difficult. Savage *et al.* (1973) report mis-classification of between twenty and thirty percent of affectives, schizophrenics, and organics for their Newcastle subjects, when using the Wechsler Adult Intelligence Scale Vocabulary, instead of the Terman Merrill, as the material for the Modified New Word Learning Test.

## INGLIS PAIRED ASSOCIATES

Inglis' (1959) original version of this test required the learning of three paired associates to a criterion of three successes with both auditory and visual presentation, as well as matching and recall tests of retention. Later studies have shown that with elderly groups the auditory form alone is highly successful at differentiating between patients without memory impairment (Caird, Sanderson, and Inglis, 1962), between organic and functional disease groups (Newcombe and Steinberg, 1964) and between ill depressives and dements (Whitehead, 1973). Altogether, the Inglis test seems to be the most useful of the diagnostic tools, although the difference between the affective and organic groups did not reach statistical significance in the Savage *et al.* (1973) study.

## PERCEPTUAL MOTOR LEARNING

The top performance on the Block Design Test of the Wechsler Adult Intelligence Scale was used by Savage *et al.* (1973) as the basis of a nonverbal learning test. The first failed design was re-presented six times and the percentage reduction in time taken to complete the design from trial one to trial six constituted the score. Savage *et al.* (1973) reported a clear-cut differentiation of scores between elderly organics and either normal aged or elderly patients with functional disorders, but the latter two groups obtained virtually identical scores on this perceptual motor learning task.

## ORGANIC BRAIN SYNDROME—PINPOINTING DEFICITS

The fundamental issue about organic brain syndrome is the degree to which its symptoms constitute an exaggeration of normal aging process and to what extent, if any, it is sui generis. The answer to the conundrum is unlikely to be straightforward, partly because elderly "organics," who are by definition elderly, would be expected to demonstrate losses found among the normal aged, in addition to other possible deficits. This is linked with the obvious, but seemingly oft-forgotten, fact that there are gradations of severity among organic groups. Further, the difficulty in establishing diagnostic criteria may, indeed, mirror a real absence of clearcut differences.

The evidence from psychometric tests suggests that the special difficulties occur during the acquisition phase, and this has been Kral's (1958) focus in distinguishing between malignant and benign memory losses. Malignant memory loss, which seems typical of organic brain syndrome patients, occurs when there is severely impaired recall of recent personal experience, and Kral argues that this represents a registration deficiency. The label of memory loss could, therefore, be a misnomer, and a more appropriate ascription might refer to inadequate acquisition or inadequate learning. A malignancy label, unfortunately, became particularly apt after Wigdor and Kral (1961) reported increased death rates among patients suffering from the acquisition deficiency. The benign variety of memory loss is mild, common in healthy elderly populations, and demonstrated by a temporary inability to recall specifics, although these become spontaneously available on later occasions. Clearly, this refers to retrieval failures (Schonfield, 1965). One objection to the implied neat solution of input failure for organics and output problems in normal aging is that members of the latter group also manifest some registration difficulties (p. 228).

A number of investigators have attempted to shed light on the exact nature of the acquisition deficit found among organic brain syndrome patients. The best culprit would be short-term memory, but against this there is indisputable evidence that memory span as such shows little, if any, loss, and that, at least in presenile dementia, the usual recency effect occurs in free recall (Miller, 1971). Inglis and his associates (Inglis, 1970) have implicated the particular aspect of short-term memory demanded in dichotic listening tasks. Following simultaneous feeding of different material to two ears, subjects will usually report all the information received in one ear before attempting to recall the information received in the other ear. Everyone tends to be poorer in their recall from the second channel than from the first, but the deficiency is much more pronounced among elderly patients with memory disorders. Results obtained by Inglis and Sanderson (1961) for a sample of the latter category and a parallel control group of patients (mean age 75) with one to four digits per ear are given in Table 10–3. Clearly, the memory-disordered group is persistently much worse on the second channel, and performs comparatively well on the first channel. It is important, however, to note that in a number of experiments Inglis (1970) has documented the fact that second channel memory loss occurs during normal aging. A study by Mackay and Inglis (1963) includes dichotic listening scores for participants belonging to the same age group as the patients tested by Inglis and Sanderson, but living in the community. The scores in that study for the 70- to 80-year-old group, as well as those obtained by participants in their twenties are included in Table 10–3 for comparison purposes. The two investigations show little difference between patients with memory disorder and community-living residents. They also indicate that elderly patients without memory disorder obtain scores superior to healthy people of the same age,

and compare quite favorably with a normal young group. Be that as it may, the special nature of the dichotic listening paradigm, with its requirement for attention switch between ears, and where even the young manage to repeat only one correct digit on average out of four on the second channel, does not seem a fertile field for producing definitive generalizations (Craik, 1977).

Insofar as a distinction between short-term and long-term memory is accepted, it seems that the search for organic-associated deficiency should be concentrated in the transfer of information from the first system to the second. The process of encoding and whatever neurological changes underlie the establishment of long-term memory traces in normal adults do not operate efficiently among the patients in question. For some of these patients, they perhaps do not operate at all. Other studies point towards the same domain. Newcombe and Steinberg (1964) repeatedly presented the same paragraph on different days to patients (mean age, 69) suffering from either organic cerebral disease or functional psychiatric illness. Recall was required not only after each presentation but also beforehand, except, obviously, on day 1. The results are depicted in Figure 10–2, and show that those suffering from functional illnesses obtain benefits which cumulate with each presentation, while the organics do not. The organics have very low scores for immediate recall, but even that amount of recollection disappears before the next presentation. Caird (1965), following a method invented by Hebb (1961), also used a repeated presentation design. The task was to recall different strings of six digits, with every third string being identical. Memory-disordered elderly psy-

**Table 10-3**   Dichotic Listening: Recall Scores for Elderly Patients, The Healthy Old and Young

| Mean Age | | PATIENTS* | | COMMUNITY LIVING** | |
| | | Memory Disordered 75.53 | Control 75.00 | 76.30 | 23.50 |
|---|---|---|---|---|---|
| Digits per ear | Channel | | | | |
| 1 | 1st | 0.98 | 1.00 | 0.91 | 1.00 |
| | 2nd | 0.47 | 0.95 | 0.31 | 1.00 |
| 2 | 1st | 1.83 | 1.95 | 1.66 | 1.59 |
| | 2nd | 0.09 | 1.80 | 0.23 | 1.40 |
| 3 | 1st | 2.42 | 2.90 | 2.41 | 2.22 |
| | 2nd | 0.05 | 2.15 | 0.19 | 1.63 |
| 4 | 1st | 2.82 | 3.63 | 2.86 | 2.60 |
| | 2nd | 0.09 | 0.95 | 0.04 | 1.15 |

*Adapted with permission from Inglis and Sanderson (1961). Copyright 1961 by the Amer. Psychol. Assoc. Reprinted by permission.
**Adapted with permission from Mackay and Inglis (1963) and S. Karger AG, Basel.

chiatric patients showed little improvement on the repeated digits, whereas the control patients had far better scores on those. It is also, perhaps, pertinent to mention an experiment by Whitman, Brown, and Gantt (1961) on differential conditioning, where one tone was always followed by shock and another tone was not. Even after being told that this was the case, no chronic brain syndrome patient showed evidence of learning, although most of the controls (median age 68) responded differentially to the two conditioned stimuli. These investigations all suggest that repetition, or what used to be called exercise, do not increase the probability of responding correctly. Something funny happens on the way to long-term memory; the schema exchange does not operate, and the nonconsumer of information is created (see p. 219).

The idea of schema exchange has important implications for understanding acquisition deficiencies, since it emphasizes that long-term memories have potent influence at a very early stage of any cognitive process. Relevant aspects of long-term memory circulate *into* short-term memory and do not merely act as a repository of output *from* the short-term memory system. For that reason, Broadbent's (1958) nomenclature of a p-system—limited capacity perceptual system—is more descriptive than short-term memory. The meaning

of whatever is in the forefront of attention depends on contact with existing memory schemata. However, success in understanding and acting demands the abstraction of appropriate aspects of a stored schema and suppression of the remaining aspects. Also, whatever is at the forefront of attention should direct the route from one schema to another, rather than the routes being determined by haphazard existing links. As Bartlett stated long ago: "A new incoming impulse must become not merely a cue setting up a series of reactions all carried out in a fixed temporal order, but a stimulus which enables us to go direct to that portion of the organized setting of past responses which is most relevant to the needs of the moment" (Bartlett, 1932, p. 206). There must be control of the schema and not control by the schema. What is now suggested is that such control is diminished, or lost, in organic brain syndrome patients—the ability to inhibit the irrelevant memories is missing. Even among this group, long-term memory provides a dominant semantic or contextual or formal association with the incoming stimulus, but from thereon, the organism seems at the mercy of prepotent and fortuitous existing links with other episodic or generic memories. These now come to the forefront of attention, but have only tenuous logical connections with the original stimulus. Perhaps because of the absence of a supporting cast of relevant associations, new information does not readily transfer to secondary memory or, if it does, the representation is isolated and fragmented. The schema exchange has ceased to function efficiently.

The lines of this highly sketchy and underdeveloped picture have been drawn to accord with reported observations about organic syndrome patients, such as their rambling talk, and with results obtained from empirical studies. Relatively good showing on the vocabulary and information tests (Erickson and Scott, 1977) demonstrate that the appropriate semantic memory is usually aroused for verbal material. However, even on such tests, which are wholly dependent on old stored information, organic groups do not perform as well as the normal aged (Botwinick and Birren, 1951; Savage *et al.,* 1973). "Organics" lose the point and, as Whitehead (1973) showed in a learning experiment, they make what she categorized as random errors. On the other hand, the demonstration by Warrington and Weiskrantz (1968) of learning and retaining the meaning of fragmented words or pictures by amnesic patients might be due to the absence of a prepotent interfering schema. Perhaps memories can be established when an original stimulus evokes no meaning, and a gradual build-up of new associations is encouraged.

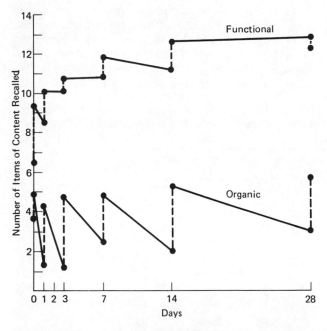

**Figure 10–2** Immediate and delayed recall scores for functional and organic patients. See text for explanation. Adapted with permission from Newcombe and Steinberg (1964, p. 492), and J. of Gerontol.

The proposed faulty schema exchange hypothesis is, in a sense, an alternative way of describing inefficient coding. That characterization is espoused by Miller (1975), who seems to suggest that presenile dements use an initial letter code rather than a semantic code for long-term storage. The idea is based on his finding that there was little difference between presenile and control patients (mean age 59) in recall of word lists when initial letters were provided as cues, although large differences occurred in free recall and recognition. However, his data show that the control group hardly benefited at all from the cues, but that the presenile group, even with the cues, managed to recall only 3.4 words out of 10. In any case, the present proposal could encompass the possibility of occasional coding according to formal characteristics, since that might well be the prepotent initial association produced from the long-term memory store.

## PSYCHOLOGICAL THERAPIES

### APPLIED SETTINGS

The emphasis in this section is on relatively straightforward and readily replicable types of therapeutic intervention, which involve articulated aims about desired changes in specific behaviors. What is omitted are the traditional lengthy psychotherapies, and their concern with underlying dynamics or conflicts, since those approaches are far removed from the learning and memory issues discussed in this chapter. It can be assumed, however, that the outcome of reducing unsuitable conduct is not necessarily circumscribed, but may affect reactions from members of the immediate social group and, ultimately, alter psychosocial generic memories (p. 220). The effects of changing from an incontinent to a continent person, for example, are likely to modify attitudes of other people to the cured individual, as well as the individual's self-schemata.

Most of the relevant studies have taken place in hospital and nursing home settings, where, overtly or covertly, patients are often categorized as unable to change their behavior. This verdict of hopelessness has been assigned without adequate evidence and serves as an excuse for a warehouse, custodial approach. Providing the best care, but treating symptoms as incurable, often seems to have become the ideal situation. That ideal is praiseworthy, given the horrendous stories of patient care in some institutions, and yet it creates a nihilistic atmosphere. But, even if learning were

impossible, it might be better to have tried and lost, than not to have tried at all. A focal aim—management by objectives—is likely to improve the social milieu. In fact, however, quite a lot of the evidence reported in the literature of successful learning by the elderly has been obtained from subjects residing in institutions. It is best to assume that every patient has at least minimal learning ability, and, as has been shown in earlier sections, that there are also important methods of retarding and accelerating the speed of acquisition.

### BEHAVIOR THERAPY

The techniques used in many attempted interventions have been firmly embedded in the traditions of behavior therapy, with a stress on consistent environmental manipulation through rewards. Behavior therapy, as Lazarus (1977) points out, nowadays covers a broad spectrum of approaches and is not confined to the primitive, radical faith of its founders. The influence of thought, under a camouflage label of cognitive mediation, has ceased being anathema. Nevertheless, some experimenters continue in the old tradition of omitting to tell subjects what actions are to be rewarded. As was implied in discussing Bellucci and Hoyer's (1975) experiment (p. 223) the interpretation of situations by those involved has to be taken into consideration. When a participant is not told why rewards are provided and withheld, a problem-solving study may have been created. The desire to solve the problem is, of course, based on the assumption that the reward is wanted. From the subject's perspective, it is not a question of an experimenter conditioning a subject, but the subject conditioning the experimenter to produce the rewards. Even discriminitive classical conditioning (Whitman *et al.*, 1961; Zaretsky and Brucker, 1976) can be viewed as a problem-solving paradigm when human beings are involved. Indeed, quite a strong argument could be made for the view that the ultimate reinforcements derived from learning are not rewards and punishments provided by an experimenter, but the establishment of generic schema which permit more veridical predictions about, and control of, the environment (see p. 219).

Elderly patients often belong to only one social environment—the institution in which they reside—and, therefore, interactions with others are of pivotal concern. Increasing the number of communications is an obvious target for change, and behavioral therapists have tackled this problem at various levels. Pettigrew and Keith (1975) report a demonstration study with, what they called, two geriatric populations—four nursing home patients and five active members of a senior citizens club (age ranges 66–83 and 57–90, respectively). Participants were seen individually and were told to say as many words as they could. The experimenter attempted to increase the number of consecutive words with S as an initial letter by saying "very good"—the reinforcement—every time this occurred. There were two fifteen-minute sessions a day for fourteen days, the first two days establishing a base line, followed by six days of reinforcement, four days of extinction without responses from the experimenter, and another four days of reinforcement. Results clearly indicated that the patients did not increase their output of alliterative S words. The healthy elderly alliterated appropriately and were not much affected by the so-called extinction procedure. Pettigrew and Keith interpreted their results as showing that in the institution "reinforcing contingencies contributed to a decrement or inhibition of new verbal behavior," whereas "a senior citizens group may importantly contribute to providing an adequate supportive milieu in which increments in operant behavior by geriatric subjects can be achieved" (Pettigrew and Keith, 1975, p. 260). The conclusions may well be true, but for a variety of reasons the results do not justify them. Firstly, the objectively defined reinforcement "very good" may be more rewarding for active volunteers who have donated twenty-eight sessions to a gerontological study than for captive patients. Secondly, spontaneous utterance by patients of alliterative S words may have been so infrequent that the opportunity for reinforcement was rare. Data are not provided for differences between the two groups on producing nontarget words, but it could be guessed that the patients were more taciturn. Thirdly, the problem-solving component may have been paramount, with the sick being less proficient than the healthy in this regard. In fact, after the sessions ended, most of the noninstitutionalized subjects showed that they were aware of the cue for approval, but only one of the patients had even noticed that "very good was said by the experimenter at indeterminant intervals" (Pettigrew and Keith, 1975, p. 261). If the aim is to discover whether someone can produce consecutive alliterative S words, the obvious first method to explore is to ask the person to do just that. Paraphernalia transported from the experimental laboratory may defeat the aim of therapeutic intervention.

The introduction of specific external reinforcement, and even more an ensuing extinction procedure, can of itself produce a conflict between the aim of overcoming a disability and the aim of pure science. Rewarding and withholding rewards might well be interpreted as signifying that social approval for the desirable behavior is confined to situations where the rewards are given. For example, Hoyer, Kafer, Simpson, and Hoyer (1974) report successful attempts to increase the frequency of spoken words among untalkative or mute chronic schizophrenics aged over sixty. In one experiment, two of four members of a group received a penny for each word uttered, whereas the other two participants received nothing. The nonreinforced pair of subjects increased their word output at least as much as the reinforced pair. When the reinforced pair were being extinguished, the nonreinforced pair talked less than during their own baseline session. Hoyer *et al.* explain this in terms of the nonreinforced subjects modeling the behavior of the reinforced, although the nonreinforced produced more words overall at each session than the reinforced. A more likely interpretation is that the rewards to the reinforced pair provided the clue to the nonreinforced pair for solving the problem of what was desired behavior. The real issue is whether a sequence of reinforced and unreinforced sessions might restrict the desired increased talking to situations where concrete rewards are offered. Without extinction sessions, Mueller and Atlas (1972) found some carry-over of increased conversation to the ward, following dynamic re-motivational game playing in a pleasantly furnished room, with refreshments available. Tokens were presented as rewards for social interactions, the tokens being exchangeable for candy and cigarettes. A simpler form of increasing social participation during ongoing recreational activities was reported by Linsk, Howe, and Pinkston (1975). They encouraged a group worker to talk less herself and to pose task-related, specific questions of patients (age range 68–96). When extinction procedures were introduced—the worker talking more—not very surprisingly, the patients talked less.

The literature includes accounts of attempts to change a variety of target behaviors, with a variety of patients and methods. Libb and Clements (1969) increased the time spent on an exercise bicycle in three out of four patients with chronic brain syndrome by having marbles delivered automatically for wheel revolutions, their marbles being exchangeable for goodies of choice. MacDonald and Butler (1974) managed to persuade two patients (aged 92 and 85) to forego using their wheelchairs and to walk to the dining room, by asking them to do just that, and rewarded them both with praise and a chat en route. When the patients were told not to walk and the reinforcement was withdrawn, they reverted to the wheelchair. Geiger and Johnson (1974) were successful in getting six patients (age range 65–91) to finish their meals by allowing a choice of a reasonable gift each time this occurred. There was a slight relapse with one patient, who chose extra desserts, but then discovered that she was sometimes too full to consume the desserts immediately after the meal. The question of individual differences in the effectiveness of different reinforcers was explored by Ankus and Quarrington (1972) with a large group of memory-disordered patients (age range 55–86). It was found that pennies were more effective as rewards among females, and a liquid reward—type of liquid according to choice—tended to be more effective for males in increasing the frequency of lever pushing.

Incontinence is a severe problem among elderly patients, and successful intervention has rarely been reported. One difficulty is the appropriate timing for immediate reinforcement of desirable behavior. Going to the toilet following incontinence cannot really be considered as a target movement, but rewarding the minute-by-minute occurrence of continence is impossible. Ankus (1969) successfully reduced the incidence of incontinence in two female patients, aged 72 and 70, with an edible of each patient's choice as reinforcers every time the toilet was used. A remark by one of the patients that she was sick of candy implies that it might be better to offer a smorgasbord of reinforcements rather than to adhere rigidly to the subject's original choice. Ankus suggested that a change in the kind of attention provided by the staff to the two experimental subjects may have been as potent an influence as the chosen reward. Ankus' study also showed the importance of control groups for analyzing the outcome of intervention, since her controls demonstrated significantly improved scores on an adjustment scale during the course of the experiment. Both experimental and control subjects had been hospitalized for many years, and one could presume that their behavior had stabilized unless some form of new treatment was introduced. Grosicki (1968) was unsuccessful in reducing incontinence among patients (age range 63–74) at a veterans' hospital. Her reinforcement for using the toilet were tokens valued at one cent and a type of social interaction reward consisting of three-minutes conversation when the patient was dry at hourly checks. Surprisingly, the control group in this experiment showed a significant increase of continence. On the other hand, Atthowe (1972) completely eliminated enuresis among twelve hospitalized veterans (age range 42–77). Even during the two-month baseline period, there was considerable improvement, and by the

end of the succeeding aversive phase, also lasting two months, the battle was won for almost all participants. The aversive phase was a noncontingent treatment, involving the placement of patients in an overcrowded ward, turning lights on four times a night, thus disturbing everybody, and escorting the experimental group to the bathroom, whether they were dry or wet. During the ensuing reinforcement period, not wetting was rewarded step by step through tokens, through not being taken to the bathroom, through a move to better sleeping quarters, and constantly through expressions of approval by the staff. After that, all the patients were cured, and the persistence of continence over a period of years demonstrated that the results were not a mere flash in the pan.

The location of many of these investigations in hospitals raises the general issue of successfully isolating specific forms of behavior for reinforcement in such environments. The experimenters' intentions regarding behavior to be rewarded may not parallel the impressions received by participants. Not only is the staff showing approval and disapproval, but the reactions of other patients, especially in a veterans' hospital, cannot be ignored. This complicates the assessment of differences between experimental and control groups. In Filer and O'Connell's (1964) veterans' hospital study, control subjects who were not receiving reinforcement for conduct rewarded among the experimental subjects, asked about this. It may well be the case that the control subjects hoped or expected that they, too, would eventually receive identical rewards. Filer and O'Connell had matched pairs of patients (age range 62–90) and randomly assigned one member of a pair to the experimental group and the other to the control group. Members of both groups were told at the outset of the investigation about a variety of behavior requirements, that conduct would be evaluated and report cards provided each fortnight. The only difference in treatment was the variety of rewards promised to and received by the experimental subjects, if they met expectations. Results showed significant beneficial effects of rewards, but both groups improved greatly. The melioration among controls may have been due to the trust felt by the veterans in the eventual fair apportioning of the kitty. An alternative hypothesis to explain the improved behavior of the control group is that clearly defined expectations with knowledge of results produces a Hawthorne effect. Whatever the cause, the important lesson is that difficult and objectionable behavior should not necessarily be regarded as unchangeable because of the presence of illness or advanced age. However, it must always be remembered that patients are an amorphous group, and successful learning in one study does not guarantee success elsewhere.

## INTERACTIONS WITH ALCOHOL

Often, it is not so much new behavior that a therapist wishes an elderly patient to acquire, but rather the reinstatement of previous behavior. An attack on the obstacles preventing such reinstatement is, therefore, a reasonable approach. The reputation of alcohol as a disinhibitor in social intercourse makes it a likely agent to overcome a virtual absence of personal relationships in many geriatric wards. Promoting social interactions in a hospital setting serves not only as an end on its own, but also acts as a means of increasing environmental stimulation. Further, alcohol can be viewed as a reinforcement from a behavior therapy perspective, and has certain advantages over the traditional rewards mentioned in the previous section. With a different setting in mind, Ogden Nash (1975) aptly stated that candy was dandy, but liquor was quicker.

Kastenbaum (1964, 1972) has the credit for persuading United States hospital authorities to introduce wine and beer therapy. His first study was with two groups of males (age range 68–96), who were provided with wine at specified daily times in two club-type rooms. At first, the main social intercourse was between the participant observer and individual patients, but eventually small groups were formed, and the club meetings persisted for more than a year following the cessation of the alcoholic incentive. Beneficial social effects of wine over grape juice were definite within the group situation, although there was minimal transfer of socialization to the patients' own wards. Further studies showed that beer was as satisfactory a medium as wine, that a mixed male-female group caused some problems, and that a ladies-only group was least successful. Approval by medical and nursing staff of the venture and their resulting cooperative attitude were found to be the sine qua non for progress. Among later investigators, Lysak, Fisher, and Shedletsky (1977) demonstrated the value of an English-type pub with the spooneristic title of The Boar's Head. Chien (1971) reported that social therapy combined with beer had statistically significant advantages over social therapy combined with thioridazine or fruit punch among patients suffering from organic brain syndrome, while Burrill, McCourt, and Cutter (1974) found no advantage for beer over soda in a similar group of patients.

## REALITY ORIENTATION

Reality orientation (Taulbee and Folsom, 1966) is the only treatment specifically designed for confused and memory disordered chronic brain syndrome patients. The approach adopted is in some sense the opposite of the usual, superficially considerate, method of leaving these unfortunate people in peace. As its name implies, reality orientation therapy attacks the manifested disorientation by constantly reiterating basic personal and current information. When someone has forgotten where he lives, the date, his name, and so on, the best chance of relearning these, it is assumed, is by hearing and repeating them. All staff, with whom a patient is in contact, become involved in the therapy and are instructed to use their normal contacts to remind the patient about simple aspects of the immediate environment, as well as to state in words any activity of a patient. The patient is always requested to repeat statements. Constant signs of approval for success and active friendliness by staff are combined with firmness. Clear responses are encouraged, and tendencies to digress are checked. The twenty-four-hour-milieu therapy is supplemented by more formal daily classroom sessions with a few patients at a time. A variety of visual aids are used, with a focus on a noticeboard where daily information (date, weather, menu) and permanent information (location, names) are displayed in large print.

The earlier practitioners of reality orientation reported great success with the technique, even to the extent of many "graduates" of the programme returning to the community (Folsom, 1968; Stephens, 1970). More recent claims have been somewhat tempered, although the general reaction is still enthusiastic. Barnes (1974) confined his treatment to a reality classroom for six weeks, and the director of nursing noted improvements in each of the six patients (mean age 81) involved, with a relapse within one week after sessions terminated. However, a test devised by Barnes failed to show a significant increase of scores. Citrin and Dixon (1977) provide statistically significant evidence to demonstrate the effectiveness of their combined twenty-four-hour-milieu and classroom procedure for an experimental group as compared to a control group (mean ages 83 and 84, respectively). The staff attending to the controls were specifically forbidden to use the reality orientation approaches with their patients, and that type of directive could have an adverse effect on the quality of care. In fact, the untreated controls showed a slight decline in scores during the course of the investigation on the measuring instruments used. A similar criticism can be made of Brook, Degun, and Mather's (1975) study, which attempted to assess the contribution made by the therapist in a reality classroom. Members of their experimental group not only received instruction, but were always given a warm welcome on entering the room, whereas members of the control group were given what amounted to the cold shoulder. The findings show greater overall improvement of the experimental group, and there is really little doubt that someone suffering from senile dementia left to his own devices in a classroom is unlikely to fare as well as someone who interacted with a therapist. Nevertheless, the difference in reception by the therapist amounts to unequal treatment, apart from the independent variable under consideration. Harris and Ivory (1976) used carefully designed measuring instruments to demonstrate the advantage of behavior therapy over traditional hospital care, but that, too, can be faulted in that the patients were rated by psychiatric aides, who also were involved in the therapy. The foregoing rather picky criticisms show that pitting an experimental group against a control group in an institutional setting is fraught with difficulties. Nevertheless, the relevant studies taken together justify the conclusion that reality orientation techniques lead to some improvement in at least some chronic brain syndrome patients.

The successes of reality orientation constitute clear evidence for learning and remembering, but what exactly has changed in the course of therapy and why the changes have occurred are not readily apparent. Treatment seems directed towards the reestablishment of generic rather than episodic memories, but a better understanding of the cognitive processes stimulated by the techniques await controlled variations of the learning material bombarded to participants. Comparision of possible differences between reacquiring immutable specific facts and an organized set of data certainly deserves investigation. The proper answer to the question, "What is your name?" does not change during a stay in hospital, whereas the correct answer to, "What is today?" will be incorrect tomorrow. Ability to reply to the former question could depend on the strengthening of a simple stimulus-response connection, but correctly identifying the day of the week seems to demand suppression of yesterday's strengthened association. According to the hypothesized faulty schema exchange of organic brain syndrome patients, it would be especially difficult to learn to inhibit a strong association, such as yesterday's date. Outside a hospital

setting, many younger people are unaware of the date, but it is linked with a wide network of schemata—all the happenings of yesterday and the day before, the order of seasons, bithdays of relations, and so on. Knowing the date would be more difficult without this network. It may be that patients' success in giving the date depends on a stimulus-response connection—the stimulus being the calendar displayed prominently in a reality-orientation setup. Another problem worthy of consideration is the value, use, or cost benefit of information acquired, such as date and names of other patients. Retrieval of names causes difficulty, even for those with only "benign" memory loss, and perhaps other knowledge could be learned with less difficulty. A scientific approach with two experimental groups pitted against each other would be the sophisticated way of investigating these issues. Nevertheless, reports of therapists' own impressions should not be denigrated. Gerontologists must not allow themselves to be completely brainwashed by the worshippers at the altar of statistical significance.

## EPILOGUE

Gaps in our knowledge, conflicts in our approaches, fallacies in our arguments and contradictory conclusions have, perhaps, been overemphasized in this chapter. The criticisms, however, merely reflect the complexity of problems confronting past and future investigators in these heterogeneous areas. The fact that so many advances have been made during the short history of gerontological research, notwithstanding intractable logistics and methodology, is, therefore, all the more commendable.

One theme which constantly comes to the fore is the drawback of rigid adherence to methods developed for dealing with nongerontological problems. Since no experiment settles any issue forever, an investigator has to make a judgment on priorities among many potential objections to a proposed study. The importance of a specific methodological challenge is not necessarily invariant across different studies. Even within gerontology, a theoretical perspective and an applied perspective may require different levels of sophistication. Attempts to answer problems confronting today's older generations need not be put aside, because some future older generations may have different problems. During the early stages of a new discipline, tolerance of ambiguity is a valuable characteristic for investigators.

To what extent age-related deficits in learning and remembering can be attributed to underlying physiological changes and to what extent these are due to environmental or experiential causes will not be readily settled. It is unnecessary to set up a straw neanderthal man who is purported to have thought that all age changes are biologically based. No responsible theorist seems to have taken that position. It is unwise to go to the other extreme and to suggest that all deficits will vanish, just because there is evidence that some disabilities can be made to disappear. The results of classical conditioning experiments, for example, are unlikely to be generation-linked. And, if the hookup of connections, inhibition of irrelevant memories, and retrieval of specific memory items do indeed cause increasing problems with increasing age, the appropriate response is not a hopeless shrug of shoulders, but a search for compensatory devices. Future research in learning and remembering areas will benefit from the increased pressure for ecological validity. We will soon have to come to grips with what exactly are the benefits of experience and how the wisdom of aging individuals can best be put to use, not only for the sake of each individual's mental health, but also in the interests of the community at large.

# REFERENCES

American Psychiatric Association. 1968. *Manual of Mental Disorders*. Washington, D.C.: American Psychiatric Association, 2nd edition, DSM–II.

ANDERS, T. R., FOZARD, J. L., AND LILLYQUIST, T. D. 1972. Effects of age on retrieval from short-term memory. *Developmental Psychology, 6*, 214–217.

ANKUS, M. 1969. *Operant control of incontinence in female geriatric patients: A pilot study*. Whitby, Ontario: Whitby Psychiatric Hospital.

ANKUS, M., AND QUARRINGTON, B. 1972. Operant behavior in the memory disordered. *Journal of Gerontology, 27*, 500–510.

ARENBERG, D. 1973. Cognition and aging: Verbal learning, memory, problem solving and aging. *In*, C. Eisdorfer and M. P. Lawton (eds.), *The Psychology of Adult Development and Aging*, pp. 74–97. Washington, D.C.: American Psychological Association.

ARENBERG, D., AND ROBERTSON-TCHABO, E. A. 1977. Learning and aging. *In*, J. E. Birren and K. W. Schaie (eds.), *Handbook of the Psychology of Aging*, pp. 421–449. New York: Van Nostrand Reinhold.

ATTHOWE, J. M. 1972. Controlling nocturnal enuresis in severely disabled and chronic patients. *Behavior Therapy, 3*, 232–239.

BABCOCK, H. 1930. An experiment in the measurement of mental deterioration. *Archives of Psychology, No. 117*.

BARNES, J. A. 1974. Effects of reality orientation classroom on memory loss, confusion and disorientation in geriatric patients. *Gerontologist, 14*, 138–142.

BARTLETT, F. C. 1932. *Remembering*. Cambridge, England: Cambridge University Press.

BELBIN, E., AND BELBIN, R. M. 1972. *Problems in Adult Retraining*. London: Heinemann.

BELBIN, R. M. 1965. *Training Methods*. Paris: Organization for Economic Cooperation and Development.

BELBIN, R. M. 1969. *The Discovery Method*. Paris: Organization for Economic Cooperation and Development.

BELLUCCI, G., AND HOYER, W. J. 1975. Feedback effects on the performance and self-reinforcing behavior of elderly and young adult women. *Journal of Gerontology, 30*, 456–460.

BENTON, A., AND SPREEN, O. 1964. Visual memory test performance in mentally deficient and brain damaged patients. *American Journal of Mental Deficiency, 68*, 630–633.

BIRREN, J. E. (Ed.) 1959. *Handbook of Aging and the Individual*. Chicago: University of Chicago Press.

BIRREN, J. E., AND SCHAIE, K. W. (Eds.) 1977. *Handbook of the Psychology of Aging*. New York: Van Nostrand Reinhold.

BOTWINICK, J. 1973. *Aging and Behavior*. New York: Springer.

BOTWINICK, J., AND BIRREN, J. E. 1951. Differential decline in the Wechsler-Bellevue sub-tests in the senile psychoses. *Journal of Gerontology, 6*, 365–368.

BOTWINICK, J., BRINLEY, J. F., AND ROBBIN, J. S. 1958. The interaction effects of perceptual difficulty and stimulus exposure time on age differences in speed and accuracy of response. *Gerontologia, 2*, 1–10.

BOTWINICK, J., AND KORNETSKY, C. 1960. Age differences in the acquisition and extinction of the GSR. *Journal of Gerontology, 15*, 83–84.

BRAUN, H. W., AND GEISELHART, R. 1959. Age differences in the acquisition and extinction of the conditioned eyelid response. *Journal of Experimental Psychology, 57*, 386–388.

BROADBENT, D. E. 1958. *Perception and Communication*. London: Pergamon Press.

BROOK, P., DEGUN, G., AND MATHER, M. 1975. Reality orientation, a therapy for psycho-geriatric patients: A controlled study. *British Journal of Psychiatry, 127*, 42–45.

Burrill, R. H., McCourt, J. F., and Cutter, H. S. 1974. Beer: A social facilitator for PMI patients? *Gerontologist, 14,* 430–431.

Caird, W. K. 1965. Memory disorder and psychological test performance in aged psychiatric patients. *Diseases of the Nervous System, 26,* 499–505.

Caird, W. K. 1966. Conditioning, learning and reflex excitability in memory disordered geriatric patients. *Proceedings 7th International Congress of Gerontology,* Vienna, 27–34.

Caird, W. K., Sanderson, R. E., and Inglis, J. 1962. Cross-validation of a learning test for use with elderly psychiatric patients. *Journal of Mental Science, 108,* 368–370.

Canestrari, R. E. 1963. Paced and self-paced learning in young and elderly adults. *Journal of Gerontology, 18,* 165–168.

Canestrari, R. E., and Eberly, B. W. 1964. CS-UCS interval and avoidance conditioning in older subjects. *Newsletter for Research in Psychology, 4,* 10–11.

Cantor, N., and Mischel, W. 1977. Traits as prototypes: Effects on recognition memory. *Journal of Personality and Social Psychology, 35,* 38–48.

Cauthen, N. R. 1977. Extension of the Wechsler Memory Scale norms to older age groups. *Journal of Clinical Psychology, 33,* 208–211.

Chatfield, S. V. 1977. *Directed forgetting, interference and age.* Unpublished Master's thesis, University of Calgary.

Chien, C. 1971. Psychiatric treatment for geriatric patients. *American Journal of Psychiatry, 127,* 1070–1074.

Citrin, R. S., and Dixon, D. N. 1977. Reality orientation: A milieu therapy used in an institution for the aged. *Gerontologist, 17,* 39–43.

Costello, C. G. 1970. Classification and psychopathology. *In,* C. G. Costello (ed.), *Symptoms of Psychopathology,* pp. 1–26. New York: John Wiley.

Craik, F. I. M. 1977. Age differences in human memory. *In,* J. E. Birren and K. W. Schaie (eds.), *Handbook of the Psychology of Aging,* pp. 384–420. New York: Van Nostrand Reinhold.

Craik, F. I. M., and Lockhart, R. S. 1972. Levels of processing: A framework for memory research. *Journal of Verbal Learning and Verbal Behavior, 11,* 671–684.

Downs, S. 1965. Age in relation to part and whole learning. *Journal of Gerontology, 20,* 479–482.

Eisdorfer, C. 1968. Arousal and performance experiments in verbal learning and a tentative theory. *In,* G. A. Talland (ed.), *Human Aging and Behavior,* pp. 189–216. New York: Academic Press.

Eisdorfer, C., Nowlin, J., and Wilkie, F. 1970. Improvement of learning in the aged by modification of autonomic nervous system activity. *Science, 170,* 1327–1329.

Erickson, R. C., and Scott, M. L. 1977. Clinical memory testing: A review. *Psychological Bulletin, 84,* 1130–1149.

Eriksen, C. W., Hamlin, R. M., and Daye, C. 1973. Aging adults and rate of memory scan. *Bulletin of the Psychonomic Society, 1,* 259–260.

Eysenck, H., and Halstead, H. 1945. The memory function. *American Journal of Psychiatry, 102,* 174–180.

Filer, R. N., and O'Connell, D. D. 1964. Motivation of aging persons. *Journal of Gerontology, 19,* 15–22.

Folsom, J. C. 1968. Reality orientation for the elderly mental patient. *Journal of Psychiatry, 1,* 291–307.

Gagné, R. M. 1965. *The Conditions of Learning.* New York: Holt, Rinehart and Winston.

Geiger, O. G., and Johnson, L. A. 1974. Positive education for elderly persons: Correct eating through reinforcement. *Gerontologist, 14,* 432–436.

Gendreau, P., and Suboski, M. D. 1971. Intelligence and age in discrimination conditioning of the eyelid response. *Journal of Experimental Psychology, 89,* 379–382.

Gilbert, J. G. 1935. Mental efficiency in senescence. *Archives of Psychology, No. 188.*

Goldenberg, H. 1977. *Abnormal Psychology: A Social/Community Approach.* Monterey, California: Brooks/Cole.

Graham, F. K., and Kendall, B. S. 1960. Memory-for-designs test: Revised general manual. *Perceptual and Motor Skills, 11,* 147–188.

Grosicki, J. P. 1968. Effect of operant conditioning on modification of incontinence in neuro-psychiatric geriatric patients. *Nursing Research, 17,* 304–311.

Harris, C. S., and Ivory, P. B. C. B. 1976. An outcome evaluation of reality orientation therapy with geriatric patients in a state mental hospital. *Gerontologist, 16,* 496–507.

Hebb, D. O. 1961. Distinctive features of learning in the higher animal. *In,* J. F. Delafresneye (ed.), *Brain Mechanisms and Learning,* pp. 37–46. Oxford, England: Blackwell.

Hilbert, N. M., Niederehe, G., and Kahn, R. L. 1976. Accuracy and speed of memory in depressed and organic aged. *Educational Gerontology, 1,* 131–146.

Howard, A. R. 1966. A fifteen-year follow-up with the Wechsler Memory Scale. *Journal of Consulting Psychology, 30,* 175–176.

Hoyer, W. J., Kafer, R. A., Simpson, S. C., and Hoyer, F. W. 1974. Reinstatement of verbal behavior in elderly patients using operant procedures. *Gerontologist, 14,* 149–152.

Hulicka, I. M. 1966. Age differences in Wechsler Memory Scale scores. *Journal of Genetic Psychology, 109,* 135–145.

Hulicka, I. M., and Wheeler, D. 1976. Recall scores of old and young people as a function of registration intervals. *Educational Gerontology, 1,* 361–372.

INGLIS, J. 1959. A paired-associate learning test for use with elderly psychiatric patients. *Journal of Mental Science, 105,* 440–447.

INGLIS, J. 1970. Memory disorder. *In,* C. G. Costello (ed.), *Symptoms of Psychopathology,* pp. 95–133. New York: John Wiley.

INGLIS, J., AND SANDERSON, R. E. 1961. Successive responses to simultaneous stimulation in elderly patients with memory disorder. *Journal of Abnormal and Social Psychology, 62,* 709–712.

KASTENBAUM, R. 1972. Beer, wine, and mutual gratification in the gerontopolis. *In,* D. P. Kent, R. Kastenbaum, and S. Sherwood (eds.), *Research Planning and Action for the Elderly,* pp. 365–394. New York: Behavioral Publications.

KASTENBAUM, R., AND SLATER, P. E. 1964. Effects of wine on the interpersonal behavior of geriatric patients: An exploratory study. *In,* R. Kastenbaum (ed.), *New Thoughts on Old Age,* pp. 191–204. New York: Springer.

KATKIN, E. S. 1971. *Instrumental Autonomic Conditioning.* New York: General Learning Press.

KAUSLER, D. H. 1970. Retention-forgetting as a nomothological network for developmental research. *In,* L. R. Goulet and P. B. Baltes (eds.), *Life Span Developmental Psychology,* pp. 305–353. New York: Academic Press.

KAY, H. 1951. Learning of a serial task by different age groups. *Quarterly Journal of Experimental Psychology, 3,* 166–183.

KAY, H. 1966. The retrieval of information by older subjects. *Proceedings 7th International Congress of Gerontology,* Vienna, *8,* 7–20.

KEAR-COLWELL, J. J. 1973. The structure of the Wechsler Memory Scale and its relationship to "brain damage." *British Journal of Social and Clinical Psychology, 12,* 384–392.

KELLETT, J. M., COPELAND, J. R. R., AND KELLEHER, M. J. 1975. Information leading to accurate diagnosis in the elderly. *British Journal of Psychiatry, 126,* 423–430.

KELLY, G. A. 1955. *The Psychology of Personal Constructs. Volumes 1 and 2.* New York: Norton.

KENDRICK, D. C., PARBOOSINGH, R. C., AND POST, F. 1965. A synonym learning test for use with elderly psychiatric patients: A validation study. *British Journal of Social and Clinical Psychology, 4,* 63–71.

KIMBLE, G. A., AND PENNYPACKER, H. S. 1963. Eyelid conditioning in young and aged subjects. *Journal of Genetic Psychology, 103,* 283–289.

KLONOFF, H., AND KENNEDY, M. 1965. Memory and perceptual functioning in octogenarians and nonagenarians in the community. *Journal of Gerontology, 20,* 328–333.

KLONOFF, H., AND KENNEDY, M. 1966. A comparative study of cognitive functioning in old age. *Journal of Gerontology, 21,* 239–243.

KRAL, V. A. 1958. Senescent memory decline and senile amnesic syndrome. *American Journal of Psychiatry, 115,* 361–362.

KRAMER, M. 1969. Cross-national study of diagnosis of the mental disorders: Origin of the problem. *American Journal of Psychiatry, Suppl. 125,* 1–11.

LAIR, C. V., AND MOON, W. H. 1972. The effects of praise and reproof on the performance of middle aged and older subjects. *Aging and Human Development, 3,* 279–284.

LAWTON, M. P. 1977. The impact of the environment on aging and behavior. *In,* J. E. Birren and K. W. Schaie (eds.), *Handbook of the Psychology of Aging,* pp. 276–301. New York: Van Nostrand Reinhold.

LAZARUS, A. A. 1977. Has behavior therapy outlived its usefulness? *American Psychologist, 32,* 550–553.

LEECH, S., AND WITTE, K. L. 1971. Paired-associate learning in elderly adults as related to pacing and incentive conditions. *Developmental Psychology, 5,* 180.

LEY, P. 1970. Acute psychiatric patients. *In,* P. Mittler (ed.), *The Psychological Assessment of Mental and Physical Handicaps,* pp. 205–236. London: Methuen.

LIBB, J. W., AND CLEMENTS, C. B. 1969. Token reinforcement in an exercise program for hospitalized geriatric patients. *Perceptual and Motor Skills, 28,* 957–958.

LINSK, N., HOWE, M. W., AND PINKSTON, E. M. 1975. Behavioral group work in a home for the aged. *Social Work, 20,* 454–463.

LYSAK, A., FISHER, R. H., AND SHEDLETSKY, R. 1977. The Boar's Head. *Proceedings,* Canadian Association on Gerontology, Montreal, p. 21.

MACDONALD, M. L., AND BUTLER, A. K. 1974. Reversal of helplessness: Producing walking behavior in nursing home wheelchair residents using behavior modification procedures. *Journal of Gerontology, 29,* 97–101.

MACKAY, H. A., AND INGLIS, J. 1963. The effect of age on a short-term auditory storage process. *Gerontologia, 8,* 193–200.

MARKUS, H. 1977. Self-schemata and information processing about the self. *Journal of Personality and Social Psychology, 35,* 63–78.

MARSH, G. R., AND THOMPSON, L. W. 1977. Psychophysiology of aging. *In,* J. E. Birren and K. W. Schaie (eds.), *Handbook of the Psychology of Aging,* pp. 219–248. New York: Van Nostrand Reinhold.

MILLER, E. 1971. On the nature of memory disorder in presenile dementia. *Neuropsychologia, 9,* 75–81.

MILLER, E. 1975. Impaired recall and the memory disturbance in presenile dementia. *British Journal of Social and Clinical Psychology, 14,* 73–79.

MONGE, R., AND HULTSCH, D. 1971. Paired-associate learning as a function of adult age and the length of the anticipation and inspection intervals. *Journal of Gerontology, 26,* 157–162.

MOWRER, O. H. 1960. *Learning Theory and Behavior.* New York: John Wiley.

MUELLER, D. J., AND ATLAS, L. 1972. Resocialization of regressed elderly residents: A behavioral management approach. *Journal of Gerontology, 27,* 390–392.

NASH, O. 1975. *I Wouldn't Have Missed It—Selected Poems of Ogden Nash.* New York: Little, Brown.

NEISSER, U. 1976. *Cognition and Reality.* San Francisco: W. H. Freeman.

NEWCOMBE, F., AND STEINBERG, B. 1964. Some aspects of learning and memory function in older psychiatric patients. *Journal of Gerontology, 19,* 490–493.

PETTIGREW, L. E., AND KEITH, L. T. 1975. New learning by geriatric subjects. *Language and Speech, 18,* 255–263.

POSTMAN, L., AND UNDERWOOD, B. J. 1973. Critical issues in interference theory. *Memory and Cognition, 1,* 19–40.

RABBITT, P. M. A. 1965. An age decrement in the ability to ignore irrelevant information. *Journal of Gerontology, 20,* 233–238.

ROBERTSON-TCHABO, E. A., HAUSMAN, C. P., AND ARENBERG, D. 1976. A classical mnemonic for older learners: A trip that works! *Educational Gerontology, 1,* 215–226.

ROSS, E. 1968. Effects of challenging and supportive instructions on verbal learning in older persons. *Journal of Educational Psychology, 59,* 261–266.

SACCUZZO, D. P. 1977. Bridges between schizophrenia and gerontology: Generalized or specific deficits. *Psychological Bulletin, 84,* 595–600.

SAVAGE, R. D., BRITTON, P. G., BOLTON, N., AND HALL, E. H. 1973. *Intellectual Functioning in the Aged.* London: Methuen.

SAVAGE, R. D., AND HALL, E. H. 1973. A performance learning measure for the aged. *British Journal of Psychiatry, 122,* 721–723.

SCHONFIELD, D. 1965. Memory changes with age. *Nature, 208,* 918.

SCHONFIELD, D. 1975. Delineating the loci of loss. *In,* L. W. Poon and J. L. Fozard (eds.), *Design Conference on Decision Making and Aging,* pp. 1–12. Cambridge, Mass.: National Institute on Aging and Veterans Administration.

SCHONFIELD, D., AND ROBERTSON, B. A. 1966. Memory storage and aging. *Canadian Journal of Psychology, 20,* 228–236.

SCHONFIELD, D., AND STONES, M. J. 1979. Remembering and aging. *In,* J. F. Kihlstrom and F. J. Evans (eds.), *Functional Disorders of Memory.* Hillsdale, N.J.: Erlbaum.

SCHONFIELD, D., TRUEMAN, V., AND KLINE, D. 1972. Recognition tests of dichotic listening and the age var-

iable. *Journal of Gerontology, 27,* 487–493.

SHAPIRO, M. B., AND NELSON, E. 1955. An investigation of the nature of cognitive impairment in cooperative psychiatric patients. *British Journal of Medical Psychology, 28,* 239–256.

SHAPIRO, M. B., POST, F., LOFVING, B., AND INGLIS, J. 1956. Memory function in psychiatric patients over sixty, some methodological and diagnostic implications. *Journal of Mental Science, 102,* 233–246.

SHMAVONIAN, B. M., MILLER, L. H., AND COHEN, S. I. 1968. Differences among age and sex groups in electrodermal conditioning. *Psycho-physiology, 5,* 119–131.

SHMAVONIAN, B. M., MILLER, L. H., AND COHEN, S. I. 1970. Differences among age and sex groups with respect to cardiovascular conditioning and reactivity. *Journal of Gerontology, 25,* 87–94.

SHMAVONIAN, B. M., YARMAT, A. J., AND COHEN, S. I. 1965. Relationships between the autonomic nervous system and central nervous system in age differences in behavior. *In,* A. T. Welford and J. E. Birren (eds.), *Behaviour, Aging and the Nervous System,* pp. 235–258. Springfield, Ill.: Charles C Thomas.

SIMON, J. R. 1967. Reaction time as a function of SR correspondence, age and sex. *Ergonomics, 10,* 659–664.

SMITH, A. D. 1977. Adult age differences in cued recall. *Developmental Psychology, 13,* 326–331.

SMITH, S. L. 1974. *Age differences in part and whole learning.* Unpublished Doctoral thesis, University of Calgary.

SOLYOM, L., AND BARIK, H. C. 1965. Conditioning in senescence and senility. *Journal of Gerontology, 20,* 483–488.

STEPHENS, L. P. (Ed.) 1970. *Reality Orientation.* Washington, D.C.: American Psychiatric Association Hospital and Community Psychiatry Service.

TAULBEE, L. R., AND FOLSOM, J. C. 1966. Reality orientation for geriatric patients. *Hospital and Community Psychiatry, 17,* 133–135.

THORNDIKE, E. L., BREGMAN, E. O., TILTON, J. W., AND WOODWARD, E. 1928. *Adult Learning.* New York: Macmillan.

TOLMAN, E. C. 1949. There is more than one kind of learning. *Psychological Review, 56,* 144–145.

TULVING, E. 1972. Episodic and semantic memory. *In,* E. Tulving and W. Donaldson (eds.), *Organization of Memory,* pp. 382–403. New York: Academic Press.

UNDERWOOD, B. J. 1964. The representativeness of rote verbal learning. *In,* A. W. Melton (ed.), *Categories of Human Learning,* pp. 48–78. New York: Academic Press.

WALTON, D., AND BLACK, D. A. 1959. The predictive validity of a psychological test of brain damage. *Journal of Mental Science, 105,* 807–810.

WARRINGTON, E. K., AND WEISKRANTZ, L. 1968. A new method of testing long-term retention with special reference to amnesic patients. *Nature, 217,* 972–974.

WECHSLER, D. 1945. A standardized memory scale for clinical use. *Journal of Psychology, 19,* 87–95.

WELFORD, A. T. 1958. *Ageing and Human Skill.* London: Oxford University Press.

WELFORD, A. T. 1977. Motor performance. *In,* J. E. Birren and K. W. Schaie (eds.), *Handbook of the Psychology of Aging,* pp. 450–496. New York: Van Nostrand Reinhold.

WHITEHEAD, A. 1973. Verbal learning and memory in elderly depressives. *British Journal of Psychiatry, 123,* 203–208.

WHITMAN, J. R., BROWN, C. C., AND GANTT, W. W. 1961. Application of conditioning procedures in the study of aging. *In,* J. Wortis (ed.), *Recent Advances in Biological Psychiatry,* pp. 54–57. New York: Plenum Press.

WIGDOR, B. T., AND KRAL, V. A. 1961. Senescent memory function as an indicator of the general preservation of the aging human organism. *Proceedings of Third World Congress of Psychiatry,* pp. 682–686. Toronto: University of Toronto.

WILLIAMS, M. 1970. Geriatric patients. *In,* P. Mittler (ed.), *The Psychological Assessment of Mental and Physical Handicaps,* pp. 319–339. London: Methuen.

WOODWORTH, R. S. 1958. *Dynamics of Behavior.* New York: Henry Holt.

ZARETSKY, H. H., AND BRUCKER, B. S. 1976. Verbal discrimination learning as a function of brain damage, aging and institutionalization. *Journal of General Psychology, 95,* 303–312.

# 11

# Drives
# and Motivations
# with Aging

*Blossom T. Wigdor*

## INTRODUCTION

The topic of drives and motivation in humans has been one of the most difficult for students of human behavior owing to the complexity of the variables involved and the lack of a comprehensive theoretical framework. The problem is even more complex when one attempts to look at the human adult in the late years of the life span. The variety of past experiences as well as individual differences in the physiological changes with age create a condition which does not lend itself easily to generalization for a group of middle-aged or aged individuals or about the process of growing old. No attempt will be made in this chapter to cover the animal research on drives and motivation except to cite some studies which may have a direct bearing on understanding motivation in the older adult. Similarly no pretense is made to cover the entire motivation literature or the various theories which tend to lead to different approaches to this topic. The understanding of motivation in the older adult is of importance in changing situations to maintain involvement and prevent the withdrawal which damages the functioning of the individual both physically and mentally. It has been shown that individuals who remain involved tend to have greater life satisfaction and better general functioning. Furthermore, better understanding of motivational changes with aging would be useful in developing programs and environments which would result in optimal functioning.

A review of the literature makes it quite clear that there is a paucity of empirical research on drives and motivation of the human adult and certainly little in terms of the relationship between motivation and aging. One concludes, as did Neugarten (1977) in relation to personality, that motivation influences aging, and aging influences motivation. This means that the way in which the individual interacted in terms of his physiological condition and cognitive-perceptual processes throughout his lifetime will have had an effect on the way adaptation took place. Adequate adaptation in terms of mental and physical health will have played a part in determining the aging process. In addition, good mental health will be crucial in determining the perceptual appreciation of actual situations, and thus in interacting with the physical condition of the individual to determine motivation in the later years.

### DEFINITIONS

Terms like motivated behavior or motivation are sometimes used loosely. In this chapter, *motivation* refers to the energizers of behavior and the sources of energy in a particular set of responses that keep them dominant over others and account for continuity and direction of behavior (Hebb, 1955). *Needs, drives, incentives* and *goals* are all included under this general heading. *Drive* is seen as the energy impetus arising from a basic physiological or psychological need and external stimulation which results in heightened arousal. Drive tends to result in activity but interacts with incentives to determine choice of activity. *Incentives* are sometimes used interchangeably with goals and are significantly affected by learned behavior, habit patterns, or the development of a hierarchy of secondary needs, or even a functional autonomy of motives.

## THE BASIC DRIVES AND CHANGES WITH AGE

### HUNGER AND THIRST

The debate over basic drives in humans continues as it becomes increasingly difficult to describe at what level the human organism is pushed to activity as well as the form of that activity. The role of incentives and habit patterns as well as the properties of reinforcers is still open to investigation. However, it is generally accepted that hunger and thirst are primary drives that must be satisfied. On a physiological basis, with advancing age there is a slowing in the functioning of the central nervous system and consequently of the general somatic metabolism. Thus, in animal studies there is some evidence of reduced drive for activity when related to amount of consumption. There is a decreased need on a physiological level for food and drink in aging humans as well. However, behavior related to the satisfaction of these basic drives and needs cannot be explained in terms only of lowered physiological drive. It is clear that learning, both in terms of direct conditioning and vicarious learning, results in behavior which does not reflect the reduced physiological need (Bandura, 1969). For example, many older individuals do not modify their eating habits unless there is some significant change in their external environment. If they associate eating heartily with good health they may actually overeat in terms of actual need. If, however, they find there is a weight gain, they may modify behavior if there are other incentives such as compelling cosmetic or physical reasons. On the other hand, the secondary social incentives are often lacking for the aged and many of the elderly suffer from malnutrition and various physical complications because there is no incentive to prepare food even if there is no economic deprivation. If one defines motivation as the impulse to action, the motivation to eat or drink with aging seems more related to established habit patterns or learned social behavior and the immediate social situation than to basic needs associated with fundamental drives.

### HOMEOSTASIS

Even for homeostasis, in terms of maintaining body temperature or in terms of other systems coping with adjustments to the environment, there is evidence of the slower responsiveness of the aging organism. However, early life experiences seem to condition the organism in terms of its ability to adjust for or compensate for environmental changes. For example, animal studies show that rats raised under extreme conditions of cold adapted better to living conditions of old age (Margolin and Bunch, 1940).

There is evidence that the changes in the hypothalamus reduce the reliability of homeostatic control in the aged. Everitt and Burgess (1976) suggest that the hypothalamus is less sensitive in reading blood levels and other input and that it is less efficient in bringing about necessary somatic adjustments, for example, blood glucose levels. Exton-Smith and Grimley Evans (1977) have shown that humans are not able to maintain body temperature in the face of extreme high or low temperatures, and attribute this to reduced sensitivity of the hypothalamus in regulating or effecting the necessary adjustments. Thus, if indeed the feedback mechanisms from the hypothalamus and pituitary are slow and inadequate, the ability of the individual to adapt to changing environmental and somatic circumstances is restrictive with advancing age. Consequently, advance planning may be more important for the aged to allow for compensatory behavior. The aged individual may make adjustments to change more slowly or in a limited way.

## SEX

There is some tradition to view sex as a primary drive or need in humans, although among the basic drives the expression and fulfillment of this drive is most subject to learning and the influence of social conditions. In most animals, but particularly in primates, sexual behavior is changed or modified by early environment, habit patterns, and learned preferences (Harlow, 1962). With advancing age, there is evidence in animal studies of diminution of strength of drives and higher levels of arousal. That is, the older animals need a higher level of stimulation to achieve arousal. Available studies suggest that these changes are also characteristic of humans (Masters and Johnson, 1966; Pfeiffer and Davis, 1972). However, the learned behavior, past history, and present physical and social situation obviously play an even more important role in the actual motivation of the elderly to act in terms of fulfilling this need. There is some evidence to support the contention that, in this area as well as in relation to food and drink, early habits influence the manifest behavior to fulfill this basic drive. Individuals who have been active in early life and have maintained high levels of interest and activity show a tendency to maintain sexual activity longer and more frequently. There is, however, a significant problem from a mental health point of view in that it may be more difficult to satisfy this need with increasing age because of social taboos, loss of marital partners, reduction in novelty, and possible habit patterns regarding sexual expression which may not be adaptive relative to the changed capacity of the older person. The interdependence of mood, feelings of anxiety and performance, or the thwarting of expression and resulting frustration are particularly important in the expression of the sexual drive. (For fuller discussion see chapters in this Handbook by Comfort and by Corby and Solnick).

## EXPLORATORY DRIVE

Activity, exploration, and curiosity have been the focus of various theoretical approaches in attempts to resolve the basic nature of these drives. However, Hebb (1955), Heron (1966), and others have shown that activity and exploratory behavior seem to be basic drives of the healthy organism, particularly evident when survival needs are fulfilled. Here again the strength of the drives seems reduced in older animals and also in elderly humans. Physiological changes, in terms of slowing of the organism and a lowered general energy level, may provide only a partial explanation. In the elderly, lowered energy level may mean that a higher proportion of the available energy is utilized to fulfill the basic needs for food, shelter, and thirst, and there may be little left for exploratory behavior. The question of satiation or lack of novelty is again raised as an element in arousing the organism to action. Nevertheless, the evidence suggests that the healthy individual tends to seek activity and stimulation even when aged, and shows better life satisfaction under these conditions (deCharms and Muir, 1978; Maddox, 1968).

The tendency to reduce activities and the actual degree of change in drive in the older individual are difficult to assess and to separate from the habit patterns developed over the lifetime and from the presence or absence of sufficiently strong incentives. The rewards for activity may actually be so small compared to the energy involved that this may tend to inhibit activity. However, rather than a diminution of a wide range of activities, there seems to be a substitution process, either because of external circumstances or by choice (Dawson and Baller, 1972; Hearn, 1972; Maddox, 1968). Decline in activity is usually dictated by poor health or perceived poor health and by economic constraints (Sherman, 1974; Tissue, 1971; Youmans, 1968). For the most part, healthy individuals substitute activities or change their strategy. The concept of perceived health status is important to consider here since there is evidence that actual state of health may be less of a factor in maintaining activities than perceived health (Kral and Wigdor, 1957). In the study just mentioned, of a group of elderly presenting themselves to a multidisciplinary clinic in a general hospital, it was striking to note that there was a significant percentage of patients who had organic deficits and who carried on their daily activities of living well, compared to a group of less impaired individuals who showed much poorer functioning. Thus, some intervening variables seem to play a role, and one could attribute this to motivation, incentive, or personality.

There is, however, evidence that both young and old animals will perform in order to produce a change in level of stimulation (Elias and Elias, 1977). In humans, the need for stimulation is evident and is reflected in the frequent complaints of boredom and frustration in older adults. However, this need does not always lead to action.

It is now recognized that there is a need for the organism to adapt to, learn about, and control the environment (Buck, 1976). Drive theory in the classical sense was questioned by investigators who showed that healthy animals are not inactive when their bodily needs are met. They show curiosity, explore the environment, and seem to seek stimulation. Sensory deprivation studies showed that in isolation subjects suffered boredom, restlessness, irritability, and apparent hunger for stimulation (Bexton, Heron, and Scott, 1954). The concept of exploratory drive involves the acceptance of the idea that under some conditions drive reduction involves an increase in stimulation. Berlyne (1960) explains curiosity, exploratory behavior, and the effects of sensory deprivation by assuming that the relationship between drive and the variety and complexity of stimulation is curvilinear; that is, both very high and very low levels of stimulation can be associated with high drive. Hebb (1955), approaching the subject from the point of view of arousal theory, argues that there is an optimal level of drive and that when there is a high level of drive a response that decreases it will be reinforced. Thus, the original state of the organism will be important in determining what will be reinforced. Individual differences in energy level and learned patterns will thus account for much of the variation of behavior in the elderly. However, the negative effects of nonstimulation, such as irritability, boredom, and restlessness, are seen frequently in the elderly and may be mistaken for mental illness or ignored if they are perceived as part of the normal aging process.

## NEED FOR ACHIEVEMENT AND COMPETENCE

The development of a need for achievement and competence is argued by some as a primary need which may be thwarted or distorted by lack of reinforcement or negative feedback. By others, it is seen as a secondary need, determined by learning in a society which values competitive striving and achievement as an important element in self-esteem. In the search for clarity, there is some evidence that need for competence should be separated from need for achievement. It is easier to justify need for competence as a primary drive, while need for achievement may be seen as more dependent on learning and social reinforcement.

Cognitive functioning plays an important role in the drive for competence and, although there is an interaction with physiological functioning, it is not clear from current research the extent to which behavior is actually determined by the cognitive versus the physiological changes in the so-called healthy aged individual. It is possible that decrease in achievement motivation and lower levels of aspiration may be reactions to poorer cognitive functioning or general performance (Chown, 1977; Schaie and Strother, 1968). In laboratory studies where attempts were made to look at the relationship between the differences of performance and the meaningfulness of material, it was found that with increased meaningfulness age differences diminished although they did not disappear completely (Craik and Masani, 1967; Elias and Elias, 1977; Powell, Eisdorfer, and Bogdonoff, 1964; Shmavonian and Busse, 1963). However, the assumption of Shmavonian and Busse (1963) that increased galvanic skin response (GSR) activity was a reflection of increased cognitive involvement may be questioned. Others (Craik and Masani, 1967), using an experimental design manipulating the meaningfulness of English words, found that there was an increase in the difference between young and old in the task performance, These studies do not give a clear answer, but methodological problems also contribute to the confusion. It is difficult to separate meaningfulness in the experimental task from complexity, and to separate possibly increased arousal from the question of interference by anxiety. In their review of this literature Elias and Elias (1977) point out that the evidence in comparing old and young subjects is that the elderly do consistently more poorly than young groups on paired-associate learning tasks under most conditions, but that increased meaningfulness usually results in better performance for both groups. However, the difference between the groups may be increased in favor of the young if the material lends itself to organization. The seemingly contradictory results in studies (Craik and Masani, 1967; Wittels, 1972) in this area appear to be related to methodological difficulties in separating meaningfulness from task difficulty and complexity.

Nevertheless, there seems no doubt that a cognitive factor relating to meaningfulness both of the material and of the situation plays an important part in determining the incentive to respond to stimuli.

Conditioning experiments (Braun and Geiselhart, 1959; Kimble and Pennypacker, 1963) show greater difficulty in conditioning the aged, but recent work suggests there is little evidence that classical conditioning decreases with increasing age in the rat (Arenberg and Robertson-Tchabo, 1977). In a study in which preparatory signals were used to set subjects to respond to a stimulus, both young and old subjects improved their performance (Botwinick, Brinley, and Robbin, 1959). The implication of this finding for motivation is that the older subjects behaved similarly to younger subjects depending on conditions of learning. They may perform less well, but obviously cognitive appraisal of situations has an important role to play in the functioning of the aged. This is not independent of the physiological changes, but exists in interaction with them.

The healthy or normal aging process seems to indicate that all the mechanisms that operate to maintain incentive or motivation in the younger organism continue to do so as the organism ages, in spite of the fact that there seems to be a general reduction in the strength of the various drives. The incentive for each individual will be modified by previous learning, habit patterns, and cognitive appraisal of the actual situation in which the individual is functioning. Pathological conditions, either physiological or functional, due either to changes in the central nervous system or to the frequent psychological disorders found in the aged, such as excessive anxiety or depression, will significantly affect the drives and motivation of the elderly.

Of course, this is true of young individuals as well. The significant difference is the number of necessary adaptations which affect secondary needs in the adult who is entering middle or old age. The elderly adult is more likely to be faced with negative situations involving losses, little positive reinforcement, and decreased physical capacity. In particular, our society tends to offer fewer rewards to the aged for exploratory behavior and to create more barriers to achievement and to fulfillment of feelings of competence. A condition of motivation may also be perception of future opportunities, which may be diminished in the aged. This is more likely to give rise to feelings of frustration and withdrawal avoidance behavior. As Elias and Elias (1977) point out, decreases in exploratory behavior with advancing age may apply only to specific strains and for specific periods of the life span. It may also be that these are transition periods and are affected more significantly by personal and social circumstances.

## PHYSIOLOGICAL CHANGES IN THE CENTRAL NERVOUS SYSTEM AND THEIR RELATION TO MOTIVATION

A consideration of the physiological basis of need and motivation revolves about the functioning of the central nervous system (CNS) and particularly the various levels of "brain" function. No attempt will be made to review this material comprehensively here. The reticular system, diffuse thalamic system, and hypothalamus are still not fully understood in terms of their role in motivation. However, they seem to be central to the functioning of those systems which are most closely related to the needs and drives which underly much that is covered by motivation. If one considers that there is fairly conclusive evidence of slowing of the CNS and some atrophy of cortical and subcortical structures with aging, the amount of stimulation needed for arousal is probably higher in the aged. Furthermore, the endocrine system, and particularly the adrenal cortical responses, are slower. Thus, related lowered ability to cope with stress may be reflected in withdrawal and avoidance behavior, and consequently in a reduction of activity. This reduction of activity can be interpreted as lowered motivational drive.

One may speculate too that pathological changes as well as normal changes with age in the hypothalamic, limbic, or reticular systems of the brain, as well as cortical changes in the temporal and frontal regions, may lower drive. Furthermore, changes in the frontal area, which involves mechanisms which trigger or initiate behavior and many emotional reactions, may account for some of the difficulty in initiating behavior seen in the elderly. These changes may be thus partly due to organic changes as well as to psychological or social reasons.

The work of Strelau (1970) suggests that the more aroused the nervous system, the less the excitation produced by a given stimulus, and that therefore a less aroused nervous system may be relatively reactive to stimulation and a highly aroused nervous system relatively resistant to stimulation. The healthier CNS may be insensitive to weak stimuli but able to cope with strong stimuli, while the weak type is effective in dealing with weak stimuli but cannot cope with intense or massed stimulation (Sales, 1971). Thus, exploratory or stimulus-seeking behavior may vary considerably depending on the state of the individual. Therapeutic approaches may have to vary to arouse the individual to an optimal level. The importance of relating cognitive appraisal of situations to this behavior cannot be overlooked. Studies have indicated that the same stimulus may or may not be stressful, depending on the individual's cognitive appraisal. This appraisal is determined not only by the physiological capacity of the individual, but by situational, personality, and cultural factors (Lazarus and Opton, 1966).

The concept outlined by Bindra (1976), of viewing goal-directed behavior as the resultant of the interaction of the organismic state of the individual and the situational incentives, seems to account for much of the behavior of the aged. The parameters and limits of the possible resultant behavior are not yet clear.

## INTERPERSONAL AND CULTURAL INFLUENCES

The primary drives are sometimes difficult to separate from the secondary and even more complex motivators which develop out of a hierarchy of secondary needs. These secondary needs develop for the individual out of the learning that takes place at the interpersonal level, leading to particular motivational situations for the individual, as well as from the general societal reinforcers which stem from cultural influences. The individual's value system stems from reinforcement at both these levels and will be central to the kinds of motives the individual responds to and the activities he engages in. Thus, level of drive will depend to some extent on the general level of arousal of the organism, and the learning throughout the life span. A particular situation will either maximize the drive level or operate to reduce it.

The way individuals have learned to satisfy their primary needs is most important in the adaptation to the aging process. The eating and drinking habits of a lifetime are based on both interpersonal relationships and the patterns of the society. Much socializing is associated with eating and drinking in our society. They are symbols of acceptance and love and of belonging to some group, and thus are related not only to the need to satisfy hunger and thirst, but to the needs for affiliation, recognition, self-esteem, and affection.

Our society tends to reinforce the need for achievement, competence, competitiveness, and acquisition. It tends to value technological advance and productivity in a material sense and to measure these in terms of speed and financial reward. The major reinforcers in our culture tend to develop habit patterns and emphasize incentives for activity which may not be adaptive or appropriate to the changing life situations with advancing age. Loss of spouse and friends due to illness, death, or geographic relocation may make it increasingly diffi-

cult to maintain a social group, either in terms of a family situation or in terms of purely social activities. Therefore, the motivation for many of the activities surrounding eating and drinking may diminish or disappear. With retirement, the structure which reinforced our needs for achievement, recognition, self-esteem, and competence are for many withdrawn. It is also difficult to simply internalize these needs and satisfy them in alternative ways, since our society has no formal roles for satisfying these needs for the older individuals. Other economic and social factors may also interfere. In fact, the public image tends to portray the senior citizen as incompetent in most public roles except perhaps for isolated political activities.

## ADAPTIVE CHANGES IN MOTIVATION WITH AGING

### NOVELTY AND CURIOSITY VERSUS MEANINGFULNESS AND CREATIVITY

As stated previously, novelty in motivating behavior or in serving as an incentive is probably related to a general exploratory-curiosity-manipulatory drive which essentially is a tendency to seek varied stimulation (Hebb, 1955). This can be related to the curiosity drive of Berlyne (1960) where a modicum of fear seems to stimulate activity. However, if a stimulus goes beyond an optimal level of arousal it may acquire a negative value (Hebb, 1955).

In the aged, novelty may not be an effective drive stimulus if it is threatening and arouses anxiety or produces a stressful situation. This may be similar to the factors operating in learning experiments where Eisdorfer, Nowlin, and Wilkie (1970) showed that motivation increased beyond an optimum level for efficiency might account for decrements in performance (Arenberg and Robertson-Tchabo, 1977). Paré (1969) showed that age differences were abolished in a learning task when discrimination complexity was decreased. The Eisdorfer studies (Eisdorfer *et al.*, 1970; Eisdorfer, Conner, and Wilkie, 1968; Troyer, Eisdorfer, Bogdonoff, and Wilkie, 1967; Troyer, Eisdorfer, Wilkie, and Bogdonoff, 1966) attempted to clarify the conditions in which performance decrements appear. They found that errors of omission exceeded errors of commission and that both types of error were increased when the rate of task pacing was high (Eisdorfer *et al.*, 1968; Troyer *et al.*, 1967). Eisdorfer postulated from his data that the omission errors were a response inhibition due to heightened situational anxiety. Some support for this hypothesis was found in the observation that the performance of elderly improved significantly when taskpacing was reduced. Of particular importance was a greater improvement for omission errors than for commission errors. Thus, the data were consistent with the idea that the rapid task-pacing induced increasing anxiety. To test this hypothesis further, a measure of arousal independent of performance measure was necessary. Eisdorfer and his group then employed free fatty acid (FFA) levels and measures of heart rate as well as galvanic skin response (GSR) to indicate level of arousal. In a serial learning task the older group exhibited higher FFA levels than the younger group and performed more poorly (Powell, Eisdorfer, and Bogdonoff, 1964).

In a second study with only elderly subjects, degree of arousal was related to performance in a curvilinear manner (Troyer *et al.*, 1966). However, this did not prove a cause and effect relationship, although it did indicate that the task was more stressful for the older subjects. Consequently, Eisdorfer *et al.* (1970) used a drug (propranodol) which had an autonomic nervous system blocking action, but which had a minimal effect on the central nervous system activation or deactivation, to test for support of the original hypothesis. Older men were given the propranodol and compared with a control group who were administered a placebo. The two groups were compared on a rote learning task performance and on FFA, heart rate, GSR, the Wechsler Adult Intelligence Scale, the Taylor Anxiety Scale, and a test of organic brain impairment. There was a significant difference between the groups only in the decrease in total number of errors for the older group. The older men also showed a decrease in FFA after drug administration as compared to the control (placebo) group who showed a rise in FFA. Heart rate and GSR changed in same direction but not as significantly. These data provide some support for the view that the autonomic nervous system activation associated with task requirements may contribute to performance decrement. As Elias and Elias (1977) pointed out, a finding that errors of omission were even more favorably affected by drug treatment than errors of commission would have provided better evidence in support of the anxiety arousal interpretation. In addition, the use of a younger comparison group would have helped distinguish between motivational and cognitive factors as important determinants of age difference in performance. Thus, although not definitive, the Eisdorfer *et al.* studies give some support to the idea of overarousal interfering with performance in investigations of aging. Consequently, a degree

of novelty in the aged may act as an incentive but overarousal may impair performance. The problem of optimal limits is thus of importance in this regard. Shift of incentives from novelty and curiosity to meaningfulness and creativity is suggested, but difficult to support empirically. Shmavonian and Busse (1963) showed that both old and young tend to show better performance with increase in task meaningfulness, but older persons seem to be disproportionately more affected by decreases in task meaningfulness than young persons. However, it was not clear in their study that task meaningfulness was separated from task difficulty.

In assessing or predicting behavior in actual situations, it seems quite clear that meaningfulness may be very idiosyncratic but that it plays a role in activating the organism. Creativity, if one limits its definition to the emergence of a most important insight, diminishes with aging, but measures of creative productivity do not show such clear age differences. Lehman (1953) showed an early peaking in the thirties for some fields but, for most, creative productivity continued, based on individual differences. Wayne Dennis (1966) examined creative productivity between the ages of 20 and 80 years by an examination of bibliographies and found that scholars were as productive in their 70s as in their 40s, and were actually more productive in their 60s. For scientists there was a slight decline from their 40s through their 50s and 60s but a sharp drop in their 70s. The decline in the arts is greater since there is a contrast between the steady output of scholars and steep decline in the arts. Dennis (1966) suggested that this greater decline in the arts was because production in this area might depend more on individual creativity while scholars and scientists might depend on a greater accumulation of data and learning and more group effort. A study by Alpaugh and Birren (1977) found age differences in divergent thinking, transformations, and preference for complexity which were congruent with the age changes found in the number of highly creative productions by Lehman (1953). These differences were also found to be more important than differences in intelligence, and thus may be more viable explanations for the changes in creative contributions. The Alpaugh and Birren (1977) study also suggests that two tests such as the Guilford Test of creativity and the Barron-Welsh Art Scale, although both purporting to measure creativity, may actually measure significantly different aspects of creativity. The former may relate more directly to intellectual function and creative problem-solving activity, and the latter scale may reflect a nonaptitude trait such as interest or motivation, and both may be important components of creativity. Thus, the older age group may show decrease in creative production for either one or both of these factors.

In terms of motivation or incentive an examination of the goal-directed behavior in these areas shows continued activity until late in life if the health of the organism is maintained at a reasonable level. It also suggests that with increasing age the individual is more dependent on external stimuli. An unpublished study (Wigdor and Eisenberg, 1975) of retired professors suggests continued productivity but at a slower pace. Senior citizen centers have found as well that the opportunity to engage in new and creative activities was enthusiastically espoused if there was adequate encouragement. Staff enthusiasm and openness seem to be a factor.

The literature on desire or need to work arouses much controversy in terms of "disengagement" versus "activity." The theory of disengagement as proposed by Cumming and Henry (1961) as a reflection of decreased motivation to remain attached or involved has come under heavy fire. Maddox (1968) and others have found that even after retirement, given good health, activity levels tend to be maintained and to be associated with greater life satisfaction. Palmore (1968) also found a clear tendency for aged persons to persist with the same relative levels of activities and attitudes as they grow older. In a study of attitudes to work and leisure in later life, Pfeiffer and Davis (1971) found a disproportionately high percentage of men in the 66–71 age group complained about too much free time, and almost all the men aged 66–71 indicated a preference for continued employment. Some caution should be exercised in generalizing these findings to all retirees.

## CAUTIOUSNESS AND RISK-TAKING

From an examination of the foregoing, the incentive to engage in activities seems to be maintained throughout the life span, but the approach to activities or the barriers to participation may be of considerable importance. There is evidence of increased caution with aging and a tendency to avoid risk-taking. In many studies it is difficult to separate increased caution from decreased competence. To test this, Birkhill and Schaie (1975) examined the performance of elderly individuals under high and low risk conditions. Their elderly showed less reluctance to respond to low-risk situations only when failure to register a response was not penalized. These results suggest that the cautiousness operated least under conditions of low anxiety combined with low risk, but was also

minimized under conditions of high anxiety given that the risk was also high. The results of this study suggested that the performance of the elderly on the Primary Mental Abilities Test could be enhanced markedly by programming of reinforcement conditions. This lends support to the hypothesis that ability-extraneous factors may be crucial in determining the performance of elderly people (Botwinick, 1977; Furry and Baltes, 1973). In addition, the perception of the personal importance of meaning of a situation must be considered as affecting motivation.

In a study which attempted to relate choice in a risk-taking problem to life situations for peer groups, Botwinick (1966) found older subjects more cautious than young subjects. The older subjects made decisions which tended to avoid a risky course of action, regardless of the likelihood of outcome. They seemed to be disinclined to make decisions or were satisfied with conditions which were far from ideal. When the alternatives were equally balanced with respect to risky and safe alternatives, then the problems concerning the aged were solved with less caution than the problems concerning the younger adults by both the young and elderly population. This may reflect a belief that the aged have less to lose than the young with a gamble that goes badly. However, in studies of risk-taking in actual situations such as job turnover with older workers, there seems to be a greater caution and less risk-taking because it seems the perception is one of having more to lose. The differences in various studies are probably attributable to the actual situation and possibly to differences between "young-old" and "old-old" groups. Some gerontologists have noted the acceptance by the old of stereotypes associated with being old and seeing themselves as "worthless" (Butler and Lewis, 1973).

## ENERGY AND PROBLEM-SOLVING

Related to the question of caution and risk-taking is the one of impaired problem-solving ability. The difficulties experienced by older people in problem-solving seem to be a combination of factors involving cognitive changes, including changes in memory, learning, information, processing rate, attention, and perceptual integration among others (Rabbitt, 1977). In terms of incentive or drive the perceived goal or reward in problem-solving may not involve sufficient satisfaction to justify the effort (or pain) of the energy output required in view of more limited resources.

The data arrived at by various approaches indicate that the interaction between the state of the organism and the perceived reward, modified by lifelong patterns, will determine the goal-directed behavior of the older person. The model suggested by Bindra (1976) conceptualizes goal-directed behavior as resulting from an interaction between the organismic condition of the individual and the strength of the same incentives which have operated for that individual throughout a lifetime of developing secondary needs or habit systems and relating them to specific conditions. According to this model, the aging organism would respond in terms of a decreased organismic capacity, varying in degree with the individual, perceived incentives, and present situation. Individual performance or activity will thus vary in light of the strength of the factors mentioned and the demands of the situation. The limits of the effectiveness of these incentives is not known, and therefore it is difficult to answer questions about optimal stimulation. Certainly the evidence is clear that deprivation or overloading may cause decrement of performance whether they occur on a cognitive level or because of fear or anxiety. Birren (1969) pointed out in a study of successful professionals who remained engaged that there is an important reorientation in goals and values with aging. It may be useful to examine the goals, values, and attitudes that may influence the balance between the condition of the individual and the incentives which are likely to result in action.

## ATTITUDES, VALUES, AND GOALS

The adaptive style of the aging individual is probably of prime importance in the type, as well as the number, of goals which are pursued. The energy level of the individual is often seen as identical with the motivational level; but this author postulates that it is more meaningful in the study of aging to see energy as associated with the organismic condition of the individual, including level of arousal, with motivation resulting from this and the existence and strength of meaningful goals or incentives. If one takes this approach, then the adaptation the individual makes will depend on his or her energy level and personal value system as well as that of the social or cultural group in which the individual is functioning (see also Chown, 1977).

In the previously mentioned study of 100 successful professionals, Birren (1969) found that they defined their problems differently from the young and tended to change their goals. The successful professionals recognized both this change in goals and the need to maintain some flexibility in setting shorter-term goals. The older professionals showed an awareness of a need for greater discipline, and

for "control of affect" towards colleagues and juniors, and this tolerance was reflected in how they defined their goals. They seemed to compensate for their limitations and were able to seek advice, conserve time and energy, and distinguish between critical and extraneous tasks. Lowenthal (1972) and Lowenthal, Thurnher, Chiriboga, and Associates (1975) point out that individuals who have been goal-directed may have a temporary period of low morale followed by a substitution of new goals, and that those who are self-protective continue to function without change if their defenses are unchallenged. In a comparison of preretirees and adolescents, Lowenthal and Chiriboga (1973) found that in the older group those with the lowest resources and the lowest deficits were the happiest, while the happiest adolescents had the highest resources and the highest deficits. They conclude that qualities associated with good adjustment at one period of life may make it more difficult to adjust at another period. The crucial variable seemed to be the ability to adapt or change in the face of changing personal circumstances. A recent unpublished study suggests that elderly individuals who are more dependent on inner control than on external control showed greater persistence on a frustrating task and greater degree of life satisfaction (Wigdor and Yankofsky, 1977). There is also considerable evidence that higher education and higher socioeconomic level are positively correlated to high morale and life satisfaction. It is also possible that many extremely creative and goal-directed individuals may experience greater stress during middle age, with resulting breakdown involving depression, cardiovascular disease, and possible earlier mortality. Thus, the older successful group with positive adaptation may be a survivor group (Troll, 1975).

The mental health of the older individual is affected by lifelong coping skills and the appropriateness of the changes made with age. Satisfactory past achievement is more likely to have created a positive personal social environment and will thus facilitate the necessary changes. However, this culture does create stresses because of its emphasis on competitiveness and achievement, and because of the low esteem with which individuals who no longer behave in terms of achievement-related goals are regarded. The stress will also be greatest for those who have difficulty in setting personal goals and defining personal roles, since society has few goals or roles for the older individual except for maintenance roles and goals. Breakdown in mental health may be postulated to occur at old age, as in earlier periods, when adaptation cannot be made because of the inappropriateness of goals in view of the realities of both the cultural climate and the individual capacity. Since social and cultural values seem to be changing rapidly, future cohorts may show differences.

If one accepts Festinger's (1957) theory of cognitive dissonance, then some adaptive behavior of the aged, characterized by withdrawal, avoidance, and reduced involvement, may be due to the recognition of the futility of combating the realities of compulsory retirement, the greater vigor of younger individuals, and the negative value placed on the aged. Breakdown in mental health, in terms of depression or severe anxiety, may occur when it is not possible to reduce the dissonance between the two cognitions. The reaction may be inappropriate behavior and accompanying stress, or lack of goal-directed behavior because of the weak incentive. Some of the most compelling incentives in our culture are associated with power, money, social status, and recognition. Once developed, the individual's incentives tend to remain fairly consistent throughout life, but the goals just mentioned are hard to satisfy in old age. Some of these goals may have been fulfilled and are no longer operative. Nevertheless, in terms of most habit patterns and incentives developed over a lifetime, the same incentives operate but the level of arousal and the level or means of satisfaction may change.

## INTERESTS AND ACTIVITIES

In the concept of successful aging, there is an assumption that a person should be able to look back on his life with a feeling of satisfaction of having reconciled lifetime goals with achievement. If such is the case, achievement needs may diminish with age, but the need for recognition and a sense of personal worth, which has been associated with achievement in our culture, tends to remain. More present-oriented and shorter-term goals may have to be substituted to influence activities and interests. In addition, the condition of the organism and the possible satiation of certain incentives play a part in making some activities more appealing than others.

In reality the individuals who have developed a variety of interests or true involvement in an area tend to maintain these interests, although the behavior in regard to the interest may change somewhat. In a study of retired university professors (Wigdor and Eisenberg, 1975), the retirees reported continuing involvement in professional and research activities. Schaie and Strother (1968) showed some evidence for continuity as well. There is some tendency for men to become more passive in their pursuits and women more assertive in pursuing their own interests (Neugarten and Gutman, 1958). In our clinical experience, women in their later years show some tendency to move away from other-directed, nurturant activities to those more involved with personal satisfaction.

Changes in demographic factors and environment may make the cohort differences more significant than age changes. Schaie and Gribbin (1975) point out the relative strength of cohort and environmental factors in assessing cognitive ability; individual patterns of change over time may reflect increment, decrement, or maintenance of intellectual level regardless of cohort membership, even though maintenance or increment is more characteristic of the more recent than of the older cohorts. Similarly, stability of personality traits tends to be the rule rather than the exception. This may not be due to lack of change, but rather to changes that occur as a function of specific early socialization experiences, commonly shared generation-specific environmental impact, and particular sociocultural transactions (Schaie and Parham, 1976).

## INFLUENCE OF CHANGES IN TIME CONCEPT

The realization in late middle age that life is finite, and that one has a shorter time left to live than one has lived, tends to influence individuals differently. Those who still have a high level of arousal and unfulfilled goals may be spurred to activity—even frenetic activity—to complete a life work. On the other hand, the realization that there may not be enough time to embark on long-term goals may create barriers to activity. The capacity to substitute sufficiently arousing short-term goals for more future-oriented goals is one of the tasks of the later years. The better adapted individuals will find rewarding short-term goals. There has been little or no research on the degree to which individuals shift because of a conscious recognition of a change in the available time frame.

A few studies have been carried out, but little support has been found for the idea that the subjective rate of time passage increases with age. This hypothesis may be based on the results of studies of adults who experience many varied situations and who may have heavy demands on their time. Time which is filled and which involves a variety of experience passes more quickly and seems longer in retrospect. However, it has been hypothesized that older adults value time more, either because they perceive that there is less of it left, because they are anticipating an unpostponable dreaded event, or, conversely, because they are happy. Kuhlen and Monge (1968) studied males and females from the 20s to the 80s, using both a Time Metaphor Test and direct questions, and found that estimates of passage of time did not seem to be related to age per se. For both males and females, the direct measure of passage of time correlated with relative speed of time, not enough spare time, high degree of felt time pressure, past year of life more exciting, and higher present happiness. Thus, sense of speed of time passage seemed related to the extent to which time was filled and to the degree to which events that filled it were viewed as having a positive effect. This study supported the supposition that males in their 40s and 50s felt under greater time pressure than did both the younger and older decades, and that the degree of future orientation, subjective happiness, and excitement were inversely related to age. The trends were similar for females, but only the relationship between age and future orientation was significant. Thus, it may be assumed that for the significantly older group time is less filled, less exciting, and less future-oriented, but that time pressure may be felt because of the awareness of finitude.

Marshall (1975) examined the question of the individual's awareness of time left as an inverse function of age. This hypothesis was clearly supported in that older individuals estimated less time available before death than younger individuals; however, estimates were not in absolute terms but were related to the association between an individual's own age to age-at-death of both their parents. Awareness of finitude was also more related to how individuals perceived their health than to age alone. Lehr (1967) had previously reported that there was great variability with respect to attitudes to the future. Older males in general tended to have more positive attitudes to the future than females, and for all categories of subjects above average intelligence, satisfaction with current life, high activity level, general responsiveness, and positive mood or affect were related to positive attitude to the future. For men and women in the younger (60–65) group, good health and high socioeconomic status were predictive of a positive attitude to the future. For males only, general adjustment and ego control correlated with attitude to the future. Thus, the behavior of the elderly in terms of time left will probably be a function of their perceived health, time pressure, and their previous habits and needs, which may have a functional autonomy and may carry on throughout the life span even if the drives are somewhat decreased.

There seems to be a highly personal time perspective when individuals rate the importance of the past, present, and future. Young adults view the present as better than the past and expect the future to be much better than the present (Bortner and Hultsch, 1972). This trend continued with decreasing difference in the perception of the past, present, and future, but by the 60s the past, present, and future were rated equally, and the 70s saw individuals rating the past better than the present and the present better than the future.

Sex differences in time perception with regard to time left to live in relation to time since birth were also reported by Neugarten (1968) and Back (1971). These differences are probably related to the different life expectancies of the sexes, but one can also speculate on the effect of the life patterns and roles of men and women for those who are already old in our society. It seems clear that factors such as variety of experience, and time pressure were greater for males than females. The differences are probably more significant the higher the education, the greater the intellectual level, and the higher the socioeconomic status. It is likely that the differences in activities in men and women in the higher socioeconomic groups will differ most significantly and that the more highly educated men may have a better opportunity of carrying over a variety of activities which were related to earlier achievement motives. In view of the changing role of women and the upward mobility in North American society, future generations will probably show a different pattern of activity as they reach old age.

## EFFECTS OF PHYSICAL ENVIRONMENT

The preceding discussion about activity and motivation in later years must be taken in the context of assumed good health and a supportive physical environment. This involves adequate income, social relationships, and housing. If the research on motivation in the work place (Herzberg, Mausner, and Snyderman, 1959) has some validity, it should come as no surprise that, if the so-called "hygienic factors" (basic needs related to income and physical surrounding) are out of reach, then the secondary motives will not be effective in influencing goal-directed behavior except for those that may be necessary for survival. In fact, there is some evidence that the level of nutrition in many elderly is extremely poor, and that apathy and depression may take over to the extent that even those activities necessary for survival are not undertaken.

There is significant evidence that housing and/or social isolation have significant effect on the well-being of individuals and on their motivation to be active. The results reported by Carp (1967) have tended to be supported by other studies (Lawton, Nahemow and Teaff, 1975; Schooler, 1970). Demographic, biographic, attitudinal, and other psychological variables were studied in a group of 352 applicants for new public housing (Carp, 1967). The applicants were males and females with a median age of 72 years. The applicants were studied before moving in and 12–15 months after occupying the new residence. A control group consisted of matched applicants who could not move into the new housing. Both males and females showed significant improvement in that residents showed significant increase in level of "happiness," feelings about accomplishment in life, number of leisure activities, activities compared to those engaged in at age 55, present social activities, number of close friends, attitude to family, attitudes to health, and rating of health. The residents showed significant decrease in the number of major health problems, neurotic problems, time on health care, sleeping, and "lost" time. The nonresidents' scores consistently showed no change or decrements. The increase in activity levels is reported in all studies and bears directly on the effects of housing, community identity, and opportunities for social contact.

Elderly individuals living in substandard conditions often rate their condition as satisfactory. Carp (1967) has postulated that this may be due to the need to defend against anxiety or cognitive dissonance. Some support for this was found in the number of applicants for new public housing when it became available.

In a study of institutionalized disabled veterans, even those who showed significant deterioration improved significantly on a program of behavior modification (Filer and O'Connell, 1964). They conclude that elderly disabled individuals in institutions function below their capacity, and that their functional levels rise when they are exposed to greater opportunity, increased expectancy, and increased attention. There are supporting studies showing declines in institutional settings, but some must be interpreted with care as all variables are not equally well controlled. However, there is enough evidence to suggest that age bias may attribute behavior to age alone which is due to the physical and social environment in which individuals find themselves.

Activities may be limited by the lack of economic resources or by a physical environment which does not offer any reward or incentive for independence or creative productivity. Most "protected" environments, such as nursing homes and institutions, tend to foster dependence and conformity and do not reward independent behavior. These factors tend to lead to apathy, regression, and depression. Poor housing or poorly conceived housing and institutions may reduce both sensory and cognitive stimulation, and thus also further impair the capacity to maintain incentive systems, drives, or activity.

In the foregoing, we have linked physical and social environment insofar as most physical environments involve a social interaction factor. This is particularly important since most incentives involve a degree of interpersonal interaction. For incentives to operate, a reward or goal must be seen as attainable. Experimental housing in which appliances were available to facilitate independent living for the handicapped has shown that many will opt for this rather than for institutions even when it requires considerable effort. However, if no such option is available, the motivation for independent living decreases significantly.

The effect of no choice or possibility of satisfying a drive is particularly evident in the relation to sexual activity. Most institutions do not allow privacy for heterosexual living and in fact have negative sanctions against interaction between the sexes. Thus, availability of resources and peer group individuals and possibilities of satisfying a need seem to be important in determining the utilization of opportunities by the elderly. It is difficult to examine the activities of the elderly only in terms of drive and incentive. For example, transportation that is accessible and convenient may be more important than location of housing for the elderly.

Lack of definite studies of the effects of institutions over time, coupled with variation in selection and health of individuals who are admitted, as well as the difficulty in finding adequate control groups, make assessment of the effects of institutionalization very difficult. Consequently, until better studies are found, it is probably safe to conclude that the effect on the individual will depend on how closely an institutional situation meets an individual need at a particular time. Inappropriate institutionalization for social reasons seems bound to have negative effects on morale and motivation. Poor physical surroundings or a poor social environment which removes all rewards for activities previously seen as rewarding is bound to lead to a decrease in motivation. On the other hand, environments that enhance one's sense of worth and provide stimulation will offer incentive for activities which have been part of a previous life-style or are a new discovery.

## MENTAL HEALTH AND MOTIVATION

There has been both the implicit and explicit assumption in this chapter than morale and life satisfaction are intimately associated with level of drive or arousal of the individual and thus with the likelihood that incentives will be operative in producing goal-directed behavior. Furthermore, mental health includes the subjective feeling of well-being as well as clinical diagnoses of either functional or organic mental disease. It is quite clear that the mental state of the elderly individual is even more closely related to his physical state than in the earlier years and that physical health will effect mental health. More research is pointing out that mental health will also effect physical health not only in old age but also over the life span. In a comparison of the medical histories over a 20-year period of a group of male subjects treated for depression and a matched group of male paranoid subjects, Wigdor and Morris (1977) found a significantly higher number of medical conditions in the depressed group. The disorders were primarily cardiovascular. A further comparison in the same population showed significantly more medical disorders in the depressed group than in a nonpsychiatric group.

It seems clear that the individual in good mental health is moved to activities based on incentives that were operative throughout a lifetime. Schaie and Parham (1976) showed some stability in personality traits of their subjects over the life span, although this did not mean there was no change. A change related to age alone and not to cohort differences was an increase in humanitarian concern with increasing age. The continuance of activity and satisfactory interpersonal relationships tend to keep the individual aging as successfully as possible, physically as well as mentally.

The effects of apathy and withdrawal on physical capacities, because of malnutrition and lack of exercise, are well known. If one eliminates the organic conditions, disturbances in old age tend to be predominantly of the type that specifically impair goal-directed behavior. The most common mental disorders in the aged tend to be depression, anxiety, or a related condition, hypochondriasis (Pfeiffer, 1977). The very nature of these disturbances tends to reduce drive and make the usual incentives seem remote or nonoperative because they appear unattainable or because the person feels worthless and incompetent. Pfeiffer (1977) points out that epidemiological studies show the incidence of mental disorders in the elderly as ranging from 50 to 60 per cent if one includes "mild" emotional disturbances. The high incidence of these "mild" disturbances is reflected in the lowered drive level of this age group; and this lower drive level is frequently attributed to the aging process itself rather than to treatable mental conditions of the elderly. There seems to be no argument about the reactions of young subjects when they are faced with goals which they perceive as unattainable, with negative feedback, or with being in a "hopeless" or "no choice" situation, yet this is frequently the position of the aged. The maintenance of motivated or goal-directed behavior then is determined by the level of mental health as well as the physical capacity of the individual. Indeed, mental health may be more important than physical health (except for markedly incapacitating conditions), since it has been shown that individuals with good mental health show higher levels of activity in spite of some physical incapacity (Kral and Wigdor, 1957). Interest and plans for the future go with well-being and happiness, except for the very old (Lehr, 1967; Spence, 1968).

There is evidence that the actual life situation of some aging individuals precipitates mental breakdown even in individuals who previously functioned fairly well. It may be that the incentive system which some individuals develop is more adaptive than others. Thus, if an attractive woman bases her self-esteem, achievement needs, and feelings of worth entirely on physical appearance, the ability of the individual to fulfill these needs through beauty care will become less and less feasible with time. A breakdown is more likely for this woman than for an individual whose needs were fulfilled in a variety of ways that were better adapted to the changes that occur with age. The ability to cope with change and to make adaptations seems to be developed throughout the life span and will determine the likelihood of maintaining good mental health in the later years.

Particularly important in maintaining mental health is the ability to replace losses, to have a sufficiently satisfying self-image, to cope with the life-review, to substitute activities, and to maintain meaningful contacts so as to remain active and functional. Breakdown may result from an accumulation of stresses in a particular individual, but the availability of a support system is also likely to depend on previous life-style or adjustment. Stress in the aged may come from maladaptive overcompensatory behavior as well as from frustration and withdrawal. The aspects of aging which decrease the ability of the individual to cope include not only intrinsic factors (health, previous adjustment) but also extrinsic factors such as negative stereotypes of the aged, lack of meaningful or valued roles, poverty, and the particular role of women in our society.

Women may adapt to aging fairly well until widowhood, since role change is not as directly related to chronological age as, for example, is forced retirement from work. However, the position of the single woman in our culture is extremely stressful and unrewarding. Social and cultural forces

(Butler and Lewis, 1973) have contributed to the particular problems of aged women who, if they are single, frequently find no real acceptance in our society. In the past, the scarcity of women in the labor force for long periods also tended to place them at an economic disadvantage. However, the changing role of women in our society will probably be extremely important in affecting the future aged, and these cohort differences must be emphasized. This is extremely important when one realizes that, owing to the differential in life expectancy, the aged population is predominantly female. Unless one can find significant ways of improving both the life satisfaction of elderly women and their opportunity for meaningful involvement, the motivation of these individuals to remain independent and active is likely to be impaired. Schaie and Gribbin (1975) report that differences in life satisfaction may well reflect cohort membership and that widowhood may not be the significant variable.

Even in extreme cases of deteriorated capacity to function, as in cases of severe organic brain syndrome, functioning improves when individuals are able to respond to the increased expectation of those around them. The needs developed in earlier years remain basically the same for the elderly, but the relative strength of these drives in relation to the external environment is critical.

## QUALITATIVE CHANGE IN INCENTIVES

Although admittedly sparse, the evidence that is available in this area is that the basic needs or the incentives for the individual do not actually change significantly over the adult life span. However, there are qualitative changes which relate to intensity and the ordering of priorities, and which tend to change the quality of the incentives. The individual who has aged successfully and reconciled his past and present achievements may adapt his achievement needs from recognition of his present achievement to that of his past achievement, from more externally dependent criteria to more internal ones, from recognition by the total community to recognition by family and friends. Rituals around eating may be simplified because of changed needs, but a change in routine or an expected welcome guest will act as an incentive. Individual interests seem to be remarkably stable over a lifetime (Palmore, 1968; Stone and Norris, 1966), but the aged are often fearful and anxious about reaching out to find ways of satisfying these interests. Fear of failure or rejection are inhibiting (Davis, 1967; Krugman, 1959). As is frequently the case where there is underlying anxiety, the aged seem to be more preoccupied with themselves and satisfying

their own needs than with the needs of others. Women appear to become less nurturant but often experience guilt or rejection because of this and thus cannot achieve acceptance and love and at the same time satisfy their need for self-assertion. These are but a few examples of needs that tend to change in strength and priority. The aged must perceive that there are choices in finding ways of satisfying their needs.

## ASSESSMENT OF MOTIVATION

The question of assessment of motivation in relation to aging involves two very different problems. The first problem deals with the better understanding of the factors involved in contributing to the arousal level of the aging organism, and the quantitative and qualitative changes in drive, incentives, or goals. The extreme complexity of the problem is indicated in the difficulty in understanding the relative effects of the physical, social, and psychological elements of a particular situation. Recent studies of particular relevance suggest that there is considerable consistency in the adaptive capacities and effectiveness of coping styles throughout the life span. However, there has been relatively little work on assessing the relationship of these lifelong patterns to motivation in the aged (Schaie, 1978). There is a real necessity to carry out careful studies of the viable incentives in the elderly under a variety of conditions. Too often there is a tendency to project the incentives of earlier years to late life or to make judgments on the basis of preconceived notions as to what is appropriate and valued in the elderly. The conditions under which these studies are carried out are often too varied to conclude what would happen under optimal situations for the healthy aged.

The second, completely different problem related to assessment is the role of motivation on performance. Some of the studies cited in this chapter illustrate this problem. Many decrements in performance have been attributed to lack of motivation. However, there are few studies which support this contention. What has become apparent is the fact that the decrements in performance are more likely attributable to factors other than motivation. Awareness of the meaning of the situation for the individual and perception of the outcome is of importance in assessing the incentive value of a particular situation. It seems evident that the condition and situation of the individual will affect the level of motivation to respond. For example, it has been the experience of the author that frequently the attention, novelty, and concern of the experimenter is sufficient incentive for a maximum effort on the part of elderly subjects. In the same vein, if assessment is perceived to be in some way threatening, then anxiety and avoidance tend to interfere with performance.

Motivation in the older subject can basically be assessed by using many of the methods applicable in studying younger subjects. However, the conditions under which the studies are carried out have to be more carefully considered and understood. In our preoccupation with measurement, there also seems to have been too little use made of the insights produced by the elderly themselves. A better understanding might develop from a more systematic examination of material such as reminiscences, autobiography, introspective insights, and life review.

### ISSUES FOR RESEARCH ON MOTIVATION

The problems that have haunted researchers on motivation in humans are multiplied many times in older subjects by the factors outlined in the preceding discussion. However, the actual attempts at research with the aged in this area have been few indeed. In writing this chapter, it has been necessary to extrapolate from work with young subjects and to draw from clinical experience. It is clear that one of the priorities is to assess activity and incentives under a variety of conditions by developing an appropriate methodology and seeking a model that explores the limits of behavior rather than only the individual situation. The ability to understand motivation and incentive in aging is important for research, not only on drive and motivation per se, but also in terms of the effect of these factors on the validity of the results of research on many aspects of the performance of the elderly.

Some of the crucial questions in this area still revolve about the motivation related to work and the differentiation between work and activity. Furthermore, as pointed out by deCharms and Muir (1978), the problem for motivation is to understand the determinants of change in the stream of action as well as to discover what drives impel specific behaviors. Another question that should be further addressed is the elucidation of factors that determine the capacity of some individuals to compensate for large losses and change, while others cannot cope with even minor change. The role of diminishing energy has not yet been fully demonstrated. A better understanding of the crucial factors which facilitate adaptations in aging while maintaining involvement and activity is still to be achieved through further study. One of the most obvious gaps in methodology is the availability of samples for study representing the well aged who have remained integrated in the community.

In spite of the meager conclusive research in this area, the model of drive or directed behavior which depends on the achievement of a balance between the actual state of the organism and the environmental conditions relative to the incentive system of the individual seems to be most promising. The same basic incentives seem to operate fairly consistently through adult life, although the quality of goals and expectations may change. Motivation for an immediate task can be conceived of as a function of the relationship of the task to the life-space of the actor and to future events and opportunities (deCharms and Muir, 1978). Thus the paradigm seen as most useful is that of regarding the organism as adapting to changes in a variety of spheres, both internal and external. The final outcome of behavior is hardly explained by any one change such as selective reinforcement, reduction in biological drives, other changes in condition of the organism or the consequences of preexisting personality traits or coping styles. Assessment of the interaction of changes in the organism's condition and incentive system with a perceived situation is crucial to a better understanding of drives and motivation with aging. Deeply implicit in the maintenance of goal-directed behavior is the good mental health of the individual.

# REFERENCES

ALPAUGH, P. K., AND BIRREN, J. E. 1977. Variables affecting creative contributions across the adult life span. *In*, K. F. Reigel and H. Thomae (eds.), *Human Development*, pp. 240–248. Basel: Karger.

ARENBERG, D., AND ROBERTSON-TCHABO, E. 1977. Learning and aging. *In*, J. E. Birren and K. W. Schaie (eds.), *Handbook of the Psychology of Aging*, pp. 421–449. New York: Van Nostrand Reinhold.

BACK, K. W. 1971. Metaphors as a test of personal philosophy of aging. *Sociol. Focus, 5* (1), 1–8.

BANDURA, A. 1969. *Principles of Behavior Modification.* New York: Holt, Rinehart and Winston.

BERLYNE, D. E. 1960. *Conflict, Arousal and Curiosity.* New York: McGraw-Hill.

BEXTON, W. H., HERON, W., AND SCOTT, T. H. 1954. Effects of decreased variation in the sensory environment. *Can. J. Psychol., 8,* 70–76.

BINDRA, D. 1976. *A Theory of Intelligent Behavior.* New York: Wiley.

BIRKHILL, W. R., AND SCHAIE, K. W. 1975. The effect of differential reinforcement of cautiousness in intellectual performance among the elderly. *J. Gerontol., 30,* 578–583.

BIRREN, J. E. 1969. Age and decision strategies. *In*, A. T. Welford and J. E. Birren (eds.), *Interdiscipl. Top-*

*ics Gerontol.* Vol. 4, pp. 23–26. Basel: Karger.

BORTNER, R. W., AND HULTSCH, D. F. 1972. Personal time perspective in adulthood. *Developmental Psychology,* 7, 98–103.

BOTWINICK, J. 1966. Cautiousness with advanced age. *J. Gerontol., 21,* 347–352.

BOTWINICK, J. 1977. Intellectual Abilities. *In,* J. E. Birren and K. W. Schaie (eds.), *Handbook of the Psychology of Aging,* pp. 580–605. New York: Van Nostrand Reinhold.

BOTWINICK, J., BRINLEY, J. F. AND ROBBIN, J. S. 1959. Further results concerning the effect of motivation by electrical shocks in reaction-time in relation to age. *Amer. J. Psychol., 72,* 140.

BRAUN, H. W., AND GEISELHART, R. 1959. Age differences in the acquisition and extinction of the conditioned eyelid response. *J. Exp. Psychol., 57,* 386–388.

BUCK, R. 1976. *Human Motivation and Emotion.* New York: Wiley.

BUTLER, R., AND LEWIS, M. 1973. *Aging and Mental Health.* St. Louis: C. V. Mosby Company.

CARP, F. M. 1967. The impact of environment on old people. *Gerontologist, 7,* 106–108 and 135.

CHOWN, S. M. 1977. Morale, careers and personal potentials. *In,* J. E. Birren and K. W. Schaie (eds.), *Handbook of the Psychology of Aging,* pp. 676–691. New York: Van Nostrand Reinhold.

CRAIK, F. I. M., AND MASANI, P. A. 1967. Age differences in the temporal integration of language. *Brit. J. Psychol., 58,* 291–299.

CUMMING, E., AND HENRY, W. E. 1961. *Growing Old.* New York: Basic Books.

DAVIS, R. W. 1967. Social influences on the aspiration tendency of older people. *J. Gerontol., 22,* 510–516.

DAWSON, A. M., AND BALLER, W. R. 1972. Relationship between creative activity and the health of elderly persons. *J. Psychol., 82,* 49–58.

deCHARMS, R., AND MUIR, M. S. 1978. Motivation: Social approaches. *Annual Rev. of Psychol., 29,* 91–113.

DENNIS, W. 1966. Creative productivity of persons engaged in scholarship, the sciences and the arts. *J. Gerontol., 21,* 1–8.

EISDORFER, C., CONNER, J. F., AND WILKIE, F. L. 1968. The effect of magnesium pemoline on cognition and behavior. *J. Gerontol., 23,* 283–288.

EISDORFER, C., NOWLIN, J., AND WILKIE, F. 1970. Improvement of learning in the aged by modification of autonomic nervous system activity. *Science, 170,* 1327–1329.

ELIAS, M. F., AND ELIAS, P. K. 1977. Motivation and activity. *In,* J. E. Birren and K. W. Schaie (eds.), *Handbook of the Psychology of Aging,* pp. 357–383. New York: Van Nostrand Reinhold.

EVERITT, A. V., AND BURGESS, J. A. 1976. *Hypothalamus, Pituitary and Aging.* Springfield, Ill.: Charles C Thomas.

EXTON-SMITH, A. N., AND GRIMLEY EVANS, J. (eds.), 1977. *Care of the Elderly: Meeting the Challenge of Dependency.* London: Academic Press, and New York: Grune & Stratton.

FESTINGER, L. 1957. *A Theory of Cognitive Dissonance.* Stanford: Stanford Press.

FILER, R. N., AND O'DONNELL, D. D. 1964. Motivation of aging persons. *J. Gerontol., 19,* 15–24.

FURRY, C. A., AND BALTES, P. B. 1973. The effect of age differences in ability-extraneous performance variables on the assessment of intelligence in children, adults and the elderly. *J. of Gerontol., 28,* 73–80.

HARLOW, H. F. 1962. The heterosexual and affectional system in monkeys. *Amer. Psychologist, 19,* 1–9.

HEARN, H. L. 1972. Aging and the artistic career. *Gerontologist, 12,* 357–362.

HEBB, D. O. 1955. Drives and the C.N.S. (Conceptual Nervous System). *Psychol. Rev., 62,* 243–254.

HERON, W. 1966. The pathology of boredom. *In,* S. Coopersmith (ed.), *Frontiers of Psychological Research,* pp. 282. San Francisco: Freeman.

HERZBERG, F., MAUSNER, B., AND SYNDERMAN, B. 1959. *The Motivation to Work.* New York: Wiley.

KIMBLE, G. A., AND PENNYPACKER, H. S. 1963. Eyelid conditioning in young and aged subjects. *Genetic Psychol., 103,* 283–289.

KRAL, V. A., AND WIGDOR, B. T. 1957. Psychiatric and psychological observations in a geriatric clinic. *Can. Psychiatric Assoc. J., 2,* 185–189.

KRUGMAN, A. D. 1959. A note on level of aspiration behavior and aging. *J. Gerontol., 14,* 222–225.

KUHLEN, R. G., AND MONGE, R. H. 1968. Correlates of estimated rate of time passage in the adult years. *J. Gerontol., 23,* 427–433.

LAWTON, M. P., NAHEMOW, L., AND TEAFF, J. 1975. Housing characteristics and well-being. *J. Gerontol., 30,* 601–607.

LAZARUS, R. S., AND OPTON, E. M., JR. 1966. The study of psychological stress: A summary of theoretical formulations and experimental findings. *In,* C. D. Spielberg (ed.), *Anxiety and Behaviour,* pp. 225–262. New York: Academic Press.

LEHMAN, H. C. 1953. *Age and Achievement.* Princeton: Princeton University Press.

LEHR, W. 1967. Attitudes toward the future in old age. *Human Development, 10,* 230–238.

LOWENTHAL, M. F. 1972. Some potentialities of a life cycle approach to a study of retirement. *In,* F. M. Carp (ed.), *Retirement,* pp. 307–336. New York: Behavioral Publications.

LOWENTHAL, M. F., AND CHIRIBOGA, D. 1973. Social stress and adaptation: Toward a life-course perspective. *In,* C. Eisdorfer and M. P. Lawton (eds.), *The Psychology of Adult Development and Aging,* pp. 281–310. Washington, D.C.: American Psychological Association.

LOWENTHAL, M. F., THURNHER, M., CHIRIBOGA, D., AND ASSOCIATES, 1975. *Four Stages of Life: A Comparative*

*Study of Women and Men Facing Transitions.* San Francisco: Jossey-Bass.

MADDOX, G. L. 1968. Persistence of life-style among the elderly: A longitudinal study of patterns of social activity in relation to life satisfaction. *In,* B. L. Neugarten (ed.), *Middle Age and Aging,* pp. 181–183. Chicago: University of Chicago Press.

MARGOLIN, S. E., AND BUNCH, M. E. 1940. The relationship between age and the strength of hunger motivation. *Comp. Psychol. Monogr., 16,* 1–34.

MARSHALL, V. W. 1975. Age and awareness of finitude in developmental psychology. *Omega, 6,* 113–129.

MASTERS, W. H., AND JOHNSON, V. E. 1966. *Human Sexual Response.* Boston: Little, Brown.

NEUGARTEN, B. L. 1968. The awareness of middle age. *In,* B. L. Neugarten (ed.), *Middle Age and Aging,* pp. 93–98. Chicago: University of Chicago Press.

NEUGARTEN, B. L. 1977. Personality and Aging. *In,* J. E. Birren and K. W. Schaie (eds.), *Handbook of the Psychology of Aging,* pp. 626–649. New York: Van Nostrand Reinhold.

NEUGARTEN, B. L., AND GUTMAN, D. L. 1958. "Middle age: A thematic apperception study." *Psychol. Monographs, 72,* 1–33.

PALMORE, E. B. 1968. The effect of aging on activities and attitudes. *Gerontologist, 8,* 259–263.

PARÉ, W. P. 1969. Interaction of age and shock intensity on acquisition of a discriminated conditioned emotional response. *J. Comp. Physiol. Psychol., 68,* 367–369.

PFEIFFER, E. 1977. Psychopathology and social pathology. *In,* J. E. Birren and K. W. Schaie (eds.), *Handbook of the Psychology of Aging,* pp. 650–671. New York: Van Nostrand Reinhold.

PFEIFFER, E., AND DAVIS, G. C. 1971. "Use of leisure time in middle life." *Gerontologist, 11,* 187–195.

PFEIFFER, E., AND DAVIS, G. C. 1972. Determinants of sexual behavior in middle and old age. *J. Amer. Geriat. Soc., 20,* 151–158.

POWELL, A. H., EISDORFER, C., AND BOGDONOFF, M. D. 1964. Physiologic response patterns observed in a learning task. *Arch. Gen. Psychiatry, 10,* 192–195.

RABBITT, P. 1977. Changes in problem solving ability in old age. *In,* J. E. Birren and K. W. Schaie (eds.), *Handbook of the Psychology of Aging,* pp. 606–625. New York: Van Nostrand Reinhold.

SALES, S. 1971. Need for stimulation as a factor in social behaviour. *J. Pers. Soc. Psychol., 19,* 124–134.

SCHAIE, K. W. 1978. External validity in the assessment of intellectual development in adulthood. *J. Gerontol.,* in press.

SCHAIE, K. W., AND GRIBBIN, K. 1975. The impact of environmental complexity upon adult cognitive development. Paper presented at the 3rd Biennial Conference of the International Society for the Study of Behavioral Development, Guilford, England.

SCHAIE, K. W., AND PARHAM, I. A. 1976. Stability of adult personality traits: Fact or fable. *J. Pers. Soc. Psychol., 34,* 146–158.

SCHAIE, K. W., AND STROTHER, C. R. 1968. Cognitive and personality variables in college graduates of advanced age. *In,* G. A. Talland (ed.), *Human Behavior and Aging: Recent Advances in Research and Theory,* pp. 281–308. New York: Academic Press.

SCHOOLER, K. K. 1970. Effect of environment on morale. *Gerontologist, 10,* 194–197.

SHERMAN, S. R. 1974. Leisure activities in retirement housing. *J. Gerontol., 29,* 325–335.

SHMAVONIAN, B. M., AND BUSSE, E. W. 1963. The use of psychophysical techniques in the study of the aged. *In,* R. H. Williams, C. Tibbetts, and W. Donahue (eds.), *Process of Aging, Social and Psychological Perspectives,* pp. 160–183. New York: Atherton Press.

SPENCE, D. L. 1968. The role of futurity in aging adaptation. *Gerontologist, 8,* 180–183.

STONE, J., AND NORRIS, A. H. 1966. Activities and attitudes of participants in the Baltimore longitudinal study. *J. Gerontol., 21,* 575.

STRELAU, J. 1970. Nervous system type and extraversion-introversion. A comparision of Eysenck's theory with Pavlov typology. *Pol. Psychol. Bull., 1,* 17–24.

TISSUE, T. 1971. Disengagement potential: Replication and use as an explanatory variable. *J. Gerontol., 26,* 76–80.

TROLL, L. E. 1975. *Early and Middle Adulthood.* Monterey: Brooks/Cole Publishing Company.

TROYER, W. G., EISDORFER, C., BOGDONOFF, M. D., AND WILKIE, F. L. 1967. Experimental stress and learning in the aged. *J. Abnorm. Psychol., 72,* 65–70.

TROYER, W. G., EISDORFER, C., WILKIE, F. L., AND BOGDONOFF, M. D. 1966. Free fatty acid responses in the aged individual during performance of learning tasks. *J. Gerontol., 21,* 415–419.

WIGDOR, B. T., AND EISENBERG, S. 1975. Age changes in a group of intellectually superior men. Paper presented at the Fourth Annual meeting of the Canadian Association on Gerontology, Toronto, Canada.

WIGDOR, B. T., AND MORRIS, G. 1977. A comparison of twenty-year medical histories of individuals with depressive and paranoid states: A preliminary note. *J. Gerontol., 32* (2) 160–163.

WIGDOR, B. T., AND YANKOFSKY, L. 1977. Successful adjustment to old age as a function of persistence and effectence coping and locus of control. Unpublished undergraduate thesis, McGill University.

WITTELS, L. 1972. Age and stimulus meaningfulness in paired associate learning. *J. Gerontol., 27,* 372–375.

YOUMANS, E. G. 1968. Objective and subjective economic disengagement among older rural and urban men. *J. Gerontol., 21,* 439–441.

# 12

# Intelligence and Problem Solving

*K. Warner Schaie*

Some of the major characteristics of the well-adapted person, considered to be in optimal mental health during the prime of life, relate to the concepts of intellectual competence and the ability to solve complex problems. Indeed, failure to perform within the average range of measured behaviors deduced from these concepts at least implicitly raises questions as to the presence of psychopathology. The popular stereotype, however, suggests that with advancing age, decline in intellectual abilities and problem-solving capabilities is a commonly observed phenomenon, even if not universal or inevitable. This stereotype is supported by a substantial research literature most recently reviewed by Botwinick (1977) and Rabbitt (1977). The mental health professional, in attempting diagnostic assessment of the elderly, is therefore in the position not only to identify apparent deficit of function by comparison to appropriate normative data, but also to specify what proportion of behavioral deficit must be attributed to the "normal" ravages of time and tide, and what proportion should be attributed to psychopathology, which may or may not be age-related.

It is frequently forgotten that older individuals are prone to all the physical and psychological trauma which might face younger individuals, in addition to those more specific problems which are concomitant with the increasing fragility and role restrictions occurring with advanced age. In addition we must note that the older client has an experiential history which is much longer than for other life-stage groups, often extending beyond the personal experience of the professional serving that client. As a consequence, it becomes important to differentiate ontogenetic changes occurring within the individual (whether related to normal aging or individual pathology) from obsolescence phenomena which reflect the individual's inability to keep pace with the rapid sociocultural and technological changes of the past half century (cf. Schaie, 1977b). The former must, of course, be noted for their limitations upon the client's effective behavior, the latter call for appropriate programs of remediation.

In this chapter I will try to sort out the myths and realities about intellectual decline and decreasing problem-solving abilities with aging. I will also attempt to show how a reasonable view of the current state of the art affects assessment and diagnostic practice for mental health professionals working with the elderly. To do so, it will first be necessary to characterize certain methodological issues related to the internal and external validity of the data base to be reviewed (cf. Baltes, Reese, and Nesselroade, 1977; Schaie, 1977b, 1978b). Next, the evidence on intellectual decline will be reviewed for the period from middle age to early old age, where there seems to be little evidence of serious decline in most, and for the period of advanced old age when decremental change becomes all too real. Before taking such changes too seriously, I will examine the issue of the practical significance (in contrast to statistical reliability) of observed age decrement, and contrast such decrement with the much more serious problem of the intellectual obsolescence of the elderly. A similar analysis will be made for problem-solving ability, with an immediate extension to the question of how problem-solving ability seems to apply to the everyday problems of the elderly, and to the necessary concerns of mental health personnel with the attributes of specific criterion situations within which intelligent behavior is thought or desired to occur.

## METHODOLOGICAL ISSUES

I will not bore the reader here with a detailed account of the various design problems which bedevil the research literature on the psychology of aging. Nevertheless, attention needs to be called to a number of matters essential to understanding why certain research findings must be heeded with respect while others can be dismissed as interesting but trivial. More detailed accounts of such matters which are relevant to this chapter may be found in chapters by Birren and Renner (1977), Botwinick (1977), and Schaie (1973, 1977a).

Campbell and Stanley (1966) have distinguished for us two major types of design problems. The first is concerned with the internal validity of studies, that is, whether or not there are equally plausible explanations for the outcomes of experiments which have not been properly controlled for. In our case, for the study of intellectual processes and problem-solving behavior in old age, such alternatives are presented in particular by the noncomparability of young and old with respect to formal education and many socioeconomic variables, but also because of the differential effects of assessment practices in modifying the behavior to be assessed, and the tricky matter of nonrandom attrition in panel studies used to describe normal age functions.

The second type of problem, called external validity, deals with the question of generalizability of findings from specific samples to other population groups. For the mental health practitioner, such issues revolve often about the applicability of sample-specific norms to individual clients having different population characteristics, the generalizability of findings across different behavioral settings, conditions under which assessment occurs, and the appropriateness of the task used to measure the constructs of interest to the clinician (Schaie, 1978b).

### INTERNAL VALIDITY ISSUES

Descriptive and normative studies of age changes or differences in cognitive processes are special cases of the traditional pretest-posttest paradigm, where the "treatment" is assumed to be the aging of the individual. In such studies Campbell and Stanley (1966) suggest the possibility of eight different threats to internal validity. These are the effects of history, maturation, testing, instrumentation, statistical regression, mortality, selection, and the selection-maturation interaction.

*History.* Longitudinal findings of age changes may be suspect because environmental events occurring between successive longitudinal measurements may either mask true age changes, if such intervenors are favorable, or create the impression of age changes where there are none if the intervention is unfavorable. Because of the potency of changing environmental circumstances upon performance on cognitive tasks, we have therefore questioned whether data from unreplicated, single-cohort, longitudinal studies can be accepted as meaningful evidence for behavioral age functions (cf. Baltes *et al.,* 1977; Schaie, 1972).

*Maturation.* This variable is no threat to aging studies per se. However, we need to worry about cross-sectional studies in which the effects of aging are unwittingly controlled by equating groups for such variables as response speed, educational attainment, or other variables where there is a strong relationship between the covariate and chronological age. It might be mentioned in this context also, that since maturational effects are to be expected in an aging study, the proper hypothesis to be tested quite often is not the null, but rather an alternative hypothesis specifying a given magnitude of the expected age difference.

*Testing.* In longitudinal studies, experience gained on the first test occasion may result in gain or compensate for maturational decrement due to practice effects. Although this effect is particularly serious over short time periods, it may also impair the validity of results from intermediate-range longitudinal studies (cf. Schaie and Parham, 1974). In addition, however, experience gained in testing, relatively new for many older individuals, may well generalize to performance on other cognitive tasks. Examples of these kinds of testing transfer effects have been found in a number of recent cognitive training studies (e.g., Labouvie-Vief and Gonda, 1976; Plemons, Willis, and Baltes, 1978).

*Instrumentation.* In both cross-sectional and longitudinal studies, the assumption is made that the measurement instrument or process is identical for all age groups or all occasions. Such equivalence may not often be possible over wide age ranges because of simple logistic reasons as well as differences in response sets and the differential efficiency of peripheral sensory and motor systems at different ages. Less obvious, when whole test batteries are given, are the possible shifts in the latent constructs (factors) estimated by the same observable operations at different ages. Similar concerns are, of course, equally applicable in cross-sex comparisons (e.g. Cohen, Schaie, and Gribbin, 1977).

*Statistical Regression.* Unless our test instruments have nearly perfect reliability, it is probable that high scorers at the first test will show lower scores upon the subsequent test with the opposite true for low scorers. Such regression effects, depending upon the range of talent sampled, as well as whether individuals were examined under optimal or marginal conditions, may either enhance or mask true maturational change (cf. Baltes, Nesselroade, Schaie, and Labouvie, 1972; Furby, 1973).

*Mortality.* Longitudinal panel studies must contend with the problem of dropouts. In aging studies experimental mortality includes death, disappearance, and failure to cooperate for the second and subsequent test (cf. Baltes, Schaie, and Nardi, 1971; Riegel, Riegel, and Meyer, 1967; Schaie,

Labouvie, and Barrett, 1973). Fortunately, attrition effects seem to be most pronounced after the first test, and fairly random with respect to the dependent variables thereafter, but the relationship of the residual sample to the structural characteristics of the parent population is always problematic (Gribbin and Schaie, 1978). Differential mortality, of course, is a problem also for cross-sectional and independent random-sample sequential studies because cohorts sampled at older ages, by definition, must have a proportionately greater number of long-lived members.

*Selection.* Most normative studies of aging are based on volunteer samples. In addition to the general problems in obtaining comparable samples of volunteers (Rosenthal and Rosnow, 1975), there is evidence of differential recruitment rates by age (Schaie, 1959). On the other hand, there do not seem to be any sampling effects by age upon cognitive variables, whether or not monetary incentives have been used in participant recruitment (Gribbin and Schaie, 1976).

*Selection-Maturation Interaction.* Although one would not consciously control for maturation in aging studies, there is again the possibility that differential selection at particular ages might have the effects of masking or enhancing maturational effects. Indeed much of the controversy in the literature to be discussed in this chapter hinges upon the fact that normal aging effects can or cannot be demonstrated, depending upon the conditions under which study samples were selected.

EXTERNAL VALIDITY ISSUES

The observations upon which the results of any particular study must be based always represent a unique combination of a person, a treatment variable, the setting, the measurement variables, and the specific point in time when the observations were taken. When normative data are to be applied to individuals other than those included in the normative study, each of the variables listed above poses obstacles, and limits valid interpretations (cf. Baltes *et al.*, 1977). We will briefly identify the implications of each of these threats to the applicability of the current research literature on cognitive functioning.

*Experimental Units (the person variable).* Psychologists have often been accused of basing their behavioral principles upon the study of the albino rat and the college sophomore psychology major. Similarly, studies of human aging have often been based on readily available populations such as the members of senior centers, residents of nursing homes, or V.A. domiciliaries, and the like. But a more pressing issue for the study of intellectual functioning in old age is the question of the generalizability of age functions across cohorts. The question simply asks whether there can be any reasonable permanence in age norms under circumstances where there are rapid changes in population and environment characteristics. The problem is complicated by the facts of differential pathology across cohorts (Hertzog, Schaie, and Gribbin, 1978), and of differential levels and slopes of ontogenetic change for successive generations (Schaie, 1979). Explicitly, since cross-sectional studies typically used for the development of age norms (cf. Matarazzo, 1972) must compare individuals belonging to different cohorts at *one* point in time, one cannot be sure that the next cohort when it reaches the next age bracket in the table of norms will indeed perform at the the same level as did the former cohort. Longitudinal data, on the other hand, are not terribly useful for the development of age norms for adults, since the test's usefulness will likely have become seriously impaired by sociocultural obsolescence before data over long time intervals become available (cf. Gribbin and Schaie, 1977). What is needed then is information from either short-term longitudinal or replicated cross-sectional studies over many adult age intervals. Once cohort trends are known, it is then possible to provide estimates of how normative data are likely to change in the proximal future because of changes in level and slope across successive cohorts (for an example of such data see the *Manual for the Test of Behavioral Rigidity* [Schaie and Parham, 1975]).

*Experimental Settings.*   In contrast to studies with children where the prediction of educational attainment may be the most important goal for the use of intelligence tests, we find that for adults there are always multiple criteria for the expression of behavioral competence. We would expect therefore that the validity of intelligence measures will be limited by the behavioral setting towards which one wishes to predict. Although it might be argued that such criterion settings are as many as there are opportunities for the expression of competent behaviors, nature is fortunately more parsimonious. Scheidt and Schaie (1978), in an analysis of over 300 different situations generated by elderly individuals, were able to identify four bipolar dimensions along which situations could be classified. These dimensions order situations as to whether they are common or uncommon, supportive or

depriving, involve solitary or social activities, and whether they require an active or passive role by the individual. A total of sixteen classes were thus found sufficient to index situations in which older individuals engage in intelligent, problem-solving behavior.

*Treatment Variables.*   Formal intelligence tests or structured laboratory paradigms used to measure problem-solving capability in themselves serve as treatments which may obscure or magnify developmental changes in performance. Several recent studies suggest that intelligence test performance can be affected by manipulating reinforcement schedules. For example, Hoyer, Labouvie-Vief, and Baltes (1973) showed that the speed with which older adults performed on ability tests could be increased markedly by rewarding participants with trading stamps. And Birkhill and Schaie (1975) demonstrated substantial effects on performance on the Primary Mental Abilities test in individuals in their seventies by introducing reinforcement schedules which minimized or maximized risk taking and guessing behavior.

Not to be overlooked are the incidental effects upon performance by anxiety-arousing aspects of the test situation or laboratory setting, which may interact with differential levels of autonomic nervous system integration (Eisdorfer, Nowlin, and Wilkie, 1970), or with personality traits known to be related to various learning parameters (Schaie and Goulet, 1977).

*Measurement Variables.*   Here we are concerned with the fact that measures which may be most appropriate for the assessment of a particular construct in the young (e.g., visuo-spatial behavior) may become nothing more than a measure of test-taking behavior in the old (cf. Marquette, 1976). In addition we know that the old tasks must be meaningful to elicit their best performance (Schaie, 1977/78; Sinnott, 1975). The latter issue is certainly not a new one. Some twenty years ago, Demming and Pressey (1957) pioneered a number of interesting procedures which they selected in terms of their relevance to the life experience of older individuals. However, if different measures are to be valid for comparision of individuals across age, they must not only be relevant to the population to which they are applied, but they must also be relevant to a structure or intellect model which can at least in theory extend across ontogeny. This is an approach which has best been demonstrated in the area of personality development by the successive series of questionnaires assessing the same latent factors by instruments suitable at appropriate age levels (Cattell and Kline, 1977). In the area of intellectual ability, similar work has been done only for single factor models (e.g., Terman and Merrill, 1937), but we know that single factor models have little promise in adulthood (cf. Reinert, 1970, regarding differentiation-de-differentiation of intellectual structures). However, work in this author's laboratory is progressing to develop alternate test forms for the Primary Mental Abilities which are specifically designed to deal with the requirements of older adults while maintaining relevance to established frameworks of ability measurement. An early report on these studies was presented by I.K. Krauss and K. W. Schaie at the 1976 meeting of the American Psychological Association in Washington, D.C..

*Time of Measurement.* What has been well described as a period effect in sociology (Riley, Johnson, and Foner, 1972) seems equally important in the measurement of intellectual abilities. Any single behavioral observation is, of course, simply a reflection of the person-environment interaction prevalent at a particular historic point in time. From a dialectic point of view (cf. Riegel, 1976), individuals shape the influences that affect the expression of intelligent behavior, and such environmental influences in turn affect all or most individuals present in the environment. This effect is different from the cohort succession referred to above, in that it affects equally all individuals exposed to the particular influences occurring during a given period. In intelligence measurement, this variable is particularly important with respect to the obsolescence of tests, and to the introduction of environment support systems which will compensate for developmental changes which in the past would have been described as deficit phenomena.

# DOES INTELLIGENCE DECLINE IN OLD AGE?

The reader has now been prepared to understand why it is necessary in the following section to interpret the research literature most cautiously, to reinterpret the conclusions drawn by some, and to ignore the work of others outright, either because it is based on inadmissible data bases or because the data are not really relevant to the questions to be asked. We will now carefully examine the evidence, first for the limited changes which occur in midlife and then for the more important ones occurring in old age. In both instances we will distinguish between age changes within individuals

and generational (cohort) differences. We will then try to come to some conclusions regarding the practical significance of statistically reliable findings with particular emphasis upon what such changes might mean to the mental health professional.

## SOME PREFATORY COMMENTS

In his chapter in the *Handbook of the Psychology of Aging,* Botwinick (1977) alerts us that the controversy regarding the facts of intellectual decline with age depend upon inconsistencies in five areas: (1) what part of the age spectrum are we looking at; (2) what kind of tests do we use; (3) how do we define intelligence; (4) what are the sampling techniques; and (5) what are the pitfalls of the specific research designs used? The last two topics have already been addressed in the methodologic introduction to this chapter, but the remaining three items deserve some attention.

*The Age Period of Interest.* The house of Gerontology encompasses both scientists who are interested in the process of adult development and those interested in the end product of this development, the elderly. It is not surprising, therefore, that the former group of investigators would be interested in changes occurring past a maturational asymptote, say in the early twenties, and would pursue such changes until that stage, perhaps no later than the early seventies, where study populations can be found that are reasonably free from confounding pathology. The latter, on the other hand, would perhaps wish to start with individuals in their fifties and continue to that age level where any assessable subjects can still be found. Botwinick (1977) suggests therefore that researchers who focus on the earlier "developmental" ages will also argue for "no decline," while those who focus primarily on the later years will propose that "decline" is to be found.

Matters are not quite that simple, however, because the question is not just whether it is possible to demonstrate decline for some variables for some individuals, for indeed it is. What we need to recognize instead is that there may also be some variables on which there is little or no decrement and that there are some individuals who show no decrement on most variables into very old age (Baltes and Schaie, 1976; Schaie, 1974). Unfortunately it is most difficult to obtain data on normative aging beyond the late sixties, since most available samples will not be comparable in terms of education, health status, and other demographic variables to younger populations. Separate studies with measures validated for the old are therefore needed to build appropriate normative bases (cf. Schaie, 1978b), but such studies have only begun and do not as yet allow firm conclusions. With respect to currently available data then, we must perforce take a conservative position and regard normative "decline" data with a due amount of suspicion.

*Types of Tests Used.* The answer to our question whether or not decline occurs will differ markedly depending upon the tasks employed. There is no question that speed of response declines with age on almost any performance measure (Welford, 1977), and some authors argue that speed is an important component of intellectual performance (e.g., Botwinick and Storandt, 1974). But there is a serious question whether speeded tests can be justified in the assessment of adult intelligence, unless speed of response is an essential component of the criterion situation to be predicted (cf. Green, 1969; Schaie and Parr, 1979b). Normative data from cross-sectional studies are affected by different generational change patterns for those variables which involve knowledge acquisition and utilization (crystallized intelligence) and for those which involve the study of relationships (fluid intelligence). Complex tests such as the Wechsler Adult Intelligence Scale (WAIS), moreover, may measure different constructs at different ages (Reinert, 1970).

Particular caution should be exercised in interpreting linear composites of various subtest scores, and in particular the so-called global IQ scores obtained from tests developed for children or young adults. For all of its advantages over a mental-age measure, Wechsler's deviation IQ still has the property of being a composite of apples and oranges. As such it may have some meaning within a single reference group, but it is of no use whatsoever in comparing individuals across age groups or for monitoring changes within individuals. Currently available IQ measures most certainly do not even come close to matching the requirements for any meaningful assessment of functional age (see Schaie and Parr, 1979a, for a detailed discussion of the latter concept).

*Definitions of Intelligence.* What is it that we seek to measure? We surely have overcome the illusion that we can ever assess what may be the biologic limits of adaptive intelligent behavior, or intellectual capacity. What we do measure is the individual's ability to perform on a set of tasks which are our operational definition of the expression of intellectual ability. Nevertheless, we must still make one further distinction and that is between intellectual ability and competence. Connolly and Bruner (1973) define competence as that aspect of intelligence which involves "*knowing how* rather than simply *knowing that* (authors' italics)." What we often wish to predict is this competence which refers to specific behaviors in specific situations, but what we measure, of course, are laboratory tasks of intellectual ability which are hopefully generalizable across situations, although some specific permutation of abilities might best predict competence in a given situation. As indicated above it is these building blocks of intelligence, the profile of abilities which would best be able to characterize the performance of a given individual (cf. Schaie and Schaie, 1977a), rather than a measure of general intelligence which would be indicative of very little and predictive of less.

In contrast to Botwinick (1977), we hold that ability tests which are useful measures must refer directly to a given construct and not to the manner in which the construct is measured in confound. Thus it becomes quite critical to know and to apply appropriate adjustments in clinical situations for the fact that educational level accounts for a greater proportion of variance in major measures of intelligence than does age (Birren and Morrison, 1961; Granick and Friedman, 1973; Green, 1969). And other ability-extraneous variables, such as test fatigue (Furry and Baltes, 1973), are not implicit either in intellectual performance on a particular construct. They are implicated only in the particular way in which a particular construct is measured. That is, test fatigue is an implicit part of test performance only if the criterion variable is affected by fatigue as well.

## MIDLIFE CHANGES

I will follow Botwinick's (1977) lead and ignore the earlier cross-sectional studies (for reviews see Botwinick, 1967; Jones, 1959). My analyses will deal primarily with cross-sectional work conducted as part of the WAIS standardization studies (Doppelt and Wallace, 1955) and my earlier cross-sectional studies with the Primary Mental Abilities test (PMA) (Schaie, 1958), and I will then try to clarify the results by further reference to my longitudinal-sequential work with the PMA (Schaie, 1970; 1979).

Let us first examine the work with the commonly used Wechsler tests, a battery comprising 11 measures, six of which involve primarily verbal behaviors and are called a Verbal Scale, and five of which involve some manipulative performance of a primarily nonverbal nature and are summed to arrive at a Performance Scale. Although the

Wechsler tests first appeared in 1939, normative data for individuals beyond age 60 were not published until 1955. Figure 12-1 illustrates several points. First, it may be noted that the Verbal Scale shows less of an age trend than does the Performance Scale. The full scale score, being a sum of the two components, is a rather meaningless average and should best be ignored. Note that until 60 or so there is virtually no drop for the Verbal Scale. On the other hand, there is quite a sharp drop on the Performance Scale. A more analytic picture is presented by Table 12-1 (adapted from Matarazzo, 1972, p. 354) which presents age differences from early adulthood to late middle age. Considering that the mean of the standardization reference group is 10 and its standard deviation 3, none of the differences are particularly remarkable, but they are consistent indeed. All of the differences which approach significance involve measures which are speeded, that is, a constant time interval will, with successive age groups, become more and more inadequate to assess the psychological construct of interest in an equitable manner. For the power tests—Information, Comprehension, Arithmetic, Similarities, and Vocabulary—there are obviously no significant changes over the entire midlife period.

The Wechsler subtests themselves are factorially complex. An even clearer picture may therefore be obtained by considering age differences for the factorially less complex Primary Mental Abilities test (Thurstone and Thurstone, 1949). Results of the first parametric study of this test covering

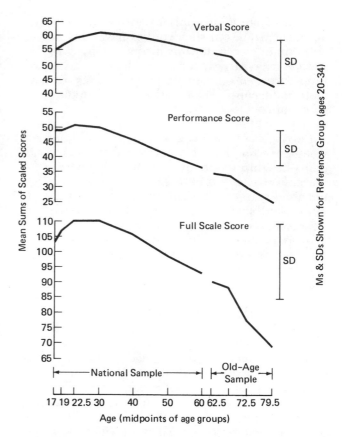

**Figure 12–1** Verbal, Performance and Full Scale scores as a function of age. (From: Doppelt and Wallace, 1955. Copyright © 1955 by the American Psychological Association. Reproduced by permission).

**Table 12-1** Mean Scores by Age for Subtest Performance on the WAIS During Middle Adulthood (Each mean is based on N = 200)

| Subtest | 20–24 | 25–34 | 35–44 | 45–54 | 55–64 |
|---|---|---|---|---|---|
| VERBAL SCALE | | | | | |
| Information | 9.8 | 10.3 | 10.3 | 9.9 | 9.9 |
| Comprehension | 10.0 | 10.2 | 10.2 | 9.9 | 9.6 |
| Arithmetic | 10.0 | 10.1 | 10.2 | 9.8 | 9.4 |
| Similarities | 10.2 | 10.1 | 9.2 | 9.0 | 9.0 |
| Digit Span | 9.9 | 10.0 | 9.6 | 9.0 | 8.4 |
| Vocabulary | 9.6 | 10.3 | 10.4 | 10.1 | 10.1 |
| | | | | | |
| PERFORMANCE SCALE | | | | | |
| Digit Symbol | 10.1 | 9.9 | 8.5 | 7.5 | 6.3 |
| Picture Completion | 10.1 | 10.0 | 9.8 | 8.6 | 8.0 |
| Block Design | 9.9 | 10.0 | 9.4 | 8.5 | 7.7 |
| Picture Arrangement | 10.5 | 9.7 | 9.1 | 8.0 | 7.3 |
| Object Assembly | 10.1 | 10.0 | 9.3 | 8.5 | 7.8 |

Adapted from Wechsler's "Measurement and Appraisal of Adult Intelligence" by Joseph D. Matarazzo, 5th and enlarged edition. Copyright © 1939, 1941, 1944, 1958 by David Wechsler; 1972 by Oxford University Press, Inc. Reprinted by permission of the author and publisher.

the age range from early adulthood to early old age (Schaie, 1958) are shown in Figure 12-2. These data come from a study of 25 men and 25 women in each five-year interval from 20 to 70, who were randomly selected from the membership of a large metropolitan prepaid health-care plan. This sample also provides the base for the sequential studies to be presented later on. Five abilities were systematically sampled. These were *Verbal Meaning,* a measure of recognition vocabulary; *Space,* the ability to visualize mentally the rotation of geometric objects; *Reasoning,* a measure of the ability to identify rules and serial principles; *Number,* a test of numerical skills; and *Word Fluency,* a measure of vocabulary recall.

Inspection of Figure 12-2 once again shows only insubstantial age differences until about age 50 for Space, Reasoning, and Verbal Meaning and until about age 60 for Number and Word Fluency. For the latter abilities, even at age 70 the drop from peak does not exceed one standard deviation. Note also that peaks are obtained for most abilities in the 31- to 35-year-old group.

As was pointed out earlier, the basic flaw of cross-sectional studies is the fact that they confound age changes with generational differences. It behooves us therefore to look at age trends determined from samples of individuals who have been followed over time, duly minding the fact that

such attrited samples are likely to yield findings characteristic for the more stable and environmentally favored segments of the total population.

Of relevance here are a number of intermediate-range longitudinal studies. Bayley and Oden (1955) followed children who had been included in Terman's study of gifted children (Terman and Oden, 1947), over the age range from 29 to 41 and showed increment in performance. Similar findings have been reported by Kangas and Bradway (1971) for both WAIS Verbal and Performance scores from ages 30 to 42. But in a study of the Army General Classification Test (AGCT) from ages 30 to 43, Tuddenham, Blumenkrantz, and Wilkin (1968) found minor decrement in one nonverbal subtest. Over an even longer period of time, Owens (1953; 1966) reported follow-up findings on the Army Alpha Test given in 1919 to 363 Iowa State College students at age 19. Owens was able to retest 127 of these students at age 49 and of the latter 96 at age 61. Most of the Army Alpha subtests are speeded tests of a largely verbal nature. At age 49 all but one arithmetic problem test showed significant increments, and by 61 there were few further changes suggesting a plateau, with some further increment for the verbal and minor decrement for the numerical components of the battery. Cunningham and Birren (1976) followed a group of 143 USC alumni first tested at age 20 and retested

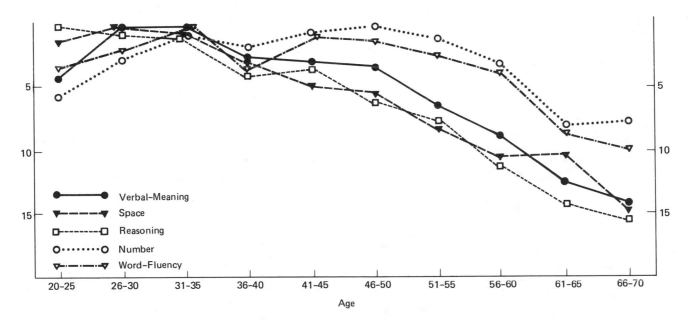

**Figure 12-2**   Cross-sectional performance differences on the Primary Mental Abilities Test from young adulthood to early old age. (From Schaie, 1958. Copyright © 1958 by the American Psychological Association. Reproduced by permission).

at age 47. In this study there was gain for the Verbal factor, stability for the Number factor and decrement for the Relations factor. In addition, cohort effects were detected for the variables influenced by educational experience, and a period effect for the Relations factor.

The apparent discrepancies between some of these studies, notably, the cross-sectional and longitudinal findings, can be addressed directly when sequential studies following several cohorts over the same age range are employed. An example of such data is given in Figure 12-3 for the Space subtest of the Primary Mental Abilities test (Thurstone and Thurstone, 1949). This figure combines results from three stages of our longitudinal-sequential studies of adult intelligence (Schaie, 1979; Schaie and Labouvie-Vief, 1974). The upper left quadrant of Figure 12-3 provides data on 301 individuals first tested in 1956 and retested in 1963; the lower left quadrant has similar data for 409 individuals first tested in 1963 and retested in

1970. In both instances the cross-sectional data (solid lines) show linear decrement from young adulthood on, but the seven-year longitudinal data (dotted lines) show substantial change in both studies only beyond age 67. The right side of Figure 12-3 shows data for 161 subjects tested in 1956, 1963, and 1970. The upper right quadrant pictures the cross-sectional comparisons at those three points in time while the lower quadrant gives the 14-year longitudinal data for the seven cohorts sampled in this study. Note that for comparable ages there is an upward trend for successive cohorts, but that changes within cohort are quite trivial until the age interval from 74 to 81 years.

Further detailed analyses to which we shall return in the next section make it clear that the normal midlife pattern is stability or increment until the sixties for measures where speed is not substantially implicated, with a possibly slight drop in the sixties for measures involving the induction

SPACE

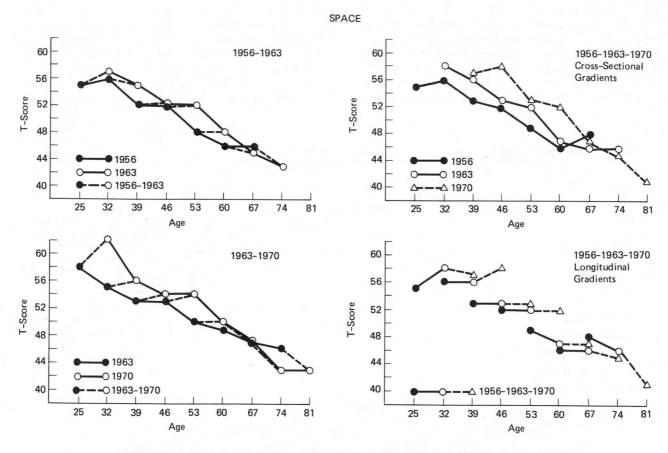

**Figure 12–3**  Cross-sectional age differences and seven- and fourteen-year longitudinal age changes from ages 25 to 81 on the Primary Mental Abilities Space test. (From: Schaie and Labouvie-Vief, 1974. Copyright © 1974 by the American Psychological Association. Reproduced by permission).

of relationships and a modest drop in the fifties for measures which are highly speeded.

## CHANGES IN OLD AGE

When we turn to intellectual change beyond the sixties we begin to see evidence of apparent decline. Again we must alert the reader to the fact that many measures used in past research may well be inappropriate and invalid for the comparisons made. And more important, attention must be given to the practical significance of what may be statistically reliable decrements. In this section we will briefly review the pertinent empirical literature and then return to the question of the practical significance of the decremental findings which have been reported.

*Wechsler Adult Intelligence Scales.* Norms for the WAIS for ages 65 and older were reported by Doppelt and Wallace (1955). These norms do show a significant drop, even for the verbal scales, past the age of 70. Substantial drop is most noteworthy again for the performance (speed-implicated) measures. The discrepancy between verbal and performance measures seems well replicated and has been found across the sexes, racial groups, and different socioeconomic levels (Eisdorfer, Busse, and Cohen, 1959). Greater than average drop in performance IQ has been implicated as a predictor of survival (Hall, Savage, Bolton, Pidwell, and Blessed, 1972). In another study Harwood and Naylor (1971) matched a group of subjects in their sixties and seventies with young adult control groups in terms of the overall WAIS IQ. For the sixtyish group, Information, Comprehension, and Vocabulary was higher than for the matched young, while Digit Symbol, Picture Completion, and Picture Arrangement were lower. The same pattern held for the older group except that Object Assembly was also lower than for the young adult controls. But for some of the elderly, relaxation of time limits may change this pattern (Storandt, 1977).

While cross-sectional comparisons of the WAIS clearly implicate speed-related age decrements beyond the fifties, it has generally been maintained that verbal performance continues unimpaired into old age. This notion has recently been challenged by Botwinick and Storandt (1974) who gave the WAIS Vocabulary test to individuals ranging in age from 62 to 83 years matched on quantitative scores on that test. Qualitative scoring then revealed that the younger subjects excelled in superior synonyms (the only scoring category yielding an age difference). But in a similar later study

(Botwinick, West, and Storandt, 1975), the authors concluded that qualitative and quantitative age differences in Vocabulary performance did not differ except for fine meaning nuances.

Eisdorfer and Wilkie (1973) have reported longitudinal data on changes in WAIS scores over a 10-year period for groups of subjects in their sixties and seventies, each tested four times. A small number of subjects had three further tests over an additional 5-year period. The 10-year loss between the sixties and seventies was statistically significant but amounted only to an average of 2 score points for the Performance and 2.6 for the Verbal Scales. From the seventies to the eighties there was a loss of 7.3 score points, equally divided between Verbal and Performance Scales. Similar decline from the mid-sixties into the eighties was reported in a 20-year study by Blum, Fosshage, and Jarvik (1972). By contrast, there have been some reports on highly selected groups which show little or no drop on Vocabulary even into very advanced age (Gilbert, 1973; Green, 1969).

*Primary Mental Abilities.* Major data here come from our longitudinal-sequential studies begun in 1956, which involve the study of persons from the twenties to the eighties arranged in 7-year age groups over 7-year intervals. Although 21-year follow-up data have now been collected, data thus far have been reported on replicated 7-year and 14-year intervals (Schaie, 1978a, 1979). Data have been reported for groups in which the same individuals were measured repeatedly (Schaie and Labouvie-Vief, 1974) as well as for the comparison of random samples of individuals from the same birth cohorts sampled over successive 7-year periods (Schaie, Labouvie, and Buech, 1973).

These data have been critically analyzed by Botwinick (1977), who argues that our findings show that cross-sectional and longitudinal data differ quantitatively but not qualitatively, but that decrement occurs for most abilities at an advanced age. He also argues that the repeated measurement data must be taken with particular caution because successive measurement points involve ever more favorably selected subjects, leading in some instances (cf. Botwinick, 1977, Figure 3) to age difference reversals. Botwinick also argues that the observed cross-sectional differences may be larger than the longitudinal differences simply because we have followed the same subjects longitudinally for only 14 years while our cross-sectional comparisons extend over more than 40 years (also see Botwinick and Arenberg, 1976).

While some of Botwinick's points are well taken, exceptions must be raised to others. Contrary to Botwinick's assumptions, selective dropout appears to effect *level* of performance primarily rather than slope of change (cf. Schaie, Labouvie, and Barrett, 1973). And our data on changes within panels involve the same individuals at all comparison points (albeit, of course, the group of persons surviving to the last comparison points). As to the disparity in time span for cross-sectional and longitudinal data, we have addressed this issue in a recent reanalysis utilizing the cohort-sequential approach, in which we have compared two successive 7-year cohorts over each 7-year age range from 25 to 81 (Schaie and Parham, 1977). Table 12-2 identifies the ages (for both panel and independent sample data) where reliable 7-year age decrements are first detected. Note that for the panel data reliable decrement is first found for Word Fluency (the most highly speeded task) at 53; for Space, Reasoning and Number at 74; and for Verbal Meaning no reliable decrement occurs even between the ages of 74 and 81. Earlier decrement occurs for the random samples comparison. Here Word Fluency shows early decrement at 39, but once again for the other variables decrement onset is late and for one variable (Reasoning) no reliable decrement is detected at any age in the study.

What about the discrepancy between the panel and random sampling data? The first involves, of course, a more highly selected panel with better health and education, but the data obtained from the panel are probably quite characteristic of middle-class and above individuals. The random sample data on the other hand might provide us with more useful guidance for a less well educated, average lower-middle-class population.

*Adult-relevant tests.*   Although work on such tasks is only beginning to enter the literature there is one recent study which deserves special attention. Gardner and Monge (1977) conducted a cross-sectional study of a large sample of men and women between the ages of 20 and 79 years who were given specially devised, adult-relevant tests of vocabulary and information as well as the Adult Basic Learning Examination (Karlsen, Madden, and Gardner, 1967), a test of formal educational skills. Age differences characteristic of the above-reported findings on the WAIS and PMA were reported with decrement first occurring in the sixties on the school-related tests. However, no such decrement was found on adult-relevant tests such as knowledge of transportation, facts on death and disease, and knowledge about finance. These data suggest that older individuals seem to perform better even on cross-sectional comparisons when material is presented which has some direct life relevance.

*Piagetian Tasks.*   Similar findings occur when Piagetian tasks are presented to older individuals in their classical as well as more meaningful content form. In the latter case substantially higher performance is found and age differences disappear or are substantially diminished (e.g., Sinnott, 1975). Although earlier studies have implied the possibility of regression from formal operations to lower levels of cognitive function (Papalia and Bielby, 1974; Storck, Looft, and Hooper, 1972), there is recent work to suggest that when suitable paradigms are used, such observations may be attributed to individuals never having attained the level of formal operations in the first place. In a study of 42 community-dwelling males aged 65 to 92 (Protinsky and Hughston, 1978), it was found that all subjects could conserve mass, better than three-fourths of all subjects conserved surface, and over 90 percent conserved volume. It seems then that previous attempts to apply Piaget's model to life-span development have ignored the interplay between operational structures and the individual's increasing awareness (Sinnott, 1975), a view further explicated by Schaie (1977/78).

## IS ADVANCED AGE KINDER TO THE MORE ABLE?

Miles and Miles, as early as 1932, suggested that age differences in intelligence increase with advancing age to the disadvantage of those less well endowed. More recently this issue was addressed by Riegel and Riegel (1972) in their study of verbal behavior. They contrasted their lowest and highest 15 percent and computed average age trends for these extremes. They concluded that the more able maintained function on tests involving relatively unfamiliar material, but that there was convergence between the two ability groups on tasks involving familiar concepts such as providing synonyms and antonyms. The former finding agrees

**Table 12-2**   Ages at Which Reliable Decrement Over a 7-year Period is First Shown

|  | REPEATED MEASUREMENT STUDY | INDEPENDENT RANDOM SAMPLES STUDY |
|---|---|---|
| Verbal Meaning | – | 74 |
| Space | 74 | 67 |
| Reasoning | 74 | – |
| Number | 74 | 60 |
| Word Fluency | 53 | 39 |
| Intellectual Aptitude | 67 | 67 |
| Educational Aptitude | 74 | 74 |

From: Schaie and Parham, 1977. Copyright © 1977 by the American Psychological Association. Reproduced by Permission.

with Raven's (1948) report of divergence between ability groups, but the latter finding goes in the opposite direction. Both of these studies are difficult to interpret because they involve cross-sectional data and therefore do not permit controlling for the effects of statistical regression.

The first objection was handled by Owens (1959) when he divided his 30-year retest group into five ability levels. He did not find any relationship between the amount of gain or loss and initial level of function. The issue of statistical regression was considered in a study by Baltes, Nesselroade, Schaie, and Labouvie (1972). Subjects ranging in age from 21 to 70 and retested after seven years were divided into three ability groups at first test. Data were analyzed for three derived factor scores: crystallized intelligence, cognitive flexibility, and visualization. For crystallized intelligence, all three groups went up, but the lowest ability group showed the greatest increment. However, for both cognitive flexibility and visualization, there was sharp increment for the low ability group, but sharp decrement for the high ability group. To test the regression model, data were rearranged by dividing subjects into three ability levels in terms of scores at the second measurement point and then computing group averages for the first test occasion. When this was done patterns remained quite similar for the crystallized intelligence score, but reversal occurred for cognitive flexibility and visualization factors; that is, in the time-reversed analysis the low ability group showed loss while the high ability group showed gain. The middle group on the other hand had very similar patterns for both analyses. These results suggest that reported differences in ability pattern-related ontogenetic change are due primarily to error of measurement and not to the graceful aging of the more able (cf. also Berkowitz and Green, 1963).

While age may not be kinder to the more able per se, there are other conditions often related to high ability level which do seem to relate to the maintenance or loss of intellectual functioning (cf. Hertzog, Schaie, and Gribbin, 1978; Schaie and Gribbin, 1975; Wilkie and Eisdorfer, 1973b). Thus, we do know that cardiovascular disease seems implicated in modest intellectual decrement, as does low socioeconomic status, and even more important, low active involvement in activities which are intellectually stimulating.

Practical Significance of Age Decrement

Whatever the evidence on the statistical reliability of age changes and differences in intelligence, the mental health professional will have to apply some criteria as to the practical importance of the magnitude of change observed within a given client, or his difference from a younger criterion group. I have given this issue considerable thought and will here attempt to provide some simple guidelines and examine the consequence of such guidelines for some group data (cf. also Schaie and Parham, 1977; Schaie, 1979).

Neither absolute raw score changes nor changes on standardized measures will be of help here, because what we really want to know is the absolute amount of change on a variable of interest as a function of the performance of a specific reference group. We think that we have solved this problem by first computing cumulative age changes (within-cohort age changes averaged across two seven-year cohorts) for each seven-year interval from 25 to 81, and then expressing these cumulative changes as proportions of performance level at age 25. As stated above, regression effects tend to point changes in a downward direction when scores are fallible. Changes cumulated without regard to the reliability of difference terms will therefore result in conservative estimates favoring decrement, particularly since older cohorts will also be at disadvantage from greater interference by construct-extraneous variables affecting their test performance (Schaie, 1979).

The practical significance of the cumulative age change can then be evaluated by applying as our standard the traditional psychometric assumption that one Probable Error (P.E.) about the mean constitutes the middle 50 percent (average) range of performance, under the assumption that mental abilities are normally distributed in the population (Matarazzo, 1972). I shall now argue that a decrement in performance across age attains practical importance whenever the cumulative loss for the older sample brings the performance of that sample below the level at one P.E. below the mean (25th percentile) of the young adult reference base.

Table 12-3 provides values for an Index of Age Change (IAC) with a standard of 100 for the average performance at age 25 for mean ages 32 to 81 as well as the 25th percentile level for this index (lower bound of average range) at age 25. Estimates are provided in that table from data yielded by a favorably attrited panel measured repeatedly (R) and from independent random population samples measured only once (I). It will be noted from this table that average within-cohort performance drops below the midrange of 25-year-olds in the panel study only at 67 for Word Fluency and at 81 for Inductive Reasoning and the Index of Intellectual Aptitude. No such drop was observed for Verbal Meaning, Space, or Number. The independent random samples study by contrast showed drops below the 25-year-old mid-range for Inductive Reasoning and Work Fluency at age 53, for Space and the Index of Intellectual Ability at 67, for Verbal Meaning and Educational Aptitude at 74, but again no such drop for Number.

The above data can provide some guidelines for clinicians in evaluating whether or not a particular client's performance is both below the expected normal change at the client's age, as well as whether it should be considered of practical significance in having fallen below the average range of a young normal comparison group.

### Practical Significance of Intellectual Obsolescence

Comparison of cross-sectional and longitudinal data bases in sequential studies has suggested that a major proportion of observed differences in test performance between young and old must be attributed to their difference in experiential backgrounds and other population characteristics which have changed across generations. It is possible to provide some guidelines for the extent of these cohort differences pretty much in the same manner as described above for the evaluation of age changes. To do so it is necessary to estimate cumulative cohort differences as a proportion of the performance of an appropriate young adult reference cohort. Once again we suggest that an older

cohort should be considered suffering from obsolescence if its average performance drops below the value which is one P.E. below the mean (25th percentile) of the reference cohort.

Table 12-4 presents data for an Index of Cohort Differences which indicates the proportion of performance of seven-year cohorts with mean birth years from 1889 to 1931, expressed as the proportion of performance for each cohort with respect to a standard cohort with mean birth year 1938. As for the age data, cohort differences are more pronounced for the random samples from the general population than for the better educated and more favorably endowed repeated measurement panel. By our criterion (25th percentile of the reference cohort), cohort obsolescence was observed in the panel data for as recent a cohort as that born in 1924 for Inductive Reasoning. Evidence of significant cohort obsolescence was found for all other variables except for Word Fluency (and Number in the panel data).

The above data may be useful in appraising the extent to which lower levels of performance found in older persons may be attributable to obsolescence (or failure to acquire certain skill levels in the first place) rather than age-related decrement. Such obsolescence is most likely that portion of behavioral variance which is amenable to intervention strategies involving both formal and informal educational processes (cf. Plemons, *et al.* 1978; Schaie and Willis, 1978).

**Table 12-3**  Index of Age Change (Base: Age 25 = 100) Rounded to Integers

|  |  | AGE | | | | | | | | −1 P.E @ Age 25 |
|---|---|---|---|---|---|---|---|---|---|---|
|  |  | 32 | 39 | 46 | 53 | 60 | 67 | 74 | 81 | |
| Verbal Meaning | R | 107 | 112 | 116 | 119 | 120 | 117 | 110 | 103 | 84 |
|  | I | 102 | 102 | 100 | 95 | 95 | 89 | 80 | 74 | 83 |
| Spatial Visualization | R | 113 | 114 | 117 | 118 | 117 | 110 | 97 | 77 | 71 |
|  | I | 98 | 90 | 89 | 82 | 81 | 68 | 58 | 55 | 71 |
| Inductive Reasoning | R | 94 | 97 | 97 | 95 | 96 | 91 | 82 | 74 | 80 |
|  | I | 97 | 90 | 84 | 76 | 72 | 64 | 58 | 53 | 79 |
| Number | R | 110 | 114 | 115 | 116 | 120 | 116 | 103 | 89 | 71 |
|  | I | 116 | 119 | 121 | 115 | 115 | 106 | 98 | 85 | 74 |
| Word Fluency | R | 100 | 96 | 95 | 89 | 86 | 74 | 63 | 52 | 83 |
|  | I | 96 | 89 | 85 | 77 | 74 | 60 | 50 | 46 | 82 |
| Intellectual Ability | R | 107 | 108 | 110 | 109 | 109 | 103 | 93 | 81 | 84 |
|  | I | 103 | 99 | 97 | 90 | 88 | 79 | 70 | 63 | 84 |
| Educational Aptitude | R | 107 | 112 | 116 | 117 | 118 | 115 | 108 | 101 | 85 |
|  | I | 101 | 100 | 97 | 92 | 91 | 84 | 76 | 70 | 83 |

From: Schaie, K. W., and Parham, I. A. Cohort-sequential analysis of adult intellectual development (extended version of Schaie & Parham, 1977). NAPS # 03170.

**Table 12-4**   Index of Cohort Differences (Base: Cohort 1938 = 100) Rounded to Integers

| | | MEAN BIRTH YEAR | | | | | | | −1 P.E @ BASE YEAR 1938 |
| | | 1931 | 1924 | 1917 | 1910 | 1903 | 1896 | 1889 | |
|---|---|---|---|---|---|---|---|---|---|
| Verbal Meaning | R | 93 | 96 | 90 | 92 | 88 | 81 | 73 | 87 |
| Meaning | I | 100 | 101 | 94 | 86 | 78 | 70 | 70 | 83 |
| Spatial | R | 85 | 87 | 81 | 75 | 68 | 59 | 57 | 74 |
| Visualization | I | 87 | 86 | 81 | 73 | 66 | 58 | 57 | 75 |
| Inductive | R | 85 | 82 | 70 | 72 | 71 | 65 | 62 | 84 |
| Reasoning | I | 90 | 87 | 76 | 68 | 60 | 52 | 55 | 80 |
| Number | R | 84 | 82 | 80 | 85 | 88 | 79 | 79 | 76 |
| | I | 100 | 101 | 93 | 83 | 76 | 67 | 68 | 72 |
| Word Fluency | R | 94 | 98 | 102 | 119 | 129 | 127 | 128 | 86 |
| | I | 100 | 106 | 106 | 106 | 95 | 95 | 103 | 83 |
| Intellectual | R | 88 | 89 | 95 | 90 | 90 | 84 | 82 | 88 |
| Ability | I | 97 | 98 | 92 | 84 | 80 | 76 | 74 | 85 |
| Educational | R | 91 | 95 | 86 | 87 | 85 | 78 | 71 | 88 |
| Aptitude | I | 98 | 92 | 85 | 77 | 69 | 60 | 61 | 84 |

From: Schaie, K. W., and Parham, I. A. Cohort-sequential analyses of adult intellectual development (extended version of Schaie & Parham, 1977), NAPS # 03170

Before leaving this topic it would be well to remind the reader once again that the facts of obsolescence require us to apply different yardsticks for comparisons of individuals of different ages at the same point in time (the cohort problem) than where within-client age changes are to be considered. In the first case, we need up-to-date norms for the cohort levels to be compared, while in the latter we need data appropriate to within-cohort change for the client to be assessed (cf. also Schaie and Schaie, 1977b). I have recently suggested (Schaie, 1979) that clinicians interested in the intellectual assessment of older people should include estimates of a peer comparison quotient (PCQ) and a base comparison quotient (BCQ).

The PCQ is analogous to the well-known Wechsler deviation IQ in that it would describe how a given client compares with his age peers. However, in contrast to traditional approaches, the PCQ requires normative data not just classified by age, but by age *within* cohort for those variables where different age trends are known to exist for successive cohorts. This procedure requires, of course, that test authors provide estimates for their tests for both age and cohort trends (e.g., Schaie and Parham, 1975). If such age-cohort data are available, it is then possible to compute the PCQ by the conventional formula:

$$ PCQ = \frac{X - \bar{X}_{ac}}{\sigma_{ac}} \times 15 + 100 $$

where the subscript *ac* refers to cohort-specific means and standard deviations for each age of interest. I would assume that corrections for cohort change might suffice if they were made for each five- to ten-year period for age norms up to the early seventies. Because of the very rapid changes in the characteristics of the very old, more frequent updates may be required for persons in the late seventies and beyond.

The second proposed index, the BCQ, indicates how a particular individual compares with a reference cohort judged to be at the optimal performance level for a particular variable. It is similar to Wechsler's EQ, but differs in that the younger reference cohort is not fixed, but is determined at the point in time when the clinician wishes to make the comparison. Computation of the BCQ requires knowledge of the means and standard deviations of the age-cohort to be used as the comparison, e.g., those age 25 at the time the comparison is to be made, and the standard deviation of the age-cohort to which the person to be assessed belongs. The BCQ can then be computed as follows in a form comparable to the PCQ described above:

$$ BCQ = \frac{X - \bar{X}_{bc}}{\sqrt{\sigma_{ac} \quad \sigma_{bc}}} \times 15 + 100 $$

where the subscript *ac* again refers to the age-cohort of which the client is a member and *bc* refers to the comparison base age-cohort. Both the PCQ and BCQ can be interpreted in a fashion similar to the conventional deviation IQs; i.e., the range from 90 to 110 would represent the middle 50 percent of the comparison population, etc. A number of other additional indices which would be more useful than those currently fashionable have been proposed in relation to work on functional aging. These have recently been described elsewhere (Schaie and Parr, 1979a).

## PROBLEM-SOLVING ABILITY IN OLD AGE

We began our discussion of intellectual abilities by distinguishing between intelligence and competence. We could have elected in that discussion to use the concept of problem solving as a mediator. That is, we might have argued that competence not only involves a particular permutation of intellectual abilities, but additional factors such as memory, selective attention, and rates of information processing. It is the latter set of constructs (and perhaps others) that have in the past been considered in discussions of complex problem solving (see recent overviews on problem solving such as Anderson and Bower, 1973; Gregg, 1974; and Newell and Simon, 1972). There has been some lack of continuity, however, in the aging literature between the work of those who try to relate directly to the psychometric tradition and those who extend the problem-solving literature on children into adulthood (cf. Rabbitt, 1977). It seemed best therefore to address this literature separately and in particular try to distinguish between two major trends, that concerned with problem solving along information-processing lines and the other concerned with concept formation and classification ability. We will then attempt to come full circle and try to speculate how this literature may be of relevance to the clinician in assessing and understanding everyday behavior of the elderly.

### PROBLEM-SOLVING ABILITY AND INFORMATION PROCESSING

Possible difficulties encountered by the elderly in complex problem solving may be related both to changes in the rate with which information is processed and to the strategies used in integrating components of information. We shall first consider the effects of slowing of the central nervous system with respect to rates of information processing. In particular we are interested here in examining the speed with which decisions are made in terms of the units of information obtained from each decision.

*Speed, Accuracy, and Perceptual Organization.* There is no question that older individuals exhibit slowed reaction time (Welford, 1977) and are found to be less accurate under certain but not all conditions (Rabbitt, 1968). Clay (1954) studied the relationship between speed and accuracy with advancing age in a matrix task in which cells had to be filled with numbered counters to yield prescribed row and column totals. She found that her subjects were able to retain accuracy until about age 50 but with increasing expenditure of time. By age 70, however, there was a tendency to "give up" after a reasonable length of time at the price of accuracy. Welford (1958) interprets these findings by noting that the amount of time taken on complex problem-solving tasks interacts with memory load. That is, the longer the individual spends on a given task, the higher the probability that essential information held in memory may be forgotten, thus contributing to lack of accuracy.

In a subsequent experiment, Clay (1956) varied the perceptual organization of her matrices. She found that under some conditions there were no age differences, while other conditions put her old subjects at disadvantage. Since many everyday problem-solving tasks involve processing of information from complex displays, the issue of perceptual complexity as related to problem solving becomes of considerable importance. There is research on simple perceptual organization which may be relevant. Welsh, Laterman, and Bell (1969) showed that old people recognize words less well than the young when speech is presented through either high or low bandpath filters. Rabbitt (1977) interprets these findings to mean that old people either require additional information which is redundant for the young or that old people cannot integrate information presented in an unfamiliar way. What must be kept in mind, of course, is that with advanced age there are sensory changes as well (see Corso, 1977). This means that both quantity and quality of sensory information available to the older individual may be reduced, even if there is relatively little central change in the precision of sensory coding associated with perceptual organization.

Certain compensating strategies are, however, of benefit to the older person. Kinsbourne (1973), in a study of letter span showed that sequential redundancy improved memory for both young and old. But the older subjects were unable to make use of redundancy at fast rates of presentation. That is, older persons must be given not only redundancy of information but also the time to recognize the redundancy. Further, the old appear to benefit when the material to be organized has meaning (Cooper-Howell, 1972).

*Guessing Behavior and Willingness to Respond.* Rates of information processing may also be affected by certain motivational variables. A number of studies have shown that older people tend to evaluate probabilities of success differently from the young and thus tend to be more cautious and less willing to respond quickly in situations where they perceive the risk of failure or loss to be high. An interesting study by Botwinick (1966) presented both young and old adults with a variety of life situations that were described either as rewarding and risky or as less rewarding but safe. The older adults (ages 67–80) were found to prefer the safer alternative. In a follow-up study (Botwinick, 1969), however, when the subjects were asked to choose between different levels of risk (not having the opportunity for a risk-free alternative), no differences in cautiousness were found between young and old.

Rabbitt (1977) raises the question whether old people may require more constraints before being able to make a decision because they may have less information and thus have greater difficulty in working out appropriate solutions. It is of interest to note here that even highly intelligent young people have very different conceptions of probabilistic odds from those inherent in a given decision situation (Kahneman and Tversky, 1973).

Birkhill and Schaie (1975) furthermore found that subjects aged 62 to 86 performed better under a low-risk condition only when they had the option of responding or not responding on a particular task item. And further complications are introduced by the fact that older individuals may have both long-range goals and tactical insights on how these can best be maximized (Birren, 1969). Their response in decision situations may well be affected by considerations intruding from their long life experience which must differ from those found in the young.

A number of laboratory studies of probability matching may also be relevant here. In these studies subjects are typically expected to predict the probability of the occurrence of a subsequent signal in a series with unequal presentation rates for different signals. Several of these studies report virtually no differences in accuracy between young and old adults (Griew, 1968; Sanford, Griew, and O'Donnell, 1972). However, Sanford and Maule (1973) found that even though their older subjects could estimate fault probabilities as well as their young comparison group, the older persons were less able to use this information in a situation where they were testing faults of different pieces of mechanical equipment. Sanford (1973) argues that this effect may be due to older individuals either becoming more random in their behavior, or narrowly focusing on the correct prediction of a particular outcome to the neglect of other essential elements of the situation.

## CONCEPT FORMATION AND CLASSIFICATION ABILITY

Laboratory studies of concept formation usually require subjects to identify a classification rule which permits them to sort a variety of complex objects (whether these are pictures, common household objects, or geometric shapes) into a number of unspecified or prescribed subsets (cf. Kendler and Kendler, 1962; Wason and Johnson-Laird, 1972). As part of such a task it is necessary to remember both a variety of features of the stimuli to be sorted and the classification rule (whether arbitrary or not) once it is adopted. Consequently, if there are a great many such aspects to be remembered, performance will become increasingly inefficient. Of importance also for older people seems to be whether the task involves presentation of a positive or negative instance of the concept to be grasped (Arenberg, 1970). Since concept formation requires the learning and memorization of rules, all of the variables which interfere with learning and memory in the aged also have an effect upon concept formation (for reviews of these topics see Arenberg and Robertson-Tchabo, 1977; and Craik, 1977). Three areas of experimentation give us some clues, however, of the performance characteristics of the elderly on concept formation tasks. These include work on transfer in concept formation, categorization behavior, and the application of training strategies.

*Transfer in Concept Formation.* The basic design here is to train individuals to apply a particular rule in one task and then examine what happens on another task where the first rule is no longer appropriate. Since there is some evidence that elderly individuals are more rigid and show greater perseveration (Chown, 1961; Schaie, 1958), one might argue that the older person would be affected particularly when reversal shifts are required. However, Coppinger and Nehrke (1972) did not obtain such results. They do point out, however, that previous experience with the dimensions across which shifting is demanded is critical, and further alert us to the fact that older individuals may do as well as the young in informationally simple tasks, but not necessarily when the going becomes more complex (Arenberg, 1970; Nehrke 1973; Rogers, Keyes, and Fuller, 1976). There is a popular stereotype that many previously learned and perhaps now inappropriate learning strategies interfere with the concept learning of the elderly. But left-right reading habits which are known to effect paired associate learning in the young do not seem to interfere any more in old than in young persons (Monge and Hultsch, 1971).

Another interesting experiment on the ability of older people to shift is a study using Wicken's "release from proactive inhibition" task. The assumption here is that in order to learn a new concept, it is necessary to be released from a previously learned association. Mistler-Lachman (1977) compared college students, community elderly, and elderly rest home residents on this task. She found that the college students and community elderly had comparable recovery on the shift task, while the rest-home subjects did much more poorly, suggesting that it may not be age but other disabilities which produce the shifting problems in the institutionalized aged.

The possibility remains that older people can shift on familiar tasks but are particularly disabled when new problems are to be learned. This alternative was first suggested by Ruch (1934), who required older individuals to suppress previously learned rules in remembering nonsense equations. But Boyarsky and Eisdorfer (1972) failed to demonstrate greater negative transfer in the older than in the young, a difference that would be essential to account for the contention that earlier learning interferes in new learning by the elderly. Once again, most clinicians will feel uncomfortable in trying to generalize data from laboratory tasks which are so remote from everyday life experiences. Nevertheless in more life-related studies (e.g., Speakman, 1954), similar findings lead to the conclusion that, where both simple and more complex procedures are available, the old will tend to use the simpler, but not necessarily more efficient, solutions (Rabbitt, 1977).

*Classification Behavior.*   Three dimensions of classification have been studied. The first concerns the accuracy with which an individual can use a given classification system. The second is the number of categories individuals will use when they are free to form their own classes. And the third concerns the level of complexity used in forming classes, such as abstractness, establishment of category hierarchies, etc. Denney and Lennon (1972) studied free classification in middle-aged and elderly subjects. Only 28 percent of the elderly but 97 percent of the middle-aged sorted the geometric objects used according to similiarity on an attribute such as color, size, or shape. The balance of the elderly tended to sort so as to make a design. Because many of their subjects were foreign-born, a second study was done (Denney, 1974). This time all subjects between 35 and 59 sorted according to similarity, while as many as 89 percent of the 60- to 79-year-olds and 90 percent of the 80-to 95-year-olds sorted in that manner. The authors therefore question whether the egocentric response in the first study represents preference rather than loss of sorting ability.

Kogan (1973, 1974) asked college students and older individuals ranging in age from 62 to 85 to sort line drawings of common objects into categories. The older subjects used fewer categories, and tended to prefer categories which involved functional or thematic relationships between objects over categories which shared a common physical attribute or where each object is an example of a superordinate concept. The Kogan study was replicated over a larger age-span by Cicirelli (1976). The latter found that categorical-inferential responses increased from childhood to age 65 and then declined, while relational categories decreased until 20 and then increased systematically into old age.

## APPLICATION OF TRAINING STRATEGIES

Another clue to the understanding of problem solving is an examination of the kind of training strategies that will lead to improved performance in the elderly. Age differences in performance might be reduced, for example, if older individuals can be taught more appropriate learning strategies which are readily available to the young (Goulet, 1972). When this is done successfully, however, it may be premature to suggest that it is the learning strategy which has helped per se. Rather, what may have occurred is that the more efficient organization of the material has led to greater retention (Kintsch, 1970). Rabbitt (1977) argues that all we have done is to make it unnecessary for the individual to remember as much, or, via better organization, to remember more of the essential elements. One cannot take much exception to this position other than reminding the reader that memory is, or course, an essential component of all organized behavior, but that there is one inherent circularity in the argument, since more efficient concept formation, whether spontaneous or otherwise, is going to lead to both memory improvement and improved problem solving (also see Labouvie-Vief and Gonda, 1976; Plemons *et al.* 1978).

## APPLICATION OF PROBLEM-SOLVING ABILITY TO THE EVERYDAY PROBLEMS OF THE ELDERLY

What do all the above studies mean for our understanding of what is normal or pathological in the way old people handle complex problems? At this time all the cautions that were raised in the section of intellectual abilities must again be raised here, and perhaps more so, because the problem-solving literature reviewed above is virtually *in toto* based upon cross-sectional comparisons. We must at least speculate that there are substantial generational differences in experience with complex problem-solving strategies and tendencies towards cautiousness and risk taking, as well as in decision-making skills which relate to the individual's level of formal education. But these generational differences are quite real, and the clinician must take due note and avoid attributing apparent performance deficits to potential psychopathology when such apparent deficits reflect no more than differential experience and levels characteristic of a generation of individuals who are much older than the clinician evaluating them.

Another consideration is of importance here, and that is to ask whether the problem-solving capability of the average older person does not suffice to deal with the needs of his current life-stage. I have argued that the life-stage during which individuals respond to the demands of the environment which require complex problem solving is largely that of midlife, and that problem-solving activities in old age become increasingly oriented towards much more egocentric goals (Schaie, 1977/78). There is considerable literature to support this point of view, stemming from the analysis of creative productivity in outstanding individuals, a literature which, strictly speaking, is not longitudinal, but could be described as archival-archeological reconstruction. But this literature (notably the work of Lehman, 1953, 1962, 1965; and of Dennis, 1966), also tells us that while the most intensive productivity occurs in midlife, there are vast differences between fields. Those fields that require little experience seem to peak in both quantity and quality in early middle age, while other fields (notably history, literature, and philosophy) tend to peak towards the end of the midlife period.

What is most amazing to the careful observer is not that old people asked to perform by criteria raised for their juniors perform somewhat less well, but rather that most older people are capable of quite impressive problem solving and decision making. Again, attention should be called to studies such as those by Birren (1969) and by Schaie and Strother (1968) which ask questions about the performance of highly intelligent older people who seem to cope so well, and who, in spite of obvious physiological changes, manage to adapt to the demands of their daily existence in a resourceful and satisfactory manner.

When all is said and done, we conclude this section in a rather similar vein to what we have proposed in our discussion of the intellectal abilities. There seems to be little change until midlife, except for the need to take somewhat more time to achieve equal levels of accuracy. Slowing sensory and perceptual processes may make it likely that older people, particularly those beyond the early seventies, will tend to make mistakes by simplifying their conceptual frameworks even when this is maladaptive and by failing to spend as much time as their central nervous system requires to obtain adequate solutions because of real or perceived external pressures "to get on with it." For today's generation of elderly, there is the further disadvantage of obsolescence with respect to problem-solving strategies appropriate to an increasingly complex environment and the perpetuation of perhaps depression-engendered attitudes about risk taking, even when it is the older problem solver who needs to take increasing risks to survive and to survive well.

## SOME CONCLUDING THOUGHTS

It was not the purpose of this chapter to assess the adequacy of measures of intelligence and problem solving for purposes of clinical assessment (see Schaie and Schaie, 1977a, 1977b, and Chapter 23, this volume, for full discussions of that issue). Nevertheless, the literature reviewed here must provide the baseline data for the work of the clinician in distinguishing between normal aging and psychopathology. I will therefore close by summarizing the conclusions which I feel represent a fair assessment of the current state of the art.

First, intellectual decrement and decline in problem-solving abilities within individuals, when occurring before the late fifties, is pathological rather than normal. Second, from the early sixties to the mid-seventies there is normal decline on some but not all abilities, for some but not all individuals, but beyond eighty decrement is the rule for most individuals. Third, for most individuals there is decrement beginning in the fifties for those abilities which implicate speed of response, and abilities which are sensitive to relatively modest impairment of the peripheral nervous system. Fourth, decrement is also frequently found on most abilities for individuals with severe cardiovascular disease at any age, and for individuals living in relatively undifferentiated or socially deprived environments beginning with the late fifties or early sixties. Fifth, because of the enormous pace of sociocultural change, most persons now in their late fifties and beyond are to some extent suffering from obsolescence effects, and therefore compare poorly with their younger peers, even though they may currently function as well as they ever have. Sixth, it is essential for clinicians to distinguish between individual decline and personal disadvantage due to obsolescence, since the former may require therapeutic intervention while the latter calls for remedial education. And seventh, data on complex problem solving are not yet very clear because our knowledge is based mostly on cross-sectional studies, but there is little reason to suspect that matters will differ much from what has been said about intellectual ability.

Finally, I would like to caution clinicians once again that most of what we know about intelligence and problem solving in the elderly has been learned using instruments and techniques developed for children and young adults. We are only at the beginning of charting adult functioning with techniques which are truly indigenous to the elderly. It is quite possible, therefore, that what appears as disadvantage when compared with the young, may simply represent a regrouping and reexpression of function which might be quite appropriate and adaptive for the old. Research now in progress in a number of laboratories will hopefully shed light on this major issue in time for a future revision of this Handbook.

# REFERENCES

ANDERSON, J. R., AND BOWER, G. H. 1973. *Human Associative Memory.* Washington, D.C.: V.H. Winston.

ARENBERG, D. 1970. Equivalence of information in concept identification. *Psychological Bulletin, 14,* 355–361.

ARENBERG, D., AND ROBERTSON-TCHABO E. A. 1977. Learning and aging. *In,* J. E. Birren and K. W. Schaie (eds.), *Handbook of the Psychology of Aging* pp. 421–449. New York: Van Nostrand Reinhold.

BALTES, P. B., NESSELROADE, J. R., SCHAIE, K. W., AND LABOUVIE, E. W. 1972. On the dilemma of regression effects in examining ability-level related differentials in ontogenetic patterns of intelligence. *Developmental Psychology, 6,* 78–84.

BALTES, P. B., REESE, H. W., AND NESSELROADE, J. R. 1977. *Life-span Developmental Psychology: Introduction to Research Methods.* Monterey, Ca.: Brooks/Cole.

BALTES, P. B., AND SCHAIE, K. W. 1976. On the plasticity of intelligence in adulthood and old age: Where Horn and Donaldson fail. *American Psychologist, 31,* 720–725.

BALTES, P. B., SCHAIE, K. W., AND NARDI, A. H. 1971. Age and experimental mortality in a seven-year longitudinal study of cognitive behavior. *Developmental Psychology, 5,* 18–26.

BAYLEY, N., AND ODEN, M. H. 1955. The maintenance of intellectual ability in gifted adults. *Journal of Gerontology, 10,* 91–107.

BERKOWITZ, B., AND GREEN, R. F. 1963. Changes in intellect with age. I. Longitudinal study of Wechsler-Bellevue scores. *Journal of Genetic Psychology, 103,* 3–21.

BIRKHILL, W. R., AND SCHAIE, K. W. 1975. The effect of differential reinforcement of cautiousness in the intellectual performance of the elderly. *Journal of Gerontology, 30,* 578–583.

BIRREN, J. E. 1969. Age and decision strategies. *In,* A. T. Welford and J. E. Birren (eds.), *Interdisciplinary Topics in Gerontology,* Vol 4, pp. 23–36. Basel: S. Karger.

BIRREN, J. E., AND MORRISON, D. F. 1961. Analysis of the WAIS subtests in relation to age and education. *Journal of Gerontology, 16,* 363–369.

BIRREN, J. E., AND RENNER, V. J. 1977. Research on the psychology of aging: Principles and experimentation. *In,* J. E. Birren and K. W. Schaie (eds.), *Handbook of the Psychology of Aging,* pp. 3–38. New York: Van Nostrand Reinhold.

BLUM, J. E., FOSSHAGE, J. L., AND JARVIK, L. F. 1972. Intellectual changes and sex differences in octogenarians: A twenty-year logitudinal study of aging. *Developmental Psychology, 7,* 178–187.

BOTWINICK, J. 1966. Cautiousness in advanced age. *Journal of Gerontology, 21,* 347–353.

BOTWINICK, J. 1967. *Cognitive Processes in Maturity and Old Age.* New York: Springer.

BOTWINICK, J. 1969. Disinclination to venture response versus cautiousness in responding: Age differences. *Journal of Genetic Psychology, 115,* 55–62.

BOTWINICK, J. 1977. Intellectual abilities. *In,* J. E. Birren and K. W. Schaie (eds.), *Handbook of the Psychology of Aging,* pp. 580–605. New York: Van Nostrand Reinhold.

BOTWINICK J., AND ARENBERG, D. 1976. Disparate time span in sequential studies of aging. *Experimental Aging Research, 2,* 55–61.

BOTWINICK, J., AND STORANDT, M. 1974. Vocabulary ability in later life. *Journal of Genetic Psychology, 125,* 303–308.

BOTWINICK, J., WEST, R., AND STORANDT, M. 1975. Qualitative vocabulary test responses and age. *Journal of Gerontology, 30,* 574–577.

BOYARSKY, R. E., AND EISDORFER, C. 1972. Forgetting in older persons. *Journal of Gerontology, 27,* 254–258.

CAMPBELL, D. T., AND STANLEY, J. E. 1966. *Experimental and Quasi-Experimental Designs for Research.* Chicago: Rand McNally.

CATTELL, R. B., AND KLINE, P. 1977. *The Scientific Analysis of Personality and Motivation.* New York: Academic Press.

CHOWN, S. M. 1961. Age and the rigidities. *Journal of Gerontology, 16,* 353–362.

CICIRELLI, V. G. 1976. Categorization behavior in aging subjects. *Journal of Gerontology, 31,* 676–680.

CLAY, H. M. 1954. Changes of performance with age on similar tasks of varying complexity. *British Journal of Psychology, 45,* 7–13.

CLAY, H. M. 1956. An age difference in separating spatially contiguous data. *Journal of Gerontology, 11,* 318–322.

COHEN, D., SCHAIE, K. W., AND GRIBBIN, K. 1977. The organization of spatial ability in older men and women. *Journal of Gerontology, 32,* 578–585.

CONNOLLY, K. J., AND BRUNER, J. S. 1973. Competence: Its nature and nurture. *In,* K. J. Connolly and J. S. Bruner (eds.), *The Growth of Competence,* pp. 3–10. New York: Academic Press.

COOPER-HOWELL, S. 1972. Familiarity and complexity in perceptual recognition. *Journal of Gerontology, 27,* 364–371.

COPPINGER, N. W., AND NEHRKE, M. F. 1972. Discrimination learning and transfer of training in the aged. *Journal of Genetic Psychology, 120,* 92–102.

CORSO, J. F. 1977. Auditory perception and communication. *In,* J. E. Birren and K. W. Schaie (eds.), *Handbook of the Psychology of Aging,* pp. 535–553. New York: Van Nostrand Reinhold.

CRAIK, F. I. M. 1977. Age differences in human memory. *In,* J. E. Birren and K. W. Schaie (eds.), *Handbook of the Psychology of Aging,* pp. 384–420. New York: Van Nostrand Reinhold.

CUNNINGHAM, W. R., AND BIRREN, J. E. 1976. Age changes in human abilities: A 28-year longitudinal study. *Developmental Psychology, 12,* 81–82.

DEMMING, J. A., AND PRESSEY, S. L. 1957. Tests indigenous to the adult and older years. *Journal of Counseling Psychology, 4,* 144–148.

DENNEY, N. W. 1974. Classification abilities in the elderly. *Journal of Gerontology, 29,* 309–314.

DENNEY, N. W., AND LENNON, M. I. 1972. Classification: A comparison of middle and old age. *Developmental Psychology, 7,* 210–213.

DENNIS, W. 1966. Creative productivity between ages of 20 and 80 years. *Journal of Gerontology, 21,* 1–8.

DOPPELT, J. E., AND WALLACE, W. L. 1955. Standardization of the Wechsler Adult Intelligence Scale for older persons. *Journal of Abnormal and Social Psychology, 51,* 312–330.

EISDORFER, C., BUSSE, E. W., AND COHEN, L. D. 1959. The WAIS performance of an aged sample: The relationship between verbal and performance IQ's. *Journal of Gerontology, 14,* 197–201.

EISDORFER, C., NOWLIN, J., AND WILKIE, F. 1970. Improvement of learning by modification of autonomous nervous system activity. *Science, 170,* 1327–1328.

EISDORFER C., AND WILKIE, F. 1973. Intellectual changes with advancing age. *In,* L. F. Jarvik, C. Eisdorfer, and J. E. Blum (eds.), *Intellectual Functioning in Adults,* pp. 21–29. New York: Springer.

FURBY, L. 1973. Interpreting regression toward the mean in developmental research. *Developmental Psychology, 8,* 172–179.

FURRY, C. A., AND BALTES, P. B. 1973. The effect of age differences in ability-extraneous performance variables on the assessment of intelligence in children, adults and the elderly. *Journal of Gerontology, 28,* 73–80.

GARDNER, E. F., AND MONGE, R. H. 1977. Adult age differences in cognitive abilities and educational background. *Experimental Aging Research, 3,* 337–383.

GILBERT, J. G. 1973. Thirty-five year follow-up study of intellectual functioning. *Journal of Gerontology, 28,* 68–72.

GOULET, L. R. 1972. New directions for research on aging and retention. *Journal of Gerontology, 27,* 52–60.

GRANICK, S., AND FRIEDMAN, A. S. 1973. Educational experience and maintenance of intellectual functioning in the aged: An overview. *In,* L. F. Jarvik, C. Eisdorfer, and J. E. Blum (eds.), *Intellectual Functioning in Adults,* pp. 59–64. New York: Springer.

GREEN, R. F. 1969. Age-intelligence relationship between ages sixteen and sixty-four: A rising trend. *Developmental Psychology, 1,* 618–627.

GREGG, L. W. 1974. *Knowledge and Cognition.* Potomac, Md. L. Erlbaum.

GRIBBIN, K., AND SCHAIE, K. W. 1976. Monetary incentive, age and cognition. *Experimental Aging Research, 2,* 461–468.

GRIBBIN, K., AND SCHAIE, K. W. 1977. The aging of tests: A methodological problem in longitudinal studies. Paper presented at Annual Meeting of the Gerontological Society, San Francisco.

GRIBBIN, K., AND SCHAIE, K. W. 1978. Selective attrition

effects in longitudinal studies: A cohort-sequential approach. *XIth International Congress of Gerontology. Abstracts for Sectional Sessions*, pp. 174–175. Tokyo: Scimed Publications.

GRIEW, S. 1968. Age and the matching of signal frequency in a 2-channel detection task. *Journal of Gerontology, 23*, 93–96.

HALL, E. H., SAVAGE, R. D., BOLTON, N., PIDWELL, D. M., AND BLESSED, G. 1972. Intellect, mental illness, and survival in the aged: A longitudinal investigation. *Journal of Gerontology, 27*, 237–244.

HARWOOD, E., AND NAYLOR, G. F. K. 1971. Changes in the constitution of the WAIS intelligence pattern with advancing age. *Australian Journal of Psychology, 2*, 297–303.

HERTZOG, C., SCHAIE, K. W., AND GRIBBIN, K. 1978. Cardiovascular disease and changes in intellectual functioning from middle to old age. *Journal of Gerontology, 33*, 872–883.

HOYER, W. J., LABOUVIE-VIEF, G., AND BALTES, P. B. 1973. Modification of response speed deficits and intellectual performance in the elderly. *Human Development, 16*, 233–242.

JONES, H. E. 1959. Intelligence and problem-solving. *In*, J. E. Birren (ed.), *Handbook of Aging and the Individual*, pp. 700–738. Chicago: University of Chicago Press.

KAHNEMAN, D., AND TVERSKY, A. 1973. On the psychology of prediction. *Psychological Review, 80*, 237–251.

KANGAS, J., AND BRADWAY, K. 1971. Intelligence at middle age: A thirty-eight year follow-up. *Developmental Psychology, 5*, 333–337.

KARLSEN, B., MADDEN, R., AND GARDNER, E. G. 1967. *Manual for Adult Basic Learning Examination*. New York: Harcourt Brace Jovanovich.

KENDLER, H. H., AND KENDLER, T. S. 1962. Vertical and horizontal processes in human problem solving. *Psychological Review, 69*, 1–18.

KINSBOURNE, M. 1973. Age effects on letter span related to rate and sequential dependency. *Journal of Gerontology, 28*, 317–319.

KINTSCH, W. 1970. *Learning, Memory and Conceptual Processes*. New York: John Wiley.

KOGAN, N. 1973. Creativity and cognitive style: A life-span perspective. *In*, P. B. Baltes and K. W. Schaie (eds.), *Life-span Developmental Psychology: Personality and Socialization*, pp. 146–179. New York: Academic Press.

KOGAN, N. 1974. Categorization and conceptualizing styles in younger and older adults. *Human Development, 17*, 218–230.

KRAUSS, I. K., AND SCHAIE, K. W. 1976. Errors in spatial rotation in the elderly. Paper presented at the Annual Meeting of the American Psychological Association, Washington, D.C.

LABOUVIE-VIEF, G., AND GONDA, J. N. 1976. Cognitive strategy training and intellectual performance in the elderly. *Journal of Gerontology, 31*, 327–332.

LEHMAN, H. C. 1953. *Age and Achievement*. Princeton, N.J.: Princeton University Press.

LEHMAN, H. C. 1962. The creative production rates of present versus past generations of scientists. *Journal of Gerontology, 17*, 409–417.

LEHMAN, H. C. 1965. The production of master's works prior to age 30. *Gerontologist, 5*, 24–30.

MARQUETTE, B. W. 1976. Limitations on the generalizability of adult competence across situations. Paper presented at the Annual Meeting of the Western Psychological Association, Los Angeles, Ca.

MATARAZZO, J. D. 1972. *Wechsler's Measurement and Appraisal of Adult Intelligence* (5th ed.), Baltimore: Williams & Wilkins.

MILES, C. C., AND MILES, W. R. 1932. The correlation of intelligence scores and chronological age from early to late maturity. *American Journal of Psychology, 44*, 44–78.

MISTLER-LACHMAN, J. L. 1977. Spontaneous shift in encoding dimensions among elderly subjects. *Journal of Gerontology, 32*, 68–72.

MONGE, R., AND HULTSCH, D. 1971. Paired associate learning as a function of adult age and length of anticipation and inspection intervals. *Journal of Gerontology, 26*, 157–162.

NEHRKE, M. F. 1973. Age and sex differences in discrimination learning and transfer of training. *Journal of Gerontology, 28*, 320–327.

NEWELL, A., AND SIMON, H. A. 1972. *Human Problem Solving*. Englewood Cliffs, N.J.: Prentice-Hall.

OWENS, W. A., JR. 1953. Age and mental abilities: A longitudinal study. *Genetic Psychology Monographs, 48*, 3–54.

OWENS, W. A., JR. 1959. Is age kinder to the initially more able? *Journal of Gerontology, 14*, 334–337.

OWENS, W. A., JR. 1966. Age and mental abilities: A second adult follow-up. *Journal of Educational Psychology, 51*, 311–325.

PAPALIA, D. E., AND BIELBY, D. 1974. Cognitive functioning in middle and old age adults. *Human Development, 17*, 424–443.

PLEMONS, J. K., WILLIS, S. L., AND BALTES, P. B. 1978. Modifiability of fluid intelligence in aging: A short-term training approach. *Journal of Gerontology, 33*, 224–231.

PROTINSKY, H., AND HUGHSTON, G. 1978. Conservation in elderly males: An empirical investigation. *Developmental Psychology, 14*, 114.

RABBITT, P. M. A. 1968. Age and the use of structure in transmitted information. *In*, G. A. Tallend (ed.), *Human Aging and Behavior*, pp. 75–92. New York: Academic Press.

RABBITT, P. M. A. 1977. Changes in problem solving ability in old age. *In*, J. E. Birren and K. W. Schaie (eds.), *Handbook of the Psychology of Aging*, pp. 606–

625. New York: Van Nostrand Reinhold.

RAVEN, J. C. 1948. The comparative assessment of intellectual ability. *British Journal of Psychology, 39,* 12–19.

REINERT, G. 1970. Comparative factor analytic studies of intelligence throughout the human life-span. *In,* L. R. Goulet and P. B. Baltes (eds.), *Life-span Developmental Psychology: Research and Theory,* pp. 468–485. New York: Academic Press.

RIEGEL, K. F. 1976. *Psychology of Development and History.* New York: Plenum.

RIEGEL, K. F., AND RIEGEL, R. M. 1972. Development, drop, and death. *Developmental Psychology, 6,* 306–319.

RIEGEL, K. F., RIEGEL, R. M, AND MEYER, G. 1967. A study of the dropout rates of longitudinal research on aging and the prediction of death. *Journal of Personality and Social Psychology, 5,* 342–348.

RILEY, M. W., JOHNSON, W., AND FONER, A., (eds.), 1972. *Aging and Society (Vol. 3): A Sociology of Age Stratification.* New York: Russell Sage.

ROGERS, C. J., KEYES, B. J., AND FULLER, B. J. 1976. Solution shift performance in the elderly. *Journal of Gerontology, 31,* 670–675.

ROSENTHAL, R., AND ROSNOW, R. L. 1975. *The Volunteer Subject.* New York: John Wiley.

RUCH, F. L. 1934. The differentiative effects of age upon human learning. *Journal of Genetic Psychology, 11,* 261–286.

SANFORD, A. J. 1973. Age-related differences in strategies for locating hidden targets. *Gerontologia, 19,* 16–21.

SANFORD, A. J., GRIEW, S., AND O'DONNELL, L. 1972. Age effects in simple prediction behaviour. *Journal of Gerontology, 27,* 259–264.

SANFORD, A. J., AND MAULE, A. T. 1973. The allocation of attention in multi-source monitoring behaviour: Adult age differences. *Perception, 2,* 91–100.

SCHAIE, K. W. 1958. Rigidity-flexibility and intelligence: A cross-sectional study of the adult life span from 20 to 70. *Psychological Monographs, 72,* No. 462. (Whole No. 9).

SCHAIE, K. W. 1959. Cross-sectional methods in the study of psychological aspects of aging. *Journal of Gerontology, 14,* 208–215.

SCHAIE, K. W. 1970. A re-interpretation of age-related changes in cognitive structure and functioning. *In,* L. R. Goulet and P. B. Baltes (eds.), *Life-span Developmental Psychology: Research and Theory,* pp. 485–507. New York: Academic Press.

SCHAIE, K. W. 1972. Can the longitudinal method be applied to psychological studies of human development? *In,* F. Z. Moenks, W. W. Hartup, and J. DeWit (eds.), *Determinants of Behavioral Development,* pp. 3–22. New York: Academic Press.

SCHAIE, K. W. 1973. Methodological problems in descriptive developmental research on adulthood and aging. *In,* J. R. Nesselroade and H. W. Reese (eds.), *Life-span Developmental Psychology: Methodological Issues,* pp. 253–280. New York: Academic Press.

SCHAIE, K. W. 1974. Translations in Gerontology—from lab to life: Intellectual functioning. *American Psychologist, 29,* 802–807.

SCHAIE, K. W. 1977a. Quasi-experimental designs in the psychology of aging. *In,* J. E. Birren and K. W. Schaie (eds.), *Handbook of the Psychology of Aging,* pp. 39–58. New York: Van Nostrand Reinhold.

SCHAIE, K. W. 1977b. Aging: Research methods. *In,* B. B. Wolman (ed.), *International Encyclopedia of Neurobiology, Psychiatry, Psychoanalysis, and Psychology* (Vol I), pp. 376–379. New York: Aesculapius Publishers.

SCHAIE, K. W. 1977/78. Toward a stage theory of adult cognitive development. *Journal of Aging and Human Development, 8,* 129–138.

SCHAIE, K. W. 1978a. Cohort-sequential research on intelligence in aging: Implications for theories of intelligence. *XIth International Congress of Gerontology. Abstracts for Plenary Sessions and Symposia,* p. 79. Tokyo: Scimed Publications.

SCHAIE, K. W. 1978b. External validity in the assessment of intellectual development in adulthood. *Journal of Gerontology, 33,* 695–701.

SCHAIE, K. W. 1979. The primary mental abilities in adulthood: An exploration of psychometric intelligence. *In,* P. B. Baltes, and O. G. Brim, Jr., (eds.), *Life-span Development and Behavior* (Vol. 2), pp. 67–115. New York: Academic Press.

SCHAIE, K. W., AND GOULET, L. R. 1977. Trait theory and verbal learning processes. *In,* R. B. Cattell and R. M. Dreger (eds.), *Handbook of Modern Personality Theory,* pp. 567–584. New York: Hemisphere/Halsted Press.

SCHAIE, K. W., AND GRIBBIN, K. 1975. The impact of environmental complexity upon adult cognitive development. Paper presented at the 3rd Biennial Conference of the International Society for the Study of Human Development, Guildford, England.

SCHAIE, K. W., LABOUVIE, G. V., AND BARRETT, T. J. 1973. Selective attrition effects in a fourteen-year study of adult intelligence. *Journal of Gerontology, 28,* 328–334.

SCHAIE, K. W., LABOUVIE, G. V., AND BUECH, B. U. 1973. Generational and cohort-specific differences in adult cognitive functioning: A fourteen-year study of independent samples. *Developmental Psychology, 9,* 151–166.

SCHAIE, K. W., AND LABOUVIE-VIEF, G. 1974. Generational versus ontogenetic components of change in adult cognitive behavior: A fourteen-year cross-sequential study. *Developmental Psychology, 10,* 305–320.

SCHAIE, K. W., AND PARHAM, I. A. 1974. Social responsibility in adulthood: Ontogenetic and sociocultural change. *Journal of Personality and Social Psychology, 30,* 483–492.

SCHAIE, K. W., AND PARHAM, I. A. 1975. *Manual for the Test of Behavioral Rigidity* (2nd ed.). Palo Alto, Ca.: Consulting Psychologists Press.

SCHAIE, K. W., AND PARHAM, I. A. 1977. Cohort-sequential analyses of adult intellectual development. *Developmental Psychology, 13,* 649–653.

SCHAIE, K. W., AND PARR, J. 1979a. Concepts and criteria for functional age. *In,* M. Marois (ed.), *"Aging: A Challenge to Science and Social Policy."* Oxford: Oxford University Press.

SCHAIE, K. W., AND PARR, J. 1979b. Intellectual development. *In,* A. W. Chickering (ed.), *The Future American College,* San Francisco: Jossey-Bass.

SCHAIE, J. P., AND SCHAIE, K. W. 1977a. Psychological evaluation of the cognitively impaired elderly. *In,* C. Eisdorfer and R. O. Friedel (eds.), *Cognitive and Emotional Disturbances in the Elderly: Clinical Issues,* pp. 55–73. New York: Yearbook Medical Publishers.

SCHAIE, K. W., AND SCHAIE, J. P. 1977b. Clinical assessment and aging. *In,* J. E. Birren and K. W. Schaie (eds.), *Handbook of the Psychology of Aging,* pp. 692–723. New York: Van Nostrand Reinhold.

SCHAIE, K. W., AND STROTHER, C. R. 1968. Cognitive and personality variables in college graduates of advanced ages. *In,* G. A. Talland (ed.), *Human Aging and Behavior,* pp. 281–303. New York: Academic Press.

SCHAIE, K. W., AND WILLIS, S. L. 1978. Life-span development: Implications for education. *In,* L. Shulman (ed.), *Review of Research in Education, 6,* pp. 120–156. Itasca, Ill.: F. E. Peacock.

SCHEIDT, R. J., AND SCHAIE, K. W. 1978. Taxonomy of situations for the aged: Generating situational criteria. *Journal of Gerontology, 33,* 848–857.

SINNOTT, J. D. 1975. Everyday thinking and Piagetian operativity in adults. *Human Development, 18,* 430–443.

SPEAKMAN, D. 1954. The effect of age on the incidental relearning of stamp values. *Journal of Gerontology, 9,* 162–167.

STORANDT, M. 1977. Age, ability level, and methods of administering and scoring the WAIS. *Journal of Gerontology, 32,* 175–178.

STORCK, P. A., LOOFT, W. R., AND HOOPER, F. H. 1972. Interrelationships among Piagetian tasks and traditional measures of cognitive abilities in mature and aged adults. *Journal of Gerontology, 27,* 461–465.

TERMAN, L. M., AND MERRILL, M. A. 1937. *Measuring Intelligence.* Cambridge, Mass.: Houghton-Mifflin.

TERMAN, L. M., AND ODEN, M. H. 1947. *The Gifted Child Grows Up: Volume IV, Genetic Studies of Genius.* Stanford, Ca.: Stanford University Press.

THURSTONE, L. L., AND THURSTONE, T. G. 1949. *SRA Primary Mental Abilities.* Chicago: Science Research Associates.

TUDDENHAM, R. D., BLUMENKRANTZ, J., AND WILKIN, W. R. 1968. Age changes on AGCT: A longitudinal study of average adults. *Journal of Consulting Clinical Psychology, 32,* 659–663.

WASON, P. C., AND JOHNSON-LAIRD, P. N. 1972. *Psychology of Reasoning.* London: Batsford.

WELFORD, A. T. 1958. *Aging and Human Skill.* Oxford: Oxford University Press.

WELFORD, A. T. 1977. Motor performance. *In,* J. E. Birren and K. W. Schaie (eds.), *Handbook of the Psychology of Aging,* pp. 450–496. New York: Van Nostrand Reinhold.

WELSH, O. L., LATERMAN, D. M., AND BELL, B. 1969. The effects of aging on responses in filtered speech. *Journal of Gerontology, 24,* 189–192.

WILKIE, F., AND EISDORFER, C. 1973a. Intellectual changes: A 15-year-follow-up of the Duke sample. Unpublished manuscript read at the 26th Annual Meeting of the Gerontological Society, Miami, Florida.

WILKIE, F., AND EISDORFER, C. 1973b. Systemic disease and behavioral correlates. *In,* L. F. Jarvik, C. Eisdorfer, and J. E. Blum (eds.), *Intellectual Functioning in Adults: Psychological and Biological Influences,* pp. 83–93. New York: Springer.

# 13

# Personality and Adjustment
# to Aging

*Hans Thomae*

A behavioral pattern of "an energic restriction" was attributed to old age by a sample of lower-middle-class people (Aaronson, 1966). Old people are "stubborn," "touchy," "bossy," or "apt to complain excessively" according to the opinion of a high percentage of graduate students and of a representative sample of the United States population (McTavish, 1971). According to findings obtained from a sample representative for West Germany (Schneider, 1970), any active and outgoing life style is attributed to the age groups below 50 years. Old people are incompetent, dependent, and passive according to stereotypes presented to German schoolchildren in their textbooks (Viebahn, 1971). They are rigid, irritable, and extreme in their expression of formerly appropriate behavioral patterns according to psychiatric experts (Braceland, 1972; Gruhle, 1938; and Müller, 1967). From her phenomenological analysis of life in old

age, Simone de Beauvoir (1970) believes that boredom, indolence, resignation, and lack of trust are traits characterizing old people.

It is not easy to trace the origins of these stereotypes about the aged personality. If we take the psychiatrist's and the novelist-philosopher's image of old people as an example, we can hypothesize that the majority of these descriptions of elderly people are outcomes of overgeneralized observations on very specific samples or cases. De Beauvoir (1970) quotes outstanding French poets, politicians, and scientists regarding their reactions to loss of roles in old age. The generation-gap and its psychological effects (critical especially for eminent persons) is generalized for all aged men by De Beauvoir, although we do know that the feelings of "isolation," "boredom," or "resignation" are reactions of a minority of aged persons to the social situation of the aged (Lehr, 1977; Shanas, Townsend, Wedderbrun, Friis, Milhoj, and Stehouwer, 1968). Another source for overgeneralization is the problem case seen by psychiatrists and/or neurologists. The states of deterioration and irritation observed by them in their patients are sometimes described as generally representative for older people (Cohen, 1976).

It should be remembered, too, that until very recently many psychological studies were based on institutionalized subjects—a very small minority of the aged population. In West Germany, only 2.8 percent of the men and women over 65 years of age live in homes for the aged or in similar institutions. However, as it is often very difficult to get the cooperation of community aged for psychologic testing, the temptation is always present to focus research on institutionalized persons and to generalize from findings related to the problems of this small group. On the other hand, studies on community samples often are biased in terms of socioeconomic status (SES) by an overrepresentation of aged persons from the middle class.

Data on "normal" personality aging are not as available as data on problem cases or special groups (like old artists or very active centenarians). When relating mental health policies to problems of the aged personality, a decision must be made either to orient toward problem groups or toward normal community aged. Focusing on the small minority of institutionalized aged may help improve the life conditions of dependent persons and those in need, whereas orientation toward normal aging may promote the development of preventive measures and methods. I suggest that normal as well as special forms of aging be included in our considerations, but there still remains the problem of establishing a standard for definition of these varieties.

Two types of approaches to this problem exist in personality research. The trait-centered approaches to personality will define the aged by the similarity or differences of trait scores measured in persons of different age groups at the same measurement point, or in the same person at different measurement points. Another type of approach focuses on the processes that constitute "the aging personality."

The process-centered approach in personality research has a long tradition in dynamic theories like those of Freud or Jung. *Personality* is defined as a system of different, often conflicting forces or drives and of adjustive mechanisms. Understanding the process by which adjustment to the complicated situation of the aged is achieved or not achieved is one of the main objectives of this approach.

Trait-centered as well as process-centered approaches to the aged personality face the common problem of generalizing observations and/or experimental findings from a restricted sample to the whole group of the aged. When we define *old age* as a certain stage in development, we expect generalizations to some degree. Any research worker in the field of personality however is primarily interested in interindividual differences (see Cronbach, 1957; Guilford, 1959; and Rotter, 1966) rather than in global statements. This conflict between the generalizing orientation of the developmental psychologist and the individualizing or differentiating orientation of the personality psychologist is no longer unsolvable. Due especially to the findings of longitudinal studies, interindividual differences in development became a major issue in theory as well as in research on childhood, adolescence, maturity, and old age (Havighurst, 1975; Kessen, Williams, and Williams, 1961; McCall, 1977). In this chapter a critical review of psychogerontologic findings on personality traits or personality dynamics demonstrates that variation in these findings is related more to variables such as sex, education, or SES, than to age itself. The concluding section of this chapter will discuss patterns of the aging personality and their explanation, prediction, and control.

## TRAIT APPROACHES TO THE AGING PERSONALITY

A major group of research workers defines *personality* as a unique pattern of traits (Guilford, 1959). In terms of this approach the aged personality is defined by differences in scores for traits measured in aged and younger adults or adolescent populations. Many believe that this dimensional or trait model is the most common conceptual approach employed in studies of the aged person (Costa and McCrae, 1976). Contrary to the prevailing fictional, public, and, in some cases, professional stereotypes of the aged personality, there is no universal trend toward change in personality traits in the transition from middle to old age, as indicated by research based on studies of the great majority of healthy aged persons living outside of institutions (Reichard, Livson, and Peterson, 1962; Britton and Britton, 1972). This model of the stable aging personality has been confirmed by Schaie and Parham (1976) who used a sequential design and stated that such stability did not reflect a lack of change after adolescence.

Although some problems exist in the interpretation of cross-sectional as well as of longitudinal data (Schaie, 1965), I shall review existing evidence for stability as well as for change in personality traits before I analyze findings from more complex studies.

## ACTIVITY

Very often a decrease of activity or vitality is expected with increasing age (von Bracken, 1952). However Palmore (1970) found only a nonsignificant decrease between the 1st and the 12th measurement points of the Activity-Inventory-Scores of the Duke Study Subjects. Stone and Norris (1966) noted a high degree of consistency in their findings in the Baltimore study. Men over 60 years of age reported the same degree of both participation in activities and satisfaction with an active life as those between 20–59 years of age. The authors attribute this continuity and satisfaction to the occupations and social background of study subjects, 80 percent of whom had college training. The same explanation may be valid for Palmore's finding.

A great degree of consistency in activity was also observed in less biased samples, such as those of the Bonn Longitudinal Study of Aging (BLSA) (Thomae, 1976). Only a minority of this sample (12 percent) had college training, and the majority belonged to the lower-middle class. The measures for activity in this study were not derived from responses to questionnaires, but were based on one week of observation of the overt behavior of the study subjects, and measured by rating scales. At the first measurement point (1965), the activity of the two cohorts included in the study (born 1890–95 or 1900—1905) did not differ significantly during the week of observation. Data on activity in social roles and in leisure time also does not differentiate between aged people in their early sixties and those in their seventies (Olbrich, 1976; and Schmitz-Scherzer, 1977) although loss of roles and increasing health problems might be expected to decrease these activities. Health and SES were correlated to activity in a significant way. Schmitz-Scherzer (1974) compared the leisure time activity of the two cohorts of BLSA with that of samples 55–65 years old, and found no significant differences explained by age. The same was true for a sample of 60–90-year-old residents of a low-income urban housing development program (Nystrom, 1974). Comparing the leisure activities of a sample of middle-aged and old study subjects, Gordon, Gaitz, and Scott (1973) found that numerous factors like age, sex, education, and income correlated with quantitative and qualitative indices of leisure activities.

Consistency of activity from middle to old age supports the activity theory of aging as a valid alternative to the disengagement theory of aging (Cumming and Henry, 1961). Many regional, national, and cross-national studies showed that life satisfaction is positively related to social action or activity (Lehr and Rudinger, 1969; Neugarten, 1977; Neugarten and Havighurst, 1969; Shanas et al., 1968). Only if the elderly can remain active in everyday life will satisfaction be attained.

Even a major loss like that of spouse does not alter this readiness for activity, as was shown by Heyman and Gianturco (1973) in a study on long-term adaptation to bereavement. The widows interviewed by these writers reported a consistently high degree of activity before and after widowhood.

Studies on predictors of longevity also point to the role of activity as well as SES and education, as a factor in longevity. Behavioral activity rated by trained observers and reported in terms of leisure-time activities based on the BLSA showed a significant relationship to survivorship (Lehr and Schmitz-Scherzer 1976). Activity is undoubtedly a very complex trait determined by both biological and cultural influences.

In a study of social and leisure-time activities based on a seven-year observation period Schmitz-Scherzer (1977) found that family-related activities as well as activities related to neighborhood increases whereas activities in roles as club member, friend, or citizen decreased. Leisure time activities such as looking at television, reading newspapers, and going to pubs increased. These changes reflect alterations in cultural and economic factors and indicate the attractiveness of mass media.

## MOOD AND HAPPINESS

The increasing frequency of depression in elderly patients has been generalized by some medical experts into a depressive syndrome basic to the aging personality. Busse and Dovenmuehle, in a paper presented to the 1958 meeting of the Gerontological Society, found a depressive symptom in 54 percent of a sample of community aged in Durham, North Carolina. Depressive reactions were also responsible for a majority of the diagnoses of neuroses in this sample. Although other experts rate the frequency of depressive reactions in aged persons in a less dramatic way (Lauter, 1973; Oesterreich, 1975), the expectation of depressive mood and low morale is commonly associated with attitudes toward old age (Lehr, 1964). Nonpsychiatric instruments for assessing mood and morale include questionnaires and interviews as well as behavior ratings. The Depression Score of the Minnesota Multiphasic Personality Inventory (MMPI) was higher in men beyond 56 years of age, according to Hathaway and McKinley (1956) and according to the findings of the Bethesda Study of healthy elderly men (Kornetsky, 1963). In the latter study, only the scores of this subscale of the MMPI differed significantly from those of the general population.

A nonpsychiatric approach to the assessment of mood uses different instruments to measure happiness. Cameron (1967a) asked his study subjects to characterize their affective state during the prior half-hour as happy, neutral, or sad. There was no age difference in the tendency to report more happy moods than sad ones, and no significant difference in the degree in which the older and the younger subjects (age 18–40 years) assigned themselves happy or unhappy states. Although the subsample of hospitalized aged reported mainly neutral states, the difference was not significant. In a longitudinal study on elderly women, Graney (1975) found a close relationship between social participation and happiness; in the oldest group, change in social activities was the most important determiner of happiness.

Another approach to the assessment of mood is defined by rating procedures which use observations on expressive behavior. In the BLSA (Thomae, 1976) I used a nine-point scale (from depressive to gay) for rating each of the seven one-week waves. While there was no difference between the two cohorts in the study, older subjects had a tendency to rate toward the middle of the scale whereas the younger subjects were more positive. However these differences were not significant. This may reflect a tendency toward a neutralization of mood with age. Affecting this, however, are many factors related to perceived health, attitude toward others, degree of social participation, and degree of perceived frustration and failure in life (Grombach, 1976).

## LIFE SATISFACTION AND MORALE

Operational definitions of mood which are not trait-oriented are morale, life satisfaction, and adjustment; these are outcomes of process-centered approaches to the aging personality (Havighurst, 1963). The instruments used in this approach are characteristic of the trait-centered approach and research on these constructs is of the correlational-psychology type (Cronbach, 1957). Measures for these variables correlate with each other in a significant way (Lohmann, 1977). We should remember however, that, life-satisfaction or morale are the outcomes rather than the conditions of ad-

justment processes. Life satisfaction therefore is an index of a successful aging (Havighurst, 1963), which is defined as the ability of the individual to recover from disturbances in this affective-emotional state.

In an analysis of the literature, Adams (1971) found approximately 60 correlates of life satisfaction, including health (objectively assessed and/or perceived by study subject), SES, degree of social participation, perceived extension of life space, availability of transportation, and religious affiliation (see also Cutler, 1975, and Schonfield, 1973). A correlation of age and life satisfaction was found in some studies, but not in others. A reanalysis of Cantril's data (1965) from the Gallup-sample done by Bortner and Hultsch (1970) demonstrated that self-ratings which reflected opportunities to select goals and access to means for achieving goals were most predictive of life satisfaction. However, according to Moriwaki (1973) the number of significant others (close personal relationships) was the most important variable. Edwards and Klemmak (1973) identified SES and family income, together with perceived health and nonfamilial social activities, as the most decisive determinants of life satisfaction. Bild and Havighurst (1976) found that life satisfaction (LS) was most highly correlated with health and income. There is a growing tendency to stress the economic aspect of LS. According to Chatfield's (1977) evaluation, income was the most decisive factor in influencing life satisfaction. The higher satisfaction of those living in a family and those still working could be related to their higher income. Even the impact of health problems in the lower income groups indicated lower LS.

Chatfield (1977) stressed the need for longitudinal studies to clarify the role of the different determinants of satisfaction. Palmore and Kivett (1977) provide this information with a four-year longitudinal study on community aged (age 47–70). Although they reported a considerable consistency of LS scores from measurement point I to IV, a quarter of the cases showed a decrease or increase. The best predictor of change was self-rated health at the first measurement point followed by sexual enjoyment and social activity. Apparently the middle-class structure of the Duke sample reduced the probability of the income variable appearing as a determinant. In any case the diversity of the more recent findings confirms Adam's (1971) analysis of the very complex network of variables related to LS.

Cameron (1967a) found that morale as another measure of successful aging is lower in older study subjects. However Granick (1973) found that perceived health and personality measures were the only variables which were significantly correlated to morale. Age, education, and cognitive and medical status failed to correlate significantly. According to Kutner, Fanshel, Togo, and Langner (1956), health had a profound effect on morale only in persons of low socioeconomic status. The morale of the aged who were living in better economic conditions did not differ regardless of their state of health, while persons of lower SES who were in poor health had significantly lower morale scores than those in good health. Birren and Renner (1977) believe that high SES is accompanied by a sense of optimism and well-being, which gives considerable psychological immunity to potentially handicapping health problems of the later years.

The complexity of predictors of morale in the aged was also found in studies comparing different cultural groups. Sauer (1977) could not confirm any independent relationship between morale and SES, race, age, marital status, voluntary associations, or interactions with friends. A comparison of predictors of morale revealed only two significant factors for black aged, namely health and participation in solitary activities. Health, solitary activities, interaction with family, and sex contributed to the prediction of morale for whites (Sauer, 1977). Apparently the racial composition of the samples is a major factor in the definition of the variables involved. Morgan (1976), in a reexamination of the relationship between widowhood and morale, found that Mexican-American widows had lower morale than their married peers if family interaction was low; this variable was not important in black or white widows. Although Morgan (1976) confirmed previous reports of a lower morale among the widowed, the findings of his regression analysis suggest that there are important situational factors such as lower income, lower work involvement, less family interaction, and cross-cultural marital status differences which explain morale scores in some ethnic groups.

Similar to the belief that there is lower morale among widows, retirement is also expected to have an impact on morale. Lower morale is expected as a result of role loss (of that of worker, of colleagues, etc.). However, an examination of this hypothesis showed that most of the variation in the morale of retired and employed men was explained by perceived health, age, income, and functional disability (Thompson, 1973).

Obviously the results of different studies on correlations of morale must be interpreted very carefully. Failure to identify sample characteristics, differences in the instruments used, and the lack of sufficient multivariate research may contribute to the somewhat unsatisfactory results obtained

thus far. However, the repeated appearance of income and perceived health in most of the studies indicate that they may be major factors influencing morale.

## ADJUSTMENT

Adjustment to the situation of the aged will influence degree of life satisfaction and mood. In addition to this emotional-affective outcome, adjustment is also reflected in the manner in which the organism's behavior corresponds to challenges of its environment. This functional aspect of adjustment cannot be evaluated by responses of a subject to a questionnaire. It can be measured only by psychiatrically or psychologically trained personnel. Psychiatric evaluations of degree adjustment in elderly persons are used in different studies on psychiatric-neurological epidemiology. Estimates of the incidence of psychopathology in the population of the community aged vary from less than 10 percent to more than 60 percent in the studies or guesses presented in the literature. Bergener (1975) doubted that any reliable data exist on the incidence of psychopathology in old age. I should add, too, that these data either do not exist for other age groups or, if they are presented, point to higher rates of psychopathology in adolescence and young adulthood than in old age.

Communication by language is a specifically human adjustment, as demonstrated by Vygotsky (1966) and Leontjew (1964). Therefore adjustment to a series of interviews and tests administered by psychologists can be regarded as a valid measure. The scores for adjustment of the BLSA study subjects varied from average to slightly above average. There was a small insignificant decrease during the first seven years of observation, but more important was the consistently significant relationship between adjustment and a positive attitude toward others, and between adjustment and health (Grombach, 1976). It should be mentioned also that adjustment to aging as defined by a complex pattern of indicators (Schonfield, 1973) was related to health, amount of daily activities, transportation, and usefulness. Personality variables such as expectation for internal control also contribute to positive adjustment to the life situation of the aged (Wolk and Kurtz, 1975).

Personality-environment interactions are regarded as decisive for adjustment. In a comparison of elderly women living in a nursing home outside of town versus those living in a public housing program, Abdo, Dills, Sheetman, and Yanish (1973) found a highly significant (p < .001) statistical difference in the personal and social adjustment of these two groups, with the public housing study subjects achieving higher mean scores. Although there were differences in the criteria for admission to both housing facilities, the authors point especially to the nursing home's comparative lack of privacy, and the availability of independence of action, and nearness to friends, relatives, and community in the public housing project as factors affecting the differences observed.

The different variables which are related to adjustment in these studies demonstrate its multidimensional character. It is very likely that these conditions will change from situation to situation. Personality variables which are helpful in adjustment in one situation may have negative effects in other ones. A striking example for this was offered by Turner, Tobin, and Lieberman (1972). Adjustment to relocation stress in institutionalization was defined in this study by survival after one year. The particular trait cluster found to be associated with successful adaptation loaded highly on activity, aggression, and narcissistic body image. The authors admit that this cluster may vary from one relocation situation to the other one. This person-situation interaction is one of the reasons why process-centered approaches have some advantages compared to trait theories.

## EXTRAVERSION—INTROVERSION

Although the differentiation of outer-and inner-orientated personality types has a long history, it was not given an operational definition before midcentury. Especially according to Eysenck, extraversion—introversion is one of the main dimensions which explain the most fundamental differences between persons. Eysenck previously adopted some of the criteria defined by C. G. Jung (1925) for this dimension from middle to late life, and it was hypothesized that there should be a continuous change with age from extraversion to introversion (Cameron, 1967b). This was related to modes of survival; extraversion was equivalent to survival by expansion, and introversion was identical with internal control of behavior and reduction of all externalities.

The same type of thinking was prevalent in the disengagement theory of aging, which hypothesized not only a mutual withdrawal or disengagement between the aged and others, but also changes in personality that "cause and result in decreased involvement with others and increased preoccupation with himself" (Cumming and Henry, 1961, p. 15). As mentioned already, a general tendency toward disengagement as the optimum state in old age was not confirmed in more recent studies. Conflicts involving the activity theory of aging

have been resolved by reference to personality variables (Lehr and Rudinger, 1969; Neugarten, 1977; Olbrich, 1976). Differential aspects were also implicated by studies using the original Eysenck questionnaires for measuring extraversion. Cameron (1967b) found an increase of introversion only in women and explained this by invoking a higher degree of strain placed upon women in the U.S. This interpretation did not take into account the 1960 revision of the extraversion-introversion construct presented by Eysenck (1967) and Eysenck and Eysenck (1969). According to his biological theory of personality, the variability in this personality trait is explained by hereditary differences in the arousal level of ascending reticular activating system (ARAS), with introverts presumably having higher arousal levels. While this hypothesis is consistent with findings of higher EEG activity in aged subjects, it is not supported by those findings which point to lower conditioning rates in aged study subjects (Shmavonian, Yarmat, and Cohen, 1965). According to Eysenck introverts have higher conditioning rates compared to extraverts. Therefore the construct of introversion as an indicator of cortical and subcortical arousal is not supported by conditioning studies.

The ambiguity of existing evidence for higher introversion scores in aged study subjects, together with the controversial discussions about a general tendency toward disengagement, may be one of the reasons why gerontological research on this personality dimension was almost discontinued in the seventies. Cattell's factor A as measured by the 16 Personality Factors Questionnaire (PFQ) or equivalent instruments (Schaie and Parham, 1976) is close to C. G. Jung's conception of the introversion-extraversion dimension. No age differences in the factor "reserved vs outgoingness" were found in a study by Angleitner, Schmitz-Scherzer, and Rudinger (1971) in a sample of 50-90-year-old residents of a middle-class home for the aged whereas, according to Schaie and Parham (1976), the oldest cohort in their study was the "least outgoing."

## RIGIDITY

In several studies (Riegel, 1959; Schaie, 1958) rigidity is shown to increase with increasing age. Factor-analytical studies demonstrated that there are many rigidities (Chown, 1961; Riegel, 1959). Lack of fluidity in problem-solving must be discriminated from attitudinal rigidity which is measured by scales (Riegel and Riegel, 1960). Angleitner (1972) demonstrated that SES is a major component of variance in these rigidity measures. Angleitner (1976) also analyzed the data on rigidity in the BLSA for a period of seven years. He found no significant overall change in the scores of the Riegel scales. While general statements pointed to a decrease in rigidity, personalized statements suggested a slight increase. As rigidity is closely related to intelligence, according to Angleitner (1972), these findings must be interpreted with caution.

Evidence for stability of rigidity across longer sections of the life span is provided by Schaie's and Parham's (1977) cross-sequential analysis of cognitive development. Aside from intelligence scales they administered a Behavioral Rigidity Test (Schaie and Parham, 1976) at three measurement points (1956, 1963, 1970) to a sample of 723 study subjects. Within-cohort change was measured in the form of an index with a value of 100 at age 25. Motor-cognitive and personality-perceptual rigidity did not drop below the 25-year average range. However the authors found differences with some of older cohorts being more rigid. Together with the findings on cognitive performance, these results indicate the greater impact of intergenerational change compared to age on degree of behavioral rigidity.

## DIFFERENTIATION

According to theories of development such as those of Werner (1957) changes in personality can be defined as increasing differentiation followed by a tendency toward de-differentiation of functions and processes in old age. One set of arguments in favor of this proposition is related to the number of factors defining cognitive performance (Reinert, 1970). Rudinger (1976) questioned the validity of studies which found changes in the number of factors defining intellectual performance. If uniform extraction, rotation, and interpretation criteria are applied, all factor studies on intelligence yield only two factors.

A more promising way to test the differentiation hypothesis is defined by the work of Witkin, Dyk, and Fatterson (1962). The cognitive style of differentiation is defined operationally by the Perceptual Index as well as by characteristics of self concept, preferences for coping versus defense mechanisms against threat, and a precise socialization history. While there is evidence for increasing differentiation from childhood to postadolescence (Witkin et al., 1962), stability is expected for the adult years. In old age, scores for differentiation (field-independence) decrease (Markus and Nielsen, 1973; Schwartz and Karp, 1967). Comalli (1965), however, found higher scores for differentiation in a group of 80 to 90-year-old men than Schwartz and Karp found in their younger group. This finding does not indicate a reversal of a hy-

pothesized developmental trend. It may be explained by correlations between activity, field-independence (differentiation), and survivorship (Schwartz and Karp, 1967).

A relationship between activity, independence of living arrangement, and differentiation in terms of Witkin et al. (1962) is also suggested by findings on institutionalized aged persons who have lower scores for field independence than do the community aged (Markus and Nielson, 1973). The greater similarity of life conditions for men and women after retirement may explain the fact that the sex differences in differentiation reported by Witkin et al. (1962) for children and adolescents could not be confirmed for the aged sample of Markus and Nielson (1973).

The extension of the construct of field-independence to the cognitive style of an analytical versus a global field approach as proposed by Witkin et al. (1962) using factorial analysis of perceptual and intelligence test data of children and adolescents, could not be confirmed in aged study subjects (Erlemeier, Schreiner, and Schnürer, 1972). They found three factors which were not identical to those extracted by Witkin et al. (1962). Another study by Schreiner, Erlemeier, and Glasmacher (1973) analyzed correlations between differentiation (as defined by Embedded Figures Test and Rod Frame Test) and personality measures in the sample of BLSA (Thomae, 1976). The results of their factor analysis pointed to a relationship between field-independence and emotional balance and satisfaction. No correlations between field-independence and a more active-expansive life style could be identified.

## LOCUS OF CONTROL

The construct "locus of internal versus external control" was introduced by Rotter (1966) in the framework of a cognitive social learning theory of personality. This dimension refers to a consistent generalized expectation of the person that he or she controls events, whereas "external control" study subjects believe that they are completely dependent on the decisions, plans, or actions of others. Lao (1974) administered Rotter's I-E-scale to 277 white males (age 15–85 yrs). He found an increase in internal locus of control from 15–39 years of age and a stabilized sense of internal control in middle age. The hypothesis that a decrease of internal control accompanies loss of autonomy and mastery in persons over 60 years was not supported. The finding of stability of scores for internal control from middle to old age was confirmed by Ryckman and Malikosi (1975). These authors believe that stereotypes of the elderly as powerless and dependent on others for subsistence in a threatening and unreliable environment are questioned by gerontological research on Rotter's construct. Kuypers (1972) could not find any age differences between "internals" and "externals." The "internals" had more years of formal education and preferred more active coping styles. Other variables relating to perceived internal versus external control are self-rated health (Levinson, 1975), self-esteem, ego strength, and absence versus presence of mental disorders (Kivett, Watson, and Busch, 1977).

Internality in terms of Rotter's general expectation dimension is related to positive self concept, especially in men living in institutions (Reid, Haas, and Douglas, 1977). Expectation of internal control was related to nurses' ratings of subjects' happiness and self-ratings of contentment and happiness. It correlated negatively with length of residency in home, and age. The authors of this study believe that the construct of "locus of control," if defined operationally according to the context of a specific life situation (e.g. being institutionalized), may help to understand the psychological impact of adjustment to old age. Expectation for internal control may be higher in the years before old age. The many physical and social changes perceived from middle to old age may reduce the sense of control and effectiveness elderly persons may wish to have in their everyday life. In some men, however, this expectation is maintained even in institutions, apparently according to specific socialization conditions.

## ANXIETY AND CAUTIOUSNESS

Clinical as well as research work with the aged pointed to the relevance of anxiety or cautiousness in the behavior of the aged. According to Oberleder (1964) and Eisdorfer (1967), anxiety or cautiousness are a major intervening variable in cognitive functioning of the aged. Anxiety may raise the arousal level beyond its optimal level and elicit erroneous responses. On the other hand, anxiety can result in cautiousness which delays decision processes and reactions. Even in these situations, generalizations concerning adult age differences are unwarranted. Okun and Elias (1977) showed that elderly people are more cautious in risk-taking tasks with a constant pay-off structure. If size of pay-off is contingent upon the rise of the risk, older adults were not found to be more cautious than young adults.

Another context in which anxiety is increased among the aged is related to the high crime rate directed against elderly persons in some metropolitan areas of the US (Lebowitz, 1975). However,

in these situations persons under 40 and over 60 years of age did not differ in their responses to the question if they would be afraid of going out in their neighborhood at night. Forty percent of the respondents reported being fearful. Generally women, those living alone, the poor, and those who reside in large urban areas were the most fearful (Lebowitz, 1975).

## VALUES

In agreement with philosophies of personality change, Ryff and Baltes (1976) found a value transition from middle to old age which is defined by the sequence of change in preference for instrumental values (like "ambitious," "capable") to a preference for "terminal" values ("freedom," "happiness," "accomplishment"). This finding is based on a female sample, but Tismer and Struck (1971) found lower need achievement (n ach) scores in older men and women compared to a sample of young adults (see also, Smith, 1970).

Values like work, leisure, and achievement appeared to be considerably less important to aged study subjects than to younger subjects in a statewide survey in North Carolina (Christenson, 1977). While the devaluation of work as well as of leisure needs further clarification (Christenson, 1977), the lower need achievement scores of the other study subjects may indicate a structural change in motivation so that achievement-related values are supplemented or substituted by social humanitarian concerns. This interpretation of Tismer and Struck (1971) is in agreement with Christenson (1977) and with Schaie and Parham (1976) who found an increased humanitarian concern in their oldest age group.

Another approach to the study of values was used by Tismer-Puschner and Haacke (1972). They asked 468 study subjects (ages 17–77 years) to order photographs (showing girls and boys, young men and women, and old men and women) within each age and sex group according to their preferences. The researchers then analyzed the reasons given by the study subjects for their choices. While apparel and mood of the person on the photograph were the main reasons given by the youngest age groups, norm-orientated characteristics dominated in the older age groups. Among these norm-orientated reasons, items like reliability, efficiency, obedience, and similar traits were regarded as negative values by the younger groups, and as positive values by the oldest age groups. This change in values appeared in men over the age of 50 and in women over the age of 60. It is very likely that this finding is very cohort-specific and that longitudinal analyses of the younger age groups would point to a rather high degree in the evaluation of certain conformity-linked traits.

## STRUCTURAL CHANGE

For some of the authors who regard the dimensional or trait model as the "most common conceptual approach in the study of adult and aging personality" (Costa and McCrae,1976), covariance of traits within and across different age groups is a major question. The consistency or change of factor structures replaces that of single traits. With the increasing awareness of the pitfalls in measuring change (Baltes, 1968; Harris, 1963; Rudinger, 1972), the analysis of factor structures across age groups or measurement points is regarded as one possible alternative in cross-sectional as well as in longitudinal studies. One of the first studies on structural change in the aged personality is that of Craik (1964) who found that emotional adjustment and sociability are differently related in men and women of different age. Costa (1973) found significant age differences in the factor structures as defined by the 16 personality factors (PF) (Cattell). These data can be supplemented by a study of Angleitner, Schmitz-Scherzer, and Rudinger (1971) who showed that there are age-and sex-related differences in the relationships of 16 PF factors with variables like "ergic tension," "radicalism-conservatism," or "dominance-submission," etc.

In a more recent study, Costa and McCrae (1976) used cluster analysis to demonstrate structural change in 16 PF factors across three age groups of men (young: 25–34; middle-aged: 35–54; old 55–82 years). Two clusters (adjustment-anxiety and introversion-extraversion) showed similarity of structure across the whole age range. The third cluster, however, had a different structure in the age groups studied. In the younger group this cluster is related to openness, feelings, and aesthetic sensibility, and in the middle-aged group to an "openness to new ideas and values." In the old group, the third cluster includes openness to affective as well as cognitive experiences. Costa and McCrae (1976) believe that they can relate their conclusions to C. G. Jung's theory that individualization, as the ultimate goal of personality development in human life, is defined as the integration of two fundamental psychological "functions" namely, "feeling and thinking."

In her analysis of multivariate approaches to aging in the context of personality, Neugarten (1977) questioned the contributions made by this group of scientists especially with regard to the definition of the direction of change over time. The distinction between a more emotional young adulthood and a more rational middle adulthood may reflect popular stereotypes rather than scientific enlightening.

# PROCESS-CENTERED APPROACHES TO THE STUDY OF AGING

## SITUATIONISM VS. STRUCTURALISM IN PERSONALITY RESEARCH

Due to the complex interaction between calendar age, sex, social conditions, biological age, and disease on the one hand and the behavior of the individual on the other, trait-centered approaches have a limited value for the study of aging in personality. Any prediction of the behavior of the aged based entirely on expected correlations between age and trait scores must fail if the interaction of other variables cannot be calculated. As data for such a calculation can be only partially provided, process-centered approaches are relevant alternatives. These approaches study personality in the context of the individual's history and the present situation, and look for regularities in the ways in which the elderly adjust to their situation.

This interaction became the focus of approaches stemming from cognitive social learning theory and clinical experience (Ekkehammar, 1974; Mischel, 1968; 1973). They criticize trait models for their underestimation of situation—specific inconsistencies of behavior and of the discriminative facility of the human actor. This discriminative facility contributes much to the adjustment of the person, whereas rigid across-situational consistency of behavior may cause conflict or maladjustment. As the situation is defined by the idiosyncratic social learning history of the individual, the theory could end up with an idiographic concept of the uniqueness of personality like that of G. W. Allport (1937) and with a conceptualization of behavior as idiosyncratic in terms of person, situation, and the specific meaning of this situation. Prediction of behavior no longer would be one of the objects of this kind of personality psychology and a replacement of tests by "the analysis of naturally occurring behaviors observed in the interactions among people in real settings."

These propositions have not yet been applied to a study on aging and personality[1]. Process-

---

[1] For the evaluation of intellectual performance, Schaie and his coworkers have discussed the person-situation-task interface (Schaie, 1978) and have developed a taxonomy of situations for the elderly (Scheidt and Schaie, 1978).

centered approaches to the aging personality always had to take regard of the health, family, or housing conditions of the elderly. Indeed there exist some similarities in the social changes, gains, and losses the elderly experiences in his career from employment to retirement and through many stages into the nursing home. So far Mischel's empirical work is mainly concerned with studies on self-control in children, but the incorporation of the person-situation-interactions as defined by Mischel (1973) and others may also serve as tools for reconceptualization of the aging personality in the future.

Actually many of the ideas of interactionism influenced process-centered approaches to the aged personality long before the work of Mischel. Implicitly and/or explicit, most of these approaches were based on certain hypotheses regarding the situations of the aged and their impact on the behavior of the individual. Very often these hypotheses or expectations refer to changes in the biological situation and especially in the social situation from middle to old age. These changes often are characterized as loss of physical and mental capacity, of availability of resources, of roles and social ties, etc. (Loeb, 1973; Rosow, 1973; Streib, 1976).

Expectations which are too much oriented on experiences with clinical cases or with social welfare recipients can lead to overgeneralizations. However, defining the situation as a problem or something involving loss helps to assess the organism-environment relationships in an adequate way so that the active role of the person is taken into account. Furthermore, we should remember that many of these process-centered approaches to the aging personality are integrated into some conceptualization of the life cycle. Therefore the ideas of loss, problem, and crisis are not restricted to old age. They are present in different forms and degrees in each of the main stages of life. This is true for Erikson's (1950) theory of the growth of the healthy personality, which defines the whole human life as a sequence of problems which have to be solved. Alternative conceptualizations of the process of aging in middle and old age were offered by Peck (1956) and Havighurst (1963; 1975). Discrepancies between desired and achieved goals, between hetero- and autostereotypes, and between social norms and own norms for age-appropriate behavior (Neugarten, 1977) and similar conflict situations are stressed in these approaches. More recent conceptualizations point to analogies between the social situation of the aged and a "social break down syndrome" (Kuypers and Bengtson, 1973) or define aging as a system of stressors (Lazarus and Cohen, 1976; Tallmer and Kutner, 1969).

From these points of view, process-centered approaches to the aging personality implicitly and explicitly define the problems the aged person has to cope with, the ways in which these problems are perceived, the selection of the responses to these problems, and the efficiency of these responses. Personality variables like traits, cognitive styles, or defense or coping mechanisms are involved in the perception of the situation and the selection of responses. However, their role may be different in different persons as well as in different situations.

## PERSONALITY DYNAMICS AND THE PRINCIPLES OF HOMEOSTASIS

Problems in the life of the aged can be conceptualized as divergencies from an optimal state of well being, whether this divergence is caused by health problems, or by loss of social roles, economic resources, or significant others (like spouse or friend). Therefore the process of adjustment to the aged's situation is another example of homeostatic regulation (Cannon, 1932). There are some doubts if homeostatic principles are sufficient to explain all of human behavior (Weiner, 1972). However, as far as there exist divergencies between a certain level of equilibrium and the present state of affairs, the homeostatic model has some advantages. It enables us to formalize biological, medical, psychological, and sociological aspects of the situation to a degree that changes in any of these aspects can be treated in equivalent ways. Any loss is deprivation and any decrease in capacity is equivalent to deprivation and disequilibrium.

In sociology the main problem of the aged is that of loss of roles and of economic resources (Rosow, 1967). This loss of roles leads to a systematic status loss for an entire cohort, to devaluation and to a negative self-concept (Rosow, 1973). These social contexts of the aging self must be taken into account if the psychologic situation of the elderly is to be assessed (Riley, Finer, and Heb, 1968). Kent (1966) believed that the social situation of the aged could be defined as one of social alienation. The aged "becomes a stranger in a society that is both his and of his making. Yet he no longer belongs nor can he participate."

This social alienation is regarded as the main problem for social gerontology. Support for this view also comes from studies on stereotypes of the aged (Lehr, 1979) and on agism (Butler, 1969, Neugarten 1969). Another source of stress and discomfort for the elderly is loss of spouse or close friends. Many studies have tried to assess the psychological and social implications of widowhood, especially in elderly women (Lopata, 1972).

Degree of economic deprivation is different

for different social classes and countries. However, even in industrial societies with a highly developed system of pensions and insurance companies there exists a larger group, composed mainly of elderly women, who live in poverty (Geibler, 1975; Rosenmayr, 1976). There is evidence that these economic restrictions result in poor housing conditions (Dringenberg, 1975) and lack of transportation and availability of open-air leisure-time facilities.

Another major source for divergence from a desirable level of well-being are health problems, sensory and motor disabilities, dental problems, etc. According to Tallmer and Kutner (1969), health was the "stressor" which had a more powerful effect on engagement than any other factor, like age, widowhood, or retirement. Although the health status of the aged has improved since 1961, health problems may limit mobility and activity among the aged (Palmore, 1976).

These are only some examples of the arguments raised by process-centered approaches to the aging personality. It is a matter of convenience if we take stress or problem as the label by which we define the situation of the aged. In any case, a divergence from a moderate level of well-being will (according to homeostatic principles) arouse overt and/or covert behavior to decrease the divergence between the real and the desired state of affairs. The problem inherent in this approach is the emphasis on deficiencies and disturbances which can contribute to a reinforcement of negative stereotypes of old age.

However the main emphasis within all these theories is on the way in which the aged cope with these problem situations, and the majority of the approaches stress the competence with which the aged cope with their problems.

This is especially true for a new conceptualization of the homeostatic model of behavior for adaptation in old age, as formulated by Kuypers and Bengtson (1973). They hypothesize a social breakdown syndrome as the instigating event for the process of adaptation. This social breakdown is initiated by the social changes inherent in transition from middle to old age and is especially defined by loss of roles and status. According to Kuypers and Bengtson (1973), this social reorganization results in a negative cycle of events which end up in the labeling of the elderly as incompetent first by society and finally by the elderly themselves. Originally, social breakdown syndrome theory was supposed to explain the development of mental illness (Zusman, 1966). The application of this theory in a process theory of personality and aging faces the risk of inadequate generalizations based on findings in psychopathology. As long as we take Kuypers' and Bengtson's interpretation of the situation of the elderly as an *analogy* to susceptibility to maladjustment and incompetence, it is another conceptualization of the homeostatic sequence in adjustment to the situation of the aged. Susceptibility to incompetence is equivalent to the instigating nature of the unbalanced situation. The sequence of actions leading to new competence is equivalent with restoration of equilibrium. As far as the theory suggests the development of new competences, it goes beyond Cannon (1932) and Hull (1952): it attributes capacity for self-actualization to the new constellation of personal and social systems postulated in this theory.

## COGNITIVE THEORY OF PERSONALITY AND ADJUSTMENT TO AGING

A critical point inherent in homeostatic interpretations of behavior as well as in Social Breakdown Syndrome Theory or in Role Theory refers to the difference between the objective situation and that perceived by the person involved. According to cognitive theories of personality (Baldwin, 1969; Bolles, 1974; Thomae, 1968; 1970), the first stage in the chain of events initiated by the stimulus situation and resulting in the behavioral act is the construction of a cognitive representation of the situation. The uniqueness of personality according to Kelly (1955) is to be defined by their constructions of events. Unfortunately, personal construct theory is more interested in the results of these construction processes and the formal qualities of these constructs. The same is true for Rotter's concept of generalized expectations (such as locus of internal versus external control, basic trust versus basic mistrust). These constructs were transformed into traits and cognitive approaches offered concepts for the design of trait theory studies. The same is true of most conceptualizations of cognitive styles which originally were conceived as approaches to the assessment of cognitive representations of the situation.

### PERCEPTIONS OF CHANGE IN HEALTH

Cognitive theories related to age-change relationships such as cognitive theories of aging and personality emphasize especially perceptions of change. Therefore cognitive theory of personality as related to a theory of aging postulated that perceived change rather than objective change is related to behavioral change (Thomae, 1970). Evidence for this relationship is offered in those cases of malignant disease which do not influence the patient's well-being and efficiency until the doctor advises him to undergo surgery. The obvious change in the morphological structure had no effects as long as it was not perceived. Even if the full truth is withheld, the perception of the situation changes the individual completely until some new balance has been attained.

In the second year of the BLSA (1966) one part of a semi-structured interview was related to change perceived by the individual in his own personality in general and in his health and cognitive and occupational efficiency in particular (Tismer, 1971). Although the health of the older cohort (born 1890–95) received poorer rating scores by the doctor than that of the younger cohort (born 1900–1901), there was no difference in the perceived change regarding health between the cohorts. Complaints regarding health did not differentiate between the two groups either. At least for the older group, this means a definite divergence between perceived change in health and objectively assessed health. According to Schmitz-Scherzer (1979) only a quarter of the BLSA men and a third of the women rated their health as good or as bad as did the doctor. Generally there was tendency, especially by men, to rate their health better than the doctor did. The discrepancy between objective and subjective health assessment was smaller in the study subjects of the Duke Gerontological Study (Maddox, 1970).

This may be explained by the higher social status of the Duke sample. However there is the same tendency for a more positive evaluation of own health in male study subjects as in the Bonn sample. In both studies many attitudinal correlates of perceived health were stated. In any case the dynamics of subjective health perception cannot be explained exclusively by defense mechanisms. There are many factors involved which demonstrate the complex motivational conditions of perception and appraisal of the situation.

Tornstam (1975) found that subjective health status is influenced mainly by symptoms of disease like aches, serious illness, visible impairment, and vascular disease, and, to a lesser degree, by mobility and social interaction. These symptoms were reported by respondents given a checklist of medical symptoms. This design explains the unusually high correlation between objective and perceived health as reported in Tornstam's (1975) study. In any case the Swedish study shows that subjective health status is also influenced by perception of physical symptoms, which were not as influential in other studies.

A major contribution of Tornstam is related to a motivational variable included by Tornstam— the construct "aspiration level regarding health" which decreased with increasing age. Therefore the same level of subjective health may be attained in ill aged persons as in less ill, younger persons. Tornstam points to the dynamics of cognitive evaluation and motivational tendencies directed to consistency of self-perception.

Other determinants of perceived health were shown by comparisons of two groups of BLSA study subjects; one group reported no perceived change in their general condition, while the other group reported poorer health (personal communication, Fisseni). From some characteristics of these groups, Fisseni defined the no-perceived change group as subjectively young, and the other group as subjectively old. However, the calender age of the subjectively old study subjects was younger than that of the subjectively young. This subjectively young group included more women and more single persons and was assessed by the doctor as being in poorer health. This group also reported less stress in other areas of life. They showed an increasing feeling of being needed and consistently higher life satisfaction scores. Therefore we might wonder if this group was not influenced by a general tendency to distorted perceptions. This interpretation may be supported by the behavioral tendency as rated by the trained psychologists at each of three measurement points. From these ratings Fisseni believes that the personality correlates of the change-perceivers can be summarized by a greater sensibility and responsiveness. They more often showed changes in mood or happiness, and in the longitudinal perspective, a tendency toward more depressed mood. Their scores in WAIS decreased during the years of observation. However, they were still open to many activities. The no-change perceivers were characterized by a tendency toward desensitization. They were happier and more adjusted to the specific demands of the situation (i.e., the interview, testing program, or informal group meetings), and felt more secure during the testing procedures, but became less responsive and less active during the years of observation.

It would be risky to identify these two groups, defined by different degrees of readiness to perceive change in vital aspects of their own situation, with well-known cognitive styles like repressors or sensitizers. The major point of this study brought out the complex determination of the ways in which the aged perceive their situation and the divergencies and convergencies of these perceptions from reality (see also, Fisseni, 1976).

The relevance of the cognitive theory of behavior to intervention in institutional settings was demonstrated by Langer and Rodin (1976) in a field experiment. A group of nursing home residents was given communication emphasizing their responsibility for themselves, whereas the control group was given a communication stressing the staff's responsibility for them. Activity rated before and three weeks after the communication was received was significantly different in the experimental group and pointed to a decisive effect of perceived responsibility. The control group's activity and well-being decreased in a significant way during the same time. The manipulation of the perception of the situation to include freedom and responsibility in the experimental group even had effects on cognitive functioning, which improved in the experimental group and decreased in the control group.

## PERCEPTIONS OF ECONOMIC SITUATION

Thomae (1975) and Maderna (1977) reported a very positive appraisal of their own economic situation by many aged persons in Western Germany and Italy, respectively, who actually lived in or close to poverty. Maderna believes that this is a reaction specific to the cohorts under study. Thomae (1975) pointed to the two currency reforms (1923 and 1948) and the time of complete political and economic breakdown of Germany which served as reference points for the appraisal of the present situation by aged persons interviewed between 1965 and 1970. In any case the perception of economic situation is a variable dependent on the life history of the subjects and on many cultural and generational influences. This is shown, too, by study of Tissue (1972) on the perception of income by welfare recipients in the US. There existed a considerable degree of dissatisfaction with their own economic situation and a significant relationship between perception of money problems and morale. The welfare income seemed most unsatisfactory to those whose age, behavior, and self-image were characteristic of a youthful life style. The difference between this finding and those of Maderna (1977) and Thomae (1975) may be explained by the fact that the European studies included the general population. Also, the socialization histories of the elderly in the US emphasized far more attitudes of asking for more rights during their young and middle adulthood compared to their European age peers, who at those times learned to follow the rules of a dictatorship. Finally, the differences in the perception of welfare income in Tissue's (1972) sample between those who identified with their own age group and those who did not point to the complex determinants of perceptions which very often are neglected in cognitive theories of behavior.

## HOUSING CONDITIONS: REAL AND PERCEIVED

In studies coming mainly from the US the difference between stimulus quality and evaluative perception has been demonstrated with reference to housing conditions. Aged persons living in very unsufficient and even inappropriate environments very often evaluated them as fair or even good (Hamovitch and Peterson, 1969; Winiecke, 1973). Some authors believe that this is due to some socialization effects. Britton (1966), Carp (1975), and Lawton, Kleban, and Carlson (1973), however, hypothesized that this positive image of the own home was due to mechanisms of ego defense against the threatening awareness of the inevitability of the situation. Carp (1975) tested this hypothesis by interviewing aged persons living in very bad housing conditions: one group was offered alternative apartments and help in moving, etc.; the control group consisted of those who were not rated as eligible for the rehousing program. A majority of the study subjects of the first group shifted to more negative evaluations of the present housing conditions after the alternative was presented. The interpretation offered by Carp (1975) is related to the theory of cognitive consistency. Perceptions of housing conditions which are not consistent with the view of oneself as a worthwhile human being are distorted or at least changed to a positive direction.

## PERCEPTION OF FUTURE AND ADJUSTMENT

Future time perspective is an important dimension in the individual's life space (Lehr, 1961, 1967; Lewin, 1951; Nuttin, 1964; Schreiner, 1970, 1971). Whether there is a general restriction of future time perspective in old age may be doubted from more recent research (Munnichs, 1979). Some studies could not find a correlation between calendar age and extension of future time perspective (Kastenbaum, 1963); others point to the increasing relevance of the near future (Kuhlen and Monge, 1968; Thomae, 1970; Nuttin and Grommen, 1975). Schonfield (1973) compared the future commitments (defined by plans for the next seven days) of a random sample and of special groups of aged persons. Successful aging defined by a tri-scale approach was related to future commitments, which were less frequent among nursing home aged and among those receiving meals on wheels.

Schreiner (1970; 1971) analyzed the data on future time perspective of the BLSA study subjects from their responses to the question related to number and kind of plans in the year following the interview. There was no difference in the extension of future time perspective between the two cohorts (1890–05; 1900–05) and, following a drop from the first to the third measurement points there was no significant change for four years. Perceptions of present life situation (well-balanced versus unbalanced), and personality variables like activity, responsiveness, and self-reliance showed significant correlations with extensity and quality of future plans in most of the measurement points. Perceived health and concern about death were not related to future time perspective as defined in this study.

Specific forms of the future time perspective are defined by expectations which may be used as models for analyzing the perceptions of the actual situation. Lehr (1966) and Neugarten, Wood, Kraines, and Loomis (1963) showed that unfavorable expectations of menopause rather than menopause itself arouses the climacteric crisis. Studies on adjustment to retirement gave evidence for the role of a realistic anticipation of retirement for adjustment to this stage (Ash, 1966; Davidson and Kunze, 1965; Lehr and Dreher, 1969). Unrealistic or negative anticipations served as personal constructs which aroused conflict or dissonance between expectation and attained status. Glamser and De Jong (1975) showed that discussion groups in preretirement education can prevent anxiety as they facilitate more accurate anticipations of the future.

## SELF-PERCEPTION AND SELF-CONCEPT

Self-concept is an organized, coherent, and integrated pattern of self-related perceptions. According to Rogers (1959) and many other writers, it is that section or part of the perceived life space which is most decisive in determining consistency and change in behavior. For clinical work the processes which prevent the inclusion of perceptions into the self-concept are the most relevant ones.

The same aspect is important for any discussion on personality and aging, which in Western culture has major effects on the self-concept as it shifts from independent to dependent and from aspiring to declining (Rose, 1965). Research findings do not confirm this negative self-concept generally. Using a semantic differential technique, Bergler (1968) found in a sample of West Germans 19–69 years of age, that the elderly still perceive of themselves as active, self-controlled, and competent. They believe they are more sensitive and irritable, and more cautious, controlled, serious, fact–minded, and reserved than younger persons.

On the other hand, there is some thought that this positive self-concept is based on distorted perceptions or on exclusions of experiences from the self-concept. From their work with fatally ill patients, Weisman and Hackett (1967) have pointed to the role of denial as a major instrument in dealing with threats to the self-concept. Studies on everyday behavior also can point to the very complex dynamics by which perceptions and experiences are admitted to or excluded from the self-concept of aged persons. Such interpretations are suggested by the findings of a survey on behaviors and attitudes of elderly pedestrians (Thomae, Mathey, Knorr, 1977). A majority of the 220 respondents (65–95 years) reported frequent participation as pedestrians even during traffic rush hours. More than 85 percent of them stated that they did not have any difficulties in crossing streets, even in crowded areas. On the other hand, 95 percent of them agreed that almost all elderly persons have a great deal of anxiety when going on the streets. There were some indications that these respondents did not identify themselves with the social group of the aged. Belonging to this group would mean identification with a low-status group. Therefore, there is denial of one's own age and denial of problems in facing traffic, too. As this reaction was found in almost all men, and as old men are next to children as the highest risk group in German traffic, we might regard their perception of the traffic situation as a distortion caused by mechanisms of ego defense. If we consider the very detailed observations on traffic situations made by the same study subjects, we would hesitate to label the cognitive structuring of their perception in such a way. We should also mention that the respondents named elderly pedestrians more frequently than drivers of cars as causes of traffic accidents. The main topic to be stressed here is the complex pattern of perceptions of the same situation which may be present in the same person, and which may change corresponding to threats or enhancements of their self-concept.

The same aspect is important for any discussion on personality and aging, as acceptance of oneself as old or rejection of this perception is one of the developmental tasks which face the aging person. This process of identification of oneself as old will depend on the quality of the person's existing self-concept. If an individual's self-concept has been positive, positive elements of the stereotype of old will be accepted, and the individual will still hold a positive self-concept when defining himself as old (Brubaker and Powers, 1976). If the previous self-concept was negative, negative elements of the stereotype of old will be accepted and thereby produce a negative self-definition. These conclusions drawn from existing research seem to reflect a very smooth process in the transformation of self-concept. From experience with fatally ill patients, Weisman and Hackett (1967) have pointed to the role of denial as a major instrument in dealing with threats to self-concept.

The decisive role of sex in shaping the self-concept of the aged has been demonstrated by Angleitner (1975), Back (1971) and Markson and Grevert (1972). Markson and Grevert (1972) found some confirmation for the hypothesis that sex role differences, socialized especially deeply for the cohorts around the turn of century, are mirrored in the self-concepts of the aged. Men, regardless of mental state, feel themselves as independent more often than do women, and are even more likely to stress independence when confronted by a female interviewer. It is concluded that differences between men and women reflect role behavior which persists even after work and parental roles have been abandoned. Analyzing data from the first wave of the Duke Longitudinal Study of Aging, Back (1974) reported that women in middle age define themselves in terms of personal background, such as family relations and demographic characteristics. Cohorts beyond 60 however referred more often to personal values and achieved positions. These values and occupational achievements had already been the reference points in middle-aged men. According to Back (1974), among women neither retirement nor separation from children affected the self-concept as much as age. The impact of these two life-crises were visible however with regard to discrepancy between real self-concept and appearance of self. For men especially, this discrepancy between their own self-concept and what they imagine other people think about them caused many problems. The age-related changes in the self-concept of women are defined mainly by shifts from relationships with others to their own abilities and feelings. The authors interpret the findings as a hypothesized feeling of freedom from family obligations and of being accepted for their own sake. They furthermore hypothesize a general and enduring involvement of men with the work role. Separation from children will make them even more dependent on work role, and in this way will increase the problematic aspects in this stage of their life.

The self-concept as defined by the Interpersonal Checklist (ICL) of La Farge and Suczek (1955) discriminates between old men and women mainly on the basis of health (Angleitner, 1975). Relatively healthy men describe themselves as more "rebellious–distrustful" than men in worse health. Women perceive themselves as most "re-bellious-distrustful" when in poor health. Both the difference in the theoretical background of the instruments for measuring self-concept and the difference between samples do not enable us to make any summarizing comments on these sex differences in self-concept. In any case the differences mentioned so far raise doubt regarding any theory of a universal development of self-concept from middle to old age. As the self-concept is the result of relevant previous and simultaneous experiences, it is subject to many different influences. We should therefore be careful about any generalization.

Measurement problems can also confound comparisons of results. Theissen (1970) showed that there exists very little correspondence between different measures of the self-concept of aged persons. Even self-concepts derived from the same instrument, a structured interview, can turn out very differently when introduced in a different way. Self-concepts derived from interviews on everyday behavior pointed to a self-concept in which social and occupational competence was the most striking aspect. If the same interview was introduced by questions dealing with change in behavior and performance, the self-concepts had a greater tendency towards incompetence and declining ability. Although we observed similar reactions in younger adults (Lehr and Thomae, 1958), the differences between these two self-concepts expressed by the same persons over a period of one day were more striking. They point at least to one aspect which is universal: the delicate equilibrium among the constituents of a fairly balanced self-concept in old age.

## PERSONALITY DYNAMICS AND PATTERNS OF AGING

Many findings from recent studies in gerontology point to the complex network of variables which are related to consistency and change in behavior and performance from middle to old age. Chronological age no longer is regarded as the decisive determinant of behavioral change in old age. Due to the same findings, the science of aging now deals with the different patterns of aging, the conditions of these patterns, and the prediction and prevention of adverse forms of aging.

### LEVELS OF COMPETENCE AS PATTERNS OF AGING

As a very preliminary instrument for orientation we can define five main patterns of aging:
   1) *Elite aging* (as defined by studies on cen-

tenarians or professional people with continued activity and engagement even in the seventies and eighties).

*2) Survivorship in longitudinal studies,* with its correlates of higher intelligence, better education, continued activity, and adjustment to life in community (Lehr and Schmitz-Scherzer, 1976; Palmore, 1974; and Pfeiffer, 1974).

*3) Normal aging,* studied in cross-sectional samples which are representative for the age groups studied. According to comparisons of findings of the BLSA with a cross-sectional study in the same area of Western Germany, differences between these two groups are not sizeable, and there are even many varieties of both these main patterns which point to gradual transitions from pattern 2 to pattern 3. However there may be larger differences between longitudinal studies which are biased in terms of SES or health and cross-sectional studies which cover the full range of social and health levels.

*4) Institutionalized aging,* as defined by the disabilities and social losses which motivate most aged people to ask for admission into institutions and by the deprivating effects of life conditions which exist in many homes for the aged. The high percentage of institutionalized aged persons who show serious defects in temporal and local orientations and altered states of consciousness, is considered by Jansen (1971) to be a consequence of unprepared transfer to a home for the aged, but these conditions may have been etiological factors for the transfer, rather than a result. However there seems to exist clear evidence for negative changes in the self-concept of the institutionalized (Lieberman and Lakin, 1963; Pollack, Karp, Kahn, and Goldfarb, 1962). Anderson (1967) however confirmed her hypothesis that degree of interaction as provided inside or outside of institutions is related more closely to self-esteem than institutionalization itself. Within the institution those identifying with the residential community had higher self-esteem than those who did not have this identification.

Findings like these indicate that living in an institution involves many environmental variables which have different effects on different persons. According to several studies, adjustment to relocation is dependent on personality variables like depression, aggression, and anxiety (Brody, Kleban, and Moss, 1974) or activity and aggression (Turner *et al.*, 1972).

Therefore within the category of institutionalized persons, there is a wide range of interindividual differences. This is due to the variety of institutions and to the social and biographical conditions leading to the institutional career. Our label

for this group is a very unspecific one and the overlap between group (3) and (4) may be rather large.

*5) Impaired aging,* refers to mental deviation due to illness or pathology requiring psychiatric treatment and hospitalization or reference to a nursing home. From studies on intervention we learned that this group is by no means homogeneous and that characteristics of this group are also dependent on the care or intervention received during institutionalization (Baltes, 1973; and Salter and Salter, 1975).

## PATTERNS OF NORMAL AGING

The largest group of elderly people certainly is that characterized by normal aging with its close connections to survivorship in longitudinal studies. One of the main aims of a policy for the aged should be to orient all specialists involved in planning a better future for the aged toward these two patterns, rather than toward the last two patterns. Unfortunately, the general public very often is informed on aging only in terms of patterns included in the last group.

One of the main tasks for gerontology—theoretical as well as applied—is the study of the conditions by which the second and third aging patterns characterized by a high degree of social competence, can be attained by as many aged persons as possible. Biological (e.g., health) as well as social conditions (e.g., education, occupation, socio-economic status, degree of social integration, motivation, and ecology) interact with each other in the shaping of the individual patterns of aging. Therefore one can differentiate a variety of subforms from among the main patterns.

From trait-oriented approaches these subforms might be defined in terms of differences on trait scores like internal locus of control versus external locus of control. So far personality research on aged study subjects has stressed the comparison of mean or median scores obtained for different age groups. The major contributions to a classification of different patterns of aging are coming from process-centered approaches, which refer to the process of adjustment, to the situation of the aged itself, to outcomes of this adjustment process, and to process-outcome relationships.

## PATTERNS OF ADJUSTMENT TO CRISIS AND STRESS

Adjustment to the situation of the aged is often defined in terms of preferences for coping or defense. This classification of the different adjustment mechanisms has its roots in psychoanalysis and ego psychology (A. Freud, 1936) and has been subsequently modified (Ford, 1965; Haan, 1977; Parsons and Shils, 1951). From a longitudinal study on Harvard University graduates whom Vaillant (1977) followed for 30 years, a hierarchical model of ego mechanisms was deduced, with psychotic mechanisms at the lowest and mature mechanisms at the top level of the hierarchy. The differentiation between coping and non-coping is defined by Vaillant (1977) in terms of the pathological character of an adaptive mechanism. This pathological nature is evaluated within the context of the person's life situation rather than by labeling a certain reaction as pathological or non-pathological. Denial which is classified as a psychotic mechanism can be pathological if it prevents a patient from undergoing surgery, whereas it can be adaptive after the necessary treatment has been applied (Cohen and Lazarus, 1973; Vallaint 1977, p.51; see also Weisman and Hackett, 1967). From this point of view the classification of aged persons according to the level of their preferred adaptive mechanisms would have to be supplemented by an evaluation of the relationship of these mechanisms to their situation.

From the process by which the elderly attain a balance between the individual and the social system, Williams and Wirths (1965) identified two fundamental patterns of aging. They assert that an autonomy-dependency dimension defines the degree and the manner of attaining or restoring the balance between the person and the social system. An autonomous person is a person who is in balance or who is maintaining a balance by more en-

ergy output. A dependent person requires more input from others to maintain a balance.

In a series of studies on the way juvenile delinquents (Thomae, 1953), physically disabled persons (Hambitzer, 1962), displaced persons (Haupt, 1959), and community aged (Thomae and Simons, 1967) reacted to the problems and stresses on their lives, we identified a group of techniques used in coping with these situations. They are defined in a descriptive rather than in the interpretative way done in psychoanalytical perspective (Thomae, 1968).

In the BLSA we tried to get reports on life stresses on the economic, familial, health, and housing conditions of our study subjects from the post World War II years until 1977. We analyzed especially the ways in which our study subjects reacted to their situations and we developed a classification system indicating different reaction patterns for the time of extreme deprivation (1948) and for the 1960s and 1970s. (see Table 13-1).

The analysis of the reactions between 1965–1977 suggested the hypothesis that persistent and unavoidable stress situations ask for adjustment patterns which we define as cognitive restructuration of the situation rather than ego defense. Rather than distorting the perception, this reaction to stress structures the situation in a way which may give meaning and relevance to failure and loss. There are, however, many interindividual differences.

Ongoing research will differentiate between those preferring achievement-related behavior from those who preferred adaptation to the habits and expectations of others up to the late 70s. Main em-

**Table 13–1**  Rank order of adjustment patterns to occupational problems reported by men (age 60–75) for 1948 and 1965.

| 1948 | 1965 |
|------|------|
| (1) Achievement orientated behavior. | (1) Achievement orientated behavior. |
| (2) Adjustment to the institutional aspects of the situation. | (2) Identification with the aims and/or successes (eventually failures) of children and grandchildren. |
| (3) Adjustment to the habits and/or needs of others. | (3) Seeking and/or cultivating social contacts. |
| (4) Establishing and/or cultivating social contacts. | (4) Accepting situation as it is. |
| (5) Using chance opportunities. | (5) Adjustment to the habits and/or needs of others. |
| (6) Active resistance to obstacles. | (6) Evasive reactions. |
| (7) Accepting situation as it is. | (7) Adjustment to the institutional aspects of the situation. |
| (8) Hope for help from others. | (8) Hope for help from others. |
| (9) To rely on others. | (9) Active resistance to obstacles. |
| (10) Aggressive reaction. | (10) Depressive reaction. |
| (11) Asking others for help. | (11) Aggressive reaction. |
| (12) Depressive reaction. | (12) To rely on others. |
| (13) Resignation in favor of others. | (13) To disengage from situation. |
| (14) Identification with the aims and/or successes— (eventually failures) of children. | (14) Resignation in favor of others. |
| (15) Evasive reaction. | (15) Using chance opportunities. |

tau (Kendall II) = 0.276; p>0.05.

phasis will be given to the dynamics of cognitive restructuring as this pattern of reactions is related to adaptation to situations which no longer can be solved by achievement related activity, external adaptation (to institutions or to habits and expectations of others) or by aggression.

An intervening variable between perception of life stress and selection of response is expectation of unchangeability of unfavorable situations in old age. Especially the expectations of unchangeability of serious health problems can influence this selection in favor of more unadjusted behavior (Thomae 1979).

Still another approach to the classification of patterns of aging in relation to stress reaction was proposed by Birren and Renner (1977). In an analysis of relationships between stress and illness in the aged they introduced personality as an intervening variable. From existing evidence on the different consequences of stress related to illness, they hypothesized that personality may intervene in four ways between stress and illness. Some persons may seek or create stress (environmental stress amplifiers), while others will avoid or minimize stress (environmental stress dampeners). While these two behavioral tendencies can be related to the primary appraisal of stressors in terms of the cognitive model of stress reaction (Lazarus, 1974), the two remaining personality types refer to differences in coping style. Internal stress amplifiers are excessively aroused and will remain so even to small incidents, whereas internal stress dampeners minimize stress by their preferred coping style. These reaction tendencies are related to cognitive restructuring of the situation as identified in the analysis of reactions to life stress in the BLSA (Thomae, 1976).

## PATTERNS OF SOCIAL PARTICIPATION OR "LIFE STYLES"

An alternative way of classifying patterns of aging in terms of the process of adjustment is related to different degrees and ways of social participation (Peppers, 1976). Havighurst and De Vries (1969) analyzed interview data on adjustment to retirement coming from six cities (Chicago, Duisburg [Rhine], Milano, Nijmegen [Netherlands], Vienna, and Warsaw). They identified seven life styles in terms of social participation, seven patterns of free-time activity, and five types of formal and informal social relations. The samples of retired teachers and steelworkers studied in this project showed different profiles in these patterns. Teachers more often continue with a part-time worker's role into their seventies or they become more active in church, club, or civic-political activity. Steel-

workers who substitute for loss of the worker role very often do so by increasing their family-role activity. Classifying the different patterns of social participation and leisure-time activity in terms of engagement or disengagement, Havighurst and De Vries (1969) more often found an engaged aging pattern in teachers and a disengaged aging pattern in steelworkers.

Patterns of social participation in a longitudinal perspective were also indentified by Olbrich (1976) from data of seven years of the BLSA. He found that patterns of change in agreement with disengagement theory were far less frequent in the different roles than those in agreement with activity theory of aging. On the other hand, he demonstrated that there is a considerable number of aged persons who have greater satisfaction with decreasing social participation as described by Cumming and Henry (1961).

In an integration of his former approaches to a classification of patterns of aging, Havighurst (1975) defined eight personality types in old age:

1. *Re-organizers*: "competent people engaged in a wide variety of activity."
2. *Integrated-focused*: "they tend to be selective in their activities and gain satisfaction from this concentration on one or two roles."
3. *Successful disengaged:* "persons with low role activity and high satisfaction."
4. *Holding-on pattern:* "they hold as long as possible to the activities of middle age."
5. *Constricted pattern:* "they have reduced their role activity presumably as a defense against aging."
6. *Succor-seeking:* "they are successful in getting emotional support from others."
7. *Apathetic:* "they have low role-activity combined with mediums of low life satisfaction."
8. *Disorganized:* "they have deteriorated thought processes and poor control over their emotions."

Havighurst (1975) assumes that these patterns are established and predictable by middle age. He believes that patterns of aging are consequences of individual choices rather than outcomes of social, biological, and biographical constellations. Alternative classifications of life styles of old men and women in terms of social participation and early adulthood antecedents of these styles are presented by Maas and Kuypers (1974), based on the data of Berkeley Child Guidance and Oakland Growth Study.

## TYPES OF ATTAINED ADJUSTMENT

Havighurst's final classification combined process as well as outcome aspects. In the San Francisco study orginally directed by Else Frenkel-Brunswick, Reichard and her co-workers (1962) took the result of the adjustment process as the criterion for the definition of five patterns of adjustment to aging, with the mature person as the most successful one and the angry individual and the self-haters as the least successful ones. The records evaluated by this research group give evidence for a history of these adjustment types going back into childhood. The mature persons had a happy childhood and reached adulthood without undue emotional stress. They also glided smoothly into old age. They showed the least tendency towards defensive mechanisms. The rocking-chair person who fits very well into the disengagement theory type of successful aging had very easy-going fathers and dominant mothers. The characteristics given by Reichard *et al.* (1962) point to similarities of this adjustment pattern and preferences for oral defense mechanisms. The angry men were the largest group of aged persons defined. Most of them were not retired and they were not adjusted to aging. They were hostile, intolerant, and constantly alert for hostility in others. There were many indications that they had not led satisfying lives.

The greatest problem of the classification done by Reichard is the small number of persons included in each of the groups. The angry group consisted of 16 men; the mature group was made up of 14 persons. Each of the three remaining groups did not exceed seven persons (e.g. self-haters were identified by only four persons). Of the 87 aging men included in Reichard's study, only 47 could be categorized in terms of the five types mentioned here. From this point of view the classification of patterns of aging can be regarded only as an instrument for an individual specific approach. However, gerontology cannot consist solely of idiographic case-histories, and some methods of generalization are essential.

## CONCLUSIONS

One of the main reasons I do not summarize our findings by a list of types is because developments in personality theory raise doubts regarding the trait-centered approaches in personality research and stress interactionistic (Rotter) and situation-centered (Mischel) approaches. From these trends in personality theory, we should regard the different principles for classification of patterns of aging as instruments for the assessment of the individual life course in late adulthood. From our findings on consistency and change of psychological functioning and adjustment in old age we should define patterns of aging in terms of biological, social, and perceptual-motivational processes. Patterns of this kind might support theoretical as well as applied research. Any kind of prediction

of adjustment to aging and of planning services and support for the aged would require a systematic assessment of the different subsystems which define the aging process in a given individual-environment interaction. Ten of these subsystems can be defined as follows:

1. Nature-nurture constellation at the beginning of the aging process (e.g., heredity, educational history, habits regarding physical and mental activity, nutrition, smoking, cultivating interests, and social contacts).
2. Recent changes in the biological system (health, insensory functions regarding primary process of aging, short-term memory, etc.).
3. Recent changes in the social role system (retirement, loss of spouse or other relatives, or friends, new friendships, substitute roles).
4. Socioeconomic and ecological situation (e.g., income, social security, housing, transportation, availability of medical care, and of preventive measures, etc.).
5. Consistency and change in different aspects of cognitive functioning.
6. Consistency and change in personality (activity, interest, mood, creativity, adjustment, ego-control).
7. Individual life space (self-concept; concept of significant others; perceived socioeconomic, political, and historical situation; general belief-value system, [religion, attitude toward death].
8. Life satisfaction or degree of attained balance between individual needs and perceived life situation.
9. Capacity for restoring balance by active coping (achievement-orientated behavior, adjustment, cognitive restructuring).
10. Social competence as a global measure for the individual's capacity to meet social and biological demands and the society's capacity to meet individual needs and capacities.

Patterns of aging (as defined from these ten dimensions or subsystems) are outcomes of the complex interaction between these subsystems. In terms of this complex network there is not one way to successful aging. Any recommendation for interventions and services in support of successful aging have to be evaluated in terms of the great variability, which can disturb and restore the balance of internal and external milieu, and in terms of the effects of this restoration on increased social competence of the aging individual.

## REFERENCES

AARONSON, B. S. 1966. Personality stereotypes of aging. *Journal of Gerontology, 21,* 458–462.

ABDO, E., DILLS, J., SHEETMAN, H., AND YANISH, M. 1973. Elderly women in institutions versus those in public housing: Comparison of personal and social adjustment. *Journal of the American Geriatrics Society, 21,* 81–87.

ADAMS, D. L. 1971. Correlates of life satisfaction. *Gerontologist, 11* (4, Part II), 64–68.

ALLPORT, G. W. 1937. *Personality: A Psychological Interpretation.* New York: Harper.

ANDERSON, N. 1967. The significance of age categories for older persons. *Gerontologist, 7,* 164–167.

ANGLEITNER, A. 1972. *Rigidität im Alter.* Unpublished doctoral dissertation. Bonn.

ANGLEITNER, A. 1975. Affects of health and sex in self-perception as measured by the ICL. *Proceedings Tenth International Congress of Gerontology,* Vol. I., pp. 233–235. Jerusalem.

ANGLEITNER, A. 1976. Changes in personality observed in questionnaire data from the Riegel Questionnaire on rigidity, dogmatism, and attitude toward life. *In,* H. Thomae (ed.), *Patterns of Aging,* pp.68–80. Basel-New York: Karger.

ANGLEITNER, A., SCHMITZ-SCHERZER, R., AND RUDINGER, G. 1971. Altersabhängigkeit der Persönlichkeit im Sinne von R. B. Cattell. *Actuelle Gerontologie, 1,* 721–729.

ASH, P. 1966. Pre-retirement counseling. *Gerontologist, 6,* 61–64.

BACK, K. W. 1971. Transitions to aging and the self-image. *Aging and Human Development, 2,* 296–304. Reprinted in E. Palmore (Ed.) Normal Aging II. Durham, N.C.: Duke University Press, 1974, pp. 207–216.

BALDWIN. A. L. 1969. A cognitive theory of socialization. *In,* D. Goslin (ed.), *Handbook of Socialization Theory and Research,* pp. 325–345. Chicago: Rand McNally.

BALTES, P. B. 1968. Longitudinal and cross-sectional sequences in the study of age and generation effects. *Human Development, 11,* 145–171.

BALTES, P. B. 1973. Strategies for psychological intervention in old age. *Gerontologist, 13,* 4–6.

BERGENER, M. 1975. Zumheutigen Stand der gerontopsychiatrischen Grundlagenforschung. *Actuelle Gerontologie, 5,* 365–376.

BERGLER, R. 1968. Selbstbild und Alter. *In,* R. Schubert (ed.), *Bericht I. Kongress Deutsche Gesellschaft für Gerontologie,* pp. 156–169. Darmstadt: Steinkopff.

BILD, B. R., AND HAVIGHURST, R. J. 1976. Senior Citizens in Great Cities. The Case of Chicago, *Gerontologist, 16,* No. 1, Pt II, 3–82.

BIRREN, J. E., AND RENNER, V. J. 1977. Health, behavior, and aging. *In,* J. E. Birren, J. M. Munnichs, and H. Thomae (eds.), *Institut de la Vie: Proc. World Conference on Aging: A challenge to science and policy.* Section: Behavioral Sciences, Oxford: Oxford University Press (in press).

BOLLES, R. C. 1974. Cognition and motivation. Some historical trends. *In,* B. Weiner (ed.), *Cognitive Views of Human Motivation,* pp. 1–20. New York: Academic Press.

BORTNER, R. W., AND HULTSCH, D. F. 1970. A multivariate analysis of correlates of life satisfaction in adulthood. *Journal of Gerontology, 25,* 41–47.

BRACELAND, F. J. 1972. Senescence: The inside story. *Psychiatric Annals, 2* (Part 1), 48–62.

BRACKEN, H. V. 1952. Wandlungen der menschlichen Persönlichkeit im mittleren und höheren Alter. *Studium Generale, 5,* 306–315.

BRITTON, J. H. 1966. Living in a rural Pennsylvania community in old age. *In,* F. M. Carp (ed.), *Patterns of living and housing of middle-aged and older people.* Washington, D.C.: US Government Printing Office.

BRITTON, J. H., AND BRITTON, J. O. 1972. *Personality changes in aging.* New York: Springer.

BRODY, E., KLEBAN, U. H., AND MOSS, M. 1974. Measuring the impact of change. *Gerontologist, 14,* (4), 299–305.

BRUBAKER, T. H., AND POWERS, E. A. 1976. The stereotype of old. *Journal of Gerontology, 31,* 441–447.

BUSSE, E. W., AND DOVENMUEHLE, R. H. 1958. *Patterns of successful aging.* Paper presented at the Symposium on patterns of successful aging at the 1958 meeting of the Gerontological society.

BUTLER, R. N. 1969. Ageism. *Gerontologist, 9,* 243–246.

CAMERON, P. 1967[a]. Ego strength and happiness of the aged. *Journal of Gerontology, 22,* 199–202.

CAMERON, P. 1967[b]. Introversion and egocentricity among the aged. *Journal of Gerontology, 22,* 465–468.

CANNON, W. B. 1932. *The Wisdom of the Body.* New York: Norton.

CANTRIL, H. 1965. The pattern of human concerns. New Brunswick, N.J.: Rutgers University Press.

CARP, F. M. 1975. Ego-defense or cognitive consistency effects on environmental evaluations. *Journal of Gerontology, 30,* 707–711.

CHATFIELD, W. F. 1977. Economic and sociological factors influencing life satisfaction of the aged. *Journal of Gerontology, 32,* 593–599.

CHOWN, S. 1961. Age and the rigidities. *Journal of Gerontology, 16,* 353–362.

CHRISTENSON, J. A. 1977. Generational value differences. *Gerontologist, 17* (No. 4), 367–374.

COHEN, G. D. 1976. Mental health services and the elderly: Needs and options. *American Journal of Psychiatry,* 65–68.

COHEN, F., AND LAZARUS, R. S. 1973. Active coping processes, coping dispositions, and recovery from surgery. *Psychosomatic Medicine, 35* (5), 375–389.

COMALLI, P. 1965. Cognitive functioning in a group of 80-90 years old men. *Journal of Gerontology, 20,* 14–17.

COSTA, P. J. 1973. *Age differences in the structure of 16 PF surface traits.* Paper presented at the 81st Annual Meeting of the American Psychological Association, Montreal.

COSTA, P. T., AND MCCRAE, R. R. 1976. Age differences in personality structure. A cluster analysis approach. *Journal of Gerontology, 31*, 564–570.

CRAIK, F. I. M. 1964. An observed age difference in responses to a personality inventory. *British Journal of Psychology, 55*, 453–462.

CRONBACH, L. J. 1957. The two disciplines of psychology. *American Psychologist, 12*, 224–232.

CUMMING, E., AND HENRY, W. E. 1961. *Growing old. The Process of Disengagement.* New York: Basic Books.

CUTLER, S. J. 1975. Transportation and changes in life satisfaction. *Gerontologist, 15*, 155–159.

DAVIDSON, W. R., AND KUNZE, K. R. 1965. Psychological, social, and economic meanings of work in modern society; their effects on the worker facing retirement. *Gerontologist, 5*, 129–133.

DE BEAUVOIR, S. 1970. *La Vieillesse:* Paris: Editions Gallimard.

DRINGENBERG, R. 1975. Neure Aspekte der Wohnforschúng. Z. *Gerontologist, 8*, 383–399.

EWARDS, J. N., AND KLEMMAK, D. L. 1973. Correlates of life satisfaction: a reexamination. *Journal of Gerontology, 28*, 497–502.

EISDORFER, C. 1967. New dimensions and tentative theory. *Gerontologist, 7*, 14–18.

EKKEHAMMAR, B. 1974. Interactionism in personality from a historical perspective. *Psychological Bulletin, 81*, 1026–1048.

ERIKSON, H. E. 1950. Growth and crises of the health personality. *In*, M. Senn (ed.), *Symposium on the Healthy Personality*, pp. 91–146. New York: Macey Foundation.

ERLEMEIER, N., SCHREINER, M., AND SCHNÜRER, H. 1972. Beziehungen zwischen Intelligenz und kognitivem Stil (Witkin) im höheren Alter. *Zeitschrift für Entwicklungspsychologie u. Pädagogische Psychologie, 3*, 183–193.

EYSENCK, H. J. 1947. *Dimensions of personality.* London: Routledge and Kegan.

EYSENCK, H. J. 1967. *The biological basis of personality.* Springfield, Ill.: Thomas.

EYSENCK, H. J., AND EYSENCK, S. B. G. 1969. *Personality Structure and Measurement.* London: Routledge & Kegan.

FISSENI, H. J. 1976. Perceived life space. Patterns of consistency and change. *In*, H. Thomae (ed.), *Patterns of Aging*, pp. 93–112. Basel-New York: Karger.

FORD, C. S. 1965. Ego adaptive mechanisms of older persons. *Social case work, 46*, 1, 16–21.

FREUD, A. 1936. *Das Ich und die Abwehrmechnismen.* Wien-London: Imago.

GEISSLER, J. 1975. *Neue Soziale Frage.* Bonn: Dokumentation CDU.

GLAMSER, F. D., AND DE JONG, G. F. 1975. The efficiency of preretirement preparation programs for industrial workers. *Journal of Gerontology, 30*, 595–600.

GORDON, C., GAITZ, C. M., AND SCOTT, J. 1973. Value priorities and leisure activities among middle aged

and older Americans. *Diseases of the Nervous System, 34*, 13–26.

GRANEY, M. J. 1975. Happiness and social participation in aging. *Journal of Gerontology, 30*, 701–706.

GRANICK, S. 1973. Morale measures as related to personality cognitive and medical functioning of the aged. *Proceedings of the 81st Annual Convention of the American Psychological Association*, Vol. 8, pp. 785–786. Montreal, Canada.

GROMBACH, H. 1976. Consistency and change of personality variables in late life. *In*, H. Thomae (ed.), *Patterns of Aging*, pp. 51–67. Basel-New York: Karger.

GRUHLE, H. 1938. Der Einfluss des Alterns auf den Ablauf seelischer Störungen. Z. *Alternsforschung, 1*, 209–221.

GUILFORD, J. P. 1959. *Personality.* New York-London: McGraw-Hill.

HAAN, N. 1977. *Coping and Defending. Processes of self-environment organization.* New York: Academic Press.

HAMBITZER, M. 1962. *Schicksalsbewältigung und Daseinsermöglichung bei Körperbehinderten.* Bonn-Bouvier.

HAMOVITCH, M. B., AND PETERSON, J. E. 1969. Housing needs and satisfactions of the elderly. *Gerontologist, 9*, 30–32.

HARRIS, C. W. 1963. *Problems of Measuring Change.* Madison, Wisc.: University of Wisconsin Press.

HATHAWAY, S. R., AND, McKINLEY, J. C. 1956. Scale 2 (Depression). *In*, G. S. Welsh and W. G. Dahlstrom (eds.), *Basic readings on the MMPI in psychology and Medicine*, pp. 73–80. Minneapolis: University of Minnesota Press.

HAUPT, K. 1959. Formen der sozialen Eingliederung Vertriebener. *Vita Humana. 2*, 35–64.

HAVIGHURST, R. J. 1963. Successful aging. *In*, R. H. Williams, I. Tibbitts, and W. Donahue (eds.), *Processes of Aging*, Vol. I, pp. 299–320. New York: Williams.

HAVIGHURST, R. J. 1975. Life styles transitions related to personality after age fifty. Paper presented at the International Society for Study of Behavioral Development Symposium. *The problem of transitions in the human life cycle.* Kibbutz Kiravim, Israel.

HAVIGHURST, R. B., AND DE VRIES, A., 1969. Life styles and free time activities of retired men. *Human Development, 12*, 34–54.

HEYMAN, D. K., AND GIANTURCO, D. J. 1973. Long term adaptation by the elderly to bereavement. *Journal of Gerontology, 3*, 359–362.

HULL, G. L. 1952. *A behavior system.* New Haven: Yale University Press.

JANSEN, W. 1971. Die Vorbereitung auf das Altenheim. *Actuelle Gerontologie, 1*, 285–289.

JUNG, C. J. 1925. *Psychologische Typen.* Zurich: Rascher.

KASTENBAUM, R. 1963. Cognitive and personal futurity in later life. *Journal of Individual Psychology, 19*, 216–222.

KELLY, G. 1955. *The Psychology of Personal Constructs*, Vols. 1 and 2. New York: Norton.

KENT, D. K. 1966. Social and cultural factors influencing the mental health of the aged. *American Journal of Orthopsychiatry, 36*, 680–685.

KESSEN, W., WILLIAMS, E. J., AND WILLIAMS, J. P. 1961. Selection and test of response measures in the study of the human new born. *Child Development, 32*, 7–24.

KIVETT, V. R., WATSON, J. A., AND BUSCH, J. G. 1977. The relative importance of physical, psychological and social variables to locus of control orientation in middle age. *Journal of Gerontology, 32*, 203–210.

KORNETSKY, C. 1963. Minnesota Multiphasic Personality Inventory Results on an aged population. *In,* J. E. Birren, R. N. Butler, S. W. Greenhouse, L. Sokoloff, and M. R. Yarrow (eds.), *Human Aging*, pp. 253–256. Bethesda, Md.: Department of Health, Education and Welfare.

KUHLEN, R. G., AND MONGE, R. H. 1968. Correlates of estimated rate of time passage in the adult years. *Journal of Gerontology, 23*, 427–433.

KUTNER, B., FANSHEL, D., TOGO, A. M., AND LANGER, T. A. 1956. *Five Hundred Over Sixty*. New York: Russell Sage Foundation.

KUYPERS, J. A. 1972. Internal-External locus of control, ego functioning, and personality characteristics in old age. *Gerontologist, 12*, 168–173.

KUYPERS, J. A., AND BENGSTON, V. L. 1973. Social breakdown and competence. A model of normal aging. *Human Development, 16*, 181–201.

LA FARGE, R., AND SUCZEK, R. F. 1955. The interpersonal dimension of personality III. An interpersonal checklist. *Journal of Personality, 24*, 94–112.

LANGER, E. J., AND RODIN, J. 1976. The effects of choice and enhanced personal responsibility for the aged. A field experiment in an institutional setting. *Journal of Personality and Social Psychology, 34*, 191–198.

LAO, I. 1974. The developmental trend of the locus of control. *Personality and Social Psychology Bulletin, 1*, (1), 348–350.

LAUTER, H. 1973. Altersdepressionen - Ursachen, Epidemiologie, Nosologie. *Actuelle Gerontologie, 3*, 247–252.

LAWTON, M. P., KLEBAN, M. H., AND CARLSON, D. 1973. The inner city-resident: To move or not to move. *Gerontologist, 13*, 443–448.

LAZARUS, R. S. 1974. Psychological stress and coping in adaptation and illness. *International Journal of Psychiatry in Medicine, 5*, 321–333.

LAZARUS, R. S., AND COHEN, J. B. 1976. Theory and Method in the Study of Stress and Coping in Aging Individuals. Paper prepared for the 5th WHO Conference on Society-Stress and Disease: Aging and Old Age. Stockholm.

LEBOWITZ, B. D. 1975. Age and fearfulness: Personal and situational factors. *Journal of Gerontology, 30*, 696–700.

LEHR, U. 1961. Veränderung der Daseinsthematik der Frau im Erwachsenenalter. *Vita Humana, 4*, 193–228.

LEHR, U. 1964. Einstellungen zu einzelnen Lebensaltern. *Vita Humana, 7*, 201–227.

LEHR, U. 1966. Zur Problematik des Menschen im reiferen Erwachsenenalter-eine sozialpsychologische Interpretation der Wechseljahre. *Psychiatrie, Neurologie, Medizinische Psychologie, 18*, 59–62.

LEHR, U. 1967. Attitudes toward the future in old age. *Human Development, 10*, 230–238.

LEHR, U. 1977. *Psychologie des Alterns*. Heidelberg: Quelle and Meyer. (Rev. ed.).

LEHR, U. 1979. Stereotypes of aging and age norms. *In,* J. E. Birren, J. M. Munnichs, and H. Thomae (eds.), *Proceedings World Conference of Institute de la Vie*, Aging: A challenge to science and policy. (Vichy, France 1977). Behavioral Sciences Section. Oxford: Oxford University Press (in press).

LEHR, U., AND DREHER, G. 1969. Determinants of attitudes toward retirement. *In,* R. J. Havighurst, J. M. M. Munnichs, B. L. Neugarten, and H. Thomae (eds.), *Adjustment to Retirement. A Crossnational Study*. Assen: van Gorcum.

LEHR, U., AND RUDINGER, G. 1969. Consistency and change in social participation in old age. *Human Development, 12*, 255–267.

LEHR, U., AND SCHMITZ-SCHERZER, R. 1976. Survivors and non survivors—Two fundamental patterns of aging. *In,* H. Thomae (ed.), *Patterns of Aging*, pp. 137–156. Basel-New York: Karger.

LEHR, U., AND THOMAE, H. 1958. Eine Längsschnittuntersuchung bei 30–50 jährigen Angestellten. *Vita Humana, 1*, 100–110.

LEONTJEW, A. N. 1964. *Probleme der Entwicklung des Psychischen*. Berlin: Volk u. Wissen.

LEVINSON. E. J. 1975. Correlates of the internal-external locus of control scale in an aging population. Paper presented at meeting of Gerontol Society. Louisville.

LEWIN, K. 1951. *Field Theory in Social Science*. New York: Harper.

LIEBERMANN, M. A., AND LAKIN, M. 1963. On becoming an institutionalized person. *In,* R. H. Williams, C. Tibbitts, and W. Donahue (eds.), *Processes of Aging*. Vol. I (Social and Psychological Perspectives), pp. 475–503. New York: Atherton.

LOEB, R. 1973. Disengagement, activity, or maturity. *Sociology and Social Research, 57*, 367–382.

LOHMANN, N. 1977. Correlates of life satisfaction, morale and adjustment measures. *Journal of Gerontology, 32*, 73–75.

LOPATA, H. 1972. *Widowhood in American Society*. Chicago: Schenkman.

MAAS, H. J., AND KUYPERS, J. A. 1974. *From Thirty to*

*Seventy*. San Francisco: Jossey-Bass.

MADDOX, G. L. 1970. Self-assessment of health status. *In*, E. Palmore (ed.), *Normal Aging, I*, pp. 356–363. Durham, N.C.: Duke University Press.

MADERNA, A. M. 1977. Medical and psychological problems of aging and senility: Results of psycho-social and psycho-clinical researches carried out in Northern Italy. Paper read at the fourth Biennial Meeting of ISSBD. Pavia (Italy).

MARKSON, E., AND GREVERT, P. 1972. Circe's terrible island of change: Self perceptions of incapacity. *Aging and Human Development, 3*, 261–271.

MARKUS, E. J., AND NIELSEN, M. 1973. Embedded figures test scores among five samples of aged persons. *Perceptual and Motor Skills, 36*, 455–459.

McCALL, R. 1977. Challenges to a science of developmental psychology. *Child Development, 48*, 333–344.

McTAVISH, D. G. 1971. Perceptions of old people: A review of research methodologies and findings. *Gerontologist, 11*, (4), Part II, 90–102.

MISCHEL, W. 1968. *Personality and Assessment*. New York: John Wiley.

MISCHEL, W. 1973. Toward a cognitive social learning reconceptualization of personality. *Psychological Review, 80*, 252–283.

MORGAN, L. A. 1976. A re-examination of widowhood and morale. *Journal of Gerontology, 31*, 687–695.

MORIWAKI, S. Y. 1973. Self-disclosure, significant others, and psychological well-being in old age. *Journal of Health, 14*, 226–232.

MÜLLER, C. 1967. *Alterspsychiatrie*. Stuttgart: Thieme.

MUNNICHS, J. M. A. 1979. Chronological, social and psychological time. *In*, J. E. Birren, J. M. Munnichs, and H. Thomae (eds.), *Proceedings of World Conference on Aging: a challenge to science and policy*. (Institut de la Vie, Vichy 1977) Behavioral Sciences Section. Oxford (UK): Oxford University Press (in press).

NEUGARTEN, B. L. 1969. The old and the young in advanced industrialized societies. *Proceedings, Eighth International Congress of Gerontology*. Vol. I. 448–450. Washington.

NEUGARTEN, B. L. 1977. Personality and Aging. *In*, J. E. Birren (ed.), *Handbook of the Psychology of Aging*. New York: Van Nostrand Reinhold.

NEUGARTEN, B. L., AND HAVIGHURST, R. J. 1969. Disengagement reconsidered in a cross-national context. *In*, R. J. Havighurst, J. M. Munnichs, B. L. Neugarten, and H. Thomae (eds.). *Adjustment to retirement. A crossnational study*, pp. 138–146. Assen: Van Gorcum & Comp. N.V..

NEUGARTEN, B. L., WOOD, V., KRAINES, R. J., AND LOOMIS, B. 1963. Women's attitudes toward the menopause. *Vita Humana, 6*, 140–151.

NUTTIN, J. R. 1964. The future time perspective in human motivation and learning. *Acta Psychologica, 23*, 60–82.

NUTTIN, J. R., AND GROMMEN, R. 1975. Future time perspective in three socio-economic groups. U. Leuven (Belgium): *University of Leuven/Louvain Psychological Reports*, No. 5, 1–17.

NYSTROM, E. P. 1974. Activity patterns and leisure concepts among the elderly. *American Journal of Occupational Therapy, 28*, 337–345.

OBERLEDER, M. 1964. Effects of psychological factors in test results on aging. *Psychological Reports, 14*, 383–387.

OESTERREICH, K. 1975. *Psychiatrie des Alters*. Heidelberg: Quelle u. Meyer.

OKUN, M. A., AND ELIAS, C. S. 1977. Cautiousness in adulthood as a function of age and payoff structure. *Journal of Gerontology, 32*, 451–455.

OLBRICH, E. 1976. Der ältere Mensch in der Interaktion mit seiner sozialen Umwelt. Inter-und Intraindividuelle Unterschiede. Unpublished doctoral dissertation. Bonn.

PALMORE, E. 1970. The effects of aging on activities and attitudes. *In*, E. Palmore (ed.), *Normal Aging, I*, pp. 332–341. Durham, N.C.: Duke University Press.

PALMORE, E. 1974, Predicting longevity: A new method. *In*, E. Palmore (ed.), *Normal Aging, II*, pp. 281–285. Durham, N.C.: Duke University Press.

PALMORE, E. 1976. The future status of the aged. *Gerontologist, 16*, (4), 297–302.

PALMORE, E., AND KIVETT, V. 1977. Change in life satisfaction: A longitudinal study of persons aged 46-70. *Journal of Gerontology, 32*, 311–316.

PARSONS, T., AND SHILS, E. (Eds.). 1951. *Toward a General Theory of Action*. Cambridge, Mass.: Harvard University Press.

PECK, R. 1956. Psychological developments in the second half of life. *In*, J. E. Anderson (ed.), *Psychological Aspects of Aging*, pp. 47–53. Washington, D.C.: American Psychological Association.

PEPPERS, L. G. 1976. Patterns of leisure and adjustment. *Gerontologist, 16*, 5, 441–446.

PFEIFFER, E. 1974. Survival in old age. *In*, E Palmore (ed.), *Normal Aging, II*, pp. 269–280. Durham, N.C.: Duke University Press.

POLLACK, M., KARP, E., KAHN, R., AND GOLDFARB, A. I. 1962. Perception of self in institutionalized aged subjects. *Journal of Gerontology, 17*, 405–408.

REICHARD, S., LIVSON, F., AND PETERSON, P. G. 1962. *Aging and personality. A study of 87 older men*. New York: John Wiley.

REID, D. W., HAAS, G., AND DOUGLAS, H. 1977. Locus of desired control and positive concept of the elderly. *Journal of Gerontology, 32*, 441–450.

REINERT, G. 1970. Comparative factor analytic studies of intelligence throughout the life-span. *In*, L. R. Goulet and P. B. Baltes (eds.), *Life Span Developmental Psychology Research and Theory*, pp. 468–484.

New York: Academic Press.

RIEGEL, K. F. 1959. Personality theory in aging. *In*, J. E. Birren (ed.), *Handbook of Aging and the Individual*, pp. 797–851. Chicago: University of Chicago Press.

RIEGEL, K. F., AND RIEGEL, R. M. 1960. A study on changes of attitudes and interests during later years of life. *Vita Humana, 3*, 177–206.

RILEY, M. W., FINER, A. B., AND HEB, A. H. 1968. *Aging & society. An Inventory of Research Findings*, Vol. 1. New York: Russell Sage Foundation.

ROGERS, C. 1959. A theory of therapy, personality, and interpersonal relationships as developed in the client-centered frame-work. *In*, S. Koch (ed.), *Psychology. A study of Science*, Vol. 3, pp. 184–256. New York: McGraw-Hill.

ROSE, A. M. 1965. The sub-culture of aging: a framework of research in social gerontology. *In*, A. M. Rose and W. A Peterson (eds.), *Older People and Their Social World*, pp. 3–16. Philadelphia: Davis.

ROSENMAYR, L. 1976. Die soziale Benachteiligung alter Menschen. *In*, W. Doberauer (ed.), *Scriptum Geriatricum*, pp. 203–219. München-Wien: Urban and Schwarzenberg.

ROSOW, I. 1967. *Social Integration of the Aged*. New York: Free Press.

ROSOW, I. 1973. The social context of the aging self. *Gerontologist*, 1 (1), 82–83.

ROTTER, J. 1966. Generalized expectancies for internal versus external control of reinforcement. *Psychological Monographs, 80*, (whole No. 609).

RUDINGER, G. 1972. Methoden der Langsschnittforschung I. *Z. Gerontologie, 5*, 397–423.

RUDINGER, G. 1976. Correlates of changes in cognitive functioning. *In*, H. Thomae (ed.), *Patterns of Aging*, pp. 20–35. Basel-New York: Karger.

RYCKMAN, R. M., AND MALIKOSI, M. X. 1975. Relationship between locus of control and chronological age. *Psychological Reports, 36*, 655–658.

RYFF, C. D., AND BALTES, P. B. 1976. Value transition and adult development in women. The Instrumentality - Terminality Sequence Hypothesis. *Developmental Psychology, 12*, 567–568.

SALTER, C., AND SALTER, C. A. 1975. Effects of an individualized activity program on elderly patients. *Gerontologist, 15* (5), 404–406.

SAUER, W. 1977. Morale of the urban aged. A regression analysis by race. *Journal of Gerontology, 32*, 600–608.

SCHAIE, K. W. 1958. Rigidity—flexibility and intelligence: A cross-sectional study of the adult life span from 20 to 70 years. *Psychological Monographs, 72*(No.9.).

SCHAIE, K. W. 1965. A general model for the study of developmental problems. *Psychological Bulletin, 64*, 92–105.

SCHAIE, K. W. 1978. External validity in the assessment of intellectual development in adulthood. *Journal of Gerontology. 33*. 695–701

SCHAIE, K. W., AND PARHAM, I. A. 1976. Stability of adult personality traits. Facts or fable? *Journal of Personality and Social Psychology, 34*, 146–158.

SCHAIE, K. W., AND PARHAM, I. A. 1977. Cohort-sequential analyses of adult intellectual development. *Developmental Psychology, 13*, 649–653.

SCHEIDT, R. J., AND SCHAIE, K. W. 1978. A taxonomy of situations for the elderly: Generating situational criteria. Unpublished manuscript.

SCHMITZ-SCHERZER, R. 1974. Socialpsychologie der Freizeit. Stuttgart: Kohlhammer.

SCHMITZ-SCHERZER, 1977. Zur Veränderung des Freizeit-und Sozialverhaltens. *Z. Gerontologie, 10*, 300–321.

SCHMITZ-SCHERZER, R. 1979. Health, self-perceived and assessed by a physician, and behavior. Paper presented at Institute de la Vie (Paris) World Conference on Aging: A challenge to science and policy (Vichy) France.

SCHNEIDER, H. J. 1970. *Soziale Rollen im Erwachsenenalter*. Frankfurt: Thesen Verlag.

SCHONFIELD, D. 1973. Future commitments and successful aging. I. The Random Sample. *Journal of Gerontology, 28*, 189–196.

SCHREINER, M. 1970. Zur zukunftsbezogenen Zeitperspektive älterer Menschen. *Z. Entwicklungspsychol. Pädagogische Psychologie, 2*, 28–38.

SCHREINER, M. 1971. Dimensionen der Gegenwarts- und Zukunfts- orientierung bei alteren Menschen. *Actuelle Gerontologie, 1*, 715–720.

SCHREINER, M., ERLEMEIER, N., AND GLASMACHER, J. 1973. Persönlichkeit und kognitiver Stil (Watkin) im höheren Alter. *Zeitschrift für Entwicklungs-psychologie u. Pädagogische Psychologie, 5*, 29–41.

SCHWARTZ, I., AND KARP, S. 1967. Field dependence in a geriatric population. *Perceptual and Motor Skills, 24*, 495–504.

SHANAS, E., TOWNSEND, P., WEDDERBRUN, D., FRIIS, H., MILHOJ, P., AND STEHOUWER, J. 1968. *Old People in Three Industrial Societies*. New York-London: Routledge and Kegan.

SHMAVONIAN, B. M., YARMAT, A. J., AND COHEN, S. I. 1965. Relationships between the autonomic nervous system and central nervous system in age differences in behavior. In, A. I. Welford and J. E. Birren (eds.), *Behavior, Aging and the Nervous System*, pp. 235–258. Springfield, Ill.: Charles C Thomas.

SMITH, J. N. 1970. Age differences in achievement motivation. *British Journal of Social and Clinical Psychology, 9*, 175–176.

STONE, J. L., AND NORRIS, A. H. 1966. Activities and attitudes of participants in the Baltimore Longitudinal Study. *Journal of Gerontology, 21*, 575–580.

STREIB, G. F. 1976. Social stratification and age. *In*, R. Binstock and E. Shanas (eds.), *Handbook of Aging and the Social Sciences*, pp. 160–185. New York: Van Nostrand Reinhold.

TALLMER, M., AND KUTNER, B. 1969. Disengagement and the stresses of Aging. *Journal of Gerontology, 24*, 70–75.

THEISSEN, C. 1970. Untersuchungen zum Selbstbild älterer Menschen. Unpublished doctoral dissertation, University of Bonn.

THOMAE, H. 1953. Daseinstechniken sozialauffälliger Jugendlicher. *Psychol. Forschung, 24*, 11–33.

THOMAE, H. 1968. Das Individuum u. seine Welt. Eine Persönlichkeitstheorie. *Göttingen Verlag f. Psychologie.*

THOMAE, H. 1970. Cognitive theory of personality and theory of aging. *Human Development, 13*, 1–10.

THOMAE, H. 1975. Perceptions of and reactions to the economic situation in middle and old age. *Proceedings Tenth International Congress of Gerontology, I*, 353–354. Jerusalem.

THOMAE, H. (ed.). 1976. *Patterns of Aging. Contributions to Human Development.* Vol. 3. Basel-New York: Karger.

THOMAE, H. 1979. Reaktionen auf gesundheit liche Belastung. *Zeitschrift für Alternsforschung, 33*, (in press).

THOMAE, H., MATHEY, F. J., AND KNORR, F. 1977. Verhaltensweisen und Einstellungen älterer Menschen im StraBenverkehr Schriftenreihe des Bundesministers für Jugend, Familie und Gesundheit. Bd. 50, Bonn-Bad Godesberg.

THOMAE, H., AND SIMONS, H. 1967. Reaktionen auf Belastungssituationen höheren Lebensalter. *Zeitschrift für Experimentelle u. Angewandte Psychologie. 14*, 290–312.

THOMPSON, G. B. 1973. Work versus leisure roles: An investigation of morale among employed and retired men. *Journal of Gerontology, 28*, 339–344.

TISMER, K. G. 1971. Leistungsfähigkeit in der Sicht älterer Menschen. *Actuelle Gerontologie, 1*, 153–157.

TISMER, K. G., AND STRUCK, E. 1971. Leistungsmotivation im 7. u. 8 Lebensjahrzehnt. *Actuelle Gerontologie, 1*, 739–745.

TISMER-PUSCHER, I., AND HAACKE, I. 1972. Die Beachtung normbezogener Eigenschaften und Verhaltensweisen bei Mannern und Frauen des 2.-8. Lebensjahrzehnts. *Actuelle Gerontologie, 2*, 461–468.

TISSUE, T. 1972. Old age and the perception of poverty. *Sociology and Social Research, 56* (3), 331–344.

TORNSTAM, L. 1975. Health and self-perception. A systems-analytical approach. *Gerontologist, 15*, 264, 270.

TURNER, B. F., TOBIN, S. S., AND LIEBERMAN, M. A. 1972. Personality traits as predictors of institutional adaptation among the aged. *Journal of Gerontology, 27*, 61–68.

VAILLANT, G. E. 1977. *Adaptation to Life.* Boston-Toronto: Little, Brown and Co.

VIEBAHN, W. 1971. Das Bild des alten Menschen im westdeutschen Schullesebuch. *Actuelle Gerontologie, 1*, 711–714.

VYGOTSKY, L. S. 1966. Development of the higher mental functions. *In*, A. N. Leontjev, A. R. Luria, and A. Smirnow (eds.), *Psychological research in the USSR*, Vol. 1. pp. 11–46. Moscow: Progress.

WEINER, B. 1972. *Theories of Motivation.* Chicago: Markham.

WEISMAN, A. D., AND HACKETT, TH. P. 1967. Denial as a social act. *In*, S. Levin and R. T. Kahana (eds.), *Psychodynamic Studies on Aging*, pp. 79–110. New York: International University Press.

WERNER, H. 1957. The concept of development from a comparative and organismic point of view. *In*, D. B. Harris (ed.), *The concept of development*, pp. 125–148. Minneapolis, Minn.: University of Minnesota Press.

WILLIAMS, R. H., AND WIRTHS, C. G. 1965. *Lives through the years.* New York-London: John Wiley.

WINIECKE, L. 1973. The appeal of age segregated housing to the elderly poor. *Aging and Human Development, 4*, 293–306.

WITKIN, H. A., DYK, R. B., AND FATTERSON, H. F. 1962. *Psychological Differentiation.* New York-London: John Wiley.

WOLK, S., AND KURTZ, I. 1975. Positive adjustment and involvement during aging and expectancy for internal control. *Journal of Consulting and Clinical Psychology, 43*, 173–178.

ZUSMAN, I. 1966. Some explanations of the changing appearance of psychotic patients: Antecedents of the social breakdown syndrome concept. *Millbauk Memorial Fund Quarterly*, Vol. *64*.

# 14

# Stress:
# Physiological and
# Psychological Mechanisms

*V. Jayne Renner & James E. Birren*

The purpose of this chapter is to link the topics of stress, mental health, and aging by reviewing the relevant research literature and by suggesting some pathways whereby environmental stressors become translated into undesirable outcomes for the mental and physical well being of the aging individual. It is suggested that one of the pathways to poor mental and physical health, and their interaction, is the accumulation of the consequences of acute stress and chronic stress over the life span.

There are several difficulties with the development of this chapter. Since there have been few attempts to place the components of stress into a comprehensive conceptual thesis one is faced with a fragmented and, in instances, a parochial treatment of the particular aspects of stress. Also, most attention has been directed to the effects of stress on the young animal or young adult human, with the topic of aging relatively unexplored. The re-

view by Eisdorfer and Wilkie (1977) represents perhaps the only previous attempt to present an integrated approach. The requirements for presenting a synthesis of the subject are severe. The investigator needs to embrace four different areas of measurement or observation: (1) the nature, organization, and intensity of the stressors that face us in daily life; (2) the psychological mechanisms in the individual which mediate the environmental stressors and the internal responses; (3) the physiological mechanisms which mobilize the organism in response to stress; and (4) the expression of the physiological response which has consequences for physical and mental health.

This chapter will primarily emphasize the middle two of these areas, that of the psychological and physiological mechanisms which act as a filter or mediator between the stressors and their consequences, though both the stressor exposure of the organism and the disease consequences will be commented upon.

One of the frustrations in developing the topic of stress is its wide scope. An avalanche of publications on the subject has appeared in a wide range of journals leaving the impression that stress is a universal phenomenon. Perhaps because of its apparent ubiquity it is not a very satisfactory construct to use in explaining differences in mental health and in the ways individuals grow old. However, the topic of stress has been durable and the concept seems to be plausible in explaining some human phenomena. One view of stress is that its chronic effects can deplete the organism and lead to the appearance of mental and physical changes. An analysis of the literature on sequelae of the extress stress of war and other disasters leaves the clear impression that there can be a depletion of the organism which is later expressed as delayed disease (Lφnnum, 1969). Thus, in addition to dealing with the conceptual problem of the nearly universal character of stress, there is also the issue that extreme stress at an earlier period of life may have a "sleeper effect" which is expressed years later as an increase in morbidity from a wide range of diseases. The possibility of many years elapsing before there is a delayed expression of stress reactions stretches our limits of observation as individual investigators and taxes our sensitivity to protracted cause and effect relationships. Yet we should take seriously the observations that large numbers of individuals exposed to the conditions of prisoner of war camps and concentration camps of World War II appeared to "age prematurely." Premature aging in this instance refers to the early appearance of diseases found most commonly in late life.

Several of the nations of Europe, for example, France, Netherlands, Austria and Norway, have given individual pensions based upon the premise that protracted wartime stresses damaged the individual in ways not expected of the normal endogenous changes of advancing age (Lφnnum, 1969). This suggests a widespread acceptance of the principle that individuals exposed to extreme stress show permanent sequelae. A Norwegian Medical Commission examining concentration camp survivors found a constellation of mental health disturbances which included tenseness, anxiety, despair and indignation about events. Also reported were depressive reactions, gradual social withdrawal, and complete mental unresponsiveness (Strom, 1968).

Admittedly the extreme stresses of wartime concentration and prisoner of war camps are unusual but they provide examples of an extreme of a continuum. They also establish the point that

differences in the exposure to stress contribute to outcomes in mental and physical health. To the variable of exposure differences must be added the resistance and resiliency of the host which is exposed to stress. The thought is added that the manner of responding and adapting to stress modulates the physiological outcomes. A diagrammatic view of stress relationships is seen in Figure 14–1.

The experience of a stressful or traumatic stimulus interacts with both physiological and psychological processes to evoke responses from the organism which influence his physical and mental state. Figure 14–1 illustrates schematically the relationship between stressors and the state of a person's physical and mental health.

These stressors have been viewed by others as constituting some form of aversive environmental stimuli (Appley and Trumbull, 1967), or threat, or anticipated harm (Lazarus, 1966). Such stressors may be physical or psychological. No attempt will be made in this chapter to define the term *stressor* in a manner rigorously consistent with the demands of a particular theory of stress. Instead, a working definition is offered which will facilitate a coherent discussion of a wide range of research with different orientations. A stressor implies a threat to the organism. In human terms such a stressor may be life threatening, status threatening

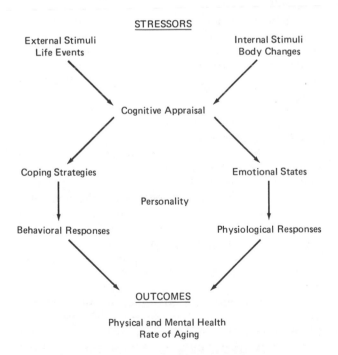

**Figure 14–1** Schematic diagram illustrating relationships between stressors and the behavioral and physiological responses. The feedback loops are not included.

or portend a loss of a relationship or object, or represent an attack on one's belief system. Stressful situations imply that the individual may not simply avoid the stressor or attack and direct anger against it, and because of this and the noxious quality of the stressor there is a sustained state of arousal which is catabolic. The term catabolic implies that the sustained physiological mobilization of the organism has biochemical outcomes which predispose the organism to disease. The result of being exposed to a stressor is that it puts the body into a state of protracted emotion and physiological preparation for physical exertion, the direct expression of which is often blocked.

Stressful internal or external stimuli, such as stressful life events impose themselves on the individual. How the individual manages external or internal stressors depends on his cognitive appraisal of each particular situation which in turn is largely dependent on past experiences and emotional state. In addition, the individual's subsequent adaptation behaviors will also depend on his emotional state and his personality organization, which includes his defense mechanisms and his various coping strategies. These in turn are determined by genetics and his past experiences, especially his early experiences. These coping mechanisms involve both physiological and psychological processes.

The word stress has a long history, having been widely and persistently used in medicine, biology and the social sciences. In addition, there is widespread controversy regarding the meaning of the term. According to Mason (1975a), Walter Cannon throughout a lot of his work used the term both in a physiological and a psychological sense, emphasizing both the physical stimuli and the emotional factors which place a strain on the homeostatic systems of the organism. However, it was with the work of Selye that the term became popularized. In an extensive paper on the General Adaptation Syndrome, to be described later, Selye used the term stress in the sense of it being a stimulus, those external forces which impose themselves as alarming or "evocative" stimuli on the organism (Selye, 1946). Later, Selye (1950a, 1950b) used the term stress to denote a condition within the organism that was a reaction or a response to evocative alarming stimuli which he now termed *stressors*. This typology persisted in his later work when Selye (1955/1974) still used the term stress in the sense of it being a response. "Stress is the non-specific response of the body to any demand made upon it" (Selye, 1974, p. 14). Selye (1975) believes that much of the confusion could be eliminated from this controversial area if the word

stressors was used to refer to those noxious stimuli which lead to a stress response "the non-specific biological reaction."

Although, as this chapter will show, there is a dispute on the non-specificity of the stress response, the distinction between the stress stimulus and the stress response is the tradition in which this chapter is written. Stressors may be physical or psychosocial, and indeed, much of the literature to be cited in this paper deals with psychosocial stimuli which may lead to both psychological and physiological stress reactions.

## LIFE EVENTS AND DISEASE

### CRISES AND DISEASES

Numerous studies have found a significant relationship between an elevation of life crisis units and the outcome of certain diseases.

Wolff (1950) postulated that a great variety of stressors induced a wide range of physiological responses which are mediated through a large number of biological mechanisms. When an individual is confronted with stressors that present a threat, cause frustration or demand dealing with crises or emergencies, certain physiological or psychological reaction patterns are set up to allow the individual to adapt and protect himself. Such adaptive patterns vary, depending on the individual's cognitive and emotional apparatus, his past experiences, and also the type of situation he is confronted with.

Furthermore, Wolff postulated that the organ involved in the disease process is not necessarily inherently weak, but that repeated prolonged use of a particular organ in the adaptive process may result in structural damage. For instance, continual feelings of anger or feelings of emotional deprivation and lack of support, whether it be real or experienced because of some past associations, are often felt in the stomach, where the feeling state set up is one of a readiness to eat. This is because the earliest aggressive behavior patterns set up during infancy are associated with hunger. Thus "gastric hyperfunction" (Wolff, 1950, p. 1064) may occur when in later life a person feels threatened. A variety of gastrointestinal disorders may finally result due to the prolonged adaptive use of the gastrointestinal tract to cope with provoking or threatening situations.

Other bodily adaptive patterns may result in cardiovascular disease, circulatory inefficiency, hypertension, respiratory disorders, a variety of metabolic disorders and other diseases. Such diseases of adaptation, which commonly today are termed psychosomatic disorders, are postulated by Wolff to be more likely to occur in societies that are undergoing rapid cultural change, thus engendering a greater degree of insecurity against which people develop particular protective responses which, with persistent use, may finally become maladaptive or diseased.

Wolff also suggests that "it is not the particular nature of the forces or pressures or preferences that constitute stress for the individual in any particular society but the amount of conflict which is either directly or indirectly engendered in him by his cultural medium" (1950, p. 1088).

This particularly happens when value systems within a culture become incongruous with environmental demands. Hypertension, for example, tends to increase with age in cultures undergoing cultural transition, compared to more primitive societies (Cassel, 1975). Cassel reviews evidence from a study investigating blood pressure in a sample of Polynesian males and females living on two different Pacific island atolls. It was found that the group who lived on an island where a great deal of urban cultural transition was occuring, and who were thus exposed to the conflicting demands of a primitive and urban environment had higher blood pressures during their lifespan than their counterparts who lived on an isolated atoll where traditions remained intact.

This general formulation of life stressors being associated with bodily diseases has been confirmed in a wide variety of studies using the scale of Holmes and Rahe (1967) or a modification of it. Such studies in the more general area of illness include Rahe, Meyer, Smith, Kjaer, and Holmes (1964); Rahe, McKean, and Arthur (1967); Rahe (1968); Rahe, Gunderson, and Arthur (1970); Rahe, Mahan, and Arthur (1970); Wyler, Masuda, and Holmes (1971); Cline and Chosy (1972); Bramwell, Masuda, Wagner, and Holmes (1975); and Marx, Garrity, and Bowers (1975). A comprehensive review on the use of this scale and the onset of diseases was compiled by Rahe (1972).

We now turn to consider the relationship of stressful events and two specific psychosomatic disease states, the incidence of which tends to increase with age, diabetes mellitus, and cardiovascular disorders.

*Diabetes Mellitus.* Hinkle and Wolf (1950, 1952), Treuting (1962), Danowski (1963), and Kravitz, Isenberg, Shore, and Barnett (1971) are among the investigators who have found that there is an association between stressful events and an exacerbation of the symptoms of diabetes mellitus. Fur-

thermore, there is the possibility that stress may trigger the initial metabolic imbalances in pre-disposed individuals. For instance, Hinkle and Wolf (1952) found from over 50 diabetic case histories that they studied, that the onset of the disease nearly always occurred "after a period of environmental and interpersonal stress characterized by the loss of persons, objects, relationships, or cultural values which the patient has regarded as indispensable to his total security, both psychological and physical" (Hinkle and Wolf , 1952, p. 566).

The authors in the two papers cited propose that the metabolic pattern, which characterizes the diabetic, represents an adaptive reaction to "carbohydrate starvation." During infancy food is identified with physical and emotional security which becomes strongly reinforced during childhood and some experiences during later adult life. In pre-disposed individuals there are some who in later years respond to cumulative stressors which involve lack of security or emotional attachment as if they represented a threat of starvation. Further, such stressful events in those who have developed the disease may result in hyperglycaemia and ketonemia associated with diabetic ketoacidosis.

*Cardiovascular Disease.* Similar such findings have been found with other age-related diseases, although the studies themselves have not been concerned with the elderly. Thus Weiss, Dlin, Rollin, Fischer, and Bepler (1957) found emotional distress to be associated with 37 percent of a group of patients who had suffered coronary occlusion. Syme, Hyman, and Enterline (1964) found that coronary heart disease had a higher rate of incidence among white men with American urban backgrounds, were white-collar workers and who were subject to geographical and occupational mobility, as compared to rural or non-white-collared workers with less mobility.

Theorell and Rahe (1971) and Rahe and Paasikivi (1971) gave the Schedule of Recent Experience to myocardial patients, finding that there had been significantly more life changes in this group when compared to a control group. Theorell, Lind, Fröberg, Karlsson, and Levi (1972) in a longitudinal study of 21 subjects who had survived a myocardial infarction found that catecholamine excretion was raised when there was a build-up of psychosocial stress, and that serum triglyceride levels were higher in those subjects observed to be depressed than those patients who were not depressed.

Rahe and Bennett (1974) used the Schedule of Recent Experience in a Helsinki population to evaluate recent life changes among 279 survivors who had suffered myocardial infarctions. Spouses of 226 cases of sudden coronary deaths were also interviewed to provide life change data on the coronary death victims. With the exception of a small group of persons who had had no prior illnesses two years prior to their death which had occurred less suddenly than the remaining cases, a significant build-up of life changes was seen in both the myocardial infarction group and the group that had died suddenly of coronary disease. In both these groups, elevations in life change unit scores occurred six months prior to the infarction or death, compared to the life changes that had occurred during the same time interval one year prior to this. Similar findings were arrived at in a longitudinal study by Theorell and Rahe (1975) who found among a group of myocardial infarction patients that there was a significantly greater number of life changes that occurred among the group who did not survive, than among those who did survive.

All these studies thus confirm the hypothesis, that an increase in life change unit scores, or in the number of stressors which confront an individual, are closely associated with subsequent illnesses. Many of these studies, however, suffer from the handicap of being retrospective in nature. As Hurst, Jenkins, and Rose (1976) point out, recall decreases with time, which may account for the increase in reported life changes that are made a few months before the onset of an illness. Furthermore, the results are less reliable if a control group is not included (Hurst, Jenkins, and Rose, 1976). As an example of this, Theorell, Lind, and Floderus (1975) found no difference in reported life change units among a group of myocardial infarction patients and a control group.

Past and current stressful life experiences may act as catalysts to alter a person's susceptibility to stress-related diseases, and this susceptibility presumably increases with age. However, the investigator should be wary of concluding that there is a simple one-to-one relationship between stressors or life changes and disease outcomes.

Indeed, the emotional response or what Hurst, Jenkins, and Rose (1976, p. 305) termed the "systemic emotional arousal" response which is idiosyncratic to each individual, may be the most significant contributing psychological factor. Lundberg, Theorell, and Lind (1975), for example, found that the distinguishing difference between their myocardial infarction patients and a control group was in the assessment of the degree of emotion felt by the subject in a stress associated event. Greater emotive content in prior-life changes was experienced by those who became ill. In other words, myocardial infarction patients rated their

life changes as more "upsetting" than the controls. Perlman, Ferguson, Bergum, Isenberg, and Hammarsten (1975) found, from patient and family interviews, that 49 percent of a group of congestive heart failure patients, as compared to 24 percent of controls (i.e., those with no history of cardiovascular difficulties) had experienced what they had perceived as an emotional crisis three days prior to hospitalization. The difference between the two groups was significant.

Recent reviews of the relationship between emotional stress, risk factors, and cardiovascular disease has recently been written by Eliot (1977) and Glass (1977).

It is pertinent to emphasize that a fruitful area for future research is to investigate certain life events and the emotional significance attached to these changes by the individuals concerned, particularly in older populations where there is a dearth of information.

*Stressors, Life Events, and Daily Hassles.* Stressors are the internal or external stimuli that cause trauma to the organism. These range from internal irritants, such as the stress of a broken limb, to troublesome external life events. External life events have been measured by certain life event scales. Holmes and Rahe (1967) constructed a scale of recent life events assigning certain life crisis units to each event. These items from the social readjustment rating scale are presented in Table 14–1.

The Holmes and Rahe (1967) scale has been criticized on the grounds that it concerns major life events which may be of less importance in terms of disease outcomes than the occurence of "chronic daily hassles," especially with older age groups. The term chronic daily hassles was coined by Lazarus and Cohen (1977).

Lazarus and Cohen (1977) developed a hassles scale where most of the items concern themselves with irritants that may occur on a more frequent basis than those events in the social readjustment rating scale of Holmes and Rahe. Items in this scale range from major pressures or problems, such as retirement to comparatively minor annoyances, such as inconsiderate smokers. Further such examples of the type of question asked on this scale are misplacing or losing things, concerns about getting credit, planning meals, concerns about the meaning of life, not enough money for food, being lonely, physical illness, legal problems, not enough personal energy, and regrets over past decisions.

It is just recently that pilot data are being collected on this scale. In a sample of 124 Canadian adults, consisting of a group of professionals, mostly nurses with an average age of 45, the mean number of hassles checked from a possible total of 119 was 22. Among a sample of 43 college students, with an average age of 21, the mean number of hassles checked was 36 (Lazarus, 1977, personal communication). The most frequent hassles checked by the professional group were, in descending order, troubling thoughts about the future, health of a family member, concerns about weight, and too many things to do. Among the college students the most frequent hassles were troubling thoughts about the future, inconsiderate smokers, not getting enough sleep, and misplacing or losing things (Lazarus, 1977, personal communication).

An unpublished study using this scale has just been completed at the University of Southern California by Renner, Gekowski, Knox, and Birren where it is predicted that in a sample of healthy

**Table 14–1**  Social Readjustment Rating Scale.

| RANK | LIFE EVENT | MEAN VALUE |
|---|---|---|
| 1 | Death of spouse | 100 |
| 2 | Divorce | 73 |
| 3 | Marital separation | 65 |
| 4 | Jail term | 63 |
| 5 | Death of close family member | 63 |
| 6 | Personal injury or illness | 53 |
| 7 | Marriage | 50 |
| 8 | Fired at work | 47 |
| 9 | Marital reconciliation | 45 |
| 10 | Retirement | 45 |
| 11 | Change in health of family member | 44 |
| 12 | Pregnancy | 40 |
| 13 | Sex difficulties | 39 |
| 14 | Gain of new family member | 39 |
| 15 | Business readjustment | 39 |
| 16 | Change in financial state | 38 |
| 17 | Death of close friend | 37 |
| 18 | Change to different line of work | 36 |
| 19 | Change in number of arguments with spouse | 35 |
| 20 | Mortgage over $10,000 | 31 |
| 21 | Foreclosure of mortgage or loan | 30 |
| 22 | Change in responsibilities at work | 29 |
| 23 | Son or daughter leaving home | 29 |
| 24 | Trouble with in-laws | 29 |
| 25 | Outstanding personal achievement | 28 |
| 26 | Wife begin or stop work | 26 |
| 27 | Begin or end school | 26 |
| 28 | Change in living conditions | 25 |
| 29 | Revision of personal habits | 24 |
| 30 | Trouble with boss | 23 |
| 31 | Change in work hours or conditions | 20 |
| 32 | Change in residence | 20 |
| 33 | Change in schools | 20 |
| 34 | Change in recreation | 19 |
| 35 | Change in church activities | 19 |
| 36 | Change in social activities | 18 |
| 37 | Mortgage or loan less than $10,000 | 17 |
| 38 | Change in sleeping habits | 16 |
| 39 | Change in number of family get-togethers | 15 |
| 40 | Change in eating habits | 15 |
| 41 | Vacation | 13 |
| 42 | Christmas | 12 |
| 43 | Minor violations of the law | 11 |

From Holmes and Rahe, 1967, p. 216.

older adults, who were the subjects of this study, the number of hassles checked will be less than those recorded by younger people. Because of reduced life space of older persons it is expected that the number of daily hassles to which they are exposed declines with age. However, it is also expected that a smaller magnitude of the stressor can induce the same level of physiological response compared to the young. Also, since the older person has already accrued much of the consequences of stress, stress related diseases which are cumulative, may be already present. That fewer stressful events are experienced by older people was also predicted by Eisdorfer and Wilkie (1977). However, this has yet to be confirmed on large numbers of older adults.

At least one study did not find a relationship between either Holmes and Rahe's recent life events or Lazarus and Cohen's hassle scale and disease outcomes in 179 healthy, married, educated, employed, middle-class white males ranging in age from 25 to 50 (Noffsinger, 1977). Some of the difficulties in interpreting this investigator's results involve the lack of precise measurement and analysis of how these subjects dealt with the stressors. Cognitive appraisal was only measured by how each subject subjectively rated the events as stressful, the degree of his personal adjustment, subjectively assessed, and how well he felt he coped. The amount of stress experienced may have been relatively mild, although the author did not discuss this. However, only 5 percent of the subjects scored over 300 in the life event scale of Holmes and Rahe. In addition, the degree of emotion experienced by each individual in this study, with the stressful situations may have been fairly mild although the author again does not discuss this either. Furthermore, specific coping strategies were not measured.

More work needs to be done on analyzing the specific stressors, the degree of emotion involved, and the specific coping strategy mechanisms. Certainly there should also be a continued effort to measure clusters of stressful stimuli although Selye (1950a, 1950b, 1975), for example, sees the stress reaction emerging in response to non-specific stimuli.

This non-specificity of the stress stimulus, however, may merely reflect the fact that a variety of stimuli can lead to the stress reaction. Such stimuli include psychic shock, burns, surgery, external life events, etc.

*Chronic Stress: Alienation and Anomie.* Consideration should also be given to as yet more abstract concepts such as alienation and anomie (Durkheim, 1951; Seeman, 1959, 1976) or loss of the cultural canon, that is, the loss of a value system (Henry and Ely, 1976; Henry and Stephens, 1977). Seeman (1976), for example, found six parameters of alienation which could be assumed as being stressful. These were feelings of powerlessness, meaninglessness, normlessness, cultural estrangement, social isolation, and self-estrangement. Using these parameters Martin, Bengston, and Acock (1974) found that these stressors were higher in old age than during middle age, although lower in value than scores from the young. However, it is possible that the degree of stress associated with the feelings of alienation are more severe in later adulthood when there is a concomitant decline in physical and psychological resources, and because death of loved ones and friends are a more abrupt and erosive loss of support. A review of the literature on alienation, anomie, and age has been given by Birren and Renner in Chapter 1 of this handbook.

*Desirability versus Undesirability of Life Changes.* Finally, with respect to the question of stressors, it is important to evaluate the desirability and undesirability of life change events as well as their significance to the individual concerned, and their emotive content. The Hassles Scale of Lazarus and Cohen (1977) to some extent embraces these concepts, by getting the examinee to rate the frequency and severity of each stressor he checks. Other investigators have made further such attempts. Most of these attempts have concerned themselves with the Social Readjustment Rating Scale of Holmes and Rahe (1967).

However, the authors of this Social Readjustment Rating Scale are not oblivious to its shortcomings. As Holmes and Masuda (1974) specifically explain:

> There was identified, however, one theme common to all these events. The occurence of each event usually evoked, or was associated with, some adaptive or coping behavior on the part of the involved individual. Thus, each item was constructed to contain life events whose advent is either indicative of, or requires a significant change in, the ongoing life pattern of the individual. The emphasis is on change from the existing steady state and not on psychological meaning, emotion, or social desirability (p. 46).

Mechanic (1975) points out that the experimental findings, which claim the existence of or a relationship between life changes and illness, cannot resolve the issue as to whether it is "life changes in general or primarily adverse life changes" which "affect the occurence of illness" (p. 44). In other words, as the Social Readjustment Rating Scale

stands, the type of changes which affect people adversely, cannot be determined. Furthermore, stimulus intensity as subjectively experienced, decreases over time, as suggested by Hurst, Jenkins, and Rose (1976) and experimentally demonstrated by Horowitz, Schaefer, and Looney (1974).

An effort to construct such a scale in which adverse events could be identified, was made by Paykel, Prusoff, and Uhlenhuth (1971) who asked a heterogeneous sample of 373 subjects, aged between 17 and 70, to rate 61 life events in terms of the degree to which they were upsetting to them. Considerable consistency and reliability was attained, where those events which were regarded as the most distressing were major catastrophic events, such as death of child or spouse. Arguments with members of a family were of moderate concern, and certain events, such as beginning an education, or having a child married with parental consent, were of little import in terms of distress.

This technique has been extended further by Tennant and Andrews (1976) who derived 67 life event items from the questionnaire of Paykel *et al.* (1971) and that of Holmes and Rahe (1967). Two scales were derived from this instrument. One involving a "ratio method of scaling" (Tennant and Andrews, 1976, p. 28) permitted an evaluation of cumulative life stress and its relationship to illness. The other scaling involved scoring in terms of the amount of distress each item engendered.

Aware that the significance of life events varies from one culture to another, Tennant and Andrews (1976) emphasize that their scale is so constructed as to be suitable for an Australian urban population. However, within such demographic limits, it is an instrument which permits Mechanic's (1975) objections to be overcome, and to determine whether it is life events and changes as such, or upsetting distressing events in particular, which are related to illness onset. In this way Selye's concept of the non-specificity of the stress response, that life changes in general cause physiological arousal and increase susceptibility to disease (Selye, 1946, 1950a, 1950b, 1955, 1974, 1975, 1976) can be examined with more scrutiny. What is suggested is a contrast between a non-specific aggregation of life events and an event-specific evocative intensity.

Recently Rahe (1978) pointed out his objections to the new scaling methods, claiming that classifying events as desirable or undesirable, etc., have methodological difficulties also, since different individuals have quite different evaluations in this matter. The introduction of a Subjective Life Change Unit scaling system, he found, presented difficulties in predicting future illnesses, because subjective evaluations tended to contaminate the significance of events as such. Rahe (1978) concludes that in order to distinguish and estimate "environmental stress" as against "subjective stress," "a simple counting of recent life changes" is more valuable (p. 97). Such a conclusion had also been reached in a study of Dohrenwend (1973) who found in a sample of 124 persons, ranging in age from under 30 to over 60, that stressfulness was better measured in terms of life changes than in terms of their desirability.

The difficulty in allowing subjective evaluations to enter the picture or to depend on established undesirable-desirable scales, and so on, is emphasized by Horowitz, Schaefer, Hiroto, Wilner, and Levin (1977). As predicted, time tended to reduce the significance of an event in their study, in that recent events were rated as more stressful than past events. This is an especially important variable to consider when measuring the stressors among an older population, since many of them will have already faced some of the major crises that people have to face over a life time, such as divorce, loss of spouse, or retirement several months or even several years ago. Although the age-span was not great in this study, Horowitz *et al.* did find that younger people rated items as more stressful than older people, and furthermore women tended to rate life changes as more stressful than did men.

Age, marital status, sex, socioeconomic status, ethnicity, level of education, culture, and even whether a person has experienced the event or not are all important variables, which must be accounted for in rating the significance of stressful life changes (Masuda and Holmes, 1978).

The importance of accounting for these variables in predicting the onset of psychiatric, as well as the psychosomatic disorders has not always been well documented. However, there is evidence that an increase in stressful life events is associated with psychiatric disorders.

*Stressors and Psychiatric Disturbance.* In an age-related study, Lowenthal, Berkman, and Associates (1967) found that no one single variable, such as physical illness, physical disability, retirement, decline in the standard of living, widowhood, or social isolation accounted for mental illness in the old. Rather, psychiatric impairment tended to be associated with "multiple deprivation" (Lowenthal *et al.,* 1967, p. 264), so that a spiralling of events tended to produce spiralling effects.

This cumulative effect of the influence of life events on mental status has also been found in other studies not so specifically age-related (Brown, Sklair, Harris, and Birley, 1973; Dekker and Webb,

1974; Myers, Lindenthal, and Pepper, 1971; Paykel, 1974; Payne, 1975; Reavley, 1974; Uhlenhuth and Paykel, 1973a).

Interestingly, a further analysis of the study done by Uhlenhuth and Paykel, outlined in another paper (Uhlenhuth and Paykel, 1973b) found that, although the intensity of the psychiatric symptoms was associated with the magnitude or cumulation of life stress, symptom configuration was not so related. Irascibility and compulsiveness were characteristic of both upper socioeconomic class people and males. Females tended to show more depression. Lower socioeconomic class patients tended to show more anxiety. Anxiety was also more typical of white populations, whereas black populations tended to report more physical symptoms. There were also age related differences. Younger people manifested more anxiety, while older patients were more typically depressed.

Despite the shortcomings in using measures which evaluate the desirability and undesirability of life events, some studies have looked at the relationship of stressful events and psychiatric impairment, and have found that emotional disturbances are more likely to occur when the stressor is undesirable. Thus, Vinokur and Selzer (1975) found that undesirable life changes such as deterioration in working conditions (as contrasted with the more desirable life changes such as improvement in working conditions) were more highly related to reported experiences of tension or anxiety, emotional disturbances such as depression, paranoia, suicidal feelings or anxiety, and behavioral transgressions such as excess drinking and traffic accidents.

Similar tendencies were found by Paykel, Myers, Dienelt, Klerman, Lindenthal, and Pepper (1969) and Paykel (1976). Although a relationship between the genesis of depression and cumulative stressful events, six months prior to the onset of illness, was found, the distinguishing feature between the depressed group (which had an age range between 21 and 65) and matched controls was whether these events were desirable or undesirable. In particular, experienced losses of some sort, or an exit from a desirable social field characterized the depressed patients but not the controls.

An accumulation of life events also characterized a group of attempted suicide patients ranging in age from 18 to 65, from two matched control groups (Paykel, Prusoff, and Myers, 1975; Paykel, 1976). Whereas the suicide attempters reported significantly more undesirable events than the depressed controls or the general population, they also reported about the same number of desirable events as the general population. Paykel (1976) points out that what characterizes the suicide patient is that a marked peaking in the number of threatening events occurs, one month before the attempt is made, so that the attempted suicide is a response to a crisis, which implies that crisis intervention techniques for these patients would be beneficial and could be used at the time, threatening events begin to peak.

There is thus a wide body of evidence to suggest that there is a link between stressors and mental and physical disease. The suggestion made by the present authors is that this is not merely a one-to-one relationship but rather certain physiological and psychological mechanisms intervene to translate the stressful experiences and thereby introduce individual differences, into maladaptive physiological and/or psychological responses.

## PHYSIOLOGICAL MECHANISMS OF STRESS

Our knowledge of the mechanisms which take place after experiencing a stressful situation comes from the two disciplines, physiology and the behavioral sciences. The physiology of the stress response stems from the work of Claude Bernard, Walter Cannon, and particularly the ideas and research of Hans Selye.

Bernard (1945) stressed the importance of the organism's ability to maintain a constant internal environment or milieu interior for survival. Cannon (1929) emphasized the maintenance of a steady state of the organism for coordinated physiological activities, a process he named homeostasis. He was also responsible for being the first to systematically describe the role of epinephrine as an immediate physiological response which occured during flight or fight responses.

Hans Selye has also, in more recent years, applied the concept of stress to the aging process. In this connection, particularly, stress represents "the rate of wear and tear to which a living being is exposed at any moment" (Selye, 1970, p. 669). In contrast, aging is defined as that which reflects "the sum of all the stresses which have acted upon the body during a life-span" (Selye, 1970, p. 670). In this sense, Selye and many other investigators believe that stress accelerates aging. Such a concept has been part of Selye's repertoire for a long time. In 1956 he made the analogy which described the individual as having only a certain quantum of energy available, like one has money available in a bank. However, unlike a bank account, this available energy could be withdrawn, but new energy could not be deposited. Indeed, in this same book Selye (1956) went so far as to say:

It is as though at birth, each individual inherited a certain amount of adaptation energy, the magnitude of which is determined by his genetic background, his parents. He can draw upon this capital thriftily for a long but monotonously uneventful existence, or he can spend it lavishly in the course of a stressful, intense, but perhaps more colorful and exciting life. In any case, there is just so much of it, and he must budget accordingly (p. 66).

While such an analogy is attractive it fails to recognize that built into the body are powerful regenerative processes, and that living is a balance between breakdown and regeneration. Molecular parts of the organism are constantly being broken down and just as constantly these parts are being replaced by the cell machinery involved in protein synthesis. Such regenerative processes require energy. Death is not a breakdown of the parts of the body per se. Rather, death is due to a breakdown of machinery that is required for the continuous regeneration of vital parts of the body. Regulation of protein synthesis and energy production is mediated by specific hormones (Munro, 1970). Hormonal output is, in turn, regulated by the central nervous system, particularly by the hypothalamus and pituitary.

### HYPOTHALAMIC AND PITUITARY REGULATION AND AGING

Recent evidence suggests that at least part of the regulation of the aging process may be centered in the hypothalamus and the related pituitary-endocrine axis (Everitt and Burgess, 1976). Thus, the declining ability of the organism to undergo regenerative processes which are necessary to combat the continuous breakdown of the body's parts, is related to less efficient regulatory processes in the central nervous and hormonal systems. Such breakdown phenomena are concomitant with aging and are accelerated under chronic or persistent stress.

In identifying the hypothalamus as one of the major regulators of the aging process Frolkis (1976) claims that "with age the sensitivity of the hypothalamus to a number of hormonal factors increases" (p. 623). These hormonal factors, which, in Frolkis' experimental system, were directly injected into the hypothalamic area of young and old rabbits, included epinephrine, nor-epinephrine and acetylcholine. In addition, Frolkis found in his experiments with young and old animals that there was a more sensitive and overt reaction to stress with epinephrine stimulation in the older group. Epinephrine is one of the stress hormones. Interestingly, the functional activity of some of the hypothalamic neurosecretory elements decrease with age, in a number of different animal species, although there is also an accumulation of some neurosecretory substances with age (Frolkis, 1976). Frolkis (1976) concludes that the "accumulation of neurosecretion is due not to its increased production but to retarded secretion" (p. 618).

The hypothalamus is the central regulator of the autonomic nervous system (ANS), of various cycles of metabolism, adaptive processes, and homeostatic mechanisms, and of certain behaviors, so that it becomes a primary candidate for explaining the changes in adaptive capabilities of the organism that occur with age and indeed of the aging process itself. In addition to the increased sensitivity of the hypothalamus to certain substances, such as the catecholamines, leading to a more overt stress response, the aging process may also be influenced by "an age-related elevation to the hypothalamic threshold to feedback suppression in the three main homeostatic systems of higher organisms: energy, reproduction and adaptation systems" (Dilman, 1976, p. 634). By this is meant that the stability of the internal environment of the organism is disturbed by the fact that the hypothalamus in older animals is less sensitive than that of younger animals to the endogeneous peripheral hormonal substances which by feedback mechanisms inhibit the output of the CNS regulatory factors. Consequently, there is an increased output of hormonal substances in the peripheral endocrine organs in the older organism to maintain "the feedback mechanism under the conditions of enhanced hypothalamic activity" (Dilman, 1976, p. 634). This has yet to be elucidated in more detail, for in man the *secretion* of most hormones decreases in old age, when compared with younger age groups "except where compensatory changes increase the secretion" (Everitt, 1976, p. 676). This need not imply a contradiction of the above, but merely point out that under even minor stressful conditions, the older person has to put out more hormonal substances than the young to maintain the same degree of homeostais. One of the reasons for this greater work load would be due to a higher hypothalamic threshold for the operation of feedback processes which occur with aging.

Furthermore, it would seem that the changes in the hypothalamus limit "the activation range of protein biosynthesis" in the older organism (Frolkis, 1976, p. 626) and hence render less effective the essential regenerative machinery, which includes the genetic apparatus. More specifically, the hypothalamus, through both the hormonal and neural systems, influences genetic induction which in turn affects protein synthesis. Experiments which have stimulated the hypothalamus in old and younger adult animals have shown that there is decreased genetic enzymic induction with age in the liver and kidney although the spleen remains relatively unaffected (Frolkis, 1977).

Frolkis (1976) talks of these various changes as "functional 'disregulation' " of the hypothalamus and of "hypothalamic misinformation of the organism" (p. 630) which not only reduces the adaptive abilities of the organism but can lead to the age-related pathological disorders such as hypertension, myocardial infarction, atherosclerosis and diabetes mellitus.

The importance of the pituitary should also be emphasized, since age-related changes occur here as well as in its target organs, thus altering the output of certain hormones and influencing the aging process (Everitt, 1976). The anterior pituitary releases such diverse hormones as adrenocorticotropic hormone (ACTH), growth hormone (GH), follicle stimulating hormone (FSH), luteinizing hormone (LH), thyroid stimulating hormone (TSH), and prolactin. The release of these hormones in turn is regulated by the hypothalamus. Thus, the CNS plays a major role as the pacemaker of homeostatic physiological responses, psychological behavioral patterns and of the processes of aging.

The executive regulator of the stress reaction also lies in the higher centers of the nervous system so that an understanding of the mechanisms of the stress response will enable us to further understand the aging and disease processes. If there is a decreased regulatory effectiveness in the CNS and ANS systems, then continued subjection to stressful psychosocial stimuli which impose their effects on declining physiological structures will account for disease as well as decremental performance patterns such as slower reaction times, decline in learning ability, or decreased cognitive abilities, rather than the factor of age per se.

*Other Endocrine Disorders.* Ordy and Kaack (1976, p. 290) make an even more complete list involving the endocrine disorders which tend to increase with age. Endocrine changes involving the hormone insulin may result in diabetes mellitus which increases in incidence with age. Other endocrine disorders may also occur in older people involving vascular and metabolic complications which may be due to changes in the thyroid hormones. Osteoporosis is also listed as involving the parathyroid hormones and estrogens. Abnormalities in the adrenal cortical hormones are related to such disorders as Cushing's syndrome. The climacteric for the female involving both changes in the estrogen and progesterone hormones may also lead to heart disease and breast cancer. For the male the climacteric involves changes in testosterone and may induce prostatic hypertrophy or cancer. Lipid metabolism disorders also increase with age. Insulin, epinephrine, glucagon, thyroid hormones, growth hormone, and the glucocorticoids may be involved, and obesity or atherosclerosis may result.

Blood pressure increases with age which as Ordy and Kaack (1976) point out may result in hypertension with subsequent coronary arterial disease or cerebral vascular disease. Although a variety of hormones may be involved, these include renin, angiotensin, and aldosterone (Ordy and Kaack, 1976). Cross-linkages in collagen, changes in elastin or an increase in lipofuscin which may involve the thyroid hormones are listed as resulting in structural changes in connective tissue and an increase in pigmentation. Progeria or premature aging and certain types of tumors involve the pituitary hormones, such as ACTH.

The important point is that these are not merely age-related diseases. They are also stress-related diseases which tend to have a greater incidence among older people. The hormones involved are the hormones of stress. Thus, these illnesses are not just the expression of peripheral constitutional effects but heavily involve the endocrine and neuroendocrine systems. In turn, exacerbation of these diseases is modulated by stressful events and the management of external events and their internal consequences. Furthermore, not only may the individual's emotional or mental health state affect the onset of these diseases, for example, hypertension is commonly associated with high tension and anxiety levels, but the existence of these diseases in individuals may also affect the mental states of the people concerned.

## PITUITARY ADRENAL CORTICAL RESPONSE TO STRESS

Selye is credited with the discovery of the pituitary adrenocortical response, the release of ACTH from the anterior pituitary which activates the release of corticosteroids from the adrenal cortex, during the stress response. Such a response Selye claimed was universal in all higher organisms and occured after exposure to a diverse and variable number of stressors. This over-emphasis on the adrenocortical response tended to allow him to minimize the importance of epinephrine, although he did acknowledge this hormone as a stressor. This omission in Selye's arguments is particularly corrected for in Bessman's model of 1976 for he discussed the first phase of the stress response as being mediated by the hormone epinephrine and

as responsible for the catabolic breakdown of glycogen and fats.

Stressors which were defined by Selye as non-specific stimuli of sufficient magnitude to disturb internal equilibrium or homeostasis produced what Selye called the General Adaptation Syndrome (the GAS) which he described as having three states (Selye, 1946, 1950a, 1950b, 1955, 1974, 1976). "The *alarm reaction* (A-R) is defined as the sum of all non-specific phenomena elicited by sudden exposure to stimuli, which affect large portions of the body and to which the organism is quantitatively or qualitatively not adapted," (Selye, 1950a, p. 10). He describes two phases of the A-R, the phase of shock where general systemic damage to the organism occurs and the phase of counter-shock where the organism physiologically defends itself against the shock phase by amongst other things, releasing corticosteroids into the bloodstream This is followed by the second stage of stress which Selye called the stage of resistance which he defined as representing "the sum of all non-specific systemic reactions elicited by prolonged exposure to stimuli to which the organism has acquired adaptation" (Selye, 1950a, p. 11). In this stage the organism is able to marshall his physiological resources to put up resistance to the stressor(s). The third and final stage is called the stage of exhaustion which Selye defines as representing "the sum of all non-specific systemic reactions which ultimately develop as a result of prolonged overexposure to stimuli to which adaptation has been developed but could no longer be maintained," (Selye, 1950a, p. 12). In this final stage the ability of the organism to adapt to the stressors is weakened. Such conditions of chronic, persistent stress imposing this continual wear and tear on the organism is responsible according to Selye for the aging process, can result in disease and in extreme circumstances cause death.

## AGING AS EXHAUSTION

The discovery and description of the triphasic general adaptation syndrome led to the concept that the organism was born with a finite amount of adaptation energy and that rate of aging was a function of the expenditure of this energy (Selye and Tuchweber, 1976, 1978). Selye suggests that the triphasic GAS is similar to the three stages of the life-span. During childhood there is an over reaction to stimuli and resistance to stressors is low. Adulthood is a time when there is an increase in resistance, and the body has learned to adapt to most stressors. Senility, on the other hand, represents the stage of exhaustion, when there is a gradual loss in the ability to adapt, and finally death results. This loss in the capacity for adaptation to change is reflected in an increased susceptibility to disease (Selye and Tuchweber, 1976, 1978).

One of the important implications of this stress theory is that the process of aging will be accelerated with continued exposure to stressful stimuli, for every encounter with such an event utilizes up furthur adaptation energy of which there is only a fixed amount. This acceleration process is particularly important the older an individual gets, for with increasing age the ability to adapt to changed environmental conditions declines. It should be noted that the implication of senescent decline in capacity to respond, implies that an older person may show stress related disease in a period in which the stressful events themselves may decline in frequency or intensity. In the later phase of life a little stress may go a long way.

The mechanisms which mediate this decline in adaptability are not yet fully understood, although Selye and Tuchweber (1976, 1978) claim that neuro-endocrine mechanisms, particularly the pituitary adrenal cortical system, play a major role. Several age-related and stress-related diseases are explained in this way. Such explanations do not in themselves explain the process of aging but do describe some of its pathological consequences.

This conceptualization of aging is not necessarily, for Selye, a pessimistic one. For him the ongoing processes of life should be accepted and enjoyed. Although, according to Selye, loss of adaptation is inevitable as the individual grows older, he distinguishes in his later works, stress which is distressing and stress which is not. Life, he feels, can be prolonged and enjoyed if one indulges in activity which is successful and fulfilling, no matter how intense it is (Selye, 1974).

However, the emphasis made by Selye with respect to stressors is their non-specificity. Furthermore, Selye (1975) claims that although the stress response is specific for each individual, depending on his genetic endowment and past experiences, the reaction in general is a non-specific one. Mason (1975a, 1975b) has been among those to critically analyze several of Selye's concepts. Other theories also have taken issue with some of Selye's points, in particular by emphasizing the role of the sympathetic adrenal medullary system and describing the stress response in more specific terms.

## SYMPATHETIC ADRENAL MEDULLARY RESPONSE

Henry (1976), Henry and Ely (1976), and Henry and Stephens (1977) invoke the amygdala as the CNS area responsible for initiating the aggressive or the fight reaction. The amygdaloid nuclei in turn are regulated by the frontal lobes of the brain. From the amygdala, nerve impulses are relayed to the hypothalamus. Via the hypothalamus the sympathetic adrenal medullary system becomes aroused leading to the release of the hormones norepinephrine and epinephrine. Physiological consequences of these reactions include an increase in cardiac output, heart rate and blood pressure. Henry and his colleagues found a relationship between these physiological responses and an increase in the catecholamine synthesizing enzymes, although they fail in their theory to elaborate on the physiological and biochemical consequences of the raised level of these enzymes during stress. In particular, Henry and his group found raised levels of tyrosine hydroxylase, responsible for the conversion of the amino acid tyrosine to Dopa, and PNMT (phenylethanolamine N-methyltransferase) which is responsible for the conversion of norepinephrine to epinephrine. Epinephrine is the hormone responsible for modulating several biochemical responses which occur during stress, including a rise in blood sugar and free fatty acids (Bessman, 1976). There is some evidence in rodents that although tyrosine hydroxylase activity in the adrenal medulla increases with age, PNMT is reduced by 60 percent (Reis, Ross, Brodsky, Specht, and Joh, 1976). Dopa decarboxylase, the enzyme mediating the conversion of dopa to dopamine, is also reported to increase with age. This leads the investigators to conclude that in the peripheral tissues of rodents at least, there is an increased ability to synthesize dopamine which is counterbalanced by a declining ability to synthesize epinephrine. Under these circumstances there would be a decreased ability to physiologically cope with stressors.

## ADRENAL HORMONAL BALANCE: AGGRESSION OR DEFEAT

Arousal of the fight response occurs if the stressor is seen as an avoidable threat to the individual's status or value system. Henry (1976), Henry and Ely (1976), and Henry and Stephens (1977) postulate that an opposite arousal pattern to that of aggression is evoked when the organism perceives the stressor or threat to involve defeat, failure, loss of status, inability to fulfill expectations, or loss of control. Under these circumstances these investigators claim that the predominating physiological response does not involve the sympathetic adrenal medullary chain but rather the pituitary adrenal cortical system. Impulses from the hippocampal and septal region are set up which are relayed to the anterior pituitary via the median eminence of the hypothalamus, so that ACTH from the anterior pituitary is released. The release of this hormone is regulated by the adrenocorticosteroid hormone releasing factor in the median eminence of the hypothalamus which stimulates the anterior pituitary to regulate ACTH secretion. The target organ for ACTH is the adrenal cortex. Under stressful situations where the individual is subordinated or withdraws, there is an increased output of corticosteroids from the adrenal cortex. This is also an increase in hypothalamically mediated parasympathetic activity, especially vagal activity, an increase in pepsin activity in the stomach, and an increase in gluconeogenesis. Gluconeogenesis involves the formation of glucose from noncarbohydrate sources which involves in particular the breakdown of proteins and the use of amino acids for this purpose. There is also a rise in blood pressure and a decrease in the functioning of the reticuloendothelial system, meaning that an individual will be more susceptible to infections, a feature frequently seen in those people who are under a lot of stress and strain. The increase in blood pressure in this case is claimed to involve, in particular, the reninangiotensin system.

Henry and his colleagues claim that either the sympathetic adrenal medullary system or the pituitary adrenal cortical response predominates under stressful conditions, depending on how the individual cognitively and emotionally appraises the situation. Furthermore, Henry (1976) claims that with age there is a shift in the type of response which is evoked. Namely, this involves the adrenal cortical response associated with subordination, which gradually predominates over the adrenal medullary reaction associated with aggression. Henry cites evidence which shows that in colonies of CBA mice, this alteration in the predominating pattern of the stress response does occur, namely, the shift to the pituitary adrenal cortical axis. He also cites human studies which have the same implication. As a person ages "the stimulus may shift from a preponderance of the active, acting-out, sympathetic adrenal medullary mode toward a greater participation of the adrenal cortical mode. This shift would be an expression of a decreasing sense of control, of subordination with diminishing aggressiveness, and of an increased bottling up of emotions as aging progresses" (Henry, 1976, p. 67).

The reduction of aggressive behavior in old age, which Henry is suggesting, implies that there is a decrease in the amount of epinephrine released from the adrenal medulla. This fits in with the evidence of Reis, *et al.* (1976) cited earlier in this chapter, that the level of PNMT in the adrenal medulla decreases with age. This evidence empha-sizes the need for stress research to take into consideration the factor of age when interpreting one's results, concerning the balance of responses which occur under stress, a practice which is unfortunately all too rare.

## PHYSIOLOGICAL REACTIONS OF DEPRESSION

The reduction of aggressive behavior with age as discussed in the previous section implies a kind of withdrawal or retreat. Most commonly this may be manifested psychologically in the form of depression.

Biochemical findings are controversial when we consider depression among the aged. Perhaps the most popular hypothesis with respect to the etiology of depression concerns altered metabolism in brain amines (Baldessarini, 1975; Lipton, 1976; Maas, 1975). The most important of the amine metabolites so far investigated are 3-methoxy-4-hydroxy phenylglycol (MHPG) and homovanillic acid (HVA). MHPG is derived from the methylation and reduction of norepinephrine in the brain. HVA is derived from dopamine metabolism. Although findings are still disputable, it seems that in cerebrospinal fluid, MHPG and HVA are lower in depressed patients than in controls (Gordon and Oliver, 1971; Mendels, Frazer, Fitzgerald, Ramsey, and Stokes, 1972; Papeschi and McClure, 1971).

From the indoleamines, the metabolic end product of serotonin, 5-hydroxyindoleacetic acid (5 HIAA) has been found by some to be lower in the cerebrospinal fluid during depression (Ashcroft, Crawford, Eccleston, Sharman, MacDougall, Stanton, and Binns, 1966; Mendels *et al.*, 1972; Praag, Korf, and Puite, 1970) although others have found no change (Ashcroft *et al.*, 1966; Wilk, Shopsin, Gershon, and Suhl, 1972).

Platelet monoamine oxidase levels have also been reported to be higher in depressed patients than in normal ones (Nies, Robinson, Ravaris, and Davis, 1971) and monoamine oxidase levels increase with age (Robinson, Davis, Nies, Ravaris, and Sylvester, 1971; Robinson, Davis, Nies, Colburn, Davis, Bourne, Bunney, Shaw, and Coppen, 1972).

Finally, it is possible that the levels of the widely distributed inhibitory neurotransmitter gamma-aminobutyric acid may alter during certain psychiatric and neurological disorders including depression (Roberts, 1974a, 1974b). It is suggested that in depression the excessive inhibition manifested in impaired cognitive and affective behaviors may be due not only to the deficiency in certain biogenic amine systems but in an overactivity of the inhibitory GABA system which may be reflected in raised levels of this neurotransmitter in the CSF.

## Toward a General Theory of the Physiology of Stress

Bessman (1976) goes beyond these theories stating that under all conditions of stress there are biphasic, specific, ubiquitous, physiological, and biochemical reactions which occur to some degree in all individuals. These reactions are due to the release of epinephrine which mediates the first phase of the stress response, and the anterior pituitary hormones, especially growth hormone (GH) and ACTH which modulate the second phase of the stress response. It is noteworthy that both these systems are under the regulatory control of the hypothalamus. The first phase is short and immediate in its biochemical effects. The second phase takes longer to exert its effects on the organism and is more prolonged since the biochemical consequences from the pituitary and adrenal cortical hormonal effects persist for several days. It is for these reasons Bessman (1976) describes the biochemical processes which occur under stress to be biphasic in nature. More specifically, Bessman's theory, which essentially describes the physiological chemistry of emotion, proposes the following. In the first phase, which is rapid and reversible, the following five stages occur:

1. Activation of the phosphorylase system causes liberation into the blood of glucose resulting in elevated blood glucose levels.
2. Activation of the lipase system results in the liberation into the blood of free fatty acids resulting in elevated free fatty acid levels.
3. Excess free fatty acids are converted into ketone acids by the liver resulting in elevated ketone body blood levels.
4. Ketone acids react with bicarbonate resulting in decreased blood bicarbonate levels.
5. Decreased bicarbonate levels cause a consequent reduction in pH.

The pathological consequences of this first phase include hyperglycaemia, ketonemia, and eventually diabetic ketoacidosis.

The second phase of stress called the peptide-steroid hormone phase may begin at the same time as the catecholamine phase, but takes much longer to express itself metabolically and persists for a greater length of time. This phase involves the peptide and steroid hormones such as:

1. ACTH release from the anterior pituitary which acts on the adrenal cortex to release corticosteroids and testosterone.

2. Growth hormone release from the anterior pituitary which acts directly on target organs.

These hormones cause an increase in the net synthesis of key enzymes involved in gluconeogenesis (glucose 6 phosphatase, fructose 1–6 diphosphatase, PEP carboxykinase, pyruvate carboxylase, and pyruvate kinase). There is also an increase in proteolytic activity or the breakdown of protein.

Consequences, therefore, of the second phase of stress are:

1. Breakdown of protein.
2. Liberation of amino acids which enter the pathway of gluconeogenesis thereby causing elevated blood sugar levels.
3. Conversion of most of the carbon of essential amino acids to ketone bodies causing elevated blood ketone levels.
4. Excess ketone bodies which are not oxidized react with bicarbonate resulting in decreased blood bicarbonate levels.
5. Decreased bicarbonate levels cause a consequent reduction in pH.

Again, the pathological consequences of the second phase include hyperglycaemia, ketonemia, and in the extreme case diabetic ketoacidosis. Yalow, Aharon-Varsano, Echemendia, and Berson (1969) found experimental evidence in human subjects which showed that a variety of stressful stimuli, including surgical procedures, electroconvulsive therapy, and insulin-induced hypoglycaemia produced differential hormonal effects. The secretion of either growth hormone or ACTH depended on the specific stressor; for example, there was always a rise in ACTH after electroconvulsive therapy, but there were no significant changes in the levels of growth hormone observed. Under mild conditions of hypoglycaemia, no significant increases in ACTH occurred, but there were significant increases in growth hormone. More severe conditions of hypoglycaemia will initiate the release of ACTH also. During surgery the results varied. Depending on the individual either ACTH or growth hormone were elevated or both were elevated. These authors concluded that under non-specific stressful conditions the release of ACTH or growth hormone does not share a common neuroendocrine pathway, although as Bessman's 1976 theory shows, the actions of both these hormones are similar in their effects on gluconeogenesis.

The recent discovery and elucidation of several hypothalamic factors including somatostatin make this an exciting area of research. For recent reviews on the nature of these factors see Gerich,

Charles, and Brodsky (1976); Reichlin, Saperstein, Jackson, Boyd, and Patel (1976); and Schally, Kastin, and Arimura (1977).

A number of studies can be found to support the hypothesis that due to the output of stress hormones, disease may develop or existing disease may be exacerbated. Henry and his colleagues, for example, cite hypertension as supporting the thesis that via either the sympathetic adrenal medullary pathway or the anterior pituitary adrenal cortical pathway, cardiovascular diseases, which increase in incidence with age, can develop. Cannon (1942) cited evidence that showed how stressful situations could cause death, such as voodoo death, and speculated that such death was due to cardiac failure. Lown, Verrier, and Corbalan (1973) and Lown, Verrier, and Rabinowitz (1977) elucidated the physiological mechanisms involved in such deaths. They presented considerable evidence to show that death caused by stress, involved neurophysiological pathways especially the hypothalamus, which in predisposed animals and people could trigger an arrhythmia. In particular, a ventricular fibrillation could be set up in the heart, via the hypothalamus, the sympathetic nervous system, and the inferior cardiac nerves, and could result in cardiac death.

Bessman (1976) describes the uncontrolled mechanisms of the biphasic processes of stress, as simulating the condition of diabetic ketoacidosis. Hinkle and Wolf (1950, 1952) in a series of experiments, found that stressful situations exacerbated the diabetic condition which could result in diabetic ketoacidosis. These authors considered that the onset of diabetes could be related to stressful conditons. Events in the life situation which directly or through their symbolic meaning threaten the security and well-being of an individual may also call forth a state of hypermetabolism and an increase in the possibility of ketonemia particularly in the diabetic. It is as if a perception and appraisal of a threat leads to a metabolic preparation to meet the threat. Since the metabolic machinery becomes less adaptive and efficient with age (Andres and Tobin, 1977; Burgess, 1976; Dilman, 1976) this theory of Bessman has a particular applicability to aging individuals, who under very stressful situations are more likely to be precipitated into this diabetic stressful state.

## PHYSIOLOGY OF STRESS AND PSYCHIATRIC DISORDERS

The previous discussion is by no means a complete description of all of the stress theories which have been proposed. However, one other theoretical approach that should be included because of its direct relevance to psychiatric disorders is that evolved by Gellhorn and Kiely. Utilizing the basic work of Hess who recognized as early as 1925 that alterations in the autonomic nervous system are also associated with changes in the central nervous system, Gellhorn (1968), Gellhorn and Kiely (1973), and Kiely (1974, 1976) extended this work of Hess by elaborating on two opposing but reciprocal neurobiological systems termed the ergotropic and trophotropic units. The use of such units allows the somatic and autonomic systems to be integrated.

Both the ergotropic and trophotropic systems have CNS, ANS and neuroendocrine components, but whereas the ergotropic system leads to arousal with its concomitant behavioral consequences of elevated levels of activity and emotional responsiveness, the trophotropic system is associated with diminished arousal which may lead to inactivity, drowsiness, or sleep.

In a logical way the creators of this theory systematically trace the different neural and endocrine pathways, and the neurotransmitters associated with each system, noting that a balanced dynamic state or "tuning" between these two systems is required to maintain homeostasis. Whereas the ergotropic system is associated with the release of the biogenic amines, norepinephine and dopamine, as their neurotransmitters, the trophotropic system is characterized by the release of 5-hydroxytryptamine (serotonin) and acetylcholine.

When stress, challenges, or threats are imposed upon the individual and have been cognitively appraised, the individual may approach the stimulus as characterized by the ergotropic or "Go" system or withdraw and avoid as characterized by the trophotropic or "No Go" system. Alternately, both systems may discharge simultaneously. Mediated by changes in the reticular formation, hypothalamus, the limbic system and the higher cortical regions the ergotropic system "is characterized by alerting, arousal, excitement, increased muscle tone, and sympathetic nervous activity, and the release of catabolic hormonal products." (Kiely, 1974, p. 518). In contrast the trophotropic system in order to conserve energy and permit withdrawal raises its perceptual stimulus threshold and is thus characterized by "decreased skeletal muscle tone, increased parasympathetic nervous function, and the circulation of anabolic hormones" (Kiely, 1974, p. 518).

A number of psychosomatic and psychiatric disorders are explained by utilizing the mechanisms of these two systems (Gellhorn and Kiely, 1973; Kiely, 1976). For instance, overstimulation of the trophotropic system may lead to peptic ulcers, whereas overstimulation of the ergotropic system may lead to hypertension. In particular, the psychiatric symptoms encountered represent either opposing forces of the two systems acting independently or simultaneously, in an attempt to make some kind of adaptive response. If the trophotropic system dominates, acute fearfulness may result. If the ergotropic system is dominant, chronic tension is manifested. If the two systems simultaneously discharge, anxiety, agitated depression, delirium, or what is termed "acute schizophreniform psychotic disintegration" (involving hallucinations, delusions or thought disorders, without loss of consciousness or memory) may eventuate (Kiely, 1976, p. 2759).

While any of these symptoms can appear in any age group, the middle aged and the elderly, because of their increased susceptibility to cardiac, pulmonary, or renal failure, which may lead to cerebral inefficiency, are more prone to delirium symptoms (Kiely, 1976). Other psychiatric disorders among the elderly may also occur because of an imbalance between the ergotropic and trophotropic systems and indeed this approach to mental diseases in the aged is a most promising one.

Although this concludes the present discussion concerning the physiological mechanisms involved during the stress response and disease outcomes, the reader should be aware that other experimental and theoretical descriptions involving neuroendocrine mechanisms and physiological or psychological states exhibited under conditions of stress have been given by Bridges (1974), Mason (1968) and Yuwiler (1976). Both the biological and psychological states as they relate to aging have recently been reviewed by Stenback (1975). The present authors now concern themselves with a discussion of the psychological mechanisms which may be involved in dealing with stressful situations.

## PSYCHOLOGICAL MECHANISMS MEDIATING STRESS

### COGNITIVE APPRAISALS AND EMOTIONAL STATES

Progress in the behavioral sciences has been slow in clarifying the sequence of psychological processes which occur under stressful conditions. The terms cognitive appraisal, emotional states, and psychological coping mechanisms or strategies are used to designate the processes whereby an individual adapts to or manages the stressful situation or stressors.

Important in the translation of such stressors into physiological responses is the individual's cognitive appraisal of the situation. Via the process of cognition, appraisal of the event occurs which leads to the individual either minimizing or magnifying the phenomena. Such appraisal is linked with other psychological processes which simultaneously occur, namely, the initiation of coping strategies which also play a significant part in dictating the subsequent physiological reactions.

Cognitive appraisal involves evaluation processes, an attachment of meaning to the stressors, and these processes have cogitable, perceptual, and emotional components. Grinker and Spiegel in speaking of the strictly cognitive aspects of this appraisal defined it in the following way: "appraisal of the situation requires mental activity involving judgment, discrimination, and choice of activity, based largely on past experience" (Grinker and Spiegel, 1945, p. 122). Lazarus described the involvement of cognitive processes during stress by stating that in order for a threat to be experienced "an evaluation must be made of the situation, to the effect that a harm is signified. The individual's knowledge and beliefs contribute to this. The appraisal of threat is not a simple perception of the elements of the situation, but a judgment, an inference in which the data are assimilated to a constellation of ideas and expectations" (Lazarus, 1966 p. 44).

Lazarus and his colleagues have been, perhaps, the major proponents of the issues concerning cognitive appraisals, the involvement of emotional states and coping processes (Lazarus, 1966, 1967, 1968, 1974, 1975a, 1975b; Lazarus, Averill, and Opton, 1970; Lazarus and Cohen, 1978a, 1978b; Lazarus and Launier, 1978). As the theoretical state of the art now stands there are two components of cognitive appraisal. Primary appraisal involves a cognitive evaluation of the "transaction" between a person and his/her environment, to determine whether the event is threatening or stressful, as a benign or positive challenge situation, or as an irrelevancy. Secondary appraisals, which may or may not precede the primary appraisals, involve an evaluation by the person of his/her coping capabilities, coping resources, or the *options* that may be open to him/her. These secondary appraisals subsequently modify the coping behavior exhibited and also shape the primary appraisal processes.

A central factor to these processes of cognitive appraisal is the emotional state of the individual. Indeed, there is a cause and effect relationship between coping and emotion, where the emotional state may be the independent or dependent variable. In other words, the emotional feelings may precede or follow the appraisal or coping. The appraisal processes may be altered by changing the emotional state, *or* coping processes may precede the emotions which are subsequently experienced by the individual. Many reactions to potential stressors are anticipatory. The work of Lazarus and his colleagues place great emphasis on the individual's ability to self-regulate his or her emotional state. When Lazarus writes of the self-regulation of emotions he means "control not only over the overt behavior associated with an emotion (e.g., the expressive gestures and postures and instrumental action) but of the entire organized state that is subsumed under the emotion construct" (Lazarus, 1975a, p. 57). Extending this proposal further, Lazarus suggests that this "self-regulation also dampens, eliminates, or alters the quality of emotional states, depending on its successfulness. This would in fact follow from the theoretical dependence of emotions and coping processes on cognitive appraisal and reappraisal processes. . . ." (Lazarus, 1975a, p. 57). Thus, the current emotional state of the individual effects the cognitive appraisal and the adaptation or coping mechanisms, and the emotional state may also arise as a consequence of the appraisal processes or as consequences of coping.

While the present authors agree that there are these interactions and feedback loops between cognitive, emotional, and coping processes, this approach does not sufficiently separate the variables of appraisal, emotion, and coping, either for descriptive or experimental purposes. Figure 14-1, of this chapter, therefore, for the purposes of clarity, does not include the feedback loops between the different components. Further research needs to concentrate on measuring the different individual variables that intervene between the stressors and the stress response or outcome. The issue of cognitive appraisals, for instance, needs elaboration. One aspect of this is the question of what cognitive options does the individual have, and how do these options change with age.

A recent study suggests that over a life-span, an individual may reduce his cognitive options by becoming more convergently biased in his thinking (Renner, Alpaugh, and Birren, 1978). In this study divergent thinking tests were given to a group of elementary school children, young adults, and older adults. Although older adults had lower scores on all parameters of fluency, flexibility, and originality, compared with children and young adults, the particular reason for this seemed to be in the older individual's comparative lack of ability to shift between major categories of ideas. The older subjects shifted less well compared with the young who shifted their focus of attention with greater facility. Furthermore, older adults tended to restrict themselves to conventional practical solutions rather than perceive the more imaginative, fanciful possibilities which were more characteristic of the young. The tendency toward more conventional, conforming answers with age, those that reflect the possible rather than a probable, may reflect more caution in the thinking of older adults as has been found, for example by Arenberg and Robertson (1977), Botwinick (1973), and Klein (1972).

However, the decline in divergent thinking ability scores in the study of Renner, Alpaugh, and Birren (1978) was already observed in young adults, as compared to the elementary school children, particularly in their sub-scores of originality (which were based on frequency ratings of flexibility scores). Thus, it may be more reasonable to argue that reduced divergent scores are due to educational practices and subsequent environmental and job experiences or demands, especially those which force an individual to become increasingly specialized, so that a person's thinking tends to become more convergently biased (Alpaugh, Renner, and Birren, 1975; Renner, 1978; Renner *et al.*, 1978). In terms of how an older individual copes with stressful situations this means that the number of options or solutions that he or she can perceive will be reduced, compared with the younger person.

Although, as already mentioned, much more research needs to be done into these questions of cognitive appraisals, emotional states, and coping processes, the important point is that psychological mechanisms do intervene between the inputs of stressful stimuli and the eventual stress response. Furthermore, these psychological mediators may affect the physiological response. A study by Gray, Ramsey, Villarreal, and Krakauer (1955) revealed that general anesthesia by itself does not induce a significant adrenal cortical physiological response. Symington, Currie, Curran, and Davidson (1955), in examining the effect of stressful conditions on the adrenal cortical reaction in matched groups, found that there was a difference in the appearance of the adrenal cortex, as assessed during autopsies, between those who remained conscious and those who were unconscious during extensive fatal injuries. A "normal" appearance of the adrenal cortex occurred in those patients who died without regaining consciousness, while in those patients who remained conscious before dying, pathological adrenal cortical changes were observed. While this evidence is only tentative, it does suggest that psychological processes may participate in the mediation of the physiological response. Thus, all of the elements in Figure 14-1 of this chapter, interact, although the remainder of this chapter concerns itself with behavioral responses and coping mechanisms as separate issues.

## Disease Predisposing Behavior

Personality coping styles or types of defense mechanisms play a significant role in determining how one deals with stressful circumstances, and the degree of emotion or psychological significance one associates with particular events. The type of coping style used has also been found to be related to manifestations of organic and/or psychiatric illness (Piorkowski, 1972; Schwartz, 1972; Schwartz, Krupp, and Byrne, 1971). Renner and Birren (in press) in a recent review of this research concluded, however, that the defense style of many psychiatric patients was still largely unknown.

Some studies have been influenced by traditions in psychiatry (e.g., Hinkle and Wolf, 1950, 1952). These have been largely descriptive and in explanations of behavioral phenomena have sometimes invoked the use of psychoanalytical ego defense mechanisms, such as projection or repression, and very often have been confined to detailed case-study descriptions. These will not be discussed here. Other studies have looked at personality variables that may be related to general illness or certain designated diseases. These have been numerous and very few of them have been related to aging. In particular, most of studies that do have relevance to aging have been concerned with cardiovascular diseases. These have been recently reviewed by Eisdorfer and Wilkie (1977), Glass (1977), Rowland and Sokol (1977), and Weiss (1975).

As an extension of these reviews, the present authors briefly review those studies related to psychosomatic and psychiatric disorders which have examined two specific personality dimensions, namely those of repression and sensitization. These two parameters have been investigated in terms of the possibility that they represent two types of coping strategies which pre-dispose the individual to certain diseases. An extensive review of the personality variables associated with stress, aging, and disease has recently been compiled (Renner and Birren, in press).

The individual who uses sensitization as a coping strategy resorts to intellectualization, obsessional thinking, continuous worrying, rumination, or overt concern when confronted with a stressful situation. Repression, on the other hand

is the type of coping strategy, whereby avoidance behavior, denial, and suppression are the characteristic reactions to stress (Byrne, 1964; Byrne, Barry, and Nelson, 1963; Chabot, 1973; Schwartz, 1972; Schwartz et al., 1971). To measure such traits, 127 items derived from the Minnesota Multiphasic Personality Inventory have been used. One of the values claimed from using such a scale is that there are significant relationships between the pattern of test responses, and the presence of medical or psychiatric disturbances. The generalized trend of the results of a number of investigations has been that there are significant relationships found between the pattern of test responses and the presence of medical or psychiatric disturbances (see for example, Byrne, Steinberg, and Schwartz, 1968) From the studies already cited the findings have been that repressors and sensitizers differ in the type of medical diagnoses, the former receiving more organic diagnoses, and the sensitizers more psychiatric diagnoses. For instance, in one of the few age-related studies, Schwartz, Krupp, and Byrne (1971) investigated 360 patients from both sexes, representing three age groups (20–29 years; 40–49 years; and 60–69 years) and categorized according to three repression-sensitization levels (repressors, neutrals, and sensitizers). They found that repressors, the people who tend to use denial as a defense, had from their medical records, significantly more organic illnesses. More significantly, although the number of organic illnesses increased with age, there did not seem to be a shift in the mode of adaptation, in terms of repression or sensitization, with age.

Stuart (1977) found apparently contradictory evidence in a study of older females, in that sensitizers reported more organic illnesses. However, the Cornell Medical Index, which is a test allowing subjective evaluations of one's health, was used in this study, which may explain the results, since repressors would tend to deny their symptoms.

Birren and Renner (in press) and Renner and Birren (in press) extended the repression-sensitization conceptual approach by suggesting that personality in relation to the development of disease due to stress, should be looked upon as having four potentials: (a) the personality which seeks stress; (b) the personality which avoids stress; (c) the personality which on being exposed to a stressful stimulus, however trivial, amplifies the distressing situation; and (d) the personality which on being exposed to a stressful stimulus, however severe, tends to dampen its significance.

From these possibilities, four categories of personalities are suggested. First, there are the *Environmental Stress Amplifiers* who are those individuals who appear to "approach" stressful circumstances, or magnify and amplify the stressful implications surrounding even trivial circumstances. Second, there are the *Environmental Stress Dampeners or Insulators,* those individuals who avoid events which may be stressful or who, by their behavior, minimize the significance of any stressful events. These two categories refer to the observable responses of people. They refer to the individual's behavioral tendencies or his/her overt coping strategies. The second two categories relate to the individual's internal or physiological response, which may be maximized or minimized, and will depend on his/her coping strategies. The *Internal Stress Amplifiers* are those individuals whose coping styles lead to heightened emotional arousal which can be of long duration, even in response to apparently minor crises. In contrast, there are the *Internal Stress Dampeners or Insulators* whose coping style allows them to reduce the intensity and duration of physiological arousal in response to stress. Thus, in those studies that have investigated the repression-sensitization dichotomy, repressors would represent those individuals who are environmental stress dampeners but internal stress amplifiers, whereas sensitizors are people who typify the environmental stress amplifiers but internal stress dampeners.

## COPING STRATEGIES

There have been those studies which have investigated actual coping strategies that an individual would use or uses in specific stressful situations. Work in this area has been largely descriptive. The focus of such studies has been to emphasize the actual coping response per se. Rahe (1974), for example, shifted from his original position which conceptualized a one-to-one relationship between stressors and disease. In this paper he conceded that there was a pathway of different filters intervening between life crisis units and illness. The life changes which a person is exposed to, may be filtered or modified by past experiences of similar or parallel life changes. The next filter or modifier in the pathway represents the individual's psychological defenses or his ego defense mechanisms. The type of psychological defenses used will regulate the amount of autonomic nervous system (ANS) arousal, so that those who are able to internally dampen stress will have less arousal than those who internally amplify stressful stimuli (Birren and Renner, in press). Heightened ANS arousal, particularly if it is prolonged, will not only impair performance (Eisdorfer, 1968; Eisdorfer, Nowlin, and

Wilkie, 1970) but also increase susceptibility to physiological damage and disease (Henry, 1976; Henry and Ely, 1976; Henry and Stephens, 1977). Prolonged autonomic arousal will have greater deleterious effects among older people who after stressful experiences, take longer to return to basal homeostatic levels. This last statement reinforces earlier statements that age should be a major factor in stress research and that a wise way to approach the problem of stress is to take a lifespan approach. One of the early, significant studies made in the area of coping strategies was made by Birren (1969). Birren described some of the successful strategies or mechanisms used by adults when making complex decisions. He used the term "strategies" to denote "planful aspects of human behavior" (p. 23).

The subjects for the study reported by Birren (1969) were 100 men and women aged 30 to 60 years who were successful in their careers of a professional or executive nature. They were interviewed about several important areas of life experience: work and career, family relationships, body, health and appearance, friendships, activities in clubs and associations, and relations to time and death. The interview material was analyzed with respect to reports of changing goals with age; long ranged plans which were in effect; and the tactics of living. The latter comprise what are regarded as strategies or coping mechanisms. The study identified 19 strategies that the individuals used in managing their life activities. Several of the findings are relevant to this chapter. The middle-aged adults seemed to be very well aware of the strategies they used in pursuing their long ranged goals. One of the goals of middle age appears to be a reduction of "load" in order to gain or maintain effectiveness. Another major point was the fact that the successful middle-aged and older adults seem to be increasingly effective in their careers as a result of the concepts or abstractions they form. They reduce the information load by chunking information. By developing a map of major life events, larger units of information can be dealt with instead of an overload of details. The successful middle-aged or older adults appear to conserve their energies. Unlike young adults they seem to be under a lesser load by virtue of the "map of life" they have developed and the strategies they have evolved in managing their lives and the attendant stressors.

Recent investigations into the area of coping strategies has been and is currently being done by Lazarus and his colleagues (Lazarus, 1966, 1967, 1968, 1974, 1975a, 1975b; Lazarus and Cohen,

1978a, 1978b; Lazarus and Launier, 1978). These investigators emphasize the cognitive appraisal aspect of coping and the specific coping mechanisms that individuals use when confronted with a stressful situation. Lazarus (1977) has developed a coping strategy scale which in a descriptive fashion asks the individual how he copes with certain tense, anxiety provoking situations. Examples of such situations may involve frustration, such as not getting something you need or deserve, concern about doing well, disappointment with a person, being criticized or rejected, fighting or arguing, dealing with a difficult person, or losing something or someone. Specific responses which the individual might use as a way of coping are also included. Examples from this part of the coping questionnaire which require either a yes or no response include the following: "criticized or lectured yourself," "went on as if nothing had happened," "kept your feelings to yourself," "slept more than usual," "got mad at the people or things that caused the problem," "accepted the next best thing to what you wanted," or "let your feelings out somehow."

The coping questionnaire emanates from the theoretical rationale of Lazarus and his colleagues that both the cognitive appraisal and the emotional state are important in determining the type of coping strategies that are used by each individual. The extent to which any event can be negatively stressful depends on the balance of power within the individual between the self-assessed demands of the situation and the resources of the individual. According to Lazarus and his colleagues, there are four types of processes which can occur when the individual tries to cope with stress. These are the following:

1. An information search of the environmental event to sum up the situation both cognitively and emotionally.

2. Direct action on the part of the individual concerned to attempt to change the situation. This can take the form of attack or withdrawal.

3. Inhibition of action.

4. Intrapsychic modes of action which include denial, avoidance, intellectual detachment, humor, an attempt to put a positive light on the situation, rationalization, or looking towards religious support.

As to which of these mechanisms are actually used in any specific situation depends on the degree of uncertainty, the degree of threat that an individual perceives and experiences, the presence or absence of a conflict, and the experience or felt degree of helplessness (Lazarus and Launier, 1978). The approach of these investigators, to furthering our understanding of the psychological coping processes that are involved, when individuals are confronted with conflicts or stressful situations, is a most promising one. At the present time, it still awaits empirical support, and in particular data to determine its applicability to specific age groups.

Finally, Thoresen and his colleagues have developed a behavioral working model to not only investigate how people manage in stressful situations, but how to teach them to cope better (Thoresen, 1978; Thoresen and Coates, 1976; Thoresen, Kirmil-Gray, and Crosbie, 1977). Their cognitive social learning model emphasizes the cognitive processes which come into play when certain environmental events impose themselves on the individual, and the interaction of those two variables with behavioral actions. The intention of such therapies is to enable the individual to manage stressful situations without damaging consequences, or as Selye (1974) puts it to handle "stress without distress."

Selye (1974) offered the following motto which seems a fitting conclusion to this section: "Fight for your highest attainable aim, but never put up resistance in vain" (p. 112.).

## IMPLICATIONS FOR INTERVENTION AND RESEARCH

Being a somewhat vague concept it is tempting to either dismiss the topic of stress as not being important in mental health and aging or to impart to it an overly magical importance that can explain too much. It seems temperate at this point to regard stress as at least modifying the appearance of disease. Exposure to stressors and the inability to effect appropriate control over events seems to bring out the weaknesses in the psychophysiology of mankind. That is, stress seems to exacerbate our tendencies to certain afflictions such as heart disease and depression. For example, mortality data on the United States population indicate that there are large differences in mortality from cardiovascular diseases associated with socioeconomic levels whereas mortality from malignant neoplasms show small effects of social class influences (Kitagawa and Hauser, 1973). Also, the high rate of cardiovascular disease in survivors of war-time prisoner and concentration camps suggests that in a general way the level of cardiovascular disease in middle age is a rough index of the level of stress in human society. Middle age is emphasized rather than late life because socioeconomic differences in mortality due to vascular disease are greatest in middle age and in old age disappear or are small.

With the above thought in mind, the large sex differences in mortality due to cardiovascular disease in midlife are appropriately a cause for concern and a focus for research. To what extent is the male organism more prone to over react to threat and sustain physiologically debilitating effects or to what extent is the male more exposed to threatening circumstances in his occupational life? Such important issues cannot be answered at present but warrant research since the sex differences in mortality is the highest in the United States of any technologically developed country.

The topic of aging implies long periods of observation and one question that arises is that of selecting the important variables to track over a life-span. One important variable in the present context is that of depression for depression seems to be associated with a high incidence of chronic disease. Depressed affect appears to be both a subjective reaction to loss or threat which one cannot avoid or conquer and also it is an indicator of catabolic processes which, if sustained, have their outcomes in degenerative disease. The stress response is one of mobilizing the organism to defend itself, a group of survival mechanisms which are organized as a result of evolution of the species. It is the chronic and intense evoking of the stress mechanisms which is undesirable. Thus, tracking individuals who have shown a disposition to depression may prove to be a way of early detection of somatic disease and also of identifying those persons who may be either over exposed to environmental stressors or whose cognitive organization is such as to intensify and protract the stress response.

The classical teaching of psychiatry suggests that clinical depressive disorders increase in prevalence and intensity with age (Butler and Lewis, 1973; Klerman and Barrett, 1973; Post, 1962; Roth, 1955). It is possible that depression may increasingly become an age phenomenon; that depression will become an even greater problem amongst the elderly to be, in the next century, since clinical depression, as seen by psychiatrists since World War II, is increasing in prevalance among adolescents and young adults (Klerman, 1976).

It is predicted from current epidemiological data that at least 10 to 20 percent of young people will at some time during their adult lives suffer a clinical depression (Lehmann, 1971). Klerman (1976) goes so far as to predict that "we will be entering a new age of melancholy as a successor to the age of anxiety" (p. 323).

Although methodological issues are still the major problem to solve in understanding the relationship of age and depression, its frequency and type (Gurland, 1976), depression is the most common psychiatric disorder that the physician is likely to encounter when dealing with an older patient, and is most likely to be overlooked or misdiagnosed (Epstein, 1976).

Pfeiffer and Busse (1973) claim that amongst hospitalized elderly patients and older residents in community centers, the frequency of affective disorders range from 10 to 65 percent. Using the criteria of a psychiatric diagnosis, for both neurotic and psychotic depressions, from a variety of surveys, suggests that although the disorder may have its highest prevalence in those in their middle years, its prevalence in the elderly groups is still high, and may go unrecognized. In addition, surveys are likely to take into account only the most recent episode of depression, and previous episodes, which may have occurred in the past, are forgotten. If, however, symptoms of depression are taken as a criteria, rather than clinical diagnosis, then depressive symptoms are most frequent in older age groups (Gurland, 1976).

In 1970, 31.5 percent of the total number of known successful suicides in the US were committed by people who were 65 years or more (Pfeiffer, 1977), yet this age group makes up only 10 percent of the population. Recognizing or diagnosing depressive illnesses in the elderly is important, because with appropriate treatment and therapeutic measures, the prognosis is favorable (Epstein, 1976). A life-span study of depression would seem an urgent priority.

Another implication of this chapter on stress, mental health, and aging is the matter of sensitizing professional personnel to the potential outcomes of stress in the older person. Given what may be narrower limits of adaptive capacity a small amount of stress may have stronger and more protracted impact upon the older person.

With regard to the psychological mechanisms in the management and response to stress, more research needs to be done on the situation specific nature of stressors. That is, given the symbolic nature of threat, the circumstances which evoke a stress response may vary considerably from individual to individual and also within the individual. Coping devices may, therefore, be narrow or broad in their range of effectiveness. However, the stressor and situation specific character of coping mechanisms is a subject for investigation. In a similar manner, the physiological stress response requires analysis in terms of the relative ease of evoking it. This is equivalent to asking the question as to whether or not there are individual differences in temperament or physiological liability such that a large portion of the phenomena of stress is explained by a generalized responsiveness of the individual rather than by the evocative intensity of the situational variables. To some extent this raises a type of "nature-nurture question" with regard to stress, i.e., does the individuation result from differences in the responsiveness or from the generalization among stressors that may come from learning.

We can expect more differentiation of the phenomena of stress as a result of physiological investigations. Many issues remain unclear at present such as the different roles of epinephrine and norepinephrine on responding tissues and also their role in regional brain metabolism. We may also expect that there will be a further differentiation in neuroendocrines when more substances are discovered and more specific modes of action are identified for those already known. It is quite possible that such knowledge will enable a more effective pharmacology to be developed which could be used to dampen the consequences of acute and chronic stress.

Parallel with our expectations that further research will lead to a more specific pharmacology of stress we may also expect that behavioral research will produce methods for the control of stress responses which will be both more adaptable to individual needs and have fewer undesirable side effects. Thus, research on the effects of jogging and meditation may lead to more specific knowledge of their mode of action in promoting relaxation. At the level of society more study needs to be done on the mortality and incidence of various stress related diseases in relation to e.g., occupation, education, mobility, and habits of diet, drinking, smoking, sleep, and recreation. By joining the results of such population studies with the findings of laboratory research we would perhaps be able to develop ways of reducing the mortality rates of sub-populations of high risk and generally improve the health and well being of the population.

It would seem that in our studies to date we have but scratched the surface of the phenomena of stress, aging, and mental health. Older adults experience psychosocial losses and disappointments which, because of their implications for a life long pattern of behavior, are not easily set aside. As yet we must be tentative in our suggestions as to how best to minimize acute shock and chronic effects. The gradual acceptance of changed life conditions is as important for the old as the young adult. However, to extract satisfaction, meaning, and optimistic anticipation of the future may be more of an art in the aged after a long life, than it is in the young adult whose life styles and commitments are in the process of formation. The more we seek answers to all aspects of stress phenomena implies that we may offer relief and better "mental health" to all individuals whatever their age.

# REFERENCES

ALPAUGH, P. K., RENNER, V. J., AND BIRREN, J. E. 1975. Age and creativity: Implications for education and teachers. *Journal of Educational Gerontology, 1,* 17–40.

ANDRES, R., AND TOBIN, J. R. 1977. Endocrine systems. *In,* C. E. Finch and L. Hayflick (eds.), *Handbook of the Biology of Aging,* pp. 357–378. New York: Van Nostrand Reinhold.

APPLEY, M. H., AND TRUMBULL, R. 1967. On the concept of psychological stress. *In,* M. H. Appley and R. Trumbull (eds.), *Psychological Stress: Issues in Research,* pp. 1–13. New York: Appleton-Century Crofts.

ARENBERG, D., AND ROBERTSON, E. A. 1977. Learning and aging. *In,* J. E. Birren and K. W. Schaie (eds.), *Handbook of the Psychology of Aging,* pp. 421–449. New York: Van Nostrand Reinhold.

ASHCROFT, G. W., CRAWFORD, T. B. B., ECCLESTON, D., SHARMAN, D. F., MACDOUGALL, E. J., STANTON, J. B., AND BINNS, J. E. 1966. 5-Hydroxyindole compounds in the cerebrospinal fluid of patients with psychiatric or neurological diseases. *Lancet, II,* 1049–1052.

BALDESSARINI, R. J. 1975. The basis for amine hypotheses in affective disorders. A critical evaluation. *Archives of General Psychiatry, 32,* 1087–1093.

BERNARD C. 1945. *Introduction à l'étude de la Médecine Experimentale.* Paris: Flammarion.

BESSMAN, S. P. 1976. The philosophic basis for the artificial pancreas. *Excerpta Medica International Congress Series No. 403 Endocrinology. Proceedings of the V International Congress of Endocrinology.* Amsterdam, Excerpta Medica, 2, 576–577.

BIRREN, J. E. 1969. Age and decision strategies. *In,* A. T. Welford and J. E. Birren (eds.), *Decision Making and Age,* pp. 23–36. New York: S. Karger.

BIRREN, J. E., AND RENNER, V. J. *Health, behavior and aging.* Paper presented at the Conference of the Institute de la Vie, Vichy, France, April 1977. (In press).

BOTWINICK, J. 1973. *Aging and Behavior.* New York: Springer.

BRAMWELL, S. T., MASUDA, M., WAGNER, N. N., AND HOLMES, T. H. 1975. Psychosocial factors in athletic injuries. *Journal of Human Stress, 1,* 6–20.

BRIDGES, P. K. 1974. Recent physiological studies of stress and anxiety in man. *Biological Psychiatry, 8,* 95–112.

BROWN, G. W., SKLAIR, F., HARRIS, T. O., AND BIRLEY, J. L. T. 1973. Life events and psychiatric disorders. *Psychological Medicine, 3,* 74–87.

BURGESS, J. A. 1976. Diabetes mellitus and aging. *In,* A. V. Everitt and J. A. Burgess (eds.), *Hypothalamus, Pituitary, and Aging,* pp. 497–510. Springfield, Ill.: Charles C Thomas.

BUTLER, R. N., AND LEWIS, M. I. 1973. *Aging and Mental Health, Positive Psychosocial Approaches.* St. Louis: C. V. Mosby.

BYRNE, E. 1964. Repression-sensitization as a dimension of personality. *Progress in Experimental Personality Research, 1,* 169–220.

BYRNE, D., BARRY, J., AND NELSON, D. 1963. Relation of the revised repression-sensitization scale to measures of self-description. *Psychological Reports, 13,* 323–334.

BYRNE, D., STEINBERG, M., AND SCHWARTZ, M. 1968. Relationship between repression-sensitization and physical illness. *Journal of Abnormal Psychology, 73,* 154–155.

CANNON, W. B. 1929. *Bodily Changes in Pain, Hunger, Fear and Rage.* New York: Appleton and Company.

CANNON, W. B. 1942. "Voodoo" death. *American Anthropologist, 44,* 169–181.

CASSEL, J. 1975. Studies of hypertension in migrants. *In,* P. Oglesby (ed.), *Epidemiology and Control of Hypertension,* pp. 41–58. New York: Stratton Intercontinental Medical Book Corporation.

CHABOT, J. A. 1973. Repression-sensitization: A critique of some neglected variables in the literature. *Psychological Bulletin, 80,* 122–129.

CLINE, D. W., AND CHOSY, J. J. 1972. A prospective study of life changes and subsequent health changes. *Archives of General Psychiatry, 27,* 51–53.

DANOWSKI, T. S. 1963. Emotional stress as a cause of diabetes mellitus. *Diabetes, 12,* 183–184.

DEKKER, D. J., AND WEBB, J. T. 1974. Relationships of the social readjustment rating scale to psychiatric patient status, anxiety and social desirability. *Journal of Psychosomatic Research, 18,* 125–130.

DILMAN, V. M. 1976. The hypothalamic control of aging and age-associated pathology. The elevation mechanism of aging. *In,* A. V. Everitt and J. A. Burgess (eds.), *Hypothalamus, Pituitary and Aging,* pp. 634–667. Springfield, Ill.: Charles C. Thomas.

DOHRENWEND, B. S. 1973. Life events as stressors: A methodological inquiry. *Journal of Health and Social Behavior, 14,* 167–175.

DURKHEIM, E. 1951. *Suicide: A Study in Sociology.* (Translated by J. A. Spaulding and G. Simpson.) New York: The Free Press.

EISDORFER, C. 1968. Arousal and performance: Experiments in verbal learning and a tentative theory. *In,* G. A. Talland (ed.), *Human Aging and Behavior,* pp.189–216. New York: Academic Press.

EISDORFER, C., NOWLIN J., AND WILKIE, F. 1970. Improvement of learning in the aged by modification of autonomic nervous system activity. *Science, 170,* 1327–1329.

EISDORFER, C., AND WILKIE, F. 1977. Stress, disease, aging and behavior. *In,* J. E. Birren and K. W. Schaie (eds.), *Handbook of the Psychology of Aging,* pp. 251–275. New York: Van Nostrand Reinhold.

ELIOT, R. S. 1977. Stress and cardiovascular disease. *European Journal of Cardiology, 5,* 97–104.

EPSTEIN, L. J. 1976. Depression in the elderly. *Journal of Gerontology, 31,* 278–282.

EVERITT, A. V. 1976. Aging and its hypothalamic-pituitary control. *In,* A. V. Everitt and J. A. Burgess (eds.), *Hypothalamus, Pituitary and Aging,* pp. 676–701. Springfield, Ill.: Charles C Thomas.

EVERITT, A. V., AND BURGESS, J. A. (eds.), 1976. *Hypothalamus, Pituitary and Aging.* Springfield, Ill.: Charles C Thomas.

FROLKIS, V. V. 1976. The hypothalamic mechanisms of aging. *In,* A. V. Everitt and J. A. Burgess (eds.), *Hypothalamus, Pituitary and Aging,* pp. 614–633. Springfield, Ill.: Charles C Thomas.

FROLKIS, V. V. 1977. Aging of the autonomic nervous system. *In,* J. E. Birren and K. W. Schaie (eds.), *Handbook of the Psychology of Aging,* pp. 177–189. New York: Van Nostrand Reinhold.

GELLHORN, E. 1968. Central nervous system tuning and its implications for neuropsychiatry. *Journal of Nervous and Mental Disease, 147,* 148–162.

GELLHORN, E., AND KIELY, W. F. 1973. Autonomic nervous system in psychiatric disorder. *In,* J. Mendels (ed.), *Biological Psychiatry,* pp. 235–261. New York: John Wiley.

GERICH, J. E., CHARLES, M. A., AND GRODSKY, G. M. 1976. Regulation of pancreatic insulin and glucagon secretion. *Annual Review of Physiology, 38,* 353–388.

GLASS, D. C. 1977. *Behavior Patterns, Stress, and Coronary Disease.* Hillsdale, N.J.: Lawrence Erlbaum Associates.

GORDON, E. K., AND OLIVER J. 1971. 3-Methoxy-4-hydroxyphenyl-ethylene glycol in human cerebrospinal fluid. *Clinica Chimica Acta, 35,* 145–150.

GRAY, S. J., RAMSEY, C. G., VILLARREAL, R., AND KRAKAUER, L. J. 1955. Adrenal influences upon the stomach and the gastric response to stress. *In,* H. Selye and G. Heuser (eds.), *Fifth Annual Report on Stress, 1955–56,* pp. 138–160. New York: M.D. Publications.

GRINKER, R. R., AND SPIEGEL, J. P. 1945. *Men Under Stress.* New York: McGraw-Hill.

GURLAND, B. J. 1976. The comparative frequency of depression in various adult age groups. *Journal of Gerontology, 31,* 283–292.

HENRY, J. P. 1976. Understanding the early pathophysiology of essential hypertension. *Geriatrics, 31,* 59–72.

HENRY, J. P., AND ELY, D. L. 1976. Biologic correlates of

psychosomatic illness. *In*, R. G. Grenell and S. Galay (eds.), *Biological Foundations of Psychiatry*, pp. 945–985. New York: Raven Press.

Henry, J. P., and Stephens, P. M. 1977. *Stress, Health and the Social Environment. A Sociobiologic Approach to Medicine.* New York: Springer-Verlag.

Hinkle, L. E., and Wolf, S. 1950. Studies in diabetes mellitus: Changes in glucose, ketone and water metabolism during stress. *In*, H. G. Wolff, S. G. Wolf and C. C. Hare (eds.), *Life Stress and Bodily Disease. Proceedings of the Association for Research in Nervous and Mental Diseases*, pp. 338–389. Baltimore: Williams & Wilkins.

Hinkle, L. E., and Wolf, S. 1952. A summary of experimental evidence relating life stress to diabetes mellitus. *Journal of the Mount Sinai Hospital, XIX*, 537–570.

Holmes, T. H., and Rahe, R. H. 1967. The social readjustment rating scale. *Journal of Psychosomatic Research, 11*, 213–218. N.Y.: Pergaman Press, Ltd.

Holmes, T. H., and Masuda, M. 1974. Life change and illness susceptibility. *In*, B. S. Dohrenwend and B. P. Dohrenwend (eds.), *Stressful Life Events: Their Nature and Effects*, pp. 45–72. New York: John Wiley.

Horowitz, M. J., Schaefer, C., and Looney, P. 1974. Life event scaling for recency of experiences. *In*, E. Gunderson and R. H. Rahe (eds.), *Life Stress and Illness*, pp. 125–133. Springfield, Ill.: Charles C Thomas.

Horowitz, M., Schaefer, C., Hiroto, D., Wilner, N., and Levin, B. 1977. Life event questionnaires for measuring presumptive stress. *Psychosomatic Medicine, 39*, 413–431.

Hurst, M. W., Jenkins, C. D., and Rose, R. M. 1976. The relation of psychological stress to onset of medical illness. *Annual Review of Medicine, 27*, 301–312.

Kiely, W. F. 1974. From the symbolic stimulus to the pathophysiological response: Neurophysiological mechanisms. *International Journal of Psychiatry in Medicine, 5*, 517–529.

Kiely, W. F. 1976. Psychiatric syndromes in critically ill patients. *Journal of the American Medical Association, 235*, 2759–2761.

Kitagawa, E. M., and Hauser, P. M. 1973. *Differential Mortality in the United States: A Study in Socioeconomic Epidemiology.* Cambridge, Mass.: Harvard University Press.

Klein, R. L. 1972. Age, sex and task difficulty as predictors of social conformity. *Journal of Gerontology, 27*, 229–236.

Klerman, G. L., and Barrett, J. E. 1973. The affective disorders: Clinical and epidemiological aspects. *In*, S. Gershon and B. Shopsin (eds.), *Lithium: Its Role in Psychiatric Treatment and Research*, pp. 201–236. New York: Plenum.

Klerman, G. L. 1976. Age and clinical depression: Today's youth in the twenty-first century. *Journal of Gerontology, 31*, 318–323.

Kravitz, A. R., Isenberg, P. L., Shore, M. F., and Barnett, D. M. 1971. Emotional factors in diabetes mellitus. *In*, A. Marble, P. White, R. F. Bradley and L. P. Krall (eds.), *Joslin's Diabetes Mellitus, 11th Edition*, pp. 767–782. Philadelphia: Lee and Febiger.

Lazarus, R. S. 1966. *Psychological Stress and the Coping Process.* New York: McGraw–Hill.

Lazarus, R. S. 1967. Cognitive and personality factors underlying threat and coping. *In*, M. H. Appley and R. Trumbull (eds.), *Psychological Stress: Issues in Research*, pp. 151–169. New York: Appleton-Century-Crofts.

Lazarus, R. S. 1968. Emotions and adaptation: Conceptual and empirical relations. *In*, W. J. Arnold (ed.), *Nebraska Symposium on Motivation*, pp. 175–266. Lincoln: University of Nebraska Press.

Lazarus, R. S. 1974. Cognitive and coping processes in emotion. Paper given at AAAS Symposium: Cognitive Views of Motivation (organized by Bernard Weiner). San Francisco, Sheraton-Palace (February 27).

Lazarus, R. S. 1975a. The self-regulation of emotions. *In*, L. Levi (ed.), *Emotions—Their Parameters and Measurement*, pp. 47–67. New York: Raven Press.

Lazarus, R. S. May 1975b. Psychological stress and coping in adaptation and illness. *In*, S. M. Weiss (ed.), *Proceedings of the National Heart and Lung Institute Working Conference on Health Behavior*, (Basye, May 12–15, 1975), pp. 199–214. DHEW Publication No. (NIH) 76–868.

Lazarus, R. S. 1977. *Coping Questionnaire*, Stress and Coping Project. Berkeley, Ca.: University of California.

Lazarus, R. S., Averill, J. R., and Opton, E. M., Jr. 1970. Towards a cognitive theory of emotion. *In*, M. Arnold (ed.), *Feelings and Emotions*, pp. 207–232. New York: Academic Press.

Lazarus, R. S., and Cohen, J. B. 1977. *The Hassles Scale*, Stress and Coping Project. Berkeley, Ca.: University of California.

Lazarus, R. S., and Cohen, J. B. 1978a. Theory and method in the study of stress and coping in aging individuals. *Paper presented at Symposium No. 5, Society, Stress and Disease.* (June, 1976, Stockholm, Sweden).

Lazarus, R. S., and Cohen, J. B. 1978b. Environmental stress. *In*, I. Altman and J. F. Wohlwill (eds.). *Human Behavior and the Environment, Vol. 1, Current Theory and Research.* New York: Plenum.

Lazarus, R. S., and Launier, R. 1978. Stress-related transactions between person and environment. *In*, L. A. Pervin and M. Lewis (eds.), *Internal and External Determinants of Behavior.* New York: Plenum.

Lehmann, H. E. 1971. Epidemiology of affective disorders. *In*, R. Fieve (ed.), *Depression in the 70's*, pp. 21–30. Princeton, N.J.: Excerpta Medica.

LIPTON, M. A. 1976. Age differentiation in depression: Biochemical aspects. *Journal of Gerontology, 31,* 293–299.

LØNNUM, A. 1969. *Delayed Disease and Ill-health.* Oslo: The Norwegian Association of Disabled Veterans.

LOWENTHAL, M. F., BERKMAN, P. L., AND ASSOCIATES. 1967. *Aging and Mental Disorder in San Francisco.* San Francisco: Jossey-Bass, Inc.

LOWN, B., VERRIER, R., AND CORBALAN, R. 1973. Physiologic stress and threshold for repetitive ventricular response. *Science, 182,* 834–836.

LOWN, B. VERRIER, R. L., AND RABINOWITZ, S. H. 1977. Neural and psychologic mechanisms and the problem of sudden cardiac death. *American Journal of Cardiology, 39,* 890–902.

LUNDBERG, U., THEORELL, T., AND LIND, E. 1975. Life changes and myocardial infarction: Individual differences in life change scaling. *Journal of Psychosomatic Research, 19,* 27–32.

MAAS, J. W. 1975. Biogenic amines and depression. *Archives of General Psychiatry, 32,* 1357–1361.

MARTIN, W. C., BENGTSON, V. L., AND ACOCK, A. C. 1974. Alienation and age: A context-specific approach. *Social Forces, 53,* 266–274.

MARX, M. B., GARRITY, T. F., AND BOWERS, F. R. 1975. The influence of recent life experience on the health of college freshmen. *Journal of Psychosomatic Research, 19,* 87–98.

MASON, J. W. 1968. Organization of psychoendocrine mechanisms. *Psychosomatic Medicine, 30,* 565–808.

MASON, J. W. 1975a. A historical view of the stress field. *Journal of Human Stress, 1,* 6–12.

MASON, J. W. 1975b. A historical view of the stress field. *Journal of Human Stress, 1,* 22–36.

MASUDA, M., AND HOLMES, T. H. 1978. Life events: Perceptions and frequencies. *Psychosomatic Medicine, 40,* 236–261.

MECHANIC, D. 1975. Some problems in the measurement of stress and social readjustment. *Journal of Human Stress, 1,* 43–48.

MENDELS, J., FRAZER, A., FITZGERALD, R. G., RAMSEY, T. A., AND STOKES, J. W. 1972. Biogenic amine metabolites in cerebrospinal fluid of depressed and manic patients. *Science, 175,* 1380–1382.

MUNRO, H. N. (Ed.) 1970. *Mammalian Protein Metabolism* (Vol. 4). New York: Academic Press.

MYERS, J. K., LINDENTHAL, J. J., AND PEPPER, M. P. 1971. Life events and psychiatric impairment. *Journal of Nervous and Mental Disease, 152,* 149–157.

NIES, A., ROBINSON, D. S., RAVARIS, C. L., AND DAVIS, J. M. 1971. Amines and monoamine oxidase in relation to aging and depression in man. *Psychosomatic Medicine, 33,* 470.

NOFFSINGER, E. B. 1977. Psychosocial stress and illness.

Doctoral Dissertation, Berkeley, Ca.: University of California.

ORDY, J. M., AND KAACK, B. 1976. Psychoneuroendicronology and aging in man. *In*, M. K. Elias, B. E. Eleftheriou and P. K. Elias (eds.), *Special Review of Experimental Aging Research: Progress in Biology*, pp. 255–299. Ellsworth, Maine: Ellsworth American.

PAPESCHI, R., AND McCLURE, D. J. 1971. Homovanillic and 5-hydroxyindoleacetic acid in cerebrospinal fluid of depressed patients. *Archives of General Psychiatry, 25,* 354–358.

PAYKEL, E. S. 1974. Life stress and psychiatric disorder. *In*, B. S. Dohrenwend and B. P. Dohrenwend (eds.), *Stressful Life Events: Their Nature and Effects*, pp. 135–149. New York: John Wiley.

PAYKEL, E. S. 1976. Life stress, depression and attempted suicide. *Journal of Human Stress, 2,* 3–12.

PAYKEL, E. S., MYERS, J. K., DIENELT, M. N., KLERMAN, G. L., LINDENTHAL, J. J., AND PEPPER, M. P. 1969. Life events and depression. *Archives of General Psychiatry, 21,* 753–760.

PAYKEL, E. S., PRUSOFF, B. A., AND MYERS, J. K. 1975. Suicide attempts and recent life events. *Archives of General Psychiatry, 32,* 327–333.

PAYKEL, E. S., PRUSOFF, B. A., AND UHLENHUTH, E. H. 1971. Scaling of life events. *Archives of General Psychiatry, 25,* 340–347.

PAYNE, R. L. 1975. Recent life changes and the reporting of psychological states. *Journal of Psychosomatic Research, 19,* 99–103.

PERLMAN, L. V., FERGUSON, S., BERGUM, K., ISENBERG, E. L., AND HAMMARSTEN, J. F. 1975. Precipitation of congestive heart failure: Social and emotional factors. *Annals of Internal Medicine, 75,* 1–7.

PFEIFFER, E. 1977. Psychopathology and social pathology. *In*, J. E. Birren and K. W. Schaie (eds.), *Handbook of the Psychology of Aging*, pp. 650–671. New York: Van Nostrand Reinhold.

PFEIFFER, E., AND BUSSE, E. W. 1973. Mental disorders in later life-affective disorders; paranoid, neurotic and situational reactions. *In*, E. W. Busse and E. Pfeiffer (eds.), *Mental Illness in Later Life*, pp. 107–144. Washington, D.C.: American Psychiatric Association.

PIORKOWSKI, G. K. 1972. Relationship between repression–sensitization and psychiatric symptoms. *Journal of Clinical Psychology, 28,* 28–30.

POST, F. 1962. *The Significance of Affective Symptoms in Old Age: A Follow-up Study of One Hundred Patients.* London: Oxford University Press.

PRAAG, H. M. VAN, KORF, J., AND PUITE, J. 1970. 5-Hydroxyindoleacetic acid levels in the cerebrospinal fluid of depressive patients with probenecid. *Nature, 225,* 1259–1260.

RAHE, R. H. 1968. Life-change measurement as a predictor of illness. *Proceedings of the Royal Society of*

*Medicine, 61,* 1124–1126.

RAHE, R. H. 1972. Subjects' recent life changes and their near-future illness reports. *Annals of Clinical Research, 4,* 250–265.

RAHE, R. H. 1974. The pathway between subjects' recent life changes and their near-future illness reports: Representative results and methodological issues. *In,* B. S. Dohrenwend and B. P. Dohrenwend (eds.), *Stressful Life Events: Their Nature and Effects,* pp. 73–86. New York: John Wiley.

RAHE, R. H. 1978. Life change measurement clarification. *Psychosomatic Medicine, 40,* 95–98.

RAHE, R. H., AND BENNETT, L. 1974. Recent life changes, myocardial infarction, and abrupt coronary death. *Archives of Internal Medicine, 133,* 221–228.

RAHE, R. H., GUNDERSON, E., AND ARTHUR, R. J. 1970. Demographic and psychosocial factors in acute illness reporting. *Journal of Chronic Diseases, 23,* 245–255.

RAHE, R. H., MAHAN, J. L., AND ARTHUR, R. J. 1970. Prediction of near-future health change from subjects' preceding life changes. *Journal of Psychosomatic Research, 14,* 401–406.

RAHE, R. H., MCKEAN, J. D., AND ARTHUR, R. J. 1967. A longitudinal study of life-change and illness patterns. *Journal of Psychosomatic Research, 10,* 355–366.

RAHE, R. H., MEYER, M., SMITH, M., KJAER, G., AND HOLMES, T. H. 1964. Social stress and illness onset. *Journal of Psychosomatic Research, 8,* 35–44.

RAHE, R. H., AND PAASIKIVI, J. 1971. Psychosocial factors and myocardial infarction—II. An outpatient study in Sweden. *Journal of Psychosomatic Research, 15,* 33–39.

REAVLEY, W. 1974. The relationship of life events to several aspects of "anxiety." *Journal of Psychosomatic Research, 18,* 421–424.

REICHLIN, S., SAPERSTEIN, R., JACKSON, I. M. D., BOYD, A. E., AND PATEL, Y. 1976. Hypothalamic hormones. *Annual Review of Physiology, 38,* 389–424.

REIS, D. J., ROSS, R. A., BRODSKY, M., SPECHT, L., AND JOH, T. 1976. Changes in catecholamine synthesizing enzymes in ganglia, adrenal medulla and brain of aged rats. *Federation Proceedings, 35,* 486.

RENNER, V. J. 1978. Effects of different methods of administration on performance in convergent and divergent "tests". Doctoral disseration, University of Adelaide, South Australia.

RENNER, V. J., ALPAUGH, P. K., AND BIRREN, J. E. 1978. Divergent thinking over the life-span. *Paper presented at the National Gerontological Society Meeting,* (Dallas, Texas, November 1978).

RENNER, V. J., AND BIRREN, J. E. Objectives and new directions in the study of stress, disease and aging. *Paper presented at Symposium No. 5, Society Stress and Disease* (Stockholm, Sweden, June 1976) (in press).

ROBERTS, E. 1974a. Disinhibition as an organizing principle in the nervous system—The role of gamma-aminobutyric acid. *Advances in Neurology, 5,* 127–143.

ROBERTS, E., 1974b. Gamma-aminobutyric acid and nervous system function—A perspective. *Biochemical Pharmacology, 23,* 2637–2649.

ROBINSON, D. S., DAVIS, J. M., NIES, A., COLBURN, R. W., DAVIS, J. N., BOURNE, H. R., BUNNEY, W. E., SHAW, D. M., AND COPPEN, A. J. 1972. Aging, monoamines, and monoamine-oxidase levels. *Lancet, 1,* 290–291.

ROBINSON, D. S., DAVIS, J. M., NIES, A., RAVARIS, C. L., AND SYLVESTER, D. 1971. Relation of sex and aging to monoamine oxidase activity of human brain, plasma and platelets. *Archives of General Psychiatry, 24,* 536–539.

ROTH, M. 1955. The natural history of mental disorders in old age. *Journal of Mental Science, 101,* 281–301.

ROWLAND, K. F., AND SOKOL, B. 1977. A review of research examining the coronary-prone behavior pattern. *Journal of Human Stress, 3,* 26–33.

SCHALLY, A. V., KASTIN, A. J., AND ARIMURA, A. 1977. Hypothalamic hormones: The link between brain and body. *American Scientist, 65,* 712–719.

SCHWARTZ, M. S. 1972. The repression–sensitization scale: Normative age and sex data on 30,000 medical patients. *Journal of Clinical Psychology, 28,* 72–73.

SCHWARTZ, M. S., KRUPP, N. E., AND BYRNE, D. 1971. Repression-sensitization and medical diagnosis. *Journal of Abnormal Psychology, 78,* 286–291.

SEEMAN, M. 1959. On the meaning of alienation. *American Sociological Review, 24,* 783–791.

SEEMAN, M. 1976. Empirical alienation studies: An overview. *In,* R. F. Geyer, and D. R. Schweitzer (eds.), *Theories of Alienation,* pp. 265–305. Leiden, Germany: Martinus Nijhoff Social Sciences Division.

SELYE, H. 1946. The general adaptation syndrome and the diseases of adaptation. *Journal of Clinical Endocrinology, 6,* 117–230.

SELYE, H. 1950a. *The Physiology and Pathology of Exposure to Stress.* Montreal: Acta, Inc. Medical Publishers.

SELYE, H. 1950b. Adaptive reactions to stress. *In,* H. G. Wolff, S. G. Wolf, and C. C. Hare (eds.), *Life Stress and Bodily Disease,* pp. 3–18. Baltimore: Williams & Wilkins.

SELYE, H. 1955. General physiology and pathology of stress. *In,* H. Selye and G. Heuser (eds.), *Fifth Annual Report on Stress, 1955–56,* pp. 25–103. New York: M. D. Publications.

SELYE, H. 1956. *The Stress of Life.* New York: McGraw-Hill.

SELYE, H. 1970. Stress and aging. *Journal of the American Geriatrics Society, 18,* 669–680.

SELYE, H. 1974. *Stress Without Distress.* New York: New American Library.

SELYE, H. 1975. Confusion and controversy in the stress field. *Journal of Human Stress, 1,* 37–44.

SELYE, H. 1976. *Stress in Health and Disease.* Boston: Butterworth.

SELYE, H., AND TUCHWEBER, B. 1976. Stress in relation to aging and disease. *In,* A. V. Everitt and J. A. Burgess (eds.), *Hypothalamus, Pituitary and Aging,* pp. 553–569. Springfield, Ill.: Charles C Thomas.

SELYE, H., AND TUCHWEBER, B. 1978. Stress and aging. *Paper presented at Symposium No. 5, Society, Stress and Disease,* (Stockholm, Sweden, June 1976).

STENBACK, A. 1975. Psychosomatic states. *In,* J. G. HOWELLS (ed.), *Modern Perspectives in the Psychiatry of Old Age,* pp. 269–289. New York: Brunner/Mazel.

STROM, A. 1968. *Norwegian Concentration Camp Survivors.* Oslo: Oslo University Press.

STUART, D. M. 1977. The relation between stressful events, age, personality and illness. Doctoral dissertation, University of Southern California.

SYME, S. L., HYMAN, M. M., AND ENTERLINE, P. E. 1964. Some social and cultural factors associated with the occurrence of coronary heart disease. *Journal of Chronic Diseases, 17,* 277–289.

SYMINGTON, T., CURRIE, A. R., CURRAN, R. C., AND DAVIDSON, J. N. 1955. The reaction of the adrenal cortex in conditions of stress. *In,* G. E. W. WOLSTENHOLME and M. P. CAMERON (eds.), *Ciba Foundation Colloquia on Endocrinology, Vol. 8, The Human Adrenal Cortex,* pp. 70–87. Boston: Little, Brown.

TENNANT, C., AND ANDREWS, G. 1976. A scale to measure the stress of life events. *Australian and New Zealand Journal of Psychiatry, 10,* 27–31.

THEORELL, T., LIND, E., AND FLODERUS, B. 1975. Life events and prospective near-future serious illness with special reference to myocardial infarction studies on middle-aged building construction workers. Stockholm: Laboratory of Clinical Research, Karolinska Institute (Mimeographed)

THEORELL, T., LIND, E., FRÖBERG J., KARLSSON, C., AND LEVI, L. 1972. A longitudinal study of 21 subjects with coronary heart disease: Life changes, catecholamine excretion and related biochemical reactions. *Psychosomatic Medicine, 34,* 505–516.

THEORELL, T., AND RAHE, R. H. 1971. Psychosocial factors and myocardial infarction—I: An inpatient study in Sweden. *Journal of Psychosomatic Research, 15,* 25–31.

THEORELL, T., AND RAHE, R. H. 1975. Life change events, ballistocardiography, and coronary death. *Journal of Human Stress, 1,* 18–24.

THORESON, C. E. 1978. Behavior therapy in stress management. Paper presented to the Stress Management Conference (Los Angeles, February, 1978).

THORESON, C. E., AND COATES, T. J. 1976. Behavioral self-control: Some clinical concerns. *In,* M. HERSON, P. EISLER, AND P. MILLER (eds.), *Progress in Behavior Modification,* pp. 307–352. New York: Academic Press.

THORESEN, C. E., KIRMIL-GRAY, K., AND CROSBIE, P. 1977. Processes and procedures in self-control: A working model. *The Canadian Counselor, 12,* 66–75.

TREUTING, T. F. 1962. The role of emotional factors in the etiology and course of diabetes mellitus: A review of the recent literature. *American Journal of the Medical Sciences, 244,* 93–109.

UHLENHUTH, E. H., AND PAYKEL, E. S. 1973a. Symptom intensity and life events. *Archives of General Psychiatry, 28,* 473–477.

UHLENHUTH, E. H., AND PAYKEL, E. S. 1973b. Symptom configuration and life events. *Archives of General Psychiatry, 28,* 744–748.

VINOKUR, A., AND SELZER, M. L. 1975. Desirable versus undesirable life events: Their relationship to stress and mental distress. *Journal of Personality and Social Psychology, 32,* 329–337.

WEISS, E., DLIN, B., ROLLIN, H. R., FISCHER, H. K., AND BEPLER, C. R. 1957. Emotional factors in coronary occlusion. *Archives of Internal Medicine, 99,* 628–641.

WEISS, S. M. (ed.) 1975., *Proceedings of the National Heart and Lung Institute Working Conference on Health Behavior.* (Basye, Va. May 12–15, 1975), DHEW Publication No. (NIH) 76–868.

WILK, S., SHOPSIN, B., GERSHON, S., AND SUHL, M. 1972. Cerebrospinal fluid levels of MHPG in affective disorders. *Nature, 235,* 440–441.

WOLFF, H. G. 1950. Life stress and bodily disease—A formulation. *In,* H. G. WOOLF, S. G. WOLF, AND C. C. HARE (eds.), *Life Stress and Bodily Disease. Proceedings of the Association for Research in Nervous and Mental Diseases,* pp. 1059–1094. Baltimore: Williams & Wilkins.

WYLER A. R., MASUDA, M., AND HOLMES, T. H. 1971. Magnitude of life events and seriousness of illness. *Psychosomatic Medicine, 33,* 115–122.

YALOW, R. S., AHARON-VARSANO, N., ECHEMENDIA, E., AND BERSON, S. A. 1969. HGH and ACTH secretory responses to stress. *Hormone and Metabolic Research, 1,* 3–8.

YUWILER, A. 1976. Stress, anxiety and endocrine function. *In,* R. G. GRENELL AND S. GALAY (eds.), *Biological Foundations of Psychiatry,* pp. 889–943. New York: Raven Press.

# 15

# Tasks and Crises of the Second Half of Life: The Interrelationship of Commitment, Coping, and Adaptation

*Marjorie Fiske*

This chapter will explore the tasks, problems, and crises of middle and later life from two perspectives: theoretical and conceptual views of psychosocial change in adulthood, and empirical studies. These viewpoints are not necessarily mutually exclusive. Theories range from the abstractions and semi-abstractions of philosophy to those of psychoanalytic, psychological, sociological, and anthropological tradition, often borrowed by the empirical investigator because he feels comfortable with them as an acceptable mode of ordering complex data. Most importantly, if the investigator is sufficiently courageous and open-minded, he or she may undertake studies initially designed to be purely descriptive. Such research often generates middle-range theories which, with an insistence of their own, challenge prior and often more global theories.[1]

[1]Dr. David Chiriboga kindly reviewed the penultimate version of the manuscript and I am most appreciative of his suggestions, many of which are herewith incorporated.

The first section of the chapter is devoted to the more theoretical approaches. In the two ensuing sections, research results are examined in terms both of so-called "objective" measures and those designed to assess the perspectives and assessments of the individuals participating in the studies. These two sections of the chapter will be drawn, in considerable part, from two large scale interdisciplinary studies conducted by the Human Development and Aging Program at the University of California (San Francisco) over the past twenty years, supplemented by material from studies conducted elsewhere in this country and abroad. In the concluding section, we shall re-examine the results of these studies in terms of their implications for educational, diagnostic, therapeutic, and policy approaches to mental health and illness in later life, and propose a multidimensional, rather than the more linear medical model of health and illness. Particular attention will be paid to changes in styles of coping with stress, self-concept, close interpersonal relationships, commitments, and the complexities of adaptation, further developing concepts proposed in two of the other recent Handbooks (Lowenthal and Robinson, 1976; Lowenthal, 1977).

## THEORETICAL AND CONCEPTUAL PERSPECTIVES ON PSYCHOSOCIAL CHANGE

There are three primary sources from which stem current approaches to issues of psychosocial change in later life. At two extremes are scholars who have moved forward and those who have moved backward in their examination of the adult life course. Many of the former adapt their perspectives from those generated by psychoanalytic theories of development in infancy and childhood; the latter, fewer in number, apply theories and concepts first evolved in studies of the elderly. In between are a small, but increasing number, of researchers who are beginning to apply a life course perspective to fields in which they have long specialized, such as stress and coping, achievement and power, gender roles, personality, psychophysiology and behaviorism. Reflecting, perhaps, the continuing strength of the older field of child development, the literature is becoming increasingly permeated with "stage" extensions to studies of adulthood, often with developmental crises, special tasks, or dichotomized alternatives characterizing each stage. Other investigators are deliberately cautious, on the grounds that to impose a map drawn from studies of childhood onto the relatively uncharted territory of middle and later life is premature.

In passing, the continuing, if not so dramatic influence of the preceding generation of theorists, most of whom also drew on empirical materials, should be acknowledged. These include, among others, Kurt Goldstein, Gordon Allport, Abraham Maslow, Katherine Wolf, and Charlotte Bühler, whose work might be categorized under the rubric of self-actualization or self-realization. They were more process than stage-oriented, and the implications of their work for middle and especially late life remain rather more implicit than otherwise. This writer is indebted to all of them.

### Developmental and Stage Frameworks

The work of the majority of stage theorists is strongly influenced by that of Freud and Piaget—though not necessarily in conjunction. The stages of both are "classical," in the sense that they are sequential and, for Piaget, irreversible. By far the most productive and influential of those concerned with development in adult life is, of course, Erikson, whose life course stages were first introduced in *Childhood and Society* (1950/1963). Indeed, after Jung, he is clearly the most dedicated and productive of all scholars who have become interested in psychosocial change in adult life. Unlike some colleagues whose interest in the field is more recent, Erikson is becoming quite flexible about his stages, allowing for regression, stagnation, and the possibility of continuing conflict between the polar extremes within each stage. He has also redefined some of his stages: in middle age, for example, the polar opposite of generativity becomes rejectivity; in late middle age, integrity vs. despair has become integrity vs. disdain (including self-disdain). Most recently, he has become concerned with the broader applications of the societal parallels to these polarities.

Generativity has long been a favorite concept of Erik Erikson's, although it has proved not a simple one to describe in terms, for example, that are readily researchable. In his discussions of generative middle-aged people, at least two interwoven capacities can be traced. One, perhaps the essential prerequisite, combines productivity and mastery, which *enables* the individual to offer support to others. A second is the middle-aged equivalent of procreativity: commitment to support for oncoming generations and the sharing of one's experience, no matter how humble, to that end. The middle-aged person who no longer is either productive or generative in any way stagnates, and has little to offer even if he or she were so inclined. The individual who continues to grow but does not share experience, or limits sharing in a way suggesting "exclusivity" is, in Erikson's terms, a *rejecting* person.

Similarly, the concept of integrity which Erik Erikson considers appropriate to late-middle and old age, incorporates two qualities: wholeness and honorable sincerity. As with generativity, the presupposition is that the person is *centered* in himself or herself. In his earlier dichotomy, he defined despair as the opposite of integrity but he has now revised (or expanded) the term to include disdain, which may be for one's self or for particular or generalized others. This writer finds it difficult to envisage clear (that is to say, researchable) distinctions between the generativity stage and that of integrity, for would it be possible to be truly generative unless one were a person of integrity?

Stressing the importance of wider identities and broader world views, Erikson now adds to each stage a dimension of ritualizations and ritualisms, in order more precisely to relate change in the individual to the sociohistorical developments within which he or she lives and is a part. The processes which integrate the person with his broader world are defined as ritual*izations*, which he constrasts with the ritual*ism*. The caring of the middle aged for the generations which come after them (ritualization) stands in opposition to authoritarianism (ritualism). The more philosophical and open modes, in other words, are the opposite of dogmatism (Erikson, in press). While he speaks of life stages and of "crises" associated with them, Erikson does not assign ages to the stages of adulthood, and the crises, if such there be, are interwoven processes of self-appraisal and changes in thinking and behavior. His penetrating study of Gandhi presents a beautiful and convincing case for the applicability of these somewhat abstract concepts to at least one genius of the Eastern world (Erikson, 1969).

Longitudinal studies of long and short duration have provided the raw material on which a few investigators have imposed or derived sequences rather similar to those postulated by Erikson, to whom they gladly acknowledge indebtedness. But before briefly reviewing some of them, we should note that in one of the oldest series of longitudinal studies, those conducted at the Institute of Human Development at the University of California (Berkeley campus), successive "generations" of participating scholars rarely applied stage concepts to their analyses of change once the participants in the study had reached adulthood (Block and Haan, 1971; Haan, 1972). The Berkeley studies began when many of its subjects, who are now middle and late middle-aged, were young children. While neo-Freudian analyses were conducted on their stages of development through adolescence, the principal emphasis of the initial group of researchers was on the formation and consistency of personality characteristics, and on the longterm effects of early familial and related influences (Jones and Bayley, 1941). However, in the follow-up studies, conducted when the respondents were in various stages of adulthood, some of those who had had the most unfortunate childhoods and least promising personalities turned out to be among the healthiest, most at ease with themselves, and often among the more creative in the group (Block and Haan, 1971). In the Berkeley samples, the change is often in a growth-improvement-development direction, but there is at once both less predictability and more change than anticipated by the original investigators, and the results justify as much attention to socio-situational circumstances as to intra-psychic characteristics. This rapidly accumulating evidence of the importance of socio-situational factors is also reinforcing the growing awareness of the need to loosen up disciplinary boundaries in the study of psychosocial change in adulthood.

Studies characterized by a stage approach to change in adult life include longitudinal ones, mostly of shorter duration than the Berkeley studies, as well as those focusing simultaneously on one or more age groups. Among others are the works of Kohlberg (1973), mainly with young adults growing somewhat older; Levinson and his colleagues who studied 40 men between the ages of 35 and 45, from a rather broad spectrum of socioeconomic backgrounds (Levinson, Darrow, Klein, M. Levinson, and McKee, 1978); Gould, who supports a concept of "transformations" with selections from life histories and clinical studies (1978). While the stages and "transformations" occasionally seem highly selective, the middle-aged reader accustomed to self-assessment is likely to have a sense of recognition at times. Indeed, some of these investigators have reported that their own interest in a midlife (often a "crisis") stage was sparked by a change in their own lives. For the most part, they are reporting on very well educated and privileged people, as is true of recent popular books on "the midlife crisis" (Sheehy, 1976; Mayer, 1978).

It is my (not very agreeable) conviction, however, that developmental stage theory, appealing though it is, does not stand up well to replication testing, especially among mainstream (middle and lower middle class) adult Americans here and now. Some stage theorists, including Piaget in his brief excursion into later life (1972), Loevinger, whose work on ego development has primarily been undertaken with women (1976), McClelland (1975), and Lifton (1976), are quite explicit in stating that the later, and especially the "highest," stages may be manifest in a variety of content and structures and are difficult to assess with the kinds of replicable measures applied to early stages. Piaget, for example, in writing about later life, unapologetically (but perhaps somewhat uneasily) provides a far looser definition of formal operations "in different areas according to their aptitudes and their professional specializations" than he does for his other stages (1972, p. 10). Lifton uses terms such as "transcendence." Such concepts are used much less abashedly in the recent book of another newcomer to stage theory, that of the philosopher Norton (1976), whose stages are similar to those of Erikson in that they can and should lead to self-knowledge and fulfillment and to the support of growth in others.

As a firm believer in the philosophical roots of the study of man (and there was a time when psychology was primarily taught in departments of philosophy), my intent is to applaud these distinguished theorists and investigators. At the same time, the reader must be aware that the upper reaches of human development require a shift in perspective, from stages that can to some extent be explored through empirical evidence, to higher reaches of human potential that one may agree with (and hope for), but which are not often found in our culture, except among an exceptional few whom we can only hope will serve as inspirations for a better society.

The cross-cultural studies conducted among middle-aged and old men by David Gutmann (1969, 1977), elaborate on a stage theory which evolves from empirical data. His interest was in mastery styles, and his stages progress from active to passive to magical. Unlike the work discussed thus far (with the exception of Kohlberg's), Gutmann's is based on projective methods, and originated in findings from the ten year longitudinal studies conducted at the University of Chicago (Neugarten and Gutmann, 1968). The later cross-cultural studies, however, were of men only, and were not systematically longitudinal. That cross-sectional studies of a limited age range and one sex may prove somewhat misleading is suggested by the fact that a replication and elaboration (in consultation with Professor Gutmann) of his approach is revealing some pronounced fluctuations between active and passive mastery styles over a five year period among Americans ranging from late adolescence up to the early seventies, and notable differences between men and women (Hodges, forthcoming). Men originally interviewed when they were high school seniors, for example, declined dramatically in active mastery over the next five years, whereas there was no change among women in the same cohort. While the dominant style among men facing retirement was indeed one of passive mastery, among women in this late middle-aged group, active mastery was the principal style. Five years later (average age 63), these sex differences still held. Active mastery was still the preferred style among women, passive among men, though some women shifted from active to "magical" mastery. Gutmann's thesis, that there is a progression from active to passive mastery among men, is then supported by the current study. It seems to begin quite early in life among the lower middle-class American men studied by Hodges. While active mastery is prevalent in men in their late twenties, passive mastery is the dominant mode of men who have reached even the early forties. Women in their forties seem rather conflicted, but those a few years older outrank, on active mastery, even the youngest men. Thus, the findings from the "Kansas City" card (Neugarten and Gutmann,

1968) revisited, with another projective measure, not only re-emphasized the criss-crossing trajectories of older men and women in regard to mastery, but do much to counter this researcher's (mild) skepticism about projective research methods.

## ADAPTATION, COPING, AND LIFE SATISFACTION

As in most attempts to impose order, the schema used here for presenting the modes of assessing psychosocial change in adulthood is somewhat arbitrary. The emphasis in this section is on work which is not firmly placed in either a developmental or stage-oriented framework. There is no press to prove that growth or "positive" development across the life course is, or could become, the norm, much as most of us would like to see such a thesis supported. Nor are stages of adulthood chronologically defined. Rather, the investigators discussed here suggest that, while there are individuals who clearly attain higher forms of wisdom, more effective means of coping and adaptation, and *ergo* a more fulfilling life as they grow older, it is not necessarily the prevailing pattern. Some of these researchers do, and some do not, utilize one or another variation of the medical model. We shall first elaborate a bit on current pros and cons of the efficacy of this rather traditional approach in assessing psychological adaptation.

It was Freud's (possibly apocryphal) dictum that the criteria for mental health (I would prefer the word maturity) are the capacities for love and for work. The quotation, if it be one, has not greatly influenced his fellow physicians. For most, health is the absence of illness, physical or mental, and gradations within "health" are irrelevant. Recently, especially in mental health fields, the need to take the individual's resources, as well as degree of "impairment," into account has been acknowledged by many behavioral and social scientists (but as yet by relatively few clinical researchers). We are still a long way from clear definitions of mental health resources, however; "emotional maturity," "well-rounded personality," "strength of character," or a "cheerful disposition" and "sense of humor" make for "good adaptation," but how do we define and measure such attributes? It is small wonder that some workers have expressed skepticism about the feasibility of doing so, to say nothing of clarifying the concept of psychological health. Lewis offers a particulary telling, albeit rather one-sided complaint:

> A rather silly but often repeated truism says that the aim of psychiatric treatment is to promote mental health. It is hard to tell what the latter

phrase means. Mental health is an invincibly obscure concept. Those who have attempted to define it in positive terms have twisted ropes of sand, telling us, for example, that a man's mental health consists in: (a) active adjustment or attempts at mastery of his environment as distinct both from his inability to adjust and from his indiscriminate adjustment through passive acceptance or environmental conditions; (b) unity of his personality, the maintenance of a stable, internal integration which remains intact not-withstanding the flexibility of behavior which derives from active adjustment; and (c) ability to perceive correctly the world and himself. This clutter of words is groping toward an ideal, a sociobiological ideal, but much of it can have no operational referents and it abounds in terms which are undefined and at present undefinable (Lewis, 1958, p. 173).

Of course every individual harbors both deficits and resources (and many characteristics that are neither of these) within his psychic makeup. Some degree of what mental health professionals label psychopathology exists, for example, in most seemingly well-adapted people (see Barron, 1963; Lowenthal, Berkman, and Associates, 1967; Singer, 1963). Age has a great deal to do with how some symptoms are diagnosed: at twenty-two, a woman may be having a post-partum depression; at forty-four, a menopausal one; and at sixty-six, the same symptoms are frequently (and erroneously) diagnosed as senile brain damage (A. Simon, personal communication, 1978).

We must learn much more about the adaptive coexistence of both deficits and resources because one "strong" resource may offset or counter-balance several deficits. The balance sheet, in short, contains different degrees of strengths and deficits (or symptoms) on each side of the ledger, and we can no longer afford not to weigh them. Labeling, either in terms of age, psychological types, neuroses, or mental and emotional illness, is insidious, and flies in the face of what we are learning about the extent of psychosocial change in adulthood. For the layman, perhaps most misleading of all are the self-administered "psychological" tests often found in highly respectable magazines and newspapers. Statistical norms may tell the reader how he resembles or differs from some (usually ill-defined) majority of people today—but the category he finds himself in would likely be very different had he taken the test yesterday or even later today. Further, what is the norm of health, and to whom does it apply? Does the reader know he may be trying to compare an apple-self with people who are oranges?

In an ongoing longitudinal study of a broad age spectrum of the "middle majority," several of us are now trying to assess the balance between inner resources and deficits among men and women at different stages of the life course, and the relationship between these dimensions to the personal sense of well-being.[2] Looked at separately, the two dimensions are related to life satisfaction in an entirely expectable fashion. People with the most resources (such as the capacity for mutuality, growth, competence, hope, and insight) tend to be satisfied with themselves and their lives, and those with deficits (psychological symptoms, including anxiety, hostility, and self-hatred) the least so. But these expectable results are found among fewer than a third of the people being intensively studied. Among others in the sample, a *combination* of many "positive" and many "negative" attributes seems to enhance the sense of well-being. (Bradburn, 1969, also reports on the importance of such ratios for the sense of "happiness".)

What such findings suggest is that reliance solely on "degree of impairment" or number of symptoms, does an injustice to the complexity of human beings, for when we look closer at people who harbor a rather complex array of characteristics on both sides of the ledger, it appears that they are deeply involved in their worlds, and cope well with the diversity of stress which in-depth encounters with work and with people involve (Chiriboga and Lowenthal, 1975). In some ways, they resemble people who have been selected for study because they are exceptionally creative. Rothenberg (1971), for example, finds that "Janusian thinking," or the ability to conceive and deal with opposing ideas simultaneously, is central to the creative process. Perhaps such people are also exceptionally tolerant of ambiguities within themselves. For the individual, the ability to recognize conflicting messages from within and from the outer world, and to synthesize the two, is the mark of creativity. For the behavioral scientist it is an indication of the fact that most people are complex and contradictory. The next step is to realize that conflicting drives, anxieties, hopes, and impulses are normal.

Among the primarily lower middle class people in the Transitions Study, the harboring of both conflicts and inner weaknesses and strengths, is adaptive for young and middle-aged people. They tend to feel good about themselves. Among the older middle-aged (average age 58), however, it is the more "simplistic," those having relatively few

[2]The Longitudinal Study of Transitions (also referred to as the Transitions Study) being conducted at the Human Development and Aging Program, University of California at San Francisco, was initially supported by Grant #HD05941, National Institute of Child Health and Human Development, and later by the National Institute on Aging, Grant #AG00002.

resources and relatively few deficits, who report themselves as happy. The more complex among the late middle-aged grow older gracefully and comfortably only if they have the kinds of open options, alternatives, and choices usually more readily available only in more privileged sectors of our society. It is most regrettable that such complex and challenged people become, as they reach late middle and old age, deprived of the arenas in which they find satisfaction for themselves and—by the same token—can continue to serve as role models for the generations coming after them.

The potentially enriching mixture of opposites is discussed from a cross-cultural point of view by British social scientist Peter Marris, in his skillfully interwoven collection of essays on *Loss and Change* (1975). He reports intriguing similarities in effective ways of coping with a variety of personal and social changes in several cultures, and illustrates the concept of a dual approach to adaptation in a somewhat different way. The interplay, and the conflict, in his terms, is mainly between the conservative impulse and the innovative. The aim of maintaining a degree of equilibrium between the two is the achievement of a sense of continuity. Marris believes "... that the impulse to defend the predictability of life is a fundamental and universal principle of human psychology" (1975, p. 3). This impulse is seriously threatened by changing events and processes as varied as bereavement, slum clearance, colonization, revolution, the accelerating advances of the sciences—and, in some social arenas, the erection of barriers against middle-aged and older people. It is important to realize that most such changes involve losses of the familiar and predictable, even though intrinsically they represent gains or improvements (as in slum clearance), and we should expect to be temporarily distracted and unsettled, which is to say, emotionally and mentally distressed, when they occur.

Interpreting Marris' work from a somewhat different perspective, we might conclude that if the individual recognizes and anticipates that major changes, good or bad, will be disruptive, and if he allows for a moratorium for self-repair, he is likely to emerge the stronger for it. Innovation (change) has outbalanced the sense of continuity, and such moratoria provide the opportunity to rearrange and to recenter one's inner resources. In this way, the individual finds within himself or herself the sense of continuity which is the chief bulwark against the onslaught of change and conflict in both his personal milieu and in the wider world which interlace with the more private ones. Without taking this kind of process into account, temporary distraughtness might tempt a clinician

who has not previously seen a particular patient to make a "degree of impairment" diagnosis, unaware that next week or the week after his assessment might be quite different.

The recent work of Vaillant (1977) reporting on psychosocial change in adulthood falls within an adaptation/coping/life satisfaction framework. While not adopting stage theory per se, the approach does examine levels of maturity. Neuroticism is viewed as a kind of level through which a sizeable proportion of adults do not find their way to maturity (as the author conceives it). His sample consists of male graduates of an "elitist" university who have been followed from college years to, thus far, an average age of 52. Vaillant is psychiatrist and professor at Harvard Medical School, and has organized the data of this longitudinal study around the themes of mental health and adaptation. While he agrees with Erikson that under some optimal circumstances many persons grow (which is to be expected in such a sample) and does apply some assessments in hierarchical form, he does not link any movement through these levels to specific ages or stages—indeed, his data seem to prevent him from so doing. Nor does he conclude that there are tasks and crises common to given periods. His fundamental interests are in learning how these men cope, in various spheres of life; what spheres of living are or become most important to them; and the kinds of problems that demand to be coped with under a variety of circumstances. His points of departure and his conclusions are within the framework of ego mechanisms, including the defenses. As his analysis demonstrates, a given mode may change from adaptive to maladaptive depending on changing situations and circumstances in which it is utilized.

Robert and Pauline Sears' follow-up of the men and women first studied as "gifted children" by Terman in 1922, when their average age was 11, focuses in large part, following Terman, on the predictability of certain characteristics for satisfaction and coping at later periods of life. As Robert Sears remarks in reporting on the men in the study (1977), these are global terms. They are measured, however, by precise and replicable indices, and, again following Terman, satisfactions pertain particularly to work and to family life. Among other interesting and rather unexpected results is that among these men (at an average age of 62), family life satisfaction was more closely related to overall life satisfaction than was satisfaction in work.

Among the Terman women, somewhat fewer than half work, and most of those who do have professional careers. The working women report more satisfaction with their lives in general than those who do not. Non-working women are less satisfied with their family lives than the working women are, and less so than the men (Sears and Barbee, 1977), and many of these non-working women would now opt for a career were they to relive their lives. Considering that their average age when last seen was 62, and the volumes of research studies reporting on the guilt problems of married working mothers, one wonders whether these women would have felt the same way, or more importantly, felt free to make such confessions prior to the latest wave of women's liberation literature. While thus far the Sears' have not published comparisons between the men and women in their study, having a working wife is evidently not conducive to a happy family life for men. Men whose wives worked, are more likely than men whose wives did not work, to be divorced or separated by the time they had reached their early sixties. It would appear then, that men of this age are influenced negatively, if at all, by the women's liberation movement, while non-working women wish they could start over again. That the working women, married and otherwise, tend to find great satisfaction in their family lives, in their work, and in life in general, is apparently more difficult for many late middle-aged men to understand and accept than it is for their non-working female counterparts.

Unlike many other longitudinal studies, the group being studied by the Sears' has a phenomenal 916 participants out of an original sample of 857 boys and 671 girls who were in the third to eighth grade between 1921 and 1923. As in most such studies, the nature of research assessments and measures change through the years, and subsequent investigators face the dilemma of using rather outmoded indices and thus maintaining continuity vs. more adequate (or different) ones which might well produce richer data. It appears that Professor Terman thought that females should be measured and evaluated differently from males, and comparisons between the sexes may well be difficult. Despite these limitations, these rich materials are an invaluable resource for further study. We hope the Sears' and their colleagues and graduate students will soon give us more information, especially concerning comparisons between men and women where feasible, and how people are reacting to the opening up of more balanced lifestyles for women.

Vaillant (1977) reports interesting differences between the quite exceptional sample of men in the Grant Study and those people initially chosen by Terman on the basis of their high scores on intelligence tests (they were estimated to be rep-

resentative of the upper one percent of the population). Many of the Terman Study participants went on to college, and beyond; some did not. The recently analyzed samples of these two longitudinal studies are still sufficiently large to warrant a potentially interesting comparison between the Vaillant and Sears' men in terms of capacity for change, adaptation, and life satisfaction among those who went to elitist colleges (both studies), those who went to schools that were less elitist (Sears' Study), and those who had no advanced education (Sears' Study). On the average, there is about a 10 year age difference between the men in the two studies, and therefore these cohorts no doubt experienced notably different motivations and pressures in regard to the importance of a college education. The majority of participants in the Grant Study reached the age of decision regarding higher education in the late 1930s and early 1940s, when it was for the most part taken for granted that the middle class male would go to college, and were selected from classes to graduate between 1942 and 1944. The men in the Terman sample would have made the decision for college or no college in the late 1920s and early 1930s, a period when American admiration for self-made men was still very much alive and college was not as much of a must for the middle and even upper-class male as it has subsequently become. The challenge of comparing these two cohorts should be particularly appealing for scholars interested in trying to begin to sort out the influence of sociocultural change on psychosocial change, with a rare opportunity to hold many other factors constant (such as intelligence and socioeconomic status).

More importantly, the often neglected issue of gender differences could be further explored. As we have noted, in the Chicago Studies, which fortunately included both sexes, the life trajectories of men and women were often unexpectedly divergent (Neugarten and Gutmann, 1968). In the current study of transitions in adult life, from youth to old age, on most measures the differences between men and women within a given stage are greater than those between the young and the old of each gender (Lowenthal, Thurnher, Chiriboga, and Associates, 1975). Material that would lend itself to comparisons between the gifted Terman group and "typical" Americans would be quite accessible in the Human Development and Aging Program (UC San Francisco) and the Institute of Human Development (UC Berkeley) data banks. Such analyses could go far toward testing the dialectic theories of change in adulthood proposed by Klaus Riegel (1977), and others. If Vaillant's data are also accessible, the four studies combined would provide a rare opportunity to respond to Neugarten's plea (1977) for a rapprochement among clinical, personality, and developmental approaches. The Institute of Human Development Studies, it will be recalled, started out with (child) developmental and personality trait approach, Vaillant has a clinical/adaptive orientation, the HD/UCSF Study adopts a process rather than a developmental/stage approach, and the Terman Study was designed to explore comparative life satisfaction in the spheres of work and family.

Among relative newcomers to the field of psychosocial change in adulthood is Richard Lazarus[3], who is now pursuing his longstanding interest in stress and coping in an intensive study of middle and later middle-aged men and women who are being followed up frequently and regularly. Not only is his a highly innovative study focusing on chronic, day-to-day stress (to this writer's knowledge, the first to do so), but Professor Lazarus' study is also promising in its systematic efforts to untangle the interweave between cognitive and emotional factors in stress appraisal and response. The material provides for some interesting comparisons between assessment and coping with chronic as compared with acute stress. Utilizing a stress typology developed earlier (Lowenthal and Chiriboga, 1973), one objective in this study will be to determine the extent to which the customary stance, being challenged vs. being overwhelmed by more acute stresses, for example, is influenced by long periods of chronic stress, such as boredom on the job or incompatibility in marriage (Lazarus, 1977, personal communication). The potential significance of this and the related studies is aptly summarized in the final paragraph of "Stress, Disease, Aging and Behavior" (Eisdorfer and Wilkie, 1977, p. 270):

> The implications of a relationship between stress, disease, aging, and behavior goes beyond theoretical interest. An understanding of the nature of these variables and the interactions involved, carries with it the potential for intervention not only at the behavioral level but at the somatic level as well. It is clear that stress, a physiological event, may have social and psychological antecedents as well as physical etiologies. The potential consequences of mediating stresses throughout the life span is fascinating to contemplate.

[3]Professor Lazarus is conducting his study within the more general framework of a group of projects on stress and adaptation in the Human Development and Aging Group (UCSF), which includes the Transitions Study, the Divorce Study (Chiriboga), and a study of treated and untreated people undergoing acute stress (Horowitz).

For some people, effective coping with stress and other adaptive and maturing processes continue through late life, perhaps at the current historical moment more so among women than men. While their lives may be clearly punctuated by certain normative or idiosyncratic stages and events, these processes of growth are unique to each individual, and not easily grouped into a set sequence that most people experience. There are, of course, the "expectable" transitions of life, such as completing school and leaving home, starting to work, getting married, having a first child, the departure from home of the youngest child (the "empty nest"), retirement from work. We shall have more to say about these later, but suffice it for now to say that by no means everyone conceives of these as major turning points in their lives. Many people find that less expectable events, and internal experiences, or sometimes a very sudden one, have far more impact on their thoughts, feelings, and actions. Included among these are falling in love, reaching some desired peak of achievement which might range from being highest scorer on the high school basketball team, finding the most satisfactory and comfortable way to present oneself to the world, to becoming chairman of the board or making one's first million. At the other extreme are such negative events as unanticipated bereavement, divorce (at all ages), or the development of chronic illness or impairment in one's self or a loved one.

We should be cautious not to overgeneralize about middle and old age, nor to attempt to connect their beginnings and ends with particular stages or ages. Though the recent spurt of publicity about the perils of various periods of adulthood, and, at the moment, especially middle age, is almost certainly influencing the way most of us think of ourselves and our futures, it seems pretty clear for now that the idea of stages, with particular ages attached to them, is not something most of us plan our lives around. To be sure, in the United States and several other countries (including Japan and Western Europe) such measures as Social Security, Medicare, and forced retirement at a certain age (55 in Japan), combined with a general awareness of the increase in life expectancy, have officially established some period ranging between 55 to 65 as the beginning of "old age," all too often having a devastating effect on the self-concepts of people as they attain these socially down-graded ages and stages. Palmore (1975) mentions the re-hiring of retirees in Japan, but not the fact that they are generally re-hired at lower status, lower pay, and loss of fringe benefits, and that they lose union membership as well (Kiefer, personal communication, 1978). Such compromises are often accepted by retirees in the United States as well — including professors. The obvious query is whether we should not have laws against exploitation of the old as we now have against child labor. The youngest recruit to the labor force is now made aware of the post-retirement period as a life stage each time a paycheck is received, which was certainly not true of his grandparents. We can only hope today's young are preparing to rebel early and not wait too long before they begin to resent this kind of age-grading, for age-grading (to borrow Neugarten's term) is *de*grading, as can be readily observed in the demeanor and conversation of residents in many middle and upper middle class "adult" and "retirement" communities.

There is considerable evidence that most working people consider themselves middle-aged until they become concerned with (and usually anxious about) planning for a retirement period beginning in the next few years. If the forced retirement age in the United States becomes 70, or is eliminated altogether, will such self-definitions of becoming old be postponed, or is the whole idea of life stages irrelevant to that high proportion of adults who just live each day as it comes, without attaching labels or noting milestones? Does a 45 or 50 year old man who marries a 30 year old and starts a family (or a new family) think of himself as middle-aged? Does a woman who has had her first child at 40 consider herself entering "old age" at 60 when she is only a few years post PTA?

A number of other psychological and sociological theories, frameworks and concepts addressed to issues of adaptation, coping, and life satisfaction should not be overlooked. Their potential and shortcomings have been expertly presented by, among others, Baltes and Willis (1977); Maddox and Wiley (1976); Neugarten (1977); and Rosow (1976) in the recently published handbooks on aging. This writer has found no more recent work that would alter the cogent conclusions these authors drew at the time of their writing. While theoretical approaches such as the dialectic theory of Klaus Riegel (1975 a,b; 1977) and the systems theory of Parsons and Shils (1962) may not seem manageable frameworks to some investigators, the trend is eminently clear. With very few exceptions, most scholars are expressing the need for a transcendence of disciplinary bonds if future progress is to be made in our understanding of how adults adapt, cope, and to a greater or lesser degree acquire some sense of worth, fulfillment, or satisfaction as they move through their allotted time. Few are pressing for a "global" theory. Riegel, for example, proposes role theory, to be interrelated with the more psychologically derived theories, as a promising and feasible first move toward synthesis. Neugarten, as mentioned earlier, hopes for a closer integration of personality, clinical, and developmental frameworks and concepts. Many rightly urge more integration of cross-cultural views (Clark, 1967; Kiefer, 1974; Shanas and Maddox, 1976; and Streib 1976, among others). In the light of this widespread interest, contributions by anthropologists to the handbooks referenced here are conspicuous by their absence. Further, particularly in relation to longitudinal studies of adults, and more specifically to mental health and aging with which the present volume is concerned, the need for theoretical, conceptual, and methodological orientations of social historians is also self-evident. Finally, the need for a humanistically oriented philosophy, as exemplified in Norton's recent work (1976), is also a pressing one. While he does adopt a (rather loose) stage framework, in distinguishing between them, Norton assumes a kind of blending at the beginning of each "stage exchange." The change taking place is not in whole-hearted commitment, or what he calls eudaimonia, for this is the lifelong task of the individual. While he sees the "intuition of new conditions" as "illumination marking stage exchange" and the "recognition that new requirements apply," the fulfillment of the new requirements is a continuing envolvement throughout the years of the new stage (Norton, 1976, p. 169). The new stage is thus not clearly defined for or by the individual until well toward its end. In maturity, one learns eventually to *choose* what must be done, wholeheartedly and in terms of one's ultimate possibility. It is the *process* of choosing that determines choices and ultimately gives them meaning.

> "The individual who strives in accordance with his innate inclination does all that he does out of love. ... The individual whose striving is at variance with his innate inclinations lacks the moving power of love, and acts on such surrogate motivations as need, desire, ... vanity, guilt, shame or extrinsically imposed 'duty'" (Norton, 1976, pp. 189–190).

While, in Norton's view, the beginning of adulthood begins with the revelation "someday I must die," right choices made during the long ensuing process of maturation do not fade away. They enable the chooser to confront and live throughout the last stage, the one "without a future," to rediscover that "his common humanity" is the foundation of that mode of love, termed "sympathy" or "fellow feeling," which affirms all "humankind" (Norton, 1976, p. 209).

This kind of old age encourages the "right" choices, and thereby also encourages the self-actualization of those accompanying and following us. As we can see, then, the kind of symbolic generativity Erikson assigns as the major task of middle age, Norton sees as the fulfillment of old age. In Norton's view, this actualization is the result of achieving integrity in middle age, while Erikson's stage framework puts integrity in the last stage and generativity in midlife. I believe the reasoning of both confirms an earlier point: integrity and generativity are not developmental stages, but essentially co-existing qualities of the individual. Neither quality can be a genuine one without the other.

## THE OBJECTIVE AND SUBJECTIVE NATURE OF TASKS AND CRISES OF LATER LIFE AND HOW THEY ARE MANAGED

In turning now to the results of studies more specifically related to aging and mental health, one of the major sources will be the interdisciplinary research program initiated in the late 1950s, in the Human Development and Aging Program at the University of California (San Francisco). This work is drawn upon both because it remains one of the more comprehensive of its kind (Shanas and Maddox, 1976), and is eminently familiar to the author of this chapter.

This interdisciplinary group has learned much about the crises and the less dramatic stresses of maturing and growing old in our society, and the kinds of resources and impediments, internal and external, that foster growth or stagnation, health or illness, in these processes.[4] Perhaps most notably, we have learned that becoming mature is hard work, and few achieve it. Growing old in good health, with dignity and a sense of social worth, perhaps especially in post World War II Western society, is becoming increasingly difficult; for many, often for reasons beyond their control, impossible (Butler, 1975). In a period of staggering and unprecedented social change, it is now often said that maintenance of integrity in the latter half of life is possible, but only through a continuing series of "identity crises," a term which, twenty years ago, was generally limited to the maturing of adolescents (Erikson, 1968). Stress and adaptation, in short, becomes a major framework of choice in assessing change in adulthood and old age.

The relationship among life stress, assessment of stress, coping, and health has been revived with gusto in the past decade and a half, after an hiatus following the important work done during and immediately following World War II. The revival, drawing in part on the wartime work of R. Grinker (Grinker and Spiegel, 1945), and Selye (1956), was given further impetus by the work of Holmes and Rahe (1967), both then at the University of Washington. The emphasis of their work has been on the effects of "life changes" on physical health, including both "positive" (such as marriage) and "negative" stresses (such as retirement or loss of work for other reasons). It is of some interest that, with the exception of a recent semi-popular work of Selye (1974), the issue of too little change, or stress, has not been a concern in most research conducted within the stress/physical illness paradigm, except for boredom, which has been considered a possible stress by a few investigators.

Our ten-year study of mental health and aging among persons sixty and older, which began, in 1958, with a deliberately eclectic approach, was subsumed within a stress/adaptation framework not long after exploratory analyses of highly detailed information on a community sample of 600 and a hospitalized sample only slightly smaller had been reduced to some semblance of order. The conviction that stress and psychological disorder were interrelated (though not inextricably) emerged before the resurgence of interest in stress and health had become widespread. Langner and Michael's (1963) findings on life stress and mental illness among community-resident adults *under* age sixty were also presented within such a framework. Their study of Midtown Manhattan was published in 1963, after the research group at UCSF had made its independent decision that life stress was a promising framework for studying mental health and illness in older people, though their major publications came later. This coincidence is a useful illustration of how an eclectic approach, and a certain similarity of problems, perhaps especially in a new field, may result in two or more investigators independently adopting similar conceptual frameworks. Once more, the data seemed to impose their own requirements for order and theory.[5]

After considerable thought, the mode adopted for presenting the material which follows has turned out to be a rather unorthodox one. The

[4]See, for example, Clark and Anderson (1967); Lowenthal (1964); Lowenthal (1977); Lowenthal, Berkman and Associates (1967); Lowenthal and Haven (1968); Lowenthal and Robinson (1976); and Simon, Lowenthal, and Epstein (1970).

[5]Subsequent to the writing of this chapter, Dr. Leo Srole presented a most interesting report on a twenty-year follow-up study of this large Manhattan sample (initially ranging in age to 60, now, of course, to 80). His report was presented at a symposium of the 31st Annual Scientific Meeting of the Gerontological Society, Dallas, November, 1978.

earlier short-range longitudinal study discussed first, was based on a cohort which was older to begin with (60 to over 90) than those to be discussed later (18 to an average of 58 at the outset). This heuristic approach has two advantages. It illustrates how an eclectic interdisciplinary study (as the older study to be reported on was), in a comparatively new field (aging and mental health), may lead to the location of more relevant problems in the field than those structured primarily by prior theories, or by the particular area of expertise of an individual investigator. And perhaps of even more significance, it reveals some of the ways in which the study of a particular life phase, stage, or age group may be enriched by knowledge of sociohistorical developments occurring both before and after the period of particular research concern.

## TASKS AND CRISES AMONG OLDER PEOPLE ARRIVING ON PSYCHIATRIC WARDS

The sample for the hospitalized group in the Normal and Abnormal Aging studies[6] consisted of a near-universe of 534 persons admitted for the first time at age sixty or over to the psychiatric screening wards of a general hospital. The community-resident group, drawn from a locating survey of 2,473 persons, was a random, stratified sample of 600 persons, sixty and older. All were San Franciscans. The hospitalized patients were studied exhaustively, with detailed, open-ended (as well as structured) interviews with both patients and their relatives, friends, and others who were informed about them or involved in some way in the decision-making process leading to the psychiatric ward. Needless to say, the majority of all concerned viewed the situation as a crisis. Physical examinations were administered to patients by interns, mental-status and clinical interviews by psychiatrists, a variety of psychological tests by psychologists, and detailed interviews by psychologists, psychiatric social workers and professionals in related fields. The community subjects were studied in a more limited fashion—the methods resembling those of a community survey, which relies heavily on pre-structured questions. However, some open-ended material was gathered at the first round, and it proved so useful that it was introduced in more detail during the second and third contacts, after new concepts and hypotheses had emerged from analysis of the initial data. (There

were two follow-ups of both samples, about a year apart, and two more of the hospitalized.)

Three years following the initial contact, intensive life history interviews were conducted with a subsample of 40 each in the hospital and community groups. These interviews often extended over a period of several days, and included thorough physical and psychiatric examinations, as well as the administration of a battery of laboratory and psychological tests. A fifth year follow-up was conducted with 46 patients still in state hospitals, and a study of deaths (11 years later) was subsequently undertaken. The results of this series of studies have been reported in four books and well over 100 articles in professional journals and book chapters. While much of this material directly relates to tasks and crises, and to the intra- and interpersonal resources and impediments to adaptation in later life, there is space here to highlight only a few of the findings. *Crisis and Intervention* (Simon, Lowenthal, and Epstein, 1970) describes in detail the condition of these patients at the time of admission. These 500 people confronted with the crisis of psychiatric hospitalization (for the first time in their lives) during the first year of the study differed from other 600 randomly sampled San Franciscans sixty and older mainly in being closer to the poverty level, with more living alone, including proportionately many more women over seventy-five than in the general population, and, even among the younger males, in not having worked for many years. About as many were married, had children in the vicinity, and had religious affiliations as among their age-peers in the community at large. In the program psychiatrists' judgment, 87 percent of these elderly patients were severely impaired and needed twenty-four hour supervision, and the rest were in need of considerable care, though not necessarily on an around-the-clock basis. Older patients were not more severely ill than were younger, and men and women tended to be equally impaired, except that women in the middle age range (70–79) were more ill than either the younger or the older women, and also more so than men in the same age group.

In explaining why these elderly people were brought to the psychiatric wards, their relatives and other informants mentioned physical health problems in three-fourths of all cases (Lowenthal, 1964). These (usually) lay appraisals, were generally confirmed by program psychiatrists and other physicians. While their physical health was not as severely impaired as was their mental and emotional condition, it is obvious that the majority of elderly patients who require emergency psychiatric care in a given year are seriously in need of general

[6]Studies in Normal and Abnormal Aging, conducted at the Human Development and Aging Program, University of California at San Francisco, was supported by the National Institute of Mental Health Grant #MH09145.

medical as well as psychiatric treatment. At the time of their admission, about one–fifth were suffering from congestive heart failure, and another fourth showed signs of marked malnutrition (of the latter, more than a third had a diagnosis of acute alcoholism). Others had respiratory disorders, strokes, hearing loss, hypertension, or serious visual impairment. Physical improvement rates during the stay on the screening wards closely resembled those found for psychiatric improvement, and those who improved physically were the most likely to improve psychiatrically. Those whose physical condition improved tended to have been admitted for acute alcoholism, acute brain syndrome, or both, or patients recovering from a suicide attempt with overdoses of drugs. While "crises" may not be the appropriate word except in obvious cases such as suicide attempts and the D.T.s, for the majority of all concerned the situation was serious.

For the analysis of change in the patients' conditions between the initial assessment and the second follow-up (a period of about two years), the sample was divided into four groups on the basis of their outcomes: (1) fifty-two patients who first went to state hospitals from the screening wards and were later discharged to the community; (2) thirty-five who were sent to institutions other than state hospitals; (3) thirty-seven who were discharged directly from the psychiatric screening wards and interviewed in the community at both follow-ups; (4) 125 remaining in the state hospitals. The findings testify to the appropriateness of the second-round location of these patients a year after their admission to the screening wards. Those who were sent to and remained in a state hospital were in the worst condition mentally, remaining about the same as at the baseline period, although there was a slight trend toward improvement in physical condition due to the generally good quality of physical care and treatment at the California state hospitals at that time.

The group residing in nursing homes, old age homes, and similar facilities had been in only slightly better psychological condition than those sent to state hospitals after the baseline interview, but showed considerable improvement during the follow-up periods. Although they had had more physical problems at the outset, they improved physically more than did those remaining in state hospitals, as they also did in the ability to care for themselves. Patients in this group were far more likely to have been diagnosed as having acute brain syndromes at the time of admission. Since these syndromes have a physical basis, and consequently more than half had spent some time in a general hospital between the baseline and the second fol-

low-up interviews, a picture emerges of a sizeable cohort whose chief problems were physical.

From former patients' self-appraisals as well as professional assessment, there is evidence suggesting that the state hospital experience was beneficial for the discharged group. While those who remained there tended to show little improvement in mental, and only slightly more so in physical, condition by the time of the second follow-up interview, patients who were discharged from state hospitals and living in the community at round three were very much better, some nearly normal on both counts. They were also in better condition at the follow-up than the group that had been directly discharged back to the community from the screening wards (Lowenthal and Trier, 1967). One cannot help but wish that a new study of older mentally ill persons will soon be undertaken among a new cohort of sixty and older people whose primary source of help is now vested in community mental health programs. Though lacking hard evidence, this writer is convinced that we would find a sadly neglected group of people.

## COMPARISONS WITH THE COMMUNITY-RESIDENT ELDERLY

The mentally and otherwise impaired within the community cohort of 600 provided evidence of impressive resiliency and capacity for change. The psychiatrically impaired among them differed from their psychologically more robust peers mainly in having more deprivations and stresses (physical, social, and economic). As was also noted in the Langner and Michael (1963) mental health study of younger subjects, the effects of such deprivations are cumulative. At the same time, comparisons between the psychiatrically impaired community-resident subjects and a matched subsample from the hospitalized group yielded strong evidence for the prevalence of considerable familial and community tolerance for eccentric or overtly pathological behavior in older persons, so long as they are able to take care of themselves physically. The community-resident aged who were psychiatrically impaired differed from hospitalized patients not so much in degree of disturbances in thought, feeling, or behavior as in their capacity for taking care of their personal needs such as dressing and eating (Lowenthal *et al.*, 1967). For elderly people, in fact, taking care of one's self may be the functional and social equivalent of work performance among younger people.

Overviews of both samples from social and cultural perspectives serve to illustrate certain commonalities among the mentally ill aged. In terms of objective social factors, for example, some association between socioeconomic status and psychiatric impairment among the community-resident mentally impaired was found, and as among the hospitalized this association was stronger among men than women, suggesting that men in our culture may attach a greater value to the instrumental roles they can no longer fill. Among both men and women, however, the correlation between socioeconomic status and mental impairment *decreases* with advancing age, possibly reflecting increasing rejection of the prevailing values placed on economic achievement and its accoutrements. Among women, psychiatric impairment was most significantly associated with low self-esteem, and with very little social interaction.

That socioeconomic status is also related to the nature of treatment for mental illness is as true for older people as any other age group; those hospitalized on the screening wards of a county hospital or in a state hospital are far more likely to be poverty-stricken than those treated in private facilities. But contrary to our expectations, the absence of social supports, such as living alone, not having children or other close relatives in the vicinity, or lack of religious or other types of organizational affiliations, did not necessarily distinguish between community-resident and the hospitalized impaired groups, nor did these characteristics influence whether patients were sent from the screening wards to a state mental hospital. In fact, the opposite was true, suggesting that those who did not become hospitalized had acquired a degree of "social invisibility." That is to say, the elderly individual may stay out of the hospital despite even quite bizarre symptomatology if he or she lives in a tolerant milieu and can avoid the attention of potentially responsible or decision-making persons. This, however, is possible only if the disturbed person is capable of elementary self-maintenance, thus avoiding the arousal of guilt or anxiety in others.

Even before the three rounds of contact with the 1100 elderly people over a three-year period had been completed, it became very obvious that the then prevailing concept among policy-makers that families of the elderly were "railroading" them into institutions was highly inappropriate. In the first place, only 5 percent of the population (sixty-five years and older) were in institutions of any kind, a national proportion which has remained fairly stable. Second, about half of the aged then crowding the state mental hospitals had grown old there, thanks in part to advances in physical medicine. And finally, in the community group, there were very seriously impaired older people sus-

tained by their families or others, often by dint of extraordinary sacrifices in time, energy, and money (Clark and Anderson, 1967; Lowenthal, 1964). In those pre-Medicare days, private institutional care was out of the question for the majority, while state hospitals were viewed by many as "snakepits," which of course was close to the truth in some areas of the country. In California and a few other states, however, such hospitals were not only devoting themselves to the treatment of the mentally ill, but, as previously noted, maintained excellent facilities for the care of physical illnesses and disabilities as well. Indeed one of the more unfortunate consequences of the subsequent move toward phasing out such institutions is that there are no longer adequate facilities where older people can be simultaneously assessed and treated for disorders in both the physical and psychological spheres, which are in any event closely related and become more so with advancing age (Lowenthal *et al.*, 1967).

In conclusion, initial findings from the community sample and follow-up contacts at one and two year intervals did much to undermine the myth that from sixty or so on all changes are downhill.

## ANTICIPATION AND ACTUALITY OF TASKS AND CRISES OF LATER LIFE AMONG MIDDLE AND LATE MIDDLE-AGED COHORTS

In the ongoing longitudinal studies of younger cohorts (Lowenthal *et al.*, 1975), a number of indicators of crises and tasks in later life are being explored in terms both of expectation and those that actually occur over a period of several years. As was true of participants in the aging studies, few of the people who, at the outset of the study, were middle and late middle-aged, anticipated mental illness as one of the crises they might face, reflecting the realities of often well-publicized statistics. There is, however, considerable concern about physical health emerging with sharp clarity among these two older groups in the 18-month and fifth and seventh year follow-up interviews, more so among women than men. Hand in hand with this realistic concern is an often expressed anxiety about becoming dependent, financially, physically, or both, on relatives, expecially their grown children. These possibilities, rather than anxieties about growing old *per se*, appear very threatening at the seven year follow-up, the younger of the two groups averaged age fifty-five, the older sixty-five. Women, again realistically, had often become increasingly preoccupied with the state of their husbands' health, many expressing frustration about their spouses' indifference to medical or media-promulgated advice about living patterns to be avoided to insure a long and healthy life. Aging widows, like aging divorcees, are not much in demand in either the economic or the social life of our society, and these women hope to avoid such a denigrated status. (Some, though not the majority, also love their husbands very much, and expressed their worries in affectionate terms.)

The sense of responsibility for aging parents proves to be even stronger than that gleaned from the reverse perspective provided by earlier studies. This is true whether it is anticipation or reality that is being explored. When anticipation becomes reality, as it often did during the periods between contacts with the informants, responsibilities were met, usually at great emotional, physical, and economic consequences. Both the physical and the emotional burdens fall primarily on the wife's shoulders, whether the parents are his, hers, or theirs—or all four as sometimes happens. While this sample represents a lower middle class, strongly family-oriented segment of our society, similar findings have been reported from the longitudinal study of a very large cross-section study being conducted by Lieberman and Pearlin at the University of Chicago, which also is finding that young adults are at least as concerned about their middle-aged parents as are the middle-aged about their old ones (G. Lieberman, 1976).

Some of these findings were anticipated in the earlier work of Shanas (1962). In the opinion of this author, educators, clinicians, and policy-makers alike have not been sufficiently responsive to this cumulative body of data, which clearly indicates that the problem of aging parents is likely soon to become one of the most pressing of our time. In the fields of prevention and education, one of the first priorities should be to foster discussion groups on the responsibility for, and the care of, aging parents and parents-in-law. No doubt, it would primarily be women who attend, because most of their spouses, working or retired, view care-taking as woman's role, no matter whose parents are the ones who need it. Perhaps, with support from other women in like situations, participants in such groups will be encouraged to persuade their husbands to share the burden a bit. While the capacity for change or growth in men in this life stage, at least in middle and lower middle socioeconomic and educational groups, short of being jolted by a wife-instigated divorce (which does occur for this reason though thus far not often) is not inspiring, they do spend a great deal of time viewing television, and more public education on the emerging facts (present and projected) might touch a few of them. Such infor-

mation would also reach younger people who, when they become middle and late middle-aged, are going to have even more crises in this sphere of family relationships.

The normative or expectable role losses that most middle-aged and older people undergo generally had little, if any, influence on the mental health status or adaptive level of the large sixty and older populations studied in the early 1960s. As these older people looked back on their lives, the normally anticipated "losses" of later life were sometimes experienced with a pleasant sense of relief, rarely, except for widowhood, as a crisis. Reality, by and large, confirmed their expectations. More idiosyncratic, unexpected events, such as the experience of the death of a close other (especially in childhood or young adulthood), or a conversion, religious or otherwise, loomed larger in their recollection of psychosocial changes requiring major reorientation and redefinition of tasks and lifestyles.

The Longitudinal Study of Transitions (Lowenthal *et al.*, 1975) was designed in part to study this rather unanticipated finding about so-called decremental role changes of later life, in greater depth than heretofore. While the normative role changes or transitions between late adolescence and old age provided the design frame for this later research program, participants in the study, other than the high school seniors, were not told that they had been selected for this reason, nor was the issue of the pending transitions directly approached in the interviewing process. Rather, they were queried in depth and in a semi-structured Rogerian fashion (Merton, Fiske, and Kendall, 1948/1955), in order to evaluate the salience of these transitions (for the two older groups they involved status and role "loss") in relation to other tasks and crises of their lives. The results confirmed the impression from the earlier studies, that it is not role loss *per se* that poses problems. Among those whose youngest child was about to graduate from high school, three-fifths of the men ignored that imminent event and focused on their own retirement, some ten or fifteen years in the future. Their anxiety, however, was about financial issues, not the retirement status *per se*. All men within two or three years of retirement mentioned it as the next major change in their lives, and although nearly a quarter of them still had children at home, few mentioned the "empty nest." Most of these older men (average age 58) were looking forward to retirement with pleasant anticipation. The majority of the middle-aged women mentioned the pending departure of the youngest child in a rather routine way, and a third of them also referred to the future retirement of their husbands, though they expressed no anxiety about either status or financial problems. Although half of the women in early and late middle age worked, none of the younger middle-aged mentioned their own retirement as an event that would be an important change in their lives.

Among the younger middle-aged people, two and five years later, there was relatively little work change. A few men had changed jobs and were less anxious about money for their future retirement. Those at the same jobs (and the majority were routine ones) continued to be as bored with their work as they had been earlier. In the light of the rather negative prevailing theories about role loss (Rosow, 1974; 1976), that half of the younger middle-aged and three-fourths of the later middle-aged men looked forward to retirement, often with eagerness, suggests the possibility of a change in attitude toward this stage of life. Many men voluntarily retired early, and others would have could they have afforded to. Some of the women, on the other hand, were worried about the impact on their own lives of having their husband "under foot" all day. As one woman remarked, "My life is with my girl friends—I don't want to have to babysit him all day."

The women in this cohort, when first seen at average age 48, were, by their own standards as well as by objective measures, neither coping well nor satisfied with their lives. Two and five years later, they proved to have found two divergent resolutions to their very obvious conflicts. One group may best be characterized as having become resigned, and in the process they had lost some of their many symptoms of agitation. A second, largely through their own efforts, had made major changes in their lives, ranging from divorce to new jobs. They were, in their own terms, well satisfied (Fiske, 1979).

The men who were close to retirement when we originally talked with them subsequently proved to be even more pleased with its reality than with its anticipation. The majority were happily relaxing in what they consider to be a well-deserved phase of comfort, complete with more pampering by their wives than might have been expected in light of what was learned about the restlessness of the younger middle-aged women. From their own reports, many of them seemed to welcome becoming the strong shoulder on which their mellowing spouses could now allow themselves to lean (Fiske, 1979; Thurnher, 1977).

We shall have more to say about modes of coping among these men and women in the next section. There, as in this one, it will be shown that several hypotheses about middle age generated by

the aging studies have been supported. Others have not. There proves to be, for example, considerably less continuity in values, goals, commitments, and self-concept than we were led to expect in the retrospective protocols of the earlier studies. Two processes seem to account for this—one is the rather well-documented need to impose order on one's life (Butler, 1963; M. Lieberman, 1970), and the second the effect on individual lives of the increasing velocity of sociohistorical change (Lowenthal, 1977; Riegel, 1977).

## RESOURCES AND IMPEDIMENTS IN COPING

### INTERPERSONAL

*Among the Hospitalized and the Community-resident Aged.* Though they interacted with others less than their unimpaired counterparts in the community, those elderly persons hospitalized on the psychiatric wards were not notably worse off in terms of social resources available in a time of crisis. To be sure, about one-tenth of them were true isolates having no friends or relatives anywhere, and about the same proportion were semi-isolates—that is, they did have friends or relatives but, for geographical or other reasons, they were not available at the time of crisis. Further, it is important to note, these proportions of isolates and semi-isolates did not differ from those found among the community-resident sample. During the period before and after hospitalization, four-fifths of the patients had relatives or friends who were involved in the decision-making process leading up to it, or who served as interviewees in the study (most often both), thus disproving the then prevalent assumptions about isolation and mental illness (Lowenthal, 1964).

There were few indications of recent social losses as the precipitators of admission. Many of these patients–in fact the majority of them —had indeed retired, lost a spouse, or both, but for most these changes had taken place in the distant past, generally more than ten years prior to their arrival on the psychiatric screening wards. In short, admission to the screening ward was not, for most, related to deterioration in interpersonal supports. Indeed, the availability of genuine social support may well be conducive to admission to the hospital. In fact, lack of such support, or a degree of social invisibility, may provide a certain amount of protection against hospitalization once mental or emotional difficulties develop.

The crucial question is whether such invisibility, usually a reflection of isolation, is conducive to the development of mental illness in old age. This study indicates that it is not, for while a number of those who became hospitalized for mental illness in old age had indeed lived isolated lives since late adolescence or young adulthood, a similar proportion of such lifelong isolates was found among the community-resident aged, and they manifest no signs of mental illness, unless isolation itself is so defined (Lowenthal, 1965). Most such people choose to live alone, perpetuating a lifelong pattern of non-intimate, primarily instrumental, social relationships. Our sample of 600 community residents did not include hotels, but there is little reason to believe that more mentally impaired persons would have been located had they been included (Eckert, 1977; Felton, Lehmann, and Burgio, 1977; Stephens, 1975).

The lack of relationship between a lifelong pattern of social isolation led to the hypothesis that the habitual isolates may in fact avoid the social losses of aging so critical to others. They do not suffer from the lack of interpersonal and group relationships, because they never had, or have long since renounced, them. Rather, it is people who have often tried and failed to establish close relationships who are most likely to become mentally ill in old age—particularly those who blame themselves for their failure. The elderly male isolates usually had left their parental homes early, because of parental dissension or lengthy absences, deaths, or divorces. These men were notably courteous, confident, and often charming in a turn of the century manner. Even those ill enough to be made in the sample of people who were admitted to psychiatric screening wards were touchingly eager to please, frequently in a witty, self-deprecating fashion. If they missed the intimacies of wife, children, or close friends of either sex, the consequences did not show up among these lifelong isolates on any of the usual measures of adaptation. Female counterparts of such men were less visible. Some had made notably *unsuccessful* escapes from difficult situations in their parental homes into very early marriages. In the generations represented in these aging studies (born between 1870 and 1900), female counterparts of isolated or "distancing" men had often devoted themselves to a commitment to white collar jobs, sometimes involving deep, well-sublimated, commitment to their bosses. Some of those who escaped unhappy childhoods into very early marriages eventually became by no means unhappy widows.

The then prevalent notion that age-linked role losses such as widowhood and retirement trig-

ger mental illness found little substantiation in this research. True, as we have noted, most of the hospitalized were retired, and a very high proportion were widowed, but these events had occurred many years before hospitalization. The few bits of evidence that did link such social losses to psychiatric illness point to some rather unanticipated differences between men and women: it was among men that the most traumatic, often very long-lasting reactions to loss of a spouse developed, and among (usually single) working women that there were most likely to be psychological disturbances associated with retirement. This finding was both unexpected and intriguing. We therefore studied gender differences in relation to work and retirement in the longitudinal phases of our current Transitions Study (Lowenthal *et al.*, 1975) with remarkably similar results. Among both men and women, conflicts about sex roles, unattained personal life goals, and certain personality characteristics such as a tendency to self-blame, proved to be important correlated factors. Under such circumstances, widowhood or retirement are experienced as a threat to one's integrity and self-esteem, and therefore a threat to psychic equilibrium, rather than as a blow inflicted by an impartial fate or by a social system over which one has no control, which is the more usual reaction. What we are suggesting here is that it is inner conflict that threatens the ego's integrity and leads to psychic breakdown in old age (and possibly at any age), whereas social losses that are envisaged as stemming from external forces or norms do not so severely threaten the ego's defenses.

Only recently has the relationship between retirement and adaptation for women been given much attention. Streib and Schneider (1971) appear to the the first to have looked at the retirement process for *both* men and women in some depth. Later, Atchley (1976) found older women to be as work-oriented as older men and, as in the aging studies reported here, to become more psychologically stressed after retirement. Jaslow (1976) found better morale among older working women than the retired, but the women who had never worked had the lowest morale of all. The recent work of Pauline Sears and Ann Barbee (1977) confirms these conclusions: among the women in the original Terman "gifted children"study, followed up at age sixty-two, many of those who had not had careers expressed regrets, and their satisfaction with life was notably less than that of women who had both work and family commitments. That for the most part age-linked social losses do not appear to be causally related to mental illness should not be taken to mean that such deprivations have no bearing on general adaptation. On the contrary, widowhood or retirement may have a very strong, usually temporary, impact on the sense of well-being and morale. This impact can best be illustrated by a brief summary of a study of voluntary as compared with involuntary social withdrawal among the community-resident elderly sample (Lowenthal and Boler, 1965). Stimulated by the conflicting views of interaction and disengagement theories, change in levels of social interaction over a two-year period and its effect on morale was analyzed. In this period, 15 percent had reduced their social contacts, and more than two-fifths of those who had done so were more satisfied with their lives than they had been previously. While this was not quite as high a level as prevailed among those who had not withdrawn, it indicated that voluntary social withdrawal is not conducive to low morale. To explore the circumstances that could presumably be influencing the relation between social withdrawal and morale, those who had reduced their social interaction and those who had not were subdivided in terms of whether they had experienced the age-linked losses of recent widowhood, retirement, or physical illness in the intervening two years. Thus four groups were delineated: the withdrawn who had experienced these stresses and those who had not; and those who had not withdrawn, subdivided between those who had experienced one or more of these three stresses and those who had not. An examination of change in morale among these four groups clearly indicated that it was the age-linked stresses themselves, rather than any consequent social withdrawal, that was decisive. Those who had not become widowed, retired, or ill maintained high morale whether or not they reduced their interaction with others. In passing we should note that a serendipitous discovery was made about these social disengagers who maintained high morale, one which has subsequently been supported in a variety of contexts: they were far more likely to have a confidant than those whose morale had been adversely affected.

*Comparisons with Middle and Late Middle-aged People.* In our discussion of the anticipation in relation to the actuality of tasks and crises in later life, we saw that while the majority of middle-aged men and women were optimistic and realistic in their anticipations, a few were very anxious. The reasons for anxiety differed between men and women, but among both seemed often to reflect inadequate coping styles adopted early in life, in turn related to deprivation in childhood or adolescence. In the Transitions Study it has become clear that loss or absence of one or both parents during an early

period continues to influence the adaptive level of women throughout life, or at least until the early sixties, the age of the oldest group when we first became acquainted with them. Among men, the effects of early parental deprivation wear off by middle age. Among high school seniors and newlyweds, men and women closely resemble each other in that those who have experienced early deprivation have many more adaptive problems than those who have not.

As was true in our study of an older generation, some of the middle-aged and older women reported that they had married and had children in their late teens or early twenties mainly to run away from what they perceived to be the misery of their own parental homes. Most had had little or no exposure to the world beyond their parental families, high school, and their own families. In such circumstances, it is perhaps not surprising that emotional problems generated early in life are perpetuated in their relationships with their husbands and children. Though many of these women work, their socialization to the world of adults is generally at one remove, at first via their husbands, later through their adolescent and adult children.

Psychoanalytic traditionalists may welcome such finding as support for the "no-growth-for-women" thesis expounded in Freud's essay on "Femininity" (1933/1965), later to be modified by Erikson (1963; 1975). That some of the women we are studying longitudinally were beginning to expand their horizons five years after we first saw them is no doubt a reflection of the intervening freeing up of norms in regard to woman's place. We have therefore an unusual opportunity to study what appears to be a developmental phenomenon heretofore stifled, especially among women in the more tradition and family-oriented segments of our culture. Jung long ago noted that men and women tended to change their values in rather opposing directions in the second half of life, observations no doubt based on a rather elitist sample of patients. As we have noted, the subsequent empirical work of Neugarten and Gutmann (1968) lends support to his clinical insight in terms of attitudinal if not behavioral assessments. And, as we have also noted, indications of attitudinal change among the late middle-aged women in the Terman sample are also very clearly in the "liberating" direction (Sears and Barbee, 1977).

Among middle and late middle-aged men, the interpersonal resources helpful in coping are interrelated with their perceptions and assessments of stress. That amount and nature of stress has a bearing on adaptation in middle age, as all through the life course, is indisputable. The nature of this relationship, however, is highly controversial, in part because insufficient attention has been paid to a variety of dimensions. The *timing* of stressful events and circumstances, for example, accounts for variations in the way people respond to them. Important time dimensions include stresses of early life; slowly accumulating chronic stress; waves of new, concurrent pressures occurring at the same time; sudden (or "precipitating") stress; and the anticipation of stresses to come.

In most studies of stress and mental health, from Emile Durkheim's classical work on suicide (1897/1951) through contemporary epidemiological and clinical studies, relatively little attention has been paid to timing—chronic, cumulative, multiple, concurrent stresses, and whether expectable and potentially stressful events are "on or off schedule" (Neugarten, 1968a). Similarly, until recently, little has been learned about the consequences of similar types of stresses, such as divorce, when they occur at successive life stages (Chiriboga, 1978). A low socioeconomic status, for example, may be construed as chronic stress, but it is more stressful for younger men in our society than for older. If additional stresses, chronic or acute, pile up, some people reach a breaking point (physical, psychological, or both), while others become strengthened to face the multiple stresses that are often the lot of the late middle-aged and even more so the elderly. It is people who have recently undergone a barrage of serious problems and events in several spheres of their lives who are thought to be most susceptible to what psychiatrists and other physicians refer to as a "precipitating stress," that is, a particular event, on top of many others, which triggers mental disturbance or physical illness, otherwise known as the last straw. Life events likely to have such a *precipitating* effect are often rather sudden and unanticipated, such as bereavement, sudden loss of income, or residential moves required by sudden changes in work, physical condition, or monetary loss. Unexpected events are more stressful than those which can be planned for. The fifty-five year old skilled worker whose company, with little advance notice, lowers its retirement age to sixty is obviously going to be far more distressed, at least for a time, than he would be had the firm adhered to its earlier policy of sixty-five. And Mrs. A. R., a forty-four year old participant in the Transitions Study (who had four young sons) was, needless to say, under much greater strain when her husband was seriously injured in a car accident and eventually died than the much older widows studied by Zena Blau (1961) and Helena Lopata (1973).

Another kind of precipitating stress would be a sudden awareness of one's self as middle-aged (or old). At this writing, however, it is simply one more intriguing question which we still know all too little about. When and if such shocks of awareness occur, whether or not they originate in interpersonal situations is almost certain to be a prime consideration. It seems reasonable to suppose that an internal clue (such as an accidental and at first unrecognizable view of one's self in a mirror or department store window, or inability to run for the bus as fast as one did before) is easier to cope with than an attitudinal or behavioral change in others. Further, one would expect to find that a signal from a close other would be more traumatic than one emanating from a broader social sphere. For example, during the late 1960s it was no doubt easier to laugh at a TV or newspaper report about the then prevalent slogan of the activist young that "no one over thirty is worth listening to" than to confront a similar statement from one's own child.

Studies of soldiers in the field and in laboratories during World War II could scarcely avoid taking *anticipation* of stress into account, since "war neuroses" often developed before any real experience of it. Yet only a few subsequent studies of stress have taken "anticipatory stress" into account. Notable exceptions are the works of Lieberman, Prock, and Tobin (1968) and Chiriboga and Lieberman (1970) at the University of Chicago; Streib and Schneider (1971) at Cornell University; Lazarus (1966) at the University of California; and Janis at Yale (1958). From them we have reliable evidence that people who "work through" the anticipated event, be it retirement, a stressful movie in a lab, or serious surgery, are likely to cope with it far more effectively than those who avoid thinking about the pending occurrence.

In addition to various aspects of the timing of stresses, there remains the equally crucial issue of considerable variation among people as to the kinds of events and circumstances they consider stressful. From time to time, various groups of professional people, usually physicians and/or behavioral scientists, have drawn up weighted lists of what they consider to be stressful events or situations. Probably the majority of laymen would agree with their assessments; yet there are many who would not, and this is the important, and often overlooked, fact. For example, using a modified and expanded version of the most frequently used measure (Holmes and Rahe, 1967), we found in the Transitions Study that whether people report many or few recent or more remote situations or circumstances in this revised "stress events" list is not necessarily reflected in their current sense of well-being.

People who have been exposed to many stresses seem to differ from those who have experienced few. They are, for example, more "complex," both in their inner and outer lives. They have many inner and outer resources, but at the same time, they also have more personal and social handicaps and deficiencies. They have broader perspectives, on both themselves and society, than do the lightly stressed, and are more growth-oriented, insightful, and competent. In other words, they are the kinds of people who seek out a challenging lifestyle, which is bound to be stressful on occasion. For example, Vaillant, in a tone of both relish and surprise, reports that among the intelligent and often gifted people in his study (1977), there is a highly stressed, productive and gifted writer (in his fifties) whom he assessed as neurotic and in other ways "poorly adapted"—he drinks too much, his love life is erratic, he has a very unorthodox schedule, and the like. But at the same time, Vaillant the psychiatrist and researcher suggests that this maladapted man is a wise and generous person. Indeed, he values this man's insights so highly that he sought him out to check his own assessments of other, usually "well-adjusted," men in the study.

Persons who have experienced little presumed stress, on the other hand, have more limited perspectives (on themselves, time, and the rest of the world); they also have fewer psychological and social handicaps, and fewer inner and outer resources. Unlike people who have had a great many stressful experiences, they have long since adopted lifestyles which protect them from stress. When we divide these two groups between those who are and who are not very preoccupied with whatever stresses they are or were exposed to, we have a typology of four kinds of people:

| | PREOCCUPATION WITH STRESS | |
|---|---|---|
| PRESUMED STRESS | Considerable | Little |
| Frequent and/or severe | Overwhelmed | Challenged |
| Infrequent and/or mild | Self-defeating | Lucky |

The *overwhelmed* beset by many ostensibly stressful situations, dwell on them at length in discussing the ups and down of their present and past lives; many, in fact, seem still to be living them through, even though their difficult experiences may have been in the remote past. The *challenged,* similarly besieged by many presumptive stresses or a few severe ones, are, in contrast, not excessively preoccupied with them. In recounting the histories of their lives, they simply report, and perhaps briefly describe, such events and circumstances, and then quickly move on to other topics which interest them more. The *self-defeating,* although they recount few stressful experiences, weight their life reviews heavily with themes of loss and deprivation, which they, like the *overwhelmed,* seem to be reliving with much of the original turmoil. On the other hand, the *lucky* who also have, and have had, few or mild stresses, rarely discuss them, and loss is not a theme in their life stories. A few even report that they feel mysteriously protected, or that Lady Luck has been on their side. While the more prosaic simply say "I've been lucky, I guess," others speak of fate, the stars, or God, feeling that there must be some mystical or magical "reason" out there that is protecting them. (In this context, it is perhaps important to recall that, according to recent surveys, a third of the people in this country consider themselves to be "born again Christians" [Vidal, 1978], and the proportions who report ESP experiences, consult astrologists, regularly read their horoscopes, or visit palm readers and other fortune tellers regularly are equally impressive.)

About three-fifths of the "typical American" groups participating in the Transitions Study have expectable reactions to the situations judged stressful by the series of researchers who developed the "life events" schedule we used. A few more than half of the people who have had little stress are of the *lucky* type (i.e., they pay little attention to whatever stress they do experience), and a slight majority of those who have experienced a great deal are *overwhelmed,* that is, they have been highly stressed by normative standards, and dwell upon it at length. But this leaves a great many "deviants": about two-fifths of those who have experienced a great many of the presumed stresses are *challenged* by it, while among those with very little, a similar proportion speak as though their lives were an unending series of problems; they are the kinds of people we call *self-defeating.* The following table shows the distribution of the four stress types

**Table 15-1**  STRESS TYPES AMONG THE YOUNG AND THE MIDDLE-AGED (percentages)

| | YOUNGER (AVERAGE AGE 21) | | OLDER (AVERAGE AGE 55) | |
|---|---|---|---|---|
| | *Men* | *Women* | *Men* | *Women* |
| **CONSIDERABLE PRESUMED STRESS** | | | | |
| Challenged | 16 | 21 | 30 | 7 |
| Overwhelmed | 36 | 27 | 21 | 40 |
| **LIGHT PRESUMED STRESS** | | | | |
| Lucky | 32 | 21 | 31 | 32 |
| Self-Defeating | 16 | 31 | 18 | 21 |
| Total | 100 | 100 | 100 | 100 |

among the younger and older men and women we are studying. As we can see, middle-aged men are far more likely to be *challenged* by considerable stress than are younger men, while both young and older lightly stressed men consider themselves *lucky*. Severely stressed young women are more *challenged* than middle-aged women (the ratio is 3 to 1). Lightly stressed young women, unlike young men, react more negatively to little stress, whereas lightly stressed middle-aged women, like the middle-aged and the young men, tend to be in the *lucky* group. Given considerable stress, while many men rise to the occasion and are *challenged*, women seem to lose their stress tolerance: the great majority of the more severely stressed middle and late middle-aged women are *overwhelmed*. It is such sizeable and important exceptions to the presumed norm that makes it necessary to remind ourselves—and often—that stress *can* be conducive to the strengthening of a healthy attitude toward life, as exemplified by middle-aged men. As the pioneer stress researcher Hans Selye has recently observed, without stress there is no life (1974).

A critical question, obviously, is what happens to middle-aged women. To repeat: among the young exposed to considerable apparent stress, men are more likely to be *overwhelmed* than women. Middle-aged men with a great deal of stress are most likely to be *challenged*, while nearly all of the highly stressed women in this life stage are *overwhelmed*. We have seen that these middle-aged women, compared with their male cohorts, have more limited contacts with the world outside of the family in which their commitments are vested. Other arenas and opportunities for self-expression rarely are cultivated. Even those women who have avoided severe stress, while they have come to appreciate that they are indeed *lucky*, are not growing and expanding the way the *challenged* men are at this life stage. A look at some of the other characteristics of the people representing the four types of stress response helps us to understand why this is so.

Lightly stressed, *lucky* men have strong masculine self-images, and do not speak freely or in detail about their past. The *lucky* of both sexes also give less thought to death than any other of the three stress types. In contrast to the *self-defeating* (lightly stressed but preoccupied with it), they describe themselves as having the "positive" characteristics which are stereotypically desirable in our culture, and they seldom acknowledge any negative ones at all. *Lucky* men and women alike also appear to be minimally involved with others; for instance, their responses to a projective test picture showing a couple embracing were notably shallow

and brief. Altogether, of the four groups in the stress typology, the *lucky* are the most clearly delineated. There are fewer differences between men and women in this group than among the other three. Their offhand relationships with others and the flatness of their emotional lives suggest minimal involvement with life, perhaps consciously or unconsciously adopted because of a very deep-seated sense of insecurity which makes it impossible for them to withstand criticism. Genuine involvement, which always carries with it a certain risk of failure, would threaten their carefully constructed self-images. To borrow Erich Fromm's (1966) term, the "life plot" of the *lucky* seemed to be to pursue a stress-avoidant life style; to accomplish this they must carefully construct a public-self and distance themselves from others to avoid disclosure of their real-selves. We might sum them up as rather simplistic, perhaps superficial, people.

The most distinguishing characteristic of the *self-defeating* (little stress, highly preoccupied with it) is excessive preoccupation with death. These defeated, or "poor me," people not only anxiously brood about death more often than most, but they also have more complex thoughts about it (and this is true of young and middle-aged alike). They differ from the *lucky* in that, for example, the *self-defeating* men, in particular, harbor very negative images of themselves. Unlike the assertive "Look at me, listen to me, and tell me how wonderful I am" stance of the *lucky*, *self-defeating* men and women rank low on self-ratings which are in any way suggestive of assertive traits. *Self-defeating* women are also notably preoccupied with the past, and have often convinced themselves that old and often remembered humiliations cause their present misery. They rarely recall being as loved and protected as they had wished to be when very young. Life-stage differences, especially among the *self-defeating* women, provide further insight into the *self-defeating* process. The young of this type report problems in relating to their age peers of both sexes. Middle-aged *self-defeating* women tend to be depressed about their marriages, which they believe to be deteriorating. In many ways, their preoccupation with (little) stress resembles the response to acute stress characterized by intrusive, repetitive thoughts and emotions, as noted in clinical studies of persons who have sought psychiatric help as a consequence of sudden onsets of serious stress (Horowitz and Becker, 1972). Such patients, however, many of whom were undergoing catastrophic stresses, usually recover, while among the *self-defeating* men and women in our study negative thoughts and feelings become the principal mode of experiencing life.

Among the heavily stressed, we find that intrapersonal characteristics, such as negative self-image and preoccupation with death, which so clearly distinguished between the two lightly stressed groups, do not differentiate between the *challenged* (mainly men) and the *overwhelmed*. In the face of the reality of considerable stress, perhaps resulting from a way of life that they to some extent deliberately chose, it is close interpersonal relationships—or their absence—that influences their degree of preoccupation with stressful experiences. On ratings of mutuality and emotional involvement with family, the *challenged* rank the highest among the four stress types, and the *overwhelmed* the lowest. This difference is found most strikingly in the young men. *Challenged* middle-aged men are not notable for their capacity for mutality, reciprocity, or the capacity for intimacy, but among late middle-aged *challenged* men these characteristics emerge as a major resource in coping with stress.

In some ways, *challenged* men resemble the "Type A" reported by Friedman and Rosenman and their colleagues (1974), populations at risk of heart attack or stroke. They are intelligent, open to new experience, and the least likely to have developed self-protective (or stress-avoidant) lifestyles (we did not assess competitiveness directly—a major characteristic of "Type A"). Some, while "well-adapted" psychologically, are suffering from rather severe physical impairments. At the same time, their own assessments of their health status are far more optimistic than is true for those men whom we call *overwhelmed*, exposed to much stress and dwelling on it at length. *Challenged* men, in fact, seem to be denying to themselves and others that they had any problems at all. One might conclude that their stress reactions are in the physical sphere, whereas those more likely to dwell on their problems at length may be of a verbal response type (Lazarus, 1970).

For the most part, the middle-aged women in this study do have close interpersonal relationships, and confidants who may or may not be their spouses. Although having such a resource is of considerable importance to our *challenged* men, it does not seem to provide strength for women, few of whom are in the *challenged* category, and many of whom are defeated by little stress. Having close relationships does not prevent a proliferation of symptoms which many of those confronting the post-parental stage report. Why? At this point, we can only speculate that sex and class differences in the impact of social change may prove to be a major explanation. Middle-aged (as well as younger) women in our society—perhaps as never before—

are expressing their needs for autonomy and self-assertion. But among the middle and lower middle class groups we are studying, there may well be more suppression than expression of such needs. If a woman's closest confidant is her husband, she is likely to get little support, because he is a firm upholder of traditional sex roles, and his needs are changing in the direction of closer relationships, though perhaps more toward receiving than giving nurturance and support. If another woman is her closest confidant, they may well reinforce each other's conflicts and sense of hopelessness and resignation (Fiske, 1979).[7]

## INTRAPERSONAL RESOURCES—AND LACK THEREOF

*Among the Elderly.* The Normal and Abnormal Aging studies located many, often impaired, elderly people who were living alone, some quite isolated (regardless of socioeconomic status) but clinging to life with a strength of determination that usually was dignified and sometimes heroic. Those of us who knew our informants at first hand were intrigued with the question as to why some who had few or no supportive networks or interpersonal relationships could transcend, or at least cope with, the pain, burdens, and frailties of old age, while others succumbed to alcohol, depression, or—especially if male—to suicide. The life histories of the intensively studied subsamples were searched for explanations. One of the more important hypotheses emerging from this analysis was that styles of coping with stress developed in earlier stages of their lives may be a continuing source of strength, an hypothesis which later led to the development of the stress typology in the Transitions Study, which we have just discussed. One 84 year old man, for example, was rightly proud of his skill in housing and feeding himself well on $40.00 a month (this was, the reader should be hurriedly reminded, in the very early 1960s), a feat which challenged him—and accomplishing it made him feel exuberant, as had coping with similar problems during the Great Depression three decades earlier. Conversely, having had very little stress in earlier life appeared to ill-prepare the elderly for coping with those of old age, and aroused our interest in the time-dimensions of stress.

[7]For more detailed analyses of intimate relations, and of friendship and other networks as resources in coping with the problems of later life, the following references and their respective bibliographies may be helpful: Lowenthal and Weiss, 1976, pp. 10–15; Weiss and Lowenthal, 1975; Weiss, 1978; Lowenthal and Robinson, 1976.

In examining the relationship between other intrapersonal characteristics such as self-concept, time perspective and morale, and mental health or illness on the one hand and morale or sense of well-being on the other, unexpected variations appeared. Low morale was by no means necessarily associated with a diagnosis of mental impairment (Clark and Anderson, 1967; Lowenthal, 1968; Lowenthal *et al.*, 1967; Simon, Lowenthal, and Clark, 1970). Nor was self-concept, which does almost always show a very strong association with morale. The sense of inner control, which we conceive as an important dimension of self-concept, was one of the personal characteristics associated with high morale. Unfortunately, the concept of inner vs. outer control, though a popular one, is beset by shortcomings, especially, although not only, methodological ones. That the sense of personal control was well worth further effort was, then, another important conclusion drawn from our studies of the elderly. While some old and very old people felt that they were buffeted about by others or by fate, the best adapted often reported that growing old provided opportunities for decisions and choices about the uses of their time, energy, and other interests and resources which the demands of middle age had, in retrospect, almost eliminated from their lives. But such recollections and retrospections, as we know, often change (and quite interestingly so) with changing life circumstances.

Our assessment of the detailed life histories also generated the hypothesis that continuity in basic values is a very important source of inner strength. In discussing how they reared their children, many of these people, who were "young-old" or "old-old" in the early 1960s, spoke with pride and satisfaction of how they had adhered to the values of their own parents. Although a few of them felt that one or more of their offspring had eluded them, they found great satisfaction in having tried. Many of these eventual San Franciscans had themselves been reared in rural areas or small towns across the country, and while there were some confessions about having been unruly as adolescents, they were nostalgic, and envied their own parents for having lived in settings where the transmission of traditional values was easier. Their emphasis, unlike that of today's middle-aged parents, was more on change in setting than on "changing times."

There were, then, a number of findings in the aging studies bearing on consistency and inconsistency in intrapersonal adaptive modes and resources that served as hypotheses guiding the design of the Longitudinal Study of Transitions.

Particularly challenging was the opportunity to explore whether continuity of coping modes are paralleled by continuity in adaptive level, or whether certain coping styles become obsolete at sequential life stages. Examining people in earlier life stages in the light of what we first learned from old people, also enabled us to begin to develop further insight into developmental as contrasted with cohort or sociohistorically induced differences between generations. From this perspective, analysis of the in-depth interviews conducted for the Transitions Study gave rise to strong suspicion that there is a widening gap between the values and life styles of, say, artists and intellectuals and "mainstream" Americans, and that it has become far wider than it was before, and perhaps during, World War II. One critical difference seems to be in the opportunity to be alone, which the nature of their work forces upon teachers, researchers, and artists of various kinds, at least from time to time, but far less so on the vast majority of urban dwellers. Among others, Barron (1963), in his studies of creativity and creative people, and Maslow (1954/1970) in his early work on the "self-actualizing" (whom he had a great deal of difficulty in tracking down), have noted stronger needs for periodic solitude than is found among others. For most Americans, the shift from a primarily rural to a dominantly urban society, and the rapid growth of the mass media in the late 1930s and throughout the 1940s may well have reduced not only the opportunity but the capacity for being alone, and along with it the kind of occasional introspection and self-assessment essential to self-knowledge and growth, however modest.

*The Intrapersonal Resources of the Middle and Late Middle-Aged.* The hypothesis that stability of values and goals is a significant component of good adaptation (Lowenthal, 1971) is not supported among the middle and late middle-aged cohorts studied in this more recent historical period (1969 and on, compared with 1960–68 for the previously studied older groups). Quite the contrary, in fact, though a moderate trend toward stabilization of values and goals does seem to occur among people in the Transitions Study who are in their sixth decade (Thurnher, publication pending).

In the initial (cross-sectional) analyses of these cohorts, we found that the values of the two younger groups (high school seniors and newlyweds) were in an expansive, growth-oriented direction. The late middle-aged differed from those about ten years younger primarily in a trend toward valuing a comfortable lifestyle. Among the younger middle-aged men, values relating to work and family were associated with a sense of well-being; among the older, it was the self-protective and more self-centered values relating to ease and contentment (Lowenthal *et al.*, 1975) that were associated with a sense of satisfaction with life. These older men were about the same age as the men in the Grant Study, recently followed up by Vaillant (1977), and on the average ten years younger than the Terman gifted men restudied by R. Sears (1977). Unlike the more privileged men in the Grant and Terman samples, the men in the Transitions Study show few signs of growth. Indeed, the subjective sense of growth was not highly valued, nor did it relate to adaptive level in any of our assessments (Thurnher, 1975). These findings reflect important differences between "elitist" and "typical" samples, and may well explain why it has proven difficult to replicate research using developmental stage frameworks in the study of psychosocial change in adulthood (Lowenthal, 1977; Neugarten, 1977; Riegel, 1977; Simpson, 1974).

Because the meanings and values we invest in life are reflected by our commitments, we shall explore in some detail what we are learning in the Transitions Study, with special emphasis here on intrapersonal commitments such as integrity. As we have suggested, changes not associated with growth and meaning are satisfying and comfortable for many middle-aged people, especially those who are overwhelmed or defeated by the stresses of their lives; they are relieved to be able to adopt increasingly self-protective modes of living. Many believe they deserve rest and relaxation, and on the basis of their evidence, there is little reason to disagree with them. Others continue to feel challenged by life, and retain vital concerns not directed toward the avoidance of stress, self-protectiveness or indulgence, or living a long time, as ends in themselves.

Let us first define the individual's commitments as the patterning or configuration, sometimes hierarchical, of the fundamental concerns he or she harbors at a particular time. This inner gestalt is drawn upon, consciously or otherwise, in organizing one's thoughts, and in turn allots priority to one kind of choice, decision, behavior, or activity in preference to another. The commitment pattern thus influences one's disposition of time. After close study of, or listening to, a life history, sometimes including those collected as "first interviews" for therapeutic purposes, an insightful reader or listener can usually trace the pattern of these inner concerns and priorities, whether or not the person telling his life story is aware of them. In the in-depth study of people in the Transitions Study, we thus far have traced four domains of

commitment: (1) a cluster which includes curiosity, mastery, and creativity; (2) commitment to other people, which we have discussed under interpersonal resources in the preceding section; (3) to concerns which transcend the self-in-present-networks and emanate from an awareness of the importance of nurturing integrity in one's self and others; and (4) to self-protectiveness, including lifelong psychopathological self-centeredness or extreme narcissism, but more often, in this sample, a concern which becomes strengthened in the course of aging.

Among the more clear-cut patterns of commitment we have found in our ongoing study is one we call the diversified, manifest among people about equally committed to the three substantive spheres of their lives we are examining. At the other extreme are those who put nearly all of their eggs into one commitment basket. The surprise came, however, when we assessed change in commitment patterns five years after the initial contact.

Despite the fact that most people in each stage had experienced the same kind of life course transition in the intervening years, there was a great deal of variation in the ways in which they had rearranged their configurations of commitment. We were surprised because, in line with our hypotheses, we had expected to find considerable consistency over time, and because each group had experienced the same kind of "typical" transition for their life stage—to the empty nest in one, for example, and to retirement in another. The following graphs for particular individuals illustrate the great variability of the changes which actually took place in five years. It is no doubt of some relevance that both the middle-aged woman and the man whose commitment changes we more or less randomly selected to graph happened to have changed jobs in the interval.

When we first talked with her, 42-year-old Mrs. M. R. had been divorced for a few years, her son, who lived with her, was a senior in high school, and she held a very responsible secretarial job. She was also studying for a professional degree and was highly committed both to her son's welfare and to her new, self-chosen field. Disillusioned by a difficult early marriage and a later unhappy love affair, she was also highly protective of herself, in hope of achieving a more satisfying life through a new career. Five years later, she was close to her objectives, having been offered an interesting and prestigious new job, and no longer feeling responsible for her son who was happily married and pursuing his own goals. As her chart shows, her positive commitments had become more balanced, and she had become dramatically less self-protective.

Mr. F. C., a 45-year-old former navy career man, had a small business of his own when we first met him. His major concern had long been financial security, and at that time he was achieving it to his own satisfaction. Five years later, he had bought a new, smaller business and was doing very well financially. Despite his success in work, and the fact that difficulties in his relationship with one of his daughters had straightened out, he had become much more cynical—and he was also bored. He has all along found his marriage "not the greatest," though he does not seem to mind spending time with his wife. In the five-year interval, he reports, he had been hard hit by the realization that his life was quite empty despite the security and material comfort he had achieved. He regrets not having had a professional career, finds his work "not worthwhile," and now says "the money doesn't mean a goddam thing . . . . I'm just not a happy person." His decline in all commitments except the self-protective is the most drastic in this middle-aged

group. We are eager to see him again, because at the time represented in his chart, he was healthy, not yet fifty, and equipped with a sense of humor (though to be sure a cynical one). Is he in a midlife crisis which he will resolve, or in a permanent slump?

Another way to examine such changes is to place each individual within the context of his or her life stage group. For example, we have graphed the change in commitment to mastery among late middle-aged (late fifties) women, and one showing changes in this same commitment among men in the somewhat younger (late forties) "empty nest" stage. The late middle-aged women were more likely to have increased their self-assertive, mastery commitments than to have relinquished them. Many increased their concern with such self-expression to a very significant extent. By contrast, men in the somewhat younger empty-nest phase rarely showed such dramatic increases in mastery.

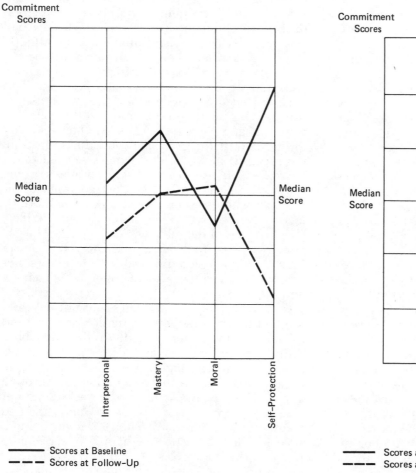

——— Scores at Baseline
− − − Scores at Follow-Up

**Figure 15–1**  Empty-nest Female (subject #31)

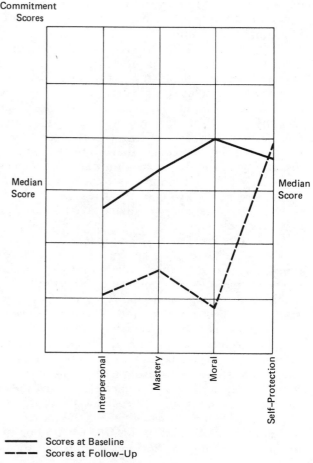

——— Scores at Baseline
− − − Scores at Follow-Up

**Figure 15–2**  Empty-nest Male (subject #27)

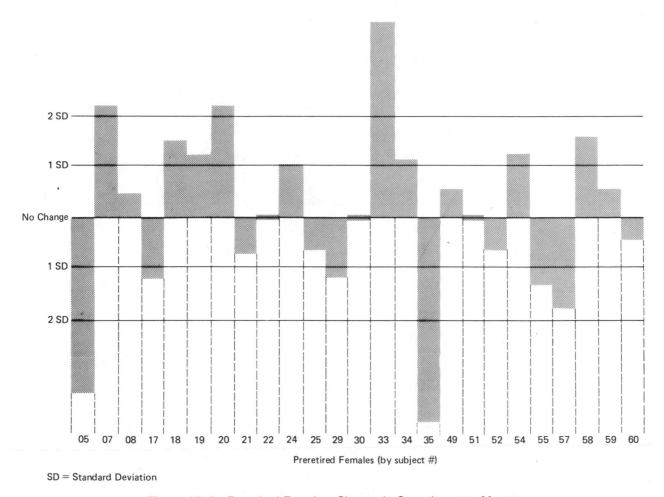

**Figure 15–3**  Preretired Females: Change in Commitment to Mastery

Among middle-aged men, the commitments to mastery and competence may or may not be readily realized in the work arena. In the still male-dominant occupational structures of our society, men usually have few conflicts, and at least some work satisfactions, up until the time they reach their occupational "peak." When the peaking occurs, in the late thirties and early forties as it does for the majority of men in our culture, it is followed by many years of boredom on the job, if not, as in the case of Mr. F. C., sheer hatred of it. Some time after occupational peaking, the eventual retirement stage becomes a pervasive theme in the thoughts and conversations of these men, even though the actual event may be twenty years in the future. Many say they are anxious about money, but this is not always a realistic worry. Children of the Great Depression, many chose their jobs in large part because of the security their pensions and other benefits provide. Though not accustomed to speaking in such terms, some of them are

worried about a quite different problem; what, when the time comes, are they going to be able to do to retain a sense of self-esteem? On the other hand, is there anything they really want to do? That their conflicts are only partly conscious is suggested in projective materials, where strong *inter*-personal needs emerge. Not only the "middle majority" people of our Transitions Study, but the highly educated, self-appraising, and often very successful men in the Vaillant (1977) and Sears (1977) studies begin, in middle or late age, to value their interpersonal relationships at least as much as their work. Underlying motives for this change, however, may vary. The upper-middle and middle class men of the latter two studies seem to express a need for better balance in their lives, and to nurture as well as to be nurtured. Many men in the Transitions Study appear to wish to be taken care of, indulged, and supported.

Women in the Transitions Study, as they seek more self-assertion, become less committed in the

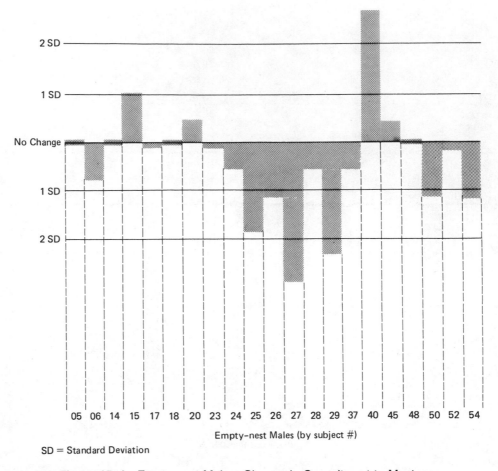

2 SD ———

1 SD ———

No Change

1 SD

2 SD

05 06 14 15 17 18 20 23 24 25 26 27 28 29 37 40 45 48 50 52 54

Empty–nest Males (by subject #)

SD = Standard Deviation

**Figure 15–4** Empty-nest Males: Change in Commitment to Mastery

interpersonal domain. Among women in Terman's gifted group, however, no such trend is apparent (P. Sears and Barbee, 1977). Few of our women are committed to their occupations, if they have one, and at middle age many became aware of a need for more satisfying outlets. These criss-crossing directions of change in commitments among "middle majority" men and women in middle life may or may not result in, or exacerbate, marital discord, depending in part on timing. If wife and husband become aware of the change in their needs at about the same time, the conflicts within each of them (as well as between them) may become difficult, if not impossible, to resolve. They come to fear that a resolution which would meet the needs of one would frustrate those of the other, and threaten the marriage. Some women in the Transitions Study find a compromise solution: they stay home and become increasingly assertive there, and, instead of responding to their husbands' increasing needs for nurturance and affection, they

become more "bossy," as many middle and late middle-aged husbands are quick to complain.

Looking at our findings in terms of changes in the intrapersonal resource which includes mastery, competence, and effectance, we see that middle and lower-middle class men come to invest less and less of themselves in this domain because of work frustrations and boredom of long duration. At the same time, many of their female counterparts are trying to strengthen and express their potential for self-expression. While some come quickly to feel frustrated and resigned as a result of opposition from their husbands and lack of outlets in their milieux, for the determined few who find appropriate arenas the sense of competence and achievement becomes a major intrapersonal resource.

Our concept of that domain of commitment which transcends self-interest resembles those of generativity and integrity, though not in sequence as proposed in Erik Erikson's well-known chart.

Indeed, systematic studies of many lives, lived in many walks of life, have disposed me to the view that commitment to one's own integrity, and respect and support for that of others (generativity) may become a major commitment very early in adulthood, perhaps even as early as adolescence. The *maturing* of this commitment, like those to other people, and to mastery/competence, is a *continuing* process which evolves in a variety of arenas, which themselves may change with normative and idiosyncratic transitions of adulthood. During this process, some people embrace commitments which extend beyond self-expression and concern with close others. Through the capacity of love for particular others, such people develop concern for, and a sense of unity with ever-widening circles of humanity. In our culture and our time, such altruistic commitments rarely become the principal domain of life, and the Eleanor Roosevelts are few—perhaps in all cultures and all times. Still, many people, in all walks of life, recognize this kind of concern, and on occasion sense it in themselves. My own preliminary studies have thus far convinced me that this domain of living, small or all-embracing, represents one commitment, not two, as envisaged by Erikson and, more recently, Norton.[8]

The kinds of choices and behaviors that are the observable (and, we believe, measurable) reflection of this commitment (and others) change with the varying arenas of the adult life course. The extent to which these arenas inhibit, tolerate, or foster the expression and fulfillment also varies with time. A genuine commitment to the fostering of integrity in others, for example, may have to be expressed differently in successive historical periods. For example, our concept of the commitment to integrity of self and generalized others would embrace what Erikson calls generativity, a sense of responsibility for the next and succeeding generations. The expression of commitment, however, becomes more difficult as the rapidity of social change widens the gap between generations and even sub-generations. Since the Middle Ages, at least in the Western part of the world, the conscious task of many university students has been not only to learn but to question the heritage of wisdom bequeathed them by their elders. The middle-aged and older leaders in those societies did not feel particularly threatened in their own

commitments, because such changes as came about in value systems were usually very gradual. There was no instant communication from town to town, and no near-instant travel from country to country. In more recent times, questioning by the young has moved with quicker, pendulum-like swings, especially since World War I and the ensuing Great Depression. During and after those two periods there was considerable dis-ease and some rebellion, not only among the young (many now grandparents of adolescents) but *their* parents, the great-grandparents of today's young, as well. There was an outburst of "liberation" and of remarkable creativity in the arts, often with strong political messages. The message, however, was little heeded by politicians of the West, except for a few (Woodrow Wilson, for example) who soon came to be dubbed dreamy-eyed idealists.

World War II had a quite different impact on young adults. At its end, family and tradition-centered norms were again accepted, and with evidence of relief, by the majority of the then young (the children of World War I veterans), and this was true in countries as different in their recent history as the United States and Germany (Fried and Fiske, 1949). Remember all the child-centeredness and family togetherness features flooding the women's journals of the late 1940s and early 1950s? The world was shrinking, impinging, and World War II had made those of us who were the young adults then, realize, as the majority of the young of former generations had not, that it could be unbelievably brutal and cruel as well. Home became the refuge, and the more pre-World War I values we could muster, the safer and more sheltered we would feel in our snug havens. The other side of the coin, of course, was what sociologists soon came to label as "anomie," the individual's sense that he or she can do little or nothing in the face of such overwhelming forces of evil and terror as those unleashed in Germany, Italy, Japan, and, as it turned out, the Soviet Union as well. The anomie was confounded with frustration engendered by mushrooming layers of bureaucracy and baffling new technologies especially, but not only, computers, succeeding each other every year or two. Most of us also became aware of the growing power of the military and industrial complexes in many Western countries, combines which were rapidly acquiring political influence, national and international, and which have further undermined the individual's sense of potency as a citizen. When the locus of control shifts away from the majority of people in a country, and now internationally as well, the effect is not limited to our roles as citi-

[8]The philosopher Norton (1976) also conceives two developmental stages or "states," one called integrity and one generativity. While Erikson identifies generativity as a stage prior to that of integrity. Norton's schema reverses this order.

zens—it pervades family and work spheres, shakes our self-confidence, and makes inroads on our zest for life (Crespi, 1966).

Then came Korea and Vietnam, and the student rebellions of the 1960s. After the anomie and retreatism of most of those young in the late 1940s and early 1950s, the renewed activism among youth was heady, for themselves and for many of their elders as well, including some parents and teachers of university students (certainly not the middle-aged parents in the Transitions Study). Whether or not they agreed with the philosophies and actions of their offspring and students, at least they were doing something, and that was far better, for most liberals at least, than the passivity of the young in the previous decade. And now in the 1970s: no hippies in the Haight; studious and ambitious young people in the professional schools, as well as in all academic programs. In one twenty-year generation, then, we have had three quite different "generations" of young people, only the oldest of which is now middle-aged and late middle-aged. While the shrinking of "generations" may be occurring even more rapidly in some developing countries, in most Western societies, it proceeds at a far more rapid pace than when today's late middle-aged people were entering adulthood. Today's parents of adolescents are not cast beyond the pale in the way "over-thirty" people were in the 1960s. But five years from now, there may be yet another swing of the pendulum. If another economic disaster—or a war—occurs in the 1980s, *that* decade's adolescents and young adults may well rebel, though perhaps differently from those who were young in the 1960s.

At such a pace, we might ask, what salience can "generativity" or "legacy" (Butler, 1970) have in the transmission of commitments and values? Some say the best one can do is teach the young to be flexible enough to bow with whatever winds of change may blow. Others believe that we are once more witnessing a change toward the strengthening of traditional values. While *Roots* (Haley, 1976) portrays the quest of a black man for identity, it may be symbolic of a long overdue trend toward renewal of awareness of continuity in history, through which we hope to find anchorage, meaning, and purpose, and a sense of continuity in our own lives and the generations before and after us. The fact that there were millions of readers and TV viewers of Haley's message may testify to a growing recognition that in tracing the paths from the past to the present, and assessing the latter in terms of the former, we strengthen our faith in ourselves—and our children—as molders of the future, but it is much too soon to say whether the seeming change is a trend or a passing fancy.

The conviction that one's life has meaning—harbored by most people committed to something other than, or in addition to, their own welfare, is the foundation of hope. Lowenthal *et al.* (1967) found such concepts to be remarkably well-supported in the previously discussed longitudinal study of six hundred people ranging in age from sixty to the early nineties. If it was true of those who were old and very old in the 1960s, the middle-aged and old of today have little reason for sloughing their major responsibility, despite the manifold and often traumatic changes they have confronted. In Norton's words:

> The object of whole-hearted commitment is not the world but oneself, as the moral task of self-actualization. This must be stressed because of the frequency with which persons in the situations of choice objectify the determinants of choice and neglect themselves. In effect such persons look to the world to make the choice for them. . . . They forget that what is to be decided is not what is, but what is to be done by themselves. . . . The possibilities of choice are not first in the world but initially in persons. . . . What one chooses whole-heartedly is the self one shall strive to become, *a becoming that contributes to the world* (1976, p. 195, italics supplied.)

In short, in doing our utmost to maintain the integrity of our own commitments, we foster and nurture that of others.

Lest this illustration of how personal change in one commitment domain is interwoven with societal change have too philosophical a conclusion for a scientific handbook, I should like to complete this section with as concise a statement as possible, at this writing, as to how a commitment paradigm may be translated into research methodology. Our commitments become observable in our choices, decisions, and behaviors. As we move through adulthood and old age, these commitment-linked behaviors change. By assessing such change, we can re-trace the commitment configuration and thereby the direction of change (i.e., toward growth/expansion, stagnation, or regression/constriction). The commitment paradigm is thus not a developmental model, although it provides for development. Being "open," it also accommodates a broad spectrum of socioeconomic and cultural samples. Moreover, since the commitment domains delineated thus far (interpersonal, self-expressive/assertive, altruistic, self-protective) are similarly manifest in changing choices, decisions, and behaviors in a variety of sociopolitical arenas, the paradigm also provides for a linkage between personal and societal change.

# TOWARD THE PRESERVATION
## OF MENTAL HEALTH IN LATER LIFE

Several suggestions for much-needed research have been made in the preceding sections. In the following, the emphasis will be on educational and clinical, as well as research, reorientations which might well enhance the possibilities for growth, dignity, and a sense of fulfillment in the latter part of life.

### STRENGTHENING THE RESOURCES OF THE ELDERLY

Consciously or not, many health professionals have acquired for themselves, or absorbed from their former teachers, a stance of therapeutic nihilism toward both the "young old" and the very old: the person who becomes mentally disturbed for the first time in later life is suffering from senile (or arteriosclerotic) brain damage, such brain damage is irreversible, ergo, some form of sedation, institutionalization (or both) is the best we can offer. Findings from the previously discussed Normal and Abnormal Aging studies conducted at UC San Francisco in the early 1960s, and of subsequent research in various centers across the country, demonstrate that this is an unwarranted assumption. To be sure, somewhat over a third of those hospitalized on the psychiatric screening wards were to die within a year, but these were generally people who suffered from serious and irreversible physical illness at the time of admission, with an accompanying Acute Brain Syndrome, which unfortunately accounted for the fact that they were not sent to medical wards. Of the survivors, after a few days on the screening wards, many resumed community living, and among those who were sent to state hospitals, nearly a quarter returned to the community within a year. Their improvement, physical, psychiatric, and in the capacity to take care of themselves, was often impressive. Even among those who remained in state hospitals, nearly as many improved as deteriorated, and in several respects.

While the possibility that time alone may have been responsible for improvement in the patients who spent some time in the state hospitals cannot be disproven, it can be pointed out (a) that time was not as kind to those who returned to the community directly from the screening wards; and (b) that many patients themselves attributed their improvement to physical and psychiatric treatment received at the hospital. That some with chronic brain syndrome might have benefited as much or more from different procedures is suggested by the follow-up study of a subsequent cohort of elderly patients who had the advantage of the services of the San Francisco Geriatric Screening Unit team which was developed in response to the needs made clear by the original research (Simon, Lowenthal, and Epstein, 1970). The fate of these patients suggests that older, like younger, people may experience periodic crises. And despite their age, their often poor physical condition, and the possible presence of chronic brain damage, many of the symptoms associated with such crises prove to be reversible or modified by appropriate treatment. Further, and most important to the improvement of clinical care, it is clear that severe depression often imitates chronic brain damage as assessed by customary mental performance tests and therefore is not treated. Finally, there is no doubt that if brain damage is present, an accompanying depression, which is by no means infrequent, severely aggravates its symptoms, which could be allocated.

The psychiatric improvement often noted following good, comprehensive medical (nonpsychiatric) treatment and care strongly indicated the need for geriatric acute treatment wards staffed by internists as well as psychiatrists. The symptoms of neglect subsequently found among the marginal group which was discharged from psychiatric screening wards back to the community dramatize with equal forcefulness the need for medical and psychiatric outpatient services for the elderly which were non-existent in 1959. In 1979, there is no indication of change, at least in the metropolitan area where the research was undertaken. A few private hospitals have asked this writer to serve on advisory planning boards for such an endeavour, but the professional barriers (and prejudices) between clinicians dealing, respectively, with mental and physical disorders have evidently thus far proven impenetrable.

The remarkable record of the medical/psychiatric screening unit team in practically eliminating geriatric first admissions to state hospitals within a very short time suggests two considerations vital for social planning. The first is that such mobile teams able to visit prospective inpatients in their homes can often alleviate crises and thus prevent the necessity for any type of institutionalization. The second, familiar to us all, is that boarding and family care home services need considerable expansion and considerable upgrading in the quality of the services provided to bring them up to the standards elderly psychiatric patients received at state hospitals. The media, in the past few years, have dramatized this need valiantly, but they have thus far focused mainly on nursing homes, and even in that segment, with appallingly few legislative results.

Theoretically, one way to improve mental health services for the elderly is through the recently required continuing education curricula for health professionals, which could provide a forum for a vigorous attack on therapeutic nihilism. In actuality, however, observation in sessions accredited for continuing education in this sphere soon makes it all too clear that the vast majority of participants find aging a boring or frustrating medical field, and though physically present at such "courses," their minds are clearly elsewhere. Their therapeutic nihilism is partly learned in medical schools (Spence, Feigenbaum, Fitzgerald, and Roth, 1968), and is thence spread to other health professionals and, all too often, to social planning bodies. Probably only the teaching physician can change this attitude, drawing upon known facts. It is to be hoped, too, that whether in psychiatry or internal medicine, such teachers will begin to break down their disciplinary barriers when dealing with the elderly, where the interdigitation of psyche and soma, and of person and milieu, becomes dramatically apparent (Lowenthal and Zilli, 1969).

Some persons suffering from psychogenic or organic disorders clinically appraised as serious, and exhibiting bizarre behavior and thought processes which are socially viewed as deviant, manage to survive, without treatment, in the community because they are capable of at least marginal self-maintenance. Were they to become dependent on others for the essentials of self-maintenance, or were they to come to the attention of a "decision-maker" in some official or semi-official capacity, they might well be sent to nursing homes. In the early 1960s, it was estimated that such persons comprised somewhere between two and three percent of the elderly population of the metropolitan area from which the community sample of the Normal and Abnormal Aging study was drawn. The closing of many state hospitals in the interim has probably doubled this percentage, at the very least, and the need for comprehensive physical and psychiatric outpatient services is therefore more acute than ever.

Among elderly people primarily suffering from organic brain disease (often in conjunction with physical illnessess or handicaps), outpatient facilities often do not suffice. It is among this group that supportive services, such as visiting nurses, home-making services, meals on wheels, but most importantly, visiting physicians and psychiatric social workers are urgently needed. Among community-resident aged who develop symptoms of the reversible acute brain syndrome, a frequent

occurrence among those suffering from alcoholism, heart disorders, or poor nutrition, hospitalization for two to four weeks should be insisted on, and their care should be provided in the as yet non-existent geriatric medical/psychiatric wards. We can only hope that former HEW Secretary Califano's "likes" (hopes? plans?) will find support in funding and action:

> At the peak of the State asylum system, it was easy to fix responsibility for meeting the needs of chronic patients. Despite their inadequacies, massive hospitals were in the business of providing the whole gamut of life-supporting services. We'd like to see a community-based system developed which is responsive to the needs of deinstitutionalized persons (Califano, 1977, p. 6).

Among the mentally ill and healthy alike, the prevalence of chronic physical impairment is considerable. Medical research can be expected to proceed apace, and it is to be hoped that the non-fatal illnesses of old age—often at least as stressful as terminal illness—will receive greater attention instead of an off-hand "to be expected at your age, just learn to live with it." If social policy becomes more oriented to providing older people with the means for access to the benefits not only of medical advances, but the "hows" of learning to live with disabilities, more of our elderly would enjoy at least somewhat better physical health which, in turn, our data suggest, will reduce their risk of mental illness. But the provision for easier access to clinic services for medical care, and to outpatient services for psychiatric care (which now, by and large, ignore the elderly) will not be enough. It has been shown, for instance, that those who were discharged from the county hospital screening wards and who were usually in the poverty ranks did not seek the medical care they obviously needed. Much more effort must be directed to informing and guiding older people, for a distressingly high proportion of them cannot be expected to take initiative themselves.

As dozens of mental health surveys and clinical observations testify, the distinction between mental health and illness is hazardous even among younger populations.[9] Among the elderly, the effort to make such a distinction is confounded by three other circumstances: (1) the perpetuation and proliferation of stereotypes about "normal" aging, which influence the self-perceptions of the older person and those of others in the milieu; (2) the fact that we are dealing not only with psychogenic disorders, but often with organic brain dam-

---

[9] For an excellent review of several perspectives on normality, see Offer and Sabshin, 1974.

age as well, the symptoms of which are often confusingly intermingled with emotional and behavioral responses to such damage; and (3) that, as already noted, symptoms of depression frequently resemble those of chronic brain damage, and the assumption of many clinicians is that the latter is the diagnosis of choice for persons over sixty.

The findings of the studies reviewed in this chapter and, a year or two earlier, in the *Handbook of Aging and the Social Sciences* (Binstock and Shanas, eds., 1976) and the *Handbook of the Psychology of Aging* (Birren and Schaie, eds., 1977) leave no doubt that the great majority of older people live independent and often productive lives even at advanced ages. Despite the increased risk of organic brain damage with age, their susceptibility to other kinds of psychiatric impairment is probably not notably greater than that of younger people, except for depression, which increases very markedly with age. The lack of notable increase in other kinds of psychiatric impairment in the sixties and early seventies may have a twofold explanation: "survival of the fittest" in the community (persons suffering severe psychogenic impairment, are, or at least were, likely to be institutionalized long before they are sixty); and the fact that some psychogenic disorders, including schizophrenia, "burn themselves out" with advancing age.

Insights into what may comprise "normal" aging are derivative at best, relying on self-reports which may reflect prevailing expectations rather than realistic self-appraisal, and they show considerable fluctuation, for better and for worse, over very short periods of time. Clinical judgements, which are also subject to change with the various and constantly changing frames of reference of most clinicians, are equally disputable, even among themselves. Decline in memory and energy may be normal aging symptoms. Such self-reports increase steadily with advancing age, but there is some evidence that they are primarily a reflection of internalization of cultural stereotypes. In view of the progressive decline in physical strength demonstrated in laboratory studies, to say nothing of the unanimity of introspective reports from forty- and even many thirty-year-olds, it seems reasonable to give more weight to the possibility that this type of loss may indeed be a "normal" one in aging. It will be interesting to see, as the exercise mania continues to spread through nearly all age levels of our society, whether older people of the 21st century complain less about energy loss.

There are some indications in the studies of Normal and Abnormal Aging that adjustment to health decline or other losses may be more gradual for women than for men. One explanation may be that most middle-aged and older women have already experienced considerably more physical and role changes such as pregnancies, child-births, menopause, the empty nest, and widowhood, than most men of their age, and these have conditioned them to adapting to change. The lack of association (among both sexes) between age-linked role loss and mental illness (as compared with low morale) in old age exercised a strong influence on the direction of our theoretical speculations. The morale measures showed reactions to losses in what Williams has called "position," defined as including the status and social-influence components of social roles (Williams, 1960). To the extent that an individual's former roles and status provide him or her with little prestige in their social milieux of old age may exacerbate the decline in the sense of well-being. That such losses, while causing low morale and "normal" depression, are not similarly related to the onset of mental illness in old age supports the possibility that ego-integrative tasks of the older person may be focused more on internal than on external reality (Neugarten, 1968b).

Many characteristics did prove to be associated with psychiatric impairment in later life, however, and the data themselves evoked the concept of "multiple deprivation." A potentially valuable contribution of future social/behavioral science and clinical research would be to separate those stresses which logically could be causative or predisposing to late life mental illness, such as physical illness, and those which could be either causative or consequential (such as low social interaction), and to avoid commingling measures of more or less objective circumstances (such as socioeconomic status) and subjective states (such as self-image).

## REDUCING THE HAZARDS AMONG THE MIDDLE AND LATE MIDDLE-AGED

From preventive, educational, therapeutic and research viewpoints, the changing and often conflicting needs of men and women in middle-to-late middle age present a challenge. In the lower middle class, it is the women within a year or two preceding and following the emptying of the nest who display a proliferation of symptoms, often for reasons they cannot explain, and they rarely receive much understanding from either their spouses or their adult children. Well-programmed and publicized educational programs may help, but it is going to take a long "out reach" indeed to help such women to escape entrapment for another twenty or more years in which they can expect to live in good health (and growth if they are sufficiently stimulated). An unprecedented new, often long, life stage has caught them—and us—all unaware. Meanwhile distressing proportions of these women, freed-up from child-rearing, and experiencing urges toward self-expression, are confronted with increasing demands for care and nurturance not only from their spouses, but from their parents and often their parents-in-law as well, a situation which, as we have noted, soon will worsen in geometric progression. With increasing frequency, too, adult children are returning home for free bed and board, often with their young children, after separations or divorces, and this circumstance proves far more stressful to most middle and late middle-aged parents than did the initial "on-time" emptying of the nest.

In the Longitudinal Study of Transitions, with three completed follow-up contacts and more to come, we have traced some of the influences of social change on women in this life stage. Among others are the now widely publicized shifts in traditional sex roles, which rapidly accelerated during this period, albeit mainly emanating from intellectuals (including graduate students) and popularized by the media. When the four groups of women were first studied, respectively, as seniors in high school, newlyweds, persons facing the empty nest, and those facing retirement (their husbands', their own, or both) toward the end of the 1960s, the women's liberation movement in the more privileged segments of our society was well under way. It had not yet flooded the press, radio, and television, and even younger women in the study either ignored or were unaware of it. In fact, the newlyweds, for example, were more likely than older women to report that their husbands were the "bosses" in their families (Thurnher, 1976). While such findings would support the Freudian hypothesis (Freud, 1933/1965) that women, unlike men, do not develop very much after young adulthood, this writer believes that to the extent that such a discrepancy exists, it has little to do with genetic or biological limitations. This statement is not meant to exclude the very strong possibility of biological-hormonal-instinctive drives for "nesting," but this normally entails merely a time lag in the development of self-generating commitments to spheres of life other than child-rearing, as is demonstrated especially by our women graduate students. Among girls and women in conservative, family-centered, and not highly educated segments of our society, sociocultural expectations and strictures are still major barriers. Among tradition-oriented women entering the post-parental phase, the mere possibility of new choices creates a turmoil of conflict.

Compared with the other groups in this study, the women whose last child was about to leave home had diffuse, ambivalent, and sometimes very negative concepts of themselves, and many psychiatric symptoms. Their child-bearing and child-rearing roles being nearly completed, they were confronting the question, sometimes acutely perceived, more often dimly, as to whether they had other potentialities which might yet be developed. In many ways they seemed to be undergoing identity crises or, in Erikson's terms, identity "diffusion" as severe as those usually attributed to adolescents. Some were desperately hoping to achieve greater intimacy with their husbands after their youngest child left home, as though sensing a need for an enhancement of themselves as individuals after what most considered to be the major, often self-sacrificing tasks of their lives had been completed. Eighteen months later, however, only about a third of them could report that their marital relationships had changed for the better. Under these circumstances, it is not surprising that they continued not to like themselves very much, nor to be satisfied with their lives. Some, not achieving closer relationships with their husbands after their youngest child departed, developed new commitments in ensuing five years, usually involving a new undertaking which may or may not have involved others. Those who did so, when interviewed five years after the initial encounter, had a much better opinion of themselves and were also much happier than those who made no changes in their lives. It was as though, their romantic dream of a second honeymoon unrealized, they had to realize themselves (though a few divorced and remarried and achieved the second honeymoon).

The plights of both the men (who, it will be recalled, were generally bored with their work) and women in this middle and lower middle class group suggests that we have an insufficiently researched puzzle, namely: When, if at all, does too little stress in itself become, so to say, stressful? The majority of working men and women (including housewives) in our society fill very routine jobs, physical or otherwise. Many become bored and resigned some 10 to 20 years before they retire, most often at whatever time in their lives they come to the realization that they are unlikely to be promoted. We all recognize boredom and its accompanying lassitude when we experience it, and conversely the stimulation of rising to a stressful or otherwise stimulating occasion. Boredom is one of the increasing hazards of growing older, but it has pretty much been ignored by social and behavioral scientists. It is, to be sure, a difficult concept to study, because the interplay between personal predispositions, boredom (or dullness) and situational context, makes it difficult to know where to start, with the person, the situation, the social milieu, or the social structure. The too little vs. too much stress issue should, nevertheless, have a high research priority, because it will help us to get at the fundamental question as to why some people maintain a zest for life and growth throughout their years, while others become resigned, stagnate, or wallow in self-pity. Thus far, we can only speculate about what the explanation is, but we do know that the increase in early, voluntary retirement among the majority of workers portends a late-middle and old-aged population whose primary stimulation is second hand, via the mass media. And we also know that vicarious mastery, while perhaps now and then providing a restful escape from the challenges of real living, can soon become a substitute for life.

We know that there are self-generating and evolving people at all ages and in all walks of life. But in comparing those growing older now with those who were growing older and very old 20 years ago, there appear to be fewer of them now. On the surface, it might appear that this change (a change in national character?) is similar to that noted years ago by David Riesman in *The Lonely Crowd* (1950), a further shift from inner to what he called other-directedness. But it is different from what he was in 1950. The nature or substance of this "other" to which we are directed is becoming a kind of socially constructed substitute for being *inner*-directed. Judging from their popularity, middle-aged as well as young people seem increasingly to want to be *told*—through encounter groups, "consciousness-raising," charismatic "religious" leaders, and the media which reports on them, what we "should" want, know, feel, and believe, as though drained of thoughts and feelings of their own.

That the more complex people in the Transitions Study, unlike those with less potential, had fewer satisfactions and lower morale as they grew older is a sobering fact, especially for those of us familiar with the optimistic concepts of self-actualization theorists such as Allport, Bühler, Goldstein, and Maslow. These scholars, however, (except for Goldstein) were generalizing from studies of the more privileged sectors of society, in which avenues for self-fulfillment are more accessible. For the potentially "self-realizing" lower middle class segment of our population, much more energy, initiative, and innovation is required on their part, and challenges from the outer world, if they are to grow from within. It is the anticipated fate of these complex "middle majority" people

that prompted our examination of the waxing, waning, and interplay of commitments at various adult life stages. In a society which blocks off new avenues of self-expression and growth for people beyond early middle age unless they are rich, powerful, or creative, we found that complexity and depth of commitment is sustained by very few.

One of the few serious educational groups in the country designed for middle-aged and older people, in part as a consequence of the findings of our Aging studies of the 1960s, testifies to the powerful appeal of an opportunity to continue to learn and grow. At the Fromm Institute for Lifelong Learning at the University of San Francisco, with its small but impressive faculty of emeriti scholars, hundreds of "students" have to be turned away each year. It should serve as an educational model for social planners as they become aware of the fact that there are still people who do not need to be told what to do, think, and feel, but to learn for themselves. History and philosophy, it should be added, are the most popular subjects of this Institute. As was true of the people providing the data for our pointing out the need for such opportunities, the student body includes many of keen curiosity but comparatively little education.

In fostering the commitment to learning, the middle and late-middle-aged strengthen their resources for coping with old age. For in very old age, many are left with only the commitment which was earlier the foundation of all others, namely the attribution of meaning to one's life—and thereby to other lives. Something more than a biological instinct or personal need for survival, this commitment, in later life, is manifest in the eagerness to live and to love, because, despite the infirmities that may prevent active pursuit of other commitments, their significance continues. Older people who know what they value, what is worth striving for, and how to love are a living symbol for the generations following them, even though the substance of their own concerns may differ. For such old people, life remains dignified, and death, while perhaps viewed with regret or sadness, holds no terrors, for they have truly lived their lives.

If we are to persuasively convey such messages as the need for opportunity for continued learning to educators, clinicians and policy makers, we researchers, young, middle-aged, and old, must work harder to translate the language we all too often use in talking and writing to each other into English as most of our countrymen know it. Our research archives are beginning to contain important messages, and as our population continues to shift its axis, there will be more educators, clinicians, and policy-makers willing, if not eager, to read and to listen to what we are learning. For our student researchers, I should like to conclude with a personal message: when you finish writing your dissertation take a month off, if you can, and then sit down and write it in twenty pages, without the superstructure we teachers most often require, and then send it to the president of your university, your doctor, and your congressman. The response—and there will usually be one—will prove propitious for the rest of your professional life.

# REFERENCES

ATCHLEY, R. C. 1976. Selected social and psychological differences between men and women in later life. *Journal of Gerontology, 31* (March), 204–211.

BALTES, P. B., AND WILLIS, S. L. 1977. Toward psychological theories of aging and development. *In,* J. E. Birren and K. W. Schaie (eds.), *Handbook of the Psychology of Aging,* pp. 128–154. New York: Van Nostrand Reinhold.

BARRON, F. 1963. *Creativity and Psychological Health.* New York: Van Nostrand Reinhold.

BINSTOCK, R. H., AND SHANAS, E. (Eds.). 1976. *Handbook of Aging and the Social Sciences.* New York: Van Nostrand Reinhold.

BIRREN, J. E., AND SCHAIE, K. W. (Eds.). 1977. *Handbook of the Psychology of Aging.* New York: Van Nostrand Reinhold.

BLAU, Z. S. 1961. Structural constraints on friendship in old age. *American Sociological Review, 26* (June), 429–439.

BLOCK, J., in collaboration with Haan, N. 1971. *Lives Through Time.* Berkeley, Ca.: Bancroft Books.

BRADBURN, N. M. 1969. *The Structure of Psychological Well-Being.* Chicago: Aldine.

BUTLER, R. 1963. The life review: An interpretation of reminiscence in the aged. *Psychiatry, 26* (February), 65–76.

BUTLER, R. 1970. Looking forward to what? The life review legacy and excessive identity vs. change. *American Behavioral Science, 14,* 121–128.

BUTLER, R. N. 1975. *Why Survive? Being Old in America.* New York: Harper and Row.

CALIFANO, J. A. 1977. Quoted in "Deinstitutionalization: The federal government joins the fray." *Behavior Today, VIII* (49), December 19, 6.

CHIRIBOGA, D. A. 1978. Evaluated time: A life course perspective. *Journal of Gerontology, 33,* 388–393.

CHIRIBOGA, D. A., AND LIEBERMAN, M. A. 1970. Relocation stress in the aged: A replication study. Paper presented at the 23rd Annual Meeting of the Gerontological Society, Toronto.

CHIRIBOGA, D. A., AND LOWENTHAL, M. F. 1975. Complexities of adaptation. *In,* M. Fiske Lowenthal, M. Thurnher, D. A. Chiriboga, and Associates, *Four Stages of Life: A Comparative Study of Women and Men Facing Transitions,* pp. 99–121. San Francisco: Jossey-Bass.

CLARK, M. 1967. The anthropology of aging: A new area for studies of culture and personality. *Gerontologist, 7*(1), 55–64.

CLARK, M., AND ANDERSON, B. G. 1967. *Culture and Aging: An Anthropological Study of Older Americans.* Springfield, Ill.: Charles C Thomas, 1967.

CRESPI, I. 1966. Some observations on the dimensions of satisfaction in the U.S. and other countries around the world. Paper presented at the American Association for Public Opinion Research Meetings, Swampscott, Massachusetts.

DURKHEIM, E. [1897] 1951. *Suicide,* (G. Simpson, ed.; J. A. Spaulding and G. Simpson, trans.). New York: Free Press.

ECKERT, J. K. 1977. Health status, adjustments, and social supports of older people living in center city hotels. Paper presented at the 30th Annual Scientific Meeting of the Gerontological Society, San Francisco (Novermber).

EISDORFER, C., AND WILKIE, F. 1977. Stress, disease, aging and behavior. *In,* J. E. Birren and K. W. Schaie (eds.), *Handbook of the Psychology of Aging,* pp. 251–275. New York: Van Nostrand Reinhold.

ERIKSON, E. H. [1950] 1963. *Childhood and Society.* New York: Norton.

ERIKSON, E. H. 1968. *Identity: Youth and Crisis.* New York: Norton.

ERIKSON, E. H. 1969. *Gandhi's Truth.* New York: Norton.

ERIKSON, E. H. 1975. *Life History and the Historical Moment.* New York: Norton.

ERIKSON, E. H. Themes of adulthood in the Freud-Jung correspondence. *In,* N. Smelser and E. Erikson (eds.), *Themes of Work and Love in Adulthood.* Cambridge: Harvard University Press (in press).

FELTON, B., LEHMANN, A. A., AND BURGIO, M. 1977. Social supports and life satisfaction among old and young SRO hotel tenants. Paper presented at the 30th Annual Scientific Meeting of the Gerontological Society, San Francisco (November).

FISKE, M. 1979. *Middle Age: The Prime of Life?* Life Cycle series, L. Kristal (ed.), London and New York: Harper and Row.

FREUD, S. [1933] 1965. Femininity. *In,* J. Strachey (trans. and ed.), *New Introductory Lectures on Psychoanalysis,* pp. 112–135. New York: Norton.

FRIED, E., AND FISKE, M. 1949. The dilemma of German youth. *Journal of Abnormal Psychology* (January).

FRIEDMAN, M., AND ROSENMAN, R. H. 1974. *Type A Behavior and Your Heart.* New York: Knopf.

FROMM, E. 1966. The problem of the Oedipus complex.

Paper presented at Langley Porter Neuropsychiatric Institute Conference, University of California, San Francisco.

GOULD, R. 1978. *Transformations: Growth and Change in Adult Life.* New York: Simon and Schuster.

GRINKER, R. R., AND SPIEGEL, J. P. 1945. *Men Under Stress.* Philadelphia: Blakiston Co.

GUTMANN, D. 1969. *The country of old men: Cross-cultural studies in the psychology of later life. Occasional Papers in Gerontology,* No. 5. Ann Arbor, Michigan: Institute of Gerontology, University of Michigan-Wayne State University.

GUTMANN, D. 1977. The cross-cultural perspective: Notes toward a comparative psychology of aging. *In,* J. E. Birren and K. W. Schaie (eds.), *Handbook of the Psychology of Aging,* pp. 302–326. New York: Van Nostrand Reinhold.

HAAN, N. 1972. Personality development from adolescence to adulthood in the Oakland Growth and Guidance studies. *Seminars in Psychiatry, 4,* 399–414.

HALEY, A. 1976. *Roots.* New York: Doubleday.

HODGES, R. Forthcoming. Ego mastery styles and the adult life course. Ph.D. dissertation, University of California, San Francisco.

HOLMES, T. H., AND RAHE, R. H. 1967. The social readjustment rating scale. *Journal of Psychosomatic Research, 11,* 213–216.

HOROWITZ, M. J., AND BECKER, S. S. 1972. Cognitive response to stress: Experimental studies of a "compulsion to repeat trauma." *Psychoanalysis and Contemporary Science, 1,* 258–305.

JANIS, I. L. 1958. *Psychological Stress: Psychoanalytic and Behavioral Studies of Surgical Patients.* New York: John Wiley.

JASLOW, P. 1976. Employment, retirement, and morale among older women. *Journal of Gerontology, 31* (March), 212–218.

JONES, H., AND BAYLEY, N. 1941. The Berkeley Growth Study. *Child Development, 12,* 167–173.

KIEFER, C. W. 1974. *Changing Cultures, Changing Lives: An Ethnographic Study of Three Generations of Japanese Americans.* San Francisco: Jossey-Bass.

KOHLBERG, L. 1973. Continuities in childhood and adult moral development revisited. *In,* P. B. Baltes and K. W. Schaie (eds.), *Life Span Developmental Psychology.* New York: Academic Press.

LANGNER, T. S., AND MICHAEL, S. T. 1963. *Life Stress and Mental Health: The Midtown Manhattan Study,* (Vol. 2). New York: The Free Press of Glencoe.

LAZARUS, R. S. 1966. *Psychological Stress and the Coping Process.* New York: McGraw-Hill.

LAZARUS, R. S. 1970. Cognitive and personality factors underlying threat and coping. *In,* S. Levine and N. A. Scotch (eds.), *Social Stress,* pp. 143–164. Chicago: Aldine.

LEVINSON, D. J., DARROW, C. N., KLEIN, E. B., LEVINSON, M. H., AND MCKEE, B. 1978. *Seasons of a Man's Life.* New York: Knopf.

LEWIS, A. 1958. Between guesswork and certainty in psychiatry. *Lancet, 1* (January 25), 170–175.

LIEBERMAN, G. 1976. The impact of parent concern on adult children. Paper presented at the 29th Annual Scientific Meeting of the Gerontological Society, New York.

LIEBERMAN, M. A. 1970. Crisis of the last decade of life: Reaction and adaptations. Invited paper, presented in Symposium on Mental Health of the Aged, 1970 Summer Institute, Gerontology Center, University of Southern California, Los Angeles.

LIEBERMAN, M. A., PROCK, V. N., AND TOBIN, S. S. 1968. Psychological effects of institutionalization. *Journal of Gerontology, 23* (July), 343–353.

LIFTON, R. J. 1976. *The Life of the Self.* New York: Simon and Schuster.

LOEVINGER, J. 1976. *Ego Development: Conceptions and Theories.* San Francisco: Jossey-Bass.

LOPATA, H. Z. 1973. *Widowhood in an American City.* Cambridge, Mass.: Schenkman.

LOWENTHAL, M. FISKE. 1964. Social isolation and mental illness in old age. *American Sociological Review, 29* (February), 54–70.

LOWENTHAL, M. FISKE. 1965. Antecedents of isolation and mental illness in old age. *Archives of General Psychiatry, 12* (March), 245–254.

LOWENTHAL, M. FISKE. 1968. The relationship between social factors and mental health in the aged. *In,* A. Simon and L. Epstein (eds.), *Aging in Modern Society,* Psychiatric Research Report 23, pp. 187–197. Washington, D. C.: American Psychiatric Association.

LOWENTHAL, M. FISKE. 1971. Intentionality: Toward a framework for the study of adaptation in adulthood. *Aging and Human Development, 2* (May), 79–95.

LOWENTHAL, M. FISKE. 1977. Toward a sociopsychological theory of change in adulthood and old age. *In,* J. E. Birren and K. W. Schaie (eds.), *Handbook of the Psychology of Aging,* pp. 116–127. New York: Van Nostrand Reinhold.

LOWENTHAL, M. FISKE, BERKMAN, P. L., AND ASSOCIATES. 1967. *Aging and Mental Disorder in San Francisco: A Social Psychiatric Study.* San Francisco: Jossey-Bass.

LOWENTHAL, M. FISKE, AND BOLER, D. 1965. Voluntary vs. involuntary social withdrawal. *Journal of Gerontology, 20* (July), 363–371.

LOWENTHAL, M. FISKE, AND CHIRIBOGA, D. A. 1973. Social stress and adaptation: Toward a life-course perspective. *In,* C. Eisdorfer and M. P. Lawton (eds.), *The Psychology of Adult Development and Aging,* pp. 281–310. Washington, D.C.: American Psychological Association.

LOWENTHAL, M. FISKE, AND HAVEN, C. 1968. Interaction

and adaptation: Intimacy as a critical variable. *American Sociological Review, 33*(1), 20–30.

LOWENTHAL, M. FISKE, AND ROBINSON, B. 1976. Social networks and isolation. *In,* R. Binstock and E. Shanas (eds.), *Handbook of Aging and the Social Sciences,* pp. 432–456. New York: Van Nostrand Reinhold.

LOWENTHAL, M. FISKE, THURNHER, M., CHIRIBOGA, D. A., AND ASSOCIATES. 1975. *Four Stages of Life: A Comparative Study of Women and Men Facing Transitions.* San Francisco: Jossey-Bass.

LOWENTHAL, M. FISKE, AND TRIER, M. 1967. The elderly ex-mental patient. *International Journal of Social Psychiatry, XIII*(2, Spring), 101–114.

LOWENTHAL, M. FISKE, AND WEISS, L. 1976. Intimacy and crises in adulthood. *In.* J. N. Whiteley (ed.), *Counseling Adults,* special issue of *The Counseling Psychologist, 6*(1), 10–15.

LOWENTHAL, M. FISKE, AND ZILLI, A. (eds.). 1969. *Interdisciplinary Topics in Gerontology: Colloquium on Health and Aging of the Population,* (Vol. 3). New York and Basel: S. Karger.

MADDOX, G. L., AND WILEY, J. 1976. Scope, concepts and methods in the study of aging. *In,* R. Binstock and E. Shanas (eds.), *Handbook of Aging and the Social Sciences,* pp. 3–34. New York: Van Nostrand Reinhold.

MARRIS, P. 1975. *Loss and Change.* New York: Doubleday/ Anchor Books.

MASLOW, A. H. [1954] 1970. *Motivation and Personality.* New York: Harper and Row.

MAYER, N. 1978. *The Male Midlife Crisis: Fresh Starts After 40.* New York: Doubleday.

MCCLELLAND, D. 1975. *Power: The Inner Experience.* New York: Irvington Publishers.

MERTON, R. K., FISKE, M., AND KENDALL, P. [1948] 1955. *The Focused Interview.* Glencoe, Ill.: The Free Press.

NEUGARTEN, B. L. (ed.). 1968a *Middle Age and Aging.* Chicago: University of Chicago Press.

NEUGARTEN, B. L. 1968b. Adult personality: Toward a psychology of the life cycle. *In,* B. L. Neugarten (ed.), *Middle Age and Aging,* pp. 137–147. Chicago.: University of Chicago Press.

NEUGARTEN, B. L. 1977. Personality and aging. *In,* J. E. Birren and K. W. Schaie (eds.), *Handbook of the Psychology of Aging,* pp. 626–649. New York: Van Nostrand Reinhold.

NEUGARTEN, B. L., AND GUTMANN, D. L. 1968. Age-sex roles and personality in middle age: A thematic apperception study. *In,* B. L. Neugarten (ed.), *Middle Age and Aging,* pp. 58–71. Chicago: University of Chicago Press.

NORTON, D. L. 1976. *Personal Destinies: A Philosophy of Ethical Individualism.* Princeton, N.J.: Princeton University Press,

OFFER, D., AND SABSHIN, M. 1974. *Normality: Theoretical and Clinical Concepts of Mental Health* (Revised edition). New York: Basic Books.

PALMORE, E. 1975. *The Honorable Elders.* Durham, N.C.: Duke University Press.

PARSONS, T., AND SHILS, E. A. (eds.). 1962. *Toward a General Theory of Action.* New York: Harper Torchbooks.

PIAGET, J. 1972. Intellectual evolution from adolescence to adulthood. *Human Development, 15*(1), 1–12.

RIEGEL, K. F. 1975a. Toward a dialectical theory of development. *Human Development, 18,* 50–64.

RIEGEL, K. F. 1975b. Adult life crises: A dialectic interpretation of development. *In,* N. Datan and L. H. Ginsberg (eds.), *Life Span Developmental Psychology: Normative Life Crises,* pp. 97–124. New York: Academic Press.

RIEGEL, K. F. 1977. History of psychological gerontology. *In,* J. E. Birren and K. W. Schaie (eds.), *Handbook of the Psychology of Aging,* pp. 70–102. New York: Van Nostrand Reinhold.

RIESMAN, D., WITH DENNEY, R., AND GLAZER, N. 1950. *The Lonely Crowd.* New Haven, Ct.: Yale University Press.

ROSOW, I. 1974. *Socialization to Old Age.* Berkeley, Ca.: University of California Press.

ROSOW, I. 1976. Status and role change through the life span. *In,* R. Binstock and E. Shanas (eds.), *Handbook of Aging and the Social Sciences,* pp. 457–482. New York: Van Nostrand Reinhold.

ROTHENBERG, A. 1971. The process of Janusian thinking in creativity. *Archives of General Psychiatry, 24* (March), 195–205.

SEARS, P., AND BARBEE, A. 1977. Career and life satisfaction among Terman's gifted women. *In,* J. Stanley, W. George, and C. Solano (eds.), *The Gifted and the Creative: A Fifty Year Perspective,* pp. 28–65. Baltimore: Johns Hopkins University Press.

SEARS, R. 1977. Sources of life satisfactions of the Terman gifted men. *American Psychologist, 32* (February), 119–128.

SELYE, H. 1956. *The Stress of Life.* New York: McGraw-Hill.

SELYE, H. 1974. *Stress Without Distress.* New York: New American Library/Signet Books.

SHANAS, E. 1962. *The Health of Older People: A Social Survey.* Cambridge, Mass. Harvard University Press.

SHANAS, E., AND MADDOX, G. 1976. Aging, health, and the organization of health resources. *In,* R. Binstock and E. Shanas (eds.), *Handbook of Aging and the Social Sciences,* pp. 592–618. New York: Van Nostrand Reinhold.

SHEEHY, G. 1976. *Passages: Predictable Crises of Adult Life.* New York: E. P. Dutton.

SIMON, A., LOWENTHAL, M. F., AND CLARK, M. 1970. Summary of studies in normal and abnormal aging. Final report to the National Institute of Mental Health (March 6).

Simon, A., Lowenthal, M. F., and Epstein, L. 1970. *Crisis and Intervention: The Fate of the Elderly Mental Patient.* San Francisco: Jossey-Bass.

Simpson, E. L. 1974. Moral development research: A case study of scientific cultural bias. *Human Development, 17* (2), 81–106.

Singer, M. T. 1963. Personality measurements in the aged. *In,* J. E. Birren, R. N. Butler, S. W. Greenhouse, L. Sokoloff, and M. R. Yarrow (eds.), *Human Aging,* pp. 217–249. Washington, D.C.: U.S. Government Printing Office.

Spence, D. L., Feigenbaum, E. M., Fitzgerald, F., and Roth, J. 1968. Medical student attitudes toward the geriatric patient. *Journal of the American Geriatrics Society, 16,* 976–983.

Stephens, J. 1975. Society of the alone: Freedom, privacy, and utilitarianism as dominant norms in the SRO. *Journal of Gerontology, 30*(March) 230–235.

Streib, G. 1976. Social stratification and aging. *In,* R. H. Binstock and E. Shanas (eds.), *Handbook of Aging and the Social Sciences,* pp. 160–185. New York: Van Nostrand Reinhold.

Streib, G. F., and Schneider, C. J. 1971. *Retirement in American Society: Impact and Process.* Ithaca, N.Y.: Cornell University Press.

Thurnher, M. 1975. Continuities and discontinuities in value orientations. *In,* M. F. Lowenthal, M. Thurnher, D. Chiriboga, and Associates, *Four Stages of Life: A Comparative Study of Women and Men Facing Transitions,* pp. 176–200. New York: Van Nostrand Reinhold.

Thurnher, M. 1976. Midlife marriage: Sex differences in evaluations and perspectives. *International Journal of Aging and Human Development, 17*(2), 129–135.

Thurnher, M. 1977. Becoming old: Perspectives on women and marriage. *In,* Symposium: Socialization to Become an Old Woman, 85th Annual Convention of the American Psychological Association, San Francisco (August).

Thurnher, M. Value change across the adult life course: A longitudinal study. (*Journal of Personality and Social Psychology.* (Publication pending, Human Development and Aging Program, University of Calif., San Francisco.)

Vaillant, G. 1977. *Adaptation to Life.* Boston: Little, Brown, and Co.

Vidal, G. 1978. Burt and Labelle and Jimmy and God. *The New York Review* (June 29), 21.

Weiss, L. 1978. Interpersonal intimacy and adaptation to stress throughout the adult life. Unpublished doctoral dissertation, University of California, San Francisco.

Weiss, L., and Lowenthal, M. F. 1975. Life course perspectives on friendship. *In,* M. F. Lowenthal, M. Thurnher, D. Chiriboga, and Associates, *Four Stages of Life: A Comparative Study of Women and Men Facing Transitions,* pp. 48–61. San Francisco: Jossey-Bass.

Williams, R. H. 1960. Changing status, roles and relationships. *In,* C. Tibbitts (ed.), *Handbook of Social Gerontology,* pp. 261–298. Chicago: University of Chicago Press.

# IV
# Society and Aging

# 16

# Age Stratification
# and the Life Course

*Pauline K. Ragan & Jeffrey B. Wales**

Age stratification involves the distribution of society's resources, power, and prestige on the basis of age, and therefore shapes the meaning of being old in a given society at a given time. Some age groups, such as the middle aged, command greater resources and influence, while others, such as children and the aged, seem to command little. The intent of this chapter is to describe the ways in which age stratification manifests itself and to consider the implications for the quality of life of the aging individual.

Gerontologists have not directed a great deal of attention to age stratification. The topic is at times complex, abstract, and difficult to document empirically. Recently, however, age stratification has gained increasing attention because it is recognized as central to the study of how well the aged fare in the distribution of society's valued resources. Furthermore, studying the aged in the context of the structure of society bears directly on the individual's taking on the status of old age, since age-stratified norms direct his behavior as an older person. If he exits from the work role, if his income drops, and if he faces a new experience of large blocs of discretionary time, these will all be stratification factors which affect his well-being.

Theories of *age* stratification borrow the conceptual language of theories of *social* stratification and the class structure. Later in this chapter, the essentials of these social stratification theories as they have developed historically are reviewed for their contribution to the understanding of age as a stratum variable like class, race, or sex. Analyses of the outcomes of the interaction of age with class, race, and sex, and analyses of age stratification it-

*The authors are grateful to Gordon Streib for his helpful suggestions on an earlier version of this chapter.

self are then reviewed, as preparation for the presentation of the major themes of this chapter.

Society is stratified by age in that it can be demonstrated that there are identifiable age strata or levels (e.g. young adults, middle aged, older people) which share unequally in the allocation of valued roles such as work, in the distribution of scarce resources such as income, and in the assignment of norms and responsibilities. The differential distribution, we will suggest, works to both the relative advantage and disadvantage of the aged. There are sets of shared beliefs about aging which provide the ideological support for such differentiation.

Analysis of age stratification is basically cross-sectional (at a single point in time) and at the macro (societal) level, but it can elucidate the change-over-time aspects of the individual's life course mobility through successive age strata, and the potential for problems as the individual experiences a transition to old age.

Along with a cross-sectional view of age strata and a processual view of the individual's progression through those strata over the life course, a third dimension of aging is presented, namely the shifts over time in the age stratification system itself. Even as the individual moves toward old age, the definitions, boundaries, and expectations attached to old age are themselves changing, so that the individual's life trajectory intersects the shifting old age stratum at an uncertain chronological age and with ambiguous expectations. The implications of these three dimensions—age strata, life course, and social change—are explored in relation to the mental health of the individual and intervention at the structural level of society. Stratification according to age is a universal phenomenon, but its particular manifestations are specific to societies and time periods; the discussion here is directed to the current age stratification system in the United States.

## STRATIFICATION THEORIES

Social stratification is the broad theoretical framework on which an age stratification perspective is based, and can be defined as a system of regularized social inequality (Roach, Gross, and Gursslin, 1969, p. 11). Society's resources are not distributed equally; some people have more valued resources such as wealth, power, prestige, and knowledge, and others have less. Those who, on the basis of some shared characteristic (e.g., class), share similar amounts of valued resources form a stratum with distinctive life chances and life styles, and the stratum differs from other strata which have more or less of what is valued. Stratification is a major feature of social organization, and as such, social scientists seek to describe it and explain its origins and consequences.

The two major classical theorists on stratification are Karl Marx (1818–1883) and Max Weber (1864–1920). Marx argued that the causes of institutionalized inequality could be found in the inner workings of the capitalistic economy. Classes arise "on the basis of the different positions or roles which individuals fulfill in the productive scheme of society" (Tumin, 1967, p. 4). People who own the means of production and those who have only their labor to sell stand opposed to each other. To the owners flow the profits—income above and beyond what it costs to maintain the workers—widening the gap between workers and owners and resulting in a two-class society. Social institutions which legitimate and perpetuate inequality are manifestations of this fundamental *economic* inequality.

Weber granted Marx's assessment of the importance of fundamental economic relations in the causes of the development, definition, and persistence of social inequality, but he added two important dimensions, power and prestige. Weber saw property, power, and prestige as three separate though interacting bases on which hierarchies are created in any society. Property differences generate classes; power differences generate political parties; and prestige differences generate status groupings or strata (Tumin, 1967, p. 6).

The most prevalent modern theory of social stratification is known as structural-functionalism. According to this approach, stratification is inevitable and universal because it serves an important function in the maintenance of the social order; it is a necessary response to the need for coordination and integration in society. As Davis and Moore (1945) argue, the functioning of society depends upon the satisfactory performance of various roles within it. Since some of these positions are more important than others and require more costly and extended periods of training, then society's more capable members must be induced to undergo such training and assume such roles by being offered a greater share of society's scarce rewards such as income, power, and prestige. The origins of institutionalized inequality and social strata are thus explained.

Other modern theories include conflict theory, which rejects the notion of functionally related segments of society used in functional theory, arguing instead that stratification is the result of domination of some groups by others, based upon force and constraint. The hierarchy of differentially valued conflict groups finds its origin in the unequal distribution of authority (Dahrendorf, 1957). Members of one group are like each other in that they share common interests or political goals, and are different from members of other groups because goals and interests are conflicting.

Lenski (1966) attempted to avoid the undue emphasis on order by functionalism and on coercion by conflict theory by drawing the salient characteristics from each to build a synthetic theory. For example, like the functionalists, he assumes that "men will share the product of their labors to the extent required to insure the survival and continued productivity of those others whose actions are necessary or beneficial to themselves" (Lenski, 1966, pp. 44–45). But unlike the functionalists, he sided with conflict theorists when he stated that "power will determine the distribution of nearly all of the surplus possessed by a society" (Lenski, 1966, pp. 44–45).

The writings of Marx, Weber, Davis and Moore, Dahrendorf, and Lenski represent major attempts to explain social stratification. The work of Riley and Streib discussed below represents current efforts to describe and explain *age* stratification. These two categories of literature are bridged by those social stratification analyses of the effects of social class status on aging and those theories which deal with age as one of the major stratum variables.

## THE EFFECTS OF SOCIAL STATUS ON AGING

Whereas our focus is on *age* stratification, with age as the stratum characteristic of interest, it is useful first to review the important work that has been undertaken on the interaction of social class stratification factors with age. Streib (1976), for example, analyzed various status combinations and showed how individual aging modifies class position and prestige and political, financial, and family power. Attributing primary importance to economic criteria as the basis for the overall stratification system, he nevertheless stresses the importance of other status criteria (e.g., race) that are largely derived from economic status, and criteria which intervene between economic class position and individual circumstances, such as age and sex. One essential benefit from this viewpoint is the appreciation of the complexity of the stratification system and heterogeneity of the older age stratum, in which members are differentially distributed on other status variables such as income and occupational prestige.

Henretta and Campbell (1976) also begin

with social stratification rather than age stratification; they extend the usual sociological treatment of life cycle effects on socioeconomic status attainment beyond the preretirement adult span, into old age. Their analysis demonstrates the persistence into old age of the relationship between other socioeconomic variables and income.

Other gerontologists have examined the implications of social stratification for an understanding of aging. Bengtson, Kasschau, and Ragan (1977) took location in the social structure, as indexed by socioeconomic status, racial/ethnic identity, and sex, and examined the effects of such status characteristics on patterns of aging. Differences among older people in life expectancy, health status, living arrangements, life satisfaction, social ties, and self identification as "old" were some of the patterns of aging that were shown to vary with economic class, race, and sex. In that study, older and younger strata were not contrasted on differential distribution of resources, as in age stratification, but rather social class, race, and sex strata were being contrasted on outcomes in aging. With location in the social structure on the basis of class, race, and sex as the independent variables, aging patterns were analyzed as the dependent variable.

## AGE AS A MAJOR STRATUM VARIABLE

Theories about social organization have acknowledged from the outset that society is organized by age strata as well as by economic classes. Linton (1936) and Parsons (1954) saw age as basic to the organization of society, with many of society's rights, duties, and responsibilities defined on the basis of age. Age categories help define kinship structure, formal education, occupation, and community participation.

Sorokin (1947) introduced the concept of *age groups* as opposed to age categories. People of like chronological age share similar biological, sociological and psychological traits, drawing them together in age groups which manifest their own values and norms. It follows, then, that people of different age groups react differently to the same social phenomenon; it is here that we see the basis of the generation gap.

Eisenstadt (1971) recognized the role of age in social stratification, but considered it a "weak link," the foundation for "partial stratification." Nevertheless, every human passes through various age stages characterized by different capacities and the performance of different tasks vis-a-vis other members of society. Consequently, *roles* can be thought of as being differentially allocated on the basis of age. Beyond this, according to Eisenstadt, an age category is evaluated on the basis of the kind of work society requires from it, some work being more highly valued than others.

Duberman (1976) made a stronger statement than many, claiming that the aged constitute a "lower caste group" because membership in an old age category is ascribed and unchangeable. In addition, there are signs in society's treatment of the aged of ascriptive membership, segregation, restrictions on social mobility, identifiable subgroup norms, and awareness of status.

An example of current theory comes from Jeffries and Ransford (1979), who posit a "multiple hierarchy" model of social stratification. Class is important, but ethnicity, sex, and age must also be examined as hierarchies of institutionalized inequality. It is the interrelationships of these separate dimensions which result in outcomes such as political attitudes, life-style, and aspirations. Age groups in society are ranked: the middle aged are ranked highest followed by young adults and youth, and the elderly and children are ranked lowest. As individuals progress through the life-cycle, they undergo changes in power, privilege, and prestige depending upon their age group.

## AGE STRATIFICATION THEORIES

The development in the recent past of a general interest in *age* in the social sciences, with attention to old age in particular, has generated the analysis of age stratification. Cain (1964) was one of the first sociologists in the field of gerontology to articulate age as a criterion of status within the social structure. He perceived the life course as "those successive statuses individuals are called upon to occupy in various cultures and walks of life as a result of aging," and age status as "the system developed by a culture to give order and predictability to the course followed by individuals" (p. 278). In contrast to our view of age stratification as a hierarchical system of unequal strata which characterize a society at a given point in time (as developed further below), Cain's scheme appears to be more of a horizontal system of statuses through which the individual proceeds over time.

Riley (1976) and Riley, Johnson, and Foner (1972) have provided the major theoretic contribution to the study of age stratification. Their contribution includes: (1) viewing both the population and also roles and norms as stratified by age as well as by social class and sex; (2) attention to the shifting age structure over time; and (3) the resulting interplay between individual aging (as the life course sequence of roles) and structural change,

which results in individuals' aging in different ways over time.

There are a few differences in emphasis between Riley's model and the presentation in this chapter. Riley's model is more abstract and explanatory rather than descriptive, and involves a series of feedback loops accounting for the emergence of an age stratification system. The discussion is limited largely to the allocation by age strata of *roles* (and the norms, rights, and privileges attached to roles), in contrast to our emphasis on the distribution of resources and responsibilities per se in addition to roles. Finally, the emphasis of Riley's model is more on *differences* between strata than on inequalities, and on a horizontal rather than a hierarchical arrangement of strata; as such it is not tied as closely to the conceptual framework of social stratification. It is possible, as in Cain's and Riley's models, to describe age strata as different stages of the life cycle without emphasizing the invidious distinctions implicit in our discussion of unequal distribution of resources to age strata at a given point in time.

Palmore and Manton (1973) discuss much of what we are calling age stratification in the terminology of *ageism*. In order to compare the relative effects of ageism, racism, and sexism, they devised a measure of actual differences in income, occupation, and education, called the "Equality Index." Describing inequalities in these socioeconomic factors on the basis of age, they found the aged to be inferior on all three measures. They then went on to analyze equality according to race, sex, and age, finding for example that for income, age inequality is greater than race inequality but less than sex inequality. The effects of combinations of low status based on age, sex, and race were found to be additive for all combinations. The emphasis in Palmore and Manton (1973) and in an earlier piece by Palmore and Whittington (1971) on the hierarchical ranking of age strata places these works clearly in the area of age stratification as presented in this chapter. In a projection of the future status of the aged, Palmore (1976) adopts the terminology of age stratification, disputing theories of the decline of the relative status of the aged and increasing stratification according to age.

Foner (1975) followed up the earlier work by Riley, Johnson, and Foner (1972) with a brief but explicit statement of age stratification as a hierarchical system of the distribution of the "desiderata" of society—roles and rewards. Neugarten and Hagestad (1976) have similarly provided a statement of the central concepts of age stratification and a review of the age status literature in introducing their material on life course processes; they point out the complexity of the concept of hierarchical age status. Neugarten's earlier work with Moore and Lowe (1968) has laid some of the foundation of an understanding of age norms. Whereas Neugarten and Hagestad (1976) seem to distinguish between *stratification* (as social ranking with its distribution of valued resources) on the one hand, and *role differentiation* and the division of labor on the other hand, this chapter incorporates both aspects in the construct of age stratification.

## AGE STRATIFICATION: A CROSS-SECTIONAL VIEW

### AGE STRATA IN THE SOCIAL STRUCTURE

It can be demonstrated that age is a stratum variable that is similar to, and in some important ways dissimilar from, the stratum variables of class, race, and sex. Age stratification involves the hierarchical arrangement of individuals according to age categories (strata), with certain resources, responsibilities, and roles distributed unequally according to age stratum. This "institutionalized social inequality" is legitimated by shared beliefs, values, and norms, and maintained by social institutions.

Age is, however, a particularly complex stratum variable. Chronological age appears to be a variable arranged hierarchically from young to old, as in Blau's use of age as a "graduated parameter" (1974), but the distribution of resources by age does not involve a simple linear increase or decrease of advantage with age. Neither does it involve an arrangement such as that of Jeffries and Ransford (1979), in which the middle aged are clearly at the top, youth in the middle, and children and older people at the bottom of the hierarchy. Unlike other stratification variables, in which there is a general agreement that the advantages go to the upper classes over the lower classes, to whites over blacks, and to males over females, advantages by age depend to a greater extent on the particular resource or domain of activity under consideration. The aged as a category are in crucial ways disadvantaged, as in the domain of work, by losing out on occupational roles and income as important resources. In other domains, such as leisure, the aged have a greater share of discretionary time. In the following sections we will attempt to analyze the variety of roles, resources, and responsibilities that are distributed by age to both the advantage and disadvantage of the aged.

The demonstration of stratification by age can be carried out as long as we are able to show the actual and unequal distribution of valued resources and roles by age category, along with the existence of supporting beliefs, values, norms, and institutions. It is not necessary to demonstrate that the distribution is inequitable (unjust), or even that it is carried out against the wishes and preferences of the individuals involved. The very fact that stratification systems involve shared beliefs, values, and norms operates to insure that the system will often proceed without conflict and even without awareness by members of the system.

### AGE STRATA AND BOUNDARIES

The phenomenon of age stratification is predicated on the existence of age strata, and recognized age categories are so integral to social life that there can be no argument about their relevance for all forms of social behavior. By contrast, the demonstration of the reality of social classes in social stratification theory confronts the difficulty of recognizing such classes; in fact, because of the total lack of clear boundaries between socioeconomic strata, socioeconomic status can be better conceptualized as a continuum rather than as discrete categories. The identification of childhood, adolescence, middle age, and old age as distinct age categories, on the other hand, is built into our daily vocabulary.

The conceptualization of age strata, however, is not without some difficulties. One source of confusion is in our conventionally vertical conceptualization of age strata, in which we array age groups chronologically with children at the bottom, adolescents, young adults and middle aged next, and the old at the top. Such a vertical arrangement does not fit the *hierarchical* distribution of resources intrinsic to age stratification theory. One of the major propositions of this chapter is that age is a highly complex stratum variable, and that the particular age stratum at the top of the distribution hierarchy (at greatest advantage) depends on whether we are discussing work roles, free time, or special privileges.

A second source of confusion is that precise boundaries are unclear for some age categories. The ambiguity of the entry boundary for old age is discussed later, but the very fact that this unclear boundary constantly calls for clarification is a demonstration that an age category exists.

Age strata are social constructions, the products of the institutional forms of society, as Riley (1976, p. 191) has stated: "Partitions of the population by age acquire meaning as age strata only as they index socially significant aspects of people and roles." The ultimate evidence that strata and their boundaries are socially determined is that they vary in response to changing social conditions

(Neugarten and Moore, 1968). The emergence of adolescence in our recent social past is a well-noted case in point, as this new age category became labeled and defined by expectations and privileges. Old age is a universally meaningful age stratum, but the boundaries of old age and the expectations attached to it vary historically, and in fact show rapid and radical shifts within our own span of observation (Fischer, 1977). Of course, only the lower or entry boundary of old age is variable; exit is determined by death alone.

Age strata can be contrasted in several ways in addition to the chronological age ranges they represent. The population distribution is displayed conventionally in an age-sex pyramid, as in Figure 16-1. The age-sex pyramid shows the size of each five-year category relative to others, and, by contrasting population distributions for different time periods, shows the relative size of each category as it changes over time. The bulges and indentations that appear on the 1970 pyramid represent such important phenomena as the increased proportion of the aged in the population, the postwar baby boom that is now entering the adult stratum, and the baby "bust" that follows. As Riley *et al.* (1972) have clearly pointed out in their model of age stratification, roles (such as jobs) and resources (such as service delivery programs and educational slots) are allocated to particular age strata, and when the number of individuals moving into an age stratum does not match the number of positions open, problems such as unemployment and shortages-excesses of classrooms and teachers arise.

In addition to the relative size of five-year age categories, the age-sex pyramid also displays shifts in the male/female distribution of age categories. The predominance of females in the older age stratum has increased since 1900 (Figure 16-1).

Constant attention is paid to the implications of the increasing old-age dependency ratio (the ratio of the 65+ population to the 18–64 population) and the strains imposed on the system by these shifts. The aged dependency ratio is conventionally calculated only on the basis of the relative size of age strata, rather than on the working status of individuals within strata, thus demonstrating a strictly age stratification approach to the analysis of economic dependency (Cutler and Harootyan, 1975). (Sheppard and Rix, 1977, discuss an alternative method of calculation.)

Age stratification involves a cross-sectional view of society, in which the age strata existing at given points in time can be identified. The labels assigned to age categories (such as young, middle aged, and "senior citizens") and the corresponding self-identifications reveal strata to be social realities and not merely statistical categories.

## ROLES, RESOURCES, AND RESPONSIBILITIES

The demonstration of age stratification calls for description of the actual distribution of the important resources of a society according to age. If we take a cross section of society and divide it into

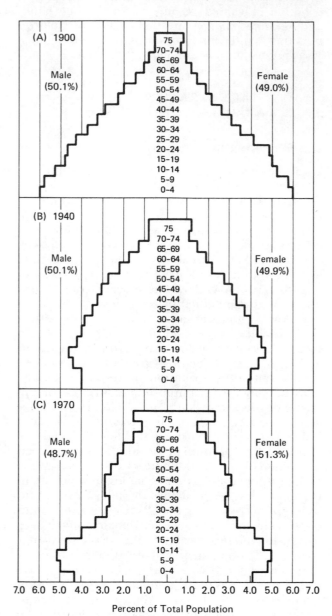

**Figure 16–1** Age-sex pyramids for the United States: 1900, 1940, 1970. (United States Bureau of the Census. *Census of Population: Characteristics of the Population*, 1940, 1970.) Reprinted from N. E. Cutler and R. E. Harootyan, "Demography of the aged," pp. 31–69 in D. S. Woodruff and J. E. Birren (eds.), *Aging: Scientific Perspectives and Social Issues*, © 1975 by Litton Educ. Publ., Inc. Reprinted by permission of D. Van Nostrand Co.

socially meaningful age categories, we can observe in which strata certain roles and resources are *generally* located; we should pay particular attention, in this stratification analysis, to those distribution factors that appear to be maintained by social institutions and belief systems.

*Roles.* The single most important differentiation between the older age stratum and the stratum of younger adults is in the allocation of the work role. In 1975 only 14 percent of the 65+ population were in the labor force (Sheppard and Rix, 1977). Policies regarding mandatory retirement are in flux, with its recent abolishment in federal employment and with the shift from age 65 to 70 in most other employment. Nevertheless, the principles hold that most employers may require retirement at an arbitrary age, that Social Security benefits are contingent on giving up the work role, and that a system of norms and beliefs supports the institution of retirement. Almost all other features of the age stratification system as it affects older adults (for example, income, economic transfers, and prestige) are understandable only in the context of the work/retirement differentiation. It is not clear what are the expected behaviors and prerogatives of the substitute role, be it the "retirement role" or the "leisure role," or if in fact these can be considered roles. Some of the problems emanating from the lack of role definitions are considered in the following section.

As with work and retirement, most important roles in society are allocated by age stratum. The family role of spouse tends to continue into old age for males (two-thirds of males 65+ are married), but not for females (one-third of females 65 + are married). Marital status in the older age stratum is determined not only by biological factors of longevity but also by norms and regulations which affect remarriage and the relative ages of older marriage partners (Treas, 1976). The parent role ends with the empty nest, and the grandparent role begins in the middle years, actually well before old age for most people, but the active grandparent role is part of the expectations we hold for older people.

The active sexual role is in many ways negatively sanctioned for older persons by our commonly mistaken set of beliefs and norms about sexual behavior and interest among the aged (Solnick, 1978; Wales, 1974). Here the proscription of a role does not follow from economic or physiological constraints, and it is not clear whether the image of asexual older persons follows from their devalued status in society or contributes to that devalued status, or both.

*Income.* The distribution of income follows from the distribution of occupational roles, with postretirement Social Security, pension, and other forms of income much lower than earned incomes of the middle years. The lower income of older persons who do continue to work follows from the combination of age discrimination in the allocation of kinds of work and the decline in some older individuals in the physiological ability to work. In the mid-1970s the median income of men 65+ and of families with heads of household 65+ was less than half that of their counterparts aged 55–64 (US Bureau of the Census, 1974). One of the hazards, however, of comparing strata by median levels of income is that such a statistical summary conceals the great variability within strata (Schultz, 1976). Strumpel's (1973) analysis of national survey data shows greater income inequality among the aged than among the rest of the population. On each of several measures of income inequality, family heads 65 and over showed greater inequality (within age group) than family heads of other age groups.

Streib (1976) has pointed out the phenomenon of the concentration of great wealth in the aged stratum, in direct contrast to the usual emphasis in stratification analyses on the disproportionate poverty of the aged. He reports data from a study showing that the median age of the wealthiest group in the United States, made up of 66 centimillionaires, was 65 years of age (Louis, 1968). Comparing median incomes of strata oversimplifies the actual within-stratum distributions of income and deemphasizes the poverty of many younger adults and the wealth of many older adults, but it does accurately portray the stratification phenomenon of the distribution of much lower incomes to the older stratum *as a whole*.

*Health Care.* Because of the combination of the greater health needs and lower incomes of the aged population, public expenditures for health care go disproportionately to the older age stratum. Per capita health care expenditures from public funds (1973) amounted to $48 for the under 19 age group, $104 for the 19–64 group, and $679 for the 65+ group (US Public Health Service, 1975). The status quo of allocation of health care funds to the aged goes largely unquestioned, but from time to time the consideration of a different manner of distribution comes up. Recent Congressional testimony, for instance, included this comment:

> One issue is whether it is more effective to allocate additional research funds for heart disease or cancer.... One should decide whether it is more desirable to maintain the life of very sick, extremely

aged persons at all costs or to apply some of these funds for preventive purposes to younger adults. The latter course could, in the long run, be more effective in improving the average quality of life among the elderly and equalizing death rates of the sexes. For example, it might be more cost-effective (in terms of years of life added) to spend a larger share of community funds on mobile cardiac units, use of which might prevent the death of many middle-aged husbands and fathers, and less on drastic mechanical methods of life prolongation for extremely aged persons who are already very seriously ill (Siegel, 1978, p. 31).

The differential distribution of life-prolonging health care might be considered the ultimate in the unequal allocation of resources. In fact, in ancient times life itself was systematically distributed by age when in the face of the most stringent shortages of vital resources, infanticide and gericide were practiced (Kastenbaum, 1978). The inequality at present works to the relative advantage of the aged, at least in dollar amounts of expenditures, but reallocation is conceivable.

*Other Economic Transfers.* Federal expenditures on behalf of the aged, counting all outlays of programs directed entirely or to a major extent to the older population, have been estimated to be about one-fifth of the total federal budget (Brotman, 1971). Methods of estimating dependency costs are admittedly debatable, but one estimate places the 1975 per capita cost of major public social programs for the aged (65+) at three times that for youth under 18 (Sheppard and Rix, 1977). Chronological age has been the single criterion for eligibility for most of the publicly financed programs which benefit the aged. The entire age stratum is thus defined as having the right to certain benefits. The use of chronological age rather than need in determining eligibility for most programs is both humane and administratively efficient, but what are the implications of defining an entire age stratum as eligible for special benefits? One implication is that the stratum is defined as dependent, and that dependent status may contribute to the overall devalued status of the aged. The minimum age for benefits is set variously at 55, 60, or 65, thus on the one hand setting some boundaries for the old age stratum, and on the other hand contributing to the confusion of what the *specific* age boundary is.

The dual processes of relinquishing roles and resources (the work role and income levels, for example) and claiming rights (benefits based on chronological age) are obviously related. The present circumstance of the raising of involuntary retirement age provides a natural laboratory for observing the redefinition of age stratum boundaries. Will there be pressure to raise the minimum eligibility age for benefits as well (Cain, 1976)?

*Time.* Discretionary time is a resource allocated distinctly by age, but not often figured into the equation of resources along with income, power, and age-specific benefits. "Discretionary time" is used here as free time, involving some choices by the individual regarding its use, following Moore (1963). Kreps (1976) has described time as a "major potential resource," but notes that its utility as leisure, when all time is free of work, is zero. Time is the paradoxical resource—the working person never has enough time, and many retired persons have too much "time on their hands." Nevertheless, unconstrained time is defined in our system of values as highly desirable, and is a resource which is gained by trading the work role for the retirement role. Belief in the advantages of free time is essential to the ideology surrounding the institution of retirement.

*Political Power.* Many analyses of the status of the aged portray the older population as politically powerless and "disenfranchised," but in fact persons 65 and over are more likely to register and to vote than younger persons (US Bureau of the Census, 1974). (Among the very old the rate of voting is curtailed by difficulties of getting out to vote.) The franchise is not distributed by age, except for minimal voting age, although there have been discussions from time to time of the advisability of setting an upper age limit for voting (Ragan, 1977). The citizen role may be the *only* role that is not age-specific (except for the requirement of reaching majority) in its allocation and performance.

Like great wealth, great political power may cluster in the older age stratum (Streib, 1976). Hudson and Binstock (1976) document the phenomenon of the advanced age of the incumbents of key political offices. In early 1978 the mean age of standing committee chairmen of the US Senate was 68. The older age stratum is not curtailed politically as far as individual voting behavior and its share of key political offices is involved, but what about wielding political clout as an age stratum? At least 15 million older persons (55+) are said to belong to age-based associations which represent them in lobbying efforts; and although they do not appear to be forming a political bloc of voters, their influence is often felt on specific issues (Pratt, 1976). These activities are sanctioned in public opinion; in a recent survey of Los Angeles County residents (aged 45–74), 73 percent agreed that

"Older people should form an active political group to influence policies that affect them" (Ragan and Bengtson, 1977). At both the individual and group level, the older age stratum is not disadvantaged politically.

*Responsibilities.* It is not difficult to recognize those major age-specific responsibilities that are assigned to youth—to obey parents and to attend school. Responsibilities are age specific at the other end of the age continuum also, and they appear to be assigned mainly to the middle aged rather than to the older age stratum. The heavy burden of taxes on the middle aged is perhaps the most often acknowledged age-specific responsibility. Older persons also pay taxes, of course, but much of their income (Social Security, for example) is not taxed, and the age stratum is allowed special exemptions on income and property taxes.

The middle aged stratum is often described as the generation caught in the middle, with the concern not only for the support of self but also for the emotional and sometimes for the financial support of young adult children and older parents. By comparison, responsibilities specifically assigned to the older age stratum are minimal.

*Norms.* The normative structure is basic to all aspects of age stratification, and in the case of formalized norms (laws and regulations) it is easy to see that age is a condition of the distribution of many benefits and obligations. Informal norms which affect everyday behavior are also often age-specific (Neugarten, *et al,* 1968; Neugarten and Hagestad, 1976). Standards of dress, recreation, friendship, and sexual behavior are all tied to age status. The mandate to "act your age" can be used to encourage mature behavior among the young or to inhibit behavior in older people that is permissible for other adults. The informal but powerful negative sanction of making older people feel ridiculous if caught in inappropriate behavior is effective in distributing prescribed and proscribed behaviors by age group.

*Prestige.* The construct of social stratification has always included the element of prestige or honor. In addition to describing the actual unequal distribution of advantageous roles and resources by age stratum, we can observe the phenomenon of the generally devalued status of the aged. The low status of the aged is not independent of their disadvantaged position on such important resources as occupation and income, but it encompasses more than these considerations. Moore (1963) calls the "accent on youth" both genuine and general, and

Rosenberg (1970) observes these dominant American outlooks: "admiration for those who could remain active, independent, and self-sufficient; our high valuation of youth; and our stress on the struggles of achievement."

In the recent Harris survey on aging, the aged were described by most of the general public as not particularly bright and alert, open minded and adaptable, or good at getting things done (although they were acknowledged to be friendly, warm, and wise from experience). The aged themselves were similar in their negative images of older people, but they did not even consider most older people to be friendly and warm (National Council on Aging, 1975). It has been demonstrated repeatedly that society's image of the aged is in many regards negative, and that the aged share that negative image of themselves as an age group (Kuypers and Bengtson, 1973).

The low status of the aged, real or imagined, inhibits their social interaction and contributes to isolation from younger segments of society. When older persons perceive that they are not welcome in or even eligible for social organizations, public entertainment, and some kinds of housing, they usually acquiesce to such age-based restrictions of social interaction. Interaction opportunities must be considered to be one of the prime resources distributed in society according to age.

Whereas youth is highly valued, old age is devalued on the basis of such factors as physical signs of aging, dependency, loss of health, senility, and impending death. But what of the honored role of elder in this society? It may persist most noticeably in some traditional subcultures within the society, but it is also easily observable in informal social interaction in all quarters of society, in the deference and respect paid to older persons, and in the outrage with which the public responds to reports of mistreatment of the aged. It is perhaps primarily the more attractive, cheerful, and healthy older persons who receive such positive treatment; deference may often be more paternalistic than respectful; but it does belie an overly simplistic image of the society as stigmatizing old age per se. The extent to which the aged as a category are negatively valued and in turn hold negative self-images is crucial in considering the implications of age stratification for the well-being of the older individual. (These implications will be discussed.)

*Overall Status of Aged.* In summary, the distribution of roles, resources, and responsibilities by age stratum is reflected in the *deprivation* of the aged stratum of work roles, family and sexual roles, income, and positive societal images. On political power the aged cannot be said to be disadvantaged. Advantages that are distributed unequally to the *advantage* of the aged are discretionary time, health care, other economic transfers, and freedom from responsibilities.

Having observed some of the ways in which age stratification operates to effect an unequal distribution of valued resources according to age, we can recapitulate some of the ideas that are basic to our discussion of age stratification: (1) age is a stratum variable; (2) age stratification is a complex system, in which the aged are disadvantaged in some respects but advantaged in others; and (3) overall, the aged occupy a lower status than other adults in the age stratification system in that they are the losers on the two resources most highly valued in this society, *work* (and its attendant occupational prestige) and *income*.

## SOCIAL INSTITUTIONS
## MAINTAINING AGE STRATIFICATION

It has been stated above that social differentiation by age strata is maintained by *social institutions*. The term "social institution" is an abstraction for "a comparatively enduring configuration of prescriptions which through the general consensus of the society is regarded as essential for the maintenance of its structure and basic values"; major institutions are the familial, religious, educational, economic, and political sectors of society (Lundberg, Schrag, Larsen, and Catton, 1968, p.709). This century has seen the development of *retirement* as the major institutional factor in age stratification. Norms, rules, regulations, and laws mandate if and when individuals of certain ages may be voluntarily or forcefully retired. Social Security retirement benefits and most public and private pension arrangements are contingent on retirement from work and provide an income to substitute for earnings.

The economic sphere includes other institutional forms of age stratification as well as retirement rules and benefits. The tax structure exempts persons 65 and over from some income and property tax obligations. The private sector occasionally provides some discounts for older consumers, e.g. in theaters and restaurants. The public sector, of course, provides benefits such as Medicare and special transportation, nutrition, recreation, and other programs for the elderly.

The *family* as one of the major institutions of society is the setting for the allocation of roles by generation, and thus by relative age. The family as we witness its current development often in-

volves four and five generations, and rights and obligations are attached to generational position within families (Brody, 1979). Older parent and grandparent role obligations and prerogatives are not entirely clear in a period of rapid social change, but the roles attached to such age-related positions are important even when they are ambiguous. In fact, the very ambiguity of age-specific roles such as older parent or grandparent is a potential source of interpersonal conflict.

Other social institutions maintain differentiation by age, both informally and by formal rules. Seniority privileges and the process of accumulation of power in office skew influence in the polity toward the aged. In religious groups, most forms of religious activity outside of formal worship services are organized by age groups, and esteem and privilege often accrue to the elders. Important educational resources such as professional training are largely allocated to the young, with only marginal and recreational educational activities set aside for older strata. In a variety of forms the social institutions of the economy, the family, religion, and education provide for differential allocation of roles and resources according to age strata.

## BELIEFS ESSENTIAL TO AGE STRATIFICATION

One of the essential characteristics of a stratification system is that there is a set of beliefs which explain and justify the differential distribution of resources and responsibilities. Is there evidence for such a set of beliefs, values, and norms which support age stratification?

A cross-cultural comparison of systems provides an example of supportive beliefs about retirement. In Eastern European countries, in which there is an acute shortage of manpower, workers are encouraged to stay on the job rather than retire (Streib, 1976). In the USSR, for example, continued working in old age is valuable because it provides the older worker a continuity of roles and a sense of pride, and because it alleviates society's shortage of skilled labor (*Ageing International*, 1977, p. 2). In the United States, on the other hand, with the opposite problem of unemployment, the belief that older workers slow down and are less effective is often put forth; the norm is that workers deserve a relief from work, and years of leisure (Sheppard, 1976), and that workers ought to retire to make room for younger workers. Such norms are widespread although there is not total consensus on them; half of the population agreed in the Harris poll on aging that "Older people should retire when they can, so as to give younger people more of a chance on the job" (National Council on Aging, 1975).

The reduced incomes of retired persons, even up to one-half reduction, is countered by the belief that such reduced incomes are adequate inasmuch as retired persons' costs for housing, child care, commuting, capital investments, etc. are much less than before retirement. Streib (1976) documents the public and bureaucratic justification for reduced incomes. (Poverty levels or retirement income, on the other hand, are unacceptable in public opinion.)

The status of the aged is attributed in large part to the physiological decrements which accompany aging. The error occurs first in exaggerating the physical decrements of the 65+ age stratum, and secondly in overlooking the ways in which the stratification system, through social institutions, allocates roles and resources far beyond biological constraints. Foner (1975) observes that the process of attributing age status differences to age-related biological incompetence is similar to the process of justifying the situations of blacks and females by citing biological genetic inadequacies.

Disengagement theory in gerontology provided a functional explanation of the situation of the aged—they disengaged from roles because it was necessary for society and beneficial for the individual (Cumming and Henry, 1961). Public perceptions of the aged reflect the disengaged image to some extent; in the Harris poll, two-thirds of those surveyed thought that "most people" over 65 spend a lot of time watching television and sitting and thinking, but only one-third of the 65+ respondents said that they spend a lot of time in these pastimes (National Council on Aging, 1975). Disengagement explanations among both scientists and the general public are the clearest example of ideological systems which accompany and support age stratification.

The dependency of the aged stratum on government benefits has clearly been integrated into the normative system. In the Los Angeles community survey, over half of those questioned about housing, health, and transportation needs of the aged attributed responsibility for meeting those needs to government (Ragan and Grigsby, 1976); similar findings came from the Harris poll (National Council on Aging, 1975).

The dependency of the aged is greatly exaggerated by the public. The Harris poll revealed that over half of the public believes that "most people over 65" experience the following *very* serious problems: poor health, not having enough money to live on, and loneliness. In fact, only 21 percent, 15 percent, and 12 percent (respectively) of the 65+

public in that poll reported these three areas as very serious problems (National Council on Aging, 1975). The percent of the older population that is ill, senile, or institutionalized is consistently and grossly exaggerated by the public and policymakers alike. In a recent survey of decision-makers, one in ten estimated that 50 percent or more of the older population is institutionalized; in fact, only 5 percent are (McConnell and Davis, 1977).

Butler (1975, p. 12), using the term "ageism" to denote negative stereotypes about the aged, states that "At times ageism becomes an expedient method by which society promotes viewpoints about the aged in order to relieve itself of responsibility toward them." Beliefs and norms about the benefits and duties of retirement, the reduced need for income after retirement, the functional necessity of disengagement, and the physiological decrements and the dependency of the aged buttress the age stratifications system as it operates in this society.

## CHRONOLOGICAL AGE AND STRATIFICATION

Why should age, as it has in all times and places, be a key marker for differentiation in society's resources and roles? In itself, age perhaps explains nothing, being merely an indicator of elapsed time since birth, but there are important universal correlates of chronological age which help us to understand its primacy in social systems. Particular correlates discussed below are biological change, functions of the passage of time, and age as an indicator of cohort membership as well as life stage.

*Biological Parameters.* Closely tied to the unfolding of the individual life span are physiological changes which form the essential limits within which variations of age stratification can be played out (Cain, 1964). The most obvious parameters are events in the reproductive cycle, as when menarche and menopause form the outer boundaries within which childbearing takes place. It is notable, however, how far removed from its biological limits is the actual period of childbearing, because social institutions constrain the timing of marriage and fertility in all societies.

The status of the aged cannot be understood apart from the inevitability of physiological decline which accompanies very old age, but as with reproductive functions, we can see that the social institutions surrounding old age go far beyond meeting the need of society to replace individuals in important roles because of health losses. Retirement from occupational roles occurs generally during an age span when only about 26 percent of the individuals in that age span (60–64) experience some work disability (US Bureau of the Census, 1974). (By contrast, in unique occupations such as professional athletics, physical decline does provide the immediate key to retirement age.) Serious cognitive declines, such as the loss of memory and intelligence functions and, at the extreme, organic brain syndrome, do occur in a minority of the older population and even then primarily among the *very* old, so the incidence of these disorders cannot account for the status of the population 65 and older. Although physical and mental decline set limitations on the allocation of roles and responsibilites to the aged, it is more likely to be economic factors which dictate actual patterns of allocation.

Death is the ultimate boundary of old age, and death is becoming increasingly specific to old age. Both aspects shape the status of the aged. The necessity to replace those individuals near death in crucial roles has been well noted (Cumming and Henry, 1961), although it might also be observed that the key statesmen in society often die in office, while the general working population is retired (at 65) with an average of another 18 years left to live (Metropolitan Life, 1977). A more subtle bearing of the fact of death on the status of the aged may be attributed to the dread of death, its denial in our culture, and the stigma attached to the dying, all of which contribute to an avoidance of and negative status for the aged in general (Streib, 1976).

Differential mortality patterns are biological factors which structure age statuses, as in the effect of female longevity advantages on the sex ratio of the older population. About 70 percent of all older persons are female, and the lower relative status of females in this society, in combination with their predominance among the aged, affect stereotypes of the aged in general and how well they fare in the stratification system.

Superficial appearances are visible indicators of age, and although appearance is not closely correlated with chronological aging, gross age differences among individuals are immediately observable. Age, then, belongs with race and sex as stratum variables that are observable; incumbents of these strata can be identified and differentiated when it is appropriate, for example in informal social interaction. Biological changes in appearance with age, such as balding, greying, and wrinkling, are not intrinsic biological parameters limiting the possibilities of age stratification, unlike reproductive functions, physical decline, and mortality, but do facilitate social diferentiation by age.

In an attempt to correct the mistaken emphasis on biological aspects of old age as the necessary and inevitable determinants of the status of the aged, many of us have tended to deny the very real constraints which biological aspects of aging place on stratification systems. A balanced view is needed.

> Age, like sex, is a biological characteristic of the human species that no society can disregard. In both cases, however, the physiological phenomena set limits on social definitions of position and role but never adequately account for the actual cultural definitions and practices (Moore, 1963, p. 55).

*Time Functions.* Whatever advantages or disadvantages accrue to an individual as a function of the passage of time itself will be reflected in an age stratification system. In the area of information and knowledge, for example, the aged gain honor to the extent that knowledge of enduring value, or wisdom, is only accumulated and never lost over time, and to the extent that such knowledge is an important asset in a given society. The aged will have lost status in a system of knowledge such as ours wherein information becomes obsolete.

Certain kinds of wealth appreciate over time, and it is not coincidental that the small number of individuals of very great wealth cluster in the older age stratum (Streib, 1976). The low income status of a large proportion of the elderly reflects in part the opposite process, the erosion of savings and fixed incomes over time due to inflation.

Some higher statuses by definition reflect the passage of time as a necessary status factor, as when seniority in employment and in unions denotes privileges, promotions, wage increases, and other benefits. Seniority in the military and class position in the university also reflect increments of status advantage over time and are highly correlated with greater age; in fact they may be thought of as "organizational age" (Moore, 1963).

The United States Congress observes customs of seniority which result in the most powerful positions in Congress accruing to the very oldest members (Riley *et al.*, 1972; Streib, 1976). Campbell (1971, p. 116) comments:

> The greatest difference [between age cohorts] lies in the possession of political power, which is largely preempted by people of middle age or beyond and is almost entirely withheld from the very young. This is a difference which depends on age itself, partly because the statutes require a minimum age for high office, partly because political advancement is typically a step-by-step process which requires an extensive period of time and partly because the public associates age with maturity and is reluctant to entrust high responsibility to what they consider an immature person.

It may then be that gerontologists claim too little for the explanatory power of chronological age when they state, as we have above, that age in itself explains nothing, being merely an indicator of elapsed time, since time itself is an important factor in the attainment of some statuses.

*Cohort Membership.* Some differences between the middle aged and older age strata are not the effects of age stratification, with social institutions and belief systems maintaining differential distribution of resources, but rather are the accumulated effects of cohort differences (Riley *et al.*, 1972). These differences can best be understood as the effects of the current older age stratum having matured in an historical period in which important advantages were less prevalent than at later periods. Only about one third of the current older population have completed a high school education. Occupational statuses formerly held by the older generation were lower in rank than current occupational statuses; for example the current aged were more likely to have been blue collar workers. A disproportionate fraction (one-third) of all the foreign born in the United States are in the 65+ age stratum, because of that cohort's unique immigration history (Uhlenberg, 1977). Health is another example of the long-range effects of early experiences, with the health decrements of the older age stratum reflecting in part inadequate medical and dental care and hazardous environments in their younger years.

Although we have stressed that these cohort membership factors are conceptually distinct from age stratification effects, to the extent that individuals and categories of individuals are evaluated in terms of education, occupational status, nativity, physical functioning, and appearance, the older age stratum suffers a devalued image and status on the basis of these cohort characteristics.

Cohort characteristics, then, like the biological parameters of reproduction, morbidity, and mortality discussed above, are correlates of aging which work mainly to the disadvantage of the aged. Some time functions, such as obsolescence, are disadvantageous, while others, such as seniority, work to the advantage of the status of the aged.

## LIFE COURSE MOBILITY THROUGH AGE STRATA

In *social* stratification theory, although individuals are grouped into hierarchically arranged social class strata, with each stratum manifesting different behavior styles, attitudes, and control of scarce resources, individuals do not necessarily remain in the socioeconomic stratum to which they were born. Through individual achievement, social change, or both, some individuals demonstrate upward mobility into a higher social class or downward mobility into a lower class. They must then adopt the norms of the new stratum and relinquish their adherence to the norms of the old one. Mobility calls for adaptation by the individual, as well as by the groups which he is departing and entering. The process can produce stress for the individual as he strives to adapt, and the social system itself can undergo strain when individuals or large groups change their position within the system.

There are parallel processes in age stratification. As individuals age, they enter new age strata appropriate to their advancing age, and exit those held previously when they were younger. Accompanying this age mobility is the need to adapt to new age norms. Traversing the age strata can be an expected and uneventful process for the individual, or it can create difficulties with implications for physical and emotional well-being. The social system can undergo strain when a cohort entering an age stratum has more or fewer members than there are positions allocated to the age stratum, as when the baby-boom cohort first required the school system to expand rapidly and then passed through, leaving it overextended (Riley *et al.*, 1972).

### THE PROCESS OF AGE MOBILITY

Age mobility (an individual's movement through age strata) can be defined as the sequencing of role entrances and exits accomplished by socialization, regulated by social institutions, and accompanied by shared meanings and values. This definition does not rest upon ontogenetic assumptions or posit the notion of intrinsic stages of development. The trajectory that one takes through successive age statuses, and the number and identification of age statuses themselves, are socially determined.

Neugarten *et al.* (1968) attempted to verify empirically the existence of age strata. They assumed that there is a span of years within which any given behavior pattern is deemed appropriate; when the behavior occurs outside that span of years, it is considered to be inappropriate and is negatively sanctioned. Statements were constructed on various age-related behaviors, for example the best age for a man to marry, when most people should become grandparents, and the best age to finish school work. A high degree of consensus was found among their subjects, indicating shared conceptions of age norms which cluster to define an age stratum and the boundaries between strata.

Age stratum boundaries are often flexible and ambiguous, so it is seldom entirely clear when an individual takes on a new, older age status; what is clear is that he *will* enter that status sooner or later. Certain rituals such as bar mitzvah or legal transitions such as reaching voting age can be indicators of passages through childhood, adolescence and young adulthood.

The transition between middle and old age, on the other hand, might be marked only by slight shifts in others' behavior toward the aging individual which signals him that the transition is approaching. These might include suggestions to slow down, a reduction in responsibilities, or proffered discussion on retirement planning. In general, the boundary will be marked by some disturbance in the interaction patterns between the aging individual and those around him as both struggle to adapt to the expectations of the new status. When both the individual and others agree that he is no longer middle aged but old, new interaction patterns may emerge which are free of the earlier disturbance; at this point, the transition is complete.

As an individual ages, then, he will move through several age statuses, each of which is characterized by different normative expectations and styles of life. When boundaries are vague, ill-defined, and not marked by any particular event (as is often the case from adolescence to young adulthood or from middle to old age), then the transition can be drawn-out and troublesome. Expectations of both adjacent age statuses compete until such a time when the norms which define the next older status gain prominence and those of the previous status become less salient.

MECHANISMS OF AGE STRATIFICATION
MOBILITY

One aspect of age stratification mobility concerns the mechanisms by which age status transition is accomplished. In social stratification, one might experience mobility between social classes due to dividual achievement, as with occupational advancement; in age stratification, personal achievement is not a significant factor. Instead, mobility from middle to old age is associated primarily with advancing age, and triggered by events such as retirement, widowhood, or failing health. Since everyone ages and dies, mobility through age statuses is "universal, unidirectional and irreversible" according to Riley (1971).

Several investigators have studied *socialization*

as a mechanism of age status change. Riley (1976, p. 200) suggests that the role of socialization in age stratification is to "teach individuals at each stage of the life course how to perform new roles, how to negotiate procedures, how to adjust to changing roles and how to relinquish old ones." Through the socialization process, one learns the appropriate norms of behavior for any given age group, comes to see these behaviors as normal, and adopts the behavior appropriate to his own age group.

Rosow (1974) contends that although this argument might hold for age status changes in the earlier part of the life cycle, individuals are not effectively socialized to old age. "Aging poses a special case of socialization to a devalued status in which restitutive and social control functions are minimal" (Rosow, 1974, p. xiv). Most rites of passage from one age status to another are characterized by social gains including greater responsibility, independence, and autonomy. When passing into old age, however, there are no rites of passage, and there are usually declines in autonomy, status, and responsibility.

One mechanism of a change from middle to old age is the *labeling* of an individual as "old" by those around him. If others define the individual as old, based upon certain cues from the aging individual and the social environment, it is likely these labeling reactions will eventually cause the individual to adopt the status being imputed to him.

In a study of air traffic controllers (Wales, 1976), it was hypothesized that certain nonvisual cues would arise in a structured occupational setting that might cause others to label an aging colleague "old" as a prelude to his age status change. It was found that if an air traffic controller had high status relative to others, he was less likely to be labeled old, and therefore not as likely to proceed to the older age status. Also, if an aging individual belonged to a task-oriented work group which was told that it had performed poorly, it was much more likely that he would be labeled old. These results suggest that *when* and *to whom* an age status change occurs are the results of a complex interaction of personal characteristics and socioenvironmental factors.

VARIATIONS IN AGE STRATIFICATION
MOBILITY PATTERNS

Everyone who ages will move through the various age strata. There is, however, considerable variation among individuals along two basic dimensions. The first concerns the pattern and pacing of age strata mobility. When in the life course age strata are entered and exited, and how they are experienced vary among individuals according to characteristics such as sex, socioeconomic status and ethnicity. The second dimension concerns problems experienced as the result of leaving one age stratum and entering another. Age strata mobility may be smooth and uneventful, or it might cause disruption.

*Patterns and Pacing.*  Bengtson, Kasschau and Ragan (1977) describe how patterns of aging vary according to individuals' location in the social structure, with location defined by gender, SES (Socioeconomic status), and race or ethnicity. For example, women are perceived to reach the status of old age at an earlier chronological age than men, with physical changes and family situations providing the cues more often for men (National Council on Aging, 1975). Women also outlive men by almost eight years (US Bureau of the Census, 1974), so they enter old age earlier and maintain the status longer. Gender probably accounts for more variation in the timing of age status transfers than any other characteristic.

Similarly, SES (indexed by income, education, or occupation) influences the timing of entry into old age. Low SES has been observed to be associated with feeling old (Riley and Foner, 1968, p. 305); and in a study of air traffic controllers it was found that subjects of high SES entered old age (a low status stratum) later than those of low SES (Wales, 1976).

Minority groups also tend to vary from the majority regarding the pace of their social aging. For example, Bengtson, Cuellar, and Ragan (1977) found in their Los Angeles community survey that at given chronological ages Mexican Americans were likely to see themselves as older and blacks were likely to see themselves as younger than whites.

Status transitions from middle age to old age depend for their timing and cues on such individual characteristics as gender, SES, and race. Although the boundary of old age is ambiguous in this society, much of the variation in status transitions is itself patterned according to these other status characteristics.

## MOBILITY AND DISRUPTION

Entering a new age stratum such as old age requires the adoption of new norms, values, and life styles and the relinquishing of old ones. Significant disruptions in self concept, behavior, and emotional state may occur in response to the status loss of the transition, the discontinuity of roles, the lack

of age status boundary clarity, inadequate socialization, and deviance from age norms.

*Status Loss.*  In spite of the advantages, as well as the disadvantages, that accrue to the older age stratum, the overall status and prestige of the aged is recognized as lower than the status of young and middle aged adults. (Butler, 1975; Rosow, 1974). Several aspects of the status of the old have been discussed, such as the loss of work role and drop in income, shifts of power and responsibility to younger adults, the dependent status of the older stratum, and the general value placed on youthful vigor and appearance. The self-esteem of the individual older person may reflect his identification with a social stratum of perceived lower status.

*Role Continuity.*  Whether the roles of adjacent strata are continuous or disjunctive is another stress factor in aging. As Riley (1976, p. 208) states:

> The transfer from one stratum to the next can be either sharp or gradual, sometimes taking place by stages. Exit from work can occur through tapering off or it can consist of a complete break between the last full day of work and the first full day of complete retirement.

Although some roles such as work and marriage may be discontinuous in old age because of such role exits as retirement or widowhood, other roles such as homemaking, parenting and grandparenting, friendship, and leisure roles may be carried over into old age, although with some modifications. Gradual role transitions and the continuity and similarity of role sets from one stratum to the next may contribute to an easy transition.

*Boundary Definition.*  Over time the age stratification system itself changes (see discussion which follows). Newly defined age strata emerge, as in the case of adolescence in our recent history; the "old-old" are becoming a newly defined age sub-stratum or stratum. The boundaries which delineate adjacent strata are often in flux, as when the age of reaching adult status shifts from 21 to 18; similarly, recent legislation shifting the chronological age used in mandatory retirement from 65 to 70 will be followed by other redefinitions of old age.

How does an individual know when he is about to be identified as old? Age strata and their boundary definitions shift, and in addition the cues to old age lack synchronization, that is, they vary from one social domain to another (Cain, 1964). A man may become a grandfather at 44, go bald at 49, become eligible for Social Security at 62, retire at 65, retain his good health and sexual desire until 73, remain mentally alert until 77, and die at 78; when did he become old? Ambiguity of age status transitions increases the individual's uncertainty about his own identity and society's expectations for his behavior.

*Socialization.* Individuals entering a new stage of the life course, such as adulthood, learn the expected behaviors and attitudes of their new age status through informal means of induction, or processes of socialization (Brim and Wheeler, 1966; Rosow, 1974). It is Rosow's thesis that "people are not effectively socialized to old age" (p. xii). Clear rites of passage are missing. Passage to earlier life course stages is marked by social gains (independence, leadership, autonomy, responsibility, and status), but the transition to old age is the exception to such status gains. Since "aging poses a special case of socialization to a devalued status" (Rosow, 1974, p. xiv) and since the expectations in old age are unclear, mobility into the stratum of old age carries a potential for personal disorientation.

*Timing of Transitions.* Most people of similar location in the social structure share a common understanding of when it is proper for an age status passage to occur (Neugarten *et al.*, 1968). Age norms define a chronological age range in which certain events such as marriage, parenthood, and retirement are considered appropriate. If one marries approximately at the same age as his peers, he is "on-time"; if the marriage occurs when he is too young or too old, he is "off-time." The significance of this on-time/off-time distinction is that "role transitions, while they call for new adaptations, are not ordinarily traumatic if they occur on time because they have been anticipated and rehearsed. Major stresses are caused by events that upset the expected sequences and rhythms of life" (Neugarten and Hagestad, 1976, p. 51). Very early retirement, romance or remarriage at an advanced age, or attempting a new career in old age are all examples of off-time events that conflict with norms of the appropriate pattern of mobility into old age. Blau (1973, p. 229) states that "To be out of phase, in short, places an individual in a deviant position vis-à-vis others in his own age group. Therefore it is likely to have some invidious effects on the person's associational life and self-concept." Deviance from the norms is a potential source of trouble for the individual, but conforming to the constraints of age norms, on the other hand, may inhibit the individual's own self-fulfillment.

Following this discussion of the mechanisms and variations of age mobility and the potential personal disruptions involved in moving from the middle aged to the older age stratum, we will now turn to a consideration of the implications of social change for an understanding of age stratification and the mental health of aging individuals.

## SOCIAL CHANGE, AGE STRATIFICATION, AND LIFE COURSE PROCESSES

Age stratification has been presented basically as a cross-sectional view; at a given point in time we can observe differences among age strata. In fact, age stratification is a function of three dynamic, change-over-time processes (Riley, *et al.*, 1972). First, the continual *succession of new birth cohorts* provides the incumbents of the youngest age stratum. Secondly, as the individuals in the youngest stratum proceed through the *life course* and follow the maturational sequence of age stratum exits and entrances, they become the occupants of successively older strata. Third, as successive cohorts proceed through the age strata, the age stratification system itself is being modified through the processes of *social change*.

Each cohort approaches the status of old age differently. The individual in a cohort born at the turn of the century has entered an old age stratum which is a different phenomenon from anything that existed when he was growing up. The intersection of that individual's life course trajectory with the changing age stratification system results in ambiguity about the meanings attached to being old. Since the pace of social change only increases, individuals will continue to anticipate and enter a period of old age with uncertainty about the future.

Since the turn of the century, old age has been transformed through a number of social changes: an entirely new social phenomenon, "retirement" as we know it, became a major institutional aspect of old age (Sheppard, 1976; Streib and Schneider, 1971); the age of 65, or slight variations in one direction or the other, became mandated as the age of entry into old age (Sheppard and Rix, 1977); the lengthy postparental "empty nest" period emerged as a distinctly new family cycle phase (Treas, 1975); more people survive to old age; the life expectancy of women has substantially exceeded that of men; ageism became a social issue. Even as individuals anticipate their own old age, old age itself becomes something different. Rosow (1974), Neugarten and Hagestad (1976); and Bengtson and Cutler (1976) have pointed out the social change aspects of age status transitions; Cain (1968) has also discussed this social change phenomenon, as follows:

> Society...calls upon these same older people to be socialized into ever-shifting patterns for old age status; in fact, in some ways the aged themselves are called upon to invent their own prospective status, then socialize themselves into it (p. 253).

Not only do the definitions of old age and the roles and responsibilities attached to the status change over time, but the boundary between middle age and old age is subject to shifts (Foner, 1975). We are witnessing many individuals electing to retire at increasingly earlier ages, and at the same time the permissible mandatory age of retirement rising from 65 to 70. Complex and often conflicting social trends over time contribute to the confusion over the age at which one enters the older age stratum (as discussed previously in the context of stratum mobility). Cues to self-identification are therefore confusing.

This chapter has not dealt with the question of changes in the relative status of the aged in society over time, whether measured by income or prestige, but others have considered the historical dimension in the status of the aged (Hendricks and Hendricks, 1977; Palmore and Whittington, 1971; Pampel, 1977). Losses that occur over time in the relative status advantages of the aged, in addition to changes in definitions and boundaries of old age, may contribute to the negative feelings which younger individuals attach to their own future selves.

One particular trend in the definition of the older age stratum is critical for an understanding of the age stratification system, namely the recent tendency to partition old age into distinct subcategories. Neugarten (1974) suggested labels for these emerging categories of the aged, the "young old" (55–74) and the "old old" (75+), and although the specific chronological age demarcations vary, her labels have gained wide use in gerontological disciplines. We noted previously that the very fact of identifying age strata by labeling is a piece of evidence that the strata are social realities. There is some evidence that these two subcategories, young old and old old, are taking on the characteristics of separate age strata. Statistics are increasingly reported on the differences between the young old and the 75+ age groups—the 75+ are poorer, in worse health, more likely to be institutionalized, and more likely to be female and widowed. The Federal Council on the Aging (1977) has taken the 75+ age group to represent the "frail elderly," the subgroup which the Commission has identified for priority in government programs. It is as if the 75+, or the "old-old," were coming to be defined as the *real* old age stratum.

A younger age category also deserves attention in the context of aging and social change, perhaps to be defined for the purpose of discussion as the 50–64 year olds. The individuals who are not yet old share many indicators of aging, such as the empty nest, menopause, grandparenthood, widowhood, some of the greying and wrinkling indicia of approaching old age, and in some cases retirement, and yet they have not emerged as an identifiable stratum. Old age benefit categories, such as for publicly assisted housing, often extend downward to include them. They are treated as the "pre-retirement" set for purposes of counseling and planning, but they have not emerged as a group distinct from other middle aged persons with specific expectations, norms, mandated privileges, or consumer interests. The most revealing evidence that they do not yet form a distinct stratum is that there is no label which is consensually applied to the category. This older middle age contingent bears watching as a group with shared age related psycho-social needs, but not yet emergent as a distinct age stratum.

Even if substantial changes in definitions and boundaries of the old age stratum were not occurring, successive cohorts would experience old age status differently because of their own differences from preceding cohorts. The current stratum of older persons, 65 and older, making up 23 million and 11 percent of the population, has moved into an age stratum which was formerly occupied, in 1900, by 3 million and 4 percent of the population; a strain on allocated resources naturally has occured. The current older cohort is better educated, in better health, and has higher expectations than earlier cohorts. The idea of successive cohorts entering different situations of old age and bringing with them different perspectives and experiences is similar to Mannheim's (1952[1928]) concept of younger generational units, each encountering society with a fresh perspective and therefore with a different social change outcome (Bengtson and Cutler, 1976). Cohorts in the immediate future will encounter old age with outcomes that are unique. We can speculate about the effects of rapid social change on the experiences of the future aged. Such developments as the extensive entry of middle-age women into the labor force, the emphasis on physical fitness, the value attached to leisure pursuits, openness toward sexuality, and experiences with political protest can lead us to expect a different set of problems, and resources for coping with those problems, among the aged in the near future.

Inadequate attention has been paid to the effects of economic development, changes in mortality and fertility patterns, and other social change patterns on shifts in the definition of the older age stratum (or strata). Elder (1975, p. 168) notes on the occasion of reviewing the literature on social change and life course differences that "very little is known about historical events and cycles in the modification of age criteria and categories." The implications of social change in the age stratification system for the older person's well-being are nevertheless significant; they are discussed further in the following section.

# CONCLUSION

## ADVANTAGES AND PROBLEMS OF AN AGE STRATIFICATION PERSPECTIVE

By taking a macro approach and using cross-sectional observations of society, we can observe the dynamics of the age stratification system. It is in periods of radical change that we can observe the stratification system most clearly. For example, now that the specific age of mandatory retirement has been shifted upward, and abolished altogether for Federal government employees, our attention is drawn to the enunciation of belief systems and the structure of laws surrounding the stratification of work roles according to age. The rapid change in laws provides a natural laboratory for observing stratification in process.

An age stratification perspective offers some advantages in understanding aging, but can it be said that age is in fact a stratum variable? Age is a stratum variable in that age strata are identifiable, resources are distributed differentially by age strata, and the distribution is institutionalized and supported by normative systems and by sets of beliefs. Some problems exist in the conceptualization of age as a stratum variable, however. Many resources, roles, and responsibilities are primarily distributed according to the other stratum variables of class, race, and sex, so the distribution by age is the basis of only a "partial" system (Eisenstadt, 1971); the great variability *within* age strata weakens the age stratification argument. Furthermore, the boundary between the strata of middle age and old age, although clear for some purposes such as mandatory retirement or age-mandated benefits, is not clearly perceived by the general public; the age at which an individual becomes "old" lacks consensus (National Council on Aging, 1975). Individuals' *self* definitions as old are even

more open to confusion than definitions of the general boundaries of old age. Partly related to the lack of self-identification as old is the lack of group solidarity within the aged stratum, one of the elements of the concept of "class" (Streib, 1976). Heterogeneity within age strata, ambiguity of stratum boundaries, and the lack of group solidarity, then, are limitations on the usefulness of viewing age categories as strata.

The use of the conceptual language of social class has proved to illuminate the status of the aged, but we can point to several errors that often occur as the age stratification concept is increasingly adopted. First, the interpretation is often made that the aged as a category are in *all respects* systematically disadvantaged relative to younger groups; the data presented in this chapter contradict that interpretation. Second, the age stratification approach is exaggerated to the extent that characteristics (such as median income) are attributed to the aged as an aggregate, without acknowledging the great variation within the aged stratum. The range of differences on income and education within the older stratum, for example, reminds us to analyze the coexistence of several stratification systems—age, SES, race, and sex. Third, the same tendency of comparing aggregate statistics of strata also conceals the concentration of important resources, such as great wealth and political power in the older stratum. An emphasis on strata characteristics is revealing, but needs to be tempered with attention to the heterogeneity within a category such as the older population (Ragan and Davis, 1978).

## IMPLICATIONS FOR SOCIAL GERONTOLOGY

In spite of some limitations in the conceptualization of age strata, there are real advantages to an age stratification analysis. One can go beyond the conventional gerontological approach of studying the individual's adjustment to becoming old in a given social system, and focus rather on the characteristics of the system itself that impinge on the status of the aged. In a period of claims and counterclaims for scarce resources by older and younger age strata, we can be sensitized to the possibilities of potential strain and conflict emerging in the system, in contrast to an order-consensus model that has tended to dominate gerontological studies.

## IMPLICATIONS FOR THE AGING INDIVIDUAL

If the aged do occupy a relatively lower status overall, what are the effects of that devalued status on the older individual? An obvious possibility is that he will identify himself as old, recognize the low status of the aged, and experience a loss of self-esteem (Kuypers and Bengtson, 1973). It is interesting to note, however, that in the NCOA survey the older respondents did indeed hold low opinions of the aged as a group (even lower than younger respondents), but their self-conceptions did not include the negative characteristics they attributed to *other* older people (National Council on Aging, 1975).

Another possibility is that the low status of the aged may cause the aging individual to postpone the identification of himself as old, despite transition events he experiences and cues he receives from other persons and from his social environment that he has become old. In the face of mounting evidence of old age, he needs to exert greater effort to deny himself and to others that he is growing old.

Movement from a higher to a lower status age stratum may have little impact on persons who do not experience the loss of roles and resources of most individuals in the older stratum. The retired physician, for example, may carry into retirement his occupational prestige and financial resources, and therefore be little affected by the group status of the aged. Individual variations in the internalization of age group status are crucial for a balanced perspective on the effects of stratification.

The lower status of the aged affects younger persons as well. The younger person on a life course trajectory toward old age faces a devalued status of his own self in the future; there may be a kind of alienation (self-estrangement) at work in that process. Younger persons may also limit their social interaction with older persons because of the devalued status of the elderly; the implications for the isolation of the aged from other age strata are clear. In fact, avoidance of other older persons because of lowered status may take place within the older population itself; the NCOA survey found that only 25 percent of the 65+ respondents themselves, compared to 82 percent of the younger public, thought that most people over 65 were "very friendly and warm" (National Council on Aging, 1975).

What does the future hold for the status of the aged? On the one hand, future cohorts of older persons will carry with them into old age characteristics which will benefit their overall status. Compared to earlier cohorts of older persons, they will be better educated, in better health, and will be more experienced and assertive in the protection of their economic status (Sheppard, 1977). On the other hand, the old age stratum may come to be defined by a higher age entry, for example age 75,

if there are not in fact two recognized age strata, the young old and the old old. Between 1980 and 1990 there will be about a 25 percent increase in the 75+ population (from 9.1 to 11.4 million) (US Bureau of the Census, 1976). The combination of political forces such as the raising of the age of mandatory retirement and the emphasis on federal programs for the 75+ "frail elderly" may contribute to the redefinition of the older stratum as the 75+. In that case the differential allocation of work, income, roles, and responsibility by age stratum will be much more dramatic than it is at present, and we might predict that the relative status of this newly defined older age stratum will be much lower overall. The transition to the status of old old may carry more serious implications of loss of self-esteem and stigmatization.

In addition to the low status of the aged, other features of the age stratification system have been discussed above which may create problems for the aging individual. The lack of clear definition of the entry boundary of old age has been discussed as a problem in the transition to old age in that it creates "ambiguity" about age statuses. It can, however, be viewed positively, as allowing for "flexibility." Cain suggested that the ambiguity of the status of old age may have positive aspects, in that it can contribute to the potential for creativity in persons making the transition to old age. Similarly, Bengtson (1973, p. 25) reinterpreted the problem of the loss of norms and roles as "a gain in freedom" and "potential opportunity" for wider choices. From a cross-cultural study of aging in Tanzania, Yugoslavia, Mexico, and the United States, the following generalization comes forth:

> ...where social discontinuity is marked, social norms concerning aging and the aged are shifting and ambiguous. Norms are fluid, and maximum opportunities exist for individual innovation, exploitation, and experimentation. Resourcefulness of individuals may be maximally exercised and often becomes very influential in accounting for differential success in aging as a career (Simic, 1978, p. 21).

This chapter has considered the effects of the system of age stratification, and social change in that system, on the aging individual. The overall low status and dependent status of the aged, the ambiguity of age status boundaries and ineffective socialization to old age, all contribute to the anxieties and uncertainties which some individuals experience. Further study is needed of the effect of death, as the exit from the stratum of old age, on the emotional life of those anticipating and occupying old age. Further attention needs to be paid to specific locations in the social structure where age intersects with race and gender to effect the extreme deprivations in old age. For example, very old women, and old minority women in particular, occupy the most disadvantaged position in the stratification system, and their emotional well-being cannot be considered without attention to basic survival needs of income, housing, and adequate nutrition.

Even when we gain some perspective on the meaning of old age by viewing individuals in the context of their location in the age stratification system, we realize that social change is immediately presenting us with the challenge of unique cohorts entering old age, and facing quite different social situations. Our approach to understanding and assisting aging individuals requires constant reappraisal.

IMPLICATIONS FOR SOCIAL POLICY

The cross-sectional description of age stratum differences that has been presented here begins not with assumptions or assertions about *inequities* (injustices) in the system, but rather with an analysis of *inequalities* (Riley, 1976, p. 211). By viewing the differential distribution by age of the valued resources in society from this inequality perspective, it becomes apparent that in certain important respects (work roles, income, and prestige) the aged are systematically disadvantaged, while in other respects (political power, discretionary time, categorical benefits, and obligations) the aged are not disadvantaged.

Advocates for the aged need to start with such a structural approach and may choose to use information about differences, or inequalities, as a base for their arguments about the need to correct inequities. A stratification perspective will be useful in attempts to secure social justice for the aged, but on the other hand it will caution us against the potential hazards of advocacy. The lowered prestige of the aged which we protest may even be in part a latent consequence of the benevolent intentions of spokespersons who call attention to the low status of the aged (as we have done above). Continued generalizations about the low status of the aged may contribute to its becoming a social reality.

With a view of both the advantages and disadvantages that accrue to an age stratum, which might be thought of as "trade-offs," it becomes necessary to consider the implications that change in one factor of distribution may have for change in other factors (Cain, 1976). The raising of the involuntary retirement age was accompanied by

arguments that it is not fair to deprive individuals of the work role on the arbitrary basis of chronologic age alone (and presumably the assumption that the age of 70 is less unfair and more appropriate than the age of 65 for such treatment). Will this legislation be followed by a trend to raise the age of eligibility for age-mandated benefits, or perhaps to challenge chronological age as the basis for distribution of benefits altogether?

The definition, the boundaries, and the relative status of age strata are flexible and may change rapidly due to socioeconomic changes and purposive policy intervention (Cain, 1964). Those who would shape social policy to intervene in the determination of the status of the aged will recognize that the age boundary between the old and not-yet-old is flexible. It has moved up to 70 to protect more individuals from involuntary retirement and it has moved down to as low as 50 to include more individuals in service delivery programs. The identification of the boundary of the aged stratum (the age at which persons become old) is ambiguous, in flux, and subject to redefinition through policy determinations.

We can observe some policy efforts to redefine the aged stratum, for the purposes of benefit programs, as the very old, the "frail elderly," usually designated as 75+ (Federal Council on the Aging, 1977). It is not difficult to imagine that the age stratification system in the future will be based on separate strata for the young old and old old. The wide age range in the 65+ population includes vast differences in behavior, attitudes, physical functioning, and cohort experiences, and it is not useful to attempt to plan programs that meet the needs of such a broad age group. Furthermore, the older population cannot be expected to share mutual interests or enjoy mutual social attractiveness from the youngest to the oldest of the "old."

Although the aged are seen to gain some advantages in the existing differential distribution of resources, such as discretionary time, leisure, and freedom from obligations, it is the allocation of the *most valued resources* in society, such as work and income, which determines the overall relative status of a stratum. Greater emphasis on the less valued roles, such as recreation and volunteerism, will not raise the status of the aged to the extent that reallocation of highly valued work roles will (Hendricks and Hendricks, 1977, p. 111). Current discussions of the reallocation of work and leisure, with periods of each dispersed throughout the life span, are important here. Even the resource of discretionary time is relevant in this regard; seriously valued pursuits in this society, such as political activity, public service, and higher education carry more prestige than recreational activities.

To the extent that a negative image or low status of the aged is pervasive, that image can probably best be modified by changing economic distributive arrangements; values and ideas, such as the stereotypes of the aged, are most clearly understood as resulting from economic circumstances rather than determining them. Direct attempts to change attitudes toward the aged, therefore, are less than promising.

The potential for altering the status of the aged indirectly through policy intervention is more apparent from a stratification point of view. Beyond the recognized effects on the status of the aged of economic forces such as industrial development, unemployment and inflation, we can see how the status of the aged is deliberately modified by legislation. Kreps (1976) speaks of such "distributional decisions":

> These macroeconomic influences set the stage within which the status of any age group is determined. Allocative patterns dictate the relative positions of youth, the middle-aged, and the elderly by specifying how each will share in total output. (p. 273).

The implications of an age stratification view for social policy rest on several themes that have been emphasized in this chapter. The differential distribution of valued resources is institutionalized, i.e. the system is maintained by norms, rules, regulations, and indeed by *law*. Economic factors are primary in the determination of relative status in all social ranking systems (Streib, 1976). Changes in the definition of age strata and in their relative ranking in the distribution system are responsive not only to long-range socioeconomic trends but also to ideas about fairness and to deliberate changes in social policy.

This chapter has dealt with a topic which has only recently received systematic attention from gerontologists. The study of age stratification, the distribution of society's scarce resources on the basis of age, holds promise as a vehicle for understanding some of the complex forces which bear upon the well-being of the older person. All people age, and as they do so they move through a sequence of age strata that affect the norms they are expected to follow, the resources they command, the roles they are called upon to play, and the prestige accorded them. The final age stratum to be occupied in the life course sequence is unique in the hazards and the potentials it holds for the individual anticipating, entering, and experiencing old age.

# REFERENCES

*Ageing International.* 1977. Vol. I, No. 3.

BENGTSON, V. L. 1973. *The Social Psychology of Aging.* Indianapolis: Bobbs-Merrill.

BENGTSON, V. L., CUELLAR, J. B., AND RAGAN, P. K. 1977. Stratum contrasts and similarities in attitudes toward death. *Journal of Gerontology, 32,* 76–88.

BENGTSON, V. L., AND CUTLER, N. E. 1976. Generations and intergenerational relations: Perspectives on age groups and social change. *In,* R. H. Binstock, and E. L. Shanas (eds.), *Handbook of Aging and the Social Sciences,* pp. 130–159. New York: Van Nostrand Reinhold.

BENGTSON, V. L., KASSCHAU, P. L., AND RAGAN, P. K. 1977. The impact of social structure on aging individuals. *In,* J. E. Birren, and K. W. Schaie, (eds.), *Handbook of the Psychology of Aging,* pp. 327–353. New York: Van Nostrand Reinhold.

BLAU, P. M. 1974. Presidential address: Parameters of social structure. *American Sociological Review, 39,* 615–635.

BLAU, Z. S. 1973. *Old Age in a Changing Society.* New York: New Viewpoints.

BRIM, O. G., AND WHEELER, S. 1966. *Socialization After Childhood: Two Essays.* New York: John Wiley.

BRODY, E. M. 1979. Aged parents and aging children. *In,* P. K. Ragan (ed.), *Aging Parents,* pp. 267–287. Los Angeles: University of Southern California Press.

BROTMAN, H. B. 1971. *Facts and Figures on Older Americans: Federal Outlays in Aging, Fiscal Years 1967–72.* DHEW Publication No. (SRS) 72–20183. Washington, D.C.: US DHEW AoA.

BUTLER, R. N. 1975. *Why Survive? Being Old in America.* New York: Harper & Row.

CAIN, L. D., JR. 1964. Life course and the social structure. *In,* R.E.L. Faris (ed.), *Handbook of Modern Sociology,* pp. 272–309. Chicago: Rand McNally.

CAIN, L. D., JR. 1968. Aging and the character of our times. *Gerontologist, 8,* 250–258.

CAIN, L. D, JR.1976. Aging and the law. *In,* R. H. Binstock and E. L. Shanas (eds.), *Handbook of Aging and the Social Sciences,* pp. 342–368. New York: Van Nostrand Reinhold.

CAMPBELL, A. 1971. Politics through the life cycle. *Gerontologist, 11,* 112–117.

CUMMING, E., AND HENRY, W. 1961. *Growing Old: The Process of Disengagement.* New York: Basic Books.

CUTLER, N. E., AND HAROOTYAN, R. A. 1975. Demography of the aged. *In,* D. S. Woodruff and J. E. Birren (eds.), *Aging: Scientific Perspectives and Social Issues,* pp. 31–69. New York: Van Nostrand Reinhold.

DAHRENDORF, R. 1957. *Class and Class Conflict in Industrial*

*Society*. Stanford: Stanford University Press.

DAVIS, K., AND MOORE, W. E. 1945. Some principles of stratification. *American Sociological Review, 10,* 242–249.

DUBERMAN, L. 1976. *Social Inequality: Class and Caste in America*. Philadelphia: Lippincott.

EISENSTADT, S. N. 1971. *Social Differentiation and Stratification*. Glenview, Ill.: Scott, Foresman.

ELDER, G. H. 1975. Age differentiation and the life course. *In,* A. Inkeles (ed.), *Annual Review of Sociology, Vol. I.,* pp. 165–190. Palo Alto: Annual Reviews.

Federal Council on the Aging. 1977. *Annual Report to the President, 1976*. DHEW Publication No. (OHD) 77–20957. Washington, D.C.: DHEW.

FISCHER, D. H. 1977. *Growing Old In America*. New York: Oxford Press.

FONER, A. 1975. Age in society. *American Behavioral Scientist. 19*(2), 144–165.

HENDRICKS, J., AND HENDRICKS, C. D. 1977. *Aging in Mass Society: Myths and Realities*. Cambridge, Mass.: Winthrop.

HENRETTA, J. C., AND CAMPBELL, R. T. 1976. Status attainment and status maintenance: A study of stratification in old age. *American Sociological Review, 41,* 981–992.

HUDSON, R. B., AND BINSTOCK, R. H. 1976. Political systems and aging. *In,* R. H. Binstock and E. L. Shanas (eds.), *Handbook of Aging and the Social Sciences,* (pp. 369–400). New York: Van Nostrand Reinhold.

JEFFRIES, V. AND RANSFORD, H. E. 1979. *Multiple Hierarchy Stratification: Class, Ethnicity, Sex, Age*. Boston: Allyn and Bacon.

KASTENBAUM, R. 1978. Essay: Gerontology's search for understanding. *Gerontologist, 18,* 60.

KREPS, J. M. 1976. The economy and the aged. *In,* R. H. Binstock and E. L. Shanas (eds.), *Handbook of Aging and the Social Sciences,* pp. 272–285. New York: Van Nostrand Reinhold.

KUYPERS, J. A., AND BENGTSON, V. L. 1973. Competence and social breakdown: A social-psychological view of aging. *Human Development, 16*(2), 181–201.

LENSKI, G. E. 1966. *Power and Privilege: A Theory of Social Stratification*. New York: McGraw-Hill.

LINTON, R. 1936. *The Study of Man*. New York: Appleton-Century-Crofts.

LOUIS, A. M. 1968. America's centimillionaires. *Fortune, 77,* 152–157.

LUNDBERG, G. A., SCHRAG, C. C., LARSEN, O. N., AND CATTON, W. R. 1968. *Sociology,* 4th edition. New York: Harper & Row.

MCCONNELL, S. R., AND DAVIS, W. J. 1977. Decision-maker report. Los Angeles: Andrus Gerontology Center, University of Southern California.

MANNHEIM, K. 1952. The problem of generations. *In,* P. Kecskemeti (ed.), *Essays on the Sociology of Knowl-*

*edge,* pp. 276–322. London: Routledge and Kegan Paul. (Originally published, 1928.)

Metropolitan Life, 1977. *Statistical Bulletin, 58,*(July-August).

MOORE, W. E. 1963. *Man, Time, and Society*. New York: John Wiley.

National Council on Aging. 1975. *The Myth and Reality of Aging in America*. Washington, D.C.: NCOA.

NEUGARTEN, B. L. 1974. Age groups in American society and the rise of the young-old. *Ann. Amer. Acad.,* (September), 187–198.

NEUGARTEN, B. L., AND HAGESTAD, G. O. 1976. Age and the life course. *In,* R. H. Binstock and E. L. Shanas (eds.), *Handbook of Aging and the Social Sciences,* pp. 35–57. New York: Van Nostrand Reinhold.

NEUGARTEN, B. L., AND MOORE, J. W. 1968. The changing age-status system. *In,* B. L. Neugarten (ed.), *Middle Age and Aging: A Reader in Social Psychology,* pp.5–21. Chicago: University of Chicago Press.

NEUGARTEN, B. L., MOORE, J. W., AND LOWE, J. C. 1968. Age norms, age constraints, and adult socialization. *In,* B. L. Neugarten (ed.), *Middle Age and Aging: A Reader in Social Psychology,* pp.22–28. Chicago: University of Chicago Press.

PALMORE, E. 1976. The future status of the aged. *Gerontologist, 16,* 297–302.

PALMORE, E., AND MANTON, K. 1973. Ageism compared to racism and sexism. *Journal of Gerontology, 28,* 363–369.

PALMORE, E., AND WHITTINGTON, F. 1971. Trends in the relative status of the aged. *Social Forces, 50,* 84–91.

PAMPEL, F. C. 1977. Social indicator models of changes in the status of the aged: Labor force, occupation and income. Unpublished Ph.D. dissertation, University of Illinois at Urbana-Champaign.

PARSONS, T. 1949. Age and sex in the social structure of the United States. *In,* T. Parsons (ed.), *Essays in Sociological Theory* (revised ed.), pp. 218–232. Glencoe, Ill.: Free Press.

PRATT, H. J. 1976. *The Gray Lobby*. Chicago: University of Chicago Press.

RAGAN, P. K. 1977. Another look at the politicizing of old age: Can we expect a backlash effect? *Urban and Social Change Review, 10*(2), 6–13.

RAGAN, P. K., AND BENGTSON, V. L. 1977. *Aging Among Blacks, Mexican Americans and Whites: Development, Procedures and Results of the Community Survey*. Final report to NSF (RANN).

RAGAN, P. K., AND DAVIS, W. J. 1978. The diversity of older voters. *Society, 15,* July/August, pp. 50–53.

RAGAN, P. K., AND GRIGSBY, J. E. 1976. Responsibility for meeting the needs of the elderly for health care, housing, and transportation: Opinions reported in a survey of Blacks, Mexican Americans and whites. Paper presented at the meeting of the Western Gerontological Society, San Diego.

RILEY, M. W. 1971. Social gerontology and the age stratification of society. *Gerontologist, 11*, 79–87.

RILEY, M. W. 1976. Age strata in social systems. *In,* R. H. Binstock and E. Shanas (eds.), *Handbook of Aging and the Social Sciences*, pp. 189–217. New York: Van Nostrand Reinhold.

RILEY, M. W., AND FONER, A. 1968. *Aging and Society, Volume I: An Inventory of Research Findings*. New York: Russell Sage.

RILEY, M. W., JOHNSON, M., AND FONER, A. 1972. *Aging and Society. Volume Three: A sociology of age stratification*. New York: Russell Sage.

ROACH, J. L., GROSS, L., AND GURSSLIN, O. (eds.) 1969. *Social Stratification in the United States*. Englewood Cliffs, N.J.: Prentice-Hall.

ROSENBERG, G. S. 1970. *The Worker Grows Old*. San Francisco: Jossey-Bass.

ROSOW, I. 1974. *Socialization to Old Age*. Berkeley, California: University of California Press.

SCHULTZ, J. H. 1976. *The Economics of Aging*. Belmont, Cal.: Wadsworth.

SHEPPARD, H. L. 1976. Work and retirement. *In,* R. H. Binstock and E. L. Shanas (eds.), *Handbook of Aging and the Social Sciences*, pp. 286–309. New York: Van Nostrand Reinhold.

SHEPPARD, H. L. 1977. Testimony before the Senate Select Committee on Aging's Subcommittee on Federal, State, and Community Services, on "Aging in the World of Tomorrow." September 27.

SHEPPARD, H. L., AND RIX, S. E. 1977. *The Graying of Working America: The coming crisis in retirement-age policy*. New York: The Free Press.

SIEGEL, J. S. 1978. Prospective trends in the size and structure of the elderly population, impact of mortality trends, and some implications. Statement before the House of Representatives Select Committee on Aging and Select Committee on Population, May 24.

SIMIC, A. 1978. Introduction: Aging and the aged in cultural perspective. *In,* B. G. Myerhoff and A. Simic (eds.), *Life's Career-Aging: Cultural Variations on Growing Old*, pp. 9–22. Beverly Hills: Sage.

SOLNICK, R. L. (ed.) 1978. *Sexuality and Aging*, Revised edition. Los Angeles: University of Southern California Press.

SOROKIN, P. A. 1947. *Society, Culture, and Personality: Their Structure and Dynamics*. New York: Harper and Brothers.

STREIB, G. F. 1976. Social stratification and aging. *In,* R. H. Binstock and E. L. Shanas (eds.), *Handbook of Aging and the Social Sciences*, pp. 160–185. New York: Van Nostrand Reinhold.

STREIB, G. F., AND SCHNEIDER, S. J. 1971. *Retirement in American Society: Impact and Process*. Ithaca: Cornell University Press.

STRUMPEL, B. 1973. The aged in an affluent economy. *In,* C. Eisdorfer and M. P. Lawton (eds.), *The Psychology of Adult Development and Aging*, pp. 657–698. Washington, D.C.: American Psychological Association.

TREAS, J. 1975. Aging and the family. *In,* D. S. Woodruff and J. E. Birren (eds.), *Aging: Scientific Perspectives and Social Issues*, pp. 92–108. New York: Van Nostrand Reinhold.

TREAS, J. 1976. Marriage and remarriage rates among older Americans. *Gerontologist, 16*, 132–136.

TUMIN, M. M. 1967. *Social Stratification*. Englewood Cliffs, N.J.: Prentice-Hall.

UHLENBERG, P. 1977. Changing structure of the older population of the USA during the twentieth century. *Gerontologist, 17*, 197–202.

US Bureau of the Census. 1974. Current Population Reports, Special Studies, Series P-23, No. 57. Social and economic characteristics of the older population. Washington, D.C.: USGPO.

US Bureau of the Census. 1976. Current Population Reports, Special Studies, Series P-23, No. 59. Demographic Aspects of Aging and the Older Population in the United States. Washington, D.C.: USGPO.

US Public Health Service. 1975. *Health: United States, 1975*. DHEW Publication No. (HRA) 76-1232. Rockville, Maryland: USDHEW.

WALES, J. B. 1974. Sexuality in middle and old age: A critical review of the literature. *Case Western Reserve Journal of Sociology*, Vol. VI (May), 82–105.

WALES, J. B. 1976. Age status change in an occupational setting: A small group, ecological study of age labelling among air traffic controllers. Unpublished Ph.D. dissertation, Case Western Reserve University.

# 17

# The Changing Family Context
# of Mental Health and Aging*

*Vern L. Bengtson & Judith Treas*

It might appear self-evident that mental health is linked to family relations, especially for older individuals. Families frequently provide direct assistance in meeting needs resulting from the normal dependencies of aging. The family has long been regarded as the social institution to deal with the physical, social and economic problems of elderly individuals —ameliorations which have obvious implications for their psychological well-being.

Family interaction also provides input to one's sense of self. Mental health, according to most personality theories, is dependent on a positive sense of self which is formed through and reinforced by social interaction. Most social roles through life are taken on, carried out, and exited from within the context of the primary family group. Thus, family members' continual evaluations of an individual's performance in the intricate network of social roles provide repeated input to his or her self-concept.

Finally, families provide a context of meaning for the changes associated with aging. In negotiating the uncharted career of old age, definitions of what is proper or inappropriate, usual or uncommon, valued or profane, are greatly influenced by family norms.

In this century, however, a number of remarkable changes have occurred which appear to alter traditional assumptions concerning family life, mental health, and aging.

First, demographic trends indicate greater numbers and proportions of individuals surviving into the seventh, eighth, and ninth decades of life. At the same time, fertility for younger cohorts has

*Preparation of this chapter has been assisted by grants from the Administration on Aging: #90–A–1015 (Judith Treas, Principal Investigator) and #90–A–1297 (Fernando Torres-Gil and Stephen McConnell, Principal Investigators). We wish to acknowledge the assistance of Ken Schoenholz, JoAnn Maze, and Judy Pinal in its formulation and preparation.

dropped. Such population trends imply that families increasingly may be taxed in providing for their elderly members.

A second and equally remarkable change involves the growth of public service bureaucracies. Their expansion suggests that other institutions, for better or worse, are taking over some traditional family functions in meeting needs of older persons. Furthermore, the rapid pace of technological and cultural change has occasioned much comment on the decline of the American family as a primary social institution, especially with regard to the needs or desires of the older generation.

Thus, the changing context of aging and family relations represents a dilemma for mental health professionals. On the one hand, it is assumed that family relationships are important in meeting needs and providing emotional support; on the other hand, it appears that social change has altered traditional relationships and responsibilities of families toward aged kin.

What are the changes that have taken place in family structure and interaction? What does current research suggest concerning the family context of older Americans? What implications may be drawn from these facts for mental health policy and practice?

In this chapter we will argue that an understanding of demographic configurations and historical contrasts is crucial to assessing the contemporary context of family life and aging. We will suggest that demographic changes have occasioned both greater problems and greater potentials for intergenerational family life.

We will observe that a principal feature of intergenerational relations involves negotiating the delicate balance between change and continuity over time—adaptations mirroring, in many respects, the challenge aging brings to individual well-being. We will note that burgeoning public service bureaucracies can supplement, rather than supplant, family relationships and enhance intergenerational family life. To summarize, this chapter is concerned with implications of change: developmental changes confronting individual families over the course of the life cycle, and historical changes confronting the institution of the family over time, for the mental health of older family members.

## DEMOGRAPHIC PERSPECTIVES: POPULATION CHANGES AND FAMILY CHALLENGES

In the Twentieth Century, a phenomenal growth in the population of older individuals has occurred. The number of older Americans not only

has increased, but their proportion relative to other age groups also has grown dramatically. In 1900, 4,901,000 Americans were 60 years of age or older; 70 years later 28,751,000 were in this age group (US Bureau of the Census, 1976). During this period, the 60 plus age group grew from 6.4 percent to 14.8 percent of the population.

Much attention has been given recently to the consequences which shifts in the US age structure will have for public policy, as evidenced by the current debate over the financing of Social Security (Kreps, 1976). Only recently has discussion centered on implications for individual families (Shanas and Hauser, 1974; Treas, 1977) and for the mental health support network.

TIPPING THE GENERATIONAL SCALE: FERTILITY DECLINES AND AGED DEPENDENCIES

Population changes in twentieth century America have registered several effects on family intergenerational relations. First, because of improvements in mortality, today's middle-aged offspring is more likely to have an aging parent than were his counterparts in previous decades. Second, the aging parent, having raised fewer children, may have fewer descendants to call upon for help than did his own parent. Third, younger adults, having grown up in smaller families, may have fewer brothers and sisters to lend a hand in the support of aging parents. Each of these developments has implications for the changing family context of mental health and aging.

Gradual improvements in health, sanitation, diet and medical services have swelled the ranks of the older population. Although infants have benefited most from reductions in mortality, adults also can expect longer lives.

Survival into old age (which we virtually take for granted today) was less commonplace during previous historical periods when mortality rates were higher. Given death rates prevailing in the US in 1900, for example, only 63 percent of women surviving to childbearing years (say, age 20) could expect to reach a 60th birthday (Preston, Keyfitz, and Schoen, 1972). The mortality schedule of 1973 suggests that fully 88 percent of women living to age 20 could expect to reach this threshold of old age (National Center for Health Statistics, 1975). These developments mean that more middle-aged adults today have elderly parents alive than ever before in our history.

Increasingly, an aging parent is very old. In 1930, for example, 29 percent of Americans 65 years or older were aged 75 or older. By 1975, 38 percent of the old were of these advancing years

(US Bureau of the Census, 1976). While the "old-old" may enjoy greater health and vigor today than in the past, it is clear that more older Americans than ever are in the age range associated with declining health and capacities. It is these frail elderly who are most dependent on the resources of kin. Such changes in the older population itself may tax the capacities of family members to provide companionship, counsel, services, and financial support to aged kin.

The *proportionate* growth of the older population reflects long-term declines in fertility. Because successive generations of women have had fewer children than did their mothers, the ratio of young to old has fallen. Table 17–1 shows the completed fertility of birth cohorts of women ages 60 to 64 in selected years. Between 1931 and 1971, the percent of these older women who had borne four or more children dropped markedly, from 47.1 to 20.7, while the percent childless varied only slightly over the forty-year period. To some extent, declines in fertility have been offset by the surer survival of those children born, but other evidence points to an overall decline in the numbers of children available to parents in later life. Not the least of this evidence is the widening sex differential in mortality which today implies that a mother has a one-in-four chance of surviving her son (Metropolitan Life, 1977).

Consequences of fertility for family life in old age can be seen in the next few years. The cohort entering old age in 1981 includes parents of the celebrated baby boom. These women were slightly more likely to have had large families than those of the preceding Depression decade (29.6 percent compared with 20.7 percent). More importantly, they were less likely to have borne no children (13.9 percent versus 21.4 percent). Their greater numbers of offspring may stand them in better stead in later life, but this cohort seems likely to offer only a brief reversal of the long run trend toward smaller families and fewer descendants in old age. In fact, the baby boom cohort itself, their children, is registering record low fertility.

Another implication of fertility trends in the past 20 years involves siblings. If smaller families mean fewer descendents for the aged, they also mean fewer siblings for the middle-aged. Preston (1976) has emphasized that the average family size of parents is not the same as the average family size of children, because children in big families weigh more heavily in the distribution of sibling numbers. Nonetheless, changes in proportions childless and in the distribution of family size suggest that even baby boom children grew up in smaller families, on the average, than did cohorts before them (Preston, 1977). This trend toward fewer brothers and sisters is important, because it suggests that successive generations may have fewer siblings with whom to share the sometimes considerable burden of aging parents. Declining numbers of descendants seem to be on a collision course with the surer survival of aging kin, and these facts pose questions about the continuing effectiveness of family support systems for the aged.

In short, we confront today an aged population of unprecedented size. Despite the improved health and economic well-being of older Americans, the composition of the older population has tipped toward the very old, a group especially dependent on the resources of others. Despite the growing numbers and needs of aging parents, their children (born into smaller families) may have fewer brothers and sisters to share responsibility for the support of older relatives.

These facts illustrate the new demands and dilemmas confronting kin today. It is likely that demographic developments have already altered age relations within families. The growing numbers of older persons living apart from kin are a case in point. For example, the percent of women 65 and older who head a household containing no kin has increased dramatically from 18 percent in 1950 to 39 percent in 1975 (US Bureau of the Census, 1976). While few can doubt that a rising tide of affluence has fostered separate living, Kobrin (1976) has argued that the increasing population of older widows has compromised many social customs of multigenerational residence; there are simply too many older women for offspring to absorb into their homes.

**Table 17–1** Fertility of Cohorts, Women Age 60–64, 1931–1981, based on cumulative birth rates for groups of cohorts.

|  | 1931 | 1941 | 1951 | 1961 | 1971 | 1981 |
|---|---|---|---|---|---|---|
| Percent of Women with No Children | 19.8 | 21.8 | 20.7 | 19.7 | 21.4 | 13.9 |
| Percent of All Women With 4 or More Children | 47.1 | 40.9 | 35.2 | 26.5 | 20.7 | 25.5 |
| Percent of Mothers with 4 or More Children | 58.8 | 52.2 | 44.4 | 33.0 | 26.4 | 29.6 |

Source: US Department of HEW Publication No. (HRA) 76–1152, Fertility Tables for Birth Cohorts by Color, United States, 1917–73, Table 7A.

In light of demographic constraints on family support systems, we must entertain the conclusion of Shanas and Hauser (1974) that "those aspects of housing, recreation, health care, and income maintenance now provided by younger generations to their elderly parents and grandparents will need to be provided by society at large."

## NEW OPTIONS IN THE MIDDLE YEARS: RECHARTING THE LIFE COURSE

The demographic trends we have cited have suggested new challenges for kin in the physical and emotional support of aging family members. No account of the constraints on intergenerational relations would be complete without consideration of the changing social roles of mid-life Americans. New options for men and women have created aspirations and obligations which in turn may compete with duties toward aging kin.

Changes in the social and economic roles of women have been especially striking. Their pertinence to age relations lies in the fact that women have long been the mainstay of family support systems for the aged. A sexual division of labor in the care of older relatives is well documented. Lopata (1973) reports that Chicago area widows found sons helpful in managing funeral arrangements and financial affairs while daughters got high marks for fostering close emotional ties through visiting and providing services. Devoted though sons may be, the major responsibility for the psychological and physical maintenance of the aged has fallen traditionally to female members of the family. It is they who take widowed mothers into their households, share confidences, run errands, and provide nursing and custodial care.

New roles for women, however, lead us to question the continued willingness and ability of women to meet fully and personally the needs of aging relatives. First, mature women today are more likely to have married and to have borne children than women of earlier eras. A husband and children (even grown children) make demands on a woman's time, and the needs of aging in-laws may conflict with the needs of one's own aging kin. The maiden aunt, devoting herself exclusively to the needs of one set of aging parents, perhaps in exchange for some small financial consideration after their deaths, appears to be a vanishing breed (Treas, 1977).

Second, paid employment represents another claim upon the time and energy of women. Half of wives, 45 to 54, are in the labor force today compared with only 11 percent in 1940 (US Bureau of the Census, 1973). Regardless of their personal satisfactions in their work, most women admit that they work because they and their families need the money. Unfortunately, work cuts into the time available to run errands for shut-in kin or to provide nursing care.

Although vigorous older people may furnish valuable assistance with household chores, parents needing care can require considerable attention. One study found that two-fifths of offspring caring for elderly parents in their homes devoted the equivalent of a full-time job (with overtime) to custodial tasks (Newman, 1976). No one knows how many women might be willing to quit their jobs to nurse older relatives. We do know that a third of mothers of preschool children are in the labor force (US Bureau of the Census, 1973). If so many mothers are willing to trust the care of small children to others in order to hold a job, women are probably willing to delegate responsibility for the care of elderly parents, too.

A third trend threatening family responsibility for the day-to-day care of older relatives is an emerging social movement for mid-life options. Growing numbers of middle-aged Americans indicate that it is never too late to launch second careers, return to college, revive romance in marriage, or vacation abroad. Doubtless, this *joie de vivre* reflects a postparental era free of the personal and financial responsibilities of childrearing, a consequence of the trend toward early childbearing and small families. Many, however, must choose between a dream too long deferred and the very real needs of aging parents. This dilemma is all the more poignant for the realization that offspring of the aged may themselves be older, retired persons hoping to enjoy the reward of carefree leisure time.

## THE DEMOGRAPHY OF FAMILY LIFE: PROBLEMS AND OPPORTUNITIES

As documented before, demographic changes have increased the demands on family support systems for the aged. Parents are likely to survive into old age, and a surviving parent is more likely to be very old and in need of family attention. At the same time, the burden of parental needs has been more sorely felt, because there are fewer siblings to share the care and because middle-aged offspring, especially women, confront more competing responsibilites and aspirations in their lives. These developments would seem to imply greater difficulties in intergenerational relations, as middle-aged children must marshal their resources toward conflicting needs of parents, offspring, and themselves.

Although demographic changes may be viewed

as having occasioned gerontological problems in family life, it may also be argued that they have made possible intergenerational family life with all its attendant benefits. Demographic changes have eliminated some of the hazardous unpredictability which characterized family life in earlier eras and have increased the span of lifetimes shared by family members.

We have commented on the increasing probability of living to old age. Declining death rates of adults are also seen in declining proportions of children who are orphaned. Estimates by Bane (1976) indicate that almost 11 percent of American children born at the turn of the century had lost their mother before age 18. For children born fifty years later, the figure was only 3 percent. In part, this decline in orphanhood reflects changes in nuptiality and fertility as well as mortality. Marrying younger, bearing fewer children earlier, and spacing them more closely together, mothers (and fathers) today have found themselves still in the prime of life when the youngest child leaves home. Along with surer survival, this narrowing age gap between generations has permitted more offspring and parents to share overlapping years of vigorous adulthood. We speculate that the closer ages of parents and children may have made possible reciprocal helping and shared recreation unknown to many nineteenth century families. Similarly, the grandparent-grandchild relation may have benefited from the overlap in their lifespans.

If mortality and advanced ages at parenthood robbed the young of their parents' presence, so, too, demographic factors placed the postparental family outside the grasp of many. Uhlenberg (1974) documents that successive cohorts of women have been more and more likely to follow a "preferred" life cycle—surviving from 15 to 50 immune to spinsterhood, childlessness, widowhood, or divorce. Comparing the 1890–1894 and 1930–1934 birth cohorts, Uhlenberg concludes that the percent experiencing the preferred life course will rise from 42.5 to 64.5 among whites and from 18 to 35 percent among blacks. If we consider the white woman, we find that early deaths claimed 17 percent of the earlier group versus 5 percent of their successors. For the 1890–1894 group, 8 percent never married, and 18.5 percent married, but bore no children; comparable figures for the 1930–1934 group were only 4.5 and 5.5 percent, respectively. Not only are more recent cohorts more likely to survive past middle years, but they are also more likely to share the second half of life with a surviving spouse and with offspring. Although an older person may average fewer offspring, she is more likely to have at least *some* surviving children.

Today's intergenerational relations are unprecedented both in their scope and their predictability. Whatever the depth of feeling and frequency of contact between generations (and sections below show them to be considerable), intergenerational relations are feasible in strictly demographic terms in a way not possible in previous historical eras. Because generations now count on sharing most of their lifespans, they are in a position to share leisure, love, and aspirations—qualities which are often assumed to be important to mental health. Although demographic changes have occasioned some gerontological problems, they may have increased the affective resources which families may draw upon.

## HISTORICAL PERSPECTIVES: FILIAL PIETY IN MYTH AND REALITY

We have argued that demographic changes of the past century have increased the number of aging kin as well as the years of overlap in the lives of parents and children. Some observers may object, however, that the greatest changes in intergenerational relations have been qualitative rather than quantitative. It is true that many Americans believe that a degeneration of family ties has taken place and that older family members fared much better in earlier eras than they do today. Peter Laslett (1976) calls such historical romanticism the *"world we have lost* syndrome."

Many assumptions about the relationship of grown children and aging parents have been colored by a patina of the past. Accounts of biblical patriarchs honored by descendants, stories of closely-knit European peasant communities, and our own memories summon forth rich images of filial piety. We envision aging kin in the warm embrace of multigenerational households, filling useful social roles and enjoying the love and respect of descendants.

Emerging from the work of contemporary social historians, however, is a picture of the past which challenges our notions of a golden era of cross-age relations (Laslett, 1976). Historical research documents the rarity of three generation families in earlier times, the instance of bitter family conflict, and the impoverished neglect suffered by some older persons. Familiarity with the reality of the past (as it is being gleaned from legal records, household censuses, parish registries, and the yellowed writings of social commentators) can serve to expand our understanding of the dynamics in contemporary intergenerational relations. Not only does historical evidence rid us of delusions that today's gerontological problems have sprung forth from a degeneration of family ties, but also comparative data alert us to the extent to which age relations are shaped by social, economic, and demographic considerations.

This is not to say that contemporary historical ·esearch has generated sweeping generalizations to supplant rosy myths of aging and family in earlier times. Indeed, the mixed findings arising from the study of different eras and various locales reveal not only the limitations of historical data, but more importantly the historical idiosyncracy of age relations themselves. The proportion of the aged might fluctuate startlingly over several decades, the popularity of intergenerational living arrangements might vary from one nation to the next, and family change might show a marked lack of syncronization with such massive societal transformations as industrialization (Laslett, 1977). While such ambiguities do not offer the comfort of a homogenized past, they do furnish valuable insights into present day relations between generations.

## INTERGENERATIONAL HOUSEHOLDS

Considerable evidence indicates that the togetherness of previous generations derived from economic necessity rather than from tender sentiment. What some people today take for a breakdown in family life may merely reflect the fact that affluence permits families to forgo intergenerational arrangements which didn't always work to everyone's satisfaction. Multigenerational households are a case in point.

Perhaps the most persistent misreading of the past is the widespread belief that three-generation households were once a dominant mode of living arrangements. In his study of 18th Century Austrian peasants, Berkner (1972) shows that even where multigenerational living was the custom, few households at any one time could contain both married offspring and aging parents; such arrangements existed only briefly during the life cycle of a family, from the time a soon-to-be-wed heir took over the farm from his aging father until the parents' deaths.

In the US and much of Western Europe, custom has long dictated that young marrieds set up housekeeping on their own rather than joining the parental household. Similarly, parents typically have maintained separate living arrangements rather than being absorbed in the households of grown children. Apparently, this generational segregation derived from preference. Indeed, widowed parents were more likely to live apart among the wealthy English classes than among the poor

(Laslett, 1977). Among those of more limited means, separate domicile of aged kin typically was maintained, sometimes through practices which no longer find favor. Rather than live with children, the aged couple or widow might take in complete strangers as boarders and lodgers to make ends meet (Anderson, 1971; Modell and Hareven, 1973). They might reside in poorhouses or other institutions, sometimes with kin paying for their keep (Anderson, 1977; Laslett, 1977).

This is not to deny the existence of multigenerational living among the aged in earlier eras. In the absence of social insurance programs, kin were an enormous resource against such vicissitudes of life as disability, widowhood, unemployment and old age. However, it is essential to understand that higher death rates limited the availability of aged kin and that social custom supported their separate residence. While separate residence may have always been preferred, it is true that intergenerational households have been on the decline in the United States in recent decades (Kobrin, 1976). To explain the growing numbers of aged women living alone, many would point to a deterioration of filial obligation. So simple an explanation is inadequate in light of other factors. A major consideration has doubtless been the improved economic circumstances of aged Americans; Social Security has permitted the old to maintain their own homes apart from kin. As Kreps (1977) has observed, income transfers from young to old remain important, but they now occur on a society-wide basis through Social Security and other old age programs. This changing economic context serves to point out a major difference between past and present family life. We argue below that intergenerational family life may have been made less strained (and less compulsory) by the advent of modern social welfare provisions.

## EXCHANGES BETWEEN UNEQUALS

Doubtless, motives based on love and concern have always firgured in intergenerational relations, but mounting evidence suggests that the cement binding earlier generations was economic necessity as much as intergenerational affection. Decisions to shelter aging parents may have been based on rational calculation of their costs and contributions to the household. Such economic formulations of household formation have been shown to provide useful explanations of contemporary living arrangements (Becker, 1976; Duncan and Morgan, 1976). It is hardly surprising that notions of rational choice governed living arrangements in our less affluent past.

Historical records document the willingness of offspring to take in an older parent who might be a contributing member of the household; such records also document the reluctance to shelter kin who represented a net liability to the family. Laslett (1977, p. 178) has discussed the usefulness of the aged grandmother in childrearing and housekeeping. Anderson (1977, pp. 51–52) points to nineteenth century English commentators who noted that modest demands and valuable service made the old woman more welcome than the old man as a household member; indeed, such old women might even find homes with nonrelatives who lacked grandmothers of their own. Accounts from the turn of the century reveal that poorhouse inmates might live with their children in summer, doing fieldwork or providing childcare for a mother in the fields, only to be returned to the institution in the winter (Anderson, 1976, p. 55).

Pensions and poor relief to the aged might also raise their stock within families. It may be hard for us today to appreciate the importance of small sums of money in an earlier age of widespread urban poverty and rural subsistence. An Irish farmer in this century voiced the following sentiment about the old-age pension (Arensberg and Kimball, 1968, p. 120):

> To have old people in the house is a great blessing in these times because if you have one, it means ten bob a week and, if you have two, it means a pound a week coming into the house. You take a man like O'D--- and every Friday he will go to Corrofin [town] to collect his ten bob and he may buy a couple of bottles of porter, but spends the rest on things for the house and then come home with a few shillings which will go into the common fund.
>
> Not only that but it adds at least ten years to a man's life because the anticipation of each Friday he is to get ten shillings will cheer him up and keep him keen. Any house which has one old person is well off in the last few years, and if there are two, it is a great blessing.

While noting that pensions from the colliery disaster funds even induced nonrelatives to care for elderly widows, Anderson (1976) documents the lamentable fact that Victorian poor-relief was often unavailable to indigent aged residing with kin. Indeed, much family friction was born of the legal responsibility of children to support aged parents (Anderson, 1976, pp. 53–54).

Of course, the aging parent most assured of offspring's devotion was neither the factory worker nor the landless laborer. Most secure in old age was the prosperous merchant or farmer who could ex-

pect an income from assets even when he himself was too old to work (Wrigley, 1977, p. 62). Control of economic resources assured parents of continuing control over the lives of grown offspring. Where day-to-day subsistence and even the chance to marry depended on parents' willingness to provide dowries to daughters and to turn over the family farm or business to sons, parental power was formidable. Typically, parents transferred property to adult children in exchange for promises of support in old age. It seems that even then intergenerational affection was not seen as sufficient guarantee of parental support, for legal contracts between generations were often invoked (Arensberg and Kimball, 1968; Berkner, 1972; Demos, 1973; and Homans, 1942).

In a study of nineteenth century farming families in Andover, Massachusetts, Greven (1973) details one way in which aging fathers perpetuated control of grown sons. Although a son might marry and settle upon family land, a father retained the property deed until his death. Lacking clear title to sell the land, offspring couldn't leave Andover without parental approval. Even the last will and testament which transferred land ownership might bind the heir to his filial responsibility, since wills typically stipulated the conditions for support of the surviving widow: a room in the house, a garden, firewood. Parental control of potential heirs was insured by the ultimate threat, disinheritance.

We might expect occasional conflict to mark social relations imposed by economic necessity rather than by strictly voluntary choice. Many historical accounts attest that this was the case. Intergenerational tensions are not solely a phenomenon of the twentieth century. For example, the diary of a wealthy Virginia planter, Landon Carter, reports his bitter quarrels with a forty-year-old son chafing impatiently at the father's authority. So acrimonious did their relations become that the elder Carter took to wearing a pistol in the house, exclaiming to his diary, "Good God! That such a monster is descended from my loin (Fischer, 1977, pp. 73–75)." Or consider the case of Oliver Mather's father. Old, sick and unable to fend for himself, he was driven from his son's Minnesota home in the winter of 1868 (Fischer, 1977, pp. 52–53). While we may feel sympathy for abused parents, we may also recognize the emotional toll they may exact upon offspring forced to stint on their own children to support aged kin, upon daughters forgoing marriage to nurse parents in their last years, upon sons subject to parental caprices even in middle-age.

Whatever intergenerational relations may have been in earlier times, they fall short of the ideal against which we often judge contemporary family affections and behavior. Demographic data make clear that aging parents have only recently become widespread fixtures of American families. Historical evidence challenges the notion that age relations have ever been completely free of conflict and calculating self-interest. It would appear that social, demographic and economic change have permitted an unprecedented level of intergenerational contact. At the same time, rising affluence has made intergenerational interaction more voluntary, less compulsory. A new cultural context has posed some new problems in age relations at the same time as it has alleviated some traditional barriers to rewarding family life in old age.

## SOCIOLOGICAL PERSPECTIVES: CONTEMPORARY PATTERNS OF INTERGENERATIONAL SOLIDARITY

Despite historical evidence to the contrary, many Americans believe that family life has significantly changed and that the position of elderly members is being jeopardized by these changes. There are other commonly accepted beliefs which may be questioned in light of contemporary data from family sociology. One is that most older people today live alone, apart from families. A second is that most older people do not have frequent contact with offspring because of frequent geographic mobility and the general weakening of family ties. A third concern involves the existence of the "generation gap," that there are serious strains in family ties between generations. A fourth notion is that older persons are primarily recipients in intergenerational exchanges, receiving more than they give.

Each of these beliefs is a commentary on popular perceptions of contemporary family relations and of the well-being of today's elderly family members. Are they myths or are they accurate generalizations? How can one characterize the intricate bonds of connectedness and the tensions between generations? What are the relevant concepts, variables, and perspectives that inform answers to these questions?

In answering these specific issues, it is useful to begin with one of the more basic observations of classical social analysis. An important determinant of the process and product of any human group is the solidarity or cohesiveness among individual members. The family, of course, is a special type of small group, so there is considerable interest in the extent to which family members like each other, do things with each other, and agree with one another. These dimensions of cohesiveness have significant implications for the individuals who comprise a family. A useful term to describe the parent-child dyad as it develops and changes through time is *solidarity*, a concept drawing from the works of the earliest sociologists down to the present.

Intergenerational solidarity can be conceptualized as comprised of several elements: *association* ("objective" interaction or shared interactions); *affect* ("subjective" interaction, the degree of sentiment between members); and *consensus* (agreement in values or opinions). These concepts serve as a way to organize the emerging literature concerning intergenerational relations involving older family members (see Bengtson, Olander, and Haddad, 1976).

We find it useful to examine family solidarity, particularly with reference to implications for psychological well-being, in terms of five dimensions implicit in the aforementioned beliefs about the family life of the aged:

1. the *structure* of the family: number of individuals in each generation; their geographic proximity; the household's composition;
2. *interaction* between family members: the frequency and type of shared activities;
3. *affect* between members: the negative or positive sentiment, and mixtures thereof, with which family members regard each other;
4. *exchanges* of assistance and support;
5. *norms* regarding family life, expectations or prescriptions regarding what *should* be the case in relations among members of that family.

Contemporary patterns of intergenerational family solidarity can be assessed in a variety of ways. Census tabulations provide evidence concerning family structure and household composition. Large-sample survey data present information concerning interaction, affect, and norms or expectations within families. Legal data draw on testamentary declarations for insight into rewards and punishments between generations. These will be reviewed below as they reflect dimensions of intergenerational solidarity.

### FAMILY STRUCTURE AND HOUSEHOLD COMPOSITION

The first dimension of solidarity involves the structure and composition of the group: how many members, what characteristics, what relation to each other? In previous sections we documented some demographic trends which have implications for family structure and composition. These include gradual increases in life expectancy through this century, resulting in larger numbers of aged individuals; and reduced fertility, resulting in fewer family members per successive generation. The implications of these trends for the family structure of aging individuals become more clear when we examine data on marital status, household composition, and presence of children, all of which reflect the potential primary group support system for older people.

Marital status is one characteristic of family structure reflecting horizontal dimensions of family composition. Table 17-2 shows trends from 1890 to 1970 in the marital status of individuals age 65 and over. For males and females there has been a slight increase in the proportion reporting themselves never married or divorced. On the other hand, the proportion widowed has decreased slightly. Due to these offsetting trends, the proportion married has remained about the same in the past 80 years.

There are, however, striking differences by sex in marital status for Americans over age 65. In 1970, females were half as likely to be currently married (36.5 percent compared to 72.4 percent)

and three times as likely to be widowed (52.2 percent to 17.1 percent). These figures reflect the tendency for men to marry women younger than themselves, as well as greater longevity for females than males. With remarriage rates much lower for older women than for older men (Treas and VanHilst, 1976), the prospect is for greater numbers of older women without spouses in the next several decades. This will be true particularly for those individuals above the age of 75.

Differences in marital status are reflected in differences in living arrangements (Table 17-3). In 1975, almost half (47.3 percent) of noninstitutionalized white females over age 75 lived as "primary individuals" with no relatives in the household. For white males the same age, the proportion was only 21 percent, for black males a mere 11.3 percent. In the younger 65 to 74-year-old age group, there were only slightly less marked sex contrasts.

The trend toward living alone has increased in the past 25 years (Table 17-4). In 1950, 10.3 percent of males and 18.1 percent of females lived as "primary individuals;" in 1975, the proportions increased to 15.4 and 39.4 percent, respectively. It is likely that this increase will continue. While these data suggest that women are increasingly

**Table 17-2**  Marital Status by Sex for Persons 65 and Older, 1890–1970.

| MARITAL STATUS AND SEX | 1890 | 1900 | 1910 | 1920 | 1930 | 1940 | 1950 | 1960 | 1970 |
|---|---|---|---|---|---|---|---|---|---|
| *Males 65 and Older* | | | | | | | | | |
| Never married | 5.6 | 5.7 | 6.2 | 7.4 | 8.5 | 9.8 | 8.2 | 7.7 | 7.5 |
| Married | 70.6 | 67.3 | 65.9 | 64.9 | 63.8 | 63.8 | (65.5) | (70.7) | (72.4) |
| Spouse present | | | | | | | 61.9 | 66.8 | 68.3 |
| Spouse absent | | | | | | | 3.6 | 3.9 | 4.1 |
| Widowed | 23.4 | 27.2 | 27.2 | 27.0 | 26.6 | 25.1 | 24.3 | 19.2 | 17.1 |
| Divorced | 0.4 | 0.7 | 0.7 | 0.7 | 1.1 | 1.3 | 1.9 | 2.3 | 3.0 |
| TOTAL* | 100.0 | 100.0 | 100.0 | 100.0 | 100.0 | 100.0 | 100.0 | 100.0 | 100.0 |
| *Females 65 and Older* | | | | | | | | | |
| Never married | 5.6 | 6.0 | 6.3 | 7.1 | 8.1 | 9.3 | 8.9 | 8.5 | 8.1 |
| Married | 35.4 | 34.3 | 35.1 | 34.0 | 34.7 | 34.3 | (35.6) | (37.3) | (36.5) |
| Spouse present | | | | | | | 33.2 | 34.6 | 33.9 |
| Spouse absent | | | | | | | 2.5 | 2.7 | 2.6 |
| Widowed | 58.7 | 59.5 | 58.2 | 58.5 | 56.6 | 55.6 | 54.4 | 52.1 | 52.2 |
| Divorced | 0.3 | 0.3 | 0.4 | 0.4 | 0.5 | 0.7 | 1.1 | 2.0 | 3.2 |
| TOTAL* | 100.0 | 100.0 | 100.0 | 100.0 | 100.0 | 100.0 | 100.0 | 100.0 | 100.0 |

*Totals may not add to 100.0 due to rounding error. Source: US Bureau of the Census. 1975 *Historical Statistics of the United States, Part 1.* Washington, D.C.: Government Printing Office, p. 21.

**Table 17–3**  Marital Status and Living Arrangements of Noninstitutionalized Older Americans; Age, Sex and Race: 1975.

| LIVING ARRANGEMENT<br>*Age*<br>65–74 | MALES | | FEMALES | |
|---|---|---|---|---|
| | *White* | *Black* | *White* | *Black* |
| In Families[a] | 87.5 | 72.3 | 64.0 | 64.1 |
| Primary Individuals | 12.2 | 22.4 | 35.0 | 34.3 |
| Others[b] | 0.4 | 5.3 | 1.1 | 1.6 |
| TOTAL[c] | 100.0 | 100.0 | 100.0 | 100.0 |
| | | | | |
| *Age*<br>*75 and over* | | | | |
| In Families[a] | 78.3 | 74.8 | 51.2 | 57.3 |
| Primary Individuals | 21.0 | 11.3 | 47.3 | 39.6 |
| Others[b] | 0.7 | 13.9 | 1.5 | 3.1 |
| TOTAL[c] | 100.0 | 100.0 | 100.0 | 100.0 |

Source: US Bureau of the Census. Current Population Reports, March, 1975. Population Characteristics: Marital Status and Living Arrangements, Table 2.

[a]Includes those in secondary families—lodgers, resident employers and their relatives living in a household.

[b]Includes lodgers, guests or resident employers with no relations in the household.

[c]Totals may not equal 100.0 due to rounding.

more likely to live alone than are their male counterparts, it should be emphasized that families are the most common living arrangement regardless of age, sex, or race. Usually such "families" consist only of an aged man and wife.

As data on marital status indicate, the companionship of marriage is a tenuous link of family life which is often broken by the death of one partner. For this reason, intergenerational linkages between older and younger family members are of special concern. To what extent do elderly individuals live with their children or grandchildren?

It appears that most older people prefer to live in their own homes and maintain independent residential arrangements (Laslett, 1976; Lopata, 1973; Townsend, 1968; and Troll, 1970). But "living apart from each other" does not mean living very far from each other. Data from a 1962 three-nation survey of older people and their families (Shanas, Townsend, Wedderburn, Friis, Milhaj, and Stehouwer, 1968) indicated that 33 percent of older Americans lived within 10 minutes of a child. Only 23 percent live more than 30 minutes distance from their children. These percentages were similar to those in Denmark and Great Britain.

A more recent survey in a metropolitan area revealed similar patterns of living arrangements and preference, but with significant differences among ethnic groups. This Los Angeles area study of blacks, Mexican Americans and anglos (Bengtson and Manuel, 1976) found that, of the sample of 62 and older, larger numbers of Mexican American respondents lived with children (46 percent

compared to 18 percent of blacks and 13 percent of anglos). There were also striking ethnic group contrasts in terms of housing preference: When asked, "Would you prefer to live with your children, or in a separate residence?", 72 percent of the Mexican Americans replied "separate residence," compared with 83 percent of the blacks and 98 percent of the anglos.

The preference for private living arrangements is not unique to the old, for the young, too, have moved increasingly out of parental homes to bachelor quarters. The old are quick to point out the drawbacks to intergenerational living. The widows surveyed by Lopata (1973) noted the rowdiness of grandchildren, the difference in life style, the

**Table 17–4**  Primary Individuals[1] as a Percent of the Total Population 65 and older, by Sex, 1950–1975.

| | 1950[a] | 1960[b] | 1970[c] | 1975[d] |
|---|---|---|---|---|
| Male<br>Primary<br>Individual | 10.3 | 12.7 | 15.6 | 15.4 |
| Female<br>Primary<br>Individual | 18.1 | 25.4 | 33.4 | 39.4 |

[1]Prior to 1950 "primary individual" was not a separate category—they were included with "Head of Private Household."

[a]1950 US Bureau of Census: 1950 Population Special Report PE No. 20 "Marital Status" Table 1.

[b]1960 US Bureau of Census: 1960 Final Report. Subject Reports PC (2)–4B "Persons By Family Characteristics" Table 2.

[c]1970 US Bureau of Census: 1970 Census of Population. Subject Reports PC (2)–4B "Persons By Family Characteristics" Table 2.

[d]1975 US Bureau of Census: Current Population Reports: Population.

desire to be the boss in one's own kitchen, as reasons they chose not to live with their offspring. Given these sentiments, it is not surprising that the aged who reside with their children are apt to be widowed and very old, very sick and/or very poor. In other words, they are persons with high needs, limited personal resources, and few options. The children with whom they reside tend to be daughters, not sons, and single, not married.

## ASSOCIATIONAL SOLIDARITY BETWEEN GENERATIONS

A second dimension of family solidarity involves the activities or encounters which characterize interaction between members. The popular stereotype depicts older family members as having infrequent contact with children due to geographic mobility and gradual weakening of family ties. While it is true that few aging parents today share living quarters with offspring, this does not imply infrequent interaction.

Survey data suggest there is, in fact, a high degree of interaction between generations in contemporary families. For example, in the three-nation survey conducted in 1962, only one in ten older Americans with surviving children reported he/she had *not* seen one of his/her children within the past 30 days (Shanas *et al.,* 1968). The corresponding figures for Denmark and Great Britain were lower (6 percent). Eighteen percent reported seeing children within the past two to seven days. Of those in the American sample who lived apart from their children, 52 percent said they had seen one of their children today or yesterday (Shanas *et al.,* 1968, p. 197).

Such high frequency of contact may be surprising in view of popular stereotypes, but these findings are typical of other studies. In the 1974 Los Angeles community survey, interaction with children during the past day was reported by 56 percent of the Mexican Americans, 40 percent of the anglos and 33 percent of the blacks (Bengtson and Manuel, 1976). In New York, a cross-ethnic survey found even higher contact (Cantor, 1976).

Sussman (1965, 1976, 1977) has argued that such data indicate the persistence of an extended family kinship structure which has special salience for the elderly. In the face of rapid social and technological change with high geographic mobility, the kinship structure provides many supports to its members. The ongoing contact between adult children and their parents, their sharing of social activities, and the exchange of material and non-material aid reflect what Litwak (1960) has called the "modified extended family."

Differentials exist in the kind and nature of intergenerational contact. Sex is one such differentiating characteristic. For example, married daughters tend to have closer ties to parents than do married sons (Sussman, 1965, p. 82). This is particularly true for widowed mothers (Lopata, 1973), who see daughters as providers of emotional closeness and comfort, and sons as more task-oriented (and less frequent) supporters. Middle-aged daughters have been identified as the more salient "kinkeepers" in terms of both type and frequency of contact by a number of researchers (Adams, 1968; Hill, Foote, Aldous, Carlson, and MacDonald, 1970; Shanas, 1962).

Marital status is a second differentiating characteristic. Widows, for example, are more dependent on kin than are the married aged. Unmarried offspring also maintain closer ties to aging parents, being more likely to share housing with the older generation than are married children.

Social class represents a third important differentiating characteristic. Hill *et al.* (1970) found that working class men engaged in more intergenerational contact than did white-collar males. Adams (1968) noted that occupational stratum of the parent affected patterns of contact; upwardly mobile males appeared the most likely to give tangible aid to working class parents. Downward mobility among males has the effect of decreasing contact with kin, while upward mobility may increase contact (Schoenholz, 1978).

From one study involving 2,044 members of three-generation family lineages (sample described in Bengtson, 1975) come several suggestions concerning associational solidarity involving older family members. Reports from both the elderly and middle-aged concerning the nature and frequency of intergenerational interaction yielded three dimensions of interaction or "objective solidarity" (Bengtson and Black, 1973): informal activities (recreation, conversation, talking about important matters), ceremonial or family ritual activities (large and small family gatherings, reunions, birthdays) and exchange of assistance (helping and being helped).

Both generations reported relatively high levels of both types of activities. No significant general differences appeared between the reports of the middle-aged and the elderly in the perception of frequency of contact, although one specific difference concerned the giving and receiving of help. When estimating the amount of help given by the middle-aged child, the child himself reported a higher level than did his parent. Moreover, the parents reported giving less help to the children than the children reported receiving. The old tend to downplay the practical exchanges between generations; they tend to emphasize the affectual or sentimental aspects of family life, as discussed below.

## AFFECTUAL SOLIDARITY BETWEEN GENERATIONS

The third major dimension of parent-child relations across the lifespan concerns subjective judgments of the *quality* of interaction. Often this is referred to as "closeness" or "warmth;" affectual solidarity may be defined as "mutual positive sentiment among group members and their expressions of love, respect, appreciation, and recognition of others" (Bengtson and Black, 1973). We have seen that many studies indicate a high degree of contact or shared activities between middle-aged children and their aged parents. Less research has been carried out on the affectual dimensions of such contact, their subjective quality for the participating generations (Bengtson *et al.*, 1976). Popular stereotypes hold that there is a "generation gap" with differences between generations leading to feelings of conflict and distance.

One analysis suggested that the problem of generations impinges on contemporary older individuals in two ways (Bengtson, 1971). First is evidence of differences between the behaviors and standards of the aged individual's own peers and those of younger age groups or cohorts. These contrasts can be attributed to differences in levels of maturation (aging) and to contrasts in historical experience, as was discussed in previous sections. Born during a particular period in history and sharing certain demographic and sociopolitical events, those individuals who are over 65 have orientations that are often perceived as contrasting with those of younger members of the society. To paraphrase the popular jargon, this may be termed a "cohort gap."

Second are differences between generations within the family. Here, possibly, the differences are more personally relevant, since they are related to the wishes and fulfillment that parents often seek for children and grandchildren. Within the family, the aging individual may see the currents of change and conflict in the broader society as impinging on him personally and as questioning lifelong principles that have governed his behavior. Such family differences may be termed a "lineage gap."

One survey offers some data which tap perceptions across generational boundaries in both cohort and lineage terms (Bengtson, 1971). In this study three parameters of person perception were examined: a) age of the *perceiver;* b) age of the *referent* or *target group;* and, c) the *social context* of the perceiver-referent relationship (primary group versus generalized collectivity). Respondents were asked to evaluate the closeness of the relationship between members of various referent groups (youth-middle aged, middle aged-elderly, youth-elderly) in two social contexts: the "broader society" (cohort) and "your own family" (lineage).

The results suggest three things. First, the "cohort gap" perceived between generations in the broader society is considerably larger than the "lineage gap" perceived within the respondent's own family. Second, the age of the *perceiver* makes some difference in the degree to which a "gap" is perceived between the youth and the elderly than between the other dyads.

The principal conclusion, then, is that the nature of cross-generation perceptions varies depending on several factors, the primary factor being the context of the referent group (primary relationship versus broader collectivity). "Yes, there *is* a generation gap, but not in my family."

A variety of explanations have been offered to account for the contrasts attributed to differing generations. Summarizing some of these factors, one set consists of *sociocultural disparities* between cohorts. (a) Each generation is born into a different historical period, shaped by different social events, and each cohort may vary in size and composition from its predecessor. (b) Social institutions change over time, and thus the various developmental roles sequentially experienced during the life course (student, parent, provider, etc.) have different meanings for members of successive generations. (c) Status in social institutions tends to increase with the years, giving the older person both greater rewards and a greater stake in the *status quo.*

A second set of factors includes *biological and psychological* factors associated with life course development: a) changes with advancing maturity in the relative importance of various needs; b) changes in perception, cognition, and sensation with advancing age; and, c) changes in life outlook and response to social stimuli, brought about by the personalistic ways in which each individual experiences the events of his life.

At a higher level of abstraction, these sets of life changes taken together can be said to give each generation a different *developmental stake* in the other (Bengtson and Kuypers, 1971). Parents and children have an investment ("stake") in their relationship which varies according to how the relationship enables the attainment of personal goals. In the case of the adolescent and his middle-aged parent, the parent may be concerned with the creation of social heirs. Aware of his own mortality and fearing that his contribution or significance may be lost, the parent may wish to perpetuate valued ideals and institutions in his offspring. To this end, the older generation may tend to deny or minimize evidence of intergenerational differences. By contrast, the younger generation is concerned with developing distinctiveness, a personal identity of one's own. The goal of youth is to create values and institutions for themselves, and their elders' attempts to perpetuate existing values and institutions may be perceived as an imposition rather than well-intentioned advice. Youths' developmental stake causes them to exaggerate or maximize intergenerational differences.

Based on the observation that different generations have contrasting perceptions of their common relationship, the developmental stake perspective represents an application of Waller's (1938) "principle of least interest" as developed in studies of dating behavior: the actor with the least commitment for maintaining the relationship will be in the best position to bargain for influence, for he has the least to lose if the relationship is broken. By contrast, the actor with the greatest commitment must often make concessions to the will of the other in order to avoid an implied threat of severance. This principle has interesting implications for the position of older members of the generational relationship; the exercise of parental authority carries with it an implied threat to the stability of the relationship, and so parents may tend to minimize differences (Bengtson and Black, 1973). In the case of the older family member, it may lead to a reluctance to request assistance from adult children, as has been shown in several studies (Streib, 1965), because such demands put the older family member at an even greater disadvantage in terms of exchange.

But what of the level of sentiment or liking expressed between dyad members? In the three-generation study described above, parents and children were asked to report their perceptions of affect toward the dyad partner and from the dyad partner. These were assessed on each of five issues (degree of understanding, trust, fairness, respect, and affection) which the individual felt characterized the relationship.

The analysis of these data produce two notable findings. First, relatively high levels of perceived solidarity are exhibited by both dyad members. The mean for the elderly parents is 50.9 and for middle-aged children, 48.1, on a scale from 10 to 60. Second, the data reveal a slightly higher perception of subjective solidarity on the part of the

elderly parent. Family members think of their relations as warm, and this is especially true of the oldest generation.

In summarizing these two dimensions of solidarity, it appears that the elderly parents report higher levels of both giving and receiving help (objective solidarity). This is consistent with the developmental stake concept discussed above which implies that each member of the dyad has a differential investment in the dyad which colors his perception of the relationship. While the elderly report higher levels of affection, they minimize the amount of assistance or exchange of services. This is congruent with their greater "stake" in the relationship, in which the dimension of affect or sentiment is more important than the instrumental dimension of assistance or help. This may also reflect the fact that declining health or income may prevent them from helping kin as much as they might wish.

## EXCHANGES OF ASSISTANCE AND SUPPORT BETWEEN GENERATIONS

A fourth dimension of intergenerational solidarity, the exchange of assistance and support between older persons and their children, has been a topic of much research on intergenerational relations (Adams, 1968; Hill *et al.*, 1970; Kreps, 1965; Lopata, 1973; Rosow, 1969; Townsend, 1968; Troll, 1970). In an earlier review, Sussman (1965) summarized empirical data on mutual aid collected since the 1950s, noting a general tendency for families to turn to kin rather than to outside agencies in times of trouble (p. 70). He depicted routine day-to-day exchange of services (i.e., shopping, childcare, provision of shelter) as well as financial help. The pattern of financial aid described in this article was usually from parents to children, especially during the early years of the child's marriage (p. 69).

In their three-generation study, Hill *et al.* (1970) found that in a crisis situation, all three generations saw kin as their preferred source of assistance (p. 69). Exchange of help within these three generations was greater than all other sources of help, including that from more distant kin and from outside agencies. Over a one-year period, 65 percent of help received by grandparents was familial; for the parent generation, 53 percent was familial and for the married child generation, 44 percent was familial (p. 66).

Patterns of mutual aid were the second most frequent activity between generations in Adams' study. Sex and occupational status influenced exchanges of help in this as well as in Rosow's study.

In the latter, the social class of the *parents* influenced the type of help received. Middle class parents tended to receive moral support and working class parents were the recipients of slightly more material help (p. 150). In Rosow's study, the most powerful predictor affecting whether or not children do aid their parents is the gender of the nearest child. This factor was even more salient than social class. Lopata's study revealed that sex, birth order, and age of children were important variables.

The fourth frequently-assumed belief about the family life of older people, that the elders are primarily dependent recipients of intergenerational exchanges, is not supported by contemporary data. Consider the three-nation study of Shanas *et al.* (1968). Although three-fifths of older Americans reported they received help from their children, over half reported they gave help. A 1974 Harris poll reports similar results, as do data from the Southern California study of generations.

A 1969 survey of Americans aged 58 to 63 (Murray, 1976) provides data on intergenerational support. For those respondents with parents alive, many reported sharing a household with the elderly or furnishing other support. Although 27 percent of married men shared with the aged, fully 54 percent of men and 43 percent of women without spouses did so. These figures may be compared with those for respondents with living children. Thirty-five percent of married persons, 25 percent of single men and 10 percent of single women provided total or partial support to the younger generation. In short, those on the threshold of old age are givers. At least at this stage of life, they make few financial claims on offspring, for the percent receiving contributions *from* children varies from only 2 percent of couples to 13 percent of single women. While these findings are suggestive, more remains to be known about the accuracy of data on financial transfers *between* households. Also under-studied is the way in which family income is allocated *within* households to elderly kin and others (Moon, 1977).

## NORMS AND THE TRANSFORMATION OF INTERGENERATIONAL TRANSFERS

A fifth dimension of solidarity within families concerns norms, the expectations and obligations one generation holds for the other. Though there are many general norms, each shaped by the context of subcultural influences and circumstances surrounding a particular family, we will focus on the specific norm of inheritance as illustrating the changing context of intergenerational exchange and control. A frequent (if cynical) observation is

that filial piety, concern for an aging family member, is motivated by the sanction of economic reward through monetary legacy. To what extent is this, too, a myth?

Age relations in a society may be characterized as a system of exchanges in which the old have declining resources to secure the compliance of others (Dowd, 1975). If we accept this useful formulation, we might ask first whether recent social changes have strengthened or weakened the aged's hand in bargaining with other generations and second whether such sanctions are relevant. We will argue that societal forces limiting some older people's power over descendants may well have been offset by economic changes obviating the need for such control.

As was noted in the second section of this chapter, control of inheritance has long enabled the propertied old to dominate the lives of grown children. However, historical changes have operated to reduce the economic clout which parents might exercise over adult offspring. Today material legacies figure less prominently in offsprings' financial success and security. In contemporary American society, one's livelihood typically derives from a job rather than from a family farm or family business. Occupational success hinges largely on educational credentials (Blau and Duncan, 1967). To be sure, middle-aged parents promote their children's success by making substantial investments in their children's schooling. When the parents are old, they have no way of revoking their generous investments, even if they might wish to do so. They must rely on such tender sentiments as gratitude to insure their offsprings' cooperation, because grown children in established careers and independent lives can resist whatever financial threats or inducements their parents might be able to muster.

This is not to argue that inheritance has lost all importance. Rising affluence means that more parents will have a legacy, no matter how small, to leave to their children. If the financial significance of inheritance has declined, its symbolic salience remains intact. Sussman, Cates, and Smith (1970) document the contemporary practice of writing wills which reward the dutiful and punish the shirkers. Few bequests are so large as to change the economic fortunes of heirs, but they do constitute a public and final judgment on parent-child relations. As such, disinheritance (or a special consideration shown a favored child) may generate extreme hostility among survivors, if such allocation is seen as "unfair." This psychologic dimension of inheritance is also seen in symbolic bequests. As Rosenfeld (1974) notes, the treasured memento or family heirloom, items of sentimental as opposed to monetary value, are cherished as signs of special intimacy.

In short, inheritance now embodies norms of emotional ties which have supplanted economic bonds or sanctions between family members. Instead of being motivated by the economic coercion of disinheritance, attention paid aging kin springs from sentiments such as affection, guilt, gratitude, or a wish for parental approval. Shorter (1975) has gone so far as to argue that tender familial feelings were not to be found in "pre-modern" families where economic sanctions were more important. Whether or not one accepts this interpretation, it is clear that economic motives must figure less prominently in the exercise of norms concerning filial piety today. Although the declining importance of inheritance may have diminished the familial control by some aged, sentimental ties continue as a powerful resource in intergenerational exchange.

While we have emphasized societal changes liberating offspring from the economic control of parents, it is worth noting that other forces have reduced aging parents' dependency on grown children. While financial support of the old once rested largely with younger family members, today this generational burden is institutionalized through social security systems (Kreps, 1977). Given governmental transfers, the elderly can count on some minimal standard of living regardless of the warmth of their own family relationships, a fact limiting the control which kin can exercise over the aged.

If the institutionalization of old-age support has eliminated some sanctions for intergenerational cooperation, it has also eliminated a potent source of tension. On the one hand, a basis for coercion has been removed. On the other hand, the onus of abject dependency has been lifted from the aging parent. After all, older people endorse self-reliance: they are more likely to hold that the old should provide for themselves in old age and less likely to attribute responsibility to children than do either the general public or the children of the aged (Ragan, 1976; Shanas, 1962, pp. 133–134). The "earned right" notion of social security with its blurred lines of intergenerational support is consistent with older people's beliefs that parents should help children rather than children helping parents.

Social security and public services have largely eliminated the need for the old to take from their children. This fact may be especially important to the self-image of older people in an era when they have less basis for reciprocal exchange with kin.

Child-tending functions of elderly grandparents have fallen victim to the demographic forces which have made small grandchildren a phenomenon of mid-life, not later years. Separate residence of the aged has also reduced the opportunity for a day-to-day exchange of services between generations. (See Treas [1979] for a cross-cultural contrast.)

While one may be inclined to lament this generational separation, it is important to remember that Social Security and overall prosperity have permitted the old to enjoy a degree of privacy sought even by earlier generations. Chicago-area widows studied by Lopata (1973, pp. 114–123) were quick to point out the sources of potential friction in multigenerational households, the differences of life style, the conflicts over authority, and the admonitions against two women in the kitchen. In summary, societal provision for the elderly are seen to have eliminated the imposed togetherness of families and with it many likely sources of intergenerational tensions.

Given this decline in economic dependency between generations, the reader may be posing a question well phrased by Juanita Kreps (1977, p. 22): "But when it is no longer necessary for grandparents, parents and children to join forces and work through the process of allocating family resources, will a joining of forces actually occur? Except for periods of psychological stress, illness, and the like, will there be a sufficient mutuality of interest to hold the three groups together on a continuous basis?"

We have documented the high frequency of contact and communication between generations. As a closing remark to this discussion of social change, we note the revolution in communication technology which has marked this century (Black and Bengtson, 1977). Universal literacy, the development of reliable and inexpensive postal service, the ubiquitous telephone, the family automobile, the expansion of the highway system, the discount airfare have all made kin accessible in a way unheard of in earlier generations. Much has been made of the mobility of modern American society, and geographical distance indeed may preclude much day-to-day, face-to-face interaction between generations. Nonetheless, kin are today accessible in an unprecedented way.

In summary, we have examined four frequently-expressed beliefs about the contemporary family life of older people. Current research suggests each is a misconception. Most older individuals do not live alone, isolated from their families; they do tend to have frequent contact with children. Relations between generations appear warm and close, at least within the older respondent's own family; and the older individual is frequently the donor, as well as the recipient, of intergenerational exchanges of assistance and support. Norms of filial piety are not the result of fears concerning economic sanctions through disinheritance. These findings suggest that many stereotypes about the decline of intergenerational solidarity in modern society are unfounded.

## CASE PERSPECTIVES: FAMILY DYNAMICS AND THE NEGOTIATION OF CHANGE

Mental health practitioners are confronted by specific problems reflecting the negotiation of change. A particular individual or family, for instance, may be attempting to deal with some crisis or disability (Alpaugh and Haney, 1978). Indeed, a number of popular volumes have appeared recently which are designed to counsel families to anticipate and respond to age-related changes (see Otten and Shelley, 1976; Ragan, 1979; Schwartz, 1977; Silverstone and Hyman, 1976). We have suggested that the idiographic perspective of the clinician and client can be more adequate if informed by an understanding of broader social patterns. We have examined some demographic, historical and interactional perspectives of family relations which have implications for the psychologic well-being of older individuals.

We turn now to a consideration of specific changes encountered by aging individuals and the role played by families in the negotiation of change. As individuals grow older, they face many transitions, some of which are predictable from the standpoint of the life cycle but unanticipated by the individual. Many involve changes in the composition of the older individual's family. It may also involve other family members' adaptation to the normal transitions of aging, reactions which may either facilitate or make more difficult the older person's adjustment to change.

### AGING AS A CAREER: CHANGE, CONTINUITY, AND SOCIALIZATION

To begin with, it is well to emphasize the inevitability of change in the developing biography of an individual. Normal aging involves the negotiation of continual alterations: in the individual's own body, self, and roles; in his or her interpersonal network; and in the broader society or culture. Mitigating these changes are forces which effect continuity. Behavior at any one time is the product

of the individual's personal history of adaptation, shaped by the interpersonal and social context in which he or she has developed.

Similarly, the normal course of family life involves inevitable change. As each family member grows and develops with the passage of time, there must be alterations in the relationships among members. The negotiation of resulting changes, sometimes stormy, sometimes subtle, takes place in the context of forces tending toward continuity. Age status positions ("mother" and "child"), norms and values transmitted from one generation to the next, family traditions or identities, the place of this family within the broader social system, all are factors lending elements of continuity to the negotiation of change.

What is the process by which individuals and families negotiate change with the passage of time? The term most often used to characterize microsocial adaptations is *socialization*, which may be defined as the learning of new behaviors and orientations appropriate to a new position or role. Two perspectives are useful in analysis of socialization and its mechanisms. The first involves a focus on the efforts of the social system and its institutions (often called "socialization agents") to prepare the individual for his new role. This is seen in studies of parents with young children, of schools, and of the organization of prisons, mental hospitals and military induction camps. The second focuses on processes in the individual by which he learns the new roles and adapts to the new expectations. Such terms as imitation and modeling, identification and internalization, are often used in analysis, but these terms do not do justice to the active restructuring that the individual usually engages in when moving into a new position. People often create new positions or carry out an established role in a novel way. At any rate, socialization should properly be regarded as a process of continuous and bilateral negotiation between the individual and the social system as he or she moves into new positions through time. Both the goals and efforts of the social system, and the individual's active integration of the new roles and expectations, should be kept in mind (Bengtson and Black, 1973; Hagestad, 1977).

Socialization is most obvious during childhood, the period of most apparent acqustion of the necessities of social behavior. One must learn to say "please," to talk only at appropriate times in class, to write, to avoid certain words. But socialization also occurs in middle and old age. Whenever one moves into a different social position, there are new behaviors which must be learned in order to fill that position in accord with the expectations of others. One important contrast, however, between early and later socialization concerns the degree of input from the social system. In childhood, one is helped and even forced to learn the new behaviors by agencies of socialization, such as the school; in late adulthood, one finds few such institutionalized mechanisms to teach new roles and new expectations. This is, perhaps, what makes the normal transitions of aging so difficult. How does one learn the behaviors necessary in order to become a happy retiree? a valued grandfather? a graceful widow?

In a sense, then, aging can be viewed as a career which involves the successful negotiation of changes in social positions. Long ago Max Weber observed that a career is comprised of a series of related jobs, arranged somewhat in a hierarchy, through which persons move in a sequence. Although career is used primarily to describe an occupational trajectory in a wage-earning setting, this limits the term too much; the "life plan" of middleclass mothers. Mannheim observed many years ago, involves a succession of rather predictable jobs related to the ages of their children. So, too, old age has attributes of a career. Transitions from worker to retiree, from caretaking mother to mother-in-law, from spouse to widow, from healthy and independent to sick and dependent—these are the more-or-less expectable transitions of aging, each with its "job" in terms of performance and expectations, each representing a part of a sequence, each involving some form of learning or socialization. Many of the career changes involve family roles, and many of the transitions embrace the family as a socializing agent.

## EXPECTABLE TRANSITIONS IN OLD AGE: FOUR CRISES TO WELL-BEING

The career of old age is frequently marked by four events which involve significant transitions for the individual and for the family. These events, expectable in the sense that one only has to live long enough and they will probably be encountered, include (a) independence of children or the "empty nest;" (b) retirement from a paid job; (c) incapacitating illness requiring institutionalization; (d) disruption of the family unit through death or divorce. Each of these events requires adjustment to change; each implies socialization, the learning of behavior and feelings appropriate to the new social position. Each involves other family members as willing or unwitting participants in the negotiation of change.

The first transition is the most expectable, if least discussed: most Americans who have children

can expect to survive to see them "launched" and living away from the parental home. For some women in our society, this may represent a major role transition with consequences for changes in self-worth and a sense of usefulness. It is an expectable transition with often unanticipated consequences in mental health or psychological well-being.

Pauline Bart (1968) has related the manifestations of psychiatric disorder among middle-aged women to the physical and emotional leave-taking of children. In her study of 533 women hospitalized for the first time for mental illness, she found a high incidence of depression among "empty nest" females whose lives had been that of the traditional mother and housewife and whose self-conception had been threatened by the loss of the maternal role: "Because the most important roles for women in our society are the roles of wife and mother, one might predict that the loss of either of these roles could result in loss of self-esteem—in the feeling of worthlessness and uselessness that characterizes most depressives" (Bart, 1968, p. 189). She quotes Sara, a 61-year-old Jewish woman diagnosed with "involutional depression," speaking about her role as mother:

> I don't . . . I don't . . . I don't feel like. I don't feel like I'm wanted. I don't feel like I'm wanted. I just feel like nothing. I don't feel anybody cares, and nobody's interested, and they don't care whether I do feel good or I don't feel good. I'm pretty useless . . . I feel like I want somebody to feel for me but nobody does.

Mental health, or a feeling of well-being, is dependent on positive self-concept. An individual's self-concept is learned by selecting certain roles from his or her role repertoire as more characteristically "him" than other roles. Self-esteem stems from role adequacy in the most salient social positions (Turner, 1962). Bart (1974) notes that women whose identity, whose sense of self, is derived mainly from their role as mothers, rather than their roles as wives or wage earners, are in a difficult position when their children leave and former patterns of interaction are displaced. These women's self-conceptions must change, but some of them have personalities too rigid to enable them to make this change. Some may turn to the "sick role" as an alternative to normlessness and confusion which result, as is demonstrated by one of Bart's cases:

> A middle-aged woman, upon hearing that her daughter was living with and planning to marry a Mexican unemployed "Communist," thought she was dying, that her heart was failing, and was ad-

mitted to the medical ward of a hospital under the care of a cardiologist . . . While she recognized that the cause of her illness was psychological, since her daughter had "broken her heart," she defined herself as physically ill and in need of medical rather than psychiatric care. She received no support in this definition. Her cardiologist and her family interpreted the behavior psychodynamically, and upon her release from the hospital where she was treated with sedatives and diagnosed as having tachycardia, she entered psychotherapy (Bart, 1967, p. 8).

Middle years may represent a difficult transition: "For women whose lives have not been child-centered and whose strong marital ties continue, for those whose children set up residence near them, the transition to middle age may be buffered. Child-centered women note that the relationship with their children is non-reciprocal, that all they are entitled to is 'respect.' A child once reaching maturity in our culture need honor and look after his/her mother only on Mother's Day, unless she is widowed... Our emphasis on youth and our stipulation that mothers-in-law should not interfere and grandmothers not meddle makes the middle years a time of stress for many thousands, if not millions, of American women" (Bart, 1975, p. 159). As put by Sara, age 61:

> I don't want to be alone, and I'm going to be alone, and my children will go their way and get married...of which I'm wishing for...and then I'll still be alone, and I got more and more alone, and more and more alone (Bart, 1975, p. 156).

Of course, the leave-taking of children can be a welcome opportunity, as is documented by Hagestad (1977), or it may be unrelated to dimensions of happiness (Bremer and Ragan, 1977). In fact, though the empty nest portends negative psychological outcomes for some women with intense investments in mothering, the majority of women face no such crisis when their children leave home. Evidence from a large national survey (Glenn, 1975) suggests that, if anything, women in the postparental stage experience higher morale than do those with children still at home. Neither should we wish to argue that men are untouched by family life cycle transitions. A study by Estes and Wilensky (1978), for example, noted that unemployed professionals short on money registered lower morale if they still had dependents in the home than if their children were launched.

Men's self-esteem has also been thought to be affected by retirement from occupational roles, and women's growing work force involvement may point to more problematic labor force transitions for them as well. A 55-year-old steel worker who had just retired expressed the mixture of relief and uncertainty which marked his new role:

> I'm glad to be through with work because I couldn't take it any more. But now my friends don't know what to call me. They kid me about being an old man, and I don't feel it... My wife doesn't know what to do with me, says I get underfoot being around the house all the time...I guess I've got to find something to do. A man my age shouldn't just sit around (Bengtson, 1973, p. 18).

A 69-year-old wife in the Southern California study of generations sample commented on her husband's retirement:

> The only tension in our family is because of my husband's retirement! He got restless and irritable because work has been his main outlet in life. I didn't know what to do until he went out and got another job. I don't know what will happen if he loses that. I know I'll go crazy!

It should be noted that studies of adaptation to retirement have not documented the purported high incidence of trauma stereotypically associated with leaving work. That is, few mental disorders are attributable to retirement (Atchley, 1975) and successful negotiation of this role change appears to be the rule, not the exception (Streib and Schneider, 1972). Although the consequences of retirement may not be directly linked to mental health disorders (Nadelson, 1975), it is obvious that retirement represents a significant transformation in the ordering of schedule, the interpersonal contact network, and the sense of self, in addition to changing consumption patterns. As described most pessimistically by Cavan:

> At the point of compulsory retirement...the means of carrying out the social role disappears: the man is a lawyer without a case, a bookkeeper without books, a machinist without tools. Second, he is excluded from his group of former co-workers: as an isolated person he may be completely unable to function in his former role. Third, as a retired person, he begins to find a different evaluation of himself in the minds of others from the evaluation he had as an employed person. He no longer sees respect in the eyes of former subordinates, praise in the faces of former superiors, and approval in the manner of former co-workers. The looking glass composed of his former important groups throws back a changed image: he is done for, an old-timer, old fashioned, on the shelf (Cavan, 1962, pp. 527–528).

A third expectable transition with old age is the loss of spouse through death. Increasingly, this end of marriage has been preempted by divorce. Though the two events are obviously different, they share common features in terms of bereavement and adaptation. Each involves loss, adaptation to living alone, psychological processes of bereavement, and an altered sense of self. Living alone is an increasingly likely condition in old age (Table 17-4). By age 65, three out of five women in America are without spouses, and by age 75 the figure is more than four out of five. About one in three men over age 75 is a widower.

The normal process of bereavement includes anger, guilt, depression, anxiety and obsession (Parkes, 1972). Bereavement may represent a relatively short-term decline in feelings of well-being or it may linger. Lopata (1973) found in her study of widows that 48 percent said they were "adjusted" to their husband's death by the end of the first year, while 20 percent reported they had not gotten over it and did not expect to. A longitudinal study of bereavement found that those who reacted by becoming depressed were more likely than others to report poor health a year later (Bornstein, Clayton, Halikas, Maurice, and Robins, 1973).

Dealing with bereavement is a family process. Having lost a parent, it may be equally painful for the middle-aged child to witness the surviving parent's continuing preoccupation with the death of her spouse. One respondent in the Southern California study of generations, when answering "What do you and your parent disagree about most?", noted:

> It may be strange, but we argue most about what she should do now that dad's gone. It's been two years now and she still sits and broods over it. She's an attractive woman at 66 and there are lots of men who belong to her church that show interest in her. But she won't do anything and won't even go to church except if we take her.

Her mother, in answering the same question about family disagreements, presented the issue from her perspective:

> My daughter keeps trying to get me to forget the past. I had a wonderful marriage to a man and the Lord took him Home. I'm not interested in anyone else.

Although kin represent a resource in bereavement, it is well to note that the relations among surviving family members may be altered by the loss of one of their own. Lifelong relationships with in-laws may fade with the loss of the living link between families. Without parental intervention, sibling rivalries may escalate into bitter breaches. A surviving parent may turn to children in place of the spouse, calling upon them as confidantes, helpers, or beneficiaries of well-meaning ministrations. In short, death demands both personal adjustment and interpersonal adaptation.

Chronic health disabilities are a fourth transition in the aging process. A 1972 national survey compared the lives of the disabled and nondisabled (Franklin, 1977). Not only did this study document the greater disability of the older population, but also it pointed out the unfortunate correlates of poor health. The disabled reported that their participation in household activities (such as shopping, chores and money handling) had declined, along with their participation in the work force. Similarly, they reported that they devoted less time to hobbies and to social activities inside and outside the house than they had done before their health problems developed. Day-to-day activities of the disabled were altered markedly by their changing health, a situation with potentially serious ramifications for mental health and well-being. There was little evidence, however, that the families of the disabled were able to compensate for their loss of good health. Although respondents tended to report spending more time with the spouse than in the past, there is no indication that the extended families of the disabled provided more money, household services, or companionship than did families of those in good health.

Incapacitating illness, resulting in hospitalization and then institutionalization, is one aspect of this expectable transition in the career of growing old. At a given point in time, half of Americans over the age of 65 have a major health incapacity, although less than five percent are institutionalized (Shanas and Maddox, 1976). The longer one lives, however, the greater the likelihood of serious illness and institutionalization.

Taking an aging parent into one's home continues to be an alternative solution for some families, but it is clear that both arrangements pose problems along with benefits. A national study surveyed grown children who had parents living with them and grown children who had parents living in an institution (Newman, 1976). One-third of each group identified at least one problem with the parent's living arrangement. Those with parents in their home mentioned interpersonal conflicts and restrictions on privacy and freedom, while those with institutionalized kin mentioned that the distance between family home and nursing home discouraged visits, that they felt guilty about not having the older person at home, and that they worried about the relative. Interestingly, those who had chosen the nursing home were less certain that they had made the right decision. For both groups, the principal determinant of satisfaction with the parent's living arrangement was the *parent's* satisfaction with the situation. Thus, from the perspective of mental health, parental incapacity poses challenges not only for the parent, but also for concerned family members.

Although the thrust of many services for the aged is to maintain the independence of the elderly in the community, it is not clear that community living is always to be preferred over institutional living. For example, a large study of older persons in Manitoba reported a surprising discovery (Myles, 1978). Given comparable levels of illness and disability, the institutionalized aged were less likely to report themselves to be in poor health than were other older persons. The author suggested that the institutionalized aged maintain this perception of their good health, because nursing homes are organized so as to minimize the disruptive potential of physical incapacity.

The precursors of institutionalization and its outcome in terms of feelings of well-being doubtless reflect a complex interplay between the needs and capacities of aging parent and grown child. Consider the following account by a 64-year-old daughter of her 92-year-old mother's pathway toward institutionalization. It illustrates the interplay between sudden physical incapacity and emotional well-being, the tension between filial piety in caring for a dependent parent and responsibilities to oneself and to other family members. The elderly woman has been in a home for the aged for five months:

> Before that time, she had lived with us for fourteen years, having her separate quarters but in daily contact with us at mealtime, and was always included in family activities. A year ago she fell and broke her pelvis, and after her return from the hospital, we moved her into our home. She needed considerable help and supervision; we hired someone to live in who was to take care of mother's needs.
>
> It didn't work out well. We hired "sitters" for those occasions when I, or we, had to be away, even for short excursions. My preoccupation with my mother's welfare put a strain on my relationship with my husband. Mother's constant presence became a burden to me, too; I dreaded hearing the sound of her slippers shuffling to the kitchen each morning. Her occasional criticisms bothered me more and more, but I tried to maintain a reasonable manner. One day, after five or six months, I blew. I said harsh and hurtful things. I was a wreck emotionally.
>
> During the next couple of weeks no mention was made of our confrontation, but mother seemed to become disturbed, coming into our bedroom at night, turning on lights, calling me in the wee hours. The paranoia increased until one morning she became extremely agitated, wanting to leave the house because "someone" wanted to get rid of us; indeed, was trying to kill us.
>
> Aware that it would be agonizingly difficult for me to make the first move to place mother in a retirement home, I seized the opportunity. With her approval, I arranged for her to move into an excellent place that very day, allowing her to make the decision to stay there after we were shown the premises. She has been there since last November except for a few weeks in the hospital after she had another fall and fractured her wrist. She has been on medication that corrects the paranoid symptoms and is presently behaving quite normally.
>
> We see mother four or fives times a week, often taking her for a drive and to lunch, spending an average of three hours each time. Much of my time away from her is concerned with "doing" for her in some way. My own projects are neglected. However, the depression I felt this past year has lessened somewhat so that I hope for an eventual return to equilibrium and some insight as to better ways to handle the traumatic aspects of aging.

This woman went on to list some concerns she felt about the relationship with her own children, aged 42, 32 and 26, concerns doubtless reflecting experiences with her own aging mother:

> That they may feel dislike, resentment, and anger toward me, and are unable to express these feelings appropriately.... That they may have to help with my support and are therefore strained or deprived economically.... That their personal lives might be disrupted.

She concluded with some observations on guilt and personal needs in what she termed the "unexplored territory of being a child to an aging parent":

> The guilt feelings suffered by so many children have different sources: that the individual isn't living up to his or her ego-ideal, some ethical concept of filial behavior that directs one to be loving, attentive, patient, and dedicated to the parent's care. In conflict with that is the natural need for one's own growth and survival which, when frustrated, results in resentment, anger, even hatred which is turned inward. The resulting depression hampers further the healthy handling of the situation.

This letter, written in response to a request in the American Association of Retired Persons newsletter for input to a conference on "You and Your Aging Parents," illustrates several important points regarding transitions in old age. First, change is inevitable; it is to be expected that transitions will occur which represent significant contrasts in the older individual's personal and social life. Many create alterations in self-images and feelings of well-being. Second, the older person's family is inevitably involved in these changes, and they represent a source of continuity and healing, as well as an impetus to many changes (Dobrof and Litwak, 1977). Third, intergenerational negotiation characterizes most role transitions in old age: parents and children are in continuous and bilateral negotiation regarding roles and norms, rights and duties, desires and fears, as these change with the passage of time. This is the normal career of aging.

## COPING WITH CHANGE: FAMILIES, SOCIALIZATION, AND THE CAREER OF AGING

If change is inevitable and often painful and if negotiation between generations is a continual if unacknowledged part of family life, what are some of the characteristic issues as families deal with the career of aging? Socialization to old age is a process which involves both the aging parent and his or her family, just as socialization is bilateral at other stages of the life cycle. Characteristic issues of family socialization involve tensions of autonomy versus dependency, connectedness versus separateness, and openness versus privateness.

Problems of autonomy and dependency can be seen at each stage of personal development, and the family represents a socialization agent for moderating or adjudicating an appropriate blend of each pole. Adolescents frequently act out extremes of each as teenagers first demand authority, then deny responsibilities seen by others as appropriate. Erikson (1950) has characterized this dilemma as reflecting psychosocial crises of indentity versus role diffusion and intimacy versus isolation. He notes that these are recurrent issues in the life cycle...never completely resolved once and for all.

In the transitions of old age, one also sees the tension between autonomy and dependency as a previously independent mature adult encounters dependency brought on by retirement, widowhood, or sickness. Coping with these changes involves socialization into a new configuration of one's social position, the definition of which engages both the individual and the family. Often symbolic exchanges are the medium by which the

older person attempts to maintain some degree of autonomy:

> A 102-year-old man was admitted to the hospital with a broken hip. He had fallen off the ladder while attempting to clean out the gutters of his daughter's house—a seasonal task which he had carried out for years.

> He began living with his daughter at the age of 61, when he was recovering from a cardiac arrest and glaucoma. He had no financial resources and no pension. From the beginning he had insisted on doing three things: gardening, washing dinner dishes, and occasionally making the family breakfast. Carrying out these tasks, he felt, represented some exchange for the living he received from his daughter.

> For 42 years he had lived with his daughter, and for 42 years he had maintained tenaciously his "role" as gardener, dishwasher, and cook—despite frequent efforts of the family to "retire" him. Tremorous hands chipped the dishes as he washed them, and cataracts made the breakfasts he cooked an unending source of surprise, but until his fall he insisted on "doing his part." Recognizing the importance of these activities to his sense of justice and autonomy, his family reluctantly went along. Together they negotiated the preservation of autonomy in the face of dependency (Bengtson, 1979).

The struggle for autonomy involves both generations and is frequently the source of conflict. Often it reflects a second characteristic issue in later life socialization, the tension between connectedness (to one's family) and separateness (maintaining an identity or style of life that is uniquely one's own). Hess and Handel (1959) suggest this is the major psychosocial agenda in family socialization during adolescence. But the issue of family connectedness versus individual separateness persists through later life. In the American Association of Retired Persons (AARP) request for input to the "You and Your Aging Parents" conference, a 69-year-old mother sent a copy of a letter from her 40-year-old daughter who was in the process of separation from her husband, with the comment, "I sincerely hope this example of the extreme breach in family relations will be of benefit in your discussions":

> Your invidious letter arrived. Henry and I agree that it is gross.

> Over the years you have called me everything from a slut to a psychopath and obviously are under the impression that you can continue to do so with

impunity. However, this letter is to inform you that I shall no longer have any contact with you.

To make sure that you understand why I have made this decision, the reasons are as follows: you have denied my validity and integrity as a person; you have attempted to destroy my self-respect and belief in myself; you have undermined my emotional strength and stability; and, most importantly, you have shown me no love and understanding, even in moments of greatest crisis. In short, you have not been a mother to me for the last twenty-three years and I have reached the conclusion that you are both unwilling and unable to ever be a mother to me again.

You say that you feel sorry for Henry [her estranged husband] and me, but, most of all for the children. Well, we feel sorry for you—sorry that you do not realize that unconditional love and understanding are what make good parents and not the perpetuation of a defunct relationship between a man and a woman. Henry and I are committed to being good parents, by our definition, and that obligation transcends any other commitment. Also, we regret your inability to fathom the pain and despair we went through in deciding to dissolve our marriage. How foolish of us to try to protect you from being hurt by our decision!

As you have so consistently pointed out to me over the past twenty years, self-preservation is a basic law of life. Therefore, I will never again put myself in a position where you can devastate me emotionally. I want nothing whatever to do with you forever more. If you write to me, I will destroy the letter. If you call me, I will hang up. If you come to my house, I will refuse to see you.

Such dramatic expression of the need for intergenerational separateness and autonomy is undoubtedly rare, but this example provides a useful reminder that the negotiation of individuation persists far beyond adolescence (Alpaugh and Haney, 1978). Another respondent in the AARP survey, a mother of a 45-year-old son who lives with her 94-year-old mother, noted that:

As a "child" I feel guilt often. Why? I think because my mother dominated and still dominates me. I have always felt that I must do as she says. She feels that children are duty bound to care for their parents. Thus now that I have her to care for I feel resentment and bitterness at having to give up all these years while I am growing old, too. I am caught between two generations.

Her solution to this problem, in retrospect, involves greater separateness and less assumption of dependency on the part of aged family members:

It is hard to strike a happy medium (Between offering too little or too much support). I think I tried to "help" too soon. My parents could have managed without me much longer and we would both have been happier.

Other respondents to the AARP survey focused on communicating the need for separateness from the standpoint of the older generation:

Parents want and need independence from their grown children. They want it to be a physical and financial independence.... [If they are] it makes a much better relationship with their children.... The parents should not expect too much from their children.... There should be some understanding when they frankly tell each other what they wish in the relationship and neither party is hurt by frankness and a clearing of wants and needs (74-year-old woman).

First and foremost there is a deep need by the parents to keep in contact with the child. At the same time the child and the parent must each carry his own responsibilities, be independent, and each live his own life with his own interests and activities.... [Parents should] become involved in groups outside the family so in later years when one is alone there will be groups of friends and individual close friends (65-year-old woman).

Related to dilemmas of autonomy and separateness is a third issue characterizing families and socialization as individuals negotiate the career of aging. Transitions involving new social roles, widow, retiree, "empty nest" parent, may occasion changes in definitions of what is good or bad, moral or immoral. Often it is supposed that other family members will disapprove, and thus a shroud of secrecy may be involved which is the source of puzzlement for the family:

Aunt Martha began acting strangely a year ago, shortly after her husband's death following a long illness. Not only would she refuse invitations to go out Sundays, but she seemed very reluctant to allow us to go to her home any more. One day I stopped by to see her anyway. While she was downstairs, I happened to go into her bedroom. To my surprise, I saw she had replaced her twin bedroom set with a gigantic king-size bed!

I teased her about it: "What is a 74-year-old widow doing with a new king-size bed?" She got very angry and said she didn't think it was anyone's business but hers. She was sick and tired of the family's moral judgments which she had endured all her life! Then she calmed down and told me: The man next door, a retired physician whose wife had died several years before, had begun "calling" on her. She felt so good about it: "I was a loyal wife for 53 years and it wasn't no picnic, believe me, especially when Andy got sick. Now I'm having some fun for a change." She seemed glad to be able to tell someone, for she had no close friends, but she was concerned about the consequences: "Don't you dare tell the family about it," she said, "they'd just get all upset. It's my business." When I left she added with a laugh, "If anyone asks about my new bed I guess I'll just say my doctor prescribed it for my health."

Privacy may become an increasingly precious commodity to older family members facing new dependencies in old age. Retirement, widowhood, institutionalization create affronts to privacy and a sense of separateness:

Now that I'm retired it seems that everyone has something to say about what I do. I have to get out and take long walks just to get away from them fussing because I'm not "doing something constructive" (Bengtson, unpublished manuscript).

I knew there would be many problems after my husband died but I didn't know I would have to put up with too much attention. My daughter means well but she thinks I'm lonely when I'm not, and I can't bring myself to tell her I'd just as soon do "my own thing."

The problem around here (a nursing home) is you can't get away from people you don't want to see. They want to run your life (Cuellar, 1977).

But perhaps more often is the plea for more openness between generations. Respondents in the AARP survey mentioned this frequently in answering the question, "What concerns do parents have about relationships with their middle-aged children?"

Lack of communication with parents about personal affairs, i.e. surprise marriages—break-ups—parents last to know. Often the last one they go to when they should be the first. Do not take advantage of experience of parents in many areas of life (70-year-old woman).

The first concern is that children cannot be relied upon...because the children do not give parents that assurance in words.... Children who marry at an early age or who live away from home never have the experience of knowing their parents as friends. They remember parents as authority figures only [which] stops the growth of the parent-child relationship before the friendship level is reached. My response is: Show interest in what your parents are doing. Be a good listener. Treat them with the same courtesies, respect, civ-

ilities you would give to neighbors, fellow workers, your peers. In other words act toward one another openly, as equal personalities (an "unmarried, older sister").

The normal course of family life involves negotiation between generations as each develops and changes with the passage of time. Negotiation often embodies conflict, or at least disagreement. In many American families, conflict is feared as an indication of disruption. But coping with change, and socialization into the new positions of old age, requires negotiating the normal and inevitable tensions that surround recurrent issues of autonomy versus dependency, connectedness versus separateness, openness versus privateness.

## IMPLICATIONS FOR MENTAL HEALTH POLICY AND PRACTICE

In charting historical and developmental changes in family life, we have noted that family relations may influence the well-being of older family members, because families are a source of assistance and because families provide a context in which the self-concept is shaped. In the public mind, the relationship between family life and the mental health of the aged is unequivocal; the notion that close intergenerational ties promote happiness is widely accepted. To be sure, many older Americans derive satisfaction from interaction with their kin, but there are others who have no families or who have families who are either a sore spot or a subject of indifference to them.

Despite a cultural bias toward cordial and intimate family life, there is little evidence that older people without such a supportive kin network are at a psychological disadvantage. Indeed, research has shown that intense interaction need not lead to greater happiness for older family members. For example, Kerckhoff's (1966) study of retired couples found that husbands and wives who lived close to their offspring had lower morale than those who lived farther away. In a large national survey of Americans 58 to 63, married men living with kin were less likely to report themselves "happy" than were those who shared housing only with a wife (Murray, 1973). In a South Carolina survey of older widows, Arling (1976) reported no association between morale and contact with kin, especially contact with children; contact with friends and neighbors, on the other hand, did serve to reduce loneliness while increasing feelings of usefulness.

How are we to reconcile our intuitive sense that families are important to the mental health of older people with the recurrent findings that morale is either unaffected or depressed by intergenerational contact? Doubtless much thinking about the family's influence on the aged has been too simplistic in that it has failed to recognize factors that mediate the impact of intergenerational relations on the aged. Three such factors warrant attention. The first factor returns to our earlier discussions of the family as a context for the development of positive or negative self-concept. The second has to do with the expectations for intergenerational life which are held by parent and offspring. The third deals with the economic bases of family living.

Let us turn first to the family's part in the development of self-concept—the delicate and continual process of negotiation described at length above. As was evident in earlier discussions, the outcome of this process—with respect to self-esteem, functional capacity, and overall mental health—may be either positive or negative. For example, "family solidarity," the bonds of interaction and affection between generations, is a two-edged sword, reinforcing mental health or breeding mental illness. Clinicians have come increasingly to recognize that the emotional dependency and day-to-day togetherness of families may foster pathology in members over whom no other primary group can possibly assert a comparable influence. Indeed, family interaction may even be predicated on the pathological behavior or agreed-upon inadequacies of individuals. Only an assessment of family dynamics can indicate whether frequent visiting provides an older family member with on-going evidence of kin's high regard or whether such interaction offers a forum for less positive messages. Do visits to grandmother's confirm her independence or do they serve to point out reasons why she is no longer competent to live alone? Unfortunately, many of the conventional ways of gauging family closeness fail to tap the content of family interaction.

If the aging of family members may be described in terms of continuity and change, it is clear that the family context for the construction of self is also subject to such patterning. Births, deaths, marriages, the splitting-offs and doubling-ups of family life all serve to alter the structure of families just as age serves to alter the roles and capacities of family members. Although the internalization of family communication may insure that some behavioral adaptations transcend (for better or worse) the family constellations which spawned them, this continuity may be contrasted with the opportunities for change which are posed by the course of the family life cycle.

Take widowhood as an example. Death of a spouse means the loss of a major source of expectations for, and evaluations of, one's self, and the loss of this kinship link may require a reordering of other family relationships as well. A new family constellation may call forth new behavioral patterns on the part of survivors. Kin may encounter heretofore unknown fears and dependency in the widow or marvel at her unsuspected resilience and resourcefulness. Neither continuity nor the direction of change are entirely predictable in response to changes in the family context.

If the family serves to evaluate the older person, it is also true that the older person evaluates the family—approving or faulting the performance of kin in the intergenerational network. These evaluations of others may also affect the well-being of the old. If others are viewed as failing in filial duties or family responsibilities, this reflects not only on them, but also on the older family member. For better or worse, values and behavior of younger generations may be thought to reflect not only on parenting, but also on the respect and affection that they hold for parents. In this respect, parental satisfaction with intergenerational family life may be seen to contribute to morale and mental well-being.

In this regard, expectations represent a second factor which mediates the impact of intergenerational relations on the aged (Treas, 1978). Even warm and frequent contact between aging parents and grown children need not result in higher morale if parents hold even higher expectations for the relationship. This observation came to attention in the University of Southern California study of middle-aged and older persons in three ethnic groups in Los Angeles (Bremer and Ragan, 1977). Mexican-American women in the sample were found to have much more frequent contact with offspring than did their black and anglo counterparts. However, they were also more likely to report that they didn't see their children as much as they would like, and their morale was lower. More recently, Seelbach and Sauer (1977) reported similar findings for a Philadelphia sample of low-income aged. Lower morale was found among those with high filial responsibility expectations. That is, those who felt children should live close, visit often, and feel responsible for parents had lower morale than older persons who did not hold such high expectations. Previously cited research by Pauline Bart (1975) on the causes of depression in middle-aged women is also pertinent. Recall that the empty nest was an invitation to mental illness for those women whose intense mothering had fostered unrealistically high expectations of what their children owed them.

These disparate findings indicate that considerable intimacy and interaction may still fall short of parental preferences, and this disparity between expectations and reality may lead to lower psychological well-being. Of course, most older people do not seem to hold excessive expectations for their children. We know that older people are more likely to believe that older folks should support themselves and less willing to assign responsibility to children than is either the public at large or the children of the aged (Shanas, 1962). While one survey reported that four-fifths of the elderly thought children should keep in touch by writing or visiting, only a minority believed children were obligated to live nearby or to entertain parents often (Streib and Thompson, 1965).

Even if most aging parents make only modest demands, some older people may hold expectations which their children are hard put to fulfill—expectations which make family life a disappointment instead of a comfort in old age. Certainly, notions of what is reasonable have changed over time. As we have noted, demographic trends seem to have made it more and more difficult for grown children to meet aging parents' needs for emotional support or physical care. If expectations regarding what children owe parents are changing, the burden will fall harder on some older people than on others. Some ethnic groups have traditionally emphasized filial responsibility, and it may be that foreign-born parents will adhere to more traditional expectations than will their more "Americanized" offspring. Elderly mothers also seem to have higher expectations than do elderly fathers. For example, they are more likely to believe that older people should live with children if they cannot live alone (Seelbach, 1977).

In the future, we can expect that fewer of the aged will be foreign-born. However, the persistent sex differential in mortality suggests that more and more of the future elderly will be women. Older women with such expectations may feel disappointed and neglected despite the well-intentioned efforts of their children, because recent trends suggest that few older women will find homes with offspring in the future. For women 65 and older, projections have indicated that the percent living alone will continue to rise from 38 to 43 percent between 1976 and 1984 (Glick, 1977). At this rate, half of the older women would be living alone before the year 2000! Now there is nothing wrong with solitary living. Recall that most of the widows in Lopata's study valued their independence and privacy over the potential hassles of multigenerational living. For those who harbor expectations that they will make homes with grown offspring, however, these trends portend real disappointments.

A third factor mediating the influence of intergenerational relations on the aged has to do with the economic basis of kin interaction. We would hardly expect family togetherness to be especially satisfying to older family members if it were imposed by economic necessity or created financial hardships. If a family must live together to make ends meet despite its members' preferences for more independent lives, we might expect some of the joy to go out of kin interaction. If taking an aging widow into the home puts middle-aged offspring in a financial pinch, intergenerational living may take an emotional toll on everyone concerned.

As we have noted previously, the growth of private pensions and government programs such as Social Security have made it feasible for more older persons to maintain independence and privacy from kin. Although some would argue that the concomitant decline in three-generation families has been to the detriment of the old, one is hard put to criticize developments which have mitigated the emotional strains of imposed togetherness. Family members who don't get along together can go their own ways, and personal privacy and independence can serve to keep intergenerational differences from looming large. Surely, this freedom can represent a contribution to mental health, rather than a burden on well-being.

In sum, we have argued that family relations contribute to the mental health or sense of well-being of older persons in two ways. First, families represent a support system, actual and potential, in the provision of needed services for older members. In some ways the support is direct, by giving financial assistance, helping with tasks, assisting during illness, or providing a place to live. In other ways the support is indirect, by helping the older person make contact with service agencies which can meet a specific need: Social Security, Medicare, Meals-on-Wheels, or private pension offices.

Second, families represent an important element in self-concept as it develops through time. From a social interactionist perspective, mental health, or feelings of well-being, is dependent on a favorable self-concept which is formed by and reinforced through social interaction. The family is the first and perhaps most pervasive context of social interactions, and the evaluations of family members as one carries out various social roles are incorporated into the self-concept (Turner, 1962). Thus, the positive or negative impact of the family on the mental well-being of the older person must be examined on both instrumental and socio-emotional levels.

We have examined the changing context of the family as a support system for older individuals. We noted that in earlier periods of American history, family support systems were regarded as the most appropriate—perhaps the only—protection against the misfortunes of sickness, widowhood, unemployment, and disabilities of old age. Today social insurance programs and public agencies increasingly provide services to those in need, obviating the need for imposed togetherness with all its stresses and strains. But family relations continue to be important to the well-being of most older persons in socio-emotional, as well as instrumental, concerns.

It is clear that the kin network in many families runs the risk of being overburdened by cross-generational demands. It is also clear that many American taxpayers are concerned about burgeoning governmental service provisions, such as those to the aged. We have documented the increased survival of aging parents, the declining number of descendants who might lend support, and the new expectations of the middle-aged which may compete with filial responsibilities. Thus, it appears that future public policy and practice must emphasize the ways in which families may be enhanced as support systems for the elderly, meeting both the subsistence and the emotional needs of aged kin.

# REFERENCES

ADAMS, B. N. 1968. *Kinship in an Urban Setting.* Chicago: Markham.

ALPAUGH, P., AND HANEY, M. 1978. *Counseling the Older Adult: A Training Manual for Paraprofessionals and Beginning Counselors.* Los Angeles: University of Southern California Press.

ANDERSON, M. 1971. *Family Structure in Nineteenth Century Lancashire.* London: Cambridge University Press.

ANDERSON, M. 1977. The impact on the family relationship of the elderly of changes since Victorian times in governmental income maintenance provision. *In,* E. Shanas and M. Sussman (eds.), *Family, Bureaucracy and the Elderly,* pp. 36–39. Durham, N.C.: Duke University Press.

ARENSBERG, C. M., AND KIMBALL, S. T. 1968. *Family and Community in Ireland.* Cambridge: Harvard University Press.

ARLING, G. 1976. The elderly widow and her family, neighbors and friends. *Journal of Marriage and the Family, 38,* 757–768.

ATCHLEY, R. C. 1975. *Sociology of Retirement.* Boston: Schenkman.

BANE, M. J. 1976. *Here to Stay: American Families in the Twentieth Century.* New York: Basic Books.

BART, P. 1967. Depression in middle-aged women: Some sociocultural factors. Unpublished dissertation UCLA. Ann Arbor, Mich.: University Microfilms.

BART, P. 1968. Social structure and vocabularies of discomfort: What happened to female hysteria? *Journal of Health and Social Behavior, 9,* 188–193.

BART, P. 1974. The Sociology of Depression. *In,* P. Roman and H. Trice (eds.), *Explorations in Psychiatric Sociology,* pp. 139–157. Philadelphia: F. A. Davis Co.

BART, P. 1975. The loneliness of the long-distance mother. *In,* J. Freeman (ed.), *Women: A Feminist Persepctive,* pp. 156–170. Palo Alto, Calif.: Mayfield.

BECKER, G. S. 1976. A theory of marriage. *An Economic Approach to Human Behavior,* pp. 205–250. Chicago: University of Chicago Press.

BERKNER, L. K. 1972. The stem family and the developmental cycle of the peasant household: An 18th century Austrian example. *American Historical Review, 77,* 398–418.

BENGTSON, V. L. 1971. Inter-age differences in perception and the generation gap. *Gerontologist,* Part II, 85–90.

BENGTSON, V. L. 1973. *The Social Psychology of Aging.* Indianapolis, Ind.: Bobbs-Merrill.

BENGTSON, V. L. 1975. Generation and family effects in value socialization. *American Sociological Review, 40,* 358–371.

BENGTSON, V. L. 1979. You and your aging parent: Research perspective on intergenerational interaction. *In,* P. Ragan (ed.), *Aging Parents,* pp. 41–68. Los Angeles: University of Southern California Press.

BENGTSON, V. L., AND BLACK. K. D. 1973. Intergenerational relations and continuities in socialization. *In,* P. Baltes and K. W. Schaie (eds.), *Life-Span Developmental Psychology: Personality and Socialization,* pp. 207–234. New York: Academic Press.

BENGTSON, V. L., AND KUYPERS, J. A. 1971. Generational differences and the developmental stake. *Aging and Human Development, 2,* 249–260.

BENGTSON, V. L., AND MANUEL, R. 1976. *Ethnicity and family patterns in mature adults: Effects of race, age, SES and sex.* Paper presented at the annual meetings of the Pacific Sociological Association, San Diego.

BENGTSON, V. L., OLANDER, E., AND HADDAD, A. 1976. 'The generation gap' and aging family members: Toward a conceptual model. *In,* J. G. Gubrium (ed.), *Time, Self, and Roles in Old Age,* pp. 237–263. New York: Human Science Press.

BLACK, K. D., AND BENGTSON, V. L. 1977. Implications of telecommunications technology for old people, families and bureaucracies. *In*, E. Shanas and M. B. Sussman (eds.), *Family, Bureaucracy and the Elderly*, pp. 174–195. Durham, N.C.: Duke University Press.

BLAU, P. M., AND DUNCAN, O. D. 1967. *The American Occupational Structure.* New York: John Wiley.

BORNSTEIN, P. E., CLAYTON, P. J., HALIKAS, J. A., MAURICE, W. L., AND ROBINS, E. 1973. The depression of widowhood after thirteen months. *British Journal of Psychiatry, 122,* 561–566.

BREMER T., AND RAGAN, P. K. 1977. *Effect of the empty nest on morale of Mexican-American and white women.* Paper presented at the annual meetings of the Gerontological Society, San Francisco.

*Business Week.* 1976. Caring for the elderly in your family. February 7, 83–88.

CAIN, L. D. 1967. Age status and generational phenomena: The new old people in contemporary America. *Gerontologist, 7,* 83–92.

CANTOR, M. H. 1976. *The configuration and intensity of the informal support system in a New York city elderly population.* Paper presented at the Gerontological Society meeting in New York.

CAVAN, R. 1962. Self and role in adjustment to old age. *In*, A. Rose (ed.), *Human Behavior and Social Processes: An Interactionist Perspective*, pp. 526–536. Boston: Houghton Mifflin.

CUELLAR, J. B. 1977. El Oro de Maravilla: An Ethnographic Study of Aging and Age Stratification in an Urban Chicano Community. Dissertation presented at U. C. L. A.

DEMOS, J. 1973. Infancy and childhood in the Plymouth colony. *In*, M. Gordon (ed.), *The American Family in Social-Historical Perspective*, pp. 180–191. New York: Martin Press.

DOBROF, R., AND LITWAK, E. 1977. *Maintenance of Family Ties of Long-Term Care Patients: Theory and Guide to Practice.* US Department of Health, Education and Welfare. Publication No. (ADM) 77–400.

DOWD, J. J. 1975. Aging as exchange: A preface to theory. *Journal of Gerontology, 30,* 585–594.

DUNCAN, G. J., AND MORGAN, J. N. (eds.). 1976. *Five Thousand American Families—Patterns of Economic Progress*, Vol. IV. Survey Research Center, Institute for Social Research, the University of Michigan.

ERIKSON, E. H. 1950. *Childhood and Society.* New York: Norton.

ESTES, R. J., AND WILENSKY, H. L. 1978. Life cycle squeeze and the morale curve. *Social Problems, 25,* 277–293.

FISCHER, D. 1977. *Growing Old in America.* New York: Oxford University Press.

FRANKLIN, P. A. 1977. Impact of disability on the family structure. *Social Security Bulletin, 40,* 3–18.

GLENN, N. D. 1975. Psychological well-being in the postparental stage: Some evidence from national surveys. *Journal of Marriage and the Family, 37,* 105–110.

GLICK, P. 1977. *A demographer looks at the family.* Paper presented at the Gerontological Society meetings, San Francisco.

GREVEN, P. J., Jr. 1973. Family structure in seventeenth century Andover, Massachusetts. *In*, M. Gordon (ed.), *The American Family in Social-Historical Perspective*, pp. 77–99. New York: Martin Press.

HAGESTAD, G. 1977. Role change in adulthood: The transition to the empty nest. Unpublished manuscript, Committee on Human Development, University of Chicago.

HESS, R. D. B., AND HANDEL, G. 1959. *Family Worlds.* Chicago: University of Chicago Press.

HILL, R., FOOTE, N., ALDOUS, J., CARLSON, R., AND MACDONALD, R. 1970. *Family Development in Three Generations.* Cambridge: Schenkman.

HOMANS, G. F. 1942. *English Villages of the Thirteenth Century.* Cambridge, Mass.: Harvard University Press.

KAMERMAN, S. B. 1976. *Developing a Family Impact Statement.* New York: Foundation for Child Development.

KERCKHOFF, A. 1966. Family patterns and morale in retirement. *In*, I. H. Simpson and J. C. McKinney (eds.), *Social Aspects of Aging.* Durham, N.C.: Duke University Press.

KOBRIN, F. E. 1976. The fall of household size and the rise of the primary individual in the United States. *Demography, 13,* 127–138.

KREPS, J. 1965. The economics of intergenerational relationships. *In*, E. Shanas and G. Streib (eds.), *Social Structure and the Family*, pp. 267–289. Englewood Cliffs, N.J.: Prentice-Hall.

KREPS, J. 1976. The economy and the aged. *In*, R. Binstock and E. Shanas (eds.), *Handbook of Aging and the Social Sciences*, pp. 272–285. New York: Van Nostrand Reinhold Company.

KREPS, J. 1977. Intergenerational transfers and the bureaucracy. *In*, E. Shanas and M. Sussman (eds.), *Family, Bureaucracy, and the Elderly*, pp. 21–34. Durham, N.C.: Duke University Press.

LASCH, C. 1977. *Haven in a Heartless World: The Family Besieged.* New York: Basic Books.

LASLETT, P. 1976. Societal development and aging. *In*, R. H. Binstock and E. Shanas (eds.), *Handbook of Aging and the Social Sciences*, pp. 87–116. New York: Van Nostrand Reinhold.

LASLETT, P. 1977. *Family Life and Illicit Love in Earlier Generations.* Cambridge: Cambridge University Press.

LITWAK, E. 1960. Reference group theory, bureaucratic career and neighborhood primary group cohesion. *Sociometry, 23,* 72–84.

LOPATA, H. 1973. *Widowhood in an American City.* Cambridge: Schenkman.

MANNHEIM, K. 1952. The problem of generations. *In*, P. Kecskemeti (ed.), *Essays on the Sociology of Knowledge*, pp. 276–322. London: Routledge and Kegan Paul

(1928).

Metropolitan Life Insurance Company. 1977. Current patterns of dependency. *Statistical Bulletin, 58,* January.

MODELL, J., AND HAREVEN, T. K. 1973. Urbanization and the malleable household: An examination of boarding and lodging in American families. *Journal of Marriage and the Family, 35,* 467–479.

MOON, M. 1977. *The Measurement of Economic Welfare.* New York: Academic Press.

MORONEY, R. M. 1977. The need for a national family policy. *The Urban and Social Change Review, 10,* 10–14.

MURRAY, J. 1976. Family structure in preretirement years. *In,* M. Irelan *et al., Almost 65: Baseline Data from the Retirement History Study,* pp. 82–101. Washington, D.C.: US Government Printing Office.

MYLES, J. F. 1978. Institutionalization and sick role identification among the elderly. *American Sociological Review, 43,* 508–521.

NADELSON, T. 1975. A survey of the literature on the adjustment of the aged to retirement. *Journal of Geriatric Psychiatry, 3,* 3–20.

National Center for Health Statistics. 1975. Vital statistic of the United States, 1973, life tables. Rockville, Maryland.

NEUGARTEN, B. L. 1975. The future and the young-old. *Gerontologist, 15,* 4–9.

NEWMAN, S. 1976. Housing Adjustments of Older People: A Report from the Second Phase. Ann Arbor: Institute for Social Research, University of Michigan.

OTTEN, J., AND SHELLEY, F. D. 1976. *When Your Parents Grow Old.* New York: Funk and Wagnalls.

PARKES, C. M. 1972. *Bereavement.* New York: International Universities Press.

PRESTON, S. 1976. Family sizes of children and family sizes of women. *Demography, 13,* 105–114.

PRESTON, S. H. 1977. Reply to comment on 'Family sizes of children and family sizes of women.' *Demography, 14,* 375–377.

PRESTON, S. H., KEYFITZ, N., AND SCHOEN, R. 1972. *Causes of Death: Life Tables for National Populations.* New York: Seminar Press.

RAGAN, P. K. 1976a. *Another look at the politicizing of old age: Can we expect a backlash effect?* Paper presented at the Society for the Study of Social Problems, New York.

RAGAN, P. K. 1976b. *Ethnic contrasts in styles of aging.* Paper presented at the meetings of the Gerontological Society, New York.

RAGAN, P. K. (ed.). 1979. *Aging Parents.* Los Angeles: University of Southern California Press.

RETHERFORD, R. 1975. *The Changing Sex Differential in Mortality.* Connecticut: Greenwood Press.

ROSENFELD, J. P. 1974. Inheritance: A sex-related system of exchange. *In,* R. L. Coser (ed.), *The Family: Its Structures and Functions,* pp. 400–411. New York:

St. Martin's Press.

ROSOW, I. 1967. *Social Integration of the Aged.* New York: The Free Press.

SCHOENHOLZ, K. 1978. *Occupational mobility and kin interaction: A reconceptualization.* Paper presented at the meetings of the American Sociological Association, San Francisco.

SCHWARTZ, A. N. 1977. *Survival Handbook for Children of Aging Parents.* Chicago: Follett.

SEELBACH, W. C. 1977. Gender differences in expectations of filial responsibility. *Gerontologist, 17,* 421–425.

SEELBACH, W. C., AND SAUER, W. J. 1977. Filial responsibility expectations and morale among aged parents. *Gerontologist, 17,* 492–499.

SHANAS, E., AND HAUSER, P. M. 1974. Zero population growth and the family of older people. *Journal of Social Issues, 30,* 79–92.

SHANAS, E., AND MADDOX, G. L. 1976. Aging, health and the organization of aging health resources. *In,* R. H. Binstock and E. Shanas (eds.), *Handbook of Aging and the Social Sciences,* pp. 542–618. New York: Van Nostrand Reinhold.

SHANAS, E., AND SUSSMAN, M. B. 1977. *Family, Bureaucracy and the Elderly.* Durham, N.C.: Duke University Press.

SHANAS, E., TOWNSEND, P., WEDDERBURN, D., FRIIS, H., MILHAJ, P., AND STEHOUWER, J. 1968. *Old People in Three Industrial Societies.* London: Routledge and Kegan Paul.

IORTER, E. 1975. *The Making of the Modern Family.* New York: Basic Books.

SILVERSTONE, B., AND HYMAN, H. K. 1976. *You and Your Aging Parent.* New York: Pantheon.

STREIB, G. 1965. Intergenerational relations: Perspectives of the two generations on the older parent. *Journal of Marriage and the Family, 27,* 469–476.

STREIB, G., AND SCHNEIDER, C. J. 1971. *Retirement in American Society.* Ithaca, N.Y.: Cornell University Press.

STREIB, G. F., AND THOMPSON, W. 1965. The older person in a family context. *In,* E. Shanas and G. F. Streib (eds.), *Social Structure and the Family: Generational Relations.* Englewood Cliffs, N.J.: Prentice-Hall.

SUSSMAN, M. S. 1965. Relationships of adult children with their parents in the United States. *In,* E. Shanas and G. Streib (eds.), *Social Structure and the Family: Generational Relationships,* pp. 62–92. Englewood Cliffs, N.J.: Prentice-Hall.

SUSSMAN, M. B. 1976. The family life of old people. *In,* R. H. Binstock and E. Shanas (eds.), *Handbook of Aging and the Social Sciences,* pp. 218–243. New York: Van Nostrand Reinhold.

SUSSMAN, M. 1977. Family, bureaucracy, and the elderly individual: An organizational/linkage perspective. *In,* E. Shanas and M Sussman (eds.), *Family, Bureaucracy and the Elderly.* Durham, N.C.: Duke

University Press.

SUSSMAN, M. S., CATES, N., AND SMITH, D. 1970. *The Family and Inheritance.* New York: Russell Sage Foundation.

TOWNSEND, P. 1968. Isolation, desolation, and loneliness. *In*, E. Shanas *et al.* (eds.), *Old People in Three Industrial Societies*, pp. 258–287. London: Routledge and Kegan Paul.

TREAS, J. 1977. Family support systems for the aged: Some social and demographic considerations. *Gerontologist, 17*, 486–491.

TREAS, J. 1978. Hindsight, foresight, and all's right: The intergenerational life of the aged. Proceedings of the Distinguished Speakers in Aging Series. Manhattan, Kansas: Kansas State University.

TREAS, J. 1979. Socialist organization and economic development in China: Latent consequences for the aged. *Gerontologist, 19*, 34–43.

TREAS, J., AND VANHILST, A. 1976. Marriage and remarriage rates among older Americans. *Gerontologist, 16*, 132–136.

TROLL, L. E. 1970. Issues in the study of generations. *Aging and Human Development, 1*, 199–218.

TURNER, R. H. 1962. Role taking: Process vs. conformity. *In*, A. M. Rose (ed.), *Human Behavior and Social Processes*, pp. 20–40. Boston: Houghton Mifflin.

UHLENBERG, P. 1974. Cohort variations in family life cycle experiences of U.S. females. *Journal of Marriage and the Family, 36*, 264–292.

US Bureau of the Census. 1973. Census of population: 1970. Subject reports final report PC(2)-6A. *Employment Status and Work Experience*. Washington, D.C.: US Government Printing Office.

US Bureau of the Census. 1976. Demographic aspects of aging and the older population in the United States. Current Population Report PC-23, No.59. Washington, D.C.: US Government Printing office.

WALLER, W. 1938. *The Family: A Dynamic Interpretation.* New York: Dryden.

WRIGLEY, E. A. 1977. Reflections on the history of the family. *Daedalus*, Spring, 71–85.

# 18

# Observations on Culture
# and Mental Health
# in Later Life

*David Gutmann*

## CONCEPTUAL DEFICIENCIES

This chapter must begin with the admission that very little can be said about culture and mental health in late life. The blunt truth is that there have been very few attempts, using standard measures and standard instruments, to study variations in the mental health of older individuals, across disparate cultures, or sub-cultures.

One can understand this paucity of research. It is hard enough for investigators to study mental health in their own cultures, where the indications of that state are at least intuitively known; the task becomes much harder as investigators move out into societies which maintain different definitions—if they have them at all—of mental health. By the same token, what is normal behavior in one society may be regarded as pathologic in another; and we do not know the transformational rules

which would allow us to convert particular cultural standards into universally applicable criteria for mental health and illness. The difficulties are doubled when we limit our concern with mental health to the period of later life, since even *within* cultures the criteria for mental health and illness may vary for each life period: the young man's madness may be the old man's amusing eccentricity. Under such conditions, the psychological investigator would have to do a thorough ethnography of the belief systems around mental health and illness, as well as the age grading of such systems, before a sophisticated study of the emotional health of the older residents of a particular society could even begin.

However, despite the lack of hard research, we sense that some societies are more supportive of the psychological health of the aged than others; and we further sense that this variation is orderly, and that it has to do with observable and recurrent aspects of social life. Lacking an adequate cross-cultural theory, as well as an extensive body of cross-cultural research, we can only make educated guesses as to the relationships between social phenomena and the psychological well-being of older individuals in various societies. But common sense does lead us to believe that social factors, particularly those that have clear meaning for the individual—for example, status, access to power, family bonds, and the content of age-grading systems—can influence mental health in later life. Accordingly, despite the lack of cross-cultural studies relating social phenomena to psychological outcomes, we can at least hypothesize that factors of social prestige, strong family bonds, and economic security, singly or in combination, will contribute to (even if they do not guarantee) the emotional well-being of seniors in most human communities. For the purposes of this chapter, we will take a further leap of faith, and assume that the hypothesis has been demonstrated. Accordingly, we will treat social and emotional conditions as though they were interchangeable terms: we will regard any report concerning the social fate of the aged as though it also predicted to the psychological status of the aged in that society. This admittedly crude procedure will at least allow us to develop some testable generalizations concerning the distribution of those sociocultural factors that may be linked to mental health in later life.

A *caveat* is called for at this point: while we agree that aspects of social nurture do have an important bearing on the psychological well-being of elders, we do not grant that such social factors have the status of independent variables in relation to the mental life. We would also hold that the effects of powerful social variables on the psyche are not standard across all communities, and that their impact is modified by ambient ecological conditions, as well as by aspects of human nature (i.e., personality and developmental variables).

Furthermore, though the assignment of this chapter is to explore the relations between culture and mental health in later life, "culture" is most certainly among those social constructs most ambiguous in its definition, as well as being extremely variable and unpredictable in its effects on individual psychology. Indeed, while cultural theorists might agree that the various ideational counterparts of social living—mores, linguistic forms, "world view," rituals, "shared understandings"—are all properly grouped under the rather vague heading of "culture," the definition of this construct is as ambiguous as the definition of "mental health" (as attested by the fact that each cultural

anthropologist seems to generate his own unique definition of culture). However, despite their many disagreements as to the meaning of this variable, cultural anthropologists are fairly unanimous in assuming that "culture" is the primary factor in determining social behavior. For them, it determines, as an independent variable, the psychological constitution of all properly socialized individuals. Thus, from this perspective, the positive, benign values and beliefs maintained by a society, e.g., its culture, are a necessary precondition for the mental health of its members. In the main, psychologists are very prone to accept this social environmentalism, and to agree with the anthropologists as to the unilateral flow of causation, from the contents of culture to the contents of the psyche. In large part, this chapter will question the largely unexamined "culturalist" assumption, particularly as it refers to older adults.

## THE SOCIAL BASES OF CULTURE

Indeed, even a cursory review suggests that culture, regarded in its content aspect as a *corpus* of understanding shared by a community, does not predict inner psychological states or even overt conformity to cultural norms. Thus, the recent student "revolt" against the middle-class achievement ethic was primarily instigated by the affluent cohort that had been most exposed to that ethic in the course of early socialization. By the same token, the positive, benign, "official" norms that our society maintains toward the aged do not guarantee either their contentment or their mental health. Indeed, under certain conditions the favorable cultural propositions might even provoke despair, as the older individual compares his real condition to the formal ideology of his society. And like ours, most societies profess respect for the aged; but the actual degree of honor, as manifested in daily behavior, elderly prestige, and old age compensation varies greatly among these same societies. "Practice what you preach" is a frequent admonition of the elderly toward the young.

In point of fact, this author (Gutmann, 1967) has studied a society—the Highland Maya of the Chiapas region—in which the aged enjoy a great deal of titular prestige, and hold the highest posts in the political and religious life of the village. Young men go in some awe of them, and when meeting lower their heads for the elder's touch of blessing. But the positive bent of the Mayan culture toward the aged does not protect them from crippling anxiety, as they have particular reasons to fear the effects of the corrosive envy which—

though it is not overtly sponsored or even much acknowledged in the annals of the local culture—is the major undertone of human relationships in Chiapas.

Clearly then, the modal personality of a community may mediate between the cultural respect systems and their psychological consequences for the aged. Aspects of social ecology, quite independent of the cultural value systems toward the aged, may play a similar moderating role. Thus, this author (Gutmann, 1971) has studied the life of aged men along the folk-urban axis of the Druze and Navajo societies, and has observed that, while the *content* of the cultural ideas concerning the aged remains constant, the treatment that they receive from younger individuals changes markedly along this continuum. In the high mountain village, or in the remote sheep camp, the cultural scenarios call for and determine respectful behavior toward the aged. There, the cultural ideas are *internalized* within individuals, and they direct behavior; but closer to the city, the same body of belief and understanding does not generate the same respectful sentiments of behavior. Again, it is not the *idea* of respect and care for aging relatives that varies with the form of community organization in these two very disparate societies. What varies is the degree to which the gerontophilic beliefs and values are internalized by individual actors—those who must actually provide the necessary care. In the remote countryside, the positive consensus in regard to the aged is unquestioned, and *idealized*; to act against such values is to risk not only social censure, but also internal guilt and even terror. But as we approach the more urbanized habitats, the cultural ideas in favor of the aged, while *known* to individual actors, are neither *loved* nor idealized—they lack the affective investment that would make them powerful within personality and directive over behavior.

Thus, it may well be that the *structural* aspect of culture, having to do with its acceptance by individuals, is more important than the content aspect in determining the status, the contentment—and ultimately, the mental health—of the aged. Thus far, culture-personality researchers have concentrated, with little success, on the relationships between cultural content and personality functioning, but it is clear that the power of cultural ideas to sway individual psychology depends on the mediating influence of those *structural* factors which determine the degree to which cultural conceptions will be idealized, internalized within individuals, and dispersed across the community. Clearly, the absorption (internalization) and dispersion of cultural ideas has to do with structural

aspects of collective life that may bear little relation to the content *per se* of cultural value systems.

## AGING AND CULTURE IN THE FOLK SOCIETY

In this regard, it appears clear that the psychosocial ecology of the small, face-to-face, traditional folk society provides optimal conditions for the idealization, absorption, and dispersion of those ideas which protect the aged, and sponsor their emotional stability. This observation accords with the conclusions drawn by commentators on the status of the aged across a wide variety of societies. Thus, Simmons (1960) notes that "advancing age has been barely possible and quite intolerable without a sustaining social order." In Simmons' view, that sustaining order involves permanent residence, stable food supply, herding, the cultivation of the soil, and the increase of closely knit family relationships—in short, the typical features of the preliterate, traditional folk society. Similarly, Cowgill (1968) notes that the status of the aged is inversely proportional to their numbers, and is highest in static folk societies, declining with modernization. And the equality index designed by Palmore and Manton (1974) to estimate the status of the aged relative to the non-aged in various societies indicates that elderly prestige in the areas of employment, occupation, education, and socio-economic position is highest in underdeveloped countries. Clearly, if we assume some rough correlation between mental health and social prestige in later life, then it is predictable that the aged of preliterate societies would score high, relative to their urban peers, on any valid index of psychological functioning.

Both Simmons (1945) and Cowgill (1971) account for the near-universal phenomenon of preliterate gerontocracy in the most parsimonious terms. As they see it, in the small, static society, old age leads naturally to social power: it is only the aged who have lived long enough to accumulate the property, exploits, ritual power, and "wisdom" on which their prestige is based. The preliterate society is, in effect, a participatory gerontocracy in which prestige accrues to the old man who has had more time to acquire the spiritual, mental, and economic goods that are valued by young and old alike.

Clearly, this explanation of preliterate gerontocracy refers to that which is valued—hence, to the *value* aspect of culture. But again, such "content" conceptions overlook those *structures* of the small society which underwrite and institutionalize the values that in turn favor the aged. Thus, the slowly accruing cross-cultural evidence suggests that it is not their material possessions, but their special association with the sacred systems of society that may be the true key to the traditional elders' prestige. Abarbanel (1972), analyzing the relationship between the prestige of older persons and their access to cultural resources in 62 societies, found that older persons are *less* (rather than more) apt to control resources that have to do with pragmatic, economic production; but, by the same token, their grip over the ritual sources of sacred power increases with age.

Goody (1962) also notes the pattern of moving from control of production and material resources to control of ritual as men age in preliterate and traditional societies: "In the simpler societies, retirement in the sense of the transfer of control is rare. Aging invariably lessens one's ability to perform the productive tasks, leading to a measure of withdrawal, even though other important jobs still remain in the hands of the elderly. In the noneconomic domains, especially those dominated by ideas of kinship or religion (where selection is delegated to, or sanctioned by, one's forebears or one's gods), individuals generally continue to perform their offices and roles until the end."

## AGING AND RITUAL POWER

Thus, the association between economic affluence and advanced age does not appear to be guaranteed in the folk society; but the integration of senescence to the sacred order *is* predictable in these settings—and this linkage also guarantees the special powers of the traditional aged.

Thus, while Levine (personal communication) asserts that older men move to the ritual track in order to compensate for failures in their productive and political life, Kracke (1977) disputes this: "The spiritual realm is not, as it is sometimes pictured, an avenue to self-esteem for those unable to obtain political power. It is a separate realm of at least equal significance in its own right." Thus, Kagwahiv (Amazonian Brazil) "who reach old age are highly respected, not only for their knowledge of tradition, but also for the spiritual strength that has permitted them so long a life. This is recognized in the relaxation of food tabus, for an old person is considered to have the spiritual strength to withstand the power even of such meats as paca and curassow." The Kagwahiv aged are awesome in the eyes of their juniors, and they also seem to sense in themselves a core of special power and

privilege: thus, "old people also seem to take more liberties in asserting their wishes; old men are apt to ask for things with an abrupt and demanding air, and may complain sharply if not given what they want..."

In effect, we find a generational rule of some universality that compensates the traditional aged for their losses of physical-muscular power with the acquistion of supernatural power. Typically, young men kill with edged weapons; but older men can kill with a curse. Thus, Levy-Bruhl (1928) observed that in the preliterate folk society, the old man is "encircled by a kind of mystic halo," an essence so pervasive that his body parts and even his excrement can become the residence of *tabu* power. By the same token, Simmons (1945) argues, "it was not strength or brawn alone that won in battle or staved off bad luck or healed the dreaded disease; it was a special power, mysterious and most potent in the hands of old men and old women who have survived all these dangers...not *all* magicians were old, but superannuation and the supernatural were very commonly and closely linked."

Briggs (1977), writing on the Inuit, gives us a clear example of the powers that are ascribed to traditional aged of an Eskimo society, as well as the resentment that these powers can generate in the young.[1] However, such powers are great enough to protect the Inuit aged against any envy that they might stimulate: "Longevity itself is valued; it indicates vigor. If an old person gives his or her name to a baby who seems likely to die, the baby may acquire the strength to live. Old people should be, and often are, treated with deference, sometimes because they are genuinely respected and loved, and sometimes because people wish to avoid arousing their resentment...The strength of an old person's *isuma* is feared. An old person's resentful brooding can make others sick or even kill them."

The same veneration of the traditional aged was found by Ikels (1975) in the Far East, where, again, it is based on the special tie that the aged maintain with the supernatural agencies, in this case the ancestors: "In ceremonies paying respect to the ancestors, the ritual leader was the senior male of the senior generation. Since he himself

---

[1]In human prehistory the aged may have been hated for their powers, rather than their weakness. Thus, while the special powers of the aged can add to their prestige, they can also add to their risk. While studying the Highland Maya, this author was told that the *Naguales* (the animal familiars) of older men meet in covens on the mountaintops to decide who shall die and who shall be spared. Accordingly, when epidemics and deaths increase, particularly among the young, the aged men come under suspicion and are sometimes killed in revenge.

would soon become an ancestor, this role seemed especially fitting."[2]

To repeat, there appears to be an assured, organic linkage—a "deep structure"—that bonds the older traditional persons and the sacred systems of their culture as these are represented in theology, in myth, and in ritual. This special bonding between the sacred and the geriatric leads to traditional gerontocracy, to special privilege and esteem for the aged, based on their special access to spiritual resources. We can also hypothesize, with confidence, that this linkage between the aged, the sacred order, and social prestige systems would lead to superior mental health, by any reliable indicators. That is, if mental health is linked to self-esteem, the sense of special resource centered within the self, then the older preliterates, with their privileged access to awesome power, clearly possess an important ingredient of psychological well-being.[3]

Meanwhile, this hypothesis concerning the spiritual bases of psychological health among the traditional aged is supported by one of the few studies which contrasts aged men in the preliterate and modernized sectors of an Amerindian society. Thus, Boyer, Klopfer, Boyer, Brawer, and Kawai (1965) used Rorschach measures to study variations in ego strength across the traditional-modern axis of the Mescalero and Chiricahua Apache groups. Their findings point to a clear advantage in ego strength among the most traditional elderly men, those aged 50 and over. The authors speculate that their shamanistic practices give the traditional elders special routes for focusing hostility of the sort that are unavailable to the more modernized Apache—whether young or old—who must instead rely on strong drink to rationalize their aggressive acts. However, this author would hold that shamanism does not only give the older Apache a way of managing aggression; in effect,

it provides him with more aggressive power to manage.[4]

This notion, that the religious life contributes to the vitality and, quite possibly, the mental health of the traditional person, is further borne out by the evident association, observed in Turkey, between religious activity and longevity. Thus Beller and Palmore (1974), who studied the life of longevous Turkish peasants, noted that most villagers aged 90 and over continue to regularly observe religious rituals (in contrast to only one half of the younger control group). Indeed, it may be that those who have been inducted into the service and representation of traditional ways are particularly contented in later life, even in relatively sophisticated contexts. Thus, Maduro (1975) finds a widening and deepening of spiritual life, and the continuing cultivation of artistic creativity, in older male Brahmin folk painters of India.

## THE AGED: BRIDGEHEADS TO THE SACRED

This author has come to some tentative conclusions concerning the observed isomorphism between the elderly and the sacred, in the traditional folk society. Their special psycho-ecological niche is created by a special cosmology, recurrent in preliterate societies, that divides the universe bicamerally, into sacred and profane domains. In addition, folk theologies typically conceive of interfaces between these domains: certain aspects of existence are mundane and pragmatic; others are clearly *tabu*, and sacred; and there are agents which, while they move and act within the daily life, are also metaphors and extensions of the sacred domain, charged with the power of their totemic sponsors. Typically, in the preliterate mind, these intermediaries are the bridgeheads of the unordinary domain within the ordinary world; they freight in the vital power

[2]Ikels (1975) also points out how much the gerontophilic ideas are distributed in a small community, as well as the great power possessed by the majority to ensure conformity to these cultural ideas under such conditions: "...the forces of public opinion in the small, stable village where everyone knew everyone else made life difficult for any young man who chose to defy convention by neglecting his parents. He would find it difficult to obtain a wife or to maintain his business relationships. He would find his opinions ignored in public discussion and would either have to reform or attempt to survive as a social isolate."

[3]The task of testing such a hypothesis would be a reasonable one for workers in the slowly emerging field of cross-cultural gerontology. However, the work had best be done quickly, before the traditional enclaves are obliterated by the advance of modernization and urbanization.

[4]A study by Barker and Barker (1968) underlines the tendency of the aged, across social settings and societies, to move toward the "ritual track," even in relatively non-traditional, "modern" settings, so long as a vestige of the religious option is made available to them. Thus, the authors identified the various "behavior settings" of two small communities, one in the Midwestern US and one in England, and found that "the old people of both communities overinhabit behavior settings where religion and art are prominent and underinhabit settings where education, physical health, government, social interaction, and recreation are prominent." In effect, the aged of both societies have shifted their investment from those behavior settings that stress physical activity, competitive political engagement, and authority over the young, in favor of settings which stress submission to a higher sacred authority.

that literally keeps the mundane world alive. They are the sources of luck, success in battle, ripeness in crops, fatness in herds, and health in children. Many agents can fit this special niche: the dead (particularly, the enemy dead), the madman, the hero or champion—and the aged. All these agents have in common the fact that they, like the sacred world whose fringes they touch, are unordinary, of this world and yet not familiar, and carrying with them the aura of the *stranger*. Thus, while the aged perform usual, natural functions within this world, yet they have one foot in the next; they represent, within life, the awesome transformation into death that they will soon endure. For some cultures, the aged are linked to power by virtue of their weakness: they are passive, humble, compliant before the gods; having already endured the forces that waste and weaken men, they have nothing to lose, and can place themselves without fear in the socket of dangerous power. For other cultures, the aged inhabit the niche of power not because of weakness, but because of their unique strengths; their life trajectories have intersected the major storehouses of power—*they* knew and trafficked with the spiritualized ancestors; *they* were part of the pivotal events that shaped the present. In such constructions, the aged link the mythic past to the ordinary present (just as their imminent death will elevate them to the powerful ancestral status). Specially endowed, they alone can tolerate the fearful contact with god-power, contain it, neutralize it, and render it into usable forms for the community and its ecosystem.

In sum, whether by virtue of their special weakness or their special strength, the aged are *elected*: where young men live on the physical perimeter of the community, to contain and harvest the forces of physical nature, the old men move out onto the spiritual perimeter, there to fend off the bad power and to harvest the good power of the gods. Inevitably, as wardens of *tabu* power, the aged also become *tabu*; and social power, prestige (even perhaps, mental health) follows sacred power.

## SOCIAL BOUNDARIES AND CULTURAL CONSENSUS

We can understand, on other than "rational" economic grounds, that a culture of gerontophilic ideas would develop in traditional, preliterate societies, those which usually maintain a bicameral cosmology. But while we can understand the generation of these ideas, how do we understand their deep absorption *within* individuals, as well as their wide and uniform dispersion *across* individuals of

the folk society? Again, we look to structural conditions, particularly those having to do with the nature of individual and community boundaries, for an answer.

We have proposed that gerontophilic ideas develop in the folk society as a consequence of the rigid boundaries that are drawn between the sacred and the profane, between the pragmatic and supernatural communities; we further propose that the general dispersion of these ideas has to do with the relative lack of *interpersonal* boundaries *within* the folk community.

In such face-to-face societies major life events are standardized and redundant, and individuals who have gone through the same orienting experiences tend to be intuitively comprehensible to each other. Through self-examination, each member of the society can understand and predict, quite accurately, the actions, beliefs, and feelings of his or her age/sex peers across a wide range of situations. Under such conditions, interpersonal boundaries are diffuse and osmotic; the other is experienced as a version of the self and takes on the tonus of familiarity. Narcissistic investments are not fixed on the boundaried, individuated self, but extend outward, toward those self extensions who share the same basic life experiences, the same basic dress, the same kinship name, and live under the same cultural constraints. In the folk society, one does not experience a clear "I" distinct from others, but a "we," the true humans, distinct from the not quite human strangers. Under these conditions, ideas discovered in other minds can easily be confounded with one's own; they easily acquire the coding of familiarity, of self-ness, and become the furnishing of the inner self. Thus, under structural conditions that promote low individual boundaries, there is high *absorption* of the ideas that originate in powerful individuals, such as the aged: to take in their ideas is to take in their strength. By the same token, ideas emanating from any powerful source will disperse rapidly across all minds within the social setting in which this power is recognized, to become the culture of that society. The aged will, in their turn, be susceptible to the same conditions which foster the internalization and diffusion of cultural ideas favorable to their cohort. In their case, as these ideas are absorbed into the self, they should become an important basis of elderly self-esteem.

In sum, under certain optimal conditions of folk, rural life, the culture that they help to generate will tend to support the aged. By the same token, changes in structural and ecological conditions of a society—its location within the sacred and natural world, and the ordering of its parts—

should bring about changes which affect the degree to which gerontophilic ideas are internalized and disseminated, without necessarily affecting the contents of the ideas themselves. This distinction, between the *absorption* of ideas *within* individuals and their spread throughout the society, is important to maintain, as it is likely that, under conditions of modernization, ideas remain widely distributed in a society, even as they lose their "absorbtive" properties, their power to strongly affect individual behavior. Thus, as in our case, it is possible for the majority of individuals in a "modern" society to retrieve and report gerontophilic ideas as *ideas*, but no longer as unquestioned predicates of social existence.

## THE EROSION OF GERONTOCRACY

Most commonly, it is the loss of rural isolation that causes the first shock to established, unquestioned gerontocracy. Clearly, cultural ideas are more likely to be idealized, hence strongly internalized and universally distributed, if they reign supreme in their special social niche. So long as beliefs and values remain uncontested by alternate world views, particularly those emanating from more developed societies, they avoid the fate of being relativized, and questioned. But when a society moves out of its isolation—or is moved out of it, by conquest or colonization—the people are automatically brought into contact with contrasting and even conflicting conceptions as to the nature of good and bad, possible and impossible, holy and impure. Despite such disorienting contact, the emerging society may retain much of the *ideational* contents of its culture; but the *structural* relationship between the people and this culture content must change as a result. The contact with foreign conceptions eventually brings home to the people of the once isolate society, the realization that their system of cultural ideas is only one member of a set of such systems, some of which may be more powerful or more proximate to the truth than their own. Their ideas become relativized; worse yet, they become revealed as *ideas* that may or may not approach the ultimate reality; and they lose their tonus as the unquestioned and unchallenged coordinates of existence. Under such conditions, the cultural conceptions may still be widely distributed, known to most affiliates of the society; but now they are known as symbols and not as substance; they are not the basic, power compelling axioms of the universe.

Thus, under conditions of prolonged and intensive contact among societies, cultural ideas tend to lose their mythic status; they are less apt to be idealized, and hence less apt to be internalized. As regards the gerontophilic ideas, they will remain current in the society as ideal prescriptions for behavior, but more honored in the breach than in the observance—the ideas are given lip service, but they lose their compelling power to influence behavior in favor of the aged.

Similar effects occur as the modernizing society expands and loses its face-to-face, neighborly character. As the range of social experience broadens and diversifies, then members of the society can no longer automatically understand the other through self-reference. There is less immediate, "mechanical" basis for empathy, and members of the same society lose the quality of being self-extensions to each other. The hitherto unquestioned identity between the social and the personal, between the individual and the group, breaks down. As the individual in the developing society generates boundaries between the social and the personal, and begins to recognize and make data out of a realm of inner, private experience, he begins to recognize that the cultural ideas come from outside the self, and he no longer confounds them with the inward subjectivity. While he can cite the ideas, he knows them as "outside" entities, and is less likely to internalize them as fundamental structures of self. Again, to the degree that the aged are the beneficiaries of the traditional ideas, their status will suffer, and with it, perhaps, their mental health.

But perhaps the most important change occurs as the modernizing society, through its contact with other, more advanced societies, generates a new economics, as well as new conceptions of economic power and of power in general. Typically, the modernizing society provides a labor pool for the developed world, and the young men, instead of staying home to work their father's tillage, will leave the traditional village to find wage employment in the plantations, mines, mills, and armies of the more developed sectors. As a consequence, or side effect, the younger men discover an economic base of power to which *they* have privileged access, and which is not under the control of their fathers. They no longer have to look to him for the bride price, or for the economic substance that will change them from boys into men. The confirmatory power now comes from outside the precincts of the community, rather than from within it. Thus, in the Asian sector, Rowe (1961) finds that village gerontocracy has eroded as a result of Indian modernization. The young men find wage work in the cities, and return home impatient with tradition, with the rule of the father, and with the slow paced village life. Furthermore, the wealth that they bring back undercuts the traditional association between affluence and advanced age, and further corrodes the status of the aged. Press and McKool (1972) find a similar effect in the villages of Mayan Mexico when the *avanzado* elements of the traditional village draw on outside funding to build the small village factories that will produce new forms of capital. Shifting from agricultural to wage work, the young men can now buy their own land before their father is ready to surrender the family holdings to them. In his dotage, the father now comes to live in the son's house, rather than granting the son's family a place in the patriarchal compound. In the author's terminology, such decline in the acquired statuses, based on control of resources, leads to a decline in the *residual* statuses that automatically accrue with age. As a possible result, the once mighty *principales* are degraded, and aging fathers who hold on to their land, refusing to recognize this shift of power, are sometimes murdered by their own sons.

Modernization also takes nonfinancial forms of power, such as knowledge, out of the old traditional's hands, and locates it in the extra-communal sector; it is now the job of young men to acquire that power, *via* education, for the sake of the community. Thus, Levy (1967) finds that, with the advent of federal boarding schools, the Navajo traditionalist loses his reputation for superior intellectual power, and the educational role that goes with it. His grandchildren now go to the Indian agency boarding schools to learn the "white man's knowledge," the access to white man's power that old traditionals lack. Similar changes are noted by Okada (1962), who found that the Japanese rural family was a successful gerontocracy in the past: the elder maintained and increased his property, turning the patrimony over to his older son at a time of his own choosing. But now, as farming becomes more mechanized, and is based on non-traditional skills and powers, control passes earlier to the son because of his superior technical sophistication.

This shift in the bases of financial power has similar effects in Africa: in one of the few cross-cultural studies linking mental illness to loss of elderly prestige, Arth (1968) finds that young Ibo, who now acquire independent wealth from wage work, no longer rely on their fathers for the bride price. In consequence the father's prestige declines, and the author finds that "psychosenility" is prevalent among the elderly casualties of Ibo modernization. By the same token, the old men of the African Chagga are angry over ·the conse-

quences of modernization, stating quite explicitly that it has deprived them of their chance to dominate their society in the manner of their fathers.

In a recent longitudinal study of the aging Druze of the Golan Heights this author has noted similar fallout from the economics of modernity in a traditional and classically gerontocratic village. During ten years of Israeli hegemony, the young Druze, who used to work their fathers' land while waiting to inherit, now find wage work in the kibbutzim and industries of the Jewish sector. Again, they are less dependent for resource on their father's whim or generosity; and their exposure to modern people who do not respect or fear their father gives them further reason to doubt his hitherto unquestioned power. Furthermore, much as on the Japanese farm, affluence and modernization means machinery: in Majd-al-Shams, the donkey has largely been replaced by the tractor, and while the old men might understand donkeys, it is the young men with their trade·school and army experience who understand tractors. They can command the exotic power of the machine, and make it available for the general purposes of the Druze. The net result is that there is notably less deference toward the aged on the part of the Golan young, who begin to resemble the young men of the less traditional sectors of Druze society. A "generation gap" has occurred, such that their manner toward older traditional relatives begins to be patronizing and insulting, and there is some crime in the village.

Thus, in Majd-al-Shams, as the culture is relativized for the young men, as life experience becomes more heterogeneous for them, and as they develop independent access to secular modes of power, respect for the elderly *aqil* in some cases gives way to scorn, and flagrant—by Druze norms—disrespect.[5] Concurrently, potentially divisive issues between the generations come to the fore: we

---

[5]Shlewet (1975), an Arab social worker, corroborates this author's Druze observations with parallel observations of Israeli Arabs in their rapidly modernizing villages. She notes that the young, until recently financially dependent on and therefore respectful to their elders, have now become financially independent as they find a place in industry. Despite Social Security, which allows the elders to remain financially independent, their social and emotional situation has degraded: "Our elderly today are feeling more and more deprived of the power they once had over their children, as well as of their children's care and respect. Children are getting married and leaving their parents' home. The power of the mother-in-law is diminishing. Daughters-in-law are turning less and less for help to their mothers-in-law. Grandmothers are becoming lonely...Unfortunately, some of the new houses are being built only for young couples without any consideration for the elderly."

noted, for example, more frequent arguments between fathers and sons, based on the son's "Oedipal" demand for sexual freedom.

Finally, in our own country, Achenbaum (1974) finds that the historic movement toward American modernity had the same consequences for the aging that are brought about by modernity, generally. Thus, prior to the Civil War, in the period 1790-1850, the aged are presented in public prints as venerable, and as socially, morally, and economically useful. Furthermore, they were repositories of wisdom, guardians of the revolutionary spirit. Commonly, they were portrayed as having one foot in heaven and one in this world. Significantly, there is no concept of senility appearing before 1880.

After the Civil War, older people are no longer seen as the repositories of public health, nor the guardians of virtue. Now older people are apt to be presented as unkempt and irritable, as no longer useful, and as occasional victims of satyriasis—the "dirty old man" image now makes its first appearance. During this period the young appear for the first time in an idealized image, as repositories of virtue.

This decline in the status of old people in America does not appear to be a consequence of early industrialization, and it occurs before the demographic changes that increased the proportion of aged in the population. It seems to reflect an early secularization of the society, as well as the loss, by the aged, of a particular form of mythic protection: as the founding generation, the aged were special; but when the revolutionary cohort died out, the aged lost the special aura that devolved from their connection to the mythic past. They lost the special grace that is required to protect the aging from stigmatization.

## MODERNIZATION AND POWER

In discussing the changing fate of the aged in the modernizing society, most authors focus on the changing economic relations between the generations, brought about by the new opportunity structures which result from modernization, and which make independent sources of wealth, of the sort that their fathers cannot reach or control, available to the young men. However, the various examples cited here of modernizing societies make it clear that money is only one factor in a changing conception and distribution of power. With modernization, the traditional culture, which stresses the

ritual access to power, loses its commanding position within a special preserve, even as the new forms of power made available and relevant by modernization take on some of the *mana* that the traditional forms have lost. Power becomes secularized: represented by cash, by machines, by the products of machines (and even by beverage alcohol).

In effect, as the distinction between totemic and secular power phases out, the "power" boundary is reset; it no longer divides the sacred from the ordinary world, but instead stands between the "underdeveloped" community and the "modern" or "Western" world. The aged are the monitors and heroes of the old power frontier that faced the gods; but it is young men who cross the new frontier to bring back power, in the form of wealth and technology, for themselves and their community. This is a role for the Promethean young and not for the cautious elders. If anything, the role of the old men on the new frontier is a reactionary and even destructive one. They tend to distrust the new sources of power; and, because of their traditionalism, they impede development, and the flow of significant power from its "modern" reservoirs into the still relatively powerless emerging community. These changes, of course, occur slowly: the old man may be feared as a sorcerer long after he ceases to be respected as a healer—witchcraft beliefs are always the last to go. But as regards the self-esteem of the aged, the important change has taken place—the older individual is no longer a benefactor, a source of good rather than bad strength.

As the aged lose their cosmic connection, they also lose the power to control the cultural imagery in their favor. New images and new myths, based on the power of aliens, and of contemporary heroes who stole alien power, fill the cultural space. The young can interpret and relate to these myths, for they have been in the place of the alien: they have endured his power, and they have—like Prometheus—captured some small part of it in the form of wages, technical knowledge, and even weapons. The young begin to take on some of the glamor of those who have danced before the gods and have survived the awesome contact with strange power. As the young take on the functions *vis-à-vis* alien power that the aged once performed, the prestige of the young is elevated; and the prestige of the traditional aged declines. While the images and beliefs that once supported the prestige of the aged might still remain current in the society, they are no longer doorways to or metaphors of power; no longer idealized, these ideas are less likely to be

internalized or widely distributed. Losing their capacity to create individual character and social consensus, the gerontophilic ideas lose their power to
influence the collectivity in favor of the aged—just
as they lose their power to influence the aged in
favor of themselves. Thus, the deep changes in the
structure of culture that result from modernization
bring about, as a general rule, a potent decline in
the outer status and the inner well-being of the
aged.

While there is paucity of research concerning
the psychological effects of modernization on the
aging, there is some Druze evidence which suggests
that social development may affect the soma before
it affects the psyche. Thus, a Druze doctor, practicing in Majd-al-Shams, informed this author that
the oldest men, perhaps buffered by their religious
affiliations, are not likely to suffer from stress-related
diseases. Indeed, rheumatism, and the various effects of being overweight, are the chief complaints
of the old *aqil*. There are only a few cases of cardio-vascular disorder among the older generation,
who do not tend to suffer from drawn out degenerative disease, but rather die suddenly, usually in
their seventies, from a stroke or a sudden heart
attack. In fact, chronic heart disease is more prevalent among the middle-aged—those who drink
and smoke, and who are not folded into the traditional religion—than among the religious aged.
Other stress diseases, such as ulcers, similar gastrointestinal disorders, and hypertension, are also
more common among the younger adults, who are
more open to and vulnerable to the enticements
and pressures of the modern, extra-Druze world.[6]

These conceptions are supported by surveys
of aged status under various social conditions.
Thus, Palmore and Manton (1974) used the Equality Index (E.I.), to estimate gerontic status relative
to the young. The E.I. indicates reduced status for
the aged in the more modern countries, as opposed
to the less advanced. However, the relationship
between the E.I. and modernization is "J" shaped,
rather than linear; early modernization brings
about a sharp decline in E.I., with some resurgence
in countries that have reached the later stages of
development.[7]

[6]The possibility that older women might better survive
the translation from rural to urban settings than older men is
suggested in a study by Datuk (1975), who investigated awareness of menopausal symptoms among older women in an urbanized village of metropolitan Delhi. Both pre- and postmenopausal women in the sample showed no awareness of
physical or psychological stress for this period, and whatever
symptoms are present are not perceived as being related to the
menopause.

[7] However, the evidence for decline in the modernizing
sector is probably more trustworthy than the evidence for re-

A more sophisticated statement comes from
Sheehan (1976) who sought to establish what, if
any, correlation existed between type of society and
esteem of senior persons. The survey data on 47
primitive societies indicate that maximal socioeconomic complexity corresponds with maximal
power and positive treatment for the aged. The
seniors are particularly powerful as long as socioeconomic complexity is a feature of the society itself, but not a feature of its relations with other
societies. A *settled*, non-nomadic traditional society
provides the best ecology for the aged: under these
conditions there is an intellectual and cultural life,
there is folklore to be guarded and handed down
by seniors, and there is religious thought, cosmic
ceremony, and *rites de passage* through which they
are linked to the gods. But as societies modernize
technologically, and ramify their socio-economic
connections to the outer world, younger persons
gradually achieve economic and social autonomy
and senior esteem declines.

Meanwhile, Bengtson, Dowd, Smith, and Inkeles (1975) would qualify any generalization that
linked gerontic decline to societal development.
Their findings from the comparative study of
5,450 young males in six developing nations argue
that a distinction must be made between modernization (the level of societal development) and *modernity* (the *individual's* exposure to technology and
urban social experience). Modernization does indeed correlate with negative perceptions of aging,
while modernity does not. Thus, in only three of
the six countries studied did the occupational
group least exposed to modernizing experiences—
the cultivators—have the greatest proportion of
respondents choosing the traditional deferential
response to the aged. In the other three countries,
factory workers are as likely as agriculturalists to
favor the aged. However, while these results may
cast doubts on the model proposed here, they do
not adequately test it, in that they do not make a
distinction between the absorption and the dispersion of the cultural ideas. Thus, young men who
migrate from the rural village to the factory town
may retain their cognitive *awareness* of gerontophilic ideas, such that they can retrieve them for
investigators; what has not been tested is the degree to which such ideas have been idealized, internalized, and compounded with action. Are these

covery among the elders of industralized nations. Status does
not have comparable origins in the two social conditions. In the
industralized case, the prestigeful elders are not—as they would
be in the traditional society—participatory gerontocrats; rather,
they are more likely to be powerful old men who have gained
their laurels while they were still young.

sentiments carefully dissociated from behavior or are they unquestioned prescriptions for attitude, sentiment, and action? As long as this issue is not dealt with, Bengtson *et al.* have not, despite their claims, successfully disputed what they call the "conventional aging and modernization postulate."

## URBANIZATION AND THE AGED: THE BENIGN CITY

Urbanization is not necessarily the end product of modernization. Modernization implies the contact with a culture that is conceded by the emerging society to be higher or better than the native life-ways. But when cities evolve from the ethnically homogeneous folk society, as the urban expression of a coherent culture, there is not necessarily a sharp distinction between urban and rural forms of mentation and behavior, particularly as regards the institutions and practices that directly affect the aged. Thus, when cities are not imposed by foreign conquerors, and are not the entry point for waves of foreign immigration, the city is not necessarily the adversary of culture or of tradition. On the contrary, when the city and the rural sector are part of a joint social evolution, then they come to share common traditions, and a common cultural heritage. In the city, culture is preserved by relatively impersonal institutions (e.g., the emperor figure, in Japan) rather than the extended family of the countryside; but these nonetheless provide some continuity, and the bases of honor for the aged. Thus, we find that Oriental cities, indigenous to the land, and established long before the contact with the West, preserve the forms of patriarchy, traditional practice, extended family, and respect for the aged, that are usually confined to the countryside in Western settings.

Thus, there exist special Oriental enclaves, sacred cities, where religious traditions and urban forms of association co-exist, and even facilitate each other. In such settings, the "high culture" that typically flowers in the city is devoted to exploring and making art out of the deeper meanings of the common culture, particularly its religious aspects; and under these special conditions, tradition seems to play the same role in sponsoring the psychological development of the urban aged as it regularly does in rural settings. Thus, Levy (1977) studied the high culture of the Newars of Nepal, in their sacred city of Bhaktapur. Quoting him, the Newars "have many compensations for men's voluntary relinquishment of the householder stage...The old Newar man of middle or upper caste (and economic class) enters a busy, fascinating, and ex-

tremely sustaining period of learning of deep religious mysteries; authoritative involvement in corporations engaged in religious activities; much family show of honor; and a preparation for the adventure of death, an undertaking which requires much active involvement and responsibility on the part of the dying and newly dead man."

Palmore (1975) tells us of another Oriental society where traditional respect for the aged man survives the transition to modernity. He asserts, "The most general thing we can learn about aging from the Japanese is that high status and integration can be maintained in a modern industrialized society." Respect for the elders in Japanese urban life goes beyond mere show: over 75 percent of all Japanese men over 65 continue to be in the labor force (as compared to 29 percent of men in the United States over 65). Apparently, the persistence of the traditional patriarchal Japanese culture, that is a feature of urban as well as rural life, and is most marked in the institution of emperor worship, has important consequence for the social status and the psychic well-being of the Japanese aged.

Ikels (1975) also cites the example of an Oriental city, Hong Kong, where the younger people are not about to abandon the senior generation: "Those elderly who are presently in needy circumstances are disproportionately those who either have no surviving close relatives in Hong Kong, or whose close relatives are so economically limited themselves that they cannot offer adequate assistance."

The gerontocratic city is even found outside the Far East, in Yugoslavia, on the borders of the Middle East. Thus, Simic (1977) rejects the idea that urbanization is necessarily bad for the aged, citing in evidence his own studies contrasting intergenerational relationships in rural and urban America to rural and urban Yugoslavia. While his American studies do indicate the degradation of family ties as one moves toward the city, this is not true in Yugoslavia, where strong kinship ties are maintained in all social settings. Because kinship bonds are by definition cross-generational, and mandate important filial obligations, the aged—both men and women—continue to receive important endowments of affection and material support, even in the modern, socialistic cities of Yugoslavia: "Intense affection and respect typify the relationship of children of all ages toward their parents, and this positive affect is reciprocated within the bonds of the authoritative roles assigned to mothers, and particularly fathers." In effect, then, the Yugoslavs also carry over into the city the relational patterns that are usually exclusive to the countryside: patriarchy, strong cross-generational kinship ties, deference to the aged, and the playing down of the intra-generational romantic bond between mates.

## URBANIZATION AND THE AGED: THE NOXIOUS CITY

It appears then, that the slowly maturing provincial or stabilized city can provide a relatively benign environment for the aged; it may be the rapid pacing of change that is noxious to the elders, rather than urbanism *per se*. Thus, when we consider the special troubles of the urban aged, we are perhaps referring to those cities wherein urbanization is confounded with modernization and rapid change. Accordingly, the ensuing comments will focus on the consequences, not of urbanism *per se*, but rather, the consequences of the rapidly changing, *modernizing* city for the mental health of the older individual. We are referring now to the kind of city which is a continuing center of modernizing influences, as well as the product of a prior, historic process of urban growth. This kind of city, because of its own rapid growth, draws young men from the village, fills their heads with contra-traditional ideas, and sends them home to challenge the local gerontocrats. By the same token, it should be remembered that the city, particularly during its period of rapid gestation, in itself represents the outcome of a revolution against the rule of the rural elders. The massive youthful migration from rural hinterlands to cities is one of the most pronounced cross-cultural phenomena: during their "growth spurt," cities are in large part founded and settled by young people, and especially by young men, refugees from village gerontocracy. Historically, the city is a magnet for young men who go there not only in search of wage work, but also in search of adventure, and in search of a milieu where they can experiment with forbidden lifestyles, without making final choices among them. But finally, they go to the city as a kind of revolution against gerontocracy, against patriarchy, and against the omnipresent extended family—the ring of monitoring, critical, gossiping elders. Accordingly, the psychic dispossession of the elders (and particularly older men) in the city, may represent more than an accidental side effect of urban social ecology. It is perhaps no accident that the structures of city life function so as to prevent the recurrence of male gerontocracy, and also function so as to give fuller expression and social power to the oppressed constituencies of the patriarchal village—women, and young people of both sexes.

Besides functioning so as to stigmatize the once mighty gerontocrats, it may be that the lifeways of the growing city have the effect of *revealing* a pre-existing stigma, which, while it is chronically associated with the aged, is masked and neutralized by the customs and institutions of the gerontocratic village.

The following discussion of elderly stigmatization is based on a profound observation by De Beauvoir (1972) who points out that the aged, in that they can represent the stranger, the "other," are always at risk, even under the most benign cultural circumstances.[8] Universally, whether he appears in the guise of the enemy, the corpse, the madman, or the elder, the stranger always calls up strong feelings, a mixture of awe and revulsion. As we have seen, in the traditional society, the aged, *precisely because they are strange*, are told off to face the ultimate strangers, the gods. In this syncretic mingling of two kinds of otherness, the aged are to some degree compounded with the gods, and automatically receive some of their power. Under such conditions, strangeness is an *asset*, a precondition for the endowment of power; and as a consequence, awe toward the aged predominates over revulsion in the traditional, preliterate society.

## URBANISM AND THE AGING STRANGER

In the traditional society the aged are protected against the stigmatized meanings of their strangeness not only by particularly favorable cultural conceptions, but also by the institution of culture itself. We have seen that the traditional society sponsors the generation, absorption, and diffusion of gerontophilic ideas; but it also sponsors the vitality of culture *per se*, as a set of regulations which, because they are *idealized*, ensure their internalization by individuals, as well as standard, predictable group behavior in conformity to the cultural prescriptions. As a consequence, within the traditional so-

---

[8] This quality of "eeriness" that attends the aging is caught by Briggs (1977) as she describes the reactions of young Inuit Eskimos, who generally venerate the aged, to photographs of unfamiliar old people. The typical exclamation is "frightening!," a reaction reminiscent of the way Inuit react to mention of the *tunrait*, the evil spirits. Parenthetically, the word for spirit-fear is the same as that used to express fear of old people. Indeed, some older Inuit attempt to master their alienation by turning it into a weapon: thus, some old people "seem to enjoy being feared; they make frightening faces at children, speak to them in scary voices, and laugh when the children run away or cry...still others enjoy playing teasing games with children, frightening them, but then reassuring them, afterward." By contrast, "other old people take pains to reassure children who are frightened by their elderly appearance, and are very gentle and mild-mannered. Of course, the fear felt toward old people increases the distance between them and others."

ciety, familiarity tends to be automatic, and does not require direct interpersonal association: the subjective tonus of "we-ness" is extended to those individuals, of any age, who live according to the group consensus. The true stranger is found outside and not within the community. Thus, the cultural system of the traditional society, irrespective of its agenda of particular beliefs, plays the great role of making even potential strangers familiar to each other; and the resulting endowment of protection extends to the aged. So long as they are included under the umbrella of "we-ness," the aged can preserve their humanity.

We have seen that the modernizing society weakens the particular cultural ideas that locate the aged at the pivot of sacred power. This de-mystification of the aged is necessary if the backward society is to tap, at first through its young men, the technological power that is being made available to it. However, modernization brings more than electricity to the village—it brings the sense of the vital, expansive city. Even though it may be distant from the village, and connected to it only by tarred roads and creaky buses, as modernization progresses the city becomes part of the mental landscape of the village. And the rapidly growing city is inimical not only to particular cultural ideas, but to culture itself. The expanding city may support the *high* culture—the arts, the sciences, as well as the *literati* and intellectuals who serve them—but it does not, by and large, support the common culture of shared understanding and values, nor the myths from which cultural rules derive their legitimacy. Thus, the urban environment does not as a rule collectivize and standardize personal experience so as to support the basic postulate of culture—that the other can be *predicted*: either through reference to shared custom, or through reference to the self. Where the village society creates familiars, people who *know* each other even though they are not *known* to each other, the city pools strangers: those who remain *unfamiliar* and *unpredictable*, despite years of physical proximity.

In effect then, where modernization erodes the cultural ideas that favor the aged, rapid urbanization, which undercuts the standardizing and familiarizing power of culture *per se*, may destroy the second great defense of the aged against their possible estrangement. In the countryside, the aged are made familiar, and their quotient of strangeness is converted, *via* the sacred system, into awe and reverence; but in the city, where culture loses its power to ensure familiarity, urbanites move toward the condition of estrangement. There, the "stranger" potential of the aged is maximized,

and that strangeness does not imply a connection with sacred power. Thus, where awe of the aging stranger predominates in the traditional countryside, revulsion against the aging stranger tends to predominate in the city.

Besides culture, the extended family is the second great structure that maintains the humanity of the aged, and preserves their familiarity. Within the confines of the extended family, the drift toward old age and alienation takes place slowly, almost imperceptibly. Generally, extended family members do not experience in the elderly relative the immediacy of withered and uncanny old age; rather, they experience an overarching history that they and that relative have shared in common. The continuity of the extended family, in its place, lends continuity and "sameness" to all of its members, young or old. Thus, like culture, the extended family of the rural, traditional setting buffers the aged against their potential fate, as strangers.

But, while the extended family is generally preserved even in the modernizing village, it fares less well in the city. Thus, Burgess (1960) states that the "roleless role" of the aged reflects shifts from home to family production; from rural to urban residence, from the extended to the conjugal family. Kooy (1962) makes the same point in regard to Holland, where he finds that the urban-proximal regions provide less status to the aged than do the urban-remote enclaves, those where the extended family predominates. Similarly, Baumert (1962) finds more multigenerational, co-residential families in farming areas of Germany, and less exclusion of rural elders.

A study by Helland, Solem, and Traeldal (1974) has illustrated, in the Scandinavian context, the relationship between the social integration and the life satisfaction of the elderly in six local areas of Norway. Two of these are neighborhoods within central Oslo; two are either suburban or exurban to Oslo; and two are large towns, Arendal (pop. 20,000) and Flekkefjord (pop. 8,000), distant from Oslo and in rural areas. They found that, whereas attendance at organizational meetings declined with age in the Oslo area, the frequency of attendance does not decline in the two smaller towns. Indeed, Flekkefjord, the smallest and most remote community, "distinguishes itself as the area with highest frequency of attendance at meetings by all age groups and especially the elderly." By the same token, occupation of elected offices by the elderly is highest in Arendal and Flekkefjord. Informal participation matches formal association: "We find that the elderly in the center of Oslo have the least frequent contact with their children over given distances while the elderly in Flekkefjord have the most such contact; and it is mainly in the three Oslo areas that the elderly report their lack of participation in leisure time activities."

Level of life satisfaction is found to be generally correlated with the degree of political and familial integration: thus, life satisfaction is generally lower in Oslo than in the outlying areas.

## THE URBAN SPONSORSHIP OF MATRIARCHY

However, while the life satisfaction of the aged may decline in step with the attrition of family bonds, these do not—contrary to the conventional wisdom—completely disappear from urban precincts. Thus, the coherent extended family of the countryside is to some degree retained in the city as the modified-extended family, and it provides what Rosenmayr (1973) terms "intimacy at a distance." But while the extended family of the countryside is patriarchal, the modified-extended family of the city tends to be matrilocal; as such, it provides less by way of security and guarantees against estrangement for men than it does for women. Thus, Youmans (1967) concludes that men are likely to be the recipients of emotional supplies in rural areas, and that this pattern is reversed in the cities. And Burgess (1960) notes that the matrilocal and modified-extended family can function in stable working class neighborhoods as the urban equivalent of the patriarchal extended family of the countryside. The urban family is based on strong bonds between grandmothers, mothers, and daughters. In the city, Burgess says, "Men have friends, women have relatives." This observation is echoed by Young and Geertz (1961) who asserted, following a review of family ties in San Francisco and London, that "The mother-daughter bond is the central nexus of kin ties in industrial societies." In sum, the modified-extended family may substitute for culture in preserving the humanity and, by extension, the mental health of older urban women; but it does not play the same role for older urban men: they tend to lose the protection of culture—particularly after their retirement from the work society—as well as the protection of the extended family.

This implication, that the dehumanizing pressures of the city impact more heavily on older men than on older urban women, is borne out by the mortality statistics: thus, Kooy (1962) discovers that, *save in rural areas*, older Dutch women outnumber older Dutch men. By the same token, Chevry (1962) reports that the proportion of aged men, particularly widowers, increases in step with the agricultural character of the French munici-

pality. And Jackson's (1971) comparisons of rural and urban American blacks also suggests a correlation between later life survival and the nature of familial bonds. Again, rural black men outlive their women; but the urban shift toward superior female longevity is accompanied by a corresponding shift in the patterning of affectional ties. In the city, these are strongest between mothers and daughters; and this close female bond pays off in the form of greater direct assistance to the aging black mother at all social class levels. Not surprising then, in the urban American setting men die earlier than women, and men are more likely than women to commit suicide at any age (see DeGrazia, 1961), with the male lead in this regard increasing steadily over successive age groups.

There are few studies that shed light on the specific psychological vulnerabilities that are released by urbanization and modernization in the men of hitherto traditional communities. However, studies by this author (Gutmann, 1971) indicate that the changes run deep, and have consequences for the fundamental, appetitive strata of the personality. Thus, oral-incorporative imagery increases at much the same rate in the fantasy and self-report data of Druze and Navajo men as a function of age; but also as a function of their closeness to cities. The orality index has validity as a register of passive-dependency: it correlates with passive themes in dreams and the Thematic Apperception Test (TAT). More to the point, orality correlates positively with Navajo alcoholism, with the severity of physical illness, and with emotional vulnerability. This evidence, gleaned from the folk-urban continua of two very different cultures, again points up the value of cross-societal comparisons made in the context of social structure, rather than cultural content. And it also adds psychological weight to the sociological evidence, which suggests that the urban milieu can be detrimental to masculine mental health, particularly in later life. Indeed, since oral incorporativeness increases in men on two independent axes, age, and the closeness to cities, there is some basis for the statement that urbanization within cultures replicates, at least for men, the psychological effects of aging, across cultures. In any event, the index of male passive-dependency—hence, of psychic vulnerability—appears to rise in step with the residential proximity to cities.[9]

Superior female longevity is sometimes taken

[9] Thus, Cantor (1977) finds that New York City is mainly valuable to those elderly for whom amenities and services are more important than opportunities for economic advancement. In this case at least, the city is the favored habitat for the more passive, less achievement- and exploit-centered individual.

as a sign of women's biological superiority over the male; but this difference may reflect nurture rather than nature—it may register the peculiarly troubling effects that the urban environment seems to have on the mental health of men.

## AGING AND URBAN NARCISSISM

The erosion of culture in the city threatens to transform the aged into the stranger, into a phobic object for others; but it also deprives the aged themselves of important routes to self-transcendence, and thus makes it more difficult for them to overcome the losses and insults that are normal parts of the aging process. That is, as a coherent system of idealized rules, culture provides the socialized individual with potent reasons for transforming personal egocentricity—for example, the sense of being personally *central* in the scheme of things—in favor of extra-personal social bonds, collective ideals, and collective purposes. But when culture is weakened (as in the city), and loses its power to provoke the reality of myth, then the decultured individual loses the rationale for transforming egocentricity and narcissism into the idealizations that sustain the community, the social order, and ultimately the self. A de-idealized culture gives the individual little reason to sacrifice his own narcissism in favor of social needs and projects. Narcissism conserved for the self and for personal projects can be the *sine qua non* of creativity—accordingly, the high culture, the culture of original artistry, flourishes in the city—but it can also be a recipe for personal vulnerability, and even breakdown.

This author found that the aged Druze, who have transformed narcissism into worship, can look unflinchingly, and with dignity, on the prospect of their death, saying only, "This is Allah's will; to complain about my sickness or death would be to dispute his will." The aged Druze have found a posture, based on their idealization of their god, which permits them to transcend, without much sense of insult, their personal demise. But what of the deculturated elder, who remains in the egocentric position, without the possibility of transforming idealizations, and at a time when he or she is in the period of maximum loss in the somatic, cosmetic, work, social, and existential spheres? If the centrality of the self is maintained in late life, then the result is an increasing sense of vulnerability which transforms the "normal" losses of aging into insults, outrages, and terrors. Depression and hypochondriasis, as well as strained attempts to deny the various decrements are a too frequent result. Thus, we note in our own clinical researches

that many psychopathological manifestations of later life represent attempts to overcome the sense of insult and depression, on the part of older individuals who have not relinquished the conviction of their own centrality and omnipotentiality. In those cases where psychiatric breakdown has occurred, the need to deny loss and insult—or to project the responsibility for imperfection—is so strong that reality is abandoned in favor of the defense. Thus, denial of loss and threat, often taking the form of manic psychosis, is a major characteristic of the older patient. By the same token, paranoid states in which the sense of blemish—or the responsibility for the blemish—is projected onto others, is another major development. Severe depression, alcoholism, and even suicide can result when these primitive defenses fail. In a real sense, psychosis in later life represents a hectic attempt to find the bases of self-esteem that are normally supplied to elders by a "transformative" culture.

The urban aged do not only suffer from their own narcissism, but from the narcissism of others. Again, because it is antagonistic to the supportive structures, the urban environment retards absorption and even disperson of all cultural ideas. The aged, who depend on the inner controls of younger, stronger individuals and on the external social controls that are maintained by a cultural consensus, suffer accordingly. The reduction in culture turns them into strangers, and it also brings about an increase in the numbers of those who would victimize them, because of their estrangement.

When urban culture loses its power to bind and transform narcissism to the collective weal, then egocentricity tends increasingly to become the general coinage of social relations—to the detriment of all vulnerable populations, including the aged. Under conditions of high egocentricity, the bases of association tend to change, such that individuals tend to group not according to the "social" and generation-transcending categories of family and class, but according to the most visible and tangible categories of skin color, sex (or sexual preference), and age. The motto of affiliation becomes, "I love those who are, indisputably, most like myself." Thus, the politics of the city become the politics of narcissism: Youth Liberation, Women's Liberation, Black Liberation, or Gay Liberation. These politics and the boundaries that they define introduce profound cleavages even into those social institutions—particularly the family, and certain professional enclaves—in which age distinctions are normally overlooked in favor of some higher principle of kinship solidarity or ideological affiliation. Thus, the "generation gap" that is strikingly absent in the village and folk society bisects the heart of the nuclear and modified-extended family in the city. De Beauvoir (1972) has observed, "A surer protection—than magic or religion—is that which their children's love provides their parents." Clearly, the narcissistic *ethos* of the city tends to weaken that great protection, and to increase the vulnerability of the aged, thereby making loss and deprivation the great theme of mental illness in later life. In the city, the abandonment of the aged by their children reaches the point where the provision of extra-familial and institutional forms of care to the aged becomes a major social task—and problem. More and more, society is called upon to provide the physical and even the emotional security that city children are less willing to provide their own parents. As undisguised narcissism tends increasingly to become the coinage of urban social relations, then all unproductive, dependent cohorts—children as well as the aged—are at risk: ageism and child abuse both increase in the city, and perhaps at the same rate. When the *motif* of human relations becomes "me first," then the weak and needy tend to go under.[10]

## URBAN SUB-CULTURES AND ELDERLY SELF-TRANSCENDENCE

Thus far, we seem to be suggesting that healing self-transcendence in later life can only be accomplished within the setting of the traditional, rural community. But this meaning is not intended. This essay has a diagnostic purpose, aimed at isolating and identifying those aspects of communal living that have served the aged well, across cultures and across history. If these can be identified and abstracted from the traditional-folk setting, then perhaps their functional equivalents can be discovered

[10]Turnbull's (1972) powerful portrayal of the Ik tribe of Kenya provides a chilling example of the human disaster that ensues when society loses culture. The Ik had recently lost their ancient hunting preserves, and this dispossession undercut and invalidated the predicates of their culture: in effect, if the gods could not protect them, then the gods were dead—and with them died the cultural principles that the gods had sacralized, and legitimized. When the cultural rules were no longer idealized, they were at best only weakly absorbed; and they lost their power to bind narcissism and aggression to the social weal. In consequence, unmodified narcissism is the major theme of human relationships among the Ik, to the point where children are literally evicted from the parental home at the age of three. If they are lucky, they can become part of a juvenile food gathering band; and they may survive to adulthood. Again, the fate of the relatively useless Ik aged parallels that of the children: they have no honor, no secure place within ritual or within the family, and they are left to die when they can no longer fend for themselves.

and sponsored within the urban setting as well. Again, research into these matters is almost nonexistent, but it does begin to appear that certain religious and professional subcultures, enclaves within the larger secular and urban society, do preserve gerontophilic conceptions that are both internalized within and dispersed across their memberships. We already have reason to believe that church affiliation heightens the life satisfaction of aging members, even in the city; and the bases of this belief were set forth earlier in this chapter. But it is also likely (though this is a worthwhile subject for future research) that those secular professions which nevertheless maintain a traditional armature—for example, the law, medicine, academia, the priesthood, the arts, and the military—may sponsor the special status, self-esteem, and self-transcendence of their older members.

Conceivably, the traditional professions, those which maintain a strong consensus as to ethical purpose and ethical performance, provide norms and standards that the older practitioner can *best* represent. In a real sense, the traditionalist profession is an urban equivalent of the folk society, in that both maintain a bicameral ordering of norms. The folk society makes a strong distinction between the sacred and the secular; and the traditional profession is similarly bimodal in its normative structure: it maintains norms that govern routine performance, but it also maintains "sacred" norms as to the ethical meanings and goals of daily practice. To some important degree these two normative orders are kept distinct: the pragmatic norms derive from practical experience and current technology; while the ethical norms are *mythic* in their origin—they refer to principles expounded by the founding heroes and martyrs of the profession. Such traditional professions maintain two tracks for advancement, corresponding to the bicameral division of norms: one can be successful in terms of the practical norms, but that success is transient, lasting only so long as practice and technology remain unchanged; or one can be successful and esteemed in terms of the ethical norms, known as one who is unfailingly moral, courageous, or objective, in the manner of the mythical founders. To an important degree, generational cohorts are coordinated with these two quite distinct normative orders: thus, it appears that younger professionals are most responsive to the pragmatic norms, those having to do with the mundane and agentic aspect of the profession; while older practitioners are more responsive to those norms which refer to the mythic origins and which define the ethical limits of performance. The older professionals, possibly for "developmental" reasons (see Gutmann, 1975), are less interested in production and worldly advance, and in consequence they are less identified with the norms that guide immediate practice in the marketplace. But by the same token, they feel better represented by—and can better represent—those norms which derive from the history, the enduring goals, and the legendary antecedents of the enterprise. When the older practitioner speaks, he may not be *au courant* with the latest techniques, but the historic distillate of the profession announces itself through his words. In effect, the bicameral organization of norms serves the same function for the older professional that the bicameral ordering of the universe serves for the folk traditionalists. In the folk society the elder is fitted into the socket of numinous power; in the professional sub-culture he can be a living reminder of the special moral theme of the enterprise, that lifts it above the pettiness of the marketplace. In both cases, he is the interface, the bridgehead to mythic origins and mythic powers.

The older practitioner is best qualified to carry on the moral business of the profession because, for better or for worse, he has already made his mark: he has no career to build at the expense of others. If he espouses some particular moral position, or calls for sacrifice or restraint, he can be trusted as a personally disinterested spokesman for the course that he advocates. He cannot easily be accused of advancing himself through claiming to advance some principle. Thus, where the younger professional's moral rebuke can be discounted as special pleading, the older practitioner's rebuke has some of the power of the shaman's curse: it is charged with the *mana* that derives from the totemic figures of the profession.

The above assertion is not meant to be a pollyannaish consolation to the aged; recent events in the legal profession, for example, have demonstrated again the special and enduring power of even the secular aged in a secular profession. Thus, it was Joseph Welch, an aging lawyer, who almost single-handedly broke the seemingly irresistible power of a notable demagogue, Senator Joseph McCarthy. When, during the Senate hearing of 1953, Welch rebuked McCarthy publicly, his anathema was not substantially different from other attacks in the media, or from those essayed in person by younger men. But Welch's words had all the power of an ancient curse. McCarthy withered before them, his condemnation by the Senate followed shortly, and he subsequently—while still holding on to his official powers—lost his morale, his sobriety, his health, and finally his life.

It is also a remarkable but unremarked aspect of the Watergate drama that Richard Nixon was in large part brought down by the dedicated efforts of old lawyers and legislators, most of them in their seventies and even eighties.[11] Younger men were spear-bearers in both camps, but the old politicians were mainly arrayed against Nixon. These senior lawyers had in effect been *freed* by their aging to discover and fight for the moral *objects* of the law, those which were perhaps less obvious to them when they were involved in the sweat of daily practice and the struggle for self-advancement. In effect, as in the traditionalist folk society, they had moved to the ritual domain, the spiritual perimeter of their sub-culture; and as they sat in judgment on Richard Nixon, their audience no longer saw tired old men, but the numinous entity of the law itself, in a human guise. Mustering the powers lodged in that great representation, they could bring a President down. Clearly, they had transcended their momentary condition as aged men who were soon to die: through them, the wrinkled mask of advanced age was transformed into the majestic visage of the law. This transubstantiation of the aged lawyer, through his privileged alignment with the supra-ordinary entity of the law, creates a culture of ideas which favor the aged, and these are—much as in the folk society—to a large degree internalized and dispersed within the ranks of the legal profession. And the special perspectives that they represented were absorbed and distributed across the country as a whole, so that this heterogeneous nation became, briefly, a coherent community, engaged in the collective and revolutionary business of bringing down a President.

This is not to argue that we can only benefit the aged by returning to traditional folk ways. It is too late for that; and besides, we have seen that traditional gerontocracy implies the disenfranchisement of women, and of the young. Rather, the task is to find within the secular society (and the elders can help in this) those special enclaves, organized around special principles and progeni-

---

[11]Thus, Judge Sirica, perhaps Nixon's major nemesis, was in his seventies. Senator Sam Irwin, who initiated and presided over the original Watergate hearings, was in his early eighties. His performance illustrates well the distinction between norms of practice and "norms of virtue": his actual management of the hearings was often inept; his great effect derived from his evident love of the Constitution, and from his hatred of the mere men who would traduce that sacred document. Furthermore, this moral fervor was unimpeachable: Sam Irwin was clearly beyond the age of worrying about re-election. Jaworski, the special prosecutor who replaced the sixty-year-old Cox after the "Saturday night massacre," stated the generational point very clearly. He was reputedly an ally of the Nixon forces, and in some quarters his appointment was seen as a continuation of the Watergate cover-up. Accused of this, Counselor Jaworski answered scornfully, "I am 69 years old; do you really think that I still have a career to build?"

tors, out of which sub-cultures can be built—sub-cultures that, because of their usefulness to the larger society, can also provide psychic sustenance to the aged. Our definitions need not be elitist: the older industrial worker who fought in his youth to build a union has as much linkage to great principles and a heroic past as an elderly doctor, or lawyer.[12]

The common culture of our society is fragmented; but perhaps the fragments themselves will provide the nuclei of new sub-cultures that can provide identity and emotional security—mental health, if you will—to at least a significant portion of our elderly population.

[12] There are hopeful signs that this remedial reculturation is actually taking place. The *Gray Panthers*, for example, are recruiting elders to become social activists, and not only in causes that benefit the elderly. They have taken, as their motto, the principle that makes the elderly trustworthy as moral advocates: "We have nothing to lose." In so doing, the *Gray Panthers* have translated loss, usually the passively endured trauma of aging, into the basis for an age appropriate version of active mastery.

# REFERENCES

ABARBANEL, J. 1972. Aging, family phase, and intergenerational relations in an Israeli farming cooperative. Paper presented at the December 1972 meetings of the American Gerontological Society, San Juan, Puerto Rico.

ACHENBAUM, W. A. 1974. *Old Age in America*. Unpublished doctoral dissertation, University of Michigan, Ann Arbor.

ARTH, M. 1968. Ideals and behavior. A comment on Ibo respect patterns. *Gerontologist, 8,* 242–244.

BARKER, R. G., AND BARKER, L. S. 1968. I. The psychological ecology of old people in Midwest, Kansas and Yoredale, Yorkshire. *In,* B. Neugarten (ed.), *Middle Age and Aging,* pp. 453–460. Chicago: University of Chicago Press.

BAUMERT, G. 1962. Changes in the family and the position of older person in Germany. *In,* C. Tibbetts and W. Donahue (eds.), *Social and Psychological Aspects of Aging: Aging Around the World,* pp. 415–425. New York: Columbia University Press.

BELLER, S., AND PALMORE, E. 1974. Longevity in Turkey. *Gerontologist, 14,* 373–387.

BENGTSON, V. L., DOWD, J. J., SMITH, D. H., AND INKELES, A. 1975. Modernization, modernity, and perceptions of aging: A cross-cultural study. *Journal of Gerontology, 30,* 688–695.

BOYER, B., KLOPFER, B., BOYER, R., BRAWER, F., AND KAWAI, H. 1965. Effects of acculturation on the personality traits of the old people of the Mescalero and Chiricahua Apaches. *International Journal of Social Psychiatry, 11,* 264–272.

BRIGGS, J. L. 1977. Paper prepared for the symposium on the Cultural Phenomenology of Adulthood and Aging. Harvard University, Cambridge, Massachusetts.

BURGESS, E. 1960. Aging in western culture. *In,* E. Burgess (ed.), *Aging in Western Societies,* pp. 3–28. Chicago: University of Chicago Press.

CANTOR, N. 1977. Life space and the social support system of the inner city elderly of New York. *Gerontologist, 15,* 23–27.

CHEVRY, G. 1962. One aspect of the problem of older persons: Housing conditions. *In,* C. Tibbetts and W. Donahue (eds.), *Social and Psychological Aspects of Aging: Aging Around the World,* pp. 98–110. New York: Columbia University Press.

COWGILL, D. 1968. The social life of the aging in Thailand. *Gerontologist, 8,* 159–163.

COWGILL, D. 1971. A theoretical framework for consideration of data on aging. Paper delivered at meetings for the Society for Applied Anthropology, Miami, Florida, April 1971.

DATUK, F. 1975. The aging woman in India: Self-perceptions and changing roles. *In,* A. deSouza (ed.), *Women in Contemporary India.* pp. 84–98. Delhi: Manohar.

DEBEAUVOIR, S. 1972. *The Coming of Age.* New York: J.P. Putnam's Sons.

DEGRAZIA, S. 1961. The uses of time. *In,* R. Kleemeier (ed.), *Aging and Leisure,* pp. 113–154. New York: Oxford University Press.

GOODY, J. 1962. *Death, Property and the Ancestors.* Stanford: Stanford University Press.

GUTMANN, D. 1967. Aging among the Highland Maya: A comparative study. *Journal of Personality and Social Psychology, 7,* 28–35.

GUTMANN, D. 1971. Navajo dependency and illness. *In,* Palmore (ed.), *Prediction of Life Span,* pp. 181–198. Lexington, Mass.: Heath.

GUTMANN, D. 1975. Parenthood: Key to the comparative psychology of the life cycle? *In,* N. Datan and L. Ginsberg (eds.), *Life Span Developmental Psychology,* pp. 167–184. New York: Academic Press.

HELLAND, H., SOLEM, P., AND TRAELDAL, A. 1974. Integration of the elderly in six local areas in Norway. *Norwegian Gerontological Institute Report No. 2,* pp. 1–36.

IKELS, C. 1975. Old age in Hong Kong. *Gerontologist, 15,* 230–235.

JACKSON, J. 1971. Sex and social class variations in black aged parent-adult child relationships. *Aging and Human Development, 2,* 96–107.

KOOY, G. 1962. The aged in the rural Netherlands. *In,* C. Tibbitts and W. Donahue (eds.), *Social and Psychological Aspects of Aging: Aging Around the World,* pp. 501–509. New York: Columbia University Press.

KRACKE, W. 1977. Some frequent crises in Kagwahiv adulthood. Paper prepared for the symposium on The Cultural Phenomenology of Adulthood and Aging, Harvard University, Cambridge, Massachusetts.

LEVY, J. 1967. The older American Indian. *In,* E. Youmans (ed.), *The Older Rural Americans,* pp. 231–238. Lexington, Ky.: University of Kentucky Press.

LEVY, R. 1977. *Notes on being adult in different places.* Unpublished paper, University of California, San Diego.

LEVY-BRUHL, L. 1928. *The "Soul" of the Primitive.* New York: Macmillan.

MADURO, R. 1975. Artistic creativity and aging in India. *International Journal of Aging and Human Development, 5,* 303–329.

OKADA, Y. 1962. The aged in rural and urban Japan. *In,* C. Tibbitts and W. Donahue (eds.), *Social and Psychological Aspects of Aging: Aging Around the World,* pp. 454–458. New York: Columbia University Press.

PALMORE, E., AND MANTON, K. 1974. Modernization and the status of the aged: International correlations. *Journal of Gerontology, 25,* 205–210.

PALMORE, E. 1975. What can the U.S.A. learn from the Japanese about aging. *Gerontologist, 15,* 64–67.

PRESS, I., AND MCKOOL, M. 1972. Social structure and status of the aged: Toward some valid cross-cultural generalizations. *Aging and Human Development, 3,* 297–306.

ROSENMAYR, L. 1973. Family relations of the elderly. *Zeitschrift Fur Gerontologie, 6,* 272–283.

ROWE, W. 1961. The middle and later years in Indian society. *In,* R. Kleemeier (ed.), *Aging and Leisure,* pp. 104–112, New York: Oxford University Press.

SHLEWET, L. 1975. Application of modern social services for the aged in Israeli-Arab villages. *Gerontologist, 15,* 560–561.

SHEEHAN, T. 1976. Senior esteem as a factor of socioeconomic complexity. *Gerontologist, 16,* 433–440.

SIMIC, A. 1977. Aging in the United States and Yugoslavia: Contrasting models of intergenerational relationships. *Anthropological Quarterly, 50,* 53–64.

SIMMONS, L. 1945. *The Role of the Aged in Primitive Society.* New Haven: Yale University Press.

SIMMONS, L. 1960. Aging in preindustrial societies. *In,* C. Tibbitts (ed.), *Handbook of Social Gerontology,* pp. 62–91. Chicago: University of Chicago Press.

TURNBULL, C. 1972. *The Mountain People.* New York: Simon and Schuster.

YOUMANS, E. 1967. Disengagement among older rural and urban men. *In,* E. Youmans (ed.), *The Older Rural Americans,* pp. 97–116. Lexington, Ky.: University of Kentucky Press.

YOUNG, M., AND GEERTZ, H. 1961. Old age in London and San Francisco: Some families compared. *British Journal of Sociology, 12,* 124–141.

# 19

# Minority Issues
# in Mental Health
# and Aging

*Frances S. Kobata, Shirley A. Lockery, & Sharon Y. Moriwaki*

## INTRODUCTION

The problems of ethnic minority elderly in American society were brought to the forefront in the 1971 White House Conference on Aging.[1] Since that time the problem has had greater visibility, with few viable solutions for adequately responding to these needs. For example, a growing number of books, monographs and articles are being written about minorities in American society; however, the literature yields little that deals with the mental

---

[1]Although, in 1970 there were only 2.5 million minority elderly (see Table 19-1), the rapid growth of this segment of the population has brought increased attention to the needs of these people. Although the elderly population increased in general between 1960 and 1970, the increase was greatest for those in the most vulnerable age category (75 + years) and particularly so for the nonwhite population, where there was an increase of 99.2 percent in the number of elderly.

health needs of minority elderly per se. Because of the scanty data on the subject, much of what is proffered in this chapter must be largely inferential. Although generalizations are made from existing sources available on the subject, the reader is cautioned to avoid the pitfall of rigidly applying these generalizations in working with the different ethnic elderly groups. Intra-and inter-group diversity and variation are key words throughout the chapter.

Issues are raised here which may stimulate further exploration of the complex world of the minority elderly and the resultant implications for their mental health. The first section deals with the minority experience in America, that is, what do we mean by the term "minority", and how is it related to one's ethnic and cultural background. The second section examines the definitions of mental health and current assessment instruments and their applicability for minority elderly. The third section deals with the subject of prevention and treatment; and the final section provides some implications for research, training and service programs.

## WHAT IS A MINORITY?

Minority status connotes categorical and differential treatment. According to Louis Wirth (1945):

> "We may define a minority as a group of people who, because of their physical or cultural characteristics, are singled out from the others in the society in which they live for differential and unequal treatment, and who therefore regard themselves as objects of collective discrimination. The existence of a minority in a society implies the existence of a corresponding dominant group with higher social status and greater privileges. Minority status carries with it the exclusion from full participation in the life of the society.

Statistical underrepresentation does not, in itself, account for groups being considered a minority in the sociological sense. It is not even a necessary condition (Rose, 1964). Those groups that have unequal access to power, that are considered in some way unworthy of sharing power equally, and that are stigmatized in terms of assumed inferior traits or characteristics are minority groups (Mindel and Habenstein, 1976).

It is clear that the salient variables defining minority status refer to patterns of relationship, the distribution of power and assumed differences in character traits.

Any discussion of aging as a social process in America would be deficient if some attention were not given to the experiences of the minority elderly

who make up a small but significant segment of the total aging population. For the purposes of our discussion, "minority" status will be limited to those groups whose language and physical and cultural characteristics make them visible and identifiable—the people of color—blacks, Hispanics (Mexican Americans/Chicanos, Puerto Ricans, Cubans, and Latin Americans), Native Americans, and Asians (Japanese, Chinese, Filipino, Korean, and Pacific Islanders). Each of these groups has experienced a unique history in the United States, and each has developed its own method of coping with the inherent conflicts between traditional and adopted life styles. As Kent (1971) points out in referring to these major groups, "Each of the groups is a minority and exhibits many of the characteristics associated with minority status. Each encounters discrimination; each has developed coping behavior that together with a physical separation has given rise to distinctive subcultures. The unity among these groups lies in the fact of minority position; the diversity between groups lies in the fact of minority position; the diversity between groups lies in the distinctive patterning of life." The vulnerabilities and the strengths resulting from the shared experience have led to negative and positive consequences for the mental well-being of the minority elderly.

THE SIGNIFICANCE
OF THE MINORITY EXPERIENCE
FOR MENTAL HEALTH

Moore (1971) argues that most research in aging has been based on limited samples, primarily of middle-majority Anglos, from which over generalizations have been made. She further argues for an examination of what is inherent in the minority

**Table 19-1** COMPARISON OF WHITE AND NONWHITE ELDERLY POPULATION—1960 AND 1970.

| AGE | WHITE | | | NONWHITE | | |
|---|---|---|---|---|---|---|
| | 1960 | 1970 | % Increase | 1960 | 1970 | % Increase |
| Total Population 60+ | 21,478,576 | 26,193,850 | 22.0 | 1,840,558 | 2,556,250 | 38.9 |
| 60–64 | 6,519,629 | 7,834,302 | 20.2 | 592,268 | 814,629 | 37.5 |
| 65–69 | 5,668,320 | 6,290,291 | 11.0 | 518,443 | 693,050 | 33.7 |
| 70–74 | 4,312,863 | 4,985,511 | 15.6 | 348,273 | 463,245 | 33.0 |
| 75–79 | 2,759,955 | 3,581,952 | 29.8 | 217,392 | 288,106 | 32.5 |
| 80–84 | 1,420,987 | 2,120,102 | 49.2 | 97,219 | 163,821 | 68.5 |
| 85+ | 796,822 | 1,381,692 | 73.4 | 66,963 | 133,399 | 99.2 |

Source: 1970 Census of Population—Volume 1, Part 1, United States Department of Commerce. (Taken from Table 189).

situation that is important to the study of aging, rather than focusing on minority status per se, and feels that such inquiry can begin to contribute substantially to the understanding of aging in general. She presents five characteristics of the minority situation that are relevant to aging:

1. Each minority group has a *special history.*
2. The special history has been accompanied by *discrimination.*
3. A *subculture* has developed.
4. *Coping structures* have developed.
5. *Rapid change is occurring.*

The impact of the minority experience on a personal level is described by Kramer (1970) as leading to a certain self-consciousness and uncertainty about one's status, and it is, in fact, this self-consciousness which may remain as a telltale trace that reveals minority member status when other signs have faded:

> I think the thing that irks us most is the teasing uncertainty of it all. Did the man at the box office give us the seat behind the post on purpose? Is the shopgirl impudent or merely nervous? Had the position really been filled before we applied for it?

These lines, written in 1922 by Jessie Fauset quoted in Davie, 1949, a black novelist, might be expanded to include "teasing uncertainties" about being turned away from housing in more desirable neighborhoods with the oft-repeated, "sorry, it was just rented," or, "it was just sold." What about the closed doors to certain clubs, organizations, and institutions? Was the promotion denied for lack of competence, or would visibility in the position be bad for business? The world of the minority elderly has been shaped by such individual experiences as well as by group responses that have been passed along in the stream of culture. The social and psychological consequences of repeated rejection, denial, segregation and exclusion extending over the life cycle to old age has not been sufficiently studied or explored. The lack of data severely impedes our understanding of the implications of long term societal neglect and its effect on the aging minority member's mental health. Carter (1972) stresses the need to take a hard and honest look at cultural issues as they affect in particular the black aged patient, but the admonition might be applied to all minorities who have experienced the cumulative effects of racism. We can safely assume that each comes bearing the scars of long-neglected medical and emotional problems which have caused a certain healthy paranoia necessary for survival.

## THE MINORITY EXPERIENCE

An examination of the minority experience will provide insights to some of the situational factors affecting mental health. This section presents historical group experiences including both positive and negative consequences—and their implications for mental health practitioners.

### HISTORICAL KALEIDOSCOPE: A COLLECTIVE EXPERIENCE

The history of the United States has been a history of diverse groups. As each new nationality arrived from abroad, it was met with hostility for one or two generations, but eventually its members climbed out of the slums, took on better paying occupations, and acquired social respect and dignity. This has not been true of such nonwhites as the blacks, Asians, Hispanics, and Native Americans. Many of today's elderly are immigrants from other countries. At least 1.6 million are persons of minority backgrounds (Butler and Lewis, 1977; Maykovich, 1972). Kent (1971) goes on to say that this diversity long has been a source of pride in America. Few nations have been so varied, and even fewer have permitted or encouraged the preservation of variant cultural patterns in which subcultures abound, creating a variety of patterns of aging. According to Butler and Lewis (1977), there are two major and distinctly separate issues which need to be kept in mind when considering the minority group elderly: the unique culture of each group which affects its life style, and the effects imposed on the lives of the elderly as a consequence of living in a majority culture. A general conclusion is drawn by Carter (1972) that there is usually a direct relationship between social status and the type, as well as intensity, of mental illness.

Solomon (1977) cites Novak as answering the question "What is an ethnic group" in rather lyrical terms. "It is a group with historical memory, real or imaginary. One belongs to an ethnic group in part involuntarily, in part by choice . . . Ethnic memory is not a series of events remembered, but rather a set of instinct, feelings, intimacies, expectations, patterns of emotion and behavior; a sense of reality; a set of stories for individuals—and for the people as a whole—to live out." The historical memory for each group has been unique. Conquest, prolonged conflict, and annexation are antecedents linking the history of the Native Americans and the Mexicans; dehumanizing enslavement and its special institutional forms in America are unique to the blacks; varied immigration and migration patterns for the Asians and Hispanics resulted in a cycle of recruitment, exploitation, and exclusion.

Our country was being settled at the very time that racial cleavages began to be drawn. Kramer (1970) and Simpson and Yinger (1965) recount in some detail the consequences of deculturation of the American Indian and blacks through conquest and enslavement. "The humiliation of a people without a culture is perhaps more exquisite than that of the man without a country, whatever his sensibility. The real issue is, nevertheless, the particular—and peculiar—history that impels each . . . As a result of their respective histories, Indians and Negroes feel the need to prove something to themselves . . . . The impulse toward self-validation exists not so much because of their categorical status, but because of the reason for that status" (Kramer, 1970).

A variation on the theme of historical memories is the cycle of immigration and migration patterns among the Asian and Hispanic groups over the years, joined more recently by others. Particularly on the West Coast the period prior to and immediately following the turn of the century saw a new phase or an extension of racial cleavages being applied to immigrants from Asia, initially with the influx of the Chinese, who were later followed by the Japanese and Pilipino[2] groups. As each new group grew in number and began to compete economically, forces were mobilized to enact restrictive legislation to exclude further immigration from these countries. Federal legislation in 1882 and 1892 sealed off further immigration from China; the enactment of the Alien Land Laws of 1913 and 1920, combined with the Alien Exclusion Act of 1924, virtually brought to a halt all immigration from Japan. Pilipino curtailment followed in 1935. Throughout the 1920s and the 1930s, a massive repatriation effort was directed against the Mexicans (Daniels and Kitano, 1970; Simpson and Yinger, 1965). The significant factor to be recognized in these campaigns for restriction and exclusion is that many of today's minority elderly are a unique cohort whose isolation from further contact with their counterparts in their countries of origin has created a subculture of men and women who belong to a vanished era. Newcomers entering the United States following the lifting of restrictions in 1965 have been members of a younger generation who grew up in a different

era, in which the values of over a half century ago have undergone many changes.

Since social interaction requires mutual intelligibility, the frustration of the incommunicability of experiences not shared exacerbates the sense of alienation and isolation among the minority elderly. Solomon (1972) cautions that it is unrealistic to assume that the black aged constitute a homogeneous group, as though they all had had the same life experiences. On the other hand, Golden (1976) cites Jackson as arguing that race is indeed a reality and that black old people should not be treated as though they were the same as white old people, because they are not. Jackson believes racism has adversely affected the black's preparation for old age. In essence, all minority groups can share in the sentiments of these writers.

The historical events recounted above are not in the too distant past for many of the ethnic minorities of today. For some it has become an ethnic memory, for others the experiences are still vividly imprinted upon their minds and souls, and for still others life continues to bring daily reminders of separateness which bring into question their identity. "Musings of a Hyphenated American" written by Sata (1973) poignantly describes the lonely quest for indentity:

> As may be true with other minorities, my earlier quest for self-identity was best characterized by aimless wandering down many blind alleys and dead ends. A place in the sun for most tends to obscure the reality that for minorities that place may be in the shadows. Until that reality is reconciled, the quest for self-identity is punctuated with repeated disappointments and failures. Perhaps it is less an issue of a place in the sun as it is the process through which it takes place that deserves further attention . . . . Without conscious awareness, I began to function as a human chameleon, sensitive and adaptive to the response of others. More often than I care to remember, I have attempted to relate with others honestly and openly, only to discover that, when I least expected it, either my racialness would be denied, which is to deny an important aspect of my identity, or I would be reminded that, because of my racialness, I was less than equal.

The life style emerging from this type of hyper-vigilance (suspicious, cautious, and guarded) has been a form of cultural paranoia which many minorities have adopted as a mechanism to deal with the external world. The issue is whether it has been adaptive. As Moore (1971) points out, the examination of the special histories of minority groups could help illuminate our understanding of what

---

[2]"Pilipino" is used throughout this report in reference to persons whose place of origin is the Philippine Islands. There is no "f" sound in the Pilipino language and the Pilipino community prefers that the spelling be with a "P."

factors affect continuities or discontinuities that might be related to successful aging.

## DISCRIMINATION AND STEREOTYPES

Moore (1971) contends that in all cases of minority situations discrimination and stereotyping are to be found. Literature abounds with analyses of the patterns of prejudice, discrimination, segregation, and even annihilation, yet viable solutions for the elimination of such practices are far from being realized for many of today's elderly who have been the victims of the acting out of group hatred. The danger of institutionalized discrimination is that it pervades the entire system, so that those with racial prejudices find validation for their prejudgments (Allport, 1958; Daniels and Kitano, 1970; Kramer, 1970; Rose, 1964; Simpson and Yinger, 1965). Discrimination in its most common forms has been experienced in various arenas of housing, employment, educational or recreational opportunities, churches, health care, or other social privileges. All groups have come in for their share of discriminatory practices in varying degrees of intensity. From the perspective of this chapter, the temptation to take an approach of "let's compare scars" or quantify experience by each ethnic group will be resisted. According to Butler and Lewis (1977), our historical gifts to minority citizens have been poverty, poor housing, and lack of medical care and education.

A concomitant feature of discrimination is the emergence of stereotypes growing out of our need to justify hostilities, order our complex world, or simplify the categories we assign to groups. Labels such as "the inscrutable Oriental" or the "happy go lucky blacks" and epithets of "lazy," "filthy," or "sneaky and sly," have had deleterious effects on the self-concept of minority groups. Although not all stereotypes are always negative, in most instances the attributes assigned to groups classify them as inferior, physically or mentally.

Assumptions are frequently made about a particular group based on inaccurate stereotypes which, when acted upon, can lead to further disenfranchisement of their basic human rights. For example, it has long been a common belief that "Asians take care of their own." The myth failed to take into account the fact that for many Asians, especially elderly Chinese and Pilipino men who were denied opportunities to establish families because of the above mentioned exclusion acts, the care system does not exist. Consequently, in acting upon the stereotypic notion that problems do not exist, it follows that little attention and resources are directed to these groups. Needless suffering

goes unnoticed and unattended. Sotomayor (1977) elaborates on the importance of the relationship between having a positive self-perception and function adequately and comfortably in one's environment:

> Psychologically, the self-concept is the most vulnerable component in the transactions between minorities of color and majority populations. Negative stereotypes, for example, aim at the perpetuation of the depreciation and undermining of the self-worth. The self-concept can suffer irreparable damage if the socialization process prevents significant and familiar symbols to be present and reinforced at various levels of experience (p. 196).

Based on the patterns of discrimination and stereotyping, one outcome is the selective association among minority groups, giving rise to the formation of subcultures, and, more particularly, informal ethnic networks to buffer against such assaults on the individual.

## NATURAL CARE AND SUPPORT SYSTEMS

Although many commonalities related to the minority experience exist among different ethnic groups and subgroups, their heterogeneity cannot be overemphasized. In general, there is no definitive research which addresses such issues as the minority elders' interpretation of care and support in their later years. Historically, the family, the church, and the community have usually been viewed as the major support systems for these groups.

*Family.* The world of the minority elderly to a large extent has been limited to the ghetto, barrios, reservations, and enclaves, cut off from any interaction with the dominant group. Especially has this been true for those in the rural areas of the South and Southwest, where reverence and attachment to the land placed a value on the importance of the extended family and the roles assigned to older members (Maldonado, 1975).

Familial support and expectations vary within each ethnic group, social class, and subculture. A review of the literature on minority groups provides strong evidence that the role of the family and extended family is still a viable support for many of the ethnic communities (Alvarez and Bean, 1976; Bell, Kasschau, and Zellman, 1976; Bengtson, 1976; Kitano and Kikumura, 1976; Price, 1976; Solomon, 1976). For each minority group the family has played an important role in transmitting cultural values, beliefs, customs, and practices and has given relative stability and served as a sanctuary in a hostile world. The values of filial piety among the Asians; the idealized role given to the extended family among Mexican Americans in which relatives and *compadres* (godparents) play an important role; the extended or augmented families in the black communities which provide support in maintaining continuity in lives of its members; and the kinship system and its lines of descent which still function among the Native Americans are all ways in which subcultural indentities are maintained and preserved.

For example, in discussing the traditional Japanese family, Kitano (1969) describes filial responsibility "as a reciprocal obligation from parent to child and child to parent." Within this cultural framework the elders would obviously expect their children to assume total responsibility for parental needs in old age. Other first-generation minority elders with similar traditional cultural beliefs are likely to have similar expectations of their children.

Trinidad (1977) clearly states that Spanish-speaking elderly on the East Coast turn to their families for assistance, and that "their sense of belonging is provided to them by their primary group, the family, which is very closely knit...." This is also true in the Mexican-American culture where the family system or alternative systems, which includes the family, curanderos (folk healers), and church, provide the needed support in the event of mental illness (Andrulus, 1977; Padilla, Carlos, and Keefe, 1976).

Reliance on the extended family for support and guidance is indigenous to the black elderly. In fact, a more recent exploratory study on "Support Services and Aged Blacks" found that in spite of the marital or employment status of those surveyed, "the family is the primary source of support ..." (Anderson, 1978). However, it is still not uncommon to hear the black elderly say that they pray to God that they won't become an economic or social burden to their children.

*Church.* Ethnic churches have played a major role in most of the minority communities from their inception, usually being the first institution to be built. Kramer (1970) states that for many of the immigrants their religion was the only experience which they could carry unchanged from their old home to their new life. The church was the only institution that was completely transferable, and it provided a source of comfort for the first generation who were experiencing stress from uprooting and isolation.

As a primary social institution in the minority community, the church offers a great deal of psychic support to its members in general, and to the elderly in particular. A study of mental health services for Spanish-speaking/surnamed populations (Padilla, Ruiz, and Alvarez, 1975) noted that individuals with emotional or "spiritual" problems were more likely to seek out or be referred by family members or friends to clergymen for comfort and reassurance rather than to mental health professionals.

Kitano (1969) cites a similar religiosity among the Issei for those whose average age is now in the middle 80s who attend both the Buddhist and Christian churches in large numbers and appear to be seeking reassurance in the face of aging and death. He notes that prayer- and study groups are well attended.

As for the black elderly, the church and religion continue to be an important aspect of their lives. This was amply stated by Carnella Barnes (Newquist, 1977) who said, "The church is the one institution to which older blacks turn .... Blacks have found faith, social support, Christian nurturance, and recreation through the church ... which has contributed a great deal to human survival." Furthermore, Solomon (1976) suggests that we look at the role of the black church and its significance as a natural support in the community. The black church has had a pervasive influence on the community ... "encompassing issues beyond salvation and sin all the way to politics and economic development." Plumpp (1972) proposed that the black church is the only institution for instilling a sense of self-determination for blacks, and that it can be a major force for change. It is further suggested by Solomon that the church may be the most viable mechanism for service delivery, in view of the fact that it is the most stable organization in black communities.

Studies by Jackson and Wood (1976) and Swanson and Harter (1971) corroborate the importance of the church. The church and religion can be seen as a source of strength in old age.

*Community.* Identifiable and visible minority communities as we know them today had their origins in the ghettos of the first generation. The uprooted immigrants and displaced groups formed their ethnic enclaves to meet the needs of their alien status. Within the boundaries of these communities, which are to some extent physically segregated and socially isolated, a parallel subsystem evolved. The support subsystem as described by Moriwaki (1976) served as a buffer against the acts of discrimination and the strange language and customs of the dominant society. Kramer (1970) and Kitano (1969) note that in the process of developing a subculture as a reaction to the external pressure from a hostile society, the cultural insulation served to strengthen the cohesiveness of the community. The practice of closure functioned to perpetuate distinctive values, beliefs, and norms held by the group. Similar language, food preferences, and common experiences were further sources of establishing communal strength and cohesion. But a price is exacted, for in the adaptation to a subculture, participation in the larger society is impeded. Another view presented by Maykovich (1972), particularly in reference to the Japanese elderly, although some generalization may be made for other similarly integrated communities, is that, despite the alienation from American society, the integration within an ethnic community in which values are affirmed compensates for loss and mitigates against experiencing alienation. An important factor to be recognized is that the emergence of a minority community, especially for the immigrants, is not a re-creation of the original community or village in the old country, but an adaptation to minority status (Kramer, 1970).

Solomon (1976) points out the difficulty in specifying what constitutes the black community. Geographical boundaries alone do not constitute a community. The involuntary and forced nature of limiting residential options has created ghetto centers rather than integrated communities in which major functions are carried out by social organizations over which one has some control. According to Solomon, an important ingredient in defining community is the presence of a degree of personal intimacy among the residents of a particular physical space. The incorporation of children into other than nuclear families, especially those headed by older women, as well as the taking in of relatives is seen as an evidence of intimacy and a feeling that indeed a community does exist.

The Japanese and Chinese communities (Little Tokyos and Chinatowns), by contrast, developed an elaborate network of associations and institutions to support their members. The early immigrants who are today's elderly viewed themselves as sojourners who always expected to return to their homeland, however long their residence in the United States. Such an orientation strengthened ethnic solidarity, giving rise to the exclusive association with kinship groups (Kramer, 1970). As discrimination and prejudice intensified, the ethnic community provided a certain degree of refuge and security. In time, associations to perform familial and welfare functions developed: *kenjin-kais*, or Japanese prefectural organizations, benevolent societies, ethnic churches, language schools, athletic leagues, and merchants' associations. A community within a community developed in which cultural values were reinforced to encourage ingroup solidarity. For the Japanese, the social organization was severely dislocated with the wartime evacuation in 1942. Recreated communities have emerged following the war, which increasingly feel the strains of no longer being able to fulfill the total needs of their members (Kitano, 1969).

In response to categorical status and the emergence of variant subcultures, minority members have had to come to terms with the social deprivation and psychological derogation imposed upon them. Kramer (1970) illustrates the importance of the function of the institutional structures within minority communities which help members to cope with the inherent frustrations with varying degrees of effectiveness. "The fact that they live in communities provides them with the social support that permits constructive action" (Kramer, 1970).

Finally, while community support and cohesiveness vary and may range from total support to nothing much more than the comfort that comes from being with people who look like oneself and talk like oneself, after a lifetime of prejudice and discrimination on "the outside" it is still significant to the minority elderly (Moore, 1971).

Language patterns of ethnic elders are crucial but often overlooked aspects of the minority community. Among the major subcultural groups, a significant number are handicapped by the inability to speak English. Asian elderly and the Spanish-speaking elderly are particularly vulnerable because of the lack of proficiency in the dominant language. Lack of language ability contributes to a sense of estrangement and isolation.

At the same time, it is the shared language patterns that have contributed toward preservation of the subcultural patterns and the maintenance of segregated communities. Numerous works have been written on the role of language in the formulation and perception of the world view (Giglioli, 1972; Hall, 1959; Kramer, 1970; Lynd, 1958; Sotomayor, 1977). "The world view, also seen as the intermediary world of a language, was perceived as inherent in language itself. It is through this unique and complex relationship that language was seen to play a decisive role in shaping the attitudes of individuals and groups and, by extension, their personalities and behaviors" (Sotomayor, 1977, p. 197). If we apply this principle to the language patterns of the minority elderly under discussion, we will find a mosaic of patterns which view experiences through multiple lenses.

Special words are used to convey nuances of meaning unknown to outsiders; certain gestures, facial expressions, and bodily attitudes communicate meaning and messages. Maretzki (1974) states that prediction is a crucial part of human communication, and that to share a life style or culture implies efficiency in predicting the behavior of others. "This ability to predict is a natural, even unconscious, factor in the interaction of members of the same cultural group and is important to effective communication within the group."

## IMPLICATIONS—CHANGING CULTURES AND CHANGING VALUES

In his study of health problems among the black, Chicano, Japanese and Pilipino communities, Weaver (1976) describes the importance of recognizing and developing ways to use social structures within the ethnic communities to alleviate problems. The social network is conceptualized as an explanation of behavior and attitudes, for it takes into account the interaction of structural and psychological relations within a specific population. The implication is that social and economic relations alone are not the determining factors, but rather that binding ties exist within the groups which influence attitudes and behaviors. As an example, Weaver points out that although the Japanese may limit much of their business, social, and cultural activities to the ethnic community, "it is the *strength* of the community as a reference group, a source of values and criteria for evaluating and controlling their behavior, that provides the durability and continuity conceptualized as social network". However, changes are taking place at all levels of society which threaten the more traditionally bound family characteristics and the roles of its elderly. These impinge upon the lives of all elderly in varying degrees. We would suggest that the impact of these changes on the lives of the minority elderly may bring into question the viability and relevance of much of the traditional values, beliefs, and supports thought to be inherent elements of ethnic groups and communities.

With succeeding generations, what will be the prognosis for the future of the variant subcultures? Kramer (1970) notes an interesting aspect by stating that the hard core of the minority community is its lower middle class. Those of higher status move out and become peripheral to the community by virtue of increased contact with the majority group, while those of very low status move to the periphery due to increased dependency on the larger society for basic sustenance. These factors, compounded by social isolation, produce the phenomenon of a middle-class minority community. Many would argue that, given the present racial cleavages, economic mobility alone would not obliterate ghettos, barrios, and the like. A continual re-creating process, different with each succeeding generation, yet still identifiable, is more likely taking place. Regional differences as well as rural and urban differences exist among the various groups. Some of the major changes occurring are sources of stress, resulting in dislocation from familiar surroundings, increased isolation, and changing roles.

First, with the increased mobility and economic independence of the younger generations among the different minority groups, there has been a gradual but consistent upward and outward movement from formerly insulated ethnic communities. Beginning with the major thrusts in migration of the blacks and Mexican-Americans during and immediately following World War II, the trend has continued for the Native Americans and other Spanish-speaking and Spanish surnamed groups in the ensuing years. Not all migration patterns to the urban centers included taking the aged family members, although for many the uprooting did take place, causing a sense of alienation for those cut off from familiar knowledge and skills more appropriate to an agrarian society. For those left behind, especially in the South and Southwest regions of the country, the vulnerabilities of old age have increased and greater dependence is placed upon surrogate families made up of friends, neighbors, and churches. The same pattern of upward and outward mobility has transformed many of the tightly knit enclaves of the Asian communities, especially among the Japanese and Chinese. Acculturation with each succeeding generation of American-born offspring of the immigrants has modified the structure of the institutions and organization of the ethnic communities in which the traditional supports were predictable and forthcoming. Remnants of formerly insulated ethnic communities are still visible in parts of major cities such as Los Angeles and San Francisco, but the predominance of older members in these communities is evident. A phenomenon of more recent times is that of the new immigrants arriving from Asian countries, replicating in many ways the earlier patterns of settlement based on language, culture, and ethnicity.

Secondly, the rapid changes occurring affect intergenerational relationships on several levels. Among many minority families, it is not uncommon to find members who are virtually cut off from any meaningful and effective communication with one another. For example, among the monolingual elderly (Chinese, Japanese, Mexican-American, and Native American) who, in most cases, did not master proficiency in the English language, a communication gap exists with their grandchildren. The traditional role of transmitting cultural values, beliefs, and rituals is denied them, resulting in a sense of mutual loss. Solomon (1970) also points up an important fact which is cause for some concern. Very often what occurs is that the younger generation of blacks hold stereotypes of elderly blacks in somewhat the same manner that whites have stereotyped all blacks. At the same time that distance is occurring between the younger generation and the elderly, an equally disturbing gap is occurring because of the socioeconomic mobility of the middle generation. The hold on the newly acquired status of "middle class" is a precarious one according to Solomon, and one which puts constraints upon the material resources which were once shared with dependent parents. "The black elderly may in fact have had a more secure family status when things were worse for black people."

Another aspect of intergenerational conflict and confusion is the bilingual and bicultural nature of many of the ethnic minorities. Living on the fringe of both cultures can cause what Kiefer (1974) calls "acculturative stress." The bicultural individual very often experiences a high degree of stress due to a lack of predictability in the face of a number of socializing agents and conflicting norms for behavior. Emotional isolation for the elderly Japanese is further perpetuated by the inability of the American-born offspring to communicate in their parent's native tongue. The reliance on subtle facial, postural, and gestural cues to communicate feelings is a skill which many of the second and third generations increasingly lack. A countervailing force at work, especially among the Mexican Americans, is the affirmation of cultural and linguistic identification as a way of easing the internal stress caused by external political and socioeconomic derogation. A rebirth of ethnic pride is emerging as a strategy for a renewed sense of self-acceptance and self-worth (Sotomayor, 1977).

Finally, as perceptively observed by Moore (1971), the kinship supports and supportive networks of ethnic communities are precarious at best in the face of rapidly changing situations. How supportive are ethnic communities and how supportive will they be in the future? Conventional wisdom and assumptions about ethnic communities as strongholds for preservation of values and culture, and their capability for maintaining the well-being of all their members, are brought into

question at the present time. Kramer describes the limiting dimensions as follows:

> The functions of the minority community are not without concomitant dysfunctions for its members. Its enclosure is sheltering, of course, but it may also be limiting. Minority members may not explore the changing reality of the larger society as a result . . . can be stifling . . . too little variation in the group because of its emphasis on unity (Kramer, 1970, p. 264).

Kitano (1973) further elaborates upon the above by stating, "That the tightly knit ethnic community is a completely healthy development can be questioned. There is the risk of encapsulation, of a slowness of acculturation, of self-imposed isolation, restricted communication. . . ." As long as patterns of discrimination, prejudice, and segregation continue to isolate large numbers of ethnic minority citizens from full participation in the dominant society, the ability to gain skills in competing and maneuvering beyond the ghetto and barrio walls is denied. A "we and they" dichotomy becomes entrenched, and future elderly will live out their lives within the self-limiting confines of minority communities. The utter sense of powerlessness, the lowered expectations, and the cycle of poverty, poor health, poor housing, and lack of education may be a continued legacy for many.

A model for empowerment of the powerless is proposed by Solomon (1976), holding forth a possibility for ameliorating historical inequities. Empowerment refers to a process by which the powerless and stigmatized collective become engaged in identifying those obstacles or power blocks which have kept them from developing the knowledge, skills, and resources necessary for effective performance in social roles. The engagement in problem-solving is seen as a critical strategy or technique for empowerment. The removal of stigma from the powerless role to one of a causal force in effecting change instills a sense of empowerment for many who have historically only known nonpower. Perhaps in the redefinition and re-creating of minority communities this sense of empowerment can be achieved to some degree of success for the forthcoming generations of ethnic elderly.

How then does one attempt to understand or assess the positive and negative consequences of the life circumstances of this group? Perhaps due to the miniscule number of minority elderly entering the mental health system, little has been done to accurately assess their past and current life situations and needs. The next section deals more specifically with these issues and suggests areas for further development.

## DEFINITIONS
## OF MENTAL HEALTH AND ILLNESS

This section deals with the definitions of mental health and illness as they affect the ethnic minority elderly. It will examine the issues of defining mental health among ethnic minority elderly, devising assessment instruments, and obtaining valid data for accurate assessments.

### NOSOLOGY: DEFINITIONS OF MENTAL ILLNESS

We do not know much about the mental health status of our ethnic minority elderly. Statistics providing a demographic profile are available (although their accuracy is questionable), but there is no information on the health status, and particularly the mental health status, of these diverse minority elderly groups. For estimates of mental health status, we might examine mental hospital admission rates, but the limited scope of these data have been discussed elsewhere (Kitano, 1969). However, these data indicate, at best, admission rates by age only and do not specify the various ethnic group distributions. What these statistics do tell us, though, is that the elderly in general, and the ethnic minority elderly in particular, are underrepresented in the mental health care system.

We cannot assume that these elderly do not have problems—we know merely that they do not enter the mental health system. They face life changes—physical deterioration and losses, widowhood, marital conflicts, retirement—as well as interpersonal crises. Those who speak only their mother tongue cannot communicate and, therefore, cannot transmit their heritage to their grandchildren. Rapid social changes only exacerbate their isolation, alienation, and sense of loss. Many are coping in the community—some alone, others with families—never to enter the rolls of the mental health register. To them, the numerous federal, state, and local helping programs are not a resource to which they can turn.

The low priority given to elderly and to minorities in the mental health care system is reflected in the nosology used by the practitioner. Diagnostic classifications are used for convenience and statistical purposes rather than as a tool for recommending appropriate treatment. Thus, the International Classification of Diseases (ICD), which

should be used as a classification system for mental disorders, is sometimes mistakenly used to classify patients. If diagnosis is to be useful for treatment, categories and accompanying symptoms should be precise; and precision would result in a proliferation of types of disorders. Such "fine-tuning" of categories is lacking in the usual diagnosis of the elderly. Among the twenty categories of mental disorders cited in the Professional Activity Study of 1965, which surveyed patient records from 357 nonfederal short-term hospitals in the Western United States, the elderly were disproportionately classified into only three categories—Acute Organic Brain Syndrome, Chronic Organic Brain Syndrome, and Involutionary Melancholia (Commission on Professional and Hospital Activities, 1976). It is important to note that these illnesses usually result in custodial-type treatment in the system. For minority elderly, especially for those who do not speak the language, this type of treatment is even more disastrous and precludes improvement and discharge. Is it not, therefore, understandable that the minority elderly underutilize the services which are available and enter such facilities only when problems have become so severe and irreversible that no other recourse is possible?

Mental illness in minority elderly is easily detectable. The bizarre behaviors found among other age and ethnic groups which become intolerable to family and friends precipitate admission. However, of more importance is the other end of the continuum—the mental health of minority elderly. Very little is known about what constitutes mental health, adjustment, self-esteem, or happiness. No norms are available for what constitutes acceptable behavior for various ethnic groups or for their elderly. One attempt to examine normative behavior in ethnic groups was the Hawaii Normal Adjustment Study (Sanborn and Katz, 1977).[3] A sample of 932 "normal" Honolulu community residents from five ethnic groups (Japanese, Caucasian, Hawaiian, Pilipino, and Chinese) were asked to rate a relative's behavior on the Katz Adjustment Scale. The study attempted to develop normal baseline data on each of the ethnic groups. Although the study resulted in norms for each group on a number of dimensions such as hyperactivity, negativism, anxiety, and so on, it did not yield sufficient analyses of how each group evaluated the various behaviors, that is, as healthy or maladjusted. Although cultural factors were attributed to the dif-

[3]Unpublished report of a grant from the National Institute of Mental Health. Copies may be obtained from the authors at the Institute of Behavioral Sciences, 250 Ward Avenue, Suite 226, Honolulu, Hawaii 96814.

ference in behavior found among these ethnic groups, the utility of these results for assessing mental health is minimal because of the lack of the ethnic groups' assessment of whether the dimensions included in the scale were in fact valid indicators of mental health or illness.

Another study by Edgerton and Karno (1971), which examined the mental health characteristics of the Mexican-American community in Los Angeles, found that in definitions and perceptions of mental illness, there were greater differences between generations of Mexican-Americans (particularly among those who spoke English and those who did not) than between Mexican-Americans and Anglos. Thus, there is even greater need to look at intragroup variations, particularly for ethnic elderly who are dependent on their English-speaking children, who are usually the determining influence on decisions regarding institutionalization.

If mental health is seen as the...

> ...optimal state for each individual, including such factors as age, economic status, social setting, and cultural surroundings...[then] Mental illness, conversely, implies a deviance in behavior, which is foreign to that expected of a person of a certain age, a certain sex, in a certain social setting and with a particular cultural background (Stoller, 1969, p. 5).

In assessing the mental health status of ethnic minority elderly, the practitioner must examine the total person—not only his current presenting problem, but his life situation, his social and personal world, his values, and his life history.

The need for more research and understanding of the factors which lead to optimal or dysfunctional behaviors and to well-being is urgent yet not new. In 1966, a number of Asian and Western psychiatrists and social scientists met to discuss their methods and findings in identifying psychiatric disorders cross-culturally (Caudill and Lin, 1969). Their major concern was with understanding the similarities and diversity of mental health and mental illness in varying cultures. Transcultural psychiatrists are still wrestling with these issues today. However, their data consist primarily of official statistics, using the standard psychiatric nosology mentioned previously. Empirical work in examining what constitutes stress for the individual and its relationship to coping has been minimal. The elderly have also been neglected. However, ethnic elderly, with their varied histories and experiences, can provide the insight into positive as

well as negative coping strategies (some of which are derived from their cultural background) which have contributed to their survival.

### INSTRUMENTS

If the concepts of mental health and illness are ill-defined for the ethnic minority elderly, then indicators to assess these states appropriately are nonexistent. Yet outreach workers who canvass neighborhoods find many elderly who are coping, sometimes minimally, but who refuse help. These workers intuitively feel that these elderly need professional help and are constantly asking for assessment guides to properly evaluate and refer such older people. An instrument such as the Katz Adjustment Scale, discussed earlier, is lengthy and requires sophisticated interpretation, and is also beset with problems of validity for ethnic elderly, particularly for those without families and living alone. For example, 24 items ranging from "acted as if he had no interest in things" and "spoke so low you could not hear him" to "felt that people did not care about him" are used to determine psychopathology. These items could very well be real for an elderly Japanese immigrant who has never learned the language and is living alone in a hotel room. Strong cultural traditions of family interdependence and filial piety as expectations for his old age, rapid social changes in the environment surrounding him, and minority status and fear of the larger white society may all impinge on the individual to cause psychopathology. On the other hand, the individual could be coping quite well with his life situation, perhaps with a strong personality developed over the years, and with his life routinized so that his daily walks in the mornings and afternoon, his job as a janitor at the local school, and his health become his forte in survival. Thus, once again, it must be reemphasized that the instruments used in diagnosis should be aids to observe the total person, including the cultural, social and personal factors (Moriwaki, 1976).

A short, easily administered scale for outreach workers is the Mental Status Questionnaire (Kahn, Goldfarb, Pollack, and Peck, 1960) consisting of 10 items which can be used for screening and cursory diagnosis. But even here it is important to examine thoroughly the items and their applicability to the individual. For example, the questions such as "Who is the President of the US?" or "Who was the President before him?" might be irrelevant and unknown to a minority older person. In this case, for greater validity, the practitioner could substitute other more local figures which would be common knowledge for the particular group.

## DATA GATHERING—THE ASSESSMENT INTERVIEW

Even more critical for appropriate assessment of the individual is the process of eliciting information for evaluation. A major effort in helping mental health workers to elicit and understand variations of behavior among ethnic groups was published in 1974 (Tseng, McDermott, and Maretzski, 1974). Although limited somewhat by its examination of eight ethnic groups in the context of Hawaiian society, this volume does include cultural dimensions which are helpful in understanding more fully the behaviors of our ethnic elderly. For example, in both the chapters on the Chinese and the Japanese, the authors (Tseng and Char, 1974; Kinzie and Furukawa, 1974) cite the avoidance of expressing inner negative thoughts, feelings, and personal problems—the crux of our traditional treatment modalities. This alerts practitioners to follow up on the somatic manifestations of internal conflicts. Tseng and Char (1974) explain that the traditional culture suppresses unacceptable thoughts and feelings; however physical illness is acceptable and results in attention and positive concern. In addition, traditional Chinese medication links emotion to specific viscera, for example the heart to happiness and the liver to anger and nervousness. Such beliefs help to clarify further the importance of looking more closely at somatic complaints among this group. It is interesting to note that cries for help are much more restrained among Asians, with the emphasis being on proper situation-oriented behavior. Suicide, alcoholism, and violence would merely compound the stress, for the individual would be alone with his problem with no support from family or peers.

Similarly, the Philipino elderly have difficulty relating to the expression of emotions, having come from a country with a history of centuries of occupation by other cultures and thus beset with enduring a lifetime of minority status. Such conditions would also affect one's self-esteem negatively (Ponce, 1974). These cultural factors have also imprinted the belief that to acknowledge emotion is a sign of weakness. Thus, the elderly may view the mental health worker with alarm, and may prefer not to discuss the introspective concerns of the therapist. Much more concrete and pragmatic strategies for problem-solving may be the means by which to develop rapport and trust in such a case.

These examples point to the essential ingredient of data-gathering interviews, *i.e.*, trust. A major question is whether the practitioner must be from the same ethnic group as the client. Brown, Stein, Huang, and Harris (1973) found in their intervention program in Los Angeles Chinatown that a worker, to be most effective, had not only to speak the same language and be of the same ethnic background, but also should live in the same community. Corroborating evidence of the preference for therapists of the same ethnic background was found by Wolkon and Moriwaki (1973) among black students at UCLA. They report that, regardless of class, black students preferred a therapist of the same social and racial background.

However, there are exceptions. In Honolulu, one of the agencies providing outreach and counselling services to the elderly, many of whom were from the various ethnic minority groups discussed here, found significant success in using a white psychiatrist in their home visitation program. Initially withdrawn, seclusive, and hesitant to see anyone or even speak of mental disturbance, many Pilipino elderly men opened their doors to this psychiatrist, for he is sensitive to their backgrounds and life circumstances, and talks with them as persons rather than as "bodies" to be treated. With his warmth and patience, distance, fear, and suspicion have gradually dissipated over time. He is perceived as a friend who can help. However time-consuming, this psychiatrist's work exemplifies the importance of developing trust in helping relationships. What is universal among all cultural and ethnic groups is the need to develop *trust*; what may differ is the means by which we develop and establish that trust.

Once data are gathered, the practitioner must analyze and decide on the problem and treatment. Cultural elements influencing the diagnostician are involved. For example, Katz, Cole, and Lowery (1969) found differences in perceptions of pathology among American and British psychiatrists, reflective of differences in national norms as to what constitutes deviant behavior. If differences are prevalent among these two groups, we would expect even less agreement among those who are from more divergent backgrounds. Kendall (1968) found that psychiatrists in a southern state were in fact biased against blacks, reporting greater pathology among blacks than whites. He suggests that psychiatrists, in using their white, middle class framework as a standard, would perceive black behaviors as deviant, regardless of whether these behaviors might in fact be positive coping strategies for this group.

## PREVENTION AND TREATMENT

A primary issue in assessing mental health services to the minority elderly demands examination of society's provisions to insure the development, implementation, and delivery of preventive mental health services to its citizens.

### PREVENTION

Norman J. Finkel (1976) has delineated the following types of preventive therapy in the mental health arena: "Primary prevention seeks to block the development of disorders and to promote psychological health. Secondary prevention seeks to prevent a mild disorder from worsening."

Within this framework, the major focus is usually on primary and secondary prevention. This is further supported by Hendricks and Hendricks (1977), who view primary prevention as extensive attempts at reinstructing the public to the significance of aging in the total maturational process, and secondary prevention as being more concerned with increasing positive mental health through the utilization of appropriate treatment modalities based on the character of the illness. Others feel "that primary prevention is generally unattainable and that we do enough to wrestle with secondary prevention . . . which consists of identifying and decreasing mental illness" (Martin, 1970).

In terms of primary intervention, little or nothing has been done for the minority elderly.[4] Suffice it to say that public insurance programs supported by the federal and state governments, such as Medicare and Medicaid, are restricted and therefore limited in their responsiveness in the provision of mental health services for the poor or near poor. In fact, these programs have done little to facilitate preventive mental health and outpatient programs for the population they serve.

In the sixties, as part of the "Great Society," the community mental health movement emerged as a potential vehicle for strengthening mental health services, alleviating social problems, and improving the quality of life for the total community.

---

[4]Little, in fact, has been done for the elderly population in general. Cohen (1976), for example, reported that those 65 years and older have a higher incidence of mental health problems but fewer than 4 percent constitute all psychiatric outpatients seen in private practice or at community mental health centers. The norm has usually been to relegate this segment of the population to custodial care.

Congress passed the Community Mental Health Centers Act of 1963, with an Amendment in 1965. The Act itself provided funds for construction while the Amendment allocated resources for personnel.

> The centers envisioned by this legislation were to include in-patient and out-patient facilities, day and night care services, halfway houses and foster home placement services, 24-hour emergency services, and consultation and educational programs. . . . More specifically, the Act emphasized the linkage of the mental health field with urban based social planning which took socioculturally defined communities as its strategic unit of analysis (Marx, Rieker, and Ellison, 1974).

Although the centers were to provide comprehensive services to the total community, in 1975 an Amendment was necessary to insure specialized services for specific populations, such as the elderly.

As it relates to ethnic elders, Butler (1975) found that:

> In general, community mental health centers have not been a great success . . . partly because their staffs do not have the perception, training and resources to deal with the inner-city poverty, racism and agism that affect the patients who come to them; and . . . because of poor linkage to the poverty areas in which many of the elderly reside.

Poverty, racism, and agism are interrelated factors that cannot be ignored in terms of their consequences on the mental health of minority elders. Furthermore, there is a general belief that socioeconomic and environmental determinants contribute to negative adjustment and are therefore significant in the expansion of mental illness among the poor. For the most part, prevention as a concept or practice has not been a significant aspect of ethnic elders' life styles. Popular misconceptions about the treatability of mental illness continues to support these groups' reliance on emergency services in the event of crisis situations. Preventive mental health services have not addressed the needs of this population.

### TREATMENT

In the framework developed by Finkel (1976), tertiary treatment is that of reducing the negative consequences of more severe disorder, requiring professional intervention and treatment.

Butler and Lewis (1977), in addressing institutional care of ethnic elders, cited black elders as constituting less than 3 percent of the nursing home and home for the aged population. The only consistently accessible accommodations have been the state mental hospitals. However, no specific data were mentioned in relation to the Mexican-American, American Indian, or Asian-American elderly. This omission in and of itself would seem to indicate the underrepresentation of these groups in mental health treatment facilities.

A growing body of literature is beginning to address the treatment and utilization patterns of the different ethnic groups in the mental health system. Although the underrepresentation of the elderly in most instances precludes accurate generalizations, the information is useful for this discussion.

For example, Yamamoto, James and Palley (1968) conducted a study of the Psychiatric Outpatient Clinic of the Los Angeles County General Hospital to determine the outcome of treatment to blacks, Mexican-Americans, and Asian-Americans. The authors found that, in comparison to the white population, the ethnic minority clients were more likely to be terminated or given a minimal amount of corroborative psychotherapy.

In another project in Seattle, Sue's (1977) analysis showed that "the services received by minority clients in 17 community health facilities suggested that blacks received differential treatment and poorer outcomes than whites. However, Asian Americans, Chicanos, and Native American clients who tended to receive treatment equal to that of white clients also had poorer outcomes as measured by premature termination rates." Other studies (e.g., Andrulis, 1977; Karno and Edgerton, 1969; Padilla, Ruiz, and Alvarez, 1975; Sue and McKinney, 1975) support these findings. In general, ethnic minorities under-utilized the available services, received fewer referrals, and remained in treatment for significantly shorter periods than their Anglo counterparts.

More specifically, in keeping with traditional cultural values, "Asians may fail to utilize professional services since an admission of emotional problems and inability to work out one's problems would arouse shame and would reflect poorly on the family name" (Sue and McKinney, 1975). Or, as cited by Trinidad (1977) in an article addressing the special characteristics of the Spanish-speaking elderly on the East Coast, "The Spanish-speaking person at any age and certainly at a later stage in life, will not be oriented toward looking for help in a need situation through an agency." Other ethnic issues of this nature are important factors in the service utilization patterns of minority elders.

## ISSUES OF PREVENTION/INTERVENTION

A key issue in the delivery of mental health services to minority elders is related to Community Mental Health Centers (CMHC) which in spite of the legislative intent, have done little to address the needs of this population. In a survey of services for the aged in eight CMHCs, Patterson (1976) observed that preventive or treatment provisions were only directed to those elders who actively sought out the Center's services. It is obvious that there exists among most CMHC staff a "lack of belief in appropriateness of mental health assistance" to the older population. For the minority aged this is compounded further by racism. The issue then becomes one of educating the center staff to dispel these myths and prejudices.

To promote the acceptance and better utilization of services to ethnic minority elders, bilingual workers, facilities located in or near the ethnic community, utilization of existing ethnic community organizations, and the strengthening and support of family networks are but a few of the viable alternatives available to mental health service providers. Practitioners must acknowledge and demonstrate an understanding of the cultural backgrounds and beliefs of different ethnic groups.

For example, Padilla et al., (1975), in their study of mental health services for the Spanish-speaking population, suggest that under-utilization can be attributed to the inaccessibility of services, which are usually located at the farthest distance possible from the neighborhood of the group in highest need. In addition, there are communication problems due to monolingualism of professional staff, inaccurate diagnosis based on middle class values, social distance between the practitioner and client, and racial prejudice. For the purpose of this paper, there is also "agism."

In another study (Sue and McKinney, 1975), a mental health facility was established in an Asian community. Through widespread publicity, the use of a bilingual therapist, and the ability of the therapist to understand the need and lifestyle of Asians in the community, the number of Asians seen in 12 months was greater than the total number seen at 17 facilities over a period of 36 months. Similar findings were observed by Phillipus (1971) in a Spanish-speaking urban population study. In addition, Phillipus found that service utilization was facilitated by having the services in the neighborhood to be served, seeing the client immediately upon his request for service, and having a staff capable of offering "functionally useful services" through their knowledge and use of other community resources. Another positive factor was the community involvement, which was encouraged through a board of community representatives who were instrumental in reflecting the needs of the population to be served. The meaning of ethnic cultural values is stressed even further by Weaver (1976) who found that "Japanese, regardless of age or degree of acculturation, tend to seek out Japanese physicians, dentists, and other health care providers."

Furthermore, many ethnic elderly defer to "expert" opinion and therefore take a less active part in the treatment process, which may be construed by some as a lack of motivation. In line with this, a review of the literature by Padilla, *et al.* (1975) found that low-socioeconomic-status patients seem to expect the therapist to assume a more active role.

The extended family network is, in most instances, a natural resource on which ethnic elders rely for support and guidance to varying degrees. Because of this, families should be assisted in their endeavors to maintain the older relative in the home through various economic mechanisms, such as tax incentives or supplemental income programs when necessary. This support could be bolstered through the provisions of culturally relevant supportive services, such as, home health, homemakers, meals-on-wheels, day-care centers, senior centers, and so forth.

For those elders without relatives, other programs should be encouraged in support of their positive mental health. For example, a study pertaining to the mental health of the black aged where no family members were available demonstrated the need for service workers to act as family surrogates, going into clients' homes as if they were close relatives or friends, to help them make use of available community resources and personal relationships (Faulkner, Heisal, and Simms, 1975). Might not this concept be expanded and utilized with other ethnic groups?

In terms of community, the national trend towards urban redevelopment oftentimes creates a weakening of the usual social and cultural supports of many ethnic elders. A primary prevention program was suggested by Gerald Caplan in 1964. It was his contention that advanced planning should be undertaken "to rehouse extended families and friendship groups near each other and if their traditional social, recreational, and religious agencies are also housed nearby . . . to . . . safeguard social ties and permit people to support each other . . ." such planning would avoid unnecessary mental health crises. This is extremely important for ethnic elders who have spent a lifetime in inner-city

communities, such as "Little Tokyo" or "Chinatown".

As stated previously, the church is a major institution in the lives of a large segment of the ethnic aged. Because of this, and because of the aged's tendency to turn to their clergymen with their mental health problems, we should evaluate the feasibility of using these facilities as a base for the delivery of more culturally relevant mental health programs.

In summary, as suggested by Sue (1977), "changes could be made within the existing services, i.e., training of mental health care providers for minority groups and hiring of ethnic specialists to serve as a bridge between ethnic group clients and the institution; use of non-professionals; consumer advocacy; consultation, etc., could be initiated; establishment of independent but parallel services, especially communities where minority groups represent large numbers, and centers that respond to minority communities should be rewarded and encouraged in their efforts." These then are some of the issues which must be considered in the delivery of mental health services to ethnic minority elders.

## IMPLICATIONS FOR RESEARCH, TRAINING, AND PROGRAMS

The issues presented here have yet to be untangled and understood. They are important for enabling us to provide appropriate care and treatment in relieving the personal disturbances and facilitating optimal functioning and well-being among elderly minorities. With the goal of quality care for our elderly—majority and minority alike—the need is great for valid research sensitive to the group being studied.

In June, 1976, the National Institute of Mental Health conducted a national conference on minority research, calling together researchers to identify priority areas for further investigation. Two of the many recommendations were to develop definitions and paradigms sensitive to minorities (rather than the traditional models currently being imposed on minorities) and to develop and test alternate modalities for treating ethnic minorities more effectively.

For example, one of the authors had the experience of working with Mr. M., an older Japanese gentlemen, who, after his wife's death, was admitted to a care home since he had no family to attend to him. He was adjusting quite well, although gradually, to his wife's death by visiting and developing interests in calligraphy, tutoring, and lecturing to students at the local university. However, he did have sporadic depressive events during the holiday season, being alone for the first time without his wife. A white, perhaps overzealous, graduate student had befriended him and provided support during this period. However, when called upon by the care home to help them deal with his garrulousness, she immediately set up an appointment with a psychiatrist without disclosing the nature of this appointment with Mr. M., even after his many queries as to the kind of doctor to whom she was referring him. Regardless of being a graduate of a gerontology masters program, she demonstrated further lack of sensitivity and skill by telling Mr. M. that he was "manic-depressive." It was then that Mr. M. came to the author to verify that, in fact, he was *not* crazy. Such lack of sensitivity of "do-gooders" to those unempowered—usually minority and elderly—can have very real and devastating effects. In this case, the gentleman, who was perfectly capable of handling his own affairs and who had previously not shown signs of maladjustment (other than eccentricity), began to exhibit aberrant behavior. He felt that since the student had befriended him, he must accept (in his words "acquiesce") the verdict she had administered. As he stated, "when someone gives you a gift, you must accept it, even if you don't like it . . .." Although Mr. M. spoke English very well, he was perceiving his world as a Japanese, that is, accept what cannot be changed. He thus unwillingly accepted the misdiagnosis of "crazy," and began to exhibit those behaviors. The consequence was destructive. The home began fearing his behavior, now labeling him as a psychiatric case and pulling all support which had previously been given him and which he needed even more at this time. Thus began the "social breakdown syndrome" (Gruenberg, 1967; Sarbin, 1968), which occurs so often as a result of labeling.

Particularly among English-speaking minority elderly, we must be careful in diagnosis, for their fluency in English may cloud their true feelings and perceptions. Their behaviors must be assessed in light of their meaning for the individual. The consequences of misdiagnosis (and erroneous labeling) are far-reaching. Helping agencies, if they are truly to help, must assess each individual with caution and seek to understand the client's behavior in both his past cultural and current social situation. The complexity of the individual precludes hasty labeling. Regardless of the severity of the crisis he is in, the individual's dignity must never be thwarted.

For those working with minority elderly, concentration on pathology misdirects energy toward finding solutions which are ineffective and short-term. Practitioners must begin to assess the various coping strategies—both positive and negative—as well as the stresses which elicit these coping mechanisms. Research which analyzes this process and its outcomes would be a step toward identifying critical variables in defining and assessing mental health among minority elderly. However, we also should be remiss were we to neglect an intergenerational focus among ethnic minorities, particularly those groups which are our most recent immigrants and for whom the problem of the transmission of culture and traditions is most problematic.

The current status of curricula in aging which address minority concerns is perhaps dampened by the lack of adequate research (Moriwaki, 1978). At best, we have more minority students being recruited for gerontology careers, with one or two special courses related to minority groups. What is needed is a curriculum founded on a solid knowledge base along with practical experience, allowing students to develop more responsive models and to test them in the community. Only then will students learn, but more importantly, apply, the sensitivity, understanding, and skills to effectively guide clients in maintaining their dignity in the process of attaining emotional and mental well-being. Some audiovisual resources that are helpful in understanding the cultural variations in aging are listed in Appendix B.

To accomplish these ends in our future professionals, it must be reemphasized that research should be closely tied to training as well as to service, so that the practitioners can test new theories and modalities developed to benefit the current and future elderly. Current problems in research on the mental health of the ethnic elderly stem from their feelings of mistrust and of being exploited, because the purpose of the research and its benefits are not usually explained (Kalish and Moriwaki, 1973). If results could be tested in demonstration programs serving minority elderly, more cooperation would be forthcoming.

Programs and delivery models to serve the ethnic minority elderly should be encouraged via funding sources for model projects as well as by service providers themselves. Those programs which are found to be successful should be disseminated to schools and training programs to build a knowledge base and to develop those skills most appropriate for serving the ethnic elderly. One such model worth examining more closely for the Japanese elderly is Morita psychotherapy as described by Reynolds and Yamamoto (1973). Based on cultural values of service to one's family and nation as well as familiar activities such as experiential learning, mnemonic phrases, and concrete illustrations, this therapeutic modality has been successful in breaking the "cycle of hypersensitive introspection and social failure" (neurosis). Adapting such modalities, which take into consideration the cultural values of the individual, may prove beneficial in meeting the goal of retaining one's self-worth and, at the same time, adjusting to a majority society with dissimilar values.

Results from various studies (Pacific Asian Elderly Research Project, 1978; Monographs and Technical Report Series, 1978) indicate the viability and importance of the family and informal social networks. Advocacy organizations within the minority communities are another viable resource to develop relevant and ethnic-sensitive programs. A limited list of such organizations is presented in Appendix A. Future exploration of the functions of these informal supports, as well as of the conditions necessary to maintain and utilize these supports, will be crucial in the delivery of services. Agencies should consider developing models, with accompanying policy recommendations, which would utilize these supports in delivering services to the elderly.

In summary, we have much to learn from our ethnic minority elders, and service providers and future professionals must be open to societal and individual variations, as well as to alternative and creative strategies for enhancing the well-being of not only our current, but also our future, elderly.

# APPENDIX A

MINORITY ORGANIZATIONS/RESOURCES (LIMITED SELECTION)

National Center on Black Aged
1730 M Street, N.W., Suite 811
Washington, DC 20020

National Association for Spanish Speaking Elderly
(ASOCIACION NACIONAL PRO
PERSONAS MAYORES)
3875 Wilshire Blvd., Suite 401
Los Angeles, CA 90005

1801 K. Street, N.W., Suite 1021
Washington, DC 20026

National Indian Council on Aging
P.O. Box 2088
Albuquerque, NM 87103

Spanish Speaking Mental Health Research Center
Franz Hall
University of California at Los Angeles (UCLA)
Los Angeles, CA 90024

Pacific/Asian Coalition
1760 The Alameda, Suite 210
San Jose, CA 95126

Asian American Mental Health Research Center
7th Floor, I.I.D.D. Building
1640 West Roosevelt Road
Chicago, Ill. 60608

Center on Aging
San Diego State University
School of Social Work
349 Cedar Street
San Diego, CA 92101

Asian American Community Mental Health Training Center
1300 W. Olympic Blvd., Suite 310
Los Angeles, CA 90015

# APPENDIX B

AUDIO VISUAL RESOURCES (LIMITED SELECTION)

*Asian American:*

1. ON LOK — Where the old keep on growing. Sponsored by Social Rehabilitation Services, DHEW available via: National Audio Visual Center, Sales Branch, Washington, D.C., 20036.

2. SAM
   Producer: Indiana University. Available via: University of California, Extension Media Center, Berkeley, CA 94720.

3. WATARIDORI: Birds of Passage
   Producer: Visual Communications. Asian-American Studies Central, Inc. Available via: Amerasia Bookstore, 338 East 2nd St., Los Angeles, CA 90012.

*Black American:*

1. A MAN NAMED CHARLIE SMITH
   Producer: N. H. Comines
   Available via: (MacMillan) Audio Brandon
   1619 North Cherokee Street
   Los Angeles, CA 90028

2. A WELL SPENT LIFE
   Producer: Les Blank and Skip Gerson
   Available via: Flower Films, 11305 Q-Ranch Road
   Austin, TX 78757

3. FANNIE BELL CHAPMAN: Gospel Singer
   Producer/Distributor: Center for Southern Folklore
   1216 Peabody Avenue, Memphis, Tennessee 38104

4. I'M THE PRETTIEST PIECE IN GREECE
   Producer: Richard Wedler

Available via: North Texas State University Gerontological Film Collection, Main Library, Denton, TEX 76203

5. ME AND STELLA
Producer: Geri Ashur
Available via: Phoenix Films, 470 Park Avenue South, New York, NY 10016

6. NEW WINGS FOR ICARUS
Producer: Luthern Television, Box 14572, St. Louis, MO 63178

7. OLD, BLACK, AND ALIVE!!
Released by: The New Film Co., Inc., 331 Newberry St., Boston MA 02115

8. TAKING CARE OF MOTHER BALDWIN
Producer: Perspective Films
Available via: Viewfinders, P.O. Box 1665, Evanston, IL 60204

9. UNCOMMON IMAGES
Producer: Evelyn Barron
Available via: Filmmaker Library, Inc., 290 West End Avenue, New York NY 10023

10. WITH JUST A LITTLE TRUST
Producer: Teleketics Films (Tony Frangakis)
Available via: Teleketics, Franciscian Communications Center, 1229 South Santee, Los Angeles, CA 90015

*Hispanic:*

1. AGUEDA MARTINEZ
Available via: Educational Media Corp.
2036 Lemoyne Avenue
Los Angeles, CA. 90026

2. MANUEL JIMENEZ — Wood Carver
Producer: Judith Bronowski
Available via: The Works, 1659 — 18th Street, Santa Monica, CA 90404

3. MARIO SANCHEZ: Painter of Memories
Producer: Jack Ofield
Available via: Bowling Green Films, Inc., Box 384-D, Hudson, NY 12534

4. PEDRO LINARES — Folk Artist (Artesano Cartonero)
Producer: Judith Bronowski
Available via: The Works, 1659 — 18th St., Santa Monica, CA 90404

5. SABINA SANCHEZ AND THE ART OF EMBROIDERY
(*Artesana Bordabora*)
Available via: The Works, 1659 — 18th St. Santa Monica, CA 90404

*Native American:*

1. ALICE ELLIOTT
Producer: Extension Media Center, University of California, Berkeley, CA 94720

2. ANNIE AND THE OLD ONE
A Greenhouse Films Production from a book by Miska Miles (Little, Brown & Co.).
Available via: BFA Educational Media, 2211 Michigan Avenue, Santa Monica, CA 90404

3. LEGEND DAYS ARE OVER
Producer: Robert Primes
Paulist Productions, P.O. Box 1057, Pacific Palisades, CA 90272

# REFERENCES

ALLPORT, G. W. 1958. *The Nature of Prejudice.* Garden City, New York: Doubleday.

ALVAREZ, D., AND BEAN, F. D. 1976. The Mexican American family. *In*, C. H. Mindel and R. W. Habenstein (eds.), *Ethnic Families in America: Patterns and Variations*, pp. 271–287. New York: Elsevier Scientific Pub.

ANDERSON, P. 1978. Support services and aged blacks. *Black Aging, 3*(3), pp. 53–59.

ANDRULIS, D. P. 1977. Ethnicity as a variable in the utilization and referral patterns of a comprehensive mental health center. *Journal of Community Psychology, 5,* 231–237.

BELL, D., KASSCHAU, P., AND ZELLMAN, G. 1976. *Delivering services to elderly members of minority groups: A critical review of the literature.* Santa Monica: Rand Corporation.

BENGTSON, V. 1976. Families, support systems and ethnic groups: Patterns of contrast and congruence. Paper presented at The Gerontological Society, New York.

BROWN, T. R., STEIN, K. M., HUANG, K., AND HARRIS, D. E. 1973. Mental illness and the role of mental health facilities in Chinatown. *In*, S. Sue and N. Wagner (eds.), *Asian-Americans: Psychological Perspectives*, pp. 212–231. Ben Lomand,Ca.: Science and Behavior Books.

BUTLER, R. N. 1975. *Why Survive? Being Old in America.* New York: Harper & Row.

BUTLER, R. N., AND LEWIS, M. I. 1977. *Aging and Mental Health: Positive Psychosocial Approaches.* St. Louis: C V. Mosby.

CAPLAN, G. 1964. *Principles of Preventive Psychiatry.* New York: Basic Books.

CARTER, J. H. 1972. Psychiatry, racism, and aging. *Journal of the American Geriatrics Society, 20,* 343–346.

CAUDILL, W., AND LIN, T. 1969. *Mental Health Research in Asia and the Pacific.* Honolulu: East-West Center Press.

COHEN, G. D. 1976. Mental health services and the elderly: Needs and Options. *American Journal of Psychiatry, 133*(1), pp. 65–68.

Commission on Professional and Hospital Activities, 1976. Length of stay in PAS Hospitals, by Diagnosis, United States and Western Region, 1975. Ann Arbor, Michigan: Commission on Professional's and Hospital Activities.

DANIELS, R., AND KITANO, H. H. L. 1970. *American Racism.* Englewood Cliffs, N.J.: Prentice -Hall, Inc.

DAVIE, M. R. 1949. *Negroes in American Society,* N.Y.: McGraw-Hill, p. 439. Quote from J. Fauset.

EDGERTON, R. B., AND KARNO, M. 1971. Mexican-American bilingualism and the perception of mental illness. *Archives of General Psychiatry, 24,* 286–290.

FAULKNER, A. O., HEISAL, M. A., AND SIMMS, P. 1975. Life strengths and life stresses: Explorations in the measurements of the mental health of the black aged. *American Journal of Orthopsychiatry, 45*(1), 102–110.

FINKEL, N. J. 1976. *Mental Illness and Health.* New York: Macmillan.

GIGLIOLI, P. P. 1972. *Language and Social Context.* New York: Penguin.

GOLDEN, H. M. 1976. Black agism. *Social Policy, 7*(3), 40–42.

GRUENBERG, E. M. 1967. The social breakdown syndrome—some origins. *American Journal of Psychiatry, 123*(12), 1481–1489.

HALL, E. T. 1959. *The Silent Language.* Greenwich, Conn.: Fawcett.

HENDRICKS, J., AND HENDRICKS, C. D. 1977. *Aging in Mass Society: Myths and Realities.* Cambridge: Winthrop.

JACKSON, M., AND WOOD, J. L. 1976. *Aging in America: Implication for the Black Aged.* Washington, D.C.: National Council on Aging, Inc.

KAHN, R. L., GOLDFARB, A. I., POLLACK, M., AND PECK, A. 1960. Brief objective measures for determination of mental status of the aged. *American Journal of Psychiatry, 117,* 326–328.

KALISH, R. A., AND MORIWAKI, S. 1973. The world of the elderly Asian American. *Journal of Social Issues, 29*(2), 187–209.

KARNO, M., AND EDGERTON, R. 1969. Perception of mental illness in a Mexican-American community. *Archives of General Psychiatry, 20*(2), 233–238.

KATZ, M., COLE, J., AND LOWERY, H. 1969. Studies of the diagnostic process: the influence of symptom perception, past experience, and ethnic background on diagnostic decisions. *American Journal of Psychiatry, 125*(7), 937–947.

KENDALL, R. E. 1968. An important source of bias affecting ratings made by psychiatrists. *Journal of Psychiatric Research, 6,* 135–141.

KENT, D. P. 1971. The elderly in minority groups: Variant patterns of aging. *Gerontologists, 11* (1), 26–29.

KIEFER, C. W. 1974. *Changing Cultures, Changing Lives: An Ethnographic Study of Three Generations of Japanese Americans.* San Francisco: Jossey-Bass Publishers.

KINZIE, J. D., AND FURUKAWA, E. P. 1974. The Japanese of Hawaii. *In,* W. Tseng, J. F. McDermott and T. W. Maretzski (eds.), *People and Cultures in Hawaii,* pp. 56–64. Honolulu:Department of Psychiatry, University of Hawaii, School of Medicine.

KITANO, H. H. L. 1969. *Japanese Americans: The Evolution of a Subculture.* Englewood Cliffs, N.J.: Prentice-Hall, Inc.

KITANO, H. H. L. 1973. Japanese-American Mental Illness. *In,* Sue S. and N. N. Wagner (eds.), *Asian-Americans Psychological Perspectives,* pp. 181–201. Palo Alto: Science & Behavior Books.

KITANO, H. L., AND KIKUMURA, A. 1976. The Japanese American family. *In,* C. H. Mindel and R. W. Habenstein (eds.), *Ethnic Families in America: Patterns and Variations,* pp. 41–59. New York: Elsevier Scientific Pub.

KRAMER, J. R. 1970. *The American Minority Community.* New York: Thomas Y. Crowell.

LYND, H. M. 1958. *On Shame and the Search For Identity.* New York: Harcourt, Brace & World.

MALDONADO, D. JR. 1975. The Chicano Aged. *Social Work, 20* (8), 213–216.

MARETZKI, T. W. 1974. Culture and the individual. *In,* W. Tseng, J. F. McDermott, and T. W. Maretzki (eds.), *People and Cultures of Hawaii,* pp. 1–7. Honolulu: Department of Psychiatry, University of Hawaii, School of Medicine.

MARTIN, L. E. 1970. *Mental Health/Mental Illness: Revolution in progress.* San Francisco: McGraw-Hill.

MARX, J. H., RIEKER, P., AND ELLISON, D. L. 1974. The sociology of community mental health: Historical and methodological perspectives. *In,* P. M Roman and H. M. Trice (eds.), *Sociological Perspectives on Community Mental Health,* pp. 9–39. Philadelphia: Davis.

MAYKOVICH, M. K. 1972. *Japanese American Identity Dilemma.* Tokyo: Waseda University Press.

MINDEL, C. H., AND HABENSTEIN, R. W. 1976. *Ethnic Families in America.* New York: Elsevier Scientific Pub.

Monographs and Technical Report Series. 1978. *A Cross-Cultural Study on Minority Elders in San Diego.* Grant number AoA 90-A-317. San Diego: The Campanile Press.

MOORE, J. W. 1971. Situational factors affecting minority aging. *The Gerontologists, 11,*(1), 88–93.

MORIWAKI, S. 1978. Minority curriculum: disappointing. *Generations,* Summer, 29–30.

MORIWAKI, S. Y. 1976. Ethnicity and aging. *In,* I. M. Burnside (ed.), *Nursing and the Aged,* pp. 543–558. New York: McGraw-Hill.

NEWQUIST, D. 1977. Interview with Carnella Barnes, A WGS Pioneer. *Generations, 2*(2), 18–19.

*Pacific Asian Elderly Research Project. Final Report.* 1978. Los Angeles: Special Service for Groups, Inc.

PADILLA, A. M., RUIZ, R. A., AND ALVAREZ, R. 1975. Delivery of community mental health services to the Spanish-speaking/surnamed population. *American Psychologist, 30*, 892–905.

PADILLA, A., CARLOS, M. L., AND KEEFE, S. 1976. Mental health service utilization by Mexican-Americans. *In*, M. Mirranda (ed.), *Psychotherapy with the Spanish-Speaking: Issues in Research and Service Delivery*, pp. 9–20. Los Angeles: Spanish Speaking Mental Health Research Center.

PATTERSON, R. D. 1976. Services for the aged in community mental health centers. *American Journal of Psychiatry, 133*(3), 271–273.

PLUMPP, S. 1972. *Black Rituals*, Chicago: Third World Press.

PHILLIPUS, M. J. 1971. Successful and unsuccessful approaches to mental health services for an urban Hispano-American population. *Journal of Public Health, 61*(4), 820–830.

PONCE, D. E. 1974. The Filipinos of Hawaii. *In, W. Tseng, J. F. McDermott, and T. W. Maretzski (eds.), People and Cultures in Hawaii*, pp. 34–43. Honolulu: Department of Psychiatry, University of Hawaii, School of Medicine.

PRICE, J. A. 1976. North American Indian Families. *In*, C. H. Mindel and R. W. Habenstein (eds.), *Ethnic Families in America: Patterns and Variations*, pp. 248–269. New York: Elsevier Scientific Publishing Company, Inc.

REYNOLDS, D. K., AND YAMAMOTO, J. 1973. Morita psychotherapy in Japan. *Current Psychiatric Therapies, XIII*, 219–227, Jules H. Masserman (ed.).

ROSE, P. I. 1964. *They & We*. New York: Random House, Inc.

SANBORN, K. O., AND KATZ, M. 1977. *Hawaii Normal Adjustment Study*. Unpublished report, Institute of Behavioral Sciences, Honolulu, Hawaii.

SARBIN, T. R. 1968. Notes on the transformation of social identity. *In*, L. M. Roberts, N. S. Greenfield, M. H. Miller (eds.), *Comprehensive Mental Health: The Challenge of Evaluation*, pp. 97–115. Madison: University of Wisconsin Press.

SATA, L. S. 1973. Musings of a hyphenated American. *In*, S. Sue and N. N. Wagner (eds.), *Asian-Americans: Psychological Perspectives*, pp. 150–156. Palo Alto, California: Science and Behavior, Inc.

SIMPSON, G. E., AND YINGER, J. M. 1965. *Racial and Cultural Minorities*. New York: Harper & Row.

SOLOMON, B. B. 1976. *Black Empowerment: Social Work In Oppressed Communities*. New York: Columbia University Press.

SOLOMON, B. 1970. "Ethnicity, Mental Health and the Older Black Aged," *Ethnicity, Mental Health and Aging*. Summary of Proceedings of a 2-day workshop, Los Angeles: The Gerontology Center, University of Southern California.

SOLOMON, B. 1972. Social and protective services. *Community Services and the Black Elderly*, Richard H. Davis (ed.), Monograph, pp. 1–11. Ethel Percy Andrus Gerontology Center, University of Southern California.

SOLOMON, B. 1977. Better planning through research. Paper presented at Fourth National Institute on Minority Aging, Center on Aging, California State University at San Diego.

SOTOMAYOR, M. 1977. Language, cultures, and ethnicity in developing self-concept. *Social Casework, 58*, 195–203.

STOLLER, A. 1969. Parameters of mental illness and mental health: A public health approach. *In*, W. Caudill and T. Lin (eds.), *Mental Health Research in Asia and the Pacific*, pp. 3–20. Honolulu: East-West Center Press.

SUE, S. 1977. Community mental health services to minority groups: Some optimism, some pessimism. *American Psychologist*, 616–623.

SUE, S., AND MCKINNEY, H. 1975. Asian-Americans in the community mental health care system. *American Journal of Orthopsychiatry, 45*(1), 111–118.

SWANSON, W. C., AND HARTER, C. L. 1971. How do elderly blacks cope in New Orleans? *Aging and Human Development, 2*, pp. 210–216.

TSENG, W., AND CHAR, W. F. 1974. *In*, W. Tseng, J. F. McDermott and T. W. Maretzski (eds.), *The Chinese of Hawaii, People and Cultures in Hawaii*, pp. 24–33. Honolulu: Department of Psychiatry, University of Hawaii, School of Medicine.

TSENG, W., MCDERMOTT, J. F. and MARETZSKI, T. W. (eds.), 1974. *People and Cultures in Hawaii*, Honolulu: University of Hawaii, School of Medicine.

TRINIDAD, L. L., 1977. The Spanish-Speaking Elderly. *In*, B. L. Newsome (ed.), *Insights on the Minority Elderly*, pp. 30–32. Washington, D. C.: National Center on Black Aged, Inc. and University of the District of Columbia.

WEAVER, J. L., 1976. *National Health Policy and the Underserved: Ethnic Minorities, Women and the Elderly*. Saint Louis: C. V. Mosby Co.

WIRTH, L. 1945. The problem of minority groups. *In*, R. Linton (ed.), *The Science of Man in the World Crisis*, pp. 347–372, New York: Columbia University Press.

WOLKON, G. H., AND MORIWAKI, S. Y., 1973. Race and social class factors in the orientation toward psychotherapy. *Journal of Counseling Psychology, 20*(4), 312–316.

YAMAMOTO, J. JAMES, Q. C., AND PALLEY, N. 1968. Cultural problems in psychiatric therapy. *Archives of General Psychiatry, 19* (1), 45–49.

# 20

# The Residential Environment and
# Its Impact on the
# Mental Health of the Aged

*Stanislav V. Kasl & Sarah Rosenfield*

Our task is to review the relevant evidence so that we may describe the causal influences of the "independent" variable, the residential environment, on the "dependent" variable, mental health of the elderly. We will also consider additional evidence which would enable us to better characterize the intervening processes and modifying variables, and which would thereby make the presumed causal influences more intelligible.

The task is difficult because of a number of fundamental problems which get eagerly sucked into the vortex-created vacuum as one begins to stir up the many ideas, formulations, and studies. The most troublesome issue concerns the *conceptualization and measurement of the environmental variables*. In many of the studies, it is difficult to establish what the "independent" variable actually is, particularly when one is trying to separate the

physical parameters of the residential environment from the primarily psychological and experiential aspects. But this difficulty is itself a part of a secondary, larger controversy (e.g., Stokols, 1978) regarding whether or not such a separation is possible or useful, and how our theory or metatheory should deal with it, and which component should be the more prominent one. Moreover, the very phrase "residential environment" becomes so elusive that it fails to convey any information about the boundaries of this review or its most appropriate structure and organization. The second problem, of course, concerns the *conceptualization and measurement* of the "dependent" variable, *mental health*. The studies reviewed easily reveal the many problems which plague this domain of social science research: (a) lack of consensus on concepts, definitions, and boundaries, and (b) a plethora of measures which cover highly disparate content and which are often inadequate from the psychometric, test-construction viewpoint. These two fundamental issues will be discussed at greater length in the next two sections of this chapter.

There are two additional problems found in this research literature, but they are less overwhelming and more typical of many other domains of social research; they both deal with limitations and gaps in our knowledge. One stems from the fact that many of the studies do not concern themselves with possible *intervening processes* and thus their results fail to illuminate the probable links in the presumed causal chain. Outcomes are frequently linked to residential factors by interpretive speculations or theories formulated after the results are obtained, and few studies specifically set out to test a priori notions about possible intervening processes. A reviewer is thus forced to fall back on less direct evidence, that is, on results of other studies which do not deal with residential factors but appear to document relevant links, such as between level of social interaction and aspects of mental health. The second problem stems from the fact that just about all of the studies to be reviewed are based on various *quasi-experimental designs*, in Campbell's terminology (Cook and Campbell, 1976), and do not represent true experiments in field settings. This naturally limits the permissible causal inferences which can be drawn, sometimes quite severely, such as when cross-sectional comparisons of contrasting residential settings are involved. A related limitation is that the majority of such field studies represent opportunistic research on elderly subjects, where the access to them was made available through one agency or another which is involved in dealing with some social-residential problem: institutionalization and institutional transfer, urban renewal and relocation, opening up of federal housing for elderly, and so on. The consequence of this quite understandable research opportunism is a sporadic and spotty accumulation of scientific knowledge. For example, much more information is available on apartment dwelling urban elderly coming to the attention of some social agency, than on rural elderly or elderly homeowners; representative samples of elderly seen in their original residential setting and followed through as they make their residential moves are a rare exception (e.g., Schooler, 1969a, and 1976). Such research opportunism also means that the investigator does not study a well defined and circumscribed "independent" residential variable of his choosing, but a broad social-residential experience with uncertain components and boundaries. Agency selection practices and nu-

merous self-selection factors contribute to the inability to be precise about just what exactly was studied and on what specific subgroup of the elderly.

## IMPRESSIONS FROM RECENT REVIEWS

The published literature contains several recent reviews on the impact of housing and living environment on the aged, written by distinguished investigators in this field (Carp, 1976a; Lawton, 1977; Lawton and Nahemow, 1973). It is appropriate that the present chapter build on the contribution of these reviews and that it avoid duplication of coverage or redundancy in organization and perspective. However, since two of the reviews are quite recent, it is not possible to take these reviews as given and simply accept the task as one of updating the literature.

The Carp and Lawton reviews are an excellent entrée into the whole literature on the residential environment of the aged, and they give the reader a good grasp of the major themes and concerns, the major findings and their limitations. It seems to us, first of all, that there is obvious consensus that the effects of the residential environment (that is, defined in physical terms and encompassing housing and neighborhood parameters, including services and facilities) cannot be understood in isolation, but must be seen in complex interaction with the characteristics of the individual and the characteristics of his/her social environment. This consensus at the metatheoretical level has led to some convergence regarding needed theoretical formulations in this field. These formulations go under different labels—person-environment congruence, adaptation theory, stress theory—but they all deal with the relationship of environmental demands and resources to the needs and competencies of the aged individual. However, it seems to us that there is much less consensus on how to translate this metatheoretical orientation into effective research designs, or what specific dimensions of the environment and of the person one needs to study. Furthermore, there is no particular agreement on what should be optimally encompassed by the notions of "residential environment" or "living environment." The distinction between physical and social environmental dimensions tends to be blurred, both conceptually, in the formulations of many investigators, and operationally, in specific studies of the impact of some environmental event or condition.

The Carp and Lawton reviews give also a good indication of the major types of studies which have been carried out: (a) impact of new housing

or planned housing, and of various aspects of this, such as structural characteristics, location, and services; (b) impact of institutionalization and institutional environments; (c) consequences of relocation or involuntary residential moves; (d) impact of special residential settings, particularly retirement communities. Among social-environmental variables most frequently included in such studies are the presence of age peers, and the presence of (or distance to) friends and family. The most popular impact criteria are social-leisure activities or interactions, and various aspects of satisfaction (residential, life); indices of physical and mental health and of "adjustment" represent the bulk of the remainder of impact criteria.

The reviews also reveal some of the significant limitations in our knowledge. For example, it would seem that too much work is based on studies of special populations, such as recent inmovers to public housing for which they met some agency criteria and which they in some sense chose or preferred. Our feeling is that needed studies include: (a) prospective studies of individuals experiencing various social-residential events (institutionalization, moves from private homes to apartments, geographically distant moves to retirement communities, and so on), which are sufficiently long-range prior to the event as well as in follow-up, so that one has a better handle on the biases due to self-selection and selective attrition, and so that one can document both short-term and long-term impact; (b) impact of lack of residential mobility on those who wish to move but cannot; (c) studies of the adaptive process to misfit between residential preferences and needs and actual residential characteristics, including the role of changed aspirations; (d) the interactive effects of residential changes with other "life events" including retirement, widowhood, reduced income, and increased disability.

## THE SCOPE AND OBJECTIVES OF PRESENT REVIEW

The above comments represent our impressions of the Carp and Lawton reviews and of the literature which they bring together. The present chapter builds on these two reviews and is distinct from them in the sense that it represents a narrowing down of focus, a more detailed examination of a narrower range of issues. On the independent variable side, we shall be concerned with environmental dimensions, or residential events and experiences, which link up, directly or indirectly, with *physical properties of the environment;* environmental variables which are only "in the head" (Wohlwill, 1973) or which represent purely the social environment will not be viewed as relevant. For example, a study which relates reports of having a "confidante" to life satisfaction is deemed outside of the scope of the review, but a study showing that the presence of a confidante buffers the adverse effects of a forced residential move is seen as eminently relevant. On the dependent variable side, the focal concern is with mental health, albeit very broadly defined; studies of environmental cognitions, esthetic preferences, housing values, and so on, as pure outcome variables will not be reviewed, although studies in which the selfsame variables act as intervening or modifying influences will be included, if they exist. Purely descriptive survey data on various representative national or community samples of elderly will also be omitted as long as they only deal with the living conditions of the elderly but not their mental health, or only with giving an epidemiological profile of their mental health, but not dealing with residential variables.

In general, it is assumed that the primary audience for this chapter are scholars and investigators who have an interest in the elderly, in residential environments, and in determinants of mental health. Planners with similar interests will find the chapter less relevant to them and are expected to refer to other publications (e.g., Gelwicks and Newcomer, 1974; Lawton, 1975; Lawton, Newcomer, and Byerts, 1976; Newman, 1972; Schwartz, 1975) which address their concerns more directly and explicitly. The reader will find that the chapter does not shy away from methodological critique, and that it deals heavily with issues of evidence and permissible inferences from it. Whether or not the evidence supports a particular theory or a particular current practice among architects and planners will be of much lesser concern.

## CONCEPTUALIZATION AND MEASUREMENT OF THE RESIDENTIAL ENVIRONMENT

In *Slums and Social Insecurity,* Schorr (1963) painted a broad picture of the presumed adverse effects of poor housing and "slum" neighborhood settings on physical and mental health of the residents, including assertions about effects on self-perceptions, pessimism, and passivity. At about the same time, Wilner published the results of his classical study of improved housing (Wilner, Walkley, Pinkerton, and Tayback, 1962). The findings revealed minimal benefits of improved housing on mental health (mood, nervousness, general morale, self-esteem, general anxiety), on aspirations, and on various self-promotive activities. However, Wilner has been criticized (e.g., Pynoos, Schafer, and Hartman, 1973) for using a much too limited a notion of housing (heat and plumbing, more dwelling space, structural safety, modernity) and for not attempting "to improve other dimensions of the housing services bundle, such as the social environment, status, and location" (p. 132).

The above captures the essence of the *dilemma* and of the *controversy* regarding the effects of residential environment on mental health: (a) the apparent cultural bias toward ecological determinism, that is, the a priori belief that the physical-residential environment influences mental health and behavior (e.g., also Gilbertson and Mood, 1964; Rosow, 1961); (b) the empirical evidence, which falls considerably short of such beliefs (e.g., Hinkle and Loring, 1977; Kasl, 1976); and (c) the broadening of the concept of residential environment to include a whole array of psycho-social dimensions, and thereby sidestep the issue of negative evidence, since it now pertains to an "inappropriately" narrow conception of the residential environment.

The broad view of housing is perhaps best seen in The Report of the President's Committee on Urban Housing (1969). There, the position is taken that "The most successful programs for bettering housing conditions and economic opportunities cannot, in themselves, produce better environments. Good neighbors are vital for preserving good neighborhoods" (p.2). However, since it is also asserted that "decent housing is essential in helping lower-income families help themselves achieve self-fulfillment in a free and democratic society" (p.3), one can discern the underlying metatheory: poor housing is an obstacle, but remedying poor housing is not enough.

There are a number of possible disadvantages to broadening the concept of the residential environment to include, beyond the physical parameters, the psycho-social dimensions as well. When the two become inextricably mixed, we can no longer tell how the two sets of dimensions interact with each other or, even, whether the observed impact in fact may not be due solely to the social dimensions, and the physical parameters have no impact, neither independent or interactive. Furthermore, interventions in the psychosocial environment may be much more difficult to implement than those in the physical-residential environment, but with data on impact coming from studies using a very broad operational definition of residential environment, the design-oriented planner or architect may not be able to infer what the called-for modifications of the physical parameters are, if any.

In short, just because it is agreed that the impact of the physical parameters of the residential setting must be studied in a rich network of psycho-social-environmental variables, this does not mean that the operational definition of the residential environment should inextricably confound the physical and psychosocial components. A reading of the literature on residential environments (e.g., Gutman, 1972; Hinkle and Loring, 1977; Kasl, 1976; Michelson, 1976) suggests that there are probably two major ways in which *physical and psychosocial parameters may interact*: (1) the effect of a particular physical residential parameter is distinct for different subgroups of residents (whether they are defined in socio-demographic and life cycle terms, or along various dimensions of needs and aspirations); and (2) the effect of a particular physical residential parameter is dependent on how the resident responds to it (cognitively, behaviorally) and the way it is used. However, both of these interactions call for a clear separation, at the operational level, of the physical and psychosocial parameters.

It is likely that in many studies the use of an independent residential variable which confounds the physical and the psychosocial parameters is inadvertent rather than intentional. However, it poses problems of interpretation nonetheless. Consider, for example, the well-known study of Victoria Plaza (Carp, 1966) which appeared to demonstrate striking benefits of improved housing on the elderly—benefits that seem to last up to 8 years of followup (Carp, 1975b, 1975c, 1975d, 1977). In this study, the impact of new housing is inferred from differential outcomes for applicants who became tenants, compared to applicants who were rejected. There are two primary issues to consider: (1) The reasons for desiring to move which included, aside from search for better housing: cheaper rent; better location; companionship; and interpersonal stress. (2) Differences between successful and unsuccessful applicants which revealed (on self-report and interviewers' ratings) the future tenants to be: more alert; with better memory; with stronger interest in "mental stimulation," in personal contacts, and in group activities; less antisocial, "eccentric," bitter, complaining, fussy, fault-finding, moody, irritable. Interestingly, future tenants were also rated as higher on "negative talk about the past."

The above data suggest that there were a substantial number of successful applicants who, on the one hand, were dissatisfied with the purely social and interpersonal aspects of their living conditions and who, on the other hand, were particularly alert, active, socially outgoing, and in possession of many socially desirable interpersonal traits. It is a very plausible alternate hypothesis that the benefits they derived from the move depended on improvements in their inadequate social conditions (e.g., reduced social isolation or interpersonal stress) and that the concomitant improvements in the physical parameters of their residential environment were irrelevant and without impact. There are other alternate hypotheses which could explain the differential outcomes but which do not implicate the physical aspects of housing: (a) The selection-screening process separated the total pool of applicants into two unlike groups who were going to have differential outcomes in the mental health-life satisfaction domain even if none of them moved to Victoria Plaza; (b) the poorer outcomes of the unsuccessful applicants reflect a general impact of blocked goals and aspirations, of frustration and failure at not being able to implement important life plans.

Other reservations about the striking benefits of moving to Victoria Plaza have been expressed. For example, Riley and Foner (1968) suggest that the observed benefits could also have been due to "a situation that involved a group of older people encountering common problems of adapting to a new environment at the same time" (p. 142). Lawton (1977) has suggested that issues of cognitive dissonance reduction and desire to please the interviewer and the administrator could have biased the results. In view of the long term benefits noted (Carp, 1975b, 1975c, 1975d, 1977), these criticisms appear less relevant than when applied to the original one year follow-up (Carp, 1966). Carp (1976a) herself has some reservations about the results, but they concern primarily the issue of generalizability, i.e., that the study dealt with a select population in special circumstances. However, she does not seem to question the basic impact of the physical-residential environmental change. (The Victoria Plaza findings will be described in greater detail in a later section of this chapter.)

The above discussion is meant to illustrate the *difficulty of conceptualizing, analyzing into components, and properly attributing the impact of a particular residential experience.* Voluntary moves by people with a wide range of choices may be particularly ambiguous regarding interpretation of impact. For example, housing moves to the suburbs are accompanied by changes which are best interpreted as "intended" changes, i.e. the reasons for which the move was made in the first place (e.g., Gans, 1963 and 1967): increased satisfaction with housing (especially with amount of space), increased social life,

and so on. Gans has summarized the findings as follows: "In short, the community itself does not shape people's ways of life as significantly as has been proposed by ecological and planning theory. The major behavior patterns are determined rather by the period of the life cycle, and the opportunities and aspirations associated with class position" (Gans, 1963, p. 193). Thus while the life satisfaction and social activities of people living in the suburbs may be different, this appears to be primarily due to self-selection. But does this mean that the physical-residential environment has no impact? Perhaps the best way to conceptualize this situation is to see the role of the residential environment as a facilitator: it permits certain outcomes to take place but does not initiate or stimulate them. (By analogy: medical schools may have no impact on choosing medicine as career, but they still have something to do with becoming a doctor.) Thus, for example, working class individuals do not adopt middle class life styles after moving to the suburbs (Berger, 1960). This conceptualization suggests that we should turn our attention more on the interplay of current set of residential factors, goals and aspirations to change these, and inability to make a residential move. Studies of desire to move among those who don't move are not common (e.g., Drettboom, McAllister, Kaiser, and Butler, 1971; Kasl and Harburg, 1972; Schooler, 1975) and the link of such desires to mental health may be quite tenuous (Kasl and Harburg, 1975).

Many investigators within the broad field of environmental psychology conceptualize and study purely psychological or psycho-social environments (Stokols, 1978). There is, of course, nothing wrong with this and it would be surprising if it were otherwise. On the other hand, we should not be misled into thinking that their results establish any kind of a link to the physical parameters of the residential environment. This is especially true if these investigators deal with respondent's cognitions and perceptions of the psycho-social environment rather than with "objective," independent assessments (e.g., as determined by the investigator, as obtained from significant others, etc.). For example, Esser (1973) discusses crowding as the subjective experience of not being able "to have one's way," as a failure to "complete the man-environment transaction in which the subject is engaged." Altman (1975) and Margulis (1977) define privacy in terms of control over access to the self or control over the transactions between the person and others. However, the problem is, as Archea (1977) points out, that the environment thus conceived has "no existential status independent of the uses to which it is put" and linking it to the various arrangements of the physical environment becomes extremely difficult.

Conceptualizations of institutional environments, especially of "institutional totality" (Bennett, 1963; Bennett and Nahemow, 1965a; Goffman, 1961) similarly tend to be heavily psychosocial; conceptual emphasis is on scheduling of activities, standardization of rewards and punishments, decision-making about use of personal property, and so on. Such an approach tends to miss the opportunity of investigating the interplay between the purely psycho-social and organizational variables and the physical-residential parameters of the institution; for example, to what extent can the impact of certain aspects of regimentation of institutional life be modified by various physical arrangements of living conditions? Similarly, the recent studies on experimental manipulation of perceived choice, control, responsibility, and predictability among institutionalized aged (Langer and Rodin, 1976; Schulz, 1976) represent purely psycho-social interventions and one would like to know something about the environmental specificity-generality of such findings.

*Dimensionalizing the residential environment* and/or developing an *adequate taxonomy* has always been a difficult problem. At present there is no empirical approach or conceptual schema which would give us a definitive classification, useful for a variety of purposes. To be sure, certain distinctions are fairly obvious and well entrenched. For example: dwelling vs. neighborhood; types of dwelling, such as single family, high-rise apartment, etc.; by various structural and spatial characteristics of the dwelling unit; by services and resources available in the neighborhood; by social characteristics of neighborhood. Dimensions and classifications have been developed on the basis of environmental cognitions, residential preferences, sources or areas of satisfaction-dissatisfaction, and violations of building codes or public health codes. Theoretical approaches, such as the person-environment congruence model (Kahana, 1974), have also generated ways of dimensionalizing the environment. However, none of these approaches can as yet make any exclusive claims on our attention. Kahana's formulation, though very elaborate, is in fact tied to the institutional setting, deals only with psychosocial dimensions, involves horrendous problems of operationalization, and includes various ad hoc "environmental" dimensions formulated only because the theory demands that for every dimension of the person there be a parallel environmental dimension.

Perhaps the most ambitious and best thought-through classification schema of properties of the built environment, relevant to social behavior, has been developed by Geddes and Gutman (1977). This classification schema consists of 48 categories of environments, based on the conjunction of six levels of environmental scale and eight "properties" of environments. The six levels are: building, site plan, neighborhood layout, local community, region, and macro-region. The eight environmental properties are: spatial organization, circulation and movement systems, communication systems, ambient properties, visual properties, amenities, symbolic properties, and architectonic properties. The authors also offer a very useful discussion of the desiderata or requirements of an environmental classification, given from the perspective of the planner or builder concerned with the impact of the built environment on health and behavior.

One particularly troublesome way of generating environmental dimensions is that which is used in certain *"urban ecology"* studies and which depends on aggregating individual characteristics over some geographical unit, such as census tract. When such a study goes on to run *ecological correlations* between aggregated data on various indices of "social disorganization" (crowding, percent unemployed, percent female head of household, juvenile delinquency and adult crime rates, fire calls, etc.) and rates of various pathologies (usually based on agency records or treatment data), we get impressive associations which fail to illuminate anything about environmental factors in the etiology of such pathologies (e.g., Dunham, 1966; Weinberg, 1967). Aside from the methodological criticism known as the ecological fallacy (Robinson, 1950), and the issue of disentangling the influence of highly correlated variables, the main question here is: does aggregating individual data create thereby an ecological or environmental variable which impacts on the outcome? For example, does the ecological correlation between percent divorced and psychiatric treatment rates represent simply a summary shorthand for the association between the individual characteristics of being divorced and being in treatment, and would it show up if we aggregate over any unit of analysis, however silly? Or does it mean that living in neighborhood areas with many divorced people impairs one's mental health? Ecological correlations cannot answer this and many ecological studies of so called community conditions (e.g., Gruenberg, 1954) probably reflect no more than the impact of aggregated individual characteristics. However, there is a perfectly good use of such aggregate data, but the analysis has to be done on individuals. This is the approach used in studies investigating the so-called "social fit" or "social homogeneity" hypothesis (e.g., Wechsler and Pugh, 1967): persons with a certain social characteristic, living in an area where the characteristic is less common, will have higher rates of pathology than people with the numerically dominant social characteristic. For example, Rosenberg (1968) found that the greatest isolation from friends was experienced by older, poor men whose socio-demographic or racial characteristics were different from the dominant characteristics of the local residents of the neighborhood.

This section of the chapter has discussed a number of issues pertaining to the general topic of conceptualization and measurement of the residential environment. Some of the issues, such as dimensionalizing the residential environment, are somewhat less relevant to the actual evidence to be reviewed later, since so many of the studies deal with the impact of a global residential experience, which is difficult to define precisely and from which the separate effects of individual parameters certainly cannot be isolated.

## CONCEPTUALIZATION AND MEASUREMENT OF MENTAL HEALTH

Since the whole handbook deals with mental health, this chapter on the residential environment is not the proper place for a detailed discussion of the many relevant issues here. The comments which follow are thus restricted to that part of our thinking on this topic which will make the remainder of the review more intelligible. In general, we feel that the recent searching examinations of the issue of conceptual definition and measurement of mental health and mental illness (Clausen, 1969; Dohrenwend, 1973; Dohrenwend, Dohrenwend, and Cook, 1973; French and Kahn, 1962; Jahoda, 1958; Scott, 1958; Sells, 1969; Smith, 1961; Spitzer and Wilson, 1975; Srole, 1975) have failed to provide theoretical or methodological convergence of opinion—except to emphasize the necessity for multiple definitions and multiple measurement. Indeed, it is quite clear that any single measure which might be chosen (such as hospitalization in a mental institution or a psychiatrist's rating) is always going to be too narrow and too broad; too narrow because it will not reflect all of the underlying dimensions which have been proposed as indicative of mental health, and too broad because it will be "contaminated" by other influences as well —reporting biases in questionnaire measures, readiness for self-referral in treatment-based indices, and so on.

The large set of possible criteria of mental health can be grouped as follows: (a) indices based on treatment; (b) psychiatric signs and symptoms, indices of "impairment" or "caseness", psychiatric diagnoses; (c) indicators of moods and affects, of well-being and distress, satisfaction indicators; (d) indices of functional effectiveness and role performance; and (e) indices derived from notions of "positive mental health" (e.g., growth and self-actualization, adequacy of coping, etc.).

This grouping of mental health criteria does not represent any kind of a theory, though collectively they may be viewed as representing a working definition of mental health. The categories represent different viewpoints or approaches: societal, social-psychological, intrapersonal, transactional (mental health as interaction between the person and his environment), and clinical. No one category is meant to stand by itself or to have a preeminent status. Furthermore, the categories should not be seen as additive, with some kind of a summary index averaging all the components. Instead, the components are better treated in a profile approach, with a person characterized by a pattern of high and low scores on the various indices.

One of the more troublesome concepts within the field of mental health of the aged has been the notion of "adjustment." Some investigators use it very broadly, as synonymous with mental health; others use it very narrowly, equivalent to meeting specific demands of the environment, mostly institutional demands; still others, particularly those with a sociological orientation, conceive of adjustment as an index of functional effectiveness. But some authors (e.g., Rosow, 1963) have argued that adjustment among the aged is difficult to conceptualize and measure since there are, in their view, no clear roles and expectations for the aged. In point of fact, however, there are always individuals on whom role performance or functional effectiveness in certain roles cannot be assessed (e.g., work role among students, parental role among the childless, spouse role among the widowed) and the aged are not unique. Moreover, adjustment thus conceived is not the sole or preeminent indicator of mental health, just one of many, and we are not prevented from assessing most of the other aspects of mental health of the aged. Thus the suggestion that adjustment measures among the elderly must primarily reflect the continuity of life patterns (Rosow, 1963) needs to be rejected as too idiosyncratic and narrow. On the other hand, there is good reason to believe (Bortner and Hultsch, 1970; Thurnher, 1974) that measures which reflect opportunities to select goals and access to means for achieving goals will be particularly sensitive indicators of adjustment and well-being among the elderly.

Certain recent developments within the field of social indicators and the emphasis on perceived life quality and subjective measures of well-being (Andrews and Withey, 1974; Brenner, 1975; Campbell, Converse, and Rodgers, 1976; Mann, 1977; Sheldon and Parke, 1975) have exerted further pressure on enlarging the scope of "mental health and well-being" to include evaluative perceptions of the environment and some very general and very subjective measures of happiness and well-being. We shall include these variables as legitimate impact criteria without committing ourselves to the notion that these additional variables should also be viewed as indicators of mental health. However, this non-commital attitude should not prevent us from examining the behavioral meaning (validity) of these various perceptual, attitudinal and evaluative variables.

It is not as easy to sidestep methodological concerns regarding many of these measures. For example, Riemer (1951) long ago pointed to a number of limitations of the various measures of housing preferences and satisfactions: (a) Housing attitudes are related to the housing conditions with which the respondent is familiar and/or to the conditions to which he aspires; (b) Preferences are not absolute or permanent; (c) As some needs are satisfied, other needs become paramount; (d) Housing attitudes are not based on full information; (e) Housing attitudes and satisfactions are more volatile after rehousing. Similarly, Rainwater (1966) has noted that for slum residents, satisfactions and dissatisfactions center on basic concerns with safety and space while for working class individuals, their satisfactions and dissatisfactions center on creating a pleasant, cozy, convenient home environment and on living in a "respectable" neighborhood.

Investigators working with the elderly have noted that residents' perceptions and evaluations of their living environments tend to show poor agreement with observers' ratings and that, on the whole, the elderly residents are considerably more optimistic (Carp, 1975a; Pincus and Wood, 1970). The finding that elderly persons selected to move to better housing become more negative in their evaluations of current housing, while applicants not so selected don't change (Carp, 1975a), has been interpreted in terms of cognitive dissonance reduction. However, an equally compelling interpretation is in terms of raised level of aspiration among those selected. The recent volume on *The Quality of American Life* (Campbell et al., 1976) rep-

resents one of the most detailed explorations of the relation of housing satisfaction to levels of aspiration, expectation, and adaptation and reveals much about the general dynamics of satisfaction measures. The study shows that as subjects get older, the distance between present living conditions and either those aspired to or those expected five years hence, gets smaller; that is, aspirations and expectations go down with age. Of course, none of these analyses can reveal to us whether or not these levels of aspirations are influenced by defensive maneuvers (either conscious or unconscious distortion), or what the mental health penalty of such defensive maneuvers might be.

Even though in this section we have adopted a very broad, eclectic approach to mental health and well-being, the actual studies to be reviewed in the next sections are typically much narrower in their assessments of mental health. The kind of careful and detailed measurement of mental health found in good community studies (e.g., Dohrenwend, 1973; Srole, 1975; Srole, Langner, Michael, Opler, and Rennie, 1962) is simply not in evidence; moreover, morale and satisfaction type of measures tend to dominate, while symptom-based indicators are much less common.

Before turning to the actual review of the various studies, we wish to remind the reader that it is necessary to see the residential environment as only one of several influences on the mental health and well-being of the elderly, and that this influence does not appear to be the major one. For example, in the national survey done by Campbell et al. (1976), the frequencies of the respondents' ratings of various domains as "extremely important" were as follows: a happy marriage, 74 percent; being in good health, 70 percent; a good family life, 67 percent; a house/apartment that you like to live in, 35 percent. Similarly, data from several national surveys of hopes and fears of U. S. adults (Cantril and Roll, 1971) reveal housing-residential issues to be infrequently mentioned. Specific examinations of the various influences on overall well-being and happiness (Campbell et al., 1976; Wessman, 1956; Wilson, 1967) reveal family life and spare-time activities to be the most important ones. In a characteristic viewpoint, Donahue and Ashley (1965) list the following influences on good adjustment of the elderly: health and personal security, independent action, social experience and group membership, and useful activity. Since the residential environment is not included in the list, it would follow from this viewpoint that its impact, if any, must be through its effects on these primary influences. That, in a nutshell, is the most common theoretical framework (explicit or implicit) of the studies to be reviewed.

## EFFECTS OF VOLUNTARY RESIDENTIAL MOVES

If we are seeking to describe the *benefits of improved housing* on the mental health of the elderly, then the most compelling evidence should be available to us from studies possessing the following characteristics: (a) a prospective, before-after design; (b) the improvement is substantial rather than small (see Glazer, 1967); (c) self-selection factors are minimal; (d) social uprooting and social change effects are minimal; (e) case-control comparisons involve a contrast only on the desired housing factors. In actuality, it is difficult to tell if a particular study under review possesses any one or more of the specified characteristics. Even the first requirement is more complex than it would appear: we may be able to tell that longitudinal data are being analyzed, but in view of the strong likelihood of anticipation effects (e.g., Carp, 1975a; Schooler, 1975), can one really tell we have "before" data, representing "baseline" conditions? Typically, little information is provided about the specifics of improvement in residential conditions, less on possible social uprooting factors. The requirement of minimal self-selection factors is contradictory to our desire to study voluntary moves, and the subjects studied are typically applicants who survived one or more undocumented stages of selection and self-selection. As a result, the last requirement, representing a fundamental concept in experimental research, is impossible to satisfy in these field studies, and the investigator is generally studying in his independent variable more than he wishes to, without being sure how much more. These points have to be kept in mind, as we evaluate the evidence.

It is generally agreed (Carp, 1976a; Golant, 1977; Goldscheider, 1966; Lawton, 1975 and 1977) that elderly people are less likely to make residential moves, less likely to desire such moves, and are less successful in anticipating their mobility behavior. Mobility is lower among owner-occupants, and higher among those who are retired and widowed or divorced (Riley and Foner, 1968). Desire to move is related to dissatisfaction with housing and neighborhood and to economic circumstances; the specifics of these influences, however, may be highly dependent on local circumstances (Lawton, 1977). The preference for living in a house is near-universal and includes the elderly (Louis Harris and Associates, 1976). Overall, these data suggest that residential moves for the elderly, unless

they are made away from highly distressed urban centers (e.g., Lawton, Kleban, and Singer, 1971) will, under most circumstances, carry some likelihood of being stressful experiences even if representing improvement in housing.

Let us begin with the study which found the most impressive benefits of improved housing, the *Victoria Plaza study* (Carp, 1966) and the various follow-up results (Carp, 1974, 1975b, 1975c, 1975d, 1976b, 1977). At the end of one year, applicants who moved in, in contrast to applicants who were rejected, showed the following changes: a much higher level of housing satisfaction; a more positive evaluation of the neighborhood; a reduced felt need for services; increase in membership in organizations and in social groups; more visiting with friends; listing more neighbors as "best friends"; a more positive self-concept; less likely to indicate "present time as unhappiest."

At the end of eight years of follow-up, the benefits of moving to Victoria Plaza appeared to persist. The residents, in contrast to the unsuccessful applicants, were: happier (on a number of questions), more satisfied with life's accomplishments, more optimistic about the future, more satisfied with their use of time, and more active socially. On various self-assessments of health (global self-rating, health as a major problem, number of health problems), they presented a more positive picture. Reports of days in bed, days of restricted activity, and remaining indoors because of illness, were consistently in favor of the residents. In fact, even mortality rates (actually, those "dead or dying") revealed a more favorable outcome (26 percent) for residents than for unsuccessful applicants (36 percent). There were only three results which departed from the overall set of findings: residents were more dissatisfied with shopping facilities, they were less "satisfied" with their health (in spite of the above differences), and the much more positive evaluation of their neighborhood at one year follow-up had disappeared, yielding essentially no difference after eight years. Overall, Carp has concluded that these data document more than a "honeymoon" effect of improved housing and that they show that the determinants of short- and long-term adjustment are similar (Carp, 1974).

There seems to be agreement (e.g., Carp, 1976a; Lawton, 1977) that these powerful benefits are unique and not replicated by other studies. Thus as long as social gerontologists and planners do not expect to obtain such benefits routinely, in other settings and at other times, there would seem to be relatively little urgency for us here to try to distinguish between two viewpoints: (a) the benefits are genuine (i.e., attributable to physical changes in housing) but the circumstances were highly unusual; and (b) various research design and methodological aspects of the study conspired to produce or exaggerate the apparent benefits due to housing. In an earlier section of this review, we have already discussed some fundamental questions about the design and interpretation of findings. To this we might add some concern with loss to follow-up: about 16 percent of surviving residents and 33 percent of surviving non-residents were not interviewed eight years later. This is, of course, very respectable, but it is possible that selective losses might have increased the difference between the two groups: the least satisfied residents of Victoria Plaza who move out would be expected to be lost to follow-up, as would be those unsuccessful applicants who were able to move on their own and to improve their original inadequate residential circumstances. It might be also noted that the presentation of results is consistently very unsophisticated and one cannot even tell whether a comparison of results at initial contact and then at follow-up is based only on respondents for whom data are available on both occasions, or whether the initial results include respondents later lost to follow-up. It would also be useful to know whether the many benefits reflect independent effects, or whether the various items are highly intercorrelated and essentially one result is being reported.

It is likely that the results of the Lawton and Cohen (1974) study are more representative of the impact on older people moving to planned highrise apartments for elderly. Essentially, tenants at five housing sites were studied before and 12 months after occupancy, and compared to three groups of community residents who had not applied for planned housing. The data analysis was rather sophisticated, involving multiple regressions, where the initial level of a particular variable was always entered in first. The most variance accounted for due to housing was on perceived change for better (8.1 percent) and satisfaction with status quo (6.7 percent). No significant benefits on morale were demonstrated, once one controlled for initial level of the variable, demographic data, and initial health status. On "functional health" (frequency and vigor of performing various tasks) the rehoused group was worse off than the community controls. No differences were seen on loner status, orientation to children, and continued breadth of activity.

Other investigations of older community living persons moving to highrise apartments (Storandt and Wittels, 1975; Storandt, Wittels, and Botwinick, 1975) also suggest quite limited effects.

For example, the move was found to have no significant impact on: cognitive-psychomotor functioning; various mental health indicators (hostility, neuroticism, depression, life satisfaction); self-rating of health; and activities. However, the methodology here is rather precarious, with various problems of selection and self-selection (including participation in the study), small numbers, difficult-to-compare groups, and relatively minor residential moves. In a Vermont study of persons moving to a low income elderly housing project (Larson, 1974), no significant changes in alienation could be detected. Data on morbidity and mortality associated with voluntary intra-community moves (Lawton and Yaffe, 1970; Wittels and Botwinick, 1974) failed to reveal an average impact, though the Lawton study suggests that movers may have more variable outcomes, i.e., that they may be at greater risk both for improvements and declines in health status.

Lawton and his collaborators (Brody, 1978; Brody, Kleban, and Liebowitz, 1975; Kleban and Turner-Massey, 1978; Lawton, 1976; Lawton, Brody, and Turner-Massey, 1978) have also examined the differential impact of different residential moves. In one study, older persons moving to "traditional" housing for elderly were compared with those moving to "congregate" housing, which included enhanced services such as an activity program, a hot midday meal, and a nurse's office (Lawton, 1976). After one year's residence, the traditional housing environment had a greater impact on involvement with the external world, while the congregate housing had a greater impact on morale, reduction in loner status, and housing satisfaction. Several additional indices of well-being showed no differential impact. The second study carried out by the Philadelphia Geriatric Center group involved an evaluation of the impact of moving to Intermediate Housing (later called Community Housing), which consisted of one-family semi-detached homes in a residential neighborhood that were converted to apartments. Some 87 elderly, who wanted to move because of fear, isolation, and loneliness in their high crime neighborhood, became the applicant pool, from which 24 were randomly assigned to the Intermediate Housing. By six months' follow-up the remainder had self-selected themselves into two sub-groups, those who moved somewhere else (22) on their own and those who didn't move (41). The non-moving controls experienced a decline in morale and were extremely dissatisfied with the housing and neighborhood. The moving controls and the experimental group experienced similar increase in satisfaction with neighborhood; but on satisfaction with living arrangements, lesser fear of crime, and greater closeness to friends, the experimental group showed the greater benefits. An overall multivariate analysis of changes in well-being in relation to changes in environmental characteristics (Lawton *et al.*, 1978) revealed greatest effects on housing satisfaction, lesser effects on activity participation and rated functional ability (where improvement was associated with change to a smaller unit), and no significant effects on morale.

*Overall*, the results in this section point to relatively *modest benefits of voluntary residential moves which represent improvement* in housing; the Victoria Plaza study, however, remains a tantalizing exception. The benefits are strongest on indices of well-being which deal specifically with residential parameters and weakest on the more traditional indicators of mental health; benefits of intermediate magnitude are seen for indices of social activity and general evaluations of one's current life circumstances.

Lawton *et al.* (1978) conclude that "improved housing stands on its own as a goal for all people, whether or not gains are seen in indices of behavioral well-being" (p.137). This statement, we suspect, echoes both the voice of an optimistic and committed humanist as well as of a disappointed investigator whose assessment of the cumulative evidence prevented him from sounding an unduly loud clarion call for action.

## CROSS-SECTIONAL STUDIES OF THE IMPACT OF HOUSING CHARACTERISTICS

The previous section dealt with longitudinal data from studies of voluntary housing moves and the general conclusion was one of a modest impact on most indicators of mental health. In this section we want to examine mental health correlates of housing characteristics, obtained from cross-sectional studies, in order to see if the above general conclusion can be sustained. Admittedly, such studies represent weaker designs in which possible confounding and biasing variables are more difficult to rule out.

Studies of elderly, dealing with physical parameters of housing are relatively rare. For example, Struyk (1977) has reported data from the 1973 National Housing Survey, including incidence of key indicators of housing problems among the elderly. But the link between such indicators and various aspects of mental health and well-being remains to be systematically investigated. As a result, only sporadic evidence is available. For example, Bell (1976) compared patterns

of interaction and life satisfaction between two samples of married elderly, those living in congregate (i.e., age-concentrated) housing and those living in independent residential units. None of the six interaction variables produced significant differences, but the independent residents were found to be higher on life satisfaction, a difference which remained after various statistical controls on age, sex, social status, health, and residential duration. However, attributing the difference to the differential living conditions, rather than to (unknown) self-selection factors, appears too risky. In another study (Woodward, Gingles, and Woodward, 1974), feelings of loneliness among elderly were not found to differ significantly by type of housing (apartments, housing complexes, own homes, living with friends/relatives). Low satisfaction with housing was related to loneliness, but such an association, in the absence of any relationship to type of housing, is quite ambiguous and suspect, and includes, of course, the possibility that loneliness influences low housing satisfaction.

Lawton, Nahemow, and Teaff (1975) have recently reported the results of their study of 2457 elderly subjects living in some 154 federally-assisted housing projects. Four environmental variables were examined (sponsorship, building size, community size, and height of building) for their impact on several indices of well-being, controlling for age, sex, race, marital status, length of residence, welfare status, and self-reported health. On three of the variables (morale, mobility, and family contact), the environmental factors failed to account for more than 1 percent of the variance. For the other three variables (friendship in housing, housing satisfaction, and activity participation), the variance accounted for was a little over 4 percent. However, only two of the four environmental factors deal specifically with physical parameters of housing, and only one "notable" finding involving these two factors was obtained: housing satisfaction is higher among those living in projects with fewer floors in the residence building (1.2 percent of variance).

The Schooler study of a probability sample of some 4000 US elderly (Schooler, 1969a and 1969b; Schooler and Bellos, 1977) does not offer any kind of a simple picture of the association between several environmental factors (distance to facilities, condition of dwelling unit, features at the dwelling, size of dwelling, etc.) and a number of health, morale, life satisfaction, and anomie factors. The associations are generally quite weak, not particularly consistent across various subgroups, and influenced by interactions with social factors. For example, the association between the environmental factor called "condition of dwelling" and a general health factor (self-rated health, chronic health problems, restriction of activities, etc.) is seen in path analysis as mediated by a couple of social relations factors (groups and organizations membership, contact with children) and morale factors (anomie, sustained unhappiness). The simple association between this environmental factor and general health is weak (r = 0.102) and the estimated direct effect from path analysis is smaller (0.044).

The social gerontological literature on residential environments contains many more studies of social parameters than of the physical dimensions. Many of the social characteristics actually involve the scale of neighborhood and are discussed in the next section. The one social characteristic involving the dwelling itself is *age context*, or the distinction between *age-integrated vs. age-segregated housing*. The findings of Rosow's (1967) classic study are too well known to require much detailed discussion. Essentially, Rosow found that buildings which contained a larger proportion of units with older tenants represented a significant advantage for friendship-formation and socialization. This effect of age-peer density was stronger for working class subjects, women, and the very old. Moreover, those characterized by various "role losses," such as illness, widowhood, reduced income, and retirement were also more sensitive to age-peer density. (However, residential proximity did not seem to stimulate friendships across generations.) Morale among the elderly did not show an overall association with age-peer density, but more complex interactions with Rosow's typology of subjects were suggested: (a) "Isolated" respondents (low contact with neighbors, want more friends) had lower morale in higher density dwellings; (b) "Sociable" respondents (high contact, don't want more) showed no association between morale and age-peer density; (c) "Insatiable" respondents (high contact, want more) had somewhat higher morale in higher density dwellings. Rosow also found that complaints about care in events of illness were not related to density nor to socialization, suggesting perhaps that solitary people may develop more independence, as well as lowering their expectations of help.

Messer's (1967) findings also suggest an interaction between age-peer density, social interaction, and morale: in age-segregated settings, which had higher levels of social interaction, no significant association between activity and morale was found, while in the age-integrated settings, the usual association (see Larson, 1978) between high activity and high morale was obtained.

The recent analysis of data on a national probability sample of 1875 elderly living in 153 public housing sites (Teaff, Lawton, Nahemow, and Carlson, 1978) found that subjects living in age-segregated environments were higher on: participation in organized activities within the housing environment, morale, housing satisfaction, and mobility in their neighborhood. No associations were found for contact with family and with friends. Again, however, it was seen that these effects were quite small: for none of the outcomes did the independent variable, degree of age-segregation, account for as much as 2.0 percent of the unique variance, when certain background, social, and physical-environmental variables were also entered into the multiple regression. Teaff *et al.* (1978) also discuss the point that in public housing age-integration may, in fact, mean presence of children and teenagers from problem families, with the consequent fear for personal security among the elderly. In short, we must be careful how we interpret the apparent benefits of age-segregation. Carp (1976a) raises a similar caution when she discusses the limits of generalizability of the Rosow findings.

We must also not forget the self-selection factors which may be operating in cross-sectional comparisons, such as those between age-segregated and age-integrated housing. In a study of interest in age-segregated public housing soon to be available (Winiecke, 1973), those aged welfare recipients indicating interest were different from those expressing no desire to live in such a setting. The interested respondents were more likely to be: renters, living alone, with more friends and with more frequent contacts with friends and with children. Renters reporting loneliness or boredom as a problem were particularly likely to indicate interest in age-segregated housing. In most studies, of course, the investigator is unaware of the nature or extent of the possible biasing influence of such self-selection factors.

## STUDIES OF THE IMPACT OF NEIGHBORHOOD PARAMETERS

It is traditional to discuss the residential environment in terms of two major components, housing and neighborhood. While it is difficult to assess the relative importance of housing satisfaction vs. neighborhood satisfaction, there appears to be some agreement that for the elderly, the characteristics of the neighborhood are the more important ones in influencing overall residential satisfaction (Carp, 1976a; Hamovitch and Peterson,

1969; Havinghurst, 1969); for younger adults, the order of importance is apparently reversed (e.g., Foote, Abu-Lughod, Foley, and Winnick, 1960). Among the various aspects of the neighborhood which influence its evaluation, the elderly are most concerned with access to facilities and services (Hamovitch, Peterson, and Larson, 1969; Lawton, 1969), while other adults are more concerned with social characteristics of neighbors and the level of maintenance in the neighborhood (Foote *et al.*, 1960; Lansing and Marans, 1969; Zehner, 1971).

A good deal of the literature on *neighborhood facilities and services* (e.g., Lawton, 1977; Niebanck and Pope, 1965; Regnier, 1975) is concerned with determining which are the needed ones and what is their optimal or "critical" distance from elderly housing. The studies which are concerned with the impact of their relative availability on mental health and well-being restrict themselves generally to only one indicator, satisfaction. There is no doubt from this literature (e.g., Donahue and Ashley, 1965; Hamovitch and Peterson, 1969; Lawton, 1969; Niebanck and Pope, 1965) that proximity to such services as shopping facilities, transportation, and medical services is a major determinant of the elderly's residential satisfaction. However, tracing the more distal impact of relative proximity is more difficult. For example, distance to grocery and to some form of transportation influences the frequency and type of shopping, and there is some evidence that this may, in turn, affect the adequacy of nutrition of the aged (Howell and Loeb, 1969). Similarly, the decline in church attendance among the elderly—even as their religious feelings and attitudes grow stronger—is largely due to problems of accessibility of the church (Gray and Moberg, 1962; Moberg, 1968). However, the mental health impact of involuntary reduction in church attendance among the elderly has not been documented.

A particular facility may satisfy different needs and thus its impact may be more complex. For example, Newcomer (1973) gives an illustration of a differential use of a park by older people: those who came from apartments came to socialize because these had no public spaces, while those who came from a nearby retirement hotel came to be alone since their place of residence had several public places.

*Transportation* occupies a special role as a "facility," since access to adequate transportation can mitigate the impact of relative inaccessibility of other services and facilities. The issue of transportation has received a fair amount of attention (see Cantilli and Shmelzer, 1971; Carp, 1976a; Lawton, 1977) but very little of it deals with the impact on

morale or mental health. In general, it would appear (Ashford and Holloway, 1972; Golant, 1976) that transportation needs of elderly are not that atypical, once one removes travel to and from work; however, there is tendency to underestimate the demand for mobility among the elderly. In a study of availability of a car for personal use, carried out in a city without public transportation (Cutler, 1972), it was found that life satisfaction of the elderly was higher among owners of cars. However, additional controls on socioeconomic status, subjective health, and distance of residence from center of the city, revealed that the original association remained significant only for those who lived farther away from the city and who were lower on SES or in poorer health (no more than some 13 percent of the total sample). In a follow-up study, Cutler (1975) showed that the tendency for elderly to decline in life satisfaction over a 30 month period was greater among those who had been without a car throughout or those who had lost access to a car in the meantime; effects of health, income, age, sex, and residential location were controlled in this analysis.

Lawton, Nahemow, and Yeh (in press) have reported the results of their study of a national area probability sample of two types of housing environments, federal low-rent public housing and the lower middle-income Section 202 housing programs which are under private non-profit sponsorship. Six indices of well-being (activity participation, housing satisfaction, mobility, morale, friendship behavior, family contact) were related to a number of independent variables in a hierarchical multiple regression which entered them in the following order: personal characteristics (sex, age, marital status, race, length of residence welfare status, self-rated health) and type of sponsorship went in first as controls, followed by community size, age segregation (of housing), administrator-rated crime risk, active vs. quiet neighborhood, distance to medical services, distance to church and recreational facilities, distance to shopping, and interviewer-rated neighborhood quality. Some results of interest, involving specifically neighborhood characteristics and increasing the variance accounted for by at least 1.0 percent, were as follows: (a) Rated high quality of neighborhood was related to housing satisfaction (1.2 percent); (b) Active (vs. quiet) neighborhood was related to lower mobility (1.2 percent); (c) Few medical services were related to more activity participation (1.6 percent); (d) High crime risk was related to low housing satisfaction (2.2 percent). Distance to church and recreational facilities and distance to shopping did not account for even 0.5 percent of variance on any of the outcome variables. Similarly, morale was not accounted for by any of the neighborhood environmental variables. Overall, the six neighborhood variables plus community size and age-segregation of housing accounted for the following amounts of variance: housing satisfaction, 8.3 percent; friendship behavior, 5.2 percent (mostly due to community size); activity participation, 4.0 percent; mobility, 3.2 percent; morale, 1.6 percent; contact with relatives, 1.6 percent. Once again we see that the largest impact (but still only a modest one) of the residential environment is on housing satisfaction, less on social interaction, and least on morale.

*Risk of crime* and *fear of crime* have become a recent but growing concern of social gerontologists dealing with the residential environment. The elderly are more likely to be found residing within the central city of a metropolitan area (Kennedy and DeJong, 1977), which is where the majority of crimes take place; crime rates in local neighborhoods which contain housing projects for elderly also tend to be above national average (Lawton, Nahemow, Yaffe, and Feldman, 1976). The nature and the extent of crime as a "problem" for the elderly had become a matter of some controversy initially but the component issues appear to have been identified and clarified. Thus, there is a good agreement (Conklin, 1976; Goldsmith and Goldsmith, 1976; Lawton, Nahemow, Yaffe, and Feldman, 1976; Sykes, 1976) that the elderly are less likely to be victims of crime, but that certain crimes are over-represented among the elderly (robbery with injury, larceny with personal contact); these crimes are more likely to take place in the dwelling than in "public" places (Conklin, 1976; Sykes, 1976). However, it is generally conceded that older people are more vulnerable to the impact of crime and that their fear of crime can be greater even if their actual exposure to crime is below average. It is also acknowledged that their lower rate of victimization could be the result of defensive maneuvers which severely restrict their mobility and life space and adversely affect the quality of life.

Studies of fear of crime and concerns over safety do reveal an association with age. In a national survey of adults (Louis Harris and Associates, 1976), older people were more likely to list crime in the streets as one of the two to three "most serious problems in their neighborhood." In another national study of adults (Lebowitz, 1975), older people expressed greater fear about walking alone at night in some areas of their neighborhood than did younger adults; this age effect was par-

ticularly seen for those living alone, living in metropolitan or suburban areas, and those with low income. In a study of reactions to crime among residents of high and low crime rate communities (Conklin, 1976), perceptions of crime were not associated with age, while perceptions of safety were lower among older residents in both areas. Willingness to report crimes was also found to be lower among older residents.

Older residents generally feel safest in their dwelling unit, less safe within the multiunit building, less safe in outdoor spaces of the housing unit, and least safe in the neighborhood (Lawton, Nahemow, Yaffe, and Feldman, 1976). Feelings of safety are the lowest in age-integrated housing and the highest in retirement communities and age-segregated housing (Sherman, Newman, and Nelson, 1976; Sundeen and Mathieu, 1976). The latter study also found a modest negative association between a sense of dependence on neighbors and sense of solidarity with the community, on the one hand, and fear of burglary and of robbery, on the other hand. This finding thus provides some support for Gubrium's (1974) hypothesis that elderly living in areas of extensive friendships experience greater social support which will act to diffuse their fears of crime. Incidentally, this hypothesis may be reasonably stated as applying to other age groups as well. For example, Wolfe, Lex, and Yancey (1968) found that perception of human dangers in the neighborhood was strongly related to the level of the respondent's integration into informal networks; persons who were not integrated were more likely to express concern over allowing children out of the house, felt more vulnerable to strangers entering the neighborhood, and felt unsafe on the street at night.

Crime is a neighborhood parameter which interacts not only with social variables (e.g., social support) but also with physical aspects of the dwelling. Newman (1972), in his influential book, *Defensible Space*, has argued that certain elements of design (such as territorial definition of space to reflect areas of influence, or position of window to allow natural surveillance) can make it possible for both inhabitants and strangers to perceive that an area is under an undisputed influence of a particular group. "Defensible space is a model for residential environments which inhibits crime by creating the physical expression of a social fabric that defends itself" (p.3). The crime data which Newman presents, and the evidence from other studies (e.g., Sherman, Newman, and Nelson, 1976), are as yet too meager and inconclusive to permit an evaluation of his conceptualization of defensible space and of the interaction of social and design factors. Of particular interest is the question whether Newman's conceptualization offers an adequate explanation of high-rise public housing disasters such as Pruit-Igoe (Rainwater, 1967 and 1970) where the social fabric within was weak and fragmented.

The above studies of victimization and fear of crime among the elderly do not extend to an examination of the empirical link to mental health and well-being. One exception is the already discussed study by Lawton, Nahemow, and Yeh (in press) in which the rated risk of crime was not related to any of the indices of well-being, except housing satisfaction. Similar findings have been obtained from a Detroit study (Kasl and Harburg, 1972 and 1975), where perceived danger from crime and respondent's ratings of the safety of the neighborhood were strongly related to various indices of housing and neighborhood satisfaction and desire to move, but only weakly and sporadically (i.e., only in some race-sex-residential area subgroups) to indicators of mental health. The Detroit study did not deal specifically with elderly but with a cross-section of married adults; however, additional analyses which we have recently done on the original data do not reveal that controlling on age modifies the above conclusion in any way. It is also interesting to note from this recent analysis that among the adults living in the high "stress" areas (i.e., low social class and high rates of crime and instability), the older respondents were less likely to dislike the neighborhood and less likely to want to move out; even on their evaluations of safety of the neighborhood and of the possibility of being robbed, the older respondents were slightly more optimistic but these differences were no longer significant. It must be noted that this study dealt with respondents who were married and had relatives (at least a sibling) living in the Detroit area.

This review might concern itself with other aspects of the neighborhood residential environment, such as *noise and air pollution*. However, the studies which would be relevant for this review, that is, those which deal with the impact on the mental health of the elderly, just do not seem to exist. For example, the literature on effects of noise (e.g., Goldsmith and Jonsson, 1973; Kryter, 1970) reveals one relevant report (Abey-Wickrama, Brook, Gattoni, and Herridge, 1969). This study found a greater number of admissions to a mental hospital from the residential area around Heathrow airport with the greatest amount of noise, than from other surrounding areas. The excess in admissions was specific to one category of people: women over 45

who were widowed, divorced, or unmarried. Of course, this study is only suggestive, but it is possible that noise affects well-being and mental health via curtailment of valued activities, including social contacts and socializing. Less mobile groups, such as the elderly (especially the relative social isolates among them), may be less able to cope with such adverse effects of noise.

## SOCIAL INTERACTION IN THE RESIDENTIAL SETTING

Social characteristics of the neighborhood—the "supra-personal environment" (Lawton, 1977)—continue to hold the interest of many investigators. The two issues most frequently examined are distance to relatives and friends, and the similarity of respondents' socio-demographic characteristics to neighbors' characteristics. There is good agreement that the elderly prefer what has been called "independent propinquity" (Sheldon, 1954), "supported independence" (Shanas, Townsend, Wedderburn, Friis, Milhøj, and Stehouwer, 1968), and "intimacy par distance" (Rosenmayr and Kockeis, 1966); that is, they want to live alone but near their children and relatives (Beyer and Woods, 1963; Kleemeier, 1963; Niebanck and Pope, 1965; Shanas, 1962). They also seek proximity to their own peers (Hamovitch and Petersen, 1969; Kleemeier, 1963). In addition to the agreement of the evidence regarding these housing preferences, there is also good evidence that contact with friends and close kin is important and that there is a positive association between the amount of such contact and life satisfaction-morale (Burgess, 1960; Larson, 1978; Streib, 1958; Townsend, 1967).

In spite of the plentiful evidence on the above issues, it is difficult to find studies which establish the full link from (a) distance to friends and relatives, to (b) amount of social interaction, to (c) mental health and well-being. The work of Rosenberg (1967, 1968, and 1970) contains evidence regarding the first link only. For example, among a group of working-class respondents, there was an average of five visits with close kin during the week prior to the interview if they lived within the same block, but only an average of one weekly visit if the distance was six blocks or more. Rosenberg also found that "neighborhood contextual dissonance" (i.e., the dominant socio-demographic characteristics of the neighbors being unlike those of the respondent) increased the probability of social isolation among the older working-class men. Conner and Powers (1975) did examine community age density together with age-graded interaction and life satisfaction in a small study. Essentially, no association of age density with the other two variables was found; only interaction and life satisfaction showed a small association.

The correlational data linking social interaction and life satisfaction suggest, but do not establish, that residential parameters which influence social interaction would also affect life satisfaction, were the latter to have been studied as well. But some gerontologists have questioned the direction of causality in such associations. For example, some (e.g. Lowenthal and Boler, 1965; Palmore, 1968; Shanas, 1962; Tallmer and Kutner, 1969) have argued that decreases in social interaction are most often the result of concomitant stresses, such as ill health, widowhood, or retirement, and that low morale is more likely a function of these stresses than of the reduced social interaction. Nelson and Winter (1975) have, indeed, shown that the consideration of moving is associated with the occurrence of major life disruptions and with a low level of personal independence. Thus it is prudent to conclude that residential parameters appear to affect social interaction, but that the more distal effect on morale and life satisfaction is only suggested. The later section on involuntary relocation will enable us to re-examine this issue.

## THE IMPACT OF RETIREMENT COMMUNITIES

Our review of the empirical literature for this section will be relatively brief. There are several reasons for this. First, there are not that many recent relevant studies to review. Second, the major concerns of these studies, on the independent variable side, are age-segregation vs. age-integration and provision of services and facilities. These concerns, however, have already been adequately explored in the previous sections and the literature on retirement communities does not add anything new. Third, these studies yield results which are particularly difficult to interpret from the viewpoint of what they may indicate, if anything, about the impact of the residential environment.

The reason for this ambiguity of the results is the problem of self-selection. Moving to a particular retirement community setting represents for most elderly a deliberate choice among various alternatives which include: different types of retirement settings with varying facilities, clientele, and costs; intra- and inter-state geographical moves; moves to housing for elderly within the subject's city or neighborhood; not moving at all. In contrast, most of the studies so far dealt primarily with respondents who typically had, at best, two choices:

to move or not to move into some federal housing for the elderly, typically the only one available in the area. There are two main consequences of this self-selection: (1) Obtained differences in satisfaction and mental health by different settings can reflect the various differential characteristics which the individuals "brought in" with them; (2) Obtained differences can reflect the result of an idiographic comparison between the goals, plans, and aspirations for a specific retirement setting and the individual's assessment of what he/she actually got. The influence of fulfilled vs. unfulfilled expectations and goals on adjustment and well-being of the elderly is, as was noted earlier, a powerful one (Bortner and Hultsch, 1970; Thurnher, 1974). We must also note that the first effect of self-selection can be somewhat reduced by the usual control or matching on socio-demographic and background variables, but such a statistical control does nothing to the second consequence of the self-selection process.

The work of Bultena (Bultena, 1969 and 1974; Bultena and Wood, 1969) is based on a study of retired males who had moved from the Midwest to Arizona an average of four years prior to data collection; migrants to three age-integrated communities were compared with migrants to four planned retirement communities. The men in the latter group were higher on occupational status, educational attainment, and income; their self-reported health was considerably better. Interestingly, the two groups were also different on contact with children: 50 percent of men in age-integrated communities but only 16 percent of those in planned retirement communities reported weekly (or more frequent) contact with an offspring. The main results were as follows. Men in retirement communities: had higher life satisfaction (even after statistical controls for SES and perceived health); were more satisfied with retirement living in Arizona; were less likely to report a decline in close friends and to be dissatisfied with the number of new friends. A special analysis of friendship formation in the retirement communities (Bultena, 1969) revealed that new friends were selected from similar occupational strata. In view of the previous discussion, it is difficult to know what differences, if any, can be interpreted as the impact of the differential residential environment; only the life satisfaction data were adjusted for initial SES and health differences.

The work of Sherman and her collaborators (Sherman, 1972, 1974, 1975a, 1975b, 1975c; Sherman, Magnum, Dodds, Walkley, and Wilner, 1968) is based on a study of residents of six retirement housing sites: a retirement hotel and an apartment tower, both located in a downtown urban area; a rental village of single-story buildings, located in a suburban area; two suburban retirement villages (one single family houses, one a co-op) primarily for married couples; a life-care home in an urban area, licensed to give personal care and protective services. Controls were elderly living in age-integrated housing and were matched to residents of each of the six retirement sites on the usual socio-demographic variables (but not health status). The six retirement settings were obviously vastly different on a number of residential parameters, as well as in the social characteristics of the clientele. Residents and controls were interviewed twice: some one to two years after having moved into the sites, and two years later (if still living there).

Some of the results—and their limitations—can be summarized as follows: (1) Site residents had less interaction with their children than did controls; however, this difference disappeared if one controlled for distance to children; (2) Help received from children or given to children was lower among site residents than controls; however, among the strongest reported motivations for moving to any retirement site was to avoid dependence on children; (3) Mutual help among neighbors was higher than for controls at some sites (e.g., life care home) and lower than controls at other sites (e.g., retirement hotel) with no overall differences between sites and controls; (4) The hypothesis that mutual help with neighbors and with children are compensatory was not supported: those higher on mutual help with children were also higher on such help with neighbors; (5) Site residents reported more new friends and more frequent visiting with neighbors; however, it is not clear to what extent this is strictly a recency effect, since the site residents were relatively new in their settings.

Overall, there were few findings which could be interpreted as an impact of the residential environment. For example, at one site (a mountain desert area), there was lower satisfaction, easily attributed to relative inaccessibility of services. Residents were less likely to perceive their medical needs as easy enough to care for, and as a result tended to worry more about their health and to have somewhat lower morale. (These residents were also more likely to be out-of-state migrants.) But since the literature relating dissatisfaction to inaccessibility of services is plentiful, a finding such as this adds little to our knowledge. Sherman's own conclusion is a forceful reminder of how little we have learned from these types of studies regarding environmental impact: "Thus, one can draw no general conclusion other than the obvious one that

there is no one right kind of housing; rather the person will be most satisfied with the housing that best fits his requirements and conditions" (Sherman, 1972, p. 363). Instead of continuing cross-sectional comparisons of hopelessly disparate retirement residential settings (e.g., Wolk and Teleen, 1976), we must turn to better designed prospective studies if we are to learn something truly useful about retirement communities.

## INVOLUNTARY RELOCATION WITHIN THE COMMUNITY

At this point we are ready to examine studies which, although still dealing with the impact of the residential environment, are best seen from a "social stress" perspective. That is, they are studies where the social experience, rather than the residential one, seems to be the primary "independent variable" under study. This includes unplanned or involuntary residential moves, and transfer from community to an institution or between institutions (discussed in the next section). Many of the relevant studies through 1970 have been reviewed in an earlier paper (Kasl, 1972).

Since social ties to people and to the community are the most powerful reasons for the older person's unwillingness to make a residential move (e.g., Langford, 1962; Niebanck and Pope, 1965; Riley and Foner, 1968), we might presume that adverse effects of unplanned moves would be the greatest among elderly with strong social ties to their residential settings. In addition, it has also been hypothesized (Schulz and Brenner, 1977) that adverse effects will be greater if: (a) there is little or no choice; (b) the nature of the new environment is unpredictable; and (c) the change in before-after environments is relatively large. The authors also postulate that those elderly who see themselves as in control of their own fate will have adverse effects to the extent that the move is beyond their control and/or they are moving into a more controlling environment.

Fried's influential work on *urban renewal* (Fried, 1963, and 1965), while not specifically dealing with elderly subjects, has become an implicit idealized paradigm for the study of involuntary residential moves: elderly residents in an old intact neighborhood, where they have lived for many years and where rich and strong social ties exist, are forced out because of urban renewal or highway construction. They receive no help with relocation; they scatter throughout the city, finding available housing which is seldom as good as where they had lived previously, and generally costs more. But can this phenomenon still be studied? It is likely that the following picture is more current: The elderly residents are already somewhat social isolates, living in neighborhoods which are undergoing various piecemeal changes, usually for the worse. The residential move, though forced on them by various circumstances, may be welcomed by many of them. They may receive assistance with the move and they generally go into federally subsidized elderly housing, which in fact represents a residential improvement without the usual financial penalty. Certain services may be more readily available (e.g., a medical clinic on premises) and the potential for new friendships with other elderly may be great.

There are a couple of implications of this historical trend in the nature of the phenomenon of involuntary relocation. One is that the evidence from older and more recent studies may not be quite consistent. The other is that operationalizing the dimension "voluntary vs. involuntary" becomes more difficult, and, in a particular study, one cannot be necessarily sure how "involuntary" the experience was, or how it differed on this dimension for various identifiable subgroups. In a recent study of forced relocation (Kasl, Ostfeld, Brody, Snell, and Price, in press), relocation agencies in three cities provided names of poor older persons who were moving because of urban renewal, eviction, condemned or substandard housing, fire, and extreme financial hardship. Yet subjective descriptions of the move at initial interview just prior to the move revealed that approximately two-thirds of the respondents saw the move as voluntary ("wanted to move, choice is respondent's"), as desirable ("How much look forward to the new move—very much"), with little regret ("How much will miss the neighborhood, that part of the city—not at all"), and easy to adjust to ("How long before feel at home and settled in a new place—a week or so"). However, there was some worry about the move, especially about what to expect. It is possible that negative aspects of such residential moves are more closely linked to uncertainty and worry than to "involuntariness."

The early literature has been summarized by Niebanck (Niebanck, 1966 and 1968; Niebanck and Pope, 1965) and the following picture emerges. The relocated elderly are generally those who have been less mobile and who have lived in the old neighborhood longer than the average person (see also Stutz, 1976). For the elderly, the move frequently represents an added financial hardship because their economic circumstances are already quite precarious. The old neighborhood which they are forced to leave has two major advantages for which the better housing condition (for some) of the new location cannot adequately compensate: the extensive friendship ties and the convenience to many facilities (grocery, drug store, church, transportation, etc.). The strength of the social ties to the old neighborhood relate to dissatisfaction with the new neighborhood (Langford, 1962) and to a more severe "grief" reaction (Fried, 1963). Those who are able to maintain old contacts with friends from the old neighborhood show the least emotional distress. The loss of friends creates not only loneliness but also a certain amount of insecurity, inasmuch as the elderly depend partly upon their friends for help in case of some emergency (Shanas, 1962). In studies not restricted to elderly, the evidence suggests that the older people are more vulnerable to the adverse effects of the involuntary relocation. Key (1967), for example, found more intense depression, sadness, and negative feelings among the older persons who were forced to move because of urban renewal or highway construction.

A couple of the more recent studies utilize a retrospective design. Kasteler, Gray, and Carruth (1968) found 48 subjects aged 55 and older, who had been relocated because of highway construction during the previous five years, and compared them to some 268 subjects selected at random from the community. The relocated persons scored consistently less adjusted and more dissatisfied on a number of established attitude and adjustment scales. This would seem to suggest that adverse effects of relocation are long-lasting. However, it is extremely doubtful that a random sampling of the total community will yield subjects comparable to those who had lived in areas vulnerable to highway construction (no education, occupation, or income data are given for the controls). Moreover, it is impossible to tell if the 48 relocatees studied were in any way representative of all those who were originally displaced. Another recent study (Brand and Smith, 1974) located some 71 older persons who had survived an involuntary relocation, associated with urban renewal from two years before. Compared to controls in the community, the relocatees had lower life satisfaction (in particular women and those in poor health) and less social interaction with family and friends. Again, it is not clear to what extent the community controls were appropriately comparable.

The remainder of this section will be devoted to a brief summary of selected findings, mostly unpublished, from a recently completed study of forced relocation (Kasl et al., in press). As noted already, the phenomenon actually studied was a residential change experience which no more than one-third of the subjects perceived as at least somewhat involuntary, undesirable, or socially uprooting. The study represents a prospective inquiry into the behavioral, psychological and health consequences of a relocation experience which at least in some sense was imposed upon the elderly. Four sets of variables were assessed: health, psychological state, physiological data, and social behavior. Data were collected on four occasions over two years on some 225 elderly who were forced to move and 173 matched neighborhood controls who had not moved. Interviews with cases (relocatees) were scheduled around the date of the move, and at 3, 12, and 24 months; controls were interviewed at comparable intervals. The cases were all poor elderly (62 and over) in three Connecticut communities who were forced to move within a specified period and came to the attention of a relocation agency; 79 percent of eligible subjects agreed to participate. All cases moved to federally subsidized housing for the elderly which was located in the urban (rather than suburban) areas of these communities; none of the cases had to make a move which represented a distance of more than about three to four miles.

Data on perceptions of the neighborhood and of the dwelling unit clearly revealed that the cases saw the move as an improvement in their residential environment. Data on social networks and social interaction reflected a mixed picture regarding the hypothesis that such moves are socially disrupting. For example, cases reported an increase in "number of neighbors knows well enough to call on," but there was no change in frequency of visiting with neighbors. There was a decrease in mutual visits with friends, but there was also a decrease in percent of subjects who felt they were not getting together enough with people they enjoyed. The percent reporting having a "confidant" and the frequency of getting together with the confidant remained unchanged. Interestingly, only about one-eighth of the cases reported initially before the move that the confidant lived in "the same building," while one year after the move, one third of the cases listed a confidant in "the same building." This suggests that a confidant for some elderly need not be as much "a dear, old friend," as a person one can depend on for help in distress and emergencies.

Physical health data reflected more adverse outcomes among relocatees than among controls during two years of follow-up. For example, cases had significantly more hospitalization events (percent hospitalized, mean number of hospitalizations, hospitalizations also involving an operation) and more nursing home admissions. Incidence of

new disease revealed an excess of stroke and angina pectoris among relocatees, but no differences on intermittent claudication. Global self-ratings of health revealed more negative changes among cases. On the other hand, the mortality experience of the two groups was not significantly different; physiological data (blood pressure, serum cholesterol, serum uric acid, casual blood sugar) also failed to reveal any lasting impact of the experience above and beyond some modest anticipation effects.

Data based on the Multiple Affect Adjective Checklist (Zuckerman and Lubin, 1965) revealed only a small impact: cases showed some drop in anxiety (initial to three month interview), hostility (initial to one year interview), and depression (initial to two year follow-up); controls showed only non-significant fluctuations and very small trends upward over time. The Index of Life Satisfaction (Neugarten, Havinghurst, and Tobin, 1961) failed to separate cases and controls at any time and appeared insensitive to the relocation experience.

We also constructed several indices of severity of the relocation experienced based on: (a) anticipatory perceptions (involuntary, unexpected, socially uprooting, worrisome, unknown, long time to adjust, big life change); (b) relative change in before-after evaluations of the neighborhood and of the apartment; and (c) relative change in before-after social interaction. In general, more adverse physical health outcomes (hospitalizations, incidence of cardiovascular disease) were more common among those with more negative anticipatory perceptions and those with smaller positive changes in evaluations of the neighborhood and the apartment; the social interaction-based indicator of severity did not relate to frequency of adverse physical health outcomes. Analysis of mental health indicators (anxiety, hostility, depression, anomie, life satisfaction) in relation to anticipatory perceptions revealed considerably poorer mental health at initial interview among those with more severe experience (not surprisingly), but a sharper "recovery" during the two-year follow-up.

An analysis of predictors of physical health outcomes (mortality, incidence of cardiovascular disease) revealed that certain relocatees were at greater risk, were more vulnerable. These indicators of greater vulnerability (from the initial interview only) included higher levels of depression and anomie, and greater social isolation, such as no assistance from family and not knowing many neighbors well enough to call on.

The last-mentioned finding raises interesting problems for our theoretical formulations. Essentially, we have two notions of vulnerability. Elderly who have few friends, know few neighbors, and get together with them infrequently, may be viewed as social isolates who do not have much social support available to them as a buffer in difficult, stressful times (e.g., Kaplan, Cassel, and Gore, 1977; Cobb, 1976). On the other hand, we have a notion of vulnerability based on severity of the relocation experience, and the data suggest (e.g., Fried, 1963, 1965) that the experience will be more severe among those who had a strong pre-relocation commitment to the neighborhood, who had a greater number of close friends in the area, and who had positive feelings about their neighbors. In this instance the two plausible and data-based notions of vulnerability lead to mutually contradictory predictions, since the social isolates are more vulnerable by the first notion and less vulnerable by the second. If both notions are plausible and do, in fact, represent ongoing processes, one may well find no differences since the two effects will cancel each other out. We need more probing research designs and more subtle measures in order to begin to disentangle such possibly complex dynamics.

## THE IMPACT OF INSTITUTIONALIZATION AND INSTITUTIONAL TRANSFER

Lawton (1977) has expressed astonishment that "to date no complete longitudinal control-group study allowing a critical test of the effects of institutionalization has been reported" (p. 293). Given the recency of Lawton's observation, the reader may well imagine that the statement can be repeated in this review without much fear of contradiction. The study design which Lawton has probably in mind would be a prospective, longitudinal study which would begin to clarify the dynamics and the impact of the several (hypothetical) stages of institutionalization: (a) The decision-making process, especially its selective factors and its timing aspects, whereby certain elderly persons, living in the community, become applicants to an institution. (b) The stage of anticipation of change where the elderly, still living in the community, are awaiting their turn to enter the institution (the waiting list stage). (c) The short-term adjustment stage, presumably reflecting mainly the impact of the environmental change from community to the institution. (d) The long-term adaptation stage during which the elderly person comes to terms with the environment of the institution and which presumably reflects mainly the impact of living in the institution. Given this complexity of the phenomenon, it can be readily seen that cross-sectional comparisons at one point in time or another will be quite inadequate in demonstrating an impact of the institutional setting per se. (The reader is referred to two recent reviews of the institutionalization literature [Kasl, 1972; Lieberman, 1969] for a more detailed discussion of the various methodological issues involved.)

It is not difficult to document the fact that in the vast majority of instances there is a higher *mortality* of aged subjects within the first year (or some shorter period) of hospitalization or institutionalization in a state hospital, nursing home, or old age home (see Rowland, 1977, for the most recent review of these data). How this fact should be interpreted is another matter altogether. The assumption that this reflects the stress consequences of a profound environmental change (e.g., Kent, 1963) is at best premature in the face of the powerful alternative explanation due to self-selection, i.e., individuals who are in a seriously debilitated or incapacitated condition are largely the ones who get admitted. Logic also demands that a second alternative explanation be entertained, i.e., that it is not the environmental change as such, but the exposure to some noxious aspect of the institutional environment (poor diet, infections, poor medical care, sensory deprivation, etc.) which raises the mortality rates. The plausibility of this second alternative depends on additional considerations, such as: Are the elevated rates during first year in comparison to pre-institutionalization baselines (or general population data), or in relation to later years of institutionalization? Are the effects of these noxious elements of the institutional environment cumulative over the years, or do they go down with time because of a "the survival of the fittest" (to that peculiar environment) kind of phenomenon?

Studies of aged individuals *transferred from one institutional setting to another* represent a natural experiment in which it is possible to zero in better on the single issue of interest, environmental change. However, even in this simple situation, there are at least two aspects which can influence the impact and thus yield different results across different studies: (a) the institutional transfer may represent moves across highly similar or highly dissimilar institutional environments, with the latter, of course, being changes either for the better or for the worse; (b) variations in the way the relocation process is managed may also influence the outcome. It goes without saying that, in addition, methodological flaws in such studies (primarily, lack of initial comparability of transferred vs. nontransferred subjects) would also affect or obscure outcomes.

There are several early studies (Aleksandrowicz, 1961; Aldrich and Mendkoff, 1963; Jasnau, 1967; Killian, 1970) which showed an increase in mortality rates after transfer, compared to rates either before transfer or to controls. The Jasnau study actually showed that only patients who are mass-moved within the hospital, with little or no preparation, have the increased mortality rate; those who received individualized attention (case-work service, pschological support) showed a lower than expected death rate following the move. A number of mostly later studies (Goldfarb, Shahinian, and Burr, 1972; Gutman and Herbert, 1976; Markson and Cumming, 1974 and 1975; Markus, Blenker, Bloom and Downs, 1970 and 1971; Novick, 1967; Zweig and Csank, 1975) have failed to find any elevations in mortality after transfer. At least three of these (Gutman and Herbert, 1976; Novick, 1967; Zweig and Csank, 1957) specifically note that the transfer was carried out with careful planning and supportive services in order to prevent any adverse impact on health. One study (Markson and Cumming, 1974) appeared to have selected only healthier patients for transfer, while in another study (Gutman and Herbert, 1976) the transfer was to a radically improved environment. Finally, one set of investigators (Markus *et al.*, 1970, and 1971) claim to have found significantly elevated rates, where, in fact, simple chi square calculations of observed to expected rates reveal that this cannot be so; however, their bizarre significance testing might lead some reviewers to classify their outcome with the studies showing some effects.

Perhaps most intriguing are two reports (Boureston and Tars, 1974; Zweig and Csank, 1976) which suggest that the elevated rates may occur during a period prior to the transfer (anticipation effect) as well as after the transfer. This is a little distressing since it is bound to produce a flood of articles based on recalculations of the mortality rates in the older studies. It also would imply that some of the casework and preparation for the move needs to be done earlier, probably at the time of the first announcement.

Lieberman (1974a) has criticized much of this research for "the over-preoccupation with death rates," which he labels a "near idiocy." Actually, it seems to us that the weakness of these studies is not in the choice of the outcome variable, but in the choice of the most impoverished and simple-minded goal of the studies: does the transfer affect mortality? Given the enormous variability of the phenomenon and of the subjects involved in these studies, it is inevitable that the results will be all over the place and that the question is really so general as to be meaningless. And it does not help much that some investigators actually appear to be testing a complex "null hypothesis," i.e., that stress of transfer increases mortality but that their protective intervention effectively wiped out any effects of such stress. Overall, then, no general conclusions are possible, particularly in view of the possibility that the rates may be elevated prior to the transfer. It does appear, however, that the transfer experience is not such an overwhelmingly powerful phenomenon so that its impact on mortality comes through irrespective of the many individuating circumstances.

There have been some attempts to advance our understanding of the impact of the transfer experience by studying patient characteristics which relate to *differential outcomes*. For example, Aldrich (1964) suggests that survivors of the relocation were more likely to be patients whose adjustment to the institution prior to the news of relocation were characterized as "satisfactory" or "angry, demanding" (vs. "neurotic, depressed, psychotic"), and whose reaction to the news of relocation was judged to be "philosophical, angry, anxious, or regression" (vs. "depression, denial, psychotic"). Other attempts at personality predictors of survival have failed upon attempted replication (Markus, Blenker, Bloom, and Downs, 1972). Men and those in poor physical or mental health are also at greater risk for post-relocation mortality (Goldfarb *et al.*, 1972; Kral, Grad, and Berenson, 1968; Markus *et al.*, 1970 and 1971); however, it is not clear to what extent this is because these are general predictors, whether or not an institutional transfer has taken place. However, the fact that only men showed elevated levels of plasma cortisol after relocation (Kral *et al.*, 1968) does suggest a genuine sex difference. In a study of privacy preferences among relocated elderly, Pastalan (1975) reported that those who subsequently died by 12 months post-relocation had a much greater readiness to agree that if "they had curtains around the bed they would keep them closed most of the time"; however, it is difficult to tell if such an attitude taps depression or a severely debilitated physical state.

There are a couple of studies (Costello and Tanaka, 1961; Lieberman, 1961) which have compared mortality of subjects on a waiting list (accepted to an institution but not yet admitted) to mortality after institutionalization. While this may take care of the self-selection problem, it doesn't provide adequate baseline data, since the anticipation period also appears associated with higher mortality (Boureston and Tars, 1974; Zweig and Csank, 1976). Moreover, waiting periods of different lengths will produce different attrition rates among the ill on the waiting list and thus different groups of survivors will be entering the institution. In addition, admission criteria may favor leaving healthier persons on the waiting list longer. In any case, the results are inconclusive. Lieberman (1961) found a slightly lower waiting-list mortality (once one correctly recomputes his data on an annual basis) while Costello and Tanaka (1961) got somewhat higher rates for the waiting list subjects.

The work of Lieberman and his collaborators (Lieberman, 1966, 1969, 1971, 1974b; Lieberman, Prock, and Tobin, 1968; Miller and Lieberman, 1965; Tobin and Lieberman, 1976; Turner, Tobin, and Lieberman, 1972) represents a prominent part of the literature on institutionalization and institutional relocation. This group uses both cross-sectional and longitudinal designs and utilizes various community and waiting-list comparison groups. Overall, one gets the impression that as they became more thoughtful and sophisticated methodologically, they became more skeptical about being able to document the impact of institutionalization and tended to switch more toward the goal of understanding the predictors of adjustment and outcome. Some of the early work (e.g., Lieberman *et al.*, 1968; Miller and Lieberman, 1965), intended to document the impact of the institutionalization experience, used carefully selected, physically and psychologically intact subjects, which ultimately undermined the objective of describing a generalizable impact of the experience. For example, the 1968 study used three cross-sectional samples of community, waiting-list, and institutionalized elderly who were chosen with so many intentional and unintentional selection biases that any differences among the three groups can only be seen as a direct outcome of the elaborate selection process. Thus, the institutionalized group excluded those who: had lived there less than one year or more than three, were non-ambulatory, could not speak English well enough, had deteriorated since admission, had more than three errors on the Mental Status Questionnaire, and scored poorly on the Self-Care Index. Surely such a study becomes an unwitting reaffirmation of the need for fully prospective studies of unselected populations.

Predictors of outcome of institutionalization can be conceptualized in at least three different ways: (a) those characteristics which reflect the capacity of the individual to adapt to new situations and new demands; (b) those pre-institutional characteristics which will be most congruent with the particular institutional environment; and (c) institutional environmental variables, such as the variation in the "totality" of the institution. Beyond these, we also have generalized predictors, such as poor physical health or depression, which reflect temporal associations in any group of people, whether or not they are experiencing a particular

life stress. The Lieberman group has contributed a good deal to our understanding of these issues. For example, Turner *et al.* (1972) studied the predictors of successful adaptation (i.e., not showing a decline in physical, mental, or behavioral functioning) among a group of waiting-list elderly persons re-assessed one year after institutionalization; characteristics reflecting a vigorous, somewhat hostile-narcissistic pre-admission style predicted successful adaptation and were interpreted as pre-institutional traits congruent with the institutional environment.

Lieberman (1974b) has summarized the results from several of his studies which pertain to environmental characteristics which are associated with successful adaptation (excluding mortality as outcome). In general, "good" environments are those which: foster autonomy and more personalization of patients; are more integrated into the community; allow privacy and leave locus of control to a greater extent with the patient; are not permissive regarding deviant behavior and are rather low on care giving. Resource richness of the institutional environment appears to make little difference. The reader must remember, of course, that such a description of "good" environment has validity only for the specific criteria of adaptation which are used; such criteria themselves represent a choice involving the investigator's theory and values. Predictors of mortality tend to be restricted to initial physical health status, cognitive ability, and level of responsiveness to the environment (Lieberman, 1971, 1974b).

The most recent work (Tobin and Lieberman, 1976) follows a group of waiting list aged up to one year after institutionalization, and compares them to a small community sample and an institutionalized sample who had been in an institution one to three years. The community sample is clearly superior on mental health and cognitive functioning; the subjects have also experienced fewer recent adverse changes (illness, economic, residential, social). The waiting list group is reasonably comparable to the institutional sample, except for scoring poorer on mental health. After three months of institutionalization, the subjects showed some decline in hopefulness, in sense of capacity for self-care, in affiliation, and an increase in body preoccupation. The decline on the Mental Status Questionnaire is primarily due to subjects not knowing the exact date or street address of the institution. After one year, 49 percent of the institutionalized subjects showed "extreme deterioration" (including death) compared to 18 percent for the community sample follow-up. Given the lack of comparability of the two groups, the authors

490 The Residential Environment and Its Impact on the Mental Health of the Aged

are right in noting, somewhat wistfully, that "these findings are difficult to interpret" (Tobin and Lieberman, 1976, p. 175). In a search for psychological characteristics which could be interpreted as specific predictors of morbidity or mortality (i.e., those which are not also predictors of outcome in the other two comparison samples), only one variable was identified: passivity increased the risk for deterioration.

There are other studies which deal with differences in adjustment to an institutional setting, but they are better seen as reflecting continuity of psychological and social functioning than as predicting outcome. For example, Bennett and Nahemow (1965b) show rather nicely that those residents in a home for the aged who prior to entry had had only a few social contacts in the community had, subsequently, few social contacts in the home and had a harder time learning about the norms and the ways of the home. Similarly, the finding that the aged persons most likely to have adjustment difficulties during the first month after admission are those who, prior to admission, had poor capacity for interpersonal relationship, had severe chronic brain syndrome, had often been referred for psychiatric evaluation before admission, etc., etc., (Rodstein, Savitsky, and Starkman, 1976) hardly represents a leap of great predictive power.

Circumstances surrounding the institutionalization remain a fairly unexplored area for understanding the later impact of institutionalization. Schulz and Brenner (1977) hypothesize that voluntary moves from community to institution should have a lesser impact than involuntary ones, but it is exceedingly difficult to operationalize the "voluntariness" aspects of an institutionalization experience (Lieberman, 1974b). Ferrari (1963) has reported that among the elderly who were institutionalized, those who had no choice but to be placed in an institution had higher mortality rates after admission than those for whom other alternatives were also available. (However, it is not clear to what extent initial differences in health status are confounding these mortality differences.) Morris (1975) has noted that the decline in morale may be smaller among those for whom residency at an institution is judged to be clinically appropriate than among those for whom it is judged less appropriate. The distinction between institutionalization from home vs. from another institutional setting has also been examined. Schulz and Aderman (1973) showed that among those admitted to a facility which provided long term care for indigent patients with terminal cancer, persons admitted from hospitals lived twice as long (60 days)

as those admitted from home (32 days); it does not appear likely that severity of the disease at admission can explain this difference. Smith and Brand (1975), on the other hand, found a lesser impact (as reflected in higher life satisfaction) among institutionalized patients who had been admitted from home, compared to those admitted from medical care institutions. However, the former were also in much better health and of higher social status, variables which were left uncontrolled.

Cross-sectional comparisons between community-living and institution-living elderly continue being done (e.g., Abdo, Dills, Shectman, and Yanish, 1973; Dudley and Hillery, 1977), and they continue being of marginal interpretability. Cross-sectional comparisons of waiting-list samples with institutional samples are beginning to converge with their evidence (e.g., Anderson, 1967; Kasl, 1972; Tobin and Lieberman, 1976) of only small differences between the two groups. However, we cannot as yet tell to what extent one or more of the following are involved: (a) a common self-selection process; (b) "stressfulness" of waiting-list status is comparable to institutional environmental impact; (c) attrition processes and administrative practices create a spurious equivalence. Cross-sectional comparisons of contrasting institutional environments (e.g., Bennett and Nahemow, 1972; Pincus and Wood, 1970) continue being eminently worthwhile, provided one can adequately control for extraneous factors which correlate both with institutional environmental conditions and with pre-institutional characteristics of the residents. The emphasis on social interaction-social isolation (e.g., Bennett, 1973) appears fully appropriate in view of its crucial link to subjective well-being (Larson, 1978), but criteria of institutional adjustment continue to pose some problem of the investigator's selective value judgment.

The dream of a fully prospective study with the investigator having experimental control over assignment to conditions remains just that. The only tantalizing study of this kind which we have found (Blenker, 1967) involved very small numbers, but very suggestive results. In an experiment designed to test the effects of social work and public health nursing services for non-institutionalized aged, participants were randomly assigned to three service programs, ranging from minimal (providing information and direction) to maximal (intensive program of direct service). At six month follow-up, the death rate in the maximal program group was the highest and in the minimal program, the lowest. The suggested explanation for this surprising outcome was that frequently the maximal service was directed toward securing the necessary care in settings other than the person's home. The "better" medical care thus involved uprooting from familiar surroundings.

## SOME CONCLUDING COMMENTS

In this chapter we have reviewed a number of content areas which pertain to the issue of the impact of the residential environment on the mental health of the elderly. However, because the boundaries of the topic of this chapter are indefinite—they represent our own construction of what can be reasonably managed in an effort of this kind and what are the major topics that need to be covered—it is well to remind the reader of the limitations of our chosen level and scope of inquiry. On the one hand, we have omitted the larger setting of the housing and neighborhood variables, that is, the level of the total community and beyond. Traditionally, this would include a concern with the rural-urban distinction, with regional differences, and even international or cross-cultural comparisons. On the other hand, we have also omitted a more microscopic level of analysis, one which would deal with the possible intervening processes involved in the overall associations. This literature falls into two primary categories. One is the concern with the proximate physical residential environment and its impact on behavior, the domain of proxemics (Stokols, 1978). Typical studies here are those which relate facility design and spatial proximity to social interaction (e.g., Cluff and Campbell, 1975; Friedman, 1966; Snyder, 1973). A more microscopic level of analysis is also seen in the Lawton, Patnaik, and Kleban (1976) study, which related the experience of intrainstitutional room transfer to various behaviors and activities (e.g., leaving the door to one's room open) and their location. The primary justification for leaving out the proxemics studies is that they do not deal directly with mental health outcomes (Hinkle and Loring, 1977; Stokols, 1978), though it is acknowledged that they may deal with significant behavioral precursors which ultimately link up with variations in mental health status.

The other category of literature omitted from this review is the theoretical writing on man-environment relations. Particularly important here are the notions of person-environment fit, either in their general form (e.g., French, Rodgers, and Cobb, 1974) or those specific to a particular setting such as an institution (e.g., Kahana, 1974). The primary justification for omitting this literature is that the recent reviews of the residential environ-

ment of the aged (Carp, 1976a; Lawton, 1977; Lawton and Nahemow, 1973) all have an excellent exposition of these theories, and the field simply has not moved that fast since then to require any updating.

It would be foolish to attempt to summarize the content of this review, since any further distillation of such a large set of studies only invites a less balanced, more idiosyncratic perspective that usually goes along with such brevity. Nevertheless, we are tempted to offer three parting observations.

**(1)** The impact of the residential environment on mental health of the elderly certainly does not appear to be overwhelming. The impact is greatest on housing satisfaction and evaluative perceptions, less on social and leisure activities, less on evaluation of current life circumstances, and least on more traditional indicators of mental health. The reader is invited to decide for himself/herself whether such "soft" indicators of "quality of life" as housing satisfactions are to be viewed as mental health indices. Social interaction, in most studies, is seen as a worthwhile impact criterion of its own, though its causal link to traditional mental health indices is more problematic than the plethora of observed cross-sectional correlations would suggest.

**(2)** Social and physical environmental variables obviously interact in their impact, most prominently in the joint influence of physical proximity and social homogeneity on social interaction. In many other instances, the fusion of these two classes of variables is problematic since it prevents the investigator from disentangling their separate and interactive effects; this is because many of such studies are based on housing interventions which are also always social interventions, whether intentionally or unintentionally. The strongest negative impact of the residential environment appears to be associated with certain life experiences which have in them embedded a residential change. Since some of these changes are across comparable residential environments, it is difficult to avoid conceptualizing such experience primarily in social terms.

**(3)** Social gerontological research on the residential environment of the aged is typically opportunistic and cross-disciplinary. Both characteristics are desirable, inevitable. We hope that this review will contribute to a greater selectivity from among the obvious research opportunities, and a more diligent search for the less obvious opportunities which would, however, permit a more definitive examination of the various issues (almost always prospective and longitudinal). We also hope that cross-disciplinary research will less often involve the lowest common denominator from the several disciplines involved, and more often the borrowing of the best methodology available from each discipline.

# REFERENCES

ABDO, E., DILLS, J., SHECTMAN, H., AND YANISH, M. 1973. Elderly women in institutions versus those in public housing: Comparison of personal and social adjustments. *J. Amer. Geriat. Soc., 21*, 81–87.

ABEY-WICKRAMA, I., BROOK, M. E. A., GATTONI, F. E. G., AND HERRIDGE, C. F. 1969. Mental-hospital admissions and aircraft noise. *Lancet, II*, 1275–1278.

ALDRICH, C. K. 1964. Personality factors and mortality in the relocation of the aged. *Gerontologist, 4*, 92–93.

ALDRICH, C. K., AND MENDKOFF, E. 1963. Relocation of the aged and disabled: a mortality study. *J. Amer. Geriat. Soc., 11*, 185–194.

ALEKSANDROWICZ, D. R. 1961. Fire and its aftermath on a geriatric ward. *Bull. Menninger Clinic, 25*, 23–32.

ALTMAN, I. 1975. *The Environment and Social Behavior.* Monterey, Ca.: Brooks/Cole.

ANDERSON, N. N. 1967. Effects of institutionalization on self-esteem. *J. Gerontol., 22*, 313–317.

ANDREWS, F., AND WITHEY, S. 1974. Developing measures of perceived life quality: Results from several national surveys. *Social Indicators Research, 1*, 1–26.

ARCHEA, J. 1977. The place of architectural factors in behavioral theories of privacy. *J. Social Issues, 33*(3), 116–137.

ASHFORD, N., AND HOLLOWAY, F. M. 1972. Transportation patterns of older people in six urban centers. *Gerontologist, 12*, 43–47.

BELL, B. D. 1976. The impact of housing relocation on the elderly: An alternative methodological approach. *Int. J. Aging and Human Develop., 7*, 27–37.

BENNETT, R. 1963. The meaning of institutional life. *Gerontologist, 3*, 117–125.

BENNETT, R. 1973. Living conditions and everyday needs of the elderly with particular reference to social isolation. *Int. J. Aging and Human Develop., 4*, 179–198.

BENNETT, R., AND NAHEMOW, L. 1965a. Institutional totality and criteria of social adjustment in residence for the aged. *J. Social Issues, 21*(4), 44–78.

BENNETT, R., AND NAHEMOW, L. D. 1965b. The relation between social isolation, socialization, and adjustment in residents of a home for aged. *In*, M. P. Lawton and F. G. Lawton (eds.), *Mental Impairment of the Aged*, pp. 88–105. Philadelphia: Philadelphia Geriatric Center.

BENNETT, R., AND NAHEMOW, L. 1972. Socialization and social adjustment in five residential settings for the aged. *In*, D. P. Kent, R. Kastenbaum, and J. Sherwood (eds.), *Research Planning and Action for the Elderly*, pp. 514–524. New York: Behavioral Publications, Inc.

BERGER, B. 1960. *Working Class Suburb: A Study of Autoworkers in Suburbia.* Berkeley: University of California Press.

BEYER, G. H., AND WOODS, M. E. 1963. *Living and Activity Patterns of the Aged.* Ithaca, N.Y.: Center for Housing and Environmental Studies, Cornell University.

BLENKER, M. 1967. Environmental change and the changing individual. *Gerontologist, 7*, 101–105.

BORTNER, R. W., AND HULTSCH D. F. 1970. A multivariate analysis of correlates of life satisfaction in adulthood. *J. Gerontol., 25*, 41–47.

BOURESTON, N., AND TARS, S. 1974. Alterations in life patterns following nursing home relocation. *Gerontologist, 14*, 506–510.

BRAND, F.N., AND SMITH, R. T. 1974. Life adjustment and relocation of the elderly. *J. Gerontol., 29*, 336–340.

BRENNER, B. 1975. Quality of affect and self-evaluated happiness. *Social Indicators Research, 2*, 315–331.

BRODY, E. M. 1978. Community housing for the elderly, the program, the people, the decision-making process, and the research. *Gerontologist, 18*, 121–128.

BRODY, E. M., KLEBAN, M. H., AND LIEBOWITZ, B. 1975. Intermediate housing for the elderly: Satisfaction of those who moved in and those who did not. *Gerontologist, 15*, 350–356.

BULTENA, G. L. 1969. The relationship of occupational status of friendship ties in three planned retirement communities. *J. Gerontol., 24*, 461–464.

BULTENA, G. L. 1974. Structural effects on the morale of the aged: A comparison of age-segregated and age-integrated communities. *In*, J.F. Gubrium (ed.), *Late Life: Communities and Environmental Policy*, pp. 18–31. Springfield, Ill.: Charles C Thomas.

BULTENA, G. L., AND WOOD, V. 1969. The American retirement community: Bane or blessing? *J. Gerontol., 24*, 209–217.

BURGESS, E. W. 1960. Family structure and relationships. *In*, E. W. Burgess (ed.), *Aging in Western Societies*, pp. 271–298. Chicago: University of Chicago Press.

CAMPBELL, A., CONVERSE, P. E., AND RODGERS, W. L. 1976. *The Quality of American Life.* New York: Russell Sage.

CANTILLI, E. J., AND SHMELZER, J. L. (eds.) 1971. *Transportation and Aging: Selected Issues.* Washington, D.C.: US Government Printing Office.

CANTRIL, A. H., AND ROLL, C. W., Jr. 1971. *Hopes and Fears of the American People.* New York: Universe Books.

CARP, F. M. 1966. *A Future for the Aged.* Austin: University of Texas Press.

CARP, F. M. 1974. Short-term and long-term prediction of adjustment to a new environment. *J. Gerontol., 29,* 444–453.

CARP, F. M. 1975a. Ego-defense or cognitive consistency effects on environmental evaluations. *J. Gerontol., 30,* 707–711.

CARP, F. M. 1975b. Housing and living arrangement. *In,* L. E. Brown and E. O. Ellis (eds.), *Quality of Life: The Later Years,* pp. 168–176. Acton, Mass.: Publishing Sciences Group.

CARP, F. M. 1975c. Impact of improved housing on morale and life satisfaction. *Gerontologist, 15,* 511–515.

CARP, F. M. 1975d. Long-range satisfaction with housing. *Gerontologist, 15,* 68–72.

CARP, F. M. 1976a. Housing and living environments of older people. *In,* R. H. Binstock and E. Shanas (eds.), *Handbook of Aging and the Social Sciences,* pp. 244–271. New York: Van Nostrand Reinhold.

CARP, F. M. 1976b. User evaluation of housing for the elderly. *Gerontologist, 16,* 102–111.

CARP, F. M. 1977. Impact of improved living environment on health and life expectancy. *Gerontologist, 17,* 242–249.

CLAUSEN, J. A. 1969. Methodological issues in the measurement of mental health of the aged. *In,* M. F. Lowenthal and A. Zilli (eds.), *Colloquium on Health and Aging of the Population,* pp. 111–127. Basel: S. Karger.

CLUFF, P. J., AND CAMPBELL, W. H. 1975. The social corridor: An environmental and behavioral evaluation. *Gerontologist, 15,* 516–523.

COBB, S. 1976. Social support as a moderator of life stress. *Psychosom. Med., 38,* 300–314.

CONKLIN, J. E. 1976. Robbery, the elderly, and fear: An urban problem in search of a solution. *In,* J. Goldsmith and S. S. Goldsmith (eds.), *Crime and the Elderly,* pp. 99–110. Lexington, Mass.: Lexington Books.

CONNER, K. H., AND POWERS, E. A. 1975. Structural effects and life satisfaction among the aged. *Int. J. Aging and Human Develop., 6,* 321–327.

COOK, T. D., AND CAMPBELL, D. T. 1976. The design and conduct of quasi-experiments and true experiments in field settings. *In,* M. D. Dunnette (ed.), *Handbook of Industrial and Organizational Psychology,* pp. 223–326. Chicago: Rand McNally.

COSTELLO, J. P., AND TANAKA, G. M. 1961. Mortality and morbidity in longterm institutional care of the aged. *J. Amer. Geriat. Soc., 9,* 959–963.

CUTLER, S. J. 1972. The availability of personal transportation, residential location, and life satisfaction among the aged. *J. Gerontol., 27,* 383–389.

CUTLER, S. J. 1975. Transportation and changes in life satisfaction. *Gerontologist, 15,* 155–159.

DOHRENWEND, B. P. 1973. Some issues in the definition and measurement of psychiatric disorders in general populations. *In,* National Center for Health Statistics, *Proceedings of the 14th National Meeting of the Public Health Conference on Records and Statistics,* DHEW Publication No. (HRA) 74-1214, pp. 480–489. Washington, D.C.: US Government Printing Office.

DOHRENWEND, B. S., DOHRENWEND, B. P., AND COOK, D. 1973. Ability and disability in role functioning in psychiatric patient and non-patient groups. *In,* J. K. Wing and H. Hafner (eds.), *Roots of Evaluation,* pp. 337–360. London: Oxford University Press.

DONAHUE, W., AND ASHLEY, E. E., 3rd. 1965. Housing and the social health of older people in the United States. *In,* A. A. Katz and J. S. Felton (eds.), *Health and the Community,* pp. 149–163. New York: The Free Press.

DRETTBOOM, T., JR., MCALLISTER, R. J., KAISER, E. J., AND BUTLER, E. W. 1971. Urban violence and residential mobility. *J. Amer. Inst. Planners, 37,* 319–325.

DUDLEY, C. J., AND HILLERY, G. A., JR. 1977. Freedom and alienation in homes for the aged. *Gerontologist, 17,* 140–145.

DUNHAM, H. W. 1966. Epidemiology of psychiatric disorders as a contribution to medical ecology. *Arch. Gen. Psychiat., 14,* 1–19.

ESSER, A. H. 1973. Experiences of crowding: Illustration of a paradigm for man-environment relations. *Representative Research in Social Psychology, 4,* 207–218.

FERRARI, N. A. 1963. Freedom of choice. *Social Work, 8,* 105–106.

FOOTE, N. N., ABU-LUGHOD, J., FOLEY, M. M., AND WINNICK, L. 1960. *Housing Choices and Housing Constraints.* New York: McGraw-Hill.

FRENCH, J. R. P., JR., AND KAHN, R. L. 1962. A programmatic approach to studying the industrial environment and mental health. *J. Social Issues, 18*(3), 1–47.

FRENCH, J. R. P., JR., RODGERS, W. L., AND COBB, S. 1974. Adjustment as person-environment fit. *In,* G. V. Coelho, D. A. Hamburg and J. E. Adams (eds.), *Coping and Adaptation,* pp. 316–333. New York: Basic Books.

FRIED, M. 1963. Grieving for a lost home. *In,* L. J. Duhl (ed.), *The Urban Condition,* pp. 151–171. New York: Basic Books.

FRIED, M. 1965. Transitional functions of working-class communities: Implications for forced relocation. *In,* M. B. Kantor (ed.), *Mobility and Mental Health,* 123–165. Springfield, Ill.: Charles C Thomas.

FRIEDMAN, E. P. 1966. Spatial proximity and social interaction in a home for the aged. *J. Gerontol., 21,* 566–570.

GANS, H. J. 1963. The effects of the move from city to

suburb. *In*, L. J. Duhl (ed.), *The Urban Condition*, pp. 184–198. New York: Basic Books.

GANS, H. J. 1967. *The Levittowners*. New York: Pantheon Books.

GEDDES, R., AND GUTMAN, R. 1977. The assessment of the built-environment for safety: Research and practice. *In*, L. E. Hinkle, Jr., and W. C. Loring (eds.), *The Effect of the Man-Made Environment on Health and Behavior*, pp. 143–195. Center for Disease Control, Atlanta: DHEW Publication No. (CDC) 77–8318.

GELWICKS, L. E., AND NEWCOMER, R. J. 1974. *Planning Housing Environments for the Elderly*. Washington, D.C.: National Council and the Aging.

GILBERTSON, W. E., AND MOOD, E. W. 1964. Housing, the residential environment, and health—A re-evaluation. *Amer. J. Pub. Health, 54*, 2009–2113.

GLAZER, N. 1967. The effects of poor housing. *J. Marriage and Family, 29*, 140–145.

GOFFMAN, E. 1961. *Asylums*. New York: Doubleday.

GOLANT, S. M. 1976. Intraurban transportation needs and problems of the elderly. *In*, M. P. Lawton, R. J. Newcomer, and T. O. Byerts (eds.), *Community Planning for an Aging Society*, pp. 282–308. Stroudsburg, Pa.: Dowden, Hutchinson, and Ross.

GOLANT, S. M. 1977. The housing tenure adjustments of the young and the elderly; policy implications. *Urban Affairs Quart., 13*, 95–108.

GOLDFARB, A. I., SHAHINIAN, S. P., AND BURR, H. T. 1972. Death rate of relocated nursing home residents. *In*, D. P. Kent, R. Kastenbaum, and S. Sherwood (eds.), *Research Planning and Action for the Elderly*, pp. 525–537. New York: Behavioral Publications, Inc.

GOLDSCHEIDER, C. 1966. Differential residential mobility of the older population. *J. Gerontol., 21*, 103–108.

GOLDSMITH, J., AND GOLDSMITH, S. S. 1976. Crime and the elderly: An overview. *In*, J. Goldsmith and S. S. Goldsmith (eds.), *Crime and the Elderly*, pp. 1–4. Lexington, Mass.: Lexington Books.

GOLDSMITH, J. R., AND JONSSON, E. 1973. Health effects of community noise. *Amer. J. Public Health, 63*, 782–793.

GRAY, R. M., AND MOBERG, D. O. 1962. *The Church and the Older Person*. Grand Rapids, Mich.: Eerdmans.

GRUENBERG, E. M. 1954. Community conditions and psychoses of the elderly. *Amer. J. Psychiat., 110*, 888–896.

GUBRIUM, J. F. 1974. Victimization in old age: Available evidence and three hypotheses. *Crime and Delinquency, 20*, 245–250.

GUTMAN, G. M., AND HERBERT, C. P. 1976. Mortality rates among relocated extended-care patients. *J. Gerontol., 31*, 352–357.

GUTMAN, R. (ed.) 1972. *People and Buildings*. New York: Basic Books.

HAMOVITCH, M. B., AND PETERSON, J. E. 1969. Housing needs and satisfactions of the elderly. *Gerontologist, 9* 30–32

HAMOVITCH, M. B., PETERSON, J. A., AND LARSON, A. E. 1969. Perceptions and fulfillment of housing needs of an aging population. Paper presented at the 8th International Congress of Gerontology, Washington, D.C.

HAVINGHURST, R. J. 1969. Research and development goals in social gerontology. A report of a special committee of the Gerontological Society. *Gerontologist, 9*, 1–90.

HINKLE, L. E., JR., AND LORING, W. C. (eds.) 1977. *The Effect of the Man-Made Environment on Health and Behavior*. Center for Disease Control, Atlanta: DHEW Publication No. (CDC) 77-8318.

HOWELL, S. C., AND LOEB, M. B. 1969. Nutrition and aging: A monograph for practitioners. *Gerontologist, 9*(3,Pt.II), 7–122.

JAHODA, M. 1958. *Current Concepts of Positive Mental Health*. New York: Basic Books.

JASNAU, K. F. 1967. Individualized versus mass transfer of nonpsychotic geriatric patients from mental hospitals to nursing homes, with special reference to the death rate. *J. Amer. Geriat. Soc., 15*, 280–284.

KAHANA, E. 1974. Matching environments to needs of the aged: A conceptual scheme. *In*, J. F. Gubrium (ed.), *Later Life: Communities and Environmental Policy*, pp. 201–214. Springfield, Ill.: Charles C Thomas.

KAPLAN, B. H., CASSEL, J. C., AND GORE, S. 1977. Social support and health. *Med. Care, 15*(No. 5, Supplement), 47–58.

KASL, S. V. 1972. Physical and mental health effects of involuntary relocation and institutionalization—a review. *Amer. J. Pub. Health, 62*, 377–384.

KASL, S. V. 1976. Effects of housing on mental and physical health. *In, Housing in the Seventies, Working Papers 1*, pp. 286–304. Washington, D.C.: US Department of Housing and Urban Development.

KASL, S. V., AND HARBURG, E. 1972. Perceptions of the neighborhood and the desire to move out. *J. Amer. Inst. Planners, 38*, 318–324.

KASL, S. V., AND HARBURG, E. 1975. Mental health and the urban environment: Some doubts and second thoughts. *J. Health and Soc. Behav., 16*, 268–282.

KASL, S. V., OSTFELD, A. M., BRODY, G. M., SNELL, L., AND PRICE, C. A. In press. Effects of "involuntary" relocation on the health and behavior of the elderly. *In, Proceedings of the Epidemiology of Aging Conference*. Bethesda: National Institute of Aging.

KASTELER, J. M., GRAY, R. M., AND CARRUTH, M. L. 1968. Involuntary relocation of the elderly. *Gerontologist, 8*, 276–279.

KENNEDY, J. M., AND DEJONG, G. F. 1977. Aged in cities: residential segregation in 10 USA central cities. *J. Gerontol., 32*, 97–102.

KEY, W. H. 1967. *When People Are Forced to Move.* Topeka, Kansas: The Menninger Foundation.

KENT, E. A. 1963. Role of admission stress in adaptation of older persons in institutions. *Geriatrics, 18,* 133–138.

KILLIAN, E. C. 1970. Effect of geriatric transfers on mortality rates. *Social Work, 15,* 19–26.

KLEBAN, M. H., AND TURNER-MASSEY, P. 1978. Short-range effects of community housing. *Gerontologist, 18,* 129–132.

KLEEMEIER, R. W. 1963. Attitudes toward special settings for the aged. *In,* R. H. Williams, C. Tibbits, and W. Donahue (eds.), *Processes of Aging,* (Vol. II), pp. 101–121. New York: Atherton Press.

KRAL, V. A., GRAD, B., AND BERENSON, J. 1968. Stress reactions resulting from the relocation of an aged population. *Canad. J. Psychiat. Assoc. J., 13,* 201–209.

KRYTER, K. D. 1970. *The Effects of Noise on Man.* New York: Academic Press.

LANGFORD, M. 1962. Community aspects of housing for the aged. *Research Report No. 5.* Ithaca, N.Y.: Center for Housing and Environmental Studies, Cornell University.

LANGER, E. J., AND RODIN, J. 1976. The effects of choice and enhanced personal responsibility for the aged: A field experiment in an institutional setting. *J. Pers. & Soc. Psychol., 34,* 191–198.

LANSING J. B., AND MARANS, R. W. 1969. Evaluation of neighborhood quality. *J. Amer. Inst. Planners, 35,* 195–199.

LARSON, C. J. 1974. Alienation and public housing for the elderly. *Int. J. Aging and Human Develop., 5,* 217–230.

LARSON, R. 1978. Thirty years of research on the subjective well-being of older Americans. *J. Gerontol., 33,* 109–125.

LAWTON, M.P. 1969. Supportive services in the context of the housing environment. *Gerontologist, 9,* 15-19.

LAWTON, M.P. 1975. *Planning and Managing Housing for the Elderly.* New York: John Wiley.

LAWTON, M. P. 1976. The relative impact of congregate and traditional housing on elderly tenants. *Gerontologist, 16,* 237–242.

LAWTON, M. P. 1977. The impact of the environment on aging and behavior. *In,* J. E. Birren and K. W. Schaie (eds.), *Handbook of the Psychology of Aging,* pp. 276–301. New York: Van Nostrand Reinhold.

LAWTON, M. P., BRODY, E. M., AND TURNER-MASSEY, P. 1978. The relationships of environmental factors to changes in well-being. *Gerontologist, 18,* 133–137.

LAWTON, M. P., AND COHEN, J. 1974. The generality of housing impact on the well-being of older people. *J. Gerontol., 29,* 194–204.

LAWTON, M. P., KLEBAN. M. H., AND SINGER, M. 1971. The aged Jewish person and the slum environment. *J. Gerontol., 26,* 231–239.

LAWTON, M. P., AND NAHEMOW, L. 1973. Ecology and the aging process. *In,* C. Eisdorfer and M. P. Lawton (eds.), *The Psychology of Adult Development and Aging,* pp. 619–674. Washington, D.C.: American Psychological Association.

LAWTON, M. P., NAHEMOW, L., AND TEAFF, J. 1975. Housing characteristics and the well-being of elderly tenants in federally assisted housing. *J. Gerontol., 30,* 601–607.

LAWTON, M. P., NAHEMOW, L., YAFFE, S., AND FELDMAN, S. 1976. Psychological aspects of crime and fear of crime. *In,* J. Goldsmith and S. S. Goldsmith (eds.), *Crime and the Elderly,* pp. 21–29. Lexington, Mass.: Lexington Books.

LAWTON, M. P., NAHEMOW, L., AND YEH, T.-M. In press. Neighborhood environment and the well-being of older tenants in planned housing. *Int. J. Aging and Human Development.*

LAWTON, M. P., NEWCOMER, R. J., AND BYERTS, T. O. (eds.), 1976. *Community Planning for an Aging Society.* Stroudsburg, Pa.: Dowden, Hutchinson & Ross.

LAWTON, M. P., PATNAIK, B., AND KLEBAN, M. H. 1976. The ecology of adaptation to a new environment. *Int. J. Aging and Human Develop., 7,* 15–25.

LAWTON, M. P., AND YAFFE, S. 1970. Mortality, morbidity, and voluntary change of residence by older people. *J. Amer. Geriat. Soc., 18,* 823–831.

LEBOWITZ, B. D. 1975. Age and fearfulness: Personal and situational factors. *J. Gerontol., 30,* 696–700.

LIEBERMAN, M. A. 1961. Relationship of mortality rates to entrance to a home for the aged. *Geriatrics, 16,* 515–519.

LIEBERMAN, M. A. 1966. Factors in environmental change. *In,* F. M. Carp and W. M. Burnette (eds.), *Patterns of Living and Housing of Middle-Aged and Older People,* pp. 117–125. Washington, D.C.: U.S. Dept. of Health, Education and Welfare, Publication No. 1496.

LIEBERMAN, M. A. 1969. Institutionalization of the aged: Effects on behavior. *J. Gerontol., 24,* 330–340.

LIEBERMAN, M. A. 1971. Some issues in studying psychological predictors of survival. *In,* E. Palmore and F. C. Jeffers (eds.), *Prediction of Life Span,* pp. 167–179. Lexington, Mass.: Lexington Books.

LIEBERMAN, M. A. 1974a. Relocation research and social policy. *Gerontologist, 14,* 494–501.

LIEBERMAN, M. A. 1974b. Relocation research and social policy. *In,* J. F. Gubrium (ed.), *Late Life: Communities and Environmental Policy,* pp. 5–17. Springfield, Ill.: Charles C Thomas.

LIEBERMAN, M. A., PROCK, V. N., AND TOBIN, S. S. 1968. Psychological effects of institutionalization. *J. Gerontol., 23,* 343–353.

LOUIS HARRIS AND Associates, Inc. 1976. A study of public attitudes toward federal government assistance for housing for low income and moderate income families. *In, Housing in the Seventies, Working Papers 2,* pp. 1433–1481. Washington, D.C.: U.S. Dept. of Housing and Urban Development.

LOWENTHAL, M. F., AND BOLER, D. 1965. Voluntary vs. involuntary social withdrawal. *J. Gerontol., 20,* 363–371.

MANN, S. H. 1977. The use of social indicators in environmental planning. *In,* I. Altman and J. F. Wohlwill (eds.), *Human Behavior and Environment, Vol. 2,* pp. 307–330. New York: Plenum Press.

MARGULIS, S. T. 1977. Conceptions of privacy: current status and next steps. *J. Social Issues, 33*(3), 5–21.

MARKSON, E. W., AND CUMMING, J. H. 1974. A strategy of necessary mass transfer and its impact on patient mortality. *J. Gerontol., 29,* 315–321.

MARKSON, E. W., AND CUMMING, J. H. 1975. The post-transfer fate of relocated mental patients in New York. *Gerontologist, 15,* 104–108.

MARKUS, E., BLENKER, M., BLOOM, M., AND DOWNS, T. 1970. Relocation stress and the aged. *In,* H. T. Blumenthal (ed.), *Interdisciplinary Topics in Gerontology, Vol. 7. The Regulatory Role of the Nervous System in Aging,* pp. 60–71. Basel: S. Karger.

MARKUS, E., BLENKER, M., BLOOM, M., AND DOWNS, T. 1971. The impact of relocation upon mortality rates of institutionalized aged persons. *J. Gerontol., 26,* 537–541.

MARKUS, E., BLENKER, M., BLOOM, M., AND DOWNS, T. 1972. Some factors and their association with post-relocation mortality among institutionalized aged persons. *J. Gerontol., 27,* 376–382.

MESSER, M. 1967. The possibility of an age-concentrated environment becoming a normative system. *Gerontologist, 7,* 247–251.

MICHELSON, W. 1976. *Man and His Urban Environment: A Sociological Approach,* 2nd ed. Reading, Mass.: Addison-Wesley.

MILLER, D., AND LIEBERMAN, M. A. 1965. The relationship of affect state and adaptive capacity to reactions to stress. *J. Gerontol., 20,* 492–497.

MOBERG, D. O. 1968. Religiosity in old age. *In,* B. L. Neugarten (ed.), *Middle Age and Aging,* pp. 497–508. Chicago: University of Chicago Press

MORRIS, J. N. 1975. Changes in morale experienced by elderly institutional applicants along the institutional path. *Gerontologist, 15,* 345–349.

NELSON, L. M., AND WINTER, M. 1975. Life disruption, independence, satisfaction, and the consideration of moving. *Gerontologist, 15,* 160–164.

NEUGARTEN, B. L., HAVINGHURST, R. J., AND TOBIN, S. S. 1961. The measurement of life satisfaction. *J. Gerontol., 16,* 134–143.

NEWCOMER, R. 1973. Environmental influences on the older person. *In,* R. H. Davis (ed.), *Aging: Prospects and Issues,* pp. 178–189. Los Angeles: University of Southern California Press.

NEWMAN, O. 1972. *Defensible Space.* New York: Macmillan.

NIEBANCK, P. L. 1966. Knowledge gained in studies of relocation. *In,* F. M. Carp and W. M. Burnette (eds.), *Patterns of Living and Housing of Middle Aged and Older People,* pp. 107–116. Washington, D.C.: U.S. Dept. of Health, Education and Welfare, P.H.S. Publication No. 1496.

NIEBANCK, P. L. 1968. *Relocation in Urban Planning: From Obstacle to Opportunity.* Philadelphia: University of Pennsylvania Press.

NIEBANCK, P. L., AND POPE, J. B. 1965. *The Elderly in Older Urban Areas.* Philadelphia: University of Pennsylvania, Institute for Environmental Studies.

NOVICK, L. J. 1967. Easing the stress of moving day. *Hospitals, 41*(16), 64–74.

PALMORE, E. B. 1968. The effects of aging activities and attitudes. *Gerontologist, 8,* 259–263.

PASTALAN, L. A. 1975. Privacy preferences among relocated institutionalized elderly. *In,* D. H. Carson (ed.), *Man-Environment Interactions: Evaluations and Applications, Part II.,* pp. 73–82. Stroudsburg, Pa.: Dowden, Hutchinson & Ross.

PINCUS, A., AND WOOD, V. 1970. Methodological issues in measuring the environment in institutions for the aged and its impact on residents. *Aging & Human Develop., 1,* 117–126.

PYNOOS, J., SCHAFER, R., AND HARTMAN, C. W. (eds.), 1973. *Housing Urban America.* Chicago: Aldine.

RAINWATER, L. 1966. Fear and the house-as-haven in the lower class. *J. Amer. Inst. Planners, 32,* 23–31.

RAINWATER, L. 1967. The lessons of Pruit-Igoe. *The Public Interest,* Summer, 116–126.

RAINWATER, L. 1970. *Behind Ghetto Walls.* Chicago: Aldine.

REGNIER, V. 1975. Neighborhood planning for the urban elderly. *In,* D. S. WOODRUFF AND J. E. BIRREN (eds.), *Aging: Scientific Perspectives and Social Issues,* pp. 295–312. New York: Van Nostrand, Reinhold.

RIEMER, S. 1951. Architecture for family living. *J. Social Issues, 7*(1–2), 140–151.

RILEY, M. W., AND FONER, A. 1968. *Aging and Society. Vol. I. An Inventory of Research Findings.* New York: Russell Sage.

ROBINSON, W. S. 1950. Ecological correlations and the behavior of individuals. *Amer. Sociol. Rev., 15,* 351–357.

RODSTEIN, M., SAVITSKY, E., AND STARKMAN, R. 1976. Initial adjustment to a long-term care institution: Medical and behavioral aspects. *J. Amer. Geriat. Soc., 24,* 65–71.

ROSENBERG, G. S. 1967. *Poverty, Aging, and Social Isolation.* Washington, D.C.: Bureau of Social Science Research, Inc.

ROSENBERG, G. S. 1968. Age, poverty, and social isolation

from friends in the urban working class. *J. Gerontol., 23,* 533–538.

ROSENBERG, G. S. 1970. *The Worker Grows Old.* San Francisco: Jossey-Bass.

ROSENMAYR, L., AND KOCKEIS, E. 1966. Housing conditions and family relations of the elderly. *In,* F. M. Carp and N. M. Burnett (eds.), *Patterns of Living and Housing of Middle-Aged and Older People,* pp. 29–46. Washington, D.C.: U.S. Dept. of Health, Education and Welfare, P. H. S. Publication No. 1496.

ROSOW, I. 1961. The social effects of the physical environment. *J. Amer. Inst. Planners, 27,* 127–133.

ROSOW, I. 1963. Adjustment of the normal aged. *In,* R. H. Williams, C. Tibbitts, and W. Donahue (eds.), *Processes of Aging Vol. II,* pp. 195–223. New York: Atherton Press.

ROSOW, I. 1967. *Social Integration of the Aged.* New York: The Free Press.

ROWLAND, K. F. 1977. Environmental events predicting death for the elderly. *Psychol. Bull., 84,* 349–372.

SCHOOLER, K. K. 1969a. The relationship between social interaction and morale of the elderly as a function of environmental characteristics. *Gerontologist, 9*(1), 25–29.

SCHOOLER, K. K. 1969b. On the relation between characteristics of residential environment, social behavior, and the emotional and physical health of the elderly in the U.S. Paper presented at the 8th International Congress of Gerontology, Washington, D.C.

SCHOOLER, K. K. 1975. Response of the elderly to environment: A stress-theoretical perspective. *In,* P. G. Windley, T. O. Byents, and F. G. Ernst (eds.), *Theory Development in Environment and Aging,* Washington, D.C.: The Gerontological Society.

SCHOOLER, K. K. 1976. Environmental change and the elderly. *In,* I. Altman and J. Wohlwill (eds.), *Human Behavior and Environment: Advances in Theory and Research,* Vol. 1, pp. 265–298. New York: Plenum.

SCHOOLER, K. K., AND BELLOS, N. 1977. Residential environment and health of the elderly: Use of research results for policy and planning. *In,* L. E. Hinkle, Jr., and W. C. Loring (eds.), *The Effect of the Man Made Environment on Health and Behavior,* pp. 263–300. Center for Disease Control, Atlanta: DHEW Publication No. (CDC) 77–8318.

SCHORR, A. L. 1963. *Slums and Social Insecurity.* Washington, D.C.: Social Security Administration Research Report No. 1.

SCHULZ, R. 1976. Effects of control and predictability on the physical and psychological well-being of institutionalized aged. *J. Pers. and Soc. Psychol., 33,* 563–573.

SCHULZ, R., AND ADERMAN, D. 1973. Effect of residential change on the temporal distance to death of terminal cancer patients. *Omega, 4,* 157–162.

SCHULZ, R., AND BRENNER, G. 1977. Relocation of the aged: A review and theoretical analysis. *J. Gerontol., 32,* 323–333.

SCHWARTZ, A. N. 1975. Planning micro-environments for the aged. *In,* D. S. Woodruff and J. E. Birren (eds.), *Aging: Scientific Perspectives and Social Issues,* pp. 279–294. New York: Van Nostrand, Reinhold.

SCOTT, W. A. 1958. Research definitions of mental health and mental illness. *Psychol. Bull., 55,* 29–45.

SELLS, S. B. (ed.) 1969. *The Definition and Measurement of Mental Health.* PHS Publication No. 1873. Washington, D.C.: U.S. Government Printing Office.

SHANAS, E. 1962. *The Health of Older People.* Cambridge: Harvard University Press.

SHANAS, E., TOWNSEND, P., WEDDERBURN, D., FRIIS, H., MILHØJ, P., AND STEHOUWER, J. 1968. *Old People in Three Industrial Societies.* New York: Atherton Press.

SHELDON, E., AND PARKE, R. 1975. Social indicators. *Science, 188,* 693–699.

SHELDON, J. H. 1954. The social philosophy of old age. *Lancet, II,* 151–155.

SHERMAN, E. A., NEWMAN, E. S., AND NELSON, A. D. 1976. Patterns of age integration in public housing and the incidence and fears of crime among elderly tenants. *In,* J. Goldsmith and S. S. Goldsmith (eds.), *Crime and the Elderly,* pp. 67–73. Lexington, Mass.: Lexington Books.

SHERMAN, S. R. 1972. Satisfaction with retirement housing: Attitudes, recommendations, and moves. *Aging and Human Develop., 3,* 339-366.

SHERMAN, S. R. 1974. Leisure activities in retirement housing. *J. Gerontol., 29,* 325–335.

SHERMAN, S. R. 1975a. Mutual assistance and support in retirement housing. *J. Gerontol., 30,* 479–483.

SHERMAN, S. R. 1975b. Patterns of contacts for residents of age-segregated and age-integrated housing. *J. Gerontol., 30,* 103–107.

SHERMAN, S. R. 1975c. Provision of on-site services in retirement housing. *Int. J. Aging and Human Develop., 6,* 229–247.

SHERMAN, S. R., MAGNUM, W. P., JR., DODDS, S., WALKLEY, R. P., AND WILNER, D. M. 1968. Psychological effects of retirement housing. *Gerontologist, 8* (3,Pt.I), 170–175.

SMITH, M. B. 1961. Mental health reconsidered: A special case of the problem of values in psychology. *Amer. Psychologist, 16,* 299–306.

SMITH, R. T., AND BRAND, F. N. 1975. Effects of enforced relocation on life adjustment in a nursing home. *Int. J. Aging and Human Develop., 6,* 249–259.

SNYDER, L. H. 1973. An exploratory study of patterns of social interaction, organization, and facility design in three nursing homes. *Int. J. Aging and Human Develop., 4,* 319–333.

SPITZER, R. L., AND WILSON, P. T. 1975. Nosology and

the official psychiatric nomenclature. *In,* A. M. Freedman, H. I. Kaplan and B. J. Sadock (eds.), *Comprehensive Textbook in Psychiatry II., Vol. 1,* pp. 826–845. Baltimore: Williams and Wilkins.

SROLE, L. 1975. Measurement and classification in sociopsychiatric epidemiology: Midtown Manhattan Study (1954) and Midtown Manhattan Restudy (1974). *J. Health and Soc. Behav., 16,* 347–364.

SROLE, L., LANGNER, T. S., MICHAEL, S. T., OPLER, M. K., AND RENNIE, T. A. C. 1962. *Mental Health in the Metropolis: The Midtown Manhattan Study.* New York: McGraw-Hill.

STOKOLS, D. 1978. Environmental psychology. *Ann. Rev. Psychol., 29,* 253–295.

STORANDT, M., AND WITTELS, I. 1975. Maintenance of function in relocation of community-dwelling older adults. *J. Gerontol., 30,* 608–612.

STORANDT, M., WITTELS, I., AND BOTWINICK, J. 1975. Predictors of a dimension of well-being in the relocated healthy aged. *J. Gerontol., 30,* 97–102.

STREIB, G. F. 1958. Family patterns in retirement. *J. Soc. Issues, 14*(2), 46–60.

STRUYK, R. J. 1977. The housing situation of elderly Americans. *Gerontologist, 17,* 130–139.

STUTZ, F. P. 1976. Adjustment and mobility of elderly poor amid downtown renewal. *The Geographical Rev., 66,* 391–400.

SUNDEEN, R. A., AND MATHIEU, J. T. 1976. The urban elderly: Environments of fear. *In,* J. Goldsmith and S. S. Goldsmith (eds.), *Crime and the Elderly,* pp. 51–66. Lexington, Mass.: Lexington Books.

SYKES, R. E. 1976. The urban police function in regard to the elderly: A special case of police–community relations. *In,* J. Goldsmith and S. S. Goldsmith (eds.), *Crime and the Elderly,* pp. 127–137. Lexington, Mass.: Lexington Books.

TALLMER, M., AND KUTNER, B. 1969. Disengagement and stresses of aging. *J. Gerontol., 24,* 70–75.

TEAFF, J. D., LAWTON, M. P., NAHEMOW, L., AND CARLSON, D. 1978. Impact of age integration on the well-being of elderly tenants in public housing. *J. Gerontol., 33,* 126–133.

The Report of the President's Committee on Urban Housing. 1969. *A Decent Home.* Washington, D.C.: U.S. Government Printing Office.

THURNHER, M. 1974. Goals, values, and life evaluations at pre-retirement stage. *J. Gerontol., 29,* 85–96.

TOBIN, S. S., AND LIEBERMAN, M. A. 1976. *Last Home for the Aged.* San Francisco: Jossey-Bass.

TOWNSEND, P. 1957. *Family Life of Old People.* London: Routledge and Kegan Paul.

TURNER, B. F., TOBIN, S. S., AND LIEBERMAN, M. A. 1972.

Personality traits as predictors of institutional adaptation among the aged. *J. Gerontol., 27,* 61–68.

WECHSLER, H., AND PUGH, T. F. 1967. Fit of individual and community characteristics and rates of psychiatric hospitalization. *Amer. J. Sociol., 73,* 331–338.

WEINBERG, S. K. 1967. Urban areas and hospitalized psychotics. *In,* S. K. Weinberg (ed.), *The Sociology of Mental Disorders,* pp. 22–26. Chicago: Aldine.

WESSMAN, A. E. 1956. *A Psychological Inquiry into Satisfaction and Happiness.* Princeton, N.J.: Princeton University, unpublished doctoral dissertation.

WILNER, D. M., WALKLEY, R. P., PINKERTON, T. C., AND TAYBACK, M. 1962. *The Housing Environment and Family Life.* Baltimore: The Johns Hopkins Press.

WILSON, W. 1967. Correlates of avowed happiness. *Psychol. Bull., 67,* 294–306.

WINIECKE, L. 1973. The appeal of age segregated housing to the elderly poor. *Int. J. Aging and Human Develop., 4,* 293–306.

WITTELS, I., AND BOTWINICK, J. 1974. Survival in relocation. *J. Gerontol., 29,* 440–443.

WOHLWILL, J. F. 1973. The environment is not in the head. *In,* W. F. E. Preiser (ed.), *Environmental Design Research: Vol. 2, Symposia and Workshops,* pp. 166–181. Stroudsburg, Pa.: Dowden, Hutchinson & Ross.

WOLFE, A., LEX, B., AND YANCEY, W. L. 1968. *The Soulard Area: Adaptations by Urban White Families to Poverty.* St. Louis: Washington University, Social Science Institute.

WOLK, S., AND TELLEEN, S. 1976. Psychological and social correlates of life satisfaction as a function of residential constraint. *J. Gerontol., 31,*89–98.

WOODWARD, H., GINGLES, R., AND WOODWARD, J. C. 1974. Loneliness and the elderly as related to housing. *Gerontologist, 14,* 349–351.

ZEHNER, R. B. 1971. Neighborhood and community satisfaction in new towns and less planned suburbs. *J. Amer. Inst. Planners, 37,* 379–385.

ZUCKERMAN, M., AND LUBIN, B. 1965. *Multiple Affect Adjective Checklist.* San Diego: Educational and Industrial Testing Service.

ZWEIG, J. P., AND CSANK, J. Z. 1975. Effects of relocation on chronically ill geriatric patients of a medical unit: Mortality rates. *J. Amer. Geriat. Soc., 23,* 132–136.

ZWEIG, J. P., AND CSANK, J. Z. 1976. Mortality fluctuations among chronically ill medical geriatric patients as an indicator of stress before and after relocation. *J. Amer. Geriat. Soc., 24,* 264–277.

# V
# Pathology: Diagnosis and Assessment

# 21

# An Approach to the Neurology
of Aging

*David A. Drachman*

## INTRODUCTION

Among the elderly, symptoms and signs of neurologic dysfunction are commonplace. Impairment of memory, intellect, strength, sensation, balance, and coordination are well-known. Caird and his colleagues have shown that neurologic disorders are the most common causes of disability in the elderly, accounting for almost half of the incapacitation beyond the age of 65, and over 90 percent of serious dependency. (Akhtar, Broe, Crombie *et al.*, 1973; Broe, Akhtar, Andrews *et al.*, 1976.) (In addition to the references cited later in the text, see Brewis, Poskanzer, Rolland *et al.*, 1966; Gilbert and Levee, 1971; Jerome, 1959; and Kinsbourne, 1977.)

Why should the nervous system, more than any other organ, be susceptible to debilitating deterioration in the aged? In large part, this is be-cause the nervous system consists of exclusively post-mitotic neuronal elements; every neuron present in the octogenarian was present at the time of his birth (Strehler, 1975). We know somewhat less about the persistence of neural connections and their replaceability during life, although the axons and dendrites, too, are likely to be relatively permanent components of the nervous system (Raisman, 1978). Strehler has pointed out the teleologic advantage of this arrangement, which permits an individual to retain information that has been acquired (Strehler, 1975). If the neural elements were constantly replaced, the possibility of accumulating lasting memories would be markedly diminished.

One of the consequences of this otherwise useful arrangement is the inevitable deterioration of the system over time. Elements that wear out cannot be replaced; nor can those that are damaged. Even in a system with a large "safety factor", or excess of neural elements, the ability to compensate for losses — either present or past — declines as its reserve diminishes (Laurence and Stein, 1977; Stein and Firl, 1976).

For these reasons, neurologic deterioration in the elderly should be viewed as the cumulative summation of four factors

1. *"normal" neuronal attrition (involution over time);*
2. *previous neural damage, occurring in the past;*
3. *decline in neural reserve, or "plasticity"; and*
4. *specific disease of the nervous system present at the time of evaluation.*

Among different individuals, the rate of involutional change, the burden of previous damage, the amount of neural reserve, and the presence or extent of current nervous system disease may vary considerably. Clinical neurologic disorders become evident when any or all of these factors reach some *threshold of clinical deficit*. In practice, this threshold may depend not only upon the initial endowment of the individual and the summation of his neural losses, but also upon the demands of the particular situation in which a deficit becomes apparent. Thus, a clinically-apparent deficit may be the result of rapidly-advancing involution alone; specific disease alone (e.g., a major stroke); previous traumatic injury combined with "normal" involution; or a mild new disease process (e.g., a vascular lacune) combined with other factors, etc.

Some of the difficulties in assessing the neurologic status of the elderly, then, are due to the simultaneous operation of multiple factors in producing clinical deterioration; some the result of variability in the rate of involution among different individuals; some due to differing histories of nervous system exposure to injuries that were unnoticed or long-forgotten; and some stem from the differing physical and mental challenges with which aged individuals attempt to cope.

In approaching the neurologic problems of the elderly, the physician must adopt strategies appropriate to both the variations in individual performance and the multiple factors contributing to the deficits. First, he must be able to distinguish between *normal* and *abnormal* neurologic function commensurate with the individual's age. Second, he must determine whether a *specific disease state* exists, or whether the degree of neurologic impairment present is the result of *neural attrition*, *previous damage*, or *loss of neural reserve*. Finally, he must attempt to identify those features of the patient's condition that contribute to his disability, and attempt to improve function by modifying as many of the limiting problems as possible. While ideal treatment would specifically prevent or reverse neural involution, this is possible in only a few conditions; further, involution is only a part of the total picture of neurologic deterioration in the aged individual.

## NORMAL AND ABNORMAL FUNCTION: HEALTH AND DISEASE

"Normal" function, most simply, is regarded as the mean performance on a given test, $\pm 2$ standard deviations, for individuals of a given age. As reasonable as this concept of *normal* —that is equivalent to average —may seem, it presents many problems(Andres, 1967). First, there is much scatter of function in the aged compared with young adults, leading to a less homogeneous pattern of performance. Certain findings commonly seen in the aged (e.g., decreased glucose tolerance; diminished ankle jerk reflexes) are considered to be abnormalities or even diseases in the young. Indeed, the observation that 75 percent of the individuals over the age of 65 have at least one serious chronic illness(Confrey and Goldstein, 1960) makes it impossible to equate normal (= average) function in the elderly with a state of health, or the absence of disease.

The difficulties arising from this concept of normality have led to two other definitions of normal function. The first of these changes the definition of *normal* to restrict it to the average performance of *healthy* aged individuals; that is, those functioning independently, and free of known disease. Although a useful compromise, the difficulty of defining a *healthy* person, and the circular, self-fulfilling nature of the definition give it limited value. The second defines *normal* function in the elderly as equivalent to *ideal* function for all healthy adults. Viewed in this way, findings that occur even quite frequently in an aged population may be considered *abnormal* if they fail to reach some definable minimum standard.

All three concepts of normality must be considered in order to evaluate the neurologic status of aged individuals, and to attempt to distinguish neurologic *disease* from *non-disease*. The physician must recognize that in some aged patients normal involution masquerades as a disease state; while in others, actual disease is concealed in the guise of the normal aging process. Since specific diseases are often treatable, while involution usually is not, this distinction is of central importance in the neurologic assessment.

# THE NEUROLOGICAL EVALUATION

The neurological evaluation of any adult, young or old, includes a history, neurological examination, and a series of laboratory tests (Adams and Victor, 1977; DeJong, 1969; Mayo Clinic, 1976). However, in the elderly a different range of problems is likely to be encountered. The implications of a numb hand or a Babinski (extensor toe) sign are therefore quite different in the 75 year old compared with the 25 year old patient.

## NEUROLOGICAL HISTORY

Every medical history includes the patient's *chief complaint* and a series of *general questions* regarding the present illness: how long it has been present; what makes it better; what makes it worse; is it improving; what medications have been tried; etc. These questions are quite nonspecific and apply equally to complaints of headache, chest pain, or constipation. Non-physicians are often unaware of the subsequent process of inquiry: based on the initial information, the physician must form a *series of hypotheses* and ask pointed questions that help to discriminate among the possibilities. Here, a knowledge of the range of neurologic disorders seen particularly in the elderly becomes important (See Table 21–1). Headache in the young adult, for example, most frequently implies muscle tension or migraine; a new headache in the elderly patient might suggest a subdural hematoma, brain tumor, or temporal arteritis. Where vertigo would suggest inner ear disease or multiple sclerosis in the young adult, the possibility of a cerebrovascular event must be considered in the elderly.

Certain disorders unique to an older population provide an especially difficult history. In the dementing disorders particularly, the patient himself may be either unaware of his intellectual deficits or may deny them; and the history is then obtainable only from the patient's family (Paulson, 1977). Paradoxically, those patients who do complain of memory loss or intellectual impairment are less likely to be significantly demented; more often they are suffering from a depressive state.

Because families' expectations of elderly patients' performance may vary widely, their judgment regarding intactness or degree of impairment may be misleading: the patient who is "very sharp" may be considered so because he remembers his grandchildren's names; while the aged person with a "poor memory" may no longer be able to make as astute business decisions as he once did, though otherwise functioning at a high level.

For this reason it is especially important to ask questions ranging from the ability of the patient to care for his personal needs to his competence in playing bridge or discussing world events. Impairment of memory is most frequently recognized by both patients and their families as the initial deficit in most forms of dementia. If it is determined that a degree of dementia exists, additional questions can help to clarify the nature of the underlying disorder. The abrupt or gradual onset of symptoms, the course of the deterioration, and the association of dementia with other neurologic symptoms may be especially valuable in identifying the underlying condition. Finally, the patient's mood, energy, interests, sleep pattern, and appetite help to determine whether depression is a contributing factor in the impairment of cognitive function.

A similar range of questioning is necessary to differentiate among possible causes of most complaints of the elderly, from dizziness to gait disorders, back pain to hearing loss. The rate of decline of each function is of value in assessing the *pace of involutional processes*. A past history of neurologic injury (e.g., head trauma, minor stroke, encephalitis, etc.) indicates the extent of *previous neural losses*. Finally a *review of the neurologic system should be carried out*, covering the use of alcohol or other drugs, episodes of loss of consciousness, and

**Table 21–1**  Neurological History.

HEAD AND MENTAL FUNCTION
  Headaches
  Dizziness
  Mental or memory change
  CVA
  Head trauma
  Seizures
  Loss of consciousness
  Alcoholism

CRANIAL NERVES
  Loss of smell
  Visual blurring or loss
  Diplopia
  Numbness or weakness of the face
  Hearing loss, tinnitus
  Difficulty in swallowing or speaking

MOTOR AND COORDINATION
  Difficulty in walking
  Clumsiness
  Weakness of an arm or a leg

REFLEXES
  Involuntary spasms of legs

SENSATION
  Numbness or abnormal sensation in limbs

specific inquiries into cranial nerve, motor, and sensory functions.

### NEUROLOGICAL EXAMINATION

The neurological examination of the elderly patient assesses the integrity of the central and peripheral nervous system by a series of maneuvers that can be performed in the office or at the bedside (See Table 21–2). Mental status; cranial nerve functions; gait, motor performance and coordination; reflexes; sensory function; and cranial vasculature are the areas evaluated. The standards of performance must be adjusted in accordance with the patient's age.

*Mental Status.* Assessment of mental function begins with an evaluation of the patient's *state of consciousness*. Several levels of consciousness are recognized, ranging from alertness through lethargy, obtundation, stupor, and coma. In alert patients, orientation for time, place, and person should be specifically tested, and not assumed to be normal based on casual conversation. Adequacy of *information* is evaluated in relation to the patient's educational and cultural background. Questions re-

lating to current events, job, friends, hobbies, etc., should be individually adapted. The evaluation of *memory* may be divided into immediate memory span, storage, long-term memory, and retrieval from old store. Assessment of storage ability is especially valuable. It is roughly evaluated by testing the patient's recall of a list of four items, after five minutes have elapsed. Similar information can be derived by asking the patient about events of the past day, meals, etc. Immediate memory span and long-term memory are often preserved even when storage is seriously impaired. *Calculation* is traditionally tested by asking the patient to subtract sevens serially from 100, then from the remainder, etc. Intactness of *language* function is readily evaluated by having the patient write a test phrase such as, "This is a lovely day in the month of May"; or repeat orally, "no ifs, ands, or buts" Almost all patients with aphasic disorders will have difficulty with one or both of these tasks. Finally, the patient is asked to copy two simple designs (Figure 21–1); a variety of omissions, rotations, etc., are characteristic of certain organic brain disorders.

**Table 21–2**   Neurological Examination

MENTAL STATUS
    State of consciousness
    Orientation
    Information
    Memory
    Calculation
    Language function
    Special testing for aphasia, apraxia, or agnosia

CRANIAL NERVES
    Sense of smell
    Visual acuity, visual fields, optic fundi, ocular motility, pupillary response
    Facial sensation, corneal reflexes, jaw movement, jaw jerk
    Facial movement and symmetry, taste
    Hearing (air, bone conduction), gag reflex, swallowing, phonation
    sternocleidomastoid and trapezius movement
    Tongue motion

MOTOR AND COORDINATION
    Gait, station, walking on heels and toes, tandem gait
    Direct testing of strength, tone and coordination in extremities

REFLEXES
    Deep tendon reflexes, plantar reflexes, abdominal reflexes

SENSATION
    Primary (touch, pinprick, vibration, and position sense)
    Cortical (face-hand, DSS, etc.)

VASCULAR
    Carotid palpation, auscultation for bruits

**Figure 21–1**   Sample design to be copied by a patient during testing.

*Cranial Nerve Functions.* The neurological examination includes evaluation of the functions of the 12 paired cranial nerves; details of the techniques of examination are available in standard neurologic texts (Adams and Victor, 1977, DeJong, 1969). Attention to vision, ocular motility, hearing and speech is especially important in the examination of the aged.

*Gait, Motor Performance and Coordination.* The gait of the elderly is commonly impaired, and may be particularly revealing of any neurologic deterioration. Aged patients should be observed walking in a natural manner, with special attention to the placement of the feet, length of stride, arm swing, balance, ease of turning, freedom of head movement on executing a turn, ability to walk tandem (one foot in front of the other along a straight line), and to walk on toes and heels. The patient is asked to hop on either foot, with the examiner providing balance by holding the patient's hand. Tone in the axial (trunk) musculature is evaluated by rotating the standing patient's shoulders from side to side, observing the degree of passive resistance. Limb tone is assessed by passive flexion and extension of the forearms and wrists, and by flexion and extension of the knees. Tremor should be searched for by having the patient first hold his arms outstretched with the fingers abducted; then attempt to bring the pointing forefingers to a nearly-touching position without actual contact. Writing, and drawing a spiral with closely wound lines, also help to reveal a tremor. Finally, cerebellar coordination and strength in individual muscle groups are assessed in a standard fashion (Mayo Clinic, 1976).

*Reflexes.* Testing of deep tendon and superficial reflexes is well described elsewhere (DeJong, 1969, Mayo Clinic, 1976). Examination of the aged should include special attention to the so-called "frontal release" reflexes — grasp and suck; to the briskness of the ankle jerk reflexes compared with other deep tendon reflexes; and to the plantar reflexes, for the presence of an extensor toe sign. Any asymmetries of other reflexes, their absence or marked increase, should also be noted.

*Sensation.* Although touch, pinprick, position sense and temperature sense are also routinely tested, vibratory sensation distally in the lower extremities, tested with a 128 Hz tuning fork, is most likely to be revealing in elderly patients. Certain cortical sensory tests, particularly including the Face-Hand test (Bender, Fink, and Green, 1951), and other tests of simultaneous perception of symmetrically placed stimuli (pin, touch) are also of special value.

*Cranial Vasculature.* Auscultation of the major cranial vessels should be performed by placing the bell of a stethoscope over the carotid, subclavian, vertebral and ophthalmic arteries.

LABORATORY STUDIES

In Table 21–3, a number of laboratory studies are listed which are useful in the evaluation of aged patients with a variety of complaints. It is by no means complete; yet, even a superficial discussion of the techniques and interpretations is far beyond the scope of this chapter. The specific applications of certain of the tests will be discussed below.

Of all the studies listed, the one that has clearly most altered the neurologic evaluation is computerized axial tomography — the CT scan (New and Scott, 1975). While it is in no sense a substitute for careful neurologic assessment, it permits the visualization of reconstructed radiologic "slices" through the brain. It is capable of visualizing the anatomic appearance of brain sections including details such as the ventricles, gyri and sulci, gray and white matter structures. It is capable

**Table 21–3.** Some Neurological Laboratory Tests Useful in the Aged.

NEURORADIOLOGICAL PROCEDURES
*Non-invasive*
CT scan
Radioisotope scan
Skull x-rays
Spine x-rays

*Invasive*
Angiogram
Myelogram
(Pneumoencephalogram)

ELECTROPHYSIOLOGICAL TESTS
Electroencephalogram
Nerve conduction velocities; Electromyography
Audiometry: Electronystagmography

PSYCHOMETRIC TESTS
WAIS
WMQ
MMPI
Rorschach
Reitan battery, etc.

VASCULAR TESTS
Oculoplethymography (OPG)
Ophthalmodynamometry (ODM)
Phonoangiography
Doppler flow studies

NEURO-OPHTHALMOLOGICAL TESTS
Visual acuity
Visual fields
Slit lamp

LUMBAR PUNCTURE

of revealing lesions (tumors, strokes, etc.) smaller than a centimeter in diameter. Because it is "non-invasive"— that is, entails no procedural risk to the patient — it has become a highly useful means of detecting gross anatomic disorders of the brain.

Other tests listed in Table 21–3 provide the means of evaluating the aged patient's intellectual performance, hearing, visual acuity, cerebral blood flow, etc. Numerous other studies are often needed to evaluate the effects of the cardiac, renal, respiratory, and other systems on neurologic functioning.

## NEUROLOGY OF THE AGED IN THE ABSENCE OF DISEASE

Clinical neurologic changes occurring with age in an undiseased population can be attributed to neurobiologic deterioration. Details of these changes are discussed in chapters 4, 5, and 7 but a brief overview of the biological substrate for nervous system deterioration is presented below.

### NEUROBIOLOGICAL CHANGES WITH AGE

Anatomical, biochemical, physiological, pharmacological, and support-system changes appear to underlie the progressive involution of the nervous system with age. Of all the changes, the anatomic have been most extensively studied and are best understood (Brody, 1975; Corsellis, 1976; Terry and Wiesniewski, 1975, 1977; Tomlinson, 1977; and Tomlinson and Henderson, 1975). Grossly, the weight of the brain declines with age, normally decreasing by about 10 percent from its maximum weight in early adult life to the ninth decade (Corsellis, 1976). There is enlargement of the ventricles and sulci, while both gray and white matter appear to decrease in volume. Neurons are said to be lost at the rate of approximately 100,000 per day. By the 80s, 30 to 50 percent of cortical neurons are lost in certain areas, (Brody, 1955; and 1975) although brainstem neurons (with some exceptions) remain intact. The dendritic branches of the cortical neurons decrease in number and extent, particularly the horizontal dendrites which comprise cortical pathways (Scheibel and Scheibel, 1975; Scheibel, Lindsay, Tomiyasu, et al., 1975). Synaptic connections between neurons also decline as evidenced by the loss of both dendritic spines (Feldman, 1975) and synapses (Bondareff and Geinisman, 1976; Cragg, 1975). Senile plaques, representing degraded dendrites and axons, begin to appear with increasing frequency and in increasing numbers

with advancing age, as do neuro fibrillary tangles—presumably relics of degenerate microtubules (Tomlinson, 1977; Tomlinson and Henderson, 1975). The total number of motor units (anterior horn cells of the spinal cord and their related muscle fibers) decreases, and the number of muscle fibers declines as well. It is of interest that peripheral nerve fibers remain essentially unchanged with advancing age (Gutmann and Hanzlikova, 1972).

The biochemical basis for neurologic deterioration is less well understood. (See Bowen, Smith, White, Goodhardt et al., 1977; Bowen, Smith, White, Flack et al., 1977; Iqbal, Grundke-Iqbal, Wísniewski et al., 1976; McNamara and Appel, 1977; Meier-Ruge, Reichlmeier, and Iwangoff, 1975; Orgel, 1963; and Shelanski, 1975). It has been hypothesized that neuronal proteins are inaccurately synthesized due to "transcription failure"; i.e., errors in the copying from DNA to ribosomal RNA (Orgel, 1963). When important structural protein "building blocks" are inaccurately produced, the structure of the nerve cells becomes degraded (Meier-Ruge et al., 1975). Other biochemical mechanisms deteriorate as well; these include diminution of energy metabolism, and the accumulation of lipofuscin. Physiologically, there is evidence that axoplasmic flow decreases with age (Geinisman, Bondareff, and Telser, 1977). Cerebral blood flow and cerebral metabolic rate of oxygen diminish, although not remarkably (Thompson, 1975). Central synaptic delays in reflex arcs are increased in the elderly (Botwinick, 1975), and evoked potential responses have prolonged latencies (Celesia and Daly, 1977). In aged subjects, the overall amount of spontaneous physical activity is reduced, a clinical observation that has been reproduced by determining "activity levels" in aged vs. young rats (Gutmann and Hanzlikova, 1972). Pharmacologic changes occur with aging, but in many cases only indirect measures of neurotransmitter function have been carried out in detail. It is known that cortical cholinergic receptors decrease with age (White, Goodhardt, Keet et al., 1977); and cholinergic neural function has been shown to be closely related to cognitive function (Drachman, 1978). Enzymes involved in catecholamine and GABA synthesis diminish with age (McGeer and McGeer, 1975), while monoamine oxidase, which is concerned with catecholamine degradation, increases (Nies, Robinson, Davis et al., 1973); it is not surprising that catecholamine levels decrease in the basal ganglia. Since the nervous system depends upon other organs for its life support, it is important to note that there is also diminution of a wide variety of other supporting functions, from cardiac output to basal metabolic rate, as detailed elsewhere in this volume.

*Neurology of "Normal" Aging.* As a result of these and other involutional processes, in the absence of disease, a variety of neurologic changes occur; some are clinically evident to the patient, while others may be detected only by the examining neurologist. Not only is the midpoint of the normal distribution curve shifted in the elderly, but the variance seems to increase considerably. As a result, the separation between the low end of normal function and a disease-induced abnormality becomes indistinct. The neurologist must often decide whether his findings represent a disease or simple involution, based on the *context* in which the signs appear. Thus, Babinski signs may be seen in the absence of disease in the elderly; but if they occur asymmetrically, and in the presence of weakness, they are most likely part of a disease process rather then merely involutional. It is in this light that neurologic changes in the elderly should be interpreted.

*Mental Status.* Many elderly individuals complain of impairment of memory. (Kahn, Zarit, Hilbert, *et al.,* 1975). This complaint may actually include other disorders of cognitive function (Horn, 1975), but it is difficult for most patients to frame complaints about such aspects of mental performance as problem-solving, etc. Immediate memory tends to be spared in the aged, as is retrieval by category; however, the ability to store new information (acquistion) clearly proceeds at a slower pace in the aged (Caird, 1966; Drachman and Leavitt, 1972; Gilbert, 1941; Gilbert, 1973; Kral, 1966; and Schneider, Gritz, and Jarvik, 1975). There is still some controversy as to whether the difficulty lies in retrieval of newly-learned information (Laurence, 1967; and Schonfield, 1967), or in its storage, but the latter seems more likely (Drachman and Leavitt, 1972). Both the solving of complex novel problems (Schaie and Gribbin, 1975) and rapid responses under time constraints (Botwinick, 1975; Jones, 1959; Welford, 1959) are also impaired in the normal aged. *Fluid intelligence*—the type required for solving novel problems—is more often impaired than *crystallized intelligence*—the manipulation of previously-learned information (Horn, 1975). Many standard tests have been used to measure intellectual function in both aged and young adults; the more "difficult" ones (Reitan, 1967) tend to show the greatest differences. In the Wechsler adult intelligence scale, which has been perhaps most widely used. the subtests of the Performance scale are notably impaired, while those of the Verbal scale remain largely intact. Nonetheless, the extent to which the cerebral horsepower of the aged is diminished overall is illustrated by the fact that, at age 75, one need obtain only about half as many correct answers on the age-corrected scale to achieve an IQ of 100, as at age 21! (Wechsler, 1955). Other observations indicate that the aged have diminished energy, tend to be cautious, and show decreased initiative (Botwinick, 1975).

It is often valuable, in assessing the aged patient's mental function, to oberve *both* his performance in direct tests of mental status, and his ability to function operationally within his own setting. Thus, the patient should be able to manage his personal, family, and financial affairs; to maintain knowledge of world events; and to keep up appropriately with his contemporaries in conversation, card games, etc. Any significant change in interactions with close family members is also noteworthy; for example, the previously dominant husband who now turns to his wife for answers to questions, and no longer trusts his memory or judgment. Finally, it is important to recognize that *depression*, common in the elderly, may often present as a cognitive disorder (pseudodementia); and a high index of suspicion should be maintained for this functional disorder (Kiloh, 1961).

In many instances where the extent of mental deterioration, *or its absence*, requires documentation, it is useful to obtain a battery of psychometric tests as quantitative and objective measures. In addition to the WAIS, the Wechsler Memory Quotient, Bender-Gestalt, Raven's Matrices, Trailmaking test, Halstead-Wepman and Benton Visual Retention tests may be of value in assessing cognitive capacity and performance; and the MMPI, Rorschach and others in evaluating affective disorders (Wells and Buchanan, 1977). Reitan has developed a standard battery of tests which have proven of value in assessing cognitive functions (Reitan, 1967). Compared with these tests, the clinical impression of the skilled physician may be, paradoxically, both cruder and more subtle. A skillful interview and mental status examination may detect minor disorders that affect objective tests minimally if at all; or may miss surprisingly gross deficits of isolated cognitive functions in patients whose alertness and energy is retained.

*Sleep patterns* frequently change in the elderly, who complain of insomnia. Typically, the total sleep time per night does not change; but aged individuals spend more time awake in bed than do young adults, and awaken more frequently (Feinberg, 1975). The percent time spent in various EEG-determined stages of sleep shifts with age, delta-wave deep sleep (stage 4) decreasing, while stage 3 increases. There is probably no significant change in the number or duration of REM cycles (Williams, Karacan, and Hursch, 1974) although some studies have suggested a decrease in REM sleep.

*Cranial Nerves.* Significant alterations are seen in cranial sensory functions in the elderly. With age, impairment of visual accommodation for near objects is nearly universal; and distant vision also requires correcting lenses by age 70 in most individuals (Botwinick, 1975). Dark adaptation diminishes with age (Weiss, 1959), and greater illumination is needed for accurate vision (Weale, 1965). Yellowing of the lens impairs color vision for the blue end of the spectrum (Gilbert, 1957). Centrally, visual evoked responses are delayed, suggesting slowing in the central visual pathways (Celesia and Daly, 1977). Pupillary responses are diminished or even absent in the elderly, and pupil size decreases on the average (Howell, 1949; and Weiss, 1959). Ocular motility tends to be slowed, and upward gaze is often limited. *Perception* of visual stimuli also diminishes in the elderly: Critical flicker fusion frequency declines with age (Weiss, 1959), and, for example, embedded figures are less easily extracted from confusing pictures (Basowitz and Korchin, 1957). Hearing is similarly diminished in the aged, beginning about age 50 (Weiss, 1959). High frequencies are chiefly affected, and the suggestion has been advanced that this may be due to acoustic trauma suffered over a lifetime (Rosen, Plester, El-Mofty, *et al.*, 1964). Dichotic auditory stimuli are less often correctly identified simultaneously (Drachman, 1977); this observation suggests that central processing of auditory information becomes limited with advancing age. Diminution of the senses of taste and smell has been noted, but is less well documented (Botwinick, 1975; and Weiss, 1959). Impairment of other cranial nerve functions may be seen with specific disease entities but is not common in the normal aging process. Occasionally, the distinction between neurogenic dysarthria and that due to oral pathology (ill-fitting dentures, e.g.) may be difficult.

*Motor System.* Second to impairment of mental function, deterioration of gait and motility are the most frequent neurologic concomitants of the aging process (Hobson and Pemberton, 1955). In the elderly, the characteristics of the gait change, the confident stride of youth altering to a hesitant, broad-based, small-stepped gait that has many of the characteristics of incipient Parkinsonism: stooped posture, diminished arm-swing, turns performed

en bloc, etc. (Barbeau, 1973; and Critchley, 1956). The demarcation between this gait change and various clinical disorders described below may be a shaded difference of degree, although from a pragmatic viewpoint it is the ability to walk without serious limitations or falling that distinguishes dysfunction from a normal aged gait. This change is believed to be due to central (probably extrapyramidal) deterioration (Barbeau, 1973), since the peripheral changes seen in normal aging—minor decrease in nerve conduction velocity, no change in anterior horn cells, decrease in muscle mass (Gutmann and Hanzlikova, 1972)—are not sufficient to account for the disability. Tremor, although often regarded as a normal concomitant of the aging process, will be discussed later; its infrequency—less than 2 percent of the elderly (Hobson and Pemberton, 1955)—suggests that it should be regarded as a neurologic dysfunction rather than a normal finding. Increased tone is often seen, however (Critchley, 1956); this may be in the form of mild axial rigidity, slight limb rigidity (resistance to passive stretch), or mild paratonic rigidity, the latter in association with other evidence of frontal lobe signs. The role of mechanical changes involving arthritic joints, inelastic tendons or ligaments or other musculoskeletal restraints is difficult to assess; undoubtedly they contribute in a significant way to the restricted motility of the elderly (Critchley, 1956; and Hobson and Pemberton, 1955).

*Reflexes.* The reflex change most commonly noted in the aged is diminution or absence of the ankle jerks, which may occur in about 10 percent of patients (Hobson and Pemberton, 1955). Whether this reflects a simple degenerative change, or the frequency of accumulation of any of a variety of neuropathies (e.g., diabetic) is uncertain. However, the finding may occur in the absence of otherwise typical neuropathy. Plantar reflexes may be neutral or extensor in about 5 percent of the aged (Hobson and Pemberton, 1955), and superficial abdominal reflexes are often absent. This latter finding is often attributed to obesity, abdominal surgery or multiparity (Critchley, 1956). Suck and grasp reflexes, often regarded as signs of general cerebral or frontal lobe damage, occur in many elderly patients; and the snout reflex, a "corticobulbar" sign, is also frequently present (Paulson, 1977).

*Sensation.* Vibratory sensation is regularly diminished or lost in the lower extremities, the proportion increasing from about 10 percent at age 60 to a third to a half beyond 75 (Hobson and Pemberton, 1955). An increase in the thresholds for touch and pinprick may be found, but is not ordinarily present at the level of clinical testing, and may be due to changes in skin and connective tissue (Weiss, 1959). The face-hand test, a measure of cortical perceptual ability, shows extinction of the hand stimulus in the elderly (Bender, Fink, and Green, 1951); but other measures of cortical perception (stereognosis, graphesthesia, double simultaneous stimulation, etc.) ordinarily remain intact.

## ELECTROENCEPHALOGRAPHIC CHANGES

During normal aging slowing of the background rhythm in the EEG characteristically occurs with a shift of the mean alpha frequency of 11 to 12 Hz to 7 to 8 Hz in the elderly (Wilson, Musella, and Short, 1977). In addition, temporal theta activity increases, particularly on the left side, and sharp waves may be seen in the same regions. By the age of 65 these findings are present in more than half of otherwise normal subjects. Drachman and Hughes (1971) have found that in normal "healthy" aged volunteer subjects, temporal sharp and slow activity correlates significantly with psychological evidence of cognitive deterioration, while not reflecting specific disorders of the underlying hippocampal complexes.

## COMPUTERIZED AXIAL TOMOGRAPHY

CT scans show mild enlargement of the ventricular system and widening of the sulci with advancing age (Pear, 1977; Lowry, Bahr, Allen, et al., 1977). The CT scan is useful in determining whether the degree of atrophy is excessive, and likely to be related to dementia, although there is considerable overlap in the CT findings between normal and demented patients. In one study, for example, 60 percent of demented patients showed atrophy while 15 percent of normal aged patients showed the same degree of change on CT scan (Huckman, Fox, and Topel, 1975). In the detection of other destructive or space-occupying lesions, however, the CT scan remains of great value in the evaluation of the aged patient.

## NEUROLOGICAL DYSFUNCTION DUE TO INVOLUTION: DISABILITY WITHOUT DISEASE

Even in the absence of specific disease states, normal attrition of neural function may lead to a significant degree of disability in some individuals. This is the no-man's land in the neurology of aging: a statistical inevitability situated between normal involution and specific disease. Several conditions are worth noting because of their frequency of occurrence in a non-diseased population: *normal dementia; dizziness; gait disorders; and cervical spondylosis.*

*Normal Dementia.* Much has already been said about the cognitive changes occurring with normal aging. Here, it should be stressed that the condition is not always benign (Kral, 1962) even when occurring in the absence of disease. In fact, the very question of where normal neuronal attrition ends and Alzheimer's disease begins, is exceedingly difficult—perhaps more a philosophical than a medical problem. Tomlinson and his colleagues have shown that the relationship between senile plaques and normal or impaired mental functions in the elderly is a quantitative one; and that senile plaques and neurofibrillary tangles accumulate in increasing numbers with advancing age in a nondiseased population (Tomlinson, 1975; and Tomlinson and Henderson, 1975). It is clear that some individuals at 65 are no longer able to compete intellectually with their younger colleagues; while past 75 only the exceptional individual is still able to perform at an intellectual level that permits him to remain employed. While not a specific disease-state, the cognitive impairment may prove disabling in the context of the patient's usual social or occupational requirements; it may then be termed the "normal dementia of aging."

*Dizziness.* Dizziness, an exceedingly common complaint in the elderly, is commonly the result of involutional changes involving multiple sensory modalities (Drachman and Hart, 1973). We have indicated elsewhere that normal spatial orientation requires accurate visual, vestibular, proprioceptive, tactile and auditory perceptions (Drachman, 1977). Impairment of several of these orienting functions is perceived by patients as "dizziness", an elusive complaint that results from the patient's *uncertainty of his position or motion in space.* The elderly individual complaining of dizziness typically walks with a broad-based unsteady gait, with particular difficulty turning, or walking on uneven ground. Carrying a cane or holding someone's arm provides some improvement in balance. This multi-sensory dizziness appears to result from a combination of diminished sensation in several spheres: visual, vestibular, cervical proprioception, and peripheral nerve modalities. Each deficit may be the result of involutional changes occurring with age; it is only when several occur simultaneously that the patient complains of dizziness, rather than a primary sensory problem.

There are, of course, many other causes of

dizziness in the aged. Visual distortion produced by using supplementary lenses after cataract extraction produces spatial disorientation, and dizziness in the aged. A mild degree of positional vertigo also occurs with increased frequency in the elderly. And, since postural blood pressure adjustments occur more slowly in the aged, transient orthostatic hypotension on rapidly arising is common. Finally, pathologic causes of dizziness due to specific disease states are also frequent, ranging from Meniere's disorder to brain stem cerebrovascular accidents, etc.

*Disorders of Gait.* When disorders of gait interfere with the elderly patient's independence, the distinction between an involutional process and a specific disease state must be closely considered. In the absence of specific disease, gait disturbances produce disability in 13 percent of an aged population (Akhtar, *et al.*, 1973). It is often the combination of an extrapyramidal syndrome, Bruns' frontal lobe gait apraxia, multi-sensory dizziness and mechanical impairment due to joint degeneration, that leads to significant disability. The gait may have characteristics of each of the components: small steps, stooped posture, a broad base, loss of balance or turning, retropulsion, and an entalgic component. Added to this composite picture is the patient's acquired cautiousness, often developed as a result of frequent falls. Neurologic examination may reveal increased axial and limb tone, grasp and suck reflexes, and Meyerson's glabellar sign, as well as the features of multi-sensory dizziness described above.

Diagnostically, it is important to determine whether any aspect of this combination of conditions may be due to a specific disease state. In particular, diseases of the frontal lobes (brain tumor, subdural hematoma), normal pressure hydrocephalus, drug intoxication, and cerebellar disorders should be ruled out with appropriate studies. The course of the gait disturbance should be followed long enough to confirm that no additional disease process is evolving.

*Cervical Spondylosis.* Degenerative changes of the cervical spine, and resulting symptoms, occur so commonly that they deserve mention in the neurologic assessment of the aged. Radiologically, more than 80 percent of individuals over the age of 55 show evidence of cervical disc degeneration, and by 75 the finding is virtually universal (Brain and Wilkinson, 1967). Osteoarthritic changes of the zygapophyseal joints are almost as common as disc disease. Roughly half the patients with evidence of cervical spondylosis may experience symptoms of local cervical pain, nerve root or spinal cord compression. In all, signs of cervical spinal cord compression are uncommon; but some degree of bony degeneration of the cervical spine and accompanying pain can be expected as a frequent consequence of the aging process.

## SPECIFIC NEUROLOGICAL DISEASES OF THE AGED

Clearly, the range of neurological diseases capable of affecting the aged is far beyond the scope of this chapter. Instead, a few of the more common, important, or illustrative conditions will be briefly discussed. The reader is referred to standard textbooks of neurology for more detailed descriptions and a broader spectrum of pathologic entities.

*Alzheimer's Disease/Senile Dementia.* Of all the neurologic disorders affecting the aged, Alzheimer's disease, or senile dementia, (now regarded as synonymous) is among the most frequent, and is clearly the leading cause of dementia (Katzman, 1976; Tomlinson and Henderson, 1975; and Wang, 1977). It is estimated that almost 5 percent of the surviving population over age 65 will be totally disabled by dementia, while another 11 percent are dependent because of dementia. Of these patients, at least half owe the major cause of their cognitive impairment to Alzheimer's disease. At this point, it is unclear whether this condition represents a specific disease process, the end result of preprogrammed deterioration, or both. The pathology is well recognized, however, and has been described with care from the gross to the ultrastructural levels (Corsellis, 1978; Terry, 1975; Terry and Wisniewski, 1977; Tomlinson, 1977; and Tomlinson and Henderson, 1975). Further details of the neuropathology of this condition may be found in chapter 24. Briefly, it is characterized by the occurrence of neurofibrillary tangles in neurons, particularly in the hippocampal regions; cortical senile plaques, consisting of an amyloid core surrounded by degenerating neurites (dendritic and axonal processes); granulovacuolar degeneration of hippocampal neurons; and perhaps loss of dendritic spines.

Clinically, Alzheimer's disease often begins as a "lucid dementia," with impaired cognitive function but no change in the sensorium, or state of consciousness. Subtle changes in judgment, decisiveness and memory are often the earliest symptoms of this condition. Loss of interests and energy occur as well, overlapping with the symptoms of depression, which may accompany the patient's awareness of his failing intellect. Cognitive decline is rapid, and within two or three years most patients are unable to care for themselves independently. Focal neurologic findings, such as hemiparesis, sensory deficits, visual impairment or asymmetric reflexes are not a feature of Alzheimer's disease. With progression, bradyphrenia and psychomotor retardation are often seen. Frontal lobe release signs, including suck and grasp reflexes, are common, and occasionally Babinski signs may be present. Although the neurologic condition itself is not lethal, most patients with Alzheimer's disease die within five to ten years as a result of debility, inanition, intercurrent infection, etc.

Laboratory findings are of limited help in establishing the diagnosis. The CT scan often shows cortical atrophy, with enlargement of the ventricles and widening of the sulci (Lowry, *et al.*, 1977; Pear, 1977). While this is of value in distinguishing Alzheimer's disease from dementia produced by multiple infarcts, a subdural hematoma or a frontal tumor, for example, the degree of atrophy may not exceed that seen in aged individuals without dementia (Huckman, Fox, and Topel, 1975). Lumbar puncture, skull x-rays, brain scan and radioisotope cisternogram are all normal; the EEG shows mild diffuse slow-wave activity without focal features. Psychological testing is often of value in documenting the extent of the intellectual impairment, and in assessing the contributing role of depression.

Recently, further information regarding the possible etiology and pathogenesis of Alzheimer's disease has come to light. The possibility of a viral origin has been raised by transmission of a spongiform encephalopathy from two cases of familial Alzheimer's disease to primates (Traub, Gajdusek, and Gibbs, 1977). A genetic or chromosomal origin has been suggested for some cases by the finding of increased aneuploidy in the lymphocytes of patients with familial Alzheimer's disease (Cook, Ward, Austin, *et al.*, 1978). And, in the last several years, a disorder of central cholinergic neuronal function has been demonstrated (Boyd, Graham, White, Blackwood, *et al.* 1977; Davies and Maloney, 1976; Drachman, 1977, 1978; Drachman and Leavitt, 1974; Nies, *et al.*, 1973; Perry, Perry, Blessed, *et al.*, 1977; and White, *et al.*, 1977). A strong likelihood remains, however, that Alzheimer's disease may be the end-stage of more than one pathogenetic mechanism.

*Arteriopathic Dementia.* Although in the past most dementias were thought to be due to arteriosclerosis of cerebral vessels, it is now evident that this is the case in only a minority of patients with dementia. Tomlinson and his colleagues estimate that 15-20 percent of dements are suffering primarily from *multi-infarct dementia*, and impairment of intellectual function due to diffuse and multicentric cerebral ischemia (Tomlinson, 1977; and Tomlinson and Henderson, 1975). Pathologically, an estimated 50 ml of cerebral softening will result in dementia in 90 percent of elderly patients, although the sites of involvement are also contributory to the dementing effects of infarction (O'Brien, 1977). Further, the combination of multiple cerebral softenings with Alzheimer-type pathological changes results in a combined etiology of dementia in another 20 percent of patients. Dementia of this type is characterized by the history of a stroke at the onset, with focal neurologic deficits such as impairment of speech, use of a hand, or balance, or the occurrence of dizziness. Although the initial events may be discrete, subsequent intellectual decline is often gradually progressive, without recognized focal events. This pattern is particularly common in patients with hypertension who develop a *lacunar state*, with multiple small areas of softening in the thalamus, basal ganglia and adjacent white matter.

Neurologic examination often reveals, in addition to dementia, focal deficits, such as impairment of language function, asymmetric reflexes, a Babinski sign, or a mild hemiparesis. Frontal lobe release signs are common, as in many dementing disorders. CT scanning may reveal one or more areas of cerebral softening, particularly if the lesions are of sufficient size (1/2 to 1 cm) to be visualized by this technique. Some degree of diffuse cerebral atrophy is often present as well. The EEG shows focal or asymmetrical areas of slowing, frequently referred to the temporal or frontal leads. The lumbar puncture and radioisotope brain scan are of varying usefulness, depending on the duration since the most recent infarction.

*Treatment* is palliative, with antidepressant (stimulant) agents such as methlyphenidate providing some benefit in patients with psychomotor retardation. *Prevention* of additional infarction is important in patients with identifiable underlying causes, such as hypertension, stenosis of extracranial arteries, hyperlipidemias, etc.

*Normal Pressure Hydrocephalus.* This syndrome, described more than a decade ago by Adams and his colleagues, (Adams, Fisher, Hakim, *et al.*, 1965), has been widely sought but infrequently found since its initial description. Certain patients with progressive dementia, apraxia of gait and urinary incontinence have been noted to have "compensated hydrocephalus" of late onset. In most cases the cause of the hydrocephalus has been failure of absorption of cerebrospinal fluid (CSF) by the arachnoid granulations over the cerebral convexity, resulting in ventricular enlargement. The absorptive failure is believed to be due to fibrotic changes occurring in the meninges and arachnoid granulations following subarachnoid hemorrhage, trauma, meningeal inflammation, etc. (Katzman, 1977). It has been theorized that, within the closed and unyielding confines of the skull, the ventricles enlarge at the expense of cerebral tissue, until the pressure stabilizes at an equilibrium between the production and absorption of CSF. When demented patients with this disorder are identified, surgical shunting of CSF from the ventricles to the peritoneal cavity can relieve the hydrocephalus and restore normal neurologic function.

Numerous diagnostic procedures have been tried to identify patients with this condition, including CT scanning, radioisotope cisternography, pneumoencephalography, pressure measurements of CSF during infusion of saline, etc. (Katzman, 1977). Unfortunately, none has reliably predicted the success of CSF shunting procedure. Nonetheless, patients who show the typical clinical features of this condition, along with ventricular enlargement on CT scanning and failure of absorption of a radioisotope from the subarachnoid space, are appropriate candidates for consideration of emplacement of a shunt.

*Extrapyramidal Dementia.* Some patients with dementia manifest a number of clinical findings indicating involvement of the extrapyramidal system (Drachman and Stahl, 1975). These include axial and limb rigidity, a mild tremor of the hands, increasing on attempts to draw a spiral (Archimedes' screw), masked facies, and Meyerson's sign (failure to inhibit blink on repeated tapping of the glabella). Although such patients are akin to those with Parkinsonism, they lie at the opposite end of what is probably a spectrum: manifestations of dementia are prominent while extrapyramidal findings are minimal. The features of a diffuse dementing disorder may also be prominent, including frontal lobe signs, Bruns' apraxia of gait and urinary incontinence. The pathogenesis of this clinical syndrome is not yet clear; some may have extrapyramidal signs along with Alzheimer's disease or arteriopathic dementia. The value of recognizing this syndrome lies in the apparent benefits both to mobility and to cognitive functioning in some patients treated with L-DOPA alone or combined with DOPA-decarboxylase-inhibitor (carbidopa). In two studies, a number of patients have shown considerable benefits from treatment (Drachman and Stahl, 1975; Lewis, Ballinger, and Presly,

1978). Additional studies, and further definition of the syndrome are needed.

*Other Causes of Dementia.* Many other conditions may cause dementia (Haase, 1977), as indicated in Table 21-4. Some of these are treatable: brain tumors, subdural hematomas, syphilis, etc. It is worth stressing that the clinical manifestations of the "treatable dementias" may be virtually indistinguishable clinically from the common ones that are presently untreatable. Various estimates suggest that 10–30 percent of patients with dementias have identifiable conditions other than Alzheimer's disease or arteriopathic dementia (Freemon, 1976); these should be vigorously sought by appropriate diagnostic studies. Despite the relatively low yield, the penalties for missing a treatable dementing condition are high both for the patient and his family, and for society.

*Cerebrovascular Disease.* Cerebrovascular disease producing strokes—infarctive or hemorrhagic—is clearly the single most common neurologic disorder of the elderly. Stroke is a rare event before the age of 55. From 55 to 65 the annual incidence is about 400 per 100,000, rising sharply to 5,000 per 100,000 at age 85 (Hutchinson and Acheson, 1975;

**Table 21-4**   Etiologies of Dementia

I. PRIMARY NEUROLOGICAL DISEASES
  A. Common
    Alzheimer's disease (senile dementia)
    Arteriopathic dementia

  B. Treatable
    Normal pressure hydrocephalus
    Extrapyramidal dementia
    Tumors
    Subdural hematoma
    Drug intoxication
    Lues
    Alcoholic dementia
    Depressions

  C. Other
    Korsakoff's psychosis
    Post-encephalitic
    Huntington's chorea
    Creutzfeldt-Jacob disease
    Pick's disease

II. SYSTEMIC DISEASES
    Myxedema
    Pernicious anemia
    Hyponatremia
    Uremia
    Dialysis dementia
    Remote malignancy
    Lupus erythematosus
    Hepatic encephalopathy
    Hyperparathyroidism
    Recurrent hypoglycemia, anoxia

and Kurtzke, 1976). Furthermore, strokes are more lethal in an older population: the mortality in several studies shows a marked rise from 10–15 percent in patients under 60 to more than 60 percent in patients in the 8th or 9th decades. The clinical manifestations of stroke are well-described elsewhere in standard textbooks (Adams and Victor, 1977; and Mayo Clinic, 1976), and monographs (Hutchinson and Acheson, 1975; and Toole and Patel, 1974). Briefly, strokes may be ischemic, that is, due to inadequate flow of blood with deprivation of oxygen and nutrients; or hemorrhagic, with forceful leakage of blood into the substance of the brain, causing mechanical destruction of surrounding tissue. Classically, they are categorized into *thrombotic, embolic, intracerebral hemorrhagic* and *subarachnoid hemorrhagic* events. The precise neurologic manifestations depend on the site of ischemic or hemorrhagic damage, involving the territories of the carotid arteries and their branches (middle and anterior cerebral) or the basilar-vertebral arterial system (posterior cerebral; brainstem and cerebellar vasculature). In the majority of cases, the abrupt onset of a neurologic deficit in an elderly individual is likely to be due to a stroke; a detailed neurological examination will usually indicate the site of the damage. Many diagnostic techniques are of benefit in further identifying both the location and the pathogenesis of the stroke; these include CT scanning, radioisotope scanning, and EEG, for localization. Intracerebral hemorrhage is often visible on the CT scan; lumbar puncture is helpful in identifying intracerebral and subarachnoid hemorrhage. Patency of the carotid arteries can be evaluated noninvasively by the use of oculoplethysmography (OPG), or ophthalmodynamometry, techniques which measure the arrival time of the cardiac pulse wave and the pressure, respectively, in the ophthalmic arteries. Arteriography, with injection of radio-opaque material into the carotid or vertebral arteries, permits direct roentgenographic visualization of the major cerebral vessels and their branches. Other studies, not detailed here, permit the neurologist to determine whether the stroke may have been due to emboli arising from the carotid artery or heart, to abnormal coagulability of blood, to inflammatory diseases of the arteries, etc.

Completed strokes are, at this time, essentially untreatable. Emphasis is therefore placed on the identification of particularly susceptible individuals and the prevention of occurrence of strokes. Hypertension, obesity, hyperlipidemia, heart disease, cigarette smoking, and a positive family history are all risk factors; patients at high risk can help to avoid strokes by minimizing the control-lable factors with diet, exercise, control of hypertension, etc. In some patients transient ischemic events lasting less than 24 hours warn of the possibility of an impending permanent stroke; when these are due to a narrowed carotid artery, surgical removal of the obstruction by endarterectomy may be of benefit.

In all, the problem of cause and prevention of strokes in the elderly is not well understood. It will remain a major problem until the pathogenesis of arteriosclerosis is better known.

*Parkinson's Disease.* Parkinsonism is a neurologic syndrome of unknown etiology, manifest as a disorder of movement (Adams and Victor, 1977; Mayo Clinic, 1976; Martin, Loewenson, Resch, *et al.*, 1973). Although it may appear at any time after 30, the median age of onset is the 7th decade. The earliest symptoms are usually slowness of movement, stooped posture and a small-stepped gait (marche-a-petits-pas). The face becomes masked, with infrequent blinking; the voice becomes a soft monotone; and a 4–6 Hz tremor of the extremities (often asymmetrical) develops. Patients have difficulty initiating movement (bradykinesia), and often have impaired balance resulting in accelerating backwards (retropulsion) or forwards (propulsion) once they begin to walk. Fine movements are tremulous and clumsy; for example, the handwriting becomes small, slow and shaky. Axial rigidity interferes with such activities as rolling over in bed or sliding over in an automobile seat. Impairment of mental function occurs in a proportion of patients varying from 25 to 80 percent (Loranger, Goodell, McDowell, *et al.*, 1972). Untreated, the symptoms of typical Parkinsonism progress at a variable rate, usually resulting in disability in 3–5 years.

In addition to these classic manifestations of Parkinsonism, a large proportion of elderly patients will show fractional forms of an extrapyramidal syndrome. This clinical picture consists of a stooped posture and small-stepped gait, slowness of movement, and a mild increase in tone, often accompanied by frontal lobe release signs. Tremor is usually absent or minimal. The pathogenesis of this condition is not entirely clear; some authors have called it "arteriosclerotic Parkinsonism," although the role of vascular disease has been disputed by others (Adams and Victor, 1977).

The diagnosis of Parkinsonism is established by the neurologic examination, which reveals the features noted above. Axial and cogwheel rigidity and Meyerson's glabellar sign are present. The absence of muscular weakness is striking in a patient whose rigidity, clumsiness, and tremor prevent effective purposeful motor performance. Diagnostic tests are usually unremarkable.

Parkinsonism, although idiopathic in most cases, can be caused by encephalitis, phenothiazine drugs, manganese toxicity, etc. Pathologically, the substantia nigra is consistently lacking in pigmented cells; and biochemically, the basal ganglia are depleted of dopamine. Treatment of Parkinsonian patients with L-DOPA, a precursor of dopamine, has effectively diminished the morbidity of this condition, both initially and in long-term follow-up (Cotzias, Papavasiliou, and Gellene, 1969). Other agonists of dopamine, such as amantadine and bromocriptine, have also been shown to be beneficial.

*Senile Tremor.* "Essential" tremor may occur at almost any age, occurring with or without a family history. When it develops in the elderly, it is called "senile tremor," although it is morphologically identical to earlier-onset forms (Critchley, 1949; and Larsson and Sjogren, 1960). This tremor is most typically 4–6 Hz, but may be rapid as well (12 Hz). The hands are usually affected, but the jaw, tongue, head, or other areas may also be involved. By history, the tremor is usually reduced by drinking alcoholic beverages. The tremor is exaggerated in many patients by maintaining the arms and hands extended (postural tremor), or by approximating the index fingers to each other or to the patient's nose without actually touching. Efforts to write may produce a dramatic exaggeration of the tremor, resulting in a grossly tremulous, *large*, handwriting (macrographia), in contradistinction to Parkinsonism. The occurrence of such a tremor in the absence of rigidity, bradykinesia, or the other signs of Parkinsonism is diagnostic. Treatment with beta-adrenergic blocking-drugs, such as propranolol, is often effective in reducing the tremor; minor tranquilizers such as chlordiazepoxide are also useful. Recognition of senile tremor is important for several reasons: to eliminate the question of Parkinsonism; and to institute appropriate treatment where the tremor causes disability or embarrassment.

*Depression.* Although not strictly a neurologic disorder, the effects of depression in the aged may mimic the symptoms of dementia or aggravate its manifestations. Jarvik (1975) has pointed out that in England depression is diagnosed five times as frequently as in the United States, among elderly patients first admitted to psychiatric hospitals. The decreased psychomotor activity, interests and energy, and disordered sleep pattern in depressive patients resemble the manifestations of aging and dementia. McHugh (1978) and others have noted that psychometric testing of elderly depressed patients may show a pattern suggesting organic dementia, which is reversible when the depression has been satisfactorily treated. Thus, as a primary disorder of the aged, or as a complicating factor, depression must be considered in the neurologic assessment of the aged. The fact that it is often successfully treated with pharmacologic antidepressant agents makes its recognition especially important.

*Head Trauma in the Elderly.* Head injuries of apparently comparable degree result in far more serious and lasting neurologic deficits in the aged than in young adults (Overgaard, Hvid-Hansen, Land, et al., 1973). Following a closed head trauma it is extremely rare for older patients with evidence of brainstem damage to recover normal function, although under the age of 30 normal recovery may take place in similarly injured patients. The ability to recover function following injury—termed plasticity—probably depends on several factors; a reserve of undamaged neural tissue, and a greater margin of safety in the functioning of individual neural elements.

*Dementia Pugilistica.* Dementia pugilistica, or the "punch-drunk syndrome" (see Corsellis, 1978; Mawdsley and Ferguson, 1963; Spillane, 1962) is mentioned here because it illustrates a principle of some importance. Young, healthy prize fighters who sustain repeated head injuries may be relatively free of symptoms for a number of years; yet as they age, dementia develops in 17 percent (Corsellis, 1978), and cerebellar ataxia and extrapyramidal movement disorders appear. Although the exact mechanism of this phenomenon is uncertain, it appears likely that early damage to neurons and their connections becomes clinically manifest later, when the combination of normal neuronal attrition and prior damage summate to reach a threshold of clinical dysfunction. It is of interest that pathologically, the brains of punch-drunk fighters show neurofibrillary tangles similar to those of Alzheimer's disease, although without an excess of senile plaques (Corsellis, 1978).

## NEUROLOGICAL MANIFESTATIONS OF SYSTEMIC DISEASE

Numerous diseases of other organ systems result in clinical neurological deficits. The scope of these diseases is too broad to discuss here; but the manifestations range from exceedingly common peripheral neuropathies seen in, for example, diabetes, to the ataxia of hypothyroidism; from the cerebellar degeneration of remote malignancy to the myopathies occurring with collagen disorders. In assessing disease of the nervous system at any age, although particularly in the elderly, it is important to keep in mind the range of diseases in which the nervous system is *secondarily* involved, although the first evidence of disease is seen as neurologic dysfunction.

## ASSESSMENT AND MANAGEMENT OF NEUROLOGICAL DISORDERS OF THE AGED

Unlike the situation in the young healthy adult, where neurological signs generally indicate significant disease, special care and judgment are required for the assessment and management of neurological findings in the elderly. As has already been indicated, the neurologic status of the aged patient reflects the summation of multiple processes; some due to specific disease, some the result of involutional changes; some that are curable or treatable, some that are not; some that can be named, and some that are nameless. How should the physician respond to this confusing array of complaints and signs, where the specific combination of findings is often unique to the individual's genetic background and life history, as well as his present disease state?

The purpose of the neurological assessment must be sharply focused: *First,* the identification of specific disease processes, particularly those that are treatable or curable; *second,* the explanation of abnormal neurologic symptoms or signs; *third,* relief or reduction of disability, whatever the cause. A final goal is the careful observation of presently untreatable conditions to derive insights, where possible, into the mechanism of the disorder, for the development of future rational treatments.

A few examples may serve to illustrate these points: In the dementing disorders, the majority of neurological disorders are due to Alzheimer's disease, and a second large group to arteriopathic (multi-infarct) dementia. Fewer than a fourth of these disorders are due to treatable disease; and in some populations fewer than 10 percent. How far should an investigation be carried out, when the probability of identifying a treatable disease, such as a subdural hematoma, normal pressure hyrocephalus, extrapyramidal dementia or depression, is relatively small? Aside from the humanitarian considerations, the cost of caring for a single patient in a nursing home environment for several years far exceeds that of *many* well-planned clinical

evaluations. The overall benefits of reasonable investigations are therefore substantial, even when many patients are found to have disappointingly untreatable conditions. It is likely that the chance of a successful outcome probably exceeds that of the patient who is comatose following cardiac resuscitation, again at a fraction of the cost.

Explanation of the cause of symptoms or signs is often of great value as well. For example, the concerned professional who is disabled by fears that his memory is declining at 60, may be restored to normal function by assurance (based on an adequate evaluation) that his mental function is still superior compared with his coevals; and that he does not have a brain tumor or dementing process.

The reduction of disability due to noncurable disease, involution, or both, is also of importance. In multisensory dizziness, for example, where the underlying neuropathy, cervical spondylosis, and vestibular impairments cannot be cured, patients may often be restored to independent function by attention to details: the use of a cervical collar to eliminate excessive mobility and false proprioceptive inputs; training in cane-trailing to substitute hand sensation for impaired lower extremity sensation; and the use of contact lenses in patients who have undergone cataract extractions, etc.

The ultimate goal of this neurologic approach is not to attempt to eliminate the inevitable deterioration that must occur with aging. Rather, it is to maintain sufficient neural integrity in aging individuals, so that they may function with acceptable independence and satisfaction although the entire human machine wears down—a human counterpart of the Holmesian "wonderful one horse shay."

## REFERENCES

ADAMS, R. D., AND VICTOR, M. 1977. *Principles of Neurology,* New York: McGraw-Hill.

ADAMS, R. D., FISHER, C. M., HAKIM, S., OJEMANN, R. G. AND SWEET, W. H. 1965. Symptomatic occult hydrocephalus with "normal" cerebrospinal-fluid pressure. *New England Journal of Medicine, 273,* 117–126.

AKHTAR, A. J., BROE, D. A., CROMBIE, A., MCLEAN, W. M. R., ANDREWS, G. R., AND CAIRD, F. I. 1973. Disability and dependence in the elderly at home. *Age and Aging, 2,* 102–110.

ANDRES, R. 1967. Relation of physiologic changes in aging to medical changes of disease in the aged. *Mayo Clinic Proceedings, 42*, 674–684.

BARBEAU, A. 1973. Aging and the extrapyramidal system. *Journal of the American Geriatrics Society, 21*, 145–149.

BASOWITZ, H., AND KORCHIN, S. J. 1957. Age differences in the perception of closure. *Journal of Abnormal and Social Psychology, 54*, 93–97.

BENDER, M. B., FINK, M., AND GREEN, M. 1951. Patterns of perception on simultaneous tests of face and hand. *Archives of Neurology and Psychiatry, 66*, 355–362.

BONDAREFF, W., AND GEINISMAN, Y. 1976. Loss of synapses in the dentate gyrus of the senescent rat. *American Journal of Anatomy, 145*, 129–136.

BOTWINICK, J. 1975. Behavioral Processes. *In*, S. Gershon and A. Raskin (eds.), *Aging*, Vol. 2, pp. 1–18. New York: Raven Press.

BOWEN, D. M., SMITH, C. B., WHITE, P. FLACK, R. H. A., CARRASCO, L. H., GEDYE, J. L., AND DAVISON, A. N. 1977. Chemical pathology of the organic dementias. II. *Brain, 100*, 427–453.

BOWEN, D. M., SMITH, C. B., WHITE, P., GOODHARDT, M. J., SPILLANE, J. A., FLACK, R. H. A., AND DAVISON, A. N. 1977. Chemical pathology of the organic dementias. I. *Brain, 100*, 397–426.

BOYD, W. D., GRAHAM-WHITE, J., BLACKWOOD, G., GLEN, J., AND McQUEEN, J. 1977. Clinical effects of choline in alzheimer senile dementia. *Lancet* (letter), *2*, 711.

BRAIN, R., AND WILKINSON, M. 1967. *Cervical Spondylosis.* Philadelphia: W. B. Saunders.

BRAUN, H. W. 1959. Perceptual processes. *In*, J. E. Birren (ed.), *Handbook of Aging and the Individual*, pp. 543–561. Chicago: University of Chicago Press.

BREWIS, M., POSKANZER, D. C., ROLLAND, C., AND MILLER, H. 1966. Neurological disease in an English city. *Acta Neurologica Scandinavica*, Suppl. 24, *42*, 1–89.

BRODY, H. 1955. Organization of the cerebral cortex. III. A study of aging in the human cerebral cortex. *Journal of Comp. Neurol., 102*, 511–556.

BRODY, H. 1975. The effects of age upon the main nucleus of inferior olive in the human. *Journal of Comparative Neurology, 155* (1), 61–66.

BRODY, H. 1976. An examination of cerebral cortex and brainstem aging. *In*, R. D. Terry and S. Gershon (eds.), *Aging*, Vol. 3, pp. 177–181. New York: Raven Press.

BROE, G. A., AKHTAR, A. J., ANDREWS, G. R., CAIRD, F. I., GILMORE, A. J. J., AND McLENNAN, W. J. 1976. Neurological disorders in the elderly at home. *Journal of Neurology, Neurosurgery and Psychiatry, 39*, 362–366.

CAIRD, W. K. 1966. Aging and short-term memory. *Journal of Gerontology, 21*, 295–299.

CELESIA, G. G., AND DALY, R. F. 1977. Effects of aging on visual evoked responses. *Archives of Neurology, 34*, 403–407.

CONFREY, E. A., AND GOLDSTEIN, M. S. 1960. The health status of aging people. *In*, C. Tibbitts (ed.), *Handbook of Social Gerontology*, pp. 165–207. Chicago: University of Chicago Press.

COOK, R. H., WARD, B., AUSTIN, J. H., AND ROBINSON, A. 1978. Familial Alzheimer disease: Its relation to cytogenetic abnormality and transmissible dementia. *Neurology* (Abstract), *28*, 353.

CORSELLIS, J. A. N. 1976. Aging and the dementias. *In*, W. Blackwood and J. A. N. Corsellis (eds.), *Greenfield's Neuropathology*, 3rd ed., pp. 1–42. Chicago: Year Book Medical Publishers.

CORSELLIS, J. A. N. 1978. Post-traumatic dementia. *In*, R. Katzman, R. D. and K. L. Bick (eds.), *Alzheimer's Disease: Senile Dementia and Related Disorders*, pp. 125–133. New York: Raven Press.

COTZIAS, G. C., PAPAVASILIOU, P. S., AND GELLENE, R. 1969. Modification of parkinsonism-chronic treatment with L-DOPA. *New England Journal of Medicine, 280*, 337–345.

CRAGG, B. G. 1975. The density of synapses and neurons in normal, mentally defective and ageing human brains. *Brain, 98*, 81–90.

CRITCHLEY, M. 1949. Observations on essential (heredofamilial) tremor. *Brain, 72*, 113–139.

CRITCHLEY, M. 1956. Neurologic changes in the aged. *Journal of Chronic Diseases, 3*, 459–477.

DAVIES, P., AND MALONEY, A. J. F. 1976. Selective loss of central cholinergic neurons in Alzheimer's disease. *Lancet* (letter), *2*, 1403.

DEJONG, R. N. 1969. *The Neurologic Examination*, 3rd ed. New York: Paul B. Hoeber, Inc.

DRACHMAN, D. A. 1975. Dizziness and vertigo. *In*, P. B. Beeson and W. McDermott (eds.), *Textbook of Medicine*, 14th ed., pp. 621–626. Philadelphia: W. B. Saunders.

DRACHMAN, D. A. 1977. Memory and the cholinergic system. *In*, W. S. Fields (ed.), *Neurotransmitter Function, Basic and Clinical Aspects*, pp. 353–372. Miami: Symposia Specialists.

DRACHMAN, D. A. 1978. Central cholinergic system and memory. *In*, M. A. Lipton, A. Dimascio, and K. F. Killam (eds.), *Psychopharmacology: A Generation of Progress*, pp. 651–662. New York: Raven Press.

DRACHMAN, D. A., AND HART, C. W. 1973. Multisensory dizziness. *Neurology, 23*, 434.

DRACHMAN, D. A., AND HUGHES, J. R. 1971. Memory and the hippocampal complexes, III. Aging and temporal EEG abnormalities. *Neurology, 21*, 1–14.

DRACHMAN, D. A., AND LEAVITT, J. 1972. Memory impairment in the aged: Storage versus retrieval deficit. *Journal of Experimental Psychology, 93*, 302–308.

DRACHMAN, D. A., AND LEAVITT, J. 1974. Human memory and the cholinergic system. A relationship to aging? *Archives of Neurology, 30*, 113–121.

DRACHMAN, D. A., AND STAHL, S. 1975. Extrapyramidal dementia and levodopa. *Lancet, 1*, 809.

FEINBERG, I. 1976. Functional implications of changes in sleep physiology with age. *In*, R. D. Terry and S. Gershon (eds.), *Aging*, Vol, 3. pp. 23–41. New York: Raven Press.

FELDMAN, M. L. 1976. Aging changes in the morphology of cortical dendrites. *In*, R. D. Terry and S. Gershon (eds.), *Aging*, Vol. 3, pp. 211–227. New York: Raven Press.

FOLSTEIN, M. F., AND McHUGH, P. 1978. Dementia syndrome of depression. *In*, R. Katzman, R. D. Terry and K. Bick (eds.), *Alzheimer's Disease, Senile Dementia and Related Disorders*, pp. 87–93.

FREEMON, F. R. 1976. Evaluation of patients with progressive intellectual deterioration. *Archives of Neurology, 33*, 658–659.

GEINISMAN, Y., BONDAREFF, W., AND TELSER, A. 1977. Transport of ($^3$H) fucose labeled glycoproteins in the septo-hippocampal pathway of young adult and senescent rats. *Brain Research, 125*, 182–186.

GILBERT, J. C. 1941. Memory loss in senescence. *Journal of Abnormal and Social Psychology, 36*, 73–86.

GILBERT, J. G. 1957. Age changes in color matching. *Journal of Gerontology, 12*, 210–215.

GILBERT, J. G. 1973. Thirty-five-year follow-up study of intellectual functioning. *Journal of Gerontology, 28*, 68–72.

GILBERT, J. G., AND LEVEE, R. F. 1971. Patterns of declining memory. *Journal of Gerontology, 26*, 70–75.

GUTMANN, E., AND HANZLIKOVA, V. 1972. Age changes in the neuromuscular system. Bristol: Scientechnica.

HAASE, G. R. 1977. Diseases presenting as dementia. *In*, C. E. Wells (ed.), *Dementia*, 2nd ed., pp. 27–68. Philadelphia: F.A. Davis.

HOBSON, W., AND PEMBERTON, J. 1955. *The Health of the Elderly at Home*, pp. 68–80. London: Butterworth.

HORN, J. L. 1975. Psychometric studies of aging and intelligence. *In*, S. Gershon and A. Raskin (eds.), *Aging*, Vol. 2, pp. 19–43. New York: Raven Press.

HOWELL, T. H. 1949. Senile deterioration of the central nervous system. *British Medical Journal, 1*, 56–58.

HUCKMAN, M. S., FOX, J., AND TOPEL, J. 1975. The validity of criteria for the evaluation of cerebral atrophy by computed tomography. *Radiology, 116*, 85–92.

HUTCHINSON, E. C., AND ACHESON, E. G. 1975. Strokes, *Natural History, Pathology and Surgical Treatment*, p. 283. London, Philadelphia: W. B. Saunders.

IQBAL, K., GRUNDKE-IQBAL, I., WIŚNIEWSKI, H., KORTHALS, J., AND TERRY, R. 1976. Chemistry of neurofibrous proteins in aging. *In*, R. D. Terry and S. Gershon (eds.), *Aging*, Vol. 3, pp. 351–360.

JARVIK, L. F. 1975. The aging nervous system: Clinical aspects. *In*, H. Brody, D. Harman, and J. M. Ordy (eds.), *Aging*, Vol. 1, pp. 1–9. New York: Raven Press.

JEROME, E. A. 1959. Age and learning—Experimental studies. *In*, J. E. Birren (ed.), *Handbook of Aging and the Individual*, pp. 655–699. Chicago: University of Chicago Press.

JONES, H. E. 1959. Intelligence and problem-solving. *In*, J. E. Birren (ed.), *Handbook of Aging and the Individual*, pp. 700–738. Chicago: University of Chicago Press.

KAHN, R. L., ZARIT, S. H., HILBERT, N. M., AND NIEDEREHE, G. 1975. Memory complaint and impairment in the aged. *Archives of General Psychiatry, 32*, 1569–1573.

KATZMAN, R., 1976. The prevalence and malignancy of Alzheimer disease. *Archives of Neurology, 33*, 217–218.

KATZMAN, R. 1977. Normal pressure hydrocephalus. *In*, C. E. Wells (ed.), *Dementia*, 2nd ed., pp. 69–72. Philadelphia: F. A. Davis.

KILOH, L. G. 1961. Pseudo-dementia. *Acta Psychiatrica Scandinavica, 37*, 336–351.

KINSBOURNE, M. 1977. Cognitive decline with advancing age: An interpretation. *In*, W. L. Smith and M. Kinsbourne (eds.), *Aging and Dementia*, pp. 217–235. New York: Spectrum Publ.

KRAL, V. A. 1962. Senescent forgetfulness: Benign and malignant. *Canadian Medical Association Journal, 86*, 257–260.

KRAL, V. A. 1966. Memory loss in the aged. *Diseases of the Nervous System, 27*(7), 51–54.

KURTZKE, J. F. 1976. An introduction to the epidemiology of cerebrovascular disease. *In*, P. Scheinberg (ed.), *Cerebrovascular Diseases*, pp. 239–253. New York: Raven Press.

LARSSON, T., AND SJÖGREN, T. 1960. Essential tremor. *Acta Psychiatrica et Neurologica Scandinavica*, Suppl. 144, *36*, 1–176

LAURENCE, M. W. 1967. Memory loss with age: A test of two strategies for its retardation. *Psychonomic Science, 9*, 209–210.

LAURENCE, S., AND STEIN, D. G. 1978. Recovery after brain damage and the concept of localization of function. *In*, S. Finger (ed.), *Recovery from Brain Damage: Research and Theory*, pp. 369–407. New York: Plenum.

LEWIS, C., BALLINGER, B. R., AND PRESLY, A. S. 1978. Trial of levodopa in senile dementia. *British Medical Journal, 1*, 550

LORANGER, A. W., GOODELL, H., McDOWELL, F. H., LEE, J. E., AND SWEET, R. D. 1972. Intellectual impairment in Parkinson's Syndrome. *Brain, 95*, 405–412

LOWRY, J., BAHR, A. L., ALLEN, J. H., JR., MEACHAM, W. F., AND JAMES, A. E., JR. 1977. Radiological techniques in the diagnostic evaluation of dementia. *In*, C. E. Wells (ed.), *Dementia*, 2nd ed., pp. 223–245. Philadelphia: F. A. Davis.

MARTIN, W. E., LOEWENSON, R. B., RESCH, J. A., AND

BAKER, A. B. 1973. Parkinson's disease. *Neurology, 23,* 783–790.

MAWDSLEY, C., AND FERGUSON, F. R. 1963. Neurological disease in boxers. *Lancet, 2,* 795–801.

Mayo Clinic and Mayo Foundation. 1976. *Clinical Examinations in Neurology,* 4th ed. Philadelphia: W. B. Saunders.

MCGEER, E., AND MCGEER, P. L. 1975. Neurotransmitter metabolism in the aging brain. *In,* R. D. Terry and S. Gershon (eds.), *Aging,* Vol. 3, pp. 389–403. New York: Raven Press.

MCHUGH, P. 1978. "Differentiation of Alzheimer's disease from depression and other psychiatric disorders of the senium. *In, Alzheimer's Disease, Senile Dementia, and Related Disorders.* New York: Raven Press.

MCNAMARA, J. O., AND APPEL, S. H. 1977. Biochemical approaches to dementia. *In,* C. E. Wells (ed.), *Dementia,* 2nd ed., pp. 155–168. Philadelphia: F. A. Davis.

MEIER-RUGE, W., REICHLMEIER, K., AND IWANGOFF, P. 1975. Enzymatic and enzyme histochemical changes of the aging animal brain and consequences for experimental pharmacology on aging. *In,* R. D. Terry and S. Gershon (eds.), *Aging,* Vol. 3, pp. 379–387. New York: Raven Press.

NIES, A., ROBINSON, D., DAVIS, J., AND RAVARIS, C. L. 1973. Changes in monoamine oxidase with aging. *In,* C. Eisdorfer and W. E. Fann (eds.), *Psychopharmacology and Aging,* pp. 41–54. New York: Plenum.

NEW, P. F. J., AND SCOTT, W. R. 1975. *Computed Tomography of the Brain and Orbit.* Baltimore: Williams & Wilkins.

O'BRIEN, M. D. 1977. Vascular disease and dementia in the elderly. *In,* W. L. Smith and M. Kinsbourne (eds.), *Aging and Dementia,* pp. 77–90. New York: Spectrum Publ.

ORGEL, L. E. 1963. The maintenance and the accuracy of protein synthesis and its relevance to aging. *Proceedings of the National Academy of Science, 49,* 517–521.

OVERGAARD, J., HVID-HANSEN, O., LAND, A. M., PEDERSEN, K., CHRISTENSEN, S., HAASE, J., HEIN, O., AND TWEED, W. 1973. Prognosis after head injury based on early clinical examination. *Lancet, 2,* 631–635.

PAULSON, G. W. 1977. The neurological examination in dementia. *In,* C. E. Wells (ed.), *Dementia,* 2nd ed., pp. 169–188. Philadelphia: F. A. Davis.

PEAR, B. L. 1977. The radiographic morphology of cerebral atrophy. *In,* W. L. Smith and M. Kinsbourne (eds.), *Aging and Dementia,* pp. 57–76. New York: Spectrum Publ.

PERRY, E. K., PERRY, R. H., BLESSED, G., AND TOMLINSON, B. E. 1977. Necropsy evidence of central cholinergic deficits in senile dementia. *Lancet* (letter), *1,* 189.

RAISMAN, G. 1978. What hope for repair of the brain? *Annals of Neurology, 3,* 101–106.

REITAN, R. M. 1967. Changes with Aging and Cerebral Damage. *Mayo Clinic Proceedings, 42,* 653–673.

ROSEN, S., PLESTER, D., EL-MOFTY, A., AND ROSEN, H. V. 1964. High frequency audiometry in presbycusis; A comparative study of the Mabaan tribe in the Sudan with urban populations. *Archives of Otolaryngology, 79,* 18–32.

SCHAIE, K. W., AND GRIBBIN, K. 1975. Adult development and aging. *Annual Review of Psychology, 26,* 65–96.

SCHEIBEL, M. E., LINDSAY, R. D., TOMIYASU, U., AND SCHEIBEL, A. B. 1975. Progressive dendritic changes in aging human cortex. *Experimental Neurology, 47,* 392–403.

SCHEIBEL, M. E., AND SCHEIBEL, A. B. 1975. Structural changes in the aging brain. *In,* H. Brody, D. Harman, and J. M. Ordy (eds.), *Aging,* Vol. 1, pp. 11–37. New York: Raven Press.

SCHNEIDER, N. G., GRITZ, E. R., AND JARVIK, M. E. 1975. Age difference in learning, immediate and one week delayed recall. *Gerontologia, 21,* 10–20.

SCHONFIELD, D. 1967. Memory loss with age: Acquisition and retrieval. *Psychological Reports, 20,* 223–226.

SHELANSKI, M. 1975. Neurochemistry of aging: Review and prospectus. *In,* R. D. Terry and S. Gershon (eds.), *Aging,* Vol. 3, pp. 339–350. New York: Raven Press.

SPILLANE, J. D. 1962. Five boxers. *British Medical Journal, 2,* 1205–1210.

STEIN, D. G., AND FIRL, A. C. 1976. Brain damage and reorganization of function in old age. *Experimental Neurology, 52,* 157-167.

STREHLER, B. L. 1975. Introduction: Aging and the human brain. *In,* R. D. Terry and S. Gershon (eds.), *Aging,* Vol. 3, pp. 1–22. New York: Raven Press.

TERRY, R. D., AND WIŚNIEWSKI, H. M. 1975. Structural and chemical changes of the aged human brain. *In,* S. Gershon and A. Raskin (eds.), *Aging,* Vol. 2, pp. 127–141. New York: Raven Press.

TERRY, R. D., AND WIŚNIEWSKI, H. M. 1977. Structural aspects of aging of the brain. *In,* C. Eisdorfer and R. O. Friedel (eds.), *Cognitive and Emotional Disturbances in the Elderly,* pp. 1–9. Chicago: Year Book Medical Publishers.

THOMPSON, L. W. 1975. Cerebral blood flow, EEG, and behavior in aging. *In,* R. D. Terry and S. Gershon (eds.), *Aging,* Vol. 3, pp. 103–120. New York: Raven Press.

TOMLINSON, B. E. 1977. Morphological changes and dementia in old age. *In,* W. L. Smith and M. Kinsbourne (eds.), *Aging and Dementia,* pp. 25–56. New York: Spectrum Publ.

TOMLINSON, B. E., AND HENDERSON, G. 1975. Some quantitative cerebral findings in normal and demented old people. *In*, R. D. Terry and S. Gershon (eds.), *Aging*, Vol. 3, pp. 183–204. New York: Raven Press.

TOOLE, J. F., AND PATEL, A. N. 1974. *Cerebrovascular Disorders*, 2nd ed. New York: McGraw-Hill.

TRAUB, R., GAJDUSEK, D. C., AND GIBBS, C. J., JR. 1977. Transmissible virus dementia: The relation of transmissible spongiform encephalopathy to Creutzfeldt-Jacob disease. *In*, W. L. Smith and M. Kinsbourne (eds.), *Aging and Dementia*, pp. 91–172. New York: Spectrum Publ.

WANG, H. S. 1977. Dementia in old age. *In*, C. E. Wells (ed.), *Dementia*, 2nd ed., pp. 15–25. Philadelphia: F. A. Davis.

WEALE, R. A. 1965. On the eye. *In*, A. T. Welford and J. E. Birren (eds.), *Behavior, Aging and the Nervous System*, pp. 307–325. Springfield, Ill,: Charles C Thomas.

WECHSLER, D. 1955. *Manual for Wechsler Adult Intelligence Scale*. New York: The Psychological Corporation.

WEISS, A. D. 1959. Sensory functions. *In*, J. E. Birren (ed.), *Handbook of Aging and the Individual*, pp. 503–542. Chicago: University of Chicago Press.

WELFORD, A. T. 1959. Psychomotor performance. *In*, J. E. Birren (ed.), *Handbook of Aging and the Individual*, pp. 655–699. Chicago: University of Chicago Press.

WELLS, C. E., AND BUCHANAN, D. C. 1977. The clinical use of psychological testing in evaluation of dementia. *In*, C. E. Wells (ed.), *Dementia*, 2nd ed., pp. 189–204. Philadelphia: F. A. Davis.

WHITE, P., GOODHARDT, M. J., KEET, J. P., HILEY, C. R., CARRASCO, L. H., WILLIAMS, I. E. I., AND BOWEN, D. M. 1977. Neocortical cholinergic neurons in elderly people. *Lancet, 1*, 668–670.

WILLIAMS, R. L., KARACAN, I., AND HURSCH, C. J. 1974. *EEG of Human Sleep*. New York: John Wiley.

WILSON, W. P., MUSELLA, L., AND SHORT, M. J. 1977. The electroencephalogram in dementia. *In*, C. E. Wells (ed.), *Dementia*, 2nd ed., pp. 205–222. Philadelphia: F. A. Davis.

# 22

# Cognitive Assessment
# of the Older Adult

*Edgar Miller*

In the eyes of many clinical psychologists psychological assessment has become more than a little passé. The early practice of clinical psychology was substantially based upon the use of psychometric tests and related procedures, such as the projective tests, to describe and classify patients. The present trend is very much towards the psychologist's involvement in therapeutic procedures. Assessment is more and more neglected if not actually rejected. It is for this reason that the writer, like others who have recently attempted a similar task (e.g. Schaie and Schaie, 1977), feels constrained to justify his continuing emphasis on the importance of assessment. This justification also has the additional merit of leading discussion to the important preliminary question of what assessment is intended to achieve. This point is overlooked all too often and it is argued that if appropriate goals are set for assessment then worthwhile results can be obtained.

It would require far too long a detour to go into the reasons for the current scepticism with regard to assessment. It is sufficient to state that, in this writer's opinion, many of the criticisms directed against psychological assessment as traditionally practiced (e.g. Goldfried and Kent, 1972) are substantially valid. Nevertheless it is too simple minded to jump from the amply justified criticisms of many assessment procedures to the conclusion that all psychological assessment is worthless and should be abandoned. In the first place the use of psychological techniques in the therapy or management of a person's problems assumes some sort of assessment of the situation in order to decide how to treat that particular client. Assessment is still crucial although it may be covert and based upon information rather different from that obtainable from traditional assessment procedures.

Another important point is that it is illogical to lump all assessment together as though it were unitary activity carried out in one particular way and for a single purpose. This is obviously not the case. Instead of worrying whether psychological assessment is useful or not in very general terms much more specific questions need to be asked. The value of assessment will depend upon the procedures used, the population to which they are applied and the purpose for which the assessment is carried out. In this chapter the population involved is already fixed: the mentally disturbed aged. The different types of assessment technique will be dealt with in relation to the problems presented by the individual case and the psychological assessment which might be used. These problems will now be briefly outlined.

Traditionally psychological assessment of the mentally disturbed elderly seems to have been directed towards two major questions. The first of these is the measurement of decline. Deterioration in intellectual functioning occurs in many conditions found in the elderly but especially in dementia. Establishing whether such deterioration has occurred and measuring its extent is of relevance to diagnosis and could have implications for management.

The second type of question centers around differential diagnosis. Accurate diagnosis in the elderly can have important implications. Functional disorders, in particular depression, can be very difficult to discriminate from dementia, yet the two conditions are managed differently and the prognosis is very different (Roth, 1955). Differential diagnosis is thus not an empty, academic exercise.

Further problems can be added to these more traditional concerns. The increasing interest in pharmacological agents that might retard or even reverse cognitive decline in demented patients calls for suitable measures that will be sensitive to induced changes in cognitive functioning. The recent development of social and psychological techniques designed to enhance the functioning of elderly people, together with the realization that even those with dementing illnesses may show some favorable response (e.g. Barns, Sack, and Shore, 1973; Miller, 1977a; Woods and Britton, 1977), emphasizes the need to find ways of predicting which patients will respond to the different techniques and in what way. Finally there is the problem of finding ways to assess the very deteriorated demented patient who is unable to cooperate adequately with the more usual forms of psychological assessment.

Before passing to the more detailed issues it is sensible to consider the more general difficulties which arise in the psychological assessment of the elderly patient. In addition to providing further general orientation to what follows this will also avoid the repetitive raising of some points in later sections.

## GENERAL DIFFICULTIES IN THE ASSESSMENT OF THE ELDERLY SUBJECT

In general terms there are of course no issues involved in assessing the elderly that do not arise in other groups as well. Age alone does not make the elderly subject more difficult to handle in the assessment situation. There are merely some difficulties which are particularly prominent in this population. These problems involve both the personal characteristics of the elderly individual, especially those with pathological disturbances which form the subpopulations most likely to be in need of assessment, as well as technical problems with the instruments that are available.

A number of elderly patients are disoriented and mildly confused. As a result they are likely to take longer to adjust to new surroundings and new demands that are placed upon them. The person carrying out the assessment therefore needs to take more care than might otherwise be the case in establishing a good rapport with the subject and take greater pains in explaining what he is trying to do. Taking care and a little time over the preliminary interactions with the patient will enable the examiner to judge whether there are any of the more obvious signs of confusion or intellectual deterioration. Adapting the assessment accordingly may avoid running into an unexpected failure of the patient to understand what is required of him. An early disturbance of this type may upset the patient and lower the level of cooperation.

Some elderly patients can present problems of motivation and cooperation. It has sometimes been assumed that the elderly as a whole may do less well on psychological measures at least partly because of reduced motivation. Experimental studies that have manipulated motivational levels in younger and older subjects have consistently failed to obtain results suggesting lowered motivation in the elderly (e.g. Botwinick, Brinley, and Birren, 1958; Ganzler, 1964). Even where studies have involved the mentally impaired aged comments about the good level of motivation have been made (Katz, Neal, and Simon, 1960). Poor motivation is therefore not the general problem in assessment that might be feared. Lack of motivation, and hence low levels of cooperation, can be encountered occasionally but this is a significant problem in only a small proportion of elderly subjects. Sometimes this seems to be in individuals who perceive, correctly or otherwise, that their intellectual deficiencies are likely to be shown up. The depressed elderly patient may also be very reluctant to take part in assessment. Such individuals can often be assessed quite adequately but they need handling with considerable tact and skill. As with the patient who tires easily, several short sessions may be preferable to one or two long ones. The fact that the performance of elderly patients on intellectual tasks appears to be modifiable by the use of incentives may also be of relevance in working with poorly motivated subjects (e.g. Hoyer, Labouvie, and Baltes, 1973).

A final set of complications related to the elderly individual are the physical changes and diseases which become more common with advancing age. Sensory impairments are common and a significant proportion of the elderly have a serious enough loss of sight or hearing to be a potential source of real difficulty in communication. Although spectacles and hearing aids may give a reasonable correction for these deficits this does not guarantee that individuals, especially if mentally impaired, will have managed to acquire adequate prostheses. A number of investigations have shown that the presence of sensory impairments, especially in the auditory modality, has an inverse correlation with measures of psychological functioning (Birren, Butler, Greenhouse, Sokoloff, and Yarrow, 1963; O'Neill and Calhoun, 1975).

Other physical problems can affect cognitive status. Cardiovascular disease becomes increasingly prevalent with advancing years. Patients with such conditions have been shown to have lowered intellectual performance (Abrahams and Birren, 1973; Wilkie and Eisdorfer, 1971). Common infections, such as those of the urinary tract, can produce confusional states in the elderly which may not be pronounced enough to be clinically obvious yet may still reduce scores on intellectual tests. Because of the marked interaction between physical and psychological states in the elderly (and many other examples could be cited of physical conditions which may have psychological consequences) it is sound practice to check on the recent physical health of elderly patients that are being assessed.

These practical problems are not the only complications that need to be taken into account in the assessment of the elderly. There are a number of technical difficulties which relate to the assessment procedures that are used. Many tests of potential value for use with the elderly do not have norms that extend far enough up the age scale. Even where test constructors have attempted to extend norms to the elderly their derivation is often not as soundly based as it is for younger subjects. This appears to be the case for the much used Wechsler Adult Intelligence Scale (Eisdorfer and Cohen, 1961).

Even a test that appears to have soundly based norms for the elderly may be misleading especially if these norms have not been recently established. There are reasons for believing that as time passes from the point at which the standardization was carried out, so the test may start to overestimate the intellectual level of elderly subjects. The argument underlying this statement is as follows. There is substantial evidence that cross-sectional studies whereby groups of elderly subjects are directly compared with younger subjects will exaggerate the decline in cognitive functioning that occurs as a result of normal aging (e.g. Botwinick, 1977; Miller, 1977b; Savage, 1973). An important cause of this is that in such comparisons the older group may differ from the younger in other variables besides age. The older group will have been born at a time when good ante- and post-natal care were less common, infant nutrition may have been less adequate, and educational opportunities were not so extensive. Successive generations would be better placed for these things and thus would be expected to do better on intellectual tests when they reach old age. This expectation has been supported in that there are indications that the age at which intellectual decline starts to become manifest is increasing generation by generation (Schaie and Gribbin, 1975). The likely upshot is that a test such as the Wechsler Adult Intelligence Scale standardized in 1955 is likely to have norms for elderly subjects based upon a mean level of performance which is below that of similar subjects tested two to three decades later.

## MEASUREMENT OF DECLINE

A common goal in the assessment of the elderly is to measure decline in cognitive functioning. This has diagnostic significance since dementia is expected to produce intellectual deterioration. It is still an occasional topic of debate as to whether functional disorders, particularly depression and schizophrenia, produce any intellectual deficit.

(W.R. Miller, 1975; Payne, 1973). This could conceivably be a source of confusion in using estimates of cognitive decline as an indicator of dementia. Fortunately if intellectual deterioration does occur in functional disorders it is quite small and very much out of proportion with that found in organic states. The measurement of decline, or rate of decline, has other potential uses especially in evaluating therapeutic or management procedures. Any drug of benefit in slowing down the process of dementia, or any other condition having adverse effects on the intellect, ought to reduce the measured rate of intellectual decline.

The ideal way of measuring intellectual deterioration is by comparing the patient's present level of performance with that established prior to the illness. Unfortunately this is rarely possible. For very few patients are there data available from a previous testing on a useful instrument which is both recent enough to be considered reliable and not too close to the onset of the condition to be possibly contaminated by it. Direct measurement of decline is usually feasible from the point at which the patient comes into contact with the service. The patient can be tested initially and then retested after a suitable interval. In this way any further decline can be measured and this is sometimes useful where a diagnosis of dementia remains in doubt or in patients with confusional states to see if improvement has occurred.

Although simple in conception the attempt to compare the results of psychometric testing on two occasions is fraught with technical difficulties. The test used needs to be highly reliable; otherwise a very large change will need to occur by the second testing in order to be considered significant. In addition a subject's score may change with retesting as a result of factors such as practice effects which have nothing to do with whether the true level on the variable being measured has actually changed. Such changes can sometimes be quite large. In order to compare results from two separate testings with the same test it is highly desirable that test-retest data are available. Such information is extremely sparse even for the most commonly used tests. Some indication of likely changes on retesting together with test-retest correlations can be obtained from Gerboth (1950) and Hamister (1949) for the Wechsler-Bellevue Scales; from Guertin, Rabin, Frank, and Ladd (1962) and Matarazzo, Wiens, Matarazzo, and Monaugh (1973) for the Wechsler Adult Intelligence Scale; from Desai (1952) for Raven's Progressive Matrices; and from Schaie and Labouvie-Vief (1974) for the Primary Mental Abilities. Only the last of these studies used elderly subjects and so the rest have to be treated

with caution because of this. The simple statistical procedures required to use test-retest data to the best effect are described by Payne and Jones (1957).

Because of the difficulties in the direct measurement of intellectual decline there have been a number of attempts to devise indirect means. These are invariably based upon the assumption that some aspects of intellectual functioning are more prone to decline with age or as a result of neurological disease than are others. Those aspects resistant to change can be used to estimate premorbid levels of functioning while those intellectual measures most likely to decline can be used to indicate the present level. These two levels can then be compared to give an estimate of the amount of deterioration.

One popular assumption is that vocabulary scores are highly resistant to decline both as a consequence of normal aging and as a result of brain disease. Test of mental deterioration using vocabulary to estimate premorbid functioning have been the Babcock Examination for the Efficiency of Mental Functioning (Babcock, 1930), the Hunt Minnesota Test for Organic Brain Damage (Hunt, 1943), the Shipley Institute of Living Scale (Shipley, 1940) and their later modifications and developments. The use of vocabulary as an index of premorbid functioning in such scales is based on a number of assumptions. The most detailed discussion of these has been provided by Yates (1956) although Lezak (1976) and Miller (1977b) also discuss the issues involved. It is clear that vocabulary scales do correlate quite highly with overall measures of general intelligence, as well, if not better, than most other scales measuring specific abilities. The problem is that the correlation is not high enough to avoid an appreciable margin of error in estimating intelligence on the basis of vocabulary alone (Yates, 1956). The stability of vocabulary following pathological changes in the brain is also open to dispute. Although there are a few negative results, vocabulary has been shown to decline in many studies (e.g. Acklesberg, 1944; Miller, 1977b; Nelson, 1953) although the amount of decline may be less than that shown by other types of test. It also appears that the sensitivity of vocabulary tests to pathological decline is a function of the criteria used to determine whether the subject has defined the word adequately (Yates, 1956).

Another source of confusion with indirect measures of decline is that subjects in their premorbid states are not always equally good (or bad) at all kinds of intellectual tests. Some people will start off with relatively higher scores on vocabulary tests than on the sort of reasoning and visuospatial tests used by instruments like the Babcock to indicate the present level of functioning. Such subjects will emerge as having "intellectual deterioration" even before they start to dement. Other subjects will have the reverse pattern of abilities and thus will be unusually resistant to showing decline in intellect.

Thus it can be seen that the use of vocabulary as an indication of premorbid intellectual status in the measurement of intellectual decline is based upon a number of assumptions which, to a greater or lesser degree, are only approximations to what is really the case. The distorting effect of these deviations from the assumptions is likely to be cumulative and this means that this general technique is unlikely to produce results that are accurate enough for use with individual patients. This is borne out by empirical studies of the ability of these scales to distinguish between normal subjects and those with organic conditions known to be associated with intellectual deterioration (Yates, 1954). The group means do differ in the expected direction but the amount of overlap between them is so large as to preclude making reliable decisions about individuals.

A recent development of a similar rationale has been described by Nelson and O'Connell (1978). They built upon a previous finding that reading ability in adults correlated highly with intellectual level. They also claim that reading remains relatively intact in dementia and is less likely to be affected than the vocabulary scale of the WAIS. Using a specially devised reading test they publish regression equations with relatively small standard errors enabling the various WAIS IQs to be predicted from errors in reading. Nelson and O'Connell also attempted to validate their work by looking at the measured amount of intellectual decline in a group of controls and a group with cerebral atrophy. The degree of discrimination was quite impressive although there was still some overlap between the groups. Although the use of the Nelson and O'Connell reading test may have overcome some of the difficulties inherent in the previous use of vocabulary as an index of premorbid level it has not entirely eliminated them. It remains to be seen if others can cross-validate the procedure and still maintain the same discriminatory power.

Another indirect method of measuring intellectual deterioration has been the use of various combinations of subtest scores from the Wechsler intelligence scales to form a "deterioration index." Wechsler (1958) made use of the fact that scores on the different subtests of the WAIS tend to decline as a function of age at different rates. In effect

Wechsler's index uses four of the subtests showing least decline with age as indicators of premorbid level and four subtests more susceptible to decline to give the present level. The formula then compares the two to estimate the extent of intellectual decline. A number of alternative deterioration indices based upon the Wechsler subtests have been proposed using slightly different rationales or derived purely on an empirical basis (e.g., Crookes, 1974; Hewson, 1949).

In general these deterioration indices involve similar assumptions to those discussed with regard to the instruments which use vocabulary scores to indicate premorbid levels. Again these assumptions are only approximately true (Miller, 1977b). The ultimate criterion is of course how well they work out in practice. The evidence is not impressive and indices that seem to work well on first publication do not stand up to cross-validation. Few of these studies have been carried out using elderly subjects but one of the rare exceptions is described by Savage (1971). He compared a normal group of elderly subjects with elderly "organics" who ought to have undergone intellectual deterioration on Wechsler's (1958) index. The two groups were well separated in terms of their mean scores. Unfortunately there was considerable overlap in the distributions and a quarter of the allegedly deteriorated organic group appeared to have less deterioration than the average normal subject. Again the problem seems to be that there is some basis to the use of deterioration indices based on the Wechsler intelligence scales but the results are too unreliable to enable decisions to be made about individual patients.

A final possible way of estimating deterioration is to use the subject's past history, educational level and occupational record as an indicator of premorbid IQ. The basic difficulty with this method is the considerable variation in IQ found amongst individuals of given occupational or educational levels (Harrell and Harrell, 1945). This problem is greatest amongst those with lower attainments because having, say, a particular professional qualification may guarantee a minimum level of ability (often lower in IQ terms than many might think) while having only the minimal level of education and an unskilled job does not preclude a person from being highly intelligent.

The measurement of intellectual deterioration in the individual patient is far from satisfactory at present. For very few patients encountered in clinical practice is there any reliable information about premorbid level, so direct measurement is precluded except for the measurement of further decline following the initial assessment. Even in the latter case there are technical difficulties due to the scarcity of test-retest data on suitable instruments. The indirect methods of measuring deterioration are too inaccurate for use with individual cases, because the assumptions involved are only rough approximations of the real state of affairs. A possible exception is the use of a reading test to estimate premorbid levels as advocated by Nelson and O'Connell (1978) but the history of work in this field cautions against accepting their results at face value until cross-validation has been achieved. There also appear to have been no attempts to try to find ways of measuring the amount of decline in any cognitive functions other than general intelligence in a way that would be applicable to the individual patient.

The measurement of the extent of cognitive decline is a somewhat more difficult task than just establishing that a change has occurred. This latter issue is more relevant to the question of differential diagnosis that is to be discussed below. It may be that in the future some of the techniques discussed in the next section could be adapted to the measurement of decline.

## DIFFERENTIAL DIAGNOSIS

As already indicated, the differential diagnosis of the mentally disturbed elderly patient is not merely of academic interest but has important implications for treatment and management. An important distinction is that between the functional disorders and the organic states, especially dementia. Depression and dementia can be particularly difficult to discriminate on clinical grounds since both can present a picture of neglect, lack of verbal communication, and apparent low affect. Cognitive testing may be used to help differentiate between the different types of organic disorder. A number of elderly patients who appear demented may turn out to have toxic confusional states and a few may even have other types of neurological disorder (Marsden, 1978).

Before actually describing the tests and other techniques that may be of use in differential diagnosis some preliminary points need to be made. The first is that measures that discriminate reliably between groups of subjects of different kinds are not necessarily of much value in making decisions about individual cases. For example, if suitable groups of men and women were selected at random then the mean height of the men would almost certainly be significantly higher than that of the women. Despite the fact that this finding could be readily replicated and achieve a very high level

of statistical significance, measuring a new client's height would not be a very accurate way of determining his or her sex. Not only would this lead to an unacceptably high level of errors but there are better ways of making this decision. In a related way, differences between groups are often demonstrated on groups containing readily diagnosed examples of the conditions being examined. It is those cases that are not so clearcut that cause the biggest diagnostic problems and for these the demonstrated group differences may not be so relevant.

Another important point relates to antecedent probabilities or base rates (Gathercole, 1968; Meehl and Rosen, 1955). In trying to distinguish between two possible diagnoses such as depression and dementia it is unlikely that the two diagnoses will be equiprobable. In British psychogeriatric units it has been found that incoming patients are about twice as likely to be depressed as demented (Glaister, 1971; Kendrick, 1965). These proportions will be prone to vary as a result of local conditions, admission policies, etc. Intuitively it can be seen that if one diagnosis is more likely on a statistical basis than another, then it might be possible to get quite an impressive "hit rate" just by saying that every patient has this diagnosis. The more extreme the base rate, the more this is so, and the more powerful any test needs to be to improve upon chance levels. Ideally local base rates should always be established and the appropriate correction applied to any diagnostic tests that are used. Meehl and Rosen's (1955) paper makes it clear how this can be done.

An important qualification is that the important base rate is not necessarily the overall one for admissions to the unit in which the test is being used. The critical rate is that in the population for which the test is being used. It could be, for example, that the unit admits two depressed patients for every dement. Only half the depressions may be referred for psychological assessment because the other half are considered to be adequately identified on purely clinical grounds. All the new dements might be referred. The referral base rate would then be 50:50 and not 67:33 as the overall admission figures would suggest.

### DEMENTIA VS. FUNCTIONAL DISORDERS

Most clinicians would probably start by administering a test of general intelligence, preferably the Wechsler Adult Intelligence Scale, to a patient presenting this problem in differential diagnosis. Unless the dementia is so marked that the diagnostic question would not need posing in the first place it is unlikely that the WAIS alone would give any firm indication. It is improbable that the obtained IQs would be unequivocally below those anticipated on the basis of the subject's previous occupation and educational attainments. A lower Performance than Verbal IQ and higher scores on the Vocabulary and Picture Completion subtests have been alleged to be more typical of dementia but these features can also be found in a substantial proportion of cases with functional disorders (McFie, 1975; Miller, 1977b). In fact Whitehead (1973) was unable to discriminate between elderly depressives and dements on the basis of the pattern of WAIS subtest scores. Probably the most useful result of administering a highly reliable test of general intelligence, like the WAIS, is that it gives a good basis for the measurement of any decline should diagnosis remain in doubt.

In general patients with dementia (e.g. senile or arteriosclerotic dementia) tend to do badly on test of learning or memory. Depressed patients may also show some impairment on such tests but the reason for this seems to be an alteration in the response criteria adopted by the subject rather than poor memory per se (Miller and Lewis, 1977). A large number of approaches have been used in the clinical examination of memory and many of these might be of potential value in the present context. Erickson and Scott (1977) have recently provided an extensive review of clinical memory tests but present discussion will concentrate on those that have been particularly used in the discrimination of dementia.

One of the earliest learning/memory tests to be devised specifically for use with the elderly is the Inglis Paired Associate Learning Test (Inglis, 1959). This has two parallel forms and requires the subject to learn three pairs of otherwise unrelated words. Inglis (1959) found that it gave a worthwhile level of discrimination between elderly patients with and without clinically evident dementia. Cross-validation studies by Caird, Sanderson, and Inglis (1962) and Parsons (1965) have substantially confirmed Inglis' results.

A common principle in learning tests has been to take a set of words that the subject is unable to define and teach him their meanings by a set procedure. This idea was first proposed by Shapiro and Nelson (1955) but the first successful use of this principle was by Walton and Black (1957). In the Walton-Black, the test proper is based on the first ten consecutively failed words from the vocabulary scale of one of the major intelligence tests. The subject is then taught the meanings of these words by a standard procedure (which could do with being specified in a little greater detail). Sub-

sequently the scoring system has been simplified and further work has confirmed that the test has a useful level of diagnostic validity (Bolton, Savage, and Roth, 1967; Walton, White, Black, and Young, 1959). It correctly discriminates a high proportion of those with functional disorders although it does less well in classifying those with brain disease. A limitation of this test, which it shares with other similar tests, is that it starts to misclassify the non-organic subjects when used with patients whose intelligence is getting down towards the levels associated with mental retardation.

A rather more sophisticated development specifically designed for use with geriatric populations is the Synonym Learning Test (Kendrick, Parboosingh, and Post, 1965). The SLT is based on the Mill Hill Vocabulary Scale but extra words are provided in case the subject can define too many words in the Mill Hill. The procedure for teaching the words to the subject is also less ambiguously described than in the Walton-Black. The SLT does not stand on its own but is administered together with a simple test of motor speed, the Digit Copying Test (DCT).

In developing his small test battery Kendrick has made use of Bayesian statistics (Kendrick, 1965). The Bayesian model enables the test constructor and user to take base rates into account. Kendrick made the assumption that in psychogeriatric populations for which the differential diagnosis between depression and dementia is appropriate there is an antecedent probability that about a third will be demented. This proportion was derived from psychogeriatric admissions to the Bethlem Royal Hospital, a prestigious teaching unit linked to the Institute of Psychiatry in London. Glaister (1971) has found that this proportion is about right for a much more typical British psychiatric hospital.

The original validation of the test and a further cross-validation by Kendrick (1967) have shown that an extremely high level of diagnostic discrimination can be obtained when the SLT and DCT are each administered on two occasions six weeks apart. This amounts to a diagnostic efficiency of over 90 percent. Other reports (e.g., Whitehead, 1971) have not been quite so encouraging.

A particular problem with learning tests, and especially the SLT, is that subjects (and hence administrators) can find it stressful and an appreciable minority of elderly subjects will refuse to carry on until the learning criterion is reached. This has led Kendrick and his colleagues to devise an alternative to the SLT known as the Object Learning

Test (Gibson and Kendrick, 1976). The OLT requires subjects to remember pictures of common objects. It is quicker to administer than the SLT, is not similarly stressful, and subject refusal is rare. A full and detailed report has yet to appear but preliminary results of a study in which the OLT replaced the SLT in a battery administered to over a hundred psychogeriatric patients indicates a diagnostic discrimination accuracy exceeding 90 percent (Kendrick, Gibson, and Moyes, 1978).

The tests described so far are only a few of those that have been suggested as clinical measures of verbal learning and memory. In view of their success in differentiating between dementia and functional disorders in the older patient it would be worthwhile exploring the use of many more clinical tests of memory in this population (see Erickson and Scott, 1977). Experimental studies of memory in dementia (e.g. Miller, 1971) have also used measures (in this case free recall) which discriminate well between groups and which might have diagnostic potential. The tendency for some depressed patients to be misclassified because of poor scores on memory tests could possibly be compensated for by using recognition testing thus allowing the effects of response bias to be partialled out (Miller and Lewis, 1977).

The various design copying tests have also been used in the diagnosis of dementia. The principal examples are the Visual Motor Gestalt Test (Bender, 1946), the Revised Visual Retention Test (Benton, 1963) and Graham and Kendall's (1960) Memory for Designs Test. Unfortunately attempts to validate these tests have usually been concerned with the rather more general question of their potential value in discriminating between "organics" and "non-organics" of all types. They do appear to have some validity in the present context but this is less impressive than that demonstrated for the verbal learning tests (Brilliant and Gynther, 1963; Crookes and McDonald, 1972). These tests do not place the same stress upon the subject as the verbal learning tests. Better validational data obtained from elderly subjects is necessary to gain a full understanding of their usefulness.

Neuropsychological assessments can also be useful in discriminating dementia from functional disorders. Although detailed studies of neuropsychological functions in dementia are sparse (Miller, 1977b) it is well documented that dements can show a wide range of neuropsychological disturbances while functional disorders should not. A detailed account of many forms of neuropsychological assessment can be found in Lezak (1976) but Warrington's (1970) account of some basic procedures is still a useful starting point for those unfamiliar with this field.

Although early cases of dementia may be quite well oriented, failure to give an adequate answer to the usual kinds of questions relating to orientation in time and place must raise strong suspicions of an organic disorder (Williams, 1970). The person with severe depression may be unwilling or slow to respond but is reasonably well aware of his situation in time and place. Demented patients are often particularly impaired on tests of spatial perception and praxis (Pearce and Miller, 1973). Simple tests such as asking the patient to draw a house, clock face, or cube can show quite gross distortions and inadequacies. Unfortunately the more formal tests of constructional apraxia, such as block and stick construction tasks (see Lezak, 1976; Warrington, 1970) do not appear to have been applied systematically to groups of older subjects and so it is difficult to state how often the various abnormalities appear.

Speech disturbances are another feature of dementia that should not be manifest in functional disorders. In many clinical accounts of dementia these are described as aphasic. The objective evidence, such as it is, implies that dementia of the Alzheimer's or senile dementia type which is characterized by cerebral atrophy, gives speech disturbances which are qualitatively different from those associated with aphasia as a result of focal lesions (Miller, 1977b; Rochford, 1971). Errors and delays in naming are the best documented abnormalities of speech in dementia (Barker and Lawson, 1968; Lawson and Barker, 1968). It appears that, unlike cases with dysphasia produced by focal lesions, naming errors in dementia are at least partly the result of a failure to adequately recognize the object or picture that is to be named. Asking the demented patient to name easily recoginzed things, like parts of the body, produces an improvement in naming that is not found in the true aphasic (Rochford, 1971).

Psychophysiological measures are also related to cognitive deterioration in dementia and so may be useful in diagnosis. There are a large number of psychophysiological variables and a recent general review of the psychophysiology of aging has been provided by Marsh and Thompson (1977). On the EEG the amount of slow wave activity is particularly related to dementia (e.g Barnes, Busse, and Friedman 1956; Wang, Obrist, and Busse, 1970). Changes in slow wave activity do not seem to be present in those with functional psychoses (Frey and Sjögren, 1959; Obrist and Henry, 1958). Obrist and Busse (1965) have argued for the value of the

EEG in discriminating between organic and functional disorders but others, such as Levy (1978), stress the appreciable amount of overlap in EEG findings between pathological and normal groups.

Many other psychophysiological variables might be of interest in this context but as Levy (1978) points out most studies have focused upon organic mental deterioration and there is little data relating to subjects with functional disorders. It may be that measures that discriminate those with organic disorders from those with normal controls may not be so effective in discriminating organics from functional disorders, which is the more important diagnostic question. In his own work Levy has examined motor nerve conduction and has found that slowing is related to intellectual deterioration. Measures of motor nerve conduction velocity do discriminate between depressed and demented elderly subjects. Where hospitalized dements are used, the level of discrimination is quite impressive but the use of outpatient dements (presumably not such advanced cases) appreciably increased the amount of overlap with the depressed group.

Levy, Isaacs, and Behrman (1971) reported on the somatosensory evoked potentials obtained from electrical stimuli applied to the ulnar nerve. The latencies of various peaks in the response were slower in cases of senile dementia than in those with depression. Somewhat similar results had been found earlier by Straumanis, Shayass, and Schwartz (1965) with visual evoked potentials. It is interesting that in Straumanis *et al.*'s study the effects of normal aging were particularly marked in the first 100 milliseconds of the response. Subjects with chronic brain syndromes typically showed changes in those components occurring after the first 100 milliseconds.

Another possible approach to differential diagnosis is to use automated testing procedures (Gedye and Miller, 1970; Perez, Hruska, Stell, and Rivera, 1978). These are visual displays with responses indicated by the subject pressing a button or the window in which the appropriate stimulus is displayed. Such automated systems offer the possibility of higher reliability because of a greater standardization in the presentation and recording of test stimuli and the ability to make more extensive use of information such as response latencies (Gedye and Miller, 1970). So far only a limited range of test formats have been used, usually a form of matching to sample task, and detailed examinations of the clinical effectiveness of such procedures have been lacking. Preliminary indications of possible diagnostic validity are encouraging (Perez *et al.*, 1978).

## DIFFERENTIATION BETWEEN TYPES OF ORGANIC DISORDER

Although dementia is common it is by no means the only form of brain disease that may afflict the elderly. Some have claimed to be able to distinguish between Alzheimer's or Senile Dementia on the one hand and dementia produced by multiple infarcts on the other by means of cognitive tests. For example, Perez and coworkers (Perez, Gay, Taylor, and Rivera, 1975a; Perez, Rivera, Meyer, Gay, Taylor, and Matthew, 1975b) administered the Wechsler Memory Scale and six subtests of the WAIS to subjects with Alzheimer's disease, multi-infarct dementia and vertebrobasiliar insufficiency. Using the various subscales and complex methods of multivariate analysis they claimed to be able to get quite an impressive level of discrimination between the different types of subject and especially between those with dementia due to vascular and non-vascular causes. The major difficulty with this type of study is that it is all too easy to apply a set of measures to different groups of subjects and produce a formula to discriminate between the groups which merely capitalizes upon chance variations in the various measures. Cross-validation is therefore essential before such results are taken at face value.

In general terms this writer remains to be convinced that cognitive assessment has a great deal to contribute to the problem of differentiating between conditions that have diffuse cerebral pathology, although certain findings may direct suspicion one way or the other. The history of the development of the cognitive impairment may be of interest (Pearce and Miller, 1973). The Alzheimer's or atrophic type of dementia usually has an insidious onset with a slow, gradual deterioration. Dementia as a result of multiple infarcts may have a more obvious step like progression with sudden exacerbations. A careful neuropsychological examination, although unlikely to be definitive, may also yield some indicators. Cerebral atrophy is likely to give a more global and generalized range of impairments while dementia as a result of cerebrovascular disease is more likely to produce focal impairments. However, it must be remembered that the issue is complicated by the fact that cases with cerebral atrophy can give apparently focal disturbances especially in language and praxis. A final complication is that multi-infarct dementia is relatively uncommon and may well account for less than 20 percent of all cases of dementia (Marsden, 1978). This figure is low enough to cause difficulty with all but the most reliable of discriminators because of a low base rate (see the brief discussion of base rates in the previous section).

The discrimination between dementia and organic brain disease of other types (e.g. tumors or strokes) is much easier and depends upon the demonstration of neuropsychological impairments relating to the appropriate part of the brain. The appropriate techniques are well described elsewhere by Lezak (1976), Warrington (1970) and Walsh (1978) and are substantially the same as used with younger subjects.

## COMMENT

Cognitive assessment can make a useful contribution to differential diagnosis especially when this involves the discrimination between functional and organic disorders. A summary of the various assessment procedures together with their values and limitations is provided in Table 22-1. On the debit side it must be stressed again that a good diagnostic indicator is much more than a measure that can be shown to give significantly different results when applied to the appropriate groups. Research into diagnostic tests needs to take into account such things as base rates and the exact characteristics of the subjects in order to ensure that they carefully match those with whom the instrument will be used for diagnostic purposes (Parsons and Prigatano, 1978). Both direct and indirect contamination whereby the criterion groups are partly derived from measures that are the same as, or highly related to, those being investigated need to be eliminated from investigations of diagnostic efficiency

(Shapiro, Post, Löfring, and Inglis, 1956). Finally note needs to be taken of the fact that the diagnosis of dementia is subject to some inaccuracy (e.g., Nott and Fleminger, 1975) and ideally studies of diagnostic efficiency should also follow up the samples of subjects used in order to confirm that the original classification was accurate. In the light of these criteria few of the techniques discussed above can be considered to have been adequately explored as diagnostic procedures and the most satisfactory is the work of Kendrick and his associates on the Synonym Learning Test.

## PREDICTION OF OUTCOME

A common use of psychometric tests in general has been as predictors of various kinds of outcome. In the case of the elderly it is appropriate to comment upon the prediction of two kinds of outcome. A number of studies have examined the relationship between cognitive performance and mortality. A second, and potentially more fruitful goal of assessment, is in the prediction of the effects of management or therapeutic procedures. Evidence is accumulating that social and psychological manipulations can have an effect on the level of functioning of elderly individuals, including those with definite intellectual deterioration (Barns *et al.*, 1973; Miller, 1977a; Woods and Britton, 1977). The use of management or therapeutic programs presupposes some kind of assessment in order that they can be appropriately designed and applied.

**Table 22–I**   Cognitive Measures and Differential Diagnosis

| PROCEDURE | INFORMATION GAINED | COMMENTS |
| --- | --- | --- |
| Intelligence test (possibly Wechsler) | Not usually diagnostic itself but gives base from which to measure change. Low IQ may also contaminate other tests. | Norms may be out of date. Shortage of good test-retest data. |
| Verbal learning tests | Good discrimination between functional disorders and dementia. | May be stressful for subject. Unreliable for subjects with IQ< 80. |
| Design copying tests | Some discrimination between functional and organic disorders but not as good as verbal learning tests. | Quick and easy to administer with high level of subject acceptability. |
| Neuropsychological examination (for aphasia, apraxia, etc.) | Deficits indicate organic disorder. May help to distinguish diffuse pathology from focal lesions. | Tests of orientation, praxis, and language probably most useful. |
| Psychophysiological techniques (EEG, etc.) | May be of use in discriminating between functional and organic disorders and in deciding the type of organic disorder. | Studies of psychophysiological variables often show large overlaps between groups. |

## MORTALITY

Sanderson and Inglis (1961) administered the Walton-Black New Word Learning Test and the Inglis Paired Associate Learning Test to elderly subjects and found that survival at a 16-month follow-up was related to scores on these tests but not to clinical judgments that had been made about the subjects. Hall, Savage, Bolton, Pidwell, and Blessed (1972) showed that decline in intelligence as measured by the WAIS predicted mortality in all elderly subjects, while within a subgroup who had dementia, a verbal learning impairment was also adversely related to survival. Many other examples of similar findings could be cited which show an apparent association between cognitive status and mortality.

Particular attention has been given to the fact that a decline in cognitive ability seems to occur just before death. Jarvik and Falek (1963) gave various cognitive tests to elderly subjects over a prolonged period. Each subject was tested at least three times and subjects were then followed up after the last testing. A much higher mortality was found amongst those subjects whose scores declined from one testing to the next. Similar results have been claimed by others. For example, Lieberman (1965) tested subjects every few weeks over a two-and-one-half year period. He claimed that those who died showed a decline in cognitive test performance which occurred as early as six to nine months prior to death.

Work in this tradition has led to discussions of "terminal decline" and "terminal drop." Palmore and Cleveland (1976) point out that much of this work has been unsatisfactory in a number of ways. There is terminological confusion and many investigators have used poor methodology with wide-ranging conclusions being drawn on the basis of a small number of subjects. Palmore and Cleveland distinguish between "terminal decline," considered to be a steady linear decline before death, and "terminal drop," a curvilinear accelerating deterioration. They examined the effects of these two possible factors using complex regression analyses of data obtained from the first Duke longitudinal survey. When the effects of age were partialled out only a few of the large number of measures showed a terminal decline and only two a terminal drop. Intelligence was in evidence in both of these. Nevertheless the authors claim that the overall impact of the results point to the most powerful effect being that of age alone.

Palmore and Cleveland (1976) are certainly correct in drawing attention to the terminological inaccuracy and inadequate methodology in the work that is often cited on this topic. However, their own study is not immune from criticism in that it is unsatisfactory to partial out age first since this will also tend to remove all time dependent variance whether or not it is related to age. There are also some investigations using designs not so open to Palmore and Cleveland's criticisms. Riegel and Riegel (1972) started with a large sample (N = 380) who were tested and retested after a five year interval and then followed up for a further five years. This study yielded clear evidence of lower scores on intellectual tests in subjects within five years of death. Riegel and Riegel further suggest that the apparent decline in intellectual levels in older adults is the consequence of the samples containing an increasing proportion of subjects who are showing the terminal decline prior to death.

Terminal decline and drop are interesting concepts and need further exploration. If they are substantiated as powerful effects they open up the way for the use of cognitive tests in the prediction of mortality. On the other hand, it could be argued that psychological research would be much more humanely and usefully applied in trying to find ways to improve the quality of life for the elderly rather than in predicting their demise.

## ASSESSMENT FOR MANAGEMENT

The growing use of active intervention procedures with the elderly patient presumes some way of assessing individuals in order to decide what goals should be set and what is the best way to set about achieving them. In general this type of assessment of the elderly has been almost entirely neglected. What is particularly required are techniques for determining impairments that are of practical significance in reducing the elderly individual's ability to function as an independent unit in society. Also required are means of measuring change in such variables.

Certain developments in thinking about assessment which have occurred in clinical psychology in general may also be of considerable potential relevance to work with the elderly. The recent concern with "behavioral assessment" in relation to behavior therapy has arisen because of this same need to identify problems, derive suitable therapeutic interventions and monitor change. The general principles and many of the techniques of behavioral assessment would transfer readily to work with the aged. An outline of the present state of behavioral assessment can be found in Ciminero, Calhoun, and Adams, (1977) but the most relevant aspect is probably the work on direct observational methods.

The nearest that work with the elderly has

come to providing techniques for this purpose has been the development of various behavior rating scales. A number of these have been reviewed by Salzman, Shader, Kochansky, and Cronin, (1972). Probably the best known and studied of these is the Stockton Geriatric Rating Scale (Meer and Baker, 1966; Taylor and Bloom, 1974). Although these scales often contain some items relevant to the problem of defining areas of functioning that might provide a focus for therapeutic intervention they are invariably not designed with this in mind. They are more concerned with the problem of discriminating the mentally impaired aged from the rest and therefore do not systematically cover all the areas of functioning that might be of relevance in the planning of intervention programs. The development of more comprehensive scales possibly using a criterion referenced rather than a norm referenced approach would be valuable (Popham and Musek, 1969; Ward, 1970).

The principles governing social and psychological intervention with the elderly are not different from those pertaining to younger subjects. To that extent similar solutions to the problem of assessment in relation to intervention are also appropriate. Any change in emphasis arises from the fact that the behavioral problems that often arise in older subjects (e.g. confusion, wandering, incontinence, impaired memory) are not the same as those commonly found in young adults. As a result there is some need to modify or adapt existing techniques to meet the specific needs of working with old people.

## THE UNTESTABLE PATIENT

An occasionally encountered difficulty in the assessment of the elderly patient is in dealing with the one who is "untestable." By this is usually meant the person who, for various reasons, cannot be assessed by means of the conventionally used procedures dealt with in the major part of this chapter. While many elderly patients may be "untestable" in this sense, there is certainly no conscious individual who cannot be assessed psychologically in some way or other. It is useful to distinguish two main reasons why the usual methods of assessment may not be possible. The first is the patient who probably could do what is asked of him but refuses to cooperate. This is "test refusal." The second is the subject who is incapable of meeting the minimum requirements for giving a measurable performance on the test or procedure (e.g., the person who cannot even understand the instructions). To

a certain degree the approach to these two types of difficulty will be different.

Test refusal does occur from time to time with elderly clients and a certain incidence is probably unavoidable. It can be minimized by taking particular care in developing a good rapport with the patient, by being painstaking in explaining why the assessment is being carried out, and in being sensitive to the kind of fears and suspicions that subjects may have about undergoing the assessment procedure. Attempting to administer the tests patients find most acceptable first can also help in that it may mean that an inevitable refusal does not occur until some data have been obtained. For example, design copying tests give less trouble in this way than the Synonym Learning Test which some patients find quite stressful. Experience also suggests that backing off at the first hint of refusal and continuing something that the client does find acceptable (e.g., asking further questions about his history) may lead to cooperation later. It is also possible to let things rest and try again later although in this case it is probably best to avoid finishing one session in such a way that the subject's last contact with the examiner has an unpleasant connotation. Forcing the issue with an unwilling subject is rarely satisfactory. At best it only gets grudging compliance for a while and it tends to make further approaches more difficult. If refusal is determined, it is always possible to fall back upon the types of assessment applicable to those who are incapable of cooperating with the conventional procedures.

The demonstration that performance on intellectual tests can be influenced by training, particularly operant conditioning procedures (Hoyer et al., 1973; Plemons, Willis, and Baltes, 1978), has implications for dealing with the subject whose level of cooperation is less than adequate. Test performance can be improved and modified and it may even be possible to shape up the behavior necessary for subject participation in assessment.

Those who are incapable of taking part in the usual forms of assessment present other difficulties. These are generally the more intellectually deteriorated and the goal of assessment will not be a differential diagnosis because this will have been decided previously or will have become obvious. The concern will therefore be with trying to assess the remaining functional capacity or in measuring change as a consequence of some form of intervention. The behavior rating scales mentioned in the previous section are applicable to this type of patient. The limitations of those developed so far have also been described so they do not need to be dealt with further.

Automated testing systems (Gedye and Miller, 1970; Levy and Post, 1975; Perez *et al.*, 1978) have proved very acceptable to old people and are capable of satisfactory use with many who would be unable to cope with the more usual psychometric tests. The automated tests developed so far have often been based upon a "matching-to-sample" format. A "sample" stimulus is shown and two or more "match" stimuli. The subject then has to make a response, pressing a button or the panel on which the stimulus is shown, to indicate the "match" stimulus that corresponds to the "sample." The inspiration for this technique has come from the animal laboratory where testing has to be carried out with non-verbal subjects who are also incapable of responding satisfactorily on standardized tests!

A major advantage of the "matching-to-sample" procedure is that it is basically a very simple task for the subject to understand yet the difficulty level can be varied over a very wide range. From having very simple stimuli such as a "sample" consisting of a patch of color with two simultaneously presented "matches," the difficulty level can be manipulated along several different dimensions. The complexity of the stimuli may be increased, a greater number of "matches" can be provided, and delays can be introduced between "sample" and "match," if necessary, with distracting stimuli introduced into the interval. Not only can automated test systems record the accuracy of responses but latencies can also be measured.

Preliminary work has shown that automated testing is quite promising (Levy and Post, 1975; Perez *et al.*, 1978). In particular it has been found that a sample of long-term residents in a geriatric hospital could all give some measurable response to an automated test system while a substantial proportion of the same group were unable to be assessed by means of conventional psychometric tests (Gedye and Miller, 1970). The wide variation in difficulty that it is possible to utilize should mean that automated testing will be sensitive to change in cognitive status down to quite low levels of functioning.

Another, and even more flexible, approach to assessing the deteriorated elderly patient is by means of observational techniques. In clinical psychology direct observation and recording of behavior has been most exploited by those involved in behavior modification procedures (e.g., Kazdin, 1975) although there is no reason why it should be confined to those with a specifically operant approach. In general direct observation depends upon selecting target behaviors of particular interest and systematically recording such things as when the behavior occurs, its frequency and du-

ration. Since patients typically cannot be observed closely all the time or on all relevant occasions, some form of sampling has to be used. Direct observation also involves a number of methodological problems most of which have been discussed in detail by Kent and Foster (1977).

Direct observation has some particular benefits as a method of assessment when working with moderately to severely handicapped groups such as the mentally retarded or the intellectually deteriorated elderly. With such patient groups the overriding problem is that of management and appropriate management is closely linked to the individual's ability to cope with the needs of everyday living. The use of observational techniques readily allows assessment to be directly related to these practical issues in living and the techniques are easily adapted to the particular assessment needs of individual patients.

## CONCLUDING COMMENTS

Assessment, in its wide context, is central to work with the mentally disturbed elderly. Any decision presupposes some form of assessment of the situation in relation to which the decision is made. The commonly occurring problems to which assessment needs to be directed involve the measurement of change (whether this relates to the amount of intellectual decline or change in behavior in response to some intervention), the need to make differential diagnoses, and the prediction of outcome. The value of any assessment procedure can only be considered in the light of the problem that it is designed to resolve and procedures that are useful in one context may be of little or no worth in another.

An issue that has repeatedly been encountered in the foregoing discussion concerns the fact that the development of suitable instruments for assessment involves a number of complications that are not present in other types of research. This is particularly so if the need is to make reliable decisions about individuals. These relate to many things. Measures that discriminate well between groups need not have precise implications for individual members of these groups, base rates need to be taken into account in some forms of assessment, and the detailed characteristics of the subjects on which the instrument is developed need to match very closely those of the patients on whom it will be used.

It can be seen that much of the work covered in this chapter does not meet these criteria. Methodologically the work on the use of tests of verbal learning and memory in the discrimination of the organic states from those with functional psychiatric disorders is probably the most sophisticated. It is probably significant that in terms of established validity in the assessment situation, the verbal learning and memory tests also emerge as some of the most useful of the assessment procedures that are available.

In this writer's opinion the future development of assessment in this field will be maximally useful if it has three features. First, assessment research must pay much greater attention to the methodological needs of research in this field. Second, it should be much more widely based in the kind of problems that it aims to solve. The questions of differential diagnosis and the measurement of intellectual decline have received considerable attention. The problems of assessment as they relate to the needs of management have been relatively neglected. An example of this is the prediction of which patients are likely to show the best response to certain kinds of intervention procedure or the measurement of response to such procedures.

Third, work on assessment needs to continue to look beyond the traditional approach in clinical psychology which is to see assessment as being almost synonymous with psychometrics. The growing general literature on the nature of mental disfunction in old age is replete with examples of findings which could have implications for assessment. An example is the use of psychophysiological procedures as mentioned above in the section on differential diagnosis. Automated testing systems with their links to the animal laboratory are also a development of considerable potential value. Other developments in psychological assessment as applied to client groups other than the elderly also need to be examined for their possible usefulness. Examples here are criterion-referenced scales and behavioral assessment techniques.

# REFERENCES

ABRAHAMS, J. T., AND BIRREN, J. E. 1973. Reaction time as a function of age and behavioral predisposition to coronary heart disease. *J. Gerontol., 28,* 471–478.

ACKLESBERG, S. B. 1944. Vocabulary and mental deterioration in senile dementia. *J. Abnorm. Soc. Psychol., 39,* 393–406.

BABCOCK, H. 1930. An experiment in the measurement of mental deterioration. *Arch. Psychol.,* No. 117.

BARKER, M. G., AND LAWSON, J. S. 1968. Nominal aphasia in dementia. *Br. J. Psychiat., 114,* 1351–1356.

BARNES, R. H., BUSSE, E. W., AND FRIEDMAN, E. L. 1956. The psychological functions of aged individuals with normal and abnormal encephalograms. II. A study of hospitalized individuals. *J. Nerv. Ment. Dis., 124,* 585–593.

BARNS, E. K., SACK, A., AND SHORE, H. 1973. Guidelines to treatment approaches: modalities and methods for use with the aged. *Gerontologist, 13,* 513–527.

BENDER, L. 1946. *Instructions for the Use of the Visual Motor Gestalt Test.* New York: American Orthopsychiatric Association.

BENTON, A. L. 1963. *The Revised Visual Retention Test.* Iowa City: State University of Iowa Press.

BIRREN, J. E., BUTLER, R. N., GREENHOUSE, S. W., SOKOLOFF, L., AND YARROW, M. R. 1963. *Human Aging: A Biological and Behavioral Study.* U.S. Public Health Publication No. 9861. Washington D.C.: National Institute of Mental Health.

BOLTON, N., SAVAGE, R. D., AND ROTH, M. 1967. The Modified Word Learning Test and the aged psychiatric patient. *Br. J. Psychiat., 113,* 1139–1140.

BOTWINICK, J. 1977. Intellectual abilities. In, J. E. Birren and K. W. Schaie (eds.), *Handbook of the Psychology of Aging,* pp. 580–605. New York: Van Nostrand Reinhold.

BOTWINICK, J., BRINLEY, J. F., AND BIRREN, J. E. 1958. The effect of motivation by electric shocks on reaction time in relation to age. *Amer. J. Psychol., 71,* 408–411.

BRILLIANT, P. J., AND GYNTHER, M. D. 1963. Relationship between performance on three tests for organicity and selected patient variables. *J. Consult. Psychol., 27,* 474–479.

CAIRD, W. K., SANDERSON, R. E., AND INGLIS, J. 1962. Cross validation of a learning test for use with elderly psychiatric patients. *J. Ment. Sci., 108,* 368–370.

CIMINERO, A. R., CALHOUN, K. S., AND ADAMS, H. E. (eds.), 1977. *Handbook of Behavioral Assessment.* New York: John Wiley. Crookes, T. G. 1974. Indices of early dementia on the WAIS. *Psychol. Rep., 34,* 374.

CROOKES, T. G. 1974. Indices of early dementia on WAIS, *Psychological Reports, 34,* (3, Pt. 1), 734.

CROOKES, T. G., AND McDONALD, K. G. 1972. Benton's Visual Retention Test in the differentiation of depression and early dementia. *Br. J. Soc. Clin. Psychol., 11,* 66–69.

DESAI, M. 1952. The test-retest reliability of the Progressive Matrices Test. *Br. J. Med. Psychol., 25,* 48–53.

EISDORFER, C., AND COHEN, L. D. 1961. The generality of the WAIS standardization for the aged. *J. Abnorm. Soc. Psychol., 62,* 520–527.

ERICKSON, R. C., AND SCOTT, M. L. 1977. Clinical memory

tests: a review. *Psychol. Bull., 84,* 1130–1149.

FREY, T. S., AND SJÖGREN, H. 1959. The electroencephalogram in elderly persons suffering from neuropsychiatric disorders. *Acta. Psychiat. Scand., 34,* 438–450.

GANZLER, H. 1964. Motivation as a factor in the psychological deficit of aging. *J. Gerontol., 19,* 425–429.

GATHERCOLE, C. E. 1968. *Assessment in Clinical Psychology.* Harmondsworth, Middlesex: Penguin.

GEDYE, J. L., AND MILLER, E. 1970. Developments in automated testing systems. *In,* P. J. Mittler (ed.), *The Psychological Assessment of Mental and Physical Handicap,* pp. 735–760. London: Methuen.

GERBOTH, R. 1950. A study of the two forms of the Wechsler-Bellevue Intelligence Scale. *J. Consult. Psychol., 15,* 365–370.

GIBSON, A. J., AND KENDRICK, D. C. 1976. The development of a visual learning test to replace the SLT in the Kendrick Battery. *Bull. Br. Psychol. Soc., 29,* 200–201.

GLAISTER, B. R. 1971. An ordinate comparison method of calculating brain damage probability. *Br. J. Soc. Clin. Psychol., 10,* 367–374.

GOLDFRIED, M. R., AND KENT, R. N. 1972. Traditional versus behavioral personality assessment: a comparison of methodological and theoretical assumptions. *Psychol. Bull., 77,* 409–420.

GRAHAM, F. K., AND KENDALL, B. S. 1960. *Memory-for-Designs Test: Revised General Manual.* Perceptual and Motor Skills Monograph Supplement No. 11.

GUERTIN, W. H., RABIN, A. L., FRANK, G. H., AND LADD, C. E. 1962. Research on the Wechsler Intelligence Scale for Adults, 1955-1966. *Psychol. Bull., 59,* 1–26.

HALL, E. H., SAVAGE, R. D., BOLTON, N., PIDWELL, D. M., AND BLESSED, G. 1972. Intellect, mental illness, and survival in the aged. *J. Gerontol., 27,* 237–244.

HAMISTER, R. C. 1949. Test-retest reliability of the Wechsler-Bellevue. *J. Consult. Psychol., 13,* 39–43.

HARRELL, T. W., AND HARRELL, M. S. 1945. Army General Classification Test scores for civilian populations. *Educ. Psychol. Meas., 5,* 229–239.

HEWSON, L. R. 1949. The Wechsler-Bellevue Scale and the substitution test as aids in neuropsychiatric diagnosis. *J. Nerv. Ment. Dis., 109,* 158–183.

HOYER, W. J., LABOUVIE, G. V., AND BALTES, P. B. 1973. Modification of response speed deficits and intellectual performance in the elderly. *Hum. Develop., 16,* 233–242.

HUNT, H. F. 1943. A practical, clinical test for organic brain damage. *J. Appl. Psychol., 27,* 375–386.

INGLIS, J. 1959. A paired associate learning test for use with elderly psychiatric patients. *J. Ment. Sci., 105,* 440–448.

JARVIK, L. F., AND FALEK, A. 1963. Intellectual stability and survival in the aged. *J. Gerontol., 18,* 173–176.

KATZ, L., NEAL, M. W., AND SIMON, A. 1960. Observations of psychic mechanisms in organic psychoses of the aged. *In,* P. H. Hoch and J. Zubin (eds.), *Psychopathology of Aging,* pp. 160–181. New York: Proceedings of the American Psychopathological Association.

KAZDIN, A. E. 1975. *Behavior Modification in Applied Settings.* Homewood, Ill.: The Dorsey Press.

KENDRICK, D. C. 1965. Speed and learning in the diagnosis of diffuse brain damage in elderly subjects: a Bayesian statistical approach. *Br. J. Soc. Clin. Psychol.,4,* 141–148.

KENDRICK, D. C. 1967. A cross validation study of the use of the SLT and DCT in screening for diffuse brain pathology in elderly subjects. *Br. J. Med. Psychol., 40,* 173–178.

KENDRICK, D. C., GIBSON, A. C., AND MOYES, I. C. A. 1978. The Kendrick battery: mark II. *Bull. Br. Psychol. Soc., 31,* 177–178.

KENDRICK, D. C., PARBOOSINGH, R. C., AND POST, F. 1965. A synonym learning test for use with elderly psychiatric subjects: a validation study. *Br. J. Soc. Clin. Psychol., 4,* 63–71.

KENT, R. N., AND FOSTER, S. L. 1978. Direct observational procedures: methodological issues in naturalistic settings. *In,* A. R. Ciminero, K. S. Calhoun, and H. E. Adams (eds.), *Handbook of Behavioral Assessment,* pp. 279–328. New York: John Wiley.

LAWSON, J. A., AND BARKER, N. G. 1968. The assessment of nominal dysphasia in dementia. *Br. J. Med. Psychol., 41,* 411–414.

LEVY, R. 1978. Neurophysiological disturbances associated with psychiatric disorders in old age. *In,* A. D. Isaacs and F. Post (eds.), *Studies in Geriatric Psychiatry,* pp. 169–187. Chichester: John Wiley.

LEVY, R., ISAACS, A. D., AND BEHRMAN, J. 1971. Neurophysiological correlates of senile dementia II. The somatosensory evoked response. *Psychol. Med., 1,* 159–165.

LEVY, R., AND POST, F. 1975. The use of an interactive computer terminal in the assessment of cognitive functions in elderly psychiatric patients. *Age and Ageing 4,* 110–115.

LEZAK, M. D. 1976. *Neuropsychological Assessment.* London: Oxford University Press.

LIEBERMAN, M. A. 1965. Psychological correlates of impending death: some preliminary observations. *J. Gerontol., 20,* 181–190.

MARSDEN, C. D. 1978. The diagnosis of dementia. *In,* A. D. Isaacs and F. Post (eds.), *Studies in Geriatric Psychiatry,* pp. 95–118. Chichester: John Wiley.

MARSH, G. R., AND THOMPSON, L. W. 1977. Psychophysiology of aging. *In,* J. E. Birren and K. W. Schaie (eds.), *Handbook of the Psychology of Aging,* pp. 219–248. New York: Van Nostrand Reinhold.

MATARAZZO, R. G., WIENS, A. N., MATARAZZO, J. D., AND

MONAUGH, T. 1973. Test-retest reliability of the WAIS in a normal population. *J. Clin. Psychol., 29,* 124–197.

McFIE, J. 1975. *Assessment of Organic Intellectual Impairment.* London: Academic Press.

MEEHL, P. E., AND ROSEN, A. 1955. Antecedent probability and the efficiency of psychometric signs, patterns or cutting scores. *Psychol. Bull., 52,* 194–216.

MEER, B., AND BAKER, J. A. 1966. The Stockton Geriatric Rating Scale. *J. Gerontol., 21,* 392–403.

MILLER, E. 1971. On the nature of the memory disorder in presenile dementia. *Neuropsychologia, 9,* 75–78.

MILLER, E. 1977a. The management of dementia: a review of some possibilities. *Br. J. Soc. Clin. Psychol., 16,* 77–83.

MILLER, E. 1977b. *Abnormal Ageing.* Chichester: John Wiley.

MILLER, E., AND LEWIS, P. 1977. Recognition memory in elderly patients with depression and dementia: a signal detection analysis. *J. Abnorm. Psychol., 86,* 84–86.

MILLER, W. R. 1975. Psychological deficits in depression. *Psychol. Bull., 82,* 238–260.

NELSON, H. E. 1953. *An Experimental Investigation of Intellectual Speed and Power in Mental Disorders.* London University: Unpublished Ph.D. Thesis.

NELSON, H. E., AND O'CONNELL, A. 1978. Dementia: the estimation of premorbid intelligence levels using the new adult reading test. *Cortex, 14,* 234–244.

NOTT, P., N., AND FLEMINGER, J. J. 1975. Presenile dementia: the difficulties of early diagnosis. *Acta Psychiat. Scand., 51,* 210–217.

OBRIST, W. D., AND BUSSE, E. W. 1965. The encephalogram in old age. *In,* W. P. Wilson (ed.), *Applications of Electroencephalography in Psychiatry,* pp. 185–205. Durham, N.C.: Duke University Press.

OBRIST, W. D., AND HENRY, D. E. 1958. Electroencephalographic findings in aged psychiatric patients. *J. Nerv. Ment. Dis., 126,* 254–267.

O'NEILL, P. M., AND CALHOUN, K. S. 1975. Sensory deficits and behavioral deterioration in senescence. *J. Abnorm. Psychol., 84,* 579–582.

PALMORE, E., AND CLEVELAND, W. 1976. Aging, terminal decline and terminal drop. *J. Gerontol., 31,* 76–81.

PARSONS, O. A., AND PRIGATANO, G. P. 1978. Methodological considerations in clinical neuropsychological research. *J. Con. Clin. Psychol., 46,* 608–619.

PARSONS, P. L. 1965. The mental health of Swansea's old folk. *Br. J. Prev. Soc. Med., 19,* 43–58.

PAYNE, R. W. 1973. Cognitive abnormalities. *In,* H. J. Eysenck (ed.), *Handbook of Abnormal Psychology,* pp. 420–483. London: Pitman.

PAYNE, R. W., AND JONES, H. G. 1957. Statistics for the investigation of individual cases. *J. Clin. Psychol., 13,* 117–121.

PEARCE, J., AND MILLER, E. 1973. *Clinical Aspects of Dementia.* London: Baillière Tindall.

PEREZ, F. I., GAY, J. R. A., TAYLOR, R. L., AND RIVERA, V. M. 1975a. Patterns of memory performance in the neurologically impaired aged. *Canad. J. Neurol. Sci., 2,* 347–355.

PEREZ, F. I., RIVERA, V. M., MEYER, J. S., GAY, J. R. A., TAYLOR, R. L., and MATTHEW, N. T. 1975b. Analysis of intellectual and cognitive performance in patients with multi-infarct dementia, vertebrobasilar insufficiency with dementia and Alzheimer's disease. *J. Neurol. Neurosurg. Psychiat., 38,* 533–540.

PEREZ, F. I., HRUSKA, N. A., STELL, R. I., AND RIVERA, V. M. 1978. Computerized assessment of memory performance in dementia. *Canad. J. Neurol. Sci., 5,* 307–312.

PLEMONS, J. K., WILLIS, S. L., AND BALTES, P. B. 1978. Modifiability of fluid intelligence in aging: a short-term longitudinal training approach. *J. Gerontol., 33,* 224–231.

POPHAM, W. J., AND MUSEK, T. R. 1969. Implications of criterion referenced measurement. *J. Educ. Measurement, 6,* 1–9.

RIEGEL, K. F., AND RIEGEL, R. M. 1972. Development. drop, and death. *Develop. Psychol., 6,* 306–319.

ROCHFORD, G. 1971. A study of naming errors in dysphasic and in demented patients. *Neuropsychologia, 9,* 437–443.

ROTH, M. 1955. The natural history of mental disorder in old age. *J. Ment. Sci., 101,* 281–301.

SALZMAN, C., SHADER, R. I., KOCHANSKY, G. E., AND CRONIN, D. M. 1972. Rating scales for psychotropic drug research with geriatric patients. 1. Behavior ratings. *J. Amer. Geriat. Soc., 20,* 209–214.

SANDERSON, R. E., AND INGLIS, J. 1961. Learning and mortality in elderly psychiatric patients. *J. Gerontol., 16,* 375–376.

SAVAGE, R. D. 1971. Psychometric assessment and clinical diagnosis in the aged. *In,* D. W. Kay and A. Walk (eds.), *Recent Developments in Psychogeriatrics,* pp. 51–61. London: Royal Medical Psychological Association.

SAVAGE, R. D. 1973. Old age. *In,* H. J. Eysenck (ed.), *Handbook of Abnormal Psychology,* pp. 645–688. London: Pitman.

SCHAIE, K. W., AND GRIBBIN, K. 1975. Adult development and aging. *Ann. Rev. Psychol., 26,* 65–96.

SCHAIE, K. W., AND LABOUVIE-VIEF, G. V. 1974. Generational versus ontogenetic components of change in adult cognitive behavior: a fourteen year cross-sectional study. *Develop. Psychol., 10,* 305–320.

SCHAIE, K. W., AND SCHAIE, J. P. 1977. Clinical assessment of aging. *In,* J. E. Birren and K. W. Schaie (eds.), *Handbook of the Psychology of Aging,* pp. 692–723. New York: Van Nostrand Reinhold.

SHAPIRO, M. B., AND NELSON, E. H. 1955. An investigation

of the nature of cognitive impairment in co-operative psychiatric patients. *Br. J. Med. Psychol., 4,* 205–280.

SHAPIRO, M. B., POST, F. LÖFVING, B. AND INGLIS, J. 1956. "Memory function" in psychiatric patients over sixty: some methodological and diagnostic implications. *J. Ment. Sci., 102,* 233–246.

SHIPLEY, W. C. 1940. A self-administering scale for measuring intellectual impairment and deterioration. *J. Psychol., 9,* 371–377.

STRAUMANIS, J. J., SHAYASS, C., AND SCHWARTZ, M. 1965. Visually evoked response changes associated with chronic brain syndromes and aging. *J. Gerontol., 20,* 498–506.

TAYLOR, H. G., AND BLOOM, L. M. 1974. Cross validation and methodological extension of the Stockton Geriatric Rating Scale. *J. Gerontol., 29,* 190–193.

WALSH, K. W. 1978. *Neuropsychology: A Clinical Approach,* Edinburgh: Churchill-Livingstone.

WALTON, D., AND BLACK, D. A. 1957. The validity of psychological test of brain damage. *Br. J. Med. Psychol., 20,* 270–279.

WALTON, D., WHITE, J. G., BLACK, D. A., AND YOUNG, A. J. 1959. The modified word learning test—a cross validation study. *Br. J. Med. Psychol., 22,* 213–220.

WANG, H. S. OBRIST, W. D., AND BUSSE, E. W. 1970. Neurophysiological correlates of the intellectual function of elderly persons living in the community. *Amer. J. Psychiat., 126,* 1205–1212.

WARD, J. 1970. On the concept of criterion referenced measurement. *Br. J. Educ. Psychol., 40,* 314–323.

WARRINGTON, E. K. 1970. Neurological deficits. *In,* P. J. Mittler (ed.), *The Psychological Assessment of Mental and Physical Handicap,* pp. 261–288. London: Methuen.

WECHSLER, D. 1958. *The Measurement and Appraisal of Adult Intelligence.* Baltimore: Williams & Wilkins.

WHITEHEAD, A. 1971. *An Investigation of Learning in Elderly Psychiatric Patients,* London University: Unpublished Ph.D. Thesis.

WHITEHEAD, A. 1973. The pattern of WAIS performance in elderly psychiatric patients. *Br. J. Soc. Clin. Psychol., 12,* 435–436.

WILKIE, F., AND EISDORFER, C. 1971. Intelligence and blood pressure in the aged. *Science, 172,* 959–962.

WILLIAMS, M. 1970. Geriatric patients. *In,* P. J. Mittler (ed.), *The Psychological Assessment of Mental and Physical Handicaps,* pp. 319–339. London: Methuen.

WOODS, R. T., AND BRITTON, P. G 1977. Psychological approaches to treatment of the elderly. *Age and Ageing, 6,* 104–112.

YATES, A. J. 1954. The validity of some psychological tests of brain damage. *Psychol. Bull., 51,* 359–379.

YATES, A. J. 1956. The use of vocabulary in the measurement of intellectual deterioration—a review. *J. Ment. Sci., 102,* 409–440.

# 23

# Personality Tests
# and Their Uses
# with Older Adults

*M. Powell Lawton, William M. Whelihan,*
*& Janet Kaplan Belsky*

Before reviewing the uses of specific personality tests with older adults, it is necessary to discuss the question of the rationale for wishing to make such an assessment in the first place. The most general answer leads in two directions: research purposes and clinical practice. Of course, these are far from mutually exclusive directions. The development of personality tests in general psychology has had such dual roots. Clinical psychological assessment has characteristically been at least partially guided by the results of empirical testing of the utility of personality assessment devices. In some cases tests originally developed for research purposes have become incorporated into clinical assessment batteries.

A related duality may be seen in the distinction between the theory-based and the purely empirical assessment device. There is room for both of these approaches, and there are successful and unsuccessful tests of both types. While there are obvious advantages to basing a test on a strong conceptual framework, such an approach by no means guarantees a test's usefulness either for research or clinical practice. Even more importantly, the current lack of a rich variety of theory regarding the adult development process limits greatly the possibility of a correspondingly rich store of theory-based personality assessment devices. Thus, while some of the personality test repertoire is purely empirical for good reasons (e.g., diagnostic or selection purposes), much is empirical simply by default.

The kinds of questions that can be fruitfully posed by the clinical geropsychologist do not differ appreciably from those addressed by the general clinician. That is, one may diagnose, assess the level of psychopathology, examine personality strengths and weaknesses, describe the structural and cognitive aspects of personality, explore psycho-dynamics or pursue the many other goals of psychological assessment. However, usefulness of personality tests for these purposes in older clients has by no means been established by either the acclamation of clinicians or empirical tests. Because the evidence is skimpy and application infrequent, it may even be appropriate to ask whether personality testing has *any* clinical utility (compared, for example, to the clinical interview, as suggested by Sheldon Tobin [personal communication]). The suggestion made here is that increased experience will lead to an affirmative response, but in the meantime, the verdict must be stated as "unproven."

While earlier reviews (Chown, 1968; Costa and McCrae, 1978; Kuhlen, 1959; Savage, Gaber, Britton, Bolton, and Cooper, 1977; Schaie and Marquette, 1972; Schaie and Schaie, 1977) have included sections on personality tests used with older people, it cannot be said that a technology for personality assessment for the aged in a clinical situation currently exists. Clinical psychology has selectively ignored the problems of older people (Lawton, 1970; Lawton and Gottesman, 1974) and, as will be documented later, the last five years have seen little improvement in the production of research relevant to the problems involved in traditional clinical personality assessment. Some recent signs, however, suggest that the next decade will see a great deal of trial-and-error behavior designed to find appropriate evaluation tools for older clients. Because we know so little about how older people respond to some of the traditional tests, we shall experience a certain amount of *déjà vu* in the repetition with older study subjects of research that was originally performed on younger subjects. We shall also probably see some of the special-purpose research tests adopted for use in clinical assessment. Other tests may be developed or refined for use in research only. This review will attempt to collate existent knowledge relevant to all of these uses of personality tests. Clinical application will be considered in the opening section, which discusses problems associated with testing some older subjects.

K. W. Schaie and his coworkers have sensitized researchers to the ambiguity inherent in findings regarding age-related personality changes that are based on cross-sectional studies. For the purpose of this chapter, which is focused on the empirical usefulness of personality tests rather than on theoretical issues in personality development, such cross-sectional age differences constitute less of a problem. In most clinical situations it is important to know whether a test finding that deviates from the norm does so because of psy-

chopathology or because of the age of the subject. Should the "deviance" be characteristic of an age cohort, it is less important to know whether the origin of the difference is in chronological age or the historical cohort. On the other hand, as suggested by Schaie and Schaie (1977) time-of-testing effects constitute a potentially important source of error in longitudinal studies, where changes in attitudes or standards for social acceptability may be wrongly interpreted as age or cohort effects. For clinical purposes, a set of test norms derived 10 or 20 years ago may no longer be applicable. If there are tests whose usefulness endures over several generations, it would be highly desirable to replicate the norm-derivation process periodically (see Pearson, Swenson, and Rome, [1965] for examples of time-related response changes). The use of age-appropriate norms is critically important, yet such norms are rarely available. Thus, reports that utilize large or representative samples whose characteristics are fully described will be highlighted in this review.

## PROBLEMS IN THE USE OF PERSONALITY TESTS WITH OLDER PEOPLE

The avoidance of older people as mental health clients is not solely attributable to professional attitudes of therapeutic nihilism regarding the ability of older people to change. The scarcity of research reports on personality testing with the aged is in part based on the fact that it is simply more difficult to test older people. The busy clinician finds it inconvenient to prolong a group testing session for an older person who works very slowly or to spend the additional time required to convince him or her that responding to inkblots is something other than child's play. A number of factors that are statistically more prevalent among older people in our society may limit the meaningfulness of test results and should be considered by the user prior to embarking on a testing venture.

Impairment in cognitive skills such as orientation, memory, abstract thinking, and judgment may grossly limit the usefulness of many personality tests. While the prevalence of organic brain syndrome (OBS) is relatively low in the general community-resident aged population (Gunner-Swenson and Jensen, 1976), clients in many service situations will be more likely to suffer from this type of impairment, especially those in long-term care facilities where almost 60 percent are estimated to be confused some or all of the time (National Center for Health Statistics, 1977). In general, these types of deficits will often rule out the use of many personality tests. For example, questionnaires demand that the subject be able to read, remember past experiences, and indicate responses on a recording form, and any of these tasks may lie beyond the ability of the OBS patient. On a test like the Thematic Apperception Test (TAT), the extensive directions for taking the test and the requirement to produce a logical story may make excessive demands on a person of marginal intellectual competence. It seems clear that a thorough cognitive evaluation should precede the decision to use personality tests in a clinical situation. For research purposes, a brief measure of cognitive skill (such as the Mental Status Questionnaire [Kahn, Pollack, and Goldfarb, 1961]) would be helpful in screening out some for whom personality testing would not be productive.

Far more prevalent than OBS are sensory and motor impairments, which can penalize the older person on personality measures and in some cases can make the task almost impossible. The Minnesota Multiphasic Personality Inventory (MMPI) booklet forms, especially when used with answer forms structured for computer scoring, are difficult to use (although some improvement may be achieved in card-sorting test formats). The Rorschach is a highly visual test that may elicit low-quality responses because of sensory rather than psychological deficits.

Hearing deficits can clearly influence any test performance if directions are not properly understood. Eisdorfer (1960a), for example, found that hearing impairment was associated with several Rorschach indicators of low developmental level, though, paradoxically, the same deficits were not associated with visual loss. Motor difficulties can lead to incorrect psychological interpretations of performance on such tests as the Bender-Gestalt or Figure Drawing.

Educational deprivation, social subgroup differences, and cohort-specific cultural norms may also be sources of response and interpretation problems. Today's older population averages less than a tenth-grade education, and about 10 percent learned English as a second language. These factors may limit task understanding and verbal productivity, particularly in projective tests. Older people as a group may construe the testing situation quite differently from the way high school students do, not having undergone early socialization at a time when the school psychologist and *Psychology Today* were commonplace elements of the social milieu. It may therefore be very difficult to explain the rationale for psychological testing in such a way as to motivate some psychologically

naive older people to comply with test instructions. Some personality tests often require self-revelation in areas that are still taboo for older persons, such as sexuality, overt aggressive impulses, or personal hygiene. Many tests constructed for the general population or college students contain items whose content is inappropriate to the present lives or future goals of the elderly—for example, vocational goals, dating behavior, active sports, and so on. The older subject may see such content as irrelevant and be quick to reject the entire test or battery.

Attention, concentration, and energy expenditure have been frequently noted as sources of test-taking deficiencies, although empirical data are not at hand to support the assertion that these factors differ systematically by age of subject. Nonetheless, many refusals, breakoffs, and incomplete protocols probably are related to a lack of energy secondary to mental or physical fraility, and possibly also to some of the less pathological manifestations of simple chronological age, including visual strain, susceptibility to tiring of muscles used in writing or maintaining a particular body posture, psychophysiological fatigue, maintaining perceptual vigilance to test stimuli, and so on.

Finally, some personality traits such as rigidity, cautiousness, and denial that have been asserted to be age-related (with varying degrees of empirical support) may have effects on test taking and the kinds of responses produced. While personality rigidity does not appear to be strongly age-related, as compared to cognitive rigidity, responsiveness to projective tests is likely to be somewhat constricted in the rigid individual. The extensive literature documenting the increase in errors of omission as a function of age in cognitive tasks (Botwinick, 1973) suggests that a similar problem will occur in personality testing. For example, the usefulness of a test protocol may be minimal when the subject rejects many Rorschach cards or gives an inordinate number of "cannot say" responses to the MMPI.

There is often a tendency for older persons to respond in a more limited manner than younger persons when addressing personal, emotional issues. Extensive discussions of the use of denial by older people may be found in Carp (1975) and in Campbell, Converse, and Rodgers (1976). Carp has referred to this as the "sweet-lemon" phenomenon. The latter authors discuss in detail some of the factors that may be involved in the relative lack of correlation (even opposite-direction correlations in some instances) between objective indicators of quality of life and subjective evaluations of the same qualities by older people themselves. Klassen, Homstra, and Aderson (1975) found a consistent increase in social desirability scores with age. Denial may be a positively adaptive mechanism that the older person uses to maintain some sense of well being in face of the many deprivations that accompany aging in our society. It is highly probable that such positive thinking and the related tendency to respond in socially desirable ways introduce a significant degree of error into responses to objective personality tests and to some extent in responses to projective tests.

These sources of test-taking difficulty will combine to reduce the number of subjects in studies involving the elderly. Table 23–1 shows all studies where the percentage of untestable people was reported. While most investigators regrettably neglected to report this useful datum, the percentages shown in Table 23-1 suggest that the yield is better with shorter instruments and with less impaired subjects. The relatively large percentage of attempted but incomplete Mini-Mult protocols reported by Fillenbaum and Pfeiffer (1976) should alert the researcher to seek ways of reducing this bothersome missing-data problem. While it is often asserted that projective tests elicit better cooperation, only one instance was found where the completion rate was reported for any projective test (Kahana, 1978).

The above discussion has highlighted some test comprehension and response problems to which older people are subject. It must be emphasized that few of these problems are likely to be experienced by a majority of older people. In general, the healthier, more economically secure, and more culturally privileged the older subject the less likely are such problems to occur.

OPTIMAL TESTING PROCEDURES

The first requirements for the successful use of personality tests with the aged are persistence, patience, and a willingness to be flexible on the part of the examiner both during the period of pretest preparation and during the process of testing. Before introducing the tests, the examiner must take great pains to present the rationale for the testing, whether it be for research or clinical purposes, since the older person of today does not accept the value of such testing as self-evident. It is essential to realize that many older people will interpret the testing situation as one designed to lay bare their "senility." The examiner's clinical skills should be exercised to the fullest to allay this anxiety and to provide encouragement if "failure" is experienced. Test instructions will require pacing according to the sensory and cognitive status of the individual, frequently requiring an uncomfortably slow speech for the examiner. Engaging eye contact with the subject, clear enunciation, repetition of instructions, and, if in doubt, asking the subject to restate instructions, will help. Needless to say, proper illumination and auditory privacy are essential. Where possible, multimodal stimuli are desirable, as in a verbal test administered orally where the subject can read silently if wished. A testing session of one hour can be tolerated by most people under most conditions, though the motivated and vigorous subject may continue much longer. Some tests lend themselves to departures from standard procedures, such as the examiner making an inquiry immediately after each Rorschach response, possibly rephrasing some instructions if necessary, and interpolating rest periods or changes of tasks. In order to monitor the degree of compliance with instructions and quality of responses, it is always advisable for the examiner to be available while self-administering tests are being done and to check the finished product before the subject leaves.

## SPECIFIC PERSONALITY TESTS USED WITH THE AGED

The discussion of specific tests is organized into sections dealing with objective and projective tests. Each includes tests constructed for general use or

**Table 23–1** Reported Proportions of Testable Older People.

| TYPE OF SUBJECTS | TEST | % TESTABLE | REFERENCE |
|---|---|---|---|
| VA domiciliary patients | MMPI | 50 | Apfeldorf and Hunley (1971) |
| "Normal" community residents | MMPI (Mini-Mult) | 94[a] | Fillenbaum and Pfeiffer (1976) |
| Community and institutional residents | MMPI | 48 | Swenson (1961) |
| "Normal" community residents | Maudsley PI | 62 | Gilmore (1972) |
| 20 "mild organic" community residents | 16 PF | 30 | Savage et al. (1977) |
| Community and institutional residents | Figure Drawing | 76 | Kahana (1978) |

[a]64 percent produced complete records.

for younger people, tests constructed or adapted for clinical use with older people, and tests that were constructed primarily for research purposes but are considered to be potentially useful in clinical situations as well. Wherever possible, an effort is made to indicate if each test is widely used, judging by the number of reports found; if age norms or samples large enough to provide some frame of reference for interpretation are available; if age-specific reliability estimates exist; and if reported or implied interpretations are valid.

## OBJECTIVE TESTS

Despite a decline over the past decade in reports using the *Minnesota Multiphasic Personality Inventory* (MMPI), this test has been the most frequently-used personality test for older subjects. Since the test contains 550 items and the language of the questions is often difficult, it is probably that the published reports are based on highly nonrepresentative samples of older people. Nonetheless there are many reports in which the test has been successfully used, including one by Swenson, Pearson, and Osborne (1973) with an astounding sample size of 13, 748 people over the age of 60; the fact that these subjects were obtained from Mayo Clinic patients suggests that this test is maximally useful with people of above-average education and socioeconomic status.

The MMPI was constructed on a purely empirical basis in order to diagnose psychopathology. Thus it could be very important to know if older people in general respond differently than younger people. Age differences have been extensively investigated by comparing subject groups of differ-

ing ages for score values within the same study, by comparing older study subjects with standardization-group norms, and by high-point code analysis. Table 23–2 shows these age comparisons. In general, where age comparisons were made within the same basic subject pool (i.e., the 50,000 Mayo Clinic patients reported by Swenson *et al.*, 1973), the elderly appear to have shown less deviant scores, while by comparison with standardization-group norms their scores are elevated.

Table 23–2 suggests that depression is clearly elevated among the elderly—a finding that is consistent with other evidence (Butler and Lewis, 1973). Similarly it is not surprising that the incidence of Hypochondriasis is frequently elevated among the aged, with their many physical illnesses. The "acting-out" scales (Pyschopathic Deviate and Hypomania) are clearly lower; the consistency of this finding should alert the clinician to even mildly elevated scores on these scales among older clients, in terms of possible emotional lability or poor control. The "psychotic triad" scales (Paranoia, Psychasthenia, and Schizophrenia) were either similar to or lower than scores of younger people; the only exceptions were the Newcastle-upon-Tyne community residents of Britton and Savage (1966), whose elevations were minor. Thus it seems that the minor neurotic symptoms may occur more frequently among the aged, but other types of deviance are probably the same or even less frequent than among the younger population. It must be emphasized that these are only gross age differences. Closer examination of sex-specific item distributions by age revealed a number of items that were curvilinearly distributed (Pearson, Swenson, and Rome, 1965), suggesting that different items

**Table 23–2** MMPI Clinical Scale Score Ranks of Elderly as Compared to Younger People.

| TYPE OF SUBJECTS | HS | D | HY | PD | PA | PT | SC | MA | REFERENCE |
|---|---|---|---|---|---|---|---|---|---|
| Community residents, psychiatric patients, all ages | | High | | Low | | | | | Aaronson (1958) |
| Older community residents | High | High | High | | High | High | High | Low | Britton and Savage (1966) |
| TB patients, all ages | High | High | | | | | | | Calden and Hokanson (1959) |
| Psychiatric inpatients, all ages | | | | Low | Low | | Low | Low | Gynther and Shimkunas (1966) |
| Healthy older community residents | | High | | | | | | | Kornetsky (1963) |
| Male offenders, all ages | | | | Low | | | | | McCreery and Mensh (1977) |
| Young and old psychiatric patients | | | | | Low | Low | Low | | Postema and Schell (1967) |
| Older community residents | | | | Low | | | | Low | Scarr and Slater (n.d.) |
| Older community and institutional residents | High | High | | | | | | | Swenson (1961) |
| Medical patients, all ages | | | | Low | Low | Low | Low | Low | Swenson et al. (1973) |
| Job applicants, ages 19–56 | | | | | Low | Low | | | Thumin (1969) |

may have different meanings for people of different ages.

Scattered findings relevant to the validity of the MMPI for older people are at hand, but few were explicitly generated for this purpose. Fillenbaum and Pfeiffer (1976) derived basic psychometric data on the Mini-Mult (Kincannon, 1968), a 71-item short form of the MMPI that is included as part of the Duke Older Americans Resources and Services (OARS) assessment package (Pfeiffer, 1975). Contrary to expectation, the small number who by their own self-reports on other OARS items (many items had no clear relationship to mental health) were classified as "superbly well" in terms of mental health, generally did not differ from the remainder of their large community sample in Mini-Mult scale scores. However, when 69 study subjects were examined by psychiatrists one year after taking the Mini-Mult, the subjects judged to be in the best mental health by this external criterion showed less pathological scores on six of eight clinical scales. All scale scores except Hypomania (Ma) were elevated in comparison with standardization-group norms and several were comparable to older mental patient means reported by Swenson (1961). Fillenbaum and Pfeiffer thus question if the Mini-Mult may overestimate pathology, as compared to the standard form.

Using the standard MMPI both Postema and Schell (1967) and Swenson (1961) found the profiles of elderly psychiatric patients to be elevated on all scales as compared with normal aged; most scales also differentiated between normal community residents and those with a psychological problem (Britton and Savage, 1966).

In conclusion, while most of these studies to some extent affirm the validity of the MMPI in diagnosing psychopathology, the body of evidence is very slim and clearly in need of augmentation if the test is to be used with confidence among older people. Notable by their absence are studies of nonpsychotic elderly psychiatric patients.

We found only two reliability studies, and these were less than satisfactory. Uecker (1969) administered the MMPI in two modes (order counterbalanced) to 30 mildly organically impaired hospitalized psychiatric VA patients. One mode was an oral tape-recorded version, the other a card form with large type on five-by-eight-inch cards. While there were no scaled-score differences between the two modes, scale reliabilities ranged from 0.43 to 0.70, with median of 0.60. Using the Mini-Mult twice on 30 study subjects with a median interval of five weeks, Fillenbaum and Pfeiffer (1976) found a median scale reliability of 0.38 (range 0.10 for Paranoia [Pa] to 0.75 for Hypo-chondriasis [Hs]). Excessive demands on the test's reliability were undoubtedly made, in the one case by using OBS patients and two different modes, and in the other using the grossly foreshortened Mini-Mult. Nonetheless, confidence in the clinical or research utility of the MMPI is not strengthened by these findings; at best, the need for more systematic reliability studies is indicated.

Three factor analyses of MMPI scale scores were located (Britton and Savage, 1969; Coppinger, Bortner, and Saucer, 1963; Slater and Scarr, 1964). Since these studies used widely varying scales, subject populations, and modes of factoring, any search for similarity of factor structure among the studies is probably unrealistic. Each study found a generalized psychopathology factor, but the component scales differed considerably.

The MMPI is likely to see continued use for both research and clinical purposes. It seems clear that the full scale should be limited to study subjects who are of above-average intelligence, in full physical and mental vigor, and who are motivated to complete an arduous task. Shortened versions may be more useful—the Mini-Mult, because of the illuminating research on it reported by Fillenbaum and Pfeiffer (1976), seems the most likely candidate. However, their discouraging work on its reliability raises the question if the differential use of subscales can be fruitful when the length is reduced so severely. It may be that further work on specific item characteristics (Brozek, 1955; Hardyck, 1964; Pearson *et al.*, 1965; Swenson *et al.*, 1973) leading to more usable and reliable single-score estimates of general pathology (Britton and Savage, 1967) is the most productive direction for further development. It is important to note that validity findings relate primarily to mental health rather than to personality. Considering the totally atheoretic basis of the test, its item content, and the pathological criterion-group validation of the original scale, it is suggested that the MMPI be used as a diagnostic device rather than as an aid to understanding the dynamic aspects of personality. Given the insoluble psychometric problems of item overlap among scales, it is unlikely that further factor-analytic work with scale scores will lead to any appreciable enlightenment.

The clearly preferred objective personality test in the United Kingdom is the *Maudsley Personality Inventory* (MPI, Eysenck, 1959), a 48-item questionnaire with two second-order factored scales measuring Neuroticism and Introversion-Extraversion. These scales have been highly stable and replicable over many diverse samples. The largest sample of older (60+) study subjects (N = 200) was reported by Gutman (1966). Because there are only two factor scales, a short form of 12 items is likely to be fairly reliable and useful with the elderly (Eysenck, 1958). The only information on the yield of usable records was given by Gilmore (1972), who reported that only 40 out of 65 normal community residents (ages 65+) were able to totally complete even the short form without problems. Gilmore then administered a special form of the MPI developed to be understood by people of low intelligence (Eysenck, 1969) to 75 new study subjects. With individualized inquiries to each subject to make certain each item was understood, comprehensibility was largely unproblematic with this simplified version. Thus the choices for the researcher or clinician who wishes to measure these two basic personality dimensions seem varied enough to meet most needs, though no report has been located that examines the relationships among the three versions for an elderly population. Few notable age differences were found by Gutman (1966).

The only direct validity test of the MPI is that of Hare and Shaw (1965), in which they found significant agreement between study subjects' neuroticism scores and interviewers' ratings (interviewers were, of course, aware of the study subjects' inventory responses). Bolton and Savage (1971) found minimal differences among elderly normals and hospitalized organics, schizophrenics, and affective disorders.

Thus, unlike the MMPI, age differences associated with MPI scores appear to be few, and this test appears useful if based on general population norms. Further, the short and simplified versions of the MPI add some flexibility for the user. Despite the elaborate theory behind the MPI, its usefulness seems to be primarily in its ability to measure neuroticism in a clinical situation. No other age-specific predictive validity information is available.

While its origins were purely empirical, Cattell's Sixteen Personality-Factor Questionnaire (16 PF, Cattell, Eber, and Tatsuoka, 1970) has been used extensively as a trait measure, rather than a measure of psychopathology. Theory-based findings have been extensively reported by one research group, the Boston Veterans Administration Normative Aging Study, and others have used it as well. Parallel Forms A and B contain 187 items each, yielding scores on 16 factor-derived scales. A short Form C contains 105 items. In distinction to the symptom focus of the MMPI, the item content consists primarily of personality traits and attitudinal and behavioral items. Many of the scales are labeled in neologistic fashion, which authors often "translate" for the reader. Regrettably, no information is available on older people's test-taking problems with the 16 PF, though the Normative Aging Study did successfully test a large number of older veterans on both of the long forms.

Tests of age differences in fair-sized samples show enough convergence to suggest that the user should be aware of possible age or cohort variation. Table 23-3 shows the results of age-group comparisons (either among study subjects of different ages within the same study or by comparison with standardization-group norms). By no means did all studies report the same age differences. However, among 12 scales where age differences were reported by three or more investigators, the directions of the differences were uniform in 10 scales. This promising degree of concordance suggests the value of pursuing further the establishment of age norms, with the understanding of the psychological meaning of these differences, and possibly the use of the 16 PF among high-functioning clinical subjects.

Notable for their absence are any attempts to test the validity of 16 PF scales in terms of their match with external ratings of the same traits in

**Table 23–3**  16 PF Scale Score Ranks of Older as Compared to Younger Subjects.

| TYPE OF SUBJECTS | A | B | C | E | F | G | H | I | L | M | N | O | Q₁ | Q₂ | Q₃ | Q₄ | REFERENCE |
|---|---|---|---|---|---|---|---|---|---|---|---|---|---|---|---|---|---|
| Older veteran domiciliary pts. | L | L | L |  | L | H | L |  | L |  |  | H | L |  | L | L | Bortner (1962) |
| Community residents, all ages |  | L |  | L |  | H | L |  |  | H |  |  |  |  |  |  | Botwinick and Storandt (1974) |
| Older veteran domiciliary residents | L | L | L |  | L | H | L | H | L |  |  | H | L | H |  |  | Davol (1958) |
| Community-resident veterans, all ages |  | L |  | L | L | H |  | H |  |  | H |  |  | H | H |  | Fozard and Nuttall (1971) |
| 82 old community residents | L |  | L |  | L | H | L |  | H |  | H | H | L | H |  | H | Savage et al. (1977) |
| Community residents, all ages |  | H |  | L | H |  |  | H |  |  |  |  |  |  |  |  | Sealy and Cattell (1965) |

older study subjects. On the other hand, a number of convergent and discriminant relationships have been reported from the Normative Aging Study. Relationships between 16 PF factor scores and job satisfaction (Rose, 1973), cognitive functioning (Costa, Fozard, McCrae, and Bossé, 1976), vocational interests (Costa, Fozard, and McCrae, 1977), field independence (Costa and McRae, in press) and values (Costa *et al.*, 1977) have been reported.

Reliability over a 10-year period was high for two 16 PF second-order factors (see below), ranging from 0.58 for anxiety in the younger group to 0.84 for extraversion in the older group, although individual scale-score reliability was lower, with median retest reliability of about 0.50 (Costa and McCrae, 1978; Costa and McCrae, in press).

The factor structure of the 16 PF across three broad age groups (young [mean age = 31.7], middle-aged [43.7], and old [60.3]) was investigated by Costa and McCrae (1976). The usual second-order factors, anxiety and introversion-extraversion, were found in all three age groups, plus a third factor, called "openness to experience."

The psychometric properties of the 16 PF may be superior to those of the MMPI, and most of the factors portray personality traits that are meaningful as descriptors of people. However, there is almost nothing in the literature to suggest how this test could be useful in a clinical situation; it seems likely that it will continue to be used primarily for research purposes.

The *Edwards Personal Preference Schedule* (EPPS, Edwards, 1953) measures 15 Murray (1938) needs by 225 paired-comparison statements, where the subject chooses one of two different need-revealing statements that best applies. The EPPS is an "ipsative" scale, in the sense that a subject's score profile reflects the hierarchy of that particular individual's needs. Qualitative experience with older people completing the test indicates that the length is a problem, and the recurrence of many items (in different paired-comparisons) is annoying and confusing to this age group, and sometimes leads to omissions because of their feeling that they have already responded to that item. Nonetheless, three

studies successfully tested significant numbers of older people.

Age differences were tested by Gannon (1965), Schaie and Strother (1968), and Spangler and Thomas (1962) (Table 23-4). All three studies found an increase in Deference and a decrease in Heterosexuality as age increased. Allowing for the probability that the highly diverse subject source introduced an unknown amount of error, the general agreement for some needs suggests that age differences should be borne in mind when the test is applied to older study subjects.

No report was found that estimated reliability. Virtually none was found that tested validity, unless one considers that some of the replicated age differences confirm to some degree popular suppositions regarding generational personality differences.

Peckens (n.d.) factored EPPS scores for each of six age-sex groups. While he concluded that factor structure was fairly stable across age groups, the ipsative nature of the test makes questionable the application of the principal-axes factoring method.

Research using the EPPS has been directed to too few of the standard psychometric issues to warrant firm conclusions regarding its utility with the elderly. To a mild degree, its apparent ability to reflect age/cohort differences suggests that it may be worthwhile to explore further, though because of test-taking problems it is likely to be useful with only a limited segment of the older population.

*Adjective checklists* have been used by Apfeldorf and Hunley (1971a; 1971b), Bloom (1961), Culbertson, Pomeroy, and Cunningham (n.d.), Hess and Bradshaw (1970), and Tobin and Lieberman (1977). The adjective checklist format may be easier for the older subject to complete than a full questionnaire and it is possible that it may be useful in many situations. The most promising evidence is from the relatively short lists focusing on mood adjectives reported by Culbertson *et al.*

The *Guilford-Zimmerman Temperament Survey* (Guilford and Zimmerman, 1949) was used on people from young through middle age (Bendig,

**Table 23–4**   EPPS Scale Score Ranks of Older as Compared to Younger Subjects.

| TYPE OF SUBJECTS | NEED SCALES | | | | | | | | | | | | | | | REFERENCE |
|---|---|---|---|---|---|---|---|---|---|---|---|---|---|---|---|---|
| | ACH | DEF | ORD | EXH | AUT | AFF | INT | SUC | DOM | ABA | NUR | CHG | END | HET | AGG | |
| Psychiatric inpatients ages 15–59 | H | H | L | | | | | | H | | L | H | | L | L | Gannon (1965) |
| Young graduate students and retired professors | H | H | L | | | | | L | H | | | H | L | | | Schaie and Strother (1968) |
| Old community residents and chronic disease hospital patients age 40–79 | H | | | H | H | | | | | | | | | L | | Spangler and Thomas (1962) |

1960). It was also used by Douglas and Arenberg (1977) in the only full cross-sequential study using a standard objective personality test.

Scattered reports have appeared on several other objective tests with older people or across age groups, such as the *Heron* (1956) *Personality Inventory* (Craik, 1964; Heron and Chown, 1967); Cattell's (1955) *Objective-Analytic Personality Test* (Clark, 1960); the *Comrey* (1961) *Personality Inventory* (Edwards and Wine, 1963); and the *Behavioral Rigidity Test* (Schaie and Parham, 1975), which has age norms across a wide age range.

While many self-report measures of morale, life satisfaction or adjustment have been devised explicitly for older people (Nydegger, 1977), there appear to be almost no old-age-specific tests for self-reported personality trait measurement in the objective test area.

*Objective Tests for Research Use.* A category of personality characteristics that may be termed "personality style" has appeared fairly frequently in gerontological research, including such traits as locus of control (Rotter, 1966), field dependence or psychological differentiation (Witkin, Lewis, Hertzman, Machover, Meissner, and Wapner, 1954), constricted versus flexible control (Gardner, Holzman, Klein, Linton, and Spence, 1959), repression/sensitization (Byrne, 1964), sensation-seeking (Zukerman and Link, 1968), leveling-sharpening (Gardner *et al.*, 1959), preference for simplicity/complexity (Berlyne, 1960), and augmentation/reduction (Petrie, 1967). Presumably these styles act as regulators of the manner in which the individual processes or reacts to stimuli from within or from the external environment. In the general psychological literature, individual differences in these styles have been found to be correlated with a variety of other personal characteristics. Yet their discriminant validity remains uncertain, since many of them are as highly correlated with intelligence, socioeconomic status, or psychopathology as they are with their presumed validity criteria.

A summary of studies of personal styles in older study subjects is presented in Table 23-5. For any such test to be useful, the basic question as to whether test scores add anything to prediction independent of background characteristics, health, cognitive ability, and adjustment will first need to be answered much more clearly.

PROJECTIVE TESTS

Most of the studies using projective techniques with older people were done from the late 1940s through the 1960s. This trend matches the general

decline of interest in projective techniques among clinical psychologists in recent years.

*The Rorschach Test.* Few studies report on the acceptability of the Rorschach to older people, although both Ames (1966), Wolk (1972), and Oberleder (1964) found it easy for the elderly to respond to. While Caldwell (1954) warned about the effect of visual impairment on Rorschach responses, Eisdorfer (1960a,b) found no measurable effect of such impairment on several measures of quality.

Rorschach's (1942) early observations on the constriction, stereotypy, and low perceptual clarity of old people's responses were generally upheld by a large number of studies. The weight of reported results is clearly on the side of fewer responses, higher *W%*, higher *F%*, fewer *M* and *C* (and constricted experience balance), and more rejections (Ames, 1966; Ames, 1974; Ames, Metraux, Rodell, and Walker, 1973; Klopfer, 1946; Kuhlen and Kiel, 1951; Light and Amick, 1956; Singer, 1963).

Few of these studies meet the standards of currently acceptable research methodology, however. Many of them compared the average response of an older group to the "normal" levels asserted by Rorschach and later writers on the subject. Those that did include subjects of different ages in their own studies either did not attempt to match subjects on important background characteristics or used grossly mismatched groups of young and old (Ames, 1966; Light and Amick, 1956). Particularly bothersome was the reliance of most of the studies on institutionalized older people, with no attempt to control for health or other variables that conceivably could be causally related to both institutionalization and Rorschach response quality. In the only study to compare institutionalized and community subjects Ames *et al.* (1973) found the typical signs of aging to occur more frequently among those in institutions, despite the fact that they were preselected for good health.

Another substantial defect in most studies was their failure to include cognitive ability in their data-analytic designs. The importance of intelligence was demonstrated in Eisdorfer's (1963) finding that Rorschach indicators were minimally related to age in a community sample of 242 subjects ranging in age from 60–94, but systematically related to measured IQ; in his results the "typical" pattern of decline with old age described above characterized the lower-IQ groups but not the highest. A parallel finding when subjects were classified by socioeconomic status was reported by Ames *et al.* (1973); "typical" aging patterns were found at lower SES levels. Ames *et al.* (1973) and Ames (1974) identified aged subgroups whose summary scores did not differ from the ranges accepted as normal, suggesting at least that the age-decline pattern is not inevitable. More recent studies that controlled for intelligence and used only community-resident samples failed to find the classical pattern (Erlemeier, 1968; Poitreneau and Moreaux, 1975).

Ames (1960; 1966) reported the only longitudinal findings with older subjects over periods of four to five and three years, respectively. While some scores changed in the predicted direction, more did not, and her studies did not agree on which scores change.

Like the general Rorschach literature, studies of older subjects have been lacking in successful validity tests. In fact, the only convincing correlations with other types of measures have involved broadly cognitive skills, such as Wechsler IQ (Eisdorfer, 1963), clinically judged "senile quality"

(Singer, 1963), and a battery of cognitively-loaded visual-motor tests (Ames, 1974). Inasmuch as the Rorschach is asserted to be a personality test and is used clinically to draw conclusions regarding psychodynamic processes, it is discouraging to see its validity demonstrated primarily with cognitive processes. Furthermore, there is no evidence to suggest that it is as, or more, useful then the explicitly cognitive measures in general use for this purpose.

Klopfer (1974) suggested that age-related changes in Rorschach scores may be explained in terms of Birren's (1964) concept of "cognitive load-shedding;" that is, if individuals are required to make discriminations beyond their capacities, they feel inner tension and a desire to escape from the situation. Many of the classic Rorschach changes imputed to aging may reflect this motivation, though it remains to be seen whether cognitive capacity, the presence of organic brain syndrome, poor physical health, sociocultural background, in-

**Table 23–5**  Summary of correlates of personal styles found in research using older subjects.

| PERSONALITY | BRIEF DEFINITION | AGE DIFFERENCES | MEASURES USED | BASIC CORRELATES | OTHER CORRELATES |
|---|---|---|---|---|---|
| Augmentation vs. reduction (Petrie, 1967) (A-R)[a] | Tendency to diminish (R) or amplify (A) intensity of incoming stimulation | | Kinesthetic after-effect | | High interpersonal involvement (R); high responsiveness in interview (R); plans ahead (R); sleeps less (R); past and future life less "rough" (R), (Mishara and Baker, 1974) |
| Constricted vs. flexible control (Gardner *et al.*, 1959) (C-F) | Ability to articulate stimulus fields containing contradictory elements (F) | Older (C), (Eisner, 1972) | Stroop Color-Word Test | Good health (F), Birren *et al.*, (1963) | Institutionalization (C), (Comalli, Krus, and Wapner, 1965) |
| Leveling vs. sharpening (Gardner *et al.*, 1959) (L-S) | Obliviousness (L) or vigilance (S) to stimulus variation | None (Warren and Staines, 1974) | Size judgment test | | |
| Repression vs. sensitization (Byrne, 1964) (R-S) | Denial of (R) vs. vigilance (S) for conflict, threat, and emotionally disturbing situations | Older (R), (Andrew, 1973; Schwartz, 1972) | R-S scale (MMPI); Sentence Completion | Female (S), Physical illness (R), Psychiatric illness (S), (Schwartz and Krupp, 1971) | Older Ss with poorer memory (R), older Ss with better memory (S), Andrew (1973) |
| Sensation-seeking (Zuckerman and Link, 1968) (SS) | Preference for new, novel, stimulating situations (SS) | Older low SS, (Dibner, 1973; Sterns, 1974) | Sensation-Seeking Scale | | Better efficiency in psychomotor speed and incidental learning, high egocentrism (SS), (Dibner, 1973; Sterns, 1974) |
| Preference for simplicity vs. complexity (Berlyne, 1960) (S-C) | Preference for simple (S) vs. complex (C) stimuli | Old (S) (Dibner, 1973) | Visual displays (dots, figures, photos); questionnaire | | No relationship to egocentrism, stimulus seeking, or cognitive-motor performance, (Dibner, 1973) |

[a]Letters in parenthesis refer to one or the other polarity of a given style

stitutional status, or other factors may explain away all such apparent age differences.

In the meantime, a revival of research with updated methodology seems necessary before any conclusion may be drawn regarding the Rorschach's usefulness. In terms of clinical practice, the personal preferences of the clinician (and perhaps his or her age cohort!) may well be the primary determinant of whether it is used or not. By comparison with the longer objective tests, the Rorschach is unquestionably easier to use, and this fact alone may warrant continued use among the coming generation of clinical geropsychologists.

A more systematically-constructed inkblot test is the *Holtzmann Inkblot Technique* (Holtzman, Thorpe, Swartz, and Herron, 1961). Age differences up to age 61 were not remarkable in a study by Witzke, Swartz, and Drew (1971) but did appear, in somewhat irregular form, among an older VA domiciliary group (Overall and Gorham, 1972). The latter study revealed that responses in old age differed from those of younger age, along with a continuum quite different from that which separated organic brain syndrome patients from normal aged groups.

*The Thematic Appreception Test (TAT) and Related Techniques*   In contrast to the Rorschach, there is no single generally-accepted scoring system and therefore no norms to guide the clinician using the TAT as an overall personality measure with any age group. Psychologists generally make their own subjective interpretations of the stories a patient produces. They also administer the TAT in a less standardized way than many other personality tests. For example, it is considered perfectly acceptable to probe if the content of the story is too sparse. Few clinicians administer the full twenty-card set. Instead, cards are chosen in line with the examiner's personal preference and a judgment as to what will be most meaningful to a particular subject.

Thus studies of older subjects have typically used one to 12 cards and have frequently introduced special-purpose cards not from the Murray (1938) set. Deviations from the usual instructions or inquiry were reported to be necessary by Gutmann (1964) and Britton and Britton (1972) in order to encourage responses beyond a descriptive level. Since no other problems in obtaining stories have been reported, it would seem that older adults can relate to the test in a meaningful way. Most, but not all, subject samples have been relatively intact cognitively, and of somewhat higher than average socioeconomic status.

Most research using thematic stories has had a very clear theoretical focus, which in turn has led to idosyncratic scoring systems. Rosen and Neugarten (1960) defined ego energy in terms of the introduction of nonpictured characters into stories, the introduction of conflict, and the activity level ascribed to the characters in five TAT cards. A significant cross-sectional decrease in ego energy was observed with age, but none with sex or socioeconomic status. Parallel longitudinal changes were found four to five years later (Lubin, 1964). Another dimension, ego mastery, was derived from the same larger study, as an indicator of quality of involvement with the environment, ranging from active mastery to magical mastery (Gutmann, 1964). Again, older male age groups were found to move cross-sectionally from active toward magical mastery. Gutmann (1969) found these age differences replicable in three nonindustrialized cultures, and concluded that the changes from active to less active styles of dealing with the environment as age increases were relatively free of cultural context. Cumming and Henry (1961) found the above results on ego energy and ego mastery to be consistent with their disengagement theory of aging.

Given the theoretical focus of the Chicago studies, the reported age effects may be seen as one affirmation of the validity of the TAT for older people. Other validity indicators have been reported. Gutmann (1964) found that ego mastery scores were related as predicted to one of three measures of social-interactional reward sources, to interviewer ratings of social presentation during the interview, and to life satisfaction ratings among males, but not among females. Shukin and Neugarten (1964) found that two of three TAT-derived dimensions (concern with causality and concern with learning) were related to social-behavior measures (though this relationship dissipated when age was controlled). Cumming and Henry (1961) reported significant relationships between ego energy scores and two of three measures of social behavior, though the size of these relationships varied radically by sex, with no compelling rationale for this finding; these results were not analyzed to control for age. Lieberman, Prock, and Tobin (1968) used the Dana (1955) perceptual organization score, the ego energy score, and three other TAT-derived indices (heterosexual futurity, future events, and meaning of others) in testing differences among community residents, a community-resident institutional waiting-list group, and institutional residents. Of the 10 comparisons between community residents and the other two groups, nine were significant in the expected direction, i.e., the community group was superior. Two of the five tests of one of their major hypotheses (that waiting-list subjects would show poorer ego function than institutional subjects) were upheld by the TAT analyses. Britton and Britton (1972) used a TAT-derived index of adjustment in their longitudinal study of small-town residents. These scores were not related to "reputation" ratings elicited from other subjects, but in a subset of 25 who were known to selected informant-judges, TAT adjustment correlated 0.80 with mean peer ratings. They found no relationship between change in TAT adjustment and change in health, social involvement, activity, or number of sources of support.

The net of this body of research using the TAT appears to have been substantial in adumbrating the psychological correlates of age viewed cross-sectionally, and moderately successful in demonstrating some validity with respect to external criteria. It is important to call attention to the great care taken by the Chicago investigators to define TAT concepts in terms of their relationship to the theory underlying their research. Even more impressive were the pains taken by this group and the Brittons to train judges in the difficult process of coding and to report interjudge reliability measures, which have been quite acceptable. The stability over time of the TAT adjustment measure used by Britton and Britton (1972) was lower than in the case of other measures used in their study; further exploration of retest reliability seems desirable. In conclusion, the lack of use of the TAT in recent years seems unwarranted. By contrast to the Rorschach literature, TAT results appear to be more directly relevant to clinical concerns and their research use apparent. Conspicuously absent is knowledge about how cognitive functioning is related to the age and validity-criterion relationships of the TAT scores that have been discussed, and whether the TAT would be useful with the cognitively impaired. While the claims that the TAT is relatively resistant to conscious bias and taps deeper levels of the personality have not been formally tested with the aged, it seems likely that it is less subject to the denial widely reported in the gerontological literature.

With the exception of the special-purpose cards used by Chicago investigators, the published literature gives little reason for the user to prefer alternative apperceptive tests now available. The *Gerontological Apperception Test* (GAT) is presented as allowing easier identification with pictured age peers and portrays typical life situations of older people (Wolk and Wolk, 1971). Yet Fitzgerald, Pasewark, and Fleisher (1974) found no difference in the ability of the TAT and GAT to elicit selected themes. The *Senior Apperception Test* (SAT) (Bellak

and Bellak, 1975) has not been formally compared with other sets. Both the GAT and the SAT suffer from negatively stereotyped presentation of older people and their situations, so that the negative stimulus "pull" may overshadow the subject's own projections.

*Sentence Completion Test.* A few reports have appeared using various sentence-completion forms. Relationships between sentence completion dimensions and cognitive functions were found by Andrew (1973), Dibner (1973), and Singer (1963). Normal middle-aged and elderly community residents judged high and low in personal adjustment were differentiated by responses to 10 items (Peck, 1959). Carp (1967a,b) found a revision of Peck's form to be usable with low-income housing applicants. Scores based on the positive or negative mental-health connotations of self-referent responses showed several concurrent relationships to other tests. Similar scores for content related to other people showed predictive validity in terms of several measures of social adjustment one year later. Scoring reliability was tested and found satisfactory. Tobin and Lieberman (1977) found community residents, as predicted, to score more highly than waiting-list or institutionalized subjects on sentence completion items relating to the ability to extend oneself into the future and on anxiety and depression scores. Body preoccupation was found to increase following institutionalization, and survival among the total group was significantly predicted by three S.C. test scores.

*Human Figure Drawing Test.* The major conclusion from the few reports on human figure drawings among the elderly is that the test is related to other measures of cognitive functioning (Gilbert and Hall, 1962; Lorge, Tuckman, and Dunn, 1954; Singer, 1963). However, Cumming and Henry (1961) found a relationship between figure drawing scores and the TAT-derived score of ego energy (Rosen and Neugarten, 1960). Lakin (1958) found that drawings of older people were judged to be more negative in affective tone than those of children.

SELECTION OF PERSONALITY TESTS
FOR USE WITH THE ELDERLY

Many of the deficiencies of the personality tests discussed in this chapter are not related to the age of client, but are rooted in the most general problems of personality assessment: the very distressing lack of convincing data on reliability, validity, and subgroup norms. These problems are compounded for the elderly client by the many limitations discussed above: test length; demands on attention, concentration, and energy expenditures; and the differences statistically related to age, such as sensory, motor, and cognitive functioning and educational, social, and cultural background.

Where the known characteristics of a subject population or an individual client include few of these limitations, the entire array of personality tests used with younger populations is at least theoretically available, provided the user takes proper account of generational meanings of stimuli, the probable lack of age-specific norms, and so on. For intact and relatively well-educated older people, then, the researcher and clinician are free to use their own preferences in choosing appropriate test batteries.

For subjects of less than optimum capability, modifications will be necessary, based first on the endurance of both user and subject. The voluminous battery used successfully with marginally competent subjects by Tobin and Lieberman (1977) attests to the feasibility of in-depth assessment with proper pacing and timing of test sessions.

For diagnostic purposes and the measurement of psychopathology, the MMPI is still the method of choice, because of the more extensive list of studies indicating its validity. Because of the full MMPI's length problem, the Mini-Mult may be more useful in practice. If a measure of neurotic anxiety alone is wished, the MPI Neuroticism scale unquestionably has the strongest psychometric qualities, with the important exception of established age-specific validity. Again, however, MMPI "neurotic triad" subscales (hypochondriasis, depression, hysteria) may perform just as well as or better than the MPI Neuroticism scale.

For the clinician wishing to explore the personality structure and dynamics of the individual, the 16PF, EPPS, Guilford-Zimmerman, and Gough Adjective Check List (Gough and Heilbrun, 1965) at least have the advantage of producing scores with appropriate trait names. Their length consigns them to use with the elite subject, however. Furthermore, to date there is very little research evidence to suggest that these test scores agree with any other independent characterization of the named personality dimension in older people. For research purposes, the 16PF in particular has positive psychometric qualities; the work of Costa and associates in determining other test and demographic correlates of 16PF scores, and particularly in exploring the theoretical meaning of 16PF factors, is exemplary. Much more such research is necessary to make these inventories useful in clinical situations, however.

Among the projective tests, the TAT is far and away the best-developed test for use with older people. The results in the research reviewed here (when pursued with a firm grounding in theory) provides at least suggestive support for its clinical use. The sentence completion deserves further use for research and exhibits a certain amount of validity for clinical purposes. For the Rorschach, no comparable research support is found, outside the sphere of cognitive processes (where frankly cognitive tests would clearly provide more efficient measures). Yet, clinical research has neglected the Rorschach performance of the elderly; for this reason, as well as because of the continued attachment of some clinicians to the Rorschach, improved methods should be applied to exploring the validity of this test with older people.

These and other projective tests in the hands of a skilled clinician should be no less useful for the elderly than for people of younger ages. The need is clear for more research directed at the psychometric characteristics of the tests themselves. Only after more basic work is completed will one feel confident in suggesting that projective tests be used as measures of important variables in personality research.

## CONCLUSION

The only conclusion possible from the review of the literature in personality testing is that the current state of the art is not encouraging. It is just as clear, however, that where coherent theory, judicious test choice, and careful methodology have been applied, knowledge has been advanced. Therefore, a renewed effort to extend theoretical knowledge in this manner appears warranted. The growing number of clinicians who work with the elderly will find familiarity with the best of existing research and the improved quality of future research a necessary basis for the development of a better clinical practice of geropsychology.

## REFERENCES

AARONSON, B. S. 1958. Age and sex influences on MMPI profile peak distributions in an abnormal population. *Journal of Consulting Psychology, 22*, 203–206.
AMES, L. B. 1960. Age changes in the Rorschach re-

sponses of institutionalized elderly subjects. *Journal of Genetic Psychology, 97,* 287–315.

AMES, L. B. 1966. Changes in Rorschach response throughout the human life span. *Genetic Psychology Monographs, 74,* 89–125

AMES, L. B. 1974. Calibration of aging. *Journal of Personality Assessment, 38,* 507–519

AMES, L. B., METRAUX, R., RODELL, J., AND WALKER, R. 1973. *Rorschach Responses in Old Age.* New York: Brunner/Mazel.

ANDREW, J. M. 1973. Coping style and declining verbal abilities. *Journal of Gerontology, 28,* 179–183.

APFELDORF, M., AND HUNLEY, P. J. 1971. Personality assessment of the aged with the adjective check list. Paper presented at the annual meeting of the American Psychological Association, Washington, DC.

APFELDORF, M., AND HUNLEY, P. J. 1971b. The adjective check list approach to older institutionalized men. *Journal of Personality Assessment, 35,* 457–462.

BELLAK, L., AND BELLAK, S. S. 1975. *The TAT, CAT, and SAT in Clinical Use.* New York: Grune & Stratton.

BENDIG, A. W. 1960. Age differences in the interscale factor structure of the Guilford-Zimmerman Temperament Survey. *Journal of Consulting Psychology, 24,* 134–138.

BERLYNE, D. E. 1960. *Conflict, Arousal, and Curiosity.* New York: McGraw-Hill.

BIRREN, J. E. 1964. *The Psychology of Aging.* Englewood Cliffs, N.J.: Prentice-Hall, Inc.

BIRREN, J. E., BUTLER, R. N., GREENHOUSE, S. W., SOKOLOFF, L., AND YARROW, M. 1963. *Human aging.* Public Health Service Publication No. 986. Washington, DC: National Institute of Mental Health.

BLOOM, K. L. 1961. Age and the self-concept. *American Journal of Psychiatry, 118,* 534–538.

BOLTON, N., AND SAVAGE, R. D. 1971. Neuroticism and extraversion in elderly normal subjects. *British Journal of Psychiatry, 118,* 473–474.

BORTNER, R. W. 1962. Test differences attributable to age, selection processes and institutional effects. *Journal of Gerontology, 17,* 58–64.

BOTWINICK, J. 1973. *Aging and Behavior.* New York: Springer.

BOTWINICK, J., AND STORANDT, M. 1974. *Memory, related functions, and age.* Springfield, Il.: Charles C Thomas.

BRITTON, J. H., AND BRITTON, J. O. 1972. *Personality Changes in Aging.* New York: Springer.

BRITTON, P. G., AND SAVAGE, R. D. 1966. The MMPI and the aged—Some normative data from a community sample. *British Journal of Psychiatry, 112,* 941–943.

BRITTON, P. G., AND SAVAGE, R. D. 1967. A short scale for the assessment of mental health in the community aged. *British Journal of Psychiatry, 113,* 498.

BRITTON, P. G., AND SAVAGE, R. D. 1969. The factorial structure of the MMPI from an aged sample. *Jour-*

nal of Genetic Psychology, 114, 13–17.

BROZEK, J. 1955. Personality changes with age: An item analysis of the Minnesota Multiphasic personality inventory. *Journal of Gerontology, 10,* 194–206.

BUTLER, R. N., AND LEWIS, M. I. 1973. *Aging and Mental Health.* St. Louis: C. V. Mosby.

BYRNE, D. 1964. Repression-sensitization as a dimension of personality. *Progress in Experimental Personality Research, 1,* 169–220.

CALDEN, G., AND HOKANSON, J. E. 1959. The influence of age on MMPI responses. *Journal of Clinical Psychology, 15,* 194–195.

CALDWELL, B. McD. 1954. The use of the Rorschach in personality research with the aged. *Journal of Gerontology, 9,* 316–323.

CAMPBELL, A., CONVERSE, P. E., AND RODGERS, W. L. 1976. *The Quality of American Life: Perceptions, Evaluations, and Satisfactions.* New York: Russell Sage.

CARP, F. 1967a. The applicability of an empirical scoring standard for a sentence completion test administered to two age groups. *Journal of Gerontology, 22,* 301–307.

CARP, F. 1967b. Attitudes of older persons toward themselves and toward others. *Journal of Gerontology, 22,* 308–312.

CARP, F. M. 1975. Ego defense or cognitive consistency effects of environmental evaluation. *Journal of Gerontology, 30,* 707–716.

CATTELL, R. B. 1955. *The Objective-Analytic Personality Test Batteries.* Champaign, Illinois: Institute for Personality and Ability Testing.

CATTELL, R. B., EBER, H. W., AND TATSUOKA, M. M. 1970. *Handbook for the Sixteen Personality Factor Questionnaire.* Champaign, Ill.: Institute for Personality and Ability Testing.

CHOWN, S. M. 1968. Personality and aging. *In,* K.W. Schaie (ed.), *Theory and Methods of Research on Aging.* Morgantown, W.V.: University Press.

CLARK, J. W. 1960. The aging dimension: A factorial analysis of individual differences with age on psychological and physiological measurements. *Journal of Gerontology, 15,* 183–187.

COMALLI, P. E., KRUS, D. M., AND WAPNER, S. 1965. Cognitive functioning in two groups of aged: One institutionalized, the other living in the community. *Journal of Gerontology, 20,* 9–13.

COMREY, A. L 1961. Factored homogeneous item dimensions in personality research. *Educational Psychology Measurement, 21,* 417–431.

COPPINGER, N. W., BORTNER, R. W., AND SAUCER, R. T. 1963. A factor analysis of psychological adjustment. *Journal of Genetic Psychology, 103,* 23–43.

COSTA, P. T., FOZARD, J. L., AND McCRAE, R. R. 1977. Personological interpretation of factors from the Strong Vocational Interest Blank Scales. *Journal of Vocational Behavior, 10,* 231–243.

COSTA, P. T., FOZARD, F. L., McCRAE, R. R., AND BOSSÉ,

R. 1976. Relations of age and personality dimensions to cognitive ability factors. *Journal of Gerontology, 31*, 663–669.

Costa, P. T., and McCrae, R. R. 1976. Age differences in personality structure: A cluster-analytic approach. *Journal of Gerontology, 31*, 564–570.

Costa, P. T., and McCrae, R. R. 1978. Objective personality assessment. *In*, M. A. Storandt, I. C. Siegler, and M. F. Elias (eds.), *Clinical Psychology in Gerontology*, pp. 119–144. New York: Plenum.

Costa, P. T., and McCrae, R. R. In press. "Hold" and "no-hold" domains of personality: Studies in validity, stability, and change. *International Journal of Aging and Human Development*.

Craik, F. I. M. 1964. An observed age difference in responses to a personality inventory. *British Journal of Psychology, 55*, 453–462.

Culbertson, K. L., Pomeroy, E. L. and Cunningham, W. R. No date. Age and the measurement of mood. Mimeo report, University of Southern California, Andrus Gerontology Center.

Cumming, E., and Henry, W. 1961. *Growing Old*. New York: Basic Books.

Dana, R. H. 1955. Clinical diagnoses and objective TAT scoring. *Journal of Abnormal and Social Psychology, 50*, 19–25.

Davol, S. H. 1958. Some determinants of sociometric relationships and group structure in a Veterans Administration domiciliary. Unpublished doctoral dissertation, University of Rochester.

Dibner, A. S. 1973. Behavioral correlates of preference for complexity in the aged. Paper presented at the annual meeting of the Gerontological Society, Miami Beach, November.

Douglas, K., and Arenberg, D. 1977. Age differences, cohort differences, and cultural change on the Guilford-Zimmerman Temperament Survey. Mimeo report. Baltimore: National Institute on Aging, Gerontology Research Center.

Edwards, A. E., and Wine, D. 1963. Personality changes with age: Their dependency on concomitant intellectual decline. *Journal of Gerontology, 18*, 182–184.

Edwards, A. L. 1953. *Manual for the Personal Preference Schedule*. New York: Psychological Corporation.

Eisdorfer, C. 1960a. Developmental level and sensory impairment in the aged. *Journal of Projective Techniques, 24*, 119–132.

Eisdorfer, C. 1960b. Rorschach rigidity and sensory decrement in a senescent population. *Journal of Gerontology, 15*, 188–190.

Eisdorfer, C. 1963. Rorschach performance and intellectual functioning in the aged. *Journal of Gerontology, 18*, 358–363.

Eisner, D. A. 1972. Developmental relationships between field independence and fixity-mobility. *Perceptual and Motor Skills, 34*, 767–770.

Erlemeier, N. 1968. Rorschachbefunde im höheren alter. *Zeitschrift für Gerontologie, 1*, 296–310.

Eysenck, H. J. 1958. A short questionnaire for the measurement of two dimensions of personality. *Journal of Applied Psychology, 42*, 1–10.

Eysenck, H. J. 1959. *Manual of the Maudsley Personality Inventory*. London: University of London Press.

Eysenck, S. B. 1969. *Manual of the Eysenck-Withers Personality Inventory for Subnormal Subjects*. London: University of London Press.

Fillenbaum, G., and Pfeiffer, E. 1976. The Mini-Mult: A cautionary note. *Journal of Consulting and Clinical Psychology, 44*, 698–703.

Fitzgerald, B. J., Pasework, R. A., and Fleisher, S. 1974. Responses of an aged population on the Gerontological and Thematic Apperception Tests. *Journal of Personality Assessment, 38*, 234–235.

Fozard, J. L., and Nuttall, R. L. 1971. Effects of age and socioeconomic status differences on the Sixteen Personality Factors Questionnaire scores. *Proceedings of the 79th Annual Convention*, American Psychological Association, *6*, 597–598.

Gannon, E. F. 1965. Changes in Edwards Personal Preference Schedule needs with age and psychiatric status. *Journal of Clinical Psychology, 21*, 194–196.

Gardner, R. W., Holzman, P. S., Klein, G. S., Linton, H. B., and Spence, D. P. 1959. Cognitive control: A study of individual consistencies in cognitive behavior. *Psychological Issues*, 4. New York: International Universities Press.

Gilbert, J. G., and Hall, M. R. 1962. Changes with age in human figure drawings. *Journal of Gerontology, 17*, 397–404.

Gilmore, A. J. J. 1972. Personality in the elderly: Problems in methodology. *Age and Ageing, 1*, 227–232.

Gough, H. G., and Heilbrun, A. B. 1965. *The Adjective Check List Manual*. Palo Alto, Ca.: Consulting Psychologists Press.

Guilford, J. P., and Zimmerman, W. S. 1949. *The Guilford-Zimmerman Temperament Survey: Manual of Instructions and Interpretations*. Beverly Hills, Ca.: Sheridan House.

Gunner-Swenson, F., and Jensen, K. 1976. Frequency of mental disorders in old age. *Acta Psychiatrica Scandinavica, 53*, 283–297.

Gutman, G. 1966. A note on the Maudsley Personality Inventory: Age and sex differences in extraversion and neuroticism in a Canadian sample. *British Journal of Social and Clinical Psychology, 5*, 128–129.

Gutmann, D. L. 1964. An exploration of ego configurations in middle and later life. *In*, B. L. Neugarten (ed.), *Personality in Middle and Late Life*, pp. 114–148. New York: Atherton Press.

Gutmann, D. L. 1969. *The Country of Old Men: Cross Cultural Studies in the Psychology of Later Life*. Ann Arbor, Mi.: University of Michigan, Wayne State Institute of Gerontology.

GYNTHER, M., AND SHIMKUNAS, A. 1966. Age and MMPI performance. *Journal of Consulting Psychology, 30,* 118–121.

HARDYCK, C. D. 1964. Sex differences in personality changes with age. *Journal of Gerontology, 19,* 78–82.

HARE, E. H., AND SHAW, G. K. 1965. *Mental Health on a New Housing Estate.* London: Oxford University Press.

HERON, A. 1956. A two-part personality measure for use as a research criterion. *British Journal of Psychology, 47,* 243–251.

HERON, A., AND CHOWN, S. 1967. *Age and Function.* Boston: Little, Brown.

HESS, A. L., AND BRADSHAW, H. L. 1970. Positiveness of self-concept and ideal self as a function of age. *Journal of Genetic Psychology, 117,* 57–67.

HOLTZMAN, W. H., THORPE, J. S., SWARTZ, J. D., AND HERRON, E. W. 1961. *Inkblot Perception and Personality: Holtzman Inkblot Technique.* Austin, Texas: University of Texas Press.

KAHANA, B. 1978. The use of projective techniques in personality assessment of the aged. *In,* M. Storandt, I. C. Siegler, and M. F. Elias (eds.), *Clinical Psychology in Gerontology,* pp. 145–180. New York: Plenum.

KAHN, R. L., POLLACK, M., GOLDFARB, A. I. 1961. Factors related to individual differences in mental status of institutionalized aged. *In,* P. H. Hoch, and J. Zubin (eds.), *Psychopathology of Aging,* pp. 104–113. New York: Grune & Stratton.

KINCANNON, J. C. 1968. Prediction of the standard MMPI scale scores from 71 items: The Mini-Mult. *Journal of Consulting and Clinical Psychology, 32,* 319–325.

KLASSEN, D., HOMSTRA, R. K., AND ADERSON, P. B. 1975. Influence of social desirability on symptom and mood reporting in a community survey. *Journal of Consulting and Clinical Psychology, 43,* 448–452.

KLOPFER, W. G. 1946. Personality patterns of old age. *Rorschach Research Exchange, 10,* 145–166.

KLOPFER, W. G. 1974. The Rorschach and old age. *Journal of Personality Assessment, 38,* 420–422.

KORNETSKY, C. 1963. Minnesota Multiphasic Personality Inventory: Results obtained from a population of aged men. *In,* J. E. Birren, *et al. Human Aging.* U.S. Public Health Service Publication No. 986. Washington, DC: National Institute of Mental Health, pp. 253–256.

KUHLEN, R. G. 1959. Aging and life adjustment. *In,* J. E. Birren (ed.), *Handbook of Aging and the Individual,* pp. 852–900. Chicago: University of Chicago Press.

KUHLEN, R. G., AND KIEL, C. 1951. The Rorschach performance of 100 elderly males. *Journal of Gerontology,* Supplement to No. 3, *6,* 115 [Abstract].

LAKIN, M. 1958. Affective tone in human figure drawings by institutionalized aged and by normal children. *Journal of the American Geriatrics Society, 6,* 495–500.

LAWTON, M. P. 1970. Gerontology in clinical psychology and vice versa. *Aging and Human Development, 1,* 147–159.

LAWTON, M. P., AND GOTTESMAN, L. 1974. Psychological services to the elderly. *American Psychologist, 29,* 689–693.

LIEBERMAN, M. A., PROCK, V. N., AND TOBIN, S. S. 1968. Psychological effects of institutionalization. *Journal of Gerontology, 23,* 343–353.

LIGHT, B. H., AND AMICK, J. H. 1956. Rorschach responses of normal aged. *Journal of Projective Techniques, 20,* 185–195.

LORGE, I., TUCKMAN, J., AND DUNN, M. B. 1954. Human figure drawings by younger and older adults. *American Psychologist, 9,* 420–421 [Abstract].

LUBIN, M. I. 1964. Addendum to J. L. Rosen, and B. L. Neugarten. Ego functions in the middle and later years. *In,* B. L. Neugarten (ed.), *Personality in Middle and Late Life,* pp. 102–104. New York: Atherton Press.

MCCREERY, C. P., AND MENSH, I. N. 1977. Personality differences associated with age in law offenders. *Journal of Gerontology, 32,* 164–167.

MISHARA, B. L., AND BAKER, A. H. 1974. Stimulus intensity modulation: A perceptual cognitive approach to life style in the elderly. Paper presented at the annual meeting of the American Psychological Association, New Orleans.

MURRAY, H. 1938. *Explorations in Personality.* New York: Oxford University Press.

National Center for Health Statistics. 1977. Profile of chronic illness in nursing homes. DHEW Publication No. (PHS) 78–1780, Series 13, No. 29. Hyattsville, Md: Department of Health, Education, and Welfare.

NYDEGGER, C. (ed.), 1977. *Measuring Morale: A Guide to Effective Assessment.* Washington, DC: Gerontological Society.

OBERLEDER, M. 1964. Effects of psychosocial factors on test results of the aging. *Psychological Reports, 14,* 383–387.

OVERALL, J. E., AND GORHAM, D. R. 1972. Organicity vs. old age in objective and projective test performance. *Journal of Consulting and Clinical Psychology, 39,* 98–105.

PEARSON, J. S., SWENSON, W. M., AND ROME, H. P. 1965. Age and sex differences related to MMPI response frequency in 25,000 medical patients. *American Journal of Psychiatry, 121,* 988–995.

PECK, R. F. 1959. Measuring the mental health of normal adults. *Genetic Psychology Monographs, 60,* 197–225.

PECKENS, R. No date. A factor analytic study of Edwards Personal Preference Schedule need scores as a function of age and sex. Mimeo report. Texas Womens University, Psychology Department.

PETRIE, A. 1967. *Individuality in Pain and Suffering.* 1967. Chicago: University of Chicago Press.

PFEIFFER, E. 1975. *Multidimensional Functional Assessment: The OARS Methodology.* Durham, N.C.: Duke University Center for the Study of Aging.

POITRENEAU, J., AND MOREAUX, C. 1975. Réponses données au test de Rorschach par un groupe de sujets agés, cliniquement normaux. *Revue de Psychologie Appliquee, 25,* 267–283.

POSTEMA, L. J., AND SCHELL, R. E. 1967. Aging and psychopathology: Some MMPI evidence for seemingly greater neurotic behavior among older people. *Journal of Clinical Psychology, 23,* 140–143.

RORSCHACH, H. 1942. *Psychodiagnostics.* New York: Grune & Stratton.

ROSE, C. L. 1973. Age role expectations, personality and job satisfaction. Paper presented at the annual meeting of the American Psychological Association.

ROSEN, J., AND NEUGARTEN, B. 1960. Ego functions in middle and later years. *Journal of Gerontology, 15,* 62–67.

ROTTER, J. B. 1966. Generalized expectancies for internal versus external control of reinforcement. *Psychological Monographs, 80,* No. 1 (whole No. 609).

SAVAGE, R. D., GABER, L. B., BRITTON, P. G., BOLTON, N., AND COOPER, A. 1977. *Personality and Adjustment in the Aged.* London: Academic Press.

SCARR, H. A., AND SLATER, P. E. n.d. Age and introversion. Mimeo report. Brandeis University, Psychology Department.

SCHAIE, K. W., AND MARQUETTE, B. W. 1972. Personality in maturity and old age. *In,* R. M. Dreger (ed.), *Multivariate Personality Research: Contributions to the Understanding of Personality in Honor of Raymond B. Cattell,* pp. 612–632. Baton Rouge, La.: Claitor's Publishing Division.

SCHAIE, K. W., AND PARHAM, I. A. 1975. *Manual for the Test of Behavioral Rigidity* (2nd revised edition). Palo Alto, Ca.: Consulting Psychologists Press.

SCHAIE, K. W., AND SCHAIE, J. P. 1977. Clinical assessment and aging. *In,* J. E. Birren, and K. W. Schaie (eds.), *Handbook of the Psychology of Aging,* pp. 692–723. New York: Van Nostrand Reinhold.

SCHAIE, K. W., AND STROTHER, C. R. 1968. Cognitive and personality variables in college graduates of advanced age. *In,* G. Talland (ed.), *Human Aging and Behavior,* pp. 281–308. New York: Academic Press.

SCHWARTZ, M. S. 1972. The Repression-Sensitization Scale: Normative age and sex data on 30,000 medical patients. *Journal of Clinical Psychology, 28,* 72–73.

SCHWARTZ, M. S., AND KRUPP, N. E. 1971. Repression-sensitization and medical diagnosis. *Journal of Abnormal Psychology, 78,* 286–291.

SEALY, A. P., AND CATTELL, R. B. 1965. Standard trends in personality development in men and women of 16–70 years, determined by Sixteen Personality Factors Questionnaire measurements. Paper presented at British Psychological Society Conference.

SHUKIN, A., AND NEUGARTEN, B. L. 1964. Personality and social interaction. *In,* B. L Neugarten (ed.), *Personality in Middle and Late Life,* pp. 149–157. New York: Atherton Press.

SINGER, M. T. 1963. Personality measurements in the aged. *In,* J. E. Birren, R. N. Butler, S. W. Greenhouse, L. Sokoloff, and M. Yarrow (eds.), *Human Aging,* pp. 217–249. Washington, DC: National Institute of Mental Health. Public Health Service Publication, No. 986.

SLATER, P. E., AND SCARR, H. A. 1964. Personality in old age. *Genetic Psychology Monographs, 70,* 229–269.

SPANGLER, D. P., AND THOMAS, C. W. 1962. The effects of age, sex, and physical disability upon manifest needs. *Journal of Counseling Psychology, 9,* 313–319.

STERNS, H. L. 1974. Developmental differences in the evaluation of visual complexity. Paper presented at the annual meeting of the American Psychological Association, New Orleans.

SWENSON, W. M. 1961. Structured personality testing in the aged: A study of the gerontic population. *Journal of Clinical Psychology, 17,* 302–304.

SWENSON, W. M., PEARSON, J. S., AND OSBORNE, D. 1973. *An MMPI Source Book: Basic Item, Scale, and Pattern Data on 50,000 Medical Patients.* Minneapolis, Minn.: University of Minnesota Press.

THUMIN, F. J. 1969. MMPI scores as related to age, education, and intelligence among male job applicants. *Journal of Applied Psychology, 53,* 404–407.

TOBIN, S., AND LIEBERMAN, M. A. 1977. *Last Home for the Aged.* San Francisco: Jossey-Bass.

UECKER, A. E. 1969. Comparability of two methods of administering the MMPI to brain-damaged geriatric patients. *Journal of Clinical Psychology, 25,* 196–198.

WARREN, W. G., AND STAINES, J. W. 1974. Levelling-sharpening in aged persons. *Psychological Reports, 35,* 181–182.

WITKIN, H. A., LEWIS, H. B., HERTZMAN, M., MACHOVER, K., MEISSNER, P. B., AND WAPNER, S. 1954. *Personality Through Perception.* New York: Harper & Row.

WITZKE, D. B., SWARTZ, J. D., AND DREW, C. J. 1971. Level of perceptual development of normal adults as measured by the Holtzman Inkblot technique. *Proceedings of the 79th American Psychological Association Annual Convention, 6,* 609–610.

WOLK, R. L. 1972. Refined projective techniques with the aged. *In,* D. P. Kent, R. Kastenbaum, and S. Sherwood (eds.), *Research Planning and Action for the Elderly,* pp. 218–251. New York: Behavioral Publications.

WOLK, R. L., AND WOLK, R. B. 1971. *The Gerontological Apperception Test.* New York: Behavioral Publications.

ZUCKERMAN, M., AND LINK, K. 1968. Construct validity for the sensation seeking scale. *Journal of Consulting and Clinical Psychology, 32,* 420–426.

# 24

# Organic Brain Syndrome*

*R. Bruce Sloane†*

## CLASSIFICATION

The very term *organic* brain syndrome, acute and chronic, smacks of the Cartesian duality that has bedeviled medicine for many years. Nowhere, perhaps, is this mind/body problem better exemplified than in such terms. Neurologists have never had any difficulty with the robust term "dementia" and undoubtedly have looked tolerantly upon psychiatric classification until it came to its senses. Fortunately, in the proposed new American Psychiatric Association classification, DSM-III (Diagnostic and Statistical Manual of the American Psychiatric Association, 1978), dementia and delirium are central. This accords with the new emphasis on descriptive criteria rather than putative mechanisms to make diagnoses.

In the past, in the United States, diagnosis has been confounded by the tendency to attribute most disorders in the aged to organic psychosis. The wide disparity in the rate of first admissions to hospitals for senile and arteriosclerotic psychosis in the UK and US was first pointed out by Roth (1959), who has provided so much seminal work in his area. He suggested this was most likely due to the fact that, in essence, a wider range of mental disorders were diagnosed as organic psychosis in the United States than Great Britain. This has since been confirmed by comparative diagnostic studies (Duckworth and Ross, 1975; Kelleher, Copeland, Gurland, and Sharpe, 1976).

*I am most grateful to: Jytte Busk, Ph.D., for her help in preparing this chapter; Jeff Boyd, M. S., who was invaluable in searching for references; Mary Luben, B.A., for incomparable manuscript typing.

†During 1978-79, Dr. Sloane received a Senior Fellowship from the Foundation Fund for Research in Psychiatry.

Roth and his colleagues (Roth and Morrissey, 1952) showed that the mental disorders in old age could be classified on the basis of their psychiatric features into five groups:

   I. Affective disorder
  II. Late paraphrenia
 III. Acute or subacute delirious states
 IV. Senile psychosis (dementia)
  V. Arteriosclerotic psychosis

These groups had widely different outcomes after admission to hospital. Follow-up studies seven to eight years after admission to hospital revealed the differences shown at 6 and 24 months between the groups still to be clearly evident, despite mortality blurring the picture. The distinction of the groups from one another was further supported by the results of formal psychological testing (Hopkins and Roth, 1953; Roth and Hopkins, 1953). The causes of death were also found to differ in the different groups. In affective and paranoid illness, death was more often due to some specific illness, in contrast to ill-defined causes such as "old age" in arteriosclerotic and senile psychoses (Kay, 1962).

Such diagnostic separation is crucial to the understanding of the diseases of the aged. Eighty-six percent (15.4 million) of people 65 years and older and 72 percent (28 million) of those from 45 to 64 are estimated to have one or more chronic conditions. High blood pressure, arthritis, diabetes, heart disease, and arteriosclerosis are but a few examples. Multiple ailments in the same individual are common (Butler, 1975). Roth has stressed how important it is to formulate a separate symptomatological and etiological diagnosis in the case of the aged. Although concordance will generally be found between the two kinds of diagnoses, discrepancies will appear for an important minority of patients. Psychogenic aspects, whether neurotic, depressive or paranoid, may often respond to treatment, in contrast to the organic process, which may progress.

Harris (1972) has pointed to the direct relationship between organic brain disease and physical status. Numerous studies in the medical literature support a direct relationship in the elderly between poor physical status and organic brain disease with psychiatric impairment. Simon (1968) reported that four-fifths of 534 geriatric patients hospitalized permanently for chronic brain syndrome and senile brain disease also suffered physical impairments severe enough to interfere with their daily functions. In his series, the most com-

mon physical illnesses, in descending order of frequency, were malnutrition, congestive heart failure, stroke, hypertension, serious respiratory infection, peripheral neuritis (often associated with alcoholism), and cancer. Hader, Schulman, and Faigman (1965) uncovered physical illness in 90 percent of the mentally ill patients they examined in a geriatric mental hygiene clinic. Libow (1973) has drawn attention to the failure to diagnose reversible brain syndromes, which may be variously due to malnutrition, anemia, congestive heart failure, infection, drugs, head trauma, alcohol, cerebrovascular accidents, dehydration, reactions to surgery and many other causes. These are all too easily attributed to chronic brain disease but, if untreated, may, in fact, progress to irreversibility, quite apart from the failure to diagnose underlying physical problems.

Conversely, as Roth has pointed out in his magnificent text (Slater and Roth, 1977), minor neurological signs abound in the elderly, including rigidity, diminished reflexes, doubtful plantar responses and slow reactions, irregularity of the pupil, and impaired vibration sense. Without harder neurological signs or definite history of a cerebrovascular accident, they should not be allowed to influence the choice of treatment. This is especially important in predominantly psychogenic conditions. Also, minor defects of memory, such as disorientation for time and place, are commonly found in healthy old subjects. The prognostic significance of these is somewhat uncertain. Parsons (1965) described marked impairment of memory in half the women aged 80 years and over investigated in the course of a community survey. Kay, Bergmann, Garside, and Roth (1966) suggested that many memory impairments in elderly people were benign.

Although the DSM-III (1978) classification is only being field-tested at this time and may well be changed, it appears to be logical and helpful, and its excellent descriptions are quoted throughout this chapter. The organic brain syndromes can be grouped into six categories:

1. Delirium and dementia with relatively global cognitive impairment.
2. Amnestic syndrome and hallucinosis with relatively selective cognitive impairment.
3. Organic delusional syndrome and organic affective state with features resembling schizophrenic or affective disorders.
4. Organic personality syndrome.
5. Intoxication and withdrawal associated with drug ingestion or cessation.
6. Other organic brain syndromes.

The organic mental disorders display a great deal of variability, both between subjects and in the same subject over time. Thus, a dementia may have a super-imposed delirium, an organic personality syndrome may follow a delirium, and other combinations and permutations may occur.

In both acute and chronic brain disorders, that is in delirium or dementia, the primary symptoms are of *intellectual impairment*, the most important varieties of which are as follows:

1. Impairment of all intellectual functions, including comprehension, calculation, knowledge, learning, and others. Ideation tends to be impoverished and concrete and associated with stereotyped repetition (perseveration) and compensatory fabrications (confabulation). This leads to:
2. Impairment of orientation, most marked for time, less for place and person.
3. Impairment of memory, most marked for recent events, less so for those of the remote past.
4. Impairment of judgment, conscience, and ability to plan for the future.
5. Shallowness or lability of affect and emotional response (Gregory, 1968).

In a delirium, it is usual to stress the temporary, reversible change of brain cell function, in contrast to the permanent, irreversible damage of dementia. Such irreversibility is, of course, not hard and fast. Myxedema is potentially irreversible though it is usually classified as a dementia.

Delirium and dementia are often intertwined. Nevertheless, there is a tendency for most persons to react to acute brain damage with the clinical syndrome of delirium or stupor and to chronic brain syndrome with a clinical syndrome of dementia. Delirium is usually characterized by a clouded sensorium with oftentimes imaginary experiences that are more illusional than delusional or hallucinatory, and which frequently embrace objects around the person. There is usually distractibility and increased or decreased psychomotor activity. In dementia, in contrast, there is more usually an obtundity or slowing of mental grasp, which does not have the characteristic perplexity of the clouding of delirium and its associated disorders of perception.

Although the primary defect in both is a cognitive one, it is often impossible to separate the primary cognitive impairment from the associated symptoms, which might be regarded as secondary. Such secondary features run the gamut of the idiosyncratic emotional reactions of an individual. These are heavily influenced by the previous personality structure and accustomed modes of reaction of the person. They can span the whole range of personality disorders, from neuroses and affective disorders to delusions which often take a paranoid form.

Although it is not necessary, and is often irrelevant to treatment to make a distinction between the cognitive defect and the associated features, it is usually important to assess the relative influence of both, especially where the cognitive impairment is mild. Where the associated illness, such as depression, is of severity, it may be necessary to treat it first, before appropriate intellectual assessment can be made.

The associated reactive features include the full spectrum of functional psychopathology, such as neurotic anxiety, depressive or manic disorders, schizophrenic or paranoid manifestations, sociopathic behavior, sexual deviation, and addiction to drugs. These reactions are clearly a compound of the awareness of the patient of failing function, his/her interpretation of its meaning, and associated judgmental defects. Anxiety, depression, irritability, shame, and anger are all as common as mere apathy. The depression may be heightened to a psychotic suicidal degree. Perfectionistic patients may be particularly disturbed by their lack of control and may show obsessive-compulsive symptoms, sometimes for the first time in their lives. Increased orderliness is not uncommon—for example, the keeping of a diary and the completion of tasks while they are still remembered. The aging executive who starts to clear his desk first thing in the morning may not be so much efficient as aware of his progressive loss of memory. He does as many things as possible before he forgets what it was he had to do—the so-called "organic orderliness."

Suspiciousness, which may become referential and even reach delusional paranoid intensity, is very common. Dementing patients may accuse others of stealing or hiding their possessions and are often particularly protective of food and money.

Associated judgmental defect may lead to disinhibition of impulses and social judgment. These may be sexual, appetitive, aggressive, or acquisitive and may result in sexual advances, stealing, unawareness of other people's feelings, and gauche, eccentric, or bizarre behavior. Even in medical communities it is sometimes surprising how much "eccentricity" is tolerated.

A fortyish urological surgeon who had always been noted for his brusqueness and failure to follow accepted procedures was referred for care of his "depression" when he got into the habit of dropping his surgical glove on the operating room floor, picking it up, replacing it on his hand, and proceeding with the operation. When he was examined, his presenile dementia had already led to severe intellectual impairment and disorientation.

Since relatively global cognitive impairment results in either delirium or dementia, a fuller generic description will be given of these disorders and also of their variations under their specific etiologies.

# DELIRIUM

Characteristically, there is a rapid impairment of intellectual functioning, and it is usually caused by widespread disturbance of brain metabolism. It has been suggested by Posner (1975) that it might better be termed "acute exogenous metabolic encephalopathy." This is in keeping with the British classification of symptomatic psychoses.

Nevertheless, as Roth (Slater and Roth, 1977) suggests, although Bonhoeffer introduced order out of chaos by classifying the symptomatic psychoses as forms of "exogenous reactions" with a universality independent of their underlying cause, much was lost in the process. Careful clinical observations have been forgotten, and new material is not being gathered. Nevertheless, the brain is not a jelly bag, and those who lump diagnostic categories run the risk of losing valuable heuristic distinctions.

The majority of elderly delirious patients lack many of the positive features of delirium which are found in younger ones (Roth, 1976). Older patients show mostly a disorientation for time and place, impaired consciousness, retardation, and exhaustion. Involuntary movements, especially coarse tremors or choreiform ones, may occur.

## General Description

### Appearance

The patient often looks unwell. He may show signs of an accompanying disease, such as fever, shortness of breath, and other systemic signs. He may be restless or verging on stupor. Fluctuation of both motor and sensorial function is common, as is rapid change from somnolence to agitated restlessness. The so-called "picking delirium" of infectious fevers in which the near-stuporous patient picks restlessly at the bedclothes is less commonly seen nowadays than in earlier times.

### Attention

There is characteristically a perplexity and clouding of attention, with associated difficulty of focus and maintenance. There may be hyper- or hypovigilance with increased or decreased reactivity to stimuli. Such stimuli and the associated information are poorly, and often aberrantly, integrated.

### Orientation

Awareness of surroundings and self is reduced, and orientation of time is invariably affected. Personal identity is usually retained, but ability to identify the place is often defective, with misidentification and a tendency to confuse illusional perceptions with illusional falsifications and imaginary experiences and dreamlike sequences. There may be "twilight states" similar to those of epilepsy.

### Talk

There may be very little or diffuse chatter. Frequently, the patient mistakes unfamiliar places and persons for familiar ones, and his talk may be concerned with this or may rapidly degenerate into merely a "muttering delirium."

### Mood

The mood is labile and often varies from euphoria through anxiety to terror. In general, it is a dysphoric one.

### Thought Processes

These are slowed, diminished, and sometimes speeded, but invariably disorganized. Coherent and rational thought is difficult or impossible.

### Delusions, Illusions and Hallucinations

There is a dreamlike quality to the patient even when awake, and he finds difficulty in distinguishing between his dreams and illusions and what is actually happening. Illusions may take the form of poorly organized and fleeting delusions. Illusions and hallucinations in any sensory modality may occur; visual ones are the most common. These may vary from simple and unformed to complex thoughts. Often the hallucinations are linked to delusions, especially fearful, paranoid ones.

### Memory

Memory is always impaired to a greater or lesser extent. In particular, there is difficulty in new learning, which often leads to an amnesia, both antrograde and retrograde. There may be islands of memory for experiences during the delirium after resolution of the illness. Occasionally, but unusually, there is a total recall of a vivid "movielike" sequence which tends to fade as time goes by.

*Insight*

This is usually lacking and the patient is unaware of what he is suffering from and of how he will get better.

*Judgment*

Judgment is usually impaired, with inappropriate behavior which is dependent on illusional, hallucinatory, or delusional experiences.

*Sleep*

Sleep is always disturbed, with drowsiness and sleep at some times during the day, wakefulness at night, or combinations of these; nightmares are common.

CLINICAL COURSE

There may be prodromal symptoms in which restlessness, dreams, nightmares, hypersensitivity to stimuli, some problems in thinking, and restlessness at night, with poor sleep and somnolence during the day, predominate. However, the onset is usually rapid, within a matter of hours or days. Often, the first symptoms occur at night.

The fluctuation of sensorial clouding and cognitive impairment is characteristic. At night, there is usually worsening, which is often associated with impaired circulatory or pulmonary function or disorientation due to a darkened room. Fluctuation during the day is common, with lucid intervals of rational thought and behavior. The degree of impairment may range from slight to total incapacity. Suicidal attempts, and even homicidal ones, may occur. Usually, the illness improves in a week; where a fever is prolonged, the delirium may continue.

As a rule, there is a full recovery from delirium. If there is a serious coincidental illness there may be death, although continuing pathology may also lead to dementia. However, the marked fluctuations of cognitive impairment and lucid intervals with normal orientation and mentation distinguish delirium from dementia. Roth (1976) suggests, then, that it might be expected that a number of persons with chronic recurrent delirious states arising from progressive systemic disease, such as cardiac or respiratory failure, would show a transition to demented states. However, in practice this is very rare and the brains of such persons show cerebral damage within the range found in mentally well-preserved old people. As he comments, it may be possible that such patients do not survive long enough for cerebral anoxia and other effects of systemic disease to cause cerebral damage sufficient to produce progressive deterioration. Wolff

and Curran (1935) have pointed to the occasional persistence of residual delusional and paranoid attitudes after a delirium. Moreover, they found that the clinical picture was markedly influenced by the underlying personality.

*Predisposing Factors*

Delirium is more common in children and the aged than in persons of middle age, and in existing brain impairment from any origin, or prolonged sleep deprivation, as well as impaired cerebral circulation and physical illness, all predispose to the condition.

THE ETIOLOGY OF DELIRIUM

The delirious response is only the final common pathway for a multitude of causes. Posner (1975) wisely says that "few situations in clinical medicine confuse and upset the physician so much as when he confronts a patient whose state of consciousness is rapidly changing." Here the physician's "task" is "both enormous and exacting. First he must decide which of three major categories of disease is responsible for the patient's condition:

1. Structural brain disease (e.g., brain tumors, subdural hematomas, cerebral infarctions);
2. 'Functional' brain disease (e.g., schizophrenia, manic-depressive psychosis);
3. Metabolic brain disease or delirium."

This diagnostic dilemma is even more complicated in aged delirious patients, who lack many of the positive features of delirium in the younger ones. All too often the diagnostic process is abandoned and the patient is consigned to senile psychosis. Libow (1973), who draws attention to the acute, potentially reversible mental changes which he calls pseudosenility, points to the study of Epstein and Simon, where, in a general hospital, of those patients over 60 years admitted for psychiatric screening because of abnormal function, 13 percent had acute brain syndrome and 33 percent had combined acute and chronic brain syndrome (Epstein and Simon, 1967). According to Libow, who discusses the matter more fully in this volume, the following are the most important causes of delirium:

*Medications*

The forgetfulness of the elderly lends itself unkindly to self-administration of multiple medications they are often prescribed (Libow and Mehl, 1970; Schwartz, Wang, Zeitz, and Goss, 1962). The need for calendar packs has been emphasized by many researchers and, hopefully, the pharmaceutical companies will introduce them, just as they have for contraceptive pills. The "paper bag test" is often used; elderly patients are invited to bring all their medications with them and the paper bag is sometimes quite a large sack.

All drugs that act on the central nervous system, especially sedatives, are likely to cause delirium, especially in the presence of marginal cerebral oxygenation. L-dopa, indomethacin, and steroids may produce delirium, as may diuretics, through dehydration.

## Metabolic Imbalance

Inadequate fluid intake in a severely ill or mentally impaired patient leads to electrolyte disturbances. Azotemia and uremia may be accompanied by delirium; and, not infrequently, a urinary infection, which may or may not be associated with an underlying chronic mild pyelonephritis, may usher in the syndrome. In elderly males obstruction of urine, secondary to benign prostatic enlargement, is also quite common.

Either hyperglycemia or hypoglycemia in diabetes, where there is a diminished food intake related to physical or mental illness or reduced hepatic or renal function may lead to delirious symptoms.

Abnormality of thyroid, either hypothyroidism, referred to as "myxedematous madness", or hyperthyroidism may present as a delirium. In the elderly, this latter may present with apathy and depression, the so-called apathetic hyperthyroidism.

## Malnutritional States

As Libow points out, these occur in at least 10 percent of older people in the United States. In particular, there is a deficiency of at least three of the four important vitamins (thiamine, riboflavin, ascorbic acid, and vitamin A).

## Intracranial Tumors

Metastatic tumors originating mostly from the lung and breast account for almost half of all brain tumors seen in a general hospital. Focal signs are often slow to develop because of the enlarged intracranial space due to cerebral atrophy. Thus, subdural hematoma in older persons is frequently insidious and, as Perlmutter (1961) points out, a person who has been merely increasingly drowsy over a period of days may suddenly slip into an irreversible coma. Also, papilledema occurs in only 11 percent of brain tumor cases in the elderly. Nevertheless, the brain scan often gives positive results in an intracerebral tumor in 94 percent of cases and in subdural hematoma in 86 percent (Friedman and Odom, 1972). Similarly, patients

with questionable or mild atrophy may be shown to have other potentially treatable illnesses, such as hyperthyroidism and pernicious anemia (Jacob, Topel, and Huckman, 1975).

## Cirrhosis of the Liver or Hepatitis.

## Cardiovascular Disease

Any condition causing diminished cardiac output, whether due to heart failure or arrhythmia, will precipitate delirium. Profound anemia is a potential contributor to cerebral hypoxia.

## Cerebrovascular Accidents

These are dealt with more fully under multi-infarct dementia; they frequently are ushered in by a delirium.

## Fever.

## Pulmonary Disease

Emphysema is one of the most common.

## Acute Alcoholic Intoxication

This is often superimposed on chronic alcoholism, with or without a persisting dementia. Alcoholism is common in the elderly, and one-third of older patients considered for commitment to state psychiatric hospitals have a background of excessive drinking (Epstein and Simon, 1967).

The differential diagnosis of delirium encompasses a large part of the practice of medicine, but the insidious onset of the so-called "silent symptoms of disease" in the elderly further obfuscates the picture. Barbiturate or alcohol withdrawal symptoms and acute liver necrosis may cause an agitated delirium, in contrast to uremia, pulmonary disease, and anoxia, where there is a quiet and apathetic withdrawal. The more rapid the illness, the more likely, in general, is there to be agitation. When the causes are not clear, the first conditions to consider are *hypoxia, hypoglycemia,* and *metabolic acidosis.* Posner (1975) points out that unless all three are promptly treated they are potentially rapidly lethal and, in the first two cases, very quickly damage the brain irreversibly.

Rarely is there a single cause for delirium in the aged. Usually there are multiple defects, some of which produce the delirium. A common example is the elderly patient with mild congestive heart failure, anemia, and hypoxia who is given diuretics and sedative drugs for agitation, thus causing an electrolyte imbalance. In patients who have symptoms of relatively short duration, or where there is a minor head injury involved, a subdural hematoma should always be considered.

Postoperative delirium is not infrequent in

the aged. Metabolic imbalance, fever, anoxia, post-anesthetic effects and disorientation from unfamiliar surroundings all contribute to its genesis. To all this may be added the specific defects of deafness or loss of sight, such as the familiar post-cataract confusional state.

## EXAMINATION OF THE PATIENT IN DELIRIUM

The province of deliria is obviously that of the internist. Nevertheless, more and more such patients stray into the fold of mental health facilities. The history from a reliable informant, particularly that of the medical illnesses and all drugs taken, prescribed or not, is most important. General physical examination should look particularly for evidence of trauma, systemic illness, and the state of respiratory ventilation.

Posner stresses the importance of the presence of focal weakness or abnormal movements. Tremor in delirious patients is coarse and irregular, usually at a rate of about 8 to 10 per second. It is usually absent at complete rest and is not specific. However, asterixis and multiple myoclonus, especially if bilateral, is rare and seldom seen, except in deliria. *Asterixis* is described by Posner as an abnormal involuntary jerking movement elicited in the hands by asking the patient to dorsaflex the wrist and spread the extended fingers; the movements may also involve the feet and tongue. Such movements need to be distinguished from tardive dyskinesia. *Multifocal myoclonus* consists of sudden, non-rhythmic, non-patterned gross muscle contractions in a resting person. The movements are most common in the face and jaws but can occur elsewhere in the body. It is seen most commonly in cases of uremia, hypercarbicanoxic encephalopathy, and penicillin overdose, but can occur in most metabolic encephalopathies.

Seizures, weakness, and hyperactive stretch reflexes frequently accompany severe metabolic brain disease. These are usually generalized, and the motor abnormalities are usually symmetrical. Nevertheless, focal pareses and focal seizures may occur, but they are usually fleeting.

Pupillary light reactions are preserved in metabolic coma, and the absence of a pupillary light reaction strongly suggests a structural lesion. However, anticholinergic drugs may produce fixed dilated pupils, which are also seen in severe anoxia or asphyxia.

## INVESTIGATIONS

Posner's (1975) summary of the essential tests is presented in Table 24–1. Those performed immediately establish the presence of life-threatening metabolic defects; others may be done later if the diagnosis is unclear.

### Electroencephalogram

There is non-specific bilateral symmetrical slowing. There may frequently be superimposed bilateral synchronous paroxysmal bursts of one-to three-per-second activity upon a background of mildly slow five-to-seven cps. A normal EEG is incompatible with severe delirium, and an EEG with focal or unilateral slow activity strongly suggests a structural disease (Engel and Romano, 1959).

### TREATMENT

As Posner points out, metabolic brain disease can be definitively treated only by correcting the systemic disorder responsible for the delirium. How effective this treatment is, in turn, determines the prognosis of the delirium. However, this delirium is somewhat slower in clearing than is the systemic illness. He points to certain general therapeutic measures applicable to all delirious patients. These are (1) to ensure oxygenation, (2) to maintain circulation, (3) to give blood glucose, (4) to restore acid base balance, (5) to treat infection, (6) to control body temperature, and (7) to stop seizures.

An adequate airway and oxygenation must be assured, and extra oxygen should be given to mildly hypoxic patients; transfusions should be given to those with significant anemia. An intake and output chart of both food and fluid is essential; parenteral fluid and glucose may be necessary. Vital signs and state of consciousness must be checked frequently and charted.

**Table 24–1**   Laboratory Evaluation of Metabolic Brain Disease

| TEST | REASON FOR TEST |
| --- | --- |
| *Immediate* | |
| Glucose | Hypoglycemia, hyperosmolar coma |
| Na+ | Osmolar abnormalities |
| Ca++ | Hyper- or hypocalcemia |
| BUN | Uremia |
| pH, $Pco_2$ | Acidosis, alkalosis |
| $Po_2$ | Hypoxia |
| Lumbar puncture | Infection, hemorrhage |
| *Later:* | |
| Liver function tests | Hepatic coma |
| Sedative drug levels | Overdose |
| Blood and CSF culture | Sepsis, encephalitis, meningitis |
| Full electrolytes, including Mg++ | Electrolyte imbalance |
| EEG | |

*General Measures*

A quiet, single room away from the unfamiliar noises and activity of a general ward is helpful. A single sitter, who may be a relative or friend, helps delirious patients orient themselves. Physicians and nurses can reassure the patient by introducing themselves and telling him the time and where he is. Rooms should be well-lighted and the light should be kept burning at night, because darkness accentuates disorientation and hallucinations.

## DEMENTIA

Dementia, although usually defined as an irreversible decline of mental functions, is not necessarily so clear-cut. Thus, cerebral tumor, hypothyroidism, and neurosyphilis may all cause dementia which may be arrested or even reversed. Dementia is more a descriptive term for a clinical syndrome than an etiological or prognostic diagnosis. Most important is to distinguish the *treatable* causes of dementia from the *untreatable* ones, and here early diagnosis is both critical and difficult. This has led Kiloh (1961) to observe that "any suggestion that the illness is of short duration virtually eliminates the possibility of dementia; and exceptions to this rule are rare." The problem lies in the fact that early, subtle changes in mental function can only be seen in comparison to the individual's premorbid function. In his superb book on dementia, Wells (1977) borrows "the finest first-hand description of the onset and progression of a dementing process published"—a daughter's account of her father.

> Here she points to the elusiveness of symptoms and signs which vanished when she tried to pin them down. 'I was left with a feeling of uneasiness which I could not justify. In the beginning, I became gradually aware that the fine edge of his intellect was becoming dulled. He was less clear in discussion, less quick to make the jump from a new piece of evidence to its possible significance ... Later, he remained himself, but a self that was subtly devitalized.'

There are many definitions of dementia. As good a one as any is "dementia is a symptom arising from cerebral disease, often progressive, which is characterized by a decline of intellect and personality, which reflects a disturbance of memory, orientation and capacity for conceptual thought and often of affect" (Pearce and Miller, 1973).

Gustafson and Hagberg (1975) well summarized the various symptoms of dementia:

1. *Amnesia.* Reduced learning, retention, and recall of recent events and remote past. Confabulation.
2. *Disturbances of attention and concentration.*
3. *Lack of initiative and spontaneity.*
4. *Reduced stock of ideas.* Stereotypy and impoverishment of thoughts and associations.
5. *Increased reactivity. Extreme selectiveness of stimuli.* Inability to survey, integrate and analyze information. Tendency toward catastrophic reactions.
6. *Disturbances of consciousness.*
7. *Disorientation.*
8. *Affective disturbances.* Emotional shallowness. Reduction of general interests and awareness of own illness. Affective bluntness. Euphoria. Affective lability. Increased irritability.
9. *Suspiciousness and paranoid tendencies.*
10. *Aphasia.* Various disturbances of language.
11. *Agnosia.* Inability to understand nonverbal symbols.
12. *Apraxia.* Incapacity for carrying out purposeful movements.

By using a formal rating scale in 57 patients with presenile dementia, they were able to divide such clinical symptoms into a number of factors which they considered were useful both for qualitative and quantitative descriptions. In fact, these symptom clusters were correlated with regional cerebral blood flow. Thus, in "psychomotor overactivity-euphoria," which represented disinhibition and loss of insight and was found in the most deteriorated patients, there was a low blood flow in the frontal region and a relatively high post-central flow. In contrast, paranoid symptoms, which were independent of cognitive reduction, revealed a low flow in the temporo-occipital area and a higher flow in the frontal region.

Roth points to the seminal work of Goldstein (1942) in illuminating thought processes in brain damage. He describes two "attitudes"—(1) a concrete one in which "we are bound" to the immediate experience, object or situation, and (2) the abstract one in which we are oriented to a conceptual point of view "determined not so much by the objects before us as by what we think about them."

This abstract attitude allows planning ahead and thinking symbolically. Whereas the normal person can assume either mind set and shift voluntarily, the demented patient is relatively incapable of assuming the abstract attitude and cannot shift at will from the concrete to the abstract. However, loss of abstract thinking is not specific of brain damage, nor can the effects of brain damage be simplified into mere disturbance of abstract thinking (Zangwill, 1964).

Goldstein's concepts, although possibly outdated, are helpful in day-to-day dealings and accord a distinction that has been used between "fluid" and "crystallized" intelligence in Cattell's 1943 terminology (Cattell, 1943). Similarly, Halstead (1943) found that tests that showed greatest impairment were those in which the subject could not use old mental habits and had to adapt to new and unfamiliar situations and ways of thinking. However, later work by Hopkins and Post (1955) showed that very few elderly subjects with functional psychiatric disorders and few even of elderly normals were able to produce consistently abstract sorting. This suggests that concrete thinking may not, in any sense, merely be specific to the aging demented patient but only to differ in degree from his normally aged peer.

Finally, to such cognitive shifts are added changes in behavior as the patient attempts to master his awareness of his defects. Paradoxically, the more partial the defect, the more difficult it is for the person to suppress it (Goldstein, 1942).

## CLINICAL MANIFESTATIONS OF DEMENTIA

It is not easy to provide a clinical description, which perforce has to be a longitudinal one, of a disease with insidious onset. As in so many clinical descriptions, the usual presentation will be a "forme fruste," in which only part of the whole is seen. Nevertheless as Gurland emphasizes in this volume, longitudinal observations are crucial to the differential diagnoses of the dementias.

### Appearance

The patient may be as neat and spruce as ever but neglect some minor detail in his clothing. The classical Scottish sign, adapted to the new world, is "porridgium vestitutum," which loosely translated might be "porridge on the vest." Occasional spots of soup on the tie of the previous immaculate professional man may be more revealing than careful examination. An accentuation or alteration of premorbid personality traits may lead to a caricature of the person: the stubborn man, stubborner; the taciturn one, more silent; the garrulous one, more talkative. Father is the same as ever only more so.

It is very common for there to be a lack of energy, enthusiasm, interest, and concern for work, family, or recreation.

### Orientation

There is often an increasing impairment with retention of personal identity but with time frequently being misidentified. The ordering of the calendar for a retired or aged person assumes much less significance than for a younger. As many dementias are ushered in by a change in the life,

such as the death of a relative or a new illness or an inability of the relatives to care for the person, sudden social change may well lead to the difficulty of orienting to a new place.

### Affect

Lability of affect is common but usually there is a lowered frustration level and some increase in anxiety. Most notable and most difficult in the differential diagnosis is the presence of depression. Depression is not infrequently associated with dementia and this is discussed more fully under differential diagnosis.

Goldstein (1942) emphasized how the "catastrophic reaction" modifies the reaction. Thus, the patient, when exposed to situations with which he cannot cope, easily becomes anxious, agitated, sullen, angry or evasive. He characteristically seeks to remove himself from such situations, which may lead to solitary withdrawal. The anger often is excessive and slow to subside.

### Memory

Although this is cardinal to this disorder and is usually an impairment of new learning, it is seldom complained of by the patient. Far more common is the complaint a symptom of depression (Gurland, Fleiss, Goldberg, Sharpe, Copeland, Kelleher, and Kellet, 1976; Kahn, Zarit, Hilbert, and Niederehe, 1975). If the memory impairment is also slow and insidious, it may be overlooked by relatives.

### Thinking Process

There is often an increased preoccupation with self, with much hypochondriasis. Again, it is difficult to distinguish such hypochondriacal preoccupation from depressive illness of the aged. Usually in the latter there is associated loss of weight, appetite and impairment of sleep and, frequently, a diurnal rhythm of symptoms. More importantly, the relatives believe that the patient is sad, in contrast to some subtle differentiation of not being themselves, which may be more a blunting of drive, enthusiasm and personal warmth. The commingling of depression with dementia makes the differentiation extremely difficult at times.

### Delusions

With progression of the disease, the impairment of memory and difficulty of integrating information may lead to delusions, which may be changing and unorganized and commonly fearful and concerned with robbery or deprivation.

*Obsessive-compulsive symptoms* may become manifest, often for the first time in a person's life.

"Organic orderliness," in which a person orders their own life or even the life of their family because of their own recognition of their failing memory, may be present even in the early stages.

### Insight

Awareness of failing function and especially of memory is rare in patients, except in very early stages.

### Judgment

The incapacity to pay attention and to learn the new details of life lead increasingly to faulty and impaired and sometimes grossly aberrant decision making.

### CLINICAL COURSE

Dementia is seldom abrupt, unless ushered in by a cerebral catastrophe, but is more usually gradual and progressive. It may, however, become relatively static and progress intermittently. Appropriate behavior becomes rarer, and the affect of the patient is often labile, with easy shifting from sadness to equanimity or anger. Disinhibition of emotions and impulses often leads to socially embarrassing behavior.

Thinking often becomes increasingly disruptive with suspicion heightening into paranoid delusions. There is increasing self-centeredness, increased obtundity and decreased understanding. The patient may become easily lost and gradually has trouble either understanding or following directions and often loses his train of thought. Some patients become restless and overactive, but more commonly, there is a lethargy and a general withdrawal.

To this scene are added the specific defects of neurological function whereby apraxia, aphasia and signs of motor and sensory impairment compound the picture.

In the end stage, the patient is mostly apathetic, grossly disoriented in place and time, with defective memory in all phases, and unable to care for his personal appearance or even such simple functions as eating. They are often doubly incontinent.

### DIFFERENTIAL DIAGNOSIS

### Delirium

If global cognitive impairment has persisted unchanged or has increased for one month or longer, the diagnosis of dementia, which of course may be ushered in by a delirium, is usually made.

In the delirium are fluctuations in the level of consciousness, in contrast to the more stable impairment of dementia. Hallucinations are more common in delirium. Continued or increasing intellectual deficits in the presence of a normal or normalizing electroencephalogram suggest dementia.

### Affective Disturbance

In the earlier stages of dementia, anxieties and depression may suggest a neurotic disturbance. Although the neurotic person may complain of impaired memory, there is usually no loss of new learning on testing, nor of orientation. The judgmental defect is different in the two. In dementia, this is usually the result of the inability to grasp the varying aspects of a problem, which are necessary to reach a decision. In a neurotic disturbance of old age, it is more likely that emotional preoccupation merely handicaps the patient in paying attention to details of which he or she is quite aware. The vagueness and apathy of early dementia, before precise demonstration of disturbance of intellectual functioning, may mimic depressive illness.

As the dementia progresses, the differentiation from a serious depression may be extremely challenging (Kiloh, 1961). Usually, a depressive illness is more sudden in onset, with a clearer history of a recent deterioration. In most cases, orientation and new learning can be demonstrated to be unimpaired. However, this is difficult when the patient is very retarded, and Sternberg and Jarvik (1976) have demonstrated marked impairment in short-term memory in depression. Biological features of a depression, such as loss of appetite, loss of weight, poor sleep, early morning awakening, constipation and dry mouth, are more pronounced in depression. The mood disturbance tends to be more marked but may be masked by the patient's preoccupation with the physical aspects of his illness. At times the diagnosis is so obscure that it may be necessary to treat the patient for depression before assessing whether there is or not an underlying dementia. This has even led Snowdon (1972) to suggest that all demented patients be treated with antidepressants. This suggestion is based on the fact that the 25 percent of patients with dementia who may be depressed may be identified by a trial of therapy and, perhaps more importantly, can be successfully treated. Mattis (1976) suggests that a useful diagnostic strategy lies in repeated psychological evaluation. Demented patients, after three to six months, almost invariably show regression in psychological function. In contrast, the depressed patient either is stable or shows improved functioning. Fleiss, Gurland, and Des Roche (1976) have shown that their Geriatric Mental Status Interview effectively discriminated those with organic brain disease from those with functional psychiatric disorder. The former scored significantly higher on impaired memory, disorientation, and incomprehensibility, and lower on depression and somatic concerns. Gurland, in this volume, discusses the diagnostic value of mood scales, preferring the Zung Self Rating Depression Scale to others.

An hysterical reaction is the most common neurotic syndrome to complicate dementing processes. Sixty percent of Slater's series of 85 patients given a diagnosis of hysteria at a neurological hospital (Slater, 1961) proved to have a neurological illness.

Duckworth and Ross (1975) have shown that there is a tendency in the United States to diagnose most elderly psychiatric patients as demented, in contrast to diagnostic patterns seen in Toronto or London. In the United States functional psychoses were overlooked, in particular affective illness, mainly depression. However, with appropriate treatment, an excellent outcome is possible. The authors comment that such poor diagnostic habits deny the patient appropriate treatment for curable ills. Nevertheless, Kelleher *et al.* (1976) showed that although elderly patients with affective disorder were less likely to be given antidepressants in American than in British hospitals, the outcome of the American patient was as good, if not better, than the British ones. This illustrated the "natural recuperative powers" of the elderly depressed patients and, of course, the good prognoses of most depressions. It is reassuring to know that a common illness gets better in spite of misdiagnosis.

It is also important to remember that some 10 percent of cases of depression in old age are ushered in with a short-lived confusional or delirious phase which subsides within a relatively short time to reveal the underlying affective disorder (Slater and Roth, 1977). Often, this is due to some associated febrile or metabolic disturbance, which in itself may be complicated by under-nutrition.

Physical illness is frequent in all psychiatric disabilities in the aged (Kay and Roth, 1955; Roth and Kay, 1956). It may be difficult to diagnose with inconspicuous and muted symptoms and, thus, attributed merely to the mental disturbance.

Kahn *et al.* (1975) showed that the complaint of disturbed memory was more related to the level of depression than the actual degree of cognitive impairment. In some instances, persons who complained about memory actually functioned better than those who did not. Post (1975) cites a number of long-term follow-up studies, including his own, which show that few depressions in the old proceed to dementia (Post, 1962; Post, 1972; Roth, 1955).

*Schizophrenia*

Differentiation from schizophrenia is somewhat easier. In the schizophrenic who has grown old and suffers a coincidental dementia, there is usually a history of the nuclear symptoms of schizophrenia. More difficult is the schizophrenia of late onset, the so-called paraphrenia. Here, those patients whose symptoms resemble paranoid reactions may merely be suffering from an accentuation of their previous suspicious personality with irritability, bad temper and hypochondriasis. In others, more overt disturbance of thought, delusions and hallucinations are present in a setting of clearer consciousness and greater fluidity than usually occurs in dementia. Again, it is important to diagnose this group, as the majority respond well to antipsychotic drugs (Post, 1975). Post, in this volume, more fully reviews this syndrome.

THE ETIOLOGY OF DEMENTIA

All etiological classifications of the diseases presenting as dementia tend to be approximate. A definite diagnosis can be reached only in about half of all demented patients, despite comprehensive investigation (Marsden and Harrison, 1972). In Marsden's series, some 15 percent of the patients suffered from conditions which were amenable to treatment. Even pathological study does not necessarily always provide positive identification (Hughes, Myers, Smith, and Torack, 1973).

McDonald (1969) has pointed out that controversies center around whether to define dementia by its social criteria—namely, failures of activities of everyday life, or in global impressionistic terms—mental decay—or in terms of subfunctions, such as intellectual capacity and memory, or the supposed etiology.

Karasu and Katzman (1976) consider that if Alzheimer's disease is the primary cause of intellectual deterioration in both presenile and senile brain disease and also in those patients with mixed vascular and Alzheimer's picture, then almost from 90–100,000 deaths per year could be attributed to it. This would make the disorder the fourth or fifth most common cause of death—causing about the same number of deaths as those due to accidents but less than the number attributed to heart disease, cancer or stroke. Thus, they emphasize that in this disorder, one is dealing with a disease that is responsible for a significant portion of the morbidity and early mortality of the aged.

The next most frequent cause is vascular disease. Although this was held to be common in the past, better interpretation of the pathological changes has downplayed its role. Malamud and Waggoner (1943) showed that, amongst 1225 cases of organic brain disease autopsied in a mental hospital, 42 percent had senile disease (Alzheimer's), 29 percent had arteriosclerotic brain disease, and 23 percent had a mixed senile and arteriosclerotic disease picture. However, the much better, later study of Tomlinson (Tomlinson, Blessed, and Roth, 1970) showed that, in a study of 50 consecutive demented elderly patients coming to autopsy, Alzheimer's disease accounted for 50 percent of the cases, contributed equally with infarction in 8 percent, and possibly played some role in 10 percent. Cerebral changes due to arteriosclerosis, on the other hand, accounted definitely for only 12 percent, probably for an additional 6 percent, and contributed equally with Alzheimer's disease in 8 percent, and possibly played some role in 10 percent. Thus, degenerative disease played a far more important role in the genesis of dementia than did vascular disease. Wells (1978) points out that this has also been corroborated in three recent clinical studies, and in only 8 percent of these patients was vascular disease identified as the cause of dementia. Fifty-one percent were diagnosed as having atrophy of unknown causes, either presenile or senile Alzheimer's in most cases. Haase (1977), in his excellent and comprehensive review of diseases presenting as dementia, delineates the wide range of potential causes. Karasu and Katzman (1976) have noted how rarely, in reality, many of these cases reach the psychiatrist and neurologist. While this is undoubtedly so, it is salutary to remember Wells' warning that Geschwind has been recently quoted as estimating that perhaps 40 percent of chronically hospitalized psychiatric patients suffer primarily from unrecognized physical "brain disorders" (Clark and Gosnell, 1976)! Seltzer and Sherwin (1978) showed that in 80 randomly picked patients suffering from organic brain syndrome in a VA hospital, there was a wide range of diagnoses. Although senile dementia and alcoholic dementia and Korsakoff's syndrome were commonest, there was enough diversity of other diagnoses to give second thoughts to the classification. Marsden and Harrison (1972) found that of 106 patients admitted with presumptive diagnosis of dementia, only 84 were conclusively demonstrated to be so. Of the 15 who were discovered not to be demented but to have some other illness, depression was found most commonly, followed by drug toxicity. Of the 84 demented patients, 48 were shown to have cerebral atrophy of unknown cause, followed by in-

tracranial mass lesions, arterial disease and alcoholism. Freemon (1976) showed that 18 (30 percent) of 60 consecutive patients with progressive intellectual deterioration had treatable disease. Of these, seven had normal pressure hydrocephalous; five, chronic drug toxicity; two, resectable intracranial mass lesions; one, a depressive illness; one, syphilis of the central nervous system; one, hepatic failure; and another, hyperthyroidism. Further, 16 patients (27 percent) were specifically diagnosed as follows: five with multi-infarct dementia, four with alcoholic dementia, and four with Huntington's chorea. Of three others, one had anglio blastoma, one had mental changes following severe head trauma, and the other had herpes simplex encephalitis. The remaining 26 patients were accorded no specific diagnosis and suffered, presumably, Alzheimer's disease. Freemon emphasized the value of the radioisotope brain scan discovering the cases of subdural hematoma with the pneumoencephalogram discovering the normal pressure hydrocephalus (these would now be replaced by tomography), the thyroid function screen and the liver function studies.

These two studies reveal that, although common things occur commonly, uncommon things should not be forgotten, especially when they are not all that uncommon.

Thus, the diseases to be aware of are, certainly, normal pressure hydrocephalus, drug or alcoholic toxicity, subdural hematomas and depressive illness. Rarer are the dementias associated with hyper- or hypothyroidism, subacute combined degeneration of the cord, other intracranial mass lesions, or herpes simplex encephalitis. Diseases causing well-marked neurological symptoms, such as Creutzfeldt-Jakob or Huntington's, are not likely to be missed. However, in the present climate of interest and frequency of tardive dyskinesia, Huntington's chorea may be misdiagnosed as this disease.

## Diffuse Parenchymatous Diseases of the Central Nervous System

### Alzheimer's Disease and Pick's Disease

Katzman (1976) argues that both Alzheimer's disease and senile dementia are progressive dementias, with similar changes in the mental and neurological signs that are indistinguishable by careful clinical analyses (Neumann and Cohn, 1963; Newton, 1948). The pathological findings, he says, are identical: atrophy of the brain, minor loss of neurons, neurofibrillary tangles, granulovacuolar changes and neuritic (senile) plaques. Ultrastructural studies, he says, have established the identity of the neurofibrillary tangle with its twisted tubule, and senile plaque with its amyloid core and degenerating neurites, in the brains of patients with Alzheimer's disease (under the age of 65) and senile dementia (over the age of 65). He continues that the evidence on which the distinction between senile dementia and Alzheimer's disease can still be argued is the genetic analysis of Larsson, Sjogren, and Jacobson (1963). In their analysis of the kindred of patients with senile dementia, numerous relatives were found with senile dementia, but none with the diagnosis of Alzheimer's disease. However, the incidence of the Alzheimer's senile dementia complex is strongly age related, even amongst the elderly. Larsson had suggested a predisposing autosomal dominant gene with age related penetrance, reaching a penetrance of 40 percent at age 90. Therefore, the absence of any relatives with "Alzheimer's disease" might be related to its relative infrequency in patients under 65. Moreover, in a genetic study carried out in Switzerland, Constantinidis, Garrone, and Ajuriaguerra (1962) encountered two of these diseases in the same family. Katzman urges that, although further studies are clearly indicated, the majority of workers in the field should now accept the identity of the two diseases (Fisher, 1968).

Slater and Roth (1977), while agreeing to a unitary theory of Alzheimer's and senile dementia, caution that final conclusions must await further systematic observation. In support of their homogeneity, they suggest that Sjogren's (Sjogren, Sjogren, and Lindgren, 1952) concept of "threshold phenomenon" may explain the clinical differences between normal senescence, senile dementia, and Alzheimer's disease; as the accumulation of pathological changes reaches certain levels, qualitatively distinct phenomena may make their appearance. These could also be expected to show some variation with the age at which the condition becomes manifest. They believe that disorders of this group are best defined in clinical terms. If the conditions which produce highly specific neurological signs, such as Creutzfeldt-Jakob disease and Huntington's chorea, are set aside, they say, the remaining disorders mainly fall into the two fairly clearly defined groups of Pick's and Alzheimer's disease. Most of these commence between the ages of 40 and 60.

Roth maintains the distinction of Pick's disease in both its specific pathology, its causation by a dominant autosomal gene (Sjogren *et al.*, 1952), and its clinical manifestations. He stresses that amnesic aphasia, apraxia, and agraphia are less frequent in Pick's than Alzheimer's. On the whole, he

says, the picture in Alzheimer's disease tends, in the earliest stage, to be dominated by parietal lobe symptoms and, in Pick's disease, by frontal lobe symptoms. The vague resemblance of the former to senile dementia and the latter to dementia paralytica (neurosyphilis) also helps distinction. Disturbances of gait and muscle tone, typical in Alzheimer's and rare in Pick's, are reliable in distinguishing between them, and the occurrence of epileptic seizures is also uncommon in Pick's disease.

Haase (1977), however, is somewhat skeptical. He cites the extensive body of literature claiming differences which are either based on a small series of cases or disputed by other writers. Moreover, he points out that the clinician confronted with a patient with dementia in middle life will not receive much assistance from these indicators. Thus, he concludes that criteria to separate these diseases on clinical grounds (Alpers, 1936; Sim and Sussman, 1962; Sjogren *et al.*, 1952; Stevens and Forster, 1953) are not universally accepted, and the possibility of separation on the basis of clinical and neuroradiological features is denied or described as extremely difficult by others (Alpers and Mancall, 1971; Merritt, 1973; Neumann and Cohn, 1953). Pick's is certainly a much rarer disease, and there are few psychiatrists or neurologists who have much first hand experience. As Terry (1976) points out:

> Most American neurologists do not differentiate clinically between Alzheimer and Pick disease, but the European clinicians often do. The lack of parietal lobe signs in Pick disease is said to be most helpful. At least in the American Northeast, this disease seems to be scarcely one-fiftieth as common as Alzheimer pre-senile dementia, so the differential diagnosis must, at least statistically, be heavily weighted toward the latter.

He adds:

> Most recent observers of the histological changes, either electron or light microscopists, have been remarkably reticent about drawing pathogenetic inferences from their findings.

Patients with Down's syndrome appear to have a high incidence of Alzheimer's disease, especially if they survive beyond 40. Familial occurrence has been described in both diseases; usually Alzheimer's is regarded as multifactorially inherited, in contrast to Pick's, where there is suggested a dominant autosomal motive inheritance (Sjogren *et al.*, 1952). Heston and Mastri (1977) found that the relatives of probands with histologically confirmed Alzheimer's disease not only had excessive morbidity from Alzheimer's disease itself but also

Down's syndrome and hematological malignancy. This has been reported previously and the histopathological changes of the two syndromes are indistinguishable. There is also a twenty-fold increase of the incidence of leukemia in Down's syndrome. Heston suggests a unitary genetic etiology, possibly expressed through disorganization of the microtubules. Stam (Op Den Velde and Stam, 1973) points to the significantly increased HP1[1] gene frequency in patients with Alzheimer's disease and senile dementia compared with normal individuals. Persons of the HP1[1] genotype also have a greater incidence of leukemia and a poorer immune response than persons of the HP2 genotype (Nevo and Sutton, 1968), and the incidence of trisomy 21 (Down's syndrome) is excessive amongst relatives of patients with Alzheimer's disease. Such findings, he suggests, point to a multifactorial genesis of Alzheimer's disease with the HP1[1] gene considered as a facilitative factor in the etiology of the disease. Harman (Harman, Heidrick, and Eddy, 1977) postulates that endogenous free radical reactions which are impaired in aging may contribute to this poorer immune response.

So-called familial Alzheimer's disease has twice been transmitted to lower animals (Gajdusek and Gibbs, Jr., 1975). This suggests either a different form of Alzheimer's disease or a variant of a type of Creutzfeldt-Jakob disease, which may be familial.

Emotional disturbance in the two illnesses follows the general signs of dementia. Both may develop slowly or proceed rapidly. In Pick's, a blunting of emotion and diminution of drive with fatuous euphoria, diminution of self-restraint and impairment of insight is said to be more characteristic, but a similar picture may occur in Alzheimer's and, in fact, this was found by Sjogren in 15 of his 18 cases at an early stage, in contrast to hyperactivity. Dysphasic defects are less common and occur at a later stage in Pick's than Alzheimer's. In the latter, other parietal lobe symptoms, such as apraxia and agnosia, are commonly associated so that it is difficult to distinguish the separate disabilities. Both expression and comprehension are affected in speech which becomes rapidly disrupted. In both illnesses, the patient may find difficulty in naming. Sentences are left incomplete and words and phrases are jumbled up, and this may lead to an incoherent aphasic jargon. There may be severe dysphasia with other functions well preserved. Varying degrees of dyspraxia are also common and sometimes apraxia is present early. There may be inability to use a knife and fork and loss of other long accustomed actions. Such apraxic symptoms depend upon lesions of the parietal cortex and its deeper connections, especially those with the corpus callosum and comissural fibres.

Agnosic defects are also common with disturbance of spatial orientation. This may lead to distortion of the body image ad difficulty for the individual in finding his way around his own house. Such a patient may get lost in previously familiar surroundings. Apraxia also may depend, in part, upon an agnosic disturbance of space and body image. Such gross focal signs of apraxia and agnosia without generalized intellectual impairment are more commonly the result of a stroke or tumor than cerebral atrophy.

### Motor Disturbances

There may be an early increase of muscle tone or the rigidity of extrapyramidal type. Sometimes, this is described as cogwheel and, sometimes, as a combination between cogwheel and clasp-knife (Sjogren et al., 1952). The gait may become slow, unsteady and clumsy (Sjogren et al., 1952). Such disturbances of gait and muscle tone are much rarer in Pick's disease, as is the incidence of convulsive seizures (Sourander and Sjogren, 1970). Later in the disease, the gait in Alzheimer's may take on the character of "marche à petits pas".

### Course of Disease

In both, as the disease progresses, patients show a profound dementia with apathy, emotional blunting, meaningless speech, and often they present without movement or expression.

### The Diagnostic Value of Neurological Symptoms and Signs

In Alzheimer's disease, particularly, progress of intellectual deterioration is often accompanied by a variety of neurological changes, such as gait disturbances, incontinence, focal weakness, abnormal reflexes, dysphasia, dyspraxia, seizures, myoclonic jerks and, rarely, blindness (Coblentz, Mattis, Zingesser, Kasoff, Wisniewski, and Katzman, 1973).

In considering the diagnostic specificity of the dementias in addition to the loss of memory, deterioration of intellect, change of personality and affective disorder already described, the neurological symptoms become of major importance.

Seltzer and Sherwin (1978) have pleaded for more of a neurological approach leading to greater specificity of diagnosis in so-called organic brain syndromes. "Organic brain syndrome," they maintain, is not a specific neurological diagnosis, although it remains a standard diagnostic category. Thus, they instance the many differing neuropathological processes leading to such a syndrome and the naive belief that such *diverse* processes would express themselves in more or less the same way. This echoes the criticism of the Bonhoeffer-Kraepelin controversy of the generality of the so-called acute exogenous reaction versus the specificity of individual pathogens. They urge that fractionating the diagnosis of organic brain syndromes into more specific categories is essential "if we are to learn more about this group of diseases." "Organic brain syndrome," they suggest, might be considered a term analogous to "heart failure" or "end stage kidney failure." The conjunction of senile dementia and post-traumatic encephalopathy is likely, to produce a syndrome different from the combination of alcoholic dementia and post-traumatic encephalopathy.

Geschwind (1975) has also criticized the tendency to lump organic disorders into categories of acute and chronic brain syndromes. He suggests that such categories are as unacceptable for the brain as would be the diagnosis of chronic myocardiopathy for all forms of chronic heart disease. He emphasizes that "there is no single feature common to all forms of organic brain disease with behavior disorder." He believes that the ability to maintain a fully classical *agitated* depression almost always excludes organic disease. Apathy, however, he points out, is an important feature of many organic disorders and is frequently misinterpreted as a depression. He stresses that incontinence of urine or feces is a major danger signal as it almost never occurs in functional disorders. Although he sums up his chapter as a negative one, he underlines that his intention is to point out that disease of the brain is an important and often treatable cause of behavior disorders.

Lipowski (1975) echoes this approach by urging that selective brain syndromes be labeled according to their predominant psychological impairment or abnormality. They are clearly distinct from the more extensive global syndromes and they point toward focal rather than diffuse cerebral pathology and, thus, have a limited diagnostic value. Moreover, such labeling narrows the range of etiological factors to look for. Finally, and perhaps most importantly, he argues that each syndrome may require specific therapeutic measures to help the patient compensate for and cope with a given circumscribed defect. His suggestions are, of course, embodied in part in the new DSM-III draft classification (1978).

Disturbances of language are important and common in dementia (Critchley, 1964; Stengel, 1943; Stengel, 1964). This usually begins with a general poverty of vocabulary and range of expression leading to speech which becomes concrete, circumlocutory and repetitious. However, definite dysphasic signs may also appear. Stengel (1964)

has suggested that nominal dysphasia occurring in dementia is unlike that occurring in aphasia due to focal lesions, in which the patient usually gives a strong impression that he knows what the object is but just cannot find the right word to apply to it. Critchley (1964) has argued that the demented patient's poverty of speech is due to the inaccessibility of words in his vocabulary. However, this may be merely a function of slowed thought. There also may be ideational perseveration in which phrases and themes tend to appear again and again in spontaneous speech.

Language has certainly been much neglected in psychiatry as a diagnostic aid. Put at its simplest with only a few exceptions, the presence of a language disorder, namely aphasia, indicates disease or destruction of some part of the cerebrum and, specifically, damage to the left hemisphere in the vast majority of people (Geschwind, 1975). For most people, the left hemisphere is essential for verbal tasks, including speech and comprehension of spoken language, reading and writing—namely, aphasia, alexia and agraphia. Sherwin and Geschwind (1978) point to the usefulness of the classification devised by members of the Aphasia unit of the Boston Veterans Administration Hospital. In this scheme, the aphasia is divided according to whether repetition of verbal material is normal or abnormal. Probably, the psychiatrists of the future need to know *how* something is said as much as for many years they have listened carefully to *what* is said.

Thus, differences between speech and language are complicated. As Benson (1975) points out, a patient with a speech disorder knows exactly what he wants to say but mechanical (neuromuscular or nervous) disturbances interfere with his saying it. Writing may or may not be simultaneously involved.

In contrast, language disorders, he says, may be characterized as abnormalities of verbal output in which the patient has difficulty in manipulating the semantic and syntactic structures necessary to express his ideas. Both differ from thought disrder where speech and language are intact but abnormal ideas are expressed.

It is indeed true that the present generation of psychiatrists have tended to shy away from the more specific neurological signs which might have rendered better diagnostic differentiation.

Special Investigations of Dementia
The electroencephalogram does not show specific abnormalities. Absence or reduction of alpha activity is more common in Alzheimer's disease, and there may be theta and delta wave activ-

ity, sometimes in bursts (Gordon and Sim, 1967; Letemendia and Pampiglione, 1958; Liddell, 1958). The EEG may be normal in Pick's disease (Gordon and Sim, 1967; Swain, 1959).

Cerebrospinal fluid is usually normal in both illnesses.

Computerized axial tomography delineates the degree of cortical atrophy and ventricular enlargement and helps rule out other central neurological disease. The pneumoencephalogram may show cerebral atrophy by increased width of sulcal markings and by ventricular enlargement, particularly of the anterior and temporal horns.

Psychological testing is discussed elsewhere in this volume; however, Schreiber, *et. al* (Schreiber, Goldman, Kleinman, Goldfader, and Snow, 1976) have suggested that the Halstead Battery may complement the localization of the clinical diagnosis.

### Senile Dementia

As already described, the clinical picture is similar to, if not indistinguishable from, Alzheimer's disease, although, by definition, its onset is later in life. There is global disintegration of personality, in which impairment of memory is followed by deterioration of intellect and change of personality, with or without focal neurological symptoms and associated affective disorder. The syndrome is contrasted with the more limited changes of intellect and personality of normal aging.

The many controversies between the evidence or not for a qualitative difference in psychological tests in dementia are covered elsewhere in this volume (see chapters by Schonfield, Schaie, and Miller). Kral has argued that two types of memory disturbance can be found in old age (Kral, 1962; Kral, 1966). These he refers to as "benign" and "malignant", the former relatively mild and consisting of the occasional inability to recall certain details of information. In contrast, "malignant" memory impairment is more marked for items of the recent past and whole sequences are lost rather than just details. The malignant form leads to greater progression and females predominate. Kral believes that the benign type is due to difficulties in recall whereas the malignant involves reduction of registration of information. Miller (1977) criticizes this, pointing out that the clinical data do not convincingly demonstrate that he is dealing with two distinct types of memory disorder, but rather, merely describing the milder and more advanced forms of the same process. Certainly, the demonstrations by both Kay *et al.* (1966) and Wigdor and Kral (1961) of increased mortality in those

suffering the benign forgetfulness suggests a progressive organic disorder.

### Etiology

Kay, Beamish, and Roth (1964) found advanced age to be the main etiological factor. However, extracerebral disease sometimes was a primary cause of mental symptoms or aggravated those due to other causes. Nevertheless, sensory defects and inadequate diet due to poverty and isolation seemed to be more part of the age itself than major causes of the illness. Similarly, in only a small number of cases did social isolation seem to have aggravated the mental state.

There is a strong suggestion of a hereditary factor, and Larsson, Sjogren, and Jacobson (1963) showed that sibs, parents and children of subjects of senile dementia showed a morbid risk for this condition 4.3 times greater than any corresponding segment of the general population.

The significance of the pathological changes found in the senile brain and their relationship to dementia is discussed more thoroughly by Adams in this volume. In general, it can be said that the changes of arteriosclerotic cerebrovascular disease and senile dementia are distinct, any overlap occurring by chance in two common conditions (Blessed, Tomlinson, and Roth, 1968; Corsellis, 1962). Moreover, Roth, Tomlinson, and Blessed (1967) and Blessed *et al.* (1968) found a highly significant correlation between deterioration of intellectual functioning on psychological tests and the mean plaque count found in those who came to post-mortem. This involved patients with a variety of psychiatric disorders and normal elderly subjects and suggested that the plaque was related to psychological deterioration and cut across diagnostic categories. However, as Adams discusses, such changes cannot be regarded as specifically due to age alone.

There are a few patients with dementia in both presenium and senium in whom neither significant Alzheimer changes nor evidence of major cerebrovascular or other pathology is present. The term simple senile atrophy has been recommended (McMenemey, 1966).

### Clinical Features

Usually, the onset is after the age of 70 and is more common in females, which may be partly due to their high rate of survival.

The progress is gradual and shows the general features of dementia. The patient dwells more on the past and shows greater forgetfulness and apathetic interest in day to day events. The previous avid reader of the newspaper and watcher of television sits idly in front of the unread paper or aimlessly in front of the television screen whose program content he ignores. The preoccupation with the past may lead to misidentification of present familiar surroundings with those of childhood. Often, there is a logical plausibility in this, as though visual engrams are retained in the brain— the low hills of coastal California being confused with those of the lowlands of Scotland, six thousand miles and nearly a century apart. This stage may rapidly progress to a disorientation for house and neighborhood and, eventually, even of the room in which the person spends the most time. At this time, there are often other agnosias and apraxias, especially of dressing.

Loss of urinary control often occurs early, to be followed by fecal incontinence. It is very characteristic for such persons to "deny" or to be "unaware" of such incontinence. Frequently, there are implausible explanations, such as, "The cat wet the bed," or "The rain came through the roof," which may serve to preserve the person's face in their own eyes. Wells (1977) underlines how necessary such defenses are to the patient whose mind is disintegrating. Denial is therapeutic, he says, and should be aided by the physician. Of course, it is usually not the physician on whom the brunt of the care falls but rather the family or nursing attendants. They, in turn, need support and reassurance that occasional expostulations at "bad behavior" are quite understandable.

Post (1965) comments on the psychological mechanisms operating in elderly patients. Many of these reactions are responses to stress either in a test or real life situation. He quotes the studies of Katz (Katz, Neal, and Simon, 1961), who conceptualizes the mechanisms as:

1. Warding off or anticipatory control;
2. Time buying delaying tactics to allow the patient time to come up with the correct answer;
3. Coping with failure, failure rarely being accepted but instead being rationalized and explained away; reminiscence as frequent substitute response or, where there was even more anxiety, inappropriate behavior or defenses, such as that "Well, I don't pay attention to that" or "Ask my husband, son, daughter"; disturbed and disruptive responses which are similar to the catastrophic reactions described by Goldstein; and even disintegrative responses, such as delusions, illusions, hallucinations.

Post expands on such defenses into the relationship between the symptomatology of dementia and the previous personality. In one study, only 30 of 79 consecutive admissions for senile or arteriosclerotic dementia had normal previous personalities, and only eight of this group with normal personalities had psychotic symptoms in addition to the dementia (Post, 1944).

The narrowing of interest and diminution of energy, with blunting of affect or shallow depression, may episodically be replaced by irritability, disinhibition and temper tantrums. Hoarding of food and possessions often occurs and, frequently, suspicions due to misplaced objects or food lead to ideas of reference or paranoid delusions.

Gradually, and sometimes rapidly, the patient becomes more muddled, with increasing slowness, apathy and physical feebleness. Speech is often impaired by dysphasic errors, and the inability to remember names, either in thought or speech, often leads to irritable importunity. More focal signs of gross aphasia, apraxia or agnosia are sometimes present but usually not marked or severe in degree. An apraxic disturbance for complex sequential tasks involving the arms, such as dressing or walking, is, however, not uncommon.

Most notable is the easy fatigue and tiring of the patient with lack of a span of attention. However, islands of memory will be recaptured and surprising revitalization occurs with the advent of an old friend or relative with whom the patient can reminisce. Ehrentheil (1957) has suggested a series of subtypes:

1. Simple deterioration
2. Depressed and agitated
3. Delirious and confused
4. Hyperactive with motor restlessness and loquaciousness
5. Paranoid

These seem more expository than of value, and usually there is a combination of the full range of the symptoms of dementia.

Presbyophrenia, in which memory impairment is present in a patient with cheerful extroversion, is usually due to superficial disinhibition with underlying serious dementia.

Sudden changes in life, whether of crisis proportion or not, often precipitate serious worsening. Death of relatives, moves of house, an acute infection, fracture of hip may all turn a slow insidious dementia into an acute delirium. At this time, mortality is high (Roth and Morrissey, 1952). Roth, moreover, emphasizes the poor prognosis of patients admitted to mental hospitals, with 60 percent being dead within six months of admission and 80 percent within 24 months. While death often occurs from an intercurrent infection or injury, there is usually a loss of weight and activity and lowering of vital functions.

## Differential Diagnosis

General differentiation from secondary dementias has been discussed. In dementia due to vascular disease, the course is more acute, remitting and fluctuating with general better preservation of personality and retention of insight.

## Treatment

In addition to general principles, old persons are better cared for at home, with hospital admission being reserved for episodic crises. The relatives all too often view admission to the hospital as a terminal event. They should be told that, really, it is merely for a short time, and they will be expected to take their relative back. However, it is also important to remember that, in the inchoate state of cities, many lack family or community support. Here the mental hospital, which so often refuses the merely "senile" patient, can serve a valuable function. Feldshuh, Sillen, Parker, and Frosch (1973) found that nearly half of the patients seen by the Geriatrics Unit at Bellevue were diagnosed as "simply senile." Although they had "nonpsychotic" organic brain syndrome, they needed admission to hospital for both diagnosis and planning. Some had, in fact, suffered sufficient impairment to require long-term compulsory residential care.

Recent findings of cholinergic deficiencies in Alzheimer's disease (Bowen, Smith, White, Flack, Carrasco, Gedye, and Davison, 1977; Davies and Maloney, 1976; Perry, Gibson, Blessed, Perry, and Tomlinson, 1977; Spillane, White, Goodhardt, Flack, Bowen, and Davison, 1977; White, Goodhardt, Keet, Hiley, Carrasco, Williams, and Bowen, 1977) have led Ferris, Sathananthan, Gershon, and Clark (1977) to try deanol. This substance (2-dimethylaminoethanol), which is assumed to increase brain acetylcholine, produced global improvement in 10 of 14 patients. However, neither the clinical ratings nor an extensive pre- versus post-treatment series of cognitive tests revealed changes in memory or other cognitive functions.

Similarly, findings of impaired metabolism of dopamine and 5-hydroxytryptamine (Gottfries, Kjällquist, Pontén, Roos, and Sandbärg, 1974) led Meyer (Meyer, Welch, Deshmukh, Perez, Jacob, Haufrect, Mathew, and Morrell, 1977) to treat ten patients with severe dementia due to Alzheimer's disease (AD) or multi-infarct dementia (MID) or both with the precursor amino acids of the neurotransmitters, serotonin and dopamine. One patient with MID and one with AD+MID showed clinical and psychologic improvement, but the others did not improve. Analysis of the cerebrospinal fluid for HVA and 5-HIAA before and after the pro-benecid test indicated some improvement in the metabolic turnover of these acid metabolites of serotonin and dopamine after administration of their precursor amino acids.

### Huntington's Chorea

Although this disease is uncommon, probably affecting some 50 per million in this country, its interest far outweighs its frequency.

It is transmitted by a single autosomal dominant gene (Sjogren, 1935). Half the offspring of the affected person can, therefore, be expected to develop it, and there is a manifestation rate of almost 100 percent, and hardly ever does the condition skip a generation. Thus, there is an increasing interest in a search for biochemical anomalies which may provide a genetic marker. An abnormal protein has been discovered (Stahl and Swanson, 1974) and abnormal amounts of histone-like compounds (Iqbal, Tellez-Nagel, and Grundke-Iqbal, 1974). Also, with the increasing frequency of tardive dyskinesia, to differentiate it from this is important. This is particularly so because, although the "neurological features" of the disease lend overt color to it, they are, in fact, dominated by the psychological ones. In fact, Panse (1942) found that the most common misdiagnosis of the disease was schizophrenia. He showed that for years before there was any detectable neurological signs, the patient might have shown a schizophrenic syndrome, usually paranoid and in every way typical. Thus, any patient developing tardive dyskinesia should certainly be investigated for Huntington's chorea.

### Manifestations

The mean age of onset is in the middle 40s but its occurrence in childhood, although rare, is well documented (Falstein and Stone, 1941; Jervis, 1963; Markham, and Knox, 1965). It can also manifest in the 70s.

Psychiatric symptoms usually precede the neurological symptoms and signs by a considerable period of time. It is not clear whether individuals who will later develop the disease are perfectly normal prior to the onset of clinical symptoms. In the presymptomatic stage, Goodman, Hall, Terango, Perrine, and Roberts (1966) detected mild deficits in psychomotor and verbal functioning and visual retention. Moreover, 10 of the 13 offspring of a family they studied were not well-adjusted. This was true whether or not they were judged to be organic. In maturity, an emotional disturbance seemed to characterize all the offspring, which may have been due to their nonnurturent and repressing mothers. Additional characteristics of hostility, depression and incompetence were primarily characteristic of the offspring judged organic.

In general, the psychiatric symptoms span a wide range, often with increased sensitivity and irritability, bad temper and mood swings. Alcoholism, criminality, impulsive and unpredictable behavior, violence and sexual promiscuity have frequently been recorded as preceding the appearance of the disease. There may also be apathy and slowness.

There is a mild familial tendency to suicide (Bickford and Ellison, 1953). With the increasing development of the disease, there may be psychotic signs with an ill-sustained depression which, nevertheless, may lead to impulsive suicidal attempts. There may be ideas of reference leading to paranoid delusions. As the dementia progresses, there may be apathy and agnosia with loss of initiative, and the characteristic distractibility superimposed on this is restlessness and irritability. Later, there may be a simple euphoric mood. Memory has been said to be well retained. It is important to remember that dementia may occur without choreiform movements (Curran, 1930) or that chorea may occur without the mental symptoms (Bell, 1934). Exceptionally, Parkinsonian rigidity takes the place of the involuntary movements (Campbell, Corner, Norman, and Urich, 1961).

### Movement Disorder

The involuntary movements usually occur in the face and upper limbs. At first, they may seem only to be normal fidgetiness. This restlessness usually develops a jerking quality with abrupt movements in the proximal part of the limbs. Voluntary movements may lead to jerkings and muscular contractions. Later, there is a writhing of the face, dysarthria and ataxia of the gait. Sometimes, this jerky gait draws first attention to the illness. Involuntary movements are often converted into unnecessary but apparently purposeful voluntary movements to conceal them.

Later, voluntary movement becomes increasingly disorganized. Both breathing and speech become irregular and the jerking expression becomes dominated by involuntary contractions of the face, producing hideous expressions. It is perhaps no wonder that this combination of grotesqueness and dementia led to the claims that some of the earlier sufferers in New England were burned at the stake as witches.

### Investigation

In addition to psychological tests, Klawans, Paulson, Ringel, and Barbeau (1972) have suggested provocation of chorea by L-dopa. About a third of the people genetically at risk of developing the disease produced dyskinetic movements. It has been questioned whether or not it is ethical to provoke or carry out this procedure in a disease without treatment (Gaylin, 1972).

The EEG sometimes shows abnormalities a few years before clinical signs are present with a flat low voltage record (Patterson, Bagchi, and Test, 1948).

Other laboratory studies usually yield normal values, although sometimes the protein level of the cerebrospinal fluid is raised. Pneumoencephalogram or tomography may show enlargement of the ventricles with loss of the shadow of the caudate nucleus and evidence of cortical atrophy. Claims that intracellular levels of magnesium and calcium are elevated in Huntington's chorea have not been confirmed. The progression of the disorder is slow and the average survival state is usually about 15 years.

### Differential Diagnosis

Differentiation from senile chorea, which may be disassociated with dementia and is not familial, is necessary. Where chorea is not present, the dementia needs to be differentiated from any other cause of dementia in mid or late life. With the increasing interest in and frequency of tardive dyskinesia combined with the presence of symptomatic schizophrenia in Huntington's, this syndrome needs to be carefully differentiated. Tardive dyskinesia usually involves the mouth and tongue more, and relatively spares the upper face and gait (Brandon, McClelland, and Protheroe, 1971; Degkwitz, 1969). Tardive dyskinesia in its buccolingual masticatory components is, in fact, indistinguishable from spontaneous oral-facial dyskinesia. Such dyskinesia is frequently associated with advanced age, cerebrovascular disease and the edentulous state. The latter, however, is usually confined to the mouth, in contrast to the more general choreoathetosis of tardive dyskinesia.

### Treatment

Genetic counseling is important. Keeping the patient out of an institution and in work is also helpful. Antipsychotic medication of the phenothiazine or other groups have been used and aid both the involuntary movement and disinhibition or psychotic manifestations if present. Thioridazine in doses of up to 200 mg/day or Thiothixene in doses of 6-10 mg/day are helpful. These may be given divided at first with eventually a nocturnal loading dose. They are probably the two medications least likely to give Parkinsonian secondary effects which are prominent in this disease, especially if rigidity dominates.

Reduced levels of GABA (Perry, Hansen, and Kloster, 1973) and the GABA-synthesizing enzyme glutamic acid decarboxilase (Bird and Iversen, 1974) in the basal ganglia have suggested that GABA-mimetic drugs might alleviate the movement disorder (Enna, Bird, Bennett, Jr., Bylund, Yamamura, Iversen, and Snyder, 1976).

*Parkinson's Disease*

Variable degrees of dementia and intellectual deterioration have been seen in all forms of Parkinson's disease (Pollock and Hornabrook, 1966). Pearce (1974) describes a tetrad of (1) Parkinsonism, (2) dementia of varying degree, (3) primitive reflexes, and (4) cerebral atrophy. This forms a distinctive clinical syndrome seen in the advancing or late cases of Parkinson's disease. It is not exclusive to this disease and can be found in Alzheimer's. Martilla and Rinne (1976) found a prevalence of 29 percent in the 444 patients they studied. Rigidity and hypokinesia were positively correlated with the degree of dementia. The signs of apathetic obtundity were in keeping with subcortical dementia (Albert, Feldman, and Willis, 1974) and not improved by levodopa (Markham, Treclokas, and Diamond, 1974).

## Normal Pressure Hydrocephalus

Katzman (1977) has recently given an excellent review. This progressive dementia with a communicating hydrocephalus with normal or nearly normal pressure of the cerebrospinal fluid has aroused great interest because of the possibility of its treatment since its first description by Hakim and Adams (Adams, Fisher, Hakim, Ojemann, and Sweet, 1965; Hakim and Adams, 1965). The characteristic clinical symptoms of a slowly progressive dementia, gait disturbance, ataxic or apractic in nature, and incontinence without elevation of the CSF pressure has resulted in almost a thousand cases being reported. The condition may develop idiopathically without any apparent cause or may follow subretinal hemorrhage, trauma or chronic meningitis or neoplasm.

Other signs of dementia are nonspecific; usually slowness, apathy and withdrawal; sometimes irritability and paranoid ideas or depression are present. The syndrome is usually dominated by the gait disturbance.

Improvement has been reported in approximately 55 percent of all patients treated surgically, with better results in the secondary group of 65 percent improvement than in the primary or idiopathic where only 41 percent were improved. It is generally agreed that the surgical outcome is also better where the clinical pattern conforms most closely to the classical triad.

Katzman points out that many of the features thought to be characteristic of communicating hydrocephalus are more a feature of ventricular enlargement than obstruction (James, Jr., Burns, Hor, Strecker, Merz, Bush, and Price, 1975). Thus, the venticular enlargement associated with Alzheimer's disease may mimic the CSF dynamics of this condition. Nevertheless, the majority of Alzheimer's patients do poorly after shunting (Coblentz *et al.*, 1973; Stein and Langfitt, 1974).

## Vascular Disorders

*Repeated Infarct Dementia*

Fisher (1968), a long-time worker in the field, says, "In brief, cerebral vascular dementia is a matter of strokes, large and small. In most instances, it will be evident from the events combined with the occurrence of paralysis, sensory loss or visual field defect, that a stroke has occurred." Thus, the proposed new DSM-III classification of "repeated infarct dementia" to replace the DSM "organic brain syndrome with cerebral arteriosclerosis" is in keeping with the general belief that the severity of the disorder appears to relate to repeated infarcts of the brain rather than to the extent of the cerebral arteriosclerosis. The term multi-infarct dementia is also used and, in those patients in whom over 50 cc of brain tissue has been lost, there is usually general intellectual impairment as well as focal neurological signs (Hachinski, Lassen, and Marshall, 1974). Often, the patient is hypertensive, and there is a high correlation between the presence of hypertension and stroke. Vascular disease is the primary cause of the dementia in only a few cases and significantly contributes to only a minority (Tomlinson, Blessed, and Roth, 1970).

Moreover, the degree of correlation between systemic, retinal and cerebral arteriosclerosis is of low order (Alpers, Forster, and Herbert, 1948; Raskin and Ehrenberg, 1956). Raskin and Ehrenberg (1956) found no difference in the character, location and degree of arteriosclerotic changes between demented and nondemented elderly persons. Butler, Dastur, and Perlin (1965) suggested that factors other than diminished blood supply contribute to dementia in the primary degenerative group. Hachinski, Lassen, and Marshall (1974) showed the cerebral blood flow per hundred grams of brain per minute was normal in the primary degenerative group but low in the multi-infarct group. This suggested the blood flow was adequate for the metabolic needs of the brain in patients with primary degenerative dementia but inadequate for those with multi-infarct dementia. There was no correlation between the degree of dementia and cerebral blood flow in the primary degenerative group, but an inverse relationship existed in the multi-infarct group. Their "ischaemic score" used features such as acute onset, focal neurological signs, relative preservation of personality and lability of mood. They assigned two points to abrupt onset, history of strokes, focal neurological symptoms and focal neurological signs, and one point to stepwise deterioration, nocturnal confusion, relative preservation of personality, depression, somatic complaints, emotional incontinence, history of hypertension, evidence of associated arteriosclerosis. Ten patients scoring seven and above were classed as having multi-infarct dementia, and 14 patients scoring four and below were labeled as having primary degenerative dementia. The means of the dementia information scores did not differ significantly between the two groups, indicating that they were impaired to the same degree. More sensitive intellectual testing by Perez, Rivera, Meyer, Gay, Taylor, and Mathew (1975) did, however, reveal significantly lower scores on the Wechsler Adult Intelligence Scale in patients with Alzheimer's disease than with multi-infarct dementia. O'Brien and Mallett (1970) also showed that, in contrast to the normal cerebral cortex perfusion rate in patients with primary dementia, that of patients with dementia caused by vascular disease was considerably reduced.

Thus, these studies suggest that, whatever the controversies of terminology, the distinction of cerebrovascular dementia from senile and other causes is based on well-marked and well-known clinical features, *namely, the presence of cerebrovascular lesions, a markedly remittant or fluctuating course, the preservation of the personality, a large measure of insight until a relatively late stage, explosiveness or incontinence of emotional expression, and epilepticform attacks.* These features make this a fairly well-defined syndrome with clinical utility. The incidence in males is about double that of females.

Sourander and Walinder (1977) have described a small cluster of "hereditary" multi-infarct dementias affecting a family. The age of onset is in the early 30s with survival for 10–15 years.

### Clinical Features

The onset is stepwise, fluctuating, and remitting, rather than insidious. Deficits tend to be patchy—that is, frequently, certain cognitive functions are rapidly affected while others are unimpaired. The condition, beginning in the 60s or 70s, sometimes as early as the middle 40s, may be ushered in by a delirium or following one or a number of cerebrovascular accidents. When a single, small stroke is followed by rapid deterioration, it is usually due to an associated senile dementia.

In the initial delirium, the patient may show clouding of consciousness and considerable disorientation, but in a few weeks, he may appear to be much improved, and only careful testing shows a residual intellectual disability. Similarly, the delirious clouding of consciousness may occur at night or from day to day or even hour to hour. However, underlying these acute episodes is often a steady personality deterioration with a gradual caricature of personality traits taking place. The general changes of intellectual deterioration occur with memory, concentration and comprehension all being affected, leading eventually to loss of drive and initiative. The important distinguishing feature is the preservation of insight and, often, apparent preservation of personality. Both relatives and other physicians often misinterpret the syndrome because of this superficial fabric of intactness until some florid social or other misdemeanor brings the matter to light.

Emotions are often labile—so-called "emotional incontinence." There may be fleeting or longer-lived depressive episodes, usually without the cardinal signs or persistence or autonomy seen in primary depression.

Often, where there is associated hypertension, many of the traits ascribed to that disease may be evidenced—anxiety, easy fatigueability, palpitations, difficulty in sleeping, hypochondriasis, irritableness, and changeability. There may be more localized signs, such as headache, giddiness, or discomfort in the chest.

Epileptic seizures, either grand mal or, more rarely, Jacksonian or other focal seizures, occur in some 20 percent of patients. Eventually, permanent neurological lesions of corticospinal tracts lead to hemiparesis, aphasia and, sometimes but rarely, apraxic symptoms. When multiple strokes have occurred, there may be the so-called pseudobulbar palsy, which is accompanied by explosive laughing and crying. Where, in addition, there is bilateral corticospinal involvement, there is a tendency to a masklike face, poverty of movement and shuffling gait. This state mimics Parkinsonism. Minor neurological signs, such as unequal deep tendon reflexes and, occasionally, extensor plantar responses, may be found.

The fluctuating course of the disease is characteristic, but, eventually, there is progression toward the severe dementia seen in the senile variety.

### Differential Diagnosis

Despite characteristic clinical features, the condition needs to be distinguished from other dementias. Cerebral tumors, whether primary or secondary, and subdural hematoma are the most important to exclude, although Alzheimer's type of dementia is the most frequently encountered.

Where hypertension is present, any serious primary cause, such as phaeochromocytoma or renal disease, must be excluded.

### Treatment

Those patients with hypertension should be given hypotensive medication and investigated for the possibility of a primary disease.

Bilateral carotid disease occurred in only 17 percent of 370 cases angiographically studied because of suspected cerebrovascular disease (Drake, Jr., Baker, Blumenkrantz, and Dahlgren, 1968), and these patients showed the greatest incidence of general intellectual loss. However, the results of thromboendarterectomy in either bilateral or unilateral occlusion had no great effect on their survival, but did sometimes produce an intellectual improvement and, certainly, a reduction of the frequency of transient and residual strokes. Probably, the problem is that disease of the extracranial vessels rarely exists independently of intracerebral disease (Stein, McCormick, Rodriguez, and Taveras, 1962). In general, the place of endarterectomy remains somewhat controversial despite reports of beneficial results (Paulson, Kapp, and Cook, 1966; Williams and McGee, 1964).

Anticoagulants are usually not indicated and may increase morbidity (Hill, Marshall, and Shaw, 1960).

Antipsychotic drugs may be necessary for acute disturbed states, and Thiothixene in divided doses between 2–8/day and Haloperidol in similar doses are probably the safest.

## Infections:

### Acute:

#### Viruses:

*Meningitis, Encephalitis, and Encephalomyelitis.* The enteroviruses and mumps usually lead to a benign meningitis, whereas the arboviruses and herpes simplex virus are more likely to produce severe encephalitis and continuing disability (Meyer, Jr., Johnson, Crawford, Dascomb, and Rogers, 1960). Although persisting effects are commoner in children, the St. Louis encephalitis causes greater mortality and morbidity over the age of 40 years of age. Smith (1958) found that 60 percent of older patients showed memory deficiency persisting a year after their acute illness.

Herpes simplex virus encephalitis is not uncommon and may give rise to focal neurological signs, a severe amnestic syndrome, or more generalized dementia (Miller and Ross, 1968). It is usually not associated with visceral or cutaneous herpes.

The electroencephalogram (EEG) may show repetitive periodic sharp and slow waves against a diffuse slow background activity. The CSF may show a raised white cell count and protein.

### Subacute

#### Creutzeldt-Jakob Disease (CJD)

This rare disease, occurring about one per million of the population, usually begins in the fifth and sixth decades of life (Gajdusek and Gibbs, Jr., 1975; Traub, Gajdusek, and Gibbs, Jr., 1977). Like Huntington's disease, its interest far outweighs its frequency. It is usually classed as non-inflammatory. However, the disease is transmissible and its agent appears to be similar to the scrapie agent (Gajdusek and Gibbs, Jr., 1975). Some 10 percent of cases may be familial (Gajdusek and Gibbs, Jr., 1975).

Traub *et al.* (1977) excellently review the relationship of transmissible virus dementia and spongiform encephalopathy to Creutzfeldt-Jakob disease and Alzheimer's disease. Sixteen of the 126 patients that suffered with CJD had so-called senile amyloid containing plaques. Six of these were patients who had transmissible virus disease, and 10 were those whose disease had still not been transmitted. Their present opinion is that CJD and Alzheimer's disease represent distinct entities, but the CJD agent may, perhaps, affect a brain already damaged by Alzheimer's disease. Others continue to question whether Alzheimer's disease is, in fact, transmissible. Wells also raises the possibility of other chronic neuropsychiatric disorders being due to similar transmissible agents. The absence of clinical and pathological signs of inflammation in CJD certainly disarms suspicions of infection and this speculation remains, at least, an intriguing one. In fact, a cluster of CJD and presenile dementia have recently been reported by Mayer, Orolin, and Mitrová (1977) in southeast Slovakia.

The three most common symptoms of CJD are a rapidly progressive dementia, myoclonus and a characteristic EEG with diffuse slowing and periodic sharp wave complexes (Burger, Rowan, and Goldensohn, 1972). In addition, there are a variety of neurological changes involving both pyramidal, extrapyramidal, cerebellum and lower motor neurons.

There may be epileptic seizures and choreoathetoid movements and tremor. There may be hallucinations, illusions or an overt delirium.

Treatment: No satisfactory treatment, despite use of antiviral agents and immunotherapeutic drugs, has been evolved.

*Chronic*

Post-encephalitic Parkinsonism

The worldwide pandemic of encephalitis lethargica left many sequelae. Often, there were latent intervals as long as 5–25 years before symptoms of the chronic illness manifested, and, frequently, there was no history of an acute illness. Whether such disabilities will follow the other encephalitides with any frequency is not known. It is probable that they will be much rarer.

The illness took many forms. In addition to the characteristic Parkinsonian features of immobility of the face, poverty of motor movement with cogwheel rigidity, loss of associated limb movements and salivation, there were other more specific features. Respiration was often disorganized in its rhythm and increased in rate. Forced upward deviation of the eye and other oculogyric crises occurred. Compulsive movements with tics and spasms were common.

The thoughts were dominated by obsessive-compulsive phenomenon and tended to be stereotyped, but there was usually not a loss of intellectual capacity. Depression was common, including suicide.

Neurosyphilis

It is customary nowadays to regard neurosyphilis as a dead disease. This seems foolhardy; at best, it may only be lurking. Undoubtedly, neurosyphilis is very rare in many parts of the country and more likely to present in regions and populations where there was inadequate treatment of primary syphilis some 20 years ago.

Thus, Hooshmand, Escobar, and Kopf (1972) reported on 241 cases seen in a five year (1965–70) period at one university hospital. The outstanding feature was that the patients were not brought to the hospital with a classical picture of tabes dorsalis, general paralysis of the insane (GPI), or meningovascular syphilis. In fact, neurosyphilis presented in a most atypical fashion and was often discovered incidentally on routine medical examinations. They found that nontreponemal serological tests for syphilis (STS) were not sensitive enough and up to 39 percent of tests could be negative in the late stages of syphilis (Smith, 1969;

Harner, Smith, and Israel, 1968). They found GPI in 12 cases, organic brain syndrome in 9, depression in 12, mania in 8, and personality changes in 5. They suggested that all these psychiatric diagnoses, totalling almost one-fifth, may have been "formes frustes" of GPI.

Kofman (1956), more than 20 years ago, pointed to the changing pattern of neurosyphilis in which he suggested that penicillin therapy had altered the general picture to produce a greater incidence of monosymptomatic cases and so-called formes frustes of the various clinical patterns. It is probable that this trend has continued in the intervening years. He also emphasized the well-known fact that neurosyphilis may continue to progress clinically in spite of inactivity of the cerebrospinal fluid, either spontaneously or after therapy.

*Meningovascular Syphilis.* This is most likely to lead to episodes of delirium or sensorial clouding. Occasionally, there may be manic attacks. There may be generalized or focal epileptic seizures and other signs of local CNS involvement. More rarely is there diffuse cortical involvement with dementia.

*Parenchymatous Syphilis.* This is usually known under the term of general paralysis or general paralysis of the insane (GPI). The onset is usually gradual, with from 5 to 25 years between the primary infection and the first symptoms. There may be early personality changes with alterations in conduct and errors of judgment; and various physical symptoms, such as headache and restlessness and poor sleep.

More usually, the illness presents as a dementia. This is predominantly a simple or euphoric dementia, the latter of which may reflect a predominant involvement of the frontal lobe, but often lacks the infectious gaiety of the idiopathic manic illness. Depression is, in fact, quite common, with a swinging mood and a shallowness of affect. There may be paranoid ideas associated with grandiosity and hallucinations.

Physically, there are usually signs of a neurological disease, with pupillary changes of small unequal pupils failing to react to light, ataxia, dysarthria and long tract signs, even hemiplegia. The illness may be ushered in by epileptic fits. All these signs may, however, be muted, but the serological tests for syphilis in blood and spinal fluid are nearly always positive, although several negative cases have been reported (Ch'ien, Hathaway, and Israel, 1970).

The most important aspect of the syndrome is that it should not be forgotten and, second, that it is treatable, and up to 20 mega-units of penicillin have been advocated. Often, there is surprising improvement, although GPI can continue to worsen despite the treatment, which is seldom seen in other forms of neurosyphilis.

### Brain Abscess
A brain abscess is rare and its features, dementing or otherwise, resemble those of brain tumors.

## CEREBRAL TUMORS

The symptoms of cerebral tumors are dealt with more specifically elsewhere (Brain and Walton, 1969). In general, they will depend upon the site and the focal neurological symptoms caused. Any may be ushered in by seizures either focal or generalized.

### Frontal Lobe Syndrome
There is characteristically a reduction of drive and initiative with euphoria or apathy.

### Parietal and Occipital Lobe Syndromes
There are a variety of agnostic, agnosic and apraxic symptoms, and temporal lobe epilepsy may be present.

### Metastatic Tumor
Usually, such metastases are multiple. Pulmonary carcinoma is the most common source and, as other systemic cancers frequently metastasise in the lungs, an X-ray of the chest should be routine.

It is important to remember that two very common sites, namely the frontal and temporal lobes, are areas where focal signs will occur only at a late stage. Similarly, in meningioma, a frequent tumor, there is compression of the brain without focal signs, except in the suprasellar and sphenoidal regions.

The general somatic symptoms are headache, vomiting, epileptic fits (focal or general) and papilloedema. All are less common in the aged than younger patients.

Sensorial clouding is more common than a well-established dementia, and the amnesic syndrome may be produced by tumors in or near the floor of the third ventricle.

Other symptoms, such as hysterical, depressive and schizophreniform, have been described but are rare. Hysteria for the first time in the aged should be thought of as due to organic disease, especially a tumor. As meningiomas are frequently missed in mental patients (Patton and Sheppard,

1956) and may be detected by focal convulsions, they should be borne in mind.

### Differential Diagnosis
The characteristic features of repeated infarct dementia and senile and presenile dementia have been described. A cerebral tumor or metastasis may present as a depressive illness. However, here there is more an apathy than depression, and the characteristic features of an endogenous depression are usually missing, with or without some organic features. Epilepsy of late onset is always a danger sign.

Although many authors have sought to attribute specific mental symptoms to the various sites of cerebral tumors, this is unlikely (Walther-Büel, 1961). If the disease is of rapid onset, there is likely to be a disturbance of sensorium, proceeding to stupor. If it is of slower onset, there may be more prominent memory disturbance and insidious dementia (Soniat, 1951).

## SUBDURAL HEMATOMA

Any neurological signs due to increased intracranial pressure are less prominent because of the widened subarachnoid space. The most common finding is a diminution of responsiveness and obtundity (Munro, 1942).

Increasing drowsiness is an important sign, but other vital signs, such as an increase of blood pressure, slowing of the pulse, irregularity and stentorous respirations may often be surprisingly unaltered in elderly patients (Perlmutter, 1961). X-rays of the skull usually show no evidence of a fracture, but the pineal gland is seen to be displaced in a few cases. Arteriography or tomography establish the diagnosis of a condition which very closely mimics dementia (Friedman and Odom, 1972).

## DEMENTIA DUE TO CHRONIC DRUG AND ALCOHOL ABUSE

### THE AMNESTIC SYNDROME

This syndrome, although by no means specific, is common to both chronic drug and alcohol dependence. Its importance is that it may be reversible. The essential features are clinical and dominated by the inability to retain memory for events for more than a few minutes. There is an inability to consolidate information to permanent memory stores, with a loss of past memories. There is preservation of intellect and personality. It occurs in a number of conditions, all of which affect the regions of the hippocampus-fornix-mammilary memory body system bilaterally (Marsden, 1978). It is more generally recognized in chronic alcoholism and known as Korsakoff's syndrome. Some claim that it may progress into a full-blown dementia, although this is controversial and is, of course, only one of the several symptom patterns of brain disorders which may be present in chronic alcoholism.

Short-term memory is also mildly impaired but intelligence is usually unchanged. Thus, there is usually some disorientation for time, defects in perception, and impaired concept formation. Lack of initiative and emotional blandness are common. Confabulation, that is, filling the memory gaps with false facts, is common but not invariably present.

Insight into the presence of memory defects is often lacking, and they may be explicitly denied by the patient, despite incontrovertible evidence. Awareness of self and surroundings is typically intact.

The patients are usually apathetic, but not overtly depressed.

The commonest causes of such a condition are chronic alcoholism or chronic barbiturate dependence or malnutrition. In the aged, such a syndrome may be due to cerebrovascular damage with or without chronic alcoholism. An amnestic syndrome may predominate in the early stage of presenile or senile dementia and in encephalitis and other inflammatory and degenerative diseases, especially where there is particular involvement of the temporal lobe or in the presence of a temporal lobe or diencephalic tumor or trauma.

As Marsden (Marsden and Harrison, 1972) points out, an interesting but unexplained amnestic syndrome may occur episodically in otherwise normal people, the so-called transient global amnesia. This may represent (Fisher and Adams, 1964) focal bilateral transient ischaemia in posterior cerebral artery distribution affecting the medial temporal regions.

However, a purely amnestic syndrome is very rare in the course of a dementia due to cerebrovascular disturbance, but the cognitive defect may be largely confined to memory for a relatively long period. In pure form, it may be seen in ischaemia, in the distribution of both posterior cerebral arteries, as in vertebra-basilar disease.

### Course of the Illness

Depending on the underlying pathology and treatment, the syndrome remits completely, partially, or not at all. Recovery may be protracted and take up to two years and occasionally longer. In the most common amnestic syndromes, mainly those due to alcohol and barbiturate abuse, the mental symptoms are usually irreversible.

### Differential Diagnosis

Usually, there are not the global cognitive defects present in dementia or delirium, and intelligence estimates are normal or only slightly lowered.

## ALCOHOLISM

It has been estimated that more than 80 million people in the United States use alcoholic beverages. Six percent are considered excessive users and probably problem drinkers (Joling, 1975). More patients with alcoholism survive into old age as a result of more effective treatment. In addition, alcoholism may well develop for the first time in a person's later life, as a reaction to bereavement, loneliness or other life changes. Simon, in this volume, deals with the subject more fully.

### Syndromes:

#### Alcoholic Personality

Lability of mood with irritable depression varying with noisy cheerfulness and much self-deception may eventually merge into organic personality changes. There may be impaired control of emotions and impulses, social judgment and disinhibition. Narrowing and restrictions of energy and aims in life are common. Emotional lability with euphoria and temper outbursts are frequent. There may be suspiciousness and paranoid sensitivity. Morbid jealousy may exist with or without alcoholism. Such changes embrace terms such as "alcoholic deterioration," "intermediate stage of alcoholic brain disease," and "subclinical organic brain disorder" (Horvath, 1975). Brewer and Parrott (1971) found in 33 well-nourished heavy drinkers, all under 60, that the pneumoencephalogram was abnormal in 70 percent, the Wechsler Adult Intelligence Scale and Benton Visual Retention Test in 58 percent of the cases, but there was only one case of clinical organic brain syndrome. Kleinknecht and Goldstein (1972) reviewed the neuropsychological indices of subclinical brain damage in alcoholics. They concluded that there was a loss of abstract attitude and impairment of complex perceptual-motor abilities. They suggested that these effects were consistent with the thesis that the effect of chronic excessive ingestion of alcohol was to hasten and accentuate the aging process of the brain.

As such changes progress to Korsakoff's syndrome, they are indistinguishable from those of senile dementia (Plutchik and DiScipio, 1974).

Victor, Adams and Collins (1971) dispute this. They believe that in the alcoholic patient, Wernicke's disease and Korsakoff's psychosis are all one disease. As the acute phase of Wernicke's passes off, it is replaced by a stage of amnesic-confabulatory (Korsakoff's) psychosis. This, if severe, ends as a permanent amnesic defect without confabulation. This state is, they believe, often misdiagnosed as "alcoholic dementia" or as "deteriorated state". In a relatively small proportion of patients, Korsakoff's psychosis is evident at the time the patient is first seen and rarely it may occur in the absence of ocular or ataxic signs (Victor, Adams, and Collins, 1971).

### Delirium Tremens

Delirium may be precipitated by sudden cessation of drinking, a reduction of heavy consumption, or coincidental illness, such as infection, poor nutrition, or injuries.

The acute attack may be preceded by anxious nightmares and illusions or hallucinations. As the delirium develops, such illusionary experiences involve common objects in the environment.

The acute attack may be ushered in by an epileptic fit and status epilepticus may intervene with life threatening results.

In addition to the general signs of delirium, there is often a coarse and persistent tremor of the hands, great restlessness, fear, and overactivity. Sensorial clouding varies from mild to near stupor. Most characteristic are the rapid shifts of mood from overcheerfulness to terror. Such changes are often associated with the hallucinations, which may take the form of animals or merely formless shapes.

Auditory hallucinations are rare.

There may be a rise of temperature and signs of peripheral neuritis may be present. In general, the patient is dry mouthed and sick looking.

Although the condition may spontaneously remit after three to seven days, it is often life threatening, especially in the aged. There may be complicating pneumonia, cardiovascular illness or infections.

Treatment: This should routinely be regarded as a medical emergency and the patient admitted to hospital. Kaim (1974) reviews VA studies showing that chlordiazepoxide, paraldehyde, perphenazine, and sodium pentobarbital all produced similarly favorable results in the treatment of uncomplicated delirium tremens (Kaim and Klett, 1972). In an earlier study, chlordiazepoxide was significantly better in preventing delirium or convulsions than chlorpromazine, hydroxyzine, thiamine, or placebo (Kaim, Klett, and Rothfeld, 1969). Although the therapeutic mechanism of these drugs other than sedation remains unclear, chlordiazepoxide possibly has a slight edge over the others, perhaps because of its anticonvulsant action. It should be given intramuscularly in a dose of 20–40 mg, which may be repeated every four to six hours. If the patient has a prior history of seizures, diphenylhydantoin 300–400 mg/day should be given. Electrolytes, especially potassium, and intravenous fluids are often necessary. An initial dose of 100–200 mg of intramuscular thiamine with folic acid 1–5 mg daily, vitamin B complex by mouth, and a daily multivitamin supplement is recommended (Greenblatt and Shader, 1975).

### Alcoholic Hallucinosis

Auditory illusions or hallucinations commonly occur during a period of withdrawal but may recur again with drinking. They are usually accusatory and threatening and may become organized into a complete paranoid system. The hallucinations may have a compelling quality. There are marked resemblances to schizophrenia, but there is usually no formal thought disorder. Usually, the condition is short-lived. However, the relationship to schizophrenia has always been controversial. In the patients studied by Victor and Hope (1958), the majority recovered, but in eight of 76, hallucinations persisted for months and in four, symptoms of schizophrenia developed.

### Alcoholic Psychosis

Alcoholic dementia, the progressive mental deterioration resulting from alcohol abuse, leads to a dementia that is in no way distinguishable from other ones, although a delusion of marital infidelity is particularly common.

It may also be associated with dysarthria, tremor, sluggish pupillary reactions to light, and muscular weakness. All the symptoms of alcoholic polineuritis may be present but, even when this is absent, tendon reflexes are likely to be lost in the lower limbs, especially the ankle jerks.

Epileptic attacks are quite common and they are indistinguishable from the convulsions of idiopathic epilepsy. They may occur either at the height of drinking or after a period of withdrawal. Horvath (1975) found that dementia was a relatively common complication of alcoholism, occurring in about 9 percent of cases of a total sample of 1100 alcoholics. Its incidence rose with age, and it affected relatively more women than men. The condition had a poor prognosis for itself and for alcoholism.

However, it is important to remember that alcoholic dementia is not synonymous with Korsakoff's psychosis, which is merely one of the syndromes within the wider context of chronic alcoholic brain disorders. Other syndromes include frontal, parietal, frontal-parietal, and global disorders.

The psychosis which was described by Korsakoff often follows an acute episode of Wernicke's encephalopathy. Certainly, Wernicke's encephalopathy is caused by a thiamine deficiency and probably Korsakoff's also. They tend to be linked in most descriptions as Wernicke-Korsakoff syndrome. Wernicke's itself may be found in the terminal stage of chronic illnesses, such as intestinal carcinoma, pernicious anemia, or starvation. It may be ushered in by loss of appetite, nausea and vomiting, poor sleep, and giddiness. Most notable are the eye signs, nystagmus invariably, and ocular palsies, especially of the external rectus. Ataxia of gait is common, and 90 percent show mental symptoms and 80 percent polyneuropathy.

Mentally, there is usually a disturbance of consciousness with apprehension and excitement or apathy. Disorientation is almost invariable, and confabulations or hallucinations may be present (Victor, Adams, and Collins, 1971).

Two essential features of Korsakoff's syndrome seem to be retrograde amnesia, namely an inability to recall some events that occurred before the onset of the disease, and antrograde amnesia, namely the inability to form new memories. The patients are otherwise alert, show no apraxia or other cortical signs, and their social behavior is normal within the limits of their memory impairment. At times, there is a mild perceptual and/or conceptual disorder which is usually only detectable with psychological testing. This may only be present in alcoholic cases of the amnesic syndrome.

Confabulation is not universally present and is more common in the early delirious or stuporose phase than in the chronic one. The emotions of such patients are at first fluctuating, followed by a rather flat detached apathy. Behavior is usually distractible and variable. Usually the onset is in delirium with or without the features of Wernicke's encephalopathy, but half the patients improve considerably, usually within the first three months.

Talland (1965) found that capacity to recall the past was often as severely impaired as the ability to learn new material. However, reasoning and judgment often were unimpaired, in contrast to concept formation. He considered that the basic defect was one of conation, the patients lacking the capacity to match and test new information with that already stored. However, Seltzer and Benson (1974) used a multiple choice questionnaire about well-known public events of the past five years. With this, they showed that patients with Korsakoff's disease, although they performed very poorly on recent events, improved to levels of the normal controls on more remote events.

As Rankin (1975) has pointed out, while there is substantial agreement that chronic consumption of alcohol is associated with brain damage, the etiology is a matter of debate. It is clear that in the chronic alcoholic, a thiamine deficiency alone can cause irreversible changes in the diencephalon, brain stem, and cerebellum, which are manifested by the Wernicke-Korsakoff syndrome and alcoholic cerebellar disease respectively. It is, however, unclear whether alcohol alone can produce neuronal injury and death, as well as to what extent other factors may be important in either precipitating or aggravating the brain damage due to alcohol and/or thiamine deficiency. These factors might include trauma, anoxia, genetic inheritance, and the use of other drugs.

## Chronic Abuse of Sedative Drugs

Barbiturates provide the paradigm of chronic sedative-hypnotic abuse. About 20 percent of individuals receiving 600–800 mg of secobarbital or pentobarbital for one to two months will show serious symptoms of withdrawal, including convulsions (Wikler, 1968). In doses larger than this, they will also suffer delirium. Doses of chlordiazepoxide of 300–600 mg for some months or diazepam from as little as 100 mg to 1.5 grams may both lead to tolerance, habituation, and withdrawal symptoms.

The symptoms of withdrawal of barbiturates or other sedative-hypnotics are similar to those following alcohol withdrawal. There may be tremulousness, anxiety, poor sleep, loss of appetite, nausea and vomiting and, in some cases, convulsions and delirium. There may also be grand mal convulsions, fever, electrolyte abnormalities, and even cardiovascular impairment.

The EEG shows increased fast activity with a spikey pattern.

In either acute or subacute intoxication, ataxia, nystagmus, and hypotonia are all frequent.

In chronic usage, there may be some slurring of the speech, with irritability, restlessness, and sometimes euphoric overactivity and loquaciousness, which may have a sticky perseverative quality.

With prolonged usage, in addition to nystagmus, opthalmoplegia may occur, together with somnolence. Barbiturates and sedative hypnotics, in general, may cause an amnestic syndrome, indistinguishable from that of alcoholism. Frequently, both classes of drugs are abused together.

Older people are particularly in danger of having such drugs prescribed to induce sleep when their normal reduced sleep pattern is misdiagnosed by the physician as insomnia. Because of the slower effect of hypnotics in the aged, one taken at the hour of retirement may not have acted an hour or two later, leading to a second dose with consequent increased danger of both habit formation and hangover the following day. Although flurazepam is said not to cause disturbance of the sleep architecture, there are already reported dependencies.

Treatment: Gradual withdrawal of the addicting drug, often substituting phenobarbital or pentobarbital and reducing the dose by a 10th daily, is a usually recommended course (Wikler, 1968).

### Chronic Analgesic Abuse

Murray (Murray, Greene, and Adams, 1971) showed neurofibrillary change in four and senile plaques in six of seven phenacetin abusers. These patients had analgesic neuropathy, and no abnormalities were found in two patients who had taken aspirin only. In all the phenacetin cases, senile plaques were present in the frontal, temporal, and occipital regions, but they were always most obvious in the hippocampal gyrus. Granular-vacular degeneration was identified in only one case. Evans (1975) raises the question whether the prolonged abuse of a powerful oxidizing agent may inhibit the antioxidant protection of the brain, leading to accelerated deposition of neuronal lipofuschin and the formation of neurofibrillary tangles and senile plaques.

Evans also points to the striking impression in clinical practice with both alcohol and drug dependents of the frequent occurrence of "general dilapidation of the personality and loss of higher cerebral functions, suggesting accelerated aging of the brain."

## ASSESSMENT TECHNIQUES FOR ORGANIC MENTAL DISORDER

### History and Examination

The more systematized and standard the history and examination taking is, the more likely is it not to be influenced by the observer's bias. This is covered more fully by Gurland et al. (1976). He and his co-workers have carefully designed questionnaires which not only provide historical informa-

tion but also provide testing, for example, of memory and the discrimination of bilateral consensual stimulation. Use of the Geriatric Mental Status allows functional psychiatric disorders to be distinguished from organic brain syndrome and their change with treatment to be assessed. Their comprehensive assessment and referral evaluation (CARE) reliably lists, records, grades, and classifies information on the health and social problems of the older person. It also can be used for evaluating the effectiveness of service and treatment given. To these, Kuriansky and Gurland (1976) have added a performance test of activities of daily living which subjectively measures the self-care capacity of geriatric psychiatric patients, and Shannon, a measurement of the fulfillment of health needs by means of systematized observation in hospital. Gurland extensively reviews the whole field in this volume.

Undoubtedly, such systematized approaches will become more common. In the meantime, Arie (1973) provides sensible down-to-earth advice for the clinician. He suggests seeing the relatives before the patient and nowhere is this more essential than in the mental illnesses of the aged. He emphasizes that the state of the household is a good indicator of the capacity for self-care.

The ability to ask the right questions forms the basis of management, he points out:

Does the patient live alone?
How long since he/she was normal or competent?
Was the change sudden or gradual?
What has been the subsequent course, steady or intermittent?
Is the patient mobile?
Does he/she go out of the house?
What can he/she do for herself—toileting, washing, dressing, cleaning, shopping, cooking?

What other undesirable behavior is present?

Does he/she wander?
Is he/she incontinent?
Is he/she up at night?
Does he/she make paranoid accusations?
Is he/she aggressive or destructive?

Examination of the mental state has often paid no more than lip service to higher cortical functioning, just as, sometimes, examination of the neurological state has made short shrift of psychological functioning. There are, however, a number of existing formats, such as the Maudsley notes on eliciting and recording clinical information (Department of Psychiatry Teaching Committee, 1973), which outline systematic examination. In this, it is emphasized that testing must not be hurried, that the patient may tire easily and several sessions may be needed for complete examination. It also advises adhering to a simple routine at the start of the examination in which is evaluated the level of conscious awareness, language function, memory (especially the ability to store new information), and the use of simple screening tests for spatial and constructional ability. The language function can be rapidly assessed by

1. estimating the patient's verbal ability during conversation and history taking;
2. asking him to name a series of objects;
3. presenting him with a series of written commands to point to specific objects; and
4. asking him to write down the names of objects to which you point.

Spatial and constructional ability can be tested by asking the patient to execute simple drawings and copy simple designs, such as a square, circle and triangle and line drawings of greater complexity, such as a three dimensional cube. Pearce and Miller (1973) describe a simplified scheme which can be carried out in 30 to 40 minutes with a cooperative patient.

To the normal mental status examination with emphasis on the quality of mood should be added the following essentials:

1. *A complete medical and neurological examination.* The former should cover especially the systems liable to lead to secondary dementia. The latter should pay special attention to the cranial nerves, which should include fields of vision by consensual confrontation. Weakness, tone, and abnormality of long track signs are important.

Diffuse brain dysfunction may be revealed by the presence of abnormal reflexes, such as the sucking or snout reflex. Focal signs may provide localizing value.

2. *The state of consciousness* with precise recording of the orientation not only should be the name, place and person, but if the person is disoriented in place, do they understand the quality of where they are? Often the precise calendar date is not of great significance to elderly people but, do they understand the time of the year, season, or have some approximate orientation? Personal identity is lost only in advanced disease but marital names of women may often be forgotten.

3. *Memory impairment* is often noted by the relatives and comparisons between their account and the patient's may be helpful. In general, however, memory is best tested as an estimate of the disturbance in new learning. The examiner's name can be given early in the interview until it is learned

and asked again at later times during the interview. In the same way, a disoriented person may be told the name of hospital and ward they are in and asked to remember this and recall it later.

More systematically, a short name and address and message is repeated as many times as is required to learn it accurately and then recalled in five minutes or longer. A sentence of unusual syntax may be used. Zangwill (1943) emphasized the inability to correct errors through the learning trials of the Babcock sentence (Babcock, 1930; Wells and Martin, 1923)—"One thing a nation needs in order to become rich and great is a large, secure supply of wood." Unfortunately, such a test is heavily influenced by culture and educational achievement. Nevertheless, a slight advantage of such relatively unstandardized tests as this is that they allow an opportunity to assess grasp of information. However, for many years before giving it up, the only meaningful comment I ever obtained from laboriously reading out "The Cowboy Story" was, "It's either a bloody stupid story or a bloody stupid dog." Fortunately, this story, which concerned an unhappy dog who did not recognize his cowboy master when he changed his clothes, is no longer in the Maudsley questionnaire, undoubtedly to the relief of new generations of Maudsley registrars.

In Britain, the Gresham Ward questionnaires (Department of Psychiatry Training Committee, 1973) of orientation, past and recent memory, and general information are given. This is longer but more comprehensive than the short portable mental status questionnaire described by Pfeiffer (1975). This 10 item questionnaire has been standardized and validated and consists of the date, the day of the week, the name of this place, the telephone number of the patient, his street address, his age, when he was born, who is the president of the US now, who was the president just before him, what was your mother's maiden name, subtract three from 20 and keep subtracting three for each new number all the way down. The scoring is standardized and adjustment can be made for both education and race. Anything over four errors suggests moderate to severe intellectual impairment. Gurland, in this volume, discusses the high correlation of this questionnaire with the Mental Status Questionnaire which serves as the paradigm of such analog scales.

Haglund and Schuckit (1976) concluded that a combination of the SPMSQ and the Face-Hand Test (FHT) were the most empirically useful tests.

Serial subtraction of numbers is more a test of attention and concentration than memory. In the same way, although digit repetition forwards and backwards is constantly used, there have been

HESTON, L. L., AND MASTRI, A. R. 1977. The genetics of Alzheimer's disease: Associations with hematological malignancy and Down's syndrome. *Arch. Gen. Psychiat., 34*(8), 976–981.

HILL, A. B., MARSHALL, J., AND SHAW, D. A. 1960. A controlled clinical trial of long-term anticoagulant therapy in cerebrovascular disease. *Quat. J. Med., 29*, 597–609.

HOOSHMAND, H., ESCOBAR, M. R., AND KOPF, S. W. 1972. Neurosyphilis: A study of 241 patients. *J. Amer. Med. Assoc., 219*(6), 726–729.

HOPKINS, B., AND POST, R. 1955. The significance of abstract and concrete behavior in elderly psychiatric patients and control subjects. *J. Ment. Sci., 101*, 841–850.

HOPKINS, B., AND ROTH, M. 1953. Psychological test performance in patients over 60. II. Paraphrenia, arteriosclerotic psychoses and acute confusion. *J. Ment. Sci., 99*, 451.

HORVATH, T. B. 1975. Clinical spectrum and epidemiological features of alcoholic dementia. *In*, J. G. Rankin (ed.), *Alcohol, Drugs and Brain Damage*, pp. 1–16. Ontario: Addiction Research Foundation of Ontario.

HUGHES, C. P., MYERS, F. K., SMITH, K., AND TORACK, R. M. 1973. Nosologic problems in dementia: A clinical and pathologic study of 11 cases. *Neurology* (Minneap.), *23*, 344–351

INGLIS, J. 1966. Memory disorder. *In, The Scientific Study of Abnormal Behavior*, Chicago: Aldine.

IQBAL, K., TELLEZ-NAGEL, I., AND GRUNDKE-IQBAL, I. 1974. Protein abnormalities in Huntington's chorea. *Brain Res., 76*, 178–184.

JACOB, H. F., TOPEL, J. L., AND HUCKMAN, M. S. 1975. Use of computerized tomography in senile dementia. *J. Neurol. Neurosurg. Psychiat., 38*, 948–953.

JAMES, A. E., JR., BURNS, B., FLOR, W. F., STRECKER, E. P., MERZ, T., BUSH, M., AND PRICE, D. L. 1975. Pathophysiology of chronic communicating hydrocephalus in dogs (Canis familiaris). Experimental studies. *J. Neurol. Sci., 24*, 151–178.

JAVEL, A. F. 1978. Diagnostic guidelines for demented patients (letter to the editor). *Amer. J. Psychiat., 135*(7), 870.

JERVIS, G. A. 1963. Huntington's chorea in childhood. *Arch. Neurol., 9*, 244–257.

JOLING, R. J. 1975. Sociomedical and legal aspects of alcohol and alcoholism. *In*, S. Israelstam and S. Lambert (eds.), *Alcohol, Drugs and Traffic Safety*, pp. 855–859. Ontario: Addiction Research Foundation of Ontario.

KAHN, R. L., ZARIT, S. H., HILBERT, N. M., AND NIEDEREHE, G. 1975. Memory complaint and impairment in the aged. The effect of depression and altered brain function. *Arch. Gen. Psychiat., 32*, 1569.

KAIM, S. C. 1974. Prevention of delirium tremens: Use of phenothiazines versus drugs cross-dependent with alcohol. *Adv. in Biochem. Psychopharmacology, 9*, 685–690.

KAIM, S. C., AND KLETT, C. J. 1972. Treatment of delirium tremens: A comparative evaluation of four drugs. *Quart. J. Stud. Alc., 33*, 1065–1072.

KAIM, S. C., KLETT, C. J., AND ROTHFELD, B. 1969. Treatment of the acute alcohol withdrawal state; a comparison of four drugs. *Amer. J. Psychiat., 125*, 54–60.

KARASU, T. B., AND KATZMAN, R. 1976. Organic brain syndromes. *In*, L. Bellak and T. B. Karasu (eds.), *Geriatric Psychiatry: A Handbook for Psychiatrists and Primary Care Physicians*, pp. 123–140. New York: Grune & Stratton.

KATZ, L., NEAL, M. W., AND SIMON, A. 1961. Observations on psychic mechanisms in organic psychosis of the aged. *In*, P. H. Hoch and J. Zubin (eds.), *Psychopathology of Aging*. New York: Grune & Stratton.

KATZMAN, R. 1976. The prevalence and malignancy of Alzheimer disease. *Arch. Neurol., 33*, 217–218.

KATZMAN, R. 1977. Normal pressure hydrocephalus. *In*, C. E. Wells (ed.), *Dementia*, pp. 69–92. Philadelphia: Davis.

KAY, D. W. K. 1962. Outcome and cause of death in mental disorders of old age: A long-term follow-up of functional and organic psychoses. *Acta Psychiat. Scand., 38*, 249.

KAY, D. W. K., BEAMISH, P., AND ROTH, M. 1964. Old age mental disorders in Newcastle upon Tyne. Part II. A study of possible social and medical causes. *Brit. J. Psychiat., 110*, 668–682.

KAY, D. W. K., BERGMANN, K., GARSIDE, R. F., AND ROTH, M. 1966. A four-year follow-up study of a random sample of old people originally seen in their own homes. A physical, social and psychiatric enquiry. Comm. to the IVth Wld. Congr. Psychiat., Madrid, Sept., 1966.

KAY, D. W. K., AND ROTH, M. 1955. Physical accompaniments of mental disorder in old age. *Lancet, 2*, 740.

KELLEHER, M., COPELAND, J., GURLAND, B., AND SHARPE, L. 1976. Assessment of the older psychiatric inpatient. *Int'l. J. Aging and Human Development, 7*(4), 295–302.

KILOH, L. G. 1961. Pseudo-dementia. *Acta Psychiat. Scand., 37*, 336.

KLAWANS, H. L., JR., PAULSON, G. W., RINGEL, S. P., AND BARBEAU, A. 1972. Use of L-dopa in the detection of presymptomatic Huntington's chorea. *N. Engl. J. Med., 286*, 1332–1334.

KLEINKNECHT, R. A., AND GOLDSTEIN, S. 1972. Neuropsychological deficits associated with alcoholism: A review and discussion. *Quart. J. Stud. Alc., 33*, 999–1020.

KOFMAN, O. 1956. The changing pattern of neurosyphilis. *Canad. Med. Assoc. J., 74*, 807–812.

KRAL, V. A. 1962. Senescent forgetfulness: Benign or

malignant. *Canad. Med. Assoc. J., 86,* 257–260.

KRAL, V. A. 1966. Memory loss in the aged. *Dis. Nerv. Syst., 27,* 51–54.

KURIANSKY, J. AND GURLAND, B. 1976. The performance test of activities of daily living. *Int'l. J. Aging & Human Develop., 7,* 343–352.

LARSSON, T., SJOGREN, T., AND JACOBSON, G. 1963. Senile dementia. *Acta Psychiat. Scand., 39*(suppl. 167), 3–259.

LETEMENDIA, F., AND PAMPIGLIONE, G. 1958. Clinical and electroencephalographic observations in Alzheimer's disease. *J. Neurol. Neurosurg. Psychiat., 21,* 167.

LIBOW, L. S. 1973. Pseudosenility: Acute and reversible organic brain syndrome. *J. Amer. Geriat. Soc., 21,* 112–120.

LIBOW, L. S., AND MEHL, B. 1970. Self-administration of medications by patients in hospitals or extended care facilities. *J. Amer. Geriat. Soc., 18,* 81.

LIDDELL, D. W. 1958. Investigations of EEG findings in presenile dementia. *J. Neurol. Neurosurg. Psychiat., 21,* 173.

LIPOWSKI, Z. J. 1975. Organic brain syndromes: Overview and classification. *In,* D. F. Benson and D. Blumer (eds.), *Psychiatric Aspects of Neurologic Disease,* pp. 11–35. New York: Grune & Stratton.

MALAMUD, N., AND WAGGONER, R. W. 1943. Genealogical and clinical-pathological study of Pick's disease. *Amer. Med. Assoc. Arch. Neuro. Psychiat., 50,* 288–302.

MARKHAM, C. H., AND KNOX, J. W. 1965. Observations on Huntington's chorea in childhood. *J. Ped., 67,* 46–57.

MARKHAM, C. H., TRECLOKAS, L. J., AND DIAMOND, S. G. 1974. Parkinson's disease and levodopa. A five year follow-up and review. *West. J. Med., 121,* 188–206.

MARSDEN, C. D. 1978. The diagnosis of dementia. *In,* A. D. Isaacs and F. Post (eds.), *Studies in Geriatric Psychiatry,* pp. 95–118. Chichester, New York: John Wiley.

MARSDEN, C. D., AND HARRISON, M. J. G. 1972. Outcome of investigation of patients with presenile dementia. *Brit. Med. J., 2,* 249–252.

MARTILLA, R. J., AND RINNE, U. 1976. Dementia in Parkinson's disease. *Acta Neurol. Scandinav., 54,* 431–441.

MATTIS, S. 1976. Mental status examination for organic mental syndrome in the elderly patient. *In,* L. Bellak and T. B. Karasu (eds.), *Geriatric Psychiatry: A Handbook for Psychiatrists and Primary Care Physicians,* pp. 77–121. New York: Grune & Stratton.

MAYER, V., OROLIN, D., AND MITROVA, E. 1977. Cluster of Creutzfeldt-Jakob disease and presenile dementia. *Lancet, 2,* 256.

MCDONALD, C. 1969. Clinical heterogeneity in senile dementia. *Brit. J. Psychiat., 115,* 267–271.

MCMENEMEY, W. H. 1966. The dementias and progressive diseases of the basal ganglia. *In,* W. Blackwood *et al.* (eds.), *Greenfield's Neuropathology,* 2nd ed. Baltimore: Williams & Wilkins.

MERRITT, H. H. 1973. *A Textbook of Neurology,* 5th ed. Philadelphia: Lea & Febiger.

MEYER, H. M., JR., JOHNSON, R. T., CRAWFORD, I. P., DASCOMB, H. E., AND ROGERS, N. G. 1960. Central nervous system syndromes of "viral" etiology. A study of 713 cases. *Amer. J. Med., 29,* 334–347.

MEYER, J. S., WELCH, K. M. A., DESHMUKH, V. D., PEREZ, F. I., JACOB, R. H., HAUFRECT, D. B., MATHEW, N. T., AND MORRELL, R. M. 1977. Neurotransmitter precursor amino acids in the treatment of multi-infarct dementia and Alzheimer's disease. *J. Amer. Geriat. Soc., 25*(7), 289–298.

MILLER, E. 1977. *Abnormal Aging: The Psychology of Senile and Presenile Dementia.* London: John Wiley & Sons.

MILLER, J. D., AND ROSS, C. 1968. Encephalitis: A four-year survey. *Lancet, 1,* 1121–1126.

MUNRO, D. 1942. Cerebral subdural hematomas: Study of 310 verified cases. *N. Engl. J. Med., 227,* 87–95.

MURRAY, R. M., GREENE, J. G., AND ADAMS, J. H. 1971. Analgesic abuse in dementia. *Lancet, ii,* 242–245.

NEUMANN, M. A., AND COHN, R. 1963. Incidence of Alzheimer's disease in a large mental hospital. *Arch. Neurol., 69,* 615–636.

NEVO, S. S., AND SUTTON, H. E. 1968. Association between response to typhoid vaccination and known genetic markers. *Amer. J. Human Genetics, 20,* 461–469.

NEWTON, R. D. 1948. The identity of Alzheimer's disease and senile dementia and their relationship to senility. *J. Ment. Sci., 94,* 225–249.

O'BRIEN, M. D., AND MALLETT, B. L. 1970. Cerebral cortex perfusion rates in dementia. *J. Neurol. Neurosurg. Psychiat., 33,* 497–500.

OP DEN VELDE, W., AND STAM, F. C. 1973. Haptoglobin types in Alzheimer's disease and senile dementia. *Brit. J. Psychiat., 122,* 331–336.

PANSE, F. 1942. Die Erbchorea. Leipzig.

PARSONS, P. L. 1965. Mental health of Swansea's old folk. *Brit. J. Prev. Soc. Med., 19,* 43.

PATTERSON, R., BAGCHI, B. K., AND TEST, A. 1948. The prediction of Huntington's chorea, an electroencephalographic and genetic study. *Amer. J. Psychiat., 104,* 786–797.

PATTON, R. B., AND SHEPPARD, J. A. 1956. Intracranial tumors found at autopsy in mental patients. *Amer. J. Psychiat., 113,* 319–324.

PAULSON, G. W., KAPP, J., AND, COOK, W. 1966. Dementia associated with bilateral carotid artery disease. *Geriatrics, 21,* 159–166.

PEARCE, J. 1974. Mental changes in Parkinsonism. *Brit. Med. J., 2,* 445.

Pearce, J., and Miller, E. 1973. *Clinical Aspects of Dementia*. London: Baillière, Tindall.

Perez, F. I., Rivera, V. M., Meyer, J. S., Gay, J. R. A., Taylor, R. L., and Mathew, N. T. 1975. Analysis of intellectual and cognitive performance in patients with multi-infarct dementia, vertebrobasilar insufficiency with dementia, and Alzheimer's disease. *J. Neurol. Neurosurg. Psychiat., 38*(6), 533–540.

Perlmutter, I. 1961. Subdural hematoma in older patients. *J. Amer. Med. Assoc., 176*(1), 212–214.

Perry, E. K., Gibson, P. H., Blessed, G., Perry, R. H., and Tomlinson, B. E. 1977. Neurotransmitter enzyme abnormalities in senile dementia. *J. Neurol. Sci., 34*, 247–265.

Perry, T. L., Hansen, S., and Kloster, M. 1973. Huntington's chorea: Deficiency of y-aminobutyric acid in brain. *N. Engl. J. Med., 288*, 337–342.

Pfeiffer, E. 1975. A short portable mental status questionnaire for the assessment of organic brain deficit in elderly patients. *J. Amer. Geriat. Soc., 23*(10), 433–441.

Plutchik, R., and DiScipio, W. J. 1974. Personality patterns in chronic alcoholism (Korsakoff's syndrome), chronic schizophrenia, and geriatric patients with chronic brain syndrome. *J. Amer. Geriat. Soc., 22*(11), 514–516.

Pollock, M., and Hornabrook, R. W. 1966. The prevalence, natural history and dementia of Parkinson's disease. *Brain, 89*, 429–448.

Posner, J. B. 1975. Delirium and exogenous metabolic brain disease. *In*, P. B. Beeson and W. McDermott (eds.), *Textbook of Medicine*, Vol. I, Ed. 14, pp. 544–552. Philadelphia: Saunders.

Post, F. 1944. Some problems arising from the study of mental patients over the age of 60 years. *J. Ment. Sci., 90*, 554.

Post, F. 1962. *The Significance of Affective Symptoms in Old Age*. Maudsley Monographs 10. London: Oxford University Press.

Post, F. 1965. *The Clinical Psychiatry of Late Life*. Oxford: Pergamon Press.

Post, F. 1972. The management and nature of depressive illnesses in late life: A follow-through study. *Brit. J. Psychiat., 121*, 393–404.

Post, F. 1975. Dementia, depression, and pseudodementia. *In*, D. F. Benson and D. Blumer (eds.), *Psychiatric Aspects of Neurologic Disease*, pp. 99–120. New York: Grune & Stratton.

Rankin, J. G. 1975. Introduction. *In*, J. G. Rankin (ed.), *Alcohol, Drugs and Brain Damage*, pp. V–IX. Ontario: Addiction Research Foundation of Ontario.

Raskin, N., and Ehrenberg, R. 1956. Cerebral arteriosclerosis. *Amer. Pract. Digest Treatment, 7*, 1095–1096.

Roth, M. 1955. The natural history of mental disorders in old age. *J. Ment. Sci., 101*, 281–301.

Roth, M. 1959. Mental health problems of aging and the aged. *Bull. Wld. Hlth. Org., 21*, 527.

Roth, M. 1976. The psychiatric disorders of later life. *Psychiatric Annals, 6*(9), 57–98.

Roth, M., and Hopkins, B. 1953. Psychological test performance in patients over 60. I Senile psychosis and the affective disorders of old age. *J. Ment. Sci., 99*, 439.

Roth, M., and Kay, D. W. K. 1956. Affective disorders arising in the senium. II. Physical disability as an aetiological factor. *J. Ment. Sci., 102*, 141–150.

Roth, M., and Morrissey, J. D. 1952. Problems in the diagnosis and classification of mental disorder in old age. *J. Ment. Sci., 98*, 66.

Roth, M., Tomlinson, B. E., and Blessed, G. 1967. The relationship between quantitative measures of dementia and of degenerative changes in the cerebral grey matter of elderly subjects. *Proc. Roy. Soc. Med., 60*, 254.

Schreiber, D. J., Goldman, H., Kleinman, K. M., Goldfader, P. R., and Snow, M. Y. 1976. The relationship between independent neuropsychological and neurological detection and localization of cerebral impairment. *J. Nerv. Ment. Dis., 162*(5), 360–365.

Schwartz, D., Wang, M., Zeitz, L., and Goss, M. E. W. 1962. Medication errors made by elderly chronically ill patients. *Amer. J. Publ. Hlth., 52*, 2018.

Seltzer, B., and Benson, D. F. 1974. The temporal pattern of retrograde amnesia in Korsakoff's disease. *Neurology, 24*, 527–530.

Seltzer, B., and Sherwin, I. 1978. "Organic brain syndromes": An empirical study and critical review. *Amer. J. Psychiat., 135*(1), 13–21.

Sherwin, I., and Geschwind, N. 1978. The neural substrates of behavior. *In*, A. M. Nicholi (ed.), *Harvard Guide to Modern Psychiatry*, pp. 59–80. Cambridge–London: Harvard University Press.

Sim, M., and Sussman, I. 1962. Alzheimer's disease: Its natural history and differential diagnosis. *J. Nerv. Ment. Dis., 135*, 489–499.

Simon, A. 1968. The geriatric mentally ill. *Gerontologist, 8*(II), 7.

Sjogren, T. 1935. Genetical investigations of Huntington's chorea in a Swedish peasant population. *Z. mensche. Vererb.-u. Konstit.-Lehre, 19*, 131.

Sjogren, T., Sjogren, H., and Lindgren, A. G. H. 1952. Morbus Alzheimer and morbus Pick: Genetic, clinical and patho-anatomical study. *Acta Psychiat. Scand.*, Suppl. 82.

Slater, E. 1961. Hysteria 311. *J. Ment. Sci., 107*, 359.

Slater, E., and Roth, M. 1977. *Clinical Psychiatry*, 3rd ed. Baltimore: Williams & Wilkins.

Smith, J. E. 1958. St. Louis encephalitis: Sequelae. *Neurology* (Minneap.), *8*, 884.

Smith, J. L. 1969. *Spirochetes in Late Seronegative Syphilis,*

*Penicillin Not-withstanding.* Springfield, Ill.: Charles C Thomas.

SNOWDON, J. 1972. When is dementia presenile? *Brit. Med. J., 2,* 465.

SONIAT, T. L. L. 1951. Psychiatric symptoms associated with intracranial neoplasm. *Amer. J. Psychiat., 108,* 19–22.

SOURANDER, P., AND SJOGREN, H. 1970. The concept of Alzheimer's disease and its clinical implications. *In,* G. E. W. Wolstenholme and M. O'Conner (eds.), *Alzheimer's Disease and Related Conditions.* London: J. & A. Churchill.

SOURANDER, P., AND WALINDER, J. 1977. Hereditary multi-infarct dementia. *Lancet, 1,* 1015.

SPILLANE, J. A., WHITE, P., GOODHARDT, M. J., FLACK, R. H. A., BOWEN, D. M., AND DAVISON, A. N. 1977. Selective vulnerability of neurones in organic dementia. *Nature, 266,* 558–559.

STAHL, W. L., AND SWANSON, P. D. 1974. Biochemical abnormalities in Huntington's chorea brains. *Neurology* (Minneap.), *24,* 813–819.

STAM, F. C. 1977. Can normal aging be explained by the immunological theory? *Geriatrics, 32,* 111.

STEIN, S. C., AND LANGFITT, T. W. 1974. Normal-pressure hydrocephalus. Predicting the results of cerebrospinal fluid shunting. *J. Neurosurg., 41,* 463–470.

STEIN, B. M., McCORMICK, W. F., RODRIGUEZ, J. N., AND TAVERAS, J. M. 1962. Postmortem angiography of cerebral vascular system. *Arch. Neurol.* (Chic.), *7,* 545–569.

STENGEL, E. 1943. A study of the symptomatology and differential diagnosis of Alzheimer's and Pick's diseases. *J. Ment. Sci., 89,* 1–20.

STENGEL, E. 1964. Psychopathology of dementia. *Proc. Roy. Soc. Med., 57,* 911–914.

STERNBERG, D. E., AND JARVIK, M. E. 1976. Memory function in depression. Involvement with antidepressant medication. *Arch. Gen. Psychiat., 33,* 219.

STEVENS, H., AND FORSTER, F. M. 1953. Effect of carbon tetrachloride on the nervous system. *Arch. Neurol. Psychiat., 70,* 635–649.

SWAIN, J. M. 1959. Electroencephalographic abnormalities in presenile atrophy. *Neurology* (Minneap.), *9,* 722.

TALLAND, G. A. 1965. *Deranged Memory.* New York: Academic Press.

Task Force on Nomenclature and Statistics of The American Psychiatric Association, *Diagnostic and Statistical Manual of Mental Disorders,* 3rd ed., 1978 (April 15). Draft.

TERRY, R. D. 1976. Dementia: A brief and selective review. *Arch. Neurol., 33,* 1–4.

TOMLINSON, B. E., BLESSED, G., AND ROTH, M. 1970. Ob-

servations on the brains of demented old people. *J. Neurol. Sci., 11,* 205–242.

TRAUB, R. D., GAJDUSEK, D. C., AND GIBBS, C. J., JR., 1977. Transmissible virus dementias: The relation of transmissible spongiform encephalopathy to Creutzfeldt-Jakob disease. *In,* L. Smith and M. Kinsbourne (eds.), *Aging and Dementia.* New York: Spectrum.

VICTOR, M., ADAMS, R. D., AND COLLINS, G. H. 1971. *The Wernicke-Korsakoff Syndrome.* Philadelphia: Davis.

VICTOR, M., AND HOPE, J. M. 1958. The phenomenon of auditory hallucinations in chronic alcoholism. *J. Nerv. Ment. Dis., 126,* 451–481.

WALTHER-BÜEL, H. 1961. Die psychiatrie der hirngeschwülste. *Acta Neurochir.* (Suppl. 2).

WELLS, C. E. 1977. *Dementia,* 2nd. ed. Philadelphia: F. A. Davis Co.

WELLS, C. E. 1978. Chronic brain disease: An overview. *Amer. J. Psychiat., 135*(1), 1–12.

WELLS, F. L., AND MARTIN, H. A. A. 1923. A method of memory examination suitable for psychotic cases. *Amer. J. Psychiat., 3,* 243–276.

WHITE, P., GOODHARDT, M. J., KEET, J. P., HILEY, C. R., CARRASCO, L. H., WILLIAMS, I. E. I., AND BOWEN, D. M. 1977. Neurocortical cholinergic neurones in elderly people. *Lancet, 1,* 668–671.

WIGDOR, B. T., AND KRAL, V. A. 1961. Senescent memory function as an indicator of the general preservation of the aging human organism. Proc. Third World Congress, Psychiatry, University of Toronto, Toronto, Canada.

WIKLER, A. 1968. Diagnosis and treatment of drug dependence of the barbiturate type. *Amer. J. Psychiat., 125,* 758–765.

WILLIAMS, M., AND McGEE, T. E. 1964. Psychological study of carotid occlusion and endarterectomy. *Arch. Neurol., 10,* 293–297.

WILSON, W. P., MUSELLA, L., AND SHORT, M. J. 1977. The electroencephalogram in dementia. *In,* C. E. Wells (ed.), *Dementia,* 2nd. ed., pp. 205–221. Philadelphia: Davis.

WOLFF, H. G., AND CURRAN, D. 1935. Nature of delirium and allied states. *Arch. Neurol. Psychiat.* (Chic.), *33,* 1175.

ZANGWILL, O. L. 1943. Clinical tests of memory impairment. *Proc. Roy. Soc. Med., 36,* 576–580.

ZANGWILL, O. L. 1964. Neurological studies and human behaviour. *Brit. Med. Bull., 20,* 43.

ZARIT, S. H., MILLER, N. E., AND KAHN, R. L. 1978. Brain function, intellectual impairment and education in the aged. *J. of Amer. Geriat. Soc., XXVI,* No. 2, 58–67.

# 25

# Paranoid, Schizophrenia-like, and Schizophrenic States in the Aged

*Felix Post*

## INTRODUCTION

### TERMINOLOGY

When encountered among the elderly, the conditions comprising the title of this chapter are almost entirely characterized by delusions of self-reference or of actual persecution, as well as by content-related hallucinations in the majority of cases. There are hardly ever any true autochthonous delusions (Berner, 1972): most can be derived from other mental content. Most so-called delusions are actually delusion-like phenomena or delusional ideas, which are secondary to and derivable from illusionary perceptions and experiences, hallucinations, or affective disturbances. Thus, paranoid, rather than paranoiac, syndromes are seen in the elderly.

The problematic nature of distinctions of this kind was illuminated in historical perspective by Aubrey Lewis (1970). He concluded that *paranoid* was a descriptive term which, unlike *paranoiac*, did not carry any implications concerning prognosis or etiology. Following Kolle, Lewis defined a *paranoid syndrome* as one in which there were delusions of self-reference, which might be concerned with persecution, grandeur, litigation, jealousy, love, envy, hate, honor, or the supernatural. Tangential to our subject are Lewis's opening remarks: After explaining the derivation of the terms *paranoia* and *paranoid* from the Greek words for "crazy" or "out of his mind" (as used by classical dramatists and philosophers), Lewis reports that, "Several other writers put it in a context where it denotes senile deterioration, justifying action by the patient's son, according to Attic law."

The term *schizophrenic states* will be applied to patients who exhibit Schneider's (1959) first-rank symptoms, that is, clinical phenomena whose presence should (according to that author) be regarded as mandatory before making a firm diagnosis of schizophrenia. In the case of elderly patients, the more important of Schneider's first-rank symptoms are delusions of passivity or influence, withdrawal or induction of thoughts, thought-echoing, and voices discussing the patient or commenting on his actions. Though one is naturally reluctant to accept this kind of dogmatic pronouncement, the presence of "first-rank symptoms" will be shown to have considerable practical importance in the case of elderly patients.

By contrast, *schizophrenia-like* is a much softer term, and will be used to describe patients with delusional and hallucinatory symptoms, that are not depressive, manic, or first-rank schizophrenic. Schizophrenia-like has also been used by others to categorize conditions in which schizophrenic symptomatology was related to organic-cerebral disorders, for example, temporal lobe epilepsy. In the age group over 60 as well as in younger patients the matter is further complicated by some subjects with confirmed cerebral pathology exhibiting first rank schizophrenic symptoms. It will be shown that similar difficulties have been encountered in using the term *schizo-affective*. This term will be employed to signify disorders in which competent psychiatrists tend to define both schizophrenic and affective symptoms either concurrently or in succession.

Before closing this section on terminology, misunderstandings relating to the term *senile* or *late paraphrenia* should also be clarified. These terms are also largely of historical importance. In 1913, Kleist reported ten case histories of patients who had fallen ill with a paranoid illness between the ages of 40 and 54, and who had been followed into their 60s and 70s. He named the condition *Involutions-paranoia*, and in a footnote he suggested that some of his cases belonged among those "to which Kraepelin quite recently referred as paraphrenics."

Now, Kraepelin's paraphrenics, who were characterized by paranoid delusions and hallucinations in a setting of well-preserved personality functions and absence of "dementia," have subsequently been shown to become indistinguishable from paranoid schizophrenics with time (summarized by Fish, 1960, and also by this author, 1966).

Roth (1955) resurrected the term *late paraphrenia* for descriptive purposes, "because the clinical picture of most cases has many similarities to the paranoid illnesses described by Kraepelin under the heading of paraphrenia (later shown to be a relatively late form of schizophrenia)." The respectability of the term *late paraphrenia* has possibly been enhanced by the finding that all seven senile schizophrenics discovered by Fish (1960) in Edinburgh could be classified as different kinds of paraphrenics in terms of the Leonhard (1957) classi-

fication. Most writers have, however, found a far greater variety of clinical pictures. Janzarik (1957), in particular, pointed out that patients tended to pass from one type of textbook schizophrenic symptomatology to another, and that at times there might be considerable difficulties in excluding depressive illnesses with paranoid features. For all these reasons, and for others discussed in the section on symptomatology, the present writer prefers to continue to use the term *persistent persecutory states of the elderly*, but to avoid monotony, the terms *late paraphrenia* or *late schizophrenia* will also be employed.

The following should be remembered: while clear-cut definitions for terms such as paranoid, schizophrenic, schizophrenia-like, or schizo-affective are useful for communication between author and reader, or among psychiatrists comparing their experiences informally or in research settings, in the present state of our ignorance they should not be mistakenly regarded as evidence for the existence of more fundamental knowledge.

## AGE AND PARANOID SYNDROMES

Most psychiatrists agree that paranoid attitudes, ideas, and delusions are not encountered in childhood and adolescence, but become increasingly common with increasing age. Surly suspiciousness is regarded as a frequent component of senile personality change. Along with hypochondriacal and poverty-delusions those with paranoid content are commonly seen to accompany many of the more severe mental disorders of the aged. Among the impressionistic but plausible discussions is that of Bostroem (1938), in which he speculated on the paucity of delusional symptoms in children. He quoted earlier authors who stated that children are too distractable and changeable for delusional ideas to take root: also, that the child's world is simple and characterized by a naive atmosphere of trust in others. Of course children do suffer from bogies, but these are never incorporated into any sort of persecution system.

In the psychoses of adolescents, states akin to delusional moods do occur, but they are characterized by perplexity rather than by structured and persistent delusional ideas. In the course of hebephrenic and catatonic schizophrenic illnesses of young adults, paranoid delusions and hallucinations have been reported, but again they have usually been described as fleeting and not subject to further elaboration. Real paranoid delusions are said to establish themselves only in patients falling mentally ill after the age of 35 or 40.

It has been pointed out previously (Post, 1973) and supported by some data (Birren, 1964) that with increasing age, slowness and learning difficulties increase, and related to this is a tendency to withdraw from situations which require adaptation. Therefore, a shift toward a more introverted attitude results, which has been regarded to be responsible for an age-related increase of habitual preoccupations with the interior of the body (hypochondriacal orientation), anxiety, self-devaluation and, as a kind of reaction-formation, suspiciousness, and hostility toward others (Bosch, 1972).

More recently, it has again been pointed out that, in Piagetian terms, paranoid delusions could arise only after the age of six, as only then do children begin to overcome an entirely egocentric orientation, and become able to appreciate the self in relationship to others. Bosch illustrates this point by referring to two autistic children observed from the age of five, who only in later childhood developed a delusional mood, hallucinations, and delusions of being poisoned. However, these symptoms were fleeting and transient. Similarly, sensitive reactions to real or imagined slights do occur in adolescents (Meyer, 1972), but possibly because the adolescent easily removes himself (geographically and psychologically) from the scene of real or imagined humiliation, these reactions do not lead to paranoid or querulant developments.

Less impressionistic research concerning the relationship between aging and paranoid symptomatology will be recounted in later discussions of the effects of aging on the life course of schizophrenics. Only one comparative study of delusions in schizophrenia as a function of chronological age could be discovered: referring to an unpublished doctoral thesis, Albee (1950) reports very briefly on a study of two groups of schizophrenics. Members of one group had been below the age of 25 at the time of admission, and those of the other group had been over 40. None of the patients had been ill for more than three years before admission. Abstracting from the case notes, five principal kinds of delusions emerged: bizarre depersonalization and derealization; self-condemnatory; persecutory; wish-fulfilling; and grandiose. The two age groups were compared with regard to incidence of each type of delusion. A relationship between age and type of delusion was discovered, and this was significant in the case of self-condemnatory and persecutory delusion: paranoid delusions were more common in older patients, self-condemnatory delusions in younger patients.

## HISTORICAL BACKGROUND

I will attempt to present a brief survey of the manner in which psychiatric thinking concerning paranoid and schizophrenic disorders in later life has taken its present shape. The more recent literature will be discussed later in the chapter where relevant.

Until lately, the average clinician avoided making a diagnosis of schizophrenia in persons beyond the age of 40 or 50. Whenever paranoid symptoms arose for the first time in life beyond that age range, and whenever they were not clearly related to a depressive or manic illness, cerebral organic factors were almost always postulated. And yet, a very organically oriented psychiatrist, Kraepelin (1913) reported that 5.6 percent of his series of over 1,000 cases had an onset at the age of 40 years or more, with 0.2 percent occurring beyond the age of 60. Similar or slightly larger proportions of late-onset schizophrenics are reported by other earlier workers (see Fish, 1960).

The more specialized study of late-onset schizophrenia was ushered in by Manfred Bleuler's (1943) report based on 126 schizophrenics falling ill for the first time after the age of 40. Only five had become ill after 60, while 40 had fallen ill between the ages of 50 and 60. With regard to his sample, Bleuler wondered whether late-life schizophrenia had not been underdiagnosed in an excessive endeavor to exclude patients with suspected cerebral pathology. In fact, 17 women in his series came to necropsy, and brain changes coinciding with the onset of the psychosis were discovered in only 3 patients. In a review of 355 cases admitted after age 65 to the Heidelberg University Clinic, Lechler (1950) allocated 30 patients to the schizophrenic category. Of these, 12 had fallen ill before the age of 65, mainly between 40 and 50. A wrong diagnosis of dementia had been made initially in only 2 of these 12. By contrast, a wrong (and mainly organic) diagnosis had been made in all but 4 of the 18 patients first falling ill after the age of 65.

There are a number of other studies, reviewed elsewhere (Post, 1966), which are mainly concerned with patients who have fallen ill between the ages of 40 and 50, and rarely after 60. Here we shall only comment on two of these studies. Schimmelpenning's (1965) report is interesting because of its high reported incidence of cerebral arteriosclerosis developing in the course of the patients' illness. Knoll's (1952) results foreshadow many findings reported by later workers: he studied a sample of 21 men and 83 women with paranoid-hallucinatory menopausal or involutional psychoses (only 33 percent of whom had fallen ill after the age of 50). Premorbid personalities were mainly schizoid. Marriage rates were very low, falling between those of schizophrenics and manic-depressives. Knoll pointed out that in this group of late-onset patients, failure to marry had obviously occurred in the setting of their premorbid personality characteristics rather than in the setting of the psychosis itself. At first, symptomatology (though mainly paranoid) was not clearly schizophrenic, but it tended to become so especially in patients followed over longer periods. Depressive features were often encountered during the early part of the illness. At the same time, the study of other members of the families pointed to largely schizophrenic genetic factors. On the other hand, pyknic body build was registered more frequently than in early-onset schizophrenics, and Knoll suggested that the delayed onset of schizophrenic disorders in his sample was due to some modifying manic-depressive genetic influences. In a few patients there was, in confirmation of this suggestion, evidence for abortive schizophrenic attacks in early life.

Increasing interest in the psychiatric disorders of late life has led to studies of mental patients admitted to the hospital after the age of 60 or 65. Examining the records of 150 consecutive patients admitted to a mental hospital after the age of 60, Roth and Morrissey (1952) discovered only 12 patients with schizophrenic symptoms without depression or organic cerebral decline. For all of these, the onset had been after the age of 60. In a later sample of 450 cases, Roth (1955) discovered the same condition in 46 cases, three-fourths of whom (according to their case records) had fallen ill after age 60. Janzarik (1957) also reported on 50 late-onset schizophrenics. According to Fish (1960), only 7 of 264 Edinburgh admissions were schizophrenics with onset after the age of 60. The studies of Kay and Roth, (1961), of Kay (1963), Funding (1963), Herbert and Jacobson, (1967), and that of this author's (1966) which describes, among other things, the impact of phenothiazine treatment, all form the basis of much that is known about late-life schizophrenia at the present time, and will be discussed later on.

## DESCRIPTIVE PSYCHOPATHOLOGY

### GENERAL SURVEY

In elderly persons paranoid disturbances of mental content are encountered in a variety of clinical settings. They may strongly color the symptomatology of brain failure (Isaacs and Caird, 1976), either in its acute or subacute forms (acute confusional states or brain syndromes), or of the less-advanced stages of chronic brain failure (chronic brain syndromes). Paranoid phenomena are, of course, the leading features of the so-called late paraphrenias, but they are also common in the more severe depressions

of the elderly, and in schizo-affective conditions.

Aged persons in the throes of an acute brain syndrome or (in old fashioned terminology) of a senile delirium, are almost always physically ill. Probably for this reason, there seem to be no systematic investigations into the condition's psychopathology. But, the picture is well known from numerous descriptive accounts: in a setting of variable impaired awareness, the patient tends to misidentify people, and under the impact of disorientation and mainly visual and olfactory hallucinations he may develop persecutory ideas, which are always fleeting and fluctuating, and which are not exaggerated into any system of paranoid beliefs. The paranoid experiences may, however, become very frightening to the patient, and may be responsible for aggressive or agitated panic behavior. Rather more prolonged paranoid states with little impairment of awareness, but with auditory as well as with olfactory and visual hallucinations may occur at all ages as part and parcel of a subacute brain syndrome. Especially when the causative physical disorders cannot be reversed, these states may gradually shade over into those associated with persistent cerebral failure. The causes of this type of failure are numerous, but in the elderly the most important ones are excessive or prolonged doses of numerous drugs; prolonged hypoxia, especially that related to cardiopulmonary disease; hypothyroidism; and the recovery phase of cerebral infarcts.

Structural cerebral changes such as those due to repeated cerebral infarctions or due to Alzheimer-type degenerations are associated with progressive and eventually with irreversible cerebral failure. The earlier stages of these dementing disorders of late life may be complicated by a paranoid symptomatology (discussed below).

Most authors investigating the paranoid disorders of the elderly have attempted to exclude patients with transient or persistent cerebral pathology. Roth and his fellow workers (Kay and Roth, 1961; Roth and Morrissey, 1952) obviously thought there was no difficulty in defining and recognizing groups of paranoid patients over the age of 60 in whose cases the delusions were not part and parcel of a depressive illness or of either acute or chronic organic psychoses. Instead, the "paraphrenic delusions" occurred in a setting of a well-preserved intellect and personality. In patients of this kind the delusions were often "primary" in character, and usually were associated with "the passivity feelings or other volitional disturbances and hallucinations in clear consciousness, pathognomonic of schizophrenia."

Later workers were more indefinite and imprecise, possibly because they realized that diagnostic classifications based on the study of case notes mostly recorded by other psychiatrists might not be very reliable. Fish (1960), for instance, extracted from the records 264 patients over the age of 60 who were consecutively admitted to Edinburgh psychiatric facilities, 41 of whom had "marked paranoid symptoms." These 41 patients could be categorized as follows: 9 schizophrenics with onsets before 60; 7 schizophrenics with onsets after 60; 6 paranoid depressives; 16 organic psychotics; 3 patients with psychogenic paranoid reactions.

Similarly, Funding (1963) collected 148 patients admitted consecutively to the Aarhus State Hospital (Denmark) with paranoid psychoses commencing after the age of 50 (only 25 percent became psychotic after the age of 65). However, he personally followed almost all surviving patients, and his diagnostic groupings were based on personal observations. Organic psychotics were excluded, and he judged that 26 percent of his 148 paranoid subjects were manic depressives, and that 37 percent suffered from psychogenic and atypical psychoses. The remaining 37 percent of his series were classified as schizophrenics, paraphrenics, or paranoid psychotics.

All these authors give only few or no details of their patients' clinical characteristics: diagnostic labels are attached or at best a few symptoms are mentioned in short-hand terms. Unless the reader has knowledge of the usages of the particular author or his school, it is difficult to be sure what precisely the patients were like.

I attempted a phenomenologically oriented study of a consecutive series of patients. They had all been admitted under my care, and personally interviewed by me on many occasions: I followed most for at least three years. The sample consisted of almost 100 patients over the age of 60 who were suffering from persistent persecutory states commencing after the age of 50. Excluded were paranoid patients with essentially affective illnesses, in terms of course and response to treatment. This differentiation was certainly not entirely reliable, and the matter will be taken up again in the section on so-called schizo-affective illnesses. Included in the sample under investigation were patients with persistent paranoid symptomatology in a setting of cerebral disease or deterioration. As the monograph (Post, 1966) in which this investigation was reported is no longer easily obtainable, many of the findings will be restated in this chapter without giving repeated references to the original publication. Stated briefly, there emerged three different and distinctive ways in which paranoid symptomatology tends to persist over long periods of time and in a variety of clinical settings.

The first type of paranoid picture is characterized by a strictly limited symptomatology: the patients suffer from one or a few delusional beliefs, experiences, or auditory hallucinations. In the second type, the psychotic symptomatology is widespread and always involves hallucinatory, mainly auditory, phenomena although hallucinations of taste, smell and less commonly of sight also occur. It has been found useful for very practical purposes to subdivide patients exhibiting this type of symptomatology into two subgroups: a schizophrenic one, so classed because Schneider's (1959) first-rank symptoms are present, and a schizophrenia-like one without features regarded by Schneider to be of first-rank significance. Patients with clinical pictures restricted to a narrowly confined paranoid hallucinosis, as well as those with schizophrenia-like psychoses frequently lose their active symptoms on transfer to more sheltered and supportive environments, while the disturbances of patients with a schizophrenic ("Schneider-positive") type of disorder fail to respond to environmental changes.

Since these distinctions were suggested, clinical experience has not led to a modification of these rigid, and therefore dubious, formulations; neither have they been contradicted by other workers. It is not known whether these three reaction types represent stages of the same disorder. This writer is not aware of any sample of elderly paranoid patients who have been followed with repeated careful mental state assessments since this distinction between paranoid hallucinosis, schizophrenia-like psychosis, and late paranoid schizophrenia was suggested. Almost all patients followed since then have received treatment leading to the cessation or modification of their symptomatology, and possibly for this reason the writer has gained a strong impression of syndrome stability. This is confirmed by retrospective accounts of the development of the disorder, which tends to acquire rapidly the form in which it presents at the first psychiatric consultation.

However, one of the earlier writers, Janzarik (1957), who reported on 50 late schizophrenics with an average age of onset of 67 years who were investigated before treatment with major tranquilizers had been introduced, stated that patients tended to pass from one type of schizophrenic symptomatology to another. There was a trend for illnesses to start with paranoid delusions with a later gradual development of hallucinations. Three of his patients exhibited catatonic symptoms at one time or other, and another feature in 6 late paraphrenics (described also by other authors) was the occurrence of remissions. Other earlier writers (including Knoll, 1952) recorded that paranoid symptomatology often assumed a frankly schizophrenic character only later in the illness, and that depressive features were prominent in the early stages.

## CLINICAL DESCRIPTIONS

The three types of clinical pictures seen in elderly subjects with persistent persecutory symptoms will now be described in detail.

### SIMPLE PARANOID PSYCHOSIS

This type of paranoid illness tends to be the least disruptive, and may remain entirely unnoticed. I was once given the barely credible account of an old man's family learning of his delusions of being followed in the street only when they found his diary after his death. Frequently an old woman's psychotic condition is detected only after her husband's death, and it is then learned that he had covered up or sometimes shared her beliefs for many years. Probably, only a small proportion of persons with this type of paranoid disorder are seen by physicians, usually after creating public scenes or persistently complaining to the police.

There is a strong impression (not confirmed by my study) that a simple hallucinosis is unduly frequently associated with deafness, and the patient may complain solely of hearing music or other meaningful sounds. In many deaf persons this may simply present an illusion relating to tinnitus, but this view is obviously not tenable when, as is sometimes the case, the patient also begins to hear spoken language, and (of more importance) starts to respond to hallucinated remarks or commands.

More often, the patient feels herself to be molested by talk believed to emanate from next door or from upstairs or from rooms underneath her dwelling. Unpleasant remarks are shouted, obscenities are heard, or the patient believes that threats are being uttered against her. She may report that the voices tell her that she is dirty, that she had been a whore in the past, that she had committed murder, or they may threaten a break-in, a beating, etc. A proportion of patients do not complain about "voices," but only about noises which are produced to annoy them: machinery has been installed for this specific purpose. Finally, there may be a complete absence of auditory phenomena, but the patient believes that her home is entered during her absence for the commission of thefts. Sometimes there is only a complaint of in-

terference with the patient's belongings: objects have been displaced, wardrobes and drawers have been opened, etc. In this group seem to belong the much more rarely seen old men who accuse their wives of unfaithfulness, find stains on their clothing, or hear suspicious noises at night.

On the whole, it is unusual for patients in the older age group to develop sudden and autochthonous delusional beliefs. They seem to become gradually preoccupied with the sounds they believe they hear or with imagined changes in their domestic arrangements which seem to indicate outside interference. Soon they suspect certain persons in their environment, usually neighbors, to be their persecutors or false accusers. They feel that these accusations are entirely undeserved. There is no guilt; on the contrary, the patients feel themselves envied because of their superior social status or that of their relatives. For this reason, they had kept apart from their neighbors, who are now retaliating by trying to take possession of their apartment and drive them away. Special difficulties are caused by old people who come to believe that a member of their families is attempting to defraud them of their money, or that they are acting or speaking meanly behind their backs. (Testamentary capacity may be impaired, or such impairment may be alleged later by persons excluded from a newly drawn will.)

As was indicated earlier, many patients with these simple paranoid illnesses never come to medical notice. They do not become impaired in self-care and there is no striking change in conduct or appearance, and as we shall see later many have already been somewhat eccentric for many years. In some patients, complaints to the police, angry scenes with neighbors, barricading themselves in their homes, and an increasingly inadequate diet (fear of shopping) will lead to medical and eventually perhaps to psychiatric consultation. Common sense social measures may then be applied, and the patient may be encouraged to change apartment or move into a retirement home. Similarly, if relatives are not targets of the patient's paranoid beliefs, a temporary removal into their care may be advised. Under these circumstances, almost always the patient's active symptoms will cease. No more voices will be heard, no more noises: the patient's state of fear, which may have been considerable, will abate. The same will happen if (because of even greater distress and urgency) the patient had to be admitted to the hospital. However, the patient will remain "deluded"; and will maintain that all experiences were real, and that trouble will start again if returned home. Claims that permanent changes of surroundings without pharmacologic treatments will affect lasting cures have never been tested, nor is it known how often and how soon active paranoid symptoms recur in changed and more sheltered surroundings. Possibly a few lasting remissions may be achieved by social measures alone.

The main characteristics of a simple senile paranoid illness which sharply differentiate this condition from schizophrenia-like, and paranoid schizophrenic psychoses, may be restated as follows: (*a*) The patient suffers from only one or two delusional beliefs which are commonplace, (*b*) These may or may not be associated with largely auditory hallucinations of related content, (*c*) Personality functioning is not usually seriously disrupted but may be in an occasional crisis, (*d*) The condition can be improved at least temporarily by social measures to such an extent that only careful questioning may reveal continuing paranoid beliefs.

## SCHIZOPHRENIA-LIKE ILLNESSES

The clinical pictures presented by these conditions and those associated with paranoid-schizophrenic states are both characterized by a more general disturbance of mental functioning, which certainly in urban society will sooner or later be brought to medical attention. Patients become increasingly distressed by hallucinatory experiences and paranoid delusions which tend to be only loosely thrust together. It is often impossible to decide whether the delusional beliefs arose from hallucinatory experiences or presented delusional perceptions. The nature of these beliefs and experiences tends to be (like in simple paranoid illnesses) what Klages (1961) called "banal," that is, commonplace, domestic, and in keeping with the patient's social and educational background. The patient's ideas and experiences are understandable without recourse to any kind of in-depth psychology.

At the same time, the symptoms of schizophrenia-like states are more florid and bizarre than those of a simple paranoid psychosis. There are not just delusions of theft, but beliefs that gas and electricity supplies are being interfered with, false money has been planted on the patient, the television set no longer works properly. Food is poisoned, unpleasant smells are produced, gases are pumped into the room. Cars circle the block, their headlights shine into the apartment. Insulting remarks are hurled at the patient, who is being observed through the ceiling or photographed in embarrassing situations, while undressing, or in the lavatory. Insulting words relating to the patient's past (but often in reality absent) sex life are heard; the room has been wired, loudspeakers and microphones are hidden. There are vibrations from underneath the floorboards, or the cries of small children are heard.

Usually several experiences of this kind affect the patient at the same time, and he or she soon becomes very distressed, calling for help, etc. The nature of the persecutors behind these experiences tends to be more diffuse and indefinite than in simple paranoid psychoses; not just scheming relatives or envious neighbors, but gangs of thieves, or persons holding a grudge from some past encounter.

## PARANOID SCHIZOPHRENIA STATES

Finally, a paranoid illness of late life may display the same symptomatology as a schizophrenic or paraphrenic psychosis in persons first falling ill at an earlier age, for example between 30 and 50 years. There may be a narrowly confined area of delusional beliefs as in simple paranoid psychoses, or more widespread psychotic ideas and experiences as in the schizophrenia-like mental illnesses. However, in addition, the patient will be found to exhibit some of the psychopathologic phenomena that many psychiatrists might require to be present before making a firm diagnosis of schizophrenia (World Health Organization, 1973). Many of the symptoms which are now generally regarded as indicators of some basic disturbance of psychologic functioning in schizophrenia are not seen in late-onset patients: blatant affective incongruity is not encountered, though it is true that the apparently affectless recital of psychotic beliefs and experiences may suggest affective flattening. Most patients are, however, very upset by their disordered perceptions and thought content, and as we shall see, a depressed affect is very common early in the illness. Thought blocking and various degrees of verbal incoherence reflecting a formal schizophrenic disorder of thinking are certainly not very marked in patients with late paraphrenia. Many of these old and often deaf people speak indistinctly or tend to trail off in their verbal communication. Close enquiry into their delusional beliefs may meet with elliptical answers or odd, almost neologistic explanations. However, the more severe and obvious speech disturbances of schizophrenia are never observed in our group of patients. I have seen catatonic symptoms on only two occasions: once in a patient who died very soon after several cerebrovascular accidents, and a second in the setting of an atypical manic-depressive rather than schizophrenic illness. Grimacing and manneristic movements are also difficult to differentiate from oral dyskinesias and akathesias, which may occur in the elderly without a history of phenothiazine medication. I recall a patient who made gyrating movements of the whole body which he attributed to the force of the sun!

Schneider (1959) did not include any of the phenomena mentioned just now among his symptoms of first-rank significance in making a diagnosis of schizophrenia, not because he did not accept their importance, but because he felt (especially perhaps in recently ill patients) that they were often too indefinite to serve as a basis for a firm clinical judgment. He included in his first-rank symptoms only those which the patient was able to describe spontaneously or on skilled exploration.

First-rank phenomena are, in fact, fairly frequently encountered in elderly paranoid patients, and the most common and most striking are third person singular auditory hallucinations: the person reports that he or she overhears conversations referring to him or her by name or more often by the term "he" or "she." Typically, one voice maligns the patient while the other defends him. As in the other types of paranoid psychoses seen in the elderly, the purpose of the voice is to deprive the patient of his home or to obtain revenge for some past slight. Equally common, the two or sometimes more voices discuss the patient's actions and provide continuous commentary on them, spiced with uncomplimentary remarks.

Where the voices repeat or anticipate the patient's thoughts we enter the area of symptoms that are based on a dissolution of ego boundaries: thought-reading, thought-withdrawal, and influence and passivity phenomena are not infrequently described by late paraphrenics, and are often sexual in nature. For female patients, it is usually not possible to discover whether the man involved in these experiences was once actually known to the patient, but the somatic hallucinations consist of sexual feelings and coital vaginal sensations. These are produced by telepathic means often from great distances (e.g., the Bishop of Cape Town in a patient in London!). More commonly perhaps, the telepathic interferences are directed "by electricity" or consist of "penetrating stabs" from closer at hand.

The content of many of these symptoms, in which the barrier between the ego and the non-ego appears to be disrupted is no longer of a commonplace or domestic type, but much more like the "out-of-this-world" content of the younger schizophrenic's delusional beliefs and experiences. This becomes even more marked in the few patients exhibiting a veritable *paraphrenia phantastica*, taking part in complex hallucinated television programs, influencing the size and appearance of persons around them, regarding themselves as reincarnations of historic personalities, conversing intimately with the "Archangel Michael" or the "Heavenly Father," etc.

As was pointed out earlier, patients with simple paranoid and with schizophrenia-like psychoses not infrequently calm down considerably when moved from their home surroundings. Their hallucinosis may disappear completely, and for the time being they may cease to complain of ongoing persecutions without gaining any retrospective insight. By contrast, patients exhibiting a schizophrenic picture with auditory hallucinations in the third person which comment on the patient's actions, and with features indicative of a dissolution of ego boundaries, will fail to experience any remission on removal to a hospital or to other sheltered situations. Among 93 patients over the age of 60 with persistent persecutory states first arising after the age of 50 there were 21 with simple paranoid psychoses, 37 with schizophrenia-like illnesses, and 34 who exhibited symptoms of paranoid schizophrenia. Based on follow-up of approximately three years and on further experience, the symptomatology of individual patients remained constant, and once established was not in any way progressive. (Post, 1966).

## AFFECTIVE SYMPTOMATOLOGY

*Paranoid Features of Affective Psychoses.* Purely depressive and anxious-depressive states are not infrequently associated with ideas of reference. The patient feels that people are looking at him in the street, that things are said of him that are derogatory or critical. He feels that his unhappy appearance is noticed and commented upon by others. However, patients suffering from relatively mild affective disturbances will unhesitatingly explain that they realize how absurd these ideas are: their experiences seem to haunt them, but they fully realize their imaginary nature. Insight is lost to a variable and often varying extent in persons with more severe mood disorders, and in view of the special propensity of the middle-aged and elderly to deploy paranoid mental mechanisms, it is not surprising that both retarded and agitated melancholic depressions of the so-called involutional and senile kind are so often complicated by paranoid delusions and hallucinations. In one series of elderly persons with affective symptoms sufficiently severe to warrant inpatient care, 38 percent exhibited paranoid features, and these took the form of clear-cut delusions and hallucinations in 9 percent (Post, 1962).

Classically, the persecutory content of thought in patients with severe affective illnesses is kata-thymic in type, this is, clearly arising out of the disorder of mood. Depressed mood is associated with diminished self-esteem, guilt, and fears of impending doom. Thus, the depressed patient with paranoid symptoms feels himself justly accused pursued, or threatened with punishment. He has cheated the tax authorities or committed some other property offence, to give a common example, and whether this belief represents the revival of a real memory or more often an exaggeration, the patient now believes that the police are following him.

Equally typically, hypochondriacal delusions, especially those of venereal disease or cancer may be accompanied by paranoid experiences: the patient is avoided or rejected because of his smell or of his imaginary uncleanness or involuntary excretions. In manic patients, persecutory content is usually derived from the patient's grandiose feeling of being envied, or it is an understandable reaction to attempts made at restraining the patient's activities. Many elderly manics can be shown to have rapid swings or admixtures of a depressive mood, and this may often show itself in the presence of paranoid phenomena.

The choice of the treatment most likely to provide long-lasting help to patients of this kind can be very difficult. The disturbed state of over-active and elated patients with paranoid symptoms is likely to be terminated by the use of major tranquilizers regardless of whether the patient's condition has been manic or paraphrenic. It will, however, be advisable to discontinue medication soon after symptoms have remitted. In the case of manic patients, there may be no recurrence of any disorder for considerable time, but in the case of paraphrenics, there will be an early reappearance of schizophrenic symptomatology. The choice of agent for maintenance therapy will thus depend on the condition that emerges after the acute attack has been systematically treated. With patients exhibiting paranoid symptoms in a depressive-retarded or agitated setting, antidepressant remedies are likely to be employed for those patients who feel persecuted, inferior, guilty, or worthless. All the same, not infrequently patients of this kind respond immediately, and show long-term response only when major tranquilizers or other "anti-schizophrenic" drugs are administered. The special problems of patients presenting with schizo-affective disorders will be discussed later in this section, but an examination of the meaningfulness of diagnostic differentiation will be left to the end of the chapter.

*Affective Symptoms in Paraphrenic Illness.* All patients had been excluded from the 1966 research sample (patients with persistent persecutory states) whose progress with treatment had been in keeping with an affective diagnosis: a few came to be regarded in retrospect as hypomanics with paranoid ideations, but most were paranoid depressives.

Among the 93 patients with confirmed persistent persecutory disorders of a simple paranoid, a schizophrenia-like, or a paranoid-schizophrenic type, 57 percent displayed some affective symptoms: these were well marked in 23 percent. Patients who showed only anxiety in relation to their psychotic experiences were not rated as exhibiting affective symptoms, as such symptoms were usually of a more generalized agitated depressive, and rarely of an elated type. In this last group, it was often difficult to distinguish a paranoid tirade from a flight of ideas in an overly talkative patient. When depression was marked, patients might feel themselves persecuted from a position of inferiority, related to a sense of guilt, self-blame, poverty, etc. If it had not been for the additional presence of features belonging to the schizophrenic reaction type, and for their response to phenothiazine treatment, they might well have been classified as paranoid depressives. Affective symptomatology was associated with all types of paraphrenia. An especially strong association between affective disturbance and schizophrenia-like symptomatology did not meet tests of statistical significance. The frequency of suicidal attempts was, unfortunately, not noted, and impressionistic ratings of the extent to which the patient's psychomotor behavior (e.g., facial expression), rather than verbal behavior, transmitted affective disturbance may not be very reliable. For what it is worth, poor communication of affect was rare in simple paranoid and schizophrenia-like states: 16 of the 22 patients receiving a rating of inadequate affective display belonged to the paranoid-schizophrenic group.

## PERSISTENT ORGANIC PARANOID PSYCHOSES

Paranoid symptoms occur in a proportion of patients suffering from one of the late-life dementias. Paranoid interpretations of occurrences, the construction of systems of paranoid belief, experiencing auditory hallucinations of a meaningful content—all these pathologic phenomena cannot arise in patients suffering from the more severe kinds of cerebral deterioration. Therefore, structured and persistent paranoid symptoms occur only during the less-advanced stages of dementia, and probably most frequently in persons with, in some respects, abnormal previous personalities.

The classical example is presented by the domineering, emotionally cold or brittle, suspicious, and aloof type of woman, who in old age and in a setting of increasing memory impairment and domestic disorganization hides what to her are precious objects, cannot find them again, and then develops delusions of theft. Similarly, such a person may believe that some entirely honest and straightforward suggestions regarding his or her financial affairs are part of a conspiracy to cheat them. Men may develop ridiculous delusions of jealousy, and may become dangerous to their wives. There is a strong clinical impression that in relation to senile dementia the most common psychotic picture is a simple paranoid one, often without a hallucinosis.

However, when experience is based on samples of hospital patients, as was the case in my (1966) study, these relatively manageable forms of the disorder are underrepresented, and more seriously disruptive psychotic symptoms are seen unduly frequently. Among 93 patients with persistent persecutory states, the additional presence of defects due to brain disease or deterioration was confirmed on follow-up in 16, of the sample, in almost 17 percent. In four patients the underlying cerebral conditions were rather unusual ones (Jakob-Creutzfeld disease, Alzheimer's presenile dementia, the late effects of neurosyphilis, and the aftermath of cerebral thrombophlebitis). The remaining 12 were thought to be suffering from one of the dementias of old age, but as only few came to postmortem, a subdivision into senile and multi-infarct dementia would be misleading. Of the 16 patients with confirmed cerebral conditions, 6 exhibited a simple paranoid symptomatology, 6 had schizophrenia-like symptoms, and 4 had paranoid-schizophrenic ones. As may be expected, one-half of these patients with cerebral disorders died during a three-year follow-up period, while the death rate among the remaining 77 patients without confirmed brain changes was only just under 9 percent.

In view of the small number of patients studied and the absence of other publications concerning dementing disorders of late life with paranoid or schizophrenic symptomatology, response to treatment may be briefly mentioned here, rather than in the section in the treatment of late-paraphrenic illnesses. During the 1966 study a strong impression arose that a complete and lasting response of the paranoid symptoms to phenothiazine therapy was occasionally seen, but that satisfactory long-term control of psychotic symptoms was less common than in patients without cerebral impairment. The impression gained since then would suggest that the use of small doses of major tranquilizing drugs is usually successful in the case of organic paranoid patients living with relatives who make themselves responsible for continuing the treatment. On the other hand, symptoms frequently disappear on transfer of the old person to sheltered surroundings.

In the context of the present section, I will also consider the extent to which the first appearance of paranoid or paraphrenic symptoms might signal the onset of one of the dementing conditions of late life. Reporting on patients with schizophrenic symptoms developing after the age of 40, continental authors tend to stress the considerable frequency of cerebral complications during the later part of the illness. For instance, Schimmelpenning (1965) claimed the appearance of cerebral arteriosclerotic phenomena in over one-half of his patients; however, these were rarely cerebral infarcts, but more often raised blood pressure, sclerotic peripheral vessels, dubious intellectual impairment, etc. Gabriel (1974a, b) found evidence of organic mental impairment in some three-quarters of similar patients, though to a severe extent in a much smaller proportion. By contrast, Kay (1963) found in a long-term follow-up of late paraphrenics that only 20 percent had developed senile dementia; this is a figure in good accord with the incidence of dementing conditions expected in any sample of elderly people followed over a similar (16–25 years) period. In the course of three years of observation while confirming the presence of psycho-organic disorders in 16 of 20 patients labeled as "organic" at the time of admission (Post, 1966), I thought that there was doubtful evidence in an additional 13 patients after three years had passed. So there was the possibility of a developing dementia in some 22 percent of elderly paraphrenics, a figure very similar to that emerging from Kay's (1962) case-note review of Stockholm material.

The key to the discrepancy between the continental and the British workers seems to be that I had been unable to decide whether 22 percent of my paraphrenic patients were dementing even after personal observation extending over three years. This kind of uncertainty at the end of a follow-up period had hardly ever arisen in the case of elderly depressives (Post, 1962). In the case of the elderly subjects with persecutory syndromes, these were persons who were often deaf, who, as we shall see later, had frequently exhibited long-standing personality and social deviations, and who belonged perhaps rather more frequently to the lower social classes. In addition, these patients were often on phenothiazine drugs, and, in spite of them, the patients continued to have symptoms of a schizophrenic or related type. In other words, there were considerable problems in communication. Even if psychologic tests had been applied to these people, the interpretation of the results would have been debatable. Now, Gabriel (1974b) found that the later occurrence of what he thought were psycho-organic developments did not correlate with the presence or absence of delusional symptoms or of affective admixtures. There was, however, a significant correlation between organic mental changes and a chronic deteriorating course, as well as with the presence of formal thought disorders of a schizophrenic type. Patients with this kind of clinical picture are especially difficult to assess for the presence of intellectual deterioration, and it is suggested that for this reason continental workers tend to overestimate the prevalence of organic mental deterioration, especially if it is characterized as existing in a milder or incipient form. It had been shown that in the case of elderly persons with affective conditions doubtful or "early" dementia was hardly ever confirmed on follow-up. When depressive patients were confirmed to be dementing, the evidence for this had been quite obvious at the time they were first seen by psychiatrists (Bergmann, Kay, Foster, McKechnie, and Roth, 1971; Post, 1971b).

In conclusion, it may be stated that the paraphrenic illnesses of late life are unrelated to disorders caused by gross brain changes, and that the later occurrences of one of the late-life dementias are no more common in late-paraphrenics than they are in mentally healthy old people. On the other hand, simple paranoid, schizophrenia-like, or paranoid-schizophrenic symptoms quite often complicate acute, subacute, and in a more lasting fashion, persistent and progressive brain failure. However, whenever an independent account of the illness is available, it will (in my experience) always emerge very clearly that disorders of memory and orientation, as well as decline in other mental abilities, had preceded the first emergence of persecutory delusions or related phenomena by months, if not years. As these paranoid features are far more disruptive, and mild intellectual changes tend to be overlooked, their earlier presence may require special and determined inquiry.

## SCHIZO-AFFECTIVE ILLNESSES

The nosologic status of the term *schizo-affective* has recently been very fully reviewed and discussed by Procci (1976). He concluded from an extensive study of the literature that there was no consensus regarding the theoretical or clinical validity of the term. He pointed out, however, that there was also no clear-cut distinction between the two major

(schizophrenic and affective) psychoses on the basis of the existence of two separate acute symptom complexes: there was a continuum of symptomatology. Furthermore, neither schizophrenias nor affective psychoses were in themselves homogeneous disorders. "With fuzziness surrounding the boundaries of both schizophrenic and affective disorders, it is understandable that the borderland schizo-affective state cannot be precisely defined." Procci accordingly went on to extend his survey to studies that investigated the schizo-affective concept, not just from a descriptive-symptomatic viewpoint, but also in relation to family studies, epidemiologic research, response to treatment, and outcome, both short-term and long-term. The conclusions at the end of Procci's essay are indefinite: possibly there is a group of young acutely ill schizo-affective patients who might require further study. Otherwise, there arose the suggestion that schizo-affective psychosis was itself "a heterogeneous entity that included a number of different pathologic states"!

Procci's conclusions have little relevance to the present section, as he has only one reference to a study of elderly patients—my own (Post, 1971a). This was based on patients selected over a three-year period from consecutive hospital admissions. The sample consisted of all patients for whom doubts existed (about a week after admission) concerning the differential diagnosis between an affective or a schizophrenic illness. A few patients were added at a later stage because diagnostic doubts had arisen. Far more frequently, the initial problems concerning the differential diagnosis were resolved soon after the initial assessment, and only some 4 percent of consecutively admitted patients (only 29 persons) formed the sample of schizo-affective patients. Surviving members of this group were reassessed by me on several occasions in the course of 3 to 7 years (average length of follow-up period being 4.5 years). Information concerning earlier psychiatric illnesses was also obtained, largely from hospital records.

Follow-up revealed that a mixed paraphrenic-affective clinical picture became firmly established in 14 of the 29 patients. The remainder either exhibited a mixture of symptoms intermittently over short periods, or passed through succeeding episodes characterized by purely affective or purely paraphrenic symptomatology. Schizophrenia-like symptoms predominated, but there were also a few patients in whose case the late-paraphrenic symptomatology took the form of a simple hallucinosis or of a classical paranoid schizophrenia.

An attempt was made to discover in what respect these schizo-affective elderly patients differed from nearly 200 patients over 60 years of age who were admitted to the same unit with affective illness or with persistent persecutory states (late-paraphrenias). As will be discussed later, in comparison with depressives elderly paraphrenics were significantly more often women, had a poorer past sexual adjustment, had more frequently remained unmarried, and tended to have lower socioeconomic status. On the other hand, paraphrenics had less affective heredity, more rarely frank psychologic ill health before the age of 50, and far less evidence for event-related precipitation of illness.

In terms of all these variables, schizo-affectives assumed an intermediate position, which in most instances was statistically beyond chance. On the other hand, significantly more frequently schizo-affective patients had first-degree relatives suffering from psychiatric disorders (76 percent) than did elderly depressives (62 percent) or paraphrenics (40 percent). More specifically, schizo-affective heredity was discovered in 9 percent of the probands with late paraphrenia, in 3 percent of the depressives, and in 17 percent of the schizo-affectives. These differences were, however, statistically insignificant. Evidence for a specific hereditary factor for schizo-affective psychosis of the elderly is thus not very strong. While in the case of younger patients Perris (1974) reported "a high degree of homotypical hereditary loading through several generations and no more than occasional loading for other psychoses (schizophrenia and manic-depression)," the striking finding in elderly schizo-affectives was the high family incidence of all kinds of psychiatric conditions, that is, heterotypical heredity.

It seems very likely that the occurrence of a variety of psychiatric disorders in the families of three-quarters of schizo-affective patients is, in both hereditary and early-environmental terms, related to the high prevalence of marked personality deviations. These were recorded in 86 percent of elderly schizo-affectives, compared to 63 percent of depressives, and 68 percent of paraphrenics. To a smaller extent, confirmed cerebral pathology was associated with schizo-affective disorders more frequently than with purely affective or paraphrenic clinical conditions.

In keeping with the greater loading of schizo-affectives with those factors usually regarded as prognostically unfavorable, the results of their management and treatment were more disappointing than those results achieved in other elderly persons with functional psychiatric conditions. Only one of 25 surviving patients remained symptom-free after discharge from the hospital compared to 26 of 100 depressives, and 12 of 21 paraphrenics cooperating in maintenance treatment. With schizo-affectives, it proved difficult to find the most effective type of therapy. Major tranquilizers and antidepressive measures were used in the same patient at different times; in a few, combined therapy seemed to produce optimal results.

In conclusion, there does seem to exist a small number of patients who, for the first time late in life, develop disorders displaying characteristics of both the affective and the schizophrenic reaction types either simultaneously or in quick succession. Following a theoretical discussion, which does not deserve to be rehearsed here, I concluded in my 1971 paper that schizo-affective patients should not be regarded as suffering from a separate disease, or from both schizophrenia and an affective psychosis at the same time, but that they should be conceptualized as occupying the central portion of a continuum of persons (Post, 1971a). In these persons, biological faults associated both with affective and with schizophrenic disorders had facilitated mental breakdown in relation to emotional stress, physical illness, cerebral disorder, but also perhaps "normal" mental age changes.

## SENILE RECLUSES

This term refers to a group of persons who exhibit a very specific type of paranoid behavior. They come to be noticed because of severe deterioration in hygiene and self-care, which has developed out of an increasing self-imposed social isolation. Senile recluses have withdrawn from all contacts with other people, sometimes to the extent of barricading themselves in their homes, papering over their windows, etc. A few will allow access to one relative or some other old eccentric, but most refuse all help. Finally, complaints from neighbors accumulate, or the health authorities arrange for the old person's compulsory removal after his or her physical collapse.

I have had only sporadic clinical contact with this kind of problem, and have found only a few references in the literature. Earlier surveys of old people living in their homes (e.g., the one by Sheldon, 1948) referred to some 4 percent of subjects as lonely eccentrics, who struck the observer as vigorous, independent, and apparently happy old people. It is not known whether and to what extent these eccentrics might at some stage have begun to show deterioration of self-care. Granick and Zeman (1960) attempted to study the phenomenon from newspaper cuttings describing, often in sensational terms, the discovery and background of 105 senile recluses. In their sample were as many men as women, and 42 percent had never married, leading to their suggestion that social isolation had started early in life. As has been confirmed in later studies, adopting the role of recluse with severe neglect of hygiene, diet, etc. was not related to poor housing conditions, poverty, or low intelligence. On the contrary, members of the upper social classes were overrepresented. Considerable sums of money were frequently found hidden away under the filth and disorder of the home.

Of the later studies, one was carried out from the geriatrician's viewpoint (Clark, Mankikar, and Gray, 1975) and the other one by two psychiatrists with public health interest (MacMillan and Shaw, 1966). The geriatric study concerned 30 admissions evenly divided between men and women, often in the last stages of neglect with an immediate death rate of 46 percent, so that full evaluation was possible in only half the subjects. The psychiatric study was designed and funded specifically to study senile breakdown in personal and environmental-cleanliness standards. With the help of family doctors and social workers, 72 old recluses were traced and investigated in their own homes, and an annual incidence of 0.5 cases per 1,000 people over 60 years of age was suggested. There were far fewer men than women in this community sample, and the widowed rather than the never-married state predominated. Just over one-half of subjects were diagnosed as psychotic, and most were labeled as suffering from senile dementia of the paranoid type, with a few diagnosed as schizophrenics, paraphrenics, depressives, and deteriorated alcoholics. However, no details of diagnostic methods are given, and only a few of the patients had had previous contact with psychiatry. However, "normals" and "psychotics" had exhibited the same kind of personality earlier in life, and a reconstruction of the course by which the social deterioration had occurred was identical for members of both groups: a domineering, quarrelsome, and independent individual with a suspicious and secretive cast of mind would gradually reject all contacts with others, and abandon the accepted standards of the neighborhood. Sometimes there was evidence that bereavement had initiated the process, but occasionally two people were affected (husband and wife or two siblings), and following the removal of one to the hospital, the other one might rehabilitate him- or herself, much as occurs following the admission of the dominant partner in folie à deux. In some patients rehabilitation in a day-hospital rather than a residential setting was successful. The geriatric paper (Clark, et al. 1975) did not attempt

any psychiatric diagnosis of the surviving patients, but again one-half were regarded as "mentally normal" with above-normal (measured) intelligence, but with certain deviant character traits.

It seems doubtful to me whether the picture presented by senile recluses in states of severe personal neglect should be called a "syndrome." Rather it would seem to represent the consequence of a number of different psychiatric conditions, particularly character disorders and intellectual senile decline. It is interesting that the personalities of senile recluses are very similar to those of elderly people with persistent paranoid disorders.

## EPIDEMIOLOGY

### INCIDENCE AND PREVALENCE

In both a Swedish and an English mental hospital, patients with paraphrenic illnesses commencing after the age of 55 formed some 10 percent of all first admissions after the age of 60 (Kay and Roth, 1961). Rather lower percentages have been given for admission after 65 in England and Wales (5.6 percent) and in the United States (3.2 percent). In other words, late paraphrenic illnesses are a rare cause of admission to psychiatric facilities.

The prevalence of the condition in the community seems very similar: 4 paraphrenics among 228 people over 65 in a Welsh town (Parsons, 1964); 2 among 200 in a Scottish study (Williamson, Stokoe, Gray, Fisher, and Smith, 1964). The Newcastle survey of 309 persons over 65 living in their own homes (Kay, Beamish, and Roth, 1964) failed to bring to light a single case of paraphrenia, but 8 persons with this diagnosis had been admitted from the surveyed area to mental institutions at some earlier time. Eight of 300 consecutive clients over 70 brought to the notice of the welfare services of a London borough were found to be suffering from paranoid disorders compared to 3 with clinical depression, and 30 with organic brain syndromes (Goldberg, 1970).

Thus, in terms of incidence and prevalence, clearly recognized paranoid disorders of late life would seem to be of only minor significance, but because of the nature of the condition almost every sufferer is likely to create considerable problems sooner or later.

### SEX DISTRIBUTION AND CIVIL STATUS

Up to the age of 35 schizophrenia occurs more frequently in males. After that age, females begin to predominate to an increasingly extent, and far in excess to the proportion of females in the general population (Kay, 1972). In Stockholm, for instance, instead of an expected 21 males and 36 females, there were only 9 male and 48 female late-paraphrenic patients (Kay and Roth, 1961). Other workers have reported a similar preponderance of female patients among late-onset schizophrenics. Quite independently, Sternberg (1972), ascertained that among late-schizophrenics registered at a Moscow dispensary the ratio between female and male patients was 3:1, compared to 2:1 in the general population of the same age.

There is similar interstudy agreement on the low marriage rate of late-paraphrenics, which, while higher than in younger schizophrenics, is considerably lower than that of elderly depressives and the general population (Post, 1966). It has also been pointed out that late and infertile marriages are unduly frequent, as are marital separations.

Social class membership is notoriously difficult to determine in old persons. In my series (Post, 1966), 62 percent of patients with persistent persecutory states had practiced semi- and unskilled occupations earlier in life, compared to 12 percent of elderly depressives, whose social class distribution was very similar to that of younger patients of the same hospital. Among the late-paraphrenics there was no evidence of a downward drift, as has been suggested for younger patients. To what extent this apparent link between late-paraphrenia and low social class is genuine, or rather is the result of higher-class patients' greater ability to evade detection and treatment, remains to be investigated. Kay, Cooper, Garside, and Roth (1976) have recently also reported an unduly frequent membership of unskilled and semiskilled occupational classes for those patients first developing schizophrenic and paraphrenic illnesses after the age of 50. Interestingly, this greater-than-"expected" lower class membership was found only in divorced and never-married patients.

## ETIOLOGY

It seems hardly necessary to stress that the causes of schizophrenia-like and paranoid-schizophrenic illnesses of late life are as little known as those of the typical schizophrenias of younger people. There are certain features of the internal and external milieu that are found more frequently in patients with late-paraphrenic illnesses than in other elderly psychiatric subjects, and for this reason, these may be of etiologic significance.

### HEREDITARY FACTORS

At first sight, these look unimportant: Klages, (1961) reported 8 affected first-degree relatives for 53 probands: Funding (1963) dealt with 148 patients with paranoid illnesses of various types and reported 21 secondary cases with a schizophrenic diagnosis. Eight secondary schizophrenics were found by Herbert and Jacobson (1967) among 47 late-paraphrenics. There were 6 secondary cases among my 93 probands (these included "organic" patients) (Post, 1966). The highest figure comes from the study that was probably the most thoroughly and expertly executed, that of Kay (1963) using Scandinavian material and facilities. Among 57 Stockholm patients he reported 13 secondary cases of schizophrenia (2 parents, 8 siblings, and 2 children). Like Funding (1963), he concluded that the risks of siblings developing schizophrenia were significantly lower in the aged than was the case with younger schizophrenics, but still significantly higher than in the general population. Kay (1972) has more recently compared risks for late-paraphrenics with those for younger schizophrenics reported in a Swedish study with the results shown in Table 25–1.

These calculations (Table 25–1) were based on risk periods extending only to an age of 45 or 50, and there is a strong impression among some workers that late-paraphrenics have an unduly large proportion of secondary cases with illnesses commencing after age 50; other workers disagree. A related disagreement concerns the extent to which late-paraphrenia "breeds true." Kay (1963) stressed that he discovered among the first-degree relatives of his patients only a few rather atypical cases of affective psychosis. Others (e.g., Herbert and Jacobson, 1967; Post, 1966) commented on the considerable frequency of affective illnesses, personality disorders, and other psychiatric conditions in the families of their late-paraphrenics.

In conclusion, the outstanding finding of all these family studies seems clear: patients with persistent persecutory syndromes of late life show

**Table 25–1**   Risks of developing schizophrenia for siblings and children of various patient groups.[a]

| PATIENT GROUP | STRICT DIAGNOSTIC CRITERIA (%) | DOUBTFUL CASES INCLUDED (%) |
|---|---|---|
| General Population | 0.8 | 1.6 |
| Late Paraphrenics | 3.4 | 5.4 |
| Early Schizophrenics | 5.8 | 8.5 |

[a]Data taken from Kay, 1972.

stronger evidence for schizophrenic heredity than do members of the general population. At the same time, there is the suggestion that hereditary factors are less in evidence than they are in early-onset typical schizophrenics. As has been pointed out most recently by Kay (1972), this is the sort of finding that is in keeping with a polygenic hypothesis for schizophrenia, i.e., that patients with few affected relatives have fewer genetic factors, and therefore tend to develop their psychoses later in life.

## PERSONAL AND INTERPERSONAL FACTORS

The title of this subsection has been chosen to stress that a person's psychologic functioning and personality cannot be assessed solely as a collection of traits, but only as seen in action with other persons. The prepsychotic functioning of late-paraphrenics has been addressed in the literature at two levels: first, there have been general descriptions which include estimates of the frequency of various personality deviations. The main references to this level of research will be found in the previously quoted publications by Kay and Roth (1961), Post (1966), Herbert and Jacobson (1967), and Sternberg (1972). These researches refer to patients investigated in Sweden, England and Russia.

Second, attempts have been made to define personality and relationship factors more precisely by statistical analyses of personality comparisons of late-paraphrenics with other late-onset psychiatric patients. A start was made by this writer (1966), but the recent study by Kay *et al.* (1976) was carried out with incomparably greater expertise. It would be tedious to paraphrase the relevant sections of all of these papers, and to label each statement with the appropriate reference, except on the few occasions where there have been differences of opinion. Instead, an attempt will be made to communicate the present state of knowledge in a more summarized and simplified fashion.

Even those who maintain that personality structure is genetically determined would not deny that early family influence must also play an important role in personality formation. In contrast with younger schizophrenics, there have, for obvious reasons, not been any studies of the childhoods of late-paraphrenics, though Retterstöll (1966) has attempted to investigate factors in the childhood and adolescence that might have predisposed to paranoid illnesses in later life. However, only some 10 percent of his patients fell ill after 50.

As far as the patient's adult life experience is concerned, it is only rarely possible to obtain reliable accounts of previous personality functioning from the spouses or relatives of late-paraphrenics. Usually, one can learn only about the patient as he appeared in the recent past, when he might have already begun to show early symptoms of his illness.

With this proviso, it may be stated that favorable accounts of the previous personalities of late-paraphrenics are given by their relatives or friends in only a minority of cases (between 10 percent and 30 percent in various reports). In the great majority, quite serious deviations are related by such sources. As far as their prepsychotic personalities were concerned, patients tended to fall into a number of subtypes such as quarrelsome-aggressive-hostile, egocentric-obstinate-domineering, suspicious-jealous-persecuted, or shy-sensitive-withdrawn. In addition, many displayed characteristics such as vegetarianism, herbalism, membership in esoteric religious sects, etc. There has also been an impression that more serious personality deviations have been most prominent in patients with purely paranoid rather than schizophrenic illnesses. The paranoid psychosis (usually without an hallucinosis) impressed observers as an accentuation of the previous personality. Personality defects tend to be regarded as the source rather than the result of the much-reported low marriage rate and social isolation of late-paraphrenics. Even in a sample of voluntarily admitted, and for this reason probably less frequently deprived patients, one-third had always been withdrawn and suspicious with no or only hostile human contacts, and only one-third had had mainly pleasant, though rather superficial, relationships limited to family members. In contrast with younger schizophrenics, work records had usually been good, and patients had apparently been able to relate adequately to the work situation. Failure had, however, almost always occurred in the area of more intimate relationships. The relatively low marriage rate of late-paraphrenics has already been commented on. In addition, some workers have reported an increased frequency of delayed marriages (to an unusually late age), or failure to marry despite the birth of illegitimate children. Ever-married patients tend to have fewer-than-"expected" surviving children, but whether this is due to decreased fertility of the patients or to excessive mortality of the children remains uncertain (Kay *et al.*, 1976). It has obviously been very difficult to obtain reliable information on past sexual adjustment in these paranoid old people. In my experience, presumably satisfactory sexual adjustment had been achieved by only 33 percent of late-paraphrenics as compared with 55 percent of elderly depressives.

In view of the brittle or absent relationships that had existed for many years between most of the patients and their significant others, it was not surprising that in my experience, interpersonal events such as bereavements hardly ever appear to have precipitated the illness. This opinion is, at the first sight at least, contradicted by the more recent findings of Kay *et al.* (1976). Comparing consecutively admitted patients with either paranoid or affective psychoses commencing after the age of 50, "events or situations which were regarded by the patients or relatives as important" were recorded for 77 percent of depressives, but also for 50 percent of the paranoid cases (Kay *et al.*, 1976). However, events that could be regarded as entirely independent of the patients (i.e., not even partly created by the patient) occurred in 46 percent of the affectives and in only 18.5 percent of the paranoid subjects of the enquiry. These emotionally disturbing life events were mainly bereavements, physical illnesses, and separations from children. In my experience, psychotic-paranoid symptoms were not infrequently initially alleged to have appeared following bereavement or separation from children, but on closer enquiry it almost always emerged that the psychosis had predated these events by months or years, and that spouses or children had managed to conceal the patient's disorder. Sometimes, there was evidence of the deceased spouse having shared the patient's beliefs within a framework of folie à deux.

Important differences between late-onset depressives and late-paraphrenics emerged when investigating the patients' earlier mental health. In the case of paraphrenics it was rather remarkable that phobic, obsessional or hypochondriacal trends or states hardly ever played a role in the earlier life history, and this contrasted strongly with the accounts obtained in the case of most elderly depressives (Post, 1962). On the other hand, episodes of other minor psychologic disturbances had been reported in a sizeable proportion of paraphrenics (e.g., 37 percent by Post, 1966). These events had been regarded as being of the anxious-depressive type, and had usually not required any special psychiatric treatment. Obviously, patients would not have been included in these studies if the earlier attacks had been regarded as schizophrenic. However, Sternberg (1972), who had also discovered minor disturbances during the earlier life of many of his late-onset paranoid patients, thought there was sufficient evidence to class these episodes as thrusts or shifts of a schizophrenic process. Such

an interpretation is obviously very much in line with the Soviet concept of latent or creeping schizophrenia. Even in the rare instances in which good earlier case notes are available, it must surely be difficult to distinguish in retrospect between largely neurotic and mild schizophrenic conditions occurring in schizoid personalities. All the same, in the last section of this chapter the possible relationship between late-paraphrenia and a mild schizophrenic disorder dating from early life will have to be considered.

## SOMATIC FACTORS

Regarding physical constitution, earlier writers had frequently remarked on the tendency of paranoid schizophrenics, whose illnesses usually commence a decade or two later than other forms of schizophrenia, to exhibit the pyknic type of body build. This was on an impressionistic basis. Exact anthropometric evaluations of samples of elderly depressives and late-paraphrenics (Lodge-Patch, Post, and Slater, 1965) showed that these patients did not exhibit any of the physical differences that have been found to exist between younger schizophrenics and depressives.

While transient paranoid symptomatology is not infrequently encountered in relation to potentially reversible brain syndromes of physical causes, bodily health is more often than not outstandingly satisfactory in late-paraphrenics. In keeping with this, their death rate has been found to be similar to that of the age-matched general population (Kay, 1962). However, there has come to light a good deal of evidence for an association between late paranoid symptomatology and the presence of sensory defects, especially deafness, but possibly also visual impairment.

The meaning of being deaf, hard of hearing, or socially deaf; and the relationship between auditory defects and mental health generally, and between such defects and paranoid symptomatology more specifically have been recently illuminated by Cooper (1976). In late-paranoid illnesses, most writers have reported a more frequent occurrence of hearing defects when compared to the general population and with elderly depressives (Cooper, Garside, and Kay, 1976; Kay and Roth, 1961; Post, 1966). The association between aural pathology and paranoid illnesses of late life has been more searchingly investigated by Cooper, Kay, Curry, Garside, and Roth (1974) by comparing 65 paraphrenics with 37 patients with primary affective illnesses. Members of both groups had for the first time become psychotic after the age of 50, and had been assessed as suffering from social deafness. Almost all the subjects were, after re-mission of their acute symptoms, examined by the otologist of the investigating team. After allowing for a number of relevant variables, it was concluded that patients with paranoid psychoses had a more severe hearing loss and were more often socially deaf than were patients with affective illnesses. Furthermore, a far higher proportion of paranoid patients had longstanding, usually severe, bilateral deafness of a middle-ear type rather than nerve deafness. In a more specific report (Cooper *et al.*, 1976), 27 deaf paranoid patients (average age of 67 years) were compared with 18 deaf affective patients (average age of 69 years). Deaf paranoid patients had audiograms typical of conductive deafness, while deaf affective patients had audiograms indicating nerve deafness—the common form of deafness found in relation to advancing age. The causes of conductive deafness found in the paranoid patients were most commonly chronic suppurative otitis media, but oto-sclerosis and tympanosclerosis were also found, and these conditions were highly significantly more frequent in the paranoid than in the affective patients. Over and above this, deafness was more severe (measured by audiometry) in the deaf paranoids than in the deaf affectives. In other words, while the elderly depressives, like so many mentally normal persons, suffered almost entirely from hearing impairment due to age changes, the paranoid subjects showed evidence of ear disease and deafness dating from an early age.

In the previously quoted papers and in a more recent publication reporting a comparison of deaf and nondeaf patients with paranoid and affective psychoses, respectively (Cooper, Garside, and Kay, 1976), Cooper and his associates speculate on the role of deafness in the development of paranoid symptoms in late life. Deafness appeared to emerge as an etiologic factor rather more suggestively in relation to the findings that deaf paraphrenics had fewer other predisposing factors for schizophrenia, such as family histories of the disorders and schizoid personalities. As a causal mechanism in late-paraphrenia these workers favor deafness as producing changes in psychologic functioning and social adaption slowly, rather than regarding deafness as a precipitating factor acting via sensory deprivation.

The etiologic role of visual impairment is far less well defined. Probably, visual defects are more common in paranoids than in depressives. In addition, there may be an association of deafness and cataracts in paranoid patients. However, in the relevant study (Cooper and Porter, 1976), considerable difficulties were encountered in fixing the du-ration of visual defects and thus their etiologic significance.

An attempt to synthesize the causal factors for late-paraphrenia described in this section will be postponed to the end of the chapter.

## DYNAMIC PSYCHOPATHOLOGY

A search of the literature for psychodynamic studies in late-paraphrenia and related conditions proved unsuccessful. A single study (Haase, 1963), does include the term *psychodynamic* in its title, but in actual fact it is (without any clear-cut results) concerned with the etiologic role of social isolation in paranoid-hallucinatory psychoses of middle-aged and elderly women.

It must be remembered that persons with paranoid illnesses, especially when psychotic in degree of severity, are barely accessible to psychodynamic exploration. Freud's classical analysis of the well-known Schreber case had to be carried out on the case history alone. Even when prolonged conversations with paranoid subjects are possible, attempts to gain a dynamic understanding can be made only by reading between the lines. The life histories and symptomatologies of patients with late-paraphrenia frequently lend themselves to obvious and plausible interpretations, because the delusions and hallucinatory experiences are almost always characterized by a strikingly obvious banality.

While younger schizophrenics tend to have experiences with mystical or religious contents, those of late-paraphrenics are almost always very much earth-bound. The content of these late-life psychoses is almost exclusively centered around themes of personal possessions and sexuality. Most commonly, psychotic experiences refer entirely to interference with objects in the home or to a threat against possession of the home itself. The erection of delusional systems is very rare. At the very most, patients explain their having become targets of persecution in terms of revenge by the neighbors for the patient's aloofness or elevated social status.

Sexual delusions and hallucinations tend to be coarse, concrete, and undisguisedly genital. The homosexual undercurrent discerned in the mental content of many younger paranoid schizophrenics is displaced by a largely heterosexual coloring: the phantom lover produces vaginal sensations by telepathic means; the patient believes herself observed by special apparatus during intimate functions. Visual hallucinations are often of an obvious phallic kind (an elongated balloon appears in the sky; a ray penetrates into her room, etc.). When religious themes do occur, they tend to be of a concrete quality (God touching her head with a feather to show she is good).

The wish-fear basis and the projection of barely unconscious material seems very clear in elderly paraphrenics, even when they use mental mechanisms in common with young schizophrenics, like dissolution of ego-boundaries or third-person-singular auditory hallucinations. These patients have, in reality, harbored hostile feeling towards others and have felt themselves to be superior. It is almost always those without any or with only unsatisfactory experiences, who suffer from sexual delusions and hallucinations.

The concreteness and banality of the psychotic experiences of late-schizophrenics has been explained in terms of senile emotional flattening and intellectual impoverishment, but I wonder whether it might not be an indication of the relative mildness of those schizophrenic disorders that first arise in an aged person, and of the relatively minor disintegration of personality functioning in this setting. Related to this, a recent and interesting contribution was made by Gillièron (1976). He compared two groups of elderly women with paranoid psychoses: in one, the illness had started before the age of 45; in the other, only after the age of 65. The early-onset schizophrenics had had far more disturbed and autistic personalities and had showed far more disintegration in terms of a richer and more typically schizophrenic symptomatology.

## PROGNOSIS AND TREATMENT

### OUTLOOK BEFORE THE USE OF MAJOR TRANQUILIZERS

Until fairly recently there had been a strong impression that the outlook was poor for elderly patients with paranoid disorders, unless they occurred in a setting of either mania or melancholia. In the absence of cerebral pathology, duration of life was not significantly shortened (Kay, 1962). It was common for many old people to survive for long periods in the community despite highly disturbing delusional beliefs and consequent behavior disorders: the few who finally required hospital admission had to remain under long-term hospital care for many years. There was an impression that in a few instances delusions might become "encapsulated," or that the paranoid illness could take a fluctuating and remitting course. During my follow-up study (Post, 1966), there was, in fact, only one patient who defaulted early on in drug therapy, and who appreared to have made a sponta-

neous remission. However, she relapsed after a couple of years and then responded well and lastingly to treatment.

### OUTLOOK AFTER THE INTRODUCTION OF PSYCHOPHARMACOLOGIC TREATMENT

The response of patients with paranoid delusions and hallucinations in the setting of schizophrenia-like or schizophrenic illnesses to major tranquilizing drugs (originally largely chlorpromazine was so striking that no reports of double-blind therapeutic trials were ever published or demanded. In a series of 45 patients admitted to a regional mental hospital between 1958 and 1961, only 16 had to remain for long-term care. Apart from 8 patients who died, the rest could be discharged after treatment and most of them did not require readmissions (Herbert and Jacobson, 1967).

Dealing only with voluntarily admitted patients, and comparing outcome before and after the introduction of phenothiazine therapy, I (Post, 1966) reported that 24 patients admitted before the introduction of specific therapy all remained psychotic, while among a subsequent consecutively-admitted and drug-treated sample of 37, only 4 remained unchanged, 8 patients experienced partial remissions, and 25 made complete recoveries. In a later sample, which for the first time included subjects treated only in an out-patient setting, 2 of 32 defaulted early, 2 showed no response, 18 made immediate complete recoveries, and 10 only partial immediate recoveries.

### THERAPEUTIC TECHNIQUES

Treatment of elderly paraphrenics can now be planned with considerable confidence of success, provided that adequate amounts of major tranquilizing drugs can be administered. Unfortunately this provision is not always fulfilled.

During my 1966 study, 71 patients were treated, apparently adequately, largely with trifluoperazine or thioridazine: 6 of them failed to respond completely; 22 continued to have abnormal experiences or to entertain delusional beliefs, but the intensity of symptoms did not prohibit their discharge from hospital and successful reentry into the community; and 43 patients ceased to have ongoing symptoms. However, only about half of these 43 gained insight, that is, admitted that their past beliefs and experiences might have been, or had definitely been, part and parcel of a mental breakdown. With a greater choice of preparations, and especially with the introduction of depot injections, there is a strong impression that complete failure of response is now even more rarely encountered.

A systematic account of the use of major tranquilizing drugs in the treatment of elderly psychotics can be found in Chapter 30. From my experience, chlorpromazine has been found to be effective, but because of the frequency with which it seems to precipitate jaundice in elderly women, thioridazine is now preferred. Trifluoperazine and other drugs requiring only low dosages (5–30 mg. daily) tend to produce much more severe neurologic side effects, and are reserved for patients not responding to a slowly increasing dosage of thioridazine (50–600 mg daily). When there is remission or no further improvement (usually with a daily dose of 100–200 mg) maintenance treatment at a lower dose (usually in the region of 50 mg) is instituted. Attempt should be made to discontinue maintenance therapy at least once a year whenever this is possible to avoid dyskinetic syndromes due to the long-term use of phenothiazines and other preparations. The relative success of drug therapy is best presented in table form, and requires no comment (Figure 25–1).

Obviously the largest obstacle to the successful treatment of old people with paranoid illnesses stems from the nature of the disorder: these patients are most unlikely to accept even the possibility of being ill rather than being persecuted. However, most old persons, in Britain at any rate, see their physicians regularly for somatic problems. If the doctors are skilled and experienced, they will not (like friends and relatives) argue with the patients about their beliefs and experiences. Instead, the doctor will listen and admit he cannot deal with the patient's environment. Instead, he will offer to protect the patient's overstressed nervous system through the use of suitable medication. It is surprising how many insightless patients can be made to cooperate in drug therapy by doctors displaying a psychotherapeutically sophisticated attitude promoting rapport and trust. All the same, refusal of treatment will be resolute in a minority of cases. For these patients and those whose tablet-taking cannot be satisfactorily supervised, hospital admission is required. Such an admission need only be temporary, but in the case of treatment refusers will have to take the form of compulsory commitment. As favorable results are expected, it may be possible to overcome the contemporary reluctance of some relatives and most social agencies "to lock up old people." Needless to say, maintenance treatment of patients who have had to be treated against their will or who continue to be unreliable tablet-takers, will have to make use of intramuscular depot injections.

## LONG-TERM OUTCOME

There are few hard data documenting the course pursued by old people with paraphrenic illnesses who were either never admitted, or who could be discharged after a period of hospital care. As stated, a proportion of senile recluses are thought to suffer from schizophrenic psychoses, but it is not known how frequently paranoid old people continue to exist in their own home without ever coming to medical notice.

Long-term outcome has been analyzed in considerable detail elsewhere (Post, 1966). But as that study dealt with patients who had permitted themselves to be brought into treatment informally, and in relation to this still had fairly strong family ties, and were thus rather atypical, the results will be summarized only briefly. Numbers refer to patients who were followed for three years and who had survived the first year of the observation period. There were 21 patients treated before the introduction of specific drug therapy. Few needed readmission, but only 6 caused no further problems; most had apparently learned to live with their continuing preoccupations. By contrast, there

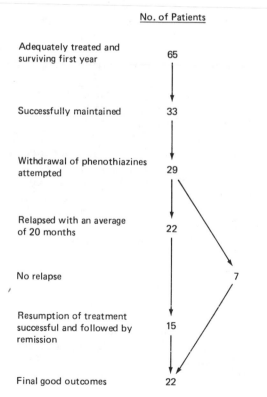

No. of Patients

|  |  |
|---|---|
| Adequately treated and surviving first year | 65 |
| Successfully maintained | 33 |
| Withdrawal of phenothiazines attempted | 29 |
| Relapsed with an average of 20 months | 22 |
| No relapse | 7 |
| Resumption of treatment successful and followed by remission | 15 |
| Final good outcomes | 22 |

**Figure 25-1**   Results of drug therapy.

were 65 patients who had been treated initially and adequately with one of the phenothiazine drugs. Of this number, 34 percent remained symptom-free and without psychiatric disabilities throughout the follow-up period, while 28 percent remained continuously psychotic. Varying periods of intermittent mental disturbances were experienced by the remaining 38 percent and these were usually related to fluctuating cooperation in maintenance drug therapy.

At a statistically highly significant level, those subjects who did well had become completely asymptomatic during the initial treatment episode, and had gained at least a modicum of "insight." At a similar level of significance, patient success corresponded to the extent to which they and their families continued to cooperate in maintenance drug therapy. As might be expected, this continued cooperation was positively associated with preservation of reasonably good relationships between the patient and his "significant others,"—including his psychiatrist.

Though not to a statistically significant extent, several other characteristics were associated with good long-term cooperation and outcome. These characteristics are all ones that appear to favor preservation of personal relationships: relatively young age, being married, working class membership, mild rather than markedly deviant personality traits in the past, relatively good sexual adjustment, and short duration of paranoid symptoms prior to treatment. By contrast, deafness and cerebral deterioration might be expected to impair interpersonal relationships, and they were in fact associated with poorer cooperation in treatment and with unfavorable outcome.

In a sample of elderly depressives, social adjustment tended to improve long-term in relation to a clinically favorable course; by contrast, hardly any late-paraphrenics regardless of clinical progress were able to improve their relationship patterns or their social activities during the follow-up period. In fact, some patients who did well as far as their symptoms were concerned, continued to decline in social adjustment. It was suggested that processes of increasing social withdrawal, which had preceded overt illness, continued despite the removal of symptoms by drug therapy.

Experience over the last 10 years has not changed earlier impressions that adequate drug therapy removes the symptoms of a late-schizophrenic syndrome, restoring previous adjustment to the level of continuously and slowly progressive deviant personality functioning. Provided a patient accepting treatment has some home supervision, admission to the hospital is now rarely necessary.

It has recently been claimed (Baker and Byrne, 1977) that elderly paranoid persons, even when living on their own, can be successfully treated in a day-hospital setting.

## THE AGING SCHIZOPHRENIC

A full account of the influence of aging on the schizophrenic syndrome throughout the life span would require a separate chapter. Within the framework of a handbook of mental aging, it seems more appropriate to confine the discussion to studies that have concerned themselves with schizophrenics who have survived into late middle life and old age either in the hospital or in the community. Incidental insights obtained into the natural history of schizophrenia will not be withheld.

LITERATURE

The earlier references concerning old schizophrenics were summarized by Müller (1959). His main discovery showed that schizophrenics surviving into old age tended to become very much less psychotic so far as the severity of their symptoms was concerned, and that for this reason they were able to make better social adjustments than at an earlier age. These findings have since been confirmed by a number of other workers. Diminution of affective incongruity and of affective disturbance as a whole was reported in a rather impressionistic paper by Ruemke (1963).An amelioration of the psychosis was reported by Wenger (1958), and using psychometric quantification, by Lawton (1972), among others. Many of M. Bleuler's (1972) patients were followed beyond the age of 60, but the definitive study of schizophrenics followed beyond 65 is that of Ciompi and Müller (1976). Before we look at their conclusions in detail, we shall mention briefly that they confirmed most of the findings concerning the long-term course of schizophrenic patients obtained by Bleuler (1972, 1974) during his investigations of personal patients followed over at least 20 years.

A certain number of facts are clear and striking. At the beginning of the century some 10 percent of young schizophrenics pursued what Bleuler called a "catastrophic course": the acute schizophrenic breakdown was followed by a steady and severe progress of deterioration, chronicity, or sometimes early death. (In fact, the mortality of schizophrenics has remained higher than that of the age-matched general population, mainly due to a more frequent occurrence of suicide (during all stages of the disorder) and of other unnatural deaths.)

Only 6 percent of Ciompi and Müller's cases, some of whom had been originally treated before 1930, were recorded as having deteriorated by the time they were followed after the age of 65 as compared to their status at initial admission. However, in a more recently treated sample, Bleuler (1972) no longer encountered a rapidly and irreversibly deteriorative course. This improvement in the prognosis of schizophrenia would seem to be due to improved patient management, but whether related to insulin coma and convulsive therapies or to improved sociotherapeutic atmosphere of the mental hospital, which went forward hand-in-hand with the introduction of somatic therapies, can no longer be determined. In both investigations, some 20 percent of patients made complete and apparently permanent recoveries from their first and only attacks. The remainder suffered either recurrent illness episodes with good adjustment between attacks or stabilized in a state of psychosis. Permanent hospitalization, however, was required for only 10 percent (Bleuler, 1974) to 23 percent (Ciompi and Müller, 1976) of patients. Most importantly, increasing deterioration of the mental condition is no longer seen after five years post onset of the psychosis. Thus there is no modern evidence for the role of a deteriorative, perhaps cerebral-organic "process" in schizophrenia. On the contrary, schizophrenics reveal good preservation of intellect and affect beneath their symptomatology again and again, especially when under physical or psychologic stress. In addition, the long-term course of even permanently hospitalized, chronic schizophrenics tends toward a certain amount of improvement as senility is reached.

Bleuler, Ciompi and Müller thought that the use of psychopharmacologic preparations or of electroconvulsive therapies (i.e., of tranquilizing or stimulating treatments) might cut short the first acute attack and subsequent exacerbations, but would not affect long-term outcome. However, the main and perhaps only weakness of both studies lies in the fact that Bleuler saw his patients almost only when they were ill, and Ciompi and Müller only at follow-up. Thus the effects of active aftercare and maintenance drug therapy, which might have improved prognosis even more, were not investigated.

## THE LAUSANNE STUDY

Ciompi and Müller (1976) studied 1,642 case records of patients who before the age of 65 had been admitted to the Lausanne Clinic during their first attack of schizophrenia (primarily between the years 1920 and 1940). At follow-up, the patients' ages varied from 65 to 90. However, only 347 were still alive, and personal examination as well as interviews with relatives and consultation of documents were possible in only 305 cases. On the other hand, the diagnosis of schizophrenia was unconfirmed in only 16 of the cases (patients with borderline and atypical diagnoses had been discarded from the original research sample). Because patients with severe and especially with catatonic symptomatologies had a high death rate from complicating physical disease, the study does not tell us anything about outcome in old age in patients with the more severe forms of schizophrenia, that is, patients who today may well survive in greater numbers.

During an observation period averaging 37 years, 47 percent of patients spent less than one year (including the index admission) in a hospital, 10 percent spent 1–3 years in hospital, and as mentioned earlier, 23 percent remained in a hospital for more than 20 years. As expected, continued hospital stay tended to correlate with severely incapacitated end states, though decrease in severity and number of symptoms was the rule with schizophrenics reaching late life. In the course of the illness, differences in symptomatology (e.g., between catatonic and hebephrenic pictures) tended to disappear, and in this sample of patients selected by survival into old age, the evidence for the existence of concepts like nuclear, phasic, reactive, or atypical schizophrenia was not forthcoming. It was confirmed that an acute onset, a rich and variable psychopathology, and affective responsiveness were favorable prognostic indicators as compared with a slow development of less obviously disruptive symptoms. However, the future of the schizophrenics surviving into late life was much more influenced by the level of personality integration they had achieved before their first attack; this also related to late-life social adjustment.

The investigators looked into the possible role of "institutional neurosis" in producing poor social adjustment. Many patients had been admitted during the earlier part of the century when hospital management had been restrictive and unstimulating. Analysis of the data showed that this had not affected long-term outcome if the original admission had been short term. Patients with extended first admissions had remained more severely ill for longer periods, but to what extent this was related to severity of illness or to institutionalization could not be disentangled in retrospect. However, it should be pointed out that only 33 percent of these patients had had prolonged hospital stays (and only a proportion of them "in the bad old days"), so that the deleterious role of institutional care in causing chronic schizophrenic deterioration may have been overstressed in the past.

Perhaps the most chastening finding of the Lausanne study lies in the assessment of social outcome. Though most patients had remained in the hospital for only short periods, at an average age of 75 only 55 percent had ever married, and only 15 percent of those married were found living with their spouses. In fact, only two-fifths of subjects lived outside institutions of one type or another. In comparison with psychiatric patients with other diagnoses similarly followed into old age during the "Enquête Lausanne," three-quarters of schizophrenic subjects had noticeably fewer social contacts and outlets. Even so, three-fifths had some satisfying relationships, and there was an impression that, in keeping with decreasing severity of symptoms, the interpersonal adjustment of many patients had improved as they had grown older. Despite this, however, a satisfactory global social adjustment was achieved by only one-third of these schizophrenics.

Addressing the supervention of intellectual changes in life-long schizophrenics due to abnormal aging, earlier workers had sometimes hoped that these subjects' sheltered existence might protect them from the ravages of senile and arteriosclerotic dementia. Ciompi and Müller (1976) could not confirm this. On the contrary, they found a somewhat increased occurrence of these conditions in their subjects. They did not, however, employ any psychometry, but relied on patient responses during interviews and accounts given by others. In view of the difficulties encountered in the intellectual assessment of paraphrenic old people, which might only be surmounted by precisely quantified serial assessments, the reported agreement of two interviewers in 75 percent of cases need not point to a correct assessment. It seems more likely that schizophrenics surviving into late life show a similar incidence of pathologic brain changes as do mentally healthy old people of comparable age.

## CONCLUDING SYNTHESIS

The reported findings in elderly people with paranoid, schizophrenia-like, or schizophrenic breakdowns on the one hand, and the results of the follow-up into late life of schizophrenics with earlier onsets of their illness on the other hand, invite a synthesis.

In the past there seems to have been two contrasting attitudes to the question: "What is schizophrenia?" For many years the dominant approach assumed that schizophrenia was a disease and a "somatosis" (i.e., a psychosis of somatic origin) to boot. The case for the somatosis hypothesis of schizophrenia has been recently and most cogently argued by Huber (1976). Many workers have, however, become increasingly disenchanted with the search for a cause of the disease, either in terms of a "toxin," or in more modern times, in terms of a "neurobiologic cerebral enzyme disorder." Paraphrasing a well-known dictum, most researchers would suggest that there is no schizophrenia, only schizophrenics. These would be regarded as human beings displaying deviant, maladaptive, and sometimes even "psychotic" personality features to varying degrees. As is well known, some workers have even gone so far as to suggest that "patients" are often less "sick" than others in their families to whom they are trying to adapt by developing schizophrenic symptoms. Other investigators (among them Bleuler, 1963, 1972), have reminded us that ways of schizophrenic experiencing and thinking occur in the mental lives of many people who never develop any psychoses, and perhaps especially in apparently healthy relatives of schizophrenics. The genetic-hereditary factors found in the families of schizophrenics were not so much genetic faults associated with a familial disease called *schizophrenia*, but might be thought to operate by causing flaws in personality development. It is suggested that the resulting defects of personality may facilitate the emergence of schizophrenic symptomatology under the impact of emotionally significant life experiences. Well-known precipitating events in younger schizophrenics are, of course, a first love affair or the birth of a child, but earlier adverse emotional factors arising from faulty communications within the family have been described in numerous and well-known publications.

In addition, this writer suggests that when one looks at late-life paranoid–schizophrenia-like and schizophrenic developments in relation to the life course of schizophrenics with earlier breakdowns, there emerges a picture that accords very well with a third approach to the nature of schizophrenia, namely the *spectrum concept* recently expounded by Reich (1976), and defined as follows:

> This concept designates a theory that proposes that there exists a cluster or spectrum of psychopathologic states, some characterized by psychosis and others not, which share a genetic etiology with schizophrenia, and which, therefore, constitute together with classical schizophrenia itself a "spectrum of schizophrenic disorders."

First of all, this spectrum concept accords well with the hereditary facts discovered for early-life and late-life schizophrenics. We may recall that a family history of schizophrenia is less frequent in late-onset than in early-onset schizophrenics, but even so is more frequent than in the general population. In both groups there is in addition a good deal of psychopathology, especially in the form of various personality disorders and atypical psychiatric conditions.

The second way in which the spectrum concept may be usefully applied relates to schizophrenics followed throughout a lifetime into old age. We saw in the Lausanne study that some had suffered only one psychotic breakdown followed by complete and lasting recovery; others had several attacks in a lifetime with or without complete remissions; others remained mildly ill and disabled for the rest of their lives; and others remained severely schizophrenic throughout life. Features were described, especially in this last group, that might be of cerebral-organic origin. Such features have been proposed as occurring in chronic schizophrenics by workers such as Huber (summarized in 1976) and Johnstone, Crow, Firth, Husband, and Kreel (1976), who employed serial tomography of the brain (EMI scanning). In other words, the patients followed by Bleuler (1972, 1974), over at least 20 years, and those followed by Ciompi and Müller (1976) for an average of 37 years, exhibited a spectrum of schizophrenic disorders of various types and degrees of severity when analyzed in longitudinal section.

Third, the writer's own patients, all commencing their illnesses after the age of 50, were followed for only short periods (Post, 1966), and they presented a spectrum of schizophrenic disorders in cross-section, which ranged from classical ("Schneider-positive") paranoid-schizophrenia, through schizophrenic-like illnesses, to what were described as simple paranoid psychoses. The excellent response of all these patients to modern drug therapy (whenever it could be consistently applied) would also suggest that they belonged within the schizophrenic spectrum.

Fourth, a number of workers have suggested that personality descriptions of late-paraphrenics point to a life-long abnormality, or life-long membership in the spectrum of schizophrenic disorders. Possibly due to an attenuated genetic loading, these patients had broken down with an overt psychosis only relatively late in life.

Recently some evidence has begun to appear that suggests that life stresses may play an additional role to factors in the patient's make-up. Moreover these external factors (stresses) are of a kind easily seen to be potentiated by aging. First, age-related cerebral disease and deterioration were occasionally seen to precipitate paranoid, schizophrenia-like, or paranoid-schizophrenic symptomatology. Second, we reviewed the impressive work on deafness, and found that only the longstanding middle-ear type was of etiologic significance. More recently Cooper *et al.* (1976) have discussed the possible influence of deafness on the shaping of prepsychotic personality. Third, quite independently of the severity of previous personality deviations, late-paraphrenics have been shown to be disadvantaged by (a) lower social class membership, (b) remaining unmarried, (c) living in isolation, and (d) having fewer surviving relatives more often than have late-onset depressives.

At the present time a spectrum concept of schizophrenia would seem to provide a useful framework for further work on late-life paranoid, schizophrenia-like, and schizophrenic illnesses. With a much-attenuated hereditary predisposition, impairment of certain aspects of personality development may occur and result in personality deviation within the schizophrenic spectrum. Long-term stresses related to aging, as well as to brain changes, deafness, perhaps blindness, and various kinds of social deprivation may lead to the emergence of a variety of conditions which, in conjunction with the antecedent personality disorder, are much more centrally placed within this schizophrenic spectrum. No doubt, better management of deafness in earlier life would reduce the frequency of late-paraphrenic illnesses, but it seems unlikely that prepsychotic personality developments could be prevented by psychotherapy or by social measures in a significant proportion of the population. More realistically, prophylactic research might be directed toward age changes that cause a schizophrenic, schizophrenic-like or paranoid syndrome to emerge, and my guess is that these changes will be found to occur in cerebral enzyme activities.

## REFERENCES

ALBEE, G. W. 1950. Delusions in schizophrenia as a function of chronological age. *J. Consult. Psychol.*, *14*, 340–342.

BAKER, A. A., AND BYRNE, R. J. F. 1977. Another style of psychogeriatric service. *Brit. J. Psychiat.*, *130*, 123–126.

BERGMANN, K., KAY, D. W. K., FOSTER, E. M., MC-KECHNIE, A. A., AND ROTH, M. 1971. A follow-up study of randomly selected community residents to assess the effects of chronic brain syndrome and cerebro-vascular disease. Paper read at Fifth World Congress of Psychiatry, Mexico City.

BERNER, P. 1972. Paranoide syndrome. *In*, K. P. Kisker, J. E. Meyer, M. Müller, E. Strömgren (eds.), *Psychiatrie der Gegenwart*. 2nd Ed., Vol. II/I. Berlin, Heidelberg, New York: Springer-Verlag.

BIRREN, J. E. 1964. *The Psychology of Aging*. Englewood Cliffs, N.J.: Prentice-Hall.

BLEULER, M. 1943. Die spaetschizophrenen Krankheitsbilder. *Fortsch. d. Neurol. & Psychiat., 15*, 259.

BLEULER, M. 1963. Conception of schizophrenia within the last fifty years and today. *Proc. Roy. Soc. Med., 56*, 945–952.

BLEULER, M. 1972. *Die schizophrenen Geistesstörungen*, Stuttgart; Thieme.

BLEULER, M. 1974. The long-term course of the schizophrenic psychoses. *Psychol. Med., 4*, 244–254.

BOSCH, G. 1972. Psychosen des Kindesalters. *In, Psychiatrie der Gegenwart*, Vol. II/I. pp. 873–920. Berlin, Heidelberg, New York: Springer-Verlag.

BOSTROEM, A. 1938. Die verschiedenen Lebensabschnitte in ihrer Auswirkung auf das psychiatrische Krankheitsbild. *Arch. Psychiat. Neurol., 107*, 155–171.

CIOMPI, L., AND MÜLLER, C. 1976. *Lebensweg und Alter der Schizophrenen*. Berlin, Heidelberg, New York: Springer-Verlag.

CLARK, A. N. G., MANKIKAR, G. D., AND GRAY, I. 1975. Diogenes syndrome. A clinical study of gross neglect in old age. *Lancet, 1*, 366–373.

COOPER, A. F. 1976. Deafness and psychiatric illness. *Brit. J. Psychiat., 129*, 216–226.

COOPER, A. F., GARSIDE, R. F., AND KAY, D. W. K. 1976. A comparison of deaf and non-deaf patients with paranoid and affective psychoses. *Brit. J. Psychiat., 129*, 532–538.

COOPER, A. F., KAY, D. W. K., CURRY, A. R., GARSIDE, R. F., AND ROTH, M. 1974. Hearing loss in paranoid and affective psychoses of the elderly. *Lancet, ii*, 851–861.

COOPER, H. F., AND PORTER, R. 1976. Visual acuity and ocular pathology in the paranoid and affective psychoses of later life. *J. Psychosom. Res., 20*, 107–114.

FISH, F. 1960. Senile schizophrenia. *J. Ment. Sci., 106*, 938–946.

FUNDING, T. 1963. Paranoid psychoses in later life. *Acta. Psychiat. Scand., 39*, Supp. 169, 356–361.

GABRIEL, E. 1974a. Der langfristige Verlauf schizophrener Späterkrankungen. *Psychiat. Clin., 7*, 172–180.

GABRIEL, E. 1974b. Ueber den Einfluss psychoorganischer Beeintraechtigung im Alter auf den Verlauf sogenannter Spaetschizophrenien. *Psychiat. Clin. 7*, 358–364.

GILLIÈRON, E. 1976. *Etude comparative de deux groupes de syndromes paranoides apparaissant à des âges différents*, MD. Thesis, Lausanne, Orell Füssli, Zürich.

GOLDBERG, E. M. 1970. *Helping the Aged: A Field Experiment in Social Work*, London: George Allen & Unwin.

GRANICK, R., AND ZEMAN, F. D. 1960. The aged recluse—an exploratory study with special reference to community responsibility. *J. Chron. Dis., 12*, 639–642.

HAASE, H. J. 1963. Zur Psychodynamic und Pathoplastik paranoider und paranoid—halluzinatorischer Psychosen bei alleinstehenden Frauen. *Fortschr. Neurol. Psychiat., 31*, 308–322.

HERBERT, M. E., AND JACOBSON, S. 1967. Late paraphrenia. *Brit. J. Psychiat., 113*, 461–469.

HUBER, G. 1976. Indizien für die Somatosehypothese bei den Schizophrenien. *Fortschr. Neurol. Psychiat., 44*, 77–94.

ISAACS, B., AND CAIRD, F. I. 1976. 'Brain failure': A contribution to the terminology of mental abnormality in old age. *Age and Ageing, 5*, 241–244.

JANZARIK, W. 1957. Zur Problematik schizophrener Psychosen im hoeheren Lebensalter. *N. Arzt, 28*, 535–541.

JOHNSTONE, E., CROW, T. J., FIRTH, C. D., HUSBAND, J., AND KREEL, L. 1976. Cerebral ventricular size and cognitive impairment in chronic schizophrenia. *Lancet, ii*, 924–926.

KAY, D. W. K. 1962. Outcome and cause of death in mental disorders of old age: A long-term follow-up of functional and organic psychoses. *Acta. Psychiat. Scand., 38*, 249–276.

KAY, D. W. K. 1963. Late paraphrenia and its bearing on the etiology of schizophrenia. *Acta. Psychiat. Scand., 39*, 159–169.

KAY, D. W. K. 1972. Schizophrenia and schizophrenia-like states in the elderly. *Brit. J. Hosp. Med., 8*, 369–376.

KAY, D. W. K., BEAMISH, P., AND ROTH, M. 1964. Old age mental disorders in Newcastle-upon-Tyne. *J. Ment. Sci. 110*, 668–682.

KAY, D. W. K., COOPER, A. F., GARSIDE, R. F., AND ROTH, M. 1976. The differentiation of paranoid from affective psychoses by patients' premorbid characteristics. *Brit. J. Psychiat., 129*, 207–215.

KAY, D. W. K., AND ROTH, M. 1961. Environmental and hereditary factors in the schizophrenias of old age ("late paraphrenia") and their bearing on the general problem of causation in schizophrenia. *J. Ment. Sci., 107*, 649–686.

KLAGES, W. 1961. *Die Spaetschizophrenie*, Stuttgart: Enke.

KLEIST, K. 1913. Die Involutionsparanoia. *Allg. Z. Psychiat., 70*, 1–134.

KNOLL, H. 1952. Wahnbildende Psychosen der Zeit des Klimakteriums und der Involution in klinischer und genealogischer Betrachtung. *Arch. Psychiat. Nervenkr., 189*, 59–92.

KRAEPELIN, E. 1913. *Psychiatrie*, Vol. 3: Leipzig.

LAWTON, P. 1972. Schizophrenia forty-five years later. *J. Genet. Psychol., 121*, 133–143.

LECHLER, H. 1950. Die Psychosen der Alten. *Arch. Psychiat. Nervenkr., 185*, 460–465.

LEONHARD, K. 1957. *Die Aufteilung der endogenen Psychosen*, Berlin.

LEWIS, A. 1970. Paranoia and paranoid: A historical perspective. *Psychol. Med., I*, 2–12.

LODGE-PATCH, I. C., POST, F., AND SLATER, P. 1965. Constitution and the psychiatry of old age. *Brit. J. Psychiat., 111*, 405–413.

MACMILLAN, D., AND SHAW, P. 1966. Senile breakdown in standards of personal and environmental cleanliness. *Brit. Med. J., II*, 1032–1037.

MEYER, J. E. 1972. Psychopathologie und Klinik des Jugendalters. *In, Psychiatrie der Gegenwart.* Vol. II/I. pp. 823–858. Berlin, Heidelberg, New York: Springer-Verlag.

MÜLLER, C. 1959. *Über das Senium der Schizophrenen.* Basel: Karger.

PARSONS, P. L. 1964. Mental health of Swansea's old folk. *Brit. J. Prevent. Soc. Med., 19*, 43–47.

PERRIS, C. 1974. *A study of cycloid psychoses. Acta. Psychiat. Scand.*, Supp. 253.

POST, F. 1962. *The Significance of Affective Symptoms in Old Age.* Maudsley Monographs 10. London: Oxford University Press.

POST, F. 1966. *Persistent Persecutory States of the Elderly.* Oxford: Pergamon Press.

POST, F. 1971a. Schizo-affective symptomatology in late life. *Brit. J. Psychiat., 118*, 437–445.

POST, F. 1971b. The diagnostic process. *In*, D. W. K. Kay and A. Walk (eds.), *Recent Developments in Psycho-*

geriatrics. *Brit. J. Psychiat.* Special Publication No. 6.

POST, F. 1973. Psychiatric disorders. *In*, J. C. Brocklehurst (ed.), *Textbook of Geriatric Medicine and Gerontology.* Edinburgh and London: Churchill Livingstone.

PROCCI, W. R. 1976. Schizo-affective psychosis: Fact or fiction? *Arch. Gen Psychiat., 33*, 1167–1178.

REICH, W. 1976. The schizophrenic spectrum: a genetic concept. *J. Nerv. Ment. Dis., 162*, 3–12.

RETTERSTÖLL, N. 1966. *Paranoid and Paranoiac Psychoses.* Oslo: Universitetsforlagöt.

ROTH, M. 1955. The natural history of mental disorders in old age. *J. Ment. Sci., 101*, 281–301.

ROTH, M., AND MORRISSEY, J. D. 1952. Problems of diagnosis and classification of mental disorders in old age. *J. Ment. Sci., 98*, 66–80.

RÜEMKE, H. C. 1963. Über alte schizophrene. *Schweiz. Arch Neurol. Psychiat., 91*, 201–210.

SCHIMMELPENNING, G. W. 1965. Die paranoiden Psychosen der zweiten Lebenshaelfte. *Biblothe. Psychiat. Neurol., 128*, Basel: Karger

SCHNEIDER, K. 1959. *Clinical Psychopathology.* (Transl. 1953). New York: Grune & Stratton.

SHELDON, J. H. 1948. *The Social Medicine of Old Age.* London: Oxford University Press.

STERNBERG, E. 1972. Neuere Forschungsergebnisse bei spätschizophrenen Psychosen. *Fortschr. Neurol. Psychiat., 40*, 631–664.

WENGER, P. A. 1958. A comparative study of the aging process in groups of schizophrenics and mentally well veterans. *Geriatrics, 13*, 367–370.

WILLIAMSON, J., STOKOE, I. H., GRAY, S., FISHER, M., AND SMITH, A. 1964. Old people at home: Their unreported needs. *Lancet, 1*, 1117–1120.

WORLD HEALTH ORGANIZATION. 1973. *Report of the International Pilot Study of Schizophrenia.* Vol. I., Geneva: WHO.

# 26

# Depression and Suicidal Behavior in Old Age

*Asser Stenback*

## CLINICAL DEPRESSION

Depression is a major mental health problem. If the annual prevalence of depressive disorders is estimated to be nearly 3 percent, there may be about 100 million people in the world each year who develop clinically recognizable depression (Sartorius, 1975). Because there are findings indicating a much higher rate in the aged population, depression deserves a particular emphasis in research and health services involving the aged.

### DEFINITION

The concept of clinical depression is difficult to define in a precise way. A person is said to be depressed when he describes his feeling state as low-spirited, "blue," sad, grievous, or unhappy. This

mood change, however, is not a sufficient ground for making a diagnosis of clinical depression. In fair accordance with old psychiatric tradition, *A Psychiatric Glossary* (American Psychiatric Association 1975), states: "Slowed thinking and decreased purposeful physical activity accompany the mood change when the term is used diagnostically. This definition indicates that depression is a state of both mood change and reduced activity. Persistent grief feelings make up a clinical depression only when accompanied by marked reduction in activity. In many severe cases this reduction involves the above-mentioned obvious slowing of thinking and movements. In other cases, often equally severe, the diminution of activity is only related to withdrawal from previous fields of interest."

This definition of depression, involving markedly reduced activity in connection with depressive mood, excludes self-accusations and somatic symptoms from the constituents of the depressive disorder. Marked sadness without depressive behavior, reported by Hogarty and Katz (1971) as making up a notable minority in the normal population, is also excluded from the realm of clinical depression. The depressive character, a diagnosis applied to individuals with habitual depressive mood, does not prevent normal activities. The classification of depression as an affective disorder, or a mood disorder, obscures the nature of depression as a comprehensive personality disorder. In addition to the affective and psychomotor (conative) aspects, cognitive changes, as strongly advocated by Beck (1967) are a common element of clinical depression.

Normal grief, low morale (Kutner, Fanshel, Togo, and Langner, 1956), and low life satisfaction (Neugarten, Havighurst, and Tobin, 1961) do not necessarily include marked diminution of activity and hence are not synonyms of depression, although they frequently overlap with mild depression.

Depression may be viewed as a reactive mood disturbance accompanied by failure at adaptation, as well as a disease in the sense that its manifestations are deviations from normal biological functions (Hill, 1968; Klerman, 1974). Disregarding the tricky question about etiology vs. secondary consequence, in many cases of depression with a prolonged course, a development takes place towards increasing somatization which reenforces the disease character of a depression.

This presentation of depression in old age will proceed from description of some general aspects of depression and aging, to involutional melancholia as the depression of middle age, before going to old age depressions. Proper background material for understanding the specific features of old age depression will be presented, not only in the introductory sections but also later in association with discussing the main factors and phenomena of old age depressions.

## CLASSIFICATION

Mental disturbances are divided up into psychoses and neuroses (and other nonpsychotic mental disorders). Many authors find it difficult to uphold a qualitative difference between psychotic and neurotic depression and view the difference as a question of severity. From the beginning of scientific psychiatry, psychosis was considered to be due to genetic and/or metabolic disturbances. Only gradually has the reactive origin of a psychosis been

recognized. The International Classification of Diseases (ICD-8) and the Diagnostic Nomenclature of the American Psychiatric Association (DSM-II) put forward the following diagnostic categories for depression: major affective disorders, psychotic depressive reaction, depressive neuroses, and cyclothymic (or affective) personality disorders. The category "major affective psychoses" consists of several subcategories including manic disorders. The depressive subcategories are involutional melancholia; manic-depressive illness, depressed type; and manic-depressive illness, circular type.

Two other approaches to classification of depressive disorders have recently aroused considerable interest: those of bipolar vs. unipolar classification, and primary vs. secondary classification. The *bipolar-unipolar* distinction follows the proposal of Leonhard (1959) to separate depressed patients with a history of manic episodes (the bipolar group) from those patients who have had only recurrent episodes of depression (the unipolar group). There is a bulk of evidence for the existence of a distinct category of bipolar depression. No agreement about the distinctive features of a unipolar depression has been reached, unless all nonbipolar depressions are allocated to the unipolar group.

In order to avoid the ambiguities related to the concepts of endogenous vs. reactive and psychotic vs. neurotic, Robins and Guze (1972) have put forward the distinction *primary* vs. *secondary* affective disorders based on two criteria, chronology and the presence of associated illnesses. Primary affective disorders refer to the disorders in patients who have been well or whose only previous episodes of psychiatric disease were mania or depression. Secondary affective disorders may occur in persons who have had or have another psychiatric illness. Robins and Guze themselves point to two difficulties related to this categorizing. The patient may have had a previous undiagnosed psychiatric (e.g., neurotic) reaction. In addition, depressions developing in association with physical disease are difficult to allocate.

In psychiatry, the term "endogenous" is used in an ambiguous way. On one hand, in accordance with its etymological sense, endogenous means "of internal origin," the opposite of "reactive." On the other hand, endogenous denotes a particular syndrome. Endogenous stands for a "psychotic" syndrome of depressive mood, retardation and diurnal rhythm. In this sense, the opposite of endogenous is neurotic. Endogenous depressions in these two senses correlate but are not identical (Klerman, 1971). It seems impossible to refrain completely from use of this term. In order to avoid semantic ambiguity, it seems best to qualify "endogenous" by saying either "endogenous in the etiologic sense" or "endogenous in the symptomatological sense."

## PRIMARY SYMPTOMS

*Depressive Mood.* For describing the crucial feature of the depressive mood, many adjectives have been employed: sad, dejected, dysphoric, blue, in mental pain, listless, guilty, unworthy, lonely, fatigued, apathetic, helpless, hopeless etc. Some of these adjectives more properly describe the object to which the feeling refers rather than the feeling tone proper. Depressive mood or dysphoria are perhaps the most appropriate terms.

*Reduced Behavior.* The psychomotor aspect of reduced activity has received too much attention as a main characteristic of depression. As an adequate term, reduced activity is preferred to psychomotor retardation and agitation, because reduced activity is the factor underlying the psychomotor disturbances, and, in addition, reduced activity also encompasses withdrawn apathetic behavior. The pattern of reduced activity can be considered as "given-up" behavior subsequent to loss and failure at adaptation. Reduced activity is the external manifestation of lowered self-esteem and helplessness ("I am bad, I can't do anything") as well as of hopelessness ("there is no point in trying").

## SECONDARY SYMPTOMS

For a long time *guilt* has been considered a central symptom in depression. Nevertheless guilt is not a universal feature of depression. Guilt feelings develop when the individual asks himself who is to be blamed for the loss or failure. People differ from each other in their propensity to blame oneself or others. Persons with strong conviction about their own responsibility for their life may feel strongly guilty, which to a high degree can worsen their depression. People who typically blame others direct their *aggressiveness* towards the environment, deepening in this way the feeling of bitterness and loneliness. *Anxiety* is a regular concomitant of depression, sometimes preceding the depression (Wolpe, 1971), but mostly present as a part of the pessimistic outlook and hopelessness.

*Cognitive Disturbances.* (Depressive delusions, pessimistic thoughts, self-blame) have long been viewed as consequences and not as causes of the depressed

mood. Beck (1967) has strongly argued that the depressive ideation frequently precedes the depression. Obviously, thought and affect are always interwoven in an intricate way in a reciprocal feedback system. In some cases pessimistic and self-depreciating thoughts predominate in the development of depressive mood and activity; in other cases, the reverse may be true.

*Somatic Symptoms.* In addition to the classical symptom of psychomotor retardation and agitation, loss of appetite, loss of libido and sleep disturbance are common somatic symptoms. Anxiety and aggression give rise to vegetative disturbances characteristic of these two feeling states.

A pervading somesthetic (or cenesthetic) feeling of fatigue and fatigability is frequently an integrated part of the depressive affect; listlessness and inability to take a strong interest are experienced as inability to make efforts and to work. Although depression frequently manifests itself as changes in appearance and in somatic symptoms, there are many patients who, particularly in a brief encounter with other people, present themselves without any external depressive manifestations.

## ETIOLOGY: PSYCHOSOCIAL ASPECTS

When clinical depression is characterized as a mood disturbance and a reduction of activity related to the mood disturbance, the etiology has to be sought in factors influencing both mood and activity. *Loss* of external love objects is in all quarters recognized as a principal etiological factor. Disagreement exists only concerning the scope and sufficiency of loss as a factor causing depression. By loss is commonly meant an observable deprivation of an object that is of high value for the subject, an object that is, as psychoanalysis puts it, cathected. Others also include in the concept of loss the minute losses belonging to normal life, which are frequently observable only for the subject himself. However, in order to preserve loss as a concept useful for research and clinical work, loss has to be defined as deprivation of a major love object, such as a person, thing, or activity. When estimating the emotional impact of a loss, the personal meaning of the loss and its consequences must be taken into account.

Most people can cope with a loss. The crucial question is therefore: why is the prospective depression patient unable to rise after the smarting blow? Normally after a period of mourning, new or old objects of interest get even more attention, and gradually the mental pain abates. When depression ensues, a number of psychic processes take place. The lost object remains a cathected object; in his inner world the patient has not accepted the loss. This implies that thinking and feelings are still directed towards the lost object. Under the emotional impact of the loss, withdrawal from external reality takes place, reducing the opportunities for finding new external cathected objects. But the seeking of new sources of satisfaction starts sooner or later. When this seeking fails, anxiety, despair, helplessness, and aggressiveness of various degrees ensue. The premorbid personality is a crucial factor in this failure to deal with the loss.

This presentation of the etiology of depression as due to loss is in accordance with Freud's view on grief as a process related to depression. However, man is not only a "haver" but also a "doer." Loss of possession of highly valued objects initiates an existential crisis. But of equally great significance to some persons is *failure* in carrying out central life tasks. This failure in many quarters is recognized as a factor leading to depression. When analyzing papers on endogenous depression, it is easy to detect that a pervading theme is the patient's inability to feel and act. The inability to act is due to an overwhelming feeling of listlessness, pain, fatigue, and guilt. The patient's guilt feeling arises from the conviction that the depressive condition is due to his own badness and will. This view of depression is supported by the premorbid personality studies which reveal two main personality types: the extractive-manipulative type who suffers particularly from loss of narcissistic supplies, and the obsessive-perfectionistic type who is vulnerable to perceived failure (Chodoff, 1973). This twofold way to depression is supported by animal depression research, involving the loss-separation model (Harlow, Harlow, and Suomi, 1971; Kaufman, 1973; McKinney, Suomi, and Harlow, 1973) and the helplessness model (Seligman, 1974). (Rather than a learned helplessness, the state of Seligman's rats can be characterized as emotional dullness and inability to act.)

Although in this way, two etiological paths can be discerned, the common final path is *failure in restitution* of normal emotionality and activity. After loss or failure in activity, compensatory efforts are carried out. When these attempts at restitution fail, depression ensues. This failure constitutes the difference between grief and depressive mood. Lewinsohn's (1975) view of deficient social skill as the crucial deficiency in depression is in accordance with this conception. As will be discussed later in some detail, in old age there is not only deficient social skills but also scarcity of appropriate social situations.

## BIOLOGICAL ASPECTS

As early as the fifth century BC, Hippocrates explained depression as due to a biological factor, black bile (melan, black; chole, bile; melancholia). After decades of intensive study of a number of biological processes, the present state of research in depression points to the crucial role of biogenic amines, particularly norepinephrine, dopamine, and serotonin. Many agents which affect the metabolism of biogenic amines also have a pathogenic or therapeutic effect upon depression; these agents include reserpine, monoamine oxidase inhibitors, levodopa, and 1-tryptophan. There are also numerous reports of a decrease in norepinephrine, serotonin, or their metabolites in persons suffering from depression. Another biological disturbance related to depression is intraneuronal sodium accumulation with subsequent lowering of the resting membrane potential in the neuronal receptor cells.

In spite of the overwhelming evidence in favor of the combined catecholamine and serotonin hypothesis, the results obtained in studies of depressive subjects are in some respects equivocal and controversial. This is partly due to the etiological heterogeneity of depression, despite considerable similarity in symptomatology; Akiskal and McKinney (1975) view depressive illness as a "psychobiological final common pathway." Another cause for the divergent results may be the different neurobiology in different phases of the depressive disorder. Especially in unipolar and bipolar depressions with only a slightly disturbed premorbid personality, disturbances of monoamine metabolism have been found (van Praag, 1977).

An attractive hypothesis is put forward by Prange and his coworkers (Prange, Wilson, Lynn, Alltop, Strikeleather, and Raleigh, 1974). According to their hypothesis, a genetic predisposition to low serotonin level results in reduced excretion of catecholamines, which may cause depression. Akiskal and McKinney (1975) called attention to the role of norepinephrine in the "reward" part of the diencephalic reinforcement system. In addition to this experience of pleasure, with norepinephrine and its precursor dopamine participating in psychomotor functioning, disturbances in the metabolism of these catecholamines may be as crucial in the genesis and course of depression. Decrease in catecholamine stores may be brought about by prolonged high activity (Weiss, Stone, and Harrell, 1970).

As emphasized earlier, a sense of prolonged failure in central life tasks is a psychosocial factor in the etiology of depression. Failure and effort are closely related to catecholamines, and the disturbances in the catecholamine metabolism is obviously a cause and/or a consequence of the depressive illness.

The shock effect inherent in the loss experience of a significant person implies reduced behavioral activity and its concomitant reduced catecholamine synthesis. With the exception of phases of protest, despair, and agitation, which are frequently accompanied by increase in 17-hydroxycorticosteroids and catecholamine secretion, the depressed process involves apathy and dejection, with concomitant low values of catecholamines.

The loss factor in the etiology of depression cannot, however, be explained by the monoamine hypothesis. The feelings of sadness and mental pain brought about by a loss arise subsequent to appraisal of the meaning of the event. Arnold (1970) has described the neurophysiology of this affective appraisal. An important link in this process is the affective memory in which bereavements experienced from early childhood and throughout life are coded. In this affective appraisal catecholamine metabolism is not a decisive factor. Instead, the activity of the limbic brain as a whole has to be considered.

In the biological treatment of depression, pharmacological agents stimulating catecholamine metabolism have a good therapeutic effect. Dopamine stimulates motor activity and norepinephrine acts on motor activity and on the experience of pleasure or "reward" associated with activity (Olds, 1958). But the depressing memories will not be deleted by chemicals. The spontanous gradual recovery typical of many depressions is partly due to fading away of painful memories. The beneficial effect of electroconvulsive treatment of depression is mainly due to the transitory blunting effect upon affective memory (Stenback, Viitamäki, and Kukkonen, 1957).

Biological factors also act in the effect of cerebral and extracerebral diseases. The depression-evoking effect of the physical diseases may take place by means of direct influence upon the cerebral function or through the medium of psychological reactions to the deteriorated physical state. These mechanisms will be discussed in some detail later when dealing with the factors characteristic of old age depression.

## AGING FACTORS

Depression in the latter part of life is due partly to individual events, and partly to biological, psychological, social, and cultural factors characteristic of this life phase. In order to understand the development of depression in old age, some relevant facts about aging have to be presented.

### BIOLOGICAL FACTORS

The effect of biological aging upon depression has been estimated to be so great that the concept of involutional depression has been formed. The basis of this diagnostic category is the supposition that the transition from middle age to senescence is bound up with specific biological processes which sometimes can produce depression. The best illustration of this notion is the climacteric as the supposed cause of involutional depression. However, there is no evidence indicating that endocrinological changes around the menopause are the main cause of depression in the menopausal period. The marked decline in production of estrogens is only one of a number of physiological declines in this life period.

The studies of Shock (Shock, 1962) demonstrated a progressive fall in a large number of physiological parameters between the ages of 30 and 70 years; the percentage of decline in various functions was between 16 and 50 percent. A certain cautiousness in interpreting these findings is wise because a considerable decline in all parameters was not discovered when the aged in poor health were deliberately excluded from the study population (Birren, Butler, Greenhouse, Sokoloff, and Yarrow, 1963). However, autopsy reveals a decrease in the weight due to loss of cells in most organs; particularly important are the changes in brain and skeletal muscles. These anatomic-physiological age changes constitute a biological basis for the fatigability frequently reported by elderly people.

The impact of biological aging upon affectivity is not yet clarified. There is a scarcity of experimental work with animals dealing with the relationship of motivation to aging. A general agreement exists concerning the reduction of "vitality" or "vital potential" with old age. By using the TAT-test, Shaw and Henry (1956) showed that 50-year old businessmen reacted with less intensity and effectiveness than their 30-year-old colleagues. In a TAT-study, Rosen and Neugarten (1960) observed age-related decline both in activity-energy level and affect intensity. Dean (1962) observed a similar reduction of anger and irritation. No relevant studies have related these psychological changes to anatomic and physiological deterioration.

Depression of physiological and psychological processes does not directly cause clinical depression. But when depression as briefly outlined above ensues as a result of a multiple interaction of factors, many a factor which alone is not able to give rise to depression can do so in interaction with others.

Fatigue and fatigability can prevent the individual from seeking new cathected objects after a loss. To the disinterest and apathy brought about by the loss will be added this age-specific reluctance to enter into new enterprises. After the loss, decline in affective intensity can mitigate the mental pain, but the weakened affectivity is also likely to make the cathecting of new objects more difficult. The age-related reduction of affect intensity may be the main reason for the observed milder character of depressions in old age. (Ciompi and Lai, 1968; Kay, Beamish, and Roth, 1964a; Stenback, Kumpulainen, and Vauhkonen, 1979). Physical diseases not related to aging per se but occurring frequently in old age, are in many cases a conspicuous component in the etiology of depression in old age. This will be discussed in detail later in this chapter.

## SOCIAL FACTORS

Life involves interaction with cathected objects and activity for replacing lost ones. To some degree aging always implies loss of objects such as *cathected people, goals,* and *social roles.*

The loss of cathected people takes place through death of friends, migration (own, family members, and friends), and retirement from work and community activities. The loss of goals may occur in many ways; e.g., retirement may exclude one from gainful work. In many subcultures, retirement from work tends to imply an obligation to withdraw from positions of trust in organizations (except pensioners' own organizations). Loss of people and goals always involves loss of social roles and activity. A widow may suffer more from the loss of some daily household activities than from the loss of a beloved spouse. Retirement also means breaking up close peer relationships. In addition, reduced income implies less opportunity for participation in a number of social activities.

It stands to reason that this reduction of social life-space (an apt term by Lewin, applied to aging by Williams, 1959) can powerfully influence the development of depression. Thus both processes implicated in the etiology of depression, loss and failure in activities, will be affected by the social changes that occur with age.

The relationship between depression and poverty cannot be clarified by studies of treated depression (e.g., Hollingshead and Redlich, 1958). On the other hand, the gloomy and pessimistic life style common in poverty-stricken areas (e.g., Harrington, 1962) is more characteristic of the depressive personality than of clinical depression. Nevertheless, field studies (Leighton, Harding, Machlin, MacMillan, and Leighton, 1963; Warheit, Holzer, and Schwab, 1973) have brought forth evidence for a correlation between depression and low socioeconomic status. Poverty occurring in adult life may contribute more to mental illness than lifelong poverty (Brill, Weinstein, and Garratt, 1969).

## CULTURAL FACTORS

Every culture contains views on life from birth to death, which create attitudes to aging and old age. In the Western culture, negative attitudes, prejudices, and stereotypes about old age prevail. *Agism* is used as a term to denote these attitudes and views.

Lowered self-esteem is frequently emphasized as a depression symptom. When youth and early middle-age are glamorized, old age is automatically disparaged, resulting in low self-esteem in the aged. Self is an important cathected object for everybody. When self-esteem has fallen below a certain level, feelings of inferiority ensue. Without a sufficient amount of self-reliance, the individual cannot enter into the efforts required for the postloss restitution of internal equilibrium. All relevant feelings and attitudes are maintained or weakened by the prevailing culture.

## PSYCHOLOGICAL FACTORS

The main task of man's psychological inner-life is to cope with the external world, consisting of the biological, social, and cultural factors of each particular moment. This coping capacity is acquired throughout the whole life. Characteristics of this coping capacity coincide to a high degree with aspects of the premorbid personality. There are some coping functions particularly needed in old age.

Gradual physical decline weakens the emotionality of the aged. Material things, social status and sexuality also lose their attractiveness to some extent. They will to some degree be replaced by intrapsychic values (Neugarten and associates, 1964) or interest in their own body. If they are not replaced, depression, general apathy, and functional dementia may develop. To a certain extent, withdrawal from previous activity and interaction with people takes place. In this way, disengagement (Cumming and Henry, 1961) and giving up (Engel, 1968; Schmale, 1958) are characteristics of aging.

Loss of significant persons through death and migration, loss of work owing to retirement, loss of social opportunities, and loss of self-esteem through "ageism" in the prevailing culture, all of these things require cathecting of new objects. Rigidity or incapacity to shift interest from one object to another is an important hindrance in maintaining a positive mood.

The most conspicuous feature of aging is the changing *time perspective*. In his time perspective, the aged tends to see himself as increasingly ailing and disabled. He may observe the passing away of family members and old friends. His own death stands out more and more as an inevitable fate. Many feel that life has irrevocably run out; others entertain an unshakeable belief in a life after death. However, death and death-fear are not major factors conducive to depression. More depression-provoking is the looking back at the past life. Butler (1963) has drawn attention to this reminiscing of previous life events and has emphasized that this reminiscing is, to a high degree, a reorganization of life events sometimes resulting in a deeper and maturer "ego integrity" (Erikson, 1950), and sometimes resulting in depression with reality-based and/or imagined guilt feelings.

## INVOLUTIONAL MELANCHOLIA

Classification and understanding of depressive disorders in old age are not possible without clarification of the controversial nature of involutionary melancholia. At the end of the last century, when Emil Kraepelin (d. 1926) created his nosological system of mental disorders, which still is the main basis of the present classification, he separated manic-depressive disorder from cases of depression occurring at later age. Making use of the old Greek word for depression, he termed these depressions "involutional melancholia." Prompted by results from investigations of the course of diagnosed involutional melancholias (Dreyfus, 1907), Kraepelin later changed his stand and included involutional melancholia in the group of manic-depressive disorders. Particularly in the Anglo-American countries, involutional melancholia has been held as a separate diagnostic entity which together with the manic-depressive illness makes up the diagnostic category of endogenous depression. In the American A Standard Classified Nomenclature of Diseases, published in 1933, involutional melancholia was classified under "psychoses due to disturbances of metabolism, growth, nutrition, or endocrine functions." Not until 1968, in the second edition of Diagnostic and Statistical Manual,

Mental Disorders (DSM-II), was involutional melancholia entered among major affective disorders. DSM-II gives the following description of involutional melancholia:

> This is disorder in the involutional period and characterized by worry, anxiety, and severe insomnia. Feelings of guilt and somatic pre-occupations are frequently present and may be of delusional proportions. This disorder is distinguishable from *manic-depressive illness* (q.v.) by the absence of previous episodes; it is distinguished from *Schizophrenia* (q.v.) in that impaired testing is due to a disorder of mood; and it is distinguished from *Psychotic depressive* reaction (q.v.) in that the depression is not due to some life experience. Opinion is divided as to whether this psychosis can be distinguished from the other affective disorders.

### INVOLUTION, MIDDLE AGE, AND DEPRESSION

In the psychiatric literature, it is difficult to find a clear explanation of involution and the involutional period. Obviously, involution is an obsolete term for aging processes. By using the changes in the ovaries as a model, it is assumed that in man's life there is a period of "involution" before settling down to a new stable level of functioning, the senescent state. Although biological gerontology has refuted this view, it is retained as a concept. From a biological point of view there is, however, no involution preceding senescence but only a continuum of aging. Use of a term, originally biological in meaning and without proved application is questionable. Emphasizing the arbitrariness, Ey (Ey, Bernard, and Brisset, 1967) declared expressively that by use of habitual distinction one can divide senescence into two parts: (1) presenescence or *involution period* which can be put between 45 and 65 years, and (2) aging proper over 65 years. This categorizing seems more plausible than that of Henderson, Gillespie, and Batchelor (1969) who, after stating that "the involutional period is a physiological epoch common to men and women, bringing in its train certain mental and bodily changes," indicate that "roughly, it ranges from 40 to 60 years in women, and from 50 to 65 years in men." In my opinion the term "involutional" ought to be dropped altogether and be replaced by "middle age" (Stenback, 1963). In dealing with involutional melancholia in great detail, Ford (1975) strongly maintains that the symptomatology of involutional melancholia is not markedly different from that of a cross-section of the middle-aged stratum in the general psychiatric population.

## INVOLUTIONAL OR MIDDLE AGE DEPRESSION

Refutation of the concept of involution does not, however, do full justice to all the valuable work done by the proponents of a separate psychiatric disease entity named involutional melancholia. In order to understand this question, one has to realize that when a diagnostic classification system was created for the first time, only the severest cases of depression were admitted to hospitals, where the clinical studies pointed to distinct disease entity. The clinician could not help but notice that there were a great number of depressive patients who, by their agitated mood and behavior, differed from the typically retarded manic-depressive patients. When it was discovered that these patients were mostly in the older age group and when, according to the prevalent view, the etiology had to be allocated exclusively to biological causes, "involution" was resorted to. Later studies have shown that agitation can also be a symptom of depression in younger patients. The same is true of other symptoms described as characteristic of involutional depression: rigid personality, hypochondriasis, nihilism, paranoid thoughts, guilt feelings, and despair. Nevertheless, traditional involutional melancholia represents the first serious attempt to study the relationship between depression and aging.

Stenstedt (1959) made a crucial contribution to the undermining of the concept of involutional melancholia as a distinct disease entity. Stenstedt's findings showed that involutional melancholia patients constitute a heterogeneous group, consisting of late cases of manic-depressive illness and cases of mainly exogenous symptomatic or reactive depression. In order to be qualified as a disease entity, the clinical picture should have: (1) characteristic symptoms and signs; (2) characteristic epidemiology and etiology; and (3) characteristic course and outcome. Involutional melancholia does not meet these requirements and, hence, ought to be dropped as a diagnostic category.

The designation of involutional melancholia as "middle-age depression" does not imply inclusion of this term in the official nomenclature. Involutional melancholia is "a late-occurring psychotic depressive reaction" (Beck, 1967). Because of its connotation of recency, "reaction" is not a completely adequate term. According to DSM-II, a criterion of psychotic depressive reaction is that the depressive mood is "attributable to experience." This "experience" may to a large extent be all those factors and events that have contributed during the whole life to the formation of a personality that breaks down in a depression after a major loss or after failure in activities. If lifelong personality formation is included in the concept of reaction, "involutional melancholia" can be called a "depressive reaction." In addition the denotation as a reaction should not imply exclusion of the biological aspect of the reacting individual. Weitbrecht's (1952) term "endoreactive dysthymia" expresses a view that emphasizes the interplay of biological personality (endogenous), and reactive factors in depressive disorder.

The denotation of involutional melancholia as middle age depression indicates that "late age depressions" are generally not included in involutional melancholias. The background thinking behind the concept "involution" presupposes a period of transition from normal adult life to senescence proper. This transition period has been named "involution." Lehman (1959) pointed out that a correct differential diagnosis between involutional depression, manic-depressive psychosis, and late schizophrenia can be made only when there is certainty that the depression will not recur, because by definition involutional depression as a depression of a transitional period cannot come again.

## FEATURES OF DEPRESSIONS IN MIDDLE AGE

The syndrome described as involutional depression, consisting of "depression without retardation, anxiety, a feeling of unreality, and hypochondriacal delusions" (Gillespie, 1929), does exist as a subtype but seems to be definitely rare in current populations (Rosenthal, 1968). Most depressions in middle age are late manic-depressive illness and neurotic or psychotic-depressive reactions. The involutional depression is a subtype of psychotic depressive-reaction.

It is an interesting question whether there are specific etiological characteristics of the depressions in the middle-age years. Losses of cathected persons are common to all ages but are more numerous after the age of 40. It is frequently observed that repeated losses of persons are sometimes more than a subject can stand. The social situation of the aged with their narrowed social life-space makes the efforts to replace the lost person more difficult than earlier in life. Loss of spouse and loss of work, including workmates, are many times irreplaceable.

The increased frequency of physical diseases from the fifth decade on deprives the individual of an important source of satisfaction and of an instrumental means necessary for attempts of restitution of the emotional well-being.

By pointing to the significance of commitment, Becker (1964) has drawn attention to a process greatly influencing aging and depression in the later part of life. A person is said to be committed when he is pursuing a consistent line of activity in a sequence of varied situations. This observable behavior is due primarily to highly valued goals and interests. Melges and Bowlby (1969) have discussed the intimate relationship between failure in carrying out such life plans and the development of depression. The rigid and obsessional personality often discovered in middle-age depression patients may in some cases be interpreted as "overcommitment" to a certain life style.

In gerontology the question concerning particular age-related "developmental tasks" has drawn much interest. Modifying the suggestions made by R. C. Peck (1956), the following tasks are characteristic of middle age (for detailed explanation the reader is referred to the original paper): cathectic flexibility vs. cathectic impoverishment, mental flexibility vs. mental rigidity, ego differentiation vs. work-role preoccupation, body transcendence vs. body preoccupation. In order to avoid depression, flexibility in thinking, emotional reactions, and application of social skills are particularly needed. In view of approaching retirement, ego differentiation and lively interest in home and community activities are of considerable importance.

The life tasks presented here as belonging to middle age are not fully encountered by particularly active and healthy persons until old age. Hence, involutional or middle-age depression, as a depression subtype developing under the impact of the characteristics of the middle-age life tasks, is a depression subtype which may also be met in old age.

## OLD AGE DEPRESSIONS

### SYMPTOMATOLOGY

Like other branches of medicine, geriatric psychiatry has developed in hospitals. It stands to reason that particularly severe cases are the first to be admitted to hospital care. This implies that clinical studies refer primarily to severe morbidity. Applied to depression in old age, this means that clinical studies are primarily studies of and reveal the symptomatology of *severe* depressions.

In a study of 100 elderly patients with affective symptoms (seven patients suffered from mania), Post (1969) found anxious-agitated affect in four-fifths. Nearly half the patients had feelings of guilt or self-reproach. An even larger proportion, two-

thirds, had hypochondrial preoccupations. Ideas of poverty were present in 27 percent. Severe psychotic symptoms (hallucinations, delusions, etc.) were found in 14 percent. Obsessional symptoms were observed in 15 percent. Noting that the average age in most research samples is around 68, Post (1968) stated that there is a strong impression that symptomatology and outcome of depression in the oldest age groups are not essentially different from that of patients in their late 60s. However, Leighton *et al.* (1963) observed that overall psychiatric morbidity in the 70 years and over age group was clearly lower than among the 60–69 year age group. Ciompi and Lai (1968) studied all depression patients who had been admitted to the university hospital in Lausanne prior to the age of 65, and who were alive and over 65 at the time of study. The mean age at the first admission was 53 years and at the catamnestic examination, 73.5 years. They found that one-third had not suffered from depression after the age of 65, one-third had shorter and milder attacks, and the remaining third had similar or more severe depressive symptoms. Because these patients had suffered from recurrent depressive attacks, the bulk of these patients may be considered to have unipolar depressions, although the investigators have not tried to sort out the patients with at least three episodes (a criterion put up by Perris (1966) for unipolar depressions).

Ciompi and Lai stated that the often-expressed opinion that depression aggravates with increasing age is not true. They maintained that the climacteric-involutional period, rather than old age, is the most typical depression period in life. Psychomotor retardation and agitation, frequently present prior to 65 years of age, had mostly disappeared in higher age. The same was true of paranoid symptoms. When a depression developed in late life, symptomatology had lost its stenic character, had become more flat and monotonic, and had moved from the ideo-affective level (e.g., less self-blaming) towards the somatic level (e.g., hypochondriac complaints and fatigue). This decrease in typical depressive symptomatology was counterbalanced by development of "minor" affective symptoms in more than a half of the subjects; these symptoms included general dissatisfaction, irritability, aggressiveness, hypochondria, and psychosomatic troubles. In a fifth of the subjects, this transformation was associated with a progressive loss of the "elan vital," zest of life, and by a contraction of personality, interests, and activities.

On the basis of these and other studies, the following overview of the symptomatology in severe old age depressions may be developed. Typical manic-depressive disorders (bipolar and unipolar) are also seen in old age. In normally active and physically well old subjects, depressions similar to those seen in middle age can develop. The symptomatology covers deep sadness or dysphoria, retardation, guilt feelings, depressive delusions, and dicernal variation. The typical involutional (middle age) depression, with agitation, hypochondria, and some paranoid ideation, is also occasionally seen in old age. The most frequent type of depression in old age is characterized by dysphoria, loss of interest in outside matters, and somatic illness, or fatigue. It is most appropriately understood as a severe and usually chronic form of those depressions loosely characterized as mild. The depressions dealt with so far can be designated as endogenous in the symptomatological sense.

The elucidation of the symptomatology of *mild* depression has taken place not in hospitals but in field studies of mental morbidity in old age. The Newcastle field study of mental disorders in old age under the leadership of Sir Martin Roth (Garside, Kay, and Roth, 1965; Kay, Beamish, and Roth, 1964a; Kay, Beamish, and Roth, 1964b) is a landmark in the development of geriatric psychiatry. Old-age mental disorders were studied in a random sample from the electoral register in the seaport and industrial town of Newcastle-upon-Tyne in Northern England. The main finding was the high frequency (26.5 percent) of affective and neurotic disorders. Another major finding was the preponderance of moderate and mild cases (Kay *et al.*, 1964a). Owing to the frequent coexistence of depressive mood and anxiety in functional mental disorders in old age, no attempts were made in the study to sort out the depressive patients from the combined group of affective and neurotic disorders.

Investigating 985 subjects aged 65 and over, living in their homes, Balier (1968) found depressive and neurotic disorders in 30 percent. He stated that old age depression frequently remains unnoticed behind a barrier of social isolation, pessimism toward existence, passivity, and complaints concerning the somatic condition, all of which are wrongly considered as part of normal aging. Balier particularly emphasized the classic picture presented of neurasthenia dominated by perpetual fatigue and symptoms from the gastrointestinal system, such as anorexia, epigastric distress, and constipation.

The attribute "mild" may confer a feeling of uncertainty and doubt as to the truly depressive nature of the depressions so designated. In order to qualify for the diagnostic category of depression, the case, however, must fulfill the two criteria of depressive mood disturbance and reduced activity. The patients with mild depression mostly have a dysphoric mood and have withdrawn from pre-depressive activities. Only rarely do they show retardation or agitation, mostly only resignation, apathy, and passivity are seen.

Three types of mild depression can be distinguished. These are reactive, neurasthenic-hypochondriacal, and neurotic depression. A depression is *reactive* (in the symptomatological sense) when the patient complains of grief and sadness which he closely links to an event that incessantly occupies his mind. It is mostly seen subsequent to loss of a significant person, retirement, or discovery of a severe illness. If not adequately treated, the reactive depression frequently will be transformed into a neurotic or neurasthenic-hypochondriacal depression. *Neurasthenic-hypochondriacal* is a somewhat awkward term for designating a depression type, conferring the notion that body preoccupation is not always of a hypochondriacal nature. Neurasthenia is a psychiatric diagnosis which, although it has a long history, is nevertheless not accepted in all quarters. According to the current Diagnostic and Statistical Manual of Mental Disorders (DSM-II), neurasthenia is characterized by "complaints of chronic weakness, easy fatigability, and sometimes exhaustion." The DSM-II adds that neurasthenia differs from depressive neurosis in the moderateness of the depression and in the chronicity of its course. As mentioned earlier, a person can react with depression to the deteriorating and life-threatening character of physical illness. In addition, the fatiguing effect of an illness can exaggerate the feeling of helplessness and can act as a reason for withdrawal. Typical of the neurasthenic type of depression is the almost complete absence of classical depression symptoms. This depression type is not characterized by loss or failure, but is a fatigue depression. Because the somatic complaints predominate in the neurasthenic-hypochondriacal depression, it is in many respects similar to *masked depression*.

Many authors (e.g., Balier, 1968) state that the most characteristic feature of old age depression is the hypochondriacal complaints. The disturbances and attitudes subsumed under the heading of hypochondria are large and pertain to man's attitude to his body. This attitude is more multifaceted than can be adequately described by the concept of hypochondria. In the definition of hypochondriacal neurosis offered by DSM-II, there are two main components: preoccupation with the body, and preoccupation with fear of presumed diseases of various organs. In the author's opinion, it would be appropriate to retain the old definition of hypochondriasis as fear of presumed disease. Preoccupation with the body is a much larger matter. Particularly in old age, active interest taken in personal preventive health care and tenacious care of a chronic disease are adequate and necessary "preoccupations" with the body. When body stamina decreases and the body becomes ailing, foreboding disability and death, depressive preoccupation with the body has to be deemed normal rather than neurotic. When speaking about the developmental tasks in old age, R. C. Peck (1956) links the mastery of "body transcendence vs. body preoccupation" to the realm of value systems. Unquestionably, mental pathology adds aspects to this task which nevertheless transgress the boundaries of psychiatry.

Busse (1970) is to be credited with having carried out pioneering research on hypochondriasis in the elderly. In a group of elderly subjects in the community, 33 percent were found to have hypochondria. A much greater number showed what Busse aptly called "high bodily concern." In a community study (Stenback, Kumpulainen, and Vauhkonen, 1979), a much lower frequency of hypochondria (4 percent) was observed. The difference is obviously due not only to a stricter definition of hypochondria but also to different sampling. In the latter study the subjects investigated were taken from a birth register, whereas in the Duke study the sample consisted of volunteers; it is highly likely that hypochondriacal subjects volunteer for medical investigation. Three of the four hypochondriac subjects in the Stenback *et al.* series of 102 septuagenarians were also diagnosed as depressive. In an additional 10 cases of depression, somatic illness without hypochondriacal preoccupation was diagnosed as the main etiological factor.

It is difficult to find an unobjectionable terminology. Distinction of *neurotic* from reactive and neurasthenic-hypochondriacal depressions can be objected to. However, most typical of a neurosis are the personality conflicts arising from early childhood. In coping with the normal losses and the typical sociocultural situation of the aged population, the neurotic depressive fails due to personality factors. Low self-esteem, pessimistic outlook, bitter resignation, sometimes with a paranoid taint, and feelings of not being needed are typical of neurotic depression. Feelings of abandonment, loneliness, and alienation are often experienced. Included in the dysphoric mood is a low-grade anxiety, more properly called anxiousness. Guilt feelings and self-blame are replaced by feelings of insufficiency and inferiority. Retardation is absent. Withdrawal from social life is markedly reduced but seldom complete.

Summarizing, the symptomatology of depressions in old age can be described as severe depressions (endogenous in the symptomatological sense) and mild depressions. Severe depressions are in many respects similar to bipolar, unipolar, and involutional (middle-age) depressions. Mild depression consists of three types: reactive, neurasthenic-hypochondriacal, and neurotic.

## CLASSIFICATION

Like other fields of science, psychiatry has a need of classification. Criteria used are mostly etiological or symptomatological, or both. The starting point for classification consists of some obvious clinical observations. First, there are depression cases characterized by an intense feeling of sadness resulting from a loss or failure which is still vividly in mind. One cannot avoid attaching the label *reactive* to such a state. There are other cases with a life-long history of anxiety, pessimism, and withdrawal. When they become depressed as a result of a common life adversity one cannot refrain from assuming that this depression is *neurotic*, because the neurotic personality looms large in the development of the mental disorder. Then there are subjects who have been without personality disorders prior to the depressive disorder, which started without any obvious cause. The label *endogenous* seems an appropriate name for these cases. In addition, there are some peculiar features in a great number of depressions which arise after the age of 40. Confronted with life-span problems and biological deterioration, these subjects develop a depression which seems to require a descriptive term of its own. Unfortunately (in my opinion), "involutional" has been chosen. This *involutional* (middle age) type seems to predominate in frequency, particularly due to the symptomatological homogenization which takes place when the depression follows a chronic course.

The four types above are included in the International Classification of Diseases, 8th edition (World Health Organization) and the Diagnostic and Statistical Manual, II edition (American Psychiatric Association).These two classification systems are almost identical, and they subsume under the headings "Psychosis affectiva" respectively major affective disorders, the two "endogenous" disorders: manic depressive illness (bipolar and unipolar, also manic attacks), and involutional melancholia. In addition, "depressive reaction" and "depressive neurosis" are included in the classifications. DSM-II has also included under the heading Schizophrenia "schizo-affective, depressed type."

The differentiation of depression into *psy-chotic* and *neurotic* categories is a much debated question. When the symptomatology also covers delusions and frequently refers to guilt, there is no uncertainty as to the correctness of the attribute "psychotic." When experience of reality is grossly distorted only because of severe sadness, a depression can be characterized as "psychotic," but there is as much justification for describing such a depression only as "severe." Post (1972) presents a classification according to which the depressions are divided into severe, intermediate, and neurotic.

## DIFFERENTIAL DIAGNOSIS

*Dementia.* Until the 1950s, aged psychiatric patients were almost without exception regarded as suffering from dementia or chronic brain syndrome. In an influential paper, Roth (1955) reported that about one-half of all admissions aged 60 and over to an English mental hospital were suffering from depression. A considerable number of depressed patients manifest symptomatology of "pseudodementia" (Hemsi, Whitehead, and Post, 1968; Post, 1976). In many cases, cerebral pathology and depression coexist. In psychological testing, the depressives may show results similar to those of demented patients. Due to the agitation or retardation, many patients prove untestable. Post (1976) maintains that simple clinical assessment is useful in most cases. Memory and cognitive impairment noted before depression, evasive or perseverative replies, dysphagias, dysgnosias, and dyspraxias point to the likelihood of progressive failure being present. The correct evaluation of the proportion of depressive and demental pathology has significance for the choice of therapeutic measures.

*Schizophrenia.* There is no agreement as to the concept of schizophrenia. According to the stand taken by the author, schizophrenia is a personality disorder characterized by chronic delusions penetrating most areas of psychic function. Acute schizophrenia is a contradictory term, and hence does not exist. Acute psychosis is a suitable term for psychic disorders with disturbances of the level of consciousness. Delusions frequently cover only a circumscript sector of personality and as such do not influence the whole personality. In these cases the diagnosis of paranoia is preferred to schizophrenia. Kay and Roth (1961) have adopted "late paraphrenia" as a suitable term for late life paranoia. In many cases of mental disorder, concurrence of depressed mood and paranoid content of

thought and experiencing can be found. The differential diagnosis should be based upon the premorbid presence of nondepressive delusions.

*Schizo-affective Disorder.* In the current classification systems, schizo-affective disorder is to a high degree a synonym of schizophreniform psychosis and acute schizophrenia. I prefer the label "acute reactive psychosis." Acute psychosis may develop on a reactive and/or an organic basis. Post (1971) reported on 29 patients diagnosed as schizo-affective. In these patients depressed mood and delusions were present with acute breakdown of psychological functioning. Etiology involved hereditary factors, emotional stresses, physical illnesses, and cerebral disorders. Post suggested that this schizo-affective disorder (in my terminology, acute psychosis) would be considered as a syndrome rather than a disease entity.

*Neurosis.* The observations made by many investigators indicate that the typical symptomatology of neurosis tends to alleviate or disappear and will be replaced by somatic complaints and mild affective disturbances (Ernst, 1962). The boundary between depression and neurosis in old age is so diffuse that almost all cases of neurosis can be considered as mild depressions. It is pointless to try to sort out the few cases of true neurosis without depressive symptomatology. In practice it usually pays off to treat depression first, as in a large majority of patients their neurotic difficulties will cease to be a problem once their affective state has been normalized (Post, 1976).

## EPIDEMIOLOGY

No satisfactory epidemiological study of affective disorders has been carried out. Psychiatric field studies have primarily covered depressions which are severe or endogenous in the symptomatological sense. The findings in a number of epidemiological studies have indicated the prevalence of depression among the elderly (percentages) as follows: 0 (Bremer, 1951), 0.45 (Essen-Möller, 1956), 1.2 (Nielsen, 1963) and 0.48 (Bollerup, 1975). All these findings are approximately of the same size and show that the prevalence of severe or endogenous depression in subjects aged 65 or older is about 1 percent. The period prevalence of depressive disorders has been estimated to be nearly 3 percent per annum (Lehman, 1971; Sartorius, 1975).

The scope of depression, however, does not cover only severe depressions. The question how to deal epidemiologically with the mild depression is not yet resolved. The problems concerning classification and measurements are considerable. In many cases, neuroses with anxiety also have a depressive aspect. Frequently, an anxiety neurosis gradually merges into a depressive state. Not only chronic neuroses but also "late-onset neuroses" often make their appearance as depressive neuroses. Bergmann (1970) speaks of the late-onset neuroses as consisting of "tension and/or depression."

An epidemiological study which also deals with *mild* depression is the well-known prevalence study of old age mental disorders in Newcastle-upon-Tyne (Kay, Beamish, and Roth, 1964a). Realizing the almost insurmountable task of sorting out, in a field study, the nondepressive neuroses from the affective disorders, the investigators established the category of "Affective disorders and neuroses." To this diagnostic category was allocated 25.1 percent of the sample: 8.9 percent were considered as moderate/severe cases and 16.2 percent as mild cases. "The illness consisted of an admixture of depression and anxiety, usually in response to environmental or physical stress."

Another study covering mild depressions was carried out in Paris (Balier, 1968). In a study of 985 residential subjects aged over 65 years, he found a 4 percent incidence of cases with moderate classical neuroses and a 26 percent incidence of mild cases of mainly depressive and hypochondric symptoms.

In order to get a sample unbiased even by the migration factor, a cohort of 200 men and 200 women born in 1903 were traced and studied in 1973 and 1974 (Stenback *et al.*, 1979). Out of the 125 still alive and not registered as moved abroad, 106 subjects, or 84.8 percent were investigated. Eight cases of moderate and 17 cases of mild depression were diagnosed. The diagnostic criteria was the presence of sadness and withdrawal related to emotional disturbance.

All these epidemiological studies which include mild depressions point to a prevalence of 20 to 25 percent of depressive states in the old population. Only exceptionally is a depression in old age severe enough to require hospitalization. Watts (1966), a general practitioner particularly interested in psychiatric problems, reported that 31.5 per cent of his community patients aged over 65 were manic-depressive and 10.0 percent were in anxiety states.

These studies, which point to a high prevalence of functional mental disorders, are in keeping with the epidemiological studies showing high prevalence of functional mental disorders in the age group 45 to 64 (Leighton, 1959; Srole, Langner, Michael, Opler, and Rennie, 1962; Väisänen,

1975). It is unlikely—although not unthinkable—that passing the age limit of 65 would imply a drastic decrease in functional mental disorders including depression.

In a study of depressive symptomatology in a random sample of 1,645 adults in a Southeastern county in the US (Schwab, Holzer, and Warheit, 1973; Warheit, Holzer, and Schwab, 1973) found a particularly high frequency of depression both in subjects aged 70 and over and in those aged 19 and under. This surprising result, indicating that depression is as frequent in young people as in old, can first be criticized because of the small number of respondents aged 19 and under. But more importantly, the result questions the capacity of a questionnaire test to measure the prevalence of clinical depression. As stated in a previous section, clinical depression is characterized by depressive mood and failure at restitution, or readaptation. Only in a personal interview can certainty be obtained about adaptational failure connected with depressed mood. Interestingly, Katz (1971) found high scores on the depressive mood factor both in the depressed normals and in subjects with clinical depression. It was the behavior, and not the mood, that distinguished normal depression and clinical depression.

## ETIOLOGY AND DEVELOPMENT

In order to understand old age depressions, it is appropriate not only to examine the various etiological factors but to unravel the intricate interaction of these factors in the origin and subsequent course of a depression. Table 26–1 presents a list of factors and mechanisms involved in the development of depression.

The depressive process starts with a personal loss, failure, stress, physical disease, or some other biological process which in Table 26–1 are linked together under the noncommittal heading "Significant life events." Because everybody more or less experiences such significant events, the course towards depression is determined by the biological and psychological make-up of the individual and his social and cultural environment. Sufficient attention has not been paid to the metamorphosis a depression undergoes as time passes on.

*Significant Life Events.* From theoretical point of view, it is difficult to believe that such a profound psychic change as depression can take place without environmental factors playing a role in its genesis. Life is a constantly ongoing interactive process between individual and environment. The role of causative external factors is emphasized by the patient's spontaneous reporting that the depression ensued after or because of some event. In many cases of endogenous depression where no etiological event was discovered, a more thorough investigation revealed preceding events of the same nature as are found in reactive depressions (Leff, Roatch, and Bunney, 1970; Matussek, Halbach, and Troeger, 1965). But there are also a substantial number of cases where the patient is personally involved in the crucial event to such a degree that he is unconscious of his real life situation (Matussek *et al.*, 1965). Instead, he experiences his depression as a bodily disease without any etiological connection with his life situation. Three categories of significant life events can be differentiated: losses of personal relationships or things, physical disease, and failures in personally significant pursuits.

In his study of 100 patients with affective symptoms, Post (1962) found that 20 patients had experienced recent *losses* of persons: 11 had experienced actual bereavements, four, the removal of relatives, and five, a severe threat of loss in the form of a spouse's severe illness. Losses of things had occurred in 16 instances: loss of home in three, of money or other property in five. Including in these losses, the loss of health or job, and upsetting events, Post found a precipitating factor in 65 percent of the cases; in the remaining 35 percent no precipitating factor could be discovered. In a random series of 65-year-old hospital patients suffering from depression, Stenback (1965) found precipitating factors in 19 of 24 cases (79 percent), similar to the rate observed by Chesser (1965).

*Physical disease* is in many respects related to affective disorders. In many cases, physical disease, particularly mild chronic illness, may be viewed as a factor that generally weakens the individual and his coping capacity, his ego strength. In other cases, physical disease along with physiological derangements are partly caused by depression. But in many cases physical disease is a "significant life event" to which the individual reacts. The disease is a threat to the individual's survival, his working ability, his

ability to pursue his interests, his free motor activity, and his feelings of well-being. In most cases, these effects of physical disease are intertwined with other factors, but for understanding the development of depression it is of importance to consider these aspects separately. In many studies, no attempt to differentiate the ego-strength reducing effect of physical disease from the physical disease as a precipitating factor has been carried out.

Because of difficulty in operationalizing the concept of *failure*, not only minor personal failures but also many major failures cannot be included among the "life changes" now intensively studied in the wake of Holmes and Rahe's original work (1967). After retirement, man can stay "committed" (Becker, 1964) to a consistent pattern of behavior, to value-based goals. Minor failures, particularly if repeated, may have a strong frustrating impact upon the aged who otherwise lead an outwardly rewarding life. Repeatedly occurring minor losses may have a similarly damaging effect, if the psychological predisposition is particularly vulnerable. Discussing depressive neurosis, Nemiah (1975) says that when a person with a reasonable degree of self-confidence finds himself disliked he can easily turn to another, whereas a person highly dependent on other people experiences a real decrease in friendliness which is much more threatening, frequently because of the often extremely restricted number of such close persons. When interviewing in depth, Nemiah also found sexual impotence generally viewed as a consequence and not as a cause of depression. The same is true of assaults to the self-esteem. In subjects with persistent feelings of unworthiness, this may precipitate a depressive reaction. If the self-esteem is lowered as the result of failing to achieve a goal, a feeling of others being critical and rejecting may ensue.

Matussek *et al.* (1965) described "performance personalities" who feel themselves accepted only when they can perform in the right way and in sufficient amount. Sexual impotence acts for this

**Table 26–1**   Factors in development of depression

| ENVIRONMENT | INDIVIDUAL | SIGNIFICANT LIFE EVENTS | BIOLOGICAL AND PSYCHOLOGICAL REACTIONS |
| --- | --- | --- | --- |
| Social, e.g., retirement, poverty, social life pace | Biological factors, e.g., genetic, biological aging, physical diseases | Losses | Symptomatology of clinical depression |
| Cultural, e.g., agism, alienation | Psychological factors, e.g., personality make-up, psychological aging | Physical diseases | |
| Physical, e.g., housing, transport, climate | | Failures | |

patient as an external proof of his inability to love. Although in all these cases, the narcissistic or insecure personality plays the crucial role, the significance of the frustrating experiences cannot be entirely overlooked.

There has been a wide-spread belief in *retirement* as the cause of depression in old age. The finding of mental illness in the retirees was uncritically explained as due to retirement. More thoughtful research showed that retirement only occasionally was the main etiological factor (Friedmann and Orbach, 1974).

When considering the impact of retirement on depression, the two principal components of depression, feelings of loss and failure at restitution, have to be dealt with. The loss of work produces feelings of loss according to the significance of work for the particular individual. The more central work is in life, instrumentally and expresively, the more severely will the loss of work be felt. These intense feelings of loss hinder the restitution process from starting.

Most elderly have a positive attitude to being relieved from the burden of regular work. In spite of simultaneous feelings of discomfort, the immediate impact of retirement is mainly positive. Only gradually does the retiree become conscious of the satisfaction associated with the job as an outlet for a general need of activity. When the subsequent seeking of new activities, involving attempts at restitution of inner equilibrium and satisfaction, fails, a state of "low morale" (Kutner *et al.*, 1956) ensues. The decrease in self-esteem, a characteristic of depression (Bibring, 1953) found subsequent to retirement (Back, 1974), acts in the same direction. Low morale can be viewed as a state of at least slight dissatisfaction with life and reduced motivation for striving and efforts. In this way, low morale can constitute a predepressive phase prior to the helplessness and hopelessness of depression proper. In the international study of old people in Denmark, Great Britain, and the United States (Shanas, Townsend, Wedderburn, Friis, Milhoj, and Stehower, 1968), the retired men were asked what they enjoyed in retirement. The percentage of answers indicating "nothing" was depressingly high. Interestingly, the lowest percentage was in the United States, and if "rest" was added to the "nothing" group, the total percentage was 52 in the United States compared to 75 in Denmark and 83 in Great Britain. Such an emptiness in interests, if not producing depression, nevertheless prepares the ground for it.

*The Individual.* In the sections on depression and aging, some aspects of the *biological factors* were

discussed. It is self-evident that, in various degrees, the same factors which produce depression earlier in life also contribute to development of depression in old age. But it is also to be expected that there are biological factors specifically related to old age depressions.

All recent investigators agree upon an inverse relationship between the age at first attack and the strength of *hereditary-genetic factors* of affective illness. In late onset depressions, the incidence of positive family histories is significantly lowered (Hopkinson, 1964; Post, 1962; Stenstedt, 1959). Although the evidence against strong genetic disposition seems convincing, Post (1968) offered another explanation of the low incidence of depressions in the families of late onset depressives: they have fewer affected relatives because many of them do not live to the age at which their genetic predisposition might have appeared as an actual illness. Post put forth the hypothesis that the genetic basis is made up of subtle age changes in the brain which may be the main reason why depressions occur with increasing frequency with rising age, and why they are so often seen for the first time late in life in persons without previous serious psychiatric disorders. According to Post, these subtle age changes would manifest themselves as a decrease in cerebral excitability and as inhibition of cerebral arousal after anxiety-producing experiences. This interesting but not verified hypothesis has a close resemblance to the old notion of involutional depression.

Another hypothesis with emphasis upon physiological factors was proposed by Wolpert (1975), who viewed manic-depressive illness and recurrent depressive disorder as due primarily to lack of physiological energy. According to Wolpert the effect of lithium is due to its ability to normalize the physiological affective system of manic-depressives so that the periodic excesses and lack of physiological energy no longer occur.

Frolkis (1975) has shown that the aging of hypothalamus and the hormonal system involves decreases in many functions and compensatory increases in others. The overall effect is a decrease in hypothalamic function with concomitant diminished ability to cope with stress. The synthesis of catecholamines proceeds at a lower rate, and the monoamine oxidase activity is increased (Robinson, Davis, Nies, Ravaris, and Sylvester, 1971; Robinson, Nies, Davis, Bunney, Davis, Colburn, Bourne, Shaw, and Coppen, 1972). The adrenogenic function of the adrenal cortex decreases progressively with age. The outcome of all these changes is a reduced ability to withstand depression-evoking events.

Although *extracerebral diseases* in many cases have a systemic character, involving in part cerebral diseases, it is convenient to deal separately with diseases of primary extracerebral location and diseases of a cerebral nature. In most studies of relationship between physical disease and depression, the high proportion of physical diseases in the aged has been overlooked. The highly influential paper of Roth and Kay (1956), who found physical illness and/or sensory disability in 62 percent of the men and 51 percent of the women with affective disorder, did not present reliable information concerning physical morbidity in the general aged population. In the US, about 86 percent of people aged 65 and over in 1967 were estimated to have one or more chronic conditions (National Center for Health Statistics, 1968). Most studies of the relationship of depression and physical disease come up with even lower percentages of physical disease. No conclusions can be made by concentrating on the mere number of depressive persons with physical disease.

It is also impossible to draw any confident conclusions from studies based upon hospital admissions because of the national and regional differences in criteria for admission and the availability of hospital beds. Convincing statistical evidence of an etiological relationship between depression and physical illness can be obtained only by comparing a random sample of physically ill people with a corresponding sample of phsyically well subjects. If this inquiry results in a higher frequency of depression in the physically ill population, this would demonstrate an etiological link between physical disease and depression.

Field studies with truly random samples fulfill these criteria. In such a study of mental illness in the aged of Newcastle-upon-Tyne (Kay, Beamish, and Roth, 1964b), moderate or severe physical disability was found in 41 percent of the subjects in the functional group (mostly depressions) compared to 16 percent among normals. Deafness, mostly mild, was observed in 39 percent of the subjects, and defects of vision in 30 percent; the corresponding figures concerning normals were 31 percent and 22 percent. Only 12.5 percent of the functional group did not complain of any physical disability, including sensory defects, compared with 21 percent of the normals.

In a study of psychiatric impairment in a random community sample of 600 subjects aged 60 years and over in San Francisco, (Lowenthal, Berkman, and Associates, 1967) 15 percent were found to be severely or moderately psychiatrically disabled. Almost half of these subjects were judged to be suffering from psychogenic disorders. More

than 10 percent of the psychiatrically well subjects, however, reported symptoms which may point to mild depression. Decreased energy was reported by 53 percent of the well subjects. Both in this community sample and in a hospital sample of 534 mental patients, the most common mental disease diagnosed in physically ill persons was chronic brain syndrome (Simon and Talley, 1965).

Some interesting findings were reported by Anderson and Davidson (1975). In a Scottish study of the mental health of people 55 years and older, emotional disturbance regarded as outside the normal reaction to the vicissitudes of life was observed in 13 percent of 400 physically healthy men and in 17.8 percent of 404 physically healthy women. In physically ill people the corresponding figures were 31.2 percent in 250 physically ill men and 38.2 percent in 178 women with physical illness.

In a field study of septuagenarians (Stenback et al., 1979), 13 of the 25 depressive subjects reported physical disease as the cause of their mood disorder. Ten cases reported a chronic illness and in three cases an acute illness was mentioned. Among the 25 depressive subjects, 18 or 72 percent considered themselves physically ill whereas the corresponding figures for the 77 nondepressive subjects were 13 percent and 19.4 percent.

Psychiatric examination of depression patients will point out the role of physical disease in the etiology of depression. When two events occur closely in time, when the subject in question feels that the two events are causally linked together, and when a trained investigator considers this link plausible, the etiological link may be considered proven. Roth and Kay (1956) found acute physical stress at the start of depression in 18.2 percent of 231 depression patients. Total physical ill-health (acute and chronic) was greater in males (the same finding was made by Lowenthal et al., 1967), particularly among those males with the first attack occurring after the sixtieth birthday. This finding was confirmed by Gibson (1961) in a study carried out in the north of England, but it was not confirmed in a study of patients admitted to a geriatric unit in London (Post, 1969).

The diseases most commonly found as etiological factors in depression are the same as those generally found in the old population (Gibson, 1961; Post, 1962; Roth and Kay, 1956; Simon and Talley, 1964). The extracerebral diseases act partly as precipitating factors, partly as "functional cerebral diseases" which influence those hormonal and metabolic processes in the brain which are related to mood and activity. Simon (1970) found that, in many cases, physical illness was a critical antecedent to late-developing isolation of elderly persons and to subsequent mental illness. Vulnerability to protracted reactions after bereavement was dependent upon the presence of other deprivations such as physical illness.

There are two *cerebral diseases*, common in old age and frequently occurring subclinically, which may have a causal relationship with depression: chronic brain syndrome and parkinsonism.

Depression in old age has been explained as due to incipient, latent chronic brain syndrome. Nevertheless, the notion of old age depression as generally caused by organic brain changes has been refuted. In a study of 175 patients with affective disorder, Kay and coworkers (Kay, Roth, and Hopkins, 1955) did not observe new cases of cerebral arteriosclerosis or senile dementia during the follow-up 20 months later. Although the follow-up time was short, the study points to the absence of marked cerebral degeneration. These findings got support from a study of outcome in a long-term follow-up carried out later by Kay (1962) and from a follow-up study by Post (1962). Neuropathological studies (Corsellis, 1962) support the distinction between organic and functional mental disorders in old age.

In these clinical studies, a considerable number of patients with "mixed syndromes" were observed. The onset of organic brain disease appeared in some cases to have activated an existing predisposition for depression. Post (1962) and Ciompi and Lai (1969) found that the etiological link between depression and cerebral arteriosclerosis was one of precipitation. Self-observation of a progressive loss of intellectual faculties can bring about a reactive depression. When the chronic brain syndrome becomes severe, there is such a severe loss of psychological capacity including mood reactivity that the individual is deprived of his capacity to react with depression.

In a hospital sample of 111 patients suffering from parkinsonism, (mean age of 63.7 years), Brown and Wilson (1972) found the incidence of clinical depression to be 52 percent. Because of the conflicting reports of both the alleviation and the worsening of depression with l-dopa, a lively interest has been taken in the unraveling of this relationship. The equivocal results in a treatment experiment with l-dopa (Goodwin, Brodie, Murphy, and Bunney, 1970) do not constitute convincing evidence against the depression-evoking role of a decrease in dopaminergic activity. The psychobiology of an established depression is different than that of an incipient depression. The effect of l-dopa depends upon the psychobiological condition of each particular type (Riklan, 1972).

Obviously, parkinsonism not only has depression-precipitating effects but it also brings about a decrease of neural transmitters necessary for maintenance of normal mood.

Along with biological factors, *psychological factors* have to be considered. An analysis of the *personality* classifications system points out the similarity of the main differentiating criteria. The concepts employed are not identical but overlap to a high degree (Table 26-2). Man's world is twofold: internal psyche and external environment. Due to the difficulty of focusing simultaneously upon inner life and outer reality, a preponderance of one at the expense of the other ensues, i.e. relative introversion or relative extraversion. Due to biological and social factors, the theoretically possible case of an even amount of introversion and extraversion does not exist; differentiation always takes place (Witkin, Dyk, Paterson, Goodenough, and Karp, 1962).

When discussing the premorbid depressive personality, Chodoff (1974) concurs with three often expressed opinions: an *obsessive* personality is predisposed to the development of involutional depressions, manic depressive patients have an *oral* character, and the unipolar depressives are marked by a greater degree of a rather nonspecific *neuroticism*. When discussing the psychodynamics of senescent depressive patients, Lai (Lai, 1968) grouped the personalities into three clusters: anal, oral, and "unstable-polymorphous." Obviously they are the same as presented by Chodoff. Interestingly, Ciompi and Lai (1969) found a fourth personality type with good therapeutic outcome: the emotional, choleric, impulsive personality.

Life is ongoing interaction between individual and environment. In this interactive process the obsessive, introverted, inner-directed, field-independent personality attempts to realize his inner demands and convictions. The oral, extraverted, other-directed, and field-dependent personality

**Table 26–2** Related opposite concepts describing personality.

| | |
|---|---|
| Extraversion (*Jung*) | Introversion |
| Oral (*Freud*) | Anal |
| Getting (*Adler*) | Ruling |
| Global (*Witkin*) | Analytical |
| Field dependent (*Witkin*) | Field independent |
| Other-directed (*Riesman*) | Inner-directed |
| Adjusted (*Riesman*) | Autonomous |
| Conforming | Creative |
| Expressive | Instrumental |
| Environmental | Innerpsychic |
| External objects | Internal objects |

builds his equilibrium upon adapting to desires of significant others. These two personality types are usually able to achieve an equilibrium, but the third type, the "unstable-polymorphous," is not able to find an equilibrium because there is no firm center in the personality.

When not suffering from clinical depression, all these four personality types are not afflicted with depressive symptoms. On the contrary, *the depressive personality* (Nemiah, 1975) is characterized by habitual depressive mood and pessimistic outlook; this personality does not often develop into a case of clinical depression.

As hinted earlier, both extraverted and introverted personalities are disposed to depression. When Neugarten (1973) maintains that with increasing age people move from active involvement with the world to a more introversive, passive and self-centered position, this does not necessarily imply a change in predisposition to depression, only that the vulnerability to particular stimuli increases.

Prior to the emphasis on *cognitive distortions* in the etiology of depression put forward by Beck (1967), depression was viewed as an exclusively affective disorder. Most clinicians still do not state that depression is a cognitive disorder. However, the cognitive factor in depression is now recognized to be of primary importance. When the cognitive triad—a negative view of future, environment, and self—is the basis of the evaluation of the experienced loss, the impact of the cognitive distortions is greater than that of the loss, according to Beck (1967). When discussing the origin of this "negative cognitive set," Beck (1974) pointed to parental loss prior to the age 16 and to the general tendency to appraise situations in extreme terms: either good or bad.

Common views of old people indicate that Beck's cognitive triad is characteristic of old people. There is an abundance of gerontological literature corroborating this opinion (e.g., Butler, 1975). If Beck's view concerning the significance of cognitive factors in depression is even partly true—and there is much in favor of it—the cognitive predisposition to depression is much stronger in old age than in middle age. The high frequency of mild and moderate depressions in old age may be due to this cognitive attitude. How much this negative view is "cognitive distortion" and not a realistic standpoint is difficult to resolve in face of isolation and severe physical disease.

The *shortened time perspective* is not only an objective fact but also in many cases an important psychological factor. Although in many respects interrelated, shortened time perspective is differentiated from death and attitude to death and dying. The time perspective refers to the consciousness of finitude of life and to the length of lifetime left.

As many times emphasized, depression is the result of experienced loss and failed restitution. Old age not only is a time of losses but also offers a shortened time for restitution. In addition, a septuagenarian has statistically speaking about one decade of lifetime left; however, according to the common view, an elderly person has no time left and consequently often feels that it isn't worthwhile to attempt to find new love objects, new goals, and new plans. The depressed old person tends to remain depressed.

When encountering crises of various types, including imminent death, some old persons resort to the life review described by Butler (1963). In some of the aged the result of this process is serenity and wisdom; in others this reminiscing may bring up guilt and frustrations, and so contribute to the occurrence of depression.

The relationship between depression and the approaching death is manifold. In his essay on death and neurosis, Meyer (1973) draws attention to death as the many times hidden cause of hypochondria. Another way of furthering depression is the feeling that time is short and all attempts to start again after a severe blow are of no avail. The attitude to death will be analyzed in some length in the section dealing with suicide in old age.

*Environment.* When conceptualizing the genesis of depression, attention is usually focused on the individual living under the depressing impact of some significant life events. Such a "precipitating" event is in many cases a distressing and deplorable change in the individual's environment. When attention is paid to such a pronounced "loss" in the life of the individual, many smaller unpleasant and annoying occurrences remain unnoticed. The plight of the aged is that they—in contrast to the young and middle aged—live in an environment replete with multiple small losses. The aged person is taught—and this is an inherent, mostly unchallenged part of the prevailing culture—that repeated losses fall to his lot up to the time of the final loss of the bodily existence. He has to cope with the idea of aging as a life period of continuous losses.

As it is emphasized repeatedly, depression is not the outcome of loss and subsequent sadness but the outcome of failure in replacing the experienced loss. Old age is characterized by scarcity of opportunities for this readaption. No new roles are offered to the aged. On the contrary, he is discouraged from making serious attempts at restitution of the intrapsychic and intrapersonal equilibrium. He ought to withdraw, to take the depressive position (Hill, 1968). A society and a culture setting the stage for development of hopelessness are depression promoting (Melges and Bowlby, 1969).

So far the facts and considerations presented primarily refer to depressive symptomatology in Western industrial countries. The *transcultural* study of depression in developing countries is still in its incipiency. Because the average life expectancy is low (before 1960 it was less than 40 years in East Africa [German, 1972]) the scope and study of psychogeriatric problems is almost nonexistent. Nevertheless, extrapolation from the scarce findings concerning depression in lower age can be made.

Two decades ago, the available evidence pointed to rareness of depressive disorders in preliterate societies (Carothers, 1953; Stainbrook, 1954; Tooth, 1950). In his essay on the rarity of depressive disorders in preliterate and developing societies, Kiev (1972) strongly emphasized that, because a depressive attitude of apathy and lassitude is in many societies part of the cultural background, mild depressive disorders go unrecognized. Lambo (1956) and Field (1960) pointed out that depression might be missed because of a veneer of psychosomatic and hypochondriacal symptoms. In 1972, German dared to maintain that depression is as common in Africa as in Europe. The symptom pattern is however somewhat different. Self-blaming is rare; persecutory delusions, hypochondriasis, and somatic complaints predominate. These dissimilarities to the Western nosographic entities of depression were not found by Yap (1965) in the Chinese society of Hong Kong.

In 1972, the World Health Organization undertook the coordination of an international collaborative project on depressive disorders. The study started in four countries: Canada, Iran, Japan, and Switzerland. Subsequently, other study centers in both developing and developed countries joined the project. The preliminary results showed no differences in symptomatology between the four countries (Sartorius *et al.*, 1977). The main finding was corroboration of the old differentiation in "endogenous" and "non-endogenous" depressive disorders. From the psychogeriatric point of view, the most interesting finding was that the endogenous group had higher factor scores on age, whereas the non-endogenous group scored higher on abnormal premorbid history and personality. This finding was made in all collaborating countries regardless of differences in culture.

*Psychological and Biological Reactions.* In a previous section, losses of persons and things, physical ill-

ness, retirement, failures and frustrations were described as significant life events conducive to development of depression. The first three events can be grouped together as losses in a wider sense; all of them involve the loss of something valuable that is the property of the individual. Failures refer to something not existing, an anticipated, hoped-for result of striving and activities.

The effects subsequent to loss are sadness and mental pain. Failures and frustrations elicit discouragement and dejection. The emotions after loss and frustration arise mostly immediately in relation to affective memory (Arnold, 1970). For example, a loss of a spouse is felt immediately as a strong sadness, without preceding conscious structuring of this experience, as maintained by Beck (1967). The cognitive appraisal—distorted or undistorted—tends to increase or to alleviate the emotional reaction.

After the emotional shock has abated, the individual starts to build up his emotional equilibrium again. In this restitution phase, the cognitive appraisal of himself and his situation is of predominating significance. In seeking new objects to cathect, his view of himself and his life situation has a crucial impact. Here the "cognitive distortions" so ably studied and described by Beck (1967) have a pronounced influence. Not only personal cognitive distortions but also similar conceptions inherent in the prevailing culture act upon the individual. Social factors—scarcity of personal contacts, lack of roles, and poverty—add to this restriction of opportunities. In many cases ill health worsens the situation. These reciprocally reinforcing factors may bring about failure in the attempts at restitution. To the original feelings of sadness and discouragement, feelings of helplessness and hopelessness will be added. In considering his own role in the development of the present situation, the individual develops guilt and lowered self-esteem. The typical symptoms of depression (affective anesthesia, inability or reduced ability to react emotionally to environment) ensues.

The field-dependent, global, oral, extraverted personality type is predisposed to all-or-nothing reactions. When significant persons or central life tasks are lost, all is lost. The reaction is a total reaction of body and mind without elaborated psychic work-up. The ensuing depression is that of endogenous depression in the symptomatological sense. These depressions are frequently bipolar.

The field-independent, analytical, obsessive, introverted personality type is more intrapsychically oriented, which implies that memories, fears, idiosyncratic concepts, and failure in carrying out life plans play a considerably bigger role in the ensuing depression. This depression is called "neurotic" which, generally speaking, implies a preponderance of these intrapsychic processes. Increasing introversion (Neugarten, 1973) will further the development of depression of the neurotic (and unipolar) type.

The biological reactions obviously develop in close relationship with the biological changes that commonly take place in depression and to the biological aging factors described earlier in this chapter. Features characteristic of the biology of the aged depressive are largely uninvestigated, but one remarkable finding is the previously mentioned age-related increase in monoamine oxidase level (Robinson *et al.*, 1971; Robinson *et al.*, 1972).

## Course and Prognosis

Only a few studies regarding the course and prognosis of depressive illness in old age have been carried out. The most serious attempts to study changes in symptomatology and factors correlating with these changes were made by Post (1962, 1972) and Ciompi and Lai (1969). Post's two studies cover followups of two patient groups aged 60 and over admitted to a geriatric unit around 1950 and 1966, with a followup period of over 6 years and three years, respectively. In the followup study of Ciompi and Lai (1969) all depressive patients who were admitted to a psychiatric university clinic at age less than 65, were studied after the age of 65. The followup period was one to 52 years, the mean being 20.5 years. Although not exclusively focusing upon old age, Matussek and coworkers, (Matussek *et al.*, 1965) have also brought forward pertinent findings.

Out of the wealth of observations in these studies only a few can be presented here. Post (1962) concluded that in only 19 percent of his 100 patients did the affective illness have no detrimental longterm effects; in a further 35 percent their later lives remained tolerable in spite of subsequent, sometimes protracted, periods of mental illness, and in the remaining 46 percent the illness had ushered in a sustained decline, which in 18 percent had been very severe. In spite of more active treatment, the outcome in the 1966 series (Post, 1972) was about the same. This disappointing result was attributed to better preadmission treatment available in 1966, resulting in admission of more ill patients. The following characteristics tended to point to a good prognosis: age below 70, positive family history of affective disorders, recovery from earlier attacks before the age of 50, extraverted personality, social ties and activities

extending beyond the family, absence of dysthymic or cyclothymic trends and an absence of severe affective symptomatology, including schizo-affective features. Prognostically unfavorable were patients with physical senility (especially in women over 70) or physical defects and disabilities.

In their study of aged former depression patients, Ciompi and Lai (1969) found that only 33.9 percent did not suffer from depression after the age of 65. At the followup study, 66 percent showed no depressive symptoms (i.e. about 50 percent of the depressive episodes after the age of 65 had had a favorable outcome, a finding similar to Post's observations). Analyzing the statistically significant factors, Ciompi and Lai found that present physical health was significant in 100 percent of the cases; this was followed by present activity level (93 percent of the cases), present social milieu (67 percent), premorbid personality (32 percent), age (26 percent), heredity (26 percent), sex (20 percent), constitution (20 percent) and civil status (20 percent). In contrast to Roth (1955) who claimed that onset of affective illness after the age of 60 pointed to a more favorable prognosis, Post (1962) found that patients first falling ill after 60 tended to have unfavorable outcome though this observation did not reach statistical significance (p>0.10). These conflicting results can be interpreted as support for Ciompi and Lai's observation that there was no difference in prognosis between manic-depressive illness and involutional depressions, with only reactive and neurotic depressions having more favorable outcome.

Referring to Sattes (1955), Matussek *et al.* (1965) described the depressive symptoms as "ego-close" and "ego-remote" or "body-close." Between the two extremes of exclusively ego-close and body-close, the depressive symptoms can be ranked: vital feelings, agitation, inhibition, anxiety, guilt feelings, rumination, suicidal ideation, and suicidal attempts. With increasing age and number of episodes, the symptomatology moves more and more towards the body-close pole, which means that the patient experiences his depression more and more as a disease which has befallen him. This increasing "vitalization" of the depression implies less depressive ideation, and more of emotional hypoaesthesia, listlessness, hypochondria and fatigue.

Closely related to this increased somatization of depression in old age is the *depletion* state (Cath, 1965) encountered in old age. Cath's description of the depletion is somewhat ambiguous. On one side, depletion is described as the internal and external changes related to aging. On the other side (relevant for our discussion of the course of depression) depletion is a state of emptiness and decline, helplessness, and loss of interests and energy subsequent to depression. "One might say that beyond depression is depletion."

The evolution described by Cath as depletion, is dealt with by Ernst (Ernst, 1962; Ernst and Ernst, 1965) as *"residual state."* Ernst had observed that chronic neuroses in many cases change into a mental state characterized by attenuation of the specific neurotic symptoms and simultaneous reduction of the level of general psychological functioning, narrowing of interests and activities, and decrease in the "vital potential." This residual state was observed subsequent not only to chronic neurosis but also to schizophrenia and manic-depressive illness (Angst, 1966). In their study of aging of previous depression patients, Ciompi and Lai (1969) found the same attenuation in intensity of depressive symptoms, which had been partly replaced by an increase in hypochondria and by new affective symptomatology of aggressiveness, vindictiveness, resentment, and hysterical behavior. In addition, with age there is also an increase in physical diseases, organic brain symptoms, and social difficulties. Ciompi and Lai emphasized that this residual state is not so much a state after a depression as it is due to factors concomitant with aging. Weissman and Paykel (1974) have showed how much these sequels could be observed in 40-year-old depressed women 20 months after clinical recovery. How much more this may be true in the age over 60 when the adaptive capacity is reduced!

In a paper on manic-depressive disorder, Ey (1954) stated that recovery is the most frequent outcome, but when on a chronic course, manic-depressive disorder evolves on four lines: demential, schizophrenic, delusional, and neurotic. These deteriorating courses of severe depression are even more probable in old age than earlier in life. The demential course is primarily due to the damaging effect of the depressed mood upon the intellectual activities. The schizophrenic development implies a change into late paraphrenia. Resembling late paraphrenia is the delusional development, in particular the delusion of negation, which in the literature goes under the name of Cotard's symptom; the patient believes in the nonexistence or disappearance of body organs, his entire body, his mind, God, etc. The neurotic development is in many respects similar to these depletion and residual states.

As a state of emotional strain and increased activity, depression can act as a psychosomatic etiological factor, the effect of which varies according to the predisposition of the patient. Post (1962) assumed that chronic depression and cardiorespiratory disorders are psychosomatically linked in a process of pathological aging. His patients, like those of Ciompi and Lai (1969), had a higher death rate from extracerebral causes than did other elderly people of the same age distribution. Cardiorespiratory disorders do have a deteriorating effect upon the brain and thus add an organic factor to the functional deteriorating effect of depression upon intellectual abilities.

When discussing the dynamics of hypochondria, Pfeiffer and Busse (1973) made use of the notion of the "sick role" which the hypochondriac adopts in a characteristic way. In my opinion, it is fruitful to view the chronically depressed elderly as a person who has adopted the "depressed role of the old." In our society, the life of the aged is viewed as sick, tired, listless, and depressed. Due to this prevailing notion a depressed elderly person is often unsure that his life can be changed. Hence, when treating old depressives, it is advantageous to apply, along with medical measures, the educational model suggested by Mechanic (1977) as applicable to the treatment of illness behavior.

## THERAPY

Reluctance and pessimism have long been typical of the attitude toward therapy in old age. After research has established that depression in many ways is not due to normal aging nor to senile dementia, a positive change has taken place. In some quarters an unrealistic optimism has replaced the previous negative attitude. This over-optimism is, however, to be found only among gero-psychiatrists with the bulk of psychiatrists, internists and social welfare workers remaining pessimistic. In a field study of depression in septuagenarians, an evaluation of the treatability of the 25 depression cases was attempted (Stenback *et al.*, 1979). These old age depressions were easily divided up in two groups: depressions with severe physical illness and depressions without any physical illness or with mild physical illness. Thirteen subjects were allocated to the former group. These patients were to a high degree resistant to therapy. The severe physical illness caused a decrease in vitality already reduced by depression. In addition, a reactive factor was at play: the subjects anticipated further deterioration, more suffering, and eventual death. Only general medicine, not psychiatry, can render these patients substantial help. The remaining 12 subjects were somatically in a better condition. A reactive factor was also involved in these subjects, but contrary to the first group, the event to which they reacted was in the past and not currently operating.

In old age, psychological and biological disturbances are even more intertwined than earlier in life. In many cases old-age depression is neurasthenic-hypochondriacal, permeated by feelings of weakness and fatigue. Reduction of vitality can be observed in old age without clear-cut diseases. The depletion state (Cath, 1965) and old age neurasthenia require improvement of the physical state. Latent or obvious physical disease has to be treated energetically. Antidepressive medication is indicated in many cases. The psychopharmacological aspects of antidepressive therapy are dealt with elsewhere in this book. Emphasized here is the need for coordination of medical, psychopharmacological, sociotherapeutic, and psychotherapeutic measures. Electric convulsive treatment can have good therapeutic effect, particularly in depression with strong guilt feelings, but the number of treatments has to be kept low to avoid organic brain changes.

Some old persons are so psychologically and socially similar to middle-age persons that their problems and therapeutic methods are the same. They are capable of transference, insight, working-through, cathecting, and social adaptation. Most old persons, however, have old-age problems, and their attitude to psychotherapy is also somewhat different. The motivation for deeper psychotherapy is weak and the capacity for transference is often hampered by a certain superficiality of affectivity. Goldfarb (1967) and Peck (1966) described the transference most desired by the elderly as a help-seeking relationship to an omnipotent paternal figure.

Crisis intervention is not a depression therapy but, if carried out in an adequate way, is one of the most effective preventive measures against depression. Its aim should be restoration of the precrisis activity level, or depression will easily ensue.

In addition to crisis intervention, other forms of brief therapy should be given to old people. These therapies should contribute to cathecting new objects after experienced loss and to relieving bitterness, low self-esteem, and feelings of hopelessness. Persons with a deep sense of failure in life need help in forgetting the past and in adopting new goals that are at the same time inspiring and realistic. In many cases psychotherapy will encourage joining small community groups in which the patient will get the benefits involved in group fellowships. Psychotherapy often lends itself to promote the "life review" (Butler, 1963) meditation. Only rarely in old age does psychotherapy aim at reconstruction of personality. Working through childhood conflicts may be useful for identifying the major patterns in life and personality, but Adlerian and Jungian finalistic psychotherapy

aiming at creating new futurity is in many cases more useful than analysis of the past on Freudian lines.

Cognitive psychotherapy (Beck, 1967) focusing on the patient's depression-generating cognitions is a significant new acquisition to the therapeutic arsenal. Thomae (1976) states that "cognitive restructuration" is one of the main instruments for restoring the internal balance in aged persons, who very often are faced with situations which can be changed in the way they are perceived but not in reality. However, one wonders if these cognitive methods do not sometimes overstrain the ordinary patient's capacity to permanently improve and recover. Most people are more field dependent (Witkin et al., 1962) and need new interpersonal relationships and social activities in addition to "cognitive restructuration." The new therapeutic approaches by Lewinsohn (1974) and Seligman (1974) have shown that the depressive can learn to interact with the environment in a therapeutically helpful way.

The findings concerning several different personality types related to "successful aging" (Neugarten et al., 1964) have to be applied to psychotherapy. Before starting the therapy proper the therapist should find out whether the patient's basic personality is autonomous (Riesman, Glazer, and Denney, 1950), analytically minded, field independent (Witkin et al., 1962), creative (Wolff, 1959) or adapting (Riesman et al., 1950), global, field dependent (Witkin et al., 1962) or conforming carriers (Wolff, 1959). The therapy is then to be carried out in accordance with the constructive potentialities in the patient's basic personality and within his characteristic life-style.

In spite of its subjective character ("psychotherapy is an art"), psychotherapy has to stay close to scientifically established facts. This implies a restrictive and cautious attitude to "cognitive restructuration" when facing existential meaninglessness, suffering, and death for otherwise psychotherapy becomes a secular belief system.

## SUICIDE AND ATTEMPTED SUICIDE

From time immemorial the study of suicide (from Latin, *sui*, of oneself, *-cide*, from *caedere*, to cut, kill, killing) has exerted uncanny attraction. During the last few decades the scope of behaviors related to suicide has largely expanded. Inspired by Freud's theory of a death-instinct, Karl Menninger (1938) wrote his highly influential treatise *Man Against Himself*. Viewing suicide as direct self-destruction, he described a vast array of behaviors as forms of indirect self-destruction: ascetism, martyrdom, neurotic invalidism, alcohol addiction, antisocial behavior, psychosis, self-mutilations, malingering, polysurgery, purposive accidents, impotence, frigidity, and physical disease. These citations from the list of contents in *Man Against Himself* indicate the vast scope of indirect self-destruction, a much discussed subject in current suicidology. All unhealthy and harmful behaviors can be included in "indirect self-destruction." This in many respects fruitful concept is, however, diffuse and will not be dealt with in this presentation.

Erwin Stengel (1973) has made a major contribution to the present generally accepted differences in the psychodynamics of suicide and attempted suicide. A purpose of self-destruction is not always inherent in the suicidal act. Instead the suicidal attempt serves as an alarm signal and has the effect of an appeal for help. The persons who attempt suicide and those who commit suicide represent essentially two different, although overlapping, populations (Stengel and Cook, 1958).

Stengel (1973) put forward the definition: "A suicidal act is any deliberate act of self-damage which the person committing the act could not be sure to survive." Attempted suicide and suicidal attempt are used as synonyms although the terms have different connotations: suicide may really be attempted but in many cases the attempt may only have a suicidal character.

FREQUENCY

In the literature on suicide of the elderly it is often stated that the frequency of suicide rises with age. Although true in many countries, as a general statement, it is, however, not correct.

In a study of suicides during the period 1950–1971, Ruzicka (1976) discerned three types of typical age-related suicide rates for both males and females. For males, the first type (A) is represented by continuously increasing suicide rates with age. The majority of countries (e.g., Austria, Czechoslovakia, France, Hungary, Japan, Mexico, and United States) belong to this type. The second type (B) has suicide rates gradually or steeply increasing to a peak, generally at ages around 50 to 60 years, and declining thereafter. Canada, Finland, Norway, and Poland belong to this group. The third type (C) is a modification of type B: the rates around 50 to 60 years are followed by a decline but subsequently turn up again at the age 75 and over. This type is represented by Denmark, Scotland, Sweden, and Switzerland. Japan makes up a type of its own: very high rate at the youngest age group (15–24), rapidly declining to middle age (35–45), and steeply rising thereafter.

Suicide rates for females in the 30 countries studied also exhibited three well-discernible age patterns. The first one is identical with the male type (A), that is, gradual growth of suicide rates with increasing age. Interestingly, rather few countries belong to this type, which holds the majority of male suicides. Instead, the second type (B), similar to the one identified for males, with decline in old age, was most frequently found. Austria, Czechoslovakia, France, Hungary, Italy, Netherlands, Portugal and West Germany represent the type A, whereas Australia, Belgium, Canada, Denmark, England and Wales, Finland, Israel, New Zealand, Norway, Poland, Sweden, Switzerland and United States belong to the type B. The third female type C differs from the male type C: suicide rates are high at the younger ages, descend to a trough of various lengths, and thereafter resume an upward trend progressively rising with age. This type of suicide rate is found in Bulgaria, Greece, Japan, Singapore, and Yugoslavia.

If the rates per 100,000 are compared in the age groups 65–74 and 45–54 in the 41 countries which have reported to the World Health Organization on deaths due to "suicide and self-inflicted injury" in 1974 (WHO 1977), the following observations can be made. The rates for males age 65 and over increased in 26 countries and were about the same or decreased in 15 countries. For females in this category, the rates increased in 22 countries and decreased or remained the same in 19. The increases in rates were marked in 12 countries for males and in 11 countries for females. These rates for one year corroborate the overall picture of no regular relationship between higher rates and higher age.

The suicide statistics in the United States provide interesting evidence for the absence of a connection between suicide and age. Analyzing the US suicide rates for the period 1933–1968, Diggory (1976) found that among white males, the highest suicide rates were in the age group 75 and older, whereas the US white female suicide rate was at a maximum in the 50–54 year age group with a tendency to become increasingly lower at higher ages. During 1933–1968, the maximum suicide rates of nonwhite males occurred in the 60–64 year age group. For nonwhite females this age group had rates similar to the 30–34 year age group. Diggory remarked that sex and race have greater bearing upon suicide rates than does age.

The US has seen a decrease in suicide rates of the aged during the last decades (Diggory, 1976). Rates in the 65–69 age group have fallen from about 45 per 100,000 in 1933 to about 20 per 100,000 in 1968. A similar decrease has been observed in England (Sainsbury, 1973). For Swedish males, the rates for this age group in 1921 remained about 55 per 100,000 from 1921 to 1960, and then fell to 48 per 100,000 in the decade 1961 to 1969. A gradual rise took place for females from 11 in 1921–1930 to 16 in 1961–1968 (Bolander, 1972).

From the practical point of view, rates are not the only way to visualize the scope of the problem of suicide among the aged. The proportion of suicides to the total deaths in an age group indicates the significance of suicide among the aged. In 1974 in the US in the 45–54 year age group there was one suicide out of 34.5 deaths, whereas in the age groups 65–74 and 75 and over the corresponding figures were one in 176.7 and one in 471.3 respectively (WHO, 1977).

The absolute number of suicides also reflects the quantitative aspect of suicides. It can be calculated that if the distribution of suicides and age groups were geographically even (which is not the case) in a US city of 500,000 inhabitants the total annual number of suicides would be about 60, out of which 10 would occur in those aged 65 or older. In West Berlin (pop. 2.1 million) the percentage of males and females over 60 years of age is 22.2 and 35.7 percent respectively, and the absolute numbers of suicides for the years 1973 and 1974 were 264 males and 353 females; this results in an annual rate of 308.5 suicides per year, or 73.5 suicides per 500,000 population, obviously the highest suicide frequency for the aged in the world (WHO, 1977). Although Finland has a markedly higher suicide rate than the US, in the years 1970 and 1971 no more than 33 suicides (10.5 per year) occurred among persons aged 65 and over in the city of Helsinki (pop. 500,000) (Lönnqvist, 1977).

The frequency of *attempted suicide* is difficult to estimate because many unsuccessful attempts do not reach the attention of the recording authorities. There is reason to assume that only the more dramatic or almost successful attempts will be reported and recorded, such as the "aborted successful suicidal attempts" described by Weiss, Nunez, and Schaie (1961).

Shneidman and Farberow (1961) traced 5906 attempted suicides in Los Angeles county in 1957, whereas the number of committed suicides was 768, according to the official records of the coroner's office. This yields a ratio of 7.69 attempted suicides to one committed suicide. Twenty-seven percent of the committed suicides and 6 percent of the attemped suicides occurred in the age group 60 and over, whereas 64 percent of the attempted

suicides and 30 percent of the committed suicides occurred before age 40. Parkin and Stengel (1965) made a two-year survey covering the hospitals and general practitioners in Sheffield, an English industrial town, and found four attempts to one suicide in the age group 60 and over, and 20 attempts to one suicide in the population aged under 40. The ratio of nonfatal to fatal suicidal acts doubled between 1960 and 1970 (Smith, 1972). In 1970, the rates for attempted suicide in the 20–24 age group in Edinburgh were about 400 per 100,000 for males, and about 450 per 100,000 for females. The corresponding rate for both males and females aged 65 and over was about 80 per 100,000 (Kreitman, 1972). In a random sample of attempted suicides admitted to an emergency clinic in West Berlin, Grüneberg (1977) found that the rate for attempts was eight times higher in males and females aged 26 to 30 than in the age group 66 to 75.

## TWO TYPES OF SUICIDE

Without explicit reference to Durkheim's (1951) classification of four types of suicides (egoistic, anomic, altruistic and fatalistic), Ovenstone and Kreitman (1974) presented evidence for two types of suicide which correspond to a high degree to Durkheim's egoistic and anomic types. In a series of 106 consecutive suicides they were able to differentiate two subgroups according to absence or presence of previously attempted suicides. One subgroup, the "non-parasuicide group," comprised individuals who had led stable if precariously adjusted lives until dislocation occurred; they then reacted with a relatively brief depressive episode, sometimes associated with excessive drinking, and soon after killed themselves. The second group, the "para-suicide group," consisted of individuals with long-standing and severe personality problems, commonly with chronic alcoholism, who had a history of at least one attempted suicide, and who eventually committed suicide in a setting of interpersonal chaos frequently associated with events and problems that were dependent on their own behavior.

There are a number of studies pointing to the validity of these two subgroups. Studying 134 successful suicides, Robins, Murphy, Wilkinson, Gassner, and Kayes (1959) found that most cases were suffering either from manic depressive depression or chronic alcoholism. Prior to the study of Ovenstone and Kreitman, Seager and Flood (1965) and McCulloch, Philip and Carstairs (1967) also brought forward evidence for two subgroups to which most suicides could be allocated.

There is a dearth of information concerning the personality structure of the aged suicides. The few pertinent studies indicate that most aged suicides belong to the group with stable personalities. This may be due to selective factors: most people surviving to old age are more or less free from manifest character disorder. Barraclough (1971) found only one case of chronic alcoholism among 30 elderly suicides. Patel (1972) found that for those without a previous history of attempted suicide, suicide occurred most commonly in the sixth decade. In detailed descriptions of characteristics of suicide in old age, Ringel (1969) and Seidel (1969) made no reference to asocial personalities and alcoholism.

This evidence indicates that the suicides of the aged belong to Ovenstone and Kreitman's "non-parasuicide group," or are egoistic rather than anomic according to the terminology of Durkheim.

## MENTAL ILLNESS

In the studies of suicides, the percentages of suicides suffering from mental illness vary from 20 to 94 (WHO, 1968). There are only a few systematic studies aimed at establishing a psychiatric diagnosis of the deceased subjects. Robins *et al.* (1959) found that nine out of 134 suicides were "apparently clinically well," whereas the numbers of manic-depressives and chronic alcoholics were 42 and 27 respectively. In his study of suicides in London, Sainsbury (1955) concluded that mental disorders were the principal factor in 37 percent and a contributory factor in a further 10 percent. Referring to later studies, Sainsbury (1973) stated that nearly all suicides are psychiatrically ill. According to diagnoses made independently by three consultant psychiatrists, over two-thirds had a depressive illness, 13 percent were alcoholics, and eight percent suffered from other mental illness. Analyzing the 30 elderly suicides in this study group Barraclough (1971) found 26 persons with depression, one chronic alcoholic, one possible confusional state, and four who were deemed not mentally ill. In a study of the 31 suicides committed by persons aged 65 and over in Helsinki in 1970 and 1971, Lönnqvist (1977) found that 14 were severely mentally ill, 13 had mild mental symptoms, and no mental symptoms were discovered in four.

The role of organic brain factors in the etiology of suicides in elderly is of particular interest. Sainsbury (1955) reported that between 15 and 20 percent of suicides over 60 had signs of intellectual deterioration before death.

The observed frequencies of mental illness in suicides of old age are related to diagnosis of depression. If the diagnosis of depression is considered justified only when there are severe symptoms (deeply depressive mood associated with retardation or agitation), the incidence of depression in suicides will remain at around 20 percent (WHO, 1968). But if a wider diagnosis of depression is employed, the percentage of depression preceding suicide will rise almost to 100, as stated by Sainsbury (1973). In many cases chronic alcoholism may lead to depression. The core of depression is the hopelessness subsequent to repeated failures at restitution. Suicide can be viewed as an act carried out to relieve this state of hopelessness.

In the consideration of mental illness and attempted suicide, the preponderant role of depressions also comes to the fore. Batchelor and Napier (1953) diagnosed depressive illness in 80 percent and organic syndrome in 10 percent of attempted suicides. The corresponding figures reported by O'Neal, Robins, and Schmidt (1956) were 47 percent and 42 percent, by Kreitman (1976) 58 percent and 8 percent, and by Feuerlein (1977) 50 percent and 14 percent.

Neither acute confusional states nor late paraphrenia seem to play a conspicuous role in attempted suicide in old age. In a study of 34 attempted suicides in persons aged 60 years or over, Sendbuehler and Goldstein (1973) found organic brain syndrome in 18 cases, or 53 percent compared with an incidence of 5 to 10 percent in the normal population. In most cases the organic brain syndrome coexisted with other mental diseases, mostly depression (with only one case of character disorder). In many cases a diagnosis of "life crisis" or acute depression seems most appropriate, seen not infrequently in association with psychopathic or hysterical traits.

There is slight evidence for a higher incidence of chronic alcoholism among aged people who attempt suicide, compared to aged people who complete the act. In studies of attempted suicides, Batchelor and Napier (1953) reported 10 percent chronic alcoholism, O'Neal *et al.* (1956) 11 percent, Böcker (1975) 15 percent, Kreitman (1976) 12 percent or 26 percent if only men were considered, Feuerlein (1977) 15 percent among men, and Grüneberg (1977) 23.5 percent among men and 6 percent among women. The frequency of chronic alcoholism among the elderly who attempt suicide is clearly less than in persons under 65 years of age who do so (Feuerlein 1977; Kreitman 1976).

## PHYSICAL ILLNESS

Because of the high frequency of chronic physical diseases in old age, the mere finding of physical ill-health in suicides and attempted suicides is of no import without a simultaneous estimation of the personal significance allocated to the illness. Sainsbury (1955) estimated that physical illness contributed to the suicide in 35 percent of the elderly cases, compared with 27 percent in the middle-aged and 10 percent in young people. Analyzing 80 cases of suicides committed by persons over 65 years, Hedri (1967) found the most common factor was the attitude to somatic illnesses. Making a comparison between 30 suicides over 65 and 30 accidental deaths of the same age, Barraclough (1971) found 17 important physical disorders in the suicides compared to nine in the accidental deaths. Studying suicidal notes Kulawik and Decke (1973) found physical illness most frequently mentioned, particularly by elderly female suicides. In his study of 31 completed suicides aged 65 and over, Lönnqvist (1979) found severe physical illness in 16 cases.

Comparing attempted and committed suicides Shneidman and Farberow (1961) found that physical illness played a lesser role in attempted suicide than in committed suicide. In fair agreement with this finding, Böcker (1975), Feuerlein (1977), and Grüneberg (1977) established a heavy preponderance of interpersonal problems compared to illness problems among elderly who had attempted suicide. Dorpat, Anderson, and Ripley (1968) found physical illness to be the most common precipitating factor in completed suicide, whereas no statistically significant relationship between age and prevalence of physical illness could be established in the attempted suicides.

*Hypochondria.* Hypochondria is part of man's attitude to his body. Man views his body and physical illness in many ways: adequately, with "high bodily concern" (Busse, 1970), with denial of illness, with an unfounded fear of suffering from a disease (hypochondriac fear), or with a conviction to the same effect (hypochondriac delusion). It stands to reason that fear of being ill fights against illness and death, including suicide. Accordingly, no hypochondriac fear was discovered in a randomly selected series of suicides committed by mental hospital patients (Stenback, Achté and Rimón, 1965). In a randomly selected series of 80 alcohol addicts, hypochondria was found in only three subjects, none of whom belonged to 12 subjects who had attempted suicide (Stenback and Blumenthal, 1964). This incompatibility of suicide and hypochondriac fear is not found in cases with hypochondriac delusions. In these cases the risk of suicide is high, because a hypochondriac delusion acts psychologically like a physical disease. The finding of De Alarcón (1964) of more attempted suicides among aged depressive patients with hy-

pochondria points to the seriousness of depressive delusions with hypochondriac content.

SOCIAL FACTORS

*Social Isolation and Loneliness.* Along with social disintegration and social disorganization, social isolation and loneliness are frequently mentioned in the analysis of causes of suicidal behavior in the aged (Böcker, 1975; Gardner, Bahn, and Mack, 1964; Sainsbury, 1962; Stengel, 1965). Social isolation and loneliness are treated as corollaries of living alone. Frequently many aspects of isolation and loneliness do not get the attention they deserve.

In a study of isolation, loneliness, and suicidal ideation, Bungard (1977) differentiated three dimensions of isolation: objective quantitative isolation, subjective quantitative isolation, and qualitative isolation. Objective quantitative isolation indicates frequency of weekly social contacts. Subjective quantitative isolation is the subject's self-estimation of the frequency of his social contacts. Based on the concept of intimacy put forward by Lowenthal and Haven (1968), qualitative isolation is a measure of intimacy experienced in the social contacts. According to responses given by 134 subjects aged 65 and over who lived alone, 15.7 percent were highly isolated, 11.9 percent regarded themselves as isolated, and 18.7 percent were "qualitatively isolated" (Bungard, 1977). When asked about feelings of loneliness, only half of the quantitatively isolated reported that they suffered from loneliness. This loneliness correlated clearly with loss of intimacy and not with the other measures of isolation. The percentage of suicidal ideation was no higher in these 134 subjects than in 271 subjects who were not living alone. The highest correlation was found between qualitative isolation and suicidal ideation. An unsatisfactory marriage and poor relationship to children proved to be the most crucial factors in qualitative isolation with suicidal ideation. This study of Bungard has been reported in some length in order to illustrate the intricate interplay between social and psychological factors.

*Marital Status.* The suicide rates for single men are double that for married men (Monk, 1975). In a study of 2,064 suicides comprising all suicides in the adult population 25 years of age and older in Finland during 1969–1971, Lönnqvist, Koskenvuo, Sarna, and Kaprio (1979) found that the rates for single women in the 25–44 age group were almost three times higher than the rates for married women, but in the age group 65 and over the rates of single and married women were almost the same. The rates for widows and divorcees in the age group 65 and over were higher than those for the married women, but were less than the rates for the age group 45–64. Thus living alone, widowhood, or marital separation contribute to suicides among the elderly but to a lesser degree than among the young and middle-aged.

*Bereavement.* As reported above, the rates of suicide are higher among the widowed than among the married. A reasonable supposition is that the event of bereavement may predispose to suicide. MacMahon and Pugh (1965) compared 320 widowed suicides with the same number of widowed persons having died of other causes. Deaths from suicide clustered in the first four years of widowhood, particularly in the first year. This was more marked in the older age groups, especially among males. For example, there were 12 suicides within one year of widowhood among males 70 years and over, where only two would have been expected on the basis of the comparison deaths. In a study of all suicides aged 65 and over in Helsinki during 1970–1971, Lönnqvist (1977) found that out of 11 widowers and widows, three men and one woman had lost their spouse within six months prior to suicide.

Bunch, Barraclough, Nelson and Sainsbury (1971) found a high proportion of bereavements of mothers among suicidal single males aged 50 and over. In addition to marital break-up, the death or admission to hospital of a friend or relative was the reason for living alone on the day of suicide in 34 percent of 30 aged suicides studied by Barraclough (1971). Moss and Hamilton (1956) found that among the aged, the loss or death of close relatives occurred twice as often for a group of attempted suicides as for a control group. Finding simultaneous mental illness, particularly depression, in the bereaved suicides, Barraclough (1971) referred to the obvious fact that bereavement acts through the mental illness, mostly through the depression that it elicits.

*Living Alone.* In his study of suicide in London, Sainsbury (1955) found that the percentage of suicides living alone was as high as 29.7 percent. The percentage of suicides 60 years and over living alone was even higher, 39.0 percent. In 10 percent of cases the loneliness was considered as a contributory factor. In an ecological study of suicide in England and Wales, Whitlock (1973a, 1973b) showed that unfavorable social factors had considerably less impact upon suicides aged 65 and over except for loneliness in men. Whitlock (1973b) concluded:

> There is good reason to regard suicide in old age as a distinct phenomenon, compared with suicide

by younger persons. When one examines the intercorrelations between the suicide rates for men and women in the three age samples (15–44, 45–64, and 65+), there are no significant correlations between suicides of those aged 65 and over with the younger age groups, whereas both the younger age groups correlate highly significantly with each other and with the general suicide rate for all ages. Hence, one might conclude that social environmental circumstances have greater impact on younger suicides than they do on the oldest age group.

When emphasizing the high percentage among the elderly of suicides living alone, the high percentage of persons living alone aged 65 and over is frequently overlooked. In the study of Lönnqvist (1977) six men (33 percent) and four women (31 percent) were living alone, the corresponding percentages in the normal population being 19 percent and 50 percent respectively. In a less urbanized sample, Barraclough (1971) found that nearly half of the elderly suicides were permanently living alone whereas only 20 percent of the old population lived in one-person households.

*Moving House.* In his analysis of precedents to suicide, Sainsbury (1973) took considerable interest in the bearing of moving house. He found that suicides had moved more often than controls. Analyses by age indicated that elderly men and middle-aged women are the groups most vulnerable to the effects of moving house. Most frequently the suicides took place within two years after the move.

*Retirement.* The impact of retirement on suicidal behavior is difficult to estimate because an event taking place after the age of 65 is not necessarily due to the retirement at 65. There is no evidence indicating that the "retirement shock" is a common cause of suicide. According to the "status integration theory" (Gibbs and Martin, 1964), suicide is associated with moving from one occupational status to another. Retirement implies moving from the status of a gainfully employed worker to a nonworker status void of meaningful roles. It seems plausible to assume that such a change, which may have only a minor immediate effect, can in the long run have weighty consequences, particularly when retirement involves less income and less prestige in addition to loss of work and workmates. Having observed that the rates of suicides had decreased in the retirees belonging to higher classes and increased in the lower status groups, Sainsbury (1962) hypothesized that the capacity to retire to opportunities for more varied interests and outlets may protect the higher class aged against suicide.

However Lönnqvist *et al.* (1979) found a decrease in suicide rates of the age group 65 and over in all social classes.

*Social Class.* According to a highly extant opinion, suicide is more common among the higher social classes. However, the only evidence found for this idea is the higher suicide rates of males aged 20–64 in social classes I and II in England and Wales (Sainsbury, 1963). Sainsbury's own study of suicide in London (Sainsbury, 1955) did not provide an answer to this question. It is important to make the distinction between ecological and individual correlation with social class. By ecological correlation is meant that suicide rates correlate with the proportion of the upper social classes in the population. There is evidence of such correlation in England (Bagley, Jacobson, and Palmer, 1973; Whitlock, 1973a, 1973b) but not in Buffalo, N.Y. (Lester, 1970). Ecological correlations with social classes I and II (i.e., more suicides were committed in regions with higher proportion of people in these social classes) were found for males and females in the age groups 15–44 and 45–64 but not in the age group 65 and over (Whitlock, 1973a, 1973b). In studies of individuals, a strong correlation between suicide and lowest social class was found (Achté, 1962; Breed, 1963; Lalli and Turner, 1968; Maris, 1967; Yap, 1958). Studying suicide in New Haven, Connecticut, Weiss (1954) found that after the age of 65, the rates for lower-class males were considerably higher than those for upper-class males. Differentiating the suicides according to marital status (single, married, widowhood and divorce), age (25 to 44, 45 to 64, and 65 and over), and social class (I to IV), Lönnqvist *et al.* (1979) found the highest rate for men aged 65 and over in social class IV. For women, the highest rate was in social class I but the result was not statistically significant. In general, the figures for males 65 and over showed an overall small decrease from the rates for the 45–64 age group in almost all social classes and marital status groups. The rates for women 65 and over were mostly lower than in the 45–64 age group in all social classes and marital status groups.

*Poverty* is related to social class, because social class is primarily constructed on the basis of occupation and associated income. Sainsbury (1962) very strongly emphasized that "wealth, not poverty, is associated with suicide." However, he recognized the significance of secondary poverty, the condition of becoming poor after having been well-to-do. The low rate of suicide in the Southern blacks points to the minor role of poverty as such. The role of economic misery however is stressed by the finding that 40 percent of black suicides in New Orleans had worried about debts (Swanson and Breed, 1976).

Sainsbury (1963) argued that old-age pension systems have not reduced suicide frequency in the elderly. He based this statement upon the equal rise in frequency both in countries with the most comprehensive old-age pension schemes and in countries with the least. Kruijt (1960), basing his conclusions on the WHO statistics, pointed out that the old-age regression in suicide rates was most apparent in Great Britain and Scandinavia and in the white populations of the commonwealth countries, where the health and social status of old people were better than in countries not showing such a decline in the suicide rates.

As mentioned previously, the decrease of suicide rates in the population 65 years and over in the U.S. went from 45 per 100,000 in 1933 to about 20 per 100,000 in 1968, whereas the decrease for all ages was only from 15.9 to 10.7 per 100,000 (Diggory, 1976). This relatively greater decrease for the aged can be related to the Social Security developed just during this time period.

*Social Disorganization.* Suicides are more frequent in urban than in rural areas, and in central city than in suburban areas. To a high degree this is due to selective migration. A community can be considered as having an optimal social organization when its population is a balanced cross-section of the national population. Conversely, a community can be regarded as disorganized when its share of children, persons living alone, old people, men, and women is uneven. An additional dimension in social disorganization is the proportion of old dilapidated buildings lacking continuous repair and new buildings considered by the residents as good residences. Social disorganization as a structural term has to be differentiated from social integration or social functioning. In his ecological study of suicide in London, Sainsbury (1955) emphasized that districts with a high proportion of lodging-houses, hotels, and flatlets had high suicide rates. In his study of high- and low-risk areas within a city, Lönnqvist (1977) found that the areas characterized by absence of slum formation and with a high proportion of retired old women had low suicide rates, i.e., there were only few suicides in districts where old people lived quietly by themselves.

## CULTURAL FACTORS

The impact of culture, including religion, upon suicide is two-fold. Culture has a direct impact through the creation of concepts on life and death, life after death, old age, suicide, personal responsibility, and other values. An indirect effect is seen in the influencing of society and other modes of social life, resulting in social integration or disintegration.

Durkheim (1951) strongly emphasized that religion has a prophylactic effect upon suicide and that this effect is related to the social integration religion brings about:

> If religion protects man against the desire for self-destruction, it is not that it preaches the respect for his own person to him with arguments sui generis; but because it is a society. What constitutes this society is the existence of a certain number of beliefs and practices common to all the faithful, traditional and thus obligatory. The more numerous and strong these collective states of mind are, the stronger the integration of the religious community, and also the greater its preservative value. The details of dogmas and rites are secondary. The essential thing is that they be capable of supporting a sufficiently intense collective life.

However, "details of dogmas" are part of the cognitive structure of culture. The impact of culture upon suicidal behavior has to be estimated according to the role allocated to cognitive factors in human behavior. Thomae (1976) views human personality as highly influenced by cognitive processes, and according to Beck (1967) cognitive factors are more crucial in the development of depression, the mental state preceding suicide, than is generally believed. Obviously, the obstacles related to the study of cognitive factors in suicide hinder the acquisition of adequate knowledge about the cognitive aspects of culture, including religion.

In the interaction between social factors proper and cultural factors, the adverse social situation may override the prophylactic effect of culture. In his report on suicide in Hong Kong, Yap (1958) presented the figures for suicides in Peking in 1917. In contrast to the increased suicide rates for old Chinese in Hong Kong in the early 1950s, the rates for the aged in Peking in 1917 were about the same as for the younger adult population. Yap interpreted these findings in the light of the traditional culture with its great emphasis on filial piety and respect for the aged. This culture could not, however, protect the old in the social upheaval characteristic of Hong Kong in the fifties. In their explanation of the high suicide rates in Japan, Iga and Tatai (1975) also allocated more weight to social defects than to cultural attitudes accepting or even idealizing suicide.

Cultures disapproving suicide overtly or covertly take a more permissive stand concerning suicide in old age than suicide committed in young or middle age. An old person is regarded entitled to relieve himself—and his relatives—from the burden of chronic illness, loneliness, and feelings of uselessness. The present discussion of euthanasia exemplifies this. Nevertheless, a negative attitude to suicide in old age is still prevalent in most cultures.

In his overview on suicide, Sainsbury (1973) formulated four "strands" in his explanation of suicide: psychological predisposition, social predisposition, personal crisis, and the attitudes to death and self-destruction prevailing within a society and its institutions, particularly its religious ones. He believes that if a church anathematizes suicide, its practicing members will be protected simply on this account. In addition, following Durkheim's line of thought, Sainsbury allocates great significance to religion's capacity to strengthen the social cohesiveness of its members. In his study he found that nearly half of the controls but only 25 percent of the suicides were somewhat religiously active.

## Some General Aspects

*Suicide as an Act, not a Symptom.* Only in extreme cases can suicide be viewed as a pure symptom of a psychiatric disturbance characterized by confusion and autoaggressiveness. Dementia and confusion generally weaken the ability to act with the sufficient intentionality required to commit a suicide. According to the degree of psychological intent, Weiss (1974) divided the suicidal acts into serious acts, gestures, or gambling with death. The proportion of completed suicides to attempted suicides is higher in old age. This is taken to indicate that the use of suicidal acts for appeal (Stengel, 1973) is not common in old age. Evidence to the effect that suicidal attempts are, nevertheless, not rare in the elderly population was provided by Grüneberg (1977), who found that two-thirds of the attempted suicides in persons aged 60 and over in West Berlin could be classified as gestures or gamblings. Although suicide is an act and not a symptom in the proper sense, it is not an act of free will. Weiss (1974) has clearly stated this point: "The evidence indicates that suicidal behavior is most often a symptom (or a terminating act) of biologically, psychologically and culturally determined psychiatric disorder, not a free moral choice."

*Aggression.* According to psychoanalytical thought, suicide is caused by aggression directed toward the self (Menninger, 1938; Ringel, 1952). Autoaggression can be implicated in the cases when depression and suicidal thoughts are linked with guilt feelings, indicating that the subject views himself as the source and cause of his failure and emotional distress. But, as dealt with elsewhere, depressions in old age are mostly not distinctly guilt depressions. Judging from the low rate of aggressive delinquency in old age (Riley and Foner, 1968), the aggressive potential of old people is markedly low.

If aggression inappropriately loses its connotation of hostile, emotionally forceful activity and becomes a verbal expression for any form of forceful activity, aggression can be said to play a role in every suicide. The higher rates of male suicides can be attributed not to aggression as such but to men's particular position in culture and society and to the biologically and culturally stronger disposition in men to settle difficulties by action.

*Impulse and Purpose.* Man's behavior can in a general sense be classified as impulse behavior and purpose behavior. The bulk of studies provide evidence indicating that the proportion of impulse suicides—almost identical with anomic, psychopathic and hysteric suicides—decreases with age. The typical suicide of old age is a suicide seriously planned and carried out. Nevertheless, the very execution of the frequently long-harbored purpose often has the psychological features of impulse behavior. A tiny incident may put the suicidal idea into execution. Nevertheless, this impulse behavior in the last crucial phase does not contradict the premeditated, deliberate character of the suicide in the aged.

*Old Age Suicide Is "Egoistic."* In many ways, evidence indicates that the suicide of the aged is of the type Durkheim (1951) called "egoistic." Egoism or excessive individualism, as Durkheim also put it, involves deficient commitment to the cultural, ethical or religious values of the society in which the individual lives. In addition, egoism in Durkheim's sense implies that emotional bonds tying the individual to other people are few, frequently resulting in social isolation. The individualistic withdrawal makes it difficult for the supporting social networks, if they exist at all, to build up the reality and feelings of social integration badly needed in the times of losses and failures.

*Five Main Factors.* Although aging in many cases is associated with factors conducive to suicide, it is not plausible to consider, as was done by Seidel (1969), the general biological and psychosocial characteristics of aging as the crucial causes of suicide. The main factors contributing to the suicidal behavior can be condensed as follows: first, general

and age-specific losses and failures which cause depression with hopelessness and despair; second, an "egoistic" or excessively individualistic personality, emotionally shallow or cold; third, a society unable to create social integration by means of family bonds, community interest groups, or supporting social services; fourth, a personality trait of resolving problems by action and not by passive adaptation; fifth, a suicide-promoting environment, either personal (e.g., suicides in the family) or cultural (e.g., acceptance and idealization of suicide).

TREATMENT

Shneidman (1969) introduced the concepts of prevention, intervention, and postvention of suicide. Prevention is roughly synonymous with the concept of prevention in public health and preventive medicine. Intervention and postvention equal the old notion of treatment, including followup treatment. The aim of treatment is early identification of prospective cases of suicide and attempted suicide, and prevention.

As discussed earlier, physical and mental illness have a great impact upon suicidal behavior in old age. This fact indicates that the doctor who treats the elderly for the physical illness (usually a general practitioner) is the key person in the treatment of mental illness, including the suicidal intent. The presence of depression, particularly if hopelessness is a pronounced symptom (Minkoff, Bergman, Beck, and Beck, 1973), should alert the doctor to the possibility of suicide. The treatment of a presumptive suicide is basically the same as the treatment given to a person suffering from depression. This includes drug treatment, psychotherapy, and sociotherapy. In a psychologically appropriate way, although not too cautiously, the therapist has to search for suicidal ideation and explicitly discuss the nature of suicide and its consequences. Because a truly significant personal relationship, a "confidant" (Lowenthal and Haven, 1968), may be the crucial life-saving thing, the treating person (doctor, social worker, psychologist, or minister) has the moral obligation to see to it that the help-seeking person finds such a helper or friend. Although the general practitioner has to first deal with the physical ailments, he also is obliged to treat the presuicidal state. He should try to get family members, friends, and social welfare personnel to help the patients. In addition to the humane obligation to relieve elderly persons from loneliness, the concrete provision of continuing medical services and home care is of crucial significance. The old person will almost always take recourse to suicide only when he feels himself abandoned. Particular attention should be paid to acute crises during which the elderly person, who has long harbored a suicide intent, may put intent into execution.

In addition to the emergency telephone service, The Samaritans in Great Britain have established a "befriending" service within which ordinary people befriend lonely people (Fox, 1976). In towns where the Samaritans had been in operation for at least two years, Bagley (1968, 1971) found a decrease of 58 percent in the suicide rate compared with a rise of 19.8 percent in matched control towns. However, the proportion of old people making use of "suicide prevention centers" was low. The Samaritan Organization had fewer old clients of both sexes than expected, amounting to 6 percent of the total against an average of 13 percent in the general population. "It seems universally the experience of helping agencies that the elderly are likelier to suffer, stoically, in silence." (Fox, 1976).

It seems obvious that treatment of the suicidal aged must take place primarily in hospitals, outpatient clinics, social welfare agencies, and other places where the aged seek help for their diverse needs, rather than in community suicide services, although they are also highly necessary for the older age groups.

### Prevention

In connection with suicide, prevention describes the measures to be taken for preventing an individual from committing suicide. This is in contrast to public health and preventive medicine, where prevention is mainly "primary prevention," group-directed activity aimed at reducing morbidity. Because of the central role physical and mental disorders have in the etiology of suicide in old age, an important preventive measure is provision of good medical care, including good mental health services. Studying the effect of introduction of community-oriented mental health services, Walk (1967) found evidence indicating that the community care may have protected some elderly patients from suicide. A similar project in a more rural area failed to repeat these results (Nielsen and Videbeck, 1973).

Health services are intimately interwoven with the social services and good personal relationships. Prevention of suicide in old age can succeed only by a combination of macrosocial measures (pension, housing, transport, etc.) and microsocial action (family, friend, social case work, group work, leisure activities, etc.). As an overall aspect, "community organization" can describe the whole spectrum of community activities which must be put to bear on the situation of the aged.

Information on the suicide problem has to be given to all professional groups dealing with old people. In addition, the general public should be informed about the risks involved in letting old people with chronic disorders live in isolation. The organizations for aged people could have a considerable preventive role. Of particular significance is a culture that allocates general esteem to the elderly and creates meaning and optimism for the last decades of life.

In his essay on self-destruction, Menninger (1938) pointed to the close relationship between alcohol addiction and suicide. As was discussed earlier, one of the two types of suicide put forward by Ovenstone and Kreitman (1974) was characterized by a chronic alcoholism. In a study of committed suicides among clients at the Los Angeles Suicide Prevention Center, Litman and Wold (1976) found that the cases who did not respond to the center's "crisis intervention" suffered from chronic alcoholism to a high degree. Suicide prevention has to face the challenge of a culture favoring self-destruction by means of alcohol. Nevertheless, the basic problem is not alcohol but a hedonistic life-style which does not view bodily integrity as a basic value and as a means for using life for self-fullfilment and for service of fellow men and cultural goals.

Durkheim's comprehensive view of suicide as caused by disturbances in structure and function of society still has relevance. Prevention of suicide in old age has to make possible the integration of the old into society on all levels, not least on the personal level. In the words of Litman and Wold (1976), "extended personal relationships are the most potent of anti-suicide remedies." Failures and losses are burdens easier to bear when a friend is at hand.

# REFERENCES

Achté, K. 1962. Sosiaalinen tutkimus Helsingissä 1958–1960 tehdyistä itsemurhista. *Duodecim, 78,* 677–682.

Akiskal, H. S., and McKinney, W. T. 1975. Overview of recent research in depression. *Arch. Gen. Psychiat., 32,* 285–305.

American Psychiatric Association. 1975. *A Psychiatric Glossary.* New York: Basic Books Inc.

ANDERSON, W. F., AND DAVIDSON, R. 1975. Concomitant physical states. *In*, J. G. Howells (ed.), *Modern Perspectives in the Psychiatry of Old Age*, pp. 84–106. New York: Brunner/Mazel.

ANGST, J. 1966. *Zur Aetiologie und Nosologie endogener depressiver Psychosen*. Monograph. Neurol. Psychiat., Heft 112. New York: Springer-Verlag.

ARNOLD, M. B. 1970. Brain function in emotion: a phenomenological analysis. *In*, P. Black (ed.), *Physiological Correlates of Emotion*, pp. 261–285. New York: Academic Press.

BACK, K. W. 1974. Transition to aging and self-image. *In*, E. Palmore (ed.), *Normal Aging II*, pp. 207–216. Durham, N.C.: Duke University Press.

BAGLEY, C. 1968. The evaluation of a suicide prevention scheme by an ecological method. *Soc. Sci. Med., 2*, 1–14.

BAGLEY, C. 1971. An evaluation of suicide prevention agencies. *Life-Threatening Behavior, 1*, 245–259.

BAGLEY, C., JACOBSON, S., AND PALMER, C. 1973. Social structure and the ecological distribution of mental illness, suicide, and delinquency. *Psychol. Med., 3*, 177–187.

BALIER, C. 1968. Les états névrotiques chez les personnes agées. *Gazette Medicale de France, 75*, 3415–3420.

BARRACLOUGH, B. M. 1971. Suicide in the elderly. *In*, D. W. K. Kay and A. Walk (eds.), *Recent Developments in Psychogeriatrics*, pp. 87–97. Brit. J. Psychiat. Special Publication No. 6. Ashford, Kent: Hedley Bros. Ltd.

BARRACLOUGH, B. M., NELSON, B., BUNCH, J., AND SAINSBURY, P. 1970. The diagnostic classification and psychiatric treatment of 100 suicides. *In*, R. Fox (ed.), *Proceedings of Fifth International Conference for Sucide Prevention*. Vienna: I.A.S.P.

BATCHELOR, I. R. C., AND NAPIER, M. B. 1953. Attempted suicide in old age. *Brit. Med. J., 2*, 1186–1190.

BECK, A. T. 1967. *Depression*. New York: Hoeber Medical Division, Harper & Row.

BECK, A. T. 1974. The development of depression: a cognitive model. *In*, R. J. Friedman and M. M. Katz (eds.), *The Psychology of Depression: Contemporary Theory and Research*, pp. 3–27. New York: Winston & Sons.

BECKER, H. S. 1964. Personal change in adult life. *Sociometry, 27*, 40–53.

BERGMANN, K. 1970. *Sex differences in the neurotic reaction of the aged*. J. Biosoc. Sci. Suppl., 2, 137–145.

BIBRING, E. 1953. The mechanism of depression. *In*, P. Greenacre (ed.), *Affective Disorders*, pp. 13–48. New York: International Universities Press.

BIRREN, J. E., BUTLER, R. N., GREENHOUSE, S. W., SOKOLOFF, L., AND YARROW, M. (Eds.). 1963. *Human Aging: A Biological and Behavioral Study*. National Institute of Health, PHS Publication No. 986. Washington, D.C.: U.S. Government Printing Office.

BÖCKER, F. 1975. Suizidhandlungen alter Menschen, *Münch. med. Wschr. 117*, 201–204.

BOLANDER, A-M. 1972. Nordic suicide statistics. *In*, J. Waldenström, T. Larsson, and N. Ljungstedt (eds.), *Suicide and Attempted Suicide*, pp. 57–88. Stockholm: Nordiska Bokhandelns Förlag.

BOLLERUP, T. R. 1975. Prevalence of mental illness among 70-year-olds domiciled in nine Copenhagen suburbs. *Acta Psychiat. Scand., 51*, 327–339.

BREED, W. 1963. Occupational mobility and suicide among white males. *Amer. Sociol. Rev., 28*, 179–188.

BREMER, J. 1951. *A Social Psychiatric Investigation of a Small Community in Northern Norway*. Acta Psychiat. Scand. Suppl. 62.

BRILL, N. Q., WEINSTEIN, R., AND GARRATT, J. 1969. Poverty, and mental illness: patients' perceptions of poverty as an etiological factor in their illness. *Amer. J. Psychiat., 125*, 1172–1179.

BROWN, G. L., AND WILSON, W. P. 1972. Parkinsonism and depression. *Southern Med. J., 65*, 540–545.

BUNCH, J., BARRACLOUGH, B., NELSON, B., AND SAINSBURY, P. 1971. Suicide following bereavement of parents. *Soc. Psychiat., 6*, 193–199.

BUNGARD, W. 1977. Isolation, Einsamkeit und Selbstmordgedanken im Alter. *Aktuelle Gerontologie, 7*, 81–89.

BUSSE, E. W. 1970. Psychoneurotic reactions and defense mechanisms in the aged. *In*, E. Palmore (ed.), *Normal Aging*, pp. 84–90. Durham N.C.: Duke University Press.

BUTLER, R. N. 1963. The life review: an interpretation of reminiscence in the aged. *Psychiatry, 26*, 65–76.

BUTLER, R. N. 1975. *Why Survive? Being Old in America*. New York: Harper & Row.

CAROTHERS, J. C. 1953. *The African Mind in Health and Disease. A Study in Ethnopsychiatry*. Geneva:WHO, Monograph Series.

CATH, S. H. 1965. Some dynamics of middle and later years: a study in depletion and restitution. *In*, M. A. Berezin and S. H. Cath (eds.), *Geriatric Psychiatry: Grief, Loss, and Emotional Disorders in the Aging Process*, pp. 21–72. New York: International Universities Press, Inc.

CHESSER, E. S. 1965. A Study of Some Aetiological Factors in the Affective Disorders of Old Age. Unpublished dissertation. Institute of Psychiatry, London.

CHODOFF, P. 1973. The depressive personality: a critical review. *Int. J. Psychiat., 11*, 196–217.

CHODOFF, P. 1974. The depressive personality: a critical view. *In*, R. J. Friedman and M. M. Katz (eds.), *The Psychology of Depression: Contemporary Theory and Research*, pp. 55–70. New York: Winston & Sons.

CIOMPI, L., AND LAI, G. P. 1969. *Dépression et Vieillesse*. Bern: Editions Hans Huber.

CORSELLIS, J. A. N. 1962. *Mental Illness and the Ageing Brain*. London: Oxford University Press.

CUMMING, E., AND HENRY, N. E. 1961. *Growing Old*. New York: Basic Books.

DE ALARCÓN, R. 1964. Hypochondriasis and depression in the aged. *Geront. Clin., 6*, 266–277.

DEAN, L. R. 1962. Aging and the decline of affect. *J. Geront., 17*, 440–448.

DIGGORY, J. C. 1976. United States suicide rates 1933–1968: An analysis of some trends. *In*, E. S. Shneidman (ed.), *Suicidology: Contemporary Developments*, pp. 25–69. New York: Grune & Stratton.

DORPAT, T. L., ANDERSON, W. F., AND RIPLEY, H. S. 1968. The relationship of physical illness to suicide. *In*, H. L. P. Resnik (ed.), *Suicidal Behaviors*, pp. 209–219. Boston: Little, Brown and Company.

DREYFUS, G. L. 1907. *Die Melancholie; ein Zustandsbild des manisch-depressiven Irrenseins*. Jena.

DURKHEIM, E. 1951. *Suicide*. New York: The Free Press.

ENGLE, G. L. 1968. A life setting conducive to illness. The giving-up-given-up complex. *Ann. Int. Medicine, 69*, 293–300.

ERIKSON, E. 1950. *Childhood and Society*. New York: W. W. Norton.

ERNST, K. 1962. Neurotische und endogene Residualzustände. *Arch. Neurol. Psychiat., 203*, 61–84.

ERNST, K., AND ERNST, C. 1965. 70 zwangigjährige Katamnesen hospitalisierter neurotischer Patientinnen. *Arch. Neurol. Psychiat., 95*, 359–415.

ESSEN-MÖLLER, E. 1956. *Individual Traits and Morbidity in a Swedish Rural Population*. Acta Psychiat. Scand. Suppl. 100.

EY, H. 1954. *Etudes Psychiatriques*, Vol. 3. Paris: Desclée de Brouwer & Cie.

EY, H., BERNARD, P., AND BRISSET, C. 1967. *Manuel de Psychiatrie*. Paris: Mason et Cie.

FEUERLEIN, W. 1977. Ursachen, Motivationen und Tendenzen von Selbst-mordhandlungen im Alter. *Aktuelle Gerontologie, 7*, 67–74.

FIELD, M. J. 1960. *Search for Security: An Ethnospychiatric Study of Rural Ghana*. Evanston, Ill.: Northwestern University Press.

FORD, H. 1975. Involutional melancholia. *In*, A. M. Freedman, H. I. Kaplan, and B. J. Sadock (eds.), *Comprehensive Textbook of Psychiatry*, Vol. 1, pp. 1025–1042. Baltimore: Williams & Wilkins.

FOX, R. 1976. The recent decline of suicide in Britain: The role of the Samaritan suicide prevention movement. *In.*, E. S. Shneidman (ed.), *Suicidology: Contemporary Developments*, pp. 499–524. New York: Grune & Stratton.

FRIEDMAN, E. A., AND ORBACH, H. L. 1974. Adjustment to retirement. *In*, S. Aricti (ed.), *American Handbook of Psychiatry*, pp. 609–645. New York: Basic Books.

FROLKIS, V. V. 1975. Physiological aspects of aging. *In*, H. P. von Hahn (ed.), *Practical Geriatrics*, pp. 1–20. Basel: S. Karger

GARDNER, E. A., BAHN, A. K., AND MACK, M. 1964. Suicide and psychiatric care in aging. *Arch. Gen. Psychiat., 10*, 547–553.

GARSIDE, R. F., KAY, D. W. K., AND ROTH, M. 1965. Old age Mental disorders in Newcastle-upon-Tyne. Part III: A factorial study of medical, psychiatric and social characteristics. *Brit. J. Psychiat., 111*, 939–946.

GERMAN, G. A. 1972. Aspects of clinical psychiatry in Sub-Saharan Africa. *Brit. J. Psychiat., 121*, 461–479.

GIBBS, J., AND MARTIN, W. T. 1964. *Status Integration and Suicide*. Eugene, Ore.: The University of Oregon Press.

GIBSON, A. C. 1961. Psychosis occurring in the senium. *J. Ment. Sc., 107*, 921–925.

GILLESPIE, R. D. 1929. The clinical differentiation of types of depression. *Guy. Hosp. Rep., 79*, 305–344.

GOLDFARB, A. 1967. Geriatric psychiatry. *In*, A. M. Freedman, H. I. Kaplan, and H. S. Kaplan (eds.), *Comprehensive Textbook of Psychiatry*, pp. 1564–1587. Baltimore: Williams & Wilkins.

GOODWIN, F. K., BRODIE, H. K. H., MURPHY, D. L., AND BUNNEY, W. E. 1970. L-dopa, catecholamines and behavior: a clinical and biochemical study in depressed patients. *Biolog. Psychiat., 2*, 341–366.

GRÜNEBERG, F. 1977. Suizidalität bei Patienten einer geriatrischen Abteilung. *Aktuelle Gerontologie, 7*, 91–100.

HARLOW, H. F., HARLOW, M. K., AND SUOMI, S. J. 1971. From thought to therapy: lessons from a primate laboratory. *Amer. Sci., 59*, 538–549.

HARRINGTON, M. 1962. *The Other America: Poverty in the United States*. New York: MacMillan Co.

HEDRI, A. 1967. Selbstmord im höheren Alter. *Schweiz. Arch. Neurol. Neurochir. Psychiat., 100*, 179–202.

HEMSI, L. K., WHITEHEAD, A., AND POST, F. 1968. Cognitive functioning and cerebral arousal in elderly depressives and dements. *J. Psychosom. Res., 12*, 145–156.

HENDERSON, D. K., GILLESPIE, R. D., AND BATCHELOR, I. R. C. 1969. *Textbook of Psychiatry*. London: Oxford University Press.

HILL, D. 1968. Depression: disease, reaction, or posture. *Amer. J. Psychiat., 125*, 445–457.

HOLLINGSHEAD, A. B., AND REDLICH, F. C. 1958. *Social Class and Mental Illness: A Community Study*. New York: John Wiley.

HOGARTY, G., AND, KATZ, M. M. 1971. Norms of adjustment and social behavior. *Arch. Gen. Psychiat., 25*, 470–480.

HOLMES, T. H., AND RAHE, R. H. 1967. The social readjustment scale. *J. Psychosom. Res., 11*, 213–218.

HOPKINSON, F. J. 1964. A genetic study of affective illness in patients over 50. *Brit. J. Psychiat., 110*, 244–254.

IGA, M. AND TATAI, K. 1975. Characteristics of suicides

and attitudes toward suicide in Japan. *In*, N. L. Farberow (ed.), *Suicide in Different Cultures*, pp. 255–280. Baltimore: University Park Press.

KATZ, M. M. 1971. The classification of depression: normal clinical and ethnocultural variations. *In*, R. R. Fieve (ed.), *Depression in the 1970s*, pp. 31–40. Amsterdam: Excerpta Medica.

KAUFMAN, I. C. 1973. Mother-infant separation in monkeys: an experimental model. *In*, J. P. Scott and E. C. Senay (eds.), *Separation and Depression*, pp. 33–52. Washington, D.C.: American Association for the Advancement of Science.

KAY, D. W. K. 1962. Outcome, and cause of death in mental disorders of old age: a long-term follow-up of functional and organic psychoses. *Acta Psychiat. Scand., 38*, 249–276.

KAY, D. W. K., BEAMISH, P., AND ROTH, M. 1964a. Old age mental disorders in Newcastle-upon-Tyne. Part I: A study of prevalence. *Brit. J. Psychiat., 110*, 146–158.

KAY, D. W. K., BEAMISH, P., AND ROTH, M. 1964b. Old age mental disorders in Newcastle-upon-Tyne. Part II: A study of possible social and medical causes. *Brit. J. Psychiat., 110*, 668–682.

KAY, D. W. K., AND ROTH, M. 1961. Environmental and hereditary factors in the schizophrenias of old age ("late paraphrenia") and their bearing on the general problem of causation in schizophrenia. *J. Ment. Sci., 107*, 686–691.

KAY, D. W. K., ROTH, M., AND HOPKINS, B. 1955. Affective disorders arising in senium. I. Their association with organic cerebral degeneration. *J. Ment. Sci., 101*, 302–316.

KIEV, A. 1972. *Transcultural Psychiatry*. New York: The Free Press.

KLERMAN, G. L. 1971. Clinical research in depression. *Arch. Gen. Psychiat., 24*, 305–319.

KLERMAN, G. L. 1974. Depression and adaptation. *In*, R. J. Friedman and M. M. Katz (eds.), *The Psychology of Depression: Contemporary Theory and Research*, pp. 127–145. Washington, D.C.: Winston & Sons.

KREITMAN, N. 1972. Aspects of the epidemiology of suicide and "attempted suicide" (parasuicide). *In*, J. Waldeström, T. Larsson, and N. Ljungstedt (eds.), *Suicide and Attempted Suicide*, pp. 45–52. Stockholm: Nordiska Bokhandelns Förlag.

KREITMAN, N. 1976. Age and parasuicide ("attempted suicide"). *Psychological Medicine, 6*, 113–121.

KRUIJT, C. S. 1960. *Zelfmoord*. Utrecht: van Gorum.

KULAWIK, H., AND DECKE, D. 1973. Letzte Aufzeichnungen—eine Analyse von 223 nach vollendeten Suiziden hinterlassenen Briefen und Mitteilungen. *Psychiat. Clin., 6*, 193–210.

KUTNER, B., FANSHEL, D., TOGO, A. M., AND LANGNER, T. S. 1956. *Five Hundred over Sixty: a Community Survey on Aging*. New York: Russell Sage.

LALLI, M., AND TURNER, S. H. 1968. Suicide and homicide: a comparative analysis by race and occupational levels. *J. Criminal Law, Criminol. and Police Sci., 59*, 191–200.

LAMBO, T. A. 1956. Neuro-psychiatric observations in the Western region of Nigeria. *Brit. Med. J., II*, 1385–1392.

LEFF, M. J., ROATCH, J. F., AND BUNNEY, W. E. 1970. Environmental factors preceding the onset of severe depressions. *Psychiat., 33*, 293–311.

LEHMAN, H. E. 1959. Psychiatric concepts of depression: nomenclature and classification. *Canad. Psychiat. Ass. J., Suppl. 4*, 1–12.

LEHMAN, H. E. 1971. Epidemiology of depressive disorders. *In*, L. R. Fieve (ed.), *Depression in the 70's*, pp. 21–31. Amsterdam: Excerpta Medica.

LEIGHTON, A. 1959. *My Name is Legion*. New York: Basic Books.

LEIGHTON, D. C., HARDING, J. S. MACHLIN, D. B., MACMILLAN, A. M., AND LEIGHTON, A. H. 1963. *The Stirling County Study, Vol. III, The Character of Danger*, New York: Basic Books.

LEONHARD, K. 1959. *Aufteilung der endogenen Psychosen*. Berlin: Akademie Verlag.

LESTER, D. 1970. Social disorganization and completed suicide. *Soc. Psychiat., 5*, 175–176.

LEWINSOHN, P. M. 1975. The behavioral study and treatment of depression. *In*, M. Hersen, R. M. Eisler, and P. M. Miller (eds.), *Progress in Behavior Modification*, pp. 19–64. New York: Academic Press.

LEWINSOHN, P. M. 1974. A behavioral approach to depression. *In*, R. J. Friedman and M. M. Katz (eds.), *The Psychology of Depression: Contemporary Theory and Research*, pp. 157–178. Washington, D.C.: Winston & Sons.

LITMAN, R. E., AND WOLD, C. I. 1976. Beyond crisis intervention. *In*, E. S. Shneidman (ed.), *Suicidology: Contemporary Developments*, pp. 525–546. New York: Grune & Stratton.

LÖNNQVIST, J. 1977. *Suicide in Helsinki*. Helsinki: Psychiatria Fennica.

LÖNNQVIST, J. 1979. Personal communication.

LÖNNQVIST, J., KOSKENVUO, M., SARNA, S., AND KAPRIO, J. 1979. Social status and suicide. In manuscript.

LOWENTHAL, M. F., BERKMAN, P. L., AND ASSOCIATES 1967. *Aging and Mental Disorder in San Francisco*. San Francisco: Jossey-Bass.

LOWENTHAL, M. F., AND HAVEN, C. 1968. Interaction and adaptation: intimacy as a critical variable. *Amer. Sociol. Rev., 33*, 414–420.

MacMAHON, B., AND PUGH, T. F. 1965. Suicide in the widowed. *Am. J. Epidemiol., 81*, 23–31.

MARIS, R. 1967. Suicide, status and mobility in Chicago. *Social Forces, 46*, 246–256.

MATUSSEK, P., HALBACH, A., AND TROEGER, U. 1965. *En-*

*dogene Depression.* München-Berlin: Urban and Schwarzenberg.

McCulloch, J. W., Philip, A. E., and Carstairs, G. M. 1967. The ecology of suicidal behavior. *Brit. J. Psychiat., 113,* 313–319.

McKinney, W. T., Suomi, S. J., and Harlow, H. F. 1973. New models of separation and depression in rhesus monkeys. *In,* J. P. Scott and E. C. Senay (eds.), *Separation and Depression,* pp. 53–66. Washington, D.C.: American Association for the Advancement of Science.

Mechanic, D. 1977. Illness behavior, social adaptation, and the management of illness. A comparison of educational and medical models. *J. Nerv. Ment. Dis., 165,* 79–87.

Melges, F. T., and Bowlby, J. 1969. Types of hopelessness in psychopathological process. *Arch. Gen. Psychiat., 20,* 690–699.

Menninger, K. 1938. *Man Against Himself.* New York: Harcourt, Brace and Company.

Meyer, J. E. 1973. *Tod und Neurose.* Gottingen: Vandenhoek & Ruprecht.

Minkoff, K., Bergman, E., Beck, A. T., and Beck, R. 1973. Hopelessness, depression and attempted suicide. *Amer. J. Psychiat., 130,* 455–459.

Monk, M. 1975. Epidemiology. *In,* S. Perlin (ed.), *A Handbook for the Study of Suicide,* pp. 185–211. New York: Oxford University Press.

Moss, L. M., and Hamilton, D. M. 1956. Psychotherapy of the suicidal patient. *Amer. J. Psychiat., 112,* 814–820.

National Center for Health Statistics. 1968. *Limitation of Activity and Mobility Due to Chronic Conditions— United States (July 1965–June 1966).* Public Health Service Publication No. 1000, Series 10, No. 45. Washington, D.C.: U.S. Government Printing Office.

Nemiah, J. C. 1975. Depressive neurosis. *In,* A. M. Freedman, H. I. Kaplan, and B. J. Sadock (eds.), *Comprehensive Textbook of Psychiatry,* pp. 1255–1264. Baltimore: Williams & Williams.

Neugarten, B. L. 1973. Personality change in late life: a developmental perspective. *In,* C. Eisdorfer and M. P. Lawton (eds.), *The Psychology of Adult Development and Aging,* pp. 311–335. Washington, D.C.: American Psychological Association.

Neugarten, B. L., Havighurst, R. J., and Tobin, S. S. 1961. The measurement of life satisfaction. *J. Geront., 16,* 134–143.

Neugarten, B. L. and Associates. 1964. *Personality in Middle and Late Life.* New York: Atherton Press.

Nielsen, J. 1963. Gerontopsychiatric period-prevalence investigation in a geographically delimited population. *Acta Psychiat. Scand., 38,* 307–330.

Nielsen, J., and Videbeck, T. 1973. Suicide frequency before and after introduction of community psy-

chiatry in a Danish island. *Brit. J. Psychiat., 123,* 35–39.

Olds, J. 1958. Self-stimulation of the brain. *Science, 127,* 315–324.

O'Neal, P., Robins, E., and Schmidt, E. H. 1956. A psychiatric study of attempted suicide in persons over sixty years of age. *Arch. Neurol. & Psychiat., 75,* 275–284.

Ovenstone, I. M. K., and Kreitman, N. 1974. Two syndromes of suicide. *Brit. J. Psychiat., 124,* 336–345.

Parkin, D., and Stengel, E. 1965. Incidence of suicide attempts in an urban community. *Brit. Med. J., 2,* 133–138.

Patel, N. S. 1972. Life style of the completed suicide. *In,* R. E. Litman (ed.), *Proceedings 6th International Conference for Suicide Prevention,* pp. 158–164. Los Angeles: International Association for Suicide Prevention.

Peck, A. 1966. Psychotherapy of the aged. *J. Amer. Geriat. Soc., 14,* 748–753.

Peck, R. C. 1956. Psychological developments in the second half of life. *In,* J. E. Anderson (ed.), *Psychological Aspects of Aging,* pp. 44–49. Washington, D.C.: American Psychological Association.

Perris, C. 1966. A study of Bipolar (manic-depressive) and Unipolar Recurrent Depressive Psychoses. *Acta Psychiat. Scand. Suppl.* 194.

Pfeiffer, E., and Busse, E. W. 1973. Mental disorders in later life—affective disorders; paranoid, neurotic, and situational reactions. *In,* E. Pfeiffer and E. W. Busse (eds.), *Mental Illness in Later Life,* pp. 87–95. Washington, D.C.: American Psychiatric Association.

Post, F. 1962. *The Significance of Affective Symptoms in Old Age.* Maudsley Monograph, 10. London: Oxford University Press.

Post, F. 1968. The factor of aging in affective illness. *In,* A. Coppen and A. Walk (eds.), *Recent Developments in Affective Disorders,* pp. 105–116. Br. J. Psychiat. Spec. Pub. No. 2. Ashford, Kent: Hedley Brothers Ltd.

Post, F. 1969. The relationship to physical health of the affective illnesses in the elderly. *8th International Congress of Gerontology Proceedings, 1,* 198–201. Washington, D.C.

Post, F. 1971. Schizo-affective symptomatology in late life. *Brit. J. Psychiat., 118,* 437–445.

Post, F. 1972. The management and nature of depressive illnesses in late life. *Brit. J. Psychiat., 121,* 393–404.

Post, F. 1976. Diagnosis of depression in geriatric patients and treatment modalities appropriate for the population. *In,* D. M. Gallant and G. M. Simpson (eds.), *Depression: Behavioral, Biochemical, Diagnostic and Treatment Concepts,* pp. 205–231. New York: Spectrum.

PRAAG, H. M van. 1977. *Depression and Schizophrenia.* New York: Spectrum.

PRANGE, A. J., WILSON, I. C., LYNN, C. W., ALLTOP, L. B., STRIKELEATHER, R. A., AND RALEIGH, N. C. 1974. L-tryptophan in mania. *Arch. Gen. Psychiat., 30,* 52–62.

RIESMAN, D., GLAZER, N., AND DENNEY, R. 1950. *The Lonely Crowd.* New York: Doubleday.

RIKLAN, M. 1972. An l-dopa paradox: bipolar behavioral alterations. *J. Amer. Geriat. Soc., 20,* 572–575.

RILEY, M. W., AND FONER, A. 1968. *Aging and Society. Volume one: An Inventory of Research Findings.* New York: Russell Sage.

RINGEL, E. 1952. *Der Selbstmord.* Vienna: Maudrich.

RINGEL, E. 1969. Neue Gesichtspunkte zum präsuizidalen Syndrom. *In,* E. Ringel (ed.), *Selbstmordverhütung,* pp. 51–116. Bern: Verlag Hans Huber.

ROBINS, E., MURPHY, G. E., WILKINSON, R. H., GASSNER, S., AND KAYES, J. 1959. Some clinical considerations in the prevention of suicide based on a study of 134 successful suicides. *Amer. J. Public Health, 49,* 888–899.

ROBINS, E., AND GUZE, S. B. 1972. Classification of affective disorders: the primary-secondary, the endogenous-reactive, and the neurotic-psychotic concepts. *In,* T. A. Williams and M. M. Katz (eds.), *Recent Advances in the Psychobiology of the Depressive Illnesses,* pp. 283–293. Washington, D.C.: U.S. Government Printing Office.

ROBINSON, D. S., DAVIS, J. M., NIES, A., RAVARIS, C. L., AND SYLVESTER, D. 1971. Relation of sex and aging to monoamine oxidase activity of human brain, plasma, and platelets. *Arch. Gen. Psychiat., 24,* 536–539.

ROBINSON, D. S., NIES, A., DAVIS, J. N., BUNNEY, W. E., DAVIS, J. M., COLBURN, R. W., BOURNE, H. R., SHAW, D. M., AND COPPEN, A. J. 1972. Aging, monoamines, and monoamine-oxidase levels. *Lancet, 1,* 290–291.

ROSEN, J. L., AND NEUGARTEN, B. L. 1960. Ego functions in the middle and later years: a thematic apperception study of normal adults. *J. Geront., 15,* 62–67.

ROSENTHAL, S. H. 1968. The involutional depressive syndrome. *Amer. J. Psychiat., 124,* 21–35.

ROTH, M. 1955. The natural history of mental disorder in old age. *J. Ment. Sci., 101,* 281–301.

ROTH, M., AND KAY, D. W. K. 1956. Affective disorder arising in the senium. II. Physical disability as an aetiological factor. *J. Ment. Sci., 102,* 141–150.

RUZICKA, L. T. 1976. Suicide, 1950 to 1971. *World Health Statistics Report, 29,* 396–413.

SAINSBURY, P. 1955. *Suicide in London.* London: Chapman and Hall Ltd.

SAINSBURY, P. 1962. Suicide in late life. *Geront. Clin., 4,* 161–170.

SAINSBURY, P. 1963. Social and epidemiological aspect of suicide with special reference to the aged. *In,* R. H. Williams, C. Tibbitts, and W. Donahue (eds.), *Processes of Aging. Vol. II,* pp. 153–175. New York: Atherton Press.

SAINSBURY, P. 1973. Suicide: opinion and facts. *Proc. Roy. Soc. Med., 66,* 579–587.

SARTORIUS, N. 1975. Epidemiology of depression. *WHO Chronicle, 29,* 423–427.

SARTORIUS, N., DAVIDIAN, H., ERNBERG, G., FENTON, F. R., GASTPAR, M., GULBINAT, W., JABLENSKY, A., KIELHOLZ, P., LEHMANN, H. E., NARAGHI, M., SAKURAI, Y., SHIMIZU, M., SHINFUKU, N., AND TAKAHASHI, R. 1977. International agreement on the assessment of depression. Paper prepared for the VI World Congress of Psychiatry, Honolulu, Hawaii. 28 August-3 September 1977.

SATTES, H. 1955. *Die hypochondrische Depression.* Halle: VEB Carl Marhold Verlag.

SCHMALE, A. 1958. Relationship of separation and depression to disease. *Psychosom. Med., 20,* 259–277.

SCHWAB, J. J., HOLZER, C. E., AND WARHEIT, G. J. 1973. Depressive symptomatology and age. *Psychosomatics, 14,* 135–141.

SEAGER, C. P., AND FLOOD, R. A. 1965. Suicide in Bristol. *Brit. J. Psychiat., 111,* 919–932.

SEIDEL, K. 1969. Die eigenständige innere Dynamik des Alters Suizids. *Aktuelle Fragen Psychiat. Neurol. Vol. 9,* pp. 42–62. Basel: S. Karger.

SELIGMAN, M. E. P. 1974. Depression and learned helplessness. *In,* R. J. Friedman and M. M. Katz (eds.), *The Psychology of Depression: Comtemporary Theory and Research,* pp. 83–113. Washington, D.C.: Winston & Sons.

SENDBUEHLER, J. M., AND GOLDSTEIN, S. 1977. Attempted suicide among the aged. *J. Amer. Geriat. Soc., 25,* 245–248.

SHANAS, E., TOWNSEND, P., WEDDERBURN, D., FRIIS, H., MILHOJ, P., AND STEHOWER, J. 1968. *Older People in Three Industrial Societies.* New York: Atherton Press.

SHAW, L. C., AND HENRY, N. E. 1956. A method for the comparison of groups: a study in thematic apperception. *Genet. Psychol. Monogr., 54,* 207–253.

SHNEIDMAN, E. S. 1969. Suicide, lethality, and the psychological autopsy. *Int. Psychiat. Clin., 6,* 225–250.

SHNEIDMAN, E. S., AND FARBEROW, N. L. 1961. Statistical comparisons between attempted and committed suicides. *In,* N. L. Farberow and E. S. Shneidman (eds.), *The Cry for Help,* pp. 19–47. New York: McGraw-Hill.

SHOCK, N. W. 1962. The physiology of aging. *Sci. Am., 206,* 100–135.

SIMON, A. 1970. Physical and socio-psychologic stress in the geriatric mentally ill. *Comp. Psychiat., 11,* 242–247.

SIMON, A., AND TALLEY, J. 1965. The role of physical illness in geriatric mental disorders. *In, Disorders in the Aged*, pp. 154–170. Manchester: Geigy (U.K.) Ltd.

SROLE, L., LANGNER, T. S., MICHAEL, S. T., OPLER, M. K., AND RENNIE, T. A. C. 1962. *Mental Health in Metropolis.* New York: McGraw-Hill.

STAINBROOK, E. 1954. A cross-cultural evaluation of depressive reactions. *In,* P. H. Hoch and J. Zubin (eds.), *Depression*, pp. 39–50. New York: Grune & Stratton.

STENBACK, A. 1963. On involutional and middle age depressions. *Acta Psychiat. Scand. Suppl., 169*, 14–32.

STENBACK, A. 1965. Object loss and depression. *Arch. Gen. Psychiat., 12*, 144–151.

STENBACK, A., ACHTÉ, K. A., AND RIMÓN, R. H. 1965. Physical disease, hypochondria, and alcohol addiction in suicides committed by mental hospital patients. *Brit. J. Psychiat., 111*, 933–937.

STENBACK, A., AND BLUMETHAL, M. 1964. Relationship of alcoholism, hypochondria and attempted suicide. *Acta Psychiat. Scand., 40*, 133–140.

STENBACK, A., KUMPULAINEN, M., AND VAUHKONEN, M-L. 1978. Illness and health behavior in septuagenarians. *J. Geront., 33*, 57–61.

STENBACK, A., KUMPULAINEN, M., AND VAUHKONEN, M-L. 1979. Depression in septuagenarians. *Aktuelle Gerontologie, 9*, 112–121.

STENBACK, A., VIITAMÄKI, R. O., AND KUKKONEN, S. 1957. Personality changes in electroconvulsive treatment. *Acta Psychiat. Neurol. Scand., 32*, 345–359.

STENGEL, E. 1965. The prevention of suicide in old age. *Z. Präventivmed, 10*, 474–481.

STENGEL, E. 1973. *Suicide and Attempted Suicide.* Harmondsworth: Penguin Books.

STENGEL, E., AND COOK, N. G. 1958. *Attempted Suicide.* Maudsley Monographs, No. 4. Oxford: Oxford University Press.

STENSTEDT, Å. 1959. Involutional Melancholia. *Acta Psychiat. Psychiat. Neurol. Scand.*, Suppl, 127.

SWANSON, W. C., AND BREED, W. 1976. Black suicide in New Orleans. *In,* E. S. Shneidman (ed.), *Suicidology: Contemporary Developments*, pp. 99–128. New York: Grune & Stratton.

THOMAE, H. 1976. Patterns of "successful" aging. *In,* H. Thomae (ed.), *Patterns of Aging*, pp. 147–161. Basel: S. Karger.

TOOTH, G. 1950. *Studies in Mental Illness in the Gold Coast.* Colonial Research Publication No. 6. London: H. M. Stationary Office.

VÄISÄNEN, E. 1975. *Mielenterveyden Häiriöt Suomessa.* Helsinki: Kansaneläkelaitoksen julkaisuja AL:2. Helsinki: Kansanelakelaltos.

WALK, D. 1967. Suicide and community care. *Brit. J. Psychiat., 113*, 1381–1391.

WARHEIT, G. J., HOLZER, C. E., AND SCHWAB, J. J. 1973. An analysis of social class and racial differences in depressive symptomatology: a community study. *J. Health. Soc. Beh., 14*, 291–299.

WATTS, C. A. H. 1966. *Depressive Disorders in the Community.* Bristol: John Wright & Sons Ltd.

WEISS, J. M. A. 1954. Suicide: an epidemiological analysis. *Psychiat. Quart., 18*, 225–282.

WEISS, J. M. A. 1974. Suicide. *In,* S. Arieti (ed.), *American Handbook of Psychiatry. Vol. III.*, pp. 743–765. New York: Basic Books.

WEISS, J. M. A., NUNEZ, N., AND SCHAIE, K. W. 1961. Quantification of certain trends in attempted suicide. *In, Proceedings of the Third World Congress of Psychiatry*, pp. 1236–1240. Montreal: University of Toronto Press and McGill University Press.

WEISS, J. M., STONE, E. A., AND HARRELL, N. 1970. Coping behavior and brain norepinephrine level in rats. *J. Comp. Physiol. Psychol., 72*, 153–160.

WEISSMAN, M. M., AND PAKEL, E. S. 1974. *The Depressed Woman.* Chicago: The University of Chicago Press.

WEITBRECHT, H. J. 1952. Zur Typologie depressiver Psychosen. *Fortschr. Neur., 20*, 247–267.

WHITLOCK, F. A. 1973a. Suicide in England and Wales 1959–63. Part 1: The county boroughs. *Psychol. Med., 3*, 350–365.

WHITLOCK, F. A. 1973b. Suicide in England and Wales 1959–63. Part 2: London. *Psychol. Med., 3*, 411–420.

WILLIAMS, R. H. 1959. Changing status, roles, and relationships. *In,* C. Tibbitts (ed.), *Handbook of Social Gerontology*, pp. 261–297. Chicago: The University of Chicago Press.

WITKIN, H. A., DYK, R. B., PATERSON, H. F., GOODENOUGH, D. R., AND KARP, S. A. 1962. *Differentiation. Studies of Development.* New York: John Wiley.

WOLFF, K. 1959. *The Biological, Sociological, and Psychological Aspects of Aging.* Springfield, Ill.: Charles C Thomas.

WOLPE, J. 1971. Neurotic depression: experimental analog, clinical syndromes and treatment. *Am. J. Psychother., 25*, 362–368.

WOLPERT, E. A. 1975. Manic-depressive illness as an actual neurosis. *In,* E. J. Anthony and T. Benedek (eds.), *Depression and Human Existence*, pp. 199–221. Boston: Little, Brown and Company.

World Health Organization. 1968. *Prevention of Suicide.* Public Health Papers No. 35. Geneva.

World Health Organization. 1977. *World Health Statistics Annual. Vol. I. Vital Statistics and Causes of Death.* Geneva.

YAP, P. M. 1958. Suicide in Hong Kong. *J. Ment. Sci., 104*, 266–301.

YAP, P. M. 1965. Phenomenology of affective disorder in Chinese and other cultures. *In,* A. V. S. de Reuck and R. Porter (eds.), *Transcultural Psychiatry*, pp. 84–108. London: J. and A. Churchill.

# 27

# The Neuroses, Personality Disorders, Alcoholism, Drug Use and Misuse, and Crime in the Aged

*Alexander Simon*

Classical forms of neurosis rarely arise for the first time in old age. More commonly, earlier neurotic conflicts and manifestations, perhaps suppressed and compensated for a long time, are reactivated under the stresses of old age. The effect of the aging process itself on preexisting neuroses is little understood; it has been noted that these may become exaggerated with old age, but for the most part such symptoms become less intense (Ciompi, 1969; Müller, 1967).

Nevertheless, even though it is uncommon for authentic neuroses to appear for the first time in old age, many neurotic-like disturbances do become apparent for the first time in later life. Indeed, such reactions are the most common disorders of nonhospitalized older patients seen in clinics and in family practice settings. Very few of these patients exhibit the classical pictures of phobic reactions, anxiety reactions, obsessive compul-

sive neuroses, and the like, that are characteristic of younger neurotic patients. The majority show depression of greater or lesser degree, some of the leading symptoms in older patients being feelings of loneliness and rejection, anxiety about illness or the possibility of illness, somatic complaints or hypochondriacal fears, irritability and attention-seeking or apathy and withdrawal. Depression, then, is a central problem in definition and diagnosis for the clinician treating older patients who manifest neurotic symptoms. These patients rarely are seen by psychiatrists and rarely are referred to psychiatrists by family physicians (Post, 1974).

The usual psychiatric nosologic and diagnostic considerations are complicated for older patients by the aging process, which involves a complex network of physical, psychological, interpersonal, family, and socioeconomic factors that have a crucial effect on the mental and emotional

653

functioning of the aged person. The clinical picture presented by the aged patient may require careful investigation in order to differentiate, for example, neurotic depression from an underlying manic-depressive type depression, or from depression associated with somatic illness or physiological decompensation, or from depression associated with the early stages of an organic brain disease, or from depression related to the use of certain drugs (Gurney, Roth, Garside, Kerr, and Schapira, 1970; Gurney, Roth, Garside, Kerr, and Schapira, 1972; Ibor-López, 1972; Lesse and Mathers, 1968; Prusoff and Klerman, 1974; Weissman and Klerman, 1977).

Accurate diagnosis may be difficult but is essential, for more often than not these patients exhibit multiple physical and psychological symptoms that may mimic or mask a great variety of disorders. The accuracy of the diagnosis will determine the appropriateness of the treatment and indicate the prognosis. Diagnosis and prognosis have important implications not only for the course of the aged patient's illness but also for his overall management and placement, and thus for the quality of his life (Goldfarb, 1967).

## EPIDEMIOLOGY

The relatively few epidemiological studies that indicate psychiatric morbidity in the aged have been carried out in Great Britain and the Scandinavian countries. Most of these have been general medical and social community investigations, and the comparison of results is difficult because of differences in the cultural and social characteristics of the populations studied, the methods and diagnostic categories used, the aims of the investigators, and the form in which the results are presented, whether as prevalence, incidence, morbidity risk, or on some other basis.

In the Northern European countries where these studies were done, the tendency is to keep the aged at home rather than in institutional settings of one kind or another. The populations studied are largely community resident or, in some cases, community resident plus hospitalized patients, and most are from well defined overall populations such as the inhabitants of an island, a village, or a small town. The "aged" in these populations usually are defined as aged sixty and older or sixty-five and older.

The epidemiological findings with regard to neurosis and character disorder in the aged from nine of these community studies are summarized in Table 27-1.

Although hospital admissions for neurosis generally decline with advancing age from a peak in early maturity, the community studies confirm a relatively high prevalence among the aged in the community for neurosis and character disorder, often considered to be closely allied to neurosis (Blau and Berezin, 1975), and often not listed separately. The figures are similar in the various areas studied, whether rural or urban, in spite of inevitable differences in diagnostic concepts and criteria relating to normal vs. abnormal, psychosis vs. neurosis, etc. In summary, from 5 to 10 percent of the aged population are found to be suffering from fairly definite neurosis, or 8 to 17 percent when less clear-cut conditions related to personality factors are included.

Other studies have suggested a similar prevalence of neurotic disorder in the aged (Abrahams and Patterson, 1978/79; Gurland, 1976; Kessel and Shepherd, 1962; Nielsen, Hømma, and Biorn-Henriksen, 1977; Spicer, Hare, and Slater, 1973). Symptoms of anxiety and depression severe enough to be incapacitating were found in approximately 14 percent of one community sample of old people (Kay, Bergmann, Foster, McKechnie, and Roth, 1970). Another random sample of 300 aged subjects revealed 51 percent to be suffering from mild to moderately severe neurotic symptoms, 24 per-

**Table 27-1**   Neurosis in the Aged: A Summary of Nine Community Studies*

|  | SHELDON (1948) N=369 ENGLAND | BREMER (1951) N=119 NORWAY | ESSEN-MÖLLER (1956) N=443 SWEDEN | PRIMROSE (1962) N=222 SCOTLAND | JENSEN (1963) N=546 DENMARK | NIELSEN (1962) N=978 DENMARK | KAY et al. (1964 a,b) N=297 ENGLAND | PARSONS (1965) N=228 ENGLAND | BOLLERUP (1975) N=626 DENMARK |
|---|---|---|---|---|---|---|---|---|---|
| Neuroses | 9.4% | 5.0% | 1.4% | 10.4% | 1.4% | 4.0% | 8.9% | 4.8% | 4.2% |
| Character disorders | 3.2 | 12.6 | 10.6 | 2.2 | — | 4.7 | 3.6 | — | 3.2 |
| Neuroses + character disorders | 12.6 | 17.6 | 12.0 | 12.6 | — | 8.7 | 12.5 | — | 7.4 |

*See chapter references for exact citations.

cent late onset, 21 percent chronic, and 6 percent personality disorders (Bergmann, 1971).

## THE CLINICAL SYNDROMES

The classical diagnosis of neurosis, with the various specific disorders grouped under that general heading, is not included in the DSM-III classification. However, the older categorization is a useful one for considering these disorders in the aged. The subtypes of neuroses are not disease entities but are types of reaction that may have multiple causation and almost always, especially in the aged, appear not as "pure" types but as mixtures. The aged, neurotic patient may show depressive, anxious, hysterical, obsessional, and hypochondriacal manifestations in varying degrees at different times.

### Etiological Considerations

Neurotic disorders may be considered as arising from the individual's attempts to deal with psychological problems and stresses that arouse anxiety. The symptoms may reveal the anxiety directly or may represent the person's defenses against anxiety (for example, dissociation, conversion, displacement, or phobic manifestations). In a neurosis there is both a feeling of anxiety and the formation of repetitive unconscious techniques to control the anxiety. Neurotic symptoms may not be significant in themselves, but are indications that there are anxiety-producing situations that are upsetting to the individual. The form of the neurosis is determined by the type of defensive measure the patient uses to control anxiety.

Many neurotic patients show mixed features rather than a single defensive picture. The patient does not recognize the relationship between his emotional problems and the disturbed personality functioning associated with his neurotic symptoms. For example, he may experience anxiety attacks when he is in a crowd and develop somatic symptoms that prevent his having to venture out where he might have to be in a crowd, yet he does not realize that his somatic symptoms serve the function of protecting him from anxiety. In general, a neurotic person's inner problems do not result in outer behavior as disturbed as that of a psychotic person, who suffers a much greater disorganization of personality and disruption of social functioning. Also unlike the psychotic person, the neurotic usually is very much aware that he is ill and wants his suffering relieved.

Roth (1976) has noted that "to a considerable extent, the mental disorders of the aged are those of early life under different conditions" (p.443). There is really no great difference between the neurotic patterns of early life and those of old age. The same general mechanisms operate, although they may be modified as a result of biologic aging and the influence of socioeconomic factors related to the position of the aged in a particular society and the individual's efforts to cope with age-related stresses and changes in his life (Zinberg and Kaufman, 1963).

The individual carries with him from earlier life into old age his general personality characteristics and patterns of adaptation to his life circumstances and to physical and sociopsychologic stress. He also may carry with him various mental and emotional disorders, including personality and behavioral disorders, neuroses, psychoses, alcoholism, and psychophysiological illness. The conflicts of childhood and adolescence may persist with some intensity into old age. Like younger persons, the aged person who has difficulty in meeting the demands placed upon him by his life circumstances may develop symptoms such as fatigue, vague somatic complaints, irrational anxieties and fears, hysterical manifestations, or depression.

Decreases in strength and stamina, waning sexual abilities, increasing frequency of physical illness, especially chronic illness such as diabetes, arthritis, cardiopulmonary disease, emphysema, urinary infections, decreased vision and hearing, and so forth, may precipitate efforts at adaptation expressed in somatization of symptoms. There may be complaints of easy fatigability, weakness, pain (especially visceral discomfort), constipation, headaches, etc., or over-compensatory (counterphobic) efforts of the aging person to prove to himself or others that he is as good as ever. Should these fail, anxiety, depression, and hypochondriasis may develop. Failing vision and hearing cannot always be compensated by glasses or hearing aids and lead to deprivation of pleasures and diversions of great importance to the individual. Isolation may develop, sometimes associated with increasing suspicion and misinterpretation. Loneliness, feelings of uselessness, and anxiety-panic reactions may occur.

Threatened loss of economic independence, forced dependency because of physical handicaps from arthritis, fractured hip, cardiopulmonary disease, stroke, and the like, constitute threats to self-esteem and independence and may well lead to symptoms of depression and anxiety, with or without somatic preoccupations. The loss of a spouse, involuntary relocation, especially for financial reasons, a move to unfamiliar surroundings away from friends and acquaintances, may precipitate a reactive tense, anxious, hypochondriacal depression. To move in with a daughter or son and daughter-in-law may raise problems of prestige, status, and authority to which an older person may react with anger or withdrawal and depression.

Retirement can offer many rewards, providing there are adequate financial resources, relatively good health, and freedom of activities with release from former responsibilities and perhaps from a monotonous, uninteresting job. Too often, however, retirement means serious reduction in income, loss of prestige, a change in the sense of personal identity, loss of externally imposed routine, and a feeling of being unwanted and unnecessary. Surprisingly, retirement seldom precipitates an acute depression, although adjustment to the "retirement shock" after work stops may take several months.

Grief reactions have been studied extensively, but only a few studies have given attention specifically to grief reactions, including bereavement, in old age, although this is a frequently encountered stress among the aged. One study (Clayton, Halikas, and Maurice, 1972) of widows and widowers, average age sixty-one years, found 35 percent to have symptoms similar to those common in depressed psychiatric patients. "Normal" depression of widowhood has been found not to be more common in either women or men, and not to be more associated with psychiatric illness in the individual or in the family history. Older bereaved persons do show some differences from those in younger age groups, including a lesser tendency to guilt feelings related to the deceased person, a greater tendency to develop somatic illness as depressive equivalents, and a tendency toward a shorter recovery time (Smith, 1978; Stern, Williams, and Prados, 1951; Vachon, 1976).

The older person does have to adapt to significant changes within and outside of himself, and although the aged are sometimes thought to be incapable of learning and using new ways of dealing with stress, this is a matter of individual differences, as it is for younger persons. The older person uses the same kinds of coping mechanisms that he did in younger years—mature acceptance of reality, compensation (counterphobic reactions), somatization, denial, projection, depression, dependency, isolation and withdrawal (Cameron, 1956).

The situation is additionally complicated by the occurrence in later life of mental and behavioral disorders associated with age-linked organic brain disease such as cerebral arteriosclerosis and senile brain disease and with certain presenile brain diseases. These organic brain syndromes have in the past received most of the attention of those dealing with mental illness in the aged, with the unfortunate consequence that until very recent years any neurotic symptoms manifested by an old person too often were regarded as evidence of brain disease, inevitable and untreatable. Such therapeutic nihilism is unwarranted, although cerebral impairment certainly may influence the development and manifestation of neurotic reactions. A breakdown of compensating mechanisms may result from impairment of cerebral function, or focal cerebrovascular disease may produce neurologic signs that serve as a stress leading to neurotic symptomatology.

A nocturnal neurosis has been described (C. Cohen, 1976) that is characterized by nocturnal increase in symptoms in older persons who isolate themselves in their rooms at night, for fear of being assaulted on the street if they go out. Their social supportive system ceases to function at night, and a mixed depressive, anxious, hypochondriacal neurosis may develop. A syndrome characterized by gross self-neglect has been called the "Diogenes syndrome" (Clark, Mankikar, and Gray, 1975). These patients have personality traits of aloofness, suspiciousness, emotional lability, and may become acutely ill as a result of deficiency states stemming from their living alone in squalor, with minimal funds for support.

Nevertheless, the neuroses of old age, like those that occur in earlier years, appear clinically as patterns of maladaptation to individual life circumstances (Cameron, 1956). In view of the burden placed upon older people by the aging process itself and the stresses associated with it, it is not surprising that they should manifest considerable neurotic symptomatology, although it should be remembered that despite the near-universality of these stresses with aging, some 75 to 80 percent of the aged do not react with neurotic illness.

The physical and psychological characteristics of the person, and his life experiences, may be of significance in his development of mental illness in later life, and in some instances may be the determinants of his breakdown. However, we still know too little about the causal and other relationships that may exist among hereditary factors, lifelong personality characteristics, psychogenic or functional disorders that occur during the early, middle, and later years, and the organic mental disorders of old age. Whether functional illness arises primarily as a reaction to the aging process, or as the culmination of lifelong conflicts in particularly vulnerable individuals, or as a combination of these remains an open question (Lowenthal, Berkman, and Associates, 1964).

Bergmann (1971) studied a random sample of aged persons in the community, in an attempt to define possible "causes" of neurotic reactions. Such common stresses as poverty, bereavement, social isolation, and low socioeconomic status, together with certain abnormal personality traits and various types of physical disability, were investigated. The results suggested that the factors most distinguishing neurotic from "normal" old people were personal vulnerability and physical health. Those who were anxiety-prone and had histrionic personality traits seemed to be more vulnerable to neurotic and depressive symptoms. Bergmann (1978) has also noted that social stress does not have a strong relationship to the development of neurotic reactions in later life. Retirement, for example, is more likely to be a result of than a cause of poor health. Even bereavement does not have a clear-cut relationship to the occurrence of neurotic and depressive reactions in later life, as has been noted by other studies (Parkes, 1964).

Most studies of premorbid personality in depressed patients have failed to demonstrate a personality specific to depression. One study (Paykel, Klerman, and Prusoff, 1976) found that patients with premorbid neuroticism showed a neurotic rather than endogenous depression symptom pattern. Depressives with neurotic rather than endogenous symptom patterns showed more evidence of oral dependent personality and less obsessional characteristics. Patients with hysterical personalities tended to be less severely ill and displayed a clinical picture of mixed depression and hostility, and less evidence of anxiety.

It may not be easy to establish a diagnosis of neurotic illness in an older patient, especially when depression is a major component of the clinical picture, as it so often is. Careful investigation will include complete and thoughtful history-taking (including history of any medication being taken), thorough physical and neurological examinations, and the use of any indicated special procedures, including biochemical and radiological studies, psychological tests, and perhaps various assessment scales and questionnaires. Precipitating and predisposing factors must be considered, including physical health, stress of all kinds, the premorbid personality and life adjustment, and the family history and relationships (Post, 1978).

## PSYCHOPATHOLOGY AND CLINICAL FEATURES

The most common patterns of neurotic reaction in the aged are depression, anxiety states, hypochondriacal concerns, and chronic fatigue states.

Whatever the pattern, there are likely to be important depressive features, although these may be hidden, and most older patients who have physical health problems will have some degree of depression associated with these. A clear distinction between neurotic depression and other depressive illnesses cannot always be made with certainty, and there are certain depressions of slow onset that become severe in later stages but in the beginning demonstrate neurotic symptomatology. These present a special suicide risk (de Alarcon, 1964) and point up the need for determining the presence of depression in any older patient who exhibits neurotic symptoms, especially hypochondriacal ones.

Bergmann (1975) has outlined the characteristics of late onset neurotic disorder as:

1. It is compatible with a relatively undisturbed early history.
2. In later life there is a greater association with physical ill health, especially cardiovascular disorder.
3. The longstanding elderly neurotic seems to suffer relatively little from his disorder, even when symptoms are florid.
4. The late onset elderly neurotic suffers more acutely from loneliness, difficulty in self-care, and lack of hobbies and recreation. The clinical picture is less florid and usually is a mixture of depression and anxiety.
5. Phobic features may be present arising out of irrational extension of limitations imposed by physical ill health.
6. The main characteristic of neurotic disorder arising in the senium is that it remains relatively silent, manifesting itself mainly by social disabilities and a stepwise reduction in the quality of life.

He has also noted two types of late-onset neurosis: (1) that associated with moderate or severe physical disability (with no sex difference in diagnosis) and (2) that seen in the "physically well," a group in which women predominate.

By and large, preexisting neurotic and depressive symptomatologies tend to improve during senescence (Ciompi, 1969), although they often are replaced by minor affective disorders and residual states. When signs of cognitive impairment appear in older persons with depressive symptomatology, this may not be the result of organic brain disease but instead a secondary effect of the depression. In patients with early senile or arteriosclerotic dementia who are depressed, as the deteriorative process continues the depressive aspects are more or less overwhelmed by the picture of dementia.

Little information is available concerning the changes that take place with aging in persons with personality and behavioral disorders. It has been noted that some of these individuals may gain a better equilibrium in old age while in others exacerbations of abnormal personality traits lead to poorer adjustment (Semke, 1965).

As Ernst (1959) and others have pointed out, anxiety neurosis is the most persistent of the neuroses, while it is rare to see persistent hysterical (conversion and dissociative) illness manifested in old age (Diethelm and Rockwell, 1943) or severe obsessional states (Pollitt, 1957). Phobic anxiety does occur in old age, both as longstanding, florid, chronic phobic anxiety states and as acute attacks of phobic anxiety that begin in later life. Such attacks may be dramatic and often occur in response to severe physical illness (especially myocardial infarction) and surgery (such as the removal of cataracts). Depressive symptoms are often found. In fact, Bergmann (1971) found that 75 percent of respondents with late onset neurotic reactions of moderate severity were considered to be suffering from neurotic depression.

Old persons with early mild dementia may exhibit neurotic symptoms. Manipulative, dissociative, and hysterical behavior, sudden anxiety symptoms, and depressive reactions all may mask an early organic brain syndrome. Intellectual impairment on an organic basis does not seem to be significantly related to neurotic disorder in later life, but there is a relationship between lifelong low intelligence and the capacity to face the stresses of old age. Nunn, Bergmann, Britton, Foster, Hall, and Kay, (1974) found below average intelligence to be one of several factors contributing to the development or persistence of neurosis in old age.

### DEPRESSIVE REACTIONS

The definition of "neurotic depression," and indeed the very existence of such a diagnostic entity, has been a subject of dispute since the early years of psychiatric consideration of depression (Kendall, 1968; Kiloh, Andrews, Neilson, and Bianchi, 1972; McDonald, 1967; Roth, 1972). The term has been used both as synonymous with reactive depression and to cover all depressive illness other than psychotic depression. It has been widely held by those who distinguish "endogenous" from "neurotic" depression that the diagnosis of a neurotic depression can be made on the basis of a poorly adjusted premorbid personality (Klerman, 1971; Winokur, Clayton, and Reich, 1969). Post (1965) has used neurotic depression to denote depressive illness associated with longstanding mixed anxiety, phobic, obsessional, or hysterical features.

However, such depressive reactions are less often seen in older patients than are mixtures of anxiety, depression, and hypochondriasis.

A neurotic depressive reaction generally arises as a reaction to a loss of some kind—a stress to which the aged are particularly vulnerable (Wilson and Lawson, 1962). The symptoms may include feelings of sadness, discouragement, self-depreciation, loneliness, pessimism, loss of interest in others, irritability, fatigue, loss of appetite, insomnia, and complaints of difficulty in thinking and memory. In fact, depressed persons are very likely to complain of poor memory even though memory tests may show no deterioration, the complaint being related to the depth of depression (Kahn, Zarit, Hilbert, and Niederehe, 1975).

### ANXIETY REACTIONS

An anxiety reaction is characterized by feelings of fear and apprehension, often anticipatory and frequently associated with a variety of somatic symptoms. The anxiety often is a free-floating anxiety, generalized and persistent and associated with evidence of chronic autonomic overactivity, increased motor tension, and apprehensive expectation. There may be complaints such as sweating, palpitation of the heart, cold clammy hands, dry mouth, dizziness, tingling or "pins and needles" sensations of hands and feet and around the lips, nausea, "butterflies in the stomach," diarrhea, frequency of urination, lump in the throat, and rapid breathing (hyperventilation). Increased motor tension may lead to feeling shaky and jittery, tremors, feelings of tension and of being keyed up, muscular aches, easy fatigue, restlessness, easy startle reaction, and sighing respiration. There is a sense of apprehension, of anticipation of something bad or terrible occurring (what, is not always clear), a fear of dying, of loss of control, of fainting. Increased tension may be associated with difficulties in concentration, poor memory, insomnia, restless sleep, and feelings of fatigue.

Anxiety reactions may be so intense as to constitute panic reactions manifested by recurrent attacks of anxiety that vary in intensity, often with a sudden onset of fear and apprehension, sometimes amounting to sheer terror and panic and associated with a fear of dying or of impending doom, often without an apparent stimulus. An attack may be brief, lasting only a few minutes, or it may go on for many minutes. Anxiety attacks may occur in association with medical illnesses such as hyperthyroidism, hyperglycemia, pheochromocytoma, drug withdrawal, and alcohol withdrawal.

### PHOBIC REACTIONS

A phobic person experiences a feeling of intense fear and/or apprehension that he recognizes as resulting from no real danger. Still, he reacts with fear and associated somatic symptoms such as palpitations, faintness, numbness, tingling, nausea, tremor, or panic. The condition may be episodic or chronic, with avoidance behavior secondary to fears of a situation, activity, or object. The patient usually recognizes the fear as silly and out of proportion to the stimulus.

Some persons attempt to lessen the intensity of their anxiety by using sedatives or minor tranquilizers, and become dependent upon these. The condition is more frequently diagnosed in women than in men.

Phobic symptoms with or without associated panic reactions or pervasive anxiety may be part of an episodic depressive reaction, an obsessive-compulsive neurosis, or a schizophrenic reaction.

## HYSTERICAL REACTIONS

The traditional hysterical disorders (Woodruff, Clayton, and Guze, 1971) are reclassified in DSM-III, so that conditions that suggest physical illness but in which psychological factors are important are redefined according to certain fundamental distinctions (Hyler and Spitzer, 1978).

These disorders are characterized by a loss or disturbance in function of a psychogenic character. The symptoms sometimes may be changed by strong suggestion. In the *conversion* type of hysterical neurosis, the special senses such as vision, hearing, touch, etc., may be affected, or some aspect of the voluntary nervous system, as in paralysis, anesthesia, paresthesia, dyskinesia. In the *dissociative* type of hysterical neurosis, there is an alteration of identity or state of consciousness, as in amnesia, fugue, or multiple personality.

## BRIQUET'S SYNDROME

Briquet's syndrome is a chronic disorder, fluctuating in intensity, usually beginning early in life, and may extend into old age. It is characterized by recurrent and multiple somatic complaints that are not caused by any physical illness. Complaints involve many organ systems and patients often are involved with many physicians (Morrison, 1978). The most common somatic complaints are headache, fatigue, fainting, nausea, vomiting, abdominal pain, bowel problems, urinary symptoms, allergies, menstrual and sexual problems, and conversion symptoms.

Depressive and anxiety features are common and may be accompanied by suicidal threats and attempts. Abuse of alcohol and other drugs is common. Patients experience a wide range of interpersonal difficulties. The onset is often in the teens and almost always before the age of twenty-five

years. It is more commonly seen in women and is said to be rare in men. It may resemble a depressive disorder or even a schizophrenic reaction, and may or may not be associated with a histrionic personality.

Patients usually believe they have been ill for most of their lives, or they present pseudoneurological symptoms such as paralysis, blindness, aphonia, loss of sensation, or report attacks of abdominal pain and vomiting, or complain of dysmenorrhea and other menstrual problems more frequently and of more severe character than most women experience, or complain more than most persons of sexual indifference and lack of pleasure or of back and joint pain or headaches.

## OBSESSIVE-COMPULSIVE REACTIONS

Unwanted thoughts or actions persistently intrude and the patient is unable to stop them. Anxiety develops if the patient is prevented from completing his ritual or train of thought. The condition usually is chronic, although episodic exacerbations of varying duration and intensity may occur (Kringlen, 1965). The obsessions are regarded as ideas that invade consciousness and the individual experiences them as ego alien. When efforts are made to ignore or suppress them, anxiety is aroused. Compulsions are behavior that is regarded as ego alien and resisted by the individual. The patient appreciates the silliness or senselessness of the behavior (compulsion) or obsession (thinking).

## HYPOCHONDRIACAL REACTIONS

Hypochondriasis has been considered to be a separate nosologic entity, and Pfeiffer and Busse (1973) hold it to be of particular importance among the neuroses of old age. This view can be disputed on the basis of findings in a number of studies (de Alarcon, 1964; Bergmann, 1971; Kay and Bergmann, 1966; Kreitman, Sainsbury, Pearce, and Costain, 1965) that relate hypochondriasis to depression (Jacobs, Fogelson, and Charles, 1968) and other psychiatric symptoms and to actual physical ill health (Meyer, 1974; Kenyon, 1976).

General conclusions drawn by Bergmann (1978) on hypochondriasis include: (1) Hypochondriasis is an important sign, (2) lifelong hypochondriacal tendencies combined with personality disorder can be distinguished from hypochondriacal complaints that arise in later life, and (3) when hypochondriacal complaints do arise in later life, they may be an indicator not only of depression and increased risk of suicide but also of serious and perhaps unrelated underlying physical disease of which the patient is otherwise unaware.

These patients with multiple somatic complaints become the "rotating" patients of medical practice (Lipsitt, 1968/69). The internist may be unwilling to treat them because they have no specific organic disease and the psychiatrist may consider them unsuitable for treatment. They wander from physician to physician, clinic to clinic, or perhaps develop a relationship with an institution. Their major defenses are denial and somatization, but the multiple somatic complaints may hide an underlying depression (Earley and Von Mering, 1969).

## THE SIGNIFICANCE OF PHYSICAL ILLNESS

The complex interrelationship of physical and mental health in the aged has been noted many times in the literature (Anderson, 1971; Anderson and Davidson, 1975; Clow and Allen, 1951; Post, 1962; Roth and Kay, 1956; Salzman and Shader, 1978; Simon and Talley, 1965; Stenback, Kumpulaenin, and Vauhkonen, 1978; Wigdor and Morris, 1977). The aging process is associated with pathological changes that affect the brain and many other organ systems, and mental illness in the aged often is associated with physical illness. Busse, Dovenmuehle, and Brown, (1960) found that neurotics may not differ from "normals" in physical disability but they have more physical complaints. However, exaggerated somatic complaints in old age may, in fact, represent serious physical illness. Mortality has been found to be significantly higher for patients with functional disorders than for normal subjects (Kay and Bergmann, 1966). The association between physical illness and functional disorder in old age seems to be real and cannot be explained only in terms of hypochondriasis or depression.

Nevertheless, it has been found that a significant proportion of old people whose ill health continues, do recover from their neurotic disorders, so the physical illness was not in itself a necessary and sufficient cause for the neurotic illness (Bergmann and Eastham, 1974). Increasing interest is being directed toward the question of whether neurotic illness can actually contribute to physical illness, in some cases, or even can be a manifestation of a yet undiagnosed physical illness.

## PERSONALITY DISORDERS

Personality disorders are characterized by an exaggeration of or a deficiency in certain elements of personality structure, resulting in severely maladaptive behavior patterns and associated with impairment of interpersonal relationships. There have been no detailed studies of the effect of aging on a personality disorder that has been present since adolescence or early adulthood, but clinical experience suggests that in some individuals symptoms probably lessen with age, and in others that disturbed personality pattern becomes more exaggerated. Nevertheless, it probably is the case the deviant personality patterns, like "normal" patterns, remain characteristic of the individual throughout the life span. Life circumstances, especially the presence of stress, will have a great deal to do with the ways in which and the extent to which any existing personality disorder will be manifested in later life. Certainly, the antisocial personality is not often diagnosed for the first time in old age, nor are the most severe forms of any personality disorder. Depressive manifestations and phobic and anxiety symptoms, on the other hand, are quite commonly diagnosed for the first time in old age. Personality disorders related to alcoholism and other problems with drug misuse also constitute a significant clinical category of older patients.

Certain well known personality changes take place with aging, and these perhaps can help to explain the characteristic features of personality disorder in old age (Post, 1965). For example, the tendency of the older person to turn inward may be related to the lessening of acting-out behavior and of hysterical conversion reactions. At the same time, sensitive and restrictive personality traits, and phobic and obsessive symptom formation may become more overt because of the tendency toward age-related withdrawal from outward concerns.

The personality disorders that are more likely to be seen in older patients are the depressive, paranoid, obsessive-compulsive, dependent, schizoid, and histrionic personalities.

Established personality patterns both influence the expression of depressive symptoms and also may predispose individuals to depressive episodes, although our current state of knowledge about the relationship or premorbid personality and depression is very limited (Chodoff, 1972). The person with a "depressive personality" may be described as quiet, tending to be pessimistic and self-depreciating and to have feelings of inadequacy and hopelessness, to be perfectionistic, overconscientious, and easily discouraged. A basic sense of insecurity may be revealed by indecision and excessive caution. Such an individual tends to become depressed easily, and it is obvious that someone with such a personality who must cope with the stresses attendant upon aging is likely to suffer even more than in earlier life from feelings of loneliness, regret, discouragement, hopelessness, and associated depression.

Old people with lifelong paranoid personalities also are likely candidates for an increased expression of their personality disorder. These persons are stubborn, suspicious, overly sensitive about the attitudes of others toward them, and tend to misinterpret the behavior of others as being directed against them. They tend to be irritable, argumentative, and often threatening.

Symptoms associated with obsessive-compulsive personality patterns are relatively common in old age. These rigid, inhibited, perfectionistic, stubborn, and self-doubting individuals tend to have difficulty making decisions and to suffer from chronic tension in relation to the demands they place upon themselves. The stress imposed by the physical and other limitations associated with aging can be severe for such persons, and the exaggeration of their obsessive-compulsive traits may reach the proportions of a neurosis.

A person whose personality has been of a dependent type tends to be overwhelmed by feelings of helplessness and indecision. Passive and fearful, he may suffer from considerable anxiety and require much reassurance. The characteristic lack of self-reliance, immaturity, and irresponsibility can easily become exaggerated in old age, when the dependency is likely to have some basis in reality.

The schizoid personality, characterized by feelings of loneliness, isolation, inferiority, self-consciousness, and suspiciousness, also can become exaggerated in old age.

The hysterical personality is marked by traits of self-centeredness and self-indulgence, associated with self-dramatization, histrionic behavior, and exhibitionism (Chodoff, 1974). This personality type has been said to be more common among women than men. There is a characteristic emotional lability and capriciousness, and a tendency toward emotional outbursts. The picture is one of attention-seeking behavior that masks a dependent need. The personality type has been described in men, too, however (Luisada, Peele, and Pittard, 1974).

The symptomatology of personality disorders represents the individual's attempts to adapt to the physical, psychological, and social forces affecting his personal situation. He may try to deny the truth of the situation, to retreat from a difficult situation, to cope with anxiety, or to otherwise deal with stress. In old age, with its increasing stresses and vulnerability, the person will continue to use the mechanisms he has resorted to in earlier life in order to avoid anxiety and to function in his unique circumstances. These mechanisms may or may not continue to serve his needs adequately as his situation changes, but his basic personality is unlikely to appear to change drastically unless severe illness intervenes and he falls victim to an organic brain syndrome or a psychotic disorder.

## ALCOHOLISM

An alcoholic is a person whose dependence upon alcohol has reached a degree such that it interferes with his health, interpersonal relationships, social adjustment, and economic functioning. Few studies have been made of alcoholism in the aged. The available epidemiologic data are, for the most part, from studies of admissions to psychiatric hospitals and outpatient clinics, and these show a peak in the age group 35–50 years. Nevertheless, although the incidence of alcoholism may decline with age (Cahalan, 1970; Cahalan, Cisin, and Crossley, 1969; and Knupfer and Room, 1964), the number of alcoholics in the older age groups is significant. Estimates are that as many as 10 percent of those aged 60 and older are heavy drinkers, and alcoholism and related physical illness are an important problem in those aged who are hospitalized for psychiatric disorders (Gaitz and Baer, 1971). In San Francisco, Simon, Epstein, and Reynolds, (1968) found that of 534 patients aged 60 and older admitted to a psychiatric screening unit, 28 percent had serious drinking problems, 5 percent being heavy social drinkers and 23 percent having diagnoses of alcoholism. In a general municipal hospital population, McCusker, Cherubin, and Zimberg, (1971) classified 60 percent of male patients and 34 percent of female patients of all ages as moderate to severe alcoholics. For those aged 70 and older, 56 percent of the males were alcoholic. Whittier and Korenyi (1961) found that of 540 males aged 60 and older admitted to a state mental hospital for the first time, 20 percent suffered from severe chronic alcoholism. A study in a community mental health center found that 17 percent of the patients aged 65 and older showed evidence of alcohol abuse (Zimberg, 1974).

Some evidence is available, also, on elderly community residents. A household survey of alcoholism in a health district of New York showed two peaks for alcoholism—one in the age group 45–54 and the other 65–74 (Bailey, Haberman, and Alksne, 1965).

Alcoholism is a significant factor in arrests of older persons. Zax, Gardner, and Hart (1964) found the peak of arrests for public drunkenness to be in the age group 50–59, but white males aged 60 and older had a rate of 100/10,000. A study done in San Francisco (Epstein, Mills, and Simon, 1970) of the frequency and causes of arrests of persons aged 60 and older found that four out of five (82 percent) of arrests in this age group were for drunkenness, whereas only one out of two (46 percent) of all adult arrests during the study period were for this offense.

Alcoholism in an aged person may be of long standing, present since earlier adulthood, or it may have arisen only in middle or old age. The late onset alcoholics probably are reacting to age-related stress, especially physical illness and depression (Droller, 1964; Rosin and Glatt, 1971). In a great many cases, when they receive help for these difficulties, their need for alcohol lessens (Zimberg, 1974).

Alcoholism in women often has been attributed to a specific stressful life situation, one of which has been described as the "empty nest syndrome" (Curlee, 1969). Some women who are very dependent on husband and children for their identity react with depression when the children leave the home. The precise relationship between early experiences and psychosocial adjustment and mental illness in later life is hard to establish, but some studies suggest that women alcoholics are emotionally traumatized and maladjusted personalities with a clear tendency toward depressive illness, independent of their alcoholism (Rathod and Thomson, 1971).

Mortality from alcoholism in the United States is substantial, although statistics are not entirely reliable because of undoubted underreporting of alcoholism as a cause of death (Lipscomb, 1959; Metropolitan Life Insurance Company, 1977). Mortality varies with age, the highest rates being in the age groups 50–59 and 60–69, and a considerably lower mortality over age seventy years. The high mortality in the younger years has been cited as a possible explanation for the apparent decline in alcoholism with aging.

Another possible explanation (Drew, 1968) is that alcoholism is a self-limiting disease. A significant part of the decrease in alcoholism in the older age groups may be the result not of treatment or of mortality in younger age groups, but of spontaneous recovery brought about, in part, by such age-related factors as decreasing drive and changing social pressures.

## Characteristics of Aged Alcoholics

Elderly alcoholics are not a homogeneous group. Some are younger alcoholics grown old; others are old people who have become alcoholic. There are more men, more Caucasians, and more persons of lower educational status among older than among younger alcoholics and medical problems are more common in late onset alcoholics (Schuckit, 1977).

Personality traits of older alcoholics of long-standing are similar to those of younger alcoholics—neuroticism, egocentricity, deviant behavior (Rosin and Glatt, 1971). The heavy drinking of late onset alcoholism is more often associated with illness or age-related environmental stresses such as bereavement, retirement, and loneliness leading to depression. However, one must be careful about drawing conclusions as to causality. It has not been established that such stress causes alcoholism in these elderly persons. As Schuckit (1977) has warned, just because something makes sense, it is not necessarily true.

The late effects of alcoholism—social isolation, falls, malnutrition, general physical deterioration, dementia—may be mistaken for the effects of age and chronic illness and attributed to senility, and it is important to be aware of the possibility of alcoholism.

## Alcoholic Brain Disorders

The neurologic and psychiatric disorders caused by alcoholism are closely interrelated (Bennett, 1977). The alcoholic brain disorders can be classified as acute brain syndromes (including withdrawal syndromes and delirium tremens) and chronic brain syndromes (including alcoholic deterioration and various stages of advanced brain disease such as Korsakoff/Wernicke's syndrome) and perhaps an intermediate stage of alcoholic brain disease, described by Bennett, Mowery, and Fort (1960). Classification systems include both phenomenological and etiological elements, and none thus far has fully satisfied the need to include neuropathologic knowledge in a useful way.

Withdrawal syndromes include early, partial withdrawal conditions, impending delirium tremens, and alcoholic hallucinosis, up to alcoholic convulsions and delirium tremens. These syndromes can be considered as release phenomena from the depressive effects of alcohol (S. Cohen, 1976). Symptoms associated with early withdrawal conditions include tremulousness and shakiness, sleep disturbances, muscle aches, agitation, nausea, anxiety, and depression. Impending delirium tremens includes shakiness, sweating, and low-grade fever, and may constitute the entire withdrawal experience for many persons. Grand mal convulsions can occur in association with impending delirium tremens. More advanced syndromes include alcoholic hallucinosis, with auditory hallucinosis, a clear sensorium, and intact orientation. The hallucinatory content frequently is paranoid, with voices making accusatory or persecutory remarks. This syndrome can develop within a day after drinking stops.

Delirium tremens is a late manifestation of alcohol withdrawal, approximately three to four days following stopping drinking, and the condition is accompanied by visual and auditory hallucinations, confusion, disorientation, gross and irregular tremors, and perhaps high fever, tachycardia, and high blood pressure. Delirium tremens can be life-threatening to the aged alcoholic, with hyperthermia or peripheral vascular collapse the usual causes of death (S. Cohen, 1976).

The Korsakoff/Wernicke's syndrome is not strictly speaking a withdrawal syndrome, but may appear following a withdrawal state. It may be associated with evidence of severe B avitaminosis.

Chronic brain syndromes are relatively common in alcoholism, especially with advancing age. They are associated with longstanding heavy drinking and antecedent delirium tremens and general malnutrition, as well as specific deficiency disorders such as Wernicke's encephalopathy, cerebellar degeneration, and peripheral neuropathy.

"Alcoholic deterioration" often is used interchangeably with "early dementia," and usually is related to deterioration of conduct rather than symbolic function (Horvath, 1975). Orientation may be normal but there is memory impairment and deterioration of social judgment and abstractive capacity. Overt neurologic signs generally are absent.

Bennett *et al.* (1960) described an intermediate stage of alcoholic brain disease that has a clinical picture similar to that of alcoholic deterioration—sociopathic behavior, emotional lability, frequent amnesic episodes, and exaggeration of preexisting personality disorders. He noted a gradual clinical improvement in these patients after long periods of abstinence, and even some cases of apparently severe Korsakoff's syndrome seemed to be partly reversible. The personality changes of patients with intermediate stage alcoholic brain disease include hostility, poor judgment, emotional lability, lack of insight, pathologic lying, and rationalization of drinking. Physiologic reactions include blackouts, withdrawal reactions, and, in some, delirious or convulsive episodes. There may be such system complications as fatty liver, cirrhosis, and polyneuritis.

Progressive mental deterioration undoubtedly is associated with progressive cerebral atrophy. The clinical picture is one of a person who has lost "moral and ethical values," has become careless about personal hygiene and social customs, insensitive to the feelings of others, crude in behavior, and shows gross impairment in intellectual functioning, including defects in memory, judgment, and insight (Cutting, 1978). This condition is irreversible, although there may be some slight improvement with treatment (vitamins and improved nutrition).

A number of studies using pneumoencephalographic and pathologic examinations (and, more recently, computed axial tomography) have found that chronic alcoholism may be associated with evidence of cerebral atrophy (Carlen, Wortzman, Holgate, Wilkinson, and Rankin, 1978). Of eight chronic alcoholics who received repeated computed axial tomography scans (CAT), four patients maintained abstinence and showed functional improvement and partially reversible cerebral atrophy. Two abstinent and two other nonabstinent patients who displayed functional improvement before the first scan was taken displayed no change in cerebral atrophy. The changes in the scans were not considered to be artifacts or to result from systematic variation in location of the cuts, to water or electrolyte imbalance, to derangement in cerebrospinal fluid pressure, or to altered cerebral blood flow. The authors offered the hypothesis that regrowth of damaged neurons may occur with abstinence, with concomitant psychological improvement. A decrease in ventricular size with maintained abstinence may be the result of remyelination rather than regrowth of axons.

Advanced brain disease, Korsakoff/Wernicke's syndrome, appears after a long history of drinking, in association with malnutrition and vitamin deficiency. There are spotty memory defects, with confabulation and emotional lability, from depression to euphoria. Or, there may be simple progressive dementia, without delirium but with paranoid ideation. A peripheral neuropathy often is noted. The essential features of Korsakoff's psychosis are retrograde amnesia and anterograde amnesia. These patients are otherwise alert and show the so-called amnestic syndrome. Their emotional state is characteristically euphoric early, with a detached state of apathy in the later stages. The onset of the psychosis may be marked by a classical delirium, and about half the patients show a significant recovery within the first few months. Ocular palsies may be present and indicate Wernicke's syndrome (Malamud and Skillicorn, 1956).

Studies of aging and of alcoholism have led some investigators to suggest a parallel between the two conditions such that "premature aging" might be a cause of alcoholism (Blusewicz, Dustman,

Schenkenberg, and Beck, 1977). Results of such studies generally reveal a decline in neuropsychological functioning with aging and suggest a similar tendency with alcoholism, particularly with regard to short-term memory and abstract reasoning. However, a number of methodological problems are inherent in such studies, as well as problems of interpreting results when applying criteria of brain dysfunction to aged populations, where both age-related neuropsychological changes and neurological damage may be involved.

### PERSONALITY FACTORS

There is no single personality pattern in alcoholism. Only recently have there been studies attempting to determine systematically what can be found out about the stages of alcoholism, specific patterns of response to heavy drinking, and rates of spontaneous remission (Pattison, 1977). In general, alcoholics can be viewed as reactive or addictive alcoholic persons, with marked differences in premorbid personality, life patterns, and course of illness. However, much remains to be learned about demographic, social, behavioral, and personal correlates of alcoholism in the aged.

## DRUG ABUSE AND MISUSE IN THE AGED

For all the concern of social and medical institutions with drug use and abuse, few studies have ever been made of the aged drug user and abuser. It is generally recognized that drug abuse and medication misuse among the elderly is a significant problem, but the qualitative studies done in very recent years have few accurate prevalence studies for support. Certainly, the overlapping of problems with alcoholism, drug abuse, and medication misuse, including misuse of psychoactive agents, makes this an area of grave concern in geriatric medicine (Bozzetti and MacMurray, 1977; Zawadski, Glazer, and Lurie, 1978). The literature reflects a problem that is central in the field of drug studies, and that is the lack of a standard definition for drug use and abuse, except in reference to legal and illegal use and misuse.

Older persons use far more drugs than do younger people. Approximately one-fourth of all prescriptions written in 1967 were written for persons in the older-age groups, and their use of over-the-counter drugs undoubtedly was as large (Task Force on Prescription Drugs, 1968). Drugs most commonly are prescribed for heart disease, hypertension, arthritis, and mental and nervous conditions. Among the ten most prescribed drugs for persons aged 65 and older are four psychotropic substances (chlordiazepoxide, glutethimide, phenobarbital, and diazepam), and the older age groups are the largest regular users of sedatives, hypnotics, and major and minor tranquilizers. In contrast, there is a heavy concentration in younger age groups of the use of marijuana, LSD, other psychotogens, methedrine, heroin, and cocaine.

Because of this high usage of drugs by the aged, it seems likely they would have a high rate of misuse or abuse, but there are very few data to support such an assumption. Older patients are somewhat underrepresented among drug users seeking emergency medical care for drug-induced reactions and most often are seen for reactions to legally available drugs. Drug misuse among the aged thus seems to be associated with drugs that are prescribed for them. Drug-related problems in older patients include excessive self-medication, drug interactions, and side effects.

As to illegal drugs, the most visible addicts (especially to opiates) in the United States are young adults, with persons aged 60 and older accounting for less than 4 percent of those admitted to the US Public Health Service Hospital in Lexington, Kentucky, in 1963 (Petersen and Whittington, 1977). It has been suggested that a "maturing out" process, with the reaching of an "emotional homeostasis" in the thirties, or a "burning out" of addiction, or death or debility of addicts may account for the low incidence of such addiction in older patients (Winick, 1962). However, there is mounting evidence that many older addicts do in fact exist but may not come to official attention (Capel, Goldsmith, Waddell, and Stewart, 1972; Pascarelli, 1972).

Little is known about the response of aged patients to treatment for drug-related conditions or about how they manage their problems in the community, if, indeed, there are many such drug users hidden in the community who do not seek help.

## CRIME AMONG THE AGED

It has long been held that crime rates decrease gradually with advancing age (Pollak, 1941; Moberg, 1953), with a sharp drop in the proportion of arrestees in the 55–59 age category. However, arrests for index crimes (generally considered the felony offenses), has a proportion of total arrests that has risen steadily since 1964. By 1974 that proportion had increased by 43 percent for all age groups, but for the 55 and over population arrests for index crimes had increased by 224 percent (from 3.7 to 8.3 percent), (Shichor and Kobrin, 1978). These arrests of persons aged 55 and older show a pattern of crimes of violence, the largest single category being aggravated assault, and next, larceny theft.

Misdemeanor offenses in the older age group include gambling, driving under the influence of alcohol, drunkenness, disorderly conduct, and vagrancy, with the highest proportion of arrests being poor skid row phenomena (drunkenness and vagrancy). Nevertheless, there was a substantial decrease in such arrests over the ten year period from 1964–1974.

Robbery is one of the most infrequent of the offenses for which older persons are arrested. Serious property crimes are usually of the larceny theft kind. The proportion of arrests for drunkenness has significantly declined and this probably represents a shift from penal to civil forms of response to the problems associated with alcoholism—a shift away from the "revolving door" form of management of these offenses.

The trend, then, is for a gradual decline in the proportion of all arrests but an increase in proportion of index arrests (especially for aggravated assault and murder) of the age group 55 and older. Misdemeanor offenses are most prominently associated with alcohol consumption. This pattern was seen also in a San Francisco study (Epstein *et al.*, 1970) in which the frequency and causes of arrests of individuals aged 60 and older was investigated. It was found that adults aged 60 and younger in San Francisco (three-fourths of all adults in the population) are five times more likely to be arrested than are adults over age 60. Four out of five arrests of elderly persons are for drunkenness, which is true for only one out of two of all adult arrests. It was noted that arresting officers, jail personnel, and court officials tended not to see the aged alcoholic as a law breaker but rather as a sick person, arrested only when this seemed the best or only way to assure protection and care for the helpless old person.

Characteristics of elderly offenders have received little study, although scattered investigations have focused on such aspects of criminality among the aged as differences in the types of crime and the nature of punishment for crime among the aged in comparison with young offenders, the life history of younger criminals as they age, the etiology of crime appearing for the first time in later life, and the effects of social class and cultural background on the nature of the crimes committed by the aged (Keller and Vedder, 1969; Rodstein, 1975). A study reported by Whiskin (1967/68) was based on a group of older offenders seen in a Court Clinic. Among the broad questions taken up was whether intrapsychic factors long latent caused the commission of the delinquent act or whether broader age-related factors were predominant, and to what extent the aging person's troubles with the law were related to organic brain disorder.

McCreary and Mensh (1977) used psychological testing to investigate personality differences between older and younger law offenders, to clarify suggestions that older offenders show more psychological and sociopathic disturbances. The results were consistent with earlier findings that the elderly show more neurotic and fewer psychotic symptoms and are in greater need of rehabilitation programs than offenders in general. An extensive study done in Israel (Bergman and Amir, 1973) examined deviant behavior of the elderly by studying recorded crimes by persons age 60 and older during the period from 1960 to 1964. An "experience survey" was conducted of a selected group of persons directly involved with problems of the aged or problems of crime. Areas of interest explored included the subjects' knowledge of and contact with aged persons and problems of old age, particularly the problems of aged immigrants to Israel (including economic, health, ethnic, family, and cultural problems) and experience with criminality among the aged. The general findings suggested that, as with younger offenders, personal, physical, and environmental factors can explain the criminality of the minority of the aged who become involved in deviant behavior.

The question of what happens to persons whose behavior patterns bring them into conflict with society has been debated but little studied. Robins (1966) found significant remission in such behavior in a substantial minority of such persons as they aged. Weiss (1972) used computer techniques to study relationships among somatic and psychosocial problems, personality characteristics, and patterns on psychological tests in various age groups. Results indicated that antisocial tendencies generally tended to decrease in each succeeding age group, lending support to the thesis that serious psychopathic behavior and attitudes show improvement in a substantial minority of such persons as they grow older.

In the San Francisco study on antisocial behavior among the elderly (Epstein *et al.*, 1970) it was noted that out of a total of 256 sexual offenses by adults, only five were by individuals over age 60 years. Two were for indecent exposure, two for sexual advances to children, and one was a woman over age 65 arrested for "committing a lewd act in a public place." Informal discussions with the police indicated that in several cases of indecent exposure by older men in a school neighborhood, the police tried to allay the anxiety of the parents of the children and urged the families of the old men to give closer supervision. These authors also reported that psychiatric hospitalization was not used as a substitute for arrest for sexual offenses of the aged; where such behavior was noted it occurred at home and was not regarded as dangerous or a sexual offense, and only rarely did it involve a child.

A study by Hirschmann (1962) of a group of elderly sex offenders reported that most offenses were committed against children, but these seldom involved sexual intercourse. Most commonly, exhibitionism, fondling, kissing, and sexual play occurred. If satisfactory to the older man and not resisted by the child, this often was repeated. Such behavior usually was not associated with evidence of cognitive impairment and senile dementia with loss of or diminished inhibitory control. The offenders most often were men who when younger had prided themselves on their sexual abilities but with advancing years were unable to achieve satisfactory intercourse with women and so turned to sexual play with children, who would not reject them.

## CONCLUSION

Community surveys indicate a high prevalence among the aged of neurotic and personality problems of at least moderate severity (12.5 percent of the population); almost half of these began after the age of 60. Cases of dementia, depression, and neurosis, in particular, are likely to be undetected by the family doctor (Williamson, Stokoe, Gray, Fisher, Smith, McGhea, and Stephenson, 1964). If this is as true today as it was in the mid-sixties, it may be because of inappropriate or inadequate education and training in geriatric medicine and psychiatry in medical school or during postdoctoral training; too little interest by professional health workers in the aged (another manifestation of ageism); lack of recognition that somatic complaints are often "the chief complaint" in cases of early dementia, depression, and depressive neurosis; too little recognition of the social and interpersonal factors that bring an older person to the physician's

office; or too much attribution of symptoms and behavioral changes to "old age." Health professionals need to become aware of the importance of recognizing neurotic-like syndromes in the elderly. Educational programs emphasizing this must be developed for the various health disciplines.

Clearly, there are a number of areas in which research is needed to clarify issues relating to neurotic illness, personality disorders, alcoholism and other drug abuse and misuse, and crime in the aged.

There is increasing interest in those aged persons who are at risk of institutional placement, who show varying degrees of severity of impairment of their ability to cope with day-to-day living—the "frail" or vulnerable elderly. It is becoming increasingly important to define such persons, to determine their numbers and the services they require, particularly home health care and home supportive care services that may keep them out of institutions. Some can be rehabilitated, some will deteriorate into states requiring 24-hour-a-day care, and some can remain at home if provided with appropriate supportive services.

What are the health, social, family, economic, and behavior factors included in the definition of the "frail" elderly? What factors must be considered in determining the prognosis with home care compared to institutional care? How many are in need of psychiatric treatment? How can home care and day care supplement each other in a program of comprehensive care? Does this group of patients consist primarily of persons suffering from chronic brain syndromes or of those with functional psychosyndromes (often diagnosed as depression or depressive neurosis)? Do such patients require primarily psychiatric or medical care, home help, or supportive services? How successful are efforts to disengage such patients from supportive services once it is decided that independence should be encouraged?

It has often been said that with the onset of early mild dementia, neurotic symptoms such as anxiety, depression, hypochondriasis, manipulative and histrionic behavior may become manifest and that such symptoms may hide the evidence of mild intellectual impairment. While it is possible for a dementing illness to be ushered in by neurotic-like symptoms, it is probably more common for individuals who show symptoms of anxiety and depression to complain of poor memory and of difficulties in thinking and concentration, and for this reason they may be erroneously diagnosed as suffering from an organic brain syndrome. A long-term follow-up of persons diagnosed as suffering from mild dementia (especially those who have also been diagnosed by means of computed axial tomography as suffering from mild cerebral atrophy) should be made. The diagnosis of "mild dementia" needs more specificity.

It has been stated that hypochondriacal symptoms arising for the first time late in life may be in reality a "masked depression," but that such symptom pictures may be indicative of underlying and unrecognized serious physical illness. Additional studies are needed to determine the validity of such views and the frequency of such clinical occurrences.

There are contradictory reports in the literature regarding the relationship of physical illness (especially cardiac disease) and the frequency and severity of reactive depression or neurotic depression. What is the natural history of such reactions and how are they best treated? Further studies are needed to determine the extent and severity of emotional reactions to both acute and chronic illness in the elderly—the coping mechanisms utilized, whether these are situationally-engendered or exaggerations of longstanding premorbid personality traits, and what the natural history of the symptoms may be; whether psychological symptoms vary with the system involved (cardiac, pulmonary, gastrointestinal, sensory—visual or hearing, or neurological) or with premorbid personality or situational, interpersonal, or social factors.

Old age is filled with social and personal stresses such as decreased income, retirement, loss of a spouse, sibling, or friends. How often do neurotic reactions appear in such circumstances? Or is it cumulative stress over a period of years that is the stressor producing the neurotic reactions?

Criminal behavior among the elderly has received comparatively little attention from researchers in criminology—why criminals become less involved with crime as they grow older is still not clear, and to what extent changing attitudes on the part of the police and the justice system may affect the statistics is still unknown (Bittner 1967). Certainly, the frequency of anxiety does not decrease with aging, but it is possible that the concept of the "burn-out" syndrome may apply to crime as it is said to apply to narcotic addiction, or older persons may learn to avoid trouble with the law as they disengage with increasing age. Longitudinal studies may help to clarify these issues. Why is it that earlier reports on sex offenders among the aged include such a large sample labeled as "senile" or "chronic brain syndrome?" Seldom is the degree of severity of the cognitive impairment or intellectual deterioration mentioned. It could well be that many of these are cases of pseudodementia or of "pseudo-organic syndrome."

# REFERENCES

ABRAHAMS, R. B., AND PATTERSON, R. D. 1978/79. Psychological distress among the community elderly: Prevalence, characteristics, and implications for service. *Int. J. Aging and Hum. Develop., 9*, 1–18.

DE ALARCON, R. 1964. Hypochondriasis and depression in the aged. *Geront. Clin., 6*, 266–277.

ANDERSON, W. F. 1971. The inter-relationship between physical and mental disease in the elderly. *In*, D. W. K. Kay and A. Walk (eds.), *Recent Developments in Psycho-Geriatrics, A Symposium*, pp. 19–24. Brit. J. Psychiatry Special Publication No. 6.

ANDERSON, W. F., AND DAVIDSON, R. 1975. Concomitant physical states. *In*, J. G. Howells (ed.), *Modern Perspective in the Psychiatry of Old Age*, pp. 84–106. New York: Brunner/Mazel.

BAILEY, M. B., HABERMAN, P. W., AND ALKSNE, H. 1965. The epidemiology of alcoholism in an urban residential area. *Q. J. Stud. Alc., 26*, 19–40.

BENNETT, A. E. 1977. *Alcoholism and the Brain.* New York: Stratton Intercontinental Medical Book Corp.

BENNETT, A. E., MOWERY, G. L., AND FORT, J. T. 1960. Brain damage from chronic alcoholism; the diagnosis of intermediate stage of alcoholic brain disease. *Amer. J. Psychiatry, 116*, 705–711.

BERGMANN, K. 1971. The neuroses of old age. *In*, D. W. K. Kay and A. Walk (eds.), *Recent Developments in Psycho-Geriatrics, A Symposium*, pp. 39–50. Brit. J. Psychiatry Special Publication No. 6.

BERGMANN, K. 1978. Neurosis and personality disorder in old age. *In*, A. D. Isaacs and F. Post (eds.), *Studies in Geriatric Psychiatry*, pp. 41–75. Chichester, New York, Brisbane, Toronto: John Wiley.

BERGMANN, K. 1975. Nosology. *In*, J. G. Howells (ed.), *Modern Perspectives in the Psychiatry of Old age*, pp. 170–187. New York: Brunner/Mazel.

BERGMANN, K. AND EASTHAM, E. J. 1974. Psychogeriatric ascertainment and assessment for treatment in an acute medical ward setting. *Age and Ageing, 3*, 174–188.

BERGMAN, S., AND AMIR, M. 1973. Crime and delinquency among the aged in Israel. *Geriatrics, 28*, 149–157.

BITTNER, E. 1967. The police on skid row: A study of peace keeping. *Am. Socio. Rev., 32*, 699–715.

BLAU, D., AND BEREZIN, M. A. 1975. Neuroses and character disorders. *In*, J. G. Howells (ed.), *Modern Perspectives in the Psychiatry of Old Age*, pp. 201–233. New York: Brunner/Mazel.

BLUSEWICZ, M. J., DUSTMAN, R. E., SCHENKENBERG, T., AND BECK, E. C. 1977. Neuropsychological correlates of chronic alcoholism and aging. *J. Nerv. Ment. Dis., 165*, 348–355.

BOLLERUP, T. R. 1975. Prevalence of mental illness among 70-year-olds domiciled in nine Copenhagen suburbs. *Acta Psychiatrica Scand., 51,* 327–339.

BOZZETTI, L. P., AND MacMURRAY, J. P. 1977. Drug misuse among the elderly: a hidden menace. *Psychiat. Ann., 7,* 98–107.

BREMER, J. 1951. A social psychiatric investigation of a small community in northern Norway. *Acta Psychiatrica Neurologica Scand.* Suppl. 62. Copenhagen: Munksgaard.

BUSSE, E. W., DOVENMUEHLE, R. H., AND BROWN, R. G. 1960. Psychoneurotic reactions of the aged. *Geriatrics, 15,* 97.

CAHALAN, D. 1970. *Problem Drinkers.* San Francisco: Jossey-Bass.

CAHALAN, D., CISIN, I. H., AND CROSSLEY, H. M. 1969. *American Drinking Practices.* New Brunswick, N.J.: Rutgers University Press.

CAMERON, N. 1956. Neuroses of later maturity. *In,* O. J. Kaplan (ed.), *Mental Disorders in Later Life,* 2nd ed. Stanford, Ca.: Stanford University Press.

CAPEL, W. C., GOLDSMITH, B. M., WADDELL, K. J., AND STEWART, G. T. 1972. The aging narcotic addict: An increasing problem for the next decades. *J. Gerontol., 27,* 102–106.

CARLEN, P. L., WORTZMAN, G., HOLGATE, R. C., WILKINSON, D. A., AND RANKIN, J. G. 1978. Reversible cerebral atrophy in recently abstinent chronic alcoholics measured by computed tomography scans. *Science, 200,* 1076–1078.

CHODOFF, P. 1972. The depressive personality. A critical review. *Arch. Gen. Psychiatry, 27,* 666–673.

CIOMPI, L. 1969. Follow-up studies on the evolution of former neurotic and depressive states in old age. *J. Geriatric Psychiatry, 3,* 90–106.

CLARK, A. N. G., MANKIKAR, G. D., AND GRAY, I. 1975. Diogenes syndrome. A clinical study of gross neglect in old age. *Lancet,* February 15, 366–368.

CLAYTON, P. J., HALIKAS, J. A., AND MAURICE, W. L. 1972. The depression of widowhood. *Brit. J. Psychiatry, 120,* 71–78.

CLOW, H. E., AND ALLEN, E. B. 1951. Manifestations of psychoneuroses occurring in later life. *Geriatrics, 6,* 31–39.

COHEN, C. I. 1976. Nocturnal neurosis of the elderly: failure of agencies to cope with the problem. *J. Amer. Geriatrics Soc., 24,* 86–88.

COHEN, S. 1976. Alcohol withdrawal syndromes. *Drug Abuse and Alcoholism Newsletter* (Vista Hill Foundation), *5*(5), 3 pp.

CURLEE, J. 1969. Alcoholism and the "empty nest." *Bull. Menn. Clin., 33,* 165–171.

CUTTING, J. 1978. The relationship between Korsakov's syndrome and "alcoholic dementia." *Brit. J. Psychiatry, 132,* 240–251.

DIETHELM, O., AND ROCKWELL, F. V. 1943. Psychopath-

ology of aging. *Amer. J. Psychiatry, 99,* 553–556.

DREW, L. R. H. 1968. Alcoholism as a self-limiting disease. *Q. J. Stud. Alc., 29,* 956–967.

DROLLER, H. 1964. Some aspects of alcoholism in the elderly. *Lancet,* July 18, 137–139.

EARLEY, L. W., AND VON MERING, O. 1969. Growing old the outpatient way. *Amer. J Psychiatry, 125,* 964–967.

EPSTEIN, L. J., MILLS, C., AND SIMON, A. 1970. Antisocial behavior of the elderly. *Compr. Psychiatry, 11,* 36–42.

ERNST, K. 1959. *Die Prognose der Neurosen.* Monographien Heft 85. Berlin, Stuttgart, Heidelberg: Springer Verlag.

ESSEN-MOLLER, E. 1956. Individual traits and morbidity in a Swedish rural population. *Acta Psychiatric Neurologica Scand.,* Suppl. 100.

GAITZ, C. M., AND BAER, P. E. 1971. Characteristics of elderly patients with alcoholism. *Arch. Gen. Psychiatry, 24,* 372–378.

GOLDFARB, A. I. 1967. Geriatric psychiatry. *In,* A. Freedman and H. I. Kaplan (eds.), *Comprehensive Textbook of Psychiatry,* pp. 1564–1587. Baltimore: Williams & Wilkins.

GURLAND, B. J. 1976. The comparative frequency of depression in various adult age groups. *J. Gerontol., 31,* 283–292.

GURNEY, C., ROTH, M., GARSIDE, R. F., KERR, T. A., AND SCHAPIRA, K. 1970. The bearing of treatment on the classification of the affective disorders. *Brit. J. Psychiatry, 117,* 251–255.

GURNEY, C., ROTH, M., GARSIDE, R. F., KERR, T. A., AND SCHAPIRA, K. 1972. Studies in the classification of affective disorders. The relationship between anxiety states and depressive illness. I and II. *Brit. J. Psychiatry, 121,* 147–161, 162–166.

HIRSCHMANN, J. 1962. Zur Kriminologie der Sexualdelikte des alternden Mannes. *Gerontol. Clin. Additamentum,* pp. 115–119.

HORVATH, T. B. 1975. Clincal spectrum and epidemiological features of alcoholic dementia. *In,* J. C. Rankin (ed.), *Alcohol, Drugs, and Brain Damage,* pp. 1–16.

HYLER, S. E. AND SPITZER, R. L. 1978. Hysteria split asunder. *Amer. J. Psychiatry, 135,* 1500–1504.

IBOR-LÓPEZ, J. J. 1972. Masked depressions. *Brit. J. Psychiatry, 120,* 245–258.

JACOBS, T. J., FOGELSON, S., AND CHARLES, E. 1968. Depression ratings in hypochondria. *N.Y. State J. Med.,* Dec. 15, 3119–3122.

JENSEN, K. 1963. Psychiatric problems in four Danish old age homes. *Acta Psychiatrica Scand., Suppl. 169,* pp. 411–419.

KAHN, R. L., ZARIT, S. H., HILBERT, N. M., AND NIEDEREHE, G. 1975. Memory complaint and impairment in the aged. The effect of depression and altered brain function. *Arch. Gen. Psychiatry, 32,*

1569–1573.

KAY, D. W. K., BEAMISH, P., AND ROTH, M. 1964a. Old age mental disorder in Newcastle-upon-Tyne. Part I. A study of prevalence. *Brit. J. Psychiatry, 110,* 146–158.

KAY, D. W. K., BEAMISH, P., AND ROTH, M. 1964b. Old age mental disorders in Newcastle-upon-Tyne. Part II. A study of possible social and medical causes. *Brit. J. Psychiatry, 110,* 668–682.

KAY, D. W. K., AND BERGMANN, K. 1966. Physical disability and mental health in old age. *J. Psychosom. Res.* (Lond.), *10,* 3–12.

KAY, D. W. K., BERGMANN, K., FOSTER, E., MCKECHNIE, A. A., AND ROTH, M. 1970. Mental illness and hospital usage in the elderly: a random sample followed up. *Compr. Psychiatry, 1,* 26–35.

KELLER, O. J., AND VEDDER, C. B. 1969. The crimes that old persons commit. *Gerontologist, 9*(II), 43–50.

KENDALL, R. E. 1968. *The Classification of Depressive Illnesses.* London: Oxford University Press.

KENYON, F. E. 1976. Hypochondriacal states. *British Journal of Psychiatry, 129;* 1–14.

KESSEL, N., AND SHEPHERD, M. 1962. Neurosis in hospital and general practice. *J. Ment. Sci., 108,* 159–166.

KILOH, L. G., ANDREWS, G., NEILSON, M., AND BIANCHI, G. N. 1972. The relationship of the syndromes called endogenous and neurotic depression. *Brit. J. Psychiatry, 121,* 183–196.

KLERMAN, G. L. 1971. Clinical research in depression. *Arch. Gen. Psychiatry, 24,* 305–319.

KNUPFER, G., AND ROOM, R. 1964. Age, sex, and social class as factors in amount of drinking in a metropolitan community. *Social Problems, 12,* 224–240.

KREITMAN, N., SAINSBURY, P., PEARCE, K., AND COSTAIN, W. R. 1965. Hypochondriasis and depression in out-patients at a general hospital. *Brit. J. Psychiatry, 111,* 607–615.

KRINGLEN, E. 1965. Obsessional neurotics, a long-term follow-up. *Brit. J. Psychiatry, 111,* 709–722.

LESSE, S., AND MATHERS, J. 1968. Depression sine depression (masked depression). *N. Y. State J. Med., 68,* (4), 535–543.

LINN, M. W., LINN, B. S., AND GREENWALD, S. R. 1975. The alcoholic patient in the nursing home. *Aging and Hum. Develop., 3,* 273–277.

LIPSCOMB, W. R. 1959. Mortality among treated alcoholics. A three-year follow-up study. *Q. J. Stud. Alc., 20,* 596–603.

LIPSITT, D. R. 1968/69. The "rotating" patient: a challenge to psychiatrists. *J. Geriatric Psychiatry, 2,* 51–61.

LOWENTHAL, M. F., BERKMAN, P., AND ASSOCIATES. 1964. *Aging and Mental Disorder in San Francisco.* San Francisco: Jossey-Bass.

LUISADA, P., PEELE, R., AND PITTARD, E. 1974. The hysterical personality in men. *Amer. J. Psychiatry, 131,* 518–522.

MALAMUD, N., AND SKILLICORN, S. A. 1956. Relationship between the Wernicke and the Korsakoff syndrome. *Arch. Neurol. Psychiatry, 76,* 585–596.

MCCREARY, C. P., AND MENSH, I. N. 1977. Personality differences associated with age in law offenders. *J. Gerontol., 32,* 164–167.

MCCUSKER, J., CHERUBIN, C. E., AND ZIMBERG, S. 1971. Prevalence of alcoholism in general municipal hospital populations. *N. Y. State J. Med., 71,* 751–754.

MCDONALD, C. 1967. The pattern of neurotic illness in the elderly. *Aust. N. Z. J. Psychiatry, 1,* 203–210.

Metropolitan Life Insurance Company. 1977. Mortality from alcoholism. *Statistical Bulletin, 58.* 3–7.

MEYER, J. E. 1974. Psychoneuroses and neurotic reactions in old age. *Journal of American Geriatrics Society, 22* (6), 254–257.

MOBERG, D. O. 1953. Old age and crime. *J. Crim. Law, Criminology, and Police Science, 43,* 764–776.

MORRISON, J. R. 1978. Management of Briquet syndrome (hysteria). *West. J. Med., 128,* 482–487.

MÜLLER, C. 1967. *Alterspsychiatrie.* Stuttgart: Thieme.

NIELSEN, J. 1962. Geronto-psychiatric period-prevalence investigation in a geographically delimited population. *Acta Psychiatrica Neurological Scan., 38,* 307–330.

NIELSEN, J., HOMMA, A., AND BIORN-HENRIKSEN, T. 1977. Follow-up 15 years after a geronto-psychiatric prevalence study. *J. Gerontol., 32,* 554–561.

NUNN, C., BERGMANN, K., BRITTON, P. G., FOSTER, E. M., HALL, E. H., AND KAY, D. W. K. 1974. Intelligence and neuroses in old age. *Brit. J. Psychiatry, 124,* 446–452.

PARKES, C. M. 1964. Recent bereavement as a cause of mental illness. *Brit. J. Psychiatry, 110,* 198.

PARSONS, P. L. 1965. Mental health of Swansea's old folk. *Brit. J. Prev. Soc. Med., 19,* 43–47.

PASCARELLI, E. 1972. Alcoholism and drug addiction in the elderly. *Geriatric Focus, 11,* 1, 4–5.

PATTISON, E. M. 1977. Ten years of change in alcoholism treatment and delivery systems. *American Journal of Psychiatry, 134* (3), 261–266.

PAYKEL, E. S., KLERMAN, G. L., AND PRUSOFF, B. A. 1976. Personality and symptom pattern in depression. *Brit. J. Psychiatry, 129,* 327–334.

PETERSEN, D. M., AND WHITTINGTON, F. J. 1977. Drug use among the elderly: a review. *J. Psychedelic Drugs, 9,* 25–37.

PFEIFFER, E. AND BUSSE, E. W. 1973. Affective disorders. *In,* E. W. Busse and E. Pfeiffer (eds.), *Mental Illness in Later Life,* pp. 199–232. Washington, D.C.: American Psychiatric Association.

POLLAK, O. 1941. The criminality of old age. *J. Crim. Psychopath., 3,* 213–235.

POLLITT, J. 1957. Natural history of obsessional states. *Brit. Med. J., 1,* 194–198.

POST, F. 1962. *The Significance of Affective Symptoms in Old Age.* London: Oxford University Press.

POST, F. 1965. *The Clinical Psychiatry of Later Life*. London: Pergamon Press.

POST, F. 1974. Diagnosis of depression in geriatric patients and treatment modalities appropriate for the population. *In*, D. M. Gallant and G. M. Simpson (eds.), *Depression: Behavioral, Biochemical, Diagnostic and Treatment Concepts*, pp. 205–231. New York: Spectrum.

PRIMROSE, E. J. R. 1962. *Psychological Illness: A Community Study*. Springfield, Ill.: Charles C Thomas.

PRUSOFF, B., AND KLERMAN, G. L. 1974. Differentiating depressed from anxious neurotic outpatients. *Arch. Gen. Psychiatry, 30*, 302–309.

RATHOD, N. H., AND THOMSON, I. G. 1971. Women alcoholics, a clinical study. *Q. J. Stud. Alc., 32*, 45–52.

ROBINS, L. N. 1966. *Deviant Children Grown Up*. Baltimore: Williams & Wilkins.

RODSTEIN, M. 1975. Crime and the aged. 1. The victims. 2. The criminals. *J.A.M.A., 234* (5), 533–534, *234* (6), 639.

ROSIN, A. J., AND GLATT, M. M. 1971. Alcohol excess in the elderly. *Q. J. Stud. Alc., 32*, 53–59.

ROTH, M. 1972. Studies in the classification of affective disorders: The relationship between anxiety states and depressive illness. *Brit. J. Psychiatry, 121*, 147–161.

ROTH, M. 1976. The psychiatric disorders of later life. *Psychiatric Annals, 6*, 417–445.

ROTH, M. AND KAY, D. W. K. 1956. Affective disorders arising in the senium. *J. Ment. Sci., 102*, 426–485.

SALZMAN, C., AND SHADER, R. I. 1978. Depression in the elderly. I. Relationship between depression, psychologic defense mechanisms and physical illness. II. Possible drug etiologies; differential criteria. *J. Amer. Geriatrics Soc., 26*, 253–260; 303–308.

SCHUCKIT, M. A. 1977. Geriatric alcoholism and drug abuse. *Gerontologist, 17*, 168–174.

SEMKE, V. Y. 1965. Paranoid reactions and development of paranoid syndrome in psychopaths in old age (in Russian). *Zh. Nevropat. Psikhiat.* 65, 593. (Abstract in Excerpta med. (Amst.), Sect. XX, 9, 73.

SHELDON, J. H. 1948. *The Social Medicine of Old Age: Report of an Inquiry in Wolverhampton*. London: Oxford University Press.

SHEPHERD, M., AND GRUENBERG, E. M. 1957. The age for neuroses. *Milbank Memorial Fund Quarterly, 35*, 258–265.

SHICHOR, D., AND KOBRIN, S. 1978. Note: Criminal behavior among the elderly. *Gerontologist, 18*, 213–218.

SIMON, A., EPSTEIN, L. J., AND REYNOLDS, L. 1968. Alcoholism in the geriatric mentally ill. *Geriatrics, 23*, 125–131.

SIMON, A., AND TALLEY, J. E. 1965. The role of physical illness in geriatric mental disorders. *In, Psychiatric Disorders in the Aged*, pp. 154–170. Manchester, England: Geigy UK.

SMITH, W. J. 1978. The etiology of depression in a sample of elderly widows. *J. Geriatric Psychiatry, 11*, 81–83.

SPICER, C. C., HARE, E. H., AND SLATER, E. 1973. Neurotic and psychotic forms of depressive illness; evidence from age-incidence in a national sample. *Brit. J. Psychiatry, 123*, 535–541.

STENBACK, A., KUMPULAENIN, M., AND VAUHKONEN, M. L. 1978. Illness and health behavior in septuagenarians. *J. Gerontol., 33*, 57–61.

STERN, K., WILLIAMS, G. M., AND PRADOS, M. 1951. Grief reactions in later life. *Amer. J. Psychiatry, 108*, 289–294.

Task Force on Prescription Drugs, 1968, D.H.E.W. 1971. *The Drug Users and the Drug Prescribers*. Washington, D.C.: U.S. Government Printing Office.

VACHON, M. L. S. 1976. Grief and bereavement following the death of a spouse. *Can. Psychiatr. Ass. J., 21*, 35–44.

WEISS, J. M. A. 1972. The natural history of antisocial attitudes: what happens to psychopaths? *J. Gerontol. Psychiatry, 5*, 236–242.

WEISSMAN, M. M., AND KLERMAN, G. L. 1977. The chronic depressive in the community: unrecognized and poorly treated. *Compr. Psychiatry, 18*, 523–532.

WHISKIN, F. E. Delinquency in the aged. 1967/68. *J. Geriatric Psychiatry, 1*, 242–252.

WHITTIER, J. R., AND KORENYI, C. 1961. Selected characteristics of aged patients: A study of mental hospital admissions. *Compr. Psychiatry, 2*, 113–120.

WIGDOR, B. T., AND MORRIS, G. 1977. A comparison of twenty-year medical histories of individuals with depressive and paranoid states. *J. Gerontol, 32*, 160–163.

WILLIAMSON, J., STOKOE, I. H., GRAY, S., FISHER, M., SMITH, A., MCGHEA, A., AND STEPHENSON, E. 1964. Old people at home—their unreported needs. *Lancet, 1*, 117–1120.

WILSON, L. A., AND LAWSON, I. R. 1962. Situational depression in the elderly. A study of 23 cases. *Gerontol. Clin., Additamentum*, pp. 59–71.

WINICK, C. 1962. Maturing out of addiction. *Bull. Narc., 14*, 1–7.

WINOKUR, G., CLAYTON, P., AND REICH, T. 1969. *Manic Depressive Illness*. St. Louis: C. V. Mosby.

WOODRUFF, R. A., CLAYTON, P. J., AND GUZE, S. B. 1971. Hysteria: Studies of diagnosis, outcome and prevalence. *J. A. M. A., 215*, 425–428.

ZAWADSKI, R. T., GLAZER, G. B., AND LURIE, E. 1978. Psychotropic drug use among institutionalized and noninstitutionalized Medicaid aged in California. *J. Gerontol., 33*, 825–834.

ZAX, M., GARDNER, E. A., AND HART, W. T. 1964. Public intoxication in Rochester: A survey of individuals charged during 1961. *Q. J. Stud. Alc., 22*, 669–678.

ZIMBERG, S. 1974. The elderly alcoholic. *Gerontologist, 14*, 222–224.

# 28

# The Assessment
# of the Mental Health Status
# of Older Adults*

*Barry J. Gurland*

## PROCESSES OF ASSESSMENT

Continuum of structure, operationalism, and empiricism: Three main processes are involved in completing an assessment of the older person's mental health, namely (1) gathering relevant information, (2) storing the information for immediate and long-term analysis and (3) interpreting its implications for the state of the subject's mental health. In practice, these processes are conducted with widely varying degrees of reliability. At one extreme, the gathering of information may be haphazard and patchy, depending mainly on the spontaneous complaints of the patient or a family member, most of the information may go unrecorded and the conclusions reached may be largely determined by the interviewer's prejudice. At the other extreme, the information may be gathered along prescribed and structured guidelines, the record

entered according to an inventory of precoded and precisely defined items, and the interpretation based on reference to a store of empirical data. Between these two extremes lies a continuum of degrees of structuring in the gathering of information, of precision in the operational definition of the recorded information and of empiricism in the interpretation of its implications for mental health. It is customary to place the clinical interview towards the less structured, less precise and less empirical end of the continuum of assessment techniques and to place laboratory tests towards the other end, with psychological tests falling somewhere in between.

The style and scope of the clinical interview

*Roni Gurland D.B.O. assisted in the literature research for this paper. Literature Research Assistant, Department of Geriatrics Research.

may vary among clinicians and among interviews by the same clinician. Clinicians may differ in their manner of conducting interviews particularly if they have been trained in different schools of psychiatric thinking and also because their personal experience may lead them to a set of topics that they have found useful to explore in reaching a diagnosis and a manner of probing those topics with which they feel comfortable. Furthermore, the same clinician may vary the manner of interviewing for different patients, following clues that are suggested by the emergence of diagnostically significant information. In the interests of efficiency the physician may seek evidence during the interview which will quickly refute or confirm one or another probable diagnoses suggested by the information obtained up to that point in the interviewing process.

The length and completeness of the clinical interview will very likely depend on the decisions that must be reached then and there. In cases of attempted suicide, for example, little information may be required to determine that the patient needs immediate admission, and other information gathering will be deferred. In the case of suspected dementia, however, the clinician may request an extended series of interviews with the patient and other informants, with observation and examination during a hospital stay, as well as a trial treatment, all as part of the process of assessment prior to reaching a definitive diagnosis and management decision. Thus the style, content, duration and number of interviews may vary widely depending on the clinician's past experience, the way he sees the primary purpose of the interview and the most efficient method for pursuing that purpose and the point at which he believes the goal of the interview has been reached.

Laboratory tests, and to a lesser extent psychological tests, have procedural guidelines which are intended to enable the verbal or non-verbal stimuli to be administered in a consistent way by different practitioners on every occasion. The range of responses recognized as relevant is narrow compared with the range covered in the clinical interview and each response is carefully defined. Responses which cannot be carefully defined are excluded during the development of the test. The responses are quantifiable and are interpreted by relating the results on an individual subject to previously derived normative standards, to establish relationships with important criteria such as clinical diagnosis and response to treatment, and to statistically derived patterns reflecting independent psychological functions.

Relative merits of clinical and psychological

techniques: Assessment methods on the clinical end of the structured-operational-empirical continuum have certain obvious disadvantages relative to those on the laboratory or psychological test end. Clinical assessments are prone to be distorted by many factors including any prejudice on the interviewer's part towards aged patients, by the theoretical stance of the clinician, and by cultural and personal attitudes of the patient towards the interview situation and towards their own symptoms. Some of the consequences of such flaws in the assessment are that misdiagnoses may occur, communication about patients between clinicians may be confounded by misunderstanding, and it may be difficult to relate the findings on an individual patient on a specific occasion to a body of knowledge about patients in general or to previous findings on that patient.

However, the comparison between the clinical and the laboratory or psychological methods is not by any means all favorable to the latter. The flexibility of the clinical method permits its use under conditions which might preclude laboratory or psychological testing such as in emergency situations, where the patient is very disturbed, has a perceptual deficit which interferes with testing, or where a communication problem based on a physical disorder, cultural differences or poor education exists. Moreover, the clinical method allows review of a wide range of issues relevant to a patient's particular problem whereas the laboratory-psychological tests tend to focus on a limited number of mental functions. Furthermore, recognition of the relative merits of the clinical and the laboratory-psychological methods of assessment has led to attempts to find new ways of moving the clinical interview nearer to the laboratory or psychological test end of the continuum of structure-precision-empiricism. The latter effort is epitomized by the development of semistructured clinical interviewing. This technique is based on the observation that certain skilled clinicians have developed or adopted a style of interview and a set of questions for patients that they apply with consistency and effectiveness in eliciting psychopathology, that many of these questions have wide currency among skilled psychiatrists, and that the symptoms identified by these clinicians are discriminating with respect to diagnosis and can be defined in great detail. From this observation it is a logical step to record the questions used as clinical probes by skilled psychiatrists and to place such questions in a script with an orderly sequence of topics which can be rehearsed and applied by other psychiatrists or allied health professionals to their own patients. The discriminatory symptoms elicited by these means are recorded on an inventory of a mutually exclusive and jointly comprehensive set of items each of which is carefully defined and precoded. The information arising from the interview can also be classified in a global fashion according to set criteria. Such interviews are capable of good reliability and can be statistically analyzed, yet have clinical flexibility in that the order of questioning and the exact wording of the question can be modified to cope with any difficulties of comprehension and cooperation posed by a patient. In addition the interviewer is allowed some room for judgment in applying the definitions of symptoms.

The clinical, psychological and laboratory methods of assessing mental health each have their distinctive advantages and disadvantages, none of which are sufficiently outstanding to make the choice between methods self-evident. All these methods and their combinations therefore require consideration in choosing the best method for a given assessment task. A major determinant in making that choice will be the particular purpose of that assessment.

## PURPOSES OF ASSESSMENT

### EMOTIONAL SUPPORT

It is surprisingly easy to overlook the fact that the primary purpose of mental health assessment should be dictated by the needs of the client rather than the professional curiosity of the interviewer. From the viewpoint of the elderly patient the crucial quality of a method of assessment is the degree to which it conveys to the patient a sense that someone in the health profession is concerned and taking the trouble to understand the patient's problems. Patients may feel supported and reassured by a good assessment interview even where no substantial therapeutic program follows, while conversely, even the most energetic treatment program may be rejected by patients if they feel it is based upon an inadequate or unsympathetic assessment of their problems. Thus the foremost purpose of the assessment process should be to instill in the patient a sense of confidence in the therapist.

### VULNERABILITY

The clinical decisions that may constitute the purpose of an assessment interview will vary with the point on the mental health service pathway at which the assessment is carried out. At the earliest point, prior to the subject being a candidate for

entry into the mental health system (i.e., before the subject is overtly mentally ill) the decision will revolve around whether there exists a state of vulnerability to mental illness which calls for preventive intervention. Such interviews are likely to be conducted at routine annual examinations, senior citizen centers, in congregate dwellings for the elderly, in social service agencies, or in other locations outside the mental health system. Interviews in these circumstances must be more than usually tactful and in no way threaten subjects with questions or tests that appear to be placing their sanity in doubt. The subject is often reassured on this score when the mental health questions are presented in the context of a full health inquiry. Other indicators of vulnerability to mental ill health that should be assessed include previous history of mental illness, perceptual impairment (especially deafness of longstanding duration), a recent cluster of life events with high stress values, the absence of a confidante or other elements of a supportive network and the presence of chronic physical illness in the subject or someone who is dependent on the subject. All these conditions are associated with increased incidence rates of mental illness.

### MORBID QUALITY

The next point along the mental health service pathway is reached when an older person complains of distress or a change in pattern or level of function but is not yet labeled as a patient in the mental health system. The purpose of mental health assessment at this point is to determine first whether the symptoms are part of the normal spectrum of behavior, feeling and thinking or are morbid in quality, and second, whether the symptoms, if morbid, belong in the domain of mental health as opposed to physical health. In order to reduce the chances that the assessment will reinforce a hypochondriacal tendency in a patient it is essential that it be persuasively thorough and followed soon after by an understandable explanation of the findings.

### URGENCY

Those persons judged to be mentally ill require an assessment of how they should progress further along the mental health service pathway. The identification of the need for emergency treatment now becomes the main purpose of assessment. Features that obviously will be sought are suicidal or other dangerous impulses which can best be determined by routine but gentle questioning of patients as well as informants. Less obvious is the urgent need for treatment in acute confusional states which would be recognized by inquiry regarding the recent onset of a fluctuating state of impaired alertness, with episodes of disorientation and lapses in memory, restlessness, fearfulness and possibly hallucinations or misinterpretations. The assessment would include a search for the underlying cause of the acute confusion such as drug interactions, infections, vomiting, diarrhea and dehydration, fecal impaction, trauma and a variety of other conditions. Arie (1978) remarks that "we all know the accepted list of potential causes of acute confusion or delirium in old people: they encompass practically every condition in medicine and some not within the traditional confines of medicine at all."

Where emergency admission is indicated as it would be in the instances cited above, completion of the assessment will probably be left until after admission to hospital at which time the assessment will extend beyond interview techniques to include various laboratory tests and physical examinations.

SELECTION OF TREATMENT

Putting aside emergency decisions, the assessment of the need for treatment will depend ideally on identifying syndromes of mental ill health which have a poor chance of spontaneous recovery but a good chance of a favorable response to a known and safe treatment. The late onset persistent paranoid states of old age known as paraphrenia, characteristically are chronic and such persons live bitter, isolated and distressed lives because of their symptoms, frequently causing problems for neighbors and authorities and progressively eroding the security of their niche in the community by their behavior. Appropriate psychopharmacological treatment, for example with phenothiazines, often alleviates symptoms provided the patient complies with treatment. Severe clinical depressions also do distinctly better with treatment than without. By way of contrast, persons suffering from a reaction to bereavement may have as good a chance of recovery (if not a better one) without being admitted to the mental health system, while cases of senile dementia of the Alzheimer type may follow a steady deteriorating course not substantially altered by attempts at curative treatment. Thus, at this stage of passage along the mental health service pathway the critical purpose of assessment is that of differential diagnosis (or differential classification to use a broader concept) for the purpose of instituting therapeutically effective treatments. For this purpose clinical, psychological and laboratory testing may all be invoked. In addition, characteristics besides diagnosis that aid prediction of

spontaneous outcome and response to treatment must be assessed.

PSYCHODYNAMICS

Good treatment almost always includes a consideration of the personal preoccupations, attitudes and sensitivities and unique reactivity of the individual; and sometimes the treatment may center on these psychodynamic characteristics. For this purpose of assessment it is quite usual for the clinician to begin with expectations or assumptions based on theory or experience and to assess their relevance to the patient by unstructured interviewing or by the response of the patient to management consistent with the clinician's understanding of the causes of undesired behaviors. The approach to the treatment of hostile-dependent aid seeking behavior (Goldfarb, 1967, 1968) is an example of this form of assessment. More systematic methods are also applied to the purpose of psychodynamic assessment such as projective tests and the personal exploration exercises of the life review type of therapy (Butler and Lewis, 1973).

OUTCOME

Once treatment is instituted the purpose of mental health assessment becomes that of monitoring the response to treatment. The features of mental ill health that serve to discriminate the different diagnostic categories are not necessarily the most sensitive to change during the course of treatment so that change measures may be different from diagnostic or predictive measures. Failures of treatment may direct the assessment along still different lines, for example to determine the blood levels of a prescribed medication or the state of thyroid activity in the case of failure to respond to tricyclic antidepressants.

PLACEMENT

Where a favorable response to treatment is either not forthcoming or not to be expected, or when residual chronic symptoms remain after treatment, the purpose of assessment may focus on the need for long term supportive care and for intensified efforts at rehabilitation. The patient's current and potential capacity for basic self-care and for managing the necessary instrumental roles of independent living will be a pivotal concern of assessment. The patient's needs in these respects will have to be matched to available supportive environments preferably at home, but if necessary in a sheltered or institutional setting. The type and amount of personal assistance needed by the patient and available from family members, home care services, or in institutions offering various levels of care, will be an overriding issue and eligibility for reimbursement in these settings will also be important. In predicting the person's likely response to rehabilitation, an assessment of positive mental health will be helpful with special attention to previous ability to cope with health crises, cooperativeness, energy, tolerance of discomfort, extent and depth of interests, social manner and intelligence.

## EVALUATION

All the above purposes of assessing mental health revolve around the needs of the individual patient at various stages of the pathway along the mental health service system. However, there are also needs for assessment to serve programs of further research in mental health in order to make the mental health system more effective and less costly. Evaluation of therapeutic programs such as new drugs or varieties of psychotherapy require assessment techniques which are highly reliable, used by as many investigators in that area as possible, sensitive to change, and covering not only the parameters of mental health which are the targets of experimental therapy but also those parameters which might deteriorate for lack of treatment or because of side-effects of treatment. Since the effectiveness of treatment might be viewed differently by various parties who are involved with the patient it may be necessary to assess changes in mental health both by objective behavioral changes as well as by reports from the patient, the family, and the staff who are attending the patient; all these parties may have a legitimate claim to have their vantage point reliably assessed as part of the overall evaluation of the usefulness of a new therapy.

## PLANNING

The planning and modification of mental health systems and their components to make them more efficient and more responsive to the needs of the consumer is facilitated by a knowledge base which includes mental health assessments of both existing and potential clients. Epidemiological studies of communities within a mental health system, or of groups at high risk for mental illness, are examples of assessments whose main purpose may be the formulation of new policies or plans for development of mental health services. The assessment must take note not only of the typical symptoms and disabilities that identify cases in need of specific treatments but also of atypical presentations of psychiatric disorder that because of this characteristic frequently go without appropriate treatment, for example depressive disorder which is marked by somatic symptoms.

## RESEARCH INTO ETIOLOGY

The most difficult and complex purpose of assessment of mental health has been left to the last, namely to advance understanding of the etiology and mechanisms of mental disorder. Such research is of necessity innovative and assessments may have to be equally innovative. Nevertheless, certain approaches to assessment have been found to be fruitful in this area of research and will certainly continue to be utilized in the foreseeable future. These approaches include the assessment of phenomenological psychopathology on a multi-dimensional and typological basis requiring the exploration of the following symptoms: depressed moods; phobic anxiety; vegetative (somatic) symptoms; disorder of thinking; auditory and visual hallucinations; paranoid, grandiose and depressive delusions; motor and speech retardation; obsessions; depersonalization; drug and alcohol abuse; hypochondriasis; lack of insight; apathy and withdrawal; concentration; antisocial behavior; and disturbances of memory, orientation and judgment. It is not enough to determine the mere presence or absence of these symptoms but their detailed characteristics (e.g., the diurnal variation in depressed mood) are necessary as well. Additions to this essentially cross-sectional picture of the patient's condition should be the features of the previous personality, prior episodes, interval state, onset and course and response to treatment of the condition, the family history, precipitation events, situational reinforcers, and associated physical health findings. With these assessments in hand it is possible to relate the patient's condition to a body of knowledge about its causes and mechanisms and for research to proceed from that solid foundation.

## INTERVIEWING THE OLDER PERSON

It might be expected that the participants in a mental health assessment interview usually agree about the need for accurate communication. There are of course occasions which would tempt the patient to engage in deception and dissimulation such as when the interviewer is engaged in a commitment procedure or in determining the need for surrogate management. However, even when the interviewer has the best of intentions the patient may appear to be uncooperative and to reject the role of a good informant. The interview may then fail to produce important information because of the patient's denial of symptoms, evasiveness, tendency to ramble, rhetorical replies, or frank hostility. The interviewer may regard such behavior as senile cantankerousness, as evidence of organic brain syndrome or as lack of insight due to a functional psychiatric disorder. Yet, very often, an unproductive interview is a result of a poor interview technique.

The interviewer must from the outset be aware of the common anxieties that older persons harbor about having their mental health assessed. Since chronic illnesses occur very frequently in the elderly, their comfort and the security of their health may depend heavily upon receiving good medical care and they may feel threatened by a minimization of the physical nature of their symptoms, seeing this as a rejection by the physician. Furthermore, whereas physical disorder may be regarded as inevitable accompaniment of old age which can be met as a challenge or can justify dependency, mental disorder is often viewed by the patient as heralding a final disintegration and a loss of control over the self and the environment. If there are still some members of the health professions who believe that mental disorders in old age are usually irrecoverable it is not surprising that patients are prone to make the same mistake. Moreover, the elderly cohorts of today remember the days when there was no effective treatment for mental illness.

If the interviewer does not take account of the anxieties of the patient the quality of the interview may quickly deteriorate. The more anxious the older patient becomes the more likely is the patient to hesitate in responding, to be overly cautious and thus vague in replies and to have difficulty in completing tasks which test intellectual ability; in other words, to be an inefficient interviewee because of an excessive level of arousal. Under these circumstances the interviewer's impatience or concern about the patient's poor performance may make the patient still more anxious so that matters go from bad to worse.

The patient may have a sense of helplessness arising out of a state of depression, from disability whether physical or psychiatric, or from the diminished status of being labeled mentally ill or old. Anger or manipulative behavior displayed by the patient during the interview can be a reaction to this sense of helplessness; a defensive attempt to show strength or gain control, or a fearful response to the anticipation of being abandoned in time of need. Here again the interview may be disrupted if the interviewer also becomes irritable or loses interest thus increasing the patient's fear or sense of rejection.

The anxiety of the patient and his sense of helplessness can be considerably allayed by good interview technique, which will also increase the patient's confidence in the interviewer and the associated therapeutic team. The mental health questions are best set in the context of a thorough general health and social problem interview so that the interviewer can assure the patient that there is concern for all the patient's problems (rather than a focus of finding out how mentally ill the patient is). If the patient should show concern about the implication of a particular item, the examiner can offer the assurance that the questions are routine and put to all patients. Tests of intellectual capacity should be dispersed throughout the interview rather than massed since the latter approach may indicate to the patient that the interviewer is attempting to prove a point. Specific tests of memory and orientation can be inconspicuously interwoven with questions on census and demographic information that conventionally introduce almost any kind of interview. There should be an unhurried air about the pace of the questions and patients should be allowed ample time to respond; it is surprising how often correct and informative replies are forthcoming after a long interval of hesitation. Where patients are given insufficient time to respond appropriately to a question, the examiner may be misled by the reply or lack of it and the patients may be made to feel that they have failed in their attempts at communication. The patient is also reassured about the adequacy of communication if the interviewer opens and closes with an opportunity for the patient to talk spontaneously about his or her problems while the interviewer records what the patient says so as to show that it is being taken seriously. Restating aloud the patient's report from time to time will indicate that the interviewer is listening attentively. The interview should end with a clear explanation as to what will be the next step in the assessment or treatment process. The examiner should indicate an understanding of the patient's plight though it is usually not a good idea to attempt a summary of that understanding since patients may be concerned about the inconclusiveness of the account rather than its highlights.

Distressing issues should not be raised towards the end of the interview unless the patient volunteers such matters. It is crucial at this phase of the interview not to overstress the patient either by raising emotionally laden topics or by testing of cognitive functions. Control of the interview is very often best left to the patient in the last few minutes. The interviewer should indicate how well the patient has handled the task of reporting problems and should convey a clear message that the information and understanding obtained by the interviewer will allow the next step to be satisfactorily undertaken. The attitude to be projected is that the patient has done a good job and now the interviewer can also do a good job in the patient's best interests.

Patients who are agitated, suffering from depressive retardation, intellectually impaired or physically ill may not tolerate a lengthy interview. It is important that the interview should not exceed the limits of the patient's attention and tolerance since beyond this point the patient's errors in communication will increase rapidly. Several brief interviews may be required. However, most elderly patients can accept and will appreciate the same length of interview that is suitable for younger persons.

Communication and perceptual impairments, especially partial deafness, may impose difficulties on the interview. Interviewers can learn to speak slowly, clearly and firmly, but without shouting, and with their lips plainly visible to the patient, directing their voice to the 'best ear,' and introducing more than the usual amount of redundance into their speech. A quiet room without echo or background noise is helpful. If the person has a hearing aid it should be checked to see if it is in good working order. For patients with difficulty in seeing, large print test charts are available for certain tests. Expressive communication impairments, including dysphasias and dysarthrias, will sometimes require a good deal of patience on the part of the interviewer in learning to interpret the patient's style of communication.

In most instances of difficulty in communicating with patients, whether because of agitation, intellectual impairment, or expressive and receptive impairments, the communication can be greatly improved by a good match between the interviewer's and the patient's attention. In order to effect this, the interviewer should signal the delivery of a question by use of body movements (e.g., leaning forward and looking into the patient's eyes), and should ensure that the patient's attention is focused on the question at least long enough to formulate a reply, by use of alerting stimuli such as addressing the patient by name or hand-holding. It is possible to monitor the patient's level of attention by watching his face and eyes, which will also help to fasten the interviewer's attention on the patient's responses.

A good assessment interview is both searching and comprehensive. Touchy topics such as suicidal feelings and sexual problems are not avoided. All information of significance is double-checked wherein doubt by questioning of a reliable informant, if one is available. Yet, at the end of the interview, the patient will usually feel a sense of accomplishment and a reduction in anxiety.

## ASSESSMENT OF THE FINAL COMMON PATHWAYS OF MENTAL DISORDERS

There are many causes of mental disorder yet their effects on the patient can for some purposes be usefully classified into a relatively limited range of categories. These final common pathways of mental disorder are arbitrarily derived by selecting effects which are of special importance in eliciting a helping response from formal sources (e.g., the health services) or informal sources (e.g., the family or significant others). Thus the range of categories is limited by several factors: the repertoire of inherited or acquired behaviors, the nature of the mental disorder, the methods currently available to detect abnormalities of behavior, and the targets of helping responses by formal and informal agents. Mental health assessment of older persons, especially in a clinical setting, generally begins with an examination of each of these final common pathways. They are as follows: cognitive impairment; depression; excessive dependence on others; disruptive or dangerous behavior; bizarre behavior; somatic disturbance and social maladjustment.

There are a large and perhaps overwhelming number of assessment instruments available for most of these final common pathways. Yet many of these instruments are merely variations on a common theme while others which are ostensibly different from each other in content nevertheless accomplish the same specific task of assessment. In order to simplify this review of available instruments, for each of the areas of interest, a single instrument or test is featured and used as a standard against which to compare some other relevant measures. The featured measure is selected on the grounds that it is clinically practical; that is to say, relatively brief and straightforward to administer, feasible for the clinician to apply, based on clearly defined observations or tests or with wording that is easy for the patient to understand, requiring only a moderate level of cooperation from the patient, and capable of being administered without benefit of complex technology or a laboratory setting.

## COGNITIVE IMPAIRMENT

The cognitive impairments which arise as a final common pathway of a wide variety of dementing processes are sometimes referred to as an organic brain syndrome and are most usefully divided into those characteristic of the chronic brain syndrome and of the acute brain syndrome. In both cases the core symptoms involve disorientation and impairments of recent memory and new learning. The most widely used test of the cognitive impairments in an organic brain syndrome, the Mental Status Questionnaire (MSQ), focuses on these core symptoms.

The MSQ consists of 10 items winnowed by means of discriminant function analysis from a larger pool of thirty-one items designed to identify elderly patients with organic brain syndrome (Kahn, Goldfarb, Pollack and Peck, 1960). None of these items is unfamiliar to the clinician since they are taken from the repertoire of common clinical practice but the MSQ standardizes the format for their administration and quantifies the responses of the patient in terms of an error score; simply a score of one for each error.

There have been many modifications of the MSQ by other research workers (e.g. disorientation factor [Lawson, Rodenburg and Dykes, 1977], SPMSQ [Pfeiffer, 1975a], and the Orientation Test [Irving, Robinson and McAdam, 1970]), sometimes in an effort to adapt the items for settings other than the long term care institutions where the items were first developed. As a basis for comparison, a table is provided in which the MSQ items are listed next to corresponding items from similar scales. Many of the items in the other scales are shared in common with the MSQ and the remaining items are in a similar domain of mental functioning. Thus it is possible to regard these scales as more or less interchangeable and for the purposes of further discussion, the validity and utility of the MSQ will be judged from data collected on the MSQ itself or on any of the MSQ analog scales. In fact, the correlation between scores on one analog scale, the SPMSQ, and on the MSQ (original 31 item inventory) has been noted to be as high as .84 (Haglund and Schuckit, 1976).

*Reliability.*   Wilson, Roy and Bursil (1973) gave the MSQ four times a week at three week intervals to 55 elderly patients selected because their condition was likely to be stable; three-quarters of the scores changed by one or less. Pfeiffer (1975a) reports the test-retest reliability of the (MSQ analog) SPMSQ given at 4 weekly intervals as .82 in one group of elderly subjects and .83 in another. He points out that there is no significant practice effect under these circumstances. Stonier (1974) also found little evidence of a learning effect for the MSQ.

*Diagnostic Validity.*   The validity of the MSQ and analog scales can be judged first of all against the criterion of an expert clinician's diagnosis of dementia. In the Goldfarb-Kahn series of studies, when patients made no errors on the MSQ, the diagnosis of chronic organic brain syndrome was independently made by a geriatric psychiatrist in only 6 percent of such cases, whereas when patients made as many as 10 errors (the maximum possible) they were independently diagnosed as suffering from chronic organic brain syndrome in 95 percent of cases. Irving, Robinson and McAdam (1970), found the Orientation Test to agree with clinical diagnosis in the distinction between functional and organic brain syndromes in 82 percent of cases. Birkett and Boltuch (1977), employing clinical tests of verbal memory and orientation from the Maudsley Tests of Sensorium, noted that the tests and clinical classification agreed in 37 out of 50 cases. This latter series of cases is distinguished by clear-cut criteria for clinical classification and the independence of the criteria from the information entering into the psychological tests.

*Prognostic Validity.*   In general, senile dementia, the major cause of chronic organic brain syndrome, is a progressive disorder with a high mortality rate, considerably shortening the expected duration of life at the age at which it is diagnosed. In a study of 1,280 persons over 64 years of age randomly sampled from long term care institutions in New York City, it was found that within one year after examination, 11 percent of cases scoring 0-2 errors on the MSQ were dead but about three times as many of those scoring 9-10 errors were dead (Goldfarb, Fisch and Gerber, 1966). The MSQ has been shown to decline in octogenarians in institutions who were selected on the basis of scoring more than 6 errors at the initial examination and were followed for two years (Kleban, Lawton, Brody and Moss, 1976). In predicting the status five months after admission to a geriatric service in 36 consecutive admissions, Neiditch and White (1976), calculated that the MSQ improved the accuracy of prediction over that predicated on base rates by 42 percent.

*Levels of Disability.*   In a study comparing activities of daily living with dementia scores, Liisa Ferm (1974), used Isaacs and Walkey's (Isaacs and Walkey, 1964) MSQ analog test of dementia in a modified version. One hundred and twenty-four patients in psychogeriatric wards of a geriatric hospital in Scandinavia were examined and activity and dementia scores were made independently. The patient's observed ability to correctly orient herself within the hospital correlated highly (.76) with the MSQ analog score. Ability to communicate (express needs and follow orders) and recognition of others also correlated highly with the MSQ analog score. In fact, apart from sleep disturbance and

**Table 28–1**  A Comparison of the MSQ and Similar Scales

| MENTAL STATUS QUESTIONNAIRE (MSQ) | DISORIENTATION FACTOR FROM A DEMENTIA RATING SCALE | SHORT PORTABLE MENTAL STATUS QUESTIONNAIRE (SPMSQ) | THE ORIENTATION TEST | A SIMPLIFIED MSQ | AN ABBREVIATED MENTAL TEST SCORE | CLIFTON ASSESSMENT SCHEDULE: INF/ ORIEN SECT |
|---|---|---|---|---|---|---|
| COMMON ITEMS | | | | | | |
| 1. What is the name of this place? | Where are you now? Are you in a school, a church, a hospital, or a house? | What is the name of this place? | What is the name of this place? What is the name of the ward you are on? | What is the name of this place? | Name of hospital? | Hospital/Address? Ward/Place? City? |
| 2. Where is it located? (address) | | What is your street address? OR What is your telephone number? | | | | |
| 3. What is today's date? | What is the day of the week? | What is the date today? What day of the week is it? | What day is it? | What day is it? | | Day? |
| 4. What is the month now? | What is the month? | | What month is it? | What month is it? | | Month? |
| 5. What is the year? | What is the year? | | What year is it? | What year is it? | Year? | Year? |
| 6. How old are you now? | Disorientation to age (error of at least 5 years) | How old are you? | How old are you? | What age are you? (error more than 1 year) | Age? | Age? |
| 7. When were you born (month)? | | When were you born? | | In what month is your birthday? | Date of birth? | Date of birth? |
| 8. When were you born (year)? | | | | In what year were you born? | | |
| 9. Who is the President of the United States? | | Who is the President of the United States now? | | | Name of present monarch? | Prime Minister? U.S. President? |
| 10. Who was the President before him? | | Who was the President before him? | | | | |
| ITEMS NOT HELD IN COMMON | | | | | | |
| | What is the time of day (morning, afternoon, or evening)? Inability to find bathroom Wandering Disorientation to people: Inability to distinguish patients from staff | What was your mother's maiden name? Subtract 3 from 20 and keep subtracting 3 from each new number all the way down | What time is it? What were you doing before coming to this room? What is my name? (as given at beginning of the interview) What did you have for breakfast/lunch? When did you last have a visitor? | What time is it? (error more than 1 hour) How long have you been here? (error more than 25%) | Time to nearest hour? Address given and recall at end of test Year of 1st World War Count backwards 20 - 1 Recognition of two persons | Name? Color of British Flag? |
| AUTHORS | | | | | | |
| Kahn, R. et al. (1961) Kahn, R. et. al. (1960) | Lawson, J. S. et al. (1977) | Pfeiffer, E. (1975) | Irving, G. et al. (1970) | Isaacs, B., & Walkey, F. (1963) | Hodkinson, H. et al. (1972) | Patie, A. H., and Gilleard, C. J. (1975) |

noisy behavior, all other behaviors measured had positive correlations with the MSQ analog score.

Insofar as inferences about progression can be made from the cross-sectional data in the Ferm study reported above, it would appear that as the MSQ analog scores get worse the patient first loses the capacity to maintain usual hobbies, then fails to participate spontaneously in group activities; the next stage in deterioration is loss of the ability to wash and dress; then orientation, recognition of persons, communication and control of the bladder and bowels is lost; finally the ability to eat and to move disintegrates when the MSQ concept scores reach their maximum levels of severity.

One can therefore gauge to a fair extent the level of nursing needs from the MSQ score, all other factors being equal. The presence of physical handicaps will of course alter the relationship between the MSQ score and the disability; so may the specific characteristics of the quality and type of care in an institution. The effect of such intervening variables is an important area of research. Nevertheless, there appears to be a basic orderliness in the sequence of abilities which are lost as the dementing process steadily advances and the MSQ scores get worse.

Wilson, Grant, Witney and Kerridge (1973), selected for study 100 female geriatric patients who were "not unduly impeded by blindness, deafness, dysphasia, apraxia, paralysis, sensory loss, arthritis or general debility," though they did have multiple physical problems and about half used walking aids. Several simple tests of intellectual function were used including serial 7s, proverb interpretation and the MSQ. Occupational therapists independently assessed the patient's capacity to carry out a variety of activities of daily living (ADL) tasks (household tasks and self-care activities) in a standard workshop. The MSQ was found to be the test that correlated best with ADL capacity of the patient. Those who made five or fewer errors on the MSQ almost invariably did well on the ADL tasks. Those who made six or more errors frequently but not always did poorly on ADL. Levels of depression or anxiety had no bearing on ADL performance. In these patients it was the cognitive impairment measured by the MSQ that was the main impediment to performance on ADL. The authors speculate that some patients with poor MSQ scores can nevertheless do well on the ADL because they were drawing on a reservoir of trained competence. Thus, those with poor MSQ scores should be carefully tested for ADL incapacity before, for instance, discharge plans are drawn up. However, those with good MSQ scores did not need elaborate ADL tests

unless they had a physical condition that might be incapacitating.

*Neurological Status.*   The MSQ also correlates highly with classification based on electroencephalography ($x^2 = 20.6$, p< .001) according to Irving, Robinson and McAdam (1970).

Roth (1971) points out that there is a close relationship between cognitive functioning and the histological changes associated with senile dementia (plaques and neurofibrillary tangles). Roth suggested that the relationship between cognitive impairment and the neuropathology of senile dementia can only be convincingly demonstrated by quantitative measure of both impairment and pathology. In the series of studies along these lines that Roth and his colleagues have conducted, the quantitative measure of pathology is primarily the number of plaques per unit area in samples of cerebral cortex taken at post mortem from the frontal, occipital, temporal and parietal lobes; a technique shown to have very high reliability. The measure of the severity of the cognitive impairment was, for the purpose of our present discussion, "scores allocated for the patient's performance in a number of simple psychological tests for orientation, recent memory, remote memory and concentration." These tests are MSQ analogs.

Patients from psychiatric, geriatric and general hospital wards were studied (cases with any signs of an ischemic lesion being excluded) and results in 60 subjects were reported by Roth, Tomlinson and Blessed in 1967. The correlation between MSQ analog score and mean plaque count was found to be .591 (p<.001) and when acute confusional states were eliminated the correlation rose to .626. The correlation between plaque counts and a measure of social incompetence (in personal, domestic and social activities) was even higher (.77) than for the MSQ score. For both types of measures of cognitive performance the correlation with plaque counts was significant except in the most severely demented subjects.

Roth (1971), adds that a threshold effect may exist with respect to the intensity of neuropathological change. Although there is a continuum of pathological levels it is only above a certain threshold that the organic brain syndrome becomes diagnosable and the MSQ scores begin to show abnormal levels.

*Comparisons with Other Measures.*   It appears from the data given above that the MSQ and its analogs are valid tests of organic brain syndrome in that they correlate highly with clinical diagnosis, are predictive of the course of illness which would be expected in most cases of chronic organic brain syndrome, and relate to biological indices of degenerative brain change. There are other psychological and laboratory tests that do the same and the question arises as to whether these other tests give different results than do the MSQ or its analogs and whether they are more or less accurate. Irving, Robinson and McAdam (1970), found that the MSQ analog Orientation Test agreed with clinical diagnosis in the assignment of cases to categories of functional or organic brain syndrome in about the same proportion of cases as did the Progressive Matrices (Raven, 1938), Face-Hand Test (Fink, Green and Bender, 1952) and Names Learning Test; and all of those tests did better than the Paired Associate Learning Test (Inglis, 1959). Haglund and Schuckit (1976), carried out a regression analysis of the (MSQ analog) Short Portable Mental Status Questionnaire or SPMSQ, Face-Hand Test and Memory for Designs Test (Graham and Kendall, 1960) (as well as the MSQ in its old 31 item version but which will be ignored because the SPMSQ is closer to the final version of the MSQ); by far the largest portion of variance was explained by the SPMSQ and the other two tests added little. Lawson, Rodenburg and Dykes (1977), factor analyzed their (MSQ analog) Dementia Rating Scale and found that the Disorientation factor was more highly discriminating between functional and organic brain syndrome groups than were the factors of Activities of Daily Living, Affective Lability and Communication Disorder. Birkett and Boltuch (1977), using the (MSQ analog) Maudsley Tests of Sensorium were able to correctly classify cases as often as with Kendall's Memory for Design. Pattie and Gilleard (1976), examined the power of diagnostic discrimination of the three sections of the Clifton Assessment Schedule and of the Stockton Geriatric Rating Scale, and concluded that the (MSQ analog) Information/Orientation questions "offered the best diagnostic classification for the individual case."

Wilson and Brass (1973) compared the MSQ with serial 7 subtraction, cash calculations, digit span retention forward and backwards and proverb interpretation in a study of the elderly in domiciliary consultation. The MSQ was completed at a higher rate (207 out of 230 cases) than the other tests. Furthermore, the MSQ correlated with a dementia rating made by a physician more strongly (.82) than the other tests or combination of tests with the exception of the combination of MSQ with Reverse Digit Span (.86). The latter result might have been produced by chance according to the

authors. Lloyd-Evans, Brocklehurst and Palmer (1978) found the MSQ to be significantly and highly correlated with the object-naming and span tests, orientation test and set test; they conclude "this confirms the MSQ as a particularly satisfactory single test for use in drug trials . . .".

Not only in relation to diagnostic discrimination but also in predicting outcome, the MSQ compares favorably with other tests. The (MSQ analog) orientation and memory sections of the Brief Psychiatric Rating Scale and the Modified Minimal Social Behavior Scale predicted outcome of hospitalization at five months better than all the other sections of these scales, or the Depression Status Inventory, Clinical Global Impressions, and all the sections of the Geriatric Rating Scale with the exception of the rating of incontinence (Neiditch and White, 1976).

*Limitations.* When the MSQ results conflict with clinical judgments the clinician will correctly back the clinical rather than psychometric result (Denham, 1978). This will apply especially to minor or early states of dementia or where difficulties in administration or understanding by the patient exist, or in the presence of depression. The clinician will also, of course, need to pursue the diagnosis of any cognitive impairment which is uncovered by the MSQ. The MSQ relates to the degree of brain failure, regardless of cause (Lloyd-Evans, Brocklehurst and Palmer, 1978).

*Place in a battery of tests.* The trend of this discussion so far has been to suggest that the MSQ or its analogs are the first choice as a practical, clinical aid to the assessment of organic brain syndrome. This leaves open the question of what additional tests can usefully be employed for this purpose. In Haglund and Schuckit's study (1976), the variance in clinical diagnosis was accounted for largely by the MSQ analog SPMSQ (40 percent) while the Face-Hand Test and the Memory for Designs Test added less than 5 percent additional explained variance. On the other hand, Neiditch and White (1976), applied the lamba statistic to short-term prediction of the outcome of hospitalization of elderly subjects and determined that whereas the improvement of prediction over use of base rates was 42 percent for MSQ and 37 percent for a measure of incontinence taken separately, the use of the two measures together improved over base rate prediction by 75 percent.

Unfortunately, the usual method of analysis employed for comparing the effectiveness of psychological tests in the elderly is to examine the relative predictive or discriminant power of each test in relation to the other tests. Rarely does one find that multiple regression analysis has been applied; so that there remains uncertainty as to the contribution of each test to the predictive or discriminant power of the test battery as a whole. Thus one must base a conclusion on the value of test batteries on relatively little evidence. It is possible that longer or more extensive testing might be more sensitive to minor changes in cognitive states (Silver, 1978). However, a tentative suggestion is that for most purposes the MSQ or its analogs provide the *majority* of information to be gained from available psychological tests with respect to assessing cognitive impairment as a basis for the detection of organic brain syndrome, the prediction of the outcome of the syndrome and the monitoring of the course of cognitive impairment over time.

It is regrettable that so many variations on the theme of the MSQ exist. As Seltzer (1975) put it, after examining a wide range of 1968 research publications in gerontology and geriatrics, "a lack of comparability in . . . . methods of measuring has resulted in our being able to say little which is definitive about age related changes."

## DEPRESSION

The term depression is applied to a wide variety of concepts both in professional and lay usage. It may refer to a serious clinical disorder, to a normal variation in mood or to a persistent state of demoralization. Depression as a serious clinical disorder may refer to a symptom of abnormal mood, to a syndrome or pattern of symptoms associated with a disturbance in mood (even sometimes with the abnormal mood concealed); or to a specific disorder such as minor or major affective disorder, or unipolar or bipolar depression, with a characteristic course, treatment and assumed etiology. The distinction between these conditions may require skilled differential diagnosis. In this section, however, we are concerned only with depression as a final common pathway and for this purpose it is necessary to address two concepts in particular: the syndrome of depression and of demoralization.

In general, the depression syndrome when fully developed consists of pervasively negative changes in mood, self-image and evaluation of the personal past and future; somatic symptoms and changes in physiological behavior patterns; and distortions of perception and thinking consistent with a depressive viewpoint. Demoralization may refer to attitudes of alienation, dissatisfaction or despair bearing upon the person's membership of a low status group, location in a deprived situation,

or loss of health and power; the concept includes a lack of well-being, but does not characteristically include somatic or biological symptoms nor perceptual or thinking distortions. Lawton (1972), defines the concept of morale in similar terms (but from a positive viewpoint). Pierce and Clark (1973), cluster analyzed responses from 435 elderly subjects and concluded that the clusters bearing most closely on the concept of morale were characterized by three aspects: (1) satisfaction with one's life, (2) composure, and (3) anticipation of the future.

The depression syndrome indicates a state that requires careful clinical appraisal to determine the need for treatment, frequently along the lines of the medical approach. Genetic, biochemical and neurophysiological models have been usefully applied to understanding the etiology and treatment of conditions giving rise to the depressive syndrome (see van Praag, 1977). This is in obvious contrast to the situation with normal mood variation and, less obviously, to the approach to understanding and alleviating demoralization. In the latter case socio-ecological models and approaches appear more useful (Carp, 1975).

The features of the syndrome of depression have been fairly well mapped out with the result that instruments for assessing this syndrome now have a great deal in common with each other. Little has been added over the past two decades to the universe of items selected by Beck, Ward, Mendelson, Mock and Erbaugh in 1961 for their assessment inventory. Nevertheless, the number of instruments for assessing depression have proliferated. Salzman, Kochansky, Shader and Cronin (1972) reviewed mood scales for geriatric subjects in psychopharmacological research and despite this restricted focus and fairly stringent standards of suitability they made favorable comments on no less than eleven depression inventories. Among the scales designed specifically for this syndrome and shown to be useful with older populations, the Zung Self-Rating Depression Scale (Zung, 1965, 1967) ranks with the best and most practical (within the limitations of a self-administered test).

Salzman, Kochansky, Shader and Cronin (1972) reviewed mood scales suitable for geriatric subjects in psychopharmacological research. In addition to the Zung scale, they comment favorably on the following depression inventories: Hamilton Rating for Depression (Hamilton, 1960); Beck Depression Inventory (Beck, Ward, Mendelson, Mock and Erbaugh, 1961); Depressive Scale (Cutler and Kurland, 1961); Psychiatric Judgment of Depression Scale (Overall, Hollister, Pokorny, Casey and Katz, 1962); Longitudinal Observation of Behavior (Bunney and Hamburg, 1963); Depression Rating Scale (Overall, Hollister and Meyer, 1964); Depression Adjective Checklist (Lubin, 1965); NIMH Collaborative Depression Mood Scale (Raskin, 1965; SAD-GLAD (Simpson, Hackett and Kline, 1966); and the Dynamic Depression Scale (Hunt, Singer and Cobb, 1967). Subsequent to that review the Geriatric Mental State Interview was published (Gurland, Copeland, Sharpe and Kelleher, 1976) and contains a depression scale. The content of many of these scales appears similar and this impression is confirmed by cross-correlation studies and comparison of their factorial structure (Zung, 1965; Levitt and Lubin, 1975; Bailey and Coppen, 1976).

Those scales with content similar to the Zung Scale tend to rely on the self-report of the subject, to be state rather than trait measures, and have better than adequate levels of reliability. Where they chiefly differ is in the manner of administration (by a clinician, by structured interview, by presentation to the subject or by self-administration), the length of the interview, whether the responses are dichotomized or scaled, whether the questions are balanced or not for number of negatively and positively oriented items, whether or not the depression scale is part of a multi-dimensional instrument, and in the number of factors that have been extracted from data collected with that instrument.

The Zung Scale is self-administered, brief, balanced for positive and negative responses, state rather than trait related, and has a four point scale of severity for each item. It covers a wide variety of symptoms in depression but is necessarily not as inclusive as longer scales. Where the rater administered test is desired or a self-administered test is not within the subject's capacity (e.g. because of frailty, perceptual problems or lack of sophistication) the depression scale of the Geriatric Mental State Interview, a semi-structured technique, can be used or reliance can be placed on information gathered from nurses' observations as in the Bunney and Hamburg (1963) method.

For the purpose of present day classification of depression a scale should contain at least items bearing upon the general factor areas of depressed mood, physiological or somatic symptoms of depression (e.g. appetite and sleep disturbance), anxiety, motor retardation and irritability. In addition, classification of depressive disorders requires more than a description of the current depressive symptoms; a history of the symptoms of mania, previous episodes of mental illness, the presence of physical illness, family history, age of

onset, and evidence of a preceding stress must all be taken into account. The depression scale may serve as a screening test to detect possible cases of serious depression, or for estimating the prevalence and associations of depression in a population, or for evaluating response to a therapeutic regimen; but for diagnosis the depression scale itself does not provide sufficient information.

The accuracy with which these depression scales can reflect the presence or severity of depression is quite impressive. In an early study by Beck, Ward, Mendelson, Mock and Erbaugh (1961), it was shown that a cutting score established for the Depression Inventory on one series of patients was able to distinguish in another series of patients between categories of 'no depression' and 'severe depression' as independently assessed by clinicians with an agreement rate of 91 percent between clinical and inventory classification.

The depression scales described above have many items with common content and are generally descriptive of the clinical syndrome of depression. There are, however, other scales which (1) reflect depression without asking directly about symptoms or (2) are indicative of depression as a (persistent) trait rather than a (temporary) state. In the first domain occur tests in which the subject selects from a list of adjectives those which are most syntonic with his present mood (for example, the Depression Adjective Checklist of Lubin, 1965). In the second domain are tests which are constructed to examine more or less persistent attitudes towards one's life situation.

Lubin (Levitt and Lubin, 1975) reports that his DACL Scale correlates significantly at the 1 percent level (.43 to .63) with the three factors of the Zung Scale when tested on groups of patients and normals. The DACL also correlates .5 to .6 with the D Scale of the MMPI and the Beck Depression Inventory.

Demoralization syndromes are measured by such instruments as the Life Satisfaction Index (Neugarten, Havighurst and Tobin, 1961), and Philadelphia Geriatric Center Morale Scale (Lawton, 1975), which tap attitudes to the quality of the past, present, and future phases of the person's life; the Affect Balance Scale (Bradburn, 1969) which focuses on negative and positive mood; or the Self-Concept Scale of Schwartz and Tangri (Robinson and Shaver, 1973). The qualities covered include interest, rewards, happiness, energy, self-respect and other satisfactions. Life satisfaction has been found to be influenced by level of income (Chatfield, 1977), developmental task accomplishment (Kurtz and Wolk, 1975), family relationships (Duval, 1971), occupational role (Miller, 1965), involvement in activities (Cutler, 1973), self-perception of health (Edwards and Klemack, 1973), self-image (Hulicka, Morganti and Cataldo, 1975) and locus of control (Reid, Haas and Hawkins, 1977) among other factors.

The relationship between the various measures of the quality of life was examined further by Lohmann (1977). The following frequently used instruments were applied to 259 subjects aged 60 years and over: the Cavan Adjustment Scale (Cavan, Burgess and Havighurst, 1949), the Kutner Morale Scale (Kutner, Fanshel, Togo and Langner, 1956), the Dean Scale (Cumming, Dean and Newell, 1958), the Life Satisfaction Indexes A and B (Neugarten, Havighurst and Tobin, 1961), and the Philadelphia Geriatric Center Morale Scale (Lawton, 1972). Various modifications of these instruments were also utilized. The modifications correlated very highly with their originals. The lowest correlations were obtained with a global question on satisfaction with life but there was a high level of correlation among most of the other pairs of measures. The author concludes that many of these measures are directed toward a common underlying construct.

The majority of instruments designed to assess demoralization require a fairly high level of understanding and cooperation from the patient. An exception is the Morale Inventory developed by Maroney, Gurel and Davis (1969), and modified by Watson (1976), and which is suitable for use with nursing home patients, many of whom may have intellectual impairment. It is completed by a rater during a semistructured interview and the validity of the patient's responses is judged by the rater. The content covers satisfactions or dissatisfactions with the nursing home environment, staff and treatment. This instrument has been shown by Watson (1976) to be sensitive to changes in the outlook of geriatric patients when placed in outpatient rather than inpatient settings.

Direct comparisons of scales aimed at assessing morale with those aimed at the depression syndrome show conceptual overlap between these domains. Morris, Wolf and Klerman (1975), administered a morale inventory (the Philadelphia Geriatric Center Morale Scale or PGCMS) and two depression inventories (including the Zung Self-Rating Depression Scale) to 120 state hospital patients with a mean age of 53 years. They found 'considerable informational or conceptual overlap' between the morale and the depression scales. Independent components were, in the Zung scale, the items representing Self-satisfaction (subjective estimates of appetite, thinking, efficiency, opti-

mism, decisiveness, usefulness, interest and enjoyment), and, in the PGCMS, the items representing Life Progression (subjective opinion that things get worse with age, less pep this year, bothered by little things more this year, less useful with age, life isn't worth living, less happy than when young). The remaining items were mathematically similar and focused on Clinical Depression (subjective feeling of being a failure, causing suffering or harm to others, deserving of punishment, guilty, distant or isolated from people, losing mind, fearful, more angry than before, life is hard, downhearted and blue, crying spells or feeling like crying, restlessness, and others would be better off if subject were dead).

Bloom (1975), expressed his view, in an editorial, that quality of life measures are of unsatisfactory validity in terms of both what they measure and what they predict. Insofar as the measures of morale, life satisfaction or adjustment overlap with those of the depression syndrome, efforts at separation of the demoralization and depression concepts would seem necessary. Gurland (1976), showed that the age specific distribution of the prevalence of the clinical type of depression syndrome is diametrically opposed to the distribution for depression as a symptom or attitude. The latter aspects of depression are akin to the concepts measured by the quality of life scales. Thus there is epidemiological as well as clinical evidence that depression and demoralization are distinctly different conditions. For the assessment of mental health it is important to further refine the distinction between depression and demoralization because they have presumably different modes of presentation, priorities for health services, remedies and etiologies.

## DEPENDENCE

Dependence is here taken to mean the need for personal intervention by another in order to sustain life and maintain living arrangements. Dependence on another is regarded as excessive when it is above the norm for a healthy adult. By this definition excessive dependence may arise in an old person for mental health reasons (e.g., cognitive impairment, disorder of reasoning or volition, preoccupation by distress or troubling thoughts, or feelings of insecurity and powerlessness) but also for reasons of physical ill-health or the frailty of old age. Dependence is thus the final common pathway of several mental and non-mental disorders. Of the mental disorders, senile dementia of the Alzheimer type is the most common cause of dependence in old age.

The importance of assessing dependence is that it is a pivotal concept with respect to the old person's capacity to remain in the community or his need for placement at a specific level of care within an institution. The degree of dependence will heavily influence services required by the patient and thus the cost of home or institutional care, whether in the form of public or private payments or in terms of the sacrifices made by the supportive care-givers. The degree of dependence is also an indicator of the severity of the causal mental disorder and changes in dependence can be used to plot the course of the underlying disorder. Finally, there is a high correlation between the presence of dependence and of depression (Gurland, Dean, Gurland and Cook, 1978).

The major determinant of dependence is inability to carry out certain basic self-care tasks or to fulfill the instrumental roles required for subsistence in the community. The prime assessment instruments in this area are the Index of Independence in Activities of Daily Living (ADL) developed by Katz (Katz, Ford, Moscowitz, Jackson and Jaffe, 1963; Katz and Akpom, 1976), and the Instrumental Activities of Daily Living Scale (IADL) developed by Lawton and Brody (1969).

The Index of ADL assesses performance in bathing, dressing, toileting, transfer, continence and feeding. Each function is carefully defined as is the type of assistance identifying dependence in that area of function. These functions are hierarchically related with increasing dependence successively involving the functions in the order listed above. A seven point Index of Independence is constructed based on the number and type of functions impaired.

The Instrumental ADL Scale assesses ability to telephone, shop, prepare food, keep house, do laundry, use transportation, manage medication and handle finances. The rating of each task is based on the degree of success in completing the task and the amount of assistance required.

Both the ADL and IADL have been shown to be valid and reliable as described in the papers cited above. Judging by the results obtained by Lawton and Brody (1969), between the IADL and an ADL analog (the Physical Self-Maintenance Scale; Lawton and Brody, 1969), the correlation between the IADL and ADL is about .61.

There are a vast number of scales and multidimensional instruments that incorporate modified versions of the ADL and IADL. There are none that have shown any advantage over the versions described above. Some of the modified versions reintroduce functions (such as mobility, walking, stair-climbing) that were tested and dropped

because they were found psychometrically unsatisfactory in developing the original scales.

The ADL and IADL and its variants are generally completed by a trained social worker or nurse who questions the patient and informants or observes the patient directly over an extended period of time. There are some drawbacks to this system of data collection. Informants who are staff members may vary in the accuracy of their reporting and thus bias comparisons between different institutions; and patients may receive assistance because the staff or family members are overprotective or the patient is undermotivated rather than because the patient is impaired in the capacity to fulfill the tasks. Where it is desirable to obtain a direct assessment of the patient's capacities, an assessment instrument such as the Performance Test of Activities of Daily Living or PADL (Kuriansky and Gurland, 1976), may be used. The PADL consists of a 20 minute test in which the patient is given 16 tasks within the ADL-IADL scope. Errors and omissions in completing the tasks are scored. The PADL scores have been shown to correlate with the physical health, mental status and outcome of hospitalization of psychogeriatric patients; while informant and patient reports within the ADL-IADL scope correlated less well with the above criteria.

For the purposes of planning and monitoring the delivery of supportive services to the dependent elderly it is useful to assess dependency not only along the ADL-IADL parameter but also in terms of the amount and type of services required. A two-dimensional assessment based on 5 levels of skill and 5 levels of hours of service delivered has been recently presented by Gurland and his colleagues (Gurland, Dean, Gurland and Cook, 1978). The scores obtained on this assessment grid can be converted to a cost equivalent by attaching the hourly rate of pay for a given level of skill.

There is no clear-cut and objective way to assess the degree to which overprotectiveness of others, institutional policy, poor motivation of the patient or emotional needs contribute to a given level of observed dependency. Mental health assessment of such issues as these is sometimes indistinguishable from treatment since the clinician may proceed to treat the patient on the basis of a clinical hypothesis and perhaps an emotional impediment to independence and the hypothesis will be to some extent tested by the patient's response to treatment. Furthermore, some clinicians may regard dependency as an adaptation of the aging person to diminished mastery over sources of gratification and may encourage dependency in a therapeutic relationship as a means of aiding adaptation (Goldfarb, 1977). Therefore, nothing in this section on dependency should be taken to mean that a full assessment of its mental health implications can be accomplished by resorting to ADL-IADL measures. The latter are the backbone but not the whole of assessment of excess dependency.

## DISRUPTIVE, BIZARRE AND DANGEROUS BEHAVIORS

There is a cluster of behaviors which results from a variety of mental or physical disorders and which is characterized by a marked rejecting, suppressive or supportive response from significant others, health professionals or society. This cluster consists mainly of disruptive, bizarre or dangerous behaviors. These behaviors often precipitate admission of the old person into acute care when they arise de novo or after a long symptom free period; or into a long term care facility if they are added to a chronic mental disorder. Particularly in institutions, these behaviors account for a substantial proportion of the major psychotropic medications which are administered. Where there is not an immediate response to medication, this cluster of behaviors may make heavy demands upon the staff time and be upsetting to staff, family and other residents of the institution alike. Thus the assessment of this cluster of behaviors is crucial, not only because of diagnostic implications, but because they often call for important management decisions.

The most common disruptive behaviors in geriatric subjects include shouting, perseverative exclamations, wandering, messy or unkempt manners, incontinence of urine and feces, hoarding and stealing, destroying objects, negativistic and uncooperative reactions and indecent behavior or advances. There are many rating scales which include items for these disruptive behaviors, such as the NOSIE (Honigfeld and Klett, 1965), or the Plutchik Geriatric Rating Scale (Plutchik, Conte, Lieverman, Bakur, Grossman and Lehrman, 1970). Such scales are useful for evaluating the effects of treatment. However, for making management decisions about treatment, a very detailed assessment of a disruptive behavior is required in order to counterbalance the common tendency to suppress annoying symptoms without adequately examining their cause. Several of the behaviors listed here may result from interpersonal conflicts or misunderstandings between patient and staff; some may result from acute confusional states or undetected physical defects; and some may be reinforced unwittingly by the responses of the supportive personnel. Urinary incontinence, for example, may be precipitated by diuretics, bladder infections, pro-

lapse of the bladder wall, sedation or polyuria; a careful analysis of the type of incontinence and associated symptoms or laboratory findings will be helpful in determining the cause. Similarly, in the case of fecal incontinence, a distinction must be drawn between incontinence resulting from the patient's disorientation and that resulting from, or aggravated by, fecal impaction, diarrhea, immobility, peripheral neurological disorder, and a poor match between toilet schedules and natural bowel rhythms.

Bizarre behaviors include abnormal posturing, asocial speech or incoherence, reactions to, or expressions of, delusions and hallucinations, grimacing, inappropriate laughing, mutism and outlandish dress. These behaviors are usually more helpful for arriving at a diagnosis but less disturbing to others than are the disruptive behaviors. Fairly sophisticated mental state interviews such as the Present State Examination (PSE) (Wing, Birley, Cooper, Graham and Isaacs, 1967), and its modification, the Geriatric Mental State (GMS) interview (Gurland, Copeland, Sharpe and Kelleher, 1976), are needed to properly assess the mental health implications of the bizarre behaviors since such symptoms as delusions and hallucinations have specific qualities that help to identify the underlying mental disorder. For example, hallucinations with a depressive content would suggest an underlying depressive disorder, or with an inappropriate affect would suggest schizophrenia, while fleeting and changing hallucinations accompanied by anxiety would suggest an acute confusional state.

Dangerous behaviors most obviously include suicidal and homicidal impulses but also lighting fires, leaving gas taps on and taking unnecessary risks. The very high rate of suicide among depressives, those with physical illness, and elderly white males makes its assessment important in this age group. Whereas suicidal attempts can be generally assessed through informants and observation, the presence of suicidal impulses can only be adequately determined by routinely asking the appropriate questions. A clear distinction should be made between resignation to death, which is very common among the elderly, and an active desire to die which is ominous and should not be ignored.

It sometimes occurs that far-reaching actions are taken as a result of a report that an old person has exposed himself and others to danger, for example, by virtue of leaving a gas stove lit and unattended. It is sometimes taken for granted that this is a token of progressive dementing process. A full mental health assessment may prove its value by revealing in many cases that such behaviors are due to a reversible condition such as depression. The associations between, on the one hand, reports of poor concentration and attention or lapses of memory, and, on the other hand, the symptoms of clinical depression have been demonstrated by Gurland and his colleagues (Gurland, Fleiss, Goldberg, Sharpe, Copeland, Kelleher and Kellett, 1976), and others. It can also be borne in mind that normal healthy young adults may have similar lapses of attention without provoking much concern either on their part or in others. Thus a systematic examination of the mental state of the old person may equally show that an apparently dangerous act was a normal accidental lapse for that person.

## SOMATIC AND SEXUAL SYMPTOMS

Somatic symptoms are common among the elderly either as a result of physical illness, medication side-effects, aging changes or mental disorder. Among the latter are included the somatic symptoms of depression (e.g., sleep, appetite and weight disturbance, constipation, slowness and fatigue, and ill-defined aches and pains), of anxiety (e.g., palpitations, faintness, sweating, trembling and abdominal discomfort) and hypochondriasis (e.g., undue and maladaptive preoccupation with a real or imagined illness). In younger age groups where chronic physical illness is not frequent, or in a psychiatric setting from which patients with physical illness have been excluded, the presence of somatic symptoms without obvious cause is usually attributable to mental disorder. However, since about 80 percent of the general population of elderly persons have at least one chronic disorder, the origin of somatic symptoms is often difficult to discern in this age group even where clearcut mental disorder co-exists. Therefore the assessment of somatic symptoms which could possibly be due to mental disorder but could equally be due to physical disorder must always be conducted with great care in the old person.

Putting aside other diagnostic steps, which involve a full physical and mental examination and history, the assessment of the somatic symptom itself can be revealing. Difficulty in falling asleep accompanied by brooding thoughts while lying awake, or waking a couple of hours before the accustomed time in the morning, are generally attributable to mental disorder while wakefulness due to pain or discomfort, or waking several times at night to empty the bladder but being able to return to sleep are characteristic of physical disorder. Loss of weight secondary to loss of appetite but without nausea, pain or general debility is more likely to have a mental origin than is loss of weight without preceding loss of appetite which is strongly suggestive of a physical disorder. Faintness occurring when tired or under pressure, or accompanied by sighing over-breathing, and experienced as a sense of unsteadiness and a fear of collapse is often a mental symptom but if associated with a distinct impression that the body or the room is spinning, or if precipitated by rising quickly from the sitting position then a physical cause should be suspected. These examples serve to illustrate the manner of assessing somatic symptoms for their mental health implications in the elderly. The information derived in this way is often just as useful as that forthcoming from a physical examination and laboratory tests.

The assessment of somatic distress in the hypochondriacal patient can be viewed as part of the treatment of that condition. A thorough mental and physical evaluation followed by an immediate and understandable plan which does not threaten the dependency needs of the patient but reassures him or her about the non-progressive nature of the disorder is a good way to begin treatment.

Most mental health professionals will find themselves fairly comfortable with inquiry into somatic as well as mental symptoms. However, many still find it difficult to probe for sexual problems among elderly patients, or may believe that such problems have little relevance for the elderly. However, up till their middle 70s, the majority of elderly continue to have active and valued sexual lives and even beyond 80 an important minority remain sexually active. Depression, anxiety, non-specific stress and enforced abstinence may all compromise the sexual capacity of the older person and should be part of an assessment of any sexual problem. Assessment should also cover those parameters of sexual arousal expected to show changes with age (e.g., in the male, delayed excitement, reduced strength of orgasm and demand for ejaculation, more rapid resolution and lengthened refractory period; in the female, delayed excitement, reduced lubrication, heightened clitoral sensitivity), as well as the signs of overreaction to age changes as seen in psychological impotence or despair. In the absence of radical surgery or gross physical disease it is likely that sexual problems in the elderly arise from ignorance and anxieties about the normal age changes, failure to take simple remedies such as unhurried techniques or use of lubricants when necessary, self-fulfilling stereotypes or failure to develop alternative modes of gratification. These problems should be uncovered in routine mental health assessments.

## SOCIAL MALADJUSTMENT

The assessment of somatic distress and sexual problems, as examples of distress and impairment of function respectively, illustrates the recurring themes in assessment of distinguishing between normal age change, and physical and mental disorder. This was evident also in the assessments of cognitive impairment and excessive dependency on others. These distinctions are perhaps the most difficult to draw in assessing the mental health implications of adjustment or maladjustment in the elderly. Graney and Graney (1973), point out the difficulties in merely obtaining consensus on the conceptual domain of adjustment in the gerontological literature. The affective aspects of adjustment have been discussed from a mental health viewpoint in the section dealing with demoralization syndromes. The performance aspects have been partially covered under activities of daily living and also under sexual problems. However, there is an aspect of adjustment which requires particularly subtle assessment and has not yet been mentioned, namely the inappropriateness of a lifestyle, where inappropriate lifestyles are defined as those associated with the presence or risk of mental problems. Isolation as defined by Bennett (Granick and Nahemow, 1961), and disengagement by Cumming and Henry (1961), are germane to this issue.

Isolation is commonly regarded as mentally unhealthy because of an alleged high risk of depression, a vulnerability to the consequences of stress, or a tendency towards paranoid disorders among such persons. However, Townsend (1962), has shown that it is recent loss of significant others (desolation) not isolation that is associated with depression, while Bennett (Bennett and Nahemow, 1965), has clearly defined four types of isolates, one of which, the recent involuntary isolate, is at high risk for developing interpersonal difficulties but another type, the lifelong voluntary isolate, is able to deal effectively with other people. More recently Brown (Brown, Bhrolchain and Harris, 1975), and Lowenthal (Lowenthal and Chiriboga, 1973), have emphasized the critical role of a confidante in enabling a person to weather a stressful event. Thus, the presence or absence of isolation in the sense of numbers of contacts with others has little bearing on mental health unless the history and nature of the person's patterns of social relationships are carefully assessed.

The evolution of a narrowed range and depth of social relations and activities generally implied by the term disengagement has been the subject of well-aired controversy with respect to its mental health implications. Withdrawal from social contacts can be a sign of mental illness. However, it is the history of the development of disengagement that needs to be unravelled in order to determine whether it may signify vulnerability to, or the prodrome of, mental illness or neither. Features which are ominous it these respects are suddeness of onset, accompanying tiredness, irritability, loss of appetite, libidinal changes or increase of vague somatic symptoms, or evidence of overt mood disturbance or fearful suspicions.

## TEST BATTERIES

In certain circumstances it is useful to assemble a test battery or multidimensional instrument to assess patients or their disorders, for example in research or clinical investigations into the neuropsychological structure of dementia, or where sensitivity to fine changes in a patient's condition over time is important, or where comprehensive assessment of a wide variety of mental disorders and related problems is required.

Test batteries within the domain of cognitive impairment usually include tests to assess disorientation or memory impairment, e.g., MSQ or Kahn-Goldfarb (Kahn, Goldfarb, Pollack and Peck, 1960), Wechsler Memory Scale (Wechsler, 1955); motor-perceptual disability, e.g., Bender Gestalt (Bender, 1938); sensory discrimination, e.g., Face-Hand Test of Fink-Kahn (Fink, Green and Bender, 1952); difficulty with verbal new learning, e.g., Modified Word Learning Test (Walton and Black, 1957) or the Paired Associate Learning Test (Inglis, 1959); difficulty with nonverbal learning, e.g., Block Design Learning Test (Savage and Hall, 1973); delayed reaction time; altered attention, e.g., digit span and digits backwards; inaccuracy in speeded tests, e.g., Minnesota Rate of Manipulation Tests (Betts, 1946) or Trail Making Test of Reitan (Reitan, 1958); and diminution of general intelligence, e.g., Short WAIS (Britton and Savage, 1966). This partial list of test functions and examples indicates the extensive choice of psychological tests available in this area. An example of an assembled test battery shown to be suitable for psychopharmacological research in geriatrics is provided by the work of Branconnier and Cole (1978). They derived an overall Impairment Index from a battery which included tests for spatial orientation; concept formation; motor performance; memory (orientation, information, mental control, logical memory, digits total, visual reproductions, associated learning, perceptual trace, short-term memory); mood; secondary visual fields; figure-ground separation; and logical-grammatical relationship. Tests requiring more complex apparatus can be added such as those for short term memory and asymmetrical brain impairment (e.g., dichotic listening tasks) or for isolating defects of central brain processing (e.g., Disjunctive Reaction Time of Ferris, Crook, Sathananthan and Gershon, 1976).

## LABORATORY TESTS

Laboratory tests, as defined earlier in this chapter and excluding any tests dependent on a voluntary motor or verbal response from the subject, may be added to, or substituted for, the battery of psychological tests. They are strictly 'additional' when they are intended to identify conditions which can mimic, aggravate or precipitate mental disorder; for example, the wide repertoire of blood and urine tests that are essential in the investigation of actue confusional states. Laboratory tests are 'substitutive' when they are intended to detect evidence of the same brain dysfunctions targeted by psychological tests.

An important example of a substitutive laboratory test is electroencephalography which has been used for many years to reflect general brain impairment of the Alzheimer type by diffuse slow activity in the theta or delta range (Busse and Wang, 1965) and in the later stages by disorganization and sharp and slow wave complexes (Muller and Kral, 1967). Regional variations in EEG slow wave activity can be related to verbal or performance disabilities respectively. Muller (1978) finds that "despite a marked lability in its appearance which can be caused by various systemic influences, the geropsychiatric EEG is of great practical help in the diagnosis of Senile Alzheimer disorder." He also emphasizes its value for predicting survival (diffuse slowing is highly correlated with death within 5 years) and reflecting progress over time. Autopsy findings of Alzheimer's disease correlate significantly with abnormal EEG tracings. Unfortunately, systemic physical illness or drugs can confound the interpretation of EEG patterns. However, Verwoerdt (1976) concludes that "EEG changes are not pathognomic (of brain failure) and because of the wide variations among old persons of comparable age and health, a single EEG tracing has limited value." Much the same could be said of perhaps all currently available laboratory tests such as pneumoencephalography, echoencephalography, brain scan, angiograms and tests of cerebral blood flow. As tests additional to the psychological battery, they may reveal a localized lesion which is crucial to the diagnosis and management of the patient but as substitutive indicators of cognitive impairments where clinical and psychological testing is ambiguous they may be helpful but are often fallible and some of the procedures such as pneumoencephalogram and cerebral angiogram carry undesirable risks.

Recent developments in non-invasive techniques and in computer applications have given laboratory testing renewed potential for assessing brain dysfunction. Non-invasive techniques allow, for example, the estimation of cerebral blood flow by tracking the passage through the brain of a harmless radioactive labeled gas ($^{133}$Xenon) which is administered by inhalation (Obrist, Thompson, King and Wang, 1967). Echoencephalography is another example of a non-invasive technique relying on ultrasonic waves as the probe for exploring changes in brain structure. Computer methods of analyzing data from non-invasive exploration of the brain have been even more promising and two examples will be briefly mentioned: Computerized Tomography (Emiscan or CT-scan) and Neurometric Analysis.

The CT-scan relies on low voltage multiple radiographic exposures of the skull as the source of data which are then computer analyzed to reconstruct images of serial sections of the brain. Widening of the cortical sulci and dilation of the lateral ventricles as well as other features of brain atrophy can be identified.

Scores on the Crichton Geriatric Behavioral Rating Scale (Robinson, 1961) were found to correlate significantly with measures of ventricular dilation in the CT-scan on 66 elderly patients, 17 of whom were normal and the remainder of whom had varying degrees of dementia (Caird, 1977). However, overlap between the groups was considerable and the author concludes that it is still not clear whether the CT-scan is a research tool or a routine clinical procedure in dementia. The enhancement of CT-scanning by the addition of intravenous dyes, by inhalation of labeled gases and by proton emission techniques is likely to expand the contribution of this procedure to mental health assessment.

Neurometrics (John, Karmel, Corning, Easton, Brown, Ahn, John, Harmony, Prichep, Toro, Gerson, Bartlett, Thatcher, Kaye, Valdes and Schwartz, 1977) is the application of computer methods to the quantitative analysis of the EEG and sensory-evoked potentials in order to reveal subtle details of these tracings and to derive, through numerical taxonomy, distinctive electrophysiological profiles with implications for identification of cognitive dysfunction. The neurometric method of classification is claimed to be potentially more powerful for selecting treatment than psychological tests because it may distinguish different brain dysfunctions underlying similar psychological dysfunctions. John and his colleagues examined 60 cognitively impaired patients and 60 demographically matched normals over 60 years of age, excluding those with other neurological or physical disorders (Gerson, John, Koenig and Bartlett, 1976). They concluded that "normal and cognitively impaired elderly groups revealed marked neurometric differences not apparent in the conventional EEG, and showed a graded relation between abnormal neurometric indices and abnormal behavior, and these findings were replicated well in an independent sample."

## MULTIDIMENSIONAL INSTRUMENTS

Multidimensional assessment instruments, like test batteries, are constructed to measure a range of independent functions in an individual and produce a profile of levels of impairment of the various functions. Whereas test batteries usually refer to psychological and laboratory tests, multidimensional instruments are usually inventories of items dealing with self-report or observations of psychiatric, medical and social problems. The rationale for multidimensional assessment in the elderly is that the latter generally have a multiplicity of problems and that global measures of general ill-health do not provide the specificity required for many of the purposes of referral, clinical work, research, or policy and planning. The key issue obscured by global measures but illuminated by multidimensional assessment is the identification of which problems vary or are present together in a given treatment or casual context, and which are independent of each other.

Health service research is particularly dependent on multidimensional assessment because services are delivered not to disembodied problems but to people who have a multiplicity of problems. Similarly, the evaluation of drugs administered to the elderly in institutions is properly based on all the dimensions of behavior or feeling that affect the status and management of the patient and not only on the target dimension of the drug employed.

From the viewpoint of mental health, the dimensions of cognitive impairment, depression and dependence on others are crucial measurements since they tap the major mental disorders of old age and their consequences. In fact, in one form or another, these dimensions do constitute the bulk of items relevant to mental health in most multidimensional instruments. However, these three dimensions are only a small proportion of those which have been established to be derivable by factorial methods from data on mental health in the

elderly. For example, the data gathered by the Geriatric Mental State Schedule on hospitalized geriatric patients was resolvable into over a dozen dimensions within the domain of mental status alone (Gurland, Copeland, Sharpe and Kelleher, 1976); and that did not include dimensions which emerge from the history and course of the mental illness. Furthermore, within the domains of physical and social problems there are many dimensions of relevance to mental health. Thus the term multidimensional should be applied with reserve to an assessment instrument unless it sets out to be fairly exhaustive in scope.

For the purpose of determining mental health needs in a general population of elderly a multidimensional instrument should identify primarily those needs for which there is a potential service or treatment and should distinguish mental health needs from each other insofar as they require referral to different clinical settings or require different treatment approaches. Thus the instrument should allow recognition of at least the following conditions: psychiatric emergencies (e.g. suicide risk, lighting of fires), major affective disorders, minor affective disorders (acute and chronic), low morale, malignant dementia, benign dementia, acute confusional states, persistent paranoid states of late onset, chronic schizophrenia, anxiety states, alcohol and drug abuse, hypochondriasis, other neuroses, and specific management problems whether or not part of the above syndromes (e.g., sleep or appetite disturbance, withdrawal and apathy, wandering, incontinence, dependence). The multiple dimensions required for defining these conditions are to some extent self-evident and others will be surmised from descriptions of these conditions in this and other chapters in this handbook. The dimensions include those on depressed mood, vegetative signs of depression, elated mood, somatic concerns, autonomic signs of anxiety, suicidal feelings, lack of insight, somatic and grandiose delusions, delusions of control, auditory and visual hallucinations, incoherence, disorientation and memory disturbance, alcohol and drug intake and degrees of dependence on others. Also required are the dimensions of previous episodes, onset and course, and the presence of major stressors such as bereavement, relocation or serious physical illness. Finally, other dimensions relevant to serving need may be required such as current service utilization, chronicity of accompanying physical illness, medication interaction, the informal support system, finances, housing, transport and other environmental factors.

It might appear that the technology of the multidimensional approach to mental health assessment, as described here, is overwhelming.

However, it need not be overly difficult or costly either in data collection or in analysis and in any event the benefits of applied health service research are likely to be underwhelming without use of such technology. Interviewers without professional qualifications but with special training in assessment techniques can collect the data required to assess the required multiple dimensions. Computer programs and specified criteria are available for translating the dimensional data into the categories of the conditions nominated as relevant to the mental health services. The cost of data collection is in any event a small proportion of the resources wasted by operating or planning a mental health service without adequate data on the population which is served.

A large number of multidimensional assessment instruments have been constructed and used with geriatric populations. The following is a list of a few multidimensional instruments whose psychometric properties have been described: Sandoz Clinical Assessment-Geriatric or SCAG (Shader, Harmatz and Salzman, 1974), which is intended mainly for psychogeriatric pharmacological studies and covers 18 symptom areas relevant to senile dementia and depressive disorders; Patient Appraisal and Care Evaluation or PACE, from the HEW Office of Long Term Care, which covers physical functions, psychosocial problems, impairments (including decubitus ulcers, sensory-speech defects, dental problems, amputations and paralyses), medical risk status, care being received and sociodemographic status, and is particularly suited for use in long-term care facilities; Crichton Geriatric Behavioral Rating Scale (Robinson, 1961), aimed at monitoring treatment programs and covering 11 areas of behavior including orientation, self-care, mood and communication; London Psychogeriatric Rating Scale (Hersch, Kral and Palmer, 1978), with items in the areas of mental disorganization-confusion, physical disability, socially irritating behavior and disengagement, and reported to be predictive of diagnosis, outcome, placement, and response to treatment. Other widely used multidimensional instruments include the Stockton Geriatric Rating Scale (Meer and Baker, 1966) and the Physical and Mental Impairment of Function Evaluation or PAMIE Scale (Gurel, Linn, and Linn 1972). Two recent instruments developed for use with the community elderly, with semi-structured interview guides, are the Older American Resources and Services Program or OARS Multidimensional Functional Assessment Questionnaire (Pfeiffer, 1975b) and the Comprehensive Assessment and Referral Evaluation, or CARE (Gurland, Kuriansky, Sharpe, Simon, Stiller and Birkett, 1977). The CARE contains more information of relevance to psychiatric dimensions and diagnosis than the other multidimensional instruments mentioned above. A potential user should check not only the dimensions available from a given instrument but also the degree to which these dimensions are psychometrically sound (rather than ad hoc rational lists) and the manner of converting the dimensions into relevant typologies (e.g. the presence or absence of a given condition or need) or levels of severity. In addition, it is important to determine whether the interview guide, if any, flows in a way that will be acceptable and understandable to the subjects and will maintain the subject's interest through the quite lengthy interview required for adequate assessment.

## SPECIAL PURPOSE ASSESSMENT

Specific problems in assessment may require modifications of the general scheme of assessment. In this section we discuss problems that arise in relation to the use of mental health assessments for the purposes of screening, for use with populations that include very deteriorated as well as intact subjects, for determining positive mental health and in the determination of the need for surrogate management.

*Screening.* This term refers to the use of an assessment schedule to identify subjects likely to have positive (psychopathological) findings on a full mental health assessment and to exclude subjects likely to have negative findings. This kind of screening is often used on general populations of elderly persons, in high risk groups and in annual routine health examinations. Generally the rationale for use of a screen rather than a full mental health assessment is that the former is more economical and feasible to use on large numbers of subjects and can save the expense of the skilled professional and longer time required for full assessment. "A plan to use the services of trained interviewers to screen and separate into two classes (with and without apparent psychopathology) a large preliminary sample in order to conserve the time of the psychiatrist, by letting him test mainly cases that are almost surely afflicted with psychopathology, is appealing whenever the cost per case is much lower for the screening than for the psychiatric examination" (Deming, 1977).

According to Cochrane and Holland (1972), a screen, to be useful, must be simple and cheap to administer and interpret, acceptable to subjects both on initial examination and on repeat testing, sensitive (able to correctly identify the criterion positives) and specific (able to correctly identify the criterion negatives). Deming (1977), has pointed out that screening achieves the greatest cost reduction when the criterion disorder has a low prevalence, when the sensitivity and (especially) the specificity is high and where costs for the screen are greatly less than for the full examination. He emphasizes that the properties of the screen must be accurately known and "in the absence of sound information about screening.....it is perhaps best to use no screening at all."

Powell and Crombie (1974), constructed a screen intended to be used by a health visitor to detect a comprehensive set of problems in the elderly at home. Two hundred and sixty randomly selected persons over 70 years of age were screened, the psychiatric component being a series of questions on depression and anxiety and the Set Test of Isaacs and Akhtar (1972), for memory impairment. The criterion was the opinion of the family doctor and of a research geriatrician. The mental health ratings showed a sensitivity of 94 percent and a specificity of 97 percent. The refusal rate was 14 cases. The reliability of the screen in the hands of different health visitors was not established. The authors point out that it disclosed a number of cases whose needs were unknown to the family doctor.

Simon (1970), pointed out the value of screening for ensuring an appropriate fit between need and level of care whether at home or with respect to placement in various types of institutions. This, he believes, can integrate hospital and community resources and help to reduce rates of admission to institutions. He lists the key agencies, professionals and sites for screening including mobile screening units, clergymen, lawyers and law enforcement officials. In a study conducted by him and his colleagues on 164 subjects, 65 years and older, from institutional and community settings, they found that 15 items provided a 91 percent sensitivity and an 80 percent specificity for mental impairment. This compares quite well with the Savage-Britton 15-item incidence index for functional illness in the elderly; the latter index showed a 95 percent sensitivity and 81 percent specificity on the derivation sample and these figures were 88 percent and 86 percent respectively on the replication sample. Simon does not report a replication sample for his index.

From these data there appear to be some promising instruments developed for geriatric screening purposes.

*Deteriorated Cases.* Quite apart from the quite understandable refusal of some old persons to cooperate in a procedure aimed at assessing their mental health there is a further proportion who are unable to cooperate even with the best of intentions. For example, Isaacs and Walkey (1964), went to considerable pains to develop a battery of simple mental tests which would be suitable for the population of a geriatric hospital and yet "of the 522 patients who were offered the test, 117 were unable to complete it because of blindness, deafness, speech defect, physical handicap or illness." If this is the situation with tests it is clear that it is much worse with questionnaires involving self-report items on mood, thinking, and behavior. Certain laboratory-type tests (e.g. the Neurometric Analysis of John, 1977) attempt to reduce the degree of cooperation needed from the subject by resort to stimuli which are deliverable with minimum attention from the subject example, directly observable responses and analysis of evoked cortical responses. However, a common procedure is to limit a study to patients who can cooperate with the assessments or to limit the complexity and content of the assessment to the level suitable for the most deteriorated subjects. Another possibility, as yet not well explored, is the use of a basic test administerable to almost all subjects no matter how deteriorated (e.g. the Performance Test of Activities of Daily Living, Kuriansky and Gurland, 1976), and a more complex additional assessment for those capable of responding to detailed questioning. Such a system would, however, require a reliable and operational decision tree for determining the eligibility of subjects for the level of complexity of the test. For example, it is not known, though it is theoretically ascertainable, at what level of cognitive impairment a patient's response to questions about mood becomes unreliable or internally inconsistent. This and similar links in the assessment procedure do not yet exist.

*Positive Mental Health.*  The assessment of mental health, notwithstanding the implied emphasis, is usually explicitly an assessment of ill health. Yet the concept of positive mental health has been well established for many years (see Jahoda, 1958). Clausen (1969) specified some of the necessary areas for evaluating positive mental health in old age, namely, interpersonal relations, personal resourcefulness, control over life activities, and accuracy of self-perception. Dohrenwend, Egri and Mendelsohn (1971), working with a non-elderly population, have found that community subjects with psychopathology are less likely to be judged to be cases when they show signs of positive mental health. This is consistent with clinical lore that when disease processes can be quantified (for example, by the neuropathology of Alzheimer's dementia) the degree of resulting disability or illness behavior varies between different subjects in a way that is not entirely accounted for by the degree to which the disease has advanced; and positive mental health is considered to be one of the intervening variables accounting for the above imperfect correlation. In Zubin's (1976) theory of vulnerability, emphasis is placed on factors which alter the threshold for developing disease or illness in the face of stress and his concept of vulnerability explicates many important issues in its mirror image, positive mental health. Rehabilitation efforts in the chronic disorders of the elderly may be aided in an important manner by the positive mental health assets of the patient. Thus from a variety of viewpoints, positive mental health is an important quality to assess but an adequate technique for accomplishing this assessment has not yet been devised.

Ego psychology, work on aging capacity, life cycle longitudinal research, and studies on personality and heart disease or cancer prevalence have all contributed to knowledge about positive mental health. However, in the absence of a well accepted method for assessing positive mental health, the clinician will want to at least cover some of the relevant topic areas in an assessment, namely: levels of satisfaction, achievement and functioning in work, interpersonal relations, sex and intimacy; reactions and recovery in the face of past crises; intelligence and problem-solving ability; realistic but favorable and optimistic evaluations of present and future opportunities; energy levels; ability to comply with regimes either self-selected or medically instructed; warmth and charm; and the patient's valuation of the details of the full pageant of his own life.

*Surrogate Management.* The role of the mental health assessor in determining legal issues of competency is the subject of much skeptical debate (e.g. Bazelon, 1964; Wooton, 1968). The reliability of the mental health assessment in contributing to such decisions is at issue as is the primacy of the mental health expert in the decision-making process. With respect to the special case of deciding the need for surrogate management in the elderly, a full airing of the issues is provided by Alexander and Lewin (1972), in their monograph, "The Aged and the Need for Surrogate Management." Several of the points which follow on assessment are taken from their work (though the opinions expressed are this author's responsibility).

Surrogate management involves the appointment of a legal administrator to manage the subject's estate in the subject's own best interests within the law, when the subject is incapable of doing so because of mental incapacity. It is not the type of mental incapacity that is in question but its existence and its effects upon the subject's competence to manage ordinary business affairs. This legal process is vulnerable to abuse, therefore the mental health assessment should be as meticulous as possible. A clear causal line should be drawn between mental impairment, mental disability and incompetence in ordinary business affairs. The psychiatrist does not need to consider whether the level of incompetency meets the legal standards for incompetency. That is for the judicial authorities to do.

The establishing of mental impairment should be the most straightforward step for the psychiatrist in this role. Clearly, if mental impairment is sufficient to cause incompetence then it must be independently diagnosable and should not be inferred from the incompetence in question. Chronic organic brain syndrome and schizophrenia or paraphrenia will be the usual relevant mental impairments in the aged. Recourse to systematic techniques such as the Kahn-Goldfarb MSQ for cognitive impairment, and a structured interview for psychotic symptoms might give unequivocal results with or without other components of a test battery. If the results are dubious then clinical judgment must of course prevail but under those circumstances it is hard to see that a psychiatrist can proceed to give confident evidence of mental impairment; and without mental impairment, the next two steps of the decision process (disability and incompetence in business affairs) are not within the psychiatrist's specialist capacity. It is doubtful whether such issues as disability-incompetence due to old age or prolonged institutional residence are well understood by psychiatrists, and, if anyone, social gerontologists would seem better prepared than psychiatrists to explicate these areas.

If mental impairment is clearly present then the related disability may be systematically assessed by applying ADL-IADL measures; since informants may be biased, a directly observed performance measure is desirable. Difficulty in communicating should be carefully measured in all perceptual channels and a general physical, neurological and laboratory examination should be carried out so as to detect remediable types of cognitive impairment and specific neurological defects not involving reasoning or thought disorder and possibly responsive to rehabilitation with a return to an adequate level of competence in business affairs.

The final line of logic linking signs of incompetence to the conduct of ordinary business affairs should not be difficult at this stage. Problems principally arise when incompetence in business is taken as the point of departure for assessment on the assumption that if it exists it is a sign of mental impairment. This tautology leads to the abandonment of stringent criteria for diagnosis which are independent of the legal issues.

# CLASSIFICATION

## PURPOSES

Classification serves to summarize the data of assessment and relate them to what is already known about mental health and to what can be garnered by further research. It is true that the mental problems of an individual are to some extent unique and to that extent the origin and the treatment of that person's condition cannot be inferred from what is known about other individuals. However, to the extent that persons or their mental conditions can be placed in a category that reflects shared characteristics of importance to cause, course, control or cure, knowledge can be accumulated from the study of some of the persons in that category and applied to the benefit of the remainder of persons in that category.

## ATTRIBUTES OF DIAGNOSIS

Clinical diagnosis is a form of classification whose major purpose is to allow delivery of appropriate treatment. Thus, diagnosis should indicate something about the natural (untreated) course of a disorder, about the outcome of the disorder with existing treatments, about the origins of the disorder so that preventive treatments can be attempted or developed, and about the mechanisms producing the symptoms and disability associated with the disorder so that improved treatments can be found. Where diagnosis has these attributes, the recognition of a diagnosis in an individual or the plotting of its distribution in a population will promote optimal allocation of individual treatment, service development and research.

The classification of clinical psychiatric diagnosis in the elderly has many but not all of the attributes of the ideal system. Martin Roth and his colleagues (Roth, 1971, 1976), and others, have demonstrated characteristic contrasts in the natural course of senile dementia (progressive deterioration, markedly shortened life-expectancy, duration of stay in an institution of several years), acute confusional state (death or recovery within 6 months or so), affective disorder (high rate of spontaneous recovery, slightly increased mortality), and late onset paranoid disorders (chronicity but no reduction in life expectancy). The treated outcome of these conditions is generally, for senile dementia, little alteration in the progressive nature of the disorder though life expectancy may be increased by intensive care (Gruenberg, 1977), for acute confusional state a dramatic reduction in mortality and often a return to the pre-episode state of functioning, for affective disorder a recovery rate not dissimilar from that obtained with younger persons, and for late onset paraphrenia a satisfactory recovery rate provided treatment is maintained during the interval state. A specific treatment has not been established for senile dementia, but is distinct for the other conditions; medical approaches for the underlying condition in acute confusional states, antidepressants or ECT for the affective disorders and phenothiazines or related drugs for the paraphrenias. Origins and mechanisms, as far as can be judged by neuropathological evidence, are quite different between senile dementia, acute confusional states and the functional disorders (affective disorder and paraphrenia). There appear also to be neurochemical differences between affective disorder and paraphrenia. Genetic evidence supports the distinction between senile dementia, affective disorder and paraphrenia. A similar, but not necessarily as complete an argument could be made for other diagnoses in geriatric psychiatry: alcohol and drug abuse, unipolar and bipolar depression, major and minor affective disorder, early and late onset paranoid states, certain subtypes of dementia such as Jakob-Creuzfeldt disease, and some of the neuroses. These diagnoses can be as reliably made for older as for younger patients and convey a great deal of information relevant to clinical purposes.

The limitations of clinical diagnosis show up particularly outside the range of the kind of diagnoses mentioned above. For example, as yet not well established is the reliability of such diagnoses as arteriosclerotic as opposed to Alzheimer's dementia, the various types of personality disorder, hypochondriacal neurosis, reactive as opposed to endogenous depression; while certain other conventional diagnoses such as involutional melancholia have been discarded as not fulfilling the attributes of clinical diagnosis. Roth (1976) provides a thorough review of the diagnostic features of the psychiatric disorders of later life.

## DIMENSIONS

However, some dimensional characteristics of mental disorder have relevance for a specific aspect of treatment and are thus useful for describing a patient's condition even though these dimensions may not justify separate diagnostic categories: for example, retardation or agitation in depression, florid symptomatology or withdrawal in paranoid states, the medication response of blood relatives with disorder similar to the one the patient has, previous history of medication response, the course of the illness (speed of onset, rate of progress, continuity or intermittency of symptoms, etc.), reinforcement history or situational precipitants of symptoms and levels of neurotransmitter metabolites in the blood, CSF or urine. Similarly, certain background characteristics of the patient such as the basic personality of the individual, psychodynamic responses (predominant defense mechanisms, level of regression, ego strength, etc.), the level of functioning achieved prior to the onset of the illness, the general physical health of the patient, the capacity of the body to absorb and metabolize medications, the possibility of drug interactions, or the strength of the patient's supportive network may be helpful mainly in determining treatment while conveying little else about the attributes of clinical diagnosis.

## ITERATION

Diagnosis or other means of classification must also serve as a tool for the discovery of better treatments or prevention. In this respect, the more homogeneous and specific (with respect to any of the attributes of clinical diagnosis) the cases which fit a diagnostic category, the more useful it is likely to be for research purposes. For example, where a diagnostic group is homogeneous for prognosis the evaluation of response to a new treatment is made the easier; where homogeneous and specific for treatment response the search for the underlying mechanisms maintaining symptoms can be better focused. One way of increasing the chances that cases in a diagnostic category are homogeneous and specific with respect to a critical but unknown attribute (e.g. etiology) is to progressively adjust the diagnostic criteria until all known attributes are homogeneous (for example, course, symptoms, physiological behavior, treatment response, etc.). Serial adjustment of this kind has been dubbed the iterative technique (Sutton, 1973; Gurland, 1973).

## CRITERIA

Clinical diagnosis, whether used for the immediate purposes of selecting treatment, planning services, or communicating with other professionals, or for the more remote goals of discovering new treatments, is likely to be useful only if used reliably. Unreliability in clinical diagnosis (or any other form of classification relying on the same sources of information) can be apportioned to inconsistencies on the part of the patient or between patients in reporting or demonstrating symptoms and signs, or on the part of the clinician or between clinicians in eliciting, interpreting and classifying that information. The use of structured interviewing, or psychological and laboratory tests in controlling some of these inconsistencies has already been discussed. A recent innovation designed to reduce inconsistencies in classification is the systematizing of explicit criteria for diagnosis (Feighner, 1972), which technique will be incorporated into the official nomenclature (DSM-III) of the American Psychiatric Association. The inclusion and exclusion criteria set firm boundaries to the diagnostic categories unlike the diagnostic definitions in the previous nomenclature (DSM-II) which described the typical symptoms of each category but gave little guidance as to where to draw the line in admitting or excluding atypical cases. The categories in DSM-III are yet to be finalized and the extent to which its use will lead to more reliable diagnoses in clinical practice is yet to be established; to say nothing about the effect on the validity of diagnoses. However, it is important to emphasize that the criteria in DSM-III are based on the recognition of specific symptoms or symptom complexes (e.g. impairment in judgment, personality change, flight of ideas, delusions of being controlled) which might be the source of major variability between assessors.

The recognition of symptoms and the assignment of their cause to mental disorder is particularly difficult with the elderly because the norms for behavior in the elderly are not well known to many clinicians; the changes in the environment, social role and resources of the elderly affect the norms for their behavior; physical disease frequently coexists with mental disorder and produces symptoms which are often hard to distinguish from those of mental disorder; and the elderly may not communicate their symptoms as clearly as do younger patients. Thus there is still no substitute for careful systematic assessment and skilled judgments in classifying the person's responses into those which are or are not abnormal (or diagnostically significant), then, if abnormal, into the type of symptom or symptom complex involved. In the final process of classification into the diagnostic categories the criteria in DSM-III will be found useful as a guide. Schuckit, Miller and Hahlbohm (1975), applied research diagnostic criteria by personal structured interviews and chart interviews to 50 males over 65 consecutively admitted to a medical-surgical ward and whose admitting evaluation did not note a specific psychiatric illness. Twelve patients met the research criteria for psychiatric illness which had not been noted or treated in hospital.

## AXES

For the most part classification for clinical or research work deals with conditions, not individuals. The condition from which an individual is suffering may, as previously described, give only part of the information required to adequately treat the individual and for this reason multiaxial descriptions will be used to supplement clinical diagnosis in DSM-III. Although multiaxial classifications focus attention on the individual, the number of axes that can be used must be limited since the combinations and permutations of even a large number of axes may place individuals in a category which is unique to them and hence of no value for the transfer of information to or from other patients. For an older person the four axes that are probably most important in addition to diagnosis are current ADL-IADL incapacity, duration of illness, strength of family support and the degree to which symptoms are attributable to concurrent medical disorder. Whether the DSM-III axes will be well adapted for the diagnosis of elderly subjects is yet to be seen.

Whereas diagnosis is for the most part eclectic with respect to relevance to treatment modalities, from the viewpoint of specific classes of treatment the additional dimensions and background characteristics mentioned above can be more useful: levels of neurotransmitter activity for psychopharmacology; ego strength for psychotherapy; the reinforcement history for behavioral methods of treatment; types of isolation for resocialization approaches, and so on.

## CASENESS

Whichever classification is chosen of mental disorder or its synonyms (emotional disorder, mental health, psychiatric, or psychological problems, etc.) there is an assumption that all the persons who are being classified are 'cases'; yet the definition of a case is in itself complex and controversial. The modal type of case can be recognized by the clustering of certain features. "There is a high consensus of opinion that psychopathology is being manifested when an old person contemporaneously expresses distress, disturbs others, is incompetent, and shows a change from his previous state (especially when this change is rapid and marked); when this constellation of events is not commonly seen in subjects of that age; when the causes of these events are seen to originate in the subject rather than in his circumstances; when the events are judged to be maladaptive; and when a treatment is available to slow down, or reverse, the progress of these events" (Gurland, 1973). Each of these features may carry a different rationale for identifying caseness, and Gurland (1973), has discussed these features and their rationale in detail. In the final analysis, it should not be forgotten that the definition of caseness has many purposes and thus many possible definitions.

## CONCLUSION

In this chapter, the view has been taken that the ultimate purpose of classification, and of mental health assessment in general, is the improvement or preservation of the individual's well being and functioning. Thus, a definition of caseness would be, in these terms, the identification of individuals who can benefit more from mental health expertise than from other more readily available or cost-effective approaches. Correspondingly, the roles of assessment and classification have been evaluated on the basis of their contribution to the current or potential application of treatment or management modalities. The welfare of the patient has also been held paramount in assessing the assessments relevant to the mental health of older persons and precedence has been given to those which are least strenuous for the patient without undue sacrifice of thoroughness and accuracy.

## REFERENCES

ALEXANDER, G., AND LEWIN, T. 1972. *The Aged and the Need for Surrogate Management.* New York: Syracuse University Press.

ARIE, T. 1978. Confusion in old age. *Age & Ageing,* 7(Supplement), 72–76.

BAILEY, J., AND COPPEN, A. 1976. A comparison between the Hamilton Rating Scale and the Beck Inventory in the measurement of depression. *Brit. J. Psychiat., 128,* 486–489.

BAZELON, D. L. 1964. Interface of law and behavioral sciences. *New England J. Med., 271,* 1141–1145.

BECK, A. T., WARD, C. H., MENDELSON, M., MOCK, J., AND ERBAUGH, J. 1951. An inventory for measuring depression. *Arch. Gen. Psychiat., 4,* 561–571.

BENDER, L. 1938. *A Visual-Motor Gestalt Test and its Clinical Use.* New York: American Orthopsychiatric Association.

BENNETT, R., AND NAHEMOW, L. 1965. The relations between social isolation, socialization and adjustment in residents of a home for the aged. *In*, M. P. Lawton (ed.), *Proceedings of Institute on Mentally Impaired Aged*, pp. 88–105. Philadelphia: Maurice Jacob Press.

BETTS, G. 1946. *Manual, Minnesota Rate of Manipulation.* Minneapolis: Educational Test Bureau.

BIRKETT, D. P., AND BOLTUCH, B. 1977. Measuring dementia, *J. Am. Geriat. Soc., 25*, 153–156.

BLOOM, M. 1975. Discontent with contentment scales, *Gerontologist, 15*, 99.

BRADBURN, N. 1969. *The Structure of Psychological Well Being.* Chicago: Aldine.

BRANCONNIER, R., AND COLE, J. 1978. The Impairment Index as a symptom-independent parameter of drug efficacy in geriatric psychopharmacology, *J. Geront., 33*, 217–223.

BRITTON, P., AND SAVAGE, R. 1966. A short form of the WAIS for use with the aged, *Brit. J. Psychiat., 112*, 417–418.

BROWN, G., BHROLCHAIN, M. N., AND HARRIS, T. 1975. Social class and psychiatric disturbance among women in an urban population, *Sociology, 9*, 225–254.

BUNNEY, W. E., AND HAMBURG, D. A. 1963. Methods for reliable longitudinal observation of behavior, *Arch. Gen. Psychiat., 9*, 280–294.

BUSSE, E., AND WANG, H. 1965. The value of electroencephalography in geriatrics, *Geriatrics, 20*, 906–924.

BUTLER, R. N., AND LEWIS, M. 1973. *Aging and Mental Health.* St. Louis, Missouri: C. V. Mosby.

CAIRD, F. I. 1977. Computerized tomography (Emiscan), *Age & Ageing, 6*(Supplement), 50–51.

CARP, F. 1975. Impact of improved housing on morale and life satisfaction, *Gerontologist, 15*, 511–515.

CAVAN, R. S., BURGESS, E. W., HAVIGHURST, R. J., AND GOLDHAMER, H. 1949. *Personal Adjustment in Old Age.* Chicago: Science Research Associates.

CHATFIELD, W. 1977. Economic and sociological factors influencing life satisfaction in the aged, *J. Geront., 32*, 593–599.

CLAUSEN, J. A. 1969. Methodological issues in the measurement of mental health in the aged. *In*, M. F. Lowenthal, and A. Zilli (eds.), *Interdisciplinary Topics in Gerontology: Colloquium on Health and Aging of the Population.* New York: Karger.

COCHRANE, A. L., AND HOLLAND, W. W. 1972. Validation of screening procedures, *Brit. Med. Bull., 27*, 3.

CUMMING, E., DEAN, L. R., AND NEWELL, D. S. 1958. What is "morale"? A case history of a validity problem, *Human Organization, 17*, 3–8.

CUMMING, E., AND HENRY, W. 1961. *Growing Old.* New York: Basic Books.

CUTLER, R. P., AND KURLAND, H. D. 1961. Clinical quantification of depressive reactions, *Arch. Gen. Psychiat., 5*, 280–285.

CUTLER, S. J. 1973. Voluntary association participation and life satisfaction: A cautionary research note, *J. Geront., 28*, 96–100.

DEMING, W. E. 1977. An essay on screening, or on two-phase sampling, applied to surveys of a community, *Int'l. Stat. Rev., 45*, 29–37.

DENHAM, M. J. 1978. Assessment of mental function, *Age & Ageing, 7*(Supplement), 137–138.

DOHRENWEND, B. P., EGRI, G., AND MENDELSOHN, F. 1971. Psychiatric disorder in general populations: A study of the problem of clinical judgement, *Am. J. Psychiat., 127*, 1304–1312.

DUVAL, E. M. 1973. Aging family members: Roles and relationships. *In*, White House Conference on Aging, 1971, *Toward a National Policy on Aging: Proceedings.* Washington, D.C.: U.S. Government Printing Office.

EDWARDS, J. N., AND KLEMMACK, D. L. 1973. Correlates of life satisfaction: A reexamination, *J. Geront., 28*, 497–502.

FEIGHNER, J. P., ROBINS, E., GUZE, S. B., WOODRUFF, R. A., WINOKUR, G., AND MUNOZ, R. 1972. Diagnostic criteria for use in psychiatric research, *Arch. Gen. Psychiat., 26*, 57–63.

FERM, L. 1974. Behavioral activities in demented geriatric patients, *Geront. Clin., 16*, 185–194.

FERRIS, S., CROOK, T., SATHANANTHAN, G., AND GERSHON, S. 1976. Reaction time as a diagnostic measure in senility, *J. Am. Geriat. Soc., 24*, 529–533.

FINK, M., GREEN, M., AND BENDER, M. 1952. The Face-Hand Test as a diagnostic sign of organic mental syndrome, *Neurol., 2*, 46–58.

GERSON, I. M., JOHN, E. R., KOENIG, V., AND BARTLETT, F. 1976. Average evoked response (AER) in the electroencephalographic diagnosis of the normally aging brain: A practical application, *Clin. EEG, 7*, 77–91.

GOLDFARB, A. I. 1967. Masked depression in the old, *Am. J. Psychother., 21*, 791–796.

GOLDFARB, A. I. 1968. Clinical perspectives, *Psychiat. Res. Rep., No. 23*, 170–178.

GOLDFARB, A. I. 1977. Psychotherapy of the aged. *In*, S. Steury and M. Blank (eds.), *Readings in Psychotherapy with Older People*, pp. 182–191 (DHEW Publ. No. (ADM)77–409). Washington, D.C.: U.S. Government Printing Office.

GOLDFARB, A. I., FISCH, M., AND GERBER, I. 1966. Predictors of mortality in the institutionalized elderly, *Dis. Nerv. Syst., 27*, 21–29.

GRAHAM, F. K., AND KENDALL, B. S. 1960. Memory for Designs Test: revised general manual, *Percep. Mo-*

*tor Skills, 30,* 319–326.

GRANEY, M., AND GRANEY, E. 1973. Scaling adjustment in older people, *Int'l. J. Aging & Hum. Develop., 4,* 351–359.

GRANICK, (BENNETT), R., AND NAHEMOW, L. 1961. Preadmission isolation as a factor in adjustment to an old age home. *In,* P. Hoch, and J. Zubin (eds.), *Psychopathology of Aging,* pp. 285–302. New York: Grune and Stratton.

GRUENBERG, E. 1977. The failures of success, *Milbank Mem. Fund Q., 55*(1), 3–24.

GUREL, L., LINN, M. W., AND LINN, B. S. 1972. Physical and mental impairment-of-function evaluation in the aged: The PAMIE Scale, *J. Geront., 27,* 83–90.

GURLAND, B. J. 1973. A flexible approach to psychiatric classification. *In,* M. Hammer, K. Salzinger, and S. Sutton (eds.), *Psychopathology: Contributions from the Social, Behavioral, and Biological Sciences,* pp. 409–426. New York: Wiley.

GURLAND, B. J. 1976. The comparative frequency of depression in various adult age groups. *J. Geront., 31,* 283–292.

GURLAND, B. J., COPELAND, J. R. M., SHARPE, L., AND KELLEHER, M. J. 1976. The Geriatric Mental Status Interview (GMS), *Int'l. J. Aging & Hum. Develop., 7,* 303–311.

GURLAND, B. J., DEAN, L., GURLAND, R. V., AND COOK, D. 1978. Personal time dependency in the elderly of New York City: Health service implications. *In,* Community Council of Greater New York (ed.), *Proceedings of the Research Utilization Workshop, March 23, 1978.* New York: Community Council of Greater New York.

GURLAND, B. J., FLEISS, J. L., GOLDBERG, K., AND SHARPE, L. (U.S. team) with COPELAND, J. R. M., KELLEHER, M. J., AND KELLETT, J. (U.K. team). 1976. A semi-structured clinical interview for the assessment of diagnosis and mental state in the elderly: the Geriatric Mental State Schedule II. A factor analysis, *Psychol. Med., 6,* 451–459.

GURLAND, B. J., KURIANSKY, J., SHARPE, L., SIMON, R., STILLER, P., AND BIRKETT, P. 1977. The Comprehensive Assessment and Referral Evaluation (CARE)-Rationale, development and reliability, *Int'l. J. Aging & Hum. Develop., 8,* 9–42.

HAGLUND, R., AND SCHUCKIT, M. 1976. A clinical comparison of tests of organicity in elderly patients, *J. Geront., 31,* 654–659.

HAMILTON, M. 1960. A rating scale for depression, *J. Neurol. Neurosurg. Psychiat., 23,* 56–62.

HERSCH, E., KRAL, V., AND PALMER, R. 1978. Clinical value of the London Psychogeriatric Rating Scale, *J. Am. Geriat. Soc., 26,* 348–354.

HODKINSON, H. M., EVANS, G. F., AND MEZER, A. G. 1972. Factors associated with misplacement of elderly patients in geriatric and psychiatric hospitals. *Geront. Clin.* 14/5, 267–273.

HONIGFELD, G., AND KLETT, C. J. 1965. The Nurses' Observation Scale for Inpatient Evaluation (NOSIE): A new scale for measuring improvement in chronic schizophrenia, *J. Clin. Psychol., 21,* 65–71.

HULICKA, I., MORGANTI, J., AND CATALDO, J. 1975. Differences in perceived latitude of choice between elderly institutionalized and non-institutionalized women, *Exper. Aging Res., 1,* 27–40.

HUNT, S. M., JR., SINGER, K., AND COBB, S. 1967. Components of depression, *Arch. Gen. Psychiat., 16,* 441–447.

INGLIS, J. 1959. A paired-associate learning test for use with elderly psychiatric patients, *J. Ment. Sci., 105,* 440–443.

IRVING, G., ROBINSON, R., AND MCADAM, W. 1970. The validity of some cognitive tests in the diagnosis of dementia, *Brit. J. Psychiat., 117,* 149–156.

ISAACS, B., AND AKHTAR, A. 1972. The set test: A rapid test of mental function in old people, *Age & Ageing, 1,* 233–238.

ISAACS, B., AND WALKEY, F. A. 1964. Measurement of mental impairment in geriatric practice, *Gerontologia Clinica, 6,* 114–123.

JAHODA, M. 1958. *Current concepts of positive mental health.* New York: Basic Books.

JOHN, E. R., KARMEL, B., CORNING, W., EASTON, P., BROWN, D., AHN, H., JOHN, M., HARMONY, T., PRICHEP, L., TORO, A., GERSON, I., BARTLETT, F., THATCHER, R., KAYE, H., VALDES, P., AND SCHWARTZ, E. 1977. Neurometrics, *Science, 196,* 1393–1410.

KAHN, R. L., GOLDFARB, A. I., POLLACK, M., AND PECK, A. 1960. Brief objective measures for the determination of mental status in the aged, *Am. J. Psychiat., 117,* 326–328.

KATZ, S., AND AKPOM, C. 1976. A measure of primary sociobiological functions, *Int'l. J. Health Services, 6,* 493–508.

KATZ, S., FORD, A. B., MOSKOWITZ, R. W., JACKSON, B. A., AND JAFFE, M. W. 1963. Studies of illness in the aged: The index of ADL, a standardized measure of biological and psychosocial function, *J.A.M.A. 185,* 914–919.

KLEBAN, M., LAWTON, M. P., BRODY, E., AND MOSS, M. 1976. Behavioral observations of mentally impaired aged: Those who decline and those who do not, *J. Geront., 31,* 333–339.

KURIANSKY, J., AND GURLAND, B. J. 1976. The Performance Test of Activities of Daily Living, *Int'l. J. Aging & Hum. Develop., 7,* 343–352.

KURTZ, J., AND WOLK, S. 1975. Continued growth and life satisfaction, *Gerontologist, 15,* 129–131.

KUTNER, B., FANSHEL, D., TOGO, A., AND LANGNER, T. S. 1956. *Five Hundred Over Sixty.* New York: Russell Sage Foundation.

LAWSON, J. S., RODENBURG, M., AND DYKES, J. 1977. A dementia rating scale for use with psychogeriatric patients, *J. Geront., 32,* 153–159.

LAWTON, M. P. 1972. The dimensions of morale. *In,* D.

Kent, R. Kastenbaum, and S. Sherwood (eds.), *Research Planning and Action for the Elderly: The Power and Potential of Political Science*, pp. 144–165. New York: Behavioral Publications.

LAWTON, M. P. 1975. The Philadelphia Geriatric Center Morale Scale: A revision, *J. Geront., 30*, 85–89.

LAWTON, M. P., AND BRODY, E. 1969. Assessment of older people: Self-maintaining and instrumental activities of daily living, *Gerontologist, 9*, 179–186.

LEVITT, E., AND LUBIN, B. 1975. *Depression: Concepts, Controversies and Some New Facts*. New York: Springer Publishing Company.

LLOYD-EVANS, S., BROCKLEHURST, J., AND PALMER, M. 1978. Assessment of drug therapy in chronic brain failure, *Gerontology, 24*, 304–311.

LOHMANN, N. 1977. Correlations of life satisfaction, morale and adjustment measures, *J. Geront., 32*, 73–75.

LOWENTHAL, M. F., AND CHIRIBOGA, D. 1973. Social stress and adaptation: Toward a life-course perspective. *In*, C. Eisdorfer, and M. P. Lawton (eds.), *The Psychology of Adult Development and Aging*, pp. 281–310. Washington, D.C.: American Psychological Association.

LUBIN, B. 1965. Adjective Checklists for measurement of depression, *Arch. Gen. Psychiat., 12*, 57–62.

MARONEY, R., GUREL, L., AND DAVIS, J. 1969. Patient's perception of nursing home placement, *Geriatrics, 24*, 119–124.

MEER, B., AND BAKER, J. 1966. The Stockton Geriatric Rating Scale, *J. Geront., 21*, 392–403.

MILLER, S. J. 1965. The dilemma of a social role for the aging, *Papers in Social Welfare, 8*, 3–4.

MORRIS, J., WOLF, R., AND KLERMAN, L. V. 1975. Common themes among morale and depression scales, *J. Geront., 30*, 209–215.

MÜLLER, H. 1978. The electroencephalogram in senile dementia. *In*, K. Nandy (ed.), *Senile Dementia: A Biomedical Approach*, pp. 237–250. New York: Elsevier.

MULLER, H., AND KRAL, V. 1967. The electroencephalogram in advanced senile dementia, *J. Am. Geriat. Soc., 15*, 415–426.

NEIDITCH, J., AND WHITE, L. 1976. Prediction of short-term outcome in newly admitted psychogeriatric patients, *J. Am. Geriat. Soc., 24*, 72–78.

NEUGARTEN, B., HAVIGHURST, R., AND TOBIN, S. 1961. The measurement of life satisfaction, *J. Geront., 16*, 134–143.

OBRIST, W., THOMPSON, H. K., JR., KING, C. H., AND WANG, H. S. 1967. Determination of regional cerebral blood flow by inhalation of 133-Xenon, *Circ. Res., 20*, 124–135.

OVERALL, J. E., HOLLISTER, L. E., AND MEYER, F. 1964. Imipramine and thioridazine in depressed and schizophrenic patients. Are these specific anti-depressant drugs? *J. A. M. A., 189*, 605–608.

OVERALL, J. E., HOLLISTER, L. E., POKORNY, A. D., CASEY, J. F., AND KATZ, G. 1962. Drug therapy in depressions: Controlled evaluation of imipramine, isocarboxazide, dextroamphetamine-amobarbital and placebo, *Clin. Pharmacol. Therap., 3*, 16–22.

PATIE, A. H., AND GILLEARD, C. J. 1975. A brief psychogeriatric assessment schedule: validation against psychiatric diagnosis and discharge from hospital. *Brit. J. Psychiat., 127*, 489–493.

PATIE, A. H., AND GILLEARD, C. J. 1976. The Clifton Assessment Schedule—further validation of a psychogeriatric assessment schedule, *Brit. J. Psychiat., 129*, 68–72.

PFEIFFER, E. 1975a. A Short Portable Mental Status Questionnaire for the assessment of organic brain deficit in elderly patients, *J. Am. Geriat. Soc., 23*, 433–441.

PFEIFFER, E. (Ed.) 1975b. *Multidimensional Functional Assessment:The OARS Methodology*. Durham, North Carolina: Center for Study of Aging and Human Development.

PIERCE, R., AND CLARK, M. 1973. Measurement of morale in the elderly, *Int'l. J. Aging & Hum. Develop., 4*, 83–101.

PLUTCHIK, R., CONTE, H., LIEVERMAN, M., BAKUR, M., GROSSMAN, J., AND LEHRMAN, N. 1970. Reliability and validity of a scale for assessing the functioning of geriatric patients, *J. Am. Geriat. Soc., 18*, 491–500.

POWELL, C., AND CROMBIE, A. 1974. The Kilsyth Questionnaire: A method of screening elderly people at home, *Age & Ageing, 3*, 23–28.

RASKIN, A. 1965. *N. I. M. H. Collaborative Depression Mood Scale*. Washington, D.C.: National Institute of Mental Health.

RAVEN, J. C. 1938. *Progressive Matrices*. London: H. K. Lewis.

REID, D.W., HAAS, G., AND HAWKINGS, D. 1977. Locus of desired control and positive self-concept of the elderly, *J. Geront., 32*, 441–450.

REITAN, R. M. 1958. Validity of the Trail Making Test as an indicator of organic brain damage, *Percept. Motor Skills, 8*, 271–276.

ROBINSON, J., AND SHAVER, P. 1973. *Measures of Social Psychological Attitudes*. Ann Arbor, Michigan: Institute for Social Research.

ROBINSON, R. A. 1961. Some problems of clinical trials in elderly people, *Gerontologia Clinica, 3*, 247–257.

ROTH, M. 1971. Classification and ætiology in mental disorders of old age: Some recent developments. *In*, D. W. K. Kay, and A. Walk (eds.), *Recent Developments in Psychogeriatrics: A symposium, Brit. J. Psychiatry Special Pub. No. 6*, pp. 1–18. Ashford, Kent: Headley.

ROTH, M. 1976. The psychiatric disorders of later life, *Psychiatric annals, 6*, 417–444.

ROTH, M., TOMLINSON, B., AND BLESSED, G. 1967. The relationship between quantitative measures of dementia and of degenerative changes in the cerebral grey matter of elderly subjects, *Proceedings Royal Soc. Med., 60*, 254–259.

SALZMAN, C., KOCHANSKY, G., SHADER, R., AND CRONIN, D. 1972. Rating scales for psychotropic drug research with geriatric patients. II. Mood ratings, *J. Am. Geriat. Soc. 20*, 215–221.

SAVAGE, R., AND HALL, E. 1973. A performance learning measure for the aged, *Brit. J. Psychiat., 122*, 721–723.

SCHUCKIT, M., MILLER, P., AND HAHLBOHM, D. 1975. Unrecognized psychiatric illness in elderly medical-surgical patients, *J. Geront., 30*, 655–660.

SELTZER, M. 1975. The quality of research is strained, *Gerontologist, 15*, 503–507.

SHADER, R., HARMATZ, J., AND SALZMAN, C. 1974. A new scale for clinical assessment in geriatric populations: Sandoz Clinical Assessment-Geriatric (SCAG), *J. Am. Geriat. Soc., 22*, 107–113.

SILVER, C. P. 1978. Tests for assessment of mental function, *Age & Ageing*, 7(Supplement), 12–21.

SIMON, A. 1970. The psychiatrists and the geriatric patient: Screening of the aged mentally ill, *J. Geriat. Psychiat., 4*, 5–22.

SIMPSON, G. M., HACKETT, E., AND KLINE, N. S. 1966. Difficulties in systematic rating of depression during out-patient drug treatment, *Canad. Psychiat. Assoc. J., 11*, 116–122.

STONIER, P. 1974. Score changes following repeated administration of mental status questionnaires, *Age & Ageing, 3*, 91.

SUTTON, S. 1973. Fact and artifact in the psychology of schizophrenia. *In*, M. Hammer, K. Salzinger, and S. Sutton (eds.), *Psychopathology: Contributions from the Social, Behavioral, and Biological Sciences*, pp.

TOWNSEND, P. 1962. *The Last Refuge: A Survey of Residential Institutions and Homes for the Aged in England and Wales*. London: Routledge Kegan and Paul.

VAN PRAAG, H. M. 1977. Significance of biochemical parameters in the diagnosis, treatment, and prevention of depressive disorders, *Biolog. Psychiat., 12*, 101–131.

VERWOERDT, A. 1976. *Clinical Geropsychiatry*. Baltimore: Williams & Wilkins.

WALTON, D., AND BLACK, D. A. 1957. The validity of a psychological test of brain damage, *Brit. J. Med. Psychol., 30*, 270–279.

WATSON, C. 1976. Inpatient care or outplacement: Which is better for the psychiatric medically infirm patient? *J. Geront., 31*, 611–616.

WESCHLER, D. 1955. *Manual for the Weschler Adult Intelligence Scale*. New York: Psychological Corp.

WILSON, L. AND BRASS, W. 1973. Brief assessment of the mental state in geriatric domiciliary practice. The usefulness of the mental status questionnaire, *Age & Ageing, 2*, 92–101.

WILSON, L., GRANT, K., WITNEY, P., AND KERRIDGE, D. 1973. Mental status of elderly hospital patients related to occupational therapist's assessment of activities of daily living, *Gerontologia Clinica, 15*, 197–202.

WILSON, L., ROY, S., AND BURSILL, A. 1973. The reliability of the mental status questionnaire in geriatrics. (To be published).

WING, J. K., BIRLEY, J. L., COOPER, J. E., GRAHAM, P., AND ISAACS, A. 1967. Reliability of a procedure for measuring and classifying "Present Psychiatric State", *Brit. J. Psychiat., 113*, 499–515.

WOOTON, B. 1968. Social psychiatry and psychopathology: A layman's comments on contemporary developments. *In*, J. Zubin, and F. Freyhan (eds.), *Social Psychiatry*, pp. 283–299. New York: Grune & Stratton.

ZUBIN, J. 1976. The role of vulnerability in the etiology of schizophrenic episodes. *In*, L. J. West, and D. E. Flinn (eds.), *Treatment of Schizophrenia: Progress and Prospects*, pp. 5–33. New York: Grune & Stratton.

ZUNG, W. 1965. A Self-rating Depression Scale, *Arch. Gen. Psychiat., 12*, 63–70.

ZUNG, W. 1967. Depression in the normal aged, *Psychosomatics, 8*, 287–292.

# 29

# The Interrelationship of Mental and Physical Status and Its Assessment in the Older Adult: Mind-Body Interaction*

*Beni Habot & Leslie S. Libow*

Mental change is one of the most common components of the stereotype of being "old." Yet mental change in late life is often a reflection of bodily illnesses which may occur at any age, but which, when occurring in the elderly, produce mental deterioration. Conversely, severe mental change in the elderly is often the catalyst for rapid physical decline.

## BRAIN FUNCTION AND AGE

The older mind has strengths and weaknesses not present in the young. The healthy elderly possess a larger vocabulary and more general information skills than the healthy young college student. On the other hand, intelligence skills related to speed of response decline with age (Bellak, 1976; Botwinick and Birren, 1971; Carp, 1969; and Patterson, Freeman, and Butler, 1971).

There does not appear to be any significant decline in cerebral blood flow or cerebral oxygen consumption with normal aging, though glucose utilization by the brain does decline (Dastur, Lane, Hansen, Kety, Butler, Perlin, and Sokoloff, 1971).

Endocrine changes with age may reflect primary changes in brain function or secondary effects of gland dysfunction. Much attention has focused on biogenic amines and cerebral function. In animals, there appears to be a decline with age in brain dopamine, norepinephrine and serotonin, while the enzyme monoamine oxidase is increased (Kent, 1976). Certain other hormone secretion rates and responses to stimuli change with age. Growth hormone concentration in plasma may

*The authors thank Dr. F. Charatan and Mr. H. Spierer for their editorial assistance and suggestions, and Mrs. Donna Burke, and Mrs. Isabel Vader for their technical assistance.

decrease with age, and there is a decreased response to stimulation of growth hormone release. Thyrotropin-releasing hormone has a diminished effect in initiating TSH thyrotropin stimulating hormone release in older men. Serum levels of triiodothyronine (T3) decrease with age (particularly in men), while T4 levels do not change with age. Many other serum hormone levels decline with age, for example, aldosterone, epinephrine, testosterone and estrogen. Serum insulin levels increase with age while glucagon levels do not change. Thus, age is a variable which, along with metabolism, must be taken into consideration when evaluating endocrine functions (Gregerman and Bierman, 1974).

Electroencephalographic (EEG) patterns change with age, showing a slower peak occipital frequency (Obrist, 1971). Though not statistically significant, a lower peak occipital frequency and a greater percentage of fast activity relates to shortened survival in the healthy elderly (Libow, Obrist, and Sokoloff, 1971). The aged brain shows neuronal loss, neurofibrillary tangles, and "senile" plaques. Grossly, there is loss of cortical tissue and widened ventricles. These changes are found in both normal aged brains and the brains of patients with the late-life Alzheimer-type dementia, but there appear to be more plaques and tangles in the brain of demented patients (Terry, and Wisniewski, 1977).

In summary, though there are obvious anatomical and physiological changes of the human brain with age, these brain changes cannot be clearly correlated with the behavioral and/or intellectual functions of the older brain. Thus, the mechanisms for normal mental change and/or for the senile dementias are unclear and not simply related to the observed anatomical changes.

## CLINICAL EVALUATION OF THE CENTRAL NERVOUS SYSTEM

In the older adult population, mental status evaluation is of great importance. It is an essential part of the clinical evaluation. Prompt recognition of deterioration of mental function should stimulate further investigations to elucidate the cause. Successful treatment in some cases will enable the older adult to remain in the community. Too often the mental status of the older patient is evaluated cursorily and with insensitive indicators of organic mental syndromes (Jacobs, Bernhard, Delgado, and Strain, 1977).

The tests used in mental status evaluation are affected by the patient's physical and/or mental status, his/her intelligence level, language, education, verbal skills, sensory acuity, willingness to cooperate with the examiner, etc. If the patient-physician interaction is handled insensitively, resistance to the examiner may develop, leading to uncooperativeness and incomplete or guarded answers. The final result of any mental status test depends on the examiner's skills and his familiarity with the test. Since mental status may change within the course of one day, one week or month, it is important to do more than one evaluation before reaching a diagnosis. There are many clinical tests of mental function in the elderly (Jacobs, Bernhard, Delgado, and Strain, 1977; Kahn, Goldfarb, Pollack, and Peck, 1960; Libow, 1977; Perlin, and Butler, 1971; Pfeiffer, 1975).

The sensitive areas in diagnosing organic brain syndromes are memory, orientation and intellectual function. All of the above mentioned tests focus on these abilities. The approach used in our program evaluates the overall mental and social function as well as the parameters of judgement and emotional state (Libow, 1977). This technique uses an acronym *FROMAJE,* with each letter representing one aspect of mental function. This mnemonic device is easy to remember, and the test has been used with a high degree of accuracy by physicians, nurses, medical students and laymen. Concordance with the ratings of a gero-psychiatrist range from 80 to 90 percent. The rating format is flexible, and the final rating is a product of the examiner's subjective assessment. The test takes 10 to 15 minutes for an experienced interviewer and approximately 20 minutes for an inexperienced one, and has been described in detail elsewhere (Libow, 1977). It is briefly summarized here.

F — unction
R — easoning
O — rientation
M — emory
A — rithmetic
J — udgment
E — motional state

The letter *F* stands for function. For an accurate rating, the interviewer has to ask the relative, friend, nurse, etc., about the patient's mental function in the last weeks or months. By function, we refer to the mental ability of the individual to maintain himself or herself in the community or to return home if he/she is an individual in an institution. Specifically, this relates to hygiene, bill payment, nutrition, etc. Adequate mental abilities from this point of view will be rated +1, meaning that no home support will be necessary. Mild impairment will be rated +2, indicating need for some at-home support (part of the day or week). More severe mental impairment will be rated +3, meaning that there is a need for support or supervision 24 hours a day, seven days a week.

The letter R stands for reasoning. The person interviewed is asked the meaning of proverbs. The interviewer should be aware of language or educational or cultural problems. It may be necessary to use an interpreter, and it is, of course, important to use proverbs familiar to the patient. The person interviewed will be rated +1 for a proverb well explained with general connotation given; +2 for partial explanation or connotation; or +3 for complete inability to describe the meaning or a completely concretized explanation.

The letter O stands for orientation. The questions on orientation relate to time, place and self. Specific questions include: date, location, name and age, etc. General accuracy will be rated +1; a rating of +2 will be given for errors in one area—time, place or self; +3 will be given for errors in two of three areas.

The letter M stands for memory. The patient will be asked to remember three numbers (i.e., 2, 11, 18). Then, specific areas of memory will be tested. Distant memory: What is the name of the President of the US during World War II? (answer: Roosevelt; Truman). Recent memory: have you had breakfast? lunch? and so on. Immediate memory: what did I ask you about the President of the US? What numbers did I ask you to remember?

The letter A stands for arithmetic. The patient is asked to count from 1 to 10 and backwards from 10 to 1 and to subtract 7 from 100 and to continue to subtract. The score will be +1 for complete accuracy; +2 for one significant error; and +3 for two or more significant errors.

The letter J stands for judgment. Typical questions in use are as follows: If you need help at night, how do you obtain it? If you see fire in your wastepaper basket, what action would you take? A rating score of +1 will be given to generally sensible responses; +2 demonstrates some poor judgment and +3; extremely poor judgment.

The letter E stands for emotional state. The interviewer has to observe the patient's manner during the interview as well as to ask about crying, sadness, depression, optimism, future plans, etc. The score of +1 is given for reasonable and appropriate emotional state; +2 for grandiosity, anxiety or depression, paranoia, and so forth; and +3 for inappropriate ideas, severe depression, etc.

The total score of 7 or 8 reflects no significant mental dysfunction. A total score of 9 to 10 shows minimal mental dysfunction; a score of 11 or 12

shows moderate mental dysfunction; and a score of 13 or more shows a severe mental dysfunction.

The FROMAJE responses are recorded for comparison with a later reevaluation so as to gauge the response to adaptation, to therapy or to time.

The aphasic or dysphasic patient cannot be well evaluated by the FROMAJE scale. An emotional state ("E") score of 3, while the rest of the functions are rated 1, will produce a total score of 9. This score will be a false positive one for dementia, but will highlight, for the inexperienced interviewer, an emotional illness.

In conclusion, FROMAJE is a global interview emphasizing many areas of mentation, including overall social function and emotional state. It is easy to remember and administer and correlates accurately with clinical conclusions. The experienced interviewer does not need to apply any numerical ratings, but merely uses this acronym to assure a reasonably complete and smooth interview. (The whole area of mental status questionnaires is dealt with by Gurland [Chapter 28], in this volume.)

## NEUROLOGICAL EXAMINATION*

(The Neurological component of this chapter was co-authored by N. Basavaraju.)‡

The neurological examination of the older adult should take into consideration the physiological changes of normal aging. For example, there is a decreased vibratory senation at the ankles; pain and touch sensitivity are also reduced; and the ankle jerks are often absent (Paulson, 1977). The examination should include testing for primitive reflexes and sensory perceptual tests which reflect diffuse cerebral dysfunction. When evaluating an aged person, the examiner should take into consideration the possibility of decreased hearing, slow motor responses, weakness, decreased memory, fright, diminished vision, language barrier, etc.

As part of the overall neuropsychiatric examination of the older adult, the neurological examination should include evaluation of primitive reflexes and perceptual sensory tests. These can

---

*The part of this paper on primitive neurological reflexes and perceptual sensory tests is reprinted with the kind permission of Basavaraju, N. G., Paraskevas, K., and Libow, L. S., 1977. Initially presented at the 30th annual meeting of the Gerontological Society, San Francisco, Nov. 1977. In preparation, now, for publication.

‡N. Basavaraju, M. D. Attending Physician Jewish Institute for Geriatric Care and Assistant Professor of Medicine State University of New York at Stony Brook.

provide a useful guide to diffuse impairment of cerebral function, a territory common to the neurologist, geriatrician, internist, psychiatrist and all primary care physicians. The primitive reflexes such as palmomental (Magnusson and Wernstedt, 1935; Parmelee, 1963), snout, sucking and grasp (Bieber, 1940) are physiological and universally present in the human infant. They disappear with maturation of the central nervous system and development of inhibitory mechanisms in adults. They may reappear in advanced age, dementia, and certain neurological disorders (Bender, 1975).

Similarly, perceptual function develops in infancy and early childhood and becomes a part of the permanent intellectual and behavioral characteristics of the youth and adult. Discriminative functions tend to decline in late life both in visual and cutaneous perceptual modalities. This can be demonstrated by the method of double simultaneous stimulation and by the face-hand tests and the large-small figure test (Bender, 1975). From a study done in our institution (Basavaraju, Paraskevas, and Libow, 1977), it is clear that there is a statistically significant increase in the incidence of certain primitive reflexes with age, and even more so in patients with dementia. The study was done using four comparative groups (see Table 29–1).

**Table 29–1**  Description of the groups used in the study.

| NO. | GROUP | AGE RANGE | MEAN AGE |
|---|---|---|---|
| 50 | Organic brain syndrome in institution (O.B.S.) | 70–96 | 82.6 |
| 50 | Neurologically impaired elderly in institution (N.I.E.) | 52–91 | 77.1 |
| 50 | Healthy elderly (H.E.) | 65–81 | 73.6 |
| 50 | Healthy young adults (H.Y.A.) | 20–55 | 38.3 |

Reproduced with permission of Basavaraju, N., Paraskevas, K., Libow, L.S., from a paper presented at the 30th Annual Gerontological Society meeting in San Francisco, Calif., November, 1977.

## PRIMITIVE REFLEXES

*The Palmomental Reflex.*  This consists of contraction of the ipsilateral mentalis muscle (muscle of the chin, which, when contracting, causes the skin on the chin to wrinkle) in response to stroking the thenar eminence of the hand. The great distance between the sensory stimulus and motor response makes it a clinical curiosity, as first described by Marinesco and Radovici (1920). Results are described in Table 29–2. Thirty-two percent of healthy elderly had a positive bilateral palmomen-

tal reflex compared to 54 percent for organic brain syndrome patients and 52 percent for neurologically impaired elderly, a statistically significant difference.

**Table 29–2**  The Palmo-Mental reflex.

| | O.B.S. | N.I.E. | H.E. | H.Y.A. |
|---|---|---|---|---|
| Positive Unilateral | 6% | 28%[++] | 2% | 0% |
| Positive Bilateral | 54%[+] | 52%[+] | 32% | 0% |
| Negative | 40% | 20% | 66% | 100% |

[+]p <.001 (compared to H.E.)
[++]p <.005 (compared to O.B.S.)

Reproduced with permission of Basavaraju, N., Paraskevas, K., Libow, L.S., from a paper presented at the 30th Annual Gerontological Society meeting in San Francisco, Calif., November, 1977.

*The Snout Reflex:*  The snout reflex consists of a brief puckering movement of the lips due to contraction of the orbicularis oris evoked by a sharp tap on the closed lips. The results are presented in Table 29–3. Though 36 percent of healthy elderly and 24 percent of healthy young adults had a positive snout reflex, the OBS and neurologically affected patients showed a 72 percent and 76 percent positive response, a statistically significant difference.

**Table 29–3**  The snout reflex.

| | O.B.S. | N.I.E. | H.E. | H.Y.A. |
|---|---|---|---|---|
| Positive | 72%[+] | 76%[+] | 36% | 24% |
| Negative | 28% | 24% | 64% | 76% |

[+] p <.001 (compared to H.E. and H.Y.A.)

Reproduced with permission of Basavaraju, N., Paraskevas, K., Libow, L.S., from a paper presented at the 30th Annual Gerontological Society meeting in San Francisco, Calif., November, 1977.

*The Sucking Reflex.*  The sucking reflex consists of sucking movement of the lips, tongue and jaw when the oral region is stroked. This reflex was demonstrated, surprisingly, only in one OBS patient.

*The Grasp Reflex.*  The grasp reflex is a flexor response of the fingers and hand elicited by stimulation of the skin of the palmar surface of the hands and fingers, especially the region between the thumb and index finger. Results are presented in Table 29–4. None of the healthy elderly or healthy young adults have a grasp reflex, while 26 percent of the OBS group showed bilateral grasp.

**Table 29–4** The grasp reflex.

| | O.B.S. | N.I.E. | H.E. | H.Y.A. |
|---|---|---|---|---|
| Unilateral | 8% | 12% | 0% | 0% |
| Bilateral | 26%[++] | 6%[+] | 0% | 0% |
| Negative | 66% | 82% | 100% | 100% |

[+]p <.001 (compared to H.E.)
[++]p <.005 (compared to N.I.E.)

Reproduced with permission of Basavaraju, N., Paraskevas, K., Libow, L.S., from a paper presented at the 30th Annual Gerontological Society meeting in San Francisco, Calif., November, 1977.

## PERCEPTUAL SENSORY TESTS

*Face-Hand.* The face-hand test, as performed by us, has the patient looking at the examiner's face. A side of the patient's face and the dorsum of the contralateral hand are simultaneously touched. The patient is asked about the number of stimuli and asked to localize these stimuli. If only one stimulus is reported by the patient, the test is repeated two or more times. The test is repeated by simultaneous stimulation of the opposite side of the face and contralateral hand. Then the test is modified so that the examiner touches his own face, for example, patient's left hand and examiner's right face, and the patient is asked to localize the stimuli.

*Pattern of Responses.* Identification of both stimuli represent a normal response. The healthy elderly and the dementia group demonstrate "extinction" of the hand in 16 and 18 percent of the cases, (see Table 29–5) while this was true in only 2 percent of the healthy younger adults. Thus, this test does not appear to be a sensitive indicator of organic brain syndrome. However, "extinction" coupled with "displacement" (projection of the stimulus elsewhere than where applied) may have some dif-

**Table 29–5** Face-hand test.

| | O.B.S. | N.I.E. | H.E. | H.Y.A. |
|---|---|---|---|---|
| Extinction | 16% | 18% | 18% | 2% |
| Other type responses‡ | 72% | 60% | 0% | 0% |
| Negative (Normal) | 12% | 22% | 82% | 98% |

‡These responses are being further studied. In particular, extinction with displacement to the examiner's body or to space, appears to be significantly increased in the OBS group (Basavaraju, Silverstone, Paraskevas, & Libow, 1979).

Reproduced with permission of Basavaraju, N., Paraskevas, K., Libow, L.S., from a paper presented at the 30th Annual Gerontological Society meeting in San Francisco, Calif., November, 1977.

ferentiating value, and this data will soon be reported (Basavaraju, Silverstone, Paraskevas, & Libow, 1979).

Other methods of scoring this test and its relationship to other estimates of cognitive function are discussed in this volume by Sloane, Chapter 24. In our opinion, this battery of simple neurological tests should be included in the clinical-neurological examination of older adults suspected of suffering from dementia. It takes a few minutes at bedside or in an office setting, and several of those tests, when positive, further clarify the clinical impression of dementia.

## THE APPROPRIATE LABORATORY INVESTIGATIONS OF THE OLDER ADULT PATIENT PRESENTING WITH MENTAL CHANGES

In Table 29–6 is presented a list of the obligatory and elective tests. Though most are self-explanatory, the reader is referred elsewhere for more detail (Libow, 1977). The computerized axial tom-

**Table 29–6** Laboratory Tests for the Investigation of the Elderly Patient Presenting with Mental Function Disturbances.

OBLIGATORY TESTS
    Complete blood count
    Erythrocyte sedimentation rate
    Serum Na+, K+, Cl−, CO2, BUN, Glucose (SMA 6)
    Serum Ca++, PO4, liver function tests, creatinine (SMA 12)
    Serologic test for syphilis (VDRL, etc.)
    Serum folate and B12
    Thyroid function tests, i.e. total serum thyroxine concentration (T4) tri-iodothyroxine resin uptake (T3) and/or radioimmuno assay, serum free T4 and T3
    Resting electrocardiogram (EKG)
    Chest x-ray
    Computerized axial tomography (CAT scan); appropriate in most cases of dementia.
ELECTIVE TESTS (To be done on specific indications)
    Spinal tap and cerebro-spinal fluid (CSF) examination (in the absence of signs of increased intracranial pressure such as papilledema or erosion of dorsum sellae, etc.)
    Electroencephalogram (EEG)
    Skull x-ray
    Brain scan
    Isotope cisternography
    Cerebral aniography.
Because of the potential morbidity and because of the wide use of the CAT scan, the pneumoencephalogram is not to be used in the evaluation of the elderly patient.

Adapted from Libow, L.S.: Senile Dementa and "Pseudosenility"; Clinical Diagnosis, in Eisdorfer, C. and Friedel, R.O. (eds.): *Cognitive and Emotional Disturbance in the Elderly.* Copyright © 1977 by Year Book Medical Publishers, Inc. Chicago. Used by permission.

ogram (CAT) should be used in all new cases of dementia and in appropriate chronic cases. However, it is essential to emphasize that the diagnosis of senile dementia cannot be made with the CAT. The greatest value of this new and remarkable test is in the search for the 5 to 10 percent of dementias related to focal neurological abnormalities (Weisberg and Nice, 1977). But, even here, false negatives occur (Tentler and Palacios, 1977).

## SYSTEMIC DISTURBANCES PRODUCING POTENTIALLY REVERSIBLE MENTAL CHANGES— "PSEUDOSENILITY"

It is essential to seek out the potentially reversible organic brain syndromes (Lipowski, Z. J., 1967 & 1978; Libow, L. S., 1973; Wells, C. E., 1977). Table 29–7 presents an overview of the multiple causes of pseudosenility.

**Table 29–7\*** Causes of Potentially "Reversible" Mental Changes in the Elderly\*\*

I. MEDICATIONS
 a) Errors in self-administration.
 b) Polypharmacy causing drug interactions; (propranolol-insulin; digitalis—diuretics; phenothiazines—barbiturates).
 c) Abuse of non-prescription drugs.
 d) L-dopa, indomethacin, steroids, gentamicin, propranolol, digitalis, procainamide, benzodiazepines, can induce psychosis.
 e) Diuretics lead to subtle dehydration and electrolyte imbalance.
 f) All drugs with a primary CNS-desired action, e.g. phenothiazines, barbiturates, tricyclic antidepressants, diphenylhydantoin.
 g) Chlorpropamide (Diabinese) morphine, vincristine, clofibrate, cyclophosphamide and tricyclic antidepressants causing inappropriate ADH secretion leading to water intoxication.
 h) Antihypertensive medications, i.e. methyldopa, clonidine.
 i) Drugs leading to confusion, i.e. histamine $H_2$ receptor antagonist (cimetidine) flurazepam (Dalmane), lithium.
II. METABOLIC IMBALANCE
 a) Hypercalcemia secondary to:
  1) Carcinoma of lung, breast, and other tissues.
  2) Primary hyperparathyroidism.
  3) Multiple myeloma.
  4) Paget's disease coupled with immobilization.
  5) Thiazide administration.

\*The authors thank Rein Tideiksaar RPA-C, Jewish Institute for Geriatric Care and Clinical Instructor, Health Science Center, State University of New York at Stony Brook for his significant contribution to the development of this table.

\*\*Table adapted with permission of the American Geriatric Society from Libow, L.S. "Pseudo-Senility," J. Am Geriatr. 12:112, 1973 and Libow, L.S.: Senile Dementia and "Pseudosenility" in *Cognitive and Emotional Disturbance in the Elderly* (eds) Eisdorfer, C. and Friedel, R. O. Yearbook Medical Publishers, Inc., 1977.

  6) Vitamin D intoxication.
  7) Milk—alkali syndrome.
  8) Addison's disease
  9) Thyroid dysfunction.
 b) Hypocalcemia secondary to:
  1) Malabsorptive states.
  2) Renal failure.
  3) Hypoparathyroidism: post-thyroidectomy or idiopathic.
 c) Hyperglycemia
  1) Easily recognized: ketoacidosis.
  2) Less easily recognized
   a) Lactic acidosis; look for the "anion gap."
   b) Nonacidotic hyperosmolarity syndrome; blood sugar above 600 mg/100ml; serum bicarbonate normal; no urinary ketones.
 d) Hypoglycemia secondary to insulin or sulfonylureas.
 e) Hypothyroidism: "subacute" onset; low PBI, serum thyroxine (T4), T3 resin uptake, and 24-hour I[131] uptake by thyroid gland; high SGOT, LDH, and CPK; high TSH if primary hypothyroidism.
 f) Hyperthyroidism: may be present in the elderly as depression and/or apathy; termed "apathetic hyperthyroidism;" may also present as dementia.
 g) Hypernatremia: a hyperosmolarity syndrome secondary to
  1) Inadequate fluid intake in very ill or disoriented patients.
  2) Cerebral concussion.
  3) Iatrogenic factors: administration of hypertonic saline by intravenous or intraperitoneal route or tube feeding of high-protein mixtures.
  4) Excessive sweating without increased water intake.
 h) Hyponatremia: a hypo-osmolarity syndrome secondary to increased antidiuretic hormone secretion; bronchogenic carcinoma; cerebrovascular accident; skull fracture; postoperative period; Tb; pneumonias; brain tumors; hypothyroidism; congestive heart failure; liver cirrhosis, etc.
 i) Azotemia
  1) Low cardiac output.
  2) Hypovolemia secondary to medication induced dehydration or bleeding.
  3) Hypokalemic nephropathy.
  4) Worsening of a chronic mild nephritis by a urinary tract infection.
  5) Pyelonephritis.
  6) Glomerulonephritis.
  7) SLE (systemic lupus erythematosus).
  8) Aminoglycoside induced nephritis.
  9) "Obstructive uropathy."
   a) Benign prostatic hypertrophy.
   b) Neurogenic.
    1) Diabetes Mellitus.
    2) Anticholinergics.
    3) Antihypertensives: reserpine, ganglionic blockers, hydralazine.
    4) Adrenergics: ephedrine, dextroamphetamine.
    5) Antihistamines.
    6) Isoniazid.
  10) Potent diuretics causing acute bladder overload.
   a) Furosemide (Lasix).
   b) Etharcrynic acid (Edcrin).
  11) Urate precipitation in treatment of lymphoma or leukemia.
  12) Calcium precipitation in hypercalcemia syndromes.
  13) Dialysis dementia.
  14) Phosphorus depletion secondary to hemodialysis and antacid consumption (i.e. amphogel).
III. DEPRESSION OR ACUTE EMOTIONAL STRESS; usually related to "losses," institutionalization, prolonged immobilization, or medications (i.e. reserpine).

IV. NUTRITION:
   More than 10% of elderly have simultaneous deficiencies of at least four of five important vitamins: thiamine, riboflavin, ascorbic acid, vitamin A, and nicotinic acid deficiency. Deficiencies may play a role in CNS dysfunction and may be due to inadequate intake or secondary to chronic illness. Pernicious anemia, too, may have CNS manifestations.
V. NEUROLOGICAL
   a) Tumors.
      1) Intracranial:
         a) Gliomas 50—60% of all CNS tumors, mostly malignant.
         b) Metastatic, 20—50%; lung, breast, others.
      2) Remote effects of distant cancer: lymphoma, lung.
   b) Aphasia.
   c) Normal pressure hydrocephalus.
   d) Parkinsonism.
   e) Infections of CNS: meningitis, brain abscess, herpes simplex encephalitis.
VI. GASTROINTESTINAL
   a) Constipation.
   b) Intestinal obstruction (i.e. volvulus, rectosigmoid cancer).
   c) Gastrointestinal bleeding secondary to diverticulosis.
VII. HEPATIC CONDITIONS
   a) Cirrhosis; onset between ages 40 and 70 years.
   b) Hepatitis; not uncommon in the elderly.
VIII. CARDIAC CONDITIONS
   a) Decreased cardiac output secondary to arrhythmia, congestive heart failure, or pulmonary emboli.
   b) Acute myocardial infarction; 13% of patients have confusion as the major symptom.
   c) Infective endocarditis.
   d) Cardiogenic dementia.
IX. VASCULAR CONDITIONS
   a) Transient ischemic attacks and cerebrovascular accidents.
   b) Subdural hematoma; 20% of all intracranial masses in the elderly.
   c) Hypertension.
X. ANY FEBRILE CONDITION
XI. PULMONARY CONDITIONS:
   chronic lung disease (emphysema) with hypoxia and/or hypercapnia; pulmonary emboli; pneumonia
XII. SURGERY
   a) Post-surgical dementia (i.e. postanesthesia; post cataract removal).
XIII. POST-TRAUMA DEMENTIA
   a) Accidents.
   b) Assaults.

## MEDICATIONS

Although older adults represent one-tenth of the US population, they receive approximately one-fourth of all prescriptions written. They are thus the leading consumers of medications in this country. The most frequently prescribed drugs in recent surveys were tranquilizers, for example, diazepam (Valium), chlordiazepoxide (Librium) and the non-narcotic analgesic propoxyphene (Darvon) (Petersen and Thomas, 1975).

Iatrogenic disease related to drugs is very common in the elderly. Organ efficiency of the body lessens with age. For certain drugs, the me-tabolism, detoxification, excretion and, occasionally, the absorption change with increasing age (Hall, 1973). Mental deterioration is seen quite often among the complications generated by errors in self-administration of medications in the elderly (Libow and Mehl, 1970; Schwartz, Wang, Zeitz, and Goss, 1962). Many medications have the potential to cause confusion and/or dementia. These include digitalis (Gupta, Singh, and Gupta, 1974), benzodiazepines (Preskorn, S. H., Lee, D. J., 1977), antidepressants, lidocaine, pentazocine (Talwin), cimetidine (Schentag, J. J., Calleri, G., et al., 1979), gentamicin (Kane, F. J., Byrd, O., 1975), propranolol (Fraser, H. S., Carr, A. C., 1976) and others (Glickman, L., Friedman, S. A., 1976).

Anticholinergic drugs can induce dementia. Drachman (1977) has shown that scoplamine produced cognitive impairment in the ability of young volunteers to store new information, thereby resembling the changes of normal aging. Antihypertensive drugs are well known to induce depression and/or confusion and reserpine, methyldopa (Dubach, V. C., 1963), and clonidine are the most likely to do so (Bant, 1973; Fleming, 1973; Hodkinson, 1973; and Pariente, 1973).

Drugs that occasionally produce inappropriate secretion of the antidiuretic hormone or enhance its activity can produce dementia via hyponatremia, hypo-osmolarity and/or water intoxication. These drugs include chlorpropamide, carbamazepine (Flegel and Cole, 1977; and Henry, Lawson, Reavey, and Renfrew, 1977), morphine, barbiturates, vincristine, clofibrate, cyclophosphamide and tricyclic anti-depressants. Diuretic therapy, so often used in the elderly, can produce mental deterioration through a mechanism of dehydration and hyperosmolarity, uremia, hyperglycemia, hypopotassemia or hyponatremia. Lithium is a drug used in the elderly for psychiatric disorders, such as manic states and cyclic mood disorders. The drug has a longer half-life in the elderly and a lower daily dose has to be used than in younger aged patients. Despite precautions, the drug frequently produces acute organic brain syndrome as the predominant sign of toxicity (Foster, Gershell, and Goldfarb, 1977).

The metal aluminum may induce dementia (Berlyne, 1976; Crapper, Krishnan, and Quittkat, 1976; Duckett, 1976; Editorial, Feb. 1976; Editorial, June 1976; and Flendrig, Kruis, and Das, 1976).

These are but a few examples of drugs and chemicals that can induce a deterioration of the mental function in the older adult group of patients.

## METABOLIC DISTURBANCES AND THEIR INFLUENCE ON MENTAL FUNCTION

### ELECTROLYTE IMBALANCE

*Sodium abnormalities*—Hypernatremia is a hyperosmolar state with adverse effects on the brain function. The hypernatremic state in the older adult can be caused by many factors, such as inadequate fluid intake, excessive water loss (dehydration) due to excessive perspiration, diarrhea, vomiting, burns, cerebral concussion, administration of hypertonic saline, increased salt intake (accidental or iatrogenic ingestion) diabetes insipidus, hypokalemic nephropathy, hypercalcemia, and primary hyperaldosteronism following acute diuretic phase of renal failure recovery (Jana and Jana, 1973). A serum sodium level of more than 160 mg. indicates a serious water deficit producing confusion, disorientation, neuromuscular irritability and hypotension. The situation can progress to stupor, coma and even to death.

Hyponatremia represents a hypo-osmolar syndrome. A serum sodium concentration below 133 mg. is a frequent finding among hospitalized elderly population (Rosen, 1976). The symptoms of hyponatremia are not specific and include confusion, lethargy, mental sluggishness, anorexia, headache, nausea and can progress to convulsions, coma and death. Hyponatremia may be due to inappropriate secretion of anti-diuretic hormone (ADH). Earlier, we gave a list of drugs that can produce the inappropriate secretion of this hormone. Bronchogenic carcinoma, tuberculosis, other pneumonias, cerebrovascular accident, primary and secondary brain tumors, skull fracture, hypothyroidism, congestive heart failure, liver cirrhosis and solid tumors can produce inappropriate anti-diuretic hormone secretion.

### CALCIUM ABNORMALITIES

Hypercalcemia is another metabolic disturbance with potential influence on mental function. There does not always exist a strict correlation between the abnormal plasma level of calcium and the presence of mental deterioration. One patient will have completely normal mental function, with a level of 14 to 15 mg. plasma calcium per hundred ml. and another may become confused having a plasma level of calcium of 12 to 13 mg. per hundred ml. The variation may relate to the rapidity of the change of serum level.

Causes of hypercalcemia include hyperparathyroid excess, vitamin D intoxication, bone metastases from malignancies, medications such as the diuretics, immobilization, thyroid dysfunction, milk-alkali syndrome, Addison's disease, multiple myeloma, etc. (Roof and Gordan, 1978).

### PHOSPHORUS ABNORMALITIES

Phosphate depletion was claimed to induce encephalopathy in hemodialysis patients (Pierides, Ward, and Kerr, 1976).

### DIABETES MELLITUS

Diabetes mellitus is common in the elderly, and its peripheral complications include defects in vision, in the nervous system and vascular tree. The diagnosis of diabetes mellitus may present difficulties in the older adult. "Elevated" levels of 2 hours postprandial blood sugars in the older adult are frequent in late life and it is often difficult for the clinician to decide where aging and disease differ. This disease and treatment influences mental status in different ways by inducing confusion, lethargy or dementia. Hypoglycemic states may be mild and undiagnosed clinically, producing mental deterioration and, if they are more severe, prolonged and/or repeated, may produce irreversible brain damage. Hypoglycemia is caused by insulin or by oral hypoglycemic drugs possibly accompanied by inadequate food intake related to physical or mental illness. The hyperosmolar nonketotic coma is an entity specific almost to the elderly, with confusion and coma accompanying severe hyperglycemia occurring in the absence of ketosis (Williams, 1978). Usually this syndrome develops gradually and unrecognized in a patient undiagnosed as diabetic or in a diabetic previously well controlled.

The mental changes occurring with hyperglycemia in ketoacidotic states are usually easily recognized and don't present diagnostic problems. Lactic acidosis syndrome is often induced by biguanide oral hypoglycemics, such as phenformin (DBI), and is less easily diagnosed. The specificity of the disease is the presence of acidosis showing an anion gap that is filled by lactic acid in the absence of ketosis. The syndrome is less common today, since biguanide prescription has been restricted.

The older adult diabetic is often controlled without such hypoglycemic agents as insulin or oral hypoglycemic, and good control is achieved by diet and some exercise (Williams, 1978). In treating the diabetic with oral hypoglycemics, one has to keep in mind the potential of drug-drug interactions, with compounds such as aspirin, phenylbutazone, oral anticoagulants, sulfizoxazole, etc.

## KIDNEY DYSFUNCTION

Uremia is another frequent cause of mental deterioration in the older adult patient. The coexistence of nutritional deficiencies can include Korsakoff psychosis and Wernicke's encephalopathy. The mental changes are usually reversible if the cause of uremia is treatable (Haase, 1977).

Renal function (renal bloodflow, glomerular filtration, etc.) declines by about 50 percent by the time one attains the age of 65 years. The creatinine is somewhat maintained at younger adult levels by the reduction of muscular mass (Rosen, 1976).

Prerenal causes of uremia are multiple and include low cardiac output, gastrointestinal bleeding, dehydration, all those factors leading to a reduced effective blood volume with the consequence of reduction of the glomerular filtration rate. The intact kidney will produce a urine with low sodium content or high osmolality. The renal causes of uremia are multiple, including infections (pyelonephritis), immune reactions (glomerulonephritis), autoimmune collagen diseases (lupus erythematosus, periarteritis nodosa), vascular atheromatosis and vascular occlusion, and drug induced (aminoglycoside, antibiotics, analgesics, etc.). Calcium and urate deposition are other causes of renal dysfunction of BUN (Rosen, 1976).

Postrenal causes ("obstructive") are multiple and include neurogenic disorders, use of anticholinergics, antihypertensives (reserpine, ganglion blockers, hydralazine, adrenergics, antihistamines, izoniazide, etc.). Bladder outlet obstruction, too, can cause uremia.

An interesting kind of dementia is the so-called dialysis dementia. This type of dementia is not infrequently seen in dialysis centers and is often fatal to the patient within three to eighteen months after the first symptoms develop (Sullivan, Murnaghan, and Callaghan, 1977). These patients show high concentration of aluminum within the brain tissue, on postmortem examination (Editorial, Feb. 1976). Cases of curability of the disease after parathyroidectomy (Ball, Butkus, and Madison, 1977) or after renal transplantation (Sullivan, Murnaghan, and Callaghan, 1977) have been reported. The cause of dialysis dementia remains unknown.

## VITAMINS

At least 10 percent of the older adult population of Great Britain have deficiency in Vitamin A, ascorbic acid, thiamine and riboflavin and these deficiencies may be accompanied by mental changes.

A small percentage of the elderly population present with B12 or folic acid deficiencies, too. A deficiency of B12 certainly may cause dementia while the role of folic acid in dementia is unclear. Vitamin B12 deficiency may cause mental changes even in the absence of anemia (Glickman and Friedman, 1976).

Thiamine deficiency can induce apathetic confusion, ataxia and oculomotor disturbances (Wernicke's triad). Another syndrome induced by the thiamine deficiency is Korsakoff's, characterized by memory deficit and confabulation (Glickman and Friedman, 1976).

Mental changes (depression, apathy, irritability, confusion and delirium as well as dementia) are found in nicotinic acid deficiency, together with diarrhea and dermatitis, the so-called pellagra triad (Haase, 1977).

## ALCOHOLISM

Chronic alcoholism is a common problem in the older adult population and can produce mental changes (Arie, 1973). The older alcoholic is often labeled as a mental patient, admitted to a mental hospital and then does not get the proper care (McCuan and Bland, 1975). Brain function is affected by the direct toxic effect of the alcohol or by its withdrawal in the patient who is physically dependent (Glickman and Friedman, 1976). Alcoholism is dealt with more fully by Simon, Chapter 27, in this volume.

## ENDOCRINE

In a previous section we discussed hypercalcemia and its influence on the brain function. Hyperparathyroidism is one of the causes of hypercalcemia, with a relatively high incidence in the elderly. In this age group the symptoms of the disease develop insidiously and are often attributed to other pathological processes (Roof and Gordan, 1978). Organs affected in hyperparathyroidism include bones, kidneys, gastrointestinal tract and central nervous system. The incidence of radiologically overt bone involvement in this age group is approximately 10 percent (Steinbach, Gordan, Eisenberg, Crane, Silverman, and Goldman, 1961). The incidence of renal lithiasis is less than in younger adult population.

Thyroid disease is common in the elderly. Toxic nodular goiter is much more common in the elderly than diffuse toxic goiter. The clinical presentation is often different from that found in the younger adult. Cardiovascular disturbances (arrhythmias) without obvious hypermetabolic effects, are frequent. Weight loss, if present, is often accompanied by anorexia rather than increased appetite, and constipation may be more common than diarrhea. As mentioned earlier in the chapter, the mental impairment of hyperthyroidism may present as depression, dementia or apathy (Ingbar, 1978; Libow, 1977). Tri-iodothyroxine (T3) thyrotoxicosis seems to be more common in the older adult than in the younger group (Ingbar, 1978). In general, the therapy of choice in this age group is radio-iodine.

Hypothyroidism is the classic clinical situation in which the elderly patient is often incorrectly labeled as having dementia. Depression and apathy, lethargy, constipation, cold intolerance, loss of mental and auditory acuity, drying of the skin, dementia and coma (Ingbar, 1978) are the characteristic symptoms of this disease and are often overlooked in mild cases. The treatment of the condition will improve the physical and mental status in many of the cases while in others the mental status will remain unchanged. It is unknown if this persistent dementia is due to effects of thyroid deprivation or to a simultaneously present senile dementia. The treatment is usually replacement with thyroxine. One should start with a low dose, increasing the dose slowly, trying to avoid the cardiovascular complications which can threaten the patient's life. Tri-iodothyroxine should not be used as replacement therapy, unless one is treating a patient with myxedema coma.

## RESPIRATORY SYSTEM AND ITS INFLUENCE ON MENTAL FUNCTION

Pulmonary infections can be present as confusional states (Dunn and Arie, 1972). Mild mental deterioration can worsen during an episode of pneumonia and improve again after the lung condition is treated. A chronic infection can present an insidious mental and bodily decline, which presents diagnostic problems (Hodkinson, 1973). The mechanism that explains the influence on mental status is complex. Carcinoma of the lungs can induce mental deterioration by metastasis, endocrine effects, or by remote effect demyelinating (Haase, 1977). Chronic obstructive pulmonary disease (COPD) or emphysema with hypoxia and/or hypercapnea may also present with confusion or dementia (Dunn and Arie, 1972; Libow, 1977), as may pulmonary embolism.

## CARDIOVASCULAR PATHOLOGY AND ITS INFLUENCE ON MENTAL STATUS

Cardiogenic dementia may result from heart failure and/or dysrhythmias. At times, correction of the cardiac state will produce an obvious improvement in mental status (Editorial, Jan. 1977). The mechanism of mental deterioration is through diminished cardiac output. The only clinical presentation of acute myocardial infarction may be mental deterioration (Librach, Schadel, Seltzer, Harth, and Yellin, 1976). Subacute bacterial endocarditis can also cause mental deterioration (Hodkinson, 1973).

As already indicated, the integrity of the vascular tree is very important for a normal mental function. Mental changes may be encountered during transient ischemic attacks or cerebrovascular accidents.

Vasculitis is another, though infrequent, cause of mental deterioration. Vascular inflammatory disease can be caused by rheumatoid arthritis, lupus erythematosus (Karasu and Katzman, 1976), or by giant cell arthritis (and/or polymyalgia rheumatica).

Hypertension can present as elevation of diastolic pressure and/or systolic pressure, the latter being of greatest prevalence in old age.

What is the relationship of hypertension to mental function? The mean blood pressure and the systolic pressure were found to be higher in depressed than in non-depressed elderly. Even subtle depression in otherwise healthy and well-integrated individuals is accompanied by increased levels of blood pressure (Libow, 1971a).

Hypertension is one of the major contributory factors included as causes of atherosclerosis, which, in turn, has obvious pathologic effects on brain function. Further, the treatment of hypertension may adversely influence mental status, via mechanisms such as orthostatic hypotension, drug-drug interaction, direct effect on brain function, etc.

## NEUROLOGICAL DISTURBANCES

Intracranial tumors present with behavioral alterations in 50 to 70 percent of the cases (Dunn and Arie, 1972; Haase, 1977). The symptomatology in the elderly is often delayed because of the increased intracranial space available as a result of the cerebral atrophy in the elderly. The presence of papilledema is encountered in approximately 11 percent of the space occupying lesions in the older adult patient. Almost half of all brain tumors seen in this age group are metastases originating from carcinoma of the lung and breast. A nonmetastatic impairment of brain function caused by extracranial carcinomas is known as a paraneoplastic syndrome or remote effect of carcinoma. Lymphoma, carcinoma of the lung, ovary, prostate, rectum and breast are known to produce neurological as well as mental deterioration. The central nervous system mechanism is by demyelinization, particularly in the subthalamic and brain stem nuclei. In the majority of the cases pathological examination fails to show abnormalities capable of explaining the mental picture (Haase, 1977).

Subdural hematoma is largely related to falls in the elderly. The incidence is higher among alcoholics. Confusion and aggressiveness may be the only clinical presentation. Fluctuating confusion or consciousness may increase clinical suspicions and, together with a history of falls, may be the clue for diagnosis (Dunn and Arie, 1972). Organic mental syndrome may be the presentation of other intracranial diseases such as subarachnoid hemorrhage, as well as meningitis, brain abscess or herpes simplex encephalitis (Karasu and Katzman, 1976). Aphasia must be recognized clinically, and not attributed to an organic mental syndrome. Post-traumatic confusional states or senile dementia are encountered also in the elderly patient even when the trauma does not result in subdural hematoma and even if the trauma is unrelated to the head. These are often irreversible and present a mystery (Karasu and Katzman, 1976; Libow, 1977).

Normal pressure hydrocephalus presents as a progressive dementia with incontinence and ataxia and is a relatively infrequent disease in the elderly (Libow, 1977). The cerebro-spinal fluid reveals normal pressure. The condition may appear as idiopathic or can follow trauma, subarachnoid hemorrhage, chronic meningitis, or may accompany neoplasms. The diagnosis is aided by isotope cystenography and CAT scan. The mental status occasionally improves following shunt procedures.

Central nervous system syphilitic involvement is still seen. The characteristic feature is a personal disintegration, e.g, errors in judgement, instability, depression and intellectual, social and moral deterioration. The disease may appear 10 to 30 years after the initial luetic infection, and is more common in men than women (Haase, 1977).

Parkinson's disease presents with accompanying mental deterioration in an impressive number of cases. L-Dopa treatment may improve the mental status as an accompaniment of the general physical improvement, but the improvement is temporary. Dementia is also a possible adverse effect of L-Dopa (Haase, 1977).

## HEMATOLOGICAL

Anemia in the older adult patient may develop with a slow insidious and nonspecific symptomatology, such as confusion, apathy, giddiness, clumsiness; symptoms which can be considered unrelated to anemia in the elderly (Lewis, 1976). One has to keep in mind that anemia always represents a pathological feature and is not a concomitant of age. The incidence of anemia among elderly patients admitted to a hospital is about 30 percent (Thomas, 1973). The classification of anemia does not differ from the younger adult. The most common anemia in this age is iron deficiency anemia (Lewis, 1976). The causes leading to anemias are numerous, including occult gastrointestinal bleeding, chronic infections, atrophic gastritis, carcinomatous diseases, renal diseases, B12 and/or folic acid deficiency, etc. (Thomas, 1973).

## GASTROINTESTINAL

Liver diseases, with their influence on mental function, are not a rarity in the older adult patient. Cirrhosis, inflammatory diseases of the liver, obstruction of the bile ducts with a consequent elevation of plasma bilirubin as well as surgical portocaval shunt—all may present with mental status deterioration (Haase, 1977; Libow, 1977).

Chronic active hepatitis is an entity seen in young females. The presence of the disease in elderly is unusual, but exists and affects the older adult female. The disease may present atypically, the only symptom being a confusional state (Woolf, Boyes, Leeming, and Dymock, 1974). When the situation is warranted, the diagnosis is made, as in the younger adult female, by liver biopsy that shows disruption of limiting plates, rosette formation, bile duct proliferation and piecemeal necrosis, antinuclear antibody, lupus erythematosus cells, and antimitochondrial antibody are seen in some of the patients. Steroid therapy may produce a marked improvement.

Intestinal obstruction may present with mental confusion (Editorial, Dec. 1977). Though the obstruction is usually related to adhesions, hernias, neoplasms, etc., an occasional case is due to fecal impaction. This is especially so in a chronically ill, not too mobile, elderly person.

Approximately one-third of the older adult

patients with rectosigmoid cancer present with intestinal obstruction as the first presentation of the disease (Steinheber, 1976). Cecal volvulus, most often seen in women, and sigmoid volvulus, most seen in men, are other important causes of intestinal obstruction in this age (Steinheber, 1976). Mental changes, especially depression, are one of the puzzling presentations of carcinoma of the pancreas.

Gastrointestinal bleeding from upper and lower intestinal tract exist unrecognized for a long time, and the patient can present with mental deterioration as the only clinical symptomatology (Editorial, Dec. 1977; Steinheber, 1976).

The most common cause of upper gastrointestinal bleeding is benign peptic ulcer. Aspirin-induced hemorrhagic gastritis or gastric ulcer is found also, as well as bleeding esophageal varices. Colonic cancer, ischemic colitis and diverticulosis are the most commonly encountered causes of lower gastrointestinal bleeding (Steinheber, 1976).

## SURGERY

Major surgical interventions can occasionally lead to mental changes in a patient who had normal brain function prior to the surgery. The mental deterioration is usually seen when the surgical intervention was done using general anesthesia. The mechanism of production of the dementia is unknown. Not all patients will recover to their premorbid mental state (Libow, 1977). Minor surgical procedures, such as cataract surgery, can be accompanied by confusion, thought to represent anticholinergic toxicity (Summers and Reich, 1979).

## DEPRESSION AND OTHER PSYCHOLOGICAL CHANGES

Depression, a disease common in the older adult, is often difficult to distinguish from chronic organic mental syndrome. Being a treatable dementia, the differentiation of depression is crucial for the patient's future. Symptoms of insomnia and hypochondriasis may lead one to think about the diagnosis as well as recent acute social, psychological or economic losses. Medication, too, can precipitate a confusional state that finally turns out to be depression. Most cases of depression will respond to tricyclic antidepressant medications. Electroshock therapy is usually successful in cases resistant to medication (Dunn and Arie, 1972).

Institutionalization and prolonged immobilization are mentally and physically detrimental for the older adult patient. Prolonged immobilization produces metabolic changes that will adversely influence all organ functions. Organic brain syndrome, if previously present, may worsen after prolonged immobilization. Depression, fear, and panic are commonly seen in the patient who is immobilized. Increasing apathy and even stupor may result. These patients may present regressive behavior with social withdrawal, unintelligible speech patterns, or complete loss of speech. These regressive syndromes are often reversible and, where appropriate, rehabilitation efforts should be made to return these patients to their previous physical and mental status (Miller, 1975).

Life changes in the older adult population are frequently found in association with changes in behavior, mood and thinking. Successful suicide efforts in men increase with age and, in the eighth decade of life, are three times more frequent than in the third decade of life. Depression and suicidal thoughts are often precipitated by losses such as the death of a spouse, children marrying and moving away, loss of health, or retirement (Glickman and Friedman, 1976).

The physician who is evaluating a patient with recent personality changes has to be aware of the suicidal risk to which the older adult patient is prone (Murphy, 1975).

## BRAIN INFLUENCE ON BODILY FUNCTION

Though unrelated to age, the most dramatic example of mental status influencing the somatic function is the so-called "Voodoo" death (Cannon, 1942). Spells, sorcery, or black magic apparently have the power to produce illness and even death. Such is the evidence reported in observation of the primitive populations among the natives of South America, Africa, Australia, New Zealand, and the Islands of the Pacific, as well as among the blacks of Haiti. Voodoo death was reported by competent observers, including physicians. A bone pointed by the chief or the medicine man is enough to kill the intended victim. Another form of Voodoo death is by "taboo" among the New Zealand natives. Cannon's explanation of the mechanism of death was that the intense stress of fear produced a discharge of catecholamines which somehow results in shock and death.

Modern civilized society is not protected from mechanisms possibly similar to voodoo death. The "broken heart" is a figure of speech with important significance among the older adult population. In a nine-year follow-up study on about 5,000 widowers, 213 died during the first six months of bereavement (Parkes, Benjamin, and Fitzgerald, 1969). The death rate was 40 percent more than the expected rate for married men of the same age. The main cause of death was coronary thrombosis and other arteriosclerotic and degenerative heart disease. Another interesting finding was that 22.5 percent of the deaths were in the same diagnostic group as the cause of death of the wife. After six months, the death rate fell gradually and achieved the same level as that of married men. This study suggests that grief is killing and that the most important mechanism is cardiac.

There are differences in survivor morbidity between anticipatory grief of a lengthy chronic fatal illness and a shorter chronic fatal illness. The aged bereaved survivor of a lengthy chronic fatal illness occurring in the spouse does worse than the bereaved of a shorter fatal chronic illness death. In addition, widowers show more medical problems than do widows (Gerber, Rusalem, Hannon, Battin, and Arkin, 1975).

The relationship between stress, behavior, life changes, and coronary disease has been highlighted in recent years (Friedman, 1969). In coronary prone behavior pattern, Type A is represented by highly competitive individuals who are involved in multiple activities, many of which are characterized by time restrictions or deadlines. They are highly alert and like to set their own work pace. Type B behavior is the absence of the overt manifestations of Type A. Type A behavior is significantly more associated with coronary heart disease than is Type B.

Another study focused on "life changes" and myocardial infarction. "Adjusting" and "upsetting" were the criteria used to describe life changes. The myocardial infarction group had a higher total "life changes" score than the control group during the one year before the infarction occurred (Lundberg, Theorell, and Lind, 1975). Other studies seem to show the same results when dealing with the influence of psychosocial factor on coronary heart disease (Rahe and Lind, 1971; Theorell and Rahe, 1971).

Social and emotional factors were found to play a role in precipitating heart failure. Among a group of older patients with congestive heart failure, a significantly greater percentage had stressful emotional factors occurring in the few days prior to the acute heart failure than did a control group of age-matched patients (Perlman, Ferguson, Bergum, Istenberg, and Hammarsten, 1971).

Another mechanism of cardiac sudden death is represented by electrical instability of the conduction system and a predisposition to ventricular fibrillation. Psychological stress was shown to reduce the threshold of the ventricle for repetitive response in canine experiments (Lown, Verrier, and Corbalan, 1973).

Severe stress has been shown to have influence on the immune system. Twenty-six bereaved spouses were checked two and six weeks after bereavement. They were evaluated for T and B cell function number. Six weeks after bereavement the widows showed a decreased response of the lymphocytes to phytohemaglutinin as well as to concovalin A reflecting diminished T cell function. The mechanisms linking these psychologic stresses to decreased immune function are unclear (Bartrop, Luckhurst, Lazarus, Kiloh, and Penny, 1977). Depression, hopelessness, and undischarged grief may be significant precursors to the development of cancer (LeShan, 1959).

In evaluating the older patient, the physician is challenged more than by any age group. Here there is the interplay, not only between body and mind, but also between time and disease.

# REFERENCES

ARIE, T. 1973. Dementia in the elderly: Diagnosis and assessment. *B.M.J.*, *4*, 540–543.

BALL, J. H., BUTKUS, D. E., AND MADISON, D. S. 1977. Effect of subtotal parathyroidectomy on dialysis dementia. *Nephron*, *18*, 151–155.

BANT, W. 1973. Methyldopa and depression. *B.M.J.*, *4*, 553.

BASAVARAJU, N. G., PARASKEVAS, K., AND LIBOW, L. S. November, 1977. Primitive reflexes and perceptual sensory tests in the elderly—their usefulness in dementia. Presented to the Annual Meeting, Gerontological Society, San Francisco, Cal.

BASAVARAJU, N. G., SILVERSTONE, F., PARASKEVAS, K., AND LIBOW, L. S. 1979. Primitive reflexes and perceptual sensory tests in dementia and normal aging. In preparation.

BARTROP, R. W., LUCKHURST, E., LAZARUS, L., KILOH, L. G., AND PENNY, R. 1977. Depressed lymphocyte function after bereavement. *Lancet*, *1*, 834–836.

BELLAK, L. 1976. Psychological aspects of normal aging. *In*, L. Bellak and T. B. Karasu, (eds.), *Geriatric Psychiatry—A Handbook for Psychiatrists and Primary Care Physicians*, pp. 21–29. New York: Grune & Stratton.

BENDER, M. B. 1975. The incidence and type of perceptual deficiencies in the aged. *In*, W. S. Fields (ed.), *Neurological and Sensory Disorders in the Elderly*, pp.

15–31. New York: Stratton Intercont. Book Corp.

BERLYNE, G. M. 1976. Aluminum toxicity. *Lancet, 1*, 589.

BIEBER, I. 1940. Grasping and sucking. *J. Nerv. Ment. Dis., 91*, 31–36.

BOTWINICK, J., AND BIRREN, J. E. 1971 (reprinted 1976). Mental abilities and psychomotor responses in healthy aged men. *In,* J. E. Birren, R. N. Butler, S. W. Greenhouse, L. Sokoloff, and M. R. Yarrow (eds.), *Human Aging, A Biological and Behavioral Study,* pp. 97–108. Washington, D.C.: Publication No. (HSM) 71–9051, US Government Printing Office.

CANNON, W. B. 1942. Voodoo death. *American Anthropologist—New Series, 44*, 169–181.

CARP, F. M. 1969. The psychology of aging. *In,* R. R. Boyd and C. G. Oakes (eds.), *Foundations of Practical Gerontology,* pp. 100–116. Columbia, S.C.: The University of South Carolina Press.

CRAPPER, D. R., KRISHNAN, S. S., AND QUITTKAT, S. 1976. Aluminum, neurofibrillary degeneration and Alzheimer's disease. *Brain, 99*, 67–80.

DASTUR, D. K., LANE, M. H., HANSEN, D. B., KETY, S. S., BUTLER, R. N., PERLIN, S., AND SOKOLOFF, L. 1971. Effects of aging on cerebral circulation and metabolism in man. *In,* J. E. Birren, R. N. Butler, S. W. Greenhouse, L. Sokoloff, and M. R. Yarrow (eds.), *Human Aging, A Biological and Behavioral Study,* pp. 59–76. Washington, D.C.: Publication No. (HSM) 71–9051, US Government Printing Office.

DRACHMAN, D. A. June, 1977. Systematic analysis of the cognitive effects of blockade and facilitation of central cholinergic function. Presented in the Workshop Conference on Alzheimer's Disease, Senile Dementia and Related Disorders at The Clinical Center of the National Institutes of Health, Bethesda, Maryland.

DUBACH, V. C. Jan. 26, 1963. Methyldopa and depression. *B.M.J., 1*, 261–62.

DUCKETT, S. 1976. Aluminum and Alzheimer disease. *Arch. Neurol., 33*, 730–731.

DUNN, T., AND ARIE, T. 1972. Mental disturbance in the ill old person. *B.M.J., 2*, 413–416.

Editorial, Feb. 14, 1976. Dialysis dementia: Aluminum again? *Lancet, 1*, 349.

Editorial, June 12, 1976. Aluminum and Alzheimer. *Lancet, 1*, 1281–1282.

Editorial, Jan. 1, 1977. Cardiogenic dementia. *Lancet, 1*, 27–28.

Editorial, Dec. 10, 1977. Uncovering physical illness in elderly patients with dementia. *B.M.J., 4*, 1499–1500.

FLEGEL, K. M., AND COLE, C. H. 1977. Inappropriate antidiuresis during carbamazepine treatment. *Ann. Int. Medic., 87*, 722–723.

FLEMING, H. A. 1973. Methyldopa and depression. *B.M.J., 2*, 232.

FLENDRIG, J. A., KRUIS, H., AND DAS, H. A. 1976. Aluminum and dialysis dementia. *Lancet, 1*, 1235.

FOSTER, J. R., GERSHELL, W. J., AND GOLDFARB, A. I. 1977. Lithium treatment in the elderly—clinical usage. *J. Geront., 32*, 299–302.

FRASER, H. S., AND CARR, A. C. 1976. Propranolol psychosis. *Brit. J. Psychiat., 129*, 508–12.

FRIEDMAN, M. 1969. The possible and general causes of coronary artery disease. *In,* M. Friedman (ed.), *The Pathogenesis of Coronary Artery Disease,* pp. 68–135. New York: McGraw-Hill.

GERBER, I., RUSALEM, R., HANNON, N., BATTIN, D., AND ARKIN, A. 1975. Anticipatory grief and aged widows and widowers. *J. Geront., 30*, 225–229.

GLICKMAN, L., AND FRIEDMAN, S. A. 1976. Changes in behavior, mood or thinking in the elderly—diagnosis and management. *In,* S. A. Friedman and F. D. Steinheber (Guest eds.), *Geriatric Medicine,* pp. 1297–1313. *the Med. Clin. N. Amer.* Philadelphia: W. B. Saunders.

GREGERMAN, R. I., AND BIERMAN, E. L. 1974. Aging and hormones. *In,* R. H. Williams (ed.), *Textbook of Endocrinology,* Fifth Edition, pp. 1059–1070. Philadelphia: W. B. Saunders.

GUPTA, O. P., SINGH, S., AND GUPTA, H. M. 1974. Psychosis—A feature of digitalis intoxication. *Ind. Heart J., 27*, 69–70.

HAASE, G. R. 1977. Diseases presenting as dementia. *In,* Ch. E. Wells (ed.), *Dementia,* 2nd Edition, (Contemporary Neurology Series) pp. 27–67. Philadelphia: F. A. Davis.

HALL, M. R. P., 1973. Drug therapy in the elderly. *B. M. J., 4*, 582–584.

HENRY, D. A., LAWSON, D. H., REAVEY, P., AND RENFREW, S. 1977. Hyponatremia during carbamazepine treatment. *B.M.J., 1*, 83–84.

HODKINSON, H. M. 1973. Non-specific presentation of illness. *B.M.J., 4*, 94–96.

INGBAR, S. H. 1978. The influence of aging on the human thyroid hormone economy. *In,* R. B. Greenblatt (ed.), *Geriatric Endocrinology Aging,* Vol. 5, pp. 13–31. New York: Raven Press.

JACOBS, J. W., BERNHARD, M. R., DELGADO, A., AND STRAIN, J. J. 1977. Screening for organic mental syndromes in the medically ill. *Ann. Int. Med., 86*, 40–46.

JANA, D. K., AND JANA, L. R. 1973. Hypernatremic psychosis in the elderly: Case reports. *J. Am. Geriatr. Soc., 21*, 473–477.

KAHN, R. L., GOLDFARB, A. I., POLLACK, M., AND PECK, A. 1960. Brief objective measures for the determination of mental status in the aged. *Am. J. Psychiatry, 117*, 326–328.

KANE, F. J., AND BYRD, O. Oct., 1975. Acute toxic psychosis associated with gentamicin therapy. *Southern Med. J., 68*, 1283–85.

KARASU, T. B., AND KATZMAN, R. 1976. Organic brain syndromes. *In*, L. Bellak and T. B. Karasu (eds.), *Geriatric Psychiatry: A Handbook for Psychiatrists and Primary Care Physicians*, pp. 132–140. New York: Grune & Stratton.

KENT, S. 1976. Neurotransmitters may be weak link in the aging brain's communication network. *Geriatrics, July*, 105–111.

LeSHAN, L. 1959. Psychological states as factors in the development of malignant disease: A critical review. *J. Nat. Cancer Inst., 22*, 1–18.

LEWIS, R. 1976. Anemia—a common but never a normal concomitant of aging. *Geriatrics, Dec.*, 53–60.

LIBOW, L. S., AND MEHL, B. 1970. Self administration of medications by patients in hospital or extended care facilities. *J. Am. Geriatr. Soc., 18*, 81.

LIBOW, L. S. 1971a (reprinted 1976). Medical investigation of the processes of aging. *In*, J. E. Birren, R. N. Butler, S. W. Greenhouse, L. Sokoloff, and M. R. Yarrow (eds.), *Human Aging I: A Biological and Behavioral Study*, pp. 37–56. Washington, D.C.: Publication No. (HSM) 71–9051, US Government Printing Office.

LIBOW, L. S., 1971b (reprinted 1974). Medical factors in survival and mortality of the healthy elderly. *In*, S. Granick and R. D. Patterson (eds.), *Human Aging II: An Eleven-Year Follow-Up Biomedical and Behavioral Study*, pp. 21–39. Washington, D.C.: DHEW Publication No. (HSM) 71–9037, US Government Printing Office.

LIBOW, L. S., OBRIST, W. D., AND SOKOLOFF, L. 1971 (reprinted 1974). Cerebral circulatory and electroencephalographic changes in elderly men. *In*, S. Granick and R. D. Patterson (eds.), *Human Aging II: An Eleven-Year Follow-Up Biomedical and Behavioral Study*, pp. 41–48. Washington, D.C.: DHEW Publication No. (HSM) 71–9037, US Government Printing Office.

LIBOW, L. S. 1973. Pseudo-senility: Acute and reversible organic brain syndrome. *J. Am. Geriatr. Soc.*, 112–120.

LIBOW, L. S. 1977. Senile dementia and pseudosenility: Clinical diagnosis. *In*, C. Eisdorfer and R. O. Friedel (eds.), *Cognitive and Emotional Disturbance in the Elderly*, pp. 75–88. Chicago: Year Book Medical Publishing.

LIBRACH, G., SCHADEL, M., SELTZER, M., HARTH, A., AND YELLIN, N. 1976. The initial manifestations of acute myocardial infarction. *Geriatrics, July*, 41–46.

LIPOWSKI, Z. J. 1967. Delirium, clouding of consciousness and confusion. *J. Nerv. Ment. Dis., 145*, 227.

LIPOWSKI, Z. J. 1978. Organic brain syndrome, A refor-

mulation. *Comp. Psychiat., 19*, 309.

LOWN, B., VERRIER, R., AND CORBALAN, R. 1973. Psychologic stress and threshold for repetitive ventricular response. *Science, 1&2*, 834–836.

LUNDBERG, U., THEORELL, T., AND LIND, E. 1975. Life changes and myocardial infarction. Individual differences in life change scaling. *J. Psychosom. Dis., 19*, 27–32.

MAGNUSSON, J. H., AND WERNSTEDT, W. 1935. The infantile palmo-mentalis reflex. *Acta. Poed.*, (Suppl. 1)*17*, 241–245.

MARINESCO, G., AND RADOVICI, A. 1920. Sur un reflexe cutane nouveau reflexe palmomentonnier. *Rev. Neurol., 27*, 237–240.

McCUAN, E. R., AND BLAND, J. 1975. A treatment typology for the elderly alcohol abuser. *J. Am. Geriatr. Soc., 28*, 553–557.

MILLER, M. B. 1975. Iatrogenic and nursigenic effects of prolonged immobilization of the ill aged. *J. Am. Geriatr. Soc., 23*, 360–369.

MURPHY, G. 1975. The physician's responsibility for suicide II—errors of omission. *Ann. Int. Med., 82*, 305–309.

OBRIST, W. D. 1971 (reprinted 1976). The electroencephalogram of healthy aged males. *In*, J. E. Birren, R. N. Butler, S. W. Greenhouse, L. Sokoloff, and M. R. Yarrow (eds.), *Human Aging I: A Biological and Behavioral Study*, pp. 79–93. Washington, D.C.: Publication No. (HSM) 71–9051, US Government Printing Office.

PARIENTE, D. 1973. Methyldopa and depression. *B.M.J., 2*, 110–111.

PARKES, C. M., BENJAMIN, B., AND FITZGERALD, R. G. 1969. Broken heart: A statistical study of increased mortality among widowers. *B.M.J., 1*, 740–743.

PARMELEE, A. H. 1963. The palmo-mental reflex in premature infants. *Develop. and Med. Child Neuro., 5*, 381–387.

PATTERSON, R. D., FREEMAN, L. C., AND BUTLER, R. N. 1971. (Reprinted 1974). Psychiatric aspects of adaptation, survival and death. *In*, S. Granick and R. D. Patterson (eds.), *Human Aging II: An Eleven-Year Follow-Up Biomedical and Behavioral Study*, pp. 63–94, Washington, D.C.: DHEW Publication No. (HSM) 71–9037, US Government Printing Office.

PAULSON, G. W. 1977. The neurological examination in dementia. *In*, Ch. E. Wells (ed.), *Dementia*, 2nd Edition (Contemporary Neurology Series), pp. 169–188. Philadelphia: F. A. Davis.

PERLIN, S., AND BUTLER, R. N. 1971 (reprinted 1976). Psychiatric aspects of adaptation to the aging experience. *In*, J. E. Birren, R. N. Butler, S. W. Greenhouse, L. Sokoloff, and M. R. Yarrow (eds.), *Human Aging I: A Biological and Behavioral Study*, pp. 159–191. Washington, D.C.: Publication No.

(HSM) 71–9051, US Government Printing Office.

PERLMAN, L. V., FERGUSON, S., BERGUM, K., ISTENBERG, E. L., AND HAMMARSTEN, J. F. 1971. Precipitation of congestive heart failure; social and emotional factors. *Ann. Int. Med., 75,* 1–7.

PETERSEN, D. M., AND THOMAS, CH. W. 1975. Acute drug reactions among the elderly. *J. Geront., 30,* 552–556.

PFEIFFER, E. 1975. A short portable mental status questionnaire for the assessment of organic brain deficit in elderly patients. *J. Am. Geriatr. Soc., 23,* 433.

PIERIDES, A. M., WARD, K. M., AND KERR, D. N. S. 1976. Hemodialysis encepholopathy: Possible role of phosphate depletion. *Lancet, 1,* 1234–1235.

PRESKORN, S. H. AND LEE, D. J. 1977. Benzodiazepines and withdrawal psychosis. *JAMA, 237,* 36.

RAHE, R. H., AND LIND, E. 1971. Psychosocial factors and sudden cardiac death. *A Pilot Study of Psychosom. Res., 15,* 19–24.

ROOF, B. S., AND GORDAN, G. S. 1978. Hyperparathyroid disease in the aged. *In,* R. B. Greenblatt, (ed.), Geriatric Endocrinology, *Aging,* Vol. 5 pp. 33–79. New York: Raven Press.

ROSEN, H. 1976. Renal disease in the elderly. *In,* S. A. Friedman and F. D. Steinheber (Guest eds.), *Geriatric Medicine,* pp. 1105–1119, The Med. Clin. N. Amer. Philadelphia: W. B. Saunders.

SCHENTAG, J. J., AND CALLERI, G. *et al.* Jan. 27, 1979. Pharmacokinetic and clinical studies in patients with cimetidine-associated mental confusion. *Lancet,* 177–181.

SCHWARTZ, D., WANG, M., ZEITZ, L., AND GOSS, M. E. W. 1962. Medication errors made by elderly, chronically ill patients. *Am. J. Public Health, 52,* 2018.

STEINBACH, H. L., GORDAN, G. S., EISENBERG, E., CRANE, J. T., SILVERMAN, S., AND GOLDMAN, L. 1961. Primary hyperparathyroidism: Correlation of roentgen, clinical and pathologic features. *Am. J. Roentgenol. Rad. Ther. Nucl. Med., 86,* 329–343.

STEINHEBER, F. W. 1976. Interpretation of gastrointestinal symptoms in the elderly. *In,* S. A. Friedman and F. U. Steinheber (guest eds.), *Symposium on Geriatric Medicine,* pp. 1141–1157. Philadelphia: W. B. Saunders.

SULLIVAN, P. A., MURNAGHAN, D. J., CALLAGHAN, N. 1977. Dialysis dementia: Recovery after transplantation. *B.M.J., 3,* 740.

SUMMERS, N. K., AND REICH, T. C. 1979. Delirium after cataract surgery: Review and two cases. *Am. J. Psychiat., 136,* 386–391.

TENTLER, R. L., AND PALACIOS, E. 1977. False negative computerized tomography in brain tumor. *J.A.M.A., 238,* 339–340.

TERRY, R. D., AND WISNIEWSKI, H. M. 1977: Structural aspects of aging of the brain. *In,* C. Eisdorfer and R. O. Friedel (eds.), *Cognitive and Emotional Disturbance in the Elderly,* pp. 3–9. Chicago: Year Book Medical Publishers.

THEORELL, T., AND RAHE, R. H. 1971. Psychosocial factors and myocardial infarction-1: An inpatient study in Sweden, *J. Psychosom. Res.* 15:25–31.

THOMAS, J. H. 1973. Anemia in the Elderly. *B.M.J., 4,* 288–290.

WEISBERG, L. A., AND NICE, CH. N. 1977. Intracranial tumors simulating the presentation of cerebrovascular syndromes—early detection with cerebral computed tomography (CTT). *Am. J. Med. 63,* 517–524.

WELLS, C. B. 1977. Diagnostic evaluation and treatment in dementia. *In,* Wells, C. E. (ed.), *Dementia,* 2nd ed. Philadelphia: F. A. Davis, Cr., 247–276.

WILLIAMS, T. F. 1978. Diabetes mellitus in the aged. *In,* R. B. Greenblatt (ed.) Geriatric Endocrinology *Aging,* Vol. 5, pp. 103–113. New York: Raven Press.

WOOLF, I. L., BOYES, B. E., LEEMING, J. T., AND DYMOCK, I. W. 1974. Active chronic hepatitis in the elderly. *Age and Ageing, 3,* 226–228.

# VI
# Treatment and Prevention

# 30

# Symptomatic Behaviors in the Elderly*

*Irene Mortenson Burnside*

How to grow old is the master work of wisdom and one of the most difficult chapters in the great art of living.
    Amiel

The purpose of this chapter is to treat symptomatic behaviors of the elderly from the point of view of the caretakers from many disciplines who will interact with these people. The literature on these behaviors has been reviewed, lacunae have been noted, and some interesting questions have been examined.

## SCOPE OF THE PROBLEM

In 1974, there were 3,300,000 "mentally ill aged" over 65 — this is more than the total population of the aged (3,000,000) in 1900. Of the millions of elderly chronically ill, at least 2.5 million are out of the mainstream of life and are in mental institutions (111,000). Home care is required by 1.5 million and constant care by 0.5 million. There are 113,218 patients in nursing homes, of whom approximately one-half have lived in a nursing home over one and one-half years and receive only routine nursing or personal care. Approximately 40 percent of nursing home residents have a mental disorder or impairment (U.S. Dept. of Health, Education, and Welfare, 1976).

## SYMPTOMATIC BEHAVIORS

Symptomatic behaviors which may occur in late life make growing old difficult, not only for the older person but also for relatives, peers, and staff mem-

*The author gratefully acknowledges the pharmacological suggestions by Ronald C. Kayne, Pharm.D., and thanks to Marion Kalkman for her reading of this chapter.

bers. This is true whether the old person resides in an institution or in the community. This chapter describes quite diverse behaviors and states which demand frequent and skillful interventions by caretakers — interventions which must be concomitantly psychosocial and physical. The chapter is weighted towards institutionalized elderly since there is a larger body of knowledge on that group. This chapter will focus on: (1) aggression, (2) confusion and disorientation, (3) loneliness, (4) incontinence, (5) insomnia, and (6) wandering. These conditions, whether alone or combined, place heavy demands of care, responsibility, and increased stress on families, staff persons, and/or even neighbors.

These behaviors can hasten the burn-out of a staff, which may be manifested by frustration, short tempers, low morale, despair and overwork. Mutual support and understanding of problems by all of the disciplines working on the health team can help reduce or prevent some of the burn-out of persons working specifically with geriatric patients. Burn-out of this specialized group of caretakers has not yet been described in the literature, but is easily observed in long-term care settings where low morale, low pay, low status, and overwork are prevalent. It is also not uncommon for depression to occur in workers new to the field of mental health and aging. Students especially will need guidance and support at the onset of their clinical experiences; supervisors and preceptors should be alert for signs of depression, frustration, and/or feelings of helplessness in the student (Burnside, 1978).

Butler and Lewis (1977) listed problems frequently presented to them by nursing staffs when professional help was sought by nursing homes and homes for the aged. These problems include: depression; confusion, or other symptoms of acute or chronic brain syndrome; paranoid delusions; noisiness; restlessness or wandering; combativeness; inappropriate dependency on staff; persistent talk of a wish to die; incontinence; and families who are critical or demanding of the institution. This list is included for readers who are developing linkages between community mental health centers and long-term care facilities. York's (1977) manual is recommended reading for guidelines for cooperative programs.

## NEGATIVE SEMANTICS REGARDING THE AGED

The negative connotations of words synonymous with aging comprise a large and interesting vocabulary, and Kassel (1965) has compiled a long list indicating the pervasive pessimism regarding the elderly. The negativeness continues and the list has not decreased much in the years since Kassel itemized, "aged, ancient, anile, antiquated, archaic, arteriosclerotic, autumn years; centenarian, codger, crock, crone; dean, decline, decrepit, deteriorated, doddery, dodo, dotard, dowager; elder; fading, failing, feeble, fogey, fossil, frail; gaffer, geezer, gerontic, golden ager, grandfather, grandmother, granny, gray, graybeard, grisard; hag, hoary; infirm; matriarch, mature, mellow, moldy, mossback, motheaten; nonagenarian; obsolete, octogenarian, old, old salt, oldster, old timer; patriarch, pop, professor; rusty; sage, second childhood, senator, senescent, senile, senior, senior citizen, septuagenarian, sexagenarian, superannuated; time worn, trot, twilight years; venerable, veteran, waning, winter years, wrinkles." One might disagree on a few terms he chose — especially those nouns or adjectives which accurately place the individual in the life span (e.g., "centenarian" is a decent term and surely "senescent" has a softer tone than others on the list). However, the negative attitude and/or therapeutic nihilism soars if the word "confused," "disoriented," "incontinent," or "wanderer" is used to describe an old person.

## INCONGRUITY: SEMANTICS AND PSEUDOADVOCACY

An incongruity frequently observed in a classroom, workshop, medical rounds, or the work setting, is a speaker assuming the advocacy role but consistently using words like "old hag," "old codger," "old duffer," etc. — a good example of pseudoadvocacy. The choice of semantics can negate any statement made about the aged. At a conference, a participant posed a question to the speaker about an elderly client, and when the speaker asked the age of the client, the reply was, "Oh, he was *just* a geriatric."

The familiar cliché, "you have to treat them like children" is the bane of dedicated caretakers but unfortunately is still a common admonition. One common example which prolongs this philosophy is the giving of dolls or stuffed toys to elderly women. This intervention is one way to withhold human interaction and, although a blatant offense in psychosocial care, is still being done. See Figure 30-1.

Pervasive and perjorative attitudes regarding treatment and intervention of mentally-impaired elderly include one recorded by Gubrium (1975). "It's a waste of time. Why not leave them in their own little world? They're happy, so leave them be." Such phrases are sung so often by nihilistic choirs that they carry great impact through sheer repetition, especially to neophytes in the field of aging.

Four behaviors—confusion, disorientation, incontinence, and wandering—require consistent, constant, and patient intervention. The sheer, dogged, hard work and patience necessary to intervene must be acknowledged. Whitehead (1974) described "dangerous symptoms" which are "likely to result in the individual being rejected by society and consequently put away in an institution." Among these symptoms, he included violence, restlessness, wandering, incontinence, and suicidal thoughts.

## INTERVENTION: DEFINITION AND CAUTIONS

Webster's Dictionary (1977) defines an intervention as "a state of coming or being between; interpositions . . . any interference in the affairs of others." Old people may indeed see interventions in just that light.

An important point Kahn makes is to *keep the intervention minimal.* Kahn (1975) states:

> Intervention can be harmful as well as helpful. Although resources for intervention should be available when needed, it is best to follow a policy of *minimal* intervention; that is, intervention that is least disruptive of usual functioning in the usual setting. Thus, it would be more sensible to provide care in the home or in the day-care center than in the hospital; in the storefront rather than in the clinic, etc. . . . Minimal intervention is a positive concept and must be differentiated from neglect. It must also be differentiated from 'maximal-minimal' intervention, in which the person is removed from his community, then placed in an institution that provides no psychological or social compensatory measures.

It is well for caretakers to remember Blenkner's (1968) findings about community-based aged persons and all their needed services. She found that the elderly who received the most services had the highest rates of both institutionalization and death, and attributed this finding to the damage done by professionals and their interventions. Simon (personal communication) says that persons who stay in the community are skillful in eluding the clutches of caretakers such as nurses, social workers, doctors, policemen, etc. Lowy, in his chapter of this volume, describes a wide array of mental health services in the community.

In an effort to be helpful to older people, caretakers often intervene too quickly, with too little data about the individual, group, or family; or they intervene to meet a pressing need of their own. For example, learning needs of students at times disregard the well-being, energy level, and needs of the old person. Working with old people frequently requires intervenors to be still — if for no other reason than to better pace one's self, and to allow time for the old person to move, either physically or psychologically, on his own. One young doctor always sits back early in the history taking to see what the patient actually can do; for example, how easily can he remove his coat or shoes? (R. Mangel, personal communication).

"Life is made up of choices both large and small, being old should not preclude the right to make them" (Tobin, Davidson, and Sack, 1976). Intervention, as used in this chapter, is geared towards the individual, not groups of aged persons.

**Figure 30–1.**   Giving elderly women dolls or stuffed animals to hold is one way caretakers can avoid the responsibility of substituting for the loss of significant others. The photo above poignantly depicts such an example. (Source: Magnum Photos, Inc. Photo credit: Abigail Heyman)

One constant problem in interacting with the aged is communication and the obtaining of an accurate, complete data base. Langley (1975) believes that the problem of obtaining relevant information is due to communication problems. Good interviewing technique is important (Burnside, 1973). There is a "self-erected barrier of classification . . . fitting the observed symptoms and signs into a system," and "no psychiatric diagnosis or treatment is better than the quality of the information on which it is based" (Langley, 1975). Simple questions about the immediate environment are likely to be more productive for examiners than a reliance on many of the hallowed tests. See other chapters in this volume for discussions of assessment of the elderly client.

"To make adequate personal contact with an elderly, easily fatigued, perhaps forgetful, apathetic, deaf, and partially sighted patient and to elicit the depth of information required for a psychiatric diagnosis and appraisal can be a stern test of *clinical* technique and dispassionate patience. For the unwary or hasty, diagnostic error is most likely to be in the direction of underestimating the capacity and/or distress of the patient, to his ultimate detriment" (Langley, 1975). This is as true for nurses and other health workers as it is for doctors.

In summary, the symptomatic behaviors such as aggression, confusion, disorientation, loneliness, incontinence, insomnia, and wandering can cause difficult caretaking problems for family, staff, and peers, whether the aged individual is in an institution or in the community. Unfortunately, negative terminology and pseudoadvocacy still persist in the caretakers. *Interventions need to be kept to a minimum and should be based on current data about the aged. Interventions should not be based on personal needs of the intervenor.* Adequate personal contact, skillful interviewing, and careful assessments are the basis for effective caretaking of aged individuals. A conscientious effort must also be made to identify and reduce or prevent burn-out in the caretakers who care for the frail aged.

## AGGRESSION AND HOSTILITY

Literature on aggressive, violent behavior is scattered throughout books and journals, but there are still few articles geared toward the elderly client. Weinberg (1975) reminds caretakers that behavior of an individual should be of great interest, but the covert meaning of that behavior should also be intriguing. It is the understanding of behavior that

can help to ascertain the proper responses in dealing with it and ensuing problems. Understanding aggression in the aged is not easy, partially because staff members are usually not sophisticated in psychodynamics and psychiatric interventions. Mental health workers tend not to understand normal aging, or to know how to interact with the older client. Also, the flexibility of handling aggressive old people is stifled because of stereotypic expectations of personnel, that is, little old women and men are often expected to be sweet, slow and subdued. Their violent outbursts in nonpsychiatric settings tend to catch staff members off guard. On the other hand, ex-state hospital patients, whether in the community or in the nursing home, are expected to behave as they did in the state hospital. If they had violent episodes in previous hospitalizations, some workers anticipate they will repeat that behavior, even though some are schizophrenics who grew old in the state hospital and have left such behavior behind them.

*In acute hospitals and nursing homes, the use of restraints is still a too common intervention when aggressive behavior occurs.* The physiological basis for mental problems, including aggression, is often not well understood by caretakers. *Application of restraints often increases resistance and agitation instead of calming or quieting the older patient.* The other common solution caretakers resort to is transfer of the patient. If this strategy is effective in reducing aggression, it may be that the old person is in a confused state which has been increased by the sudden move or mover, and by the influx of all the personnel who descend in such situations, or it may be that the old person simply gives up, realizing how little control she/he has in the institution.

The following is an example of applying restraints to an old man, with the intervention subsequently backfiring. It is also an example of an intervention without adequate data about the patient or communication with him.

### Case Example

Mr. W., a 74-year-old white male, was hospitalized for a prostatectomy and placed in a four-bed ward. He was alert, oriented, but had some hearing deficit and did tend to talk loudly. A new patient was admitted to the room and complained of feeling chilled. Mr. W., an empathic man, who had several blankets on his bed, said, "I have more blankets than I need," and threw one blanket across to the young man. At that same time a nurse's aide walked into the room. She immediately reported to the head nurse that Mr. W. was throwing things and was noisy. He was quickly placed in two point restraints (both wrists); he then became really noisy, and began yelling and demanding to see his doctor. His doctor was called, he came and talked to Mr. W., and ordered the restraints removed.

## IRRITABILITY AND HOSTILITY

Irritability and/or hostility are signs of tension found more often in the aged paranoid patient than in any other group, but *hostility is also a common reaction to a decline in competence in the aged person* (Stotsky, 1968). Weinberg (1975) wrote eloquently about the dynamics of loss as experienced by the aged, and stated that losses in the aged may be handled by denial, over-compensatory mechanisms or projections. Caretakers are prone to take over functions for the aged, and the aged are robbed of their own important control and their mastery. They respond with rage or accusations, and tenaciously hang on to any semblance of control. Denial is also a mechanism which causes difficulty for most staff persons and family. *Reality testing, when done to excess, can strip the aged person of the mechanism of denial, which he is using to cope with the situation.* The reader is referred to "Behavioral Problems" in *Workshop on Aging* (Sandoz, 1977).

## INTERVENTION IN AGGRESSION

Stotsky (1968) suggested that one way to deal with hostility is to accept the patient's complaints; another way to handle hostility is to seek out one particular cause which can be treated, for example, a physical illness. Stotsky further stated that it is helpful to give hostile, aged patients plenty of room and that they should be moved to another area if they are being provoked and teased by other residents. This move will allow them physical space to "blow off steam," and will also help to release the tensions easily caused by communal living. While it may also be necessary to restrict the activity of the resident and/or to isolate him, seclusion per se is frowned upon by modern psychiatrists. *Seclusion of elderly persons in an isolated room may increase sensory deprivation.* In the face of so many losses, seclusion may be the least effective therapeutic intervention.

## INTERVENTION IN VIOLENT BEHAVIOR

Anders (1977) describes how staff can handle a violent patient, and confirms what Stotsky (1968) wrote about the potentially violent patient needing space between himself and others. Some suggestions by Anders include helping the patient to identify the anxiety that triggered the angry behavior or outburst. A potentially violent or aggressive patient senses that she/he is about to lose control and needs the reassurance that the behavior can be handled. The person should be offered alternatives so self-esteem can be recovered. Anders spelled out several practical interventions: "It seems like you are really upset about something, and I am afraid you might injure someone if you do use that cue stick" (identifying the anxiety). "I would like to help you control your behavior . . . I cannot allow you to injure yourself or someone else" (providing reassurance). "Let's sit down and talk it over. How about a cup of coffee?" (providing alternatives). "Now, what happened to make you so angry?" (encouraging verbalization rather than acting-out).

Restraints should be the last alternative. Anders' article describes the best way to apply four-point restraints (restraining all four limbs). The article is recommended reading for those who must handle severely disturbed and physically strong elderly.

## CASE EXAMPLE

A staff nurse working in a nursing home was surprised to see a rather frail, slow, 103-year-old man quickly pick up a chair to crack over the head of a man whom he mistakenly thought was wearing his hat. She was able to talk him out of the act, and walked with him to help him find his hat which he had left in the lounge.

## CASE EXAMPLE

A nurse was attacked and hit by a feisty, disturbed little lady. A helpful visitor from another ward kept splashing Holy Water on both of them. The nurse kept asking her to get help from the next ward, to no avail. Finally another patient went for help.

## CASE EXAMPLE

A friendly visitor saw a 90-year-old woman in San Francisco every week. The elderly woman finally completely discouraged her visits because the volunteer had the presumptuous habit of sampling the woman's colognes and perfumes (M. Kalkman, personal communication).

The strength of even the tiniest agitated woman, or man, will often surprise caretakers and catch them quite off guard. Ignoring needs for privacy and violating the aged person's obvious "no trespassing" signs by moving into their territory can cause volatile reactions (Burnside, 1979).

In home settings, the health worker must never forget that the worker is a guest and can be thrown out of the home, if not bodily, then psychologically.

Sometimes illusions may also cause angry reactions (e.g., mistaking a person for another person). *The sensory deficits raise havoc with old people's reality.* Staff members, whether based in the community or institution, will need to improve their understanding and interventions regarding the sensory processes of the aged person.

Another consideration in aggressive behavior is the life style and the personality of the aged. The person may have always been mean, surly, and abusive. The chronic drinker who becomes abusive and surly is another major problem for many mental health workers. One clever old man with a drinking problem, who was in a nursing home, absolutely would not wear the prosthesis for his leg. It was some time before the prosthesis was discovered to be a cache for his whiskey!

A staff member's description of abusiveness and hostility occasionally must be checked out. Staff mores often cannot let them tolerate any cursing or swearing. Swearing may be verbally assaultive, but it is not as destructive as other behavior. If one cannot physically dispel one's anger, all that remains for any release is to curse those in one's way.

Anticipation of abusive behavior may encourage it, and, at times, provocative, cruel, teasing behavior can push an older person much too far. Interpretations of "teasing" and other such interactions need to be carefully discussed during in-service training of home health aides, nursing assistants, psychiatric technicians and perhaps even relatives.

PHARMACOLOGICAL DRUGS

Pharmacological drugs used for agitated, tense, hostile, and excited geriatric patients include: chlorpromazine (Thorazine[R]), meprobromate (Miltown[R]), perphenzine (Trilafon[R]), trifluoperazine (Stelazine[R]), chlordiazepoxide (Librium[R]), thioridazine (Mellaril[R]), and others. Reserpine (Serpasil[R]), once commonly used, is now not widely used for treatment of agitation because of the serious depressive states which may occur as side effects. Compazine[R], also a once popular drug for agitated, tense, elderly clients, is now used almost exclusively as an antiemetic.

Instead of inducing sleep, barbiturates and chloral hydrate may agitate and confuse aged patients (Stotsky, 1968). As a result, the aged individual may become even more disturbed and require additional sedation. During the evening hours, many patients become hyperactive, confused, and aggressive because of the noise volume in a nursing home at night (Stotsky, 1968). Night staff personnel have long been notorious for the multiple, raucous sounds they create! *Measures to reduce the confusion so prevalent at night should include increasing environmental cues, especially at night. These are paramount for the confused elderly.*

At least one clinician (Butler, 1971) suggests thioridazine (Mellaril®) as a major tranquilizer of choice, but there are, of course, different choices for varying circumstances of elderly clients. (Chapter 31 in this volume discusses pharmacologic approaches to treatment and prevention of the mental health problems of older adults.) Table 30–1 indicates drug usage in aggressive, hostile behavior among the elderly and gives the pharmacist's comments. The chart does not include specific dosage recommendations and ranges because there are many considerations for each patient. *There is a great need to individualize dosage regimens in the old patient, taking into consideration patient characteristics, disease states and history, other drugs currently being taken,* and so on. Drugs, while they are helpful and an important adjunct to therapy, need to be coupled with "people therapy," to use E. Pfeiffer's (1973) term. The drugs must be carefully monitored.

Guidelines for diagnosis, rehabilitation, and intervention in aggression in the aged person are presented in Table 30–2.

## CONFUSION AND DISORIENTATION

The literature in the study of confusion and disorientation in the elderly is steadily increasing. The best source of articles can be found in the literature from the United Kingdom. Lately, *The Gerontologist,* a multidisciplinary journal, has featured controversial articles. A fascinating article by Hellebrandt (1978) is especially recommended to the reader.

The mental health problems of the elderly occur in the community, in the acute care hospital, and in the nursing home. The extent of mental health problems of the elderly in the community is not known, as Lowy has stated in his chapter of this volume. Table 30–3 lists chronic conditions and impairments and indicates that "senility" is at the top of the list for all residents of nursing homes and also heads the list of primary diagnosis at last examination. The fact that "senility" still stands as a primary diagnosis indicates that we have much educating to do. In a doctoral study, Frankfather (1976) found older people who resided in the com-

**Table 30–1**  Drugs Commonly Used For Aggressive Behavior Among Elderly Clients[1]

| | POTENCY | EQUIVA-LENT DOSES | ANTICHOLINERGIC EFFECTS | HYPERSENSITIVITY | SEDATION | HYPOTEN-SION[7] | EXTRA-PYRAMIDAL EFFECTS[8] |
|---|---|---|---|---|---|---|---|
| | | | Dry mouth, tachycardia, constipation, adynamic ileus (lack of bowel motility), fecal impaction causing obstruction, blurred vision,[6] and urinary retention. | Rash (5%), agranulocytosis (rare), cholestatic jaundice (less than 1-2%, and occurring in the first four weeks of treatment.) | | | |
| Antipsychotics[2] Phenothiazines, e.g., | | | | | | | |
| Chlorpromazine (Thorazine[R]) | low | 25mg[5] | yes | yes | high | moderate | moderate |
| Thioridazine (Mellaril[R]) | low | 25mg | yes | yes | prominent | moderate | lowest (seldom) |
| Trifluoperazine (Stelazine[R]) | high | 1mg | yes | yes | low | low | high (motor restlessness prevalent) |
| Butyrophenones Haloperiodol (Haldol[R]) | high | 0.5mg | yes | yes | relatively non-sedating | seldom | very high |

Anti-anxiety and Sedative-Hypnotics (See Table 30–5)
Barbiturates[3]
Benzodiazepines,[4] e.g. Chlordiazepoxide (Librium[R]); Diazepam (Valium[R])

## Notes on Pharmacological Drugs

1. The appearance of agitation, combativeness, confusion, or delirium should not suggest that a psychoactive drug be immediately instituted, but rather that an underlying cause be sought. Important mechanisms in the production of acute and reversible mental changes in the aged include: (1) an abrupt reduction in cerebral blood flow occurring secondary to acute hypotension, congestive heart failure, or cardiac arrhythmias, (2) hypoxia secondary to pneumonia or severe anemia, (3) hypoglycemia, (4) dehydration or electrolyte disorders, (5) head injuries, (6) nutritional deficiencies, (7) drug withdrawal (e.g., alcohol), and (8) fever. Frequently, confusion is induced by drugs such as tranquilizers, insulin, or oral hypoglycemics, corticosteroids, digitalis, or anticholinergics, analgesics, e.g. Pentazocine (Talwin[R]).

2. In psychotic patients, antipsychotic drugs ameliorate the underlying thought disorder responsible for such manifestations as aggressive behavior, hyperactivity, parnoid symptoms, or delusions. All are potent and sometimes toxic. Their use is not without risk. In nonpsychotic individuals, antipsychotic drugs produce variable, nonspecific sedation depending upon the particular drug and the patient's sensitivity to it. To use antipsychotics for inducing sedation in normal individuals, rather than conventional sedative-hypnotics is unjustified given the attendant risks and higher cost. Patients with chronic brain syndrome of any etiology who are agitated, hyperactive, and delusional often respond to phenothiazine drugs used cautiously in small doses. Antipsychotic drugs should be used for what they do best, and not for uses that other potentially less toxic drugs may serve equally well or better (Hollister, 1973).

3. Management of nonpsychotic, acutely agitated and aggressive patients may be best accomplished by judicious use of a rapidly-acting barbiturate (e.g., pentobarbital or amobarbital). Even highly agitated, aggressive schizophrenics might best be treated with a barbiturate along with an antipsychotic drug.

4. The benzodiazepines (e.g., diazepam [Valium[R]]), may be used to manage anxiety and aggressive behavior in nonpsychotic

patients. In psychotic patients, the benzodiazepines have no effect on disordered thinking and other psychotic manifestations, although attendant anxiety and agitation may be improved in some cases. Their absorption from intramuscular sites tends to be less predictable, less timely, and less complete than orally administered doses; this may limit their usefulness in some cases.

5. The intramuscular route of administration is at least several times more potent than the oral route. In starting therapy, divided doses are generally useful to minimize the initial impact of many of the unwanted pharmacologic effects (e.g., sedation or hypotension) and allow for better titration of the dosage. However, due to the intrinsically long duration of activity, no basis exists for divided daily dosage on a continuous basis. A practice becoming increasingly more common is once-daily maintenance dosing rather than the traditional divided dosage schedules of three to four times daily. Once daily dosing is equal in efficacy to a divided dosing schedule and offers four distinct advantages: (1) There is better patient compliance with prescribed instructions, and/or lessened nursing time and reduced risk of medication administration error. (2) The sedative properties of many antipsychotic drugs can be utilized to promote a better night's sleep and the patient is not drowsy during the daytime. (3) Peak blood levels are reached while the patient sleeps so that unwanted sedation, and extrapyramidal and some anticholinergic effects occur during sleep. (4) Once-daily dosing with tablets precludes the need for the more expensive capsule dosage forms.

6. Some package inserts state that the systemic use of anticholinergic drugs is contraindicated in patients with glaucoma. Although systemic anticholinergic drugs can cause dangerous elevation in intraocular pressure in patients with or without glaucoma who have an abnormally narrow angle between the iris and the cornea, no significant rise in intraocular pressure is reported to occur in patients with a normal (wide) angle, even in those under treatment for glaucoma. Systemic anticholinergic drugs are therefore usually considered to be safe for patients with open-angle glaucoma, the most common form of the disease.

**Table 30–1** continued

7. Aged patients receiving postural hypotensive-inducing drugs such as chlorpromazine, should be cautioned against rising too rapidly, or if appropriate, protected from doing so. This is especially important in the morning, following a hot bath, or for those patients who have to get up once or more during the night to urinate (e.g., elderly males with benign prostatic hypertrophy). Such patients should arise from bed in stages over several minutes, with assistance if appropriate. They should arise slowly from a lying to a sitting position, then dangle their legs over the side of the bed, and then finally stand up. Fainting may occur when the initial symptoms of dizziness or weakness are ignored. Falls occurring secondary to hypotensive episodes are potentially catastrophic in the aged client.

8. Drug-induced parkinsonism is a troublesome but common patient complaint that interferes with ambulation and self-care. It is characterized by: (1) muscle rigidity including cogwheel rigidity (a type of muscle hypertonicity which gives way in a series of small jerks when the muscle is passively stretched), changes in speech and handwriting, and drooling due to rigidity of tongue muscles and decreased swallowing. (2) Dyskinesias (difficulty in performance of voluntary muscles), including akinesia (lack of normal muscle movements), or

akathesia (constant restlessness and movement). (3) A rhythmic, pill-rolling tremor (the patient moves his thumb across his fingers as if he were rolling a pill), which occurs at rest, increases with excitement or anxiety, and is lessened or absent with intentional movement and during sleep. (4) Abnormal posturing or gait disturbances including a propulsive or hastening gait (a gait in which the patient moves with short hurried steps, often on tip toes, with his trunk inclined forward and his arms and hands hanging in front of him). Tardive dyskinesia represents a major, drug-induced adverse effect of all antipsychotic drugs. It is characterized by involuntary repetitive movements of the tongue, face, mouth, or jaw (e.g., tongue protrusion, licking of the lips, smacking and sucking lip movements, chewing and jaw deviations, facial grimacing and eye blinking), but may involve involuntary movements of the extremities as well. It may appear at any time during treatment with these drugs, or after drug therapy has been stopped. The risk appears to be greater in aged patients treated with high doses for prolonged periods, especially women. The symptoms tend to be persistent and often irreversible. There is no known effective treatment. The most effective course is prevention by avoiding long-term, high-dose use of antipsychotic drugs, especially in the aged, unless the need for such therapy is clearly indicated.

Source: Ronald C. Kayne, Pharm. D.

munity and were labeled as mentally impaired or senile were better described as confused. He felt the uniformed network (policemen, firemen, postmen, etc.) were more helpful to these people than were mental health agencies.

Researchers in New York City studied residents of a low income housing facility and found that, on the basis of a psychiatric examination, 22 percent of the residents had clinical evidence of chronic brain syndrome (Fisch, Goldfarb, Shahinian, and Turner, 1968). The reader is referred to Chapters 22, 24, and 28 of this text for information on assessment of organic brain syndrome (OBS), and to a fine article by Libow (1973). Another succinct helpful resource is the section on organic brain syndromes in *Workshop on Aging* (Sandoz, 1977).

DIAGNOSTIC ISSUES

Lurie (1977) includes the following characteristics as diagnostic for chronic brain syndrome:

(1) Memory, especially for recent events, is impaired; (2) Data perception and integration deteriorated. In advanced stages, disorientation for time may occur, and later for place and person; (3) A loss of judgment may occur (poor conduct in social situations and difficulties with interpersonal relationships resulting from insensitivity to others); (4) Emotional expression is defective; either emotional lability or a general flattening of affect; (5) Some impaired ability to solve intellectual problems (such as simple mental arithmetic);

(6) Abstract thinking is impaired; patients may have difficulty in their abilities to understand subtleties of language, with shades of meaning, or with symbolization; (7) Affective and thinking disorders may be superimposed on the chronic brain syndrome. Anxiety, depressive, or paranoid thinking may add to the disability produced by the brain damage.

Ankers and Quarrington (1972) have written about operant behavior in the memory-disordered. The term they coined for chronic brain syndrome, *memory-disordered*, although not widely used, is far less pejorative than *senile*.

Wershow (1977) says:

However discouraging, even frightening, the problem of senility may be, its implications must be faced squarely and dealt with. It should be recognized that much of what we practice and advocate in the psychosocial area may be inappropriate in treatment of Organic Brain Syndrome (OBS). So far, we have been markedly unsuccessful in reversing OBS by either organic or sociopsychological therapies. Most factors implicated in the genesis of OBS are not readily amenable to prophylactic intervention, e.g. alcoholism and atherosclerosis.

Weinberg (1970) describes three types of symptoms manifested by older persons: (1) exclusion of stimuli; (2) conservation of energy; and (3) regression; and states, "Memory defect in the aged

**Table 30–2** The Abusive/Combative Patient.

| DIAGNOSTIC ISSUES: | REHABILITATION ISSUES AND SUGGESTIONS: |
|---|---|
| 1. Is there a legitimate reason for the patient to be angry (has he/she been waiting two hours for breakfast?) | 1. Firmness and limit-setting should be employed. Restraints are rarely necessary and should be used only as the absolute last resort. |
| 2. Is the hostile behavior a way the patient defends himself from feeling either depressed or dependent on other people? | 2. The worker should listen respectfully regarding the basis of the hostility, try to clarify the patient's complaint, and respond without being defensive. |
| 3. Do explosions of rage in a particular patient occur with particular staff members or with everyone? (The interactions between such patients and staff should be examined in detail if the patient is usually manageable with other staff members.) | 3. Try to get beyond the anger to some sort of human and personal level of communication. |
| 4. Is a medical condition making the particular patient more irritable? A medical consultation may be in order. | 4. Low doses of tranquilizers (e.g., valium, mellaril) may help reduce the irritability or impulsivity of some patients. Avoid barbiturates whenever possible because of their addicting and oversedating properties. |

Source: Discussion Guide for the film entitled, "The Disturbed Nursing Home Patient," produced by Hugh James Lurie, M.D., University of Washington, Seattle, Washington. Funded by an NIMH-PS grant to the Bureau of Mental Health, DSHS, Olympia, Washington.

**Table 30–3** Reported chronic conditions and impairments, primary diagnoses at last examination and at admission for both sexes.

| CONDITION | TOTAL NO. OF RESIDENTS | ALL AGES | UNDER 65 YRS. | 65–74 YEARS | 75–84 YEARS | 85 YEARS and over |
|---|---|---|---|---|---|---|
| **Primary diagnosis at last examination** | | | | | | |
| Senility, old age, other symptoms and ill-defined conditions | 146,800 | 136.5 | 20.6 | 85.2 | 140.9 | 184.6 |
| Heart attack | 55,700 | 51.8 | * | 41.1 | 53.3 | 64.1 |
| Stroke | 113,400 | 105.4 | 94.0 | 138.0 | 120.6 | 81.5 |
| Hardening of the arteries | 241,800 | 224.7 | 36.6 | 151.7 | 237.2 | 293.9 |
| Diseases of the circulatory system other than hardening of the arteries, stroke, and heart attack | 39,400 | 36.6 | * | 31.4 | 39.9 | 40.4 |
| Accidents, poisonings, and violence | 49,300 | 45.8 | 39.6 | 35.8 | 45.8 | 51.4 |
| Mental disorders | 115,800 | 107.6 | 395.8 | 185.1 | 72.1 | 30.5 |
| Diseases of the musculoskeletal system and connective tissue | 73,100 | 67.9 | 48.3 | 58.5 | 70.7 | 74.4 |
| Endocrine, nutritional, and metabolic disease | 48,100 | 44.7 | 44.0 | 59.5 | 46.9 | 37.1 |
| Diseases of the respiratory system | 22,200 | 20.6 | * | 33.3 | 22.9 | 13.7 |
| Neoplasma | 25,600 | 23.8 | 27.9 | 29.4 | 23.6 | 20.7 |
| Diseases of the nervous system and sense organs | 64,200 | 59.7 | 156.0 | 78.4 | 49.3 | 35.4 |
| Diseases of the digestive system | 20,500 | 19.0 | * | 18.6 | 17.9 | 20.1 |
| Infective and parasitic diseases | * | * | * | * | * | * |
| Diseases of genitourinary system | 15,600 | 14.5 | * | * | 16.7 | 15.1 |
| Diseases of skin and subcutaneous tissues | 6,000 | 5.6 | * | * | 6.1 | * |
| Diseases of blood and blood-forming organs | 7,600 | 7.1 | * | * | 7.6 | 8.8 |
| Congenital anomalies | 3,100 | 2.9 | 19.1 | * | * | * |
| Other diagnoses | 16,100 | 15.0 | 22.1 | 15.9 | 15.0 | 12.6 |
| Unknown diagnoses | 9,600 | 8.9 | * | * | 9.3 | 9.8 |

Source: National Center for Health Statistics

Final estimates from the 1973–74 National Nursing Home Survey

*Figure does not meet standards of reliability or precision, i.e. relative standard error exceeds 25%.

implies an attempt to conserve energy." Confusion commonly seen among the aged is due to fragmentation of the ego and the intrusion into consciousness of unconscious irrelevancies (Linden, 1956).

Assessment and management of the confused, disoriented elderly person (these elderly are also often labeled "difficult") can be trying and may be poorly accomplished by staff personnel for a variety of reasons—lack of staff for surveillance, lack of equipment, lack of empathy, etc. Emotional lability in terms of aggression or tearfulness may be present (Godber, 1976). The confused behavior or disorientation may be most marked late in the day and at night; such behavior is called sundowner's.

## CASE EXAMPLE

Mr. D., in his late 80's, was hospitalized on a medical ward in a Veterans Hospital. Although a sweet, gentle old man during the daytime, he was into much mischief, albeit confusedly so, during the night. His three roommates complained bitterly that they could not sleep because of his antics. One night he was found trying to urinate in the sink in the corner of the room, complaining that "the toilet was too high." Very late on another evening, when the ward was apparently quiet, a rash of lights began flashing. All patients had the same complaint, "Some old guy was in here stealing my slippers." Mr. D. later appeared at the nurses' station, placed six mismatched bedroom slippers on the desk and said, "For you nurse," and shuffled off. The nursing staff, busy with increased evening care routines for very ill patients, admitted that they never had adequate time to spend with Mr. D.

Nurses comment on the capricious behavior, wandering or sexual aggression which results and/or increases when patients receive less attention than usual. Disorientation may occur in three spheres: (1) time; (2) person; or (3) place. Night time routines and noises can disorient the elderly who are not sure where they are when they have been moved to a new setting.

An unidentified man, who had once been a missionary in Brazil, listened to a lecture which discussed disorientation of the elderly. He approached the speaker afterwards and said that he now better understood a term he had heard the natives use often, "disnortesdo," which meant unnorth, or the inability to find the north direction. He had never really quite understood the term until he associated it with disorientation in the specific sphere of place.

## ILLUSIONS AND CONFUSION

Earlier in the chapter, illusions were mentioned. I have become increasingly aware of the great number and variety of illusions experienced by older persons (Burnside, 1980), although the literature discusses little about the problems created by illusions of the aged. Current literature in the field of illusions has been written only by nonmedical researchers (Castaneda, 1972; Gibson, 1966; Gregory and Gombrich, 1973; Neisser, 1976; Segall, 1966).

Gregory and Gombrich (1973) point out that a deviation may be an illusion or a discrepancy. Specific kinds of illusions can be generated through misplaced strategies: for example, through inappropriate data processing; through failure to derive object hypothesis from patterns; through misleading laws; through mislinking data and facts; through ambiguity (inadequate data); through paradox; and through creativity. Among the elderly, illusions arising from misplaced strategy, especially illusions generated by ambiguity or inadequate data, seem to be a problem.

Neisser (1976) wonders how illusion and error are possible "if perception is simply the pickup of information that is already available and specific." The perception of old people makes errors not only possible but very likely because the information is not readily available to them, and often is not specific enough. For example, cardiac monitors resemble televisions, an intravenous standard resembles a person standing by the bed, and shadows of tree branches outside a window at home resemble a prowler.

## SUGGESTIONS FOR INTERVENTION

Often, misinterpretation of the immediate environment can lead to ideas of persecution ("they're trying to poison me" is a very common one) or will be exacerbated by visual hallucinations. Reality testing is of paramount importance during times of misperception (Burnside, 1977). The following are terse guidelines for reality testing: Remember that reality testing is an urgent intervention. Explain all that is unfamiliar. Be a fanatic about consistency. Give explanations with empathy and great patience. Remember that the pacing of the caretaker is important. Do what you can to allay fear and apprehension. Touch the person during reality testing. Help the person to keep familiar objects. Design interventions to improve self-esteem. Do not argue. Take care of yourself. Have accurate information before you begin reality testing. Record information in detail and accurately.

## CASE EXAMPLE

A newly admitted woman in a nursing home could not sleep and a night nurse finally heard her fears. The elderly woman's window faced out onto a parking lot. She believed that the night crew coming on duty (with car doors slamming, talking, etc.) were morticians who drove into the parking lot to pick up the dead bodies of people who had died during the day. She was afraid to go to sleep. A sensitive nurse reality-tested with her; she put her in a wheel chair and took her outside to view the change-of-shift scene (Burnside, 1976).

MacKinnon and Michels (1971), suggest that it is helpful to conduct brief interviews; to recognize the patient as a person; to allow the patient time to respond; to stimulate memory chains; to aid in reality testing; and to take an interest in physical complaints.

To summarize some of the care aspects, a list of suggestions for caretakers of chronic brain syndrome is given by Lurie (1977): (1) Assign one or two staff members who will care for the resident on a regular basis; (2) Keep a predictable routine. Use visual aids, such as signs about place, date, activities, the names of personnel, etc.; (3) Begin reality orientation programs; (4) Provide structures and limits for safety of patients, which may sometimes include locked doors; (5) Leave lights on at all times because some patients have more disorientation with poor lighting; (6) Remember that familiar objects help to maintain the orientation of some residents; (7) Rectify auditory or visual impairment when possible; (8) Look for any mild illnesses or medical changes such as fever or constipation, which could cause the recent change in mental status; (9) Avoid disruption of routine or surroundings whenever possible; (10) "Borderline" functioning patients may regress and withdraw, so stimulation and activities are crucial; (11) These individuals will respond best to gentle reminders; do not use insistent demands or confrontations; and (12) Uncontrolled high blood pressure tends to accelerate the mental decline. Consider antihypertensive medication to arrest rapidity of deterioration.

## LONELINESS IN LATE LIFE

"It's a lonely life, you know, with nothing to do and plenty of time to do it in," said an elderly woman in one long-term care facility (Townsend, 1963). Loneliness has long been a popular theme in poetry, novels, and literature, and has been a constant theme in poetry especially in haiku (Bownas, 1966; Henderson, 1958; Blyth, 1966). Osborn (1975), discussing expression of psychopathology in art, especially paintings, stated that Rembrandt was an outstanding and perceptive painter of old people; his portraits revealed the isolation and sadness of his subjects.

The problem of loneliness among the aged is apparent to community workers, particularly public health nurses, visiting nurses, home health aides, and Friendly Visitors. The aged client clings to the worker and tries to hold them with conversation, coffee, or unfinished tasks. While there are no specific studies about loneliness per se, loneliness appears in studies which have some other focus in community residents. Current media describes the problem, for example, in the films, "Minnie Remembers"* and "Passing Quietly Through."†

## OVERVIEW OF THE LITERATURE

In spite of the pervasiveness of the condition, loneliness has received little professional attention. In recent years the literature on the loneliness in the aged person has increased slightly. Fromm-Reichman (1959b) noted that psychiatric textbooks fail to mention loneliness. Weiss (1973) said that professionals who work in research and treatment may prefer not to change their own current emotional balance. It would be uncomfortable to consider that loneliness is a potential problem in the day-to-day life of everyone. He further states, "Loneliness is not simply a desire for company, any company,—rather it yields only to very specific forms of relationships. . . . is often uninterrupted by social activity. . . . However, the responsiveness of loneliness to just the right sort of relationship with others is absolutely remarkable." Caretakers of old persons will have to analyze their own behavior and responses to determine what comprises the right sort of relationship.

Gaev (1976) wrote about the psychology of loneliness; her analysis was based on the classic writings of Buber (1970), Fromm (1941), Fromm-Reichman (1959a,b), Horney (1937), Maslow (1970), May (1953), Sullivan (1953), and Tillich (1963). Factors I have observed which contribute to loneliness in the aged include: geographical loneliness; language barriers; cultural loneliness experienced by many foreign-born patients; life-style loneliness; loneliness of illness and/or pain; loss loneli-

---

*Produced by K. Henderson, P. Arnold, and W. Smith. 1976. Baltimore: Norton and Company.

†Produced by D. McCarthy. 1970. New York: Grove Press Film Division.

ness; and loneliness caused by impending death (Burnside, 1971).

Weiss (1973) suggested reasons why there has been so little research on loneliness (and wryly notes that loneliness has had more attention from songwriters than from social scientists). Loneliness is rarely studied because there is no theory to cope with its presence (Leiderman, 1969); it is so painful people avoid it (Fromm-Reichmann, 1959b); and those who are not lonely will have little empathy for those who are. Weiss states there is still a lack of solid taxonomy of the types of loneliness.

Linden (1956), in a seldom found statement, described the loneliness of the chronic-brain-syndrome individual, which he feels "develops out of loss of real objects...and improves greatly when fantasy objects take over supremacy..." In an earlier paper the same author wrote, "Perhaps nowhere, not even in the other psychoses and neuroses, is there to be found a greater degree of loneliness than in senility" (Linden, 1953).

There is a need to learn about the frequencies of loneliness, the differing intensities, durations, and distributions of symptoms, and the conditions under which loneliness is avoided. There is also a need to find better ways to establish that loneliness exists, other than by use of the single question on a survey (Weiss, 1973). The same author wonders if there is any physical damage because of extended stress induced by loneliness. Is sleep affected? Is tension or irritability increased during states of loneliness? Weiss (1973), states, "It is reasonably well-demonstrated that loneliness is a deficit condition, a response to the absence of specific relational provisions. The deficit is always one of a specific provision or provisions." He names two deficit states which exist in loneliness—emotional isolation and social isolation—which, in his opinion, occur with the same frequency in our society. He wonders if loneliness can be expected to fade with time, since loneliness is a deficit state. He suggests that it is possible for individuals to change their standards for evaluating both their situations and their feelings, "and, in particular, that standard might shrink to conform more clearly to the shape of a bleak reality."

Hyams (1969), noted, "Loneliness (a subjective feeling not necessarily related to physical isolation) is very common in the elderly and can exert a profound influence in aggravating the emotional components of an illness by leading to feelings of insecurity; later, apathy may develop."

Some old ones cope with loneliness by withdrawal and a drastic reduction in communication. (Townsend, 1963). These old persons found it difficult to form new friendships, had little materially

to give others, and were discouraged from physically assisting other residents. *The universal need to be needed comes through loudly and clearly in working with the aged.* The subjects were also lonely for someone who knew their past life. Often in group work with the elderly, members will learn that someone lived near a place they once did, or that they had a mutual acquaintance. Such knowledge invariably will brighten up the members and is an important aspect of group leadership ability. Group leaders need to maximize such opportunities. The reader is referred to *Working With the Elderly: Group Process and Techniques* (Burnside, 1978).

Townsend (1963), said:

The resident may *appear* in time to become more resigned, apathetic, or contented but this probably means only that, as his familiarity with the institutional regime grows, he conforms to the rules of the game to obtain certain limited ends, which are to be left in peace, or given an extra cup of tea or piece of cake because he is a "model" resident. He may not preserve his pride and self-respect outwardly, only inwardly. He presents an amiable, submissive self to the outside world while retaining his own very difficult personal feelings. Despite outward appearances and the experiences of a communal life, many individuals appear to cling tenaciously to individual identity and ideals. If this is so, then the task of rehabilitation may be easier than is often supposed.

This reminds one of Jung's (1964) writings about individuation being one of the tasks of late life.

One only has to consider all the ways that the aged express, and perhaps flaunt, their identity—favorite hats and jewelry, for example. The writer once observed a bedridden woman in a nursing home, who was in her eighties, who clung to her own stay-clean brand of individuality with one of the few possibilities left to her—washcloths! Each day, the nurses' attendant patiently gave her eight washcloths—one for her forehead, one for her wrist, neck, etc. While her appearance was ludicrous, the ability of the staff to meet her needs so cheerfully was commendable.

Busse and Pfeiffer (1969), Bennett (1973), and Townsend (1968) noted the isolation of residents in nursing homes. Faunce (1969) described loneliness of women in a nursing home and listed six difficulties she observed: grief, homesickness, loss of outside contacts, loss of health, financial insecurity, and uselessness.

Bennett and Nahemow (1965) studied four nursing homes and noted that the nursing home administrators seemed to expect little from the residents and that the residents expected little from the facility or from each other. A resident subsystem did not exist, and most residents said they knew no one in the home. They said this was the best way for them to keep out of trouble. Such low expectations add to the loneliness and isolation of aged, institutionalized residents.

Palmore (1977), flatly states, "The majority of old people are not isolated and lonely." This writer does not agree for several reasons. Denial is often operant when an old person says he is not lonely. Old people often have difficulty expressing feelings and their behavior better describes their plight than their words. A mental health worker will be faced with lonely old people, whether the worker is based in the community or in the institution.

Some of the loneliest old people live their last years of life in nursing homes and are verbal about their loneliness. Mr. S. was one such person.

## CASE EXAMPLE

Mr. S. was a 103-year-old white male in a county home for the aged in a western state. He articulated his loneliness by projecting it onto the interviewer saying he thought she came to visit him because she was lonely. "We all get lonely, you know." While they were discussing the growing-old theme of the opening quote of this chapter, he replied, "I don't know how to grow old gracefully, but I do know how to grow old quietly" (Burnside, 1979).

## LONELINESS AMONG WIDOWS

Lopata (1976) listed five short-range needs of widows "regardless of typology or life circumstances." These needs were: grief work; companionship; solution of immediate problems; building of competence and self-confidence; and help in reengagements. Lopata, in her study of widows, found that even phone calls did not offset feelings of loneliness. The whole profile of the women described referred to loneliness as a second problem in widowhood. They lacked a satisfactory level of interpersonal contact with other people in a similar position; they were lonely for human contact. Yet they were ambivalent—they wanted remarriage, yet felt it would cause them trouble; they were lonely for people, yet they listed "peace of mind" as the most important compensation in the new role of widow.

Discussing the establishment of relationships, Weiss (1973) says, "loneliness will vanish abruptly and without a trace, as though it never had existed. There is no gradual recovery, no getting over it bit by bit. When it ends, it ends suddenly; one was lonely, one is not any more." But it is hard to fit this statement into the proverbial loneliness of some old people. It seems that the loneliness after death of spouse in the aged may also imbue a certain acceptance of a lonely state. Given the difficulty of meeting people (often of either sex), there may be a greater acceptance of lonely moments. The inability to replace lost persons due to the lack of energy to move out and mix with others is commonly seen. The loneliness of those in communal living settings seems to continually surprise new persons who witness it; yet it is well-documented in the literature.

There is not any time in one's life when loneliness ceases to be a threat; however, one of the risks of aging is that one becomes more vulnerable to loneliness (Weiss, 1973) because of the risk of losing relationships. What can be done to cope with loneliness? What can be done for those who seem likely to embark on loneliness? Weiss disagrees with Moustakas (1960) who says that one should cherish one's loneliness and that it can be strengthening. Weiss (1973) suggests that, "To dwell on one's loneliness may overburden one's relationships with those who are not lonely." This seems to be especially true of the aged lonely person. "Minnie Remembers" (Swanson, 1976), a very brief poem, subsequently filmed, poignantly deals with loneliness in the aged who are widowed.

The lonely often do feel anger—especially in the grief work stage—which may be expressed against a deceased spouse. Riesman (1973), feels that "so great is the shame of the lonely, (they) withdraw further out of fear of additional experiences of loss...a bit like Groucho Marx who believed that any club that admitted him could not be worth joining."

The loneliness of the dying aged person is best expressed in this case example.

## CASE EXAMPLE

A private duty nurse described Mrs. K., an elderly woman who was dying in an acute hospital. Mrs. K. was alert and participated in her own care and her dying until she became comatose. When the nurse went on the case, Mrs. K. was content to have only one private duty nurse, from 4:00 p.m. to midnight. Her husband stopped taking his high blood pressure medication soon after she was admitted to the hospital. He knew she was terminally ill and he subsequently suffered a massive stroke and died in the same hospital. Mrs. K. planned her husband's memorial service, selected hymns, casket, etc. (by then she was on intravenous feedings).

She asked the nurse to attend the funeral and report back to her, which the nurse did.

Mrs. K. openly discussed her fears—not the fear of dying but the loneliness of death—dying alone at night in her room. Mrs. K. agreed to the nurse's suggestion that she have a private nurse with her from dusk to daylight. Mrs. K. died at 1:00 a.m. several weeks later with a compassionate night nurse holding her.

In summary, guidelines for interventions in loneliness might include: (1) Carefully observe the patient for signs of apathy or resignation (Townsend, 1963); (2) Try to find persons to converse with who may have been familiar with aspects of the patient's past life (Townsend, 1963); (3) Do not discourage older people from helping one another, or from feeding pets, or birds; (4) Set up situations which make it easier for the older person to make new friends; (5) Be alert to the fact that loneliness can aggravate emotional components of an illness (Hyams, 1969); (6) Keep in mind that loneliness is a deficit condition; intervene accordingly (Weiss, 1973); (7) Be able to deal with your own lonely states; (8) Consider your own empathy; caretakers may have little empathy for clients who are lonely (Weiss, 1973); (9) Remember that lonely persons may feel anger; (10) Remember that there is not a gradual recovery from loneliness; when it ends, it ends suddenly (Weiss, 1973) so do not foster dependency on you; and (11) Give exquisite care to the dying; they, too, will express feelings of loneliness.

## INCONTINENCE: ISSUES AND INTERVENTIONS

The reader now must shift mental gears as we move from loneliness to incontinence! Newman (1962) wrote, "It will not be much good looking up incontinence in the textbooks because they are written by people who do not have any problem with it. The dictionary definition of incontinence includes failure to restrain sexual appetite, unchastity, and inability of the body to control the evacuative functions. In most circles the word has the negative connotation described earlier and certainly is not used to indicate unrestrained sexual desires!" Willington (1976), adds, "The word incontinence conjures up a sense of frustration, disgust, and even despair. It has all the stigmata of failure resulting as it does now from the use of a restricted sense of a negative term."

### DEFINITION

The usual definition of urinary incontinence is, "the voiding of urine at unsuitable times and elsewhere than in a suitable receptacle" (Agate, 1970). The condition of incontinence may be temporary or it may be permanent as a result of a severe injury, central nervous system disease, chronic infections, etc. Incontinence which is temporary and reversible may be related to anxiety, pain, hostility or inadequate attention. Incontinence provides some elderly with an easy revenge on those they wish to provoke or annoy. Willington (1975) reminds us that the topic is hardly discussed with medical students, and taught in a sketchy fashion to nursing students and others. A very fine research study on the problems of the geriatric hospitalized patient, including incontinence, was done in England (Norton, McLaren, and Exton-Smith, 1975).

### SCOPE OF PROBLEM

Incontinence causes great unhappiness and many problems for both the aged and their families. Urinary incontinence is more common than fecal incontinence and can be one reason for seeking hospitalization. The problem can also prevent discharge from the hospital (Anderson, 1971). During childhood and adult life, incontinence is considered to be in the purview of urologists and gynecologists since surgical treatment is often used, but in the elderly surgery is less likely and the problem is more prone to have a medical etiology (Willington, 1975).

### OVERVIEW OF THE LITERATURE

The work on incontinence has primarily been done by the English medical and nursing professionals: Adams and McIlwraith (1963); Brocklehurst and Dillane (1967); Exton-Smith, Norton, and McLaren (1962); and Willington (1975). Surveys in the United Kingdom showed incidences of incontinence which may be in excess of 20 percent if one includes all types and degrees of cases (Brocklehurst, Fry, Griffiths, and Kalton, 1971; Milne, Williamson, Maule, and Wallace, 1972). In a country with 6.9 million elderly people, the figure of 1.3 million people incontinent is staggering. Brocklehurst (1951) studied 2,000 hospital patients and found the incidence of incontinence to be 23 percent. Isaacs and Walkey (1964) found 63 percent of 522 patients to be incontinent. Willington (1969) studied 900 consecutive hospital admissions over 60 years of age and found 33.6 percent were incontinent. Eckerstrom (1955) in Sweden estimated 25 percent.

Agate (1971) considered incontinence one of the most challenging problems in the field of geriatric medicine; of all the patients who enter geriatric hospital wards, one-third will probably develop incontinence at some time during their hospitalization, probably when they are gravely ill or in a disturbed condition.

Newman (1962) felt that mental deterioration did not play a part in the genesis of incontinence. Agate (1970) felt that the most intractable causes of incontinence were due to cerebral damage and mental change. Others have demonstrated the greatly increased mortality of incontinent patients, (Brocklehurst, 1962; Isaacs, 1964). Urinary incontinence is the cause of more than 20 percent of admissions to geriatric units (Shuttleworth, 1970). The first definitive study was done by Wilson (1948). He studied 36 old people, 21 of whom were incontinent. The author concluded that a common urinary dysfunction in the aged is increased frequency and precipitancy of micturition, often accompanied by incontinence. The cause was overactivity of the neuromuscular mechanisms of the bladder—rarely sphincteric weakness. The findings were confirmed and futher amplified by Brocklehurst (1951).

In nursing research in the United States, one nursing study discusses incontinence and elderly patients (Grosicki, 1968). The researcher used behavior therapy as a mode of intervention with elderly incontinent geriatric veterans. She used social and material reinforcers, with prolonged effects lasting three months after withdrawal of the reinforcers.

The social stigma and disgrace of incontinence has not been thoroughly studied. The reader is referred to an excellent chapter on the psychology of incontinence by Sutherland (1976). Following are case examples of social stigma.

## CASE EXAMPLE

In a nursing home it was apparent that one elderly couple, over a period of a year or so, had developed an intimate and important relationship. The staff personnel carefully avoided barging into Mrs. A.'s room when her door was closed and Mr. T. was in her room. However, it became apparent to one of the nurses one day that Mr. T. was no longer going to her room and was spending his time sitting in the lounge staring out the window or watching television. The nurse asked him if he had had a spat with Mrs. A. With a note of dejection in his

voice, he replied, "Not really, but she has started wetting the bed now, and she never used to do that."

## CASE EXAMPLE

An elderly farmer and his wife sold their farm in the midwest and moved to town. The couple entertained relatives, friends, and neighbors, particularly for birthdays, anniversaries, and so forth. However, the elderly gentleman, when in his 80s, began urinating in the living room. The rug was impossible to keep odor-free. The wife was humiliated by his incontinence, and the entertaining, including visits by some of the relatives, stopped when his unacceptable behavior began.

## THE PSYCHODYNAMICS OF INCONTINENCE

Sutherland (1976) has tidily categorized the psychological mechanisms into three categories: psychological mechanisms in the aetiology of incontinence; psychological reactions of the patient to incontinence; and the psychodynamics of the caretaker. Under psychological mechanisms of the patient he has included regression, dependency, rebellion, insecurity, attention seeking, disturbance of conditioned reflex, sensory deprivation, and symptom selection. Subsumed under psychological reactions to incontinence by the older person are depressive reaction, insecurity, and apathy.

## REACTIONS OF CARETAKERS

The psychodynamics of the caretakers include reactions of disgust or revulsion. Healthy disgust is not detrimental in itself; the serious problem is guilt at one's own disgust, writes Sutherland (1976). Sutherland does not mention the anger displayed by staff when they encounter the lazy patient, or the one who may be protesting and making the staff irate. Geriatric nursing places great stress on the increased work load in caring for incontinent aged persons, yet little has been done to examine this area in the United States. Adams and McIlwraith (1963) and Exton-Smith et al. (1962) noted comparable times for the amount of nursing time spent in dealing with incontinent patients, which included handling of bedclothes, garments, and linens, as well as bathing the patient. The 24-hour routine can quickly bring on a burn-out of workers.

Gubrium (1975) described nursing attendants' reaction. He described bowel work as a "feature of bed-and-body routines," and states, "Aides use a variety of techniques to expedite bowel work.

For example, an aide who finds that one of her patients has somehow smeared stool over much of his clothing and body is not likely to painstakingly 'clean it all bit by bit.' Rather, she virtually 'hoses him down.'" As one aide described it, "We strip 'em bare. Then we get the shower chair and put 'em in it. Then we wheel 'em down the hall to the shower and hose 'em down."

The Jury brothers (1976) graphically described the toileting problems encountered with their grandfather. Gubrium (1975, p. 139) describing nursing home care wrote, "Bowel work and talk is part of Manor routine . . . Although it is an integral part of bed-and-body work, nurses and aides take little precautions to make bowel work less obnoxious. Some handle stool delicately. Some try to avoid continual eye contact with it, preferring to 'look just enough to know what you're doing.' A few even defend themselves with perfume. 'I didn't put my perfume on today. When I work upstairs (patient floors), I have the habit of putting perfume on my tits so that when I have to stoop over to clean, I smell the perfume and not the BM." (BM is the abbreviation for bowel movement).

### DEFENSE MECHANISMS OF CARETAKERS

Defense mechanisms used by caretakers to deal with incontinence may include avoidance, rationalization, projection, and denial. Sutherland (1976) points out that the most dangerous defense mechanisms used by caretakers are projection and displacement, and, though these mechanisms do not occur only in the caretakers of the incontinent, they are instrumental in providing disharmony and conflicts in staff members. Table 30-4 indicates characteristics of commonly used diuretic drugs.

Bladder training programs need to be coordinated with the drug regime: for example, when can the aged person on diuretics be expected to void? If nocturia is present then diuretics should not be given close to bedtime.

### FECAL INCONTINENCE

Verwoerdt (1976), in accordance with the British writers, agrees that incontinence is a major concern, with one reason being that cleaning up requires so much personnel time. He lists causes of fecal incontinence: (1) "local pathology, prolapse rectum, malignancies, etc."; (2) neuromuscular incoordination of central origin, organic brain syndrome; (3) acute confusional states; e.g., resulting from "transplantation shock;" (4) intentional incontinence, e.g., spiteful behavior; and (5) constipation, fecal impaction. Fecal impaction may be due to reduced activity and anticholinergic effects of psychotropic drugs. Caretakers should take note of vomiting, bending over to one side, or increasing agitation, lethargy, or confusion.

### METHODS OF MANAGEMENT

Methods of management depend on the causes of the pathologic conditions affecting micturition. The causes include acute cerebrovascular accident, chronic brain syndrome, toxic confusional states, lesions of spinal cord, stress, and prostrate obstruction.

Isaacs (1965) states that *incontinence occurring for the first time in a seriously ill patient indicates impending death.* Goldfarb (personal communication) also indicated that incontinence should be considered a serious omen. Hospital-induced incontinence may be caused by too few toilets, great distance to walk, narrow toilets which do not accommodate wheel chairs, overcrowded wards,

**Table 30-4**  Characteristics of Commonly Used Diuretic Drugs.

| DRUG | USUAL DOSAGE SCHEDULE | ONSET OF EFFECT | PEAK EFFECT | DURATION |
|---|---|---|---|---|
| Chlorothiazide (Diuril<sup>R</sup>) | 500–1000mg/day | 1–2 hours | 3–6 hours | 6–12 hours |
| Hydrochlorothiazide (HydroDiuril<sup>R</sup>) | 50–100mg/day | 1–2 hours | 3–6 hours | 6–12 hours |
| Triamterene (Dyrenium<sup>R</sup>) | 100–300mg/day | 2 hours | 6–8 hours | 12–16 hours |
| Spironolactone (Aldactone<sup>R</sup>) | 25mg 4 times/day | gradual onset | 2–3 days after starting therapy | 2–3 days after stopping therapy |
| Furosemide (Lasix<sup>R</sup>) | 40–120mg/day | Oral: 1 hour Intravenous: 5 min. | 1–2 hours 30 minutes | 8 hours 2 hours |

Source: Ronald C. Kayne, Pharm. D.

too few signs, poor equipment, too few nurses, inadequate training, and too rigid hospital rules and regulations (Pinel, 1975).

Incontinence "implies an indignity to the social integrity of the individual" (Wilson, 1948). The most important aspects of treatment are the attitudes of the person himself, those around him, and those caring for him. Wilson reminds the reader of the importance of data regarding the disability and suggests considering the following therapeutic interventions: treatment of urinary infection, treatment of senile vaginitis, therapeutic cystometry, treatment of prostatic enlargement, drug therapy treatment, and physiotherapy.

Fine (1969) notes that older persons who have urgency or lack of control fear that they might wet the bed. During the first night of an admission to an institution, they can be found wandering in search of the toilet because of bladder discomfort. (Then they are often labeled by the night staff as a "wanderer." Few hospitals have adequate indications where the toilets are, and the lighting is poor en route to and inside the toilet area. Wells (1975) and Abbey (personal communication) remind us that the distance to the toilet should be short.

A great amount of work falls on the nursing personnel in caring for incontinent bed patients, who may develop decubitus lesions and infections of the skin. One of the first aims in treating such patients is to get them out of bed as soon as possible.

## THE INCONTINENT PERSON WHO HAS HAD A STROKE

Stroke ranks third as primary diagnosis of the last examination and as cause for admission on a National Nursing Home survey. The number of residents who reside in nursing homes and who have suffered strokes can be seen in Table 30–3.

Schultz (1974) recommends that a bowel and bladder program be initiated in a person who has suffered a stroke, even if the patient is unconscious. A bowel and bladder program, to be successful, requires that the caretaker: (1) determine prior bowel and bladder habits; (2) develop a program of offering the bedpan at regular intervals; (3) discuss the plan with the patient, family, and members of the nursing team; (4) develop a schedule for forcing fluids; (5) determine if the patient has a fecal impaction; (6) maintain an accurate record of the intake and output; (7) keep the patient dry; (8) encourage activity; (9) insure privacy; and (10) consult with the dietitian.

## INTERVENTION FOR THE COMMUNITY-BASED AGED PERSON

Caird and Judge (1974) state:

It is most distressing to find a patient who has become incontinent of urine solely because he is unable to reach adequate toilet facilities. Many old people are, however, faced with a toilet situated on a flight of stairs, up or down from the living area. Such a toilet may even be communal, outside the house, or indeed at the bottom of the garden. It may be quite inaccessible to anyone suffering from a neurological or locomotor disorder. Where an old person can reach such a toilet, he may be reluctant to go to it because of embarrassment, distaste of the state of the toilet itself, or, in wintertime, dislike of the temperature.

It is not surprising that bowel habits may become disordered or indeed that fecal impaction may even result. Such toilets rarely have handwashing facilities, with the consequent hazard of cross-infection. The size of the toilet is also of great importance to a disabled person, particularly if a walking aid or wheel chair is used; there must be adequate room to get in and out. Sometimes the provision of a simple aid such as a handrail or a grip may make all the difference between recurrent misery and a reasonable existence.

One family's struggles with an elderly incontinent relative with organic brain syndrome is described.

The time we all dreaded, but knew was inevitable, came without warning—Gramp lost control of his bowels completely. In one incredible day, the Tugend house became a military-like operation of diapers, rolls of toilet paper, and a well-orchestrated platoon system for getting him cleaned off and before the next 'accident' happened.

The crisis was so unexpected and the pace so hectic that none of us realized that the intolerable time had undoubtedly arrived. On that day, Nan voiced the feelings of everyone when she said, to no one in particular, 'Gosh, it's an awful ordeal.'

Gramp was as bewildered as anyone at the turn of events. At each recurring accident, he'd react with a startled grunt. During the umteenth trip to the bathroom (we'd quit counting when he hit nine before noon), Dee said, 'Oh, no, Gramp, you didn't go in your pants again, did you?'

'No,' replied Gramp, 'that other guy did' (Jury and Jury, 1976).

In summary, guidelines for intervention in incontinence include: (1) The caretaker should remember that incontinence may be a reason for seeking hospitalization and can also prevent discharge (Anderson, 1971). (2) Psychological mechanisms to consider in the etiology of incontinent persons include regression, dependency, rebellion, insecurity, attention seeking, disturbance of condition reflex, sensory deprivation, and symptom selection (Sutherland, 1976). (3) The caretaker should be alert to psychological reactions of the incontinent person which might include depressive reaction, insecurity, apathy (Sutherland, 1976). (4) The caretaker should be cognizant of his or her own reactions, which may include disgust, revulsion, and/or guilt regarding the disgust (Sutherland, 1976). (5) Decrease incidences of incontinence because incontinence is destructive to staff morale (Anderson, 1971). (6) Coordinate bladder training programs with the drug regimen of the incontinent person. (7) Be sure old people have adequate toilet facilities (Caird and Judge, 1974). (8) In dealing with the problems of incontinence, sit down with the patient and discuss the problem and express the view that you intend to be helpful (Kick, unpublished manuscript).

# INSOMNIA

Guy de Maupassant wrote, "The bed, my friend, is our whole life. It is there we are born, it is there that we love, it is there that we die," but he forgot to add it is there we lie awake. Insomnia has troubled people from the earliest of times. There is an ancient Egyptian hieroglyphic which rank orders the three great living hells: (1) to be in bed and sleep not; (2) to want the one who comes not; and (3) to try to please and please not (Dunkell, 1977).

## SCOPE OF THE PROBLEM

A 1973 Los Angeles study described by Dunkell (1977) showed that 32 percent of the population suffered some type of insomnia. It is estimated that more than thirty million Americans do have severe sleep problems. In a stress-ridden world insomnia is understandable, but one has to wonder why the insomnia rate is so high in a population supposedly living in a safe, protected environment?

## TYPES OF INSOMNIA

Dunkell (1977) described three general types of insomnia: (1) The first is sleep-onset insomnia in which the individual has trouble going to sleep. The person may be awake for hours ruminating about that day, or what will happen the next day. (2) The second is sleep-maintenance insomnia, which is the most common of the three and affects about 50 percent of the insomniacs. This type of

insomnia occurs frequently during the night, with awakenings of varying durations. This type of sleep pattern allows no profound rest and is a fragmented sleep experience. (3) Finally, there is terminal insomnia, in which the insomniac will awaken at an early hour and be unable to go back to sleep.

Different amounts of sleep are required by different individuals. Physical makeup as well as personality type is to be considered in one's sleep needs. Youths who loll in bed until noon have trouble understanding why grandparents arise with the fowls, and vice versa. Circadian rhythm is still blatantly ignored in the psychosocial care of the elderly. In a book based on observations made in a nursing home, the early morning rituals carried out by staff personnel in nursing homes are well described (Gubrium, 1975).

## OVERVIEW OF THE LITERATURE

Dunkell's (1977) main point about sleep positions is that the way we sleep reveals the way we live. "In the night world, each of us becomes the pantomimist of his own personal saga." He calls the characterological sleeping stance the omega position.

There is a common theme in the literature about the importance of presleep rituals (Dunkell, 1977; Zelechowski, 1977; Raskind, 1977). "Although there is sometimes an eccentric aspect to our presleep rituals, they are important for several reasons. For one thing, their habitual, automatic nature assists us in withdrawing ourselves and our thoughts from the activities of the day world" (Dunkell, 1977). Omega position, Dunkell points out, will change in altered physical conditions; e.g., a cardiac patient may sit up to sleep, but persons with ulcers, kidney stones, hernias, etc. may change sleep positions to diminish painful pressure around inflamed or tender parts of the body. Caretakers should be alert to such changes in sleeping positions of the elderly.

## NORMAL SLEEP PATTERNS FOR THE AGING

There is a change in sleep pattern for the normal aging person: Light sleep only, awakening several times at night, can return to sleep after awakening, and several daytime catnaps. It is advised not to interfere with normal sleep patterns of old individuals (Pfeiffer, 1977).

Insomnia among the aged can be due to a variety of problems, including: (1) illness; (2) pain; (3) too much sleep during the day; (4) poor sleeping arrangements—uncomfortable bed, too hot, too cold room; (5) anxiety; (6) fear (for example, of death); (7) drugs; (8) translocation shock; (9)

noisy environment; and (10) depression. In depressive states generally the agitated person sleeps less in the latter half of the night. But insomnia may be a symptom in other emotional reactions: grief, anxiety, anger and "even a result of sexual deprivation" (Butler and Lewis, 1977). The relationship of insomnia to depression should be underscored (Raskind, 1977).

Raskind (1977) in a concise, practical manner, delineates steps to improve sleep for older persons. He ends with a provocative line, "The middle of the night may be a good time to do something you've always wanted to do but never found the time for it."

## HOSPITALIZED PATIENTS

"Most hospitalized patients have difficulty sleeping. The possibility or reality of serious organic disease, the prospect of an uncomfortable diagnostic procedure or just the novelty of the hospital environment, can provoke enough emotional discomfort to disrupt sleep. Because medical care is a round-the-clock endeavor, hospitals are inherently unconducive to normal sleep. Physicians and nurses take vital signs, perform physical examinations, give medications and draw blood samples at all hours of the night. Paging systems blare, monitors beep, respirators hiss and chest tubes gurgle with no regard for bedtime" (Greenblatt and Miller, 1974).

Webb and Swinburne (1971) conducted a sleep study on a small sample of elderly patients in a self-care ward in England. Subjects spent almost half of their time in bed, sleep was often interrupted by wakefulness, almost all took one or more naps, and the length of naps was unrelated to the length of night sleep. The reader is referred to a comprehensive monograph, *Research on Sleep and Dreams* (National Institute of Mental Health, 1976) for more specific information on sleep and dreams.

Dunkell (1977) states, "Among those who do suffer from distinct sleep problems, some find them more upsetting than others. Studies have shown that younger males are the least likely to complain about their insomnia, while people over sixty who are having these difficulties most commonly find them disturbing enough to consult their physicians. In this older group, insomnia is sexist and affects more women than men." However, there are more older women than older men and therefore the studies need to be critically reviewed.

*Insomnia is considered to be chronic if it lasts longer than three months*, but whether it is transient or chronic most people handle it by reaching for a pill bottle. However, the "remedy" may create even more serious sleep problems.

Some commonly used antianxiety drugs are included in Table 30-5. They differ from the sedative-hypnotics in that they are used primarily as daytime sedatives to treat anxiety, while the latter are used to induce sleep at bedtime. They are included in Table 30-5 because they possess many of the same characteristics—notably sedation and the potential for inducing confusion—of those drugs used as "sleepers."

In an excellent article two drugs are recommended to relieve the symptomatic insomnia so indicative of depression: doxeprin (25 – 100 mg at bedtime) or amitriptyline (25 – 100 mg hs) (Raskind and Eisdorfer, 1977).

Transient insomnia occurs during periods of stress, is highly individualized, and may last only a few nights. Persons newly admitted to institutions very often have difficulty "settling in" and their nighttime wandering—searching for home or husband or wife—is common.

Sleeping pill addiction due to the improper management of transient insomnia is a large problem in geriatric medicine and nursing. But self-medication with over-the-counter drugs is also dangerous. Aged persons should be advised that, though they may be tired and not as effective for a few days, they will not be greatly harmed by getting only a few hours of sleep per night. Figure 30-2 indicates precautions which need to be given to elderly clients concerning the drugs listed on Table 30-5.

Old persons, whether in acute hospitals or nursing homes, may fear the nights, and some express fear about dying alone. A line from the poet Shelley (1901) describes the fear, "Till death like sleep might steal on me." Dunkell (1977) describes that fear, "since sleep takes the individual out of the day world into an unknown new world each night, many older people become acutely aware of the 'deathlike' aspects of the sleep universe and resist letting go of the reassuringly familiar surroundings of waking existence." The same author points out that retirement may also rob retirees of sleep because of the worry about their health and reduced income.

## MANAGEMENT OF INSOMNIA

### IMPORTANCE OF SLEEP HISTORY

Zelechowski (1977), wrote, "The vital first step in managing patients who have trouble sleeping is to take a careful sleep history. If you know how pa-

738 *Symptomatic Behaviors in the Elderly*

tients sleep at home, you can often maintain some of the conditions in the hospital." Twelve basic rules to be followed include:

(1) Take a thorough sleep history, (2) Try to maintain room conditions, such as temperature, ventilation, and lighting, that patients find conducive to sleep, (3) Help patients observe their 'bedtime rituals,' (4) If time permits, relax patients by giving bedtime nourishment and backrubs, (5) Try to schedule treatments, procedures, and routines for times when patients are awake, (6) Schedule exercise periods for those patients who can exercise, (7) Use common sense nursing methods to promote sleep—not hypnotics, (8) When hypnotics are necessary, use those that minimize disruption of normal sleep patterns, whenever possible, (9) At night, observe patients who are asleep (as well as those who are awake) to see who is not sleeping well, (10) Talk to patients who have trouble sleeping. Can you help them? (11) Be aware of physiological changes that might disturb patients during sleep, such as increased gastric secretion, and try to minimize any discomfort, and (12) Be sure to keep unnecessary noise to a minimum.

## Case Example

A woman in her late 70s was widowed by the suicide of her husband. He shot himself in the head one night while she slept in another bedroom. The bedroom was sealed off by the police department during the investigation. She was left alone with a constant reminder of the tragic death—police bringing the gun and then removing the seal, bloody linen to dispose of, and the funeral plans. During the initial shock period relatives were available, but when they left the old woman was alone at night and afraid to go to sleep. She was afraid because she was almost deaf (she had thought the gunshot blast was a car backfiring). She had been a baby sitter for many years, so one of her clients asked if she would like one of the children (who were 12–14 years of age) to spend the night with her. The two children who alternated evenings sleeping there, had also been to the funeral parlor to see the dead man and so they clearly understood what had happened. The children were old enough to be considerate and helpful, and her cooking the evening meal and breakfast for them kept her eat-

**Table 30–5**  Commonly Used Anti-Anxiety and Sedative-Hypnotic Drugs[1,2,3]

| | |
|---|---|
| Benzodiazepines<br>  Anti-anxiety Agents<br>    Chlordiazepoxide (Librium[R])<br>    Diazepam (Valium[R])<br>    Oxazepam (Serax[R])<br>    Chlorazepate dipotassium (Tranxene[R])<br>  Hypnotics<br>    Flurazepam (Dalmane[R])<br>Barbiturates<br>  Sedative-Hypnotics<br>    Phenobarbital<br>    Amobarbital (Amytal[R])<br>    Pentobarbital (Nembutal[R])<br>    Secobarbital (Seconal[R])<br>Barbiturate-like Hypnotics[4]<br>  Glutethimide (Doriden[R])<br>  Methyprylon (Noludar[R])<br>  Methaqualone (Quaalude[R])<br>  Ethchlorovynol (Placidyl[R])<br>Miscellaneous Sedative-Hypnotics<br>  Chloral Hydrate<br>Miscellaneous Anti-Anxiety-Sedatives<br>  Meprobamate (Miltown[R], Equanil[R])<br>  Antihistamines<br>    Hydroxyzine (Vistaril[R], Atarax[R]) | 1. Subtle distortion of mood, impaired judgment and impaired motor skills may persist for many hours after administration. For example, the duration of effect of barbiturates used for hypnotic (sleep inducing) purposes is longer than generally assumed. Secobarbital, a "short-acting" compound, has been shown to impair performance in multidimensional tests for as long as 10 to 22 hours. Likewise, the effects of the benzodiazepines (oxazepam is an exception) tend to persist for 24 hours or longer. Thus, repeated daily dosage of these drugs can lead to cumulative clinical effects.<br><br>2. Clients may react to usual doses of these drugs with excitement, agitation, confusion, or depression. Erratic responses, including a paradoxical increase in aggressive behavior, with attendant hostility and rage, occur more frequently in the aged. (This effect is not seen with the antipsychotic drugs.)<br><br>3. The concurrent ingestion of more than modest amounts of alcohol with therapeutic doses of the above drugs—all of which depress the central nervous system to some degree—may be expected to enhance the depressant effects of alcohol. These effects predominantly include the impairment of mental performance and judgment, reduction of motor skills and coordination, and increased drowsiness and sleepiness. In addition to the obvious hazards this presents to the aged client driving an automobile, mobility in the pedestrian is impaired and the risk of a catastrophic fall increased. Aged clients and their caretakers, if appropriate, should be warned about the dangers of taking combinations of sedative drugs and of mixing sedative drugs with alcohol.<br><br>4. Many drugs promoted as non-barbiturate hypnotics, such as glutethimide, methyprylong and methaqualone, carry liabilities equal to, or greater than, those of barbiturates. |

Source: Ronald C. Kayne, Pharm. D.

ing also. There were also other ears to hear the phone, and to answer it, and for a couple of weeks she was not afraid to go to sleep. When she stated she was no longer afraid, she decided she "would have to learn to go it alone."

In summary, the sleep patterns as well as the dreams of the elderly could well be suitable grounds for study. Daytime sleeping interferes with night-

time sleeping; therefore, in studying insomnia in the elderly, baseline data must include the circadian rhythm and the sleeping patterns in a 24–hour period, sleeping patterns across the life span, and causes of the most common disruption in patterns.

## WANDERING

There is only one article in the current literature on wandering behavior of older persons (Cornbleth, 1978). Yet, it is a common behavior which is difficult to manage and can ultimately cause serious consequences—death from auto accidents, serious falls, or exposure to very cold or very hot weather. Restlessness, either during the day or night, is a pervasive problem in nursing homes but also occurs in the acute setting or in the home. Even residents in wheel chairs wander—sometimes quite far from the facility or ward. Perhaps it is not viewed as wandering, however.

Gubrium (1974), makes the point that anyone considered "senile" who appears unaccompanied is defined by staff as "escaping," and that, if such an individual is left unaccompanied, they are often whisked away by another staff person.

> One aide (Sharon) occasionally takes patient (Mike) down to the employees' lounge for a soda. When it is time for her break, she readies him, and they proceed down the elevator to the lounge together. If there should happen to be other staff members present in the lounge, Sharon mentions to Mike in a clear and distinct voice that is obviously meant for everyone in the room, "Now, let's have a soda and sit down for awhile, Mike." This signifies to those present that she, after all, is in control of the situation, and it accounts for Mike's presence there. Without it, those in the lounge would wisk him away to his proper place on the fourth floor.

> On such occasions, a slapstick series of events may follow that does not always rectify matters to everyone's satisfaction. To one aide, a patient's been found; to another, he's 'escaped' and to the patient, his change of scene has been rudely cut short. His objections, of course, go unheeded as he's warned to 'stay put.'
> Patients and residents considered by the staff to be alert receive a different treatment in staff places. As long as they can provide a legitimate account for their presence in such places, the places are public to them. The range of acceptable accounts, however, is usually fairly narrow.

Institutionalized residents lack exercise and although they may pace in agitation as a caged

---

DRUG NAME:

_____

 No. _____

This information sheet tells you how to use this medicine safely. Because this drug makes some people sleepy or dizzy, you should be careful not to drive a car, use machinery, or perform any dangerous tasks until you see how this medicine affects you.

This drug may also worsen the effects of alcohol and may make the effects of alcohol last longer. Alcohol should be avoided or used with caution when you are taking this medicine.

This drug may be dangerous if you are taking another medicine. Ask your family pharmacist before taking other medicines, or if you have any questions. The pharmacy name and phone number are on the prescription label.

 **academy**

**Clinical Practice**

Produced as a public service by your family pharmacist and the California Pharmaceutical Association, a non-profit professional society of pharmacists dedicated to public awareness of health care.

© California Pharmaceutical Association, 1977

**Figure 30–2** Information Sheet on drug usage created by California Pharmaceutical Association, 1977. Such drug information should be read and carefully explained to an older client. A large print version should be sent home with the client to read again later, or given to relatives if client does not comprehend. Permission to use granted by California Pharmaceutical Association.

animal might, they also could be walking out of sheer boredom. Gottesman, Quarterman, and Cohen (1973), wrote, "Most sit from arising to bedtime with only meals to punctuate their day." The need for exercise among the elderly who led active lives, and who may walk as though in a self-assigned exercise program, is observed in long-term care units. Older persons, most especially those with organic brain damage, often will be found walking aimlessly at night. If the brain damage is compounded with sensory deficits, the problems can be enormous.

Wandering creates concern, worry and problems for both staff and family members. In spite of the frequency of the problem, and the implications, it is an unstudied area in the literature. In the community, police often have to return aged wanderers to home or to a long-term care facility. If the aged person does not have identification on him/her, he/she may sit in the police station for some time before being reported missing. Old persons often see policemen in a way the youth do not. They are often flattered by the attention the "nice young officer" gave them, either in the police station or in the police car when being returned to the facility.

## CASE EXAMPLE

A man in his 80s lived with his daughter in the suburbs of a large city. He loved to gamble at the horse races but he never saved money for bus fare to take him back home—a 20-mile trip. He solved his financial embarrassment easily by simply pulling his hat down over his ears, slouching, and starting to walk aimlessly (wandering behavior) down the side of the freeway near the race track. He knew he would be picked up, and although he always knew his address, but not how to get there, he was treated as an incompetent, wandering, confused old man by the highway patrol.

In rural areas and small towns, the aged person is often well known and is returned to home base by friends or neighbors. The life style needs to be considered. Many old people have no transportation and are forced to walk when they want to go to town or to the store. Also, if they lose their driver's license in late life, many resort to walking more and are not really wandering.

Stotsky (1960) mentions a special kind of wanderer—the elderly who still retain a driving license and may drive aimlessly getting into accidents. A poignant example is recounted in *Gramp* (Jury and Jury, 1976).

Stotsky (1968) suggests that "the elderly may suddenly experience a desire to travel in search of new experiences and to find means of tension relief

and reduction." Boredom is no small problem. Incidents of boredom among the institutionalized aged are described in *Nursing and the Aged* (Burnside, 1980). Clow (1953) has beautifully described his individualized care plan for a wanderer.

## CASE EXAMPLE

A 96-year-old man had participated in a group demonstration at a conference. The second day of the conference, the director of nurses described the nonagerian's behavior, "He tried to run away—kept saying he wanted to go back to 'that class with the pretty women in it'; he would not take his name tag off—the one the group leader had put on him." The behavior, though a positive reaction to his experience, was reported in negative terms and as undesirable behavior, "He's a wanderer."

In summary, the following guidelines for interventions in wandering are suggested. (1) For daytime wanderers increase activity available in daytime, to prevent wandering. (2) Study the aged person's behavior—is it actually wandering, that is, undesirable behavior, or does the person really have a place he or she wants to see and visit again? (Burnside, 1977). (3) Consider the impact of transportation changes in the aged person's life; for example, loss of driver's license. (4) Evaluate the exercise program for a person who worked hard all of his/her life; this may be an overlooked factor in the wandering behavior. (5) Interventions for nighttime wanderers who have chronic brain syndrome include: leaving the lights on in bathrooms, firm management, careful administration of medication, adequate lighting, properly chosen night activities, napping in a comfortable chair, especially if the individual is afraid in room, staying up (if not disturbing other residents), and reality test. (6) Focus on the basis of wandering. Is it the boredom, ennui, monotony in the institutional life? and (7) For community-based residents it is well to remember that old people can "wander" in wheel chairs, in cars, and also on city buses or street cars.

While intervention is necessary in unacceptable symptomatic behaviors, three questions must be asked: To whom is the behavior unacceptable? Why is the behavior unacceptable? What needs of the intervenor are being met? On the fly leaf of a novel the reviewer wrote of the old people in the book, "(they) are to themselves as actual, as alive, as passionately in life as they have ever been. They refuse to write themselves off; they cling to hopes, which are often fantastic; they suffer needs, which are seldom met. Above all, they feel. And . . . each of them takes on the force of personality that gives each an unyielding selfhood" (Wright, 1975). Caretakers may consider how they will encourage "unyielding selfhoods" rather than expecting older persons to conform rigidly. As Weinberg said, "disordered chaos" may be a way of coping and organizing strength for the aged, and forbearance should be our stance (Weinberg, 1975).

## QUESTIONS FOR CARETAKERS

We have discussed a diverse array of behaviors or states in the elderly in this chapter and have noted lacunae in the literature regarding symptomatic behaviors, wandering behavior, loneliness in old age, illusions, reality testing, and interventions in the frail elderly. What are some of the questions to ask about future research and about some of the existing problems which are not adequately covered in the United States literature?

1. After the behavior or state is identified, these questions must be asked: Why is the behavior considered symptomatic, and/or unacceptable? Why is it unacceptable? If so, to whom?

2. What types of research can be initiated to better understand the psychodynamics of wandering?

3. When and where does wandering of the elderly occur most frequently and what are the greatest hazards?

4. What precisely is wandering behavior; is it always concomitant with confusion?

5. When and where is loneliness most prevalent in the aged population?

6. What are the psychodynamics of loneliness in the aged?

7. What is the relationship of severe loneliness to depression and/or suicide in the elderly?

8. When and where do illusions in the aged most commonly occur?

9. Are the illusions fairly consistent or do they change from time to time, place to place, person to person?

10. What research could be initiated to study illusions and so improve interventions with the aged? (For example, when and how often are illusions described by the aged person interpreted by caretakers as confusional states, crazy talk, or disorientation?)

11. What research could be initiated to study visually impaired elderly to better understand illusions and relationship to pathology of the eyes?

12. What conditions in the environment are especially conducive to causing illusions in the old person?

13. How can research on illusions done by cognitive psychologists be incorporated into improved care and understanding of the aged person who experience illusions?

14. Can peer help groups be studied for their effectiveness in reality testing with their cohorts?

15. How can linkages be increased among community services, nursing homes, and community mental health centers?

16. Double or triple jeopardy exist in some aged, but the aged person is in "quadruple jeopardy" if he/she has the stigma of being confused, a wanderer, or incontinent. What in-service, continuing education, and mental health curricula will ultimately improve the care of those in "quadruple jeopardy"?

17. What responsibility or educational programs can drug companies assume to control and monitor use of drugs that precipitate behaviors described in this chapter?

18. What community supports best help to maintain the elderly with the above symptoms in their homes?

19. Would a national campaign on hypertension be effective to help slow the progressive deterioration of some chronic brain syndrome individuals?

20. How can such an affluent nation as ours place men on other planets and have so few solutions for better care and equipment for incontinent old people?

21. How can we develop a system of well elderly clinics to continuously monitor health problems *before* the oldster is wandering, or incontinent, or confused or desperately lonely?

## SUMMARY

This chapter comprises a potpourri selection and a discussion of common symptomatic behaviors/symptoms in the elderly which cause nursing problems. An overview of the literature on each behavior/symptom is presented; guidelines for interventions gleaned from the search of the literature are given for utilization by the caretakers of the aged. Behaviors described include: (1) reactive depression; (2) aggressivity; (3) confusion and disorientation; (4) loneliness; (5) incontinence (both urinary and fecal); (6) insomnia; and (7) wandering. Drug tables are included in the areas of aggressivity, confusion/disorientation, and incontinence.

Apropos to the closure of this chapter are the following remarks of Verwoerdt and Willington. Verwoerdt (1976), wrote, "Anyone who has done clinical work in the field of aging is confronted with arduous tasks, including the necessity to relinquish one's reserve fantasies, to be faced with death or despair, to struggle for value and meaning, and to keep the humanitarian and the scientist within . . . in dynamic equilibrium. If some measure of personal maturation results from this, a proper sense of humility will be part of it. Surprisingly many can be our rewards: the challenge of work in what is very much a terra incognita, the excitement of the team effort, and the therapeutic response of our patients."

Willington's (1976) words are, "A society cannot mature fully if the unsatisfactory, and untidy aspects of life are removed immediately from its midst, so that compassion, and the understanding of its less fortunate members are lost."

# REFERENCES

ABBEY, J. 1973. Physiology of Aging. Lecture at Andrus Gerontology Center, University of Southern California.

ADAMS, G. F., AND, McILWRAITH, P. M. 1963. *Geriatric Nursing*. Fair Lawn, N.J.: Oxford University Press.

AGATE, J. 1971. Special hazards of illness in later life. *In*, I. Rossman (ed.), *Clinical Geriatrics*, pp. 461–471. Philadelphia: J. B. Lippincott.

AGATE, J. 1970. *The Practice of Geriatrics*. London: William Heinemann Medical Books.

ANDERS, R. L. 1977. When a patient becomes violent. *American Journal of Nursing, 77,* 1144–1148.

ANDERSON, W. F. 1971. *Practical Management of the Elderly*, Second Edition. Oxford: Blackwell Scientific Publications.

ANKERS, M., AND QUARRINGTON, B. 1972. Operant behavior in the memory-disordered. *Gerontologist, 27,* 500–510.

BENNETT, R., AND NAHEMOW, L. 1965. A two-year follow-up study of the process of social adjustments in residents of a home for the aged. Paper presented at the meeting of the Gerontological Society, Los Angeles.

BENNETT, R. 1973. Living conditions and everyday needs of the elderly with particular reference to social isolation. *International Journal of Aging and Human Development, 4,* 179–198.

BLENKNER, M. 1968. The place of the nursing home among community resources. *Journal of Geriatric Psychiatry, 1,* 135–144.

BLYTH, R. H. 1966. *Haiku Volume 3*. Tokyo: Hokuseido.

BOWNAS, G. 1966. *The Penguin Book of Japanese Verse*. Baltimore: Penguin Books.

BROCKLEHURST, J. C. 1951. *Incontinence in Old People*. Edinburgh: E. and S. Livingston.

BROCKLEHURST, J. C. 1962. Letter in *British Medical Journal, 1,* 115–116.

BROCKLEHURST, J. C., AND DILLANE, J. B. 1967. Studies of the female bladder in old age—drug effects in urinary incontinence. *Gerontologia 'Clinica, 9,* 182–189.

BROCKLEHURST, J. C., FRY, J., GRIFFITHS, L., AND KALTON, G. 1971. Dysuria in old age. *Journal American Geriatric Society, 19,* 582–592.

BUBER, M. 1970. *I and Thou*. New York: C. Scribner's Sons.

BURNSIDE, I. M. 1971. Loneliness in old age. *Mental Hygiene, 55,* 391–397.

BURNSIDE, I. M. 1973. Interviewing the aged. *In*, I. M. Burnside (ed.), *Psychosocial Nursing Care of the Aged*, pp. 3–14. New York: McGraw-Hill.

BURNSIDE, I. M. 1980. *Nursing and the Aged,* 2nd ed. New York: McGraw-Hill.

BURNSIDE, I. M. 1977. Reality testing: An important concept. *Association of Rehabilitation Nurses, 2,* 3–7.

BURNSIDE, I. M. 1978. *Working With the Elderly: Group Process and Techniques*. North Scituate, Mass.: Duxbury Press.

BURNSIDE, I. M. 1979. Loneliness in the aged. *In*, I. M. Burnside, P. R. Ebersole, and H. E. Monea (eds.), *Psychosocial Caring Throughout the Life Span*, pp. 508–512. New York: McGraw-Hill.

BUSSE, E. W., AND PFEIFFER, E. 1969. *Behavior and Adaptation in Late Life*. Boston: Little, Brown and Company.

BUTLER, R. N. 1971. Clinical psychiatry in late life. *In*, I. Rossman (ed.), *Clinical Geriatrics*, pp. 439–459. Philadelphia: J. Lippincott.

BUTLER, R. N., AND LEWIS, M. I. 1977. *Aging and Mental Health*. St. Louis: C. V. Mosby.

CAIRD, F. I., AND JUDGE, T. G. 1974. *Assessment of the Elderly Patient*. London: Pitman Medical.

CASTANEDA, C. 1972. *Journey to Ixtlan*. New York: Simon and Schuster.

CLOW, H. E. 1953. Individualizing the care of the aging. *American Journal of Psychiatry, 110,* 460–464.

CORNBLETH, T. 1977. Effects of a protected hospital ward area on wandering and nonwandering geriatric patients. *Journal of Gerontology, 32,* 573–577.

DUNKELL, S. 1977. *Sleep Positions: The Night Language of the Body*. New York: William Morrow.

ECKERSTROM, S. 1955. Urinary incontinence in old persons. *Geriatrics, 10,* 83–85.

EXTON-SMITH, A. N., NORTON, D., AND McLAREN, R. 1962. *Geriatric Nursing Problems in Hospital*. London: Nat. Corp. Care of Old People.

FAUNCE, F. A. 1969. Loneliness in a nursing home. *In*, R. J. Hill, Jr. (ed.), *The Nursing Home Visitor*, pp. 4–6. Nashville: Abingdon Press.

FINE, W. 1969. Sphincteric disorders in the elderly. *Nursing Mirror, 130,* 30.

FISCH, M., GOLDFARB, A. I., SHAHINIAN, S. P., AND TURNER, H. 1968. Chronic brain syndrome in the community aged. *Archives of General Psychiatry, 18,* 739–745.

FRANKFATHER, D. 1976. Senility in the aged—confusion in the community. *Dissertation Abstracts International, 37(A),* 3184–3185. Waltham, Mass.: Brandeis University.

FROMM, E. 1941/1969. *Escape From Freedom*. New York: Rinehart (1941). Reprinted: New York: Avon, 1969.

FROMM-REICHMANN, R. 1959a. Loneliness. *Psychiatry, 22,* 1–16.

FROMM-REICHMANN, F. 1959b. On loneliness. *In*, D. M. Bullard (ed.), *Psychoanalysis and Psychotherapy: Selected Papers of Frieda Fromm-Reichmann*. Chicago: University of Chicago Press.

GAEV, D. M. 1976. *The Psychology of Loneliness*. Chicago: Adams Press.

GIBSON, J. J. 1966. *The Senses Considered as Perceptual Systems*. Boston: Houghton Mifflin Company.

GODBER, C. 1976. The confused elderly. *Nursing Times (Care of the Elderly Supplement), 72*, vii–viv.

GOODRICH, M., AND SCHWARTZ, D. 1959. Some changes in the sleeping and eating patterns of fifty patients with long-term illnesses. *Journal of Chronic Diseases, 9*, 63–73.

GOTTESMAN, L. E., QUARTERMAN, C. E., AND COHEN, G. M. 1973. Psychosocial treatment of the aged. *In*, C. Eisdorfer and M. Powell (eds.), *The Psychology of Adult Development and Aging*. Washington, D.C.: American Psychological Association.

GREENBLATT, D. J., AND MILLER, R. R. 1974. Rational use of psychotropic drugs. *American Journal of Hospital Pharmacy, 31*, 990–995.

GREGORY, R. L., AND GOMBRICH, E. H. 1973. *Illusion in Nature and Art*. New York: C. Scribner's Sons.

GROSICKI, J. P. 1968. Effect of operant conditioning on modification of incontinence in neuropsychiatric geriatric patients. *Nursing Research, 17*, 304–311.

GUBRIUM, J. F. 1975. *Living and Dying at Murray Manor*. New York: St. Martin's Press.

HELLEBRANDT, F. A. 1978. The senile dement in our midst: A look at the other side of the coin. *Gerontologist, 18*, 67–70.

HENDERSON, H. G. 1958. *An Introduction to Haiku, Garden City*. New York: Doubleday.

HORNEY, K. 1937. *The Neurotic Personality of Our Time*. New York: Norton and Company.

Human Relations Media Center (Producer). 1976. *Gramp*. Baltimore: Mass Media Ministries. (Film)

HYAMS, D. E. 1969. Psychological factors in rehabilitation of the elderly. *Gerontologica Clinica, 11*, 129–136.

ISAACS, B. 1964. Morbidity in old people. *In*, B. Isaacs (ed.), Current *Achievements in Geriatrics*, pp. 84. London: Cassell.

ISAACS, B., AND WALKEY, F. A. 1964. A survey of incontinence in elderly hospital patients. *Gerontologia Clinica, 6*, 367–371.

ISAACS, B. 1965. *An Introduction to Geriatrics*. London: Bailliere, Tindall and Cassell.

JUNG, C. G. 1964. *Man and His Symbols*. London: Aldus Books, Ltd.

JURY, M., AND JURY, D. 1976. *Gramp*. New York: Grossman Publishers.

KAHN, R. L. 1975. The mental health system and the future aged. *Gerontologist, 15*, 24–31.

KASSEL, V. 1965. Senility a definition. *Rocky Mountain Medical Journal, 62*, 51–52.

LANGLEY, G. E. 1975. Functional psychoses. *In*, G. Howells (ed.), *Modern Perspectives in the Psychiatry of Old Age*, pp. 326–355. New York: Brunner/Mazel.

LIBOW, L. S. 1973. Pseudo-senility: Acute and reversible organic brain syndromes. *Journal of the American Geriatrics Society, 20*, 112–120.

LINDEN, M. E. 1956. Geriatrics. *In*, S. R. Slavson (ed.), *The Fields of Group Psychotherapy*, pp. 129–152. New York: International Universities Press.

LINDEN, M. E. 1953. Group psychotherapy with institutionalized senile women: Study in gerontologic human relations. *International Journal of Group Psychotherapy, 3*, 150–170.

LOPATA, H. Z. 1976. Excerpts from widowhood in an American city. *In*, B. B. Hess (ed.), *Growing Old in America*, pp. 219–249. New Brunswick: Transaction Books.

LURIE, H. J. 1977. Discussion guide for film, *The Disturbed Nursing Home Patient*. Seattle: University of Washington.

MACKINNON, R. A., AND MICHELS, R. 1971. *The Psychiatric Interview in Clinical Practice*. Philadelphia: W. B. Saunders.

MASLOW, A. 1970. *Motivation and Personality*, Second Edition. New York: Harper & Row.

MAY, R. 1953. *Man's Search for Himself*. New York: Norton.

MILNE, J. S., WILLIAMSON, J., MAULE, M. M., AND WALLACE, E. T. 1972. Urinary symptoms in older people. *Modern Geriatrics, 2*, 198–205.

MOUSTAKAS, C. E. 1960. Communal loneliness. *Psychologica, 3*, 188–190.

National Institute of Mental Health. 1976. *Research on Sleep and Dreams*. Bethesda, Md.: National Institute of Mental Health.

NEISSER, U. 1976. *Cognition and Reality*. San Francisco: W. H. Freeman and Co.

NEWMAN, J. L. 1962. Old folks in wet beds. *British Medical Journal, 7*, 1824–1828.

NORTON, D., McLAREN, R., AND EXTON-SMITH, A. N. 1975. *An Investigation of Geriatric Nursing Problems in Hospitals*. Edinburgh: Churchill Livingstone.

OSBORN, M. L. 1975. Expression of psychopathology in art. *In*, J. G. Howells (ed.), *Modern Perspectives in the Psychiatry of Old Age*, pp. 584–604. New York: Brunner/Mazel.

PALMORE, E. 1977. Facts on aging: A short quiz. *Gerontologist, 17*, 315–320.

PFEIFFER, E. 1973. Drugs and the elderly. Paper presented at conference, Andrus Gerontology Center, Los Angeles.

PFEIFFER, E. 1977. The patients of geriatric psychiatry. *Career Directions, 5*, 20–38.

PINEL, C. 1975. Disorders of micturition in the elderly. *Nursing Times, 71*, 2019–2021.

RASKIND, M. A. 1977. Why you don't sleep like you used to. *Drug Therapy, 7*, 51–52.

RASKIND, M. A., AND EISDORFER, C. 1977. When elderly patients can't sleep. *Drug Therapy, 7*, 44–50.

RIESMAN, D. 1973. Foreword. *In*, R. W. Weiss (ed.), *Loneliness: The Experience of Emotional and Social Isolation*, pp. ix–xx. Cambridge, Mass.: Massachusetts Institute Technology Press.

Sandoz Pharmaceuticals. 1977. Behavioral problems. *In, Workshop on Aging.* East Hanover, N. J.: Sandoz Pharmaceuticals.

SCHULTZ, L. C. 1974. Nursing care of the patient with a stroke. *In,* V. Christopherson *et al.* (eds.), *Rehabilitation Nursing, Perspectives and Applications,* New York: McGraw-Hill.

SEGALL, M. H. 1966. *Influence of Culture on Visual Perception.* Indianapolis: Bobbs-Merrill.

SHELLEY, P. B. 1901. Stanzas written in dejection near Naples. *In,* P. B. Shelley and G. E. Woodberry (eds.), *The Complete Poetical Works of Shelley,* Cambridge Edition. Boston: Houghton Mifflin.

SHUTTLEWORTH, K. E. D. 1970. Urinary tract diseases, incontinence. *British Medical Journal, 4,* 727–729.

STOTSKY, B. A. 1968. *The Elderly Patient.* New York: Grune & Stratton.

SULLIVAN, H. S. 1953. *The Interpersonal Theory of Psychiatry.* New York: Norton.

SUTHERLAND, S. S. 1976. The psychology of incontinence. *In,* F. S. Willington (ed.), *Incontinence in the Elderly,* pp 52–69. London: Academic Press.

SWANSON, D. 1976. Minnie Remembers. *In,* J. T. Grana (ed.), *Images: Women in Transition,* Nashville: Upper Room.

TILLICH, P. 1963. *The Eternal Now.* New York: C. Scribner's Sons.

TOBIN, S. S., DAVIDSON, S. M., AND SACK, A. 1976. *Effective Social Services for Older Americans.* Institute of Gerontology, University of Michigan at Wayne State.

TOWNSEND, P. 1963. *The Last Refuge.* London: Routledge & Kegan Paul, Ltd.

TOWNSEND, P. 1968. Isolation, desolation and loneliness. *In,* E. Shanas (ed.), *Old People in Three Industrial Societies,* New York: Atherton Press.

U. S. Department of Health, Education and Welfare. 1976. *Excerpts From Health, United States, 1975.* DHEW, PHS, Health Resources Administration, National Center for Health Services Research of National Center for Health Statistics.

VERWOERDT, A. 1976. *Clinical Geropsychiatry.* Baltimore: Williams & Wilkins Co.

WEBB, B., AND SWINBURNE, H. 1971. An observational study of sleep of the aged. *Perceptual and Motor Skills, 32,* 895–898.

*Webster's New Twentieth Century Dictionary.* 1977. Cleveland: Collins-World.

WEINBERG, J. 1970. Understanding mentally confused persons. *Postgraduate Medicine, 47,* 116–119.

WEINBERG, J. 1975. Psychopathology. *In,* J. G. Howells (ed.), *Modern Perspectives in the Psychiatry of Old Age,* pp. 234–252. New York: Brunner/Mazel.

WEISS, R. S. 1973. *Loneliness: The Experience of Emotional and Social Isolation.* Cambridge, Mass.: Massachusetts Institute of Technology.

WELLS, T. 1975. Promoting urinary continence in the elderly in hospital. *Nursing Times, 71,* 1908–1909.

WERSHOW, H. 1977. Comment: reality orientation for gerontologists. *Gerontologist, 17,* 297–301.

WHITEHEAD, J. G. 1974. *Psychiatric Disorders in Old Age.* New York: Springer.

WILLINGTON, F. L. 1969. Problems in urinary incontinence in the aged. *Gerontologia Clinica, II,* 330–356.

WILLINGTON, F. L. 1975. Incontinence: The significance of incontinence in personal sanitary habits. *Nursing Times, 71,* 340–341.

WILLINGTON, F. L. 1976. *Incontinence in the Elderly.* London: Academic Press.

WILSON, T. S. 1948. Urinary incontinence in the aged. *Lancet, 255,* 374–377.

WRIGHT, R. 1975. *Rocking.* New York: Harper & Row.

YORK, J. L. 1977. *Community Mental Health Centers and Nursing Homes: Guidelines for Cooperative Program.* Lansing, Michigan: St. Lawrence Hospital.

ZELECHOWSKI, G. P. 1977. Helping your patient sleep: Planning instead of pills. *Nursing '77, 7,* 63–65.

# 31

# Geriatric
# Psychopharmacology

*Robert Hicks, H. Harris Funkenstein,*
*Maurice W. Dysken, & John M. Davis*

## INTRODUCTION

This chapter concerns itself with the principles, issues, problems and other details involved in the psychopharmacologic management of the elderly, with some comments on somatic therapies as well.

Lehmann and Ban have proclaimed (1969) that geriatric psychopharmacology has become a "discipline in its own right." Indeed, it has been subject to attention—at one time or another—by many leading psychopharmacologists (for example, these two authors and: Cole and Stotsky, 1974; Davis, 1974; Hollister, 1977; Salzman, Shader, and Harmatz, 1975; van Pragg, 1977; and others below), with some authorities (Fann and Eisdorfer, 1979; Gershon and Raskin, 1975; Jarvik, 1978) especially associated with the field. This is not surprising, since the elderly constitute an increasing proportion of the population (Butler, 1975), and

since there is an increasing concern over drug reactions in general (Hurwitz, 1969; Seidl, Thornton, Smith, and Cluff, 1966), with evidence that the elderly are particularly sensitive (Hicks and Davis, 1979, 1980; Hurwitz, 1969; Miller and Greenblatt, 1976; Seidl *et al.*, 1966).

Interest in geriatric *psycho*pharmacology, however, is not only a result of the above, but is also related to increasing evidence that psychotropic medications are widely dispensed in both the general population (Parry, Balter, Mellinger, Cisin, and Manheimer, 1973) and often even more in the older age groups (Butler, 1975; Guttmann, 1978; Parry *et al.*, 1973). It is also the result of the increasing attention that has been paid to the adverse effects which psychoactive agents may produce when given to the elderly (Bender, 1964; Hicks and Davis, 1980; Miller and Greenblatt, 1976; Salzman, Shader, and Harmatz, 1975). (The increasing awareness of potential psychotropic drug interactions probably is also a factor, and will be discussed below.)

## FOCUS

Since there are many reviews, chapters, and portions of books (e.g., Lipton, DiMascio, and Killam, 1978) available in addition to those mentioned above, and since exhaustive reviews (Stotsky, 1975) exist, *this chapter will take the approach of trying to impart principles*, rather than to provide another encyclopedic review in the face of the excellent ones already available. For this reason, there is much emphasis on pharmacokinetics and little on various trials of one agent (or class of agents) versus another.

## AGE-RELATED CHANGES IN BRAIN MORPHOLOGY, PHYSIOLOGY, AND FUNCTION

Bender (1964) concluded early that the "central nervous system is perhaps the system most sensitive to alterations in drug activity with age." Hamilton (1966) concluded that the neuronal loss due to aging was the "primary change responsible for the altered reactivity and sensitivity of the aged to neurogenic drugs." While these early and widely-quoted observations might seem slightly simplistic in their terminology, their basic concepts seem to have held up.

We have provided elsewhere (Funkenstein, Hicks, Dysken, and Davis, 1980) a brief review which describes the age-related CNS pathophysiological changes that can alter the cognitive function of the older individual. We noted in that same review some of the clinical and research problems in assessing such morphological, physiological, and functional changes. These areas are covered elsewhere in this volume in greater detail, especially in the chapters by Adams, Bondareff, and Gurland.

## NEUROPSYCHIATRIC PROBLEMS IN GEROPSYCHIATRY SECONDARY TO MEDICATION

Before proceeding further, it seems worthwhile to remind the clinician that a myriad of neuropsychiatric problems may be *produced* in the elderly by many drugs, both those given for strictly medical reasons as well as those with psychotropic function.

Confusional states that occur on propranalol (see below), analgesics, and sedative-hypnotics (e.g., Stotsky, 1970) are well known. Such conditions occurring with antituberculosis medication should (but may not to the *younger* physician) be common knowledge. As a potential cause of confusion, anticholinergic agents should always be of concern to the geriatric physician. Since most psychotropic medications, including perhaps even the benzodiazepines, have anticholinergic effects (see *Anticholinergic agents versus physostigmine* in the *OTHER IMPORTANT DRUG INTERACTIONS* section further on), this is of even greater relevance, especially in view of the probably already compromised cerebral function in the elderly (Bender, 1964; Hamilton, 1966; Salzman *et al.*, 1975).

One should also note here the proclivity, reported by Guttmann (1978), for the elderly to take over-the-counter (OTC) agents (67 percent of 447 patients studied—versus 10 percent in the general population noted by Parry *et al.*, 1973). In only about one-sixth of Gutmann's group was the primary physician informed by the patient about the use of such agents. Related to this is what appears to be either an increased incidence or a greater awareness of drug abuse problems (especially alcoholism) in the elderly (see *DRUGS OF ABUSE*).

## GENERAL PRINCIPLES AND TERMINOLOGY OF PHARMACOKINETICS

Since this chapter will stress principles, a discussion of geriatric pharmacokinetics is in order. We have already discussed this topic in detail elsewhere (see especially Hicks and Davis, 1980). The following is, therefore, an abbreviated review, essentially to clarify terms as they will be used in this chapter. (For other discussions of basic pharmacokinetics see Gibaldi and Perrier, 1975; Greenblatt and Koch-Weser, 1974; and Smith and Rawlins, 1973. Other good reviews of geriatric pharmacokinetics are Crooks, O'Malley, and Stevenson, 1976; Triggs and Nation, 1975; and Shader and Greenblatt, 1979).

*Pharmacokinetics* is basically a mathematical analysis of the way the body handles pharmacologic agents. Specifically, it involves the study of drug *absorption, distribution, biotransformation* (into *inactive* and/or *active metabolites*), and the subsequent *excretion* from the body of the "parent" drug and/or its metabolites. The site of a drug's absorption is dependent upon its *route of administration*, essentially either *oral (enteral)* or *parenteral (intramuscular, subcutaneous, or intravenous)*. (Rectal, pulmonary, or "topical"—from the skin or mucous membranes—routes are rarely employed for any drug, and are of essentially no relevance to this chapter. Hydergine[R] [see below] is often administered by the sublingual route.) In common practice, however, the oral and parenteral routes are virtually the only ways in which psychotropic agents are administered with any age group.

Biotransformation usually occurs in the *liver microsomal enzyme system(s)*, although other tissues can contribute. These usually include the soluble portion of the liver, but also the GI tract, kidneys, and lungs. In fact, these last three tissues may occasionally be more active than the liver. Excretion is usually via the kidneys but can occur in other ways. (*Metabolism* is usually synonymous with biotransformation, but the term is occasionally used more loosely to include some or all of the other steps in pharmacokinetics just listed.)

With oral administration, the absorption of a drug is determined by two important factors: first, the relative ease or difficulty with which the drug crosses the gastrointestinal mucosa; second, the degree of the drug's biotransformation(s) prior to its appearance in the systemic circulation. Such biotransformation(s) may occur within the GI tract by the gut flora, within the GI wall, or—most importantly—during the drug's *first-pass* (Gibaldi,

Boyes, and Feldman, 1971) through the liver (which the drug reaches via the *portal* circulation prior to the drug's appearance in the *systemic* circulation). A substantial portion of the oral dose of many drugs fails to reach the systemic circulation following first-pass metabolism (up to 80 percent in the case of propranolol—see below). (There are a few reports of an at least partial GI wall metabolism of some psychotropic agents—see Hicks and Davis, 1980—such as chlorpromazine, imipramine, and flurazepam. Technically this is also a "first-pass" metabolism. However, "first-pass" is used commonly only to refer to the biotransformation that occurs in the liver during the initial phases of the GI absorption of a drug.)

The most important pharmacokinetic parameters of absorption are the *rate* and *completeness*, the latter being the total amount of drug absorbed, regardless of the rate. These are ascertained, in many studies, by plotting a curve of plasma levels obtained over time following a single oral and/or intramuscular dose. The completeness of drug absorption is calculated from the total *area under the curve* (AUC) (see Figure 31–1), which is measured by an appropriate numerical integration procedure and expressed as the product of concentration and time. These data are compared to the curve produced by a single intravenous injection

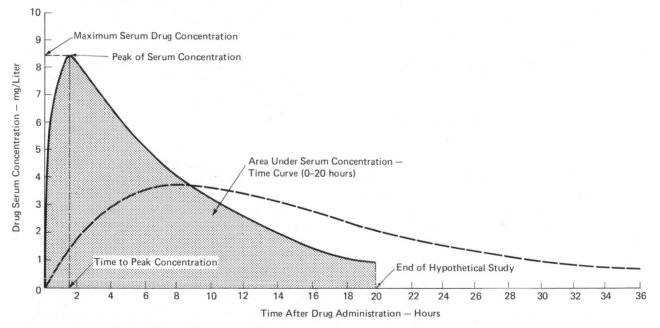

**Figure 31–1**   Serum concentration-time curve after oral administration of a hypothetical drug. Dotted line indicates impaired *rate* but normal *completeness* of absorption (as judged by the AUC at 36 hours, [AUC-36] but not as judged by the AUC-20).

of the same drug at the same dose (which is 100 percent "absorbed"). Obviously, a reduction in the AUC (and thus the total absorption) of an orally administered agent can be the result of either impaired GI absorption or first-pass metabolism (to which the i.v. dose is not subject) or both. However, many drugs are not metabolized extensively enough on the first-pass to make this distinction necessary. In addition, pharmacokinetic models (discussion of which is beyond the scope of this chapter) have been developed to factor out extensive first-pass effects. It is essential that the AUC be determined over a sufficiently long period of time; otherwise, it would be influenced not only by absorption completeness but also the rate. (For example, if the absorption rate of the hypothetical drug in Figure 31–1 were impaired, resulting in, say, a peak serum concentration at 9 instead of 1¾ hours, its completeness of absorption could still be unchanged. The result would simply be a "flatter" curve, with significant serum concentration still evident after 9 hours, with no change in the total area under the curve. If the study did not extend beyond 20 hours, however, this could not be demonstrated.) The rate of absorption can be ascertained by the time it takes to reach peak serum concentration (see again Figure 31–1). It is, however, more commonly expressed as the time required for the completeness of absorption to be 50 percent accomplished (the *absorption half-life* or t½a).

Absorption of a drug may depend on whether it is given orally or intramuscularly. Contrary to popular belief, the intramuscular route is *not* always the more reliable, especially in the case of diazepam and chlordiazepoxide, discussed below (see *Benzodiazepines* in ANTI ANXIETY AGENTS AND HYPNOTICS).

*Clearance* (i.e., from the plasma compartment, unless otherwise defined) of a drug *is* therefore *inversely proportional to its elimination half-life* ($t_{1/2\beta}$) and *directly proportional to the apparent volume of distribution* ($V_d$).

In actual practice (and in some absorption studies) drugs are given in repeated doses, at a fixed *dosage interval*. Administration of most drugs at their usual clinical dosage intervals results in some *accumulation* until a *steady-state concentration* is reached. The *rate* at which steady-state is attained depends almost entirely upon the $t_{1/2\beta}$ and is independent of the dosage interval. The *extent* of accumulation depends on the relationship between the dose and/or dosage interval and the $t_{1/2\beta}$ (see Figure 31-2).

At a fixed dose (with no change in pharmacokinetics) giving a drug at intervals equal to $t_{1/2\beta}$ will result, after only five doses, in a serum concentration that is 95 percent of that of steady-state (Greenblatt and Koch-Weser, 1975). The drug will *not* continue to accumulate after steady-state equilibrium is reached if the dose, dosage interval, and body pharmacokinetics remained fixed. However, pharmacokinetic changes are common, especially those involving enzyme changes that affect biotransformation (and ultimately $t_{1/2\beta}$). Likewise, age may affect all the pharmacokinetic parameters in ways that are remarkably variable.

The ultimate pharmacokinetic behavior of a drug involves many physiologic functions that occur simultaneously and which contribute to the determination of drug distribution and elimination. For example, "biotransformation" (or "metabolism" in the strictest sense) refers to many enzymatically-mediated chemical tranformations. Also, there are large *interindividual differences* in pharmacokinetics, which may be genetically determined, at least in part. Vesell (1977) has recently discussed the problem of assessing the relative roles of *genetic* versus *environmental* factors in determining these metabolic differences.

Many drugs are lipid-soluble, weak organic acids or bases. They are usually not readily eliminated from the body because of their binding to plasma and tissue proteins, their affinity for body fat, and the ease with which the kidney reabsorbs them (by diffusion through the renal tubular cells). To be excreted, these drugs must be biotransformed into less lipid soluble metabolites. Some of these metabolites are pharmacologically active (sometimes more than the "parent" drug), while others are not. If a metabolite is active, termination of action takes place by further biotransformation(s) or by excretion of the active metabolite(s) (Drayer, 1974; see also the review by Shader and Greenblatt, 1979).

## GENERAL PRINCIPLES OF PHARMACODYNAMICS

*Pharmacodynamics* (see the review of Fingl and Woodbury, 1975) involves the study of drug *action* (the initial consequence of drug-cell interaction) and *effect* (the subsequent events that follow from this). This is a less widely-used term, with drug action and effects often imprecisely subsumed under the general heading of "pharmacokinetics." Drug action, by this definition, implies the existence of *target organs* containing drug *receptor-sites*, which may vary in sensitivity to a given drug concentration. (Age-related changes in pharmacodynamics will be discussed in this chapter.)

## DRUG INTERACTIONS—PRINCIPLES AND TERMINOLOGY

### GENERAL DEFINITION(S) AND PRINCIPLES

"Whenever two or more drugs are administered simultaneously therapeutic and/or toxic effects may be enhanced mutually or unilaterally. One drug may diminish the therapeutic efficacy of another, or they may not interact to a clinically significant degree. For practical purposes, the mechanisms responsible for *such interactions can be arbitrarily divided into two principal subdivisions, pharmacokinetic and pharmacologic [pharmacodynamic]*" (Shader, Weinberger, and Greenblatt, 1978; our italics).

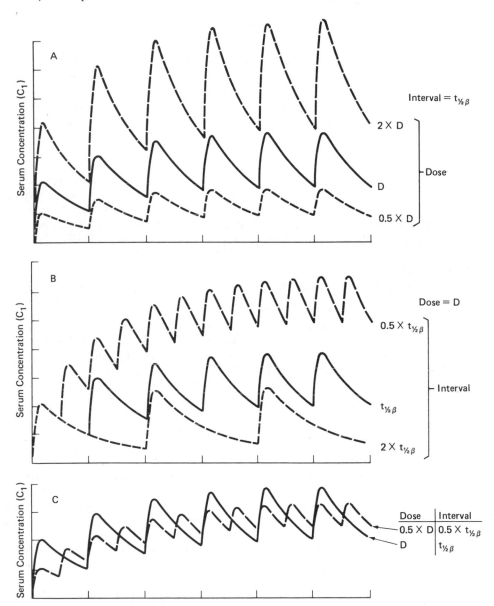

**Figure 31–2**   Effect of varying doses and dosage intervals on drug accumulation during repeated administration.
A. Varying the dose while keeping the dosage interval constant.
B. Varying the dosage interval while keeping the dose constant.
C. Halving both the dose and the dosage interval reduces the amount of fluctuation but leaves the mean steady-state serum concentration unchanged.
Modified from: Greenblatt D. J., Koch-Weser, J. 1975. Clinical pharmacokinetics (II). *New England Journal of Medicine* 293, 964–970, p. 767. (Reprinted by permission of the authors and the *New England Journal of Medicine*.)

(1) PHARMACOKINETIC INTERACTIONS:

"Drug interactions may occur at any of five broadly defined pharmacokinetic steps: absorption, binding to plasma proteins distribution to active sites, metabolism, and excretion. Alterations in any one of these steps may have important clinical implications. Other factors involved include: drug dose, age of the patient, complicating diseases or metabolic derangements, plasma protein abnormalities, and hepatic or renal disorders..." (Shader, Weinberger, and Greenblatt, 1978).

(2) PHARMACOLOGIC (PHARMACODYNAMIC) INTERACTIONS:

"Two or more drugs may interact additively, synergistically, or antagonistically at the same or different receptor sites. These interactions are usually dose-related" (Shader, Weinberger, and Greenblatt, 1978).

## GENERAL PRINCIPLES OF GERIATRIC PHARMACOKINETICS

Triggs and Nation (1975) summarize the *age-related physiologic changes in the body which affect pharmacokinetics* as follows:

1. Cardiac output decreases by 30–40 percent; renal and splanchnic flow also decrease.
2. Glomerular filtration rate decreases, as does creatinine clearance, although the serum creatinine level may remain normal due to a decrease in body muscle mass.
3. There is direct evidence in animals (and indirect in humans) that hepatic enzyme activity, in both microsomal and soluble portions, also decreases.
4. The concentration of albumin relative to globulins decreases.
5. Sugars, fats, and vitamins are less well absorbed by the GI tract.
6. Drug distribution is altered as fat replaces lean mass in the aging process.

Shader and Greenblatt (1979) summarize the *pharmacokinetic effects of age-related changes in bodily function* as:

1. Prolongation of drug elimination half-life ($t_{1/2\beta}$).
2. Reduction in total drug clearance.
3. Inconsistent changes in the volume of distribution ($V_d$).
4. Occasional increases in the unbound drug concentration due to lower serum albumin (although there is probably no change with aging in the affinity of drugs for serum proteins).

5. For drugs excreted by the kidneys, decreased clearance with age.

Other workers have made the generalization that, while absorption of actively transported substances in the elderly may decrease, many medications are passively absorbed, so there are *essentially no age-related changes in GI drug absorption* (Crooks *et al.*, 1976).

Much of the research in geriatric pharmacokinetics—and much of this review—has proceeded along these lines, demonstrating how these age-related bodily changes affect absorption, distribution, biotransformation, and excretion of psychotropic medications. However, one should always bear in mind that, in addition to *age-related changes in pharmacokinetics*, there are also probable *age-related changes in pharmacodynamics* and thus in *receptor-site sensitivity* (see reviews of Hicks and Davis, 1980; Shader and Greenblatt, 1979; Triggs and Nation, 1975). In addition, there are specific *drug interactions that are more likely to occur in the elderly* and that can also affect either pharmacokinetics or dynamics as discussed and specifically cited below (in the *IMPORTANT DRUG INTERACTIONS* section).

## SPECIFIC AGENTS

We will next discuss the age-related pharmacokinetic changes of several specific psychotropic agents. We will follow the usual categorization (Raskind and Eisdorfer, 1976) of geropsychiatric medications, *antipsychotic, antidepressant, antimanic, antianxiety and hypnotic,* and *"cognitive-acting."*

### ANTIPSYCHOTIC AGENTS (AND "ANTIPARKINSONIAN" DRUGS)

*Chlorpromazine* (Thorazine[R], Largactil[R]). Studies have noted a reduction in urinary and plasma chlorpromazine (CPZ) levels with antacid therapy (Aludrox[R], a magnesium trisilicate-aluminum hydroxide compound; (see *Antacids* in *OTHER IMPORTANT DRUG INTERACTIONS* below). Rivera-Calimlim and her colleagues have noted extensively that co-administration of the strongly anticholinergic trihexyphenidyl (see Table 31-1) can impair the GI absorption of CPZ, probably by a delay in gastric emptying (e.g., Rivera-Calimlim, 1976). Her group has also reported work which suggests impairment of L-DOPA absorption by imipramine, a tricyclic antidepressant with "moderate" anticholinergic effects (Table 31–1) (Morgan, Rivera-Calimlim, Sundareson, and Trabert, 1975).

Several other studies exist (see our review—Hicks and Davis, 1980) suggesting similar effects of anticholinergic agents on other drugs, for example, impaired GI absorption of phenylbutazone by desipramine, a tricyclic with relatively "low" anticholinergic properties compared to the other TCA's (Consolo, Morselli, Zaccala, and Garattini, 1970).

These studies suggest that co-administration of agents with strong anticholinergic effects could impair the GI absorption of many drugs. The actual clinical relevance of this is not clear, but it is conceivable that such a drug interaction might be of consequence, especially in the elderly, whose GI tract absorption of certain substances such as vitamins is already impaired (Triggs and Nation, 1975; see above). There is some poorly-documented evidence for an age-related decrease in the GI absorption of diazepam and chlordiazepoxide (see *Benzodiazepines* in *ANTIANXIETY AGENTS AND HYPNOTICS*, further on). Splanchnic blood flow decreases with age (Triggs and Nation, 1975), which might add to impairment of GI absorption (see *Antacids and food* in the *OTHER IMPORTANT DRUG INTERACTIONS* section). The elderly are more likely to use more antacids, which could decrease GI absorption (see *Antacids and food*). The tendency of the old to use more analgesics (see *DRUGS OF ABUSE)* might also compound the problem, if opiate-like agents further delay gastric emptying. This, however, all remains—to our knowledge—yet to be shown clinically relevant. However, studies of age-related changes in the GI absorption of drugs have been sparse; in addition, those that have been carried out have only recently begun to take into account the above possible interactions and the possible effects of such "gastrointestinal polypharmacy."

We suggest that these possibilities are good reasons to discourage the routine use of the highly anticholinergic (see Table 31–1) "anti-parkinsonian agents" (e.g., *trihexyphenidyl* [Artane[R]] and *benztropine* [Cogentin[R]]). (Other reasons to avoid these agents are an increased risk of tardive dyskinesia when these agents are given along with neuroleptics [see *Clinical Choice of Antipsychotic Medication in the Elderly* just below] and the potential confusion such agents can cause [see "Anticholinergic Agents Versus Physostigmine" below]).

Rivera-Calimlim's group also studied the effect of age on CPZ plasma levels. They found that increased age was associated with elevated steady-state plasma levels. Her group felt that this effect was possibly the result of differential gut absorption or decreased metabolism of CPZ (Rivera-Calimlim, Nasrallah *et al.*, 1977).

This one study, however, does not imply nec-

essarily greater clinical efficacy in the older patient, since a relation between CPZ plasma levels and clinical response has yet to be established (Davis, Erickson, and Dekirmenjian, 1978), depite the fact that CPZ was the first of the modern antipsychotics introduced (Delay, Deniker, and Harl, 1952). As we reviewed (Davis *et al.*, 1978), the problem in correlating plasma chlorpromazine (and many other antipsychotic) levels with clinical effect is a

**Table 31–1**  Antimuscurinic Potency of CNS Agents

| AGENT | EC$_{50}$(nM)[a] | K$_d$(nM)[b] |
|---|---|---|
| Scopolamine | 0.3 | – |
| Atropine | 0.4 | 2 |
| Trihexyphenidyl (Artane) | 0.6 | – |
| Benztropine (Cogentin) | 1.5 | – |
| Amitriptyline (Elavil, etc.) | 10 | 100 |
| Doxepin (Sinequan) | 44 | 300 |
| Nortriptyline (Aventyl) | 57 | 1,000 |
| Imipramine (Tofranil, etc.) | 78 | 400 |
| Protriptyline (Vivactil) | – | 2,000 |
| Desipramine (Norpramin, etc.) | 170 | 2,000 |
| Clozapine (Leponex) | 26 | 3 |
| Thioridazine (Mellaril) | 150 | 60 |
| Promazine (Sparine) | 650 | 60 |
| Chlorpromazine (Thorazine, etc.) | 1,000 | 2,000 |
| Triflupromazine (Vesprin) | 1,000 | – |
| Acetophenazine (Tindal) | 10,000 | 4,000 |
| Perphenazine (Trifalon) | 11,000 | 4,000 |
| Fluphenazine (Prolixin) | 12,000 | 2,000 |
| Trifluoperazine (Stelazine) | 13,000 | 20,000 |
| Haloperidol (Haldol) | 48,000 | 7,000 |
| Iproniazid (Marplan) | 100,000 | – |
| Nialamid (Niamid) | 100,000 | – |
| Phenelzine (Nardil) | 100,000 | – |

[a]Data are half-maximally effective concentrations (EC$_{50}$) of drugs which compete for the binding to tissue of the labeled test agent, $^3$H—QNB—an avid and selective muscarinic antagonist, [$^3$H]—3—quinuclidinylbenzilate—as estimated in rat brain homogenates. Concentrations are in units of nM (nanomolar, or $10^{-9}$M). Adapted from Baldessarini, 1977(1) based on data of Snyder, Yamamura, and Greenberg, 1974(2) and 1977(3).

[b]From data of Richelson and Divinetz-Romero, 1977(4), based on the potency of the test drugs in blocking the formation of cyclic guanosine 3′, 5′—cylic-monophosphate (cyclic GMP by carbonylcholine (a stable acetylcholine analogue), using cultured mouse neuroblastoma cells. Data are reported as dissociation constants (K$_d$ in units of nM). The two methods are best compared by the rank-order of potencies, disregarding the absolute values obtained.

(1) Baldessarini, R.J. 1977. *Chemotherapy in Psychiatry*, p. 103. Cambridge, Mass.: Harvard University Press.

(2) Snyder, S.H., Greenberg, D., and Yamamura, H.I. 1974. Antischizophrenic drugs and brain cholinergic receptors: Affinity for muscarinic sites predicts extrapyramidal effects. *Arch. Gen. Psychiatry, 31*, 58–61.

(3) Snyder, S.H., and Yamamura, H. 1977. Antidepressants and the muscarinic acetylcholine receptor. *Arch. Gen. Psychiatry, 34*, 236–239.

(4) Richelson, E., and Divinetz-Romero, S. 1977. Blockade of psychotropic drugs of the muscarinic acetylcholine receptor in cultured nerve cells. *Biol. Psychiatry, 12*, 771–785.

From: Baldessarini R.J., The clinical pharmacology and toxicology of antipsychotic drugs. Part II. Actions and neurological side-effects, *Weekly Psychiatry Update* (Lesson 40): 1–8, 1978. Published by Biomedia, Inc., Princeton, N.J. Reprod. by permission.

result of technical difficulties in the assay and of complex pharmacokinetics (e.g., CPZ produces so many metabolites that to determine exactly which are active and which are inactive remains impossible, despite over a quarter century of clinical use).

*Other Antipsychotics and Age-related Pharmacokinetic Changes.* We were able to find age-related pharmacokinetic studies on only two other antipsychotics. A single study on *haloperidol* (Haldol[R]) showed no change in pharmacokinetics with age (Forsman and Öhman, 1977). Two studies on *thioridazine* (Mellaril[R])—Martensson and Roos (1973) and Axelsson and Martensson (1976)—were conflicting and only tangentially addressed to age-related pharmacokinetic changes.

*Clinical Choice of Antipsychotic Medication in the Elderly.* Most comparative studies of antipsychotic medications in the elderly tend to compare the "high" potency agents (e.g., haloperidol, piperazine phenothiazines such as *trifluoperazine* [Stelazine[R]] or *fluphenazine* [Prolixin[R], Permitil[R]]) with the "low" potency agents (e.g., chlorpromazine, thioridazine). A recent example was the study by Branchey, Lee, Amin, and Simpson (1978), who gave both fluphenazine hydrochloride and thioridazine to 30 elderly chronic schizophrenic patients. Through a cross-over design, each patient received both drugs with an intervening washout period. Although both drugs produced a "similar" degree of antipsychotic improvement on roughly equipotent doses, they had different "side-effect profiles." Fluphenazine caused slightly more extrapyramidal effects than thioridazine, while the latter caused more weight gain, orthostatic hypotension, and markedly greater EKG changes (including QT interval prolongation in 9 of the 30). The study's authors recommended high-potency neuroleptic agents for elderly schizophrenics.

This study, however, presents a number of problems. First, as with CPZ, the pharmacokinetics of both thioridazine and fluphenazine are poorly understood, especially when aging is factored in. Hence the EKG changes are hard to evaluate, since effects due to pharmacokinetics (i.e., plasma levels) become hard to separate from those due to pharmacodynamics (i.e., cardiac receptor-site sensitivity) when plasma levels are not well-correlated with pharmacologic activity. Nonetheless, an association of defects in repolarization with thioridazine (usually manifest as flattening of the T wave) has long been noted (e.g., Alexander and Niño, 1969). The actual cardiotoxicity of thioridazine, however, remains unclear, since many reports of arrhythmia on this agent—which include fatal ventricular

types—have involved concomitant use of a tricyclic antidepressant (the cardiotoxic potential of which is well accepted—see below—and/or other agent). Nonetheless, there exists some clinical (e.g., Kelly, Fay, and Laverty, 1968) and *in vitro* (e.g., Landmark, 1971) evidence for a quinidine-like effect of thioridazine (although we have seen one case of atrial fibrillation possibly *secondary* to thioridazine*). Perhaps the cardiotoxicity suggested for thioridazine is not due to effects directly on the myocardium but is secondary to the orthostatic hypotension seen with both this agent and also with CPZ (see Jefferson, 1976). Also, the high anticholinergic potency of thioridazine (see Table 31–1) would obviously be more likely to cause sinus tachycardia, although the contribution of this to cardiotoxicity is obviously speculative.

Another problem with the Branchey *et al.* study is its failure to address tardive dyskinesia, a problem to which the older patient is more at risk (Ayd, 1960; Bell and Smith, 1978), presumably due to an age-related change in CNS receptor-site sensitivity (Friedhoff, Rosengarten, and Bonnet, 1978; Salzman *et al.*, 1975). Anticholinergic agents, especially the anti-parkinsonians (see Table 31–1), may exaggerate and perhaps even predispose (Tarsy and Baldessarini, 1976) to this side-effect. In recommending the high potency group, Branchey *et al.* focused on the neurologic side-effects most likely to occur relatively *early* in treatment. Concern over tardive dyskinesia, however, might cause the clinician to choose the *low*-potency neuroleptic, thioridazine, which seems to have a uniquely low propensity for causing tardive dyskinesia despite its high anticholinergic activity. (Also, the extrapyramidal effects of the high potency group predispose to reactions requiring an anti-parkinsonian, which then all too frequently is never discontinued.)

In support of the Branchey *et al.* conclusion, however, is the fact that the low-potency CPZ is quite sedating; and the highly anticholinergic thioridazine is more likely to produce confusion (see *Anticholinergic agents versus physostigmine*)—especially in the impaired aging cortex (Salzman *et al.*, 1975).

We thus conclude that, for now, no generalization can be made on the question of high versus low-potency antipsychotic agents for the elderly. Ideally, the choice of an antipsychotic regimen should be tailored to individual needs and should take into account each patient's relative susceptibility to one of the above side-effects.

---

*Dysken, M. W., Hicks, R., and Davis, J. M. Unpublished clinical observations.

ANTIDEPRESSANT AGENTS

*Tricyclic Antidepressants.* As noted above (see *Chlorpromazine*), tricyclic antidepressants have been reported to delay gastric emptying, and can thus impair the GI absorption of other oral drugs. This may have special relevance to the treatment of the elderly patient, who is more likely to be depressed (Pfeiffer and Busse, 1973) and thus on such agents. The tricyclics exert their effect on absorption via their anticholinergic activity, which is—among commonly used agents—greatest with *amitriptyline* (Elavil[R]), moderate with *imipramine* (Tofranil[R]), and least with *desipramine* (Norpramin[R], Pertofrane[R]). (The degree of anticholinergic activity of *doxepin*—Sinequan[R]—is a point of controversy since there is no agreement on what constitutes an "equipotent" antidepressant dose. That is, at 150-mg qd, its anticholinergic activity is low, but probably so is its antidepressant action, which *may* require a daily dose of 250 to 400-mg qd to be as effective as 150-mg qd of amitriptyline. Therefore, it is not surprising to find it quite high on the list [in Table 31–1] of the differential binding to important receptor-sites of various psychotropic agents.)

A more important interaction is that between the tricyclics and various neuroleptics, usually with the latter inhibiting tricyclic metabolism (Gram and Overø, 1970), although the converse has been reported (El-Yousef and Menier, 1974). Since depression in the elderly is often accompanied by disordered or delusional thinking, including paranoia (Pfeiffer and Busse, 1973), the chance of a neuroleptic-tricyclic combination is quite high and possible interactions should be kept in mind.

There has been a recent report (Nies, Robinson, Freidman, Green, Cooper, Ravaris, Ives, 1978) of a correlation between age and elevated steady-state serum imipramine and its metabolite desipramine, as well as amitriptyline. (The amitriptyline metabolite, *nortriptyline* was found in concentrations that did *not* correlate with age.) The authors suggested decreased liver enzyme activity as the cause. They encouraged lowering the tricyclic dosage by a third to a half in the elderly. This is an extremely important point, since side-effects of the tricyclics include cardiotoxicity—ranging from sinus tachycardia (secondary to anticholinergic vagolytic effects), to quinidine-like effects, to potentially fatal arrhythmias (Bigger, Kantor, Glassman, Perel, 1978). Probable age-related pharmacodynamic changes in the "target organ" (that is, in the receptor-sites of the heart) *plus* age-related changes in pharmacokinetics (that is, in the biotransformation and detoxification of these drugs)—all add up to potentially more drug

available to a more sensitive heart. Therefore, we suggest not only lowering the dose in the elderly, but also dividing it (e.g., into qid, instead of the common practice of giving all the daily dose qhs). This is suggested to diminish the effect of sudden vagolytic loading. We also suggest choosing the least anticholinergic tricyclic possible (although there is no clear evidence yet that tricyclic-induced sinus tachycardia contributes significantly to cardiotoxicity). (In addition to erroneously being thought quite low in anticholinergic properties, doxepin has been reported to impair cardiac conduction less than other tricyclics [e.g., Vohra, Burrows, and Sloman, 1975]. However, Bigger *et al.,* suggest that such findings were obtained at plasma levels not sufficient for antidepressant action; that is, at doses not equipotent.)

Cardiovascular problems in the elderly may also arise with the concomitant use of antihypertensive and tricyclic medication. The adverse reactions that may occur are summarized in Table 31–2. The most notable interaction is the antagonism of guanethidine by the tricyclic antidepressants, which can lead to ever-increasing doses of this drug in a patient on tricyclic medication. This, in turn, can lead to fatal results following sudden withdrawal of the tricyclic compound (Cairncross, 1965; see Jefferson, 1975 for several other references). (Here, again, compared to the other tricyclics, doxepin was once thought to have special properties, that is, that it could be given concomitantly with guanethidine without an interaction. However, we found doxepin to interact with guanethidine no differently than did the other tricyclics when we gave it at equipotent dosage—Fann, Cavanaugh, Kaufmann *et al.,* 1971. We have also shown that *chlorpromazine* can have a similar interaction with guanethidine—Janowsky, El-Yousef, Davis *et al.,* 1973.)

Note that the more recently introduced clonidine (Catapres[R]) has been reported to lead to hypotension when used concomitantly with desipramine (Briant, Reid, and Dollery, 1973), which is at variance with Table 31–2. A complete review of the literature on this (and all of the potential drug interactions in the table) is beyond the scope of this presentation; the reader is, therefore, referred to reviews such as that by Jefferson (1975) for more details.

*MAO Inhibitors.* These agents are often seen as contraindicated in the case of the geriatric patient. We, however, recommend that they be considered as an alternative treatment for the elderly patient with an endogenous depression refractory to tricyclics. J.M.D. has had considerable experience

**Table 31–2** Interactions of the Antidepressants with Other Agents.

| AGENT | TRICYCLIC ANTIDEPRESSANTS | MAO INHIBITORS |
|---|---|---|
| Alcohol, anxiolytics, antihistamines | More sedation and anticholinergic effects | More sedation, decreased metabolism |
| Anesthetics | Cardiac arrhythmias[a] (?) | Potentiate |
| Barbiturates | More sedation and anticholinergic, increased metabolism of antidepressant | More sedation, decreased metabolism of MAO inhibitors |
| Narcotics, especially meperidine | Some potentiation | Dangerous CNS depression or excitation and fever |
| Anticonvulsants | Make less effective | CNS depression |
| Anticholinergics, antiparkinson agents, spasmolytics | Potentiate each other, more anticholinergic effects | Potentiate CNS intoxication; decrease metabolism of MAO inhibitors |
| L-dopa | Decrease absorption | May induce hypertension |
| Stimulants, anorexics | Potentiate, induce hypertension, decrease metabolism of tricyclics | CNS excitation hypertension, fever |
| Reserpine | Acutely, hypertension; later some inhibition; arrhythmias (?) | Paradoxical hypertension and CNS excitation acutely |
| Alpha-methyldopa | May antagonize | Paradoxical hypertension |
| Alpha-methyltyrosine | — | — |
| Guanethidine, bethanidine debrisoquine | Antagonize, severe withdrawal hypotension | Unpredictable; may induce acute hypertension with guanethidine |
| Hypotensive diuretics | — | More hypotension |
| Hypotensive smooth muscle relaxants (e.g., hydralazine) | — | More hypotension |
| Any agent with MAO inhibitory action (e.g., Eutonyl, Furoxone[R] Matulane[R]) | Seizures, hyperpyrexial(?) | Additive toxicity |
| Alpha-adrenergic agonists (e.g., norepinephrine, phenylephrine) | Potentiate | Potentiate |
| Clonidine (Catapres[R]) | Antagonize (mechanism unknown) [?potentiate[c]] | Potentiate (?) |
| Indirect sympathomines (e.g., tyramine in food) | Antagonize | Hypertension, CNS excitation, stroke |
| Alpha-adrenergic blockers (e.g., phentolamine, phenoxybenzamine) | Antagonize | Antagonize |
| Beta-adrenergic agonists (e.g., epinephrine, isoproterenol) | Potentiate | Potentiate[b] |
| Beta-adrenergic blockers | Antagonize | Antagonize acutely, potentiate later |
| Anticoagulants (e.g., coumarins and indanediones) | Minimal potentiation | Probably potentiate |
| Cardiac agents (e.g., quinidine, digitalis) | May potentiate | ? |
| Steroids | Unpredictable | ? |
| Insulin and Oral hypoglycemics | Unpredictable, may potentiate | Potentiate |
| Oral alkalis (e.g., Amphojel[R], and resins (e.g., Cholestyramine[R], Questran[R]) | Absorption of tricyclics decreased | ? |

[a]Unless otherwise stated, effects are those of the antidepressants on actions of the medical agents in the first column. Dash (—) indicates no effect known; question mark (?) indicates no effects clearly demonstrated, but should be suspected.

[b]Beware of administering dental preparations of procaine (Novocain[R]) containing epinephrephrine (adrenaline) to patients receiving MAO inhibitors.

[c]See text p. 753

Modified from: Baldessarini, R.J. 1977. *Chemotherapy in Psychiatry,* pp. 109–111. Cambridge, Mass.: Harvard University Press.
Used by permission.

with the use of these agents in older patients— some in their 80s—and has found them quite safe if proper precautions are taken. R. H. has found *pargyline* (Eutonyl[R]—an MAOI marketed as an anti-hypertensive agent) to occasionally permit the treatment—with a single agent—of a patient with coexisting hypertension and endogenous depression.*

The MAO inhibitors do, of course, have the potential for a number of adverse drug and/or food

*Unpublished clinical observations.

interactions, which can be catastrophic for the older patient, whose cardiovascular system is more likely to be compromised. Baldessarini has also put together an excellent list of drug interactions involving the MAO inhibitors (see Table 31–2). The Massachusetts General Hospital Psychopharmacology Clinics have an inclusive patient instruction list (Table 31–3) outlining foods and beverages which contain tyramine and OTC drugs which contain substances, especially sympathomimetics, that can react with the MAOIs. (No list of OTC medications is, of course, ever up to date. And it is worth reiterating Guttmann's [1978] report of the heavy use of OTC agents in the elderly—see *NEUROPSYCHIATRIC PROBLEMS IN GEROPSYCHIATRY SECONDARY TO MEDICATION* previously discussed.)

*Lithium Carbonate and Electroconvulsive Therapy (ECT).*    The issue of what constitutes the best type of maintenance treatment of affective illness, especially recurrent depression, is an area of discussion beyond the scope of this chapter (see Davis, 1976). For the elderly, the greater toxicity of the

### MEDICATIONS

Do not take *any* other medication without checking first with me. This includes especially *over-the-counter drugs,* examples of which are listed below (*which is by no means complete*):

| *Analgesics (pain medication)* | *Liquid Decongestants,* | *Nasal Decongestants (pills)* |
|---|---|---|
| Amprin | *Cough Suppressants* | Allerest |
| Percogesic | Cheracold | Contac |
| Vanquish | Coldene | Coricidin |
| Zumarin | Novahistine | Coricidin D |
| | Novahistine-DH | Coricidin |
| *Sleeping Aids* | Nyquil | Demilets |
| Dormin | Super Anahist | Coricidin Medilets |
| Nytol | Syrup | Dristan |
| Sleep-Eze | Triaminic | Ornex |
| Sominex | Triaminicol | Sinutab |
| | Trind | Super Anahist |
| *Inhalation Products* | Vicks Formula 44 | Triaminicin |
| Adrenalin | | Ursinus |
| Asthmanephrin | *Nasal Decongestants (drops and sprays)* | *Other* |
| Breatheasy | Alcon-Efrin | Tedral |
| Bronkaid Mist | Contac Spray | |
| Medihaler-Epi | Coricidin Mist | |
| Primatene Mist | NTZ | |
| Vaponefrin | Neo-Synephrine | |
| | Privine | |
| | Sinex | |
| | Dristan | |
| | Vick Va-Tro-Nol | |

From the *Massachusetts General Hospital Psychopharmacology Clinics (PPC),* Jerrold F. Rosenbaum, M.D. (Director) Prepared by Robert Hicks, M.D. (Former Director), 1977. Modified by Ross J. Baldessarini, M.D. (Chief Consultant), 1977. Modified from Appendix G: Restricted substances for patients on MAO inhibitors. In *Psychiatric Drugs: A Desk Reference* (2nd ed) (Honigfeld G., Howard A., eds), Academic Press, New York, 1978.

**Table 31–3**    MAO Inhibitor Instruction List.

#### FOODS AND BEVERAGES

To avoid serious and potentially dangerous reactions, you should not eat or drink any of the following while taking a MAO-inhibitor:

1. *Aged or strong cheeses,* such as: Camembert, Cheddar, Gruyere, Stilton, Boursalt, Emmenthal, Brie, Cracker Barrel, Bleu, Roquefort, Romano. *Permitted in small amounts* are: American cheese, Gouda, Parmesan. *Permitted* are: cottage cheese, cream, "farmer". *If you are uncertain* about a cheese, *do not eat it.*
2. *Yeast* extract and food supplements (such as Ovaltine and Bovril, used mostly in England). Baked products raised with yeast are allowed.
3. *Yogurt* (in excess of 1 cup per meal); *sour cream.*
4. *Liver,* especially chicken (and spreads prepared from liver).
5. *Canned or processed fish,* such as herring, canned sardines, anchovies, and lox.
6. *Canned or processed meats,* especially sausages and salami.
7. *Game,* such as rabbit, pheasant, goose, duck, game hens, venison (deer).
8. *Broad beans* (English bean and Chinese pea pod) or *fava beans.*
9. *Canned figs, raisins.*
10. More than one *banana* or *avocado* per day.
11. *Pickles; sauerkraut.*
12. *Soy sauce.*
13. *Beer, ale, sherry, red wine (especially Chianti);* one or two glasses of white wine per day can be permitted, but this should be discussed first.
14. Beverages including *caffeine,* such as coffee, tea, or cola may be consumed in moderation. We suggest that you not exceed 4 cups of caffeinated beverages per day.

tricyclics (and MAOIs) should be considered. However, the possible nephrotoxicity of lithium—see below—should also be weighed, especially in the geriatric patient whose baseline renal function may already be compromised. For these reasons and others, ECT is to be considered in the elderly as a sometimes safer alternative (see "Electroconvulsive Therapy" further on).

*Estrogens.*    The frequent co-occurrence of depressive symptoms and estrogen deficiency in menopausal and post-menopausal females has led some investigators to invoke a causal link and to recommend treatment of involutional depression with estrogenic compounds. Reports of younger women with improved sense of well-being while taking oral contraceptives have further buttressed this notion (Hamburg, Moos, Yalom, 1968). A possible mechanism for this mood-elevating effect has been advanced by Klaiber, Broverman, Vogel, Kobayashi, and Moriarity (1972), who observed depression of plasma MAO levels after administration of conjugated equine estrogen to endogenously depressed younger women.

Despite these promising clues, however, the results of estrogen therapy for depression have been disappointing. Ripley, Shorr, and Papanicolaou (1940) observed therapeutic results only in women with mild depressive reactions, possibly in part related to the symptoms of estrogen deficiency. Utian (1972) did a controlled study with placebo and found no preferential effect of estrogens on depressive symptoms. Based on the above studies, it might prove worthwhile to look at the responses of menopausal and post-menopausal depressed women who have inappropriately elevated MAO levels.

For now, however, the paucity of evidence for the antidepressant efficacy is inadequate to justify the increased risk of cancer produced by estrogen treatment.

### ANTIMANIC AGENTS

*Lithium carbonate* (Lithane[R], Eskalith[R], Lithonate[R]). Lithium carbonate is excreted almost entirely by the kidneys (Jefferson and Greist, 1978). Therefore, lithium clearance decreases with age and is directly correlated with creatinine clearance (see the reviews of Schou, 1968, and Jefferson and Greist, 1979). (There exists a widely-quoted study by Fyrö, Petterson, and Sedvall [1973], reporting no correlation between lithium clearance and aging, a conclusion dutifully reported in several subsequent reviews. However, close examination of the Fyrö group's data shows a modest decrease in lithium clearance with aging. This trend is not statistically significant [r = 0.28, p < .10], but is also not that much at variance with the more numerous studies finding a definite age-related decrease.)

Creatinine clearance has been found to decrease by as much as 30 percent in men between years 30 and 80 (Rowe, Andres, Tobin *et al.*, 1976a). A useful nomogram for ascertaining age- (and sex-)adjusted rank in creatinine clearance (see Figure 31–3) has recently been devised (Rowe *et al.*, 1976b).

It is, therefore, inevitable that the half-life of lithium in the body varies with aging, from about 18–30 hours in younger patients to as long as 36 hours in the elderly (see Schou, 1968). As much as a 50 percent decrease in dose may be necessary to compensate for changes in the elderly, largely, although not solely, because of decline in lithium clearance (Hewick, Newbury, Hopwood *et al.*,

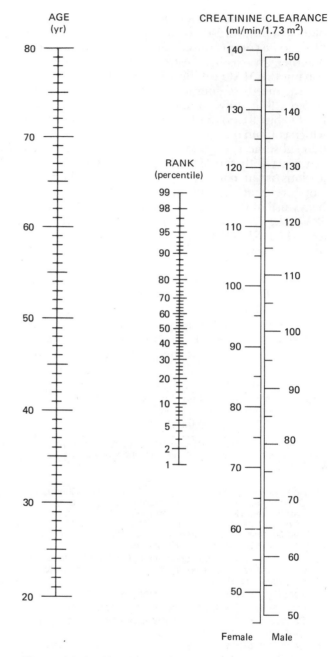

**Figure 31–3** Nomogram for ascertaining age-adjusted percentile rank in creatinine clearance. Determinations done by the automated "total chromogen" method. A line through the subject's age and creatnine clearance intersects the percentile rank line at a point indicating the subject's age-adjusted percentile rank.

From: Rowe, J. W., Andres, R., Tobin, J. D., Norris, A. H., Shock, N. W. 1976. Age-adjusted standards for creatinine clearance. *Annals of Internal Medicine 84:* 567–569, p. 568. American College of Physicians. Reprinted by permission.

1977). It should be remembered that lithium has been found to be nephrotoxic, irrespective of age (Jefferson and Greist, 1978). In late 1977, considerable alarm was caused by a report from Denmark (Hestbech, Hansen, Amdisen *et al.*, 1977) of 14 cases of patients on chronic lithium, all of whom were found on renal biopsy to have clear focal atrophy and interstitial fibrosis. There also appeared to be various decreases in creatinine clearance which correlated with these pathological changes. These findings were soon confirmed by subsequent studies, and reviews of various isolated earlier reports provided antecedent evidence (see Jefferson and Greist, 1979). These lesions did not correlate either with patient age or with length of time on lithium treatment (range: 2 to 15 years). While none of this original patient group exhibited a clinically significant reduction in creatinine clearance, it was feared that a larger series might reveal not only morphologic abnormalities but also physiologic changes sufficient to produce terminal azotemia. The most recent reports, however, are encouraging; a much more extensive patient series by the original Danish investigators suggests serious impairment of creatinine clearance to be unlikely (Vestergaard, Amdisen, Hansen, Schou, 1979).

It appears that the most common manifestation of lithium nephrotoxicity is impairment of renal concentrating ability. While this is not as potentially life treatening as impaired creatinine clearance, lithium-induced polyuria is often severe enough to disrupt daily function. Studies have found polydipsia in 40 percent of lithium-treated patients, daily urine volumes of greater than three liters in 12 percent, and nephrogenic diabetes insipidus in 21 percent. While these symptoms are usually mild and transient, urine volumes as high as 6 to 8 liters per day, with impairment of both daily activities and sleep, have been found. Polyuria of this degree is usually described as a condition which is ameliorated by reduction in the daily lithium dosage and which is fully reversible within a few weeks after total discontinuation of the drug (Baldessarini and Lipinski, 1975). Jefferson and Greist (1979), however, cite a few examples of the lithium-induced polyuria (including two patients from the Hestbech *et al.*, 1977, group) thought secondary to lithium-produced *anatomical* changes in the distal tubule. They even cite an example of lithium-induced diabetes insipidus persisting almost two years after cessation of the drug.

Despite the clear decrease with age in renal clearance of both creatinine and lithium, an age-related predilection to the above lithium nephro-

toxicity was not apparent on our review. However, common sense would seem to dictate special care, especially in regard to creatinine clearance, which—as noted—can be impaired long before the serum creatinine level (which may remain normal due to muscle breakdown) rises. For now, yearly creatinine clearance determinations (as well as tests of renal concentration), are the ideal, in all age groups on lithium. This recommendation, however, must be weighed against issues such as cost and compliance.

For some patients, particularly the elderly, concomitant use of diuretics and lithium is a drug interaction which may further complicate the issue of lithium clearance. Chlorothiazides can produce lithium retention, sometimes resulting in toxic lithium levels (Jefferson and Greist, 1978; Schou, 1976). Like sodium, 80 percent of the lithium ion is reabsorbed in the proximal renal tubules (see Schou, 1976). The reabsorption of both sodium and lithium proximally is very similar and perhaps even "identical" (Schou, 1976). The thiazide diuretics, by producing a distal diuresis of sodium, may increase the fractional reabsorption proximally of sodium, and therefore perhaps of lithium (Jefferson and Greist, 1979). This can produce as much as 24 percent increase in the reabsorption of lithium in patients chronically treated with thiazide diuretics (Peterson, Hvidt, Thomsen, and Schou, 1974). This has led clinicians to suggest extreme caution with the concomitant use of lithium and the thiazides. However, the use of these agents together has recently been proven feasible, if proper monitoring is carried out (e.g., Himmelhoch, Poust, Mallinger *et al.*, 1977). In fact, the use of lithium in patients with actual kidney disease has demonstrated that lithium may be prescribed in the most hazardous situations, provided that the kidneys retain *some* capacity to excrete lithium and that appropriate precautions are utilized, including adequate sodium intake (see, for example, Hicks and Davis, 1980; Jefferson and Greist, 1979). In fact, as far back as 1972,* R. H. was able (with the help and supervision of J. L. Lipinski) to successfully maintain on lithium a 39-year-old psychiatric inpatient at the Massachusetts General Hospital who was status-post bilateral nephrectomy and (cadaver) kidney transplantation. The relationship of diuretics other than thiazides to lithium is less well-established, although preliminary data suggest that the potassium-sparing diuretics—spironolactone, etc.—causes lithium retention, while the loop diuretics—furosemide

_____
*Unpublished clinical observations.

(Lasix[R]), ethacrynic acid (Edecrin[R])—do not (see Jefferson and Greist, 1979). Even greater caution with their use is suggested. The relevance of this to the elderly patient—more prone to congestive heart failure, cardiovascular and/or renal disorders—should be self-evident.

As mentioned above, the pharmacokinetics of a drug to not entirely account for its action. Receptor-site sensitivity must also be taken into account, particularly in the case of lithium CNS effects, about which there is some debate (see Hicks and Davis, 1980, for the complete references). For example, it is claimed that both therapeutic and toxic CNS effects occur at lower serum levels in the elderly, but it has also been reported that lithium CNS toxicity is not age-related. CNS toxicity has been correlated with pre-existing neurologic change rather than age, but this still increases the likelihood of toxicity in the elderly who are more prone to have CNS impairment (Salzman *et al.*, 1975). There are many reports of lithium CNS toxicity—in all age groups—with normal therapeutic maintenance blood levels, although many of these cases suggest pre-existing CNS disturbance. Increased toxicity has been reported in three out of 12 geriatric patients on levels less than 2.0 meq/L, with these being the only such instances of toxicity among 150 patients of all ages treated the same way (Van der Velde, 1971). It has been suggested that it is impossible to rely solely on lithium levels in establishing dosage, and that evidence for advanced age leading to increased risk for lithium CNS toxicity is lacking. There have also been reports of mild, reversible cognitive changes in normal subjects and patients given lithium. A recent study showed substantial evidence for greater organic impairment among elderly patients who were on lithium, but no explanation for this phenomenon was offered by the authors who reported it (Friedman, Culver, and Ferrell, 1977).

The question of toxicity secondary to concomitant lithium carbonate and haloperidol use is occasionally still raised (e.g., Lasagna, 1978) since a widely-publicized report that appeared in 1974 (Cohen and Cohen). This report described four patients on such a regimen (two of whom were over 60 years in age) who developed a severe encephalopathic picture, leaving two with widespread irreversible brain damage and two with persistent parkinsonism and dyskinesias. Subsequent reviews have failed to replicate this picture (e.g., Baastrup, Hollnagel, Sorenson *et al.*, 1976, and others cited in Altesman and Cole [1978] and Hicks and Davis [1980]). In fact, there are reports suggesting that lithium may *prevent* dyskinesias of the tardive type, although evidence is far from conclusive (Pert, Rosenblatt, Sivit *et al.*, 1978).

Methyldopa—Aldomet[R]—when administered concomitantly with lithium, can lower serum lithium levels yet simultaneously enhance lithium CNS toxicity, suggesting a movement of lithium from extra to intracellular compartments. The significance of this interaction is unclear, but evidence suggests that to combine these agents is "inadvisable" at present (see Schou, 1976).

There is a growing body of literature which suggests that lithium *alone* is associated with extrapyramidal symptoms of a parkinsonian type (e.g., Kane, Rifkin, Quitkin *et al.*, 1976). Lithium tremor—a fine "action" (or "postural") type (see Adams and Victor, 1977, for a lucid categorization of various tremors)—is often erroneously ascribed in the elderly to senility alone.* However, since both these neurologic conditions, by themselves, *may* be seen more often in the elderly, these observations may have special relevance (especially in view of the toxicity of propranolol—see below—which has been suggested variously as an agent to counteract lithium tremor).

There is an hypothesis that the same factors which govern the passage of lithium across the blood-brain barrier or into the CNS neuron might be "mimicked" by those involved in its uptake into the more accessible red blood cell. There is, therefore, some evidence that the erythrocyte uptake of lithium may correlate well with its CNS toxicity (e.g., Hewick and Murray, 1976). In our laboratory, there is preliminary evidence suggesting that age-related CNS toxicity may be related to RBC lithium uptake.** The clinical usefulness of such observations, however, remains to be shown.

Some other lithium drug interactions should be noted here. Lithium has been reported to help the dysphoria secondary to L-DOPA (see Jefferson and Greist, 1978) and ACTH (Falk, Mahnke, and Postkanzer, 1979). It may reduce and/or block the euphoriant effects of opiates and some CNS stimulants (Jefferson and Greist, 1978), a finding of special relevance since the elderly are often prescribed these agents (see COGNITIVE ACTING AGENTS) or come to abuse them (see *DRUGS OF ABUSE*).

---

*In fact, Adams and Victor (1977) question the association between old age and tremor, including the so-called "senile" type. They note that Charcot, in a review of 2,000 elderly patients at the Salpetrière, found only 30 with tremor.

**Dorus, E., Pandey, G. N., Schumacker, R., and Davis, J. M. Age-related variation in the red blood cell lithium/plasma ratio and lithium side-effects. Unpublished manuscript.

*Antipsychotics.* These have already been discussed. They are often a special adjunct to the treatment of acute mania. In the elderly, manic attacks would be expected to have occurred earlier in life, and thus hopefully to have been correctly diagnosed and treated with lithium already. However—for whatever reason—such attacks can occur in the elderly and thus may require the clinician to weigh the various issues already raised about the use of antipsychotics in the elderly. (Lithium carbonate may decrease the absorption of chlorpromazine via a delay in gastric emptying—Kerzner and Rivera-Calimlim, 1976.)

## ANTIANXIETY AGENTS AND HYPNOTICS

*Barbiturates.* Barbiturates not destroyed in the body are excreted in the urine (Harvey, 1975). Only barbital is dependent mainly on renal excretion, with up to 90 percent total dose appearing in the urine unaltered (vs. 50 percent for phenobarbital). However, most barbiturates are transformed, principally in the liver, to inactive metabolites. These metabolites are in turn excreted in the urine.

The effect of decreased renal clearance on barbital should be obvious. Decreased renal clearance may also affect the pharmacokinetics of the other barbiturates, even though they are detoxified by the liver. For example, Irvine, Grove, Toseland *et al.*, (1974), studied the effect of increasing age on the metabolism of amylobarbital. They used a urine and serum assay to measure a major metabolite for 48 hours after a single oral dose, in a younger and older group of subjects. At 24 hours, the mean plasma level of the elderly group was significantly greater. The authors felt that this represented decreased hepatic enzyme activity in the elderly. Triggs and Nation (1975), however, criticized the study on the grounds of not having enough data to tell whether the elevated 24-hour plasma levels were due to changes in elimination half-life ($t_{1/2\beta}$), changes in volume of distribution ($V_d$), or both. Triggs and Nation also suggested that, although specific data were not presented, the glomerular filtration rate of the older group was probably lower than that of the younger, and that the slower rate of appearance of the metabolite in the urine of the elderly might thus simply be a result of decreased creatinine clearance. (Changes in creatinine clearance, it should be noted, generally have little effect on the estimation and/or actual pharmacokinetics of drugs whose metabolism is extrarenal.)

In a study from the East German literature (Traeger, Kiesewetter, and Kunze, 1974), phenobarbital was given in a single i.m. dose to a group of young patients, 20 to 40 years in age, and two older groups, ages 50 to 60 and over 70. The $t_{1/2\beta}$ and renal excretion of unchanged phenobarbital were recorded. The $t_{1/2\beta}$ was significantly elevated in the oldest group. No significant differences in urine volume or phenobarbital concentration were noted. The authors concluded that this difference in $t_{1/2\beta}$ was due to an age-related change in hepatic biotransformation.

In general, the use of barbiturates has fallen into disrepute, especially in the elderly. This is partly because of the so-called "paradoxical" excitement (see Stotsky, 1970) alleged to occur with hypnotics, especially in the elderly and with this group of agents. (One should note, however, the Boston Collaborative Drug Survey Program data on chloral hydrate and several barbiturates—see Miller and Greenblatt, 1976—suggesting little or no age-related change in CNS side-effects with these agents.) In addition, the suppression of REM sleep seen with these agents (Greenblatt and Miller, 1974) and much less with the now-common benzodiazepine hypnotic flurazepam (Dalmane[R]—see below) may be the cause of so-called "rebound" nightmares and insomnia. The high risk of addiction and gravity of an overdose with barbiturates—especially when compared to flurazepam—has further discredited their value. These liabilities have helped lead to a public condemnation of the barbiturates and to the subsequent ascendance of flurazepam as the most prescribed hypnotic in the United States and Canada (Greenblatt, Allen and Shader, 1977).

There is, however, an even more serious cause for concern with the use of these agents: the ability of these drugs to induce microsomal enzyme activity (Conney, 1967; see also reviews of Hicks and Davis, 1980; Greenblatt and Miller, 1974; and Shader, Weinberger, and Greenblatt, 1978). This can affect plasma levels of warfarin, often with catastrophic results. The greatest danger occurs when a barbiturate is suddenly stopped in a patient on concomitant anticoagulants (which may have previously been increased to compensate for the faster metabolism by the hypnotic-induced hepatic enzymes).

Chlorpromazine and antidepressant medications may be more rapidly metabolized with concomitant use of barbiturates. However, actual clinical significance of these interactions has not yet been documented, nor has a report that barbiturates (and DPH) lower haloperidol levels (Shader,

Weinberger, and Greenblatt, 1978). In 1970, however, we showed a clear decrease in plasma CPZ levels with the addition of phenobarbital (see Figure 6 in Curry, Davis, Janowsky et al., 1970). Although not described in the text, the patient's course worsened simultaneously with the fall in plasma CPZ (J. M. D.*).

Because of all these problems, we would consider the use of barbiturates in the elderly to be contraindicated except on an acute basis (such as i.m. sedation) or as an anticonvulsant.

*Glutethimide* (Doriden[R]). This agent may be grouped with the barbiturates in terms of enzyme induction, potential for abuse, gravity of overdosage, and REM deprivation (Greenblatt and Miller, 1974). It has little use in general practice and none in geriatrics.

*Chloral Hydrate.* This old and widely-used agent may (via its metabolite trichloroacetic acid) displace acidic drugs from plasma proteins. This can result in a sudden increase in the free blood levels of the displaced agents and shortening of the elimination half-lives. With warfarin, however, this phenomenon may be of more academic than clinical significance, as clear documentation of prothrombin-time prolongation by chloral hydrate exists (Sellers and Koch-Weser, 1970) but actual relevance of this to clinical practice is questionable (e.g., Griner, Raisz, Rickles et al., 1971). Likewise a clinically significant interaction between chloral hydrate and DPH has not been demonstrated convincingly (see Shader, Weinberger, and Greenblatt, 1978).

*Other Hypnotics.* Enzyme induction by *methaqualone* (Quaalude[R]) and *ethchlorvynol* (Placidyl[R]) as has been suggested does not appear to be of significance (Greenblatt and Miller, 1974). Their addictive potential, however, in the face of no clearly unique benefits, suggests no basis for their usage, with the young or old.

*Propanediols.* This group—represented by *meprobamate* (Miltown[R], Equanil[R])—does not seem to induce enzyme changes either but has a risk of addiction, high CNS toxicity, and no particular advantage over the other sedative-hypnotics.

*Benzodiazepines.* The recent (1978) review of the benzodiazepines by Greenblatt and Shader demonstrated no "consistent evidence of differences among the benzodiazepines in clinical efficacy." Therefore, we shall discuss only the most com-

*Unpublished clinical observations.

monly used members of this group (For a more complete review of benzodiazepine pharmacokinetics with respect to age, see Hicks and Davis 1980.)

The benzodiazepines have received the most attention in terms of age-related changes in pharmacokinetics. In a particularly important study (Klotz, Avant, Hoyumpa et al., 1975) the effects of age and hepatocellular liver disease on the disposition and elimination of *diazepam* were studied. There was no correlation between clearance and the subject's age; $V_d$ was age-dependent as was $t_{1/2\beta}$ (both increased). The authors concluded that the prolongation of $t_{1/2\beta}$ was primarily dependent on an increase in the initial $V_d$, and not on a change in metabolism. However, four elderly patients had a significant reduction in the total plasma clearance, contributing to prolongation of the $t_{1/2\beta}$. The authors suggested that this might represent an age-dependent reduction in hepatic enzyme activity. They also cautioned that possible changes in receptor-site sensitivity should be taken into account as well.

*Chlordiazepoxide* pharmacokinetics have been well studied, (e.g., Greenblatt, Shader, MacLeod et al., 1978). The $V_d$ appears to increase with age, as does the $t_{1/2\beta}$. In contrast to diazepam, the clearance changes, decreasing with age. According to these studies, this is consistent with decreased hepatic transformation.

Possible age-related changes in oral GI absorption of both diazepam and chlordiazepoxide have been suggested. These reports are, however, isolated, questionable, and unexplained (see Hicks and Davis, 1979). In addition, such findings would be conspicuous exceptions to the general rule of no age-related changes in GI drug absorption (see *GENERAL PRINCIPLES OF GERIATRIC PHARMACOKINETICS*).

It has been known for some time that the intramuscular absorption of diazepam and chlordiazepoxide is *slower* than the absorption of oral preparations (e.g., Greenblatt and Koch-Weser, 1975). This phenomenon is probably the result of local tissue reaction to the diazepam solvent or to chlordiazepoxide itself (see Hicks and Davis, 1980). This is one of the only justifications—that is, on an acute basis—for barbiturate use in the elderly.

In a study of *oxazepam* and liver disease, Shull, Wilkinson, Johnson et al. (1976) noted no age-related changes in either $t_{1/2\beta}$ or clearance; $V_d$ was either unchanged or minimally elevated in the elderly, depending on the way in which it was calculated. Shull's group concluded that oxazepam metabolism changes the least in terms of age-related pharmacokinetics compared to diazepam and chlordiazepoxide. They concluded that, in the case of oxazepam, any increased sensitivity in the elderly would have to involve receptor-site sensitivity, since there appears to be essentially no age-related change in drug disposition. Greenblatt and Shader (1974), however, have suggested that "any differences between various benzodiazepines may in large part be pharmacokinetic rather than neuropharmacologic."

It should be noted here that the metabolic degradation of diazepam (DZ), chlordiazepoxide (CDX), and oxazepam (OXZ) have similarities. Greenblatt and Shader (1974) have provided a nice overall summary. DZ and CDX are both broken down initially to active metabolites, *desmethyldiazepam (DMDZ)* and *desmethylchlordiazepoxide (DMCDX)*. Both also proceed in stepwise fashion to eventually form OXZ, which itself is excreted as an inactive glucuronide. The half-life of CDX (5–30 hours)* changes markedly with age, while those of DZ (15–61 hours) and OXZ (4–11 hours) exhibit little or no change. This can be explained by the high lipid solubility of DZ, which could also explain the increased $V_d$ noted by Klotz *et al.* (1975) above in the proportionately more fatty geriatric patient. This in turn could compensate for the increased $t_{1/2\beta}$, with clearance than remaining the same as in the young. OXZ pharmacokinetics are noted to remain essentially the same in the elderly patient; any possible change in $V_d$ would be compensated for by the short $t_{1/2\beta}$. Because of this, and because of its shorter half-life, OXZ is less likely to result in toxic plasma levels in the older patient. Largely for these reasons, oxazepam may be the benzodiazepine of choice in the pharmacologic management of anxiety in the geriatric patient (a view held by several authorities—see Hicks and Davis, 1980).

The pharmacokinetics of *flurazepam* (Dalmane[R]) are unusual (Greenblatt, Allen, Shader, 1977). Even after large doses, the drug is barely detectable in the blood. However, its major metabolite, desalkylflurazepam, is immediately detectable and disappears slowly, with a half-life greater than 50 hours. (There is a possibility of the metabolism of flurazepam within the GI wall itself—see Hicks and Davis, 1980.) The influence of age on its pharmacokinetics has yet to be worked out in any detail.

Flurazepam toxicity appears low in general (found in 3.1 percent of 2,542 medical in-patients, manifesting itself almost entirely as a minor and easily reversible CNS depression). This CNS depression has been related to both dose ($X^2 =$

11.4, $p < 0.001$) and age ($X^2 = 23.1$, $p < 0.001$), with unwanted effects found in 39 percent of patients over 70 years of age who were receiving a daily dose of 30-mg or more (Greenblatt, Allen, Shader, 1977). Compared to other hypnotics, flurazepam seems to influence REM sleep less; also, it has a relative paucity of CNS effects, especially the so-called "paradoxical" excitement (Greenblatt, Allen, Shader, 1977). Flurazepam—and the other benzodiazepine hypnotics—have definite advantages, in terms of a relatively lower or negligible incidence of drug interaction, over the other sedative-hypnotics (see *Barbiturates* above).

The interactions of various benzodiazepines with antacids and food are discussed further on (in *OTHER IMPORTANT DRUG INTERACTIONS*).

*Propranolol (Inderal[R]).* This agent has come to be used more widely as an anxiolytic of late. One report (Eisdorfer, Nowlin, and Wilkie, 1970) has suggested that it showed promise as an aid to learning in the elderly, but this appears unsubstantiated or ignored. Propranolol, of course, has many non-psychiatric uses; and, it has been advocated as an agent to reduce tremor, insomnia, or agitation produced by tricyclic antidepressants and as an antidote for lithium tremor (Schou, 1976) and other action tremors (Adams, 1977). (This agent may actually *produce* neuropsychiatric disturbances when used medically, e.g., depression, confusion, and/or hallucinations, and insomnia—Greenblatt and Koch-Weser, 1974; Greenblatt and Shader, 1978). Greenblatt and Shader (1978) have reviewed recent controlled trials of the anxiolytic efficacy of the β-blockers. They concluded that comparative judgment of these studies, which they summarized as "heterogeneous in design and objective," was "difficult and tenuous." It is not surprising, therefore, that the exact role of propranolol in psychopharmacology, either of the young or the elderly, is yet to be established (Greenblatt and Shader, 1978).

The pharmacokinetics of propranolol are interesting, but beyond the scope of this chapter (see works of Evans, Wilkinson, Shand *et al.*, cited in Hicks and Davis, 1980). Over 90 percent of the circulating drug is bound to proteins. Its biotransformation occurs mostly in the liver, where 80 percent may be extracted on first-pass. Metabolism is not confined to free drug in the circulation; in fact, unlike most drugs, its metabolism may be *accelerated* by binding to elements in the blood, which could actually act as a carrier system to the liver. An active metabolite (4-hydroxypropranolol) has been identified. This appears only after oral administration. The clinical significance of this metabolite is not

*Values for these half-lives vary some in the literature; see our review (Hicks and Davis, 1980) for our sources.

clear. Greenblatt and Shader (1978) note studies showing it to have significant sedative and anticonvulsant properties in animals, while Shand (1978) considers it to play only a minor role with chronic administration of its parent, propranolol.

The effect of food on the absorption of propranolol is discussed below (see *OTHER IMPORTANT DRUG INTERACTIONS*). Large interindividual variation in propranolol absorption—but not in elimination ($t_{1/2\beta}$ = 2 to 3 hours)—has been noted.

There is an unresolved question over the site of propranolol's anxiolytic action: *peripheral* (by blockade of β-adrenergic blocking of autonomic feedback) or *central* (by a direct effect on the CNS) (Greenblatt and Shader, 1978). Indeed, there has been, and remains, a controversy over the site of anxiety itself, as Lader nicely summarized (1978). Greenblatt and Shader (1978) have reviewed evidence which suggests "that direct central effects undoubtedly play some role" in the anxiolytic action of this agent.

A study of particular relevance here is that of Castleden, Kaye, and Parsons (1975). The Castleden group studied the effect of age on plasma levels of propranolol. After a single dose of 40-mg, plasma levels were obtained in serial fashion for up to 8 hours, in an elderly and a control group. The propranolol levels in both groups peaked at 2 hours, but there was a significantly longer "decay" in the elderly group. This was attributed to "substantially reduced first-pass effect." There was, however, no data reported on $V_d$ other than matching for height and weight and "normal" serum proteins. The lack of such data makes these results hard to evaluate, especially if one accepts the suggestion that binding of propranolol to elements in the blood might shorten its $t_{1/2\beta}$ by acting as a carrier system to its site of elimination in the liver (and that this all occurs without alteration in $V_d$ or drug clearance). Hence, the lack of data in the Castelden study makes it possible to explain the longer "decay" in the elderly as perhaps šecondary to the decreased plasma binding of drugs secondary to decreased albumin.

Adverse reactions to the β-blockers is, of course, important for the clinician interested in geriatric pharmacology. Greenblatt and Koch-Weser have provided an excellent review (1974). Adverse reactions to propranolol were found to occur in 8.4 percent of 14,344 hospitalized patients. In a literature survey of 797 outpatients, the authors also found that GI symptoms were the most common (11.2 percent), followed by impairment of cardiac function (6.9 percent), and peripheral arterial insufficiency (5.8 percent). In the hospitalized patients who suffered propranolol-induced cardiac impairment, 20 out of 22 had evidence of pre-existing heart disease. Adverse reactions to β-blockers in general were found by the authors to be more common among the elderly, although the trend was not statistically significant. Sex, hospital, diagnosis, indication for use, and concomitant administration of other agents did *not* alter the frequency of adverse reactions. Also there was a lack of correlation found between adverse reaction and *dose*, and that half the adverse reactions occurred in patients taking less than 40-mg qd. This last point is particularly important since the suggested daily anxiolytic dose range is 30 to 120-mg qd and since the recommended doses for lithium tremor and tricyclic psychomotor agitation are similar (see Hicks and Davis, 1980). The dose for action tremor is slightly greater (see Adams, 1977).

## "COGNITIVE-ACTING" AGENTS

The group of agents that falls within this category is often the subject of a chapter itself, and some agents the subjects of their own chapters. Space permits only the following here, however.

Included in this group are:

1. *Cerebral "vasodilators"*: *papavarine* (Pavabid®); *isoxsuprine hydrochloride* (Vasodilan®); *cyclandelate* (Cyclospasmol®); *dihydroergotoxin* (Hydergine®); *nicotinic acid*, etc.

2. *CNS stimulants: caffeine; pentylenetetrazol* (Metrazol®); *pipradrol; methylphenidate* (Ritalin®); the *amphetamines;* and *magnesium pemoline* (Cylert®).

3. *Procaine hydrochloride* (Gerovital-H3®).

4. *Anabolic substances*.

5. *Cholinomimetic agents* (choline, arecholine, lecithin, etc.).

6. Miscellaneous: hyperbaric oxygen; piracetam (Nootropil®); vitamins; RNA-like compounds; propranolol (see above and Eisdorfer *et al.*, 1970); et alia.

As noted, we have covered these agents elsewhere in detail (see Funkenstein *et al.*, 1980). We have also discussed what we feel to be some of the methodologic problems involved in the evaluation of these drugs and in the assessment of the reports on their relative efficacy.

We have had to conclude that *no* drug thus far has demonstrated any clear efficacy in reversing the cognitive decline of old age or the cognitive failure of dementia. We concluded that certain of these agents might be useful in some individual patients, but we felt that no means of reliable patient selection exists at present.

Some of these problems can be illustrated by a brief review of the work on *Hydergine*.

This agent is a mixture of ergot alkaloids—dihydroergocristine mesylate, dihydroergokriptine mesylate, and dihydroergocornine mesylate—and is usually administered sublingually. It is probably the most frequently prescribed drug for the treatment of cognitive impairment secondary to both cerebrovascular insufficiency and senile dementia. Marketed initially as a vasodilator by virtue of its adrenolytic and direct vasomotor activity, recent evidence suggests that its actions may involve at least: stimulation of nerve cell metabolism (Emmenegger and Meier-Ruge, 1968); interference with norepinephrine uptake (Pacha and Salzman, 1970); and inhibition of phosphodiesterase activity (Cerletti, 1974). Increases in jugular pyruvate/lactate ratio suggest that increased cerebral blood flow may result from improved cerebral metabolism, rather than vice versa (Hollister, 1976).

Table 31–4 presents a total of 18 Hydergine efficacy studies that meet criteria for a carefully controlled study. Fourteen of these studies found Hydergine superior to placebo. Of the three negative studies, one employed a low daily dose of drug (Forster, Schultz, and Henderson, 1955), while the other two did not hold up in attempts at replication which, in one case (Roubicek, Geiger, and Abt, 1972), involved a longer period of study and in the other (Rehman, 1973) employed a parallel group (instead of cross-over) design.

The actual therapeutic effect of Hydergine, however, is unclear, particularly in terms of the symptoms that it is suggested to improve. For example, some of these studies (e.g., Gerin, 1969; Roubicek *et al.*, 1972; Triboletti and Ferri, 1969) specifically found no improvement in memory function, despite apparent gains in mood, confidence, and sociability. Many of these studies, moreover, do not make it possible to assess whether Hydergine actually acts by improving mood and lessening anxiety, thus improving test performance that was depressed for emotional reasons. This possibility is suggested by the observations of Shader and Goldsmith (1975), who compared Hydergine and imipramine to placebo, finding both of the former drugs superior to placebo, but only after 9 weeks of therapy—a time course suggesting antidepressant action as a possible, at least partial, basis for Hydergine's efficacy. (We have presented typical data showing that, with continuous treatment over a time-period of 12 [see Figure 31–4] to 24 [see Figure 31–5] weeks, Hydergine produces continued improvement. The longer the study, the greater the difference between improvement means. Figure 31–4 presents mean factor scores along four dimensions derived from the Sandoz Chemical Assessment Geriatric Scale [SCAGS] [Gaitz, Varner, and Overall, 1977]. The cognitive dysfunction axis is characterized by confusion, mental dullness, memory impairment, disorientation, and lack of self-care. It should be noted that this score is based on observer ratings and not on results of psychological testing. Although the drug-placebo differences are small, they appear consistently in a large number of patients, clearly giving a statistically significant difference).

As noted, studies by Bazo (1973) and by Ro-

**Table 31–4**  Summary of Adequately-Controlled Studies on Hydergine[R]

| STUDY | YEAR | N | DB/PLACEBO | MAX. DAILY DOSE and (ROUTE OF ADMIN.) | DURATION | RESULTS |
|---|---|---|---|---|---|---|
| Hofstatter *et al.* | 1955 | 35 | Yes/Yes | 3.0 mg (?) | 6 weeks | + |
| Hollister | 1955 | 25 | Yes/Yes | 4.0 mg (SL) | 8 weeks | + |
| Forster *et al.* | 1955 | 15 | Yes/Yes | 1.5 mg (SL) | ? | − |
| Gerin | 1969 | 39 | Yes/Yes | 3.0 mg (SL) | 12 weeks | + |
| Triboletti and Ferri | 1969 | 59 | Yes/Yes | 3.0 mg (SL) | 12 weeks | + |
| Grill and Broicher | 1969 | 39 | Yes/Yes | 3.0 mg (?) | 6 weeks | + |
| Ditch *et al.* | 1971 | 40 | Yes/Yes | 3.0 mg (SL) | 12 weeks | + |
| Rao and Norris | 1971 | 50 | Yes/Yes | 3.0 mg (SL) | 12 weeks | + |
| Banen | 1972 | 78 | Yes/Yes | 3.0 mg (SL) | 12 weeks | + |
| Roubicek *et al.* | 1972 | 4 | No/No | 0.6 mg (IV & SC) | 15 days | − |
| Roubicek *et al.* | 1972 | 44 | Yes/Yes | 4.5 mg (?) | 12 weeks | + |
| Jennings | 1972 | 50 | Yes/Yes | 3.0 mg (SL) | 12 weeks | − |
| Arrigo *et al.* | 1973 | 20 | Yes/Yes | 4.5 mg (?) | 12 weeks | + |
| Rehman[1] | 1973 | 40 | Yes/Yes | 4.5 mg (?) | 12 weeks | + |
| Rehman[2] | 1973 | 30 | Yes/Yes | 4.5 mg (?) | 12 weeks | + |
| McConnachie | 1973 | 52 | Yes/Yes | 4.5 mg (?) | 12 weeks | + |
| Thibault | 1974 | 48 | Yes/Yes | 6.0 mg (?) | 12 weeks | + |
| Gaitz *et al.* | 1977 | 54 | Yes/Yes | 3.0 mg (SL) | 24 weeks | + |

[1]Crossover design at 8 weeks
[2]Parallel-group study (no crossover)

sen (1975) have compared the response of Hydergine to papaverine and found a superior effect for the former drug in most aspects of patient performance. It is tempting to hypothesize that in this population papaverine lacks significant antidepressant effects, which may account for the difference. This notion is consistent with the conclusions of Shader and Goldsmith (1976), who have provided an extensive review of some of the studies on Hydergine and other "vasodilators."

In summary, it would appear that Hydergine does benefit some elderly or mildly demented subjects although it probably does not do so by virtue of any vasodilator action. Evidence in favor of this conclusion comes from the above studies, which were carried out in a number of centers, both ac-

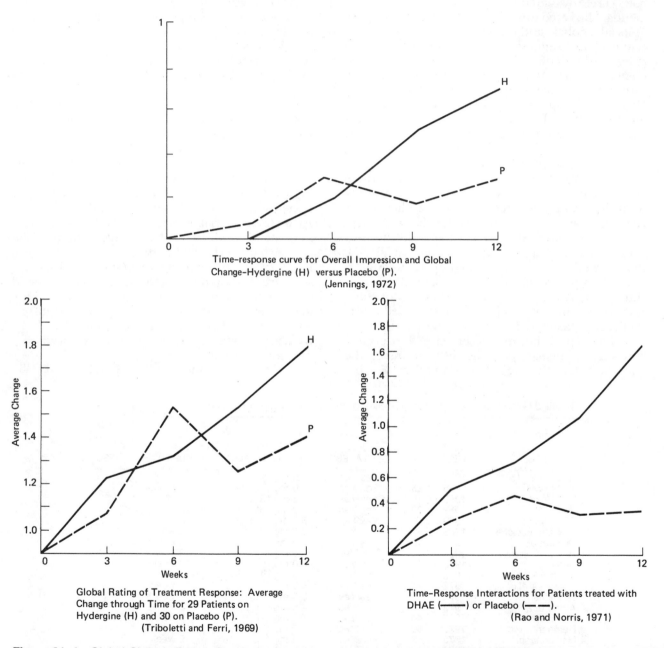

Time–response curve for Overall Impression and Global Change-Hydergine (H) versus Placebo (P).
(Jennings, 1972)

Global Rating of Treatment Response: Average Change through Time for 29 Patients on Hydergine (H) and 30 on Placebo (P).
(Triboletti and Ferri, 1969)

Time–Response Interactions for Patients treated with DHAE (———) or Placebo (— —).
(Rao and Norris, 1971)

**Figure 31–4** Global Change Rating. Time response ratings for three clinical studies of Hydergine® conducted over 12 weeks. From "Hydergine for Treatment of Symptoms of Cerebrovascular Insufficiency." in *Current Therapeutic Research,* Oct., 1969. By Rao, D. B., *et al.* Johns Hopkins Med. Journal, May, 1972. Reprod. by perm.

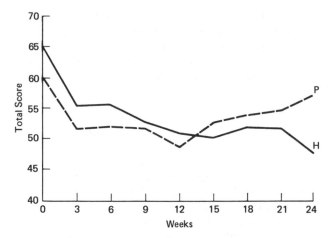

**Figure 31–5**  Time-response rating of Hydergine® over 24 weeks. From "Archives of General Psychiatry," *34*, 839–845, copyright 1977, American Medical Association. Reprod. by permission.

ademic and nonacademic, and resulted in consistent findings along a variety of objective outcome measures. Further research should attempt to define the nature of the psychological functions affected, particularly the degree to which improved attention and memory (both measurable) reflect improved mood.

We wish to emphasize, however, that while we have noted many problems with this particular group of agents, we also encourage further work. For example, we are encouraged by preliminary work suggesting that, in *early* dementias, cholinomimetic agents might prove helpful in alleviating some forms of cognitive impairment.* The reader is referred to our review (Funkenstein *et al.*, 1980) for evidence in favor of the utility of some of these other agents.

ELECTROCONVULSIVE THERAPY (ECT)

Despite its long history (see Cerletti and Bini, 1938), ECT continues to represent a viable and effective means of dealing with depressive symptoms of widely divergent cause. (Since a full discussion of the topic is beyond the scope of this chapter, see Kalinowsky and Hippius, 1969.) The use of transient anesthesia, neuromuscular blockade with succinylcholine, and unilateral nondominant application has greatly improved its safety and reduced the incidence of physiologic and psychologic sequelae. Greenblatt, Grosser, and Wechs-

*Dysken, M. W., Fovall, P., Harris, C., and Davis, J. M. Unpublished data.

ler (1962) found a superior response to ECT in older patients as compared to drugs. This is especially notable in view of the side-effects—especially cardiac—and drug interactions to which the elderly are especially sensitive. In the elderly group, ECT is an effective alternative (Royal College of Psychiatrists, 1977; Turek and Hanlon, 1977). Our unit (Dysken, Evans, Chan, and Davis) has reported (1976) the case of a 69-year-old man whose symptoms of Parkinson's disease improved in a fashion parallel to those of his depression following a course of ECT, suggesting that ECT acts by increasing catecholamine synthesis, both of dopamine and of norepinephrine. For the elderly individual with primary mood disturbance or with combination of early dementia and depressive symptoms, ECT may offer a means of improving cognitive performance by substantially improving the mood disorder.

## OTHER IMPORTANT DRUG INTERACTIONS

INTRODUCTION

The increasing interest in, and proliferation of literature on, drug interactions is growing at a rate which one author has described as an "explosion" (see Hicks and Davis, 1980, for representative references). Literature on interactions among all pharmacologic agents is prolific, as is literature on psychotropic drug interactions, in both the general and geriatric (e.g., Fann, 1973) population. Shader, Weinberger, and Greenblatt (1978) have also provided an excellent review of interactions involving drugs used in the treatment of seizures and other brain disorders.

There is also a growing literature on "polypharmacy," especially with regard to psychotropic agents in the elderly, documented most thoroughly in the work of Fracchia, Sheppard, and Merlis (e.g., 1971). (*Polypharmacy* can be defined simply as the use of more than one agent to treat the same condition.) There is concern about the escalating use of multiple geropsychiatric drugs, especially in view of studies such as that by Ingman, Lawson, Pierpaoli *et al.* (1975). These authors noted that the greatest number of prescriptions in a long-term care facility were given to patients with the *least* physical and mental impairment. This has prompted Ayd (1974) to criticize this practice and to demand a more "rational" approach. (This review has already deplored the almost automatic concomitant use of anti-parkinsonian agents with neuroleptics.)

However, it is worth noting Shader's observation (1976) that there is a clear pejorative connotation in "polypharmacy" which is not *always* justified, especially in conditions not amenable to treatment by one drug alone, such as anxious depression. (The literature on some non-psychiatric conditions such as hypertension not only tolerates but actually *encourages* combination therapy, *including* fixed-dose combinations to increase compliance, in the "real world of therapeutics . . .very different from the pharmacology laboratory"— Dollery, 1977.) The latter point is raised not to justify the abuse of multimedications—in *any* age group—but to suggest a little tolerance for the practicing physician. He may not have the logistical back-up that is enjoyed by those in academic medicine, with staff sufficient to allow a trial of one drug at a time—often after an in-patient "washout period." And he may not have the social service or visiting nurse support to help a confused patient on a medical regimen that might otherwise require the less-than-optimal fixed-dose combination to insure compliance.

Many potential interactions have been discussed; others of relevance not yet mentioned will be listed briefly.

## SPECIFIC INTERACTIONS

*Anticholinergic Agents Versus Physostigmine.*  The anti-parkinsonian agents, tricyclic antidepressants, and phenothiazines (in that order—see Table 31–1) possess anticholinergic properties. Many of the antihistamines—often prescribed for sleep—do so as well. In the elderly, therefore, one must, with the use of these agents, be especially concerned about paralytic ileus, urinary retention, glaucoma, tachycardia, and confusional states.

Confusional states are especially relevant here, since these agents—alone or in combination—can produce an *atropine psychosis* (Granacher and Baldessarini, 1975), especially in the case of the older patient, whose cerebral function may already be compromised (Salzman *et al.*, 1975). This reaction is manifest both centrally (disorientation, hyperactivity, hallucinations including visual, and sometimes seizures) and peripherally (tachycardia, mydriasis, facial flushing but decreased sweating, fever, urinary retention and decreased motility). This reaction may be easily reversed, within 15 to 30 minutes, by *physostigmine salicylate* (Antilirium[R])— 1 to 2-mg i.v. (*slowly*)—which then wears off just as quickly, with the patient returning from lucidity

and calm back to his agitated confusional state (see Granacher and Baldessarini, 1975).

An atropine psychosis may be misinterpreted by an over-worked nursing home or state hospital staff as a worsening of the condition for which these drugs were given in the first place, sometimes resulting in *more* of the toxic medication being given.

The differential potency of anticholinergic psychotropic agents in binding to clinically important receptors has been shown in Table 31–1. (Of interest here are the suggestions, cited in our review—see Hicks and Davis, 1980—that the benzodiazepines may have some anticholinergic activity, especially since the package insert for Valium[R] [diazepam] contains a warning about possible precipitation of glaucoma.)

*Antacids and Food.*  In early studies (Forrest, Forrest, and Serr, 1970; Fann, Davis, Janowsky *et al.*, 1973), plasma chlorpromazine was shown to be decreased with concomitant antacid therapy.

Of interest are findings that Maalox[R] (a magnesium and aluminum hydroxide antacid) decreases the rate (measured as the time to peak serum concentration), although probably not the completeness (measured as the AUC at 24 hours, or "AUC-24"), of oral chlordiazepoxide absorption, normally complete. This was correlated with subjective experiences on the part of volunteers. Feelings of "spaciness" and "slowed down" thinking were noted when chlordiazepoxide was absorbed at the normally rapid rate (without Maalox), suggesting the importance not only of concentration at the receptor-site (and receptor-site sensitivity), but also the rate at which this concentration takes place. A similar delay in the rate (increased $t_{1/2a}$) but not completeness (AUC-48) of diazepam absorption has been shown recently to occur with the concomitant use of Maalox and/or Gelusil[R] (also a magnesium-aluminum hydroxide antacid). Food, however, has been found to decrease the rate of diazepam absorption, but to *increase* the completeness (see Greenblatt, Shader, MacLeod *et al.*, 1978; Hicks and Davis, 1980). These findings may be of special relevance to the elderly patient, who is more likely to suffer from any disease, including those that produce GI distress. Also, the geriatric patient may be more sensitive to the CNS side-effects of sedative-hypnotics and thus perhaps to changes in absorption rate and completeness. There appears to be no data as yet on the effects of antacids on the absorption of the other common benzodiazepines. One study suggested that food had no effect on oxazepam absorption (Melander, Danielson,

Scherstén *et al.*, 1977a). This is presently an area of much work, especially involving the benzodiazepines, about which several reports may have appeared by the publication date of this chapter.

A recent study of the effect of food on the absorption of propranolol found no change in the rate (time to peak serum concentration), but an increase in the completeness (AUC-10), of absorption (Melander *et al.*, 1977b).

There exist excellent reviews of the effects of illness (Nimmo, 1976), changes in splanchnic blood flow (McLean, McNamara, duSouch, *et al.*), food (McLean *et al.*, 1978; Nimmo, 1976) and medication (Nimmo, 1976)—(specifically antacids, Hurwitz, 1977)—on the absorption of orally administered medications (see also Hicks and Davis, 1980).

Contrary to once popular belief, the stomach is not the most important *site* of drug absorption (Nimmo, 1976). Basic drugs and drugs absorbed by active transport are not absorbed to any extent by the stomach. Readily-diffusable, neutral drugs (such as ethanol) are better absorbed by the greater surface area of the small intestine. Nimmo (1976) claims that even weakly acidic drugs, which are largely lipid-soluble at gastric pH (aspirin, barbiturates), are absorbed more slowly from the stomach than from the small intestine. However, the stomach may *influence* absorption greatly. With delayed gastric emptying, absorption is usually either incomplete and/or delayed. This can be due to increased degradation in the stomach (and possibly intestine), or due to increased time for first-pass effects to take place. Increases in gastrointestinal motility usually increase absorption, but may also decrease absorption if the increase leads to less time for dissolution and adequate contact between the drug and its intestinal absorption sites.

Antacids can reduce absorption by binding drugs directly in the GI tract. Antacids with aluminum (and, to some extent, those with magnesium) may delay gastric emptying. Antacids may interfere with absorption by decreasing dissolution in the stomach. (However, certain acidic drugs may be better absorbed because of greater dissolution via change in pH around the tablet, as has been suggested for aspirin—see Hicks and Davis, 1980.) By raising urinary pH, antacids may increase or decrease urinary excretion of, respectively, acidic (e.g., barbiturate) or basic (e.g., amphetamine) drugs.

The decreased plasma levels with antacid treatment (Forrest *et al.*, 1970; Fann *et al.*, 1973) were ascribed to binding of CPZ within the GI tract itself. The delay in chlordiazepoxide absorption by antacid administration was attributed to delayed gastric emptying. The delay in diazepam absorption was partially attributed to a delay in gastric emptying caused by the antacids, as well as to decreased dissolution secondary to buffering of gastric acid (see Hicks and Davis, 1980).

Ingestion of a meal may enhance oral absorption by stimulating gastric secretion and/or delaying gastric emptying just enough to allow for greater dissolution and prolonged residence at the intestinal site of absorption. (McLean, *et al.*, 1978). Greater dissolution but delayed gastric emptying were the explanations given for the decreased rate but increased completeness of diazepam absorption (see Hicks and Davis, 1980). However, the increase in propranolol with meals was suggested to be more related to changes in hepatic blood flow or in first-pass metabolism (McLean *et al.*, 1978). This last point is particularly relevant to the elderly, who as Triggs and Nation—1975—have pointed out, have a general decrease in cardiac output and splanchnic blood flow, as well as a decreased capacity for biotransformation of many drugs. This might, therefore, partially explain the longer "decay" of the plasma propranolol levels of the older subjects in the Castleden—1975—study. It might also provide a fuller explanation for the effect of meals on diazepam blood levels noted above, especially since there is evidence of an increase in these levels by meals even when diazepam is given *intravenously* (see Hicks and Davis, 1980).

## DRUGS OF ABUSE

### Ethanol

The tendency for the old to use alcohol in greater quantities than the young is well-documented, especially in recent reports focusing on alcoholism in the older population (e.g., Schuckt, Morrissey, and O'Leary, 1977). Also, the use of medicinal alcohol (as a facilitator of social and interpersonal interactions) is well established in geriatrics (Chien, Stotsky, and Cole, 1973; Kastenbaum, 1965).

It is, therefore, worth noting here that alcohol is an inducer of hepatic microsomal enzyme activity in the chronic user. It can, however, inhibit this activity if alcohol is still in the blood. Obviously, if alcohol damages the liver markedly, metabolic biotransformation is decreased, although the degree of hepatic impairment often has to be marked for this to occur (Williams, 1972).

Vestal, McGuire, Tobin *et al.* studied age-related changes in alcohol pharmacokinetics (1977). They found the rate of ethanol elimination to be unchanged in older patients. There was, however, an increased peak concentration level in the elderly. This was demonstrated to be secondary to decreased $V_d$ in association with decreased lean body mass. It was concluded that this suggested that age-related changes in pharmacokinetics would be relevant in assessing the pharmacological effects of alcohol in the elderly patient.

These findings might have special relevance to the older person taking alcohol by prescription or through abuse. Since the elderly CNS is likely to be more sensitive to drug effect (Salzman *et al.*, 1975), good judgment would suggest care in the administration of alcohol to the geriatric patient, especially with the concomitant administration of CNS sedatives (even though there is evidence, not controlled for age, that the supra-additive effects of ethanol taken with other CNS depressants may be of exaggerated clinical relevance—see Greenblatt and Miller, 1974).

### ANALGESICS

Analgesics are relevant to our discussion since hypochondriasis is often the presenting symptom of depression in the aged (de Alarcón, 1964; Pfeiffer and Busse, 1973). Consistent with this are the findings that 55.4 percent of the OTC drugs in the Guttmann sample (1978) were analgesics. Capel and Peppers (1978) have summarized data that show that the proportion of older opiate addicts is on the increase (while the proportion of younger addicts is decreasing)—direct evidence that the concept of addicts "maturing out" of narcotic use is not a realistic one.

The effect of age on the pharmacokinetics of various analgesics is reviewed by Shader and Greenblatt (1979). They cite evidence for a decrease in erythrocyte and plasma binding of *meperidine* with increasing age, but they also cite work that either is faintly suggestive or completely negative for other age-related pharmacokinetic changes. They note work showing *acetaminophen* to have a prolonged $t_{1/2\beta}$, reduced clearance, but unchanged $V_d$ with increase in age. Their review also includes several studies of *phenylbutazone* that essentially show no consistent age-related change in pharmacokinetics.

Problems attendant with opiate use, specifically GI effects, take on a special significance in the elderly. Constipation is often a problem in the older patient, which can only be made worse by such agents. Gastrointestinal slowing produced by opiates might also delay gastric emptying and possibly impair GI absorption, already usually compromised with regard to certain vitamins (Triggs and Nation, 1975) and possibly some drugs such as diazepam and chlordiazepoxide (see Hicks and Davis, 1980).

The clinician is reminded also of the potential for a reaction of many analgesics, especially meperidine (Davis *et al.*, 1974) with MAO inhibitors (see Table 31–2). This suggests another reason (beyond cardiovascular concerns) for caution in prescribing MAOIs to the elderly.

As noted above, lithium has been reported to block the actions of many drugs of abuse, including opiates (Jefferson and Greist, 1978), which could be both an advantage—in decreasing reward—and a disadvantage—in decreasing actual analgesia.

### TOBACCO

Jusko (1978) has provided a fascinating review of the pharmacokinetics of tobacco smoke, which he notes to contain at least *3,000* chemicals. We have reviewed elsewhere (Hicks and Davis, 1980), some of the abstruse interactions that might affect the older patient. Of special note is the tendency of smoking to antagonize analgesics, especially propoxyphene (Darvon[R]), and to lower the pain threshold in the older patient. How this relates to the hypochondriasis and increased (especially self-administered) use of analgesics in the older age group is not clear.

In general, smoking increases the biotransformation rate (Jusko, 1978), including that for diazepam and chlordiazepoxide (Boston Collaborative Drug Surveillance Program, 1973), but pharmacokinetic effects of tobacco on psychotropics seem variable and minimally understood, particularly when the effects are related to age (see Hicks and Davis, 1980; Jusko, 1978).

## CONCLUSION

It would be desirable to be able to summarize all of the above material on changes in psychopharmacology with aging. However, other than our skeptical conclusion about the so-called "cognitive acting agents," generalizations are hard to make. Not only are there large interindividual variations (Vesell, 1977) in the pharmacokinetics of all drugs at any age, but Shader and Greenblatt (1979) conclude additionally that there is "no cohesive model or theory . . . yet predictive of the rate and/or extent of changes in pharmacokinetics that occur with age."

One can, however, suggest *caution* in the use of psychotropic agents in the elderly. More specifically, the clinician should keep in mind the following points:

1. The elderly patient is more likely to be sensitive to drug effects, regardless of any change in pharmacokinetics.
2. Such a patient is thus more likely to suffer from adverse drug interactions, not only because of his or her intrinsic sensitivity to drug effects, but also because (s)he is more likely to be on more than one medication, often a self-administered over-the-counter agent.
3. It is, therefore, imperative to obtain a complete record of *all* medications, keeping in mind that:
 a. The patient may be unable or unwilling to comply with this data collection because of a dementing process and/or depression.
 b. (S)he might not regard certain agents (especially OTC type) as important enough to mention.
 c. (S)he may conceal the use of an agent (such as an analgesic or sedative) with which (s)he may be self-treating a depression and/or about which (s)he does not understand the risks.
 d. (S)he may be prone to abuse alcohol and/or drugs.
4. The clinician should keep medications at a minimum.
5. The clinician should err on the side of caution and assume that the patient may have an impaired capacity to metabolize and/or excrete any drug, since the "most common finding in the literature [on geriatric pharmacokinetics] is a prolonged half-life" (Triggs and Nation, 1975).
6. Appropriate laboratory testing is essential and should be carried out *before* administration of an agent, unless the clinical situation is so dire that this is not feasible. It should be emphasized that creatinine clearance is the only reliable meaure of the GFR, since the serum creatinine may remain normal long after its renal clearance has diminished.

It should be kept in mind, however, that the aging process varies from individual to individual, and from one organ system to another within the same individual. Therefore, the concept of the "geriatric" individual as a homogeneous entity, demarcated by some age-related cut-off line, is simplistic. Lamy and Kitler (1971) suggest a direction away from the automatic classification of persons over 65 years of age as "elderly" or "geriatric," and away from the equation of "aging" with "illness." They also point out that there is not necessarily a correlation between "chronologic" and "biologic" age. In fact, Butler (1975) states that the elderly "actually become more diverse rather than more similar with advancing age."

# REFERENCES

Adams, R. D., and Victor, M. (eds.) 1977. *Principles of Neurology.* New York: McGraw-Hill.

Alexander, C. S., and Niño, A. 1969. Cardiovascular complications in young patients taking psychotropic drugs. *American Heart Journal, 78,* 757–759.

Altesman, R. I., and Cole, J. O. 1978. Lithium therapy: A practical review. *McLean Hospital Journal, 3,* 106–121.

Arrigo, A., Brown, P., Kauchtschischwili, G. M., Moglia, A., and Tartara, A. 1973. Influence of treatment on symptomatology and correlated electroencephalograph (EEG) change in the aged. *Current Therapeutic Research, 15,* 417–420.

Axelsson, R., and Martensson, E. 1976. Serum concentration and elimination from serum of thioridazine in psychiatric patients. *Current Therapeutic Research, 19,* 242–264.

Ayd, F. J. 1960. Tranquilizers and the ambulatory geriatric patient. *Journal of the American Geriatrics Society, 8,* 909–914.

Ayd, F. J. 1974. Rational pharmacotherapy: Once-a-day drug dosage. *Diseases of the Nervous System,* 183–189.

Baastrup, P. C., Hollnagel, P., Srenson, R., and Schou, M. 1976. Adverse reactions in treatment with lithium carbonate and haloperidol. *Journal of the American Medical Association, 236,* 2635–2646.

Banen, D. M. 1972. An ergot preparation (Hydergine) for relief of symptoms of cerebrovascular insufficiency. *Journal of the American Geriatrics Society, 20,* 22–24.

Bazo, A. J. 1973. An ergot alkaloid preparation (Hydergine) versus papavarine in treating common complaints of the aged: Double-blind study. *Journal of the American Geriatrics Society, 21,* 63–71.

Baldessarini, R. J., and Lipinski, J. F. 1975. Lithium salts: 1970–1975. *Annals of Internal Medicine, 83,* 527–533.

Bell, R. C. H., and Smith, R. C. 1978. Tardive dyskinesia: Characterization and prevalence in a statewide system. *Journal of Clinical Psychiatry, 39,* 39–47.

Bender, A. D. 1964. Pharmacodynamic principles of drug therapy in the aged. *Journal of the American Geriatrics Society, 13,* 387–418.

Bigger, J. T., Kantor, S. J., Glassman, A. H., and Perel, J. M. 1978. Cardiovascular effects of tricyclic drugs. *In*, M. A. Lipton, A. DiMascio, and K. F. Killam (eds.), *Psychopharmacology: A Generation of Progress*, pp. 1033–1046. New York: Raven Press.

Boston Collaborative Drug Surveillance Program. 1973. Clinical depression of the central nervous system due to diazepam and chlordiazepoxide in relation to cigarette smoking and age. *New England Journal of Medicine, 288,* 277–280.

BRANCHEY, M. H., LEE, J. H., AMIN, R., AND SIMPSON, G. M. 1978. High- and low-potency neuroleptics in elderly psychiatric patients. *Journal of the American Medical Association, 239,* 1860–1862.

BRIANT, R. H., REID, J. L., AND DOLLERY, C. T. 1973. Interaction between clonidine and desipramine in man. *British Medical Journal, 1,* 522–523.

BUTLER, R. N. 1975. Psychiatry and the elderly: An overview. *American Journal of Psychiatry, 32,* 893–900.

CAPEL, W. C., AND PEPPERS, L. G. 1978. The aging addict: A longitudinal study of known abusers. *Addictive Diseases, 3,* 389–403.

CASTLEDEN, C. M., KAYE, C. M., AND PARSONS, R. L. 1975. The effect of age on plasma levels of propranolol and practolol in man. *British Journal of Clinical Pharmacology, 2,* 303–306.

CERLETTI, A. 1974. Ramifications of ergot research and their impact on the treatment of migraine. *Archives of Neurobiology* (Madrid), *37,* Supplement, 3–8.

CERLETTI, U., AND BINI, L. 1938. L'Elettroshock. *Archivivi Generale di Neurologia, Psichiatria e Psicoanalisi, 19,* 266–275.

CHIEN, C. P., STOTSKY, B. A., COLE, J. 1973. Psychiatric treatment for nursing home patients: Drug, alcohol milieu. *American Journal of Psychiatry, 130,* 543–548.

COHEN, W. J., AND COHEN, N. H. 1974. Lithium carbonate, haloperidol and irreversible brain damage. *Journal of the American Medical Association, 230,* 1283–1287.

COLE, J. O., AND STOTSKY, B. A. 1974. Improving psychiatric drug therapy: A matter of dosage and choice. *Geriatrics, 29,* 1978.

CONNEY, A. H. 1967. Pharmacological implications of microsomal enzyme induction. *Pharmacology Review, 19,* 317–366.

CONSOLO, S., MORSELLI, P. L., ZACCALA, M., AND GARATTINI, S. 1970. Delayed absorption of phenylbutazone caused by desmethylimipramine in humans. *European Journal of Pharmacology, 10,* 239–242.

CROOKS, J., O'MALLEY, K., AND STEVENSON, I. H. 1976. Pharmacokinetics in the elderly. *Clinical Pharmacokinetics, 1,* 280–296.

CURRY, S. H., DAVIS, J. M., JANOWSKY, D. S., AND MARSHALL, J. H. L. 1970. Factors affecting chlorpromazine plasma levels in psychiatric patients. *Archives of General Psychiatry, 22,* 209–215.

DAVIS, J. M. 1974. Psychopharmacology in the aged: Use of psychotropic drugs in geriatric patients. *Journal of Geriatric Psychiatry, 7,* 145–159.

DAVIS, J. M. 1976. Overview: Maintenance therapy in psychiatry: II. Affective disorders. *American Journal of Psychiatry, 133,* 9–13.

DAVIS, J. M., ERICKSON S., AND DEKIRMENJIAN, H. 1978. Plasma levels of antipsychotic drugs and clinical response. *In,* M. A. Lipton, A. DiMascio, and K. F. Killam (eds.), *Psychopharmacology: A Generation of Progress,* pp. 905–915. New York: Raven Press.

DAVIS, J. M., SEKERKE, J., AND JANOWSKY, D. S. 1974. Drug interactions involving the drugs of abuse. *Drug Intelligence and Clinical Pharmacy, 8,* 120–141.

DELAY, J., DENIKER, P., AND HARL, J. M. 1952. Utilization en thérapeutique psychiatrique d'une phénothiazine d'action centrale elective (4560R). *Annales Médico-Psychologiques, 110,* 112–131.

DE ALARCÓN, R. Hypochondriasis and depression in the aged. 1964. *Gerontologica Clinica, 6,* 266–277.

DITCH, M., KELLY, F. J., AND RESNICK, O. 1971. An ergot preparation (Hydergine) in the treatment of cerebrovascular disorders in the geriatric patient: A double blind-study. *Journal of the American Geriatrics Society, 19,* 208–217.

DOLLERY, C. T. 1977. Pharmacological basis for continuation therapy of hypertension. *Annual Review of Pharmacology and Toxicology, 17,* 311–323.

DRAYER, D. E. 1974. Pathways of drug metabolism in man. *Medical Clinics of North America, 49,* 927–944.

DYSKEN, M., EVANS, H. E., CHAN, C. H., AND DAVIS, J. M. 1976. Improvement of depression and Parkinsonism during ECT: A case sudy. *Neuropsychobiology, 2,* 81–86.

EISDORFER, C., NOWLIN, J., AND WILKIE, F. 1970. Improvement of learning in the aged by modification of autonomic nervous system activity. *Science, 170,* 1327–1329.

EL-YOUSEF, M. R., AND MENIER, D. M. 1974. Tricyclic antidepressants and phenothiazines. *Journal of the American Medical Association, 229,* 1419.

EMMENEGER, H., AND MEIER-RUGE, W. 1968. Actions of Hydergine on the brain. *Pharmacology, 1,* 65–78.

FALK, W. E., MAHNKE, M. W., AND POSKANZER, D. C. 1979. Lithium prophylaxis of corticotropin-induced psychosis. *Journal of the American Medical Association, 241,* 1011–1012.

FANN, W. E. 1973. Some clinically important interactions of psychotropic drugs. *Southern Medical School Journal, 66,* 661–665.

FANN, W. E., CAVANAUGH, J. H., KAUFMANN, J. S., GRIFFITH, J. D., DAVIS, J. M., JANOWSKY, D. S., AND OATES, J. A. 1971. Doxepin: Effects on transport of biogenic amines in man. *Psychopharmacologia, 22,* 111–125.

FANN, W. E., DAVIS, J. M., JANOWSKY, D. S., SEKERKE, H. J., AND SCHMIDT, D. M. 1973. Chlorpromazine: Effects of antacids on its gastrointestinal absorption. *Journal of Clinical Pharmacology, 13,* 388–390.

FANN, W. E., AND EISDORFER, C. (eds.) 1979. *Psychophar-*

*macology and the Aging Patient.* New York: Spectrum Publ. (in press).

FINGL, E., AND WOODBURY, D. M. 1975. General principles [basic pharmacology] *In,* L. S. Goodman and A. Gilman (eds.), *The Pharmacological Basis of Therapeutics,* 5th ed., pp. 1–46. New York: Macmillan.

FORREST, F. M., FORREST, I. S., AND SERR, M. T. 1970. Modification of chlorpromazine metabolism by some other drugs frequently administered to psychiatric patients. *Biological Psychiatry, 2,* 53–59

FORSMAN, A., AND ÖHMAN, R. 1977. Applied pharmacokinetics of haloperidol in man. *Current Therapeutic Research, 21,* 396–411.

FORSTER, W., SCHULTZ, S., AND HENDERSON, A. L. 1955. Combined hydragenated alkaloids of ergot in senile and arteriosclerotic psychoses. *Geriatrics, 10,* 26–30.

FRACCHIA, J., SHEPPARD, C., AND MERLIS, S. 1971. Combination medications in psychiatric treatment: Patterns in a group of elderly hospital patients. *Journal of the American Geriatrics Society, 19,* 301–307.

FRIEDMAN, M. J., CULVER, C. M., AND FERRELL, R. B. 1977. On the safety of long-term treatment with lithium. *American Journal of Psychiatry, 134,* 1123–1126.

FRIEDHOFF, A. J., ROSENGARTEN, M. D., AND BONNET, K. 1978. Receptor-cell sensitivity modification (RSM) as a model for pathogenesis and treatment of tardive dyskinesia. *Psychopharmacology Bulletin, 14*(4), 77–79.

FUNKENSTEIN, H. H., HICKS, R., DYSKEN, M. W., AND DAVIS, J. M. 1980. Drug treatment of cognitive impairment in Altheimer's disease in late-life dementias. *In,* N. Miller (ed.), *Clinical Aspects of Altheimer's Disease and Senile Dementia.* New York: Raven Press (in press).

FYRÖ, B., PETTERSON, U., AND SEDVALL, G. 1973. Pharmacokinetics of lithium in manic-depressive patients. *Acta Psychiatrica Scandinavica, 49,* 237–247.

GAITZ, C. M., VARNER, R. V., AND OVERALL, J. E. 1977. Pharmacotherapy for organic brain syndrome in late life. *Archives of General Psychiatry, 34,* 839–845.

GERIN, J. 1969. Symptomatic treatment of cerebrovascular insufficiency. *Current Therapeutic Research, 11,* 609–620.

GERSHON, S., AND RASKIN, A. (eds.). 1975. *Aging, Volume 2.* New York: Raven Press.

GIBALDI, M., BOYES, R. N., AND FELDMAN, S. 1971. Influence of first-pass effect on availability of drugs in oral administration. *Journal of Pharmaceutical Sciences, 60,* 1338–1340.

GIBALDI, M., AND PERRIER, D. 1975. *Pharmacokinetics.* New York: Marcel Dekker.

GRAM, L. F., AND OVERØ, K. F. 1970. Drug interaction: Inhibiting effect of neuroleptics on metabolism of tricyclic antidepressants in man. *British Medical Journal, I,* 463–465.

GRANACHER, R. P., AND BALDESSARINI, R. J. 1975. Physostigmine: Its use in acute anticholinergic syndrome with antidepressant and antiparkinsonian drugs. *Archives of General Psychiatry, 32,* 375–380.

GREENBLATT, D. J., ALLEN, M. D., AND SHADER, R. I. 1977. Toxicity of high-dose flurazepam in the elderly. *Clinical Pharmacology and Therapeutics, 21,* 355–361.

GREENBLATT, M., GROSSER, G. H., AND WECHSLER, H. 1962. A comparative study of selected antidepressant medications and EST. *American Journal of Psychiatry, 119,* 144–153.

GREENBLATT, D. J., AND KOCH-WESER, J. 1974. Adverse reactions to β-adrenergic blocking drugs: A report from the Boston Collaborative Drug Surveillance Program. *Drugs, 1,* 118–129.

GREENBLATT, D. J., AND KOCH-WESER, J. 1975. Clinical pharmacokinetics. *New England Journal of Medicine, 293.*

GREENBLATT, D. J., AND MILLER, R. R. 1974. Rational use of psychotropic drugs: I. Hypnotics. *American Journal of Hospital Pharmacy, 31,* 990–995.

GREENBLATT, D. J., AND SHADER, R. I. 1974. *Benzodiozepenes in Clinical Practice.* New York: Raven Press.

GREENBLATT, D. J., AND SHADER, R. I. 1978. Pharmacotherapy of anxiety with benzodiazepines and β-adrenergic blockers. *In,* M. A. Lipton, A. DiMascio, and K. F. Killam (eds.), *Psycopharmacology: A Generation of Progress,* pp. 1381–1390. New York: Raven Press.

GREENBLATT, D. J., SHADER, R. I., MacLEOD, S. M., AND SELLERS, E. M. 1978. Clinical pharmacokinetics of chlordiazepoxide: A review. *Clinical Pharmacokinetics, 3,* 381–394.

GRILL, P., AND BROICHER, H. 1969. Zur Therapie der zerebralen Insuffizienz. *Deutsche Medizinische Wochenschrift, 94,* 2429–2433.

GRINER, P. F., RAISZ, L. G., RICKLES, F. R., WIESENER, F. J., AND ODEROFF, C. L. 1971. Chloral hydrate and warfarin interaction: Clinical significance? *Annals of Internal Medicine, 74,* 540–543.

GUITMAN, D. 1978. Patterns of legal drug use by older Americans. *Addictive Diseases, 3,* 337–355.

HAMBURG, D. A., MOOS, R. H., AND YALOM, I. D. 1968. Studies of distress in the menstrual cycle and postpartum period. *In,* R. P. Michael (ed.), *Endocrinology and Human Behavior,* pp. 94–116. London: Oxford University Press.

HAMILTON, L. D. 1966. Aged brain and the phenothiazines. *Geriatrics, 21,* 131–138.

HARVEY, S. C. 1975. Hypnotics and sedatives. *In,* L. S. Goodman and A. Gilman (eds.), *The Pharmacological Basis of Therapeutics,* 5th ed., pp. 102–125. New York: Macmillan.

HESTBECK, J., HANSEN, H. E., AMDISEN, A., AND OLSEN, S. 1977. Chronic renal lesions following long-term treatment with lithium. *Kidney International, 12,* 205–213.

HEWICK, D. S., AND MURRAY, N. 1976. Red-blood-cell levels and lithium toxicity. *Lancet, ii,* 473.

HEWICK, D. S., NEWBURY, P., HOPWOOD, S., NAYLOR, G., AND MOODY, J. Age as a factor effecting lithium therapy. *British Journal of Clinical Pharmacology, 4,* 201–205.

HICKS, R., AND DAVIS, J. M. 1979. Pharmacokinetics in geriatric psychopharmacology. *In,* W. E. Fann and C. Eisdorfer (eds.), *Psychopharmacology and the Aging Patient.* New York: Spectrum Publ., (in press).

HICKS, R., AND, DAVIS, J. M. 1980. The pharmacokinetics of psychotropic medication in the elderly: A review. *Journal of Clinical Psychiatry* (in press).

HIMMELHOCH, J. M., POUST, R. I., MALLINGER, A. G., HANIN, I., AND NEIL, J. F. 1977. Adjustment of lithium dose during lithium chlorthiazide therapy. *Clinical Pharmacology and Therapeutics, 22,* 222–227.

HOFSTATTER, L., OSSORIO, A., MANDL, B., KOHLER, L. H., BUSCH, A. K., AND NYMAN, A. 1955. Pharmaceutical treatment of patients with senile brain changes. Scientific exhibit, Section on Nervous and Mental Disease, 104th Annual Meeting of the American Medical Association, Atlantic City, June 6–10.

HOLLISTER, L. E. 1955. Combined hydrogenated alkaloids of ergot in mental and nervous disorders associated with old age. *Diseases of the Nervous System, 15,* 259–262.

HOLLISTER, L. E. 1976. Drugs for mental disorders of old age. *In,* D. F. Klein and R. Gittelman-Klein (eds.), *Progress In Psychiatric Drug Treatment, Vol. 2,* pp. 531–539. New York: Brunner/Mazel.

HOLLISTER, L. E. 1977. Mental disorders in the elderly. *Drug Update,* December, 37–41.

HURWITZ, A. 1977. Antacid therapy and drug kinetics. *Clinical Pharmacokinetics, 2,* 269–280.

HURWITZ, N. 1969. Predisposing factors in adverse reactions to drugs. *British Medical Journal, 1,* 536–539.

INGMAN, S. R., LAWSON, I. R., PIERPAOLI, P. G., AND BLAKE, P. 1975. A survey of the prescribing and administration of drugs in a long-term care institution for the elderly. *Journal of the American Geriatrics Society, 23,* 309–316.

IRVINE, R. E., GROVE, J., TOSELAND, P. A., AND TROUNCE, J. R. 1974. The effect of age on the hydroxylation of amylobarbitone sodium in man. *British Journal of Clinical Pharmacology, 1,* 41–43.

JANOWSKY, D. S., EL-YOUSEF, M. K., DAVIS, J. M., AND FANN, W. E. 1973. Antagonism of quanethidine by chlorpromazine. *American Journal of Psychiatry, 130,* 808–812.

JARVIK, L. S. AND FORD, C. V. 1978. Aging and psychopharmacology, *Weekly Psychiatry Update, 2,* Lesson 9.

JEFFERSON, J. W. 1975. A review of the cardiovascular effects and toxicity of tricyclic antidepressants. *Psychosomatic Medicine, 37,* 160–179.

JEFFERSON, J. W. 1976. Hypotension from drugs: Incidence, peril, prevention. *Diseases of the Nervous System, 37,* 66–71.

JEFFERSON, J. W., AND GREIST, J. H. 1978. *Primer of Lithium Therapy.* Baltimore: Williams & Wilkins.

JEFFERSON, J. W., AND GREIST, J. H. 1979. Lithium and the kidney. *In,* J. M. Davis and D. J. Greenblatt (eds.), *Psychopharmacology Update: New and Neglected Areas,* pp. 81–104. New York: Grune & Stratton.

JENNINGS, W. G. 1972. An ergot alkaloid preparation (Hydergine) versus placebo for treatment of symptoms of cerebrovascular insufficiency: Double-blind study. *Journal of the American Geriatrics Society, 20,* 407–412.

JUSKO, W. L. 1978. Role of tobacco smoking in pharmacokinetics. *Journal of Pharmacokinetics and Biopharmaceutics, 6,* 17–39.

KALINOWSKY, L. B., AND HIPPIUS, H. 1969. The convulsive therapies. *In,* L. B. Kalinowsky and H. Hippius (eds.), *Pharmacological, Convulsive and Other Somatic Treatments in Psychiatry,* pp. 160–249. New York: Grune & Stratton.

KANE, J., RIFKIN, A., QUITKIN, F., AND KLEIN, D. F. 1976. Extrapyramidal side effects with lithium treatment. *American Journal of Psychiatry, 135,* 851–852.

KASTENBAUM, R. 1965. Wine and fellowship in aging: An exploratory action program. *Journal of Human Relations, 13,* 266–275.

KELLY, H. G., FAY, J. E., AND LAVERTY, S. G. 1968. Thioridazine hydrochloride (Mellaril): Its effect on the electrocardiogram and a report of two fatalities with electrocardiographic abnormalities. *Canadian Medical Association Journal, 89,* 546–551.

KERZNER, B. AND RIVERA-CALIMLIM, L. 1976. Lithium and chlorpromazine (CPZ) interaction. Abstract, *Clinical Pharmacology and Therapeutics, 19,* 109.

KLAIBER, E. L., BROVERMAN, D. M., VOGEL, W., KOBAYASHI, Y., MORIARITY, 1972. Effects of estrogen therapy on plasma MAO activity and EEG during responses of depressed women. *American Journal of Psychiatry, 128,* 1492–1498.

KLOTZ, U., AVANT, G. R., HOYUMPA, A., SCHENKER, S., AND WILKINSON, G. R. 1975. The effects of age and liver disease in the disposition and elimination in adult man. *Journal of Clinical Investigation, 55,* 347–359.

LADER, M. 1978. Current psychophysiological theories of anxiety. *In,* M. A. Lipton, A. DiMascio, and K. F. Killam (eds.), *Psychopharmacology: A Generation of Progress,* pp. 1375–1380. New York: Raven Press.

LAMY, P. P., AND KITLER, M. E. Drugs and the geriatric

patient. *Journal of the American Geriatrics Society, 1,* 23–33.

LANDMARK, K. 1971. The action of promazine and thioridazine in isolated rat atria. 1. Effects on automaticity, mechanical performance, refractoriness and excitability. *European Journal of Pharmacology, 16,* 1–7.

LASAGNA, L. 1978. Some adverse reactions with other drugs. *In,* M. A. Lipton, A. DiMascio, and K. F. Killam (eds.), *Psychopharmacology: A Generation of Progress,* pp. 1005–1008. New York: Raven Press.

LEHMANN, H. E., AND BAN, T. A. 1969. Chemotherapy in aged psychiatric patients. *Canadian Psychiatric Association, 14,* 361–369.

LIPTON, M. A., DiMASCIO, A., AND KILLAM, K. F. (eds.). 1978. *Psychopharmacology: A Generation of Progress,* pp. 1489–1533. New York: Raven Press.

MÅRTENSSON, E., AND ROOS, B. E. 1973. Serum levels of thioridazine in psychiatric patients and healthy volunteers. *European Journal of Clinical Pharmacology, 6,* 181–186.

MCCONNACHIE, R. W. 1973. A clinical trial comparing Hydergine with placebo in the treatment of cerebrovascular insufficiency in elderly patients. *Current Medical Research and Opinion, 1,* 463–468.

MCLEAN, A. J., MCNAMARA, P. J., DUSOUCH, P., GIBALDI, M., AND LALKA, D. 1978. Food, splanchic blood flow, and bioavailability of drugs subject to first-pass metabolism. *Clinical Pharmacology and Therapeutics, 24,* 5–10.

MELANDER, A., DANIELSON, K., SCHERSTÉN, B., AND WÅHLIN, E. 1977. Bioavailability of oxazepam: Absence of influence of food intake. *Acta Pharmacologica et Toxicologica, 40,* 584–588.

MELANDER, A., DANIELSON, K., SCHERSTÉN, B., AND WAHLIN, E. 1977. Enhancement of the bioavailability of propranolol and metroprolol by food. *Clinical Pharmacology and Therapeutics, 22,* 108–112.

MILLER, R. R., AND GREENBLATT, D. J. 1976. *Drug Effects in Hospitalized Patients: Experience of the Boston Collaborative Drug Surveillance Program, 1966–1975.* New York: John Wiley.

MORGAN, J. P., RIVERA-CALIMLIM, L., SUNDARESON, P. R., TRABERT, N. 1975. Imipramine-mediated interference with levodopa absorption for the gastrointestinal tract in man. *Neurology, 25,* 1029–1034.

NIES, A., ROBINSON, D. S., FRIEDMAN, M. J., GREEN, R., COOPER, T. B., RAVARIS, C. L., AND IVES, J. O. 1978. Relationship between age and tricyclic antidepressant plasma levels. *American Journal of Psychiatry, 134,* 790–793.

NIMMO, W. J. 1976. Drugs, diseases and altered gastric emptying. *Clinical Pharmacokinetics, 1* 189–203.

PACHA, W., AND SALZMAN, R. 1970. Inhibition of the re-uptake of neuronally-liberated noradrenaline and receptor blocking action of some ergot alkaloids. *British Journal of Pharmacology, 38,* 439–440.

PARRY, H. J., BALTER, M. B., MELLINGER, G. D., CISIN, I. H., AND MANHEIMER, D. I. 1973. National patterns of psychotherapeutic drug use. *Archives of General Psychiatry, 28,* 769–783.

PERT, A. ROSENBLATT, J. E., SIVIT, C., PERT, C., AND BUNNEY, W. E. 1978. Long-term treatment with lithium prevents the development of dopamine receptor sensitivity. *Science, 201,* 171–173.

PETERSON, V., HVIDT, A., THOMSEN, K., AND SCHOU, M. 1974. Effect of prolonged thiazide treatment on renal lithium clearance. *British Medical Journal, 3,* 143–145.

PFEIFFER, E., AND BUSSE, E. Q. 1973. Mental disorders in later life—Affective disorder; paranoid, neutotic, and situational reactions. *In,* E. W. Busse and E. Pfeiffer (eds.), *Mental Illness and Later Life,* pp. 107–144. Washington, D.C.: American Psychiatric Association.

RAO, D. B., AND NORRIS, J. R. 1971. A double blind investigation of hydergine in the treatment of cerebrovascular insufficiency in the elderly. *Johns Hopkins Medical Journal, 130,* 317–324.

RASKIND, M., AND EISDORFER, C. 1976. Psychopharmacology of the aged. *In,* L. L. Simpson (ed.), *Drug Treatment of Mental Disorders,* pp. 237–266. New York: Raven Press.

REHMAN, S. A. 1973. Two trials comparing Hydergine with placebo in the treatment of patients suffering from cerebrovascular insufficiency. *Current Medical Research and Opinion, 1,* 456–468.

RIPLEY, H. S., SHORR, E., AND PAPANICOLAU, G. N. 1940. The effect of treatment of depression in the menopause with estrogenic hormone. *American Journal of Psychiatry, 96,* 905–913.

RIVERA-CALIMLIM, L. 1976. Impaired absorption of chlorpromazine in rats given trihexyphenidyl. *British Journal of Pharmacology, 56,* 301–305.

RIVERA-CALIMLIM, L., NASRALLAH, H., GIFT, T., KERZNER, B., GREISBACH, P. H., AND WYATT, R. J. 1977. Plasma levels of chlorpromazine: Effect of age, chronicity of disease, and duration of treatment. Abstract, *Clinical Pharmacology and Therapeutics, 21,* 115–116.

ROSEN, H. T. 1975. Mental decline in the elderly: Pharmacotherapy (ergot alkaloids papaverine). *Journal of the American Geriatrics Society, 23,* 169–174.

ROUBICEK, M. D., GEIGER, C., AND ABT, K. 1972. An ergot alkaloid preparation (Hydergine) in geriatric therapy. *Journal of the American Geriatrics Society, 20,* 222–229.

ROWE, J. W., ANDRES, R., TOBIN, J. D., NORRIS, A. H., AND SHOCK, N. W. 1976. The effective age on creatinine clearance in men: A cross-sectional longitudinal study. *Journal of Gerontology, 31*, 155–163.

ROWE, J. W., ANDRES, R., TOBIN, J. D., NORRIS, A. H., AND SHOCK, N. W. 1976. Age-adjusted standards for creatinine clearance. *Annals of Internal Medicine, 84*, 567–569.

Royal College of Psychiatrists. 1977. Memorandum on the use of electroconvulsive treatment. *British Journal of Psychiatry, 31*, 261–272.

SALZMAN, C., SHADER, R. I., AND HARMATZ, J. S. 1975. Response of the elderly to psychotropic drugs: Predictable or idiosyncratic? *In*, S. Gershon and A. Raskin (eds.), *Aging, Volume 2*, pp. 259–272. New York: Raven Press.

SCHOU, M. 1968. Lithium in psychiatric therapy and prophylaxis. *Journal of Psychiatric Research, 6*, 69–95.

SCHOU, M. 1976. Pharmacology and toxicology of lithium. *Annual Review of Pharmacology and Toxicology, 16*, 231–243.

SCHUCKT, M. A., MORRISSEY, E. R., AND O'LEARY, M. R. 1978. Alcohol problems in elderly men and women. *Addictive Diseases, 3*, 405–427.

SEIDL, L. G., THORNTON, G. F., SMITH, J. W., AND CLUFF, L. E. 1966. Studies on the epidemiology of adverse drug reactions. III. Reactions in patients on a general medical service. *Bulletin of the Johns Hopkins Hospital, 119*, 299–315.

SELLERS, E. M., AND KOCH-WESER, J. 1970. Potentiation of warfarin-induced hypoprothrombinemia by chloral hydrate. *New England Journal of Medicine, 283*, 827–831.

SHADER, R. I. 1976. Problems of polypharmacy in depression. *Diseases of the Nervous System, 38*, 30–34.

SHADER, R. I., AND GOLDSMITH, G. N. 1976. Dihydrogerated ergot alkaloids and papaverine: A status report on their effects in senile mental deterioration. *In*, D. F. Klein and R. Gittelman-Klein (eds.), *Progress in Psychiatric Drug Treatment, Vol. 2*, pp. 540–554. New York: Brunner/Mazel.

SHADER, R. I., AND GREENBLATT, D. J. 1979. Pharmacokinetics and clinical drug effects in the elderly. *Psychopharmacology Bulletin 15*, 8–14.

SHADER, R. I., WEINBERGER, D. R., AND GREENBLATT, D. J. 1978. Problems with drug interactions in treating brain disorders. *Psychiatric Clinics of North America, 1*, 51–69.

SHAND, D. G. 1978. Propranolol: Resolving problems in usage. *Drug Therapy (Hospital)*, August, 52–60.

SHULL, H. G., WILKINSON, G. R., JOHNSON, R., AND SCHENKER, S. 1976. Normal disposition of oxazepam in acute viral hepatitis and cirrhosis. *Annals of Internal Medicine, 84*, 420–425.

SMITH, S. E., AND RAWLINS, M. D. 1973. *Variability in Human Drug Response*. London: Butterworth & Co.

STOTSKY, B. A. 1970. Use of psychopharmacologic agents for geriatric patients. *In*, A. DiMascio and Shader (eds.), *Clinical Handbook of Psychopharmacology*, pp. 266–278. New York: Science House.

STOTSKY, B. A. 1975. Psychoactive drugs for geriatric patients with psychiatric disorders. *In*, S. Gershon and A. Raskin (eds.), *Aging, Volume 2*, pp. 229–258. New York: Raven Press.

TARSY, D., AND BALDESSARINI, R. J. 1976. The tardive dyskinesia syndrome. *In*, H. L. Klawans (ed.), *Clinical Neuropharmacology, Volume 1*, pp. 29–61. New York: Raven Press.

THIBAULT, A. 1974. A double-blind evaluation of Hydergine and placebo in the treatment of patients with organic brain syndrome and cerebral arteriosclerosis in a nursing home. *Current Medical Research and Opinion, 2*, 482–486.

TRAEGER, A., KIESEWETTER, R., AND KUNZE, M. 1974. Zur Pharmacokinetic von Phenobarbital bei Erwachsenen und Greisen. *Deutsche Gesundheitswensen, 29*, 1040–1043.

TRIBOLETTI, F., AND FERRI, A. 1969. Hydergine for the treatment of symptoms of cerebrovascular insufficiency. *Current Therapeutic Research, LL*, 609–620.

TRIGGS, E. J., AND NATION, R. L. 1975. Pharmacokinetics in the aged: A review. *Journal of Pharmacokinetics and Biopharmaceutics, 3*, 387–418.

TUREK, J. S., AND HANLON, T. E. 1977. The effectiveness and safety of electroconvulsive therapy. *Journal of Nervous and Mental Disease, 164*, 491–431.

UTIAN, W. H. 1972. The true clinical features of postmenopause and oophorectomy and their response to oestrogen therapy. *South African Medical Journal, 46*, 732–737.

VAN DER VELDE, C. D. 1971. Toxicity of lithium carbonate in elderly patients. *American Journal of Psychiatry, 127*, 1075–1077.

VAN PRAGG, H. M. 1977. Psychotropic drugs in the aged. *Comprehensive Psychiatry, 18*, 429–442.

VESELL, E. S. 1977. Factors causing individual variations of drug concentrations in blood. *Clinical Pharmacology and Therapeutics, 16*, 135–148.

VESTAL, R. E., MCGUIRE, E. A., TOBIN, J. D., ANDRES, R., NORRIS, A. H., AND MEZEY, E. 1977. Aging and ethanol metabolism. *Clinical Pharmacology and Therapeutics, 21*, 343–354.

VESTERGAARD, P., AMDISEN, A., HANSEN, H. E., AND SCHOU, M. 1979. Lithium treatment and kidney function: A survey of 237 patients in long-term treatment. *Acta Psychiatrica Scandinavica* (in press).

VOHRA, J., BURROWS, G. D., AND SLOMAN, G. 1975. Assessment of cardiovascular side effects of therapeutic doses of tricyclic antidepressants. *Australia: New Zealand Journal of Medicine, 5*, 7–11.

WILLIAMS, R. T. 1972. Hepatic metabolism of drugs. *Gut, 13*, 579–585.

# 32

# Behavioral
# and Dynamic Psychotherapy
# with the Elderly

*K. Gunnar Götestam*

## EVOLUTION OF GERONTOLOGY AND GERIATRIC PSYCHIATRY*

### DEFINITIONS USED IN THE VARIOUS FIELDS

Psychotherapy with the elderly is performed by several different kinds of professionals. There may be psychotherapists, psychoanalysts, behavior therapists, caseworkers, as well as peer and pastoral counselors and members of the nursing staff. The present text will avoid unnecessary technical dis-

*I gratefully acknowledge the assistance of several persons during the preparation of this chapter: to Boo E. A. Johansson and to the staff and reviewers of the Handbook Project for their helpful contributions to the contents of the chapter, to Sandra Bates for editorial polishing of the structure and language, and to the Faculty of Medicine, University of Trondheim, Norway for financial support. While acknowledging the help and support received, I nevertheless take sole responsibility for the final product.

cussions; however, some terms require a specific definition (see Table 32-1).

### HISTORICAL SURVEY

Gerontology, which means the study of the normal aging process, has evolved as a discipline in its own right during the 20th century. Geriatrics, meaning the care of the elderly affected by some disease, has also come into its own in recent years, whereas geriatric psychiatry (psychiatry for the elderly) has had its strongest evolution since World War II, although attempts were already being made on behalf of the elderly in the late twenties.

The first report on psychotherapy with the aged was published in 1930 by Lillien J. Martin. Since then, a long series of reports of psychoanalytically oriented psychotherapy has been published (see the extensive review of the literature in the later sections of this chapter for more detail.)

Psychoanalytically oriented psychotherapy has dominated the field of psychotherapy in general from the early works of Freud until the late 60s.

Behavioral psychotherapy, or behavior therapy was first presented by Mary Cover Jones in 1924. This was a presentation of systematic desensitization of a case of phobic anxiety (Wolpe, 1969). This type of behavior therapy has mainly been founded on classical conditioning according to Pavlov (1955). During the 60s and early 70s, Skinner's concept of operant conditioning (Skinner, 1936, 1953) has been applied to human problems (Leitenberg, 1976), and nearly every psychological or psychiatric problem has been analyzed and treated by behavior therapy, many of them with good effect. The number of publications on behavior therapy exceeded the number of publications in psychoanalysis in 1972, which is a strong indication of the amount of scientific activity in the area of behavior therapy (Hoon and Lindsley, 1974).

There have been publications on the use of behavior therapy in the field of geriatric psychiatry since 1968. The main goal in the studies reported has been behavior change of various kinds. Since 1973, however, there have also been an increasing number of studies which have used environmental change to improve the well-being and behavior of patients or residents in institutions. This work may eventually lead to the construction of better institutions, or to a kind of prosthetic environment which can support patients with a wide range of disabling handicaps. These reports will be reviewed in a later section of this chapter.

## ROLES IN THERAPY

PATIENT ROLE

Butler (1963) discussed the tendency which older people have to engage in a "life review." They progressively return to a consciousness of past experiences, in particular to the resurgence of unresolved conflicts, which can now be surveyed and integrated. Not only do they turn their thoughts to earlier years, but they also look for ways to use these memories in the time that they have left. During such reflections, they may frequently feel grief or sorrow. The death of others concerns them, often more than their own death. They are particularly apt to experience a feeling of powerlessness because their fate depends on so many elements over which they have little or no control (cf. Seligman, 1975). Other researchers have pursued this concept of life review and found that the increased and intense introspection which occurs in the first stages of late life tends to wane again as time passes. This leads to a more serene and tranquil disposition, with the dispelling of many doubts and worries. Butler (1975) considers the life review to be a fruitful phase of the individual who seeks help in the form of psychotherapy. Accordingly, he has developed a special therapeutic approach based on the concept of life review (Lewis and Butler, 1974).

*Special Problems in Psychotherapy with the Elderly.* The person who is aging is also changing a number of roles simultaneously, for example, in regards to work, family, therapy, as well as other aspects of life. In regards to work, Verwoerdt (1976) distinguishes between four patterns found in the elderly: a) involved and active, b) involved and inactive, c) uninvolved and active, and d) uninvolved and inactive. This first pattern (involved and active) does not imply a change in role, but rather a continuation of an earlier active life in the spheres of work and social activities, which continues in much the same fashion. The second pattern (involved and inactive) does not necessarily imply that activity is substantially reduced below the level of the individual's resources. Thus this level can be a sta-

**Table 32–1** Definitions used in the chapter.

GERONTOLOGY–the study of aging.
GERIATRICS–the care of diseases in the elderly.
GERIATRIC PSYCHIATRY–the care of psychiatric disturbances in the elderly.
PSYCHOTHERAPY–psychological treatment of psychiatric disturbances.
PSYCHOANALYSIS–Freud's approach to psychotherapy.
PSYCHODYNAMIC THERAPY–Freud's successors' approach to psychotherapy (although the term may also include Freud's therapy).
BEHAVIOR THERAPY–psychotherapy based on learning principles (i.e. respondent and operant conditioning).
RESPONDENT CONDITIONING–( = classical = Pavlovian conditioning)–learning through association of a new stimulus to an old stimulus, resulting in both stimuli being able to elicit the same response.
OPERANT CONDITIONING–( = instrumental = Skinnerian conditioning)–learning by the influence of situational stimuli and by the consequences following the behavior.
ADL–activity of daily life.

ble pattern without problems. The third pattern (uninvolved and active) is a kind of isolation which is quite difficult to break but which can proceed with relatively few problems. The fourth pattern (uninvolved and inactive) is the pattern which can cause problems for the person and the immediate environment. Thus this pattern may indicate a need for some kind of psychotherapy which will increase social functioning and general activity or will compensate for these areas with other non-social activities.

With regards to the family, there is also a change in role to be observed. It is often assumed that once the children have grown up and become independent, the relationship between parents and children will take on a new but finalized appearance. This is an oversimplification in several ways, however, since the relationship may very well continue to change over a longer period of time. As the parents age, adult offspring need to realize that they can no longer look to their parents for the support they once received. The parents lose the strong, omnipotent role they once had and instead become the party that needs to be taken care of.

Both areas of role change may increase the need for help, often in the form of psychotherapy. But role change may also make help more difficult to give, since the elderly often do not want to accept help.

Pfeiffer (1973) has pointed out the importance, when working with the elderly, of pacing all the steps of the program (such as taking the medical history, asking questions, or giving instructions) to the capacities of the particular older person. If elderly people are given more than one stimulus at a time, they tend to react with incorrect or inappropriate responses. Therefore it is important to maintain a slow pace in contact with elderly people.

*Motivation.* What kind of motivation does the elderly person have for receiving psychotherapy and for living in general? This question has, of course, as many answers as there are individuals it concerns. Therefore this question must be anchored in relation to the person's present environment. If there is no longer a supportive environment available for the individual who retires from his job, loses his spouse, or several of his friends, then the motivation for living may decrease sharply to zero. The only adequate way to increase the motivation is to build up new elements in a stimulating and supporting environment. Psychotherapy does not necessarily increase this motivation, but it may eventually lead to a better understanding of the situation.

As a byproduct of industrialization there have been a number of changes in the status, role and functions accorded the elderly. Furthermore, life expectancy has increased from 49.2 years in 1900 to more than 75 years today, and thus by sheer numbers the problems have increased. The day when the designation "elder" reflected a measure of respect and a recognition of wisdom and experience is gone. We have created euphemisms for old age as "senior citizen" instead of giving real status to the elderly. The best thing to do, of course, would be to give the elderly new functions in society and thereby assure them of a role and status of a more positive nature. Psychotherapy is a second-best solution which is meant to help the person adjust to the fate of growing old.

In psychotic and neurotic disturbances one can offer effective treatment, both pharmacological and psychotherapeutic, which can produce positive changes. But when it comes to organic brain disorders, which is one of the main problems in geriatric psychiatry, we have less to offer. When our offer of help has been shown to be of substantial value, then we can turn our attention to increasing the motivation of the elderly to receive help (Kanfer, 1979). Until then, we must concentrate our efforts on improving the efficacy of the treatments which we have to offer.

*Limitations.* The fact that a person has attained a great age, and statistically does not have many years left to live must not be regarded as a contraindication for treatment. Pfeiffer (1976) reports the case of a 68-year-old man, who only had 2 more years to live according to the life expectancy tables. "He woke up one morning and realized that he was 79!" He then became depressed, did not know what to do with his time, and was totally inactive. During a three-weeks hospital stay he was reoriented to his situation and the following three years he worked intensely on his autobiography and lived a rich and fulfilling life. It is often more important to ascertain a patient's mental outlook than his chronological age. Pfeiffer (1976) states that "the occurrence of disease in old age is as much an indication for intervention as it is *at any other age*." I have added the italics to that quotation as a measure of my emphatic agreement with the statement.

A general consideration in psychotherapy applies equally well to the elderly. That is the necessity of adapting treatment to the resources which the individual possesses with regards to physical and psychic capacity, memory, motivation, and other factors of importance to effective therapy.

When initiating treatment of the elderly, it is

important to have worked out a plan for treatment which states explicit goals (see the later section entitled "Treating the Elderly"), both in terms of long-term or final goals, and short-term goals on a weekly basis.

### THERAPIST ROLE

*Use of Professionals and Para-Professionals.* Traditional therapy has been exclusively in the hands of professionals. This is the case with both psychopharmacology and psychoanalysis. Psychodynamic-supportive therapy, behavior therapy and different kinds of group therapy have been increasingly utilized by different groups of paraprofessionals. The question of who will perform the treatment has often been answered by economic considerations. Another aspect of the answer to such a question has often been overlooked. When designing treatment it is well to remember that the staff on the ward as well as others, in comparison to the professional, are often very close to the patient. It is therefore quite natural to use these resources and instead to redefine the professional's role as that of therapeutic supervisor.

When it comes to the use of paraprofessionals in the therapy of the elderly, it is important that they be trained and supervised both theoretically and especially practically. A good example of such a training program is found in Goldstein (1973) who has designed a comprehensive training program for psychiatric nurses who are to serve as psychotherapists for their patients. This program has paid special attention to social-class structure, self-disclosure, empathy and even the rules, disapproval patterns and reinforcement contingencies of nurse-patient contact. Goldstein's program is termed "Structured Learning Therapy."

Significant others with whom the patient has contact are a potential source of help in treatment. Their participation is an excellent way to increase the possibility of a positive outcome of therapy. The main reason for this is that the transition from therapy to real-life situations is facilitated by these contacts at an early stage. The relatives (spouse, children, sisters or brothers) may be used solely as support or they may be used as co-therapists in the same way as paraprofessionals. Especially in regards to out-patient treatment, this is an important consideration.

When it is impossible to include relatives, or when this measure is deemed insufficent, it is wise to look for other social contacts which can be utilized in therapy. This may mean friends, acquaintances from leisure activities, social workers, or any-one in the patient's environment who is interested in the patient's welfare.

*Necessary Therapist Qualities.* Truax and his associates (Truax and Carkhuff, 1967) have demonstrated the potent effects of such therapists variables as a) self-congruence, b) accurate empathy, c) depth of interpersonal contact, and d) unconditional positive regard on treatment outcome. These measures, originally devised to test a number of assumptions of Rogerian nondirective counseling, may also very well be valid dimensions of therapist behavior in general.

A comparison between psychodynamic therapists and behavior therapists has been made by Sloane and his co-workers (Sloane, Staples, Cristol, Yorkston, and Whipple, 1975). The surprising result which they found was that behavior therapists were significantly better in terms of interpersonal contact, accurate empathy and therapist self-congruence. Both groups of therapists showed equal degrees of warmth or unconditional positive regard towards the patient. This finding is somewhat surprising in light of the fact that behavior therapy has sometimes been characterized as a rather impersonal process with little regard for the patient as a human being. A view which stands in sharp contrast to the close empathetic relationship of psychodynamic psychotherapy. Both groups, however, showed high scores in all variables and obtained the same general level of success.

It is quite clear that these factors are of great importance. But they should be regarded as prerequisites for performing psychotherapy rather than sufficient qualities in themselves for effective treatment.

*Special Problems for the Therapist.* Pfeiffer (1971) has pointed out some modifications which are necessary in a psychotherapeutic approach with the elderly. First, more activity is needed on the part of the therapist, in delineating and clarifying the nature of the psychiatric problem, and in seeking to uncover the determinants of the problem. Secondly it is important to consider if and how the losses which the person sustains during late life (income, prestige, associates, friends) can be replaced. The therapeutic relationship cannot substitute for these losses directly, but it can do so symbolically, according to Pfeiffer. Thirdly, the importance of defining goals is stated. These may be more restricted than for other groups of patients, but they should be carefully considered, nonetheless. Fourthly, Pfeiffer has examined the transference situation. This topic will be discussed in greater detail below. Finally the need for empathy is stressed, especially in regards to the concepts put forth by Truax and Carkhuff and discussed in a preceding section.

PERSONAL EXPERIENCE WITH THE ELDERLY. Younger therapists may have some difficulty in understanding the experiences of their older patients. The understanding of another person requires empathy and the ability to imagine what it would be like to be in the other person's situation. Since relatively few therapists have the experience of being old, this understanding may be difficult. However, personal experience with other older persons, such as parents, grandparents, or elderly acquaintances in the immediate environment could increase the possibility of understanding the aging person's situation.

OWN FEAR OF AGING. One result of the all too common segregation in industrialized society is an increased fear of aging. This is mainly due to a lack of knowledge regarding the conditions of aging, but also to the absence of adequate resources which could contribute to a natural and harmonious aging. A better understanding of the elderly and their situation could reduce one's own fears. This is true both for the younger person, far removed from aging himself, as well as for the elderly who find themselves in the midst of this process (Skoglund, 1977). Butler and Lewis (1973) have tried to overcome this problem in therapy and have therefore used age-integrated psychotherapy groups. Some of the unique contributions of the elderly in these groups have been "models for growing older, solutions for loss and grief, the creative use of reminiscence, historic empathy, and a sense of entire life cycle."

REALISTIC EXPECTATIONS. As mentioned earlier, it is important to formulate a treatment goal in the beginning stages of therapy. This must be related to the patient's resources, both actual and latent. Increased functioning is a general goal for the majority of patients, but beyond that it might be to aim for an active life for several more years or rather to strive for more independence for the patient and a lesser degree of institutionalized care.

## THERAPIST-PATIENT RELATIONSHIP

*Transference and Countertransference.* Transference means that the patient attributes unrealistic or nonexistent qualities to the therapist. The most common example of this in psychotherapy with the elderly is that the patient ascribes traits which his son or daughter has to the therapist, or even takes the therapist to be the son or daughter. Counter-

transference means that the therapist, in the same way, attributes traits to the patient which are unrealistic or related to the therapist's own earlier feelings or experiences with older people.

When therapist and patient become too attached to one another because of such transference and countertransference this may create problems in therapy. There has been a general trend in psychotherapy with the elderly (to a greater extent than with other groups) to accept transference and countertransference and to consider these factors as tools of treatment rather than disturbing elements in therapy (Pfeiffer, 1976; Post, 1965; Verwoerdt, 1976).

Meerloo (1955) puts forth the view that these phenomena are quite different in psychotherapy with the elderly as compared to other groups. The therapist is usually younger than the patient and because of this he does not represent a parental figure (as is common in other therapy) but rather one of the children of the patient. For the most part he often becomes a combination of parental and filial images. When the therapist takes the time and has the patience to communicate with the elderly, who often feel lost in a strange and hostile world, this may give rise to transference. But it may also lead to a remarkable clearing of mental functions in cases of chronic brain syndromes. It is important to point out that there is no therapeutic need to solve such transference. Meerloo suggests that the best form of therapy is to stick to the relationship and to serve as a substitute social contact for the patient. It is better to schedule intermittent visits with the therapist so that the contact assumes a continuous format. Those who think that they no longer have a future must be brought back to the past in order to accept the future. For them, the technique of free association is experienced as true liberation from their fear of chaos and loss of control. In a second paper, Meerloo (1961) has further elaborated on the problems and usefulness of the transference situation.

It is true that the transference situation is useful, and also that earlier experiences can be helpful in therapy, especially when it is possible to connect these experiences with the present situation. It is, however, not necessary to interpret these phenomena psychoanalytically. They may just as well be interpreted in terms of learning and memory. Again it is important to be quite clear as to the goals for treatment. The therapist must ask himself if it is realistic to expect that the patient can function on a higher level than he presently does. If the answer is yes then some planning for the future might be performed. If the answer is no, then efforts should be directed to increased understanding of the situation and exploration of the limitations.

*Replacement or Supplement to Other Social Contacts.* Grief is a common companion of old age. Apathy and emptiness are the usual sequel to the initial shock and sadness that come with the deaths of close friends and relatives. It is often observed that after the death of one's spouse the partner dies within a year. Another phenomenon which is often seen is that people who retire and thereby become relatively inactive also die within a relatively short period of time. These findings support the notion that it is important to supplement or replace losses with new social contacts. Equally important is finding ways to fill the time after retirement with some new kind of activity.

The purpose of treatment is not simply to fill in the gaps in social contacts and activity but rather to design strategies for the patient to do this on his own. It may mean that the therapist will advise the patient as to what clubs to seek, what courses to attend, or what methods can be used to make new contacts in other settings.

A danger in this situation is that the therapist may embrace this role too enthusiastically. This may result in a "rent-a-friend" situation where the patient uses the therapist for a pleasant chat on various occasions. This can often be congenial and undoubtedly reinforcing for the therapist but it is not really a solution for the patient. The best way to escape this situation is to use the established contact between therapist and patient to introduce some new person, such as a relative, friend, paraprofessional or other interested party, and then for the therapist to gradually withdraw from the scene.

## TYPES OF DISORDERS OR DIAGNOSES

Psychological disturbances may include at least four different types of signs or symptoms: 1) cognitive symptoms, 2) affective symptoms, 3) overt behavioral changes, or 4) psychosomatic changes.

Cognitive symptoms can consist of changes in thought content or process, or thoughts which can assume the character of ruminations. Perceptual disturbances can produce illusions, hallucinations, or depersonalization. There may also be disturbances in memory, vigilance, or the ability to concentrate, which eventually leads to loss of reality orientation or confusional states.

Affective symptoms can be of either a depressive or an elated nature, as in the case of depressions or manias respectively.

Several disorders manifest themselves in behavioral disorders, such as compulsions, stereotyped behaviors, hyperactivity, and addictive behaviors. Behavior changes may also be a secondary effect of other malfunctions.

A psychosomatic disorder is defined as a somatic symptom (i.e. a peptic ulcer or hypertension) which is primarily caused by psychological tension or stress. In the elderly, as with many other patient groups, it may be difficult to differentiate between strictly somatic and psychosomatic complaints.

### ORGANIC BRAIN DISORDERS

Organic brain disorders include cerebral atherosclerosis with dementia, senile dementia, and presenile dementia, all of which are related to geriatric psychiatry. Epilepsy, Huntington's Chorea, Korsakoff's disorder, and several other disorders are also included in this group, although they are of less interest in this context since they are less frequently seen.

*Cerebral Atherosclerosis.** As the designation cerebral atherosclerosis indicates, this disorder is caused by reduced capacity of certain blood vessels, primarily in the cerebral arteries, with a resulting hypoxia of the cerebral tissue and eventually damage to that tissue. This may be due to small cerebral infarctions, which can be caused by reduced arterial flow or by small emboli in the arteries, which suddenly arrest the flow of blood.

The disorder has an intermittent and fluctuating course, where periods of reduced reality orientation, hallucinations, and confusions alternate with periods of relatively intact personality. The person often has full insight into his situation in earlier stages of the disorder, which can, in turn, lead to depressive reactions. Some cases show focal signs such as aphasia or paresis. Memory functions are affected in varying degrees. In the beginning, the dysfunctions are relatively minor, and the severe disturbances do not occur until later stages. In connection with these more severe problems, there may be accompanying affective symptoms such as emotional lability, anxiety, and depression, which can in turn lead to emotional dementia.

From its onset, the course of this disorder can range from a number of days to several years, with a mean duration of four years. The prognosis is relatively poor, and these persons often die of cardiac insufficiency, especially when the atherosclerosis is not confined to the cerebral vessels, but also affects the cardiac vessels.

*More properly, cerebral athersclerosis may be called multi-infarct dementia.

Although there is no known cure, the course of the disease can be slowed down by certain specific measures. For example, if hypertension is a concurrent problem, then effective treatment to reduce blood pressure can delay the rapid course of this disorder. As with all patients, it is essential to maintain a warm, empathetic and understanding manner. Treatment should be conducted in an environment which is restful but not completely void of stimulation for those sense organs which show reduced reaction potential.

*Senile Dementia.* Even in normal aging, the brain atrophies to some extent, but this does not always affect the functioning of the brain in a manifest way. In senile dementia, there is a substantial reduction of grey matter in the cerebral cortex. A generalized damage develops, resulting in a diffuse functional decay. The onset is slow and gradual, and usually begins in the seventies, with a mean age of 75 years. More women than men are affected by this disorder (3 to 2 ratio) and while genetic factors seem to play a certain role, they appear to be of minor importance.

The main symptoms appear in relation to memory, where the short-term memory is the first to deteriorate. Later on, even the long-term memory is affected. Personal hygiene and clothing are often neglected, reality orientation decreases, and delusions may develop. Patients seldom display any insight into the situation. In addition, the individual may show emotional symptoms such as apathy, agitation, anxiety, and sometimes even euphoria. Neurological symptoms such as various forms of tremors and an unsteady gait may complicate the picture, but there are seldom any focal neurological signs to be found as is the case with cerebral atherosclerosis.

Deterioration is slow and steady, with very little fluctuation. The prognosis is poor, with the disorder lasting from 2-3 months to several years (the mean is five years). The most common cause of death is general collapse of the organism or some slight but fatal infection.

No specific treatment is known which can significantly affect the course of the disorder. As with cerebral atherosclerosis, it is essential to give these patients good care in a peaceful environment, with an optimal level of stimulation.

*Other Organic Brain Disorders.*

PRESENILE DEMENTIAS. The presenile dementias are in principle similar to senile dementia, although they can appear as early as the 40s. Since they bear such a strong resemblance to senile dementia, their description here will be brief.

Alzheimer's disease generally has its onset between the ages of 50 and 60 (mean = 56), and has a higher incidence for women than for men (3 to 2). The onset is more sudden than in senile dementia and has a rapid course, with a mean duration of four years. Once again, the prognosis is poor, and death often comes through general collapse or through some slight infection. Brain damage is diffuse in character, including general atrophy, especially of the cerebral cortex. The disorder includes a series of neurological focal symptoms and memory dysfunctions. Personal hygiene and care of clothing deteriorate rapidly, and the person becomes totally emotionally unresponsive. Nor can one expect any insight from patients with this disorder.

Pick's disease begins most often between the ages of 45 and 55 (mean = 50), with the same dominance of women as found in the previously discussed disorders. While onset is slow, the prognosis is similar to that of Alzheimer's disease. There is a lobal atrophy of the brain, and one finds so-called Pick's cells in the cerebral tissue. The patient's personality deteriorates in a manner similar to Alzheimer's disease.

Creutzfeldt-Jacob's disease begins sometime between the ages of 40 and 70, with the highest incidence being found in the 50s. This disease advances in two steps, the first step being more diffuse and characterized by fatigue, apathy, slight memory disturbances, and some deviant behavior. In the second stage, epilepsy, unsteady gait, and emotional lability are present. Eventually a psychotic picture may develop. There is a diffuse destruction of all layers of the cerebral tissue in some of the cerebral lobes. The cause of Creutzfeldt-Jacob's disease has been traced to the action of a slow-acting virus (Gajdusek, 1973).

There is no specific treatment known for the three above-mentioned presenile dementias. The same principles of case should be applied to this group as were advocated for senile dementia.

SOMATIC DISORDERS AND CONFUSIONAL STATES. In the case of the elderly, there are several somatic disorders which may cause confusional states. Examples of such disorders are commotio cerebri, hemorrhagia cerebri, trombosis cerebri, tumor cerebri, infectious diseases, deficiency states (nutritional, fluid, or vitamin), hormonal disturbances, and intoxications.

Even quite small changes in the environment may also induce a confusional state in elderly persons and thus diagnosis should not focus solely on internal causes. If there is, however, a discernible organic cause of psychological symptoms, then the remedy is, of course, elimination of that cause. This may entail measures such as surgery, antibiotic treatment, substitution treatment, or detoxification.

PSYCHOTIC DISTURBANCES

*Schizophrenia.* In elderly people, schizophrenia may occur as new acute attacks of a schizophrenia of earlier origin. But it may even arise in the form of the first schizophrenic attack encountered by the person. The most frequent form of schizophrenia in elderly people is, however, the residual form of an earlier passed acute schizophrenia.

Many patients with acute attacks of schizophrenia in early adulthood have often sought hospital care and acute treatment under quite dramatic circumstances. The acute psychotic symptoms decrease generally within a period of 20 to 30 years—regardless of the treatment applied. When these acute symptoms are no longer present, the patient shows a lack of initiative, low activity level, apathy, and occasionally some weak delusional phenomena. It is difficult to distinguish between these persisting "psychotic" symptoms and the symptoms which develop after several years of hospitalization in mental institutions. This persisting or newly developed syndrome has been termed the "social breakdown syndrome" (Gelfand, Gelfand, and Dobson, 1967). The introduction of the major ataraxic drugs has not altered the probability of developing this kind of syndrome, but it has increased the possibility of treating these patients for a shorter period of time, often with ambulatory treatment even in the acute phases.

*Affective Disorders.* The affective disorders, or manodepressive disorders, include both mania and endogenous depression. Reactive depression will also be described as it has some similarities to endogenous depression. The bipolar form of manodepressive disorders consists of episodes of both maniac and depressive type, whereas the unipolar form may include either maniac or depressive episodes.

MANIA. Less than one tenth of manodepressive episodes among elderly are maniac episodes. This may depend, in part, on the amount of attention paid to various behaviors. A depression may pass relatively unrecognized but when a person who is normally shy and timid becomes expansive, talkative, and energetic, it is generally detected.

Elation, high activity level, elevated mood, and assertiveness are important signs in a mania. Irritability and garrulousness may also become evident in some cases. Thought processes and speech are accelerated and the person seems to be inde-

fatigable and to need very little sleep. In severe cases, delirium, confusion and restlessness may also be present.

Mania has been effectively treated psychopharmocologically with lithium, both therapeutically and prophylactically.

ENDOGENOUS DEPRESSION. The term endogenous indicates an internal cause, although such an origin has not been demonstrated empirically. Since endogenous depressions generally have a psychotic appearance, it is not unusual to hear the terms endogenous depression and psychotic depression used interchangeably as synonymous concepts.

Endogenous depression is the most common form of depression in the elderly. The first symptom is often a disturbance in sleep, with an early awakening. The mood is subdued, the person seems unhappy, "down," melancholic, pessimistic, anxious, self-accusing, and has often a reduced level of motor activity. Many elderly with depression, however, are agitated and hyperactive.

Depressive symptoms may also be visible in organic brain disorders, especially in the early stages when the patient has sufficient insight to understand the condition. Conversely, a depression can also give rise to a "pseudo-dement" picture, which vanishes if the depression is adequately treated.

Suicide is much more common among the elderly than in younger age groups. In Sweden, where statistics for suicides have been carefully recorded for several years, the suicide rate is 2-3 times greater for 80-84 year olds, as compared with 25-29 year olds. About half of the suicide cases have been estimated to result from depressed states. The highest suicide rate is found among divorced and widowed individuals, with men showing a higher rate than women. People living in intact marriages, on the other hand, show the lowest rates. There are seven times more attempted suicides than successful suicides in the younger age groups, where these two categories are approximately equal in elderly people.

Endogenous depression is effectively treated by antidepressant drugs and also by electroconvulsive treatment (ECT). The antidepressants have a delayed effect of up to two weeks, whereas ECT may produce an effect within two to three days.

REACTIVE DEPRESSION. Reactive, psychogenic and neurotic depressions are three concepts which are commonly considered to be synonymous terms. It has been suggested that this kind of depression is caused by some trauma in the person's environment. Although psychotic elements may emerge, the nature of this depression is primarily neurotic.

The patient is subdued, pessimistic, and disillusioned, and even simple daily tasks become difficult to perform. Anxiety is often an important part of the picture as well.

Unlike patients suffering from endogenous depression, the reactive depressive patient can often be diverted, retains a normal level of motor activity, and may even go undetected by the casual observer, who does not notice the depressed state. Much of the inactivity and lack of initiative can be explained with the help of the theory of learned helplessness as described by Seligman (1975).

Reactive depressions may primarily be treated by psychological interventions, in an attempt to reduce or eliminate the traumatic or stressful situations. Some psychopharmacological agents, such as the benzodiazepines, may be of some help in reducing the anxiety for a limited time.

## NEUROTIC DISTURBANCES

Everyone experiences both anxiety and obsessive thoughts in some situations. There is no qualitative difference between such anxiety and the anxiety experienced by the "anxiety neurotic." Obsessions are not a special type of thought but rather ordinary thoughts which all individuals have at some time. What is it then that makes these symptoms problems?

Factors of importance which determine whether a phenomenon is a problem are the symptom's a) frequency, b) duration, c) intensity, and d) situational occurrence. High frequency, long duration, high intensity, and occurrence in a wide range of situations increase the likelihood that the symptom will be considered a problem, either by the person in question, or individuals who come in contact with him.

Certain neurotic disturbances are more frequently found among the elderly, while other disturbances are less common. The different types of neurotic disturbances to be described here are a) anxiety states, b) phobic states, c) obsessions, d) compulsions, and e) psychosomatic disorders.

*Anxiety and Phobic States.* Anxiety is characterized by nervousness, feelings of insecurity, and agitation. Often, but not always, it is accompanied by symptoms such as palpitations, sweating, muscle tension, tremors, and nausea. Anxiety is present in all kinds of neurotic disturbances and also to some degree in psychoses. It may appear as a single, isolated symptom without any obvious relation to other problems. This kind of isolated anxiety is called "free floating anxiety."

It is more common, however, that anxiety is associated with specific situations, behaviors, thoughts, or objects. This kind of anxiety is termed a phobia, and different kinds of phobias include claustrophobia (anxiety in small rooms), agoraphobia (anxiety in open places), ochlosphobia (anxiety in crowds), and aichmophobia (anxiety for pointed objects). Phobias for various animals (dogs, rats, and snakes) and social phobias are also described in the literature.

A traumatic experience in a specific situation has often been the starting point of a phobia, and it has been shown that it is possible to develop a "mini-phobia" to specific situations experimentally (Öhman, 1976).

Besides the physiological components, phobias consist of two other parts: the cognitive anxiety and the avoidance behavior of the anxiety-provoking situation. The cognitive anxiety is most effectively treated psychopharmacologically, whereas avoidance behavior is most effectively treated by behavior therapy (Solyom, Heseltine, McClure, Solyom, Ledwidge, and Steinberg, 1973). The pharmacological treatment seems to have a rapid and short-lived effect, whereas behavior therapy seems to have a delayed but more lasting effect, according to the results of the two year follow-up (Solyom *et al.*, 1973). Behavior therapy has now become the treatment of choice for phobias.

Free floating anxiety has been treated by different strategies: pharmacological, psychodynamic, and behavioral. It is clear that pharmacological intervention has a rapid effect with this syndrome, as is the case with phobias, but there is no convincing evidence that any particular strategy is most effective with this type of problem

*Obsessions and Compulsions.* It can be difficult to differentiate between obsessions and compulsions since many compulsive patients often have obsessions as well. It is less common to find the reverse, that is, obsessive patients suffering from compulsions. The cardinal symptoms in obsessive-compulsive disorders are: a) obsessive thoughts, b) compulsive rituals, c) intense doubt, d) strong temptations, and e) anxiety.

In phobias, the avoidance of anxiety-eliciting cues and situations is reinforced by a reduction in anxiety, and thus it becomes a strategy for escaping a negative state. In a similar fashion, the person with handwashing compulsions eventually reduces the anxiety by prolonged washing. Thus, this ritual becomes his own strategy for reducing anxiety. When in other stressful situations which do not contain cues which elicit handwashing, the patient nevertheless retains his anxiety-reducing ritual. Thereby, the ritual becomes more and more firmly established and resistent to change. If the patient refrains from washing his hands, the anxiety is eventually reduced but this fact is unknown or at least disbelieved by the patient.

Psychodynamic insight therapy has been used with all neurotic disturbances. The goal of treatment is to attain insight as to the cause of the problems. The results with phobias and obsessions-compulsions have not been very satisfactory. Therefore psychodynamic treatment is seldom used with these problems. Behavior therapy has been shown to be effective, especially with compulsions, and to some extent with obsessions. It is important to note that these disturbances have been among the most difficult to treat until recently. No pharmacological treatment has been shown to have a satisfactory effect.

*Psychosomatic Disorders.*  Psychosomatic disorders do not occur more often in the elderly than in other age groups but rather manifest themselves in much the same way.

Psychosomatic means that the patient has somatic complaints which are influenced by psychological factors. It is unclear, both in principle and in the individual cases, to what degree the condition is influenced by a given psychological fashion. At times it appears to play a major role while at other times it appears to be of little importance.

Psychosomatic disorders include the following systems: a) cardiovascular, b) gastrointestinal, c) respiratory, d) skin, e) genitourinary and f) sensory (cf. Lachman, 1972).

*Other Neurotic Disorders.*  Alcohol and drug dependence are often serious problems among the elderly. A contributing factor when a person starts to drink may be his/her loneliness, which in itself may be the greatest problem. Sleep disturbances are also a common complaint, and the elderly often resort to sleeping pills or alcohol for relief. The extent of this problem is unknown but it has been suggested 40 percent of elderly patients with psychological problems also have problems with alcohol.

Habits of long standing are always difficult to change, even if the person is highly motivated to break the habit. Since it has been shown to be difficult to control drinking in the natural environment, it is not surprising that health care institutions, which may be overzealous in their attempts to keep patients totally abstinent, have had problems with regards to consumption of alcohol. It would seem that there should be little danger involved in accepting a controlled drinking pattern from patients who have alcohol problems of long standing.

# TREATING THE ELDERLY

## PARAMETERS OF TREATMENT

*Goals or Purposes of Therapy.*  A general goal or purpose of therapy with the elderly formulated within gerontology is to add life to the years instead of years to the life. Thus it is more important to give content to the life of the elderly, especially those in institutions. This may also mean increased respect, self-confidence, assertiveness, and human value for the elderly. Increased functioning in one or several areas of life may also lead to an increased autonomy for the patient who may eventually be able to chose what to do, where to live, or how to use the remaining time in his life.

More specific aims with therapy are to increase the functioning in several areas: (1) insight, (2) symptom relief, (3) relief to relatives, (4) delayed deterioration, (5) adaption to present situation, (6) self-care skills, (7) activity, and (8) lower level of care.

INSIGHT. Insight has been the main goal in psychotherapy for decades. By insight it is meant that the patient should understand the origin of the problem as well as the underlying causes, and should face reality as it really is.

SYMPTOM RELIEF. Several studies which had insight as a primary goal had symptom relief as a secondary goal. This may entail a decrease in anxiety or depression. Behavioral approaches are often more problem-oriented and seek to relieve disturbing symptoms as their primary concern. Another common reliever of symptoms has been found in the use of psychopharmacological treatment forms.

RELIEF TO RELATIVES. Treatment or hospitalization of the elderly may be necessary to relieve relatives from a too heavy burden, borne for too long a period of time. Care should be taken to maintain contact with the family and, ideally, this goal should only be a temporary measure.

DELAYED DETERIORATION. The main psychiatric problem with the elderly is the chronic brain syndrome which is incurable. Regardless of the treatment administered, there is a slow, successive deterioration. Some interventions, especially psychologically-based, may decelerate or delay this deteriorative process, and therefore leave functions intact in the elderly for some time.

ADAPTION TO PRESENT SITUATION. Although hospitalization is not a desirable goal for most patients, it is a reality for all parts concerned. Thus the most feasible thing to do is to try to adapt the patient to the situation in which he finds himself.

If the hospital environment is satisfactory and if the patient's adaption is effectual, then the well being of the patient may increase.

SELF-CARE SKILLS. Self-care skills such as grooming and personal hygiene or even the so called activity of daily life functions (ADL) are important both for the patient in the natural environment and for the patient within an institution. Katz, Downs, Cash, and Grotz (1970) have designed an ADL index which contains important behaviors for the maintenance of the geriatric patient: (a) bathing, (b) dressing, (c) going to the toilet, (d) transfer (ambulatory), (e) continence, and (f) feeding.

ACTIVITY. When a person grows old and especially when he retires, the level of activity decreases. While some decrease is natural, too great a reduction is harmful to the individual. Activity at an optimal level has therefore been an important goal in treatment.

LOWER LEVEL OF CARE. The patients should be taken care of at the lowest possible level of care. Stated more clearly this does not imply a qualitative lowering of the standard of care but rather that the patient should be allowed and encouraged to be as independent as possible. Thus for some patients it may be possible to provide care in a nursing home or a home for the elderly, while others may require hospitalization. For still others, the only care necessary may be provided through out-patient services. It is important to transfer the patient to a lower level of care as soon as he is capable of more independence. Far too often the patient enters a care facility and remains there. Ultimately, then, it is often desirable to have discharge from the hospital as a treatment goal.

*Long-term vs. Short-term Therapy.* Whether or not a treatment modality is effective can not be determined by the length of time it is administered. In general, it can be said that long-term therapy is not recommendable in principle. In the treatment of the elderly, several therapists (Goldfarb, 1953; Pfeiffer, 1971) have advocated short-term therapy, often of an intensive character. Long-term therapy should only be considered when the state of the patient is so chronic that it is impossible to discharge him, regardless of the type of therapy given.

*Ambulatory vs. Institutional Care.* As was mentioned previously, it is preferable to treat a patient on an out-patient basis if at all possible. This has been repeatedly demonstrated by several different authors. Kelman (Kelman, 1962; Kelman and Muller, 1962) pointed out that increased self-care

skills in a nursing home population and increased medical services to these homes was preferable to hospital treatment for a shorter period of time for these patients.

Special day care centers have also been developed, both for ambulatory treatment and for recreational activity. Ambulatory socialization therapy was instituted by Rathbone-McCuan and Levenson (1975). Pierce (1975) described how specific activities were engaged in at a Senior Citizen center. It could be shown that persons attending this center benefited greatly from it.

*Individual, Group, and Family Settings.* Most therapeutic interventions in geriatric psychiatry have been made directly with the individual in question. During recent years, however, several group therapy approaches and several ward programs have been developed. Family therapy has been an overlooked setting until now in regards to working with the elderly.

There are both therapeutic and economic considerations to be made when choosing the setting for intervention. It is noteworthy that interventions made within the entire ward for all patients is less expensive than the sum of the costs of individual treatments. Furthermore, if it is possible to change the ward's physical environment in order to improve patients' functioning, this may generally be much less expensive and require less staff time. It is safe to assume that the increased use of group techniques has followed on the heels of reduced funding to institutions. Nevertheless the therapeutic ingenuity demonstrated in the face of economic cuts is commendable.

From a therapeutic point of view, the most important consideration is whether therapy is to be conducted in the natural environment. If the patient is to remain in the hospital environment, then the most appropriate intervention should be within that environment. If the patient will be returning to his family, then some form of family therapy is most appropriate. Not all problems can be treated on a group basis, however, and the therapist would do well to remember that the individual approach can be the best form of treatment for certain types of problems.

INSIGHT THERAPY

*Historic Survey.* In an extensive review by Rechtschaffen (1959) the following types of psychotherapy with the aged are described: a) the psychoanalytic approach, b) modified psychoanalytic techniques, c) Goldfarb's brief therapy, d) other approaches, and e) group approaches.

The first comprehensive psychotherapy program was carried out by Lillien J. Martin (1930, 1933, 1944) who founded the San Francisco Old Age Counseling Center after her own retirement. She directed this center until her death at the age of 92. Her technique was essentially directive and consisted of a series of structured interviews.

Sigmund Freud did not favor individual psychotherapy for patients over the age of 45. He believed that after that age the patient's character would be too inflexible to make the necessary personality changes which were brought about by increased insight. Memory disturbances were also believed to represent an obstacle to treatment because elderly people might not recall details of their childhood which would be important for the analysis (Freud, 1924).

In addition to Martin's early approach, several other psychoanalysts were skeptical with regard to Freud's pessimism for treating the elderly, and they therefore modified Freudian techniques. Among the most important figures were Abraham (1949) and Alexander (1944). Alexander differentiated between insight therapy and supportive therapy, and stated that, on the whole, supportive therapy was the most important form for the elderly. Grotjahn (1951) recognized the difficulties which the elderly had in looking back on a life full of neuroticism and maladjustment. He therefore suggests that it is important for the older person to integrate his past life experiences as they were rather than as they might have been.

Meerloo (1953) showed some optimism for treating the elderly and offered several suggestions for the therapist working with this type of patient. The quality of the relationship is an essential factor in successful therapy. In contrast to Freud, who saw geriatric rigidity as a defense to be dealt with therapeutically, Meerloo spoke of a decreased resistence in the elderly. Rigidity has also been discussed by Lawton (1968) who linked this attitude with the need for training in geriatric psychotherapy.

Goldfarb presented what later has been termed Goldfarb's brief therapy in several papers (see Goldfarb and Turner, 1953). This approach is largely based on psychoanalytic thinking but it is more than any other approach specifically oriented to the aged and therefore has attracted a great deal of attention. Goldfarb's major point is that the dependency of the elderly is a function of somatic changes, intellectual impairment, and socioeconomic level and personal losses. Other therapists have either discouraged or provided real gratification of dependency needs, while Goldfarb attempted to use the increased dependency as a therapeutic tool. Going into the transference situation,

where the patient takes on a parental role and the therapist takes on a filial role, Goldfarb actively encourages this misinterpretation of facts in order to give the patient the illusion of being a powerful parental figure. Once the illusion is firmly established, it is then used to provide gratification of emotional needs for punishment, affection, respect, and protection. Goldfarb claims substantial success with this technique, although no controlled study comparing it with other techniques has yet established the value of this approach.

Since the review by Rechtschaffen, several publications on psychotherapy with the elderly have appeared. Most of them are more or less extensive descriptions of modifications of therapeutic techniques but few have reported any empirical results. The most important among publications are Schulte (1961), Petrilowitsch (1962), Schulte (1965), Wittich (1966), da Silva (1966), Oberleder (1966), Peck (1966), Schulte (1967), Kahana (1967) Dodgen and Arthur (1967), Poppe (1967), Scheidlinger (1968), Kepinski (1971), Hiatt (1972), and Spoerl (1975).

Among the 11 papers reporting empirical findings, six have also used some experimental procedure which makes it possible to draw some tentative conclusions. These experimental studies will be reported in some detail, while the other empirical studies will be briefly mentioned first.

*Individual Approaches.* In 1953 Goldfarb and Turner had already reported 75 cases which had been treated by Goldfarb's brief psychotherapy technique. Among the 59 patients completing treatment (which consisted of 5 to 31 sessions lasting 15 minutes each) 28 were considered improved and 18 stabilized, while the rest were unimproved.

Butler (1960) treated 6 cases with individual intensive psychotherapy, with 4 to 5 weekly sessions for 3 months or more. He judged 1 patient to be recovered, 3 as moderately improved, and 1 as slightly improved.

Hader (1964) treated 7 cases with individual psychotherapy and considered 6 to be better after treatment.

Safirstein (1972) treated 10 cases with brief psychotherapy during 11 sessions or more during a period of 5 months. He reported that 7 of the patients could be discharged after treatment.

None of these studies made any comparison between different treatment approaches or compared the treatment with some control group. Thus it is not possible to draw any conclusions as to the effectiveness of these treatments. However, the descriptions are interesting and can serve as a starting point for further experimental evaluation.

Three studies have reported experimental evaluations of individual psychotherapy. Wolff (1963, 1971) has reported two studies, one of which is preliminary, one of which is more conclusive (apparently from the same data). It is the second study which will be described in more detail. Some of the data from both studies are listed in Table 32–2.

**Table 32–2** Experimental studies with psychodynamic orientation, where insight has been one of the main goals of therapy.

| STUDY | SETTING AND PROBLEM | NUMBER OF PATIENTS | AGE | TREATMENT TECHNIQUE | TREATMENT DURATION | TREATMENT GOAL | RESULTS | DESIGN AND ASSESSMENT |
|---|---|---|---|---|---|---|---|---|
| Wolff, 1963 | Psychoger.: 3 schiz 15 neur (11 anx, 4 depr) slight brain damage | 18 | M = 64 | Individual psychodyn. therapy | 50 min/w 3–9 mo | Insight Symptom relief | 1 recov 5 mod. impr 4 slightly improved | Clinical judgment |
| | Control pat:s | 20 | | Psychopharm (10) Mileu ther (10) | | | F-u 1 yr: 4 still discharged  Controls: all relapsed | Exp/contr groups |
| Wolff, 1971 | Psychoger.: 8 schiz 46 neur (30 anx, 16 depr) slight brain damage | 54 (46M, 8F) | M = 64 | Individual psychodyn. therapy | 50 min/w 3–9 mo | Insight Symptom relief | 3 recov 21 mod. impr 10 sl. impr (22 rel.) | Clinical judgment |
| | Control pat:s | 108 | | Psychopharm (54) Mileu ther (54) | | | Controls: all relapsed | Exp/contr groups |
| Godbole & Verinis, 1974 | Physical disabilities | 61 | M = 69 | 1. Brief psycho- therapy (20) 2. Brief supportive psychoth. (19) 3. Controls (22) | 6–12 sess. 15 min/sess | Emotional improvement | 1>2>3 | Ratings by a) nurses, b) therapists c) patients 2 Exp/ 1 cont group |
| Wolff, 1962 | Psychoger: 77 schiz 31 chr brain 2 alcohol | 110 (70M, 40F) | M = 63 | Group psycho- therapy | 50 min/w at least 6 mo | Insight Symptom relief | 44 released | Clinical judgment |
| | Controls | ? | | Mileu therapy | | | 18% released | Exp/Contr groups |
| Wolff, 1967 | Psychoger: 80 schiz 120 chr brain | 200 | M = 65 | Group psychother | 50 min/w at least 6 mo | Insight Symptom relief Adjustm. | 90% better adjusted on ward | 1 Exp/3 Control groups |
| | Controls | 1. ? 2. ? 3. 24 | | 1. Psychopharm 2. Occupational ther 3. Brief psychother | | | 15 % -"- 15 % -"- 10 improved | Clinical judgment |
| Nevruz & Hrushka, 1969 | Psychoger: 23 schiz 6 invol. psych 5 chr brain sy 2 psychopaths | 36 (18M, 18 F) | M = 70 | Group psychother (1. Structured, 2. Unstructured) | 1hr/w, 12 w | Insight Discharged | F-u 1 yr: 17 still discharged (1. 8, 2. 9) | Nurse ratings 2 Exp grs |
| Wolk & Goldfarb, 1967 | Psychoger. | 50 (23M, 27F) | over 60 | 1. Group psychother. 2. Controls a. Hospitalized more than 5 yrs b. Hosp less th 5 yrs | 1 year | Symptom relief | All exp changed, a > b, controls no change | 2 × 2 exp design Rel. 0.35– 0.90 |

Wolff (1967) treated 53 patients (46 males, 8 females) with a mean age of 64. Eight of these patients were diagnosed as schizophrenic, 45 as neurotic (30 anxiety and 16 depressive-neurotic), but all the patients displayed slight to moderate symptoms of a chronic brain syndrome, with partial disorientation, slightly impaired memory and occasional confusion. The patients received no psychopharmacological drugs during the study. Two control groups were used, one (N = 54) was treated with psychopharmacological drugs, and one (N = 54) was treated in a milieu therapy setting. These patients and their treatment are not described in any detail. The treatment given the experimental group was individual psychoanalytically oriented psychotherapy (comparable to Goldfarb's brief psychotherapy according to Wolff) during a 50 minute weekly session for 3-9 months. The goal of treatment was insight, to strengthen ego and eliminate anxiety and depression. Wolff reports that the majority of patients were able to gain some insight into their condition: 44 patients achieved partial insight, four (anxiety neurotics) gained a high degree of insight, whereas eight (schizophrenics) did not gain any insight. Since several of the patients who achieved partial insight showed remarkable resistance and increased anxiety, the goal of total insight was abandoned and therapy was directed toward ego-supporting techniques. After such treatment, of 54 patients, 20 still showed no improvement. Wolff regarded 3 patients as recovered, 21 as moderately improved as assessed through clinical judgment. The results in the two control groups (psychopharmacological and milieu therapy respectively) showed only a slight improvement of a temporary nature. All these patients, except for two depressive neuroses, relapsed to their previous condition when treatment was discontinued. It is difficult to assess the value of the treatment approach tested in this study, as there is no objective and reliable assessment of the results, but only the findings based on clinical judgment. Neither can one assume that the control groups received more than cursory treatment from the superficial descriptions included in the report.

Godbole and Verinis (1974) reported treating 61 patients in a rehabilitation hospital, all of whom had physical disabilities in addition to problems which required psychiatric consultation (although no psychiatric diagnoses are reported). The mean age of the patients was 69 and they were randomly assigned to one of the following three treatments: (1) brief psychotherapy (N = 20), (2) brief supportive psychotherapy (N = 19), or (3) no-treatment control (other than two evaluation interviews) (N = 22). The treatment groups received 6 to 12 treatment sessions of 15 minutes duration. Several rating scales were used to assess emotional improvement. The ratings were performed by (a) nurses, (b) therapists, and (c) patients. Reliability was assessed for all of the rating scales and found to be in the range from 0.39 to 0.97, with the majority over 0.70. The main difference between the two treatment conditions was that treatment by brief psychotherapy included "confrontation statements" whereas supportive psychotherapy did not contain such statements. All patients were treated in the same hospital environment. In most of the assessments, the first group showed greater improvement than the second group, which in turn improved more than the control group. According to patient ratings, the first group tended to display more feelings than the other two groups. The authors drew the conclusion that brief psychotherapy as used in the first group was helpful for this type of patient. The main effect of treatment resulted in changes in the emotional concomitant of the physical disability, as well as a decrease in neurotic symptoms and improvements in appetite and sleep patterns. The study shows a high scientific standard, but the conclusions can not be assumed to be true for a strictly psychogeriatric population, as the patient groups are dissimilar.

From a scientific point of view, it is discouraging to find that after 40 years of treating the aged individual with psychodynamic psychotherapy there are only two experimental studies which can support claims of its efficacy. And of those two studies, one was poorly run and the other was not carried out with psychiatric patients. From a clinical point of view, on the other hand, there is much that can be learned from psychoanalytic literature and practice. It may be safe to suggest that clinical experience would tend to support Goldfarb's brief psychotherapy approach for use with geriatric populations. As was mentioned earlier, it is also important to consider the effects of transference and countertransference, which may play a more important role in therapy with older people than in more traditional therapy. The main point which must be emphasized is to provide competent care in a warm and empathetic physical and psychological environment.

*Group Approaches.* The first papers to appear regarding group therapy with older psychiatric patients was presented by Silver (1950) and Linden (1953). Lair, Smith, and Deaton (1961) reported treating 50 patients twice weekly for 1 to 6 weeks.

Nine months after the completion of therapy, 27 of these patients were functioning outside the hospital. The improvements were only assessed through clinical judgments. The final results of the study must also be viewed in light of the fact that clinical interviews, conducted before discharge, form the basis for the impressive results. No control group was used.

Saul and Saul (1974) reported on the treatment of 10 patients by group therapy. The only results reported are in the form of three case examples.

Four reports on experimental evaluation of group therapy approaches are available from the literature. Wolff (1962, 1967) has studied such treatment forms and presented two reports. Although the studies are similar, different control procedures are used, which makes it less reasonable to assume that both reports apply to the same patient population. They will therefore be described separately.

In the first paper (Wolff, 1962) 110 patients with a mean age of 63 were treated by group psychotherapy for 50 minutes per week for at least six months. The treatment goal was insight as well as some symptom relief. The patients (70 males, 40 females) were divided among the following diagnoses: 77 schizophrenia, 31 chronic brain syndrome, and 2 alcoholics. A control group of unknown size was treated in a milieu therapy program. In the experimental group, 44 percent could be released from the hospital after treatment, whereas only 18 percent of the control group could be.

In the second paper (Wolff, 1967) 200 patients with a mean age of 65 received the same amount of treatment as in the first study (i.e. 50 minutes per week for at least 6 months). Eighty of these patients were diagnosed as schizophrenic while 120 suffered from chronic brain syndrome. The goal of therapy was insight, symptom reduction and improved adjustment on the ward. Three control groups were compared to this group psychotherapy approach: (1) psychopharmacological drugs, (2) occupational therapy, and (3) brief psychotherapy. Wolff stated that 90 percent of the patients were better adjusted on the ward at the completion of therapy, as compared to 15 percent of the first two control groups and 42 percent of the third control group (brief psychotherapy).

In both studies, Wolff (1962, 1967) assessed the results by means of clinical judgment, which makes it difficult to judge the results scientifically. It is clear that the treatment procedures benefit the patients in some measure, but this is insufficient evidence to evaluate the efficacy of the treatment.

Nevruz and Hrushka (1969) presented a study of 36 patients with a mean age of 70 (18 males, 18 females) and the following psychiatric diagnoses: 23 schizophrenics, 6 involutional psychoses, 5 chronic brain syndromes and 2 psychopaths. Treatment consisted of group therapy in structured or unstructured form, one hour per week for 12 weeks. The treatment goal was insight and if possible discharge. Behavioral ratings were made by the nursing staff and included such areas as anxiety, display of affect, socialization, work attitude and appearance. There was no statistical change in any of these ratings as an effect of treatment. Several of the patients were discharged from the hospital, however, and at the one-year followup a total of 17 patients (8 in the structured group and 7 in the unstructured group) had not been readmitted to the hospital.

Wolk and Goldfarb (1967) compared the effectiveness of group therapy with 50 psychogeriatric patients over the age of 60 (23 males, 27 females). Treatment duration was one year. Patients were randomly assigned to a treatment group (N = 24) or a control group (N = 26). Furthermore the patients were divided into recent admissions (N = 26) and aged in the hospital (N = 24). The four different groups thus had the following profile: Recent admissions (12 experimental, 14 control), Aged in hospital (12 experimental, 12 control). Several patients died during the course of the year, leaving a total of 35 patients, equally distributed over the four groups. The goals of treatment—symptom relief, as well as insight to some extent—were achieved by all patients in the experiment group, with those who had aged in the hospital showing the most improvement. The control group did not show any change according to the same clinical judgment. A psychological test (House-Tree-Person) revealed improvements in both experimental groups regarding depression and interpersonal relationship scales as well as for the organic mental syndrome in the aged group. These scales were reported to have an inter-rater reliability of 0.35 to 0.90.

Of the four reports on experimental evaluation of group therapy with the elderly psychiatric patient, only the last one by Wolk and Goldfarb (1967) gives any convincing clinical evidence on the effect of the procedures. The increased amount of attention paid to the experimental patients may explain a large share of the improvement shown by the patients, but that exact extent of such attention is an unknown quantity. It is, without question, this kind of concern that is of such great importance for these patients. For those who are forgotten and left on their own, one can not expect improvement.

*Family Therapy.* Only one report on family therapy with the aged has been uncovered in the review of the literature for this chapter. It is a short description by Manaster (1967) of his attempts to include family members of patients who were placed in or on the waiting list for a home for the aged. Approximately 50 percent of the families of 125 residents attended therapy sessions when invited to do so. An average of 10 persons attended each session, which focused on an awareness of what being the family of a patient at a geriatric center meant, awareness of their own feelings about "putting their parents away," as well as clearer understanding of the entire field of aging. Although the author reports positive results of this project, no data are provided to substantiate this claim.

*Environmental Stimulation.* Loew and Silverstone (1971) conducted an interesting study on intensified stimulation and response facilitation for a ward with 14 patients and a mean age of 87.5 years. The program was compared to another ward with 14 patients and a mean age of 86.5 years. The degree and distribution of physical and mental impairment was similar for both patient groups, as was the amount of confusion and disorientation displayed. All patients on both wards participated in the study. The control ward remained unchanged throughout the study while the experimental ward was changed physically, psychologically, and socially. The physical environment was colorfully redecorated, supplied with paintings, mobiles, and curtains. Live plants were placed in the windows and family pictures and other mementos were placed on the bedside table if the patient so desired. A large visible clock was installed and several daily calendars were placed about on the ward. Auditory stimulation, in the form of live musical presentations and recorded music was also introduced. Wine was served during the music periods. Psychologically attempts were made to stimulate the patients' cognitive resources and emotional responses. By conducting religious services on the ward, it was hoped that earlier cultural experiences would be recalled. The social environment included a bedside visiting program and the creation of mealtime groups. Several of the patients were also encouraged to leave the ward for outside activities.

To assess the effects of this six month program, six psychological tests were used to evaluate (a) cognitive functions, (b) affective state, and (c) social attitude. No tests of reliability were made during the program. There was some significant improvement in the experimental group as calculated by these measures. Some additional information regarding the effects of the program was also collected, indicating that the interaction between patients and staff had increased considerably. Furthermore, the patients had improved their time orientation with the help of the clock and calendars. It was reported that the staff had also increased its sensitivity to the patients' needs. These observations were also true at a limited follow-up made 10 months after the program.

This is the only environmental program reported in the literature which is psychodynamic in character, where the treatment goal is directed towards increased insight in a broad sense. Several similar programs of behavioral orientation have been made (see below) where this kind of environmental stimulation has been shown to have great impact on the patients' behaviors.

SUPPORTIVE THERAPY

*Psychodynamic Approaches.* Several authors referred to above have advocated a supportive rather than an insight-oriented psychodynamic approach. (Goldfarb and Turner, 1953; Meerloo 1953; and Pfeiffer, 1971). This approach is also an important ingredient in some of the experimental studies presented. No study, however, has designated support rather than insight as the main goal in individual therapy with the elderly.

*Milieu Therapy.* Milieu therapy, or the therapeutic community, is a psychodynamically oriented approach which is applied to entire wards. This form of therapy was first described in 1953 by Jones. It has not, however, been widely used on geriatric wards, since these patients have been assumed to lack the necessary communication skills for such therapy. Aronson (1958) briefly discussed the use of milieu therapy at a home for aged, but did not present any data. Wolff (1962, 1963, 1971) has used milieu therapy as a control condition, with quite unsatisfactory results. However, judging from the literature, one gets the impression that this form of therapy has not been given a fair chance.

*Supportive Environments.* As early as 1941 one finds descriptions of the confused wandering that senile patients often engage in during the night reported by Cameron. It was concurrently discovered that this same disorganized behavior could be produced during the daytime if the patient was placed in a darkened room. The obvious conclusion from these findings was that confusion was a function of the level of background stimulation.

Not until 17 years later were there any publications on the issue. Sommer and Ross (1958) measured the amount of social interaction in a geriatric ward with senile dementia patients. By arranging the chairs into small groups rather than having them placed along the walls they were able to increase the amount of social interaction considerably.

Bower (1967) suggested that senile dementia was the result of sensory deprivation. Consequently he exposed a group of elderly patients to "structured stimulation" for several hours per day during a 6 month period. As compared with a control group, the patients who had received additional stimulation showed certain positive changes as evaluated by clinical judges and ratings made by occupational therapists.

Ten reports appear in the literature where there has been experimental evaluation of one or more factors in the environment and the effect(s) on patients' behavior. These studies are all of a behavioral orientation and are relatively well-designed and executed. A summary of these studies is presented in Table 32–3. McClannahan and Risley (1973, 1974, 1975a, 1975b, 1979) have presented the results from a series of studies dealing with environmental changes in a nursing home for the physically disabled. The nursing home had 100 patients (33 male, 67 female) and the residents ranged in age from 33 to 100—with the mode group between 76 and 80.

In the first study (McClannahan and Risley, 1974) the goal of treatment was increased attendance at various activities scheduled for the residents. All residents participated in each of three

conditions: (1) announcement plus money, (2) money but no announcement (3) control condition. Time sampled observations were made and were shown to have a reliability of 86–100 percent. Announcements were made (a) over the home's public address system, (b) at the table during lunch, or (c) by means of a large-print sign placed at the entrance. No differences were found between these three types of announcements (a = b = c). The announcements were made at 9 sessions during a three week period. The results showed increased participation for announcement plus money (25¢) (condition 1) compared to money but no announcement (condition 2). Condition 1 resulted in a mean attendance of 32 (for one type of announcement) or 36 (if all three types of announcements were made simultaneously) as compared to 13 for condition 2. When even the money was withdrawn (condition 3) the mean attendance dropped to 2.

In the second study (McClannahan and Risley, 1975a) two separate experiments were performed, with 8 and 10 residents respectively. In the first study, equipment was available during certain daily periods for 12 days. Resident attendance was between 5 and 8 and when the equipment was available 4.41 patients were active as compared to 0.71 when there was no special equipment available. In the second experiment, different kinds of equipment, such as games and puzzles, were made available in 20 one-hour sessions. The patients were active 40 percent of the session, as measured by time-sampled observations. Practical conclusions were also drawn as to what types of equipment was most frequently used in the home.

In a third study (McClannahan and Risley, 1975b) a comparison was made among 100 resi-

**Table 32–3** Experimental studies, where the main goal has been to support the patient's activity and functioning through environmental changes.

| STUDY | SETTING | NUMBER OF PATIENTS | AGE | TECHNIQUE | DURATION | GOAL | RESULTS | DESIGN | ASSESSMENT | RELIABILITY |
|---|---|---|---|---|---|---|---|---|---|---|
| McClannahan & Risley, 1974 | Nursing home (Physically disabled) | 99 (37M, 63F) | 31–100 (mode 76–80) yrs | 1. Announcement + money 2. No ann. money 3. Control | 9 sess, 3 w | Increased activity | 1 = 2>3 | 3 conditions for all Ss | Time sampled observations | 86–100 % |
| McClannahan & Risley, 1975a | Nursing home (not ambulatory) | 1. 8 | 53–99 M = 83 | Equipment available | 12 days | Increased activity | Presence 5–8 pat:s, 4.41 active when equipm, 0.71 when not | Exp/Contr conditions for all pat:s | Observat. | |
| | | 2. 10 | ? | Diff. kinds of equipm. | 20 1 hr sessions | Increased activity | Active 40 % of time | Diff. kinds of equipm. | Observat. | |

**Table 32–3** (continued)

| STUDY | SETTING | NUMBER OF PATIENTS | AGE | TREATMENT TECHNIQUE | TREATMENT DURATION | TREATMENT GOAL | RESULTS | DESIGN | ASSESSMENT | RELIABILITY |
|---|---|---|---|---|---|---|---|---|---|---|
| McClannahan & Risley, 1975b | Nursing home (56% ambulatory) | 100 (33M, 67F) | 25–100 (mode 76–80) yrs | 1) Equipm. | 1 hr/day, 35 days | Increased activity | 1) Similar presence, 74 % active when equipm, 20 % when not | Exp/Contr conditions for all pat:s | Observat. | 90 % |
| | | | | 2) Prompting | | | 2) 74 % when equipm, 25 % when not. No diff. when prompting | -"- | -"- | 90 % |
| McClannahan & Risley, in press | Nursing home (80% physically mobile) | 100 (33M, 67F) | 25–100 (mode 76–80 yrs) | 1) Prizes | 20 w | Increased attendance | A phases: 8–12 pat:s, B phases: 16–22 pat:s | Bingo:BAB Art:ABAB Reading: ABAB | Observat. | 88–100 % |
| | | | | 2) Snacks | 20 w | Increased attendance & activity | Increased attendance and activity for snacks (1 % level) | BABA | Observat. | 97–100% |
| McClannahan & Risley, 1973 | Nursing home (55% ambulatory) | 100 (33M, 67F) | 25–100 (mode 76–80)yrs | Store | 9 mo (36 shopping days) 1 hr/day | Increased leisure activity & self-care | Store: 4 attending, 3 particip, no store: 1 attending, 0.1 partic. | 2 conditions for all pats | Observat. | |
| Salter & Salter, 1975 | Psychoger: chron brain sy, mental retard. (86% desorient.) | 21 (Male) | 60–86 M = 68 | Environmental stimulation | 30 min/day 4 mo | Increased activity | Activity increased from 14 to 76% (1% level) | AB | Observat. | |
| Wisocki, 1977 | Psychoger. | 24 | 46–94 M = 71 | Sampling recreational activities Imagery | 3 × 30 min | Increased activity | Overt 40% inc Covert 60% incr | 1 Exp/2 Contr grp | Observ. | |
| | Controls | | | 1. Discussion grp 2. No-contact | | | 1. 10% incr 2. 0% incr | | | |
| Jenkins et al., 1977 | Senile dementia | 1. 19 2. 19 | 71–100 M = 85 71–91 M = 80 | Material Interaction | 45 min/day 18 days | Increased activity | Activity increased from 2.4 to 6.1 (1), 0.7 to 4.1 (2) Attendance unchanged | 2 conditions for all pats | Observ. | 91–100% |
| Götestam & Melin, 1979 | Psychoger. Senile dementia Controls | 11 10 | 1) M = 82.1 2) M = 80.5 | Environmental changes: 1. Furniture 2. Meals 3. Material | 2 hr/day 6 w | Increased 1. Communication 2. Eating manners 3. Activity | Significant effect in all three target behaviors (1% level) | Multiple baseline design (for exp group 1), + contr grp | | 96–100% |
| Peterson et al., 1977 | Psychoger | Mean no. of pat:s = 28 | Furniture arrangement | 1–3 hr/w, 19 w | | Increase in 14 behav:s | Significant increase in talking (not in 13 other behav) | | ABCAC | 88% |

dents as to the effect of dispensing and prompting the use of activity equipment. The study ran for 1 hour per day for 35 days. When equipment was available, activity increased from 20 to 74 percent.

In a fourth study (McClannahan and Risley, 1979) prizes and snacks were used to increase attendance and activity. One experiment was performed with a BAB-design for Bingo, and ABAB design for Art and an ABAB design for Reading. Prizes were randomly awarded during the session. The program ran for a total of 20 weeks. The final results showed that 16–22 residents attended the sessions during B phases (i.e. treatment via distribution of snacks and prizes) as compared to 8–12 residents during A phases (baseline). Another experiment was conducted in a similar fashion for 20 weeks. During the last 10 minutes of each session, snacks (in the form of juice, iced tea, Kool-aid, cookies, fruit, donuts, popcorn, or candy) were served. The experiment was performed in BABA-design. There was a significant increase (at the 1 percent level) in both attendance and activity during the snack condition.

In the fifth study (McClannahan and Risley, 1973) a store was set up at the nursing home with the intention of increasing leisure activity and self-care behavior. The program was run for 9 months with 36 "shopping days" for one hour per day. The store was opened in the activity area and increased the attendance from 1–4 residents and the participation in activities from 0.1 to 3.

The studies conducted by McClannahan and Risley are well designed, with residents participating in all experimental and control conditions at different points in time. The observer reliability is high (86–100 percent) and all studies clearly show that the behaviors under study were under good experimental control and that they varied as a function of the independent variables. The authors state that withdrawal and isolation from friends and relatives are important problems for residents of nursing homes. The kind of program which the authors set up could be an important aid in designing and running this kind of home more appropriately.

Salter and Salter (1975) treated a group of 21 male patients with chronic brain syndrome by means of environmental stimulation. The goal of treatment was to increase the level of activity by means of a program which included three areas of intervention: (1) reality orientation, (2) activities of daily living (ADL), and (3) recreational activities. To increase reality orientation 30 minute sessions were held daily, posters were used to remind the staff of the basic concepts of reality orientation, large pictures of everyday objects (such as food,

cars, houses, or animals) were displayed on the ward, and signs pointing the way to the dining room and bathroom in large easily-read letters were set up. To increase ADL the patients were trained to perform necessary routines within the limits of their disabilities. Recreational activities were introduced, with a special emphasis on activity in the recreation hall, on the ward, and out-of-doors. The results showed an increase in activity from 14 to 76 percent (which is significant at the 1 percent level). No observer reliability data was reported for the assessments made.

Wisocki (1977) treated 24 psychogeriatric patients with a mean age of 71 years with a "sampling procedure" whereby a range of recreational activities were made available to the patients. The use of imagery of recreational activities was an alternative treatment form. For purposes of comparison there were two control groups, a discussion group and a no-contact control group. All patients participated in all four conditions. The duration of each treatment form was 3 sessions of 30 minutes each. There was an increased level of activity after both treatment conditions, with a 40 percent increase in the overt condition and a 60 percent in the covert condition. The discussion group control showed an insignificant increase of 10 percent, whereas the no-contact condition showed no change at all.

This is an unusually elegant study in terms of the design. All patients participated in all conditions and thus served as their own controls. The selection of target behaviors is also innovative. They were selected from those activities which each patient had consistently refused to perform in order to reduce the probability that the patient would perform the activity without any specific intervention.

Jenkins, Felce, Lund, and Powell (1977) treated two groups of senile dement patients in two homes for the elderly ($N_1 = 19$, $M_1 = 85$ years; $N_2 = 19$, $M_2 = 80$ years). Activity material was made available and the experimenters interacted with the residents and made specific suggestions for activity. The activity level was assessed by means of a time-sampled schedule. Reliability of inter-observer agreement was 91–100 percent. A control condition without special activity material or experimental interaction was also included in the study. The results showed that an average of 4 more residents participated in activities as compared to baseline conditions (an increase from 2.4 to 6.1 at the first home and 0.7 to 4.1 at the second home).

Götestam and Melin (1979) treated 11 patients with senile dementia by means of environmental changes. Another 10 patients on the same ward served as control patients. The mean age was 82.1 for the experimental group and 80.5 for the control group. Interventions were made for 2 hours per day during a 6-week period and the experimental design was a multiple baseline design where one factor at a time was altered. The three groups of changes made were (1) changed furniture arrangement, (2) changed mealtime routines, and (3) availability of activity material. The dependent measures (corresponding to these changes) were (1) communication, (2) table manners/eating behavior, and (3) activity level. The dependent measures were assessed with the help of a time-sampling procedure and inter-observer reliability was 96–100 percent. The results showed a significant increase for the experimental group in all three dependent variables as compared to pretreatment baseline conditions. There was also a significant difference between experimental and control groups for all three dependent variables during treatment conditions.

Peterson, Knapp, Rosen, and Pither (1977) treated a group of psychogeriatric patients with the total number of patients treated unspecified. The goal of treatment was to increase 14 specific behaviors. An ABCAC design was used and an interrater reliability of 88 percent was achieved. The independent variable was the arrangement of furniture. The mean number of participants during the observation periods was 28. Although the results showed a significant increase in talking, the other 13 behaviors remained unchanged.

The experimental studies reported above all made changes in one or more environmental variables and found consistent changes in some dependent variable, which was logically linked to the independent variable. This environmental or milieu approach has been the cause of much optimism in recent years, an attitude which is in strong contrast to the prevailing pessimism of the 20th century. Future treatment programs must include such variables in their strategies in order to increase their efficacy and to build up the self-confidence of the patients involved.

PROSTHETIC ENVIRONMENTS. Lindsley (1964) has suggested a model for behavioral prosthetics where the deficits of geriatric patients can be compensated for to some extent through the use of different kinds of prosthetics. Examples of such prosthetics might be signs and calendars for the disoriented, support bars for the physically disabled, or family items to enhance recollections in those patients who suffer from impaired memory. Today we have so much more knowledge than was the case in 1964, when Lindsley constructed his model, that it should be possible to consolidate the findings from numerous studies in order to create

a total prosthetic environment for geriatric patients.

Lawton (1970) has also presented a descriptive model for the different levels of social and personal functions of the aged. This model could be useful for matching individuals with a suitable environment to a greater extent than is seen today. Lawton suggests that the following components could increase the ability of the environment to enhance the functioning of the elderly: (1) capacity to provide basic life maintenance, (2) functional health provisions, (3) support for perceptual and cognitive behavior, (4) assistance in physical self-maintenance, (5) assistance in instrumental self-maintenance, (6) level of effectance, and (7) facilitation of social functioning.

McClannahan (1973) has also summarized the findings achieved in her programs and pointed to the possibility that the following three aspects should be included in prosthetic environments: (1) locomotion, (2) social interaction and (3) self-care skills.

## BEHAVIORAL CHANGE

*Psychodynamic Approaches.* Although it is seldom stated explicitly in psychodynamic reports, it is often regarded as desirable to effect some form of behavior change, in addition to the stated goal of increased insight. Some behavior changes have been reported in the results of a number of studies, in the form of symptom relief (Wolff, 1962, 1963, 1967, 1971; Wolk and Goldfarb, 1967) better adjustment on the ward (Wolff, 1967), better grooming behaviors (Meerloo, 1953) and discharge from the hospital (Wolff, 1962, 1971, Nevruz and Hrushka, 1969).

*Social Approaches.* The study by Volpe and Kastenbaum is not classic in its straightforward approach and its optimistic view of the potential of geriatric patients. Patients were given beer at mealtime and showed dramatically increased levels of activity, decreased incontinence, and reduced consumption of medication.

Carroll (1978) has taken the above procedure one step further and introduced a social hour (30 minutes) on weekdays where patients who so desired could receive alcohol (whiskey, gin, vodka, or wine). If soft drinks were preferred, they were readily dispensed to the patient. The alcohol was restricted to two drinks (½ oz. strong alcohol or 2 oz. of wine) per day. Socialization increased for the group which imbibed alcohol, but not for those taking soft drinks.

An experimental study of the effects of beer on the behavior of geriatric patients was performed by Black (1969). Ninety elderly patient with chronic brain syndrome participated in the study, with half receiving 11 oz. of beer per day for four weeks while the other half received fruit juice. After four weeks, the fruit juice group received beer instead. When a total of eight weeks had passed, beer was made available only during three days of the week. Thus the design may be said to be a combination of an ABA design and a multiple baseline. The patients' behaviors were observed via a special list with such items as social competence and interest, cooperation, personal neatness, physical condition, and irritability. The group which received beer from the start of the experiment showed improvement during the first four weeks as compared to the second group as well as reduced consumption of drugs. During the second four-week period, the other group (now receiving beer) made similar progress. At the end of the eight weeks, improvements in different areas ranged between 34.8 to 62.1 percent. For purposes of comparison with other programs which were designed to produce behavioral change, the study is included in Table 32–4. Minor alterations in the pattern of ward activities has been claimed to produce beneficial effects. Cosin, Mort, Post, Westrop, and Williams (1958) investigated the efficacy of social and occupational therapy which is often used with demented patients. The recipients of such therapy demonstrated several kinds of more appropriate behavior, the most important of which was the increased amount of communication between patients.

*Behavior Therapy.* Behavior therapy can be divided into two principally distinctive categories: (1) respondent or classical (Pavlovian) conditioning and (2) operant or instrumental (Skinnerian) conditioning.

Respondent conditioning occurs when two phenomena associated with each other (such as food and a bell), culminate in a specific response (such as salivation). The original unconditioned stimulus (food) which elicits the response (salivation) may thus be replaced in time by the conditioned stimulus (bell), which will elicit the same response (salivation). The principle of respondent conditioning has been used in systematic desensitization in the treatment of phobias and in assertive training for people who lack the necessary skills for social interaction. It has also been used in some aversive techniques where a noxious stimulus has been linked to various stimuli connected with maladaptive behavior such as alcoholism or obesity. However, these techniques have not been used in geriatrics.

Operant conditioning has three working components: (a) the situation or discriminative stimulus, (b) the behavior or stimulus, and (c) the consequence or reinforcer. The main principle underlying the operant paradigm is that human behavior is controlled by situational factors (i.e. we do certain things in specific situations but not in others) as well as by the consequences which follow after the performance of behaviors. If a behavior is followed by a positive consequence, then the probability of that behavior being repeated is increased. Likewise, a negative consequence lowers the probability of a behavior being repeated. In geriatrics, treatment has consisted of application of positive reinforcement (consequences) in order to increase adaptive behaviors. This is similar to the principle used for the kind of therapeutic environment designed by Ayllon and Azrin (1968) which is called token economy. The other application of operant conditioning has been the use of controlling stimuli for various situations. To increase the probability of certain responses, some stimuli or prompting procedures are added to the natural environment. This form of treatment has been used in some of the environmental programs mentioned above.

Quilitch (1974) introduced Bingo sessions among demented patients. As compared to an initial baseline period, this simple measure led to changes in behavior and increased "purposeful activity" (i.e., talking to other patients and staff, using recreational material, etc.). However, as soon as the Bingo sessions were discontinued, the purposeful activity returned to the same low level as found before the program started.

Brody and his co-workers (Brody, Kleban, Lawton, and Silverman, 1971; Brody, Kleban, Lawton, and Moss, 1974) compared two groups of elderly patients with chronic brain syndrome. An initial assessment of each patient sought to identify functional impairments over and above the results of organic impairment. The experimental group received individually tailored programs which were designed to reduce the functional disabilities. Unfortunately, the reports do not contain a detailed description of either the functional impairments or the treatment methods used, which makes it difficult to judge the results adequately. After one year of treatment, the experimental group showed some improvement, but after an additional nine months, the differences between the experimental and control groups disappeared.

Nine behavioral programs which have had behavioral change as a goal of treatment are found in the literature and are listed in Table 32–4. Since the treatment approaches are problem-oriented in character, it is possible to evaluate the results with a fair degree of confidence.

In an uncontrolled case report Flannery (1974) treated a patient with geriatric grief with

**Table 32–4** Experimental studies of treatment with the goal of behavior change.

| STUDY | PROBLEM AND SETTING | NO. OF PATIENTS | AGE | TREATMENT | | | RESULT | DESIGN AND ASSESSMENT |
|---|---|---|---|---|---|---|---|---|
| | | | | TECHNIQUE | DURATION | GOAL | | |
| Grosicki, 1968 | Psychoger: incontin. | 10 | 63–85 | 1. Social reinforcement | 14 w | Continence Adjustment | Controls increased continence (5% level) C > E Adjustment (communication, social, mood) E > C | $r_{xy}$ = .97–.91 Exp/Control groups |
| | Controls | 10 | | 2. Material reinforcement | 14 w | same | Controls incr cont (1% level) C > E | $r_{xy}$ = .96–.97 |
| Libb & Clements, 1969 | Psychoger: Chr br sy | 4 | 65–75 | Material rf (token economy) | 14 sessions, 5 min/sess | Increased activity (exercise) | Exercise increase (33.0, 1.95, 1.07 & 0.81 times) of baseline | AB |
| Black, 1969 | Geriatric Chr br sy | 90 (?) | ? | Beer (11 oz/d) | 8 w | General improvem. | Performance increased, less drugs | Multiple baseline (ABA) |
| | Controls | | | Fruit juice | | | no change | |
| Mueller & Atlas, 1972 | Geriatric ward (?) | 5 | 50–82 M=70 | Material rf in groups (token economy) | 11 sess | Interaction | Interaction responses incr from 0.85 to 5.88 | AB |
| MacDonald & Butler, 1974 | Nursing home | 2 | 1) 92, M 2) 85, F | Social rf | 1) 40 days 2) 35 days | Walking | Walking (in 40 feet): 0–96.3– 0–91.1 % | ABAB |
| Hoyer et al., 1974 | Psychoger: Schiz | 1) 4 (M) | over 60 | Material rf in groups (group contingent) (token economy) | 11 sessions, 45–55min/s, 5 weeks | Verbal interaction | No. of words per session: 4.75–9.75– 4.00 | ABA |
| | | 2) 4 (M) | over 60 | Material rf (direct) | 24 sessions, 12 weeks | –"– | Consistently following exp phases | ABAB $r_{xy}$ = .86–.93 |
| Pollock & Liberman, 1974 | Psychoger: Chr br sy | 6 (M) | 61–79 | Social & material rf | 5 w | Continence | No change | ABC |
| Sachs, 1975 | | 1) 1 (F) | 88 | 1) Social & material rf (te) | 1) 12 sess. | 1) walking & no-isolation | 1) 3.2–11.3 | AB |
| | | 2) 1 (F) | 64 | 2) Social & material rf (token economy) | 2) 20 sess. | 2) Walking | 2) 4.3–7.3 | AB |
| | | 3) 3 (2M, 1F) | 76, 71, 58 | 3) –"– | 3) 25 sess. | 3) Oral hygiene | 3) no eff | AB |
| | | 4) 1 (M) | 91 | 4) Soc. rf | 4) 70 sess. | 4) Social interaction | 4) Good exp control | ABAB |
| Wisocki et al., 1976 | Psychotics | 3 | 1) 85 2) 44 3) 75 | Recreational stimuli Soc. reinf. | 15 min × 3, daily, 11 mo | 1) eye contact 2) –"–, interaction, verbal beh. 3) verbal beh., no. words | Increases, 4 mo f-u, even better | ABCDED |
| Götestam, 1979 | Psychoger. Senile dementia | 5 | 70–89 M=81.4 | Reality orientation training | 1 hr/day, 23 days | Increased reality orientation (time, place, person) | Significant short effect | Multiple baseline design |

the help of a behavior contract (see Götestam and Bates, 1979) where obligations and rights of both the therapist and patient were specified. For this particular case of grief, behavior contracting seemed to provide an effective means of treatment.

Grosicki (1968) reported treating 10 patients with severe incontinence. These patients were between the ages of 63 and 85 and were compared with 10 patients of similar age. In the first stage of treatment, which lasted for 14 weeks, appropriate behavior (absence of soiling) was socially reinforced. A staff member checked each patient every hour. If the patient was soiled, the observer said nothing. If the patient was dry, the staff member spent 3 minutes with the patient, engaging in conversation if the patient so desired. During the second stage of treatment, which also lasted for 14 weeks, money was introduced as material reinforcement for appropriate behavior. Each time the patient used the commode he received a token and each time he was found soiled he had to pay one token. Observations had a high inter-rater reliability ($r_{xy} = 0.97 - 0.91$). The results were somewhat unexpected in that the control group increased its continence as compared to the experimental group during both stages of the intervention. (The results are significantly different at the 5 percent level for stage one and at the 1 percent level for stage two). The adjustment of the patients in the experimental group in terms of communication, social functioning, and mood increased during the first stage (social reinforcement) but showed no improvement in the second stage (material reinforcement).

Libb and Clements (1969) treated 4 patients between the ages of 65 and 75 years, with chronic brain syndrome, by means of material reinforcement in a token economy system. In a token economy, certain adaptive behaviors can be performed by the individual to earn tokens (money, counters, coupons, or points) which can be exchanged for certain reinforcers such as beverages, snacks, or privileges. The program described by Libb and Clements included 14 sessions of 5 minute duration where the goal was increased participation in an exercise situation. Three of the patients achieved this goal while the program was in operation as compared to the baseline condition in this AB design. The increases were 320 percent, 95 percent, and 7 percent respectively.

Mueller and Atlas (1972) treated five patients ranging in age from 50–82 years of age (mean = 70) with material reinforcers in a group within the structure of a token economy. The goal of treatment was to increase the interaction among patients as well as between patients and staff. After four baseline sessions, cigarettes and sweets were given immediately after interpersonal interaction and then tokens were gradually introduced as intermediate reinforcers. In this AB design the results showed an increase of interaction responses from 0.85 to 5.88 expressed in mean number of responses per session and patient.

MacDonald and Butler (1974) worked with two patients in a nursing home, age 92 and 85. In order to increase walking behavior in these wheelchair patients, social reinforcement was delivered for appropriate behavior for 40 and 35 days respectively. The experiment was conducted in an ABAB design. At the conclusion of the study the distance walked was a maximum of 40 feet. During each phase of the experiment, the patient's mean percentage of that distance was $0 - 96.3 - 0 - 91.1$ percent respectively.

Hoyer, Kafer, Simpson, and Hoyer (1974) treated four chronic schizophrenic patients on a geriatric ward where all patients were over the age of 60. Increased verbal interaction was the goal of this study. In the first stage, (11 sessions of 45–55 minutes spread over 5 weeks) token reinforcers were delivered on a group contingency basis. An ABA design was used and the results showed that the number of words per session were 4.75, 9.75 and 4.00 respectively. In the second stage, the patients received material reinforcement directly for verbal interaction in 24 sessions over the course of 12 weeks. This stage was conducted in an ABAB design. The results clearly showed experimental control in that verbal interaction was consistently higher during B phases (material reinforcement) than A phases (baseline).

Pollock and Liberman (1974) attempted to reduce incontinence in six male psychogeriatric patients, age 61–79. They introduced social and material reinforcement in an ABC design. However, no reduction of incontinence occurred after the interventions. The absence of positive results is discussed at great length in the study, the primary flaw being thought to lie in the patients' severe cerebral dysfunctions and memory impairment. These patients had difficulty in finding the bathroom, so it is not surprising that reinforcement failed to produce new behavior. Another factor of importance is the strategy of checking the patient at specific points in time rather than trying to pinpoint the time of the "accident." An electronic device which would alert the staff to the onset of urination could have produced better results, as it did in working with retarded individuals (Azrin and Foxx, 1971).

Sachs (1975) treated six patients with a variety of problems by social reinforcement and the implementation of a token economy. The treatment goals included walking behavior, social interaction, elimination of withdrawal behavior and isolation and improvement of oral hygiene. With the exception of oral hygiene, all target behaviors were under experimental control in the AB or ABAB designs used, that is, the dependent variables followed changes in the independent variables with acceptable consistentcy.

Wisocki, Mosher, and Korfhage (1976) treated three psychotics (ages 85, 44, and 75) for 11 months during three daily 15 minute sessions. The treatment goal was to increase eye contact, interaction, and verbal behavior. The technique used was the introduction of recreational stimuli. In one experimental condition target behaviors were reinforced both socially and materially by certain games and activities. The author used an ABCDED design, where experimental conditions produced substantial increases in target behaviors as compared to baseline conditions. The most effective reinforcers were a combination of activity and social reinforcers (phase D). At the follow-up, which was performed four months after the termination of treatment, the patients' behaviors had continued to improve, an indication that they were being reinforced in the natural environment.

Folsom (Taulbee and Folsom, 1966; Folsom, 1968) reported on the reality orientation of elderly mental patients while Gubrium and Ksander (1975) have presented a development of the concepts used in studying this topic. None of the reports, however, include any data on reality orientation training or the results obtained. Götestam (1979) treated five senile demented patients with the purpose of increasing reality orientation in regards to time, place, and person. The patients were between 70–89 years of age with a mean of 81.4. After baseline registrations, the patients were trained in a special room designed to enhance time orientation by means of a large wall clock and prominently displayed calendars (as described earlier by Loew and Silverstone, 1971). This kind of material was also placed out on the ward. During the third phase, time orientation training continued but in addition patients were exposed to training in person orientation. The patients were asked to say their own names, and to roll the ball to another patient, also pronouncing that patient's name. In the fourth phase, room orientation was added to the two other kinds of training. Maps of the town, county, and country were placed on the walls, as well as the name of the hospital, the ward, etc. Symbols were also placed at appropriate places around the ward to improve ward orientation. Assessment was made by asking the patients specific questions about time, persons, and room, both in the treatment session (within 5 minutes after the session), and on the ward outside that situation (15–30 minutes after the session). The results clearly showed an improved orientation as to time and room while the

patient was in the training situation, but there was no effect outside this situation. These results were thought to be a result of the impaired learning capacity of these patients. In specific situations, however, some functions were improved.

Brook, Gegun, and Mather (1975) applied reality orientation therapy to an experimental group for 16 weeks. Therapists actively sought to engage the patients in various tasks using materials found in the room. A control group had a similar amount of exposure to the experimental room and its materials, but the therapist remained passive. Intellectual and social functioning improved during the first two to four weeks in both groups but only the experimental group continued to show improvement. Barnes (1974) was unable to find any improvement after reality orientation therapy. These reports provide ample evidence of the need for a prosthetic environment for geriatric patients, although the work by Brook *et al.* (1975) indicates that stimulation from the physical environment is insufficient in itself. It is also important to provide the patients with psychological stimulation in order to achieve good results.

The experimental studies reported above have sound experimental designs and have demonstrated that it is possible to treat problems in geriatric psychiatry with the help of behavior methods. Incontinence and reality orientation have not yet been effectively treated however. It is possible that the addition of appropriate electronic equipment to the treatment format could produce better results. Reality orientation can be increased, although not reinstated totally, by designing more appropriate living environments for the patients.

SPECIAL THERAPY APPROACHES

*Remotivation Therapy.* A remotivation model has been described by Bowers, Anderson, Blomeier, and Pelz (1967). They advocate resocialization and facilitation of activities within the institution for the patient. They treated three groups with group remotivation therapy and measured individual behaviors and social functioning before as well as after six months of treatment. The only results reported were that there was significant improvements in all six groups in individual behavior in the group and in social functioning.

Birkett and Boltuch (1973) also reported a study of remotivation therapy as compared to conventional group therapy with 39 geriatric patients. Treatment consisted of 12 weekly sessions of one hour's duration. The results indicated improvement in both groups but no statistical difference between the groups.

Another approach to this issue is presented

by Peth (1974). He constructed eight "myths of late life" (i.e. "everyone is old except me" "old age is a disease," "to be old is to be asexual") which he based on the 11 "myths" described by Ellis (1962) as prevailing in contemporary Western society. Peth used these "myths of late life" in a form of rational-emotive therapy, or a kind of cognitive restructuring, in order to confront the patients with them and to dispel the myths. No outcome data are reported.

*Hypnosis.* Since the days of Freud, hypnosis has been extensively used in psychotherapy. Freud used it to facilitate regression, whereas in modern therapy it has been used as a relaxation technique, as a medium to achieve cognitive restructuring, and as a treatment *per se.* Hypnosis has been used in psychodynamic therapy (to achieve regression and improve insight) and in behavior therapy (to increase relaxation in systematic desensitization and in cognitive restructuring therapy). Clinically it has been of some use in psychogeriatrics although there were no reports on its use found in the literature search.

## OTHER FORMS OF TREATMENT

*Pharmacotherapy.* In general psychiatry drugs have been extensively used. This is true both for those forms of mental illness where specific pharmacologic treatment exists and for other forms where an unspecific remedy can be achieved through the use of drugs. For a comprehensive outline of pharmacological treatment, the reader is referred to Chapter 31 of this book (Hicks, *et al.,* 1980). The main groups of psychopharmacological drugs may be divided into the following categories: (1) minor tranquilizers, (2) major tranquilizers, (3) antidepressants, and (4) others.

*Occupational Therapy.* The use of occupational therapy should always be considered in the treatment of elderly people. When they have retired, elderly people often risk total inactivity, which is not only detrimental in itself but also leads to decreased mobility, poor health, and possibly an early death. The type of occupational therapy offered to these patients should be designed to increase their self-confidence rather than humiliation through menial, tedious tasks. However, many older people do not want to be active in an ordinary work situation. In such cases, individually tailored activity programs are the best solutions. Recreational therapy might be a better designation than occupational therapy. The ultimate goal of the therapy should be to resocialize the patient. Simple

domestic tasks and craft work, together with group activities, may serve this goal.

*Physiotherapy.* Some patients need physiotherapy to be able to move joints and extremities. Others simply need some form of exercise to maintain good physical condition. It is important that patients have access to such facilities near the hospital or home, or preferably, within the institution.

## CONCLUSIONS AND FUTURE DIRECTIONS

### CONCLUSIONS OF RECENT RESEARCH

*Experimental Studies.* Going through the experimental studies reported in the preceding section, the following comments seem appropriate:

INSIGHT THERAPY. The seven experimental studies (see Table 32–2) which were reported in the section above suffer from relatively poor designs. They have all used control groups for comparison of treatment effects, but these groups are described perfunctorily. The assessments of treatment effectiveness are based solely on clinical judgments, with the exception of two studies (Godbole and Verinis, 1974; Nevruz and Hrushka, 1969), where different types of ratings were performed. Measures of reliability were made in only one study (Wolk and Goldfarb, 1967). Discharge from the hospital was often used as the ultimate measure of recovery, but it can not be regarded as solely an effect criterion, since it relys mainly on the decision of the doctor. (In all studies this is likely to be the same person as administered the therapy.) No statistical evaluations of outcome were reported, but this is laudable with a thought to the quality of the assessments made. Thus no real conclusions are possible from these studies.

SUPPORTIVE THERAPY. Of the 10 experimental studies reported (Table 32–3) one compared an experimental group with a control group, eight used reversal designs (where comparisons were made between the different conditions which each patient was exposed to), and one used a combination of a multiple baseline design and a conventional group design (with both experimental and control groups). All assessments are described and well-defined, and in six of the studies satisfactory reliability measures are reported. The conclusion which can be drawn from these experiments is that environmental variables (such as activity material, announcements, or furniture arrangements) affect or control the patients' attendance, activity or communication. This conclusion can be said to rest on firm scientific evidence.

BEHAVIOR CHANGE. Among the 10 studies reported in Table 32–4 there were nine behavioral and one social study. One used a conventional design (with experimental group and control group) seven used reversal designs, and two used multiple baseline designs. Although the assessments are adequately described and defined, only two studies report satisfactory reliability co-efficients. The conclusions, therefore, must be regarded as tentative. They do, however, indicate that positive reinforcement (social or material, with or without a token economy framework) improves activity, walking, social and verbal interactions, and eye contact.

*What We Know Today.* From the body of research examined here we know that the following factors are of importance for the well-being of the elderly who suffer from psychiatric disorders: (1) physical environment, (2) psychological environment, and (3) reminiscent memories. On the contrary, the following activities do not seem to have any great or lasting importance: (4) learning new material and (5) training new skills.

The physical environment should be designed to facilitate normal functioning for people with deficits in orientation, communication, and walking, to name but a few examples. The psychological environment must include stimulation from the staff as well as other individuals in the environment. Such supportive surroundings have been called a prosthetic environment. Such an environment has been shown to maintain and even decelerate the process of deterioration. As soon as such environmental stimuli are removed, deterioration increases and the total level of functioning decreases rapidly.

Furthermore, several studies have reported the introduction of such activities as dancing, playing games, or religious services. These activities have been intended to remind the elderly of earlier experiences and thus to reactivate skills now absent. Many patients have showed marked improvement of functioning during regular attendance of such activities, however, without transfer to other settings. The use of such reminiscences could also improve the total functioning of senile demented patients and could lead to better contacts with relatives and friends under those conditions.

No efforts at teaching senile demented patients to use new materials or to engage in new activities has led to permanent improvement. This finding is hardly surprising considering the impaired memory functions of this category of patients.

*Suggestions for Clinical Work.* In working with the psychogeriatric population, the following points should be kept in mind: (1) tender, loving care (TLC), (2) stimulating environment, (3) problem-oriented therapy, and (4) ambulatory treatment.

All authors in the field have stressed the importance of the therapist's attitude and relation to the patient. Good care must include tenderness and love and these attributes are the unspecified treatment variables which every hospitalized or institutionalized individual should have the privilege to receive, equally as well as all other individuals. These qualities must therefore be regarded as an integral part of an institutional setting.

The stimulating environment mentioned above includes an interested and interesting, well-trained staff as well as the entire physical environment. The specialist would be well advised to spend the larger portion of his or her time in training the staff rather than in direct contact with the patient. This rule, of course, should be flexibly applied as to permit a variety of contacts.

If there are specific problems such as a low level of communication, absence of walking without organic cause, or neurotic and psychotic problems, then therapy should be directed to solving just those problems. Psychopharmacological drugs have been shown to be useful with some neurotic and psychotic disorders, but psychological interventions may be equally as successful in alleviating other problems. When psychological interventions are made it is essential that close contact be maintained with both staff and patient not only in treatment planning and execution, but also in maintenance of changes achieved.

One environment which can generally be relied on to be supporting and prosthetic is the patient's own home environment. Many demented patients show the most rapid deterioration when they are moved from their well-known milieu. Keeping the patient in his own familiar environment as long as possible will pay off not only for the community in terms of economic terms but also for the individual and the relatives involved in terms of emotional gains. Support in this environment is therefore an important goal. More ambulatory treatment facilities, with day care centers, outpatient units, home therapists and other help is a sound investment for the community, especially with a thought to the ever-increasing numbers of elderly patients and the increasing burden on present care facilities.

IMPLICATIONS FOR FUTURE RESEARCH

Medically oriented treatment and research have taken precedence over other forms of treatment during the major portion of this century. While this has led to some improvement for certain categories of patients, the chronic brain syndrome has been regarded as chronic and incurable. This pessimistic view of the syndrome has led to a dismal view for both staff and relatives. During the last 5-10 years, however, several psychologically oriented approaches have evolved, which in turn has given rise to a more positive and optimistic view. This revised estimation of the outlook for elderly patients may very well lead to an improvement in the entire field of geriatrics.

The main indications for future research must include a reduction of the economic burden as well as increased efficiency in the treatment given. One good investment might be to put research facilities and funding in the hands of local government in order to allow them to develop the components of a prosthetic environment of the kind first proposed by Lindsley (1964).

Several theoretical questions may have a profound effect on the field if answered in a convincing fashion. These questions deal with learning, memory and memory dysfunction. Up until now, learning has not been shown to be effective with the elderly in the long run. This has also been the case with training procedures. The exact nature of this learning disability is a scientific knot that needs untying.

Exploring the possibilities of memory reminiscences (such as singing, dancing, playing games) where motor memories seem to be retained longer than other types of memories and where these motor memories seem to be more easily recalled by specific eliciting stimuli, can yield fruitful fields for research and treatment.

Until the most recent years, research has had the character of "hit and run." Far too many researchers have been content to touch on a problem superficially and to leave the field. One reason for such tactics has been that a great deal of research has been conducted with the help of students. What is needed now is long-term research projects where the answer to one question leads to the investigation of several new questions.

## SUMMARY AND CONCLUSIONS

The chapter opens with a brief survey of the definitions used in gerontology as well as a short historical perspective of the field, followed by a discussion of the roles which exist in the therapeutic context. The patient role may be an especially difficult one to fill for the elderly, especially in regards to motivation and individual limitations. The role of the therapist requires some special qualities in this particular therapeutic context, notably experience in dealing with the elderly and consideration

of one's own fear of aging. The qualities of warmth, empathy and genuineness are equally as important in this context as in any form of therapy. The use of paraprofessionals offers several advantages and it is recommended that the main body of treatment be built around them.

Both patient and therapist should have realistic expectations concerning the potential effects of treatment, rather than indulging in false optimism or wishful thinking. Therapy with the elderly can be both rewarding and beneficial, however, and the bleak pessimism which has prevailed in the past has been detrimental to the progress of treatment and research. Also included is a short presentation of the different types of disorders or diagnoses most commonly found among the elderly.

The main section of the chapter deals with the nature of treatment of the elderly. The parameters of treatment, including the setting of treatment goals, long-term versus short-term therapy, ambulatory versus institutional care, and individual, group or family therapy, are discussed initially. Using an extensive review of the literature as a point of departure, a brief review of psychoanalytic and psychodynamic therapies is presented, as well as a number of individual and group approaches. The second topic of the section is supportive therapy, which is described through the presentation of several studies as well as milieu therapy. The more general category of supportive environments, which usually entails a number of behavioral techniques, is illustrated by several well-designed experimental studies. These studies indicate that the environment is of great importance for the elderly's situation, especially within the institutional setting. The third topic in this section examines treatments designed to produce behavioral change, primarily a number of studies using behavior therapy with good experimental designs. These studies show surprisingly positive changes in behavior.

The chapter closes with a number of suggestions that clinical work with the elderly be characterized by: tender, loving care, a stimulating environment (both physically and psychologically), problem-oriented therapy and ambulant treatment (in day care centers, outpatient units, etc). Research efforts in the future should be directed towards long-term projects which seek to reduce the costs while increasing the efficacy of geriatric care. The theoretical questions dealing with learning, memory, and memory dysfunctions in the elderly need to be studied in order to develop more effective treatment methods. Through effective and continuous research, the answers to these questions can help us build treatment programs which can greatly improve the quality of life for large numbers of the elderly.

# REFERENCES

ABRAHAM, K. 1949. The applicability of psycho-analytic treatment to patients at an advanced age. *Selected Papers of Psycho-Analysis.* London: Hogarth Press, 312–317.

ALEXANDER, F. G. 1944. The indication for psychoanalytic therapy. *Bulletin of the New York Academy of Medicine, 20,* 319–334.

ARONSON, M. J. 1958. Psychotherapy in a home for the aged. *Archives of Neurology and Psychiatry, 79,* 671–674.

AYLLON, T., AND AZRIN, N. H. 1968. *The Token Economy.* Englewood Cliffs, N.J.: Prentice-Hall.

AZRIN, N. H., AND FOXX, R. 1971. A rapid method of toilet training the institutionalized mentally retarded. *Journal of Applied Behavior Analysis, 4,* 89–99.

BARNES, J. A. 1974. Effects of reality orientation classroom on memory loss, confusion and disorientation in geriatric patients. *Gerontologist, 14,* 138–142.

BIRKETT, D. R., AND BOLTUCH, B. 1973. Remotivation therapy. *Journal of the American Geriatrics Society, 21,* 368–371.

BLACK, A. L. 1969. Altering behavior of geriatric patients with beer. *Northwest Medicine, 68,* 453–456.

BOWER, H. M. 1967. Sensory stimulation and the treatment of senile dementia. *Medical Journal of Australia, 1,* 1113–1119.

BOWERS, M. B., ANDERSON, G. K., BLOMEIER, E. C., AND PELZ, K. 1967. Brain syndrome and behavior in geriatric remotivation groups. *Journal of Gerontology, 22,* 348–352.

BRODY, E. M., KLEBAN, M. H., LAWTON, M. P., AND MOSS, M. 1974. Longitudinal look at excess disabilities in the mentally impaired aged. *Journal of Gerontology, 29,* 79–84.

BRODY, E. M., KLEBAN, M. H., LAWTON, M. P., AND SILVERMAN, H. A. 1971. Excess disabilities of mentally impaired aged: Impact of individualized treatment. *Gerontologist, 11,* 124–132.

BROOK, P., GEGUN, G., AND MATHER, M. 1975. Reality orientation, a therapy for psychogeriatric patients. A controlled study. *British Journal of Psychiatry, 127,* 42–45.

BUTLER, R. N. 1960. Intensive psychotherapy for the hospitalized aged. *Geriatrics, 15,* 644–653.

BUTLER, R. N. 1963. The life review: An interpretation of reminiscence in the aged. *Psychiatry, 119,* 721–728.

BUTLER, R. N. 1975. *Why Survive? Being Old in America.* New York: Harper & Row.

BUTLER, R. N., AND LEWIS, M. I. 1973. *Aging and Mental Health: Positive Psychosocial Approaches.* St. Louis: C. V. Mosby.

CAMERON, D. E. 1941. Studies in senile nocturnal delirium. *Psychiatric Quarterly, 15,* 47–53.

CARROLL, P. J. 1978. The social hour for geropsychiatric patients. *Journal of the American Geriatrics Society, 26,* 32–35.

COSIN, L. Z., MORT, M., POST, F., WESTROP, C., AND WILLIAMS, M. 1958. Experimental treatment of persistent senile confusion. *International Journal of Social Psychiatry, 4,* 24–42.

DA SILVA, G. 1966. Considerations sur le viellissement et la psychothérapie. *Laval Médical, 37,* 199–207.

DODGEN, J. C., AND ARTHUR, R. J. 1967. Psychotherapy of a sexagenarian. *Diseases of the Nervous System, 28,* 680–682.

ELLIS, A. 1962. *Reason and Emotion in Psychotherapy.* New York: Lyle Stuart.

FLANNERY, R. B. 1974. Behavior modification of geriatric grief: A transactional perspective. *International Journal of Aging and Human Development, 5,* 197–203.

FOLSOM, J. C. 1968. Reality orientation for the elderly mental patient. *Journal of Geriatric Psychiatry, 1,* 291–307.

FREUD, S. 1924. On psychotherapy. *Collected Papers, Vol. 1,* London: Hogarth Press.

GAJDUSEK, D. C. 1973. Kuru and Creutzfeldt-Jakob disease. Experimental models of noninflammatory degenerative slow virus disease of the central nervous system. *Annals of Clinical Research, 5(5),* 254–261.

GELFAND, D. M., GELFAND, S., AND DOBSON, W. R. 1967. Unprogrammed reinforcement of patients' behavior in a mental hospital. *Behaviour Research and Therapy, 5,* 201–207.

GODBOLE, A., AND VERINIS, J. S. 1974. Brief psychotherapy in the treatment of emotional disorders in physically ill geriatric patients. *Gerontologist, 14,* 143–148.

GOLDFARB, A. I. 1953. The orientation of staff in a home for the aged. *Mental Hygiene, 37,* 76–83.

GOLDFARB, A. I. 1953. Recommendations for psychiatric care in a home for the aged. *Journal of Gerontology, 8,* 343–347.

GOLDFARB, A. I., AND TURNER, H. 1953. Psychotherapy of aged persons. *American Journal of Psychiatry, 109,* 116–121.

GOLDSTEIN, A. P. 1973. *Structured Learning Therapy.* New York: Academic Press.

GÖTESTAM, K. G. 1979. Training in reality orientation of patients with senile dementia. *In*, L. Levi (ed.), *Society, Stress and Disease: Aging and Old Age*. London: Oxford University Press.

GÖTESTAM, K. G. AND BATES, S. 1979. Contingency contracting—principles and practice. *Behavioural Analysis and Modification, 3*, 126–134.

GÖTESTAM, K. G., AND MELIN, L. 1979. Improving well-being for patients with senile dementia by minor changes in the ward environment. *In*, L. Levi (ed.), *Society Stress and Disease: Aging and Old Age*. London: Oxford University Press.

GROSICKI, J. P. 1968. Effect of operant conditioning on modification of incontinence in neuropsychiatric geriatric patients. *Nursing Research, 17*, 304–311.

GROTJAHN, M. 1951. Some analytic observations about the process of growing old. *Psychoanalysis and Social Sciences, 3*, 301–312.

GUBRIUM, J. F., AND KSANDER, M. 1975. On multiple realities and reality orientation. *Gerontologist, 15*, 142–145.

HADER, M. 1964. Psychotherapy for certain psychotic states in geriatric patients. *Journal of the American Geriatric Society, 12*, 607–617.

HIATT, H. 1972. Dynamic psychotherapy of the aged. *Current Psychiatric Therapies, 12*, 224–229.

HICKS, R., FUNKENSTEIN, H. H., DYSKEN, M. W., AND DAVIS. 1980. J. M. Geriatric Psycho-pharmacology, *In*, J. E. Birren and R. B. Sloane (eds.), *Handbook of Mental Health and Aging*, pp. 745–774. Englewood Cliffs, N.J.: Prentice-Hall.

HOON, P. W., AND LINDSLEY, O. R. 1974. A comparison of behavior and traditional therapy publication activity. *American Psychologist, 29*, 694–697.

HOYER, W. J., KAFER, R. A., SIMPSON, S. C., AND HOYER, F. W. 1974. Reinstatement of verbal behavior in elderly mental patients using operant procedures. *Gerontologist, 14*, 149–152.

JENKINS, J., FELCE, D., LUND, B., AND POWELL, L. 1977. Increasing engagement in activity of residents in old people's homes by providing recreational materials. *Behaviour Research and Therapy, 15*, 429–434.

JONES, M. 1953. *The Therapeutic Community*. New York: Basic Books.

JONES, M. C. 1924. The elimination of children's fears. *Journal of Experimental Psychology, 43*, 382–390.

KAHANA, R. J. 1967. Medical management, psychotherapy, and aging. *Journal of Geriatric Psychiatry, 1*, 78–89.

KANFER, F. H. 1979. Self-management: Strategies and tactics. *In*, A. P. Goldstein and F. H. Kanfer (eds.), *Maximizing Treatment Gains*, pp. 185–224. New York: Academic Press.

KATZ, S., DOWNS, T. D., CASH, H. R., AND GROTZ, R. C. 1970. Progress in development of the Index of ADL. *Gerontologist, 10*, 20–30.

KELMAN, H. R. 1962. An experiment in the rehabilitation of nursing home patients. *Public Health Reports, 77*, 356–366.

KELMAN, H. R., AND MULLER, J. N. 1962. Rehabilitation of nursing home residents. *Geriatrics, 17*, 402–411.

KEPINSKI, A. 1971. Psychotherapy in geriatrics. *Przeglad Lekarzka, 27*, 193–196.

LACHMAN, S. J. 1972. *Psychosomatic Disorders: A Behavioristic Interpretation*. New York: John Wiley.

LAIR, C., SMITH, J. D., AND DEATON, A. N. 1961. Combined group recreation and psychotherapy for hospitalized geriatric patients. *Geriatrics, 16*, 598–603.

LAWTON, M. P. 1968. Social rehabilitation of the aged: some neglected aspects. *Journal of the American Geriatric Society, 16*, 1346–1363.

LAWTON, M. P. 1970. Assessment, integration, and environments for older people. *Gerontologist, 10*, 38–46.

LEITENBERG, H. (ed.), 1976. *Handbook of Behavior Modification and Behavior Therapy*. Englewood Cliffs, N.J.: Prentice-Hall.

LEWIS, M. I., AND BUTLER, R. N. 1974. Life review therapy. *Geriatrics, 29*, 165–173.

LIBB, J. W., AND CLEMENTS, C. B. 1969. Token reinforcement in an exercise program for hospitalized geriatric patients. *Perceptual and Motor Skills, 28*, 957–958.

LINDEN, M. E. 1953. Group psychotherapy with institutionalized senile women. *International Journal of Group Psychotherapy, 3*, 150.

LINDSLEY, O. R. 1964. Geriatric behavioral prosthetics. *In*, R. Kastenbaum (ed.), *New Thoughts on Old Age*, pp. 41–60. New York: Springer.

LOEW, C. A., AND SILVERSTONE, B. M. 1971. A program of intensified stimulation and response facilitation for the senile aged. *Gerontologist, 11*, 341–347.

MacDONALD, M. L., AND BUTLER, A. K. 1974. Reversal of helplessness: Producing walking behavior in nursing home wheelchair residents using behavior modification procedures. *Journal of Gerontology, 29*, 97–101.

MANASTER, A. 1967. The family group therapy program at Park View Home for the aged. *Journal of the American Geriatrics Society, 15*, 302–306.

MARTIN, L. J. 1944. *A Handbook for Old Age Counselors*. San Francisco: Geertz Printing Co.

MARTIN, L. J., AND deGRUNCHY, C. 1930. *Salvaging Old Age*. New York: Macmillan.

MARTIN, L. J., AND deGRUNCHY, C. 1933. *Sweeping the Cobwebs*. New York: Macmillan.

McCLANNAHAN, L. E. 1973. Therapeutic and prosthetic living environments for nursing home residents. *Gerontologist, 13*, 424–429.

McCLANNAHAN, L. E., AND RISLEY, T. R. 1973. A store

for nursing home residents. *Nursing Homes, 22,* 10–11.

McClannahan, L. E., and Risley, T. R. 1974. Design of living environments for nursing home residents: Recruiting attendance at activities. *Gerontologist, 14,* 236–240.

McClannahan, L. E., and Risley, T. R. 1975a. Activities and materials for severely disabled geriatric patients. *Nursing Homes, 23,* 1–4.

McClannahan, L. E., and Risley, T. R. 1975b. Design of living environments for nursing-home residents; Increasing participation in recreation activities. *Journal of Applied Behavior Analysis, 8,* 261–268.

McClannahan, L. E., and Risley, T. R. 1979. Design of living environments for nursing home residents: Additional strategies for increasing attendance and participation in group activities. *Journal of Applied Behavior Analysis.* In press.

Meerloo, J. A. M. 1953. Contribution of psychoanalysis to the problem of the aged. *In,* M. Heiman (ed.), *Psychoanalysis and Social Work,* pp. 321–337. New York: International Universities Press.

Meerloo, J. A. M. 1955. Transference and resistance in geriatric psychotherapy. *Psychoanalytic Review, 42,* 72–82.

Meerloo, J. A. M. 1961. Geriatric psychotherapy. *Acta Psychotherapeutica, 9,* 169–182.

Mueller, D. J., and Atlas, L. 1972. Resocialization of regressed elderly residents: A behavioral management approach. *Journal of Gerontology, 27,* 390–392.

Nevruz, N., and Hrushka, M. 1969. The influence of unstructured and structured group psychotherapy with geriatric patients on their decision to leave the hospital. *International Journal of Group Psychotherapy, 19,* 72–79.

Oberleder, M. 1966. Psychotherapy with the aging: An art of the possible. *Psychotherapy: Theory, Research & Practice, 3,* 139–143.

Öhman, A. 1976. Towards experimental models of "Mental Disease." *Faculty of Social Sciences at Uppsala University,* pp. 119–145. Uppsala: Almqvist & Wiksell.

Pavlov, I. P. 1955. *Selected Works.* (Transl. S. Belsky; Ed. J. Gibbons). Moscow: Foreign Languages Publishing House.

Peck, A. 1966. Psychotherapy of the aged. *Journal of the American Geriatrics Society, 14,* 748–753.

Peterson, R. F., Knapp, T. J., Rosen, J. C., and Pither, B. F. 1977. The effects of furniture arrangement on the behavior of geriatric patients. *Behavior Therapy, 8,* 464–467.

Peth, P. R. 1974. Rational-Emotive Therapy and the older adult. *Journal of Contemporary Psychotherapy, 6,* 179–184.

Petrilowitsch, N. 1962. Psychotherapie in höherem Lebensalter. *Zeitschrift für Psychotherapie und Medizinsche Psychologie, 14,* 14–29.

Pfeiffer, E. 1971. Psychotherapy with elderly patients. *Postgraduate Medicine, 50,* 254–258.

Pfeiffer, E. 1973. Interacting with older patients. *In,* E. W. Busse and E. Pfeiffer (eds.), *Mental Illness in Later Life,* pp. 5–17. Washington, DC: American Psychiatric Association.

Pfeiffer, E. 1976. Psychotherapy with elderly patients. *In,* L. Bellak and T. B. Karasu (eds.), *Geriatric Psychiatry,* pp. 191–205. New York: Grune & Stratton.

Pierce, C. H. 1975. Recreation for the elderly: Activity participation at a senior citizen center. *Gerontolgist, 15,* 202–205.

Pollock, D. D., and Liberman, R. P. 1974. Behavior therapy of incontinence in demented in-patients. *Gerontologist, 14,* 488–491.

Poppe, W. 1967. Die Möglichkeit einer Psychotherapie bei psychischen Alterskrankheiten. *Zeitschrift für Arzliche Fortbildung, 61,* 688–690.

Post, F. 1965. *The Clinical Psychiatry of Late Life.* Oxford: Pergamon Press.

Quilitch, H. R. 1974. Purposeful activity increased in a geriatric ward through programmed recreation. *Journal of the American Geriatrics Society, 22,* 226–229.

Rathbone-McCuan, E., and Levenson, J. 1975. Impact of socialization therapy in a geriatric day-care setting. *Gerontologist, 15,* 338–342.

Rechtschaffen, A. 1959. Psychotherapy with geriatric patients: A review of the literature. *Journal of Gerontology, 14,* 73–84.

Sachs, D. A. 1975. Behavioral techniques in a residential nursing home facility. *Journal of Behavior Therapy & Experimental Psychiatry, 6,* 123–127.

Safirstein, S. L. 1972. Psychotherapy for geriatric patients. *New York State Journal of Medicine, 72,* 2743–2748.

Salter, C. d. L., and Salter, C. A. 1975. Effects of an individualized activity program on elderly patients. *Gerontologist, 15,* 404–406.

Saul, S. R., and Saul, S. 1974. Group psychotherapy in a proprietary nursing home. *Gerontologist, 14,* 446–450.

Scheidlinger S. 1968. Group psychotherapy in the sixties. *American Journal of Psychotherapy, 22,* 170–183.

Schulte, W. 1961. Komminikative Psychotherapie bei Störungen im höheren Lebensalter. *Zeitschrift für Psychotherapie und Medizinische Psychologie, 11,* 159–173.

Schulte, W. 1965. Psychotherapy of emotional disturbances in the later years of life. *International Journal of Neuropsychiatry, 1,* 662–657.

Schulte, W. 1967. Psychotherapie im höheren Lebensalter unter Ausnutzung der autoprotektiven Mechanismen in der Involution. *Zeitschrift für Alterforschung, 20,* 129–133.

SELIGMAN, M. E. P. 1975. *Helplessness. On Depression, Development and Death.* San Francisco: W. H. Freeman.

SILVER, A. 1950. Group psychotherapy with senile psychotic patients. *Geriatrics, 5,* 147–150.

SKINNER, B. F. 1936. *Behavior of Organisms.* New York: Appleton-Century-Crofts.

SKINNER, B. F. 1953. *Science and Human Behavior.* New York: Macmillan.

SKÖGLUND, J. 1977. *Aging and Retirement. Studies of Attitudes Toward the Elderly in Sweden.* Uppsala: Almqvist & Wiksell.

SLOANE, R. B., STAPLES, F. R., CRISTOL, A. H., YORKSTON, N. J., AND WHIPPLE, K. 1975. *Psychotherapy versus Behavior Therapy.* Cambridge, Mass: Harvard University Press.

SPOERL, O. H. 1975. Single Session-Psychotherapy. *Diseases of the Nervous System, 36,* 283–285.

SOLYOM, L., HESELTINE, G. F. D., McCLURE, D. J., SOLYOM, C., LEDWIDGE, B., AND STEINBERG, G. 1973. Behaviour therapy versus drug therapy in the treatment of phobic neurosis. *Canadian Psychiatrist Association Journal, 18,* 25–32.

SOMMER, R., AND ROSS, H. 1958. Social interaction on a geriatric ward. *International Journal of Social Psychiatry, 4,* 128–133.

TAULBEE, L. R., AND FOLSOM, J. C. 1966. Reality orientation for geriatric patients. *Hospital and Community Psychiatry, 17,* 133–135.

TRUAX, C. B., AND CARKHUFF, R. R. 1967. *Toward Effective Counseling and Psychotherapy: Training and Practice.* Chicago: Aldine.

VERWOERDT, A. 1976. *Clinical Geropsychiatry.* Baltimore, Md: Williams & Wilkins.

VOLPE, A., AND KASTENBAUM, R. 1967. Beer and TLC. *American Journal of Nursing, 67,* 101–103.

WISOCKI, P. A. 1977. Sampling procedures: Tools for stimulating the activity and interest of institutionalized elderly. Paper presented at the *American Psychological Association,* San Francisco.

WISOCKI, P. A., MOSHER, P. M., AND KORFHAGE, M. 1976. The effect of individual attention and recreational activities on improving the social skills of institutionalized geriatric man. Paper presented at *The Tenth Annual Meeting of the Association for the Advancement of Behavior Therapy,* New York City, December, 1976.

WITTICH, G. H. 1966. The older human being in the psychotherapeutic group. *Psychiatrie, Neurologie und Medizinsche Psychologie, 18,* 145.

WOLFF, K. 1962. Group psychotherapy with geriatric patients in a psychiatric hospital: Six-year study. *Journal of the American Geriatrics Society, 10,* 1077–1080.

WOLFF, K. 1963. Individual psychotherapy with geriatric patients. *Diseases of the Nervous System, 24,* 688–691.

WOLFF, K. 1967. Comparison of group and individual psychotherapy with geriatric patients. *Diseases of the Nervous System, 28,* 384–386.

WOLFF, K. 1971. Individual psychotherapy with geriatric patients. *Psychosomatics, 12,* 89–93.

WOLK, R. L., AND GOLDFARB, A. I. 1967. The response to group psychotherapy of aged recent admissions compared with long-term mental hospital patients. *American Journal of Psychiatry, 123,* 1251–1257.

WOLPE, J. 1969. *The Practice of Behavior Therapy.* New York: Pergamon Press.

# 33

# The Use of Group Methods
# for Work with the Aged

*Margaret E. Hartford*

If old age is viewed as a period of continued growth and development, with the probability of some physical and emotional decrements and some losses of social relationships as the person progresses through the later years, then it follows that participation in groups may have many and varied uses for the improvement or sustenance of the social and mental health of older adults. Groups may facilitate continued individual social growth through the creation of new relationships and learning, provide support through crises, offer opportunities for rehabilitation when there has been breakdown, may provide a means for collective action for management of environment, or offer collective means for advocacy to change procedures of social institutions affecting the elderly. All of these functions, whether focused on individuals or the environment in which the person exists, have mental health components and affect the mental health of the elderly in the community.

The uses of group methods for work with the aged has occurred primarily in the past 35 years, reflecting the emergence of group services generally. The several strands of group work with the aged include: the services for the well elderly living in their own homes, homes of relatives, foster homes in retirement communities or other communal arrangements; group services for the frail elderly participating in day care centers or outpatient therapeutic group sessions; and group services for the frail and dependent elderly who live in homes for the aged, hospitals for chronically ill or for the mentally ill, or long-term care facilities, nursing homes or convalescent homes. The group services for each of these populations arise from somewhat different historical roots, but all use some of the same group methods focusing on one or more of the following purposes. (1) the growth, enhancement, or rehabilitation of the *individual* older participants; (2) improved *interpersonal* relationships among older people or between the elderly and their relatives or other associates; (3) *problem solving* or task achievement through collective action of elderly peers; (4) *change in the surroundings* of the living environment of the participants in the group; (5) action for change or *management of a social system* or an institution; (6) *change in attitudes*, values, or procedures of and for elderly; (7) or *change in society* for the improved quality of life for all older people. The spectrum of use of group methods for mental health of older adults includes therapy, support, crisis intervention, management and maintenance, growth, enhancement and increased self sufficiency, and social change.

This chapter will examine the findings of small group research and theory which have implications for work with the elderly; will review the historical development of methods and uses of groups which may be applied to the needs of the elderly; will explore the specific needs of well and frail elderly, living at home or in institutions, who may be assisted through group experiences; will examine various group methods; and, finally, will examine technical aspects of working with groups. The findings of research on group uses with various types of elderly populations will be examined throughout for applications.

## SMALL GROUP RESEARCH AND THEORY WITH APPLICATIONS FOR THE AGED

Small group theory had its roots in the research of several European and American sociologists in the 1890s and early 1900s (LeBon, McDougall, Simmel, Durkheim, and Cooley), and took a rapid stride forward in the 1950s and 1960s through the work of sociologists and social psychologists at Harvard, Michigan, and Chicago, followed by the group dynamicists who conducted much of their research during and immediately following World War II. The latter group was pioneered by Lewin and his followers. The rapid growth of knowledge and theory about groups was applied to practice beginning in the 1940s and use increased in the 1950s and 1960s. While some group treatment derived from individual treatment modalities, with some attempts to use Freud's writings about groups, actually most group work and group therapy tended to draw upon the group theory of the social sciences. Some of the group uses found to be helpful for treatment, growth, or action were easily applicable to practice with older people.

### SOCIALIZATION

For instance, Cooley's (1909) concepts of the use of groups for socialization, role induction, and resocialization (originally focused on socialization of children) were naturally applicable for older people with a need for induction into appropriate roles of the aging. As noted by Brim and Wheeler (1966), socialization of the individual proceeds throughout life, but the older individual must be socialized to widowhood, to a life style which is often at a lower economic level, to the many losses of friends and relatives, and to an ever-changing world about him. The instrument for socialization is the small group of peers, family, friends, or associates. Since some of these normal small groups may disappear or be distant from many older adults who retire, move out of their old communities, and lose relatives, alternative groups need to be created. If groups assist in socialization and resocialization, then it would follow that the person who must adjust to an institutional life, retirement community, long-term care facility, old age home, or hospital, can be helped to do so by being part of a group established for socialization.

### ATTITUDE CHANGE AND DEVELOPMENT

Allport (1954;) Cartwright (1961;) Festinger, Schachter, and Back (1950); and Stouffer (1949) observed that behavior, values, attitudes, and beliefs were grounded in the groups to which a person belonged. Lewin (1943) demonstrated that attitudes may change through the reinforcement of groups of peers. Therefore, it follows that groups are useful in helping older people who feel a sense of loss, who have been socialized to accept myths and stereotypes about appropriate aging behavior, and who are self-depreciating because they are socially depreciated, to have corrective experiences in groups. Guided group experiences may be geared to helping older people to change false attitudes about aging, to feel better about themselves, and to recover from some of the real losses they have experienced. The use of groups as a corrective for attitude and belief change then is a valuable purpose.

## DEVELOPMENT OF SELF-CONCEPT

From Mead's (1934) theory of the looking-glass-self, self-perception derives from the way others respond to a person. If society tends to demean or diminish older people through cultural expressions, social structure, and the access which older people have to goods and services, then older people would tend to have depreciated views of themselves. Judging from the "youth culture" and the denial of aging process, it would be natural that the self-image of many older people would be poor. With the reality of failing physical capacities and some of the decrements of aging, many older people experience strong negative reinforcement. On the other side of the same phenomenon, however, positive feedback, support, and expectations for adequate functioning may counteract this negativity if older people are part of groups of significant others who provide support. Therefore, a third use of therapy groups, group work services, and activity groups may be the provision of better self-concepts and identity in aging. Research has shown that an individual may change his self-concept in accordance with the feedback he receives from a group (Manis, 1955). Other action research has demonstrated that individuals who were helped to reflect themselves positively in groups, modified their behavior in ways that they became more effective in all of their social and interpersonal relationships (Schein and Bennis, 1965).

## LEARNING

For learning, teaching, and mastering new information, the small group helps participants to clarify ideas, reinforce each other's learning, and talk through and more clearly imprint ideas in the minds of the learner (McKeachie, 1958). For older adults, groups for learning may be used to better understand the physiological, psychological, and emotional changes of their lives. Educational groups can also be used to reduce obsolescence in a rapidly changing technological society. Educational groups may also be used to understand procedures of institutions and communal living arrangements. The mastery of learning also is a supportive, growth experience for many older people in educational groups. Along with the new knowledge is the sheer joy of companionship in the learning process and the contribution to each other's growth.

## BEHAVIORAL CHANGE

Groups are found to have profound influence on participants' behavior, as well as their beliefs and values. The use of groups to modify habits, manners, and customs has been extensively demonstrated (Hastorf, 1965; Sundel and Lawrence, 1974). Thus, behavior modification groups may help older people to change lifelong ways of feeling, behaving, and believing in order to find greater fulfillment and creativity in later life.

The participants in groups using a behavior modification method based on learning theory are rewarded by the group worker, by other group participants, and by themselves for making changes in their actions, activities, and responses. The rewards may be verbal support or acclaim, interpersonal acts, or tangible gifts (Linsk, Howe, and Pinkston, 1975).

Closely akin to the behavior modification is Reality Therapy pioneered by Glasser (1965). Especially with older people who have lost contact, have no motivation to remain connected, or have had catastrophic illnesses, reality therapy groups can help to improve current functioning (Allen, 1976).

A modification of this type of work called Reality Orientation was developed further by Veterans Administration workers dealing with moderately confused elderly who had been placed in psychiatric wards (Stephens, 1975; Allen, 1970). Reality Orientation therapy focuses on current functioning within the given environment, based on repetition and relearning. The goal is to help group participants have consistent and accurate information and to be anchored in the present set of relationships and environmental influences (Birkett and Baltuch, 1973). This method provides support, security, production, and regularity, and hopefully reduces ambiguity, disorganization, and confusion. The presence of others in the group is an effective factor in providing a motivational force for improvement (Taulbee and Folsom, 1966).

## DISCUSSION—CATHARSIS

Allport (1945) discovered that when group conversation was used for catharsis, for talking out problems, pressures, and tensions, people were then free to make use of the learning and growth experiences about them. This finding has been used consistently in group treatment, especially as a beginning activity and as tensions build up within the group or the individuals in the course of particular types of treatment or crises in the living situation. With groups of older people in the community, in day care centers, or in institutions, this conceptual approach has been used especially to deal with some of the frustrations of aging, institutionalization, and some chronic illnesses (Weiner, Brok, and Snadowsky, 1978). Getting the pressure out in the open through group conversations can therefore be useful in the progress toward working on those things which can be changed and those things which must be accepted (Abrahams, 1972).

## PROBLEM SOLVING

For problem solving, where the task requires more minds than one, or where more people have different knowledge so that they have different inputs to the common tasks or solutions, groups can be particularly effective (Hare, 1962; Murphy, 1963). Groups for residence management, for advisory committees to area agencies on aging, for planning groups for senior multi-service centers, for needs assessment, and for problem solving of community needs of the elderly, make use of this theory. The person who feels that he is contributing to the group, since his contribution is acknowledged and used, also grows in strength and stature by participating in task groups. Recognizing some of the losses felt by many elderly, one can see that participating in task and problem-solving groups may have therapeutic rewards in addition to the contribution to the common goal. Participation may not only improve the mental health of the participants, but may also prolong the feeling of adequacy and self-importance and serve as a preventive from disengagement and breakdown.

## SOCIAL ACTION

Task groups can also be a strong influence on their environment. Thus, a collection of elderly who attend a public hearing or collaborate on a piece of legislation speak louder politically than a number of disparate older individuals. Bennis, Benne, and Chin (1961) studied the value of groups for action on policy, planning, and program building. Their work in merging of small group theory with organizational theory points to the power of the organized small group in effecting change.

In the initial organization of the National Retired Teachers Association led by Dr. Ethel Percy Andrus, for instance, group pressure finally convinced insurance companies that older people were good risks for automobile, life, and health insurance. The consortium of pressure of the Grey Panthers and the groups of the National Council on the Aging apparently provided the pressure on Social Security to permit the protection of social security and other types of income checks for older adults by changing distribution procedures. Organized minority elderly caucuses apparently influenced the content and direction of White House Conferences on Aging to include minority content. While it is difficult to prove that any one small group or collection of small groups of elderly have had considerable effect to date in social policy or legislative action, there is potential for group pressure as older people become organized.

The research on the various small groups is directly applicable to the needs of the elderly. These needs include the need for self definition; for support; for opportunities to grow, learn, and become more enhanced; to improve self image; to be inducted into appropriate roles and to shed false stereotypes; to recover from illness, injury, or injustice; to replace friends, mates, families, and associates lost through various life transpositions; to keep connected with current reality and avoid obsolescence in a rapidly changing world; and to collaborate in problem solving, task achievement, and action for social change.

## SOME OF THE NEGATIVE USES OF GROUPS

It should be noted that, while the intent of this chapter is to show the uses of groups for the mental health of the elderly and to examine research and theory for their useful applications, attention should be called to the potential destructiveness of groups for the individual, for the system in which the group exists, and for society. There is very little research on the destructiveness of groups, but it is apparent that the very strengths of groups may become negatives when overused or wrongly used. For instance, the phenomenon of group support and modification of behavior, with changes in attitudes and values, may be used to devalue, to teach destructive attitudes, to socialize to greater rigidity, or to leave a person with a sense of greater defeat. Groups can socialize patients to accept poor institutional care and become compliant to harmful procedures, take away independence, or create inappropriate dependency on workers or other members. Encounter techniques used by some methodologies of group work may be overpowering and destructive to the fragile ego of an ill patient, or to one who has suffered many social losses through the normal process of aging (Lieberman, Yallom, and Miles, 1973). A very lonely person may feel more so, if he participates in a group where he becomes isolated, rejected, or even scapegoated, and where his loneliness becomes more apparent by contrast. It therefore behooves professional workers who would use group methods to be knowledgeable not only about the findings of research on group processes and group leadership techniques but also about the particular characteristics of the social, psychological, and physiological aging processes which should be considered in the deliberate use of groups for the mental health needs of the elderly (Hartford, 1978).

## HISTORICAL VIEW OF THE GROWTH AND EXPANSION OF GROUP APPROACHES WITH OLDER ADULTS

As older adults began to emerge as a visible subpopulation of need, or a population at risk in the areas of socialization, interpersonal relations, role changes, and growth, there was the accompanying recognition of this need expressed in the development of new services, particularly those using group methods. Golden age clubs, senior citizen activity programs, recreation and group work, and senior adult camping appeared. In the late 1930s, within group service centers such as settlement houses, neighborhood centers, Jewish community centers, churches, public recreation programs, and public libraries, professional workers recognized that the numbers of older people were increasing. Former members of programs who had grown old, grandparents of program participants, or elderly parents of adult members began to ask for services, or sometimes arrived at centers as observers. The professional response was to offer activity and recreational group services. The first "Golden Age Clubs" were established simultaneously by the Benjamin Rose Institute in collaboration with the Group Work department of Case Western Reserve University in Cleveland, by Dr. Oskar Schulze at Goodrich House in Cleveland, and by the Irene Kaufman Settlement in Pittsburgh in 1939 (Trecker, 1964; Woods, 1953). The time was right in the late 1930s and early 1940s for the appearance of such group programs in response to a recognized need of a sizeable population of well elderly in the communities (Kubie and Landau, 1953).

There emerged for these people, particularly in the cities of the East Coast and Midwest US, club and activity programs consisting primarily of games, parties, and some discussion groups.Viewed as a population at leisure in a work-oriented culture, the programs for older adults were geared primarily to social activities to keep people occupied and were patterned after existing leisure time programs such as folk dancing, singing, handcrafts, dramatics, card games, bingo, and other table games (Woods, 1953). Most clubs in senior programs had some basic organization such as officers or program committees, but they were primarily

managed by staff whose background was in social group work, recreation, or adult education and whose philosophy, knowledge, and skill were derived from training and work in activities. Staff approach was based on a belief that good mental and physical health derived from being busy and involved, getting out of the house, and being occupied with other people in organized activities (Kubie and Landau, 1953; Vickery, 1960).

In some cities during this period of the 1940s, welfare planning bodies began to stimulate and coordinate group work programs for the elderly through existing group services and recreational agencies. Where no such services existed, the planning bodies themselves set up direct service programs such as senior clubs or camps (Bing, 1951; Maxwell, 1962).

Senior Adult Group Workers, as a class of professionals, began to emerge in the early 1950s. They began to convene in local communities, and sometimes as sections of national professional meetings, to exchange information about methods of approach to group work with the elderly. Professional practice papers began to appear in the literature of social work, recreation, and adult education. (Bing, 1951; Mathiasen, 1951). Several national and regional conferences on group work with the elderly were held in the 1950s and early 1960s as workers began to examine the growing body of knowledge on aging processes as well as on group leadership methods (Council on Social Work Education, Aspen Conference, 1959; National Association of Social Workers, 1963).

As public and private housing for the elderly was constructed, especially in the East and the Midwest, frequently facilities were built for group services programs for the residents. Sometimes housing authorities or management employed activities directors to develop and manage group programs for older adults on the site. In others the programs were offered within the housing estates by local existing group work agencies.

In many communities, specialized group services for senior adults, called variously, "Golden Age Centers," "Senior Centers," or "Adult Recreation" were sponsored by service clubs such as Kiwanis or Rotary, or by the Chamber of Commerce, federations of churches or synagogues, the Department of Parks and Recreation, or trade unions (Boskind, 1966).

The initial programs, while developed by well-meaning professionals, were frequently based on stereotypes that old age is a time of deterioration, second childhood, slowing down, loss of memory dependency, or diminished capacity to learn. Thus the group programs were frequently developed for older people by younger staff without participation of older adults in planning, and were often patterned after children's programs. Many of the people themselves reinforced the attitude by participating passively in the group and recreation activities. More sophisticated, energetic, better educated, or more independent older adults did not participate in these programs and sought out the company of their peers in the library, at the corner tavern, or at the church doing volunteer work. They recognized the need for group association but were not satisfied with the services offered to them.

From this early activity-focus, predetermined by staff, there came pressure from some of the participants to change programs, at least in part, from entertainment and time filling, to programs of responsible action on issues and circumstances relating to themselves and their peers (Epstein, 1964). In the late 1950s and early 1960s new group approaches in the senior centers began to organize group activity for citizen action or social action. These groups worked to achieve benefits for the elderly such as reduced fares on public transportation during off-pressure hours, reduced entrance fees for entertainment, cultural arts, museums and theaters, involvement of seniors in consumer affairs, and the securing of legislation which protected and enhanced the senior adult status. Study groups were organized for world affairs, social problems, book reviews, voter issues, better housing for the elderly, and better medical facilities and services (Maxwell, 1962). Classes and courses for and by retired people were begun on such serious subjects as philosophy, history, language, art and music appreciation, current literature, and psychology, as well as lectures and tours of the community. The adult educators joined the social workers and recreation workers in these programs, as a natural evolution from their community services programs (Lowy, 1955).

From the beginnings in recreation, activity, and group work, there was a logical move to adult education, and to the use of group methods for learning and intellectually demanding activities through adult schools and continuing education. The senior adult education movement began in the 1950s but burgeoned in the 1960s and 1970s into a vast network of group programs through educational sponsorship of public school systems and private, state, and municipal universities and colleges. In most of these programs the interpersonal and group focus was as important to the participants as the content of courses. Today some educational programs are geared primarily to senior adults, while others emphasize the intergenera-

tional aspects. Some have a residential component of on-site group living (Astle, Howsdin and Arquitt, 1977), while others are based on a commuter concept, and a third type is offered in neighborhoods within walking distance. From a mental health standpoint the main objective of these educational offerings is the involvement, participation, connection, self-definition, and social meaning that result from the participation, mental stimulation, growth and sense of emotional well-being produced by the group association (Seguin and O'Brien, 1976).

A logical outgrowth of the group work, recreation, and adult education programs for the aging in the late 1960s and early 1970s was the emergence of the Senior Multiservice Centers, drawing in not only group activities but also health screening and health education, exercise physiology, and group activities for physical movement therapy, meals and nutritional programs with a social component, rehabilitation, and day care programs (Boskind, 1966; Maxwell, 1962). All of these services use a group work base and bring together the social services and health services practices. Collaborating in these programs are nurses, occupational therapists, nutritionists, physical therapists, medical doctors, dentists, recreation workers, public health administrators, public administrators, and social workers (Meredith and Amor, 1976). Many of the multiservice centers existing in the 1970s are not unlike the settlement house programs that existed from the 1890s to the 1950s, with the exception that the new programs tend to serve primarily the needs of the elderly rather than all ages. In many instances the new multiservice centers use governmental funds, under the Older Americans Act and the state and local offices on Aging, especially for their nutritional programs and their group activities and recreation. It should be noted that some senior centers have individual information and referral services, individual counselling, and individual health clinic services, but their approach is primarily through group services with a focus on social interaction, socialization, alternative role development, and the establishment of a sense of belonging for self-definition (Leanse and Wagner, 1975).

## USE OF GROUPS FOR THERAPEUTIC PURPOSES IN INSTITUTIONS

A second historical strand grew out of the movement to use groups as a means of therapy (resocialization, survival, relief of anxiety, insight and self-awareness, support, and maintenance of some independence or self-mastery) for patients in hospitals and for residents of institutions for both short-term and long-term care. Therapeutic group uses imply the existence of a problem in the person or in his relationships, which can be helped by the deliberate development of a group treatment modality. During World War II, the armed services medical corps, through social workers, psychiatrists, psychologists, and psychiatric nurses, developed group methods for therapy for both short-term crisis intervention and long-term coping. These programs were offered for patients in service-related hospitals, in veteran's hospitals, and in rehabilitation centers. The personnel trained through this experience returned to the community after the war and began a movement in the late 1940s and early 1950s to provide group work services in psychiatric hospitals, in hospitals for acute and chronically ill patients, and in custodial institutions for both long- and short-term care. Groups began to be used for therapeutic purposes with relatives, inpatients, and outpatients (Coyle, 1960; Trecker, 1956). Some of the uses of groups in these situations were to relieve anxiety and free energy for healing, to promote adaptation to diseases and illnesses where necessary, to encourage adjustment to medical procedures or the constraints of the institution, to assist in adjustment to the patient role, to aid in the maintenance of some independence of patients where possible within the limitations of the illness and prescribed care, and to prepare the patient for discharge.

It was discovered, for instance, that many people who were hospitalized or institutionalized became isolated or withdrawn, even in the presence of others (Sloan, 1953). Perhaps in part they were protecting their individuality in the face of having procedures done to, at, or for them. But it became apparent that patients and residents needed assistance in forming social connections in the institution. Patients who were in groups showed remarkable changes in the total healing process, in relief of anxiety, and in their preparation for medical procedures, for discharge, or for adaptation to physical and emotional changes resulting from illness. Patients with similar problems learned to support each other through the group experiences, and frequently formed self-help groups that continued even when the professionals were no longer present (Frey, 1966).

Task-centered groups were used for ward management or advocacy and change in long-term care facilities. In the latter case, the focus was usually on individual growth and ego support by having patients take responsibility for their surroundings and for each other as well as for improving the milieu (Saul and Saul, 1973). As this movement grew from work with armed forces personnel and veterans, and adults in psychiatric hospitals, many of whom were elderly, the methodology was naturally transferred to old age homes, nursing homes, and various institutions for the elderly (Friedman, 1975).

While the first professionals to enter these programs were military (medical and psychiatric social workers, psychologists, psychiatrists, nurses, and activities specialists from the Red Cross, Salvation Army, and USO), they were quickly joined by chaplains, occupational therapists and recreation therapists. A new set of professionals emerged, calling themselves variously hospital or institutional group workers, psychiatric group workers, group therapists, group psychotherapists, or group psychiatric nurses. They began to bring together the knowledge about small groups, which had been developing through social psychology during and immediately after World War II, with group work practice theory that had been developing during the same time period. The work of the group dynamicists, the social psychologists doing research on groups (Cartwright and Zander, 1958), the social group workers who were trying to evolve a practice theory (Hartford, 1962), and dynamic group psychotherapists, coupled with other research and practice-demonstrations, moved the group into a central position as a therapeutic tool (Hartford, 1971).

It was natural that this approach should be picked for use in settings where there were a preponderance of elderly patients. With mental patients, the advent of chemotherapy and the use of psychotherapeutic drugs rendered unnecessary and inappropriate some previously used techniques, and increased the need to promote social relationships among patients. Professionals trained and/or experienced in group methods emerged from nursing, social work, occupational therapy, recreation, psychology, and psychiatry. Their practice encompassed considerable work with the growing population of elderly in and out of psychiatric hospitals, convalescent homes, nursing homes, institutions, old age residences, and retirement communities (Brudno and Seltzer, 1968; Lazarus, 1976; Linsk, Howe, and Pinkston, 1975). By the 1970s group work programs including adult education had become so integral to the creation and maintenance of the social life of institutions for older adults, that programs of this sort were mandated for licensure or financial reimbursement of institutions in many parts of the country.

## GROUP THERAPY FOR AGING IN THE COMMUNITY

The therapeutic group methods of work with older adults used in institutions were picked up in the community in outpatient services, family counseling services, drop-in centers, retirement communities, and senior centers (Lowy and Mogey, 1966). In some services where individual counselling and casework had been the primary method, it was recognized that group approaches were more consonant with the nature of the problems of the elderly, such as lessening social isolation, loneliness, role loss, and widowhood (Larson, 1970). The group therapies of the 1960s and the 1970s (reality therapy, remotivation therapy, socialization and resocialization therapy, gestalt group therapy, transactional analysis groups, and reminiscence therapies) were practiced with the elderly in community settings as well as in institutions (Weiner et al., 1978). The settings where these approaches were used included private practice in the office of the therapist or in participant's homes, churches, the community rooms of banks, libraries, motels, conference grounds, universities, or neighborhood center lounges, as well as in the traditional counseling agencies (Rank, 1963; Rathbone-Moodan, and Levenson, 1975).

While group psychotherapy and group therapy have grown extensively since the early 1960s, only recently has attention been given by therapists of several disciplines to the problems and concerns of the aged. Today a few psychiatrists, psychologists, marriage and family counselors, and social group workers trained in group psychotherapy are including work with groups of older patients and their families in their practice. In part this is the result of the demand for services as older people are seeking the services of these practitioners, joining therapy groups at mental health centers, and struggling with some of the effects of retirement, life change, widowhood, changing life styles and social status, alternative marriage patterns, and the pressures resulting from rapid social changes. Group psychotherapists and group therapists in private practice and in community counseling services have begun to recognize that their methods are particularly appropriate for some of the problems and stresses faced by older adults in the middle and upper socioeconomic levels in young and middle old age.

Historically, then, groups have been used with, by, and for older adults by professional practitioners of many disciplines for social relationships, activities, for occupation and filling time, for staying connected with the real world and with other people, for reconnecting after disengagement due to physical or emotional problems, for personal growth and enhancement, for new learning and survival, and for enrichment. Groups have been used more recently for therapeutic purposes and for dealing with emotional and physical problems and losses resulting from life changes, crises, and death of friends and relatives. They have been used to help other adults adjust to new life styles and life situations such as institutional or communal living, or to physical changes such as loss of sight or commitment to wheelchairs and to the normal stresses of growing old in a rapidly changing society.

## GROUPS FOR SOCIAL CHANGE

More recently, groups of older adults have come into being as a source of renewed power and action for improving the quality of life for themselves and their peers. Through activist, advocacy or collective action for political and social change, or consumer protection, older people have organized (Sainer, Schwarz, and Jackson, 1973). Such groups as the Grey Panthers, National Senior Citizens Council, National Council on the Aging, National Retired Teachers Association and American Association of Retired Persons have organized at a national level, but their major activities are carried on through the small group associations at the local level. While activist groups are not new to this country, even among the elderly, there is a resurgence of them. Actually the roots of advocacy groups of senior adults began with the Townsend Plan, preceeding Social Security and Medicare, when small groups of seniors all across the country during the depression of the 1920s and 1930s were organized for the purpose of establishing health support and financial assistance for the elderly. These were militant groups of older people, but their impetus subsided after the various benefit programs for people over 65 were enacted by government.

Programs developed by the government, including Foster Grandparents, Senior Companions, and RSVP (Retired Seniors Volunteer Program), while focusing on bringing satisfaction to the individual through alternative work and family roles for older adults, also include a strong emphasis on the group component (Seguin and O'Brien, 1976). These programs call for regular group activities of the senior volunteers for exchange, support, training, and socialization. Programs created by the Older Americans Act such as Senior Centers and

Nutrition Services have a definite group approach associated with health, recreation, and food delivery. Groups of senior adults as advisory committees are also mandated as part of state and local Agencies on Aging established through the Older American Act. While the intent of these groups is the involvement of older people in behalf of themselves in the administration of services, there is the underlying notion that the interpersonal exchange and attachment is an important element in the self-maintenance and independence of the participants.

## GROUPS IN RETIREMENT COMMUNITIES

With the growth of retirement communities under either commercial auspices or nonprofit associations, religious organizations, or trade unions, the appearance of many kinds of autonomous groups has been noted (Seguin, 1973). New communities of several hundred or several thousand older people have come into being in every part of the nation, and within most of them are a myriad of groups that have arisen spontaneously including the many types of groups discussed so far in this chapter. Some are therapeutic, to help individuals in the coping processes of the crises accompanying old age. Others help with adapting and adjusting to new living arrangements. In contrast to the therapeutic and supportive groups, the majority of collectivities in retirement communities and old age homes are for activity, occupation, social relationships, and enhancement, or for the management of the community, governance, and service provision. The unique aspect of these groups as compared to similar groups in the wider community is that they tend to take account of the special status, increments and decrements, and social aspects of aging (Seguin, 1973). From an historic perspective, the creation of many groups for older people in retirement communities is a fairly recent social invention of the last 10 to 20 years.

## USES OF GROUPS FOR THE WELL ELDERLY

The deliberate development and use of groups in the human services for the well elderly has been and is for the maintenance or reestablishment of social relationships as people outlive their mates or peers, or find it necessary to move to new communities (Hennessey, 1973). Groups also have been created for continued intellectual and social growth, for prevention of obsolescence in a rapidly changing world, and for enhancement and enrichment appropriate to interests and abilities. Groups provide support through crises, such as prolonged illness of self or mate, loss of some physical capac-

ity, or facing tragedy in one's family. Also with well functioning aged, as mentioned previously, groups have been organized by professionals to help older adults engage in problem solving, action, and advocacy at the community level and in management of their surroundings in the residential areas (Ross, 1975). In these groups the focus is not only on mastery and control of one's own destiny, but also on having a vital and needed function, and in having meaningful attachments to others. At the same time these groups give the participants satisfaction in bringing about some improvement in the quality of life for other older adults.

## USES OF GROUPS WITH THE VERY OLD AND FRAIL ELDERLY

With the very old, the frail, dependent, handicapped, or ill, groups have been used for dealing with physical and emotional problems in outpatient or therapeutic services in the community or in institutions such as old age homes, nursing homes, and chronic and acute illness hospitals. In these groups the focus has been primarily on rehabilitation, restoration, or care and support. It is recognized that anxiety can be released and the emotions freed for use in healing of the individual through group discussion and activity, by playing out some of the fears, fantasies, and realities or by understanding better the nature of the problem (Burnside, 1978). Also some of the anxiety growing out of the stereotypes socialized into the older adults, such as beliefs that they may lose memory, self-control, or mastery, may be dealt with in groups (Hochschild, 1973). Understanding and coping with illness or physical and mental losses can be supported in groups (Mayadas and Hink, 1974). To some degree, groups of the frail elderly have also been used for activity, education, enhancement, and growth, just as with the well elderly, except that their physical and/or mental capacities may be different and provide certain limitations (Shapiro, 1973).

It is recognized that some of the normal or expected crises that occur in the lives of people as they reach the latter years, and some of the usual illnesses, physical disabilities, and emotional stresses are those for which a group method of care or treatment may be particularly useful. For instance, the need for social contacts, relationships, a sense of belonging, and self-definition which comes from the usual life support groups may disappear with widowhood, friends and relatives through death, or movement away from one's usual social contacts because of hospitalization or institutionalization (Hartford, 1971). By participating with peers or in mixed generation groups, new contacts may be made, and alternative relationships established. Such groups are also therapeutic in the sense that they help the person to be introspective and grow in self-awareness, explore feelings of loss and surface them in order to deal with grief, and take some responsibility for forming new relationships. These groups may also focus on coping, building personal strengths to maintain self, and master the crisis or loss. Participants may feel support, understanding, and empathy of other group members while dealing with their own griefs, mourning, and coping. They also reap the rewards of helping others who are experiencing some of the same feelings. New supportive networks may evolve (Crosby, 1978; Abrahams, 1972).

For the elderly who are not residing in institutions, groups of this nature may be found at senior centers, family service or counseling centers, or some of the special agencies for the aging, such as geriatric centers (Lowy and Mogey, 1966). Within institutions and hospitals such groups may be offered by social service, the chaplaincy, or the geriatric or psychiatric nurse practitioners.

Research and demonstration reports indicate considerable success in mental hospitals and old age homes in working with deteriorated senile people suffering from chronic brain syndrome, to bring them into contact and communication through various forms of group therapy (Reichenfeld, Csapo, Carriere, and Gardner, 1973; Allen, 1976). The use of the arts, music, films, painting, dance or movement, as well as reminiscence, conversation, or encounter techniques, have apparently been successful with deteriorated elderly in groups to help them regain some social functioning (Burnside, 1978). Various types of group therapy have been used to help the frail and deteriorated elderly remain attached or to reattach themselves to each other and to their surroundings, or to return to a higher level of social and independent functioning (Dewdney, 1973). Observation has been made of better self-image, self-management, and maintenance of deteriorated older people who participated in therapeutic groups (Maizler and Solomon, 1976). For the highly disturbed frail elderly, group programs have reportedly relieved anxiety, anger, and depression, and have improved connections and interaction (Yallom and Terrazas, 1968). In some instances the improvement has been merely during the group session (Salter and Salter, 1975), in others it has carried over for extended periods of time outside of the group (Scott and Crowhurst, 1975). Group methods used with these patients include discussion, stimulation with music or art, recreation and activities, reminiscing, rhythm orches-

tras, group games, and dance. In one program of music therapy, for instance, the investigator reported a noticeable change in establishing a sense of belonging, self-confidence, contentment, relaxation, socialization, and security as a result of group participation with other older patients (Gabelic, Breitenfeld, Grubistic, Radotic, Matakovic, and Kulcar, 1974).

## OUTPATIENT GROUP SERVICE PROGRAMS

In outpatient programs for deteriorated elderly group programs are successful in improving social functioning and patterns of living so that a large proportion of group members are able to remain out of the hospital (Liederman, Green, and Liederman, 1967). Use of life review and life cycle group therapy helps people to stay connected with self-identity and current reality, and also relieves anxiety through expression of anger and aggression in the group (Butler, 1974). With senior adults sharing adaptive methods with each other, they gain confidence, feel comfort and identification, reduce their sense of isolation, and are thereby more independent as well as interdependent (Altholz and Doss, 1973). In an outpatient group program for persons diagnosed as having chronic brain syndrome, meeting with their adult relatives using group interaction, psycho-drama, reminiscing, and socialization produced evidence of considerable recovery by elderly and better management of the problems by the relatives. In a similar program the group experience of the elderly and their families brought out the strengths of the families and the senior adult patients (Shier, 1972).

### GROUPS IN MEDICAL SETTINGS

In the medical hospital or in long-term convalescent care for physical problems, groups have proved useful in helping older adults and their relatives learn to cope with medical procedures such as kidney dialysis, respirators, use of wheel chairs, and artificial limbs (Burnside, 1971). Acceptance of physical limitations or chronic conditions resulting from illness such as stroke, heart attack, cancer, lung disease, has been facilitated by discussions and support in groups of patients with similar conditions (Rosin, 1975). Groups have also been used for helping patients adapt to the limitations of the hospital and to accept the appropriate patient role on the one hand (Remnet, 1974), and to prepare for discharge on the other (Wallen, 1970). In general these groups may use the social group work or group therapy approaches, which are practiced by social workers, nurses, psychologists, and occupational therapists.

Within the hospital, group methods used include social group work, group therapy, reality orientation, and resocialization. The latter methods are particularly useful for people who have experienced the trauma of disengagement or withdrawal due to the severity of their illness or the extent of their disability. Reality orientation is used to help group members become reconnected, especially when there may have been some brain damage or a shocking separation from the previous experience as a result of stroke, heart attack, surgery, or loss of consciousness, so that the patient needs help in becoming reoriented to current reality. The group support is useful, both for sharing with others who have had similar experiences and for meeting the demands to communicate with the therapist and with others.

Remotivation and resocialization groups may be helpful for people who are suffering from brain damage or reactive depression resulting from physical illness (Allen, 1976; Bovey, 1972; Brudno and Seltzer, 1968). The therapist in this type of group within the medical setting attempts to bring the person to a higher level of social and emotional functioning within the group in order to facilitate discharge when this is possible, or at least to stimulate the participants to a higher level of independence, self-confidence, and interaction with each other (Nevruz and Hrushka, 1969).

In addition to groups developed to support patients or to help them to handle their emotional responses to their illness or to hospitalization, there are groups designed to achieve certain tasks to bring about changes in the management and procedure of the hospital. Such groups as representative patient government, ward management, and committees to modify certain procedures in the hospital have been helpful in raising morale, especially in long-term care facilities, and in having a therapeutic effect for the patients who participated (Frey, 1966).

## DESCRIPTIONS OF METHODS OF USES OF GROUPS WITH THE ELDERLY

Work with older adults in groups, then, derives from the sources of work with all ages of people in groups in social group work, clinical psychology, psychiatric and geriatric nursing, occupational and recreational therapy, and psychiatry. Approaches include social group work, group therapy, group psychotherapy, activity group therapy (including dance, art, music, dramatics, creative writing, and games and recreation), reality orientation therapy, resocialization or socialization and remotivation therapy, family group therapy, task-centered group work, and advocacy. Each of these approaches will be defined briefly and the application and implications for group work with the elderly will be considered, as well as the contexts within which each is offered, and the nature of the aging problems for which each is applicable.

### SOCIAL GROUP WORK

Social group work is described as a method, generated originally by social workers but adopted by many other professional practitioners, which places emphasis on group development (maximizing group processes), so that the group may become the instrument in which and through which participating individuals may benefit, their interpersonal relationships may improve, and/or the participants may collaborate in improving their social conditions. While the worker in social group work is concerned with each individual member's growth, change, or rehabilitation, depending on the purpose of the group, the worker is also simultaneously concerned with developing interpersonal relationships of the group members and facilitating group processes for collective outcomes. When applied to the needs of older adults, the social group work method provides enhanced, improved, or restored sense of self and identity through positive feedback of group members to each other. The group also provides collective support through crises and trauma; induction to new roles available and appropriate for senior adults; substitute roles and relationships for older people who have left employment, families or community associational roles; and opportunities for new affiliations, new friends, new peers, or a new social circle. Lowy (1967) reminds us that relationships offer not only rewards, but also social obligations which give a person a sense of being needed and responsible. Social group work is also a useful method for making participants aware of alternative coping mechanisms for mental and physical losses through the exchange of experiences of other older adults in the group. The social group work method may provide enhancement for the individual and for the collective through intellectual as well as emotional and social stimulation, by using the mind and the emotions in problem solving and in mastering new knowledge not available on an individual basis, or learning new skills which take a group to perform.

Social group work is employed usually as part of the social service program of psychiatric and medical hospitals, long-term care facilities for chronically ill or confused patients, residences for the elderly, community centers and senior centers, mental health or family counselling centers, and sometimes universities and community colleges. Social group work is used for continued growth, development, and enhancement of older individuals; for socialization and resocialization; for the establishment of new social connections or the restoration of social relationships after withdrawal or isolation; for gaining a better sense of identity and feeling needed and responsible; for support through crises or the development of new coping mechanisms; for rehabilitation; and for collaboration with other older individuals in problem solving. The major characteristics of group work is the maximized use of the group interaction as the means for achieving specific objectives or as the context within which problems are approached.

## GROUP THERAPY FOR OLDER ADULTS

Group therapy is a form of treatment where there are defined individual problems, personal, mental, emotional, physical or relationship in nature, and where the focus is on the rehabilitation of each participant (Slauson, 1956). The therapist (who may be a clinical psychologist, social worker, psychiatric or geriatric nurse clinician, psychiatrist, or marriage and family counsellor by professional orientation) has had some training and supervised practice in therapeutic group methods. The relationship between the therapist and each individual patient is of prime importance as is the relationship of participants with each other. It is presumed that participants benefit from observing and experiencing the therapists' work with each of the participants as well as participating in work themselves. Group members learn through the process to become helpful to each other as well as to gain help for themselves from the group. The group process becomes an important part of the help.

Content of group therapy for older adults may include developing an awareness of some of the social, psychological, physical and environmental aspects of growing older and gaining of assistance in coping with the problematic aspect of these factors. Faced with some of the frustrations of aging, some people find themselves in reactive depression, with low morale or anxiety, for which therapeutic groups offer some relief and some opportunity for mastery and regaining some element of control. Therapeutic groups provide support, modified behavior, increased self-awareness and/or modified behavioral patterns and alternative personal problem solutions in coping with the

trauma of widowhood or the loss of peers and roles. Group therapy may also offer help to participants in coping with their everyday circumstances and with specific trauma associated with their lives.

Within the psychiatric and medical settings, group therapy has been used to reconnect individuals who have suffered from mental, emotional, or physical breakdown, or who have had catastrophic illnesses and developed problems of memory loss. To some degree group therapy has been used on an outpatient basis for older adults in mental health and day care centers. Some forms of group therapy include life review and reminiscence, as reported by Butler (1974), and therapeutic coping with problems reported by Yallom and Terrazas (1968). Genrally the approach of group therapy used with older adults is to provide reinforcement and support, some growing awareness of the nature of the individual problems, and guidance in finding new ways of dealing with the problems which the individual participant faces.

## GROUP PSYCHOTHERAPY

While the literature reveals some confusion among the definitions or distinctions of group work, group therapy, and group psychotherapy, and the labels are used interchangeably and imprecisely in some research and description of practice, analytic group psychotherapy at least has a distinction. In this practice the therapist, and subsequently group members, as they become versed in the method, engage in a process of helping participants become aware of the sources and meanings of their behavior, feelings, and belief systems. Not only do participants attempt to recall and reconstruct events and emotions from their past life which may have been painful or hurtful, but they also explain their current means of adapting, their coping mechanisms, and the behavior by which they appear to define or protect themselves or solve personal problems. Efforts to gain insight and therefore to move toward mastery of the individual behavior are heightened by the exploration of the participant's behavior in the group, both with the therapist and with other group members. Methods include dialogue and discussion, psychodrama, recollection, reminiscence and life review, and an analysis and interpretation of the content of the group and each individual's role in it (Scheidlinger, 1952).

While there is continuing debate as to whether psychotherapy is effective with the elderly and whether it actually provides potential for growth and self-awareness, those psychiatrists, psychologists, social workers, and psychiatric nurses who have mastered the skill of analytic group psychotherapy report measured success in dealing with certain aspects of problems with the elderly using this approach. In reviewing several approaches to analytic group psychotherapy, De Schill (1973) notes that work with the elderly in geropsychiatry is especially productive for formerly neurotic and disabled elderly patients. Colucci and Amato (1973) report that group psychotherapeutic sessions for senile patients are particularly difficult. Their reasons include the lack of trained personnel, the age of the patients, and their separation from their family. Wolff (1967), notes the questionable and problematic value of gaining insight into the psychodynamics of the geriatric patients, but he also notes that group psychotherapy offers a corrective experience in improved interpersonal relationships, resocialization, and motivation to adjust outside the hospital. Similarly Petrovic (1971) noted that group psychotherapy reduced depression, and reestablished better relationships with the milieu and among elderly patients with organic deterioration in a psychiatric hospital. Gunn (1967) reports that patients in a geriatric ward of a psychiatric hospital were observed by their nurses to have a symptom change from behavior disturbance to verbalized depressed ideas during a 12-month period when they had weekly group psychotherapy sessions. In another pscyhiatric hospital it was reported (Wolk and Goldfarb, 1967), that long-term patients (mostly with diagnosed schizophrenia), who had grown old in the hospital showed pronounced improvement as a result of group psychotherapy. New admissions of elderly patients with a diagnosis of chronic brain syndrome also showed some improvement through group psychotherapy.

On an outpatient basis, group psychotherapy has been used successfully in working with patients in the resolution of individual problems in adapting to growing older as well as in improving social interaction (Altholz and Doss, 1973). The authors note the advantage of the opportunity for exposure to problem solutions developed by other elderly people. Berger and Berger (1973) noted successful use of group psychotherapeutic approaches to the aging by providing interpersonal activity and involvement with others which diminishes isolation, regressive behavior, and despair.

## ACTIVITY GROUP THERAPY

Activity group therapy may be one of several approaches to helping people through groups, where an activity provides the major focal point for interaction and for individual growth or change.

Activities are specially selected, designed, and developed for the particular goals, taking into consideration the unique needs of the participants. Types of activities used for this sort of group therapy include drama, dance and movement, exercise, sports and games, art, music, poetry reading and writing, creative writing, autobiography and reminiscence or oral history, recreational programs, and square and folk dancing. One of the differences between activity group therapy and recreational activity generally is the therapeutic focus, characterized by the use of verbal and nonverbal expressions for approaching the problems felt by group members, and the recognition and deliberate dealing with specified objectives. It is reported, for instance, that, with activity groups used on a geropsychiatric ward of a mental health service, patients were less hostile and showed less behavioral deterioration (Reichenfeld *et al.*, 1973). The discharge rates were also higher for patients in the activity group programs. In another program of handicapped elderly women, where operant conditioning was used as a stimulus for participating in the activity group program (Blackman, Howe, and Pinkston, 1976), social interaction among patients increased noticeably. In a day care program for elderly living in their own homes (Cohen, 1973), the activity group was used to engage the participants in planning for their own activities and developing their own interests in the group.

## MUSIC THERAPY

Music therapy includes the use of instruments, singing, listening to recordings, and the creation of songs and music. Shapiro (1969) reports that in a home for the aged, instruments were assigned on the basis of physical need and preference. Participation in the rhythm orchestra relieved stiffness of arthritis, encouraged muscular movements, and led to personal satisfaction, experience in conducting, developing leadership, and increased interpersonal relationships. There was some evidence of improvement of memory and concentration and release of tensions. In the same institution group singing was used to help patients analyze lyrics of songs and express their anxiety and hostility related to their life situations.

Gabelic *et al.* (1974) report the superior value of music in geriatric treatment, both because of the promotion of a sense of belonging, self-confidence, contentment, and relaxation, and because of its use as a socialization exercise and stimulus for reality contact. Hennessey (1978) notes that music has the quality of bringing people closer together, whether listening or participating. Developing a cohesive quality in the group provides the individual participants with the feeling of belonging and a sense of creating together. Music therapy may also be used as a supplement to other group therapeutic approaches, including social group work and group therapy, and reminiscence, relaxation, and physical therapy groups.

## ART THERAPY GROUPS

While many forms of art and art appreciation are individual in nature, art therapy can be conducted in groups, and the groups used as evaluation, feedback, support, and response to individual work. In one instance where art therapy was used in a psychiatric hospital with elderly patients who had very serious illnesses (Dewdney, 1973), the geriatric patients reverted from time to time to the functioning, organized person of a previous time. Inspired sense of self-worth was noted as a result of the art therapy groups.

Many well elderly engage in a variety of art and music activities in groups as a means of finding social relationships and personal enhancement. Some of these groups are in senior centers or adult schools, or are organized through other programs specifically for older adults. While the effect of these experiences are therapeutic and preventive of social isolation, many of these groups do not have a specific goal or objective of activities group therapy. The difference is in the defined need of the participants and their state of physical and mental health.

## DRAMATICS THERAPY

Therapeutic dramatic group activity is widely used, especially with people who are well enough physically or emotionally to participate in playing roles (Gray, 1973). Play readings and play writing have been employed for the elderly in many types of settings as a means of surfacing feelings, indentifying with characters, and taking the role of another. Simple role play, enacting previous or current life experiences, playing out traumatic situations, or rehearsing alternative roles and functions which an older person would take is closely related to psychodrama, a method pioneered by Moreno (1930) and others. This approach has been used with elderly in institutions or hospitals, who are in crises or facing overwhelming losses, as a means of surfacing emotions and examining ways of coping. Psychodrama is used to probe deeper feelings and meanings through dramatized situations, by bringing them to the surface and making

them apparent in a group for feedback or evaluation by peers and the therapist. Unlike simple role play, psychodrama probes unconscious defenses or feelings of which the participant has not been previously aware. Psychodrama is widely used in family therapy as members take the roles of each other, and gain insight into the feelings of others in their role sets. Family treatment psychodrama is just coming into use in the 1970s for examination of the roles and conflicts with elderly family members and their adult children. It will no doubt prove to be a very valuable tool for family dealings with multigenerational family problems.

## DANCE THERAPY AND MOVEMENT THERAPY

The use of body movement, from elementary motions to fullfledged dance therapy, has been developed as a kind of group activity to assist in nonverbal expression. Deliberately created and introduced interpretive dance steps have been used to assist elderly women with their emotions and expressions. Merritt (1971) used dance therapy to help elderly patients to adjust physically, mentally, emotionally, and socially to their infirmities in a nursing home. Patients gained self-confidence and learned to pride themselves for responding to the music and the dancing. The value of the group is in the use of kinds of dancing and choreography which encourage self-expression, collaborative activity and support, touching and belonging, and the total social experience.

## CREATIVE WRITING, AUTOBIOGRAPHIC GROUPS, AND ORAL HISTORY AS GROUP THERAPY

Recently emphasis has been placed on creative writing (poetry, short stories, song lyrics, autobiography, oral history, playwriting, and essays) as a therapeutic means for providing older people with continuity from the past to the present. The notions of catharsis as a means of freeing oneself of burdens of the past and creativity in expressing one's reactions to the present are aspects of the therapeutic use of writing. The group factor comes from the stimulation of other participants in sharing their creations and their common linkage to the past. Group participant feedback, support, encouragement, and shared coping mechanisms are part of the therapy. The group leaders for such workshops, therapy groups, or writing, reading, and sharing sessions have been historians, librarians, language and literature teachers, as well as group therapists, social workers, psychologists, and psychiatrists. One aim of such groups is to help the participants to gain insight and self-awareness, as well as to provide recognition, support, and shared experiences that improve social interaction, socialization, and a sense of belonging.

## FAMILY GROUP THERAPY

Family therapy, pioneered by Jay Haley (1970–71) and Nathan Ackerman (1971) among others, is a fairly recent phenomenon. None of the traditional family therapists have given attention to three-, four-, and five-generation families, and the group treatment of the problems arising in these. Yet, as long ago as 1964, Wilson and Ryland (1964) focused attention on the productivity in working on specific types of problems of older people in group sessions involving all of the members of an extended family. Family group therapy consists of sessions with a therapist with all members of the family focusing on the presenting problem and the interacting aspects of the relationships, pressures, and tensions of all of the family members. Increasingly, as families include several generations, the problems of a widowed, ill, frail, dependent, or economically needful old relative becomes the crisis or family problem affecting several generations. By bringing all family members together to work on the alternative solutions, the family group therapist makes use of group dynamics knowledge and group leadership skills. This use of the group is only currently appearing as a distinct group approach (Kilpatrick, 1968). It will become more prevalent as the population shifts are more evident, and more middle-aged adults are responsible for aging parents while they are also concerned about their adult children and their adolescent grandchildren. Problems of economics, housing or living arrangements, care, and maintenance make more demands on the emotional energy and resources of families. Financial management, health care, integration or segregation of the elderly, and interpersonal stress are the problems faced by family groups which are brought to the resources of the skilled family group therapists. Some techniques used include role play and psychodrama as well as reality testing and group counselling (Kilpatrick, 1968). There is some evidence that problems are better dealt with by work with total family groups, rather than with either the elderly or the middle-aged alone (Brody, 1978; Silverstein, 1978; Silverstone, 1978).

With older family members who appeared to be hostile and disruptive, the tendency was for families to place the elderly persons in a day care center. After family group therapy sessions, where some of the conflicts were worked on and strengths that had existed in the family were reinforced, persons were rehabilitated and discharged with families reconstituted (Grauer, Betts, and Birnbom, 1973).

Multiple family group therapy (Laqueur, 1972) has also been a group method in which family members of several families having similiar problems are brought together with the defined patient (the elderly person) for discussion of their mutual concern. Shier (1972) reports on sessions of residents of a geriatric center and their families meeting together to discuss their concerns about life at the center. The sessions resulted in strong ties in the residents and their family members as well as suggestions for improving their services.

## TECHNICAL ASPECTS OF WORKING WITH OLDER ADULTS IN GROUPS

The various leadership of therapeutic approaches to use of groups has been discussed previously and encompasses active and passive group leadership; focus on the worker as central manager of individual or group; the worker as facilitator of process, of individual participation, and of group development; and the worker as adviser, reinforcer, clarifier, and acknowledger where appropriate. How the worker is perceived and his appropriate role behavior is defined by himself, his philosophical orientation, his technical skill, his theoretic orientation, his professional stance, and to some extent the context in which he is practicing. By context is meant such places as mental health centers, senior centers, psychiatric hospitals, old age homes, or convalescent hospitals. His approach as a professional practitioner is also conditioned by his perception of aging, his knowledge of social gerontology, and his attitudes toward old age. As we have seen, the various approaches in the community and in the institution have changed as group workers and group therapists have brought together their knowledge of group process and the recognition of those outcomes which groups may produce for the participants. The approaches have also changed as practitioners have grown in their knowledge of the differences among the young old, the middle old, and the very old, and among the well elderly and the frail elderly, and as workers have learned to individualize rather than stereotype the elderly. As Butler (1974) has suggested, group therapy or group work may be used both as a preventive and a therapeutic tool with older adults. Focus of groups may be upon adapting to growing old; accepting physical, emotional, psychological and social changes; modification in roles and life styles; adapting to rapid technological changes and pressures of urban living, finding and developing new social relationships; locating opportunities to be needed, valued and approved; taking responsibilities; participating with others in self-enhancing and growth-providing activities; providing preventive opportunities for emotional and social breakdown; and insuring against the risk that may accompany growing old. Therapeutic group intervention may resocialize or remotivate old people who have become ill, isolated, disengaged, confused, or disoriented. Guided group experiences may ease people through the crises of growing old, and may offer support, insight, and social connections to reestablish confidence, self-esteem, self-management, and independence, at least to some degree for some older people. Improved memory, relieved anxiety, and improved coping capacity may result for the impaired from participation in group experiences. Lowy (1962) warns, however, that groups must be seen not only as helpful but also as potentially destructive, and therefore those mental health workers who would use group practice techniques with the elderly need to be well grounded in group theory and group practice techniques with the elderly. Burnside (1978) also reinforces the need to bring into focus the knowledge of aging with the knowledge of group process. Hartford (1971) suggests that workers need to assess carefully the ego functioning capacity of the older person in considering the appropriate group approach. She further notes that with the mystique that surrounds groups, there are those who believe that convening people in a collective is sufficient. However, careful clarification of goals and objectives, sensitivy to the individual participant's needs and capacities, and guidance of the experience are crucial for the group to have beneficial effects for the participants (Hartford, 1978). This is particularly true for older adults who are in a sensitive stage of human development and who are faced with many personal, social, and physical losses.

Groups have wide usage and benefits for older adults. They may be the instrument for support, growth, rehabilitation, or collective and collaborative action. Groups are used by most of the professions in mental health and in the helping and healing arts, and are particularly beneficial because of the specific kinds of social and personal needs of the elderly. But groups created and used by naive, unskilled workers who do not have knowledge of group processes, leadership methods, therapeutic techniques, or diagnostic skills, may be harmful for people who are unready or incapable of using groups. Poorly managed groups may highlight loneliness and depression. They may trigger emotional illness for borderline patients if such

people are not protected, or if the group culture becomes punitive rather than supportive. Therefore, workers of any discipline who would use group methods should be knowledgeable of the methods and the effect of groups.

All small groups have some characteristics in common, and those professional personnel who work with groups, regardless of profession, need to keep these factors in mind. All groups are composed of people who are diverse from each other in some ways, while they are similar in others. Most older people are more diverse than similar, since they have had longer to develop, and more experiences that differ, even though they may have some similar qualities. In the development of a group from an abstract collection of individuals, the participants must connect with each other, communicate, influence, be influenced by, and take on meaning for and from each other. Since merely bringing people together does not cause interaction, or at least meaningful interaction, to take place, the person in role of the leader must take some initiative in helping people to connect with each other, with the purpose for which the group is convened, and with the capacities each person brings. People who have sight or hearing disabilities; who have emotional or psychological problems; who have a sense of low self-esteem; who are shy, withdrawn, or out of the habit of communicating; or who lack a sense of adequacy may have greater difficulty in connecting. People who are using all of their energy to cope with their own crises, or who have lost so much, fear risking further relationships; people who are very depressed may have very little energy to respond to a group. For these people, group formation is very slow and a worker may have to take an active role while at the same time exercising infinite patience and understanding of the individuals and of the group process. Whether the purpose of the group is therapy, education, activity, or task achievement, the composition may reflect any of the above individual profiles. The worker with groups of elderly people must take into account the total framework of the biological, psychological, and environmental forces that are playing upon the lives of the individuals, and the uniqueness of each individual in the group.

If groups are to be effective instruments for personal growth or change or social change, they must achieve a level of formation, cohesion, and unity. This means they must proceed through developmental stages well known to group theorists. There are preformation, introductory, and testing periods as the group is designed and participants are convened. At this stage the participants undertake careful work on goal definition, composition, and structural factors. Once the group is convened the important activity is connecting people and clarifying purposes, taking organizational steps, and getting the participants to work together for the purposes for which the group was established. After initial formation and coalescence, there is usually a period of retesting of the worker, the purpose, the setting, and each other, in a phase labeled "storming" (Tuckman, 1965) by some in social psychology. If and when this potentially destructive behavior has been resolved, the group can go forward and become reintegrated to work on its objectives, until the group moves toward termination. The termination process is very important and needs to be carefully worked through, especially with people who have felt as many losses as most elderly people have. Recognizing that all groups experience some of this phase development, the professional worker can increase his skill if he recognizes the steps he can take in using small group theory, the applications of findings of research, the nature of the aging processes, and the needs of the elderly which are amenable to group therapy.

## SUMMARY

The use of group methods with the elderly began primarily under social work auspices and through the work of social group workers trained in small group theory and group leadership methods. However, the expansion of use of group methods, particularly following World War II, extended to social psychologists, clinical psychologists, psychiatrists, psychiatric and geriatric nurses, recreation workers, occupational therapists, and adult educators who developed specific techniques for work with groups and have consequently applied these approaches to work with the elderly. Nurses in geriatric care facilities have done some of the original experimentation, teaching, and writing in this field (Burnside, 1970, 1971, 1978). In California, adult educators under the auspices of local adult schools and community colleges have been working with remotivation, reality therapy, and reminiscence groups of patients in long-term care facilities and convalescent homes. Occupational therapists and professionals in such specialities as art therapy, music therapy, dance therapy or movement therapy are offering groups for the elderly within many residential and community settings. Reports of their activities and programs give evidence that their intent is the improved social and

mental health of the participants. A concern for all of these professionals, paraprofessionals and volunteers should be that they make use of the knowledge available about small group theory, methods of work with groups, the specific nature and needs of the elderly, and the mental and emotional capacities of older people, so that their interventions may have a positive and constructive effect rather than a negative or harmful one.

A tremendous body of knowledge is available about groups and therapeutic or social methodolgies for the use of groups, as well as the social and psychological needs of the elderly which can be met through appropriate small group interventions. However, most professionals in the human services or in preparation for the helping and healing arts seem to get very little preparation either in gerontology or in group leadership methods. Apparently, there is still a myth that anyone can lead groups and one can become an instant gerontologist by reading a book. We are past the time when the findings of research permit this type of ignorance in group practice with older adults. Furthermore, the potential for destructiveness of groups or the harmful effect on the participants precludes inappropriate use. Professional schools of social work, nursing, recreation, occupational therapy, clinical psychology, and medicine/psychiatry, need to upgrade their teaching of content relative to groups and to social gerontology so that mental health professionals will undertake an educated approach to their work. The apparent lack of definitive research or group uses with the elderly, studies of groups where the elderly are subjects, textbooks in the methodology of group work practice with older adults, or examples of work with the elderly in the textbooks on group methods highlights the gap that exists.

The bibliography attached to this chapter gives evidence that there is considerable use of groups in services for the elderly. Observations of practice with older adults to improve or support their mental health suggests that there is general use of a variety of group methods. What is needed now in planning mental health work with the elderly is an organized classification of types of groups appropriate to various personal and interpersonal mental health needs, appropriate in different community and institutional settings, and appropriate with the well independent elderly and the frail dependent elderly. Research and problem classification, followed by clarified technical skills and therapeutic methodology, should be developed. Such conceptualization would lead to improved t aching of practice and improved practice.

# REFERENCES

ABRAHAMS, R. B. 1972. Mutual help for the widowed. *Social Work, 17*(5), 56–61.

ACKERMAN, N. 1971. The growing edge of family therapy. *Family Process,* (July), 123–145.

ALLEN, K. S. 1976. A group experience for elderly patients with organic brain syndrome. *Health and Social Work, 1*(4) (November), 61–69.

ALLEN, V. 1970. Motivation therapy with the aging geriatric veteran patient. *Military Medicine, 135*(11) (November), 1007–1010.

ALLPORT, G. 1945. Catharsis and the reduction of tension. *Journal of Social Issues, I,* 3–10.

ALLPORT, G. 1954. The historical background of modern social psychology. *In,* G. Lindzey (ed.), *Handbook of Social Psychology,* pp. 3–56. Reading, Mass.: Addison-Wesley.

ALTHOLZ, J., AND DOSS, A. 1973. Outpatient group therapy with elderly persons. *Gerontologist, 13*(3), 101.

ASTLE, J., HOWSDIN, J., AND ARQUITT, G. E. 1977. *Intergenerational Living: A Follow-up.* Stillwater, Oklahoma: Oklahoma State University Press.

BENNIS, W. G., BENNE, K., AND CHIN, R. 1961. *The Planning of Change.* New York: Holt, Rinehart and Winston.

BERGER, L. F., AND BERGER, M. M. 1973. A holistic group approach to psychogeriatric outpatients. *International Journal of Group Psychotherapy, 23*(4), 432–444.

BING, L. 1951. Rallying community forces in planning for the aging. *In, Selected Papers in Group Work and Community Organization,* pp. 124–131. Raleigh, N.C.: Health Publications Institute.

BIRKETT, D. P., AND BOLTUCH, B. 1973. Remotivation therapy. *Journal of the American Geriatrics Society, 21*(8), 368–371.

BLACKMAN, D. K., HOWE, M., AND PINKSTON, E. M. 1976. Increasing participation in social interaction of the institutionalized elderly. *Gerontologist, 16*(1) (February), 69–76.

BOSKIND, S. 1966. The multi-service center as a community institution for elderly people. *In,* L. Lowy and J. Mogey (eds.), *Theory and Practice by Social Work with the Aging,* pp. 112–124. Boston: University of Boston, Council on Gerontology.

BOVEY, J. A. 1972. The effect of intensive remotivation techniques on institutionalized geriatric mental patients in a state mental hospital. (Doctoral dissertation, North Texas State University.) *Dissertation Abstracts International, 32*(7–B) (January), (University Microfilm No. 72, 4064, 4201–4202.

BRIM, O., AND WHEELER, S. 1966. *Socialization After Childhood.* New York: John Wiley.

BRODY, E. M. 1978. Aged parents and aging children. Paper delivered at the *You and Your Aging Parent Conference,* Andrus Gerontology Center, University of Southern California (mimeo).

BRUDNO, J. J., AND SELTZER, H. 1968. Re-socialization therapy through group process with senile patients in a geriatric hospital. *Gerontologist, 8*(3), 211–214.

BURNSIDE, I. M. 1970. Loss: A constant theme in group work with the aged. *Hospital and Community Psychiatry, 21*(6) (June), 173–177.

BURNSIDE, I. M. 1971. Long-term group work with hospitalized aged. *Gerontologist, 11*(3) (Fall), 213–218.

BURNSIDE, I. M. 1978. *Working with the Elderly: Group Processes and Techniques.* North Scituate, Mass.: Duxbury Press.

BUTLER, R. N. 1974. Successful aging. *Mental Hygiene, 58*(3), 6–12.

CARTWRIGHT, D. 1961. Achieving change in people. *Human Relations, 4,* 381–392.

CARTWRIGHT, D., AND ZANDER, A. 1958. *Group Dynamics.* New York: Harper & Row.

COHEN, M. G. 1973. Alternative to institutional care of the aged. *Social Casework, 54*(8), 447–452.

COLUCCI, D., AND AMATO, F. 1973. Group psychotherapy and sociotherapy in geriatric psychiatry: Preventive note. *Napoli Ospedale Psichiatrico, 44*(3), 513–519.

CONRAD, W. K. 1974. A group therapy program with older adults in a high-risk neighborhood setting. *International Journal of Group Psychotherapy, 24*(3), 358–360.

COOLEY, C. 1909. *Social Organization.* New York: Charles Scribner.

Council on Social Work Education. 1959. *Social Work Education for Better Services to the Aging.* Report of the Aspen Conference, Aspen, Colorado, 1958, and New York Council on Social Work Education.

COYLE, G. L. 1960. Group work in psychiatric settings: Its roots and branches. *Using Groups in Psychiatric Settings,* pp. 7–20. New York: National Association of Social Workers.

COYLE, G. L. July, 1962. Concepts relevant to helping the family as a group. *Social Casework, 43,* 347–354.

CROSBY, C. 1978. A group experience for elderly socially isolated widows. Unpublished Masters thesis. Los Angeles: University of Southern California.

DE SCHILL, S. 1973. *Group Psychotherapy.* Paris: Presses Universitaires de France.

DEWDNEY, I. 1973. An art therapy program for geriatric patients. *American Journal of Art Therapy, 12*(4), 249–254.

DURKHEIM, E. 1951. Suicide. Translated by John A. Spaulding and George Simpson. New York: The Free Press.

EPSTEIN, H. 1964. Developing citizen action through the senior adult program of the Jewish center. *Proceedings of the National Conference on Social Welfare.* New York: Columbia University Press.

FEIL, N. W. 1967. Group therapy in a home for the aged. *Gerontologist, 7*(3), 192–195.

FESTINGER, L., SCHACHTER, S., AND BACK, K. 1950. *Social Pressures in Informal Groups.* New York: Harper & Row.

FIDLER, J. W. 1970. The relationship of group psychotherapy to therapeutic group approaches. *International Journal of Group Psychotherapy, 20*(4), 473–494.

FREY, L. A. (ed.) 1966. *Use of Groups in the Health Field.* New York: National Association of Social Workers.

FRIEDMAN, S. 1975. The resident welcoming committee: Institutionalized elderly in volunteer services to their peers. *Gerontologist, 15*(4), 362–367.

GABELIC, I., BREITENFELD, D., GRUBISTIC, M., RADOTIC, D., MATAKOVIC, M., AND KULCAR, M. 1974. Music therapy in the geriatric club. *Anali Klinicke Bolnice, 13*(3), 258–263.

GLASSER, W. 1965. *Reality Therapy.* New York: Harper & Row.

GRAUER, H., BETTS, D., AND BIRNBOM, F. 1973. Welfare emotions and family therapy in geriatrics. *Journal of the American Geriatrics Society, 21*(1), 21–24.

GRAY, P. E. 1973. Dramatics for the elderly: A survey of characteristics, problems encountered, and solutions suggested in dramatic programs in New York senior centers and residential care settings. *Dissertation Abstracts International, 33*, 4–192.

GUNN, J. C. 1967. Group psychotherapy on a geriatric ward. *Psychotherapy and Psychosomatics, 15*(1), 26.

HALEY, J. 1970–1971. Family therapy. *International Journal of Psychiatry, 9*, 233–242.

HARE, A. P. 1962. *Handbook of Small Group Research.* New York: The Free Press.

HARTFORD, M. E. (ed.), 1962. *Working Papers Toward a Frame of Reference for Social Groupwork Practice.* New York: National Association of Social Workers.

HARTFORD, M. E. 1971. *Groups in Social Work.* New York: Columbia University Press.

HARTFORD, M. E. 1973. The social and psychological expression of need for a group, in a group psychology class of older adults. Cleveland, Ohio: Case Western Reserve University, Post-retirement Institute (mimeo).

HARTFORD, M. E. 1978. Groups in the human services: Some facts and fancies. *Social Work with Groups, 1*(1), 7–13.

HASTORF, A. H. 1965. The reinforcement of individual actions in a group situation. *In,* L. Krasner and L. Ullman (eds.), *Research in Behavior Modification,* pp. 268–284. New York: Holt, Rinehart and Winston.

HENNESSEY, M. J. 1973. Group work with economically independent aged. *In,* I. M. Burnside (ed.), *Psy-chosocial Nursing Care of the Aged,* pp. 231–244. New York: McGraw-Hill.

HENNESSEY, M. J. 1978. Music and music therapy groups. *In,* I. M. Burnside (ed.), *Working With the Elderly: Group Processes and Techniques,* pp. 265–272. N. Scituate, Mass.: Duxbury Press.

HOCHSCHILD, A. R. 1973. Communal life-styles for the old. *Society, 10*(5), 50–57.

KILPATRICK, A. C. 1968. Conjoint family therapy with geriatric patients. *Journal of the Fort Logan Mental Health Center, 5*(1), 29–35.

KUBIE, S., AND LANDAU, G. 1953. *Group Work with the Aged.* New York: International University Press.

LAQUEUR, H. P. 1972. Mechanisms of change in multiple family therapy. *In,* C. Sager and H. S. Kaplan (eds.), *Progress in Group and Family Therapy,* pp. 22–45. New York: Brunner/Mazel Publishers.

LARSON, M. K. 1970. A descriptive account of group treatment of older people by a caseworker. *Journal of Geriatric Psychiatry, 3*(2), 231–240.

LAZARUS, L. W. April, 1976. A program for the elderly at a private psychiatric hospital. *Gerontologist, 16*(2), 125–131.

LEANSE, J., AND WAGNER, S. 1975. *Senior Centers, A Report of Senior Group Programs in America.* Prepared by the National Institute of Senior Centers, National Council on Aging, Washington, D.C.

LEBON, A. 1895. *The Crowd.* Translated by Fisher. London: Allan Unwin.

LEWIN, K. 1943. Forces behind food habits and methods of change. *National Research Council Bulletin* CVIII. Washington, D.C. 35–65.

LIEBERMAN, M. A., YALLOM, I. D., AND MILES, M. 1973. *Encounter Groups: First Facts.* New York: Basic Books.

LIEDERMAN, P. C. 1967. Music and rhythm group therapy for geriatric patients. *Journal of Music Therapy, 4*(4), 126–127.

LIEDERMAN, P. C., GREEN, R., AND LIEDERMAN, V. R. 1967. Outpatient group therapy with geriatric patients. *Geriatrics, 22*(1), 148–153.

LINSK, N., HOWE, M. W., AND PINKSTON, E. M. November, 1975. Behavioral group work in a home for the aged. *Social Work, 20*(6), 454–463.

LOWY, L. 1955. *Adult Education and Group Work.* New York: Whiteside-Morrow.

LOWY, L. October, 1962. The group in social work with the aged. *Social Work, 7*, 43–50.

LOWY, L. 1967. Roadblocks in group work practice with older people: A framework for analysis. *Gerontologist, 7*, 109–113.

LOWY, L., AND MOGEY, J. 1966. *Theory and Practice in Social Work with the Aging.* Boston, Massachusetts: Boston University, University Council on Gerontology.

MAIZLER, J. S., AND SOLOMON, J. R. 1976. Therapeutic group process with the institutional elderly. *Journal of the American Geriatrics Society, 24*(12), 542–546.

MANIS, M. 1955. Social interaction and the self-concept. *Journal of Abnormal and Social Psychology*, 362–370.

MATHIASEN, G. 1951. National resources for local planning for the aging. *In, Selected Papers in Group Work and Community Organization*, pp. 119–123. Raleigh, N.C.: Health Publications Institute.

MAXWELL, J. M. 1962. Helping older people through participation. *Potentials for Service Through Group Work in Public Welfare*. Chicago: American Public Welfare Association.

MAYADAS, N. S., AND HINK, D. L. 1974. Group work with the aging. *Gerontologist*, *14*(5), part 1, 440–445.

MCDOUGALL, W. 1920. The Group Mind. New York: G. P. Putnam's Sons.

MCKEACHIE, W. J. 1958. Students, groups and teaching methods. *American Psychologist*, *13*, 580–584.

MEAD, G. H. 1934. *Mind, Self, and Society*. Chicago: University of Chicago Press.

MEREDITH, G. M., AND AMOR, C. A. August, 1976. Indexing the polarization of social groups in a multi-purpose senior center. *Psychological Reports*, *39*(1), 88–90.

MERRITT, M. C. 1971. *Dance Therapy Program for Nursing Homes*. Boston: Unitarian Universalist Association.

MORENO, J. L. 1934. *We Shall Survive: A New Approach to the Problems of Human Interaction*. Washington, D.C.: Nervous and Mental Disease Publishing Co.

MURPHY, G. 1963. Group psychotherapy in our society. *In*, M. Rosenbaum and M. Berger (eds.), *Group Psychotherapy and Group Functions*, 255–267 New York: Basic Books.

National Association of Social Workers. 1963. *Social Group Work with Older People*. Report of the Seminar on Group Work with Older People, Lake Mohonk, New York, 1961. New York: National Association of Social Workers.

NEVRUZ, N., AND HRUSHKA, M. 1969. The influence of unstructured and structured group psychotherapy with geriatric patients on their decision to leave the hospital. *International Journal of Group Psychotherapy*, *19*(1), 72–78.

PETROVIC, D. 1971. Group psychotherapy with geriatric psychiatric patients. *Anali Zavoda Za Mentalno Zdravlje*, *3*(2–3), 97–100.

RANK, B. J. 1963. Content of the group experience in a day center. *Social Group Work with Older People*. New York: National Association of Social Workers.

RATHBONE-MOODAN, E., AND LEVENSON, J. August, 1975. Impact of socialization therapy in a geriatric day-care setting. *Gerontologist*, *15*(4), 338–342.

REICHENFELD, H. F., CSAPO, K. G., CARRIERE, L., AND GARDNER, R. C. 1973. Evaluating the effect of activity programs on a geriatric ward. *Gerontologist*, *13*(3), 305–310.

REMNET, V. L. 1974. A group program for adaptation to a convalescent hospital. *Gerontologist*, *14*(4) (August), 336–341.

ROSIN, A. J. 1975. Group discussion: A therapeutic tool in a chronic deseases hospital. *Geriatrics*, *30*(8), 45–48.

ROSS, H. K. 1975. Low-income elderly in inner-city trailer parks. *Psychiatric Annals*, *5*(8) (August), 86–90.

SAINER, J. S., SCHWARZ, L. L., AND JACKSON, T. G. 1973. Steps in the development of a comprehensive service delivery system for the elderly. *Gerontologist*, *13*(3), 98.

SALTER, C. D., AND SALTER, C. A. 1975. Regression among institutionalized elderly patients following interruption of a therapeutic program. *Gerontologist*, *15*(5), 85.

SAUL, S. R., AND SAUL, S. 1973. Group psychotherapy in a proprietary nursing home. *Gerontologist*, *13*(3), 57. Also printed in *Gerontologist*, 1974, *14*(5), 446–450.

SCHEIDLINGER, S. 1952. *Psychoanalysis and Group Behavior*. New York: W. W. Norton.

SCHEIN, E., AND BENNIS, W. G. 1965. *Personal and Organizational Change Through Group Method*. New York: John Wiley.

SCOTT, D., AND CROWHURST, J. 1975. Reawakening senses in the elderly. *Canadian Nurse*, *71*(10), 21–22.

SEGUIN, M. M. 1973. Opportunity for peer socialization to old age in a retirement community. *Gerontologist*, *13*(2) (Summer), 208–214.

SEGUIN, M. M., AND O'BRIEN, B. (Eds.). 1976. *Releasing the Potential of the Older Volunteer*. Los Angeles: University of Southern California, Andrus Gerontology Center.

SHAPIRO, A. 1969. A pilot program in music therapy with residents of a home for the aged. *Gerontologist*, *9*(2), (Summer), 128–133.

SHAPIRO, E. 1973. The residents: A study in motivation and productivity among institutionalized octogenarians. *Gerontologist*, *13*(1) (Spring), 119–124.

SHIER, B. R. 1972. Closer communication through interaction in groups of aged persons. *Journal of Jewish Communal Service*, *49*(2), 162–166.

SILVERSTEIN, D. 1978. New models in service and care. Paper delivered at the *You and Your Aging Parent Conference*. Los Angeles: University of Southern California, Andrus Gerontology Center (mimeo).

SILVERSTONE, B. 1978. Issues for the middle generation: Responsibility, adjustment, and growth. Paper delivered at the *You and Your Aging Parent Conference*. Los Angeles: University of Southern California, Andrus Gerontology Center (mimeo).

SIMMEL, G. 1950. The Sociology of George Simmel. Translated and edited by K.H. Wolff. New York: The Free Press.

SLAUSON, S. R. 1956. *The Fields of Group Psychotherapy*. New York: John Wiley.

SLOAN, M. B. 1953. The special contribution of therapeutic group work in a psychiatric setting. *The*

*Group, 15*(4) (April), 8–12.

STEPHENS, L. R. (Ed.) 1975. *Reality Orientation,* Revised Edition. Washington, D.C.: Hospital and Community Psychiatry Service, American Psychiatric Association.

STOUFFER, S. (Ed.). 1949. *The American Soldier, Combat and its Aftermath.* Princeton, N.J.: Princeton University Press.

SUNDEL, M., AND LAWRENCE, H. 1974. Behavioral group treatment with adults in a family service agency. *In,* P. Glasser, R. Sarri, and R. Vinter (eds.), *Individual Change Through Small Groups,* pp. 105–125. New York: The Free Press.

TAULBEE, L. R., AND FOLSOM, J. C. 1966. Reality orientation for geriatric patients. *Hospital and Community Psychiatry, 17*(5) (May), 133–135.

TRECKER, H. (ed.), 1956. *Group Work in the Psychiatric Setting.* New York: Whiteside and Morrow.

TRECKER, H. 1964. *Group Services in Public Welfare.* Washington, D.C.: Department of Health, Education and Welfare.

TUCKMAN, B. W. 1965. Developmental sequences in social groups. *Psychological Bulletin, 63,* 384–399.

VICKERY, F. 1960. *How to Work with Older People.* Sacramento, Calif.: Department of Natural Resources, Division of Recreation.

WALLEN, V. 1970. Motivation therapy with the aging geriatric patient. *Military Medicine, 135*(2), 1007–1010.

WEINER, M., BROK, A., AND SNADOWSKY, A. 1978. *Working with the Aged.* Englewood Cliffs, N.J.: Prentice-Hall.

WILSON, G., AND RYLAND, G. 1964. The family as a unit of service. Social Work Practice, 1964. *Proceedings of the National Conference of Social Welfare.* New York: Columbia University Press.

WOLFF, K. 1967. Comparison of group and individual psychotherapy with geriatric patients. *Diseases of the Nervous System, 28*(6), 384–386.

WOLK, R. L., AND GOLDFARB, A. I. 1967. The response to group psychotherapy of aged recent admissions compared with long-term mental hospital patients. *American Journal of Psychiatry, 123*(10), 1251–1257.

WOODS, J. H. 1953. *Helping Older People Enjoy Life.* New York: Harper Brothers.

YALLOM, I. D., AND TERRAZAS, F. 1968. Group therapy for psychotic elderly patients. *American Journal of Nursing, 68*(8), 1690–1694.

# 34

# Mental Health Services
# in the Community

*Louis Lowy*

## THE CONCEPT OF COMMUNITY
## MENTAL HEALTH SERVICES

It is not easy to arrive at a commonly accepted definition of community services for mental health. Wide variations exist in definition. (Kamerman and Kahn, 1976) For purposes of this chapter, community services for mental health are defined as those provisions that exist in a community geared to maintain "good" mental health, to prevent deterioration and to ameliorate conditions that have affected "good" mental health which can lead to mental and emotional illness among a segment of the population.

Services in a community consist of several types—those that are rendered out-of-home as well as in-home which are characterized by a non-institutionalized approach.

"The boundaries of the general social services are unclear and shifting. As much can be said about community development and area redevelopment efforts. Clearly some of the activities and programs listed under these efforts should be considered in relation to overall general social services programming, but some should not. The community mental health field is especially interesting in this regard. For a considerable period beginning in the mid-1960s, it concentrated on "prevention" and early intervention and thus became involved in activities and programs parallel to those in many of the general social services, including broad-scale neighborhood self-help activity through community organization." (Kamerman and Kahn, 1976, p. 17.)

Although this tendency has declined it has not completely disappeared as community mental health has tended to concentrate more on psychiatric disorder and prevention was difficult to define and assess.

Psychiatric disorders are seen as a subcategory of medicine, which is encompassed by the health system despite a constant struggle to assure in- and out-patient psychiatric programs within general health provisions and coverage for psychiatric care under various forms of insurance and other funding. "To the extent that community mental health programs continue with a broad sense of mission and to the degree that psychiatric programs generally are guided by other than medical models of causation and intervention, their programs of direct service to individuals, families, and groups and their community organization activities are not distinguishable from (and perhaps should be seen as part of) general social services. When mental health programs are more specifically psychiatric-medical, the need for linkage with and some adjunctive staffing by general social service personnel remains and is recognized. This is especially true in day treatment centers, after-care programs. and programs to deal with psychiatric emergencies." (Kamerman and Kahn, 1976, p. 18.)

## WHERE ARE THE MENTALLY ILL AGED?

Slightly less than one percent of all persons aged 65 and over are patients in public and private mental institutions. This group is about equally divided between two sub-groups: those hospitalized for senile brain disease, Alzheimer's and Pick's disease, and other disorders, such as affective disorders, psychotic episodes, paranoid states arising in old age, and long-term psychotics who have grown old in the hospital. Another five percent of all old people live in nursing homes, homes for the aged, and other institutions. Authorities estimate that perhaps half of these institutionalized elderly suffer from significant psychiatric disturbance. Thus, at most, three percent of all older people live in institutions as a result of mental illness, or suffer mental illness as a by-product of their institutionalization. Most of those affected are 75 and over.

However, surveys among non-institutionalized elderly reveal a high level of mental disorder (Coe and Brehm, 1972). One study indicated that the rate of psychosis among old people is ten times the rate of those between age 15 and 34. A composite picture of several psychiatric surveys indicates the following: perhaps five percent of old people living in the community are either psychotic or have severe mental disturbances; another fifteen percent have mild or moderate degrees of psychiatric impairment. These surveys are all cross-sectional. They do not indicate to what extent, if any, mental disturbances increase in frequency with age. Neither do they distinguish between organically-based disorders and those which originate in the older person's personality structure or living situation.

A respectable body of psychiatric opinion holds that no individual who manages to function in the community can be considered mentally ill (Goldfarb, 1973). This view does not deny that individuals suffer from emotional disturbances, or that their disturbances cause others to suffer as well. Those who take this approach simply say that "mentally ill" people have social and legal problems, not medical ones. Thus, while there are good reasons to doubt the precision of surveys of mental health care needs among old people living in the community, they do at least suggest an important area of need, the nature of which we might not fully understand (Lowy, 1979).

Mental health services for older people are scarce. The elderly either receive no psychiatric attention at all, or they are committed for long periods of time, often for life, to institutions which usually offer little more than custodial care. Old people comprise approximately thirty percent of all public mental hospital patients and eleven percent of these patients are in private institutions; however, they account for only two percent of the patients in psychiatric outpatient clinics. Private psychiatrists regard old people as unattractive patients, and many lack training in the therapeutic techniques which are especially suited to treating older people. Medicare pays for only a fraction of psychiatrists' fees, and most older people are unable to afford the cost of extended private psychotherapy.

A promising approach to better mental health treatment for older people seemed to be community-oriented, preventive services offered through community mental health centers (Gurian and Scherl, 1972). While it is not certain that psychiatric disorders can be "prevented" at any age, the social measures which have historically been most effective in raising the level of health have been preventive programs aimed at entire communities rather than individual patients. The concept of "community psychiatry" follows in this tradition. It is based on the notion that institutionalization—the traditional way to deal with disturbed persons—usually creates more problems for the patient than it can possibly solve. A flexible array of treatment, social and environmental interventions provided within the community, avoids the special problems of institutional care. They are also more likely to build on whatever resources the disturbed individual may have. These measures include out-patient services in private practice or clinics, day hospitals for patients who need more extensive daily support, walk-in-clinics and other crisis intervention, and brief hospitalization when necessary, usually in a psychiatric ward of a general hospital. However, community mental health centers serve a very small proportion of older people; they neglect them and serve them only when pressured to do so. And yet, comprehensive services offered through community mental health centers would have benefits particularly for the elderly, as many elderly are beset by multiple problems—medical, psychiatric, emotional and social. These problems are interrelated, but the existing health care system treats them separately. And so the troubled older person mostly has only the choice of entering an acute care hospital, where psychiatric care is usually unavailable or a mental hospital—and where his other needs are likely to be ignored.

Several studies report (Butler, 1975; Kastenbaum, 1964; Lowy, 1975; Riley and Foner, 1968), that negative attitudes of mental health professionals and concomitant manifestations of these attitudes in practice, facilities and programs are largely responsible for inadequate utilization of community mental health services by the elderly. In a survey conducted by a Committee of Aging of the American Psychological Association, 1957, it was reported that only one percent of all psychologists devoted their whole practice to older people; forty-one percent of psychologists did not see elderly patients; fifty-eight percent spent some time but over one-third did so only in institutional settings. The rate of people over 65 being treated in out-patient clinics did not increase between 1963 and 1971. It was 2.4 per 100,000 in 1971, compared to a 157 percent increase in services for all age groups in the same period.

When reviewing history, it seems that the encouragement of community mental health programs may indeed have been detrimental to solving the mental health needs of the older population instead of beneficial, as originally envisioned. The problems of drug dependent adolescents, marital conflicts of the middle years, or the suicide attempts of youths have not only appeared to be more urgent and socially imperative, but also more attractive and potentially capable of solution, particularly since it is usually a younger clientele who present themselves. As a consequence, older persons, in general, have not gone to such centers, staff members have not been trained to give either diagnosis or treatment to older adults, and the administrative organization of such units has not encouraged home contacts with older adults or developed institutional ties where the more seriously ill older adults reside. The community mental health centers stayed clear of any connection to state mental hospitals—as elder clients were shunted into mental hospitals. "The unresponsiveness to the aging is still reflected in the perpetuation of a categorical tightrope system which defines eligibility for care rigidly in categorical mental health and mental retardation terms, rather than in terms of the older person's health needs in their total psychosocial context." (Santore and Diamond, 1974.)

What had gone wrong with the ideal of community mental health centers when first conceived in the fifties and implemented in the sixties? Reiff (1976) speculates that community mental health centers were supposed to emphasize rehabilitation, a return to social functioning rather than to offer treatment and cure, but with lack of differently trained personnel and sufficient funding they became training grounds and practice centers for therapy skill, informed by the prevalent psychiatric ideology, and not rehabilitation, strengthened by a community support system. "This has been one of the major causes of the failure of community mental health centers to provide the appropriate community supports necessary to sustain the deinstitutionalized mentally ill in the community." (Reiff, 1976, p. 5) The focus should have been on rehabilitation to teach social skills and to organize community resources to reinforce the use of these skills. "This was the meaning of Community Support that was originally implied in the early conceptualization of community mental health as a rehabilitation enterprise." (Reiff, 1976, p. 5.)

## WHAT IS "GOOD" MENTAL HEALTH FOR OLDER PERSONS?

Jahoda (1958) offers six criteria of "good" mental health:

1. positive attitudes toward self
2. growth development and self-actualization
3. integration
4. autonomy
5. reality perception
6. environmental mastery.

However old, we must see ourselves in positive terms; it is important that we see ourselves growing and actualizing; it is important that we integrate ourselves in terms of a past and some kind of a future. We need to feel ourselves independent, masters of a tomorrow; we must be able to view our strengths or abilities and our weaknesses or disabilities within any time framework. And, wherever we are, however old we are, we must feel that, in the environment we find ourselves in, we have some kind of mastery or competence. (*Manpower and Training Needs*, 1977, p. 26.)

To be mentally healthy a person needs to be able to respond to other individuals, to love, be loved, and to cope with others in give and take relationships and to be able to manage separation from others, i.e. to be able to cope with feelings engendered by losses such as aggression and frustration.

In later life, these criteria seem to be more successfully realized in being and expanding the self by interpreting or reinterpreting what has been rather than what is about to be (*Manpower,* etc., 1977, p. 30). Birren and Renner (1977) speak of the 5 R's necessary for "good" mental health in old age: review, reconciliation, relevance, reverence, and release. As stated in the *Manpower and Training Needs Report* (1977, p. 31): "Balance between active striving and reflection should occur throughout the life span, but the shift in this balance may change over the life span."

WHAT ORIENTATIONS TO
COMMUNITY MENTAL HEALTH SERVICES
CAN BE DIFFERENTIATED?

Mental health as a field needs to be viewed from two fundamental perspectives:

1. A treatment perspective that focuses on restoration and rehabilitation of older people who have mental impairments, or who are classified and categorized as emotionally disturbed or mentally ill. This focus follows the "medical" model.
2. The perspective of a "public health" model concentrating on prevention. This second approach focuses on the environment and attempts to shape it to achieve mental health of people living in a community. Each perspective demands mental health personnel to perform in the roles of technicians, paraprofessionals, or full professionals to deliver direct services in agencies, inpatient and outpatient mental health facilities and programs, as members of home care teams, or to provide indirect services to the aged such as planning, administration, consultation, teaching, and research.

Since the time when community mental health centers were created mental health programs continued to overlap with "general social services." A central issue today is still the definition of "system boundaries" between mental health and general social services and the creation of a linkage between them.

Kahn (1973) identifies personal (general) social services that have three types of functions:

1. access and information to the total social sector
2. socialization and development
3. treatment and rehabilitation.

Each of these can also be conceptualized as having primarily a curative, preventive or an enhancing (promoting) goal orientation.

## TYPES AND NATURE OF OUT-OF-HOME COMMUNITY MENTAL HEALTH SERVICES

Basically, there are two major types of services based on the destination of service delivery: (1) Out-of-home and (2) In-home services. Under this first section therapeutic, preventive-support services and enhancement services will be listed.

THERAPEUTIC SERVICES IN VARIOUS SETTINGS

Counseling, casework and group work, protective services, crisis intervention, rehabilitative and day care services will be discussed here. They constitute the major programs in many communities that address themselves to direct treatment interventions.

*Counseling.*   Counseling is offered on a short term or a long term basis to individual people or to groups of people. Its primary goal is to provide help to older persons and, also increasingly, to members of their families—in their adaptation and

**Table 34–1**   Orientations to Community Mental Health Services (Denner and Price, 1973).

1. Traditional orientations define deviating behavior in intrapsychic terms, expect people to present themselves voluntarily at mental health centers that offer diagnostic treatment and consultation services and have policy made exclusively by professional staff members. (curative)
2. Environmentally oriented centers place emphasis upon milieu changes and offer crisis-oriented, brief treatment and community support services; they are more identified with clients/patients and involve a citizens' advisory board in policy making decisions. (preventive)
3. Social action oriented centers focus their programs upon the solution of social problems (drug dependencies, proverty, crime, racism, etc.) as causes of mental illness and involve citizen groups, including their clients/patients in action programs. (preventive—enhancing)
4. Growth-enhancing centers are educationally oriented and make use of group experiences as means to achieve self-awareness, sensitivity and self-growth to develop into mentally healthy people. (enhancing)

social functioning, in their role relationships, and in maintaining or re-establishing a psychic equilibrium. It tries to aid people in adapting their environment to changing functional abilities or in lessening external stress. Only if such adjustments are not possible or sufficient are they assisted in moving to new settings in which physical, emotional and social needs can be met more adequately. At all points the older person is helped to maintain or repair his/her environment and to be relieved of immobilizing fears and anxieties. The specific focus of counseling or casework and the specific services to be provided are generally determined by multiple, interrelated needs. A study of the whole person in his/her situation and milieu is basic to treatment. That is why counseling and casework are preceded by an evaluation that includes medical, psychiatric, emotional and social components.

The ideal counseling process, as a totality, involves the following six functions: screening, evaluation, diagnosis, treatment, rehabilitation and after care. The systematic screening and evaluation of the elderly person's physical and psychosocial current functional status is designed to elicit all pertinent information and to expedite the identification of a person's problem areas and underlying disorders. A physical examination is particularly important, since many behavioral disorders are traceable to physical health problems. All this culminates in a physio- psycho- social diagnosis. Following such diagnosis, a treatment plan is developed that, if successful, should lead to rehabilitative activities—physical, psychological and social—for the person with appropriate after care to maintain the gains made in the process.

Obviously reality interferes with such an orderly process and most therapeutic services do not follow this ideal path. Furthermore, very few communities are organized to meet such expectations, although there do exist model programs that attempt to operate according to the ideal pathways. The Texas Department of Mental Health and Mental Retardation, for example, offers such a comprehensive geriatric service program through TRIMS (Texas Research Institute of Mental Sciences). This, however, is still more the exception than the rule.

Treatment modalities include crisis intervention, milieu therapy, individual or group psychotherapy, family treatment and pharmacotherapy.

Common themes in treatment approaches to older persons are: guilt and restitution, guilt and atonement, awareness of the passage of time, disguised fears of death, autonomy vs. identity (Butler and Lewis, 1973, pp. 233–235). Behavior modification, in addition to psychoanalytic appraisals, Gestalt and transactional treatment modalities are gradually being tried in work with older persons.

Drugs, if judiciously employed, can be of supportive value in treatment of anxieties, agitation and depression. However, they should not represent the major or sole form of treatment. Unfortunately, even in community mental health programs there has been an overreliance upon drugs. Older people have been overmedicated. (See also discussion in Chapter 31.)

Settings where counseling or casework are offered include privately sponsored family service agencies, community mental health centers, well-aging clinics, general hospitals, mental health institutions, geriatric day hospitals, adult day care centers, multi-service centers for older persons, settlement houses, public health and public welfare departments and other social agencies.

The following five problems that require counseling have been identified in several studies: (1) Problems in individual adjustment and family relationships. While there were relatively few marital problems (few of their clients were still married), many of the problems concerned relationships between aged parents and their adult children that can be labeled as "intergenerational conflict" and "filial crisis" and problems of isolation and loneliness. (2) Problems of physical illness and medical planning. They were numerically most significant as there was a link between physical illness and emotional breakdown and physical illness in one of the partners, when they were still married, created heightened anxiety. (3) Acute breakdown and inability to manage their own affairs. These were problems whereby many of the people living alone could no longer fulfill their regular responsibilities and needed assistance, home care and, at times, protective services. (4) Economic problems, such as financial deprivation as well as problems with budgeting and shopping. (5) Living and housing problems. Older people found it difficult to adjust to their home and living situation or to an institutional setting. (Blenkner, 1965; Brody, 1966; United Charities of Chicago, 1966.)

Since public assistance agencies are usually the ones that have most contact with older people through the Supplementary Security Income Program, they were found to be in greatest need of becoming sensitized to the concerns of the elderly and to provide counseling services to them. Therefore special training programs for public welfare agency staffs have been developed by the Public Welfare Association. Social casework is one of the methods used in counseling. Only in a minority of cases, however, are such services available as a part of the general community service via family service agencies, public welfare departments (usually only for people qualifying for public funds), mental health clinics, Red Cross chapters, centers for the aged, and others. In several large cities, notably in New York, Chicago, Boston, Detroit, and Los Angeles, the Family Service Association of America has been active in developing special departments to provide services to older persons among its member agencies. The network of counseling resources is widespread but thinly drawn and as yet has reached relatively few older persons in the nation. The orientation is still traditional and places the initiative on the older person who comes to such counseling services or is referred through a social agency or by a treatment team. However, counseling has been in heavy demand wherever and whenever programs have been organized.

Already the Public Welfare Amendments of 1962 and 1967 had put greater emphasis on rehabilitation than on financial handouts in public assistance programs. It was anticipated that, when these would be implemented by state departments of public welfare, better qualified staff would be able to engage in counseling programs for their aged clients. However, the facts have not borne out this hope, since funding and training of personnel had been always inadequate to do the job.

The amendments to the Social Security Act of 1972 have led to a separation of income payments from social services in public welfare programs and have created a Supplemental Social Security Income category combining the former Old Age Assistance, Aid to the Permanently and Totally Disabled, and Aid to the Blind categories into a new title and guaranteeing a minimum income floor for the elderly across the nation. While laudable as a step in the right direction as far as income is concerned, the emphasis on an income strategy and the "benign neglect" of a service strategy have created an imbalance as regards to services.

Consequences resulting from these new programs have not yet been assessed systematically and await the results of empirical studies that will provide data to this effect (US Senate Special Committee on Aging, 1975).

*Group Work.*    This service has been in use for several decades. Originally performed as a spontaneous recreational activity in centers for the elderly or in golden age clubs, it has become recognized that group work demands specially trained personnel with special skills. More and more recreation centers, golden age clubs, day care centers, family agencies, general and geriatric hospitals, public welfare departments, homes for the aged,

etc. have begun to develop specialized group work services when older people find it difficult to cope with peer and social relationships. Groups are formed with the help of a social group worker and the group experience of the members is utilized for resocialization purposes. Group workers are attuned to individual needs and work with individuals in the group and also outside the group and, if necessary, make referrals to other community agencies, such as mental health clinics, where more specialized individual treatment is available. (Burnside, 1970, 1978; Lowy, 1962, 1963, 1979.)

Group work is differentiated from group psychotherapy as it focuses on the growth and development of the "normal," healthy person, rather than on the person who suffers from emotional functional disorders. Group psychotherapy uses psychotherapeutic principles and techniques from individual psychotherapy as well as techniques derived from group process, while group work makes use of the group process as it occurs, to afford each member as many growth producing experiences as possible in order to facilitate ego enhancement rather than treatment of a debilitating condition.

There are two essential aspects of the dynamics of groups: (1) the interpersonal relationships, making up the group process and (2) the task functions which constitute the group product. Interactions of members make groups go round, "sometimes fair and sometimes sour." Three basic processes are at work in interpersonal interactions: (1) inclusion: who is in and who is out; (2) dominance: who is on top, who is at the bottom and who is in-between; (3) closeness: who turns toward whom, who turns away or who turns against others. These are oversimplified versions of many theoretical concepts developed in small group research. In addition to developing interpersonal relationships the "work" of the group has to get done. The "work" (task) may be talking, feeling, learning, doing, playing. Through both, the interpersonal relationships and the tasks that people work on, a sense of "self," a self-image emerges because people incorporate the reflection of others into their own self perception.*

*Protective Services.*    These offer assistance to older people who may need help in managing their money or have fears of daily living but do not yet need the elaborate legal protection of a court-ap-

*See: William Schutz. Interpersonal Underworld. *In,* Bennis, Benne, and Chin (eds.), *Planning of Change,* pp. 293–306. New York: Holt, Rinehart & Winston, 1961. Also: D. Cartwright and A. Zander, (eds.). *Group Dynamics, Research and Theory.* Evanston, Ill.: Row, Peterson & Co., 1960.

pointed guardian or conservatorships. They are defined as a "constellation of social services; assist older people who manifest a degree of incapacity or limited mental, emotional or physical functioning which may result in harm or hazard to themselves or others, and they help individuals maintain at a level of competence and functioning that will enable them to manage their own affairs." (Lowy, 1979, p. 148.)

Protection for elderly should be sought and provided for in four areas (HEW, 1970):

1. protection of the life and property of the marginally functioning, non-institutionalized elderly
2. protection of civil liberties of these same elderly
3. protection for professional persons working in this field, to free them from burdens of anxiety about their authority and its limits
4. protection for the community from dangers posed by the incapacitated person.

The National Council on Aging (1972) originally and the National Council of Senior Citizens (1976) later spearheaded these services through their Legal Research and Services for the Elderly Project in 1968, which has resulted in legal aid services to older people in the community. In 1973, Congress added these legal services to those available under the Older Americans Act and in 1975 legal services were established by Congressional action as one of the four national priority services to be funded under Title III of the Older Americans Act. It is still a rocky road that leads from designating these services as a national priority and getting statewide programs into operation. A *Law and Aging Manual* (National Council of Senior Citizens, 1976) is to facilitate this process by drawing up model statutes, enlisting law schools, law practitioners, paralegals, and state legislators, developing senior advocacy, and obtaining funding for legal programs for the elderly that would provide legal assistance and legal protections.

*Crisis Intervention.* According to crisis theory, "a period of upset during crisis may be a potential turning point when the individual's vulnerability to immediate or eventual mental disorder may alter significantly; in a time of crisis there is increased openness and accessibility of the individual that can lead to both adverse and salutary consequences" (Bellak and Barten, 1969, p. 151). The outcome of crisis intervention is dependent on a person's constitutional resilience, precrisis adjustment, coping skills engendered by other crises, general helpfulness contained within the social network and specialized help stemming from a person's understanding of the circumstance of the cri-

sis. Several community agencies provide crisis-intervention services and crisis supports to the elderly who are often beset by physical, emotional and social crises which result from problems of poverty, disability, illness, loss of spouse, friends, etc. Delay in responding often produces far more damaging consequences than if an immediate response had been forthcoming.

TO ILLUSTRATE. For people with a sudden, severe emotional crisis, the West Philadelphia Community Mental Health Consortium offers an emergency service 24 hours a day, seven days a week. Located in the Receiving Ward of Philadelphia General Hospital, the staff offers evaluation and emergency care to the 4,200 people who come each year for help and responds to 8,000 people in crisis over the phone. On weekdays, the Consortium's Emergency Home-Visiting Team visits older people in emotional crisis at their homes, on the street or wherever the emergency occurs. And when a person's emotional problems are so overpowering that he or she cannot cope with a job, housework or other basic responsibilities, the Partial Hospitalization Program offers an intensive day treatment program designed to keep the person out of the hospital and to get him back on his feet as quickly as possible. The nine-person staff provides 30 clients many types of treatment in newly renovated facilities, which include a community room, an art and occupational theory studio, a fully equipped gymnasium, a dining room and kitchen (West Philadelphia Consortium for Mental Health, 1977).

*Rehabilitation and Restoration.* "The success of current deinstitutionalization efforts is as much dependent upon our establishment of meaningful, accessible rehabilitative and community residential services as upon any other factor" (Massachusetts Mental Health Planning Project, 1972, p. 22).

Occupational, speech and physical therapy are provided at day care and after care programs or are available as part of outpatient departments at general hospitals or in day hospitals. Rehabilitative services help restore patients to optimal functioning, both in activities of daily living and in general physical functioning. The latter applies especially to stroke victims.

Rehabilitation or restorative services also include training and socialization opportunities, work arrangements and living arrangements that are provided through ex-patient clubs, sheltered workshops, halfway houses or in psychosocial rehabilitation centers which offer comprehensive, coordinated programs that provide social, vocational and residential services under unified organizational auspices, often linked to a community mental health center program that features self-help and self-government.

For former hospital patients and for others with chronic mental illness, a number of communities provide day treatment programs and outpatient services to help people make a more successful return to the community. In addition, special restorative services for problem drinkers and drug abusers have emerged in the gerontological field during the last decade. Special programs in mental health centers, day care programs, geriatric hospitals, family agencies and in alcoholism or drug clinics have begun to operate, though the prevalence of such programs is in no way related to the incidence of these problem conditions of older persons.

> The most promising approach to better mental health treatment for older people seems to be flexible community-oriented preventive services offered through local community mental health centers. . . . the social measures which have historically been most effective in raising the level of health have been preventive programs aimed at entire communities rather than individual patients. . . . a flexible array of treatment interventions provided within the community avoids the special problems of institutional care. . . . include outpatient services in private practice or clinics, day hospitals for patients who need more extensive daily support, walk-in-clinics, and other crisis-intervention (Gurian and Scherl, 1972).

They further recommend that a center specifically for elderly patients be established, as it could provide more comprehensive services and more services for the isolated non-ambulatory patient; a drop-in center would allow for social, recreational and educational activities, and crisis intervention and counseling could be available without prior appointments by older people. In addition, a program for volunteers (young and old) would tap latent resources for engagement.

ILLUSTRATION. The Crozer-Chester Medical Center and Community Mental Health Center in Pennsylvania has provided a program for the residents of Catchment Area IV in Delaware County, Pa. since January, 1974. The population of this catchment area is 119,638. Residents over age 65 make up 8.6 percent of the population. White residents make up 76.1 percent of this population, while black residents make up 23.6 percent. According to a recent Research and Evaluation Report of Crozer-Chester CMHC (1976) the expected utilization of services by the geriatric population was estimated at 4.5 percent; the expected need

for such services was 10.8 percent. Thus far the utilization of services by the over 65 age group has been 2–3 percent of the service population—which is also reported from other community mental health centers.

Since the 1975 Community Mental Center Amendments Crozer-Chester CMHC has expanded its geriatric services to provide an integrated diagnosis and evaluation of medical, psychiatric and social aspects of illness by a multidisciplinary team, assist in implementing individual treatment plans through collaboration with physicians and other service agencies, and forge linkages with other agencies in the catchment area.

Other formats for community organizations where special attention is given to cope with emotional and mental health needs of the aged are geriatric day care centers, day hospitals, and foster home care programs.

*Geriatric Day Care Centers and Day Hospitals.* In the past few years day care centers have emerged in the US, though they have existed for quite a long time in several European countries. Day care centers are "primarily social programs for frail, moderately handicapped or slightly confused older persons who need care during the day or some part of the week—either because they live alone and cannot manage altogether on their own or, by sharing some of the responsibility for their care, to relieve their family and thereby help them to keep them at home" (Trager, 1975, p. 6).

There have been issues of priorities and dominance of components such as psychosocial, socialization, health or mental health. Robbins attempted to resolve these issues by dividing geriatric day care into four modules: Module 1 provides intensive restorative medical and health supportive services to individuals who otherwise would have remained as inpatients had this form of care not been available; Module 2 provides time-limited, intensive restorative services to the part-institutionalized home patient; Module 3 offers long term health maintenance services to a high risk population that also provides essential respite and relief to family members in their efforts to maintain the person in a home setting; Module 4 provides day care to the frail elderly who require primarily psychosocial activities in a protected environment (Robbins, 1975).

A dichotomous categorization divides day care services into those that focus more on meeting psychosocial and socialization needs and those that focus more on care for physical, organic, functional and mental impairments. An illustration of the former is the day care program at Levindale Center in Baltimore, Md.; an illustration of the latter is the geriatric day hospital program offered at Misericordia Hospital in Philadelphia. This includes therapeutic recreational programs, social services, medical examinations and other health services, as well as occupational and physical therapy. A hot noonday meal and a mid-afternoon snack is offered daily. Transportation is being provided by special paramedical service in specially equipped vehicles.

Goals of all day care centers and day hospitals include: to keep individuals out of institutions as long as possible; to provide social contact and enrichment experiences; to make the burdens lighter for the younger family, adult children who work, etc.; to provide a nutritional program and pleasant surroundings for isolated elderly; to provide transportation in some form, for travel to medical clinics, dentist and doctor's offices, recreational trips, therapists, and so on . . . over and above normal travel to and from center (Trager, 1975).

Financing of day care was made possible by the passage of the Social Security Amendments of 1972. Authorized as "an experimental program to provide Day Care services for individuals eligible to enroll in the supplemental medical insurance program established under Part B of Title XVIII and XIX of the Social Security Act in Day Care Centers which meet standards the Secretary shall by regulation establish" (Smith, B.K., 1976, p. 30), they have already become important facilities for the delivery of mental health services on a traditional basis and also have been seen as response mechanisms to provide a therapeutic milieu that enhances positive mental health in the broader interest of its definition.

*Boarding Out or Foster Home Care.* This is another arrangement for organizing community care. The Veterans Administration for example, has experimented with this alternative. Usually one to five patients are placed in a private home in the community. The most interesting feature of this setting is that, contrary to popular beliefs, the older patients and patients residing in the hospital for ten years or more tend to make the best adjustment to community life when "boarded out." Even patients with a history of erratic behavior in the hospital have created no unique adjustment problems in foster homes. Hospital behavior is not a reliable indicator of behavior in a normal setting. One possible interpretation offered is that the authoritarian and repressive atmosphere of institutions may cause "disturbed" behavior in patients who are in fact normal and will not tolerate petty restrictions and bossy attitudes (Whitehead, 1970).

*Summary.* The mental health system has recently undergone substantial reorganization. The move from the hospital to the community has had a profound impact on confused and emotionally disturbed elderly. Many of the geriatric patient population in state mental hospitals have been discharged and other aged community residents have been denied admission. Given the high positive correlation between old age and dependency (whether primarily social, economic, or psychological), state mental hospitals, the social institution of "last resort" for the deviant and displaced, have always maintained a disproportionately large geriatric population. The impact of community mental health upon the elderly has been unique and problematic. The uncertain future for hastily discharged geriatric patients, the discontinuity between hospital residence and community follow-up, the possible regularity of abuse and neglect of old people in the community who are under the jurisdiction of mental health authorities give cause for alarm. The "push out" into a community that has not been prepared to "receive" confused and emotionally disturbed older people has created untold problems, which have not been addressed sufficiently as yet by professionals and public officials.

An examination of national data on community based care indicates that, while community based care is a major component of the mental health system, very little of its resources is allocated to the elderly (Simon, 1973). Very few of the elderly who end up in mental hospitals had prior access to community based care. Most of the geropsychiatric patients discharged from hospitals either receive no psychiatric referral or go to the nursing home. The prevalence of psychiatric labeling in the nursing homes and their predominantly institutionalized atmosphere suggest that either of these alternatives is highly inconsistent with the rhetoric of the community mental health movement.

The complications of community coordination have limited the possible effectiveness of community care. Definitions of jurisdictions over patients are complicated and often overlapping, particularly when the patients are multiple problem cases as the elderly typically are. The willingness of other social agencies to service the geriatric population is equally limited. Screening clinics are an effective device for routing the flow of old people. They have significantly reduced geriatric hospital admission and diverted candidates to nursing homes. They have done little to assure that hospital rejects receive any psychiatric support in the community. Without deliberate intervention through social policy and with economic resources, the inadequate provision for the mentally ill elderly will continue.

## PREVENTIVE AND SUPPORTIVE SERVICES

Suicide prevention programs, social services, food programs, senior centers, programs that facilitate access and further mobility such as information/referral and transportation, consultation and informal networks constitute the major reservoir of preventively-oriented support services that take as their perspective the "public health" model, that is environmentally-social action oriented according to the "Denner and Price" classification schema.

*Suicide Prevention.* The highest rate of suicide occurs in white males in their 80s; the elderly, who constitute 10 percent of the population, account for 25 percent of reported suicides (5,000–8,000 yearly); this increased suicide rate in old age has been found in all Western countries. Explanations given are related to the severe loss of status that affect white men, particularly in the Western world (US Public Health Service data, 1974). Butler thinks the most preventable are suicides related to depression. "Reducing the frequency of depression and providing for its effective treatment when present are the major ways of reducing suicide in old age" (Butler and Lewis, 1973, p. 62–63).

Suicide prevention centers, many of them staffed by a small number of full-time professionals and a large number of volunteers, provide services throughout the country to potentially suicidal persons. A few such centers are located in community mental health centers. Many are operated with privately gathered funds rather than with public funding. Workers in the programs must be well acquainted with the resources of professional consultation and local community geriatric programs to which possibly suicidal older persons can be referred when indicated (Butler and Lewis, 1973, p. 76).

*Social Services.* There are two major federal acts that authorize provisions of social services: The Social Security Act and the Older Americans Act. The 1962 Amendments to the Social Security Act expanded eligibility criteria through regulations permitting former and potential welfare recipients as well as present recipients to receive services. The primary purpose of the Act's social service program for adults was to reduce dependency and promote opportunity for independent living and self-support. This objective is still among those specified in the most recent amendment to Title XX. In the case of the elderly, this means services

specifically intended to support a variety of living arrangements as alternatives to institutional care. The states were required to provide certain services while others were optional. Overall, there has been a large area of discretion at the state level, with regard to the extent and kinds of services which might be offered.

Mandatory services for the aged (also the blind and disabled) include the following: information and referral without regard to eligibility for assistance; protective services, services to enable persons to remain in or to return to their homes or communities, supportive services that would contribute to a "satisfactory and adequate social adjustment of the individual"; and services to meet health needs.

Optional services which any state might elect to include encompass three broad categories: services to individuals to improve their living arrangements and enhance activities of daily living; services to individuals and groups to improve opportunities for social and community participation; and services to individuals to meet special needs.

In 1975, Title XX was implemented. In effect, a special revenue-sharing plan with states to provide social services defined and developed by the state, Title XX is devoted to the achievement of five goals: self-support; self-sufficiency; protection; prevention of institutionalization; facilitating institutionalization if and when community care is not viable. At least one service must be provided for each of these goals and at least three services must be provided for SSI recipients. Other than this, no other services are mandated for the aged.

The other federal program providing services to the aged through the Older Americans Act (OAA), defines social services similarly, listing its six types as follows: health, continuing education, welfare, information, recreational, homemaker, counseling, or referral services; transportation services where necessary to facilitate access to social services; services designed to encourage and assist older persons to use the facilities and services available to them; services designed to assist older persons in avoiding institutionalization, including preinstitutionalization evaluation and screening, and home health services; or any other services if such services are necessary for the general welfare of older persons.

The major distinction in public service provision for the elderly is that some services are universal and some are selective. Services provided under Title XX are selective, means-tested services. Financial need and age (65 and over) are the basic criteria for eligibility for these services. At present, all recipients of SSI plus an additional percentage of those with incomes under 80 percent of median income may be eligible for services. (Under Title XX, eligibility criteria may vary with the service.) No firm data (dollars, services, number of recipients) exist as yet with regard to service utilization by older people.

In contrast, services provided by programs under the Older Americans Act are designed to be universal and not means tested, although a deliberate effort is made to direct provisions to communities in which the percentage of elderly "at risk" is highest (minorities, women, single). As much can be said about programs provided for the aged by the voluntary sector, which also tend to be regarded as universal.

In general, funding and extent of coverage of social services is limited and nowhere near adequate for the number needing and wanting them. The major congregate meals program is designed to serve about one percent of the elderly (the target population the program addresses is equal to at least 16 percent of the elderly); it is generally agreed that senior centers are overcrowded and haphazardly placed; reduced fare programs are heavily utilized but they exist in only about a hundred cities. Often, even where services may be available in the market, costs are prohibitive for the poor, the working class, and some times even the middle class. In contrast, in a number of metropolitan areas, free or reduced fare (50 percent) transportation on public transport is available to the elderly; and delivered or congregate meals may be free, priced at what the recipient wishes to pay or offered at very low, below-cost levels (Kamerman and Kahn, 1976).

Later in this chapter under the section discussing in-home services, a series of relevant social services will be reviewed and need not be duplicated here.

*Food Programs: The Congregate Meal Under Title VII.* One program that attempts to address two problems—inadequate nutrition and social isolation—is the congregate meal. In 1972 Congress enacted the Nutrition Program for the Elderly, which became Title VII of the amended Older Americans Act, whose purpose is "to provide older Americans, particularly those with low incomes, with low cost, nutritionally sound meals served in strategically located centers, such as schools, churches, community centers, senior citizens centers, and other public or private facilities where they can obtain other social and rehabilitative services. Besides promoting better health among the older segment of the population through im-

proved nutrition, such a program is aimed at reducing the isolation of old age, offering older Americans an opportunity to live their remaining years in dignity" (*Nutrition for the Elderly*, 1973).

Congregate meal sites established under this program must serve at least 100 meals daily, five days a week. Individuals 60 and over residing in a project area are eligible for the service and decide for themselves the charge for a meal. No means test is required.

Other congregate meal services are located in, or affiliated with, school cafeterias. School cafeterias may prepare food either for service to older persons after the students' lunch hour or to be delivered to other locations and served there. Some states have passed legislation reimbursing any school or nonprofit organization for the expense of serving a meal to the elderly, over a certain cost. In some programs the older people themselves help in the program as providers.

According to an Administration on Aging (AoA) Report (223-6885;1977) a total of 236,218,985 meals have been served under Title VII, since July 1, 1974 (when figures have been available for the first time) until September 30, 1977.

*Senior Centers.* A program providing a combination of services is the senior center. The first publicly supported senior center was established in New York City about thirty years ago and the number expanded gradually until about ten years ago. The expansion of this type of program was accelerated by authorizations of Title V of the Older Americans Act, which provided funds through the AoA's state programs to communities to assist them in developing center programs and, since 1976, also for construction of facilities. During this same period, public housing for the elderly was designed to include space for center programs for residents of housing developments as well as other older people from the neighboring community.

Voluntary organizations, both sectarian and nonsectarian, have also been active in developing and operating such programs. A directory of senior centers in the United States, published jointly by the AoA and the National Council on Aging (NCOA), listed 340 such centers in 1966; a recent directory published in 1975 listed 5,000, and the number keeps increasing (National Council on Aging, 1975).

Centers vary greatly in the kinds of programs and services offered and in the elaborateness and adequacy of physical settings, but each offers some contact with other elderly people and some links with needed services. Although, for the purpose of the directory, the definition of a senior center is "a program for older people provided in a designated facility open 3 or more days a week," the average center listed offered three or four recreational activities, and one or two types of counseling and community services. Among the typical services offered (and the best centers provide at least several of these) are the following: information, referral, and brief direct services; casework assessment; some counseling; service coordination; brief medical and psychosocial diagnosis; home health care; financial management; legal services and/or guardianship; transportation and/or escort services; cash for emergencies; volunteers' services; delivered meals.

A senior center seeks to create a social atmosphere that acknowledges the value of human life, individually and collectively, and affirms the dignity and self-worth of the older adult. This atmosphere provides for the reaffirmation of creative potential, the power of decision making, the skills of coping and defending, the warmth of caring, sharing, giving and supporting. The uniqueness of the senior center stems from its total concern for all older people and for the total older person. In an atmosphere of wellness it develops strengths and encourages independence, while building interdependence and supporting unavoidable dependencies. It works *with* older persons not *for* them, enabling and facilitating their decisions and their actions, and in so doing creates and supports a sense of community which further enables older persons to continue their involvement with and contribution to the larger community.

The philosophy of the senior center movement is based on the premises that aging is a normal development process; that human beings need peers with whom they can interact and who are available as a source of encouragement and support; and that adults have the right to have a voice in determining matters in which they have a vital interest. As such, the center is a major community institution that is geared to maintain "good" mental health and to prevent breakdown and deterioration of mental, emotional and social functioning of older persons.

Here are two examples of senior centers:

Hodson Center in New York City, the first publicly sponsored senior day center in the country, began in 1943 as a result of the concern of Department of Welfare social investigators for the retired and lonely men and women they met. Its first site was a shed 30-by-80 feet, which had formerly been used as a Works Progress Administration depot for the distribution of clothing. The present Hodson Center is located in a public housing project in space especially designed for day center operation.

The City of New York now has over 100 senior centers, sponsored by the city, religious organizations, unions, and other private, non-profit organizations.

A senior center with a comprehensive program is the Knowles Center in Nashville, Tenn. Built in 1966, it has 12 satellite centers. It offers 60-cent luncheons 5 days a week, regular health education programs such as classes for diabetics and people with auditory loss, small-group physical education, and paramedical services including glaucoma screenings and immunizations. A public health nurse is always available to members. The Center has rooms for recreation and social activity, a library, and an auditorium. Frequent outdoor programs and trips are scheduled.

Linkage of services between senior centers and mental health facilities in a community were first attempted in the early sixties in Cleveland (Cocozza and Wojniak, 1970). In 1966, the Bohn Golden Age Center had informally taken four older patients from the Cleveland State Hospital for weekly visits to the Center with good results. A study grant in 1967 and the cooperation of the administration of the State Hospital enabled the Bohn Center to select an experimental and control group of 24 men and women over 60, in each year of the three year project. The Center staff examined the operation of a program of community reintegration during institutionalization to help mentally ill older persons to develop positive community experiences in a relatively normal setting while they still had the security of hospital supervision. This was started on the hospital wards through the use of small groups as it was assumed that group support would offer additional protection during the period of transition into the community.

The evaluation report confirms that programming of a community based center for the aging can meet the particular needs of the institutionalized aged when activities are gradually adapted, when it takes place in a structured environment in a supportive peer-group setting, and when it provides an "intermediate experience" in the community without forcing the patient to leave the hospital altogether. The last point is particularly important as total relocation is traumatic to the institutionalized geriatrics patient. The importance of careful patient preparation before movement into the community is underlined by the findings that the patients' psychological state plays a significant role in the survival of the elderly following relocation.

*Programs to Facilitate Access: Information-Referral.* The primary purpose of specialized *information and re-*

*ferral services* is to link older people in need of help with services available to their communities. In addition, information and referral services have the potential for identifying recurrent needs and gaps in services for the elderly. For the most part, these services are provided by voluntary organizations, churches, labor unions etc. However, since the Older Americans Act includes provision of federal matching funds to state-approved information and referral projects, a growing number of special demonstration information and referral service projects have been funded.

Among the problems regarding this service is the lack of clear regulations covering the components of information and referral services. (Is it just information and referral? Does it also include follow-up? If so, how much and by whom?) Another is the tendency to assume that the service can in some way substitute for quantitative and qualitative service inadequacies. Information and referral services are of significant value only when they are defined as a way of ensuring access to other services, benefits, and rights—not as a substitute for them (*Information and Referral Services*, 1974).

Over 100 special information and referral service agencies have been organized in large communities and by community welfare councils, by their affiliated social agencies, and by councils on the aged. The nation-wide Old Age, Survivors, Disability Insurance (OASDI) program, however, does not provide a service that deals with the complicated problems people may have in using community services. Public welfare departments can provide information to public assistance clients if staff is available. Many older people find it very difficult to utilize information and referral services and the majority of the aged are not even aware of their existence. In other instances, it has been found (e.g., in Worcester, Massachusetts) when some of the older people utilized the information and referral services, they really were in need of highly skilled mental treatment services which were not available right then and there (Levinson Gerontological Policy Institute Study, 1976).

Central information and referral services can be offered as a component of health programs by a variety of public or private organizations. Or it can be an independent service cooperating with established services and agencies.

A 6-county area in Kansas and Missouri began an information and referral service as an alternative to a survey to find what services were wanted and needed. In addition to giving the desired information on referral, the staff kept records on callers so that data such as sex, age, occupation, geographic location, and service re-quested could be quickly ascertained. In spite of the fact that there were at least 450 agencies in the area meeting mental health, physical health and welfare needs, the information and referral service identified many gaps in service (Administration on Aging Publication No. 74-20112).

*Transportation.* The old age *transportation* problem stems from four main factors:

1. Many old people cannot afford the cost of transportation,
2. many live in areas which are poorly served by public transit,
3. many older people have difficulty using the public transportation system,
4. the American transportation system is based on the use of the private auto.

These factors are interrelated. Because they are poor, many old people live in areas which are not well served by public transportation. Because they do not have access to transit systems, they cannot go to work to supplement their incomes or make use of existing service programs either for recreational, social or health purposes.

A primary cause of the transportation problem is low income. One-fourth of all older people live in poverty. Most live on incomes which are severely squeezed by inflationary pressures. They must spend most of this income on food, housing, and medical care, leaving little money for "luxuries" such as a private car or even public transportation. Most older people do not drive. Another factor is a psychological reluctance. Old people are unwilling to face the uncertainties, terrors, and dangers of a bus ride.

A number of means for meeting these problems have developed in communities across the country. Some community and voluntary organizations sponsor a special bus or van to take older people on needed trips. For example, one Administration on Aging (AoA) demonstration project set up a senior citizens mobile service. This service provided transportation to more than 1,600 elderly people on a total of 30,000 trips. Forty-eight different agencies participated through referrals and requests for service and appointments for trips were scheduled a day ahead with two-way radios allowing last-minute changes when emergencies arose (US Senate Special Committee on Aging, 1975).

Despite the declared national policy that the elderly and handicapped should have access to mass transportation facilities, this has not been implemented. For one thing, implementation of this policy through the grant and loan provisions of the Urban Mass Transportation Act is discretionary for the Department of Transportation (DOT), though specific allotments have been made in the annual DOT budgets for funding of systems designed to meet special needs of the elderly and handicapped. There is also no specific legislative requirement that all grants and loans assure accessibility of the system to the elderly and handicapped before being approved for funding. Individual projects have been funded; model prototypes are being developed; but to date, no systematic implementation of the national policy on accessibility has been established (*Transportation and Aging,* 1974).

Without insuring adequate access to service programs, mental health services remain unavailable to older persons even in those communities where they do exist. This affects particularly rural elderly. Some communities have designed interesting transportation programs. For example: South Providence, RI, once a thriving area with grocery stores, banks, and doctor's offices in every block or two, has lost many of its stores, banks and doctors in recent years. To help approximately 2,000 older persons still living there to do their shopping and reach services in other parts of town, a station wagon was purchased by the Rhode Island Division on Aging. It averages 12 calls a day. Most trips are to doctor's offices, clinics and hospitals, but many people use this service to go grocery shopping. One trip usually serves several people at a time.

Because many small communities lack medical services, many trips are to doctor's offices. Other trips take senior citizens to polling places. In one instance, after almost a lifetime of residence in this country, three volunteer rides to Denver made it possible for an elderly woman to receive her US citizenship. With it, she was able to qualify for Medicare.

For some people, physical barriers in public transportation systems discourage use. These barriers include high bus steps, unsheltered bus stops, fast-moving escalators and turnstiles in subway stations. All can be overcome by thoughtfulness in the design of original equipment or replacement equipment.

*Informal Networks in the Community.* Frankfather (1977), in his study, "Confused Elderly in the Community" has found that many older persons in the community who have been labeled "senile" or "mentally impaired" would better be described as "confused." These people find more help and assistance in the "informal community network" than in the formal mental health service system. The formal system has a tendency to shut them out of service delivery by making limited if any efforts to reach them and by creating barriers which have to be overcome to take advantage of existing programs. Frankfather includes the informal network community agents such as the police, firemen, postmen, drugstore and neighborhood store owners, etc.

Smith (1975), in a model project conducted in Portland, Oregon, confirmed the significance of informal service providers as support systems for the older person in the community. She points out that:

> In their relationships with older people, informal service providers offer a number of distinctive qualities agency personnel can seldom provide. These qualities are: easy accessibility, relationships of long duration, element of choice, mutuality, variety.
>
> The informal service providers and the older people define their relationships around a friendship, proximity or long-term acquaintance, or shared interests such as church or group affiliations . . . Many younger providers prefer and enjoy the company of older people and are pleased at the opportunity these relationships offer their children . . .

*Consultation.* Consultation is a problem-solving process wherein more knowledgeable professionals give information and help to others to strengthen them in their areas of performance. The function of mental health consultation has become a vehicle through which services to older people can be extended in homes for aged, nursing homes, general hospitals, day centers; to physicians, clergymen, home-makers, home health aides, and visiting nurses; to legal protective services and to senior citizen centers and other types of agencies serving the elderly.

Types of elderly consultation contact can be administrative, programmatic, either milieu or client centered and/or didactic, that focuses on efforts to educate and sensitize staff. Consultative services are also offered to community-neighborhood agencies, schools, colleges, churches, synagogues, and to members of informal networks such as firefighters, postal workers, police, bartenders, an so on. (Caplan, 1970.)

EXAMPLE. The City of Newton in Massachusetts has enlisted the aid of postmen to be alert to elderly citizens on their routes. If they notice that mail is not picked up for several days they contact family members or physicians or friends—or whomever a person designates as a contact.

## ENHANCEMENT OR PROMOTIONAL SERVICES

These types of services include citizen action or citizen participation programs and educational activities that are designed to enrich the quality of life of older people and assist them in achieving a state of "good" mental health that conveys to them a sense of well-being and mastery over their own destiny.

*Participatory and Action Programs.* These involve activities by elders to promote their well-being in work or task groups, organizations of the elderly or in volunteer service roles under governmental or private auspices and sponsorship.

The Domestic Volunteer Service Act of 1973 makes grants available to state agencies as well as other public or nonprofit agencies to help older people to avail themselves of opportunities for volunteer service. The following are illustrative of a series of programs presently in operation in a number of communities:

SERVE (Serve and Enrich Retirement by Volunteer Experience) of New York uses groups of older volunteers in state hospitals and schools for the mentally retarded. Some work with patients, some in the office, some help with other hospital duties.

In the Foster Grandparent Program, older people with low incomes work with children in institutions such as schools for retarded or disturbed children, infant homes, temporary care centers, and convalescent hospitals. "Grandparents" do not replace regular staff, but establish a person-to-person relationship with a child, giving it the kind of love often missed in group-care settings. In return, "grandparents" receive an hourly stipend plus the affection and trust of the child.

The Green Thumb Program employs low-income men and women in rural sections to beautify public areas such as parks and roadsides, and to help local government and community services as aides in schools and libraries. Some provide outreach and Homemaker Service, make friendly visits and provide transportation.

Under another US Department of Labor contract the American Association of Retired Persons and the National Retired Teachers Association have trained many older people in new skills and helped others brush up unused skills. In most cases, training was given by community service agencies, such as the Red Cross or United Fund, with real work constituting and training mechanism. Trainees serve others while they learn.

The Good Neighbor Family Aides are women who have been homemakers most of their lives and who can offer aid to other older persons or families who need help in caring for a home. The women receive training at no cost to them in the local Red Cross chapter house. A Red Cross nurse teaches home nursing skills, the state university extension agent teaches home economics, and a local psychiatrist who specializes in geriatrics, volunteers his time to give insight on care of elderly persons (*Let's End Isolation,* 1977).

Many elderly who are involved in volunteer and service programs report gratification with their engagements (Naylor, 1972). Equally important to the mental health of older persons has been their involvement in activities of social action organizations that have adopted the slogan "senior power" to press claims for a more equitable share in the resources of our society. The National Council of Senior Citizens, the National Caucus of the Black Aged, the American Association of Retired Persons have developed a national following and have achieved considerable attention in the press and in legislative halls.

The "Gray Panthers" of Philadelphia are probably the best known social action organization that brings together old and young to advance the cause of the elderly and to advocate for the rights of older persons to reap their rewards for past and present achievement.

Involvement in these types of programs challenges stereotyped images of older people and enhances their mental and emotional being through active involvement in significant efforts on behalf of themselves and others.

*Educational Programs.* These programs are offered on formal and informal bases in two year and four year colleges and universities, in adult and continuing education programs, in neighborhood centers, farm and business organizations, in religious organizations of all denominations, in museums, and in civic associations (Grabowski and Mason, 1974; Hendrickson, 1968).

Educational programs can be divided into two types, instrumental and expressive. Instrumental programs teach skills for meeting life needs; expressive programs provide opportunities for recreation, creativity, and self-expression. Many older adults have shown a greater preference for instrumental courses (Eklund, 1969).

Today's elderly as a group have less formal education than any other group in our society. Seventy percent of them have a seventh-grade education or less. One fifth are functional illiterates; seven percent had no formal education at all. Moreover, since the recognition of the need for continuing education is relatively recent, many elderly have not benefited from it. Recency of education is also a factor in both likelihood of participation and likelihood of success (Eklund, 1969). In one study, less-educated adults indicated no preference for either instrumental or expressive courses; they seemed less interested than the college-educated adults in any educational programs.

Those adults who had more formal schooling, or had recently been involved in educational programs expressed an interest in expressive programs (Hiemstra, 1973). Active outreach programs are needed to reach those people most in need of educational programs.

Although older adults tend to respond only to those programs—formal or informal—that meet their needs, several educational problems confront them when they do respond. Poor health is a dominant inhibitor of learning. Older adults have a greater fear of failure than do children. Resistance to education may be encountered because of previous negative experiences. Therefore, learning should take place in a noncompetitive, nonanxiety provoking atmosphere. Older adults are less goal oriented than their younger counterparts; they are responding more to a "felt need" than to the desire for a credential. They seem to learn more slowly, but more accurately, than younger people. The rate of physiological changes associated with aging are very individual (Eklund, 1969).

Other problems cited by older adults as inhibitors to participation in educational programs were lack of transportation and fear of going out at night. Thus, planners must pay attention to flexible hours, convenient locations (particularly in senior citizen centers and homes), free tuition or stipends, and subsidized transportation. Television and radio are regarded by older adults as major sources of self-education (Hiemstra, 1973).

Universities, increasingly, pay attention to the older population and are moving not only to establish centers of gerontology but also to offer special learning programs for older students (*New York Times* Week-in-Review Section, Sunday Edition, Lindsay, 1978). More than 500 institutions of higher education are providing courses or services for older persons throughout the US, according to a survey conducted by the Academy for Educational Development. These range from special courses designed for an elderly audience to campus experiments in multi-generational living. At Syracuse University in New York, for example, elderly persons living in a public housing project on the campus share full use of the school's facilities. In Florida, Dade Community College offers courses to older persons in sites where many typically congregate, such as community centers, large housing projects and nursing homes.

A significant incentive to developing such educational programs has been the availability of funding from the Federal Government's Administration on Aging. Community colleges offering one- or two-year programs, have taken the initiative in serving the elderly, probably because they are more attuned to the needs of the local community and have proven themselves to be more flexible (*Aging,* 1977). In France and Switzerland special universities for members of the Troisième Age have found a tremendous response among the population over 55 years.

The US Department of Health, Education and Welfare has begun to attach educational programs to existing social services. This is an interesting focus for future programming on two counts: There is relatively little extra cost in recruiting learners for programs; they are already there and the specific instrumental focus of the program and the clientele's interest are already established: a client seeking legal aid wants legal information; a client seeking health services wants health care information.

*Summary.* Preventive and support services and promotional enhancement programs exist all over the country sporadically, piecemeal and uncoordinated. Many ingenious programs offer creative solutions to problems of aloneness, loneliness, lack of purpose, feelings of uselessness and futility to many older persons who are lucky enough to live in those communities where they exist and thrive. However, many older persons are deprived of these services and programs, because they live in communities that do not offer them. As these services and programs are frontline bulwarks to advance good mental health, they must be made available on a continuous, coordinated and comprehensive basis in every region and community through an aging network.

## TYPES AND NATURE OF IN-HOME COMMUNITY MENTAL HEALTH SERVICES

Many older people can benefit from services delivered to their own home as they are too frail or too debilitated to take advantage of out-of-home services. The provision of a battery of services in their own homes is probably one of the major tasks facing gerontology programs today and the financing of such programs is one of our most significant social policy challenges.

"Care at home offers better morale and security as long as proper services are given to provide comfort, support and direct treatment of physical and emotional ills" (Butler and Lewis, 1973, p. 187). When a request or a referral for mental health services is received, part or all of the evaluations can be done at home, including an assessment of the person's home situation and living conditions. A broad, comprehensive concept of care includes all the essential services to make it possible for the older person to function as a total person: intellectually, emotionally, mentally and socially. These include: mental health intake (screening and evaluation), physicians' services, nursing services, homemaker-home health aides, physical therapy, occupational therapy, speech therapy, dental care, nutrition programs, social services, home safety, education, enhancement, religious support, family respite services, outpatient care in various settings, protection services. In other words, all services mentioned already need to be included in a home-delivered care program. However, there are special services particularly related to in-home services that must be discussed.

EMERGENCY CARE SERVICES

These should be available on a mobile 24-hour basis to assist persons in medical and psychiatric emergencies, notably to those persons making suicide threats and attempts or for those wandering in the streets (confused elderly).* Physicians are reluctant to make house calls and, therefore, few home-delivered physicians' services exist at all today.

Nursing services can be grouped into three: (1) Public health nurses who work for tax-supported city or county health departments; they visit families in their homes, give health guidance, participate in communicable disease control programs. They may give emergency care as well as care for acute and chronic illness. (2) The Visiting Nurse Association, a voluntary organization that provides similar services as public health nurses (in some communities they have merged their staffs), but tend to have smaller caseloads. (3) Agencies that provide private duty registered nurses and licensed practical nurses for those who can afford them.

Most recently, a limited number of schools of nursing have begun to train geriatric nurses and geriatric psychiatric nurses. Increasingly, nurses perform teaching functions for patients and family members to do a variety of tasks, including physical therapy.

HOMEMAKER–HOME HEALTH SERVICES

Homemaker services originated in England and later came to the US during the 1920s. Although there has been some expansion over the years, primarily since the passage of Medicare, such services (on occasion combined with health aid services) are still not extensive. Yet they are generally defined as critical, both as preventive service and as a treatment service, in helping the aged live more com-

fortably in their homes. In the United Kingdom there are 265 homemakers per 100,000 people whereas the US has only 28.7 per 100,000 people as of December 1976 (International Council of Home Help Services Report, 1978).

Homemaker services are provided by mature, specially trained women with skills both as homemakers and in personal care. The function of this service is to help maintain and preserve a family environment that is threatened with disruption by illness, death, social maladjustment and other problems. Homemakers can assume full or partial responsibility for child or adult care and household management. Services are supposed to be performed under the general supervision of a social worker or other appropriate professional. The homemaker is neither a substitute for such professional personnel, nor is she a maid.

*Home health aid services* is a term referring to personal care services for a patient and may be used to include some of the services performed by a homemaker. The term itself was first used in the Medicare Regulations to describe the services eligible for reimbursement under that program. Among the types of duties performed by homemaker-home health aides are light housekeeping, light laundry, preparation and serving of meals, shopping, simple errands, teaching of household routine and skills to members of the family, general supervision of the children of the patient where young children are involved.

Homemaker-health services tend to be either hospital-based (hospitals extending services into the community) or community-based, with connection to other services and institutions. Services may be performed by many different kinds of private and public agencies, for example, nurse associations (voluntary, nonprofit groups delivering nursing services to the home), public health services, community agencies, and hospital-based programs. Within the community, services may be provided through a single agency such as a Homemaker-Home Health Aide Services Program or a Meals-on-Wheels program; or a multiple-service agency that arranges for two or more types of service such as homemaker, nursing, physical therapy; or a coordinated program that arranges for a wide variety of home services designed to meet the individual needs through one centralized administration. In 1969, the National Council for Homemaker-Home Health Services, Inc., was named the national standard setting body for those services provided under the program administered by HEW. A nonprofit, voluntary-membership organization whose purpose is the development of quality services in the home as part of health and welfare services, this organization has become a primary standard-

*A van equipped with emergency equipment and mental health personnel is perhaps the most mobile arrangement.

setting agency in the homemaker-home health field, stressing the development and expansion as well as implementation of such programs (Lowy, 1975b).

According to a report on home health services in the United States for the US Senate Special Committee on Aging (1975), in January 1972 there were approximately 2,850 agencies providing homemaker-home aide services in the United States: 1,300 serving families with children in health-related programs (both public and voluntary); 1375 single agencies (i.e., providing supervised homemaker-home health aide services to meet a variety of community needs); and 175 proprietary registries. In 1973, the total figure declined to 2,221 continuing a down trend that began over twenty years ago.

The estimated total number of homemaker-home health aides employed in these programs is 30,000 as against a total estimated need of 300,000. Furthermore, the report pointed out that, in addition to the decrease in the number of agencies providing such services, the ones that remain are curtailing service, narrowing coverage, and reducing the duration of care offered. Even considering the very limited number and extent of such services, distribution is poor and there are geographic areas of the country and large sections of the population having no services available. Hospital-based programs are in short supply, stress short-term intensive care, and do not have available community-based services to meet long-range needs. Community-based services are inadequate in number; all are substantially underfinanced (US Senate Special Committee on Aging, 1975).

Homemaker services are used by the aged in all groups, regardless of income or social status. Charges vary depending on whether the organization providing the service is public, voluntary, or proprietary, and depending on the particular auspice. Eligibility varies similarly, depending on the program auspices (*National Capital Area Homemaker Services Training Manual*, 1974).

In November, 1972, the Massachusetts De-partment of Elder Affairs was charged to be "the principal agency of the Commonwealth to mobilize the human, physical, and financial resources available to plan, develop, and implement innovative programs to insure the dignity and independence of elderly persons, including the planning, development, and implementation of a home care program for the elderly in the communities of the Commonwealth" (Mass. General Laws, Chapter 19A, Section 4, 1972).

In compliance with State and Federal responsibilities, the Department of Elder Affairs has set forth the following two goals: (1) to enable elders to remain in the community with dignity and independence through the provision of home care service; (2) to be an advocate for elders at the highest level of state government. The target groups for home care service are those elders "at risk" of being institutionalized due to social or physical limitations.

Home care corporations are private, non-profit corporations which act as funding magnets and administrative resources for local elder related programs. While home care corporations provide no direct services themselves, except information and referral, they subcontract with existing agencies for the provision of services and act as focal points within the community for elderly concerns. By 1978, 27 home care corporations were established in 240 communities.

In addition to the core services, home care corporations offer services that vary from location to location. Among these are housing, preventive health maintenance and rehabilitation, nutrition, legal and advocacy assistance, and emergency crisis care (Massachusetts Department of Elder Affairs, 1978).

A serious lack is the failure to include health services as part of the core program. Unquestionably, the push for their inclusion will increase here as in other states, though no major changes are likely to occur prior to the advent of a national health insurance program.

The primary funding sources for this home

**Table 34–2**   Five Core Services.

---

*Homemaker Services* include food shopping, personal errands, light housekeeping, meal preparation as necessary, and related activities.

*Chore services* help in home maintenance by providing such assistance as heavy household cleaning, minor repair services, snow removal, and relocation preparation.

*Transportation Services* provide mobility and independence through transportation to central meal facilities, medical appointments, community service agencies, and other locations.

*Case Management* reviews each person's need and eligibility for services and develops a service plan to help a person remain at home in safety.

*Information–referral* assists older persons to obtain access to programs and services and to obtain answers to their questions reeligibility criteria.

---

care program are Title III of the Older Americans Act, Title XX of the Social Security Act, and the Commonwealth of Massachusetts. Additional federal funding is provided through Title VII of the Older Americans Act for nutrition programs. City and town governments and community organizations also provide funds and in-kind contributions.

In other states and communities similar efforts have been underway. While evaluation and cost/benefit studies have been initiated and conducted to determine whether these types of programs do in fact delay, postpone or eliminate the need for institutionalization, or are cost effective, results so far are by no means conclusive. Though social policies now are more directed towards reducing unnecessary and premature institutionalization of the elderly, it has to be kept in mind that institutional care will continue to be of importance for those who actually require it and can benefit from it on a temporary or even permanent basis.

## MEALS-ON-WHEELS

These are programs providing prepared hot meals, brought to older persons' homes, usually by volunteers, from a congregate kitchen. Such home-delivered meals provide a daily link for the homebound with the outside world. They give the recipient someone to greet each day, and sometimes the volunteer stays to visit during the meal. At the present time, the service continues to be a minor provision among federal programs for the aged. Title VII of the OAA Act provides the major federal nutrition program for the aged. Ninety percent of these funds are for congregate meals and up to 10 percent may be spent for home-delivered meals from congregate centers. Most Meals-on-Wheels programs are small scale and are funded and/or operated locally by voluntary organizations (*Nutrition for the Elderly,* 1973).

## TELEPHONE REASSURANCE PROGRAMS

These programs provide a telephone contact for an older person who might otherwise have no outside contact for long periods of time. Recipients of this service are called at a predetermined time each day, often by older persons themselves. If the person does not answer, help is sent to the home. Usually in the event of no answer, a neighbor, relative, or nearby police or fire station is asked to make a personal check. Details are worked out when a person begins receiving this service. Telephone reassurance generally costs little and can be provided by callers of any age, usually volunteers, teenagers, or older people themselves (*Guidelines,* 1973).

## LIFELINE

This is a formalized telephone emergency alarm system that connects older persons with a central-station operator in case of emergency. The operator has lists of family, friends or back-up agencies to turn to for assistance. If older persons do not use their telephone in a 24 hour time period or reset the alarm, an emergency signal is automatically triggered to alert a central-station operator. This program is presently tested and studied as a demonstration project by Boston University Gerontology Center jointly with the Hebrew Rehabilitation Center for the Aged in Roslindale and funded by the Department of HEW.

## FRIENDLY VISITING

Friendly Visiting as an organized service began in Chicago in 1946. Already swamped by caseloads, social workers wished for time to stay and chat with lonely clients after their regular business was completed. The idea of asking volunteers to visit these isolated people grew out of this need. In this kind of program, volunteers visit isolated homebound older persons on a regular schedule once, or more often, a week. They do such things as play chess and cards, write letters, provide an arm to lean on during a shopping trip, and just sit and chat. The essential element is to provide continuing companionship for an elderly person who has no relative or friend able to do it.

This kind of visiting relieves loneliness of older people. Professional staff workers have observed that clients look better and take more interest in things outside themselves after receiving friendly visiting. Frequently there is improvement in actual physical condition or, at least, less absorption in illness. Although the Visitor need not be a social worker or other professionally trained person, he should receive some orientation from the sponsoring agency and some continuing supervision or consultation. Visitors come from a variety of backgrounds. Qualities that seem to mark all good friendly visitors are the ability to accept people as they are and a genuine friendliness plus commitment and reliability in visiting on a regular schedule. Older people themselves often prove most effective visitors.

*Peer-assistance.* A variation of this service, is particularly valuable in housing for the elderly; neighbors check in on one another and the more physically able help those less mobile. This is often set up in a structured fashion through the manager of a housing project. Service programs are frequently included such as meals-on-wheels, organized health clinics (e.g., blood pressure checks by visiting nurses who come to the project).

## OUTREACH

Remaining hidden from the social life and knowledge of their community, many older people do not know of service opportunities available to them. Their community does not realize their need, and indeed, sometimes it does not know they exist. For these reasons, it is necessary to seek out older people to make sure they know what services are available and where they can call for help. Outreach volunteers can be older people themselves. Often they are the most effective. Some communities pay outreach workers for time and services.

Sometimes outreach is provided by senior centers through the establishment of satellite neighborhood centers. These neighborhood offshoots can draw previously isolated older people into neighborhood activity.

Project FIND (Friendless, Isolated, Needy, or Disabled) conducted from August 1967 through November 1968 by the National Council on Aging and the Office of Economic Opportunity, made surveys of 12 communities using aides, ranging in age from 50 to 85. The aids found isolated persons and referred those who needed help to services available in the community. If needed services were not available, the aides tried to secure volunteer help, especially when the need was severe. One of the significant discoveries of FIND was that many persons eligible for Social Security were not receiving it. The fact that 28,079 referrals were made to existing services and 24,124 unavailable services were needed clearly establishes a reason for outreach (National Council on Aging, 1972).

In some communities, television and radio programs for, about, and by older people have provided a special kind of outreach. Some of these maintain a telephone answering service or include in their programming persons who will answer questions on the air. Because the older viewers have confidence in the programs, even extremely isolated individuals do seek and accept information which they would resist or not seek from a social agency which was strange to them.

## MOBILIZATION OF RESOURCES AND ADVOCACY

Mental health and social agencies must do more than offer existing services—they must also be involved in "hustling the system" to insure that older persons are reached and that services are made available and are accessible to them. Through outreach, registration drives, and through advocacy on behalf of older people, their needs and grievances have to be forcefully articulated. Older people must be mobilized on their own behalf to insure that they are heard, where it counts, in decision-making bodies of government or private organizations. If needs are not met through existing services, new services have to be created or present programs retooled, redesigned or modified. Mental health workers are service providers, service brokers and program advocates for and with the elderly.

## SUMMARY

Services are delivered in the homes of older people do exist, but they are fragmented and not universally available. Our social policy, as evidenced through its funding directions, has been "out-of-home" oriented and has offered disincentives to home-delivered programs and services (Medicare, Medicaid, Title XX). Home health care on a comprehensive basis is still not a viable program option for most older persons; curative, preventive, and support mental health services are out-of-home oriented as well as biased in favor of institutional care.

# ORGANIZATIONAL ASPECTS OF MENTAL HEALTH SERVICES

This section of the chapter addresses sanctions and auspices of mental health services in the community, issues in the delivery and evaluation of services and programs and reviews the personnel and training conditions pertaining to the design and delivery of mental health services.

## SANCTIONS AND AUSPICES

Sanctions for programs and services are based on federal and state legislation, notably the Social Security Act of 1935 with its amendments, the Older Americans Act of 1965 and its 1973 and 1975 amendments, as well as mental health legislation, particularly the Mental Health and Retardation Acts of 1963, 1973 and 1975. Among the many federal and state agencies affecting community services to the elderly, the following are the three most important ones, all located with the Department of Health, Education and Welfare: National Institute of Mental Health with its Center for Mental Health on Aging; Administration on Aging in the Office of Human Development; National Institute on Aging.

Apart from these major bodies, there continue to exist a variety of agencies scattered within the federal government that directly affect the elderly American. Over twenty agencies have statutory responsibility for programs and services for the aging and aged, and dozens of additional federal operations have considerable relevance. Most programs funded by the federal government are administered and operated by state and local government bodies. The proliferation and distribution of activities and responsibilities within the federal government requiring coordination to meet the needs of aging are exceptionally high and confusing.

Major nongovernmental bodies may be included under the following: National organizations, such as the Gerontological Society, National Council on Aging, American Association of Retired Persons, National Council of Senior Citizens which are study, training, advocacy, lobby and pressure groups, that focus on research education or policy impact.

Sectarian and nonsectarian voluntary organizations focus on direct service provision and operate programs in one of three ways: By contracts with local government bodies in order to implement means-tested programs; by contracts or grants directly from the federal government to implement, administer, and/or operate demonstration projects; by direct funding, administering and operating programs out of their funds.

There is no one pattern that describes the internal administrative structure of these programs. Most follow hierarchical patterns with a director, administrative and supervisory staff, and line staff providing direct service. Most have an advisory board and some have a policy-making board, too.

Programs funded under the OAA are linked with the State Office on Aging, the Regional HEW office, the federal AoA, area agencies, and the city and county government. At times these multiple vertical linkages result in contradictory and conflicting directives. Since July 1974, the area agency on aging has been responsible primarily to the state.

Voluntary programs are linked either to United Way (if nonsectarian and funded in part by this organization) or, if sectarian, to the relevant parent funding agencies. For these agencies also, to the extent that they receive public funds, funding requests and new program developments are subject to review by the area agency.

## DELIVERY OF SERVICES

Despite a formidable array of programs and services for the elderly, there remain serious gaps, notably around getting comprehensive services delivered to people in an acceptable and coordinated manner.

How do older people learn about what types of services exist and how they can obtain them? How accessible and acceptable are these to people? How can continuity of community care be assured in the face of fragmentation? How can mental health services become defined in more inclusive rather than in traditional, exclusive terms? How can linkages of mental health and social services be achieved that are directly interventive, preventive, and enhancing? These are questions for which there are no easy answers now, nor in the foreseeable future, as no research strategy has as yet focused upon these questions.

Kamerman and Kahn sum up their observations about the confused, confusing and crazy-quilt patterns of the service system in a community:

> The community human service system needs some treatment resources under psychiatric auspices, needs access to psychiatrists for consultation, and depends upon some psychiatric contribution to the education of professionals from a number of disciplines. These are not new or startling notions, but we do underscore our need to say "psychiatric" because the phrase "mental health" does not serve to delineate for everyone what social institution and what series of concepts is intended. The expertise involves prevention of, identification of, and intervention with moderate and severe mental disorder. While not completely operationalized (since behavior is defined as "mental disorder," not in terms of fully externalized criteria but only when the psychiatric profession expresses readiness to take responsibility for the domain), the concept of a psychiatric intervention system as a speciality within medicine facilitates social planning, since it also permits delineation of education, religion, personal social services, law enforcement, and other related human service systems or institutions in their own separatenesses. "Mental health," which is sometimes goal, sometimes service, and sometimes evaluation, is too diffuse for planning purposes requiring role differentiation and it belongs to a period of excessive expectations. A viable service system should be able to identify its core cases so as to create relatively viable boundaries with other systems and to achieve community consensus about them. The mental health conceptualization lends itself to the opposite effect (Kamerman and Kahn, 1976, p. 480).

## PROBLEMS IN SERVICE DELIVERY

Butler (1975) lists a number of reasons why service delivery is a problem: Short-sighted service organizations, the cost to the elderly, less adequate services to minority-group elderly, self-serving interests of providers—including peer-control of licensing of professionals, low morale in the "service industry," resistances by older persons toward accepting help offered in a condescending manner, and agism on the part of service providers.

Ehrlich and Ehrlich (1974) hypothesize that age-segregated needs that are met through age-segregated services result in reinforcement of negative stereotypes of elderly and their ability to function at all communal levels; but when age-segregated needs are met through age-integrated services, the aged have greater access to total community resources and greater input into their destiny. They offer a four-cell model to illustrate their hypothesis:

|  | AGE-SEGREGATED GROUPS & SERVICES | AGE-INTEGRATED GROUPS & SERVICES |
|---|---|---|
| Age Segregated Needs | 1 | 3 |
| Age Integrated Needs | 2 | 4 |

They argue that from cell 1–4, there is a progressively higher level of social power and decision making.

Cell 1 is the most characteristic type of service delivery today; elderly do have some involvement, but the level of community social power and community participatory decision making tends to be minimal and at times is mere tokenism. (E.g., one or two residents of an old age home are asked to serve on a policy committee). If, however, a community can develop and sustain a system which meets both age-segregated and age-integrated needs via age-integrated services through a community decision-making mechanism, then the potential of meaningful involvement of the elderly is greatly enhanced (Ehrlich and Ehrlich, 1974, p. 243). The activation of service in all four cells not only brings the elderly and the community into closer proximity, but recognizes the ever-changing psychosocial needs of people and provides a continuum of opportunities for the aged to meet their total needs through movement within and among the four alternatives outlined. Ehrlich and Ehrlich, 1974, p. 243). They maintain that such a model enhances the prestige of the elderly, provides better services to the community at large, enables younger people to work through feelings re their own aging process, offers a potential of intergenerational linkages and creates more positive relationships of younger persons with older people and provides more meaningful role models to the

young and old. Testing of this hypothesis should provide evidence as to the validity of these assertions.

In order to effect an optimal service delivery pattern and flow, the following dimensions have to be dealt with: Access to the service by clients; channeling of clients to providers of service or providers to clients; case-integration to insure that multiple services are "packaged" for the client through skillful case-management; program-integration that facilitates the meshing of multiple services through coordination and linking; accountability to clients, aging, and community to assure optimal quality of service at the lowest cost possible.

A cursory examination of our communities, urban and rural, yields overwhelming evidence that on any dimension they fall far short of a desirable service delivery arrangement to older persons. The task is to begin a comprehensive exploration of how a modern urban community should organize social care, for the young, old, well and frail aged, the retarded, the handicapped, and those in after-care status from institutions.

## EVALUATION OF PROGRAMS AND SERVICES

As is true of almost all social programs, there is a paucity of good evaluation studies of programs and services to the aging. Most existing studies are based on "soft" data and tend to measure inputs or throughputs rather than outputs, that is, results of interventive efforts on the quality of life patterns of older persons in the community (Sherwood, 1974).

Baseline data are rarely available for use in evaluating the impact or long-term effects of a program. Furthermore, precise delineations of target populations are hard to come by, both because of the absence of data as well as problems regarding conceptual confusion and difficulty in defining eligibility criteria, and objectives of programs which often are diffuse, unclear and potentially conflicting.

Problems continue to exist regarding efforts at costing out service programs for the purpose of cost benefit studies or cost effectiveness studies. In addition to questions which ought to be included in assessing costs of a program or service, there are complex methodological issues that need to be resolved in cost-benefit analysis studies. Hagedorn, Beck, Neubert, and Werlin (1976, pp. 252–253) have suggested a series of sequential steps to be undertaken in arriving at a methodology for determining cost outcome and cost effectiveness in community mental health programs. These are listed in the following table.

Criteria for evaluating programs or service

**Table 34–3**   Six Sequential Steps.

| | |
|---|---|
| *Step 1* | Identify (Treatment) goals. |
| *Step 2* | Identify Programs, modalities and techniques. |
| *Step 3* | Determine costs of each program, modality on a unit basis (e.g. per client). |
| *Step 4* | Determine Intervention outcome by pre and post-measurements. |
| *Step 5* | Combine cost and outcome information for each program in a matrix for analysis of individual program data. |
| *Step 6* | Compare cost outcome matrices for multiple programs to perform cost effective analysis. |

impact are almost non-existent. In the area of community-based services for the aged there are almost no standards for well-being or service quality.

> The whole field of service to the aged is relatively new; evaluation studies are difficult to implement in all service realms and, inevitably, more difficult in a field in which data are so soft and criteria for evaluation so amorphous. The impact of research on policy development remains limited. Most decisions about expanded programs continue to be made on the basis of societal preference and influence, expressed in a political arena, not on the basis of conclusions from rational analysis (Kamerman and Kahn, 1976, p. 359).

PERSONNEL AND TRAINING

Meeting mental health needs of older persons in coming decades will require increasing numbers of workers at all levels, who are adequately trained. Every effort must be made to: support a balanced program of training of geriatric specialists in all professions; enrich educational programs at all levels with the new knowledge that is gradually being acquired about human development and aging; encourage public awareness of the social and economic factors that influence mental health, as well as the psychological and physical aspects of aging; coordinate efforts to improve the quality of life of the aged now and in the future.

Available evidence in the literature repeatedly points out the lack of a coherent national training policy, but very little has been done since the White House Conference in 1971 to rectify this deficiency (Training Needs Report, 1972; US House of Representatives, 1976; US Senate Special Committee, 1975).

The predictions of demographers and actuarials suggest that for the next 40 years, manpower needs in the mental health and social services will continue to increase. This situation is due primarily to the currently retiring generation, which was the "baby boom" of World War I, and extends to include persons born during the "baby boom" of World War II. It could be estimated that practically all young human service workers now in practice and all students now in professional schools will extend at least some of their practice with or in behalf of older adults. Manpower needs will continue in the service of older adults, especially in clinical mental health areas such as working on adjustments and adaptations to changing life styles, dealing with anxieties of living in urban settings and with feelings of isolation in rural communities, attempting to maintain independent living while faced with certain physical and psychological decrements, however small; reentering the community after hospitalization for physical or emotional disorders, and adjusting to institutional living where necessary and available.

At present, the amount and quality of training in geriatric mental health is low among all categories of workers, both professional and paraprofessional, but especially among those personnel who spend, or should be spending, most of their time in direct services to aged patients. It is here that major emphasis must be placed in any manpower development programs. While it is essential to have a core of scientific and academic personnel to train graduate students in various mental health and related disciplines, it is even more essential to have trainers for on-the-job training of personnel already working in institutional and community settings, most of whom are not associated with formal educational institutions. Many of these work with the aged who lived in poverty or near poverty, where mental health problems are almost the rule, and priority must be given to training at every level of those who are willing to serve this population.

While specialized training is required, it is also important to bring an increased amount of geriatric training into the curricula of those disciplines such as psychiatry, psychology, nursing, social work, and the like, for those who will not become geriatric specialists.

Manpower and training needs must be considered at all levels: institutional (state mental hospitals, psychiatric wards in general hospitals, community mental health center inpatient services, convalescent and nursing homes, old age homes, halfway houses, board and care homes, intermediate care facilities, etc.); out-of-home and in-home (community mental health center and general hospital outpatient departments, clinics, senior centers, day care and all types of home-care programs, etc.); and academic (universities, colleges, community colleges, high schools, adult education and extension programs). Students must have opportunities to observe model programs and to be supervised by personnel who are appropriate role models for them to follow. Home visits, to see older people and their families in their own environments, as well as the utilization of case oriented teaching, critical incidents, and professional and paraprofessional personnel who will work with the aged.

Training programs must also consider the need to educate the active and mobile well aged so they, in turn, can work more effectively as volunteers and/or advocates to assist the impaired aged. In addition, high school and college students who serve as volunteers in various community and institutional settings should be given training in gerontological principles. These can be especially helpful with the aged in various ethnic and non-English-speaking groups.

Mental health workers also should be able to create new strategies to approach some of the emergent needs and demands of generations of newly retired and older aged persons, particularly those who face the triple jeopardy of being old, female and a member of a minority group. Many of the needs of the physically relatively healthy population entering their 60s and 70s fall within the category of mental health. These include adaptation to changes in life style, shift in income, loss of regularity of activity because of retirement, dissociation from work related associates, more time spent with spouse, increasing losses through death or movement to a new community of relatives, close friends, adult children and spouse, reduced participation in some community associations dependent on one's work connections, reduced functions and responsibility for children. All of these and other changes brought by retirement and aging bring on emotional stress and the need to discover alternatives. Workers should have necessary skills to counsel and to design programs and services that would involve these retired people in the creation of new interpersonal relationships and social structural designs for their own enjoyment.

Workers skilled in community planning, social problem assessment, program development and systems management and advocacy, as well as in counseling, group activities, and therapy, should have a central role in the field of mental health

care services delivery to the physically well and capable older people. Human service workers who understand the relationship between interpersonal engagement and mental health, or conversely, the association between disengagement and deterioration, and who have learned group organizational skills, can be helpful in maximizing the independence of older persons by creating supportive interdependency networks within the community.

It should be obvious that under the rubric "mental health workers" people of all ages are included, but it bears emphasis that special incentives must be provided for people in their middle and later years to provide services on a direct as well as indirect level and to act as counselors, planners, researchers, consultants, and teachers in the mental health field with appropriate training that insures quality services to young and old alike. It very well may be that the opportunity for older people to provide mental health services and consultation to others will be the best assurance of the continued preservation of mental health in the middle and later years by strengthening people's ego—in helping them to feel needed and wanted by making a meaningful contribution to the quality of American life (Excerpted from: *Manpower and Training Needs in Mental Health and Illness of the Aging*, 1977).

## CONCLUDING REMARKS

We have traversed the road of mental health services in the community and have made a series of discoveries about them that can be summarized as a series of issues and questions:

(1) We have noticed definitional and boundaries issues. What are mental health services in contrast to personal-general social services? Where do they overlap? Where are they competitive? Where are they mutually supportive?

(2) We have discovered different types of orientations to services; traditional, environmental, social action and growth-enhancing. Attitudes of mental health workers are shaped by their professional affiliations and by feelings and attitudes towards aging and the aged in our society.

(3) We have observed conflicting ideas about "people changing" vs. "structure changing" and about the nature of direct vs. indirect services to promote "good" mental health, a term whose imprecision is still confounding all attempts at designing standards and criteria that are universally agreed upon.

(4) Community care vs. institutional care has become a "straw man issue" as institutional care is

part of a continuum of care. Acceptance of the principle that in-home delivered services are reimbursable under third party payment arrangements is basic to the development of quality in-home services that concentrate on care as well as on rehabilitation.

The following questions are agenda items for the immediate future:

(1) How can the patchwork of fragmented, uncoordinated services be made responsive to the varied needs of heterogeneous older people in our different communities? How can links between programs and services be established to assure the realization of well-meaning policy principles enunciated by our national leaders?

(2) How can the federal system be adapted to preserve ethnic, racial and neighborhood affinities, local autonomies, states rights and national federation to shape a more equitable service system that is "in place" and responsive to modifications demanded by time and change?

(3) What kinds of financial support mechanisms can be forged out of the maze of funding mechanisms? How will mental health services in the community become part of a universal national health insurance scheme?

(4) What special efforts are to be designed to reduce, and eventually eradicate, the injustices of race, sex, and age discriminatory practices of the past centuries in the country, and in mental health programs in particular?

(5) How can the informal and the formal service networks—notably members of families—be integrated to effect a more humane and more effective service delivery pattern to older persons residing in the community?

(6) How can transitions from community to institution and back to the community be facilitated through the use of such combined networks? Shall we follow the pattern of Sweden and reimburse adult children for their services to their older parents?

(7) Which battery of services in the community is essential for any person to have around? Home-maker, transportation, information and referral, health, screening and emergency response services? How should they be packaged, as utilities (i.e., as rights upon consumer demand) or as case services (i.e., when needs justify their use)?

(8) How can service delivery be made more efficient through the use of technological devices such as computers, telephones, tapes, without losing the human touch?

Many issues about cost effectiveness and evaluation research directions and strategy have to be tackled if limited resources for meeting mental health needs are to be justified in the political decision making process.

Unquestionably, many more issues and questions come to mind when confronting the topic of community services, not the least of which are those related to training of providers and quality of services which is intimately linked to the preparation and further updating and upgrading of personnel. Above all, we need a sound planning process based on a conceptual framework that encompasses a continuum or spectrum of needs of the "young and old elderly" with an understanding that social care is as significant as social treatment and that both encompass an approach to the totality of mental health. Leadership is called for by the National Institutes of Mental Health and of Aging and the Administration on Aging to act as catalysts for bringing together all relevant parties of social planning that takes account of experiences in other countries and makes use of their data and knowledge for the benefit of our old and young to assure the mental health of this and future generations.

## REFERENCES

Administration on Aging, Dept. of Health, Education, and Welfare. *Report* No. 223–6885, Government Printing Office, 1977.

Administration on Aging, Dept. of Health, Education, and Welfare. *Aging,* February/March, 1977.

*Aging,* US Dept. HEW, Admin. on Aging, February/March, 1977.

*American Psychological Association Committee on Aging Survey,* 1957.

*American Public Welfare Association Training Project,* 1960.

BELLACK, L., AND BARTEN, H. (Eds.). 1969. *Progress in Community Mental Health.* New York: Grune & Stratton.

BIRREN, J. E., AND RENNER, V. J. 1977. Research on the psychology of aging: Principles and experimentation. *In,* J. E. Birren and K. W. Schaie (Eds.), *Handbook of the Psychology of Aging,* pp. 3–38. New York: Van Nostrand Reinhold.

BLENKNER, M. 1965. Social work and family relationships in later life. *In,* Shanes and Streib (eds.), *Social Structure and the Family,* Englewood Cliffs, N.J.: Prentice-Hall.

BRODY, E. 1966. The aging family. *Gerontologist, 6,* 4.

BURNSIDE, I. M. 1970. Loss, a constant theme in group work with the aged. *Hospital Community Psychiatry,* 21, 173–177.

BURNSIDE, I. M. 1978. *Working with the Elderly Group Processes and Techniques.* No. Scituate, Mass.: Duxbury Press.

BUTLER, R. 1975. *Why Survive: Growing Old in America.* New York: Harper & Row.

BUTLER, R.N., AND LEWIS, M.I. 1973. *Aging and Mental Health: Positive Psychosocial Approaches.* St. Louis: C.V. Mosby.

CAPLAN, G. 1970. *The Theory and Practice of Mental Health Consultation.* New York: Basic Books.

COCOZZA, J. J., AND WOJNIAK, E. J. 1970. A golden age center experience in providing services to geriatric mental patients in a state hospital. Cleveland: Unpublished Report.

COE, R. M., AND BREHM, H. P. *Preventive Health Care for Adults.* New Haven: College & University Press, 1972.

CROZER-CHESTER, Pennsylvania Medical Center Community Mental Health Center Grant Application, 1976.

DENNER, B., AND PRICE, R. (Eds.). 1973. *Community Mental Health: Social Action and Reaction.* New York: Holt, Rinehart and Winston.

EHRLICH, I., AND EHRLICH, P. 1974. A service delivery model for the aged at the community level. *Gerontologist, 14,* (3).

EKLUND, L. 1969. Aging and the field of education. *In,* M. Riley, J. Riley, and M. Johnson (eds.), *Aging and Society,* Vol. 2, *Aging and the Profession.* New York: Russell Sage Foundation.

FRANKFATHER, D. 1977. *Confused Elderly in the Community.* Unpublished dissertation, Brandeis University.

GOLDFARB, A. I. 1973. Integrated psychiatric services for the aged. *Bulletin of the New York Academy of Medicine,* 49, (12), 1070–1083.

GRABOWSKI, S. M. AND MASON, D. 1974. *Education for the Aging.* Eric Clearing House on Adult Education, Syracuse, N.Y.: Syracuse University.

*Guidelines for a Telephone Reassurance Program.* 1973. Report on the Michigan program, available from AoA. DHEW Publication No. (OHD) 73-202000. Washington, D.C.

GURIAN, B. S., AND SCHERL, D. J. 1972. A community-focused model of mental health services for the elderly. *Journal of Geriatric Psychiatry, 5,* (1).

HAGEDORN, H. J., BECK, K. J., NEUBERT, S. F., WERLIN, S. H. 1976. *A Working Manual of Simple Program Evaluation: Techniques for Community Mental Health Centers.* Cambridge, Mass.: Arthur D. Little.

HENDRICKSON, A. 1968. The role of colleges and universities in the education of the aging. *In, Poten-* *tialities for Later Living.* Gainesville: University of Florida Press.

HIEMSTRA, P. 1973. Educational planning for older adults: A survey of "expressive" vs. "instrumental" preferences. *International Journal of Aging and Human Development, 4,* (2).

*Information and Referral Services.* 1974. (DHEW Publication No. (OHD-AoA) 74-20232). Washington, D.C.

*International Council of Home Help Services Report* (Utrecht, Feb. 1978) Mimeographed document published by International Council of Home Help Services.

JAHODA, M. 1958. *Current Concepts of Positive Mental Health.* New York: Basic Books.

KAHN, A. 1973. *Social Policy and Social Services.* New York: Random House.

KAMERMAN, S., AND KAHN, A. 1976 (Eds.). "Community services to the aged." *In, Social Services in the U.S.* Philadelphia: Temple University Press.

KASL, S. 1972. Physical and mental health effects of involuntary relocation and institutionalization on the elderly—a review. *American Journal of Public Health,* (March).

KASTENBAUM, R. 1964. The reluctant therapist. *In,* R. Kastenbaum (ed.), *New Thoughts on Old Age.* New York: Springer.

*Let's End Isolation.* 1977. (DHEW/AoA.). Washington, D.C.

Levinson Gerontological Policy Institute Study of Home Care Services in Worcester, Mass., 1976; Waltham: Brandeis University.

LINDSAY, R. "Gerontology Comes of Age." *New York Times,* Week-in-Review, Sunday Edition, November, 1978.

LOWY, L. 1962. The group in social work with the aging. *Social Work, 7,* (4), 43–50.

LOWY, L. 1963. Meeting the needs of older people on a differential basis. *In, Social Group Work with Older People.* New York: National Association of Social Workers.

LOWY, L. 1975a. Relationship of use of mental health services to attitudes towards aging. (Available from Boston University School of Social Work, 264 Bay State Road, Boston, MA 02215.

LOWY, L. 1975b. Social welfare and the aging. *In,* M. Spencer and J. Dorr (eds.), *Understanding Aging.* New York: Appleton-Century-Crofts.

LOWY, L. 1979. *Challenge and Promise of the Later Years: Social Work with the Aging.* New York: Harper & Row.

*Manpower and Training Needs in Mental Health and Illness of the Aging.* A Report to the Gerontological Society, 1977. University of Southern California, Ethel Percy Andrus Gerontology Center.

Massachusetts Department of Elder Affairs. 1978. *State Plan.* Boston, Mass. Published by the Commonwealth of Mass. Superintendent of Documents, Mass. General Laws, Chapter 19A, Section 4, 1972.

Massachusetts Mental Health Planning Project. 1972. *Final Report.* Boston, Mass.

*National Capital Area Homemaker Service Training Manual.* 1974. Prepared by the Homemaker Service of the National Capital Area, Inc. Administration on Aging: (DHEW Publication No. (OHD) 74-20103.) Washington, DC.

National Council of Senior Citizens. 1976. *Law and Aging Manual.* Washington DC.

National Council on Aging. 1972. *The Golden Years . . . A Tarnished Myth.* Washington, D.C.

National Council on Aging. 1975. *Directory of Senior Centers and Clubs.* Washington, DC.

NAYLOR, H. H. 1972. The older volunteer in mental health. *Gerontologist,* 12, (1), 85–93.

*Nutrition for the Elderly.* 1973. Highlights of research and development projects stemming from the Older Americans Act of 1965. (DHEW Publication No. (AoA/OHD) 73-20236.) Washington, DC.

REIFF, R. 1976. Aftercare from a rehabilitation perspective. *Social Policy.* Vol. 6, pp. 1–8.

RILEY, M., AND FONER, A. (Eds.). 1968. *Aging and Society,* Vol. 1. New York: Russell Sage Foundation.

ROBBINS, E. G. 1975. Day care, a multifaceted concept. Paper delivered to HEW, Washington, DC. (October).

SANTORE, A. F., AND DIAMOND, H. 1974. The role of community mental health centers in developing services to the aging. *Gerontologist,* 14, (3).

*Serving Mental Health Needs of the Aged through Volunteer Services.* 1976, Washington, DC.: DHEW Publication No. (ADM) 1976–269. Government Printing Office.

SHERWOOD, S. (Ed.). 1974. *Long Term Care: A Handbook.* Jamaica, N.Y.: Spectrum Publ.

SIMON. A. 1973. Mental health and mental illness in aging: An overview. *In,* A. G. Feldman (ed.), *Community Mental Health and Aging: An Overview.* Los Angeles: University of Southern California, Ethel Percy Andrus Gerontology Center.

SMITH, B. K. 1976. *Adult Day Care and the Extended Family.* Austin, Texas: Hogg Foundation of Mental Health.

SMITH, S. A. 1975. *Natural Systems and the Elderly: An Unrecognized Resource.* Portland, Ore.: Model Project Report.

Social and Rehabilitation Service Dept. of Health, Education, and Welfare. "Statement on Goals for Protective Services for the Aging," 1970.

*Standards for Homemaker-Home Health Aide Services.* 1974, National Council for Homemaker Services, Inc. New York.

TRAGER, B. 1975. The need for community services. *In,* Adult Day Facilities for Treatment, Health Care, and Related Services, 94th Congress. Washington, D.C.: US Government Printing Office.

Training Needs Report. 1972. Conference sponsored by Administration on Aging. Southern Regional Board, Atlanta, Georgia.

*Transportation and Aging: Selected Issues.* 1974. DHEW Publication No. (OHD) 74-20232. Washington, DC.

*Transportation and the Elderly: Problems and Progress.* Hearings before Senate committee. Available from Senate Special Committee on Aging, Room G-225, Dirksen Senate Office Bldg., Washington, DC. 20510.

US House of Representatives Select Committee on Aging, March 3–4, 1976.

US Public Health Service *Report* of 1974, US Public Health Service, Washington, DC.

US Senate Special Committee on Aging. 1975. *Training Needs in Gerontology.* US Senate, March 7, 1975.

United Charities of Chicago, 1966. *Study of Services to Older People,* Chicago.

West Philadelphia Consortium for Mental Health. 1977. Annual report, Philadelphia.

WHITEHEAD, A. 1970. *In the Service of Old Age: The Welfare of Psychogeriatric Patients.* Baltimore: Penguin Books.

# 35

# Mental Health
# Institutions
# and the Elderly

*Sylvia Sherwood & Vincent Mor*

Mental disorders have been recognized and referred to in the earliest writings of man, although theories of causation and what should be done about such disorders have varied considerably. As pointed out by Margolis and Favazza (1977), for example, the Talmud refers to insanity as a disease to be treated by a physician. Hippocrates, also considering mental disorders as disease entities, postulated various bio-chemical causes for different types of disorders. Thus, "madness" was considered to be a function of the mixing of different types of bile, while "hysteria," a feminine disease, was thought to result from the "wandering" of the uterus. Espousing a very different view, Sprenger and Kramer, two Dominican monks reflecting the spirit of their times, believed that mental illness was caused by witchcraft and the free will acceptance of the devil (the appropriate "treatment"

being "punishment") and/or (presumably a "preventive treatment" for others) execution.

While history documents different theories of causation with different accompanying societal responses to deal with mental disorders, there is little in the way of solid knowledge concerning prevalence in the distant past of mental disorders in the elderly populations; nor is there solid evidence that can be used to estimate the prevalence of different types of mental disorders among the elderly. For that matter, the extent of congruency between times past and now with respect to the behavioral descriptors (the behaviors considered to be symptoms) of mental disorder is not very well documented. Certainly, there is no clear picture of the extent to which certain conditions—organic brain syndrome, for example, now considered as an integral part of the "mental health" problem—

were considered in the same light in time past.

Currently it is estimated that some 10 to 12 percent of the population over 65 have severely disabling mental disorders and that the rate of psychosis for the aged is greater than for the 35 to 64 year old group—40 per 1,000 for the 65 and over population as compared with 13 per 1,000 for the 35-64 year olds (Brody, 1977). According to Brody (1977), this greater rate among the elderly can be accounted for by:

> . . . the entry into the ranks of the mentally ill of those with organic mental disorders associated with the later phases of life—that is, the chronic brain syndromes of cerebral arteriosclerosis and senile brain disease, which are characterized by relatively permanent deficit in the capacity of intellectual functioning with symptoms such as confusion, impairment of orientation, memory and perception, knowledge and judgment. Old people with such disorders (and to some extent those with functional mental problems) are likely to have various forms of physical illness. Chronic brain syndrome and functional psychoses (in roughly equal proportions) account for more than 93 percent of the mental disorders of old people in mental hospitals (p. 63).

Recognizing that "larger numbers of mentally disturbed old people reside in the community than in institutions," she points out that, nevertheless, the elderly are over represented in mental hospitals relative to other age groups (Brody, 1977, p. 63).

These, then, are the elderly persons—the target population—under consideration in this chapter. While analyses of the current scene—recent developments vis-a-vis mental institutions and the elderly—constitute the bulk of this chapter, in order to place these in context, a brief historical perspective will first be presented, ranging from the colonial American scene to the present.

The remainder of this paper will deal more intensely with the current scene, focusing in particular on: (a) the development of alternate treatment settings for the care of the elderly with mental disorders; (b) an analysis of selected features of the mental health institution, particularly those considered to be relevant to patient outcome; and (c) a description of treatment modalities and their impact on the elderly. The goal is not only to present the knowledge base (including descriptive knowledge, observed relationships and results of impact studies) but, in addition, to raise salient issues and point to policy implications and directions for future research.

## AN HISTORICAL PERSPECTIVE

Little information is available specifically relating to the care of the aged, mentally ill in the colonial or early republican period in America. What information exists is primarily anecdotal in nature and must be largely deduced from accounts of the treatment of the mentally ill in general during this period. In the 17th and 18th centuries, the more well-to-do insane were supported by their families, but even harmless persons (and especially the agitated and violent) were confined or chained in attics and cellars or in small exterior buildings away from the main house.* As for the poor, the more violent were chained to cells like criminals, and the harmless were basically undifferentiated from the mass of the "pauper class" which had developed in early America. The township often paid the cost of constructing the small exterior buildings or cages in which the insane members of poor families were housed. Early Massachusetts law mandated that local communities insure that the insane members of their community not become a public menace or nuisance (Deutsch, 1949). The nonviolent insane, like all the poor, came under the jurisdiction of the "poor laws" which, like their Elizabethan forerunners, were designed to force localities to care for their own poor and indigent; as such, this regulation provided a strong incentive to exclude the settlement of all outsiders who might become an additional burden on the public purse.

Well into the 19th century, a common practice in rural areas was for the town to auction off its obligation to care for its indigent population to the lowest bidder. Another practice, common in both urban and rural settings, was to "board out" the harmless insane with other townspeople who were paid a fixed annual fee for the person's care.

As urban centers grew, however, the need for larger scale institutional solutions became obvious. Therefore, the poor, the indigent, the insane and the criminal were often grouped together in settings alternately termed "poorhouses," "workhouses," or "almshouses." This was true in New York City, New Haven and Boston. Despite the wretched conditions which prevailed in these poorhouses, Massachusetts and New York encouraged the construction of such institutions in every county, insisting that the centralization of the poverty and indigence problem offered a considerable financial savings over the boarding-out systems

---

*This appears to have been a relatively common practice well into the 19th century and was even used by institutions for the indigent and insane.

that prevailed. The poorhouses were also touted on the basis of their ability to achieve financial self-sufficiency through the labors of residents. Nonetheless, only ten years after the establishment of the Boston House of Industry in 1823, a model for other poorhouses in the State, it was described in the following terms.

> . . . Instead of being a House of Industry, the institution has become at once, a general Infirmary— an Asylum for the insane, and refuge for the deserted and most destitute children of the city. So great is the proportion of the aged and infirm, of the sick insane, idiots and helpless children in it, that nearly all the effective labor of the females, and much of that of the males, is required for the care of those who cannot take care of themselves (see Deutsch, 1949, pp. 129–130.*

A new era in care and treatment of the mentally ill began in the American colonies with the foundation of the Pennsylvania Hospital in 1751. While not designed exclusively for the insane, provisions had been made to house this group in special "cells" in the basement. Over 20 years later in Williamsburg, Virginia, the Eastern Lunatic Asylum was established as the first institution in America exclusively designated for the insane. Slowly, additional hospitals or asylums were established throughout the eastern states, so that by 1844, when the superintendents of American asylums met as a group for the first time, there were 23 institutions in the country serving the insane with a patient population of over 2,500 (Hall, Zilboorg, and Bunker, 1944).

In the pursuit of a moral treatment philosophy, certain hospitals stressed the value of occupational therapy and others the importance of classroom instruction (Hospital and Community Psychiatry, 1976). The notion was that occupying the mind either in work or in instruction would prevent the mentally ill from being absorbed in their own thoughts. While the Quakers stressed farming as the ideal form of occupational therapy, crafts and mechanical occupations were stressed at the Eastern State Asylum in Virginia.

Despite the comparative optimism prevalent from the 1830s to 1850s about the treatment and the "curability" of the insane, the existing facilities were far from adequate to accommodate the nation's "known" insane population. In 1850 less than one-third of the known insane were in mental asylums and, given the confusing definitions of insane in the population, it is likely that this percentage

*Quoted by Deutsch, 1949, from a report of the Massachusetts Legislature in 1833.

was closer to 15 percent (Deutsch, 1949). An 1854 survey conducted in Massachusetts found 2,632 insane persons in the state, only 1,141 of whom were in asylums. In the last decade before the Civil War the majority of insane were still to be found in the poorhouses, the almshouses or even local jails.

Rosenkrantz and Vinovskis (1978) have reanalyzed the raw data from the 1854 survey of the insane. This analysis has revealed that 18 percent of the insane in the general population were over 60 years of age and yet less than 10 percent of the insane in mental hospitals were aged 60 or over. Using data from the 1855 Massachusetts general population census, Rosenkrantz and Vinovskis found that the aged, those over 60, had the highest rates (735 per 100,000 for the age group 60-69 and 664 for the age group 70 and over) of insanity and yet they were proportionately least likely to be institutionalized. Not only were the aged insane less likely to have been in an institution, but among those who were in an institution, they were least likely to be in a "treatment oriented" mental institution. Rather, higher proportions of the elderly insane were found in poorhouses and jails than the insane in any other adult age group. Thus, at a time when the best, most prestigious treatment for the insane could be obtained in an institutional setting such as the State Hospital at Worcester, or the private McLean's Asylum, the aged were much less likely to have received such care.

With the growing demand for institutional placement, authorities tended to favor admission of more recent and therefore more "curable" patients. New York State was the first to establish a special facility for the chronically insane, requiring all towns to refer their mentally ill residing in local poorhouses to this facility. Despite such specialization attempts, by the latter half of the 19th century, the distinction between "recent" and "chronic" cases began to blur with the growing recognition of high readmission rates among recent cases. By 1890, some 70 percent of the nation's 106,485 estimated number of insane were in hospitals or asylums (Deutsch, 1949).

Throughout the first half of the 20th century, the state hospital populations continued to grow until, by 1945, there were 517,989 patients in 190 state, 33 veterans, 95 county and city, and 192 private mental hospitals (Deutsch, 1949). The size of these institutions varied from 50-bed private hospitals to massive complexes, the size of a city, with over 10,000 patients.

A 1945 American Psychiatric Association committee on psychiatric hospital standards found conditions generally deplorable and recommended extensive treatment and support criteria. One recommendation, of particular relevance to the elderly mental patient, was that hospitals admitting senile patients have a specially designated geriatric unit along with a special infirmary to manage the medical problems of the unit's population.

The number of hospitalized mental patients peaked in 1955 with 558,922 resident in-patients and 158,285, or 28 percent, of these were aged 65 or over (Kramer, 1975). The growth in the geriatric mental patient population had occurred as a function of: (1) the low rate of discharge of hospitalized mental patients after their first year of residence, resulting in a group of chronic patients growing old in the institution; and (2) an increase in the number of aged patients admitted with various brain syndromes associated with senile brain disease and cerebral arteriosclerosis (Kramer, Taube, and Redick, 1973; and Pollack, Person, Kramer, and Goldstein, 1959). Additionally, while substandard conditions in state and county mental hospitals had for years resulted in relatively high mortality rates among the long-stay chronic population, improved conditions in the early 1950s and "the application of advances in clinical medicine . . . resulted in a considerable saving of lives and led to an aging phenomenon among hospital patients" (Kramer et al., 1973, p. 433).

It is interesting to note that the public health and sanitation advances made during the first half of the 20th century did not reduce the aggregate death rate of the institutionalized mental patients aged 65 and over. Between 1930 and 1962 in New York State institutions, the death rates of all age groups except those over 65 decreased by over 30 percent (for some younger age groups this reduction was as much as 90 percent). For the aged population, there was a 12 percent *increase* in the death rate. At the same time the death rate for the elderly in the general New York State population decreased by 22 percent (Kramer, Taube, and Starr, 1968, p. 112). The increase in the death rate among aged state mental hospital patients, however, can be attributed almost entirely to the newly-admitted groups of brain damaged patients. Chronic schizophrenics over 65 years old with a decrease of 11 percent, shared in the general reduction in death rate between 1930 and 1962, although less than any other age group (Kramer et al., 1968, p. 113).

As the aged and chronic mental patients continued to pile up in the back wards of the state and county institutions across the country, the overcrowding assumed crisis proportions. By 1955, when the total resident population reached its peak, the system was strained to the breaking point. However, the seeds of reaction to the mental hospital as the locus of care for the mentally ill had already been sown.

## THE DEVELOPMENT OF ALTERNATIVE TREATMENT SETTINGS FOR THE CARE OF THE ELDERLY WITH MENTAL DISORDERS

### THE DECLINE OF STATE MENTAL HOSPITALS AS A LOCUS OF PSYCHIATRIC CARE FOR THE ELDERLY

While the large push to empty out the state mental hospitals came in the 1960s, the roots of this movement can be traced back at least to the 1940s. National recognition of the massiveness of the problems the states faced in maintaining mental institutions came in 1946 with Congressional authorization of the National Institute of Mental Health. Funding also became available for the development of psychiatric units in general community hospitals and out-patient clinics (Donahue, 1978). Indeed, over the last 30 years, the availability of such facilities has increased markedly (Kramer et al., 1973).

Kramer (1975) notes that in 1955 about half of the total mental health patient treatment or care "episodes" (both in-patient and out-patient cases) were accounted for by state and county mental hospitals. By 1973 they accounted for only 12 percent of the 5.2 million patient care episodes. Correspondingly, the percentage of out-patient psychiatric services more than doubled, from 23 percent in 1955 to 49 percent in 1973. The ratio of hospital-based to community-based treatments shifted from 3 to 1 in 1955 to 1 to 3 by 1973. The locus of care was totally reversed in less than 20 years. However, the degree to which such non-custodial alternate sources of care became available to the aged mental patient is considerably less than for the population in general.

The precipitating factors of this shift have been discussed by numerous authors (Aviram and Segal, 1977; Bloom, 1975; Butler and Lewis, 1973; Donahue, 1978; Kramer et al., 1973; and Stotsky, 1973). While the economic and social policy imperatives of alleviating the glaring deficiencies in state hospitals were crucial to the decision to initiate deinstitutionalization, the discovery and widespread utilization of psychotropic medications cannot be ignored as a necessary enabling condition. Without controlling the blatantly inappropriate behavioral and psychiatric symptoms of patients, it would have been impossible to consider returning them to a community which has not been over-anxious to welcome back even the controlled mental patient (*The Los Angeles Times,* 1972; Roberts, 1978).

Between 1955 and 1968, there was almost a 30 percent decrease in the number of patients in state and county hospitals and a decrease of some 24 percent for those aged 65 and over (Kramer *et al.,* 1973). However, the number of first admissions did not decline; indeed, between 1955 and 1972, there was an increase of 20,000 first admissions to state and county hospitals. At the same time the age composition of annual first admission cohorts changed markedly. In 1955, 27 percent of the 122,284 first admission patients were elderly; by 1972 only 10 percent of the 140,813 first admissions were elderly (Kramer, 1975, Table 6).

A major factor accounting for this decrease was the shift in admission policy vis-a-vis admitting patients with chronic brain syndromes. Whereas in 1946 some 44 percent of first admission patients were diagnosed as having a chronic brain syndrome, this was true for only 10 percent of first admissions in 1972 (Kramer, 1975, Table 7). In addition, since recently admitted brain damaged aged patients constitute the majority of hospital deaths, the number of deaths in mental hospitals, which had reached a high of over 51,000 in 1958, was only 16,597 by 1974 (Kramer, 1975, Table 3). Without the high number of annual admissions to replace those elderly brain damaged persons who died in mental hospitals each year, the size of the resident population of elderly had to decrease.

## The Rise of the Nursing Home Alternative

The enormous growth of the private nursing home industry since the early 1950s has provided mental hospitals with an outlet for the placement of chronic patients who are no longer seen as able to benefit from "active treatment" (Bennett and Eisdorfer, 1975; Moroney and Kurtz, 1975; and Stotsky, 1966). Data from the 1973-74 Nursing Home Survey (National Center for Health Statistics, 1977b) indicate that there are some 15,800 nursing facilities (excluding specialty chronic hospitals) housing about 1,075,800 patients. Between 1963 and 1973, there was a 130 percent increase in the number of nursing home beds available (National Center for Health Statistics, 1977a). Some 8 percent of all resident nursing home patients resided in mental hospitals prior to their admission to the nursing home (National Center for Health Statistics, 1977a). Nonetheless, of the over 86,000 nursing home patients admitted directly from a mental hospital, 37 percent were under age 65 (Zappolo,

1977, p. 27). In 1963, 53 percent of the persons 65 years and over with a mental disorder and residing in an institutional setting were nursing home patients. By 1969, some 75 percent of the institutionalized elderly with mental disorders were nursing home patients (Kramer, 1975). Goldfarb's studies in the early 1960s suggest that these figures are underestimates (1969). On the basis of clinical examinations using objective measures, he found that over 80 percent of the patients in nursing homes manifested a significant degree of chronic brain syndrome.

According to Donahue (1978), while there are no precise records, it is estimated that about 50 percent of those patients administratively deinstitutionalized over the past 20 years eventually found their way into nursing home settings. In 1969 some 38 percent of all releases from state and county mental hospitals were referred to nursing homes and homes for the aged. On the basis of the National Center for Health Statistics data presented above (NCHS, 1977b), it is difficult to determine the prevalence of aged chronic mental patients (those who grew old in mental hospitals) as opposed to the more recently psychiatrically impaired brain damaged patients admitted to nursing homes from the community or other medical facilities. While the former were discharged and admitted to nursing homes, the latter group were likely to have been excluded from admission in mental hospitals and referred to nursing home facilities for placement (Friedman and Lehrman, 1969).

## The Roles of SSI and Medicaid in the Deinstitutionalization of Elderly Mental Patients

Two major federal programs appear to have spurred both the deinstitutionalization push and the growth of the nursing and board and care home industry. The initiation of Medicaid in 1965 made it possible for the elderly indigent to "purchase" medical care services outside of the state and charitable institutions. While state institutions were also eligible for federal matching monies under Medicaid for their populations age 65 and over, the availability of alternative settings made it possible to implement institutional policy shifts aimed at reducing the mental hospital chronic patient population and refocusing the hospital toward the delivery of acute care. Medicaid was perhaps most useful in diverting potential state hospital admissions to nursing homes. In New York State this policy was widely practiced and resulted in a substantial decrease in the number of elderly admissions to the state hospital system by 1969 (Kobrynski and Miller, 1970; and Pollack and Taube, 1975).

The second major policy shift at the federal level was the implementation of the Supplemental Security Income (SSI) program in 1974. This federally funded program took over the state Old Age Assistance and Disability Assistance programs providing an income base for poor elderly persons living in the community. Whereas the states must pay for at least a proportion (up to 50 percent) of the cost of Medicaid for institutionalized aged mental patients, with SSI, so long as the patient was residing in a noninstitutional residence, the federal program absorbed the basic cost of the person's living expenses. Donahue (1978) maintains that SSI has been a major factor in the decision to "dump" aged mental patients out of state hospitals, but there is little national data available concerning increases in deinstitutionalization placements since 1974 to substantiate this. Additionally, since many states supplement federal SSI payments, it is not at all clear that a definitive financial incentive exists.

## THE DEVELOPMENT AND PREVALENCE OF OTHER ALTERNATE TREATMENT SITES FOR THE MENTALLY ILL ELDERLY

In 1946, the United States Congress established the National Institute of Mental Health and provided funds for community based mental health services. Between 1946 and 1968, the number of out-patient psychiatric clinics increased from 500 to almost 2,000 (Kramer et al., 1973). And, between 1946 and 1973, the number of patient care episodes accounted for by in-patient psychiatric units in general hospitals increased from just over 100,000 to almost half a million (Kramer, 1975). With passage of the 1963 Community Mental Health Act (Public Law 88-164), increased federal funding became available for the development of comprehensive community mental health centers (CMHC). Initial program goals targeted the creation of some 2,000 CMHCs but, at present, less than 500 have become a reality (Donahue, 1978).

Given this basic shift in the locus of delivery of mental health services, how have the elderly fared? Are they as likely to be receiving mental health services from such newly developed community based alternatives or has the pattern of limiting access to the most socially valued treatment modalities, begun a century and a half ago, persisted? There appears to be little doubt that the latter holds true. In 1968, only 2 percent of the terminations from out-patient mental health clinics were persons over 65. Only slightly more than 2

percent of the 11,000 admissions to day care or partial hospitalization programs in 1969 were accounted for by persons over 65. And, the poor record of community mental health centers in serving elderly and chronic patient populations has been well documented (Cumming, 1975; Donahue, 1978; Kramer, 1975; Kramer et al.,1973; Patterson, 1976). In 1969, only 4 percent of all admissions to CMHCs were persons over 65 years of age (Kramer et al., 1973). By 1971, the elderly still accounted for only 7 percent of all CMHC admissions, with about equal numbers of elderly admitted for affective and organic disorders (Taube and Redick, 1975). In a survey of eight CMHCs across the country, Patterson (1976) found that few elderly persons seek care and no outreach efforts are directed toward this population. Only three of the centers surveyed gave some form of special programmatic attention to the elderly and, in general, little or no consultation was made available to nursing homes by CMHC staff.

More recent data from the states of New Jersey (Arthur Bolton Associates, 1975) and Rhode Island (Sherwood, Mor, Morris, Sherwood, and Abrams, 1977), also indicate that the elderly and chronic patients are not as likely to be receiving CMHC services. The New Jersey data indicate that only 6 percent of the almost 5,000 clients served by CMHCs were rated as having a low level of community functioning, which is most characteristic of discharged elderly mental patients. A Horizon House Institute report (1977) for the state of Pennsylvania presents data indicating that only 5 percent of Pennsylvania's CMHC clients are over 65 years of age and reports that only 4–6 percent of a sample of discharged CMHC patients were elderly. The Rhode Island survey of institutional and community mental health clients served by state funded agencies (the single state hospital and 11 CMHCs), conducted for the purpose of identifying distinct client types and their associated service needs, found no overlap in the institutional and community client types. Less than 10 percent of the CMHC case load was over age 60 and less than 30 percent had ever been institutionalized. This implies that over 70 percent of the CMHC clients had never had problems which led to the level of personal and social dysfunction associated with admission to a mental hospital. Even among those CMHC clients who had been institutionalized, most had been in a mental hospital for less than a year, indicating that few, if any, of the CMHC clients were long-term deinstitutionalized patients (Sherwood, Mor, Morris, Sherwood, and Abrams, 1977).

Perhaps the most recent large scale source of

placement for the deinstitutionalized chronic and elderly mentally ill is also the oldest: foster care placement. Some type of domiciliary care programs (which is essentially a term descriptive of a variety of foster care, personal care or boarding homes and rest homes) had been instituted in all but six of the 50 states by 1975. Over 24,000 "facilities" housed some 300,000 elderly, disabled, retarded and mentally ill persons (Booz-Allen and Hamilton, 1975). According to a recent Social Security Bulletin (December, 1977), "nearly 107,000 Supplemental Security Income (SSI) recipients in 15 states with identifiable federally administered optional supplementation programs resided in domiciliary care facilities or under other supervised living arrangements in March, 1976" (p. 1). Of these, 53 percent were categorized as disabled adults (including the mentally ill), 40 percent as aged persons, and 1 percent as blind adults. However, when age by itself was used to categorize these persons (rather than categorical source of funding), about 50 percent were found to be 65 years of age or older.

A pattern of large scale discharging of marginally adjusted mental patients to foster or boarding home placements has been observed and studied in many states (Donahue, 1978). Large boarding and residential hotels in major cities around the country have been absorbing discharged mental patients and creating what Donahue has termed "psychiatric ghettos" (1978). Indeed, a number of authors have commented on a rising "counter-revolution" in the mental health field, particularly among the advocates of the aged and chronically ill long-term patients (Reich, 1973; Roberts, 1978). Even in England where a system of community based geriatric services has been available to absorb many deinstitutionalized patients, considerable concern has been expressed as to the continued feasibility of the administrative discharge policy (Rollin, 1977).

## FEATURES OF THE MENTAL HEALTH INSTITUTION

The current status of mental institutions in the United States, then, can be characterized as having a diminishing population of patients in the face of recent efforts at preventing admissions, reducing length of stay and deinstitutionalizing residents. The residual populations in most hospitals consist of short stay, acutely disturbed patients and those for whom no alternative placement has been found.

Assuming that the mental institution can have important goal-directed functions (rather than merely being a custodial domicile), then important issues arise concerning patient goals and various features of the institution. Focusing on such features, this section deals specifically with issues concerning classification and assessment of patients, patient mix, organizational structure, manpower and training needs, and potential influences of architectural design options on patient behavior and outcome (the achievement of patient centered goals).

### CLASSIFICATION AND ASSESSMENT ISSUES

A principal differentiation of mental patients of all ages is the classification of the "acute" versus the "chronic" patient. The temporal cutting point for distinguishing between an acute as opposed to a chronic patient generally varies between one and five years (Brown, Ebringer, and Freedman, 1977). The acute patient has traditionally been seen as having a better chance of achieving a full readjustment of community living than the more chronic patient. A similar *ex post facto* classification is the age at which the patient had his/her first psychiatric episode. This is particularly relevant in distinguishing between "early" and "late" onset elderly psychiatric patients. The "early" onset elderly patients in mental institutions are generally chronic patients who have been continuously institutionalized (Blau, 1970). The number of previous hospitalizations a patient has had is sometimes used as a means of classification. The multiple admission patients are sometimes known as the "revolving door" type. Such patients have frequent acute "flare-ups" of their chronic mental conditions and periodically require rehospitalization.

These three classifications are basically predicated on the premise that the patient's past behavior (regardless of the circumstances) is the best indicator of future behavior; that is, chronic patients do not respond to treatment; early onset patients have more intractable problems; and multiple admission patients are likely to be rehospitalized. In fact, considerable empirical evidence supports the validity of such a view (Davis, 1972; Lamb and Goertzel, 1971; Rawls, 1971; Weinstein, DiPasquale and Winsor, 1973). Despite the prognostic utility of such classification systems, the assumption made about the continuity of past behavior offers a very pessimistic view and may not hold true in the face of a novel intervention program. Additionally, the use of such classifications may act as a sort of self-fulfilling prophecy by diverting staff attention to patients with a better prognosis.

The classification of elderly mental patients on the basis of their psychiatric diagnoses has been the most common form of classification of state and county mental hospital patients. Among elderly mental patients, the major diagnostic groupings have been the functional, the affective and the organic disorders. Functional disorders, primarily schizophrenia (or its late onset equivalent, paraphrenia) are associated with the long-stay patients who grew old in the hospital. Affective disorders, such as depression, are fairly common among the elderly new admissions to psychiatric treatment and constitute the second largest diagnostic group of elderly admissions to out-patient clinics, CMHCs and general hospital in-patient psychiatric services (Kramer *et al.*, 1973).

While diagnostic classification is presumably based on a clinical evaluation of the full range of pathological symptoms, too often it is unreliable, subject to bias, and serves more as a means of labeling than providing insight into the suggested treatment. According to Gurland (1973), the value of skilled diagnostic classification is perhaps most apparent in considering the probable prognosis of the patient as well as the nature of the treatment to be prescribed. Unfortunately, the diagnostic sophistication available at most state and county hospitals is notoriously poor (Bulter, Dastur, and Perlin, 1965). Gurland (1973) and Goldfarb (1959, 1960) have described some of the difficulties and the clinical cues necessary to take into consideration in diagnosing aged mental patients, many of whom manifest similar symptom patterns to the untrained eye. Elderly patients with serious depression, perhaps in response to a physiological impairment, may show many of the surface signs commonly associated with chronic brain syndrome (Goldfarb, 1960).

Without comprehensive diagnostic and assessment approaches such as those advocated by Gurland and his colleagues, the power and perceived immutability of diagnostic labels can be a deterrent to effective treatment. Blau (1970) notes that "even professional workers prefer to cling to organic diagnoses in the face of symptoms that would be regarded as functional in a younger patient. Viewing all emotional disturbances in the aged as the product of organic changes seems to lend a greater air of respectability" (p. 211). An example of the prevalence of the assignment of organic diagnoses and its possible influence on staff attitudes was found during a study of the Rhode Island Medical Center Chronic Hospital for the Department of Mental Health, Retardation and Hospitals of the State of Rhode Island (Sherwood, Sherwood, Morris, Mor, McClain, and Greer, 1977). A large proportion of the hospital's patients had long histories of psychiatric problems (many were transferred from the adjacent state mental hospital). Organic Brain Syndrome was one of the major diagnoses in the records of the random sample of 200 interviewable patients under investigation. However, data resulting from clinical interviews conducted for each patient indicated that the prevalence of these conditions as measured by standardized, objective tests (the Mental Status Questionnaire [Goldfarb, 1960] and the Face-Hand Test [Fink, Green and Bender, 1952]) was substantially less than would have been expected, given the incidence of brain damage as a diagnosis.

A number of consequences were observed that may at least be partially attributed to the presence of the diagnostic label. Both administrative and ward staff grossly overestimated the proportion of patients who would not be able to respond to a structured interview. Specific patients pointed out as "uninterviewable" by the ward staff having daily contact with them were in fact found to be able to respond appropriately to the interview. Both institutional programming and staff behavior to that point were erroneously predicated on behavioral expectations based on the brain damage label in patients' charts.

There are a number of crucial issues to consider in assessing patients (Gurland, 1973). The first issue to consider, perhaps, is the assessment perspective, that is, is the intention of the assessment solely to present a picture of the patient's current functioning (regardless of the environmental constraints on his/her behavior that may be present) or to assess as well the capacity or future potential of the patient? Institutional regulations may prohibit certain kinds of independent behavior or at least not encourage their performance. Thus, measures of current functioning may tap the environmental press as much as the patient's actual condition.

Another important issue relates to the expectancies of the assessor. Frequently institutional staff find it difficult to visualize certain types of patients with given sets of problematic characteristics as capable of functioning or behaving other than in the manner they are commonly observed to function. They may not be aware of the fact that similar persons can and do function adequately in a community setting with the benefit of a supportive, prosthetic environment. Institutional environments generally do not provide the opportunity to practice a large range of social behaviors (Atthowe and Krasner, 1970). Exposing clinical assessors to patients who are in a community setting may be an important training device, adding considerable breadth to their assessment perspective.

Gurland (1973) notes a number of additional factors which should be considered in conducting psychiatric assessments for therapeutic or classification purposes. For example, the patient's social and cultural background as well as his/her recent history (such as experiences of loss of spouse) should be taken into consideration in the interpretation of the patient's behavior. The physical health and disability of a patient can also affect his/her behavior, and the presence of apparently psychiatrically pathological symptoms may disguise their primary physiological causes. Unless these and the other assessment issues discussed above are considered, it may be impossible to formulate an accurate and meaningful classification of elderly patients that is relevant to and suggestive of an appropriate treatment plan.

## PATIENT MIX

Since the passage of the Community Mental Health Act in 1963 and the growth of CMHCs, state hospitals have been increasingly drawn into the mental health system. During the 1960s and 1970s many states adopted a unit system in state hospitals with wards corresponding to particular geographically based "catchment" areas. Each state hospital serves a number of catchment areas and only residents of these communities are patients in the corresponding in-patient wards (Aviram and Segal, 1977; Dolnick and Pearsall, 1977; Horizon House Institute, 1977; Massachusetts Department of Mental Health, 1977). These units house a variety of patients with different psychiatric problems, levels of chronicity and ages. In some states there are also specialty units with different administrative structures in the hospitals. Most state hospitals now also house alcohol treatment or substance abuse units (Bloom, 1975; Bonn, Binner, and Huber, 1975), as well as units for disturbed or delinquent adolescents (Sherwood, Mor, et al., 1977).

Despite the presence of such specialty units in the midst of the geographic wards, the manner in which patient-unit assignments are made is by no means clear, particularly among the aged. Schuckit and Pastor (1978) indicate that over 10 percent of the admissions to alcohol detoxification units in state hospitals are over 55. Data from the Rhode Island survey (Sherwood, Mor et al., 1977) indicate that 20 percent of those patients on the alcohol treatment wards are over 62 years old while others with substantial alcohol abuse problems were found both in specialty (including geriatric) units and in the geographic units.

Despite the apparent confusion concerning the assignment of patients to particular units, the rationale behind the unitization is important to consider. Establishing an appropriately homogeneous patient mix with respect to a common therapeutic goal appears to be the motivating idea

(Blau, 1970). For the geographic units, while patients are indeed functionally and diagnostically heterogeneous, they are all, nonetheless, oriented toward community placement, which is presumably facilitated by a staff familiar with the resources in the patient's community (Blau, 1970; Bloom, 1975; and Dolnick and Pearsall, 1977). The specialty units have more homogeneous groupings of patients. While the therapeutic goal of the alcohol treatment and adolescent units may be clear, the question can be raised as to the dominant therapeutic goal in a geriatric specialty unit. For all intents and purposes, do such units, where they exist, serve a custodial role acting essentially as the new chronic wards of state hospitals *à la* the no treatment chronic hospitals founded in the 19th century?

Indeed, the wisdom of institutional age segregation can be questioned in light of research indicating it may be deleterious to positive outcome for the elderly patient. In studies where the degree of age segregation was experimentally manipulated when newly-admitted elderly were randomly assigned to standard geriatric intensive therapeutic or general adult mental hospital wards, results were supportive of an age integrated patient mix (Kahana, 1967; Kahana and Kahana, 1967).

## ORGANIZATIONAL STRUCTURE

Closely related to the unitization phenomena are the organizational and administrative changes which have accompanied the movement. In Massachusetts, for example, administrative and program authority for the wards is located in an area or regional mental health administrator and not the institution's superintendent (Massachusetts Department of Mental Health, 1977; Dolnick and Pearsall, 1977). Staff formerly assigned to ward patient care duties have been retrained to do community work (Stein and Corman, 1976; Stein and Test, 1976), or act as liaison between the state hospital unit and the community mental health service system. This both enables the hospital to retain follow-up responsibility and maintains a continuity of programming. Organizationally, it pulls the hospitals' focus more and more to the delivery of acute care and the building of effective community linkages. But what are the results on the residual population, housed either in a geographic or specialty unit? Are they more or less likely than previously to receive the needed attention when primary efforts are directed towards community involvement?

## MANPOWER NEEDS AND STAFF TRAINING

The mental institution system itself is in a state of flux, the shifting roles of facility staff can be seen as crucial to the issue of quality of care for elderly chronic patients. In the 1970s the need for an interdisciplinary noncustodial approach has been increasingly recognized; and a relatively large increase has been called for in the numbers and types of personnel needed to deal with the residual population of long-stay elderly as well as other patients. According to Knee and Lampson (1977) not only are "psychiatrists, nurses, social workers, and psychologists needed, but occupational therapists, industrial therapists, recreational therapists, rehabilitation counselors, psychiatric aides, mental health technicians, educators, public health personnel, teachers, clergymen, law enforcement officers, and physicians are needed" (p. 887).

Findings from the long-term care field in general are applicable to the mental institution. Hammerman, Friedsam, and Shore (1975) point out that ". . . one of the major problems in long-term care continues to be the high rate of employee turnover" (p. 189). No doubt contributing to this phenomenon, Ruchlin and Levey (1975) present data indicating that employment in long-term institutions is economically unattractive as compared with short-term institutions. Furthermore, recruitment and staff retention is further hindered by the low status that tends to be accorded to geriatric and chronic patient care (Howell, 1965; Kashmer, 1969). This low status may be accentuated as a function of increasing efforts and resources that are directed toward community liaison and follow-up responsibilities. Relative to the excitement of participating in such goal directed programming, working with long-stay patients, often viewed as needing primarily custodial care, may appear even more negative.

The need to gain knowledge concerning effective ways of enhancing the self-image of the front line mental health worker and making his/her job professionally more rewarding, then, is paramount for mental institutions. Holding promise for helping to enhance self-image and make institutional staff's work situation professionally more satisfying, perhaps, are a number of models developed for reversing some of the deleterious effects on motivation of industrial workers. These models include the concept of *job enlargement* (Kornhauser, 1965; Reif and Schoderbek, 1966)—not adding to his/her tasks, per se, but rather expanding the "life space" of the worker by allowing him/her to exercise more options and responsibility and expectancy models (Campbell, Dunnette, Lawler, and Wersh, 1970; Lawler, 1973; and Mitchell, 1974)—increasing motivation through the development of achievable goal-oriented expectations.

University based support of mental health manpower development and training programs have been sponsored by the Continuing Education Branch of the Division of Manpower and Training Programs, NIMH (see *Mental Health Continuing Education Program for Long-Term Care Providers,* 1975). Continuing education for human service professionals has been an established reality for years (Lauffer, 1977) and, more recently, the training and use of paraprofessionals and associate degree mental health workers have also increased (Fallon, Wallach, and Gallo, 1974; Gilbert, 1977; Rogowski, 1974; Young, True, and Packard, 1976). A recent study of the use of associate degree level mental health workers found them working unsupervised across the entire range of traditional mental health service functions (Young, True, and Packard, 1976).

Concern about mental health aspects of long-term care patients also led the National Institute of Mental Health to hold a national conference in 1972, bringing together leaders from gerontology, mental health and nursing home administration. Not only were continuing education and mental health aspects of the long-term care patients stressed, but at least several of the leaders stressed the necessity of directing such continuing education efforts towards all levels of staff, including the nurses and low-skilled personnel who are in continuous day-to-day contact with the residents (Friedsam, Dovenmuehle, and Shore, 1972; Gottesman, Fada, and Garrett, 1972; Gunter, 1972; and Thompson, 1972).

The need for training in the delivery of care to the institutionalized elderly mental patient is linked to the broader problem of developing training programs to deal with the chronic and elderly mental patient in general. Finkel (1978) surveyed psychiatric residency programs and concluded that "although there is a real need in a variety of settings for training psychiatrists to work with older people, a large proportion of psychiatric residency programs do not offer the opportunity for clinical experience with this age group" (p. 101). Attitudes towards working with the elderly also limit community treatment options both for the never institutionalized and for the elderly patients being discharged from the mental hospital. The relative absence of elderly clients in CMHCs and the reluctance of staff to outreach to this group indicate that the community-based staff may prefer to interact with more verbal, younger clients (Blau, 1970; Brown and Kosterlitz, 1964; Cumming, 1975; Epstein, 1975; and Gordon, 1965).

Training and manpower development geared towards the delivery of appropriate care for elderly chronic mental patients (clients) appear to be common needs of the mental institution and the CMCH. At the same time, the differences in the current staffs as well as their task assignments suggest that the types of training and manpower development needed within these two systems may differ somewhat. Differences in the current staffing patterns and task performances in these two types of settings can be illustrated by the findings from the Rhode Island study referred to previously. As part of the goal to develop a statewide manpower plan, staff in both the institution and CMHCs completed a questionnaire concerning their background, training and estimates as to how often they perform any of 192 distinct tasks. As compared with the CMHC staff, IMH staff tended to be older, (IMH staff—30 percent over 50, CMHC staff—9 percent over 50); males, (IMH staff—43 percent males, CMHC staff—34 percent males); less likely to be married, (IMH staff—52 percent married, CMHC staff—64 percent married). In addition, over 60 percent of the CMHC staff had a Master's degree or higher, while over 60 percent of IMH staff had only a high school diploma or less. As might be expected, almost all of the CMHC staff had a professional affiliation, while well over 50 percent of the institutional staff were mental health aides with no professional accreditation.

Perhaps the most startling finding related to differences in the pattern of performance of tasks. Only a minority of CMHC staff (primarily the small group of nurses employed) were performing any of the broad range of activities and tasks related to the provision or coordination of support services necessary for chronic and elderly patients and crucial for successful deinstitutionalization. The bulk of CMHC staff time is occupied in planning for and engaging in individual and group therapy. Very few CMHC staff engaged in tasks classified as supportive or rehabilitative. While psychotherapy with elderly and chronic patients should not be dismissed as inappropriate, the therapy session in and of itself is probably not sufficient to enable community reintegration.

If these findings are indeed representative of CMHC staff activities around the country, major attitudinal changes and perhaps retraining may be required in this sector of the mental health system if elderly mental patients are to be deinstitutionalized and treated in community mental health centers. If the deinstitutionalization push is to continue and if the past neglect of "dumping" unprepared patients into an unprepared community (Donahue, 1978) is to be reversed, priority must be directed to the chronic and vulnerable elderly population by the community mental health system (Patterson, 1976; Zusman and Lamb, 1977).

## INSTITUTIONAL DESIGN OPTIONS

In recent years considerable interest has been expressed in the use of architectural design (both for new construction as well as in retrofitting existing facilities) to help bring about desired patient oriented changes. For example, Rosenblatt (1970) has related the condition of a hospital's physical plant to the morale and treatment attitudes of staff. Pointing to potential negative effects of architectural features on patient outcome, in an observational study of the architectural designs of a VA hospital and a state mental hospital, Spivak (1967) found both institutions to have long corridors with no distinct visual features. When walking down the corridor time and distance were distorted, giving a feeling that they were never-ending. In addition to long corridors, Spivak stated that the walls, floors and ceilings were reflective which caused glare, resulting in visual distortions. Also, the corridors were "highly sound reflective" causing echos. Spivak concludes that these distortions must undoubtedly have a detrimental effect on the patients, especially those who were on hallucinogenic drugs. He suggests that the physical space of these facilities caused the patient to have difficulties in self-perception and in having social relations with others.

Lawton, Liebowitz, and Charon (1970) found that by creating a suite of rooms for residents, social interaction was encouraged. This, however, minimized staff-resident interaction. Apparently this architectural arrangement created a division between the residents' area and the area in which the staff work.

The importance of architectural features for those confined in an institutional setting (Baker, Davies, and Sivadon, 1959) and specifically for enhancing a "supportive" environment have also been pointed to (Architecture Research Construction, 1975). Indeed, designing for personal space for the mental patient within an atmosphere that is supportive is seen as integral to the therapeutic milieu by a number of investigators (Proshansky, Ittelson, and Rivlin, 1970; Schwartz, 1968). Observational findings in a number of studies suggest that modifications in the institutional environment in this manner can be related to positive behavioral changes in the patients. A part of the design and construction work undertaken by Architecture Research Construction (1975) at Cleveland State Hospital, behavior mapping of the patients on a locked, back ward for chronic male patients was undertaken before and after the reconstruction. The architectural modifications consisted of: increased individualization, such as private personal areas for each patient (had been open wards); brightly colored signs and walls; choices of private or open areas in the bathrooms and common or activities rooms; introduction of permanent seating fixtures (alcoves or interchange seating) to encourage interaction; and, the introduction of area specific lighting and lower ceilings to minimize the expansiveness and hollowness of the ward. The behavioral mapping data indicated that many of these back ward male patients appeared to respond very positively to the modifications. Not only did the study sample of patients manifest an increased variety of activities, but the occurrence of spontaneous interactions among patients increased significantly. While the number of patients on the ward did decrease in the interim, recent research has found that reduction in ward population, in and of itself, does not, apparently, lead to behavioral changes in the residual group of patients (Blumenthal and Carpenter, 1974). Thus, the findings of this Cleveland State redesign effort are encouraging. The patients they found to respond positively to environmental changes are the very kind of patients who constitute the chronic and elderly population in state hospitals across the country. It should be noted, however, that the possible confounding of a "Hawthorne" effect raised by the active involvement of patients in the planning and modification process clouds the meaning of the positive behavioral changes. Were the changes a function of the new design features or the consequences of additional attention?

## PATIENT OUTCOME AND INSTITUTIONAL TREATMENT PROGRAMS

The major issues and current conditions prevailing in state mental hospitals which have been discussed can be characterized as descriptive of the structural and organizational forces which impinge directly or indirectly on the chronic and elderly institutional patients. These forces constitute the macrosystem of care which forms the backdrop for the development and implementation of specific treatment programs within the institution. The mental hospital is generally a resource scarce environment (Van Horne, Secherman, and Cohen, n.d.) where allocation decisions are based on the expected outcome of various service delivery strategies. Maintenance and/or slowdown of deterioration as outcomes are often ignored. Client populations for whom no observable *gain* resulting from therapeutic intervention can be anticipated are least likely to receive such resources. Van Horne and his colleagues, in analyzing service patterns in a random sample of state hospital patients, found that the longer patients had been hospitalized (either continuously or repeatedly), the less likely they were to be receiving a resource intensive pattern of multiple services. There appears to be a general absence of clearly defined goals, both on an organizational and patient level concerning the chronic and elderly continued-stay patient.

There is nothing in the framework of goal attainment theory (Garwick, 1975; Kiresuk, 1973) that suggests that the organizational adaptation of appropriate goals cannot be set for the continued stay patients. The implementation of particular treatment programs, each with their short-range goals (with objective indices of attainment), can be conceived of as successive approximations to the long-range goal (Garwick, 1975). These goals can be geared toward the ultimate "normalization" of the patient and the environment even if the environment must be continued institutionalization (Wolfensberger, 1972). Certainly the climate of thought favors as important objectives maximization of quality of life and independence within the limits of the rehabilitative potential for the continued stay mental patient. As Gottesman and Brody (1975) have noted, "the rationale for programs of intervention lies in the fact that a gap is known to exist between the actual physical, mental, functional and social conditions of institutionalized residents and their potential" (p. 474). Thus, whether the goal is community placement or enriched care within an institution, treatment programs address the gap between the existing conditions and potential conditions.

While in practice intensive goal oriented treatment programs, particularly those involving long stay elderly mental patients, are not in abundance, specific therapeutic interventions for attaining both short-term and long-term goals have been developed that are relevant to the treatment of elderly institutionalized mental patients. Within the context of the major goal(s) associated with each of the various institutional treatment strategies that have evolved, this section reviews the research findings with respect to program effectiveness in attaining these explicit or implicit goals. It should be noted that not all research findings relevant to certain types of treatment programs have been specifically associated with aged institutionalized mental patients; they have been included, however, when the goals or theoretical formulations of the therapeutic intervention appear applicable to the elderly mental patient. Some of the treatment approaches reviewed below are being discussed in greater detail in other chapters in this book and as such will be discussed only briefly in their context as striving toward a particular goal.

## PHARMACOLOGICAL TREATMENT

The impact of psychoactive medications on the entire system of mental health care (institutional and community) cannot be overstated. The advent of community treatment of the chronic mental patient, was, in many ways, not possible until the introduction of anti-psychotic medication in the mid-1950s (Kramer, 1975). The effectiveness of anti-psychotic medication maintenance has been well documented (Davis, 1975). With anti-psychotic medication, discharged chronic mental patients have significantly lower hospital readmission rates (Davis, 1975). May (1968) found that reduced use of drugs as a part of an overall treatment program was strongly related to prolonged hospital stay. Drug-free treatment was not only related to increased length of stay but also to higher rates of subsequent rehospitalization. Sabin (1978) in an excellent review of research findings on chronic mental illness concludes that "no other established form of treatment is comparably effective in preventing relapse" (p. 84). Nonetheless, problems of non-compliance with the prescribed drug regimen among chronic patients has proven to be a continual problem leading to rehospitalization (Doulon, Rada, and Knight, 1973). The use of regular medications groups has been found to be an effective way of simultaneously monitoring medication dosage and compliance and for providing an incentive to patients to regularly see or visit the out-patient clinic (Doulon, Rada, and Knight, 1973; Isenberg, Mahnke, and Shields, 1974). Sabin (1978) concludes that such group-oriented medication monitoring is perhaps the best proven (and cost effective) method of maintaining chronic patients at an even keel in the community.

At the same time questions can be raised concerning inappropriate use and overuse of drugs. The use of psychotropic medications within the mental institution for chronic and elderly patients is certainly very widespread (Eisdorfer and Fann, 1973). Eisdorfer (1973) suggests that psychotropic agents are used as "pharmacologic straitjackets" and Butler and Lewis (1977) recommend that "the medical profession's penchant for chemotherapy with the elderly should be restrained" (p. 281). Furthermore, the potential long-term consequences to personality structure are not known, particularly in the context of a biology of aging which is not entirely known (Eisdorfer, 1973).

While the therapeutic application of a drug therapy regime has been shown to be effective in reducing pathological symptoms (Eisdorfer and Fann, 1973) and in reducing the need for hospitalization (Davis, 1975), it has been suggested that it should be used only in conjunction with other forms of therapeutic intervention (Butler and Lewis, 1977). The integration of a pharmacological approach with other therapeutic modalities can presumably help meet the more amorphous quality of life and community adjustment goals, once the more severe pathological symptoms and disturbing behavior have been eliminated.

## PSYCHOTHERAPIES

The treatment programs being grouped under the rubric of psychotherapy cover a broad spectrum of "talk" or interactional therapies. A minimum of some verbal skills are required which would tend to exclude the most regressed elderly mental patients (Kastenbaum, 1972). The form such psychotherapies take varies considerably both in goals, in structure and in process. The review which follows will point to some of these differences and compare research and experiential findings emanating from the treatment of the institutionalized aged with psychotherapy.

In 1959, Rechtschaffen (1959) provided a fairly comprehensive review of the literature on psychotherapy with the aged up to that point in time. Rechtschaffen stresses the distinctiveness of doing psychotherapy with the aged, suggesting a more active and participating role for the therapist. A more recent review of the psychoanalytic literature with regard to the treatment of the elderly was conducted by Cath (1972). A major theme both reviewers found in the early writings of therapists working with the elderly concerned the resistance to treatment. They note a tendency toward modification of the traditional insight development focus of psychoanalytical thought, generally as a function of a reluctance to dismantle the ego defense structure of the elderly patient (Busse and Pfeiffer, 1969; Cath, 1972). Cath also asserts that the minimal barriers to verbal communication and interaction experienced by the elderly led to a general reluctance of therapists to work with this age group. Additionally, the writings of Freud and other early psychoanalysts stressed the rigidity of the elderly organism (Cath, 1972).

## INDIVIDUAL PSYCHOTHERAPIES

In terms of individual psychotherapy approaches, Goldfarb (1955) describes success with a brief but actively involved psychotherapy with recently admitted psychogeriatric patients. The modified form of therapy he followed was to encourage the elderly patient to accept his/her dependent condition by allowing him/her to maintain the illusion that the therapist is the child who will take care of and support him/her. Busse and Pfeiffer (1969), however, qualify Goldfarb's position, suggesting that such a dependency encouraging approach may only be appropriate for the regressed, brain damaged institutional patient. Haas (1963) suggests that the depression and paranoia often associated with the aged at the onset of their terminal phase are related to a fear of impending death and inadequacy related to a loss of competence and control. He stresses the value of an active psychotherapeutic approach to imbue in the geriatric patient an increased valuation of his current life phase. Wolff (1971) presents clinical evidence that some 50 percent of the hospitalized geriatric patients with whom he has worked using individual psychotherapy improve, many sufficiently to be released to the community. In an earlier paper (1963a) Wolff describes more fully the therapeutic techniques and ancillary therapeutic supports used in the treatment of chronic elderly, long-stay patients, all of whom manifested moderate signs of chronic brain syndrome. During therapy, no patients received drugs, and there were no adverse effects. Wolff maintains most patients obtained some level of insight into their conditions, primarily expressing fears related to loss of competency both mental and physical. Given the reality based nature of their concerns, the goal of full insight was substituted for ego-supportive techniques in order to replace the patient's negative image of self with a more positive image of the value of maturity. The author's clinical observations indicated success in this revised therapeutic goal.

As a mechanism for facilitating the ego-supportive activities presumably required to reverse the negative image the aged mental patients have of themselves, a number of authors have advocated the therapeutic value of reminiscence (Butler, 1964; Butler and Lewis, 1977; Lewis, 1973). Lewis (1973) postulates the utility of supportive settings in which an aged person can reminisce as a mechanism for "re-establishing a secure self-identity based on past experiences" (p. 121) in order to recover from a state of dissonance brought about by the realization that advanced age made it impossible to live up to past expectations of self. While there may be need for a re-alignment of expectations of such persons, reminiscence perhaps, may not be at all appropriate for elderly patients with long histories of social and psychological dysfunction.

With regard to the long-term mentally ill,

Wolff (1963b) notes that the aged chronic schizophrenics were most recalcitrant to individual treatment. Stotsky (1973) indicates that this group of patients is perhaps best approached through an activities regimen as opposed to psychotherapy. Stotsky (1973) also points out that individual therapy with the psychotic brain damaged patient is hopeless due to the absence of even minimal intellectual resources. On the other hand, he does suggest the use of such individual therapy in the case of elderly paranoid psychotics and patients with either psychotic or non-psychotic affective disorders—but only after their pathological symptoms have been stabilized through the use of psychotropic agents.

The individual approach to psychotherapy is felt to be appropriate most often in cases of acute psychiatric disorders; but when it is considered appropriate, a modified, non-insight oriented approach is generally advocated (Busse and Pfeiffer, 1969). Assuming the validity of this approach, techniques recently developed in the area of behaviorally oriented therapies (Liberman, 1972) and goal oriented client-therapist interaction (Kiresuk, 1973) might be particularly fruitful in their application to the supportive form of psychotherapy currently practiced. Certainly it is an area worth experimental investigation.

## GROUP PSYCHOTHERAPY

Group psychotherapy has been increasingly used in the place of individual therapy among the institutionalized aged (when psychotherapy is used in any form) (Blank, 1974; Wolff, 1962). Burnside (1970) reviewed the literature on group work with the aged, much of which emanates from studies conducted on institutionalized state hospital patients. Most of the studies she reviewed presented a highly positive view of group therapy. Nonetheless, the goals of such groups are so varied that the meaningfulness of aggregating them is questionable. While some groups are formed for specific "curative" reasons (Linden, 1971), others are formed for more ameliorative forms of discussion groups (Kalson, 1965). Linden (1971) reports high rates of success (based on clinical evidence only) resulting from group psychotherapy with elderly female mental patients—after eight months of treatment, 40 percent were able to leave the hospital. Similarly, Wolff (1962) reports on six years of experience with group therapy programs on which he based his claim that 40 percent of those treated could leave the hospital within six months and another 10 percent in one year. According to the author, patients who did not receive group therapy exhibited slower and less substantial improvement. It should be pointed out, however, that Wolff purposefully selected only the "best" of the geriatric patients for this program, although all were chronic cases with longer than 20 years of continuous hospitalization.

In a small but well-controlled study, Wolk and Goldfarb (1967) studied the effects of group psychotherapy on recently admitted and chronic geriatric patients. As might be expected, the long-stay patients were mostly schizophrenic, while the recent cases had organic brain syndrome. Some 25 patients of each type were randomly assigned to a treatment and no treatment group. Although the randomization did not result in diagnostically matched groups, it was felt adequate to test the treatment efficacy. The treatment group met weekly for a year in structured, leader oriented sessions focusing on interpersonal problems and feelings. No attempt was made to develop patient insight into their psychopathology. Significant improvement was found only for the experimentals in the areas of depression, interpersonal relations and organic mental syndrome (Wolk and Goldfarb, 1967). While the treatment was effective for both functionally and organically disturbed experimentals in terms of depression and interpersonal relations, only the long-stay chronic patients showed significant improvement on the mental syndrome measure. The authors suggest that "the monotonous hospital life of these persons may contribute to apathy and unresponsiveness" which is often "mistakenly attributed to organic mental syndrome" (p. 1256). This finding is particularly encouraging in light of the earlier discussion concerning the assessment of aged mental patients suspected to have organic brain syndrome. Wolk and Goldfarb conclude that "psychotherapy alleviates depression and encourages interpersonal relationships, . . . signs of 'organicity' diminish as the patient's social behavior improves and anxiety decreases" (p. 1256).

Sabin (1978) in his review of the efficacy of therapies for the chronic patient concludes that research findings mildly support the conclusion "that group forms of treatment are associated with better patient outcome in out-patient treatment" (p. 88). Wolff (1962), too, feels that group work is more valuable than individual therapy because it helps the patient to face the reality of social situations. The apparent goal of most group psychotherapies of focusing on present problems or feelings (Blank 1974) or crisis intervention (Oberleder, 1970) is consistent with the principle of supportive rather than insight oriented psychotherapy. Past conflicts and problems are seen as useful only in-

sofar as they remind the older person of successful coping strategies employed earlier in life (Ingersoll and Silverman, 1978).

While, as with individual therapy, there are a host of settings and processes that have been used in group therapy with aged institutionalized patients (Burnside, 1970), Ingersoll and Silverman's (1978) review led them to conclude that no attempts have been made "to assess the relative efficacy of these treatment methods" (p. 201). Sabin's (1978) review of group treatment research led him to conclude that "what the therapist does with the patient(s) is less important than how the therapist is when doing it" (p. 89). According to Truax and Carkhuff (1967), the ability of the therapist to demonstrate empathic understanding appeared to be central to the process of effective therapeutic communication. Frank (1973), in synthesizing the common elements of successful psychotherapies, points out that the patient must have contact with a concerned helper in a therapeutic setting. In addition, some purpose for which the suffering has occurred must be identified and the therapeutic tasks or goals at hand must be well prescribed.

The extent to which such principles are applicable to chronic, aged populations of elderly patients is not clear. Many of the group processes and the necessary active participation of the client in the therapeutic interaction appear to require skills and characteristics not present in the bulk of the elderly populations in mental institutions (Goldfarb, 1955; Stotsky, 1973). Some indications are available, however, that the supportive context of group therapy is beneficial for chronic patients. They tend to enhance the community adjustment process of discharged chronic mental patients, although these effects are only observed in the long run (Hogarty, Goldberg, and Schooler, 1974).

The issue of continuity of treatment for the chronic and elderly patient is a finding echoed througout the literature (Burnside, 1970; Busse and Pfeiffer, 1969; Gottesman and Brody, 1975). Positive therapeutic changes, both large and small, have been found to be reversed upon withdrawal of the treatment. While this may make the value of specific temporally limited interventions questionable for certain types of patients, for persons with chronic conditions a different standard may be needed. In the field of physical health, for example, it is not expected that a one-time intervention can cure diabetes; rather it can be controlled through continual medication. Similarly, at the present time, chronic (organic) brain syndrome resulting in short-term memory loss cannot (at least at present) be cured; but ongoing programs that, on a day-to-day basis, are effective in improving the functioning and quality of life of such persons are nonetheless worthwhile. Gottesman and Brody (1975) emphasize that in the event of regression following program removal, the treatment should not be considered a failure. Rather, this phenomenon merely points to "the chronicity of the deficits of institutionalized people and the need for sustained treatment input" (p. 495). To the extent that, in order to be funded an expectation exists that a program must result in a "cure," then policymakers in the mental health field have not yet accepted the reality of the chronic care problem. Moreover, such an expectation would indicate that the goal of maximization of quality of life, which implies a sustained effort to maintain the maximum achievable potential of the patient, has not been fully accepted.

## REALITY ORIENTATION PROGRAMS

This form of treatment is designed to be used in an institutional atmosphere by all who come in contact with confused or disoriented patients. Its purpose is to arrest the mental deterioration process through continued stimulation and involvement in repetitive activities (Folsom, 1968). In addition to the 24 hour intensive orientation process, structured reality-orientation classes are held where basic information related to time, place and person is repeated (Letcher, Peterson, Scarbrough, 1974). Folsom (1968) used as a model for his program the techniques developed for the treatment of younger patients suffering brain damage from trauma.

To date, there have been primarily descriptive studies of the program's effectiveness (Folsom, 1968; Letcher, Peterson, and Scarbrough, 1974) and these using only limited measures of generalized improvement either in terms of nursing care needs or in terms of hospital discharge. Reality orientation appears related to milieu treatments in that it is a constant intervention, requiring staff cooperation and training. Folsom (1968) reports that in all three locations in which he implemented the program, staff response was universally positive. Recently Harris and Ivory (1976) reported the results of an evaluation of reality orientation which used a matched control group to determine the program's effect. The prepost outcome variables measured were ward behavior, verbal interaction and patient orientation. The findings indicated that experimentals interacted more, demonstrated better object recognition skills and were more likely to know their name, the date and the names of others. A number of serious methodological flaws such as pre-test differences between the groups and initial differences in staff expectations may,

however, mitigate the strength of inference drawn from these results.

Gottesman and Brody (1975) urged the experimental testing of reality orientation given its potential application to the institutionalized population. Although the number of brain damaged elderly patients admitted to and residing in mental hospitals has been drastically reduced over the past two decades, reality orientation might also prove beneficial to the residual chronic population. For despite the fact that they are not all brain damaged, the deprivational effects of continued institutional residence and inactivity may lead to similar consequences which may be amenable to intervention.

Recently, Carroll and Gray (1977) have suggested some modifications to the reality orientation approach. Rather than seeking to arrest the deterioration process, memory development assists mentally impaired persons to compensate for memory loss. This program also shares milieu treatment characteristics in that the environment (physical and staff) is used to constantly provide orienting cues to patients. Staff are trained to motivate patients to practice the information learned. In contrast to reality orientation which confronts the patient with the reality and dispels "unreal notions," memory development trains staff to recognize the basis for a patient's unreal perceptions and to correct the communication or perceptual error which, according to Carroll and Gray (1977), generally lead to expressions of unreality. No hard evidence exists, however, that this approach leads to the desired ends.

## MILIEU TREATMENT

The importance of the physical and social environment in which therapeutic interventions are implemented has been frequently discussed (Bennett and Eisdorfer, 1975). Milieu treatment involves deliberately designing and implementing a social system that provides favorable conditions for the achievement of therapeutic goals. Some of the early experiments involving milieu therapy stressed the development of groups or community cohesion through the common experiencing of various programmed activities. Indeed, it is sometimes difficult to differentiate among treatment programs stressing activities only and those which utilize activities as a means by which to develop a therapeutic milieu.

Among the earliest tests of the effectiveness of an activities program within a broader therapeutic milieu was the series of studies conducted by Donahue and her co-workers over a period of a decade. All of the studies dealt with the hypothesis that, in general, directed therapeutic activity and a milieu that encourages social interaction would tend to induce behavioral improvement and/or "retard psychological aging" (Donahue, 1950, p. 170). The first study showed dramatic results in terms of response to an activity program in a short period of time among even the most apathetic residents. The second study using similar activity programs in homes for the aged also indicated increased responsiveness among program recipients (Donahue, Hunter, and Coons, 1953). In a third study concentrating on a subgroup of extremely confused "senile" patients, it was found that, although response was possible, it was very difficult to maintain (Donahue *et al.*, 1953). Some time later, Gottesman, Donahue, Coons, and Ciarlo (1969) compared a sheltered workshop and structured activity program within the context of a mental hospital ward milieu and found that the chronic, geriatric patients exposed to these programs were more likely to be actively involved for substantial periods each day. In reviewing milieu therapy-activity programs, Gottesman and Brody (1975) conclude that, within the context of a therapeutic milieu environment which utilizes peer pressure to achieve conformity with stated goals of program participation and emphasizes the patient's own responsibility for his behavior, the nature of the activity is not as important as the environment in which it is performed. They point out that research findings have generally indicated that members of the patient groups have been found to interact more with one another and to participate in activities more (Gottesman and Brody, 1975, p. 480).

Sanders, Smith, and Weinman (1967) tested three groups with varying levels of structure (i.e., demands placed on patients to perform) and found the greatest therapeutic benefits to have accrued to the patients from the most structured groups. Interestingly, they found the greatest benefit among the aged group members, a fact which has been suggested to relate to increased compliance to group norms by the older, more institutionalized patients (Gottesman and Brody, 1975). Gottesman's own studies (Gottesman, Quarterman, and Cohn, 1973) also showed positive benefits of such a program with even the most regressed and disoriented geriatric patients. Statistically significant differences between experimental patients and those on a control ward were found in mental status as well as patient self-esteem (Gottesman, 1964). The major activity focus in these studies was a sheltered workshop and again, individual patient responsibility and freedom was stressed. Positive effects were found for both the long-stay chronic

geriatric patients as well as the more recent brain damaged patient (Gottesman, 1964).

Milieu therapy has also been combined with various types of behavior modification approaches. Mishara (1971) describes a program combining elements of milieu therapy and a token economy. Boettcher and Schie (1975) describe a strongly group oriented approach which stresses both individual patient responsibility and peer pressure within patient teams. Nonetheless, positive reinforcement with graduated group goal attainment steps and the corresponding punishment for lack of attainment are principles taken from behavior modification technology.

As with most such therapeutic intervention "systems," the crucial programmatic elements that are beneficial are never isolated (Gripp and Magaro, 1974). Raskin (1976) reviewed the program descriptions as milieu and found the term to have been used with three meanings:

1. A humane, noncustodial approach to patient care,
2. an approach to the management of a psychiatric ward,
3. a treatment approach utilizing the resources of a controlled environment.

Raskin (1976) concludes that there are two general approaches to the development of a treatment milieu. One uses an understanding of group dynamics, community social control, and a sense of belonging and mutual responsibility. The second is patterned more after the behavioral model which focuses more explicitly on specific goals. It would appear that this first approach is more representative of that implemented by Gottesman, Donahue and others as described in Gottesman and Brody (1975).

## BEHAVIOR MODIFICATION AND TOKEN ECONOMY PROGRAMS

Behavior modification, including token economy principles, were derived from years of experimental laboratory research in learning theory (Brown, Wienchowski, and Stolz, 1976; Skinner, 1953). Brown *et al.* (1976) summarize the history of the clinical application of learning theory to a variety of distinct populations ranging from normal children in an educational setting to severely retarded children thought incapable of any learning. Krasner (1971) categorizes the major techniques or themes that developed from the behavioral application of learning theory: positive reinforcement; desensitization; aversive stimulation; and modeling. Some or all of these techniques may be combined in a given therapeutic program which ranges from client therapist interactions which can be classified as psychotherapy (Liberman, 1972) to classical conditioning of psychotic or autistic persons for the purpose of changing the frequency of highly specific behaviors (Ullman and Krasner, 1965). The current behavioral therapies adopted by some psychiatrists and psychologists in the course of their clinical work with neurotic, phobic or merely shy persons hold great promise for more effective, short-term, out-patient treatment of such persons (Brown *et al.*, 1976), particularly in changing highly specific dysfunctional behaviors. Questions, however, may be raised concerning the extent to which such techniques are applicable to the generalized disabilities and dependencies of the long stay institutionalized elderly mental patient.

The most common technique employed in treatment strategies for chronic and geriatric patients has been positive reinforcement of one form or another. Early case studies by Ayllon (see Ullman and Krasner, 1965) and Isaacs, Thomas, and Goldiamond (1960) clearly pointed to the power of reinforcement in reducing or eliminating social abnormal behaviors as well as reintroducing desirable behaviors (verbal behavior) thought to be extinct. The apparent success of such techniques on a case specific basis led to the formulation that such procedures could be applied on a larger scale by systematically reinforcing only desirable behaviors of all patients on a ward.

In many ways the token economy program (TEP) as implemented in the chronic wards of state hospitals around the country is the application of rudimentary behavior modification principles on a large scale and in a group setting. Atthowe and Krasner (1970) report on one of the earliest such ward contingent reinforcement procedures based on a study conducted in a Veteran's Administration Hospital with chronic, generally elderly schizophrenics in 1963. They attempted to incorporate all aspects of life on the ward within a systematic contingency program. "The attainment of the 'good things in life' were made contingent upon the patient's performance" (p. 90). In order to surmount the problem of finding rewards that would be reinforcing for everyone, a system of tokens—essentially a form of money—were used. Patients were rewarded with tokens after the completion of some 'therapeutic' or desirable activity covering all phases of life, not just a specific behavior which had been the practice in most case studies to date. Using patients as their own controls, multiple observations over time revealed increases in activity level and participation in desirable activities. The results of this study also indicate that the patient's behavioral output is contingent upon the reinforcement schedule. Output went up, then stabilized and then rose and stabilized again, after an adjustment in the value of the token reinforcers. The authors also noted (although without data) a substantial diffusion effect in terms of increases in new and desirable behaviors that were not reinforced by tokens, and social interactions also increased according to clinical ratings.

Both this study and an earlier one reported by Ayllon and Azrin (1968) can be considered a model for the many programs instituted in the past decade. Perhaps the most important departure from the earlier approaches is not so much the introduction of the token system of reinforcement but rather the move to a group setting where successively complex behaviors were the targets of modification. The switch to a group setting generally meant that the patient specific behavior shaping process through reinforcement could not be as accurately monitored, leading to the question as to what exactly was it that was changing behavior (Gripp and Magaro, 1974). Positive reinforcement for all of its rigorous structure may perhaps be no more specific than the milieu approach.

An example of the more complex behavioral modification goals was a study conducted by Schaefer and Martin (1970) who used a token economy approach to reduce apathy in chronic patients. A random time sampling observational strategy was developed to study patient behavior. Baseline data were gathered for two months and then 40 patients were *randomly* assigned to an experimental or control ward. The staff selected patient specific behaviors to be systematically reinforced, using distinct reinforcement schedules for experimentals, while controls were merely attended to in the normal manner. The results showed a significant reduction in unidimensional behavior among experimentals. A review of patient records and discussions with staff confirmed these quantitative findings at the clinical level, suggesting the viability and meaningfulness of measuring apathy through observations of behavioral complexity.

Mishara and Kastenbaum (1973) evaluated the effectiveness of a token economy in reducing self-injurious behavior in the institutionalized elderly. They found that the experimentals (mostly "failures" from other wards) showed significantly less self-injurious behavior than controls (comparable in terms of age, length of stay, and major diagnoses) on two other wards. Mueller and Atlas (1972) indicate that TEPs can be effective in increasing social interaction with other patients. Mishara (1971), however, found less interpersonal helping behavior among patients randomly assigned to a TEP ward than those assigned to a ward on which enrichment programs were freely offered.

Gripp and Magaro (1974) in their review of the token economy literature indicate that TEPs have been shown to be effective in improving self care chains of behavior, reducing aggressive behavior and in reducing aberrant or abnormal behavior as reflected in clinical behavioral rating scales. However, they question the degree to which the available research actually demonstrates that it is the contingent reinforcement feature of TEPs that makes such programs effective. Atthowe and Krasner (1970) and Ayllon and Azrin (1968) raise the same issue but conclude that the behavioral output on the token economy wards conforms too closely (in the expected direction) to the withdrawal of contingent reinforcement or major alterations in the reinforcement schedule to question the effectiveness of the program. Nonetheless, the blending of multiple operational variables within the context of a single study, as has been the practice, raises important questions as to what elements in the complex TEP milieu are causing the behavioral changes reported. This problem is particularly difficult in view of the lack of studies concerning the characteristics, training, attitudes and morale of staff involved in the programs (Gripp and Magaro, 1974).

Perhaps the most crucial critique of TEPs is related to the generalization of effects. That is, what happens when the tokens are removed? Token economy programs have been shown to be effective in modifying patient behavior. However, it is impractical to maintain token reinforcement outside of the regulated ward setting. The original chain postulated for generalizability was conceived of as shaping behavior through contingency reinforcemnt via tokens, slowly increasing the reinforcement schedule to a more "natural" reinforcer for the tokens (Brown *et al.*, 1976). Although various researchers comment on their perception that some generalization has taken place (Atthowe and Krasner, 1970), Hersen and Bellack (1976) point out that, to date, little evidence is available to contradict the proposition that behavior is modified only as a means of earning tokens. Ullman and Krasner (1965) suggest that such behavioral generalization is possible through the development of secondary reinforcers, but on the whole, this process is generally accomplished through behavior shaping at the patient specific level. Thus, the dilemma is that TEPs are creating behavioral dependence on tokens that must subsequently be re-

shaped on a patient by patient basis. Perhaps if TEPs are thought of only as the first step, rather than a complete psychiatric rehabilitation system, their value as agents of behavioral change can be assessed from a different perspective.

### SELECTED BEHAVIOR FOCUSED STRATEGIES

There have been other programs which have been implemented within psychiatric hospitals aimed at the geriatric patient which either cannot be unambiguously categorized as representing the types of intervention strategies already described or have not been clearly formulated within the framework of a specific theoretically based intervention strategy. Gottesman and Brody (1975) have labeled the latter type of program as the "individualized approach." Unless there is a concerted effort for an interdisciplinary, coordinated approach, such treatment may merely represent "more of the same" or a quantitative or qualitative improvement in the pre-existing program.

While a number of the former type of programs have been incorporated within milieu therapy or other approaches, they can be implemented by themselves as well. For example, the "activity" programs discussed previously in connection with milieu therapy are of this nature. While it is difficult to differentiate between the contributions of these two elements in terms of effects on patient outcome, findings concerning such programs are certainly relevant to activities programs.

With the broad objective of enriching the quality of life of the mental patients and having a positive impact on patient functioning, a number of strategies focusing on specific behaviors have been developed, including social, recreational and work therapies, interpersonal skills training, and programs promoting physical health as well as physical and cognitive functioning.

Operating on the "activities" theory as described in the aging literature, in which decreased participation in social interaction and/or in activities (especially in institutional environments where there has been a radical disruption in the elderly person's social functioning) is assumed to be functionally related to low morale and life dissatisfaction, a host of programs have been developed to stimulate activities and social participation in the institutionalized elderly (Arje, 1971; Henley and Zeitz, 1962; Herman, 1968; Hill, 1961; Jaeger, 1961; and Katz, 1969). The use of recreational programs in mental health facilities has been discussed in the literature and numerous facilities have recreation and/or art programs as a therapeutic technique in the treatment of mental patients (Brocklehurst, 1963; Darley, 1967; Finkelstein, 1971; and Fink, Levick, and Goldman, 1973). May (1966) found that spontaneously pursued purposeful mass activities, such as participation in the tasks involved in a United Way drive, were more effective in achieving psychosocial reintegration for a population of chronic hospital patients than a more prescribed therapeutic regimen. Merril (1967) suggests that finding an appropriate and desirable activity in which the resident will want to engage is an important component of a motivational program. It should be noted however that with some exceptions, the effects of such programs have not been studied in any systematic manner. Indeed, many of the activity programs that have been studied are those that have been combined or integrated with other approaches. Milieu therapy has been cited as one such approach; remotivation therapy is another.

The proximate relationships between what is known as "remotivation therapy" (Bechenstein, 1966) and activities programs is perhaps best exemplified by the hybrid program "remocreation" devised by McGavack (1965). While this procedure was intended for the physically ill, Salter and Salter (1974) adapted it to elderly patients who were both physically and psychiatrically disabled. Combining elements of a token economy, reality orientation and a recreational program, substantial improvements in the 21 male patients studied were found between the before and after behavior of these patients, primarily in the areas of patient self care and recreational participation.

Usually having the same behavioral goals as social and recreational strategies, the use of alcohol (non-psychotropic "medicinal" forms) has also been tested and found, in certain atmospheres, to lead to positive patient outcomes. Chien (1971) found for geriatric mental patients that spending an hour each day in a hospital based pub, socializing and drinking beer without medication or any other therapy form was superior to either medication alone, socializing alone or a combination of medication and socializing in reducing pathological symptoms. Given the controlled research model and the further finding that socialization without alcohol and the "pub" environment was less effective than only medicine with no socialization, Chien's conclusion that the alcohol in and of itself was effective bears substantial consideration. Chien's findings appear to substantiate those of Kastenbaum (1972) who, in a series of related studies using alcohol as a therapeutic agent in a chronic hospital and in a mental hospital, found that the introduction of wine led to increased patient interaction and a more cohesive lively atmosphere.

Work therapy programs of various stripes have been present (to varying degrees) in mental hospitals since the first days of the moral philosophy treatment approach. Sheltered workshops stressing hand crafts were emphasized in some early facilities, while farming and gardening were the norm in others, and education and schooling was stressed in still others (Hospital and Community Psychiatry, 1975). The goal of such treatments was to awaken the faculties of the mind and to prevent the patient from incessantly reflecting on his own thoughts. Such activities were felt to be crucial in redirecting the activities of the mind from morbid inversion to concentration on the immediacy of the tasks at hand. To some extent, these goals are still adhered to today (the presence of psychotropic medication has obviously greatly facilitated the task of reducing such pathological symptoms), although considerably more stress is placed on the normalizing quality of increased social interaction associated with participation in activities programs (Gottesman, Quarterman, and Cohn, 1973).

Interpersonal-social skills training, conducted either in groups or individually, has grown out of the dual forces of behavioral therapy (Liberman, 1972) and the social psychology of interpersonal behavior (Hersen and Bellack, 1976). As the name implies, there is considerable emphasis on teaching patients of all different kinds new behaviors which are more productive in dealing with interpersonal interaction. Unlike the "milieu" approach to treatment described above, the skills training approach does not assume that the patient has the required social behaviors in his current repertoire to satisfy the demands made by the group to conform. The token economy approach, particularly where there are multiple target behaviors being reinforced, would simply not reward patients who do not interact acceptably, even though they do not know how to do so in the first place (Hersen and Bellack, 1976). In this respect, social or interpersonal skills training adds a new dimension to the treatment programs reviewed earlier, that is, it teaches patients the behaviors that are necessary for social competence.

For the most part, the therapeutic techniques for instilling these new responses in the patient's repertoire are taken from the various behavior therapy approaches such as assertiveness training, modeling, selective positive reinforcement, etc. (Ullman and Krasner, 1965). While initially designed as appropriate for persons suffering from neurotic disorders and anxiety, clinical practice, both in group and individual settings, suggests that positive responses are possible across a broad spectrum of patients with serious psychiatric disorders (Hersen and Bellack, 1976).

Hersen and Bellack (1976) reviewed the available research (much of which has been done via analogue experiments) and conclude that the skills training approach leads to significant beneficial changes in the targeted behaviors. Unfortunately, the majority of clinical studies on the effectiveness of interpersonal skills training are in case study form and none of the cases cited appear to resemble the chronic geriatric mental patient. Interestingly, in a number of cases the clinician first used a classical behavior conditioning approach through primary reinforcement to extinguish glaringly maladaptive behavior and then proceeded with the more complex skills training techniques. While, according to Hersen and Bellack (1976), the findings appear positive, they recognize the need for more thorough experimental and clinical research studies.

In a recent study which is claimed to be "the first application of a social learning model to development of complex social interaction behaviors in the elderly," Berger and Rose (1977, p. 347) report the results of a controlled study of the effects of this program on nursing home residents. They randomly assigned 40 patients to one of three groups: training; discussion; and control, and compared the groups after an eight week impact period, and an additional two month follow-up period. It was found that, on a behavior role play test (presenting simulated critical interpersonal interaction situations), the experimental training group scored significantly better than either of the two remaining control groups. Nonetheless, closer examination revealed that all of the between group differences were accounted for by only those behavioral situations for which the experimentals had been trained during the intervention. This finding indicates a lack of generalizability in the skills taught to this group of patients. It should be noted that this finding is similar to that noted by Hersen and Bellack (1976) in their review of the literature. In the few clinical studies (with the most seriously ill patients) where level of generalizability was reported, it appeared to have been minimal. (This apparently poor showing recalls a similar deficit pointed out with the token economy programs.)

The finding of poor generalizability in Berger and Rose's study (1977) is even more problematic when the characteristics of their elderly study group are considered. Most had no history of psychiatric involvement and they "represented a healthier and more cooperative group than the general population of nursing home residents" (p. 352). The applicability and effectiveness of such a therapy for the general psychogeriatric patient certainly cannot be assumed and is an area of needed investigation. For example, it is reasonable to hypothesize that the high level of existing verbal skills that appears to be required for participation in the elaborate program outlined by Berger and Rose (1977) would make participation impossible for the brain damaged geriatric patient.

The importance of physical health and physical functioning in the treatment of the mentally ill geriatric patient has also been postulated (Butler and Lewis, 1977). Williams, Kriauciunas, and Rodriques (1970) describe the establishment of a rehabilitation unit in a state hospital focusing on physical improvement and increasing instrumental competence. They report that of 67 patients treated, 63 were discharged within a year with only a small readmission rate. Unfortunately, they provide no indication of discharge destination (e.g., nursing home or a more independent setting). Earlier, Galbraith (1962) and Handford and Papathomopoulos (1962) describe similar intensive rehabilitation programs, both showing positive results in terms of both patient behavior and ultimate discharge (although neither study had control groups). Watson and Fulton (n.d.) evaluated an intensive treatment program for the psychiatrically and medically infirm at a Veterans' Administration Hospital. Using a matched control group, they found that patients who were exposed to the intensified treatment group showed greater improvements in physical functioning and were more likely to have been discharged to nursing homes. The transferred patients obviously were considered to be more manageable. What this means, as far as quality of life of such long-term psychiatric elderly persons, is an open question requiring further research.

Related to this physical rehabilitation focus, the value of physical exercise has been stressed in the treatment of chronic mental patients (Clark, Wade, Massey, and Van Dyke, 1975; Powell, 1974). Powell randomly assigned thirty geriatric mental patients to two groups and the experimentals received both exercise and standard social therapy treatment for 12 weeks, while controls only received social therapy consisting of arts and crafts, social interaction, and music therapy. Behavioral ratings and measures of cognitive function were taken before, during and after the impact period. The findings indicated the beneficial effects of the treatment program only on the cognitive measures. Powell interpreted the findings to indicate that exercise had the effect of revitalizing "mental abilities already extant, but in a state of disuse" (p. 160). Clark, Wade, Massey, and Van Dyke (1975) randomly assigned their small (N = 23) "testable" geriatric mental patient sample to three treatment groups: social, exercise, and a control group, and evaluated all patients on a series of physiological measures (heart rate, etc.) as well as total daily activity and self care functions. While after 12 weeks of treatment they found no significant treatment effects, multiple measures taken before, twice during and once after the treatment showed a significant time effect—all groups improved on total daily activity. The investigators do point out, however, that the rate of improvement for the exercise group indicates a possible beneficial treatment effect.

A related but very distinctive form of therapy with chronic mental patients is "therapeutic dancing." Since 1943 when Marian Chace was asked to try an experimental class for adult chronic mental patients at St. Elizabeth's Hospital in Washington, D.C., the field of dance therapy has burgeoned. The therapeutic use of dance has at its foundation the theory that the movement of the body expresses and communicates sentiments that cannot be verbally communicated, particularly by the withdrawn, chronic mental patient. Verbal images are expressed through body movements and postures. According to Chaiklin (1975), the trained dance therapist can respond to the impulses of the patient's movements and encourage the patient to again communicate with his/her environment more directly.

Chace (1957) reports the results of a study of the effects of dance therapy on long-term chronic schizophrenics in terms of self-evaluations as measured by projective drawing tests prior to and at the completion of a 21 session treatment. The matched controls received no treatment. Almost all experimentals showed marked improvements in body image, while controls showed no change or decreases. Observational monitoring of the program for each patient also indicated increases in both the quantity of movements during therapy sessions and their energy during the 21 sessions. Given the degree of physical exertion apparently required, it is not clear what role this form of therapy might have with an elderly group. However, its use in populations of handicapped and physically ill indicate it is amenable to the elderly mental patients.

Having a somewhat different treatment goal, an intervention strategy that appears to be clearly applicable to elderly mental patients is one which focuses on yet another aspect of physical functioning, sensory discrimination. The importance of sensory deprivation, both from an environmental perspective (Anderson, 1963) and from the perspective of physical deficits (Bower, 1967; Richman, 1969) has been documented. The results of laboratory and field experiments in younger subjects definitely point to the critical role of sensory stimuli in maintaining adequate functioning and perception (Cole, Machir, Altman, Haythorn, and Wagner, 1967; Gendreau, Freedman, Wilde, and Scott, 1968; Smith, Myers, and Murphy, 1966). Richman (1969) describes a model for training geriatric mental patients to discriminate among the varied stimuli received simultaneously through all senses. All senses are first independently and then jointly sensitized in a group setting. Richman suggests that increased sensory discrimination skills can lead to increased reception of stimuli "and thereby ameliorate some of the psychomotor dysfunction seen in geriatric patients" (p. 255). Earlier findings from a study by Bower (1967), in which he found that exposure to intensive stimuli over a six-month period among brain damaged patients is related to positive behavioral changes, further lends credibility to the sensory stimulation approach.

## THE NEED FOR STUDY

As perhaps can be seen by this brief review, findings on the effectiveness of different types of treatments applied to chronic and geriatric mental patients are less than conclusive. While a number of programs appear to have had positive effects on patient behavior, their applicability to the general population of elderly mental patients is not clear.

Furthermore, the question of what it is that is creating positive benefit (when it has been found) for different treatment programs can be raised. Bennett, Wilder, Blumner, and Furman (1977) point out that the predominance of positive effects found in the literature are either indicative of researchers not reporting negative findings or that these different types of programs are effective to varying extents. If the latter possibility is the case, then, as suggested by Gripp and Magaro (1974), the observed effects may merely be reflecting a persistent "Hawthorne" or placebo effect and not a function of any of the unique programmatic features of the treatments.

In order to determine the differential benefit of such programs large scale comparative research efforts are needed. (A randomized block design with both staff and patients randomly allocated to the various treatment forms as well as a control group could provide strong indications as to their relative effectiveness.) If all treatments were equally effective in achieving the desired results *vis-à-vis* the controls, a strong argument could be made that it does not matter what is done as long as something is done. If such is the case, then manpower requirements, feasibility and costs, which must always be taken into account in the choice of programs to be implemented, become even more paramount.

## ISSUES, TRENDS, AND FUTURE DIRECTIONS

Currently, as in the past, there are conflicting pulls of economics, on the one hand, and the philosophy of the rights of man on the other, which presumes the need for early identification and treatment of the mentally ill and emphasizes the importance of making services available when needed. From the latter perspective, the mental hospitals would function, in the words of Knee and Lampson (1977), as "therapeutic facilities, rather than resources for long-term custodial care, through adding new patient services, changing the organizational structure of the hospital, improving the physical facility, redistributing staff, and altering staff roles" (p. 885).

Seemingly lowering the economic priority, recent legal rulings on the patient's right to treatment may revolutionize the operation of mental hospitals. In a series of legal decisions (Rouse vs. Cameron, Nason vs. Superintendent of Bridgewater State Hospital and Wyatt vs. Stickney) the right of the mental patient legally committed to a state hospital to receive active therapeutic treatment was established (Stone, 1976). Additionally, failure to provide treatment by the hospital could not be justified on the grounds that the resources were not at the state's disposal. While the climate of thought favoring patients' rights is being legitimatized through such court rulings, the question can be raised: Will the right to treatment rulings force mental hospitals to implement therapeutic programs or will it cause them to abandon all maintenance patients, hastening the deinstitutionalization trend? The potential implications for the institutionalized aged, both brain damaged or chronically impaired, are obvious.

Court rulings on other questions can affect the mental institution as well. For example, for a long time legal (involuntary) rather than voluntary commitment was the most common form of admission procedure in most states (Van Horne, Secherman, and Cohen, n.d.; Stone, 1976). Interestingly, in Massachusetts when more stringent continued commitment review procedures were instituted in 1971, the proportion of new involuntary admission dropped from 50 percent to 10 percent (Van Horne *et al.*, n.d.). Exploring this point further, Stone (1976) points out that the distinction between a voluntary and an involuntary commitment for a confused elderly patient with

brain damage is rather specious. Consent to the procedure by the individual may essentially be meaningless. However, the question can be raised: Will the difficulties involved in obtaining commitment papers on the disoriented elderly result in denial of admission to mental hospitals for this population group even more firmly than has occurred to date via new admissions policies (Friedman and Lehrman, 1969)?

Indeed, perhaps even more dominant than decisions concerning in-house programming, the prevalent question in any discussion of the future role of state mental hospitals in serving the mentally ill is how far will the deinstitutionalization push go? At present the answer is still unclear. There is no question but that it still constitutes an active, perhaps major, force in current planning for state hospitals. Demone and Schulberg (1975), commenting on the future role of the state hospital, feel that the trend toward patient and organizational decentralization is irreversible. The move toward unitization with more emphasis on unit allegiance to community links than to integrated programming within the institution is but an example of this trend. There has been considerable debate over the continuation of mental institutions in any form (Becker and Schulberg, 1976; Dolnick and Pearsall, 1977) and a substantial number have closed altogether in recent years (Greenblatt and Glazier, 1975). Donahue (1978) has suggested the conversion of state hospitals into structured villages where chronic patients can "normalize" their behavior in a supportive setting. She suggests that architectural retrofitting of existing facilities is both a feasible and desirable method of providing human environments for chronic mental patients and a far superior alternative to vague "community" placements in uncontrollable mini-institutions.

The decision to either close an institution or alter its admission policies, of course, results in a residual population of patients who don't fit the new goals. What to do with such a residual population of chronic patients constitutes a serious social problem. After being in such a setting for 20 years or more, a major relocation may seem frightening to the 65, 75, or even older inmate.

Some institutions have met this situation by simply limiting the optional programs being considered as appropriate for this population. Ideally the goal of the patient assessment and transfer process is to maximize the fit between the needs of the patient and his/her potential for future development; restricting the options for elderly persons can be construed, in the absence of hard impact research data to the contrary, as an artificial impediment. Unfortunately, the restriction of options has meant that many of the discharged patients leave one closed and non-stimulating institution for another. Indeed, a variety of sources indicate that former mental patients may fare worse in nursing homes than in their former homes—the state hospital (Bennett and Eisdorfer, 1975; Epstein and Simon, 1968; Stotsky, 1966).

The situation for those being discharged to a community setting may not be much better. Professionals are concerned about social isolation and the lack of services being received by such persons (Lamb and Goertzel, 1971; Weber and Blenkner, 1975). The principal complaint of those who are advocating the cessation of the deinstitutionalization policy has been that the mental health system is neglecting its responsibility to the discharged patients (Donahue, 1978; Kobrynski, 1975).

From another perspective, the growth of foster or domiciliary care homes (boarding homes) in meeting the outpouring of discharged mental patients has generated considerable antagonism in communities not accustomed to nor terribly sympathetic with the problems of the mental patient (Donahue, 1978; Zusman and Bertsch, 1975). Certain communities have attempted to impose zoning restrictions in order to limit or prevent the development of foster homes or half-way houses. Indeed, a survey of half-way houses throughout the country indicates that the leading cause of their delayed growth or closure is community resistance (Piasecki, 1975).

Perhaps the most important factor in resolving some of these issues will be the community mental health system. Unfortunately, all current indicators are that CMHCs will continue to disregard the treatment of the chronic deinstitutionalized patients. According to Zusman and Lamb (1977), in order to reverse this pattern explicit guidelines and priorities must be established to force these community agencies to accept their responsibilities. It also seems reasonable to hypothesize that unless such guidelines and priorities are tied into funding decisions, such externally applied guidelines and priorities will be ignored.

## FUTURE DIRECTIONS AND THE ROLE OF RESEARCH

While economic and manpower constraints will undoubtedly remain major considerations in institutional programming and in admission and discharge policies, the recent court decisions by themselves give evidence of the strengthening climate of thought emphasizing "treatment goals" and the matching of services to meet the needs of the mental patient (client). Unfortunately, when the total

current picture is taken into consideration, there has been more lip service to these goals than available therapeutic programs in mental institutions and related facilities, particularly programs for the psychiatric elderly patient. Likewise, there is reason to question the extent to which admission and discharge policies of the mental hospitals are in the best therapeutic interests of the client.

Experience demonstrates that good intentions do not always produce the desired ends. In the mental health field, there is certainly insufficient knowledge to answer appropriately many of the important planning and policy questions. Issues such as the comparative costs and the relative effectiveness of various social programs on patient outcome, particularly on outcome for elderly chronic mental patients, are yet to be resolved. The same problem of gaps in knowledge exist with respect to costs and effects on patient outcome of admission policies, transfer to other institutional settings and/or deinstitutionalization to community settings. It seems clear that what is required is an expansion of "hard-nosed" (well controlled) research in this area—research which can provide a more solid foundation for interpreting study findings than has generally been the case.

The size of the problem—the *who, where, when, and how much* type of questions—as well as the manpower requirements, material resources necessary (building, equipment, land, etc.), feasibility, and costs, are all important areas of investigation. However, to make appropriate decisions based on the goal of meeting the needs of the patient, it is important for the mental hospital field *to examine the effects on patient outcome of any course of action*—whether in connection with site location, building design, organizational and staffing pattern decisions, the introduction of psychosocial interventions within the institution or decisions concerning admission, the transfer of patients to another institutional environment, or deinstitutionalization into a community setting.

In determining the impact of social programs (whether relocation into alternative settings or introducing specific psychosocial interventions), an intervention can be said to have impact—to have produced effects—only to the extent that there is sound empirically based reason to conclude that conditions at some point in time after the intervention are *different from what they would have been* without the intervention. It must be kept in mind that social interventions, even those introduced into the often sterile wards of state hospitals, do not occur in a vacuum. Changes in ward rules, hospital policy or even in staff can conceivably directly or indirectly affect a patient's behavior in unaticipated ways. Similarly, features of the community environment can affect a patient relocated into a community setting. Thus, a reliable estimate of what the recipients of the social program (the treatment group) would have been like had they not received it must be provided. Controlled studies using random assignment whenever possible or otherwise some of the more recently developed strategies (Sherwood and Morris, 1975; Sherwood, Morris, and Sherwood, 1975) are required.

Hopefully, the future will see a dramatic trend in expanding demonstrated therapeutic interventions as well as a continued search for others that may be an improvement in the existing programs and/or increase the potential rehabilitation and/or quality of life of different types of mental patients. Certainly at the present time therapeutic interventions within the institution as well as the deinstitutionalization push are still going on and a real opportunity presents itself to study such programs within an experimental framework. In this way model(s) can be developed that would maximize the chances of placing different types of elderly mental patients in the most advantageous setting and service programs.

Sherwood (1975) has suggested a beginning list of questions that need consideration in pursuing broad deinstitutionalization objectives:

1. What variables should be considered in assessing need?
2. To what extent is the potential for positive response to a program confounded by such variables as person and family attitudes, prior history of service utilization, relocation effects, scarcity of trained service givers, etc.?
3. What types of persons really do best within an institutional setting?
4. What types are better off outside an institution?
5. What types of mechanisms need to be and can be developed for monitoring the patient over time, geared to moving the patient between programs when it is deemed appropriate (e.g., transfer between different levels of care)?
6. To what extent can expressed wishes, goals and expectations of the long-term care person be built into the overall assessment process? and
7. What legal rights should the long-term care person be given to allow him to stay in the institutional setting should he so desire (Sherwood, 1975; pp. 45–46)?

Similar types of questions need to be answered in making decisions concerning features of institutional environments as well as in selecting appropriate programs within the institutional setting.

# REFERENCES

ANDERSON, S. E. 1963. *Environment and Meaningful Activity. Process of Aging*, Vol. 1. New York: Athens Press.

Architecture Research Construction. Written and copyright 1975. Michael Bakow, Janice Biederman, Richard Bozic, David Chapin, Charles Craig, Kenneth Esposito, Barbara Harford, Steven Kahn, Robert Reeves.

ARJE, R. B. 1971. Reactions of residents of a home for the aged to a selected remotivation technique. Paper presented at the 24th annual meeting of the Gerontological Society, Houston, Texas.

Arthur Bolton Associates. 1975. Analysis of residents of state and county hospitals in New Jersey. Report prepared for New Jersey Mental Health Planning Committee. Arthur Bolton Associates, Washington, DC.

ATTHOWE, J. M., AND KRASNER, L. 1970. Preliminary report on the application of contingent reinforcement procedures (token economy) on a "chronic" psychiatric ward. *In*, R. Ulrich, T. Stachnik, and J. Mabry (eds.), *Control of Human Behavior*, Vol. II. pp. 89–96.

AVIRAM, V., AND SEGAL, S. 1977. From hospital to community care: The change in the mental health treatment system in California. *Community Mental Health Journal, 13*, (2), 158–167.

AYLLON, T., AND AZRIN, N. H. 1968. *The Token Economy: A Motivational System for Therapy and Rehabilitation.* Englewood Cliffs, N.J.: Prentice-Hall.

BAKER, A., DAVIES, R. L., AND SIVADON, P. 1959. *Psychiatric Services and Architecture.* Geneva: World Health Organization.

BECHENSTEIN, N. I. 1966. Enhancing the gains; remotivation, a first step to restoration. *Hospital and Community Psychiatry, 7*, 115–116.

BECKER, A., AND SCHULBERG, H. C. 1976. Phasing out state hospitals—A psychiatric dilemma. *New England Journal of Medicine, 294*, 253–261.

BENNETT, R., AND EISDORFER, C. 1975. The institutional environment and behavior change. *In*, S. Sherwood (ed.), *Long-term Care: A Handbook for Researchers, Planners, and Providers.* New York: Spectrum Publ.

BENNETT, R., WILDER, D., BLUMNER, A., AND FURMAN, W. 1977. Evaluation of Programs, *In*, John E. O'Brien and Gordon Streib (eds.), *Evaluative Research on Social Programs for the Elderly*, HEW, AOA Publication No. OHD 77–20120, pp. 34–50.

BERGER, R. M., AND ROSE, S. D. 1977. Interpersonal skill training with institutionalized elderly patients. *Journal of Gerontology, 32*(3), 346–353.

BLANK, M. L. 1974. Raising the age barrier to psychotherapy. *Geriatrics, 29*(11), 141–154.

BLAU, D. 1970. The course of psychiatric hospitalization in the aged. *Journal of Geriatric Psychiatry, 3*(2), 210–223.

BLOOM, BERNARD L. 1975. *Changing Patterns of Psychiatric Care.* New York: Behavioral Publications.

BLUMENTHAL, R., AND CARPENTER, M. D. 1974. The effects of population density on the overt behavior of mental patients. *Journal of Psychiatric Research,* Vol. 10, pp. 89–100.

BOETTCHER, R. E., AND SCHIE, V. R. 1975. Milieu therapy with chronic mental patients. *Social Work, 20*(2), 130–134.

BONN, E. M., BINNER, P. R., AND HUBER, H. M. 1975. Evolution of a modern state hospital. The Fort Logan mental health center experience. *In,* J. Zusman and E. F. Bertsch (eds.), *The Future Role of the State Hospital,* Lexington, Ma.: D. C. Heath, pp. 239–260.

Booz-Allen and Hamilton, Inc. June 30, 1975. Overview of domicilliary care programs in each of the fifty states. Working paper. Rockville, Md.

BOWER, H. M. 1967. Sensory stimulation and the treatment of senile dementia. *Medical Journal of Australia, 22*(1), 1113–1119.

BROCKLEHURST, J. C. 1963. Mural painting in a geriatric hospital. *Hospital, 59,* 341–342.

BRODY, E. M. 1977. Aging. *In,* J. B. Turner (Ed.), *Encyclopedia of Social Work,* Vol. 1, pp. 55–78. Washington, D.C.: National Assoc. of Social Workers.

BROWN, B. S., WIENCHOWSKI, L. A., AND STOLZ, S. B. 1976. Behavior modification: Perspective on a current issue. DHEW Pub. # (ADM) 76–202. National Institute of Mental Health, Rockville, Md.

BROWN, J. S., AND KOSTERLITZ, N. 1964. Selection and treatment of psychiatric outpatients. *Archives of General Psychiatry, 11*(4), 425–438.

BROWN, W. C., JR., EBRINGER, L., AND FREEDMAN, L. S. 1977. A survey of a long-stay psychiatric population: Implications for community services. *Psychological Medicine, 7,* 113–126.

BURNSIDE, I. M. 1970. Group work with the aged: Selected literature. *Gerontologist, 10*(3), 241–246.

BUSSE, E. W., AND PFEIFFER, E. 1969. Functional psychiatric disorders in old age. *In,* E. W. Busse and E. Pfeiffer (eds.), *Behavior and Adaptation in Late Life,* pp. 183–235. Boston: Little, Brown.

BUTLER, R. 1964. The life review: An interpretation of reminiscence in the aged. *In,* R. Kastenbaum (ed.), *New Thoughts on Old Age.* New York: Springer Press.

BUTLER, R. N., DASTUR, D. K., AND PERLIN, S. 1965. Relationship of senile manisfestations and chronic brain syndromes to cerebral circulation and metabolism. *Journal of Psychiatric Research, 3,* 229–238.

BUTLER, R. N., AND LEWIS, M. I. 1973. *Aging and Mental Health: Positive Psycho-Social Approaches.* St. Louis: C. V. Mosby.

BUTLER, R. N., AND LEWIS, M. I. 1977. Second Edition. *Aging and Mental Health: Positive Psychosocial Approaches.* St. Louis: C. V. Mosby.

CAMPBELL, J. J., DUNNETTE, M. D., LAWLER, E. E., AND, WERSH, K. A. 1970. *Managerial Behavior, Performance and Effectiveness.* New York: McGraw-Hill.

CARROLL, K., AND GRAY K. 1977. Memory development: an approach for responding to the mentally impaired elderly in the long-term care setting. Paper presented at the 30th annual meeting of the Gerontological Society.

CATH, S. 1972. Psychoanalytic viewpoints on aging—an historical survey. *In,* D. P. Kent, R. Kastenbaum, and S. Sherwood (eds.), *Research Planning and Action for the Elderly.* New York: Behavioral Publications.

CHACE, M. 1957. Measurable and intangible aspects of dance sessions, *Music Therapy, 1,* 151–156.

CHAIKLIN, H. (ed.) 1975. *Marion Chace: Her Papers.* American Dance Therapy Association. Columbia, Maryland.

CHIEN, C. P. 1971. Psychiatric treatment for geriatric patients: "Pub" or "Drug"?, *American Journal of Psychiatry, 127*(8), 1070–1075.

CLARK, B. A., WADE, M. G., MASSEY, B. H., AND VAN DYKE, R. 1975. Response of institutionalized geriatric mental patients to a twelve week program of regular physical activity. *Journal of Gerontology, 30*(5), 565–573.

COLE, D., MACHIR, D., ALTMAN, I., HAYTHORN, W. W., AND WAGNER, C. M. 1967. Perceptual changes in social isolation and confinement. *Journal of Clinical Psychology, 23.*

CUMMING, J. 1975. Who will care for the chronically ill? *In,* J. Zusman and E. F. Bertsch (Eds.), *The Future Role of the State Hospital,* pp. 149–156. Lexington, Mass.: D.C. Health.

DARLEY, E. 1967. Reassurance through art. *Nursing Homes, 16*(10), 36–38.

DAVIS, A. E. 1972. The prevention of hospitalization in schizophrenia: five years after an experimental program. *American Journal of Orthopsychiatry, 42,* 375–388.

DAVIS, J. M. 1975. Overview: maintenance therapy in psychiatry: I schizophrenia. *American Journal of Psychiatry, 132,* 1237.

DEMONE, H. N., AND SCHULBERG, H. C 1975. Has the state mental hospital a future role as a human service resource? *In,* J. Zusman and E. F. Bertsch (eds.), *The Future Role of the State Hospital,* pp. 9–30. Lexington, Mass.: D.C. Heath.

DEUTSCH, A. 1949. *The Mentally Ill in America.* New York: Columbia University Press.

DOLNICK, J., AND PEARSALL, D. 1977. The Taunton state

hospital evaluation and planning project. Unpublished report to Region VII of the Mass. Department of Mental Health.

DONAHUE, W. 1950. An experiment in the restoration and preservation of personality in the aged. *In*, W. Donahue and C. Tibbetts (eds.), *Planning the Older Years*. Ann Arbor: University of Michigan Press.

DONAHUE, W. 1978. What about our responsibility toward the abandoned elderly? *Gerontologist, 18*(2), 102–111.

DONAHUE, W., HUNTER, W. W., AND COONS, D. 1953. A study of the socialization of old people. *Geriatrics, 8,* 656–666.

DOULON, P. T., RADA, R. T., AND KNIGHT, S. W. 1973. A therapeutic aftercare setting for "refractory" chronic schizophrenic patients. *American Journal of Psychiatry, 130,* 682–684.

EISDORFER, C. 1973. Issues in the psychopharmacology of the aged. *In*, C. Eisdorfer and W. E. Fann (eds.), *Psychopharmacology and Aging*, New York: Plenum.

EISDORFER, C., AND FANN, W. E. (Eds.) 1973. *Psychopharmacology and Aging*, New York: Plenum.

EPSTEIN, L. J. 1975. The elderly mentally ill: finding the right treatment. *Hospital and Community Psychiatry, 26*(5), 303–305.

EPSTEIN, L. J., AND SIMON, A. 1968. Alternatives to state hospitalization for the geriatric mentally ill. *American Journal of Psychiatry, 124,* 955–961.

FALLON, G. S., WALLACH, H. F., AND GALLO, C. L. 1974. Training mental health workers to better meet patient needs. *Hospital and Community Psychiatry, 25*(5), 299–302.

FINK, M., GREEN, M., AND BENDER, M. 1952. The face hand test as a diagnostic sign of organic mental syndrome. *Neurology, 2,* 46–58.

FINK, P. J. 1973. Art therapy: A diagnostic and therapeutic tool. *International Journal of Psychiatry, 11,* 104–118.

FINK, P. J., LEVICK, M. S., AND GOLDMAN, M. J. Art therapy: A diagnostic and therapeutic tool. *International Journal of Psychiatry, 11,* 104–118.

FINKEL, S. I. 1978. Geriatric psychiatry training for the general psychiatric resident. *American Journal of Psychiatry, 135*(1), 101–103.

FINKELSTEIN, M. 1971. Therapeutic value of arts and crafts in a geriatric hospital. *Journal of the American Geriatrics Society, 19*(4), 341–350.

FOLSOM, J. C. 1968. Reality orientation of the elderly mental patient. *Journal of Geriatric Psychiatry, 1*(2), 291–307.

FRANK, J. 1973. *Persuasion and Health: A Comparative Study of Psychotherapy*. Baltimore, Md.: Johns Hopkins University Press.

FRIEDMAN, J. H., AND LEHRMAN, N. S. 1969. New geriatric admission policy in a state mental hospital. *Journal of the American Geriatrics Society, 17*(11), 1086–1091.

FRIEDSAM, H. J., DOVENMUEHLE, R. H., AND SHORE, H.

1972. Two-level training in mental health for personnel in long-term care facilities. *Mental Health: Principle and Training Techniques in Nursing Home Care*, DHEW Publication No. (HSM) 73–9046, U.S. DHEW, Health Services and Mental Health Administration, NIMH, 32–34.

GALBRAITH, B. S. 1963. Intensive treatment for geriatric patients. *Mental Hospital, 14,* 205–206.

GARWICK, G. 1975. *Combining Short-Term and Long-Term Goals*. Minneapolis, Minn: Program Evaluation Resource Center.

GENDREAU, P., FREEDMAN, N., WILDE, J., AND SCOTT, G. 1968. Stimulation seeking after seven days of perceptual deprivation. *Perception and Motor Skills, 26,* 247–250.

GILBERT, J. G. 1977. *The Paraprofessional and the Elderly*. Panel Publishers.

GOLDFARB, A. 1960a. Psychiatric disorders of the aged: symptomatology diagnosis and treatment. *Journal of the American Geriatrics Society, 8,* (September), 9.

GOLDFARB, A. 1960b. Psychiatric disorders of the aged: symptomatology, diagnosis and treatment. *Journal of the American Geriatrics Society, 8,* 698.

GOLDFARB, A. 1959. Depression, brain damage, and chronic illness of the aged: psychiatric diagnosis and treatment. *Journal of Chronic Diseases, 9*(March), 3, 220–233.

GOLDFARB, A. 1955. Psychotherapy of aged persons. *Psychoanalytic Review, 42,* 180–187.

GOLDFARB, A. 1969. The psychodynamics of dependency and the search for aid. *In*, R. A. Kalish (ed.), *Dependencies of old people*. Occasional papers in Gerontology. Ann Arbor, Mich.: The University of Michigan-Wayne State University, Institute of Gerontology, 27–37.

GORDON, S. 1965. Are we seeing the right patients? *American Journal of Orthopsychiatry, 35*(1), 131–137.

GOTTESMAN, L. E. 1964. The community and the rehabilitated mentally ill patient. Paper presented at the annual meeting of the American Orthopsychiatric Association.

GOTTESMAN, L. E., AND BRODY, E. M. 1975. Psycho-social intervention programs within the institutional setting. *In*, S. Sherwood (ed.), *Long-Term Care: A Handbook for Researchers, Planners, and Providers*. New York: Spectrum Publ.

GOTTESMAN, L. E., DONAHUE, W., COONS, D., AND CIARLO, J. 1969. Extended care of the aged: psychosocial aspects. *Journal of Geriatric Psychiatry, 2*(2), 220–237.

GOTTESMAN, L. E., FADA, T. C., AND GARRETT, I. 1972. Integrating the case of the nursing home patient: a proposal. *Mental Health: Principle and Training Techniques in Nursing Home Care*, DHEW Publication No. (HSM), 73–9046, U. S. DHEW, Health Services and Mental Health Administration, NIMH, 45–46.

GOTTESMAN, L. E., QUARTERMAN, C. E., AND COHN, G. M. 1973. Psychosocial treatment of the aged. *In*, C. Eisdorfer and M. P. Lawton (eds.). *The Psychology of Adult Development and Aging*. Washington, D.C.: Americal Psychological Association.

GREENBLATT, M., AND GLAZIER, E. 1975. The phasing out of mental hospitals in the United States. *American Journal of Psychiatry, 132*, 1135–1140.

GRIPP, R. F., AND MAGARO, P. A. 1974. The token economy program in the psychiatric hospital: a review and analysis. *Behavior Research and Therapy, 12*, 205–228.

GUNTER, L. M. 1972. Notes on continuing education for nursing personnel. *Mental Health: Principle and Training Techniques in Nursing Home Care*, DHEW Publication No. (HSM) 73–9046, U.S. DHEW, Health Services and Mental Health Administration.

GURLAND, B. J. 1973. A broad clinical assessment of psychopathology in the aged. *In*, C. Eisdorfer and M. P. Lawton (Eds.). *The Psychology of Adult Development and Aging*. Washington, D.C.: American Psychological Association.

HAAS, A. 1963. Management of the geriatric psychiatric patient in a mental hospital. *Journal of the American Geriatrics Society, 11*, 259–265.

HALL, J. K., ZILBOORG, G., AND BUNKER, H. A. (Eds.) 1944. *One Hundred Years of American Psychiatry*. New York: Columbia University Press.

HAMMERMAN, J., FRIEDSAM, H. H., AND SHORE, H. 1975. Management perspectives in long-term care facilities. *In*, S. Sherwood (ed.), *Long-Term Care: A Handbook for Researchers, Planners and Providers*, pp. 179–212. New York: Spectrum Publ.

HANDFORD, J. M., AND PAPATHOMOPOULOS, E. 1962. Rehabilitation of the aged in a mental hospital. *Geriatrics, 17*, 809–814.

HARRIS, C. S., AND IVORY, P. B. C. B. 1976. An outcome evaluation of reality orientation therapy with geriatric patients in a state mental hospital. *Gerontologist, 16*(6), 496–503.

HENLEY, B., AND ZEITZ, L. 1962. Uses of free time by ambulatory chronically ill patients. *Journal of the American Geriatrics Society, 10*, 1081.

HERMAN, M. 1968. Activity programs in personal care homes. *Canadian Journal of Occupational Therapy, 35*, 98–100.

HERSEN, M., AND BELLACK, A. S. 1976. Social skills training for chronic psychiatric patients: rationale, research findings, and future directions. *Comprehensive Psychiatry, 17*(4), 559–580.

HILL, B. 1961. Here's what recreation can do for geriatric patients. *Geriatrics, 11*, 197.

HOGARTY, G. E., GOLDBERG, S. C., AND SCHOOLER, N. R. 1974. Drug and socio therapy in the after care of schizophrenic patients: II two year repulse rates. *Archives of General Psychiatry, 31*, 603–608.

Horizon House Institute, 1977. A rehabilitation services planning report for Pennsylvania. Vol. 1 & 2, Philadelphia, Penn.

Hospital and Community Psychiatry, 1975. (News Note) *26*(1), 51.

HOWELL, T. 1965. Morale in a geriatric unit. *Hospitals, 61*, 35–39.

INGERSOLL, B., AND SILVERMAN, A. 1978. Comparative group psychotherapies for the aged. *Gerontologist, 18*(2), 201–206.

ISAACS, W., THOMAS, J., AND GOLDIAMOND, I. 1960. Application of operant conditioning to reinstate verbal behavior in psychotics. *Journal of Speech and Health Disorders, 25*, 8–12.

ISENBERG, P. L., MAHNKE, M. W., AND SHIELDS, W. E. 1974. Medication groups for continuing care. *Hospital and Community Psychiatry, 25*, 517–519.

JAEGER, P. 1961. Better nursing care for the indigent aged. *Journal of Geriatrics Society, 11*, 197.

KAHANA, E. 1967. The effects of age segregation on interaction patterns of aged psychiatric patients. Paper presented at annual meeting of American Psychological Association, Washington, D.C.

KAHANA, E., AND KAHANA, B. 1967. The effects of age segregation on mental status and responsiveness of elderly psychiatric patients. Paper presented at the 20th annual meeting of Gerontological Society, St. Petersburg, Florida.

KALSON, L. 1965. The therapy of discussion. *Geriatrics, 20*, 397–401.

KASHMER, J. 1969. Selected factors in job termination: a study of nursing personnel in Pennsylvania nursing homes. Unpublished doctoral dissertation, Penn. State University.

KATZ, M. 1969. The role of motivational activities in the provision of nursing home care for the aged. Final Report—Contract #PH108–66–275. Department of Health, Education and Welfare (PHS).

KASTENBAUM, R. 1972. Beer, wine and mutual gratification in the gerontopolis. *In*, D. Kent, R. Kastenbaum, and S. Sherwood (eds.), *Research Planning and Action for the Elderly*, New York: Behavioral Publications, pp. 365–394.

KIRESUK, T. J. 1973. Goal attainment scaling at a county mental health service. *Evaluation, 1*(2), 12–18.

KNEE, R. I., AND LAMPSON, W. C. 1977. Mental health services. *In*, J. B. Turner *et al.* (eds.), *Encyclopedia of Social Work*, Vol. II, pp. 879–889. Washington, D.C.: National Association of Social Workers.

KOBRYNSKI, B. 1975. The mentally impaired—whose responsibility? *Gerontologist, 15*, (5), 411–415.

KOBRYNSKI, B., AND MILLER, A. D. 1970. The role of the state hospital in the care of the elderly. *Journal of the American Geriatrics Society, 18*(3).

KORNHAUSER, A. W. 1965. *Mental Health of the Industrial Worker: A Detroit Study*. New York: John Wiley.

KRAMER, M. 1975. Psychiatric services and the changing institutional scene. Paper presented to President's

Biomedical Research Panel, National Institutes of Health, Bethesda, Maryland.

KRAMER, M., TAUBE, C. A., AND REDICK, R. W. 1973. Patterns of use of psychiatric facilities by the aged: past, present and future. *In*, C. Eisdorfer and M. P. Lawton (eds.), *The Psychology of Adult Development and Aging*, Washington, D.C.: American Psychological Association.

KRAMER, M., TAUBE, C., AND STARR, S. 1968. Patterns of use of psychiatric facilities by the aged: current status, trends and implications. *In*, Psychiatric Research Report 23, pp. 89–147. Washington, D. C.: American Psychiatric Association.

KRASNER, L. 1971. The operant approach in behavior therapy. *In*, A. E. Bergin and S. L. Garfield (eds.), *Handbook of Psychotherapy and Behavior Change*, New York: John Wiley.

LAMB, H. R., AND GOERTZEL, V. 1971. Discharged mental patients—are they really in the community? *Archives of General Psychiatry, 24*, 29–34.

LAUFFER, A. 1977. *The Practice of Continuing Education in the Human Services*. New York: McGraw-Hill.

LAWLER, E. E. 1973. *Motivation in Work Organizations*. Monterey, Calif.: Brooks/Cole.

LAWTON, M. P., LIEBOWITZ, B., AND CHARON, H. 1970. Physical structure and the behavior of senile patients following ward remodeling. *Aging and Human Development, 1* (3), 231–239.

LETCHER, P. B., PETERSON, L. P., AND SCARBROUGH, D. 1974. *Hospital and Community Psychiatry, 25*(12), 801–803.

LEWIS, C. N. 1973. The adaptive value of reminiscing in old age. *Journal of Geriatric Psychiatry, 6* (1), 117–121.

LIBERMAN, R. P. 1972. *A Guide to Behavioral Analysis and Therapy*, New York: Pergamon Press, Inc.

LINDEN, M. 1971. Geriatrics. *In*, S. R. Slavson (ed.), *The Fields of Group Psychotherapy*, pp. 129–152. New York: Schocken Books.

*The Los Angeles Times*. February 6, 1972. Mental out-patient care: success or time bomb?

MARGOLIS, P. M., AND FAVAZZA, A. R. 1977. *Encyclopedia of Social Work*, Vol. II, pp. 849–860. Washington, D.C.: National Association of Social Workers.

Massachusetts Department of Mental Health. 1977. The five year state plan for mental health services.

MAY, S. 1966. Purposeful mass activity. *Geriatrics, 21*, 193.

MAY, P. R. A. 1968. *Treatment of Schizophrenia: A Comparative Study of Five Treatment Methods*. New York: Science House.

MCGAVACK, T. H. 1965. Remocreation-restoration of the chronically ill. *Journal of the American Geriatrics Society, 13*, 967–972.

Mental Health Continuing Education Programs for Long-Term Care Providers, 1975. DHEW Publication No. (ADM) 75–209.

MERRIL, T. 1967. *Activities for the Aged and Infirm: A Handbook for the Untrained Worker*. Springfield, Ill.: Charles C Thomas.

MISHARA, B. L. 1971. Comparison of two types of "milieu" programs for rehabilitation of chronic geriatric mental patients. Paper presented at 1971 Annual Meeting of the Gerontological Society, October 29.

MISHARA, B. L., AND KASTENBAUM, R. 1973. Self-injurious behavior and environmental change in the institutionalized elderly. *International Journal of Aging and Human Development, 4*(2), 133–145.

MITCHELL, I. R. 1974. Expectancy models of job satisfaction, occupational preference and effort. *Psychological Bulletin, 81*, 1053–1077.

MEULLER, D. J., AND ATLAS, L. 1972. Resocialization of regressed elderly residents: a behavioral management approach. *Journal of Gerontology, 27*(3), 390–392.

MORONEY, R. M., AND KURTZ, N. R. 1975. The evolution of long-term care institutions. *In*, S. Sherwood (ed.), *Long-Term Care: A Handbook for Researchers, Planners, and Providers*. New York: Spectrum Publ.

National Center for Health Statistics. 1977a. Utilization of nursing homes. Vital and Health Statistics Series 13; No. 28, DHEW Publication No. (HRA) 77–1779, Hyattsville, Maryland.

National Center for Health Statistics. 1977b. Nursing homes in the United States: 1973–74, Series 14, No. 17, DHEW Publication No. (HRA) 78–1812, Hyattsville, Maryland.

OBERLEDER, M. 1970. Crisis therapy in mental breakdown of the aging. *Gerontologist, 10*, 111.

PATTERSON, R. D. 1976. Service for the aged in community mental health centers. *American Journal of Psychiatry, 133*(3), 271–273.

PIASECKI, J. R. 1975. Community response to residential services for the psycho-socially disabled: preliminary results of a national survey. Paper presented at the First Annual Conference of the International Association of Psycho-Social Rehabilitation.

POLLACK, E. S., PERSON, P. H., JR., KRAMER, M., AND GOLDSTEIN, I. F. 1959. Patterns of retention, release and death of first admission to state mental hospitals: The experience during the first twelve months of hospitalization of patients admitted to eleven state hospital systems in 1954, Public Health Monogram, *58*, 1–53.

POLLACK, E. S., AND TAUBE, C. A. 1975. Trends and projections in state hospital use. *In*, J. Zusman and E. F. Bertsch (eds.), *The Future Role of the State Hospital*, pp. 31–64. Lexington, Mass.; D.C. Heath.

POWELL, R. D. 1974. Psychological effects of exercise therapy upon institutionalized geriatric mental patients. *Journal of Gerontology, 29*(2), 157–161.

PROSHANSKY, H. M., ITTELSON, W. H., AND RIVLIN, L. G. 1970. *Environmental Psychology: Man and His Physical Setting.* New York: Holt, Rinehart and Winston.

RASKIN, D. 1976. Milieu therapy re-examined. *Comprehensive Psychiatry, 17*(6), 695–701.

RAWLS, J. R. 1971. Toward the identification of readmissions and nonreadmissions to mental hospitals. *Social Psychiatry, 6,* 58–61.

RECHTSCHAFFEN, A. 1959. Psychotherapy with geriatric patients: a review of the literature. *Journal of Gerontology, 14,* 73.

REICH, R. 1973. Care of the chronically mentally ill—a national disgrace. *American Journal of Psychiatry, 130*(8), 911–912.

REIF, W. E., AND SCHODERBEK, P. P. 1966. Job enlargement: antidote to apathy. *Management of Personnel Quarterly,* Vol. 1, 3–30.

RICHMAN, L. 1969. Sensory training for geriatric patients. *American Journal of Occupational Therapy, 23,* 254–257.

ROBERTS, S. V. March 19, 1978. And another: What about the half-way home idea? *The New York Times,* p. E10.

ROGOWSKI, A. 1974. The new paraprofessional's role in mental health. *Psychiatric Annals, 4*(9).

ROLLIN, H. R. 1977. Deinstitutionalization and the community fact and theory. *Psychological Medicine, 7,* 181–184.

ROSENBLATT, D. 1970. Physical plant, staff morale and informal ideologies in mental hospitals. *In,* L. A. Pastalan and D. Carson (eds.), *Spatial Behavior of Older People.* Ann Arbor, Mich.: Institute of Gerontology, University of Michigan.

ROSENKRANTZ, B. G., AND VINOVSKIS, M. A. 1978. The invisible lunatics: old age and insanity in mid-nineteenth century Massachusetts. *Humanities.*

RUCHLIN, H., AND LEVEY, S. 1975. An economic perspective of long-term care. *In,* S. Sherwood (ed.), *Long-Term Care: A Handbook for Researchers, Planners, and Providers.* New York: Spectrum Publ.

SABIN, J. 1978. Research findings on chronic mental illness: a model for continuing care in the health maintenance organization. *Comprehensive Psychiatry, 19*(1), 83–95.

SALTER, C. DE L., AND SALTER, C. A. 1974. Effects of an individualized activity program on motivation among institutionalized male elderly patients. Paper presented at the 27th annual meeting of the Gerontological Society, Portland, Oregon.

SANDERS, R., SMITH, R. S., AND WEINMAN, B. 1967. *Chronic Psychoses and Recovery: An Experiment in Socio-Environmental Treatment.* San Francisco: Jossey-Bass.

SCHAEFER, H. H., AND MARTIN, P. L. 1970. Behavior therapy for "apathy" of hospitalized schizophrenics. *In,* R. Ulrich, T. Stachnik, and J. Mabry (eds.), *Control of Human Behavior,* Vol. II, 82–89.

SCHWARTZ, B. 1968. The social psychology of privacy. *American Journal of Sociology,* 73:741–752.

SHERWOOD, S. 1975. Long-term care: issues, perspectives and directions. *In,* S. Sherwood (ed.), *Long-Term Care: A Handbook for Researchers, Planners, and Providers.* New York: Spectrum Publ.

SHERWOOD, S., MOR, V., MORRIS, J. N., SHERWOOD, C. C., AND ABRAMS, S. 1977. Final Report: The Clinical Assessment of Interviewable Rhode Island State Mental Health Clients. Report to the Rhode Island Department of Mental Health, Retardation and Hospitals. In connection with NIMH Contract #278–76–0019 (MT).

SHERWOOD, C. C., AND MORRIS, J. N. 1975. Strategies for Research and Innovation. *Long-Term Care: A Handbook for Researchers, Planners, and Providers.* S. Sherwood, (ed.) New York: Spectrum Publications.

SHERWOOD, C. C., MORRIS, J. N., AND SHERWOOD, S. 1975. A Multivariate Non-Randomized Matching Technique for Studying the Impact of Social Interventions, *In,* E. Struening and M. Guttentag, (eds.), *Handbook of Evaluation Research,* Vol. 1, Berkeley, Ca.: Sage Publications, pp. 183–224.

SHERWOOD, C. C., SHERWOOD, S., MORRIS, J. N., MOR, V., MCCLAIN, J. W., AND GREER, D. S. 1977. The Clinical Assessment of Interviewable Rhode Island State Chronic Hospital Patients. DHEW/HRA, National Health Planning Information Center (No. HRP–0015944), Rockville, Maryland.

SHUCKIT, M. A., AND PASTOR, P. A. 1978. The elderly as a unique population: alcoholism. *Alcoholism: Clinical and Experimental Research, 2*(1), 31–38.

SKINNER, B. F. 1953. *Science and Human Behavior.* New York: Macmillan.

SMITH, S., MYERS, T., AND MURPHY, P., 1966. Vigilance During Sensory Perceptual Motor Skills Deprivation, 76–77.

Social Security Bulletin (December), 1977.

SPIVAK, M. 1967. Sensory distortions in tunnels and corridors. *Hospital and Community Psychiatry, 18,* 24–30.

STEIN, J. L., AND CORMAN, L. 1976. From institution to community mental health: a study of former Grafton State Hospital employees at the Valley Adult Counseling Service. Mimeo report of study conducted by Research Institute for Educational Problems, Inc., Boston, Massachusetts.

STEIN, L. I., AND TEST, M. A. 1976. Retraining hospital staff for work in a community program in Wisconsin. *Hospital and Community Psychiatry, 27*(4), 266–268.

STONE, A. A. 1976. *Mental Health and Law: A System in Transition.* National Institute of Mental Health Center for Studies of Crime and Delinquency, DHEW Publication No. (ADM) 76–176, Rockville, Maryland.

STOTSKY, B. A. 1966. The psychiatric patient in the nursing home: a retrospective study. *Journal of the American Geriatrics Society, 14*(7), 735–747.

STOTSKY, B. A. 1972. Social and clinical issues in geriatric psychiatry. *American Journal of Psychiatry, 129,* 117–126.

STOTSKY, B. A. 1973. Psychoses in the elderly. *In,* C. Eisdorfer and W. E. Taun (eds.), *Psychopharmacology and Aging.* New York: Plenum.

TAUBE, C. A., AND REDICK, R. W. 1975. Recent trends in the utilization of mental health facilities. *In,* J. Zusman and E. F. Bertsch (eds.), *The Future Role of the State Hospital.* Lexington, Mass.: D.C. Heath.

THOMPSON, P. W. 1972. Content for mental health training. *Mental Health: Principles and Training Techniques in Nursing Home Care,* DHEW Publication No. (HSM) 73–9046, US Health Services Administration.

TRUAX, C. B., AND CARKHUFF, R. R. 1967. *Toward Effective Counseling and Psychotherapy.* Chicago: Aldine.

ULLMAN, L. P., AND KRASNER, L. 1965. *Case Studies in Behavior Modification.* New York: Holt, Rinehart and Winston.

VAN HORNE, W., SECHERMAN, A., AND COHEN, S. (No Date). *The Metropolitan State Hospital Study.* In 1966 had a census of 2,100 most of whom were discharged to nursing homes. Unpublished collaborative research project between the Massachusetts Department of Mental Health and the Massachusetts Association for Mental Health.

WATSON, C. G., AND FULTON, J. R. (No Date). *The St. Cloud P.M.I. Unit Evaluation of the Experimental Treatment Program for the Psychiatric-Medically Infirm.* Mimeo project report from the St. Cloud, Minnesota, Veteran's Administration Hospital.

WEBER, R. E., AND BLENKNER, M. 1975. *In,* S. Sherwood, *Long-Term Care: A Handbook for Researchers, Planners, and Providers.* New York: Spectrum Publ.

WEINSTEIN, A. S. 1973. Relationships between length of stay in and out of the New York State Mental hospitals. *American Journal of Psychiatry, 130,* 904–909.

WEINSTEIN, A. S., DiPASQUALE, D., AND WINSOR, F. 1973. Relationship between length of stay in and out of the New York State Mental hospitals. *American Journal of Psychiatry, 130,* 904–909.

WILLIAMS, J. R., KRIAUCIUNAS, R., AND RODRIQUES, A. 1970. Physical, mental and social rehabilitation of elderly and infirm patients. *Hospital and Community Psychiatry, 21*(4), 42–44.

WOLFENSBERGER, W. 1972. *Normalization.* National Institute on Mental Retardation, Toronto, Canada.

WOLFF, K. 1962. Group psychotherapy with geriatric patients in a psychiatric hospital: a six-year study. *Journal of the American Geriatrics Society, 10,* 1077–1080.

WOLFF, K. 1963b. *Geriatric Psychiatry.* Springfield, Ill.: Charles C Thomas.

WOLFF, K. 1963a. Individual psychotherapy with geriatric patients. *Diseases of the Nervous System, 24,* 668–691.

WOLFF, K. 1971. Rehabilitating geriatric patients. *Hospital and Community Psychiatry, 22*(1), 24–27.

WOLK, R. L., AND GOLDFARB, A. I. 1967. The response to group psychotherapy of aged recent admissions compared with long-term mental hospital patients. *American Journal of Psychiatry, 123,* 1251–1257.

YOUNG, C. E., TRUE, J. E., AND PACKARD, M. S. 1976. A national study of associate degree mental health and human service workers. *Journal of Community Psychology, 4,* 89–95.

ZAPPOLO, A. 1977. National Center for Health Statistics. *Characteristics, Social Contacts and Activities of Nursing Home Residents,* United States 1973–74, National Nursing Home Survey, DHEW Publication No. (HRA) 77–1778.

ZUSMAN, J., AND BERTSCH, E. 1975. *The Future Role of the State Hospital,* D.C. Heath, Lexington, Ma.

ZUSMAN, J., AND LAMB, H. R. 1977. In defence of community mental health. *American Journal of Psychiatry, 134*(8), 887–890.

# 36

# Sexuality in Later Life

*Alex Comfort*

In our culture many features of individual sexual behavior, and particularly dysfunctional sexual behavior, are sustained by attitudinal and factual misinformation. Many features of "aging" as observed in the same culture are equally examples not of natural change but of role-playing, based on a combination of folklore and prejudice: old people, being "known" to be feeble, ineducable, unintelligent and asexual, are under pressure to assume these attributes as a result of chronological age, although age itself produces no such necessary effects.

In the sexual behaviors of older persons, both streams of misinformation merge, and it is only recently that, as in the case of intelligence and learning-power, the sexual capacities of older people, and their changes with age, have been objectively examined. Asexuality in later life is now known to reflect, as a rule, not loss of capacity but

absence of opportunity, particularly in older women, whose sexual capacity changes little with time, but whose social opportunities are culturally and demographically curtailed compared with those of older men.

As in all fields of sexual study, it is the male, moreover, who is so far documented. His sexual "capacity" is marked by, and dependent on, an externally obvious erection, and research has been heavily motivated by male anxiety in this regard. The excess of discussion devoted in this paper to male sexuality represents the distribution of available facts. At least one standard textbook of geriatric medicine omits the discussion of female sexuality altogether, despite the large excess of women over men at higher ages.

The most interesting feature of the changes in human sexual physiology and performance induced by age is that, apart from the programmed termination of fertility at the menopause, the changes are minimal. The folkloristic view of old age as impotent, uninterested in sexuality, and nonfunctional in this regard are the expression of a self-fulfilling prophecy.

## SEXUAL PHYSIOLOGY IN LATER LIFE

The slowing of response which is a characteristic feature of many processes in old age affects male sexuality. After the age of 50, purely psychic erection occurs with decreasing frequency: morning erection is retained, but erections during REM sleep become less frequent as age advances. Erection comes to depend increasingly on direct penile stimulation, and takes longer to induce than in young males. The angle of the erect penis to the abdominal wall becomes greater (90 degrees as against 45 degrees in youth) and the retraction of the testes by the cremaster during orgasm tends to disappear. At the same time, orgasm ceases to occur at every act of intercourse.

These changes are extremely variable in different individuals. They are commonly present by age 60, but show little further advance after that age. Their importance is that while sexually active and unanxious men, accustomed to prolonged sexual play in intercourse, experience them as a gain in control, men whose stereotype of virility depends on hurried erection followed by hurried intercourse may interpret them as loss of function, and the consequent anxiety may induce failure of erection. It can be said with confidence that impotency is never a consequence of chronological age alone. Its increasing frequency with age is due to a variety of causes—the increasing prevalence of diabetes, of which impotency may be the presenting symptom; an increase in incidence of vascular-autonomic insufficiency; the increasing prevalence of conditions such as hypertension and prostatic enlargement, which may lead to problems through the use of medications (notably reserpine and some ganglion blocking agents) of which impotency is a side effect; needlessly radical or negligent surgery; and above all the social expectation of impotence in age, reinforced by loss, ill health or aging of the partner, obesity, increased sensitivity to alcohol, and the increased incidence of depression which may readily be missed. In spite of these factors, objective organic loss of potency verified by penile plethysmography is relatively rare at high ages. What may be seen is an exacerbation of psychosexual problems common to younger males, a loss of interest in sexual activity reflecting loss of competitive self-esteem, and a

welcome excuse to abandon sexual activity in those for whom it has been a source of guilt or anxiety. High-dominance individuals, whose sexual attitudes have always been positive, normally remain both potent and active throughout life. Androgen deficiency does not appear to play any large part in declining sexual function, nor are androgen supplements usually indicated as a remedy for potency problems. Fertility may also persist in males into the tenth decade.

Erectile physiology in males is extremely complex (Weiss, 1972), involving central inhibitory control over a segmental reflex as well as autonomic pathways. At the effector level, blood is diverted into the corpora cavernosa by "polstern" in the arteriolar walls, and the venous outflow is regulated to maintain circulation in the corpus while keeping the vascular spaces full. It is this complexity which makes the search for a pharmacological or mechanical means of inducing erection extremely difficult, and provides a number of points at which drugs such as ganglion-blocking agents, and diseases of the vessels and nervous pathways, can interfere. What is striking is that the only specifically age-determined change in erectile physiology is the slowing of the general response cycle, combined perhaps with a less perfect regulation of the inflow and outflow of blood in the corpora, since the erection of older males often appears less hard than that in youth, though it is fully adequate. The final preorgasmic hardening of the glans, due to a rise in the venous pressure which precedes the discharge of semen, is also less evident with age.

Of conditions which become more common with age and may impair erection, diabetes is probably the most important. The specific organic interference is probably real, although psychogenic factors are almost invariably present and removal of these can often restore adequate function (Renshaw, 1978). The impairment is believed to be an alteration of vasomotor function rather than an effect of diabetic neuropathy, since diabetes can present an impotence. A similar function loss can occur in simple obesity, but other factors are present—in some cases, diabetes appears to produce not impotence but retrograde ejaculation (Anon, 1967).

It is important to recognize that human sexual function, especially in the male, is *highly idiosyncratic*, both in the interrelation of erectile and ejaculatory functions and in the response of these functions to drugs. Medication which produces impotence in one individual may produce nonejaculation or retrograde ejaculation in another and be without sexual effects in a third, as has been documented in the case of thioridazine (Mellaril[R]) (Kotin, Wilbert, Verburg, and Soldinger, 1976). Some of these differences may be attributable to different metabolism or accessibility of neurotransmitters, to differences in sympathetic-parasympathetic balance, or to central effects of the drugs; in general, however, idiosyncracy becomes more marked with age. It is likely that drugs similarly affect the incidence and intensity of tumescence, lubrication and orgasm in women. These changes are almost wholly undocumented, reflecting the excessive cultural concentration on male sexual physiology, where it is possible and indeed necessary to observe the outward and visible signs of an inner and spiritual grace.

Increased libido and erectile performance are relatively rare and are equally idiosyncratic effects of medication. While in women androgen administration almost invariably increases libido, some men remain potent and active in the virtual or total absence of testicular androgen; in others androgen may be highly effective in lowering the threshold of excitation, while in yet others it fails to produce any evident result. This simply reflects the fact that there is more than one cause of nonerection, since hypogonadal and so-called "climacteric" impotency respond to testosterone better than impotency that appears to be mainly a learned behavior (Cooper, Ismail, Smith, and Loraine, 1970). The role of androgen in the cycle of male excitation is not known—it is at least as likely that high levels result from, rather than cause, sexual arousal (Kraemer, Becker, Brodie, Doering, Moos, and Hamburg, 1976). The overall but irregular decline in cross-sectional androgen levels with increasing age reported by various authors represents not only endogenous reduction, but also quite probably the reduction in sexual activity imposed by a social "script" (Gagnon and Simon, 1973). Where androgen is effective, some of its effects may be due to an increase in general well-being.

It seems probable that while female arousal can be reliably mediated by androgen, the control of male arousal depends on an earlier neurohormone, probably an oligopeptide. Increased libido is consistently seen in males after administration of human chorionic gonadotrophin HCG (Amelar and Dubin, 1977) for infertility. This action probably depends upon follicle stimulating hormone (FSH) or luteinizing hormone (LH) or both, or on a specific peptide as yet unidentified, paralleling the arousal seen in animals of both sexes after intraventricular luteinizing hormone releasing hormone (LHRH) injection. This group of responses is insufficiently investigated to yield present clinical application, but the irregular response to androgen

in cases of reduced male libido clearly indicates that other mechanisms are involved. To the extent that libidinal decline is not wholly sociogenic, it may be integrated with the hypothalamic aging "clock."

One possibly important factor is the fact that in both sexes fantasy—which in humans is probably the most important single determinant of sexual arousal—is said to decline with age (Cameron and Biber, 1973). Whether the sixfold decline in speed of erection observed between the ages of 20 and 50 is involved with autonomic changes, role-playing, or both, remains to be explored (Solnick and Birren, 1977), but its importance for function is negligible in sexually educated males.

The overriding importance of social roles, social expectation, and socially propagated anxiety, together with the uniqueness of the uses of sexuality made by humans explain why comparative studies, both on age changes and on hormone effects (e.g., in rats), are not only irrelevant but often actively misleading, and have been for the most part omitted from this review. The most relevant primate findings would deal with the interrelation between sexuality and dominance in agonic species—old age has not yet been adequately observed in large hedonic apes—because of the uneasy mixture in humans of sexual components drawn from these two modes ("baboonery" and "chimpanism"). The role of the penis as a dominance signal, and erection as both invitation and dominance display, is clearly critical to the Freudian view of human psychosexual development, which is atypical in that human males are recognized as competitive when they reach walking age, and the dominance releaser is sited in the genitalia themselves, not in the secondary sexual characters (Comfort, 1960). The instability of the human erectile capacity in the face of social stress may in part represent an adaptation which favors the most dominant male, the result brought about in mice by the resorption of fetuses in pregnant females when a less-dominant mate is displaced (Bruce and Parkes, 1961). In humans, it is in the period of middle-age, when status is most threatened, that erectile physiology undergoes the most marked changes, and latent sexual dysfunctions commonly become manifest.

The persistence of sexual function in women has been less fully documented, but the evidence suggests that, excluding fertility, sexual function persists even more effectively in women than in men. There is no evidence that the capacity for orgasm declines at any age, and women are known to have become orgasmic for the first time at ages in excess of 80. Coition may be impaired by vaginal atrophy, lack of lubrication, kraurosis, and pelvic abnormalities such as cystocele and prolapse, but these are remediable conditions. The most common reasons for sexual inactivity in older women are social convention, lack of a partner, or role-playing. There is a clinical impression, unconfirmed by published statistics, that regular intercourse and orgasm are at least as effective as exogenous estrogens in preventing secretory and atrophic changes.

## STATISTICAL STUDIES OF SEXUAL ACTIVITY IN OLDER PERSONS

It has to be remembered that statistical studies of sexuality among the aged include subpopulations of people who are unanxious and sexually active, people who are already anxious, and people who have become dysfunctional at younger ages; few attempts have been made to separate these groups. Sex means very different things to different people—some regard it negatively or are relatively uninterested throughout life, while others appear to think of nothing else. One still encounters couples who have unsuccessfully attempted coitus a few times (lack of success is usually a result of vaginismus) and have remained married but abstinent without ever repeating the attempt or seeking advice. The valuation of sex in society is undergoing rapid change, chiefly in the direction of increased expectation. Some older people will retain the generally anxious or reticent valuation which they learned in their youth, while others, late in life, will be influenced by their culture to recoup experiences they have missed. Yet others, who have always ignored society's reservations, will continue to treat sex with their own valuation. The physician needs to distinguish these, in order to help the second while not impertinently evangelizing the first.

In spite of a high incidence of psychogenic dysfunction at all ages, it appears that older people have always been sexually active but have kept their own counsel. Pearl (1930) recorded nearly 4 percent of males aged 70–79 having intercourse on the average of every third day, and a further 9 percent having it weekly. The figures of Kinsey, Pomeroy, and Martin (1948) indicate a decline in coital frequency with age, but these figures were cross-sectional and unrelated to opportunity or attitude. Finkle, Moyers, Tobenkin, and Karg (1959) questioned 101 men, aged 56 to 86, who were ambulant patients with no complaint likely to affect potency, and found 65 percent under age 69 and 34 percent over 70 "still potent" on their own statement, with two out of five over 80 averaging at least 10 copulations a year. On further

inquiry it transpired that some in the sample had never had intercourse. Others, though potentially potent, had no partner. In the over-70 group, the main reasons given for inactivity were "no desire" or "no partner." Of all men over 65, only three gave as a reason "no erection." Newman and Nichols (1960) questioned both sexes aged 60–93 and found 54 percent still active. No significant decline occurred under age 75. Over the age of 75, 25 percent were still active, the decrease being chiefly a result of illness of self or spouse. "Those who rated sexual urges as strongest in youth rated them as moderate in old age: most who described sexual feelings as weak to moderate in youth described themselves as without sexual feelings in old age" (Newman and Nichols, 1960). As in Pearl's study, evidence suggested that early starters of both sexes were late finishers.

Pfeiffer, Verwoerdt, and Wang (1968) at Duke University studied 254 people of both sexes. The median age for stopping "sexual activity" (presumably coitus, not masturbation) was 68 in men (range 49–90) and 60 in women, with a high of 81, the differences being partly attributable to the age differential between spouses. The figures for regular and frequent intercourse were 47 percent between the ages of 60 and 71 and 15 percent age 78 and over. Unlike other studies, this investigation was longitudinal. Over a five-year observation period, 16 percent of propositi reported a falling-off of sexual activity, but 14 percent reported an increase. This study strongly supports the view that what we are seeing is not so much an "age change" as the experience of a mixture of high- and low-activity individuals, in whom those whose sexual "set" is low for physical or attitudinal reasons drop out early, often with recourse to age as an excuse. Social pressure, ill health, lack of a socially acceptable partner, all take some toll among the others, but among the sexually positive and active aging itself abolishes neither the need nor the capacity for intercourse. Masters and Johnson (1970) have confirmed that many aging men who believed themselves impotent could have their condition reversed using the same therapeutic means effective with impotent younger males. A generation with high sexual expectations, exposed to modern attitudes and counseling and devoid of the expectation of decrepitude, will probably score a great deal higher.

## COUNSELING OF SEXUAL DYSFUNCTION IN OLDER PATIENTS

Sexual counseling and therapy depend almost wholly on permission-giving and the correction of false or irrational attitudes towards sexuality. Sexual counseling in the old also involves the correction of false and irrational attitudes toward aging. Apart from the more rigid exclusion of physical and iatrogenic causes of impotency, and the recognition of intercurrent causes such as obesity and alcohol, the therapy of impotence in older men is the same as in younger, and depends on the removal of performance anxiety and the teaching of sexual attitudes which de-emphasize "sex" as a purely genital feat rather than an enjoyable interpersonal experience involving all parts of the body.

Sexual problems in later life include those which can occur at any age; those which have been present or latent throughout life and surface in the "middle-age identity crisis" as a result of the patient's mistaken belief that age involves automatic asexuality and infirmity; those which result from disease or its treatment; and those which arise—chiefly in women, who outlive men but are socially excluded from sexual appetency in later life—from isolation and lack of a receptive and socially approved partner. Of these, organic causes are the minority. As with other forms of activity, sexual intercourse once abandoned in later life becomes more difficult to resume. The physician needs to be aware of this risk and to avoid prescribing prolonged abstinence. This is especially true during convalescence from cardiac disease. The possibility of desexualization which may arise from the prohibition of intercourse for fear of a heart attack, contributes greatly to depression and demoralization, which is worse for the patient than the trifling exertion involved in gentle intercourse. Coition or masturbation to orgasm can be safely undertaken by any ambulatory patient, and should form a specific part of rehabilitation where inquiry shows sexual activity to have been of concern to the patient. Cardiac death or a stroke occurs more rarely during intercourse, especially marital intercourse, than during sleep. At another level of counseling, the physician will increasingly encounter older patients in good health who require advice and guidance in attempting to achieve greater sexual satisfaction than they experienced in youth, when permission and advice were less readily available. With the end of reproduction, the relational and recreational uses of sex become more, not less, important, and can enrich a period of life which society otherwise penalizes by exclusion from other value-giving activities.

Special geriatric problems are patterned by the changes in physiology already described. The male who attaches value to speed of performance or who regards direct genital stimulation as abnormal will become dysfunctional as a result of normal aging and will require reeducation. Males at all ages seem to fall into two types—those who,

when stressed or overtired, run out of potency, and those who in similar circumstances run out of orgasm. The second of these reactions is aggravated by age, and further aggravated by several drugs, including guanethidine, tricyclic antidepressants and monoamine oxidase inhibitors. (Imipramine and phenelzine are effective agents in the treatment of premature ejaculation.) The man who fails to ejaculate vaginally at every act of intercourse can usually do so if masturbation is continued, but if this is done sufficiently often to maintain his previous frequency of orgasm, sensitivity to vaginal friction may be further lowered. Nonejaculation can appear suddenly in the partner of a woman who is undergoing hormone supplementation, as a result of excessive lubrication. This calls for adjustment of the dose of medication given to the woman. Interference with potency, ejaculation, or both is probably the commonest cause of noncompliance in the use of antihypertensives; sexual function is unaltered by thiazides and rarely affected by propranolol. Alcohol and tranquilizers can also derange sexual response more in the old than in the young. One special male problem is *widower's impotency*, occurring when an elderly man remarries after the death of a first wife; this is particularly seen when the first wife had a long terminal illness during which he has abstained from sexual intercourse. This compound of disuse atrophy, unfamiliarity and anxiety over the new partner, and guilt at relief over the death of the invalid responds to the same couple-counseling as does secondary impotence at younger ages. It should be stressed to the "impotent" patient that if he ever gets an erection, on waking, at masturbation, or as demonstrated by penile plethysmography, there is nothing organically wrong with the hydraulics. *Failure to hold erection* is usually the result of haste. The patient should be advised "not to attempt a landing until the nosewheel has locked in the down position"; this may require several minutes of oral or manual stimulation, and the spouse should be instructed in older male physiology.

If penile plethysmography is accompanied by measurement both of the basal and of the coronal penile circumferences, not a few cases of "failure to maintain erection" will be found to represent irregular filling due to an undiagnosed Peyronie's plaque (Karacan, 1978). Erectile difficulty in patients receiving propranolol for long periods should be investigated because of this possibility. *Prostatectomy* when competently performed will almost always result either in retrograde ejaculation or in some alteration of the sensation of climax. Incompetently performed, especially by the perineal route, it can produce impotence by denervation, calling for a prosthetic implant if function is to be restored. In any patient (the majority) where continued potency is an important contributor to self-evaluation, radical prostatectomy should never be rashly undertaken, and loss of potency following the relief of simple prostatic enlargement justifies a malpractice suit, unless (1) an adequate sexual history was taken preoperatively, and (2) careful rehabilitative therapy is initiatied after the operation. Lack of these measures may well contribute more to prostatectomy impotence than the operative procedure. Patients should be warned to expect absence or reduction of ejaculation.

Although wholesale section of nerves and periurethral damage is responsible for impotency in perineal resection, the 5 percent —40 percent incidence of impotency after transurethral resections is harder to explain (Finkle and Prian, 1966; Gold and Hotchkiss, 1969; Holgrewe and Valk, 1964). In some cases at least, anxiety over possible injury to potency aggravates the disturbance due to surgery. In other cases, what is described as "impotence" is actually an alteration of orgasmal feeling resulting from partially or wholly retrograde ejaculation. It is interesting that in fracture of the pelvis, urethral injury is the factor correlating most highly with subsequent impotence (King, 1975). Zohar and his coworkers (Zohar, Meiraz, Maoz, and Durst, 1976) found that surgical technique seemed to have little to do with postprostatectomy impotence, but that in a prospective study it correlated highly with anxiety level, absence of explanation of the surgery, and low satisfaction with life. The problem of psychogenic versus surgically-induced impotence can be resolved by penile plethysmography during sleep, but this should be done both before and after surgery, since some apparently organic impotence predates the operation on which it is blamed.

## MANAGEMENT OF ORGANIC IMPOTENCY

If potency has been irremediably damaged, usually by injudicious surgery, but sometimes also by disease, there are two therapeutic options.

By far, the best strategy is to instruct the patient in techniques of sex which do not involve full erection. Many men fail to realize that not only extragenital orgasm, but penetration, can often be obtained without erection (with the woman in the dorsal knee-chest position, for example, and especially with a multipara).

The choice of surgery depends far more on the patient's psychological investment in erection than on the need to attain orgasm with satisfaction

to a partner. This investment is frequently great, and a prosthesis if properly inserted can sometimes abort a depressive illness or a general loss of interest in life. Insertion of a plastic rod prosthesis, which renders the penis permanently rigid, the baculum or os penis in some mammals, can make intercourse possible. The result is often cosmetic rather than truly restorative. In the very old, and in those who have vascular problems compromising healing or predisposing to thrombosis of the corpora, it can produce further problems, and the prosthesis may have to be removed. The Small-Carrion prosthesis (Small and Carrion, 1975) can be removed if function returns or problems arise from migration or buckling (Loeffler, 1977), and involves less surgery than the Furlow inflatable prosthesis where surgery is extensive (Furlow, 1977), with seven out of 36 patients requiring further surgery to correct mechanical problems. Prostheses should not be used as a cover for failure to adopt proper counseling techniques. They are best confined to patients in whom organic interference with erection has been demonstrated by plethysmography and the need for a tangibly stiff penis is paramount, since those prostheses are not without problems.

It should be reiterated that age alone is never a cause of impotency, that the management of impotency at all ages is identical, and that the only relevance of radical measures, such as the insertion of a prosthesis, to sexuality and age lies in the fact that diabetes and surgical assaults on the erectile mechanism increase in frequency at higher ages. At the same time, where potency has been damaged by a demonstrable lesion, age is not a contraindication for the attempt to restore it *secundum artem*. Even the extensive surgery involved in inserting Furlow's prosthesis has been successfully carried out in a man of 77 (Furlow, 1977). In impotence due to multiple sclerosis, the Small-Carrion prosthesis is preferable, since it does not hinder natural erection if the symptom remits (Loeffler, 1977). Penile prostheses cater, however, chiefly to male anxieties; partners have rarely been interviewed.

*Androgen therapy* has a chequered history in treating secondary impotence. Since androgen levels are rarely depressed in this condition and low androgen levels are not correlated with impotence, any action which exogenous androgens have is likely to result in lowering the threshold of response, or more probably in increasing general well-being. Administration of exogenous androgen has the disadvantage of serving to convince the patient that what is usually a behavioral problem can be cured by pills. If androgens are to be used, mesterolone ("Proviron" Schering) is probably the drug of choice, since it is not read by the hypothalamic sensor as a raised testosterone level, and does not inhibit endogenous hormone production.

*The menopause* is now known to result from the activity of the hypothalamic "clock," not exhaustion of ova. Cessation of the menses will affect sexual function adversely only in women for whom infertility is perceived as a loss of womanhood or of permission to experience sexual pleasure. In many women it marks a period of resexualization untroubled by anxiety over conception. The so-called "male menopause" is an inaccurate name for the middle-aged identity crisis general in our culture, which may affect sexual self-image but does not represent any radical change in endocrine patterns. It now seems proper to reject the cosmetic use of estrogens in menopausal women. Their value in the prophylaxis of osteoporosis is less than that of diet and exercise, and they should be reserved for the treatment of circumclimacteric symptoms such as hot flashes and given for a limited period only. When indicated for atrophic genital changes, topical application should be tried. Prolonged use of oral contraceptives can mask the menopause. Cessation of ovulation should never be assumed to have occurred, as unwanted pregnancy can occur in the fifth decade. On withdrawing the oral contraceptive for a test period, other birthcontrol means should be adopted if the spouse is fertile. In elderly women removal of pelvic impediments to coitus (caruncles, prolapsed viscera, injuries to the pelvic floor, stress incontinence) and decent and judicious cosmetic surgery can strikingly improve the sexual pleasure of both partners.

## SUMMARY

Human sexual response is normally lifelong unless compromised by ill health, anxiety, or social expectation. The role of the geriatrician is to foster the sexual response as a supportive and enriching part of continued experience without impertinent proselytizing. Patients require to be reassured against their own false expectations, the hostility of society, including children and potential heirs, and the officious interference or prudery of some health personnel. Old persons in institutions should enjoy so far as is possible the same freedom of sexual choice which adults enjoy in society at large, and should not be considered senile, or sedated, in response to the sexual anxieties of the staff.

Where a partner is not available, either temporarily or in general, masturbation has the same function which it has at all ages, that is, a relief of sexual tension, an enjoyable experience, and a means of maintaining function. Explicit discussion of its use with older patients may relieve anxiety caused by earlier prohibitions.

As with the disabled, group discussion among elderly couples and among the elderly in communal living situations is a valuable means of ventilating sexual anxieties and needs which they may otherwise lack the social permission to express. This discussion may be greatly valued, especially by those who have all their lives lacked the opportunity for rational dialogue on sexual subjects. It has to be remembered that sexual dysfunction is very common at all ages, resulting from culture-based anxiety, and that there is no age at which it is too late to restructure attitudes in this regard. There are many couples in their 70s who have for the first time achieved communication and fulfillment which had previously been denied them.

## REFERENCES

AMELAR, R. D., AND DUBIN, L. 1977. Human chorionic gonadotrophin therapy in male infertility. *J. Amer. Med. Assn., 237*, 2423.

Anon (editorial). 1967. Retrograde ejaculation in diabetes. *J. Amer. Med. Assn., 199*, 661–662.

BRUCE, H. M., AND PARKES, A. S. 1961. An olfactory block to implantation in mice. *J. Reproduct. Fertil., 2*, 195–196.

CAMERON, P., AND BIBER, H. 1973. Sexual thought throughout the lifespan. *Gerontologist, 13*, 144–147.

COMFORT, A. 1960. Darwin and Freud. *Lancet, ii*, 107–111.

COOPER, A. J., ISMAIL, A. A. A., SMITH, C. G., AND LORAINE, J. A. 1970. Androgen function in psychogenic and constitutional types of impotence. *Brit. Med. J., 3*, 17–20.

FINKLE, A. L., MOYERS, T. G., TOBENKIN, M. I., AND KARG, S. J. 1959. Sexual potency in aging males. I. Frequency of coitus among clinic patients. *J. Amer. Med. Assn., 170*, 1391–1393.

FINKLE, A. L., AND PRIAN, D. V. 1966. Sexual potency in elderly men before and after prostatectomy. *J. Amer. Med. Assn., 196*, 139.

FURLOW, W. L. 1977. Surgical management of impotence using the inflatable penile prosthesis. *Mayo Clinic Proc., 51*, 325–332.

GAGNON, J. H., AND SIMON, W. 1973. *Sexual Conduct.* Chicago: Aldine Press.

GOLD, B. M., AND HOTCHKISS, R. S. 1969. Sexual potency following simple prostatectomy. *N.Y. State J. Med., 69,* 2987.

HOLGREWE, H. L., AND VALK, W. L. 1964. Late results of transurethral prostatectomy. *J. Urol., 92,* 51–57.

KARACAN, I. 1978. Advances in the diagnosis of erectile impotence. *Med. Aspects Human Sexual., 12*(5), 85–104.

KING, J. 1975. Impotence after fracture of the pelvis. *J. Bone Joint Surg., 57A,* 1107–1109.

KINSEY, A. C., POMEROY, W. B., AND MARTIN, C. E. 1948. *Sexual Behavior in the Human Male.* Philadelphia/London: W. B. Saunders.

KOTIN, J., WILBERT, D. E., VERBURG, D., AND SOLDINGER, S. M. 1976. Thioridazine and sexual function. *Amer. J. Psychiat., 133,* 82–85.

KRAEMER, H. C., BECKER, H. B., BRODIE, H. K. H., DOERING, C. H., MOOS, R. H., AND HAMBURG, D. A. 1976. Orgasmic frequency and testosterone levels in normal human males. *Arch. Sexual Behav., 5,* 125–132.

LOEFFLER, R. 1977. Penile prostheses do not inhibit partial erectile ability. *Fam. Practice News, 6,* 125–132.

MASTERS, W. H., AND JOHNSON, V. E. 1970. *Human Sexual Inadequacy.* Boston: Little, Brown.

NEWMAN, G., AND NICHOLS, C. R. 1960. Sexual activities and attitudes of older persons. *J. Amer. Med. Assn., 173,* 33–35.

PEARL, R. 1930. *The Biology of Population Growth.* New York: Knopf.

PFEIFFER, E., VERWOERDT, A., AND WANG, H. S. 1968. Sexual behavior in aged men and women. *Arch. Gen. Psychiat., 19,* 753–758.

RENSHAW, D. 1978. Diabetic impotence—a need for further evaluation. *Med. Aspects Human Sexual., 12(4),* 18–28.

SMALL, M. P., AND CARRION, H. M. 1975. A new penile prosthesis for treating impotence. *Contemp. Surg., 7,* 29–33.

SOLNICK, R. L., AND BIRREN, J. E. 1977. Age and erectile responsiveness. *Arch. Sexual Behav., 6,* 1–9.

WEISS, H. 1972. The physiology of human penile erection. *Annals of Int. Med., 76,* 793–799.

ZOHAR, J., MEIRAZ, D., MAOZ, B., AND DURST, N. 1976. Factors affecting sexual activity after prostatectomy. *J. Urol., 118,* 332–334.

# 37

# Psychosocial and Physiological Influences on Sexuality in the Older Adult

*Nan Corby & Robert L. Solnick*

Human behavior, be it sexual or otherwise, is influenced by interactions between physiological state, physical and social environment, and individual's personal learning history, the psychological meaning one attaches to one's experiences, and the immediate situation. Human *sexual* behavior, because of the powerful role it plays in the lives of most people, is particularly susceptible to the influences of these factors.

In this chapter, the effects of many of these factors on sexuality in middle and later life will be presented in as much depth as is possible. Areas to be reviewed include physiological changes directly and indirectly related to sexual functioning, effects of disease, psychosocial factors, and sexual dysfunction and treatment. A point which should be stressed is that sexual functioning is more strongly related to the optimization of potential already existing in each individual than to what has

been or will be learned in the research laboratory. Research findings have proven invaluable in helping some individuals develop their innate sexual resources into satisfying sex lives, but those untapped resources are there to begin with, and research provides a methodology for understanding and enhancing their expression.

## PHYSIOLOGICAL CHANGES

There is no doubt that physiological changes occur as a person ages. There is, however, some question as to how much these changes influence sexual behavior, since it is very difficult to separate physiological and psychological effects. For this reason, it is important to bear in mind that the existence of physiological change does not, in itself, mean that sexual functioning will be affected detrimentally.

## HORMONAL CHANGES

There are probably few areas where the cause-and-effect issue is more confusing than in the study of hormonal changes, particularly with regard to the consequence of these changes on human sexual behavior. For example, Eisdorfer and Raskind (1975) state that for the female, "the role of estrogen in most physiologic and behavioral aspects of aging remains controversial." Persky, Lief, Strauss, Miller, and O'Brien (1978) point out that in spite of the research findings to date, "the general role of the endocrine system in human sexual behavior is not well understood." It is important to be aware of these changes, however, since there exists the possibility that with increased knowledge, the relationship between hormonal and behavioral issues may be further resolved.

### FEMALE

Many studies of women indicate that the production of estrogen and progesterone by the ovary reaches insignificant levels following menopause (Monroe and Menon, 1977; Timiras and Meisami, 1972; Vermeulen, 1976). The postmenopausal ovary does, however, continue to secrete significant amounts of androgens, as does the adrenal cortex. Current research indicates that the estrogens which are produced in postmenopausal women arise mainly from the peripheral conversion of androgens (Monroe and Menon, 1977; Vermeulen, 1976). It has also been shown that the rate of conversion increases with age (Vermeulen, 1976).

This decrease in the estrogen levels has frequently been cited as the cause of symptoms associated with menopause, which for the majority of women occurs in the late forties. These symptoms may include headaches, back aches, nervousness, hot flashes, coldness, and crying, as well as other uncomfortable responses (Stryker, 1977). Weg (1978), however, points out that the percentage of women who experience such symptoms probably has been exaggerated. In a recent health screening program, 75 percent of the sample reported no symptoms, whereas in a self-report menopausal study only 26 percent reported no symptoms (Weg, 1978). In addition, psychosocial factors appear to be related to the difficulty associated with menopause. One study, for example, showed that women who work or have additional purposive roles appear to have less difficulty than those who function solely in the role of housewife or mother (Weg, 1978). It seems reasonably safe to assume that a woman's response to menopause is a highly idiosyncratic life event.

The two physiological changes that seem to be related to the decrease in estrogen in the menopausal and postmenopausal woman are vasomotor instability and genital atrophy (Eisdorfer and Raskin, 1975). Vasomotor instability manifests itself in the form of uncomfortable hot flashes and sweats. These symptoms respond well to the use of exogenous estrogen, but there is some question as to the advisability of using such therapy in the treatment of this and other menopausal symptoms because of possible dangerous side effects (Stryker, 1977).

As used here, the term "menopause" has been defined in its strictest sense, that is, as a period in a woman's life when there is a sudden or gradual cessation of the menstrual cycle which is related to the loss of ovarian function. The term "climacteric," on the other hand, is used to describe a period which may extend over many years and which is characterized by clear morphological and physiological changes in the body. In these terms, menopause is but one event which occurs during the climacteric. Timiras and Meisami (1972) view the climacteric as the counterpart of puberty, and menopause as the counterpart of menarche. With this distinction in mind, there are changes which take place during the climacteric which may directly affect sexual functioning in the female. During the years following the cessation of menses there are gradually occurring involutional changes which affect the genitals and breasts as a result of steroid starvation. These changes will be discussed in more detail later.

### MALE

As in other areas relating to hormonal functioning, there has been some confusion regarding the decline in secretion of androgens in the male as he ages. Some authors (Timiras and Meisami, 1972) have reported a gradual decline in the secretion of androgens beginning in the late twenties. Recently these data have been questioned because of the difficulty experienced at that time in accurately measuring serum and urine testosterone, and the complexity of androgen metabolism (Eisdorfer and Raskin, 1975). Using more sensitive measurement techniques developed in recent years, Vermeulen, Rubens, and Verdonck (1972) found that plasma testosterone levels did not decline significantly until the sixth decade of life. There was, however, a very large variation among individuals. Bartuska (1977) reported a decline in plasma testosterone in males after the age of 50. She cited values ranging from 1.5–5.3 ng/ml for elderly men to 5.0–8.5 ng/ml for young men and concluded that there is a reduction in mean plasma testosterone level of approximately 40 percent for men aged 80–90 compared to men under 50.

The effect of reduced testosterone levels on sexual functioning in the male is not clear. Raboch, Mellan, and Starka (1975) measured the plasma testosterone levels in a group of 45 patients aged 36–55 years who complained of low sexual appetite or impotency. When compared to a group of 108 men aged 21 to 51 years who reported adequate coital activity, they found that the testosterone level of the dysfunctional group was significantly lower than that of the control group in the 36–40 and 41–45 year categories, but not in the 46–50 and 51–55 year categories. In addition, they found that the range of testosterone levels for the dysfunctional group was the same as that of another group aged 21–45 years who reported satisfactory coital frequency; this group had been evaluated previously. In conclusion, Raboch et al. stated that they "endorse the opinion of Cooper, Ismail, and Love (1972) that testosterone level per se is less important for potency than previously believed."

Other research which relates to the role that testosterone may play in the sexual functioning of the male concerns the effect of using exogenous androgen therapy as a method of treating impotence (Beaumont, Bancroft, Beardwood, and Russell, 1972; Cooper, Ismail, Smith, and Loraine, 1970; Sabotka, 1969). Taken in total, however, the research results do not present clear evidence that androgen therapy is effective in the long term alteration of either libido or sexual responsiveness.

## CHANGES DIRECTLY RELATED TO SEXUAL FUNCTIONING

Most of the findings regarding the physiological response changes that take place in both the female and male sexual body system comes from the research of Masters and Johnson (1966). Even though the numbers of females and males over 50 who participated in the research were relatively small (34 and 39, respectively), the research was so thorough and well executed that it still stands as the major source to date of actual physiological measurements. Where applicable, other sources of data also will be cited.

### FEMALE

*Breasts.* The one response that appeared to remain essentially intact in the aging female was nipple erection following sexual stimulation. There was, however, a marked reduction in the increase in breast size as compared to the under-50 group.

The engorgement of the aereolae, so common in younger women, also was diminished.

*Myotonia.* There is a general decrease in muscle-tension elevation to sexual stimulation for the older woman; specific examples of striated-muscle spasm were rare.

*Rectum.* Regularly occurring rectal sphincter contractions (an indication of the intensity of orgasm), also common in younger women, was rarely observed in women beyond the age of 51 years.

*Clitoris.* The vasocongestive increase in clitoral shaft diameter and the retraction of the clitoral shaft and glans as the female reached high levels of excitement did not change with age. This is particularly important when one considers the major role of the clitoris in reaching orgasm (Hite, 1976).

*Labia Majora and Minora.* The flattening, separation, and elevation of the labia majora in response to sexual stimulation are lost as the woman ages. The vasocongestive thickening of the labia minora, prevalent among younger women, is reduced in older women. The preorgasmic color change which was present in all women under 50 was reduced to 83 percent in the 51–60 group, and to 27 percent in the 61–80 group.

*Vagina.* The vagina begins to undergo considerable change approximately five years after the cessation of the menses. The walls of the steroid-starved vagina become much thinner and assume a light pinkish color as compared to the thickened, well-corrugated, reddish-purplish appearance of the well-stimulated young vagina. The vagina also undergoes a loss of length and width as well as some of its expansive ability. Vaginal lubrication is also reduced in both rate and amount.

### MALE

*Breasts.* Nipple turgidity remains in the older male as a result of sexual stimulation, although it is reduced with increasing age.

*Myotonia.* Very few older males demonstrate any involuntary muscle spasm when sexually stimulated.

*Rectum.* As the male ages, there is a reduction in the regularly occurring rectal sphincter contractions associated with orgasm. This may reflect a generalized reduction in the physiological intensity of the orgasmic experience.

*Penis.* The time required to reach full erection may be doubled or trebled for the male passing through his fifties compared to young males. Solnick and Birren (1977) found that the time rate of increase of penile diameter was about six times faster for a group of males in their twenties compared to a group in their fifties when exposed to the same erotic stimulus. Full penile erection, particularly for the male over 60, often is not attained until ejaculation is imminent. The erectile pattern of the older male is much less labile than that of the younger male, that is, regaining an erection following turgidity subsidence is not as easy for the older male (Masters and Johnson, 1966; Solnick and Birren, 1977). Along with these changes, the older male finds it easier to maintain an erection for longer periods of time before he feels the urge to ejaculate. It is not certain whether this increased ejaculatory control is due to the aging process per se or to coital experience.

The intensity of the ejaculatory process is reduced in the older male. The refractory period for the older male increases substantially in many cases, often requiring 24 hours or more before erectile capacity returns. The two-stage penile detumescence, so characteristic of the younger male, often appears as one stage for the older male, since the detumescent process occurs so much more rapidly for the older male. In the older male this interval often disappears and the ejaculation occurs as one event. In some cases, where the older male has maintained his erection for an extended period, the ejaculation results in a seepage of seminal fluid rather than an expulsion.

There has been research suggesting that the tactile sensitivity of the penis may decrease with age. Edwards and Husted (1976) found a significant correlation between both age and frequency of sexual activity in a group of males aged 19 to 58 years, that is, men with lower penile sensitivity were older and less active sexually. In another study related to responsiveness, Gaskell (1971) demonstrated that penile systolic blood pressure was consistently lower than mean brachial blood pressure for a group of impotent males, whereas penile systolic blood pressure was consistently higher than brachial mean blood pressure for a group of potent males. An erection involves a valve-shunt system supplying blood to the corpus cavernosa in a quantity so great that the flow of blood entering is greater than that leaving the penis, thereby causing engorgement (Tucker, 1971; Weiss, 1972). It may be that the age effect on erection is partially a reflection of which older men develop arterial blockage to the penis as a part of their general decrease in arterial flow.

*Testes.* Full testicular elevation, which is a highly consistent occurrence prior to ejaculation in the male under 50, is no longer the case for the older male.

In summary, it is accurate to state that there are many physiological sexual responses that appear to decline with age for both men and women, but few of these declines are total and several of them remain essentially unchanged, especially for the female, for example, the clitoral response. The crucial point is that there is much physiological potential for sexual pleasure remaining for both female and male.

## EFFECT OF DISEASE ON SEXUAL BEHAVIOR

There are many disease-related conditions which may have an effect on sexual functioning in varying degrees (Glover, 1977; Rossman, 1978). Many diseases modify, directly or through surgery or medication, the sexual capacity of both the male and female. The extent to which a disease-related disability affects the sex life of a person, however, is very much a function of the individual's approach to the problem (Zilbergeld, 1978, p. 297). No matter what effect a disease may have on a person's functioning, it is hard to imagine that he or she could not enjoy some level of sexual pleasure if there is sufficient motivation. Different people with the same disease and same physiological effect on their bodies vary tremendously in their adaptation to their condition, and in their sexual expressiveness.

### HEART AND CIRCULATORY DISEASE

The fact that entire books have been written on the subject of sex and heart disease attests to the importance of this issue (Scheingold and Wagner, 1974). Unfortunately, even with the increased emphasis that has been given to the minimal effect that heart disease should have on sexual functioning, the research indicates that many cardiovascular patients continue to function at levels below their potential. Bloch, Maeder, and Haissly (1975) studied 100 patients 11 months after an acute myocardial infarction. Their subjects consisted of 88 males and 12 females with a mean age of 58 years. They found that the mean frequency of sexual intercourse decreased from 5.2 times a month prior to the infarction to 2.7 times a month eleven months after the infarction. This decrease did not correlate with the results of the exercise tests which had been given to 91 of the patients. Eighty-nine percent of the non-retired patients had returned to work. Bloch *et al.* (1975) found that the main reason for the reduction in sexual activity was psychological. The three main factors seemed to be latent depression, fear of relapse, and fear of sudden death.

In a study by Kavanaugh and Sheppard (1977), it was pointed out that there appeared to be less stress on the heart during intercourse than during a standard laboratory test. Approximately 12 percent of the subjects reported anginal pain during intercourse compared to 36 percent during the laboratory test. According to the investigators, the principal reasons given for diminished activity were (a) patient apprehension (17 of 81), (b) apprehension of wife (19 of 81), (c) loss of desire (30 of 81), and (d) a combination of these factors (15 of 81). In another study, Stein (1977) found that an exercise program improved heart rate and oxygen comsumption during coitus.

The fear of death during intercourse still seems to be a factor which influences both patient and partner. This condition exists in spite of the finding that the heart rate is much higher during treadmill testing of cardiac patients than it is during intercourse. The death rate during treadmill testing is 1 per 100,000 tests and documented instances of death during intercourse are even more rare (Glover, 1977). A general rule for cardiac patients is that some level of sexual activity may be resumed three months after myocardial infarction (Glover, 1977). Scheingold and Wagner (1974, p. 98) state that "a person with any type of heart disease who can comfortably climb one or two flights of stairs, or take a brisk walk around the block, is ready to resume sexual activity."

In some cases where there is a severe circulatory problem, it may be necessary to perform aorto-illiac surgery, and because of the body area involved there may be nerve damage and subsequent effect on sexual functioning. Weinstein and Machleder (1975) conducted follow-up examinations on 20 patients (mean age 64 years) who underwent this surgery. Overall, they found that 30 percent complained of retrograde ejaculation and 10 percent complained of impotence. The investigators pointed out that the effect on sexual functioning can be minimized if the surgeon is thoroughly familiar with the relationship between the nerves involved in the operation and sexual response. In addition, the surgeon must of course consider the sex life of the patient to be a worthwhile consideration in planning the surgery.

## DIABETES

Research seems to indicate that approximately 50 percent of the men with diabetes mellitus will have some impairment of their erectile responsiveness. There also appears to be little doubt that peripheral neuropathy is associated with the disease (Braddom, Hollis, and Castell, 1977; Ellenberg, 1971). However, the mechanism by which the peripheral nerves are affected is not understood (Lawrence and Abraira, 1976). In addition, there are no studies indicating a clear relationship between the severity of the neuropathy and impotency. Lawrence and Abraira state that, "In general, there is no exact correlation between the severity of neuropathic morbidity and the severity or duration of clinically manifest diabetes mellitus." They do not address themselves to impotency, however. Braddom *et al.* (1977) found, in a study of 49 men and seven women (mean age: 54) that the duration of diabetes seemed to be more important than age in determining potency status. In comparing a potent group of diabetics (mean age: 54.1) with an impotent group (mean age: 55.5), they found the duration of the disease to be 6.1 years in the potent subjects and 10.4 years in the impotent subjects. Kent (1975) pointed out that the most common cause of organic impotence is diabetes and that the incidence of diabetes-caused impotence increases after the age of 60. This may be more a reflection of the duration of the disease than age itself.

At one time it was thought that impotence in diabetics was an endocrinologic problem. It now appears that this is not the case (Ellenberg, 1973; Kolodny, Kahn, Goldstein, and Barnett, 1974).

The effect of diabetes on the female is quite different from its effect on the male. Ellenberg (1977) studied 100 female diabetics, 54 with clinically demonstrable neuropathy and 46 without. The majority of the subjects were from 30 to 60 years old, and the duration of diabetes was more than 10 years for most of the subjects. The age distribution was similar in both groups. There were no differences in sexual response in terms of libido and orgasm between the groups, nor was the sexual response of either group impaired. Orgasmic response and an interest in sex were present in 81.5 percent of the subjects with neuropathy and in 79 percent of those without. These percentages are not significantly different from those found in a nondiabetic group.

How does one explain the difference in effect on male and female diabetics? One explanation may be that diabetes impairs the erectile capacity of the male but not necessarily his orgasmic capacity. Since the most obvious measure of female response is orgasmic ability, there would be no obvious indication that her response had been affected. Ellenberg (1977) points out that the erection of the clitoris should be affected and therefore this should affect the female response. He prefers to emphasize the different sexual socialization of the female as the explanation for the difference between the male and female. Essentially, he takes the position that the male sex drive is primarily physical whereas the female functions at a higher psychological and emotional level as a result of her enculturation. The final explanation of this difference will have to await the outcome of arousal measurements of the female. Heiman (1975, 1976, 1978) and others have started to make measurements on the engorgement of the vaginal tissue as a woman is exposed to erotic stimuli. This type of measurement will be much more comparable to the measurement of penile erection (Karacan, 1969) than the reporting of orgasmic response.

### PROSTATECTOMY

As life expectancy has increased, the probability that a male may require a prostatectomy also has increased. Studies indicate that 5 to 40 percent of patients subjected to transurethral prostatectomy will experience a decrease or loss of potency (Madorsky, Ashamalla, Schussler, Lyons, and Miller, 1976; Zohar, Meiraz, Maoz, and Durst, 1976). Approximately 80 to 90 percent of the patients will experience retrograde ejaculation. Zohar *et al.* (1976) found that providing a sympathetic explanation and a willingness to answer questions regarding the operation was a decisive factor in determining the postoperative sexual prognosis. None of the seven patients who received postoperative explanations about their operation became impotent, whereas five of the eight who did not receive an explanation did become impotent, and two complained of disturbances in their sexual functioning.

Using a penile plethysmograph (Karacan, 1969), Madorsky *et al.* (1976) studied 14 patients who underwent transurethral prostatectomies. Penile erections were monitored during sleep, prior to and 4 weeks after surgery. Their results differed somewhat from those found in studies based on self-report; it appears that the method used in determining the effect of the prostatectomy is an important factor in evaluating the outcome of the surgery.

In summary, it seems apparent that the effect of a prostatectomy is highly individual, is very much affected by psychological factors, and is not likely to cause total loss of potency. The various studies indicating that from 5 to 40 percent of patients undergoing transurethral prostatectomy will experience a decrease or loss of potency should be evaluated in light of these considerations.

To this point, only transurethral prostatec-tomy has been considered. There are two other surgical procedures which also are used to deal with more serious problems involving the prostate gland. These procedures utilize the perineal and abdominal approach and are more likely to involve nerve damage which may result in more serious sexual consequences. In these cases, cancer of the prostate gland is often involved.

### COLECTOMY AND ILEOSTOMY

Unfortunately, colectomies and ileostomies are not uncommon among the older population. Several studies indicate that the crucial factor in determining the effect of these surgical procedures is the amount of rectum that has to be removed (Burnham, Lennard-Jones, and Brooke, 1977; Grüner, Naas, and Fretheim, 1977; Weinstein and Roberts, 1977). Burnham *et al.* (1977), after surveying 316 ileostomists by questionnaire, found that none of the 42 men with intact rectums experienced any change in sexual functioning. Of the 118 men who had had a portion of their rectum removed, the results were quite different, and were related to age at the time of the surgery. It is not clear from their report whether all or only part of the rectum had been removed. For this group, the percentages experiencing sexual impairment in three age categories were as follows: (a) 15 percent up to the age of 35, (b) 44 percent between 35 and 45, and (c) 53 percent of those over 45. However, only 17 percent of the men over 45 developed complete erectile impotence.

Of the 57 female ileostomists with an intact rectum, the frequency of orgasm remained essentially the same before and after surgery (56 percent and 63 percent respectively—a slight improvement). For the 165 women who experienced rectal excision, 54 reported new sexual discomfort following surgery, but the proportion reporting orgasm and pleasurable sensation also increased slightly. One point of interest in this study was that only 7 percent of the patients said they received helpful advice from their doctor or any other source. Only 40 percent had been able to discuss sexual problems at all with a physician. Some 90 percent of both sexes reported being able to discuss sexual problems with a partner. While half of the patients reported feeling less sexually attractive, fewer than 10 percent of their partners agreed with them. Weinstein and Roberts (1977) found similar differences in the effects of rectal excision.

### MASTECTOMY

Approximately 7 percent of all American women will eventually develop breast cancer. It is the leading cause of death in American women between

40 and 44 years of age (Polivy, 1977), although the disease attacks many women in the later years as well. The principal treatment for breast cancer is the removal of the breast, underlying tissues, and axillary lymph nodes. This surgical procedure is called a radical mastectomy.

Many of the studies which have been conducted to evaluate the effect of a mastectomy stress the importance of the psychological issues on both the woman and her partner (Ervin, 1973; Jamison, Wellisch, and Pasnau, 1978; Polivy, 1977; Wellisch, Jamison, and Pasnau, 1978; Witkin, 1978). In a controlled study, Polivy found support for her hypothesis "that mastectomy is psychologically more traumatic than other operations, specifically due to its attack on such emotionally charged organs as the breasts, visible symbols of femininity." In addition, she found that the decline in body image and total self-image did not evidence itself until months after the surgery. This finding is understandable in the light of previous findings regarding massive denial in mastectomy patients.

There are three major recommendations that researchers have suggested: presurgical counseling, involvement of the husband in the entire process, and the need for the surgeon to be responsive to evidences of depression in the patient. Ervin (1973) recommends counseling the husband as well as the patient, and encourages the husband to change his wife's dressings in order to maximize his involvement. He also endorses the participation of the women in open-ended groups to assist them in dealing with grief reactions and other emotional adjustments. Witkin (1978), after studying 41 mastectomy patients, concluded that psychosexual counseling "appears to have significantly positive effects in facilitating psychological recovery from the trauma."

In a study of 41 women with a mean age of 52.7, Jamison *et al.* (1978) found that women under 45 rated their postmastectomy adjustment as significantly poorer than did women over 45. (One may speculate that the younger women had a higher investment in their body image than did the older women.) They also found that a fourth of the women in their study expressed suicidal ideation. In comparing the suicidal and non-suicidal groups, they found that concern over sexual adjustment was an important predictor of suicidal ideation, with those women expressing more anxiety about resuming a sexual relationship with their mates than did the non-suicidal group. Their conclusion was that "emotional suffering appears to far outweigh the physical pain in women who have undergone mastectomy."

Wellisch *et al.* (1978) studied the effect of mastectomy from the male perspective. A key factor in post-mastectomy adjustment appeared to be the man's evaluation of the marital relationship. There was a significant correlation between the influence of mastectomy on the sexual relationship and evaluation of the general relationship. The responses of the males relative to the effect of mastectomy on sexual relations were as follows: (a) 14.3 percent rated it as bad, (b) 21.4 percent as somewhat bad, (c) 57.1 percent as having no influence, and (d) 7.1 percent as having a somewhat positive influence. The researchers stressed the importance of having the husband look at his partner's body after the surgery.

## HYSTERECTOMY AND OOPHORECTOMY

Hysterectomy is a surgical procedure in which all or part of the uterus is removed, and oophorectomy is a procedure in which one or both ovaries are removed. Hysterectomies are being performed in increasing numbers, and the effect of this procedure on sexual behavior is of primary interest to the women involved. The incidence of diminished sexual functioning following surgery varied from 10 to 38 percent in several different studies. Dennerstein, Wood, and Burrows (1977) conducted a retrospective study of 89 patients to investigate the important factors relating to sexual alteration following hysterectomy and bilateral oophorectomy. The subjects' mean age was 46.3 years at the time of the study, with approximately two-thirds of them between 39 and 54 years of age. It was concluded that "psychologic factors, particularly an expectation that the operation will adversely affect sexual relations, are responsible for the deterioration in sexual relations which follow the operation. Estrogen administration may be necessary to prevent dyspareunia, but apparently has no primary effects on sexual desire or enjoyment." These findings are generally in agreement with the studies which have been cited earlier regarding the changes in sexual behavior of the postmenopausal woman and the factors associated with these changes.

## URINARY INFECTIONS

According to Ledger (1977), "vaginitis is the most common infection in elderly patients seeking gynecologic aid." Ledger also cautions that, in addition to examining the patient for the presence of bacteria, attention should be given to the presence of small lesions as well. Often these lesions are assumed to be related to the lack of estrogens when in fact they are early manifestations of vulvar or vaginal carcinoma. Kent (1975) points out that older women who are sexually active "are particularly susceptible to urologic problems because of physical and behavioral changes related to aging." These types of problems can lead to dyspareunia which would tend to discourage sexual activity. It is therefore important for the older woman to be aware of this possibility and deal with it promptly, rather than retreating from sexual contact as a solution. This is particularly important since research also has shown that the female who is more active sexually tends to experience less reduction in the body's production of estrogens (Masters and Johnson, 1966). Since estrogen levels are related to the aging effect on the external and internal genitalia, reduced sexual activity would have the effect of exacerbating female sexual problems.

## ALCOHOL

There is no question that overindulgence in alcohol may lead to an episode of impotency in the male of any age, although the older male is more vulnerable to the effect of alcohol than is his younger counterpart (Masters and Johnson, 1966). These incidences of impotency are reversible if the male does not become concerned and embark on a downward psychological spiral which will lead to psychogenic impotency. But what are the consequences of long-term use of alcohol? In a study of 17,000 patients who were treated for alcoholism, Lemere and Smith (1973) found that 8 percent of their patients complained of impotency and in half of these cases the impotency continued after years of sobriety. They attributed the persistency of impotency to the "destructive effect of alcohol on the neurologic arc subserving erection." There was no indication that the problem was psychologically related. Lemere (1976) believes that the erectile dysfunction in chronic alcoholism is comparable to that found in diabetes. He also pointed out that recent evidence suggests that liver damage resulting from alcoholism may reduce testosterone levels, which in turn may affect potency. In his opinion, the fact that few if any women alcoholics complain of sexual dysfunction tends to support his position that erectile failure for the male alcoholic is organically based.

## PSYCHOSOCIAL ISSUES

The elderly are characterized both by the ways in which they differ from those younger and by the ways in which they themselves are diverse (Barrett, 1972; Botwinick, 1973; Rubin, 1965). Some of these psychosocial differences have obvious ramifications on how or, indeed, whether an older person will express himself or herself sexually. Other differences, as have already been shown, affect the older person's physiological capacity to experience sex in the same ways that younger people do or that they themselves may have experienced it in the past.

Kinsey, Pomeroy, and Martin (1948) reported that the rate at which male sexual behavior changed in old age did not exceed the rate at which it had been changing since the age of 16. This continuous decrement has not been found in more recent research, however. In the first cross-sectional analysis of the Duke data, 54 percent of the married subjects (60 to 93 years old) reported they engaged in sexual intercourse with some degree of regularity and periodicity. The proportion of married people 75 and over who were sexually active (about one quarter) turned out to be significantly lower than that of the other age groups (60–64, 65–69, and 70–74). These three younger groups were approximately equal to one another in proportion of subjects (about 60 percent) who were sexually active (Pfeiffer, Verwoerdt, and Wang, 1968). A sharp drop in the incidence of activity in the mid-70s was also observed by Verwoerdt, Pfeiffer, and Wang (1969a). Men 72–74 showed a 71 percent activity incidence while those 75–77 showed a 20 percent activity incidence.

In the second set of Duke studies, the somewhat-younger males (45+) were asked whether and when they first observed a decline in their sexual interest or activity. The sharpest increase in awareness of a decline occurred between the 45–50 group and the 51–55 group (Pfeiffer, Verwoerdt, and Davis, 1972). Generally confirming these reports was a study of sexual behavior in Danish males. Approximately 100 subjects in each five-year age group from 51 to 95 were surveyed. While the incidence of those reporting sexual activity was higher throughout this study than was found in the previously reported studies, there was a steady decrease in coital activity from a high of 94 percent among the 51–55-year-olds to a low of three percent among those in their 90s. Masturbatory incidence declined from 60 percent to 23 percent across the age groups, with the most noticeable change being from 43 percent among those in their early 70s to 24 percent among those in their late 70s, and remaining stable from 85 to 95. The incidence of morning erections declined from 89 percent to 31 percent, and reports of sexual interest closely paralleled the morning erection rates (Hegeler, 1976).

Martin (1975) reported a study of sexual behavior in men 25 to 85 as part of the Baltimore Longitudinal Study on Aging. These men were white, married, well-educated, and urban. Among this group, he reported that the incidence of ejaculation dropped from more than 98 percent among adults up to age 60 to 77 percent among those in their 70s. Coital incidences alone were above 93 percent up to 60 years of age, at which point they, too, began dropping, reaching 62 percent in the 70s. Masturbation showed an incidence of some 60 percent in the 20s and 30s, and appeared to decline thereafter, leveling off at about 22 percent in the 60s. Among those 70–79, masturbatory activity was still reported by 23 percent.

In Italy, DeNigola and Peruzza (1974) investigated sexual activity in 53 males and 32 females between 62 and 81 years of age, all of whom were free of serious disease. They reported that 85 percent of the males were coitally active. A decrease in average frequency of intercourse was reported by age, with those 62 to 71 reporting a frequency of twice a week, and those 72 to 81 reporting a frequency of about three times a month. Subjects were asked to compare sexual satisfaction before and after age 60, and most reported sexual satisfaction after 60 to be similar to or higher than before 60. Of the 85 subjects, only 20 reported sexual satisfaction to be less.

In addition to the decreasing proportions of people who engage in sexual activities across age, those who do continue do so less often (Finkle, Moyers, Tobenkin, and Karg, 1959). The curves for male and female frequency of activity found in the Duke data (Pfeiffer, Verwoerdt, and Davis, 1972; Pfeiffer, Verwoerdt, and Wang, 1968, 1969) are similar to the curves Kinsey plotted for his older subjects (Kinsey et al., 1948; 1953). The activity levels are not the same in both studies, but the relative slopes of the curves are comparable, and indicate a diminishing frequency, which was also reported in the Italian study (DeNigola and Peruzza, 1974).

While the reports of decreasing sexual activity among males appear to be accurate, they do not tell the entire story. In intraindividual longitudinal analyses of data collected three to four years apart, different patterns of varying sexual activity have been found (Pfeiffer el al., 1969; Verwoerdt, Pfeiffer, and Wang, 1969b). One analysis showed no sexual activity at either point in time among 27 percent of the subjects. A pattern of decreasing sexual activity (activity at the first interview, none at the second) was reported by 31 percent. Equal activity at both points was reported by 22 percent. Interstingly, 20 percent indicated increasing activity. So while 58 percent of the males reported no or decreasing sexual activity, some 42 percent reported continuing or increasing sexual activity over

the three-to-four-year period (Verwoerdt et al., 1969b).

The proportion of the different patterns varied among age groups. From 66–71, sexual activity was either continuously absent or it was increasing, with 30 percent of the subjects showing each pattern. Sustained interest occurred in 25 percent of the men in this age group. From 72–77, decreasing sexuality was the most common pattern, and after 78, half of the men showed the continuously absent pattern and 30 percent showed the decreasing pattern. The increasing pattern was still found in 20 percent of those 78 or older (Verwoerdt et al., 1969b).

Danish men also showed a sharp drop in coital incidence, from a steady range of 75–78 percent among those in their 60s to 56 percent among those 71–75, then dropping to 24 percent at 76–80 and continuing downward precipitously. Masturbatory incidence diminished more gradually, from 60 percent at 51–55 to 43 percent at 71–75, then dropping to 24 percent at 76–80. From 80 to 95, it remained stable at 21–23 percent (Hegeler, 1976).

Among aging women, the research indicates something different. While there are declines across age in incidences and frequencies of coitus among women, those declines according to Kinsey, for example, are "controlled by the male's desires, and it is primarily his aging rather than the female's loss of interest or capacity which is reflected in the decline." He concluded that there is "no evidence that the female ages in her sexual capacities" (Kinsey et al., 1953). Masters and Johnson (1966) reached similar conclusions, stating that "there is no time limit drawn by the advancing years to female sexuality," especially if there is regular stimulation. Kleegman (1959) also has reported that orgasmic response, while occurring in decreasing proportions and frequency with age, still occurs in women in their 70s and older. This has been supported by a comparison of sexual activity frequencies by age of partner. Older wives with younger husbands have been found to be more sexually active than are younger wives with older husbands (Christenson and Gagnon, 1965).

While a woman's capacity for sex may remain intact throughout life, the data indicate that fewer women than men remain sexually active. Newman and Nichols (1960) found that around 40 percent of their married female subjects over 60 were sexually active, compared to 60 percent of the males. Verwoerdt et al. (1969a) reported the differences at 53 percent (males) to 20 percent (females), dropping to 39 percent and 13 percent among those same subjects seven to nine years later.

In the Duke research, complete data from all

four interviews across 10 years were available on 39 subjects, of whom 19 were women. The males' sexual-activity-level curve showed the expected decrease from 70 percent to 25 percent across 10 years. The women's however, showed a non-significant increase from 16 to 21 to 25 percent, followed by a drop to 15 percent (Pfeiffer *et al.*, 1969). The average age of the women was two years younger than the men; both were in their late 60s at the beginning of the study.

In their study of married and previously married women, Christenson and Gagnon (1965) found a coital incidence of 87.5 percent among 50-year-old married women and 37 percent among previously married women of the same age. By 60, these figures had dropped to 69.7 and 12.5 percent respectively. Half of the 65-year-old married women were coitally active, but none of the previously married women were at 65. While coitus was the modal sexual behavior for these married women, 31 percent of them also masturbated at age 50. By 65, 25 percent were still masturbating. None over 70 were. In contrast, the previously married women's masturbatory incidences were nearly double those of married women the same age: 59 percent at 50, a third at 65, and a fourth at 70.

Christenson and Johnson (1973) analyzed data from women 50 and over who had never married. The sex histories of a third of the sample gave little evidence of any development of erotic interests. In the others, both the incidence and frequency of sexual activities showed aging effects by 55. Comparing this study with their earlier study of formerly married women (Christenson and Gagnon, 1965), the never-married sample showed lower levels of sexual activity, but there were no marked differences in the patterns of sexual aging between the never-married and the previously married. Masturbation incidence decreased at about the same rate as for married and previously married women.

Of the 32 women between 62 and 81 in the Italian study, 53 percent were coitally active. There was no frequency difference reported between coitally active men and women (DeNigola and Peruzza, 1974).

Different patterns of sexual activity were found in different proportions of women by age in the Duke studies. Overall, most older women (74 percent) showed a pattern of no sexual activity; patterns of sustained activity and decreasing activity had incidences of 10 percent each. Six percent showed increasing activity. The incidences of these patterns changed with age, with no-activity rising from 50 percent at 60–65 to 100 percent at 78-plus. The increasing-activity pattern was found in fourteen percent of both the 60–65 and 66–71-

year-olds. By 72–77, 10 percent were showing decreasing activity, and none showed sustained or increasing activity (Verwoerdt *et al.*, 1969b).

Two sets of data from the Duke studies examined the reasons for ending intercourse. The loss of a partner was given as a reason by 48 percent of the women in the 1968 study (all widowed) and also by 48 percent of the women in the 1972 study (36 percent widowed, 12 percent separated or divorced). Among men, death of spouse was given by 10 percent and by none, respectively, in the two studies. Spouse illness or spouse lack of sexual interest or ability were given as reasons by 48 and 42 percent of the women, and by 30 and 29 percent of the men. Self illness or self lack of sexual interest or ability were given by 14 percent and 10 percent of the women and by 58 and 71 percent of the men (Pfeiffer *et al.*, 1968; Pfeiffer *et al.*, 1972). In examining congruence in the eight intact couples who had ceased having intercourse, six agreed that cessation was attributable to the husband, one agreed it was attributable to the wife, and one disagreed, blaming themselves, not each other (Pfeiffer *et al.*, 1969). These data confirm that the husband is usually the determining factor in whether or not a couple will continue intercourse.

### INTEREST AND IMAGINATION

The term "sexuality" is used to refer to many different things. In some cases, it refers to those sexual behaviors that result in orgasm. It can also mean some of those same behaviors whether or not they result in orgasm for one or both partners. It can refer to less obvious or more solitary activities such as masturbation, nocturnal orgasms, or morning erections. For many, non-genital touching and caressing may be extremely sexual (Weinberg, 1969).

Sexual interest is one measurement of sexuality, as are reports of the "amount" or intensity of enjoyment one receives from sex. Sexual interest has been measured by direct questions and has been inferred from reports of sexual thoughts, behaviors, dreams, and fantasies or daydreams.

Comparisons of sexual thoughts and interest between old and young subjects have indicated that fewer of the subjects 50 and older (average age: 70) had such thoughts and interest, and they had them less often, than did 18-to-40-year-olds (Cameron, 1969; Cameron and Biber, 1973). In contrast, however, Pfeiffer *et al.*, (1969) found that the proportion of healthy elderly men reporting continuing sexual interest at four interviews over a ten-year span remained fairly constant at 80, 85, 85, and 75 percent. These same men were showing significant sexual activity decreases over the same time period. Of men surviving into their 80s and 90s, about half reported sexual interest to some degree (Verwoerdt *et al.*, 1969a).

The incidence of moderate-to-strong sexual interest (as opposed to mild sexual interest) among another group of men declined from ages 46–50 (90 percent) to 61–65 (52 percent), but then showed a slight increase among 66–71-year-olds (58 percent). Mild interest was indicated by another 32 percent of this group (Pfeiffer *et al.*, 1972).

Freeman (1961) also found a gap between activity and interest among his male subjects (mean age: 71), 75 percent of whom expressed sexual desire while only 55 percent were sexually active. Hegeler (1976) reported sexual interest among his Danish male subjects ranging from 92 to 100 percent up to age 70, dropping to 35 percent among those 91–95.

Sexual dreams within the preceding year were experienced by 77 percent of the married men under 40 in Martin's study, dropping to 36 percent by the 70s (Martin, 1975). Giambra and Martin (1977) found that high and low frequencies of sexual events were related to frequencies of sexual daydreams (fantasies), and tended to persist over a major part of adulthood.

The proportions of married and previously married women having sex dreams to orgasm are similar. At age 50, 27 percent of the married and a third of the previously married women were having such dreams. The figures dropped to 19 and 10 percent at age 65 (Christenson and Gagnon, 1965).

In the Duke studies, the incidence of moderate-to-strong sexual interest among women diminished from 70 percent at 46–50 to 12 percent at 61–65 and then rose to 24 percent at 66–71. An additional 26 percent of this oldest group still reported having mild interest (Pfeiffer *et al.*, 1972). It has been suggested that this increase among the older groups of both men and women is because they constitute an "elite group" of survivors (Pfeiffer, 1970; Pfeiffer *et al.*, 1969; Pfeiffer *et al.*, 1972).

The apparently increasing gap between sexual interest and activity among men may be due to a reticence that some men may feel about admitting they no longer are interested in sex (Botwinick, 1973). There is greater pressure on males than on females to claim sexual interest. Supporting evidence for this contention comes from husband-wife congruence data reported by Pfeiffer *et al.* (1968) and by the data indicating that adolescent males receive homosocial support for sexual activity or reports of such (Simon and Gagnon, 1969).

Among women in the Duke study, sexual interest was expressed by 30 percent of the subjects at the beginning of the study, increasing to 40 percent in eight years and declining again to 35 percent at ten years. Incidences of sexual activity varied from 15 percent at year one to 20 percent at year eight and 15 percent at year ten. The meaning of these relatively small changes is uncertain, but the data for women were substantially less variable and consistently lower than those for men. Far fewer women than men were remaining sexually interested: about a third compared to around three-quarters of the men. Like the men, this proportion did not decline significantly. The gap between sexual interest and sexual activity was much smaller for women (Pfeiffer, 1969).

In discussing the comparatively low levels of sexual interest in older women, Pfeiffer and Davis (1972) have postulated a defense mechanism as the cause. They stated that "it may well be adaptive to inhibit sexual strivings when little opportunity for sexual fulfillment exists." The remedy they suggested: increasing efforts to extend a vigorous life span for men.

Theirs, however, is not the only suggestion that has been made. Other suggestions have included polygamous marriages (Berezin, 1969; Kassell, 1966), non-marital cohabitation and lesbian companionships (Cavan, 1973), marrying younger men (Dean, 1966; Sviland, 1975), making sexual services available to the aged (Ullerstrom, 1966), and, in a broader context, sex education programs for the elderly to extend the variety of their sexual activities (Felstein, 1970; Green, 1975).

## FACTORS AFFECTING SEXUAL BEHAVIOR

The single most important factor influencing human sexual behavior appears to be gender. The next-most-often-mentioned factor, for both men and women, is age.

Among men, other factors which appear to be of importance are varying issues related to health; past sexual experience; life satisfaction, adaptability, fears, and other psychological variables; and social factors such as class, income, and educational level. Marital status has been shown to have a great deal of influence on a woman's sexuality. Her partner's age is also relevant. Other determinants of sexuality among older women is how much enjoyment a woman derived from sex in her younger years and her present orgasmic capability. Having noticeable but smaller effects are religiosity and, as with men, certain socioeconomic, psychological, and health variables.

## MARITAL STATUS

While marital status has little to do with an older men's sexual activity (Pfeiffer and Davis, 1972), it has been shown to have a great deal to do with a woman's, whose heterosexual activity in later life is greatly dependent on the presence of a socially acceptable, sexually active partner (Christenson and Gagnon, 1965; Finkle *et al.*, 1959; Kinsey *et al.*, 1953; Masters and Johnson, 1966; Finkle, 1970; Newman and Nichols, 1960; Pfeiffer and Davis, 1972; Pfeiffer *et al.*, 1968; Pfeiffer *et al.*, 1969; Post, 1967; Verwoerdt *et al.*, 1969a, 1969b; Weinberg, 1969). Those partners become increasingly scarce with age.

Between 45 and 64, there are about 92 men to every 100 women in the United States. At 65 and over, that figure has dropped to 69 men per 100 women (US Bureau of the Census, 1977). This difference considerably limits the older women's opportunity for heterosexual relationships.

Presuming for the moment that marriage satisfies the desire for heterosexual relationships (as it does for many), thereby removing the married from the category of those who are seeking or are available for them, the number of people who are not married becomes of greater interest and importance. While 63 percent of all women over 65 are unmarried, only 27 percent of all men over 65 are also unmarried (US Bureau of the Census, 1977), resulting in a proportion of roughly 30 single men to every 100 single women over 65.

Further reducing the availability of single men to single women is the tendency of women to select partners older than they, or of men to select partners younger than they. The average difference in ages between older marriage partners has been reported as four years (Newman and Nichols, 1960). Broadly speaking, available partners for a woman of any age can be described as all single men older than she. For a man, available partners would be all single women younger than he. The position of reduced opportunity into which this puts women is apparent. As a practical matter, of course, people tend to choose partners whose ages are within a few years (higher for women, lower for men) of their own. This doesn't leave the older woman with much less of a disadvantage, since she is likely to outlive men her own age by seven years (Brotman, 1971).

What it does leave, among those over 65, is a female population in which some 37 percent are married, 53 percent are widowed, and 10 percent are separated, divorced, or never married. Of the male population over 65, some 73 percent are married.

To summarize the sex-and-marital-status findings: among older women, the incidence of sexual activity was found to be higher in the married than in the unmarried (Christenson and Gagnon, 1965; Kinsey *et al.*, 1953; Pfeiffer and Davis,

1972). Among women not currently married, the divorced had higher incidences of sexual activity than did the widowed (Gebhard, 1971), and together they had a higher incidence than never-married women (Christenson and Johnson, 1973). Marital status had little or no effect on sexual behavior in men (Pfeiffer and Davis, 1972). It also had no effect on sexual interest in men, and little effect on sexual interest in women, whose interest levels remained lower than men's at all ages studied (Verwoerdt *et al.*, 1969b).

## PAST SEXUAL EXPERIENCE

The effects of past sexual experience on later-life sexuality have been widely reported. Pfeiffer and Davis (1972) found that for men, past sexual enjoyment, interest, and frequency were highly correlated with present sexual interest and activity. Other reports of correlations between early- and later-life sexual frequency and daydreams have appeared in the literature (Giambra and Martin, 1977). This finding, that high levels of sexual activity while young are significantly correlated with high levels of later-life sexual activity, has given credence to the "use it or lose it" admonitions that have gained much currency. Masters and Johnson (1966, 1970) have emphasized the importance of regularity of sexual expression in maintaining sexual functioning throughout life. Pfeiffer (1969) has concluded that "persons to whom sex was of great importance early in life are more likely to continue to be sexually active late in life."

For women, past sexual enjoyment alone (not past frequency or past interest) was most highly associated with current sexual interest and frequency of intercourse (Pfeiffer and Davis, 1972). Christenson and Gagnon (1965) found that the value of early sexual experience as a predictor of post-marital sexual behavior was mediated by the capacity to experience coital orgasm fairly regularly. This appears to be a reasonable measure of sexual enjoyment, but it is by no means the only one.

Christenson and Johnson's later study (1973) confirmed the predictive value of early sex behavior, warning, however, that "early" is highly variable. Women who are "late developers," that is, whose sexual interests and activities began in their 30s, for instance, would be placed statistically in the group of women who had not developed sexual interest "early," that is, in their late teens or early 20s. This lack of early (pre-30s) activity is not predictive of their later sexual activity.

## PHYSICAL AND EMOTIONAL WELLBEING

While general health-related effects on sex have been reported extensively in the literature, and some of the specific effects have been discussed previously in this chapter and volume, there is one finding which deserves mention here: the differential effects of subjective and objective health ratings. Pfeiffer and Davis (1972) report that a number of health factors contributed independently to current sexual functioning in men. An objective health rating was correlated to present frequency of intercourse. When it came to determining sexual interest and enjoyment, however, subjective assessments of health became more important. Among women, health factors carried little weight in determining sexual functioning. The people in this study, however, were described as "biologically advantaged," and among a less advantaged sample, health may assume a different role.

Many psychological variables have been suggested as influencing sexuality (Denber, 1968; Lief, 1977; Masters and Johnson, 1966, 1970; Peberdy, 1967; Pfeiffer and Davis, 1972). There is little consensus on what these psychological factors are, however.

Pfeiffer and Davis (1972) found, basically, that present life satisfaction and, especially, anticipated future life satisfaction were important psychological predictors of sexual activity among both men and women. Religious devoutness has been shown to have an effect on the manner in which women express their sexuality, but has not so much an effect on men (Christenson and Johnson, 1973; Heltsley and Broderick, 1969; Kinsey *et al.*, 1953; Newman and Nichols, 1960).

In an analysis of the Duke data on demographic variables, race and socioeconomic status were found to be significantly related to sexual frequency, with black and low socioeconomic status subjects reporting significantly higher levels of sexual activity than did white and higher status subjects (Newman and Nichols, 1960). Later analyses indicated that the differences were probably due to socioeconomic status alone, rather than to race, since there was a high correlation between ethnic background and the socioeconomic factors (Pfeiffer and Davis, 1972).

In addition to these, two major environmental events, social isolation and changes in housing patterns, have potentially important influences on sexual behavior (Lowenthal, 1968; Rosow, 1968).

## ATTITUDES AND INSTITUTIONS

The elderly have attitudes, opinions, and beliefs about sex for themselves and for others, and those others have attitudes, opinions, and beliefs about sex for the elderly. While such social attitudes may have an important effect on all old people, the power to enforce such beliefs is most apparent among those who are in positions of direct control over the institutionalized elderly.

Frequently reported is the belief that old people are uninterested in sex, that they have no sexual feelings, and that they find sex unimportant (Golde and Kogan, 1959; LaTorre and Kear, 1977). An analysis of sexual humor has shown that attitudes toward elderly women are, in general, more negative than attitudes towards elderly men (Palmore, 1971).

Kahana (1976) found that among 124 nursing home residents, 49 percent agreed with the statement, "sex over 65 is ridiculous." He attributed that response to an internalization of society's negative evaluation of sex and the aged.

Types of sexual activities rated have some bearing on how credible sex is in the elderly. One study indicated that while masturbation among old and young alike was equally credible, intercourse among the elderly was far less credible than it was among the young (LaTorre and Kear, 1977).

Among old people themselves, men are more positive about sex than are women. When surveyed about "non-traditional" sex (pre-marital sex, extramarital sex, and homosexuality), a greater degree of intolerance was shown by women, people of lower educational and occupational levels, regular church attendees, married people, and parents. Age was a stronger predictor of intolerance than any of these, however, and tended to have a "conservatizing" effect (Snyder and Spreitzer, 1976).

In a comparison of young, middle-aged, and old people, the old people considered themselves relatively uninterested in sex, less capable of it, having fewer opportunities for it, less skillful at it, and doing it less often. The middle-aged judged themselves "average" on all counts, but were judged by younger and older people alike as the most sexually knowledgeable and skillful. Young people judged themselves as most interested in sex, making the most attempts ("trying harder"), the most physically capable of sex, and having the greatest access to and success rate at sex (Cameron, 1970).

As differences in sexual attitudes between husbands and wives have negative effects on marriage (Ard, 1977), so might differences in sexual attitudes between nursing home residents and staffs have a negative effect on life in a nursing home. An indication of this was reported by Wasow and Loeb (1977), who found positive *responses* among nursing home staff about freedom of sexual expression among the elderly residents, but little *support* for such activities in their own facility. LaTorre and Kear (1977) found nursing home staffs more negative toward sex in general than were students, but this could have been a function of social factors such as educational level. Kaas (1978) found nursing home staffs to be more accepting of sexual expression among various subgroups than were their nursing home residents, also attributing the differences to differences in education, religion, and age.

Many old people, both in nursing homes and out, appear to accept their waning sex lives as part of the normal process of aging (Lieberman, 1971; Riley and Foner, 1968). Whether this is a result of a "self-fulfilling prophecy" that comes from societal attitudes, or whether it comes from the realities of aging for some physically ill old people, will be debated for many years. Among the institutionalized elderly, however, at least a part of the decrement may be attributed to discrepancies between reported staff attitudes and actual staff behaviors (Wasow and Loeb, 1977).

A specific effect that staff attitudes and administrative policies may have on the issue of sex among nursing home residents centers around privacy (Miller, 1978; Wasow, 1977). Not only do nursing homes and other institutions not have places where their married residents can have sex (Burnside, 1975; Schlessinger and Miller, 1973), they often ignore or deny the sexual needs of their non-married residents. This is done most effectively by isolating the sexes. The introduction of a "heterosexual living space" in one such institution resulted in better social adjustments and a richer social life for both men and women, and the men became better groomed and more careful in their use of profanity. The residents made more use of the privacy they had (e.g., closing their doors while dressing). One sexual relationship occurred as well as other overt sexual contacts (Silverstone and Wynter, 1975).

Sex among the residents of a nursing home functions to add pleasure to the lives of the residents. It tends to reduce the amount of inappropriate sexual expression, and it provides immediate relief from anxiety for the resident (Wasow, 1977). Unfortunately, it has also been reported to cause an increase in anxiety among the families of some old people (Dean, 1966). Solutions to the problems of sexuality in nursing homes, which problems include assured privacy, sexual rights for residents, medico-legal issues that administrators and physicians may face, and staff education, have been proposed (Miller, 1978; Wasow, 1977).

### MID-LIFE CHANGES IN WOMEN AND MEN

*Women.* Pfeiffer and Davis (1972) found that being post-menopausal is negatively correlated with female sexual activities. While in a preceding section,

the data reported indicate no direct relationship between sexual capacity and menopause or the climacteric, folklore blames menopause for much of the decrease in sexual activity among women. It has been suggested, for example, that "some women perceive their sexual life as over when their reproductive capacity has ended" (Pfeiffer *et al.*, 1969). Surgical menopause, that is, hysterectomy, has also been viewed by some women as a castrating operation that puts an end to one's sex life (Post, 1967).

Looking at the impact of early-life sexual enjoyment on continued sexual activity (Pfeiffer and Davis, 1972), it would appear that menopause may be the excuse some women give (to themselves as well as to others) for stopping an activity that wasn't all that enjoyable anyway (Mann, 1977). Berezin (1969) was referring to the taboos on sex in old age when he made the following statement, but it might well apply to sex after menopause: "Those who failed to enjoy sex in their younger years . . . may retreat into the myth of a sexless old age."

Menopause is viewed as temporarily unpleasant and disturbing by both younger and middle-aged women. Few middle-aged women, however, view it as a particularly significant event in their lives. Younger women were more likely to label it such (Neugarten, Wood, Kraines, and Loomis, 1968). The personality changes associated with the climacteric in women have been more attributed to psychosocial events in their lives (Benedek, 1950; Denber, 1968) than to biological events.

Women's sexuality has been reported to increase in the late 30s, the exact age varying with specific sexual activities measured (Gadpaille, 1975; Kinsey *et al.*, 1953; Pressey and Kuhlen, 1957; Stanley, 1977). This premenopausal increase has been attributed to hormonal and pelvic vascular changes that increase libido, to a lessening in power of the cultural influences that inhibit sexuality in youth, and to the increased time and energy available once the physical and emotional demands associated with raising young children are gone (Stanley, 1977). In response to Stanley's comments, Eskin (1977) adds that the male's need for increased stimulation in mid-life may result in enhanced foreplay and more arousal in the female, bringing more satisfaction in sex and, therefore, more frequent intercourse.

While "fear of failure" at sex is a commonly referenced problem among men (Long, 1976; Masters and Johnson, 1966, 1970), women are not without their fears. Chief among these has to do with an image of the kind of feminine sensuous beauty that is attractive to others, and their realization that the "ravages of time" have made them unattractive and, therefore, unable to attract sex partners (Bardwick, 1971; Blood, 1955; Lieberman, 1971; Masters and Johnson, 1970).

In addition, a woman may also go through an assessment of her life at about the same time she goes through menopause, and may become aware that "her life has been either uninteresting or a terrible failure" (Denber, 1968). She may find, or label, herself "economically and educationally disadvantaged, and a sexual castoff" (Troll, 1977). This sense of personal or professional failure may be likened to that which men experience in their middle years.

*Men.* The sexual effects of mid-life psychological events are not limited to women, of course, but have also been described among men (Marmor, 1974; Masters and Johnson, 1966, 1970). These inhibitors of sexual functioning include questioning one's goals, one's effectiveness in achieving them, and one's control over one's own fate. It involves coming to grips with the realization that not all of one's youthful aspirations will come to pass (Marmor, 1974).

Masters and Johnson (1966) attribute an age-related decrease in male sexuality to six factors: monotony, career or economic preoccupation, mental or physical fatigue, overindulgence in food or drink, physical or mental infirmities of self or spouse, and performance fears associated with or resulting from the previous five factors. These "fears of failure" become more important to men as they begin to notice changes in their sexual responsiveness in their middle years (Bardwick, 1971; Liang, 1973; Lieberman, 1971; Masters and Johnson, 1966, 1970; Taylor, 1973).

*Marriage.* Close interpersonal relationships, of which marriage is often a result and is intended to be an example, have a number of functions. Among these are intimacy, social integration through shared concerns, the opportunity to be nurturant and to receive nurturance, reassurance of worth, a sense of reliable alliance, and guidance (Weiss, 1969, 1974). That all marriages do not achieve this may not be attributed to an unrealistic approach to marriage or to one's partner in the first place, but to unforeseen changes in situation, personality, or behavior occurring throughout life. Because people usually choose as their mates the others who are a "best fit" or who are closest to them in many ways at the time they marry, it should not be surprising that the changes that occur with time result in less of a match. Only occasionally, and often in unimportant ways, do changes result in greater compatibility. Marital disenchantment

may be the result, and an effect of this disenchantment is a decrease of sexual activities in the marriage (Pineo, 1968). Another result is that there are proportionately more divorces at this time (Martin, 1975). While most sexual activities still take place between marital partners, extramarital relationships may serve as an attempt to revive flagging sexual interest in devitalized or passive marriages (Cubber and Harroff, 1966).

The views of marriage in mid-life are, at best, mixed. For some, the middle years are a time of decreased marital satisfaction, intimacy, sex, and increased loneliness (Pineo, 1968). Middle-class marriages have been described as predominately either passive-congenial or devitalized-apathetic (Cubber and Harroff, 1966). Time appears to be a "corrosive" to such marriages (Blood and Wolfe, 1960), leading to diminished sexual attraction between mates (Beigel, 1952; Blood, 1955; Grant, 1957; Symonds, 1946).

On the other hand, the middle years can be a time when a couple can and do experience freedom from family responsibilities (Lowenthal and Chiraboga, 1972), when they can and do reform and improve their own self-concepts and marital relationships. The period when children have grown and left can provide, for those who remain married, a freedom from (or reduction of) financial and geographic limitations, and from a certain number of child-related chores. One can also "be oneself" rather than a model for one's children. These middle years of marriage have been called the "years of the payoff" (Deutscher, 1968.

In a longitudinal study that began with newlywed couples in 1935, those who were still married 20 years later were asked about their enjoyment of sex "during the last three years." "Great enjoyment" was reported by 70 percent of the husbands and 57 percent of the wives. "Mild pleasure" was reported by 25 percent of the husbands and 33 percent of the wives. Positive feelings about sex tended to remain stable across the years, with a slight decrease from 85 to 70 percent among the husbands, and a slight rise from 54 to 57 percent among the wives. Where there was incongruence between husbands and wives on opinions about sex, that incongruence produced negative effects in the marriage (Ard, 1977). These subjects were married in 1935, and the last data were collected in 1955. It would be interesting to compare these findings with data from couples who were married more recently and who, presumably, have had different social forces contributing to (or detracting from) their marriages.

Feldman (1964) compared middle-aged marriages and three stages of child-rearing and chronological age. The length of the marriage appeared to be more significant in predicting satisfaction than did the existence of children. In the "elderly marriage," there was a decrease in "marital interaction," but there was also more peacefulness, more satisfaction with the marriage, and less stress. From this work, Feldman identified three major events occurring in lasting marriages: the shift of focus from the parent role to the spousal role, the incorporation of the husband into the home following retirement, and widowhood.

Among the retirement-related changes and stresses occuring in marriages between ages 60 and 70 is, most likely, a self-esteem-related sexual change, especially in the male. (It is not known how much of an effect self-esteem changes will have on the sexuality of those increasing numbers of women who retire from careers that have provided the bulk of their identity.) Self-image and self-esteem are closely associated to sexuality, especially among men (Whiskin, 1968), and "even for the aged" (Sutterly and Donnelly, 1973).

Deteriorating marriages in late life may also be the result of fear or anger about physical or mental changes in one partner or the other, or of resentment of society's admonishment to "grow old gracefully." Anger, fear, and resentment can all decrease one's sexual activity (Butler, 1967), as can depression over one's life (Renshaw, 1975).

While the data have emphasized the disenchanted marriage in later life, there are many marriages that remain or become vital and romantic at that time. The more romantic the relationship, the more likely it is to endure (Rubin, 1968). Many of the middle-aged use their new-found freedom to improve and enhance their marriages (Lowenthal and Chiraboga, 1972), and still others report great satisfaction from the contentment they find (Deutscher, 1968). Among "self-actualizing" people, love and sex are both reported to improve as the relationship ages (Maslow, 1954).

*People Alone.* In late life, people are alone for the same reasons as they are alone at any other time of life—because they are divorced or separated, or their spouses have died, or they never married in the first place.

Single older adults, those who have never married, have been described as "lifelong isolates." They tend to have developed a style of personal independence and minimal social involvements that allows comparatively greater control over their participation in life. Many report that they prefer being alone. They value the long-term continuity they have developed in their lives. Significantly, they are well aware of an important advantage of

their never-married status in old age: they won't have to suffer the grief caused by the death of a spouse (Gubrium, 1974, 1975; Tunstall, 1966).

The never-married tend to be more like the married in that both are more positive about their lives and "well-being" than are divorced or widowed older people (Gubrium, 1974; Kutner, Fanshel, Togo, and Langner, 1956; Pihlblad and Adams, 1972), and both report loneliness less than half as often as the widowed (Willmott and Young, 1960).

Desolation, rather than isolation, appears to be a critical factor in loneliness (Gubrium, 1975). The recently bereaved were the loneliest in one English study (Townsend, 1957). For men, the loss of a spouse means a loss of love. It also means social changes, because often it has been the wife who links the older couple to its family and social relationships (Cumming and Henry, 1961). Many times, those relationships or their enjoyment hinge on the joint participation of a spouse (Blau, 1961). When the social isolation occurs as a consequence of the death of a spouse, it can lead to suicide, especially among widowers (Bernardo, 1968, 1970; Bock and Webber, 1972).

Among women, widowhood also usually means the loss of an intimate confiding relationship (Miller and Ingham, 1976). It involves an involuntary shift from the solidarity of marriage and the stability of oft-repeated ways of doing things, from a comfortable, or at least familiar, division of labor and mutual dependency to unfamiliar and unwanted reliance on a group of unattached women (Cumming and Henry, 1961). At the very best, this results in a loss of morale, at the worst, in suicide (Bernardo, 1968, 1970).

When confronted with severe adversity, the most powerful protection from psychiatric disturbance in women has been reported to be "an intimate, confiding relationship with a husband or boyfriend" (Brown, Bhrolchain, and Harris, 1975). Not only is widowhood the last of the three major crises in a woman's later life (Feldman, 1964), but by definition she must go through it without the psychiatric protection of a husband. There is evidence suggesting that in the year following the death of a spouse, the psychiatric and physical health of the surviving spouse is significantly related to the support he or (more often) she receives from others in his or her environment. When these supportive friendships are not there, mental and physical problems increase (Henderson, 1977; Maddison and Viola, 1968; Maddison and Walker, 1967; Miller and Ingham, 1976).

It has been stated that "women mourn, men replace" (Goodman, 1978) because widowers tend to remarry more often than widows (Treas and Van Hilst, 1976). They also remarry sooner, in about three years, while those widows who remarry do some seven years after the death of their spouses. Remarriage is more likely to occur if the former marriage was a happy one. Of the new remarriages surveyed by McKain (1969), 75 percent were rated as "successful" by interviewers. The factors which the successful remarriages had in common were, for the most part, predictable. The wife was younger, but by no more than 14 years. There was sufficient income. The rate of courtship activities was high. There was a mutuality of interests and of goals, with love and companionship more important than material acquisitions. Each partner was high in life satisfaction. Family relationships were good, and their children approved.

The reasons that remarriage occurs less often among widows are demographic and economic, not because they don't want to (although, in fact, many don't). Men tend to marry younger women. There is a disproportionate number of women compared to men in old age. Many times, there is a reduction in income from sources which pay widows so long as they don't remarry (Jacobs and Vinick, 1977).

What this results in are groups of women spending large amounts of time with other women, populating housing projects for the elderly, the "unexpected community" (Hochschild, 1973; Jacobs, 1969). This kind of community can allow easy access to the peer relationships that provide the emotional support necessary to good physical and mental functioning (Henderson, 1977; Maddison and Walker, 1967; Miller and Ingham, 1976). But it doesn't always. In a study of elderly residents of a slum hotel, Stephens (1974) found the relationships among the women there (who were in a minority) to be characterized by hostility, jealousy, and competition. The men in the hotel viewed the women as out to get an emotional and temporal commitment the men weren't willing to make, and the women viewed the men as only interested in sex. While there was cohesiveness among the men, the women provided each other with very little support, they were locked into where they were by age, economic circumstance, and a desire to maintain independence.

*Homosexuality.* Information on homosexuality and aging is of two types: the incidence of homosexual activities in a predominately heterosexual population, and the effects of aging on the person who is predominantly homosexual. It is the latter on which reasonably current data can be found. As with sex among old people in general, there are a number of stereotypes about people who are predominantly homosexual, and a number of these stereotypes are age-related. Few have to do with gay women.

Gay males have been described as "old" at 30 (Newton, 1972). They are characterized as being youth-oriented and, therefore, more negative to aging, more likely to label themselves old earlier than straight males (Hoffman, 1968; Saghir and Robins, 1973; Simon and Gagnon, 1967; Stearn, 1961; Warren, 1974; Weinberg, 1970). This view has gained credence as a result of studies which have, for the most part, obtained subjects from places such as gay bars, where interactions stress the fleeting sexual interaction rather than an ongoing relationship (Harry and DeVall, 1978; Humphreys, 1970) and where, as a result, youth and physical attractiveness are more important than personality characteristics and mutual interests. Since most heterosexual men are married, it is apparent that they cannot serve as an adequate comparison group for patrons of gay bars. The most logical group to use would be straight male patrons of singles bars (Saghir and Robins, 1973). If married heterosexuals are going to be the controls, then perhaps those homosexuals who are in long-term relationships should be the subjects.

To assess whether or not gay males do, in fact, label themselves older earlier in life, Minnigerode (1976) asked 95 homosexual men between 25 and 68 years of age to classify themselves as young, middle-aged, or old. Most men in their 20s and 30s described themselves as young; most in their 40s and all over 50 described themselves as middle-aged. The mean chronological ages given for the onset of middle-age was 41.29 years and for the onset of old age, 64.78 years. These data are similar to those of Neugarten, Moore, and Lowe (1965), whose middle-aged general sample labeled 40 to 50 years to be middle age and 65 to 75 to be old age.

In viewing partner-age preference among homosexual men, Harry and DeVall's data suggest that substantial variability exists between different segments of the gay world. While agreeing with the literature pointing to a greater youth orientedness among homosexuals, they argue that its degree has been overstated, and depends on age and social class, with middle-class gays, older gays, and those who frequent gay bars being the most youth-oriented. The working-class, the young, and those who visit gay bars less often are interested in older or same-age partners (Harry and DeVall, 1978).

Other stereotypes about gay males are that the process of aging is exceptionally stressful

(Weinberg, 1970) and that they are lonely, isolated, and despairing (Allen, 1961). The "oddities" of the aging homosexual have been commented on (Allen, 1961) and his so-called tendency to regress with age "to a point where he preys on small children" has been cited (Stearn, 1961; Whitehead, 1974).

From their interviews with ten male homosexuals over 50, Francher and Henkin (1973) concluded that adjustment to homosexuality implies an early coping with problems of loneliness and alienation, and the resultant development of a social network that helps insulate them from a certain amount of stress and pressure associated with old age. They further state that "the male social role as defined by the homosexual subculture is predicated on a greater degree of narcissism and youth orientation than the heterosexual male role. At its worst, this focus is self-limiting and may serve to intensify individual maladjustments and psychopathologies. At its best, this emancipation from the traditional male social role can provide alternative role expectations less in conflict with behavior patterns that the aging person is expected to assume." In other words, there are elements of the male homosexual social role that can be compared to the female heterosexual social role and, while these may contribute to a poorer old-age adjustment when not satisfactorily resolved, the coping skills developed in that resolution process allow for greater flexibility in dealing with life crises such as role losses.

Countering the stereotypes of the homosexual as being poorly able to cope with old age is the conclusion by Kelly (1977) that "there is little evidence . . . to suggest that being gay causes problems in old age, but there is a great deal of evidence to suggest that societal stigma causes problems *for* aging gays."

One small sign that societal stigma may be lessening with regard to aging homosexuals is their specific inclusion in Miller's discussion of administrative policies of nursing homes and the sexual practices of residents. While the inclusion of this topic is an advance in responsible consideration of the sexual rights of all nursing home residents, the statement that "written permission from families for homosexual activity should be part of the admission process" (Miller, 1978, p. 173) shows that full acceptance has a way to go.

In interviews with 70 never-married white women, Christenson and Johnson (1973) found eight with extensive homosexual histories, "extensive" meaning that the woman had had 21 or more different homosexual partners or that she had participated in homosexual activities more than 50 times. With two of these women, the homosexual activities occurred entirely before the age of 30, and both women changed to exclusively heterosexual behavior after breaks of four and ten years. In the other six women, the patterns of change varied, but homosexual activities were eventually discontinued by all subjects by the age of 50. Seven of the eight continued heterosexual activities past the time they ceased their homosexual activities. In evaluating the total sexual outlets of these eight women, Christenson and Johnson report that they showed a sexual aging pattern similar to the other sexually active women in the never-married sample.

From interviews with bisexual women during 1973–1975, several patterns of partner gender selection emerged. Many of the women interviewed had spent a very long and satisfactory period in heterosexual behaviors, only later turning to homosexual behavior. With others, it was the other way around. No coherent gender pattern was found in still others (Blumstein and Schwartz, 1976).

The homosexuality that is experienced by women in correctional institutions appears to be situational in nature, with those women who were heterosexual before imprisonment returning to heterosexuality on their release (Giallombardo, 1966; Ward and Kassebaum, 1965).

These sets of findings indicate an intransigence of partner-gender choice that has implications for older women such as those populating "unintentional communities." These older widows and divorcees have been isolated from heterosexual opportunity by demography or choice. It is worth speculating whether or not a significant proportion of them will find sexual release through situationally homosexual contacts. It is also worth wondering if the older male homosexual might turn to heterosexuality in old age when the numbers of available partners for him, too, diminish.

## SEXUAL DYSFUNCTIONS AND TREATMENT

This discussion will focus on those dysfunctions which are most likely to affect those in the middle and later years with some degree of frequency. For example, among women, dyspareunia (pain associated with intercourse) is more likely to be encountered than is vaginismis. Among men, the most common dysfunction by far is secondary impotence, which has been defined as the inability to achieve and/or maintain an erection of sufficient quality to accomplish coital connection 75 percent of the time. Masters and Johnson (1970) also estimate that 50 percent of the general population experiences some degree of sexual dysfunction. There is no reason to suspect that the older segment of the population experiences fewer problems.

## DIAGNOSIS

In most cases, sexual dysfunctions are obvious and there is no problem in making a specific diagnosis. One exception may be in the case of situational orgasmic dysfunction in women, and that difficulty is one of definition.

A second exception concerns the problem identifying the origin of impotence in the male. The diagnosis of impotence is a simple and straightforward one to make. Determining whether the impotence is psychogenic (psychologically based) or biogenic (organically based) is not quite as straightforward, but is important because of the implications for therapy. One of the simplest methods of making this determination involves the use of a penile plethysmograph to measure the male's erectile pattern during sleep. Extensive research indicates that all normally functioning males experience several erections during an eight-hour period of sleep regardless of their age (Karacan, Williams, Thornby, and Salis, 1975). By examining the recording of a male whose erectile pattern has been monitored during one or more nights, it is possible to determine, with a high degree of accuracy, whether the impotence is psychogenic or biogenic (Karacan, Scott, Salis, Attia, Ware, Altinel, and Williams, 1977).

Recently a device has been developed which is inserted into the vagina to assess the amount of vasocongestion which has taken place in the sexually aroused female (Heiman, 1975, 1976). This device contains a light source and a detector which measures the color change in the vaginal tissue. With further development and knowledge, this instrument may be capable of differentiating between organically and psychologically based sexual dysfunctions in the female. It will certainly be of value in assessing the effects of drugs and of physiological problems on the female's responsiveness.

## DYSPAREUNIA AND ORGASMIC DYSFUNCTION

The frequency with which women suffer from these disorders has not been documented. Dyspareunia is common among older women because of the changes which are taking place in the internal and external genitalia as a result of postmenopausal steroid starvation. As mentioned earlier, reduced levels of lubrication, thinning of the vaginal walls, changes in vaginal tissue tone, and shortening of both vaginal length and width may cause pain during intercourse.

Situational orgasmic dysfunction is the phrase used to describe the sexual problem of a woman who has been orgasmic at some point in her life, but is not currently consistently orgasmic. Fewer than half of the women in Hite's (1976) study were able to consistently reach orgasm without supplemental clitoral stimulation by the woman herself or by her partner. Kaplan (1974) has raised the question of whether a woman who is unable to climax during coitus but is able to reach orgasm as a result of manual stimulation is suffering from situational orgasmic dysfunction. She states that "our objective is to enhance the woman's total sexual responsiveness and help her have orgasms more easily, without, however, defining orgasm in coitus as the criterion of sexual normalcy" (Kaplan, 1974, p. 383). Masters and Johnson (1970), however, define their goal in therapy as being the consistent attainment of orgasm during intercourse. Depending on one's orientation, there is then some question regarding this diagnosis.

Whatever definition is eventually decided upon, the cause of situational orgasmic dysfunction can be complex and may involve physiological, psychological, and sociological factors. For example, dyspareunia could be a contributing physiological factor, and menopause a contributing psychological one. The woman may also be responding to the asexual stereotype (sociological) that is culturally assigned to the aging female.

## IMPOTENCE

The incidence of impotence rises rapidly as the male ages. Pearlman (1972), in a study of more than 2,800 males interviewed in a private urological practice, found the following: 5 percent were impotent by their forties, 11 percent in the fifties, 35 percent in the sixties, 59 percent in the seventies, and 85 percent were impotent after the age of 80. Kinsey et al. (1948) found the incidence of impotence to be 25 percent at age 65, 27 percent at age 70, 55 percent at age 75, and 75 percent at age 80. Pearlman's finding of more impotence is no doubt because of his use of a clinical sample, while Kinsey's sample was non-clinical. Pearlman cited several other studies which closely paralleled his own findings, but which also were based on patient samples. The data reported by Pfeiffer et al. (1969) are more like Kinsey's data. The actual incidence of impotence in the male is probably somewhere between the two ranges of numbers, which are significantly different only in the sixties and below.

## THE PHYSICIAN'S ROLE IN IDENTIFYING SEX PROBLEMS

Since the first course in human sexual functioning ever taught in an American medical school was offered at Washington University School of Medicine in 1960 (Belliveau and Richter, 1970), it is not surprising to find that many physicians are untrained and uncomfortable in the area of sexual function and dysfunction. Finkle and Finkle (1977) point out that urologists are often the first specialist that a male with sexual problems seeks out, and they have little or no training in counseling patients with sexual problems. They are trained and function primarily as surgeons. Berezin (1976) reported that almost twice as many sexual problems were uncovered by physicians asking about this subject during history-taking than by physicians who waited for the patients to raise the issue. Of the 60 physicians who participated in the study, only seven percent reported having had training in managing sexual problems while in medical school.

## THE ROLE OF MEDICATION IN SEXUAL DYSFUNCTION

Many older persons suffer from hypertension, depression, anxiety, arteriosclerosis, heart disease, and psychoses, and their treatment involves the use of medications which may affect their sexual functioning. The effects of these drugs on male sexual functioning has been well studied, and although many of the studies have not been conducted with adequate controls, there does appear to be substantial evidence that many of them cause erectile and/or ejaculatory problems (Kotin, Wilbert, Verburg, and Soldinger, 1976; Segraves, 1977). The effects of drugs on female sexual response is not at all well understood since very few studies have been conducted on the female. Segraves (1977) states that "it is unclear whether this represents a tendency for male physicians to be uninterested in female sexual experience or an actual infrequent disturbance of female sexual responsivity by pharmacological agents."

## TREATMENT

Masters and Johnson (1970) were the first to combine the research of others into an effective means for treating sexual dysfunction. Their model involves a combination of behavioral, learning, experiential, and psychodynamic approaches. The main thrust of the model is to teach the couple new ways of interacting and communicating with each other. Great stress is placed on the concept that the couple is the patient, not the individual. The treatment is conducted by a male-female therapy team during an intensive two-week treatment program, and patients must travel to St. Louis where the clinic is located. The treatment approach and results have been reported extensively in their second book (Masters and Johnson, 1970). Failure rates for women over 50 years of age have not been reported for individual dysfunctions, presumably because the number of older patients was too small. Some indication of the age effect is apparent, however, from the statistics on overall failure rates for women over 50. The failure rate for older women for all dysfunctions was approximately 41 percent, compared to 19 percent for the entire research sample. For males over 50, the failure rate for all dysfunctions was 25 percent as compared to 17 percent for the total male sample. Apparently, age is more of a factor in the case of the female than the male.

Many different treatment models have evolved since the development of the Masters and Johnson model, and most are based largely on their approach (Annon, 1974, 1975; Hartman and Fithian, 1972; Kaplan, 1974). As an example, Kaplan typically sees the patient once a week on an outpatient basis and does not insist on a male and female sex therapist team. For certain dysfunctions, for example, premature ejaculation, she is willing to see the individual without involving the partner in every session. She does not always follow a set pattern of treatment and tends to place a little heavier emphasis on the psychodynamics involved than do Masters and Johnson. In spite of these differences, Kaplan reports that her findings are essentially in agreement with those of Masters and Johnson.

Probably of greater importance to the older person are the changes in the Masters and Johnson model which have been proposed by Annon (1974, 1975) and which he calls the PLISSIT model. This is an acronym which describes Annon's hierarchical approach to the behavioral treatment of sexual dysfunctions. He takes the position that the same treatment regimen should not be followed for all patients. In his view, persons suffering from sexual problems experience their difficulties in various levels of complexity. Consequently, the treatment program should reflect this. In this model, the levels of treatment, starting with the least complex, involve *P*ermission, *L*imited *I*nformation, *S*pecific *S*uggestions, and *I*ntensive *T*herapy. Annon suggests that in the simplest cases, the sex problem can be solved by giving the patient permission to do what he or she has already been doing, thereby reducing fear and/or guilt. Other patients may simply require information regarding body anatomy and functioning and sexual myths. The last two levels of treatment essentially involve the use of the techniques developed by Masters and Johnson, but taken somewhat further for cases where persons may be severely inhibited sexually. For example, Annon may begin with desensitization to erotic terms and language. In the authors' experience, there are many older persons who do not need the more intensive levels of therapy, but are able to improve their levels of sexual pleasure as a result of receiving permission and additional information relating to their sexuality. Even with the increased emphasis being placed on disseminating sexual information to the older population, there are many older people who are poorly informed in these matters.

## GROUPS

The group treatment of patients with sexual dysfunctions is another innovation in the field of sex therapy. Barbach (1975) and Heiman, LoPiccolo, and LoPiccolo (1976) pioneered in this area by treating women suffering from both primary and situational orgasmic dysfunction in groups of six to ten participants. Their programs were based in large part on the Masters and Johnson behavior modification style of therapy plus a masturbation desensitization program developed by LoPiccolo and Lobitz (1972). The groups usually meet for approximately two hours once each week for ten weeks. Very high success rates have been reported for these groups if one considers the capacity to reach orgasm through self-stimulation as the goal (Barbach, 1975; Heiman *et al.*, 1976; Leiblum and Ersner-Herschfield, 1977). For example, Leiblum and Ersner-Herschfield report that 14 of the 16 women in their study became reliably orgasmic through self-stimulation as a result of the group program. Transfer of this ability to situations involving partners was less reliable.

Most of the women in the non-orgasmic therapy groups tended to be in the 25 to 45-year-old age category. Schneidman and McGuire (1976) conducted a study which evaluated the influence of the age on outcome results. The subjects in their study all had stable relationships with a partner and had never experienced an orgasm (primary orgasmic dysfunction). One group consisted of females 23 to 34 years of age and the other group consisted of females 35 to 48. At follow-up evaluations conducted six months after termination of the treatment program, 80 percent of the younger women and 60 percent of the older women were orgasmic. Schneidman and McGuire concluded

that "group therapy may be less successful for older women, who may be more successfully treated individually." One should certainly not eliminate the option of using group treatment, however, where the cost of individual treatment precludes its use. Group treatment which precedes individual treatment may also enhance, and thereby shorten, the individual therapy program.

Male groups have also become common in recent years, but the focus of these groups has been on the male without a partner (Lobitz and Baker, 1978; Zilbergeld, 1978). This has not been the case with groups of females. There are, of course, some females without partners who participate in the group sex therapies, but for the most part, that has not been the case. In a way this is unfortunate, since many older women do not have partners.

Although the first male groups dealt with premature ejaculation, in more recent years the emphasis has been on the treatment of other male dysfunctions. The success rate for these groups has varied from 60 percent to 70 percent; some level of improvement has been reported, however, by almost all the group participants. The format of these groups is very similar to that of the female groups.

Combined male and female groups are also being used in the treatment of sexual problems. The results obtained in these groups seem promising. Baker and Nagata (1977) reported a 78 percent improvement in sexual satisfaction of a group of six couples ranging in age from 33 to 64 years after meeting weekly for four weeks (each session lasted three hours). All of the couples entered the group with specific sexual dissatisfactions.

Sexual enhancement groups consisting of both sexes have also become popular. Sviland (1975, 1978), working with older couples individually and in groups, has reported substantial success in helping them enhance their sexual relationships. Rowland and Haynes (1978) found changes in sexual satisfaction and frequency of certain sexual activities for ten married couples, aged 51 to 70, following a six-week group sexual-enhancement program. They reported that "in general, significant increases in sexual satisfaction, frequency of certain sexual activities, and positive attitudes about marital and life satisfaction were found to occur over the course of the sexual enhancement program. These significant increases occurred either during the pre-treatment period or during some combination of phases." These results tend to confirm the previous statements regarding the benefits to be gained for many older people in the area of permission giving and information dissemination.

## HORMONE THERAPY

The use of exogenous estrogens and androgens in the treatment of sexual problems has been discussed briefly in the section on hormones. In the present atmosphere of concern over the unknown side effects of drugs used in chemotherapy, there is a definite trend to use estrogen and testosterone only in cases where there is no alternative. There are drugs available to control vasomotor instability which do not involve estrogens. When estrogen therapy seems to be the treatment of choice, the trend is to use the smallest dose for the least length of time. For the woman who is experiencing lubrication problems, for example, the physician may recommend the topical application of estrogen creams.

For the male, there is a strong resistance to the use of testosterone in treating psychogenic impotence. Only in very specific cases is the well-informed urologist likely to recommend its use. This position appears to be justified on two counts: (1) there is no conclusive evidence that testosterone is beneficial, and (2) the role of testosterone therapy in prostate cancer is uncertain (Fellman, Hastings, Kupperman, and Miller, 1975; Finkle and Finkle, 1977; Kaplan, 1974).

Although it is not a hormone, procaine (or Gerovital, of which procaine is the major component) has been reported to be beneficial in the management of some sexual dysfunctions in men and women. In reviewing the literature on this drug, Ostfeld, Smith, and Stotsky (1977) have concluded that the data are inadequate to support any conclusions regarding the benefits procaine may have on endocrine and sexual function.

## PROSTHETIC DEVICES

Many surgeons during the past few years have turned to the use of penile prostheses to solve organically caused impotency problems. There are basically two types of penile prostheses: the inflatable type developed by Scott, Bradley, and Timm (1973) which uses inflatable Silastic cylinders placed inside each corpus cavernosum and connected by tubing to a pumping mechanism implanted in the scrotal pouch, and the Small-Carrion type, which consists of two partically foam-filled silicone rods which are inserted in the corpus cavernosa. In general, good results have been obtained using both the inflatable type (Furlow, 1976; Kothari, Timm, Frohrib, and Bradley, 1972) and the semi-rigid type (Gottesman, Kosters, Das, and Kaufman, 1977; Loeffler and Iverson, 1976; Pearman, 1972). Most researchers stress the importance of both physiological and psychological evaluation prior to surgery. In addition, the surgeon must properly inform the patient as to what he should expect as a result of the operation.

## NEED FOR THERAPY

More older people are becoming interested in resolving their sexual problems (Martin, 1975; Peterson, 1973), are actively seeking treatment and enhancement of current functioning (Sviland, 1975, 1978), and are looking for more sex information (Feigenbaum, Lowenthal, and Trier, 1967). Many are becoming aware of their interest in developing late-life expressions of sexuality. Kahana (1976) has reported finding that sexual attraction in the elderly emphasizes "a confidante to talk and relate to or someone to hug and kiss rather than having a partner for genital sexuality per se." Butler (1975) talks about the imaginative and significant "second language of sex," the caressing, touching, and tenderness that are being creatively developed by many in their middle and later years, not necessarily as an alternate to genital sexuality, but as an enhancement of total sexuality.

It appears that the majority of men and women seeking treatment can be helped to resolve their sexual problems. It is the opinion of the authors that essentially all older persons can reach a higher level of sexual pleasure even though they may not attain a specific functional goal which they may have rigidly defined for themselves.

## SUMMARY

Physiological changes occur in the aging male and female and may show an effect on their sexual functioning. In some postmenopausal women, hormonal changes may cause tissue and lubrication changes leading to painful intercourse and an increase in vaginal infection. The physiological effects of menopause have no direct relationship to a woman's sexual interest levels. Women retain their physiological capacity to have and enjoy sex throughout their lives.

The effects of age-related declines in testosterone production in men are unclear, but testosterone is now thought to play less of a role in male potency than was previously believed. Aging males find that, in general, it takes longer to reach full erection and to regain an erection after detumescence occurs. The erection, once achieved, can be maintained for longer periods before ejaculation occurs in the older male.

The effects on sexual functioning of most

disease processes are largely psychological, and where they are not, can often be avoided or ameliorated by proper planning or treatment by the attending physician. One notable exception is diabetes, which appears to have an effect on sexual functioning, especially in males. The mechanisms of this effect are not fully understood.

Sexual activity in men declines with age; sexual interest, on the other hand, remains fairly constant. Among women, sexual interest and activity change less with age, but both are consistently lower than they are among men. It has been suggested that this difference is the result of a defense mechanism protecting women from the sexual frustrations inherent in their usual late-life status as widows.

The psychosocial issue having the greatest influence on female sexuality in later life is partner availability. Following that are her enjoyment of sex when younger, her present orgasmic capability, and her partner's age. Many more factors account for less of the variability in male sexuality. Some of these are health, past sexual experience, and psychological and social factors.

Some marriages that survive into middle and old age can be described as disenchanted but others are sometimes revitalized. The more romantic relationships are the ones which are more likely to endure and to survive the first two major crises of older marriages; the shift from parental to spousal role and the post-retirement incorporation of the husband into the marriage. Because of the strong effect that marital status has on female sexuality, the existance as well as the character of a marriage is important in late-life sexual expression. The final crisis of marriage—widowhood—involves an entirely different kind of shift, to "singlehood," and is most likely to be experienced by women.

Among single older people, the most positive and independent are those who never married, who have developed coping styles to deal with their single status. Similarly, elderly homosexuals also appear to have developed adequate mechanisms for coping with problems of loneliness and alienation.

Certain sexual dysfunctions are less likely to occur among the elderly, but others are more likely, for example, dyspareunia, which may occur as a result of the effects of hormonal changes on the tissues. Situational orgasmic dysfunction may also become a problem for the aging woman who must cope with psychological and sociological assaults on her sexuality. Among men, the incidence of secondary impotence rises rapidly with age. Drug effects may also contribute to sexual dysfunction, especially in males. Well-trained and sympathetic physicians and therapists can do much to enhance the older person's sexuality by utilizing present educational and therapeutic modalities that have been demonstrated to be effective, by investigating ways of helping the older person avoid sexual problems, and by developing new methods of treating those problems which do occur.

# REFERENCES

ALLEN, C. 1961. *In*, I. Rubin (ed.), *The Third Sex*, pp. 91–95. New York: New Book Company.

ANNON, J. S. 1974. *The Behavioral Treatment of Sexual Problems. Volume I: Brief Therapy.* Honolulu: Enabling Systems.

ANNON, J. S. 1975. *The Behavioral Treatment of Sexual Problems. Volume II: Intensive Therapy.* Honolulu: Enabling Systems.

ARD, B. N. 1977. Sex in lasting marriages: A longitudinal study. *Journal of Sex Research, 13,* 274–285.

BAKER, L. D., AND NAGATA, F. S. 1977. A group approach to the treatment of couples with sexual dysfunctions. Paper presented at the annual meeting of the American Association of Sex Educators, Counselors, and Therapists, San Francisco.

BARBACH, L. G. 1975. *For Yourself: The Fulfillment of Female Sexuality.* New York: Doubleday.

BARDWICK, J. M. 1971. *The Psychology of Women.* New York: Harper & Row.

BARRETT, J. 1972. *Gerontological Psychology.* Springfield, Ill.: Charles C Thomas.

BARTUSKA, D. G. 1977. Physiology of aging: Metabolic changes during the climacteric and menopausal periods. *Clinical Obstetrics and Gynecology, 20,* 105–112.

BEAUMONT, P. J. V., BANCROFT, J. H. J., BEARDWOOD, C. J., AND RUSSELL, G. F. M. 1972. Behavioral changes after treatment with testosterone. A case report. *Psychological Medicine, 2,* 70–72.

BEIGEL, H. G. 1952. *Encyclopedia of Sex Education.* New York: William Penn.

BELLIVEAU,.F., AND RICHTER, L. 1970. *Understanding Human Sexual Inadequacy.* Boston: Little, Brown.

BENEDEK, T. 1950. Climacterium: A developmental phase. *Psychoanalytic Quarterly, 19,* 1–27

BEREZIN, M. A. 1969. Sex and old age: A review of the literature. *Journal of Geriatric Psychiatry, 2,* 131–149.

BEREZIN, M. A. 1976. Sex and old age: A further review of the literature. *Journal of Geriatric Psychiatry, 9,* 189–209.

BERNARDO, F. M. 1968. Widowhood status in the United States: Perspective on a neglected aspect of the family life-cycle. *Family Coordinator, 17,* 191–203.

BERNARDO, F. 1970. Survivorship and social isolation: The case of the aged widower. *Family Coordinator, 19,* 11–15.

BLAU, A. 1961. Structural constraints on friendship in old age. *American Sociological Review, 26,* 429–439.

BLOCH, A., MAEDER, J., AND HAISSLY, J. 1975. Sexual problems after myocardial infarction. *American Heart Journal, 90,* 536–537.

BLOOD, R. O. 1955. *Anticipating Your Marriage.* Glencoe, Ill.: Free Press.

BLOOD, R. O., AND WOLFE, D. M. 1960. *Husbands and Wives: The Dynamics of Married Living.* New York: Free Press.

BLUMSTEIN, P. W., AND SCHWARTZ, P. 1976. Bisexuality in women. *Archives of Sexual Behavior, 5,* 171–181.

BOCK, E. W., and Webber, I. L. 1972. Suicide among the elderly: Isolating widowhood and mitigating alternatives. *Journal of Marriage and the Family, 34,* 24–31.

BOTWINICK, J. 1973. *Aging and Behavior: A Comprehensive Integration of Research Findings.* New York: Springer Publ.

BRADDOM, R. L., HOLLIS, J. B., AND CASTELL, D. O. 1977. Diabetic peripheral neuropathy: A correlation of nerve conduction studies and clinical findings. *Archives of Physical Medicine and Rehabilitation, 58,* 308–313.

BROTMAN, H. B. 1971. *Facts and Figures on Older Americans, Number 2. The older Population Revisted: First Results of the 1970 Census.* Washington, DC: Administration on Aging, US DHEW.

BROWN, G. W., BHROLCHAIN, M. N., AND HARRIS, T. 1975. Social class and psychiatric disturbance among women in an urban population. *Sociology, 8,* 225–254.

BURNHAM, W. R., LENNARD-JONES, J. E., AND BROOKE, B. N. 1977. Sexual problems among married ileostomists. *Gut, 18,* 673–677.

BURNSIDE, I. M. 1975. Sexuality and the older adult: Implications for nursing. *In,* I. M. Burnside (ed.), *Sexuality and Aging,* pp.26–34. Los Angeles: University of Southern California Press.

BUTLER, R. N. 1967. Reasearch and clinical observations on the psychologic reactions to physical changes with age. *Mayo Clinic Proceeding, 42,* 596–619.

BUTLER, R. N. 1975. Sex after 65. *In,* L. E. Brown and E. O. Ellis (eds.), *The Later Years,* pp.129–142. Acton, M.: Publishing Sciences Group, American Medical Association.

CAMERON, P. 1969. The "life-force" and age. *Journal of Gerontology, 24,* 199–200.

CAMERON, P. 1970. The generation gap: Beliefs about sexuality and self-reported sexuality. *Developmental Psychology, 3,* 272–273.

CAMERON, P., AND BIBER, H. 1973. Sexual thought throughout the life-span. *Gerontologist, 13,* 144–147.

CAVAN, R. S. 1973. Speculations on innovations to conventional marriage in old age. *Gerontologist, 13,* 409–411.

CHRISTENSON, C. V., AND GAGNON, J. H. 1965. Sexual behavior in a group of older women. *Journal of Gerontology, 20,* 351–356.

CHRISTENSON, C. V., AND JOHNSON, A. B. 1973. Sexual patterns in a group of older never-married women. *Journal of Geriatric Psychiatry, 6,* 80–98.

COOPER, A. J., ISMAIL, A. A. A., SMITH, C. G., AND LORAINE, J. A. 1970. Androgen function in "psychogenic" and "constitutional" types of impotence. *British Medical Journal, 3,* 17–20.

CUBBER, J. F., AND HARROFF, P. B. 1966. *The Significant Americans.* New York: Appleton Century.

CUMMING, E., AND HENRY, W. H. 1961. *Growing Old: The Process of Disengagement.* New York: Basic Books.

DEAN, S. R. 1966. Sin and senior citizens. *Journal of the American Geriatric Society, 14,* 935-938.

DENBER, H. C. B. 1968. Sexual problems in the mature female. *Psychosomatics, 9*(4), Section 2, 40–43.

DeNIGOLA, P., AND PERUZZA, M. 1974. Sex in the aged. *Journal of the American Geriatrics Society, 22,* 380–382.

DENNERSTEIN, L., WOOD, C., AND BURROWS, G. D. 1977. Sexual response following hysterectomy and oophorectomy. *Obstetrics and Gynecology, 49,* 92–96.

DEUTSCHER, I. 1968. The quality of postparental life. *In,* B. L. Neugarten (ed.), *Middle Age and Aging,* pp. 263–268. Chicago: University of Chicago Press.

EDWARDS, A. E., AND HUSTED, J. R. 1976. Penile sensitivity, age, and sexual behavior. *Journal of Clinical Psychology, 32,* 697-700.

EISDORFER, C., AND RASKIND, M. 1975. Aging, hormones, and human behavior. *In* B. E. Eleftheriou and R. L. Sprott (eds.), *Hormonal Correlates of Behavior,* p. 377. New York: Plenum.

ELLENBERG, M. 1971. Impotence in diabetes: The neurologic factor. *Annals of Internal Medicine, 75,* 213–219.

ELLENBERG, M. 1973. Impotence in diabetes: A neurologic rather than an endocrinologic problem. *Medical Aspects of Human Sexuality, 7,* 12–18.

ELLENBERG, M. 1977. Sexual aspects of the female diabetic. *The Mount Sinai Journal of Medicine, 44,* 495–500.

ERVIN, C. V. 1973. Psychologic adjustment to mastectomy. *Medical Aspects of Human Sexuality, 7,* 42–65.

ESKIN B. A. 1977. Commentary. *Medical Aspects of Human Sexuality, 11*(6), 27.

FEIGENBAUM, E. M., LOWENTHAL, M. F., AND TRIER, M. L. 1967. Aged are confused and hungry for sex information. *Geriatric Focus, 5,* 2.

FELDMAN, H. 1964. Development of the husband-wife

relationship. Preliminary report, Cornell studies of marital development. Department of Child Development and Family Relationships, New York: Cornell University.

FELLMAN, S. L., HASTINGS, D. W., KUPPERMAN, H., AND MILLER, W. W. 1975. Should androgens be used to treat impotence in men over 50? *Medical Aspects of Human Sexuality, 9*(7), 32–43.

FELSTEIN, I. 1970. *Sex and the Longer Life.* London: Penguin.

FINKLE, A. L., AND FINKLE, P. S. 1977. How counseling may solve sexual problems of aging men. *Geriatrics, 32,* 34–89.

FINKLE, A. L., MOYERS, T. G., TOBENKIN, M. I., AND KARG S. J. 1959. Sexual potency in aging males: I. Frequency of coitus among clinic patients. *Journal of the American Medical Association, 170,* 1391–1393.

FRANCHER, J. S., AND HENKIN, J. 1973. The menopausal queen: Adjustment to aging and the male homosexual. *American Journal of Orthopsychiatry, 43,* 670–674.

FREEMAN, J. T. 1961. Sexual capacities in the aging male. *Geriatrics, 16,* 37–43.

FURLOW, W. L. 1976. Surgical management of impotence using the inflatable penile prosthesis. *Mayo Clinic Proceedings, 51,* 325-328.

GADPAILLE, W. J. 1975. *The Cycles of Sex.* New York: Scribner's.

GASKELL, P. 1971. The importance of penile blood pressure in cases of impotence. *Canadian Medical Association Journal, 105,* 1047–1051.

GEBHARD, P. H. 1971. Postmarital coitus among widows and divorcees. *In,* P. Bohannan (ed.), *Divorce and After,* pp. 81–96. Garden City, NY: Doubleday.

GIALLOMBARDO, R. 1966. *Society of Women.* New York: John Wiley.

GIAMBRA, L. M., AND MARTIN, C. E. 1977. Sexual daydreams and quantitative aspects of sexual actitity: Some relations for males across adulthood. *Archives of Sexual Behavior, 6,* 497–505.

GLOVER, G. H. 1977. Sex counseling of the elderly. *Hospital Practice, 12* (6), 101–113.

GOLDE, P., AND KOGAN, N. 1959. A sentence completion procedure for assessing attitudes toward old people. *Journal of Gerontology, 14, 355–360.*

GOODMAN, E. 1978. Women mourn, men replace. *Miami Herald,* February 2, 1978.

GOTTESMAN, J. E., KOSTERS, S., DAS, S., AND KAUFMAN, J. J. 1977. The Small-Carrion prosthesis for male impotency. *The Journal of Urology, 117,* 289–290.

GRANT, V. W. 1957. *The Psychology of Sexual Emotion.* New York: Longmans, Green and Co.

GREEN, R. 1975. Human sexuality: Research and treatment frontiers. *In* S. Arieti (ed.), *American Handbook of Psychiatry,* Vol. 6, pp. 665–691. New York: Basic Books.

GRÜNER, O. P., NAAS, R., AND FRETHEIM, B. 1977. Marital sexual adjustment after colectomy. *Scand. Journal of Gastroenterology, 12* (2), 193–197.

GUBRIUM, J. F. 1974. Marital desolation and the evaluation of everyday life in old age. *Journal of Marriage and the Family, 35,* 107–113.

GUBRIUM, J. F. 1975. Being single in old age. *International Journal of Aging and Human Development, 6,* 29–41.

HARRY, J., AND DEVALL, W. 1978. Age and sexual culture among homosexually oriented males. *Archives of Sexual Behavior, 7,* 199–209.

HARTMAN, W. E., AND FITHIAN, M. A. 1972. *Treatment of Sexual Dysfunction.* Long Beach, Ca. Center for Marital and Sexual Studies.

HEGELER, S. 1976. Sexual Behavior in Elderly Danish Males. Paper presented at the International Symposium on Sex Education and Therapy, Stockholm, Sweden.

HEIMAN, J. R. 1975. The physiology of erotica: Women's sexual arousal. *Psychology Today, 8,* 91–94.

HEIMAN, J. R. 1976. Issues in the use of psychophysiology to assess female sexual dysfunction. *Journal of Sex and Marital Therapy, 2,* 197–204.

HEIMAN, J. R. 1978. Uses of psychophysiology in the assessment and treatment of sexual dysfunction. *In,* J. LoPiccolo and L. LoPiccolo (eds.), *Handbook of Sex Therapy,* pp. 126–135. New York: Plenum.

HEIMAN, J. R., LOPICCOLO L., AND LOPICCOLO, J. 1976. *Becoming Orgasmic: A Sexual Growth Program for Women.* Englewood Cliffs, N.J. Prentice-Hall.

HELTSLEY, M., AND BRODERICK, C. B. 1969. Religiosity and premarital sexual permissiveness: Reexamination of Reiss's traditionalism proposition. *Journal of Marriage and the Family, 31,* 441–443.

HENDERSON, S. 1977. The social network, support and neurosis: The function of attachment in adult life. *British Journal of Psychiatry, 131,* 185–191.

HITE, S. 1976. *The Hite Report.* New York: Macmillan.

HOCHSCHILD, A. R., 1973. *The Unexpected Community.* Englewood Cliffs: Prentice-Hall.

HOFFMAN, M. 1968. *The Gay World.* New York: Bantam Books.

HUMPHREYS, R.A.L. 1970. *Tearoom Trade.* Chicago: Aldine.

JACOBS, R. H. 1969. The friendship club: A case study of the segregated aged. *Gerontologist, 9,* 276–280.

JACOBS, R. H., AND VINICK, B. 1977. *Reengagement in Later Life.* Stamford, Conn.: Greylock Publishers.

JAMISON, K. R., WELLISCH, D. K., AND PASNAU, R. O. 1978. Psychosocial aspects of mastectomy: I. The woman's perspective. *American Journal of Psychiatry, 135,* 432–436.

KAAS, M. J. 1978. Sexual expression of the elderly in nursing homes. *Gerontologist, 18,* 372–378.

KAHANA, B. 1976. Social and psychological aspects of sexual behavior among the aged. *In,* E. S. E. Hafez (ed.), *Aging and Reproductive Physiology,* Vol. 2, pp. 89–95. Ann Arbor, Mich.: Ann Arbor Science.

KAPLAN, H. S. 1974. *The New Sex Therapy*. New York: Brunner/Mazel.

KARACAN, I. 1969. A simple and inexpensive transducer for quantitative measurements of penile erection during sleep. *Behavior Research Methods and Instruments, l,* 251–252.

KARACAN, I., SCOTT, F. B., SALIS, P. J., ATTIA, S. L., WARE, J. C., ALTINEL, A., AND WILLIAMS, R. L. 1977. Nocturnal erections, differential diagnosis of impotence, and diabetes. *Biological Psychiatry, 12,* 373–380.

KARACAN, I., WILLIAMS, R. L., THORNBY, J. I., AND SALIS, P. J. 1975. Sleep-related tumescence as a function of age. *American Journal of Psychiatry, 132,* 932.

KASSELL, V. 1966. Polygamy after 60. *Geriatrics, 21,* 214–218.

KAVANAUGH, T., AND SHEPPARD, R. J. 1977. Sexual activity after myocardial infarction. *Canadian Medical Association Journal, 116,* 1250–1253.

KELLY, J. 1977. The aging male homosexual: Myth and reality. *Gerontologist, 17,* 328–443.

KENT, S. 1975. Impotence as a consequence of organic disease. *Geriatrics, 30,* 155–157.

KINSEY, A. C., POMEROY, W. B., AND MARTIN, C. E. 1948. *Sexual Behavior in the Human Male.* Philadelphia: W. B. Saunders.

KINSEY, A. C., POMEROY, W. B., MARTIN, C. E., AND GEBHARD, P. H. 1953. *Sexual Behavior in the Human Female.* Philadelphia: W. B. Saunders.

KLEEGMAN, S. 1959. Frigidity in women. *Quarterly Review of Surgery, Obstetrics, and Gynecology, 16,* 243–248.

KOLODNY, R. C., KAHN, C. B., GOLDSTEIN, H. H., AND BARNETT, D. M. 1974. Sexual dysfunction in diabetic men. *Diabetes, 23,* 306–309.

KOTHARI, D. R., TIMM, G. W., FROHRIB, D. A., AND BRADLEY, W. E. 1972. An implantable fluid transfer system for treatment of impotence. *Journal of Biomechanics, 5,* 567–570.

KOTIN, J., WILBERT, D. E., VERBURG, D., AND SOLDINGER, S. M. 1976. Thionidamine and sexual dysfunction. *The American Journal of Psychiatry, 133,* 82–85.

KUTNER, B., FANSHEL, D., TOGO, A., AND LANGER, T. 1956. *Five Hundred Over Sixty.* New York: Russell Sage Foundation.

LATORRE, R. A., AND KEAR, K. 1977. Attitudes toward sex in the aged. *Archives of Sexual Behavior, 6,* 203–213.

LAWRENCE, A. M., AND ABRAIRA, C. 1976. Diabetic neuropathy: A review of clinical manifestations. *Annals of Clinical and Laboratory Science, 6,* 78–83.

LEDGER, W. J. 1977. Infections in elderly women. *Clinical Obstetrics and Gynecology, 20,* 145–153.

LEIBLUM, S. R., AND ERSNER-HERSCHFIELD, R. 1977. Sexual enhancement groups for dysfunctional women: An evaluation. *Journal of Sex and Marital Therapy, 3,* 139–152.

LEMERE, F. 1976. Sexual impairment in recovered alcoholics. *Medical Aspects of Human Sexuality, 10,* 69–70.

LEMERE, F., AND SMITH, J. D. 1973. Alcohol-induced sexual impotence. *American Journal of Psychiatry, 130,* 212–213.

LIANG, D. S. 1973. *Facts About Aging.* Springfield, Ill.: Charles C Thomas.

LIEBERMAN, B. 1971. *Human Sexual Behavior: A Book of Readings.* New York: John Wiley.

LIEF, H. I. 1977. Inhibited sexual desire. *Medical Aspects of Human Sexuality, 11*(7), 94–95.

LOBITZ, W. C., AND BAKER, E. L. 1978. Group treatment of single males with erectile dysfunction. *Archives of Sexual Behavior,* in press.

LOEFFLER, R. A., AND IVERSON, R. E. 1976. Surgical treatment of impotence in the male. *Plastic and Reconstructive Surgery, 58,* 292–297.

LONG, I. 1976. Human sexuality and aging. *Social Casework, 57,* 237–244.

LOPICCOLO, J., AND LOBITZ, W. C. 1972. The role of masturbation in the treatment of orgasmic dysfunction. *Archives of Sexual Behavior, 2,* 163–171.

LOWENTHAL, M. F. 1968. Social isolation and mental illness in old age. *In,* B. L. Neugarten (ed.), *Middle Age and Aging,* pp. 220–234. Chicago: University of Chicago Press.

LOWENTHAL, M. F., AND CHIRABOGA, D. 1972. Transition to the empty nest: Crisis, challenge, or relief? *Archives of General Psychiatry, 26,* 8.

MADDISON, D. C., AND VIOLA, A. 1968. The health of widows in the year following bereavement. *Journal of Psychosomatic Research, 12,* 279–306.

MADDISON, D. C., AND WALKER, W. L. 1967. Factors affecting the outcome of conjugal bereavement. *British Journal of Psychiatry, 113,* 1057–1067.

MADORSKY, M. L., ASHAMALLA, M. G., SCHUSSLER, I., LYONS, H. R., AND MILLER, G. H. 1976. Post-prostatectomy impotence. *The Journal of Urology, 115,* 401–403.

MANN, C. H. 1977. Psychosexual problems of middle age. *Medical Aspects of Human Sexuality, 11*(6), 125–126.

MARMOR, J. 1974. *Psychiatry in Transition.* New York: Brunner/Mazel.

MARTIN, C. E. 1975. Marital and sexual factors in relation to age, disease, and longevity. *In,* R. D. Wirt, G. Winokur, and M. Roff (eds.), *Life History Research in Psychopathology,* Vol. 4, pp. 326–347. Minneapolis: University of Minnesota Press.

MASLOW, A. H. 1954. *Motivation and Personality.* New York: Harper & Row.

MASTERS, W. H., AND JOHNSON, V. E. 1966. *Human Sexual Response.* Boston: Little, Brown.

MASTERS, W. H., AND JOHNSON, V. E. 1970. *Human Sexual Inadequacy.* Boston: Little, Brown.

MCKAIN, W. C. 1969. Retirement marriages. *Agriculture Experiment Station Monograph No. 3.* Storrs, Conn.:

University of Connecticut.

MILLER, D. B. 1978. Sexual practices and administrative policies in long-term-care institutions. *In*, R. L. Solnick (ed.), *Sexuality and Aging*, pp. 163–175. Los Angeles: University of Southern California Press.

MILLER, P. M., AND INGHAM, J. G. 1976. Friends, confidants, and symptoms. *Social Psychiatry, 11*, 51–58.

MINNIGERODE, F. A. 1976. Age-status leveling in homosexual men. *Journal of Homosexuality, 1*, 273–276.

MONROE, S. E., AND MENON, K. M. J. 1977. Changes in reproductive hormone secretion during the climacteric and postmenopausal periods. *Clinical Obstetrics and Gynecology, 20*, 113–122.

NEUGARTEN, B. L., MOORE, J. M., AND LOWE, J. C. 1965. Age norms, age constraints, and adult socialization. *American Journal of Sociology, 70*, 710–717.

NEUGARTEN, B. L., WOOD, V., KRAINES, R. J., AND LOOMIS, B. 1968. Women's attitudes toward the menopause. *In*, B. L. Neugarten (ed.), *Middle Age and Aging*, pp. 195–200. Chicago: University of Chicago Press.

NEWMAN, G., AND NICHOLS, C. R. 1960. Sexual activities and attitudes in older persons. *Journal of the American Medical Association, 173*, 33–35.

NEWTON, E. 1972. *Mother Camp: Female Impersonators in America*. Englewood Cliffs, N.J.: Prentice-Hall.

OSTFELD, A., SMITH, C. M., AND STOTSKY, B. A. 1977. The systemic use of procaine in the treatment of the elderly: A review. *Journal of the American Geriatrics Society, 25*, 1–19.

PALMORE, E. 1971. Attitudes toward aging as shown by humor. *Gerontologist, 11*, 181–186.

PEARLMAN, C. K. 1972. Frequency of intercourse in males at different ages. *Medical Aspects of Human Sexuality, 6*, 92.

PEARMAN, R. O. 1972. Insertion of a silastic penile prosthesis for the treatment of organic sexual impotence. *The Journal of Urology, 107*, 802–806.

PEBERDY, G. 1967. Sex and its problems. X. Sexual adjustment at the climacteric. *Practitioner, 199*, 564–571.

PERSKY, H., LIEF, H. I., STRAUSS, D., MILLER, W. R., AND O'BRIEN, C. P. 1978. Plasma testosterone level and sexual behavior of couples. *Archives of Sexual Behavior, 7*, 157–173.

PETERSON, J. A. 1973. Marital and family therapy involving the aged. *Gerontologist, 13*, 27–30.

PFEIFFER, E. 1969. Sexual behavior in old age *In*, E. W. Busse and E. Pfeiffer (eds.), *Behavior and Adaptation in Late Life*, pp. 151–162. Boston: Little, Brown.

PFEIFFER, E. 1970. Survival in old age: Physical, psychological and social correlates of longevity. *Journal of the American Geriatrics Society, 17*, 273–285.

PFEIFFER, E., AND DAVIS, G. C. 1972. Determinants of sexual behavior in middle and old age. *Journal of the American Geriatrics Society, 20*, 151–158.

PFEIFFER, E., VERWOERDT, A., AND WANG, H. S. 1968. Sexual behavior in aged men and women. I. Observations on 254 community volunteers. *Archives of General Psychiatry, 19*, 753–758.

PFEIFFER, E., VERWOERDT, A., AND WANG, H. S. 1969. The natural history of sexual behavior in a biologically advantaged group of aged individuals. *Journal of Gerontology, 24*, 193–198.

PFEIFFER, E., VERWOERDT, A., AND DAVIS, G. C. 1972. Sexual behavior in middle life. *American Journal of Psychiatry, 128*, 1262–1267.

PIHLBLAD, C., AND ADAMS, D. 1972. Widowhood, social participation and life satisfaction. *Aging and Human Development, 3*, 323–330.

PINEO, P. C. 1968. Disenchantment in the later years of marriage. *In*, B. L. Neugarten (ed.), *Middle Age and Aging*, pp. 258–262. Chicago: University of Chicago Press.

POLIVY, J. 1977. Psychological effects of mastectomy on a woman's feminine self-concept. *The Journal of Nervous and Mental Diseases, 164*, 77–87.

POST, F. 1967. Sex and its problems. IX. Disorders of sex in the elderly. *Practitioner, 199*, 377–382.

PRESSEY, S. L., AND KUHLEN, R. G. 1957. *Psychological Development Through the Life Span*. New York: Harper & Row.

RABOCH, J., MELLAN, J., AND STARKA, L. 1975. Plasma testosterone in male patients with sexual dysfunctions. *Archives of Sexual Behavior, 4*, 541–545.

RENSHAW, D. C. 1975. Sexuality and depression in adults and the elderly. *Medical Aspects of Human Sexuality, 9*, 40–62.

RILEY, M. W., AND FONER, A. E. 1968. *Aging and Society, Vol. I, An Inventory of Research Findings*. New York: Russell Sage Foundation.

ROSOW, I. 1968. Housing and local ties of the aged. *In*, B. L. Neugarten (ed.), *Middle Age and Aging*, pp. 382–389. Chicago: University of Chicago Press.

ROSSMAN, I. 1978. Sexuality and aging: An internist's perspective. *In*, R. L. Solnick (ed.), *Sexuality and Aging*, pp. 66–77. Los Angeles: University of Southern California Press.

ROWLAND, K. F., AND HAYNES, S. N. 1978. A sexual enhancement program for elderly couples. *Journal of Sex and Marital Therapy, 4*, 91–113.

RUBIN, I. 1965. *Sexual Life After Sixty*. New York: Basic Books.

RUBIN, I. 1968. The sexless older years, a socially harmful stereotype. *Annals of the American Academy of Political and Social Sciences, 376*, 86–96.

SABOTKA, J. J. 1969. An evaluation of Afrodex in the management of male impotence: A double-blind cross-over study. *Current Therapy Research, 11*, 87–94.

SAGHIR, M. T., AND ROBINS, E. 1973. *Male and Female Homosexuality: A Comprehensive Investigation*. Baltimore: Williams & Wilkins.

SCHEINGOLD, L. D., AND WAGNER, N. N. 1974. *Sound Sex*

*and the Aging Heart.* New York: Human Sciences Press.

SCHLESSINGER, B., AND MILLER, G. A. 1973. Sexuality and the aged. *Medical Aspects of Human Sexuality, 3,* 46–52.

SCHNEIDMAN, B., AND MCGUIRE, L. 1976. Group therapy for nonorgasmic women. Two age levels. *Archives of Sexual Behavior, 5,* 239–247.

SCOTT, F. B., BRADLEY, W. E., AND TIMM, G. W. 1973. Management of erectile impotence: Use of implantable inflatable prostheses. *Urology, 2,* 80–82.

SEGRAVES, R. T. 1977. Pharmacological agents causing sexual dysfunctions. *Journal of Sex and Marital Therapy, 3,* 157–176.

SILVERSTONE, B., AND WYNTER, L. 1975. The effects of introducing a heterosexual living space. *Gerontologist, 15,* 83–87.

SIMON, W., AND GAGNON, J. H. 1967. *Sexual Deviance.* New York: Harper & Row.

SIMON, W., AND GAGNON, J. H. 1969. On psychosexual development. *In,* D. A. Goslin (ed.), *Handbook of Socialization Theory and Research,* pp. 733–752. Chicago:Rand McNally.

SNYDER, E. E., AND SPREITZER, E. 1976. Attitudes of the aged toward non-traditional sexual behavior. *Archives of Sexual Behavior, 5,* 249–254.

SOLNICK, R. L., AND BIRREN, J. E. 1977. Age and male erectile responsiveness. *Archives of Sexual Behavior, 6,* 1–9.

STANLEY, E. 1977. Emergence of strong sexual drives in women past thirty. *Medical Aspects of Human Sexuality, 11*(6), 18–27.

STEARN, J. 1961. *The Sixth Man.* New York: Doubleday.

STEIN, R. A. 1977. The effect of exercise training on heart rate during coitus. *Circulation, 55,* 732–740.

STEPHENS, J. 1974. Romance in the SRO. *Gerontologist, 14,* 279–282.

STRYKER, J. C. 1977. Use of hormones in women over forty. *Clinical Obstetrics and Gynecology, 20,* 155–164.

SUTTERLY, D. C., AND DONNELLY, G. F. 1973. *Perspectives in Human Development.* Philadelphia: Lippincott.

SVILAND, M. A. P. 1975. Helping elderly couples become sexually liberated: Psycho–social issues. *The Counseling Psychologist, 1*(5), 67–72.

SVILAND, M. A. P. 1978. A program of sexual liberation and growth in the elderly. *In,* R. L. Solnick (ed.), *Sexuality and Aging,* pp. 96–114. Los Angeles: University of Southern California Press.

SYMONDS, P. N. 1946. *The Dynamics of Human Adjustment.* New York: Appleton Century Crofts.

TAYLOR, R. B. 1973. *Feeling Alive After 65.* New Rochelle, N. H. Arlington Publisher.

TIMIRAS, P. S., AND MEISAMI, E. 1972. Changes in gonadal function. *In,* P. S. Timiras (ed.), *Developmental Physiology and Aging,* pp. 527–541. New York: Macmillan.

TOWNSEND, P. 1957. *The Family Life of Old People.* London:

Routledge and Kegan Paul.

TREAS, J., AND VAN HILST, A. 1976. Marriage and remarriage rates among older Americans. *Gerontologist, 16,* 132–136.

TROLL, L. E. 1977. Poor, dumb, and ugly. *In,* L. E. Troll, J. Israel, and K. Israel (eds.), *Looking Ahead,* pp. 4–13. Englewood Cliffs, N.J.: Prentice-Hall.

TUCKER, C. E. 1971. Clinical evaluation and management of the impotent. *Journal of the American Geriatrics Society, 19,* 180–186.

TUNSTALL, J. 1966. *Old and Alone: A Sociological Study of Old People.* London: Routledge and Kegan Paul.

ULLERSTROM, L. 1966. *The Erotic Minorities.* New York: Grove Press.

U. S. BUREAU OF THE CENSUS, 1977. *Statistical Abstract of the United States: 1977* (98th ed.). Washington, DC.

VERMEULEN, A. 1976. The hormonal activities of the postmenopausal ovary. *Journal of Clinical Endocrinology and Metabolism, 42,* 247–253.

VERMEULEN, A., RUBENS, R., AND VERDONCK, L. 1972. Testosterone secretion and metabolism in male senescence. *Journal of Clinical Endocrinology and Metabolism, 34,* 730.

VERWOERDT, A., PFEIFFER, E., AND WANG, H. S. 1969a. Sexual behavior in senescence. Changes in sexual activity and interest of aging men and women. *Jounal of Geriatric Psychiatry, 2,* 163–180.

VERWOERDT, A., PFEIFFER, E., AND WANG, H. S. 1969b. Sexual behavior in senescence. II. Patterns of sexual activity and interest. *Geriatrics, 24,* 137–154.

WARD, D. A., AND KASSEBAUM, G. G. 1965. *Women's Prison: Sex and Social Structure.* Chicago: Aldine.

WARREN, C. 1974. *Identity and Community in the Gay World.* New York: John Wiley.

WASOW, M. 1977. Sexuality in homes for the aged.*Concern in the Care of the Aging, 3*(6), 20–21.

WASOW, M., AND LOEB, M.B. 1977. Sexuality in nursing homes. *In,* R. L. Solnick (ed.), *Sexuality and Aging,* pp. 154–162. Los Angeles: University of Southern California Press.

WEG, R. B. 1978. The physiology of sexuality in aging. *In* R. L. Solnick (ed.), *Sexuality and Aging,* pp. 48–65. Los Angeles: University of Southern California Press.

WEINBERG, J. 1969. Sexual expression in late life. *American Journal of Psychiatry, 126,* 713–716.

WEINBERG, M. 1970. The male homosexual: Age-related variation in social and psychological characteristics. *Social Problems, 17,* 527–537.

WEINSTEIN, M., AND ROBERTS, M. 1977. Sexual potency following surgery for rectal carcinoma. *Annals of Surgery, 185,* 295–300.

WEINSTEIN, M. H., AND MACHLEDER, H. I. 1975. Sexual function after aorto-iliac surgery. *Annals of Surgery, 181,* 787–790.

WEISS, H. D. 1972. The physiology of human penile

erections. *Annals of Internal Medicine, 76,* 793–799.

WEISS, R. S. 1969. The fund of sociability. *Trans-Action, 6,* 36–43.

WEISS, R. S. 1974. The provisions of social relationships. *In* Z. Rubin (ed.), *Doing Unto Others,* pp. 17–26. Englewood Cliffs, N.J.: Prentice-Hall.

WELLISCH, D. K., JAMISON, K. R., AND PASNAU, R. O. 1978. Psychosocial aspects of mastectomy: II. The man's perspective. *American Journal of Psychiatry, 135,* 543–546.

WHISKIN, 1968. The geriatric sex offender. *Practitioner, 22,* 199.

WHITEHEAD, J. A. 1974. *Psychiatric Disorders in Old Age.* New York: Springer Publ.

WILMOTT, P., AND YOUNG, M. 1960. *Family and Class in a London Suburb.* London: Routledge and Kegan Paul.

WITKIN, M. H. 1978. Psychosexual counseling of the mastectomy patient. *Journal of Sex and Marital Therapy, 4,* 20–28.

ZILBERGELD, B. 1978. *Male Sexuality: A Guide to Sexual Fulfillment.* Boston: Little, Brown.

ZOHAR, J., MEIRAZ, D., MAOZ, B., AND DURST, N. 1976. Factors influencing sexual activity after prostatectomy: A prospective study. *The Journal of Urology, 116,* 332–334.

# 38

# Social-Psychological Aspects
# of Death and Dying
# and Mental Health

*James A. Peterson*

Had someone suggested 25 years ago that one of the most popular and growing curriculum offerings in college would be courses on death and dying, or that the curriculum from kindergarten through the twelfth grade would be examined to test for appropriate references to death, or that US Senate hearings would be held on the death industry, or that entirely new institutional structures such as *Hospices* would appear to propitiate an appropriate death, the response would have been one of total disbelief, with the speaker questioned about his/her contact with reality. We do not assume that this mulititude of foci on death is a fad. It is rather the product of an urgent shift in the cultural awareness that an achievement-oriented society has neglected growth by its denial of death, with consequent heavy and costly mental health consequences. It is intriguing to ponder the

influence of the media in this regard. The prolonged vivid exposure to violence and death in the media may have had some influence in promoting a disquiet, an awareness of finitude, which led to insistent demands that attention be focused on coping mechanisms dealing with death.

While articles, books, television programs, and courses in the educational establishment have proliferated, basic research has not. Of all the disciplines involved in discussing death, very few have produced elegant studies, with one exception. Demography (the study of population from the viewpoints of natality, mortality, and immigration) has given us the most solid factual basis for discussion. Unfortunately demography is limited in terms of basic inferential foundations on which to look at death. This science records death, but its capacity for either theoretical or cultural reference is weak.

Most studies, such as those of psychiatrists like Kubler-Ross, Lindemann, and Weisman, are based on case analysis and are thus limited. Still, many of these have acute observations, which I shall utilize in this chapter, representing the best of current insight. Life development studies have tried to identify the reactions of persons at each stage of the life cycle, so that appropriate adjustment contexts might be provided at each stage of personality development. Anthony (1940), Nagy (1948), and Rochlin (1967), are appropriate citations in terms of this research.

The legal aspects of death and dying are receiving more attention because of critical issues having to do with formulating legal principles to guide judges in adjudicating cases involving definitions of death, living wills, and transplants. Sociologists have done little empirical research, but Kalish has written a significant article about the social context of death which produces some cross-disciplinary generalizations which are interesting and valuable (Kalish, 1977). Over all, the investigations have been segmental, factual, and case-oriented.

A mass of literature has been produced but it is severely limited both in terms of methodology and in theory. Scientific progress depends on interpreting data in terms of theoretical formulations which give meaning to statistical or case study analysis. When a theoretical framework is missing, interpretation of findings tends to be insular and without hope of formulation of more incisive theorems and hypotheses. Observations in the current literature regarding mental health aspects of attitudes towards death and the impact of death are consequently random and often idiosyncratic. This does not mean to say that progress in the analysis of death and dying to this date has been without value. Anyone who has immersed himself or herself in the discussions thus far, finds a richness of anecdotal and thoughtful analyses which are, after all, the ground on which theoretical formulations may grow.

The schema of this chapter on mental health aspects of death and dying is to investigate the contributions of researchers to date with a view to adumbrating a tentative theoretical framework. This framework can do no more than to reproduce some tentative contexts to look at death and dying, to raise some significant methodological and theoretical questions and to stimulate a more integrated and in-depth analysis in the future. The first section of the chapter addresses itself to a critique of possible theory construction in the area of investigation.

## APPROACHING A THEORETICAL BASIS FOR ANALYZING DEATH AND DYING

The development of theorems or hypotheses in the field of death and dying as related to mental health may seem at first glance to be an insurmountable problem. After all, death means extinction, which abruptly cancels any consideration of mental health. Is it possible to theoretically fashion a theory about that which means that one is not to be? Obviously not. But the process of dying and the entry into that world beyond cessation may be studied. Kubler-Ross (1969) reminds us that there is some yet undefined area of investigation dealing with *transitions* that needs further investigations. Still, the focus of any theory of death and dying must be based on a psychological and sociological analysis of persons in the death process (death trajectory) and its impact on society.

There are few clues in Hinton (1967), Shneidman (1973), Mant (1968), Kubler-Ross (1969), Weisman (1972), Saunders (1971–72), Glaser and Strauss (1968), Peterson and Briley (1977), or others as to a generalized psychological framework in which to interpret their findings. They are all dealing with an immediate and nontheoretical context. But, from the perspective of mental health, there are two theoretical contexts which have promise for the interpretation of present findings and future research. They are theories which come from an analysis of suicide.

A superficial analysis of suicide would lead to the conclusion that the decision to end one's life would indicate the lowest possible level of mental health. From a psychoanalytical point of view, suicide indicates depths of depression and hostility that one cannot cope with, so that extinction by self-destruction is the logical solution. From a social point of view, suicide indicates a loss of intimacy, supports, and love, which makes life unbearable. From the perspective of humanistic psychology or religion, suicide may involve a profound identification with group values which demands the surrender of self or, in facing the loss of function and self-esteem, a dignified and honorable exit. We think we can build on these theories to promulgate a tentative mental theory of death.

### FREUD

Freud gave a great deal of attention to suicide. Freud, from his organic approach to personality, postulated a biological death wish. His theory was in essence sociological because he thought that suicide occurred when an individual could not resolve ambivalent feelings toward another person toward whom he had both love and hate feelings. His thought was relatively straightforward. If a person had profound hate feelings against a person toward whom he could not act (destroy), he redirected that hate feeling towards himself and killed himself (Freud, 1953). Karl Menninger refined Freud's thought and identified three states of mind that led to suicide: (1) the wish to kill, (2) the wish to be destroyed, and (3) the wish to die (Menninger, 1938). The third wish is especially significant to a study of death because it derives from feelings of helplessness and dispair. Farberow and Shneidman (1973) studied Menninger's theory by analyzing 700 suicide notes. Twenty percent indicated a wish to kill, 15 percent were interpreted as the wish to be killed and 40 percent seemed to say that the person wished to die. I shall look later at the implications of this theory for a generalized theory on death and dying.

## DURKHEIM

Durkheim, a father of sociological theoretical thinking, approached suicide from a social context. He carefully analyzed European suicide rates from a sociological viewpoint and concluded that "suicide rates vary inversely with the degree of integration of the social groups of which the individual forms a part" (Durkheim, 1951). The theory is expressed as: the greater the cohesiveness of the group, the lower the suicide rate. With this law as his theoretic platform, Durkheim explicated three groups of suicidal persons. The first was the *altruistic*—those persons who were so overidentified with the group that their individual existence did not matter and they ritualistically sacrificed themselves for the welfare of the group. Examples would be Jesus and Socrates, Indian widows, or older folk in Eskimo society. In the second group were those who were labeled *egoistic*. This type of suicide occurs where persons perceive their integration in the group to be minimal and their own concern for their welfare takes priority over the group. The third type is *anomic* suicide which describes individuals who are alienated from society and who feel a profound sense of hopelessness.

I think it is possible to add a higher order of generalization to the theories of Freud and Durkheim that will contribute to a framework for looking at death and dying. However, before I am ready to suggest that formulation, it is important to consider a third contribution to our thinking, that of Edwin Shneidman (1976).

## SHNEIDMAN

Shneidman's contribution serves as a bridge between thinking purely of suicide and thinking of death in general. He thinks that there is an element of intentionality (or suicide) in many deaths. In his remarkable article, *the Death Certificate,* Shneidman adds four new functions to the original six of the death certificate (Shneidman, 1973). These are:

7. The death certificate should reflect the dual nature of death; that is, its private nature (as it is almost experienced by the decedent) and its public nature (as it is experienced and accounted for by others.)
8. It should relfect the type of death that is certified—for example, brain death (a flat electroencephalographic record) or somatic death (no respiration, heartbeat, reflexes).
9. It should include space for the specification of death by legal execution, death in war or military incursions, death by police action, and others of the sort.
10. Perhaps most important, it should abandon the anachronistic Cartesian view of man as a passive biological vessel on which fates work their will, and instead reflect the contemporary view of man as a psycho-socio-biological organism that can, and in many cases does, play a significant part in hastening its own demise. This means that the death certificate should contain at least one item on the decedent's *intention* vis-a-vis his own death. It is not enough to state that a death was natural, accidental, suicidal, or homicidal; we should know too whether it was intentioned, subintentioned or unintentioned.

It is the last suggestion that captures our attention in looking for theoretical grounds. Shneidman comments on this.

> It leaves man out. I propose we put him in . . . the item might be labeled imputed lethality . . . and I suggest that it consist of four designations: High, Medium, Low, Absent. High imputed lethality would indicate that the decedent definitely wanted to die . . . . Medium imputed lethality would indicate that the decedent played an important role in effecting his own death . . . . Low imputed lethality would indicate that the decedent played an important role in effecting his own death . . . . Low imputed lethality would indicate that the decedent played some small but insignificant role in effecting or hastening his demise . . . and when imputed lethality is absent, the decedent played no role effecting his death. . . .

Shneidman (1973) broadens the base of thinking about death because he suggests that so-called normal deaths may have some degree of intentionality associated with them. This assumption is strengthened by the research of Simonton (1978) on cancer who maintains that every person has some control over their health history and eventual lethality. The emergent holistic health movement is based on assumptions that are parallel to Shneidman's inferences.

It is possible to relate Menninger's etiological explanation of suicide (the feeling of hopelessness and despair) to Durkheim's Anomic suicidal typology which stems from feelings of alienation and hopelessness. The actions of individuals who are alienated and hopeless need not result in overt suicide. They can implement their death, as Shneidman suggests, through acting out lethal processes in their life history. But Shneidman also recognizes that deaths of millions of individuals occur through social causes where there is no imputed involvement of the actor. Thus a drunken driver careens into the car of a well-adjusted and non-death-oriented *young* man. Or the *young* man is later inducted by law into a national army which sends him to his death. The mental health of older persons depends on how they handle the anticipation of their own death and of that of loved ones. I shall deal with such death in a later part of this analysis.

In terms of the mental health of older persons another codicil must be added. Alienation results from damage to self-esteem. Self-esteem depends upon recognition from peers, fellow workers and one's social system. Self-esteem is also enhanced or destroyed by the availability of intimate others, who give support systems to cushion blows from secondary social systems. If the intimates are gone, the losses are more poignant. Age robs individuals of intimates. A careful study of stress shows that the loss of a mate results in the greatest stress, not only because of losing affectional bonds but also from losing emotional support. (Holmes and Rahe, 1967).

Thus, one has to add to Durkheim's theory a social-psychological theorem which includes the social support losses, as these impinge upon the individual's psychological balance. One would assume that any analysis of intentional aspects of lethality would include the increment of losses individuals suffer as they age. The losses of a meaningful occupational network, the intimate supports of a mate, and/or the physical aspects of sexual potency or physical mobility would be significant explanatory variables in accounting for intentionality (high or low lethality).

There is further evidence of the significance of the process of social alienation from Turner, Tobin, and Lieberman's (1972) studies in Chicago. They studied matched samples of older individuals who faced critical transitions in their environments. Some of them stayed in their homes and some of them had to face induction into intermediate medical facilities, nursing homes. A significant number of those who were facing entry into nursing homes died just before, or on entry into, the health facility as compared to those who stayed in their homes. This careful study shows that even the anticipation of separation from supports may induce a high degree of lethality. This study supports our general theorem regarding the critical nature of intimate supports (i.e. social cohension) as an important variable in understanding personal movement to or from death.

## A THEORETICAL FRAMEWORK

It may be possible now to build a theoretical framework in understanding attitudes which explain mental health. This framework, while based on observations regarding suicide, transcends that category and is applicable to many more individuals. In reviewing the evidence and comparing its implications to our two protean theories (Freud and Durkheim), I add the following dimensions:

1. A social component representing the powerful intervention of nonpersonality forces, such as those represented by strangers driving automobiles or national states decreeing participation in global war, should be added to any equation trying to explain death.

2. The impact of low social cohesion does not automatically decree a high degree of individual lethality. There is an intervening variable of *coping strength* which may often permit individuals with the highest degree of social alienation and personal losses to cope. This implies the essential evaluation of psychological profiles which may contradict both Freud and Durkheim in terms of understanding their generalizations.

3. In general, a sound theory of death and mental health will necessarily embrace both Freud's intrapersonality systems and Durkheim's social organizational analysis, but will go beyond these in accounting for the actions of a major number of individuals which, both for social and individual reasons, must be explained.

There is great strength on the part of many individuals. Their history and the personality product of their history must be taken into account. Consequently I introduce into the theoretical statement this quotient called coping strength (CS).

As modifiers of reactions to both social and social cohesion, there are three basic factors: (1) losses, (2) support networks and (3) coping strength. If we try to operationalize these terms, we would recognize that we may create scales with some exactness to measure each of them. Social loss factors would include wars, depressions, water quality, air quality, accidents, or other losses (any substantial decrements from the environment over which we have little or no control). Social cohesion would include support items such as family closeness, neighborhood supports, community agencies, religious activities and attitudes (Durkheim's measure), etc. Death or proneness to lethality, would include such items as ounces of alcohol consumed daily, cigarette smoking, stress-quotients, levels of relaxation, number of annual physical examinations, diet, exercise, speed of driving, attitudes toward health and death, etc. There is no exact measure in psychological literature to measure coping strength but a beginning could be made by a subjective judgment regarding one's life history, combined with an ego strength scale (perhaps the Barron scale from the MMPI or the D score from the MMPI) and a measure of engagement versus disengagement.

We now have a testable hypothesis which may be operationalized and which finally can be stated:

The greater the product of significant social support factors and social cohesion as modified by the coping strength of individuals, the lower the possibility of lethality proneness, that is, the greater the mental health of individuals in relationship to death and dying.

Coping strength is admittedly a vague scientific term. It begs the question of reality testing versus denial in terms of mental health. Such questions demand studies in themselves as we shall indicate when we consider psychological aspects of facing death. The equation likewise seems to measure only individual's reactions to death and not that of related individuals such as family members or friends, nor the functional value of lethality levels for society. These are subsidiary scientific operations and will be considered. It is possible to look at most of the critical areas involved in thinking about death by means of this theory.

So far the theorem has only involved death. It can encompass both suicide and lethality (individual's contributions to death). But the final term of the theorem can be modified. It has already been suggested that individuals vary widely in terms of coping strength. Some persons will respond to losses with depression which is manageable. Some with a high level of coping strength may manage good adjustment. Thus our final theory much more justifiably will combine losses, support networks, and coping strength.

## THE SENSE OF TIME AND DENIAL AS COPING STRATEGIES

One of the great losses of aging is time. Somewhere in middle age comes the realization that one's time is finite (Peterson, 1968). The shift from tennis to golf, the heart attack of the man who sat in the next office, the awful awareness of early goals not accomplished, or the night of impotence bring a realization that one is propelled toward death. One loses the exuberant confidence of youth that the future is an arena of exciting conquest and knows that one will inevitably lose that conquest. The midlife crisis is the confrontation of the inevitability of total impotence . . . total loss of self.

How one copes with the monumental change of life focus determines mental health in all the years that follow. One strategy, brilliantly documented by Bergler, is renewed assault on goals, a new burst of devotion to achievement whether in the halls of science, the market place, or the more private world of sex (Bergler, 1962). We suspect but we do not know that the anxiety associated with the realization of the limitation of time and the frenetic need to crowd old or new conquests into the few remaining months are important etiological factors in the startling heart attack rates of the industrialized western world. We have documented the incidence of those premature heart attacks but our research about the associated causative variables related to stress is mostly speculative.

A second coping strategy is psychological and social denial, both individual and on the part of the herd. The massive private and public dependence upon denial can be documented in almost every phase of the later years of life. Weisman has the most critical approach to denial and has defined denial as a process (1972). He outlines five "successive steps" in this process (Figure 38-1).

1. Acceptance of a primary and public field of perception.

   ↓

2. Repudiation of a portion of the shared meaning of that field.

   ↓

3. Replacement of the repudiated meaning with a more congenial version.

   ↓

4. Reorientation of the individual within the scope of the total meaning, in order to accommodate the revised reality.

   ↓

5. Acceptance of a primary and public field of perception means that no one can deny by himself, in utter solitude.

**Figure 38–1**   Weisman's Five Successive Steps in the Process of Denial.

Source: Weisman, A. 1976. Denial and Middle Knowledge. In, E. S. Shneidman (ed.), *Death: Current Perspectives*, p. 439. Palo Alto, Cal.: Mayfield Publishing Co.

In terms of coping with death, an individual starts out with a realization that life ends, but when threatened, repudiates that realization about the self . . . "all others may die but I won't . . . and certainly I won't die now" (i.e. this illness is not serious). This is the ultimate act of denial. Denial has been observed by most writers about death and dying. Mental health practitioners from Freud on have aimed their intervention goals at helping persons adjust to and not deny reality. We shall question the validity of that assumption when we have finished looking at the manifestations of denial itself.

Kubler-Ross (1969) based her classic observations of the death process on her insightful work with terminally ill persons in Billings Hospital at the University of Chicago. She describes stages of adjustment to death: (1) Denial and isolation: "No, not me; it can't be true." (2) Anger, resentment. "Why me?" (3) Bargaining: "If you'll only give me . . . then I'll . . ." (4) Depression: "What's the use?" (5) Acceptance: "Withdrawal and a final rest."

Kubler-Ross has been a pioneer in dealing with dying persons. But her effectivenss as a warm, relating human being and pioneer of death therapy may in the long run be more significant than her descriptions of what she heard. There is a great deal of skepticism about the inevitability of her stages of adjustment, as well as hope that someone might study in detail the fixation of persons at one or another of the stages. Shneidman and others feel that the reactions of the dying are far more fluid and complex that those described by Kubler-Ross. In summary Shneidman (1973) says:

> What of the nexus of emotions manifested by the dying person? Rather than the five definite stages discussed above, my experience leads me to posit a hive of affect, in which there is a constant coming and going. The emotional stages seem to include a constant interplay between disbelief and hope and, against these as background, a waxing and waning of anguish, terror, acquiescence, and surrender, rage and envy, disinterest and ennui, pretense, taunting and daring and even yearning for death . . . all these in the context of bewilderment and pain.

Shneidman and others have documented the remarkable facility of terminally ill persons to be able to discuss their deaths rationally during one time period and then to dismiss the reality completely and speak about being home for the graduation of a son or for a vacation trip. Weisman (1972) insists over and over that "the degrees of denial are never constant." His concept of "middle knowledge" is particularly incisive; this is an approach to death "somewhere between open acknowledgement of death and its utter repudiation." It tends to occur at important transition points such as the beginning of the death trajectory or in the "obvious equivocation among people on whom one depends." One valuable diagnostic inference is that "when a patient with a fatal illness becomes unable to draw plausible inferences about himself, slipping back into an exacerbation of denial, it is often a sign that the terminal phase is about to begin."

Weisman has delineated his degrees of denial according to three orders (1972). First-order denial is based upon the perception by the patient of the primary facts of his illness, with the minimizing or denial of symptomatology. Second-order denial "refers to the inferences that a patient draws, or fails to draw, about the extensions and implications of his illness." They may accept the primary facts but then minimize the implications. Third-order denial, and most basic, is the denial of extinction. In this mental process individuals may accept the primary facts of illness and even its "hazards" but refuse to believe that for themselves such hazards exist, that is, that their incurable illness will result in death. In any judgment regarding therapeutic intervention, a recognition of the degree or order of denial, and its validity for an individual person is essential to rapport with that patient.

A form of denial seems to pervade most medical institutions which must deal with death. Glaser and Strauss (1965) have described in detail their observations at hospitals. They report their findings in a remarkable chapter called "The Ritual Drama of Mutual Pretense." Basically the ritual involves patient, hospital staff, and medical staff in a common denial of impending death. Their interaction is in a closed system. In that system one party has to indicate a desire "to pretend that the patient is not dying." On the contrary, if the patient should indicate that he has a need for conversation about his impending doom, and the physicians or staff turn away, the patient may then elect to keep silent and honor the ritual of pretense because he has respect for the needs of others. Conversely some kindly staff members may give an invitation to the patient to discuss his future, but if that person turns away, the staff respects that decision. This is, in effect, bargaining, and thus the tone and level of future interaction is based on clues that one or another actor in the system supplies. Beyond this lies the social attitudes toward death which give a powerful incentive to reinforce the ritual of pretense.

Glaser and Strauss (1965) were able to identify the structural rules that govern such interactions. (1) Dangerous topics which involve the patient's death or what will follow death in the drama are avoided. (2) Discussion of such dangerous topics as future activities are allowable as long as no one breaks down. Illustrations given were those that indicated complete denial such as a terminal patient near death discussing a book he was going to write. (3) Conversation must not only avoid the dangerous, but must focus on safe topics: quality of food, sleeping achievements, minor symptomatology with no reference to their meaning in terms of death. (4) If something happens to betray the pretense, such as a patient's crying, it must be ignored. It is evident that each actor in the system takes responsibility for maintaining the lie. Kastenbaum (1967) has also documented this systematic kind of institutional denial. He discusses the "implicit mutual understanding" that patient and staff have with regard to death. "Institutional dynamics tend to operate against making death 'visible' and a subject of open communication."

Families of patients are also part of the ritualistic denial system. Loved ones do not want to believe that a person will die or, after they have died, that they are gone. They are also concerned that no word from the hospital staff or the physician will take away hope from the patient or cause depression. Consequently, they often reinforce the system's determination to participate in the ritual of pretense. Such common remarks as "you are looking better today"; "the nurse said you had a good night"; or "we are planning a big family get together two weeks from Sunday, and if you keep on improving you can be there" are all subtle ways family members try to convince the patient and themselves that all is going well. Beneath all of this is a dogged effort not to face the fact that the patient is dying.

What is the cost of this form of denial to the patient? Glaser and Strauss focus it when they say ". . . it may deny him (the patient) the closer relationships with staff members and family members that sometimes occurs when he allows them to participate in his open acceptance of death." It is this foreclosure of honesty, of sharing in the great adventure of death, that is the cost. But there is an equally disturbing consequence. Most of us go into our final days with a great deal of unfinished business. We have sinned against many. We have done that which we should not have done and left undone that which should have been accomplished. Much of this has to do with the family but whether it is with the family or not, an appropriate death can occur only if the shadows have been cleared. Those lifelong shadows are cleared by discussion and ventilation.

A few weeks ago I stood by the side of a dying man. He knew he was dying. He accepted the fact. He was not angry, nor depressed, nor anxious. I was curious about his peace of mind. I did not push but as we talked he told me of an event in the last three months of his life that had, he said, "cleared the way." During his childhood and youth he had always been at odds with his sister. She was the beautiful one, he the ugly. She seemed more talented; he stumbled along. He had resented the obvious favorite status their parents gave her. After they had matured he had, once he had imbibed too much, "told her off." She had not had a happy life and she resented his accusations and was deeply hurt by things she did not understand. As a result they had not spoken for 15 years. At the time of the fiftieth wedding anniversary of their parents, a family celebration was planned. He had every excuse not to go, but the separation from his sister plagued him. He resolved not only to go but also to speak with her, to ask her forgiveness and build a bridge for the future. He did, and although she was difficult at first, he persisted in his negotiations. She finally and unexpectedly told him that their distance had been a sorrow to her and that she was and would be grateful for what he had said. When he got home, he found a long letter from his sister in which she poured out all of the frustrations of her life and concluded by wishing that they might see each other often. Shortly after that he became moribund with inoperable cancer. After he had told me this story and before I could leave his room, his sister came. She greeted him with deep warmth and his response was rewarding.

Kubler-Ross has stated that the final stage of life is one of acceptance and withdrawal (1969). Kalish (1977) also speaks about the "disengagement of the last days" as a means of preparation for the final moment of separation, a kind of anticipatory step towards death itself. But sensitive nurses talk in another vein. Even when a patient is comatose and returns to consciousness for only a few moments, the nurses have experienced a sense of profound comfort on the part of the dying person if they were there to say "It's going to be all right" or simply to stroke the patient's arm.

One wonders if the disengagement is not the final surrender to the process of mutual denial that has gone on, a dismal giving-up of any hope that caring can mean closeness even to the last moments. The mutual pretense system results in depersonalization so that dying patients are not called by name but referred to as a number or by their illness. That depersonalization carries over to growing distancing between patient and staff. In some medical facilities and nursing homes, dying patients are removed to an isolated part of the facility and are visited less frequently by family, nurses, and doctors. This organizational response is simply the behavioral consequence of institutional denial.

Burial and funeral rites have long been identified as providing further evidence of the denial of death. An elaborate ritual and vocabulary have been provided to lull the survivors into a false pretense that the deceased is not really dead. The embalming, the cosmetology, and the terms such as "slumber room" are calculated to convince the survivors that death has been banished. I will discuss this later in relation to grief work, but it is important to note here that all of us have been conditioned for our own deaths by the subtle denial of any death by the "professionals" who handle death.

One should not be too hostile to the undertakers for the way they fit into the subterfuge. In two brilliant chapters that have unfortunately gone too much unnoticed, Harmer (1963) discusses "Epic Beginnings and Epic Endings" and "The World, the Flesh and the Funeral." She searches out contemporary attitudes toward denial of death and burial practices in Babylonian, Sumerian, Greek, Roman, Alexandrian, and early and later Jewish and Christian cultures, and shows the process by which men tried to "mold our desires, shape our ideals of conduct, virtue, courage, love, dignity, ambition, friendship." Appropriate burial was regarded as a triumph over death and the essential condition for entry to the good future life. The rituals of death are as old as man and the modern undertakers may be forgiven a little, despite their vulgarity, if we realize they are only marchers in a long procession of those who sought to ameliorate the sting of death.

Of course the modern undertaker rides on the tailcoat of the religious practitioner. In coping with death, the pyramid builders furnished the Pharoah with everything he needed to sustain life, and the Christian supplied man with profound faith that he would transcend the grave in a quite specific immortality. How important these beliefs are to secular, scientific man I will analyze in a succeeding analysis. The sociologist believes that customs that have characterized every culture have great significance. Perhaps the most penetrating look at the function of rituals, burial practices and hype comes from a most distinguished sociologist, W. Lloyd Warner (1965), in his article on "The City of the Dead." Warner visits the cemetery to help us understand our attitudes toward death. He gives some rationale for hope when he analyzes cemeteries as "collective representations," which "express many of the community's basic beliefs and values about what kind of society it is, what the persons of men are, and where each fits into the secular world of the living and the spiritual society of the dead." After establishing the social need of persons to solve the "scared problem . . . to provide suitable symbols to refer to and express man's hope of immortality through the sacred belief and ritual of Christianity, and to reduce his anxiety and fear about death as marking the obliteration of his personality," Warner (1965) suggests that:

> The belief in immortality, strengthened and reinforced by the funeral rite, helps correct some of the feeling of the survivor of loss of self. For the survivor to continue to see and feel himself still living in, and related to the dead life of the other it is necessary for him to reconstruct his image of the other; but in doing this he must also rethink who he himself is, at least insofar as he relates to the dead person. This constitutes an essential part of the social-psychological processes of the living during the transition of death.

In the cemetery "the time of man and the time of God are united, so that the cemetery as a collective representation repeats and expresses the social structure of the living as a symbolic replica, a city of the dead, it is a symbolic replica of the living community." All critical transition periods of life such as birth, puberty, marriage and death are marked by ceremonies. Society honors each transition period. Thus when a member of the community dies, "his social personality is not immediately extinguished" so the ritual has important connotations for continuing social cohesion.

I have recounted the history, ubiquity, and usefulness of denial as both a psychological and social phenomenon of adjustment to death. The discussion of denial is perhaps the most popular occupation of thanatologists. I would like to add two codicils to the discussion:

(1) It is unlikely that such a pervasive practice as universal denial could exist if it had no functional value to the individual and to society. Perhaps it has led to economic and social excesses. Perhaps it does not square with modern mental health practices in which one must confront reality at all costs. But I like Weisman's approach . . . that at times denial is essential to hope, to serenity, and to a good death. Individuals vary in their ability to confront the going from which there is no return. They vary in their ego strength and in their ability to cope. The therapist (and the family) truly committed to the mental health of patients have to be extraordinarily perceptive to ascertain when confrontation is essential and when it is a serious error. And they will know, as I know, that they will miss

the signals sometimes. But infinite sensitivity is demanded as we deal with those who enter the death trajectory. Sometimes they long to speak, to clear the books, but other times they wish that the ghosts of the road that they have traveled, the pain they are enduring, their uncertainties might best be forgotten (denied). There are as yet few guides to turn on the flashlight on the best path . . . we can only sense and listen and learn. In some cases the mutual pretense is not only justified; it is the best possible *modus vivendi* considering the psychological capacity of the patient, the staff, and the family. Another approach might be better, but the wise intervenor learns that sometimes the ideal is not possible, that reality determines an intermediate or conservative stance.

(2) The term *denial of death* is in some circumstances a great misnomer. Often in listening to a person nearing his or her final hours, one is struck by the lifelong denial not of death but of life. I remember one magnificent human being who discovered before Christmas that she had cancer of the brain. Her adjustment was superb but it detailed her life-style. She said:

> I don't mind but I won't get to wear that new gown I got for New Years. Do you know that it was silver brocade? I would have been a smash. I was going to dance all night, like I did last year. Oh, well, I'll miss the ball.

This woman had had three face lifts. Until the age of 75 she was the belle. She spent two hours with the hairdresser and the cosmetologist before she went to a party. At her funeral I reflected on her beauty and realized that not much had changed. The undertaker had only prolonged her life-style.

We live in a world of denial. Millions repulse the problems of urban civilization, ethnic conflict, the environment, global third-world disruptions, bussing, unemployment, or the conflict between the "free" world and the Soviets. They never lived in life on the level of reality or confrontation. How can we, at the time of their death trajectory, demand that they approach it with any style other than blindness? That is how they lived, and they will die in the same mode. To a man, their approach to death is consonant with their approach to life. It is difficult to "drink the whole cup," to enter into all of the paradoxes and contradictions of western society. And many are not able, sometimes because of their social class origins and sometimes because of their idiosyncratic histories. Society has destroyed "immortality" for them.

I remember one of my humiliating failures as a therapist. I should perhaps forget this, but it gnaws at me to know what I might have done. A physician called me because an aged woman had died and her son was in crisis over the death. He was alarmed about the son and asked me to come immediately, which I did. The son was paralyzed. He told me a story of utter dependency. His mother had made all the decisions, even the little ones of feeding and clothing him. Now he was lost. How could he face a world that was unknown and alien? For three hours I did my best to make a relationship that might be sustaining, to give him some notion of new supports available to him. Then I made an appointment with him for the next morning. But that night he put a shotgun to his mouth and pulled the trigger. He was an utter child and I did not know enough to relate to that child. His problem was not one of death but of life. Sometimes one feels that the thanatologists have forgotten developmental process, the baggage one brings to his last day, the heritage of failure and remorse.

The evidence is loud and startlingly clear. For many, religion offers no consolation. For many, life has been a frustrating and pernicious experience. For many, their last hours are not spent in "integration" but rather in doubt and ambiguity. The ancient supports are gone and only doubt remains. The "Zeitgeist" has little to offer except contradictions and doubts. Facing reality for those is only compounding confusion. Kubler-Ross may feel that there is a way to resolve those conflicts and doubts, but some others feel that reality testing is a vain pursuit. For many, their life has been one of immediate pursuit of recognition or evanescent success. Is it surprising in such a scene that one applies cosmetics in death as one has in life? I suggest that there is a more universal theme than denial of death. It is rather a lifelong constant—a denial of life itself. The turning aside from aging or death is consistent with the past history of many people, for they turned aside from the winds of time. They never walked in the corridors of history, never questioned the fates for tomorrow, never lifted a hand against injustice or evil. If they then turn aside from facing the ravages of age or the portents of death, who can tell them this is denial? It is the talisman of an urban age, the sign of those who cannot put a root down into earth because they walk only on endless ribbons of concrete. What the thanatologists have missed is the currency of the invisible mode—the way of life that often characterizes those who were born without roots and who lived without connections. They lived on an "island they never made." In this sense "denial" has been a way of life from age two upward, because in a life lived between lightning flashes and intermittent thunders, and between the dullness of sterile materialism, no one develops a higher consciousness. There are no "peak experiences." There is only the repetition of hope for some relief from boredom and ugliness in life. So the cosmetics do not disguise; they are what has been real. The lead coffin to preserve the corpse (it won't) is no more than the neurotic defenses raised in younger years to preserve a meaningless separation from reality. There is in all of this a fine consistency and we do ill when we label it denial. In an ironic sense it is fulfillment—completion of lives of emptiness.

## ANGER AND GRIEF

"Go not gently to thy . . . ."

We are still talking about responses to the loss of time or of significant others. Denial is but one alternative way of preserving some degree of mental sanity in the face of final oblivion. There is another way which is expressed in raging *anger*. Kubler-Ross discusses this as the second step on the way to developing a more mature mental adjustment to aging. But she fails to observe either the value in rage or its justification. I shall dwell upon these two points because a great many individuals never progress beyond anger at death, and perhaps they are justified in that fixation.

I had a blind patient once who was articulate in describing his reactions to his impending death. He had had two heart attacks and he knew that tomorrow a third would come and he would be gone. He said:

> So . . . you sit there and comment that I'm bitter. Of course I'm bitter . . . .do you remember what Loren Eisley described about his deaf mother? Well, my mother was blind . . .congenitally . . . and I knew I'd become blind too. And I am. But before I was blind I stored up all the sights . . . . around the world . . one was of a woman and I married her but she knew and when the darkness came she left me. And it was just when I was beginning to know her and share her needs. . . but she couldn't take it. And I had a research grant . . .you know what happened to that? Of course you do . . . . They took it away from me. I was supposed to look in a microscope and . . . . Well, I made it . . . without them. Now, despite the sightlessness I've got some things to say . . . I've finally put things together but I'll never get to share them. I'm just now able to have the big view but I won't make it . . . I'm dictating every day but every day I feel the darkness coming . . . in pangs and pain. Of course, I'm bitter. I got cheated.

I listened to that patient for five years. I heard his anger at the universe that had deprived him of love and life and sight, but he lived for five years. One reason he lived was because neither I nor those that were close to him resented his rage. He had a right to rage. Life had dealt badly with him, and hasn't it with many men and women?

I encountered a story recently that puts the matter even more directly. I was lecturing in South Dakota on "Death and Dying." I had made a comment in the lecture that probably I, myself, would not go gently to my grave—that I thought that He or She above had dealt unjustly with me because just when I got mature enough to help someone I would be taken away, mercilessly, and I resented it. After that lecture I walked to lunch with a young woman. She told me about her father, who had been an atheist all his life. On his deathbed his wife called in a Catholic priest. He was administering the last rites when her father, in his last effort, sat up in bed, looked the priest in the eye, and said, with anger, "Go to hell." (That is not exactly what he said, but the published word has some restraints.) Then he died. The young woman was worried. She was half-proud of him for maintaining his integrity and half-afraid of the possibility that he had alienated Divinity for all his future. I said to her that if I understood anything of the universe and its Ruler at all, I thought that whoever was in control up there would applaud and would say, "You got integrity, fellow" and prepare a special welcome. While that relieved two years of anxiety on the part of that daughter, it only increased awareness of the baggage that *all* of us carry through life. I went on to praise his integrity and his consistency. But I sorrowed for the burden that girl carried in life. If she could have been angry at her mother, or the priest, she would not have suffered so much, but the "shoulds" caught her and she was afraid of what her father's anger would cost him.

Anger is a perfectly legitimate response to loss. Catharsis through the expression of anger can be an integrating experience. On the contrary anger that is suppressed often becomes depression. How much of the depressions of older persons is due to repressed anger? We do not know, but we suspect it is an important etiological factor. The problem with cathartic feelings of anger is that it disturbs those about us. We are somehow made to feel guilty about such expressions. In America, especially, it is manly and good to repress any feelings that are negatively tinged. Consequently, a great many older persons hide their feelings about themselves or the way they are treated. This makes them live half-lives. If one is put in an emotional straitjacket because it is wrong to express one's negative feelings, one lives always with repression. Anger on the part of a dying person as he contemplates loss of self and loss of his loved ones may be an important way for him to come closer to dealing with the reality of his death, if we permit him an honest expression of his deepest responses. It certainly is the opposite of denial. For some persons it may be the coping mechanism of choice. Simone de Beauvoir (1966) expresses this by saying:

> All men must die. But for every man his death is an accident, and, even if he knows it and consents to it, an unjustifiable violation.

There is one final awareness or loss that influences the older person as well as his companions. It is called anticipatory grief. Generally the term is applied to the sorrow felt by loved ones for the coming loss of their beloved. But it is also a part of the awareness of the subject himself. He knows that after a time he will not laugh again with his family. There will be no tenderness, no affection because he is leaving. He may also feel that he is leaving himself. He cannot then be concious of himself. All his achievements will end. If he has unfinished business with any man it will never be completed. All lives are partial so that he may resent and regret the half that was not done. So he sorrows. He grieves over the losses to come.

In summary, I have discussed not only losses that older persons have but characteristic attitudes that are associated with those losses such as anger, denial, or sorrow.

## PERSONAL AND SOCIAL SUPPORTS

The second term in our theorem is a specification of Durkheim's notion of social cohesion. It is also an expansion of his definition, which I think was overgeneralized.

We (Peterson and Briley, 1977) have some research which provides some guidelines in specifying the kinds of supports older persons experience as strengths in the face of death. Mathieu (1975) investigated attitudes toward death from three samples, a rural sample from Montana, an urban sample from Pasadena, and a third sample from a retirement community in southern California. He wished to compare attitudes from these three diverse populations. The most relevent question to our inquiry was "What gives you comfort when you think of death?" Table 38-1 details the responses from Mathieu's three samples.

In the first response I wili consider, 25 percent of the respondents indicated that their greatest support came from their family. A further indication of this closeness came in response to a question asking them where they wanted to die. Over 90 percent of each of the three respondent groups wanted to die *at home*, and they wanted their families to be there at their death—not the doctor, nor the minister. They wanted to die naturally and with dignity, with over 85 percent of all samples rejecting any heroic means to keep them alive. Their wishes for a dignified death at home is strangely contradicted by what happens, because over 70 percent will be taken out of their homes to die in a nursing home or in a hospital, surrounded by strangers and often maintained by pipes and tubes.

It is probably this contradiction for the longing of the dying to be with their family and at home (or in a homelike environment) which has made the Hospice movement attractive. The hospice is a special caring center in London started by Cicely Saunders, who is the medical director. The staff and volunteers at the hospice are all dedicated to the task of relieving pain and bringing some joy to dying patients and their families. Some patients spend most of their time at home, some intermittently at home and hospice, and some most at the hospice. The idea has come to America and there

**Table 38–1**   Comfort Sources when thinking of death.

Which of the following comforts you most as you think of death?

| | Pasadena (N = 189) | | Laguna Hills (N = 183) | | Mountain States (N = 115) | |
|---|---|---|---|---|---|---|
| My religion | 62 | 32.8% | 58 | 31.7% | 43 | 37.4% |
| Love from those around me | 49 | 25.9% | 51 | 27.9% | 29 | 25.2% |
| Memories of a full life | 78 | 41.3% | 74 | 40.4% | 43 | 37.4% |

Source: Mathieu, James T., "Dying and Death Role Expectations." Ph.D. Dissertation, unpublished, University of Southern California Libraries, University of Southern California, Los Angeles, Calif., 1972, p. 162.

are committees exploring the possibility of starting hospices in most larger cities. Many hospices are now in operation across the country. The importance of the reference here is the quick response to a new institution that marshals the strong participation of the family throughout the entire death process. I shall discuss the meaning of this in another section when I talk about grief. I am focusing here on the individual who is dying and his mental health. It is our hypothesis that much of the fear of dying stems from a fear of isolation during the last few days—a fear of segregation in a sterile room served by strangers, and the fear of unremitted pain.

Thirty-five percent of the samples derived their support from religion. As these persons weighed their supports in the face of death, they found courage in their faith. By the term religion, I mean the way humanity's experiences have been institutionalized and preserved. The religious community has developed common symbols and time-tempered beliefs to bring solace to untold generations who have faced the gales of nature and the tempests of change.

The most hopeful answer that has been given to those who lose a loved one is that the loss is at most temporary. The Creator would not have molded the heavens and the earth and given man dominion only to abandon him. The rational Greek philosophers had their own intimations of immortality. Listen to Socrates:

> It must be so;—Plato, thou reason'st well-
> Else whence this pleasing hope, this fond desire,
> This longing after immortality . . . ?
> 'Tis the Divinity that stirs within us;
> 'Tis Heaven itself that points out a hereafter
> And intimates eternity to man . . . .
> Here will I hold. If there's power above us . . .
> And that which He delights in must be happy . . .
> The Soul, secured in her existence, smiles
> At the drawn dagger, and defies its point.
> The stars shall fade away, the Sun himself
> Grow dim with age, and Nature sink in years;
> But Thou shalt flourish in immortal youth,
> Unhurt amidst the war of elements,
> The wreck of matter and the crash of worlds.

Both the Old and the New Testaments echoed this feeling of the worth of the human spirit and the conviction that it would not perish in the dust. Generation after generation learned to say in faith and reverence:

> The Lord is my shepherd,
> I shall not want . . . .
> Yea, though I pass through the valley of the
>      shadow of death,
> I will fear no evil;
> For Thou are with me . . .

Jesus, following the tradition of the Psalmist, said it even more directly:

> Let not your heart be troubled:
> Ye believe in God, believe also in me.
> In my Father's house are many mansions:
> If it were not so, I would have told you.
> I go to prepare a place for you.

This is faith's answer to human destiny. It answered the spiritual needs of ancient man, it answered the questing philosophers of Greece and Rome, and it answered those who, having been won by the spirit of Jesus, gave their lives to Him. How important is that faith today? Does it have promise in a day of science and sophistication? We sought the answers to these questions by studying the responses of our three rural and urban populations. The result of our inquiry is found in Table 38-1, where we see that about one-third of our respondents still found their greatest comfort in their religion, either Jewish or Christian.

The third support in thinking about dying came from memories of work well done; 40 percent thought this helped them the most. There is a national drive now to discover the uniqueness of our roots, and many universities are teaching classes in autobiographical analysis. But older persons seem always to have participated in a life review. Erikson (1959), and Havighurst (1963) speak of aging as a period not only of review but also of "integration" or finding meaning in one's life experiences. We were somewhat surprised to find so many persons relying on a sense of their achievements for support. Perhaps we should not have been. As long ago as Paul we have testimony to the life satisfaction of good works:

> I have fought a good fight
> I have finished the course—
> Henceforth is laid up for me
> A crown of righteousness . . . .

## MEASURING MENTAL HEALTH

I have been able to specify some of the variables that go to explicate the terms of loss, social supports, and coping mechanisms. I have yet to furnish some measurable dimension of mental health. I think it possible to develop a scale of gradations of mental health that will complete the operationalization of our theorem. In the best of all possible mental states, the one most cherished is probably the higher consciousness described by Maslow (1959) as the "peak moments," moments of rare euphoria, insight, and joy. The utter loss of mental health is "suicide." Between euphoria and suicide are a number of intermediate states of emotional and integrative response. Moving from euphoria, we might label these as serenity, acceptance, depression, and suicide. The closer one comes on the scale toward euphoria, the higher the mental health and the closer one scores on the scale toward suicide the lower mental health.

The contribution of the factor of fear of death to the equation can be measured by weighting such items as fear of death, adequacy of denial mechanisms, depth of anticipatory grief about one's own death, frequency of morbid thoughts, etc. This factor can be entered into the total coping strength scale, and through regression analysis some notion of its impact can be determined. On a less statistical mode of inquiry the theorem makes it possible to integrate many of the important categories of inquiry about death and interpret them in a frame of reference. A simplification of the equation is achieved if one reduces the measurement of mental health to one factor, Shneidman's lethality index. Then instead of trying to make intervals between euphoria and suicide, only the degrees of lethality (no, low, medium, high, or total lethality) proneness would be used. This may be a simplification but the term "lethality" may be more difficult to measure than the more generalized terms of euphoria, serenity, acceptance, depression, and suicide. In an ideal theoretical framework, each of the lethality degrees would match a comparable descriptive measurement. But to what extent that might happen requires further investigation. And it may turn out that lethality may not be a very exact measure of mental health.

Developing any theoretical framework regarding complex social and personality factors is difficult. Undoubtedly many significant variables have not been considered in this formulation. It may prove to be quite primitive in terms of further explications of research findings. But it does offer a basis for developing hypothetical statements in an integrated context, and consequently should lead to both basic research and further critical generalization.

## MENTAL HEALTH AND BEREAVEMENT

Thus far this paper has focused on developing some framework to understand the responses of individuals toward their own death. I now turn to looking at the mental health aspects of the impact of death on those who do not die but who were related to the one who departed. The impact on the bereaved will generally be in proportion to the intensity of the relationship; mates, brothers and sisters, fathers and mothers, and children are first order; farther removed relatives, good friends, and working associates would be of a second order. The impact on the family is particularly interesting.

### THE FAMILY AND BEREAVEMENT

The family is a "unity of interacting personalities" (Burgess, 1934). The family maintains the most intensive small system organization known. The roles of family members interlock. Patterns of family interaction involve every member in a tight, well-defined way. Every family develops patterns of subordination and superordination, of power alignments, of favoritism, and of scapegoating. There is generally a family leader (the organizer) and the family therapist (the healer). The family has a well-defined set of rituals which mark its use of leisure time, its instrumental procedures, and its values. Obviously when any member of that family dies, the family is "dismembered." The loss of any member upsets the family equilibrium, changes the assignment of roles, destroys power alignments, and reorganizes task assignments. In terms of mental health every individual member reflects the equilibrium and support (or opprobrium) of the system. Death to a member destroys or at least disorganizes the system so that we speak of a loss of family mental health. We need to detail some of the significant impacts on various facets of the family system.

In a great many families, if not in all, there is the dominant, planning individual who is the leader. He may consider others but he does the decision-making. This is generally the father, but not always. He is the tower of strength. He earns the livelihood (now, when 50 percent of wives work, this is not universally true). He maintains contact with the world beyond the family, but he also maintains the boundaries of family privacy and concern. He represents security and strength to the other family members. He sets the family patterns for consumption, religious participation, leisure time participation, discipline, and mood. Because of his community position and his personality attributes (positive or negative), he has the power in the family. Others in the family may resent him, but they universally respect the cohesion and security he brings to family life. In some cases of an introvertive and weaker type male, this organizing role is played by the mother. In later years, when the salience of personality of father and mother fade along with their ability, this role may be undertaken by an older son or daughter, in a form of role reversal.

If the leader of the family dies, the degree of

disruption to the family system will depend on the age of its members and on the dependency of each member on that leader. Undoubtedly, part of the grieving process involves a profound sense of loss of this person who had previously taken care of everything, who was the keystone to the family and the long-respected architect of family patterns. The numbness that characterizes the first weeks after the death of a loved one also often reflects a sense of bewilderment as to how the family will function without that leader. The whole system has lost its synthesizer, its planner, its strength.

A case from my files illustrates this point. Harry Brown was the pillar of his community, his church, and his family. He was the first to recognize that the downtown needed refurbishing and he led the movement to modernize so the town would not lose its appeal and economic solvency. At home his antennae were always out to sense the needs of his family and to institute creative answers. His wife and his children walked only in his shadow and prospered and grew because of his care. No one ever challenged his wisdom. His word was not so much law as divine guidance. But all of this had some costs, and at 72 Harry died from a massive heart attack. Like many others, he had given no thought for tomorrow. He had no will and certainly no thought about interment, a funeral, or the situation of his family if he departed. All was chaos. Helen Brown, his wife, was not only numb and confused, she was overwhelmed by decision making. His son, Harry Jr., 39, thought he should take over but he had no facility for leadership. His mother rejected most of his ideas for a memorial service. The minister, recognizing the vacuum and disorganization, wisely took over as far as the funeral was concerned. He then recommended a lawyer to help the family sort out its financial problems. When things went from bad to worse in terms of family organization, he recognized that the depression of the wife and the anger of the children were more than he could cope with, so he recommended a family therapist and I was called in.

It is not difficult from the case description to analyze the tasks presented to the therapist: (1) to help the family recast its organizational structure so that it could function now that the pivotal lynchpin figure was gone; (2) to cope with the anger and guilt of Helen, who had often urged her husband to think about a will, and to talk with her about the family's future; and (3) to deal with the ambivalences of the children who had been fixated in a dependent role and who were now forced to become independent without a figure to help them gradually grow. In the beginning the therapist had to cope with the "what-ifs." "What-if" the family had not selfishly demanded so much from the father that he had to work so hard that it drove him to his grave? What-if Helen had not been so concerned with things like her car, membership in the country club, and on and on, that her husband had dutifully provided by his work investment.

*Guilt and the Family.* The "what-ifs" are a critical part of almost every phase of the grief process. They represent the guilt of those left behind who might have behaved otherwise. It takes months and months for some family members to recognize that a family is a system, that roles are played to maintain family solidarity and efficiency, and that the role they played was not so much their personal choice but dictated by the need to produce some system stasis. This tendency of every family member to fancy himself/herself as omnipotent in potential, to think that he/she might have changed destiny, is a commonplace presentation to every grief work counselor. While it is common-place, it is seldom analyzed. What do the "what-ifs" represent? They represent not a momentary failure to call the doctor, or an occasional exorbitant demand for a privilege. What, in reality, they represent are the little and big failures in relationships over all the years. The "what-ifs" are a cover in which the plaintiff is crying out for absolution for a hundred thousand omissions and commissions . . . for being what we all are, normal, incomplete, human beings. If a therapist has the opportunity to be confronted with the "what-ifs," he has a once-in-the-lifetime chance to help individuals adjust to the tremendous toll that the "oughts" and the "shoulds" place on us and to reconcile them to their humaneness.

The death of either the male or female who represents the leadership role of the family is perhaps the most devastating blow that death brings to a family, but family organizational structures suffer, too, when any member dies. A second consideration has to do with the family that has a power structure alignment in which each parent lines up with a child or two children against the other. In research strategy we need to pinpoint the degree to which these power alignments have power to determine the family system. Where they are major components of the system equilibrium, a death destroys the system.

A case illustrates this point. The Hendrickson family was well known to the counseling clinic before the crisis precipitated by the death of Judith, the mother of three children and the wife of John. The family had been referred by their minister because Hilda, a late teen-age daughter, was in depression, failing school, and in poor health. The notes about the case from previous family encounters can be summarized in brief by saying that the father, who had been born and raised in Holland, had honored his two sons and depreciated his daughter. She existed only because her mother, also depreciated, adored her, supported her, and buffered her against the barbs from her brothers and her father. It was their pastime to beleaguer her. When mother became seriously ill with cancer, Hilda became suicidal and the family was again called into consultation. There were consistent appointments all through Judith's death trajectory and the aftermath. Hilda survived one suicide attempt with pills, one with a knife, and numerous threats. She has now been removed from the family and is in a semisheltered environment.

If it is not clear to the reader what happened to Hilda, let us spell it out. She was a victim of a family power play. Her father and his two sons were aligned against her mother and herself. It might have been different. If Hilda had happened to look like her mother, and to grow up as a very beautiful girl, her father might have chosen her as the favorite. Then mother might have aligned herself with the boys and fought for their rights and egos against the father and his daughter. In some families the power alignment is different with the mother and father aligning themselves against the children and the children forming a conspiracy against their parents. *All kinds of variations in family power structures are encountered.* But death to one of the older, and sometimes to one of the younger, participants, throws the alignment out of symmetry, and chaos results. The "what-ifs" and the guilts proliferate. But even more important is the need to find a new family system. In Hilda's case, she had no refuge. Her only ally was gone. She was now to be a victim of the ruthless game played against her. She could not face it and became suicidal. We can conjecture that if she had been father's favorite, and he had died, she might have found herself in much the same circumstance. Then all the venom accumulated by the rejected sons and mother would descend on her. But where the alignment is between a mother and daughter the reactions can be extreme.

Another case describes a similar situation. Marlene's father had died when she was eight. In that marriage her father was weak and her mother the leader. He had been the expressive leader and had defended Marlene against her mother, but the family, as a system, survivied the father's death because the mother had been the leader. She waited two years before remarrying. At 42, the mother, hounded by her new husband, left the house to drive in the night. The drive ended in a grotesque accident in which Marlene's mother was so destroyed that the casket could not be opened at the funeral. Marlene never saw her mother after her drive off in the night, and fantasized that her stepfather had hidden her away and that her mother was not really dead. At the time, Marlene had just married, and was quickly pregnant. She had to face pregnancy, a disastrous marriage, and her mother's death all at once. Even if she detested much about her mother, that person had been her strength. Now she faced the coming of a child and a marriage by herself. She had no one, and the crisis induced her to try suicide. But she only "slept." (Ignorance of the lethality of drugs is sometimes a blessing.) Now her husband has left her, her children are alienated, and Marlene is trying to bring her life into focus and begin a new life at 41. The fact that her father and mother both died at 42 brings nightmares and sleepless nights.

Marlene is only one of dozens of case studies I could produce to testify to the devastation of family conflict and family favoritism, to the everlasting memories that operate unconsciously and consciously to determine one's coping ability and life satisfaction when death intervenes in the family. Mental health is the obverse dimension of family history.

*Other Family Dynamics.* One other aspect of family dynamics must be specified. A great many families hold together because each member transfers his or her difficulties to a selected person. While it may be the father or mother, it is generally a child that plays the role of scapegoat. Scapegoating is the process by which an individual maintains his own integrity by projecting his neurotic trends onto another. In the closely knit system of the family, it is essential that too greatly disruptive personality factors be controlled, for otherwise the system would fly apart. A mechanism for doing this is the selection of the weakest member of the system who is made to bear the various problems of all the others. Once a scapegoat is selected, the family sees to it that that person be kept in that position. A number of psychologic outcomes occur when any member of the system dies. If the scapegoat dies, and a new victim cannot be found, the family is apt to fly apart. In some cases when the scapegoat dies, the guilt of the other family members is intolerable but they generally handle this through denial. It is quite common for the family to blame the scapegoat for the death of another family member.

A somewhat poignant case describes this process. Jeannie was fourteen. She came late to the family when her father was 59 and mother 42. Her family had long established her as the scapegoat of the family. They had often told her that she was going to kill her father, who had a heart condition, by her irresponsible actions. Her actions were only those of a normal adolescent trying to cope with the unrestrained hostility and aggression of a family that had united in their defensive maneuvers to make her bear the brunt of a very sick family constellation. Inevitably the father died, and the full fury of two older brothers and the mother descended on Jeannie. Fortunately the minister in this case intervened and brought the family for family counseling. Unfortunately the need of every other member of the family for displacement of their guilt was so great that they could not stop their aggression. Jeannie was removed from the family scene, but the family split up. The boys moved away, the mother became paranoid, but Jeannie eventually made it. Scapegoating is a particularly pervasive family process. When a death occurs, the family finds it difficult to cope and, as in the case of Jeannie, it may drive the scapegoated person into a mental breakdown or suicide.

It may happen that the family does not lose cohesion through the death of a central figure. The other members may be brought closer together in their mourning and in their need for new supports. They lose a member but they gain a new closeness. They develop a new vocabulary which now includes references to the way father behaved and what he would wish for them. Rituals he loved are maintained. Some members may find themselves acting as he did. Certainly the social world of the family changes. Friends that were related to the family because of the father's business tend to drop away. There is probably some loss of social contacts no matter which member dies. In this sense family members take on new roles and new social positions.

But that closeness may be lost when the will is probated. I have encountered at least a dozen families where deep and permanent rifts occurred because of violent reactions to what they felt was an unfair distribution of the family resources. Often some members feel that they have contributed more in terms of money or care and that they should have been rewarded. For some perverse reason the family may continue to live together but never speak to one another. The bitterness is deeply engrained and throws a shadow over the family for the rest of its days. Very few families sit down before any significant member dies and plan for eventualities. If this were done, the family rifts could be avoided. But we are not well schooled when it comes to anticipating what our death and its sequelae may mean to those we leave behind.

Some acute observations have been made of the impact of death on children in a family. Maria Nagy (1948) studied the impact of the death in the family on children from three to 10 years. Children from three to five regard death as a *departure*; it is not final, and, although buried and consequently constricted, the departed person may come back. Children from five to nine *personify* death as a person, a skeleton-man, an angel, from whom one must flee. From ages 10 and on, children have a sense that death is not only final, it is inevitable. Death is universal and it happens to everyone.

## THE IMPACT OF DEATH ON MENTAL HEALTH OF CHILDREN

What impact on mental health do encounters with death have? Felix Brown, a psychiatrist, (1961) studied that impact. He looked at the relationship of childhood bereavement and later depression. He studied the life histories of 216 randomly selected psychotic patients. Approximately two out of every five depressed patients had lost a parent before they reached 15 years of age. But only one in eight of his control sample had lost a parent. For boys who had lost a father by age four, their depression rate was twice that of boys who had not lost a father. He concludes that bereavement in childhood is one of the "most significant factors" in the etiology of depression. However, he did not study the differential depression of the remaining period, its depth, or duration. From the point of view of family pathology and its influence on psychological health of children, I think this a serious omission. It is possible that the recorded impact on the psyche of the child, which later may appear as grave depression, may be more related to the way the mother and the family coped with the loss than to the actual death. Psychiatrists often neglect the impact of the support network.

Of course the experience of a long and painful death, and of a funeral may simply bring stark terror to a child. The following case illustrates this possibility. Johnny was taken by his parents to visit their grandmother, age 72. She suffered a major stroke while they were there and lay unconscious for four days before she died. For the four days the family talked in whispers and the house was full of winter gloom. When the grandmother died, she lay in her casket in the living room for two days. Friends came silently and left in tears. Johnnie had been the favorite of this grandmother and he could not tolerate her death. He did not want to go to the funeral but his father insisted. It was winter and terribly cold. After the graveyard ceremonies the casket was lowered to the ground, the wooden box was closed, and the family stayed while the friends of the family threw the frozen clods of dirt on the casket. Johnnie heard those thumps his whole lifetime. Soon after they returned home Johnnie became obsessed with death. He had nightmares in which he was dead and lying in that box with tons of dirt so that he could not get out. He would run screaming through the night to his parents in sheer terror. Things improved a little, he remembered, when one night his mother and father took him in their bed and talked a long time with him. He shared his fears of being buried alive and with no air to breathe. They promised him that when he died they would drill a hole in the casket and send a wide pipe up through the dirt so that he could breathe, and presumably, cry out, and be heard and rescued. While much has been written about allowing children to experience death, and to have it interpreted as a normal part of life, it is probably important to recognize that the child has some limits as to his capacity to endure the suffering and departures of those he loves. In terms of his future mental health, some restraints are important.

## The Adolescent

What is the reaction of adolescents to death? The adolescent is battling to achieve some integration of his adjustment to life. Kastenbaum and Aisenberg (1972) report the studies that have been made regarding a sense of futurity and death on the part of adolescents. They report that the adolescent may be so concerned with the moment that he thinks little about the "second half of his lifespan," but he may at times have thoughts of catastrophe. They summarize:

> We also see that the relationship between futurity and death can be complex within the same individual, let alone from one individual to another. For example, the same young person may (a) feel himself moving rapidly into the future, (b) look forward to this future self as being the "real me", (c) think very little about the second half of his lifespan, and (d) even be convinced that he has more future ahead than he cares to use. Additionally, his #1 expectation that he has a long life-span ahead may alternate with a strong secondary expectation that sudden, violent death will snuff out his life in the near future.

## The Widow or The Widower

The pivotal person in the family, the one who must reorganize the family and help children and adolescents to cope, is the widow or the widower. As of March, 1971 the Census Bureau says there were some ten million widows over age 55 in this country. In comparison there were some two million widowers. The death differential between men and women is enormous. There is no national organization in the United States, as there is in England, to guide widows through their grief work or to help them cope with the economic, social, and psychological problems which beset them on the death of their mates. They are a forgotten group, alone, lonely, isolated, shut out of previous social networks, and burdened with the need for a personal and a family reorganization (Peterson and Briley, 1977). One of the failures in analyzing the mental health problems of widows has been the tendency to lump them together and to over generalize.

In one study (Peterson and Briley, 1977) it was possible to look at special categories of the bereaved in order to be more explicit in terms of their reactions. These widow groups were identified as the *devastated widow*, the *merry widow*, the *not-so-merry widow*, and the *insolvent widow*. The categories may be rough but the significance of the classification calls attention to the differential way in which family history predisposes widows toward particular kinds of problems. Effective intervention depends on identifying specific kinds of grief work challenges which must be individually met if the widow or widower is to emerge a whole person with a renewed life integration. There are some studies, which, although segmental and without theoretical roots, report accurately on the reactions of persons in grief or the experience of those who have dealt with grief.

## THE PROCESS OF GRIEF WORK

Eric Lindemann (1944) added to the literature a very significant series of observations when he studied 101 persons who had lost close relatives in the Boston night-club fire. Through his interviews he was able to identify five basic characteristics of those who suffer such intimate losses. They are:

1. *The syndrome of somatic distress.* Sighing, choking, shortness of breath, exhaustion, digestive disturbances were universally present as part of grief reactions.
2. *Preoccupation with the image of the deceased.* Always the deceased occupied the main stage, and other persons seemed to recede into the background. They were not noticed and often not heard.
3. *Feelings of guilt.* This refers to a profound sense of personal culpability for the deaths of the loved one. Some of the "what-ifs" I have already spoken of are significant here.
4. *Hostile reactions, irritability, anger* and some concern that the psychological reactions were so severe that

the grieving person wondered if he could maintain their sanity in the face of such profound feelings.

    5. *Loss of pattern of conduct.* We have already spoken about the loss of family and social roles. The death of a central person is like an atomic bomb in a city. It rips apart the fabric of living so that the system is gone.

In trying to help bereaved persons adjust to the loss, Lindemann found that certain achievements were essential to good grief work:

    1. *Dealing with the pain of facing the loss.* One must cry with tears and with inner desperation.

    2. *All of the emotions, such as fear, anger, guilt must be expressed.* If one cannot die an appropriate death when one is dying, intimates cannot adjust to their most profound emotional needs if they continue to deny either the death or their basic reactions.

    3. *Eventually by admitting the separation through death, the grieving person must be free from bondage to the deceased.* The image must recede, the guilt must be conquered.

    4. *A grieving person must ultimately readjust to the social environment.* Old roles must be abandoned, new ones adopted.

    5. *New relationships must be formulated.* If a most significant member of the social support system is gone, it is obvious that he or she must be replaced. To continue to grieve over years because a dear one is dead, is to drift into depression and perhaps suicide.

A second study of 133 professional consultants ranging from ministers to psychiatrists were asked to describe the mental health aspects of grief and means of therapeutic intervention. Heimlick, and Kutscher (1970) correlated behavior patterns associated with grief. Ninety-nine percent of the consultants predicted that the loss of a mate would be followed by loss of weight, by sleeplessness, by feelings of despair, and by depression. This correlates with the somatic reactions observed by Lindemann. Ninety percent thought that the bereaved would have dreams about the deceased. While slightly different in concept, this has to do with the preoccupation of the bereaved with the image of the deceased. Seventy-four percent thought that the widowed would picture the presence of the dead person. Seventy-five percent of the consultants, on the basis of their experience, expected the bereaved to be angry over the death of the mate. If the wife had died, 75 percent of the consultants thought that the husband would experience impotence reactions, and an even greater percentage thought that he would show a diminished sexual drive. Interestingly, 73 percent thought that the widowed person would seek help of some consultant; 25 percent would try to talk with a physician and the same percentage of persons would turn to a clergyman for help.

What behaviors would be helpful to the widowed in terms of their grief work? Ninety-one percent felt that talking with another person through their depression would aid recovery. Ninety percent felt that the continuation of a work role would be helpful and 85 percent would recommend eventual remarriage. This may be sage advice, but the demographic picture of the plurality of widows over widowers does not make such advice very cogent. On the basis of this study, the authors made some specific therapeutic suggestions. They thought that:

    1. Dealing with the practical affairs relevant to the funeral and first financial problems was essential to good outcomes.

    2. A clergyman, mortician, friend or therapist who had an opportunity should discuss these "practical affairs" to help the verbalization of deep emotions and to give comfort.

    3. Thus important concerns of loneliness, anger, fears, regrets, and feelings of abandonment can surface and be faced.

    4. If the process is successful and rapport is established, negative and self-destructive thoughts can be ventilated and modified.

Peterson and Briley (1977) comment:

> We believe that it is possible to wash depression away with tears and that (although this is not all there is to the process) grief work is inescapable. If we cannot do it in the weeks and months following a great loss, we will do it one year or five years later, or perhaps a little at a time for the rest of our years.

The success of the CRUSE groups in England has stirred some significant research at the University of Southern California, Harvard University, and Loyola University in Chicago. Carol Barrett (1974) carried on an empirical study utilizing three types of groups with 42 widows at the University of Southern California. The age range was from 32 through 74, and these subjects had been widowed from 2 to 22 years. Half of the husbands had died suddenly. Their average income was just about half of what it had been when their husbands were living. The primary mental health problem of the widows was loneliness; a second problem was the need to deal with grief reactions and a third order problem was their relationships with their families (a finding somewhat presaged by our discussions of the salience of the family in grief situations). Further problems were finances and legal problems. Three different approaches were incorporated in the three groups. One was *a self-help group*; the leader only facilitated the way group members helped each other. A second group called the *confidante group* paired widows so that each pair would form an intimate and helping relationship to the other. The third group was thought of as a *women's consciousness-raising group*. This group focused on the ways that sex roles influenced their adjustment as widows. Each group met for two hours for eight weeks. Evaluation of the effectiveness of these groups depended on measures of attitudes toward widowhood, psychological functioning, and life-styles and attitudes towards sex roles measured before, during, and after the experiment. All three groups showed significant differences in "predicted future health" when compared with a control group. All groups showed increases in self-esteem and joy in being a woman. Participants in the consciousness-raising group brought the most enthusiastic response but all three groups pronounced the eight sessions helpful. The three groups had less depression, less loneliness, less financial stress, fewer family difficulties, and fewer health problems than did the control group that experienced no type of intervention. Barrett (1974) said about these various programs:

> One of the important findings of the research is that widows continue to suffer from grief as well as from the stresses that a male-oriented, youth-oriented, and couple-oriented society subjects them to long after the husband's death. Programs which focus on the problems of the recent widow, although essential, are insufficient.

## THEORETICAL CONSIDERATIONS

Previously I had generated a theory to account for the mental health of older persons as this was influenced by death and dying. But this theory was developed about dying persons. Does it have any relevance to those left behind? How can it handle family reactions to grief, or the reactions of the individual child, adolescent or widow? The general theory is applicable and has power. Note that the loss of a husband is both a prime loss and a factor in a great reduction in the support system. We have analyzed some of the ways in which the family as a major support system is smashed if the family leader, central figure in a power alignment, or scapegoat is lost. In applying this theory to account for the mental health of individual members of the family, some special operations would need to be specified to measure changes in the support systems. I do not think that CS (coping strength) would change particularly. In fact this may be the most stable term in the equation and may account for the differentials in mental health found in research on individuals. Only operationalizing the

theory in research can refine it, but it seems applicable both to measure the mental health of dying persons and of grieving persons, given some subtle specifications of what happens to support systems when a member of that system dies.

## THERAPEUTIC INTERVENTION TO PROMOTE THE MENTAL HEALTH OF DYING AND BEREAVED PERSONS

Some of the implications for intervention with dying persons have already been presented as I have considered the various losses that the dying persons must adjust to in their death trajectory. I may add some further observations. Avery Weisman's (1972) main concern is that those who must be close to dying persons should not react to stereotypes about dying or aging individuals. He lists seven fallacies that characterize the approach of physicians to the dying and thinks that these lead "physicians into inconsistencies and to judgements that confuse the clinical with the moralistic." He feels that often the management of the patient in his last hours is "primarily intended to comfort and console himself." He makes a very large point that:

> The most damaging and lethal fallacy is this, as in most other situations, is that of stereotyping people and problems. When we categorize anyone, doctor or patient, we reduce them to a least common denominator, and they become less than what they are or could be. The alternative, then, is to look for the exceptions, and meanwhile to treat everyone as a special case.

Shneidman (1973) would agree with this. He questions that the death trajectory is nicely organized and routinely goes through Ross's stages. Shneidman has some critical insights for dealing with the dying. He suggests (if we may paraphrase him):

1. That thanatological counseling is unique, although some elements such as building rapport, interviewing, communication, history taking, and silence are used in common with other psychotherapeutic situations.

2. The therapist must be prepared to deal with a "hive of affect, in which there is a constant coming and going."

3. Dreams can be used to understand a patient's emotional needs as he or she approaches death.

4. Therapists (with experience with dying persons) may be aware of the death trajectory and "thus govern the intensity of the sessions, their movement, the climaxes, the protective plateaus . . . over the projected time span."

5. Transference and countertransference, because of time-limited factors, is different. We may "love a dying person, and permit a dying person to love us,

in a meaningful way that is not possible in any other psychotherapeutic encounter."

6. "... but one should not fail to transmit one's honest feelings of interest, affection, and respect for the other's dignity ... presaging one's own real sense of grief at the loss to come."

7. A physician should seek psychiatric consultations for his patients if they are depressed about dying and for *himself* if he senses that his own equanimity has been touched.

Weisman has a further word to say to therapists with a "never-say-die" enthusiasm that is cogent in dealing with the death trajectory. He reminds us that death may be "both appropriate and acceptable as a solution to life's problems. Therapists ... may diagnose depression and denial when there is no evidence of either."

One feels a common thread running through the comments of Ross, Hinton, Weisman, Shneidman, and others who have dealt long and effectively with the dying person. One must have looked into the greyness of the night that every man passes through and not flinch in order to hold the hands of those who are making the great transition. All of the defenses and denials we ascribe to others may in reality be projections of our own in avoiding confrontation with the inevitability of our own extinction. When one has achieved some composure about his own death, he may finally be able to listen creatively with responses and silences that help others have an appropriate death.

As a final word regarding therapeutic interventions, I would like to suggest that our theoretical framework might supply therapists with a straightforward frame of reference. Dealing with the dying and grief work with families or individuals must always be an individual effort, but it is possible to help that effort by paying attention to measurement of the definitions of losses people sustain, by looking carefully at support systems during dying or grieving days, and by paying attention to coping strength. It would certainly be worth a research effort to see if efforts by intervenors which take into consideration each of these important facets might improve their efforts.

# REFERENCES

ANTHONY, S. 1940. *The Child's Discovery of Death*. New York: Harcourt, Brace and World.

BARRETT, C. J. 1974. The Development and Evaluation of Three-Group Therapeutic Intervention for Widows. Unpublished Ph. D. dissertation. University of Southern California, Los Angeles, California.

BERGLER, E. 1957. *The Revolt of the Middle Aged Man*, New York: Hill and Wang, pp. 2–5.

BROWN, F. 1961. Depression and childhood bereavement. *Journal of Mental Science, 107*, 754–777.

BURGESS, E. 1934. *The Family*. Chicago: University of Chicago Press.

DE BEAUVOIR, S. 1966. *A Very Easy Death*, New York: Putnam.

DURKHEIM, E. 1951. *Suicide: A Study in Sociology*, J. A. Spaulding and G. Simpson (eds. and translators), New York: The Free Press.

ERIKSON, E. H. 1959. Identity and the life cycle. *Psychological Issues, I*.

FREUD, S. 1953. Mourning and melancholia. *In*, E. Jones (ed.), *Collected Papers of Sigmund Freud, 4*(10), pp. 152–170. London: Hogarta Press.

GLASER, B. G., AND STRAUSS, A. I. 1965. *Awareness of Dying*. Chicago: Aldine.

GLASER, B. G., AND STRAUSS, A. I. 1968. *A Time for Dying*. Chicago: Aldine.

HARMER, R. 1963. *The High Cost of Dying*, p. 31. New York: Collier Books.

HAVIGHURST, R. J. 1963. Successful aging. *In*, R. Williams, C. Tibbitt, and W. Donahue (eds.), *Processes of Aging*, New York: Atherton Press.

HEIMLICK, H. J., AND KUTSCHER, A. H. 1970. The Families Reaction to Terminal Illness. *In*, B. Schlenberg, A. Carr, D. Perotz, and A. H. Kutscher (eds.), *Loss and Grief: Psychological Management in Medical Practice*, pp. 270–279. New York: Columbia University Press.

HINTON, J. 1967. *Dying*. Baltimore, Md.: Penguin Books.

HOLMES, T. H., AND RAHE, R. H. 1967. The social readjustment scale, *Journal of Psychosomatic Research, 11*, 213–218.

KALISH, R. A. 1977. Death and dying in a social context. *In*, R. N. Binstock and E. Shanas (eds.), *Aging and The Social Sciences*, pp. 483–507. New York: Van Nostrand Reinhold.

KASTENBAUM, R. 1967. The mental life of dying geriatric patients. *Gerontologist, 7*.

KASTENBAUM, R., AND AISENBERG, R., 1972. *The Psychology of Death*. New York: Springer.

KUBLER-ROSS, E. 1969. *On Death and Dying*. New York: Macmillan.

LINDEMANN, E. 1944. Symptomatology and Management of Acute Grief. *American Journal of Psychiatry, 101*, 141–148.

MANT, A. K., 1968. Definition of Death. *In*, A. Toynbee (ed.), *Man's Concern with Death*, New York: McGraw-Hill.

MASLOW, A. H. 1959. Cognition of being in the peak experiences. *Journal of Genetic Psychology, 94*, 43–66.

MATHIEU, J. 1975. Dying and Death Role. Unpublished

dissertation. University of Southern California, Los Angeles, California.

MENNINGER, K. A. 1938. Man Against Himself. New York: Harcourt, Brace & Company.

NAGY, M. 1948. The Child's View of Death. *Journal of Genetic Psychology, 73*, 3–27.

PETERSON, J. A., AND BRILEY, M. L. 1977. *Widows and Widowhood: A Creative Approach to Being Alone.* New York: Association Press.

PETERSON, J. A. 1968. *Married Love In The Middle Years.* New York: Association Press.

ROCHLIN, G. 1967. How younger children view death and themselves. *In*, E. A. Grollman (ed.), *Explaining Death to Children*, pp. 51–88. Boston: Beacon Press.

SAUNDERS, C. 1971–1972. St. Christopher's Hospice Annual Report. London.

SHNEIDMAN, E. S. 1973. Suicide notes. *Psychiatry, 36*, 379–394.

SHNEIDMAN, E. S. 1976. Death work and stages of dying. *In*, E. S. Shneidman (ed.), *Deaths of Man*, New York: Quadrangle.

SIMONTON, O. C. 1978. *Getting Well Again.* New York: St. Martin's Press.

TURNER, B. F., TOBIN, S. S., AND LIEBERMAN, M. A. 1972. Personality tests as predictors of institutional adaptation among the aged. *Journal of Gerontology, 27*, 61–68.

WARNER, W. L. 1965. The City of the Dead. *In, The Living and The Dead*, pp. 360–381. New Haven: Yale University Press.

WEISMAN, A. D. 1972. Common fallacies about dying patients. *In*, A. D. Weisman (ed.), *Dying and Denying: A Psychiatric Study of Terminality.* New York: Behavorial Publications.

WEISMAN, A. D., 1976. Denial and middle knowledge. *In*, E. S. Shneidman (ed.), *Death: Current Perspectives*, 439. Palo Alto, Ca.: Mayfield Publishing Co.

# 39

# Relaxation, Exercise, and Aging

*Robert A. Wiswell*

Teach us to live that we may dread unnecessary time in bed.
Get people up and we may save our patients from an early grave.

> Hymns Ancient and Modern,
> No. 23, Verse 3
> (Adams, 1977, Page 18)

The role of physical activity on the maintenance of mental health status in normal individuals or its therapeutic effects as a treatment in individuals with altered mental health is not well understood. While it is generally accepted that exercise (used in a broad sense to incorporate several types of activities, such as various relaxation techniques, as well as jogging and calisthenics) is beneficial to emotional well-being, the existing scientific evidence is at best contradictory and incomplete. Furthermore, a physiological model which might ex-

plain the possible mechanism of benefit has yet to be postulated. It is reasonable to assume that any of the following physiological adaptations to regular exercise may prove beneficial to mental function.

    1. Improved cerebrovascular circulation (brought about by regular endurance-type exercises).
    2. Increased neuroendocrine sensitivity and function (brought about most likely by endurance-type exercise as well as biofeedback and relaxation strategies).
    3. A change of emotionality (as a result of changes in body image and/or access to more positive psychosocial stimuli).

    In the following chapter the author will present basic knowledge about the changing exercise needs of the organism as it ages with specific regard to effects on mental function. It is hoped that the information in this chapter will incite questions, serve as a resource for mental health practitioners, and provide for those readers who are personally invested in exercise a list of reasonable expectations. The chapter will be organized to provide a general review of physiological decline and the possible effects of exercise on functional losses. Secondly, a review of the literature pertaining to exercise effects on cognitive function, personality, and depression will be provided. The final section will discuss stress and the role of relaxation training on stress reduction and mental function.

## PHYSIOLOGICAL EFFECTS OF AGING AND EXERCISE

### FUNCTIONAL DECLINE

Table 39-1 presents a summary of the major physiological changes that occur as a result of the aging process and which would most likely affect the individual's ability to perform physical exercise; also included is a list of possible physiological benefits of regular exercise. In this context physical exercise is defined as that activity which would require a relatively high percentage of maximal aerobic capacity over a prolonged period of time.

It is interesting to note that while these changes, when viewed as a composite, indicate major losses, they still do not limit one's potential for exercise. The changes suggest a need for decrease in exercise intensity as one ages and therefore requires individualized exercise prescriptions and, to be prudent, medical consultation. Furthermore, one must be aware of the great individual variation in functional losses with aging. For example, it is not uncommon to find several senior Olympians who have a greater functional status than the typical sedentary 25 year old.

It is apparent that all individuals will exhibit the above-mentioned changes. The important thing to note, however, is that the rate of decline may vary between individuals and may be reflective of several factors, one of which is exercise history. With regard to mental health status it may be more appropriate to ask the question of how these changes will affect the psychological state of the individual rather than the physical state. It is obvious, for example, that if one perceives these physical changes to be negative and worries about them, he or she may in fact be accelerating the deteriorative aspects of the aging process. This statement can be supported by the research of Bronson and Eleftheriou (1965) who found that the perceived fear (as measured by corticosterone levels in the serum) by a group of mice that had previous ex-

posure to aggressive fighting mice was physiologically more detrimental than the stress of actual exposure in another group of mice. In other words, if one views the aging process with apprehension and trepidation, he or she may in fact be accelerating decline in much the same way that other life events may lead to specific illness (Holmes and Rahe, 1967).

Another way in which physiological decline may prove detrimental to mental health may be seen in the changes in body image associated with functional decline. For instance, as one ages there will be a marked change in facial appearance. There will be a loss of subcutaneous fat from the face which, when accompanied with one's habitual expression pattern, will result in increased wrinkling (Rossman, 1971). There will be a marked elongation of the ear. The infolding of the mouth brought about by dentition problems and reabsorption of bone from the mandible and maxilla will cause a narrowing of the distance between the nose and the chin (Rossman, 1971). The susceptibility to certain skin disorders, such as pruritis, keratosis, skin cancer, and hyperpigmentation of the skin, increases (Kart, Metress, and Metress, 1978). Osteoarthritic changes will occur at most joints and occurs in all individuals after the age of 20, with a concomitant change in posture leading to kyphosis, a backward curvature of the spine (Grob, 1971). There is also a general flexion (bending) at each joint contributing to the loss in height which occurs with aging. There will be a decline in sensory function reducing one's ability to taste (Arey, Tremain, and Monzingo, 1935), smell (Anand, 1964), see, and hear (Kart *et al.*, 1978). While these changes are not life threatening, they can have dramatic effects on one's feelings of self worth. Kagan and Moss (1962) suggest that psychotherapy may be used to ease the problems associated with changes in body attitude; exercise can be used as well.

*Exercise.* Table 39-1 provides further scientific support for the use of exercise to reduce the rate of aging decline. However, it is beyond the scope of this chapter to provide detailed physiological explanations of the benefit of regular exercise. Suffice it to say that the effects of regular exercise are the antithesis of aging effects in normal pathology-free individuals. Unfortunately, exercise has often been viewed as dangerous and therefore is subject to misunderstanding and, in some cases, unjustified criticism. Jokl and McClellan (1971) in their text on exercise and cardiac death have helped to clarify some of these misperceptions. A point to be made, with regard to the common perceptions of most people that exercise may produce an "athletic heart" and therefore be harmful, is that gross changes in muscle appearance can be similar in disease and chronic exercise states but dissimilar in functional and structural aspects. The enlarged heart in chronic hypertension, for example, has a reduced mitochondria-myofibril ratio, rendering it more susceptible to insufficiency. The cardiac hypertrophy of chronic exercise, on the other hand, increases the proportion of mitochondria to myofibrils, thus increasing the contractile efficiency of the myocardium (Edington and Edgerton, 1976). Thus, there are similar structural responses with very different functional significance.

**Table 39–1**   Physiological Decline Associated with Aging and the Possible Benefit of Regular Strength and Endurance Exercise.

| STRUCTURAL CHANGE | FUNCTIONAL EFFECTS | EFFECTS OF EXERCISE | REF. FOR EXERCISE EFFECT |
|---|---|---|---|
| *Musculo-skeletal System* | | | |
| 1. Muscular atrophy with decrease in both number and size of muscle fibers<br>2. Neuro-muscular weakness<br>3. Demineralization of bones<br>4. Decline in joint function—loss of elasticity in ligaments and cartilage<br>5. Degeneration and calcification on articulating surface of joint | 1. Loss of muscle size<br>2. Decline of strength<br>3. Reduced range of motion<br>4. Reduced speed of movement<br>5. Joint stiffness<br>6. Declining neuromotor performance<br>7. Changes in posture<br>8. Frequent cramping<br>9. Gait characteristics affected:<br>  a. Center of gravity<br>  b. Span (height/arm length)<br>  c. Stride length, speed<br>  d. Width of stance<br>10. Shrinkage in height<br>11. Increased flexion at joints due to connective tissue change | 1. Increased strength of bone<br>2. Increased thickness of articular cartilage<br>3. Muscle hypertrophy<br>4. Increased muscle strength<br>5. Increased muscle capillary density<br>6. Increased strength of ligaments and tendons | Tipton *et al.* (1974)<br>Booth and Gould (1975)<br>King and Pengelly (1973)<br>Holmdahl and Ingelmark (1948)<br>Saltin *et al.* (1977)<br>Turto *et al.* (1974)<br>Clarke (1973)<br>Saltin *et al.* (1977)<br>Kiiskinen and Heikkinen (1973) |
| *Respiratory System* | | | |
| 1. Hardening of airways and support tissue<br>2. Degeneration of bronchi<br>3. Reduced elasticity and mobility of the intercostal cartilage | 1. Reduced vital capacity with increased residual volume<br>2. $O_2$ diffusing capacity is reduced<br>3. Spinal changes lead to increased rigidity of the chest wall<br>4. Declining functional reserve capacity | 1. Exercise has no chronic effect on lung volumes but may improve maximal ventilation during exercise and breathing mechanics | Ekblom *et al.* (1968)<br>Robinson (1938) |
| *Cardio-Vascular System* | | | |
| 1. Elastic changes in aorta and heart<br>2. Valvular degeneration and calcification<br>3. Changes in myocardium<br>  a. Delayed contractility and irritability<br>  b. Decline in oxygen consumption<br>  c. Increased fibrosis<br>  d. Appearance of lipofuscin<br>4. Increase in vagal control | 1. A diminished cardiac reserve<br>2. Increased peripheral resistance<br>3. Reduced exercise capacity<br>4. Decrease in maximum coronary blood flow<br>5. Elevated blood pressure<br>6. Decreased maximal heart rate | 1. Increased heart volume and heart weight<br>2. Increased blood volume<br>3. Increase in maximal stroke volume and cardiac output<br>4. Decreased arterial blood pressure<br>5. Increase in maximal oxygen consumption<br>6. Myocardial effects increased:<br>  a. Mitochondrial size<br>  b. Nuclei<br>  c. Protein synthesis<br>  d. Myosin synthesis<br>  e. Capillary density<br>7. Decreased resting heart rate | Ekblom (1969)<br>Liere and Northrup (1957)<br>Saltin *et al.* 1968<br>Saltin *et al.* (1968)<br>Barnard (1975)<br>Hartley *et al.* (1969)<br>Astrand (1956)<br>Barry *et al.* (1966a)<br>Pollock (1973)<br>Saltin *et al.* (1968)<br>Grimby and Saltin (1966)<br>Tzankoff *et al.* (1972)<br>Fischer and Parizkova (1977)<br>Edington and Edgerton (1976)<br>Skinner *et al.* (1964) |

PSYCHOLOGICAL EFFECTS OF EXERCISE

*Cognitive and Behavioral Characteristics.* The nature of the mind-body relationship is not adequately understood. Dunbar (1947) reviewed several hundred studies dealing with the relationship of emotion and body change and concluded that psychological dysfunction results in physical impairment and/or organic illness. Since that time a myriad of investigators have studied the effects of exercise on these relationships (Botwinick and Thompson, 1968; Clement, 1966; Folkins, Lynch, and Gardner, 1972; Gutin, 1966; Ohlsson, 1976; Spirduso, 1975; and Tweit, Gollnick, and Hearn, 1963.)

Clement (1966) reported no significant differences in intelligence of sportsmen and nonsportsmen (N = 48 pairs aged between 16–90). Each pair was tested twice at five-year intervals, and intelligence was assessed by measures of vocabulary, mental efficiency (coding), and memory. The sportsmen initially weighed less, had faster reaction times, and were more efficient on the forward digit task. When change scores on the tasks were compared over the five-year period, the sportsmen were not significantly better than nonsportsmen. In fact, there was a greater decline in coding ability in the sportsmen group.

Gutin (1966) investigated the effects of a 12-week training program on the individual's ability to perform complex mental tasks following physical and mental stress. The results indicated that increased fitness had no positive effect on the ability of the subjects to perform the tasks. Change in mental performance was, on the other hand, related to the degree of fitness improvement. The major criticisms of Gutin's work relate to his measures of fitness (push-ups, pull-ups, standing broad jump) and the type of fitness intervention (isometrics, calisthenics, and circuit training). Hypothetically one would assume that aerobic training would have yielded better results due to possible effects of circulatory improvement rather than primarily strength improvement.

Tweit *et al.* (1963) trained 26 low-fit college freshmen in a "vigorous" physical training program for six weeks. Significant improvement in reaction times was reported. This change was highly related to fitness improvement. In other words, it appears that the lower one's fitness level the greater the potential improvement in reaction time as a result of regular exercise. Since most individuals with mental decrement have lower functional capabilities, this finding suggests a greater possible benefit to such a group. Similarly, Botwinick and Thompson (1968) observed a shorter reaction time in fit younger subjects than in unfit younger and older subjects. Interestingly, no differences were observed between older subjects and the young, unfit subjects. The major import of Botwinick's work is that when reviewing the literature relating differences between young and old with regard to psychomotor performance, variations in physical fitness are seldom, if ever, considered.

Barry, Steinmetz, Page and Rodahl (1966b) more recently investigated the effects of physical conditioning on motor performance in older adults. Differences were observed in imaging and visual discrimination. The scores on tests of personality, cognition, and motivation did not change. The average age of the experimental group (5 men, 3 women) and the control group (2 men, 3 women) was 70 and 72, respectively. The sample size (only 8 exercisers) and the sexual bias of the group imposes a severe limitation on the importance of the study, however.

Spirduso (1975) and Ohlsson (1976) reported improved performance in fit versus unfit, older subjects. Both studies report faster reaction times in conditioned individuals. Ohlsson further reported that the older, more physically fit subjects in her study were significantly better in attention and were more efficient in the sorting and backward counting tasks.

The following conclusions can be drawn from the preceding review:

1. Physical exercise does have some effects on psychomotor performance.
2. The magnitude of the improvement brought about by exercise training depends on the initial fitness level of the individual.
3. There is probably no "general" activity effect on motor fitness, since different types of exercise may elicit different psychomotor responses.
4. Exercise probably does not affect all areas of cognition and behavior.

*Personality.* There have been several studies on the effects of fitness on personality. Unfortunately, most of these studies deal with specific subsets of young athletes. Hartung and Farge (1977) provide an excellent review of the literature concerning the use of the 16 Personality Factor Questionnaire of Cattell. It is obvious from this review that different sports groups have different personality profiles. For example, Darden (1972) found body builders to be silent and reflective, cautious, and uncommunicative, hardly the stereotype of the athlete. Hartung and Farge observed 48 middle-aged runners and joggers to be more intelligent, imaginative, reserved, self-sufficient, sober, shy, and forthright than the general population. Kroll (1967) found wrestling participants more tough-minded than the general population. Johnsgard, Ogilvie, and Merritt (1975), comparing football players to race drivers and skydivers, reported, as one would expect, that the divers and parachutists were more independent, while the football players were more dependent and expressive. Several other studies (Burdick and Zloty, 1973; Morgan, 1974; Morgan and Costill, 1972; Morgan and Pollock, 1976) have reported on the psychological characteristics of distance runners. The results of these studies are somewhat contradictory. For example, Burdick and Zloty found runners to be more imaginative and forthright, while Morgan reported them to be more reserved and introverted. The major difficulty in interpreting these studies is evidenced in the cross-sectional nature of the research. In other words, one has no way of knowing if certain personality types select certain sports activities or if certain sports activities mold certain personality characteristics.

To avoid the problem of cross-sectional evaluation, several training studies have been conducted to assess personality differences resulting from physical training (Buccola and Stone, 1975; Massie and Shephard, 1971; Naughton, Bruhn, and Lategola, 1968; Young and Ismail, 1976). In Buccola and Stone's study (1975) 36 older subjects participated in either a walk/jogging program or cycling. The results indicated cyclers to be more self-sufficient and less surgent (overbearing) after the intervention while there were no significant changes in the walk/joggers. Hammer and Wilmore (1973) found fit subjects more expedient and forthright; with training, the fit group became more trusting and anxious. Interestingly, they did not find age to be an important factor when appraising the effectiveness of the exercise program on psychological change. "Age was not a factor when considering the relationships of psychological traits and physiological traits and physiological alterations" (page 245). It appears, then, that psychological benefit can be accrued from regular exercise at any age. This statement must be qualified, however, since the oldest subject in the above-mentioned study was 59 years old. This is a good time to point out a major flaw in the majority of studies reviewed in this chapter. It appears that "old" refers to those individuals between the ages of 50–75, with no mention of possible benefits to individuals over the age of 75. To the author's knowledge there are no studies dealing with the psychological effects, either acute or chronic, of exercise training in normal individuals over the age of 80. This is a major limitation because many of the more severe mental health problems are most prevalent in the very old age group.

PSYCHOTHERAPEUTIC EFFECTS OF EXERCISE

*Anxiety.* The effects of exercise on anxiety have been investigated in several studies (Burton, 1976; deVries and Adams, 1972; Driscoll, 1976; Folkins *et al.*, 1972; Jette, 1970; Morgan, 1973; Morgan and Hammer, 1974; Morgan and Pollock, 1976; Morgan, Roberts, and Feinerman, 1971; Popejoy, 1968). Morgan (1973) reports:

> The actual influences of physical activity on anxiety states is quite important since ten million Americans are reported to suffer from anxiety neurosis. Furthermore, between 10 and 30 percent of those patients seen by general practitioners and internists are anxiety neurotics (Pitts, 1969), and therefore, this disease represents one of modern man's major health problems (Page 114).

There is controversy as to the effect of exercise on anxiety. In fact, there is a suggestion that exercise may induce anxiety as a result of elevated lactate production (Pitts, 1969; Pitts, 1971; Pitts and McClure, 1967). In Morgan's (1973) review of this controversy several studies are cited which both corroborate and refute the above-mentioned hypothesis. However, most of the work of Morgan and coworkers would refute such a claim (Morgan, 1973; Morgan *et al.*, 1971; Morgan and Hammer, 1974). An important factor to consider in this context is that exercise does not need to be of such an intensity to induce lactate production in order to bring about reduced anxiety in older subjects. Preliminary data in our laboratory suggest that low-intensity exercise (done in chairs) has a significant state-anxiety reducing effect in normal healthy subjects between the ages of 65–91.

It is interesting to note that exercise has both acute and chronic effects on anxiety reduction. DeVries and Adams (1972) reported that acute exercise of low intensity was effective in reducing muscle action potentials in older people. In this study, the acute effects of exercise were compared to the neuropharmocologic effects of meprobomate, a tranquilizer. The results indicate that acute exercise was more effective in reducing neuromuscular tension, in the muscle groups investigated, than was the drug.

Tredway (1978) reviewed and studied acute and chronic exercise effects on mood, hypothesizing that exercise would probably have a greater influence on expressions of mood than on more stable personality characteristics. Chronic mood effects were assessed before and after a 15-week exercise program by the State-Trait Anxiety Inventory, the Self Rating Depression Scale, and the Mood State Inventory. The results of her study suggest positive effects of exercise on mood, but the type of exercise intervention (calisthenics, aerobic conditioning, and shuffleboard) did not have a major, significant, chronic effect. In other words, the psychosocial involvement of shuffleboard evoked chronic improvements similar to the physiological and psychosocial effects of more intense exercise with the single exception of depression. Driscoll (1976) studied the acute effects of physical exertion and a positive image procedure to reduce anxiety in college students before a major examination. Anxiety was successfully reduced in individual exercise and psychotherapy sessions as well as together in groups.

*Depression.* Morgan, Roberts, Brand, and Feinerman (1970) studied the relationship between depression and measures of physical fitness on 67 male professors. In the first phase of the study, level of depression was correlated with results of a physical examination, structural recall of sleep, activities and dietary consumption. There were no significant results observed. In Phase II of the study, another 34 subjects were added and participated in one of five exercise groups (circuit training, jogging, swimming, treadmill or bicycle ergometry, control). Their findings indicate that for the total group, fitness, as measured by predicted maximal oxygen consumption (the validity of using this measure on older subjects has not been substantiated), is not directly related to depression. When the data were analyzed for the most depressed subjects, a significant improvement in depression resulted. It is also interesting to note that 85 percent of the subjects indicated that they "feel better" as a result of the exercise. Unfortunately, it has been virtually impossible to objectify the meaning and importance of the term "feeling better." In an unpublished study from our laboratory, we appraised the effects of regular exercise (calisthenics, walking and movement improvisation) on depression, anxiety, and the participant's subjective symptoms of health status. Interestingly, while there were no reported improvements in the physiological measures, there was a significant reduction in subjective symptoms; depression, as measured by the Zung self-rating depression scale; and anxiety. Holmes (1968) similarly observed reduction in chronic health complaints as a result of exercise training. The magnitude of improvement was related to exercise intensity in this study. This study is in direct support of the findings of Morgan

*et al.* (1970) that most individuals, middle aged and older, participating in regular exercise programs do, in fact, feel better. Morgan and Pollock (1976) concluded:

> . . . sedentary individuals who embark on training programs consistently experience an improved sensation of well-being following both acute and chronic exercise; this enhanced perception of well-being is associated with decrements in anxiety and depression in those subjects who are initially anxious or depressed; and changes in behavioral states such as anxiety and depression or psychological traits such as extroversion or neuroticism seldom occur in those individuals who score within the normal range from the outset (Page 3).

Morgan and Pollock (1976) reported a significant reduction in depression in a group of 19 depressed subjects over a 6-week endurance training period. Similar changes in a group (N = 20) of non-depressed subjects were not observed.

*Clinical Observations.* Several investigators have studied the effects of exercise as a therapy for mental health patients. Diesfeldt and Diesfeldt-Groenendijk (1977) administered four weeks of group gymnastics to a group of geriatric mental health patients suffering from symptoms of disorientation, apathy, inertia, incontinence, decreased ability to dress, and other such problems. The 40 subjects were divided into an exercise group (x̄ age = 80.9) and a control group (x̄ age = 82.6) and matched on dependency scores. The results indicated that exercise significantly improved total recall and that posting-box error scores, a measure of information processing capacity, changed in the hypothesized direction but were not significant. No changes were observed in mood and cooperation ratings. These results indicate a significant effect of exercise on memory performance. Their main conclusion was that "bringing about positive changes in mental functioning offers an argument against the ideas that senile demented patients are insensible to therapeutic interventions" (Page 63).

Dodson and Mullens (1969) studied the effects of jogging on psychiatric patients ("They range in age from teens to the 50s" Page 130). Eighteen subjects were assigned as controls or to initial assignment into either one or two light exercise groups or a jogging group. Exercise was performed five days a week; and each subject went through all of the exercise stages, each stage lasting three weeks. The results from the Minnesota Multiphasic Personality Inventory (MMPI) indicated a decrease in the hypochondrial and psychothenic scales. Jogging was associated with reduced concern for body processes and reduction in tension. Light exercise was associated with decreased hostilities. Body image changes were also monitored, and significant effects on self-concept were obtained in the jogging group.

Clark, Wade, Massey, and Van Dyke (1975) enrolled 23 geriatric residents of a state hospital (mean age = 69 years) in 12 weeks of exercise. Their hypothesis was that a regular program of physical activity would increase the total daily activity level of the subjects and upgrade patient self-care behavior. A control group, social group (recreational activities) and exercise group (calisthenic exercises, weight training and dancing) constituted the treatment conditions. Improvements were observed, but treatment effects were not significant. In other words, there were increases in daily activity in the exercise group as well as in the social group. This implies that the physiological involvement of the exercise program may not have made significant contributions to the increase in daily activity level. Powell (1974) also studied the psychological effects of exercise therapy on institutionalized geriatric patients. The results of this study contrast the results of Clark *et al.* (1975). Two treatment groups (social therapy and exercise therapy) and a control group were used. Cognition (progressive matrix test, Wechsler Memory Scale) improved significantly for the exercise group compared to social therapy and to the control group after the 12-week intervention. He concluded that the results indicated that "social interaction was not the most important factor in contributing to cognitive improvement found in the exercise treatment group" (Page 161).

It is not within the scope of this chapter to examine the relationship of mental health status to exercise and cardio-vascular status. Several investigators have reported these interrelationships, and the reader is directed to them if interested (Abrahams and Birren, 1973; Jenkins, 1971a, b; Rosenman and Friedman, 1971). It is obvious that relationships do exist between coronary heart disease and personality characteristics. The effect of exercise on the psychological function of post-infarcted patients was studied by McPherson, Paivio, Yuhasz, Rechnitzer, Packard, and Lefcoe (1967). The results indicated that initially cardiacs were significantly more tense, aloof, emotional, hurried, and aggressive than the regular exercising non-cardiacs who were more self-reliant and self-controlled. It is not known whether these traits appear after the cardiac accident or are long-term traits associated with the disease process. The results further indicated that the cardiac exercisers experienced a greater number of favorable changes in personality than the other exercisers or control groups. There was also a significant reduction in anxiety in the exercise group. Again, it appears that exercise is most beneficial for those individuals who demonstrate the most deviant psychological states.

## RELAXATION EFFECTS

Without entering into a discussion of possible mechanisms, it may be speculated that exercise could be effective in contributing to maintenance of mental health status by developing an increased psychological/physiological reserve. Thus, one's tolerance to stressful external stimuli is increased. Another possible mechanism used to cope with the stresses of the environment is to reduce the perceived significance of these events by controlling physiological reactions to them. In the first instance, the individual forces the same external stress to affect a smaller percentage of reserve by having increased systemic functional status. Seen from the second perspective, the individual maintains the same physiologic reserve but is able by controlled central processes to reduce the magnitude of these efferent signals, thus reducing the negative perceptions of them. In the preceding review, the possible role of exercise in increasing psychophysiologic reserve has been presented. In this section a brief discussion of the various relaxation strategies used to promote psychological stability will be provided. The various relaxation techniques to be discussed are:

1. Yoga
2. Transcendental meditation
3. Autogenic training
4. Progressive relaxation

An explanation of these techniques has been summarized recently by Benson (1975) and Hopper (1976).

*Yoga.* Yoga is an ancient philosophy teaching man how to obtain the fullest control over his mind. It teaches the control of all bodily activity as well as functioning of mind and will. This is done so that the individual, in recognizing the differences between body, mind, and will, can be liberated from them. Yoga is more recently defined as specific exercises or movements allowing for the attainment of mental control and well being. There are many variations in yoga meditation practices as well as physical movement techniques. Hathe Yoga deals primarily with postures and control of respiration. Shavasana Yogic technique, on the other hand, is used for teaching relaxation (Hopper,

1976). A review of the studies dealing with the effects of yoga is presented in Table 39-2. A general conclusion can be stated from the results: yoga can be used effectively to chronically reduce blood pressure in hypertensives and acutely in those individuals well trained in specific yogic techniques. While these studies do objectify the benefits of yoga, they are still open to speculation as to the possible subjective benefit. It is obvious that reduction in medications as well as the lowering of blood pressure could have psychological or mental health benefits as well. Presently the author is un-

aware of any study that is specific to the chronic mental health effects of such programs in non-institutionalized healthy older people.

*Transcendental Meditation.* Transcendental meditation is a form of yoga developed by Maharishi Mahesh Yogi. TM gained popularity in the 1960s when several celebrities (The Beatles, Mia Farrow) began using it (Benson, 1975). It is estimated by Benson (1975) that between 500,000 and 2,000,000 people actively practice TM today. TM involves the repetition of a secret word while in a comfortable,

**Table 39–2**   Results of Various Studies of Relaxation on Physiological Function.

| REFERENCE | TREATMENT CONDITION | RESULTS |
|---|---|---|
| *Yoga* | | |
| Anand et al. (1961) | (N = 1) Shri Ramanand Yogi sealed for 10 hours in metal box | Decrease in resting metabolism and heart rate |
| Datey et al. (1969) | (N = 22) Patients, Smavasan Yoga Technique | Decreased mean blood pressure from 134 to 107 and a reduction in medications |
| Patel (1973) | (N = 20) Hypertensives, Yoga and Biofeedback technique | Decreased mean blood pressure and 41 percent reduction in medication intake |
| Patel (1975) | (N = 40) Hypertensives resting on couch replace controls: yoga techniques | Reduction of 42 percent in medications and decreases in both diastolic and systolic blood pressures |
| Patel (1975) | (N = 32) Patients, measure recovery from exercise stress and cold pressor test after 6 weeks of treatment | Significant increase in recovery time after stress, reduced systolic blood pressure and diastolic blood pressure response to the stressors |
| Corby et al. (1978) | (N = 30) College students (age = 22.9) Comparison of trained meditators and naive subjects. Meditation was monitored under three stress-provoking situations | Meditators became "physiologically activated" during medications while controls became relaxed. The meditators also increased EEG alpha and theta power during meditation while showing a reduced skin conductance response as compared to controls |
| *Transcendental Meditation* | | |
| Wallace (1970) | (N = 15) Acute effects of TM were studied on prior TM students with 6 months to 3 years experience. | Decreased resting metabolic rate, ventilation and heart rate and increased alpha waves and skin resistance were reported. |
| Wallace et al. (1971) | (N = 36) The acute effects of meditation were studied on TM students with 2–9 years prior experience. | Lower blood lactates and oxygen consumptions were observed. |
| Reichert (1967) and Levander et al. (1972) | The acute effects of meditation on naive subjects with regard to circulation were measured. | Up to a 300 percent increase in forearm blood flow resulted from the practice of TM. |
| *Autogenic Training* | | |
| Polzien (1953) | Reported clinical observations on several hypertensive patients using autogenic techniques. | An acute reduction in systolic and diastolic blood pressure was reported |
| Schultz (1966) | Used autogenic training to lower the tropotrophic activity in subjects. | Decreased patellar reflex amplitude was demonstrated. |
| Dobeta et al. (1966) | Examined circulatory changes in subjects that were asked to concentrate on the sensation of warmth in the limbs. | Increased peripheral blood flow reported in the arms. |

**Table 39–2** (continued)

| REFERENCE | TREATMENT CONDITION | RESULTS |
|---|---|---|
| *Progressive Relaxation* | | |
| Jacobson (1938) | Reported the results of prior studies of relaxation in tense subjects. | Patellar reflex response to loud noise was reduced with relaxation. |
| Jacobson (1943) | (N = 10) Long term effects of relaxation on right quadriceps femoris was studied using EMG technique. | A significant reduction in EMG response was noted. |
| Steinhous and Norris (1964) | (N = 309) The chronic effect of progressive relaxation was studied in an 8-week intervention on students and the general population | There was a reduction in forehead tension and blood pressure but no long term effects of relaxation on heart rate or ventilatory rate. |
| Grossberg (1965) | (N = 30) Compared relaxation training to listening to music and resting using an abbreviated relaxation procedure. | No significant treatment effects were observed on the variables of EMG, heart rate or skin conductance. |
| Paul (1969) | (N = 60) Compared relaxation training to hypnosis. | Both relaxation and hypnosis produced reduction in EMG, heart rate, skin conductance and respiratory frequence. Relaxation was more effective in reducing EMG than hypnosis, however. |
| Mathews and Gelder (1969) | (N = 24) 14 phobic patients were used to observe the acute effects of relaxation training; 10 others were used to study the chronic effects of the training | No significant chronic effects were observed. Significant EMG reduction was found as an acute effect. |
| Shoemaker and Tasto (1975) | (N = 15) Used abbreviated relaxation and biofeedback techniques on hypertensive subjects. | Significant reduction in both diastolic and systolic blood pressure was observed. |
| Hopper (1976) | (N = 40) Used abbreviated relaxation technique in tense subjects during 6 weeks of training | No significant effects of training in EMG, oxygen consumption or blood flow were observed. |

Adapted in part from review of Hopper (1976).

relaxed position. This word, the Mantra, is given by a trained instructor. The goal for the student is to introspectively seek the source of thought, thus allowing the mind to transcend superficial thought and arrive at a more meaningful experience. An excellent review of literature concerning TM is provided by Kanellakos and Lukas (1974). To summarize the results in Table 39-2, it appears that the acute effect of TM is to decrease sympathetic activity in the autonomic nervous system, therefore allowing for a reduction in metabolic rate, heart rate, and ventilation. The increased forearm blood flow associated with meditation is associated with reduced sympathetic vaso-constriction in the peripheral vascular system (Dobeta *et al.*, 1966).

*Autogenic Training.* Autogenic training is a relaxation technique which consists of six mental exercises which are practiced several times daily. It is the purpose of this therapy to shift the patient from a high arousal state to a low arousal state (Hopper, 1976). The mental exercises, as devised by Shultz, require the patient to concentrate on:

1. the feeling of heaviness in the arms and legs
2. the sensation of warmth in the limbs
3. cardiac control
4. breathing
5. sensation of warmth in the upper abdomen
6. coolness in the forehead.

The results of several investigators indicate an acute effect of autogenic training of increased electromyographical activity and peripheral blood flow and decreased blood pressure. The use of autogenic training in this country has been quite limited.

*Progressive Relaxation.* Progressive relaxation, developed by Jacobson (1938), emphasizes the relaxation of all voluntary skeletal muscles. Jacobson contends that subjects, when asked to relax, still have a given level of residual tension. It is the objective of progressive relaxation to reduce the tension in muscles to the level of electrical silence. It was Jacobson's theory that relaxation states and anxiety represent opposing physiological conditions and cannot, therefore, simultaneously exist. Wolpe and Lazarus (1966) have developed an abbreviated method of progressive relaxation. Using their technique, Jacobson's original program is reduced from over an hour to approximately 20 to 30 minutes. The following example of the method is taken from Wolpe and Lazarus (1966, Page 259):

> [... as you relax like that, clench your right fist, just clench your fist tighter and tighter, and study the tension as you do so. Keep it clenched and feel the tension in your right fist, hand, forearm ... and now relax.]

After relaxation of the fist the technique continues with the arms, face, neck, shoulders, upper back, chest, stomach, lower back, hips, thighs, and calves. Progessive relaxation has been demonstrated to reduce neuromuscular tension and arterial blood pressure over prolonged training periods. Use of the abbreviated technique of progressive relaxation has not resulted in significant improvement in the dependent measures of blood pressure, electromyography (EMG), or forearm blood flow.

Another method used commonly for relaxation is biofeedback. There is an extensive literature relating to the use of biofeedback for inducing relaxation (Beary and Benson 1974; Datey, 1975; Mehearg and Eschette, 1975). However, it will not be reviewed in this chapter. Biofeedback, unlike the other methods discussed, requires a sophistication in bioelectric instrumentation; and while it is effective in stress reduction, it is not practical for general use in community health care settings. This does not imply that the other methods are superior to biofeedback. It simply implies a lack of general application.

It is interesting to note in this regard a study conducted by Staples and Coursey (1975), comparing EMG feedback with progressive relaxation and autogenic training. The results of their investigation indicated that both progressive relaxation and biofeedback methods were more effective in reducing EMG readings than was autogenic training. Subjectively the participants liked progressive relaxation and biofeedback more than those in the autogenic training group. Similarly, Sime (1977) compared exercise and meditation in reducing the physiological response to stress. Forty-eight high-test-anxiety students were assigned into one of three treatment groups (treadmill exercise, meditation, placebo pill). The results demonstrated that exercise produces a significantly greater decrease in heart rate, EMG and electrodermal response than the placebo. Furthermore, meditation produced a significantly greater decrease in EMG than the placebo. State anxiety levels were markedly reduced in both meditation and exercise groups; the

differences were not statistically significant, however. It is interesting to note that these results are quite consistent with the earlier findings of deVries and Adams (1972) that mild exercise may have a role in eliciting the relaxation response or in stress reduction.

In summary, it appears that there is good scientific support for the suggestion that individuals are able to exert, in degree, cognitive control over several physiological functions usually assumed to be regulated by the autonomic nervous system. The physiological mechanism by which exercise and relaxation training induce change is still a relatively open question.

## PHYSIOLOGICAL OR PSYCHOLOGICAL MECHANISMS FOR CHANGE

A major benefit of exercise and relaxation with regard to mental health is the potential ability of these interventions to assist older individuals in coping with stress, either physical or emotional. The psychological and physiological mechanisms of stress have been reported in a preceding chapter (see Birren and Renner). The manner in which exercise and relaxation reduce the detrimental effects of stress is not clearly understood. One may hypothesize that any of the following mechanisms may be in operation to assist the organism to maintain homeostasis when exposed to stressful situations:

1. Regular endurance activity may increase the efficiency and coordination of efferent signals from the brain. This change in efficiency may be obtained by improvements in nerve conduction velocity and/or increase receptor responsivity to similar levels of electrical and/or biochemical stimulation.

2. Regular exercise may influence cellular metabolic processes and therefore require lower secretion rates of specific hormones. Whether this could be accomplished by intercellular regulation affecting membrane sensitivity or by a neurologic feedback to the central nervous system is unknown.

3. Chronic exercise has the effect of improving peripheral vascular circulation and reducing, in part, vascular resistance. It may be that the increased vasculature serves as a buffer system by which stressor substances are utilized, thus reducing the effects of endocrine hypersecretion during stressful situations and exercise. Furthermore, if increases in central blood flow were observed, a more efficient central processing could be achieved resulting in improved psychomotor performance and, perhaps, a readjustment of the homeostatic set for stimulation of the sympathetic adrenal-medullary and pituitary adrenal-cortical systems.

4. Acute effects of mild exercise which would increase hormone utilization and/or relaxation technique

which would reduce hormone secretion could influence one's state of arousal, thereby affecting psychomotor efficiency.

It is quite easy to postulate mechanisms of control, but scientific support for such notions is not available. The acute and chronic effect of exercise on hormone secretion rates and utilization is controversial. Furthermore, interpretation of the results of studies relating to exercise and hormones can be misleading. For example, hormone concentration at any time is affected by: (a) the rate of glandular hormone production, (b) the rate of hormone destruction, (c) the rate at which hormones are taken up by the tissues, and, finally, (d) the extent to which any changes in blood volume occur (Lamb, 1978).

Lamb (1978) provides a good example of the difficulty in interpreting results of prior exercise studies:

> Accordingly, a rise in hormone concentration in the blood during exercise could be interpreted as an increased output of the hormone by its endocrine gland source, a decreased destruction of the hormone (perhaps because of reduced blood flow to the liver or kidneys), or a decreased uptake of the hormone by its target tissues. Even if it was proved that the rise in hormone concentration was because of increased production, the total adaptive effect of this increased hormone production may be insignificant if the production rate does not remain elevated long enough to allow the greater hormone levels to have any substantial effects on the target tissues. Thus, one must use great caution in the interpretation of changes in blood or urine levels of hormones with exercise. Such changes may indeed reflect some important alteration in endocrine function, or they may only reflect changes in blood flow either to target organs or to sites of hormone degradation. Unfortunately, most of the available data on endocrine changes with exercise consist only of reports of changes in blood or urine levels of the hormones in question. Until more complete information on other aspects of the metabolism of such hormones is available, one is probably wise not to place too much importance on observed changes in hormone concentrations in blood or urine (Page 305).

Due to these limitations, the author will not attempt to review the existing literature related to exercise and neuroendocrine responses. It is important to understand in this context, however, that different phases of exercise may stimulate different hormonal responses, some of which are necessary for energy liberation while others are used to prepare the body for stress. Thus, the increased hormone secretion rates of ACTH, cortisol, epinephrine and norepinephrine during the anticipatory phase of exercise relate to the perception of the difficulty of tasks and not directly to the amount of work to be performed. In this manner, the psychological effects on hormone secretion rates are additive with the increases in hormone secretion necessary for immediate energy utilization. The reduced resting levels of circulating hormones and the reduced hormone secretion rates during the anticipation phase of exercise, as well as during the initial, adaptation, exhaustion, and recovery phases of exercise that accompany chronic exercise programs, may be a result of a perceived decrease in intensity (of similar work bouts) added to an increased metabolic efficiency, if such exists. It is possible that the ability of individuals to cognitively control their perception of exertional or emotional stress is the link tying aerobic exercise and relaxation responses together as a contributor to positive mental health. In this context both exercise and relaxation may be the mediators of a central control mechanism to reduce the psychological impact of stress and to further keep the body in metabolic balance.

DeVries (personal communication, 1979) is presently investigating the hypothesis that the effects of exercise on eliciting the relaxation response may be controlled at local levels rather than centrally. In this study he is observing the effects of low-intensity exercise on monosynaptic reflex patterns. It is hoped that the results of this study will shed light on the controversy about the effects of exercise and relaxation. In this regard, it can also be assumed that a study of the chronic exercise effects on premotor and motor reaction time would elucidate a distinction between improvement in central processing time versus improved motor responsiveness (Schmidt and Stull, 1970). In this way, the change in reaction time as reported in the literature could be redefined based upon central versus local adaptations.

## IMPLEMENTATION

Although the studies on physical fitness and mental health do not yield consistent or unequivocal results, it is apparent that physical defects, illness, and systemic dysfunction are related to poor mental health and social maladjustment. Therefore, if exercise has a positive effect on improving physical health, these changes may result in improved mental health. The major problems faced by mental health practitioners are, first, how to motivate their clients to exercise and, secondly, how to determine what type of exercise or relaxation strategy is most appropriate.

A recent survey (President's Council on Physical Fitness and Sports, 1974) indicates that approximately 45 percent of the (110 million) individuals over the age of 22 in this country do not engage in physical activity for the purpose of exercise. The results further indicate that 63 percent of those who do not exercise regularly feel they get enough exercise, while only 53 percent of those who exercise regularly are satisfied with their amount of exercise. A major reason for lack of compliance to regular exercise in older adults is the negative attitude they and relatives and often health professionals have concerning the benefits and risks of such programs.

Conrad (1976) has characterized these attitudes as follows:

1. They believe their need for exercise diminishes and eventually disappears as they grow older.
2. They vastly exaggerate the risks involved in vigorous exercise after middle age.
3. They overrate the benefits of light, sporadic exercise.
4. They underrate their own abilities and capacities.

Many older people simply feel they do not need to exercise. Unfortunately this is not the case. Experts in the medical profession concur that the single most effective way to accelerate the aging process is to do nothing. The term hypokinetic (low movement) disease has been coined to describe those diseases that may be caused or accelerated by inactivity. The need for exercise does not diminish with age; the intensity of exercise and maximal potential for exercise decreases but the need does not. In fact, more than 20 percent of regularly exercising adults exercise at the suggestion of their physician.

The perception of risks constitutes a major reason older adults do not exercise. Certainly, there are occasional problems that do arise as a result of vigorous exercise. Furthermore, the news media have helped to precipitate the negative attitude by dramatizing the occasional cardiac problems occurring during exercise. It has been estimated, however, that a heart fatality will occur in jogging programs once for every 189,000 miles run. In practical terms, this means one can expect, in an exercise class of 50 people meeting three times per week, a cardiac fatality every six and one-half years.

Jokl (1971) has stated that "Even the most strenuous exercise will not cause death in subjects with normal hearts." The difficulty, then, encountered in changing one's attitude about exercise is to instill in people confidence about their medical health status. To do this a close tie is required between the person and his physician or nurse.

It should be mentioned at this time that pre-exercise medical examinations are not always practical or necessary. The necessity is based on the intensity and result expectations of the exercise program. If the exercise program is directed toward aerobic improvement, which would require a relatively high level of exercise intensity (walking, jogging, swimming, and similar activities), a medical clearance is obviously necessary. If, on the other hand, exercise is directed toward psychosocial involvement with its concomitant effects on mental health status, low intensity programs could be used successfully without requiring medical clearance. It is the author's contention in this chapter that low-intensity exercise can have as dramatic an effect on mental health status in older adults as does aerobic conditioning. In other words, while high-intensity exercise may contribute to both increased physiological status and psychological well being, low-intensity exercise may, by contributing to psychological well being, reduce specific factors contributing to accelerated physical decline. An important factor when programming for exercise as a mental health therapy is not so much what people do but what they will continue to do. Thus, both exercise of various intensities and relaxation techniques of various types have a viable role in the prevention and treatment of mental health problems of the aged.

The factors which contribute to lack of exercise motivation in the normal adult may be entirely different in the older portion of the population, especially those with some type of physical impairment. For example, women with mastectomies or individuals with colostomies most certainly can swim but for psychosocial reasons may choose not to. It is for reasons similar to this that a major consideration that must be made with regard to exercise planning on any level, institutional or home, is to recognize that trauma to the body and self-esteem must receive priority before suggesting type of exercise. Thus, concern for the individual's feelings preempts the therapist's preoccupation with a single treatment program or intervention. One should remember that there are always alternative methods for treatment which can be successful if one will just take the time to consider the individual's feelings and to review all possible alternatives.

## SUMMARY

A major result of the aging process is a decline in function of the locomotor and cardio-respiratory systems. These changes may reduce one's ability for maximal exercise but most likely will not reduce one's potential for social mobility. Unfortunately, these changes may have a dramatic effect on the individual's feeling of self-worth and body image. The attitudinal changes may cause the person to become socially isolated and inactive. This, in turn, may lead to various states of mental dysfunction, such as depression and anxiety, and contribute to an accelerated aging decline in physiological function.

It is in this context that exercise and relaxation therapy are valuable. Aside from the contribution of regular endurance-type exercise to improved physiological performance, there is a substantial literature that suggests a further role in the maintenance of and/or improvement in cognitive function, psychomotor performance, and possibly positive personality characteristics. The changes may improve the self-care potential for the older adult as well as increase the desire for maintenance of vitality. The mechanisms to explain these changes are not clear. However, it is obvious that the interrelationships of social stimulation, muscular activity, relaxation, and central processing involvement are additive and contributory to improved mental health status in patients as well as in healthy older adults. It should be stated in conclusion that there is no evidence that prudent exercise is detrimental in any way to the physical or mental health of older people. There is no reason why exercise programs and relaxation training could not and should not be part of any program, community or institution, dealing with mental health problems.

# REFERENCES

ABRAHAMS, J. P., AND BIRREN, J. E. 1973. Reaction time as a function of age and behavioral predisposition to coronary heart disease. *Journal of Gerontology*, *28*, 471–478.

ADAMS, G. 1977. *Essentials of Geriatric Medicine*. Oxford: Oxford University Press.

ANAND, B. K., CHHINA, G. S., AND SINGH, B. 1961. Studies on Shir Ramanand Yogi during his stay in an airtight box. *Electroencephalography and Clinical Neurophysiology Supplement*, *49*(I), 82–89.

ANAND, M. P. 1964. Accidents in the home. *In*, W. F. Anderson and B. Isaccs (*eds.*), *Current Achievements in Geriatrics*, p. 239. London: Cassell.

AREY, L. B., TREMAIN, M. J., AND MONZINGO, F. L. 1935. The numerical and topographical relation of taste buds to human circumvallate papillae throughout the life span. *Anatomical Records*, *64*, 9.

ASTRAND, P. O. 1956. Human physical fitness with reference to sex and age. *Physiological Reviews*, *36*, 307.

BARNARD, R. J. 1975. Long term effects of exercise on cardiac function. *In*, J. H. Wilmore and J. F. Keogh (eds.), *Exercise and Sport Sciences Reviews*, *3*, pp. 113–127. New York: Academic Press.

BARRY, A. J., DALY, J. W., PRUETT, E. D. R., STEINMETZ, J. R., PAGE, H. F., BIRKHEAD, N. C., AND RODAHL, 1966a. The effects of physical conditioning on older individuals. I. Work capacity, circulatory-respiratory function, and work electrocardiogram. *Journal of Gerontology*, *21*, 182–191.

BARRY, A. J., STEINMETZ, J. R., PAGE, H. F., AND RODAHL, K. 1966b. The effects of physical conditioning on older individuals. II. Motor performance and cognitive function. *Journal of Gerontology*, *21*, 192–199.

BEARY, J. F., AND BENSON, H. 1974. A simple psychophysiologic technique which elicits the hypometabolic changes of the relaxation response. *Psychosomatic Medicine*, *36*, 115–120.

BENSON, H. 1975. *The Relaxation Response*. New York: William Morrow.

BOOTH, F. W., AND GOULD, E. W. 1975. Effects of training and disuse on connective tissue. *In*, J. H. Wilmore, and Keogh (eds.), *Exercise and Sport Sciences Review*, *3*, pp. 84–107. New York: Academic Press.

BOTWINICK, J., AND THOMPSON, L. W. 1968. Age differences in reaction time: An artifact? *Gerontologist*, *8*, 25–28.

BRONSON, F. H., AND ELEFTHERIOU, B. E. 1965. Adrenal response to fighting in mice: Separations of physical and psychological causes. *Science*, *147*, 627–628.

BUCCOLA, V. A., AND STONE, W. J. 1975. Effects of jogging and cycling programs on physiological and personality variables in aged men. *Research Quarterly*, *46*, 134–139.

BURDICK, J. A., AND ZLOTY, R. B. 1973. Wakeful heart rate, personality and performance—A study of distance runners. *Journal of Sports Medicine and Physical Fitness*, *13*, 17–25.

BURTON, E. C. 1976. Relationship between trait and state anxiety, movement satisfaction, and participation in physical education activities. *Research Quarterly*, *47*, 326–331.

CLARK, B. A., WADE, M. G. MASSEY, B. H., AND VAN DYKE, R. 1975. Response of institutionalized geriatric mental patients to a twelve-week program of regular physical activity. *Journal of Gerontology*, *30*, 565–572.

CLARKE, D. H. 1973. Adaptations in strength and muscular endurance resulting from exercise. *In*, J. H. Wilmore (ed.), *Exercise and Sport Sciences Reviews*, l, New York: Academic Press.

CLARKE, H. H. (Ed.) 1974. National Adult Fitness Survey.

*President's Council on Physical Fitness and Sports, Physical Fitness Research Digest, 4*(2), 1–22.

CLEMENT, F. 1966. Effect of physical activity on the maintenance of intellectual capacities. *Gerontologist, 6,* 91–92, 126.

CONRAD, C. C. 1976. When you're young at heart. *Aging,* Adminstration on Aging, US DHEW, 11.

CORBY, J. C., ROTH, W. T., ZARCONE, V. P., JR., KOPELL, B. S. 1978. Psychophysiological correlates of the practice of Tantric Yoga Meditation. *Archives of General Psychiatry, 35*(5), 571–577.

DARDEN, E. 1972. Sixteen personality factor profiles of competitive bodybuilders and weightlifters. *Research Quarterly, 43,* 142–147.

DATEY, K. K. 1975. Effect of relaxation using biofeedback instruments in systemic hypertension. *Proceedings of the Biofeedback Research Society.* Monterey, California, 13.

DATEY, K. K., DESHMUKH, S. N., DALVI, C. P., AND VINEKAR, S. L. 1969. Shavasan: a Yogic exercise in the management of hypertension. *Angiology, 20* 325–333.

DEVRIES, H. A., AND ADAMS, G. M. 1972. Electromyographic comparison of single doses of exercise and meprobamate as to effects on muscular relaxation. *American Journal of Physical Medicine, 51,* 130–141.

DIESFELDT, H. F. A., AND DIESFELDT-GROENENDIJK, H. 1977. Improving cognitive performance in psychogeriatric patients: The influence of physical exercise. *Age and Aging, 6,* 58–64.

DOBETA, H., SUGANO, H. AND OHNO, Y. 1966. Circulatory changes during autogenic training. *In,* J. J. Lopez Ibor (ed.), IV World Congress of Psychiatry. Madrid, 5-11, IX. *International Congress Series,* No. *117,* 45. Amsterdam: Excerpta Medica Foundation.

DODSON, L. C., AND MULLENS, W. R. 1969. Some effects of jogging on psychiatric hospital patients. *American Corrective Therapy Journal, 23,* 130–134.

DRISCOLL, R. 1976. Anxiety reduction using physical exertion and positive images. *Psychological Record, 26,* 87–94.

DUNBAR, F. L. 1947. *Emotion and Bodily Changes.* New York: Columbia University Press.

EDINGTON, D. W., AND EDGERTON, V. R. 1976. *The Biology of Exercise.* Boston: Houghton Mifflin.

EKBLOM, B. 1969. Effect of physical training on oxygen transport system in man. *Acta Physiologica Scandinavica,* Suppl 328.

EKBLOM, B., ASTRAND, P. O., SALTIN, B., STENBERG, J., AND WALLSTROM J. 1968. Effect of training on circulatory response to exercise. *Journal of Applied Physiology, 24,* 518–524.

FISCHER, A. A., AND PARIZKOVA, J. A. 1977. A follow-up study of the effect of physical activity on the decline of working capacity and maximal °2 con-

sumption in the senescent male. *In,* R. Harris, and L. J. Frankel (eds.), *Guide to Fitness After Fifty,* New York: Plenum.

FOLKINS, C. H., LYNCH, S., AND GARDNER, M. M. 1972. Psychological fitness as a function of physical fitness. *Archives of Physical Medicine and Rehabilitation, 43,* 503–508.

GRIMBY, G., AND SALTIN B. 1966. Physiological analysis of physically well-trained middle-aged and older athletes, *Acta Medica Scandinavica, 179,* 513.

GROB, D. 1971. Common disorders of muscles in the aged. *In,* A. B. Chinn (ed.), *Working with Older People; Clinical Aspects of Aging,* Washington, D.C.: DHEW.

GROSSBERG, J. M. 1965. The physiological effectiveness of brief relaxation training in differential muscle relaxation. Technical Report No.IX, Western Behavioral Sciences, La Jolla.

GUTIN, B. 1966. Effect of increase in physical fitness on mental ability following physical and mental stress. *Research Quarterly, 37*(2).

HAMMER, W. M., AND WILMORE, J. H. 1973. An exploratory investigation in personality measures and physiological alterations during a 10-week jogging program. *Journal of Sports Medicine and Physical Fitness, 13,* 238–247.

HARTLEY, L. H., GRIMBY, G., KILBOM, A., NILSSON, N. J., ASTRAND, I., BJURE, J., EKBLOM, B., AND SALTIN, B. 1969. Physical training in sedentary middle-aged and older men. III Cardiac output and gas exchange at submaximal and maximal exercise. *Scandinavian Journal of Clinical Laboratory Investigation, 24,* 335–344.

HARTUNG, G. H., AND FARGE, E. J. 1977. Personality and physiological traits in middle-aged runners and joggers. *Journal of Gerontology, 32,* 541–548.

HOLMDAHL, D. E., AND INGELMARK, B. E. 1948. Der bau des gelenkknopels unter verschiedenen funktionellen verhaltrissen. *Acta Anatomica, 6,* 309–375.

HOLMES, H. Z. 1968. Effects of training on chronic health complaints of middle-aged men. Unpublished Doctoral Dissertation, University of Illinois, Department of Physical Education.

HOLMES, T. H., AND RAHE, R. H. 1967. The social readjustment rating scale. *Journal of Psychosomatic Research. 11,* 213–218.

HOPPER, R. T. 1976. An investigation of the chronic physiological changes due to relaxation training and practice. Unpublished Doctoral Dissertation, University of Southern California, Department of Physical Education.

JACOBSON, E. 1938. *Progressive Relaxation,* Ed. 2. Chicago: University of Chicago Press.

JACOBSON, E. 1943. The cultivation of physiological relaxation. *Annals of Internal Medicine, 19,* 965–972.

JENKINS, C. D. 1971a. Psychologic and social precursors

of coronary heart disease (Part I). *New England Journal of Medicine, 284,* 244–255.

JENKINS, C. D., 1971b. Psychologic and social precursors of coronary heart disease (Part II), *New England Journal of Medicine, 284,* 307–317.

JETTE, M. 1970. A study of long-term physical activity in sedentary middle-aged men. (Doctoral Dissertation, University of Illinois at Urbana-Champaign, 1969) *Dissertation Abstracts International, 30,* 2832A (University Microfilm No. 70–00, 889).

JOHNSGARD, K., OGILVIE, B., AND MERRITT, K. 1975. The stress seekers: A psychological study of sport parachutists, racing drivers, and football players. *Journal of Sports Medicine and Physical Fitness, 15,* 158–169.

JOKL, E. 1971. Exercise and Cardiac Death. *Journal of the American Medical Association, 247,* 1707.

JOKL, E., AND MCCLELLAN, J. T. (eds.), 1971. *Exercise and Cardiac Death. 5,* Medicine and Sport, Baltimore: University Park Press.

KAGAN, J., AND MOSS, H. 1962. *Birth to Maturity,* New York: John Wiley.

KANELLAKOS, D. P., AND LUKAS, J. S. (Eds.) 1974. *The Psychobiology of Transcendental Meditation: A Literature Review.* Menlo Park, Calif.: Benjamin, Inc.

KART, C. S., METRESS, E. S., AND METRESS, J. F. 1978. *Aging and Health, Biologic and Social Perspectives.* Menlo Park, Calif.: Addison-Wesley.

KIISKINEN, A., AND HEIKKINEN, E. 1973. Effect of prolonged physical training on the development of connective tissue in growing mice. *Proceedings of the International Symposium on Exercise Biochemistry,* 25.

KING, D. W., AND PENGELLY, R. G. 1973. Effect of running on density of rat tibias. *Medical Science Sports, 5,* 68–69.

KROLL, W. 1967. Sixteen personality factor profiles of collegiate wrestlers, *Research Quarterly, 38,* 49–56.

LAMB, D. R. 1978. *Physiology of Exercise Responses and Adaptations,* New York: Macmillian.

LEVANDER, V. L., BENSON, H., WHEELER, R. C., AND WALLACE, R. K. 1972. Increased forearm blood flow during a wakeful hypometabolic state. *Federation Proceedings, 31,* 405.

LIERE, E. J. VAN, AND NORTHRUP, D. W. 1957. Cardiac hypertropy produced by exercise in albino and in hooded rats. *Journal of Applied Physiology, 11,* 91.

MASSIE, J. F., AND SHEPHARD, R. J. 1971. Physiological and psychological effects of training. *Medicine and Science in Sports, 3,* 110–117.

MATHEWS, A. M., AND GELDER, M. G. 1969. Psycho-physiological effects of training. *Journal of Psychosomatic Research, 13,* 1–12.

MCPHERSON, B. D., PAIVIO, A., YUHASZ, M. S., RECHNITZER, P. A., PACKARD, H. A., AND LEFCOE, N. M. 1967. Psychological effects of an exercise program

for post infarct and normal adult men. *Journal of Sports Medicine, 7,* 95–102.

MEHEARG, LE. E., AND ESCHETTE, N. 1975. EMG measures and subjective reports of tension in feedback and no-feedback groups. *Proceedings of the Biofeedback Research Society.* Monterey, California, 13.

MORGAN, W. P. 1973. Influence of acute physical activity on state anxiety. *Proceedings of the National College of Physical Education Association, 76,* 113–120.

MORGAN, W. P. 1974. Selected psychological considerations in sports. *Research Quarterly, 45,* 374–390.

MORGAN, W. P., AND COSTILL, D. L. 1972. Psychological characteristics of the marathon runner. *Journal of Sports Medicine and Physical Fitness, 12,* 42–46.

MORGAN, W. P., AND HAMMER, W. M. 1974. Influence of competitive wrestling upon state anxiety. *Medicine and Science in Sports, 6,* 58–61.

MORGAN, W. P., AND POLLOCK, M. L. 1976. Physical activity and cardiovascular health: Psychological Aspects. *Ergopsychology Laboratory Report, 26,* 1–15.

MORGAN, W. P., ROBERTS, J. A., AND FEINERMAN, A. D. 1971. Psychologic effect of acute physical activity. *Archives of Physical Medicine and Rehabilitation, 52,* 422–425.

MORGAN, W. P., ROBERTS, J. A., BRAND, F. R., AND FEINERMAN, A. D. 1970. Psychological effects of chronic physical activity. *Medicine and Science in Sports, 2,* 213–217.

NAUGHTON, J., BRUHN J. G., AND LATEGOLA, M. T. 1968. Effects of physical training on physiological and behavioral characteristics of cardiac patients. *Archives of Physical Medicine, 49,* 131–137.

OHLSSON, M. 1976. Information processing related to physical fitness in elderly people. *Reports from the Institute of Applied Psychology, 71,* 1–12.

PATEL, C. H. 1975. Twelve-month follow up of yoga and biofeedback in the management of hypertension. *Lancet, i,* 62–64.

PATEL, C. H. 1973. Yoga and biofeedback in the management of hypertension. *Lancet, ii,* 1053–1055.

PAUL, G. L. 1969. Physiological effects of relaxation training and hypnotic suggestion. *Journal of Abnormal Psychology, 74*(4), 425–437.

PITTS, F. N., JR. 1969. The biochemistry of anxiety. *Scientific American, 220,* 69–75.

PITTS, F. N., JR. 1971. Biochemical factors in anxiety neurosis. *Behavioral Sciences, 16,* 82–91.

PITTS, F. N., JR., AND MCCLURE, J. N., JR. 1967. Lactate metabolism in anxiety neurosis. *New England Journal of Medicine, 277,* 1329–1336.

POLLOCK, M. I. 1973. The quantification of endurance training programs *In,* J. H. Wilmore (ed.), *Exercise and Sport Sciences Review, l,* pp. 155–188. New York: Academic Press.

POLZIEN, P. 1953. Versuche zur normalisier und der st-strecke und t-zache in EKG von der psyche her.

*Zeitschrift fuer Krieslaufforschung, 42,* 9–10.

POPEJOY, D. I. 1968. The effects of physical fitness program on selected psychological and physiological measures of anxiety. (Doctoral Dissertation, University of Illinois at Urbana-Champaign, 1967) *Dissertation Abstracts International, 28,* 4900A. (University Microfilm No 68–08, 196.)

POWELL, R. R. 1974. Psychological effects of exercise therapy upon institutionalized geriatric mental patients. *Journal of Gerontology, 29,*157–161.

PRESIDENT'S COUNCIL ON PHYSICAL FITNESS IN SPORTS. 1974. National Fitness Research Digest, Series 3, No. 2.

RIECHERT, H. 1967. Plethysmmographische untersuchungen bein knozentgrations und medialahonsubungen. *Arzliche Forchung,* 661–665.

ROBINSON, S. 1938. Experimental studies of physical fitness in relation to age. *Arbeitsphysiologie, 10,* 251–323.

ROSENMAN, R. H., AND FRIEDMAN, M. 1971. The possible role of behavior patterns in proneness and immunity to coronary heart disease. *In,* H. I. Russek and B. L. Zohman (eds.), *Coronary Heart Disease,* Philadelphia: J. B. Lippincott.

ROSSMAN, I. 1971. *Clinical Geriatrics.* Philadelphia: J. B. Lippincott.

SALTIN, B., BLOMQUIST, B., MITCHELL, J. H., JOHNSON, R. L., WILDENTHAL, K., AND CHAPMAN, C. B. 1968. Response to submaximal and maximal exercise after bed rest and training. *Circulation, 38,* (suppl. 7).

SALTIN, B., HENRIKSSON, E., NUGAARD, E., ANDERSEN, P., JANSSON E. 1977. Fiber types and metabolic potentials of skeletal muscle in sedentary man and endurance runners. *Annals of the New York Academy of Science.*

SCHMIDT, R. A., AND STULL, G. A. 1970. Premotor and motor reaction time as a function of preliminary muscular tension. *Journal of Motor Behavior, 2,*(2), 96–110.

SCHULTZ, J. H. 1966. *Das autogen Training.* Stuttgart: Konzentrative Selbstspannung (12 Aufl.)

SHOEMAKER, J. E., AND TASTO, D. L. 1975. The effects of muscle relaxation on blood pressure of essential hypertensives. *Behavior Research Therapy, 13*(1), 29–43.

SIME, W. E. 1977. A comparison of exercise and meditation in reducing physiological responses to stress.

*Medicine and Science in Sports, 9,* 55. (abstract).

SKINNER, J. S., HOLLOSZY, K. O. AND CURETON, T. K. 1964. Effects of a program of endurance exercises on physical work, *American Journal of Cardiology, 14,* 747.

SPIRDUSO, W. W. 1975. Reaction and movement time as a function of age and physical activity level. *Journal of Gerontology, 30,* 435–440.

STAPLES, R. AND COURSEY, R. D. 1975. A comparison of EMG feedback with two other relaxation techniques. *Proceedings of the Biofeedback Research Society.* Monterey, California.

STEINHAUS, A. H., AND NORRIS, J. E. 1964. Teaching neuromuscular relaxation. *Cooperative Research Project,* No. 1529. Education Resources Information Center. Washington D.C.: U.S. DHEW.

TIPTON, C. M., MATTHES, R. D., AND SANDAGE, D. S. 1974. In situ measurement of junction strength and ligament elongation in rats. *Journal of Applied Physiology, 37,* 758–762.

TREDWAY, V. A. 1978. Acute and chronic effects of exercise upon women and men, aged 52 to 85. Unpublished Doctoral Dissertation, University of Southern California, Department of Psychology.

TURTO, H., LINDY, S., AND HALME, J. 1974. Protocollagen proline hydroxylase activity in work-induced hypertrophy of rat muscle. *American Journal of Physiology, 226,* 63–65.

TWEIT, A. H., GOLLNICK, P. D., AND HEARN, G. R. 1963. Effect of training program on total body reaction time of individuals of low fitness. *Research Quarterly, 34,* 508–512.

TZANKOFF, S. P., ROBINSON, S., PYKE, F. S., AND BRAWN, C. A. 1972. Physiological adjustments to work in older men as affected by physical training. *Journal of Applied Physiology, 33,* 346–350.

WALLACE, R. K. 1970. Physiological effects of transcendental meditation. *Science, 167,* 1751–1754.

WALLACE, R. K. BENSON, H., AND WILSON, A. F. 1971, A wakeful hypometabolic physiological state. *American Journal of Physiology, 221,* 795–799.

WOLPE, J., AND LAZARUS, A. 1966. *Behavior Therapy Techniques: a Guide to the Treatment of Neuroses.* Oxford: Pergamon Press.

YOUNG, R. J., AND ISMAIL, A. H. 1976. Personality differences of adult men before and after a physical fitness program. *Research Quarterly, 47,* 513–519.

# 40

# Preventive Aspects
# of Mental Illness in Late Life

*Charles M. Gaitz & Roy V. Varner*

Proving that mental illness can be prevented, especially in aged persons, is extremely difficult—evidence for it has rarely been sought. The literature is rather rich, however, in descriptions of service-delivery systems that have been useful in alleviating or reducing specific problems of late life. Inferences may be drawn from this information and from the authors' experiences to predict or suggest what might be preventive in both a primary and secondary sense. The reports come predominantly from the area of secondary prevention: early recognition and treatment of late-life mental problems, usually at the point of being clearly identified as mental disorders of late life. One could argue that social welfare and health programs for the aged also will have a salutary effect on mental health before illness per se becomes identifiable.

## LIFE CYCLE CONSIDERATIONS AND OTHER PREDETERMINANTS OF MENTAL STATUS IN OLD AGE

Mental status in old age is a result of many factors. There is an interaction of physiological, psychological, developmental and social aspects, as shown in the following discussion.

### PSYCHOGENETIC INFLUENCES AND PERSONALITY PATTERNS

A life cycle approach offers a theoretical framework for understanding personality development and mental health status in old age (Butler and Lewis, 1977). Early relationships with parents, siblings, and other significant individuals influence one's interpersonal behavior over the years, shaping personality traits that eventually affect adjustment to the conditions of old age. Fastidious, perfectionistic individuals, for example, are probably more vulnerable to feelings of frustration and inadequacy when faced with the compromises and losses associated with old age than are persons who have been less demanding of themselves. On the other hand, persons with patterns of exaggerated dependence on others may have few other coping mechanisms and become even more dependent and withdrawn when old. Persons with lifelong suspiciousness and mistrust may become frankly paranoid, perceiving themselves as being acted upon. Individuals whose adjustments were marginal or fragile earlier in life may be further compromised when they have to deal with added stresses in late life.

Many use denial as a mechanism of coping with anxiety. Denial patterns interfere with the acceptance of aging at all life stages, but especially in old age. Aging politicians, for example, talk about "our elderly" as if they were not a part of the group. Men and women are secretive about their age and overuse hair dyes, wigs, cosmetics, etc., reflecting a personally and probably culturally determined need to appear young. Physical prowess is exaggerated and impairments are ignored. Such denials impede healthy adaptation to the reality of aging. Failure to consider the probability that one's capacities will decline eliminates the possibility of planning ahead; it may lead to a rude awakening one day to the realization that "I am old." Of course denial is promoted in any society that values youth and deprecates age, as expressed when referring to old people as "85 years young" rather than "85 years old." A person's degree of defensiveness toward his own aging, then, may be a dynamic predictor of late-life psychological adaptability.

## APPROPRIATENESS OF LIFE GOALS, RETIREMENT ATTITUDE, AND LEISURE TIME USE

For many people, late life is a time when goals have been reached, and they feel satisfied with a life well spent; those who fear they have not achieved their goals experience the anxiety of "time running out." Although goal-setting does not cease at any age, persons who carry high expectations into old age may encounter problems when accelerated losses and onset of physical debilities may limit productive activity. An "it won't happen to me" philosophy leads to an unrealistic self-appraisal of capacities and needs. To deny the inevitability of retirement and associated changes, for example, precludes

planning and makes a crisis of the event. Yet ambivalence toward retirement is understandable in a society that values work more than leisure. While some people look forward to retirement as a reward, for others it is a symbolically degrading experience, proof of socioeconomic disenfranchisement. Psychological factors may be more important than economic ones in adjusting to retirement; even financially secure persons may feel restless, useless, and guilt-ridden. Having grown up in a work-oriented culture, they may find little satisfaction in the options available to them. Furthermore, interpersonal conflicts (e.g., in marriage) and emotional conflicts related to self-esteem may have been masked by an emphasis on success in the work role and then surface only after retirement when such persons can no longer use this technique of denial.

## FAMILY RELATIONSHIPS

Marital adjustment is an important element in late-life mental harmony. For those who are happily married, support from a spouse cushions the pressures associated with late life. Consequently, a partner in such a relationship will likely experience a greater threat at the loss of his mate than would the surviving spouse in a less supportive marriage. Couples caught in completely unrewarding marriages maintained precariously over the years may not be able to cope with late-life stresses. Physical illness and increased demands for attention by one partner accentuate latent dissatisfaction and frustration. A supportive marital situation, on the other hand, may be a matrix in late life for pursuit of leisure activities, a solution to isolation and loneliness, and mutual assistance with each other's losses and infirmities. Single old persons, especially those who never married or who had few interpersonal attachments, are especially likely to be lonely.

For elderly parents and adult children, the quality and quantity of contacts often depend on experiences earlier in life. A warm, supportive relationship with children, as with a spouse, can be extremely helpful in coping with the vicissitudes of late life. Problems may arise if parent-child relationships have been arid. Aging does not insulate parents from feeling responsible for adult children who have adjustment problems, and if they have never had close relationships with their parents, adult children may find it difficult or impossible to provide moral and financial support to parents experiencing stress.

Decisions often have to be made about where elderly persons will live and how self-reliant they are. Realistically, the parents may need help from adult children, but this precipitates conflicts of, for example, loss of self-esteem versus the need for dependency gratification.

When parent-child relationships have been poor, resolution of the dependence-independence crises of late life (vis-à-vis one's adult children) becomes more difficult. Attitudes are more important than simple questions of support; aging does not desensitize parents or children to conflicts, and ultimately the outcome will be determined by the extent of mutual respect, love, and concern. Discord arises when children ignore their parents' wishes, or when the parents attempt to remain in an autonomous living situation that is no longer practical. Some children are angry when parents use up money and property (albeit their own) that might otherwise be left to the family. Hostility may be expressed in subtle or overt ways: instances of physical abuse have been recognized; attempts to have parents declared incompetent or to place them in living situations that foster more dependence than is necessary are not uncommon. The relationship with children, then, may either promote good adjustment in late life or reinforce the trend of a general psychological and physical decline for elderly parents.

Still another psychodynamic determinant of mental adaptability in late life is the elderly person's personal experience with his or her own aging parents (Kral, 1967). If the parents' old age is associated with negative experiences, one might view one's own future in such a way that faulty adaptation becomes, at least partially, a self-fulfilling prophecy. If one's parents were able to maintain good health, to meet their needs reasonably well and remain autonomous into old age, one might anticipate late life as similarly fulfilling. It is unfortunate that many persons approach late life pessimistically, even nihilistically, and consequently do not take steps that could lead to happiness and satisfaction.

## GENETIC ASPECTS AND PREVIOUS MENTAL AND PHYSICAL HEALTH STATUS

Genetic history and long-term personal mental and physical health data over the years, particularly in regard to the brain matrix of schizophrenia and major affective illness, is also pertinent to late-life mental health status. Persons with family histories of schizophreniform illness and recurrent affective disorders may not manifest such disorders until they are unable to cope with stresses peculiar to late life. Many individuals, of course, have exacerbations and remissions of functional disorders throughout their lives, and late-life stresses tend to complicate and compound these conditions. Therefore the genetic central-nervous-system heritage, as well as the previous psychiatric history, may be pertinent in predicting the type of emotional decompensation that might occur under late-life stresses. A genetic link has been established in Alzheimer's disease when it occurs in the presenium; it now appears that the same morphologic brain changes occur when symptoms are first noted late in life.

One of the difficulties in establishing a genetic link is the lack of precise information about relatives judged to have been senile. The importance of this kind of genetic loading is not clear. It may be that some of us enter later life somewhat more genetically predisposed to intellectual impairment than do others. Certainly there is more to the etiology of true late-life dementia than psychosocial stresses and faulty medical care. The disease has an irreversible biophysical or chemical brain substrate, and perhaps genetic predeterminants are important.

The foregoing applies equally to the question of physical health. The interplay between physical health status (both intra- and extracranial) and mental health status is well recognized and will be discussed later.

## EXISTENTIAL, RELIGIOUS, AND PHILOSOPHIC ASPECTS

Aging brings one closer to the end of life, to a narrowing future, and to an increased predilection to retrospection (Erikson, 1959). Butler (1974) writes about the relationship of a life review to successful aging, stressing this as an opportunity to formulate a satisfactory resolution of life that integrates past and present legacies. He points out that old age is the only stage of life when there is little future, a concept that has significant psychodynamic implications for those whose life review might reveal unresolved conflicts and guilt, unfulfilled goals and needs, and too many losses. Such a review is common in depressed older persons who not only are flooded with current stresses and losses but cannot even view their past life with a sense of accomplishment. Such situations may be psychogenetic precursors of unhappiness and dissatisfaction, if not depression, in late life.

A person's overall philosophic stance on the meaning of life, the nature of man, and religious orientation to "life after death" may have positive or negative significance in late life. Overconcern with death does not seem to be an important factor in late-life emotional adjustment, although such preoccupation often occurs as a symptom associated with depression and sense of unworthiness. In a religious sense, long life may be viewed as a temporal reward for worthiness or for living a righteous life. It may also, paradoxically, evolve into a tedious, overly stressful, unrewarding existence, so that Butler's question, "Why Survive?" (1975b) truly takes on existential meaning. Some people apparently approach life with a preconscious notion that they do not wish to be old and therefore will never grow old. The vicissitudes and realities of late life may present both a shock and an adaptational challenge to such individuals, especially to those who now are living much longer than did their parents.

## BRAIN PHYSIOLOGY

A discussion of mental status in old age must recognize that brain function is the biological basis of all behavior. Therefore, it is necessary to point out, though briefly, certain fundamental concepts of brain physiology that influence mental health status in late life. Although the aging brain is definitely a changing organ, it is not necessarily diseased (Samorajski, 1976, 1977). The brain as it ages is less adaptable to stress than it once was. Stress, whether biochemical or psychosocial, ultimately must be mediated through brain structures. Regardless of its nature, stress is likely to precipitate more manifestations of cognitive and emotional impairment, and to do so to a greater degree in the old than in the young brain. The less adaptable aging brain may be further compromised when frank disease is superimposed. This may be of vascular, senile atrophic, metabolic, or other physical origin (Meier-Ruge, 1975).

What *appears* to be cognitive impairment of late life is often a reversible phenomenon that Butler (1975a) labels *pseudodementia*, which is observed clinically in the absence of any definable brain disease. That modification of all stress systems may occur is a major philosophic and practical position for the geropsychiatric clinician to hold. Even the presence of irreversible brain disease in late life does not forecast inevitable failure or an entirely negative outcome. One can never be sure that cognitive and emotional functions will not improve somewhat when stress is relieved.

## THE STRESS SYSTEM OF LATE LIFE

Wang's (1977) model for the etiology of late-life organic brain syndromes may also be used as a loss-stress model for the etiology for all late-life mental illness, whether primarily cognitive, emotional, or a combination of these two. Wang envisions a dynamic interaction of biological, psychological, and socioeconomic stresses, set in the matrix of a stress-susceptible aging brain, and modified further by psychogenetic and cellular genetic predeterminants. With reference to prevention, the basic precept would be that of intervention in the loss-stress system at various levels over the entire course of the life cycle, and especially in late life when losses become accelerated.

The concept of cumulative losses that probably begin somewhere in midlife and accelerate into late life may be equated with the concept of stress within each of the three stress areas described above, the biological area including both intracranial and extracranial disease states. The "stress-system" concept concerns the dynamic interaction between the three components as losses occur, accumulate, and amplify the effects of each loss throughout the later course of the life cycle. The final common pathway may then be frank and absolute brain impairment, relative functional brain impairment, emotional impairment—these, again, occurring singly or together, each amplifying the clinical expression of the other. The actual losses do not need to be listed here, although it should be said that the common emotional denominator of the system is loss of self-esteem with reactive depression, often clinically definable as mental illness. In the biological sphere, the common denominator is an ultimate loss of cerebrocortical morphologic and/or functional integrity.

## INTERVENTION AFFECTING THE STRESS SYSTEM OF LATE LIFE

### IN EARLY LIFE STAGES

Primary prevention, at least theoretically, may occur at any time in life; however, it is extremely difficult to demonstrate a direct relationship between an intervention or a characteristic of an individual early in life, and mental status in late life. Nevertheless, certain presumptions seem reasonable, and an orientation toward health rather than illness is encouraged (Fuchs, 1974). Obviously, mental illness developing at any point in the life cycle should be treated energetically, with a view to follow-up and continuity of outpatient care, once the illness and need for intervention is established. Ineffectively treated mental illness of early life will often be unmasked by the additional and cumulative stresses of late life (Varner and Calvert,

1974). Proponents of early intervention argue that attention to stress systems in young persons may carry with it some future benefit (Braceland, 1972). Counseling and social interventions may mitigate the possibility of illness later, and these may be provided by nonmedical personnel in the absence of a clearly defined physical or mental illness. According to Post (1965), many emotional disorders manifested in later life—depression, paranoid disorders, personality changes, and neuroses—actually are rooted in an earlier phase of adult life or in childhood. The hope is that effective intervention early in life will minimize the possibility of a recurrence.

The mental health service system has become truly multidisciplinary; nonmedical counselors and caregivers contribute significantly to the system, and even more aid will be available as the health industry expands. Clarification of roles, standards, training requirements, and responsibilities is necessary since serious problems of funding and quality of care have already arisen. An attainable goal despite these potential barriers is the delivery of primary preventive service at least by middle age, to better prepare persons to cope with the vicissitudes of old age and to minimize the expression of mental illness late in life.

Education to prepare persons for successful adjustment in old age should begin early in life. Irrational attitudes, stereotypes, and prejudices, termed *ageism,* should be dispelled with such efforts beginning in elementary schools. Contacts with older persons, acceptance of aging with its inevitable losses and other changes, and understanding of changes in value systems and other measures help children and young adults learn about aging and its true characteristics and to overcome fears and misconceptions. Preparation for retirement also should begin early in life rather than at the last moment. The implication here is that an intellectual approach may be effective in primary prevention of mental illness in late life. An important part of the educational process is to teach persons early in life that psychotherapeutic intervention in stressful situations throughout the life cycle may be more effective than trying to solve problems alone, often in maladaptive and ineffective ways. Marital therapy might be of benefit. Expanded child- and adolescent-guidance programs carry the hope of a more satisfactory adult, midlife, and hence late-life adjustment.

## IN LATE LIFE

The concept of primary prevention at earlier life stages is also pertinent to late life. In 1942, Miles recommended that every person have a routine checkup with a psychiatrist, psychologist, or other mental health professional specializing in geriatrics—not because of illness but, as the author stated, because the older person wants a professional, objective answer to the "How am I doing?" question. This proposal may be utopian, though it makes as much sense as the annual or semiannual physical checkup. Obstacles inherent in such preventive programs relate partially to older persons' reluctance to seek help for psychiatric or psychological problems (especially as a preventive measure). But a growing number of public mental health agencies are becoming actively involved with geriatrics treatment. Some primary preventive needs are undoubtedly already being met by workers in the senior citizens centers, by nurse-therapists in some well-staffed nursing homes, by recreation therapists and counselors in prevention-oriented centers, and by family clinicians concerned about their patients' emotional as well as physical well-being.

Some secondary preventive work—early diagnosis, treatment, follow-up, and general continuity of care—is under way in the public psychiatric sector, and on a small scale so far, in various sections of the country—by us at Texas Research Institute in Houston, at the University of Washington in Seattle, at Duke University, and at the Massachusetts Mental Health Center in Boston. These programs may serve as models for various approaches to comprehensive, multidisciplinary mental-health-service delivery either within existing community programs or as separate but cooperative arrangements. Much of the problem consists of creating interest, initiative, and the reality of service delivery for older patients within existing programs that could well expand their geriatric services.

## ATTITUDES OF CAREGIVERS

Many practicing mental health professionals who are potential geriatric mental health clinicians prefer to work with younger clients because they feel that a mentally ill younger person will be more amenable to therapy and that the rewards will be greater because of the client's potentially longer useful life. Mentally ill older persons are often regarded somewhat pessimistically even by trained clinicians, including psychiatrists, who do not wish to "waste time." Cyrus-Lutz and Gaitz (1972) found that fewer than two percent of patients of private psychiatrists were older than 65.

Getting the physician, whether psychiatrist or other, to make an accurate psychiatric diagnosis is another problem. Each patient deserves a careful appraisal, not a diagnosis based on stereotypes of the elderly and prejudices of the examiner. When organic brain syndrome is misdiagnosed, too frequently the opportunity to treat depression or to alter psychosocial stresses is overlooked.

An attitudinal change is needed if mental health professionals are to have more realistic outcome expectations for their elderly clients. Many clinicians are unwilling to accept "minimal" results as favorable, even though higher expectations are often unrealistic. We need a new set of criteria for "favorable outcome," whether our preventive intervention is primary or secondary, or whether intervention is primarily medical, psychological, or social. We must accept, for example, that most true organic brain disorders of late life cannot be completely reversed. Yet a patient's disability from such disorders may be alleviated temporarily or his/her decline may be delayed. Achieving these objectives is reasonable and provides the incentive to work with persons whose prognosis is not good and may deteriorate regardless of treatment. Even in these cases we need to maintain a positive attitude, working as thoroughly as the state-of-the-art will allow. We cannot turn away from patients for whom the prospects of favorable results seem minimal (Gaitz and Baer, 1970).

We need to encourage our colleagues to provide continuity of care for elderly persons. Continuous follow-up is mandatory since losses occur and the needs of elderly clients are constantly changing, perhaps even more rapidly toward the end of life. Clinicians characteristically wish for a "cure" or almost complete reversal of pathology. This is not always attainable in psychiatry, and certainly not in geriatric psychiatry.

Goldfarb (1972) stressed the importance of the caring attitude of the caregiver; he said that thoroughness, interest, and optimism are therapeutic in themselves because they restore an elderly client's lost sense of self-esteem. As geriatric clinicians we must think in terms of *altering, modifying,* and *delaying,* rather than *curing, totally reversing,* or *completely preventing.* Both primary and secondary preventive efforts will produce more favorable results when the elderly are approached realistically. The personal rewards for the professional will be gained only when he or she modifies outcome expectations to some degree and is willing to maintain long-term and tedious follow-up. Even when continuity of care and conscientiousness of mental health professionals have been more than adequate, some patients may improve only minimally, and some patients will deteriorate. If one has reason to believe that deterioration is the nat-

ural history of a process—and this is the fate of many conditions associated with aging—therapists may take some satisfaction from efforts, primary and secondary, that delay decline.

## ATTITUDES OF ELDERLY PERSONS AND FAMILIES

Emotional problems in late life may represent a self-fulfilled prophecy for many elderly persons and their adult children who expected late life to be accompanied by some emotional and cognitive dysfunction. Consequently, early signs of depression and mild cognitive abnormalities signal what the parents and children anticipated, and they accept them as an inexorable process that cannot be altered or halted. Such persons do not realize that intervention in the stress system carries hope of favorable change. Education about the realities of aging may lead elderly persons to a more optimistic attitude and effective use of resources. This is equally true of children who should be told what may be realistically expected and what can be done to help their parents. Family members are more likely to seek services if, instead of believing that obtaining help is not worth exhausting the funds and personal resources of their parents, they have reason to expect some improvement or relief of the parents' condition.

## ROLE OF CAREGIVERS

Elderly persons often require a variety of services, more than a single individual or agency can provide. Thus services may be fragmented and uncoordinated, and there is little consistency from one community to another. A few mental health centers provide comprehensive care: social and health agencies, individual health practitioners, paraprofessionals, and volunteer agencies may provide assistance. Some agencies may have a primarily medical/psychiatric focus, others a social intervention information and referral model, and still others may provide counseling and recreational services. Rarely will a single discipline or approach be able to claim exclusive "territorial rights"—a multidisciplinary cooperative effort is required. To overcome barriers and to achieve a high level of care, a coordinator to obtain other services is required (Gaitz, 1970). Although such a person may provide services directly, he or she is perhaps more helpful in providing preventive care, obtaining help from other caregivers, providing information, and achieving full use of family and community resources. In a multidisciplinary center, one member of a treatment team assumes the coordinator role; individual practitioners provide comprehensive services to the extent possible while seeking help from others. The restrictions imposed by strict definitions of roles and responsibilities of a particular discipline or agency must be overcome for the benefit of the elderly persons being served. The coordinator's maintenance of continuity is important in preventing disability and chronicity in the client. For a hospital patient, for example, dependence and disability may be minimized by coordinating the efforts of the physician and mobilizing family and community resources to make home care feasible, thus reducing the period of hospitalization. A community that provides a range of services and settings for care obviously offers more alternatives for satisfying its citizens' needs.

Preventive measures are possible even in long-term care facilities. Good medical and nursing care, adequate attention to nutrition, and opportunities for socialization may indirectly improve or maintain functional capacity and mental health. Led by nurses, group programs for both severely and minimally disturbed nursing-home residents have proved effective in altering the residents' rate of intellectual decline and emotional withdrawal (Burnside, 1973). Physicians' assistants and nurses also may provide frontline advocacy and relay a need for medical/psychiatric intervention in nursing homes. The list of potential caregivers is long (Varner and Verwoerdt, 1975). The main requirement is a sensitivity to the requirements of elderly persons and the desire and stamina to obtain for them what they need.

## PSYCHIATRIC FACILITIES AND PROGRAMS

Community mental health centers have a mandate to provide geriatric services in addition to children's and general adult services. Unfortunately, there are only a few easily identified programs. The literature contains a number of innovative approaches, not strictly psychiatric, that might be developed in psychiatric facilities. These approaches have preventive significance in delaying, modifying or altering the course of mental decline in late life. One example would be a program that provides counseling to persons who are recently bereaved. Early and rapid intervention by a social agency, a minister, a friend or family member offers emotional relief and assistance in making appropriate socioenvironmental changes. The Group for the Advancement of Psychiatry (n. d., about 1970) suggested that nonprofessional paid workers who themselves had experienced a recent loss and worked through the subsequent grief might be es-

pecially effective as adjunctive counselors with newly bereaved persons because they could offer practical advice about financial and living arrangements. The benefit of counseling as a preventive measure is stressed by Wilson (1970), who also urges intervention when one spouse becomes terminally ill.

Most mental health centers and other psychiatric facilities do not have highly developed programs. Often limited to designating a nurse or social worker as the "geriatric coordinator," these programs have low priority and support. Physicians and psychiatrists in private practice are capable of rendering valuable preventive services, but they often lack the time, interest, and knowledge about the processes of aging to be as effective as they might be. Payment for services is, of course, a major factor since such third-party payors as Medicare often are unwilling to provide benefits for psychiatric treatment equal to those provided for medical care.

Elderly persons are prone to a combination of medical and psychiatric problems. A comprehensive treatment plan requires attention to both and thus psychiatric facilities must also be prepared to provide medical services, directly or indirectly.

If one accepts the principle that the mental health of elderly persons derives from medical, psychological and social aspects, a multidisciplinary approach to prevention and treatment follows. Having stressed this several times, let us review briefly several kinds of services that have proved the feasibility and benefits of intervention. Many approaches, in different settings, are possible.

The need for a coordinator of medical, psychological, and social services and the value of multifunctional assessment as a technique of early secondary intervention has been stressed (Gaitz and Hacker, 1970). Brody (1974) noted that multiple problems require multidisciplinary intervention and coordination called "linkages." He suggested that a health maintenance organization model might prove feasible for both primary and secondary intervention. Early medical intervention and continuity of medical care have inherent preventive aspects. Patterson (1976) surveyed a number of community mental health centers and concluded that advocates are needed not only to provide services in the center but also to encourage elderly persons to seek help. This principle holds for all types of organizations interested in delivering mental health services. Matlack (1975) described geriatric day hospitals as a locus for multidisciplinary comprehensive services. The availability of such programs shortens period of medical and psychiatric hospitalization, facilitates transition to community living, and provides care in an environment less restrictive than a hospital.

## MEDICAL APPROACHES

A close relationship between mental health and physical health has long been recognized, and many authors have stressed the importance of providing adequate mental health care (Gubrium, 1971). Anderson (1974) stressed the integration of physical and mental health preventive services as beginning in the homes of persons over 70, and that these early screening services could be provided by a home "health visitor" such as a nurse. A health center for the elderly devoted to their special problems of drug therapies, multiple drug usage, and other age-related issues such as housing and social planning (Anderson, 1975) represents a further development of community-based preventive services. Lowther, McLeod, and Williamson (1970) confirmed the advantages of early diagnosis and treatment, but Elwood and Oakes (1975) found that nonuse of a preventive health service was related to lack of education and understanding of the potential value of health screening. Ironically, elderly persons might not use a well-designed service delivery system because it is too complex or because personnel working there are less sensitive to their needs.

## PSYCHIATRIC SERVICES

Butler (1975a) stressed the need for mental health services in general, emphasizing home-care and services by workers trained in various professional disciplines. He points out problems inherent in the overuse of the concept of "senility." Kent (1975) made a similar plea for a more relevant and useful diagnostic classification as a basis for effective intervention, but he adopted an overly simplistic "organic" position on the etiology of mental illness in old age. Adopting an either-or posture as a basis for formulating diagnostic conceptualizations and interventions is dangerous for persons interested in prevention. Horsley (1966) attempted to clarify "senility" by dividing it into "normal senescence" (gradual physiological, mental, and physical decline; and gradual social disengagement) and "disease senescence" (true organic brain matrix of pathologic alteration). Roth (1963) also attempted to clarify the ideologic and diagnostic problems of late-life mental disorder. He recommended early intervention as a secondary preventive measure and opposed a do-nothing attitude that follows from a wastebasket clinical impression of "senility."

Much remains to be done in diagnosing ac-

curately the mental diseases of late life, but even with our present knowledge it is clear that early diagnosis and treatment prevent or delay the regression of older persons who are enduring multiple stresses (Todd, 1966). Like others, Todd reminds us that symptoms of senility may be reversible. Even when expectations are realistic and services available, the actual process of service delivery is complex and requires interdisciplinary education, coordination, and awareness of each participant's capability (Gaitz, 1974).

# TWO COMMON PSYCHIATRIC DISORDERS IN LATE LIFE—PREVENTIVE STRATEGIES

The two most common psychiatric disorders in late life are organic brain syndrome and depression. Active treatment and continuous care make it possible to alleviate distress and minimize disability.

## LATE-LIFE ORGANIC BRAIN SYNDROMES

Other chapters in this book deal fully with etiology, treatment, and prognosis of organic brain syndromes (OBS). A case of primary (or senile) cortical atrophy will be presented to illustrate strategies relevant to prevention, but these interventions apply as well to other categories of dementia. Some clinicians believe that true chronic late-life dementia is untreatable and therefore they do nothing; others feel that dementia would not occur at all if more attention were paid to preventive measures throughout the life cycle and if intervention were undertaken vigorously when organic mental symptoms first occurred in the aged patient. Both are extreme and unrealistic views.

Still, the question remains why an aging brain would exhibit reversible dementia when a younger brain under similar stresses would not. The answer has been alluded to earlier (Meier-Ruge, 1975). Both the early and late stages of true dementia have components of impaired mental functioning that are in fact alterable and improvable, although not curable. It is for this reason that we advocate treatment for late-life organic brain syndrome.

The following case history demonstrates application of some of the principles we have discussed.

A 72-year-old white, widowed female was committed to a private psychiatric facility because of paranoid behavior and severely deteriorated self-care. One precipitating cause of commitment was her leaving the gas range burning for hours in her apartment because she could not remember to turn it off. This and other symptoms had occurred during the process of an insidious two-year intellectual decline noticed by her daughter and other family members who lived nearby. Several attempts had been made to move the mother into the daughter's home, although the patient had ultimately insisted on the freedom to live alone. She remained in her apartment until her condition began to pose an obvious threat to her safety and general well-being.

Findings on admission included markedly impaired cognition, with a score of only 20 percent correct answers on the Pfeiffer Mental Status Questionnaire (Pfeiffer, 1975). Medical examination and laboratory tests found no focal neurologic abnormalities and no other physical abnormalities other than a nonfocal electroencephalographic tracing with rather diffuse slowing of the background rhythm. Routine brain scan Ic 99 (radio isotope scan technique) suggested mild asymmetry of carotid flow, but generally the impression was of some diffuse reduction of cerebral blood flow. She had no history of cerebrovascular accident and the intellectual decline had been gradual, constant, without fluctuation, and without much insight on her part. She acknowledged her memory deficit, but would not admit her overall self-care deterioration and was quite hostile toward the daughter for attempts at intervention. There was also evidence of a history of occasional friction between the two. Currently the daughter felt overwhelmed by guilt, partially because of the mother's uncooperativeness and overall hostility.

Under treatment with antipsychotic medication and occupational therapy in the hospital, the patient's paranoid symptoms improved greatly. After discharge she agreed to live in the daughter's house; the living arrangement seemed to pose no problems since the husband was agreeable and the children were away from home at college. The patient further agreed to attend three days a week at a daycare program run by a local nursing home. She and her daughter are seen jointly in the office every six months and the situation seems to have reached a plateau.

Although the patient obviously needs round-the-clock supervision, she is quite easily managed in a home setting. The hostile interaction between mother and daughter has almost stopped; the mother's demeanor and personal appearance would not suggest a past history of problems. A mental status examination, however, reveals clearly that her cognition is not really improved. She still scores only 10 to 20 percent correct on the Pfeiffer questionnaire but she now accepts her intellectual deficit. She is maintained on a low dosage of antipsychotic medication and is also receiving a triple ergot compound which will probably be continued indefinitely. The patient ultimately may decline cognitively as well as physically, but secondary intervention has altered the progress of the decline.

We believe that a favorable status has been achieved even though no improvement in cognitive function is noted. This is an example of a therapist's acceptance of a limited goal, whether prevention be primary or secondary. It is obvious that we were not dealing with pseudodementia, but rather with an OBS in a person whose condition probably would have worsened if the attitude that such conditions are untreatable had been taken. Preventive strategies in such cases suggest the need for a positive and vigorous assessment and treatment with limited goals. The patient is much happier now, the quality of her life has improved, and she has had an extended period of functioning at a level that enables her to remain at home.

Since this secondary preventive strategy seemed effective, one cannot help wondering whether an even more favorable outcome would have been achieved if primary preventive approaches could have been taken earlier. An educational program might have alerted this family to other family members who were known to have problems of dementia in late life—a "genetic alert" that might have prompted them to seek help earlier. Even then, at the present state of the art, the underlying cerebral process could not have been impeded, although such early intervention might have prevented the hostile-paranoid syndrome that followed and might have allowed time for living-situation planning before a crisis or a breakdown of communication occurred between the patient and her family.

## DEPRESSION

Depression is a term often misapplied even by professionals, who confuse its general descriptive connotation with its use for a specific clinical diagnostic category. Many older persons are described as being depressed, although they may or may not have developed what should be diagnosed as a clinical depression per se. Many will look depressed, or at least unhappy or grieving at some point in the late-life loss cycle; this should not indicate that true clinical depression is inevitable. Some persons clinically depressed in late life may have a more genetic and/or biochemical predisposition than others; many such disorders, however, are preventable or at least modifiable in course and outcome through earlier intervention. Even though older persons who are *unhappy* are misdiagnosed as being depressed, one could certainly conclude that their periods of existential unhappiness and/or grieving might be precursors to a clinical depression, regardless of a past history or a genetic predisposition to depression. It would follow then that recognizing that everyone suffers varying degrees of unhappiness in late life would lessen an aged person's feelings of denial and might encourage her or him to seek empathetic counseling by trained therapists. The treatment of clinical depression is covered elsewhere, and strategies of education or counseling earlier in the life cycle have been discussed in this chapter. The following case illustrates a preventive strategy.

A 71-year-old widow was followed as an office patient for four years. She initially had complaints of feeling depressed and had lost some 30 pounds and was extremely restless and tense. She would not let her husband out of her sight. Her complaints and demands had alienated her sisters. She relied on her husband to do housework and prepare meals. She occasionally had blackout spells. Her past medical history revealed several operations and she had numerous somatic complaints which had been investigated and treated over a period of 35 years or longer.

Her husband, who was the same age, had stopped working and had given up most of his own interests and activities to care for his wife. Hospitalization was recommended but she refused, saying that she just wanted to stay with her husband. Her appetite was not good and she had lost interest in everything. She reluctantly accepted hospitalization, and symptomatically improved on a regimen of supportive psychotherapy, antidepressants, and a mild tranquilizer. It was necessary to set limits so that she would not call her husband and he obviously was relieved that someone had taken over and could give him a respite from the pressure. It was learned that in desperation, he and members of her family had threatened her by telling the patient that if she did not pull herself together, her husband would leave. This plan obviously backfired and she had been even more possessive and unable to forget or forgive.

Following this hospitalization of about two-weeks' duration, the patient was followed at irregular intervals as an office patient and was encouraged to participate in a variety of programs available in the community. She began knitting and took pride in her achievements. She gained weight, began eating more foods and though she continued to have episodes of anxiety, fainting spells, somatic complaints, etc., she was more reasonable in her expectations of attention from her husband. She required much reassurance and support, but began to socialize more and had an improved relationship with family members. Her psychiatrist served as a "coordinator" directing her to various activities and medical specialists when indicated. He also shared responsibility with the husband who continued to be a major source of support. About two years after the initial visit, this patient was found to have a gastrointestinal lesion requiring surgery. This was accomplished and she had a rather slow but not too disturbing recovery. Her husband was able to return to work part-time and participate in his own activities. Sometimes his wife would go with him but often times she would remain at home. A sister who was older died suddenly and the patient managed to adapt to this without becoming depressed.

During the entire period of follow-up, this patient did not display the picture of agitated depression noted at the very beginning of her psychiatric treatment. She continued to have somatic complaints but these were usually not disabling. They were given proper attention and examinations were done and treatment undertaken when this seemed appropriate. It appeared that a balance had been struck between signals she gave for attention and the provision of attention within reasonable limits. Continuity was maintained with the psychiatrist but she would become disappointed with other doctors and consulted several during the several years she was in treatment.

She maintained an acceptable level of functioning for many months and was only seen about five times during one year, that before her husband suddenly died.

Immediately after the death of her husband, this patient was extremely upset, fearful, tense, anxious and needed a great deal of support from her daughter and family. Immediately an application was made for her admission to a home for the aged but there was a delay of about six weeks before she could be admitted. During this time she made frequent phone calls to express her concerns and apprehension but did not call the psychiatrist. The members of her family, however, were frequently in contact with him. A kind of emotional working through seemed to occur during this six-week delay, since almost immediately after her admission to the home for the aged there was a marked change in her personality and behavior. She was outgoing, sociable, talkative and had almost no complaints. There were still times when she asked for approval and reassurance but she quickly adjusted to the routines. Her tendencies to want her own way created some problems with her roommate but she showed no signs of depression. Rather than the expected role as a grieving spouse, this patient appears to have responded with a determination to find gratification of her dependency needs in an institution and could obtain bits of gratification in her contacts with many people and did not seem to be making excessive demands on any single person. This level of adjustment has continued for several months following the death of her husband.

It should be noted that there were no further episodes of depression per se in this woman following the establishment of a therapeutic arrangement with the psychiatrist, who ultimately assumed the role of a kind of permissive coordinator. Such a therapeutic position can be assumed by a therapist of any discipline who can comprehensively coordinate and supervise appropriate therapeutic modalities and services in a way that will enhance personality strengths without reinforcing weaknesses. In this case the patient displays accentuation of a probable life-long overdependent personality pattern which became the key dynamic element in the psychological management of the depression. There was constancy and continuity in terms of longitudinal follow-up, with obvious attention being paid to the medical aspects of her condition and medical treatment modalities called into play when appropriate. What appeared initially to be the beginning of a regressive personality and mood pattern gradually improved. She was encouraged, though not forced, into areas of activities wherein she could find new identities and where some of her dependency inclinations could be displaced. It is interesting that neither the death of the husband nor the delay in the process of admission to the retirement home had negative effects on her mood status. Indeed, she had a kind of "ungrief" reaction to the loss of her husband, with the delay period allowing her time to work through the loss and to adjust to the notion of a brand new arrangement of her living situation. There is no doubt that the therapist's therapeutic focus on the goals of new identities and more adaptive approaches to dependency set the stage for a more mature adjustment to this series of late-life stresses than one would have predicted from her past psychiatric history.

## CONCLUSIONS—DIRECTION OF RESEARCH

The following are general principles for a preventive approach to mental discord in late life:

1. Early diagnosis of and therapeutic intervention in both physical and mental disorders throughout the life cycle.
2. In earlier phases of the life cycle, increasing the opportunity for appropriate intervention, including education, counseling, and more readily accessible medical and psychiatric care.
3. Promoting the actual availability of medical and psychiatric facilities that are attractive and truly usable by the elderly population.
4. Reduction of chronicity (physical and mental) by more appropriate and comprehensive discharge planning from hospitals and mental facilities, with continuity of care appropriate to the rapidly changing needs of an old person.
5. Greater utilization and coordination of professionals from various disciplines who can intervene at all

phases of the life cycle, who are aware of the issues of aging and the needs of older people, who are able to work effectively with realistic therapeutic and preventive goals such as modification of mental decline and acceptance of the inevitability of the loss-stress dynamics of late life.

The greatest research need is that of measuring the effectiveness of primary preventive strategies, both psychosocial and medical, which so far cannot be absolutely proved to be of great value, although intuitively we feel that they give great promise of being able to modify the outcome of late-life mental illness. The issue of efficacy of the so-called *cerebral drugs* is far from clear. We need more data to determine the efficacy of cerebrovascular drugs in late-life organic brain syndromes as opposed to drugs which seem to have primarily a neuronal metabolic influence. Are both classes of drugs of value whether the organic etiology is vascular or neuronal? Are any of these drugs, or certain other cerebral drugs which are not in use in this country, of value in at least delaying intellectual decline in late life? Could some drug give promise of altering the "aging clock" of the brain? One also wonders about the secondary preventive validity of early diagnosis of brain impairment, even before gross intellectual dysfunction occurs, by such means as computerized electroencephalography, refined psychological tests, and further development of radiologic scanning devices.

## REFERENCES

ANDERSON, W. F. 1974. Preventive aspects of geriatric medicine. *Journal of the American Geriatrics Society, 22,* 385–392.

ANDERSON, W. F. 1975. Community medicine and geriatrics. *Public Health, 89,* 53–56.

BRACELAND, F. J. 1972. The mental hygiene of aging: Present-day view. *Journal of the American Geriatrics Society, 20,* 467–472.

BRODY, S. J. 1974. Evolving health delivery systems and older people. *American Journal of Public Health, 64,* 245–248.

BURNSIDE, I. M. 1973. Long-term group work with hospitalized aged. *In,* I. M. Burnside (ed.), *Psychosocial Nursing Care of the Aged,* pp. 202–214. New York: McGraw-Hill.

BUTLER, R. N. 1974. Successful aging and the role of the life review. *Journal of the American Geriatrics Society, 22,* 529–535.

BUTLER, R. N. 1975a. Psychiatry and the elderly: an overview. *The American Journal of Psychiatry, 132,* 893–900.

BUTLER, R. N. 1975b. *Why Survive? Being Old in America.* New York: Harper.

BUTLER, R. N., AND LEWIS, M. I. 1977. *Aging and Mental Health,* 2nd ed. St. Louis: C. V. Mosby.

CYRUS-LUTZ, C., AND GAITZ, C. M. 1972. Psychiatrists' attitudes toward the aged and aging. *Gerontologist, 12* (Summer), 163–167.

ELWOOD, T. W., AND OAKES, T. W. 1975. Failure by a group of elderly men to use a preventive health service. *Journal of the American Geriatrics Society, 23,* 74–76.

ERIKSON, E. H. 1959. Age: Ego integrity vs. despair or disgust. *In, Identity and the Life Cycle; Selected papers. Psychological Issues,* vol. 1, no. 1, monograph 1, pp. 98–99. International University Press.

FUCHS, V. R. 1974. *Who Shall Live?: Health, Economics, and Social Choice.* New York: Basic Books.

GAITZ, C. M. 1970. The coordinator: An essential member of a multidisciplinary team delivering health services to aged persons. *Gerontologist, 10,* 217–220.

GAITZ, C. M. 1974. Barriers to the delivery of psychiatric services to the elderly. *Gerontologist, 14,* 210–214.

GAITZ, C. M., AND BAER, P. E. 1970. Diagnostic assessment of the elderly: A multifunctional model. *Gerontologist, 10,* 47–52.

GAITZ, C. M., AND HACKER, S. 1970. Obstacles in coordinating services for the care of the psychiatrically ill aged. *Journal of the American Geriatrics Society, 18,* 172–182.

GOLDFARB, A. I. 1972. Multidimensional treatment approaches. *In,* C. M. Gaitz (ed.), *Aging and the Brain,* pp. 179–191. New York: Plenum.

Group for the Advancement of Psychiatry. No Date. *Report No. 81, The Aged and Community Mental Health: a Guide to Program Development,* p.78. New York: Mental Health Materials Center.

GUBRIUM, J. F. 1971. Self-conceptions of mental health among the aged. *Mental Hygiene, 55,* 398–403.

HORSLEY, S. 1966. Prophylaxis in tackling senility. *Nursing Times, 62,* 662–664.

KENT, E. A. 1975. Possible organic factors in the prevention of emotional problems of the aged. *Journal of the American Geriatrics Society, 23,* 541–544.

KRAL, V. A. 1967. Primary prevention of specific disorders in geriatric psychiatry. *In,* F. C. R. Chalke and J. D. Day (eds.), *Medical Aspects of Primary Prevention of Psychiatric Disorders: Papers Presented at the University of Ottawa, February 1967,* pp. 129–138. Published for the Ontario Mental Health Foundation by University of Toronto Press.

LOWTHER, C. P., MCLEOD, R. D., AND WILLIAMSON, J. 1970. Evaluation of early diagnostic services for the elderly. *British Medical Journal, 3,* 275–277.

MATLACK, D. R. 1975. The case for geriatric day hospitals. *Gerontologist, 15,* 109–113.

MEIER-RUGE, W. 1975. From our laboratories. *Triangle, 14,* 71–72. East Hanover, N.J.: Sandoz.

MILES, W. R. 1942. Performance in relation to age. *In, Mental Health in Later Maturity: Papers Presented at a Conference Held in Washington, D.C., May 23–24, 1941. Supplement No. 168 to the Public Health Reports.* US Public Health Service.

PATTERSON, R. D. 1976. Services for the aged in community health centers. *American Journal of Psychiatry, 133,* 271–273.

PFEIFFER, E. 1975. A short portable mental status questionnaire for the assessment of organic brain deficits in elderly patients. *Journal of the American Geriatrics Society, 23,* 433–441.

POST, F. 1965. *The Clinical Psychiatry of Late Life.* Oxford: Pergamon Press.

ROTH, M. 1963. Prophylaxis and early diagnoses and treatment of mental illness in late life. *In,* W. F. Anderson and B. Isaacs (eds.), *Current Achievements in Geriatrics,* pp. 155–170. London: Cassell.

SAMORAJSKI, T. 1976. How the human brain responds to aging. *Journal of the American Geriatrics Society, 24,* 4–11.

SAMORAJSKI, T. 1977. Central neurotransmitter substances and aging: A review. *Journal of the American Geriatrics Society, 25,* 337–348.

TODD, R. S. 1966. Early treatment reverses symptoms of senility. *Hospital and Community Psychiatry, 17,* 170–171.

VARNER, R. V., AND CALVERT, W. R. 1974. Psychiatric assessment of the aged: A differential model for diagnosis. *Journal of the American Geriatrics Society, 22,* 273–277.

VARNER, R. V., AND VERWOERDT, A. 1975. Training of psychogeriatricians. *In,* J. G. Howells (ed.), *Modern Perspectives in the Psychiatry of Old Age,* pp. 570–583. New York: Brunner/Mazel.

WANG, H. S. 1977. Dementia in old age. *In,* C. E. Wells (ed.), *Dementia,* 2nd Ed., Contemporary Neurology Series, Number 15, pp. 15–26. Philadelphia: Davis.

WILSON, F. G. 1970. Social isolation and bereavement. *Lancet, December 26,* 1356–1357.

# 41

# Prospects for
# Mental Health and Aging

*Gene D. Cohen*

## INTRODUCTION

The worst may be in sight. Perhaps paradoxical, this outlook is more positive than pessimistic. It is a response to the question about prospects for the mental health situation and care of older people. Much gloom and uncertainty has been expressed in the literature for what the future holds in this regard. Bleak pictures have been painted about the growing challenge to society created by expanding numbers of chronically ill aged individuals. Descriptions of an already strained economy and health system with yet more stress to come, add to mounting doubts about achieving effective planning and policies. But at the root of the problem lies a temporary historical unpreparedness. Contemporary societies have been caught off guard by the extraordinary growth in absolute numbers and rate of increase of the older population—the very

old in particular. A crisis has been slowly unfolding since the start of the 20th century, a crisis that could continue to unfold in America until 2030. In the year 1900, 3 million (4 percent of the population) were 65 and older. By 1975, the elderly population had reached 22 million (10 percent of the total). Current projections point to 33.2 million by 2010, and an awesome 51.6 million in 2030 as a result of the two-decade baby boom after World War II (US Department of Commerce, 1976). We have in effect a new nation (of older people) in our very midst—a nation unexpected, unplanned for. Services, social programs, manpower development, training efforts, and research have failed to keep pace with the needs of this rapidly expanding new population group.

What are some of the major mental health and mental illness issues that older persons will confront over the next few decades? To a large extent, these issues are likely to be continuations of present concerns which fall into three categories: (a) mental illness and crises, (b) service delivery problems, and (c) social issues. To elaborate:

### (a) mental illness and crises:

1. Mental illness is more prevalent with the elderly than with younger adults; 18–25 percent of older persons have significant mental health symptoms (Roth, 1976).

2. Psychosis, the most serious form of mental disorder, increases significantly after age 65—even more so beyond 75; it is more than twice as common in the over 75 year age group than in 25–35 year olds (Butler and Lewis, 1973).

3. Senile Dementia is being seen as the fourth leading cause of death (Katzman, 1976).

4. Suicide occurs more frequently among the elderly than in any other age group (Butler and Lewis, 1973).

5. Eighty-six percent of the elderly have chronic health problems of all causes; with at least a sixth of this group, problems are serious. Clearly, many of these older people experience significant psychological reactions from stress caused by such losses of health (Butler and Lewis, 1973).

### (b) service delivery problems:

1. Whereas the over 65 comprise more than 10 percent of the population with yet a greater prevalence of mental disorders than younger adults, during the mid 1970s, at best only 4 percent of patients seen at outpatient mental health clinics were 65 or older; only 2 percent at private psychiatric clinics have been in this age group. If time devoted to the elderly in these clinics were measured, the data would probably indicate that less than 1 percent of the total time given to patients would be provided for older people (a younger person, for example, may be seen weekly; an older individual might be seen once) (Cohen, 1976).

2. Whereas the elderly are underserved at outpatient clinics, a staggering 30 percent of public mental hospital patients in 1969 were over age 65 (Redick, 1974). Not the least factor here has been skewed insurance coverage (e.g., Medicare) with outpatient reimbursement for mental health care being severely restricted, thereby forcing a number of otherwise unnecessary hospitalizations. Other forms of potentially complementary aid (e.g., Title XX programs) have also been criticized as being poorly structured to offer mental health support to the elderly.

3. More than a million people over age 65 are in institutions (Brody, 1976). The risk increases with age after 65: 5 percent of the over 65 are in institutions. Ten percent of the over 75 are similarly placed; 20 percent of the over 85 are institutionalized. The absence of an adequate number and range of alternative living arrangements has made inappropriate nursing home placement unavoidable for too many older citizens.

Meanwhile, by 1978, the nursing home industry had grown to the point of consuming nearly 15 *billion* dollars annually.

### (c) social issues:

1. Isolation without adequate social supports is a critical issue. One in 7 men over age 65 lives alone. Nearly one-third of women 65 and older live by themselves (US Dept. HEW, 1978).

2. Related to isolation is the loss of significant others. Seventeen percent of men 65 and older are widowed; 30 percent in the over 75 age group. With women, 54 percent age 65 and older are widowed; a startling 70 percent of the over 75 age group have lost their spouses (US Dept. HEW, 1978).

3. The opportunity for man-woman relationships diminishes with age due to the differential mortality rates. At age 65 there are 4 women to every 3 men; by age 85, women outnumber men 2 to 1 (US Dept. HEW, 1978).

4. Income level clearly affects quality of life and one's ability to adjust. In the mid 1970s, 1 in 6 people age 65 and older were living below the poverty level (US Dept. of Commerce, 1976).

The situation is distorted when the elderly are defined as the problem. Rather, the problem is defined by those factors which have created the gulf between the needs of people and approaches to address their needs. The dramatic growth of the older population has been met by a societal failure to adequately meet either the *individual* or the *group needs* of the elderly. While programs like Social Security and Medicare attempt to respond to specific needs of the individual, comparable programs addressing such group needs as meaningful social and interpersonal involvements lag far behind. The mental health significance is obvious. Consider some of the extensive socializing opportunities that other age groups have as an integral part of our societal fabric. Infants and toddlers usually have intensive interactions with parents, siblings, and a range of significant others on a daily, if not, hourly basis. Preschool children have increasingly elaborate formal and informal organized nursery and play activities available to them. The school years generally lasting until the late teens to late twenties have an enormous part of the day filled with highly structured learning and age specific recreational events. So, too, during the work years leading up to retirement, is a large part of most days occupied by ongoing duties and continuing interpersonal interactions. These elaborate patterns have developed over significant periods of time as results of family dynamics, socioeconomic needs, and cultural values. The relative newness of the now sizeable elderly population in part explains the societal inertia in evolving comparable group oriented options for older people. But this is changing.

Among the major areas of change in the direction of expanding social or socializing networks for the elderly are the following:

1. *The Family:* As average longevity is increasing, the family is becoming a 4–5 generation unit. Hence, the number of one's living relatives will grow, allowing for more opportunities for family support and social involvement.

2. *Civic Activities:* By 1974, 20 percent of the 65 and older age group were already doing volunteer work (Havighurst, 1975). Combining considerable free time with better health and rising educational levels, the elderly are likely to assume an increasing number of community-oriented roles—including political positions. Elements of a new gerontocracy seem inevitable.

3. *Recreational Opportunities:* The burgeoning of recreational settings and activities for the elderly will continue. Many underdeveloped leisure options promise to proliferate—including a range of sports for older people.

4. *Educational Pursuits:* The demand for continuing education throughout the life cycle has never been so apparent. Quite interesting opportunities arise here— such as dynamic intergenerational exchanges in classrooms.

5. *New Forms of Work:* Retirement will become more a relative state, as older people undertake a variety of second or third careers—full and part-time.

The future, therefore, looks good in terms of the gradual growth of new opportunities, structures, and networks for meaningful social involvement and contribution on the part of older people as a group. All of this, of course, relates to a sense of purpose, the maintenance of self-esteem, and the continuation of mental health in later life.

The future is uncertain, however, in terms of how many older people requiring individualized mental health interventions will have their needs met. While the range, quality, and accessibility of services all may improve, the question is how far will they go. Services are already lagging, and face now the typical problem of catch-up. The problem is atypical in that the elderly population, as indicated, is not static; it is growing. The first challenge then is to keep the gap between needs and services from enlarging before one can get to the point of closing it. Better coordination alone will not accomplish this. Expansion of services is also necessary, since the older population in need of services is itself expanding. Given the seriousness of the economic situation, though, difficult decisions will have to be made about the magnitude of resources that society is willing to set aside to provide these services for its older members. But since the worst

is in sight—the time when the numbers in need of such services will peak—society should have a real incentive to aggressively work on what can eventually prove to be a manageable situation for the elderly. Simply stated, the extent and aggressiveness of this work will determine how soon the mental health situation and the delivery of mental health services for older individuals will get better instead of worse.

## AGING AND THE COST OF MENTAL ILLNESS: MYTHS AND FACTS

As one delineates the need for more and improved services, as well as an increase in research and training in the area of mental health and aging, cost concerns are quickly thrust forth. Costs are usually seen as the bottom line—indeed as a stop sign. But in the area of mental health there is considerable misunderstanding about actual and potential costs. This is even more true when the focus is on the mental health of older people. Consequently, options become blurred.

Several areas need to be analyzed in order to put mental health and aging cost issues into a better perspective. The direct costs of mental illness, with attention to differences by age, need to be examined. Health insurance issues as they relate to older people require clarification. Utilization of care patterns should be studied comparing the way elderly address their mental health problems with the way they approach physical health difficulties.

### THE DIRECT COSTS OF MENTAL ILLNESS

An analysis done by the National Institute of Mental Health on the 1974 cost of mental illness indicated that $14.5 billion (14 percent of the total national health expenditures that year) was spent for the direct care of the mentally ill (NIMH, 1976). What is remarkable, though, is that two-thirds of this direct care total expenditure went to institutional settings: 29.3 percent to nursing homes; 22.8 percent to state, county, and other public mental hospitals; 11.7 percent to general hospitals; 2.9 percent to private mental hospitals. Only one third of the total expenditure for the direct care of the mentally ill went to community-based programs; only 4.2 percent to community mental health centers. Specific costs for the care of the elderly are not indicated. We know that most of elderly (95 percent of the over 65) live in the community and that at best only 4 percent of patients seen at public or private mental health settings are over age 65

(Cohen, 1976). If some liberty is then taken in trying to estimate what percentage of the community-focused direct care mental illness expenditures went for care of the elderly in 1974, one might calculate 4 percent of the non-institutional care expenditures and arrive at a figure of less than $200 million or about 1.3 percent of the total direct care costs. Thus, in 1974, an estimated 1.3 percent of the total direct care mental illness funds went to the care of the community dwelling elderly—a group representing 95 percent of the over 65 population, a group with a greater prevalence of mental disorders than any other age group in the population (Cohen, 1977).

It is clearly very important to outline the above distinctions—to separate costs that apply to institutional care from those that apply to community programs. This is most important with the elderly where high costs for nursing home care, while not identified as such, are presented as evidence that tremendous outlays of funds are going toward the care of elderly with mental disorders. Though tremendous outlays do go toward institutional care of the mentally impaired elderly, markedly minimal funds are available for community programs facing mental health problems among the more than 20 million persons over 65, outside of institutions. The situation of the 5 percent should not be confused with that of the 95 percent. This discrepancy is becoming increasingly more manifest to consumers, service providers, and policymakers alike. Change is pounding on the door.

UTILIZATION OF CARE PATTERNS
OF OLDER PERSONS:
MENTAL HEALTH VS. PHYSICAL HEALTH

Before changes are considered in service systems or in health insurance reimbursement policies, planners need to have some sense as to what the political impact would be in terms of demand and utilization. The area of mental health seems to get a particularly wary eye in its scrutiny. Witness the number of insurance plans (including Medicare for the elderly) that have quite limited mental health coverage. It is not clear upon what data that restraints in the mental health area are based. This lack of clarity increases when utilization of services for other health problems is compared with utilization of services for mental problems. Are services for mental health problems used more than services for other health problems when access is equal to both? While good data focused specifically on the elderly are difficult to find, data are available from which reasonable inferences or hunches can

be drawn. To push the point, it would be particularly useful to look at utilization patterns of home visits, since this would eliminate the variable of how much trouble certain people—older people especially—have in getting to service facilities. Data from visits by Home Health agencies in Rhode Island during 1973 are instructive (Search Reports, 1975). Chronic diseases more likely to occur in the elderly have been selected from that study and compared in Table 41-1.

**Table 41-1**  Comparison of utilization of health services by patients needing home care.

| SERVICE PROGRAM | NUMBER OF PATIENTS | AVERAGE VISITS |
|---|---|---|
| Nervous System | 247 | 28.6 |
| Arthritis | 216 | 26.4 |
| Heart and Stroke | 1,715 | 22.4 |
| Injury | 540 | 17.9 |
| Diabetes | 541 | 17.8 |
| Neoplasm | 724 | 17.5 |
| Non-Communicable Infective Diseases | 2,036 | 15.5 |
| Mental Illness | 163 | 12.1 |

Given the equal access to services the differences in average visits for patients needing home care are striking. Mental Illness is far down the list, with several other common chronic illnesses requiring considerably more intervention. The Rhode Island study also revealed that patients with arthritis, nervous system disease, heart and stroke disorders, and other chronic conditions are more likely to have longer visits than those with mental illness. It would appear that expansion of services or liberalization of coverage for home mental health services would be far less costly than home health services for several other common illnesses and chronic conditions. For the vast majority of elderly patients who could appropriately benefit from home health services, this is most likely also the case.

When it comes to office visits, the above is probably even more apparent. In other words, given equal access to office-based services—in terms of both the availability of practitioners and insurance coverage—the elderly utilize mental health services less than services for other disorders with comparable disability. The low percentage of older people seen at community mental health centers where fees are not obstacles, makes a statement not only about problems in the delivery of mental health services to older people, but about difficulties on the part of older people in utilizing such services (Cohen, 1976). The point is that dramatic changes in the mental health care delivery system and in mental health insurance coverage are likely to result in less dramatic improvements in the utilization of mental health services by older people. That is to say, a promise of more supply to the elderly would probably not be met by a risk of overwhelming utilization—even though the need of older people for mental health services is large. Such a situation should facilitate gradual as opposed to unpredictable growth of mental health services for the elderly if existing programs are allowed to expand or new ones are to start. Surprises in the form of unexpected costs should be minimal or nonexistent. A partial illustration of this point can be seen in unpublished 1975 data (from the Office of the Actuary, US Civil Service Commission) on Blue Cross/Blue Shield and Aetna high option benefit payments to Civil Service workers for different types of health care utilization. At that time both plans provided essentially equal coverage for mental illness and physical illness. For example, after the deductible, an 80 percent reimbursement per outpatient psychiatric visit was provided. There was no limit to the number of psychiatric visits covered in a given year. Despite this very liberal coverage, psychiatric services continued to be underutilized by the elderly, as indicated in Table 41-2.

Though there is some distortion in the level of benefits provided since Medicare payments were also involved, the mental illness category is probably not that discrepant, due to low Medicare coverage for psychiatric problems. The point again, is that when the lid on limits for mental illness benefits was lifted, there were no out of control costs in the case of the elderly. Indeed, the costs remained quite low.

## HEALTH INSURANCE CONSIDERATIONS FOR THE ELDERLY

With the preceding as prologue, it would be surprising if a gradual and continued expansion of mental health insurance benefits for older people

fails to take place. This should certainly be true in the case of other than hospitalization coverage where even with Medicare—the national health insurance of the elderly—reimbursement for mental health services has been quite low. In fiscal year 1973, for example, psychiatric hospital care accounted for less than 2 percent of the total Medicare dollars spent on hospital care. Also during 1973, only 1.7 percent of the total receipt of community mental health centers came from Medicare (NIMH, 1973). The ramifications of this low coverage have been two-fold. Not only do the elderly have less access to health services because of limited insurance coverage, the reimbursement that is available favors hospitalization and in this sense is regressive. A third problem with Medicare, for the poor elderly in particular, has been in its failure to cover a number of other health aids that are more likely to become necessary in later life. Hearing aids are a case in point and have particular mental health relevance, since late onset loss of hearing is associated with an increased incidence of depression and paranoid ideation (Butler and Lewis, 1973).

While Medicaid has started to help out with additional benefits for the poor elderly, it too has presented a number of problems. Many elderly with low incomes may still have just enough money to disqualify them for Medicaid eligibility. Also, numerous differences exist among States in the types and levels of health benefits provided by Medicaid, making it difficult to design model mental health programs applicable to older people across the country. It would seem that reimbursement programs like Medicare and Medicaid would have to merge for the elderly in recognition of the salient interplay of medical, psychiatric, and social problems confronting older people. The elderly need insurance coverage that can provide them with the flexibility to pay for medical and mental health treatment, and for those supportive services and devices that can allow them to remain meaningfully in the community. The coming years should witness gradual progress in that direction.

**Table 41-2**  Comparison of utilization of mental illness benefits

|  | 65 AND OLDER ENROLLEES | | | 65 AND OLDER DEPENDENTS | | |
|---|---|---|---|---|---|---|
|  | Mental Illness Benefits as a % of total for all age groups | Total Health Care Benefits as a % of total for all age groups | % of population covered | Mental Illness Benefits as a % of total for all age groups | Total Health Care Benefit as a % of total for all age groups | % of population covered |
| Blue Cross/ Blue Shield | 1.4 | 5.5 | 3.4 | .5 | 1.6 | 1.3 |
| Aetna | 1.3 | 17.6 | 8.0 | .8 | not avail. | not avail. |

## ECONOMIC ISSUES

The cost of providing care for mental disorders in later life must be looked at in the context of the economic outlook for older people. In order to have a proper perspective on this situation, one must once again keep in mind that the elderly population will continue to be diverse in terms of problems and options. Thus, while it has been predicted that the economic picture of the elderly as a group will improve over the coming decades (Havighurst. 1975), many sub-groups within the overall older population will continue to experience absolute or relative economic strain (DHEW, 1978). The economic issue will be less one of the effect of financial status on self-esteem—rather, the impact of available resources on the ability to obtain necessary services and supports to maintain quality of life and psychosocial well-being.

To the extent that adequate resources are not available to the older individual, opportunities to utilize mental health services and social supports are diminished. As a consequence, there is less access to systems of care addressing prevention and early intervention. On the one hand, after adjusting for inflation between 1960 and 1970, the median income of families headed by persons over 65 rose by 33 percent (DHEW, 1978), along with growth in a variety of programs such as Social Security, Supplemental Security Income, Medicare, Food Stamps, housing subsidies, and others. On the other hand, though, "the subgroups that experienced slower rates of decline in poverty or no decline at all were the same subgroups that were growing in size most rapidly and are projected to continue growing at rapid rates: females, minorities, and those who live alone. These subgroups, women and minorities in particular, tend to have worked less in the past and to have worked in lower-paying occupations than white males, and therefore tend to have fewer financial assets to rely on after retirement (DHEW, 1978)," Most widows, for example, live alone, without automobiles, on relatively low incomes, with one-fourth relying on cash incomes below the Federal Government's poverty index (DHEW, 1978).

It should also be emphasized that the greatest rate of population growth is in the over 75 age group which has the most health care needs and therefore the highest demands on resources. In 1978 one-fourth of the elderly population was 75 and over, with a projected increase to one-third by the year 2035; the 85 and over group in 1978 constituted one of every sixteen elderly persons, with a projected increase to one in ten by 2035 (DHEW, 1978). Again, the economic forecast for the older

age group as a whole cannot be looked at in the same way as with those in advanced old age.

Attention to economics invariably raises questions about work patterns which in turn bring up the issue of retirement and its psychosocial impact. Table 41-3 indicates that with males (all races) labor force participation has diminished since 1940. With women (all races) decline has occurred since 1960.

**Table 41–3**  Labor Force Participation: Rates for Persons 65 +. US Dept. of Commerce, 1976

| PERCENT-LABOR FORCE PARTICIPATION | 1940 | 1960 | 1975 |
|---|---|---|---|
| Males (Black and Other Races) | 49.0 | 29.4 | 20.9 |
| Males (White) | 41.2 | 30.6 | 21.8 |
| Females (Black and Other Races) | 12.5 | 12.9 | 10.5 |
| Females (White) | 5.6 | 10.0 | 8.0 |

From the above table it is apparent that the percentage of older persons in full or partial retirement has been steadily increasing. Much has been stated and misstated about the effect of retirement on older people (Hendricks and Hendricks, 1977). As in so many other areas relevant to the elderly, here too, myths, stereotypes, and misinformation abound. The different orientation toward retirement of blue collar workers versus white collar workers, the sick versus the healthy, those with social options versus those without, are so seldom taken into consideration. Much research remains to be done about the health and mental health issues and sequelae of retirement, though there have already been studies along these lines. In one study perception of health was evaluated among a group (N = 500) who had not retired because of ill health. "Upon being asked whether there had been any change in their health since retirement, nearly one quarter (24.1 percent) indicated a change for the better, and only 10.4 percent indicated a change for the worse; the remainder said they had perceived no change in health status" (Sheldon, McEwan, and Ryser, 1975). In addition to identifying general patterns associated with retirement, it is clearly important to study variations as well. For instance, what groups are at risk for poor post-retirement adjustment, and what can be done for them in terms of prevention and intervention?

Relevant to the earlier discussion of economics and the elderly, full or partial retirement can obviously have an indirect impact on mental health prospects by virtue of reducing level of funds required to obtain needed services in times of psychosocial crises. A report on median income of the elderly by the Bureau of the Census (US Dept. of Commerce, 1976) is of interest: In 1974 men over 65 had less than half the income of men 55–64 years old. Women over 65 had about half the median income of men the same age, and about a third less median income than women in the 55–64 age group. Families headed by men 55 to 64 had a median income almost double that of those headed by men 65 and older. Families headed by women 55 to 64 had a median income over 20 percent higher than those headed by women 65 and older.

Given the altered economic situation of the older population as a whole and a number of its subgroups in particular, mental health prospects for the elderly, from an economic standpoint, will continue to be influenced by the state of personal, family, and societal resources as they affect access to services and social support systems. With the enormous expansion of older persons still to come, the need for responsible social planning and policies to address the economic complexities of this matter is quite apparent.

## AN EVOLVING FIELD

Is Aging and Mental Health a field? While some may anachronistically still be asking this question, others are indeed attempting to refine it into 4 fields focused on: (1) The Middle Years, (2) The Young-Old, (3) The Old-Old, (4) Death and Dying. This is not unlike what has happened at the other end of the life cycle with attention to children evolving to special interest in prenatal, neonatal, young child, adolescent, and youth events.

Part of the blockage in the past in seeing Aging and Mental Health or Geriatric Mental Health as a field has been a factor of misunderstanding its goals. Its aim has not been to build an army of mental health geriatricians or to suggest that any older person requiring mental health treatment go only to an Aging Specialist. From a practical standpoint alone, this is unfeasible, since there would never be enough specialists in this area to meet all the mental health needs of the older population.

Rather, the aims of the field are in three directions: (1) To facilitate the growth of research on the special mental health issues and problems of later life; this includes studies of those problems of younger adulthood which present under altered conditions in old age (Roth, 1976); (2) To advance the state of knowledge about optimal service structures and service delivery approaches in meeting the mental health needs of older adults; (3) To develop optimal approaches for the training of professionals (both specialist and generalists) and the education of families and older persons themselves to deal with the mental health concerns, disorders, and crises of later life.

As the field of Aging and Mental Health has evolved, a number of interesting dimensions have emerged. There is, for example, a dynamic interchange growing between those in the field who focus more specifically on the older person with those whose research is on aging itself in relation to mental health and illness. At the same time a number of other expanding fields of study are intersecting with Aging and Mental Health because of common areas of interest. Psychosomatic medicine shares much in common with geriatric mental health, since the interplay of the bio-medical with the psychological is more apparent with the elderly than any other age group.

The field of Psychopharmacology also is accelerating its attention to areas relevant to aging and older people. The concern about long-term effects of psychotropic medications is integrally related to concepts of time and aging. The serious problem of tardive dyskinesia stands out here. Phenomena of "drug-drug interactions" are more likely to be identified with the elderly, since older people use more drugs. Consequently, a focus on the elderly may be the fastest way of expanding knowledge in this area. Similarly, altered rates of drug metabolism with older people in general have attracted the curiosity of those studying the pharmacokinetics of psychotropic medications (Salzman, Van der Kolk, and Shader, 1976).

Interest in the course of mental disorders is blossoming, and here, too, the interface with Aging and Mental Health can be seen. Understanding the course of mental disorders is essential since different clinical pictures at different points in time can have highly significant, diagnostic, treatment, and prognostic ramifications. If one looks at the course of a disorder, one is clearly at the same time looking at a disorder as the individual ages. The course of depression is a case in point. Many patients with more typical depressive features in their 50s may have had a "phobic anxiety-depersonalization syndrome" in their early 20s (Roth, 1960; Detre and Jarecki, 1971). Both clinical pictures, though, are part of the same clinical/developmental continuum.

The fact that these different areas of investigation are intersecting is obviously to the advantage of each field involved. Different perspectives are energetically brought to bear on common problems. Along with this is a growth in the prestige of the field of Aging and Mental Health, for when members in one field of study see some of their own concerns also the concerns of another field, their curiosity and respect for that other field increase. Such a phenomenon is operating and will continue to unfold in the area of Aging and Mental Health as several other fields stand to benefit from what is gained by a focus on the elderly and on aging.

## SERVICES AND SERVICE DELIVERY ISSUES

Breakthroughs are needed more in the delivery of services to the elderly than in the services themselves. Much knowledge about the treatment of mental disorders in later life is already available. But settings where this knowledge can be applied through viable services are scanty and poorly developed. Federally-funded Community Mental Health Centers (CMHCs) are now specifically mandated to provide services to the elderly, but it is not yet clear as to whether CMHCs will improve on their past record where only 4 percent of people seen were over 65 (Cohen, 1976). Also, a significant percentage of the population does not have access to CMHCs.

There is considerable confusion around services for the elderly. The question, again, is not so much "what works?" Many and varied approaches work. The problem has several parts. In the first place, even when viable mental health services are set up, utilization by older people is too often low. The barriers to access have not been adequately addressed. For example, to what extent do people in general, and older people in particular, know what mental health services are all about? Perhaps an analogy can be made where a mental health clinic is looked at as a movie house. How many would go to a movie house without knowing what is playing there (what services are provided); who the cast is (something about the skills of the staff); what the critics say (the image of the clinic in the community); whether to expect a light film or a heavy one (will treatment be supportive or intensive); whether the movie is G, PG, R, or X rated (to what extent the services are geared to the under 18, over 21, 65 and older), ticket price (fees), length of film (duration of treatment); what theaters the film is being shown in (are there satellite clinics); and so forth?

Accessibility in other words is a factor of availability, visibility, appeal, and readiness to deliver. A second part of the problem has been the failure of the mental health system to adequately conceptualize the development of comprehensive services

for older people. Frequently those services which are set up are neither comprehensive in scope nor clear as to what needs of older persons are being addressed. The planning process, if it occurs at all, in the development of mental health programs for the elderly is likely to splinter off into confusion about what is best—direct services or indirect services or home visits or day hospitalization or pre-retirement counseling or treatment for OBS or something else. None of these alone is adequate.

Program planning for the elderly must have a population focus, taking into consideration the range of mental health problems older people experience, the various treatment modalities to draw upon, and the various service structures through which care is provided (Group for the Advancement of Psychiatry, 1971). The approach to mental health services development for the elderly is diagrammed in Figure 41-1.

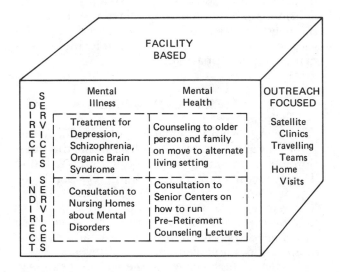

Several basic programmatic issues are addressed in Figure 41-1:

1. What should the balance be between direct services (e.g., treatment) and indirect services (e.g., consultation)?
2. What should the balance be between a mental illness focus (e.g., on depression and OBS) and a mental health focus (e.g., on prevention)?
3. To what extent should services be facility-based (e.g., at a clinic); to what extent outreach focused (e.g., home visits)?

Yet, another way of approaching program development can be appreciated from Table 41–4, where a number of programmatic concerns are expressed.

**Table 41-4** Conceptualizing Comprehensive Mental Health Programs for Older People.

| PROBLEMS DISORDERS | TREATMENT MODALITIES | SERVICES | SETTINGS FOR INTERVENTION | LIAISONS, AFFILIATES COORDINATION |
|---|---|---|---|---|
| Depression | Individual Therapy | Outpatient | Mental Health Clinics | Area Agency on Aging |
| Psychosis | Group Therapy | Inpatient | Medical Clinic | Community Health Clinics |
| Organic Brain Syndrome | Family Therapy | Partial Hospitalization | Hospitals | Social Service Agencies |
| Alcohol Abuse | Pharmacotherapy | Emergency | Nursing Homes | Local Housing Authority |
| Crises | Counseling | Consultation | Other Congregate Living Settings | Volunteer Organizations |
| Troubled Transitions | Special Techniques | Travelling Team | Senior Centers | Churches |
| Other | Other | Other | Patient's Home | Other |
| | | | Other | |

1. How does the mental health program for older adults address the range of mental disorders and other mental health problems that occur in later life (such as depression, psychosis, and organic brain syndrome)?

2. What treatment modalities does the program make available for mental health interventions in work with older persons (e.g., individual, group, and family therapy, pharmacotherapy, special techniques, etc.)?

3. What mental health services have been developed for use by the elderly (e.g., outpatient, day hospital, and home visiting services)?

4. What settings have been identified as being either sites for delivering care or places where mental health services are needed?

5. With what agencies in the community should mental health programs affiliate to better coordinate care for the elderly?

A third part of the problem, already alluded to, concerns deficiencies in reimbursement mechanisms to finance care (Butler, 1975). Medicare has provided minimal coverage for outpatient care—to the group that comprises 95 percent of the total elderly population. Medicaid and Title XX of the Social Security Act have varied from State to State in the support they have offered for mental health care and related services. Such limitations have made it uncomfortable for older people to seek services, for individual practitioners to offer services to the elderly, and for community clinics to develop mental health programs for older adults.

A fourth part of the problem concerns training. There is a growing body of knowledge focused on the elderly in the areas of needs assessment, program planning, clinical evaluation, treatment, services and service delivery design, and so on. In addition the development of an effective approach to the older patient requires special preparation. All of these aspects are training issues. Few programs that have major responsibilities for providing mental health care to older people have staff specifically trained for this purpose.

To the extent that mental health services for the elderly become more clearly defined, more accessible, more reimbursable, and provided by better trained staffs, the prospect for improved mental health care for older people will certainly improve. Policy and legislative considerations in these areas are unavoidable.

While the future will witness gradual improvements in the planning, development, and delivery of mental health services in general for older people, a number of specific areas for innovation and change will continue to emerge. Several candidates follow.

COMPREHENSIVE ASSESSMENT

Emphasis has been placed on the fact that there is a strong interplay of bio-medical and psycho-social factors affecting the mental health of older people. The high degree of misdiagnosis in separating medical from psychiatric symptoms has similarly been stressed (Agate, 1970). Nonetheless, the typical evaluation of an older patient is far from comprehensive. Most older persons in most communities across the country must make several clinical stops before a comprehensive work-up has been completed. Many do not know where to start, while others are discouraged by earlier experiences where only superficial exams took place. Particularly for those elderly with severe impairments whose situations are aggravated by difficulties in just getting to a health facility, the absence of well thought out approaches to assessment is a serious deficiency. The opportunity for prevention and early detection of insidious problems is compromised. So, too, is the opportunity to develop an orderly and comprehensive treatment plan. Health is at risk, time lost, and resources wasted when an appropriate evaluation fails to occur. Before an older person seeks a health exam, he or she really needs to be coached as to where to go, what questions to ask, what tests to demand, and how to evaluate what does or does not take place. Consumers and service providers alike are pushing to change this shortcoming in our health delivery system.

What is clearly needed is a mechanism for comprehensive assessment that builds upon existing health programs in the community. Such an assessment service could be established at any number of settings—at a general hospital, a medical clinic, a community mental health center or other important health facilities. The setting could vary in different communities, the deciding factors perhaps being where such an assessment service would be most comprehensive and most accessible.

From another perspective an exciting side benefit of such settings would be the unusual training opportunities they would provide—for medical and mental health workers alike. Such services would be rich in case material for challenging differential diagnoses. They would be similarly rich for studying the interplay of the somatic with the psychological, and in this sense would provide important research options as well. The idea that older persons of widely varying health status would be seen at such settings is also appealing from a training perspective, since too often health professionals see only the most disabled of the institutionalized elderly early in their training and get a distorted view of Geriatrics and Geriatric Mental Health. Indeed a rotation on a geriatric assessment service may be the best way for one to start his or her specialty training for work with older people. It may also be the best way for the generalist, who has limited time to learn about Geriatrics or Geriatric Mental Health, to develop skills and become familiar with issues of aging in work with older people. To the extent that medical and psychiatric training programs consider the diverse training and research opportunities that would accompany services in such a setting, University Hospitals might even visibly get into the act. And to the extent that more flexibility in health insurances and other reimbursement mechanisms is introduced to cover comprehensive assessment, the process will move forward.

## THE INTERFACE OF THE FIELDS OF MENTAL HEALTH AND MEDICINE

The question arises that since the elderly significantly under-utilize mental health services, should mental health services merge with medical services in the care of older people. The question is somewhat premature in that the mental health system has not really been tested in its capacity to respond to the needs of the elderly. Or perhaps it would be more accurate to say that the mental health system until recently has not allowed itself to be tested. Whatever, the situation is changing, and from several directions. As cohort groups among the elderly continue to change, so do attitudes of older people toward mental health services; audible demand is likely to increase. There is growing interest among mental health professionals in learning about aging and mental health; one need only look at the escalating numbers of continuing education conferences, books and other publications focused on mental health of the elderly. Health legislation is specifically mandating services for older people (e.g., Public Law 94-63, on Community Mental Health Centers). Another catalyst for positive change would also obviously come from liberalization of health insurances and reimbursement plans for mental health services.

Another consideration is that the posture of many health clinics toward the public is a passive one. That is, they are available to provide services if people come to them. They neither approach delivery of services through significant outreach nor engage in much education of the community about what services are offered. Part of the reason for this is that even with a passive posture many clinics, public ones especially, have large caseloads. It then becomes a matter of priorities. If priorities change, and if decisions are made to address other needs or other groups, then the ability to deliver on an implied promise of services becomes an issue. How much effort do public and private clinics make in encouraging older people to utilize their services? And if older people come, how much are the clinics prepared to deliver and how well can they deliver? In this sense it is not clear to what degree mental health programs have been tested or have permitted themselves to be tested in responding to the needs of older people.

This takes us back to the question of how mental health and medical services might relate to one another. In the first place the options are not just those of being totally together or totally separate. A continuum of care must be examined to better approach the issue. With assessment, as already indicated, a comprehensive evaluation demands bio-medical, psychological, and social workups. Following the initial assessment a problem oriented intervention plan should be followed. In this case, specific mental health services might be indicated and these might best be provided by a private mental health practitioner or at a mental health clinic. Having already entered the health system the older person would at this point probably be much more likely to utilize specialized mental health services because of the support and encouragement of those who carried out the assessment and established a relationship with the older individual. Whether mental health treatment that follows assessment should be carried out in the same setting where medical services are provided may or may not be a practical idea. The mental health practitioner or clinic might be more accessible, and if several appointments were necessary, accessibility certainly would be an important consideration. If the concern was one of stigma, the older person would definitely be less visible in a private psychiatrist's office than in the waiting room of a medical clinic being called to see Dr. Jones, who is known to be one of the clinic's "shrinks."

Another consideration that has an historical context to it is the concern of how viable mental health services remain if they are totally mixed with medical services. One might be cautious about swinging the pendulum back to that earlier state of undifferentiation where mental health services fared poorly. To get a sense of under what circumstances it is essential they be together for adequate and proper care may be a more useful objective. In many cases this should be obvious. The area of assessment, as one, has already been discussed. Outreach teams, especially at the point of initial contact and evaluation of the home-bound individual, should be multidisciplinary in a mental health and medical sense. Certain types of day hospitalization, depending on the nature of clinical problems that form the basis of patient selection require the medical/mental health mix. Institutional settings such as hospitals and nursing homes clearly require this mix. With repeated documentation of the high prevalence of serious mental impairment and symptomatology at nursing homes it is remarkable how little mental health input is planned by nursing homes themselves. Medical coverage, though often inadequate at nursing homes, is for the most part superior to mental health care. A better mix of the two is needed at nursing homes, but more of each of the ingredients of the mix is needed as well.

## OUTREACH

The continuing underutilization and underdelivery of mental health services to the elderly is forcing a basic re-examination of the way these services are provided to certain groups of older people (Cohen, 1976; Redlich and Kellert, 1978). Outreach is being increasingly looked at as a mechanism to alter this deficiency in the delivery system. There are a number of forms of outreach, ranging from satellite clinics spread throughout a community to improve access to services for older people, to home visits such as by traveling teams.

The full potential of outreach efforts has not been appreciated. Many have seen outreach primarily as a mechanism to reach the high-at-risk home-bound. This alone would certainly be a major contribution. But outreach can offer yet more. Many older people who are not home-bound may nonetheless be initially reluctant to seek mental health services, even though they may recognize the need for such help. This phenomenon is an entry problem, not peculiar to older people nor to mental health services, though particularly prevalent with the elderly vis-à-vis mental health care. A number of people simply experience a sense of hesitation about initiating entry into the health care system. But if the system first comes to them, ease of entry is facilitated. The individual may then feel comfortable about initiating the next steps himself or herself. This could then positively affect subsequent utilization of services.

A third advantage of outreach is one that is potentially applicable to most older persons with mental health problems. An initial home visit may be the optimal way of getting an early and optimal picture of how the older individual is coping with his or her environment, given the recognition of how important social factors are in addition to and in conjunction with psychological and medical stressors that affect mental health in later life.

Some of the multidisciplinary issues with outreach teams have already been discussed. Many combinations are possible, and will no doubt be influenced in the future by altered priorities and shifted resources within the health care delivery system and by the flexibility of reimbursement mechanisms.

## COMMUNITY SUPPORTS

The slowly awakening giant is innovation in community supports. With the 65 and older population in the community already numbering more than 20 million, and well over another 20 million likely by 2030, the need for innovations in community supports is critical. These should come in two major forms (1) new or improved resources and options for the older individual and his or her family (2) new or improved formal health maintenance programs targeted to the community dwelling. Health and mental health programs as presently designed, even if optimally implemented, would alone fall far short of meeting the needs of older persons in need of care. The sheer number of people in need of services makes this apparent. Add to the number of potential patients the number of problems each individual might experience, the challenge and gaps become even greater. Finally, continuity of care issue places enormous demands on health delivery systems, since many people—the rapidly growing over 75 group in particular—require a number of varied interventions demanding of time and dollars.

The point about dollars should be briefly addressed. Most discussions about funding requirements look at costs in relation to cost-effectiveness and/or quality of care. The missing element which is starting to peak its head out is that of values. Major societal decisions are rarely based just on cost and quality issues. Value judgments and social ideals clearly play critical roles in precipitating the choice of one program over another. The place of community supports is beginning to noticeably stir our values.

Community support innovations aimed at allowing older people and their families to help themselves need to take into consideration the dynamics and changing structure of the family itself. These innovations can take a number of directions. The Internal Revenue Service, for example, introduced such a change in 1976 (IRS, 1976). Its income tax forms that year permitted ways of paying an older family member to take care of their grandchildren, and for the parents to deduct the payments as child care expenses. Intended or not, the mental health ramifications were real for both the family as a whole and the older members as individuals. This simple adjustment in IRS rules allowed: (a) a potential strengthening of individual extended family units by providing new opportunities and incentives for family members to help one another (b) a way of keeping more money in the family itself by allowing one family member to pay another family member rather than having to hire someone outside the family and (c) an opportunity for various older persons to engage in valued activities which at the same time would be remunerative. Though this example is a simple one, it illustrates how small or basic innovations can sometimes have broader ramifications. It should be a challenge for much creativity in this area.

As the number of people over 65 escalates, so too will the number of well elderly. From the standpoint of the potential role of the informal support system where older people would assist one another, volunteer activity will undoubtedly increase. The place for incentives to involve this part of the informal support system will at the same time come under increased scrutiny. No doubt a number of research questions will arise around the issue of under what circumstances incentives to the informal support system are indicated and under what circumstances incentives might actually weaken natural support networks. An all-or-none approach hardly seems applicable. While a growing number of "senior" volunteer programs are becoming more viable, there are also situations where elderly pay other elderly for various services. Congregate living settings such as HUD supported housing for the elderly represent a case in point. At these "senior" housing projects it is not uncommon to find that in addition to many neighbors helping one another without concern about reimbursement, a number of the more impaired may pay certain residents of the building to regularly assist them with various chores, and acquisition of medications. Since the more impaired are less able to reciprocate aid from neighbors, they may feel more impelled or be under more pressure to hire specific assistance. This assistance, not infrequently, makes the critical difference that allows them to remain in the building and not have to move into a more protective setting. Different types of aid to the impaired elderly that would allow them to acquire such assistance are already getting careful attention. The future is promising.

Moving back to the formal health delivery system, a form of support already available though on a limited scale is that of Homemaker Services. Many variations on this type of assistance are possible. It is useful to consider in general what can be accomplished with only 2 hours of home assistance a day where the person providing the assistance receives periodic supervision pertaining to the client's health and mental health status:

1. Ongoing social interaction with a responsible significant other is assured.

2. If the older person has a psychotic or borderline psychotic disorder the home helper is a source of reality testing, providing support to the healthy side of the client's ego and helping to keep delusional ideas under control. By the home helper's very presence as a source of strength, the anxiety of the severely mentally disturbed home-bound elderly person can be greatly alleviated.

3. Many medications, including psychotropic medications, need to be taken only once a day. The home

helper can supervise the older person making sure he or she takes necessary medications

    4. If an exacerbation of a mental illness is starting to take place, the home helper can contact a mental health professional for early intervention, thereby helping to maintain a maximum level of functioning.

    5. Two meals a day can be prepared, with ingestion of one of them being directly supervised.

    6. The home helper can assist with up-keep of the client's home or apartment, and in helping the older person arrange certain social activities in or out of the home.

Items 5 and 6 above require the most time; items 1-4 would go on concurrently with 5 and 6. This type of intervention can make a profound difference not only in terms of quality of life, but in terms of where one lives—at home or in an institution. One home health assistant could work with 3-4 older people a day, depending on whether the clients are located in different parts of the community or in the same apartment building, and depending on the time spent with each. From a cost perspective, such services for the individual could range from 10–50 percent as expensive as care for that person in a good nursing home. The entire area of home health assistance will undoubtedly mature during the next several decades as millions of older people will be at levels of impairment for which intensive yet definitely non-heroic interventions will allow them to stay meaningfully and appropriately in the community. The level of societal commitment to this process will not be based solely on cost and/or quality considerations, but on value judgments as well.

## NURSING HOMES

The tragic irony about nursing homes is that they represent a major setting for the mentally ill, with grossly inadequate mental health attention. This shortcoming is a result of the combined failures of nursing homes, the mental health delivery system, and social policies. Nursing homes have failed by not building in a well structured mental health component despite showing a prevalence of serious mental disturbance with over 70 percent of nursing home residents (Teeter, Garetz, Miller, and Heiland, 1976). The mental health delivery system has failed in the past by not strengthening consultative ties with nursing homes either to maintain continuity of care for the newly institutionalized or to assist in developing treatment plans for elderly with new problems following entry into nursing homes. Social policies have failed by not coming to grips with the serious quality of care issues that have arisen in an industry estimated to consume

nearly 15 billion in 1978 (Senate Memorandum, 1978). What industry of this magnitude spends so little on research to improve its services and the understanding of the problems it deals with, and so little on training to improve the implementation of its basic function—the care of people?

Consider these relationships: most of those in nursing homes are elderly. But less than 4 percent of the elderly are in nursing homes; another 1 percent are in hospitals, and other institutions; 95 percent are in the community. And as mentioned, more than 70 percent of the nursing home population have serious mental disturbances. In other words the typical nursing home patient is an elderly individual with significant mental impairment or psychiatric symptomatology. This makes it even more remarkable that so little of the nursing home budget is set aside for research and training relevant to the elderly and to the mental health of the elderly. It is even more remarkable when one sees that a mere one percent of the nursing home budget in 1978 exceeded the total combined research budgets in that year for the National Institute of Mental Health (for all age groups) and the National Institute on Aging (focused on the whole elderly population). Another one percent exceeded the total training budgets in 1978 of both Institutes together. There will very likely be increased pressure for policy requirements that a percentage of nursing home funds be set aside for research and training—at least a percentage of the billions of federal dollars that go into nursing homes.

Apart from needed changes in nursing homes in areas of formal services development, problem-oriented interventions, and adequate staff training, a number of existential mental health issues must be addressed. Despite planned activities, many nursing home residents experience considerable time feeling alone. Even if staff are continually walking by them, the staff are usually quite busy and have limited time to intensively engage individual residents in highly personalized conversations. The issue is not just the quality of the interaction, but the quantity as well. In this area the potential role of the informal support system could be enormous. In many cases families alone are able to meet these needs. But many older residents of nursing homes do not have family members who are able or available to provide this type of relationship. Yet others with family or friends still are not able to get enough socializing. Such contact becomes even more important since many nursing homes patients have undergone a change in their everyday existence—from doing to being. More time becomes spent on being, than on doing or producing things. The relationship becomes then even more important.

How to fill the gap in personal relationships will then be one of the major responsibilities likely to be required of nursing homes in the future. But nursing homes cannot be left holding the bag here alone. Policy makers will have to take into consideration what incentives and/or what other kinds of programmatic assistance will be available to help nursing homes in this key mental health endeavor.

### ALTERNATIVE LIVING ARRANGEMENTS

While the earlier discussion on community supports looked at some approaches that could effect alternatives to institutionalization, the idea of alternatives deserves closer inspection. The simple dichotomy of in an institution versus in the community is obviously an illusion. A continuum separates these two points. Indeed, there are institutions and alternate institutions. What is an institution anyway? Webster says it is "an establishment, especially one of a public character"; also, "the building or buildings used by such organization" (Webster's Dictionary, 1959). Under this definition "Senior Housing" supported by HUD would be seen as an institution. It is, of course, considered "in the community." Hence the newer phraseology talking about least restrictive settings has come increasingly to the fore.

It would be understandable that policy makers might become increasingly uncomfortable with fears about whole new categories of institutions coming into existence—each with its own constituency and lobbying group. To the extent one keeps the focus on the clinical problems of concern, this whole area can be handled responsibly. The crux of the issue is that the elderly, comprising millions of people, vary greatly in their levels of impairment. If significantly different levels or categories of dysfunction can be reasonably defined, this could provide the basis for responsible programmatic innovations. From a combined mental health and medical perspective, the following groupings are offered as one way of visualizing different groups of older persons in terms of their level of dysfunction and need:

1. Those living independently with health or mental health problems who are able to make use of outpatient, ambulatory services.
2. Those living independently who are less ambulatory because of serious problems and need some home health services to avoid placement into a more restrictive setting.
3. Those whose problems make it necessary to be in a more specialized setting where protective care can

be provided from 12–24 hours a day, but on a level significantly less intensive than in a nursing home with greater numbers of highly skilled staff.
4. Nursing homes for the most seriously impaired, with 24–hour care, more intensive interventions, and highly skilled staff.

The vast majority of elderly in need of services are and will continue to be in category one. The second greatest group, but far smaller in size than the first one, is and will continue to be in category two. It is with category two that the risks for institutional care are mounting, and where creative programming and policies will probably achieve their greatest impact in allowing large numbers of older people to avoid unnecessary placement into more restrictive settings. Categories 3 and 4, though involving considerably less older people, nonetheless are and will remain significant in absolute numbers. Even, for example, if the nursing home population in category 4 numbered only 2 percent of the elderly population in 2030, one would still be dealing with over one million people—more than the number of elderly in nursing homes in 1978. If the percentage of those elderly requiring institutionalization remained constant at 5 percent where it has been for a while, one would be talking about 2.5 million in this group by 2030.

Just as the tens of millions of older persons will differ significantly from one another, so too will their problems. Options are needed—even among the more severely impaired—to match interventions with levels of impairments. Such options apply as much to living arrangements as they do to services and to the approaches for delivering services.

## TRAINING AND PERSONNEL

The proliferation of interest in training in the area of geropsychiatry or aging and mental health is becoming increasingly evident. Along the entire continuum from career training to continuing education information on mental disorders in later life is making a more frequent appearance in classrooms. Many professional schools are attempting to establish formal programs on geriatric mental health. Federal support for such efforts is more visible.

As discussed earlier in the section on aging and mental health as an evolving field, the goal is not to model the field of geriatric mental health after child mental health in the sense that older patients are encouraged to see an aging specialist the way children are referred to a child specialist.

The risks of doing disservice to older people would be great if this were the aim, since it could put up artificial barriers between the elderly and the vast number of primary care providers who represent front line contact points with troubled older individuals. And, again, it would be unrealistic to expect that there would ever be enough aging specialists to meet demand if only they saw the elderly.

Still there is an acute need for an expanding number of specialists in the field of aging and mental health. There is a common sense reason for this statement. Everyone agrees that generalists working in mental health—psychiatrists, psychologists, social workers, nurses, and para-professionals alike—need more education about aspects of aging and mental health issues of later life, as well as training for work with mentally disturbed older people. But, who is prepared to provide this training? It defies common sense to think that generalists themselves can carry out this function. What is clearly required is at least a cadre of experts on aging and mental health. Operationally, we need a number of training centers across the country for this purpose (Birren, and Sloane, 1977). Such centers would ideally be focal points for both clinical training and research training relevant to mental health and illness of older people. These centers would be places where specialists would be trained who could then go to other training programs where they would provide geriatric input into the mental health curricula of generalists. In effect, these new specialists would be the trained trainers available to help mental health professionals working with all age groups to be better prepared to provide services to older people. They would be resource people to both students and practitioners whose studies and work relate, in part or in total, to older people. They would also, in a generic educational sense, be role models for those considering varying degrees of involvement with elderly patients.

The focus of training efforts and curricula development in the field of aging and mental health is moving and will continue to move in several directions:

1. Career training for clinical work and career training for research on aging and mental health.
2. Continuing education for practitioners already in the field.
3. Inservice training for personnel working with older people in various specialized settings, where knowledge of the dynamics of the setting may be nearly as important as clinical experience with the elderly. Such settings, for example, would include nursing homes and community mental health centers with targeted programs for the elderly.

4. Training directed to the different groups of mental health professionals and paraprofessionals with attention to team approaches.
5. Multidisciplinary mental health training.
6. Geriatric Mental Health training for primary care providers working with older people.
7. Educational programs designed for the informal support system, for older people and families.
8. Problem-focused training where students and practitioners would prepare to work with certain special problems or disorders most prevalent with the elderly (e.g., Alzheimer's Disease/Senile Dementia; Organic Brain Syndrome in general).
9. Experimental training in other innovative areas.

Basic training in the clinical areas should be looked at closely. Part of the challenge facing general mental health clinical training programs is how to fit an aging component into an already overcrowded curriculum. There are no simple answers, though options exist. No option will suffice, however, unless it allows for clinical experiences. Lectures and seminars are necessary, but not sufficient. The trainee must obviously have direct clinical contact with older patients in order to develop an effective approach to treating mental disorders in the elderly. What are some of the options? Basically, the options reflect clinical/didactic rotations of varying durations and levels of intensity. A starting level, for example, might involve a trainee following 2–3 older patients (1–2 in the community, 1–2 in a nursing home) over the course of 4–6 months, with appropriate supervision and didactic balance. A higher level of training might have the trainee spending a day a week for 4–6 months working with older patients having differing degrees of impairment. Another option of yet farther breadth could provide the trainee an opportunity to work half to full-time over a 4–6 month interval with older patients in different clinical settings. Levels of still greater scope and duration (e.g., 1–2 years of full-time work with mentally disturbed elderly) could be preparing the trainee for specialization in Geriatric Mental Health.

How does one match the optimal set of clinical experiences that one should have in working with older patients with each of the different levels of training just delineated? Unfortunately, no such ideal curricula have been developed. Nonetheless, a number of logical considerations can be outlined.

Foremost conceptually is the fact that the field of Geriatric Mental Health has a population focus. It does not focus just on disorders (e.g., OBS, depression, schizophrenia), or treatments (e.g., individual, group, family, pharmacologic therapies), or services (assessment, case management, consultation), or settings (clinics, homes, institutions). Its concern is with all of these and more.

Geriatric Mental Health is, in a sense, as diverse in scope as the field of Mental Health in general. Each has a population focus. Each deals with clinical problems, treatments, services, and settings for care. Geriatric Mental Health is different from the field of Mental Health, as it relates to the younger adult, in the following ways:

1. Though the elderly patient can be troubled by any of the mental disorders found in younger adults, these disorders, as indicated earlier, may appear under altered conditions in later life. There are also those disorders which are more unique to later life (e.g., Alzheimer's Disease or Senile Dementia). The symptoms and course of a given illness, such as the atypical depression previously described, may vary with aging. The greater interplay of medical and social problems with concurrent psychological disturbance in the older patient certainly require a particular orientation and knowledge for proper intervention.

2. Treatment strategies also vary often. This is particularly common with pharmacotherapy where both the desired and the untoward effects may occur at lower dosages with older people. It is also the case with the talking therapies where the handling of dependency issues demands much skill and experience in working with the elderly.

3. Some clinical services such as assessment and consultation must assume an altered emphasis in order to adequately address the more complex mix of psychosocial and biomedical problems with which older patients present.

4. Apart from the usual settings for care, there are obviously a number of other sites specially targeted to the elderly, where direct mental health services or consultation could occur. These include nursing homes, geriatric programs at community mental health centers, senior centers, senior housing projects, nutrition sites, etc.

Thus, the magnitude of the challenge that mental health clinical training programs face in trying to incorporate an adequate Aging component into their already crowded curricula can be fully appreciated. But there is an important additional reason for making the effort, beyond the gain of learning more about the elderly and mental disorders in later life. There is another benefit—a sleeper. Knowledge gained through work with older adults may, indeed, improve the mental health worker's skill with younger patients. To illustrate, an 80-year-old patient may present the therapist with an unparalleled opportunity to look at the course of early life conflicts and problems over a period of many decades; a 70-year followup of sorts. The therapist has a chance to follow the clinical picture of a mental disorder moving across the life cycle. The older patient, as historian, can expand our understanding of the dynamic interplay of disorder and development. A focus on aging and the elderly, in other words, can better prepare us for mental health work with all age groups. With such an opportunity, if the adding of Aging to a general mental health curriculum temporarily causes a training program a little extra work, it will definitely be worth the effort for all involved.

## RESEARCH

Despite the fact that research in the area of Aging and Mental Health has been going on for a significant period of time (NIMH, 1977), the field nonetheless has a new frontier quality about it. Most of this research has been in the psychosocial and services area. Research on mental illness and the treatment of mental disorders in later life is notable by its paucity. Generally speaking, the scope and volume of aging and mental research has fallen far short of mental health research focused on other age groups. While this speaks to a tremendous gap, it also suggests a sizeable potential. It is less that many questions cannot be answered, than that many questions have not been studied. This is a phenomenon in most new fields. It also provides a basis for curiosity and excitement—both of which are current around research issues in aging and mental health.

To get a sense of where mental health research relevant to aging and the elderly might go or where areas of need might push it, one should have an understanding of different ways research in this area can be conceptualized. It can be conceptualized in terms of categories, such as the three groupings already briefly alluded to:

1. On Mental Illness in later life—etiology, diagnosis, clinical course, treatment, prevention, etc.
2. On Psychosocial factors affecting mental health and mental illness among older persons, including attention to family dynamics, one's milieu, social problems, social policy, etc.
3. On Services and the Delivery of Services for the Elderly.

Another way of looking at mental health and aging research is to ask if it will be: Short-term, immediate pay-off; Long-term, potential high pay-off; Long-term, high risk, Nobel prize aspiring research.

Short-term, immediate pay-off research encompasses a considerable number of important areas. Many questions asked about mental disorders and treatment modalities with younger adults have not been looked at as extensively with the elderly. And yet the methodologies have for the most part been developed. These questions are just waiting to be addressed, usually not requiring that much time for results. How, for example, do the clinical pictures of depression, anxiety, and schizophrenia in later life compare with the presentation of these disorders in younger adulthood? How are they altered with accompanying organic brain syndrome? How does the approach to treating the so-called functional disorders in later life compare to treatment of these disturbances with the middle-aged and youth; in this regard do the uses of individual, group, and family therapies require any basic modifications with the elderly? What about pharmacotherapy? The same questions asked about pharmacokinetics, dosage levels, side-effects, drug-drug interactions, etc., in other age groups should be studied with older persons. To be sure, some studies have already been done, and others are going on in these areas. But they are too few. Within one to three years, studies like these can have ready clinical usefulness, which is why they can be considered in the immediate, high-payoff grouping.

Long-term, potential high pay-off research similarly encompasses a multitude of areas. Many basic science and longitudinal studies could be included here. Though cross-sectional studies can provide much useful information on the course of mental disorders, longitudinal research would obviously be the ideal. Research on the impact of crises and events in the middle years on mental health in later life is a case in point. Research on suicide which reaches its highest incidence in the over 65 would cut across both the short-term and the long-term categories. Understanding and treating tardive dyskinesia may be a long-term matter.

The third grouping, long-term, high-risk, Nobel prize aspiring research addresses problems and disorders like Alzheimer's Disease/Senile Dementia whose causes have been elusive. Research moving in certain directions to find answers about etiology or intervention may wind up at a dead-end. In this sense such research may be long-term and at high risk for failure. But if it were to be successful, it would be of major breakthrough stature, a candidate for kudos as the Nobel prize.

Yet a third way of conceptualizing mental health research on older people and aging has a structural aspect to it. Does the research study have a primary or a secondary focus on aging or the elderly? A primary focus is where the predominant interest of the study is on aging or where most of the sample are older persons. A secondary focus is where only a part of the study is on aging or the

elderly. The primary/secondary dichotomy need not apply to relevance. Indeed, a study of the secondary type could be as relevant or, at times, even more relevant than the primary type; the former can add information based on comparison and contrast that the latter could not provide.

The secondary type of research may also lend itself to throwing more light on the impact of development factors on the clinical picture of mental disorders—in old age and other parts of the life cycle as well. A study of depression where the subjects would include children, young adults, middle-aged and elderly persons would reflect research where aging and the elderly would be of a secondary focus—in structure, but not relevance.

## A PIECE OF THE PUZZLE

In the discussion on Training, emphasis was placed on the value of adding a focus on aging to general curricula in better preparing mental health workers for treating all age groups—not just the elderly. A similar statement can be made in the area of Research. Including a focus on aging or the elderly in a research project might increase the chance of understanding the basic question being asked. Further clues about the problem or disorder under study might be identified. In other words, attention to aging or older people in a given study could fill in a piece of the puzzle the investigator was attempting to solve with younger subjects.

A classic example of this piece of the puzzle concept can be found in the research on biogenic amine neurotransmitters and their theorized roles in the etiology of depression. The bioamine hypothesis, most simply stated, is that depression is associated with diminished levels of biogenic amines in the brain. In elaborating this hypothesis discussions address the possible effect of monoamine oxidase (MAO) which presumably can lower levels of certain biogenic amines (Kaplan, Sadock, and Freedman, 1975). Thus, in a corollary of the biogenic amine hypothesis, if the MAO level is elevated, a clinical depression could be precipitated. Interestingly, other studies have found that MAO levels increase with age (Robinson and Davis, 1971). Extrapolating again from the biogenic amine hypothesis of depression, since MAO levels increase with age, then all older people should be depressed and increasingly so. But most older people are definitely not depressed. There is work that indicates that depression may be less frequent after age 70 than between 55-70 (Lipton, 1976). Hence, by adding a focus on aging and the elderly to the research on the relationship between brain biogenic amine levels and depression, a piece of the puzzle about depression in general was added. The new piece of information on MAO levels and aging meant that the biogenic amine theory was probably going to become more complicated before the final answer about its merits would be reached. Such information is relevant not just to the elderly, but to all age groups in the effort to understand depression itself.

The piece of the puzzle concept applies as much to social problems research as it does to mental illness studies. It speaks to a research orientation whose potential has been largely unrealized. It promises new clues, new bits of information that could be useful in contributing to an improved understanding of mental health and mental illness across the life cycle.

Given the new frontier mood in the field of Aging and Mental Health, and given the number of directions research in this field can and needs to move in, future thrust will probably be rather broad based. This should not be surprising, since, as explained before, the field has a population focus. Some fields focus on one problem (e.g., on alcohol) and even so are quite broad. But when the focus is on a population group one is looking at the myriad of problems, illnesses, treatment, services, etc.—each of which is broad—that the population deals with.

The different ways mental health and aging research has been categorized above will no doubt all be addressed through a steadily growing number of studies. Research on mental illnesses and treatment should get particular attention because of the general sparseness of studies in this area and the magnitude of mental disorders among the elderly in both community and institutional settings. At the same time, new leads that may emerge in research on aging and mental health can add to our understanding—or perhaps force us to reexamine basic theoretical constructs—of mental illness and its treatment, as well as development and growth relevant not just to the elderly, but to people in general. In other words, research on aging and later life can provide new pieces to the puzzle of the human condition.

## SPECIAL OLDER SUBGROUPS

The need to look at the particular problems of special subgroups of the elderly population was emphasized in the earlier discussion on "Economic Issues." Various special older subgroups will now be examined in more detail. The key issue that emerges is the need to develop an approach of Target Group Oriented Services. Widows, minor-

ities and those living alone will be specifically discussed.

### WIDOWS

"One experience that most elderly women will eventually have in common is the loss of their husband" (DHEW, 1978). This results from longevity (e.g. 1975 mortality data indicated white females live 77 years on the average compared to 69 for white males) coupled with the usual tendency of men to marry younger women. Even excluding the institutional population, the number of elderly widows (8.9 million in 1976) exceeded the number of elderly wives (7.8 million). At the same time, the percentage of women widowed was 23 percent for those 60–64, and 70 percent for those 75 and older. Another half million elderly widows live in nursing homes and constitute over one-half of the nursing home population. Few elderly widows remarry, and two-thirds live alone. The opportunity for man-woman relations in general has declined because of differential mortality, with women 65 + outnumbering men of the same age by over 40 percent (US Dept. of Commerce, 1976). Similarly, the disparity between the number of older widows and widowers has been growing since 1930, from a ratio of about 2 to 1 to over 5 to 1 (DHEW, 1978).

It is, therefore, obvious that future planning for aging and mental health services must involve a targeted approach for widows. The combination of aggravated psychosocial, sexual, and socioeconomic stress that elderly widows will continue to confront presents one of our greatest societal challenges.

### MINORITIES

With the predicted growth of minority populations, the need for targeted services for the various minority subgroups becomes even more evident. "Persons of races other than white are projected to grow in number about 300 percent by 2035 (compared to 115 percent for all races), increasing their proportion of the elderly population from about one-tenth (in 1978) to one-sixth in the year 2035" (DHEW, 1978). Cultural and economic issues will continue to interfere with adequate utilization and delivery of mental health services. The position of elderly minority groups has been called one of "triple jeopardy, the reference being to people who are old, poor and members of a racial or ethnic minority" (Hendricks and Hendricks, 1977).

Attempts to address the special needs of older minority groups are already in progress, and promise to evolve much further. Mental health service programs, for example, are working to improve the bilingual and bicultural capacities of staff. Mental health clinical and research training programs alike are becoming more focused on the recruitment of minority trainees and the development of curricula dealing with minority group content. Services research is examining the unique mental health problems and issues relevant to elderly minority populations, in addition to exploring more effective ways of delivering services to older minority individuals. The magnitude and momentum of these efforts, however, have a significant distance to travel.

### THE LIVING ALONE

"One of the most striking phenomena that have occurred in recent decades has been the rapid growth in the number of elderly who live alone" (DHEW 1978). From 1960 to 1976 the proportion of older persons living alone in the community rose from one-sixth to one-fourth (in numbers, from 3.8 million to 7.9 million). The increase in single-person households among the 75 and older group has been even greater—doubling the rate for the 65-74 age group, tripling the rate of the 60-64 year olds. In 1976 37 percent of all persons 75 and over lived alone, with the vast majority women. Explanations for the numbers living alone have included differential mortality rates between husbands and wives, geographical dispersal of mobile families, more financial support for the individual living alone because of the nature of restrictions in various health and income programs which paradoxically create a disincentive to change one's living status, and others.

From a mental health perspective, there can be several risks to living alone. The availability of a source of immediate social interaction and support is reduced. This has implications for both maintaining mental health and identifying the early onset of a mental disorder. While it is true that there are certain people, such as those with a schizoid personality, who may find it less stressful living alone, most men and women require a significant amount of interpersonal interaction throughout the life cycle. Where social disengagement does occur, it usually represents an undesired outcome rather than a predictable choice. In this regard the risks in living alone relate more specifically to those who are at the same time isolated or cut off from significant others.

Because of the post World War II "baby boom," new elderly cohorts will have larger families to rely upon when changes in living arrangements become considered (Neugarten, 1975). Other

dynamics such as innovations in communal living among the elderly for social and economic purposes could also alter the number living alone. "Nevertheless, elderly persons with the highest rates of living alone (women and the oldest of the elderly) are the same groups that will be growing at the most rapid rates in the future. Even if the rate of increase in living alone slows somewhat, it appears that the number of elderly living alone will continue to climb" (DHEW, 1978).

The challenge to the mental health delivery system in meeting the needs of those living alone is multifaceted. Problems may not be identified as quickly. Once identified, utilization of services is still difficult since the initiation of help is so often a factor of the nudging other who may not be as available to those living alone. Other factors such as transportation, particularly with women, add to access problems. Thus, much ingenuity and a fair amount of resources are necessary to facilitate identification of problems in those living alone, referral of these people to appropriate sources of care, and outreach to those who are both alone and isolated. As with widows, minorities, and other older subgroups, it is the target group oriented service approach that is indicated.

## POLICY, LEGISLATION

In the preceding sections a number of areas were identified where policy and/or legislative issues became apparent. Many of these issues are not new, having been raised before in a number of national studies, including the White House Conferences on Aging, the 1978 Report to the Secretary of HEW and to the Congress by the Committee on Mental Health and Illness of the Elderly, and the 1978 Report of the President's Commission on Mental Health.

To recapitulate, some of the more salient areas where policy and legislative changes are being or need to be considered follow. The list is not meant to be all inclusive.

### SERVICES

The serious underdelivery of mental health services to the elderly will continue to be a major area of policy and legislative debate. Several components are involved that affect delivery to and utilization of services by older persons. Comprehensive health assessment to assure accurate diagnosis and treatment planning is critical. Case management to facilitate coordination and continuity of services should receive increased attention given the diversity of problems with which so many older people present. For those who have difficulty getting to services, the services must get to them; mechanisms of outreach, in other words, will have to be elaborated—including a range of home services. Particularly with the old-old, if the risk of institutionalization is to be diminished, the home as a site for interventions will have to be strongly considered. Along with the old-old, other specialized subgroups (e.g., women, minorities, the isolated) will require targeting of services and mechanisms to bring this about. Policy and legislative options in these areas will probably range from categorical allocations to community-based service programs, to health insurance modifications, to various forms of direct aid to families and older persons.

## INSTITUTIONS AND COMMUNITY SUPPORTS

That a significant number of elderly, however small their percentage, will always need some degree of institutional placement seems highly likely. The challenge then is to develop a system of care where the nature of the setting and the scope of the services matches the level of need and impairment of the individual. The risk is that unnecessary new institutions will be created. But the risk must not prevent a careful approach aimed at designing a realistic continuum of options ranging from a variety of community support programs to varying levels of congregate living and congregate care.

At the same time, the institutions which already exist—the nursing home in particular whereover 70 percent of the residents have mental health problems—need to be critically re-examined. Very appropriate quality of care and ethical questions should arise with any health service industry that costs the public billions of dollars a year. The range of mental health related services provided, as well as training and continuing education for the staffs at such institutions should be addressed in terms of policies and guidelines. The idea of a percentage of dollars going into these institutions being set aside for research (e.g., a percentage of nursing home dollars designated for research on senile dementia) could also be considered.

## HEALTH AND SOCIAL SUPPORT INSURANCES

The shortcomings in major health plans where gross inequities exist between coverage for medical and mental health care have long been pointed out. This has been particularly glaring in the case of the elderly. Pressure for change for improved outpatient reimbursement, coverage for more extensive clinical assessment, and increased attention to preventive services will continue to mount.

Similarly, coverage for a variety of social supports to aid the elderly and their families will undergo more intensive scrutiny. Considerations here will probably be closely linked to a variety of community support programs aimed at keeping older persons out of more restrictive care settings.

## TRAINING AND PERSONNEL DEVELOPMENT

The immediate need for a cadre of experts in aging and mental health has been emphasized. Even if the major policy thrust were to be on gearing up the core mental health team and primary care providers to work with the elderly, geriatric mental health specialists would still be needed to carry out the required training. Policy options will have to take into consideration the range of training modes necessary for both specialty and generalist training. Balance will have to be struck along several parameters—between the development of training centers and the provision of individual fellowships, between career development and continuing education, between clinical training and research training, between training for professionals and education for the elderly and their families. A significant part of the problem of inadequate mental health service development and delivery for older persons has been the magnitude of inattention to training. That policy changes will occur in this regard is inevitable. It remains to be seen, however, how far and how rapid the push will occur.

## RESEARCH

With increasing recognition of the difference between normal aging and disease in later life has come an appreciation of the role of research to further differentiate the two. For much can be done about the latter (disease) to improve the course of the former (normal aging). While psychosocial and services research will continue to get a big push, studies of mental disorders and their treatment should get a special shove, since the prevalence of mental illness among the elderly is so high with past research activity around these disturbances so low. Senile dementia, the fourth leading cause of death and organic brain syndrome in general, because of its effect in bringing about so much institutionalization, are already receiving markedly increased attention.

With the more recent National Reports relevant to mental health and /or aging recommending considerably further research on later life, the future looks better in terms of potential breakthroughs of new knowledge for the care of older persons. Indeed, this applies to policy considerations about the field as a whole.

## FACTORS OF CHANGE

The likelihood of dynamic developments in policies and programs relevant to the mental health of older persons is increasing because of several factors. Rising consumerism is a key factor. Throughout the culture, particularly apparent since the late 1960s, has been a steadily growing expression of consumer concern about public services and products. The elderly, too, have been making their voice heard. Organized groups of older persons such as the American Association of Retired Persons, the National Council of Senior Citizens, the Gray Panthers and a multitude of others have been proliferating at national and community levels. By 1978 the American Association of Retired Persons had exceeded 10 million members. The potential influence of these organizations politically is enormous. Their potential role in improving informal support systems is similarly enormous. In both areas their impact is being and will continue to be strongly felt.

The changing picture of the over 65 population—new cohorts—is another major factor. One is looking at an increasingly educated and activist group. From 1960 to 1976, the median number of school years completed by elderly persons had risen from 8.3 to 10.3 years, with 12 years projected by 1990 (DHEW, 1978). Moreover, from 1960 to 1975 the percentage of people over 65 who completed 4 years of high school and 4 or more years of college doubled (US Dept. of Commerce, 1976). The number of well educated and action-oriented elderly, in short, has been going up yearly.

Another factor to be reckoned with is the voting presence of the older population. To illustrate, in the 1972 Presidential election, the combined elderly population (men and women of all races) had a higher voting rate than the under age 65 population.

Given the growing number of older persons with more time, energy, and know-how on hand, policies and programs relevant to the elderly will increasingly be influenced by them rather than for them. Meanwhile, the push from both directions should create no small challenge for policymakers as well as society.

## CULTURAL REEVALUATION OF OLD AGE AND THE ELDERLY

### IMPROVED PERCEPTION OF MENTAL HEALTH PROBLEMS

When myths and stereotypes of old age are clarified, problems that respond to interventions become apparent. The "old man who is getting eccentric," may in fact be manifesting the onset of an acute psychosis. The "old woman who is losing her memory because of senility," may indeed be depressed. A basic cultural change in progress is the re-examination of what should be expected in later life—of what is normal, of what is not. Older people themselves are seeking information to prevent what can be avoided, to identify what can be treated. The acceptance of negative change in health or mental health status during one's later years as an inevitable, irreversible concomitant of the aging process is increasingly being challenged. There appears to be an inverse relationship between how well old age is perceived and valued and how much society will take for granted about it. Much of what has been taken for granted is receiving careful second looks. At the same time there is a positive change taking place in the way families respond to problems of their older members. They are much less reticent to seek help, and are becoming more dissatisfied than discouraged when service and social support systems inadequately address their needs.

### NEW INTEREST IN PERSONAL, FAMILY, AND CULTURAL ROOTS

It is interesting that a reevaluation of aging is taking place at the same time that minorities and the majority alike are exhibiting marked curiosity about their personal, family, and cultural roots. The potential role of the older person in providing a link or continuity with the past has always been intellectually appreciated. But it is now being sought with affect.

Longer life and better health for the elderly have increased their availability and capacity to vigorously interact with the younger generations. In this process, younger members of a family have gained a greater opportunity to learn about the early psychological and historical dynamics that have contributed to their own, as well as their family's growth and development. It would seem more than coincidental that while the culture is romantically and intensively exploring the varying historical backgrounds of its diverse groups that those—the elderly—who have had a longer past in all the groups are receiving more empathy and attention. The converse might also be suggested—that along with a growing interest in aging has come a search into the past, a look at the old days, to try to understand our roots, our present, and our future.

## A Changing Emphasis from Producing to Experiencing

It has been common to hear that the elderly have been underappreciated or undervalued because they produce less. A general trend, though, is underway that could have a positive effect on mental health in later life, as well at other phases of the life cycle. In the simplest sense, there seems to be a changing cultural emphasis from producing to experiencing, from doing to developing—or at least toward more balance within these two dyads. Interpersonal exploration and not just occupational elevation has become important in everyday life. The former can clearly continue after retirement and lead to renegotiated family and community relationships, as well as to further personal growth.

## An Emerging Intergenerationalism

One of the most positive signs for the future of older people in America has been society's growing reevaluation of the family and intergenerational relationships. Witness television—where the fantasy life of our culture unfolds before us with wish fulfillment, escapism, and compensatory drama, but also with important trials of new or renewed social ideas. Among the latter has been a range of programs portraying—or perhaps experimenting with—various modes of family structure and interaction. Many of these families have displayed marked generational diversity. Attention to the generations on TV has not been restricted to family shows. It has been apparent in a broad spectrum, from cops and robbers shows to situation comedies. In many of these programs it is the relationship between the younger and older protagonists that is of complementary, if not primary interest. It is as if these shows are attempting to vicariously compensate for family relationships that are evading us, or else trying to explore with us new ways of restoring these relationships in real life.

TV, of course, is not the only place where intergenerational endeavors are taking place. Older people are returning to classrooms, bringing about a mix among age groups at many schools across the country. Civic and consumer organizations

(such as the Gray Panthers) draw on intergenerational strengths. Even more basic, families are extending to 4 or 5 generations, a development that is likely to significantly alter the nature of the more recent nuclear family.

In short, while the presence of older people is increasingly being felt, their role in relation to other age groups is also being expanded. The movement appears to be in the direction of continuity and reciprocity between generations rather than toward gaps.

> Youth, large, lusty, loving—
> youth, full of grace, force, fascination,
> Do you know that Old Age may come after you,
> with equal grace, force, fascination?
> Walt Whitman
> Leaves of Grass

## REFERENCES

Agate, J. D. 1970. *The Practice of Geriatrics.* Springfield, Ill. Charles C Thomas.

Birren, J. E., and Sloane, R. B. 1977. Manpower and training needs in mental health and illness of the aging. Los Angeles: Ethel Percy Andrus Gerontology Center, University of Southern California.

Brody, E. M. 1976. *A Social Work Guide for Long-Term Care Facilities.* DHEW Publication No. (ADM) 76–177.

Butler, R. N., and Lewis, M. I., 1973. *Aging and Mental Health.* St. Louis: C. V. Mosby.

Bulter, R. N., 1975. Psychiatry and the elderly: An overview. *American Journal of Psychiatry, 132* 9, 893–900.

Cohen, G. D. 1976. Mental health services and the elderly: Needs and options. *American Journal of Psychiatry, 133*, 65–68.

Cohen, G. D. 1977. Approach to the geriatric patient. *Medical Clinics of North America, 61*, 855–866.

Detre, T. P., and Jarecki, H. G. 1971. *Modern Psychiatric Treatment,* pp. 168–171. Philadelphia: Lippincott.

Group for the Advancement of Psychiatry. 1971. *The Aged and Community Mental Health: A Guide to Program Development.* New York: Mental Health Material Center.

Havighurst, R. J. 1975. The future aged: the use of time and money. *Gerontologist, 15*(1), Part II, 10–15.

Hendricks, J., and Hendricks, C. D. 1977. *Aging in Mass Society,* pp. 349–382. Cambridge, Mass: Winthrop.

Internal Revenue Service. 1976. Federal income tax forms. Department of the Treasury.

KAPLAN, H., SADOCK, B., AND FREEDMAN, A. M. 1975. The brain in psychiatry. *In,* A. M. Freedman, H. I. Kaplan, and B. J. Sadock (eds.), *Comprehensive Textbook of Psychiatry II,* pp. 162–164. Baltimore: Williams and Wilkins.

KATZMAN, R. 1976. The prevalence and malignancy of Alzheimer's Disease. *Archives of Neurology, 33,* 217–218.

LIPTON, M. A. 1976. Age differentiation in depression: biochemical aspects. *Journal of Gerontology, 31,* 293–299.

National Institute of Mental Health. 1973. Provisional data on federally funded community mental health centers. Division of Biometry and Epidemiology.

National Institute of Mental Health. 1976. Statistical note No. 125. Division of Biometry and Epidemiology.

National Institute of Mental Health. 1977. *Research on The Mental Health of the Aging.* DHEW Publication No. (ADM) 77–379.

NEUGARTEN, B. L. 1975. The future and the young-old. *Gerontologist, 15*(1), Part II, 4–9.

Report to the President from The President's Commission on Mental Health. 1978. US Government Printing Office Stock Number 040–000–00390–8.

REDICK, R. W. 1974. Patterns in use of nursing homes by aged mentally ill. Statistical Note 107. Division of Biometry, National Institute of Mental Health.

REDLICH, F., AND KELLERT, S. R. 1978. Trends in American mental health. *American Journal of Psychiatry, 135*(1), 22–28.

ROBINSON, D. S., AND DAVIS, J. M. 1971. Relation of sex and aging to monamine oxidase activity of human brain, plasma, and platelets. *Archives of General Psychiatry, 24,* 536–539.

ROTH, M. 1960. Phobic anxiety–depersonalization syndrome and some general aetiological problems in psychiatry. *Journal of Neuropsychiatry 1,* 293–306.

ROTH, M. 1976. The psychiatric disorders of later life. *Psychiatric Annals,* 6: 9, 57–101.

SALZMAN, C., VAN DER KOLK, B., AND SHADER. R. I. 1976. Psychopharmacology and the geriatric patient. *In,* R. I. Shader (ed.), *Manual of Psychiatric Therapeutics,* pp. 171–184. Boston: Little, Brown.

Search Reports, March, 1975. Nursing home care in Rhode Island.

Senate Memorandum, Special Committee on Aging, Feb. 3, 1978. Vol X. No. 1.

SHELDON, A., McEWAN, P. J. M., AND RYSER, C. P. 1975. *Retirement: Patterns and Predictions.* DHEW Publication No. (ADM) 74–49, 94–110.

TEETER, R. B., GARETZ, F. K., MILLER, W. B., AND HEILAND, W. F. 1976. Psychiatric disturbances of aged patients in skilled nursing homes. *American Journal of Psychiatry, 133*(12), 1430–1434.

US Dept. of Commerce, Bureau of the Census, September, 1976, Status, Washington, D. C., 23–38.

US Dept. of HEW, 1978. Statistical reports on older Americans:3. Some prospects for the future elderly population. DHEW Publication No. (OHDS) 78–20288.

*Webster's New Collegiate Dictionary.* 1959. Springfield, Mass: G. & C. Merriam Co.

# Author Index

# Subject Index

## A

Abducens nucleus, neuronal stability in, 76
Ability, as factor in intelligence, 272-73
Abstract thinking:
  in alcoholic brain disorders, 663, 664
  in Alzheimer's disease, 140
  in dementia, 561-62
  in personality test performance, 538
  and sensory-motor functions, 205
Acculturation, of ethnic communities, 455. *See also* Socialization
Acetaminophen, pharmcokinetics of, 768
Acetophenazine, anticholinergic effects of, 751 (table 31-1)
Acetylcholine:
  and hypothalamic aging, 105, 106
  and hypothalamic regulation, 318
  trophotropic release of, 324
Acetylcholine esterase, age changes in, 83, 90 (table 4-1)
Acetyltransferase, age changes in, 152
Achievement:
  acceptance of, 258

as consolation in death, 932 (table 38-1), 933
as factor in mood, 288
and learning process, 221, 223-24
life course perspective on, 338
and life satisfaction, 254
need for, 248-49
as reaction against death, 926
socialization into, 250, 253
in stress response, 301-2
and value changes, 292
Acoustic nerve, brainstem EP component from, 180, 181 (Fig. 8-9), 183
Acoustic neuroma, brainstem EP in, 183
Acromegaly, growth hormone secretion in, 108
ACTH. *See* Adrenocorticotropic hormone
Acting out, reflection of, in MMPI response, 541
Activities of Daily Living (ADL), encouragement of, by psychotherapy, 785, 793
Activities of Daily Living (ADL) tasks:
  assessment of dependency with, 685-86
  comparison of, to MSQ, 680, 681
  and determination of competence, 693

Activity:
  decline in, with loss, 620
  encouragement of, in behavior therapy, 871
  encouragement of, in group services, 810
  encouragement of, in milieu therapy, 869-70
  encouragement of, by psycho-therapy, 785, 791-94 (table 32-3), 795, 800
  as factor in adjustment, 289
  as factor in mood, 288
  and future orientation, 298
  v. patterns of aging, 300
  and personality differentiation, 291
  psychometric assessment of, 680
  reduction of, in depression, 616-21 passim, 625
  and responsibility, 297
  stability of, into old age, 287
  *See also* Interaction
Activity therapy:
  efficacy of, 872-73
  method of, 818-20
Acute brain syndrome, 457
  diagnosis of, 50
  as diagnostic category, 39, 568
  and drug use, 707
  incidence of, 39, 41

Curanderos, 453
Curiosity:
    and exploratory drive, 247, 248
    as motivator, 250
Cushing's syndrome, 319
Cyclophosphamide, and ADH
        secretion, 707
Cyclospasmol. *See* Cylandelate
Cylandelate, 762
Cylert. *See* Magnesium pamoline
Cytoplasmic basophilia, age changes
    in, 92 (table 4-1)
Czechoslovakia, suicide rate in, 638

## D

Dalmine. *See* Flurazepam
Dance therapy:
    efficacy of, 875
    method of, 819
    treatment of schizophrenia in, 875
Darvon. *See* Propoxyphene
Day care centers:
    consultation in, 840
    counseling in, 831
    group work in, 806, 808, 818,
        820, 832
    and maintenance of minority
        elderly, 462
    outreach of, 859
    personnel needs of, 850
    psychotherapy in, 785, 800
    rehabilitation in, 834
    services of, 834-35, 838
    as setting for intervention, 721
    social services orientation of,
        828
Day hospitals:
    counseling in, 831
    medical/mental health mix in, 981
    preventive care in, 828-29, 965-66
    rehabilitation in, 833
    services of, 835
    treatment of paraphrenics in, 610
Deafness:
    assessment of, for mental illness
        vulnerability, 673
    v. depression, 631
    effect of, on clinical interview
        responses, 677
    and hallucinations, 596
    indirect effects of, 200, 208-9
    in late paraphrenia, 606-7, 613
Deanol, treatment of Alzheimer's
        disease with, 571
Dean Scale, assessment of demoralization
    with, 684
Death:
    adjustment to, 939-40
    anger at, 931-32
    anticipation of, 395-96
    anticipation of, as stress, 121
    attitude toward, 961-62
    attitude toward, v. depression, 622, 633
    attitude toward, v. suicide, 643-44
    awareness of, 922
    bearing of, on status of elderly, 388
    bereavement over, 418, 934-38
    comprehensive theory of, 925-26, 940
    coping with, 926-33
    denial of, 926-31
    fear of, 934
    fear of, in insomnia, 737
    fear of, in intercourse, 897
    grief over, 932
    humanistic psychological view of,
        924-25
    incontinence as omen of, 734

and integration of life experiences, 28
intervention techniques with, 940-41
investigation of, 922-23
in legend, 5
and loneliness, 731-32
preoccupation with, 356, 357
psychoanalytic view of, 923-24
"quality" of, 11
realization of, 926
sacramental significance of, 434
sociological view of, 924
stress-induced, 324
supports in, 932-33 (table 38-1)
and time concept, 255
transcendence of, 443
*See also* Mortality
Death wish, 923-24
Debrisoquine, antidepressant interaction
    of, 754 (table 31-2)
Decarboxylase, age changes in, 94
    (table 4-1)
Decision making, 19
    in community services, 848
    in dementia, 563
    in families, 12-13
    in institutional admissions, 487
    in institutional environments, 473
    and life satisfaction, 24
    v. life style, 25
    monitoring of, 204
    in old age, 12-13
    and problem solving, 277, 279
    process of, 8
    and risk, 252, 277
    and slowed reactions, 202-5
Decongestants, antidepressant
    interaction of, 755 (table 31-3)
Defeat, neurochemical reactions in,
    321-22
Defense mechanisms, 327, 342
    in adjustment, 300-301
    in care of incontinence, 734
    in clinical interview response, 676
    v. maturity, 26
    mediation of stress by, 312, 328
    in neuroses, 655
    and perceived housing conditions, 297
    in senile dementia, 570
    and sexual interest, 903
    surfacing of, in group therapy, 819
Defensible space, 481-82
Deficits:
    and adaptation to stress, 355-57
    as aspect of mental health, 341
    and life satisfaction, 341-42
Degeneration, definition of, 149
Degenerative diseases, 149
    and lipofuscin deposits, 156
Dehydration:
    in delirium, 559
    and reversible brain syndrome, 555
Delirium:
    in alcoholic brain disorder, 663
    in CJD, 576
    clinical course of, 558
    and depression, 564
    differential diagnosis of, 563
    and ergotropic/trophotropic
        discharge, 325
    etiology of, 558-60
    examination of, 560
    intertwining of, with dementia, 556
    laboratory investigation of, 560
        (table 24-1)
    in meningovascular syphilis, 576
    in multi-infarct dementia, 574
    and nicotinic acid deficiency, 709
    as OBS, 554, 555
    psychological assessment of, 674

reversibility of, 558
secondary features of, 556
in sedative-hypnotic abuse, 580
symptoms of, 556-58
treatment of, 560-61
Delirium tremens:
    description of, 579, 662-63
    among psychiatric patients, 348
    treatment of, 579
Delusions:
    in affective psychoses, 598-99
    assessment of, 686
    in delirium, 556, 557, 558
    in dementia, 562
    in depression, 624, 627, 636
    in Huntington's chorea, 572
    in late paraphrenia, 592, 597, 607-8
    in organic paranoid psychoses,
        599-600, 601
    in paranoid schizophrenia, 597,
        607-8
    in paranoid states, 591, 593, 594, 595
    in schizophrenia-like states, 592,
        597
    in schizophrenic states, 592, 593
    in senile dementia, 781
    in simple paranoid psychosis, 596, 597
Dementia, 35
    and abnormal behavior, 686
    and alcoholism, 662, 663
    assessment of, in clinical
        interview, 672
    and autonomic function, 114
    and brain pathology, 157-58
    in chronic brain syndrome, 41-43
        (table 2-1)
    CT scan of, 509
    definitions of, 561
    and depression, 514
    detection of, 36, 37
    and diabetes mellitus, 708
    diagnosis of, 49-50
    differential diagnosis of, 231, 232,
        521, 523, 525-29, 563-64, 627
    discriminating among types of, 528-29
    and drug use, 707
    EP in, 171
    etiologies of, 512 (table 21-4),
        564-65
    v. functional disorders, 525-28
    identification of, 37
    and intellectual deterioration, 521, 522
    intertwining of, with delirium, 556
    and kidney dysfunction, 709
    laboratory assessment of, 689, 705-6
        (table 29-6)
    and neuroses, 656, 657, 658
    neurotransmitters and, 118
    normal, 509
    as OBS, 554, 555
    occurrence of, v. race, 49
    paraphrenic symptoms in, 599-601
    pathology of, 89
    pharmacological remedies for, 521
    prediction of mortality from, 530
    prevalence of, v. pathology, 43, 44
        (table 2-4)
    prevalence of, v. severity, 41-43
        (table 2-1)
    psychometric assessment of,
        678-80, 681, 688
    and reading ability, 524
    recognition of, with multidimensional
        tests, 690
    and respiratory disorders, 710
    reversibility in, 561
    secondary features of, 556
    and socioeconomic status, 48
    and subnormal intelligence, 50

Emphysema:
  and delirium, 559
  and mental function, 710
  and stress, 120
Empowerment, process of, 456
Empty nest, 350, 367, 393
  and alcoholism, 662
  and commitment, 359-62 (Figs. 15-1
    through 15-4)
  identity crises of, 368
  and mental health, 416-17
Encephalitis:
  as cause of Parkinsonism, 514
  in neurologic history, 503
Encephalitis lethargica, neurofibrillary
    tangles in, 156
Encephalopathies, diffuse, EEG response
    in, 165
Encephalopathies, metabolic, EEG
    response in, 166 (Fig. 8-1), 169
Encounter groups, 815
  negative potential of, 809
Endarterectomy, 513
  in treatment of multi-infarct
    dementia, 575
Endocrine disorders:
  and mental function, 709-10
  and stress, 319-20
Endocrine functions:
  and hypothalamic aging, 106, 107
  regulation of, 101-2
Endocrine system:
  age changes in, 701-2
  functional decline in, 103
  regulation of motivation by, 249.
  See also Neuroendocrine system
Endogenous depression:
  as diagnostic category, 617-18, 626
  v. personality type, 634
Energy:
  depletion of, by stress, 318, 320-21
  in depression, 514, 630
  diminished metabolism of, 506
  and exploratory drive, 247, 248
  loss of, in Alzheimer's disease, 510
  in normal aging, 367
  in personality test performance, 539
  and problem solving, 252-53
England. See United Kingdom
Entorhinal cortex, dendritic atrophy
    in, 78
Enuresis, treatment of, 237
Environment:
  exploration of, 248
  as factor in adjustment, 289-90
  as factor in personality, 632
  as factor in psychological assessment,
    861-62
  v. hereditary factors, 137, 138
  homeostatic adjustment to, 246-47
  influence of, on mental health, 11-13
  and intellect, 254
  intellectual impoverishment of, 89
  interaction of memory with, 219-20
  v. intrapsychic states, 13
  limbic response to, 100-101
  manipulation of, in behavior therapy,
    235-38
  mastery of, and anomie, 19
  mastery of, v. maturity, 26-27
  modification of, by groups, 809
  modulation of aging by, 121-23
    (Fig. 5-15)
  and motivation, 255-56, 777
  perception of, 297
  as research variable, 263, 266
  role of, in depression, 628-29,
    633-34
  in schizo-affective disorders, 602

stimulation of, in psychotherapy,
    790, 793, 800
stress effects of, 120-21, 311-12
supportive, in psychotherapy, 790-791
    793-94, 799, 800.
See also Residential environment
Enzymes:
  age changes in, 90, 94
  and hypothalamic aging, 105
EP. See Evoked potentials
Epidemiology:
  aims of, 35
  definition of, 34
  limitations of, 35
Epidemiology, method of:
  case identification in, 37-38
  definition of populations in, 35-36
  interview procedure in, 38-39
Epilepsy:
  and brain tumors, 577
  in CJD, 781
  EEG response in, 170
Epileptic seizures:
  in alcohol withdrawal, 662
  in delirium tremens, 579
  EEG response from, 168
  in general paralysis, 576
  in meningovascular syphilis, 576
  and metastatic tumors, 577
  in multi-infarct dementia, 574
  in sedative-hypnotic abuse, 580
Epinephrine:
  age changes in, 702
  antidepressant interaction of, 754
    (table 31-2)
  and endocrine disorders, 320
  and environmental adaptation, 122
  exercise effects on, 953
  in flight response, 318
  and hypothalamic aging, 106
  and hypothalamic regulation, 101, 318
  in stress reaction, 120, 121, 318
    320-23 passim, 331
  treatment of catecholamine
    deficiency with, 118
Equality Index, 380:
  and modernization, 438
  for preliterate societies, 431
Equanil. See Meprobamate
Erection:
  age changes in, 886, 896
  drug effects on, 886-87
  impairment of, 886-87, 889, 890,
    897, 898, 900, 912
  psychosexual significance of, 887
Erection, morning, incidence of, 900
Ergotropic system:
  functions of, 324
  and mental illness, 324-25
Eskalith. See Lithium carbonate
Estradiol:
  age changes in, 111 (Fig. 5-8), 123
  and environmental stress, 122
  and hypothalamic aging, 105, 106
Estrogen(s):
  age changes in, 111, 112, 702, 894
  aging effects of, 119
  and CNS development, 107
  in dyspareunia prevention, 889
  and endocrine disorders, 319
  levels of, v. sexual activity, 900
  treatment of depression with, 755-56
  treatment of sexual dysfunction
    with, 914
  use of, 891
Estrogen therapy, in menopause, 112-13,
    894
Ethacrynic acid, lithium interaction
    of, 758

Ethchlorvynol:
  pharmacokinetics of, 760
  treatment of insomnia with, 738
    (table 30-5)
Eunuchs, 114
Eutonyl. See Pargyline
Evoked potentials (EP):
  age differences in, 174-76
    (Figs. 8-5, 8-6)
  attentional factors in, 173-74
  for clinical disorders, 176-78
  computer analysis of, 689
  as diagnostic tool, 171-72, 184-85
  differential diagnosis with, 528
  technique of, 172-73 (Fig. 8-4)
  See also Brainstem evoked potentials
Exchanges:
  as aspect of solidarity, 407
  and economic necessity, 405-7
  in intergenerational interactions,
    410-11
  intergenerational patterns of, 412-13
  maintenance of autonomy through,
    420
  norms of, 413-15
  position in, 412
Exercise:
  and cardiovascular capacity, 897
  effect of, on anxiety, 947-48, 949
  effect of, on depression, 948
  effect of, on intellect, 946, 949
  effect of, on motor function, 946,
    952, 953
  effect of, on personality, 946-47
  and involution, 944-45 (table 39-1)
  mental health effects of, 943, 944,
    948-49, 953, 954
  motivation of, 953-54
  need for, 954
  risks of, 954
  and stress reactions, 952-53
  therapeutic value of, 874-75, 955
  and wandering behavior, 739-40
  See also Physiotherapy
Exertion, capacity for, vs. age, 201
Exhaustion, aging as, 320-21
Exon, in genetic structure, 136
Ex-patient clubs, rehabilitation in, 833
Expectations, about intergenerational
    relations, 423-24
Experience:
  as factor in sexuality, 904
  and generativity, 338
  integration of, 28-29
  and learning, 214, 240
  mediation of stress by, 312, 328
  and memory, 199-200
  and motivation, 245
  and problem solving, 279
  vs. production, 992
  and skill, 206
  and time concept, 254, 255
  and work efficiency, 209
  See also Life events
Experimental settings/units, as research
    variables, 264-65
Exploratory drive:
  age changes in, 247-48
  incentive to, 249
Extended auditory digit span, detection
    of multi-infarct dementia with, 168
Extended care facility, 68
Extracellular space:
  age changes in, 86-88, 93 (table 4-1),
    152
  boundaries of, 86
  composition of, 86
  function of, 87-88
  and neuronal metabolism, 89

Memory tests, differential diagnosis
    with, 526-27, 528, 533
Meniere's disease:
    brainstem EP in, 183
    dizziness in, 510
Meninges:
    amyloid deposits in, 155
    and CSF absorption failure, 512
Meningioma, 577
Meningitis, 575, 711
    as cause of normal pressure
        hydrocephalus, 573
Meningovascular syphilis, 576
Menopause, 367, 393
    anticipation of, 298
    definition of, 894
    and fertility, 886
    hormonal changes in, 111-12
    and hormonal secretion, 894
    and orgasmic dysfunction, 911
    psychosexual significance of, 891
    response to, vs. urbanization, 438 n. 6
    and sexual activity, 906-7
    symptoms of, 112, 894
Mental health:
    vs. anticipation of old age, 23
    assessment of, among minorities,
        458-59
    and bereavement, 934-38
    cross-cultural comparison of, 429-30
    and cultural determinism, 430
    and cultural relativism, 6
    definitions of, 6-7, 340-41, 474-75,
        829-30
    definition of, for minority groups,
        457-58
    effects of stress on, 311
    environmental context of, 11-13
    and family crises, 416-20
    family link to, 400-401, 422-25
    vs. family relationships, 24
    and goal orientation, 253-54
    growing attention to, 3-4
    influence of life style on, 25-26
    and integration of life experiences,
        28-29
    interactionist view of, 14
    interdisciplinary study of, 346-47
    internal-external view of, 9
    intrapsychic vs. environmental view
        of, 13-14
    vs. maturity, 26-28
    measurement of, 474-75, 933-34
    vs. mental illness, 10-11
    minority characteristics salient
        to, 449-50
    and motivation, 256-58
    multidimensional assessment of,
        690-91
    opportunities for, 8-9
    origin of concept of, 5-6
    vs. physical health, 347-48, 349,
        961, 966
    planning for, 29-30
    positive, 7-8, 692-93
    prevalence of, in old age, 367
    vs. quality of life, 23
    in residential environment, 470-71,
        475, 491
    and stereotypes of aging, 9-10
Mental Health and Retardation Acts,
    sanctioning of community
    services by, 846
Mental health associates, training
    of, 863, 864
Mental health care system:
    access to, 978
    community supports for, 981-83

comprehensive assessment in, 979-80
demands on, 980
economic issues in, 976-77
funding of, 974, 975, 979, 982
interface of, with medicine, 980-81
and mental illness prevalence, 972
multidisciplinary nature of, 963,
    964-65
outreach of, 980, 981
personnel of, 979, 980, 984-86, 990
planning for, 67-69, 675
politics of, 989-991
program development in, 978-79
    (Fig. 41-1, table 41-4)
service delivery problems in, 972
social issues in, 972-73
and special subgroups, 988-89
ties of, to nursing homes, 983
underrepresentation of minorities
    in, 457
unpreparedness of, 971
utilization patterns in, 974-75
    (table 41-1)
Mental health movement, inattention
    of, to elderly, 4
Mental hospitals:
    architecture of, 864-65
    assessment in, 861-62
    behavior therapy in, 870-75
    closing of, 366
    community alternatives to, 835
    counseling in, 831
    court decisions affecting, 876, 877
    decline in, 857-58
    elderly admissions to, 61, 62
        (Fig. 3-3), 65 (table 3-9), 70
        (app. table 3)
    expenditures on, 973
    future research on, 877-78
    goals in, 862, 863, 865, 876, 877
    group therapy in, 867-69
    group work in, 806, 807, 808, 812,
        814, 816-17
    improvement of patients in, 365
    length of stay in, 66 (Fig. 3-5), 71
        (app. table 5)
    level of care in, 349
    Medicare payments to, 975
    milieu therapy in, 869-70
    mortality rates in, 487
    organizational structure of, 862
    overrepresentation of elderly in, 972
    patient classification in, 860-62
    patient mix in, 862
    pharmacotherapy in, 866
    population of, 719, 828, 856-58
    psychotherapy in, 784, 866-69
    reality therapy in, 869
    referrals made by, 67, 68 (table 3-12)
    reorientation of, 876-78
    resident patients in, 61-62, 63
        (table 3-7)
    rise of, 856-57
    staff of, 849, 862-64
    token economy in, 870-72, 873
    treatment of aggression in, 722
    treatment of elderly in, 30
    treatment of minorities in, 461
    treatment of paraphrenics in, 609
    treatment of schizophrenics in,
        608, 611
    treatment of senile dementia in,
        571
    trends in use of, 63, 68
    use of, vs. diagnostic category, 64, 65,
        (table 3-10)
    use of, vs. gender, 64 (table 3-8), 70
        (app. table 4)

    use of, vs. marital status, 65, 66
        (table 3-11)
    use of, vs. race, 64 (Fig. 3-4), 70
        (app. table 4)
    *See also* Private psychiatric hospitals
Mental hygiene, 5
Mental illness:
    and adjustment, 289
    age-related, 103
    and alcoholism, 661
    and alienation, 15, 16, 18
    and anomie, 20
    anticipation of, 349
    assessment of, in clinical interview,
        676
    assessment of, among minorities,
        458-59
    and attempted suicide, 640
    causes of, 367
    clinical course of, 977
    among community-resident elderly,
        348-49
    correlation of, with residential
        characteristics, 473-74
    costs of, 973-74
    definition of, for minority groups,
        457-58
    demography of, 828-29
    determination of incompetence
        in, 693-94
    diagnosis of, 366-67
    diagnostic classifications for, 694-96
    early writings on, 854-55
    and environmental stress, 122
    etiological assessment of, 675
    as factor in personality styles, 545
    final common pathways of, 677-88
    as focus of community services,
        827-28, 847
    history of treatment of, 855-57
    improved perception of, 991
    and interpersonal relationships, 13
    vs. isolation, 352
    labeling of, vs. psychosocial change,
        341
    laboratory assessment of, 689-90
    manifestations of, vs. age, 986
    vs. mental health, 10-11
    non-diagnostic dimensions of, 694-95
    overgeneralization of, to elderly, 286
    percentage of, under treatment, 63-64
    vs. physical illness, 6, 257, 977
    prevalence of, 60-61, 719, 727
        (table 30-3), 854-55, 856, 972
    prevalence of, vs. age, 9
    prevention of, 959, 963, 966-68
    preventive care of, among minorities,
        460
    problem solving competence as
        indicator of, 262, 263
    psychometric testing of, 677-89
    research on, 986, 987-88, 990
    vs. role loss, 352
    screening of, 691-92
    significance of, to elderly, 676
    and somatic symptoms, 687
    and stress, 120, 121, 317-18,
        324-25, 346, 354
    and suicide, 640, 645, 646
    treatment of, 962
    treatment of, among minorities,
        460-61
    urgency of, 673-74
    utilization of services for, 974-75
        (table 41-1)
    vulnerability to, 673, 693
Mental retardation, and dendritic
    abnormality, 78-79

Narcissism, *(cont.)*
　and urbanization, 443-44
Narcotics, antidepressant interaction
　　of, 754 (table 31-2)
Nardil. *See* Phenelzine
National Caucus of the Black Aged, 841
National Council for Homemaker-Home
　　Services, Inc., 843-44
National Council of Senior Citizens,
　　841
　influence of, 991
　legal services of, 833
　sanctioning of community services
　　by, 847
National Council on Aging, 809, 813
　legal services of, 833
　outreach by, 846
　sanctioning of community
　　services by, 847
National health insurance, 68, 844, 851
National Institute of Mental Health
　　(NIMH):
　authorization of, 857, 859
　sanctioning of community
　　services by, 846, 851
　training program of, 863
National Institute on Aging,
　　sanctioning of community
　　services by, 846
National Retired Teachers Association,
　　809, 813
　training programs of, 841
National Senior Citizens Council, 813
Native Americans:
　audiovisual materials about, 465
　conquest of, 450
　intergenerational gaps among, 456
　kinship systems of, 453
　mobility of, 455
　treatment of mental illness among,
　　461
　unassimilability of, 450, 451
Nausea:
　and alcohol withdrawal, 662
　in sedative-hypnotic abuse, 580
　in Wernicke's disease, 580
Navajo, the:
　personality structures of, 442
　regard for elderly by, 431
Neighborhood:
　evaluation of, vs. voluntary
　　relocation, 476, 477-78
　facilities/services in, 480-81
　interaction opportunities in,
　　482-83
　pollution in, 482
　in residential environment, 473
　and residential satisfaction, 479-82
　safety of, 481-82
　ties to, vs. involuntary relocation,
　　484-87
Nembutal. *See* Pentobarbital
Neoplasms. *See* Tumors
Nerve cells. *See* Neurons
Nervous system:
　age changes in, 506-7
　deterioration of, 501-2
　diseases of, 510-15
　and environmental adaptation,
　　121-22, 123
　evaluation of, 502, 503-6, 515
　examination of, 504-5
　examination of, vs. differential
　　diagnosis, 527, 529 (table 22-1)
　functional decline in, 103
　laboratory studies of, 505-6
　　(table 21-3)
　medical history of, 503-4 (table 21-1)

secondary involvement of, in
　　disease, 514-15
　*See also* Autonomic nervous
　　system; Central nervous system;
　　Peripheral nervous system
Netherlands:
　family patterns in, 441
　"stress" pensions of, 311
　suicide rate in, 638
　urban matriarchy in, 442
Neural noise:
　and memory, 199
　and perception of ambiguous
　　figures, 196
　and sensory function, 194-95
　　(Fig. 9-1), 209
　and sensory-motor accuracy, 206
　and slowed reactions, 203-4
　and work intensification, 209
Neurasthenia:
　symptoms of, 625
　treatment of, 637
Neurites, degeneration of, in Alzheimer's
　　disease, 510
Neuritis, peripheral, in delirium
　　tremens, 579
Neuroendocrine deficiency hypothesis,
　　117 (Fig. 5-13)
Neuroendocrine overstimulation
　　hypothesis, 118, 119 (Fig. 5-14)
Neuroendocrine system:
　age changes in, 106-14
　and environmental adaptation, 121-22,
　　123
　exercise effects on, 943, 952-53
　functions of, 101-2
Neurofibrillary degeneration:
　and axoplasmic degeneration, 80-81
　in dentate gyrus, 77
Neurofibrillary tangles, 79, 153
　age changes in, 92 (table 4-1)
　in Alzheimer's disease, 140, 510,
　　565, 566
　appearance of, 506, 702
　and dementia, 157, 158
　in dementia pugilistica, 514
　detection of, vs. psychometric
　　scores, 680
　and granulovacuolar degeneration, 154
　and neuronal loss, 156
　and normal aging, 157, 158
　in normal dementia, 509
　in phenacetin abuse, 581
　in senile dementia, 141, 565, 566
　and senile plaques, 155
Neurofibrils:
　accumulation of, vs. dendritic
　　atrophy, 79
　in axons, 152
Neurofilaments:
　age changes in, 92 (table 4-1)
　and axoplasmic transport, 80
Neuroglia:
　age changes in, 88, 91 (table 4-1)
　metabolism of, 87
Neuroleptics, antidepressant interactions
　　of, 753
Neurometrics:
　assessment value of, 689-90
　and deteriorated cases, 692
Neurons:
　age changes in, 91 (table 4-1)
　changes in, in CJD, 575-76
　changes in, in hypothalamus, 104-5
　damage to, in dementia pugilistica,
　　514
　death of, 151
　effect of alcohol on, 663

and extracellular changes, 87
　foreign bodies in, 154
　future research on, 158
　granulovacuolar degeneration
　　in, 153-54
　Hydergine effects on, 763
　and hypothalamic disregulation, 116
　importance of, 150
　lipofuscin accumulation in, 81,
　　152-53
　loss of, 75-77, 150-51, 506, 702
　loss of, in Alzheimer's disease, 510,
　　565
　loss of, vs. cyto-vascular changes,
　　156
　loss of, vs. drug reactivity, 746
　loss of, in Huntington's chorea, 139
　loss of, in Pick's disease, 140
　loss of, in senile dementia, 141-42,
　　143, 565
　metabolism of, 82-83, 85-86, 89
　microenvironment of, 86, 88
　neurofibrillary degeneration of,
　　80-81
　organelle changes in, 152
　pathology of, 77
　post-mitotic, 501
Neuroses:
　anxiety reactions in, 658
　circumstances surrounding, 49
　and criminality, 665
　definition of, 50
　depressive reactions in, 287, 658
　detection of, 36
　diagnosis of, 653-54, 657, 694
　as diagnostic category, 37, 39
　differential diagnosis of, 563, 564,
　　627
　early development of, 963
　etiology of, 655-57, 660, 667
　evidence of, in general practice
　　studies, 39, 41 (Fig. 2-2)
　further research on, 52
　hypochondrial reactions in, 659-60
　hysterical reactions in, 659
　incidence of, 39, 40 (Fig. 2-1),
　　46-47
　obsessive-compulsive reactions
　　in, 659
　old age manifestations of, 653-54
　outcome of, 636
　phobic reactions in, 658-59
　prevalence of, 41, (Fig. 2-2), 46
　　(table 2-7), 654-55 (table 27-1)
　　666
　psychiatric services used for, 65
　　(table 3-10)
　recognition of, with multidimensional
　　tests, 690
　reflection of, in MMPI response,
　　541
　symptoms of, 657-58
　treatment of, 464, 777, 783-84, 787
　　(table 32-2), 788
　*See also* Depressive neuroses
Neurosyphilis:
　and brain syndromes, 48
　as cause of dementia, 561, 565
　description of, 576-77
　and mental status, 711
　paranoid psychosis in, 600
Neurotic depression:
　as diagnostic category, 626, 658
　differential diagnosis of, 654
　outcome of, 635
　vs. personality type, 634-35
　symptoms of, 626
Neuroticism:

many demonstrations of its inefficiency as a test of learning and merely as one of attention (Inglis, 1966). Inglis' paired associate learning test is one of the best-known of the verbal learning tasks which tap the deficit in short-term memory. They have been widely used in "organic-functional differential diagnosis" and have been reported by Kuriansky and Gurland (1976) to be highly correlated with independent measures of the patient's self-care capacity and duration of hospitalization and also the psychiatric diagnosis. In testing disturbances of new learning, it is very important to teach to a criterion (namely, until the patient learns or clearly never will do so, when the test can be abandoned) and give the patient both the time and the unstressed situation in which to learn.

4. *Language function*

(a) Motor Aspects. What is the quality of spontaneous speech and that in response to questions? Is there a disturbance of articulation, namely dysarthria or a dysphasia present? This may be indicated by wrong words or words that do not exist or words that are nearly but not exactly correct (paraphasias). Fluent dysphasias show normal or excessive output, clear articulation, normal or long phrase length, normal rhythm and inflexion and frequent paraphrasic errors produced without effort. Non-fluent dysphasias show sparse output, poor articulation, short phrase length, disturbed rhythm and inflexion, but possess meaningful content when this can be discerned and speech is produced with obvious difficulty. Impairment of word finding or nominal dysphasia may only be detected by asking the patient to name both common and uncommon objects and colors. The patient may be able to describe the usage of a pen, pencil or watch without coming up with the name. It is often necessary to make the testing more difficult, such as naming the parts of the watch—the stem or winder—to detect minimal dysfunction.

(b) Writing. Can he write spontaneously to dictation? Are numbers written more accurately than words or letters?

(c) Reading. Can he read aloud and perform simple written or printed instructions? Does he comprehend normally what he reads?

(d) Repetition of Speech. Can the patient repeat digits, words, short phrases or long sentences exactly as given? This involves both motor and sensory parts of the speech apparatus and also the connections between the two.

(e) Comprehension of Speech. Can he point correctly on command to one of several objects displayed on view? Can he signal response to simple yes/no questions? Can he carry out simple orders on request, pick up an object, show his tongue? Can he respond to more complex instruc-

tions, e.g., walk over to the door and come back again? The patient's own awareness of language disturbances should be assessed and also whether he is predominantly right or left handed.

5. *Dyspraxia.* Can the patient carry out purposeful movements to command, i.e., holding up his hand, crossing his legs, showing his teeth? Can he carry out a complex coordinated sequence (folding paper and putting it in an envelope)? Watching the patient dress or undress may reveal a dyspraxia.

Can the patient mime? Miming is more sensitive than actual performance.

Can he follow simple and complex commands involving laterality, such as touching the right ear with the first finger of the left hand? "When I raise my hand, but not before, touch the tip of the right ear with the first finger of the left hand." Such complex orders clearly involve memory. They may, however, reveal right-left disorientation or body image disturbances. They may also reveal perseveration, namely, the inability to switch rapidly from one instruction to a new one.

6. *Visual, spatial and constructual ability.* Can he clearly imitate patterns or matches or constructional drawings? Can he draw simple figures—square, circle, triangle? Does he neglect space in such a test, suggesting a parietal lesion in the absence of a field defect?

Has he visual agnosia? Can he describe what he sees and identify objects and persons?

7. *Use of numbers.* Has he the ability to handle number concepts involving addition and subtraction and simple carry over? This is often best tested by asking the patient to make simple and complex change involving carry over: the handling of money is an important guide to living alone or marketing by themselves.

Does the patient understand roughly the size of the city in which he lives and its relative size to others?

8. *Disorientation.* In addition to orientation for time, place and person, are there topographical errors? Can the patient find his way easily about around his own house or room or the hospital?

9. *The face-hand laterality test* described by Green and Bender (1952) is very sensitive. In this, the right and left cheek and the back of the right and left hand are touched in a variety of single and double ipsilateral and contralateral trials with the eyes closed. If the patient makes no errors, he is unlikely to have significant cerebral damage. In Zarit, Miller, and Kahn's 1978 study only errors after the first four tests and two learning trials were correlated with intellectual deficit as judged by the Mental Status Questionnaire and other memory tests.

Such an examination of higher cortical functioning not only provides assessment of present ability but a baseline for possible future deterioration.

Arie (1973) feels that it is not necessary in patients with a long history of progressive deterioration to pursue elaborate investigations to find one of "the rare and so-called reversible causes of dementia" when clinical evidence for them, for example, anemia, hypothyroidism, papilledema or other abnormal neurological signs, are not in evidence. He also cautions that care should be taken to avoid diagnosing dementia in:

patients in whom there is a history of depressive illness or any suggestion of it,

all patients under the age of 70 (except when there is obvious cerebrovascular disease),

patients of any age with an atypical or eccentric history (for example, too short a course in the apparently rapidly fulminating illness and/or an atypically intermittent one),

patients in whom there are other unusual features (for example, recent significant injury, intracranial illness, alcoholism or drug abuse),

patients with unexplained physical findings or,

patients whose mental status is greatly at variance from what would be expected by the history, and, finally,

patients in whom "one has a feeling that they are not quite right."

### INVESTIGATIONS

How much to investigate the patient over the age of 75 in the absence of neurological findings is questionable. Not everyone would agree with Arie. Fox, Topel and Huckman (1975) argue strongly that systematic and comprehensive studies cannot be ignored. In their series of 40 consecutive patients with the diagnosis of senile dementia, they found five with potentially treatable illness. Nevertheless, their patients suffering respectively from hypothyroidism, pernicious anemia, temporal lobe lesion and possible communicating hydrocephalus, would have been revealed by the more limited investigations suggested by Wells (1978). He recommends the smallest possible battery as a basic routine diagnostic in patients thought to have organic brain disease:

1. Urinalysis
2. Chest X-ray
3. Blood studies (complete blood count, serological test for syphilis, standard metabolic screening battery, serum thyroxin by column ($CT_4$), Vitamin B12 and folate levels)
4. CT scan

Javel (1978) questions the exclusion of examination of the CSF. Wells (1978) believes that because its diagnostic yield is low, it should only be used where there are indications such as CSF infection, early metastatic disease, or multiple sclerosis. In the absence of these, it is not justified, he says, because it is invasive, expensive in terms of time and equipment, and causes pain and post-operative headache. Not everyone would agree.

Wilson, Musella and Short (1977) point to the value of the EEG. In dementia due to degenerative diseases, metabolic disorders and normal pressure hydrocephalus, and deficiency states, the abnormality is diffuse, in contrast to cerebrovascular disease and intracranial masses, where there is a focal change. Although a normal EEG does not rule out the diagnosis of dementia, especially in its early stages, it can, nonetheless, be an important way of identifying organic processes when the diagnosis is uncertain, and in differentiating diffuse from focal cerebral lesions, and in following the course of the disease. Because it is easily performed, safe, and can be frequently repeated, they consider it is one of the more useful tools in the clinical evaluation of dementia.

Wells (1978) rightly says that he believes the psychiatrist should be the specialist best trained to meld the organic and functional aspects of the patient's problems. For the more difficult problems, a neurologist may be called in as a consultant, but the psychiatrist should firmly grasp the nettle of his or her own professional responsibility. If brain impairment can be expected to occur eventually in roughly half of the elderly who survive their 60th birthday, not only should this be the psychiatrist but every mental health professional (Gianturco and Busse, 1978)! Only then can we look to improvement of the quality of aging life despite being "sans mind, sans everything."

# REFERENCES

ADAMS, R. D., FISHER, C. M., HAKIM, S., OJEMANN, R. G., AND SWEET, W. H. 1965. Symptomatic occult hydrocephalus with "normal" cerebrospinal fluid pressure. *N. Engl. J. Med., 273,* 117–126.

ALBERT, M. I., FELDMAN, R. G., AND WILLIS, A. L. 1974. The 'subcortical dementia' of progressive supranuclear palsy. *J. Neurol. Neurosurg. Psychiat., 37,* 121–130.

ALPERS, B. J. 1936. A note on the mental syndrome of

corpus callosum tumors. *J. Nerv. Ment. Dis., 84*, 621.

ALPERS, B. J., FORSTER, F. M., AND HERBERT, P. A. 1948. Retinal, cerebral and systemic arteriosclerosis. A histopathologic study. *Arch. Neurol. Psychiat., 60*, 440–456.

ALPERS, B. J., AND MANCALL, E. L. 1971. *Clinical Neurology,* 6th ed. Philadelphia: Davis.

ARIE, T. 1973. Dementia in the elderly: Diagnosis and assessment. *Brit. Med. J., 4*, 540–543.

BABCOCK, H. 1930. An experiment in the measurement of mental deterioration. *Arch. Psychol.*, No. 117, 1–105.

BELL, J. 1934. Huntington's chorea. *Treas. Hum. Inherit., 4*, Part I.

BENSON, D. F. 1975. Disorders of verbal expression. *In,* D. F. Benson and D. Blumer (eds.), *Psychiatric Aspects of Neurologic Disease*, pp. 121–136. New York: Grune & Stratton.

BICKFORD, J. A. R., AND ELLISON, R. M. 1953. The high incidence of Huntington's chorea in the Duchy of Cornwall. *J. Ment. Sci., 99*, 291–294.

BIRD, E. D., AND IVERSEN, L. L. 1974. Huntington's chorea: Post-mortem measurement of glutamic acid decarboxylase, choline acetyltransferase and dopamine in basal ganglia. *Brain, 97*, 457–472.

BLESSED, G., TOMLINSON, B. E., AND ROTH, M. 1968. The association between quantitative measures of dementia and of degenerative changes in the cerebral grey matter of elderly subjects. *Brit. J. Psychiat., 114*, 797.

BOWEN, D. M., SMITH, C. B., WHITE, P., FLACK, R. H. A., CARRASCO, L., GEDYE, J. L., AND DAVISON, A. N. 1977. *Brain, 100*, 427–453.

BRAIN, L., AND WALTON, J. N. 1969. *Brain's Diseases of the Nervous System*, 7th ed. London, New York: Oxford University Press.

BRANDON, S., MCCLELLAND, H. A., AND PROTHEROE, C. 1971. A study of facial dyskinesia in a mental hospital population. *Brit. J. Psychiat., 118*, 171.

BREWER, C., AND PARROTT, L. 1971. Brain damage due to alcohol consumption: An aerencephalographic, psychometric, and electroencephalographic study. *Brit. J. Addict., 66*, 170–182.

BURGER, L.J., ROWAN, A. J., AND GOLDENSOHN, E. S. 1972. Creutzfeldt-Jakob disease: An electroencephalographic study. *Arch. Neurol., 26*, 428–433.

BUTLER, R. 1975. *Why Survive? Being Old in America*. New York: Harper & Row.

BUTLER, R. N., DASTUR, D. K., AND PERLIN, S. 1965. Relationships of senile manifestations and chronic brain syndromes to cerebral circulation and metabolism. *J. Psychiat. Res., 3*, 229–238.

CAMPBELL, A. M. G., CORNER, B., NORMAN, R. M., AND URICH, H. 1961. The rigid form of Huntington's chorea. *J. Neurol. Neurosurg. Psychiat., 24*, 71–77.

CATTELL, R. B. 1943. The measurement of adult intelligence. *Psychol. Bull., 3*, 153–193.

CH'IEN, L., HATHAWAY, M., AND ISRAEL, C. W. 1970. Seronegative dementia paralytica. *J. Neurol. Neurosurg. Psychiat., 33*, 376–380.

CLARK, M., AND GOSNELL, M. 1976. The brain prober. *Newsweek* (Dec. 20), 54.

COBLENTZ, J. M., MATTIS, S., ZINGESSER, L. H., KASOFF, S. S., WISNIEWSKI, H. M., AND KATZMAN, R. 1973. Presenile dementia. Clinical aspects and evaluation of cerebrospinal fluid dynamics. *Arch. Neurol., 29*, 299–308.

CONSTANTINIDIS, J., GARRONE, G., AND AJURIAGUERRA, J. 1962. L'Heredite des demences de l'age avance. *Encephale, 51*, 301–344.

CORSELLIS, J. A. N. 1962. *Mental Illness and the Ageing Brain*. Maudsley Monograph, No. 9. London: Oxford University Press.

CRITCHLEY, M. 1964. The neurology of psychotic speech. *Brit. J. Psychiat., 110*, 353–364.

CURRAN, D. 1930. Huntington's chorea without choreiform movements. *J. Neurol. Psychopath., 10*, 305–310.

DAVIES, P., AND MALONEY, A. J. F. 1976. *Lancet, 2*, 1403.

DEGKWITZ, R. 1969. Extrapyramidal motor disorders following long-term treatment with neuroleptic drugs. *In,* G. E. Crane and R. J. Gardner, Jr. (eds.), *Psychotropic Drugs and Dysfunctions of the Basal Ganglia*, pp. 22–32. Washington, DC: U.S. Public Health Service Publication No. 1938.

Department of Psychiatry Training Committee, The Institute of Psychiatry, London. 1973. *Notes on Eliciting and Recording Clinical Information*. London: Oxford University Press.

DRAKE, W. E., JR., BAKER, M., BLUMENKRANTZ, J., AND DAHLGREN, H. 1968. Surgery in occlusive cerebral vascular disease: The quality and duration of survival in bilateral carotid occlusive disease. A preliminary survey of the effects of thromboendarterectomy. *In,* J. F. Toole, R. G. Siekert and J. P. Whisnant (eds.), *Cerebral Vascular Diseases*, pp. 242–259. New York: Grune & Stratton.

DUCKWORTH, G. S., AND ROSS, H. 1975. Diagnostic differences in psychogeriatric patients in Toronto, New York and London, England. *Canad. Med. Assoc. J., 112*, 847–851.

EHRENTHEIL, D. 1957. Differential diagnosis of organic dementias and affective disorders in aged persons. *Geriatrics, 12*, 426.

ENGEL, G. L., AND ROMANO, J. 1959. Delirium: A syndrome of cerebral insufficiency. *J. Chronic Dis., 9*, 260–277.

ENNA, S. J., BIRD, E. D., BENNETT, J. P., JR., BYLUND, D. B., YAMAMURA, H. I., IVERSON, L. AND SNYDER, S. H. 1976. Huntington's chorea: Changes in neurotransmitter receptors in the brain. *N. Engl. J.*

*Med., 294,* 1305–1309.

EPSTEIN, L. J., AND SIMON, J., 1967. Organic brain syndrome in the elderly. *Geriatrics, 22,* 145.

EVANS M. 1975. Cerebral disorders due to drugs of dependence and hallucinogens. *In,* J. G. Rankin (ed.), *Alcohol, Drugs and Brain Damage,* pp. 21–42. Ontario: Addiction Research Foundation of Ontario.

FALSTEIN, E. I., AND STONE, T. T. 1941. Juvenile Huntington's chorea. *Arch. Neurol. Psychiat., 45,* 151–155.

FELDSHUH, B., SILLEN, J., PARKER, B., AND FROSCH, W. 1973. The nonpsychotic organic brain syndrome. *Amer. J. Psychiat., 130* (a), 1026–1029.

FERRIS, S. H., SATHANANTHAN, G., GERSHON, S., AND CLARK, C. 1977. Senile dementia: Treatment with deanol. *J. Amer. Geriat. Soc., 25* (6), 241–244.

FISHER, C. M. 1968. Dementia in cerebral vascular disease. *In,* J. F. Toole, R. G. Siekert, and J. P. Whisnant (eds.), *Cerebral Vascular Diseases,* pp. 232–236. New York: Grune & Stratton.

FISHER, C. M., AND ADAMS, R. D. 1964. Transient global amnesia. *Acta. Neurol. Scand., 40,* Suppl. 9, 7–83.

FLEISS, J., GURLAND, B., AND DES ROCHE, P. 1976. Distinctions between organic brain syndrome and functional psychiatric disorders: Based on the geriatric mental state interview. *Int'l. J. Aging and Human Development, 7* (4), 323–330.

FOX, J. H., TOPEL, J. L., AND HUCKMAN, M. S. 1975. Dementia in the elderly—A search for treatable illnesses. *J. Gerontol., 330* (5), 557–564.

FREEMON, F. R. 1976. Evaluation of patients with progressive intellectual deterioration. *Arch. Neurol., 33,* 658–659.

FRIEDMAN, H., AND ODOM, G. L. 1972. Expanding intracranial lesions in geriatric patients. *Geriatrics, 27,* 105–115.

GAJDUSEK, D. C., AND GIBBS, C. J., JR., 1975. Slow virus infections of the nervous system and the laboratories of slow, latent, and temperate virus infections. *In,* D. B. Tower (ed.), *The Nervous System,* Vol. 2, pp. 113–135. New York: Raven Press.

GAYLIN, W. 1972. Genetic screening: The ethics of knowing. *N. Engl. J. Med., 286,* 1361–1362.

GESCHWIND, N. 1975. The borderland of neurology and psychiatry: Some common misconceptions. *In,* D. F. Benson and D. Blumer (eds.), *Psychiatric Aspects of Neurologic Diseases,* pp. 1–9. New York: Grune & Stratton.

GIANTURCO, D. T., AND BUSSE, E. W. 1978. Psychiatric problems encountered during a long-term study of normal ageing volunteers. *In,* A. D. Isaacs and F. Post (eds.), *Studies in Geriatric Psychiatry,* pp. 1–16. Chichester, New York: John Wiley.

GOLDSTEIN, K. 1942. *After Effects of Brain Injuries in War. Their Evaluation and Treatment.* New York: Grune & Stratton.

GOODMAN, R. M., HALL, C. L., JR., TERANGO, L., PERRINE,

G. A., JR., AND ROBERTS, P.L. 1966. Huntington's chorea. *Arch. Neurol., 15,* 345–355.

GORDON, E. B., AND SIM, M. 1967. The EEG in presenile dementia. *J. Neurol. Neurosurg. Psychiatry, 30,* 285.

GOTTFRIES, C. G., KJÄLLQUIST, A., PONTÉN, U., ROOS, B. E., AND SUNDBÄRG, G. 1974. Cerebrospinal fluid pH and monoamine and glucolytic metabolites in Alzheimer's disease. *Brit J. Psychiat., 124,* 280-287.

GREEN, M. A., AND BENDER, M. B. 1952. The face-hand test as a diagnostic sign of organic mental syndrome. *Neurology, 2,* 46–58.

GREENBLATT, D. J., AND SHADER, R. I. 1975. Treatment of the alcohol withdrawal syndrome. *In,* R. I. Shader (ed.), *Manual of Psychiatric Therapeutics,* pp. 1–26. Boston: Little, Brown.

GREGORY, I. 1968. *Psychiatry: Biological and Social.* Philadelphia: Saunders.

GURLAND, B. J., FLEISS, J. L., GOLDBERG, K., SHARPE, L., COPELAND, J. R. M., KELLEHER, M. J., AND KELLET, J. M. 1976. A semi-structured clinical interview for the assessment of diagnosis and mental state in the elderly: The geriatric mental state schedule. II. A factor analysis. *Psych. Med., 6,* 451–459.

GUSTAFSON, L., AND HAGBERG, B. 1975. Dementia with onset in the research period. *Acta Psychiatr. Scand.,* Suppl. 257, 1–71.

HAASE, G. R. 1977. Diseases presenting as dementia. *In,* C. E. Wells (ed.), *Dementia,* pp. 27–67. Philadelphia: Davis.

HACHINSKI, V. C., LASSEN, N. A., AND MARSHALL, J. 1974. Multi-infarct dementia: A cause of mental deterioration in the elderly. *Lancet, 874*(2), 207–210.

HADER, M., SCHULMAN, P. M., AND FAIGMAN, I. 1965. Heightened brain syndromes as precursors of severe physical illness in geriatric patients. *Amer. J. Psychiat., 121,* 1124–1127.

HAGLUND, R. M., AND SCHUCKIT, M. A. 1976. A clinical comparison of tests of organicity in elderly patients. *J. Gerontol., 31*(6), 654–659.

HAKIM, S., AND ADAMS, R. D. 1965. The special clinical problem of symptomatic hydrocephalus with normal cerebrospinal fluid pressure: Observations on cerebrospinal fluid hydrodynamics. *J. Neurol. Sci., 2,* 307–327.

HALSTEAD, H. 1943. A psychometric study of senility. *J. Ment. Sci., 89,* 863–873.

HARMAN, D., HEIDRICK, M. L., AND EDDY, D. E. 1977. Free radical theory of aging: Effect of free-radical-reaction inhibitors on the immune response. *J. Amer. Geriat. Soc., 25*(9), 400–407.

HARNER, R. E., SMITH, J. L., AND ISRAEL, C. W. 1968. The FTA-ABS test in late syphilis: A serological study in 1,985 cases. *J. Amer. Med. Assoc., 203,* 545–548.

HARRIS, R. 1972. The relationship between organic brain disease and physical status. *In,* C. M. Gaitz (ed.), *Aging and the Brain,* pp. 163–177. New York/London: Plenum.